American Constitutional Law

American Constitutional Law

Essays, Cases, and Comparative Notes

Second Edition

Donald P. Kommers
University of Notre Dame

John E. Finn
Wesleyan University

Gary J. Jacobsohn
University of Texas, Austin

ROWMAN & LITTLEFIELD PUBLISHERS, INC.
Lanham • Boulder • New York • Toronto • Oxford

ROWMAN & LITTLEFIELD PUBLISHERS, INC.

Published in the United States of America
by Rowman & Littlefield Publishers, Inc.
A wholly owned subsidiary of The Rowman & Littlefield Publishing Group, Inc.
4501 Forbes Boulevard, Suite 200, Lanham, MD 20706
www.rowmanlittlefield.com

P.O. Box 317, Oxford OX2 9RU, UK
Copyright © 2004 by Rowman & Littlefield Publishers, Inc.

British Library Cataloguing in Publication Information Available

Library of Congress Cataloging-in-Publication Data

Kommers, Donald P.
    American constitutional law : essays, cases, and comparative notes /
Donald P. Kommers, John E. Finn, Gary J. Jacobsohn.—2nd ed.
        p.   cm.
        Includes bibliographical references and index.
    ISBN 0-7425-2687-9 (cloth : alk. paper)—ISBN 0-7425-2688-7 (pbk. :
alk. paper)—ISBN 0-7425-2693-3 (pbk. : alk. paper)
    1. Constitutional law—United States.   I. Finn, John E.   II. Jacobsohn,
Gary J., 1946–   III. Title.
KF4550.K65   2004
342.73—dc22

                                                                2003020818

Printed in the United States of America

⊗ ™ The paper used in this publication meets the minimum requirements of American
National Standard for Information Sciences—Permanence of Paper for Printed Library
Materials, ANSI/NISO Z39.48-1992.

For Nancy, Linda, and Beth

There is no remedy for love
but to love more
— *Thoreau*

Contents in Brief

Contents

Preface

This book was born of the conviction that the study of constitutional law is an integral part of—and should draw upon—a liberal arts education. In light of this, we have tried to produce a unique casebook, one that will encourage students to think critically about the principles and policies of the American constitutional order. As taught in law schools, constitutional law tends to focus on technical rules and doctrines that students are asked to apply to a given set of facts, after which they proceed to the next case. A liberal arts view, by contrast, seeks to drive constitutional doctrine and policy back to their foundation in social, moral, and political theory, prompting students to engage the great questions of political life addressed by the Constitution and constitutional interpretation. Among these issues are questions that concern the meaning of justice, liberty, equality, and America itself. We believe that our focus on these questions distinguishes this text from the standard law school book on constitutional law as well as from other texts designed for undergraduates whose main concerns are with other things.

We should note that this book centers largely, but not exclusively, on constitutional meaning as defined by the United States Supreme Court. Accordingly, judicial opinions constitute the core of its documentary materials. But this does not mean, nor do we wish to imply, that the Supreme Court monopolizes the field of constitutional interpretation. Congress, the president, governors, state legislators, and even police officers on the beat interpret the Constitution when they issue orders, pass laws, or arrest persons suspected of crime. In focusing mainly on the process of *judicial* interpretation, we have nevertheless tried to consider this broader latticework of constitutional decision-making, as several of the non-judicial materials in the appendices would indicate. Moreover, several cases reproduced in this book address the role of non-judicial institutions in the interpretation of the Constitution.

This book's major feature is the introductory essay that precedes the cases in each chapter. We have written these essays not only to situate the cases in their proper historical and political context, but also to highlight three themes or perspectives. Each theme is designed to facilitate critical thinking and draws upon knowledge and skills central to the liberal arts. Our first theme, the interpretive perspective, stresses the nature and process of constitutional interpretation. It asks students to consider how judges and other interpreters find meaning in the wonderfully elastic language of the Constitution. Accordingly, the introductory essays pay special attention to judicial modes of inquiry, styles of argument, and other approaches used by the Supreme Court in deciding constitutional disputes. Is constitutional decision-making little more than politics by another name? Is it an objective process of interpretation apart from and independent of a justice's personal values or moral commitments? Is it a matter of finding the right answer to a constitutional problem? Is there any such thing as a "right" answer in constitutional law? The notes and queries following each case, like the essays, raise these and related questions.

Our second theme, the normative perspective, prompts inquiry into the substantive values of our constitutional jurisprudence. Apart from the social, moral, and political theories—be they explicit or implicit—informing judicial rulings, the chapters of this book invite students to consider how and why constitutional argument, both at the founding and in our own time, has concentrated on three main conflicts. The first is the perennial conflict between nation and state over the limits and scope of their respective powers; the second is the conflict between the principles of democracy and constitutionalism; the third, finally, is the conflict between the values of individual liberty and those based on the claims of the larger community. Students are asked to reflect on whether the judicial resolution of these conflicts represents in some sense the "best" accommodation attainable between competing constitutional values or principles.

Our third theme, the comparative perspective, represents our belief that the study of American constitutional law should be informed by the great variety and richness of comparative materials now available in other constitutional democracies. Indeed, constitutional borrowing from other nations is an increasingly prominent theme in comparative constitutional studies. The United States Supreme Court has itself begun to cite leading decisions of other national high courts as an aid to constitutional interpretation. Needless to say, this is not a casebook in comparative constitutional law. But we believe that the limited and selective comparative materials that we have introduced—mainly in the form of boxed extracts from foreign constitutional courts—help to enrich the study of American constitutional law in several ways, not least by encouraging students to consider what, if anything, is unique in American constitutional life and what we share with other constitutional democracies. Some readers may find the inclusion of comparative materials novel, or even disquieting. We prefer to think of comparative analysis as a longstanding part of constitutional argument in the United States, one that reaches at least as far back as the *Federalist Papers*.

In most other respects, the organization of this book should seem familiar. The casebook is divided into three parts. Part I consists of original essays focusing, respectively, on the Supreme Court as a decision-making institution and on the Constitution and its interpretation. Part II contains six chapters dealing with the structures and powers of government. Part III, finally, includes seven chapters on civil rights and liberties. We trust that teachers accustomed to the canon will find much that is familiar, as well as recognize why and where our themes have led us to depart from the normal course.

It took several years to produce the first edition of this book, published in 1998. Along the way, we received the wise counsel and support of numerous colleagues and teachers of constitutional law. We also had the advice and encouragement of the forty-eight college teachers selected to participate in several National Endowment for the Humanities (NEH) Summer Seminars for College Teachers, conducted by one of us, on the topic, "American Constitutionalism in Comparative Perspective." These teachers, most of whom teach undergraduate constitutional law courses in liberal arts colleges, helped to convince us to stay the course and bring the first edition to completion.

The Second Edition

Gary Jacobsohn joins us as editor and author of the second edition of this casebook. His work in American and comparative constitutional law and jurisprudence has helped to bolster and enrich the three perspectives mentioned earlier. Readers familiar with the first edition will notice significant changes and additions to this edition. Among these are:

- A new chapter on voting and political representation.
- Updated critical essays that introduce students to the Supreme Court's most recent work.
- New materials on the Court's revival of the 11th Amendment as a limitation on state rights.
- A wider array of comparative notes, including boxed extracts from decisions of constitutional courts in India, Israel, South Africa, and Australia (along with Canada, Germany, Japan, Hungary, and the European Court of Human Rights).
- Expanded introductory essays that highlight issues of constitutional design and borrowing from other nations.
- A list of web sites for easy access to American and foreign case law as well as information on numerous foreign constitutional courts.
- An extensive set of appendices, including an updated glossary and materials on how to study Supreme Court opinions and how to research comparative materials.
- New cases and materials on the Patriot Act and other efforts to combat terrorism in the United States and abroad.

The 2nd edition also includes several changes and additions in the list of reprinted cases. Nineteen of 132 cases included in the 1st edition have been replaced with 23 new cases, not to mention the eight cases featured in the new chapter on voting. The additional cases have been selected to account for new and dramatic developments related to presidential power, state sovereignty, limits on congressional law-making, the death penalty, abortion, homosexual privacy, affirmative action, and sex discrimination. The new chapter on voting, finally, highlights the 2000 election and the controversial case of *Bush v. Gore* as well as the most recent party finance cases.

A Note on Reading the Text

For those students who may not have taken a law-related course prior to using this book, we would advise that they consult Appendix D for an account of how to understand Supreme Court opinions. In addition, at the outset of each edited case, just before the opinion of the Court, we (the editors) have written a brief summary of the facts in the background of the judicial contest, including a statement of how the dispute was decided in the lower courts. The summary concludes with a list of the justices who participated in the decision. Names appearing in italics identify the authors of dissenting, concurring, and majority or plurality opinions. (Justices whose names are set in roman type have joined one or more of these opinions.) Students will notice that selected dissenting and concurring opinions have been omitted. We omit them only if they contribute little to our understanding of a case or duplicate the reasoning of other opinions.

Acknowledgments

A book such as we have written and edited was not fashioned out of whole cloth. Years of teaching undergraduate constitutional law stands behind this enterprise: 29 years at Notre Dame in the case of Donald Kommers, 32 years at Williams College in the case of Gary Jacobsohn, and 17 years at Wesleyan University in the case of John Finn. Many of the changes and additions introduced into the 2nd edition were in response to student reactions to the 1st edition. We are deeply grateful for their comments and for suggestions made by other users of our casebook.

For their help and advice on the 2nd edition, we would like to thank Michael Tolley (Northeastern University), Theodore M. Vestal (Oklahoma State University), William Buscemi (Wittenberg University), Rodney Hero (University of Notre Dame), Nicholas Aroney (Queensland University, Australia), Peter W. Hogg (York University, Canada), Winfried Brugger (Heidelberg University, Germany), and Sotirios Barber (University of Notre Dame). Publishers' reviewers of the second edition manuscript include Martin Gruberg (University of Wisconsin at Oshkosh), Paul F. Mullen (Florida International University), Harold Pohlman (Dickinson College), and George Thomas (University of Oklahoma). First edition supporters include David Barnum (DePaul University) and Jerry Simich (University of Nevada at Las Vegas). We are also indebted to our graduate and undergraduate research assistants for their invaluable help, especially Kevin Gingras, Brendan Dunn, and Jesse Covington of Notre Dame; Justin Crowe and Hayley Horowitz of Williams College; Andrew Calica and Peter Harvey of Wesleyan; and William Adsit of the University of Connecticut Law School. We would also like to acknowledge the work of our tireless secretaries, Janet Demicco, Debbie Sumption, and Lu Ann Nate; law librarians Dwight King, Patti Ogden, and Carmela Kinslow; and the three computer wizards who liberated us from a number of frustrations, namely, Daniel Manier, Timothy Gritten, and Susan Good. Last, but not least, we are deeply grateful to Jennifer Knerr, Renee Legatt, Christopher Ruel, and Alden Perkins, all of Rowman & Littlefield, for their irreplaceable expertise and enthusiastic commitment to this book.

Finally, we owe a special word of thanks to our families for their understanding and patience during the year of this edition's preparation. Gary Jacobsohn wishes to thank his wife Beth and their three children, Vanessa, Joseph, and Matthew; John Finn his wife Linda and their two children, Alexandra and Ellery; and Donald Kommers his wife Nancy. It is only appropriate that we dedicate this book to each of our spouses.

Introduction

Our many years of teaching constitutional law have persuaded us that because of the questions it raises about the nature of our polity and the political morality of our Constitution, a course on constitutional law should be an integral part of a student's education in the liberal arts, and not simply an exercise in professional preparation. Like its predecessor, then, we began this new edition of *American Constitutional Law* with the premise that the study of constitutional law is a vital part of a student's civic education. Seen from this perspective, a constitutional law course can be—and is—no less than an extended commentary on the meaning of America. As with the first edition of this work, we have tried to produce a casebook appropriate for such a commentary, one that goes beyond the facts and rulings of particular cases to engage the great issues of constitutional interpretation and one that avoids the insularity of an exclusively domestic focus. In this new edition we take up much the same task, encouraged by the increasing relevance and importance of comparative constitutional law and the growth of international human rights law.

We think it most helpful to consider constitutional theory and Supreme Court opinions as embracing two interrelated concerns, one dealing with the forms and methods of judicial review, the other with the political theory of the Constitution as a whole. The first highlights the process of constitutional interpretation and directs attention to how judges decide cases and when they should declare legislation valid or invalid. The second concern, which emphasizes the political theory of the Constitution, emphasizes efforts to reinterpret American liberalism and to revive an older tradition of civic republicanism. Both concerns, the interpretive and the normative, promise to make the study of American constitutional cases more inviting, challenging, and relevant to the design of a stable political order in the United States.

We also think it important that students and citizens learn to view American constitutional law in a comparative light. The globalization of constitutional law is a central feature of contemporary politics, owing in part to the growth of international human rights law and to the rich and voluminous jurisprudence of foreign constitutional courts created after the Second World

War, not to mention the transnational European Court of Human Rights.[1] In recent years, for example, scholars and constitutional courts alike have engaged in an extensive discussion about the possibilities and limits of "constitutional borrowing," or the practice of seeking guidance from the constitutional experience of other democracies. In interpreting their respective constitutions, foreign constitutional courts have been consulting each other's case law, including American cases, with increasing frequency. The Constitution of South Africa (1996) even contains an interpretive provision expressly advising the court, in protecting basic rights, that it "must consider international law" and "may consider foreign law."[2] Although there are some justices on the United States Supreme Court who routinely make reference to constitutional developments elsewhere, such as Justices Breyer and Souter, in general the Court remains relatively impervious to these foreign developments. Indeed, constitutional law is one of the few areas of contemporary law and political science that remains resistant to the comparative approach. We may doubt, however, whether Americans can any longer ignore the ideas and practices of other nations with liberal constitutions similar to their own and designed for the governance of modern, secular, and pluralistic societies. So we have introduced carefully selected materials from countries and jurisdictions whose constitutional law parallels that of the United States.

Yet this book remains emphatically a text on *American* constitutional law. We have therefore introduced comparative elements in three limited ways: by including boxes featuring extracts from foreign constitutions and cases, carefully spliced into the text so as to focus on points of special interest; by reserving the concluding section of each introductory essay to discuss comparable foreign developments; and by raising comparative issues in the notes and queries following each case. Our goal is to combine these three perspectives—interpretive, normative, and comparative—into a single integrated text. The book is thus aimed at students who may welcome an approach to constitutional law that draws upon the learning they have acquired in a liberal arts curriculum. We hope to challenge and encourage these students to reflect upon constitutional law in the light both of new thinking currently taking place in American constitutional law and of comparative developments.

In reading the cases reproduced here, students will find that the interpretive, normative, and comparative perspectives interact and overlap. *How* judges interpret the Constitution often depends on their underlying vision of the kind of society or political democracy the Constitution was designed to promote, but this vision has itself unfolded within a world where ideas, values, and attitudes—constitutional and political as well as social and philosophical—easily migrate across national borders. For purposes of further clarifying the goals and concerns of this casebook, however, we shall keep the three perspectives analytically distinct in the following remarks.

---

[1] Norman Dorsen, Michel Rosenfeld, Andras Sajo, and Susannne Baer, *Comparative Constitutionalism: Cases and Materials* (St. Paul, MN: Thomson/West, 2003); David Weissbrodt, *Globalization of Constitutional Law and Civil Rights,* Journal of Legal Education (1993): 261–270. For an account of the rise and spread of judicial review around the globe see Mauro Cappelletti, *Judicial Review in the Contemporary World* (Indianapolis: The Bobbs-Merrill Company, Inc., 1971). For a more updated study see his *The Judicial Process in Comparative Perspective* (Oxford: Oxford University Press, 1989) and A.R. Brewer-Carias, *Judicial Review in Comparative Law* (Cambridge: Cambridge University Press, 1989). See also Andrzej Rapaczynski, "Bibliographical Essay: The Influence of U.S. Constitutionalism Abroad" in Louis Henkin and Albert J. Rosenthal (eds.), *Constitutionalism and Rights* (New York: Columbia University Press, 1990): 405–462; Vicki C. Jackson and Mark Tushnet, *Comparative Constitutional Law* (New York: Foundation Press, 1999); Jan-Erik Lane, *Constitutions and Political Theory* (Manchester, England: Manchester University Press, 1996).

[2] South African Constitution, 1996. Sec. 39(1)(b) and (c).

The Interpretive Perspective

In recent years, Americans have watched and participated in a fierce national debate over the source and scope of judicial power. The debate has been going on since before *Marbury v. Madison*,[3] but in recent decades, due to the robust "activism" of the Warren and Burger courts and the so-called "counter-revolution" staged by the Rehnquist Court, it has reached a level of intensity unmatched in the history of American constitutional discourse, and it shows no signs of abating.[4] At the center of this debate are two basic questions: *Who* shall be responsible for interpreting the Constitution and *how* shall it be interpreted? But there is a prior question. Before any interpretation can take place, we must know *what* we are interpreting. What, in short, is the Constitution? Is it the 7,000-word document that emerged from the Philadelphia Convention? Or does the Constitution include other foundational documents, such as the Declaration of Independence and President Lincoln's First Inaugural Address (see Appendixes A and C), or other principles, precepts, practices, rights, or theories that are not laid out in the written text? One aim of this book is to encourage students to read the opinions of the Supreme Court with these queries in mind. Another is to draw attention to the sources of information, interpretive techniques, and styles of argument used by the Court in deciding cases. Certain approaches to constitutional interpretation (e.g., historical, textual, structural, doctrinal, ethical, and prudential) compete for supremacy on and off the Supreme Court and, as the Senate hearings on the Robert Bork and Clarence Thomas nominations showed, many Americans are themselves caught up in the argument.

Although in dealing with these interpretive issues we are mainly concerned with the approaches and techniques used by the Court in construing the Constitution, institutional issues also loom large. When and under what circumstances should the judiciary, rather than the legislature or other political actors, decide a particular question of constitutional law? It is, of course, no secret that legislative and executive officials—even the police officer on the beat—also interpret the Constitution. If senators and representatives, all sworn to uphold the Constitution, have vigorously and conscientiously debated the constitutionality of a legislative bill before enacting it, should the Supreme Court then reject their judgment and declare the law unconstitutional? What deference, if any, do judicial decision-makers owe to legislators and executive officials who have made independent assessments of the constitutionality of their actions? These and related issues are brought up mainly in the notes and queries to each case.

The Normative Perspective

This casebook seeks to frame the debate over what the Constitution means within the broader context of political theory. Here too constitutional argument in our time is largely a revived and sophisticated version of a much older debate reaching back to the "founding" disputes between Federalists and anti-Federalists. This debate has traditionally focused on three central normative tensions: (1) the conflict over the

---

[3] 5 U. S. (1 Cranch) 137 (1803).

[4] A poignant example of the depth and sharpness of the debate is Sotirios A. Barber, *The Constitution of Judicial Power* (Baltimore: Johns Hopkins Press, 1993). See also Sunstein, Cass, *One Case At a Time: Judicial Minimalism On the Supreme Court* (Cambridge: Harvard University Press, 1999). For a discussion of similar issues from a comparative perspective, see Holland, Kenneth M. (ed.), *Judicial Activism In Comparative Perspective* (London: Macmillan, 1991).

limits of federal and state power; (2) the conflict between democracy (rule by political majorities) and constitutionalism (limits on majoritarian democracy); and (3) the meaning of and conflict between liberty and community. The playing out of these overlapping tensions forms the basis of the doctrinal history of American constitutional law.

These normative issues are important because they go to the heart of the kind of nation Americans aspire to be and the Supreme Court's role in defining that people. Should the Supreme Court, for example, seek to promote individualism and personal liberty, striking down laws that impinge on individual autonomy or entrepreneurialism? Or should the Court use its moral authority to protect the rights of groups and reinforce a sense of community based on widely shared and deeply held visions of the good life? Through substantial introductory essays, in the notes and queries, and by the manner in which we have edited cases, we encourage students to focus on central issues of liberty, equality, community, individualism, and personhood.

The Comparative Perspective

By introducing comparative materials into the standard course in American constitutional law, this casebook serves not only as a springboard for fresh reflection on the American Constitution, but it also anticipates an important trend in teaching constitutional law. Foreign constitutional texts and judicial opinions, along with international human rights law, are inviting targets of study, particularly if chosen to illuminate aspects of domestic constitutionalism. The outsider's perspective may furnish students with insights into their own society that would otherwise have remained invisible. In the same vein, Richard Stewart writes: "[A] glimpse into the households of our neighbors serves the better to illuminate our own, as when by pressing hard against the pane we see not only the objects on the other side but our own features reflected in the glass."[5] Carefully selected comparative references can help students better appreciate the work of our Supreme Court and enhance their understanding of the American Constitution.

A comparative perspective enriches the study of constitutional law in several ways. First, by looking at foreign models of constitutional governance or other traditions of freedom, students may begin to discern what is purely historical and contingent in the American experience and what is more universal and permanent. Second, Americans may take a great deal of pride in knowing something about the extent to which their constitutional ideals and practices are embedded in the provisions and features of other liberal democracies. Third, they may also find great value in the distinctive aspects of foreign constitutions and the sharp contrasts to American law found in foreign constitutional doctrine. For example, the idea of an "objective order of values" or an "unconstitutional constitutional amendment," or the distinction between negative and positive rights, found in the constitutional theory of Germany and India, for example, may hold fascinating implications for Americans seeking new ways of understanding their own Constitution.

For purposes of illustration, we might briefly compare *Bowers v. Hardwick*,[6] the first American homosexual sodomy case, with *Dudgeon v. United Kingdom*,[7] a similar

---

[5] *Courts and Free Markets: Perspectives from the United States and Europe* (Oxford: Clarendon Press, 1982), p. viii.

[6] 478 U.S. 186 (1986). The decision in *Bowers*, however, was overruled in *Lawrence v. Texas*, 539 U.S. _____ (2003); 123 S.Ct. 1406; 155 L. Ed. 2d 376 (2003).

[7] 4 E.H.R.R. 186 (1986).

case decided by the European Court of Human Rights. In *Dudgeon*, the European Court ruled that Northern Ireland's law prohibiting homosexual conduct between consenting adults constituted an interference with the respect for private life guaranteed by Article 8 (1) of the European Convention on Human Rights. Five years later, in 1986, the U.S. Supreme Court, in a 5–4 vote, came to the opposite conclusion. It sustained the constitutionality of a Georgia statute criminalizing homosexual sodomy even when engaged in by consenting adults.[8] That the two cases produced different results invites reflection in its own right, but the distinctive analytical approaches of the two tribunals are equally compelling. Justice White's majority opinion held that the Fourteenth Amendment's concept of due process liberty does not confer a fundamental right on homosexuals to engage in acts of consensual sodomy. Justice Blackmun, writing for the minority, held that Georgia's law violated the fundamental right to privacy implicit in the due process liberty clause of the Fourteenth Amendment. The two opinions are marked by an irreconcilable polarity. Under the majority's holding that there is no fundamental right to engage in homosexual conduct, the state won easily; had the minority prevailed, declaring that such conduct is included in the fundamental right to privacy, the individual would have won just as easily.

In sharp contrast to both of these opinions, the European Court engaged in a nuanced and sensitive balancing of the valid interests of both state and individual. The Court recognized the state's interest in regulating sexual morality, but also the individual's interest in protecting the most intimate aspects of one's private life. After examining the policies of other European nations and finding that in Northern Ireland itself there appeared to be no "pressing need" to criminalize homosexual conduct, the Court concluded that the "detrimental effects [of the legislation] on the life of a person of homosexual orientation" outweighs "the state's justification . . . for retaining the law in force."[9] There was some faint suggestion in the opinion, however, that in other circumstances and with different facts, the decision could conceivably have gone the other way.

Students may well wonder why none of the opinions in *Bowers* made reference to the European Court's opinion. Was it a conscious omission, and if so, why? Whatever the explanation, *Dudgeon* figured prominently in the recent Supreme Court decision in *Lawrence v. Texas* (2003). Writing for a 6–3 majority, Justice Kennedy explicitly overruled *Bowers,* concluding that the due process clause of the Fourteenth Amendment does protect "the full right to engage in private conduct without government intervention." In many ways *Lawrence* seems simply to replay *Bowers*, but this time with a different result. In *Bowers* the Court had characterized the issue as whether the Constitution confers upon homosexuals a right to commit sodomy. In *Lawrence*, however, Justice Kennedy rejected that formulation, writing instead that "Liberty presumes an autonomy of thought, belief, expression, and certain intimate conduct. The instant case involves liberty of the person both in its spatial and more transcendent dimensions." In dissent, Justice Scalia argued that "The Texas statute undeniably seeks to further the belief of its citizens that certain forms of sexual behavior are 'immoral and unacceptable.' . . . *Bowers* held that this was a legitimate state interest."

Unlike the *Bowers* Court, however, both the majority and the dissents in *Lawrence* made use of *Dudgeon,* as well as the case law of other jurisdictions. Justice Kennedy,

---

[8] Georgia's criminal code also punished heterosexual sodomy. For present purposes, however, it is sufficient to focus on the statute's punishment of homosexual conduct.

[9] Supra note 7, at 167.

for example, noted that *Dudgeon* is "Authoritative in all countries that are members of the Council of Europe (21 nations then, 45 nations now), [and] at odds with the premise in *Bowers* that the claim put forward there was insubstantial in our Western civilization." The Court further noted that "Other nations, too, have taken action consistent with an affirmation of the protected right of homosexual adults to engage in intimate, consensual conduct."

In dissent, Justice Scalia criticized these references to other jurisdictions, as he often does. "The Court's discussion of these foreign views (ignoring, of course, the many countries that have retained criminal prohibitions on sodomy) is . . . meaningless dicta." Quoting Justice Thomas, Scalia concluded that "this Court . . . should not impose foreign moods, fads, or fashions on Americans."

We need not decide here which of these opinions is right. Suffice to say that *Bowers* and *Lawrence* are rich for the interpretive, normative, and comparative issues they raise. First, they prompt questions about the interpretive approaches used by the Court in construing the Constitution—its reliance on history, text, precedent, structure, natural law, social utility, consensus, among other possibilities—along with the institutional question of when federal judicial power should be used to overturn majoritarian policies. Second, they revolve around the crucial normative tensions we mentioned earlier, raising important questions: What theory of liberty should inform the general meaning of the Constitution? How shall individual rights be reconciled (if they should be reconciled) with the desire to enforce the community's prevailing conception of social morality? What visions of society and human personality emerge from the case? Finally, students may be driven to wonder about the relative wisdom of the European Court's analytical approach, as opposed to those of the majority and minority opinions in *Bowers* and *Lawrence*.

We wish to reemphasize, however, that our insertion of comparative materials is extremely selective and largely for the purpose of illustrating issues and problems of *American* constitutional law. Thus we draw these materials mainly from the decisions of foreign constitutional courts in countries which face social and political problems similar to those of the United States, which share constitutional language similar to the words and phrases of the U.S. Constitution, and whose supreme judicial tribunals play roles analogous to that of the United States Supreme Court—primarily Canada, Germany, India, Israel, Japan, South Africa, and the Council of Europe. All of these jurisdictions have produced bodies of constitutional law comparable in complexity and learning to the jurisprudence of our Supreme Court, and their opinions are accessible to students unfamiliar with the complex judicial structures, legal systems, and doctrinal writings of the foreign jurisdictions. In this book we can only open the door a tiny crack to ways in which other constitutional democracies have dealt with the issues discussed in this introduction. Nevertheless, we believe that the comparative perspective, for the reasons given earlier, can offer guidance to Americans engaged in reexamining the goals and content of their own Constitution, and perhaps this book will encourage interested students to explore that perspective further.

Apart from the comparative materials, the organization of this book is fairly conventional, covering the usual topics and leading cases found in the standard course on American constitutional law. We hope, therefore, that teachers of American constitutional law accustomed to presenting the standard course materials may find this book simultaneously useful and challenging.

The casebook is divided into three parts: Part I includes two introductory chapters. Chapter 1 focuses on the organization, procedures, powers, and personnel of the United States Supreme Court. Chapter 2 introduces students to the structure and principles of the United States Constitution, describes various approaches to judicial review, and discusses competing theories of the Constitution. These chapters also compare the process of constitutional interpretation and the institution of judicial review in the United States with their variants in other advanced constitutional democracies, a discussion intended to help students think comparatively about the larger issues of liberty and community underlying particular constitutional cases and controversies in the United States.

Part II covers six chapters dealing with governmental structures and relationships. These chapters include edited cases and materials dealing respectively with the expansion of judicial power (chapter 3), divided and separated powers (chapter 4), foreign and military affairs (chapter 5), federalism (chapter 6), national regulatory powers (chapter 7), and a new chapter on elections and political representation (chapter 8). Part III includes seven additional chapters on civil rights and basic freedoms. They deal respectively with the Bill of Rights and the Fourteenth Amendment (chapter 9); liberty and property (chapter 10); liberty, life, and personhood (chapter 11); freedom of expression (chapter 12); freedom of religion (chapter 13); race, slavery, and the equal protection clause (chapter 14); and gender discrimination, and other discriminatory classifications (chapter 15). An original essay that calls attention to interpretive and normative issues raised by the edited cases and readings precedes each of these chapters. In addition, each essay describes parallel developments in selected non-American jurisdictions for the purpose of raising questions about American constitutional values and their transmission to other cultures.

Finally, we have included several appendixes. Appendixes A, B, C, and D reproduce the texts of the Declaration of Independence, the U.S. Constitution, President Lincoln's First Inaugural Address, and his Gettysburg Address, respectively. Appendix E offers tips on how to study constitutional law and includes an example of how to summarize or brief a constitutional case. Appendix F features a glossary of technical legal terms. Appendix G presents a chronological chart of the justices who have served on the U.S. Supreme Court. Appendix H discusses legal research on the World Wide Web. Finally, Appendix I reproduces the text of *The Federalist* No. 78.

Part One

Institutional and Interpretive Foundations

*T*he first part of this book (chapters 1 and 2) provides students with background on the Supreme Court and the Court's role in the American system of government as well as an overview of the process of constitutional interpretation. It locates the Court within our "dual" system of state and federal courts and focuses on its organization, composition, and decision-making procedures. Among the Court's important decisional procedures is its discretionary authority to decide only those cases it chooses to decide, a prerogative that accounts for its heavy emphasis on *constitutional* adjudication. Prior to 1950, barely 5 percent of the Court's dispositions with full opinions dealt with constitutional issues, whereas today such issues form the principal question in some 60 percent of cases decided with full opinions. Indeed, over the years, the Supreme Court has evolved, for all practical purposes, into a constitutional tribunal not unlike the specialized constitutional courts created in Western Europe after the Second World War.

Part I also offers advice on how to read Supreme Court opinions. Reading constitutional cases is not like reading P. G. Wodehouse or S. J. Perelman. Judicial opinions require close reading. They are manifestations of legal reasoning, which is not a simple thing. Felix Frankfurter once remarked that judicial opinions often "convey accents and nuances which the ear misses on a single reading, and [they] reveal meanings in silences." Unveiling these nuances and "listening" to these silences is one of the exciting intellectual challenges in reading constitutional cases.

The purpose of this volume, however, is not merely to introduce students to the policies, principles, and rulings of the Supreme Court in constitutional cases. An equally important inquiry is *how* the Court reaches its decisions. Accordingly, chapter 2 introduces students to various methods and sources of constitutional advocacy. As we shall see, constitutional arguments may be drawn from a variety of valid sources. Constitutional interpretation itself involves the various ways by which judges, and others, seek to determine what the Constitution means. Familiarity with these methods is important because a constitutional doctrine or policy enunciated by the Court may well depend on the particular judicial method or approach to interpretation. It is also important to understand that the various methods of interpretation play an important role in assisting the Court to reconcile the tension between democracy and constitutionalism. Finally, chapter 2 compares American interpretive approaches with those used by foreign constitutional tribunals. These comparisons will also be a part of all of the remaining chapters in this book, reflecting both the importance of constitutional globalization in the twenty-first century and the usefulness of looking abroad to gain valuable perspective on our own constitutional arrangements and choices.

Chapter 1

The Supreme Court

*I*n *Federalist* 78, Hamilton concluded "the judiciary is beyond comparison the weakest of the three branches. . . ." Whether Hamilton's conclusion is an accurate description of the Court's place in our constitutional life is a question we shall consider throughout this book. In 1787, Hamilton's observation was surely accurate. Today, appointment to the Court is a prize, the culmination of a career in law. President Washington, though, had to plead with friends and twist arms to find people to serve on the Court. The first Chief Justice, John Jay, left the Court after only five years, finding a more prestigious and powerful position as Governor of New York. Another justice resigned his commission in favor of a seat on the South Carolina supreme court.

When the Court first convened on 1 February 1790, it met in the Royal Exchange Building in New York City. Thereafter and until 1939, it met in a spare room in the basement of the capitol building. Today, the Court holds office in an impressive palace of white marble on the corner of First and A Streets in Washington, D.C. Inside, the justices and their clerks are surrounded by polished wood and gleaming brass. The Court has its own library, printing press, cafeteria, museum, gift shop, and even a basketball court.

The splendor of the Court's residence mirrors its prominence as an institution. The Court presides over a vast bureaucracy that includes more than one hundred lower courts staffed by over seven hundred judges. It controls a budget in excess of 30 million dollars. More importantly, the Court is at the center of public debate and policymaking in such areas as abortion, affirmative action, sexuality, gun control, and privacy. In nearly every term the Court considers cases that go to the very heart of the separation of powers, federalism, and the Bill of Rights. As Alexis de Tocqueville wrote, "there is hardly a political question in the United States which does not sooner or later turn into a judicial one."[1]

It was not always so. Under the Articles of Confederation there was no Supreme Court—indeed, no federal judiciary at all. In contrast, Article III of

---

[1] J. P. Mayer, ed., *Democracy in America.* (Garden City, NY: Doubleday, 1969), 270.

the Constitution provides "there shall be a Supreme Court and such inferior courts" as Congress may desire. To ensure the independence of the federal judiciary, it also gives judges lifetime tenure and protects against a reduction of their salaries. In broad strokes Article III also defines what kind of cases the Court can hear.

On the other hand, the text tells us nothing about who the justices should be, or how many there should be. Moreover, Article III provides no information about how the Court works, about how the Court decides which cases to hear, or how the justices should decide them. Thus, the federal court system is a product of an evolution that has been profoundly influenced by other features of the constitutional order, such as federalism, the separation of powers, and the tension between individual liberty and popular rule. And as we shall see in chapter 3, Congress, which has expanded the jurisdiction of the federal courts and given the Supreme Court greater control over its own jurisdiction, has advanced the development of the federal courts.

Article III's vagueness is due, in part, to considerable conflict at the Philadelphia Convention about whether a national judiciary was a necessary concomitant of national power. Some delegates, such as Alexander Hamilton, argued in favor of a national judiciary because "the majesty of the national authority must be manifested through the medium of the courts of justice."[2] Some of the other delegates thought a national judiciary would be a terrible threat to the sovereignty of the individual states, each of which possessed its own judiciary.

The Justices: Politics of Appointment

The appointment of a Supreme Court Justice is one of the notable events of American political life. As specified in Article II, justices are nominated by the president and must be confirmed by a majority of the Senate. If confirmed, a justice serves for life on "good behavior" and can be removed only by impeachment by the House of Representatives and conviction by the Senate.[3] On average, there is a vacancy on the Court every two years. Franklin Roosevelt made no appointments in his first term, but had nine opportunities between 1937 and 1943. President Carter made no appointments to the Court, while President Reagan made three. President George H.W. Bush made two appointments in his one term, and President Clinton two appointments in two terms. So far, President George W. Bush has made no appointments.

Presidents typically seek out Supreme Court nominees whose judicial philosophy and record are similar to the president's own political views. As often as not, however, Supreme Court justices go their own way, surprising and sometimes disappointing presidential expectations. President Eisenhower, for example, appointed both Chief Justice Earl Warren and Justice William J. Brennan. Their "liberal" inclinations on the Court disappointed Eisenhower, who later called them "the biggest damned-fool mistakes" of his presidency.[4]

---

[2] Clinton Rossiter, ed., *The Federalist Papers*. #16 (New York: New American Library, Mentor Books, 1961), 116.

[3] Only one Supreme Court justice—Samuel Chase—has been impeached. The Jeffersonians brought charges against Chase in 1805. The Senate did not convict him. For an account, see Bernard Schwartz, *A History of the Supreme Court*. (New York: Oxford University Press, 1993), 57–58.

[4] For a more detailed discussion, see Phillip Cooper and Howard Ball, *The United States Supreme Court: From the Inside Out*. (Upper Saddle River, N.J.: Prentice-Hall, 1996), 31–74. On the other hand, Professor Theodore Vestal has argued that the source of this quote is an oral history interview of Ralph H. Cake, a former Republican national committee member from Oregon and a longtime political enemy of Warren, which suggests it could be an effort to discredit Eisenhower. Theodore M. Vestal, *The Eisenhower Court and Civil Liberties*. (Westport, Conn.: Praeger Publishers, 2002), 23–24.

The nomination process has always been political and, in recent years, has often been controversial, as the nominations of Robert Bork in 1987 and Clarence Thomas in 1991 vividly demonstrate. In addition to the president and the Senate, important players in the confirmation process include the American Bar Association, which on its own initiative has chosen to evaluate nominees based on judicial experience and temperament. A wide array of interest groups and political associations are also involved, such as the American Civil Liberties Union, the National Association for the Advancement of Colored Persons, and the National Organization for Women. At times, sitting members of the Court have also tried to influence the process. The presence of so many actors testifies to the importance of the nomination process: It is one of the most important ways the community has of influencing the Court and enforcing a measure of political accountability.

Most of the people appointed to the Court have had long and distinguished careers in the law and an exemplary record of public service. Many have been members of Congress, some have aspired to the presidency, and, since 1975, all have been judges on lower courts. The overwhelming majority have been Protestant, white, and males of means. A great number have graduated from the country's most prestigious law schools, and several justices began their careers as clerks to Supreme Court justices after graduating from law school. There is, however, no constitutional requirement that a justice have a law degree or be a lawyer.

Notwithstanding this similarity of background, presidents have usually considered diversity an important factor in the Court's composition. For many years, the Court had a "Jewish" seat, and geographical and ideological diversity have also influenced the makeup of the Court. President Johnson appointed Thurgood Marshall as the first African-American on the Court in 1967. In 1981 President Reagan appointed Sandra Day O'Connor as the first woman on the Court, and he appointed Justice Antonin Scalia, the first Italian-American, in 1986.

Most nominees are confirmed without great difficulty. Between 1900 and 1967 the Senate rejected only one nominee. Since 1967, however, the Senate has rejected six nominees. On what basis may the Senate reject an appointment? There is much disagreement about how the confirmation process should work.[5] Should the Senate assess the moral character of a nominee? The nation struggled with this question during the Senate's hearings on Clarence Thomas. Should it inquire into the political or jurisprudential views of nominees? Much of the controversy surrounding Robert Bork's nomination involved these issues.

Some senators and scholars argue vehemently that the Senate's role should be limited to determining whether the nominee is "competent." They argue the Senate is a threat to judicial independence when it inquires into a nominee's substantive views.[6] Others have called for an aggressive review of a candidate's constitutional philosophy, claiming the Senate has an obligation to the people to assess the candidate's views on matters of public importance.[7] Both positions rest upon a particular understanding about the relationship between constitutionalism and democracy.

---

[5] See Susan Low Bloch and Thomas G. Krattenmaker, *Supreme Court Politics: The Institution and Its Procedures*. (St. Paul: West Publishing Company, 1994), chapter 2.

[6] Robert F. Nagel, *Advice, Consent, and Influence*, 84 Northwestern University Law Review 858 (1990).

[7] Stephen Carter, *The Confirmation Mess*, 101 Harvard Law Review 1185 (1988); Nina Totenberg, *The Confirmation Process and the Public: To Know or Not To Know*, 101 Harvard Law Review 1213 (1988); see also Lawrence Tribe, *God Save This Honorable Court: How the Choice of Supreme Court Justices Shapes Our History*. (New York: Random House, 1985).

That tension haunts nearly every area of American constitutional law and is one of the central themes of this book.

The Federal Court System

What kinds of cases may the Court hear? Article III gives us little guidance. It provides only that "the judicial Power shall extend to all Cases, in Law and Equity, arising under this Constitution, the Laws of the United States, and Treaties. . . ." The phrase presents two immediate difficulties: First, the Article refers to "judicial power" but does not say what the power is or what it includes. Second, the Court's "power" to hear cases depends upon whether it has "jurisdiction" over the particular case. As we shall see, the Court has "original" jurisdiction in a set of cases set forth explicitly in Section 2, including those affecting ambassadors and other public ministers, disputes in which the United States is a party, disputes between two or more states, and disputes between a state and citizens of another state. In all other cases the Court has "appellate" jurisdiction, with such exceptions and regulations as Congress shall make.

The great majority of the cases the Court hears come to it under its appellate jurisdiction, or on appeal from a federal or state court. The Constitution does not itself create lower federal courts, instead entrusting their creation and organization to Congress. Congress first created a system of lower federal courts in the Judiciary Act of 1789. Just below the Supreme Court were three circuit courts, each serving a group of states. Thirteen district courts served the lowest level. Although there have been substantial changes in the particular arrangements of these courts, the tripartite structure of the federal court system has remained in place ever since.

The Supreme Court is at the apogee of the system. Since 1869 the Court has had nine justices, but nine is not a constitutional command. President Washington's Court had just six justices. There have been many efforts to change the number, often as a result of straightforward political maneuvering by presidents and Congresses. President Adams tried to reduce the number to five, President Lincoln expanded the number to ten, and Franklin Roosevelt's "court-packing" plan, if it had succeeded, might have increased the number to fifteen. Sometimes sitting members of the Court have joined the fray as well. Justice Field, for example, proposed that the Court should have twenty-one justices.[8]

Directly below the Supreme Court are the United States Courts of Appeals. These twelve courts are organized by territory (except for the District of Columbia Court, which hears cases from federal administrative agencies and the District of Columbia). Each court, or "circuit," covers at least three states. The First Circuit, for example, hears cases from Maine, New Hampshire, Massachusetts, and Rhode Island. The circuit courts hear appeals from the United States District Courts and from federal agencies. Usually a three-judge panel hears cases and decides them by majority vote. On rare occasions, when an issue is especially difficult or contentious, the entire roster of judges on a circuit court may choose to hear a case *en banc*. The circuit courts hear about 40,000 cases every year.

The United States District Courts are the entry level to the federal court system. The district courts are trial courts: One judge hears criminal and civil cases, sometimes with a jury. There are ninety-four district courts, with at least one in every state. The District of Columbia also has a district court, and there is a court each for the

---

[8]Howard J. Graham, *Everyman's Constitution*. (Madison: Historical Society of Wisconsin, 1968), 136ff.

U.S. territories of Guam, Puerto Rico, the Virgin Islands, and the Northern Mariana Islands. These courts hear about 300,000 cases every year.

In addition, Congress has created a wide variety of specialized courts, including military courts, tax courts, and customs courts. Many of these courts were created by Congress under Article I and not under Article III of the Constitution. The provenance of the court is important, for unlike Article III courts, judges on Article I courts are not guaranteed lifetime tenure.

Jurisdiction: The Power to Hear Cases and Controversies

No court may hear a case unless it has "jurisdiction" over it. The Supreme Court has two kinds of jurisdiction—original, and appellate. In cases of original jurisdiction, the Supreme Court hears a case "on first impression." In other words, the litigants bypass state courts and the lower federal courts and go straight to the Supreme Court. Partly because of the Eleventh Amendment, congressional legislation, and the Court's own rules (which provide that original jurisdiction may be held "concurrently" with lower federal courts), such cases are extremely rare.

The Court's workload is therefore largely a function of its appellate jurisdiction. Although the Court is a passive, reactive institution and may not formally initiate cases, it does have great control over how many and what kinds of cases it will hear. In a typical year the Court receives approximately 8,000 petitions, or requests, by litigants to hear their appeals. The Court usually decides to hear between 120 to 150 petitions yearly.[9] In these cases, the Court will accept briefs from the parties, schedule oral arguments, and issue an opinion.

There are three kinds of appellate jurisdiction. Every case the Court hears under appellate jurisdiction follows one of these paths:

1. *Certification.* A United States Court of Appeal can "certify" to the Supreme Court that a particular case poses exceptional difficulties. When it certifies a case, the lower court asks the Supreme Court to provide instruction about how some matter of law should be settled.
2. *Appeal.* For much of its history, the Supreme Court was required to hear cases on appeal that raised certain kinds of questions about federal law. In practice, though, the Court routinely dismissed such cases, explaining that they did not present a "substantial federal question." In 1988, Congress passed legislation that sanctioned the practice, thus transforming the Court's mandatory jurisdiction in such cases into discretionary jurisdiction.
3. *Certiorari.* In most cases, a party appealing a decision files a "writ of certiorari" with the Supreme Court. A "cert" petition is a formal request by a party that the Court hear a case. The decision to accept or deny the writ is entirely within the Court's discretion.

Writs of certiorari are the primary means of access to the Court. The Court will grant the writ if four justices agree a case warrants the Court's attention. The Rules of the Supreme Court indicate under what circumstances it will be likely to grant the

---

[9]This number held more or less constant for the last fifty years. There is some indication, however, that the number of cases the Court accepts for review has steadily decreased under the leadership of Chief Justice Rehnquist. See, e.g., Bloch and Krattenmaker, supra note 5 at 334. See also, Arthur D. Hellman, *The Shrunken Docket of the Rehnquist Court*, Supreme Court Review, 403 (1996).

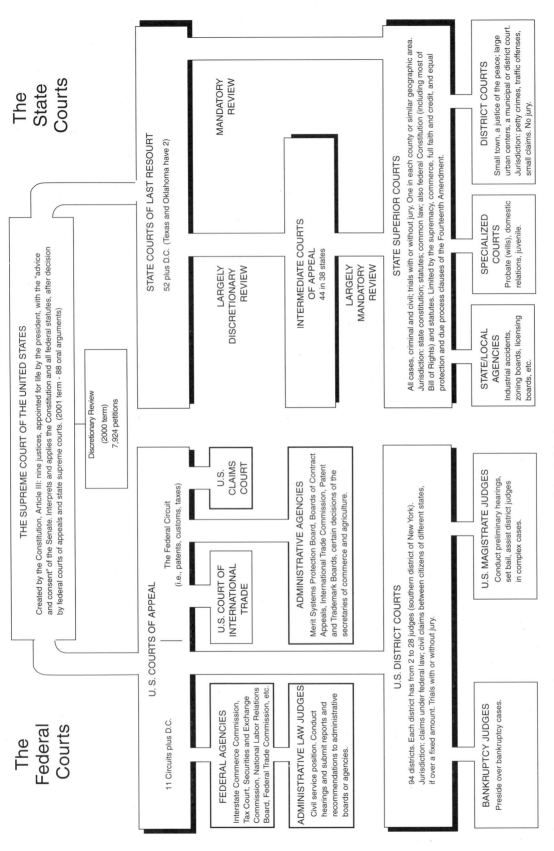

FIGURE 1.1 *Federal and state court organization and jurisdiction.*

SOURCE: Adapted from Frank M. Coffin, *On Appeal* (New York: W. W. Norton, 1994), 48–49.

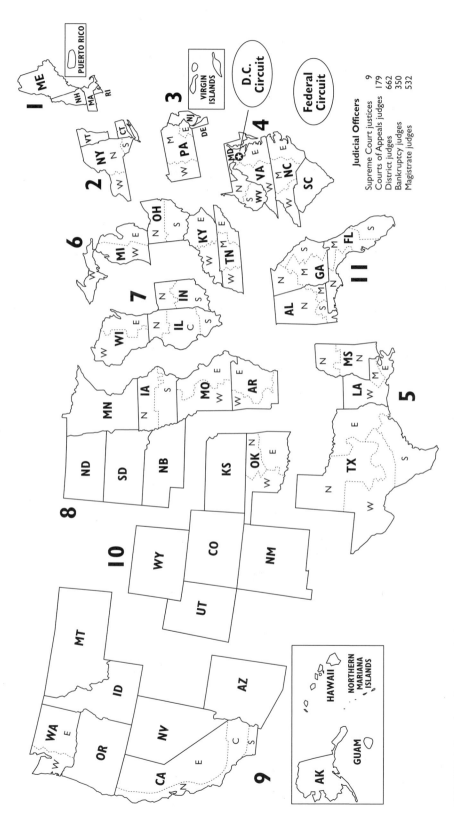

FIGURE 1.2 *The thirteen federal judicial circuits and the ninety-four U.S. district courts.*

SOURCE: Adapted from *Understanding the Federal Courts*, 2d Ed. (Washington, D.C.: Administrative Office of the Courts, 1994), 8.

Judicial Officers	
Supreme Court justices	9
Courts of Appeals judges	179
District judges	662
Bankruptcy judges	350
Magistrate judges	532

writ. Important considerations include a conflict among the Courts of Appeals on a question of law, or between a circuit court and a state supreme court, when a state court has decided a federal question in a way that conflicts with another state court or a U.S. Court of Appeals, and when a state or federal court has decided a question of federal law that the Supreme Court has not yet settled or has settled differently. In each of these instances, the Court's position at the top of the judicial hierarchy allows it to settle conflicts among lower courts and to ensure some measure of uniformity in the interpretation and application of the law.

These rules indicate when the Supreme Court has jurisdiction over a case. Whether the Court will choose to hear a case, though, is not only a function of jurisdiction. As we shall see in chapter 3, the Court has developed a number of additional devices it uses to decide whether to hear a case. Among these "prudential" considerations are the doctrines of standing, ripeness, mootness, and the political questions doctrine. Each represents a policy choice by the Court to limit its jurisdiction to avoid certain kinds of cases and issues, usually for reasons that go to the limited role of the Court in the larger political order.

Congressional Control Over Appellate Jurisdiction

Article III, Section 2 of the Constitution provides the Court shall have appellate jurisdiction "with such Exceptions, and under such Regulations as the Congress shall make." Section 2 is one of the primary means we have of assuring that the federal courts are accountable to the community. The principle of accountability, however, exists in some tension with the principle of judicial independence. As we shall see in chapter 3, Congress has exercised its power to control the Court's appellate jurisdiction on several occasions. In each case the tension between democratic accountability and judicial independence has colored the specific facts and interpretive controversies involved.

Among the interpretive issues raised by Section 2 are questions about the definition and scope of the words "Exceptions" and "Regulations." May Congress remove the Court's entire appellate jurisdiction, or would this exceed the meaning of "exception"? Are there other limits to congressional power under Section 2? If so, what are they and what is their source?

Deciding to Decide: Decision-Making Procedures

Because the Court has almost complete discretion to decide which cases it will hear, the procedures and criteria it uses to winnow 8,000 petitions to the worthy 120 to 150 are extremely important. The Court's rules give litigants some basic guidelines about what kinds of cases the Court is likely to entertain.

The first cut in the caseload is made by law clerks. Clerks are typically law school graduates with distinguished academic records. Each justice has several clerks. The clerks review every petition and prepare summaries for their justices. Some justices have asked their clerks to combine their efforts—called the cert pool—to help offset the sheer number of petitions flooding the Court every year. The clerks review the petitions in light of Rule 17 of the Court's Rules of Procedure and following whatever additional instructions they receive from their individual justices. The memos they prepare are then circulated to the justices who have chosen to participate in the cert pool.

The Chief Justice then prepares a "discuss list": a list of petitions the various justices have indicated they believe merit the Court's consideration. If a petition is not on the Chief Justice's list, or added to it by another justice, it is dismissed. Nearly three-quarters of the petitions are rejected at this stage.[10]

The justices discuss the surviving petitions in conferences soon after the Court's term begins, always on the first Monday in October. They continue to discuss petitions throughout the term, which usually ends in late June or early July. The justices have adopted a "Rule of Four" to decide which cases on the discuss list they will hear. If at least four justices do not agree to hear the case, the petition will be dismissed.

Why do some petitions attract the interest of four justices and others not? Aside from Rule 10, there are no written guidelines. As a general matter, the factors include:

1. the importance of the issue or issues the case raises;
2. the clarity of the issues involved;
3. whether the lower court has developed a clear and complete record of the case; and
4. the potential impact of the case on the Court's own credibility and prestige.

In an address to the American Bar Association, Chief Justice Vinson underscored the importance of these factors:

> *The debates in the Constitutional Convention make clear that the purpose of the establishment of one supreme national tribunal was, in the words of John Rutledge of South Carolina, "to secure the national rights and uniformity of judgments." The function of the Supreme Court is, therefore, to resolve conflicts of opinion on federal questions that have arisen among lower courts, to pass upon questions of wide import under the Constitution, laws, and treaties of the United States, and to exercise supervisory power over lower federal courts. If we took every case in which an interesting legal question is raised . . . we could not fulfill the constitutional and statutory responsibilities placed upon the Court. To remain effective, the Supreme Court must continue to decide only those cases which present questions whose resolution will have immediate importance far beyond the particular facts and parties involved.*[11]

In addition, each justice will bring to the conference individual interests and concerns. One justice might be especially interested in petitions that raise issues of federalism. Another might be on the lookout for cases that raise free exercise of religion issues. And, of course, justices will assess cases based on the likelihood that they can get four other justices to agree with their resolution of the issue.[12]

Finally, the kinds of petitions the Court accepts will be influenced by the kinds of issues—political, economic, moral, and social—that preoccupy society at the time. From the founding to the Civil War, for example, the Court's agenda was dominated by questions concerning the distribution of political power between the national government and the states. The post–Civil War period and the early twentieth century brought to the Court issues about the growth of monopoly and industrialization. In the past several decades the rapid rise of the administrative welfare state has led the Court to concentrate on issues surrounding the individual's relationship to the state.

---

[10] Cooper and Ball, supra note 4, at 112–13.

[11] Fred Vinson, speech to the American Bar Association, 7 September 1949, reprinted in 69 S.Ct. vi (1949).

[12] H.W. Perry, Jr. *Deciding to Decide: Agenda Setting in the United States Supreme Court.* (Cambridge: Harvard University Press, 1991); Doris Marie Provine, *Case Selection in the United States Supreme Court.* (Chicago: University of Chicago Press, 1980); Walter F. Murphy, *Elements of Judicial Strategy.* (Chicago: University of Chicago Press, 1964).

We may be on the cusp of yet another change: In recent years the Court has increasingly considered cases that go to the heart of concentrated power, whether political or economic. These questions present themselves in renewed debates about the limits of federal power vis-à-vis the states, as well as in cases that address the limits of the state action doctrine—or the rule that the Constitution governs only the actions of state actors, and not private persons. Similarly, rapid technological change has led the Court to consider new and intractable issues about the nature of the individual and his or her relationship to the state and community.

Once the Court accepts a case and puts it on the docket it informs the parties and schedules a deadline for them to file legal briefs. A brief is a formal legal document in which an attorney tries to persuade the Court that the relevant case law and other legal materials support his or her client's arguments. Many briefs include a great variety of nonlegal materials—such as medical information or social science—to support or to challenge the statute or policy at issue. Sometimes called "Brandeis briefs,"[13] these briefs illustrate how constitutional interpretation is not simply an academic or legal exercise, but also concerns and is shaped by conceptions of what constitutes good and wise public policy. In addition to the briefs of counsel, the Court will often receive *amicus curiae* briefs, or briefs filed by "friends of the Court." Various interest groups and other organizations that have an interest or expertise in a particular area, such as the American Civil Liberties Union, the National Organization for Women, and Citizens for Decency Through Law, prepare these briefs. The briefs often support the arguments taken by one of the parties to the case, but they sometimes raise issues or present arguments the litigants have not addressed.

More dramatic than legal briefs, but not necessarily as important to the process of decision-making, is oral argument. In a routine case, each party is entitled to one-half hour; in exceptional cases the Court may schedule more time, but no longer do the arguments run for days, as they sometimes used to in the nineteenth century. Argument in *Gibbons v. Ogden* (1824), for example, lasted five days. Opinions vary about the importance of the arguments, with some justices, such as Justice Harlan, holding that a good argument may make the difference between winning and losing.[14] Others, such as former Chief Justice Burger, complain the consistently poor quality of arguments makes them considerably less useful than the briefs. The Court hears oral argument from ten to twelve o'clock on Monday, Tuesday, and Wednesday mornings.

What are oral arguments like? It depends on the case, the justices, and the lawyers. The Rules of the Court state clearly that the Court "looks with disfavor on any oral argument that is read from a prepared text."[15] The justices frequently interrupt the lawyers—and sometimes each other—with questions. As Chief Justice Rehnquist has written, oral argument is not a "brief with gestures," but instead a conversation with "nine flesh and blood men and women."[16]

---

[13] Before he became Justice Brandeis, attorney Louis Brandeis used these kinds of materials to help persuade the Court to uphold an Oregon law that regulated the number of hours women could work. The case was *Muller v. Oregon*, 208 U.S. 412 (1908). Brandeis' tactic met with outraged disapproval in some camps. See Clement E. Vose, *The National Consumer's League and the Brandeis Brief*, 1 Midwest Journal of Political Science 267 (1957).

[14] As quoted in Anthony Lewis, *Gideon's Trumpet*. (New York: Vintage Books, 1966), 162, n. 23.

[15] Rule 10, 28 U.S.C., Rules of the Supreme Court of the United States. (1993).

[16] "Oral Advocacy: A Disappearing Art," Brainerd Currie Lecture, Mercer University School of Law, October 20, 1983, msp. 4.

Coming to Decision: Voting on Cases and Writing Opinions

The Court meets to discuss and decide cases on Wednesdays and Fridays. The meetings take place without clerks or staff. Some justices keep private records, but there is no formal or public record of the meetings, no collective record about who said what to whom or how each justice voted.

After all of the justices have shaken hands, the Chief Justice states his views on the case under discussion and indicates how he intends to vote. Then each of the other justices, in descending order of seniority, gives his or her view and intended vote. The dynamics of these discussions are a matter of conjecture. The papers of some justices, such as William O. Douglas, suggest the discussions can be heated and intense.[17] On the other hand, Chief Justice Rehnquist has said there is more presentation than persuasion in the current Court's conferences,[18] a matter of ongoing concern for some justices, including Justice Scalia.[19] Similarly, Justice Powell observed, "for the most part, perhaps as much as 90 percent of our total time, we function as nine small, independent law firms."[20] No doubt the personalities of the justices, and the leadership style of the Chief Justice, play an important role in determining how the conferences work.

After the tentative vote the justices must decide who will write the opinion. If the Chief Justice is in the majority, the opinion is his to assign. If the Chief Justice is in the minority, the power to assign falls to the senior associate justice in the majority. The assignment decision is frequently influenced by political and strategic factors. The Chief Justice, for example, may assign the majority opinion to a justice whose own vote was tentative, hoping in the process of drafting an opinion the justice may become more certain of his or her convictions.[21]

Each justice has a unique way of writing an opinion. Some rely heavily on their clerks, entrusting first drafts to them and only lightly editing thereafter. Others insist upon writing themselves and limit their clerks to research or editorial assistance. The drafting stage is often crucial to the final outcome of a case. The justices circulate opinions to each other and solicit remarks, especially if they are worried about keeping a majority or are seeking to persuade a justice who may be undecided. In short, the drafting stage is often a continuation of the conference discussions. Voting alignments often change as opinions are circulated; dissenting and concurring opinions come and go in the process of deliberation and compromise, a process that usually lasts several months.[22]

---

[17] For a general review, see Cooper and Ball, supra note 4, at 224–244.

[18] As quoted in David M. O'Brien, *Storm Center.* 6th ed. (New York: Norton, 2002), 294. See also William H. Rehnquist, *The Supreme Court: How It Was, How It Is.* (New York: William Morrow and Company, Inc.), 287–303.

[19] See Stuart Taylor, Jr., "Ruing Fixed Opinions." *New York Times*, February 22, 1988 at A1.

[20] Lewis F. Powell, Jr., *What the Justices Are Saying* . . . , 62 Amercan Bar Association Journal 1454 (1976).

[21] For a more elaborate discussion, see Murphy, supra note 4. In *Roe v. Wade* (1973), the private papers of some of the justices indicate that there was some confusion about how Justice Blackmun had voted at the conference, and likewise some doubt about whether there was a majority to strike or uphold the statute. Chief Justice Burger, who had voted to sustain the law, assigned the opinion to Blackmun. Douglas, thinking Blackmun had voted with Burger, and that Burger was in the minority, objected. Later, Douglas and Brennan decided to wait to see Blackmun's draft before pressing the issue any further. In the end, Justice Blackmun wrote the majority opinion striking the Texas abortion law. See Bernard Schwartz, *The Ascent of Pragmatism: The Burger Court in Action.* (New York: Addison-Wesley Publishing Company, 1990), 297–307.

[22] See O'Brien, note 18, 304–06.

The Court makes its decisions public on "Opinion Days." The decisions are announced to reporters and attorneys in the courtroom. The justices usually limit themselves to announcing the result in the case, but in unusual or controversial cases they may read aloud all or part of their opinions. In *Brown v. Board of Education* (1954), for example, Chief Justice Warren read the opinion in its entirety to a full and silent room. The public information office of the Court provides summaries of the decisions to reporters.

The Impact of Decisions

What happens after the Court reaches a decision? Hamilton observed in *Federalist* 78 that the Court has neither the power of purse nor sword: The Court's opinions do not enforce themselves, and the Court itself has very little power to force other actors to comply with its rulings. Consequently, in the narrowest sense, the impact of a judicial decision extends first and primarily to the parties to the case. The Court's decision thus creates a legal obligation *inter partes*, or between the parties to the case. In the great majority of cases, however, a decision has important ramifications for the polity at large. When the Court decided *Roe v. Wade* (1973), for example, its decision voided the particular Texas antiabortion law that gave rise to the case. But more broadly, it put into question the antiabortion laws of every state in the Union. When the Court decides a matter of law in ways that go beyond the particular parties of the case, it purports to create a rule of legal obligation that is *erga omnes*, or that applies to all similarly situated parties.

Whether and when a Supreme Court decision is *erga omnes* or *inter partes* is often a matter of some conflict. Unpopular decisions are likely to provoke congressional or presidential responses that seek to overturn or limit the ruling. The forms of these responses can vary from outright disobedience, as was often the case following *Brown v. Board of Education* (1954), to feigned blindness following *INS v. Chadha* (1983), to constitutional and statutory efforts to reverse specific rulings, as happened following the Court's controversial ruling in *Texas v. Johnson* (1989), the flag-burning case. More recently, in *Boerne v. Flores* (1997), the Court concluded that the Religious Freedom Restoration Act (1993), passed by Congress in reaction to the Court's decision in *Employment Div. v. Smith* (1990), was an unconstitutional infringement upon the Court's authority to determine what the Constitution means.

In some instances, as the Religious Freedom Restoration Act suggests, the Court's decisions have provoked claims by other institutional actors that they possess a coordinate and co-equal right to interpret the Constitution for themselves. As we shall see in chapter 3, President Jefferson responded to the Court's opinion in *Marbury v. Madison* (1803) by insisting "The Constitution intended that the three great branches of the government should be co-ordinate, & independent of each other. As to acts, therefore, which are to be done by either, it has given no controul to another branch."[23] Likewise, President Lincoln concluded in his first Inaugural Address (Appendix C) that

> *At the same time, the candid citizen must confess that if the whole policy of the government, upon vital questions, affecting the whole people, is to be irrevocably fixed by decisions of the Supreme Court, the instant they are made, in ordinary litigation between parties, in personal actions, the people will have ceased, to be*

---

[23] Jefferson's letter to the prosecutor in the Burr treason case, 2 June 1807.

their own rulers, having, to that extent, practically resigned their government, into the hands of that eminent tribunal.

As we shall see in chapter 2, questions about the impact and enforcement of judicial opinions inevitably raise questions of power and accountability in interpretation, questions that go to the very heart of the constitutional order.

Understanding Judicial Opinions

For most students, judicial opinions are an unusual and sometimes frustrating object of study. Filled with jargon, complicated arguments, and references to obscure legal materials, judicial opinions *are* somewhat puzzling. Most, however, follow a standard format. Learning to recognize the various parts of an opinion will make the processes of reading and understanding cases easier.

Every case includes:

• A Title. The title usually includes the names of the parties to a case. Hence, *Bowers v. Hardwick*, 478 U.S. 186 (1986), tells us that Bowers and Hardwick are the primary parties in the case. The first party—here it is Bowers—is the party that lost in the lower court. He or she is called the "appellant" or the "petitioner." The second party—usually the one seeking to have the lower court decision upheld—is the "appellee" or "respondent."

• A Citation. A string of numbers, or a citation, follows every title. In the *Bowers* case, the citation is 478 U.S. 186 (1986). The decisions of the Supreme Court (and of all federal courts) are kept in "reporters," or collections, that are organized chronologically. "478" is the volume number. The initials "U.S." tell us that the reporter is the official reporter—or collection—of Supreme Court cases. (There are also unofficial reporters prepared by private companies. The initials "L.Ed" and "S. Ct." refer to these other companies.) "186" tells us the page number where the case begins. The last number, in our example, "1986," tells us the year when the case was decided.

• Facts of the Case. Usually, although not always, the Court will begin its opinion by stating the facts of the case. Often the facts are in dispute or subject to interpretation, so concurring and dissenting opinions may also include an account of the facts.

• Questions Presented. Every case raises at least one and usually several constitutional questions. It is important to determine what those questions are. The Court will often list them near the beginning of its opinion. As with the facts, the precise nature of the questions involved—or how they are framed—is often a matter of dispute among the justices.

• The Majority Opinion. Most cases are decided by a majority of the justices. One justice, speaking for the majority, writes the Opinion of the Court. (If no opinion commands a majority, it will be a "plurality" opinion.) The majority opinion announces the holding, or the result, of the case and sets forth the reasons for the decision.

• Concurring Opinions. Sometimes one or more justices will agree with the majority's result but not entirely with its reasoning. In such cases the justice will write a "concurring opinion." Justices who joined the majority opinion may write to add to or to clarify something in the majority opinion.

• Dissenting Opinions. A justice who disagrees with the result in the case may simply note the disagreement, or he or she may choose to write a "dissenting opinion." Unlike the majority opinion, a dissent does not have the force of law. Nevertheless, it may have a considerable impact on the law, perhaps by highlighting flaws in the majority opinion or by making a forceful argument that will influence the thinking of a future Court.

As you read the opinions, you will find it helpful to assess them in light of the three themes—interpretive, normative, and comparative—we identified in the text introduction. Every opinion, for example, adopts one or more methods of constitutional interpretation. Similarly, in every opinion the justices wrestle—sometimes explicitly—with the political theory and ideals that inform the Constitution and give it meaning.

Comparative Perspectives

Although its antecedents are ancient, the practice of judicial review is essentially an American invention. The Supreme Court's power to review legislation for its constitutionality, whether a consequence of decision or evolution, has struck many observers as the very essence of constitutional democracy. Consequently, the Court has served as a model, both of attraction and repulsion, for many other countries. In *Democracy in America*, Alexis de Tocqueville praised the institution, but in the nineteenth century few Europeans shared his enthusiasm for a strong judicial body equipped with the power of constitutional review. In France and many other civil law jurisdictions the process of democratization resulted in a profound distrust of judicial power and judges, who were often associated with reactionary or aristocratic elements of society. The introduction of judicial review was easier in Latin and South America, although the transplant did not often take.

In the twentieth century, especially following World War II and later the collapse of the Iron Curtain, judicial review and constitutional courts became common. Constitutional democracy and the structures associated with it blossomed in the latter half of the century, so much so that some scholars have argued that the expansion of judicial review is one of the distinguishing features of contemporary political life.[24]

The popularity of constitutionalism has contributed to the spread of judicial review and constitutional courts. More than one hundred countries have constitutions that provide for judicial review, at least on paper. Constitutional courts exercise power, with varying degrees of success, in Canada, Germany, Spain, Italy, Austria, Israel, India, Australia, Venezuela, Japan, Ireland, South Africa, Eritrea, Uruguay, Brazil, Colombia, and in many other countries. In the former Eastern bloc countries of Europe, there are new constitutional courts in the Czech Republic, Hungary, Poland, Ukraine, and elsewhere.[25] Indeed, the idea has proven so persuasive that in Europe there are two supranational tribunals with the power of constitutional review. The European Court of Justice, established in 1952, enforces the Treaty of the European Economic Community. The European Court of Human Rights, established in 1953, enforces the European Convention on Human Rights and Fundamental Freedoms. The Court of Human Rights consists of 41 judges, equal to the number of countries that have signed on to the convention. The court sits in 4 chambers of 7 judges each, and

---

[24] C. Neal Tate and Torbjorn Vallinder, "The Globalization of Judicial Power: The Judicialization of Politics," in Tate and Vallinder, *The Global Expansion of Judicial Power.* (New York: New York University Press, 1995), 5.

[25] A form of judicial review has even made its appearance in England, the traditional bastion of parliamentary supremacy. Under the Human Rights Act of 1998, English courts have been empowered to declare laws null and void—i.e., unconstitutional—as would be possible in Germany, Canada, and the United States. When an English court makes such a ruling, the case is tossed back to Parliament, which then has the option of repealing the law or reaffirming the statute.

three judge committees conduct the initial screening of cases. Especially difficult or contentious cases are heard by a 17-judge Grand Chamber, in a process somewhat analogous to *en banc* judgments in the United States Circuit Courts. As we shall see in later chapters, the Convention includes a number of far-reaching guarantees for the protection of civil liberties, including guarantees of freedom of expression (Article 10), the right to a fair trial (Article 6), and respect for private and family life (Article 8).

Why have constitutional courts become so popular? The appeal is partly practical. Many countries have come to see judicial review as a mechanism for protecting democracy and human rights. The appeal is also political: In an era when appeals to many other forms of political legitimacy, such as communism and organic statism, have lost much of their attraction, the forms of constitutional democracy have become common currency.

Broadly speaking, we can identify two systems of judicial review—or two different kinds of constitutional courts—one based on the American experience, the other based on the European model.[26] The models differ in the structure, methods, and effects of judicial review.[27] Even within the two species, though, there is wide room for variation. Different constitutions provide for different judicial structures and kinds of organizations, for different procedures, and for different methods of appointing and removing justices. As you consider the following materials, it may be useful to consider whether these different arrangements shed light on the assumptions we make about the purposes and problems of constitutionalism, of the best way to structure the polity, and of human nature.

Generalized or Specialized Jurisdiction

The American Supreme Court is a court of general jurisdiction. It may hear a wide range of cases, many of which raise no constitutional issue at all. Its jurisdiction extends to all areas of public law, including administrative law, federal statutory law, and admiralty. It may also hear private law cases, such as torts or contracts that raise no questions of public import.

In contrast, many constitutional courts in other constitutional democracies have only special, or limited jurisdiction. These courts, such as the Federal Constitutional Court of Germany and the Italian Constitutional Court, hear only cases that raise constitutional issues. They do not hear private law cases unless they raise an issue of constitutional interpretation. Their limited jurisdiction means these courts do not have the appellate jurisdiction that makes up such a prominent part of the United States Supreme Court's jurisdiction. Similarly, they do not sit at the top of an elaborate judicial hierarchy, as does the American Court. Instead, they exist alongside or outside of the hierarchy of ordinary courts.

Which system is better suited to constitutional democracy? Some scholars have argued that the American system of generalized and diffuse review makes the Constitution more public and accessible. Others have suggested that systems of centralized and specialized review permit judges to develop a measure of expertise in questions

---

[26] See generally Mauro Cappelletti, *The Judicial Process in Comparative Perspective.* (Oxford Clarendon Press, 1989); A.R. Brewer-Carias, *Judicial Review in Comparative Law.* (Cambridge: Cambridge University Press, 1989); Louis Favoreu, "American and European Models of Constitutional Justice," in D.S. Clark, ed., *Essays in Honor of J.H. Merryman.* (Berlin: Duncker & Humblot, 1990).

[27] Favoreu, note 26 at 111–115.

constitutional, as well as a superior sense of how to achieve coherence in constitutional jurisprudence more generally.[28]

Centralized and Decentralized Systems of Constitutional Review

In the European model (sometimes called the Austrian model), only specialized constitutional courts have the power to resolve constitutional controversies. These courts usually do not share the power of review with lower courts. Hence the power of review is centralized or concentrated in a single court. The most prominent example of a centralized system with a court of specialized jurisdiction is the Federal Republic of Germany. Created in 1951, the Federal Constitutional Court has served as a model for similar courts in Hungary, Russia, Poland, and the Czech Republic.

Even within systems of centralized review there are significant differences. The German Court may hear constitutional controversies brought by various branches and officers of the state and national governments, as well as disputes submitted by individual citizens. The Italian Court, in contrast, can hear cases only if they are brought by one of the branches of government or if a judge on a lower court certifies them. The Italian model is the more common in Europe, though there are provisions for individual complaints in Austria, Belgium, Hungary, and in Spain, the latter through an elaborate procedure called an "amparo." The amparo allows individuals and "defenders of the people" to file a complaint against an administrative or judicial act (but not directly against a statute), but the Constitutional Court itself must decide that the cause raises a constitutional question.

The American model is characterized by decentralized, or diffuse, review. The Supreme Court shares its power to hear constitutional cases with other federal and state courts. Moreover, constitutional review takes place only in the context of a concrete case. Implicit in the two models are different understandings about the demands of federalism and how the relationship between the center and periphery should be moderated by judicial structures. As we saw, this issue was a source of great conflict at the Philadelphia Convention in 1789. It remains one of the great sources of conflict in contemporary constitutional regimes. As discussed in chapter 3, differences in the structure and makeup of constitutional courts and systems of constitutional review also reflect different understandings about which governmental actors bear primary responsibility for safeguarding and protecting the Constitution.

The Effects of Judicial Review

In every case that comes before a court, the court's decision is binding on the parties to the case. The decision, in other words, binds *inter partes*. If a decision binds all other actors, even those not party to the suit, we say that the decision binds *erga omnes*. As mentioned earlier, in the United States, there is always room for question about whether any particular decision is *inter partes* or *erga omnes*. In some other constitutions, the text plainly indicates whether a decision binds the parties alone. The decisions of the Federal Constitutional Court of the German Republic bind *erga omnes*, as do the decisions of the Austrian Supreme Court and the Italian Constitutional Court. The Canadian Charter provides that most decisions of the Supreme

---

[28] It may be worth noting, however, that the United States Supreme Court's increasing ability to control its own docket may, with time, have the effect of making it look more like the specialized constitutional courts of some other countries.

Court may in certain cases be overridden by the national legislature and sometimes by provincial legislatures. As the Canadian case makes clear, behind the technical issues of *inter partes* and *erga omnes* are fundamental political questions about how to weigh the balance between judicial protection of individual liberty and respect for popular rule and democratic ideals.

Differences in Judicial Opinions

In the United States, judicial opinions are often long, elaborately reasoned, and argued in unique and highly stylized ways. Judges and justices frequently write for themselves, either in concurring opinions or dissents, and they do not hesitate to criticize other opinions, sometimes very harshly. In other countries, though, it is not unusual to find very short opinions that simply announce a conclusion or provide only sparse accounts of the reasoning the justices used to reach their conclusion. Similarly, there are courts where the use of separate opinions is rare and discouraged. As we shall see in chapter 2, the interpretive styles of courts vary widely as well.

Methods of Judicial Appointment and Terms of Office

One of the most striking differences among constitutional courts is the method used for appointing and removing justices. Behind these differences are different assumptions about the purposes and limits of judicial power, and of the relationship between constitutionalism and democracy. In general, judicial appointments, especially in parliamentary systems, are an elaborate affair, entrusted in large measure to legislative bodies. The Italian Constitutional Court, for example, has fifteen judges, five nominated by the President, five by Parliament, and five by the highest state courts. The term of appointment is for nine years, with no reappointment allowed. The German Court has sixteen judges, divided into two distinct chambers. The lower house of the German legislature appoints one-half of the justices, and the upper house appoints the other half. Terms are for twelve years, with no reappointment. In Austria the President, acting upon the recommendation of the National and Federal Councils, appoints the fourteen members of the Court. There are similar processes in Belgium, Spain, and Portugal.[29]

Perhaps the most notable contrast between the foregoing systems and the United States is that the justices on these other courts do not hold life-time appointments. In the United States, life-time appointments are generally thought to be a critical means of ensuring judicial independence. It is worth considering how unusual the American practice is: Most other constitutional democracies have devised other means of ensuring judicial independence, such as immunity from prosecution, salary guarantees, autonomy over budgets and internal administrative matters, as well as prohibitions against intervention by government ministries. No less important, limited appointments reflect a judgment that judicial independence must be weighed against the equally compelling demands of democratic and popular accountability.[30]

---

[29] See generally Vicki Jackson & Mark Tushnet, *Comparative Constitutional Law* (New York: Foundation Press, 1999), 455–542.

[30] See Cappelletti, supra note 26 at 83–86.

These alternative arrangements should lead us to think about a number of assumptions most students of American constitutional law take for granted. Is life tenure really necessary to guarantee judicial independence? What, if any, are the costs of life tenure, and why have so many other constitutional democracies chosen other devices? And, perhaps more importantly, is the judicial independence won by life tenure necessarily a positive feature of American constitutionalism?

Conclusion

Although the ideas of judicial review and constitutional courts find their source in the American Supreme Court, other countries have not slavishly duplicated American practice. For the most part, the European model of specialized judicial review has been the more persuasive. In part, the aversion to the American model has stemmed from different understandings about the meaning of separation of powers and equality under law, as well as differences occasioned by the predominance of parliamentarianism rather than presidential regimes.

The prestige and influence of constitutional courts varies. Some of them, such as the German and the Canadian, have attained considerable influence and are important, persuasive voices in their countries. Other courts, especially in Latin America and the newly democratic states of Eastern Europe, are still embryonic.

All of them, however, wrestle with the same kinds of issues and questions that dominate American constitutional interpretation. The great similarity of issues and problems that dominate constitutional politics in all countries are a testimony to what is universal in human life. But if the themes are much the same, the approaches to resolving these questions vary widely in constitutional democracies. As we shall see throughout this book, an appreciation of what we share with and how we differ from others can be a powerful tool for understanding constitutional interpretation in the United States.

Selected Bibliography

Abraham, Henry J. 1999. *Justices, Presidents, and Senators.* Lanham, Md.: Rowman & Littlefield.

Barnum, David G. 1992. *The Supreme Court and American Democracy.* New York: St. Martin's Press.

Baum, Lawrence. 2000. *The Supreme Court.* 7th ed. Washington, D.C.: CQ Press.

Bloch, Susan Low and Thomas G. Krattenmaker, eds. 1994. *Supreme Court Politics: The Institution and Its Procedures.* St. Paul, Minn.: West Publishing Company.

Cooper, Phillip J. 1999. *Battles on the Bench: Conflict Inside the Supreme Court.* Lawrence: University Press of Kansas.

Cooper, Phillip J. and Howard Ball. 1996. *The United States Supreme Court: From the Inside Out.* Upper Saddle River, N.J.: Prentice Hall.

Epstein, Lee and Jack Knight. 1997. *The Choices Justices Make.* Washington, D.C.: Congressional Quarterly Press.

Gibson, J. L., G.A. Caldeira, V. A. Baird. 1998 *On the Legitimacy of National High Courts,* American Political Science Review 92: 343.

Hall, Kermit, ed. 2001. *The Oxford Guide to United States Supreme Court Decisions.* New York: Oxford University Press.

Irons, Peter H. and Howard Zinn, eds. 2000. *A People's History of the Supreme Court.* New York: Penguin Press.

Lazarus, Edward. 1999. *Closed Chambers: The Rise, Fall, and Future of the Modern Supreme Court.* New York: Penguin Press.

Malztman, Forrest, J. F. Spriggs II, P. J. Wahlbeck. 2000. *Crafting Law on the Supreme Court: The Collegial Game.* Cambridge: Cambridge University Press.

McCloskey, Robert and Sanford Levinson. 2000. *The American Supreme Court.* Rev. ed. Chicago: University of Chicago Press.

Murphy, Walter. 1964. *Elements of Judicial Strategy.* Chicago: University of Chicago Press.

Pacelle, Richard L. 2001. *The Supreme Court in American Politics: The Least Dangerous Branch.* Boulder, Colo.: Westview Press.

Perry, Barbara A., ed. 2001. *The Supremes: Essays on the Cur-*

rent Justices of the Supreme Court of the United States. New York: Peter Lang.

Perry, H. W., Jr. 1991. *Deciding to Decide: Agenda Setting in the United States Supreme Court.* Cambridge: Harvard University Press.

Provine, Doris Marie. 1980. *Case Selection in the United States Supreme Court.* Chicago: University of Chicago Press.

Rehnquist, William H. 2002. *The Supreme Court: How It Was, How It Is.* Rev. ed. New York: Vintage Books.

Schwartz, Bernard. 1993. *A History of the Supreme Court.* New York: Oxford University Press.

Tribe, Lawrence. 1985. *God Save This Honorable Court: How the Choice of Supreme Court Justices Shapes Our History.* New York: Random House.

Van Geel, T. R. 1996. *Understanding Supreme Court Opinions.* 3rd ed. New York: Longman.

Selected Comparative Bibliography

Brewer-Carias, A. R. 1989. *Judicial Review in Comparative Law.* Cambridge: Cambridge University Press.

Cappelletti, Mauro. 1989. *The Judicial Process in Comparative Perspective.* Oxford: Oxford University Press.

Jackson, Vicki C. and Mark Tushnet. 1999. *Comparative Constitutional Law.* New York: Foundation Press.

Howe, Paul and Peter H. Russell, eds. 2001. *Judicial Power and Canadian Democracy.* Montreal: McGill-Queen's University Press.

Herbert, Jacob, et al. 1996. *Courts, Law, and Politics in Comparative Perspective.* New Haven: Yale University Press.

Kavass, Igor I., ed. 1992. *Supranational and Constitutional Courts in Europe: Functions and Sources.* Buffalo: William S. Hein & Co., Inc.

Markesinis, Basil S., ed. 1998. *The Impact of the Human Rights Bill on English Law.* Oxford: Oxford University Press.

Schwartz, Herman. 2000. *The Struggle for Constitutional Justice in Post-Communist Europe.* Chicago: University of Chicago Press.

Sweet, Alec Stone. 2000. *Governing with Judges: Constitutional Politics in Europe.* Oxford: Oxford University Press.

Tate, C. Neal and Torbjorn Vallinder. 1995. *The Global Expansion of Judicial Power.* New York: New York University Press.

Chapter 2

The Constitution and Its Interpretation

The Constitution

Thomas Reed Powell once advised his first year students in the Harvard Law School not to read the Constitution because it would only confuse them. We would prefer to ignore his legendary advice and advise students to read the document before they plunge into the "why and what" of interpretation. In doing so, they should not overlook the importance of the preamble, for it lays out the broad purposes of the Constitution among which is the creation of "a more perfect union" to secure the "Blessings of Liberty" and the achievement of "justice." Nor should we overlook the significance of its opening line, "We the People of the United States," words that prompt us to ask who the framers meant by the "people"? We know they excluded some people, such as slaves. But did they exclude others? An equally important question is why we are the "we" of the preamble. Because we who live today tacitly consent to be bound by the Constitution? Because we are citizens or voters? Because we as a people are committed to a given political ideology? Or because we share certain values and want to foster preferred ways of life? (Each of these possibilities implicates the manner in which the Constitution might be interpreted.)

Related questions may be asked about the content and scope of the Constitution as a whole. Is it more than the original document ratified in 1789, along with its 27 amendments? Or does it also include extra-textual practices and traditions that define Americans as a people? Does it include values or beliefs or written sources apart from the documentary text? The Constitution, for example, was drafted in the long shadow of the Declaration of Independence, an American revolutionary confession of faith that certain self-evident truths must be respected by any government established on these shores. Should the Constitution accordingly be interpreted in the light of its values? If so, what indeed are its "truths" and what does it mean to say that Americans "hold" them and why do they regard them as "self-evident"? Whatever meaning is extracted from its terms, the Declaration is arguably an integral part of the American constitutional tradition and thus worthy of study and analysis in its own right.[1] (See Appendix A for the text of the Declaration.)

---

[1] Similarly, as Edward Corwin reminds us, principles of higher law or natural justice were commonly accepted by the founders, and many of these principles worked their way into the Supreme Court's interpretation of the original Constitution. See Edward S. Corwin, *The Higher Law Background of American Constitutional Law*, 42 Harvard Law Review 149–85; 365–409,(1928). In 1898, Justice Henry Brown

In Lincoln's memorable metaphor, it is an "apple of gold" surrounded by the Constitution's "picture of silver."[2]

On the other hand, not everything in the written text is regarded today as part of our "living" constitution. Some constitutional provisions, like muscles that have atrophied from disuse, have lost their vitality. A prominent example is the provision of the Fourteenth Amendment that requires Congress to reduce a state's congressional delegation proportionate to the number of citizens denied the right to vote in federal elections. To the extent that such provisions are ignored or unenforced, they cannot be said to have been a normative part of the Constitution.[3]

For present purposes, however, we may confine our attention to the documentary text. First, we might observe that the framers wrote the Constitution for ordinary people and thus with only a few exceptions refrained from using arcane language or the irritating "legalese" often found in statutory law, legal contracts and, alas, even in the decisions of the Supreme Court. Unlike many American state and nearly all foreign constitutions, they also shunned the minutiae of excessive detail. They produced a document distinguished not only for its graceful style but also for its judicious use of language broad and flexible enough to withstand the changes of time and circumstance. John Marshall captured the genius of the framers' accomplishment when he remarked in *McCulloch v. Maryland* that "we must never forget, that it is a *constitution* we are expounding"—that is, one marked by "its great outlines" and "important objects" unburdened by the "the prolixity of a legal code [that] would probably never be understood by the public."[4]

The original document is composed of seven articles, most of them comparatively short. The first three articles establish the branches of the national government, specifying their structures and powers, while the remaining articles lay down, respectively, the duties the states owe each other, procedures for amending the Constitution, the rule affirming the supremacy of the Constitution and laws of the United States, and the method by which the Constitution is to be ratified. These structures and procedures embody the main principles of American constitutionalism: They include federalism, separation of powers, checks and balances, the rule of law, government by consent, and republican government. (Judicial review, which is also a fundamental principle of American constitutionalism, emerged from *Marbury v. Madison* [1803] and its progeny.) In addition, the Constitution identifies three sources of power, namely, the national government, the individual states, and the people. The national

---

struck a familiar note when he wrote that "the object of the first eight amendments to the Constitution was to incorporate into the fundamental law of the land certain principles of natural justice." See *Brown v. Walker*, 161 U.S. 591 (1896). In the same vein, Supreme Court justices have often appealed to the moral and ethical values of society in resolving difficult constitutional issues.

[2] *The Collected Works of Abraham Lincoln*, Vol. IV, ed., Roy Basler (New Brunswick, NJ: Rutgers University Press, 1953), p. 169.

[3] More recently, constitutional scholars have even debated whether the Twenty-seventh Amendment, ratified in 1992, belongs in the Constitution. The provision requires a congressional election to intervene between the passage of a law raising the salaries of senators and representatives and its going into effect. Proposed in 1789, it was ratified 203 years later after some 38 states had approved the measure between 1979 and 1992. Because the proposed amendment—initially introduced by James Madison—lay dormant for nearly 200 years, some scholars urged that it had "died" and therefore could not legitimately be part of the Constitution unless proposed by a new Congress and submitted once again for ratification by the states. See the discussion of the circumstances surrounding the adoption of the 27th Amendment in Paul Brest, Sanford Levinson, Jack Balkin, and Akhil Amar, *Processes of Constitutional Decisionmaking*, 4th ed. (Boston: Little, Brown and Company, 2000), pages 393–397.

[4] 17 U.S. (4 Wheat.) 316, 407 (1819).

government is one of enumerated or limited powers while the Tenth Amendment reserves all other powers "to the States respectively, or to the people." Under the Ninth Amendment, the people alone reserve to themselves certain rights that remain unspecified in the documentary text.

As for specified rights, the first eight amendments to the Constitution include a list of personal freedoms that Congress may not infringe, including numerous procedural guarantees in criminal investigations and prosecutions. The main body of the Constitution also enhances liberty by prohibiting bills of attainder and ex post facto laws, not to mention its ban on suspending the privilege of habeas corpus unless "the public Safety may require it." Finally, ten of the seventeen amendments added to the Constitution since the incorporation of the Bill of Rights (i.e., Amendments I through X) have served either to expand the right to vote—resulting in universal adult suffrage—or to enhance the general principle of popular representation in government.

The expansion of popular government through the amendatory process has in fact transformed the American polity from what was originally a limited representative republic into a modern political democracy. Democracy, however remains conceptually in tension with the idea of constitutionalism. If the essence of democracy is universal suffrage combined with majority rule, then the people through their representatives are entitled to write their policy preferences into law. As Lincoln succinctly put it in his elegant Gettysburg Address, ours is a "government of, by, and for the people." Chief Justice John Marshall, on the other hand, regarded the Constitution as a superior legal norm that limits what the people may legislate. Lincoln's democracy and Marshall's constitutionalism may embrace each other in certain contexts but they collide in many cases before the Supreme Court. (This tension between the two ideals, as noted in our general introduction, is a major theme of this coursebook.)

The Why and What of Constitutional Interpretation

In *Texas v. Johnson* (1989), the controversial flag-burning case, Justice Anthony Kennedy wrote, "The hard fact is that sometimes we must make decisions we do not like. We make them because they are right, right in the sense that the law and the Constitution, as we see them, compel the result. And so great is our commitment to the process that, except in rare cases, we do not pause to express our distaste for the result, perhaps for fear of undermining a valued principle that dictates the decision." Justice Felix Frankfurter made a similar point when he spoke of the "awful task of judging." In the United States, unlike in some other constitutional democracies, the justices of the Supreme Court have many duties other than interpreting the Constitution, for the Court sits at the top of a hierarchy of federal and state courts. Its business as an appellate court includes responsibility for making final decisions in a wide variety of cases that ordinarily have nothing to do with the Constitution.

It is in constitutional cases, however, where the awful task of judging weighs most heavily. The burden is great in part because the responsibility is profound and far-reaching. Every year the Court must decide cases that raise issues of fundamental importance to us all. But the burden is great too because the Justices must often tease what Justice Kennedy called "right answers" from materials as enigmatic as a Jackson Pollack painting. The search for right answers would be far easier, and of less consequence, if the Constitution simply and clearly told us what they are. In many cases, the Constitution does speak clearly and precisely. It is easy to overstate its indeterminacy. A nominee for the presidency must be thirty-five or older, candidates for the Senate thirty years, and for the House twenty-five; presidential elections are held at prescribed times; and all states, large and small, are equally represented in the United States Senate.

The specificity of these provisions contrasts sharply with other parts of the text. What do the Fifth and Fourteenth Amendments mean by "due process of law"? What does "equal protection" of the law mean? When is a search and seizure "unreasonable"? What makes a punishment "cruel and unusual" or a bail "excessive"? When the Court is asked to apply these general guarantees to specific cases it is engaged in an act of interpretation—that is, an effort to discern what these expanding phrases require or prohibit in ordinary life. In this sense, constitutional interpretation is the process we use to give concrete expression to the ideals and values contained in the Constitution.

One of the difficulties in this definition of interpretation is that it tells us nothing about "the process" itself. It suggests, if it does not say, that constitutional interpretation is a routine, mechanical matter. Some justices have seemed to agree. In a well-known opinion, Justice Roberts described constitutional interpretation this way:

> *When an act of Congress is appropriately challenged in the court as not conforming to the constitutional mandate, the judicial branch . . . has only one duty; to lay the article of the Constitution which is invoked beside the statute which is challenged and to decide whether the latter squares with the former. All the court does, or can do, is to announce its considered judgment upon the question. The only power it has, if such it may be called, is the power of judgment.*[5]

One would never guess from Roberts' description that constitutional interpretation involves an element of doubt and indecision. Sometimes the "article invoked" seems to conflict with some other part of the constitutional text. Sometimes it is so hopelessly and wonderfully vague that it appears to say nothing at all—or perhaps worse, too much. In hard cases constitutional interpretation demands insight, creativity and, not least, political acumen. And if, as Justice Kennedy claimed, constitutional interpretation is really about finding "right answers," and not simply stating one's preferences, then it demands also that we have some understanding of the polity the Constitution seeks to invent. It requires, in other words, an appreciation of the ends it seeks to achieve and the means it adopts to achieve those ends. Constitutional interpretation, in this larger sense, is an ongoing act of self-definition.

For reasons we shall briefly explore, interpretation is a practical necessity. We should not forget, however, that the practice rests on an important, indeed critical assumption. When we say interpretation is necessary, we mean first that it must occur because the constitutional text gives us less than complete guidance. In such cases, we might choose simply to disregard the Constitution. When we interpret, however, we accept that the Constitution should guide our collective behavior. The act of interpretation is an act of fidelity, a decision to become citizens of the constitutional order and to order our collective affairs according to its ideals and terms.

Constitutional interpretation is thus simultaneously a choice and a necessity: a choice because we may choose not to bother; a necessity because, having chosen to be governed by the Constitution, it is not always obvious how it is to govern us. The causes of the Constitution's vagueness are not difficult to find. First, as James Madison noted in *Federalist* 37, "When the Almighty himself condescends to address mankind in their own language, his meaning, luminous as it must be, is rendered dim and doubtful by the cloudy medium through which it is communicated." Language is an imprecise and imperfect means of communication. Words have many meanings and sometimes their meanings change over time.

---

[5] *United States v. Butler*, 297 U.S. 1 (1936).

For some, this imprecision is viewed as providing judges with many opportunities to pursue the political agenda reflective of their socio-economic position in American society. Madisonian realism about the limits of linguistic precision is elaborated to describe an interpretive reality of radical indeterminacy. A text that means nothing can mean anything. Legal scholars associated with the Critical Legal Studies movement have insisted that the underlying assumptions of liberal constitutionalism—that a rationally-bounded system of written restraints could control the arbitrariness of much political decision-making—are fundamentally flawed. Moreover, they claim, it is in the interest of those who stand to gain through the malleability of legal forms to conceal the reality of indeterminacy from public view. This they do through the development of various interpretive strategies that misleadingly project the virtues of neutrality and objectivity. The accuracy of such claims is a hotly contested subject among legal theorists, and will remain so as long as ambiguity exists in the constitutional document.

But ambiguity is not simply an unavoidable consequence of imperfect communication. A second cause of imprecision is a deliberate choice by the founders to use elastic words and phrases. Conflict among the delegates about many important issues was resolved by finding language sufficiently pliant to let all parties think they might win the issue at some later point. The most litigated of these elastic phrases are contained in the Fourteenth Amendment. They include the guarantee of "equal protection" and the command that forbids the states from "depriv[ing] any person of life, liberty, or property, without due process of law." Just what "life," "liberty," and "due process" mean has bedeviled the Court for decades, and its attempt to specify what they do mean are among its most controversial decisions.

A third, and related, cause of imprecision rests in the nature of constitution making itself. Although the founders did not claim that that the new constitution would exist "in perpetuity," as had the framers of the Articles of Confederation, they were acutely aware that they were constructing a political order that would endure through time. Many of the Constitution's most important provisions, in the words of Ronald Dworkin, refer to general "concepts" and not to specific "conceptions."[6] The 8th Amendment's prohibition of "cruel and unusual punishments," for example, represents a choice by the founders to enshrine a general concept of fairness. They might have chosen instead to simply list those punishments they thought were cruel and unusual, or to give us specific conceptions about what fairness means in particular cases. Instead, each generation must find for itself what the concept means.

Another cause of vagueness is similarly related to the nature of the constitutional enterprise. Constitutional democracies are committed to a number of values. The preamble tells us, as noted earlier, that the Constitution promises the "Blessings of Liberty" and in a context of a more perfect union capable of promoting the general welfare. These goals, or ends, are not always compatible with each other. At times the general welfare is in tension with liberty. It was inevitable that a Constitution committed to these ideals would find it necessary to adopt the vague language of compromise. In addition, the founders could not have foreseen every contingency and problem, and so the text they gave us is incomplete and imperfect.

For reasons both unavoidable and desirable, then, the Constitution requires interpretation if it is to be realized. The reasons that give rise to the need for interpretation—human imperfection, the need for compromise, and a multiplicity of

---

[6] See Ronald Dworkin, *Taking the Constitution Seriously* (Cambridge: Harvard University Press, 1977), 134–36.

ideals—also make the process of interpretation difficult and complex. The complexity is heightened when we see that in the United States, especially, questions about constitutional interpretation often overlap with contentious questions about the nature and limits of judicial power in a constitutional democracy. These questions are so closely related that many students of the Constitution treat them as though they were just one question. One definition of constitutional interpretation, for example, holds that it "is concerned with the justification, standards, and methods by which a court exercises the power of judicial review."[7] There is much to commend in this definition, not least that it combines constitutional interpretation with judicial power.

We would stress, however, that constitutional interpretation is not necessarily the same thing as judicial review. When the Court exercises the power of judicial review, it does indeed interpret the Constitution, but interpretation is not an exclusively judicial function. It is a function performed also—and often—by legislators, administrative officials, police officers, constitutional scholars, journalists, and even citizens who write letters to the editor.

Matters are complicated too because constitutional interpretation takes place within a larger political environment, one that includes a great number of institutional, cultural, and social factors, any one of which can influence an interpretor. Moreover, interpretation is itself a political act—that is, an exercise of political power. One need not share the radical perspective of Critical Legal Studies proponents to appreciate that the Court is intricately caught up in the basic stuff of politics and it frequently decides who gets what, when, and how much.[8] As we saw in chapter 1, there are a variety of constitutional provisions relating to the Court that acknowledge its status as a political actor.

In a larger sense, the activity of interpretation—as opposed to its results—is also fundamentally political because it represents a collective, deliberative choice to exercise power through reason. The Court's practice of supporting its decisions with written opinions that justify and explain the result reflect a commitment, grounded in constitutional theory, to consensual instead of coercive politics. A written opinion, like a written constitution, represents an effort to engage and to persuade.

The effort to persuade tells us something, too, about the requirements of "good" or "correct" interpretation. A good interpretation must ground its reading of the Constitution *in* the Constitution or trace it to the Constitution. Some kinds of interpretive methods are surely out of bounds. An interpretation that says simply "give me that" is not an interpretation. The opinion must be expanded to include a rational basis for what is said: For example, "Give me that, it belongs to me" or "it's part of my inheritance." Constitutional jurisprudence, like the legal enterprise generally, begins when "discourse is expanded to include a rational basis for what is said."[9]

Sources and Methods of Interpretation

When we examine various methods of interpretation, it is well worth asking what we are looking for. We have seen why interpretation is necessary, but once this threshold is passed we have to ask whether we can distinguish between right and wrong, or better and worse, methods of interpretation. What criteria of interpretation shall be

---

[7] Craig R. Ducat and Harold W. Chase, *Constitutional Interpretation*, 5th ed. (St. Paul, MN: West Publishing Co., 1992), p. 82.

[8] Harold Lasswell, *Politics: Who Gets What, When, How* (New York: McGraw Hill, 1936).

[9] Robert E. Rodes, Jr., *The Legal Enterprise* (Port Washington, N.Y.: Kennikat Press, 1976), p. 22.

used and where do they come from? Surprisingly, these questions receive less attention than they deserve. To begin with, we would hope that interpretation takes seriously the fact that we have a written constitution. Second, we would hope that a
judicial opinion interpreting the Constitution is one that the public can understand.
Citizens have a right, grounded in democratic thought, to know what their judges are
saying about the Constitution's meaning and why. Finally, we would hope that in
interpreting the Constitution, judges recognize the limits of their power and find
some way to curtail their discretion.

To limit its role in deciding constitutional cases, the Supreme Court often follows
guidelines known as the *Ashwander* rules. (They are discussed in greater detail in
chapter 3.) These rules are really canons of restraint. Out of respect for the principle
of separated powers, they exhort the Supreme Court to presume the constitutionality
of legislative acts, to reach constitutional issues last not first, and never to anticipate
a constitutional question in advance of the necessity of deciding it. The rules reflect
the seriousness of any judicial decision that interprets the Constitution since there is
no way to get around a constitutional decision unless—short of noncompliance—the
Constitution is amended or the Supreme Court changes its mind. Relatedly, by observing these rules, the Court pays proper respect for the results of the democratic
political process.

Beyond these general guidelines, however, scholars and justices have developed
a number of mechanisms or methods of interpretation to discern the Constitution's
meaning. Taking a written constitution seriously means that interpretation must always begin with the constitutional text. But it must also account for omissions, con-
tradictions, and imperfections in the text. The following methods are most frequently
used in constitutional argument, both on and off the Court. We shall encounter them
as we read the cases. Justices rarely if ever commit themselves to just one of these
methods. Instead, they typically take an eclectic, pragmatic approach, using one here
and one there, or using several together, as circumstances warrant.

Textualism

Textualism is based on the unremarkable claim that constitutional interpretation must
begin with the written word. As Antonin Scalia, the justice on the current Supreme
Court most committed to this approach, has written, "The text is the law, and it is the
text that must be observed."[10] At times, the words of the Constitution are sufficiently
plain that they do provide an answer without recourse to any other source of meaning. Sometimes called the "plain words" approach, advocates of textualism claim that
we should read the words of the Constitution for their ordinary meaning and apply
them accordingly. Justice Joseph Story wrote in his celebrated *Commentaries on the
Constitution*, "It is obvious that there can be no security to the people in any constitution of government if they are not to judge of it by the fair meaning of the words of
the text."[11] Story's insistence on "plain" meaning was grounded on what Philip Bobbitt has called an "ongoing social contract, whose terms are given their contemporary
meanings continually reaffirmed by the refusal of the People to amend the instru-

---

[10] Antonin Scalia, "Common Law Courts in a Civil-Law System: The Role of United States Federal Courts in
Interpreting the Constitution and Laws," in *A Matter of Interpretation: Federal Courts and the Law*
(Princeton: Princeton University Press, 1997) p. 22.

[11] *Commentaries on the Constitution of the United States*, Vol. I (New York: De Capo Press, 1970), s. 407,
p. 390, n. 1.

ment."[12] It was grounded also—as are all theories of interpretation—in a specific conception of judicial power. As Bobbitt notes, "Story believed that this obligation to apply contemporary meanings constrained judges; one cannot appeal to superior learning to establish the meaning of a common phrase."[13]

The textual approach, however, is also profoundly limited. First, and most troublesome, is that in a great many places the words of the text are anything but clear. Indeed, it is this lack of clarity that necessitates interpretation in the first place. Or words may admit of several meanings. In such cases, which meaning is to govern? Worse, there are some provisions, such as the Ninth Amendment, that by their very terms seem to call for a method of interpretation that reaches beyond the text. The text of the Ninth Amendment, for example—once referred to by Judge Bork as an "ink blot"[14]—seems to counsel interpreters to reach beyond the text. In addition, the common sense meaning of constitutional provisions sometimes fail to catch or appreciate the way that the concepts behind those words have changed or have grown more complex with time. To put it bluntly, the common sense meanings of words are often limited or simplistic. Finally, the textual method of constitutional interpretation fails to account for the many cases where constitutional words or phrases conflict with one another.

Original History

Some judges and scholars have argued that the aim of constitutional interpretation is to discover what the founders "intended" the provision at hand to mean. Once discovered, intent governs the case. For many people, there is an intuitive appeal to the search for intent. When we seek the meaning of any text we often begin by asking, "what did the author mean"? And like textualism, appeals to intent promise to limit judicial power by putting constraints on what judges may do. Bobbitt writes that this strict intentionalist approach "draws legitimacy from the social contract negotiated from an original position."[15] If, therefore, the Constitution is in fact the supreme law of the land, it must be interpreted in terms of the original will that informs its content. This use of history is usually coupled with an argument rooted in democratic theory. Robert Bork, for example, asserts that out of respect for our political democracy judges must "accept any value choice the legislature makes unless it runs clearly contrary to a choice made in framing the Constitution."[16] Despite these obvious attractions, appeals to the founders' intent as a method of interpretation are subject to a great many reservations. As a practical matter, we have very little evidence about what the founders actually intended. No official record of the Philadelphia Convention exists. Several delegates did take notes, but often they are incomplete, subject to bias, and some may even be forged.[17] And what are we to do when, as is sometimes the case, the fifty-five delegates disagreed with each other or sought compromise. Whose intent governs and why? A similar but even more basic problem points

---

[12] Philip Bobbitt, *Constitutional Fate* (New York: Oxford University Press, 1982), p. 26.

[13] Ibid.

[14] See Walter F. Murphy et al., *American Constitutional Interpretation*, Second Edition (Westbury, NY: The Foundation Press, 1995), p. 385.

[15] Bobbitt, *Constitutional Fate*, p. 26.

[16] See Bork's *Neutral Principles and Some First Amendment Problems*, 47 Indiana Law Journal 10–11 (1971).

[17] Murphy, supra note 14, at 391.

to a fascinating question: Just who, exactly, counts as a founder? All fifty-five delegates? Some did not participate in any meaningful sense; Hamilton even quit the proceedings at one point. And why not consult the intentions of the state ratifying conventions? After all, without those conventions, the Constitution would have no binding force.

One way around some of these problems is to focus less on the founders' intent and instead to search for the "original meaning" of the words of the Constitution as they were used at the time of their drafting. Aids to interpretation would include dictionaries and etymological sources used in 1789. Like original intent, this approach—also favored by Justice Scalia—has much to be said for it. It requires judges to appeal to authoritative sources of meaning outside their personal preferences and thus to "objectify" the process of constitutional interpretation. To some extent, however, all of the difficulties that accompany the search for intent apply, albeit sometimes with less urgency, to originalism. But the move from intent to "original meaning" highlights another difficulty that attends both variations. Why should the Constitution's meaning be a function of what its authors, however broadly defined, intended it to mean? Even if intent could be objectively determined, would Americans as they moved into the twenty-first century want to be governed by prevailing attitudes and definitions of the 18th century or, as some would have it, by the "dead hand of the past."

Still there may be good reasons to undertake some effort to find out what the founders intended when they wrote the Constitution. The founders are an obvious source of great wisdom and insight into the nature and purposes of the constitutional order they created. Many of our problems—concerning the relationship between individual liberty and the common good, or the relationship between executive and legislative power—were their problems. And the basic tools we use both to formulate and to resolve many of those problems are tools they created and bequeathed to us. Consequently, it would be a great mistake not to seek their guidance. But it is important to recognize a distinction between seeking guidance and being bound, by definition, to follow their intentions.

Doctrinalism

Much of contemporary constitutional law consists of "doctrines," or verbal formulas, that the Court uses to decide specific cases. When the Court is examining state legislation that touches a "fundamental right," for example, it applies the "compelling state interest" doctrine. It provides simply that the state must have a "compelling" interest to regulate a fundamental right. But how do we know which rights are fundamental? The Court applies another doctrine—or test: Such a right is one "implicit in the concept of ordered liberty." Doctrinal tests appear in nearly every area of constitutional law, some of which consist of three or four parts.[18] The increasing importance of these doctrines is what prompted Thomas Reed Powell to tell his Harvard students not to read the constitutional text, for it would only confuse their understanding of the case law.

In its purest form, doctrinalism is both a way of deciding cases and a way of

---

[18] The following three-part test, for example, has often been used to determine whether a law violates the First Amendment's Establishment Clause: "First, the statute must have a secular legislative purpose; second, its principal or primary effect must be one that neither advances nor inhibits religion; finally, the statute must not foster 'an excessive government entanglement with religion.'" See *Lemon v. Kurtzman*, 403 U. S. 602 (1971).

organizing constitutional law. Doctrinalism attempts to impose a coherent analytical framework on an entire area of the law, such as equal protection, or no establishment of religion, and to use that overarching order to decide particular cases. The source of these doctrines is an eclectic mix of cases (precedents), logical reasoning, and judicial creativity. Its proponents insist that doctrines help to minimize judicial mischief by constraining discretion. Moreover, they allow for the orderly progression and evolution of the law by striking a middle course between respect for the past and the need for change.

Critics of the approach often begin by noting it is a simple matter to manipulate doctrine to achieve a desired result. Similarly, many of the doctrines are themselves so vague and ambiguous that, instead of providing interpretive guidance, they exacerbate the need for it. For example, what possibly would qualify—or not qualify—as a "compelling state interest" in equal protection analysis? Perhaps the most fundamental objection to doctrinalism, however, is that it may not take the Constitution seriously at all.

This may happen when doctrines and formulas dominate judicial reasoning, which is the meaning of the warning T. R. Powell gave to his students. What may be worse is that these doctrines, formulas or multi-part tests often communicate a false sense of certainty, as if to suggest a right answer will mechanically follow their invocation.[19] Doctrinalism thus runs the risk of substituting verbal tests and formulas for the Constitution. As Justice Black noted, this kind of substitution may result in the expansion of the text's meaning—an expansion Black objected to as simple judicial lawmaking—but it might also result in the contraction of meaning: "One of the most effective ways of diluting or expanding a constitutionally guaranteed right is to substitute for the crucial word or words or a constitutional guarantee another word or words more or less flexible or more or less restricted in meaning. . . ."[20] Another objection to doctrinalism recalls Justice Story's view that the interpretation of constitutional language must center on the ordinary meaning of the words. Implicit in Story's approach was his insistence that the Constitution is ultimately a public document whose meaning must be accessible to any citizen. Complex and changing verbal formulas tend to make the meaning of the Constitution less public and more remote, for few citizens will have the time or the resources to wade through a swampland of doctrine.

Precedent

Closely related to doctrinalism is a method of interpretation called *stare decisis. Stare decisis*—to stand by what has already been decided—is at bottom a doctrine built on the importance of precedent. A precedent is simply a case that has already been decided. *Stare decisis*, then, refers to a method of interpretation that decides current cases by looking at how similar cases were decided in the past. Neither doctrinalism nor precedent are unique to constitutional interpretation. Rather, they are the characteristic methods of legal reasoning in the common law tradition. The great attraction of precedent as a method of interpretation is its promise of consistency and predictability through time. These are critically important values in any system of law. In-

---

[19] Robert F. Nagel, *Constitutional Cultures: The Mentality and Consequences of Judicial Review* (Berkeley: University of California Press, 1989), 12–56.

[20] *Griswold v. Connecticut*, 381 U.S. 497, 486 (1965).

deed, one may well wonder whether the rule of law can exist without them.[21] Like doctrinalism, an appeal to precedent offers stability while leaving room for evolution and change. And like doctrinalism, it constrains judicial discretion.

Unfortunately, appeals to precedent are also subject to a great number of criticisms, some of which will seem familiar. Any good lawyer knows that there is almost always a precedent "out there" to support either side of an issue. To the extent this is true, precedents do little to guide decision-making. Similarly, it is not always clear just what principle a precedent stands for. The precedents themselves demand interpretation. Most critically, and like doctrinalism, precedent as a method of interpretation is subject to the criticism that it does not have much to do with the Constitution. Respect for the Constitution must also mean, as Justice Frankfurter argued, that "the ultimate touchstone of constitutionality is the Constitution itself and not what we have said about it."[22] For this reason, some justices have argued *stare decisis* should carry less weight in constitutional interpretation. Unlike the common law, which has no touchstone but instead develops and evolves in response to felt necessities, constitutional interpretation must revolve around a set of knowable and defined purposes, values, and rules. Especially in constitutional interpretation, therefore, it may be more important to get the case "right" than to follow a wrongly decided precedent to maintain consistency.

Prudentialism

Prudential arguments seem less of an interpretive enterprise than strategies for avoiding a decision in politically sensitive cases or balancing interests in particularly complicated ones. Prudentialism is often identified with the work of Alexander Bickel, who celebrated various "passive virtues," which Bobbitt calls "mediating devices by which the Court can introduce political realities into its decisional process."[23] In appreciation of the judiciary's limited powers under the Constitution and the caution demanded by the so-called counter-majoritarian difficulty—i.e., the problem of reconciling judicial review with democracy—Bickel advised the Court to creatively exploit jurisdictional doctrines such as ripeness, standing, and mootness, together with the judicial application of the political question doctrine. (See chapter 3 for a discussion of these jurisdictional issues.) Each of these rules is a subcategory of the basic concept of justiciability, one designed to ensure, as Chief Justice Earl Warren wrote in *Flast v. Cohen*, that "the business of the federal courts [is limited] to questions presented in an adversary context" and "to assure that the federal courts will not intrude into areas committed to other branches of government."[24]

Bickel felt that a politically unaccountable judiciary has a limited amount of moral and political capital to spend, and that if its voice were to be heeded and respected by the American people, judges should reserve their power to declare legislation unconstitutional only to vindicate the most important values at the foundation of our political system. Justices Frankfurter and Brandeis were among the most prominent of those who advocated prudentialism, though nearly every justice has used it at some point. And in "The Passive Virtues," Bickel argued that "The accomplished fact, affairs and interests that have formed around it, and perhaps popular acceptance

---

[21] See Lon Fuller, *The Morality of Law* (New Haven: Yale University Press, 1964).

[22] *Graves v. New York*, 306 U.S. 466, 491 (1939).

[23] See Bobbitt, *Constitutional Fate*, at 65.

[24] 392 U.S. 83 (1968).

of it—these are elements . . . that may *properly* enter into a decision to abstain from rendering constitutional judgment or to allow room and time for accommodation to such a judgment; and they may also enter into the shaping of the judgment, the applicable principle itself"[25] (emphasis added). The key word here is "properly." Prudentialists insist that it is appropriate that judges should account for prudential considerations in coming to a decision.

Bickel's argument has recently been refined and elaborated by Cass Sunstein, who argues strongly for "judicial minimalism." Believing that the work of the courts should not undermine the polity's commitment to democratic deliberation, Sunstein recommends that judges avoid two temptations: setting broad rules for the future and providing ambitious theoretical justification for judicial outcomes. More often than not, the decision that is narrow (focused on the particular facts of the immediate case) and shallow (uninterested in engaging broad issues of principle) will turn out to be more conducive to advancing the goals of liberal constitutionalism. Additionally, the minimalist ruling is less likely to produce the unintended and unwanted consequences that can easily result from the efforts of judges who often lack relevant information about the issues that come before them for adjudication.

If these are its strengths, the importance of such considerations is also the weakness of prudentialism. Its harshest critics suggest that prudentialism is simply consequentialism dressed in finery. Both, they argue, do violence to the Constitution because they permit the push and pull of politics—not principle, and not the Constitution proper—to determine judicial decision-making. The Constitution, or at least its text, these critics complain, become subordinate to "extraconstitutional" considerations. Moreover, the "weight" attached to these considerations and their relative importance must also be a matter of judgment, a judgment, again, that the Constitution does not speak to.

Structuralism

One of the principles of the American constitutional order is the separation of powers or, as Richard Neustadt put it more appropriately, the existence of separate institutions sharing power. The constitutional document does not contain the phrase "separation of powers," but the very structure of the text—and the larger political order it constitutes—gives life to the principle. As a method of interpretation, structuralism believes that the meaning of individual constitutional provisions can only be discerned by a thorough examination of the entire Constitution. Thus "[s]tructural arguments are inferences from the existence of constitutional structures and the relationships which the Constitution ordains among these structures."[26]

In its narrowest sense, this means we should not focus on the meaning of specific, isolated clauses, but rather on the location of the clause and its interaction with the whole text. In a somewhat broader sense, structuralism seeks unity and coherence not only in the text, but in the larger political order the text signifies. Advocates of this more expansive understanding of structuralism stress the way the constitutional document and the larger political order interact. Judicial review, for example, has been justified on structural grounds since the Supreme Court has the power to hear

---

[25] Alexander M. Bickel, *The Least Dangerous Branch*, 2nd ed. (New Haven: Yale University Press, 1986), 116.

[26] Bobbitt, *Constitutional Fate*, at 74.

cases and controversies arising under a document, one of whose provisions declares the Constitution to be the supreme law of the land.

One of structuralism's strengths is its attention to the Constitution. Unlike doctrinalism or appeals to precedent, its proponents claim, structuralism concentrates on the meaning of the Constitution and not on what has been said about it. On the other hand, structuralism does not do much to lessen the discretion of its practitioners. It is all well and good to see a provision as part of a whole, but just how it fits into the whole, and indeed just what the whole means are themselves open questions, ones that cannot be answered without interpretation. The problems multiply if structuralism moves beyond the text to the political order—that is, any effort to "read" a theory into that order must itself require an act of bold interpretation. Vincent Blasi has offered a similar objection, claiming that agreement about the existence and importance of constitutional structures, or about the desirability of structural understandings of the Constitution, does not tell us very much about what they demand in particular cases.[27] All of these criticisms share a common bond. Structuralism, its critics argue, fails one of the most basic requirements of "good" constitutional interpretation. It does not limit discretion and thus does not adequately cope with the problem of judicial power. A second objection suggests that structural arguments may work well in cases that involve structural issues and relationships, such as federalism and separation of powers, but are less useful in cases that involve constitutional liberties. Presumably, structuralism would hold that rights derive from a structural relationship between citizens and the state. On this view, citizenship is the foundation of liberties—and arguably, not a very firm foundation, if, as Professor Bickel argued, citizenship may be regulated and perhaps even taken away by the state.

Philosophical and Aspirational Argument

Our political system incorporates elements of both democratic and constitutional theory. The fundamental principles that inform our polity—including principles of self-government, of respect for liberty, and the need for limited but energetic government have their source and much of their meaning in philosophical assumptions about human nature, what constitutes the good life, and the relationship of law to politics. More particularly, constitutional commitments to republican government, or to freedom of speech, or to religious freedom, themselves rest upon larger philosophical commitments and understandings about the relationship of the individual to the community, and between state and society.

It should be no surprise then that many justices interpret the Constitution in light of these philosophical understandings, or through the lenses of democratic and constitutional theory. One might well wonder, in fact, whether any kind of constitutional interpretation is really possible without making reference—either knowingly or unknowingly—to such things. One of the advantages of philosophical approaches to constitutional interpretation is the willingness to engage fundamental questions and assumptions about constitutional democracy and to do so in ways that engage the Constitution seriously as a political text.

On the other hand, critics charge that judges are not and should not be philosophers. Part of the complaint here is a simple, straightforward recognition that judges lack the kind of expertise required to deal with sophisticated questions of moral or political philosophy. Similarly, they argue that equating or reducing constitutional

---

[27] See Vincent Blasi, *Creativity and Legitimacy in Constitutional Law*, 80 Yale Law Journal 176 (1970).

interpretation to a question of philosophy is to make the Constitution even more remote and less accessible to ordinary citizens.

A related method of interpretation is sometimes called the "aspirational" approach. This method of interpretation, sometimes promoted by Justice Brennan, argues that the Constitution is a vision of a state of affairs we hope to achieve, or that we aspire to. Individual provisions must be read in light of those aspirations and interpreted in ways that help us to realize those aspirations.[28] This can be expressed variously, as in Archibald Cox's injunction that "[T]he aspirations voiced by the Court must be those the community is willing not only to avow but in the end to live by."[29] Some justices are uncomfortable with such talk. Justices Rehnquist and Scalia, for example, have argued that judicial appeals to "aspirations" are simply ways for judges to "short-circuit" majoritarian government. There is something to such criticisms. It is also true, however, that no justice could possibly be free of relying upon "aspirations" as a tool in decision-making. The criticism of "aspirational" jurisprudence as undemocratic, for example, itself depends upon the assertion that the Constitution aspires predominantly toward democratic values.

The great difficulty, then, is that it is not always clear just what these aspirations are or whose aspirations we should incorporate into the Constitution. The abortion controversy provides an example of the difficulty. Is it the aspiration toward liberty construed as freedom of choice that we should defend, or is it the aspiration toward the protection of all human life, born and unborn, that we should protect? Since aspirations compete for ascendancy in our society, it is unclear—or, it cannot be clear without an act of interpretation—how we are to choose between or rank-order aspirations when they push in different directions. Similarly, agreement in the abstract about the nature and definition of our collective aspirations does not go very far to tell us what those aspirations mean or require in specific cases. In this respect, then, aspirational and philosophical approaches to constitutional interpretation do little to constrain judicial power and interpretive creativity.

Limits to Interpretation: An Unconstitutional Constitutional Amendment?

Now that we have reviewed several approaches to constitutional interpretation, imagine the following scenario. A constitutional amendment has been adopted through the invocation of the various procedures outlined in Article V of the Constitution. The amendment makes it possible for the government to punish someone for the act of burning the American flag.[30] The textualist sees this as irreconcilable with the clear language of the First Amendment's protection of free speech; the structuralist finds that it renders the Constitution incoherent by contradicting its core political commitments; and the aspirationalist considers the new provision offensive to the vision of constitutional development embodied in the document as a whole. Could a Supreme Court that agreed with one or all of these interpretive objections declare the amendment unconstitutional?

---

[28] For a cogent defense of the aspirational approach, see Sotirios Barber, *On What the Constitution Means* (Baltimore: The John Hopkins University Press, 1984). For another view, see Gary J. Jacobsohn, *The Supreme Court and the Decline of Constitutional Aspiration* (Totowa, NJ: Rowman & Littlefield, 1986).

[29] Archibald Cox, *The Role of the Supreme Court in American Government* (New York: Oxford University Press, 1976), pp. 117–18.

[30] In fact, such an amendment was defeated in the Congress in 1989 and 1990. It read: "The Congress and the States shall have power to prohibit the physical desecration of the flag of the United States."

Whether it could or not (it has never happened in the United States), reflecting on the pros and cons of such an exertion of judicial power can be an instructive exercise in constitutional theorizing. Not surprisingly, the question of whether there are implicit limits on the amending process has been debated by students of constitutional interpretation. Walter Murphy has pointed out that an amendment, rightly construed (that is, following the Latin *emendere*), leads to correction or improvement, not re-constitution. "Thus changes that would make a polity into another kind of political system would not be amendments at all, but revisions or transformations."[31] From this perspective the Supreme Court's decision to invalidate an amendment that, in effect, reconstituted the political order, would be entirely appropriate. Against this view is the position taken by John R. Vile, who argues that "To empower the courts not simply to review the procedures whereby amendments were adopted but also to void amendments on the basis of their substantive content would surely threaten the notion of a government founded on the consent of the governed."[32]

This debate over the limits to the amending power can be conducted through the use of arguments employing the various methods of constitutional interpretation just reviewed. For example, a textualist might point out that the language of Article V contains two explicit limits on the power of amendment, suggesting, as Vile indicates by quoting Chief Justice John Marshall in *Marbury v. Madison*, that "affirmative words are often, in their operations, negative of other objects than those affirmed." So the entire notion of implicit limits is arguably refuted by the text itself. But the real significance of the debate transcends the results flowing from this or that interpretive approach. It resides in the tension that lies at the very core of constitutional democracy. Murphy's contention that there are implicit limits on the power of amendment is consistent with his view that "A basic function of constitutionalism . . . is to restrain government, even when it accurately reflects the popular will."[33] Amendments that are procedurally correct may be substantively incorrect—and hence invalid—if they reverse the constitutional commitment to human dignity. On the other hand, Vile maintains that "[I]f the judiciary took upon itself the power to void the very substance of amendments, this branch of government could itself end up undermining such dignity."[34] In the end, then, the argument over the interpretive reach of judicial review hinges upon the outcome of a prior contest over the meaning of constitutional governance.

Griswold v. Connecticut: A Case Study in Interpretation

We have already seen that no one method of interpretation commands universal assent. Judges rarely commit to one method to the exclusion of others, and sometimes they seem unaware or profess to be uninterested in which ones they use. In part this is because the methods often overlap or complement each other. This is best illustrated by looking at a single case and making an effort to discern what methods the various justices use to interpret the Constitution. *Griswold v. Connecti-*

---

[31] Walter F. Murphy, "Merlin's Memory: The Past and Future Imperfect of the Once and Future Polity," in Sanford Levinson, ed., *Responding To Imperfection: The Theory and Practice of Constitutional Amendment* (Princeton: Princeton University Press, 1995), p.177.

[32] John R. Vile, "The Case Against Implicit Limits on the Constitutional Amending Process," in Ibid., p. 198.

[33] Walter F. Murphy, "Merlin's Memory," in Ibid., p. 187.

[34] John R. Vile, "The Case Against Implicit Limits," in Ibid., p. 199.

cut (1965), the well-known birth control case, provides us with an excellent opportunit to see how the methods work.[35] *Griswold* concerned the constitutionality of a state statute that imposed a penalty on the use of any drug or instrument for the purpose of preventing conception. Even before reaching the merits of the case, the Court was confronted with a complex issue of justiciability: Did the physician bringing the case on behalf of his patient have the necessary standing to invoke the power of the federal judiciary under the "case and controversy" requirement of Article III? A narrow application of standing, as the rigorous prudentialist might advise, would probably have resulted in the dismissal of *Griswold*.[36] That standing was granted is just one measure of the flexibility with which prudential considerations are applied in particular situations.

On the merits, most students tend to see *Griswold* as a simple case, and they usually cheer when they hear its result. In examining the case, however, we find that it contains six opinions, two of which are dissenting, and incorporates at least six interpretive approaches. In addition, the seven justices in the majority could not agree on the constitutional basis for the right they voted to uphold. No fewer than six constitutional amendments were invoked in support of *Griswold's* holding that a person's liberty interest in marital privacy is fundamental and thus protected by the Constitution.

Justice Douglas, author of the main opinion, declined to rely on the Due Process Clause of the Fourteenth Amendment which prohibits states from depriving persons within their jurisdiction of life, liberty, or property without due process of law. He was well aware of the criticism triggered by the Court's use of the Due Process Clause to strike down protective labor laws of an earlier period on the basis of a general theory of economic liberty. To deflect the charge that the Court would not similarly function as a "super-legislature," Douglas relied heavily on both textual and doctrinal analysis. He recapitulates the relevant case law under the First, Third, Fourth, and Fifth Amendments that protects aspects of personal privacy and then, arguing from the text itself he notes: "The foregoing cases suggest that specific guarantees in the Bill of Rights have penumbras, formed by emanations from those guarantees that give them life and substance." At the end of his opinion, however, Douglas felt the urge to utter what is essentially an aspiration or ethical argument well beyond the words of the Constitution itself:

> *We deal with a right of privacy older than the Bill of Rights—older than our political parties, older than our school system. Marriage is a coming together for better or for worse, hopefully enduring, and intimate to the degree of being sacred. It is an association that promotes a way of life, not causes; a harmony in living, not political faiths; a bilateral loyalty, not commercial or social projects. Yet it is an association for as noble a purpose as any involved in our prior decisions.*[37]

Douglas's ode to the wonder and majesty of marriage anticipates the arguments about to be made by Justices Goldberg, Harlan, and White.

Justice Goldberg, who joined Douglas' opinion and judgment, went on to emphasize that the concept of liberty in the Fourteenth Amendment includes not only those

---

[35] 381 U.S. 497.

[36] The Supreme Court had earlier declined to decide the constitutionality of Connecticut's birth control statute on the ground that the law was not being enforced and thus posed no harm to persons seeking contraceptive information or purchasing contraceptive devices. See *Poe v. Ullman*, 367 U.S. 497 (1961).

[37] 381 U.S. 479, 486.

personal rights confined to the specific terms of the Bill of Rights, but also those found to be "so rooted in the tradition and conscience of our people as to be ranked as fundamental." Marital privacy, he concluded, drawing now on doctrine and precedent, partakes of this fundamentality. What is new about Goldberg's argument, however, is his appeal to the "language and history of the Ninth Amendment which exist alongside those fundamental rights specifically mentioned in the first eight constitutional amendments." Goldberg's appeal to original history of the long-neglected Ninth Amendment—later in the opinion he would draw on the words of James Madison who proposed the Amendment—was designed to show that the term "liberty" was not confined to the specified rights mentioned in the Bill of Rights. In an interesting twist, Goldberg was also responding to Black, who accused him of turning "somersaults" with the Constitution. Goldberg, however, was trying to hoist Black on his own petard by focusing on the *text* of the Ninth Amendment. He used this text to validate what was essentially a structural reading—i.e., the Ninth Amendment tells us how to read other parts of the Constitution. He was thus able to conclude, on the basis of the text, that the term "liberty" in the Fourteenth Amendment included the unwritten right to marital privacy.

Justice Harlan, on the other hand, vigorously rejected the textualism of Douglas's opinion as well as the literalism advanced in the dissenting opinions of Justices Black and Stewart. Harlan, like Frankfurter before him, was a strong proponent of the view that the Due Process Clause of the Fourteenth Amendment "is not dependent on the provisions of the Bill of Rights or any of their radiations"—referring of course to Douglas's "penumbras"—but "stands on its own bottom." Justice White joined Harlan in resting squarely on the Due Process Clause. Neither justice shared Goldberg's reliance on the Ninth Amendment. For each of them the Fourteenth provided adequate standards to keep "most judges from roaming at large in the constitutional field." What the Due Process Clause requires in determining its meaning, wrote Harlan, is a "continual insistence on open respect for the teachings of history, solid recognition of the basic values that underlie our society, and [in coming close to invoking a structural argument] wise appreciation of the great roles that the doctrines of federalism and separation of powers have played in establishing and preserving American freedoms."[38]

Justice Black, dissenting, would have none of this. The Harlan-Goldberg-White approach was in his view judicial subjectivism at its worst and a blatant usurpation of the rightful power of legislatures to make law. A confirmed textualist—and the Court's leading advocate of the *total* incorporation of *all* the specified guarantees of the Bill of Rights into the Due Process Clause of the Fourteenth Amendment (validated for him incidentally by original history)—as well as one of the Court's most ardent civil libertarians, he nevertheless objected to any open-ended approach that would give judges a license to declare laws unconstitutional because they believe they are unwise, unnecessary, dangerous, or offensive to their notions of "natural justice." "I like my privacy as well as the next one," wrote Black, "but I am nevertheless compelled to admit that government has a right to invade it unless prohibited by some specific constitutional provision."

Justice Stewart was equally blunt—and succinct: "I think this [statute against the use of contraceptives] is," he wrote, "an uncommonly silly law. . . . But we are not asked in this case to say whether we think this law is unwise, or even asinine. We are asked to hold that it violates the United States Constitution. And that I cannot

---

[38] Ibid., 501.

do."[39] Needless to say, neither Stewart nor Black could find a right of married persons to use contraceptives—or the more general right of marital privacy—in the Constitution.

Comparative Perspectives

The early twenty-first century is an age of judicial review. What was generally regarded as a unique feature of the American Constitution prior to World War II is now a regular feature of numerous constitutions around the world. The proliferation of constitutional courts in Western Europe, Latin America, Asia, and, lately, in the former communist countries of Eastern Europe, is one of the most fascinating constitutional developments of our time. In truth, we live in an era of spreading democracy, but one that places elective governments under the rule of written constitutions and the guidance of courts empowered to nullify governmental actions contrary to the constitution. In the light of 20th century dictatorships, judicial review has also been seen as a potent weapon against the enemies of democracy.

The particular institutional form that judicial review takes often depends on the culture and tradition of a country's legal tradition. Germany's Federal Constitutional Court provides the model that most European countries (east and west) and, most recently, the Republic of South Africa, have adopted. As noted in chapter 1, these countries have established constitutional courts separate from and independent of the regular judiciary. In addition, only these courts are empowered to declare laws unconstitutional. Many of them, like Germany's Constitutional Court and unlike the U.S. Supreme Court, are authorized to decide constitutional disputes on the basis of what is called "abstract judicial review" (*abstrakte Normenkontrolle*), that is, outside the framework of adverse litigation or what is technically regarded as a "case or controversy" in the American sense. In Germany, for example, the federal or a state government or one-third of the members of the national parliament may request the Constitutional Court to review the validity of an enacted law even before it enters into force or becomes the object of a conventional lawsuit. In India, where the judiciary's constitutional rulings more closely follow the American model, the Supreme Court has extended the practice of judicial review to the power of amendment by explicitly embracing structuralism as a method of interpretation. In affirming such authority the Court has insisted that "the Constitution does not provide for . . . its own demise."[40] And so any proposed change in the Constitution that would alter the "basic structure" of the document could be annulled by the Court even if the change had followed the procedures prescribed by law. The list of these protected features includes judicial review itself, as well as such broader concepts of institutional design as federalism and secularism.

In the comparative section of each introductory essay in chapters 3 through 15, we discuss many of the doctrinal differences between American and foreign constitutional law, so there is no need to retrace those steps here. In this brief space, we limit ourselves to some general observations about the interpretive orientation of foreign constitutional courts that contrast most sharply with American approaches. We must caution ourselves, however, not to exaggerate these differences because principles of rationality and proportionality seem to constitute the core of judicial review wher-

---

[39] Ibid., 527.

[40] *S. R. Bommai v. Union of India*, 3 SC 1 , 237 (1994).

ever it is practiced, despite wide variations in the vigor with which the powers of judicial review are exercised.

Again it may be helpful to use Germany as an example of a contrasting—although not wholly different—approach to constitutional interpretation. One significant difference is the less important role that prudentialism appears to play in German constitutional law, probably because the counter-majoritarian difficulty, which so preoccupies American constitutional lawyers and judges, is not a major issue in German constitutional theory. One of the characteristics of the Basic Law is the normativity of all its provisions: Every provision is a legally binding norm requiring full and unambiguous implementation. In short, the Constitution may be said to represent the basic norm that governs and legitimates the entire legal order. It controls public law directly but it also influences, indirectly, the interpretation of private law. When serious doubts arise over the validity of a law or practice having the force of law, the Constitutional Court's function, in a case properly before it, is to resolve these doubts in the interest of constitutional clarity and the rule of law. This approach, which envisions the Constitutional Court as *the* guardian of the Basic Law, has little in common with the political question doctrine or the maxim that the courts reach constitutional questions last not first.

In interpreting the Basic Law, the German Court employs four classic modes of interpretation drawn from the history and practice of statutory construction. These four modes of analysis are textual, contextual or systematic, historical, and teleological. Textual and contextual analysis focus on *what is said* in the constitution, the former dwelling on the ordinary meaning of a word or its legal usage, the latter on the grammatical context or structure of a provision. Historical analysis attempts to determine *what was willed* by the framers at the time of the constitution's adoption. Teleological analysis, finally, examines the purpose—or *what was intended*—behind the various provisions of the Basic Law or the document as a whole. Like American judges, German constitutionalists have established no fixed order in which to apply these methods except that original history is less important in determining the meaning of the constitution than the other three methods, which are adhered to rigorously and used in combination. History is ordinarily used to support and not to determine constitutional meaning and carries far less weight than in the United States.

In contrast to the tendency in American constitutional analysis to focus on isolated phrases and passages of the Constitution, German constitutional theorists and practitioners place a heavy emphasis on the Basic Law as a unified structure of principles and values. In fact, the Constitutional Court has declared that "no single provision may be taken out of its context and interpreted by itself, [for] every constitutional provision must always be interpreted so as to render it compatible with the fundamental principles of the Constitution." In other instances, the Court has alluded to the Basic Law as "logical-teleological unity."[41] This accent on the Basic Law's unity has resulted in several supplementary interpretive standards among the most important of which are the principles of practical concordance (*praktische Konkordanz*), integration, and optimization.

When two or more constitutional values are in conflict, practical concordance requires the Court to harmonize these values rather than realizing one at the expense of the other. Integration instructs the Court to honor, to the extent possible, the constitutional values represented by the various parties before it and thereby to promote social and political cohesion. Optimization, finally, requires the Court to "actualize," to the extent possible, each and every value in the constitution, including those institutional values flowing from the structure of federalism and separation of powers. In

---

[41] See, for example, *Church Construction Tax Case*, 19 BVerfGE 206, 220 (1965).

each of these ways, the Court seeks to legitimate the constitution in all of its parts, reinforcing its legitimacy in the conscience of the people. One by-product of this extraordinary emphasis on the unity of the Basic Law is the doctrine of an unconstitutional constitutional amendment, which, as we have pointed out earlier, has not been embraced by the Supreme Court in the United States. On several occasions, the Federal Constitutional Court has announced its readiness to strike down any constitutional amendment that would erode the Basic Law's core principles.

The optimizing and harmonizing strategies of the Federal Constitutional Court make the balancing of obligations and rights a prominent feature of German constitutional analysis. In freedom of speech cases, for example, there is less of an effort in Germany to engage in "definitional" balancing; that is, to define a particular action or expression as an unprotected value rather than including it within the ambit of those actions or behavior requiring independent constitutional assessment. The reverse side of definitional balancing is the "preferred freedoms" approach, which has often led the Supreme Court, as in Justice Black's textualism, to renounce any balancing at all. Also noteworthy in this connection, and absent in the U.S. Constitution, are the reservation clauses that limit almost all basic rights provisions of modern constitutions. Canada's Charter of Rights and Freedoms actually contains a general reservation clause almost identical to the many reservation clauses appended to particular provisions of the European Convention on Human Rights. It reads: "The *Canadian Charter of Rights and Freedoms* guarantees the rights and freedoms set out in it subject only to such reasonable limits prescribed by law as can be demonstrably justified in a free and democratic society."

In applying interpretive provisions such as this, as noted earlier, constitutional courts almost everywhere apply the principles of rationality and proportionality. The case law of constitutional courts such as the Supreme Courts of Canada, United States, India, and Ireland as well as the European Court of Human Rights and the Constitutional Courts of Germany, Italy, and Spain, may apply the principles in dramatically different ways and with different results but the fact that all of them invoke some variation on these principles suggests that something universal is at work here. It suggests too that some degree of objectivity and determinacy informs the process of constitutional interpretation. There also seems to be a widespread tendency of constitutional courts around the world to rely in a lesser or greater extent on unwritten textual values that reflect a particular country's history and culture, an observation that recalls Justice Holmes's comment that constitutional cases "must be considered in the light of our whole experience and not merely in that of what was said a hundred years ago."[42]

Just how much of the constitutional experience of one country might be relevant to other countries is an important and fascinating question. Are constitutional mechanisms and approaches readily transferable from place to place, or do the particularities of political cultures undermine prospects for successful cross-national borrowing and transplantation?

Consider this language taken from Sec. 35 of the new South African Constitution. "In interpreting the provisions of this chapter a court of law shall promote the values which underlie an open and democratic society based on freedom and equality and shall, where applicable, have regard to public international law applicable to the protection of the rights entrenched in this Chapter, and may have regard to comparable foreign case law." These words are an invitation to judges in the post-apartheid

---

[42] *Missouri v. Holland*, 252 U.S. 416, 433 (1920).

republic to seek outside help in the structuring of a constitutional jurisprudence. They suggest a model of constitutional development that is outward looking in two related senses: first in its commitment to certain fundamental principles of democratic justice, and second in its endorsement of comparative law as an appropriate source for the adjudication of cases. The text gives new meaning to the term "nonoriginalism," which constitutional theorists sometimes use to refer to approaches that question the importance of the intentions of those who framed a legal document, but which here stands for the endorsement of foreign legal precedent as a basis for the growth of the law.

The language is noteworthy only for the explicitness of its reference to extraterritorial legal sources; the practice of searching beyond sovereign lines for legal guidance in constitutional cases is quite common. Over the years judiciaries have developed extensive histories of constitutional borrowing, usually without any official invitation to do so. All of these histories involve a mix of both acceptance and rejection of external case law. The drafting of the South African constitution deliberately followed the experience of other countries—especially Canada and Germany—and so it is perhaps not very surprising that provision was made for subsequent constitutional interpretation to seek guidance from these and other sources of inspiration. While the pressure for indigenous legal development will always be present, its practical effect may be quite limited where the animating principles behind the emergence of a constitutional tradition are essentially emulative in nature.

The words of Sec. 35 also suggests an important contemporary development: the globalization of liberal democratic institutions. It makes sense to view a system's openness to outside influence in relation to broader political trends—in this case the ascendance of liberal ideals (political and economic)—such that the transplantation of constitutional ideas and practices from one place to another projects a certain inevitability, much like what has occurred in recent years with the rapid adoption of market institutions by countries previously unfamiliar with the ways of capitalism.

Unlike the South African case, high courts in most places have not been solicited by authoritative constitutional language to employ foreign case law in their legal rulings. However, many courts have welcomed precedents imported from abroad, particularly from the United States. From these precedents judges have sought guidance and legitimacy. Nevertheless, tribunals in these countries have been highly selective in their borrowings, the pattern of usage reflecting similarities and disparities in political circumstances surrounding particular issues. To take one example, for Israeli jurists intent on pushing their legal system in the direction of Western constitutional norms, American free speech jurisprudence has proven to be an attractive model. On the other hand, the religion clauses of the First Amendment hold much less appeal for judges serving within a polity founded on very different principles of secular governance.

In the American Supreme Court, which only rarely solicits comparative materials, debates have arisen recently over the wisdom and appropriateness of utilizing such sources. On one end of the Court, Justices Breyer and Souter have argued that the experience of other countries can provide valuable lessons for American judges, whereas on the other end, Justices Scalia and Rehnquist have voiced greater skepticism over the benefits of cross-national constitutional exploration. For example, in an important federalism case, Justice Scalia responded to Justice Breyer's suggestion that the Court follow the experience of other federal systems in assessing arrangements for the administration of national law by leaving little doubt as to where he stood in these matters. "[S]uch comparative analysis [is] inappropriate to the task of interpreting a constitution, though it was of course relevant to the task of writing one."[43] For Scalia, "our federalism is not Europe's," a sentiment he has expressed in other constitutional domains as well, such as the death penalty and freedom of religion. Thus the constitutionality of executing the mentally retarded should in no way hinge upon the experience of other nations. "[I]rrelevant are the practices of the 'world community,' whose notions of justice are (thankfully) not always those of our people. We must never forget that it is a Constitution for the United States of America that we are expounding. . . ."[44]

In *The Federalist*, Publius makes clear that in considering constitutional possibilities, the framers' decisions about whether it was wise to borrow from foreign sources did not depend on an assessment of how well this or that worked in its native environment, but rather on an analysis of how well it was likely to serve the ends or vision incorporated in the constitutional aspirations of the newly emerging American polity. The contemporary debate on the Court over constitutional borrowing from foreign judicial opinions is in one sense a disagreement over these aspirations. How fixed are they? Are the justices proper agents for adapting them to new social realities, domestic and global? Different judicial approaches toward the use of experience from abroad to some extent reflect alternative stances on the role of the Court in accommodating change. Thus the disinclination of Justices Scalia and Rehnquist to incorporate foreign materials in their opinions generally supports their jurisprudential commitment to limiting opportunities for judicially derived revisions of constitutional meanings. In contrast, justices who see their role somewhat less narrowly are more likely to be open to interpretive options inspired by what they have observed of constitutional activity outside the borders of the United States.

For these justices, there are lessons from other places that can profitably inform constitutional adjudication in the United States. In some cases this will have little, if any, effect on the direction of American law, but in others—for example, with respect to what rights should be deemed fundamental under the Constitution—the impact could be considerable. In the final analysis, cross-national experience is not a quiver in the sheaf of just one side of a debate over the exercise of judicial power. Judges of all persuasions could find it a valuable resource when seeking to augment the persuasive power of their opinions. However, once we admit the experience of foreign legal systems to the arena of American constitutional adjudication, it then becomes incumbent on the judge who does so to justify the importation as reasonable in light of the relevant differences between the United States and other constitutional polities. Judges, then, must be well informed about much more than just the law. They must be conversant with their country's history and political culture, and to the extent that they wish to profit from the experience of other nations, with the diversity of these same phenomena in the world beyond their shores.

---

[43] *Printz v. United States*, 521 U.S. 898 (1997), at 921.

[44] *Atkins v. United States*, 536 U.S. 304 (2002), at 347.

Selected Bibliography

Abraham, Henry. *The Judicial Process*, 6th ed. (New York: Oxford University Press, 1993).

Ackerman, Bruce A., "Beyond Carolene Products," *Harvard Law Review* 98 (1985).

Antieau, Chester James. *Constitutional Construction* (New York: Oceana Publications, 1982).

Arkes, Hadley, *Beyond the Constitution* (Princeton: Princeton University Press, 1990).

Barber, Sotirios A., *On What the Constitution Means* (Baltimore: Johns Hopkins University Press, 1984).

Bickel, Alexander, *The Least Dangerous Branch*, 2nd ed. (New Haven: Yale University Press, 1986).

Black, Charles L. Jr., *The People and the Constitution* (Westport, Conn.: Greenwood Press, 1960).

Bobbitt, Philip, *Constitutional Fate* (New York: Oxford University Press, 1982).

————, *Constitutional Interpretation* (New York: Oxford University Press, 1991).

Cardozo, Benjamin N., *The Nature of the Judicial Process* (New Haven: Yale University Press, 1921).

Corwin, Edward S., *The Higher Law Background of American Constitutional Law*, Harvard Law Review 42 (1928).

Ducat, Craig R., *Modes of Constitutional Interpretation* (St. Paul, Minn.: West Publishing Co., 1978.

Dworkin, Ronald, *A Matter of Principle* (Cambridge: Harvard University Press, 1985).

Ely, John H., *Democracy and Distrust* (Cambridge: Harvard University Press, 1980).

Gerhardt, Michael J. and Thomas D. Rowe, Jr. (eds), *Constitutional Theory* (Charlottesville, Va.: The Michie Company, 1993).

Grey, Thomas C., *Do We Have an Unwritten Constitution?* Stanford Law Review 27 (1975).

Harris, William Fr. III, *The Interpretable Constitution* (Baltimore: Johns Hopkins University Press, 1993).

Jacobsohn, Gary, *The Supreme Court and the Decline of Constitutional Aspiration* (Totowa, N.J.: Rowman & Littlefield, 1986).

Kaplin, William A., *The Concepts and Methods of Constitutional Law* (Durham, N.C.: Carolina Academic Press, 1992).

Levinson, Sanford (ed.), *Responding To Imperfection: The Theory and Practice of Constitutional Amendment* (Princeton: Princeton University Press, 1995).

Monaghan, Henry P., *Our Perfect Constitution*, New York University Law Review 56 (1981).

Nagel, Robert F., *Constitutional Cultures* (Berkeley: University of California Press, 1989).

————, *Judicial Power and American Character* (New York: Oxford University Press, 1994).

Perry, Michael J., *The Constitution in the Courts* (New Haven: Yale University Press, 1980).

Posner, Richard A., *The Problems of Jurisprudence* (Cambridge: Harvard University Press, 1990).

Powell, H. Jefferson, *The Moral Tradition of American Constitutionalism: A Theological Interpretation* (Durham, N.C.: Duke University Press, 1993).

Rakove, Jack N., *Original Meanings: Politics and Ideas in the Making of the Constitution* (New York: Alfred A. Knopf, 1996).

Scalia, Antonin, *A Matter of Interpretation: Federal Courts and the Law* (Princeton: Princeton University Press, 1996)

Sunstein, Cass, *One Case At a Time: Judicial Minimalism On the Supreme Court* (Cambridge: Harvard University Press, 1999).

Thayer, James B., *The Origin and Scope of the American Doctrine of Constitutional Law*, Harvard Law Review 7 (1883).

Tribe, Laurence, *Constitutional Choices* (Cambridge: Harvard University Press, 1985).

Tribe, Laurence, and Michael C. Dorf, *On Reading the Constitution* (Cambridge: Harvard University Press, 1991).

Tushnet, Mark V., *Red, White, and Blue: A Critical Analysis of Constitutional Law* (Cambridge: Harvard University Press, 1988).

Wechsler, Herbert, *Toward Neutral Principles of Constitutional Law*, Harvard Law Review 73 (1959).

Selected Comparative Bibliography

Alexy, Robert, *A Theory of Legal Argumentation* (Oxford: Clarendon Press, 1989).

Barak, Aharon, *Foreward: A Judge On Judging: The Role of a Supreme Court in a Democracy*, Harvard Law Review 116 (2002).

Baxi, Upendra, *Courage, Craft, and Contention: The Indian Supreme Court in the Eighties* (Bombay: N.M. Tripathi Private Limited, 1985).

Beatty, David M. (ed.), *Human Rights and Judicial Review: A Comparative Perspective* (Dordrecht: Martinus Nijhoff Publishers, 1994).

————, *Constitutional Law In Theory and Practice* (Toronto: University of Toronto Press, 1995).

Beaudoin, Gerald A. and Errol Mendes, *The Canadian Charter of Rights and Freedoms*, Third Edition (Toronto: Carswell, 1996).

Beer, Laurence and Itoh, *Japanese Constitutional Law: 1956–1990* (Seattle: University of Washington Press, 1996).

Bryden, Philip et al., *Protecting Rights & Freedoms: Essays on the Charter's Placed in Canada's Political, Legal, and Intellectual Life* (Toronto: University of Toronto Press, 1994).

Friedrich, Carl J., *Constitutional Government and Democracy*, rev. ed. (Boston: Ginn and Company, 1950).

Henkin, Louis and Albert Rosenthal (eds.), *Constitutionalism and Rights: The Influence of the United States Constitution Abroad* (New York: Columbia University Press, 1990).

Herget, James E., *Contemporary German Legal Philosophy* (Philadelphia: University of Pennsylvania Press, 1996).

Hogan, Gerard and Gerry Whyte, *The Irish Constitution* (Dublin: Butterworths, 1994).

Holland, Kenneth M. (ed.), *Judicial Activism In Comparative Perspective* (London: Macmillan, 1991).

Janis, Mark et al., *European Human Rights Law* (Oxford: Clarendon Press, 1995).

Kommers, Donald P. *The Constitutional Jurisprudence of the Federal Republic of Germany*, 2nd ed. (Durham: Duke University Press, 1997).

————, "The Value of Comparative Constitutional Law," *John Marshall Journal of Practice and Procedure*, Vol. 9, (1976).

Lane, Jan-Eric, *Constitutions and Political Theory* (Manchester, England: Manchester University Press, 1996).

Manfredi, Christopher P., *Judicial Power and the Charter* (Oxford: Oxford University Press, 2001).

McKenna, Marian C. (ed.), *The Canadian and American Constitutions in Comparative Perspective* (Calgary: University of Calgary Press, 1993).

Murphy, Walter F. and Joseph Tanenhaus, *Comparative Constitutional Law: Cases and Commentaries* (New York: St. Martin's Press, 1977).

Singh, Mahendra P. (ed.), *Comparative Constitutional Law* (Lucknow, India: Eastern Book Co., 1989).

Starck, Christian (ed.), *Studies in German Constitutionalism* (Baden-Baden: Nomos Verlagsgesellschaft, 1995).

Trakman, Leon A., *Reasoning With the Charter* (Vancouver: Butterworths Canada Ltd., 1991).

van Wyk, Dawid et al., *Rights and Constitutionalism: The New South African Constitution* (Oxford: Clarendon Press, 1996).

Part Two

Intergovernmental Powers and Relationships

*T*he United States Constitution is a blueprint for the conduct of politics. By dividing power between federal and state governments and by placing legislative, executive, and judicial power in separate departments at the national level, the Founders hoped to combine representative democracy with limited government. They reinforced the latter by introducing a system of checks and balances into the structure of separated powers. They knew that these institutional structures and relationships would complicate the political process, but they placed a higher value on restraint and reflection than on speed and efficiency, all for the purpose of checking the abuse of power. Conflict and tension would mark interbranch and intergovernmental relations, but the Founders hoped—and expected—that these stresses and strains would engender creativity and forbearance rather than rigidity and deadlock.

Part II highlights major conflicts between levels and branches of government. The constitutional cases featured here represent the occasions on which one branch or level of government has allegedly invaded the rightful domain of another branch or level. Occasionally, too, as the cases show, creative innovations in the art of governance overstep defined competencies, as do certain well-meaning collaborative efforts between and within governments. When this happens, and adjudication ensues, the Supreme Court serves as the guardian of the spheres of authority defined by the Constitution.

The following six chapters contain important illustrations of the Court's guardianship. Chapter 3 includes cases that show how the Court has sought to confine and expand its own power under Article III, and we pay particular attention to cases in which the Court has emphasized both the finality of its rulings and the importance of its moral voice in American constitutional politics. Chapter 4 features cases that define the complex relations between the three branches of the national government. Chapter 5 continues to explore the boundary between the branches in foreign and military affairs, underscoring the strained relationship that often marks inter-branch politics in these sensitive areas of international politics. Chapter 6 shifts the scene from separation of powers to federal-state relations. Among the special subjects treated here are the scope of state power over commerce and taxation and

Eleventh Amendment restrictions on congressional power to authorize suits against the states in federal courts. Students should reflect on the extent to which arguments over state sovereignty echo those sounded in the *Federalist Papers* and in debates over the Constitution's ratification. Chapter 7 describes the powers of Congress and the checkered history of the Court's perspective on the permissible range of national power and its clash with state claims to reserved powers under the Tenth Amendment. Chapter 8, finally, deals with the American electoral process. It covers selected constitutional cases, including *Bush v. Gore*, on apportionment, campaign finance, and political parties.

Part II, like Parts I and III, includes comparative constitutional and jurisprudential perspectives. We might recall that the American Founders were themselves students of comparative constitutionalism. They looked to the experiences of Sparta, Athens, Rome, and Carthage for guidance in crafting a new constitution for the United States. But their constitution was originally crafted for a preindustrial society. Modern democratic constitutions framed after World War II and in recent years differ significantly from the American document in their structures and relationships. Many of these modern constitutions embrace mixed systems of presidential and parliamentary governments—favoring weak presidents elected by parliament or strong presidents chosen in direct popular elections. Contrasting sharply with the American system of separated powers, these constitutions feature dual executives (president and cabinet), occasionally one-house legislatures, and often popularly unaccountable institutions such as central banks and specialized constitutional courts. They seek to achieve a system of checks and balances through devices such as central financial controls, popular initiatives, the creation of ombudsmen, abstract judicial review, presidential or legislative calls for referenda, parliamentary override of constitutional court decisions, and limits on the power to dissolve parliament.

It is doubtful whether Americans would be prepared to transplant any of these practices or institutions into their constitutional system. Americans critical of the deadlock and inefficiency that often characterize policy making at the national level have often envied what appears to be the more responsible and democratic procedures of parliamentary governments.[1] Before transporting to these shores any version of parliamentary democracy, however, a new set of American constitution-makers would have to be convinced that the American presidential form is less resilient, less focused, and less democratic over the long haul than parliamentary systems, whatever the variety. Such proof does not seem to be available. And, as Robert Dahl has noted, a nation's underlying political culture is likely to be equally determinative of how politics operates as any set of constitutional structures.[2]

Were Americans given the chance to hold a new constitutional convention, they would in all probability give some thought to perfecting their democracy. A modern-day Madison, drawing on comparative knowledge, might find that the present tripartite division of power is as outmoded as it is (or sometimes seems) democratically unaccountable. Given the complexity of modern government, he or she might wish to replace the existing document with one that recognizes the critical role of administrative agencies, but which includes the two-house legislative veto—struck down by

---

[1] See, for example, Daniel Lazare, *The Frozen Republic: How the Constitution Is Paralyzing Our Democracy* (New York: Harcourt Brace & Co., 1996).

[2] Robert Dahl, "Thinking About Democratic Constitutions: Conclusions from Democratic Experience" in Ian Shapiro and Russell Hardin, eds., *Political Order: Nomos XXXIII* (New York: New York University Press, 1966), 175–202.

the Supreme Court in *INS v. Chadha* (1983)—and installs, after the pattern of Germany's Basic Law, a strong version of the doctrine of nondelegation. He or she might also be inclined to follow the lead of most modern constitutions by specifying in greater detail the powers and duties of state and local governments. In addition, our modern Madison might seek to resolve the perennial dispute between the president and Congress over their respective powers in the field of military affairs, perhaps by constitutionalizing some version of the War Powers Resolution. Finally, in the interest of democratizing major foreign policy decisions and again heeding foreign constitutional developments, he or she might shift the Senate's treaty-making power to the House of Representatives and eliminate the two-thirds vote requirement for the ratification of treaties.

Failing these reforms, the new Madison would probably consider abandoning the electoral college as an aberration among modern constitutional democracies. In a further effort to reinforce the representative character of American government, and in view of the legal changes that have taken place in Europe, Canada, South Africa, and elsewhere, he or she might also consider experimenting with compulsory voting, limiting the terms of Supreme Court justices, recognizing the constitutional role of political parties, and adopting a variation of Germany's system of modified proportional representation, an electoral system that has so impressed the world's constitution-makers that even the British are thinking of adopting it.[3] There is one other structural change—one that goes to the heart of America's national identity—that our contemporary Madison might consider if indeed he or she would wish to be guided by constitutional developments abroad. That is a tax system more in conformity with democratic communal values and one that insures a better and more equitable distribution of tax revenues between levels of government. This would entail a major redefinition of the taxing and spending power of the national government; in short, a fiscal system that announces who we Americans are and what we would like to be.[4] The time may thus be ripe, as many European constitution-makers have long recognized, to democratize, and perhaps to decentralize, the power to tax and spend.

As you read the cases and materials in Part II, you may wish to consider whether there is anything that Americans can learn from foreign constitutional developments in the interest of a better settlement than may now be available between our constitutional structures and the political democracy we claim to celebrate.

---

[3] William Rees-Mogg, "See Democracy Die in a Hail of Ballots," *The Times* (London), 27 July 1997.

[4] See generally Edward J. McCaffery, *The Political Liberal Case Against the Estate Tax*, 23 Philosophy and Public Affairs 281 (1994).

Judicial Power

The Constitution and Judicial Review

Marbury v. Madison[1] (1803, reprinted later in the chapter) is the cornerstone of American constitutional law. In this seminal case, Chief Justice John Marshall laid down the doctrine that judges are authorized to nullify and void any law that in their view violates the Constitution. The case was resourceful because Marshall enunciated the doctrine of judicial review in the absence of any constitutional provision clearly authorizing its adoption. As noted in chapter 2, the Constitution says nothing about whether the judicial power of the United States extends to the refusal to enforce laws incompatible with the Constitution. For Marshall, however, judicial review could be inferred from the Constitution's general principles.

Marshall's chain of reasoning in *Marbury* was deceptively simple: He declared that under the Constitution "it is emphatically the province and duty of the judicial department to say what the law is." In so declaring, Marshall called attention to the significance and purpose of a written constitution. "All those who have framed written constitutions," he wrote, "contemplate them as forming the fundamental and paramount law of the nation, and consequently, the theory of every such government must be, that an act of the legislature, repugnant to the Constitution, is void." It follows, therefore, that a constitution is "a law of superior obligation, unchangeable by ordinary means." From this premise, Marshall inferred the power of the judiciary to nullify a law contrary to the Constitution, a power structurally fortified in his view by the supremacy clause, the judicial oath to defend the Constitution, and the extension of federal judicial power to all cases and controversies arising under the Constitution.[2]

Marshall's decision elicited a stiff rebuke from Thomas Jefferson, and the ensuing clash of personalities was the first in a long line of historical scuffles

---

[1] 5 U.S. (1 Cranch) 137 (1803)

[2] In proclaiming the power of judicial review, Marshall was not writing on a clean slate. He reproduced the heart of the argument advanced by Alexander Hamilton in *Federalist* 78 (see Appendix I). Colonial judges were also known to have voided laws deemed contrary to their state constitutions and in an earlier case, *Hylton v. U.S.* (3 Dall.) 171 (1796), the Supreme Court implied that it could refuse to enforce unconstitutional laws or practices.

over the nature and scope of judicial power in America. The contest between judicial review and political democracy was on, and the congressional cancellation of the Supreme Court's 1801–02 term, recommended by Jefferson, was a warning shot across Marshall's bow. Jefferson was telling him to stay out of presidential affairs and to let the president run the executive branch as he sees fit. Jefferson reacted bitterly to Marshall's opinion. He described *Marbury's* view of judicial supremacy in defining the meaning of the Constitution as "an *obiter* dissertation of the Chief Justice,"[3] and he went on to recommend the impeachment of federal judges who would dare to disallow acts of the coordinate and equal branches of the federal government.

Marshall's decision met with still another rejoinder in Judge John Gibson's celebrated opinion in *Eakin v. Raub,*[4] an otherwise unremarkable case decided by Pennslyvania's Supreme Court. Like many of his contempories, Judge Gibson assumed that in the event of a collision between the Constitution and ordinary law, the latter would have to give way to the former; unlike Marshall, however, he denied that any such "collision [could] be resolved *before the Judiciary.*" Gibson's view—one that in time would be shared by Presidents Jackson, Lincoln, and Franklin Roosevelt—was that no one department or branch of the national government may conclusively interpret the Constitution for the other. The system of checks and balances overlaying the American structure of separated powers, Gibson maintained, would be sufficient to negate any exercise of unconstitutional power. He added that public opinion would serve as the only effective guard against legislative usurpation. According to Gibson, "it rests with the people, in whom full and absolute sovereign power resides, to correct abuses in legislation."[5]

Whether the framers wanted federal judges to hold laws and other governmental acts unconstitutional remains disputed. Judicial review, as such, was not discussed at the Constitutional Convention, although in the debate over a council of revision some delegates assumed that courts would have the power to overturn ordinary statutes. Yet as Hamilton remarked in *Federalist 81*, the "doctrine [of judicial review] is not deducible from any circumstance peculiar to the plan of the convention."[6] Even so, suspicious commentators examined the judiciary article and feared what they saw. Robert Yates, writing as Brutus in a preratification debate, charged that the powers vested in the judiciary would enable the federal courts "to mould the government into almost any shape they please."[7] To allay this fear, Hamilton avowed that the judiciary would always be the national government's "least dangerous" branch. Although conceding in *Federalist* 78 that the courts would have the "right . . . to pronounce legislative acts void, because contrary to the Constitution," he sought to

---

[3] Quoted in Kathleen Sullivan and Gerald Gunther, *Constitutional Law*, 14th ed. (Mineola, N.Y.: The Foundation Press, 2001), 12.

[4] 12 Sergeant & Rawle 330 (1825).

[5] Judge Gibson failed to emphasize what may be Marshall's most audacious claim, namely that the Constitution is paramount law. Paramountcy was not the main problem, however. Rather it was Marshall's uncritical claim that the Constitution should be understood essentially, if not only, as a *legal* instrument. In the understanding of many other nations at the time, constitutions were not regarded as law but rather as frameworks for the conduct of government, guidelines for political action, or counsels of aspiration that elected officials and units of government were *morally* obligated to pursue.

[6] Hamilton did say, however, that judicial review is "deducible . . . from the general theory of a limited Constitution." See *The Federalist* 81, edited by Benjamin Fletcher Wright (New York: Barnes & Noble, Inc., 1996), 506.

[7] Brutus, No. 11 (31 January 1788) in Michael Kammen, ed., *The Origins of the American Constitution: A Documentary History* (New York: Penguin Books, 1986), 337.

disarm his critics by claiming that they would "have neither Force nor Will, but merely judgment."[8] In responding to Brutus, Hamilton glossed over the substantial political power the Constitution conferred on the judiciary as well as how easily interpretation could lead to results beyond the literal language of the Constitution. Robert Yates was also aware of these perils, predicting that by a certain "latitude of interpretation," the Supreme Court would begin to dominate the legislature and render the states subservient to the national government.[9]

Equally compelling was the early clash within the Supreme Court between Justices Chase and Iredell over the substantive content of the Constitution. The year was 1798, the case was *Calder v. Bull* (reprinted in chapter 10), and the fight was over what principle or provision of the Constitution should be applied in measuring the validity of a state statute,[10] in this case a law setting aside the decree of a probate court. Both justices voted to uphold the law over the objection that it was an ex post facto measure, but they differed in their views of *what* the Constitution included. Whereas Iredell argued that the Court must confine itself to the written text of the Constitution, Chase invoked principles of natural justice, claiming that "the purposes for which men enter into society will determine the nature and terms of the social compact." As many of the cases discussed in this and subsequent chapters show, this debate continues today, unrelentingly. The perennial issue here, as in other constitutional democracies, is whether laws can or should be invalidated on the basis of principles or higher values undefined or unmentioned in the constitutional text.

The Early Struggle for Judicial Supremacy

In 1787, no one could have predicted how the Constitution would transform the system of government it created. As John Marshall noted in *McCulloch v. Maryland*, the Constitution was not a mere legal code; only its "great outlines" and "important objects" were set down in writing; the rest would be left to interpretation. What would be interpreted, however, was likely to be more than the words laid down in the documentary text. Robert McCloskey observed that "the Constitution was potentially the convergence point for all the ideas about fundamental law that had been current in America since the colonization period."[11] These ideas included the principles of popular sovereignty and government by consent; unwritten principles of liberty and freedom embedded in the idea of "higher" law; and common law doctrines relating to property, contract, and criminal procedure. Which of these principles and doctrines would be "constitutionalized" and how they would be balanced or ranked in the process of interpretation could never be known in advance. Equally uncertain was who or what branch of government would have the final word in the interpretation of the Constitution.

Whether *Marbury v. Madison* stands for the principle that the Supreme Court would have the final word depends on how broadly or narrowly the case is construed. A narrow reading could be understood as saying that the Supreme Court has the final word with respect to the meaning of Article III. *Marbury* struck down Section 13 of the Judiciary Act of 1789 because it was thought to vest the Supreme Court with original jurisdiction forbidden by Article III. In short, and consistent with the

---

[8] *The Federalist* No. 78 (see Appendix I).

[9] See Wright, *The Federalist*, 358, 335.

[10] 3 Dall. 386 (1798).

[11] *The American Supreme Court*, rev. ed. (Chicago: University of Chicago Press, 1994), 5.

view that each Jeffersonian department of government should be able to interpret for itself the powers granted to it, the Supreme Court would take charge of its *own* house. But *Marbury* could be read more broadly as vesting the Supreme Court with the authority to interpret all the Constitution's provisions.

Dred Scott v. Sandford (1856, reprinted later in the chapter and in chapter 14) appeared to vindicate the broad reading.[12] In striking down the Missouri Compromise—an act of Congress banning slavery in the Louisiana Territory—it may be said that the Supreme Court took the power of judicial review to a new level. Now, instead of reviewing a statute pertaining to the exercise of its own power under Article III, the Court invalidated a statute enacted pursuant to a grant of authority vested in Congress by Article IV (Section 3, Clause 2). The Court was telling Congress (and by implication the president) what it may or may not do under its constitutional powers. Judicial review had begun to transform itself into a principle of judicial supremacy. For its part, *Dred Scott*—the second instance in which the Court struck down an act of Congress—prompted President Lincoln to remark in his first inaugural address that "if the policy of the government, upon vital questions affecting the whole people, is to be irrevocably fixed by decisions of the Supreme Court, the instant they are made, in ordinary litigation between parties in personal actions, the people will have ceased to be their own rulers, having to that extent practically resigned their government into the hands of that eminent tribunal" (see Appendix C). The whole people did eventually take things into their own hands by ratifying the Fourteenth Amendment, a popular action that overturned the *Dred Scott* decision. This historical moment brought democracy and constitutionalism into a more perfect harmony.

Long before *Dred Scott*, however, the Supreme Court had held that its power also extended to reviewing the constitutionality of state laws. In *Fletcher v. Peck*,[13] decided seven years after *Marbury*, Chief Justice John Marshall relied on the Constitution's contract clause to invalidate a Georgia statute that nullified a corrupt land grant sale and the property rights derived from it. In so doing, he employed judicial review as an instrument of national unity. But *Fletcher* was not the first demonstration of judicial nationalism. Already in *Chisholm v. Georgia*, decided in 1793, the Supreme Court delivered a devastating blow to state sovereignty when it decided a state could be sued in federal court without the state's consent.[14] Under the Constitution, the people of the United States, not the states, were now sovereign, wrote Justice James Wilson, and it is they who ordained in Article III that the states would be "amendable to the jurisdiction of the supreme court." The decision created a firestorm, with Georgia threatening to impose the death penalty on anyone who would enforce the Court's ruling within the state. The decision angered the states, so much so that they introduced and ratified the Eleventh Amendment by 1798,[15] the first change in the constitutional text since the adoption of the Bill of Rights in 1791. The amendment reaffirmed the principle of sovereign immunity that kept states from being sued in

---

[12] 60 U.S. (19 Howard) 393 (1857). *Dred Scott* lives in infamy because it held that African Americans could not be regarded as "citizens" within the meaning of the Constitution.

[13] 6 Cranch 87 (1810).

[14] 2 Dall. (2 U.S.) 419 (1793). Article 3, Section 2, of the Constitution extends the judicial power of the United States, *inter alia*, "to controversies between a State and Citizens of another State." The Supreme Court read this language literally in allowing a South Carolina merchant to sue Georgia for its failure to pay for the supplies he sold the state in 1777.

[15] "The judicial power of the United States shall not be construed to extend to any suit in law or equity, commenced or prosecuted against one of the United States by Citizens of another State, or by Citizens or Subjects of any Foreign States." Adopted in 1795.

federal courts, but it also constituted an implicit acceptance of the proposition that only a constitutional amendment could override the Supreme Court's authoritative interpretation of a constitutional provision.

A brief discussion of *Martin v. Hunter's Lessee* (1816, reprinted later in the chapter) and *Cohens v. Virginia* (1821) will round out this discussion of the early struggle for judicial supremacy. The question presented in *Martin* was whether Congress could extend the Supreme Court's appellate jurisdiction, as laid down in Section 25 of the Judiciary Act of 1789, to the final decision of a *state* high court. Virginia's Court of Appeals held that the Supreme Court was powerless to review its ruling upholding a state policy over the objection that it violated a 1783 treaty between Great Britain and the United States. Under the terms of the Constitution, wrote Justice Story, it is the nature of the case, not the identity of the court, that determines the reach of the Supreme Court's appellate jurisdiction. Story's opinion is historically important for its unambiguous affirmation of national judicial supremacy in the interpretation of federal law and the U.S. Constitution. Similarly, *Cohens v. Virginia* held that the Supreme Court's appellate jurisdiction extended to an appeal from a defendant convicted in a state court for a state criminal offense over his objection that the state law conflicted with a federal law. Relying heavily on Story's opinion in *Martin*, John Marshall ruled that the Eleventh Amendment did not bar the Supreme Court from hearing the case to resolve a question of federal law—here whether the state law did in fact conflict with a federal statute on the same subject—even though the appeal was brought against the state after the case had been fully adjudicated in the state's judicial system.

The reference to the Eleventh Amendment prompts us to fast-forward the clock of history to 1996, when the Supreme Court declared, in *Seminole Tribe of Florida v. Florida*,[16] that the amendment prevents Congress from authorizing suits by Native American tribes against the states to enforce legislation enacted pursuant to the Indian Commerce Clause. The decision caught Congress off guard and appeared to reverse, in the opinion of the dissenting justices, the prevailing historical view, which originated with Justice James Iredell's dissenting opinion in *Chisholm v. Georgia*. In his opinion, the Eleventh Amendment did not bar Congress from creating a private federal cause of action against a state for the violation of a *federal* right. (*Seminole Tribe*, along with more recent 11th Amendment cases, will be taken up again in chapter 6 on federalism.) *Seminole Tribe* is worth mentioning because it revisits two issues central to this and other chapters in this book; namely, the relationship of the Supreme Court to a coequal branch of the federal government and the position of the states in the federal union. We cite *Seminole Tribe* not for the rightness or wrongness of its result but to underscore the current relevance of a debate that began with *Chisholm* in 1793.

Expansion of Judicial Power

The struggle for judicial supremacy has been an ongoing battle, and the Supreme Court has not always emerged victorious. We have seen that *Marbury v. Madison* was at best grudgingly accepted at the time of its deliverance. In addition, a Supreme Court decision interpreting the Constitution could be overturned by a constitutional amendment, the fate suffered by *Chisholm v. Georgia* and *Dred Scott v. Sandford*. Occasionally, however, in order to diminish the possibility of political retaliation, the Supreme Court reverses itself, as it did in 1937 with *NLRB v. Jones & Laughlin Steel*

---

[16] 134 L Ed2 252 (1996).

Corporation (reprinted in chapter 7).[17] Finally, as we shall see in the next subsection, the Supreme Court would develop a number of doctrinal strategies for limiting its power of judicial review.

Judicial review in the United States might have manifested itself in a variety of ways. First, as in *Marbury*, the Supreme Court might have limited itself, out of respect for the principle of separated powers, to holding acts unconstitutional only when necessary to defend itself against encroachments by the other branches. Second, the Court might have declared actions of the other branches incompatible with the Constitution but without ruling them null and void, effectively rendering such opinions advisory rather than obligatory. Third, the Court might have claimed for itself the right to invalidate the actions of the elected branches but only in cases where it is obvious that a violation has occurred. Finally, the Court might have claimed the power to nullify acts of the other branches but confined the enforcement of its rulings to the parties before the Court.[18] It is unclear which of these variations on judicial review would have been most acceptable to the framers, but each would have safeguarded the Court's independence.

As the cases featured in this subsection show, however, judicial power has risen to new levels of prestige and influence in the last half of the twentieth century. Three sets of constitutional cases illustrate the extent to which the Supreme Court has affected the life and law of modern America. Each set represents unprecedented exertions of judicial power. The first deals with school desegregation. *Brown v. Board of Education* (1954, reprinted in chapter 14), which struck down state-enforced segregation of the races in the nation's public schools, ushered in a new era of judicial review. In so doing, *Brown* triggered nothing less than a social revolution in America. Although *Marbury* and *Dred Scott* produced political explosions, they were nonetheless limited in their practical effects. The typical case declaring a law unconstitutional has the effect merely of rendering it unenforceable. The desegregation cases, by contrast, required positive action by the states. *Brown* and its progeny declared that schools segregated by law must be dismantled and replaced with integrated schools where white and African American children would be required to attend school together. These decisions effectively called for society's transformation. Even Americans convinced of *Brown*'s legal, political, and moral correctness would concede that the Supreme Court had lifted judicial power to a new peak.

The Supreme Court remained steadfast and unwavering in its adherence to *Brown* even in the face of massive resistance. Perhaps the most flagrant defiance of *Brown* was the refusal of the governor and legislators of Arkansas to enforce a federal court order to integrate Little Rock's public schools. *Cooper v. Aaron* (1958, reprinted later in the chapter) arose out of the state's refusal to enforce *Brown*, and the Supreme Court used the occasion to make what many acknowledge to be one of the most vigorous assertions of federal judicial power in American history. In a decision signed by all nine justices, the Supreme Court reminded Americans that "the federal judiciary is supreme in the exposition of the law of the Constitution" and thus binding not only on courts of law but also on all legislative and executive officials. *Cooper* is significant for its unambiguous claim to "judicial exclusivity in constitutional interpretation."[19] *Cooper* appeared to represent the Court's move from judicial review to judicial supremacy.

---

[17] 301 U.S. 1 (1937).

[18] For an extended discussion of these variations, see Stephen M. Griffin, *American Constitutionalism* (Princeton: Princeton University Press, 1996), 90–99.

[19] See Geoffrey Stone et al., *Constitutional Law*, 3d ed. (Boston: Little Brown and Company, 1996), 53.

The second set of cases lifting judicial review to new heights began with *Baker v. Carr* (1962, reprinted later in the chapter), a decision described by Justice Frankfurter as "a massive repudiation of the experience of our whole past." By entering the "political thicket" of legislative apportionment, he wrote, the Court was "asserting destructively novel judicial power." The decision triggered no less than a political revolution in America. *Baker* broke new ground by providing a judicial remedy for malapportioned state legislative districts. In subsequent cases, many of which are discussed in chapter 8 ("Voting and Political Representation"), the Court not only extended *Baker*'s reach to congressional and local legislative districts but laid down the rule that all legislative districts must be as equal in population as circumstances would permit. Clear also was the Court's resolve to determine whether any such circumstances warranted deviation from the rule of equal population. And so the Court installed the principle of one person–one vote as the only legitimate basis of legislative representation in America.

Roe v. Wade (1973, reprinted in chapter 11) launched the court on still another constitutional adventure. (Its detractors would call it a misadventure.) *Roe* established a woman's constitutional right to procure an abortion. The right to have an abortion, declared the Court, is a "fundamental liberty" protected against state invasion by the due process liberty clauses of the Fifth and Fourteeth Amendments. By effectively nullifying the anti-abortion statutes of nearly all the states, *Roe* inflamed passions that resisted compromise. It caused divisions between "pro-life" and "pro-choice" forces in political campaigns and became a burning issue in assessing the credentials of Supreme Court nominees. *Brown* and *Baker* also ignited passions and invited resistance to the Court's decrees, but a generation later they were seen by most Americans as landmarks in the development of their constitutional democracy. The same could not be said of *Roe*, and the controversy over its correctness and legitimacy shows no sign of abating.

The national joust over *Roe* has raged as bitterly in the Supreme Court itself as in the public at large. In dissent, Justice Byron White saw the court's vindication of the abortion liberty as "an exercise of raw judicial power."[20] From his point of view, *Baker* and *Brown* were at least rooted in logic founded respectively on the importance of the franchise to American democratic theory and on the antidiscrimination value of the equal protection clause. The right of privacy that produced the abortion liberty, however, seemed far less anchored in the Constitution's language or structure. Sixteen years later, in *Webster v. Reproductive Health Services*,[21] *Roe* narrowly escaped being overruled. The split decision prompted Justice Blackmun to end his concurring opinion on this inauspicious note: "For today," he wrote, "the women of this nation still retain the liberty to control their destinies. But the signs are evident and very ominous, and a chill wind blows."[22] The chill wind was expected to turn icy in *Planned Parenthood of Southeastern Pennsylvania v. Casey* (1992, reprinted in chapter 11). Some commentators predicted that the Court would use *Casey* to overrule *Roe*. As it turned out, *Casey* reaffirmed what the joint opinion described as *Roe*'s "essential holding," although it did qualify much of *Roe*'s original reasoning.

The focus here is not on the substantive merits of *Casey* but on the Court's understanding of its judicial role. First, *Casey* appeared to anchor the right to an abortion in a definition of liberty broader than any previous judicial pronouncement. "At the

---

[20] *Doe v. Bolton*, 410 U.S. 113 at 222 (1973).

[21] 492 U.S. 490 (1989).

[22] Ibid., at 560.

heart of liberty," said the Court, "is the right to define one's own concept of existence, of meaning, of the universe, and of the mystery of human life."[23] The language was new, the assertion untestable, and the implications boundless. Equally boundless was the Court's certitude: "Liberty finds no refuge in a jurisprudence of doubt,"[24] proclaimed the first sentence of the joint opinion. Thus, the "core" of the abortion liberty had to be protected, although the joint opinion went on to declare that states could pass legislation to protect the fetus so long as the states did not impose an "undue burden" on the right of a woman to procure an abortion.

But then the joint opinion appeared to shift the analysis from a focus on the substantive right to the abortion liberty—one that no political majority can validly interfere with—to an argument rooted in majoritarian political theory. The opinion focused now on the importance of social expectations as well as on the Court's own institutional integrity. The justices felt obligated to adhere to precedent because for two decades "people have organized intimate relationships and made choices that define their views of themselves and their places in society, in reliance on the availability of abortion in the event that contraception should fail." The joint opinion then proceeded to remind Americans of *their* responsibility to heed the voice of the Supreme Court when it decides cases "grounded truly in principle."[25] It pointed out that *Roe* is one of those "rare" cases—*Brown* being the other example—that "has a dimension that the resolution of the normal case does not carry. It is the dimension present whenever the Court's interpretation of the Constitution calls the contending sides of a national controversy to end their national divisions by accepting a common mandate rooted in the Constitution."[26] This is the closest the Court has come to instructing Americans generally to honor its judgments, even to the point of asking them to accept its vision of who they are as a people. Here, as in *Cooper v. Aaron*, the Court's judgments were said to be binding on "every state legislator and executive and judicial officer [who] is solemnly committed by oath taken pursuant to Art. VI, cl. 3, 'to support this Constitution.' "[27] Now the Court was asking Americans to share its view of the meaning of life and liberty.

As we have seen, the Court in *Casey* preoccupied itself with the legitimacy of its authority, a problem the court faces whenever it is called upon to deal with new issues on the frontiers of life and law. Examples of newer issues reaching the courts are state limits on assisted suicide, same-sex marriages, and the use of narcotic drugs. Here again the question poses itself: At what point is it proper for the courts to overturn a decision or policy of the elected representatives of the people? Should the Court take it upon itself "to confront some aspect of the general culture and to transform it by force of the superior virtue of the Constitution?"[28] What exactly is the process by which the judiciary discovers unenumerated fundamental rights? This process is by no means clear in the face of varying judicial strategies used to justify such rights. It is likely to become more problematic as the judiciary begins to decide cases in areas of national controversy that might be deemed to implicate, as in *Casey*,

---

[23] 505 U.S. 833, 851.

[24] Ibid., at 844.

[25] Ibid., at 856.

[26] Ibid., at 867.

[27] *Cooper v. Aaron*, 358 U.S. 1, 18 (1958).

[28] Robert F. Nagel, *Judicial Power and the American Character* (Oxford: Oxford University Press, 1994), 72.

"one's own concept of existence, of meaning of the universe, and of the mystery of human life."[29]

This upward spiral of judicial power might have been checked by congressional legislation limiting the appellate jurisdiction of the Supreme Court. Article III (Section 2) of the Constitution subjects the Supreme Court's appellate jurisdiction to "such Exceptions, and under such Regulations as the Congress shall make." But suppose Congress repeals a statute for the purpose of terminating pending litigation arising under it. This happened in *Ex Parte McCardle* (1868, reprinted later in the chapter), which involved a defendant seeking redress under a habeas corpus statute later repealed by Congress. In *McCardle*, the Court declined to decide the case because its jurisdiction under the statute had been withdrawn. Congress' "exceptions" power thus constitutes a powerful legislative check on the Supreme Court. But if exercised to curtail judicial review in basic civil liberties cases—*McCardle* was such a case—Congress would risk subverting the Court's historic role in protecting core constitutional values, raising doubts about the validity of such legislation even in the face of constitutional language that literally permits it. Most congressional efforts to limit the court's appellate jurisdiction have been responses to politically controversial cases. Several cases discussed in this introduction, including *Baker v. Carr* and *Roe v. Wade*, triggered efforts to repeal provisions of the judicial code under which they arose or, alternatively, to reverse the decisions by amending the Constitution. *McCardle*, however, represents one of the few instances in which Congress succeeded in limiting the Court's jurisdiction.[30]

Self-Imposed Limits on Judicial Power

Despite the expansion of judicial authority in recent decades, the Supreme Court has itself created a number of rules restricting access to the federal judiciary, prominent among which are the rules of standing, mootness, and ripeness. They are sometimes called doctrines of "justiciability." A justiciable controversy is one appropriate for judicial determination. Thus, if a dispute is deemed to be non-justiciable, a federal court will decline to decide it; it will have to be resolved politically or in some other nonjudicial way. The rules of standing, ripeness, and mootness are counsels of judicial self-restraint. They proceed from the Court's conscious effort to limit the range of its inquiry, particularly in constitutional litigation, just as they are also designed to limit the range of potential litigants capable of invoking the judicial power of the United States.

Rules of Access

Standing, mootness, and ripeness are manifestations of the Constitution's case or controversy requirement (Article III, Section 2). It limits the "judicial power of the United States" to specified "cases" and "controversies." The Supreme Court underscored the importance of these terms as early as 1793 when President George Wash-

---

[29] *Planned Parenthood v. Casey*, 505 U.S. 833, 851.

[30] The potential limits of congressional power, if any, have been the source of much speculation. See, e.g., Gerald Gunther, *Congressional Power to Curtail Federal Court Jurisdiction*, 36 Stanford Law Review 895 (1984); Michael J. Perry, *The Constitution, the Courts, and Human Rights* (New Haven: Yale University Press, 1982), 129–145; Lawrence G. Sager, *Constitutional Limitations on Congress' Authority to Regulate the Appellate Jurisdiction of the Federal Courts*, 95 Harvard Law Review 17 (1981); Henry M. Hart, *The Power of Congress to Limit the Jurisdiction of the Federal Courts*, 66 Harvard Law Review 1362 (1953).

ington asked the Supreme Court for advice on whether the Franco-American Treaty of 1778 conflicted with the recent Proclamation of Neutrality. In a letter to the President dated 8 August 1793, the Court, then led by Chief Justice John Jay, underscored its lack of power to tender such advice. The "precedent" stuck. To this day, the federal courts refuse to give advisory opinions because their jurisdiction extends only to *real* cases and controversies arising under federal law or the Constitution. This means, chiefly, that litigants appearing in the federal courts must have *standing* to sue.

As Justice Scalia pointed out in *Lujan v. Defenders of Wildlife*,[31] any person invoking the judicial power of the United States "must have suffered an 'injury in fact'—an invasion of a legally protected interest." Three elements are required: First, the plaintiff must show that his or her injury is concrete, particularized, and actual, not conjectural or hypothetical; second, the injury must flow directly from the challenged action; and third, the court must have the capacity effectively to redress the injury. *Lujan*, incidentally, involved the Endangered Species Act of 1973 which instructs the Secretary of Interior to insure that federal agencies do not engage in activities that threaten the critical habitat of animal species listed as endangered. Certain wildlife organizations challenged a rule promulgated by the Secretary exempting foreign lands from the reach of the statute. The Court denied standing to these organizations because they were capable of showing only an *interest* in studying and seeing endangered animals in foreign lands. Their interest was not enough; they would have to produce specific facts showing that the "listed species were being threatened by funded activities abroad [and also] that one or more of [their] members would thereby be 'directly' affected apart from their [particular interest in these animals]."

Standing issues are commonly adjudicated in the Supreme Court, another classic example of which is *Frothingham v. Mellon* (1923) where it was ruled that an individual taxpayer lacked standing to challenge the constitutionality of a federal spending program.[32] In short, individual citizens are powerless to initiate a federal lawsuit merely because they are convinced of a law's unconstitutionality. They must be directly affected and immediately harmed by it and in a way that differentiates their harm from the common interests of others.[33] As applied, standing means that some constitutional provisions may be judicially unenforceable. A prominent example is the provision requiring the publication "from time to time" of all receipts and expenditures of public money (Article I, Section 9, Clause 7). In 1974, the Court held that a taxpayer had no standing to challenge a statute prohibiting the Central Intelligence Agency's budget from being made public.[34] The taxpayer lacked standing because he could not differentiate his complaint from the general interest of other persons concerned and disturbed about this issue.

Mootness and ripeness are similarly concerned with limiting the Supreme Court's reach over issues and persons. A case becomes moot when the litigated complaint loses its adversarial character; that is, when the facts constituting the dispute are no longer "live" and the parties no longer have anything at stake. One such case is

---

[31] 505 U.S. 555 (1992).

[32] 262 U.S. 444, 488.

[33] The Warren Court, however, relaxed this standard for claims based on the express provisions of the Bill of Rights. For example, in *Flast v. Cohen* (1968) the Court decided that taxpayers had standing to sue in challenging aid to religious schools. Chief Justice Warren's majority opinion concluded that "the Frothingham barrier should be lowered when a taxpayer attacks a federal statute on the ground that it violates the Establishment and Free Exercise Clause of the First Amendment." 392 U.S. 83, 85.

[34] *United States v. Richardson*, 418 U.S. 166 (1974).

DeFunis v. Odegaard.[35] An unsuccessful white law school applicant sued the University of Washington for its preferential treatment of certain minorities. The applicant was later admitted to the law school under a court order while the case made its way to the United States Supreme Court. But by the time the case reached the Supreme Court, the applicant was about to finish law school with the University's blessing. This being so, the case was dismissed for being moot: there was no longer a dispute between the applicant and the University, and to render a decision in the absence of an adversary relationship, the Supreme Court noted, would be the equivalent of an advisory opinion.[36]

Finally, the requirement of ripeness is also designed to enhance the adversary character of constitutional litigation. The Supreme Court usually requires all questions of fact and law to be fully developed in cases coming before it. The facts must be hard and the issues clear; if they are not, or if there is a possibility that adjudication would not end the dispute, the Supreme Court may regard the case as unripe for review. Justice Powell's concurring opinion in *Goldwater v. Carter* (1979, reprinted later in the chapter) illustrates one use of the rule. The *Goldwater* Court dismissed a suit initiated by several United States senators against the President for his unilateral termination of an international treaty without the advice and consent of the Senate.[37] Unlike the plurality opinion—which ruled that the issue before the Court was a "political question" inappropriate for judicial resolution—Powell preferred to dismiss the complaint "as not ripe for review" because of his conviction that the conflict had yet to reach the stage of a final impasse between Congress and the president. As Powell's disagreement with the *Goldwater* plurality shows, the doctrine of ripeness, like those of standing and mootness, is anything but a rigid formula. In the hands of the Supreme Court it has been flexibly and variously applied, and for both prudential and constitutional reasons.

Political Questions

Another aspect of justiciability is the so-called "political question" doctrine. It stems largely from the Supreme Court's concern for separation of powers. The Court tends to invoke this doctrine, often for pragmatic reasons, to avoid unnecessary clashes with Congress or the Executive, or for constitutional reasons if the Court should find that the Constitution itself bars judicial review over a particular subject matter. What constitutes a political question unfit for judicial resolution, however, is a disputed issue and one about which the Supreme Court has occasionally changed its mind.

One commentator has described the political question doctrine as "the most amorphous aspect of justiciability."[38] He notes further that the doctrine is driven mainly by "underlying policy concerns" the most important of which, as we would expect, is "to avoid an improper interference with the political judgments of the other branches of the federal government."[39] *Luther v. Borden* (1849, reprinted later in the

---

[35] 416 U.S. 312 (1974).

[36] *Roe v. Wade* represents a major exception to the doctrine of mootness. A pregnant woman who initiates a complaint against a restrictive abortion law is likely not to be pregnant by the time the courts get around to her case. The birth of the child or a miscarriage would render the case moot, thus evading judicial review. The pregnancy, however, may be repeated. In this situation—where the condition is "capable of repetition yet evading review"—the doctrine of mootness will not usually apply.

[37] 444 U.S. 996 (1979).

[38] Kenneth F. Ripple, *Constitutional Litigation* (Charlottesville, Va.: The Michie Company, 1984), 96.

[39] *Ibid.*

chapter) is the classic example of a nonjusticiable political question. Writing for the Court, Chief Justice Taney held that the guarantee clause of Article IV, Section 4 of the Constitution was *judicially* unenforceable because it vested Congress with the final authority to decide whether a state has a republican form of government.

A century later, the guarantee clause would be invoked once again in legislative apportionment controversies.[40] Some litigants argued that apportionment cases were political because the guarantee clause left to Congress the decision whether malapportioned legislative districts violated the concept of "republican" government. In *Baker v. Carr* (1962, reprinted later in the chapter), the Court rejected this argument, holding that challenges to such districts were reviewable under the equal protection standards of the Fourteenth Amendment. In its labored discussion of the guarantee clause, however, the Court found it necessary to define the contours of the political question doctrine. Writing for the majority, Justice Brennan enumerated the situations in which a political question is present:

> *Prominent on the surface of any case held to involve a political question is found a textually demonstrable constitutional commitment of the issue to a coordinate political department; or a lack of judicially discoverable and manageable standards for resolving it; or the impossibility of deciding without an initial policy determination of a kind clearly for nonjudicial discretion; or the impossibility of a court's undertaking independent resolution without expressing lack of the respect due coordinate branches of government; or an unusual need for unquestioning adherence to a political decision already made; or the potentiality of embarassment from multifarious pronouncements by various departments on one question.*[41]

In applying the doctrine to specific cases, the Supreme Court does not always make clear whether it is doing so for prudential or constitutional reasons. In *Goldwater v. Carter*, the political question doctrine appeared to have been applied for prudential reasons; that is, the Court declined to interfere with a foreign policy decision of the president as a matter of propriety given the sensitive issue of international politics involved. On the other hand, in *Nixon v. United States* (1993, reprinted later in the chapter), the Court applied the doctrine because, in its view, the *Constitution* stipulated that the impeachment of a federal judge is the *sole* prerogative of the Senate. But as the various opinions show, the justices were far from unanimous over whether the impeachment of Judge Nixon was a nonjusticiable political question.[42]

Yet there is some hint in the concurring opinion of Justice White that prudential

---

[40] In 1946, the Supreme Court dismissed a constitutional challenge against Illinois' malapportioned congressional districts, partially on the ground that the question was political and thus beyond judicial resolution. *Colegrove v. Green*, 328 U.S. 549 (1946). In 1964 the Court reversed, now holding that congressional apportionments are subject to judicial review under the equal protection clause. See *Wesberry v. Sanders*, 376 U.S. 1 (1964). For a discussion of these and related cases, see chapter 8 on voting and political representation.

[41] *Baker v. Carr*, 369 U.S. 186, 217 (1962).

[42] *Goldwater v. Carter*, cited previously, provides another illustration of these differing perspectives. The Court's plurality (consisting of Chief Justice Burger and Justices Rehnquist, Stewart, and Stevens) regarded President Carter's decision to abrogate the defense treaty with Taiwan as nonjusticiable "because it involves the authority of the President in the conduct of our country's foreign relations." Justice Powell, as indicated above, thought the issue was justiciable but preferred to decline review because the complaint was not ripe for review. Justice Brennan, the only member of the Court to decide the case on its merits, ruled that the decision to abrogate the treaty "rests upon the President's well-established authority to recognize, and withdraw recognition from, foreign governments."

reasoning may have dictated the result in *Nixon*. Whether prudential rather than constitutional reasons are offered for applying the political question doctrine is largely a matter of judgment. In short, the Court may decline to decide a case if it is politically too "hot" to handle or if the justices feel, as Justice Brennan noted in *Baker*, that the exercise of jurisdiction would manifest lack of regard for the competence or judgment of another branch of government. As with most of the "passive virtues" that serve as guides to the legitimacy of judicial review, the doctrine of political questions seems to be one way, in some circumstances, of reconciling the principles of constitutionalism and democracy.

Finally, the Court has more or less adhered to various maxims of judicial restraint set forth by Justice Brandeis in his often cited concurring opinion in *Ashwander v. Tennessee Valley Authority* (1936).[43] Known as the "Ashwander rules," these maxims or "considerations of propriety," as Brandeis called them, may be summarized as follows:

1. The Court will not anticipate a question of constitutional law in advance of the necessity of deciding it, nor will the Court formulate a rule of constitutional law broader than is required by the precise facts to which it is to be applied.

2. The Court will not pass upon a constitutional question properly presented by the record if some other ground upon which the case may be disposed of is also present.

3. If a statute is challenged on constitutional grounds, the Court will first ascertain whether a construction of the statute is fairly possible by which the constitutional question may be avoided.[44]

In brief, the Court reaches constitutional questions last not first. To the extent that these rules continue to be observed, they also suggest that a constitutional decision is a serious matter, for such a decision can be overruled only by the Court itself or by a constitutional amendment—which is far more difficult to achieve. Americans tend to see these rules and other norms of constitutional adjudication discussed in this section as logical and natural ingredients of any viable regime of judicial review. The next section shows that they are uniquely American.

Judicial Review and Constitutional Amendments

To what extent may the Supreme Court review the process of amending the Constitution? We have seen that a constitutional case decided by the Court may be overturned by a constitutional amendment. But may the Court in turn consider the validity of a constitutional amendment? We noted in chapter 2 that several foreign courts have claimed the authority to declare constitutional amendments unconstitutional, but the Supreme Court has declined to arrogate to itself any such power, strongly suggesting in *Leser v. Garnett* (1922) that a constitutional amendment will not be held invalid for what it contains.[45] Amending the Constitution is a fundamental act of popular sovereignty, the ultimate democratic moment. Any amendment to the Constitution that requires a complex two-step procedure requiring a two-thirds vote in Congress

---

[43] 297 U.S. 288.

[44] Ibid., 346–348.

[45] 258 U.S. 130 (1922). Male voters in Maryland challenged the validity of the Nineteenth Amendment because, by expanding the suffrage to women, they argued that it destroyed the state's autonomy as a political body. Defining a state's electorate, they held, was not a valid subject of a constitutional amendment. Speaking for a unanimous tribunal, Justice Brandeis flatly rejected the argument and upheld the validity of the amendment.

(the proposal stage) and a three-fourths vote of the states (the ratification stage) would probably be regarded by most Americans as beyond the power of judicial review.[46]

But may the Supreme Court oversee the process of amending the Constitution? In several cases, the Court has interpreted Article V as it would any other constitutional provision. Several important cases may be mentioned: *Hollingsworth v. Virginia* (1798) established early on that the President has no role to play in the amendment process, the case having been brought to challenge the validity of the Eleventh Amendment because it had not been presented to the President for his approval.[47] In *Hawke v. Smith* (1920), the Court ruled that a state has no authority to require its legislature to submit its ratification of an amendment to a popular referendum, having made clear that a state derives its authority to ratify from the Federal Constitution which requires ratification by *legislatures*.[48] The *National Prohibition Cases*, finally, held that the two-thirds vote requirement in Congress for proposing constitutional amendments applies to two-thirds of those present and voting and not two-thirds of all the members of the two houses.[49]

On two other disputed issues, however, the Court declined to intervene. One was whether a state legislature may withdraw its ratification of an amendment; the other whether a proposed amendment loses its vitality owing to the lapse of time since its submission. *Coleman v. Miller* (1939) addressed both questions.[50] The precise issue in *Coleman* was whether the Court should restrain Kansas officials from certifying the ratification of a constitutional amendment because of its earlier rejection by the state legislature. Regarding the matter as a political question, the Court declared that the "efficacy of ratification by state legislatures" rests ultimately with "Congress in the exercise of its control over the promulgation of the adoption of the amendment."

More serious was the "lapse of time" question. Here the Child Labor Amendment had been proposed in 1924, rejected by the Kansas state legislature in 1925, and subsequently ratified in 1937. The thirteen-year interlude between submission and ratification, it was argued, stripped the amendment of its vitality. No time limitation had been imposed and, in any event, declared the Court, the question of what constitutes a "reasonable time" for ratifying an amendment was one to be decided by Congress, not the Court. This view, incidentally, governed the ratification of the Twenty-seventh Amendment on congressional pay except that here the time limit stretched into infinity. It was introduced by James Madison in 1789, buried in 1800, disinterred in 1978, and ratified in 1992. Was the ratification legal? The House of Representatives by a vote of 414 to 3 and the Senate by 99 to 0 declared the amendment adopted. *Coleman* appeared to have settled the issue; there was no judicial interference with Congress' judgment.

To what extent may the Supreme Court oversee the enforcement of an amendment? This remaining question deserves our attention in light of the decades-long controversy surrounding Congress' power to enforce the equal protection and due process guarantees of the Fourteenth Amendment. Recall that Section 5 of the Amendment authorizes Congress to enforce the Amendment "by appropriate legisla-

---

[46] See Laurence H. Tribe's discussion of unconstitutional amendments in *American Constitutional Law*, 3rd edition, Vol. 1 (New York: Foundation Press, 2000), 110–117.

[47] 3 U.S. (3 Dall.) 378 (1798).

[48] 253 U.S. 221 (1920).

[49] 253 U.S. 350 (1919).

[50] 307 U.S. 433 (1939).

tion." The Supreme Court, however, has severely circumscribed this power. In the *Civil Rights Cases* (1883, reprinted in chapter 14), the Court ruled that this power is only remedial in nature; that is, Congress may exercise the power only to repair or redress a state violation of a constitutional command, and may not decide for itself what the command actually requires. In short, the Court reserved to itself the last word on Congress' enforcement power.

In the controversial case of *Katzenbach v. Morgan* (1966),[51] the Supreme Court went even further in defining congressional power under Section 5. *Morgan* sustained the constitutionality of a federal statute—the Voting Rights Act of 1965—prohibiting the enforcement of an otherwise valid English-language literacy test against Puerto Rican voters in New York.[52] Until this case, it was widely understood that Congress could employ its enforcement power under the Fourteenth Amendment only to redress a practice found unconstitutional by the Supreme Court. Instead, Congress invalidated a state practice the Court had previously upheld as a rational means of supervising elections.[53] The *Morgan* Court appeared to be simultaneously limiting and magnifying its power of judicial review. It was limiting its power by relaxing its control over the exercise of congressional power. More significantly, however, the Court effectively ruled that while Congress may determine what state practices should be banned over and above the Court's prohibitions, it may not reverse judicial bans on such practices. In short, Congress may "ratchet" up Fourteenth Amendment protections as judicially defined but may not "ratchet" them down.

But years later, in *Boerne v. Flores* (1997, reprinted in chapter 13), the Court appeared to sing a slightly different tune. Under its Section 5 power, Congress had enacted the Religious Freedom Restoration Act (1993) to impose on the states a standard that it believed was necessary to protect the "free exercise" of religion.[54] Like the statute in *Morgan*, this exercise of congressional authority was not designed to remedy a constitutional violation. The *Boerne* Court distinguished *Morgan* by differentiating between Congress' "enforcement" of the Fourteenth Amendment and its "determination" of what constitutes a constitutional violation. The Court admitted that "the line between measures that remedy or prevent unconstitutional actions and measures that make a substantive change in the governing law is not easy to discern." This verbal dance seemed to signal the Court's unease with *Morgan* and the doubts it may have raised about its power of finality in judicial review.

Comparative Perspectives

In his classic treatise on American democracy, Alexis de Tocqueville observed that "the representative system of government has been adopted in several states of Europe, but we are not aware that any nation of the globe has hitherto organized a judicial power on the principle now adopted by the Americans."[55] He was, of course,

---

[51] 384 U.S. 641.

[52] In particular, the statute provided that no person who had successfully completed the sixth primary grade in a public or private Puerto Rican school in which the language of instruction was other than English could be denied the right to vote because of his or her inability to read or write English.

[53] *Lassiter v. Northampton County Bd. Of Election*, 360 U.S. 45 (1959).

[54] The primary purpose of the Act was to reinstate the compelling interest test in "free exercise" cases that had prevailed before the Supreme Court's decision in *Employment Div. v. Smith* (1990, reprinted in chapter 13). The compelling interest test required a state to advance a compelling reason to justify the application of an otherwise valid law that substantially impinges upon an individual's religious freedom.

[55] Alexis de Tocqueville, *Democracy in America* (London: Oxford University Press, 1952), 79.

speaking of judicial review. If Tocqueville were to observe the world today, he would be astonished to note that judicial review has emerged as a principle of governance in many if not most of the world's advanced constitutional democracies. This is mainly a post–Second World War development, to no small degree the product of American influence, and primarily in response to the excesses of prewar popular democracies.[56] Judicial review in the United States, as we have seen, was—and remains—largely a product of judicial interpretation. What is new about the emergence of judicial review in Europe, Asia, and Canada—and, most recently, the former communist countries of Eastern Europe—is not merely the broad scale on which it has been adopted, but the conscious decision of constitution-makers to place the guardianship of fundamental law in judicial hands.[57]

What accounts for this astonishing institutional development? One possible explanation—besides the historical memory of popular democracies succumbing to the totalitarian appeals—is the growth of big government and its increasing tendency to colonize areas of life and society previously consigned to the private sphere. Judicial review cannot slow the growth of government, but it can check the exercise of public power at crucial points, particularly when individual rights are implicated. Indeed, judicial review has expanded with the adoption in some countries of a constitutionally entrenched bill of rights, a most prominent illustration of which is Canada's Charter of Rights and Freedoms, adopted in 1982. Both developments—the growth of big government and the adoption of entrenched bills of rights—go hand-in-hand with the challenge that modern constitutionalism has mounted against the principle of parliamentary supremacy. Yet, as in the United States, the exercise of judicial review in other countries has also created severe tensions between the principles of constitutionalism and democracy.

The United States might be most gainfully compared in this short treatment of foreign constitutionalism to the judicial review administrations of Canada and selected European jurisdictions. Among the countries of Europe which have adopted judicial review on a scale equal to and in some instances exceeding that of the United States are Germany, France, Italy, and Spain. As we saw in chapter 1, each of these countries has housed judicial review in specialized courts of constitutional review created apart from and independent of the ordinary judicial establishment. Unlike the United States Supreme Court, these constitutional courts are not courts of general appellate jurisdiction. In common law systems such as the United States and Canada, any court may decide a constitutional issue in the normal course of litigation. In civil law systems, constitutional courts have no general appellate jurisdiction; their competence is confined to determining whether laws or other state acts having the force of law conform to the Constitution. Finally, the most prominent example of a transnational constitutional tribunal is the European Court of Human Rights, which is entrusted with the enforcement of the European Convention on Human Rights in the member-states of the Council of Europe.

---

[56] See Louis Henkin and Albert J. Rosenthal, *Constitutionalism and Rights: The Influence of the United States Constitution Abroad* (New York: Columbia University Press, 1990).

[57] See generally A.R. Brewer-Carias, *Judicial Review in Comparative Law* (Cambridge: Cambridge University Press, 1989); Lawrence W. Beer, *Constitutionalism in Asia: Asian Views of the American Influence*, Occasional Papers in Contemporary Asian Studies (Baltimore: School of Law, University of Maryland, 1988); Symposium on *Comparative Constitutionalism: Theoretical Perspectives on the Role of Constitutions in the Interplay Between Identity and Diversity*, 14 Cardozo Law Review 497–956 (January 1993); and Herman Schwartz, *The New East European Constitutional Courts*, 13 Michigan Journal of International Law 741 (1992).

Of the constitutional tribunals just mentioned, Germany's Federal Constitutional Court, created in 1951, is the oldest. The German Court is also one of the world's most powerful constitutional tribunals, rivaled in prestige and influence only by the United States Supreme Court. In fact, Germany's Constitutional Court has inspired the creation of most European constitutional tribunals, including the new constitutional courts of Hungary, Russia, Bulgaria, Lithuania, Poland, and the Czech Republic. Of course, there are significant differences in the powers conferred on these tribunals. Italy, for example, confines the competence of its constitutional court to hearing constitutional disputes between branches and levels of government. The Italian Court may also hear issues of constitutionality certified to it by judges of ordinary courts. On the other hand, France's Constitutional Council exercises what is known as "preventive" judicial review; that is, it can only examine the constitutionality of pending legislative bills and only on the request of the president, prime minister, president of one of the parliamentary assemblies, or a prescribed number of parliamentary representatives—the opposite of the U.S. rule against advisory opinions. In addition, the council is empowered to review the constitutionality of parliamentary and presidential elections as well as referenda.

Germany's Federal Constitutional Court combines all the foregoing jurisdiction along with many other competences, including the power to declare political parties unconstitutional and to hear the complaints of ordinary citizens whose constitutional rights have been infringed by any law or act of government. Even more powerful is the Hungarian Constitutional Court, recently described as "the most activist court in the former Soviet world."[58] Pursuant to the so-called "popular action"—a complaint or petition that can be brought by any citizen or public official against any law that he or she deems unconstitutional—the Court decides cases mainly on abstract judicial review. On average, the Court strikes down about one law per week and, in addition, has often ruled that parliament acts "unconstitutionally by omission" if it fails to enact a law that the Constitution requires.[59] Contrary to the canons of restraint observed by the U.S. Supreme Court, the Hungarian Court will declare a law unconstitutional if it *can be* construed as unconstitutional. The German Court, by contrast, nearly always sustains a statute if it *can be* interpreted to conform to the Constitution.

The American system of judicial review thus differs in many respects from the continental systems. We have already noted that judicial review in the United States is a power exercised by all courts but subject to "case" and "controversy" requirements, the political question doctrine, and certain prudential guidelines for avoiding a ruling on constitutional grounds—all passive virtues that would seem to be vices in Hungary and other countries. Germany's Federal Constitutional Court also finds these passive virtues unacceptable. Its approach to constitutional review has been described as follows:

> *The preservation of the constitutional state in* all *of its particulars is . . . the function of the Federal Constitutional Court. . . . [T]he Court's role is to decide constitutional issues, not to avoid them or to resolve them as a matter of last resort. When serious doubts arise over the validity of a law or practice having the force of law, the Court's function is to resolve the doubt in the interest of constitutional clarity and certainty. Gaps in the Constitution cry out for closure, for which reason all*

---

[58] See remarks of Kim Scheppele in Symposium: *Communist "Refolution" in the Ex-Communist World: The Rule of Law*, 12 American University Journal of International Law and Policy 95 (1997).

[59] *Ibid.*, 96.

issues arising under the Basic Law's provisions relating to the maintenance of peace and security appear to be justiciable. Vague constitutional terms such as "human dignity," "democracy," and "social state" have also been found to possess a sharp set of teeth capable of killing legislation and even to compel certain forms of state action if public officials are to avoid its bite. In the United States, by contrast, major constitutional provisions like the republican form of government clause . . . and the clause on the ratification of amendments to the Constitution have been relegated to the limbo of nonjusticiability.[60]

In brief, a specialized constitutional court is conceptualized as the *supreme* guardian of the constitution, its main function being to review laws of doubtful constitutionality and to annul them if they are unconstitutional. A proceeding known as abstract judicial review is, as already noted, one common method of examining such laws. In Germany, for example, upon the request of a state government or one-third of the members of the national parliament, a duty enacted and promulgated law—even before it enters into force—may be reviewed by the constitutional court. In this way, the losers in a legislative battle are able to turn a political dispute almost immediately into a constitutional controversy.

What this means in the German context is that all provisions of the Constitution are enforceable. In the United States, by contrast, some constitutional provisions are unenforceable because they give rise to "political" questions or because the plaintiff in a case lacks standing to challenge an unconstitutional action. *Constitutional* review in Europe is thus different from *judicial* review in the United States. Yet we are also seeing some kind of convergence taking place between judicial power in Europe and in the United States. First, in recent years the Supreme Court has been given total control over its own docket, allowing it to take only those cases it wishes to decide. With such discretion, the Court has been able to concentrate on constitutional issues and thus to transform itself into a virtual European-style constitutional court. Second, the political question doctrine has been subject to some narrowing in recent years, so that what was previously regarded as nonjusticiable is now open to adjudication.

Relatedly, the doctrine of standing seems to be as open or closed as the Supreme Court wishes. In addition, academic legal critics have weighed in with their own criticism of the standing cases discussed earlier. One of these critics has remarked: "When a genuine disagreement about the meaning of the Constitution erupts that affects the lives of a significant segment of the population, the Court's duty is to construe the Constitution, whether or not the disagreement can be choreographed as a classic *Marbury* dispute."[61] With regard to environmental matters, Congress appears to have had a similar model of judicial review in mind; it has often defined new injuries—e.g., interfering with recreational activities such as whale watching and outdoor hiking—and articulated chains of causation that give rise to a case or controversy where none existed before. *Lujan v. Defenders of Wildlife*, as noted earlier, involved a citizen-suit authorized by Congress for the protection of endangered species. Although the citizen-suit in *Lujan* failed, there were strong dissenting opinions to the contrary.

On the other hand, if the barriers to standing and the political question doctrine were to be dropped altogether, the Supreme Court's power would increase dramati-

---

[60] See Donald P. Kommers, *German Constitutionalism: A Prolegomenon*, 40 Emory Law Journal, 848–49 (1991).

[61] See "Justiciability, Remedies, and the Burger Court" in Herman Schwartz ed., *The Burger Years: Rights and Wrongs in the Supreme Court 1969–1986* (New York: Viking Penguin Inc., 1987), 16.

cally. This would raise significant questions about the relationship between constitutionalism and democracy. The tension between these contrasting principles seems more easily accommodated under the Canadian and German constitutions. Section 33 of Canada's Charter of Rights and Liberties contains an override provision, allowing the Parliament to declare that one of its enactments "shall operate notwithstanding" a judicial decision to the contrary. In Germany, the Federal Constitutional Court often declares a statute "incompatible" with the Constitution but declines to nullify it, a procedure which keeps the statute on the law books but allows the legislature to take a second look at it while proceeding to correct the constitutional deficiency. In addition, the German Court is unbound by the doctrine of *stare decisis* and, finally, the German Basic Law is much easier to amend than the Constitution of the United States.

Selected Bibliography

Ackerman, Bruce. *We the People.* Cambridge: Harvard University Press, 1991.

Barber, Sotirios A. *On What the Constitution Means.* Baltimore: The Johns Hopkins University Press, 1984.

Bickel, Alexander M. *The Least Dangerous Branch: The Supreme Court at the Bar of Politics.* New York: Bobbs-Merrill, 1962.

Choper, Jesse H. *Judicial Review and the National Political Process.* Chicago: University of Chicago Press, 1980.

Dworkin, Ronald. *Taking Rights Seriously.* Cambridge: Harvard University Press, 1977.

Ely, John Hart. *Democracy and Distrust: A Theory of Judicial Review.* Cambridge: Harvard University Press, 1980.

Fisher, Louis. *Constitutional Dialogues: Interpretation as Political Process.* Princeton, N.J.: Princeton University Press, 1988.

Franck, Matthew J. *Against the Imperial Judiciary.* Lawrence, Kan.: University Press of Kansas, 1996.

Harris, William F. *The Interpretable Constitution.* Baltimore: The Johns Hopkins University Press, 1993.

Jacobsohn, Gary L. *The Supreme Court and the Decline of Constitutional Aspiration.* Totowa, N.J.: Rowman & Littlefield, 1986.

Judicial Review: Blessing or Curse? Or Both? A Symposium in Commemoration of the Bicentennial of Marbury v. Madison. 38 Wake Forest Law Review 313–838 (2003)

McDowell, Gary L. *Curbing the Courts: The Constitution and the Limits of Judicial Power.* Baton Rouge: Louisiana State University Press, 1988.

Murphy, Walter F. *Who Shall Interpret: The Quest for the Ultimate Constitutional Interpreter,* 48 Review of Politics 401 (1986).

Nagel, Robert F. *Constitutional Cultures: The Mentality and Consequences of Judicial Review.* Berkeley: University of California Press, 1989.

Perry, Michael J. *The Constitution, Courts, and Human Rights.* New Haven, Conn.: Yale University Press, 1982.

Powell, Jefferson H. *The Moral Tradition of American Constitutionalism.* Durham, N.C.: Duke University Press, 1993.

Seidman, Louis Michael and Mark V. Tushnet, *Remnants of Belief.* Oxford: Oxford University Press, 1996.

Smith, Rogers M. *Liberalism and American Constitutional Law.* Cambridge: Harvard University Press, 1985.

Sunstein, Cass R. *The Partial Constitution.* Cambridge: Harvard University Press, 1993.

Tushnet, Mark. *Taking the Constitution Away from the Courts.* Princeton: Princeton University Press, 1999).

Selected Comparative Bibliography

Beaty, David M., ed. *Human Rights and Judicial Review: A Comparative Perspective.* Dordrecht, Boston and London: Martinus Nijhoff Publishers, 1994.

Brewer-Carias, A.R. *Judicial Review in Comparative Law.* Cambridge: Cambridge University Press, 1989.

Cappelletti, Mauro. *The Judicial Process in Comparative Perspective.* Oxford: Clarendon Press, 1989.

Franck, Thomas M. *Political Questions/Judicial Answers.* Princeton: Princeton University Press, 1992.

Greenberg, Douglas et al., eds. *Constitutionalism and Democracy: Transitions in the Contemporary World.* New York: Oxford University Press, 1993.

Howe, Paul and Peter H. Russell, eds. *Judicial Power and Canadian Democracy.* Montreal: McGill-Queen's University Press, 2001.

Kavas, Igor I. *Supranational and Constitutional Courts in Europe: Functions and Sources.* Buffalo, N.Y.: William S. Hein & Co., 1992.

King, Preston and Andrea Bosco, eds. *A Constitution For Europe.* London: Lothian Foundation Press, 1991.

Klug, Heinz. *Constituting Democracy: Law, Globalsim and South Africa's Political Reconstruction.* Cambridge: Cambridge University Press, 2000.

Mandel, Michael. *The Charter of Rights and the Legalization of Politics in Canada.* Toronto: Thompson Educational Publishing, Inc., 1994.

Manfredi, Christopher P. *Judicial Power and the Charter.* 2nd ed. Oxford: Oxford University Press, 2001.

McKenna, Marian C., ed. *The Canadian and American Constitutions in Comparative Perspective.* Calgary: University of Calgary Press, 1993.

Patapan, Haig. *Judging Democracy: The New Politics of the High Court of Australia.* Cambridge: Cambridge University Press, 2000.

Rogowski, Ralf and Thomas Gawron, eds. *Constitutional Courts in Comparison: The U.S. Supreme Court and the German Federal Constitutional Court.* New York: Berghahn Books, 2002.

Russell, Peter H. and David M. O'Brien, eds. *Judicial Independence in the Age of Democracy.* Charlottesville: University Press of Virginia, 2001.

Sartori, Giovanni. *Comparative Constitutional Engineering.* New York: New York University Press, 1994.

Schwarze, Jürgen ed. *The Birth of a European Constitutional Order.* Baden-Baden: Nomos Verlagsgesellschaft, 2001.

Shapiro, Martin. *Courts: A Comparative and Political Analysis.* Chicago: University of Chicago Press, 1981.

Stone, Alec. *The Birth of Judicial Politics in France: The Constitutional Council in Comparative Perspective.* Oxford: Oxford University Press, 1992.

Sweet, Alec Stone. *Governing with Judges: Constitutional Politics in Europe.* Oxford: Oxford University Press, 2000.

Marbury v. Madison

5 U.S. 137, 1 Cranch 137, 2 L. Ed. 60 (1803)

Near the end of his term of office President Adams nominated William Marbury to the office of justice of the peace in the District of Columbia. The nomination was affirmed by the Senate, the commission was signed by the president, and the seal of the United States was affixed by the secretary of state. When Adams' term of office expired, Marbury applied to James Madison, secretary of state under Jefferson, for the delivery of his commission. Jefferson maintained that the commission was not valid until delivered and ordered Madison to withhold it, whereupon Marbury applied to the Supreme Court for a writ of *mandamus.* The Court ordered Madison to show cause why the writ should not be issued. The case proceeded after a showing of no cause. Opinion of the Court: *Marshall,* Chase, Paterson, Washington. Not participating: Cushing, Moore.

Mr. Chief Justice MARSHALL delivered the opinion of the Court.

In the order in which the court has viewed this subject, the following questions have been considered and decided.

1st. Has the applicant a right to the commission he demands? . . .

It is . . . decidedly the opinion of the court, that when a commission has been signed by the President, the appointment is made; and that the commission is complete when the seal of the United States has been affixed to it by the Secretary of State. . . .

Mr. Marbury, then, since the commission was signed by the President, and sealed by the Secretary of State, was appointed. . . .

To withhold his commission, therefore, is an act deemed by the court not warranted by law, but violative of a vested legal right.

This brings us to the second inquiry; which is

2d. If he has a right, and that right has been violated, do the laws of his country afford him a remedy?

The very essence of civil liberty certainly consists in the right of every individual to claim the protection of the laws, whenever he receives an injury. One of the first duties of government is to afford that protection. . . .

3d. If they do afford him a remedy, is it a *mandamus* issuing from this court? . . .

It is then the opinion of the court,

1. That by signing the commission of Mr. Marbury, the president of the United States appointed him a justice of peace for the county of Washington in the district of Columbia; and that the seal of the United States, affixed thereto by the secretary of state, is conclusive testimony of the verity of the signature, and of the completion of the appointment; and that the appointment conferred on him a legal right to the office for the space of five years.

2. That, having this legal title to the office, he has a consequent right to the commission; a refusal to deliver which is a plain violation of that right, for which the laws of his country afford him a remedy.

It remains to be inquired whether,

3. He is entitled to the remedy for which he applies. This depends on,

    1. The nature of the writ applied for; and,

    2. The power of this court. . . .

. . . The intimate political relation subsisting between the President . . . and the heads of departments, necessarily renders any legal investigation of these acts of one of those high officers peculiarly irksome, as well as delicate; and excites some hesitation with respect to the propriety of entering into such investigation. . . .

It is scarcely necessary for the court to disclaim all pretension to such jurisdiction. An extravagance, so absurd and excessive, could not have been entertained for a moment. The province of the court is, solely, to decide on the rights of individuals, not to inquire how the executive, or executive officers, perform duties in which they have a discretion. Questions in their nature political, or which are, by the constitution and laws, submitted to the executive, can never be made in this court. . . .

This, then, is a plain case of a *mandamus*, either to deliver the commission, or a copy of it from the record; and it only remains to be inquired,

Whether it can issue from this court.

The act to establish the judicial courts of the United States authorizes the supreme court "to issue writs of *mandamus*, in cases warranted by the principles and usages of law, to any courts appointed, or persons holding office, under the authority of the United States."

The secretary of state, being a person, holding an office under the authority of the United States, is precisely within the letter of the description; and if this court is not authorized to issue a writ of *mandamus* to such an officer, it must be because the law is unconstitutional, and therefore absolutely incapable of conferring the authority, and assigning the duties which its words purport to confer and assign.

The constitution vests the whole judicial power of the United States in one supreme court, and such inferior courts as congress shall, from time to time, ordain and establish. This power is expressly extended to all cases arising under the laws of the United States; and consequently, in some form, may be exercised over the present case; because the right claimed is given by a law of the United States.

In the distribution of this power it is declared that "the supreme court shall have original jurisdiction in all cases affecting ambassadors, other public ministers and consuls, and those in which a state shall be a party. In all other cases, the supreme court shall have appellate jurisdiction."

It has been insisted at the bar, that as the original grant of jurisdiction to the supreme and inferior courts is general, and the clause, assigning original jurisdiction to the supreme court, contains no negative or restrictive words; the power remains to the legislature to assign original jurisdiction to that court in other cases than those specified in the article which has been recited; provided those cases belong to the judicial power of the United States.

If it had been intended to leave it in the discretion of the legislature to apportion the judicial power between the supreme and inferior courts according to the will of that body, it would certainly have been useless to have proceeded further than to have defined the judicial power, and the tribunals in which it should be vested. The subsequent part of the section is mere surplusage, is entirely

without meaning, if such is to be the construction. If congress remains at liberty to give this court appellate jurisdiction, where the constitution has declared their jurisdiction shall be original; and original jurisdiction where the constitution has declared it shall be appellate; the distribution of jurisdiction made in the constitution, is form without substance.

Affirmative words are often, in their operation, negative of other objects than those affirmed; and in this case, a negative or exclusive sense must be given to them or they have no operation at all.

It cannot be presumed that any clause in the constitution is intended to be without effect; and therefore, such a construction is inadmissible, unless the words require it.

When an instrument organizing fundamentally a judicial system, divides it into one supreme, and so many inferior courts as the legislature may ordain and establish; then enumerates its powers, and proceeds so far to distribute them, as to define the jurisdiction of the supreme court by declaring the cases in which it shall take original jurisdiction, and that in others it shall take appellate jurisdiction, the plain import of the words seems to be, that in one class of cases its jurisdiction is original, and not appellate; in the other it is appellate, and not original. If any other construction would render the clause inoperative, that is an additional reason for rejecting such other construction, and for adhering to the obvious meaning.

To enable this court then to issue a *mandamus*, it must be shown to be an exercise of appellate jurisdiction, or to be necessary to enable them to exercise appellate jurisdiction.

It has been stated at the bar that the appellate jurisdiction may be exercised in a variety of forms, and that if it be the will of the legislature that a *mandamus* should be used for that purpose, that will must be obeyed. This is true; yet the jurisdiction must be appellate, not original. It is the essential criterion of appellate jurisdiction, that it revises and corrects the proceedings in a cause already instituted, and does not create that case. Although, therefore, a *mandamus* may be directed to courts, yet to in effect the same as to sustain an original action for that paper, and therefore seems not to belong to appellate, but to original jurisdiction. Neither is it necessary in such a case as this, to enable the court to exercise its appellate jurisdiction.

The authority, therefore, given to the supreme court, by the act establishing the judicial courts of the United States, to issue writs of *mandamus* to public officers, appears not to be warranted by the constitution; and it becomes necessary to inquire whether a jurisdiction, so conferred, can be exercised.

Comparative Note 3.1

[Israel, like England, does not have a written constitution in the form of a single documentary text. Rather, the country's parliament, the Knesset, has enacted a number of "basic laws" rooted in the country's political culture. In 1995, Israel's Supreme Court claimed the power to declare laws or policies unconstitutional if they violate these basic laws even though the laws themselves could be repealed by a legislative majority. The Court's opinion, written by Chief Justice A. Barak, was an act of judicial creation fully worthy of Chief Justice John Marshall's reasoning in *Marbury v. Madison*.]

77. . . . The two Basic Laws contain no "supremacy clause." What is the law in this situation? It seems to me that our legal tradition requires us to conclude that the remedy for an unconstitutional law is its invalidation and that the courts have been endowed with the authority to declare it so. Just as a regulation that conflicts with a statute is void and may be declared as

such by the court, so also should be the case when a regular law conflicts with a Basic Law; the law is void and the court is empowered to declare it so.

78. The doctrine of judicial review of constitutionality is based upon the "rule of law," or, more correctly, the rule of the constitution. . . . The central role of the court in a democratic society is "to protect the rule of law. This means, inter alia, that it must enforce the law in the institutions of the government and it must ensure that the government acts according to the law." When a given legal system includes a constitution, the "rule of law" requires that the sovereignty of the constitution be protected. Thus the Knesset, in using its constituent authority, endowed the State with Basic Laws. In the normative hierarchy the Basic Laws are paramount. In order to fulfill the Knesset's directives, regular legislation that conflicts with a Basic law must be invalidated. . . .

Source: United Mizrahi Bank Ltd. V. Migdal Village, 49 (4) P.D. 221 (1995).

The question, whether an act, repugnant to the constitution, can become the law of the land, is a question deeply interesting to the United States; but, happily, not of an intricacy proportioned to its interest. It seems only necessary to recognise certain principles, supposed to have been long and well established, to decide it.

That the people have an original right to establish, for their future government, such principles as, in their opinion, shall most conduce to their own happiness, is the basis on which the whole American fabric has been erected. The exercise of this original right is a very great exertion; nor can it nor ought it to be frequently repeated. The principles, therefore, so established are deemed fundamental. And as the authority, from which they proceed, is supreme, and can seldom act, they are designed to be permanent. This original and supreme will organizes the government, and assigns to different departments their respective powers. It may either stop here; or establish certain limits not to be transcended by those departments.

The government of the United States is of the latter description. The powers of the legislature are defined and limited; and that those limits may not be mistaken or forgotten, the constitution is written. To what purpose are powers limited, and to what purpose is that limitation committed to writing; if these limits may at any time, be passed by those intended to be restrained? The distinction,

between a government with limited and unlimited powers is abolished, if those limits do not confine the persons on whom they are imposed, and if acts prohibited and acts allowed are of equal obligation. It is a proposition too plain to be contested, that the constitution controls any legislative act repugnant to it; or, that the legislature may alter the constitution by an ordinary act.

Between these alternatives there is no middle ground. The constitution is either a superior, paramount law, unchangeable by ordinary means, or it is on a level with ordinary legislative acts, and like other acts, is alterable when the legislature shall please to alter it.

If the former part of the alternative be true, then a legislative act contrary to the constitution is not law: if the latter part be true, then written constitutions are absurd attempts on the part of the people, to limit a power in its own nature illimitable.

Certainly all those who have framed written constitutions contemplate them as forming the fundamental and paramount law of the nation, and consequently the theory of every such government must be, that an act of the legislature repugnant to the constitution is void.

This theory is essentially attached to a written constitution, and is consequently to be considered by this court as one of the fundamental principles of our society. It is not therefore to be lost sight of in the further consideration of this subject.

If an act of the legislature, repugnant to the constitution is void, does it, notwithstanding its invalidity, bind the courts and oblige them to give it effect? Or, in other words, though it be not law, does it constitute a rule as operative as if it was a law? This would be to overthrow in fact what was established in theory; and would seem, at first view, an absurdity too gross to be insisted on. It shall, however, receive a more attentive consideration.

It is emphatically the province and duty of the judicial department to say what the law is. Those who apply the rule to particular cases, must of necessity expound and interpret that rule. If two laws conflict with each other, the courts must decide on the operation of each.

So if a law be in opposition to the constitution: if both the law and the constitution apply to a particular case, so that the court must either decide that case conformably to the law, disregarding the constitution; or conformably to the constitution, disregarding the law: the court must determine which of these conflicting rules governs the case. This is of the very essence of judicial duty.

If then the courts are to regard the constitution, and the constitution is superior to any ordinary act of the legislature; the constitution, and not such ordinary act, must govern the case to which they both apply.

Those, then, who controvert the principle that the constitution is to be considered, in court, as a paramount law, are reduced to the necessity of maintaining that courts must close their eyes on the constitution, and see only the law.

This doctrine would subvert the very foundation of all written constitutions. . . . That it thus reduces to nothing what we have deemed the greatest improvement on political institutions—a written constitution, would of itself be sufficient, in America where written constitutions have been viewed with so much reverence, for rejecting the construction. But the peculiar expressions of the constitution of the United States furnish additional arguments in favour of its rejection.

The judicial power of the United States is extended to all cases arising under the constitution.

Could it be the intention of those who gave this power, to say that, in using it, the constitution should not be looked into? That a case arising under the constitution should be decided without examining the instrument under which it arises? This is too extravagant to be maintained. . . .

There are many other parts of the constitution which serve to illustrate this subject.

It is declared that "no tax or duty shall be laid on articles exported from any state." Suppose a duty on the export of cotton, of tobacco, or of flour; and a suit instituted to recover it. Ought judgment to be rendered in such a case? Ought the judges to close their eyes on the constitution, and only see the law?

The constitution declares "that no bill of attainder or ex post facto law shall be passed."

If, however, such a bill should be passed, and a person should be prosecuted under it; must the court condemn to death those victims whom the constitution endeavors to preserve?

"No person," says the constitution, "shall be convicted of treason unless on the testimony of two witnesses to the same overt act, or on confession in open court."

Here the language of the constitution is addressed especially to the courts. It prescribes, directly for them, a rule of evidence not to be departed from. If the legislature should change that rule, and declare one witness, or a confession out of court, sufficient for conviction, must the constitutional principle yield to the legislative act?

From these, and many other selections which might be made, it is apparent, that the framers of the constitution contemplated that instrument as a rule for the government of the courts, as well as the legislature.

Why otherwise does it direct the judges to take an oath to support it? This oath certainly applies, in an especial manner, to their conduct in their official character. How immoral to impose it on them, if they were to be used as the instruments, and the knowing instruments, for violating what they swear to support!

Why does a judge swear to discharge his duties agreeably to the constitution of the United States, if that constitution forms no rule for his government? If it is closed upon him and cannot be inspected by him?

If such be the real state of things, this is worse than solemn mockery. To prescribe, or to take this oath, becomes equally a crime.

It is also not entirely unworthy of observation, that in declaring what shall be the supreme law of the land, the constitution itself is first mentioned; and not the laws of the United States generally, but those only which shall be made in pursuance of the constitution, have that rank.

Thus, the particular phraseology of the constitution of the United States confirms and strengthens the principle, supposed to be essential to all written constitutions, that a law repugnant to the constitution is void, and that courts, as well as other departments, are bound by that instrument.

The rule must be discharged.

Notes and Queries

1. Why was section 13 of the Judiciary Act of 1789 found unconstitutional? Where does Marshall find the power of the judiciary to declare the actions of a coordinate branch of the federal government unconstitutional? How does he differentiate the issue in this case from a political question, or one submitted to the executive, that courts cannot rule upon? What interpretive method or methods does Marshall employ in reaching his conclusion?

2. The Court concluded that "The constitution is either superior, paramount law, unchangeable by ordinary means, or it is on a level with ordinary legislative acts, and like other acts, is alterable when the legislature shall please to alter it." Is it true that there is "no middle ground" between these two alternatives? How does Marshall's insistence that the Constitution must be superior to ordinary legislation justify the practice of judicial review?

3. Marshall wrote that the question "whether an act repugnant to the Constitution, can become the law of the land, is a question deeply interesting to the United States, but, happily, not of an intricacy proportioned to its interests." Do you agree? Consider the response by Alexander M. Bickel: "Marshall's confidence . . . is understandable, since he had already begged the question- in-chief, which was not whether an act repugnant to the Constitution could stand, but who should be empowered to decide that the act is repugnant." See *The Least Dangerous Branch: The Supreme Court at the Bar of Politics* (Indianapolis: Bobbs-Merrill Educational Publishing, 1962), 3.

4. How would our system of government differ if the Supreme Court could not declare actions of Congress or the executive unconstitutional? Could individual freedom and limited government be sustained under such a system? Or do you agree with the idea expressed by Justice Oliver Wendell Holmes at the beginning of this century: "I do not think the United States would come to an end if we lost our power to declare an Act of Congress void"? Is there any support in the text or structure of the Constitution for Holmes's view?

5. Compare Marshall's opinion with that of Israel's Chief Justice featured in Comparative Note 3.1. Which opinion is the bolder exercise of judicial review?

Martin v. Hunter's Lessee
14 U.S. 304, 4 L.Ed. 97 (1816)

Lord Fairfax, a citizen of Virginia, willed his Virginia estate to his nephew, Denny Martin. In 1777, after the outbreak of the Revolutionary War, Virginia confiscated this land and other property owned by British subjects. In 1789, the state conveyed Fairfax's land to David Hunter who then sued to eject Martin, a British citizen, from the estate. Martin won in the Virginia trial court on the basis of a 1783 treaty between the United States and Great Britain protecting British-owned lands in the United States. Virginia's Supreme Court of Appeals reversed and sustained Hunter's claim on the theory that Fairfax's property had been transferred prior to the treaty's ratification. The U.S. Supreme Court reversed, but Virginia's Court of Appeals refused to obey, holding that the Supreme Court's appellate jurisdiction extends only to cases pending in the federal courts and not to the decisions of state courts. This issue—and Martin's cause—returned to the Supreme Court. Opinion of the court: *Story*, Washington, Livingston, Todd, Duvall. Concurring opinion. *Johnson.*

Mr. Justice STORY delivered the opinion of the court.

The constitution of the United States was ordained and established, not by the states in their sovereign capacities, but emphatically, as the preamble of the constitution declares, by "the people of the United States." There can be no doubt that it was competent to the people to invest the general government with all the powers which they might deem proper and necessary; to extend or restrain these powers according to their own good pleasure, and to give them a paramount and supreme authority. As little doubt can there be, that the people had a right to prohibit to the states the exercise of any powers which were, in their judgment, incompatible with the objects of the general compact; to make the powers of the state governments, in given cases, subordinate to those of the nation, or to reserve to themselves those sovereign authorities which they might not choose to delegate to either. The constitution was not, therefore, necessarily carved out of existing state sovereignties, nor a surrender of powers already existing in state institutions, for the powers of the states depend upon their own constitutions; and the people of every state had the right to modify and restrain them, according to their own views of the policy or principle. On the other hand, it is perfectly clear that the sovereign powers vested in the state governments, by their respective constitutions, remained unaltered and unimpaired, except so far as they were granted to the government of the United States. With these principles in view . . . let us now proceed to the interpretation of the constitution, so far as regards the great points in controversy.

Comparative Note 3.2

A. Article 93, German Basic Law (1949)

(1) The Federal Constitutional Court shall decide:

2. In case of differences of opinion or doubts respecting the formal or material compatibility of federal law or Land law with this Basic law, or the compatibility of Land law with other federal law, at the request of the Federal Government, of a Land government, or of one third of the members of the Bundestag.

B. Canadian Charter of Rights and Freedoms (1982)

Sec. 52. The Constitution of Canada is the supreme law of Canada, and any law that is inconsistent with the provisions of the Constitution is, to the extent of the inconsistency, of no force or effect.

C. Constitution of South Africa (1996)

Art. 167

(3) The Constitutional Court is the highest court in all constitutional matters. . . .

(4) Only the Constitutional Court may:

a. decide disputes between organs of state in the national or provincial sphere concerning the constitutional status, powers or functions of those organs of state; . . . d. decide on the constitutionality of any amendment to the Constitution; . . .

(5) The Constitutional Court makes the final decision whether an act of parliament . . . is constitutional.

The third article of the constitution is that which must principally attract our attention. The 1st. section declares, "the judicial power of the United States shall be vested in one supreme court, and in such other inferior courts as the congress may, from time to time, ordain and establish. . . ."

. . . The language of the article throughout is manifestly designed to be mandatory on the legislature. . . . The judicial power of the United States *shall be vested* (not may be vested) in one Supreme Court, and in such inferior courts as Congress may, from time to time ordain and establish. . . . The judicial power must, therefore, be vested in some court, by Congress. . . .

If, then, it is a duty of Congress to vest the judicial power of the United States, it is a duty to invest the *whole judicial power.* . . .

It being, then, established that the language of this clause is imperative, the next question is as to the cases to which it shall apply. The answer is found in the Constitution itself. The judicial power shall extend to all the cases enumerated in the Constitution. . . .

If the Constitution meant to limit the appellate jurisdiction to cases pending in the courts of the United States, it would necessarily follow that the jurisdiction of these courts would, in all the cases enumerated in the Constitution, be exclusive of state tribunals. How otherwise could the jurisdiction extend to *all* cases arising under the Constitution, laws, and treaties of the United States . . . ? If some of these cases might be entertained by state tribunals, and no appellate jurisdiction as to them should exist, then the appellate power would not extend to *all,* but to some, cases. . . .

[I]t is plain that the framers of the constitution did contemplate that cases within the judicial cognizance of the United States not only might but would arise in the state courts, in the exercise of their ordinary jurisdiction. With this view the sixth article declares, that "this constitution, and the laws of the United States which shall be made in pursuance thereof, and all treaties made, or which shall be made, under the authority of the United States, shall be the supreme law of the land, and the judges in every state shall be bound thereby, any thing in the constitution or laws of any state to the contrary notwithstanding. . . ." It is obvious that this obligation is imperative upon the state judges in their official, and not merely in their private, capacities. From the very nature of their judicial duties they would be called upon to pronounce the law applicable to the case in judgment. They were not to decide merely according to the laws or constitution of the state, but according to the constitution, laws and treaties of the United States—"the supreme law of the land."

It is a mistake that the constitution was not designed to operate upon states, in their corporate capacities. It is crowded with provisions which restrain or annul the sovereignty of the states in some of the highest branches of their prerogatives. . . . It is further argued, that no great public mischief can result from a construction which shall limit the appellate power of the United States to cases in their own courts: first, because state judges are bound by an oath to support the constitution of the United States, and must be presumed to be men of learning and integrity; and, secondly, because congress must have an unquestionable right to remove all cases within the scope of the judicial power from the state courts to the courts of the United States. . . . As to the first reason—admitting that the judges of the state courts are, and always will be, of as much learning, integrity, and wisdom, as those of the courts of the United States, (which we very cheerfully admit,) it does not aid the argument. . . . The constitution has presumed (whether rightly or wrongly we do not inquire) that state attachments, state prejudices, state jealousies, and state interests, might some times obstruct, or control, or be supposed to obstruct or control, the regular administration of justice. Hence, in controversies between states; between citizens of different states; between citizens claiming grants under different states; between a state and its citizens, or foreigners, and between citizens and foreigners, it enables the parties, under the authority of congress, to have the controversies heard, tried, and determined before the national tribunals. No other reason than that which has been stated can be assigned, why some, at least, of those cases should not have been left to the cognizance of the state courts. In respect to the other enumerated cases—the cases arising under the constitution, laws, and treaties of the United States, cases affecting ambassadors and other public ministers, and cases of admiralty and maritime jurisdiction—reasons of a higher and more extensive nature, touching the safety, peace, and sovereignty of the nation, might well justify a grant of exclusive jurisdiction.

This is not all. A motive of another kind, perfectly compatible with the most sincere respect for state tribunals, might induce the grant of appellate power over their decisions. That motive is the importance, and even necessity of uniformity of decisions throughout the whole United States, upon all subjects within the purview of the constitution. Judges of equal learning and integrity, in different states, might differently interpret a statute, or a treaty of the United States, or even the constitution itself: If there were no revising authority to control these jarring and discordant judgments, and harmonize them into uniformity, the laws, the treaties, and the constitution of the United States would be different in different states, and might, perhaps, never have precisely the same construction, obligation, or efficacy, in any two states. The public mischiefs that would attend such a state of things would be truly deplorable; and it cannot be believed that they could have escaped the enlightened convention which formed the constitution. What, indeed, might then have been only

prophecy, has now become fact; and the appellate jurisdiction must continue to be the only adequate remedy for such evils.

On the whole, the court are of opinion, that the appellate power of the United States does extend to cases pending in the state courts; and that the 25th section of the judiciary act, which authorizes the exercise of this jurisdiction in the specified cases, by a writ of error, is supported by the letter and spirit of the constitution. We find no clause in that instrument which limits this power; and we dare not interpose a limitation where the people have not been disposed to create one.

It is the opinion of the whole court, that the judgment of the court of appeals of Virginia, rendered on the mandate in this cause, be reversed, and the judgment of the district court, held at Winchester, be, and the same is hereby affirmed.

Notes and Queries

1. One of the judges of Virginia's Supreme Court of Appeals wrote: "The constitution of the United States contemplates the independence of both governments and regards the residuary sovereignty of the states, as not less inviolable, than the delegated sovereignty of the United States. . . . It has been contended that the constitution contemplated only the objects of appeal, and not the tribunals from which the appeal is to be taken; and intended to give to the Supreme Court of the United States appellate jurisdiction in all cases of federal cognizance. But this argument proves too much, and is utterly inadmissible. It would give appellate jurisdiction, as well over the courts of England or France, as over the State courts; for, although I do not think the state courts are foreign courts in relation to the federal courts, yet I consider them not less independent than foreign courts." On what theory of the nature of the Constitution is this view based?

2. What essentially is the substance of the argument advanced by Justice Story? Compare his vision of the United States with Marshall's in *Marbury v. Madison*. With Marshall's opinion in *McCulloch v. State of Maryland* (reprinted in chapter 6).

3. Here, as in *Marbury*, the Supreme Court was defining its own authority under Article III and enforcing its view against judges. Would—should—the Court's view prevail against the resistance of state legislators and governors? See in this connection *Cooper v. Aaron* (reprinted later in the chapter).

Dred Scott v. Sandford
60 U.S. 393, 19 How. 393, 15 L.Ed. 691 (1856)

Dred Scott, a slave, belonged to Dr. Emerson, a U.S. Army surgeon stationed in Missouri. In 1834 Emerson was transferred to Rock Island, Illinois, a state that forbade slavery, yet he took Scott with him. Later, Emerson was transferred to Fort Snelling in what is now Minnesota, a free territory under the Missouri Compromise of 1820, and he again took Scott with him. Emerson and Scott returned to Missouri in 1838. In 1846, Dred Scott sued for his freedom in a Missouri state court because he was brought into and had resided in a free territory. Scott won the initial case, but the Missouri Supreme Court reversed the judgment. Unsatisfied, abolitionists arranged a fictitious sale of Scott to John Sandford, a resident of New York and a relative of Emerson, so that the Federal Circuit Court could assert jurisdiction because of diversity of state citizenship. The Circuit Court ruled against Scott, and the decision was appealed to the Supreme Court on a writ of error. This extract from *Dred Scott* includes the Court's opinion on the constitutionality of the Missouri Compromise. (For that part of the opinion dealing with the citizenship of African Americans see chapter 14.) Opinion of the Court: *Taney,* Campbell, Catron, Grier, Nelson, Wayne. Concurring opinions: *Campbell, Catron, Grier, Nelson, Wayne.* Dissenting opinions: *Curtis, McLean.*

Mr. Chief Justice TANEY delivered the opinion of the Court.

. . .

We proceed, therefore, to inquire whether the facts relied on by the plaintiff entitled him to his freedom.

In considering this part of the controversy, two questions arise: 1. Was he, together with his family, free in Missouri by reason of the stay in the territory of the United States . . . ? And 2. If they were not, is Scott himself free by reason of his removal to Rock Island, in the State of Illinois . . . ?

We proceed to examine the first question.

The act of Congress, upon which the plaintiff relies, declares that slavery and involuntary servitude, except as a punishment for crime, shall be forever prohibited in all that part of the territory ceded by France, under the name of Louisiana, which lies north of thirty-six degrees thirty minutes north latitude, and not included within the limits of Missouri. And the difficulty which meets us at the threshold of this part of the inquiry is, whether Congress was authorized to pass this law under any of the powers granted to it by the Constitution; for if the authority is not given by that instrument, it is the duty of this court to declare it void and inoperative, and incapable of conferring freedom upon any one who is held as a slave under the laws of any one of the States.

The counsel for the plaintiff has laid much stress upon that article in the Constitution which confers on Congress the power "to dispose of and make all needful rules and regulations respecting the territory or other property belonging to the United States"; but, in the judgment of the court, that provision has no bearing on the present controversy, and the power there given, whatever it may be, is confined, and was intended to be confined, to the territory which at that time belonged to, or was claimed by, the United States, and was within their boundaries as settled by the treaty with Great Britain, and can have no influence upon a territory afterwards acquired from a foreign Gov-

---

Comparative Note 3.3

An individual constitutional provision cannot be considered as an isolated clause and interpreted alone. A constitution has an inner unity, and the meaning of any one part is linked to that of other provisions. Taken as a unit, a constitution reflects certain overarching principles and fundamental decisions to which individual provisions are subordinate. . . . [It is therefore the case] that a constitutional provision itself may be null and void [even though] it is part of the constitution itself.

There are constitutional principles that are so fundamental . . . that they even bind the framers of the constitution, and other constitutional provisions that do not rank as high may be null and void because they contravene these principles. From this rule of interpretation it follows that any constitutional provision must be interpreted in such a way that it is compatible with those elementary principles and with the basic values of the framers of the constitution.

SOURCE: The Southwest State Case (1951) in Donald P. Kommers, *Constitutional Jurisprudence of the Federal Republic of Germany,* 2d ed. (1997), 63.

ernment. It was a special provision for a known and particular territory, and to meet a present emergency, and nothing more. . . .

This brings us to examine by what provision of the Constitution the present Federal Government, under its delegated and restricted powers, is authorized to acquire territory outside of the original limits of the United States, and what powers it may exercise therein over the person or property of a citizen of the United States, while it remains a Territory, and until it shall be admitted as one of the States of the Union.

There is certainly no power given by the Constitution to the Federal Government to establish or maintain colonies bordering on the United States or at a distance, to be ruled and governed at its own pleasure; nor to enlarge its territorial limits in any way, except by the admission of new States. That power is plainly given; and if a new State is admitted, it needs no further legislation by Congress, because the Constitution itself defines the relative rights and powers, and duties of the State, and the citizens of the State, and the Federal Government. But no power is given to acquire a Territory to be held and governed permanently in that character.

. . . [T]he government and the citizen both enter [the territory] under the authority of the Constitution, with their respective rights defined and marked out; and the Federal Government can exercise no power over his person or property, beyond what that instrument confers, nor lawfully deny any right which it has reserved.

Upon these considerations, it is the opinion of the court that the act of Congress which prohibited a citizen from holding and owning property of this kind in the territory of the United States north of the line therein mentioned, is not warranted by the Constitution, and is therefore void; and that neither Dred Scott himself, nor any of his family, were made free by being carried into this territory; even if they had been carried there by the owner, with the intention of becoming a permanent resident.

But there is another point in the case which depends on State power and State law. And it is contended, on the part of the plaintiff, that he is made free by being taken to Rock Island, in the State of Illinois, independently of his residence in the territory of the United States; and being so made free, he was not again reduced to a state of slavery by being brought back to Missouri.

Our notice of this part of the case will be very brief; for the principle on which it depends was decided in this court, upon much consideration, in the case of *Strader et al. v. Graham* [1850]. In that case, the slaves had been taken from Kentucky to Ohio, with the consent of the owner, and afterwards brought back to Kentucky. And

this court held that their status or condition, as free or slave, depended upon the laws of Kentucky, when they were brought back into that State, and not of Ohio; and that this court had no jurisdiction to revise the judgment of a State court upon its own laws. This was the point directly before the court, and the decision that this court had not jurisdiction turned upon it, as will be seen by the report of the case.

So in this case. As Scott was a slave when taken into the State of Illinois by his owner, and was there held as such, and brought back in that character, his status, as free or slave, depended on the laws of Missouri, and not of Illinois.

Upon the whole, therefore, it is the judgment of this court, that it appears by the record before us that the plaintiff is not a citizen of Missouri, in the sense in which that word is used in the Constitution; and that the Circuit Court of the United States, for that reason, had no jurisdiction in the case, and could give no judgment in it. Its judgment for the defendant must, consequently, be reversed, and a mandate issued, directing the suit to be dismissed for want of jurisdiction.

Mr. Justice CURTIS dissenting.

I can find nothing in the Constitution which, *proprio vigore*, deprives of their citizenship any class of persons who were citizens of the United States at the time of its adoption, or who should be native-born citizens of any State after its adoption; nor any power enabling Congress to disfranchise persons born on the soil of any State, and entitled to citizenship of such State by its Constitution and laws. And my opinion is, that, under the Constitution of the United States, every free person born on the soil of a State, who is a citizen of that State by force of its Constitution or laws, is also a citizen of the United States.

I dissent, therefore, from that part of the opinion of the majority of the court, in which it is held that a person of African descent cannot be a citizen of the United States; and I regret I must go further, and dissent both from what I deem their assumption of authority to examine the constitutionality of the act of Congress commonly called the Missouri compromise act, and the grounds and conclusions announced in their opinion.

Having first decided that they were bound to consider the sufficiency of the plea to the jurisdiction of the Circuit Court, and having decided that this plea showed that the Circuit Court had not jurisdiction, and consequently that this is a case to which the judicial power of the United States does not extend, they have gone on to examine the merits of the case as they appeared on the trial before the court and jury, on the issues joined on the pleas in bar, and so have reached the question of the power of Congress to pass the act of 1820. On so grave a subject as this, I feel obliged to say that, in my opinion, such an exertion of judicial power transcends the limits of the authority of the court, as described by its repeated decisions, and, as I understand, acknowledged in this opinion of the majority of the court.

Notes and Queries

1. Does *Dred Scott* expand the power of judicial review beyond the limits of *Marbury*, as the introductory essay suggests? Chief Justice Taney wrote that the Constitution "must be construed now as it was understood at the time of its adoption." A different rule, he argued, "would abrogate the judicial character of this court, and make it the mere reflex of the popular opinion or passion of the day."

Does Taney's preferred method of constitutional interpretation therefore rest upon a particular understanding of judicial power? Is that conception of judicial power consistent with the Court's approach in *Marbury*?

2. Suppose we knew, absolutely and positively, what the Founding Fathers actually intended to include within the meaning of a given constitutional provision. Should justices today be bound by that belief? Why or why not? If not, how would they get around Chief Justice Taney's objection that "any other rule of construction would abrogate the judicial character of this court"? Does constitutional language supply any guidance to answering this question?

3. If the Supreme Court had taken the approach to constitutional interpretation described in Comparative Notes 3.2 and 3.3 might the result in *Dred Scott* have been different?

Cooper v. Aaron
358 U.S. 1, 78 S.Ct. 1401, 3 L.Ed2d 5 (1958)

The governor and legislature of Arkansas actively resisted the implementation of a Little Rock School Board plan, approved by the Federal District Court for the Eastern District of Arkansas, to begin desegregating Little Rock's public school system in the fall of 1957. Claiming that *Brown v. Board of Education* was itself unconstitutional, the governor dispatched units of Arkansas' National Guard to place Central High School "off-limits" to African American students. (In September 1957 President Eisenhower stationed federal troops at the high school to protect these students.) In early 1958 the school board, fearing more turmoil and an outbreak of violence, petitioned the district court for a postponement of its desegregation plan. The Court granted the relief requested. The U.S. Court of Appeals reversed. Opinion of the Court: *Warren, Black, Frankfurter, Douglas, Burton, Clark, Harlan, Brennan, Whittaker*. Concurring Opinion: *Frankfurter*.

The Chief Justice, Mr. Justice BLACK, Mr. Justice FRANKFURTER, Mr. Justice DOUGLAS, Mr. Justice BURTON, Mr. Justice CLARK, Mr. Justice HARLAN, Mr. Justice BRENNAN and Mr. Justice WHITTAKER delivered the opinion of the Court.

As this case reaches us it raises questions of the highest importance to the maintenance of our federal system of government. It necessarily involves a claim by the Governor and Legislature of a State that there is no duty on state officials to obey federal court orders resting on this Court's considered interpretation of the United States Constitution. Specifically it involves actions by the Governor and Legislature of Arkansas upon the premise that they are not bound by our holding in *Brown v. Board of Education* [1954]. We are urged to uphold a suspension of the Little Rock School Board's plan to do away with segregated public schools in Little Rock until state laws and efforts to upset and nullify our holding in *Brown v. Board of Education* have been further challenged and tested in the courts. We reject these contentions.

The controlling legal principles are plain. The command of the Fourteenth Amendment is that no "State" shall deny to any person within its jurisdiction the equal protection of the laws. "A State acts by its legislative, its executive, or its judicial authorities. It can act in no other way. The constitutional provision, therefore, must mean that no agency of the State, or of the officers or agents by whom its powers are exerted, shall deny to any person within its jurisdiction the equal protection of the laws. Whoever, by virtue of public position under a State government, denies or takes away the equal protection of the laws, violates the constitutional inhibition; and as he acts in the name [of] and for the State, and is clothed with the State's power, his act is that of the State. This must be so, or the constitutional prohibition has no meaning." Thus the prohibitions of the Fourteenth Amendment extend to all action of the State denying equal protection of the laws; whatever the agency of the State taking the action, or whatever the guise in which it is taken. In short, the constitutional rights of children not to be discriminated against in school admission on grounds of race or color

Comparative Note 3.4

A state, it is said, is sovereign and it is not for the courts to pass upon the policy or wisdom of legislative will. As a broad statement of principle that is undoubtedly correct, but the general principle must yield to the requisites of the constitution in a federal state. By it the bounds of sovereignty are defined and supremacy circumscribed. The court will not question the wisdom of enactments which, by the terms of the Canadian Constitution, are within the competence of the legislatures, *but it is the high duty of the court to insure that the legislature do not transgress the limits of their constitutional mandate and engage in the illegal exercise of power.*

SOURCE: *Amax Potash Ltd. v. Saskatachewan* [1977] 2 S.C.R. 576 at p. 596, 71 D.L.R. (3rd) 1.

---

declared by this Court in the *Brown* case can neither be nullified openly and directly by state legislators or state executive or judicial officers, nor nullified indirectly by them through evasive schemes for segregation whether attempted "ingeniously or ingenuously."

What has been said, in the light of the facts developed, is enough to dispose of the case. However, we should answer the premise of the actions of the Governor and Legislature that they are not bound by our holding in the *Brown* case. It is necessary only to recall some basic constitutional propositions which are settled doctrine.

Article VI of the Constitution makes the Constitution the "supreme Law of the Land." In 1803, Chief Justice Marshall, speaking for a unanimous Court, referring to the Constitution as "the fundamental and paramount law of the nation," declared in the notable case of *Marbury v. Madison* [1803] that "It is emphatically the province and duty of the judicial department to say what the law is." This decision declared the basic principle that the federal judiciary is supreme in the exposition of the law of the Constitution, and that principle has ever since been respected by this Court and the Country as a permanent and indispensable feature of our constitutional system. It follows that the interpretation of the Fourteenth Amendment enunciated by this Court in the *Brown* case is the supreme law of the land, and Art. VI of the Constitution makes it of binding effect on the States "any Thing in the Constitution or Laws of any State to the Contrary notwithstanding." Every state legislator and executive and judicial officer is solemnly committed by oath taken pursuant to Art. VI, cl. 3 "to support this Constitution." Chief Justice Taney, speaking for a unanimous Court in 1859, said that this requirement reflected the framers' "anxiety to preserve it [the Constitution] in full force, in all its powers, and to guard against resistance to or evasion of its authority, on the part of a State. . . ."

No state legislator or executive or judicial officer can war against the Constitution without violating his undertaking to support it. Chief Justice Marshall spoke for a unanimous Court in saying that: "If the legislatures of the several states may, at will, annul the judgments of the courts of the United States, and destroy the rights acquired under those judgments, the constitution itself becomes a solemn mockery. . . ." A Governor who asserts a power to nullify a federal court order is similarly restrained. If he had such power, said Chief Justice Hughes, in 1932, also for a unanimous Court, "it is manifest that the fiat of a state Governor, and not the Constitution of the United States, would be the supreme law of the land; that the restrictions of the Federal Constitution upon the exercise of state power would be but impotent phrases. . . ."

It is, of course, quite true that the responsibility for public education is primarily the concern of the States, but it is equally true that such responsibilities, like all other state activity, must be exercised consistently with federal constitutional requirements as they apply to state action. The Constitution created a government dedicated to equal justice under law. The Fourteenth Amendment embodied and emphasized that ideal. State support of segregated schools through any arrangement, management, funds, or property cannot be squared with the Amendment's command that no State shall deny to any person within its jurisdiction the equal protection of the laws. The right of a student not to be segregated on racial grounds in schools so maintained is indeed so fundamental and pervasive that it is embraced in the concept of due process of law. . . . The basic decision in *Brown* was unanimously reached by this Court only after the case had been briefed and twice argued and the issues had been given the most serious consideration. Since the first *Brown* opinion three new Justices have come to the Court. They are at one with the Justices still on the Court who participated in that basic decision as to its correctness, and that decision is now unanimously reaffirmed. The principles announced in that decision and the obedience of the States to them, according to the command of the Constitution, are indispensable for the protection of the freedoms guaranteed by our fundamental charter for all of us. Our constitutional ideal of equal justice under law is thus made a living truth.

Concurring opinion of Mr. Justice FRANKFURTER.

. . . When defiance of law judicially pronounced was last sought to be justified before this Court, views were expressed which are now especially relevant:

> The historic phrase "a government of laws and not of men" epitomizes the distinguishing character of our society. [Such a government] was the rejection in positive terms of rule by fiat, whether by the fiat of governmental or private power. . . . The conception of a government by laws dominated the thoughts of those who founded this Nation and designed its Constitution, although they knew as well as the belittlers of the conception that laws have to be made, interpreted and enforced by men. To that end, they set apart a body of men, who were to be the depositories of law, who by their disciplined training and character and by withdrawal from the usual temptations of private interest may reasonably be expected to be "as free, impartial, and independent as the lot of humanity will admit." So strongly were the framers of the Constitution bent on securing a reign of law that they endowed the judicial office with extraordinary safeguards and prestige. No one, no matter how exalted his public office or how righteous his private motive, can be judge in his own case. That is what courts are for. *United States v. United Mine Workers* [1947].

The duty to abstain from resistance to "the supreme Law of the Land," as declared by the organ of our Government for ascertaining it, does not require immediate approval of it nor does it deny the right of dissent. Criticism need not be stilled. Active obstruction or defiance is barred. Our kind of society cannot endure if the controlling authority of the Law as derived from the Constitution is not to be the tribunal specially charged with the duty of ascertaining and declaring what is "the supreme Law of the Land." Particularly is this so where the declaration of what "the supreme Law" commands on an underlying moral issue is not the dubious pronouncement of a gravely divided Court but is the unanimous conclusion of a long-matured deliberative process. The Constitution is not the formulation of the merely personal views of the members of this Court, nor can its authority be reduced to the claim that state officials are its controlling interpreters. Local customs, however hardened by time, are not decreed in heaven. . . .

That the responsibility of those who exercise power in a democratic government is not to reflect inflamed public feeling but to help form its understanding, is especially true when they are confronted with a problem like a racially discriminatory public school system. . . .

Notes and Queries

1. Does *Cooper* elevate the power of judicial review to a new plateau in American political life? Or is it simply a forthright reaffirmation of *Marbury v. Madison*? Did *Marbury* declare the "basic principle that the federal judiciary is supreme in the exposition of the law of the Constitution," as Chief Justice Warren asserts?

2. In his concurrence, Justice Frankfurter notes that the role of the Court is not to "reflect public feeling but to help form its understanding." He underscores the Court's unanimity on the moral issue of integration. Should unanimity or consensus among Supreme Court justices be considered proof of the rightness of a constitutional interpretation? Can one oppose a particular decision of the Supreme Court without being "at war with the Constitution"?

Ex Parte McCardle
74 U.S. (7 Wall.) 506, 19 L. Ed. 264 (1868)

In the aftermath of the Civil War, the Radical Republican Congress passed a series of acts imposing severe programs of reconstruction on the former states of the rebellion. McCardle, a Mississippi newspaper editor and fierce opponent of reconstruction, was held in custody by military authorities for publishing "incendiary and libelous" articles against the enforcement of the reconstruction acts. While awaiting trial, he petitioned a U.S. Circuit Court for a writ of habeas corpus and being denied the writ, he appealed to the Supreme Court. The Supreme Court's announcement that it would take the case alarmed the Radical Republicans. Fearing the fate of the reconstruction program in the hands of the Supreme Court, Congress enacted a statute taking away from the Court its power to hear appeals in habeas corpus cases. The law was passed after the Court had heard arguments in the case, but before it had handed down a decision. Opinion of the Court: *Chase*, Clifford, Davis, Field, Grier, Miller, Nelson, Swayne.

Comparative Note 3.5

Laws are not constitutional merely because they have been passed in conformity with procedural provisions. . . . They must be substantively compatible with the highest values of a free and democratic order, i.e., the constitutional order of values, and must also conform to unwritten fundamental constitutional principles as well as the fundamental decisions of the Basic law.

SOURCE: "German Constitutional Court," Kommers, *Constitutional Jurisprudence*, 318.

Mr. Chief Justice CHASE delivered the opinion of the Court.

The first question necessarily is that of jurisdiction; for, if the act of March, 1868, takes away the jurisdiction defined by the act of February, 1867, it is useless, if not improper, to enter into any discussion of other questions.

It is quite true, as was argued by the counsel for the petitioner, that the appellate jurisdiction of this court is not derived from acts of Congress. It is, strictly speaking, conferred by the Constitution. But it is conferred "with such exceptions and under such regulations as Congress shall make."

It is unnecessary to consider whether, if Congress had made no exceptions and no regulations, this court might not have exercised general appellate jurisdiction under rules prescribed by itself. For among the earliest acts of the first Congress, at its first session, was the act of September 24th, 1789, to establish the judicial courts of the United States. That act provided for the organization of this court, and prescribed regulations for the exercise of its jurisdiction.

The source of that jurisdiction, and the limitations of it by the Constitution and by statute, have been on several occasions subjects of consideration here. In the case of *Durousseau v. The United States* [1810], particularly, the whole matter was carefully examined, and the court held, that while "the appellate powers of this court are not given by the judicial act, but are given by the Constitution," they are, nevertheless, "limited and regulated by that act, and by such other acts as have been passed on the subject." The court said, further, that the judicial act was an exercise of the power given by the Constitution to Congress "of making exceptions to the appellate jurisdiction of the Supreme Court." "They have described affirmatively," said the court, "its jurisdiction, and this affirmative description has been understood to imply a negation of the exercise of such appellate power as is not comprehended within it."

The principle that the affirmation of appellate jurisdiction implies the negation of all such jurisdiction not affirmed having been thus established, it was an almost necessary consequence that acts of Congress, providing for the exercise of jurisdiction, should come to be spoken of as acts granting jurisdiction, and not as acts making exceptions to the constitutional grant of it.

The exception to appellate jurisdiction in the case before us, however, is not an inference from the affirmation of other appellate jurisdiction. It is made in terms. The provision of the act of 1867, affirming the appellate jurisdiction of this court in cases of habeas corpus is expressly repealed. It is hardly possible to imagine a plainer instance of positive exception.

We are not at liberty to inquire into the motives of the legislature. We can only examine into its power under the Constitution; and the power to make exceptions to the appellate jurisdiction of this court is given by express words.

What, then, is the effect of the repealing act upon the case before us? We cannot doubt as to this. Without jurisdiction the court cannot proceed at all in any cause. Jurisdiction is power to declare the law, and when it ceases to exist, the only function remaining to the court is that of announcing the fact and dismissing the cause. And this is not less clear upon authority than upon principle.

Several cases were cited by the counsel for the petitioner in support of the position that jurisdiction of this case is not affected by the repealing act. But none of them, in our judgment, afford any support to it. They are all cases of the exercise of judicial power by the legislature, or of legislative interference with courts in the exercising of continuing jurisdiction.

On the other hand, the general rule, supported by the best elementary writers, is, that "when an act of the legislature is repealed, it must be considered, except as to transactions past and closed, as if it never existed." . . .

It is quite clear, therefore, that this court cannot proceed to pronounce judgment in this case, for it has no longer jurisdiction of the appeal; and judicial duty is not less fitly performed by declining ungranted jurisdiction than in exercising firmly that which the Constitution and the laws confer.

The appeal of the petitioner in this case must be dismissed for want of jurisdiction.

Notes and Queries

1. Why does the Court ignore the merits of McCardle's case? Might this case fall under the Constitution's prohibition of ex post facto laws or bills of attainder?

2. What theory of judicial power is advanced in this opinion? How does it compare to that laid down in *Marbury* and *Dred Scott*?

3. The Court notes that "we are not at liberty to inquire into the motives of the legislature. We can only examine into its power under the Constitution." If the Court is to uphold constitutionalism and individual rights, should it not inquire into these motives? What might be the dangers of courts inquiring into legislative motives? How can it discover these motives if they are not obvious?

4. Are there limits on Congress' power to limit or regulate the appellate jurisdiction of the Supreme Court? Suppose Congress passed a law forbidding the Supreme Court from deciding cases on appeal dealing with abortion or freedom of speech. Could you make the case that, in this instance, Congress would have exceeded its power under the Constitution?

Luther v. Borden

48 U.S. (7 Howard) 1, 12 L.Ed. 581 (1849)

This case grew out of Thomas W. Dorr's rebellion against the government of Rhode Island, whose constitution was almost identical to the colonial charter that Charles II had granted in 1663. The constitution strictly limited the right to vote and had no provision for amendment. In 1841 Dorr and his supporters held mass meetings throughout the state, convened a constitutional convention, and drafted a new constitution that established universal manhood suffrage. Dorr was then elected governor under the new constitution. When he sought to put the new constitution into force, the state's charter government declared martial law, crushed the "insurrection," and jailed many of its support-

ers, including Luther, one of Dorr's followers. The charter government appealed to President Tyler for help, but no federal troops had to be sent. Dorr was later tried and convicted of treason, although he was eventually pardoned. In 1842 the charter government gave way to popular sentiment and a new democratic constitution entered into force.

During the rebellion, Borden and other state agents had arrested Luther after breaking into his home. Luther sued Borden for illegal entry on the grounds that the charter government was illegal and had been replaced by the new constitution. Luther had moved to Massachusetts which allowed him to bring a diversity suit against Borden, a resident of Rhode Island. The Court was called upon to decide which of the two claimants was the legal government

Comparative Note 3.6

Sec. 24 of the Canadian Constitution reads: (1) Anyone whose rights or freedoms, as guaranteed by this Charter, have been infringed or denied may apply to a court of competent jurisdiction to obtain such remedy as the court considers appropriate and just in the circumstances.

. . . s. 24 (1) of the Charter, also part of the Constitution, makes it clear that the adjudication of that question is the responsibility of a "court of competent jurisdiction." While the court is entitled to grant such remedy as it "considers appropriate and just in the circumstances," I do not think it is open to it to relinquish

its jurisdiction, either on the basis that the issue is inherently non-justiciable or that it raises a so-called "political question."

If we are to look at the Constitution for the answer to the question whether it is appropriate for the courts to "second guess" the executive on matters of defense, we would conclude that it is not appropriate. However, if what we are being asked to do is to decide whether any particular act of the executive violates the rights of citizens, then it is not only appropriate that we answer the question; it is our obligation to do so.

Source: *Operation Dismantle v. R. In the Supreme Court of Canada* [1985] 1 S.C.R. 441.

of Rhode Island. Opinion of the Court: *Taney*, Grier, McLean, Nelson, Wayne. Dissenting Opinion: *Woodbury*, Catron, Daniel. Not participating: McKinley.

Mr. Chief Justice TANEY delivered the opinion of the Court.

The fourth section of the fourth article of the Constitution of the United States provides that the United States shall guarantee to every State in the Union a republican form of government, and shall protect each of them against invasion; and on the application of the legislature or of the executive (when the legislature cannot be convened) against domestic violence.

Under this article of the Constitution it rests with Congress to decide what government is the established one in a State. For as the United States guarantee to each State a republican government, Congress must necessarily decide what government is established in the State before it can determine whether it is republican or not. And when the senators and representatives of a State are admitted into the councils of the Union, the authority of the government under which they are appointed, as well as its republican character, is recognized by the proper constitutional authority. And its decision is binding on every other department of the government, and could not be questioned in a judicial tribunal. It is true that the contest in this case did not last long enough to bring the matter to this issue; and as no senators or representatives were elected under the authority of the government of which Mr. Dorr was the head, Congress was not called upon to decide the controversy. Yet the right to decide is placed there, and not in the courts.

So, too, as relates to the clause in the above-mentioned article of the Constitution, providing for cases of domestic violence. It rested with Congress, too, to determine upon the means proper to be adopted to fulfil this guarantee. They might, if they had deemed it most advisable to do so, have placed it in the power of a court to decide when the contingency had happened which required the federal government to interfere. But Congress thought otherwise, and no doubt wisely; and by the act of February 28, 1795, provided, that, "in case of an insurrection in any State against the government thereof, it shall be lawful for the President of the United States, on application of the legislature of such State or of the executive [when the legislature cannot be convened], to call forth such number of the militia of any other State or States, as may be applied for, as he may judge sufficient to suppress such insurrection."

By this act, the power of deciding whether the exigency had arisen upon which the government of the United States is bound to interfere, is given to the President. He is to act upon the application of the legislature or of the executive, and consequently he must determine what body of men constitute the legislature, and who is the governor, before he can act. The fact that both parties claim the right to the government cannot alter the case, for both cannot be entitled to it. If there is an armed conflict, like the one of which we are speaking, it is a case of domestic violence, and one of the parties must be in insurrection against the lawful government. And the President must, of necessity, decide which is the government, and which party is unlawfully arrayed against it, before he can perform the duty imposed upon him by the act of Congress.

After the President has acted and called out the militia, is a Circuit Court of the United States authorized to inquire whether his decision was right? Could the court, while the parties were actually contending in arms for the possession of the government, call witnesses before it and inquire which party represented a majority of the people? If it could, then it would become the duty of the court (provided it came to the conclusion that the President had decided incorrectly) to discharge those who were arrested or detained by the troops in the service of the United States or the government which the President was endeavouring to maintain. If the judicial power extends so far, the guarantee contained in the Constitution of the United States is a guarantee of anarchy, and not of order. Yet if this right does not reside in the courts when the conflict is raging, if the judicial power is at that time bound to follow the decision of the political, it must be equally bound when the contest is over. It cannot, when peace is restored, punish as offences and crimes the acts which it before recognized, and was bound to recognize, as lawful.

It is true that in this case the militia were not called out by the President. But upon the application of the governor under the charter government, the President recognized him as the executive power of the State, and took measures to call out the militia to support his authority if it should be found necessary for the general government to interfere; and it is admitted in the argument, that it was the knowledge of this decision that put an end to the armed opposition to the charter government, and prevented any further efforts to establish by force the proposed constitution. The interference of the President, therefore, by announcing his determination, was as effectual as if the militia had been assembled under his orders. And it should be equally authoritative. For certainly no court of the United States, with a knowledge of this decision, would have been justified in recognizing the opposing party as the lawful government; or in treating as wrongdoers or insurgents the officers of the government which the President had recognized, and was prepared to support by an armed force. In the case of foreign nations, the government acknowledged by the President is always recognized in the courts of justice. And this principle has been applied by the act of Congress to the sovereign States of the Union.

It is said that this power in the President is dangerous to liberty, and may be abused. All power may be abused if placed in unworthy hands. But it would be difficult, we think, to point out any other hands in which this power would be more safe, and at the same time equally effectual. When citizens of the same State are in arms against each other, and the constituted authorities unable to execute the laws, the interposition of the United States must be prompt, or it is of little value. The ordinary course of proceedings in courts of justice would be utterly unfit for the crisis. And the elevated office of the President, chosen as he is by the people of the United States, and the high responsibility he could not fail to feel when acting in a case of so much moment, appear to furnish as strong safeguards against a wilful abuse of power as human prudence and foresight could well provide. At all events, it is conferred upon him by the Constitution and laws of the United States, and must therefore be respected and enforced in its judicial tribunals.

. . . Undoubtedly, if the President in exercising this power shall fall into error, or invade the rights of the people of the State, it would be in the power of Congress to apply the proper remedy. But the courts must administer the law as they find it.

Much of the argument on the part of the plaintiff turned upon political rights and political questions, upon which the court has been urged to express an opinion. We decline doing so. The high power has been conferred on this court of passing judgment upon the acts of the State sovereignties, and of the legislative and executive branches of the federal government, and of determining whether they are beyond the limits of power marked out for them respectively by the Constitution of the United States. This tribunal, therefore, should be the last to overstep the boundaries which limit its own jurisdiction. And while it should always be ready to meet any question confided to it by the Constitution, it is equally its duty not to pass beyond its appropriate sphere of action, and to take care not to involve itself in discussions which properly belong to other forums. No one, we believe, has ever doubted the proposition, that, according to the institutions of this country, the sovereignty in every State resides in the people of the State, and that they may alter and change their form of government at their own pleasure. But whether they have changed it or not by abolishing an old government, and establishing a new one in its place, is a question to be settled by the political power. And when that power has decided, the courts are bound to take notice of its decision, and to follow it.

The judgment of the Circuit Court must therefore be affirmed.

Notes and Queries

1. What reasoning does the Court use to vest in Congress—and not the judiciary—the determination of whether a state has a republican form of government?

2. Chief Justice Marshall stated in *Marbury* that "questions in their nature political, or which are, by the Constitution and laws, submitted to the Executive, can never be made by this court." How does the Court determine when a question is, in fact, political?

3. Should the judiciary have the final authority to resolve such essentially political questions? Do the political considerations cited by the Court in deferring to the other branches of government outweigh what Marshall considered the duty of the judiciary to say what the law is?

4. Can you imagine circumstances in which the application of the "political questions" doctrine would be an abdication of judicial responsibility or place at risk the principle of constitutionalism?

5. Do you find it troubling that the Court has determined that it will not or cannot enforce certain provisions of the Constitution? How can this judicial practice of refusing to intervene in political questions be reconciled with Marshall's statement that the judicial power of the United States is extended to all cases arising under the Constitution? Consider in this connection the extract from the Canadian Supreme Court in Comparative Note 3.6.

Baker v. Carr

369 U.S. 186, 82 S.Ct. 691, 7 L.Ed.2d 663 (1962)

This case arose out of a constitutional challenge to Tennessee's apportionment of its state legislative districts. The state had not reapportioned its districts since 1901, notwithstanding a provision in its constitution requiring reapportionment on the basis of population every ten years. Demographic changes over the ensuing decades had resulted in legislative districts that varied widely in population. Voters in Tennessee sued the state on the grounds that the system of representation caused by malapportionment was "utterly arbitrary" and a dilution of the strength of their votes in violation of the Equal Protection Clause of the Constitution. Citing *Colegrove v. Green* (1946), a three-judge federal district court dismissed the suit, after which the case went to the Supreme Court on appeal. Opinion of the Court: *Brennan*, Black, Clark, Douglas, Stewart, Warren. Concurring Opinion: *Clark*, Douglas, Stewart. Dissenting opinion: *Frankfurter*, Harlan. Not Participating: Whittaker.

Mr. Justice BRENNAN delivered the opinion of the Court.

. . . [W]e hold today only (a) that the court possessed jurisdiction of the subject matter; (b) that a justiciable cause of action is stated upon which appellants would be entitled to appropriate relief; and (c) because appellees raise the issue before this Court, that the appellants have standing to challenge the Tennessee apportionment statutes. Beyond noting that we have no cause at this stage to doubt the District Court will be able to fashion relief if violations of constitutional rights are found, it is improper now to consider what remedy would be most appropriate if appellants prevail at the trial.

Jurisdiction of the Subject Matter

The District Court was uncertain whether our cases withholding federal judicial relief rested upon a lack of federal jurisdiction or upon the inappropriateness of the subject matter for judicial consideration—what we have designated "nonjusticiability." The distinction between the two grounds is significant. In the instance of nonjusticiability, consideration of the cause is not wholly and immediately foreclosed; rather, the Court's inquiry necessarily proceeds to the point of deciding whether the duty asserted can be judicially identified and its breach judicially determined, and whether protection for the right asserted can be judicially molded. In the instance of lack of jurisdiction the cause either does not "arise under" the Federal Constitution, laws or treaties (or fall within one of the other enumerated categories of Art. III, s 2), or is not a "case or controversy" within the meaning of that section; or the cause is not one described by any jurisdictional statute. Our conclusion that this cause presents no nonjusticiable "political question" settles the only possible doubt that it is a case or controversy.

Standing

A federal court cannot "pronounce any statute, either of a state or of the United States, void, because irreconcilable with the constitution, except as it is called upon to adjudge the legal rights of litigants in actual controversies." Have the appellants alleged such a personal stake in the outcome of the controversy as to assure that concrete adverseness which sharpens the presentation of issues upon which the court so largely depends for illumination of difficult constitutional questions? This is the gist of the question of standing. It is, of course, a question of federal law.

We hold that the appellants do have standing to maintain this suit. Our decisions plainly support this conclusion. Many of the cases have assumed rather than articulated the premise in deciding the merits of similar claims.

These appellants seek relief in order to protect or vindicate an interest of their own, and of those similarly situated. Their constitutional claim is, in substance, that the 1901 statute constitutes arbitrary and capricious state action, offensive to the Fourteenth Amendment in its irrational disregard of the standard of apportionment prescribed by the State's Constitution or of any standard, effecting a gross disproportion of representation to voting population. The injury which appellants assert is that this classification disfavors the voters in the counties in which they reside, placing them in a position of constitutionally unjustifiable inequality vis-à-vis voters in irrationally favored counties. A citizen's right to a vote free of arbitrary impairment by state action has been judicially recognized as a right secured by the Constitution, when such impairment resulted from dilution by a false tally, or by a refusal to count votes from arbitrarily selected precincts, . . . or by a stuffing of the ballot box.

It would not be necessary to decide whether appellants' allegations of impairment of their votes by the 1901 apportionment will, ultimately, entitle them to any relief, in order to hold that they have standing to seek it. If such impairment does produce a legally cognizable injury, they are among those who have sustained it. They are asserting "a plain, direct and adequate interest in maintaining the effectiveness of their votes," [citation omitted] not merely a claim of the right possessed by every citizen "to require that the government be administered according to law. . ." They are entitled to a hearing and to the District Court's decision on their claims. "The very essence of civil liberty certainly consists in the right of every individual to claim the protection of the laws, whenever he receives an injury."

Justiciability

In holding that the subject matter of this suit was not justiciable, the District Court relied on *Colegrove v. Green* [1946]. The court stated: "From a review of these decisions there can be no doubt that the federal rule . . . is that the federal courts . . . will not intervene in cases of this type to compel legislative reapportionment." We understand the District Court to have read the cited cases as compelling the conclusion that since the appellants sought to have a legislative apportionment held unconstitutional, their suit presented a "political question" and was therefore nonjusticiable. We hold that this challenge to an apportionment presents no nonjusticiable "political question." The cited cases do not hold the contrary.

Of course the mere fact that the suit seeks protection of a political right does not mean it presents a political question. Such an objection "is little more than a play upon words." Rather, it is argued that apportionment cases, whatever the actual wording of the complaint, can involve no federal constitutional right except one resting on the guaranty of a republican form of government, and that complaints based on that clause have been held to present political questions which are nonjusticiable.

We hold that the claim pleaded here neither rests upon nor implicates the Guaranty Clause and that its justiciability is therefore not foreclosed by our decisions of cases involving that clause. . . . To show why we reject the argument based on the Guaranty Clause, we must examine the authorities under it. But because there appears to be some uncertainty as to why those cases did present political questions, and specifically as to whether this apportionment case is like those cases, we deem it necessary first to consider the contours of the "political question" doctrine.

Our discussion . . . requires review of a number of political question cases, in order to expose the attributes of the doctrine—attributes which, in various settings, diverge, combine, appear, and disappear in seeming disorderliness. . . . That review reveals that in the Guaranty Clause cases and in the other "political question" cases, it is the relationship between the judiciary and the coordinate branches of the Federal Government, and not the federal judiciary's relationship to the States, which gives rise to the "political question." . . .

The nonjusticiability of a political question is primarily a function of the separation of powers. Much confusion results from the capacity of the "political question" label to obscure the need for case-by-case inquiry. Deciding whether a matter has in any measure been committed by the Constitution to another branch of government, or whether the action of that branch exceeds whatever authority has been committed, is itself a delicate exercise in constitutional interpretation, and is a responsibility of this Court as ultimate interpreter of the Constitution. To demonstrate this requires no less than to analyze representative cases and to infer from them the analytical threads that make up the political question doctrine. We shall then show that none of those threads catches this case.

. . . Prominent on the surface of any case held to involve a political question is found a textually demonstrable constitutional commitment of the issue to a coordinate political department; or a lack of judicially discoverable and manageable standards for resolving it; or the impossibility of deciding without an initial policy determination of a kind clearly for nonjudicial discretion; or the impossibility of a court's undertaking independent resolution without expressing lack of the respect due coordinate branches of government; or an unusual need for unquestioning adherence to a political decision already made; or the potentiality of embarrassment from multifarious pronouncements by various departments on one question.

Unless one of these formulations is inextricable from the case at bar, there should be no dismissal for nonjusticiability on the ground of a political question's presence. The doctrine of which we treat is one of "political questions," not one of "political cases." The courts cannot reject as "no law suit" a bona fide controversy as to whether some action denominated "political" exceeds constitutional authority. . . .

Just as the Court has consistently held that a challenge to state action based on the Guaranty Clause presents no justiciable question so has it held, and for the same reasons, that challenges to congressional action on the ground of inconsistency with that clause present no justiciable question. In *Georgia v. Stanton* [1867], the State sought by an original bill to enjoin execution of the Reconstruction Acts, claiming that it already possessed "A republican State, in every political, legal, constitutional, and juridical sense," and that enforcement of the new Acts "Instead of keeping the guaranty against a forcible overthrow of its government by foreign invaders or domestic insurgents . . . is destroying that very government by force." Congress had clearly refused to recognize the republican character of the government of the suing State. It seemed to the Court that the only constitutional claim that could be presented was under the Guaranty Clause, and Congress having determined that the effects of the recent hostilities required extraordinary measures to restore governments of a republican form, this Court refused to interfere with Congress' action at the behest of a claimant relying on that very guaranty. . . .

We come, finally, to the ultimate inquiry whether our precedents as to what constitutes a nonjusticiable "political question" bring the case before us under the umbrella of that doctrine. A natural beginning is to note whether any of the common characteristics which we have been able to identify and label descriptively are present. We find none: The question here is the consistency of state action with the Federal Constitution. We have no question decided, or to be decided, by a political branch of government coequal with this Court. Nor do we risk embarrassment of our government abroad, or grave disturbance at home if we take issue with Tennessee as to the constitutionality of her action here challenged. Nor need the appellants, in order to succeed in this action, ask the Court to enter upon policy determinations for which judicially manageable standards are lacking. Judicial standards under the Equal Protection Clause are well developed and familiar, and it has been open to courts since the enactment of the Fourteenth Amendment to determine, if on the particular facts they must, that a discrimination reflects no policy, but simply arbitrary and capricious action.

This case does, in one sense, involve the allocation of political power within a State, and the appellants might conceivably have added a claim under the Guaranty Clause. Of course, as we have seen, any reliance on that clause would be futile. But because any reliance on the Guaranty Clause could not have succeeded it does not follow that appellants may not be heard on the equal protection claim which in fact they tender. True, it must be clear that the Fourteenth Amendment claim is not so enmeshed with those political question elements which render Guaranty Clause claims nonjusticiable as actually to present a political question itself. But we have found that not to be the case here. . . .

We conclude that the complaint's allegations of a denial of equal protection present a justiciable constitutional cause of action upon which appellants are entitled to a trial and a decision. The right asserted is within the reach of judicial protection under the Fourteenth Amendment.

The judgment of the District Court is reversed and the cause is remanded for further proceedings consistent with this opinion. Reversed and remanded.

Mr. Justice FRANKFURTER, whom Mr. Justice HARLAN joins, dissenting.

The Court today reverses a uniform course of decision established by a dozen cases, including one by which the very claim now sustained was unanimously rejected only five years ago. The impressive body of rulings thus cast aside reflected the equally uniform course of our political history regarding the relationship between population and legislative representation—a wholly different matter from denial of the franchise to individuals because of race, color, religion or sex. Such a massive repudiation of the experience of our whole past in asserting destructively novel judicial power demands a detailed analysis of the role of this Court in our constitutional scheme. Disregard of inherent limits in the effective exercise of the Court's "judicial power" not only presages the futility of judicial intervention in the essentially political conflict of forces by which the relation between population and representation has time out of mind been and now is determined. It may well impair the Court's position as the ultimate organ of "the supreme Law of the Land" in that vast range of legal problems, often strongly entangled in popular feeling, on which this Court must pronounce. The Court's authority—possessed of neither the purse nor the sword—ultimately rests on sustained public confidence in its moral sanction. Such feeling must be nourished by the Court's complete detachment, in fact and in appearance, from political entanglements and by abstention from injecting itself into the clash of political forces in political settlements.

A hypothetical claim resting on abstract assumptions is now for the first time made the basis for affording illusory relief for a particular evil even though it foreshadows deeper and more pervasive difficulties in consequence. The claim is hypothetical and the assumptions are abstract because the Court does not vouchsafe the lower courts'—state and federal—guidelines for formulating specific, definite, wholly unprecedented remedies for the inevitable litigations that today's umbrageous disposition is bound to stimulate in connection with politically motivated reapportionments in so many States. In such a setting, to promulgate jurisdiction in the abstract is meaningless. It is as devoid of reality as "a brooding omnipresence in the sky," for it conveys no intimation what relief, if any, a District Court is capable of affording that would not invite legislatures to play ducks and drakes with the judiciary. For this Court to direct the District Court to enforce a claim to which the Court has over the years consistently found itself required to deny legal enforcement and at the same time to find it necessary to withhold any guidance to the lower court how to enforce this turnabout, new legal claim, manifests an odd—indeed an esoteric—conception of judicial propriety. One of the Court's supporting opinions, as elucidated by commentary, un-

wittingly affords a disheartening preview of the mathematical quagmire (apart from diverse judicially
inappropriate and elusive determinants) into which this
Court today catapults the lower courts of the country without so much as adumbrating the basis for a legal calculus
as a means of extrication. Even assuming the indispensable intellectual disinterestedness on the part of judges in
such matters, they do not have accepted legal standards
or criteria or even reliable analogies to draw upon for
making judicial judgments. To charge courts with the task
of accommodating the incommensurable factors of policy
that underlie these mathematical puzzles is to attribute,
however flatteringly, omnicompetence to judges. . . .

We were soothingly told at the bar of this Court that we
need not worry about the kind of remedy a court could
effectively fashion once the abstract constitutional right to
have courts pass on a state-wide system of electoral districting is recognized as a matter of judicial rhetoric, because legislatures would heed the Court's admonition.
This is not only a euphoric hope. It implies a sorry confession of a frank acknowledgment that there is not under
our Constitution a judicial remedy for every political mischief, for every undesirable exercise of legislative power.
The Framers carefully and with deliberate forethought refused so to enthrone the judiciary. In this situation, as in
others of like nature, appeal for relief does not belong
here. Appeal must be to an informed, civically militant
electorate. In a democratic society like ours, relief must
come through an aroused popular conscience that sears
the conscience of the people's representatives. In any
event there is nothing judicially more unseemly nor more
self-defeating than for this Court to make *in terrorem* pronouncements, to indulge in merely empty rhetoric, sound-
ing a word of promise to the ear, sure to be disappointing
to the hope.

In sustaining appellants' claim, based on the Fourteenth
Amendment, that the District Court may entertain this suit,
this Court's uniform course of decision over the years is
overruled or disregarded. Explicitly it begins with *Colegrove v. Green*, decided in 1946, but its roots run deep in
the Court's historic adjudicatory process.

Colegrove held that a federal court should not entertain
an action for declaratory and injunctive relief to adjudicate
the constitutionality, under the Equal Protection Clause
and other federal constitutional and statutory provisions,
of a state statute establishing the respective districts for the
State's election of Representatives to the Congress. . . .
[The two opinions written by the majority] demonstrate a
predominant concern, first, with avoiding federal judicial
involvement in matters traditionally left to legislative policy making; second, with respect to the difficulty—in view

of the nature of the problems of apportionment and its
history in this country—of drawing on or devising judicial
standards for judgment, as opposed to legislative determinations, of the part which mere numerical equality among
voters should play as a criterion for the allocation of political power; and, third, with problems of finding appropriate modes of relief—particularly, the problem of
resolving the essentially political issue of the relative merits of at-large elections and elections held in districts of
unequal population. . . .

What, then, is this question of legislative apportionment? Appellants invoke the right to vote and to have their
votes counted. But they are permitted to vote and their
votes are counted. They go to the polls, they cast their
ballots, they send their representatives to the state councils. Their complaint is simply that the representatives are
not sufficiently numerous or powerful—in short, that Tennessee has adopted a basis of representation with which
they are dissatisfied. Talk of "debasement" or "dilution" is
circular talk. One cannot speak of "debasement" or "dilution" of the value of a vote until there is first defined a
standard of reference as to what a vote should be worth.
What is actually asked of the Court in this case is to choose
among competing bases of representation—ultimately,
really, among competing theories of political philosophy—in order to establish an appropriate frame of government for the State of Tennessee and thereby for all the
States of the Union.

. . . What Tennessee illustrates is an old and still widespread method of representation—representation by local
geographical division, only in part respective of population—in preference to others, forsooth, more appealing.
Appellants contest this choice and seek to make this Court
the arbiter of the disagreement. They would make the
Equal Protection Clause the charter of adjudication, asserting that the equality which it guarantees comports, if not
the assurance of equal weight to every voter's vote, at least
the basic conception that representation ought to be proportionate to population, a standard by reference to which
the reasonableness of apportionment plans may be
judged.

To find such a political conception legally enforceable
in the broad and unspecific guarantee of equal protection
is to rewrite the Constitution. Certainly, "equal protection"
is no more secure a foundation for judicial judgment of
the permissibility of varying forms of representative government than is "Republican Form." Indeed since "equal
protection of the laws" can only mean an equality of persons standing in the same relation to whatever governmental action is challenged, the determination whether
treatment is equal presupposes a determination concern-

ing the nature of the relationship. This, with respect to apportionment, means an inquiry into the theoretic base of representation in an acceptably republican state. For a court could not determine the equal-protection issue without in fact first determining the Republican-Form issue, simply because what is reasonable for equal-protection purposes will depend upon what frame of government, basically, is allowed. To divorce "equal protection" from "Republican Form" is to talk about half a question.

The notion that representation proportioned to the geographic spread of population is so universally accepted as a necessary element of equality between man and man that it must be taken to be the standard of a political equality preserved by the Fourteenth Amendment—that it is, in appellants' words "the basic principle of representative government"—is, to put it bluntly, not true. However desirable and however desired by some among the great political thinkers and framers of our government, it has never been generally practiced, today or in the past. It was not the English system, it was not the colonial system, it was not the system chosen for the national government by the Constitution, it was not the system exclusively or even predominantly practiced by the States at the time of adoption of the Fourteenth Amendment, it is not predominantly practiced by the States today. Unless judges, the judges of this Court, are to make their private views of political wisdom the measure of the Constitution—views which in all honesty cannot but give the appearance, if not reflect the reality, of involvement with the business of partisan politics so inescapably a part of apportionment controversies—the Fourteenth Amendment, "itself a historical product," provides no guide for judicial oversight of the representation problem. . . .

Manifestly, the Equal Protection Clause supplies no clearer guide for judicial examination of apportionment methods than would the Guarantee Clause itself. Apportionment, by its character, is a subject of extraordinary complexity, involving—even after the fundamental theoretical issues concerning what is to be represented in a representative legislature have been fought out or compromised—considerations of geography, demography, electoral convenience, economic and social cohesions or divergencies among particular local groups, communications, the practical effects of political institutions like the lobby and the city machine, ancient traditions and ties of settled usage, respect for proven incumbents of long experience and senior status, mathematical mechanics, censuses compiling relevant data, and a host of others. Legislative responses throughout the country to the reapportionment demands of the 1960 Census have glaringly

confirmed that these are not factors that lend themselves to evaluations of a nature that are the staple of judicial determinations or for which judges are equipped to adjudicate by legal training or experience or native wit. And this is the more so true because in every strand of this complicated, intricate web of values meet the contending forces of partisan politics. The practical significance of apportionment is that the next election results may differ because of it. Apportionment battles are overwhelmingly party or intra-party contests. It will add a virulent source of friction and tension in federal-state relations to embroil the federal judiciary in them.

Notes and Queries

1. What vision of political society animates the reasoning of the majority opinion? Does *Baker* suggest that voters are wholly autonomous persons independent of any connection with or loyalty to persons or particular communities. Does *Baker v. Carr* advance a similar view of political society? What conception of the citizen is inherent in the majority's reasoning?

2. To what ideal of representation does your answer to the previous query lead? In *Reynolds v. Sims* (1964, reprinted in chapter 8), the Court declared that the Constitution requires state legislatures to be apportioned on the principle of "one person, one vote." Does the majority opinion allow states to take into account representation of particular communities or groups when apportioning their legislatures? Should states be allowed to do so?

3. In *Wesberry v. Sanders* (1964), the Supreme Court declared that the states must also apportion their congressional legislative districts on the basis of the one person, one vote rule. Can it be plausibly argued that a challenge to malapportioned congressional districts—as opposed to state legislative districts—poses a political question that the Supreme Court should not decide?

4. Does Justice Frankfurter offer a better theory of representation? Is the fact that representation soley on the basis of population "has never been generally practiced, today or in the past," necessarily fatal to the majority's argument that the Constitution mandates states to apportion their legislatures on the basis of one person, one vote?

5. In his dissent, Justice Frankfurter wrote that "What is actually asked of the Court in this case is to choose among competing bases of representation—ultimately, really, among competing theories of political philosophy. . . ." Do you agree? Is this a proper task for judges? Are there ways for judges to ground such choices in the Constitution?

Goldwater v. Carter

444 U.S. 996, 100 S. Ct. 533, 62 L. Ed. 2d 428 (1979)

In 1979, President Carter terminated a defense treaty with Taiwan without notifying the Senate. Senator Barry Goldwater and several other Senators sued, challenging the constitutionality of the action. The Court granted certiorari, but remanded the case back to the district court with orders to dismiss the complaint without hearing oral arguments. Concurring opinion: *Rehnquist*, Burger, Stewart, Stevens. Concurring in the result: *Marshall*. Concurring in the judgment: *Powell*. Dissenting in part: *Blackmun*, White. Dissenting opinion: *Brennan*.

Mr. Justice POWELL, concurring.

Although I disagree with the result reached by the Court, I would dismiss the complaint as not ripe for judicial review.

This Court has recognized that an issue should not be decided if it is not ripe for judicial review. Prudential considerations persuade me that a dispute between Congress and the President is not ready for judicial review unless and until each branch has taken action asserting its constitutional authority. Differences between the President and the Congress are commonplace under our system. The differences should, and almost invariably do, turn on political rather than legal considerations. The Judicial Branch should not decide issues affecting the allocation of power between the President and Congress until the political branches reach a constitutional impasse. Otherwise, we would encourage small groups or even individual Members of Congress to seek judicial resolution of issues before the normal political process has the opportunity to resolve the conflict.

In this case, a few Members of Congress claim that the President's action in terminating the treaty with Taiwan has deprived them of their constitutional role with respect to a change in the supreme law of the land. Congress has taken no official action. In the present posture of this case, we do not know whether there ever will be an actual confrontation between the Legislative and Executive Branches. Although the Senate has considered a resolution declaring that Senate approval is necessary for the termination of any mutual defense treaty, no final vote has been taken on the resolution. Moreover, it is unclear whether the resolution would have retroactive effect. It cannot be said that either the Senate or the House has rejected the President's claim. If the Congress chooses not to confront the President, it is not our task to do so. I therefore concur in the dismissal of this case.

Mr. Justice Rehnquist suggests, however, that the issue presented by this case is a nonjusticiable political question

Comparative Note 3.7

. . . [O]ne must examine again the claim that determination of policy by the judge is incompatible with a democratic regime. As the argument goes, a democratic regime demands that policy be made by the people, through their elected representatives, not by the judges, who do not represent the nation and who are not accountable to it. It seems that this claim must now be seen in a different light. When a judge makes policy in the context of the fundamental values of the democracy, he does not act against the democracy but rather according to it. If democracy is a balance between majority rule and certain fundamental values, then the judge who makes policy on the basis of the fundamental values puts into effect those values that the democracy seeks to protect. A judge who adopts policy on the basis of the democracy's fundamental values makes the democracy faithful to itself. . . .

Of course, the assumption is that the judge acts lawfully within the frontiers of the zone of legitimacy. One also assumes that the legislature can at any time establish the balance that appeals to it. Yet as long as the legislature does not act and the judge operates within the limits of the zone of formal legitimacy, a determination of policy that is based on the fundamental values of the democratic regime should not be perceived as an undemocratic act. All the judge is doing is determining the borderline, as he sees it, between the power of the majority and its self-restraint. If the legislature, representing the majority, does not approve of this borderline, it has the authority to move it into the zone it believes is appropriate.

SOURCE: Aharon Barak, *Judicial Discretion*, Trans. Yadin Kaufmann (New Haven: Yale University Press, 1989), 196–97. The author is Chief Justice of Israel's Supreme Court.

which can never be considered by this Court. I cannot agree. In my view, reliance upon the political-question doctrine is inconsistent with our precedents. As set forth in the seminal case of *Baker v. Carr* (1962), the doctrine incorporates three inquiries: (i) Does the issue involve resolution of questions committed by the text of the Constitution to a coordinate branch of Government? (ii) Would resolution of the question demand that a Court move beyond areas of judicial expertise? (iii) Do prudential considerations counsel against judicial intervention? In my opinion the answer to each of these inquiries would require us to decide this case if it were ready for review.

In my view, the suggestion that this case presents a political question is incompatible with this Court's willingness on previous occasions to decide whether one branch of our Government has impinged upon the power of another. Under the criteria enunciated in *Baker v. Carr*, we have the responsibility to decide whether both the Executive and Legislative Branches have constitutional roles to play in termination of a treaty. If the Congress, by appropriate formal action, had challenged the President's authority to terminate the treaty with Taiwan, the resulting uncertainty could have serious consequences for our country. In that situation, it would be the duty of this Court to resolve the issue.

Mr. Justice REHNQUIST, with whom The Chief Justice, Mr. Justice STEWART, and Mr. Justice STEVENS join, concurring in the judgment.

I am of the view that the basic question presented by the petitioners of this case is "political" and therefore nonjusticiable because it involves the authority of the President in the conduct of our country's foreign relations and the extent to which the Senate or the Congress is authorized to negate the action of the President.

Here, while the Constitution is express as to the manner in which the Senate shall participate in the ratification of a treaty, it is silent as to that body's participation in the abrogation of a treaty.

I think that the justifications for concluding that the question here is political in nature are even more compelling than in *Coleman* because it involves foreign relations—specifically a treaty commitment to use military force in the defense of a foreign government if attacked.

The present case differs in several important respects from *Youngstown Sheet & Tube Co. v. Sawyer* (1952), cited by petitioners as authority both for reaching the merits of this dispute and for reversing the Court of Appeals. In *Youngstown*, private litigants brought a suit contesting the President's authority under his war powers to seize the Nation's steel industry, an action of profound and demon-

strable domestic impact. Here, by contrast, we are asked to settle a dispute between coequal branches of our Government, each of which has resources available to protect and assert its interests, resources not available to private litigants outside the judicial forum. Moreover, as in *Curtiss-Wright*, the effect of this action, as far as we can tell, is "entirely external to the United States, and [falls] within the category of foreign affairs." Finally, as already noted, the situation presented here is closely akin to that presented in *Coleman*, where the Constitution spoke only to the procedure for ratification of an amendment, not to its rejection.

Mr. Justice BRENNAN, dissenting.

I respectfully dissent from the order directing the District Court to dismiss this case, and would affirm the judgment of the Court of Appeals insofar as it rests upon the President's well-established authority to recognize, and withdraw recognition from, foreign governments. In stating that this case presents a nonjusticiable "political question," Mr. Justice Rehnquist, in my view, profoundly misapprehends the political-question principle as it applies to matters of foreign relations. Properly understood, the political-question doctrine restrains Courts from reviewing an exercise of foreign policy judgment by the coordinate political branch to which authority to make that judgment has been "constitutional[ly] commit[ted]." But that doctrine does not pertain when a Court is faced with the antecedent question whether a particular branch has been constitutionally designated as the repository of political decisionmaking power. The issue of decisionmaking authority must be resolved as a matter of constitutional law, not political discretion; accordingly, it falls within the competence of the Courts.

The constitutional question raised here is prudently answered in narrow terms. Abrogation of the defense treaty with Taiwan was a necessary incident to Executive recognition of the Peking Government, because the defense treaty was predicated upon the now-abandoned view that the Taiwan Government was the only legitimate political authority in China. Our cases firmly establish that the Constitution commits to the President alone the power to recognize, and withdraw recognition from, foreign regimes. That mandate being clear, our judicial inquiry into the treaty rupture can go no further.

Notes and Queries

1. Justice Powell invokes the doctrine of ripeness notwithstanding the constitutional importance of the case. Compare the doctrine of ripeness as applied by Powell

with the authority conferred on Germany's Federal Constitutional Court. See Comparative Note 3.2.

2. As Justice Brennan's opinion makes clear, discussion about the meaning and application of the political question doctrine necessarily raises questions about the proper extent of judicial power. How does Justice Brennan's un-

derstanding of that relationship differ from the other opinions?

3. Justice Powell denied that the issue in this case presented a political question. Was he correct in claiming that interpretation of the Constitution does not imply lack of respect for a coordinate branch?

Nixon v. United States
506 U.S. 224 113 S.Ct. 732, 122 L.Ed.2d 1 (1993)

Walter Nixon, a federal district court judge, was convicted of making false statements before a federal grand jury and sentenced to prison. On 10 May 1989, the House of Representatives adopted three articles of impeachment for high crimes and misdemeanors. After the articles were presented to the Senate, the Senate appointed a committee of senators to "receive evidence and testimony" under its Rule XI. The committee held four days of hearings during which ten witnesses, including Nixon, testified. Nixon and the House impeachment managers submitted extensive final briefs to the full Senate and delivered arguments from the Senate floor during the oral argument in front of the full body. The Senate voted by more than the constitutionally required two-thirds majority to convict Nixon on the first two articles, whereupon Nixon was removed from his office as United States District Judge. Nixon thereafter filed this suit arguing that the Senate Rule XI violates the constitutional grant of authority to the Senate to "try" all impeachments because it prohibits the whole Senate from taking part in the evidentiary hearings. The district court held that his claim was nonjusticiable. The court of appeals affirmed. Opinion of the Court: *Rehnquist*, Stevens, O'Connor, Scalia, Kennedy, Thomas. Concurring opinions: *Stevens*, Blackmun, *White*, *Souter*.

Mr. Chief Justice REHNQUIST delivered the opinion of the Court.

A controversy is nonjusticiable—i.e., involves a political question—where there is "a textually demonstrable constitutional commitment of the issue to a coordinate political department; or a lack of judicially discoverable and manageable standards for resolving it. . . ." But the courts must, in the first instance, interpret the text in question and determine whether and to what extent the issue is textually committed. As the discussion that follows makes clear, the concept of a textual commitment to a coordinate political department is not completely separate from the concept of a lack of judicially discoverable and manageable standards for resolving it; the lack of judicially man-

ageable standards may strengthen the conclusion that there is a textually demonstrable commitment to a coordinate branch.

In this case, we must examine Art. I, s 3, cl. 6, to determine the scope of authority conferred upon the Senate by the Framers regarding impeachment. It provides: "The Senate shall have the sole Power to try all Impeachments. When sitting for that Purpose, they shall be on Oath or Affirmation. When the President of the United States is tried, the Chief Justice shall preside: And no Person shall be convicted without the Concurrence of two thirds of the Members present." The language and structure of this Clause are revealing. The first sentence is a grant of authority to the Senate, and the word "sole" indicates that this authority is reposed in the Senate and nowhere else. The next two sentences specify requirements to which the Senate proceedings shall conform: the Senate shall be on oath or affirmation, a two-thirds vote is required to convict, and when the President is tried the Chief Justice shall preside.

Petitioner argues that the word "try" in the first sentence imposes by implication an additional requirement on the Senate in that the proceedings must be in the nature of a judicial trial. From there petitioner goes on to argue that this limitation precludes the Senate from delegating to a select committee the task of hearing the testimony of witnesses, as was done pursuant to Senate Rule XI. . . .

There are several difficulties with this position which lead us ultimately to reject it. The word "try," both in 1787 and later, has considerably broader meanings than those to which petitioner would limit it. . . . Based on the variety of definitions, however, we cannot say that the Framers used the word "try" as an implied limitation on the method by which the Senate might proceed in trying impeachments. . . .

The conclusion that the use of the word "try" in the first sentence of the Impeachment Trial Clause lacks sufficient precision to afford any judicially manageable standard of review of the Senate's actions is fortified by the existence of the three very specific requirements that the Constitution does impose on the Senate when trying impeachments: the members must be under oath, a two-thirds vote

Comparative Note 3.8

It is clear that the meaning of "unreasonable" cannot be determined by recourse to a dictionary, nor for that matter, by reference to the rules of statutory construction. The task of expounding a Constitution is crucially different from that of construing a statute. A statute defines present rights and obligations. It is easily enacted and as easily repealed. A Constitution, by contrast, is drafted with an eye to the future. Its function is to provide a continuing framework for the legitimate exercise of governmental power and, when joined by a Bill or a Charter of Rights, for the unremitting protection of individual rights and liberties. Once enacted, its provisions cannot easily be repealed or amended. It must, therefore, be capable of growth and development over time to meet new social, political and historical realities often unimagined by its framers. The Judiciary is the guardian of the Constitution and must, in interpreting its provisions, bear these considerations in mind. Professor Paul Freund expressed this idea aptly when he admonished the American courts "not to read the provisions of the Constitution like a last will and testament lest it become one."

Source: Hunter v. Southam [1984] 2 S.C.R. 145, 11 D.L.R. (4th) 641 (Supreme Court of Canada).

is required to convict, and the Chief Justice presides when the President is tried. These limitations are quite precise, and their nature suggests that the Framers did not intend to impose additional limitations on the form of the Senate proceedings by the use of the word "try" in the first sentence.

Petitioner devotes only two pages in his brief to negating the significance of the word "sole" in the first sentence of Clause 6. As noted above, that sentence provides that "[t]he Senate shall have the sole Power to try all Impeachments." We think that the word "sole" is of considerable significance. Indeed, the word "sole" appears only one other time in the Constitution—with respect to the House of Representatives' "*sole* Power of Impeachment." Art. I, s 2, cl. 5 (emphasis added). The common sense meaning of the word "sole" is that the Senate alone shall have authority to determine whether an individual should be acquitted or convicted. The dictionary definition bears this out. "Sole" is defined as "having no companion," "solitary," "being the only one," and "functioning . . . independently and without assistance or interference." If the courts may review the actions of the Senate in order to determine whether that body "tried" an impeached official, it is difficult to see how the Senate would be "functioning . . . independently and without assistance or interference."

Petitioner also contends that the word "sole" should not bear on the question of justiciability because Art. II, s 2, cl. 1, of the Constitution grants the President pardon authority "except in Cases of Impeachment." He argues that such a limitation on the President's pardon power would not have been necessary if the Framers thought that the Senate alone had authority to deal with such questions. But the granting of a pardon is in no sense an overturning of a judgment of conviction by some other tribunal; it is "[a]n executive action that mitigates or sets aside *punishment* for a crime." Authority in the Senate to determine procedures for trying an impeached official, unreviewable by the courts, is therefore not at all inconsistent with authority in the President to grant a pardon to the convicted official. . . .

Petitioner finally argues that even if significance be attributed to the word "sole" in the first sentence of the clause, the authority granted is to the Senate, and this means that "the Senate—not the courts, not a lay jury, not a Senate Committee—shall try impeachments." It would be possible to read the first sentence of the Clause this way, but it is not a natural reading. Petitioner's interpretation would bring into judicial purview not merely the sort of claim made by petitioner, but other similar claims based on the conclusion that the word "Senate" has imposed by implication limitations on procedures which the Senate might adopt. Such limitations would be inconsistent with the construction of the Clause as a whole, which, as we have noted, sets out three express limitations in separate sentences.

The history and contemporary understanding of the impeachment provisions support our reading of the constitutional language. The parties do not offer evidence of a single word in the history of the Constitutional Convention or in contemporary commentary that even alludes to the possibility of judicial review in the context of the impeachment powers. This silence is quite meaningful in light of the several explicit references to the availability of judicial review as a check on the Legislature's power with respect to bills of attainder, *ex post facto* laws, and statutes.

The Framers labored over the question of where the impeachment power should lie. Significantly, in at least two considered scenarios the power was placed with the Federal Judiciary. . . . Despite these proposals, the Convention ultimately decided that the Senate would have "the sole Power to Try all Impeachments." Art. I, s 3, cl. 6. According to Alexander Hamilton, the Senate was the "most fit depositary of this important trust" because its members are representatives of the people. The Supreme Court was not the proper body because the Framers "doubted whether the members of that tribunal would, at all times, be endowed with so eminent a portion of fortitude as would be called for in the execution of so difficult a task" or whether the Court "would possess the degree of credit and authority" to carry out its judgment if it conflicted with the accusation brought by the Legislature—the people's representative. In addition, the Framers believed the Court was too small in number: "The awful discretion, which a court of impeachments must necessarily have, to doom to honor or to infamy the most confidential and the most distinguished characters of the community, forbids the commitment of the trust to a small number of persons."

There are two additional reasons why the Judiciary, and the Supreme Court in particular, were not chosen to have any role in impeachments. First, the Framers recognized that most likely there would be two sets of proceedings for individuals who commit impeachable offenses—the impeachment trial and a separate criminal trial. In fact, the Constitution explicitly provides for two separate proceedings. The Framers deliberately separated the two forums to avoid raising the specter of bias and to ensure independent judgments. . . . Certainly judicial review of the Senate's "trial" would introduce the same risk of bias as would participation in the trial itself.

Second, judicial review would be inconsistent with the Framers' insistence that our system be one of checks and balances. In our constitutional system, impeachment was designed to be the *only* check on the Judicial Branch by the Legislature. . . . Judicial involvement in impeachment proceedings, even if only for purposes of judicial review, is counter-intuitive because it would eviscerate the "important constitutional check" placed on the Judiciary by the Framers. Nixon's argument would place final reviewing authority with respect to impeachments in the hands of the same body that the impeachment process is meant to regulate.

Nevertheless, Nixon argues that judicial review is necessary in order to place a check on the Legislature. Nixon fears that if the Senate is given unreviewable authority to interpret the Impeachment Trial Clause, there is a grave risk that the Senate will usurp judicial power. The Framers anticipated this objection and created two constitutional safeguards to keep the Senate in check. The first safeguard is that the whole of the impeachment power is divided between the two legislative bodies, with the House given the right to accuse and the Senate given the right to judge. . . . This split of authority "avoids the inconvenience of making the same persons both accusers and judges; and guards against the danger of persecution from the prevalency of a factious spirit in either of those branches." The second safeguard is the two-thirds supermajority vote requirement. Hamilton explained that "[a]s the concurrence of two-thirds of the senate will be requisite to a condemnation, the security to innocence, from this additional circumstance, will be as complete as itself can desire."

In addition to the textual commitment argument, we are persuaded that the lack of finality and the difficulty of fashioning relief counsel against justiciability. . . . We agree with the Court of Appeals that opening the door of judicial review to the procedures used by the Senate in trying impeachments would "expose the political life of the country to months, or perhaps years, of chaos." This lack of finality would manifest itself most dramatically if the President were impeached. The legitimacy of any successor, and hence his effectiveness, would be impaired severely, not merely while the judicial process was running its course, but during any retrial that a differently constituted Senate might conduct if its first judgment of conviction were invalidated. Equally uncertain is the question of what relief a court may give other than simply setting aside the judgment of conviction. Could it order the reinstatement of a convicted federal judge, or order Congress to create an additional judgeship if the seat had been filled in the interim?

In the case before us, there is no separate provision of the Constitution which could be defeated by allowing the Senate final authority to determine the meaning of the word "try" in the Impeachment Trial Clause. We agree with Nixon that courts possess power to review either legislative or executive action that transgresses identifiable textual limits. As we have made clear, "whether the action of [either the Legislative or Executive Branch] exceeds whatever authority has been committed, is itself a delicate exercise in constitutional interpretation, and is a responsibility of this Court as ultimate interpreter of the Constitution." But we conclude, after exercising that delicate responsibility, that the word "try" in the Impeachment Clause does not provide an identifiable textual limit on the authority which is committed to the Senate.

For the foregoing reasons, the judgment of the Court of Appeals is

Affirmed.

Justice WHITE, with whom Justice BLACKMUN joins, concurring in the judgment.

Petitioner contends that the method by which the Senate convicted him on two articles of impeachment violates Art. I, s 3, cl. 6 of the Constitution, which mandates that the Senate "try" impeachments. The Court is of the view that the Constitution forbids us even to consider his contention. I find no such prohibition and would therefore reach the merits of the claim. I concur in the judgment because the Senate fulfilled its constitutional obligation to "try" petitioner.

The majority states that the question raised in this case meets two of the criteria for political questions set out in *Baker v. Carr* [1962]. It concludes first that there is "a textually demonstrable constitutional commitment of the issue to a coordinate political department." It also finds that the question cannot be resolved for "a lack of judicially discoverable and manageable standards."

Of course the issue in the political question doctrine is not whether the Constitutional text commits exclusive responsibility for a particular governmental function to one of the political branches. There are numerous instances of this sort of textual commitment, e.g., Art. I, s 8, and it is not thought that disputes implicating these provisions are nonjusticiable. Rather, the issue is whether the Constitution has given one of the political branches final responsibility for interpreting the scope and nature of such a power. . . .

The majority finds a clear textual commitment in the Constitution's use of the word "sole" in the phrase "the Senate shall have the sole Power to try all impeachments." Art. I, s 3, cl. 6. . . .

. . . The significance of the Constitution's use of the term "sole" lies not in the infrequency with which the term appears, but in the fact that it appears exactly twice, in parallel provisions concerning impeachment. That the word "sole" is found only in the House and Senate Impeachment Clauses demonstrates that its purpose is to emphasize the distinct role of each in the impeachment process. As the majority notes, the Framers, following English practice, were very much concerned to separate the prosecutorial from the adjudicative aspects of impeachment. . . . Giving each House "sole" power with respect to its role in impeachments effected this division of labor. While the majority is thus right to interpret the term "sole" to indicate that the Senate ought to "functio[n] independently and without assistance or interference," . . . it wrongly identifies the judiciary, rather than the House, as the source of potential interference with which the Framers were concerned when they employed the term "sole."

The majority also claims support in the history and early interpretations of the Impeachment Clauses, noting the various arguments in support of the current system made at the Constitutional Convention and expressed powerfully by Hamilton in *The Federalist* Nos. 65 and 66. In light of these materials there can be little doubt that the Framers came to the view at the Convention that the trial of officials' public misdeeds should be conducted by representatives of the people; that the fledgling judiciary lacked the wherewithal to adjudicate political intrigues; that the judiciary ought not to try both impeachments and subsequent criminal cases emanating from them; and that the impeachment power must reside in the Legislative Branch to provide a check on the largely unaccountable judiciary.

The majority's review of the historical record thus explains why the power to try impeachments properly resides with the Senate. It does not explain, however, the sweeping statement that the judiciary was "not chosen to have any role in impeachments." Not a single word in the historical materials cited by the majority addresses judicial review of the Impeachment Trial Clause. And a glance at the arguments surrounding the Impeachment Clauses negates the majority's attempt to infer nonjusticiability from the Framers' arguments in support of the Senate's power to try impeachments.

The historical evidence reveals above all else that the Framers were deeply concerned about placing in any branch the "awful discretion, which a court of impeachments must necessarily have." . . . Viewed against this history, the discord between the majority's position and the basic principles of checks and balances underlying the Constitution's separation of powers is clear. In essence, the majority suggests that the Framers conferred upon Congress a potential tool of legislative dominance yet at the same time rendered Congress' exercise of that power one of the very few areas of legislative authority immune from any judicial review. While the majority rejects petitioner's justiciability argument as espousing a view "inconsistent with the Framers' insistence that our system be one of checks and balances," it is the Court's finding of nonjusticiability that truly upsets the Framers' careful design. In a truly balanced system, impeachments tried by the Senate would serve as a means of controlling the largely unaccountable judiciary, even as judicial review would ensure that the Senate adhered to a minimal set of procedural standards in conducting impeachment trials.

The majority also contends that the term "try" does not present a judicially manageable standard. . . .

This argument comes in two variants. The first, which asserts that one simply cannot ascertain the sense of "try" which the Framers employed and hence cannot undertake judicial review, is clearly untenable. To begin with, one would intuitively expect that, in defining the power of a political body to conduct an inquiry into official wrongdoing, the Framers used "try" in its legal sense. That intuition is borne out by reflection on the alternatives. The third clause of Art. I, s 3 cannot seriously be read to mean that the Senate shall "attempt" or "experiment with" impeachments. It is equally implausible to say that the Senate is charged with "investigating" impeachments given that this description would substantially overlap with the House of Representatives' "sole" power to draw up articles of impeachment. Art. I, s 2, cl. 5. . . .

The other variant of the majority position focuses not on which sense of "try" is employed in the Impeachment Trial Clause, but on whether the legal sense of that term creates a judicially manageable standard. The majority concludes that the term provides no "identifiable textual limit." Yet, as the Government itself conceded at oral argument, the term "try" is hardly so elusive as the majority would have it. Were the Senate, for example, to adopt the practice of automatically entering a judgment of conviction whenever articles of impeachment were delivered from the House, it is quite clear that the Senate will have failed to "try" impeachments. Indeed in this respect, "try" presents no greater, and perhaps fewer, interpretive difficulties than some other constitutional standards that have been found amenable to familiar techniques of judicial construction, including, for example, "Commerce . . . among the several States," Art. I, s 8, cl. 3, and "due process of law."

The majority's conclusion that "try" is incapable of meaningful judicial construction is not without irony. One might think that if any class of concepts would fall within the definitional abilities of the judiciary, it would be that class having to do with procedural justice. Examination of the remaining question—whether proceedings in accordance with Senate Rule XI are compatible with the Impeachment Trial Clause—confirms this intuition.

Petitioner bears the rather substantial burden of demonstrating that, simply by employing the word "try," the Constitution prohibits the Senate from relying on a fact-finding committee. It is clear that the Framers were familiar with English impeachment practice and with that of the States employing a variant of the English model at the time of the Constitutional Convention. Hence there is little doubt that the term "try" as used in Art. I, s 3, cl. 6 meant that the Senate should conduct its proceedings in a manner somewhat resembling a judicial proceeding. Indeed, it is safe to assume that Senate trials were to follow the practice in England and the States, which contemplated a formal hearing on the charges, at which the accused would be represented by counsel, evidence would be presented, and the accused would have the opportunity to be heard.

Petitioner argues, however, that because committees were not used in state impeachment trials prior to the Convention, the word "try" cannot be interpreted to permit their use. It is, however, a substantial leap to infer from the absence of a particular device of parliamentary procedure that its use has been forever barred by the Constitution. . . .

It is also noteworthy that the delegation of fact-finding by judicial and quasijudicial bodies was hardly unknown to the Framers. Jefferson, at least, was aware that the House of Lords sometimes delegated fact-finding in impeachment trials to committees and recommended use of the same to the Senate. The States also had on occasion employed legislative committees to investigate whether to draw up articles of impeachment. More generally, in colonial governments and state legislatures, contemnors appeared before committees to answer the charges against them. . . . Particularly in light of the Constitution's grant to each House of the power to "determine the Rules of its Proceedings," see Art. I, s 5, cl. 2, the existence of legislative and judicial delegation strongly suggests that the Impeachment Trial Clause was not designed to prevent employment of a factfinding committee.

In short, textual and historical evidence reveals that the Impeachment Trial Clause was not meant to bind the hands of the Senate beyond establishing a set of minimal procedures. Without identifying the exact contours of these procedures, it is sufficient to say that the Senate's use of a factfinding committee under Rule XI is entirely compatible with the Constitution's command that the Senate "try all impeachments." Petitioner's challenge to his conviction must therefore fail.

Justice SOUTER, concurring in the judgment.

I agree with the Court that this case presents a nonjusticiable political question. Because my analysis differs somewhat from the Court's, however, I concur in its judgment by this separate opinion. . . .

Whatever considerations feature most prominently in a particular case, the political question doctrine is "essentially a function of the separation of powers," existing to restrain courts "from inappropriate interference in the business of the other branches of Government," and deriving in large part from prudential concerns about the respect we owe the political departments. Not all interference is inappropriate or disrespectful, however, and application of the doctrine ultimately turns, as Learned Hand put it, on "how importunately the occasion demands an answer."

This occasion does not demand an answer. The Impeachment Trial Clause commits to the Senate "the sole Power to try all Impeachments," subject to three procedural requirements: the Senate shall be on oath or affirmation; the Chief Justice shall preside when the President is tried; and conviction shall be upon the concurrence of two-thirds of the Members present. U.S. Const., Art. I, s 3, cl. 6. It seems fair to conclude that the Clause contemplates that the Senate may determine, within broad boundaries, such subsidiary issues as the procedures for receipt and consideration of evidence necessary to satisfy its duty to "try" impeachments. Other significant considerations confirm a conclusion that this case presents a nonjusticiable political question: the "unusual need for unquestioning adherence to a political decision already made," as well as "the potentiality of embarrassment from multifarious pronouncements by various departments on one question." As the Court observes, . . . judicial review of an impeachment trial would under the best of circumstances entail significant disruption of government.

One can, nevertheless, envision different and unusual circumstances that might justify a more searching review of impeachment proceedings. If the Senate were to act in a manner seriously threatening the integrity of its results, convicting, say, upon a coin-toss, or upon a summary determination that an officer of the United States was simply "a bad guy," judicial interference might well be appropriate. In such circumstances, the Senate's action might be so far beyond the scope of its constitutional authority, and the consequent impact on the Republic so great, as to merit a judicial response despite the prudential concerns that would ordinarily counsel silence. "The political question doctrine, a tool for maintenance of governmental order, will not be so applied as to promote only disorder."

Notes and Queries

1. How does Chief Justice Rehnquist distinguish this case from *Baker v. Carr* (1962)? What sorts of analysis does Rehnquist use to determine the definition of the word "try" as used in Article I? How does he answer Nixon's arguments for a limited definition of the term?

2. Why does Rehnquist refuse Nixon's argument for judicial review of judicial impeachment proceedings? What historical materials does he use to come to this conclusion? What does he see as the potential implications if judicial review of impeachments were allowed?

3. How do the concurring opinions of Justices White and Souter differ from Rehnquist's analysis? What larger judicial oversight of impeachment proceedings would they allow?

4. According to Justice White, the issue in *Nixon* is not whether the constitutional text commits a power exclusively to one of the political branches, but whether it has given that branch "final responsibility" for interpreting the scope of such a power. Do you agree?

Chapter 4

Separation of Powers

The principle of separation of powers traces its origin back to Aristotle. The celebrated political philosopher developed the idea that government should be composed of three organs, namely, the "deliberative" (i.e., legislative), the "magisterial" (i.e., executive), and the "judicial."[1] The full implications of this distribution of public power, however, were not worked out until Locke and Montesquieu revived the doctrine in the 18th century. Both philosophers made separation of powers cardinal features of their proposed systems of modern governance, and both had a major influence on the American founders.[2] In justifying separation of powers, James Madison, following Locke, wrote in *Federalist* 47: "The accumulation of all powers, legislative, executive, and judiciary, in the same hands, whether of one, a few, or many, and whether hereditary, self-appointed, or elective, may justly be pronounced the very definition of tyranny."[3]

The View of the Framers

Madison remains America's preeminent theorist of separated powers. It is therefore important to highlight the essentials of his thought as set forth in Numbers 47 to 51 of *The Federalist Papers*. Madison advocated a new political order based on a tripartite division of powers designed to avoid the twin evils of tyranny and anarchy. The plan of the Constitution, he argued, would achieve this result by channeling power into separate departments of government, each of which would represent a will of its own. "The fundamental principles of a free constitution are subverted," he said, "where the *whole*

---

[1] *Politics*, Bk. 6, Chap. XI, Sec. 1.

[2] "Political liberty," Locke wrote, "is to be found only in moderate governments; even in these it is not always found. It is there only when there is no abuse of power. . . . To prevent this abuse, it is necessary from the very nature of things that power should be a check to power. . . . In every government there are three sorts of power: the legislative, the executive. . . . and the judicial power. . . . When the legislative and executive powers are united in the same person, or in the same body of magistrates, there can be no liberty." *Treatise on Government*, Book II, Chap. XII (1690). For Montesquieu's argument see *The Spirit of the Laws*, published in 1793. (The Legal Classics Library, 1984), Vol. 1, Book 11, Chap. 6.

[3] *The Federalist* (New York: Barnes & Noble, 1996), p. 336.

power of one department is exercised by the same hands which possess the *whole* power of another department,"[4] an insight he attributed to Montesquieu. Yet Madison was not writing on a clean slate; the constitutional experience of Massachusetts, for example, with its "watertight," or strict, separation between departments encouraged him to favor a system of shared powers at the federal level.

In defending the Constitution, Madison and the framers held that government would be most effective in protecting both liberty and democracy by incorporating a series of checks and balances into the system of separated powers, so long as each department retained its *essential* independence. The merit of the Convention's plan, Madison observed, lay in its judicious mixture of the three powers of government. "[U]nless these departments be so far connected and blended as to give each a constitutional control over the others, the degree of separation which the maxim requires, as essential to a free government, can never in practice be duly maintained."[5] Madison particularly feared the unfiltered power of public opinion and its potential sway over legislation. As it was, he remarked, "The legislative department is everywhere extending the sphere of its activity, and drawing all power into its impetuous vortex."[6] To stem the extension of this power, the Constitution vested the executive and judiciary with countervailing powers of resistance, just as they were equipped to resist the ambitions of each other. Finally, bicameralism within the legislative branch, with each House's representatives differing in their mode of selection and terms of office, would provide additional security against rash legislative action and the excesses of democracy.

Madison's theory of separated powers rooted itself in a particular vision of politics. Although he hoped that the governed and their rulers would be men and women of virtue, he expected self-interest and factional strife to dominate their behavior. He also thought that institutional power once established tends to aggrandize itself at the expense of rival centers of power. Madison deserves to be quoted in full:

> *But the great security against a gradual concentration of the several powers in the same department, consists in giving to those who administer each department the necessary constitutional means and personal motives to resist encroachments of the others. The provision for defense must in this, as in all other cases, be made commensurate to the danger of attack. Ambition must be made to counteract ambition. The interest of the man must be connected with the constitutional rights of the place. It may be a reflection on human nature, that such devices should be necessary to control the abuses of government. But what is government itself, but the greatest of all reflections on human nature? If men were angels, no government would be necessary. If angels were to govern men, neither external nor internal controls on government would be necessary. In framing a government which is to be administered by men over men, the great difficulty lies in this: you must first enable the government to control the governed; and in the next place oblige it to control itself. A dependence on the people is, no doubt, the primary control on the government; but experience has taught mankind the necessity of auxiliary precautions.[7]*

Madison—and the founders generally—rooted these forms and structures in the soil of popular sovereignty. "We, the people of the United States," reads the first line

---

[4] Ibid., at 338.

[5] Ibid., at 343.

[6] Ibid., at 343.

[7] Ibid., at 356.

of the Constitution's Preamble, "do ordain and establish this Constitution." In short, the people would rule, but they would do so indirectly through separate legislative, executive, and judicial institutions. By putting distance between the people and their ruling institutions, Madison hoped that the Constitution's governmental design would create a republic of reason in the United States, one that would reflect the voice of enlightened public opinion rather than the passions of the moment or the self-interest of private groups.[8] Madison, however, believed that neither reason nor popular sovereignty would alone be sufficient to protect liberty or a commitment to the public good. Thus "deviations . . . from the principle [of separated powers] must be admitted" in the form of "auxiliary precautions," ones that allow the separate departments to retain their essential independence but simultaneously to blend them together in a relationship of creative tension.

Separation of Powers Today

Constitutions, however, rarely work as planned. Although the formal distribution of power among the branches still prevails today, the executive branch has become dominant, largely at the expense of Congress and the judiciary. Congress and the judiciary, however, have contributed to this growth, the former by its creation of a massive federal bureaucracy and the latter by its expansive interpretation of executive power. As for the Supreme Court, it too has evolved into a much more powerful institution than originally anticipated. Moreover, it is often overlooked that Congress itself is responsible for much of the authority wielded by the Supreme Court today. For one thing, Congress has expanded the jurisdiction of the federal courts over the years; for another, Congress has given the Supreme Court complete control over its docket, virtually allowing the Court to convert itself into something like a European-style constitutional tribunal. Congress has also customarily invited the judiciary to review laws of doubtful constitutionality, thus abdicating, in the minds of some commentators, its own authority to enforce the Constitution. In addition, Congress is responsible for allowing public interest groups, with their diverging agendas, to invoke the power of the federal judiciary in overseeing the execution of federal law.[9]

Facilitated by a broad construction of its enumerated powers, Congress's authority has also increased over the decades; yet the presidency often overshadows Congress in the face of its constant visibility and the important role of the President in advancing his own legislative program. A significant change in the nature of the presidency took place in the 1820s, when the Jacksonians overthrew the congressional caucus as a method of choosing party candidates for the presidency. President Jackson turned the presidency into an office representative of the people as a whole and claimed to base much of his power on that fact, as would other presidents after him. By the middle of the twentieth century, the president would preside over an awesome federal bureaucracy, which he has never been able fully to control. The president has had even less control over the work of independent regulatory commissions whose combination of legislative, adjudicatory, and executive functions fits uneasily, if at all, into Madison's original scheme of separation of powers.

---

[8] For a detailed modern application of Madison's theory of reasoned republic, see Cass R. Sunstein, *The Partial Constitution* (Cambridge: Harvard University Press, 1993).

[9] *Lujan v. Defenders of Wildlife*, 505 U.S. 555 (1992) is a leading example, although the Court denied standing in this case. See also Steven G. Calabresi, *Some Normative Arguments for the Unitary Executive*, 48 Arkansas Law Review 48–50 (1995).

Yet, as the executive branch has expanded its powers within the more proactive affirmative state we have become, Congress found various ways to limit and obstruct the execution of federal law. The growth of the congressional committee system, the power of committee chairs, the explosive growth of congressional staffs, the development and use of the legislative veto, and the increasing tendency of the Senate to confirm cabinet secretaries subject to winning their agreement on how to construe statutes have checked the executive branch in ways unmentioned in the constitutional text. Congress has adopted these "extra-constitutional" restraints largely in response to the growth of executive power. Still, some believe these measures have undermined the unity and energy in the executive that Hamilton thought were necessary for effective and accountable government.[10] On the other hand, changes in the office of the president and presidential claims to certain prerogative powers, particularly in the field of foreign affairs (see chapter 5), have led others to speak of an "imperial" presidency capable of lording it over Congress. Further complicating this picture is the growth and operation of the American party system. When Congress and the presidency are controlled by different political parties, as in recent decades, the existing system of nontextual checks and balances serves often to exacerbate the problem of democratic control and accountability in American politics.

In reading and assessing the cases reprinted in this chapter, students should bear in mind these contemporary realities of American government. The Supreme Court has rarely made Olympian pronouncements on the meaning of separation of powers; the actual working out of the system of separated powers and checks and balances is more the result of usage, practice, and politics than of constitutional adjudication. This does not mean that separation of powers has lost all of its vitality in American constitutionalism. Actually, it has experienced a jurisprudential revival in recent years, as several cases reprinted in this chapter show. The cases are important not only for what they tell us about the changing nature of the relations between the branches of the federal government, but also of the Supreme Court's limited role in defining that relationship.

Congressional Powers and Their Limits

Before proceeding to discuss cases involving interbranch relationships, we might pause to underscore a universally accepted principle: Neither the executive nor the legislature can fully define for itself the extent of its own power. As already suggested, the Supreme Court often reserves the right to define the limits of each branch's power unless, of course, a legislative decision or an executive practice falls within the scope of the political question doctrine. In this regard it is worth recalling the tension noted in chapter 3 between judicial review as articulated by John Marshall and Jefferson's alternative departmentalism position, which would have each branch be the arbiter of the extent of its own powers. Rarely, however, does the Court intrude itself into the internal processes of the other branches of government. A major exception to this generalization is *Powell v. McCormack* (1969, reprinted later in the chapter). *Powell*, like *Baker v. Carr*, decided seven years earlier, appeared to place significant limits on the political question doctrine.

In 1967, the House of Representatives voted overwhelmingly to exclude one of its members from taking the seat to which he had been duly elected, because of impro-

---

[10] For an account of this debate see Stephen M. Griffin, *American Constitutionalism* (Princeton: Princeton University Press, 1996), esp. pp. 59–87.

prieties in his management of congressional funds in the previous session of Congress. The Congressman sued to retain his seat, arguing that his exclusion violated the provision of the Constitution (Art. I, Sec. 2, Cl. 3) that bases House eligibility on age, citizenship, and residence, all of which the member—Adam Clayton Powell—had satisfied. John McCormack, the Speaker, and other House leaders invoked in their defense the Speech and Debate Clause (Art., Sec. 6) and the political question doctrine. The Court concluded that the Speech and Debate Clause—the provision that bars senators and representatives from being questioned in any other place for any speech or debate in either House—required the removal of the Speaker and other House members as defendants, but it allowed the continuance of the lawsuit against House employees charged with enforcing the exclusion order.

The argument that the case presented a nonjusticiable political question derives from Art. I, Sec. 5. This provision makes each House the judge of its members' qualifications and empowers it to expel an already-seated member by a two-thirds vote. In affirming its authority to enforce the qualifications clause, the Court differentiated sharply between excluding and expelling a member. Members could be expelled from Congress for misconduct after being seated, but Congress could exclude them from being seated only if they failed to meet one of the three conditions laid down by the constitutional text. The Court ruled in favor of the excluded member after its long and detailed examination of the original intent behind the qualifications clause, including an historical analysis of pre-convention precedents going back to early English precedents. (Years later, in *U.S. Terms Limits, Inc. v. Thornton* [1995, reprinted in chapter 6], the Court would draw heavily on *Powell's* historical analysis to invalidate state-imposed congressional term limits.) Whether the *Powell* Court would have proclaimed an *expulsion* to have been a nonjusticiable political question remained unanswered.

In *Powell,* members of Congress successfully invoked the speech and debate clause to remove themselves as defendants. In *Gravel v. United States* (1972), however, the Speech and Debate Clause failed as a defense against a prosecution for legislative-related activities. *Gravel* warrants notice because the Court extended the constitutional privilege to the aides and assistants of senators and representatives who served as their "alter egos" in the "day-to-day" work of Congress. If the independence of the legislature is to be protected against intimidation or threats from the executive, said the Court, the privilege must be extended to such aides and assistants. To this extent, the Court faced up to the realities of the modern legislative process, the complexities of which require the assistance of large congressional staffs. In a sharply divided opinion, the majority extended the privilege only to activities that are "an integral part of the deliberative and communicative processes by which members of Congress participate in committee and House proceedings."[11] *Gravel* involved a senator who, after rising in the Senate to read from the Pentagon Papers (classified documents entitled "History of U.S. Decision-Making Process on Viet Nam Policy" stolen from the Department of State) instructed one of his aides to arrange for their private publication with the Beacon Press. The Speech and Debate Clause protected Senator Gravel against a grand jury investigation of a possible violation of federal law but did not protect, the Court ruled, his aide. Why? Because the aide's relations with the Beacon Press fell outside "the essential deliberations of the Senate." Justice Brennan, joined by Justices Douglas and Marshall, dissenting, found this view of the legislative process severely cramped. They would have extended the privilege of the

---

[11] *Gravel v. United States,* 408 U.S. 606, 625 (1972).

Speech and Debate Clause to a "legislator's duty to inform the public about matters affecting the administration of government."[12]

Here again, we find how different opinions rely on different visions of politics and the polity. The majority opinion in *Gravel* envisioned the legislative process as a rather insulated activity confined to committee hearings and debates on the floor of the House and Senate. There is merit in this view. It accords with the concept of legislators as independent decision-makers capable of making rational decisions in the public interest. It includes the view of Congress as a place of democratic representation where the people as a whole rule, in their collective sovereignty, and not an assembly of party and group interests where policy results from "unholy" compromises inimical to the general welfare. The dissenting view, on the other hand, envisions politics—i.e., legislative politics—as an open-ended process that does not end or begin with what occurs within the halls of Congress. The minority view embraces a more fluid concept of democracy, one that emphasizes the people's right to know and the importance of the media in communicating with the public. It sees the informing function of Congress as crucial to the legislative process as the enactment of laws.

Similarly, the majority and minority opinions in *Powell* represent different pictures not only of the principle of separated powers, but also of the nature of political representation. Apart from the view that Congress, as a coordinate branch of government, ought to have the right to establish and govern its own procedures, the minority opinion seems based on the conviction that democratic representation in the American polity requires men and women of integrity. The majority view, however, sees representation in a more pragmatic and, perhaps, realistic light, resting on the right of voters in any congressional district to elect who they want to represent them, whether or not he or she is a scoundrel.

Congressional Investigations

The Supreme Court has declared "that the power of inquiry—with process to enforce it—is an essential and appropriate auxiliary to the legislative function."[13] This power to ask questions is nowhere laid down in the Constitution but is implied as a matter of practical construction and historical practice. Indeed, Congress' power to investigate is as broad as its competence to legislate. Accordingly, Congress may compel the appearance and testimony of any private individual who possesses information relevant to its lawmaking authority. In short, if Congress seeks information on a matter concerning which it is authorized to legislate, Congress may require an investigation into that matter. For "a legislative body cannot legislate wisely or effectively in the absence of information respecting the conditions which the legislation is intended to affect or change."[14]

But as *Watkins v. United States* (1957) underscores, the power to ask questions is limited.[15] Watkins, who was a labor organizer and Communist activist in the 1930s, was called before the House Un-American Activities Committee to testify about his activities and to identify persons who had previously been active in the Communist Party but were no longer members. For refusing to answer questions about these

---

[12] Ibid., at 649.

[13] *McGrain v. Daugherty*, 273 U.S. 135 (1927).

[14] Ibid., at 175.

[15] 354 U.S. 178.

persons, he was tried for contempt of Congress. The Court overruled his conviction because neither Congress nor the committee before which Watkins appeared had informed him of the purpose of the inquiry. The committee's purpose appeared to be one of exposure for the sake of exposure, placing the witness "in the glare of publicity" and "subject[ing him] to public stigma, scorn, and obloquy." "No inquiry is an end in itself," said the Court. "[I]t must be related to, and in furtherance of, a legitimate task of the Congress. Investigations conducted solely for personal aggrandizement of the investigators or to 'punish' those investigated are indefensible." Because the subject of the inquiry was not clearly identified, the witness was unable to determine whether the interrogation was pertinent to a legitimate legislative objective, thus rendering him incapable of "determin[ing] whether he was within his rights in refusing to answer."[16] Accordingly, his conviction for contempt violated the Due Process Clause of the Fifth Amendment.

As with *Powell* and *Gravel*, *Watkins* embraces alternative, and largely inarticulate, visions of how a constitutional democracy is supposed to work. Here, once again, the principle of democracy and constitutionalism appear to clash. A democratic Congress in touch with the people and empowered to investigate—and operating within a system of free speech that Justice Brennan has characterized as "uninhibited, robust, and wide-open,"[17]—might be said to have the right to put witnesses "in the glare of publicity" if that person has knowledge of individuals or facts of political interest to the American people. Constitutionalism, however, embraces the principle of human dignity and, apart from any procedural right that a person may have in the context of a congressional inquiry, that principle requires that people be treated with forbearance and respect.

Executive-Legislative Relations

The Principle of Nondelegation

The doctrine that Congress may not delegate its law-making power to any other department or body derives from the principle of separation of powers. "All legislative powers herein granted," declares the Constitution, "shall be vested in [the] Congress," just as Congress is empowered "to make all laws which shall be necessary and proper" for carrying these general powers into execution. But as Madison and the founders knew from their insistence on checks and balances, the theory of separated powers would necessarily give way to the practical realities of public administration. If government were to function at all, Congress would have to confer rulemaking (i.e., legislative) authority on executive agencies lest the wheels of government grind to a halt, a self-evident proposition in the modern regulatory state.

Schechter Poultry Corporation v. United States (1935, reprinted later in the chapter), one of only two cases in which the Supreme Court has invalidated a legislative delegation of power,[18] arose out of the National Industrial Recovery Act (NIRA), the Roosevelt Administration's main weapon in coping with the Great Depression of the 1930s. The NIRA authorized various industrial groups to adopt codes of fair trade which, if approved by the president, would constitute binding law. The president

---

[16] Ibid., at 215.

[17] See *New York Times v. Sullivan*, 376 U.S. 254 (1964).

[18] *Panama Refining Co. v. Ryan*, decided four months before *Schechter*, was the one other case in which the Court invalidated a congressional delegation of authority. *Panama*, like *Schechter*, emerged from a presidential directive based on the National Industrial Recovery Act of 1933.

could, however, use his discretionary authority to modify the codes, any violation of which would be punishable by law. *Schechter* faulted Congress because it allowed the president to determine for himself the purpose and limits of the law. In effect, Congress said to the president: "Here is a serious problem; you resolve it." Accordingly, Congress had abdicated its authority by failing to establish an intelligible principle to guide the exercise of its delegated discretion. As Justice Cardozo said in his concurring opinion, the authority delegated here is "unconfined and vagrant"; it sets up "a roving commission to inquire into evils and upon discovery [to] correct them." *Schechter* teaches that Congress may authorize a governmental body to execute the law, but it must define for itself important choices of social policy and identify the boundaries within which the policy is to be carried out.

The nondelegation doctrine survives in theory but in practice it has declined into virtual obsolescence in view of the Court's apparent reluctance, since the New Deal era, to review congressional delegations of authority. (We might add, however, that a version of the nondelegation doctrine lives on in the canon of construction that says we should interpret in ways that obviate constitutional objections.) Congress regularly entrusts to agency expertise the task of discerning the purpose and boundaries of law. According to some critics, the broad discretionary authority that federal law has conferred on executive agencies has eroded both the rule of law and our representative democracy,[19] meriting in their opinion a revival of the delegation doctrine. Justice Rehnquist joined the critics in *Industrial Union v. American Petroleum Institute* (1980), which involved a statute (Occupational Safety and Health Act [OSHA]) authorizing the Secretary of Labor to promulgate standards which are "reasonably necessary or appropriate to provide safe or healthful employment and places of employment." In this case the Court set aside certain rules limiting the exposure of employees to cancer-producing chemicals, but on the ground that the Secretary of Labor's finding was unsupported by appropriate evidence. In asking the Court to "reshoulder the burden of ensuring that Congress itself make the critical policy decisions," Rehnquist was alone in deciding the case on nondelegation grounds.[20]

With his appointment to the Supreme Court, Justice Antonin Scalia joined Rehnquist in seeking to revitalize the doctrine of "unconstitutional delegation." As a law professor, Scalia had faulted Congress for delegating "vague and standardless rule-making authority" to administrative agencies.[21] He was equally critical of the "legislative veto," claiming, as the Supreme Court would hold several years later, that it invaded the authority of the president in violation of Article 2 of the Constitution (see the Legislative Veto Case *[INS* v. *Chadha]* reprinted later in the chapter). Scalia's vision of the American state is one that draws a sharp legal distinction between the powers of the three branches. It is a vision that underscores the formal allocation of function with institution that were highlighted in the Aristotelian analysis, as well as the later discussions in Locke and Montesquieu.

The Steel Seizure Case

Under the Constitution's formal distribution of power among the three branches of the federal government, Congress *makes* law, the President *executes* it, and the judi-

---

[19] See, especially, Theodore Lowi, *The End of Liberalism,* 2nd edition (New York: Norton 1979).

[20] 448 U.S. 607, at 687. In 1996, the Court once again refused to invoke the nondelegation doctrine in a constitutional challenge to a federal statute that directed the President to define the aggravating conditions that would warrant the death penalty in courts martial cases. See *Loving v. United States,* 116 S.Ct. 1737 (1996).

[21] See Richard A. Brisbin, Jr., *Justice Antonin Scalia and the Conservative Revival* (Baltimore: Johns Hopkins University Press, 1997), 26–27.

ciary *interprets* it. *Youngstown Sheet & Tube Co. v. Sawyer* (1952, reprinted later in the chapter) represents a monumental struggle over the meaning of these powers. President Truman insisted that his seizure of the steel mills was necessary to avert a strike that would shut them down in the face of a United Nation's Resolution obligating the United States to send troops into armed combat in Korea. In justifying his action, Truman invoked "the aggregate of his powers" under Article II; to wit, his general executive power, his authority as commander-in-chief, and his responsibility to "take care that the laws be faithfully executed." *Youngstown* ruled against the President because Congress had specifically denied him the authority to seize private property in the present circumstances. This denial, however, had no relevance for Justice Black, in whose view the President's action would have been unlawful even in the mere *absence* of an authorizing statute. Black's literalist approach to the interpretation of separation of powers amounted to a simple syllogism: Only Congress may provide for the taking of property; here the President took property without congressional approval; *ergo,* the President acted unconstitutionally.

Justice Frankfurter, on the other hand, resisted the temptation to define what the President could or could not do in the absence of congressional authorizing legislation. After alluding to the history of presidential seizures of property, he remarked: "Deeply embedded traditional ways of conducting government cannot supplant the Constitution or legislation, but they give meaning to the words of a text. . . . In short, a systematic, unbroken, executive practice, long pursued to the knowledge of Congress and never before questioned, engaged in by Presidents who have also sworn to uphold the Constitution, making as it were such exercise part of the structure of our government, may be treated as a gloss on 'executive Power' vested in the President by Sec. 1 of Art. II." Yet Frankfurter concurred with the result in *Youngstown* because the action of the President did "not come to us sanctioned by long-continued [congressional] acquiescence."

Like Frankfurter, Justice Jackson declined to ascertain the exact meaning of the three powers of government. He wrote: "Just what our forefathers did envision by [separation of powers], or would have envisioned had they foreseen modern conditions, must be divined from materials almost as enigmatic as the dreams Joseph was called upon to interpret for Pharaoh."[22] His opinion is noted for its flexible analytical framework for determining whether the president has acted constitutionally when he undertakes an executive action. The president's power is "at its maximum," he wrote, when he "acts pursuant to an express or implied authorization of Congress." On the other hand, if the president "takes measures incompatible with the expressed or implied will of Congress, his power is at its lowest ebb," in which case his authority must be justified by reference to one of his own powers under Article 2. But there is also a "twilight zone" where the president acts in the absence of a grant or denial of authority and where the legitimacy of his actions "depends on the imperatives of events and contemporary imponderables rather than on abstract theories of law." For Jackson, these "events" and "imponderables" were not enough to warrant the President's seizure of the steel mills.

The different views advanced in *Youngstown* focus attention on the interpretive and normative themes of this book. Certainly, they illustrate the "awful task" of interpretation that the Supreme Court faces in difficult cases. Few persons correctly predicted *Youngstown's* outcome. Chief Justice Vinson is even reported to have advised the President that the seizure of the steel mills would meet with the Court's ap-

---

[22] *Youngstown Sheet & Tube Co. v. Sawyer,* 343 U.S. 579, 634.

proval.[23] In addition, the case places in sharp relief the tension between constitutionalism and democracy. In a time of emergency, a popularly elected leader might be expected to take whatever measures he deems constitutionally necessary to avert the crisis. Yet the Constitution controls the President just as it controls the other branches of government. Indeed President Truman paid tribute to the constitutionalism incorporated in the Supreme Court's opinion by immediately bending to its will and ordering the return of the steel mills to their rightful owners. Implicitly he was acknowledging that all authority under a constitution—even the one principally charged with the responsibility of providing for the national defense—was to be constrained in his actions by limitations established in the law.

Separation of Powers Reasserted

Bowsher v. Synar (1986) featured an interesting variation on *Schechter*. *Bowsher* challenged a provision of the Gramm-Rudman-Hollings Act conferring broad authority on the Comptroller General—an official subject to removal by a joint resolution of Congress—to establish spending cuts under the statute's antideficit provisions, which the president would then be required to implement. The Court bypassed legitimate issues of delegation to decide the case on the basis of separation of powers. In as much as the Comptroller General could be removed by Congress, said the Court, he was to be regarded as a congressional official and, as such, could not constitutionally perform a function—i.e., determining spending reductions under the statute—clearly within the scope of executive responsibility. Chief Justice Burger, writing for the majority, relied heavily on *Immigration and Naturalization Service v. Chadha* (1983, reprinted later in the chapter), noting that "to permit an officer controlled by Congress to execute the laws would be, in essence, to permit a legislative veto."

Chadha, a truly historic opinion, invalidated the so-called legislative veto, a device used by Congress to monitor the execution of federal law. Congressional legislation has frequently incorporated legislative veto provisions. Normally, an agency will be required to notify the House or Senate, or both, when it promulgates a rule or issues an order, with the result that the rule or order will not go into effect if the House or Senate—or both, depending on the terms of the statute—vetos it within a specified time. By reserving to itself the power to rescind a rule promulgated by an agency under one of its statutes, Congress equipped itself with an effective check over the rulemaking powers of the federal bureaucracy. The use of the veto has a long history and, as Justice White noted in his dissent, its importance to Congress in our contemporary political system can hardly be overstated.

Yet by a seven to two vote, the Court held the legislative veto unconstitutional as violative of the presentment clauses and the principle of bicameralism. Because the legislative veto constitutes lawmaking in its own right, said the Court, the legislation in question must be presented to the President for his approval or veto. In addition, the one-house veto offended the requirement that laws be passed by both houses of Congress. More broadly, the Court held that Congress had expanded its role to one of shared administration and by doing so had encroached on the executive's duty to execute the law. Justice White thought the Court had saddled Congress with a Hobson's choice: "either to refrain from delegating the necessary authority, leaving itself with a hopeless task of writing laws with the requisite specificity to cover endless

---

[23] See remarks of Richard Schifter in *Constitutional 'Revolution' Symposium,* 12 American University Journal of International Law and Policy 131 (1997).

special circumstances across the entire policy landscape, or in the alternative, to abdicate its lawmaking function to the executive branch and independent agencies." His approach emphasized function over form, that is to say, it relied heavily on an analysis of how institutions have evolved over time in terms of their adaptation to a changing environment. In this sense it was, as we described in chapter 3, less oriented to textual fidelity and more to the broader structural configuration of the Constitution's allocation of power than was the majority opinion by Chief Justice Burger. The latter, in its attention to the specific institutional requirements set out in the Constitution, saw less urgency in the need to facilitate the efficient conduct of government than in the obligation to accommodate the formal commands of the text.

More recently, the "line-item veto" presented the Court with an opportunity to reaffirm this formalistic view of lawmaking and strict separation of powers. Long sought by presidents as a way to strengthen the executive role in the budget process, the line-item veto was finally passed by a Republican Congress in 1996, giving presidents the power to "cancel" individual items from would-be laws without having to veto the entire bill. In so doing, the president was given a power already enjoyed by the vast majority of state governors. The day after the law went into effect, six members of Congress brought suit, seeking to have the law declared unconstitutional. Although the Court, in the heavily criticized decision of *Raines v. Byrd* (1997), declined to review the act's constitutionality by denying standing under the "case and controversy" requirement, the Court would ultimately strike down the line-item veto in *Clinton v. City of New York* (1998, reprinted later in the chapter). Citing the fact that there is "no provision in the Constitution that authorizes the President to enact, to amend, or to repeal statutes," the Court, through an opinion by Justice Stevens, declared the Line Item Veto Act in violation of the Constitution's Presentment Clause.

However, in finding on the basis of the presentment clause, Justice Stevens' opinion leaves a discussion of separation of powers to Justice Kennedy's concurrence and the dissents of Justice Scalia (joined by Justice O'Connor) and Justice Breyer (joined by Justices Scalia and O'Connor). While concurring in the judgment, Justice Kennedy thought the line-item veto was not just a perversion of the "finely wrought and exhaustively considered, procedure" of lawmaking announced in *Chadha*, but a violation of separation of powers principles and, thus, a threat to individual liberty. He made it clear that, in his view, the issue came down to one of political accountability: "Abdication of responsibility is not part of the constitutional design." In dissent, Justice Breyer, following the opinion of Justice White in *Chadha*, embraced a functionalist understanding of separation of powers, urging consideration of the statute "in light of the need for 'workable government.'" Surprisingly, given his opinions in *Morrison* and *Mistretta*, Justice Scalia dissented as well, finding little evidence that the president's newly granted cancellation power was any "different from what Congress has permitted the President to do since the formation of the Union," namely, executing the law.

Appointment and Removal Power

Article II (sec. 2, par. 2) empowers the President to nominate, by and with the advice and consent of the Senate, ambassadors, judges, and "all other officers of the United States, whose appointments are not herein otherwise provided for, and which shall be established by law: but the Congress may by law vest the appointment of such inferior officers, as they think proper, in the President alone, in the courts of law, or in the heads of departments." This provision says nothing about the extent of the President's power of removing his appointees. For example, may the Senate require the president to seek its consent prior to his removal of an officer whose appointment it approved? "No," the Supreme Court answered in *Myers v. United States*.[24] Drawing on the Convention debates, the Court declared that the Founders—citing Madison in particular—intended "to give the President the sole power of removal in his responsibility for the conduct of the executive branch." If he is to "take care that the laws be faithfully executed," he must have the power to remove officials when "he loses confidence in the intelligence, ability, judgment or loyalty of any one of them [and] he must have the power to remove them without delay." The power of removal, declared the Court, is incident to the power of appointment, not to the power of advising and consenting to the appointment. With this decision, the Court underscored the importance of the unitary presidency, one that envisions the executive branch as a separate entity responsible to the President alone.

In *Humphrey's Executor v. United States*,[25] however, the Supreme Court limited the President's power to remove members of *independent* regulatory commissions. By doing so, the Court projected a less unified vision of the executive branch. In *Humphrey's Executor*, the Court faced one of the realities of modern government, namely, administrative agencies created by Congress to regulate various phases of the national economy. Vested with rulemaking and adjudicatory authority in highly specialized fields, these agencies are staffed with nonpartisan experts appointed for specified terms of office and insulated from political pressures. "Such a body," said the Court, "cannot in any proper sense be characterized as an arm or an eye of the executive. Its duties are performed without executive leave and, in the contemplation of the statute, must be free from executive control."[26] Accordingly, the Court confined the reach of *Myers*, holding that the President could remove a person from such an agency only for causes specified by statute.[27] He could not validly remove a member of an independent commission simply for reasons of policy.

Myers and *Humphrey's Executor* are rare examples of judicial interference in conflicts between the legislative and executive branches. The president and Congress have found various ways of conducting the business of government without regard to the bright lines that constitutional formalists of an earlier period had drawn between the three powers of government. Only in recent years, with decisions such as *Chadha* and *Bowsher*, has the Court returned to the formalist view of separation of powers expounded in *Myers*. This view advances "the goal of greater accountability of an energetic and efficient government to all the people it represents."[28] White's dissenting opinion in *Chadha*, on the other hand, envisions the three branches as interacting entities marked by balance and reciprocity. Justice White found nothing wrong with congressional arrangements or adaptations designed to regulate a huge modern bureaucracy in the interest of responsive and responsible government.

Executive-Judicial Relations

In *Morrison v. Olson* (1988, reprinted later in the chapter) and *Mistretta v. United States* (1989), the pendulum swung back to a more functional—as opposed to a formalist—view of separation of powers. *Morrison* deals with still another relatively

---

[24] 272 U.S. 52 (1926).

[25] 295 U.S. 602 (1935).

[26] Ibid., at 603.

[27] See also *Wiener v. United States*, 357 U.S. 349 (1958).

[28] Martin S. Flaherty, *The Most Dangerous Branch*, 105 Yale Law Journal 1732 (1966).

new phenomenon in American political life, namely, the creation of the office of an independent counsel. Congress established the office to undertake investigations of high-ranking officials accused of committing serious crimes under federal law. (The Independent Counsel Law was not renewed, having been allowed to expire at midnight on 30 June 1999.) The process of investigation and prosecution is clearly an executive function. Arguably, the President's command over this process is unconstitutionally limited when, as in *Morrison*, the right to appoint such counsel is vested in a special division of a Court of Appeals. *Morrison*, however, ruled that this arrangement did not violate the principle of separation of powers.

Another critical issue in *Morrison* was whether the independent counsel constituted a superior or inferior office of the United States. Were she a superior officer within the meaning of the Appointments Clause, she would have to be appointed by the President. Her tenure and duties were limited, however, and for this reason the Court regarded her as an inferior officer whose appointment, under the terms of the appointments clause, may be placed by Congress in the hands of the judiciary. Justice Scalia, the Court's most ardent textualist, dissented. In his view, the line between executive and judicial power must remain clear and bright. The executive power conferred on the President, he wrote, means "*all* of the executive power," and this requires total control by the executive over criminal investigations and prosecutions. The Court, he wrote, "simply *announces*, with no analysis," this major "depart[ure] from the text of the Constitution."[29]

Justice Scalia wrote an equally passionate dissenting opinion in *Mistretta*. "I dissent from today's decision because I can find no place within our constitutional system for an agency created by Congress to exercise no governmental power other than the making of laws."[30] Congress had created an independent sentencing commission within the judiciary to develop guidelines that federal judges would be obligated to follow in handing down sentences for various categories of offenses and offenders. The commission's membership included at least three federal judges, each of whom would participate in what was admittedly a legislative task. The Court acknowledged that the placement of a rulemaking commission within the judicial branch and its composition approached the borderline of constitutionality. In the end, however, the Court found that the arrangement was a practical way of dealing with the problem of disparate sentencing practices in the federal judiciary and that the work of the commission compromises neither the independence nor the integrity of either the legislature or the judiciary.

United States v. Nixon (1974, reprinted later in the chapter), however, did implicate the independence of the judiciary. This well-known decision, better known as the Watergate Tapes case, involved presidential assistants accused of conspiring to burglarize the headquarters of the Democratic Party during the presidential election campaign of 1972. The special prosecutor in charge of the investigation obtained a subpoena directing the president to produce as evidence certain tape recordings and notes of conversations held in the White House. In his defense, the President claimed executive privilege, a doctrine that refers to his discretion to withhold information of confidential communications for reasons of state. He claimed as well that the federal court lacked jurisdiction in the case "because the matter was an intrabranch dispute between a subordinate and superior officer of the Executive Branch and hence not subject to judicial resolution." The Supreme Court rejected both claims. As for execu-

---

[29] Ibid., at 711.
[30] 488 U.S. 109, at 413.

tive privilege, the Court underscored its importance in protecting the confidentiality of presidential communications, and for the first time it anchored this right in the Constitution itself. But the Court rejected the president's claim that the privilege is absolute. On the facts of this case, the Court concluded that "the ends of criminal justice would be defeated if judgments were to be founded on a partial or speculative presentation of the facts. The very integrity of the judicial system and public confidence in the system depend on full disclosure of all the facts."

The claim of presidential immunity from suit was more successful in *Nixon v. Fitzgerald* (1982).[31] Fitzgerald was discharged from his government post allegedly for his testimony on cost overruns that embarrassed his superiors, whereupon he filed a civil damage suit against President Nixon. By a 5 to 4 vote, the Court held that the president was immune from such an action. "The President occupies a unique position in our constitutional scheme," declared the Court. Any "diversion of his energies by concern with private lawsuits would raise unique risks to the effective functioning of government." Suits for civil damages, said the Court, "could distract a President from his public duties, to the detriment not only of the President and his office but also to the Nation that the Presidency was designed to serve."

Fitzgerald, however, involved the actions of a sitting president. More recently, the question has arisen whether the President is entitled to temporary immunity from a civil lawsuit for a wrong committed prior to his election as president. A former Arkansas state employee brought a sexual harassment suit against President Clinton in 1996 for an event that allegedly occurred when he was Governor. The president argued that as a sitting president he could not be required to submit as a defendant to a civil damage action directed at him personally. The argument from immunity, as suggested in *Fitzgerald*, proceeds from the view that the president is never off duty; to be required to defend himself in court would be a judicial interference with his capacity to carry out his constitutional responsibilities and thus violate the principle of separation of powers. In *Clinton v. Jones* (1997, reprinted later in the chapter), the Supreme Court held that the doctrine of separation of powers does not require federal courts to stay all private actions against the president until he leaves office. The Court rejected the claim that this case would place unacceptable burdens on the president's performance of his official duties. The Court did, however, acknowledge the burdens of the presidency and noted that these "burdens are appropriate matters for the District Court to evaluate in its management of the case."[32]

Posing a sharp contrast to a French judicial decision in 2001 granting the president of the Republic broad immunity protection and essentially deeming him "above the law,"[33] a unanimous Court, through Justice Stevens, determined that not all "interactions between the Judicial Branch and the Executive . . . necessarily rise to the level of constitutionally forbidden impairment of the Executive's ability to perform its constitutionally mandated functions." In light of the events that transpired following *Jones*, however, Justice Stevens' prediction that the Paula Jones lawsuit would not "impose an unacceptable burden on the President's time and energy, and thereby impair the effective performance of his office" seems widely off the mark. Indeed, a different decision in *Jones*—perhaps one more in keeping with Justice Breyer's concurring opinion that "once the president sets forth and explains a conflict . . . the

---

[31] 457 U.S. 731 (1982).

[32] For a summary of the argument before the Supreme Court see *New York Times*, January 14, 1997, p. 1.

[33] Suzanne Daley, "Court Shields President Chirac From Corruption Inquiries," *The New York Times*, October 11, 2001.

matter changes"—might have changed the history and legacy of the Clinton presidency. One can only guess as to whether impeachment might still have occurred if the Jones lawsuit had been postponed until after Clinton's second term expired in January 2001, but it is more than a speculative indulgence to note that the Jones lawsuit acted as an impetus and galvanizing force for much of his legal troubles over the ensuing few years.

Ultimately, the Paula Jones lawsuit, the scandalous discovery of President Clinton's sexual relationship with White House intern Monica Lewinsky, and the work of the independent counsel, Kenneth Starr, led the House of Representatives to approve articles of impeachment against William Jefferson Clinton for giving misleading testimony to and perjuring himself in front of a grand jury, obstructing justice, tampering with evidence, and impeding the independent counsel's investigation (the articles are reprinted later in the chapter). What had begun as an investigation of real estate dealings (the Whitewater controversy) ended with only the second impeachment trial of an American president in history (Andrew Johnson, in 1868, was the first), though Clinton, like Johnson before him, was acquitted (on votes closely following partisan lines) by the Senate on all counts.

Comparative Perspectives

In the interest of limiting the exercise of governmental power, all modern *constitutional* democracies include some variation on the principle of separation of powers. The independence and autonomy of the judiciary is a matter of fundamental importance. In most constitutional democracies, however, the structure of legislative-executive relations differs markedly from the American presidential system. Nearly all of the regimes with which we would wish to compare the United States have adopted parliamentary systems in which the executive and legislative branches are intermingled. In such systems, the government or the executive consists of the prime minister and the members of his cabinet, all of whom normally hold seats in the national legislature. Any such commingling of legislative and executive officialdom would violate the American principle of separated powers. Parliamentary systems also tend to divide executive authority between the head of government (i.e., prime minister, chancellor, or premier) and a head of state (usually a president), although here variations abound both in the power conferred on heads of state and in the manner of their selection.

The parliamentary executive, finally, is typically responsible to the national legislature, and the government can be brought down by a parliamentary vote of no confidence. In the United States, by contrast, the president is independent of Congress. ("[E]ach department should have a will of its own," wrote Madison.) Moreover, the president and Congress often govern with different popular mandates, a condition that breeds conflict and occasionally deadlock between the branches. In the view of many foreign critics, Congress' separation from the executive tends to frustrate majority rule and weaken electoral accountability. As the founders planned—out of their concern for liberty—American constitutionalism does indeed inhibit the smooth translation of majority opinion into public policy. Parliamentary constitutionalism, on the other hand, aspires to create legislatures more directly responsive to popular majorities and to produce governments responsible to the parliaments that elect them. The ideal of parliamentary government is to mobilize the electorate behind finding solutions to national problems and to ensure that all actions taken by government proceed from the consent of the legislature.[34]

---

[34] Harvey C. Mansfield Jr., on the other hand, has written: "The end of the [U.S.] Constitution—for which its forms are designed—is to produce an equilibrium among the separated powers, not to move the whole

Among other things, this means that while the line between legislative and executive power is less clear than it is in the United States, the line that separates judicial from legislative power is, in theory, more rigid. Thus, normatively, judge-made law should be especially problematic where the supremacy of the legislature has historically enjoyed primacy in the constitutional order. Yet as Alec Stone Sweet has pointed out in reference to parliamentary systems in Europe, "[I]t has become increasingly obvious that traditional separation of powers doctrines, however deeply embedded in consciousness we might suppose them to be, are increasingly less relevant to the realities of European governance."[35] Indeed, they are approaching obsolescence and incoherence.

The explanation for this seemingly strange development lies in the ascendance of modern constitutionalism at the expense of parliamentary sovereignty. Constitutional courts, equipped with the political resources of abstract review (which allows for judicial review without a case or controversy), have become key players in the making of public policy. With the nullifying intervention of the courts always a distinct possibility, legislators in these polities know that they must take constitutional considerations very seriously in their enactment of new laws. "The result is that judicial processes have become sites of policy-making that supplement, and at times rival, the legislature."[36] This "judicialization of politics" has probably done more to disturb traditional assumptions about the separation of powers than any other development over the last several decades. It is a phenomenon of global proportions that, ironically, has penetrated much more deeply in polities where the initial resistance to judicial review was considerably more substantial than was the case in the United States. In relative terms, then, the formal separation of judicial and legislative powers in the United States possesses a stability that exceeds what exists in many places where debates over judicial lawmaking have had a much shorter history.

Because the United States differs from other systems of government, foreign constitutional provisions and constitutional case law on separation of powers may seem to have little relevance for Americans. But when so many Americans have begun to doubt the capacity of their national government to function properly, the comparative perspective may provide some basis for rethinking the relationship among the three branches. Short of amending the Constitution, the American system of presidential government will not change, and most Americans would probably not want it to change. Still, foreign constitutional practices may help Americans to reflect more critically on their structure of separation of powers, especially as defined by certain decisions of the Supreme Court.

Such practices are observable in different settings and in various stages of constitutional development. In Europe, for example, the newly constituted democracies in the East present a vivid contrast to the established regimes in the West. Functioning within highly charged and often volatile political climates, the constitutional courts of the post-communist Eastern European republics (Poland, Hungary, and Russia, among others) understandably act cautiously when dealing with other governmental branches.[37] With the memory of Communist authoritarianism still fresh, the courts

---

government toward the solution of problems, in the direction of progress." See *The Soul of the Constitution* (Baltimore: The Johns Hopkins University Press, 1991), 6.

[35] Alec Stone Sweet, *Governing With Judges: Constitutional Politics in Europe* (Oxford: Oxford University Press, 2000), 129.

[36] Ibid., 199.

[37] For an excellent analysis of Eastern European constitutional courts, see Herman Schwartz, *The Struggle for Constitutional Justice in Post-Communist Europe* (Chicago: University of Chicago Press, 2000).

have sought to delineate the roles of respective government branches and protect a scheme of separation of powers while simultaneously working to establish their own legitimacy and independence. It has been a challenging task—in the Russian and Slovak courts especially—but it has been an important one in guaranteeing the continuance of the democratic order.

The Polish Tribunal has been particularly active in this area. In a collection of critical decisions in the late 1980s, the Tribunal limited the power of state bureaucrats, mitigated disputes between the president and the Sejm, and enhanced presidential power vis-à-vis the Sejm. In the early 1990s, the Tribunal heard the Polish equivalent of *Myers* and *Humphrey's Executor* in a case involving a 1992 Law on Radio and Television. The law gave the president the power to appoint the chairman of the Radio and Television Council, but made no mention of removal power. So when President Lech Walesa attempted to discharge the Council chairman, the Tribunal found itself confronted with a decision regarding appointment and removal powers. The ruling—that the president could only dismiss the chairman for gross violation of law and with judicial confirmation—rested on the notion that the state's power must be explicitly granted and provided for rather than merely inferred from constitutional or statutory provisions. Further decisions of the Polish Tribunal have, in the mold of *Chadha* and *City of New York*, attempted to define the nature of lawmaking and recognized, without establishing a doctrine per se, the practice of political questions. In each case, the Tribunal's goal has been to help further the separation of powers it so strongly supports; an additional result has been an enhancement of the Tribunal's own power and legitimacy to decide such thorny issues.

Other Eastern European constitutional courts have made similar attempts but only with limited success. The Hungarian Court, in particular, has generally been more reserved than its Polish counterpart in separation of powers cases. However, in one of its more momentous structural decisions, the Hungarian Court resolved a bitter dispute between the president and the prime minister, once again concerning control over public broadcast media. The president had rejected the prime minister's nominations for ministerial positions, an area where the Hungarian constitution was particularly vague on the allocation of power between the two branches. In a fractious decision in which three judges dissented, the Court ruled that the president had no power to refuse candidates suggested by the prime minister. Going beyond the details of the case to state a general constitutional principle, the Court rejected the notion of co-equal branches by interpreting the Constitution as having generally established a weak presidency within a strong parliamentary government.

More prudence (and thus less activism) has been necessary in Russia, where officials have actively fought against decisions of the Constitutional Courts. Particularly from 1991–1993, the Russian Court was forced to adjudicate under predictably harsh and threatening political conditions. Yet, even within such an unpropitious environment, the Court attempted both to resolve structural divisions as well as emphasize the necessity of obedience to law, a task requiring a deft display of political dexterity. Relying on separation of powers principles that had yet to be officially included in the Constitution, the Court (before it was suspended by President Boris Yeltsin in 1993) limited executive power against the legislature by endorsing an American conception of "checks and balances." By publicly challenging the decisions of a popular president, the Court risked the chance that Yeltsin would simply refuse to obey. Indeed, the former chairman of the Court later reported that he himself needed privately to persuade the Russian president to obey the Court's rulings.

Since the Court returned to the Russian juridical scene in 1995, it has proved more reserved in structural matters, often declining to hear politically sensitive cases or deciding such cases on narrow grounds without resolving the contentious issues at hand. In a handful of cases, however, the Court has attempted to flesh out a theory of lawmaking—its nature, limits, and the actors responsible for the process. For instance, the Court affirmed the ability of the president to reject a bill if he believed it was procedurally flawed, even if the president had yet to consider the merits of the bill. The Court has also granted the president the authority to fill in the gaps of legislation with executive action, but cautioned that Parliament may replace the presidential orders with lawmaking at any time. Finally, four years before the American Court decided *Clinton v. Jones*, the Russian Court had already reached a similar result, deciding that parliamentary immunity extended only to governmental work and not to an individual's activities before he/she entered Parliament.

By and large, the constitutional courts of Eastern Europe view separation of powers cases in connection with individual rights. After decades of enduring Communist regimes where human rights and dignity were systematically violated, these nations have developed a strong constitutional commitment to separating power in order to support and protect individuals from the potential tyranny of a single government branch. In this regard, they have much to learn from the American model—indeed many American constitutional scholars consulted in the framing of the post-Communist constitutions—but also from Germany, their influential neighbor in the heart of Europe. The German Basic Law has made the preservation of dignity the centerpiece of its constitutional project, thus making many of its features worthy objects of emulation for the newer democracies of Europe.

The Basic Law lays down separation of powers as an unamendable principle of Germany's constitutional order, a status it shares with other unalterable features of the Constitution such as the rule of law, federalism, the social state, and the multi-party state. Article 20 (2) proclaims that "all public authority emanates from the people," but then declares that "it shall be exercised . . . by specific legislative, executive, and judicial bodies." Article 79 (3) establishes the separation of these branches in perpetuity by "[prohibiting] any amendment to this Basic Law affecting the . . . principles laid down in [this] Article." This well-known "eternity clause," incidentally, is one source of the doctrine of an unconstitutional constitutional amendment, for the Federal Constitutional Court has on several occasions declared its readiness to strike down any amendment to the Basic Law that would erode the permanence of one of these principles (e.g., separation of powers). To this extent, separation of powers is more textually anchored in Germany than in the United States.

As *the* guardian of the Basic Law, the Federal Constitutional Court plays a key role in overseeing the integrity of the three branches and maintaining the proper balance among them. In fact, the Basic Law confers on the Constitutional Court express authority to settle disputes among the highest institutions of the Federal Republic—i.e., the legislature (Bundestag), Council of State Governments (Bundesrat), Chancellor, and president. Should these institutions disagree among themselves over their respective rights and obligations under the Basic Law, they may petition the Constitutional Court to resolve the conflict. As we shall see in the Military Deployment Case, this jurisdiction also extends to units of these institutions—e.g., the parliamentary parties within the Bundestag—vested with rights of their own under the Constitution. Accordingly, the Basic Law itself endorses an active judicial role in monitoring Germany's system of separated powers. No prudential canons of self-restraint or precepts such as the political-question doctrine stand in the way of a judicial ruling when a dispute between branches of the government is properly before the Court.

Some well-known cases illustrate the Federal Constitutional Court's central role in separation of powers disputes. In a case that recalls issues posed in *United States v.*

Nixon, the Court ruled that the Federal Finance and Economics Ministry was required to deliver certain corporate records to a parliamentary committee investigating illegal tax exemptions granted to a private corporation. The ministry refused to produce the documents on the ground that they contained trade and tax secrets whose confidentiality the tax code required. The Court recognized a "core sphere of executive autonomy" in which certain communications are immune to parliamentary oversight, but here the Court held that the cabinet is accountable to parliament. In the Court's unanimous view, it emphasized that parliament's right to inspect the records in this case is an essential aspect of the principle of separated powers.[38]

Two situations in particular may be of interest to Americans, namely, the delegation of legislative authority to administrative agencies and legislative-executive responsibility in the field of military affairs. As for the delegation of legislative power, Germany's constitutional court exercises more vigilance over this process than does the U.S. Supreme Court. American critics such as Theodore Lowi have viewed with dismay the post-*Schechter* decline in the vitality of the delegation doctrine (see note 19, *supra*). In Germany, by contrast, the doctrine prospers. One reason it prospers is due to the limits that the constitutional text itself imposes on the delegation of legislative authority. Article 80 (1) of the Basic Law authorizes national and state officials to issue regulations having the force of law, but specifies that "the content, purpose, and scope of any such authorization must be set forth in such laws." Statutes that confer general rulemaking power on an agency without laying down the scope and purpose of the power are likely to be viewed with distrust by the Federal Constitutional Court. As one commentator on the Basic Law notes, Article 80 represents a "conscious departure" from the practice during the Weimar Republic of conferring virtually unlimited discretion on executive officials to carry out the will of the lawmaker.[39]

The Court has declared that a "statute must regulate the agency's activity and not confine itself to articulating general principles." In its view, as critics of agency government in the United States have charged, vague delegations of legislative authority tend to encourage administrative agencies to substitute their policies for those of the legislature, risking violations of the principle of "legality" (i.e., rule of law) as well as separation of powers. On this ground, the German Court carefully reviews the validity of contested delegations of legislative power.

At the same time, the Federal Constitutional Court has not confronted parliament with the Hobson's choice that Justice White thought the majority opinion in *Chadha* imposed on Congress. In a well-known case involving Germany's Atomic Energy Act—a statute dealing with the licensing of nuclear power plants—the question was whether parliament had adequately laid down guidelines for the safe development of nuclear power. To require parliament to specify rigid safety rules in this rapidly developing field, said the Court, "would impair rather than promote technical development and adequate safeguards [for the protection of the population.]" Parliament and government must be accorded a "[measure of discretion] in making pragmatic decisions within the confines of their authority." The Court sustained the validity of the statute because it did lay down "with sufficient precision requirements for the construction, operation, and modification of nuclear installations." But this was not the end of parliament's responsibility. Since the legislation affected the basic rights of individuals under the Constitution—here the right to life and physical integrity—

---

[38] See Kommers, *Constitutional Jurisprudence*, 123.

[39] See Mahendra P. Singh, *German Administrative Law* (Berlin: Springer-Verlag, 1985), 21–22.

parliament would be constitutionally responsible for monitoring developments in the field of nuclear technology to ensure that the authority it confers on an agency conforms to the broad safety requirements of the statute.

Finally, German constitutional law may have some relevance for the seemingly unresolvable conflict between president and Congress over their respective foreign and military powers. It may suffice to focus on the recent Military Deployment Case, for this decision contrasts sharply with the U.S. Supreme Court's reluctance to enforce the War Powers Resolution. The German experience demonstrates that judicial review of military decisions taken by the executive, over the objection that such decisions have usurped the prerogatives of the legislature, need not lead to excessive judicial intervention in this sensitive field of international politics.

Germany's government had deployed its military force abroad in United Nations peace-keeping operations without explicit parliamentary approval. Ordinarily, the government (i.e., chancellor and cabinet) could count on the tacit support of a parliamentary majority. In one of the contested deployments, however—Germany's participation in the enforcement of the "no-fly zone" over Bosnia and Herzegovina—the government lacked even this tacit consent, for the operation failed to win the support not only of the opposition parties but also of the Free Democratic Party (FDP), the junior partner in coalition with the ruling Christian Democrats. In applying to the Federal Constitutional Court for a preliminary injunction against the action over Bosnia, the FDP took the unusual step of suing the government of which it was an indispensable part.

The Court held that under the Basic Law, the chancellor and his cabinet would be required to seek parliament's explicit approval prior to any deployment of the armed services even under a valid international agreement. In so ruling, the Court vindicated parliament's right to participate in cabinet decisions to deploy military units outside the area covered by NATO. In reaching this result the principle of democracy was crucial to the Court's reasoning. The government's actions were taken under treaties that constitutionally require parliamentary approval. The Court's decision was clearly a response to its concern for the principle of democratic legitimacy in military matters. In Germany, then, the unamendable principle of separation of powers combines with the equally entrenched principle of popular sovereignty and executive responsibility to produce an accountable government supported by the consent of parliament.

Selected Bibliography

Arnold, Peri E. *Making the Managerial Presidency* (Princeton: Princeton University Press, 1986).

Barber, Sotirios. *The Constitution and the Delegation of Congressional Power* (Chicago: University of Chicago Press, 1975).

Berger, Raoul. *Executive Privilege: A Constitutional Myth* (Cambridge: Harvard University Press, 1974).

———. *Impeachment: The Constitutional Problems* (Cambridge: Harvard University Press, 1973).

Calabresi, Steven G. and Prakash, Saikrishna B. *The President's Power to Executive the Laws*, 104 Yale Law Journal 541–665 (1994).

Corwin, Edward S. *The President: Office and Powers*, 4th rev. ed. (New York: New York University Press, 1957).

Craig, Barbara H. *Chadha: The Story of an Epic Constitutional Struggle* (Berkeley: University of California Press, 1990).

Fisher, Louis. *Constitutional Conflicts Between Congress and the President* (Princeton: Princeton University Press, 1985).

———. *Judicial Misjudgments About the Lawmaking Process: The Legislative Veto Case*. 45 Public Administration Review 705 (November 1985).

Flaherty, Martin S. *The Most Dangerous Branch*, 105 The Yale Law Journal 1725–1839 (1996).

Gerhardt, Michael J., *The Federal Impeachment Process: A Constitutional and Historical Analysis* (Princeton: Princeton University Press, 1996).

Hamilton, James. *The Power To Probe: A Study in Congressional Investigations* (New York: Random House, 1976).

Murphy, Walter F. *Congress and the Court* (Chicago: University of Chicago Press, 1962).

Jones, Gordon S. and Marini, John A. (eds.). *The Imperial Congress: Crisis in the Separation of Powers* (New York: Pharos, 1988).

Pierce, Richard. J. "Morrison v. Olsen, Separation of Powers, and the Structure of Government." In Gerhard Casper and Dennis J. Hutchinson, eds. *The Supreme Court Review 1988* (Chicago: University of Chicago Press, 1989).

Posner, Richard, *An Affair of State: The Investigation, Impeachment, and Trial of President Clinton* (Cambridge: Harvard University Press, 1999).

Pyle, Christopher H. and Pious, Richard. *The President, Congress, and the Constitution* (New York: The Free Press, 1984).

Ratnapala, Suri. "John Locke's Doctrine of Separation of Powers: A Reevaluation." 38 *The American Journal of Jurisprudence* 189–220 (1993).

Rohr, John. *To Run A Constitution: The Legitimacy of the Administrative State* (Lawrence: University Press of Kansas, 1986).

Shapiro, Martin. *Law and Politics in the Supreme Court*, Chapter 2 (New York: The Free Press, 1964).

Schlesinger, Arthur M. *The Imperial Presidency* (Boston: Houghton Mifflin 1973).

Stephens, Otis H. and Rathjen, Gregory J. *The Supreme Court and the Allocation of Constitutional Power* (San Francisco: W. H. Freeman and Company, 1980).

Westin, Alan F. *The Anatomy of a Constitutional Law Case* (New York: Macmillan, 1958).

Selected Comparative Bibliography

Barak, Aharon, "Foreword: A Judge On Judging: The Role of a Supreme Court In a Democracy," 116 *Harvard Law Review* 16–162 (2002).

Baxi, Upendra, *Courage, Craft, and Contention: The Indian Supreme Court in the Eighties* (Bombay: N .M. Tripathi Private Limited, 1985).

Schwartz, Herman, *The Struggle for Constitutional Justice in Post-Communist Europe* (Chicago: The University of Chicago Press, 2000).

Schechter Poultry Corporation v. United States

295 U.S. 495, 55 S.Ct. 837, 79 L.Ed. 1570 (1935)

The National Industrial Recovery Act of 1933, a major New Deal measure designed to revive and develop the national economy, authorized various trades and industries to adopt codes of fair competition. The codes, which typically covered wages, hours of work, trade practices, and labor conditions, entered into force with the president's approval. Pursuant to the act, the president approved the "Live Poultry Code" for the New York metropolitan area, one purpose of which was to prevent sellers from requiring buyers to purchase "sick" chickens along with the healthy ones offered for sale. The Schechter Poultry Company was indicted and convicted in a federal district court for violating the code's provisions. Schechter challenged the conviction, contending that the code had been adopted pursuant to an unconstitutional delegation by Congress of legislative power and that it regulated local transactions outside of Congress's authority. The following extract deals with the issue of delegation. Opinion of the Court: *Hughes*, Van Devanter, McReynolds, Brandeis, Sutherland, Butler, Roberts. Concurring Opinion: *Cardozo*, Stone.

Mr. Chief Justice HUGHES delivered the opinion of the Court.

. . . We recently had occasion to review the pertinent decisions and the general principles which govern the determination of this question. The Constitution provides that "All legislative powers herein granted shall be vested in a Congress of the United States, which shall consist of a Senate and House of Representatives." Article 1, s 1. And the Congress is authorized "To make all Laws which shall be necessary and proper for carrying into Execution" its general powers. Article 1, s 8, par. 18. The Congress is not permitted to abdicate or to transfer to others the essential legislative functions with which it is thus vested. We have repeatedly recognized the necessity of adapting legislation to complex conditions involving a host of details with which the national Legislature cannot deal directly. We pointed out in the *Panama Refining Company* [1935] case that the Constitution has never been regarded as denying to Congress the necessary resources of flexibility and practicality, which will enable it to perform its function in laying down policies and establishing standards, while leaving to selected instrumentalities the making of subordinate rules within prescribed limits and the determination of facts to which the policy as declared by the Legislature is to apply. But we said that the constant recognition of the necessity and validity of such provisions, and the wide

Comparative Note 4.1

The following considerations apply to the relationship between the legislature and the executive. In a free democratic and constitutional system, parliament has the constitutional task of enacting laws. Only parliament possesses the democratic legitimacy to make fundamental political decisions. To be sure, the Basic Law sanctions "delegated" legislation by the executive. However, the executive can legislate only within limits which the legislature prescribes. Parliament cannot neglect its responsibility as a legislative body by delegating part of its legislative authority to the executive without beforehand reflecting upon and determining the limitations of these delegated powers. If the legislature does not satisfy this requirement, then it will shift unfavorably the balance of powers presupposed by the Basic Law in the area of legislation. A total delegation of legislative power to the executive branch violates the principle of separation of powers.

. . .

To the extent that a statute delegates the authority to issue regulations to the executive, the legislative intent must provide . . . a guide for the content of the regulation. The statute must give expression to the legislative intent. It must be clear whether or not the executive confined itself to the express limits [of the delegating statute] in issuing the regulation. If the content [of the regulation] goes beyond the legislative intent, then the issuer of the regulation has overstepped the boundaries of its delegated power. The regulation is then invalid because it has an insufficient legal basis.

SOURCE: *Judicial Qualifications Case* (1972) Federal Constitutional Court (Germany) in Kommers, *Constitutional Jurisprudence*, 2nd ed., 147.

---

range of administrative authority which has been developed by means of them, cannot be allowed to obscure the limitations of the authority to delegate, if our constitutional system is to be maintained.

Accordingly, we look to the statute to see whether Congress has overstepped these limitations—whether Congress in authorizing "codes of fair competition" has itself established the standards of legal obligation, thus performing its essential legislative function, or, by the failure to enact such standards, has attempted to transfer that function to others.

The aspect in which the question is now presented is distinct from that which was before us in the case of the *Panama Company*. There, the subject of the statutory prohibition was defined. That subject was the transportation in interstate and foreign commerce of petroleum and petroleum products which are produced or withdrawn from storage in excess of the amount permitted by state authority. The question was with respect to the range of discretion given to the President in prohibiting that transportation. As to the "codes of fair competition," under section 3 of the Act, the question is more fundamental. It is whether there is any adequate definition of the subject to which the codes are to be addressed.

What is meant by "fair competition" as the term is used in the Act? Does it refer to a category established in the law, and is the authority to make codes limited accordingly? Or is it used as a convenient designation for what-

ever set of laws the formulators of a code for a particular trade or industry may propose and the President may approve (subject to certain restrictions), or the President may himself prescribe, as being wise and beneficent provisions for the government of the trade or industry in order to accomplish the broad purposes of rehabilitation, correction, and expansion which are stated in the first section of Title 1?

The Act does not define "fair competition." "Unfair competition," as known to the common law, is a limited concept. Primarily, and strictly, it relates to the palming off of one's goods as those of a rival trader. In recent years, its scope has been extended. It has been held to apply to misappropriation as well as misrepresentation, to the selling of another's goods as one's own—to misappropriation of what equitably belongs to a competitor. Unfairness in competition has been predicated of acts which lie outside the ordinary course of business and are tainted by fraud or coercion or conduct otherwise prohibited by law. But it is evident that in its widest range, "unfair competition," as it has been understood in the law, does not reach the objectives of the codes which are authorized by the National Industrial Recovery Act. The codes may, indeed, cover conduct which existing law condemns, but they are not limited to conduct of that sort. The government does not contend that the Act contemplates such a limitation. It would be opposed both to the declared purposes of the Act and to its administrative construction.

The Federal Trade Commission Act introduced the expression "unfair methods of competition," which were declared to be unlawful. That was an expression new in the law. . . . What are "unfair methods of competition" are thus to be determined in particular instances, upon evidence, in the light of particular competitive conditions and of what is found to be a specific and substantial public interest. . . .

To make this possible, Congress set up a special procedure. A Commission, a quasi judicial body, was created. Provision was made for formal complaint, for notice and hearing, for appropriate findings of fact supported by adequate evidence, and for judicial review to give assurance that the action of the commission is taken within its statutory authority.

In providing for codes, the National Industrial Recovery Act dispenses with this administrative procedure and with any administrative procedure of an analogous character. But the difference between the code plan of the Recovery Act and the scheme of the Federal Trade Commission Act lies not only in procedure but in subject-matter. We cannot regard the "fair competition" of the codes as antithetical to the "unfair methods of competition" of the Federal Trade Commission Act. The "fair competition" of the codes has a much broader range and a new significance. The Recovery Act provides that it shall not be construed to impair the powers of the Federal Trade Commission, but, when a code is approved, its provisions are to be the "standards of fair competition" for the trade or industry concerned, and any violation of such standards in any transaction in or affecting interstate or foreign commerce is to be deemed "an unfair method of competition" within the meaning of the Federal Trade Commission Act.

For a statement of the authorized objectives and content of the "codes of fair competition," we are referred repeatedly to the "Declaration of Policy" in section 1 of Title 1 of the Recovery Act. Thus the approval of a code by the President is conditioned on his finding that it "will tend to effectuate the policy of this title." The President is authorized to impose such conditions "for the protection of consumers, competitors, employees, and others, and in furtherance of the public interest, and may provide such exceptions to and exemptions from the provisions of such code, as the President in his discretion deems necessary to effectuate the policy herein declared." The "policy herein declared" is manifestly set forth in section one. That declaration embraces a broad range of objectives. Among them we find the elimination of "unfair competitive practices." But, even if this clause were to be taken to relate to practices which fall under the ban of existing law, either common law or statute, it is still only one of the authorized aims described in section one. It is there declared to be

the policy of Congress—to remove obstructions to the free flow of interstate and foreign commerce which tend to diminish the amount thereof; and to provide for the general welfare by promoting the organization of industry for the purpose of cooperative action among trade groups, to induce and maintain united action of labor and management under adequate governmental sanctions and supervision, to eliminate unfair competitive practices, to promote the fullest possible utilization of the present productive capacity of industries, to avoid undue restriction of production (except as may be temporarily required), to increase the consumption of industrial and agricultural products by increasing purchasing power, to reduce and relieve unemployment, to improve standards of labor, and otherwise to rehabilitate industry and to conserve natural resources.

Under section 3, whatever "may tend to effectuate" these general purposes may be included in the "codes of fair competition." We think the conclusion is inescapable that the authority sought to be conferred by section 3 was not merely to deal with "unfair competitive practices" which offend against existing law, and could be the subject of judicial condemnation without further legislation, or to create administrative machinery for the application of established principles of law to particular instances of violation. Rather, the purpose is clearly disclosed to authorize prohibitions through codes of laws which would embrace what the formulators would propose, and what the President would approve, or prescribe, as wise and beneficent measures for the government of trades and industries in order to bring about rehabilitation, correction and development, according to the general declaration of policy in section 1. Codes of laws of this sort are styled "codes of fair competition."

The question, then, turns upon the authority which section 3 of the Recovery Act vests in the President to approve or prescribe. If the codes have standing as penal statutes, this must be due to the effect of the executive action. But Congress cannot delegate legislative power to the President to exercise an unfettered discretion to make whatever laws he thinks may be needed or advisable for the rehabilitation and expansion of trade or industry.

To summarize and conclude upon this point: Section 3 of the Recovery Act is without precedent. It supplies no standards for any trade, industry, or activity. It does not undertake to prescribe rules of conduct to be applied to particular states of fact determined by appropriate administrative procedure. Instead of prescribing rules of conduct, it authorizes the making of codes to prescribe them. For that legislative undertaking, section 3 sets up no standards, aside from the statement of the general aims of rehabilitation, correction, and expansion described in section 1. In view of the scope of that broad declaration and of the nature of the few restrictions that are imposed, the discretion of the President in approving or prescribing codes, and thus enacting laws for the government of trade and industry throughout the country, is virtually unfettered. We think that the code-making authority thus conferred is an unconstitutional delegation of legislative power.

Mr. Justice CARDOZO, concurring.

The delegated power of legislation which has found expression in this code is not canalized within banks that keep it from overflowing. It is unconfined and vagrant, if I may borrow my own words in an earlier opinion.

This court has held that delegation may be unlawful though the act to be performed is definite and single, if the necessity, time, and occasion of performance have been left in the end to the discretion of the delegate. I thought that ruling went too far. I pointed out in an opinion that there had been "no grant to the Executive of any roving commission to inquire into evils and then, upon discovering them, do anything he pleases." Choice, though within limits, has been given to him "as to the occasion, but none whatever as to the means." Here, in the case before us, is an attempted delegation not confined to acts identified or described by reference to a standard. Here in effect is a roving commission to inquire into evils and upon discovery correct them.

I have said that there is no standard, definite or even approximate, to which legislation must conform. Let me make my meaning more precise. If codes of fair competition are codes eliminating "unfair" methods of competition ascertained upon inquiry to prevail in one industry or another, there is no unlawful delegation of legislative functions when the President is directed to inquire into such practices and denounce them when discovered. For many years a like power has been committed to the Federal Trade Commission with the approval of this court in a long series of decisions. Delegation in such circumstances is born of the necessities of the occasion. The industries of the country are too many and diverse to make it possible for Congress, in respect of matters such as these, to legislate directly with adequate appreciation of varying conditions. Nor is the substance of the power changed because the President may act at the instance of trade or industrial associations having special knowledge of the facts. Their function is strictly advisory; it is the *im-primatur* of the President that begets the quality of law. When the task that is set before one is that of cleaning house, it is prudent as well as usual to take counsel of the dwellers.

But there is another conception of codes of fair competition, their significance and function, which leads to very different consequences, though it is one that is struggling now for recognition and acceptance. By this other conception a code is not to be restricted to the elimination of business practices that would be characterized by general acceptance as oppressive or unfair. It is to include whatever ordinances may be desirable or helpful for the well-being or prosperity of the industry affected. In that view, the function of its adoption is not merely negative, but positive; the planning of improvements as well as the extirpation of abuses. What is fair, as thus conceived, is not something to be contrasted with what is unfair or fraudulent or tricky. The extension becomes as wide as the field of industrial regulation. If that conception shall prevail, anything that Congress may do within the limits of the commerce clause for the betterment of business may be done by the President upon the recommendation of a trade association by calling it a code. This is delegation running riot. No such plenitude of power is susceptible of transfer. The statute, however, aims at nothing less, as one can learn both from its terms and from the administrative practice under it. Nothing less is aimed at by the code now submitted to our scrutiny.

Notes and Queries

1. *Schechter*, along with *Panama Refining Co. v. Ryan* (1935, holding unconstitutional the NIRA's delegation of authority to the president to prohibit the transportation of petroleum products in excess of an amount provided by law but containing no definition of the circumstances and condition in which the transportation is to be allowed or prohibited) represented the height of the Supreme Court's enforcement of the nondelegation doctrine. In the sixty-three years since these two cases, the Supreme Court has invalidated no federal law on the basis of the nondelegation doctrine despite broad delegation of authority by Congress to administrative agencies. For recent, although unsuccessful, efforts to revive the nondelegation doctrine see *Industrial Union Department v. American Petroleum Institute*, 448 U.S. 607 (1980) and *Loving v. United States*, 116 S. Ct. 1737 (1996).

2. Do you detect any difference between the delegation doctrine espoused in *Schechter* and the view set forth by Germany's Federal Constitutional Court in Comparative Note 4.1?

3. Chief Justice Hughes states that the "explicit terms" of the Tenth Amendment imply that "extraordinary conditions do not create or enlarge constitutional power." Do you agree with this statement? Does this statement square with actions taken by the executive office and the legislature in wartime or with the economic legislation enacted by Congress since the New Deal (see chapters 5 and 7)? If it is admitted that the government can extend its power during a declared war, does it follow that it can do so in times of civil and economic crises as well?

4. Why should the judiciary concern itself with how Congress delegates its rightful powers? Is there something wrong with such delegation from the standpoint of democratic accountability?

5. President Roosevelt responded to the Court's decision by asking: "Does this decision mean that the United States government has no control over any national economic problem?" Roosevelt, of course, continued his efforts to rework the national economy. Among his efforts was a statute that would have established a regulatory framework for coal that was similar to the one the Court struck down in *Schechter*. In a letter to the congressional committee considering the legislation, Roosevelt wrote, "[I] hope your committee will not permit doubts as to unconstitutionality, however reasonable, to block the suggested legislation." Letter to Congressmen Hill, 6 July 1935, 4 *The Public Papers and Addresses of Franklin D. Roosevelt* (1938), 297–98. Congress passed the legislation, the Bituminous Coal Conservation Act of 1935. The Court struck it down in the case of *Carter v. Carter Coal Co.*, 298 U.S. 238 (1936).

Youngstown Sheet & Tube Co. v. Sawyer
343 U.S. 579, 72 S.Ct. 863, 96 L.Ed. 1153 (1952)

This case arose out of President Harry Truman's executive order directing the secretary of commerce to seize and operate the nation's steel mills. Other relevant facts are set forth in chapter 5 at pages 182 and 199. The following extracts feature the respective views of Justices Black and Jackson. Opinion of the Court: *Black*, Frankfurter, Burton, Jackson. Concurring opinions: *Frankfurter, Burton, Jackson, Clark, Douglas*. Dissenting opinion: *Vinson*, Reed, Minton.

Mr. Justice BLACK delivered the opinion of the Court.

We are asked to decide whether the President was acting within his constitutional power when he issued an order directing the Secretary of Commerce to take possession of and operate most of the Nation's steel mills. The mill owners argue that the President's order amounts to lawmaking, a legislative function which the Constitution has expressly confided to the Congress and not to the President. The Government's position is that the order was made on findings of the President that his action was necessary to avert a national catastrophe which would inevitably result from a stoppage of steel production, and that in meeting this grave emergency the President was acting within the aggregate of his constitutional powers as the Nation's Chief Executive and the Commander in Chief of the Armed Forces of the United States.

The President's power, if any, to issue the order must stem either from an act of Congress or from the Constitution itself. There is no statute that expressly authorizes the President to take possession of property as he did here. Nor is there any act of Congress to which our attention has been directed from which such a power can fairly be implied. Indeed, we do not understand the Government to rely on statutory authorization for this seizure.

Moreover, the use of the seizure technique to solve labor disputes in order to prevent work stoppages was not only unauthorized by any congressional enactment; prior to this controversy, Congress had refused to adopt that method of settling labor disputes. When the Taft-Hartley Act was under consideration in 1947, Congress rejected an amendment which would have authorized such governmental seizures in cases of emergency. Apparently it was thought that the technique of seizure, like that of compulsory arbitration, would interfere with the process of collective bargaining. . . .

It is clear that if the President had authority to issue the order he did, it must be found in some provision of the Constitution. And it is not claimed that express constitutional language grants this power to the President. The contention is that presidential power should be implied from the aggregate of his powers under the Constitution. Particular reliance is placed on provisions in Article II which say that "the executive Power shall be vested in a President, . . ."; that "he shall take Care that the Laws be faithfully executed"; and that he "shall be Commander in Chief of the Army and Navy of the United States."

The order cannot properly be sustained as an exercise of the President's military power as Commander in Chief of the Armed Forces. The Government attempts to do so by citing a number of cases upholding broad powers in military commanders engaged in day-to-day fighting in a theater of war. Such cases need not concern us here. Even though "theater of war" be an expanding concept, we cannot with faithfulness to our constitutional system hold that the Commander in Chief of the Armed Forces has the ultimate power as such to take possession of private property in order to keep labor disputes from stopping production. This is a job for the Nation's lawmakers, not for its military authorities.

Nor can the seizure order be sustained because of the several constitutional provisions that grant executive power to the President. In the framework of our Constitution, the President's power to see that the laws are faithfully executed refutes the idea that he is to be a lawmaker. The Constitution limits his functions in the lawmaking process to the recommending of laws he thinks wise and the vetoing of laws he thinks bad. And the Constitution is neither silent nor equivocal about who shall make laws which the President is to execute. . . .

The Founders of this Nation entrusted the law making power to the Congress alone in both good and bad times. It would do no good to recall the historical events, the fears of power and the hopes for freedom that lay behind their choice. Such a review would but confirm our holding that this seizure order cannot stand.

Affirmed

Mr. Justice FRANKFURTER, concurring.

. . . A constitutional democracy like ours is perhaps the most difficult of man's social arrangements to manage successfully. . . . The Founders of this nation were not imbued with the modern cynicism that the only thing that history teaches is that it teaches nothing. They acted on the conviction that the experience of man sheds a good deal of light on his nature. It sheds a good deal of light not merely on the need for effective power, if a society is to be at once cohesive and civilized, but also on the need for limitation on the power of governors over the governed.

To that end [the Founders] rested the structure of our central government on the system of checks and balances. For them the doctrine of separation of powers was not mere theory; it was a felt necessity. . . . The accretion of dangerous power does not come in a day. It does come, however slowly, from the generative force of unchecked disregard of the restrictions that fence in even the most disinterested assertion of authority.

The Framers, however, did not make the judiciary the overseer of our government. . . . Rigorous adherence to the narrow scope of the judicial function is especially demanded in controversies that arouse appeals to the Constitution. The attitude with which this Court must approach its duty when confronted with such issues is precisely the opposite of that normally manifested by the general public. So-called constitutional questions seem to exercise a mesmeric influence over the popular mind. This eagerness to settle—preferably forever—a specific problem on the basis of the broadest possible constitutional pronouncements may not unfairly be called one of our minor national traits. An English observer of our scene has acutely described it: "At the first sound of a new argument over the United States Constitution and its interpretation the hearts of Americans leap with a fearful joy. The blood stirs powerfully in their veins and a new luster brightens their eyes. Like King Harry's men before Harfleur, they stand like greyhounds in the slips, straining upon the start."

The path of duty for this Court, it bears repetition, lies in the opposition direction. Due regard for the implications of the distribution of powers in our Constitution and for the nature of the judicial process as the ultimate authority interpreting the Constitution, has . . . confined the Court within the narrow domain of appropriate adjudication. . . . A basic rule is the duty of the Court not to pass on a constitutional issue at all, however narrowly it may be confined, if the case may, as a matter of intellectual honesty, be decided without even considering delicate problems of power under the Constitution.

. . . Not the least characteristic of great statesmanship which the Framers manifested was the extent to which they did not attempt to bind the future. It is no less incumbent upon this Court to avoid putting fetters upon the future by needless pronouncements today.

. . . The issue before us can be met, and therefore should be, without attempting to define the President's powers comprehensively. . . . The judiciary may, as this case proves, have to intervene in determining where authority lies as between the democratic forces in our scheme of government. But in doing so we should be wary and humble. Such is the teaching of this Court's role in the history of the country.

It is in this mood and with this perspective that the issue before the Court must be approached. We must therefore put to one side consideration of what powers the President would have had if there had been no legislation whatever bearing on the authority asserted by the seizure, or if the seizure had been only for a short, explicitly temporary period, to be terminated automatically unless Congressional approval were given. . . .

To be sure, the content of the three authorities of government is not to be derived from an abstract analysis. The areas are partly interacting, not wholly disjoint. The Constitution is a framework for government. Therefore the way the framework has consistently operated fairly establishes that it has operated according to its true nature. Deeply embedded traditional ways of conducting government cannot supplant the Constitution or legislation, but they give meaning to the words of a text or supply them. It is an inadmissibly narrow conception of American constitutional law to confine it to the words of the Constitution and to disregard the gloss which life has written upon them. In short, a systematic, unbroken, executive practice, long pursued to the knowledge of the Congress and never before questioned, engaged in by Presidents who have also sworn to uphold the Constitution, making as it were such exercise of power part of the structure of our government, may be treated as a gloss on the "executive Power" vested in the President by section 1 of Art. 2.

[Frankfurter went on to hold the seizure of the steel mills unconstitutional because the President had acted contrary to the specific procedures laid down by Congress to meet the emergency in this case.]

Mr. Justice JACKSON, concurring in the judgment and opinion of the Court.

A judge, like an executive adviser, may be surprised at the poverty of really useful and unambiguous authority applicable to concrete problems of executive power as they actually present themselves. Just what our forefathers did envision, or would have envisioned had they foreseen modern conditions, must be divined from materials almost as enigmatic as the dreams Joseph was called upon to interpret for Pharaoh. A century and a half of partisan debate and scholarly speculation yields no net result but only supplies more or less apt quotations from respected sources on each side of any question. They largely cancel each other. And court decisions are indecisive because of the judicial practice of dealing with the largest questions in the most narrow way.

The actual art of governing under our Constitution does not and cannot conform to judicial definitions of the power of any of its branches based on isolated clauses or even single Articles torn from context. While the Constitution diffuses power the better to secure liberty, it also contemplates that practice will integrate the dispersed powers into a workable government. It enjoins upon its branches separateness but interdependence, autonomy but reciprocity. Presidential powers are not fixed but fluctuate, depending upon their disjunction or conjunction with those of Congress. We may well begin by a somewhat over-simplified grouping of practical situations in which a President may doubt, or others may challenge, his powers.

1. When the President acts pursuant to an express or implied authorization of Congress, his authority is at its maximum, for it includes all that he possesses in his own right plus all that Congress can delegate. In these circumstances, and in these only, may he be said (for what it may be worth), to personify the federal sovereignty. If his act is held unconstitutional under these circumstances, it usually means that the Federal Government as an undivided whole lacks power. A seizure executed by the President pursuant to an Act of Congress would be supported by the strongest of presumptions and the widest latitude of judicial interpretation, and the burden or persuasion would rest heavily upon any who might attack it.

2. When the President acts in absence of either a congressional grant or denial of authority, he can only rely upon his own independent powers, but there is a zone of twilight in which he and Congress may have concurrent authority, or in which its distribution is uncertain. Therefore, congressional inertia, indifference or quiescence may sometimes, at least as a practical matter, enable, if not invite, measures on independent presidential responsibility. In this area, any actual test of power is likely to depend on the imperatives of events and contemporary imponderables rather than on abstract theories of law.

3. When the President takes measures incompatible with the expressed or implied will of Congress, his power is at its lowest ebb, for then he can rely only upon his own constitutional powers minus any constitutional powers of Congress over the matter. Courts can sustain exclusive presidential control in such a case only by disabling the Congress from acting upon the subject. Presidential claim to a power at once so conclusive and preclusive must be scrutinized with caution, for what is at stake is the equilibrium established by our constitutional system.

Into which of these classifications does this executive seizure of the steel industry fit? It is eliminated from the first by admission, for it is conceded that no congressional authorization exists for this seizure. That takes away also the support of the many precedents and declarations which were made in relation, and must be confined, to this category.

Can it then be defended under flexible tests available to the second category? It seems clearly eliminated from that class because Congress has not left seizure of private property an open field but has covered it by three statutory policies inconsistent with this seizure. In cases where the purpose is to supply needs of the Government itself, two courses are provided: one, seizure of a plant which fails to comply with obligatory orders placed by the Government, another, condemnation of facilities, including temporary use under the power of eminent domain. The third is applicable where it is the general economy of the country that is to be protected rather than exclusive governmental interests. None of these were invoked. In choosing a different and inconsistent way of his own, the President cannot claim that it is necessitated or invited by failure of Congress to legislate upon the occasions, grounds and methods for seizure of industrial properties.

This leaves the current seizure to be justified only by the severe tests under the third grouping, where it can be supported only by any remainder of executive power after subtraction of such powers as Congress may have over the subject. In short, we can sustain the President only by holding that seizure of such strike-bound industries is within his domain and beyond control by Congress. Thus, this Court's first review of such seizures occurs under circumstances which leave Presidential power most vulnerable to attack and in the least favorable of possible constitutional postures. . . .

The Solicitor General seeks the power of seizure in three clauses of the Executive Article, the first reading, "The executive Power shall be vested in a President of the United States of America." Lest I be thought to exaggerate, I quote the interpretation which his brief puts upon it: "In our view, this clause constitutes a grant of all the executive powers of which the Government is capable." If that be true, it is difficult to see why the forefathers bothered to add several specific items, including some trifling ones.

The example of such unlimited executive power that must have most impressed the forefathers was the prerogative exercised by George III, and the description of its evils in the Declaration of Independence leads me to doubt that they were creating their new Executive in his image. Continental European examples were no more appealing. And if we seek instruction from our own times, we can match it only from the executive powers in those governments we disparagingly describe as totalitarian. I cannot accept the view that this clause is a grant in bulk of all conceivable executive power but regard it as an allocation to the presidential office of the generic powers thereafter stated.

The clause on which the Government next relies is that "The President shall be Commander in Chief of the Army and Navy of the United States. . . . " These cryptic words have given rise to some of the most persistent controversies in our constitutional history. Of course, they imply something more than an empty title. But just what authority goes with the name has plagued presidential advisers who would not waive or narrow it by nonassertion yet cannot say where it begins or ends. It undoubtedly puts the Nation's armed forces under presidential command. Hence, this loose appellation is sometimes advanced as support for any presidential action, internal or external,

involving use of force, the idea being that it vests power to do anything, anywhere, that can be done with an army or navy.

That seems to be the logic of an argument tendered at our bar—that the President having, on his own responsibility, sent American troops abroad derives from that act "affirmative power" to seize the means of producing a supply of steel for them. To quote, "Perhaps the most forceful illustrations of the scope of Presidential power in this connection is the fact that American troops in Korea, whose safety and effectiveness are so directly involved here, were sent to the field by an exercise of the President's constitutional powers." Thus, it is said he has invested himself with "war powers."

I cannot foresee all that it might entail if the Court should indorse this argument. Nothing in our Constitution is plainer than that declaration of a war is entrusted only to Congress. Of course, a state of war may in fact exist without a formal declaration. But no doctrine that the Court could promulgate would seem to me more sinister and alarming than that a President whose conduct of foreign affairs is so largely uncontrolled, and often even is unknown, can vastly enlarge his mastery over the internal affairs of the country by his own commitment of the Nation's armed forces to some foreign venture. I do not, however, find it necessary or appropriate to consider the legal status of the Korean enterprise to discountenance argument based on it.

We should not use this occasion to circumscribe, much less to contract, the lawful role of the President as Commander-in-Chief. I should indulge the widest latitude of interpretation to sustain his exclusive function to command the instruments of national force, at least when turned against the outside world for the security of our society. But, when it is turned inward, not because of rebellion but because of a lawful economic struggle between industry and labor, it should have no such indulgence. His command power is not such an absolute as might be implied from that office in a militaristic system but is subject to limitations consistent with a constitutional Republic whose law and policy-making branch is a representative Congress. . . .

In the practical working of our Government we already have evolved a technique within the framework of the Constitution by which normal executive powers may be considerably expanded to meet an emergency. Congress may and has granted extraordinary authorities which lie dormant in normal times but may be called into play by the Executive in war or upon proclamation of a national emergency. . . .

In view of the ease, expedition and safety with which

Congress can grant and has granted large emergency powers, certainly ample to embrace this crisis, I am quite unimpressed with the argument that we should affirm possession of them without statute. Such power either has no beginning or it has no end. If it exists, it need submit to no legal restraint. I am not alarmed that it would plunge us straightway into dictatorship, but it is at least a step in that wrong direction.

But I have no illusion that any decision by this Court can keep power in the hands of Congress if it is not wise and timely in meeting its problems. A crisis that challenges the President equally, or perhaps primarily, challenges Congress. If not good law, there was worldly wisdom in the maxim attributed to Napoleon that "The tools belong to the man who can use them." We may say that power to legislate for emergencies belongs in the hands of Congress, but only Congress itself can prevent power from slipping through its fingers.

The essence of our free Government is "leave to live by no man's leave, underneath the law"—to be governed by those impersonal forces which we call law. Our Government is fashioned to fulfill this concept so far as humanly possible. The Executive, except for recommendation and veto, has no legislative power. The executive action we have here originates in the individual will of the President and represents an exercise of authority without law. No one, perhaps not even the President, knows the limits of the power he may seek to exert in this instance and the parties affected cannot learn the limit of their rights. We do not know today what powers over labor or property would be claimed to flow from Government possession if we should legalize it, what rights to compensation would be claimed or recognized, or on what contingency it would end. With all its defects, delays and inconveniences, men have discovered no technique for long preserving free government except that the Executive be under the law, and that the law be made by parliamentary deliberations.

Such institutions may be destined to pass away. But it is the duty of the Court to be last, not first, to give them up.

Notes and Queries

1. Who among the three justices, in your opinion, adopts the most intellectually compelling approach to constitutional interpretation in the *Steel Seizure* case? Who among them advances the most flexible conception of the relationship between the legislative and executive branches?

2. Do you find Justice Jackson's reasoning consistent with *Schechter*? With the idea of a limited government?

What role should the long-accepted historical practices mentioned by Justice Frankfurter play in constitutional interpretation?

3. The case of *Dames & Moore v. Regan* illustrates a more recent and perhaps different conception of the president's power to act during times of congressional silence. An executive agreement was negotiated in 1981 to obtain the release of American hostages held by Iran. The agreement released Iranian assets that had been frozen in the United States and shifted all claims against Iran pending in American courts to a new Iran–United States claims tribunal for binding arbitration. The president defended the agreement on the basis of his inherent power as chief executive under Article 2 of the Constitution. Justice Rehnquist, writing for the Court, upheld the government's claim, but rested his opinion on a less expansive conception of executive power. Rehnquist noted that the agreement with Iran could be justified either by specific congressional authorization or implied congressional approval. He emphasized that "the President does have some measure of power to enter into executive agreements without obtaining the advice and consent of the Senate."

Rehnquist cited the opinions of Justices Jackson and Frankfurter in *Youngstown Sheet & Tube*. He found Jackson's three-pronged approach "analytically useful," but observed that any particular instance does not fit exactly into one of the three categories but on a spectrum from express congressional authorization to express congressional proscription. This case is a narrow one, Rehnquist stated, because Congress had not "in some way resisted the exercise of Presidential authority." He relied instead on Frankfurter's analysis, stating that, "in light of the fact that Congress may be considered to have consented to the President's action in suspending claims, we can not say that the action exceeded the President's power."

4. In what situations should the president be able to act in opposition to the expressed provisions of congressional legislation? Can this be reconciled with the presidential oath to "faithfully execute the Office of the President of the United States"? Might acting contrary to the will of Congress be necessary for the president to "preserve, protect and defend the Constitution of the United States"?

5. Did the Court review President Truman's determination that the seizure of the steel mills was necessary for national security? Is this the type of political question that is beyond the capability of the judiciary to answer? Must it decide this question in order to decide the case? Does the view of the German Constitutional Court in Comparative Note 4.1 provide any guidance in the judicial resolution of this case?

6. Do you agree with Justice Frankfurter that a "systematic, unbroken, executive practice, long pursued to the knowledge of the Congress and never before questioned, engaged in by Presidents who have also sworn to uphold the Constitution . . . may be treated as a gloss on the 'executive Power' vested in the President"?

7. In his concurring opinion, Justice Jackson wrote that "contemporary foreign experience may be inconclusive as to the wisdom of lodging emergency powers somewhere in the modern government. But it suggests that emergency powers are consistent with free government only when their control is lodged elsewhere than in the Executive who exercises them." Is this expression a simple restatement about the wisdom of separation of powers? Is the separation of powers fundamentally inconsistent with the doctrine of "inherent powers," as Jackson suggested? For a discussion of the role and limits of emergency powers in a constitutional democracy, see chapter 7. See also John E. Finn, *Constitutions in Crisis: Political Violence and the Rule of Law* (New York: Oxford University Press, 1991) and Clinton Rossiter, *Constitutional Dictatorship* (Princeton, N.J.: Princeton University Press, 1948).

Powell v. McCormack
395 U.S. 486, 89 S.Ct. 1944, 23 L.Ed. 2d 491 (1969)

In November 1966, Adam Clayton Powell was duly elected from the 18th Congressional District of New York to serve in the House of Representatives for the 90th Congress. A special subcommittee of the 89th Congress, however, found that he had falsified his expense accounts and made illegal salary payments to his wife. After further investigation and debate, and in the face of Powell's refusal to testify about matters other than his eligibility to serve in Congress under the qualifications of Article I, sec. 2 of the Constitution, the House voted 307 to 116 to exclude him from the 90th Congress and declared his seat vacant. Powell and thirteen voters from the 18th District sued the speaker (John McCormack), clerk, doorkeeper, and sergeant at arms for keeping him from taking his seat. The voters argued that they were being deprived of their representation in Congress and requested a declaratory judgment that Powell's exclusion was unconstitutional. The federal district court granted the defendants' motion to dismiss the complaint for lack of jurisdiction over the subject matter, and the court of appeals affirmed. Opinion of the Court: *Warren*, Harlan, Brennan, White, Fortas, Marshall. Concurring opinion: *Douglas*. Dissenting opinion: *Stewart*.

Mr. Chief Justice WARREN delivered the opinion of the Court.

Speech or Debate Clause

Respondents assert that the Speech or Debate Clause of the Constitution, Art. I, s 6, is an absolute bar to petitioners' action. . . .

The Speech or Debate Clause, adopted by the Constitutional Convention without debate or opposition, finds its roots in the conflict between Parliament and the Crown culminating in the Glorious Revolution of 1688 and the English Bill of Rights of 1689. Drawing upon this history, we concluded in *United States v. Johnson* [1966], that the purpose of this clause was "to prevent intimidation [of legislators] by the executive and accountability before a possibly hostile judiciary." Although the clause sprang from a fear of seditious libel actions instituted by the Crown to punish unfavorable speeches made in Parliament, we have held that it would be a "narrow view" to confine the protection of the Speech or Debate Clause to words spoken in debate. Committee reports, resolutions, and the act of voting are equally covered, as are "things generally done in a session of the House by one of its members in relation to the business before it." Furthermore, the clause not only provides a defense on the merits but also protects a legislator from the burden of defending himself.

Our cases make it clear that the legislative immunity created by the Speech or Debate Clause performs an important function in representative government. It insures that legislators are free to represent the interests of their constituents without fear that they will be later called to task in the courts for that representation. . . .

Legislative immunity does not, of course, bar all judicial review of legislative acts. That issue was settled by implication as early as 1803 [in] *Marbury v. Madison,* . . . and expressly in *Kilbourn v. Thompson* [1881], the first of this Court's cases interpreting the reach of the Speech or Debate Clause. . . . While holding that the Speech or Debate Clause barred Kilbourn's action for false imprisonment brought against several members of the House, the Court nevertheless reached the merits of Kilbourn's attack and decided that, since the House had no power to punish for contempt, Kilbourn's imprisonment pursuant to the resolution was unconstitutional. It therefore allowed Kilbourn to bring his false imprisonment action against Thompson, the House's Sergeant at Arms, who had executed the warrant for Kilbourn's arrest.

The Court first articulated in *Kilbourn* and followed in

Comparative Note 4.2

[A Japanese Prefectural Assembly expelled one of its members for grossly insulting members of the opposition party. He was expelled despite his subsequent apology. This case arose out of an effort to quash a trial court's injunction against the legislator's expulsion. The Japanese Supreme Court sustained the validity of the injunction. What follows is a dissenting opinion.]

Inasmuch as the assembly of a local public entity is like each House of the Diet, a deliberative organ, its essential mission is to deliberate. Hence . . . it has an inherent power to establish such internal rules as may be necessary for discharging this duty. . . . It goes without saying that Art. 93 of the Constitution, which provides that assemblies shall be established as the deliberative organs of local public entities, presumes the existence of the inherent power to make internal rules for internal discipline. The inherent power with respect to internal discipline is based on the principle that one can manage one's own house by one's self and means that the deliberative organ maintains the independence of its deliberative activities against outside interference. (There is no essential difference between Diet and assembly in this respect.) Since the imposition of discipline for these ends is part of the actual operation of the assembly, a disciplinary resolution is final. . . .

SOURCE: Dissenting opinion of Justice Kuriyama, *Aomori Asembly Case*, Grand Bench, 16 January 1953 in Walter F. Murphy and Joseph Tanenhaus, *Comparative Constitutional Law*, (New York: St. Martin's Press, 1977), 130.

Dombrowski v. Eastland [1967], the doctrine that, although an action against a Congressman may be barred by the Speech or Debate Clause, legislative employees [such as the Sergeant at Arms] who participated in the unconstitutional activity are responsible for their acts. . . .

That House employees are acting pursuant to express order of the House does not bar judicial review of the constitutionality of the underlying legislative decision. *Kilbourn* decisively settles this question, since the Sergeant at Arms was held liable for false imprisonment even though he did nothing more than execute the House Resolution that Kilbourn be arrested and imprisoned. . . . [W]e thus dismissed the action against members of Congress but did not regard the Speech or Debate Clause as a bar to reviewing the merits of the challenged congressional action since congressional employees were also sued. Similarly, though this action may be dismissed against the Congressmen, petitioners are entitled to maintain their action against House employees and to judicial review of the propriety of the decision to exclude petitioner Powell. . . .

Exclusion or Expulsion

The resolution excluding petitioner Powell was adopted by a vote in excess of two-thirds of the 434 Members of Congress—307 to 116. Article I, s 5, grants the House authority to expel a member "with the Concurrence of two thirds." Respondents assert that the House may expel a member for any reason whatsoever and that, since a two-thirds vote was obtained, the procedure by which Powell was denied his seat in the 90th Congress should be regarded as an expulsion, not an exclusion.

Although respondents repeatedly urge this Court not to speculate as to the reasons for Powell's exclusion, their attempt to equate exclusion with expulsion would require a similar speculation that the House would have voted to expel Powell had it been faced with that question. . . . The Speaker ruled that the House was voting to exclude Powell, and we will not speculate what the result might have been if Powell had been seated and expulsion proceedings subsequently instituted.

Nor is the distinction between exclusion and expulsion merely one of form. The misconduct for which Powell was charged occurred prior to the convening of the 90th Congress. On several occasions the House has debated whether a member can be expelled for actions taken during a prior Congress and the House's own manual of procedure applicable in the 90th Congress states that "both Houses have distrusted their power to punish in such cases." The House rules manual reflects positions taken by prior Congresses. For example, the report of the Select Committee appointed to consider the expulsion of John W. Langley states unequivocally that the House will not expel a member for misconduct committed during an earlier Congress. . . .

Finally, the proceedings which culminated in Powell's exclusion cast considerable doubt upon respondents' assumption that the two-thirds vote necessary to expel would have been mustered. These proceedings have been succinctly described by Congressman Eckhardt:

The House voted 202 votes for the previous question leading toward the adoption of the (Select) Committee

Comparative Note 4.3

[In 1985, the fervently anti-Arab religious nationalist and member of the Israeli Knesset, Rabbi Meir Kahane, submitted a motion in the legislature for an expression of nonconfidence in the Government. Kahane was a member of a party faction that had one member, himself. On receiving the motion the Chairman of the Knesset ruled that "a one-member party faction is precluded from submitting a proposal of non-confidence in the Government." In overturning the decision of a body widely perceived as exercising sovereign authority, the Israeli Supreme Court relied heavily on the American Supreme Court's ruling in *Powell v. McCormack*. What follows is taken from the judgment of the Court.]

It is precisely the respect that we have for the nation's house of representatives that obliges us to make sure that it too acts within the framework of the law. An enlightened democratic regime is one of the separation of powers. That separation does not mean that each branch of government exists in and of itself, without any consideration of the other branches. Such conception would deeply violate the foundations of democracy itself, because it implies reciprocal checks and balances among the various branches. . . . Indeed, to hermetically seal the doors of the court petitions concerning intra-parliamentary proceedings would violate the rule of law, the legitimacy of the government, and the foundations of our democratic regime.

SOURCE: Opinion of Justice Aharon Barak, *"Kach" Party Faction* v. *Shlomo Hillel, Chairman of the Knesset*, in A. Barak, J. Goldstein, B Marshall, *Limits of Law* (unpublished casebook, 1988).

---

report. It voted 222 votes against the previous question, opening the floor for the Curtis Amendment which ultimately excluded Powell.

Upon adoption of the Curtis Amendment, the vote again fell short of two-thirds, being 248 yeas to 176 nays. Only on the final vote, adopting the Resolution as amended, was more than a two-thirds vote obtained, the vote being 307 yeas to 116 nays. On this last vote, as a practical matter, members who would not have denied Powell a seat if they were given the choice to punish him had to cast an aye vote or else record themselves as opposed to the only punishment that was likely to come before the House. Had the matter come up through the processes of expulsion, it appears that the two-thirds vote would have failed, and then members would have been able to apply a lesser penalty.

We need express no opinion as to the accuracy of Congressman Eckhardt's prediction that expulsion proceedings would have produced a different result. However, the House's own views of the extent of its power to expel combined with the Congressman's analysis counsel that exclusion and expulsion are not fungible proceedings. The Speaker ruled that House Resolution No. 278 contemplated an exclusion proceeding. We must reject respondents' suggestion that we overrule the Speaker and hold that, although the House manifested an intent to exclude Powell, its action should be tested by whatever standards may govern an expulsion.

Subject Matter Jurisdiction

Respondents first contend that this is not a case "arising under" the Constitution within the meaning of Art. III. They emphasize that Art. I, s 5, assigns to each House of Congress the power to judge the elections and qualifications of its own members and to punish its members for disorderly behavior. Respondents also note that under Art. I, s 3, the Senate has the "sole power" to try all impeachments. Respondents argue that these delegations (to "judge," to "punish," and to "try") to the Legislative Branch are explicit grants of "judicial power" to the Congress and constitute specific exceptions to the general mandate of Art. III that the "judicial power" shall be vested in the federal courts. Thus, respondents maintain, the "power conferred on the courts by article III does not authorize this Court to do anything more than declare its lack of jurisdiction to proceed."

We reject this contention. Article III, s 1, provides that the "judicial Power . . . shall be vested in one supreme Court, and in such inferior Courts as the Congress may . . . establish." Further, s 2 mandates that the "judicial Power shall extend to all Cases . . . arising under this Constitution. . . ." It has long been held that a suit "arises under" the Constitution if a petitioner's claim "will be sustained if the Constitution . . . [is] given one construction and will be defeated if [it is] given another." Thus, this case clearly is one "arising under" the Constitution as the Court has interpreted that phrase. Any bar to federal courts reviewing the judgments made by the House or Senate in excluding a member arises from the allocation of powers between the two branches of the Federal Government (a question of justiciability), and not from the petitioners' failure to state a claim based on federal law.

Justiciability

Having concluded that the Court of Appeals correctly ruled that the District Court had jurisdiction over the subject matter, we turn to the question whether the case is justiciable. Two determinations must be made in this regard. First, we must decide whether the claim presented and the relief sought are of the type which admit of judicial resolution. Second, we must determine whether the structure of the Federal Government renders the issue presented a "political question"—that is, a question which is not justiciable in federal court because of the separation of powers provided by the Constitution.

General Considerations

In deciding generally whether a claim is justiciable, a court must determine whether "the duty asserted can be judicially identified and its breach judicially determined, and whether protection for the right asserted can be judicially molded." Respondents do not seriously contend that the duty asserted and its alleged breach cannot be judicially determined. If petitioners are correct, the House had a duty to seat Powell once it determined he met the standing requirements set forth in the Constitution. It is undisputed that he met those requirements and that he was nevertheless excluded.

Respondents do maintain, however, that this case is not justiciable because, they assert, it is impossible for a federal court to "mold effective relief for resolving this case." Respondents emphasize that petitioners asked for coercive relief against the officers of the House, and, they contend, federal courts cannot issue mandamus or injunctions compelling officers or employees of the House to perform specific official acts. Respondents rely primarily on the Speech or Debate Clause to support this contention.

We need express no opinion about the appropriateness of coercive relief in this case, for petitioners sought a declaratory judgment, a form of relief the District Court could have issued. . . . We thus conclude that in terms of the general criteria of justiciability, this case is justiciable.

Political Question Doctrine
Textually Demonstrable Constitutional Commitment. . . . Respondents' first contention is that this case presents a political question because under Art. I, s 5, there has been a "textually demonstrable constitutional commitment" to the House of the "adjudicatory power" to

determine Powell's qualifications. Thus it is argued that the House, and the House alone, has power to determine who is qualified to be a member.

In order to determine whether there has been a textual commitment to a coordinate department of the Government, we must interpret the Constitution. In other words, we must first determine what power the Constitution confers upon the House through Art. I, s 5, before we can determine to what extent, if any, the exercise of that power is subject to judicial review. Respondents maintain that the House has broad power under s 5, and, they argue, the House may determine which are the qualifications necessary for membership. On the other hand, petitioners allege that the Constitution provides that an elected representative may be denied his seat only if the House finds he does not meet one of the standing qualifications expressly prescribed by the Constitution

. . . [W]hether there is a "textually demonstrable constitutional commitment of the issue to a coordinate political department" of government and what is the scope of such commitment are questions we must resolve for the first time in this case. . . .

In order to determine the scope of any "textual commitment" under Art. I, s 5, we necessarily must determine the meaning of the phrase to "be the Judge of the Qualifications of its own Members." . . . When the Constitution and the debates over its adoption are . . . viewed in historical perspective, argue respondents, it becomes clear that the "qualifications" expressly set forth in the Constitution were not meant to limit the long-recognized legislative power to exclude or expel at will, but merely to establish "standing incapacities," which could be altered only by a constitutional amendment. Our examination of the relevant historical materials leads us to the conclusion that petitioners are correct and that the Constitution leaves the House without authority to exclude any person, duly elected by his constituents, who meets all the requirements for membership expressly prescribed in the Constitution.

Had the intent of the Framers emerged from these materials with less clarity, we would nevertheless have been compelled to resolve any ambiguity in favor of a narrow construction of the scope of Congress' power to exclude members-elect. A fundamental principle of our representative democracy is, in Hamilton's words, "that the people should choose whom they please to govern them." As Madison pointed out at the Convention, this principle is undermined as much by limiting whom the people can select as by limiting the franchise itself. In apparent agreement with this basic philosophy, the Convention adopted his suggestion limiting the power to expel. To allow essentially that same power to be exercised under the guise of judging qualifications, would be to ignore Madison's warning . . . against "vesting an improper & dangerous power in the Legislature." Moreover, it would effectively nullify the Convention's decision to require a two-thirds vote for expulsion. Unquestionably, Congress has an interest in preserving its institutional integrity, but in most cases that interest can be sufficiently safeguarded by the exercise of its power to punish its members for disorderly behavior and, in extreme cases, to expel a member with the concurrence of two-thirds. In short, both the intention of the Framers, to the extent it can be determined, and an examination of the basic principles of our democratic system persuade us that the Constitution does not vest in the Congress a discretionary power to deny membership by a majority vote.

For these reasons, we have concluded that Art. I, s 5, is at most a "textually demonstrable commitment" to Congress to judge only the qualifications expressly set forth in the Constitution. Therefore, the "textual commitment" formulation of the political question doctrine does not bar federal courts from adjudicating petitioners' claims.

Other Considerations. Respondents' alternate contention is that the case presents a political question because judicial resolution of petitioners' claim would produce a "potentially embarrassing confrontation between coordinate branches" of the Federal Government. But, as our interpretation of Art. I, s 5, discloses, a determination of petitioner Powell's right to sit would require no more than an interpretation of the Constitution. Such a determination falls within the traditional role accorded courts to interpret the law, and does not involve a "lack of the respect due [a] coordinate [branch] of government," nor does it involve an "initial policy determination of a kind clearly for nonjudicial discretion." Our system of government requires that federal courts on occasion interpret the Constitution in a manner at variance with the construction given the document by another branch. The alleged conflict that such an adjudication may cause cannot justify the courts' avoiding their constitutional responsibility.

. . . [W]e conclude that petitioners' claim is not barred by the political question doctrine, and, having determined that the claim is otherwise generally justiciable, we hold that the case is justiciable.

Conclusion

. . . Therefore, we hold that, since Adam Clayton Powell, Jr., was duly elected by the voters of the 18th Congressional District of New York and was not ineligible to serve

under any provision of the Constitution, the House was without power to exclude him from its membership.

Petitioners seek additional forms of equitable relief, including mandamus for the release of petitioner Powell's back pay. The propriety of such remedies, however, is more appropriately considered in the first instance by the courts below. . . .

It is so ordered.

Mr. Justice DOUGLAS.

While I join the opinion of the Court, I add a few words. As the Court says, the important constitutional question is whether the Congress has the power to deviate from or alter the qualifications for membership as a Representative contained in Art. I, s 2, cl. 2, of the Constitution. Up to now the understanding has been quite clear to the effect that such authority does not exist. To be sure, Art. I, s 5, provides that: "Each House shall be the Judge of the Elections, Returns and Qualifications of its own Members. . . ." Contests may arise over whether an elected official meets the "qualifications" of the Constitution, in which event the House is the sole judge. But the House is not the sole judge when "qualifications" are added which are not specified in the Constitution.

At the root of all these cases, however, is the basic integrity of the electoral process. Today we proclaim the constitutional principle of "one man, one vote." When that principle is followed and the electors choose a person who is repulsive to the Establishment in Congress, by what constitutional authority can that group of electors be disenfranchised?

By Art. I, s 5, the House may "expel a Member" by a vote of two-thirds. And if this were an expulsion case I would think that no justiciable controversy would be presented, the vote of the House being two-thirds or more. But it is not an expulsion case. . . .

Notes and Queries

1. What constitutional provisions does the House claim to support its power to exclude *Powell*? How does the Court determine that none of these provisions justify the House's action? Is the Court's reading consistent with the words of the constitutional text? With the constitutional structure as a whole?

2. What is the difference between exclusion and expulsion in constitutional terms? Should that difference matter?

3. Is the opinion in this case consistent with the "hands-off" stance of the majority opinion concerning the Senate's power to try impeachments in *Nixon v. United States* (1993, reprinted in chapter 3)?

4. Consider the argument advanced by Justice Kuriyama in Comparative Note 4.2. Might one plausibly have made such an argument within the text of the U.S. Constitution?

5. Consider the excerpt from the opinion by Justice Barak in Comparative Note 4.3. At the time it was written Israel had not yet legitimated the practice of judicial review. Indeed, the prevailing view was that the legislature was supreme within the political system, that sovereignty

was located in the Knesset. Nevertheless, the Israeli Supreme Court overturned the legislature's decision in a matter involving that body's internal governance. Given the status of the Israeli Court in comparison with its American counterpart, how would you account for its intervention in this inherently political domain? Does it indicate an even stronger judicial commitment to the rule of law than what was in evidence in the United States in *Powell*?

Immigration and Naturalization Service v. Chadha

462 U.S. 919, 103 S.Ct. 2764, 77 L.Ed. 2d 317 (1983)

Jagdish Rai Chadha, an East Indian born in Kenya and holding a British passport, was lawfully admitted to the United States in 1966 on a nonimmigrant student visa. His visa expired on 30 June 1972. In a subsequent deportation hearing, the Immigration and Naturalization Service (INS) allowed Chadha to apply for a suspension of his deportation. The attorney general suspended Chadha's deportation under a provision that authorizes him to do so if the lawfully admitted alien has lived in the United States for seven years, proves that he is of good moral character, and is a person whose deportation would cause "extreme hardship." The act, however, requires that such a suspension be reported to the Congress, and if either the House or the Senate vetos the suspension during the session at which a case is reported, the attorney general is obligated to deport the alien. A House subcommittee introduced a resolution opposing Chadha's continued residence in the United States, a veto that the House passed without debate or a recorded vote. Chadha then moved to terminate the proceedings against him on the ground that the legislative veto was unconstitutional. The Board of Immigration Appeals dismissed his appeal. The U.S. Court of Appeals held that the House had no constitutional authority to order the alien's deportation and the legislative veto provision violated the doctrine of separation of powers. Opinion of the Court: *Burger*, Brennan, Marshall, Blackmun, Stevens, O'Connor. Concurring opinion: *Powell*. Dissenting opinions: *White, Rehnquist*.

Chief Justice BURGER delivered the opinion of the Court.

[Both Houses of Congress challenged the authority of the Supreme Court to resolve the issue raised in this case. They contended that the Court had no jurisdiction to hear Chadha's appeal, that he lacked standing to sue, that the

case was not a genuine controversy, and that it presented a nonjusticiable political question. The Supreme Court rejected all of these contentions.]

We turn now to the question whether action of one House of Congress under s 244(c)(2) violates strictures of the Constitution. We begin, of course, with the presumption that the challenged statute is valid. Its wisdom is not the concern of the courts; if a challenged action does not violate the Constitution, it must be sustained. . . .

By the same token, the fact that a given law or procedure is efficient, convenient, and useful in facilitating functions of government, standing alone, will not save it if it is contrary to the Constitution. Convenience and efficiency are not the primary objectives—or the hallmarks—of democratic government and our inquiry is sharpened rather than blunted by the fact that Congressional veto provisions are appearing with increasing frequency in statutes which delegate authority to executive and independent agencies. . . .

"Since 1932, when the first veto provision was enacted into law, 295 congressional veto-type procedures have been inserted in 196 different statues as follows: from 1932 to 1939, five statutes were affected; from 1940–49, nineteen statutes; between 1950–59, thirty-four statues; and from 1960–69, forty-nine. From the year 1970 through 1975 at least one hundred sixty-three such provisions were included in eighty-nine laws." Abourezk, *The Congressional Veto: A Contemporary Response to Executive Encroachment on Legislative Prerogatives*, 52 Ind L Rev 323, 324 (1977). . . .

Explicit and unambiguous provisions of the Constitution prescribe and define the respective functions of the Congress and of the Executive in the legislative process. Since the precise terms of those familiar provisions are critical to the resolution of this case, we set them out verbatim. Art. I provides:

All legislative Powers herein granted shall be vested in a Congress of the United States, which shall consist of a Senate *and* a House of Representatives. Art. I, s 1. [Emphasis added.]

Comparative Note 4.4

[In this case, South Africa's new Constitutional Court ruled on the constitutional validity of a parliamentary act delegating subordinate regulatory authority to other bodies. The extracts are from the main opinion of Justice P. Chaskalson.]

. . . There is nothing in the Constitution which prohibits Parliament from delegating subordinate regulatory authority to other bodies. . . . In the United States, delegation of legislative power to the executive is dealt [with] under the doctrine of separation of powers. Congress as the body in which all federal lawmaking power has been vested must make legislative decisions in accordance with the "single, finely wrought and exhaustively considered, procedure" laid down by the United States Constitution, which requires laws to be passed bicamerally and then presented to the President for consideration of a possible veto. *INS v. Chadha.* . . . In Ireland . . . the courts have adopted a similar approach. . . . The influence of English law is referred to by Dixon J in his judgment in the Australian High Court. . . .

Seevai in his work on the Indian Constitution deals at length with the Indian jurisprudence on the power of Parliament to delegate legislative power to the executive. . . . In Canada . . . it seems to be accepted that Parliament has wide powers of delegation. . . .

This brief and somewhat limited survey of the law as it has developed in other countries is sufficient to show that where Parliament is established under a written constitution, the nature and extent of its power to delegate legislative powers to the executive depends ultimately on the language of the Constitution, construed in the light of the country's own history. . . . [But our] new Constitution establishes a fundamentally different order to that which previously existed. Parliament can no longer claim supreme power subject to limitations imposed by the Constitution; it is subject in all respects to the provisions of the Constitution and has only the powers vested in it by the Constitution expressly or by necessary implication.

SOURCE: *Executive Council of the Western Cape Legislature v. President of the Republic of South Africa and Others*, Constitutional Court Judgment of 22 September 1995, Butterworths Law Report (October 1995), 1312–17.

Every Bill which shall have passed the House of Representatives *and* the Senate, *shall*, before it becomes a Law, be presented to the President of the United States . . . Art. I, s 7, cl. 2. (Emphasis added.)

Every Order, Resolution, or Vote to which the Concurrence of the Senate and House of Representatives may be necessary (except on a question of Adjournment) *shall be* presented to the President of the United States; and before the Same shall take Effect, *shall* be approved by him, or being disapproved by him, *shall* be repassed by two thirds of the Senate and House of Representatives, according to the Rules and Limitations prescribed in the Case of a Bill. Art. I, s 7, cl. 3. (Emphasis added.)

These provisions of Art. I are integral parts of the constitutional design for the separation of powers. We have recently noted that "[t]he principle of separation of powers was not simply an abstract generalization in the minds of the Framers: it was woven into the document that they drafted in Philadelphia in the summer of 1787." *Buckley v. Valeo* [1976]. Just as we relied on the textual provision of Art. II, s 2, cl. 2, to vindicate the principle of separation of

powers, in *Buckley*, we see the purposes underlying the Presentment Clauses, Art. I, s 7, cls. 2, 3 and the bicameral requirement of Art. I, s 1, and s 7, cl. 2, guide our resolution of the important question presented in these cases. The very structure of the articles delegating and separating powers under Arts. I, II, and III exemplifies the concept of separation of powers, and we now turn to Art. I.

The Presentment Clauses

The records of the Constitutional Convention reveal that the requirement that all legislation be presented to the President before becoming law was uniformly accepted by the Framers. Presentment to the President and the Presidential veto were considered so imperative that the draftsmen took special pains to assure that these requirements could not be circumvented. . . .

The decision to provide the President with a limited and qualified power to nullify proposed legislation by veto was based on the profound conviction of the Framers that the powers conferred on Congress were the powers to be most carefully circumscribed. It is beyond doubt that law-

---

Comparative Note 4.5

Article 92

1. Regulations shall be issued on the basis of specific authorization contained in, and for the purpose of implementation of, statutes by the organs specified in the Constitution. The authorization shall specify the organ appropriate to issue a regulation and the scope of matters to be regulated as well as guidelines concerning the provisions of such act.

2. An organ authorized to issue a regulation shall not delegate its competence, referred to in paragraph 1 above, to another organ.

SOURCE: Constitution of the Republic of Poland (1997)

Article 80

1. The Federal Government, a Federal Minister or the Land governments may be empowered by the law to issue statutory orders. The content, purpose and scope of that power shall be specified in the law. Statutory orders shall contain a reference to their legal basis. Where the law provides that the power to issue statutory orders may be further delegated another statutory order shall be required to that effect.

SOURCE: Basic Law of the Federal Republic of Germany (1949)

---

making was a power to be shared by both Houses and the President. . . .

[To support this view, the Court draws heavily on Hamilton's discussion of the President's role in *The Federalist* No. 73. The Court also cites *The Federalist* No. 51 and Joseph Story's *Commentaries on the Constitution of the United States* (1858).]

Bicameralism

The bicameral requirement of Art. I, s 1, 7 was of scarcely less concern to the Framers than was the Presidential veto and indeed the two concepts are interdependent. By providing that no law could take effect without the concurrence of the prescribed majority of the Members of both Houses, the Framers reemphasized their belief, already remarked upon in connection with the Presentment Clauses, that legislation should not be enacted unless it has been carefully and fully considered by the Nation's elected officials. . . .

. . . The President's participation in the legislative process was to protect the Executive Branch from Congress and to protect the whole people from improvident laws. The division of the Congress into two distinctive bodies assures that the legislative power would be exercised only after opportunity for full study and debate in separate settings. The President's unilateral veto power, in turn, was limited by the power of two thirds of both Houses of Congress to overrule a veto thereby precluding final arbitrary action of one person. . . .

The Constitution sought to divide the delegated powers of the new Federal Government into three defined categories, Legislative, Executive and Judicial, to assure, as

nearly as possible, that each Branch of government would confine itself to its assigned responsibility. The hydraulic pressure inherent within each of the separate Branches to exceed the outer limits of its power, even to accomplish desirable objectives, must be resisted.

Although not "hermetically" sealed from one another, the powers delegated to the three Branches are functionally identifiable. When any Branch acts, it is presumptively exercising the power the Constitution has delegated to it. When the Executive acts, it presumptively acts in an executive or administrative capacity as defined in Art. II. And when, as here, one House of Congress purports to act, it is presumptively acting within its assigned sphere.

Beginning with this presumption, we must nevertheless establish that the challeged action under s 244(c)(2) is of the kind to which the requirements of Art. I, s 7, apply. Not every action taken by either House is subject to the bicameralism and presentment requirements of Art. I. Whether actions taken by either House are, in law and fact, an exercise of legislative power depends not on their form but upon "whether they contain matter which is properly to be regarded as legislative in its character and effect."

Examination of the action taken here by one House pursuant to s 244(c)(2) reveals that it was essentially legislative in purpose and effect. In purporting to exercise power defined in Art. I, s 8, cl. 4 to "establish an uniform Rule of Naturalization," the House took action that had the purpose and effect of altering the legal rights, duties and relations of persons, including the Attorney General, Executive Branch officials and Chadha, all outside the legislative branch. Section 244(c)(2) purports to authorize one House of Congress to require the Attorney General to deport an individual alien whose deportation otherwise would be canceled under s 244. The one-House veto operated in this case to overrule the Attorney General and mandate Chadha's deportation; absent the House action, Chadha would remain in the United States. Congress has *acted* and its action has altered Chadha's status.

Since it is clear that the action by the House under s 244(c)(2) was not within any of the express constitutional exceptions authorizing one House to act alone, and equally clear that it was an exercise of legislative power, that action was subject to the standards prescribed in Article I. The bicameral requirement, the Presentment Clauses, the President's veto, and Congress' power to override a veto were intended to erect enduring checks on each Branch and to protect the people from the improvident exercise of power by mandating certain prescribed steps. To preserve those checks, and maintain the separation of powers, the carefully defined limits on the power of each Branch must not be eroded. To accomplish what has been attempted by one House of Congress in this case requires action in conformity with the express prescription for legislative action: passage by a majority of both Houses and presentment to the President.

The choices we discern as having been made in the Constitutional Convention impose burdens on governmental processes that often seem clumsy, inefficient, even unworkable, but those hard choices were consciously made by men who had lived under a form of government that permitted arbitrary governmental acts to go unchecked. There is no support in the Constitution or decisions of this Court for the proposition that the cumbersomeness and delays often encountered in complying with explicit Constitutional standards may be avoided, either by the Congress or by the President. With all the obvious flaws of delay, untidiness, and potential for abuse, we have not yet found a better way to preserve freedom than by making the exercise of power subject to the crafted restraints spelled out in the Constitution. . . .

Affirmed.

Justice POWELL, concurring in the judgment.

The court's decision, based on the Presentment Clauses, Art. I, s 7, cls. 2 and 3, apparently will invalidate every use of the legislative veto. The breadth of this holding gives one pause. Congress has included the veto in literally hundreds of statues, dating back to the 1930s. Congress clearly views this procedure as essential to controlling the delegation of power to administrative agencies. One reasonably may disagree with Congress' assessment of the veto's utility, but the respect due its judgment as a coordinate branch of Government cautions that our holding should be no more extensive than necessary to decide this case. In my view, the case may be decided on narrower ground. When Congress finds that a particular person does not satisfy the statutory criteria for permanent residence in this country, it has assumed a judicial function in violation of the principle of separation of powers. Accordingly, I concur only in the judgment.

Functionally, the doctrine [of separation of powers] may be violated in two ways. One branch may interfere impermissibly with the other's performance of its constitutionally assigned function. Alternatively, the doctrine may be violated when one branch assumes a function that more properly is entrusted to another. These cases present the latter situation.

Justice WHITE, dissenting.

Today the Court not only invalidates s 244(c)(2) of the Immigration and Nationality Act, but also sounds the death knell for nearly 200 other statutory provisions in which Congress has reserved a "legislative veto." For this reason, the Court's decision is of surpassing importance. And it is for this reason that the Court would have been well-advised to decide the case, if possible, on the narrower grounds of separation of powers, leaving for full consideration the constitutionality of other congressional review statutes operating on such varied matters as war powers and agency rulemaking, some of which concern the independent regulatory agencies.

The prominence of the legislative veto mechanism in our contemporary political system and its importance to Congress can hardly be overstated. It has become a central means by which Congress secures the accountability of executive and independent agencies. Without the legislative veto, Congress is faced with a Hobson's choice: either to refrain from delegating the necessary authority, leaving itself with a hopeless task of writing laws with the requisite specificity to cover endless special circumstances across the entire policy landscape, or in the alternative, to abdicate its law-making function to the Executive Branch and independent agencies. To choose the former leaves major national problems unresolved; to opt for the latter risks unaccountable policymaking by those not elected to fill that role. Accordingly, over the past five decades, the legislative veto has been placed in nearly 200 statutes. The device is known in every field of governmental concern: reorganization, budgets, foreign affairs, war powers, and regulation of trade, safety, energy, the environment and the economy.

. . . The Court's holding today that all legislative-type action must be enacted through the lawmaking process ignores that legislative authority is routinely delegated to the Executive branch, to the independent regulatory agencies, and to private individuals and groups. . . .

This Court's decisions sanctioning such delegations make clear that Article I does not require all action with the effect of legislation to be passed as a law.

The wisdom and the constitutionality of these broad delegations are matters that still have not been put to rest. But for present purposes, these cases establish that by virtue of congressional delegation, legislative power can be exercised by independent agencies and Executive departments without the passage of new legislation. . . .

If Congress may delegate lawmaking power to independent and executive agencies, it is most difficult to understand Article I as forbidding Congress from also reserving a check on legislative power itself. Absent the veto, the agencies receiving delegations of legislative or quasi-legislative power may issue regulations having the force of law without bicameral approval and without the President's signature. It is thus not apparent why the reservation of a veto over the exercise of that legislative power must be subject to a more exacting test. In both cases, it is enough that the initial statutory authorizations comply with the Article I requirements.

The Court also takes no account of perhaps the most relevant consideration: However resolutions of disapproval under section 244(c)(2) are formally characterized, in reality, a departure from the status quo occurs only upon the concurrence of opinion among the House, Senate, and President. Reservations of legislative authority to be exercised by Congress should be upheld if the exercise of such reserved authority is consistent with the distribution of and limits upon legislative power that Article I provides.

Section 244(a)(1) authorizes the Attorney General, in his discretion, to suspend the deportation of certain aliens who are otherwise deportable and, upon Congress' approval, to adjust their status to that of aliens lawfully admitted for permanent residence. In order to be eligible for this relief, an alien must have been physically present in the United States for a continuous period of not less than seven years, must prove he is of good moral character, and must prove that he or his immediate family would suffer "extreme hardship" if he is deported. Judicial review of a denial of relief may be sought. Thus, the suspension proceeding "has two phases: a determination whether the statutory conditions have been met, which generally involves a question of law, and a determination whether relief shall be granted, which [ultimately] is confided to the sound discretion of the Attorney General [and his delegates]."

. . . Under s 244(c)(1) the Attorney General must report all such suspensions, with a detailed statement of facts and reasons, to the Congress. Either House may then act, in that session or the next, to block the suspension of deportation by passing a resolution of disapproval. s 244(c)(2). Upon Congressional approval of the suspension—by its silence—the alien's permanent status is adjusted to that of a lawful resident alien.

The history of the Immigration Act makes clear that s 244(c)(2) did not alter the division of actual authority between Congress and the Executive. At all times, whether through private bills, or through affirmative concurrent resolutions, or through the present one-House veto, a permanent change in a deportable alien's status could be accomplished only with the agreement of the Attorney General, the House, and the Senate.

Notes and Queries

1. Identify the interpretive approach used by Chief Justice Burger in this case. How does his approach differ from the reasoning of Justice White?

2. Why, according to Chief Justice Burger, is the legislative veto a legislative act and not oversight?

3. There is an old maxim that the Supreme Court should not lay down a rule of law broader than required by the facts of a case, in part out of respect for the principle of separation of powers. Does the *Chadha* majority ignore this maxim?

4. If Congress can constitutionally delegate powers under the Immigration and Naturalization Act, why shouldn't it be able to have the ultimate control of a veto upon the use of its delegated authority?

5. Justice Powell concurred with the result, but wrote separately to argue that the statue violated the separation of powers doctrine because its action was "clearly adjudicatory." The majority, however, had concluded that the congressional action was "legislative" in nature. Which of these two characterizations is correct? Does the dispute suggest that it is not always possible to clearly distinguish between the executive, legislative, and judicial powers?

6. Do you find Justice White's dissent convincing? Is Congress really faced with a "Hobson's choice" as a result of the Court's decision? Why should we not demand that Congress take more responsibility to draft statutes with clear and well-defined standards? Would it be more proper for Congress to check with the executive before rather than after executive action?

7. Powell concluded that the doctrine of separation of powers may "be violated in two ways." In the first, one branch may interfere with another's exercise of its consti-

tutionally assigned duties. In the second, a branch may assume a function the Constitution assigns to another branch. Is this a useful way to approach separation of powers cases? Which of these alternatives is implicated in *Chadha*?

8. Recall our earlier discussion of the nondelegation doctrine. In light of that doctrine, does *Chadha* stand for the proposition that Congress may delegate its power to any branch but itself?

9. Comparative Note 4.3 is an example of the guidance that constitutional courts often seek from foreign jurisdictions. Should Chief Justice Burger have consulted the experience of other constitutional democracies in deciding *Chadha*? Would the Court be well-advised to do this as a regular practice?

Morrison v. Olson
487 U.S. 654, 108 S.Ct. 2597, 101 L.Ed. 2d 569 (1988)

The Ethics in Government Act of 1978 authorized a Special Division of the United States Court of Appeals for the District of Columbia to appoint an independent counsel to investigate and, if necessary, prosecute high-ranking governmental officials for violating federal criminal law. In this case, Theodore Olson, assistant attorney general, was accused of giving false and misleading testimony to a House subcommittee investigating the activities of the Environmental Protection Agency. In accordance with the act's provisions, the chairman of the House Judiciary Committee sent a report to the attorney general requesting that an independent counsel be appointed to investigate the charges against Olson. After an inquiry by the Justice Department, the attorney general applied to the Special Division for the appointment of an independent counsel.

When Alexia Morrison, the appointee, caused a federal grand jury to issue a subpoena for the production of certain documents, Olson moved to quash the subpoena on the grounds that the act's independent counsel provisions violated the Constitution, thus invalidating the pending proceeding. The district court upheld the act, but the court of appeals reversed, holding that the act violated the Constitution's appointment clause (Art. 2, s 2, cl. 2). Opinion of the Court: *Rehnquist*, Brennan, White, Marshall, Blackmun, Stevens, O'Connor. Dissenting opinion: *Scalia*. Not participating: Kennedy.

Chief Justice REHNQUIST delivered the opinion of the Court.

This case presents us with a challenge to the independent counsel provisions of the Ethics in Government Act of 1978. . . . We hold today that these provisions of the Act do not violate the Appointments Clause of the Constitution, Art. II, s 2, cl. 2, or the limitations of Article III, nor do they impermissibly interfere with the President's authority under Article II in violation of the constitutional principle of separation of powers.

The Appointments Clause of Article II reads as follows:

The President shall nominate, and by and with the Advice and Consent of the Senate, shall appoint Ambassadors, other public Ministers and Consuls, Judges of the Supreme Court, and all other Officers of the United States, whose Appointments are not herein otherwise provided for, and which shall be established by Law: but the Congress may by Law vest the Appointment of such inferior Officers, as they think proper, in the President alone, in the Courts of Law, or in the Heads of Departments. (U.S. Const., Art. II, s 2, cl. 2.)

The line between "inferior" and "principal" officers is one that is far from clear, and the Framers provided little guidance into where it should be drawn. . . . We need not attempt here to decide exactly where the line falls between the two types of officers, because in our view appellant clearly falls on the "inferior officer" side of that line. Several factors lead to this conclusion.

First, appellant is subject to removal by a higher Executive Branch official. Although appellant may not be "subordinate" to the Attorney General (and the President) insofar as she possesses a degree of independent discretion to exercise the powers delegated to her under the Act, the fact that she can be removed by the Attorney General indicates that she is to some degree "inferior" in rank and authority. Second, appellant is empowered by the Act to perform only certain, limited duties. An independent counsel's role is restricted primarily to investigation and, if appropriate, prosecution for certain federal crimes.

Third, appellant's office is limited in jurisdiction. Not only is the Act itself restricted in applicability to certain federal officials suspected of certain serious federal crimes, but an independent counsel can only act within the scope of the jurisdiction that has been granted by the Special Division pursuant to a request by the Attorney General. Finally, appellant's office is limited in tenure. There is concededly no time limit on the appointment of a particular counsel. Nonetheless, the office of independent

Comparative Note 4.6

[In 1969 Ireland's Oireachtas (parliament) authorized its Committee of Public Accounts to investigate the diversion of public money to the IRA in Northern Ireland. If the committee found that a witness had committed a crime, it was authorized to certify that fact to Ireland's High Court with the provision that "the High Court may, after such inquiry as it thinks proper to make, punish or take steps for the punishment of that person in like manner as if he had been guilty of contempt of the High Court."]

Article 34 of the Constitution provides that justice shall be administered in courts established by law by judges appointed in the manner prescribed by the Constitution. The Committee of Public Accounts is not a court and its members are not judges. The Constitution of Ireland is founded on the doctrine of the tripartite division of the powers of government . . . and for a statute to confer on a committee of the Legislature a power to try a criminal offense would be repugnant to the Constitution. Moreover, under the Constitution the Courts cannot be used as appendages or auxiliaries to enforce the purported convictions of other tribunals. The Constitution vests the judicial power of government solely in the Courts the power to try persons on criminal charges. Trial, conviction and sentence are indivisible parts of the exercise of this power.

SOURCE: *In Re Haughey* [1971] I.R. 231, at 150.

---

counsel is "temporary" in the sense that an independent counsel is appointed essentially to accomplish a single task, and when that task is over the office is terminated, either by the counsel herself or by action of the Special Division. Unlike other prosecutors, appellant has no ongoing responsibilities that extend beyond the accomplishment of the mission that she was appointed for and authorized by the Special Division to undertake. In our view, these factors relating to the ideas of tenure, duration . . . and duties of the independent counsel, are sufficient to establish that appellant is an "inferior" officer in the constitutional sense.

This does not, however, end our inquiry under the Appointments Clause. Appellees argue that even if appellant is an "inferior" officer, the Clause does not empower Congress to place the power to appoint such an officer outside the Executive Branch. They contend that the Clause does not contemplate congressional authorization of "interbranch appointments," in which an officer of one branch is appointed by officers of another branch. The relevant language of the Appointments Clause is worth repeating. It reads: ". . . but the Congress may by Law vest the Appointment of such inferior Officers, as they think proper, in the President alone, in the courts of Law, or in the Heads of Departments." On its face, the language of this "excepting clause" admits of no limitation on interbranch appointments. Indeed, the inclusion of "as they think proper" seems clearly to give Congress significant discretion to determine whether it is "proper" to vest the appointment of, for example, executive officials in the "courts of Law." . . .

We do not mean to say that Congress' power to provide for interbranch appointments of "inferior officers" is unlimited. In addition to separation-of-powers concerns, which would arise if such provisions for appointment had the potential to impair the constitutional functions assigned to one of the branches, . . . Congress' decision to vest the appointment power in the courts would be improper if there was some "incongruity" between the functions normally performed by the courts and the performance of their duty to appoint. . . . Congress, of course, was concerned when it created the office of independent counsel with the conflicts of interest that could arise in situations when the Executive Branch is called upon to investigate its own high-ranking officers. If it were to remove the appointing authority from the Executive Branch, the most logical place to put it was in the Judicial Branch. In light of the Act's provision making the judges of the Special Division ineligible to participate in any matters relating to an independent counsel they have appointed, we do not think that appointment of the independent counsel by the court runs afoul of the constitutional limitation on "incongruous" interbranch appointments.

Appellees next contend that the powers vested in the Special Division by the Act conflict with Article III of the Constitution. We have long recognized that by the express provision of Article III, the judicial power of the United States is limited to "Cases" and "Controversies." As a general rule, we have broadly stated that "executive or administrative duties of a nonjudicial nature may not be imposed on judges holding office under Art. III of the Constitution." The purpose of this limitation is to help ensure the independence of the Judicial Branch and to prevent the Judiciary from encroaching into areas reserved for the other branches. . . .

. . . This said, we do not think that Congress may give the Division unlimited discretion to determine the independent counsel's jurisdiction. In order for the Division's definition of the counsel's jurisdiction to be truly "incidental" to its power to appoint, the jurisdiction that the court decides upon must be demonstrably related to the factual circumstances that gave rise to the Attorney General's investigation and request for the appointment of the independent counsel in the particular case.

We now turn to consider whether the Act is invalid under the constitutional principle of separation of powers. Two related issues must be addressed: The first is whether the provision of the Act restricting the Attorney General's power to remove the independent counsel to only those instances in which he can show "good cause," taken by itself, impermissibly interferes with the President's exercise of his constitutionally appointed functions. The second is whether, taken as a whole, the Act violates the separation of powers by reducing the President's ability to control the prosecutorial powers wielded by the independent counsel.

Two terms ago we had occasion to consider whether it was consistent with the separation of powers for Congress to pass a statute that authorized a Government official who is removable only by Congress to participate in what we found to be "executive powers." We held in *Bowsher* that "Congress cannot reserve for itself the power of removal of an officer charged with the execution of the laws except by impeachment." . . .

. . . [T]his case does not involve an attempt by Congress itself to gain a role in the removal of executive officials other than its established powers of impeachment and conviction. The Act instead puts the removal power squarely in the hands of the Executive Branch; an independent counsel may be removed from office, "only by the personal action of the Attorney General, and only for good cause." There is no requirement of congressional approval of the Attorney General's removal decision, though the decision is subject to judicial review. . . .

. . . We do not mean to suggest that an analysis of the functions served by the officials at issue is irrelevant. But the real question is whether the removal restrictions are of such a nature that they impede the President's ability to perform his constitutional duty, and the functions of the officials in question must be analyzed in that light.

Nor do we think that the "good cause" removal provision at issue here impermissibly burdens the President's power to control or supervise the independent counsel,

as an executive official, in the execution of his or her duties. . . . This is not a case in which the power to remove an executive official has been completely stripped from the President, thus providing no means for the President to ensure the "faithful execution" of the laws. Rather, because the independent counsel may be terminated for "good cause," the Executive, through the Attorney General, retains ample authority to assure that the counsel is competently performing his or her statutory responsibilities in a manner that comports with the provisions of the Act. . . .

The final question to be addressed is whether the Act, taken as a whole, violates the principle of separation of powers by unduly interfering with the role of the Executive Branch. . . .

We observe first that this case does not involve an attempt by Congress to increase its own powers at the expense of the Executive Branch. Unlike some of our previous cases, most recently *Bowsher v. Synar* [1986], this case simply does not pose a "dange[r] of congressional usurpation of Executive Branch functions." Indeed, with the exception of the power of impeachment—which applies to all officers of the United States—Congress retained for itself no powers of control or supervision over an independent counsel. . . .

Similarly, we do not think that the Act works any judicial usurpation of properly executive functions. . . .

Finally, we do not think that the Act "impermissibly undermine[s]" the powers of the Executive Branch or "disrupts the proper balance between the coordinate branches [by] prevent[ing] the Executive Branch from accomplishing its constitutionally assigned functions." It is undeniable that the Act reduces the amount of control or supervision that the Attorney General and, through him, the President exercises over the investigation and prosecution of a certain class of alleged criminal activity. The Attorney General is not allowed to appoint the individual of his choice; he does not determine the counsel's jurisdiction; and his power to remove a counsel is limited. Nonetheless, the Act does give the Attorney General several means of supervising or controlling the prosecutorial powers that may be wielded by an independent counsel. Most importantly, the Attorney General retains the power to remove the counsel for "good cause," a power that we have already concluded provides the Executive with substantial ability to ensure that the laws are "faithfully executed" by an independent counsel. No independent counsel may be appointed without a specific request by the Attorney General, and the Attorney General's decision not to request appointment if he finds "no reasonable grounds to believe that further investigation is warranted" is committed to his unreviewable discretion. The Act thus gives the Executive a degree of control over the power to initiate an investigation by the independent counsel. In addition, the jurisdiction of the independent counsel is defined with reference to the facts submitted by the Attorney General, and once a counsel is appointed, the Act requires that the counsel abide by Justice Department policy unless it is not "possible" to do so. Notwithstanding the fact that the counsel is to some degree "independent" and free from executive supervision to a greater extent than other federal prosecutors, in our view these features of the Act give the Executive Branch sufficient control over the independent counsel to ensure that the President is able to perform his constitutionally assigned duties.

In sum, we conclude today that it does not violate the Appointments Clause for Congress to vest the appointment of independent counsel in the Special Division; that the powers exercised by the Special Division under the Act do not violate Article III; and that the Act does not violate the separation-of-powers principle by impermissibly interfering with the functions of the Executive Branch. The decision of the Court of Appeals is therefore reversed.

Justice SCALIA, dissenting.

The principle of separation of powers is expressed in our Constitution in the first section of each of the first three Articles. . . .

But just as the mere words of a Bill of Rights are not self-effectuating, the Framers recognized "[t]he insufficiency of a mere parchment delineation of the boundaries" to achieve the separation of powers. . . . The major "fortification" provided, of course, was the veto power. But in addition to providing fortification, the Founders conspicuously and very consciously declined to sap the Executive's strength in the same way they had weakened the Legislature: by dividing the executive power. . . .

That is what this suit is about. Power. The allocation of power among Congress, the President, and the courts in such fashion as to preserve the equilibrium the Constitution sought to establish—so that "a gradual concentration of the several powers in the same department," can effectively be resisted. Frequently an issue of this sort will come before the Court clad, so to speak, in sheep's clothing: the potential of the asserted principle to effect important change in the equilibrium of power is not immediately evident, and must be discerned by a careful and perceptive analysis. But this wolf comes as a wolf.

If to describe this case is not to decide it, the concept of a government of separate and coordinate powers no longer has meaning. The Court devotes most of its attention to such relatively technical details as the Appoint-

ments Clause and the removal power, addressing briefly and only at the end of its opinion the separation of powers. As my prologue suggests, I think that has it backwards. . . .

The Court concedes that "[t]here is no real dispute that the functions performed by the independent counsel are 'executive,' " though it qualifies that concession by adding "in the sense that they are law enforcement functions that typically have been undertaken by officials within the Executive Branch." The qualifier adds nothing but atmosphere. In what *other* sense can one identify "the executive Power" that is supposed to be vested in the President (unless it includes everything the Executive Branch is given to do) *except* by reference to what has always and everywhere—if conducted by government at all—been conducted never by the legislature, never by the courts, and always by the executive. There is no possible doubt that the independent counsel's functions fit this description. She is vested with the "full power and independent authority to exercise all investigative and prosecutorial functions and powers of the Department of Justice [and] the Attorney General." Governmental investigation and prosecution of crimes is a quintessentially executive function.

. . . [W]hether the statute before us deprives the President of exclusive control over that quintessentially executive activity: The Court does not, and could not possibly, assert that it does not. That is indeed the whole object of the statute. Instead, the Court points out that the President, through his Attorney General, has at least some control. That concession is alone enough to invalidate the statute, but I cannot refrain from pointing out that the Court greatly exaggerates the extent of that "some" Presidential control. "Most importan[t]" among these controls, the Court asserts, is the Attorney General's "power to remove the counsel for 'good cause.' " This is somewhat like referring to shackles as an effective means of locomotion. . . . [L]imiting removal power to "good cause" is an impediment to, not an effective grant of, Presidential control. We said that limitation was necessary with respect to members of the Federal Trade Commission, which we found to be "an agency of the legislative and judicial departments," and "wholly disconnected from the executive department," because "it is quite evident that one who holds his office only during the pleasure of another, cannot be depended upon to maintain an attitude of independence against the latter's will." What we in *Humphrey's Executor* found to be a means of eliminating Presidential control, the Court today considers the "most importan[t]" means of assuring Presidential control. Congress, of course, operated under no such illusion when it enacted this statute, describing the "good cause" limitation as "protecting the independent counsel's ability to act independently of the President's direct control" since it permits removal only for "misconduct."

. . . Finally, the Court points out that the Act directs the independent counsel to abide by general Justice Department policy, except when not "possible." The exception alone shows this to be an empty promise. Even without that, however, one would be hard put to come up with many investigative or prosecutorial "policies" (other than those imposed by the Constitution or by Congress through law) that are absolute. Almost all investigative and prosecutorial decisions including the ultimate decision whether, after a technical violation of the law has been found, prosecution is warranted—involve the balancing of innumerable legal and practical considerations. . . . In sum, the balancing of various legal, practical, and political considerations, none of which is absolute, is the very essence of prosecutorial discretion. To take this away is to remove the core of the prosecutorial function, and not merely "some" Presidential control.

. . . It is not for us to determine, and we have never presumed to determine, how much of the purely executive powers of government must be within the full control of the President. The Constitution prescribes that they *all* are. . . .

. . . While the separation of powers may prevent us from righting every wrong, it does so in order to ensure that we do not lose liberty. The checks against any branch's abuse of its exclusive powers are twofold: First, retaliation by one of the other branch's use of *its* exclusive powers: Congress, for example, can impeach the executive who willfully fails to enforce the laws; the executive can decline to prosecute under unconstitutional statutes; and the courts can dismiss malicious prosecutions. Second, and ultimately, there is the political check that the people will replace those in the political branches . . . who are guilty of abuse. Political pressures produced special prosecutors—for Teapot Dome and for Watergate, for example—long before this statute created the independent counsel.

As I indicated earlier, the basic separation-of-powers principles I have discussed are what give life and content to our jurisprudence concerning the President's power to appoint and remove officers. The same result of unconstitutionality is therefore plainly indicated by our case law in these areas.

. . . I think it preferable to look to the text of the Constitution and the division of power that it establishes. These demonstrate, I think, that the independent counsel is not an inferior officer because she is not subordinate to any officer in the Executive Branch [indeed, not even to the President]. . . .

To be sure, it is not a sufficient condition for "inferior" officer status that one be subordinate to a principal officer. . . . But it is surely a necessary condition for inferior officer status that the officer be subordinate to another officer.

Since our 1935 decision in *Humphrey's Executor v. United States*—which was considered by many at the time the product of an activist, anti–New Deal Court bent on reducing the power of President Franklin Roosevelt—it has been established that the line of permissible restriction upon removal of principal officers lies at the point at which the powers exercised by those officers are no longer purely executive. . . .

. . . By its shortsighted action today, I fear the Court has permanently encumbered the Republic with an institution that will do it great harm.

Worse than what it has done, however, is the manner in which it has done it. A government of laws means a government of rules. Today's decision on the basic issue of fragmentation of executive power is ungoverned by rule, and hence ungoverned by law. It extends into the very heart of our most significant constitutional function the "totality of the circumstances" mode of analysis that this Court has in recent years become fond of. Taking all things into account, we conclude that the power taken away from the President here is not really too much. The next time executive power is assigned to someone other than the President we may conclude, taking all things into account, that it is too much. That opinion, like this one, will not be confined by any rule. We will describe, as we have done today . . . the effects of the provision in question, and will authoritatively announce: "The President's need to control the exercise of the [subject officer's] discretion is so central to the functioning of the Executive Branch as to require complete control." This is not analysis; it is ad hoc judgment. And it fails to explain why it is not true that—as the text of the Constitution seems to require, as the Founders seemed to expect, and as our past cases have uniformly assumed—all purely executive power must be under the control of the President.

The ad hoc approach to constitutional adjudication has real attraction, even apart from its work-saving potential. It is guaranteed to produce a result, in every case, that will make a majority of the Court happy with the law. The law is, by definition, precisely what the majority thinks, taking all things into account, it ought to be. I prefer to rely upon the judgment of the wise men who constructed our system, and of the people who approved it, and of two centuries of history that have shown it to be sound. Like it or not, that judgment says, quite plainly, that "[t]he executive Power shall be vested in a President of the United States."

Notes and Queries

1. What difference does it make to the Court whether the independent counsel is a "principal" or "inferior" officer? How does the Court determine which powers are central to the functioning of the executive branch? Can the Court, in fact, make such a determination?

2. Which opinion comes closest to the approach taken by Justice Black in the *Youngtown Sheet & Tube Co. v. Sawyer* (1952)? Which is closer to that of Justice Frankfurter? To that of Justice Jackson? Is the conception of separation of powers expressed by the Court in this case consistent with that of *Chadha*? What makes this case different? Is Justice Scalia's approach to separation of powers tenable in the modern administrative state?

3. In *Myers v. United States*, 272 U.S. 52 (1926), the Court was called upon to decide the extent of the president's power to remove government officials. The statute reviewed provided that the president could remove postmasters appointed to a four-year term only with the advice and consent of the Senate. In one of the broadest readings of presidential power, Chief Justice Taft, writing for a majority of six justices, declared that the statue invaded the power of the executive. "The power of removal," wrote Taft, "is incident to the power of appointment, not to the power of advising and consenting to appointment." The power of removal derives from the president's duty, laid down in Article II, to "take care that the laws be faithfully executed." The President's discretionary power to remove officials is absolute, for executive subordinates "must do his will." When "he loses confidence in the intelligence, ability, judgment or loyalty of any one of them, he must have the power to remove him without delay."

In two subsequent cases, however, the Court limited the President's removal power but without undermining the logic of Myers. In *Humphrey's Executor v. United* States, 295 U.S. 602 (1935), the Court held that Congress could limit the president's power to fire employees—such as the members of the Federal Trade Commission, an *independent* regulatory agency—not engaged in purely executive duties but acting "in part quasi-legislatively and in part quasi judicially." And in *Weiner v. United States*, 357 U.S. 340 (1958), by a vote of nine to zero, the Court held that the president could not remove a member of the War Claims Commission because of the "intrinsic judicial character" of his function.

United States v. Nixon
418 U.S. 683, 94 S.Ct. 3090, 41 L.Ed. 2d 1039 (1974)

In 1974, a federal grand jury indicted the attorney general and several presidential assistants for various offenses, including a conspiracy to defraud the United States and to obstruct justice. The grand jury also named President Richard Nixon as an unindicted co-conspirator. The special prosecutor caused the district court to issue a *subpoena duces tecum* directing the president to produce certain tape recordings and documents relating to his conversations with aides and advisors. The president released edited transcripts of several conversations, but refused to turn over other specified transcripts and papers. He moved to quash the subpoena, claiming that the dispute was a nonjusticiable dispute within the executive branch and that his confidential conversations within the White House were privileged communication. The district court denied the motion, and the president appealed the decision to the court of appeals. At the request of the special prosecutor, the Supreme Court expedited the matter by granting a writ of certiorari before any judgment by the court of appeals. Opinion of the Court: *Burger,* Douglas, Brennan, Stewart, White, Marshall, Blackmun, Powell. Not participating: Rehnquist.

Mr. Chief Justice BURGER delivered the opinion of the Court.

Justiciability

In the District Court, the President's counsel argued that the court lacked jurisdiction to issue the *subpoena* because the matter was an intra-branch dispute between a subordinate and superior officer of the Executive Branch and hence not subject to judicial resolution. That argument has been renewed in this Court with emphasis on the contention that the dispute does not present a "case" or "controversy" which can be adjudicated in the federal courts. . . . Since the Executive Branch has exclusive authority and absolute discretion to decide whether to prosecute a case, it is contended that a President's decision is final in determining what evidence is to be used in a given criminal case. . . . The Special Prosecutor's demand for the items therefore presents, in the view of the President's counsel, a political question . . . since it involves a "textually demonstrable" grant of power under Art. II.

The mere assertion of a claim of an "intra-branch dis-

Comparative Note 4.7

[In the following extract, the Canadian Supreme Court rejected a high public official's claim to testimonial immunity. The official invoked the Crown privilege to protect the public interest. In this leading case, the Court explored the scope of the Crown privilege.]

Once the nature . . . of [the] documents or the reasons against its disclosure are shown, the question for the Court is whether they might, on any rational view . . . be such that the public interest requires that they should not be revealed; if they are capable of sustaining such an interest, and a Minister of the Crown avers its existence, then the Courts must accept his decision. On the other hand, if the facts . . . show that . . . no such interest can exist, then such a [ministerial] declaration . . . must . . . be disregarded. To eliminate the Courts in a function with which the tradition of the common law

has invested them and to hold them subject to any opinion formed, rational or irrational, by a member of the Executive to the prejudice, it might be, of the lives of private individuals, is not in harmony with the basic conceptions of our polity. . . .

What is secured by attributing to the Courts this preliminary determination of possible prejudice is protection against Executive encroachments upon the administration of justice; and in the present trend of government, little can be more essential to the maintenance of individual security. In this important matter, to relegate the Courts to such a subserviency as is suggested would be to withdraw from them the confidence of independence and judicial appraisal that so far appear to have served well the organization of which we are the heirs.

Source: *R. V. Snyder* [1954] 4 D.L.R. 485–86.

---

pute," without more, has never operated to defeat federal jurisdiction; justiciability does not depend on such a surface inquiry. . . .

Our starting point is the nature of the proceeding for which the evidence is sought—here a pending criminal prosecution. . . . Under the authority of Art. II, s 2, Congress has vested in the Attorney General the power to conduct the criminal litigation of the United States Government. It has also vested in him the power to appoint subordinate officers to assist him in the discharge of his duties. Acting pursuant to those statutes, the Attorney General has delegated the authority to represent the United States in these particular matters to a Special Prosecutor with unique authority and tenure. The regulation gives the Special Prosecutor explicit power to contest the invocation of executive privilege in the process of seeking evidence deemed relevant to the performance of these specially delegated duties.

So long as this regulation is extant it has the force of law. . . . Here at issue is the production or nonproduction of specified evidence deemed by the Special Prosecutor to be relevant and admissible in a pending criminal case. It is sought by one official of the Executive Branch within the scope of his express authority; it is resisted by the Chief Executive on the ground of his duty to preserve the confidentiality of the communications of the President. Whatever the correct answer on the merits, these issues are "of a type which are traditionally justiciable." . . .

The Claim of Privilege

. . . [W]e turn to the claim that the subpoena should be quashed because it demands "confidential conversations between a President and his close advisors that it would be inconsistent with the public interest to produce." The first contention is a broad claim that the separation of powers doctrine precludes judicial review of a President's claim of privilege. The second contention is that if he does not prevail on the claim of absolute privilege, the court should hold as a matter of constitutional law that the privilege prevails over the *subpoena duces tecum.*

In the performance of assigned constitutional duties each branch of the Government must initially interpret the Constitution, and the interpretation of its powers by any branch is due great respect from the others. The President's counsel, as we have noted, reads the Constitution as providing an absolute privilege of confidentiality for all Presidential communications. Many decisions of this Court, however, have unequivocally reaffirmed the holding of *Marbury v. Madison* [1803], that "[i]t is emphatically the province and duty of the judicial department to say what the law is." . . .

In support of his claim of absolute privilege, the President's counsel urges two grounds, one of which is common to all governments and one of which is peculiar to our system of separation of powers. The first ground is the valid need for protection of communications between high Government officials and those who advise and assist them in the performance of their manifold duties; the importance of this confidentiality is too plain to require further discussion. Human experience teaches that those who expect public dissemination of their remarks may well temper candor with a concern for appearances and for their own interests to the detriment of the decision making process. Whatever the nature of the privilege of confidentiality of Presidential communications in the exercise of Art. II powers, the privilege can be said to derive from the supremacy of each branch within its own assigned area of constitutional duties. Certain powers and privileges flow from the nature of enumerated powers; the protection of the confidentiality of Presidential communications has similar constitutional underpinnings.

The second ground asserted by the President's counsel in support of the claim of absolute privilege rests on the doctrine of separation of powers. Here it is argued that the independence of the Executive Branch within its own sphere insulates a President from a judicial subpoena in an ongoing criminal prosecution, and thereby protects confidential Presidential communications.

However, neither the doctrine of separation of powers, nor the need for confidentiality of high-level communications, without more, can sustain an absolute, unqualified Presidential privilege of immunity from judicial process under all circumstances. The President's need for complete candor and objectivity from advisers calls for great deference from the courts. However, when the privilege depends solely on the broad, undifferentiated claim of public interest in the confidentiality of such conversations, a confrontation with other values arises. Absent a claim of need to protect military, diplomatic, or sensitive national security secrets, we find it difficult to accept the argument that even the very important interest in confidentiality of Presidential communications is significantly diminished by production of such material for *in camera* inspection with all the protection that a district court will be obliged to provide.

The impediment that an absolute, unqualified privilege would place in the way of the primary constitutional duty of the Judicial Branch to do justice in criminal prosecutions would plainly conflict with the function of the courts under Art. III. In designing the structure of our Government and dividing and allocating the sovereign power among three co-equal branches, the Framers of the Constitution sought to provide a comprehensive system, but the separate powers were not intended to operate with absolute independence. . . . To read the Art. II powers of the President as providing an absolute privilege as against a subpoena essential to enforcement of criminal statutes on no more than a generalized claim of the public interest in confidentiality of nonmilitary and nondiplomatic discussions would upset the constitutional balance of "a workable government" and gravely impair the role of the courts under Art. III.

Since we conclude that the legitimate needs of the judicial process may outweigh Presidential privilege, it is necessary to resolve those competing interests in a manner that preserves the essential functions of each branch. The right and indeed the duty to resolve that question does not free the Judiciary from according high respect to the representations made on behalf of the President.

The expectation of a President to the confidentiality of his conversations and correspondence, like the claim of confidentiality of judicial deliberations, for example, has all the values to which we accord deference for the privacy of all citizens and, added to those values, is the necessity for protection of the public interest in candid, objective, and even blunt or harsh opinions in Presidential decision making. . . .

But this presumptive privilege must be considered in light of our historic commitment to the rule of law. . . . The ends of criminal justice would be defeated if judgments were to be founded on a partial or speculative presentation of the facts. The very integrity of the judicial system and public confidence in the system depend on full disclosure of all the facts, within the framework of the rules of evidence. To ensure that justice is done, it is imperative to the function of courts that compulsory process be available for the production of evidence needed either by the prosecution or by the defense.

In this case the President challenges a subpoena served on him as a third party requiring the production of materials for use in a criminal prosecution; he does so on the claim that he has a privilege against disclosure of confidential communications. He does not place his claim of privilege on the ground they are military or diplomatic secrets. As to these areas of Art. II duties the courts have traditionally shown the utmost deference to Presidential responsibilities. . . .

On the other hand, the allowance of the privilege to withhold evidence that is demonstrably relevant in a criminal trial would cut deeply into the guarantee of due process of law and gravely impair the basic function of the courts. A President's acknowledged need for confidentiality in the communications of his office is general in nature, whereas the constitutional need for production of relevant evidence in a criminal proceeding is specific and central to the fair adjudication of a particular criminal case in the administration of justice. Without access to specific facts a criminal prosecution may be totally frustrated. The President's broad interest in confidentiality of communications will not be vitiated by disclosure of a limited number of conversations preliminarily shown to have some bearing on the pending criminal cases.

We conclude that when the ground for asserting privilege as to subpoenaed materials sought for use in a criminal trial is based only on the generalized interest in confidentiality, it cannot prevail over the fundamental demands of due process of law in the fair administration of criminal justice. The generalized assertion of privilege must yield to the demonstrated, specific need for evidence in a pending criminal trial.

Affirmed.

Notes and Queries

1. The events surrounding this case were extraordinary. After President Nixon refused to turn over subpoenaed materials to special prosecutor Leon Jaworski in March 1974, a federal district court held a trial and eventually rejected Nixon's claim to executive privilege. The president appealed to the court of appeals, but before they could rule, the special prosecutor petitioned the Supreme

Court to grant certiorari. The Supreme Court accepted Jaworski's request. The Court heard oral arguments in a special session on 8 July and handed down its opinion on 24 July. Less than a week after this decision, the House voted to impeach the President. On 9 August 1974, President Nixon resigned the presidency.

2. Was President Nixon insisting that the president has an independent authority to interpret the Constitution? Consider our discussion of judicial supremacy in chapter 3. Was President Nixon's claim unprecedented? Did the Court deny that the president has that authority?

3. The Court was careful to note that Nixon's claim of privilege did not ground itself in the need to protect sensitive information or national security. Would the Court have decided differently if the president had made such a claim? Would the presence of such claims strengthen the president's authority to interpret the Constitution to permit him to withhold such information? How should we weigh such a claim against a "demonstrated, specific need to evidence in a pending criminal trial"? Who should weigh such a claim? The Court suggested that the president's judgment must necessarily be influenced by his self-interest. Is that true of the Court's judgment as well?

Clinton v. Jones
520 U.S. 681, 137 L. Ed. 2d 945, 117 S.Ct. 1636 (1997)

Paula Corbin Jones sued President Clinton, alleging that while he was Governor of Arkansas Clinton made "abhorrent" sexual advances to her, and that her rejection of those advances led to punishment by her supervisors in the state job she held at the time. Clinton promptly advised the Federal District Court that he would file a motion to dismiss on Presidential immunity grounds, and requested that all other pleadings and motions be deferred until the immunity issue was resolved. After the court granted that request, Clinton filed a motion to dismiss without prejudice. The District Judge denied dismissal on immunity grounds and ruled that discovery could go forward, but ordered any trial stayed until Clinton's Presidency ended. The Eighth Circuit affirmed the dismissal denial, but reversed the trial postponement as the "functional equivalent" of a grant of temporary immunity to which Clinton was not constitutionally entitled. The court explained that the President, like other officials, is subject to the same laws that apply to all citizens, that no case had been found in which an official was granted immunity from suit for his unofficial acts, and that the rationale for official immunity is inapposite where only personal, private conduct by a President is at issue. The court also re-

jected the argument that, unless immunity is available, the threat of judicial interference with the Executive Branch would violate the separation of powers. Opinion of the Court: *Stevens*, Rehnquist, O'Connor, Scalia, Kennedy, Souter, Thomas, Ginsburg. Concurring opinion: *Breyer*.

Justice STEVENS delivered the opinion of the Court:

This case raises a constitutional and a prudential question concerning the Office of the President of the United States. Respondent, a private citizen, seeks to recover damages from the current occupant of that office based on actions allegedly taken before his term began. The President submits that in all but the most exceptional cases the Constitution requires federal courts to defer such litigation until his term ends and that, in any event, respect for the office warrants such a stay. Despite the force of the arguments supporting the President's submissions, we conclude that they must be rejected. . . .

I

Petitioner's principal submission—that "in all but the most exceptional cases," the Constitution affords the President temporary immunity from civil damages litigation arising out of events that occurred before he took office—cannot be sustained on the basis of precedent.

Only three sitting Presidents have been defendants in

civil litigation involving their actions prior to taking office. Complaints against Theodore Roosevelt and Harry Truman had been dismissed before they took office; the dismissals were affirmed after their respective inaugurations. Two companion cases arising out of an automobile accident were filed against John F. Kennedy in 1960 during the Presidential campaign. After taking office, he unsuccessfully argued that his status as Commander in Chief gave him a right to a stay under the Soldiers' and Sailors' Civil Relief Act of 1940, 50 U. S. C. App. s.s.501–525. The motion for a stay was denied by the District Court, and the matter was settled out of court. Thus, none of those cases sheds any light on the constitutional issue before us.

The principal rationale for affording certain public servants immunity from suits for money damages arising out of their official acts is inapplicable to unofficial conduct. In cases involving prosecutors, legislators, and judges we have repeatedly explained that the immunity serves the public interest in enabling such officials to perform their designated functions effectively without fear that a particular decision may give rise to personal liability. . . .

This reasoning provides no support for an immunity for *unofficial* conduct. As we explained in *Fitzgerald*, "the sphere of protected action must be related closely to the immunity's justifying purposes." Because of the President's broad responsibilities, we recognized in that case an immunity from damages claims arising out of official acts extending to the "outer perimeter of his authority." But we have never suggested that the President, or any other official, has an immunity that extends beyond the scope of any action taken in an official capacity.

Moreover, when defining the scope of an immunity for acts clearly taken *within* an official capacity, we have applied a functional approach. "Frequently our decisions have held that an official's absolute immunity should extend only to acts in performance of particular functions of his office." Hence, for example, a judge's absolute immunity does not extend to actions performed in a purely administrative capacity. As our opinions have made clear, immunities are grounded in "the nature of the function performed, not the identity of the actor who performed it."

Petitioner's effort to construct an immunity from suit for unofficial acts grounded purely in the identity of his office is unsupported by precedent.

II

We are also unpersuaded by the evidence from the historical record to which petitioner has called our attention. He points to a comment by Thomas Jefferson protesting the subpoena *duces tecum* Chief Justice Marshall directed to

him in the Burr trial, a statement in the diaries kept by Senator William Maclay of the first Senate debates, in which then Vice-President John Adams and Senator Oliver Ellsworth are recorded as having said that "the President personally [is] not . . . subject to any process whatever," lest it be "put . . . in the power of a common Justice to exercise any Authority over him and Stop the Whole Machine of Government," and to a quotation from Justice Story's Commentaries on the Constitution. None of these sources sheds much light on the question at hand. . . .

III

Petitioner's strongest argument supporting his immunity claim is based on the text and structure of the Constitution. He does not contend that the occupant of the Office of the President is "above the law," in the sense that his conduct is entirely immune from judicial scrutiny. The President argues merely for a postponement of the judicial proceedings that will determine whether he violated any law. His argument is grounded in the character of the office that was created by Article II of the Constitution, and relies on separation of powers principles that have structured our constitutional arrangement since the founding.

As a starting premise, petitioner contends that he occupies a unique office with powers and responsibilities so vast and important that the public interest demands that he devote his undivided time and attention to his public duties. He submits that—given the nature of the office—the doctrine of separation of powers places limits on the authority of the Federal Judiciary to interfere with the Executive Branch that would be transgressed by allowing this action to proceed.

We have no dispute with the initial premise of the argument. Former presidents, from George Washington to George Bush, have consistently endorsed petitioner's characterization of the office. After serving his term, Lyndon Johnson observed: "Of all the 1,886 nights I was President, there were not many when I got to sleep before 1 or 2 A.M., and there were few mornings when I didn't wake up by 6 or 6:30." In 1967, the Twenty-fifth Amendment to the Constitution was adopted to ensure continuity in the performance of the powers and duties of the office; one of the sponsors of that Amendment stressed the importance of providing that "at all times" there be a President "who has complete control and will be able to perform" those duties. As Justice Jackson has pointed out, the Presidency concentrates executive authority "in a single head in whose choice the whole Nation has a part, making him the focus of public hopes and expectations. In drama, magnitude and finality his decisions so far overshadow any others that almost alone he fills the public eye and ear" (*Youngstown Sheet & Tube Co. v. Sawyer*). We have, in short, long recognized the "unique position in the constitutional scheme" that this office occupies. Thus, while we suspect that even in our modern era there remains some truth to Chief Justice Marshall's suggestion that the duties of the Presidency are not entirely "unremitting," we accept the initial premise of the Executive's argument.

It does not follow, however, that separation of powers principles would be violated by allowing this action to proceed. The doctrine of separation of powers is concerned with the allocation of official power among the three co-equal branches of our Government. The Framers "built into the tripartite Federal Government . . . a self-executing safeguard against the encroachment or aggrandizement of one branch at the expense of the other" (*Buckley v. Valeo*). Thus, for example, the Congress may not exercise the judicial power to revise final judgments or the executive power to manage an airport. Similarly, the President may not exercise the legislative power to authorize the seizure of private property for public use. And, the judicial power to decide cases and controversies does not include the provision of purely advisory opinions to the Executive, or permit the federal courts to resolve nonjusticiable questions.

Of course the lines between the powers of the three branches are not always neatly defined. But in this case there is no suggestion that the Federal Judiciary is being asked to perform any function that might in some way be described as "executive." Respondent is merely asking the courts to exercise their core Article III jurisdiction to decide cases and controversies. Whatever the outcome of this case, there is no possibility that the decision will curtail the scope of the official powers of the Executive Branch. The litigation of questions that relate entirely to the unofficial conduct of the individual who happens to be the President poses no perceptible risk of misallocation of either judicial power or executive power.

Rather than arguing that the decision of the case will produce either an aggrandizement of judicial power or a narrowing of executive power, petitioner contends that—as a by-product of an otherwise traditional exercise of judicial power—burdens will be placed on the President that will hamper the performance of his official duties. We have recognized that "[e]ven when a branch does not arrogate power to itself . . . the separation-of-powers doctrine requires that a branch not impair another in the performance of its constitutional duties" (*Loving v. United States*). As a factual matter, petitioner contends that this particular case—as well as the potential additional litigation that an affirmance of the Court of Appeals judgment

might spawn—may impose an unacceptable burden on the President's time and energy, and thereby impair the effective performance of his office.

Petitioner's predictive judgment finds little support in either history or the relatively narrow compass of the issues raised in this particular case. As we have already noted, in the more than 200-year history of the Republic, only three sitting Presidents have been subjected to suits for their private actions. If the past is any indicator, it seems unlikely that a deluge of such litigation will ever engulf the Presidency. As for the case at hand, if properly managed by the District Court, it appears to us highly unlikely to occupy any substantial amount of petitioner's time.

Of greater significance, petitioner errs by presuming that interactions between the Judicial Branch and the Executive, even quite burdensome interactions, necessarily rise to the level of constitutionally forbidden impairment of the Executive's ability to perform its constitutionally mandated functions. "[O]ur . . . system imposes upon the Branches a degree of overlapping responsibility, a duty of interdependence as well as independence the absence of which 'would preclude the establishment of a Nation capable of governing itself effectively'" (*Mistretta v. United States*). As Madison explained, separation of powers does not mean that the branches "ought to have no *partial agency* in, or no *control* over the acts of each other." The fact that a federal court's exercise of its traditional Article III jurisdiction may significantly burden the time and attention of the Chief Executive is not sufficient to establish a violation of the Constitution. Two long-settled propositions, first announced by Chief Justice Marshall, support that conclusion.

First, we have long held that when the President takes official action, the Court has the authority to determine whether he has acted within the law. Perhaps the most dramatic example of such a case is our holding that President Truman exceeded his constitutional authority when he issued an order directing the Secretary of Commerce to take possession of and operate most of the Nation's steel mills in order to avert a national catastrophe. Despite the serious impact of that decision on the ability of the Executive Branch to accomplish its assigned mission, and the substantial time that the President must necessarily have devoted to the matter as a result of judicial involvement, we exercised our Article III jurisdiction to decide whether his official conduct conformed to the law. Our holding was an application of the principle established in *Marbury v. Madison* that "[i]t is emphatically the province and duty of the judicial department to say what the law is."

Second, it is also settled that the President is subject to

judicial process in appropriate circumstances. Although Thomas Jefferson apparently thought otherwise, Chief Justice Marshall, when presiding in the treason trial of Aaron Burr, ruled that a subpoena *duces tecum* could be directed to the President. We unequivocally and emphatically endorsed Marshall's position when we held that President Nixon was obligated to comply with a subpoena commanding him to produce certain tape recordings of his conversations with his aides. As we explained, "neither the doctrine of separation of powers, nor the need for confidentiality of high-level communications, without more, can sustain an absolute, unqualified Presidential privilege of immunity from judicial process under all circumstances."

Sitting Presidents have responded to court orders to provide testimony and other information with sufficient frequency that such interactions between the Judicial and Executive Branches can scarcely be thought a novelty. President Monroe responded to written interrogatories, President Nixon—as noted above—produced tapes in response to a subpoena *duces tecum*, President Ford complied with an order to give a deposition in a criminal trial, and President Clinton has twice given videotaped testimony in criminal proceedings. Moreover, sitting Presidents have also voluntarily complied with judicial requests for testimony. President Grant gave a lengthy deposition in a criminal case under such circumstances and President Carter similarly gave videotaped testimony for use at a criminal trial.

In sum, "[i]t is settled law that the separation-of-powers doctrine does not bar every exercise of jurisdiction over the President of the United States" (*Nixon v. Fitzgerald*). If the Judiciary may severely burden the Executive Branch by reviewing the legality of the President's official conduct, and if it may direct appropriate process to the President himself, it must follow that the federal courts have power to determine the legality of his unofficial conduct. The burden on the President's time and energy that is a mere by-product of such review surely cannot be considered as onerous as the direct burden imposed by judicial review and the occasional invalidation of his official actions. We therefore hold that the doctrine of separation of powers does not require federal courts to stay all private actions against the President until he leaves office.

The reasons for rejecting such a categorical rule apply as well to a rule that would require a stay "in all but the most exceptional cases." Indeed, if the Framers of the Constitution had thought it necessary to protect the President from the burdens of private litigation, we think it far more likely that they would have adopted a categorical rule than a rule that required the President to litigate the question whether a specific case belonged in the "exceptional case" subcategory. In all events, the question whether a specific case should receive exceptional treatment is more appropriately the subject of the exercise of judicial discretion than an interpretation of the Constitution. . . .

VII

Although we have rejected the argument that the potential burdens on the President violate separation of powers principles, those burdens are appropriate matters for the District Court to evaluate in its management of the case. The high respect that is owed to the office of the Chief Executive, though not justifying a rule of categorical immunity, is a matter that should inform the conduct of the entire proceeding, including the timing and scope of discovery. . . .

Nevertheless, we are persuaded that it was an abuse of discretion for the District Court to defer the trial until after the President leaves office. Such a lengthy and categorical stay takes no account whatever of the respondent's interest in bringing the case to trial. The complaint was filed within the statutory limitations period—albeit near the end of that period—and delaying trial would increase the danger of prejudice resulting from the loss of evidence, including the inability of witnesses to recall specific facts, or the possible death of a party. . . .

We add a final comment on two matters that are discussed at length in the briefs: the risk that our decision will generate a large volume of politically motivated harassing and frivolous litigation, and the danger that national security concerns might prevent the President from explaining a legitimate need for a continuance.

We are not persuaded that either of these risks is serious. Most frivolous and vexatious litigation is terminated at the pleading stage or on summary judgment, with little if any personal involvement by the defendant. Moreover, the availability of sanctions provides a significant deterrent to litigation directed at the President in his unofficial capacity for purposes of political gain or harassment. History indicates that the likelihood that a significant number of such cases will be filed is remote. Although scheduling problems may arise, there is no reason to assume that the District Courts will be either unable to accommodate the President's needs or unfaithful to the tradition—especially in matters involving national security—of giving "the utmost deference to Presidential responsibilities." Several Presidents, including petitioner, have given testimony without jeopardizing the Nation's security. In short, we have confidence in the ability of our federal judges to deal with both of these concerns.

If Congress deems it appropriate to afford the President stronger protection, it may respond with appropriate legislation. As petitioner notes in his brief, Congress has enacted more than one statute providing for the deferral of civil litigation to accommodate important public interests. If the Constitution embodied the rule that the President advocates, Congress, of course, could not repeal it. But our holding today raises no barrier to a statutory response to these concerns.

The Federal District Court has jurisdiction to decide this case. Like every other citizen who properly invokes that jurisdiction, respondent has a right to an orderly disposition of her claims. Accordingly, the judgment of the Court of Appeals is affirmed.

It is so ordered.

Justice BREYER, concurring in the judgment.

I agree with the majority that the Constitution does not automatically grant the President an immunity from civil lawsuits based upon his private conduct. Nor does the "doctrine of separation of powers . . . require federal courts to stay" virtually "all private actions against the President until he leaves office." Rather, as the Court of Appeals stated, the President cannot simply rest upon the claim that a private civil lawsuit for damages will "interfere with the constitutionally assigned duties of the Executive Branch . . . without detailing any specific responsibilities or explaining how or the degree to which they are affected by the suit." 72 F. 3d 1354, 1361 (CA8 1996). To obtain a postponement the President must "bea[r] the burden of establishing its need."

In my view, however, once the President sets forth and explains a conflict between judicial proceeding and public duties, the matter changes. At that point, the Constitution permits a judge to schedule a trial in an ordinary civil damages action (where postponement normally is possible without overwhelming damage to a plaintiff) only within the constraints of a constitutional principle—a principle that forbids a federal judge in such a case to interfere with the President's discharge of his public duties. I have no doubt that the Constitution contains such a principle applicable to civil suits, based upon Article II's vesting of the entire "executive Power" in a single individual, implemented through the Constitution's structural separation of powers, and revealed both by history and case precedent.

I recognize that this case does not require us now to apply the principle specifically, thereby delineating its contours; nor need we now decide whether lower courts are to apply it directly or categorically through the use of presumptions or rules of administration. Yet I fear that to disregard it now may appear to deny it. I also fear that

the majority's description of the relevant precedents de-emphasizes the extent to which they support a principle of the President's independent authority to control his own time and energy. Further, if the majority is wrong in predicting the future infrequency of private civil litigation against sitting Presidents, acknowledgement and future delineation of the constitutional principle will prove a practically necessary institutional safeguard. For these reasons, I think it important to explain how the Constitution's text, history, and precedent support this principle of judicial noninterference with Presidential functions in ordinary civil damages actions. . . .

The Constitution states that the "executive Power shall be vested in a President." This constitutional delegation means that a sitting President is unusually busy, that his activities have an unusually important impact upon the lives of others, and that his conduct embodies an authority bestowed by the entire American electorate. He (along with his constitutionally subordinate Vice President) is the only official for whom the entire Nation votes, and is the only elected officer to represent the entire Nation both domestically and abroad.

This constitutional delegation means still more. Article II makes a single President responsible for the actions of the Executive Branch in much the same way that the entire Congress is responsible for the actions of the Legislative Branch, or the entire Judiciary for those of the Judicial Branch. It thereby creates a constitutional equivalence between a single President, on the one hand, and many legislators, or judges, on the other.

The Founders created this equivalence by consciously deciding to vest Executive authority in one person rather than several. They did so in order to focus, rather than to spread, Executive responsibility thereby facilitating accountability. They also sought to encourage energetic, vigorous, decisive, and speedy execution of the laws by placing in the hands of a single, constitutionally indispensable individual the ultimate authority that, in respect to the other branches, the Constitution divides among many.

For present purposes, this constitutional structure means that the President is not like Congress, for Congress can function as if it were whole, even when up to half of its members are absent. It means that the President is not like the Judiciary, for judges often can designate other judges, e.g., from other judicial circuits, to sit even should an entire court be detained by personal litigation. It means that, unlike Congress, which is regularly out of session, the President never adjourns.

More importantly, these constitutional objectives explain why a President, though able to delegate duties to others, cannot delegate ultimate responsibility or the active obligation to supervise that goes with it. And the related constitutional equivalence between President, Congress, and the Judiciary, means that judicial scheduling orders in a private civil case must not only take reasonable account of, say, a particularly busy schedule, or a job on which others critically depend, or an underlying electoral mandate. They must also reflect the fact that interference with a President's ability to carry out his public responsibilities is constitutionally equivalent to interference with the ability of the entirety of Congress, or the Judicial Branch, to carry out their public obligations. . . . I concede the possibility that district courts, supervised by the Courts of Appeals and perhaps this Court, might prove able to manage private civil damage actions against sitting Presidents without significantly interfering with the discharge of Presidential duties—at least if they manage those actions with the constitutional problem in mind. Nonetheless, predicting the future is difficult, and I am skeptical. Should the majority's optimism turn out to be misplaced, then, in my view, courts will have to develop administrative rules applicable to such cases (including postponement rules of the sort at issue in this case) in order to implement the basic constitutional directive. A Constitution that separates powers in order to prevent one branch of Government from significantly threatening the workings of another could not grant a single judge more than a very limited power to second guess a President's reasonable determination (announced in open court) of his scheduling needs, nor could it permit the issuance of a trial scheduling order that would significantly interfere with the President's discharge of his duties—in a private civil damage action the trial of which might be postponed without the plaintiff suffering enormous harm. As Madison pointed out in *The Federalist* No. 51, "[t]he great security against a gradual concentration of the several powers in the same department consists in giving to those who administer each department the necessary constitutional means and personal motives to resist encroachments of the others. *The provision for defense must in this, as in all other cases, be made commensurate to the danger of attack.*" I agree with the majority's determination that a constitutional defense must await a more specific showing of need; I do not agree with what I believe to be an understatement of the "danger." And I believe that ordinary case management principles are unlikely to prove sufficient to deal with private civil lawsuits for damages unless supplemented with a constitutionally based requirement that district courts schedule proceedings so as to avoid significant interference with the President's ongoing discharge of his official responsibilities.

This case is a private action for civil damages in which,

as the District Court here found, it is possible to preserve evidence and in which later payment of interest can compensate for delay. The District Court in this case determined that the Constitution required the postponement of trial during the sitting President's term. It may well be that the trial of this case cannot take place without significantly interfering with the President's ability to carry out his official duties. Yet, I agree with the majority that there is no automatic temporary immunity and that the President should have to provide the District Court with a reasoned explanation of why the immunity is needed; and I also agree that, in the absence of that explanation, the court's postponement of the trial date was premature. For those reasons, I concur in the result.

Articles of Impeachment against President William Jefferson Clinton

[The following four articles of impeachment were approved by the Judiciary Committee of the House of Representatives on 11 and 12 December 1998. On 19 December the full House approved Articles I and III. The trial in the Senate, presided over by Chief Justice William Rehnquist, culminated on 12 February 1999 in an acquittal on both articles.]

Resolved, that William Jefferson Clinton, President of the United States, is impeached for high crimes and misdemeanors, and that the following articles of impeachment be exhibited to the United States Senate:

Articles of impeachment exhibited by the House of Representatives of the United States of America in the name of itself and of the people of the United States of America, against William Jefferson Clinton, President of the United States of America, in maintenance and support of its impeachment against him for high crimes and misdemeanors.

Article I

In his conduct while President of the United States, William Jefferson Clinton, in violation of his constitutional oath faithfully to execute the office of President of the United States and, to the best of his ability, preserve, protect, and defend the Constitution of the United States, and in violation of his constitutional duty to take care that the laws be faithfully executed, has willfully corrupted and manipulated the judicial process of the United States for his personal gain and exoneration, impeding the administration of justice, in that:

On August 17, 1998, William Jefferson Clinton swore to tell the truth, the whole truth, and nothing but the truth before a Federal grand jury of the United States. Contrary to that oath, William Jefferson Clinton willfully provided perjurious, false and misleading testimony to the grand jury concerning one or more of the following:

(1) the nature and details of his relationship with a subordinate Government employee;

(2) prior perjurious, false and misleading testimony he gave in a Federal civil rights action brought against him;

(3) prior false and misleading statements he allowed his attorney to make to a Federal judge in that civil rights action; and

(4) his corrupt efforts to influence the testimony of witnesses and to impede the discovery of evidence in that civil rights action.

In doing this, William Jefferson Clinton has undermined the integrity of his office, has brought disrepute on the Presidency, has betrayed his trust as President, and has acted in a manner subversive of the rule of law and justice, to the manifest injury of the people of the United States.

Wherefore, William Jefferson Clinton, by such conduct, warrants impeachment and trial, and removal from office and disqualification to hold and enjoy any office of honor, trust or profit under the United States.

Article II

In his conduct while President of the United States, William Jefferson Clinton, in violation of his constitutional oath faithfully to execute the office of President of the United States and, to the best of his ability, preserve, protect, and defend the Constitution of the United States, and in violation of his constitutional duty to take care that the laws be faithfully executed, has willfully corrupted and manipulated the judicial process of the United States for his personal gain and exoneration, impeding the administration of justice, in that:

(1) On December 23, 1997, William Jefferson Clinton, in sworn answers to written questions asked as part of a Federal civil rights action brought against him, willfully provided perjurious, false and misleading testimony in response to questions deemed relevant by a Federal judge concerning conduct and proposed conduct with subordinate employees.

(2) On January 17, 1998, William Jefferson Clinton swore under oath to tell the truth, the whole truth, and nothing but the truth in a deposition given as part of a Federal civil rights action brought against him. Contrary to that oath, William Jefferson Clinton willfully provided perjurious, false and misleading testimony in response to questions deemed relevant by a Federal judge concerning the nature and details of his relationship with a subordinate Government employee, his knowledge of that em-

ployee's involvement and participation in the civil rights action brought against him, and his corrupt efforts to influence the testimony of that employee.

In all of this, William Jefferson Clinton has undermined the integrity of his office, has brought disrepute on the Presidency, has betrayed his trust as President, and has acted in a manner subversive of the rule of law and justice, to the manifest injury of the people of the United States.

Wherefore, William Jefferson Clinton, by such conduct, warrants impeachment and trial, and removal from office and disqualification to hold and enjoy any office of honor, trust or profit under the United States.

Article III

In his conduct while President of the United States, William Jefferson Clinton, in violation of his constitutional oath faithfully to execute the office of President of the United States and, to the best of his ability, preserve, protect, and defend the Constitution of the United States, and in violation of his constitutional duty to take care that the laws be faithfully executed, has prevented, obstructed, and impeded the administration of justice, and has to that end engaged personally, and through his subordinates and agents, in a course of conduct or scheme designed to delay, impede, cover up, and conceal the existence of evidence and testimony related to a Federal civil rights action brought against him in a duly instituted judicial proceeding.

The means used to implement this course of conduct or scheme included one or more of the following acts:

(1) On or about December 17, 1997, William Jefferson Clinton corruptly encouraged a witness in a Federal civil rights action brought against him to execute a sworn affidavit in that proceeding that he knew to be perjurious, false and misleading.

(2) On or about December 17, 1997, William Jefferson Clinton corruptly encouraged a witness in a Federal civil rights action brought against him to give perjurious, false and misleading testimony if and when called to testify personally in that proceeding.

(3) On or about December 28, 1997, William Jefferson Clinton corruptly engaged in, encouraged, or supported a scheme to conceal evidence that had been subpoenaed in a Federal civil rights action brought against him.

(4) Beginning on or about December 7, 1997, and continuing through and including January 14, 1998, William Jefferson Clinton intensified and succeeded in an effort to secure job assistance to a witness in a Federal civil rights action brought against him in order to corruptly prevent the truthful testimony of that witness in that proceeding at a time when the truthful testimony of that witness would have been harmful to him.

(5) On January 17, 1998, at his deposition in a Federal civil rights action brought against him, William Jefferson Clinton corruptly allowed his attorney to make false and misleading statements to a Federal judge characterizing an affidavit, in order to prevent questioning deemed relevant by the judge. Such false and misleading statements were subsequently acknowledged by his attorney in a communication to that judge.

(6) On or about January 18 and January 20–21, 1998, William Jefferson Clinton related a false and misleading account of events relevant to a Federal civil rights action brought against him to a potential witness in that proceeding, in order to corruptly influence the testimony of that witness.

(7) On or about January 21, 23 and 26, 1998, William Jefferson Clinton made false and misleading statements to potential witnesses in a Federal grand jury proceeding in order to corruptly influence the testimony of those witnesses. The false and misleading statements made by William Jefferson Clinton were repeated by the witnesses to the grand jury, causing the grand jury to receive false and misleading information.

In all of this, William Jefferson Clinton has undermined the integrity of his office, has brought disrepute on the Presidency, has betrayed his trust as President, and has acted in a manner subversive of the rule of law and justice, to the manifest injury of the people of the United States.

Wherefore, William Jefferson Clinton, by such conduct, warrants impeachment and trial, and removal from office and disqualification to hold and enjoy any office of honor, trust or profit under the United States.

Article IV

Using the powers and influence of the office of President of the United States, William Jefferson Clinton, in violation of his constitutional oath faithfully to execute the office of President of the United States and, to the best of his ability, preserve, protect, and defend the Constitution of the United States, and in disregard of his constitutional duty to take care that the laws be faithfully executed, has engaged in conduct that resulted in misuse and abuse of his high office, impaired the due and proper administration of justice and the conduct of lawful inquiries, and contravened the authority of the legislative branch and the truth-seeking purpose of a coordinate investigative proceeding in that, as President, William Jefferson Clinton refused and failed to respond to certain written requests for admission and willfully made perjurious, false and misleading sworn statements in response to certain written requests for ad-

mission propounded to him as part of the impeachment inquiry authorized by the House of Representatives of the Congress of the United States.

William Jefferson Clinton, in refusing and failing to respond, and in making perjurious, false and misleading statements, assumed to himself functions and judgments necessary to the exercise of the sole power of impeachment vested by the Constitution in the House of Representatives and exhibited contempt for the inquiry.

In doing this, William Jefferson Clinton has undermined the integrity of his office, has brought disrepute on the Presidency, has betrayed his trust as President, and has acted in a manner subversive of the rule of law and justice, to the manifest injury of the people of the United States.

Wherefore, William Jefferson Clinton, by such conduct, warrants impeachment and trial, and removal from office and disqualification to hold and enjoy any office of honor, trust or profit under the United States.

Notes and Queries

1. A number of commentators have suggested that the Court was insufficiently sensitive to the political and governmental realities of the modern presidency, and thus underestimated the extent to which President Clinton would be diverted from his official duties by his legal difficulties. For example, Richard Posner (himself a federal appellate judge) wrote: "[A] closer engagement with the particulars of the case—a descent from the plane of abstract rules on which judges are happiest—might have saved the Supreme Court from committing errors harmful both to the nation and to the Court's reputation. . . . What is missing from the Court's performance . . . is an intellectual suppleness, a practicality, and a realism that judges and lawyers ought to have in a society in which disputes of high political moment are routinely submitted to courts for resolution." Richard Posner, *An Affair of State: The Investigation, Impeachment, and Trial of President Clinton* (Cambridge: Harvard University Press, 1999). What would have been a pragmatic outcome in the case? Is the familiar idea that "no man is above the law" the sort of abstract rule that requires compromise in circumstances such as this where one might have predicted that the conduct of the public's business would be seriously threatened?

2. Examine the articles of impeachment brought against President Clinton. Regardless of how you may feel about his guilt or innocence with respect to the allegations contained within them, what do they suggest about the Court's observations concerning the ability of the President to conduct the affairs of state absent a grant of temporary immunity from civil lawsuits directed against him?

3. Is the President's immunity claim supportive of the separation of powers principle or a threat to it? Is the Court's ruling required by the logic of *Marbury v. Madison*?

4. Do you agree with the Court that the decisions in *Youngstown Sheet & Tube Co. v. Sawyer* and *United States v. Nixon* argue against the President's claim that the doctrine of separation of powers does not require federal courts to stay all private actions against the President until he leaves office?

5. Justice Breyer, while concurring in this case, appears to be much more concerned than the other justices about the effects of judicial interference with the President's discharge of his public duties. There might, he suggests, be

an occasion when it would be appropriate to invoke a constitutional principle to prevent such interference in the case of civil lawsuits based upon private conduct. Can you develop a structuralist argument grounded in the "executive power" of Article II for this constitutional principle?

6. Article 68 of the French Constitution states that the President of the Republic shall not be held liable for acts performed in the exercise of his duties except in the case of high treason. What significance do you see in the fact that the immunity is explicitly provided by the text of the document? Does the absence of such language in the American Constitution reflect a different conception of the status of the executive within the legal framework of separation of powers?

Clinton v. City of New York
524 U.S. 417, 118 S.Ct. 2091 (1998)

In 1996, in a measure intended to reduce the level of federal spending, Congress passed and the President signed the Line Item Veto Act, which empowered the President to "cancel" particular budgetary lines within larger provisions that had already become law. Several members of Congress immediately brought suit, challenging the statute's constitutionality, but they were denied review because they lacked standing. When the President utilized his cancellation power over the section of the Balanced Budget Act that waived the federal government's statutory right to recoupment of $2.6 billion in taxes that the State of New York had levied against Medicare providers, the City of New York challenged the constitutionality of the Line Item Veto Act. The Court found that the plaintiff had standing and heard the case.

Opinion of the Court: *Stevens*. Concurring opinion: *Kennedy*. Concurring in part and dissenting in part: *Scalia*. Dissenting opinion: *Breyer*.

Justice STEVENS delivered the opinion of the Court . . .

IV

The Line Item Veto Act gives the President the power to "cancel in whole" three types of provisions that have been signed into law: "(1) any dollar amount of discretionary budget authority; (2) any item of new direct spending; or (3) any limited tax benefit. . . ."

. . . Moreover, he must transmit a special message to Congress notifying it of each cancellation. . . .

A cancellation takes effect upon receipt by Congress of the special message from the President. If, however, a

"disapproval bill" pertaining to a special message is enacted into law, the cancellations set forth in that message become "null and void." The Act sets forth a detailed expedited procedure for the consideration of a "disapproval bill," but no such bill was passed for either of the cancellations involved in these cases. A majority vote of both Houses is sufficient to enact a disapproval bill. The Act does not grant the President the authority to cancel a disapproval bill, but he does, of course, retain his constitutional authority to veto such a bill. . . .

In both legal and practical effect, the President has amended two Acts of Congress by repealing a portion of each. There is no provision in the Constitution that authorizes the President to enact, to amend, or to repeal statutes. Both Article I and Article II assign responsibilities to the President that directly relate to the lawmaking process, but neither addresses the issue presented by these cases. The President "shall from time to time give to the Congress Information on the State of the Union, and recommend to their Consideration such Measures as he shall judge necessary and expedient. . . ." Art. II, s.3. Thus, he may initiate and influence legislative proposals. Moreover, after a bill has passed both Houses of Congress, but "before it become[s] a Law," it must be presented to the President. If he approves it, "he shall sign it, but if not he shall return it, with his Objections to that House in which it shall have originated, who shall enter the Objections at large on their Journal, and proceed to reconsider it." Art. I, s.7, cl. 2. His "return" of a bill, which is usually described as a "veto," is subject to being overridden by a two-thirds vote in each House.

There are important differences between the President's "return" of a bill pursuant to Article I, s.7, and the exercise of the President's cancellation authority pursuant to the

Line Item Veto Act. The constitutional return takes place *before* the bill becomes law; the statutory cancellation occurs *after* the bill becomes law. The constitutional return is of the entire bill; the statutory cancellation is of only a part. Although the Constitution expressly authorizes the President to play a role in the process of enacting statutes, it is silent on the subject of unilateral Presidential action that either repeals or amends parts of duly enacted statutes.

. . . What has emerged in these cases from the President's exercise of his statutory cancellation powers . . . are truncated versions of two bills that passed both Houses of Congress. . . .

V

. . . [T]he Government contends that the cancellations were merely exercises of discretionary authority granted to the President by the Balanced Budget Act and the Taxpayer Relief Act read in light of the previously enacted Line Item Veto Act. Second, the Government submits that the substance of the authority to cancel tax and spending items "is, in practical effect, no more and no less than the power to 'decline to spend' specified sums of money, or to 'decline to implement' specified tax measures." Neither argument is persuasive. . . .

The cited statutes all relate to foreign trade, and this Court has recognized that in the foreign affairs arena, the President has "a degree of discretion and freedom from statutory restriction which would not be admissible were domestic affairs alone involved." *United States v. Curtiss-Wright Export Corp.* (1936) . . .

Neither are we persuaded by the Government's contention that the President's authority to cancel new direct spending and tax benefit items is no greater than his traditional authority to decline to spend appropriated funds. The Government has reviewed in some detail the series of statutes in which Congress has given the Executive broad discretion over the expenditure of appropriated funds. . . . It is argued that the Line Item Veto Act merely confers comparable discretionary authority over the expenditure of appropriated funds. The critical difference between this statute and all of its predecessors, however, is that unlike any of them, this Act gives the President the unilateral power to change the text of duly enacted statutes. None of the Act's predecessors could even arguably have been construed to authorize such a change.

VI

Although they are implicit in what we have already written, the profound importance of these cases makes it appropriate to emphasize three points.

First, we express no opinion about the wisdom of the procedures authorized by the Line Item Veto Act. Many members of both major political parties who have served in the Legislative and the Executive Branches have long advocated the enactment of such procedures for the purpose of "ensur[ing] greater fiscal accountability in Washington." H. R. Conf. Rep. 104–491, p. 15 (1996). The text of the Act was itself the product of much debate and deliberation in both Houses of Congress and that precise text was signed into law by the President. We do not lightly conclude that their action was unauthorized by the Constitution. . . .

Second, although appellees challenge the validity of the Act on alternative grounds, the only issue we address concerns the "finely wrought" procedure commanded by the Constitution. *INS v. Chadha* (1983). We have been favored with extensive debate about the scope of Congress' power to delegate law-making authority, or its functional equivalent, to the President. . . . [B]ecause we conclude that the Act's cancellation provisions violate Article I, s.7, of the Constitution, we find it unnecessary to consider the District Court's alternative holding that the Act "impermissibly disrupts the balance of powers among the three branches of government."

Third, our decision rests on the narrow ground that the procedures authorized by the Line Item Veto Act are not authorized by the Constitution. The Balanced Budget Act of 1997 is a 500-page document that became "Public Law 105–33" after three procedural steps were taken: (1) a bill containing its exact text was approved by a majority of the Members of the House of Representatives; (2) the Senate approved precisely the same text; and (3) that text was signed into law by the President. The Constitution explicitly requires that each of those three steps be taken before a bill may "become a law." Art. I, s.7. If one paragraph of that text had been omitted at any one of those three stages, Public Law 105–33 would not have been validly enacted. If the Line Item Veto Act were valid, it would authorize the President to create a different law—one whose text was not voted on by either House of Congress or presented to the President for signature. Something that might be known as "Public Law 105–33 as modified by the President" may or may not be desirable, but it is surely not a document that may "become a law" pursuant to the procedures designed by the Framers of Article I, s.7, of the Constitution.

If there is to be a new procedure in which the President will play a different role in determining the final text of what may "become a law," such change must come not by legislation but through the amendment procedures set forth in Article V of the Constitution.

The judgment of the District Court is affirmed.

Justice KENNEDY, concurring.

A nation cannot plunder its own treasury without putting its Constitution and its survival in peril. The statute before us, then, is of first importance, for it seems undeniable the Act will tend to restrain persistent excessive spending. Nevertheless, for the reasons given by Justice Stevens in the opinion for the Court, the statute must be found invalid. Failure of political will does not justify unconstitutional remedies.

I write to respond to my colleague Justice Breyer, who observes that the statute does not threaten the liberties of individual citizens, a point on which I disagree. The argument is related to his earlier suggestion that our role is lessened here because the two political branches are adjusting their own powers between themselves. To say the political branches have a somewhat free hand to reallocate their own authority would seem to require acceptance of two premises: first, that the public good demands it, and second, that liberty is not at risk. The former premise is inadmissible. The Constitution's structure requires a stability which transcends the convenience of the moment. The latter premise, too, is flawed. Liberty is always at stake when one or more of the branches seek to transgress the separation of powers.

Separation of powers was designed to implement a fundamental insight: concentration of power in the hands of a single branch is a threat to liberty. . . . So convinced were the Framers that liberty of the person inheres in structure that at first they did not consider a Bill of Rights necessary. It was at Madison's insistence that the First Congress enacted the Bill of Rights. It would be a grave mistake, however, to think a Bill of Rights in Madison's scheme then or in sound constitutional theory now renders separation of powers of lesser importance.

In recent years, perhaps, we have come to think of liberty as defined by that word in the Fifth and Fourteenth Amendments and as illuminated by the other provisions of the Bill of Rights. The conception of liberty embraced by the Framers was not so confined. They used the principles of separation of powers and federalism to secure liberty in the fundamental political sense of the term, quite in addition to the idea of freedom from intrusive governmental acts. The idea and the promise were that when the people delegate some degree of control to a remote central authority, one branch of government ought not possess the power to shape their destiny without a sufficient check from the other two. In this vision, liberty demands limits on the ability of any one branch to influence basic political decisions. . . .

It is no answer, of course, to say that Congress surrendered its authority by its own hand; nor does it suffice to point out that a new statute, signed by the President or enacted over his veto, could restore to Congress the power it now seeks to relinquish. That a congressional cession of power is voluntary does not make it innocuous. The Constitution is a compact enduring for more than our time, and one Congress cannot yield up its own powers, much less those of other Congresses to follow. Abdication of responsibility is not part of the constitutional design.

Separation of powers helps to ensure the ability of each branch to be vigorous in asserting its proper authority. In this respect the device operates on a horizontal axis to secure a proper balance of legislative, executive, and judicial authority. Separation of powers operates on a vertical axis as well, between each branch and the citizens in whose interest powers must be exercised. The citizen has a vital interest in the regularity of the exercise of governmental power. . . . By increasing the power of the President beyond what the Framers envisioned, the statute compromises the political liberty of our citizens, liberty which the separation of powers seeks to secure.

The Constitution is not bereft of controls over improvident spending. Federalism is one safeguard, for political accountability is easier to enforce within the States than nationwide. The other principal mechanism, of course, is control of the political branches by an informed and responsible electorate. Whether or not federalism and control by the electorate are adequate for the problem at hand, they are two of the structures the Framers designed for the problem the statute strives to confront. The Framers of the Constitution could not command statesmanship. They could simply provide structures from which it might emerge. The fact that these mechanisms, plus the proper functioning of the separation of powers itself, are not employed, or that they prove insufficient, cannot validate an otherwise unconstitutional device. With these observations, I join the opinion of the Court.

Justice SCALIA, with whom Justice O'CONNOR joins, and with whom Justice BREYER joins as to Part III, concurring in part and dissenting in part . . .

III

. . . I do not believe that Executive cancellation of this item of direct spending violates the Presentment Clause.

The Presentment Clause requires, in relevant part, that "[e]very Bill which shall have passed the House of Representatives and the Senate, shall, before it becomes a Law, be presented to the President of the United States. If he approve he shall sign it, but if not he shall return it," U.S.

Const., Art. I, s.7, cl. 2. There is no question that enactment of the Balanced Budget Act complied with these requirements: the House and Senate passed the bill, and the President signed it into law. It was only *after* the requirements of the Presentment Clause had been satisfied that the President exercised his authority under the Line Item Veto Act to cancel the spending item. Thus, the Court's problem with the Act is not that it authorizes the President to veto parts of a bill and sign others into law, but rather that it authorizes him to "cancel"—prevent from "having legal force or effect"—certain parts of duly enacted statutes. . . .

As much as the Court goes on about Art. I, s.7, therefore, that provision does not demand the result the Court reaches. It no more categorically prohibits the Executive *reduction* of congressional dispositions in the course of implementing statutes that authorize such reduction, than it categorically prohibits the Executive *augmentation* of congressional dispositions in the course of implementing statutes that authorize such augmentation—generally known as substantive rulemaking. There are, to be sure, limits upon the former just as there are limits upon the latter—and I am prepared to acknowledge that the limits upon the former may be much more severe. Those limits are established, however, not by some categorical prohibition of Art. I, s.7, which our cases conclusively disprove, but by what has come to be known as the doctrine of unconstitutional delegation of legislative authority: When authorized Executive reduction or augmentation is allowed to go too far, it usurps the nondelegable function of Congress and violates the separation of powers.

It is this doctrine, and not the Presentment Clause . . . that is the issue presented by the statute before us here. . . .

I turn, then, to the crux of the matter: whether Congress's authorizing the President to cancel an item of spending gives him a power that our history and traditions show must reside exclusively in the Legislative Branch. . . .

Insofar as the degree of political, "law-making" power conferred upon the Executive is concerned, there is not a dime's worth of difference between Congress's authorizing the President to *cancel* a spending item, and Congress's authorizing money to be spent on a particular item at the President's discretion. And the latter has been done since the Founding of the Nation. . . .

The short of the matter is this: Had the Line Item Veto Act authorized the President to "decline to spend" any item of spending contained in the Balanced Budget Act of 1997, there is not the slightest doubt that authorization would have been constitutional. What the Line Item Veto Act does instead—authorizing the President to "cancel" an item of spending—is technically different. But the technical difference does *not* relate to the technicalities of the

Presentment Clause, which have been fully complied with; and the doctrine of unconstitutional delegation, which *is* at issue here, is preeminently *not* a doctrine of technicalities. The title of the Line Item Veto Act, which was perhaps designed to simplify for public comprehension, or perhaps merely to comply with the terms of a campaign pledge, has succeeded in faking out the Supreme Court. The President's action it authorizes in fact is not a line-item veto and thus does not offend Art. I, s.7; and insofar as the substance of that action is concerned, it is no different from what Congress has permitted the President to do since the formation of the Union . . .

Justice BREYER, with whom Justice O'CONNOR and Justice SCALIA join as to Part III, dissenting.

I

. . . In my view the Line Item Veto Act does not violate any specific textual constitutional command, nor does it violate any implicit Separation of Powers principle. Consequently, I believe that the Act is constitutional.

II

I approach the constitutional question before us with three general considerations in mind. *First*, the Act represents a legislative effort to provide the President with the power to give effect to some, but not to all, of the expenditure and revenue-diminishing provisions contained in a single massive appropriations bill. And this objective is constitutionally proper.

When our Nation was founded, Congress could easily have provided the President with this kind of power. In that time period, our population was less than four million, federal employees numbered fewer than 5,000, annual federal budget outlays totaled approximately $4 million, and the entire operative text of Congress's first general appropriations law read as follows:

"Be it enacted . . . [t]hat there be appropriated for the service of the present year, to be paid out of the monies which arise, either from the requisitions heretofore made upon the several states, or from the duties on import and tonnage, the following sums, viz. A sum not exceeding two hundred and sixteen thousand dollars for defraying the expenses of the civil list, under the late and present government; a sum not exceeding one hundred and thirty-seven thousand dollars for defraying the expenses of the department of war; a sum not exceeding one hundred and ninety thousand dollars for discharging the warrants issued by the late board of treasury, and remaining unsatisfied; and a sum not exceeding ninety-six thousand dollars for paying the pensions to invalids."

At that time, a Congress, wishing to give a President the power to select among appropriations, could simply have embodied each appropriation in a separate bill, each bill subject to a separate Presidential veto.

Today, however, our population is about 250 million, the Federal Government employs more than four million people, the annual federal budget is $1.5 trillion, and a typical budget appropriations bill may have a dozen titles, hundreds of sections, and spread across more than 500 pages of the Statutes at Large. Congress cannot divide such a bill into thousands, or tens of thousands, of separate appropriations bills, each one of which the President would have to sign, or to veto, separately. Thus, the question is whether the Constitution permits Congress to choose a particular novel *means* to achieve this same, constitutionally legitimate, end.

Second, the case in part requires us to focus upon the Constitution's generally phrased structural provisions, provisions that delegate all "legislative" power to Congress and vest all "executive" power in the President. The Court, when applying these provisions, has interpreted them generously in terms of the institutional arrangements that they permit. See, e.g., *Mistretta v. United States* (1989).

Indeed, Chief Justice Marshall, in a well-known passage, explained,

"To have prescribed the means by which government should, in all future time, execute its powers, would have been to change, entirely, the character of the instrument, and give it the properties of a legal code. It would have been an unwise attempt to provide, by immutable rules, for exigencies which, if foreseen at all, must have been seen dimly, and which can be best provided for as they occur." *McCulloch v. Maryland* (1819).

This passage . . . calls attention to the genius of the Framers' pragmatic vision, which this Court has long recognized in cases that find constitutional room for necessary institutional innovation.

Third, we need not here referee a dispute among the other two branches . . .

These three background circumstances mean that, when one measures the *literal* words of the Act against the Constitution's *literal* commands, the fact that the Act may closely resemble a different, literally unconstitutional, arrangement is beside the point. To drive exactly 65 miles per hour on an interstate highway closely resembles an act that violates the speed limit. But it does not violate that limit, for small differences matter when the question is one of literal violation of law. No more does this Act literally violate the Constitution's words . . .

IV

. . . There are three relevant Separation of Powers questions here: (1) Has Congress given the President the wrong kind of power, i.e., "non-Executive" power? (2) Has Congress given the President the power to "encroach" upon Congress' own constitutionally reserved territory? (3) Has Congress given the President too much power, violating the doctrine of "nondelegation?" These three limitations help assure "adequate control by the citizen's representatives in Congress," upon which Justice Kennedy properly insists. And with respect to *this* Act, the answer to all these questions is "no."

A

Viewed conceptually, the power the Act conveys is the right kind of power. It is "executive. . . ." Conceptually speaking, it closely resembles the kind of delegated authority—to spend or not to spend appropriations, to change or not to change tariff rates—that Congress has frequently granted the President, any differences being differences in degree, not kind. . . .

If there is a Separation of Powers violation, then, it must rest, not upon purely conceptual grounds, but upon some important conflict between the Act and a significant Separation of Powers objective.

B

The Act does not undermine what this Court has often described as the principal function of the Separation of Powers, which is to maintain the tripartite structure of the Federal Government—and thereby protect individual liberty. . . .

. . . [O]ne cannot say that the Act "encroaches" upon Congress' power, when Congress retained the power to insert, by simple majority, into any future appropriations bill, into any section of any such bill, or into any phrase of any section, a provision that says the Act will not apply. Congress also retained the power to "disapprov[e]," and thereby reinstate, any of the President's cancellations. And it is Congress that drafts and enacts the appropriations statutes that are subject to the Act in the first place—and thereby defines the outer limits of the President's cancellation authority. Thus *this* Act is not the sort of delegation "without . . . sufficient check" that concerns Justice Kennedy. Indeed, the President acts only in response to, and on the terms set by, the Congress. . . .

Nor can one say the Act's grant of power "aggrandizes" the Presidential office. The grant is limited to the context of the budget. It is limited to the power to spend, or not to spend, particular appropriated items, and the power to permit, or not to permit, specific limited exemptions from generally applicable tax law from taking effect. . . . The delegation of those powers to the President may strengthen the Presidency, but any such change in Executive Branch authority seems minute when compared with the changes worked by delegations of other kinds of authority that the Court in the past has upheld.

C...

Indeed, the Court has only twice in its history found that a congressional delegation of power violated the "nondelegation" doctrine. One such case, *Panama Refining Co. v. Ryan* (1935), was in a sense a special case, for it was discovered in the midst of the case that the particular exercise of the power at issue, the promulgation of a Petroleum Code under the National Industrial Recovery Act, did not contain any legally operative sentence. The other case, *Schechter Poultry Corp. v. United States* (1935), involved a delegation through the National Industrial Recovery Act that contained not simply a broad standard ("fair competition"), but also the conferral of power on private parties to promulgate rules applying that standard to virtually all of American industry. As Justice Cardozo put it, the legislation exemplified "delegation running riot," which created a "roving commission to inquire into evils and upon discovery correct them."

The case before us does not involve any such "roving commission," nor does it involve delegation to private parties, nor does it bring all of American industry within its scope. It is limited to one area of government, the budget, and it seeks to give the President the power, in one portion of that budget, to tailor spending and special tax relief to what he concludes are the demands of fiscal responsibility. . . .

V

In sum, I recognize that the Act before us is novel. In a sense, it skirts a constitutional edge. But that edge has to do with means, not ends. The means chosen do not amount literally to the enactment, repeal, or amendment of a law. Nor, for that matter, do they amount literally to the "line item veto" that the Act's title announces. Those means do not violate any basic Separation of Powers principle. They do not improperly shift the constitutionally foreseen balance of power from Congress to the President. Nor, since they comply with Separation of Powers principles, do they threaten the liberties of individual citizens. They represent an experiment that may, or may not, help representative government work better. The Constitution, in my view, authorizes Congress and the President to try novel methods in this way. Consequently, with respect, I dissent.

Notes and Queries

1. Justice Stevens suggests that the Court did not base its ruling on the separation of powers principle; rather, it sought to rest its decision on "narrow ground," on the Presentment Clause. Would a decision based on the separation of powers principle have to be considered a broader ruling? Consider that in his concurring opinion in *INS v. Chadha*, Justice Powell urged the Court to decide the case on the "narrower ground" of separation of powers rather than on the Presentment Clause, which would produce a result the "breadth" of which "gives one pause." Are these cases so different that narrow and broad mean different things in relation to the separation of powers?

2. Justice Kennedy argues in his concurring opinion that "the separation of powers seeks to secure" the "liberty of our citizens." Does the line item veto threaten this liberty? If so, how?

3. Justice Breyer argues that the Line Item Veto Act serves to accommodate the "changing face of modern government" through adaptation rather than amendment. Justice Stevens, however, writes that the Line Item Veto Act establishes an entirely "new procedure" requiring an amendment to the Constitution. With whom do you agree? Do changes in governance require amending the Constitution rather than relying on judicial interpretation?

4. In *Morrison v. Olson*, Justice Scalia wrote in dissent advancing a strict separation of powers claim. How do you account for his broader view here? Is he inconsistent in giving Congress the latitude for granting discretion to the executive? Or is there something different about these circumstances that allows him to achieve opposite results with the same principle?

5. If, as Justices Breyer and Scalia argue, the authority granted the President under the Line Item Veto Act is indeed executive and not legislative in nature, can the Act still be found to violate the doctrine of separation of powers? On what grounds?

Chapter 5

Foreign Affairs and Constitutional Crises

I n this chapter we consider two topics of undoubted significance for the life of any constitutional democracy: the power to conduct foreign relations and the power to respond to emergencies and constitutional crises. At first glance, these might seem unlikely partners, but the problems they cause for constitutional democracy are quite similar. Moreover, as the sad events of 11 September 2001 remind us once again, threats to our collective safety come in a variety of dangerous forms. Whatever their character, though, crises always raise issues of intense constitutional conflict. One problem concerns the growth of presidential power and whether it can be squared with basic constitutional principles, such as the limitation and separation of power. A second problem concerns whether the terrible demands of war and crises can be met while maintaining our respect for constitutional principles.

First we consider the Constitution and foreign affairs. What falls under the rubric of "foreign affairs"? In the words of one scholar, foreign affairs and relations "constitute the relationship through which nations and their governments are bound together."[1] So defined, the topic covers a lot of ground. There are few issues of foreign affairs that do not also involve matters of commerce, or of federalism, or of the First Amendment and other civil liberties. Thus our study in this chapter will range across a wide variety of issues and topics.

Foreign affairs and constitutional crises are also inviting terrain for exploring the three perspectives—interpretive, normative, and comparative—we identified in the text's introduction. The interpretive theme, especially concerning questions about what the "Constitution" is and what it includes, are especially prominent in this chapter. One consequence of the Founders' failure to deal with foreign affairs at any length in the Constitution is that interpreters must make use of a great variety of nontextual sources. History and practice together, scattered with occasional quotes from the *Federalist Papers* and Madison's *Notes*, and even more infrequently with Supreme Court

---

[1] Carl J. Friedrich, *Constitutional Government and Democracy.* rev. ed. (Waltham: Blaisdell Publishing Company, 1950), 76.

opinions, provide us with the raw materials for interpretation. No student can fully understand the constitutional dimensions of foreign affairs without an appreciation of the ways in which past contests between presidents and congresses supplement the written word.[2]

Questions about what to interpret typically overlap with questions about who should interpret. We have stressed that constitutional interpretation is not coextensive with judicial interpretation. In the field of foreign affairs, especially, constitutional interpretation is not the "peculiar province" of the Supreme Court. Indeed, the Court has tended to avoid these questions, claiming lack of constitutional authority and practical expertise. The Court has used a variety of devices, such as standing, ripeness, mootness, and especially the political questions doctrine (see chapter 3), to explain its unwillingness to oversee inter-branch conflict.

The kinds of issues we have labeled "normative" also figure prominently here. We have seen in the past few chapters that the separation and distribution of power—concisely but misleadingly summed up in the phrase "checks and balances"—is a central feature of the constitutional order. The weedy growth of presidential power in the field of foreign affairs has put this principle to its strongest test. The rise of the "imperial presidency" forces us to reexamine assumptions we might otherwise take for granted. Why separate power, for example? What do we gain and at what expense? Additionally, and perhaps counterintuitively, foreign affairs issues also raise important questions about federalism, or about the horizontal distribution of power. Together, these two doctrines raise a single question: Is it possible to share power, or do the demands of foreign affairs require that the nation speak with a single, authoritative voice?[3]

Another of our recurrent themes is the tension between constitutionalism's regard for individual liberty and the democratic impulse to majoritarian politics. War highlights this tension in disturbing ways. It is often said that the first casualty of war is civil liberty. As we have suggested, the topic of foreign affairs and constitutional crises is especially useful for students of liberal arts because it forces us to confront issues of political theory and morality that we usually sidestep in other areas. To respect or to suspend the Constitution, to ignore it or to interpret it—these are ultimately questions of political morality, character, and identity. They ask us to define who we are as a people, what we believe, and why we believe it. War, observed Heraclitus, is the father of all things. If that is true, then it is also true that the demands of war pose fundamental challenges to the maintenance of constitutional democracy, demands as real in our time as they were for the Founders.[4]

---

[2] Louis Henkin, *Foreign Affairs and the Constitution.* (New York: W.W. Norton & Company, 1975), vii, 3–4.

[3] This question applies with equal force to the division of authority between the federal government and the states. In the recent case of *American Insurance Association et al. v. Garamendi* (2003), the Supreme Court struck down a California law that was intended to help Holocaust survivors collect on insurance policies issued to Jews before and during the Second World War. Writing for a 5 to 4 majority, Justice Souter concluded that the state effort was unconstitutional because it interfered with the president's authority to make executive agreements and to conduct international diplomacy. "The basic fact," the Court concluded, "is that California seeks to use an iron fist where the President has consistently chosen kid gloves. . . . [O]ur thoughts on the efficacy of the one approach versus the other are beside the point, since our business is not to judge the wisdom of the National Government's policy; dissatisfaction should be addressed to the President or, perhaps, Congress."

[4] See, e.g., John E. Finn, *Constitutions in Crisis: Political Violence and the Rule of Law.* (New York: Oxford University Press, 1991); Carl J. Friedrich, *Constitutional Reason of State: The Survival of the Constitutional Order.* (Providence: Brown University Press, 1957); Clinton Rossiter, *Constitutional Dictatorship.* (Princeton: Princeton University Press, 1948).

The Constitutional Basis and Structure of Foreign Affairs Powers

Separated and Shared Powers

Perhaps because they were intent on separating power, the Founders did not include in the constitutional document a general or comprehensive power to conduct foreign affairs. The Constitution does, however, include several provisions that relate directly to issues of foreign affairs. The most obvious of these is Article I, Section 8, which gives Congress the power "To declare War," as well as the powers to provide for the common defense and general welfare, to raise and support armies, to provide and maintain a navy, and to define and punish offenses against the law of nations. In contrast, Article II makes the president the commander in chief, as well as gives him or her the power (with the advice and consent of the Senate) to make treaties. Thus the war power, broadly defined as the power to declare, to make, and to conclude war, is both separated and shared between the legislative and executive branches. There is nothing unique here. As we saw in earlier chapters, the American constitutional order is less a system of strictly separated power than one of shared powers and separate institutions.[5]

An Invitation to Struggle: Contests for Power Between Congress and the President

A few specific provisions aside, then, the Constitution is more notable for its silence than for its clarity concerning foreign affairs. In the words of one student, "The principal difficulty has been that, from the beginning, the compromises, irresolutions, oversights, and intentional silences of the Constitution left it unclear who had sail and who had rudder, and, most important, where is command."[6] The text tells us who may make treaties, for example, but it says nothing about who may break or cancel them. Similarly, the text tells us Congress has power to declare war, but it says nothing about when the president, as commander in chief, may utilize troops without prior legislative approval.

The consequence of this silence is ongoing confusion and conflict between the branches, especially between Congress and the president. The Constitution is, in the words of the great scholar Edward Corwin, "an invitation to a struggle for the privilege of directing American foreign policy."[7] The history of that struggle begins as early as the administration of George Washington, when, in 1793, the President issued a proclamation of neutrality in the hostilities between France and Great Britain. In response, James Madison (with Jefferson, Madison favored the French) complained publicly that the decision should be the joint responsibility of Congress and the president. In this case, Madison argued, joint responsibility was required because the constitutional text had committed to Congress the power to declare war, plainly a first cousin to the power to declare neutrality.

Writing as Pacificus, Hamilton defended Washington's decision, justifying "the right of the Executive . . . to determine the condition of the nation, though it may . . .

---

[5] Richard E. Neustadt, *Presidential Power*. rev. ed. (New York: John Wiley, 1976), 101.

[6] Ibid., at 271.

[7] Edward S. Corwin, *The President: Office and Powers*. 4th rev. ed. (New York: New York University Press, 1957), 171.

affect the exercise of the power of the legislature to declare war. . . . The legislature is still free to perform its duties, according to its own sense of them. . . . The division of the executive power in the Constitution creates a *concurrent* authority in the cases to which it relates."[8] For his part, President Washington vowed in frustration that he "would be damned if he would be found in that place [the Senate] again. . . ."[9]

The Growth of the Imperial Presidency in Foreign Affairs

Whatever the Founders may have intended about shared authority and collective decision-making, the president dominates foreign relations in the United States. Presidents make war, negotiate and abrogate treaties, enter into executive agreements, and generally represent American interests in the international community. The tremendous growth of presidential power was made possible in part by the division of authority contained in the constitutional text, but it was not an inevitable result of constitutional architecture. Instead, the swell has been a consequence of the Constitution's plasticity and, no less important, the demands of modern warfare and the dizzying pace of technological change.

The very language of Article II, the source of executive authority, best exemplifies the Constitution's ambiguity. The first sentence of Article II states, "The executive power shall be vested in a President of the United States." Beyond this, however, the text has little to add. The remainder of Article II is a simple and short laundry list of specific powers that make up the "executive power" vested in the presidency. These powers include the position as commander-in-chief (itself a term whose meaning provokes argument), the power to execute the laws, the power to make treaties with the advice and consent of the Senate, to appoint ambassadors, and the responsibility to protect and defend the Constitution.

This skeletal structure stands in sharp contrast to Article I in two important ways. First, the catalog of powers entrusted to Congress, in comparison to those listed in Article II, is both long and comprehensive. Second, and of greater importance, one cannot find in Article II an explicit counterpart to Article I's necessary and proper clause. You will see that in *McCulloch v. State of Maryland* (1819, reprinted in chapter 6), that the necessary and proper clause has been an important source of "implied" legislative powers. The absence of a similar clause in Article II, coupled with the relatively sparse explicit grants of power, has led some students to conclude that Article II faithfully reflects the Founders' fears of expansive executive power. In the words of Daniel Webster, "I do not, therefore, regard the declaration that the executive power shall be vested in a President as being any grant at all; any more than the declaration that the legislative power shall be vested in Congress constitutes, by itself, a grant of such power."[10]

On the other hand, some folks argue the first sentence of Article II literally vests in the presidency all of those powers that fall under the general rubric of "executive power." John Marshall, speaking not as chief justice but as a member of the House of Representatives, similarly argued, "The President is the sole organ of the nation in its external relations, and its sole representative with foreign nations."[11] On this understanding, Article II is an expansive, general grant of power to direct foreign

---

[8] A. C. Hamilton, *Works,* Letters of Pacificus, #1 (New York, J. F. Trow, Printer, 1851), 7:76, 82–83.

[9] As quoted in Malcom M. Feeley & Samuel Krislov, *Constitutional Law.* (Glenview: Scott, Foresman), 89.

[10] *The Works of Daniel Webster.* 4 (17th ed., 1877), 186. Or, he might have added, of Article III, which provides that "The judicial Power of the United States, shall be vested in one supreme Court."

[11] 10 Annals of Congress 613 (1800).

affairs. Moreover, some proponents of presidential power have argued the president may also act even in those areas the text assigns to Congress, presumably because such grants are not entrusted *only* to Congress. Unless Congress has chosen to use its power, and in ways that are plainly opposed to the president's use of the same power, the president is free to act. President Lincoln accordingly argued that his decision to suspend the writ of habeas corpus was constitutionally proper, even though, as Chief Justice Taney observed in *Ex Parte Merryman* (1861), the location of the power in Article I implies that it is entrusted to Congress. In addition, some presidents have argued they possess an "inherent" power, sometimes called the power of prerogative, to take whatever action is necessary to protect the Union and the Constitution (though they are not necessarily one and the same or of equal weight, as Lincoln observed).

Scholarly debate has done little to resolve the conflict between these two very different understandings of Article II or the different visions of the relationship between Congress and the President that animate them. But the verdict of history is undeniable: With each decade the predominance of the executive in foreign affairs has become more complete. At least one scholar has thus concluded that the "history of the presidency is a history of aggrandizement. . . ."[12] The reasons for presidential dominance are not hard to find. As we saw in *Federalist* 70, the institutional structure of the presidency is highly conducive to leadership in a field, like foreign relations, that demands expediency, secrecy, diplomacy, political will, and "energy." In this sense, the Constitution enabled the growth of presidential power. The reasons for the expansion, however, lie in the growth of the United States as an international power and the persistence of international conflict. It is only a small exaggeration to claim that every war or armed squabble in which the United States has been engaged has resulted in the growth of presidential power.

The War Powers Resolution
Congress has alternately facilitated and challenged the rise of the imperial presidency. In 1964, President Lyndon B. Johnson sought and received from an all too willing Congress a blank check to escalate the undeclared war in Vietnam. The Tonkin Gulf Resolution authorized the president "to take all necessary measures to repel any armed attack against the forces of the United States and to prevent further aggression" by the Communist regime in Vietnam.

In 1973, Congress tried to reassert its constitutional authority by passing the War Powers Resolution over President Nixon's veto. The War Powers Resolution claims to be an effort to "fulfill the intent of the framers of the Constitution of the United States and ensure that the collective judgment of both the Congress and the President will apply to the introduction of United States Armed Forces into hostilities. . . ." The Resolution seeks to buttress congressional power by requiring the president to consult with Congress before putting American troops into hostilities "or into situations where imminent involvement in hostilities" is likely. If the president cannot consult in advance of such action, then he or she must report to Congress within forty-eight hours, and must terminate the action within sixty days of that report. Congress may extend the deadline by thirty days, or it may choose to authorize the continued use of American troops. The Resolution also permits Congress to call back the troops by a joint resolution not subject to presidential veto.

The Resolution raises important issues of constitutional theory. Many critics con-

---

[12] Edward Corwin, *The President*. 5th ed. (New York: New York University Press, 1984), 29–30.

tend that it unconstitutionally infringes upon the president's power as commander-in-chief and that it conflicts with the Court's decision in *INS v. Chadha* (1983, reprinted in chapter 4). Decisions about when to commit to troops, or when to withdraw them and why, these critics argue, are the very essence of the powers entrusted to a commander-in-chief.[13] On the other hand, the Resolution's proponents see in it, first, a renewed sense of congressional responsibility and second, a reiteration of the principle of separation of powers and collective decision-making.

In August 1990, President George H.W. Bush decided to send troops to Kuwait. The decision revived long-standing arguments about the power of the president to make war without congressional approval.[14] Fifty-four members of the House of Representatives immediately filed suit in a United States District Court, asking it to enjoin the President's decision to send troops. Judge Harold Greene rejected the request, but he did note, in language reminiscent of Madison's complaints, that "If the executive had the sole power to determine that any particular offensive military operation, no matter how vast, does not constitute war-making but only an offensive military attack, the congressional power to declare war will be at the mercy of a semantic decision by the Executive."[15]

More recently, in October 2002, President George W. Bush asked Congress for a formal resolution supporting "the use of all necessary means" to force Iraq to comply with United Nations resolutions authorizing the return of weapons inspectors to that country. President Bush was careful to note that he was *not* asking for—and did not believe he needed—congressional *approval* to use force. The request was not unlike the one President George H. W. Bush had requested just over a decade earlier. This time, however, the new resolution (reprinted later in the chapter) passed the two houses of Congress almost unanimously.

What are we to make of this continuing struggle? Two centuries of executive-legislative conflict in foreign affairs in general, and concerning the power to make war in particular, have yielded two certain truths. First, although the pendulum swings, the great trend has been toward the expansion of presidential power. Second, the constitutional text—and here text and history sing the same song—assigns no role to the judiciary in foreign affairs. With but a few exceptions, the Supreme Court has studiously avoided entering interbranch disputes over the allocation of foreign affairs powers. As this chapter's cases make clear, when the Court *has* acted, it has tended to support the growth of presidential power.

The Constitution in Crisis

The question of whether there are limits on presidential power to make war is part of a larger problem: Is it possible to square constitutionalism's insistence upon limited government with the demands of crises and emergencies? Alexander Hamilton thought not, writing in *Federalist* 23 that "The circumstances that endanger the safety of nations are infinite, and for this reason no constitutional shackles can wisely be imposed on the power to which the care of it is committed." Implicit in Hamilton's

---

[13] Robert H. Turner, *The War Powers Resolution: Unconstitutional, Unnecessary, and Unhelpful,* 17 Loyola of Los Angeles Law Review 683 (1984); Carter, *The Constitutionality of the War Powers Resolution,* 70 Virginia Law Review 101 (1984).

[14] See, for example, J. Gregory Sidak, *To Declare War,* 41 Duke Law Journal 27 (1991), and Harold Hongju Koh, *The Coase Theorem and the War Power: A Response,* 41 Duke Law Journal 124 (1991).

[15] *Dellums v. Bush,* 752 F.Supp. 1141 (D.D.C. 1990).

counsel is a frank recognition of the inherent fragility of constitutional democracy. As the terrible events of 11 September 2001 vividly demonstrate, no constitutional democracy is immune from crisis. All states must weather threats to their existence and well being, be they threats of international terrorism, war, economic instability, or crises of nature. In such cases, governments are rarely able to resist the call for emergency powers that reach far beyond what would otherwise be permissible. The United States is no exception in this regard, as we shall see when we review the USA Patriot Act and other legislative efforts to wage war on terrorism.

Crises are especially troublesome for a constitutional democracy because it is in them that the concept of limited power, so central to constitutional theory, seems of doubtful wisdom. Surely the first order of business when we are threatened must be survival and not, however glorious or principled it may appear in theory, respect for constitutional limits and parchment barriers. So, the first question we must face is perhaps the most basic and the most contentious: If it gets in the way, should we bother with the Constitution at all?

Crises and the Constitution

Nearly every constitution makes some kind of provision for crises and emergencies. The most direct provision in the United States Constitution is Article I, Section 9, which provides that in "Cases of Rebellion or Invasion" the writ of habeas corpus may be suspended if "the public safety may require it." But in contrast to almost all twentieth century constitutions, the American Constitution is largely silent on the issue of emergency powers. It says nothing about what constitutes a crisis or who determines if there is one. It does tell us that someone (presumably Congress) may suspend the writ of habeas corpus, but it says nothing about martial law, emergency or military courts, or of the suspension of elections or civil liberties.

How should we respond to a crisis? In the abstract, we have only a few options, and none of them are especially attractive. First, we might deny that there is any conflict between what necessity requires and what the Constitution permits. We can obviate the conflict between them in a number of ways. We might, for example, interpret the Constitution in ways that authorize whatever powers we think are required to resolve the crisis. Thus, we might read the Constitution to permit extensive restrictions on First Amendment freedoms if we think they are necessary to prosecute a war. Or, we might understand the Constitution to permit the president to suspend the writ of habeas corpus and to try civilians in military courts.

There are undoubtedly great advantages to using "interpretation" as a way to reconcile crises and the Constitution. By insisting that the Constitution governs all areas of our political life, we affirm our commitment to constitutional ideals, even though it may not always be possible to fully respect them. Furthermore, the continued applicability of constitutional rules and norms can provide a basis for citizens and other governmental officials to criticize and evaluate governmental policy. We thus retain a mechanism for ensuring accountability, among the most basic of constitutional ideals.

On the other hand, there are dangers with this approach as well. The first of these is one of practicality: If the Constitution may be interpreted to authorize whatever we need, whenever we need it, then what, if anything, will fall outside the pale? What are the limits to creative or expansive interpretation? The same objection has an important theoretical component as well. If we can interpret the Constitution in any way we like, what is its point? A constitution that is infinitely plastic is arguably a

Constitution that contains no limits on public power at all, arguably a contradiction in terms.[16]

A second alternative is to avoid conflict by simply ignoring the Constitution altogether. We might conclude, following Justice Jackson's dissent in *Korematsu v. United States* (1944, reprinted later in the chapter), that in some areas the Constitution does not and cannot apply. This, too, has the advantage of keeping the Constitution intact and in force (at least as regards some areas of public life), if at a subtle and dangerous cost. If the Constitution does not apply in a crisis, would it not be better, some critics ask, simply to acknowledge its limitations than to pretend there is no conflict?

A third alternative suggests we should squarely confront conflict and admit there are times when the Constitution is incompatible with the expansive governmental powers crises usually demand. This has the advantages of honesty and of maintaining respect for the integrity of constitutional ideals, instead of ignoring or warping them to fit our needs. This option, however—of suspending part or all of the Constitution—also has a terrible price. First, it means, or has seemed to mean to some scholars, that governmental power in times of emergencies is effectively without constitutional limits.[17] Second, we might wonder, having suspended the Constitution, when and if we will ever restore it. This is not an idle concern. Crises have long lives and experience teaches that governments are likely to find emergency powers addictive.

How Do Governments Respond to Crises?

At various times, all three of the approaches just described have been tried in the United States. Perhaps the most frequent course has been to ignore the Constitution. Consider, for example, the efforts of the Federal Bureau of Investigation to humiliate and discredit Martin Luther King Jr. and other leaders of the civil rights movements in the 1960s. Or earlier efforts between the two world wars to combat the "Red Menace." Whatever else may be said of the McCarthy hearings, a scrupulous regard for constitutional ideals was not one of their distinctive features.

As is true with the power of foreign affairs, the power to respond to crises has drifted to the executive branch. The growth of presidential power and the seeming inconsistency of limits on those powers raise a constitutional problem of the highest order. At least two theories have been advanced to reconcile the apparent conflict between our regard for constitutional limitations and the demands of crisis.

Inherent Powers and the Theory of Prerogative

The theory of prerogative power holds that the chief executive must have whatever authority is necessary to resolve a crisis that confronts the state. In the words of Arthur Schlesinger Jr., "Crises threatening the life of the nation have happily been rare. But, if such a crisis comes, a President must act. . . ." Consequently, he or she "must be conceded reserve power to meet authentic emergencies."[18] There are two questions we must address here. First, does the president in fact possess these pow-

---

[16] See Sotirios A. Barber, *On What the Constitution Means.* (Baltimore: Johns Hopkins University Press, 1984).

[17] One of the authors of this book has conceded the possibility of suspending the Constitution, but has insisted that constitutional democracies must still respect a set of "basic constitutional principles" that transcend individual constitutional texts. See Finn, supra note 4.

[18] Arthur M. Schlesinger, Jr., *The Imperial Presidency.* (New York: Doubleday, 1973), 17.

ers, sometimes called prerogative or inherent powers? Second, what, if any, are the limitations on these powers? The theory of prerogative dates at least from the time of the Roman Republic. Twice the Roman Senate dissolved itself and delegated the entire array of state power to Cincinnatus, an elderly farmer. On both occasions, Cincinnatus quashed the crisis and returned to his farm.[19] Thus the Republic was saved through the use of absolute and dictatorial power, the ends presumably justifying the means. The most complete modern statement of the doctrine is by John Locke, who wrote that the executive must always retain the residual power "to act according to discretion for the public good, without the prescription of the law and sometimes even against it." Hamilton's argument in *Federalist* 41 that emergency powers "ought to exist without limitation, because it is impossible to foresee or to define the extent and variety of the means which may be necessary to satisfy them" seconds Locke's observation.

American constitutional history is replete with examples of presidents who have claimed some sort of prerogative. Although he was an articulate opponent of expansive presidential power before he assumed office, Thomas Jefferson relied on some version of the theory early in his tenure in office. In 1803, presented with an opportunity to purchase the Louisiana Territory at a cut-rate price of fifteen million dollars, Jefferson searched the Constitution in vain for the authority to act. In a letter to John Breckenridge, he concluded, "The constitution has made no provision for our holding foreign territory, still less for incorporating foreign nations into our Union. The Executive in seizing the fugitive occurrence which so much advances the good of their country, have done an act beyond the Constitution."[20] Indeed, Jefferson was so convinced that the Constitution did *not* authorize him to act that he drafted a constitutional amendment that would have validated the purchase after the fact. Jefferson never acted on the amendment. He finally convinced himself he possessed the power he needed because he was obligated to protect the Union. "A strict observance of the written laws is doubtless *one* of the highest duties of a good citizen, but it is not the *highest*," he wrote in a letter to J. B. Colvin. "The laws of necessity, of self-preservation, of saving our country when in danger, are of higher obligation."[21] Hence, "a strict and rigid observation of the laws [in some cases] may do harm."[22]

Jefferson's precedent found a receptive audience in later administrations. The principle of prerogative received its most expansive treatment in the hands of President Lincoln. Lincoln's prosecution of the Civil War led him to take a number of truly extraordinary measures, such as suspending the writ of habeas corpus, calling up state militias, blocking Southern ports and harbors, and issuing the Emancipation Proclamation (which, following *Dred Scott v. Sandford* [1856] arguably took property without due process of law). None of these actions are authorized by the constitutional document. Nor were they authorized by statute, although Lincoln did later seek congressional approval for some of them. Explaining his actions to a Special Session of Congress, Lincoln argued that:

> I [understood] my oath to preserve the constitution to the best of my ability, imposed upon me the duty of preserving, by every indispensable means, that government— that nation—of which that constitution was the organic law. Was it possible to lose

---

[19] Rossiter, supra note 4, 15–19.

[20] Lyndan Ward, ed. The *Writings of Thomas Jefferson.* (Lunenburg, Vt., Stinehour Press, 1967) VIII, 244.

[21] Letter to J. B. Colvin, 20 September 1810.

[22] Finn, supra note 4, 17.

the nation, and yet preserve the constitution? . . . I felt that measures, otherwise unconstitutional, *might become lawful by becoming indispensable to the preservation of the constitution, through the preservation of the nation.*[23]

President Theodore Roosevelt advanced a somewhat narrower version of the doctrine, stating that

I declined to adopt the view that what was imperatively necessary for the Nation could not be done by the President unless he could find some specific authorization to do it. My belief was that it was not only his right but his duty to do anything that the needs of the Nation demanded unless such action was forbidden by the Constitution or the laws.[24]

Roosevelt's position seems to concede that there are some limits to the president's power, at least insofar as he may not act in ways that the Constitution explicitly forbids. The idea that there may be limits to the prerogative, however, is one that Locke and Lincoln would have denied.[25]

The Constitutional Limitations Theory

In stark contrast to the theory of prerogative, the constitutional limitations theory holds that any exercise of presidential power must be fairly traced—directly or by implication—to one of the grants enumerated in Article II. Best articulated by Chief Justice William Howard Taft (the only man to serve his country both as President and as Supreme Court justice), this position insists that any exercise of presidential power must ultimately find its source in the Constitution. "The true view of the Executive function is, as I conceive it, that the President can exercise no power which cannot be fairly and reasonably traced to some specific grant of power or justly implied and included within such express grant as proper and necessary to its exercise."[26] Hence, according to Taft, "There is no undefined residuum of power which [the President] can exercise because it seems to him to be in the public interest."[27]

Taft's position contends there are no inherent powers, free of constitutional shackles, that belong to the presidency. As you read the cases in this chapter, consider the following questions. Are Locke and Hamilton correct in their insistence that there can be no limits on the president's power to conduct war or to respond to emergencies? If no such limits exist, then in what sense, if any, can we say that such powers are consistent with constitutional democracy? Alternatively, is Taft right in claiming that the president's powers must be traceable to Article II? What limits might exist on those powers? What should a president do if he or she genuinely believes that some action—not sanctioned, or perhaps actually prohibited by the Constitution—is neces-

---

[23] John Nicolay and John Hays, eds., *The Complete Works of Abraham Lincoln.* Vol. 10 (New York: Francis D. Tandy, 1894), 65–68.

[24] Theodore Roosevelt, *Autobiography.* (New York: MacMillan, 1931), 38.

[25] Consider another version of the stewardship theory, this time offered by Franklin Delano Roosevelt: "I cannot tell what powers may have to be exercised to win this war. The American people can be sure that I will use my powers with a full sense of my responsibility to the Constitution and to my country. The American people can also be sure that I shall not hesitate to use every power vested in me to accomplish the defeat of our enemies in any part of the world where our own safety demands such defeat. When the war is won, the powers under which I act automatically revert to the people—to whom they belong." 88 Congressional Record 7044 (7 Sept. 1942).

[26] *Our Chief Magistrate and His Powers.* (New York: Columbia University Press, 1916), 139, 156–57.

[27] Ibid.

sary to save the nation? Finally, if there are limitations on the power of prerogative, then who has the authority to enforce them?

Judicial Review and Foreign Affairs

So far our discussion has concentrated on the president and Congress. The constitutional text gives no hint that the judiciary has any role to play in the area of foreign affairs. No student this far along is likely to find this omission surprising. What *is* different is that the Constitution's failure to define powers and responsibilities in the area of foreign affairs has militated strongly against *any* judicial involvement in the field. This is not to say that the Court has never acted. Still, this is an area of constitutional law and politics that has developed primarily without judicial supervision or involvement, in contrast, we shall see, to the experiences of Germany, Canada, and several other constitutional democracies.

Extraconstitutional Sources of Power

Some justices have gone so far as to suggest the field of foreign affairs has nothing to do at all with the Constitution, and hence nothing to do with judges. In the little known case of *Penhallow v. Dane* (1795), the Court addressed a conflict between two rival claimants to the legal title of a British ship seized by an American ship. Several of the justices suggested that the power to conduct war is entrusted to the national government as a principle of sovereignty. Consequently, the power to conduct war and foreign relations does not depend upon any specific provision in the Constitution.

The suggestion lingered about until 1936, when the Court heard a case that involved a challenge to a presidential proclamation that forbade the sale of arms to countries at war in South America. President Roosevelt's policy was based on a Joint Resolution of Congress, which had delegated to him the power to ban arm sales. The Curtiss-Wright Corporation was charged with selling arms to Bolivia and Paraguay, then involved in a border skirmish that eventually claimed over 100,000 lives.

Writing for the Court in *United States v. Curtiss-Wright Export Corp.* (1936, reprinted later in the chapter), Justice Sutherland sharply distinguished between the power to conduct domestic, or internal affairs, and the power to conduct foreign affairs. "The two classes of powers are different," he wrote, "both in respect of their origin and their nature. The broad statement that the federal government can exercise no powers except those specifically enumerated in the Constitution . . . is categorically true only in respect of our internal affairs." Elsewhere, reinforcing the point, Sutherland concluded "the powers to declare and wage war, to conclude peace, to make treaties, to maintain diplomatic relations, . . . if they had never been mentioned in the Constitution, would have vested in the federal government as necessary concomitants of nationality." In other words, following *Penhallow*, the source of these powers was not the Constitution, but rather the status of the United States as an independent and sovereign nation-state. Although the Court did not say so, this analysis is heavily grounded in history—Sutherland appealed repeatedly to the historical development of the nation—and in a particular political theory, that of nation-state nationalism. Can such an understanding be reconciled with the social contract theory of the founding, whether Lockean or Republican, we explored in earlier chapters?

By and large, the Court has declined to adopt the "attribute of sovereignty" theory proposed by Sutherland in *Curtiss-Wright*. But in one other respect—its assertion that "the President alone has the power to speak in this vast realm"—*Curtiss-Wright* is very much the norm. Only rarely has the Supreme Court challenged a presidential exercise of power. In *The Prize Cases* (1862, reprinted later in the chapter), for example, a majority of the Court concluded that the powers to blockade southern ports and to announce that the Southern states were in a condition of "belligerency" were entrusted to President Lincoln. The cases began when in April 1861, President Lincoln blockaded two Southern ports without seeking congressional approval. (Congress was not in session at the time.) In July, Lincoln called a special session of Congress to get approval for the blockade and for other actions he had taken on his own. In the meantime, Union forces had seized four Southern ships as prizes of war. The ships' owners filed suit, claiming the blockade proclamation, made without congressional authorization, was unconstitutional.

Writing for the majority, Justice Grier upheld the blockade and President Lincoln's decision to find the South in a state of belligerency, concluding "The President was bound to meet it in the shape it presented itself, without waiting for Congress to baptize it with a name. . . ." Concerning judicial responsibility, Grier wrote that "Whether the President is fulfilling his duties, as Commander in chief . . . is a question to be decided by him, and this court must be governed by the decisions and acts of the Political Department of the government to which this power was entrusted."

Justiciability and the Political Questions Doctrine

Justice Grier's reference to the "political departments" recalls the political questions doctrine. Many if not most of the issues involved in foreign affairs arguably are entrusted by the Constitution to the "political" branches. As we saw in chapter 3, the political questions doctrine reaches as far back as Chief Justice Marshall's opinion in *Marbury v. Madison* (1803), where he observed, "Questions in their nature political, or which are, by the constitution and laws, submitted to the executive, can never be made in this court. . . ." In *Baker v. Carr* (1962), the Court advanced an elaborate set of criteria to determine when a case raises a political question. In addressing the area of foreign relations, Justice Brennan admitted, "resolution of such issues frequently turn on standards that defy judicial application, or involve the exercise of a discretion demonstrably committed to the executive or legislature. . . ." Nevertheless, Brennan continued, not every case that "touches foreign relations lies beyond judicial cognizance."

In the seminal case of *Youngstown Sheet & Tube Co. v. Sawyer* (1952, reprinted in part in chapter 4 and later in this chapter), for example, the Court indicated that a president's claim of "war" is not always sufficient to ward off judicial scrutiny. *Youngstown* began with a threatened strike by the United Steel Workers. Fearing the strike would cripple the production of steel for the United States' war effort in Korea, President Truman issued an executive order directing his secretary of commerce to "seize" the mills and to ensure their continued operation. Under the seizure plan, the head of each plant became a "manager" under the direction of the United States government, although most of the technicalities of ownership, such as assets and liabilities, remained with the firms. Truman notified Congress of his action the next day. Congress did nothing. The owners, however, obtained an injunction against the seizure. The president won a stay of the injunction and asked the Court to grant certiorari. Just one month later the Court decided the case for the steel companies.

In his majority opinion, Justice Black wrote that Truman's action "must stem either from an Act of Congress or from the Constitution itself." No Act of Congress authorized the seizure, Black concluded, thus forcing the president to justify the seizure upon the basis of his constitutional authority. The majority concluded that the order could not be supported as an exercise of the power as commander-in-chief. In this case, at least, the "theater of war" did not extend so far as to encompass the power to take possession of private property. The majority likewise concluded that the president's aggregate of "executive" powers could not support the seizure, which was an exercise not of executive power but of the lawmaking power, plainly entrusted to Congress.

The majority opinion said little about the role of the judiciary in overseeing such conflicts. In his concurring opinion, Justice Frankfurter was more direct. "The Framers . . . did not make the judiciary the overseer of our government . . .", argued Frankfurter. "This eagerness to settle—preferably forever—a specific problem on the basis of the broadest possible constitutional pronouncements may not unfairly be called one of our minor national traits. . . . The path of duty for this Court, it bears repetition, lies in the opposite direction. . . . So here our first inquiry must not be into the powers of the President, but into the powers of a District Judge to issue a temporary injunction in the circumstances of this case."

In his influential concurring opinion, Justice Jackson also addressed the separation of powers issues involved in the case more forthrightly. "A judge, like an executive adviser," he wrote, "may be surprised at the poverty of really useful and unambiguous authority applicable to concrete problems of executive power as they actually present themselves." Noting that "the art of governing under our Constitution does not and cannot conform to judicial definitions," Jackson constructed a tripartite framework (see chapter 4) for considering the relationship between executive and congressional power. In the end, though, like Justice Frankfurter, Jackson acknowledged the limits of judicial power, much as he had in *Korematsu*. "I have no illusion," he concluded, "that any decision by this Court can keep power in the hands of Congress if it is not wise and timely in meeting its problems. . . . We may say that power to legislate for emergencies belongs in the hands of Congress, but only Congress itself can prevent power from slipping through its fingers."

Youngstown indicates that the political question doctrine is not an absolute bar to judicial intervention. In *Dellums v. Bush* (1990), U.S. District Judge Harold H. Greene reiterated the point, writing that "While the Constitution grants to the political branches . . . responsibility for conducting the nation's foreign affairs, it does not follow that the judicial power is excluded from the resolution of cases merely because they may touch upon such affairs."

When issues touch foreign affairs directly, however, the normal course is for the Court to keep to itself. On several occasions during the Viet Nam war the Court showed a reluctance to challenge the president, finding the plaintiffs lacked standing to sue or that the issues involved were political questions. In *Goldwater v. Carter* (1979, reprinted in chapter 3), the Court refused to consider a challenge to President Carter's decision to terminate our mutual defense treaty with Taiwan, again finding a political question. The hands-off policy was reiterated in the case of *Dames and Moore v. Regan* (1981). In this case, the Court upheld an order by President Carter, reaffirmed by President Reagan, which nullified the legal attachment of Iranian assets in United States banks that had been seized during the hostage crisis. Writing for the majority, Chief Justice Rehnquist noted that in this case, unlike in *Youngstown*, there was no evidence of congressional hostility to the President's actions. The action was therefore entitled to "the widest latitude of judicial interpretation."

War and Civil Liberties

No war or crisis—including the recent war on international terrorism—is long underway before there is a claim that some civil liberty, be it free speech, the right to property, or due process, is hampering the effort and must therefore be suspended or curtailed. In the Civil War, for example, the federal courts saw challenges to Lincoln's suspension of the writ of habeas corpus, which cleared the way for the military to try approximately 17,000 civilians in military courts. In 1861, Chief Justice Taney, serving as a circuit court judge in Baltimore (at the time, all of the Supreme Court justices also "rode circuit," or presided at circuit courts), received a petition of habeas corpus from John Merryman. Merryman, a civilian, had been arrested at his home by the military and charged with helping the confederate cause by blowing up several bridges. Taney issued the writ and ordered General George Cadwalader, the commander of Fort McHenry where Merryman was being held, to appear in court to explain the detention. Instead, Cadwalader sent a letter to Taney, in which he explained Merryman was suspected of treason. He justified the detention on the basis of President Lincoln's suspension of habeas corpus. In response, Taney ordered a federal marshal to arrest Cadwalader and to bring him to Court—a course of action destined to fail. Finally, in frustration, Taney wrote an opinion excoriating Lincoln, concluding that the provision in Article I regarding the suspension of habeas corpus clearly entrusted the power to Congress

> *in language too clear to be misunderstood by anyone. . . . I can see no ground whatever for supposing that the president, in any emergency, or in any state of things, can authorize the suspension of the privileges of the writ of habeas corpus . . . except in the aid of judicial power. . . . Nor can any argument be drawn from the nature of sovereignty, or the necessity of government, for self-defence in times of tumult and danger. The government of the United States is one of delegated and limited powers; it derives its existence and authority altogether from the constitution. . . .*

Taney's stinging rebuke of Lincoln is a manifesto for judicially enforceable limitations on presidential power, but it is worth considering Lincoln's response. Although he released Merryman, Lincoln staunchly ignored Taney. Later, in the special session of Congress, Lincoln defended the presidency's power of constitutional interpretation: "Now it is insisted that Congress, and not the Executive, is vested with [the power to suspend the writ.] But the Constitution itself, is silent as to which, or who, is to exercise the power. . . ." Elsewhere in the same speech, Lincoln offered a more direct challenge to Taney: "Are all the laws, *but one*, to go unexecuted, and the government itself go to pieces, lest that one be violated?" Lincoln did not invoke Locke or Jefferson by name, but he clearly defended the theory of prerogative they had promoted.

In another case, a majority of the Supreme Court aligned itself with Taney's opinion in *Merryman*. In *Ex Parte Milligan* (1866, reprinted later in the chapter), the Court was faced with a request for the writ by Lambdin P. Milligan, a civilian who had been sentenced to be hanged by a military court. In an opinion by Justice David Davis (who had helped to manage Lincoln's presidential campaign in 1864), the Court insisted that

> *The Constitution of the United States is a law for rulers and people, equally in war and in peace, and covers with the shield of its protection all classes of men, at all times, and under all circumstances. No doctrine, involving more pernicious consequences, was ever invented by the wit of man than that any of its provisions can be suspended during any of the great exigencies of government. . . . [T]he theory of necessity on which it is based is false; for the government, within the Constitution, has all the powers granted to it which are necessary to preserve its existence. . . .*

Notwithstanding this assertion of judicial power, consider two additional points. First, the Court's strong posture occurred in 1866, safely after the war was concluded. Second, even then the decision led to a direct confrontation with the Reconstruction Congress and led, ultimately, to the decision in *Ex Parte McCardle* (1868, reprinted in chapter 3). In *McCardle*, the Court upheld the constitutionality of a congressional statute that trimmed the Court's jurisdiction over habeas corpus cases. It was no secret that the statute was a slap on the Court's wrist by an angry Congress. The Court backed away from the challenge, noting, "We are not at liberty to inquire into the motives of the legislature. We can only examine into its power under the Constitution. . . ."

In the twentieth century impositions on individual liberty have been no less frequent or extensive. Many of these episodes are covered in other chapters. In chapters 12 and 13, for example, we shall consider a series of cases involving impositions on the freedoms of speech and religion justified on the basis of war. In this chapter we focus on cases that directly implicate the role of courts in mediating such conflicts, such as *Korematsu v. United States* (1944, reprinted later in the chapter), and *Zadvydas v. Davis* (2001, reprinted later in the chapter).

Korematsu began when the Japanese military invaded Pearl Harbor in 1941. A few months after the attack, a wide coalition of military, government, and civilian leaders began a campaign to intern Japanese and Japanese-Americans living on the West Coast. Ostensibly motivated by fear of espionage, the military, led by Commander General John L. DeWitt, asked the government to impose a curfew and later to intern Japanese-Americans in camps scattered throughout the West Coast. DeWitt's fears were unfounded, as he knew all too well: The FBI and the Office of Naval Intelligence had already concluded that any threat was at best minimal. Nevertheless, on 27 March 1942, President Roosevelt authorized the policy of internment.

Two years later, in the fall of 1944, Fred Korematsu—a Japanese-American citizen who did not report to the camps—was arrested by the police in Oakland, California. Fred gave a false name and a false address, but was easily found out and put in jail. With help from the American Civil Liberties Union, Fred appealed his conviction—and thus the constitutionality of internment—to the Supreme Court.

Writing for the majority, Justice Black upheld the program. Black began by noting that legal restrictions based on race are "immediately suspect" and subject "to the most rigid scrutiny." In this case, however, the legal restriction was based not on racial hostility to Japanese-Americans. If that were so, the Court said, "Our task would be simple." Instead, the policy was based on "pressing public necessity," at least as judged by the competent military authorities. "Here . . . we cannot reject as unfounded the judgment of the military authorities and of Congress. . . ."

In an impassioned dissent, Justice Murphy argued that the exclusion "Goes over 'the very brink of constitutional power' and falls into the ugly abyss of racism." Murphy conceded, "In dealing with matters relating to the prosecution and progress of war, we must accord great respect . . . to the judgments of the military authorities. . . ." Even so, Murphy continued, "it is essential that there be limits to military discretion. . . ." In another dissent, Justice Robert Jackson, later chief prosecutor at the Nuremberg war trials, added that "It would be impracticable and dangerous idealism to expect or insist that each specific military command . . . will conform to conventional tests of constitutionality. . . . The armed services must protect a society, not merely its Constitution. . . . But if we cannot confine military expedients by the Constitution, neither would I distort the Constitution to approve all that the military may deem expedient. . . ." Jackson's comments recall our discussion on pages 176–81 about how constitutional states should respond to emergencies. His suggestion that it is better not to distort the Constitution's meaning by approving everything the military deems expedient reflects a profound concern about the dangers of making the Constitution mean whatever it has to mean in an emergency.

Like President Lincoln's suspension of the writ of habeas corpus during the Civil War, *Korematsu* raises profoundly important and distressing questions about our commitment to civil liberties and whether it can be squared with the demands of war. The Court's recent decision in *Zadvydas v. Davis* (2001, reprinted later in the chapter), raises similar issues, but leaves still others unresolved. Zadvydas was a German citizen who was a resident alien in the United States. He had a criminal record, for which he was ordered deported back to Germany. Germany, however, refused to accept him, so Zadvydas was detained indefinitely in American custody. He challenged the detainment, arguing that indefinite detainment would violate the Fifth Amendment.

Writing for the majority, Justice Breyer agreed, concluding that indefinite detainment raises a "serious constitutional problem." Although it acknowledged that "ordinary principles of judicial review in this area recognize primary Executive Branch responsibility," the Court concluded "that courts can take appropriate account of such matters without abdicating their legal responsibility to review the lawfulness of an alien's continued detention." In dissent, Justice Kennedy complained loudly that the Court had "rush[ed] to substitute a judicial judgment for the Executive's discretion and authority."

The same debate over the limits of judicial and Executive authority was replayed two years later in *Demore v. Kim* (2003). In this case, however, concerning the constitutionality of the deportation of a lawful permanent resident alien, the Court stressed the need to defer to the judgment of the political branches. Although the majority admitted that permanent resident aliens have due process rights, the Court reviewed in some detail the factors and evidentiary findings that had led Congress to permit deportations in such cases. It distinguished *Zadvydas,* arguing that *Demore* was different in two substantial respects. First, in *Zadvydas* continued detention no longer served the stated goal and so was no longer practicable. In *Demore*, however, continued detention of an alien was directly related to the end—to prevent flight. Second, the Court noted that in *Demore* and similar cases the length of detention was ordinarily less than three months, whereas the detention in *Zadvydas* was indefinite and "potentially permanent."

Zadvydas and *Demore* are especially important for what they say about the relationship between the executive and the judiciary. Our study of war and civil liberties, then, much as our study earlier of foreign affairs and the growth of presidential power, is at a bottom an inquiry into the limits of judicial power and the price of constitutional ideals. And it is an inquiry as timely and as important now as it was a half-century ago.

The Constitution and the War on Terrorism

The events of 11 September 2001 have had a profound effect on American society. Among them are pervasive, far-reaching changes in the law. Within just weeks of the attacks, the attorney general of the United States had proposed and Congress had enacted a number of important changes to the law, including provisions that have greatly altered the legal rules governing such important areas as search and seizure, wiretaps, and the due process rights of aliens. The Attorney General also announced new, relaxed regulations concerning the FBI's authority to conduct domestic spying.

The centerpiece of the administration's response to international terrorism is the

USA Patriot Act (2001). Passed by Congress within one week of the attacks, the Act makes changes in some fifteen different federal statutes. For example, in the area of search and seizure, the Act gives law enforcement authorities broad new powers to conduct "sneak and peak" searches.[28] Another section of the Act expanded the FBI's authority to gain access to personal records. Although this may sound innocuous, in practice it means the FBI can force librarians to disclose what books a patron has checked out or a clerk to disclose what an individual purchased at a bookstore. Similar provisions now permit law enforcement agencies to conduct domestic spying operations, even against groups and individuals not suspected of criminal wrongdoing. The FBI, for example, may compile records of who attends the meetings of local churches or political meetings. There is no requirement that the individual or the organization be informed of these investigations. It is important to note that most of these new powers are not limited to investigations of terrorist activity, but instead apply to any and all criminal activity.

Another provision of the Patriot Act authorizes the secret detention of noncitizens based on the attorney general's uncertified, and presumably judicially unreviewable assertion that he has "reasonable grounds to believe" that a person is a threat to the national security of the United States. If a noncitizen is detained on grounds of suspected terrorism, the government must bring charges or begin deportation proceedings within seven days.

In addition to the USA Patriot Act, the administration took a number of other important steps in the war on terrorism in the weeks following the September attacks. Among the most controversial was President Bush's decision to authorize the creation of military tribunals to try noncitizen "suspected terrorists." The proposal met with intense criticism, and was slightly modified in response. As currently formulated, the commissions may try suspected terrorists under substantially relaxed rules of evidence and on penalty of death. These rules provide, among other things, that the prosecution may withhold "sensitive" evidence, that the tribunal may operate in secret and extraterritorially, and that a defendant may not appeal to a civilian court. (He or she may, however, file an appeal with the president—the same individual who ordered him detained.) In addition, the administration has argued that such defendants are not prisoners of war, but are rather "unprivileged enemy combatants." The nomenclature is important. Enemy belligerents are entitled to none of the protections of the Bill of Rights. They may be held indefinitely, and have no right to an attorney.

In drafting these proposals, the administration observed that there was some precedent for military commissions in the notable case of *Ex Parte Quirin* (1942, reprinted later in the chapter). In 1942, eight Nazi soldiers arrived on submarines and landed in New York and Florida to commit acts of sabotage. Upon their arrest by the FBI, the Attorney General placed them in the custody of the Secretary of War, to be tried by a military commission created by presidential order. They challenged the order as unconstitutional, denying that the president had constitutional or statutory authority to create the military commission. Consequently, a trial by a military commission would violate their Fifth and Sixth Amendment rights to trial by civilian courts and with the other safeguards contained in those amendments.

---

[28] A sneak and peak search allows federal agents to enter a suspect's home or place of work, and to seize materials they find, without giving prior notice to the suspect, provided they can show "reasonable necessity" for the search. This new standard of "reasonable necessity" is considerably more relaxed than the old standard of probable cause. In addition, under the old rules, government agents were required to give notice of a search and obtain a warrant.

In his opinion for the Court, Justice Stone began by noting that "We are not concerned with any question of the guilt or innocence" of the petitioners. Passing to the merits, Stone concluded that the president did have the authority to create the military commissions, but the Court stressed that it "had no occasion now to define with meticulous care the ultimate boundaries of the jurisdiction of military tribunals to try persons according to the law of war." Whether *Quirin* provides substantial support for President Bush's order is a matter of dispute. Some scholars note that the defendants in *Quirin did* have access to lawyers and to an appeal to a civilian court; such rights do not exist in the current tribunals. Moreover, *Quirin* was decided before the 1949 Geneva Conventions, which has elaborate rules governing military trials. As we go to press, there are several lawsuits challenging different aspects of the new regulations in the lower federal courts.

Ultimately, however, the constitutional questions that surround military commissions, and the USA Patriot Act, are less about fidelity to precedents than to principles. The Patriot Act and other legislative responses in the war on terrorism raise issues of the highest order for citizens and students alike. As is always the case in times of war and emergency, the trend among recent statutory efforts has been to concentrate power in the executive branch, typically at the expense of legislative and judicial accountability. The Founders might have predicated as much—Hamilton, for example, knew all too well that the exigencies of crisis demand swift and energetic action. Only the executive, he observed, could be expected to act with that kind of resolve and dispatch. "Energy in the executive is . . . essential to the protection of the community against foreign attacks."[29] But can we achieve that unity of purpose and swiftness of action without sacrificing our commitment to the principles of separation of powers and the need for democratic accountability? And consider, too: Where should we strike the balance between our need for security and our constitutional commitment to liberty? And no less fundamental: Who should strike that balance? Is there a role for Congress and the judiciary to play in considering such questions? As we go to press in the fall of 2003, the Supreme Court has agreed to take up some of these questions in two important cases that concern the legality of indefinite detentions. The litigants are all citizens of foreign countries. Some have been imprisoned for as long as two years at the U.S. Navy base in Guantanamo Bay, Cuba, without access to lawyers or family. At issue is whether U.S. courts have jurisdiction to intervene in such cases, and whether under such circumstances their detentions violate constitutional and international law. In an *amicus curiae* brief filed on behalf of Fred Korematsu (see *Korematsu v. United States,* 1944, reprinted later in the chapter), Professor Geoffrey Stone wrote that the plaintiffs are being held "without any fair hearing to determine guilt or innocence, without the assistance of counsel and without any meaningful judicial review." In contrast, the Department of Justice has argued that the men are foreign prisoners of war held beyond American borders, and thus beyond the reach of the Constitution's protections.

Finally, among the most alarming of threats to constitutional liberty posed by the war on terrorism may be the alacrity with which the measures were passed. The USA Patriot Act was passed within a week of the terrible events of September 11, leaving little time for congressional or public debate. Similarly, many of the regulations announced by the Department of Justice to govern the detention and trial of noncitizen detainees were made unilaterally and are not subject to review by other constitutional actors. At risk in such actions is perhaps the ultimate constitutional value—our tradi-

---

[29]Clinton Rossiter, ed. *The Federalist Papers.* #70. (New York: New American Library, 1961), 423.

tion of transparency in government and the consequent possibility of earnest, impassioned public debate over issues central to the constitutional life of the community.

Comparative Perspectives

The experiences of other constitutional democracies in dealing with foreign affairs and war is especially rich, in part because many of them, such as Ireland, Germany, Italy, and Canada, have constitutions that are the literally the products of war and crises. Unlike their American counterpart, most twentieth century constitutions treat these issues at length and in detail. The practice has been to follow the counsel of Machiavelli, who wrote that "[N]o republic will ever be perfect if she has not by law provided for everything, having a remedy for every emergency and fixed rules for applying it."[30]

The influence of American constitutional ideals regarding foreign affairs has also been considerable, in no small part because Americans have "participated" in the restructuring of several constitutional states, such as Germany and Japan. Sometimes this influence extended to the inclusion of specific institutions and articles. In Germany and Japan, for example, American policymakers insisted upon some kind of a supreme court with powers of constitutional review. And in both countries, Americans insisted upon the inclusion of "renunciation-of-war" clauses. Article 9 of the Japanese Constitution thus pledges that "Aspiring sincerely to an international peace based on justice and order, the Japanese people forever renounce war as a sovereign right of the nation and the threat or use of force as a means of settling international disputes."

At a general level, the influence of American constitutionalism has more to do with general norms and principles than with specific statements of policy or with the design of institutions. In the field of foreign affairs, the Founders' insistence upon principles of deliberation and accountability has been especially influential. A comparative analysis of foreign affairs and crises shows considerable variation in how various countries have attempted to realize those common ideals.

The Founders were committed to the principle that politics, and not military force, must be the primary mechanism of constitutional change in a democracy. To that end, they concluded that the powers of foreign affairs must be subject to civilian control and public accountability. Sharing powers and separating institutions were the means to accomplish that end. There is room for doubt about whether that vision has been achieved in the United States. The unchecked growth of executive power, coupled with a servile Congress and a judiciary unwilling to mediate conflict or to impose substantive limits on the president's powers, raises questions about whether there are any effective, constitutionally derived, limits on the executive's power to conduct foreign relations and to make war.

A comparative perspective, however, suggests that other constitutional democracies have succeeded, at least in part, on making good on the principle of democratic accountability. As one observer notes, "The techniques of accountability surely do vary—some techniques are embodied in written constitutions and other formal instruments, while others are unwritten or informal . . . ; some do and some do not

---

[30] Niccolo Machiavelli, *Discourses*, trans. and ed. by Bernard Crick (Harmondsworth, Eng.: Penguin Books, 1970), ch. 34.

include control through constitutional courts or other judicial bodies."[31] Although constitutions vary widely in designing methods to control the exercise of foreign affairs, the experiences of South Africa, Canada, Japan and Germany, for example, indicate that the principle of shared legislative and executive decision making can be made to work effectively.

Moreover, and perhaps in starkest contrast to American constitutional history, the experiences of these countries indicate that there may be a prominent role for constitutional courts to play in the area of foreign relations. If one of the purposes of comparative analysis is to find out what works, then Americans should pay especial attention to how other countries have tried to realize the shared ideal of deliberative decision making and public accountability. The task is complicated, however, by the lack of serious scholarship in this area. As Professor Damrosch has observed, this is an area "almost entirely ignored in comparative legal scholarship."[32]

Foreign Affairs and the German Basic Law

Like Article 9 of the Japanese Constitution, the Basic Law establishes a policy against war as a constitutional norm. Designed to facilitate Germany's peaceful inclusion in a stable international order, Article 26 provides that "Acts tending to and undertaken with the intent to disturb the peaceful relations between nations, especially to prepare for aggressive war, shall be unconstitutional." Other provisions explicitly call for the German state to participate in international arbitration and systems of mutual collective security.

The Basic Law also seeks to hold the powers of foreign affairs to a principle of accountability by simultaneously sharing and separating power. Hence, Article 32 gives to the federation the power to conduct foreign relations, although it conditions it with requirements to protect the *Länder* that far exceed any of the protections that American states receive. Article 59 gives to the President of the Republic the power to represent the state in international relations, a power that includes the authority to conclude treaties, albeit in conjunction with various state authorities. In deliberate contrast to the Weimar Republic (where the president could dismiss the Chancellor and authorize the use of expansive emergency powers), however, the great burden of executive power falls to the Prime Minister, or Chancellor, nominated by the president but chosen by the Bundestag. Thus the German system is best understood as a parliamentary, or chancellor democracy, in contrast to the presidentialism of the United States.

Article 73(1) further separates power by providing that the Federation has exclusive power to legislate regarding foreign affairs. Article 73(4) gives the Federation authority over treaties on commerce and navigation, and 73(10) power over the protection of the democratic order and the existence and security of the Federation.

In general, then, the Basic Law embodies the fundamental constitutional principle of separation of powers and embraces the principle of democratic accountability. In contrast to the United States, however, these principles are given force by a judiciary that does not hesitate to apply them. As we saw, the United States Supreme Court uses a variety of procedural devices and doctrines to avoid disputes, the most promi-

---

[31] Lori Fisler Damrosch, *Constitutional Control Over War Powers: A Common Core of Accountability in Democratic Societies?* 50 U. Miami Law Review 181, 183 (1995). Our analysis here has been heavily influenced by Professor Damrosch's pioneering article.

[32] Ibid.

nent of which is the political questions doctrine. In Germany, the doctrine has considerably less force, in part because the creators of the Federal Constitutional Court gave it expansive and far reaching authority to resolve constitutional conflicts. As one of the authors of this book has observed,

> *The Court's main task, especially with regard to direct conflicts between levels and branches of government and to separation of powers conflicts, is to clarify constitutional meaning . . . and to lay down clear rules. . . . Indeed, the Constitutional Court was established precisely to resolve disputes that the American Supreme Court would dismiss as "political." . . .*[33]

With no political question doctrine to hem it in, the Constitutional Court has developed an extensive body of case law in the area of foreign affairs. In a series of cases involving the installation of American intermediate range nuclear missiles, the Court addressed issues of critical significance to German foreign relations. In the *Missile Decision I* case, the Court heard a challenge that the decision to deploy nuclear missiles on German territory violated Article 2(2) of the Basic Law, which guarantees the right to life. Although the Court finally dismissed the complaint because "it has not been shown that there can be a possible injury to [the complainant's] lives and health . . . ," the decision was a function of its finding that the threat was from the action of foreign governments and not, as might be expected in the United States, on grounds that the matter was "political" and therefore out of bounds.[34]

In recent years a prominent source of political conflict in Germany has concerned the issue of whether the Basic Law permits units of the armed forces to participate in United Nations sanctioned peace-keeping efforts, such as those in Somalia, Kuwait, and Bosnia. Article 24(2) of the Basic Law provides that "For the maintenance of peace, the Federation may enter a system of mutual collective security. . . ." Article 87(a)(2), however, states, "Apart from defence, the Armed Forces may only be used to the extent explicitly permitted by this Basic Law." The German government's decision to participate in NATO units stationed in Bosnia and Herzegovina under United Nations authority led some members of the opposition party to file a complaint in the Federal Constitutional Court. Prior administrations had resisted participation in similar cases, claiming that it would be illegal for the state to permit active participation by military units outside of NATO, presumably because such efforts would not be primarily "defensive."

In a unanimous decision, the Court found that German participation in United Nations peacekeeping operations would not necessarily violate Article 24(2). The Court found that the Article authorizes all those tasks that normally accompany membership in such collective security arrangements.

The complainants also argued that German participation had established new international obligations, which under Article 59(2) require Parliament's consent. The Court ruled, over sharp dissents (the Court split four to four), that the Article was not violated because the action did not yet amount to a change in an old, or assumption of a new, international obligation; hence, the federal government did not need to secure parliamentary approval before committing German troops to a United Nations

---

[33] Donald P. Kommers, *The Constitutional Jurisprudence of the Federal Republic of Germany.* 2d ed. (Durham: Duke University Press, 1997), 163.

[34] For a contrast, see *Greenham Women Against Cruise Missiles v. Reagan,* 755 F.2d 34 (2d Cir. 1985), where the Court dismissed a similar challenge to President Reagan's policy on cruise missiles as a political question.

mandate. The Court did conclude, though, that unless the Parliament had already declared a "state of defense," parliamentary approval would be required for every deployment of troops in support of Security Council resolutions.

The Court's interpretation of Article 59 had the effect of insisting upon a principle of legislative decision-making and accountability, even as it upheld the executive decision in question. Consequently, the Court addressed the issues on the merits, as opposed to invoking the political questions doctrine, but did so in a way that concentrated less on the "correct" decision on the issue involved and more on the principle of shared power.[35] One commentator thus concludes, "By presenting a Solomonic judgment where both sides could claim a partial victory and did not have to lose face, the Court succeeded very well in fulfilling the integrational functions of constitutional adjudication."[36] Moreover, the Court's careful and measured opinion underscores the judgment in the *Rudolph Hess Case*, which stressed the wide degree of discretion entrusted to the government.

> *The breadth of this discretion in foreign affairs has its basis in the nature of foreign relations. . . . Such events are not governed solely by the will of the federation, but rather are dependent on many circumstances over which it has little control. . . . The Constitution confers considerable discretion on foreign affairs agencies in assessing the practicality and feasibility of certain policies or actions.[37]*

Another highly politicized area in foreign affairs has concerned Germany's participation in the European Union. After Germany signed the Maastricht Treaty on European Union in 1992, the Constitutional Court was asked to decide if the Treaty violated Article 20 of the Basic Law, which provides that the Republic is a democratic and social federal state, in which all public authority emanates from the people. Also at issue was Article 38(1), which provides that members of the German Bundestag must be elected in general, direct, free, and secret elections. The complainants argued that under Maastricht, Germany had in effect transferred part of its sovereignty to the Union, thus potentially limiting the rights of German citizens. The Court concluded the Treaty did not violate the Basic Law, but in a complicated judgment it also insisted that future delegations of sovereign power to the Union would require a "strengthening of the democratic basis of the EU itself."[38]

The German Court's willingness to undertake a substantive review of a treaty's conformity with the Basic Law stands in sharp contrast to the American Supreme Court's decision in *Missouri v. Holland* (1920, reprinted later in the chapter). We encourage you to compare the two approaches. Is one better suited to achieving a measure of democratic accountability?[39] The Japanese experience follows Holmes's lead. In the important *Sunakawa* case (1959), the Japanese Court, in addressing the possibility that it might review a security treaty, concluded that

---

[35] See, for example, the argument made by Thomas M. Franck, *Political Questions/Judicial Answers: Does the Rule of Law Apply to Foreign Affairs?* (Princeton: Princeton University Press, 1992).

[36] Markus Zockler, *Germany in Collective Security Systems—Anything Goes?*, 6 European Journal of International Law 274, 286 (1995).

[37] As quoted in Kommers, supra note 33, 164.

[38] For an insightful analysis of the decision, see Manfred H. Wiengandt, *Germany's International Integration: The Rulings of the Federal Constitutional Court on the Maastricht Treaty and the Out-of-Area Deployment of German Troops,* 10 American University Journal of International Law and Policy, 889, 896 (1995).

[39] For an excellent discussion of such questions, see Vicki C. Jackson and Mark Tushnet, *Comparative Constitutional Law.* New York: Foundation Press, 1999), 754ff.

the Security Treaty possesses a highly political nature of great importance to the very existence of our country; that a decision as to the unconstitutionality of such treaty, as a matter of principle, does not involve a decision of the judicial courts; and that, accordingly, the constitutional review of such a treaty, unless it is recognized as being "clearly and obviously unconstitutional or invalid," lies outside the scope of constitutional review.[40]

The absence of judicial review in the United States and Japan does not, of course, mean that the treaty making process is necessarily without constitutional limits. We have stressed repeatedly, and especially in this chapter, that constitutional review is not coextensive with judicial review. In Japan, for example, one commentator has argued that the absence of judicial review "is not to say that constitutional control mechanisms are absent . . . , but rather that they have taken a largely nonjudicial form. . . . The real constitutional debate occurs in the legislature, in newspapers, and in gathering places."[41] And of course, some measure of constitutional review takes place when other constitutional actors are involved in processes of treaty ratification. In the United States, this function is assigned to the Senate, which has the constitutional authority to approve or reject treaties. But a common European view is that the House, rather than the Senate, should have the power to consent to treaties to reflect the democracy we have become. For these scholars, it is scandalous that senators representing no more than 30 percent of the American people can kill a treaty. As you read the cases in this chapter, consider whether such changes in constitutional design, or more intensive judicial review, would contribute to or impede the development of public discussions of the constitutional dimensions of foreign affairs.

Accountability and the Political Questions Doctrine in Canada

The active involvement of the German Constitutional Court in foreign affairs reflects a somewhat different understanding of the doctrine of separation of powers, as well as a more expansive role for judicial review, than does American jurisprudence. The Canadian approach comes closer to German experience. In one respect, however, Canada differs from both the German and American traditions. The Basic Law and the American Constitution insist upon some form of shared legislative and executive decision making. The power to conduct foreign relations in Canada, in contrast, falls within the prerogative power assigned to the executive alone. For example, at least as a matter of constitutional necessity, the Parliament in Canada plays no formal role in the making or conclusion of treaties. Nevertheless, the principle of democratic accountability is alive and well, in part because in practice most Canadian governments have sought the approval of Parliament before concluding treaties.

Judicial Review and the Political Questions Doctrine in Canada

In the leading case of *Operation Dismantle v. The Queen* (1985), the Canadian Supreme Court explicitly refused to embrace the political questions doctrine. *Operation Dismantle* involved efforts by groups of Canadian citizens to challenge a decision by the government to permit testing of American cruise missiles in Canada. The complaint charged that the policy violated Section 7 of the Charter, which guarantees the right to life and security of the person. The Court dismissed the case, holding that the

---

[40] For a general discussion, see John M. Maki, *Court and Constitution in Japan.* (Seattle: University of Washington Press, 1964), 348.

[41] See Damrosch, supra note 31, 195

plaintiffs had failed to establish a link between the tests and an increased threat of nuclear war. Nevertheless, Chief Justice Dickson concluded that "I have no doubt that disputes of a political or foreign policy nature may be properly cognizable by the courts."

In a separate and elaborate opinion, Justice Wilson rejected a lower court's finding that the case was nonjusticiable because such issues "involve moral and political considerations. . . ." Justice Wilson responded that "I think we should focus our attention on whether the courts *should* or *must* rather than on whether they *can* deal with such matters."[42] Contrast Justice Wilson's insistence upon the normative and moral imperative of judicial review with the studied pragmatism of Justice Brennan's opinion in *Baker v. Carr* (1962, reprinted in chapter 3).

In Germany and in Canada, then, constitutional courts have been much more willing than have American courts to participate in disputes over foreign affairs. In this sense, a comparative perspective suggests that there may be institutional and structural ways to give force to principles of deliberative and shared decision-making, ways that Americans have been reluctant so far to consider. At least one scholar, for instance, has concluded that judicial involvement in such matters has had great benefits.

Among those benefits may be an improved public understanding of foreign policy and its constitutional dimensions, which has added a degree of legitimation upon the conduct of various policies.[43] These kinds of benefits help to give everyday force to basic but sometimes abstract issues of constitutional theory. They also demonstrate, once again, that issues of theory are interlaced with thorny questions about the nature and limits of judicial power.

Selected Bibliography

Ackerman, David. 2002. *Declarations of War.* Hauppauge, N.Y.: Novinka Books.

Adler, David Gray and Michael A. Genonese (eds.). 2002. *The Presidency and the Law: The Clinton Legacy.* Lawrence, KS: University Press of Kansas.

Bland, Randall Walton. 1999. *The Black Robe and the Bald Eagle: The Supreme Court and the Foreign Policy of the United States, 1789–1961.* Lanham, Md.: Austin & Winfield.

Broughton, Richard J. *What Is It Good For? War Power, Judicial Review, and Constitutional Deliberation.* Oklahoma Law Review: 54 (2001): 685.

Cole, David and James X. Dempsey. 2002. *Terrorism and the Constitution: Sacrificing civil liberties in the name of national security.* New York: New Press.

Corwin, Edward S. 1947. *Total War and the Constitution.* New York: Alfred A. Knopf.

Delahunty, Robert J., *Law and the War on Terrorism: The President's Constitutional Authority to Conduct Military Operations Against Terrorist Organizations and the Nations That Harbor or Support Them.* Harvard Journal of Law and Public Policy. 25 (2002): 488.

Ely, John Hart. 1993. *War and Responsibility: Constitutional Lessons of Vietnam and Its Aftermath.* Princeton: Princeton University Press.

Fairman, Charles. 1943. *The Law of Martial Rule.* 2d ed.; Chicago: University of Chicago Press.

Finn, John E. 1991. *Constitutions in Crisis: Political Violence and the Rule of Law.* New York: Oxford University Press.

Fisher, Louis. 2000. *Congressional Abdication On War and Spending.* College Station, TX: Texas A&M University Press.

———. 1995. *Presidential War Power.* Lawrence: University Press of Kansas.

Franck, Thomas M. 1992. *Political Questions, Judicial Answers: Does the Rule of Law Apply to Foreign Affairs?* Princeton: Princeton University Press.

---

[42] Contrast this approach with *Greenham Women Against Cruise Missiles v. Reagan,* 591 F. Supp. 1332 (1984).

[44] Franck, supra note 35, 107–25. See also Damrosch, supra note 31, 196ff.

Franklin, Daniel P. 1991. *Extraordinary Measures: The Exercise of Prerogative Powers in the United States*. Pittsburgh: University of Pittsburgh Press.

Friedrich, Carl J. 1968. *Constitutional Government and Democracy*. Waltham, MA: Blaisdell.

———. 1957. *Constitutional Reason of State: The Survival of the Constitutional Order*. Providence: Brown University Press.

Gross, Oren. *Chaos and Rules: Should Responses to Violent Crises Always be Constitutional?* Yale Law Journal 112 (2003): 1011.

Hendrickson, Ryan C. 2002. *The Clinton Wars: The Constitution, Congress, and War Powers*. Nashville: Vanderbilt University Press.

Henkin, Louis. 1990. *Constitutionalism, Democracy, and Foreign Affairs*. New York: Columbia University Press.

Koh, Harold Hongju. 1990. *The National Security Constitution: Sharing Power After the Iran-Contra Affair*. New Haven: Yale University Press.

Linn, Alexander C. *International Security and the War Powers Resolution*, 8 Wm. & Mary Bill Rts. J. 725 (2000).

Lofgren, Charles A. 1986. *Government From Reflection and Choice: Constitutional Essays on War, Foreign Relations, and Federalism*. New York: Oxford University Press.

Lurie, Jonathan. 2001. *Military Justice in America: The U.S. Court of Appeals for the Armed Forces, 1775–1980*, Revised and Abridged Edition. Lawrence, Kansas: The University Press of Kansas.

Mann, Thomas E., ed. 1990. *A Question of Balance: The President, Congress, and Foreign Policy*. Washington, D.C.: The Brookings Institution.

Mansfield, Harvey C., Jr. 1989. *Taming the Prince: The Ambivalence of Modern Executive Power*. Cambridge: Harvard University Press.

May, Christopher. 1989. *In the Name of War: Judicial Review and the War Powers Since 1918*. Cambridge: Harvard University Press.

Moore, John Norton. *Treaty Interpretation, the Constitution and the Rule of Law*. Virginia Journal of International Law 42 (2001): 163.

Neustadt, Richard E. 1976. *Presidential Power: The Politics of Leadership*. rev. ed. New York: John Wiley.

Nishimoto, Richard S. 1995. *Inside an American Concentration Camp: Japanese American Resistance at Poston, Arizona*. With an Introduction by Lane Ryo Hirabayashi. Tucson: University of Arizona Press.

Pyle, Christopher H. and Richard M. Pious, eds. 1984. *The President, Congress, and the Constitution*. New York: The Free Press.

Rossiter, Clinton. 1948. *Constitutional Dictatorship*. Princeton: Princeton University Press.

Sheffer, Martin S. 1999 *Does Absolute Power Corrupt Absolutely? Part I—A Theoretical Review of Presidential War Powers*. Oklahoma City University Law Review 24 (1999): 233.

Schlesinger, Arthur M., Jr. 1973. *The Imperial Presidency*. New York: Popular Library.

Silverstein, Gordon. 1997. *Imbalance of Power. Constitutional Interpretation and the Making of American Foreign Policy*. New York: Oxford University Press.

Smith, Jeffrey A. 1999. *War and Press Freedom: The Problem of Prerogative Power*. New York: Oxford University Press.

Smith, Page. 1995. *Democracy on Trial: The Japanese-American Evacuation and Relocation in World War II*. New York: Simon & Schuster.

Spiro, Peter J. *Globalization and the (Foreign Affairs) Constitution*. Ohio State Law Journal 63 (2002): 649.

Telman, D. A. Jeremy. *A Truism That Isn't True? The Tenth Amendment and Executive War Power*. Catholic University Law Review 51 (2001): 135.

Tiefer, Charles. *Adjusting Sovereignty: Contemporary Congressional-Executive Controversies About International Organizations*. Texas International Law Journal 35 (2000): 239.

———. *War Powers Revisited*. Stanford International Law Journal 37 (2001): 171.

Wormuth, Francis. 1939. *The Royal Prerogative 1603–1699*. Ithaca: Cornell University Press.

Selected Comparative Bibliography

Bradley, Curtis A. and Jack L. Goldsmith. 2003. *Foreign Relations Law: Cases and Materials*. New York: Aspen Publishers.

Damrosch, Lori Fisler. *Impeachment as a Technique of Parliamentary Control Over Foreign Affairs in a Presidential System?* University of Colorado Law Review 70 (1999): 1525.

———. *Constitutional Control Over War Powers: A Common Core of Accountability in Democratic Societies?* University of Miami Law Review 50 (1995): 181.

Daniels, Ronald J., et al. (eds.). 2001. *The Security of Freedom: Essays On Canada's Anti-Terrorism Bill*. Toronto; Buffalo: University of Toronto Press.

Donohue, Laura K. 2001. *Counter-Terrorist Law and Emergency Powers in the United Kingdom, 1922–2000*. Dublin; Portland, OR: Irish Academic Press.

Daniels, Ronald J., P. Macklem and K. Roach, eds,. 2001. *The Security of Freedom: Essays on Canada's Anti-Terrorism Bill*. Toronto: University of Toronto Press.

Ellmann, Stephen. 1992. *In a Time of Trouble: Law and Liberty in South Africa's State of Emergency*. Oxford: The Clarendon Press.

Kommers, Donald P. 1997. *The Constitutional Jurisprudence of the Federal Republic of Germany*. 2d ed. Durham: Duke University Press.

Wiengandt, Manfred H. *Germany's International Integration: The Rulings of the Federal Constitutional Court on the Maastricht Treaty and the Out-of-Area Deployment of Ger-*

man Troops, American University Journal of International Law and Policy. 10 (1995): 889.

Zockler, Markus. *Germany in Collective Security Systems—* *Anything Goes?* European Journal of International Law 6 (1995): 274.

State of Missouri v. Holland
252 U.S. 416, 40 S.Ct. 382, 64 L.Ed. 641 (1920)

In 1913, Congress enacted a law that placed limits on the number of certain migratory birds that could be killed by hunters. A federal district court found the act unconstitutional later that year, and the government did not appeal the decision. However, before the district court opinion was announced, the Senate passed a resolution asking President Wilson to negotiate a treaty with Canada about these hunting limits to firm the constitutional ground of the proposal. In 1916, a treaty went into effect enforcing such limits. Congress then passed new legislation to enforce the new treaty. Many states, however, saw this as an infringement on state sovereignty, and refused to enforce the new act. In 1919, the attorney general of Missouri, one of the nonenforcing states, was caught poaching. He challenged the constitutionality of the new act in district court. The district court upheld the act, and the Supreme Court granted certiorari. Opinion of the Court: *Holmes,* McKenna, Day, White, McReynolds, Brandeis, Clarke. Dissenting opinion: *Van Devanter,* Pitney.

Mr. Justice HOLMES delivered the opinion of the Court.

. . . [T]he question raised is the general one whether the treaty and statute are void as an interference with the rights reserved to the States.

To answer this question it is not enough to refer to the Tenth Amendment, reserving the powers not delegated to the United States, because by Article 2, Section 2, the power to make treaties is delegated expressly, and by Article 6 treaties made under the authority of the United States, along with the Constitution and laws of the United States made in pursuance thereof, are declared the supreme law of the land. If the treaty is valid there can be no dispute about the validity of the statute under Article 1, Section 8, as a necessary and proper means to execute the powers of the Government. The language of the Constitution as to the supremacy of treaties being general, the question before us is narrowed to an inquiry into the ground upon which the present supposed exception is placed.

It is said that a treaty cannot be valid if it infringes the Constitution, that there are limits, therefore, to the treaty-

making power, and that one such limit is that what an act of Congress could not do unaided, in derogation of the powers reserved to the States, a treaty cannot do. An earlier act of Congress that attempted by itself and not in pursuance of a treaty to regulate the killing of migratory birds within the States had been held bad in the District Court. . . . Those decisions were supported by arguments that migratory birds were owned by the States in their sovereign capacity for the benefit of their people, and this control was one that Congress had no power to displace. The same argument is supposed to apply now with equal force.

Whether the two cases cited were decided rightly or not they cannot be accepted as a test of the treaty power. Acts of Congress are the supreme law of the land only when made in pursuance of the Constitution, while treaties are declared to be so when made under the authority of the United States. It is open to question whether the authority of the United States means more than the formal acts prescribed to make the convention. We do not mean to imply that there are no qualifications to the treaty-making power; but they must be ascertained in a different way. It is obvious that there may be matters of the sharpest exigency for the national well being that an act of Congress could not deal with but that a treaty followed by such an act could, and it is not lightly to be assumed that, in matters requiring national action, "a power which must belong to and somewhere reside in every civilized government" is not to be found. . . . What was said in that case with regard to the powers of the States applies with equal force to the powers of the nation in cases where the States individually are incompetent to act.

We are not yet discussing the particular case before us but only are considering the validity of the test proposed. With regard to that we may add that when we are dealing with words that also are a constituent act, like the Constitution of the United States, we must realize that they have called into life a being the development of which could not have been foreseen completely by the most gifted of its begetters. It was enough for them to realize or to hope that they had created an organism; it has taken a century and has cost their successors much sweat and blood to prove that they created a nation. The case before us must be considered in the light of our whole experience and not merely in that of what was said a hundred years ago.

The treaty in question does not contravene any prohibitory words to be found in the Constitution. The only question is whether it is forbidden by some invisible radiation from the general terms of the Tenth Amendment. We must consider what this country has become in deciding what that amendment has reserved.

The State as we have intimated founds its claim of exclusive authority upon an assertion of title to migratory birds, an assertion that is embodied in statute. . . . The whole foundation of the State's rights is the presence within their jurisdiction of birds that yesterday had not arrived, tomorrow may be in another State and in a week a thousand miles away. If we are to be accurate we cannot put the case of the State upon higher ground than that the treaty deals with creatures that for the moment are within the state borders, that it must be carried out by officers of the United States within the same territory, and that but for the treaty the State would be free to regulate this subject itself.

As most of the laws of the United States are carried out within the States, and as many of them deal with matters which in the silence of such laws the States might regulate, such general grounds are not enough to support Missouri's claim. Valid treaties of course "are as binding within the territorial limits of the States as they are elsewhere throughout the dominion of the United States." No doubt the great body of private relations usually fall within the control of the State, but a treaty may override its power.

Here a national interest of very nearly the first magnitude is involved. It can be protected only by national action in concert with that of another power. The subject matter is only transitorily within the State and has no permanent habitat therein. But for the treaty and the statute there soon might be no birds for any powers to deal with. We see nothing in the Constitution that compels the Government to sit by while a food supply is cut off and the protectors of our forests and our crops are destroyed. It is not sufficient to rely upon the States. The reliance is vain, and were it otherwise, the question is whether the United States is forbidden to act. We are of opinion that the treaty and statute must be upheld.

Decree affirmed.

Notes and Queries

1. Holmes wrote that there are limits on the treatymaking power of the national government, "but they must be ascertained in a different way." Does he say what that way is? What limits does he identify upon the treatmaking power? Are there other limits? Consider the Court's opinion in *Reid v. Covert*, 354 U.S. 1 (1957), in which the Court ruled that an exercise of the treatymaking power could not deprive a citizen of constitutional liberties guaranteed by the Bill of Rights.

2. In the case of *Mohamed and Another v. President of the RSA and Others* (2001), the South African Constitutional Court considered whether Mohamed could be lawfully extradited, under a treaty dating from 1951, to the United States. Mohamed's objection was that his extradition had not included a guarantee from the United States government that he would not be given the death penalty. This, he claimed, constituted a violation of his rights to life, dignity and immunity from capital punishment under sections 10, 11, and 12(1)(e) of the South African Constitution. The Court ruled in favor of Mohamed, finding the South African state is under an "obligation imposed . . . by the Constitution to protect the fundamental rights contained in the Bill of Rights. . . . The Constitution also forbids it [the state] knowingly to participate, directly or indirectly, in any way in imposing or facilitating the imposition of such punishment. . . ." Consequently, "[f]or the South African government to co-operate with a foreign

Comparative Note 5.1

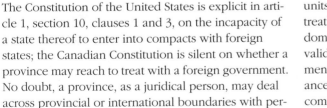

The Constitution of the United States is explicit in article 1, section 10, clauses 1 and 3, on the incapacity of a state thereof to enter into compacts with foreign states; the Canadian Constitution is silent on whether a province may reach to treat with a foreign government. No doubt, a province, as a juridical person, may deal across provincial or international boundaries with persons or private agencies, and as well with subordinate units of foreign states. . . . A province that purported to treat on its own in this way, albeit on matters within its domestic competence, could not claim international validity for any ensuing agreement, nor would implementing legislation be valid when enacted in pursuance of a non-existing power to accept international commitments.

SOURCE: Neil Finklestein, *Laskin's Canadian Constitutional Law.* 5th ed., vol. 1 (Toronto: Carswell Press, 1986), 413.

Comparative Note 5.2

[The German-Vatican Concordat of 1933 provided for the religious education of Catholic children in Germany. After the Second World War, however, the state (*Land*) of Lower Saxony enacted an education statute that violated the treaty. The issue before the Federal Constitutional Court, as in *Missouri v. Holland*, was whether the state law takes precedence over a national treaty.]

. . . [The] continued validity of the Concordat means that its terms still bind the signatories. Under the Basic Law, the Federal Republic of Germany—the Federation and (states) considered as a whole—is bound as a partner to the treaty. But, under the constitutional law of the Federal Republic, only the [states] can fulfill obligations arising from the educational provisions of this agreement. The Federation has no legislative authority over educational affairs. . . . Article 123 (2) states . . . that only those provisions of the Concordat remain in force insofar as they were valid when the Basic Law became effective, although they originate in a treaty not concluded by the [states], now exclusively competent to regulate the matter in dispute.

. . .

The supposition that Art. 123 (2) was intended to constitutionally bind [state] legislatures to treaty law, in addition to directing the continued validity of the law itself, would contradict the general relationship that the Basic Law establishes between the Federation and [the states].

Constitutionally binding [the states] to the educational provisions of the Concordat would flatly contradict their authority freely to make educational law within the limits of the Constitution.

The Constitutional principle of *Bundestreue* (federal loyalty) belongs among the constitutional standards imminent in the Basic Law . . . *Bundestreue* demands that each part take into consideration situations of interest and tension which arise in the Federation. Thus one must conclude that the [state's] obligation of loyalty toward the Federation is to be taken particularly seriously in foreign relations, where the Federation alone is competent.

Nonetheless, no obligation of (states) to the Federation to observe the Concordat's educational provisions can be derived from the principle of *Bundestreue*:

The Basic Law's choice constitutionally to limit [states] in the denominational orientation of education only by Article 7 excludes any further obligation of the [states] toward the Federation in this area.

Source: *Concordat Case* (1957) in Walter F. Murphy and Joseph Tanenhaus, *Comparative Constitutional Law* (New York: St. Martin's Press, 1977), 226–29.

---

government [in this case] is contrary to the underlying values of our Constitution." Does this decision suggest that even treaties must conform with the South African Bill of Rights, and that the Constitutional Court can enforce those commitments? Can the decision by the South African Constitutional Court be reconciled with *Missouri v. Holland*?

Similarly, in the case of *Minister of Justice v. Burns* (2001), the Supreme Court of Canada concluded that Section 7 of the Canadian Charter—which provides that "everyone has the right to life, liberty and security of the person and the right not to be deprived thereof except in accordance with the provisions of fundamental justice—requires that the Canadian government receive assurances that the death penalty will not be imposed when it extradites persons.

3. Does *Missouri v. Holland* leave the states without any substantial protection against national treaties? Some commentators have feared that such an expansive view of

the power permits the national government to use its power over foreign affairs to dramatically increase its influence over the states in domestic affairs. Such concerns, for example, lay behind Senator John Bricker's proposal for a constitutional amendment in 1954 that would have required Congress to pass legislation before any treaty could become a law in the United States. Bricker's amendment failed, but only by one vote, and hardly a session of Congress passes without the introduction of a similar amendment. Would Bricker's proposal have offered any comfort to the states?

4. What role—if any—should the states play in the making of foreign policy? As we saw in chapter 4, the Constitution also separates power horizontally, or between the national and state governments. In the field of foreign affairs, however, federalism has been less an imperative. Madison set forth the reason in *Federalist* 42, writing, "If we are to be a nation in any respect, it clearly ought to be

in respect to other nations." Article I, Section 9, thus provides that "No State shall enter into any Treaty, Alliance, or Confederation. . . ." And "No State shall, without the Consent of Congress, . . . enter into any Agreement or Compact . . . with a foreign power, or engage in War, unless actually invaded, or in such imminent Danger as will not admit of delay." Finally, the supremacy clause of Article VI provides strong support for the preeminence of national authority.

The Supreme Court reaffirmed the preeminence of national authority in *Perpich v. Department of Defense* (1990). In this case the Court rejected a challenge by a state governor to a congressional policy that authorized the training of National Guard troops (ostensibly under state control) outside of the United States. In his opinion for the Court, Justice Stevens observed, "several constitutional provisions commit matters of foreign policy and military affairs to the exclusive control of the National Government."

Nevertheless, there remain important ways in which the conduct of foreign affairs is influenced by federalism. On a theoretical level, some justices have suggested that the Constitution (in particular the Tenth Amendment) must provide some rudimentary limitations on national power, so that the national government could not, through a treaty, for example, abolish a state militia or alter the republican character of a state. On a practical level, the states may influence the conduct of foreign relations in innumerable ways, from passing "resolutions" concerning various matters of interest to them, to enforcing (or not) federal immigration or customs policies. (Henkin, 245–46).

5. Article 59(2) of the German Basic Law provides that "Treaties which regulate the political relations of the federation or are concerned with matters within the legislative competence of the federation require the consent . . . of the organs competent for the enactment of federal law in the form of federal statutes." In the *Petersberg Agreement Case* (1952) certain members of the West German parliament challenged an executive agreement between the chancellor and the Allied powers, claiming that the agreement was a treaty within the meaning of Article 59 and thus required parliamentary approval. In its decision, the Federal Constitutional Court defined a treaty as an agreement concluded with a foreign state or an equally important international agency—a status the Allied powers did not attain. The *Commercial Treaty Case* (1952) concerned the meaning of the term "political relations" in Article 59. Under that article, treaties that regulate the "political relations of the federation" require the consent or participation of appropriate legislative bodies. On the other hand, treaties that are "commercial" in nature do not need legislative approval.

Overall, then, the German Parliament has an important role to play—as does the Federal Constitutional Court—in the construction of German foreign affairs. On the other hand, Article 32(3) qualifies the power of the federal government to conduct foreign affairs by permitting the individual *Länder* to conclude treaties with foreign states in those areas where they have exclusive legislative competence, albeit subject to the approval of the national government. In the *Concordat Case* (1957)(Comparative Note 5.2), the Federal Constitutional Court intimated that the federal power to make treaties would be limited by the extent of those reserved powers.

Youngstown Sheet & Tube Co. v. Sawyer
343 U.S. 579, 72 S.Ct. 863, 96 L.Ed. 1153 (1952)

In June of 1950, North Korea invaded South Korea. President Truman authorized the use of American troops in the conflict in what he called a "policing action" rather than a war. In December 1951, several of the contracts between the United Steelworkers Union and the Youngstown Steel Company expired. The union called a strike in April 1952, during the heart of the Korean War. The strike would have halted almost the entire steel industry in the United States. Because the troops in Korea were already facing ammunition shortages, President Truman issued an executive order to seize the steel mills and place them under government control, stating the closing of the mills would

"immediately jeopardize and imperil our national defense. . . ." The day after, Truman reported to Congress the action he had taken, and stated he would abide by any action taken by Congress. Congress did not take any action, so the steel companies obtained an injunction. The opinion of the Court, by Justice Black, and the concurring opinions by Justice Frankfurter and Justice Jackson, are reprinted in chapter 4. Here we include only the dissenting opinion by Chief Justice Vinson. Opinion of the Court: *Black*, Frankfurter, Burton, Jackson. Concurring opinions: *Frankfurter; Burton; Jackson; Clark; Douglas.* Dissenting opinion: *Vinson*, Reed, Minton.

Mr. Chief Justice VINSON, with whom Mr. Justice REED and Mr. Justice MINTON join, dissenting.

Those who suggest that this is a case involving extraordinary powers should be mindful that these are extraordinary times. A world not yet recovered from the devastation of World War II has been forced to face the threat of another and more terrifying global conflict.

Plaintiffs do not remotely suggest any basis for rejecting the President's finding that any stoppage of steel production would immediately place the Nation in peril.

Accordingly, if the President has any power under the Constitution to meet a critical situation in the absence of express statutory authorization, there is no basis whatever for criticizing the exercise of such power in this case.

The steel mills were seized for a public use. The power of eminent domain, invoked in that case, is an essential attribute of sovereignty and has long been recognized as a power of the Federal Government. . . . Plaintiffs cannot complain that any provision in the Constitution prohibits the exercise of the power of eminent domain in this case. The Fifth Amendment provides: "nor shall private property be taken for public use, without just compensation." It is no bar to this seizure for, if the taking is not otherwise unlawful, plaintiffs are assured of receiving the required just compensation.

Admitting that the Government could seize the mills, plaintiffs claim that the implied power of eminent domain can be exercised only under an Act of Congress; under no circumstances, they say, can that power be exercised by the President unless he can point to an express provision in enabling legislation. This was the view adopted by the District Judge when he granted the preliminary injunction. Without an answer, without hearing evidence, he determined the issue on the basis of his "fixed conclusion that defendant's acts are illegal" because the President's only course in the face of an emergency is to present the matter to Congress and await the final passage of legislation which will enable the Government to cope with threatened disaster.

Under this view, the President is left powerless at the very moment when the need for action may be most pressing and when no one, other than he, is immediately capable of action. Under this view, he is left powerless because a power not expressly given to Congress is nevertheless found to rest exclusively with Congress. . . .

Focusing now on the situation confronting the President on the night of April 8, 1952, we cannot but conclude that the President was performing his duty under the Constitution to "take Care that the Laws be faithfully executed"—a duty described by President Benjamin Harrison as "the central idea of the office."

Much of the argument in this case has been directed at straw men. We do not now have before us the case of a President acting solely on the basis of his own notions of the public welfare. Nor is there any question of unlimited

executive power in this case. The President himself closed the door to any such claim when he sent his Message to Congress stating his purpose to abide by any action of Congress, whether approving or disapproving his seizure action. Here, the President immediately made sure that Congress was fully informed of the temporary action he had taken only to preserve the legislative programs from destruction until Congress could act.

The absence of a specific statute authorizing seizure of the steel mills as a mode of executing the laws—both the military procurement program and the anti-inflation program—has not until today been thought to prevent the President from executing the laws. Unlike an administrative commission confined to the enforcement of the statute under which it was created, or the head to a department when administering a particular statute, the President is a constitutional officer charged with taking care that a "mass of legislation" be executed. Flexibility as to mode of execution to meet critical situations is a matter of practical necessity.

. . . Faced with the duty of executing the defense programs which Congress had enacted and the disastrous effects that any stoppage in steel production would have on those programs, the President acted to preserve those programs by seizing the steel mills. There is no question that the possession was other than temporary in character and subject to congressional direction—either approving, disapproving or regulating the manner in which the mills were to be administered and returned to the owners. The President immediately informed Congress of his action and clearly stated his intention to abide by the legislative will. No basis for claims of arbitrary action, unlimited powers or dictatorial usurpation of congressional power appears from the facts of this case. On the contrary, judicial, legislative and executive precedents throughout our history demonstrate that in this case the President acted in full conformity with his duties under the Constitution. Accordingly, we would reverse the order of the District Court.

Notes and Queries

1. Immediately following the Court's decision the steelworkers called a strike that lasted for fifty-three days. No shortages ensued, in part because there was an "enormous inventory of steel on hand at the beginning of the strike. . . ." Maeva Marcus, *Truman and the Steel Seizure Case: The Limits of Presidential Power.* (New York: Columbia University Press, 1997), 252.

2. In the case of *In re Neagle*, 135 U.S. 546 (1890), the Supreme Court considered a claim of inherent presidential

powers that involved the Court itself. David Neagle, a United States marshall assigned to protect Justice Stephen Field after threats were made against the justice's life, shot and killed the man who had made the threats. California authorities arrested Neagle and charged him with murder. The federal government asked for his release, claiming Neagle had acted in the line of his authority. Nevertheless, no statute had authorized the president to appoint bodyguards for the justices. The Court held the president's power to execute the laws was not "limited to the enforcement of acts of Congress." Does the majority opinion in *Youngstown* cast doubt on the opinion in *Neagle*, perhaps by suggesting that in the field of domestic affairs, the president has no inherent or emergency powers?

3. Of what relevance was the absence of a congressional declaration of war in this case? Of what relevance was the congressional history of legislation, reviewed by Justice Black in his majority opinion, that considered but decided against giving the president the authority to seize the steel plants?

4. The various opinions in *Youngstown* utilize a wide variety of methods of constitutional interpretation. Justice Black's majority opinion begins with the claim that the president's power must stem from the Constitution itself or from an Act of Congress. How does Justice Frankfurter's concurrence differ in its understanding of the separation of powers from the majority opinion? Does it rest also upon a different understanding of judicial power? What is the source for Justice Jackson's tripartite framework for the analysis of presidential power? Does it apply to the president's power in foreign affairs, or only to domestic affairs? Does the dissent rely primarily upon statutes and precedents, or does it look to some other source for guidance?

The Prize Cases
67 U.S. (2 Black) 635, 17 L.Ed. 459 (1862)

After the Civil War began in April 1861, but before a special session of Congress was allowed to begin, President Abraham Lincoln instituted a blockade of all ports belonging to the Confederate states. During the period between this initial commencement of the blockade and the subsequent ratification of the blockade by Congress, several ships were seized and their cargoes confiscated as "prize" because they attempted to break through the blockade. The owners of these ships sued to regain their cargoes, arguing that the blockade was illegal. Questions arising from these suits were certified by the Supreme Court. Opinion of the Court: *Grier*, Wayne, Swayne, Miller, Davis. Dissenting opinion: *Nelson*, Taney, Catron, Clifford.

Mr. Justice GRIER delivered the opinion of the Court.

. . . Had the President a right to institute a blockade of ports in possession of persons in armed rebellion against the Government, on the principles of international law, as known and acknowledged among civilized States?

The right of prize and capture has its origin in the *"jus belli,"* and is governed and adjudged under the law of nations. To legitimate the capture of a neutral vessel or property on the high seas, a war must exist de facto, and the neutral must have a knowledge or notice of the intention of one of the parties belligerent to use this mode of coercion against a port, city, or territory, in possession of the other.

Let us enquire whether, at the time this blockade was instituted, a state of war existed which would justify a resort to these means of subduing the hostile force.

By the Constitution, Congress alone has the power to declare a national or foreign war. It cannot declare war against a State, or any number of States, by virtue of any clause in the Constitution. The Constitution confers on the President the whole Executive power. He is bound to take care that the laws be faithfully executed. He is Commander in chief of the Army and Navy of the United States, and of the militia of the several States when called into the actual service of the United States. He has no power to initiate or declare a war either against a foreign nation or a domestic State. But by the Acts of Congress of February 28th, 1795, and 3d of March, 1807, he is authorized to call out the militia and use the military and naval forces of the United States in case of invasion by foreign nations, and to suppress insurrection against the government of a State or of the United States.

If a war be made by invasion of a foreign nation, the President is not only authorized but bound to resist force by force. He does not initiate the war, but is bound to accept the challenge without waiting for any special legislative authority. And whether the hostile party be a foreign invader, or States organized in rebellion, it is none the less a war, although the declaration of it be *"unilateral."* . . .

This greatest of civil wars . . . sprung forth suddenly from the parent brain, a Minerva in the full panoply of *war*. The President was bound to meet it in the shape it presented itself, without waiting for Congress to baptize it with a name; and no name given to it by him or them could change the fact.

Whether the President in fulfilling his duties, as Commander in chief, in suppressing an insurrection, has met with such armed hostile resistance, and a civil war of such alarming proportions as will compel him to accord to them the character of belligerents, is a question to be decided by *him,* and this Court must be governed by the decisions and acts of the political department of the Government to which this power was entrusted. . . . The proclamation of blockade is itself official and conclusive evidence to the Court that a state of war existed which demanded and authorized a recourse to such a measure, under the circumstances peculiar to the case.

If it were necessary to the technical existence of a war, that it should have a legislative sanction, we find it in almost every act passed at the extraordinary session of the Legislature of 1861, which was wholly employed in enacting laws to enable the Government to prosecute the war with vigor and efficiency. And finally, in 1861, we find Congress . . . passing an act "approving, legalizing, and making valid all the acts, proclamations, and orders of the President, &c., as if they had been issued and done under the previous express authority and direction of the Congress of the United States."

Without admitting that such an act was necessary under the circumstances, it is plain that if the President had in any manner assumed powers which it was necessary should have the authority or sanction of Congress . . . this ratification has operated to perfectly cure the defect.

. . . [W]e are of the opinion that the President had a right, *jure belli,* to institute a blockade of ports in possession of the States in rebellion, which neutrals are bound to regard. . . .

Mr. Justice NELSON, dissenting.

. . . [T]he right of making war belongs exclusively to the supreme or sovereign power of the State.

This power in all civilized nations is regulated by the fundamental laws or municipal constitution of the country.

By our constitution this power is lodged in Congress.

Now, in one sense, no doubt this is war, and may be a war of the most extensive and threatening dimensions and effects, but it is a statement simply of its existence in a material sense, and has no relevancy or weight when the question is what constitutes war in a legal sense, in the sense of the law of nations, and of the Constitution of the United States? For it must be a war in this sense to attach to it all the consequences that belong to belligerent rights.

. . . [A]mple provision has been made under the Constitution and laws against any sudden and unexpected disturbance of the public peace from insurrection at home or invasion from abroad. The whole military and naval power of the country is put under the control of the President to meet the emergency. . . . It is the exercise of a power under the municipal laws of the country and not under the law of nations; and, as we see, furnishes the most ample means of repelling attacks from abroad or suppressing disturbances at home until the assembling of Congress, who can, if it be deemed necessary, bring into operation the war power, and thus change the nature and character of the contest.

. . . I am compelled to the conclusion that no civil war existed between this Government and the States in insurrection till recognized by the Act of Congress 13th of July, 1861; that the President does not possess the power under the Constitution to declare war or recognize its existence within the meaning of the law of nations, which carries with it belligerent rights, and thus change the country and all its citizens from a state of peace to a state of war; that this power belongs exclusively to the Congress of the United States and, consequently, that the President had no power to set on foot a blockade under the law of nations, and that the capture of the vessel and cargo in this case, and in all cases before us in which the capture occurred before the 13th of July, 1861, for breach of blockade, or as enemies' property, are illegal and void, and that the decrees of condemnation should be reversed and the vessel and cargo restored.

Mr. Chief Justice TANEY, Mr. Justice CATRON and Mr. Justice CLIFFORD, concurred in the dissenting opinion of Mr. Justice NELSON.

Notes and Queries

1. The Court appears to hold that when the country is under attack the president may "recognize" that we are in a state of war and act on the basis of his commander-in-chief powers. In all other cases, the congressional power to declare war must precede the president's action. Why did the Founders separate the power to conduct war and peace in this way? Is the separation they envisioned a constitutional impossibility in an age when international agencies and organizations play an important role in responding to conflict between countries? Is a presidential power to react but not to declare consistent with the actual practice of presidential warmaking in the twentieth century?

2. Can the *Prize Cases* be reconciled with *Ex Parte Milligan* (1866), reprinted later in this chapter?

3. Justice Grier wrote that "Whether the President in fulfilling his duties, as Commander in chief, in suppressing

Comparative Note 5.3

[In 1983 several persons filed constitutional complaints against the Federal Republic of Germany's deployment on its territory of weapons equipped with nuclear warheads. The deployment was taken under an accord of the North Atlantic Treaty Organization (NATO). The complainants charged that the presence of these weapons endangered their physical integrity and right to life in violation of Article 2 (2) of the Basic Law.]

[I]t is questionable whether the asserted violation of [the right to] life and limb by German sovereign power rises to the level of a real danger under the Basic Law. . . . Under the prevailing circumstances [we cannot make] judicially verifiable findings concerning such decisions in advance. Moreover, the possible violation of basic rights asserted [here] does not fall within the protective purview of these rights, since [basic rights] are aimed at German state action. . . .

. . . Because [we] lack legally manageable criteria [for deciding this case], the Federal Constitutional Court cannot determine whether or not the German state action challenged by complainants has any influence on decisions of the Soviet Union which may or may not trigger measures (a preventive or responsive nuclear strike) complainants fear: The federal organs responsible for the foreign and defense policy of the Federal Republic must make such evaluations. . . . To the extent that unpredictable areas of risk remain, as will often be the case, the political body constitutionally responsible for the decision must include these [considerations] in their deliberations and assume political responsibility. It is not the function of the Federal Constitutional Court to substitute its opinions for the opinions and deliberations of the competent political branch of the federation over and above standard legal handicaps in this area. This applies equally for the question of how the state should fulfill its affirmative legal duty to protect basic rights in the sphere of foreign policy and defense matter vis-à-vis foreign states.

SOURCE: *Pershing 2 and Cruise Missile Case I* (1983) in Kommers, *Constitutional Jurisprudence,* 156–57.

---

an insurrection, has met with such armed hostile resistance, and a civil war of such alarming proportions as will compel him to accord to them the character of belligerents, is a question to be decided by *him,* and this Court must be governed by the decisions . . . of the political department of the Government to which this power was entrusted. . . ." Does this mean that there can be no judicial review of such a presidential decision? What understanding of the separation of powers underlies this view? How does it differ from the dissent's understanding?

War Powers Resolution United States Code Title 50. War and National Defense Chapter 33 (1973)

s 1541. Purpose and policy

(a) Congressional declaration

It is the purpose of this chapter to fulfill the intent of the framers of the Constitution of the United States and insure that the collective judgment of both the Congress and the President will apply to the introduction of United States Armed Forces into hostilities, or into situations where imminent involvement in hostilities is clearly indicated by the circumstances, and to the continued use of such forces in hostilities or in such situations.

(b) Congressional legislative power under necessary and proper clause

Under article I, section 8, of the Constitution, it is specifically provided that the Congress shall have the power to make all laws necessary and proper for carrying into execution, not only its own powers but also all other powers vested by the Constitution in the Government of the United States, or in any department or officer thereof.

(c) Presidential executive power as Commander in chief; limitation

The constitutional powers of the President as Commander in chief to introduce United States Armed Forces into hostilities, or into situations where imminent involvement in hostilities is clearly indicated by the circumstances, are exercised only pursuant to (1) a declaration of war, (2) specific statutory authorization, or (3) a national emergency created by attack upon the United States, its territories or possessions, or its armed forces.

s 1542. Consultation; initial and regular consultations

The President in every possible instance shall consult with Congress before introducing United States Armed Forces into hostilities or into situations where imminent involvement in hostilities is clearly indicated by the circumstances, and after every such introduction shall consult regularly with the Congress until United States Armed Forces are no longer engaged in hostilities or have been removed from such situations.

s 1543. Reporting requirement

(a) Written report; time of submission and information reported

In the absence of a declaration of war, in any case in which United States Armed Forces are introduced—

(1) into hostilities or into situations where imminent involvement in hostilities is clearly indicated by the circumstances;

(2) into the territory, airspace or waters of a foreign nation, while equipped for combat, except for deployments which relate solely to supply, replacement, repair, or training of such forces; or

(3) in numbers which substantially enlarge United States Armed Forces equipped for combat already located in a foreign nation;

the President shall submit within 48 hours to the Speaker of the House of Representatives and to the President pro tempore of the Senate a report, in writing, setting forth—

(A) the circumstances necessitating the introduction of United States Armed Forces;

(B) the constitutional and legislative authority under which such introduction took place; and

---

Comparative Note 5.4

Article 40(13)

(1) Except for military exercises based on valid international agreements or peace maintenance activities performed on request of the United Nations Organization, the armed forces [Hungarian National Army and Border Guard] may cross state borders only with the prior consent of parliament. (Constitution of Hungary, 1990)

Article 26

(1) Any activities apt or intended to disturb peaceful international relations, especially preparations for military aggression, shall be unconstitutional. They shall be a criminal offense. (Basic Law, Federal Republic of Germany, 1949)

Article 87a

(1) The [German] Federation shall establish Armed Forces for defense purposes. Their numerical strength and general organizational structure shall be shown in the budget. (2) Other than for defense purposes, the Armed Forces may only be employed to the extent explicitly permitted by this Basic Law. (Basic Law, Federal Republic of Germany, as amended 1956)

Article 9

(1) Aspiring sincerely to an international peace

based on justice and order, the Japanese people forever renounce war as a sovereign right of the nation and the threat or use of force as a means of settling international disputes.

(2) In order to accomplish the aim of the preceding paragraph, land, sea, and air forces, as well as other war potential, will never be maintained. The right of the belligerency of the state will not be recognized. (Constitution of Japan, 1947)

Article 230

In case of threats to the constitutional order of the State . . . the President of the Republic may, on request of the Council of Ministers, introduce . . . for no longer than 90 days a state of emergency in a part of or upon the whole territory of the State. (Constitution of Poland, 1997)

Article 231

The President . . . shall submit the regulation on the introduction of . . . a state of emergency to the Sejm [parliament] within 48 hours of signing such regulation. The Sejm shall immediately consider the regulation of the President. The Sejm, by an absolute majority of votes taken in the presence of at least half the statutory number of representatives, may annul the regulation of the President. (Constitution of Poland, 1997)

(C) the estimated scope and duration of the hostilities or involvement.

(b) Other information reported

The President shall provide such other information as the Congress may request in the fulfillment of its constitutional responsibilities with respect to committing the Nation to war and to the use of United States Armed Forces abroad.

(c) Periodic reports; semiannual requirement

Whenever United States Armed Forces are introduced into hostilities or into any situation described in subsection (a) of this section, the President shall, so long as such armed forces continue to be engaged in such hostilities or situation, report to the Congress periodically on the status of such hostilities or situation as well as on the scope and duration of such hostilities or situation, but in no event shall he report to the Congress less often than once every six months.

s 1544. Congressional action

(a) Transmittal of report and referral to Congressional committees; joint request for convening Congress

Each report submitted pursuant to section 1543(a)(1) of this title shall be transmitted to the Speaker of the House of Representatives and to the President pro tempore of the Senate on the same calendar day. Each report so transmitted shall be referred to the Committee on Relations of the Senate for appropriate action. If, when the report is transmitted, the Congress has adjourned *sine die* or has adjourned for any period in excess of three calendar days, the Speaker of the House of Representatives and the President pro tempore of the Senate, if they deem it advisable (or if petitioned by at least 30 percent of the membership of their respective Houses) shall jointly request the President to convene Congress in order that it may consider the report and take appropriate action pursuant to this section.

(b) Termination of use of United States Armed Forces; exceptions; extension period

Within sixty calendar days after a report is submitted or is required to be submitted pursuant to section 1543(a)(1) of this title, whichever is earlier, the President shall terminate any use of United States Armed Forces with respect to which such report was submitted (or required to be submitted), unless the Congress (1) has declared war or has enacted a specific authorization for such use of United States Armed Forces, (2) has extended by law such sixty-day period, or (3) is physically unable to meet as a result

of an armed attack upon the United States. Such sixty-day period shall be extended for not more than an additional thirty days if the President determines and certifies to the Congress in writing that unavoidable military necessity respecting the safety of United States Armed Forces requires the continued use of such armed forces in the course of bringing about a prompt removal of such forces.

(c) Concurrent resolution for removal by President of United States Armed Forces

Notwithstanding subsection (b) of this section, at any time that United States Armed Forces are engaged in hostilities outside the territory of the United States, its possessions and territories without a declaration of war or specific statutory authorization, such forces shall be removed by the President if the Congress so directs by concurrent resolution.

s 1547. Interpretations from any law or treaty

Authority to introduce United States Armed Forces into hostilities or into situations wherein involvement in hostilities is clearly indicated by the circumstances shall not be inferred—

(1) from any provision of law (whether or not in effect before November 7, 1973), including any provision contained in any appropriation Act, unless such provision specifically authorizes the introduction of United States Armed Forces into hostilities or into such situations and states that it is intended to constitute specific statutory authorization within the meaning of this chapter; or

(2) from any treaty heretofore or hereafter ratified unless such treaty is implemented by legislation specifically authorizing the introduction of United States Armed Forces into hostilities or into such situations and stating that it is intended to constitute specific statutory authorization within the meaning of this chapter.

* * *

(b) Joint headquarters operations of high-level military commands

Nothing in this chapter shall be construed to require any further specific statutory authorization to permit members of United States Armed Forces to participate jointly with members of the armed forces of one or more foreign countries in the headquarters operations of high-level military commands which were established prior to November 7, 1973, and pursuant to the United Nations Charter or any treaty ratified by the United States prior to such date.

(c) Introduction of United States Armed Forces

For purposes of this chapter, the term "introduction of United States Armed Forces" includes the assignment of members of such armed forces to command, coordinate, participate in the movement of, or accompany the regular or irregular military forces of any foreign country or government when such military forces are engaged, or there exists an imminent threat that such forces will become engaged, in hostilities.

(d) Constitutional authorities or existing treaties . . . respecting use of United States Armed Forces

Nothing in this chapter—

(1) is intended to alter the constitutional authority of the Congress or of the President, or the provisions of existing treaties; or

(2) shall be construed as granting any authority to the President with respect to the introduction of United States Armed Forces into hostilities or into situations wherein involvement in hostilities is clearly indicated by the circumstances which authority he would not have had in the absence of this chapter.

s 1548. Separability of provisions

If any provision of this chapter or the application thereof to any person or circumstance is held invalid, the remainder of the chapter and the application of such provision to any other person or circumstance shall not be affected thereby.

Notes and Queries

1. Whatever its wisdom at the time, (it passed the House unanimously and the Senate with only two dissents), the Tonkin Gulf Resolution (1964) now serves as a symbol of the dangers of congressional acquiescence to presidential power. By 1967, Viet Nam was the third largest war Americans had ever participated in, at least as measured by troops abroad and the number of casualties. In many ways, the War Powers Resolution (1973) is a response to Tonkin Gulf.

2. Presidents routinely ignore the War Powers Resolution, seemingly without peril. President Ford notified but did not consult with Congress about his decision to rescue the crew of the *Mayaguez* and to evacuate Americans from Lebanon with U.S. troops. President Carter sent a military rescue force into Iran without consulting Congress, and President Reagan sent the marines into Lebanon and troops into Grenada, without conceding that the

Act applied to his action. President George H. W. Bush did notify Congress before he sent troops to Panama; he was careful, however, to make it clear that he was not asking for congressional consultation or advice. More recently, President George W. Bush received a resolution authorizing him to take military action against Iraq, following the attacks on 11 September 2001 (reprinted below).

3. Its proponents believe the War Powers Resolution is an effort to give life to one of the defining features of the American constitutional order—the principle that power should be shared and accountable. But whatever the merits of its appeal to original intent, in practice the War Powers Resolution has done little to hem in presidential power or to raise Congress to the status of a co-equal partner. Does the Resolution's failure suggest it is impossible to reconcile the "imperial presidency" with constitutional government? If constitutionalism means respect for limits on power, then what are we to make of the Resolution's failure to constrain presidential war powers?

4. Claims about respect for Founders' intent aside, how can we reconcile the Resolution with Hamilton's claim in *Federalist* 70 that "Energy in the executive is a leading character in the definition of good government. It is essential to the protection of the community against foreign attacks"? In the same paper Hamilton praises a single, energetic executive as the only branch capable of acting with "decision, activity, secrecy, and dispatch."

5. The War Powers Resolution is plainly an exercise of constitutional interpretation. To what extent are branches of government bound to respect the interpretations of coordinate branches? Does Congress's interpretation go to the limits of *its* power—or is it an interpretation about the extent of presidential power? Does it matter?

6. Do the *Prize Cases* (1862) tell us anything about the constitutionality of the War Powers Resolution? Does the Resolution authorize the president to respond to threats of attack without seeking congressional approval?

7. Both Germany and Japan include in their constitutions a renunciation of war. In both cases, however, the renunciation has done little to end oftentimes heated discussions about who has the responsibility to conduct foreign relations.

8. Consider the various constitutional provisions included in Comparative Note 5.4. Would a similar provision in the United States Constitution help to clarify or resolve disputes about the proper constitutional distribution of the power to conduct foreign affairs? Why or why not?

Iraq Resolution
107th Congress, 2d Session,
H. J. Res. 114
October 10, 2002

JOINT RESOLUTION

To authorize the use of United States Armed Forces against Iraq. . . .

Whereas Iraq both poses a continuing threat to the national security of the United States and international peace and security in the Persian Gulf region and remains in material and unacceptable breach of its international obligations by, among other things, continuing to possess and develop a significant chemical and biological weapons capability, actively seeking a nuclear weapons capability, and supporting and harboring terrorist organizations; Whereas Iraq persists in violating resolutions of the United Nations Security Council by continuing to engage in brutal repression of its civilian population thereby threatening international peace and security in the region, by refusing to release, repatriate, or account for non-Iraqi citizens wrongfully detained by Iraq, including an American serviceman, and by failing to return property wrongfully seized by Iraq from Kuwait; . . .

Whereas the attacks on the United States of September 11, 2001, underscored the gravity of the threat posed by the acquisition of weapons of mass destruction by international terrorist organizations. . . .

Whereas the Iraq Liberation Act of 1998 (Public Law 105–338) expressed the sense of Congress that it should be the policy of the United States to support efforts to remove from power the current Iraqi regime and promote the emergence of a democratic government to replace that regime. . . .

Whereas the President has authority under the Constitution to take action in order to deter and prevent acts of international terrorism against the United States, as Congress recognized in the joint resolution on Authorization for Use of Military Force (Public Law 107–40); and

Whereas it is in the national security interests of the United States to restore international peace and security to the Persian Gulf region: Now, therefore, be it Resolved by the Senate and House of Representatives of the United States of America in Congress assembled. . . .

SEC. 3. AUTHORIZATION FOR USE OF UNITED STATES ARMED FORCES.

(a) AUTHORIZATION—The President is authorized to use the Armed Forces of the United States as he determines to be necessary and appropriate in order to—

(1) defend the national security of the United States against the continuing threat posed by Iraq; and

(2) enforce all relevant United Nations Security Council resolutions regarding Iraq.

(b) PRESIDENTIAL DETERMINATION—In connection with the exercise of the authority granted in subsection (a) to use force the President shall, prior to such exercise or as soon thereafter as may be feasible, but no later than 48 hours after exercising such authority, make available to the Speaker of the House of Representatives and the President pro tempore of the Senate his determination that—

(1) reliance by the United States on further diplomatic or other peaceful means alone either (A) will not adequately protect the national security of the United States against the continuing threat posed by Iraq or (B) is not likely to lead to enforcement of all relevant United Nations Security Council resolutions regarding Iraq; and

(2) acting pursuant to this joint resolution is consistent with the United States and other countries continuing to take the necessary actions against international terrorist and terrorist organizations, including those nations, organizations, or persons who planned, authorized, committed or aided the terrorist attacks that occurred on September 11, 2001.

(c) WAR POWERS RESOLUTION REQUIREMENTS—

(1) Specific Statutory Authorization—Consistent with section 8(a)(1) of the War Powers Resolution, the Congress declares that this section is intended to constitute specific statutory authorization within the meaning of section 5(b) of the War Powers Resolution.

(2) Applicability of Other Requirements—Nothing in this joint resolution supersedes any requirement of the War Powers Resolution.

SEC. 4. REPORTS TO CONGRESS. (a) REPORTS—The President shall, at least once every 60 days, submit to the Congress a report on matters relevant to this joint resolution, including actions taken pursuant to the exercise of authority granted in section 3 and the status of planning for efforts that are expected to be required after such actions are completed, including those actions described in section 7 of the Iraq Liberation Act of 1998 (Public Law 105–338). . . .

Notes and Queries

1. President George H. W. Bush's decision to send troops to Kuwait in August 1990 revived longstanding arguments about the power of the President to make war

without congressional approval.[45] Fifty-four members of the House of Representatives immediately filed suit in a United States District Court, asking it to enjoin the President's decision to send troops. Judge Harold Greene rejected the request, but he did note, in language reminiscent of Madison's complaints in the Washington administration, that "If the executive had the sole power to determine that any particular offensive military operation, no matter how vast, does not constitute war-making but only an offensive military attack, the congressional power to declare war will be at the mercy of a semantic decision by the Executive."[46]

On 8 January 1991, four months after his decision to begin Operation Desert Storm, and a week before the deadline imposed on Iraq by the United Nations to remove all troops from Kuwait, President Bush asked Congress for a formal resolution supporting "the use of all necessary means" to give sanction to the deadline. President Bush was careful to note that he was *not* asking for— and did not believe he needed—congressional *approval* to use force. His independent authority as Commander in chief, Bush argued, provided ample constitutional support for his actions. After much scholarly and political debate, Congress gave President Bush the Resolution he had requested.

The circumstances concerning the Resolution requested by President George W. Bush were rather different. The events of 11 September 2001 cast a long shadow, and Congress showed little if any willingness to question the President when he asked for the Resolution of October 2001. The Resolution easily passed both houses of Congress.

2. Is Section 3(2)(B)'s requirement that the President report to the Speaker of the House and the President pro tempore of the Senate an unconstitutional invasion of his powers as Commander in chief?

United States v. Curtiss-Wright Export Corp.
299 U.S. 304, 57 S.Ct. 216, 81 L.Ed. 255 (1936)

In the 1930s, Bolivia and Paraguay were involved in a violent border dispute. In 1934, Congress passed a Joint Resolution authorizing the president to enforce an arms embargo against those countries if he believed it would promote peace in the region. President Roosevelt immediately issued a proclamation to that effect. The Curtiss-Wright Corporation was indicted by the Department of Justice for violating the embargo. Curtiss-Wright challenged the indictment, arguing that Congress had made an unconstitutional delegation of legislative power to the executive. Opinion of the Court: *Sutherland,* Hughes, Van Devanter, Brandeis, Butler, Roberts, Cardozo. Dissenting opinion: *McReynolds.* Not participating: Stone.

Mr. Justice SUTHERLAND delivered the opinion of the Court.

Whether, if the Joint Resolution had related solely to internal affairs, it would be open to the challenge that it constituted an unlawful delegation of legislative power to the Executive, we find it unnecessary to determine. The whole aim of the resolution is to affect a situation entirely external to the United States, and falling within the category of foreign affairs. The determination which we are called to make, therefore, is whether the Joint Resolution, as applied to that situation, is vulnerable to attack under the rule that forbids a delegation of the lawmaking power. In other words, assuming (but not deciding) that the challenged delegation, if it were confined to internal affairs, would be invalid, may it nevertheless be sustained on the ground that its exclusive aim is to afford a remedy for a hurtful condition within foreign territory?

It will contribute to the elucidation of the question if we first consider the differences between the powers of the federal government in respect of foreign or external affairs and those in respect of domestic or internal affairs. That there are differences between them, and that these differences are fundamental, may not be doubted.

The two classes of powers are different, both in respect of their origin and their nature. The broad statement that the federal government can exercise no powers except those specifically enumerated in the Constitution, and such implied powers as are necessary and proper to carry into effect the enumerated powers, is categorically true only in respect of our internal affairs. In that field, the primary purpose of the Constitution was to carve from the general mass of legislative powers then possessed by the states such portions as it was thought desirable to vest in the federal government, leaving those not included in the

---

[45] See, for example, J. Gregory Sidak, *To Declare War,* 41 Duke Law Journal 27 (1991), and Harold Hongju Koh, *The Coase Theorem and the War Power: A Response,* 41 Duke Law Journal 24 (1991).

[46] *Dellums v. Bush,* 752 F.Supp. 1141 (D.D.C. 1990).

enumeration still in the states. . . . That this doctrine applies only to powers which the states had is self-evident. And since the states generally never possessed international powers, such powers could not have been carved from the mass of state powers but obviously were transmitted to the United States from some other source. During the Colonial period, those powers were possessed exclusively by and were entirely under the control of the Crown. By the Declaration of Independence, "the Representatives of the United States of America" declared the United (not the several) Colonies to be free and independent states, and as such to have "full Power to levy War, conclude Peace, contract Alliances, establish Commerce and to do all other Acts and Things which Independent States may of right do."

As a result of the separation from Great Britain by the colonies, acting as a unit, the powers of external sovereignty passed from the Crown not to the colonies severally, but to the colonies in their collective and corporate capacity as the United States of America. Even before the Declaration, the colonies were a unit in foreign affairs, acting through a common agency—namely, the Continental Congress, composed of delegates from the thirteen colonies. That agency exercised the powers of war and peace, raised an army, created a navy, and finally adopted the Declaration of Independence. Rulers come and go; governments end and forms of government change; but sovereignty survives. A political society cannot endure without a supreme will somewhere. Sovereignty is never held in suspense. When, therefore, the external sovereignty of Great Britain in respect of the colonies ceased, it immediately passed to the Union.

The Union existed before the Constitution, which was ordained and established among other things to form "a more perfect Union." Prior to that event, it is clear that the Union, declared by the Articles of Confederation to be "perpetual," was the sole possessor of external sovereignty, and in the Union it remained without change save in so far as the Constitution in express terms qualified its exercise. The Framers' Convention was called and exerted its powers upon the irrefutable postulate that though the states were several their people in respect of foreign affairs were one.

It results that the investment of the federal government with the powers of external sovereignty did not depend upon the affirmative grants of the Constitution. The powers to declare and wage war, to conclude peace, to make treaties, to maintain diplomatic relations with other sovereignties, if they had never been mentioned in the Constitution, would have vested in the federal government as necessary concomitants of nationality. Neither the Consti-

tution nor the laws passed in pursuance of it have any force in foreign territory unless in respect of our own citizens and operations of the nation in such territory must be governed by treaties, international understandings and compacts, and the principles of international law. As a member of the family of nations, the right and power of the United States in that field are equal to the right and power of the other members of the international family. Otherwise, the United States is not completely sovereign. The power to acquire territory by discovery and occupation, the power to expel undesirable aliens, the power to make such international agreements as do not constitute treaties in the constitutional sense, none of which is expressly affirmed by the Constitution, nevertheless exist as inherently inseparable from the conception of nationality. This the Court recognized, and in each of the cases cited found the warrant for its conclusions not in the provisions of the Constitution, but in the law of nations.

Not only, as we have shown, is the federal power over external affairs in origin and essential character different from that over internal affairs, but participation in the exercise of the power is significantly limited. In this vast external realm, with its important, complicated, delicate and manifold problems, the President alone has the power to speak or listen as a representative of the nation. He *makes* treaties with the advice and consent of the Senate; but he alone negotiates. Into the field of negotiation the Senate cannot intrude; and Congress itself is powerless to invade it. As Marshall said in his great argument of March 7, 1800, in the House of Representatives, "The President is the sole organ of the nation in its external relations, and its sole representative with foreign nations."

It is important to bear in mind that we are here dealing not alone with an authority vested in the President by an exertion of legislative power, but with such an authority plus the very delicate, plenary and exclusive power of the President as the sole organ of the federal government in the field of international relations—power which does not require as a basis for its exercise an act of Congress, but which, of course, like every other governmental power, must be exercised in subordination to the applicable provisions of the Constitution. It is quite apparent that if, in the maintenance of our international relations, embarrassment—perhaps serious embarrassment—is to be avoided and success for our aims achieved, congressional legislation which is to be made effective through negotiation and inquiry within the international field must often accord to the President a degree of discretion and freedom from statutory restriction which would not be admissible were domestic affairs alone involved. Moreover, he, not Congress, has the better opportunity of knowing the conditions which prevail in foreign countries, and especially is this true in time of war. He has his confidential sources of information. He has his agents in the form of diplomatic, consular and other officials. Secrecy in respect of information gathered by them may be highly necessary, and the premature disclosure of it productive of harmful results.

The marked difference between foreign affairs and domestic affairs in this respect is recognized by both houses of Congress in the very form of their requisitions for information from the executive departments. In the case of every department except the Department of State, the resolution directs the official to furnish the information. In the case of the State Department, dealing with foreign affairs, the President is requested to furnish the information "if not incompatible with the public interest." A statement that to furnish the information is not compatible with the public interest rarely, if ever, is questioned.

When the President is to be authorized by legislation to act in respect of a matter intended to affect a situation in foreign territory, the legislator properly bears in mind the important consideration that the form of the President's

action—or, indeed, whether he shall act at all—may well depend, among other things, upon the nature of the confidential information which he has or may thereafter receive, or upon the effect which his action may have upon our foreign relations. This consideration, in connection with what we have already said on the subject discloses the unwisdom of requiring Congress in this field of governmental power to lay down narrowly definite standards by which the President is to be governed.

In the light of the foregoing observations, it is evident that this Court should not be in haste to apply a general rule which will have the effect of condemning legislation like that under review as constituting an unlawful delegation of legislative power. The principles which justify such legislation find overwhelming support in the unbroken legislative practice which has prevailed almost from the inception of the national government to the present day.

The result of holding that the joint resolution [is an] unconstitutional delegation of legislative power would be to

---

Comparative Note 5.5

[Article 9 of Japan's Constitution renounces the sovereign right of the nation to engage in war and prohibits the maintenance of "war potential." (See Comparative Note 5.4.) The present case challenged the construction of an "Air Self-Defense Force (SDF) missile base" in Hokkaido. The extracts are from the decision of Sapporo's District Court and the Japanese Supreme Court.]

. . . [We] must therefore decide the issue whether the installation of defense equipment in question is unconstitutional or not. (Arguments based on the political question doctrine) are very vague. . . . Whenever the constitutionality of a statute is questioned the matter inevitably involves a question of a more or less political nature. . . . The defendant's argument, we believe, is not compatible with the principle of government by law, nor with judicial supremacy as provided by . . . the Constitution.

The Constitution clearly sets up legal norms in its Preamble and Article 9 on the issue of [self-defense]. . . . On the basis of the organization (and) scale . . . of the Self-Defense Forces . . . it is clear that [it] is "an, organization of men and materials with the purpose of carrying out battle with force against a foreign enemy." It, therefore, falls within the meaning of the term

"armed forces" . . . whose maintenance is prohibited by Article 9, Paragraph 2 of the Forest Act. [Sapporo's High Court reversed, holding that the issue was political and hence nonjusticiable. SOURCE: Kenneth L. Port, *Comparative Law: Law and Legal Process in Japan* (Durham: Carolina Academic Press, 1996), 174.]

Whether or not the SDF corresponds to the so-called "war potential" prohibited by Article 9 of the Constitution is not a matter to be examined by the judicial branch. The question of possessing a Self-Defense Force as a means of self-defense or, if one is maintained, questions regarding the scale and levels of equipment and capability . . . are matters relating to the fundamentals of state governance; they are highly political matters . . . not ordinarily dealt with in judicial review by the judiciary, which has a purely judicial function and does not bear political responsibility to the people. . . . Even if the power of judicial review does extend to the matter of the constitutionality of the SDF, that Force is self-defense power based on our country's right of self-defense, not the "war potential" of Article 9, and is consequently constitutional. [*Naganuma Nike Missile Site Case, I* (1973)]

SOURCE: Lawrence W. Beer and Hiroshi Itoh, *The Constitutional Case Law of Japan, 1970 through 1990* (Seattle: University of Washington Press, 1996), 91.

stamp this multitude of comparable acts and resolutions as likewise invalid. And while this Court may not, and should not, hesitate to declare acts of Congress, however many times repeated, to be unconstitutional if beyond all rational doubt it finds them to be so, an impressive array of legislation such as we have just set forth, enacted by nearly every Congress from the beginning of our national existence to the present day, must be given unusual weight in the process of reaching a correct determination of the problem. A legislative practice such as we have here, evidenced not by only occasional instances, but marked by the movement of a steady stream for a century and a half of time, goes a long way in the direction of proving the presence of unassailable ground for the constitutionality of the practice, to be found in the origin and history of the power involved, or in its nature, or in both combined.

Notes and Queries

1. Two specific conclusions followed from Sutherland's analysis. First, the Court concluded that Curtiss-Wright's argument, that the congressional resolution empowering the president violated the nondelegation doctrine, was irrelevant because that constitutional limitation applies only to domestic affairs. Second, the absence of constitutional limitations on the power required the Court to abstain, for without guidance from the Constitution the Court could do nothing more than express its opinion about the wisdom of the policy involved—clearly out of the bounds of proper judicial authority. As Justice Jackson noted in *Chicago & Southern Airlines, Inc. v. Waterman Steamship Corp.* (1948),

> The very nature of executive decisions as to foreign policy is political, not judicial. . . . They are delicate, complex, and involve large elements of prophecy. They are and should be undertaken only by those directly re-

sponsible to the people whose welfare they advance or imperil. They are decisions of a kind for which the Judiciary has neither the aptitude, facilities, nor responsibility, which has long been held to be in the domain of political power not subject to judicial intrusion or inquiry.

2. What precisely does the Court hold about the source of executive power in the field of foreign affairs? The theory advanced by the Court is sometimes called the "sole organ theory": the theory that the president is the sole organ of the nation in foreign affairs. The phrase comes from a speech by John Marshall when he was in Congress. Marshall defended a decision by President John Adams to extradite a fugitive under the controversial Jay Treaty, saying "The President is the sole organ of the nation in its external relations, and its sole representative with foreign nations."

Is that power completely untethered from constitutional restraints? One commentator has suggested that the Court transformed the president's "exclusive authority to communicate with foreign nations into exclusive policy-making authority." David Gray Adler, "Foreign Policy and the Separation of Powers: The Influence of the Judiciary," in Michael W. McCann and Gerald L. Houseman, eds., *Judging the Constitution.* (Glenview, Ill.: Scott, Foresman, 1989), 160.

3. Does the majority opinion offer any guidance for distinguishing between "internal" affairs and "external" affairs? Does the distinction have any merit?

4. What conception of judicial power does the majority embrace?

5. In Comparative Note 5.5, the Japanese District Court wrote "The Constitution clearly sets up legal norms in its Preamble and Article 9 on the issue of [self-defense]." Does this suggest, in contrast to *Curtiss-Wright*, that the powers of foreign affairs are governed, at least in part, by constitutional norms and not simply or exclusively by political considerations?

Korematsu v. United States
323 U.S. 214, 65 S.Ct. 193, 89 L.Ed. 194 (1944)

On 7 December 1941, Japanese forces attacked the American naval station at Pearl Harbor. Almost immediately the Japanese forces swept across much of the western Pacific, fueling fears that an attack on the West Coast of the United States was imminent. War hysteria, simple racism, and economic competition, led local and national politicians, including Earl Warren, then attorney general for the State

of California, to clamor for the internment of local Japanese-Americans, citing the threat of sabotage and espionage. Several military leaders joined in, notably General John L. DeWitt, commander in chief of the West Coast forces, even though the Office of Naval Intelligence and the Federal Bureau of Investigation had discounted the existence of any threat. On 27 March 1942, President Roosevelt issued an executive order that gave the military authority to "relocate" Japanese-Americans to several internment camps located in the West. No formal charges were required to relocate a citizen and there was no requirement that there be any particular evidence of a citizen's disloyalty or of criminal behavior. Fred Korematsu resisted the order and was arrested and convicted. The Supreme Court granted certiorari. Opinion of the Court: *Black*, Stone, Reed, Frankfurter, Douglas, Rutledge. Concurring opinion: *Frankfurter*. Dissenting Opinion: *Roberts; Murphy; Jackson*.

Mr. Justice BLACK delivered the opinion of the Court.

It should be noted, to begin with, that all legal restrictions which curtail the civil rights of a single racial group are immediately suspect. That is not to say that all such restrictions are unconstitutional. It is to say that Courts must subject them to the most rigid scrutiny. Pressing public necessity may sometimes justify the existence of such restrictions; racial antagonism never can.

In the light of the principles we announced in the *Hirabayashi* case, we are unable to conclude that it was beyond the war power of Congress and the Executive to exclude those of Japanese ancestry from the West Coast war area at the time they did. True, exclusion from the area in which one's home is located is a far greater deprivation than constant confinement to the home from 8 p.m. to 6 a.m. Nothing short of apprehension by the proper military authorities of the gravest imminent danger to the public safety can constitutionally justify either. But exclusion from a threatened area . . . has a definite and close relationship to the prevention of espionage and sabotage. The military authorities, charged with the primary responsibility of defending our shores, concluded that curfew provided inadequate protection and ordered exclusion. They did so . . . in accordance with congressional authority to the military to say who should, and who should not, remain in the threatened areas.

Here, as in *Hirabayashi*, "we cannot reject as unfounded the judgment of the military authorities and of Congress that there were disloyal members of that population. . . ." It was because we could not reject the finding of the military authorities that it was impossible to bring about an immediate segregation of the disloyal from the loyal that we sustained the validity of the curfew order as applying to the whole group. In the instant case, temporary exclusion of the entire group was rested by the military on the same ground. The judgment that exclusion of the whole group was for the same reason a military imperative answers the contention that the exclusion was in the nature of group punishment based on antagonism to those of Japanese origin. . . . That there were members of the group who retained loyalties to Japan has been confirmed by investigations made subsequent to the exclu-

sion. Approximately five thousand American citizens of Japanese ancestry refused to swear unqualified allegiance to the United States and to renounce allegiance to the Japanese Emperor, and several thousand evacuees requested repatriation to Japan.

We uphold the exclusion order as of the time it was made and when the petitioner violated it. . . . In doing so, we are not unmindful of the hardships imposed by it upon a large group of American citizens. . . . But hardships are part of war, and war is an aggregation of hardships. Compulsory exclusion of large groups of citizens from their homes, except under circumstances of direst emergency and peril, is inconsistent with our basic governmental institutions. But when under conditions of modern warfare our shores are threatened by hostile forces, the power to protect must be commensurate with the threatened danger.

We are thus being asked to pass at this time upon the whole subsequent detention program in both assembly and relocation centers, although the only issues framed at the trial related to petitioner's remaining in the prohibited area in violation of the exclusion order. Had petitioner here left the prohibited area and gone to an assembly center we cannot say either as a matter of fact or law, that his presence in that center would have resulted in his detention in a relocation center. Some who did report . . . were not sent to relocation centers, but were released upon condition that they remain outside the prohibited zone.

Since the petitioner has not been convicted of failing to report or to remain in an assembly or relocation center, we cannot in this case determine the validity of those separate provisions of the order. . . . Some of the members of the Court are of the view that evacuation and detention . . . were inseparable. . . . The power to exclude includes the power to do it by force if necessary. And any forcible measure must necessarily entail some degree of detention and restraint whatever method of removal is selected. But whichever view is taken, it results in holding that the order under which the petitioner was convicted was valid.

It is said that we are dealing here with the case of imprisonment of a citizen in a concentration camp solely because of his ancestry, without evidence or inquiry concerning his loyalty and good disposition towards the United States. Our task would be simple, our duty clear, were this a case involving the imprisonment of a loyal citizen in a concentration camp because of racial prejudice. Regardless of the true nature of the assembly and relocation centers—and we deem it unjustifiable to call them concentration camps with all the ugly connotations that term implies—we are dealing specifically with nothing but an exclusion order. To cast this case into outlines of racial prejudice, without reference to the real military dangers which were presented, merely confuses the issue. Korematsu was not excluded from the Military Area because of hostility to him or his race. He was excluded because we are at war with the Japanese Empire, because the properly constituted military authorities feared an invasion of our West Coast and felt constrained to take proper security measures, because they decided that the military urgency of the situation demanded that all citizens of Japanese ancestry be segregated from the West Coast temporarily, and finally, because Congress, reposing its confidence in this time of war in our military leaders—as inevitably it must—determined that they should have the power to do just this. There was evidence of disloyalty on the part of some, the military authorities considered that the need for action was great, and time was short. We cannot—by availing ourselves of the calm perspective of hindsight—now say that at that time these actions were unjustified.

Affirmed.

Mr. Justice FRANKFURTER, concurring.

The provisions of the Constitution which confer on the Congress and the President powers to enable this country to wage war are as much part of the Constitution as provisions looking to a nation at peace. And we have had recent occasion to quote approvingly the statement of former Chief Justice Hughes that the war power of the Government is "the power to wage war successfully." . . . Therefore, the validity of action under the war power must be judged wholly in the context of war. That action is not to be stigmatized as lawless because like action in times of peace would be lawless. To talk about a military order that expresses an allowable judgment of war needs by those entrusted with the duty of conducting war as "an unconstitutional order" is to suffuse a part of the Constitution with an atmosphere of unconstitutionality. . . . To recognize that military orders are "reasonably expedient military precautions" in time of war and yet to deny them constitutional legitimacy makes of the Constitution an instrument for dialectic subtleties not reasonably to be attributed to the hard-headed Framers, of whom a majority had had actual participation in war. If a military order such as that under review does not transcend the means appropriate for conducting war, such action by the military is as constitutional as would be any authorized action by the Interstate Commerce Commission within the limits of the constitutional power to regulate commerce. And being an exercise of the war power explicitly granted by the Constitution for safeguarding the national life by prosecuting war effectively, I find nothing in the Constitution which denies to Congress the power to enforce such a valid military order by making its violation an offense triable in the civil courts. To find that the Constitution does not forbid the military measures now complained of does not carry with it approval of that which Congress and the Executive did. That is their business, not ours.

Mr. Justice ROBERTS.

. . . [T]he indisputable facts exhibit a clear violation of Constitutional rights. . . . [E]xclusion was but part of an overall plan for forcible detention. . . . The two conflicting orders, one of which commanded him to stay and the other which commanded him to go, were nothing but a cleverly devised trap to accomplish the real purpose . . . which was to lock him up in a concentration camp. . . . Why should we set up a figmentary and artificial situation instead of addressing ourselves to the actualities of the case?

Comparative Note 5.6

[Rudolph Hess, a cabinet minister in the Nazi government, was arrested in Britain and brought forward as an accused before the International Military Tribunal following Germany's surrender in the Second World War. He was convicted of "crimes against the peace" and sentenced to life in prison: In this case his son sought a declaration by the Federal Constitutional Court that the continuation of his imprisonment violated his rights under the Basic Law.]

The breadth of this discretion in foreign affairs has its basis in the nature of foreign relations. Such events are not governed solely by the will of the federation, but rather are dependent on many circumstances over which it has little control. In order to facilitate the realization of the federation's political goals within the framework of what is constitutionally permissible . . . the Constitution confers considerable discretion on foreign affairs agencies in assessing the practicality and feasibility of certain policies or actions.

Source: *Rudolph Hess Case* (1980) in Kommers, *Constitutional Jurisprudence*, 154.

Mr. Justice MURPHY, dissenting.

This exclusion of "all persons of Japanese ancestry, both alien and non-alien," from the Pacific Coast area on a plea of military necessity in the absence of martial law ought not to be approved. Such exclusion goes over "the very brink of constitutional power" and falls into the ugly abyss of racism.

In dealing with matters relating to the prosecution and progress of a war, we must accord great respect and consideration to the judgments of the military authorities who are on the scene and who have full knowledge of the military facts. The scope of their discretion must, as a matter of necessity and common sense, be wide. And their judgments ought not to be overruled lightly by those whose training and duties ill-equip them to deal intelligently with matters so vital to the physical security of the nation.

At the same time, however, it is essential that there be definite limits to military discretion, especially where martial law has not been declared. Individuals must not be left impoverished of their constitutional rights on a plea of military necessity that has neither substance nor support. Thus, like other claims conflicting with the asserted constitutional rights of the individual, the military claim must subject itself to the judicial process of having its reasonableness determined and its conflicts with other interests reconciled.

The judicial test of whether the Government, on a plea of military necessity, can validly deprive an individual of any of his constitutional rights is whether the deprivation is reasonably related to a public danger that is so "immediate, imminent, and impending" as not to admit of delay and not to permit the intervention of ordinary constitutional processes to alleviate the danger. . . . Being an obvious racial discrimination, the order deprives all those within its scope of the equal protection of the laws as guaranteed by the Fifth Amendment. It further deprives these individuals of their constitutional rights to live and work where they will, to establish a home where they choose and to move about freely. In excommunicating them without benefit of hearings, this order also deprives them of all their constitutional rights to procedural due process. Yet no reasonable relation to an "immediate, imminent, and impending" public danger is evident to support this racial restriction. . . .

It must be conceded that the military and naval situation in the spring of 1942 was such as to generate a very real fear of invasion of the Pacific Coast, accompanied by fears of sabotage and espionage in that area. The military command was therefore justified in adopting all reasonable means necessary to combat these dangers. In adjudging the military action taken in light of the then apparent dangers, we must not erect too high or too meticulous standards; it is necessary only that the action have some reasonable relation to the removal of the dangers of invasion, sabotage and espionage. But the exclusion, either temporarily or permanently, of all persons with Japanese blood in their veins has no such reasonable relation. And that relation is lacking because the exclusion order necessarily must rely for its reasonableness upon the assumption that all persons of Japanese ancestry may have a dangerous tendency to commit sabotage and espionage and to aid our Japanese enemy in other ways. It is difficult to believe that reason, logic or experience could be marshaled in support of such an assumption.

That this forced exclusion was the result in good measure of this erroneous assumption of racial guilt rather than bona fide military necessity is evidenced by the Commanding General's Final Report on the evacuation from the Pacific Coast area. In it he refers to all individuals of Japanese descent as "subversive," as belonging to "an enemy race" whose "racial strains are undiluted," and as constituting "over 112,000 potential enemies at large today" along the Pacific Coast. In support of this blanket condemnation of all persons of Japanese descent, however, no reliable evidence is cited to show that such individuals were generally disloyal, or had generally so conducted themselves in this area as to constitute a special menace to defense installations or war industries, or had otherwise by their behavior furnished reasonable ground for their exclusion as a group.

Justification for the exclusion is sought, instead, mainly upon questionable racial and sociological grounds not ordinarily within the realm of expert military judgment, supplemented by certain semi-military conclusions drawn from an unwarranted use of circumstantial evidence. Individuals of Japanese ancestry are condemned because they are said to be "a large, unassimilated, tightly knit racial group, bound to an enemy nation by strong ties of race, culture, custom, and religion." They are claimed to be given to "emperor worshipping ceremonies" and to "dual citizenship." Japanese language schools and allegedly pro-Japanese organizations are cited as evidence of possible group disloyalty, together with facts as to certain persons being educated and residing at length in Japan. It is intimated that many of these individuals deliberately resided "adjacent to strategic points," thus enabling them "to carry into execution a tremendous program of sabotage on a mass scale should any considerable number of them have been inclined to do so."

The need for protective custody is also asserted. The report refers without identity to "numerous incidents of violence" as well as other admittedly unverified or cumulative incidents. From this, plus certain other events not shown to have been connected with the Japanese Americans, it is concluded that the "situation was fraught with danger to the Japanese population itself" and that the general public "was ready to take matters into its own hands."

The main reasons . . . appear . . . to be largely an accumulation of much of the misinformation, half-truths and insinuations that for years have been directed against Japanese Americans by people with racial and economic prejudices—the same people who have been among the foremost advocates of the evacuation. A military judgment based upon such racial and sociological considerations is not entitled to the great weight ordinarily given the judgments based upon strictly military considerations.

No adequate reason is given for the failure to treat these Japanese Americans on an individual basis by holding investigations and hearings to separate the loyal from the disloyal, as was done in the case of persons of German and Italian ancestry. . . . It is asserted merely that the loyalties of this group "were unknown and time was of the essence." Yet nearly four months elapsed after Pearl Harbor before the first exclusion order was issued; nearly eight months went by until the last order was issued; and the last of these "subversive" persons was not actually removed until almost eleven months had elapsed. Leisure and deliberation seem to have been more of the essence than speed. And the fact that conditions were not such as to warrant a declaration of martial law adds strength to the belief that the factors of time and military necessity were not as urgent as they have been represented to be.

I dissent, therefore, from this legalization of racism. Racial discrimination in any form and in any degree has no justifiable part whatever in our democratic way of life. It is unattractive in any setting but it is utterly revolting among a free people who have embraced the principles set forth in the Constitution of the United States. All residents of this nation are kin in some way by blood or culture to a foreign land. Yet they are primarily and necessarily a part of the new and distinct civilization of the United States. They must accordingly be treated at all times as the heirs of the American experiment and as entitled to all the rights and freedoms guaranteed by the Constitution.

Mr. Justice JACKSON, dissenting.

Now if any fundamental assumption underlies our system, it is that guilt is personal and not inheritable. . . . But here is an attempt to make an otherwise innocent act a crime merely because this prisoner is the son of parents as to whom he had no choice, and belongs to a race from which there is no way to resign.

. . . [I]t is said that if the military commander had reasonable military grounds for promulgating the orders, they are constitutional and become law, and the Court is required to enforce them. [There are] several reasons why I cannot subscribe to this doctrine.

It would be impracticable and dangerous idealism to expect or insist that each specific military command in an area of probable operations will conform to conventional tests of constitutionality. When an area is so beset that it must be put under military control at all, the paramount consideration is that its measures be successful, rather than legal. The armed services must protect a society, not merely its Constitution. The very essence of the military job is to marshal physical force, to remove every obstacle to its effectiveness, to give it every strategic advantage. Defense measures will not, and often should not, be held within the limits that bind civil authority in peace. No Court can require such a commander in such circumstances to act as a reasonable man; he may be unreasonably cautious and exacting. Perhaps he should be. But a commander in temporarily focusing the life of a community on defense is carrying out a military program; he is not making law in the sense the Courts know the term. He issues orders, and they may have a certain authority as military commands, although they may be very bad as constitutional law.

But if we cannot confine military expedients by the Constitution, neither would I distort the Constitution to approve all that the military may deem expedient. This is what the Court appears to be doing, whether consciously or not. I cannot say, from any evidence before me, that the orders of General DeWitt were not reasonably expedient military precautions, nor could I say that they were. But even if they were permissible military procedures, I deny that it follows that they are constitutional. If, as the Court holds, it does follow, then we may as well say that any military order will be constitutional and have done with it.

In the very nature of things military decisions are not susceptible of intelligent judicial appraisal. They do not pretend to rest on evidence, but are made on information that often would not be admissible and on assumptions that could not be proved. Information in support of an order could not be disclosed to Courts without danger that it would reach the enemy. Neither can Courts act on communications made in confidence. Hence Courts can never have any real alternative to accepting the mere declaration of the authority that issued the order that it was reasonably necessary from a military viewpoint.

Much is said of the danger to liberty from the Army program for deporting and detaining these citizens of Japanese extraction. But a judicial construction of the due process clause that will sustain this order is a far more subtle blow to liberty than the promulgation of the order itself. A military order, however unconstitutional, is not apt to last longer than the military emergency. Even during that period a succeeding commander may revoke it all. But once a judicial opinion rationalizes such an order to show that it conforms to the Constitution, or rather rationalizes the Constitution to show that the Constitution sanctions such an order, the Court for all time has validated the principle of racial discrimination in criminal procedure and of transplanting American citizens. The principle then lies about like a loaded weapon ready for the hand of any authority that can bring forward a plausible claim of an urgent need. Every repetition imbeds that principle more deeply in our law and thinking and expands it to new purposes. All who observe the work of courts are familiar with what Judge Cardozo described as "the tendency of a principle to expand itself to the limit of its logic." A military commander may overstep the bounds of constitutionality, and it is an incident. But if we review and approve, that passing incident becomes the doctrine of the Constitution. There it has a generative power of its own, and all that it creates will be in its own image. Nothing better illustrates this danger than does the Court's opinion in this case. It argues that we are bound to uphold the conviction of Korematsu because we upheld one in *Hirabayashi*.

In that case we were urged to consider only the curfew. . . . We yielded, and the Chief Justice guarded the opinion as carefully as language will do. . . . Now the principle of racial discrimination is pushed from support of mild measures to very harsh ones, and from temporary deprivations to indeterminate ones. And the precedent which it is said requires us to do so is *Hirabayashi*. The Court is now saying that in *Hirabayashi* we did decide the very things we there said we were not deciding.

I should hold that a civil Court cannot be made to enforce an order which violates constitutional limitations even if it is a reasonable exercise of military authority. The Courts can exercise only the judicial power, can apply only law, and must abide by the Constitution, or they cease to be civil Courts and become instruments of military policy.

. . . I would not lead people to rely on this Court for a review that seems to me wholly delusive. . . . If the people ever let command of the war power fall into irresponsible and unscrupulous hands, the courts wield no power equal to its restraint. The chief restraint upon those who command . . . must be their responsibility to the political judgments of their contemporaries and to the moral judgments of history.

My duties as a justice as I see them do not require me to make a military judgment as to whether General DeWitt's evacuation and detention program was a reasonable military necessity. I do not suggest that the Courts should have

attempted to interfere with the Army in carrying out its task. But I do not think they may be asked to execute a military expedient that has no place in law under the Constitution. I would reverse the judgment and discharge the prisoner.

Notes and Queries

1. Executive Order 9066, calling for the "evacuation" of Japanese-Americans on the West Coast, resulted in the internment of over 100,000 residents. The last of the internees were released from the camps in 1946. In 1983, after years of hard work by lawyers for the American Civil Liberties Union and the Japanese-American Citizens League, among others, Fred Korematsu's conviction was "vacated" by Federal District Judge Marilyn Hall Patel. Korematsu's lawyers had used a petition of *coram nobis*—an extremely unusual procedure—to force the government to prove that there had not been a "manifest injustice" or prosecutorial misconduct in the case. Judge Patel ruled in favor of Korematsu, finding there was "substantial support in the record that the government deliberately omitted relevant information and provided misleading information" to the Supreme Court.

2. In 1980, Congress created a Commission on Wartime Relocation and Internment of Civilians to review the decision. After hearings in 1981, the Commission unanimously concluded that the internment policy was a consequence of "race prejudice, war hysteria and a failure of political leadership. . . ." It recommended that Congress reimburse each of the 60,000 or so survivors of the camps with $20,000. Congress enacted the legislation in 1988 and President Reagan signed it into law.

3. *Korematsu* involves important questions about the how and the who of constitutional interpretation. Consider: In his majority opinion, Justice Black purports to use strict scrutiny, but upholds the policy. Justice Murphy, in contrast, professes to use the lowly rationality standard, but strikes the program. What does this tell us about the integrity of these various standards of judicial scrutiny? What does it tell us about the integrity of constitutional interpretation more generally?

Similarly, Justices Black, Murphy, and Jackson approach the question of who interprets the Constitution in such cases in very different ways. Black and Murphy insist upon the principle of judicial accountability, albeit in starkly different degrees. Jackson, in contrast, cautions about the limits of judicial supervision, thus entrusting constitutional interpretation primarily to the "political branches," much as Justice Grier did almost a century earlier.

4. What theory of judicial power animates Justice

Black's opinion for the majority? How does it differ from Justice Jackson's dissent? Would Jackson—later chief prosecutor at the Nuremberg War Trials—have ruled that the executive order was unconstitutional? Or would he have refused to consider its constitutionality? Is there a difference?

5. Can the decision in *Korematsu* be reconciled with the Court's expansive language in *Ex Parte Milligan* (1866)?

6. The essential issue in *Korematsu*, of course, concerns the tension between the community and the individual. War highlights that tension better than anything else. If our collective survival is really at issue, is it not foolish to risk that survival by an overly scrupulous attention to constitutional principle? Is the Constitution a suicide pact?

7. There is a peculiar twist to *Korematsu*: It is among the very first cases to establish that "legal restrictions

which curtail the civil rights of a single racial group are immediately suspect." As we shall see in chapter 14, this test has become a cornerstone of judicial efforts to guarantee equal protection to racial minorities.

8. Canada also detained many of its citizens of Japanese ancestry. In 1945, after Japan had surrendered, the Government ordered the Labour Minister to deport any member of the Japanese race who had requested repatriation during the war. The orders included a provision authorizing the minister to deport the wife and children of a male already scheduled for deportation. In *Co-Operative Committee on Japanese-Canadian v. Attorney-General for Canada*, (1947) A.C. 87, 3 Olsmstead 458, the Privy Council upheld the orders.

9. Comparative Note 5.6 reprints an excerpt from a decision by the Federal Constitutional Court of Germany. Does the Court's decision mirror Justice Black's insistence upon deference to the military authorities in *Korematsu*?

Zadvydas v. Davis
533 U.S. 678, 121 S. Ct. 2491, 150 L. Ed. 2d 653 (2001)

This case involved two men—one, Zadvydas, born in Germany, the other, Ma, born in Cambodia—who were resident aliens in the United States. Both had criminal records and were ordered deported. In both cases the men's home countries refused to accept them, and no other willing country could be located. When they remained in custody after the removal period expired, they filed habeas actions, claiming that their indefinite detention was not authorized by statute, and would in any event violate their constitutional rights under the Fifth Amendment. Opinion of the Court: *Breyer*, Stevens, O'Connor, Souter, Ginsburg. Dissenting opinion: *Scalia*, Thomas; *Kennedy*, Rehnquist, Scalia (in part), Thomas (in part).

Justice BREYER delivered the opinion of the Court.

When an alien has been found to be unlawfully present in the United States and a final order of removal has been entered, the Government ordinarily secures the alien's removal during a subsequent 90-day statutory "removal period," during which time the alien normally is held in custody.

A special statute authorizes further detention if the Government fails to remove the alien during those 90 days. . . .

In these cases, we must decide whether this post-removal-period statute authorizes the Attorney General to detain a removable alien indefinitely beyond the removal period or only for a period reasonably necessary to secure the alien's removal. We deal here with aliens who were

admitted to the United States but subsequently ordered removed. Aliens who have not yet gained initial admission to this country would present a very different question. Based on our conclusion that indefinite detention of aliens in the former category would raise serious constitutional concerns, we construe the statute to contain an implicit "reasonable time" limitation, the application of which is subject to federal court review. . . .

The post-removal-period detention statute applies to certain categories of aliens who have been ordered removed, namely inadmissible aliens, criminal aliens, aliens who have violated their nonimmigrant status conditions, and aliens removable for certain national security or foreign relations reasons, as well as any alien "who has been determined by the Attorney General to be a risk to the community or unlikely to comply with the order of removal." It says that an alien who falls into one of these categories "may be detained beyond the removal period and, if released, shall be subject to [certain] terms of supervision."

The Government argues that the statute means what it literally says. It sets no "limit on the length of time beyond the removal period that an alien who falls within one of the Section 1231(a)(6) categories may be detained." Hence, "whether to continue to detain such an alien and, if so, in what circumstances and for how long" is up to the Attorney General, not up to the courts.

"[I]t is a cardinal principle" of statutory interpretation, however, that when an Act of Congress raises "a serious doubt" as to its constitutionality, "this Court will first ascertain whether a construction of the statute is fairly possible by which the question may be avoided." We have read

Comparative Note 5.7

[In the case of *Arjub v. Minister of Defence et al.* (1982), the Israeli Supreme Court was asked to consider whether defendants in military courts in the occupied areas of Judea, Samaria, and the Gaza strip had a right of appeal to a civilian court. The judges denied that a right of civilian appeal is "a natural right that exists even in the absence" of legislation. Moreover, the Court concluded, "there is no justification or ground for this Court's intervention as requested."]

The Court continued:

(b) The institution of a right of appeal reflects the relinquishment of extreme emergency measures that may be necessary during the initial period of a military administration, but are not justified in a military administration that has existed for over twenty years and continues to operate according to the same Governmental scheme. I shall elaborate upon this point. With respect to a right of appeal in territories under belligerent occupation, it is generally appropriate to distinguish between the beginning and later periods. When the military administration is first established, immediately after the cease-fire, the institution of a two-tier system of justice is not possible or generally practical. When the new governmental system takes over the powers of the state in the occupied territory, it must first restore the life of the inhabitants to its proper course and guarantee the public order (*l'ordre et la vie publique*) in the words of Article 43 of the 1907 Hague Regulations. At this initial stage it is essential to immediately establish one military judicial instance so as to make the population realise that the fluctuations and

upheavals of the war and accompanying licentiousness are now over, because a new government has been established and has promulgated its orders, which must be complied with strictly and immediately.

With the passage of time and the restoration of public order, however, the acute and stringent side-effects of the war and the initial organization of the new government must be gradually set aside so that life under the occupation may, as far as possible, regain the semblance of ordinary existence.

(c) The establishment of a military appellate instance would directly raise the prestige of the military justice system in the eye of the local population and all other persons, for it would thus integrate an element that enhances the competence of its judicial discretion and professional operation. The appellate instance also emphasizes the independence of the military justice system, and this is another important element in strengthening its status and prestige.

All the judges and presidents of the first military instance in our system have legal training. Some serve as part of their regular military service; and some are lawyers in civilian life who serve their reserve duty as judges. I have no doubt that they perform their judicial work faithfully and are diligent in the proper administration of justice. But, as explained above, the institution of an appellate instance would complete the structure of the legal system, bringing it into conformity with accepted notions. The military courts would thus gain an additional essential layer, reinforcing the credibility, stability and even the moral strength of the entire system."

SOURCE: 42(1) P.D. 353.

---

significant limitations into other immigration statutes in order to avoid their constitutional invalidation. For similar reasons, we read an implicit limitation into the statute before us. In our view, the statute, read in light of the Constitution's demands, limits an alien's post-removal-period detention to a period reasonably necessary to bring about that alien's removal from the United States. It does not permit indefinite detention.

A

A statute permitting indefinite detention of an alien would raise a serious constitutional problem. The Fifth Amendment's Due Process Clause forbids the Government to "depriv[e]" any "person . . . of . . . liberty . . . without due process of law." Freedom from imprisonment—from government custody, detention, or other forms of physical restraint—lies at the heart of the liberty that Clause protects. And this Court has said that government detention violates that Clause unless the detention is ordered in a criminal proceeding with adequate procedural protections, or, in certain special and "narrow" non-punitive "circumstances," where a special justification, such as harm-threatening mental illness, outweighs the "individual's constitutionally protected interest in avoiding physical restraint." The proceedings at issue here are civil, not criminal, and we assume that they are nonpunitive in purpose and effect. There is no sufficiently strong special justification here for indefinite civil detention—at least as administered under this statute. The statute, says the Government, has two regulatory goals: "ensuring the appearance of aliens at future immigration proceedings" and "[p]reventing danger to the community." But by definition the first justification—preventing flight—is weak or nonexistent where removal seems a remote possibility at best.

The second justification—protecting the community—does not necessarily diminish in force over time. But we have upheld preventive detention based on dangerousness only when limited to specially dangerous individuals and subject to strong procedural protections. In cases in which preventive detention is of potentially indefinite duration, we have also demanded that the dangerousness rationale be accompanied by some other special circumstance, such as mental illness, that helps to create the danger.

The civil confinement here at issue is not limited, but potentially permanent. The provision authorizing detention does not apply narrowly to "a small segment of particularly dangerous individuals," say suspected terrorists, but broadly to aliens ordered removed for many and various reasons, including tourist visa violations. And, once the flight risk justification evaporates, the only special circumstance present is the alien's removable status itself, which bears no relation to a detainee's dangerousness.

The serious constitutional problem arising out of a statute that, in these circumstances, permits an indefinite, perhaps permanent, deprivation of human liberty without any such protection is obvious. . . .

The Government argues that, from a constitutional perspective, alien status itself can justify indefinite detention, and points to *Shaughnessy v. United States ex rel. Mezei*, 345 U. S. 206 (1953), as support. That case involved a once lawfully admitted alien who left the United States, returned after a trip abroad, was refused admission, and was left on Ellis Island, indefinitely detained there because the Government could not find another country to accept him. The Court held that Mezei's detention did not violate the Constitution.

Although *Mezei*, like the present cases, involves indefinite detention, it differs from the present cases in a critical respect. As the Court emphasized, the alien's extended departure from the United States required him to seek entry into this country once again. His presence on Ellis Island did not count as entry into the United States. Hence, he was "treated," for constitutional purposes, "as if stopped at the border." And that made all the difference.

The distinction between an alien who has effected an entry into the United States and one who has never entered runs throughout immigration law. It is well established that certain constitutional protections available to persons inside the United States are unavailable to aliens outside of our geographic borders. . . . Indeed, this Court has held that the Due Process Clause protects an alien subject to a final order of deportation, though the nature of that protection may vary depending upon status and circumstance.

The Government also looks for support to cases holding that Congress has "plenary power" to create immigration law, and that the judicial branch must defer to executive and legislative branch decisionmaking in that area. But that power is subject to important constitutional limitations. In these cases, we focus upon those limitations. In doing so, we nowhere deny the right of Congress to remove aliens, to subject them to supervision with conditions when released from detention, or to incarcerate them where appropriate for violations of those conditions.

Nor do the cases before us require us to consider the political branches' authority to control entry into the United States. Hence we leave no "unprotected spot in the Nation's armor." Neither do we consider terrorism or other special circumstances where special arguments might be made for forms of preventive detention and for heightened deference to the judgments of the political branches with respect to matters of national security. The sole foreign policy consideration the Government mentions here is the concern lest courts interfere with "sensitive" repatriation negotiations. But neither the Government nor the dissents explain how a habeas court's efforts to determine the likelihood of repatriation, if handled with appropriate sensitivity, could make a significant difference in this respect.

Finally, the Government argues that, whatever liberty interest the aliens possess, it is "greatly diminished" by their lack of a legal right to "liv[e] at large in this country." The choice, however, is not between imprisonment and the alien "living at large." It is between imprisonment and supervision under release conditions that may not be violated. And, for the reasons we have set forth, we believe that an alien's liberty interest is, at the least, strong enough to raise a serious question as to whether, irrespective of the procedures used, the Constitution permits detention that is indefinite and potentially permanent.

We recognize, as the Government points out, that review must take appropriate account of the greater immigration-related expertise of the Executive Branch, of the serious administrative needs and concerns inherent in the necessarily extensive INS efforts to enforce this complex statute, and the Nation's need to "speak with one voice" in immigration matters. But we believe that courts can take appropriate account of such matters without abdicating their legal responsibility to review the lawfulness of an alien's continued detention.

Ordinary principles of judicial review in this area recognize primary Executive Branch responsibility. They counsel judges to give expert agencies decisionmaking leeway in matters that invoke their expertise. They recognize Executive Branch primacy in foreign policy matters. And they consequently require courts to listen with care when the Government's foreign policy judgments, including, for example, the status of repatriation negotiations, are at issue, and to grant the Government appropriate leeway when its judgments rest upon foreign policy expertise.

We realize that recognizing this necessary Executive leeway will often call for difficult judgments. In order to limit the occasions when courts will need to make them, we think it practically necessary to recognize some presumptively reasonable period of detention.

Consequently, we vacate the decisions below and remand both cases for further proceedings consistent with this opinion.

It is so ordered.

Justice SCALIA, with whom Justice THOMAS joins, dissenting.

I join Part I of Justice Kennedy's dissent, which establishes the Attorney General's clear statutory authority to detain criminal aliens with no specified time limit. I write separately because I do not believe that, as Justice Kennedy suggests in Part II of his opinion, there may be some situations in which the courts can order release. . . . A criminal alien under final order of removal who allegedly will not be accepted by any other country in the reasonably foreseeable future claims a constitutional right of supervised release into the United States. This claim can be repackaged as freedom from "physical restraint" or freedom from "indefinite detention," but it is at bottom a claimed right of release into this country by an individual who concededly has no legal right to be here. There is no such constitutional right.

. . . We are offered no justification why an alien under a valid and final order of removal—which has totally extinguished whatever right to presence in this country he possessed—has any greater due process right to be released into the country than an alien at the border seeking entry. Congress undoubtedly thought that both groups of aliens—inadmissible aliens at the threshold and criminal aliens under final order of removal—could be constitutionally detained on the same terms, since it provided the authority to detain both groups in the very same statutory provision. . . . I find no constitutional impediment to the discretion Congress gave to the Attorney General. Justice Kennedy's dissent explains the clarity of the detention provision, and I see no obstacle to following the statute's plain meaning.

Justice KENNEDY, with whom the CHIEF JUSTICE joins, and with whom Justice SCALIA and Justice THOMAS join as to Part I, dissenting.

The Court says its duty is to avoid a constitutional question. It deems the duty performed by interpreting a statute in obvious disregard of congressional intent; curing the resulting gap by writing a statutory amendment of its own; committing its own grave constitutional error by arrogating to the Judicial Branch the power to summon high officers of the Executive to assess their progress in conducting some of the Nation's most sensitive negotiations with foreign powers; and then likely releasing into our general population at least hundreds of removable or inadmissible aliens who have been found by fair procedures to be flight risks, dangers to the community, or both. Far from avoiding a constitutional question, the Court's ruling causes systemic dislocation in the balance of powers, thus raising serious constitutional concerns not just for the cases at hand but for the Court's own view of its proper authority. Any supposed respect the Court seeks in not reaching the constitutional question is outweighed by the intrusive and erroneous exercise of its own powers. In the guise of judicial restraint the Court ought not to intrude upon the other branches. The constitutional question the statute presents, it must be acknowledged, may be a significant one in some later case; but it ought not to drive us to an incorrect interpretation of the statute. The Court having reached the wrong result for the wrong reason, this respectful dissent is required.

The majority's interpretation, moreover, defeats the very repatriation goal in which it professes such interest. The Court rushes to substitute a judicial judgment for the Executive's discretion and authority. As the Government represents to us, judicial orders requiring release of removable aliens, even on a temporary basis, have the potential to undermine the obvious necessity that the Nation speak with one voice on immigration and foreign affairs matters. The result of the Court's rule is that, by refusing to accept repatriation of their own nationals, other countries can effect the release of these individuals back into the American community. If their own nationals are now at large in the United States, the nation of origin may ignore or disclaim responsibility to accept their return. The interference with sensitive foreign relations becomes even more acute where hostility or tension characterizes the relationship, for other countries can use the fact of judicially mandated release to their strategic advantage, refusing the return of their nationals to force dangerous aliens upon us. One of the more alarming aspects of the Court's new venture into foreign affairs management is the suggestion that the district court can expand or contract the reasonable period of detention based on its own assessment of the course of negotiations with foreign powers. The Court says it will allow the Executive to perform its duties on its own for six months; after that, foreign relations go into judicially supervised receivership.

It is to be expected that from time to time a foreign power will adopt a truculent stance with respect to the United States and other nations. Yet the Court by its time limit, or presumptive time limit, goes far to undercut the position of the Executive in repatriation negotiations, thus ill serving the interest of all foreign nationals of the country concerned. Law-abiding aliens might wish to return to their home country, for instance, but the strained relationship caused by the difficult repatriation talks might prove to be a substantial obstacle for these aliens as well.

In addition to weakening the hand of our Government, court ordered release cannot help but encourage dilatory and obstructive tactics by aliens who, emboldened by the Court's new rule, have good reason not to cooperate by making their own repatriation or transfer seem foreseeable. An alien ordered deported also has less incentive to cooperate or to facilitate expeditious removal when he has been released, even on a supervised basis, than does an alien held at an Immigration and Naturalization Service (INS) detention facility. Neither the alien nor his family would find any urgency in assisting with a petition to other countries to accept the alien back if the alien could simply remain in the United States indefinitely.

This rule of startling breadth invites potentially perverse results. Because other nations may refuse to admit aliens who have committed certain crimes—often the aliens who have committed the most serious crimes will be those who may be released immediately under the majority's rule. . . . Today's result will ensure these dangerous individuals, and hundreds more like them, will remain free while the Executive Branch tries to secure their removal. By contrast, aliens who violate mere tourist visa requirements, can in the typical case be held pending deportation on grounds that a minor offender is more likely to be removed. There is no reason to suppose Congress intended this odd result.

The majority's confidence that the Judiciary will handle these matters "with appropriate sensitivity," allows no meaningful category to confine or explain its own sweep-

ing rule, provides no justification for wresting this sovereign power away from the political branches in the first place, and has no support in judicially manageable standards for deciding the foreseeability of removal.

The aliens' claims are substantial; their plight is real. They face continued detention, perhaps for life, unless it is shown they no longer present a flight risk or a danger to the community. In a later case the specific circumstances of a detention may present a substantial constitutional question. That is not a reason, however, for framing a rule which ignores the law governing alien status.

As persons within our jurisdiction, the aliens are entitled to the protection of the Due Process Clause. Liberty under the Due Process Clause includes protection against unlawful or arbitrary personal restraint or detention. The liberty rights of the aliens before us here are subject to limitations and conditions not applicable to citizens, however. No party to this proceeding contests the initial premise that the aliens have been determined to be removable after a fair hearing under lawful and proper procedures. . . . They did not arrive at their removable status without thorough, substantial procedural safeguards.

That said, it must be made clear these aliens are in a position far different from aliens with a lawful right to remain here. They are removable, and their rights must be defined in accordance with that status. The due process analysis must begin with a "careful description of the asserted right." We have "long held that an alien seeking initial admission to the United States requests a privilege and has no constitutional rights regarding his application, for the power to admit or exclude aliens is a sovereign prerogative." The same is true for those aliens like Zadvydas and Ma, who face a final order of removal. When an alien is removable, he or she has no right under the basic immigration laws to remain in this country. The removal orders reflect the determination that the aliens' ties to this community are insufficient to justify their continued presence in the United States. An alien's admission to this country is conditioned upon compliance with our laws, and removal is the consequence of a breach of that understanding.

Whether a due process right is denied when removable aliens who are flight risks or dangers to the community are detained turns, then, not on the substantive right to be free, but on whether there are adequate procedures to review their cases, allowing persons once subject to detention to show that through rehabilitation, new appreciation of their responsibilities, or under other standards, they no longer present special risks or danger if put at large. The procedures to determine and to review the status-required detention go far toward this objective.

I dissent.

Notes and Queries

1. Although much of this case appears to be about issues of statutory interpretation, in fact it raises issues of profound constitutional significance. First among these is, once again, the issue of judicial power. The Court admitted, "ordinary principles of judicial review in this area recognize primary Executive Branch responsibility." Did the Court depart from those principles? How much deference does the Court owe military authorities? Is the Court's approach in this case compatible with the approach in *Korematsu*? Or, are there telling differences between the two cases, and if so, what are they?

2. The Court stated, "Aliens who have not yet gained initial admission to this country would present a very different question." Why?

3. Similarly, the Court stressed that this case applied "broadly" to aliens ordered removed for many and various reasons. The clear intimation was that an alien ordered deported because he or she was dangerous, or a suspected terrorist, might present a different case. Why? Suppose the Attorney General makes such a finding. May the Court review it?

4. Zadvydas and Ha were resident aliens. Does citizenship matter? Could the federal government hold a U.S. citizen as an "enemy combatant" indefinitely? In the recent case of *Hamdi v. Rumsfeld*, 316 F. 3d 450 (2003), the fourth circuit court of appeals ruled that President Bush has the authority to detain indefinitely any American citizen captured in a foreign battle or who participates in terrorist attacks against the United States. (The defendant Hamdi was born in Louisiana and captured in Afghanistan.) The appeals court ruled that judges owe the executive branch "great deference" when dealing with issues that arise "in the arena of combat." The court admitted that "The safeguards that all Americans have come to expect in criminal prosecutions do not transfer neatly to the arena of armed conflict," and concluded that courts are unsuited "to supervise the conduct of overseas conflict." Consequently, Hamdi had no right to visit with an attorney, no right to a formal charge, and no right to challenge—or even know—the evidence against him.

Still unresolved is at least one important question: Would it make a constitutional difference if a suspect were arrested on U.S. soil, and not abroad, as in this case? Does *Korematsu* suggest a difference? Can the *Hamdi* decision be reconciled with *Korematsu*?

5. In *Demore v. Kim* (2003), the Supreme Court addressed the constitutionality of a provision in the Illegal Immigration Reform and Immigrant Responsibility Act of 1996 that authorizes the imprisonment (without bail) and deportation of permanent resident aliens (green card holders) who have been convicted of crimes. The stated purpose of the law is to prevent flight—to make sure that the person involved actually shows up at a deportation hearing. In this case, Kim, a South Korean who had been in the United States since age 6, was arrested on a shoplifting charge and had been convicted of burglary and petty theft. Kim challenged his detention, arguing that it violated his due process rights. The Court upheld the detention and the Act, arguing that it was well within congressional power and noting, "Congress regularly makes rulings that would be unacceptable if applied to citizens."

What vision of community underlies these kinds of constitutional distinctions? Can that vision be traced to the language of the Due Process Clause of the Fourteenth Amendment?

6. In his opinion for the majority in *Demore*, the Chief Justice noted that the decision in *Zadvydas* was materially different in two important respects. First, the detention in *Zadvydas* was indefinite and "potentially permanent." In cases of the kind involved in *Demore*, however, the Chief Justice noted that detentions are usually only for a few months. Is this distinction constitutionally significant? Why? Rehnquist also noted that in *Zadvydas*, the detention was not reasonably related to the purpose of preventing flight, whereas in *Demore* it was directly related to the stated purpose. In dissent, Justice Souter wrote "This case is not about the national government's undisputed power to detain aliens in order to avoid flight. . . . The issue is whether that power may be exercised by detaining a still lawful permanent resident alien where there is no reason for it and no way to challenge it."

Ex Parte Milligan
71 U.S. (4 Wall.) 2, 18 L.Ed. 281 (1866)

Lambdin P. Milligan was arrested by federal troops in October 1864, for being part of the "Sons of Liberty," a group dedicated to freeing Confederate prisoners from Union prisons in Indiana, Ohio and Illinois. Milligan, an Indiana resident, was tried by a military tribunal, convicted, and sentenced to death by hanging. Milligan's attorney petitioned the federal circuit Court, which was still open, for a writ of habeas corpus despite President Lincoln's suspension of that privilege. The case was certified to the Supreme Court. Opinion of the Court: *Davis*, Nelson, Grier, Clifford, Field. Concurring opinion: *Chase*, Wayne, Swayne, Miller.

Mr. Justice DAVIS delivered the opinion of the Court.

The importance of the main question presented . . . cannot be overstated, for it involves the very framework of the government and the fundamental principles of American liberty.

During the late wicked Rebellion the temper of the times did not allow that calmness in deliberation and discussion so necessary to a correct conclusion of a purely judicial question. Now that the public safety is assured, this question, as well as all others, can be discussed and decided without passion.

The controlling question in the case is this: Upon the facts stated in Milligan's petition, and the exhibits filed, had the military commission mentioned in it jurisdiction, legally, to try and sentence him? Milligan, not a resident of one of the rebellious states, or a prisoner of war, but a citizen of Indiana for twenty years past, and never in the military or naval service, is, while at his home, arrested by the military power of the United States, imprisoned, and, on certain criminal charges preferred against him, tried, convicted, and sentenced to be hanged by a military commission, organized under the direction of the military commander of the military district of Indiana. Had this tribunal the legal power and authority to try and punish this man?

No graver question was ever considered by this Court, nor one which more nearly concerns the rights of the whole people; for it is the birthright of every American citizen when charged with crime, to be tried and punished according to law. The power of punishment is alone through the means which the laws have provided for that purpose, and if they are ineffectual, there is an immunity from punishment, no matter how great an offender the individual may be, or how much his crimes may have shocked the sense of justice of the country, or endangered its safety. By the protection of the law human rights are secured; withdraw that protection, and they are at the mercy of wicked rulers, or the clamor of an excited people. If there was law to justify this military trial, it is not our province to interfere; if there was not, it is our duty to declare the nullity of the whole proceedings. The decision of this question does not depend on argument or judicial precedents, numerous and highly illustrative as they are. These precedents inform us of the extent of the struggle to preserve liberty and to relieve those in civil life from military trials. The founders of our government were familiar with the history of that struggle; and secured in a written constitution every right which the people had wrested from power during a contest of ages. By that Constitution and the laws authorized by it this question must be determined. The provisions of that instrument on the administration of criminal justice are too plain and direct, to leave room for misconstruction or doubt of their true meaning. Those applicable to this case are found in that clause of the original Constitution which says, "That the trial of all crimes, except in case of impeachment, shall be by jury;" and in the fourth, fifth, and sixth articles of the amendments.

Time has proven the discernment of our ancestors; for even these provisions, expressed in such plain English words, that it would seem the ingenuity of man could not evade them, are now, after the lapse of more than seventy years, sought to be avoided. . . . The Constitution of the United States is a law for rulers and people, equally in war and in peace, and covers with the shield of its protection all classes of men, at all times, and under all circumstances. No doctrine, involving more pernicious consequences, was ever invented by the wit of man than that any of its provisions can be suspended during any of the great exigencies of government. Such a doctrine leads directly to anarchy or despotism, but the theory of necessity on which it is based is false; for the government, within the Constitution, has all the powers granted to it, which are necessary to preserve its existence; as has been happily proved by the result of the great effort to throw off its just authority.

Have any of the rights guaranteed by the Constitution been violated in the case of Milligan? And if so, what are they?

Every trial involves the exercise of judicial power; and from what source did the military commission that tried him derive their authority? Certainly no part of judicial power of the country was conferred on them; because the Constitution expressly vests it "in one supreme Court and such inferior Courts as the Congress may from time to time ordain and establish," and it is not pretended that the commission was a Court ordained and established by Congress. They cannot justify on the mandate of the President; because he is controlled by law, and has his appropriate sphere of duty, which is to execute, not to make, the laws; and there is "no unwritten criminal code to which resort can be had as a source of jurisdiction."

But it is said that the jurisdiction is complete under the "laws and usages of war."

It can serve no useful purpose to inquire what those laws and usages are, whence they originated, where found, and on whom they operate; they can never be applied to citizens in states which have upheld the authority of the government, and where the Courts are open and their process unobstructed. This Court has judicial knowledge that in Indiana the Federal authority was always unopposed, and its Courts always open to hear criminal accusations and redress grievances; and no usage of war could sanction a military trial there for any offence whatever of a citizen in civil life, in nowise connected with the military service. Congress could grant no such power; and to the honor of our national legislature be it said, it has never been provoked by the state of the country even to attempt its exercise. One of the plainest constitutional provisions was, therefore, infringed when Milligan was tried by a Court not ordained and established by Congress, and not composed of judges appointed during good behavior.

Why was he not delivered to the Circuit Court of Indiana to be proceeded against according to law? No reason of necessity could be urged against it; because Congress had declared penalties against the offences charged, provided for their punishment, and directed that Court to hear and determine them. And soon after this military tribunal was ended, the Circuit Court met, peacefully transacted its business, no military aid to execute its judgments. It was held in a state, eminently distinguished for patriotism, by judges commissioned during the Rebellion, who were provided with juries, upright, intelligent, and selected by a marshal appointed by the President. The government had no right to conclude that Milligan, if guilty, would not receive in that Court merited punishment; for its records disclose that it was constantly engaged in the trial of similar offences, and was never interrupted in its administration of criminal justice. If it was dangerous, in the distracted condition of affairs, to leave Milligan unrestrained of his liberty, because he "conspired against the government, afforded aid and comfort to rebels, and incited the people to insurrection," the law said arrest him, confine him closely, render him powerless to do further mischief; and then present his case to the grand jury of the district, with proofs of his guilt, and, if indicted, try him according to the course of the common law. If this had been done, the Constitution would have been vindicated, the law of 1863 enforced, and the securities for personal liberty preserved and defended.

Another guarantee of freedom was broken when Milligan was denied a trial by jury. The great minds of the country have differed on the correct interpretation to be given to various provisions of the Federal Constitution; and judicial decision has been often invoked to settle their true meaning; but until recently no one ever doubted that the right of trial by jury was fortified in the organic law against the power of attack. It is now assailed; but if ideas can be expressed in words, and language has any meaning, this right—one of the most valuable in a free country—is preserved to every one accused of crime who is not attached to the army, or navy, or militia in actual service.

. . . This privilege is a vital principle, underlying the whole administration of criminal justice; it is not held by sufferance, and cannot be frittered away on any plea of political necessity. When peace prevails, and the authority of the government is undisputed, there is no difficulty of preserving the safeguards of liberty; for the ordinary modes of trial are never neglected, and no one wishes it otherwise; but if society is disturbed by civil commotion—if the passions of men are aroused and the restraints of law weakened, if not disregarded—these safeguards need, and should receive, the watchful care of those intrusted with the guardianship of the Constitution and laws. . . .

It is claimed that martial law covers with its broad mantle the proceedings of this military commission. The proposition is this: that in a time of war the commander of an armed force (if in his opinion the exigencies of the country demand it, and of which he is to judge), has the power, within the lines of his military district, to suspend all civil rights and their remedies, and subject citizens as well as soldiers to the rule of his will; and in the exercise of his lawful authority cannot be restrained, except by his superior officer or the President of the United States.

If this position is sound to the extent claimed, then when war exists, foreign or domestic, and the country is subdivided into military departments for mere convenience, the commander of one of them can, if he chooses, within his limits, on the plea of necessity, with the approval of the Executive, substitute military force for and to the exclusion of the laws, and punish all persons, as he thinks right and proper, without fixed or certain rules.

The statement of this proposition shows its importance; for, if true, republican government is a failure, and there is an end of liberty regulated by law. Martial law, established on such a basis, destroys every guarantee of the Constitution, and effectually renders the "military independent of and superior to the civil power"—the attempt to do which by the King of Great Britain was deemed by our fathers such an offence, that they assigned it to the world as one of the causes which impelled them to declare their independence. Civil liberty and this kind of martial law cannot endure together; the antagonism is irreconcilable; and, in the conflict, one or the other must perish.

This nation, as experience has proved, cannot always remain at peace, and has no right to expect that it will always have wise and humane rulers, sincerely attached to the principles of the Constitution. Wicked men, ambitious of power, with hatred of liberty and contempt of law, may once fill the place occupied by Washington and Lincoln; and if this right is conceded, and the calamities of war again befall us, the dangers to human liberty are frightful to contemplate. If our fathers had failed to provide for just such a contingency, they would have been false to the trust reposed in them. They knew—the history of the world told them—the nation they were founding, be its existence short or long, would be involved in war; how often or how long continued, human foresight could not tell; and that unlimited power, wherever lodged at such a time, was especially hazardous to freemen. For this, and other equally weighty reasons, they secured the inheritance they had fought to maintain, by incorporating in a written constitution the safeguards which time had proved were essential to its preservation. Not one of these safeguards can the President, or Congress, or the Judiciary disturb, except the one concerning the writ of habeas corpus.

. . . [I]t is insisted that the safety of the country in time of war demands that this broad claim for martial law shall be sustained. If this were true, it could be well said that a country, preserved at the sacrifice of all the cardinal principles of liberty, is not worth the cost of preservation. Happily, it is not so.

It will be borne in mind that this is not a question of the power to proclaim martial law, when war exists in a community and the Courts and civil authorities are overthrown. Nor is it a question what rule a military commander, at the head of his army, can impose on states in rebellion to cripple their resources and quell the insurrection. The jurisdiction claimed is much more extensive. The necessities of the service, during the late Rebellion, required that the loyal states should be placed within the limits of certain military districts and commanders appointed in them; and, it is urged, that this, in a military sense, constituted them the theater of military operations; and, as in this case, Indiana had been and was again. . . . If armies were collected in Indiana, they were to be employed in another locality, where the laws were obstructed and the national authority disputed. On her soil there was no hostile foot; if once invaded, that invasion was at an end, and with it all pretext for martial law. Martial law cannot arise from a threatened invasion. The necessity must be actual and present; the invasion real, such as effectually closes the Courts and deposes the civil administration.

It follows, from what has been said on this subject, that there are occasions when martial rule can be properly applied. If, in foreign invasion or civil war, the Courts are actually closed, and it is impossible to administer criminal justice according to law, then, on the theatre of active military operations, where war really prevails, there is a neces-

sity to furnish a substitute for the civil authority, thus overthrown, to preserve the safety of the army and society; and as no power is left but the military, it is allowed to govern by martial rule until the laws can have their free course. As necessity creates the rule, so it limits its duration; for, if this government is continued after the Courts are reinstated, it is a gross usurpation of power. Martial rule can never exist where the Courts are open, and in the proper and unobstructed exercise of their jurisdiction. It is also confined to the locality of actual war. Because, during the late Rebellion it could have been enforced in Virginia, where the national authority was overturned and the Courts driven out, it does not follow that it should obtain in Indiana, where that authority was never disputed, and justice was always administered.

Chief Justice CHASE delivered the following opinion.

. . . [T]he opinion which has just been read . . . asserts not only that the military commission held in Indiana was not authorized by Congress; from which it may be thought to follow, that Congress has no power to indemnify the officers who composed the commission against liability in civil Courts for acting as members of it.

We cannot agree to this.

. . . Congress has power to raise and support armies; to provide and maintain a navy; to make rules for the government and regulation of the land and naval forces; and to provide for governing such part of the militia as may be in the service of the United States.

It is not denied that the power to make rules for the government of the army and navy is a power to provide for trial and punishment by military Courts without a jury. It has been so understood and exercised from the adoption of the Constitution to the present time.

Nor, in our judgment, does the fifth, or any other amendment, abridge that power.

We think, therefore, that the power of Congress, in the government of the land and naval forces and of the militia, is not at all affected by the fifth or any other amendment. It is not necessary to attempt any precise definition of the boundaries of this power. But may it not be said that government includes protection and defence as well as the regulation of internal administration? And is it impossible to imagine cases in which citizens conspiring or attempting the destruction or great injury of the national forces may be subjected by Congress to military trial and punishment in the just exercise of this undoubted constitutional power? Congress is but the agent of the nation, and does not the security of individuals against the abuse of this, as of every other power, depend on the intelligence and virtue of the people, on their zeal for public and private liberty, upon official responsibility secured by law, and upon the frequency of elections, rather than upon doubtful constructions of legislative powers?

Congress has the power not only to raise and support and govern armies but to declare war. It has, therefore, the power to provide by law for carrying on war. This power necessarily extends to all legislation essential to the prosecution of war with vigor and success, except such as interferes with the command of the forces and the conduct of campaigns. That power and duty belong to the President as commander in chief. Both these powers are derived from the Constitution, but neither is defined by that instrument. Their extent must be determined by their nature, and by the principles of our institutions.

We by no means assert that Congress can establish and apply the laws of war where no war has been declared or exists.

Where peace exists the laws of peace must prevail. What we do maintain is, that when the nation is involved in war, and some portions of the country are invaded, and all are exposed to invasion, it is within the power of Congress to determine in what states or district such great and imminent public danger exists as justifies the authorization of military tribunals for the trial of crimes and offences against the discipline or security of the army or against the public safety.

In Indiana, for example, at the time of the arrest of Milligan and his co-conspirators, it is established by the papers in the record, that the state was a military district, was the theatre of military operations, had been actually invaded, and was constantly threatened with invasion. It appears, also, that a powerful secret association, composed of citizens and others, existed within the state, under military organization, conspiring against the draft, and plotting insurrection, the liberation of the prisoners of war at various depots, the seizure of the state and national arsenals, armed cooperation with the enemy, and war against the national government.

We cannot doubt that, in such a time of public danger, Congress had power, under the Constitution, to provide for the organization of a military commission, and for trial by that commission of persons engaged in this conspiracy. The fact that the Federal Courts were open was regarded by Congress as a sufficient reason for not exercising the power; but that fact could not deprive Congress of the right to exercise it. Those Courts might be open and undisturbed in the execution of their functions, and yet wholly incompetent to avert threatened danger, or to punish, with adequate promptitude and certainty, the guilty conspirators.

There are under the Constitution three kinds of military jurisdiction: one to be exercised both in peace and war; another to be exercised in time of foreign war without the boundaries of the United States, or in time of rebellion and civil war within states or districts occupied by rebels treated as belligerents; and a third to be exercised in time of invasion or insurrection within the limits of the United States, or during rebellion within the limits of states maintaining adhesion to the National Government, when the public danger requires its exercise. The first of these may be called jurisdiction under MILITARY LAW, and is found in acts of Congress prescribing rules and articles of war, or otherwise providing for the government of the national forces; the second may be distinguished as MILITARY GOVERNMENT, superseding, as far as may be deemed expedient, the local law, and exercised by the military commander under the direction of the President, with the express or implied sanction of Congress; while the third may be denominated MARTIAL LAW PROPER, and is called into action by Congress, or temporarily, when the action of Congress cannot be invited, and in the case of justifying or excusing peril, by the President, in times of insurrection or invasion, or of civil or foreign war, within districts or localities where ordinary law no longer adequately secures public safety and private rights.

We think that the power of Congress, in such times and in such localities . . . may be derived from its constitutional authority to raise and support armies and to declare war, if not from its constitutional authority to provide for governing the national forces.

We have no apprehension that this power, under our American system of government, in which all official authority is derived from the people, and exercised under direct responsibility to the people, is more likely to be abused than the power to regulate commerce, or the power to borrow money. And we are unwilling to give our assent by silence to expressions of opinion which seem to us calculated, though not intended, to cripple the constitutional powers of the government, and to augment the public dangers in times of invasion and rebellion.

Mr. Justice WAYNE, Mr. Justice SWAYNE, and Mr. Justice MILLER concur with me in these views.

Notes and Queries

1. Can the Court's decision, particularly its claim that the "Constitution of the United States is a law for rulers and people, equally in war and peace, and covers with the shield of its protection all classes of men, at all times, and under all circumstances," be reconciled with *Korematsu* and *Zadvydas*?

2. Can the ruling against President Lincoln's orders for the trial of civilians by military courts be reconciled with the Court's earlier decision to uphold Lincoln's blockade of the Southern ports in *The Prize Cases* (1862)?

3. John P. Frank concluded that "*Ex parte Milligan* is one of the truly great documents of the American Constitution, a bulwark for the protection of the civil liberties of every American citizen." (*Ex Parte Milligan*, 44 Columbia Law Review 639 [1944]). Is he correct?

4. *Milligan* was not well received by Congress. Radical Republicans had enacted statutes that provided for military trials for some civilians. Many saw the Court's decision as a direct threat to the constitutionality of their entire program for Reconstruction. Some of those Republicans, including Congressman John Bingham, announced that if the Court did not back down Congress would propose a constitutional amendment that would call for "the abolition of the tribunal itself." The threat was real. In 1868, Congress had begun impeachment proceedings against President Johnson. Congress further reacted by depriving the Court of jurisdiction over certain classes of habeas corpus petitions. In *Ex Parte McCardle* (1868), the Court took a more cautious approach, noting that Article III, Section 2 gave Congress authority to regulate the Court's appellate jurisdiction (see chapter 3). Moreover, the Court went to great lengths to note "We are not at liberty to inquire into the motives of the legislature."

Ex Parte Quirin
317 U.S. 1, 63 S. Ct. 2, 87 L. Ed. 3 (1942)

In June 1942, four men disembarked from German submarines and paddled ashore to Amagansett Beach, Long Island. A few days later, another four men landed at Ponte Vedra Beach, Florida. They wore German military uniforms and carried explosives. Upon landing, they buried their uniforms and supplies, and proceeded, in civilian dress, to various places in the United States. All had received instructions to destroy war industries and war facilities in the United States, for which they or their relatives in Germany were to receive salary payments from the German government. The FBI arrested them. They were tried and convicted by a military commission created by President Roosevelt. Six of the men were given death sentences. On appeal to the United States Court, they argued that were entitled to be tried by civilian authorities. Opinion of the Court: *Stone*, Roberts, Black, Reed, Frankfurter, Douglas, Byrnes, Jackson; Murphy took no part in the consideration or decision of these cases.

MR. CHIEF JUSTICE STONE delivered the opinion of the Court.

The question for decision is whether the detention of petitioners by respondent for trial by Military Commission, appointed by Order of the President of July 2, 1942, on charges preferred against them purporting to set out their violations of the law of war and of the Articles of War, is in conformity to the laws and Constitution of the United States.

The President, as President and Commander in Chief of the Army and Navy, . . . appointed a Military Commission and directed it to try petitioners for offenses against the law of war and the Articles of War, and prescribed regulations for the procedure on the trial and for review of the record of the trial and of any judgment or sentence of the Commission. On the same day, by Proclamation, the President declared that "all persons who are subjects, citizens or residents of any nation at war with the United States or who give obedience to or act under the direction of any such nation, and who during time of war enter or attempt to enter the United States . . . through coastal or boundary defenses, and are charged with committing or attempting or preparing to commit sabotage, espionage, hostile or warlike acts, or violations of the law of war, shall be subject to the law of war and to the jurisdiction of military tribunals."

The Proclamation also stated in terms that all such persons were denied access to the courts.

The Commission met on July 8, 1942, and proceeded with the trial, which continued in progress while the causes were pending in this Court. On July 27th, before petitioners' applications to the District Court, all the evidence for the prosecution and the defense had been taken by the Commission and the case had been closed except for arguments of counsel. It is conceded that ever since petitioners' arrest the state and federal courts in Florida, New York, and the District of Columbia, and in the states in which each of the petitioners was arrested or detained, have been open and functioning normally.

Petitioners' main contention is that the President is without any statutory or constitutional authority to order the petitioners to be tried by military tribunal for offenses with which they are charged; that in consequence they are entitled to be tried in the civil courts with the safeguards, including trial by jury, which the Fifth and Sixth Amendments guarantee to all persons charged in such courts with criminal offenses. In any case it is urged that the President's Order, in prescribing the procedure of the Commission and the method for review of its findings and sentence, and the proceedings of the Commission under the Order, conflict with Articles of War adopted by Congress . . . are illegal and void.

The Government challenges each of these propositions. But regardless of their merits, it also insists that petitioners must be denied access to the courts, both because they are enemy aliens or have entered our territory as enemy belligerents, and because the President's Proclamation undertakes in terms to deny such access to the class of persons defined by the Proclamation, which aptly describes the character and conduct of petitioners. It is urged that if they are enemy aliens or if the Proclamation has force, no court may afford the petitioners a hearing. But there is certainly nothing in the Proclamation to preclude access to the courts for determining its applicability to the particular case. And neither the Proclamation nor the fact that they are enemy aliens forecloses consideration by the courts of petitioners' contentions that the Constitution and laws of the United States constitutionally enacted forbid their trial by military commission.

We are not here concerned with any question of the guilt or innocence of petitioners. Constitutional safeguards for the protection of all who are charged with offenses are not to be disregarded in order to inflict merited punishment on some who are guilty. *Ex parte Milligan.* . . . But the detention and trial of petitioners—ordered by the President in the declared exercise of his powers as Commander in Chief of the Army in time of war and of grave public danger—are not to be set aside by the courts without the clear conviction that they are in conflict with the Constitution or laws of Congress constitutionally enacted.

Congress and the President, like the courts, possess no power not derived from the Constitution. But one of the objects of the Constitution, as declared by its preamble, is to "provide for the common defence." As a means to that end, the Constitution gives to Congress the power to "provide for the common Defence," Art. I, s. 8, cl. 1; "To raise and support Armies," "To provide and maintain a Navy," Art. I, s. 8, cl. 12, 13; and "To make Rules for the Government and Regulation of the land and naval Forces," Art. I, s. 8, cl. 14. Congress is given authority "To declare War, grant Letters of Marque and Reprisal, and make Rules concerning Captures on Land and Water," Art. I, s. 8, cl. 11; and "To define and punish Piracies and Felonies committed on the high Seas, and Offences against the Law of Nations," Art. I, s. 8, cl. 10. And finally, the Constitution authorizes Congress "To make all Laws which shall be necessary and proper for carrying into Execution the foregoing Powers, and all other Powers vested by this Consti-

tution in the Government of the United States, or in any Department or Officer thereof." Art. I, s. 8, cl. 18.

The Constitution confers on the President the "executive Power," Art. II, s. 1, cl. 1, and imposes on him the duty to "take Care that the Laws be faithfully executed." Art. II, s. 3. It makes him the Commander in Chief of the Army and Navy, Art. II, s. 2, cl. 1, and empowers him to appoint and commission officers of the United States. Art. II, s. 3, cl. 1.

The Constitution thus invests the President, as Commander in Chief, with the power to wage war which Congress has declared, and to carry into effect all laws passed by Congress for the conduct of war and for the government and regulation of the Armed Forces, and all laws defining and punishing offenses against the law of nations, including those which pertain to the conduct of war.

By the Articles of War, 10 U. S. C. s.s. 1471–1593, Congress has provided rules for the government of the Army. It has provided for the trial and punishment, by courts martial, of violations of the Articles by members of the armed forces and by specified classes of persons associated or serving with the Army. Arts. 1, 2. But the Articles also recognize the "military commission" appointed by military command as an appropriate tribunal for the trial and punishment of offenses against the law of war not ordinarily tried by court martial. See Arts. 12, 15. Articles 38 and 46 authorize the President, with certain limitations, to prescribe the procedure for military commissions. Articles 81 and 82 authorize trial, either by court martial or military commission, of those charged with relieving, harboring or corresponding with the enemy and those charged with spying. And Article 15 declares that "the provisions of these articles conferring jurisdiction upon courts martial shall not be construed as depriving military commissions . . . or other military tribunals of concurrent jurisdiction in respect of offenders or offenses that by statute or by the law of war may be triable by such military commissions . . . or other military tribunals." Article 2 includes among those persons subject to military law the personnel of our own military establishment. But this, as Article 12 provides, does not exclude from that class "any other person who by the law of war is subject to trial by military tribunals" and who under Article 12 may be tried by court martial or under Article 15 by military commission.

From the very beginning of its history this Court has recognized and applied the law of war as including that part of the law of nations which prescribes, for the conduct of war, the status, rights and duties of enemy nations as well as of enemy individuals.

An important incident to the conduct of war is the adoption of measures by the military command not only to repel and defeat the enemy, but to seize and subject to disciplinary measures those enemies who in their attempt to thwart or impede our military effort have violated the law of war. It is unnecessary for present purposes to determine to what extent the President as Commander in Chief has constitutional power to create military commissions without the support of Congressional legislation. For here Congress has authorized trial of offenses against the law of war before such commissions. We are concerned only with the question whether it is within the constitutional power of the National Government to place petitioners upon trial before a military commission for the offenses with which they are charged. We must therefore first inquire whether any of the acts charged is an offense against the law of war cognizable before a military tribunal, and if so whether the Constitution prohibits the trial.

It is no objection that Congress in providing for the trial of such offenses has not itself undertaken to codify that branch of international law or to mark its precise boundaries, or to enumerate or define by statute all the acts which that law condemns. An Act of Congress punishing "the crime of piracy, as defined by the law of nations" is an appropriate exercise of its constitutional authority, Art. I, s. 8, cl. 10, "to define and punish" the offense, since it has adopted by reference the sufficiently precise definition of international law.

By universal agreement and practice, the law of war draws a distinction between the armed forces and the peaceful populations of belligerent nations and also between those who are lawful and unlawful combatants. Lawful combatants are subject to capture and detention as prisoners of war by opposing military forces. Unlawful combatants are likewise subject to capture and detention, but in addition they are subject to trial and punishment by military tribunals for acts which render their belligerency unlawful. The spy who secretly and without uniform passes the military lines of a belligerent in time of war, seeking to gather military information and communicate it to the enemy, or an enemy combatant who without uniform comes secretly through the lines for the purpose of waging war by destruction of life or property, are familiar examples of belligerents who are generally deemed not to be entitled to the status of prisoners of war, but to be offenders against the law of war subject to trial and punishment by military tribunals.

Such was the practice of our own military authorities before the adoption of the Constitution, and during the Mexican and Civil Wars.

But petitioners insist that, even if the offenses with which they are charged are offenses against the law of war, their trial is subject to the requirement of the Fifth Amendment that no person shall be held to answer for a capital or otherwise infamous crime unless on a presentment or indictment of a grand jury, and that such trials by Article III, s. 2, and the Sixth Amendment must be by jury in a civil court. Before the Amendments, s. 2 of Article III, the Judiciary Article, had provided, "The Trial of all Crimes, except in Cases of Impeachment, shall be by Jury," and had directed that "such Trial shall be held in the State where the said Crimes shall have been committed."

Presentment by a grand jury and trial by a jury of the vicinage where the crime was committed were at the time of the adoption of the Constitution familiar parts of the machinery for criminal trials in the civil courts. But they were procedures unknown to military tribunals, which are not courts in the sense of the Judiciary Article, and which in the natural course of events are usually called upon to function under conditions precluding resort to such procedures. As this Court has often recognized, it was not the purpose or effect of s. 2 of Article III, read in the light of the common law, to enlarge the then existing right to a jury trial. The object was to preserve unimpaired trial by jury in all those cases in which it had been recognized by the common law and in all cases of a like nature as they might arise in the future . . . but not to bring within the sweep of the guaranty those cases in which it was then well understood that a jury trial could not be demanded as of right.

Since the Amendments, like s. 2 of Article III, do not preclude all trials of offenses against the law of war by military commission without a jury when the offenders are aliens not members of our Armed Forces, it is plain that they present no greater obstacle to the trial in like manner of citizen enemies who have violated the law of war applicable to enemies. Under the original statute authorizing trial of alien spies by military tribunals, the offenders were outside the constitutional guaranty of trial by jury, not because they were aliens but only because they had violated the law of war by committing offenses constitutionally triable by military tribunal.

We cannot say that Congress in preparing the Fifth and Sixth Amendments intended to extend trial by jury to the cases of alien or citizen offenders against the law of war otherwise triable by military commission, while withholding it from members of our own armed forces charged with infractions of the Articles of War punishable by death. It is equally inadmissible to construe the Amendments—whose primary purpose was to continue unimpaired presentment by grand jury and trial by petit jury in all those cases in which they had been customary—as either abolishing all trials by military tribunals, save those of the personnel of our own armed forces, or, what in effect comes to the same thing, as imposing on all such tribunals the necessity of proceeding against unlawful enemy belligerents only on presentment and trial by jury. We conclude that the Fifth and Sixth Amendments did not restrict whatever authority was conferred by the Constitution to try offenses against the law of war by military commission, and that petitioners, charged with such an offense not required to be tried by jury at common law, were lawfully placed on trial by the Commission without a jury.

Petitioners . . . stress the pronouncement of this Court in the *Milligan* case, that the law of war "can never be applied to citizens in states which have upheld the authority of the government, and where the courts are open and their process unobstructed." Elsewhere in its opinion, the Court was at pains to point out that Milligan, a citizen twenty years resident in Indiana, who had never been a resident of any of the states in rebellion, was not an enemy belligerent either entitled to the status of a prisoner of war or subject to the penalties imposed upon unlawful belligerents. We construe the Court's statement as to the inapplicability of the law of war to Milligan's case as having particular reference to the facts before it. From them the Court concluded that Milligan, not being a part of or associated with the armed forces of the enemy, was a non-belligerent, not subject to the law of war save as—in circumstances found not there to be present, and not involved here—martial law might be constitutionally established.

The Court's opinion is inapplicable to the case presented by the present record. We have no occasion now to define with meticulous care the ultimate boundaries of the jurisdiction of military tribunals to try persons according to the law of war. It is enough that petitioners here, upon the conceded facts, were plainly within those boundaries, and were held in good faith for trial by military commission, charged with being enemies who, with the purpose of destroying war materials and utilities, entered, or after entry remained in, our territory without uniform—an offense against the law of war. We hold only that those particular acts constitute an offense against the law of war which the Constitution authorizes to be tried by military commission.

We need not inquire whether Congress may restrict the power of the Commander in Chief to deal with enemy belligerents. For the Court is unanimous in its conclusion that the Articles in question could not at any stage of the proceedings afford any basis for issuing the writ. But a majority of the full Court are not agreed on the appropriate grounds for decision. Some members of the Court are of opinion that Congress did not intend the Articles of War to govern a Presidential military commission convened for the determination of questions relating to admitted enemy invaders, and that the context of the Articles makes clear that they should not be construed to apply in that class of cases. Others are of the view that—even though this trial is subject to whatever provisions of the Articles of War Congress has in terms made applicable to "commissions"—the particular Articles in question, rightly construed, do not foreclose the procedure prescribed by the President or that shown to have been employed by the Commission, in a trial of offenses against the law of war and the 81st and 82nd Articles of War, by a military commission appointed by the President.

MR. Justice MURPHY took no part in the consideration or decision of these cases.

Notes and Queries

1. The president's authority to create a secret military tribunal in this case appears to have been grounded in a congressional statute. Are the president's independent powers under Article II sufficient, by themselves, to create such tribunals? (See note 3, below.) Does *Milligan* impose any limits upon such powers? More broadly, does *Quirin* overrule *Milligan*, perhaps by suggesting that the president may deprive a civilian of his constitutional rights simply by naming him "an enemy belligerent"?

2. Does *Quirin* suggest that a question left open in *Zadvydas*—whether a citizen arrested on U.S. soil can be tried before a military commission—must be answered in the affirmative?

3. Among the most controversial of President Bush's responses to the attacks of 11 September 2001 was his decision to authorize trial by military tribunal of any noncitizen suspected of terrorism (or other crimes "under applicable laws"), inside or outside the United States. Under the relaxed rules governing such tribunals, a defendant has no right to see or rebut certain evidence, is limited in his or her choice of counsel, and is not entitled to an appeal in a civilian court. Moreover, an individual detained under the order need not be brought to trial at all. Finally, an individual acquitted by such a tribunal need not actually be released. The order thus permits indefinite detention. Can this be reconciled with *Zadvydas*, reprinted above?

More generally, is the system of military tribunals created by President Bush consistent with *Quirin?* In *Quirin*, the defendants did receive independent counsel and an opportunity for review in a civilian court—neither is present in the current system. Do such differences have any constitutional relevance?

Chapter 6

Federalism and State Regulation

The Constitution created a *federal* system of government different from any other in history. Recall that the framers met in Philadelphia to repair the defects of the Articles of Confederation. The Articles had combined the thirteen original states into little more than a league of friendship presided over by a Congress made up of sovereign and equal governments. Congress could not enact laws: its power was limited to passing resolutions and making financial requisitions, but only with the consent of at least nine of the thirteen states. No executive or judiciary existed to enforce its authority on recalcitrant states. Congress also lacked the power to regulate interstate commerce, one of the main reasons for the summoning of a new constitutional convention. Finally, any amendment to the Articles of Confederation required the unanimous consent of all thirteen states; formal constitutional change was thus a virtual impossibility.

It is important to bear in mind that particular federal arrangements are always predicated on different visions of the good life and the polity. The Articles of Confederation flow from the view that popular government begins and ends at the local and state levels, that the people are the best keepers of their own liberty, that good government depends on active and virtuous citizens rooted in the values and interests of their communities, and that a distant government unconnected to these values and interests is the very definition of despotism. These were powerful arguments on behalf of the government created by the Articles of Confederation, and they would surface repeatedly in debates over adoption of a new constitution.[1]

The movement for a new constitutional convention was driven by the need to transform the Confederation into a stronger federal union. The framers were initially divided over the nature of the new federalism they set out to create. Two plans contested for initial acceptance in the Convention. The first, known as the Virginia Plan, proposed a radical reconstruction of the governmental system under the Articles of Confederation. More national

---

[1] For a defense of the Articles of Confederation see Merrill Jensen, *The Articles of Confederation: An Interpretation of the Social-Constitutional History of the American Revolution 1774–1781* (Madison: University of Wisconsin Press, 1948).

than federal in design, the plan would have established a government of the union with vastly increased powers, including the authority to veto state statutes deemed incompatible with national laws. To reduce the influence of the smaller states, the plan also called for the creation of a bicameral legislature, one house of which would be based on popular representation. The larger states tended to agree with this plan. The New Jersey Plan, on the other hand, would retain the basic "federal" design of the Confederation but remedy its most glaring defects. Although Congress would remain a single house with equal state representation, it would be granted enforceable lawmaking authority in the fields of taxation and commerce. To reinforce and carry out these powers, the plan proposed the establishment of a national supreme court and an executive council—albeit a relatively weak one—chosen by Congress.[2] Small states generally supported the New Jersey proposal.

The draft constitution that emerged from the Convention contained compromises between the New Jersey and Virginia Plans (as well as other compromises between the northern and southern states). The proposed new government consisted of three separate but interdependent branches that would exercise the authority, among other powers, to levy and collect taxes, to make law, and to enforce its policies. Federal law, like the Constitution itself, would be supreme law and bind the judges and officials of every state. The states, however, would retain a crucial role in the national political process. They would enjoy equal representation in the Senate, figure prominently in the election of the president, retain dispositive authority over the process of amending the Constitution,[3] and reserve to themselves all powers not given to the national government.

In the end, the Framers discarded the Articles of Confederation in defiance of the existing order of constitutional legality. Hoping to create "a more perfect union" that would avoid the potential tyranny of a unitary government as well as an arrangement that would lead to further anarchy among sovereign and independent states, they established a broadly based national government that allowed the states to continue to manage their own affairs. The Founders thought this system of divided authority would contribute to the preservation of a republican form of government while avoiding the evils of pure majority rule at the national level. The states, on the other hand, retained their traditional political identities while preserving their own distinctive cultures, values, and institutions (including slavery).

Yet no person living in 1789 could have predicted how the new federal constitution would operate in practice, for this new federalism lacked clarity. In *Federalist* 39, James Madison rejected the anti-Federalist charge that the Constitution created a strictly *national* government.[4] He claimed that the Constitution was both national and federal, and proceeded to develop a five-fold classification based on these two features. In its *foundation*, wrote Madison, the Constitution was a federal act; in the

---

[2] For a discussion of these plans, see Jack N. Rakove, *Original Meanings* (Lincoln and London: University of Nebraska Press, 1996), pp. 57–93.

[3] As for the amendatory process, the founders revised the rule of unanimity laid down in the Articles of Confederation. Under Article VII nine states would be sufficient to ratify the new constitution; similarly, Article V provides for its amendment by a vote of three-fourths of the states. For a general discussion of the Convention's proceedings see Richard B. Morris, *The Forging of the Union: 1781–1789* (New York: Harper & Row, Publishers, 1987), 267–297.

[4] Patrick Henry, among the Constitution's most vehement opponents, charged in the Virginia ratifying convention that the new government would be "one great consolidated empire," a monster wholly "incompatible with the genius of [American] republicanism." See Philip B. Kurland and Ralph Lerner, *The Founders' Constitution*, (Chicago: The University of Chicago Press, 1989), I, 289.

source of governmental power, it was partly federal and partly national; in the *opera-tion* of these powers, it was national, not federal; in the *extent* of these powers, it was federal, not national; and in the *manner* of the amendatory power, it was neither wholly federal nor entirely national.[5] Madison's scheme may have been clear to him, but different understandings of what is national and what is federal emerged in the various state ratifying conventions, just as they would in judicial interpretations of the Constitution in the years and decades ahead.

As for judicial interpretation, the question arises whether the Supreme Court should limit its power over congressional laws allegedly interfering with the rights of the states under the Tenth Amendment. The following discussion of *McCulloch v. Maryland* (1819, reprinted later in the chapter) shows that Marshall's broad interpretation of federal power won the day over Maryland's narrow interpretation. Yet, as we shall see, the Supreme Court has sometimes reserved to itself the power to strike down federal laws if they are deemed to violate the Tenth Amendment. The counter-argument holds, on the basis of representational theory, that the Supreme Court ought not to strike down national laws on federalism grounds. The Court should stay its hand in such cases, runs the argument, because all the states are fully represented in the Congress, and consequently are unlikely to vote against their own corporate interests.[6] These two arguments often—not always—run parallel with different meth-ods of constitutional interpretation. For example, the "plain words" of the Tenth Amendment approach tends to support the states in their arguments against the fed-eral government, whereas "structuralism" or the "fully represented" in Congress ap-proach tends to support the view of federal supremacy.

Enumerated, Implied, and Reserved Powers

As Chief Justice John Marshall noted repeatedly in *McCulloch v. Maryland* (1819), the national government is one of enumerated powers, whereas under the Tenth Amendment all other powers "not delegated to the United States by the Constitution, nor prohibited by it to the States, are reserved to the States respectively, or to the people."[7] This formal distribution of power would be the subject of interpretive dis-agreement throughout American history. The elusive boundary between federal and state power demanded by the Constitution's broad language would not permit any final definition. As Chief Justice Marshall emphasized in *McCulloch*, if the Constitu-tion were "to endure for ages to come [and] to be adapted to the various *crises* of human affairs," the authority of the national government would have to be broadly construed. Marshall's approach prevailed over the long term. But as *New York v. United States* (1992, reprinted later in the chapter), *U.S. Term Limits, Inc. v. Thornton* (1995, reprinted later in the chapter), and *Printz v. United States* (1997, reprinted later in the chapter) show, the historic debate over the reach of federal and state authority continues unabated today.

---

[5] *The Federalist* (New York: Barnes & Noble, 1996), p. 282–285.

[6] This argument is vigorously advanced in Jesse Choper, *Judicial Review and the National Political Process* (Chicago: The University of Chicago Press, 1984).

[7] In Madison's formulation, the proposed constitution would extend federal authority to "certain enumer-ated objects only, [leaving] to the several States a residual and inviolable sovereignty over all other objects. Ibid., 285. Among the enumerated objects that the federal government would control were matters of national importance such as interstate and foreign commerce, monetary policy, weights and measures, foreign affairs, postal administration, and the maintenance of an army and navy.

Marshall's Nationalism

The Supreme Court's contribution to our understanding of the nation-state relationship may begin with Marshall's opinion in *McCulloch v. Maryland*. In that case, Marshall sustained the constitutionality of the Second Bank of the United States. Perhaps *McCulloch's* most notable feature is the theory of the federal union that Marshall advanced to defeat Maryland's claim that the Constitution represented a *compact* among sovereign and independent states. In his reading of the preamble, Marshall claimed that the Constitution "emanated" from "we the people of the United States" and not from an agreement among the states acting in their sovereign capacities. In rejecting the compact theory of the Constitution—a rejection that would not end all future efforts to revive it—Marshall concluded that "the government of the Union . . . is emphatically, and truly, a government of the people." Hence, no one state containing a fraction of the people can disassemble what all the people in the assembled Congress have ordained in a duly passed and promulgated statute.[8]

Marshall's "emanation" theory of the Constitution helped to expand and solidify the principle of national supremacy, but it was unnecessary to justify the theory of implied power for which *McCulloch* is so famous. By examining the words and structure of the Constitution, and aided by the magnetic force of his own rhetoric, Marshall set out to show that even in the absence of any express language conferring on the national government the power to incorporate a national bank, Congress was nevertheless empowered to do so. In one of Marshall's most unforgettable passages, he reminded the world that "it is a *constitution* we are expounding"—a document that limits itself to marking government's "great outlines" and "important objects." Among these important objects—or express powers—is the power to tax and borrow money "on the due execution of which the happiness and prosperity of the nation so vitally depends." Any government entrusted with these powers, said the Chief Justice, must have "ample means for their execution" so long as they consist with the letter and spirit of the Constitution.

Note Marshall's reference to the letter and *spirit* of the Constitution. Is there any significant limit to the judgment of an interpreter who feels required to appeal to the spirit—or, for that matter, the structure—of the Constitution in his or her search for an answer to a specific constitutional problem? The question ties in to our treatment of interpretive methodology in chapter 2. Yet Marshall had it both ways. The broad construction of federal power, he noted, was fully consistent with textualism, for the last in the list of powers expressly delegated to Congress in Article I, Section 8, is that of making "all laws which shall be necessary and proper, for carrying into execution the foregoing powers, and all other powers vested by this constitution in the government of the United States, or in any department thereof." Maryland had argued for a strict interpretation of the clause (i.e., the means must be *absolutely* necessary to carry out an express power). But Marshall parried that thrust by a broad interpretation of the "necessary and proper" clause—which included an expansive definition of the world "necessary"—an approach that reinforced his conclusion that the national bank was an appropriate means for Congress to carry out its taxing and borrowing power.

Having established the bank's validity, Marshall proceeded to declare unconstitutional Maryland's tax on the operations of the federal bank within its borders. No

---

[8] Marshall was not the first to advance the emanation theory of the Constitution. He borrowed heavily from John Jay's opinion in *Chisholm v. Georgia*, 2 U.S. (Dall.) 419 (1793).

state, he wrote, is empowered to deploy its taxing authority for the purpose of undermining or destroying a federal instrumentality. In the course of his argument, Marshall conceded that the power to tax "is essential to the very existence of [a state] government" and may be exercised to the utmost extent over persons and property within the state. "The only security against the abuse of this power," said Marshall, is found in the structure of [state] government itself." But a state's right to tax the federal government cannot validly be "given by the people of a particular State." This power can only reside in "the people of the United States, [in] a government whose laws, made in pursuance of the constitution, are declared to be supreme and thus binding on all the states." Thus, *McCulloch* provided an early definition of the boundary between federal and state governments.

Dual Federalism and Judicial Dualism

In 1836, one year after Marshall's death, Roger B. Taney assumed the office of chief justice. Taney, an ardent opponent of the Bank of the United States and staunch defender of states' rights, presided over a court which by now was dominated by appointees of Andrew Jackson. Since the Jacksonians were known to loath the memory of Marshall, the old Federalists—now called Whigs—feared that the new appointees would proceed to dismantle the jurisprudential structure that Marshall had built over the previous three decades. To the surprise of the anti-Jacksonians, however, the Taney Court did not mount a constitutional revolution against the principles of Marshallian nationalism. Instead, the Taney Court vigorously affirmed the residual authority of the states—thus local majorities—to regulate their own internal affairs, a doctrinal focus that Marshall himself had sanctioned in *Gibbons v. Ogden* (1824, reprinted in chapter 7). *Gibbons* drew a bright line between interstate commerce, which Congress is empowered to regulate, and the "completely internal commerce of a state" which, Marshall proclaimed, "may be considered as reserved for the state itself" under its general police power. (See the upcoming section entitled "Local Power over Commerce.")

In its assertion of judicial power, the Taney Court was no less active than Marshall's Court. But the Court would now use this power on behalf of states' rights and local interests. Taney's Court won broad public support in sustaining the validity of local legislation designed to curtail private monopolies and provide for the public welfare.[9] But when the Court entered the slavery controversy, it was swept into the eye of a political hurricane. *Dred Scott v. Sandford* (1856), as we saw in chapter 3, was the first case since *Marbury* to declare an act of Congress unconstitutional, but *Dred Scott* invalidated a national law on the basis of a theory of dual sovereignty Marshall had rejected in *McCulloch*. In proclaiming that the United States is a "union of states, sovereign and independent," Taney revived the compact theory of the Constitution. *Ableman v. Booth* (1859), decided two years after *Dred Scott*, plunged the Court into further disrepute. When compared to *Scott*, this amounted to what Robert McCloskey called a "peculiar transvaluation of values,"[10] for *Ableman* upheld the constitutionality of a federal law—the Fugitive Slave Act—and upbraided Wisconsin for defying it.[11]

---

[9] See, for example, *Mayor of the City of New York v. Miln*, 36 U.S. (11 Pet.) 102 (1837) and *Charles River Bridge v. Warren*, 36 U.S. (11 Pet.) 420 (1837). See also the *License Cases*, 46 U. S. (5 How.) 504 (1847).

[10] Robert G. McCloskey, *The American Supreme Court*, 2nd ed., Revised by Sanford Levinson (Chicago: The University of Chicago Press, 1994), 63.

[11] *Ableman v. Booth*, 62 U.S. (21 How.) 506 (1959). See chapter 14 for a further discussion of the Fugitive Slave Act.

While the Civil War abolished slavery and gave birth to the Fourteenth Amendment—which nullified the *Dred Scott* decision—it failed to erode the power of the Supreme Court in the American governmental process. *Texas v. White* (1869) and *The Slaughter-House Cases* (1873, reprinted in chapter 9) helped to revive dual federalism. *Texas* affirmed the principle of the Union's "perpetuity" and "indissolubility"— the position championed by Lincoln in his First Inaugural Address (see appendix C)—while stating that "the Constitution in all its provisions, looks to an indestructible Union, composed of indestructible States."[12] The statement was ironic because *Texas*'s effect was to uphold the power of the national government to deprive the state of its representation in Congress and to place its people under military rule. Still, the phrase about "indestructible states" could be exploited in the future for the purpose of defending state sovereignty as much as the nation's supremacy, as Justice O'Connor's opinion in the 1992 opinion of *New York v. United States* (discussed later in the chapter) shows.

Even *Slaughter-House* celebrated the "indestructibility" of the states by exhibiting a narrow view of national "privileges and immunities" within the meaning of the Fourteenth Amendment. As noted in much greater detail in chapter 9, the Fourteenth Amendment—and, the Thirteenth and Fifteenth Amendments, as well—resulted in a revolutionary shift of power from the states to the national government. Yet, in declining to place the general rights of citizenship under the protection of the United States government—even in the face of what appeared to be the clear intent of the Fourteenth Amendment—*Slaughter-House* simply refused to tolerate "so great a departure from the structure and spirit of our institutions, when the effect is to fetter and degrade the State governments by subjecting them to the control of Congress [in matters] of the most ordinary and fundamental character."[13] One of the lessons of *Slaughter-House* is that who gets to interpret a constitutional provision may be as important, if not more so, than its author.

The theory of dual federalism flourished between 1870 and 1937, particularly in a series of reciprocal tax immunity cases, as well as in the Supreme Court's rejection of congressional efforts to regulate such matters as manufacturing, agricultural production, labor management relations, and minimum wages and maximum hours of labor—to name just four examples. The intergovernmental tax cases stood for the principle that a state government and its instrumentalities were as immune from federal taxation as the federal government was from state taxation.[14] Beginning in 1905, however, the Court would steadily narrow state immunity by upholding federal taxes on various state enterprises.[15] The Court also nullified numerous federal laws for infringing state sovereignty, decisions easily reached by its narrow interpretation of the federal commerce power. By 1937, however, the Court found that it could no longer realistically hold to a theory of dual federalism within the context of changing

---

[12] In 1866, the postwar military government of Texas initiated an original action in the Supreme Court to reclaim federal bonds that the state had seized after seceding from the Union. The bond holders argued that since Texas was not then a *state* in any constitutional sense, she was disabled from invoking the Supreme Court's original jurisdiction. See *Texas v. White*, 74 (7 Wall.) 700 (1869).

[13] *The Slaughterhouse Cases*, 83 U.S. (16 Wall.) 36 (1873).

[14] See, e.g., *Collector v. Day*, 78 U.S. (11 Wall.) 113, holding that Congress could not tax the salary of a state judge.

[15] See, e.g., *South Carolina v. United States*, 199 U.S. 437 (1905), sustaining a federal tax on South Carolina's liquor-dispensing business; *Graves v. New York*, 306 U.S. 466 (1939), upholding a federal tax on the salaries of state officials; and *New York v. United States*, 326 U.S. 572 (1946), upholding a federal tax on New York's sale of bottled mineral water. By 1988, the Supreme Court had even found that interest earned on unregistered long-term state and local government bonds did not violate the Tenth Amendment.

economic conditions. The Court would now follow rather than resist the coalition of forces that would push the principle of national supremacy to its limits.

The Revival of Implied Limits on Federal Power

As the previous discussion suggests, constitutional cases usually mirror the shifts that have taken place in the balance of power between federal and state governments. These shifts have occurred over very long periods of time. From the 1870s to 1936 the states managed their affairs as if they were as fully supreme in their own sphere of authority as the federal government was in its sphere. In the six decades since 1936, starting with the New Deal, the country witnessed a massive transfer of responsibility from the states to the national level. The Supreme Court endorsed this transfer—at first hesitantly but later willingly—by refusing to review the balance of power that the states and nation managed to forge in the political realm. It would be difficult to argue that the constitutional text dictated juridical theories of either dual federalism or national supremacy. Both theories seemed perfectly compatible with a text read in the light of changing social and economic circumstances. The judicial shift also represents changing understandings within the Court about the limits of judicial power and whether the Court shall oversee the relationship between states and the national government.

In the 1990s the pendulum began swinging back toward state power, both on and off the Court. The political shift toward decentralization found its most compelling symbol in a national law returning to the states primary responsibility for welfare, a development foreshadowed by the "new federalism" of the Reagan Administration and the sweeping rebellion against centralized government that burst forth upon the nation in the early 1990s. Judicial signs of this change showed up even earlier in *National League of Cities v. Usery* (1976). The overruling of *Usery* nine years later in *Garcia v. San Antonio Metropolitan Transit Authority* (1985) was not enough to stop the justices from seriously rethinking aspects of American federalism thought to have been long settled. Landmark cases such as *New York v. United States* (1992, reprinted later in the chapter) and *U. S. Term Limits, Inc. v. Thornton* (1995, reprinted later in the chapter) echoed the clarion call of a budding states' rights movement.[16]

New York featured a challenge to a federal statute that made the states accountable for the disposal of radioactive wastes produced within their borders. In revisiting the Tenth Amendment, the Court found that while Congress may employ various *incentives* to encourage the states to meet federal guidelines in disposing of waste material, it may not compel them to adopt a particular waste disposal system. Even while accepting a broad view of Congress' power under the commerce and spending clauses, *New York* rings with the language of states' rights. Like *Thornton*, *New York* recalls the debates over state sovereignty in the Philadelphia and state ratifying conventions. *New York* also contains echoes from the words and phrases of constitutional cases going back to the nation's beginning, an example of which is the refrain in *Texas v. White* (1869) that the United States is "an indestructible Union, composed of *indestructible states*" (emphasis added.)

The decision in *Thornton*, on the other hand, seemed to be a setback for the states' rights movement. It declared unconstitutional an amendment to Arkansas' constitution limiting the number of terms that members of the state's congressional delegation could serve. Adopted directly by the voters, the amendment limited members of

---

[16] *Usery* (1976) and *Garcia* (1985) are discussed and reprinted in chapter 7.

the House to three terms (six years) and members of the Senate to two terms (twelve years). By a five to four vote, the Court nullified these provisions under constitutional clauses (Art. I, Sec. 2, cl. 1 and Art. I, Sec. 3, cl. 3) which base eligibility for service in Congress on age, citizenship, and residency. "The right to choose representatives," declared the five justices in the majority, "belongs not to the States, but to the people," for "the Constitution creates a uniform national body representing the interests of a single people." Thus, neither Congress nor the states may alter or add to the criteria for service in the House or Senate except through a constitutional amendment.

For present purposes, however, *Thornton* is less notable for its nationalist outcome than for the debate inside the Court over the nature of the federal union. The justices stage a reenactment of the old conflict between the Federalists and anti-Federalists involving many of the interpretive and normative questions highlighted in this casebook. Relying on its decision in *Powell v. McCormack* (1969),[17] the Court started out with a detailed analysis of the original history and text of the qualification clauses. When considered in the light of "the basic principles of our democratic system"—as validated in the majority's mind by congressional experience, state practice, and the Constitution's structure—these clauses compel the conclusion that the stated qualifications may not be changed in the absence of a constitutional amendment.

The justices in the minority, on the other hand, counter with their own interpretation of the Constitution's structure and democratic principles. They found that in the absence of any constitutional language preventing the states from adopting additional standards of eligibility on congressional candidates, the *people* of the various states are entitled to prescribe them as they wish. Dissenters dusted off cases such as *McCulloch v. Maryland* (1819) and *Gibbons v. Ogden* (1824) in an effort to reveal their essential meaning for rediscovering the proper line between federal and state authority today. And no fewer than four justices appear to have adopted a modified version of the compact theory when they insisted that the federal government created by the Constitution represents an agreement of the people *of the states* and not, as Marshall insisted, an emanation of the people of the *United States*.

Two years later, in a resumption of the arguments aired in *New York v. United States*, this debate was featured prominently in the emotionally-charged case of *Printz v. United States* (1997, reprinted later in the chapter), concerning various enforcement procedures of the Brady Handgun Prevention Act. The contested provisions of the national law commanded the "chief law enforcement officer" (CLEO) of each local jurisdiction to conduct background checks on an interim basis until the national system became operative. Although Justice Scalia's finding in his opinion of the Court that Congress lacked the authority to commandeer CLEOs could not, he conceded, be supported by conclusive historical evidence, he found in "the structure of the Constitution" the evidence to derive his conclusion.

As we saw in chapter 2 (and as we shall see in the next chapter in two cases—*National League of Cities v. Usery* and *Garcia v. SAMTA*—that foreshadowed *Printz*), the strength of structuralism in constitutional interpretation resides in its attention to the document, although critics have found that it does little to limit the discretion of its practitioners.[18] Thus Justice Scalia's interpretation of the constitutional text left him

---

[17] *Powell v. McCormack*, 395 U.S. 486 (1969).

[18] As Richard A. Brisbin, Jr., has noted (borrowing from the work of William Harris in *The Interpretable Constitution*), alternative approaches to structural analysis—"transcendent" and "immanent"—were in play in *Printz*. Whereas the Scalia opinion relied on the latter (using resources from within the text), the Stevens dissent employed the former (positing fundamental forms beyond the Constitution). Richard A.

convinced that "dual sovereignty" represented the will of the Framers, who "rejected the concept of a central government that would act upon and through the states, and instead designed a system in which the state and federal governments would exercise concurrent authority over the people. . . ." On the other hand, in his dissenting opinion, Justice Stevens found that "a correct understanding of the basic structure of the Federal Government" required upholding congressional authority when used to "impose affirmative obligations on executive and judicial officers of state and local governments as well as ordinary citizens."

To emphasize what he saw as the interpretive excesses of Justice Scalia's structuralist argument, Justice Stevens appealed to the text of the Constitution, where he found no language to support "the proposition that a local police officer can ignore a command contained in a statute enacted by Congress pursuant to an express delegation of power enumerated in Article I." Moreover, he concluded that the historical record, particularly as it pertained to the intentions of the framers, was opposed to the majority's ruling; without challenging the concept of state sovereignty, Stevens denied what he characterized as the Court's assumption, "that if this trivial burden on state sovereignty is permissible, the entire structure of federalism will collapse."[19] The Court seemed to be back where it started 200 years ago, which is perhaps a way of saying that Americans are united by their common embrace of a document whose principles lend themselves to perpetual disagreement in interpretation.

State Sovereignty and the Eleventh Amendment

If the opinions in *Printz* bear some resemblance to an academic debate over political and constitutional theory, the Court's recent interpretation of the Eleventh Amendment pushes the disputation to an even more intense level. For most of our history this amendment has existed largely in the shadows of the Tenth, but in the context of the Court's developing "new federalism," it has moved to the forefront of judicial attention, both because of the substantive constitutional and policy questions involved, and the importance of the issues of judicial philosophy that are implicated.

The Amendment reads: "The Judicial power of the United States shall not be construed to extend to any suit commenced or prosecuted against one of the United States by Citizens of another State, or by Citizens or Subjects of any Foreign States." It was adopted in response to the decision in *Chisholm v. Georgia* (1793), which holds the distinction of being both the first constitutional law case decided by the Supreme Court as well as the first to engender enough negative reaction to precipitate its overturning through constitutional amendment. Its ruling, that a state could be sued by a citizen of another state, was based on Article III's language extending the jurisdiction of the Court to controversies between a state and citizens of another state. While the Eleventh Amendment unambiguously overturned the specific holding in *Chisholm*, controversy remains as to whether it also overturned the implicit larger point of that case, namely that state sovereign immunity was significantly qualified by the adoption of the Constitution.

That controversy is reflected in all of the recent Eleventh Amendment cases as well and can be framed in terms of how the Court goes about its business of constitutional

---

Brisbin, Jr., *The Reconstitution of American Federalism? The Rehnquist Court and Federal-State Relations, 1991–1997,* 28 Publius 189 (1998). In this view, choices made within the structuralist paradigm necessarily involve judicial discretion.

[19] In another dissenting opinion, Justice Souter reached the same conclusion by exclusively relying on the authority of *The Federalist*.

interpretation. Thus the text of the Amendment is clear in its limitation of the *federal judicial* power and in its application to suits by citizens of *other* states, foreign or domestic. To invoke a broad affirmation of state sovereignty as a bar to additional suits against a state, or to extend the Amendment's constraint on power to institutions other than the federal judiciary, would require a non–text based theory of interpretation. It is not surprising that this has occurred; what is, perhaps, is that the justices on the Court often identified by their determined fidelity to the language of the constitutional text have been the passionate proponents of the more expansive construction of the Eleventh Amendment.

The two sides in this struggle over federalism's meaning adduce diametrically opposed positions from the same sources in history, structure, philosophy, and precedent. Scattered comments from the Framers and English common law immunity doctrines are interpreted variously to advance alternative constitutional visions. In *Seminole Tribe of Florida v. Florida* (1996), Chief Justice Rehnquist's opinion for a soon-to-be stable and familiar five-to-four majority ruled that Congress could not violate the sovereignty of a state under the authority of the Commerce Clause. The decision overruled *Pennsylvania v. Union Gas Co.* (1989), in which a divided Court had upheld a federal environmental law permitting suits for monetary damages against states in federal courts. The Court appealed to other cases, including an important and controversial decision in 1890 (*Hans v. Louisiana*), to affirm that the Eleventh Amendment applied broadly to cases within the federal question jurisdiction of the federal judiciary, and not only, as the language of the amendment reads, to cases involving diversity jurisdiction. *Hans* supported the majority's dependence on underlying "presuppositions," rather than on a "blind reliance upon the text of the Eleventh Amendment." The most important set of presuppositions was that states in the federal system were sovereign entities, which, by virtue of the inherent nature of that status, were immune to suits instituted against them without their consent.

The further entrenchment of these presuppositions in the dominant constitutional understanding on the Court would occur in three cases—*Florida Prepaid Postsecondary Education Expense Board v. College Savings Bank, College Savings Bank v. Florida Prepaid Postsecondary Education Expense Board*, and *Alden v. Maine* (reprinted later in this chapter)—decided on the same day in 1999. Often referred to as the *Alden* trilogy, their extension of the logic of *Seminole Tribe* left no doubt that the Court was committed—fully consistent with its recent Commerce Clause decisions (see chapter 7)—to a fundamental reordering of priorities in federal-state relations.

The petitioners in *Alden* had filed suit against the state of Maine in state court claiming a violation of the Fair Labor Standards Act. This was done after two federal courts had dismissed the case under *Seminole Tribe*'s determination that Congress lacked power under Article I to abrogate the state's sovereign immunity in federal court. After unsuccessfully pressing their claims in the state courts, the plaintiffs were told by the Supreme Court that "the powers delegated to Congress under Article I of the United States Constitution do not include the power to subject nonconsenting States to private suits for damages in state courts."

Justice Kennedy's majority opinion made clear from the outset that the sovereign immunity of the states was not derived from, nor limited by, the Eleventh Amendment. Rather, it—and the state immunity from suit—was deducible from the Constitution's structure and history, as well as ample Supreme Court precedent. Despite the limited reach of its language, the Amendment was, the Court insisted, adopted to restore the original design of the Constitution; thus the failure to codify the traditional understanding of sovereign immunity was no reason to leave it subject to the destructive possibilities bound up in suits against a state. While the severance from England

and the establishment of novel republican institutions entailed a repudiation of many aspects of English political theory, at least one—the doctrine that a sovereign could not be sued without its consent—was retained and incorporated into the work of constitutional drafting and ratification. Subsequent reflection and judicial interpretation would seek to elaborate on the advantages of sovereign immunity for democratic accountability, but there is no gainsaying the fact that in *Alden*, the critical historical foundation for the Court's rejection of a suit by probation officers for alleged failures to abide by overtime provisions of the Fair Labor Standards Act was the prerogatives of the English Crown. In Blackstone's words, as quoted by Justice Kennedy: "[T]he law ascribes to the king the attribute of sovereignty, or pre-eminence. . . . Hence it is, that no suit or action can be brought against the king, even in civil matters, because no court can have jurisdiction over him. For all jurisdiction implies superiority of power. . . ."

With this precept fully accepted, and with additional structural supports found in the Constitution (as indicated in cases such as *Printz*), it followed, wrote Justice Kennedy, that "[O]ur federalism requires that Congress treat the states in a manner consistent with their status as residuary sovereigns and joint participants in the governance of the nation." These circumstances mean that states must be accorded the "dignity" befitting such a status, and so a concept that the Court has often struggled to fit within the text and framework of the Constitution—for example, in speech, privacy, and death penalty cases—had comfortably come to rest within the contours of the "new federalism."

The dissenters, of course, saw things very differently. On the critical question of sovereign immunity, they were less inclined to overlook or dismiss the silences of the constitutional text. According to Justice Souter, "While sovereign immmunity entered many new state legal systems as a part of the common law selectively received from England, it was not understood to be indefeasible or to have been given any such status by the new National Constitution, *which did not mention it* (emphasis added)." Even if not all the Framers believed it to be "an obsolete royal prerogative," the privilege, in the minority's account, was one reserved in English law for the Crown alone. Justice Souter was thus persuaded that James Wilson—Framer and Justice on the first Supreme Court—had it right in thinking "the doctrine of sovereign immunity entirely anomalous in the American Republic." The philosophical divide on the Court could not have been more starkly drawn, with the minority believing the treasured doctrine of the majority to be "an incident of European feudalism." "It would be hard to imagine anything more inimical to the republican conception, which rests on the understanding of its citizens precisely that the government is not above them, but of them, its actions being governed by law just like their own. Whatever justification there may be for an American government's immunity from private suit, it is not dignity." Ultimately what mattered most—more than the jurisprudential disagreements over "ahistorical literalism" and structural constitutional implications—was a principle affirmed in *Marbury v. Madison* and dear to the hearts of the Framers, "that where there is a right, there must be a remedy."

With *Alden*'s deeply theorized ruling, the course of Eleventh Amendment jurisprudence seems settled, at least until the next Supreme Court appointment. In *Kimel v. Florida Board of Regents* (2000), the Court held that the Age Discrimination in Employment Act of 1967 (ADEA), as amended, exceeded Congress' authority under Section 5 of the Fourteenth Amendment. In passing the measure, Congress had made clear its intent to abrogate the States' immunity from individual lawsuits based on age discrimination in hiring and firing, but the narrow Court majority concluded that the enactment was not "appropriate legislation" under Section 5, and hence the abrogation was invalid. Relying on *Boerne v. Flores* (see chapter 13), and their assessment that Congress had not identified any pattern of age discrimination by the states, the justices found the ADEA "so out of proportion to a supposed remedial or preventive object that it cannot be understood as responsive to, or designed to prevent, unconstitutional behavior." A similar outcome was achieved by the *Kimel* majority in the 2001 case of *Trustees of the University of Alabama v. Garrett*, this time involving an abrogation of state sovereign immunity in connection with the Americans with Disabilities Act of 1990.[20]

Finally, in *Federal Maritime Commission v. South Carolina State Ports Authority* (2002, reprinted later in the chapter), the Court dispelled any remaining uncertainty regarding its abandonment of textual analysis in interpreting the Eleventh Amendment. In the cases discussed above, it expanded on the text so as to have it apply to suits in *state* courts initiated by citizens from *within* the state. In this instance it ruled that Congress could not authorize suits against nonconsenting states even when their resolution occurs outside the domain of the "Judicial power," namely in a federal administrative agency.

The case arose out of a cruise ship operator's claim that the South Carolina State Ports Authority had violated the federal Shipping Act of 1984 by denying the operator berthing privileges in Charleston, South Carolina. The specific question before the Court was whether state sovereign immunity precluded the Federal Maritime Commission (FMC) from adjudicating the private complaint. The majority, in an opinion by Justice Thomas, had no difficulty answering in the affirmative, although doing so required determining whether the FMC adjudications "are the type of proceedings from which the Framers would have thought the States possessed immunity when they agreed to enter the Union." The fact that these Framers "could not have anticipated the vast growth of the administrative state" only underscored the reasons for not adhering to a literal rendering of the text. "Simply put, if the Framers thought it an impermissible affront to a State's dignity to be required to answer the complaints of private parties in federal courts, we cannot imagine that they would have found it acceptable to do exactly the same thing before the administrative tribunal of an agency, such as the FMC."

But for Justice Breyer writing in dissent, things were not quite so simple; there was no legitimate way that the "[j]udicial power of the United States" could be interpreted to mean "the executive power of the United States." Thus, even were it the case (which of course the minority would never concede) that the silence of the Constitution on the general question of sovereign immunity argued in favor of affirming such a doctrine as applied to suits in judicial proceedings, both the intentions of the Framers and the course of legal development would deny its application to administrative agencies. Indeed, according to Justice Breyer, the growth of the administrative state argues strongly against analogizing administrative enforcement pro-

---

[20] However, in *Nevada Department of Human Resources v. Hibbs* (2003), the Court ruled that the states could be sued for violating their employees' right to time off for family emergencies as provided in the Family and Medical Leave Act. While the outcome was widely reported as surprising in light of the outcomes in *Kimel* and *Garrett*, Chief Justice Rehnquist's opinion for a 6–3 majority purported to be fully consistent with the doctrinal and philosophical assumptions underlying the earlier decisions. Thus the Court stood by its commitment to state sovereign immunity, but found that Congress' goal of protecting the right to be free from gender-based discrimination was (unlike its efforts in regard to age and disability discrimination) a proper exercise of its Section 5 power under the Fourteenth Amendment. In contrast to the previous enactments, Rehnquist found the family leave provisions to be "narrowly targeted" and genuinely remedial in addressing a problem that was well documented and firmly rooted in societal stereotypes.

cedures with lawsuits brought by individuals to a court, state or federal. While the Framers may not have anticipated the administrative state, "The Court's decision threatens to deny the Executive and Legislative Branches of Government the structural flexibility that the Constitution permits and which modern government demands." From the minority's perspective, the privileging of the abstract notion of state "dignity" over the obligation to adapt institutions to rapidly changing conditions, "will undermine the Constitution's own efforts to achieve its . . . basic structural aim, the creation of a representative form of government capable of translating the people's will into effective public action."

Federal Maritime Commission is thus a case about both the separation of powers and federalism. In this regard it is not unusual; it only makes clearer than most such cases that vertical and horizontal divisions of power within the constitutional system are interconnected. Recall from our chapter on the separation of powers that an important division on the Court relates to the interpretive question of whether to apply a functional analysis to the constitutional provisions that allocate and distribute power. As the debate between Justices Thomas and Breyer over the adjudicative status of administrative decision-making illustrates, these divisions can be anticipated whenever structural issues come before the Court. But controversy over the application of the Eleventh Amendment also shows that disagreement on the relevance of functional attributes of particular institutions is often a proxy for a more profound disagreement over the meaning of the Constitution itself.

Local Power over Commerce

The cases discussed in this subsection stand on their own bottom, but they are best read in the light of *Gibbons v. Ogden* (1824) and the commerce clause cases concerning congressional power (see chapter 7). *Gibbons*, it may suffice to note, invoked the Constitution's Supremacy Clause to strike down New York's state-granted steamboat monopoly because it clashed with a federal licensing statute regulating trade and transportation in the coastal waters of the United States. However, the cases discussed later in this chapter, unlike *Gibbons*, involve judicial challenges to state laws in the absence of any conflicting or parallel national legislation—that is, when the federal commerce power remains unexercised or lies in its so-called "dormant" or negative state. One compelling issue is whether the negative or dormant commerce clause authorizes the federal judiciary to nullify state legislation affecting commerce. (After all, it is sometimes remarked, the Constitution empowers Congress, not the courts, to regulate commerce.) In addition, as we shall see, the cases raise critical issues of democratic theory.

Southern Pacific Company v. State of Arizona (1945, reprinted later in the chapter) illustrates problems of judicial role and democratic theory. Out of a legitimate concern for public safety, the state passed a law limiting the length of trains passing over its territory. States pass laws of this kind all the time, usually for a legitimate public purpose. Other examples are laws or ordinances punishing fraudulent business practices, enacting speed limits on public highways, prohibiting the sale of harmful products, and protecting the privacy of home owners against door-to-door sales pitches. As with the train-length statute, there is often no federal legislation on these issues. This absence of regulation might be taken as a sign that Congress does not want to deal with it or prefers that it be handled by the states, even though Congress could, at any time, enter the field and pass supervening legislation.

The *Arizona* Court found that the state's train-length law constituted an excessive burden on interstate commerce and thus violated the negative commerce clause.

Dissenting, Justice Black makes the case for judicial abstention on grounds of democratic theory. Judicial review of Arizona's law—and statutes like it—he suggested, turns the Court into a "superlegislature" by enmeshing it in public policy and factual issues concerning which it has little or no competence. "A century and a half of constitutional history and government admonishes this Court," he writes, "to leave that choice to the elected legislative representatives or the people themselves, where it properly belongs on democratic principles and the requirements of efficient government." He might also have emphasized the argument cited earlier in this chapter: if state law does burden commerce excessively, Congress is able to enact corrective legislation. In that case, a national majority would validly replace the decision of a local majority without any outside interference by an electorally unaccountable judiciary.

Black's theory of popular democracy is compelling, but it also invites misgivings equally rooted in democratic theory, as *City of Philadelphia v. New Jersey* (1978, reprinted later in the chapter) suggests. It also overlooks the complicated history of negative commerce clause analysis as represented by *Gibbons v. Ogden* and *Cooley v. Board of Wardens* (1851, reprinted later in the chapter) as well as modern cases like *Southern Pacific Company v. State of Arizona.*

When *Gibbons* was before the Court, two theories of the Constitution contested for judicial approval. One theory—the exclusive power theory—held that the affirmative grant of power to the national government to regulate interstate commerce was intended to give Congress sole authority over the nation's commercial life, banishing the state from any regulation of this realm. The other—the concurrent power theory—held that the states enjoyed coextensive authority with Congress to regulate all aspects of commerce within their borders not expressly denied to them by the Constitution. For practical reasons, *Gibbons* rejected both positions: the first because Congress could not be expected—and might not want—to regulate all aspects of interstate commerce, the second because the idea of a common market implicit in the commerce clause could easily be thwarted by varying state regulations. The exclusive power theory, it was argued in some circles, would have disabled the states from regulating aspects of commerce in the public interest in the event of any congressional refusal to deal with a local threat to commerce. On the other hand, giving the states a free hand to regulate their internal commerce might have led to the kind of "balkanized" economy that the commerce clause was designed to prevent. (Whether this reasoning accorded with reality is a question that deserves more attention than it has received.)

Gibbons broadly interpreted the federal commerce power to include the regulation of navigation within a state if it embraced the transportation of goods and persons across state lines. At the same time, however, Marshall affirmed the state's right to control its exclusively internal commerce and even to police the importation of goods from other states when necessary to protect the health and welfare of its people. Marshall drew a bright line between the federal commerce power and the state's police power—the general power to enact laws for the safety, comfort, and well being of the members of society. In short, the nature of the power exercised would determine its validity: only Congress could exercise the commerce power, only the states the police power. Once it was determined that New York had regulated interstate commerce in violation of a federal statute, the case was at an end.

The question *Gibbons* left open is whether, in the absence of federal law, the states may regulate aspects of commerce that Congress could regulate through legislation. This question is at the heart of *Cooley v. Board of Wardens* (1851) and ultimately all negative commerce clause cases. *Cooley* showed that *Gibbons* did not determine what aspects of commerce the states may regulate when Congress' power remains unexercised, a silence that arms the Court with with an enormous interpretive range as well as potential for doctrinal development. Accordingly, *Cooley's* analytical focus shifted from an emphasis on the origin of the power exercised—i.e., the commerce power or the police power—to the nature of the particular subject regulated. The Court in *Cooley* found that the states may regulate a subject of interstate commerce in the silence of Congress when the subject lends itself to diverse legislation at the local level. But if the nature of the subject is one that requires a uniform system of regulation throughout the nation, only Congress can legislate on it. This has become known as the *Cooley* rule.

Arizona and *Philadelphia* continued the elusive search for the limits on state power over commerce when Congress' power remains dormant. Because *Cooley* provided no guidance on which subjects of commerce required uniform regulation, its rule was as defective as *Gibbons* in divining these limits. *Arizona* represents the modern balancing approach to dormant commerce clause analysis. The Court seeks now to weigh the benefits of legitimate—and in this case nondiscriminatory—state legislation against the burden it imposes on interstate commerce. If in the Court's judgment the burden on commerce is excessive relative to the local benefit, the state law will usually be struck down.[21] Furthermore, if a state law is found to discriminate directly against interstate commerce by a regulatory—or tax—measure that prefers local over out-of-state businesses or markets, it is presumptively unconstitutional. Under this broad formula, the Court will strike the regulation unless the state can show that the public purpose advanced by the state could not have been promoted by some other means with a lesser impact on commerce. Whether the Supreme Court is more competent to make such an empirical judgment than a state legislature would seem to be an open question.

From the perspective of democratic theory, however, discriminatory state legislation is constitutionally objectionable because out-of-state concerns lack representation in the legislature, thus putting them at a competitive disadvantage. In short, the Court will use its power to oversee the state legislative process to guard against discrimination without representation. But as *Dean Milk Company v. City of Madison* shows,[22] even these cases divide the Court. *Dean Milk* involved a Madison, Wisconsin, ordinance that prohibited the sale of milk in the city unless it was pasteurized and bottled at approved plants within five miles of the city's center. A majority of the justices concluded that the statute discriminated against an Illinois milk producer barred from selling its product in Madison simply because its pasteurization plants were located outside Wisconsin. The Court recognized the valid public purpose behind the ordinance, but found that Madison could have protected its citizens against contaminated milk by a less restrictive means. Justice Black, along with Justices Douglas and Minton, disagreed with the Court's reasoning and judgment. Finding

---

[21] *Pike v. Bruce Church, Inc.*, which involved an Arizona law requiring certain fruits to be crated and packaged according to the state's standards before being shipped out of state, includes this classic statement of the Court's present analytical approach: "Where the [local] statute regulates even-handedly to effectuate a legitimate local public interest, and its effects on interstate commerce are only incidental, it will be upheld unless the burden imposed on such commerce is clearly excessive in relation to the putative local benefits. . . . If a legitimate local purpose is found, then the question becomes one of degree. And the extent of the burden that will be tolerated will of course depend on the nature of the local interest involved, and on whether it could be promoted as well with a lesser impact on interstate activities." (See 397 U.S. 137 1970).

[22] 340 U.S. 349 (1951).

that Dean Milk could easily have complied with Madison's ordinance without excessive expense or strain, he deplored this judicial interference "merely because the Court believes that alternative milk-inspection methods might insure the cleanliness and healthfulness of Dean's Illinois milk."

The Court's characterization of New Jersey's Waste Control Act as discriminatory in *City of Philadelphia v. New Jersey* (1978) poses difficult questions of fact and value. It shows more clearly the close relation between issues of policy and constitutionality. Apart from Justice Rehnquist's dissent—which is mainly a doctrinal disagreement with the majority—the case prompts inquiry into the costs and benefits of the state statute. How does the Court measure the burden on out-of-state waste producers and in-state land fill operators against the benefit to out-of-state land fill operators and in-state waste producers? What is the degree of the burden on interstate commerce relative to New Jersey's interest in protecting its environment? Equally crucial is whether the continuing availability of New Jersey landfills resulting from *Philadelphia* will postpone the development of new waste disposal technologies in northeastern urban centers. On the other hand, might the Court's ruling have prompted Congress to substitute its own rules on waste disposal for those of the states? (The national government did eventually get into the picture, as we saw earlier in the case of *New York v. United States.*)

Preemption

One can think of numerous issues over which both the nation and the state have concurrent authority. Speed limit laws provide an example. Suppose in the interest of highway safety and fuel conservation, Congress passes a national speed limit law of sixty-five miles an hour on all interstate highways. (Surely Congress possesses that power under the commerce clause.) Suppose in turn a state promulgates a fifty-five mile limit on such highways within its borders, an exercise of the local police power the legitimacy and substantiality of which is beyond dispute. Finally, suppose a trucking company challenges the state's speed limit on the ground that the federal regulation supercedes the state rule. The company, by the way, might also allege that the state rule violates the commerce clause. Who wins in such a case?

The answer depends largely on the purpose behind the federal legislation. If Congress makes clear its intent to legislate *exclusively* on a given subject, then the states are barred from enforcing their own rules on that subject. On the other hand, even conflicting state legislation may be enforced if Congress expressly permits it. If, however, Congress' intent is unclear, the Court will usually examine the structure and purpose of the federal statute to see whether it preempts a parallel state law.

Well-established judicial doctrines are available for determining whether federal preemption obtains in a specific situation. One is whether the scheme of federal regulation is so *pervasive* as to exclude by implication any coextensive state regulation. Another is whether the federal interest in a given subject is so *dominant* as to exclude the enforcement of the state legislation. Finally, state law is preempted if it cannot be enforced without simultaneously violating federal law. In *Pacific Gas & Electric v. Energy Resources* (1983), the Court concluded that the Atomic Energy Act preempts all state safety regulations dealing with the construction and operation of nuclear power plants, but that California's moratorium on the certification of nuclear power plants was not preempted because economic rather than safety concerns were at the basis of the state statute.[23] Perhaps what this and similar decisions show is the

---

[23] A more recent preemption case involved several 1986 amendments to the Occupational Safety and Health Act (OSHA), directing the Secretary of Labor to promulgate federal standards for licensing workers who handle hazardous wastes. In 1988, the Illinois legislature enacted a licensing statute of its own for

importance of constitutional structure in facilitating "teamwork" between national and state government.

Federal-State Comity

Most disputes between state and federal governments do not end in litigation before the Supreme Court. In all areas of public policy, most of the relationships between these governments are cooperative rather than conflictual. When conflicts do occur, they are usually resolved by negotiation and compromise. Teamwork, as suggested, is the *modus operandi*, particularly in such fields as education, crime control, road building, airport construction, environmental protection, and the development of nuclear power. Perhaps the most prominent example of such cooperation are federal grants-in-aid to the states for the purpose of assisting them in caring for the needs of the poor, the disabled, and the unemployed. A full description of these cooperative federal-state arrangements in the United States would fill a large volume.

Where the Supreme Court has had to *insist* on federal-state cooperation—or comity—is in the area of judicial relations. Judicial federalism, as it is sometimes called, requires the federal courts to abstain from interfering with pending state judicial proceedings even when they involve allegations of a constitutional violation. A federal lawsuit to stop a prosecution in a state court is a serious matter. Accordingly, *Younger v. Harris* (1971) laid down the doctrine of abstention. Prior to *Younger*, federal courts often issued injunctions, especially in criminal cases, to halt state court proceedings. Federal courts would intervene on the grounds that state courts were prosecuting defendants under unconstitutional statutes.[24] This practice caused a great deal of friction between federal and state courts; state judges resented the assumption that they could not be trusted to protect rights secured by the United States Constitution. Rejecting the assumption behind the practice, Justice Black invoked the principle of "comity" to limit the ability of federal courts to interfere with state criminal proceedings. In Black's view, this was a constitutional requirement stemming from "a proper respect for state functions" and the principles of "Our federalism."[25]

Comity is a cherished constitutional value (both in the United States and in most other federal systems) because it has to do with our preferred understanding about the nature of politics. Politics is—or should be—a cooperative enterprise, one that

---

such workers and their supervisors. In addition to adopting training standards similar to the federal regulation, Illinois required applicants for a hazardous waste crane operator's permit to submit "a certified record" showing that they had operated the equipment to be used in hazardous waste handling for a minimum of 4,000 hours. A waste disposal trade association asked a federal court for a declaratory judgment that OSHA preempted the Illinois statute. After examining the structure and purpose of OSHA, the Supreme Court concluded that without the Secretary of Labor's approval of a supplementary state plan, the federal statute preempts all of the state's safety and health standards on the issue of hazardous waste disposal, whether or not they conflict with the federal standards. See *Gade v. National Solid Wastes Management Association*, 505 U.S. 88 (1992).

[24] The case of *Dombrowski v. Pfister*, 380 U.S. 479 (1965), which Justice Black frequently cites, held that federal courts were empowered to enjoin state court prosecutions under overbroad statutes violative of the First Amendment. Erwin Chemerinsky writes: "Following *Dombrowski*, hundreds of cases were filed in federal courts seeking injunctions of state court proceedings." See *Federal Jurisdiction*, 2nd edition (Boston: Little, Brown and Company, 1994), p. 718. *Younger* sought to stop this process.

[25] There are of course exceptions to the *Younger* rule. As Justice Stewart remarked in his concurring opinion, the *Younger* rule would not apply where the continuance of the state proceeding would pose a threat of irreparable injury "both great and immediate" 401 U. S. 37, 56 (1965). Such a threat might be present in the face of a statute that is clearly unconstitutional or in the presence of a judge or jury who are clearly biased.

resolves disagreement through compromise or the harmonization of interests rather than by edict or judicial decree. The object of politics, which is built into the architecture of the Constitution, is political integration, which comes about through trust and mutual accommodation.

Interstate Comity

Several provisions of the Constitution require the states to treat each other with courtesy and comity to create solidarity and friendship among the states. These provisions include the full faith and credit clause, the privileges and immunities clause, and the extradition clause, all of which appear in Article IV of the Constitution. (The fugitive slave clause, which required the states to return escaped slaves to their states of origin on the demand of their owners, was repealed by the Thirteenth Amendment.) The full faith and credit clause, which obliges each state to recognize the "public acts, records, and judicial proceedings of every other state," is mentioned here because it has been invoked recently in connection with same-sex marriages. If a state grants a marriage license to a gay or lesbian couple, must that license be recognized by a state that refuses to permit such unions?

The case reprinted in this chapter—*Baldwin v. Fish and Game Commission of Montana* (1978)—deals with the privileges and immunities clause of Article IV. The clause provides that "the citizens of each state shall be entitled to all privileges and immunities of citizens in the several states." (The term "citizen" has been held to include any legal resident of a state.) A simple example of the comity required by the clause will suffice. If Wisconsin allows its own citizens to buy and sell scarce property around its northern lakes, it must extend this privilege to any resident of Illinois or New York. Even though Wisconsin would like to reserve these choice lands for its own residents and keep the price of such property from skyrocketing because of the invasion of wealthy out-of-state residents who are buying up these properties, to deny nonresidents the right to purchase land would be unconstitutional. Similarly, Wisconsin could not refuse a sturgeon fishing license to out-of-state residents while licensing its own residents to spear sturgeon during the one month—February—in which such fishing is allowed. If it wished, the state could probably ban sturgeon fishing altogether for the purpose of conserving the sturgeon population, but the policy would have to be applied equally to all persons.

In *Baldwin*, however, Montana did not deny a game license to out-of-state residents; the state simply charged them more for it. The case is important for its clarification of the nature and scope of the privileges and immunities clause. The Court divided over the constitutionality of Montana's elk-hunting license policy, but all the justices agree that the states are permitted to favor their own citizens with respect to privileges such as voting and running for political office. Another good example of a privilege a state may deny to an out-of-state resident is the right to attend its institutions of higher education. Even if out-of-state students are accepted, as they are for example at distinguished state universities in states such as Michigan, Wisconsin, California, or Texas, the state may impose substantially higher tuition rates on out-of-state residents. As the standard of judgment mentioned by Justice Brennan in his *Baldwin* dissent would seem to suggest, this practice is probably justified by the fact that it advances a substantial state interest, namely, that of preserving its limited educational resources for its own residents whose taxes and sacrifices have made these resources possible.

Comparative Perspectives

Justice Breyer's dissenting opinion in *Printz v. United States* pointed out that "[T]he United States is not the only nation that seeks to reconcile the practical need for a central authority with the democratic virtues of more local control." He then went on to challenge the majority's assertions about local control by referring to the experiences of other federal systems such as Switzerland, Germany, and the European Union. Comparative experience, he thought, should be used to instruct the Court about the consequences of different political solutions to common legal problems. On the other hand, for the majority "such comparative analysis [was] inappropriate to the task of interpreting a constitution."

Obviously this text takes the position that if used carefully comparative constitutional materials are potentially valuable resources for American courts to draw upon. Whether in *Printz* Justice Breyer was sufficiently attentive, as he states in his opinion, to the "relevant political and structural differences between [other] systems and our own," is of course a legitimate point of contention. As applied generally to the subject of federalism, these differences are most saliently related to the alternative purposes and functions that federal structures in different places are designed to serve. Countries where intractable ethnic, religious, or linguistic divisions exist, may adopt an institutional arrangement whereby identity-based representation or political autonomy can be achieved. Elsewhere concerns about the tyrannical possibilities of concentrated political power may culminate in the creation of federal structures that feature widely distributed and fragmented vertical separations of power formed without regard to who resides within subordinate jurisdictions. The United States is an example of the latter, although often polities in the former category—a good example is India—also seek constitutional safeguards against the threats to liberty posed by centralized state power.

The Indian example, however, illustrates a central point about contemporary federalism, which is that the method by which power is distributed varies widely in cross-national comparisons. Were the American model of federalism to represent the world standard, then perhaps only Switzerland and Australia would measure up to expectations. But the range of possibilities is wide; thus India's constitutional structure can be described as "*basically* federal . . . with striking unitary features."[26] This means that it displays much greater centralizing tendencies than is the experience in the United States and many other places. "It is . . . futile to try to ascertain and fit our Constitution into any particular mold. It must be understood in light of our own historical process and constitutional evolution. One thing is clear—it was not a case of independent States coming together to form a Federation as in the case of the United States."[27] One revealing textual manifestation of the difference between the two cases suggested by this Indian Supreme Court opinion is that the Indian charter actually prescribes constitutions for the individual States rather than allowing them (with one exception) to emerge out of the cauldron of local politics. Another is the authority granted the Union Parliament to reshape the federal organization, in effect reconfiguring the map of India in a manner that stands in dramatic contrast to at least one core American commitment—to "indestructible states."

We can appreciate the contrast even more by noting the Indian provision that

[26] Durga Das Basu, *Introduction to the Constitution of India* (18th ed.), (New Delhi: Prentice-Hall of India, 1998), p.51.

[27] *S. R. Bommai v. Union of India*, 3 SCC 1 (1994), p. 215.

enables the central government to dismiss duly elected state governments. Under Article 356 a regime of Presidential Rule can be installed in any State in which it has been certified that the government "cannot be carried on in accordance with the provisions of [the] Constitution." The provision has been invoked some one hundred times, most famously in a 1992 dismissal of three State governments for their failures in implementing and respecting the constitutional commitment to secularism. As was pointed out in the case that emerged from the controversy surrounding these dismissals, Article 356 "was based on Article 4, Section 4 of the American document," both of which were "not inconsistent with the Federal principle."[28] But the American Guarantee Clause (see chapter 3), unlike Article 356, has never led to the suspension or interference by the national government of a state government on the ground that the latter had fallen short of its constitutional obligations. Indeed, some abolitionists, most notably Charles Sumner, had argued that states supporting slavery could not be in possession of a "Republican Form of Government"; hence the federal government's intervention was mandated by Article IV, Section 4, in effect justifying a regime of President's Rule. That such an argument did not get very far can be explained in various ways, not the least of which is that it was too radical a challenge (even for many who agreed with Sumner about the injustice of slavery) to the American bias in favor of local self-government. The privileging of the central government in India explains the frequent use of a provision modeled after an American clause that is, for reasons partly attributable to a very different theory of federalism, never used at all.

Other federal systems with which the United States can be compared are Canada, Germany, Australia, Switzerland, and—at the transnational level—the European Union. Each of these systems embodies common features that define the core of a *federal* union: they divide power between central and state or regional governments; they provide for institutions within which state or regional governments share in making national policy; and they establish a tribunal to resolve ordinary disputes and conflicts between levels of government.[29] These federal systems, however, vary considerably. All were designed to balance unity and diversity, but each has roots in a different set of historical circumstances. For example, Canada's federation emerged from a previously unitary system, whereas Germany returned to its own pre-1933 federal models after a stormy period of unitary rule. The United States, like Australia and Switzerland, aggregated previously independent political units. The European Union, on the other hand, is in the process of merging independent nation-states into a more perfect federal union.

The governing institutions of these federal systems differ as much as their origins. The United States is a presidential system, others are parliamentary. In Germany, state administrative agencies carry out "as a matter of their own concern" laws enacted by the national government, whereas the United States has created a huge federal bureaucracy, parallel to that of the states, to execute its own laws. In each federal system the states or regions also differ in their mode of representation at the national level and the degree to which, as independent units, they are allowed to shape national policy. The structure of the judiciary is also important because it affects the relationship between federal and state courts. For example, Germany's unified judi-

---

[28] Ibid., p. 114.

[29] As A.V. Dicey once observed, "Federalism means legalism [and] the prevalence of a spirit of legality among the people [and thus] judges [are] not only the guardians but also at a given moment the masters of the Constitution." *Introduction to the Study of the Law and of the Constitution*, 9th ed. (E.C.S. Wade, 1939), pp. 173–175.

cial system, as noted in chapter 1, contrasts sharply with the dual court system in the United States. One advantage of a unified judiciary is that it avoids federal-state judicial feuds such as those that erupted in *Martin v. Hunter's Leesee* (1816), and *Cohens v. Virginia* (1821).[30]

Constitutions do not always operate as their designers intended, and all too often hastily drafted constitutional blueprints do not match actual political conditions. In several systems, federalism has evolved in directions that belie the formal division of power between levels of government. Canadian federalism, for example, has not functioned as the unifying force that might have been expected from the original constitution—i.e., the British North American Act of 1867. In Germany, the house in which the states (*Länder*) are corporately represented has evolved into a more powerful body than the constitutional text originally prescribed. In the United States, too, as this chapter has shown, the divide between enumerated and reserved powers has been replaced with cooperative arrangements and the exercise of concurrent power by state and federal governments in many areas of public policy.

Practical politics and historical necessity have produced many of these changes, yet the role of judicial review should not be underestimated. The increasing power of the German Bundesrat—i.e., the Council of State Governments—owes much to decisions of the Federal Constitutional Court. The strong centralist vision of John Marshall is also crucial to an understanding of contemporary federalism in the United States. The Canadian Supreme Court, by contrast, took a much narrower view of national power over trade and commerce, as opposed to its broad interpretation of provincial powers over civil rights and property, the effect of which hampered the national government's effort to regulate the economy. In the hands of the American Supreme Court, the Fourteenth Amendment developed into a powerful tool for nationalizing basic rights and liberties (see chapter 8), whereas the nationalization of such rights in Canada has moved forward in limited ways under the 1982 Charter of Rights and Liberties. None of these developments was inevitable, for different scenarios might have been scripted under different sets of judicial interpreters.

Under Germany's system of administrative federalism, the national government monopolizes the field of policymaking, while the states dominate the implementation of policy. In an effort to protect and fortify the few powers reserved to the states, as Comparative Notes 5.3 and 5.4 point out, the Federal Constitutional Court has narrowly interpreted the catalogue of exclusive and concurrent powers conferred on the national government. This approach, unlike the American, leaves little room for a jurisprudence of implied powers. For example, in 1962, the Constitutional Court struck down a federal law regulating the use of explosives because the statute could not be justified under the national government's concurrent power over "economic affairs." The statute had more to do with maintaining order and security, said the Court, than with furthering economic objectives. Ten years later, however, parliament amended the Basic Law to include "weapons and explosives" among the federal government's concurrent powers.

This episode is instructive when compared with similar conflicts in the United States. First, the Constitutional Court reserves for itself the power to declare with finality any and all constitutional disputes between nation and state, even those arising out of a federal law that arguably regulates the economy. We are reminded once

---

[30] There is also less chance of conflicts between federal and state courts in Canada because the Canadian Supreme court is a general court of appeal for all matters of provincial and local law as well as for cases arising under the Canadian Charter of Rights and Liberties.

again that all provisions of Germany's Basic Law are judicially enforceable. Second, and in sharp contrast to the teaching of the United States Supreme Court in *Garcia v. San Antonio Metropolitan Transit Authority* (see chapter 7) the Court does not regard the *Länder's* participation in the passage of such a law as a reason for deferring to parliament's judgment about its constitutionality. Finally, it is easier in Germany to correct a "misjudgment" of the Constitutional Court by amending the Basic Law. Amending the Basic Law is difficult—it requires a two-thirds vote of all members of the Bundestag and Bundesrat—but it is not the impossible hurdle that often prevails in the United States. Amendments of the kind mentioned in the previous paragraph seems to be a reasonable way of reconciling judicial review with political democracy.

American judicial doctrines on federalism may be compared with still other features of German and Canadian constitutional law. In each of these systems the supremacy or paramountcy of federal law has been firmly established. In the absence of federal legislation, the German and Canadian high courts are not as likely to interfere with state legislation as is the U.S. Supreme Court. But when the German government chooses to exercise one of its many concurrent powers, then federal law preempts state law altogether. In Canada, on the other hand, concurrent legislation is likely to be sustained so long as no direct conflict exists between national and provincial legislation. But in the absence of national legislation, the Canadian Supreme Court is less apt to strike down provincial legislation merely because the field could otherwise be occupied by the national government. Similarly, Canadians seldom speak of a "dormant commerce clause." In an early case, Canada's Supreme Court ruled that in the absence of national legislation over the fire insurance business, which parliament could clearly regulate as a trade, Ontario was authorized to impose its own regulation, as being a civil rights matter within provincial jurisdiction, so long as the regulation affected only the commerce of the province.[31] This remains generally the case today.

As we anticipate debates in chapter 7 over the extent of national power in the United States, it is worth noting that the German Constitutional Court has defended the so-called "core functions" (*Kernbereich*) of local government against both federal and state encroachment. For example, the Court nullified a provision of the Waste Disposal Act of 1972, enacted within the federation's concurrent powers, because it deprived a local community of its responsibility over waste disposal, thus offending the community's constitutional right to self-government. The *Kernbereich* theory echoes the federalism controversy in the United States triggered by *National League of Cities v. Usery* (1976) and *Garcia v. San Antonio Metropolitan Transit Authority* (1985), both of which are discussed in chapter 7. In *Garcia*, the Supreme Court gave up on trying to defend the states against the federal displacement of their "traditional" governmental functions. Any such determination, said the Court, would be arbitrary, for no principled standards exist for determining what is or is not a traditional function of state or local government. Hence, declared the Court, the states must look to the political process and not to the judiciary in defense of their traditional functions. It is difficult to imagine a similar decision by the Federal Constitutional Court. Perhaps the Basic Law's text encourages an active judicial role here as in most other areas of German constitutional law. After all, Article 28 (2) grants local governments explicit protection, whereas the American Tenth Amendment erects no textual barrier against

---

[31] See Neil Finkelstein, *Laskin's Canadian Constitutional Law*, 5th Ed. (Toronto: Carswell, 1986), p. 418.

displacing state authority when the national government has validly exercised one of its enumerated powers.

Finally, we would be remiss if in concluding this section on alternative models of constitutional federalism we did not draw attention to the European Union, which in its challenge to traditional notions of sovereignty, also provides a unique perspective on federalism. Although the European Union is still in its incipient stage of development, certain of its practices and priorities—most notably *subsidiarity*—are likely to endure. Under this principle, which was embraced in the 1992 Maastricht Treaty on European Union (Article 3b), the institutions of the European Community may act in areas of concurrent competence "only if and insofar as the objectives of the proposed action cannot be sufficiently achieved by the Member States." While a principle of supremacy requires that Member States abide by Community law over national law when the two are in conflict, the subsidiarity norm is designed to reassure the Union's constituent members that preference for local over central authority will be judicially enforced.

This generic preference for state over federal action may bear some resemblance to the doctrinal ascent of State sovereignty in the American Supreme Court's recent federalism jurisprudence. However, "[a]ny comparison between the United States and the Community today must of course acknowledge the fundamental difference between, on the one hand, maintaining a semblance of balance in the power relations between the federal government and the states in a system designed along federal lines from its very beginning, and, on the other hand, consciously imposing a new multi-layered legal system on a continent historically dominated by sovereign Nation-States, themselves mostly unitary in structure."[32] The aspirations for European unity cannot obscure differences among member States that are much more entrenched and enduring than are those that prevail in the United States. Additionally, the theory made popular by certain judges in the American Court, to the effect that the structure of the federal government provides adequate political safeguards for federalism (see the discussion in the next chapter), "whatever [its] strengths . . . in the United States, the theory fits the Community rather poorly."[33] Thus the European Court of Justice exercises a much more explicit constitutional mandate to protect the principle of decentralization than does its American counterpart. As the emotionally charged debate in the United States over federalism continues, it might be in everyone's interest to carefully consider the progress in constitutional development of the new experiment of the old world.

Selected Bibliography

Berger, Raoul. *Federalism: The Founders' Design.* Norman: University of Oklahoma Press, 1987.

Conference on Constitutional Federalism (symposium issue). 8 *The American University Journal of International Law and Policy* 375–454 (Winter/Spring, 1992/1993).

Corwin, Edward S. *The Passing of Dual Federalism*, 36 Virginia Law Review 1 (1950).

Diamond, Martin. *Democracy and the Federalist: A Reconsideration of the Framers' Intent.* The American Political Science Review 64 (1959).

---

[32] George A. Bermann, "Taking Subsidiarity Seriously: Federalism in the European Community and the United States," 94 *Columbia Law Review* 331 (1994), page 449

[33] Ibid., page 395

Elazar, Daniel J., *Federalism vs. Decentralization: The Drift from Authenticity*, Publius 6, no. 4 (Fall 1976): 9–19.

Elazar, Daniel J. *Exploring Federalism.* Tuscaloosa: University of Alabama Press, 1986.

McConnell, Michael *Federalism: Evaluating the Founders's Design*, 54 University of Chicago Law Review 1484 (1987).

Merritt, Deborah Jones *The Guarantee Clause and State Autonomy: Federalism for a Third Century*, 88 Columbia Law Review 1 (1988).

Ravkove, Jack N. *Original Meanings: Politics and Ideas in the Making of the Constitution.* New York: Alfred A. Knopf, Inc., 1996.

Redish, Martin H. *Abstention, Separation of Powers, and the Limits of the Judicial Function*, 94 Yale Law Journal 71 (1984).

Schmidhauser, John. *The Supreme Court as Final Arbiter in Federal-State Relations, 1789–1957.* Chapel Hill: University of North Carolina Press, 1958.

Zuckert, Michael P. *Federalism and the Founding: Toward a Reinterpretation of the Constitutional Convention.* 48 Review of Politics 166 (1986).

Selected Comparative Bibliography

Blair, Philip M. *Federalism and Judicial Review in West Germany.* Oxford: Clarendon Press, 1981.

Kommers, Donald P. "Federalism and European Integration: A Commentary." In Mauro Cappelletti et al. *Integration Through Law: European and the American Federal Experience.* Vol. 1, Book 1. Berlin: Walter de Gruyter, 1986: 603–616.

McWhinney, Edward et al. *Federalism in-the-Making: Contemporary Canadian and German Constitutionalism, National and Transnational.* Dordrecht: Martinus Nijhoff, Publishers, 1992.

McWhinney, Edward. *Comparative Federalism.* 2nd edition. Toronto: University of Toronto Press, 1965.

Taylor, Charles. *Reconciling the Solitudes: Essays on Canadian Federalism and Nationalism.* Montreal: McGill-Queens University Press, 1993.

McCulloch v. State of Maryland

17 U.S. 316, 4 Wheat. 316, 4 L.Ed. 579 (1819)

In 1816 Congress incorporated the Bank of the United Sates, which in 1817 established a branch in Baltimore. In 1818 the Maryland legislature passed an act imposing a tax on all banks or branches in Maryland not charted by the state legislature. James McCulloch, a cashier at the Baltimore branch of the Second National Bank, refused to pay the tax. A Maryland trial court upheld the state's right to collect the tax, and the state court of appeals affirmed. Opinion of the Court: *Marshall*, Washington, Johnson, Livingston, Todd, Duvall, Story.

Chief Justice MARSHALL delivered the opinion of the Court.

In the case now to be determined, the defendant, a sovereign state, denies the obligation of a law enacted by the legislature of the Union, and the plaintiff, on his part, contests the validity of an act which has been passed by the legislature of that state. The constitution of our country, in its most interesting and vital parts, is to be considered; the conflicting powers of the government of the Union and of its members, as marked in that constitution, are to be discussed; and an opinion given, which may essentially influence the great operations of the government. No tribunal can approach such a question without a deep sense of its importance, and of the awful responsibility involved in its decision. But it must be decided peacefully, or remain a source of hostile legislation, perhaps of hostility of a still more serious nature; and if it is to be so decided, by this tribunal alone can the decision be made. On the supreme court of the United States has the constitution of our country devolved this important duty.

The first question made in the cause is—has congress power to incorporate a bank? It has been truly said, that this can scarcely be considered as an open question, entirely unprejudiced by the former proceedings of the nation respecting it. The principle now contested was introduced at a very early period of our history, has been recognised by many successive legislatures, and has been acted upon by the judicial department, in cases of peculiar delicacy, as a law of undoubted obligation.

In discussing this question [of the federal bank's validity], the counsel for the state of Maryland have deemed it of some importance, in the construction of the constitution, to consider that instrument, not as emanating from the people, but as the act of sovereign and independent states. The powers of the general government, it has been said, are delegated by the states, who alone are truly sovereign; and must be exercised in subordination to the states, who alone possess supreme dominion. It would be difficult to sustain this proposition. The convention which framed the constitution was indeed elected by the state legislatures. But the instrument, when it came from their hands . . . was reported to the then existing congress of the United States, with a request that it might "be submitted to a convention of delegates, chosen in each state by the people thereof . . . for their assent and ratification." This mode of proceeding was adopted [and] the instrument was submitted to the *people*. They acted upon it in

Comparative Note 6.1

Section 91. It shall be lawful for the Queen, by and with the Advice and Consent of the Senate and House of Commons, to make Laws for the Peace, Order, and good Government of Canada, in relation to all Matters not coming within the Classes of Subjects by this Act assigned exclusively to the Legislatures of the Provinces; . . . [T]he exclusive legislative authority of the Parliament of Canada extends to . . .

1. The regulation of trade and commerce
2. The raising of money by any mode or system of taxation. . . .
3. The borrowing of money on the public credit. . . .
9. Beacons, buoys, lighthouses, and Sable Island
10. Navigation and shipping. . . .
11. Sea coast and inland fisheries. . . .
16. Savings banks. . . .
26. Marriage and divorce.
27. The criminal law, except the constitution of

courts of criminal jurisdiction, but including the procedure in criminal matters. . . .

Section 92. In each province the legislature may exclusively make laws in relation to matters coming within the classes of subject next hereinafter enumerated; that is to say,—

2. Direct taxation within the province in order to raise revenue for provincial purposes.
3. The borrowing of money on the sole credit of the province. . . .
11. The incorporation of companies with provincial objects. . . .
12. The solemnization of marriage in the province.
13. Property and civil rights in the province. . . .
14. The administration of justice in the province, including the constitution, maintenance, and organization of provincial courts, . . .
16. Generally all matters of a merely local or private nature in the province.

SOURCE: Constitution Act, 1867 (Canada).

the only manner in which they can act safely, effectively and wisely, on such a subject, by assembling in convention. It is true, they assembled in their several states—and where else should they have assembled? No political dreamer was ever wild enough to think of breaking down the lines which separate the states, and of compounding the American people into one common mass. Of consequence, when they act, they act in their states. But the measures they adopt do not, on that account, cease to be the measures of the people themselves, or become the measures of the state governments.

. . . The government [of the United States therefore] proceeds directly from the people; is "ordained and established," in the name of the people; and is declared to be ordained, "in order to form a more perfect union, establish justice, insure domestic tranquility, and secure the blessings of liberty to themselves and to their posterity."

. . . The government of the Union, then (whatever may be the influence of this fact on the case), is emphatically and truly, a government of the people. In form, and in substance, it emanates from them. Its powers are granted by them, and are to be exercised directly on them, and for their benefit.

This government is acknowledged by all, to be one of enumerated powers. The principle, that it can exercise only the powers granted to it, would seem too apparent . . . ; that principle is now universally admitted. But the question respecting the extent of the powers actually granted, is perpetually arising, and will probably continue to arise, so long as our system shall exist. In discussing these questions, the conflicting powers of the general and state governments must be brought into view, and the supremacy of their respective laws, when they are in opposition, must be settled.

If any one proposition could command the universal assent of mankind, we might expect it would be this—that the government of the Union, though limited in its powers, is supreme within its sphere of action. This would seem to result, necessarily, from its nature. It is the government of all; its powers are delegated by all; it represents all, and acts for all. Though any one state may be willing to control its operations, no state is willing to allow others to control them. The nation, on those subjects on which it can act, must necessarily bind its component parts. But this question is not left to mere reason: the people have, in express terms, decided it, by saying, "this constitution, and the laws of the United States, which shall be made in pursuance thereof," "shall be the supreme law of the land," and by requiring that the members of the state legislatures, and the officers of the executive and judicial departments of the states, shall take the oath of fidelity to it. The government of the United States, then, though limited in its powers, is supreme; and its laws, when made in pursuance of the constitution, form the supreme law of the land, "any thing in the constitution or laws of any state to the contrary notwithstanding."

Among the enumerated powers, we do not find that of establishing a bank or creating a corporation. But there is no phrase in the instrument which, like the articles of confederation, excludes incidental or implied powers; and which requires that everything granted shall be expressly and minutely described. Even the 10th Amendment, which was framed for the purpose of quieting the excessive jealousies which had been excited, omits the word "expressly," and declares only, that the powers "not delegated to the United States, nor prohibited to the states, are reserved to the states or to the people;" thus leaving the question, whether the particular power which may become the subject of contest, has been delegated to the one government, or prohibited to the other, to depend on a

fair construction of the whole instrument. The men who drew and adopted this amendment had experienced the embarrassments resulting from the insertion of this word in the articles of confederation, and probably omitted it, to avoid those embarrassments. A constitution, to contain an accurate detail of all the subdivisions of which its great powers will admit, and of all the means by which they may be carried into execution, would partake of the prolixity of a legal code, and could scarcely be embraced by the human mind. It would, probably, never be understood by the public. Its nature, therefore, requires, that only its great outlines should be marked, its important objects designated, and the minor ingredients which compose those objects, be deduced from the nature of the objects themselves. That this idea was entertained by the framers of the American constitution, is not only to be inferred from the nature of the instrument, but from the language. Why else were some of the limitations, found in the 9th section of the 1st article, introduced? It is also, in some degree, warranted, by their having omitted to use any restrictive term which might prevent its receiving a fair and just interpretation. In considering this question, then, we must never forget that it is a *constitution* we are expounding.

Although, among the enumerated powers of govern-

Comparative Note 6.2

In Germany's federal state, the unwritten constitutional principle of comity . . . governs all constitutional relationships between the nation as a whole and its [constituent] states as well as the relationship among the states. From this principle there follows a number of legal obligations rooted in the Constitution. In considering the constitutionality of the so-called horizontal financial adjustment, this Court said: "the federal principle [of comity] by its nature creates not only rights but obligations. One of these obligations consists in financially strong states having to give assistance within certain limits to financially weaker states. . . ." This legal restraint, derived from the concept of loyalty to the [federal] union, becomes even more evident in the exercise of legislative powers: "If the effects of a law are not limited to the territory of a state, the state legislature must show consideration for the interests of the federation and the other states. . . ."

The rule of comity also governs the procedure and style of the negotiations required in the constitutional

relationship between the federation and its members as well as between the states. In the Federal Republic of Germany all states have the same constitutional status; they are states entitled to equal treatment when dealing with the federation. Whenever the federation tries to achieve a constitutionally relevant agreement in a matter in which all states are interested and participating, the obligation to act in a profederal manner prohibits the federation from trying to "divide and conquer;" that is, from attempting to divide the states, to seek an agreement with only some of them and then force the others to join. In negotiations that concern all the states, that principle also prohibits the federal government from treating state governments differently because of their party orientation and, in particular, from inviting to politically decisive discussions only representatives from those state governments politically close to the federal government and excluding state governments which are close to opposition parties in the federal parliament.

Source: *Television I Case* [1961], German Federal Constitutional Court, in Kommers *Constitutional Jurisprudence*, 69.

ment, we do not find the word "bank" or "incorporation," we find the great powers, to lay and collect taxes; to borrow money; to regulate commerce; to declare and conduct a war; and to raise and support armies and navies. The sword and the purse, all the external relations, and no inconsiderable portion of the industry of the nation, are intrusted to its government. It can never be pretended, that these vast powers draw after them others of inferior importance, merely because they are inferior. Such an idea can never be advanced. But it may with great reason be contended, that a government, intrusted with such ample powers, on the due execution of which the happiness and prosperity of the nation so vitally depends, must also be intrusted with ample means for their execution. The power being given, it is the interest of the nation to facilitate its execution. It can never be their interest, and cannot be presumed to have been their intention, to clog and embarrass its execution, by withholding the most appropriate means. Throughout this vast republic, from the St. Croix to the Gulf of Mexico, from the Atlantic to the Pacific, revenue is to be collected and expended, armies are to be marched and supported. The exigencies of the nation may require, that the treasure raised in the north should be transported to the south, that raised in the east, conveyed to the west, or that this order should be reversed. Is that construction of the constitution to be preferred, which would render these operations difficult, hazardous and expensive? Can we adopt that construction (unless the words imperiously require it), which would impute to the framers of that instrument, when granting these powers for the public good, the intention of impeding their exercise, by withholding a choice of means? If, indeed, such be the mandate of the constitution, we have only to obey; but that instrument does not profess to enumerate the means by which the powers it confers may be executed; nor does it prohibit the creation of a corporation, if the existence of such a being be essential, to the beneficial exercise of those powers. It is, then, the subject of fair inquiry, how far such means may be employed.

It is not denied, that the powers given to the government imply the ordinary means of execution. That, for example, of raising revenue, and applying it to national purposes, is admitted to imply the power of conveying money from place to place, as the exigencies of the nation may require, and of employing the usual means of conveyance. But it is denied, that the government has its choice of means; or, that it may employ the most convenient means, if, to employ them, it be necessary to erect a corporation.

The power of creating a corporation, though appertaining to sovereignty, is not, like the power of making war,

or levying taxes, or of regulating commerce, a great substantive and independent power, which cannot be implied as incidental to other powers, or used as a means of executing them. It is never the end for which other powers are exercised, but a means by which other objects are accomplished.

But the constitution of the United States has not left the right of congress to employ the necessary means, for the execution of the powers conferred on the government, to general reasoning. To its enumeration of powers is added, that of making "all laws which shall be necessary and proper, for carrying into execution the foregoing powers, and all other powers vested by this constitution, in the government of the United States, or in any department thereof." The counsel for the state of Maryland have urged various arguments, to prove that this clause, though, in terms, a grant of power, is not so, in effect; but is really restrictive of the general right, which might otherwise be implied, of selecting means for executing the enumerated powers. . . .

. . . [T]he argument on which most reliance is placed, is drawn from the peculiar language of this clause. Congress is not empowered by it to make all laws, which may have relation to the powers conferred on the government, but such only as may be "necessary and proper" for carrying them into execution. The word "necessary" is considered as controlling the whole sentence, and as limiting the right to pass laws for the execution of the granted powers, to such as are indispensable, and without which the power would be nugatory. That it excludes the choice of means, and leaves to congress, in each case, that only which is most direct and simple.

Is it true, that this is the sense in which the word "necessary" is always used? Does it always import an absolute physical necessity, so strong, that one thing to which another may be termed necessary, cannot exist without that other? We think it does not. If reference be had to its use, in the common affairs of the world, or in approved authors, we find that it frequently imports no more than that one thing is convenient, or useful, or essential to another. To employ the means necessary to an end, is generally understood as employing any means calculated to produce the end, and not as being confined to those single means, without which the end would be entirely unattainable. Such is the character of human language, that no word conveys to the mind, in all situations, one single definite idea; and nothing is more common than to use words in a figurative sense. Almost all compositions contain words, which, taken in their rigorous sense, would convey a meaning different from that which is obviously intended. It is essential to just construction, that many words which import something excessive, should be understood in a more mitigated sense—in that sense which common usage justifies. The word "necessary" is of this description. It has not a fixed character, peculiar to itself. It admits of all degrees of comparison; and is often connected with other words, which increase or diminish the impression the mind receives of the urgency it imports. A thing may be necessary, very necessary, absolutely or indispensably necessary. To no mind would the same idea be conveyed by these several phrases. The comment on the word is well illustrated by the passage cited at the bar, from the 10th section of the 1st article of the constitution. It is, we think, impossible to compare the sentence which prohibits a state from laying "imposts, or duties on imports or exports, except what may be absolutely necessary for executing its inspection laws," with that which authorizes congress "to make all laws which shall be necessary and proper for carrying into execution" the powers of the general government, without feeling a conviction, that the convention understood itself to change materially the meaning of the word "necessary," by prefixing the word "absolutely." This word, then, like others, is used in various senses; and, in its construction, the subject, the context, the intention of the person using them, are all to be taken into view.

Let this be done in the case under consideration. The subject is the execution of those great powers on which the welfare of a nation essentially depends. It must have been the intention of those who gave these powers, to insure, so far as human prudence could insure, their beneficial execution. This could not be done, by confiding the choice of means to such narrow limits as not to leave it in the power of congress to adopt any which might be appropriate, and which were conducive to the end. This provision is made in a constitution, intended to endure for ages to come, and consequently, to be adapted to the various *crises* of human affairs. To have prescribed the means by which government should, in all future time, execute its powers, would have been to change, entirely, the character of the instrument, and give it the properties of a legal code. It would have been an unwise attempt to provide, by immutable rules, for exigencies which, if foreseen at all, must have been seen dimly, and which can be best provided for as they occur. To have declared, that the best means shall not be used, but those alone without which the power given would be nugatory, would have been to deprive the legislature of the capacity to avail itself of experience, to exercise its reason, and to accommodate its legislation to circumstances. If we apply this principle of construction to any of the powers of the government,

we shall find it so pernicious in its operation that we shall be compelled to discard it.

Take, for example, the power "to establish post-offices and post-roads." This power is executed, by the single act of making the establishment. But, from this has been inferred the power and duty of carrying the mail along the post-road, from one post-office to another. And from this implied power, has again been inferred the right to punish those who steal letters from the post-office, or rob the mail. It may be said, with some plausibility, that the right to carry the mail, and to punish those who rob it, is not indispensably necessary to the establishment of a post-office and post-road. This right is indeed essential to the beneficial exercise of the power, but not indispensably necessary to its existence. So, of the punishment of the crimes of stealing or falsifying a record or process of a court of the United States, or of perjury in such court. To punish these offences, is certainly conducive to the due administration of justice. But courts may exist, and may decide the causes brought before them, though such crimes escape punishment.

If this limited construction of the word "necessary" must be abandoned, in order to punish, whence is derived the rule which would reinstate it, when the government would carry its powers into execution, by means not vindictive in their nature? If the word "necessary" means "needful," "requisite," "essential," "conducive to," in order to let in the power of punishment for the infraction of law; why is it not equally comprehensive, when required to authorize the use of means which facilitate the execution of the powers of government without the infliction of punishment?

But the argument which most conclusively demonstrates the error of the construction contended for by the counsel for the state of Maryland, is founded on the intention of the convention, as manifested in the whole clause. . . . As little can it be required to prove, that in the absence of this clause, congress would have some choice of means. That it might employ those which, in its judgment, would most advantageously effect the object to be accomplished. That any means adapted to the end, any means which tended directly to the execution of the constitutional powers of the government, were in themselves constitutional. This clause, as construed by the state of Maryland, would abridge, and almost annihilate, this useful and necessary right of the legislature to select its means. That this could not be intended, is, we should think, had it not been already controverted, too apparent for controversy.

We think so for the following reasons: 1st. The clause is placed among the powers of congress, not among the limitations on those powers. Its terms purport to enlarge, not to diminish the powers vested in the government. It purports to be an additional power, not a restriction on those already granted. No reason has been, or can be assigned, for thus concealing an intention to narrow the discretion of the national legislature, under words which purport to enlarge it. The framers of the constitution wished its adoption, and well knew that it would be endangered by its strength, not by its weakness. Had they been capable of using language which would convey to the eye one idea, and, after deep reflection, impress on the mind, another, they would rather have disguised the grant of power, than its limitation. If, then, their intention had been, by this clause, to restrain the free use of means which might otherwise have been implied, that intention would have been inserted in another place, and would have been expressed in terms resembling these. "In carrying into execution the foregoing powers, and all others," &c. "No laws shall be passed but such as are necessary and proper." Had the intention been to make this clause restrictive, it would unquestionably have been so in form as well as in effect.

We admit, as all must admit, that the powers of the government are limited, and that its limits are not to be transcended. But we think the sound construction of the constitution must allow to the national legislature that discretion, with respect to the means by which the powers it confers are to be carried into execution, which will enable that body to perform the high duties assigned to it, in the manner most beneficial to the people. Let the end be legitimate, let it be within the scope of the constitution, and all means which are appropriate, which are plainly adapted to that end, which are not prohibited, but consist with the letter and spirit of the constitution, are constitutional.

. . . Should congress, in the execution of its powers, adopt measures which are prohibited by the constitution; or should congress, under the pretext of executing its powers, pass laws for the accomplishment of objects not intrusted to the government; it would become the painful duty of this tribunal, should a case requiring such a decision come before it, to say, that such an act was not the law of the land. But where the law is not prohibited, and is really calculated to effect any of the objects intrusted to the government, to undertake here to inquire into the decree of its necessity, would be to pass the line which circumscribes the judicial department, and to tread on legislative ground. This court disclaims all pretensions to such a power.

After the most deliberate consideration, it is the unanimous and decided opinion of this court, that the act to incorporate the Bank of the United States is a law made in pursuance of the constitution, and is a part of the supreme law of the land.

It being the opinion of the court, that the act incorporating the bank is constitutional; and that the power of establishing a branch in the state of Maryland might be properly exercised by the bank itself, we proceed to inquire.

2. Whether the state of Maryland may, without violating the constitution, tax that branch?

. . . [T]he very terms of this argument admit, that the sovereignty of the state, in the article of taxation itself, is subordinate to, and may be controlled by the constitution of the United States. How far it has been controlled by that instrument, must be a question of construction. In making this construction, no principle, not declared, can be admissible, which would defeat the legitimate operations of a supreme government. It is of the very essence of supremacy, to remove all obstacles to its action within its own sphere, and so to modify every power vested in subordinate governments, as to exempt its own operations from their own influence. This effect need not be stated in terms. It is so involved in the declaration of supremacy, so necessarily implied in it, that the expression of it could not make it more certain. We must, therefore, keep it in view, while construing the constitution.

The argument on the part of the state of Maryland, is, not that the states may directly resist a law of congress, but that they may exercise their acknowledged powers upon it, and that the constitution leaves them this right, in the confidence that they will not abuse it.

Before we proceed to examine this argument, and to subject it to the test of the constitution, we must be permitted to bestow a few considerations on the nature and extent of this original right of taxation, which is acknowledged to remain with the states. It is admitted that the power of taxing the people and their property is essential to the very existence of government, and may be legitimately exercised on the objects to which it is applicable, to the utmost extent to which the government may chuse to carry it. The only security against the abuse of this power, is found in the structure of the government itself. In imposing a tax the legislature acts upon its constituents. This is in general a sufficient security against erroneous and oppressive taxation.

The people of a state, therefore, give to their government a right of taxing themselves and their property, and as the exigencies of government cannot be limited, they prescribe no limits to the exercise of this right, resting confidently on the interest of the legislator, and on the influence of the constituents over their representative, to guard them against its abuse. But the means employed by the government of the Union have no such security, nor is the right of a state to tax them sustained by the same theory. Those means are not given by the constituents of the legislature, which claim the right to tax them, but by the people of all the states. They are given by all, for the benefit of all—and upon theory, should be subjected to that government only which belongs to all.

The sovereignty of a state extends to every thing which exists by its own authority, . . . but does it extend to those means which are employed by congress to carry into execution powers conferred on that body by the people of the United States? We think it demonstrable that it does not. Those powers are not given by the people of the United States, to a government whose laws, made in pursuance of the constitution, are declared to be supreme. Consequently, the people of a single state cannot confer a sovereignty which will extend over them.

That the power to tax involves the power to destroy; that the power to destroy may defeat and render useless the power to create; that there is a plain repugnance in conferring on one government a power to control the constitutional measures of another, which other, with respect to those very measures, is declared to be supreme over that which exerts the control, are propositions not to be denied. But all inconsistencies are to be reconciled by the magic of the word confidence. Taxation, it is said, does not necessarily and unavoidably destroy. To carry it to the excess of destruction, would be an abuse, to presume which, would banish that confidence which is essential to all government. But is this a case of confidence? Would the people of any one state trust those of another with a power to control the most insignificant operations of their state government? We know they would not. Why, then, should we suppose, that the people of any one state should be willing to trust those of another with a power to control the operations of a government to which they have confided their most important and most valuable interests? In the legislature of the Union alone, are all represented. The legislature of the Union alone, therefore, can be trusted by the people with the power of controlling measures which concern all, in the confidence that it will not be abused. This, then, is not a case of confidence, and we must consider it is as it really is.

If we apply the principle for which the counsel for the State of Maryland contends, to the constitution generally, we shall find it capable of changing totally the character of that instrument. We shall find it capable of arresting all the measures of the government, and of prostrating it at the foot of the states. The American people have declared their constitution and the laws made in pursuance thereof, to be supreme; but this principle would transfer the supremacy, in fact, to the states.

The question is, in truth, a question of supremacy; and if the right of the states to tax the means employed by the general government be conceded, the declaration that the constitution, and the laws made in pursuance thereof, shall be the supreme law of the land, is empty and unmeaning declamation.

It has also been insisted, that, as the power of taxation in the general and state governments is acknowledged to be concurrent, every argument which would sustain the right of the general government to tax banks chartered by the states, will equally sustain the right of the states to tax banks chartered by the general government. But the two cases are not on the same reason. The people of all the states have created the general government, and have conferred upon it the general power of taxation. The people of all the states,' and the states themselves, are represented in congress, and, by their representatives, exercise this power. When they tax the chartered institutions of the states, they tax their constituents; and these taxes must be uniform. But when a state taxes the operations of the government of the United States, it acts upon institutions created, not by their own constituents, but by people over whom they claim no control. It acts upon the measures of a government created by others as well as themselves, for the benefit of others in common with themselves. The difference is that which always exists, and always must exist, between the action of the whole on a part, and the action of a part on the whole—between the laws of a government declared to be supreme, and those of a government which, when in opposition to those laws, is not supreme.

The court has bestowed on this subject its most deliberate consideration. The result is a conviction that the states have no power, by taxation or otherwise, to retard, impede, burden, or in any manner control, the operations of the constitutional laws enacted by congress to carry into execution the powers vested in the general government. This is, we think, the unavoidable consequence of that supremacy which the constitution has declared. We are unanimously of opinion, that the law passed by the legislature of Maryland, imposing a tax on the Bank of the United States, is unconstitutional and void.

Notes and Queries

1. What theory of the Constitution is at the basis of Marshall's opinion? Identify the competing theory advanced by Maryland. Which theory is most defensible in the light of the historical record?

2. Chief Justice Marshall justified his reading of the necessary and proper clause in part on the specific location of the clause in the larger text—it is significant, he con-

cluded, that the clause appears in that section of Article I that grants rather than limits legislative power. Was this use of structuralism as a method of constitutional interpretation appropriate? Is structuralism an especially apt method of interpretation in cases concerning federalism? Why or why not? See Charles Black, *Structure and Relationship in Constitutional Law* (Baton Rouge: Louisiana State University Press, 1969).

3. Justice Frankfurter once said that Marshall's claim that "it is a *constitution* we are expounding" is the single most important utterance in the literature of constitutional law—most important because "most comprehensive and most comprehending." See *John Marshall and the Judicial Function*, 69 Harvard Law Review 217, 219 (1955). Do you agree?

4. Suppose Marshall decided this case under the terms of the Canadian Constitution as set forth in Comparative Note 6.1. Would the result be the same?

5. In discussing the issue of taxation, Marshall rejected Maryland's claim that the possibility of abuse should be combated through "confidence." Isn't confidence just another word for comity? Did the Court do damage to the principle of comity when it concluded that trust was an insufficient guarantee? See Comparative Note 6.2 for a perspective on comity between levels of government.

6. Does Marshall's definition of the word "necessary" fit with common usage of the term? Is it plausible? What notion of original intent lies behind this interpretation? Do the examples he uses make his point about Congress'

power to create a national bank? Should we read the words of the constitutional text differently from how we define those words in our everyday life? Did the Framers intend for us to read the Constitution this way? How do we know? See Laurence H. Tribe and Michael C. Dorf, *On Reading the Constitution* (Cambridge: Harvard University Press, 1991).

7. Marshall noted that Congress had twice debated the constitutionality of a national bank and on both occasions Congress voted to establish the bank, which in his view argued for its validity. But Congress also debated the constitutionality of the Judiciary Act of 1789, section 13 of which Marshall struck down in *Marbury v. Madison*. Was Marshall being inconsistent?

8. What conclusion did Marshall draw from the fact that the states are represented in Congress? How much would his case be hurt if at the time, as now, senators were directly elected by the people, rather than appointed by state legislatures? Is the mere fact of state representation in Congress sufficient to uphold the balance of power between state and federal governments? What role should the judiciary play in maintaining the federal balance? Does the Tenth Amendment demand that the Court play such a role?

9. What would the implications be—practically, politically and theoretically—on the operation of the federal government had Maryland's arguments prevailed? Could such a constrained national government have survived then? Could it survive today?

New York v. United States
505 U.S. 144, 112 S.Ct. 2408, 120 L.Ed.2d 120 (1992)

In 1985 Congress enacted the Low-Level Radioactive Waste Policy Amendments Act to deal with the scarcity of disposal sites for low-level radioactive waste. The act embodied a compromise between "sited" and "unsited" states. States having low-level radioactive waste disposal sites agreed to accept such waste from unsited states for another seven years, while unsited states agreed to end their reliance on sited states by 1992. The law contained three incentives to induce states to comply. The first was monetary: states with sites were allowed to impose a surcharge on waste received from other states. The second was an access incentive: sited states could increase the cost of access to their sites and could eventually deny access to these sites entirely. The third was a negative "take title" provision: after seven years, states failing to provide for the disposal of internally generated waste by a specific

date must, upon request of the waste's generator or owner, take possession of the waste and become liable for damages incurred by the generator or owner because of the state's failure to take prompt possession. New York sought a declaratory judgment that the act violated the Tenth Amendment. The District Court dismissed the suit, and the U.S. Court of Appeals affirmed. Opinion of the Court: *O'Connor*, Kennedy, Rehnquist, Scalia, Souter, Thomas. Concurring in part and dissenting in part: *White*, Blackmun, *Stevens*.

Justice O'CONNOR delivered the opinion of the Court.

These cases implicate one of our Nation's newest problems of public policy and perhaps our oldest question of constitutional law. The public policy issue involves the disposal of radioactive waste.... The constitutional question is as old as the Constitution: It consists of discerning the proper division of authority between the Federal Government and the States. We conclude that while Congress

Comparative Note 6.3

[The constitutionality of South Africa's national Education Policy Bill was considered by that country's Constitutional Court in 1996. The challenge to the law centered on its requirement that provincial education departments promote policies that might be inconsistent with provincial policy, and that the act illegally empowered the Minister of Education to impose national policy on the provinces. Those supporting the constitutional challenge to the law relied heavily on the United States Supreme Court's ruling in *New York v. United States*.]

[T]he powers of parliament depend ultimately upon "the language of our Constitution, construed in the light of [our] own history." Our history is different to the history of the United States of America, and the language of our Constitution differs materially from the language of the United States Constitution. . . . Unlike their counterparts in the United States of America, the provinces in South Africa are not sovereign states. They were created by the Constitution and have only those powers that are specifically conferred on them under the Constitution.

[And later in the Court's opinion. . . .]

It is . . . necessary to confront and answer the question: can an act of Parliament require a provincial head of education to cause a plan to be prepared as to how national standards can best be implemented in the province?

Where two legislatures have concurrent powers to make laws in respect of the same functional areas, the only reasonable way in which these powers can be implemented is through cooperation. And this applies as much to policy as to any other matter. It cannot therefore be said to be contrary to the Constitution for Parliament to enact legislation that is premised on the assumption that the necessary cooperation will be offered, and which requires a provincial administration to participate in cooperative structures and to provide information or formulate plans that are reasonably required by the Minister and are relevant to finding the best solution to an impasse that has arisen.

SOURCE: *Dispute Concerning the Constitutionality of Certain Provisions of the National Education Policy Bill, No. 83 Of 1995* 1996 (3) SALR 289 (CC), in Norman Dorsen, et. al., eds., *Comparative Constitutionalism: Cases and Materials* (St. Paul: Thomson/West, 2003), pp. 458, 461.

has substantial power under the Constitution to encourage the States to provide for the disposal of the radioactive waste generated within their borders, the Constitution does not confer upon Congress the ability simply to compel the States to do so. We therefore find that only two of the Act's three provisions at issue are consistent with the Constitution's allocation of power to the Federal Government.

In 1788, in the course of explaining to the citizens of New York why the recently drafted Constitution provided for federal courts, Alexander Hamilton observed: "The erection of a new government, whatever care or wisdom may distinguish the work, cannot fail to originate questions of intricacy and nicety; and these may, in a particular manner, be expected to flow from the establishment of a constitution founded upon the total or partial incorporation of a number of distinct sovereignties." *The Federalist*, No. 82. Hamilton's prediction has proved quite accurate. While no one disputes the proposition that "[t]he Constitution created a Federal Government of limited powers,"

and while the Tenth Amendment makes explicit that "[t]he powers not delegated to the United States by the Constitution, nor prohibited by it to the States, are reserved to the States respectively, or to the people"; the task of ascertaining the constitutional line between federal and state power has given rise to many of the Court's most difficult and celebrated cases. At least as far back as *Martin v. Hunter's Lessee* [1816] the Court has resolved questions "of great importance and delicacy" in determining whether particular sovereign powers have been granted by the Constitution to the Federal Government or have been retained by the States.

These questions can be viewed in either of two ways. In some cases the Court has inquired whether an Act of Congress is authorized by one of the powers delegated to Congress in Article I of the Constitution. In other cases the Court has sought to determine whether an Act of Congress invades the province of state sovereignty reserved by the Tenth Amendment. In a case like this one, involving the division of authority between federal and state governments, the two inquiries are mirror images of each other. If a power is delegated to Congress in the Constitution, the Tenth Amendment expressly disclaims any reservation of that power to the States; if a power is an attribute of state sovereignty reserved by the Tenth Amendment, it is necessarily a power the Constitution has not conferred on Congress.

It is in this sense that the Tenth Amendment "states but a truism that all is retained which has not been surrendered." As Justice Story put it, "[t]his amendment is a mere affirmation of what, upon any just reasoning, is a necessary rule of interpreting the constitution. Being an instrument of limited and enumerated powers, it follows irresistibly, that what is not conferred, is withheld, and belongs to the state authorities." This has been the Court's consistent understanding: "The States unquestionably to retai[n] a significant measure of sovereign authority . . . to the extent that the Constitution has not divested them of their original powers and transferred from those powers to the Federal Government." *Garcia v. San Antonio Metropolitan Transit Authority.*

Congress exercises its conferred powers subject to the limitations contained in the Constitution. Thus, for example, under the Commerce Clause Congress may regulate publishers engaged in interstate commerce, but Congress is constrained in the exercise of that power by the First Amendment. The Tenth Amendment likewise restrains the power of Congress, but this limit is not derived from the text of the Tenth Amendment itself, which, as we have discussed, is essentially a tautology. Instead, the Tenth Amendment confirms that the power of the Federal Government is subject to limits that may, in a given instance, reserve power to the States. The Tenth Amendment thus directs us to determine, as in this case, whether an incident of state sovereignty is protected by a limitation on an Article I power.

The benefits of this federal structure have been extensively cataloged elsewhere, but they need not concern us here. Our task would be the same even if one could prove that federalism secured no advantages to anyone. It consists not of devising our preferred system of government, but of understanding and applying the framework set forth in the Constitution. "The question is not what power the Federal Government ought to have but what powers in fact have been given by the people."

The actual scope of the Federal Government's authority with respect to the States has changed over the years, but the constitutional structure underlying and limiting that authority has not. In the end, just as a cup may be half empty or half full, it makes no difference whether one views the question at issue in this case as one of ascertaining the limits of the power delegated to the Federal Government under the affirmative provisions of the Constitution or one of discerning the core of sovereignty retained by the States under the Tenth Amendment. Either way, we must determine whether any of the three challenged provisions of the Low-Level Radioactive Waste Amendments of 1985 oversteps the boundary between federal and state authority. Petitioners do not contend that Congress lacks the power to regulate the disposal of low level radioactive waste. . . . Petitioners likewise do not dispute that under the Supremacy Clause Congress could, if it wished, pre-empt state radioactive waste regulation. Petitioners contend only that the Tenth Amendment limits the power of Congress to regulate in the way it has chosen. Rather than addressing the problem of waste disposal by directly regulating the generators and disposers of waste, petitioners argue, Congress has impermissibly directed the States to regulate in this field.

Most of our recent cases interpreting the Tenth Amendment have concerned the authority of Congress to subject state governments to generally applicable laws. The Court's jurisprudence in this area has traveled an unsteady path. . . . This litigation instead concerns the circumstances under which Congress may use the States as implements of regulation; that is, whether Congress may direct or otherwise motivate the States to regulate in a particular field or a particular way. Our cases have established a few principles that guide our resolution of the issue.

As an initial matter, Congress may not simply "commandee[r] the legislative processes of the States by directly compelling them to enact and enforce a federal regulatory program."

While Congress has substantial powers to govern the Nation directly, including in areas of intimate concern to the States, the Constitution has never been understood to confer upon Congress the ability to require the States to govern according to Congress' instructions. The Court has been explicit about this distinction. "Both the States and the United States existed before the Constitution. The people, through that instrument, established a more perfect union by substituting a national government, acting, with ample power, directly upon the citizens, instead of the Confederate government, which acted with powers, greatly restricted, only upon the States." . . .

Indeed, the question whether the Constitution should permit Congress to employ state governments as regulatory agencies was a topic of lively debate among the Framers. Under the Articles of Confederation, Congress lacked the authority in most respects to govern the people directly. . . .

The inadequacy of this governmental structure was responsible in part for the Constitutional Convention. . . . In the end, the Convention opted for a Constitution in which Congress would exercise its legislative authority directly over individuals rather than over States.

In providing for a stronger central government, therefore, the Framers explicitly chose a Constitution that confers upon Congress the power to regulate individuals, not States.

This is not to say that Congress lacks the ability to encourage a State to regulate in a particular way, or that Congress may not hold out incentives to the States as a method of influencing a State's policy choices. Our cases have identified a variety of methods, short of outright coercion, by which Congress may urge a State to adopt a legislative program consistent with federal interests. Two of these methods are of particular relevance here.

First, under Congress' spending power, "Congress may attach conditions on the receipt of federal funds." *South Dakota v. Dole* [1987, reproduced in chapter 7] was one such case: The Court found no constitutional flaw in a federal statute directing the Secretary of Transportation to withhold federal highway funds from States failing to adopt Congress' choice of a minimum drinking age.

Second, where Congress has the authority to regulate private activity under the Commerce Clause, we have recognized Congress' power to offer States the choice of regulating that activity according to federal standards or having state law pre-empted by federal regulation. This arrangement, which has been termed "a program of cooperative federalism," is replicated in numerous federal statutory schemes. . . .

By either of these methods, as by any other permissible method of encouraging a State to conform to federal policy choices, the residents of the State retain the ultimate decision as to whether or not the State will comply. If a State's citizens view federal policy as sufficiently contrary to local interests, they may elect to decline a federal grant. If state residents would prefer their government to devote its attention and resources to problems other than those deemed important by Congress, they may choose to have the Federal Government rather than the State bear the expense of a federally mandated regulatory program, and supplement that program to the extent state law is not pre-empted. Where Congress encourages state regulation rather than compelling it, state governments remain responsive to the local electorate's preferences; state officials remain accountable to the people.

By contrast, where the Federal Government compels States to regulate, the accountability of both state and federal officials is diminished. If the citizens of New York, for example, do not consider that making provision for the disposal of radioactive waste is in their best interest, they may elect state officials who share their view. That view can always be pre-empted under the Supremacy Clause if it is contrary to the national view, but in such a case it is the Federal Government that makes the decision in full view of the public, and it will be federal officials that suffer the consequences if the decision turns out to be detrimental or unpopular. But where the Federal Government directs the States to regulate, it may be state officials who will bear the brunt of public disapproval, while the federal officials who devised the regulatory program may remain insulated from the electoral ramifications of their decision. Accountability is thus diminished when, due to federal coercion, elected state officials cannot regulate in accordance with the views of the local electorate in matters not pre-empted by federal regulation.

With these principles in mind, we turn to the three challenged provisions of the Low-Level Radioactive Waste Policy Amendments Act of 1985.

The Act's first set of incentives, in which Congress has conditioned grants to the States upon the States' attainment of a series of milestones, is thus well within the authority of Congress under the Commerce and Spending Clauses. Because the first set of incentives is supported by affirmative constitutional grants of power to Congress, it is not inconsistent with the Tenth Amendment.

In the second set of incentives, Congress has authorized States and regional compacts with disposal sites gradually to increase the cost of access to the sites, and then to deny access altogether, to radioactive waste generated in States that do not meet federal deadlines. As a simple regulation, this provision would be within the power of Congress to authorize the States to discriminate against interstate commerce. Where federal regulation of private activity is within the scope of the Commerce Clause, we have recognized the ability of Congress to offer States the choice of regulating that activity according to federal standards or having state law pre-empted by federal regulation.

This is the choice presented to nonsited States by the Act's second set of incentives: States may either regulate the disposal of radioactive waste according to federal standards by attaining local or regional self-sufficiency, or their residents who produce radioactive waste will be subject to federal regulation authorizing sited States and regions to deny access to their disposal sites. The affected States are not compelled by Congress to regulate, because any burden caused by a State's refusal to regulate will fall on those who generate waste and find no outlet for its disposal, rather than on the State as a sovereign. A State whose citizens do not wish it to attain the Act's milestones may devote its attention and its resources to issues its citizens deem more worthy; the choice remains at all times with the residents of the State, not with Congress. The State need not expend any funds, or participate in any federal program, if local residents do not view such expenditures or participation as worthwhile. Nor must the State abandon the field if it does not accede to federal direction; the State may continue to regulate the generation and disposal of radioactive waste in any manner its citizens see fit.

The Act's second set of incentives thus represents a conditional exercise of Congress' commerce power, along the lines of those we have held to be within Congress' authority. As a result, the second set of incentives does not intrude on the sovereignty reserved to the States by the Tenth Amendment.

The take title provision is of a different character. This third so-called "incentive" offers States, as an alternative to regulating pursuant to Congress' direction, the option of taking title to and possession of the low level radioactive waste generated within their borders and becoming liable for all damages waste generators suffer as a result of the States' failure to do so promptly. In this provision, Congress has crossed the line distinguishing encouragement from coercion.

The take title provision offers state governments a "choice" of either accepting ownership of waste or regulating according to the instructions of Congress. Respondents do not claim that the Constitution would authorize Congress to impose either option as a freestanding requirement. On one hand, the Constitution would not permit Congress simply to transfer radioactive waste from generators to state governments. Such a forced transfer, standing alone, would in principle be no different than a congressionally compelled subsidy from state governments to radioactive waste producers. The same is true of the provision requiring the States to become liable for the generators' damages. Standing alone, this provision would be indistinguishable from an Act of Congress directing the States to assume the liabilities of certain state residents. Either type of federal action would "commandeer" state governments into the service of federal regulatory purposes, and would for this reason be inconsistent with the Constitution's division of authority between federal and state governments. On the other hand, the second alternative held out to state governments—regulating pursuant to Congress' direction—would, standing alone, present a simple command to state governments to implement legislation enacted by Congress. As we have seen, the Constitution does not empower Congress to subject state governments to this type of instruction.

Because an instruction to state governments to take title to waste, standing alone, would be beyond the authority of Congress, and because a direct order to regulate, standing alone, would also be beyond the authority of Congress, it follows that Congress lacks the power to offer the States a choice between the two. Unlike the first two sets of incentives, the take title incentive does not represent the conditional exercise of any congressional power enumerated in the Constitution. In this provision, Congress has not held out the threat of exercising its spending power or its commerce power; it has instead held out the threat, should the States not regulate according to one federal instruction, of simply forcing the States to submit to another federal instruction. A choice between two unconstitutionally coercive regulatory techniques is no choice at all. Either way, "the Act commandeers the legislative processes of the States by directly compelling them to enact and enforce a federal regulatory program," an outcome that has never been understood to lie within the authority conferred upon Congress by the Constitution.

The take title provision appears to be unique. No other federal statute has been cited which offers a state government no option other than that of implementing legislation enacted by Congress. Whether one views the take title provision as laying outside Congress' enumerated powers, or as infringing upon the core of state sovereignty reserved by the Tenth Amendment, the provision is inconsistent with the federal structure of our Government established by the Constitution.

Respondents raise a number of objections to this understanding of the limits of Congress' power. . . . [They] note that the Act embodies a bargain among the sited and unsited States, a compromise to which New York was a willing participant and from which New York has reaped much benefit. Respondents then pose what appears at first to be a troubling question: How can a federal statute be found an unconstitutional infringement of state sovereignty when state officials consented to the statute's enactment?

The answer follows from an understanding of the fundamental purpose served by our Government's federal structure. The Constitution does not protect the sovereignty of States for the benefit of the States or state governments as abstract political entities, or even for the benefit of the public officials governing the States. To the contrary, the Constitution divides authority between federal and state governments for the protection of individuals. State sovereignty is not just an end in itself: "Rather, federalism secures to citizens the liberties that derive from the diffusion of sovereign power." "Just as the separation and independence of the coordinate branches of the Federal Government serves to prevent the accumulation of excessive power in any one branch, a healthy balance of power between the States and the Federal Government will reduce the risk of tyranny and abuse from either front."

Where Congress exceeds its authority relative to the States, therefore, the departure from the constitutional plan cannot be ratified by the "consent" of state officials. An analogy to the separation of powers among the Branches of the Federal Government clarifies this point. The Constitution's division of power among the three Branches is violated where one Branch invades the territory of another, whether or not the encroached-upon Branch approves the encroachment. In *INS v. Chadha* [1983], we held that the legislative veto violated the constitutional requirement that legislation be presented to the President, despite Presidents' approval of hundreds of statutes containing a legislative veto provision. The constitutional authority of Congress cannot be expanded by the "consent" of the governmental unit whose domain is thereby narrowed, whether that unit is the Executive Branch or the States.

State officials thus cannot consent to the enlargement of the powers of Congress beyond those enumerated in the Constitution. Indeed, the facts of these cases raise the possibility that powerful incentives might lead both federal and state officials to view departures from the federal structure to be in their personal interests. Most citizens recognize the need for radioactive waste disposal sites, but few want sites near their homes. As a result, while it would be well within the authority of either federal or state officials to choose where the disposal sites will be, it is likely to be in the political interest of each individual official to avoid being held accountable to the voters for the choice of location. If a federal official is faced with the alternatives of choosing a location or directing the States to do it, the official may well prefer the latter, as a means of shifting responsibility for the eventual decision. If a state official is faced with the same set of alternatives—choosing a location or having Congress direct the choice of a location—the state official may also prefer the latter, as it may permit the avoidance of personal responsibility. The interests of public officials thus may not coincide with the Constitution's intergovernmental allocation of authority. Where state officials purport to submit to the direction of Congress in this manner, federalism is hardly being advanced.

Some truths are so basic that, like the air around us, they are easily overlooked. Much of the Constitution is concerned with setting forth the form of our government, and the courts have traditionally invalidated measures deviating from that form. The result may appear "formalistic" in a given case to partisans of the measure at issue, because such measures are typically the product of the era's perceived necessity. But the Constitution protects us from our own best intentions: It divides power among sovereigns and among branches of government precisely so that we may resist the temptation to concentrate power in one location as an expedient solution to the crisis of the day. The shortage of disposal sites for radioactive waste is a pressing national problem, but a judiciary that licensed extraconstitutional government with each issue of comparable gravity would, in the long run, be far worse.

States are not mere political subdivisions of the United States. State governments are neither regional offices nor administrative agencies of the Federal Government. The positions occupied by state officials appear nowhere on the Federal Government's most detailed organizational chart. The Constitution instead "leaves to the several States a residuary and inviolable sovereignty," reserved explicitly to the States by the Tenth Amendment.

Whatever the outer limits of that sovereignty may be, one thing is clear: The Federal Government may not compel the States to enact or administer a federal regulatory program. The Constitution permits both the Federal Government and the States to enact legislation regarding the disposal of low level radioactive waste. The Constitution enables the Federal Government to pre-empt state regulation contrary to federal interests, and it permits the Federal Government to hold out incentives to the States as a means of encouraging them to adopt suggested regulatory schemes. It does not, however, authorize Congress simply to direct the States to provide for the disposal of the radioactive waste generated within their borders. While there may be many constitutional methods of achieving regional self-sufficiency in radioactive waste disposal, the method Congress has chosen is not one of them. The judgment of the Court of Appeals is accordingly

Affirmed in part and reversed in part.

Justice WHITE, with whom Justice BLACKMUN and Justice STEVENS join, concurring in part and dissenting in part.

It is clear, therefore, that even under the precedents selectively chosen by the Court, its analysis of the take title provision's constitutionality in these cases falls far short of being persuasive. . . . Where it addresses this aspect of respondents' argument, the Court tacitly concedes that a failing of the political process cannot be shown in these cases because it refuses to rebut the unassailable arguments that the States were well able to look after themselves in the legislative process that culminated in the 1985 Act's passage. Indeed, New York acknowledges that its "congressional delegation participated in the drafting and enactment of both the 1980 and the 1985 Acts." The

Court rejects this process-based argument by resorting to generalities and platitudes about the purpose of federalism being to protect individual rights.

Ultimately, I suppose, the entire structure of our federal constitutional government can be traced to an interest in establishing checks and balances to prevent the exercise of tyranny against individuals. But these fears seem extremely far distant to me in a situation such as this. We face a crisis of national proportions in the disposal of low-level radioactive waste, and Congress has acceded to the wishes of the States by permitting local decision making rather than imposing a solution from Washington. New York itself participated and supported passage of this legislation at both the gubernatorial and federal representative levels, and then enacted state laws specifically to comply with the deadlines and timetables agreed upon by the States in the 1985 Act. For me, the Court's civics lecture has a decidedly hollow ring at a time when action, rather than rhetoric, is needed to solve a national problem.

The ultimate irony of the decision today is that in its formalistically rigid obeisance to "federalism," the Court gives Congress fewer incentives to defer to the wishes of state officials in achieving local solutions to local problems. This legislation was a classic example of Congress acting as arbiter among the States in their attempts to accept responsibility for managing a problem of grave import. The States urged the National Legislature not to impose from Washington a solution to the country's low-level radioactive waste management problems. Instead, they sought a reasonable level of local and regional autonomy consistent with Art. I, s 10, cl. 3, of the Constitution. By invalidating the measure designed to ensure compliance for recalcitrant States, such as New York, the Court upsets the delicate compromise achieved among the States and forces Congress to erect several additional formalistic hurdles to clear before achieving exactly the same objective. Because the Court's justifications for undertaking this step are unpersuasive to me, I respectfully dissent.

Notes and Queries

1. How does Justice O'Connor interpret the significance of the Tenth Amendment in this case? How might the result in this case reassert the power of state governments? In what ways is the majority's analysis similar to that of the dissent in *U.S. Term Limits, Inc. v. Thornton*? (Four of the six justices in the majority in *New York v. United States* were in the minority in *Thornton*.)

2. Should it matter constitutionally that the New York state government supported this regulation, and the state's congressional delegation voted overwhelmingly for it? Is New York merely trying to get all the benefits of the legislation with none of the costs? Besides the state government, who exactly is hurt by the take title provision? What is the purpose of the federal nature of our government? Who ultimately is it designed to protect?

3. Do you agree with Justice White's opinion that the majority view is a "formalistically rigid obeisance to 'federalism'"? Compare his opinion with his dissent in *INS v. Chadha*.

4. Is the Tenth Amendment, as Justice O'Connor concluded, "essentially a tautology"? Why? If it is not a tautology, how are judges to give it a principled meaning?

5. The use of *New York* by the South African Constitutional Court has been characterized as an example of "dialogical reasoning." This is a mode of interpretation in which "courts identify the normative and factual assumptions underlying their own constitutional jurisprudence by engaging with comparable jurisprudence of other jurisdictions." Sujit Choudry, *Globalization in Search of Justification: Toward a Theory of Comparative Constitutional Interpretation*, 74 Indiana Law Journal 801 (1999), 825. What specific assumptions of the American theory of federalism helped the South African Court to define federalism in that country?

Printz v. United States

521 U.S. 898, 117 S. Ct. 2365 (1997)

In 1993 the United States Congress passed the Brady Handgun Violence Protection Act, requiring the U.S. Attorney General to establish a national system of instant background checks for those wishing to purchase handguns. Until such a system was in place, however, the act required the "chief law enforcement officer" (CLEO) of local jurisdictions to conduct those background checks. CLEOs from Montana and Arizona sued, claiming that Congress

cannot compel state officers to enforce otherwise valid federal law. In each case, the District Court held the required check unconstitutional. The Ninth Circuit reversed on appeal.

Opinion of the Court: *Scalia*. Concurring opinions: *Thomas, O'Connor*. Dissenting opinions: *Stevens; Breyer*.

Justice SCALIA delivered the opinion of the Court.

The question presented in these cases is whether certain interim provisions of the Brady Handgun Violence Prevention Act, commanding state and local law enforcement officers to conduct background checks on prospective handgun purchasers and to perform certain related tasks, violate the Constitution. . . .

. . . The petitioners here object to being pressed into federal service, and contend that congressional action compelling state officers to execute federal laws is unconstitutional. Because there is no constitutional text speaking to this precise question, the answer to the CLEOs' challenge must be sought in historical understanding and practice, in the structure of the Constitution, and in the jurisprudence of this Court. We treat those three sources, in that order, in this and the next two sections of this opinion.

[History]

Petitioners contend that compelled enlistment of state executive officers for the administration of federal programs is, until very recent years at least, unprecedented. The Government contends, to the contrary, that the earliest Congresses enacted statutes that required the participation of state officials in the implementation of federal laws. The Government's contention demands our careful consideration, since early congressional enactments "provid[e] 'contemporaneous and weighty evidence' of the Constitution's meaning," *Bowsher v. Synar* (1986) (quoting *Marsh v. Chambers* [1983]). . . . Conversely if, as petitioners contend, earlier Congresses avoided use of this highly attractive power, we would have reason to believe that the power was thought not to exist.

The Government observes that statutes enacted by the first Congresses required state courts to record applications for citizenship, to transmit abstracts of citizenship applications and other naturalization records to the Secretary of State, and to register aliens seeking naturalization and issue certificates of registry. . . . These early laws establish, at most, that the Constitution was originally understood to permit imposition of an obligation on state *judges* to enforce federal prescriptions, insofar as those prescriptions related to matters appropriate for the judicial power. . . .

For these reasons, we do not think the early statutes imposing obligations on state courts imply a power of Congress to impress the state executive into its service. . . .

The Government points to a number of federal statutes enacted within the past few decades that require the participation of state or local officials in implementing federal regulatory schemes. Some of these are connected to federal funding measures, and can perhaps be more accurately described as conditions upon the grant of federal funding than as mandates to the States; others, which require only the provision of information to the Federal Government, do not involve the precise issue before us here, which is the forced participation of the States' executive in the actual administration of a federal program. . . . [W]e turn next to consideration of the structure of the Constitution, to see if we can discern . . . a principle that controls the present cases.

[Structure]

It is incontestable that the Constitution established a system of "dual sovereignty." Although the States surrendered many of their powers to the new Federal Government, they retained "a residuary and inviolable sovereignty," *The Federalist* No. 39. This is reflected throughout the Constitution's text, including (to mention only a few examples) the prohibition on any involuntary reduction or combination of a State's territory, Art. IV, s.3; the Judicial Power Clause, Art. III, s.2, and the Privileges and Immunities Clause, Art. IV, s.2, which speak of the "Citizens" of the States; the amendment provision, Article V, which requires the votes of three fourths of the States to amend the Constitution; and the Guarantee Clause, Art. IV, s.4. . . . Residual state sovereignty was also implicit, of course, in the Constitution's conferral upon Congress of not all governmental powers, but only discrete, enumerated ones, Art. I, s.8, which implication was rendered express by the Tenth Amendment's assertion that "[t]he powers not delegated to the United States by the Constitution, nor prohibited by it to the States, are reserved to the States respectively, or to the people."

The Framers' experience under the Articles of Confederation had persuaded them that using the States as the instruments of federal governance was both ineffectual and provocative of federal state conflict. Preservation of the States as independent political entities being the price of union . . . the Framers rejected the concept of a central government that would act upon and through the States, and instead designed a system in which the state and federal governments would exercise concurrent authority over the people . . . As Madison expressed it: "[T]he local or municipal authorities form distinct and independent portions of the supremacy, no more subject, within their respective spheres, to the general authority than the general authority is subject to them, within its own sphere." *The Federalist* No. 39.[34] . . .

---

[34] Justice Breyer's dissent would have us consider the benefits that other countries, and the European Union, believe they have derived from federal systems that are different from ours. We think such comparative analysis inappropriate to the task of interpreting a constitution, though it was of course quite relevant to the task of writing one. . . .

. . . The Constitution does not leave to speculation who is to administer the laws enacted by Congress; the President, it says, "shall take Care that the Laws be faithfully executed," Art. II, s.3, personally and through officers whom he appoints (save for such inferior officers as Congress may authorize to be appointed by the "Courts of Law" or by "the Heads of Departments" who are themselves presidential appointees), Art. II, s.2. The Brady Act effectively transfers this responsibility to thousands of CLEOs in the 50 States, who are left to implement the program without meaningful Presidential control (if indeed meaningful Presidential control is possible without the power to appoint and remove). The insistence of the Framers upon unity in the Federal Executive—to insure both vigor and accountability—is well known. That unity would be shattered, and the power of the President would be subject to reduction, if Congress could act as effectively without the President as with him, by simply requiring state officers to execute its laws.

The dissent of course resorts to the last, best hope of those who defend *ultra vires* congressional action, the Necessary and Proper Clause. It reasons that the power to regulate the sale of handguns under the Commerce Clause, coupled with the power to "make all Laws which shall be necessary and proper for carrying into Execution the foregoing Powers," Art. I, s.8, conclusively establishes the Brady Act's constitutional validity, because the *Tenth Amendment* imposes no limitations on the exercise of *delegated* powers but merely prohibits the exercise of powers "*not* delegated to the United States." What destroys the dissent's Necessary and Proper Clause argument, however, is not the *Tenth Amendment* but the Necessary and Proper Clause itself. When a "La[w] . . . for carrying into Execution" the Commerce Clause violates the principle of state sovereignty reflected in the various constitutional provisions we mentioned earlier, it is not a "La[w] . . . *proper* for carrying into Execution the Commerce Clause," and is thus, in the words of *The Federalist*, "merely [an] ac[t] of usurpation" which "deserve[s] to be treated as such." *The Federalist* No. 33 . . .

The dissent perceives a simple answer in that portion of Article VI which requires that "all executive and judicial Officers, both of the United States and of the several States, shall be bound by Oath or Affirmation, to support this Constitution," arguing that by virtue of the Supremacy Clause this makes "not only the Constitution, but every law enacted by Congress as well," binding on state officers, including laws requiring state officer enforcement. The Supremacy Clause, however, makes "Law of the Land" only "Laws of the United States which shall be made in Pursuance [of the Constitution]"; so the Suprem-

acy Clause merely brings us back to the question discussed earlier, whether laws conscripting state officers violate state sovereignty and are thus not in accord with the Constitution.

[Precedent]

Finally, and most conclusively in the present litigation, we turn to the prior jurisprudence of this Court. Federal commandeering of state governments is such a novel phenomenon that this Court's first experience with it did not occur until the 1970's, when the Environmental Protection Agency promulgated regulations requiring States to prescribe auto emissions testing, monitoring and retrofit programs, and to designate preferential bus and carpool lanes . . . After we granted certiorari to review the statutory and constitutional validity of the regulations, the Government declined even to defend them, and instead rescinded some and conceded the invalidity of those that remained. . . .

When we were at last confronted squarely with a federal statute that unambiguously required the States to enact or administer a federal regulatory program, our decision should have come as no surprise. At issue in *New York v. United States* (1992), were the so called "take title" provisions of the Low Level Radioactive Waste Policy Amendments Act of 1985, which required States either to enact legislation providing for the disposal of radioactive waste generated within their borders, or to take title to, and possession of the waste—effectively requiring the States either to legislate pursuant to Congress's directions, or to implement an administrative solution. We concluded that Congress could constitutionally require the States to do neither. . . .

* * *

We held in *New York* that Congress cannot compel the States to enact or enforce a federal regulatory program. Today we hold that Congress cannot circumvent that prohibition by conscripting the State's officers directly. The Federal Government may neither issue directives requiring the States to address particular problems, nor command the States' officers, or those of their political subdivisions, to administer or enforce a federal regulatory program. It matters not whether policymaking is involved, and no case by case weighing of the burdens or benefits is necessary; such commands are fundamentally incompatible with our constitutional system of dual sovereignty. Accordingly, the judgment of the Court of Appeals for the Ninth Circuit is reversed.

It is so ordered.

Justice THOMAS, concurring.

. . . I write separately to emphasize that the *Tenth Amendment* affirms the undeniable notion that under our Constitution, the Federal Government is one of enumerated, hence limited, powers. Accordingly, the Federal Government may act only where the Constitution authorizes it to do so.

. . . [T]he Federal Government's authority under the Commerce Clause, which merely allocates to Congress the power "to regulate Commerce . . . among the several states," does not extend to the regulation of wholly *intra*state, point of sale transactions. . . . Although this Court has long interpreted the Constitution as ceding Congress extensive authority to regulate commerce (interstate or otherwise), I continue to believe that we must "temper our Commerce Clause jurisprudence" and return to an interpretation better rooted in the Clause's original understanding. Even if we construe Congress' authority to regulate interstate commerce to encompass those intrastate transactions that "substantially affect" interstate commerce, I question whether Congress can regulate the particular transactions at issue here. The Constitution, in addition to delegating certain enumerated powers to Congress, places whole areas outside the reach of Congress' regulatory authority. The *First Amendment*, for example, is fittingly celebrated for preventing Congress from "prohibiting the free exercise" of religion or "abridging the freedom of speech." The *Second Amendment* similarly appears to contain an express limitation on the government's authority. That Amendment provides: "[a] well regulated Militia, being necessary to the security of a free State, the right of the people to keep and bear arms, shall not be infringed." This Court has not had recent occasion to consider the nature of the substantive right safeguarded by the *Second Amendment*. If, however, the *Second Amendment* is read to confer a *personal* right to "keep and bear arms," a colorable argument exists that the Federal Government's regulatory scheme, at least as it pertains to the purely intrastate sale or possession of firearms, runs afoul of that Amendment's protections. As the parties did not raise this argument, however, we need not consider it here.

Justice O'CONNOR, concurring.

. . . Our holding, of course, does not spell the end of the objectives of the Brady Act. States and chief law enforcement officers may voluntarily continue to participate in the federal program. . . . Congress is also free to amend the interim program to provide for its continuance on a contractual basis with the States if it wishes, as it does with a number of other federal programs.

In addition, the Court appropriately refrains from deciding whether other purely ministerial reporting requirements imposed by Congress on state and local authorities pursuant to its Commerce Clause powers are similarly invalid. The provisions invalidated here, however, which directly compel state officials to administer a federal regulatory program, utterly fail to adhere to the design and structure of our constitutional scheme.

Justice STEVENS, with whom Justice SOUTER, Justice GINSBURG, and Justice BREYER join, dissenting . . .

. . . The question is whether Congress, acting on behalf of the people of the entire Nation, may require local law enforcement officers to perform certain duties during the interim needed for the development of a federal gun control program. . . .

Indeed, since the ultimate issue is one of power, we must consider its implications in times of national emergency. Matters such as the enlistment of air raid wardens, the administration of a military draft, the mass inoculation of children to forestall an epidemic, or perhaps the threat of an international terrorist, may require a national response before federal personnel can be made available to respond. If the Constitution empowers Congress and the President to make an appropriate response, is there anything . . . that forbids the enlistment of state officers to make that response effective? More narrowly, what basis is there . . . for concluding that it is the Members of this Court, rather than the elected representatives of the people, who should determine whether the Constitution contains the unwritten rule that the Court announces today?

Perhaps today's majority would suggest that no such emergency is presented by the facts of these cases. But such a suggestion is itself an expression of a policy judgment. And Congress' view of the matter is quite different from that implied by the Court today.

The Brady Act was passed in response to what Congress described as an "epidemic of gun violence. . . ." Whether or not the evaluation reflected in the enactment of the Brady Act is correct as to the extent of the danger and the efficacy of the legislation, the congressional decision surely warrants more respect than it is accorded in today's unprecedented decision.

The text of the Constitution provides a sufficient basis for a correct disposition of this case.

Article I, s.8, grants the Congress the power to regulate commerce among the States. Putting to one side the revisionist views expressed by Justice Thomas in his concurring opinion in *United States v. Lopez* (1995), there can be no question that that provision adequately supports the regulation of commerce in handguns effected by the

Brady Act. Moreover, the additional grant of authority in that section of the Constitution "[t]o make all Laws which shall be necessary and proper for carrying into Execution the foregoing Powers" is surely adequate to support the temporary enlistment of local police officers in the process of identifying persons who should not be entrusted with the possession of handguns. In short, the affirmative delegation of power in Article I provides ample authority for the congressional enactment.

Unlike the *First Amendment*, which prohibits the enactment of a category of laws that would otherwise be authorized by Article I, the *Tenth Amendment* imposes no restriction on the exercise of delegated powers. . . .

. . . [T]he Amendment provides no support for a rule that immunizes local officials from obligations that might be imposed on ordinary citizens. Indeed, it would be more reasonable to infer that federal law may impose greater duties on state officials than on private citizens because another provision of the Constitution requires that "all executive and judicial Officers, both of the United States and of the several States, shall be bound by Oath or Affirmation, to support this Constitution." U. S. Const., Art. VI, cl. 3.

. . . [T]here can be no conflict between their duties to the State and those owed to the Federal Government because Article VI unambiguously provides that federal law "shall be the supreme Law of the Land," binding in every State. U. S. Const., Art. VI, cl. 2. Thus, not only the Constitution, but every law enacted by Congress as well, establishes policy for the States just as firmly as do laws enacted by state legislatures. . . .

There is not a clause, sentence, or paragraph in the entire text of the Constitution of the United States that supports the proposition that a local police officer can ignore a command contained in a statute enacted by Congress pursuant to an express delegation of power enumerated in Article I. . . .

Indeed, the historical materials strongly suggest that the Founders intended to enhance the capacity of the federal government by empowering it—as a part of the new authority to make demands directly on individual citizens—to act through local officials. . . .

This point is made especially clear in Hamilton's statement that "the legislatures, courts, and magistrates, of the respective members, will be incorporated into the operations of the national government *as far as its just and constitutional authority extends;* and *will be rendered auxiliary to the enforcement of its laws*" Ibid. (second emphasis added). It is hard to imagine a more unequivocal statement that state judicial and executive branch officials may be required to implement federal law where the Na-

tional Government acts within the scope of its affirmative powers. . . .

Bereft of support in the history of the founding, the Court rests its conclusion on the claim that there is little evidence the National Government actually exercised such a power in the early years of the Republic. This reasoning is misguided in principle and in fact. . . . [W]e have never suggested that the failure of the early Congresses to address the scope of federal power in a particular area or to exercise a particular authority was an argument against its existence. That position, if correct, would undermine most of our post–New Deal Commerce Clause jurisprudence. . . .

. . . The fact that the Framers intended to preserve the sovereignty of the several States simply does not speak to the question whether individual state employees may be required to perform federal obligations, such as registering young adults for the draft, creating state emergency response commissions designed to manage the release of hazardous substances, collecting and reporting data on underground storage tanks that may pose an environmental hazard, and reporting traffic fatalities, and missing children, to a federal agency. . . . Given the fact that the Members of Congress are elected by the people of the several States, with each State receiving an equivalent number of Senators in order to ensure that even the smallest States have a powerful voice in the legislature, it is quite unrealistic to assume that they will ignore the sovereignty concerns of their constituents. It is far more reasonable to presume that their decisions to impose modest burdens on state officials from time to time reflect a considered judgment that the people in each of the States will benefit therefrom. . . .

Far more important than the concerns that the Court musters in support of its new rule is the fact that the Framers entrusted Congress with the task of creating a working structure of intergovernmental relationships around the framework that the Constitution authorized. Neither explicitly nor implicitly did the Framers issue any command that forbids Congress from imposing federal duties on private citizens or on local officials. As a general matter, Congress has followed the sound policy of authorizing federal agencies and federal agents to administer federal programs. That general practice, however, does not negate the existence of power to rely on state officials in occasional situations in which such reliance is in the national interest. . . .

* * *

The provision of the Brady Act that crosses the Court's newly defined constitutional threshold is more comparable to a statute requiring local police officers to report the identity of missing children to the Crime Control Center of the Department of Justice than to an offensive federal command to a sovereign state. If Congress believes that such a statute will benefit the people of the Nation, and serve the interests of cooperative federalism better than an enlarged federal bureaucracy, we should respect both its policy judgment and its appraisal of its constitutional power.

Accordingly, I respectfully dissent.

Justice SOUTER, dissenting . . .

In deciding these cases, which I have found closer than I had anticipated, it is *The Federalist* that finally determines my position. I believe that the most straightforward reading of No. 27 is authority for the Government's position here, and that this reading is both supported by No. 44 and consistent with Nos. 36 and 45.

Hamilton in No. 27 first notes that because the new Constitution would authorize the National Government to bind individuals directly through national law, it could "employ the ordinary magistracy of each [State] in the execution of its laws." Were he to stop here, he would not necessarily be speaking of anything beyond the possibility of cooperative arrangements by agreement. But he then addresses the combined effect of the proposed Supremacy Clause, U. S. Const., Art. VI, cl. 2, and state officers' oath requirement, U. S. Const., Art. VI, cl. 3, and he states that "the Legislatures, Courts and Magistrates of the respective members will be incorporated into the operations of the national government, *as far as its just and constitutional authority extends;* and will be rendered auxiliary to the enforcement of its laws." *The Federalist* No. 27 (emphasis in original). . . .

Madison in No. 44 supports this reading in his commentary on the oath requirement. . . .

. . . [I] cannot persuade myself that the statements from No. 27 speak of anything less than the authority of the National Government, when exercising an otherwise legitimate power (the commerce power, say), to require state "auxiliaries" to take appropriate action. To be sure, it does not follow that any conceivable requirement may be imposed on any state official. . . . But insofar as national law would require nothing from a state officer inconsistent with the power proper to his branch of tripartite state government (say, by obligating a state judge to exercise law enforcement powers), I suppose that the reach of federal law as Hamilton described it would not be exceeded. . . .

. . . [I] do not read any of *The Federalist* material as requiring the conclusion that Congress could require administrative support without an obligation to pay fair value for it. The quotation from No. 36, for example, describes the

United States as paying. If, therefore, my views were prevailing in these cases, I would remand for development and consideration of petitioners' points, that they have no budget provision for work required under the Act and are liable for unauthorized expenditures.

Justice BREYER, with whom Justice STEVENS joins, dissenting.

I would add to the reasons Justice Stevens sets forth the fact that the United States is not the only nation that seeks to reconcile the practical need for a central authority with the democratic virtues of more local control. At least some other countries, facing the same basic problem, have found that local control is better maintained through application of a principle that is the direct opposite of the principle the majority derives from the silence of our Constitution. The federal systems of Switzerland, Germany, and the European Union, for example, all provide that constituent states, not federal bureaucracies, will themselves implement many of the laws, rules, regulations, or decrees enacted by the central "federal" body. They do so in part because they believe that such a system interferes less, not more, with the independent authority of the "state," member nation, or other subsidiary government, and helps to safeguard individual liberty as well. Of course, we are interpreting our own Constitution, not those of other nations, and there may be relevant political and structural differences between their systems and our own. *Cf. The Federalist* No. 20 (rejecting certain aspects of European federalism). But their experience may nonetheless cast an empirical light on the consequences of different solutions to a common legal problem—in this case the problem of reconciling central authority with the need to preserve the liberty enhancing autonomy of a smaller constituent governmental entity. . . . As comparative experience suggests, there is no need to interpret the Constitution as containing an absolute principle—forbidding the assignment of virtually any federal duty to any state official. . . .

. . . [T]here is neither need nor reason to find in the Constitution an absolute principle, the inflexibility of which poses a surprising and technical obstacle to the enactment of a law that Congress believed necessary to solve an important national problem. . . .

Notes and Queries

1. Compare Justice Scalia's opinion in *Printz* with his opinion in *Morrison v. Olson*, the separation of powers case involving the independent counsel provisions of the Ethics In Government Act. In both instances he eschewed

a functionalist approach in favor of a more formalistic interpretation of structural requirements mandated by the Constitution. Thus, the prohibition against congressional commandeering of state officials derives from "essential postulates" in the text and structure of the Constitution, which must take precedence over whatever governmental efficiency may result from the prescriptions of the Brady Act. In this regard, one commentator has written: "Where foundational sources of text, structure, and history provide scant guidance, interpretive formalism can easily become an exercise in undirected choice from among competing conceptions and formulations—choice that seems arbitrary because it appears neither dictated by the underlying sources, nor counseled by articulated purposes, values, or consequences." Evan H. Caminker, *Printz, State Sovereignty, and the Limits of Formalism*, 1997 The Supreme Court Review (Chicago: The University of Chicago Press, 1998), p. 201. With this in mind, are the constitutional sources clearer with regard to federalism's vertical division of powers or the document's horizontal division of powers?

2. What are the values of federalism that are affirmed by the Court's anticommandeering principle? Do they include such familiar contributions as the protection of liberty, the encouragement of diversity and innovation, and the advancement of political community?

3. In his concurring opinion, Justice Thomas questions whether Congress, even if it had the authority to regulate under the Commerce Clause, could do so within this substantive domain. He argues that the Second Amendment, much like the First's guarantees for speech and religion, limits the government's authority to regulate firearms. He suggests that perhaps in the future the Court will take up the question of the extent of the Amendment's protections for individuals, and when they do, consider the wisdom of Justice Story's description of the right to bear arms as "the palladium of the liberties of a republic." Until then, Justice Thomas appears content to rely on the Tenth Amendment to invalidate sweeping gun laws. Could a case be made that the values underlying both amendments share a similar philosophy rooted in a republican antipathy to governmental power? Should strong proponents of the Tenth Amendment also support an effort to breathe life into the Second Amendment?

4. Consider Justice Breyer's reference to the constitutional arrangements of several foreign systems that provide for state implementation of policies enacted by the central federal authority. This "comparative experience suggests [that] there is no need to interpret the Constitution as containing an absolute principle—forbidding the assignment of virtually any federal duty to any state official." In his opinion for the Court, Justice Scalia vehemently opposed judicial reliance on such experience, prompting one analysis to conclude, "[B]reyer, apparently no great fan of states' rights and Scalia, apparently no great fan of central authority, might have taken precisely the opposite positions on the use of comparative materials had their counterparts elsewhere taken precisely the opposite positions." Lee Epstein and Jack Knight, *Constitutional Borrowing and Nonborrowing*, I-Con: International Journal of Constitutional Law 2 (2003), p. 207. On this account the use of comparative materials by judges is an essentially strategic adjudicative calculation. If one were to think about the application of foreign experience in nonstrategic terms, what principled jurisprudential factors might apply to a decision regarding the employment of such materials?

U.S. Term Limits, Inc. v. Thornton

514 U.S. 779, 115 S. Ct. 1842, 131 L.Ed.2d 881 (1995)

In 1992, the voters of Arkansas approved Amendment 73 to their state constitution. The amendment prohibited a candidate for Congress from appearing on the ballot if the candidate had already served three terms in the House or two terms in the Senate. Candidates who had served the stated number of terms were not disqualified from running but could only receive "write-in" votes. An Arkansas trial court found that the amendment violated the qualifications clause of Article 1 of the Federal Constitution, and the state supreme court affirmed. Opinion of the Court: *Stevens*, Kennedy, Souter, Ginsberg, Breyer. Concurring

opinion: *Kennedy*. Dissenting opinion: *Thomas*, Rehnquist, O'Connor, Scalia.

Justice STEVENS delivered the opinion of the Court.

. . . The constitutionality of Amendment 73 depends critically on the resolution of two distinct issues. The first is whether the Constitution forbids States from adding to or altering the qualifications specifically enumerated in the Constitution. The second is, if the Constitution does so forbid, whether the fact that Amendment 73 is formulated as a ballot access restriction rather than as an outright disqualification is of constitutional significance. Our resolution of these issues draws upon our prior resolution of a related but distinct issue: whether Congress has the power to add to or alter the qualifications of its Members.

Petitioners argue that whatever the constitutionality of additional qualifications for membership imposed by Congress, the historical and textual materials discussed in *Powell* do not support the conclusion that the Constitution prohibits additional qualifications imposed by States. In the absence of such a constitutional prohibition, petitioners argue, the Tenth Amendment and the principle of reserved powers require that States be allowed to add such qualifications.

Petitioners argue that the Constitution contains no express prohibition against state-added qualifications, and that Amendment 73 is therefore an appropriate exercise of a State's reserved power to place additional restrictions on the choices that its own voters may make. We disagree for two independent reasons. First, we conclude that the power to add qualifications is not within the "original powers" of the States, and thus is not reserved to the States by the Tenth Amendment. Second, even if States possessed some original power in this area, we conclude that the Framers intended the Constitution to be the exclusive source of qualifications for members of Congress, and that the Framers thereby "divested" States of any power to add qualifications.

Contrary to petitioner's assertions, the power to add qualifications is not part of the original powers of sovereignty that the Tenth Amendment reserved to the States. Petitioner's Tenth Amendment argument misconceives the nature of the right at issue because that Amendment could only "reserve" that which existed before. As Justice Story recognized, "the states can exercise no powers whatsoever, which exclusively spring out of the existence of the national government, which the constitution does not delegate to them. . . . No state can say that it has reserved what it never possessed."

Each member of Congress is "an officer of the union, deriving his powers and qualifications from the Constitution, and neither created by, dependent upon, nor controllable by, the states. Those officers owe their existence and function to the united voice of the whole, not a portion, of the people." Representatives and Senators are as much officers of the entire nation as is the President. States thus "have just as much right, and no more, to prescribe new qualifications for a representative, as they have for a president. . . . It is no original perogative of state power to appoint a representative, a senator, or a president for the union."

We believe that the Constitution reflects the Framers' general agreement with the approach later articulated by Justice Story. For example, Art. I, s. 5, cl. 1 provides: "Each House shall be the Judge of the Elections, Returns and Qualifications of its own Members." The text of the Constitution thus gives the representatives of all the people the final say in judging the qualifications of the representatives of any one State. For this reason, the dissent falters when it states that "the people of Georgia have no say over whom the people of Massachusetts select to represent them in Congress."

Two other sections of the Constitution further support our view of the Framers' vision. First, consistent with Story's view, the Constitution provides that the salaries of representatives should "be ascertained by Law, and paid out of the Treasury of the United States," Art. I, s. 6, rather than by individual States. The salary provisions reflect the view that representatives owe their allegiance to the people, and not to States. Second, the provisions governing elections reveal the Framers' understanding that powers over the election of federal officers had to be delegated to, rather than reserved by, the States. It is surely no coincidence that the context of federal elections provides one of the few areas in which the Constitution expressly requires action by the States, namely that "the Times, Places and Manner of holding Elections for Senators and Representatives, shall be prescribed in each State by the legislature thereof." This duty parallels the duty under Article II that "Each State shall appoint, in such Manner as the Legislature thereof may direct, a Number of Electors." Art II., s. 1, cl. 2. These Clauses are express delegations of power to the States to act with respect to federal elections.

In short, as the Framers recognized, electing representatives to the National Legislature was a new right, arising from the Constitution itself. The Tenth Amendment thus provides no basis for concluding that the States possess reserved power to add qualifications to those that are fixed in the Constitution. Instead, any state power to set the qualifications for membership in Congress must derive not from the reserved powers of state sovereignty, but rather from the delegated powers of national sovereignty. In the absence of any constitutional delegation to the States of power to add qualifications to those enumerated in the Constitution, such a power does not exist.

Even if we believed that States possessed as part of their original powers some control over congressional qualifications, the text and structure of the Constitution, the relevant historical materials, and, most importantly, the "basic principles of our democratic system" all demonstrate that the Qualifications Clauses were intended to preclude the States from exercising any such power and to fix as exclusive the qualifications in the Constitution.

The Convention and Ratification Debates

The available affirmative evidence indicates the Framers' intent that States have no role in the setting of qualifications. In *Federalist Paper* No. 52, dealing with the House of Representatives, Madison addressed the "qualifications of the electors and the elected." Madison first noted the difficulty in achieving uniformity in the qualifications for electors, which resulted in the Framers' decision to require only that the qualifications for federal electors be the same as those for state electors. Madison argued that such a decision "must be satisfactory to every State, because it is comfortable to the standard already established, or which may be established, by the State itself."

The provisions in the Constitution governing federal elections confirm the Framers' intent that States lack power to add qualifications. The Framers feared that the diverse interests of the States would undermine the National Legislature, and thus they adopted provisions intended to minimize the possibility of state interference with federal elections. For example, to prevent discrimination against federal electors, the Framers required in Art. I, s. 2, cl. 1, that the qualifications for federal electors be the same as those for state electors. As Madison noted, allowing States to differentiate between the qualifications for state and federal electors "would have rendered too dependent on the State governments that branch of the federal government which ought to be dependent on the people alone." *The Federalist* No. 52. Similarly, in Art. I, s. 4, cl. 1, though giving the States the freedom to regulate the "Times, Places and Manner of holding Elections," the Framers created a safeguard against state abuse by giving Congress the power to "by Law make or alter such Regulations." The Convention debates make clear that the Framers' overriding concern was the potential for States' abuse of the power to set the "Times, Places and Manner" of elections. Madison noted that "it was impossible to foresee all the abuses that might be made of the discretionary power."

In light of the Framers' evident concern that States would try to undermine the National Government, they could not have intended States to have the power to set qualifications. Indeed, one of the more anomalous consequences of petitioners' argument is that it accepts federal supremacy over the procedural aspects of determining the times, places, and manner of elections while allowing the states carte blanche with respect to the substantive qualifications for membership in Congress.

We also find compelling the complete absence in the ratification debates of any assertion that States had the power to add qualifications. In those debates, the question whether to require term limits, or "rotation," was a major source of controversy. The draft of the Constitution that was submitted contained no provision for rotation. . . .

Regardless of which side has the better of the debate over rotation, it is most striking that nowhere in the extensive ratification debates have we found any statement by either a proponent or an opponent of rotation that the draft constitution would permit States to require rotation for the representatives of their own citizens. If the participants in the debate had believed that the States retained the authority to impose term limits, it is inconceivable that the Federalists would not have made this obvious response to the arguments of the pro-rotation forces. The absence in an otherwise freewheeling debate of any suggestion that States had the power to impose additional qualifications unquestionably reflects the Framers' common understanding that States lacked that power.

In short, if it had been assumed that States could add additional qualifications, that assumption would have provided the basis for a powerful rebuttal to the arguments being advanced. The failure of intelligent and experienced advocates to utilize this argument must reflect a general agreement that its premise was unsound, and that the power to add qualifications was one that the Constitution denied the States.

Democratic Principles

Our conclusion that States lack the power to impose qualifications vindicates the same "fundamental principle of our representative democracy" that we recognized in *Powell*, namely that "the people should choose whom they please to govern them. . . ." Additional qualifications pose the same obstacle to open elections whatever their source. The egalitarian ideal, so valued by the Framers, is thus compromised to the same degree by additional qualifications imposed by States as by those imposed by Congress.

Similarly, we believe that state-imposed qualifications, as much as congressionally imposed qualifications, would undermine the second critical idea recognized in *Powell*: that an aspect of sovereignty is the right of the people to vote for whom they wish. Again, the source of the qualification is of little moment in assessing the qualification's restrictive impact.

Finally, state-imposed restrictions, unlike the congressionally imposed restrictions at issue in *Powell*, violate a third idea central to this basic principle: that the right to choose representatives belongs not to the States, but to the people.

Consistent with these views, the constitutional structure provides for a uniform salary to be paid from the national treasury, allows the States but a limited role in federal elections, and maintains strict checks on state interference with the federal election process. The Constitution also provides that the qualifications of the representatives of each State will be judged by the representatives of the entire Nation. The Constitution thus creates a uniform national body representing the interests of a single people.

Permitting individual States to formulate diverse qualifications for their representatives would result in a patchwork of state qualifications, undermining the uniformity and the national character that the Framers envisioned and sought to ensure. *McCulloch v. Maryland* [1819], ("Those means are not given by the people of a particular State, not given by the constituents of the legislature, . . . but by the people of all the States. They are given by all, for the benefit of all—and upon theory should be subjected to that government only which belongs to all"). Such a patchwork would also sever the direct link that the Framers found so critical between the National Government and the people of the United States.

State Practice

. . . The Articles of Confederation contained a provision for term limits. As we have noted, some members of the Convention had sought to impose term limits for Members of Congress. In addition, many States imposed term limits on state officers, four placed limits on delegates to the Continental Congress, and several States voiced support for term limits for Members of Congress. Despite this wide-spread support, no State sought to impose any term limits on its own federal representatives. Thus, a proper assessment of contemporaneous state practice provides further persuasive evidence of a general understanding that the qualifications in the Constitution were unalterable by the States.

In sum, the available historical and textual evidence, read in light of the basic principles of democracy underlying the Constitution and recognized by this Court in *Powell*, reveal the Framers' intent that neither Congress nor the States should possess the power to supplement the exclusive qualifications set forth in the text of the Constitution.

Petitioners argue that, even if States may not add qualifications, Amendment 73 is constitutional because it is not such a qualification, and because Amendment 73 is a permissible exercise of state power to regulate the "Times, Places and Manner of Holding Elections." We reject these contentions.

In our view, Amendment 73 is an indirect attempt to accomplish what the Constitution prohibits Arkansas from accomplishing directly. As the plurality opinion of the Arkansas Supreme Court recognized, Amendment 73 is an "effort to dress eligibility to stand for Congress in ballot access clothing," because the "intent and the effect of

Amendment 73 are to disqualify congressional incumbents from further service." . . .

It is not our province to resolve this longstanding debate.

We are, however, firmly convinced that allowing the several States to adopt term limits for congressional service would effect a fundamental change in the constitutional framework. Any such change must come not by legislation adopted either by Congress or by an individual State, but rather—as have other important changes in the electoral process—through the Amendment procedures set forth in Article V. The Framers decided that the qualifications for service in the Congress of the United States be fixed in the Constitution and be uniform throughout the Nation. That decision reflects the Framers' understanding that Members of Congress are chosen by separate constituencies, but that they become, when elected, servants of the people of the United States. They are not merely delegates appointed by separate, sovereign States; they occupy offices that are integral and essential components of a single National Government. In the absence of a properly passed constitutional amendment, allowing individual States to craft their own qualifications for Congress would thus erode the structure envisioned by the Framers, a structure that was designed, in the words of the Preamble to our Constitution, to form a "more perfect Union."

The judgment is affirmed.

It is so ordered.

Justice THOMAS, with whom the Chief Justice, Justice O'CONNOR, and Justice SCALIA join, dissenting.

It is ironic that the Court bases today's decision on the right of the people to "choose whom they please to govern them." Under our Constitution, there is only one State whose people have the right to "choose whom they please" to represent Arkansas in Congress. The Court holds, however, that neither the elected legislature of that State nor the people themselves (acting by ballot initiative) may prescribe any qualifications for those representatives. The majority therefore defends the right of the people of Arkansas to "choose whom they please to govern them" by invalidating a provision that won nearly 60% of the votes cast in a direct election and that carried every congressional district in the State.

I dissent. Nothing in the Constitution deprives the people of each State of the power to prescribe eligibility requirements for the candidates who seek to represent them in Congress. The Constitution is simply silent on this question. And where the Constitution is silent, it raises no bar to action by the States or the people.

Because the majority fundamentally misunderstands the notion of "reserved" powers, I start with some first principles. Contrary to the majority's suggestion, the people of the States need not point to any affirmative grant of power in the Constitution in order to prescribe qualifications for their representatives in Congress, or to authorize their elected state legislators to do so. . . . When they adopted the Federal Constitution, of course, the people of each State surrendered some of their authority to the United States (and hence to entities accountable to the people of other States as well as to themselves). . . . In each State, the remainder of the people's powers—"the powers not delegated to the United States by the Constitution, nor prohibited by it to the States," Amdt. 10—are either delegated to the state government or retained by the people. . . . The Federal Government and the States thus face different default rules: where the Constitution is silent about the exercise of a particular power—that is, where the Constitution does not speak either expressly or by necessary implication—the Federal Government lacks that power and the States enjoy it.

These basic principles are enshrined in the Tenth Amendment, which declares that all powers neither delegated to the Federal Government nor prohibited to the States "are reserved to the States respectively, or to the people." . . . [T]he Amendment does make clear that powers reside at the state level except where the Constitution removes them from that level. . . .

Any ambiguity in the Tenth Amendment's use of the phrase "the people" is cleared up by the body of the Constitution itself. Article I begins by providing that the Congress of the United States enjoys "all legislative Powers herein granted," s. 1, and goes on to give a careful enumeration of Congress' powers, s. 8. It then concludes by enumerating certain powers that are *prohibited* to the States. The import of this structure is the same as the import of the Tenth Amendment: if we are to invalidate Arkansas' Amendment 73, we must point to something in the Federal Constitution that deprives the people of Arkansas of the power to enact such measures.

The majority begins by announcing an enormous and untenable limitation on the principle expressed by the Tenth Amendment. According to the majority, the States possess only those powers that the Constitution affirmatively grants to them or that they enjoyed before the Constitution was adopted; the Tenth Amendment "could only 'reserve' that which existed before.". . . . The majority's essential logic is that the state governments could not "reserve" any powers that they did not control at the time the Constitution was drafted. But it was not the state governments that were doing the reserving. The Constitution derives its authority instead from the consent of *the people* of the States. Given the fundamental principle that all governmental powers stem from the people of the States, it would simply be incoherent to assert that the people of the States could not reserve any powers that they had not previously controlled.

The majority also sketches out what may be an alternative (and narrower) argument. Again citing Story, the majority suggests that it would be inconsistent with the notion of "national sovereignty" for the States or the people of the States to have any reserved powers over the selection of Members of Congress.

The majority apparently reaches this conclusion in two steps. First, it asserts that because Congress as a whole is an institution of the National Government, the individual Members of Congress "owe primary allegiance not to the people of a State, but to the people of the Nation." Second, it concludes that because each Member of Congress has a nationwide constituency once he takes office, it would be inconsistent with the Framers' scheme to let a single state prescribe qualifications for him.

. . . [W]hile the majority is correct in that the Framers expected the selection process to create a "direct link" between members of the House of Representatives and the people, the link was between the Representatives from each State and the people of that State; the people of Georgia have no say over whom the people of Massachusetts select to represent them in Congress. This arrangement must baffle the majority, whose understanding of Congress would surely fit more comfortably within a system of nationwide elections. But the fact remains that when it comes to the selection of Members of Congress, the people of each State have retained their independent political identity. As a result, there is absolutely nothing strange about the notion that the people of the states or their state legislature possess "reserved" powers in this area.

In a final effort to deny that the people of the States enjoy "reserved" powers over the selection of their representatives in Congress, the majority suggests that the Constitution expressly delegates to the States certain powers over congressional elections. Such delegations of power, the majority argues, would be superfluous if the people of the States enjoyed reserved powers in this area.

Only one constitutional provision—the Times, Places and Manner Clause of Article I, s. 4—even arguably supports the majority's suggestion. It reads:

"The Times, Places and Manner of holding Elections for Senators and Representatives, shall be prescribed in each State by the Legislature thereof; but the Congress may at any time by Law make or alter such Regulations, except as to the Places of chusing Senators."

Contrary to the majority's assumption, however, this Clause does not delegate any authority to the States. Instead, it simply imposes a duty upon them. The majority gets it exactly right: by specifying that the state legislatures "shall" prescribe the details necessary to hold congressional elections, the Clause "expressly requires action by the States." This command meshes with one of the principal purposes of Congress' "make or alter" power: to ensure that the States hold congressional elections in the first place, so that Congress continues to exist.

I take it to be established, then, that the people of Arkansas do enjoy "reserved" powers over the selection of their representatives in Congress. Purporting to exercise those reserved powers, they have agreed among themselves that the candidates covered by s. 3 of Amendment 73—those whom they have already elected to three or more terms in the House of Representatives or to two or more terms in the Senate—should not be eligible to appear on the ballot for reelection, but should none the less be returned to Congress if enough voters are sufficiently enthusiastic about their candidacy to write in their names. Whatever one might think of the wisdom of this arrangement, we may not override the decision of the people of Arkansas unless something in the Federal Constitution deprives them of the power to enact such measures.

The majority settles on "the Qualifications Clauses" as the constitutional provisions that Amendment 73 violates.

The Qualifications Clauses do prevent the individual States from abolishing all eligibility requirements for Congress.

If the people of a State decide that they would like their representatives to possess additional qualifications, however, they have done nothing to frustrate the policy behind the Qualifications Clauses. Anyone who possesses all of the constitutional qualifications, plus some qualifications required by state law, still has all of the federal qualifications. Accordingly, the fact that the Constitution specifies certain qualifications that the Framers deemed necessary to protect the competence of the National Legislature does not imply that it strips the people of the individual States of the power to protect their own interests by adding other requirements for their own representatives.

The majority responds that "a patchwork of state qualifications" would "undermine the uniformity and the national character that the Framers envisioned and sought to ensure." Yet the Framers thought it perfectly consistent with the "national character" of Congress for the Senators and Representatives from each State to be chosen by the legislature or the people of that State. The majority never

explains why Congress' fundamental character permits this state centered system, but nonetheless prohibits the people of the states and their state legislatures from setting any eligibility requirements for the candidates who seek to represent them.

In discussing the ratification period, the majority stresses two principal data. One of these pieces of evidence is no evidence at all—literally. The majority devotes considerable space to the fact that the recorded ratification debates do not contain any affirmative statement that the States can supplement the constitutional qualifications. For the majority, this void is "compelling" evidence that "unquestionably reflects the Framers' common understanding that States lacked that power." The majority reasons that delegates at several of the ratifying conventions attacked the Constitution for failing to require Members of Congress to rotate out of office. If supporters of ratification had believed that the individual States could supplement the constitutional qualifications, the majority argues, they would have blunted these attacks by pointing out that rotation requirements could still be added State by State.

But the majority's argument cuts both ways. The recorded ratification debates also contain no affirmative statement that the States cannot supplement the constitutional qualifications. While ratification was being debated, the existing rule in America was that the States could prescribe eligibility requirements for their delegates to Congress, even though the Articles of Confederation gave Congress itself no power to impose such qualifications. If the Federal Constitution had been understood to deprive the States of this significant power, one might well have expected its opponents to seize on this point in arguing against ratification.

The fact is that arguments based on the absence of recorded debate at the ratification conventions are suspect, because the surviving records of those debates are fragmentary. If one concedes that the absence of relevant records from the ratification debates is not strong evidence for either side, then the majority's only significant piece of evidence from the ratification period is *Federalist* No. 52. Contrary to the majority's assertion, however, this essay simply does not talk about "the lack of state control over the qualifications of the elected," whether "explicitly" or otherwise.

It is true that *Federalist* No. 52 contrasts the Constitution's treatment of the qualifications of voters in elections for the House of Representatives with its treatment of the qualifications of the Representatives themselves. As Madison noted, the Framers did not specify any uniform qualifications for the franchise in the Constitution; instead, they simply incorporated each State's rules about eligibility to vote in elections for the most numerous branch of the state legislature. By contrast, Madison continued, the Framers chose to impose some particular qualifications that all members of the House had to satisfy. But while Madison did say that the qualifications of the elected were "more susceptible of uniformity" than the qualifications of electors, *Federalist* No. 52, he did not say that the Constitution prescribes anything but uniform minimum qualifications for congressmen. That, after all, is more than it does for congressional electors.

It is radical enough for the majority to hold that the Constitution implicitly precludes the people of the States from prescribing any eligibility requirements for the congressional candidates who seek their votes. This holding, after all, does not stop with negating the term limits that many States have seen fit to impose on their Senators and Representatives. Today's decision also means that no State may disqualify congressional candidates whom a court has found to be mentally incompetent, who are currently in prison, or who have past vote-fraud convictions.

In order to invalidate s. 3 of Amendment 73, however, the majority must go farther. The bulk of the majority's analysis—like Part II of my dissent—addresses the issues that would be raised if Arkansas had prescribed "genuine, unadulterated, undiluted term limits." But as the parties have agreed, Amendment 73 does not actually create this kind of disqualification. It does not say that covered candidates may not serve any more terms in Congress if re-elected, and it does not indirectly achieve the same result by barring those candidates from seeking reelection. It says only that if they are to win reelection, they must do so by write-in votes. One might think that this is a distinction without a difference. As the majority notes, "[t]he uncontested data submitted to the Arkansas Supreme Court" show that write-in candidates have won only six congressional elections in this century. But while the data's accuracy is indeed "uncontested," petitioners filed an equally uncontested affidavit challenging the data's relevance. As political science professor James S. Fay swore to the Arkansas Supreme Court, "most write-in candidacies in the past have been waged by fringe candidates, with little public support and extremely low name identification." [I]n modern times only two incumbent Congressmen have ever sought reelection as write-in candidates. One of them was Dale Alford of Arkansas, who had first entered the House of Representatives by winning 51% of the vote as a write-in candidate in 1958; Alford then waged a write-in campaign for reelection in 1960, winning a landslide 83% of the vote against an opponent who enjoyed a place on the ballot. The other incumbent write-in candidate was Philip J. Philbin of Massachusetts, who—despite losing his

party primary and thus his spot on the ballot—won 27% of the vote in his unsuccessful write-in candidacy. . . . [T]hese results—coupled with other examples of successful write-in campaigns, such as Ross Perot's victory in North Dakota's 1992 Democratic presidential primary—"demonstrate that when a write-in candidate is well-known and well-funded, it is quite possible for him or her to win an election."

. . . [T]oday's decision reads the Qualifications Clauses to impose substantial implicit prohibitions on the States and the people of the States. I would not draw such an expansive negative inference from the fact that the Constitution requires Members of Congress to be a certain age, to be inhabitants of the States that they represent, and to have been United States citizens for a specified period. Rather, I would read the Qualifications Clauses to do no more than what they say. I respectfully dissent.

Notes and Queries

1. How does Justice Stevens apply the principle of *Powell* to *Thornton*? What reading of the Constitution and conception of national/state relations does he advance in *Thornton*?

2. What significance should historical practice have on current evaluations of whether an action is constitutional? Are the historical studies in each opinion merely selective and used to support the justices' pre-existing readings of the Constitution's text and structure? Or are they used to support their intellectual or personal predilections?

3. All the opinions appeal in some way to Chief Justice Marshall's articulation of federal-state relations in *McCulloch*. Which opinion most closely approximates the spirit of Marshall's argument? Should this matter?

4. Which account seems to fit best with what you know about the behavior of Congress' members—that they serve the nation as a whole, or that they consider themselves accountable only to their electoral constituency? Which account best explains the behavior of voters? Should we make constitutional arguments from such observations of political practice? Why or why not?

5. In his dissent, Justice Thomas argued that the national government and the states "face different default rules." Why? Are these different default rules a consequence of the constitutional text? Of constitutional theory? Of judicial interpretation?

6. Justice Thomas writes: "If we are to invalidate Arkansas' Amendment 73, we must point to something in the Federal Constitution that deprives the people of Arkansas of the power to enact such measures." Do you agree?

7. The majority insists that the Constitution derives its

authority from the people *of the nation*, whereas the dissent insists that it derives its authority from the people of *the states*. Is this mere quibbling or is something very critical at stake here?

Alden v. Maine

527 U.S. 706, 144 L Ed 2d 636, 119 S Ct 2240 (1999)

In 1996 the Supreme Court ruled in *Seminole Tribe of Florida v. Florida* that even otherwise constitutional national legislation did not supercede a state's 11th Amendment "sovereign immunity" from suits in federal courts. As a "sovereign," a state, without its consent, cannot be sued by an individual seeking compliance with legitimate federal legislation. *Alden* addressed the related question; whether states can be sued by individuals in their *own* courts without consenting to the suit. A group of Maine probation officers filed suit against their employer, the State of Maine, alleging that the state had failed to comply with the overtime provisions of the federal Fair Labor Standards Act (FLSA) of 1938. The Maine Supreme Judicial Court rejected the claim on grounds of "sovereign immunity." This decision conflicted with a similar one made by the Arkansas Supreme Court. The United States Supreme Court granted certiorari to reconcile the conflict. Opinion of the Court: *Kennedy*, Rehnquist, O'Connor, Scalia, Thomas. Dissenting opinion: *Souter*, Stevens, Ginsburg, Breyer.

Justice KENNEDY delivered the opinion of the Court.

We hold that the powers delegated to Congress under Article I of the United States Constitution do not include the power to subject nonconsenting States to private suits for damages in state courts. We decide as well that the State of Maine has not consented to suits for overtime pay and liquidated damages under the FLSA. On these premises we affirm the judgment sustaining dismissal of the suit.

The *Eleventh Amendment* makes explicit reference to the States' immunity from suits "commenced or prosecuted against one of the United States by Citizens of another State, or by Citizens or Subjects of any Foreign State." U.S. Const., Amdt. 11. We have, as a result, sometimes referred to the States' immunity from suit as "*Eleventh Amendment* immunity." The phrase is convenient shorthand but something of a misnomer, for the sovereign immunity of the States neither derives from nor is limited by the terms of the *Eleventh Amendment*. Rather, as the Constitution's structure, and its history, and the authoritative interpretations by this Court make clear, the States' immunity from suit is a fundamental aspect of the sovereignty which the States enjoyed before the ratification of the Constitution, and which they retain today (either literally or by virtue of their admission into the Union upon an equal footing with the other States) except as altered by the plan of the Convention or certain constitutional Amendments.

The States thus retain "a residuary and inviolable sovereignty." *The Federalist* No. 39. They are not relegated to the role of mere provinces or political corporations, but retain the dignity, though not the full authority, of sovereignty.

. . . [T]he Court has upheld States' assertions of sovereign immunity in various contexts falling outside the literal text of the *Eleventh Amendment*.

These holdings reflect a settled doctrinal understanding, consistent with the views of the leading advocates of the Constitution's ratification, that sovereign immunity derives not from the *Eleventh Amendment* but from the structure of the original Constitution itself. The *Eleventh Amendment* confirmed rather than established sovereign immunity as a constitutional principle; it follows that the scope of the States' immunity from suit is demarcated not by the text of the Amendment alone but by fundamental postulates implicit in the constitutional design.

In this case we must determine whether Congress has the power, under Article I, to subject nonconsenting States to private suits in their own courts. As the foregoing discussion makes clear, the fact that the *Eleventh Amendment* by its terms limits only "[t]he Judicial power of the United States" does not resolve the question.

Petitioners contend the text of the Constitution and our recent sovereign immunity decisions establish that the States were required to relinquish this portion of their sovereignty. We turn first to these sources.

Article I, s.8 grants Congress broad power to enact legislation in several enumerated areas of national concern. The Supremacy Clause, furthermore, provides:

"This Constitution, and the Laws of the United States which shall be made in Pursuance thereof . . . , shall be the supreme Law of the Land; and the Judges in every State shall be bound thereby, any Thing in the Constitution or Laws of any state to the Contrary notwithstanding." U.S. Const., Art. VI.

It is contended that, by virtue of these provisions, where Congress enacts legislation subjecting the States to suit, the legislation by necessity overrides the sovereign immunity of the States.

Comparative Note 6.4

[Elections held in India in 1990 resulted in the emergence of the Bhartiya Janata Party (BJP) as the governing majority in four states. The governments of three of these states were later implicated in activities that led to the destruction of a Muslim temple in the city of Ayodhya, which in turn precipitated widespread Hindu–Muslim violence throughout India. Acting under his authority under Article 356 of the Constitution, the President of India dissolved the elected governments in the three states and declared temporary regimes of Presidential Rule. The deposed officials, arguing that the President's actions had vastly exceeded his rightful authority, appealed their cases to the Supreme Court, which issued a lengthy and important decision touching on a variety of extremely controversial issues. One of them related to the powers of the central government vis-à-vis the states. What follows is taken from one of the opinions ruling in favor of the government in New Delhi.]

Under our Constitution the State as such has no inherent sovereign power or autonomous power which cannot be encroached upon by the Centre. The very fact that under our Constitution, Article 3, Parliament may by law form a new State by separation of territory from any State or by uniting two or more States or parts of States or by uniting any territory to a part of any State, etc., militates against the view that the States are sovereign or autonomous bodies having definite independent rights of governance. In fact . . . in certain circumstances the Central Government can issue directions to States and in emergency conditions assume far-reaching powers affecting the States as well, and the fact that the President has powers to take over the administration of States demolishes the theory of an independent or autonomous existence of a State. It must also be realized that unlike the Constitution of the United States of America which recognizes dual citizenship [Section 1(1), 14th Amendment], the Constitution of India, Article 5, does not recognize the concept of dual citizenship. . . . The concept of citizenship assumes some importance in a federation because in a country which recognizes dual citizenship, the individual would owe allegiance both to the Federal Government as well as the State Government but a country recognizing a single citizenship does not face complications arising from dual citizenship and by necessary implication negatives the concept of State sovereignty.

SOURCE: *S. R. Bommai v. Union of India*, 3 SCC 1, 74–5 (1994).

As is evident from its text, however, the Supremacy Clause enshrines as "the supreme Law of the Land" only those federal Acts that accord with the constitutional design. Appeal to the Supremacy Clause alone merely raises the question whether a law is a valid exercise of the national power.

. . . We reject any contention that substantive federal law by its own force necessarily overrides the sovereign immunity of the States. When a State asserts its immunity to suit, the question is not the primacy of federal law but the implementation of the law in a manner consistent with the constitutional sovereignty of the States.

Nor can we conclude that the specific Article I powers delegated to Congress necessarily include, by virtue of the Necessary and Proper Clause or otherwise, the incidental authority to subject the States to private suits as a means of achieving objectives otherwise within the scope of the enumerated powers.

Our final consideration is whether a congressional power to subject nonconsenting States to private suits in their own courts is consistent with the structure of the Constitution.

Although the Constitution grants broad powers to Congress, our federalism requires that Congress treat the States in a manner consistent with their status as residuary sovereigns and joint participants in the governance of the Nation.

Petitioners contend that immunity from suit in federal court suffices to preserve the dignity of the States.

In some ways, . . . a congressional power to authorize private suits against nonconsenting States in their own courts would be even more offensive to state sovereignty than a power to authorize the suits in a federal forum. . . . A power to press a State's own courts into federal service to coerce the other branches of the State . . . is the power first to turn the State against itself and ultimately to commandeer the entire political machinery of the State against its will and at the behest of individuals. Such plenary federal control of state governmental processes denigrates the separate sovereignty of the States.

Underlying constitutional form are considerations of great substance. Private suits against nonconsenting States—especially suits for money damages—may threaten the financial integrity of the States. . . . [A]n unlimited congressional power to authorize suits in state court to levy upon the treasuries of the States for compensatory damages, attorney's fees, and even punitive damages could create staggering burdens, giving Congress a power and a leverage over the States that is not contemplated by our constitutional design. The potential national power would pose a severe and notorious danger to the States and their resources.

A congressional power to strip the States of their immunity from private suits in their own courts would pose more subtle risks as well.

A general federal power to authorize private suits for money damages would place unwarranted strain on the States' ability to govern in accordance with the will of their citizens. Today, as at the time of the founding, the allocation of scarce resources among competing needs and interests lies at the heart of the political process. . . . Since all cannot be satisfied in full, it is inevitable that difficult decisions involving the most sensitive and political of judgments must be made. If the principle of representative government is to be preserved to the States, the balance between competing interests must be reached after deliberation by the political process established by the citizens of the State, not by judicial decree mandated by the Federal Government and invoked by the private citizen.

. . . When the Federal Government asserts authority over a State's most fundamental political processes, it strikes at the heart of the political accountability so essential to our liberty and republican form of government.

The constitutional privilege of a State to assert its sovereign immunity in its own courts does not confer upon the State a concomitant right to disregard the Constitution or valid federal law. The States and their officers are bound by obligations imposed by the Constitution and by federal statutes that comport with the constitutional design. We are unwilling to assume the States will refuse to honor the Constitution or obey the binding laws of the United States. The good faith of the States thus provides an important assurance that "[t]his Constitution, and the Laws of the United States which shall be made in Pursuance thereof . . . shall be the supreme Law of the Land." U.S. Const., Art. VI.

Sovereign immunity, moreover, does not bar all judicial review of state compliance with the Constitution and valid federal law. Rather, certain limits are implicit in the constitutional principle of state sovereign immunity.

The first of these limits is that sovereign immunity bars suits only in the absence of consent. Many States, on their own initiative, have enacted statutes consenting to a wide variety of suits.

The States have consented, moreover, to some suits pursuant to the plan of the Convention or to subsequent constitutional amendments. In ratifying the Constitution, the States consented to suits brought by other States or by the Federal Government. A suit which is commenced and prosecuted against a State in the name of the United States by those who are entrusted with the constitutional duty to "take Care that the Laws be faithfully executed," U.S. Const., Art. II, s.3, differs in kind from the suit of an individual: While the Constitution contemplates suits among the members of the federal system as an alternative to extralegal measures, the fear of private suits against nonconsenting States was the central reason given by the founders who chose to preserve the States' sovereign immunity. Suits brought by the United States itself require the exercise of political responsibility for each suit prosecuted against a State, a control which is absent from a broad delegation to private persons to sue nonconsenting States.

. . . Although the Constitution begins with the principle that sovereignty rests with the people, it does not follow that the National Government becomes the ultimate, preferred mechanism for expressing the people's will. The States exist as a refutation of that concept. In choosing to ordain and establish the Constitution, the people insisted upon a federal structure for the very purpose of rejecting the idea that the will of the people in all instances is expressed by the central power, the one most remote from their control. The Framers of the Constitution did not share our dissenting colleagues' belief that the Congress may circumvent the federal design by regulating the States directly when it pleases to do so, including by a proxy in which individual citizens are authorized to levy upon the state treasuries absent the States' consent to jurisdiction.

Justice SOUTER, with whom Justice STEVENS, Justice GINSBURG, and Justice BREYER join, dissenting.

. . . [T]he general scheme of delegated sovereignty as between the two component governments of the federal system was clear, and was succinctly stated by Chief Justice Marshall: "In America, the powers of sovereignty are divided between the government of the Union, and those of the States. They are each sovereign, with respect to the objects committed to it, and neither sovereign with respect to the objects committed to the other." *McCulloch v. Maryland.*

Hence the flaw in the Court's appeal to federalism. The State of Maine is not sovereign with respect to the national objective of the FLSA. It is not the authority that promulgated the FLSA, on which the right of action in this case depends. That authority is the United States acting through the Congress, whose legislative power under Article I of the Constitution to extend FLSA coverage to state employees has already been decided, and is not contested here.

Nor can it be argued that because the State of Maine creates its own court system, it has authority to decide what sorts of claims may be entertained there, and thus in effect to control the right of action in this case. Maine has created state courts of general jurisdiction; once it has done so, the Supremacy Clause of the Constitution, Art. VI, cl. 2, which requires state courts to enforce federal law and state-court judges to be bound by it, requires the Maine courts to entertain this federal cause of action.

It is symptomatic of the weakness of the structural notion proffered by the Court that it seeks to buttress the argument by relying on "the dignity and respect afforded a State, which the immunity is designed to protect," and by invoking the many demands on a State's fisc. . . . [T]he Court calls "immunity from private suits central to sovereign dignity," and assumes that this "dignity" is a quality easily translated from the person of the King to the participatory abstraction of a republican State. The thoroughly anomalous character of this appeal to dignity is obvious from a reading of Blackstone's description of royal dignity, which he sets out as a premise of his discussion of sovereignty. . . .

It would be hard to imagine anything more inimical to the republican conception, which rests on the understanding of its citizens precisely that the government is not above them, but of them, its actions being governed by law just like their own. Whatever justification there may be for an American government's immunity from private suit, it is not dignity.

It is equally puzzling to hear the Court say that "federal power to authorize private suits for money damages would place unwarranted strain on the States' ability to govern in accordance with the will of their citizens." So long as the citizens' will, expressed through state legislation, does not violate valid federal law, the strain will not be felt; and to the extent that state action does violate federal law, the will of the citizens of the United States already trumps that of the citizens of the State: the strain then is not only expected, but necessarily intended.

Least of all is it to the point for the Court to suggest that because the Framers would be surprised to find States subjected to a federal-law suit in their own courts under the commerce power, the suit must be prohibited by the Constitution. The Framers' intentions and expectations count so far as they point to the meaning of the Constitution's text or the fair implications of its structure, but they do not hover over the instrument to veto any application of its principles to a world that the Framers could not have anticipated.

. . . The resemblance of today's state sovereign immunity to the *Lochner* era's industrial due process is striking. The Court began this century by imputing immutable constitutional status to a conception of economic self-reliance that was never true to industrial life and grew insistently fictional with the years, and the Court has chosen to close the century by conferring like status on a conception of state sovereign immunity that is true neither to history nor to the structure of the Constitution. I expect the Court's late essay into immunity doctrine will prove the equal of its earlier experiment in laissez-faire, the one being as unrealistic as the other, as indefensible, and probably as fleeting.

Notes and Queries

1. Read the text of the Eleventh Amendment. Should it matter that it provides very little explicit support for the ruling in this case? The majority opinion rejects "a blind reliance on the text of the Eleventh Amendment." Is such a reliance always unwise, or is there something about this case in particular that argues against a literalist approach to interpretation?

2. *Alden* has become the target of an immense amount of criticism from the scholarly community. A typical characterization asserts: "The message is that Congress does not have the capacity to govern this country with which, we supposed, the Founders endowed it, the power that Chief Justice Marshall made plain, that the Civil War paid for in blood, and that the post New Deal Court, we imagined, finally acknowledged." Louise Weinberg, *Of Sovereignty and Union: The Legends of* Alden, 76 Notre Dame Law Review (2001), p. 1181. Is this criticism fair? What would a different message be if it were based on the historical account in Justice Kennedy's opinion of the Court?

3. According to Justice Kennedy, "The generation that designed and adopted our federal system considered immunity from private suits central to sovereign dignity." What exactly does this mean? The dissenters consider the notion of dignity as attached to the phenomenon of state sovereignty to be problematic, to say the least, in a constitutional republic. Do you agree that the logic of republican institutions presupposes an understanding of dignity that connects it exclusively to individuals?

4. In speaking of the Framers, Justice Kennedy writes that "Theirs was the unique insight that freedom is enhanced by the creation of two governments, not one." Do

you agree? To what extent does Justice Souter's dissenting opinion rest on an alternative understanding of the structural requirements of freedom?

5. Consider the Indian judgment excerpted in Comparative Note 6.4. In it a distinction is drawn to the United States on the basis of the presence in that country of "dual citizenship," which differs from India's constitutional recognition of only a single national citizenship. The inference made by the Court is that the concept of state sovereignty makes no sense in the Indian context. Additionally, the power of Parliament to create new states (in ways that contrast sharply with powers available to the Congress of the United States) "militates against the view that the States are sovereign or autonomous bodies having definite independent rights of governance." Setting aside the question of whether the Indian Court has drawn the proper inferences from these distinctions, what would you say if the American Court were to draw the opposite conclusions from the comparison in order to defend the concept of state sovereignty under the American Constitution?

Federal Maritime Commission v. South Carolina State Ports Authority

535 U.S. 743, 122 S Ct 1864 (2002)

In *Seminole Tribe of Florida v. Florida*, the Supreme Court ruled that the Eleventh Amendment prevents states from being sued in federal court by private individuals, unless they consent to the suit. *Alden v. Maine* upheld the same "sovereign immunity" principle for suits initiated in state courts. Here the Court addresses the propriety of adjudication of a dispute between an unconsenting state and a private individual by an independent federal agency. After several requests to operate cruise ships from the Port of Charleston were denied by the South Carolina State Ports Authority (SCSPA), South Carolina Maritime Services, Inc. (SCMS) filed a complaint with the Federal Maritime Commission (FMC). SCMS alleged that South Carolina was in violation of the federal Shipping Act of 1984. The SCSPA filed a motion to dismiss, contending that as an arm of the state of South Carolina, it need not submit to the administrative proceeding initiated by SCMS. Opinion of the Court: *Thomas*, Rehnquist, O'Connor, Scalia, Kennedy. Dissenting opinions: Stevens; *Breyer*, Stevens, Souter, Ginsburg.

Justice THOMAS delivered the opinion of the Court.

Dual sovereignty is a defining feature of our Nation's constitutional blueprint. States, upon ratification of the Constitution, did not consent to become mere appendages of the Federal Government.

States, in ratifying the Constitution, did surrender a portion of their inherent immunity by consenting to suits brought by sister States or by the Federal Government. Nevertheless, the Convention did not disturb States' immunity from private suits, thus firmly enshrining this principle in our constitutional framework.

We now consider whether the sovereign immunity enjoyed by States as part of our constitutional framework applies to adjudications conducted by the FMC. Petitioner FMC and respondent United States initially maintain that the Court of Appeals erred because sovereign immunity only shields States from exercises of "judicial power" and FMC adjudications are not judicial proceedings. As support for their position, they point to the text of the *Eleventh Amendment* and contend that "[t]he Amendment's reference to 'judicial Power' and 'to any suit in law or equity' clearly mark it as an immunity from judicial process."

In truth, the relevant history does not provide direct guidance for our inquiry. The Framers, who envisioned a limited Federal Government, could not have anticipated the vast growth of the administrative state. Because formalized administrative adjudications were all but unheard of in the late 18th century and early 19th century, the dearth of specific evidence indicating whether the Framers believed that the States' sovereign immunity would apply in such proceedings is unsurprising.

This Court, however, has applied a presumption—first explicitly stated in *Hans v. Louisiana*—that the Constitution was not intended to "rais[e] up" any proceedings against the States that were "anomalous and unheard of when the Constitution was adopted." We therefore attribute great significance to the fact that States were not subject to private suits in administrative adjudications at the time of the founding or for many years thereafter.

To decide whether [this] presumption applies here, however, we must examine FMC adjudications to determine whether they are the type of proceedings from which the Framers would have thought the States possessed immunity when they agreed to enter the Union.

Turning to FMC adjudications . . . neither the Commission nor the United States disputes the Court of Appeals' characterization below that such a proceeding "walks, talks, and squawks very much like a lawsuit."

A review of the FMC's Rules of Practice and Procedure confirms that FMC administrative proceedings bear a re-

Comparative Note 6.5

[The 1993 Interim Constitution for South Africa provided that a provincial legislature was entitled to pass a constitution for its province by a resolution of a majority of at least two-thirds of all its members. But before acquiring the force of law the Constitutional Court had to certify that all of its provisions were consistent with the Interim Constitution. In 1996 the Legislature of the province of KwaZulu-Natal (KZN) unanimously adopted a provincial Constitution, which was subsequently found by the Court to be fatally flawed. One of these flaws involved the usurpation of national powers.]

Clause 2(1) of Chapter 5 [of the provincial constitution] proclaims that "[t]his Constitution recognizes" the exclusive legislative and executive authority of the "national Government" over certain matters and clause 2(2) similarly purports to recognize the "competence" of the "national Parliament" in certain respects. These assertions of recognition purport to be the constitutional acts of a sovereign state. They are inconsistent with the Interim Constitution because KZN is not a sovereign state and it simply has no power of authority to grant constitutional "recognition" to what the national Government may or may not do.

SOURCE: *Certification of the Constitution of the Province of KwaZulu-Natal*, 1996 (4) SALR 1098 (CC), in Norman Dorsen, et. al., eds., *Comparative Constitutionalism: Cases and Materials* (St. Paul: Thomson/West, 2003), p. 418.

---

markably strong resemblance to civil litigation in federal courts.

The preeminent purpose of state sovereign immunity is to accord States the dignity that is consistent with their status as sovereign entities.

Given both this interest in protecting States' dignity and the strong similarities between FMC proceedings and civil litigation, we hold that state sovereign immunity bars the FMC from adjudicating complaints filed by a private party against a nonconsenting State. Simply put, if the Framers thought it an impermissible affront to a State's dignity to be required to answer the complaints of private parties in federal courts, we cannot imagine that they would have found it acceptable to compel a State to do exactly the same thing before the administrative tribunal of an agency, such as the FMC. The affront to a State's dignity does not lessen when an adjudication takes place in an administrative tribunal as opposed to an Article III court. In both instances, a State is required to defend itself in an adversarial proceeding against a private party before an impartial federal officer. Moreover, it would be quite strange to prohibit Congress from exercising its Article I powers to abrogate state sovereign immunity in Article III judicial proceedings, but permit the use of those same Article I powers to create court-like administrative tribunals where sovereign immunity does not apply.

The United States . . . suggests that sovereign immunity should not apply to FMC proceedings because they do not present the same threat to the financial integrity of States as do private judicial suits.

This argument, however, reflects a fundamental misun-

derstanding of the purposes of sovereign immunity. While state sovereign immunity serves the important function of shielding state treasuries and thus preserving "the States' ability to govern in accordance with the will of their citizens," *Alden*, the doctrine's central purpose is to "accord the States the respect owed them as" joint sovereigns. See *Puerto Rico Aqueduct and Sewer Authority v. Metcalf & Eddy, Inc.* (1993).

While some might complain that our system of dual sovereignty is not a model of administrative convenience, that is not its purpose. Rather, "[t]he 'constitutionally mandated balance of power' between the States and the Federal Government was adopted by the Framers to ensure the protection of 'our fundamental liberties.'" *Atascadero State Hospital v. Scanlon* (1985) (quoting *Garcia v. San Antonio Metropolitan Transit Authority* [1985]). By guarding against encroachments by the Federal Government on fundamental aspects of state sovereignty, such as sovereign immunity, we strive to maintain the balance of power embodied in our Constitution and thus to "reduce the risk of tyranny and abuse from either front." *Gregory v. Ashcroft*. Although the Framers likely did not envision the intrusion on state sovereignty at issue in today's case, we are nonetheless confident that it is contrary to their constitutional design, and therefore affirm the judgment of the Court of Appeals.

Justice BREYER, with whom Justice STEVENS, Justice SOUTER, and Justice GINSBURG join, dissenting.

. . . Where does the Constitution contain the principle of law that the Court enunciates? I cannot find the answer to this question in any text, in any tradition, or in any relevant purpose. In saying this, I do not simply reiterate the dissenting views set forth in many of the Court's recent sovereign immunity decisions. For even were I to believe that those decisions properly stated the law—which I do not—I still could not accept the Court's conclusion here.

At the outset one must understand the constitutional nature of the legal proceeding before us. The legal body conducting the proceeding, the Federal Maritime Commission, is an "independent" federal agency. Constitutionally speaking, an "independent" agency belongs neither to the Legislative Branch nor to the Judicial Branch of Government. Although Members of this Court have referred to agencies as a "fourth branch" of Government, the agencies, even "independent" agencies, are more appropriately considered to be part of the Executive Branch. The President appoints their chief administrators, typically a Chairman and Commissioners, subject to confirmation by the Senate. The agencies derive their legal powers from congressionally enacted statutes. And the agencies enforce those statutes, i.e., they "execute" them, in part by making rules or by adjudicating matters in dispute.

The Court long ago laid to rest any constitutional doubts about whether the Constitution permitted Congress to delegate rulemaking and adjudicative powers to agencies. That, in part, is because the Court established certain safeguards surrounding the exercise of these powers. And the Court denied that those activities as safeguarded, however much they might *resemble* the activities of a legislature or court, fell within the scope of Article I or Article III of the Constitution. Consequently, in exercising those powers, the agency is engaging in an Article II, Executive Branch activity. And the powers it is exercising are powers that the Executive Branch of Government must possess if it is to enforce modern law through administration.

The upshot is that this case involves a typical Executive Branch agency exercising typical Executive Branch powers seeking to determine whether a particular person has violated federal law. The particular person in this instance is a state entity, the South Carolina State Ports Authority, and the agency is acting in response to the request of a private individual. But at first blush it is difficult to see why these special circumstances matter. After all, the Constitution created a Federal Government empowered to enact laws that would bind the States and it empowered that Federal Government to enforce those laws against the States. It also left private individuals perfectly free to complain to the Federal Government about unlawful state activity, and it left the Federal Government free to take subsequent legal action. Where then can the Court find its constitutional principle—the principle that the Constitu-

tion forbids an Executive Branch agency to determine through ordinary adjudicative processes whether such a private complaint is justified? As I have said, I cannot find that principle anywhere in the Constitution.

The Court's principle lacks any firm anchor in the Constitution's text.

Indeed, the Court refers for textual support only to an earlier case, namely *Alden v. Maine* (1999) and, through *Alden*, to the texts that *Alden* mentioned. These textual references include: (1) what Alexander Hamilton described as a constitutional "postulate," namely that the States retain their immunity from "suits, without their consent," unless there has been a "surrender" of that immunity "in the plan of the convention"; (2) what the *Alden* majority called "the system of federalism established by the Constitution"; and (3) what the *Alden* majority called "the constitutional design."

Considered purely as constitutional text, these words— "constitutional design," "system of federalism," and "plan of the convention"—suffer several defects. Their language is highly abstract, making them difficult to apply. They invite differing interpretations at least as much as do the Constitution's own broad liberty-protecting phrases, such as "due process of law" or the word "liberty" itself. And compared to these latter phrases, they suffer the additional disadvantage that they do not actually appear anywhere in the Constitution. Regardless, unless supported by considerations of history, of constitutional purpose, or of related consequence, those abstract phrases cannot support today's result.

. . . As the Court points out, the Framers may not have "anticipated the vast growth of the administrative state," and the history of their debates "does not provide direct guidance." But the Court is wrong to ignore the relevance and importance of what the Framers did say. And it is doubly wrong to attach "great" legal "significance" to the absence of 18th- and 19th-century administrative agency experience. Even if those alive in the 18th century did not "anticipat[e] the vast growth of the administrative state," they did write a Constitution designed to provide a framework for Government across the centuries, a framework that is flexible enough to meet modern needs. And we cannot read their silence about particular means as if it were an instruction to forbid their use.

The Court's decision threatens to deny the Executive and Legislative Branches of Government the structural flexibility that the Constitution permits and which modern government demands. The Court derives from the abstract notion of state "dignity" a structural principle that limits the powers of both Congress and the President. . . . In its readiness to rest a structural limitation on so little evidence and in its willingness to interpret that limitation so broadly, the majority ignores a historical lesson, reflected in a constitutional understanding that the Court adopted long ago: An overly restrictive judicial interpretation of the Constitution's structural constraints (unlike its protections of certain basic liberties) will undermine the Constitution's own efforts to achieve its far more basic structural aim, the creation of a representative form of government capable of translating the people's will into effective public action.

This understanding, underlying constitutional interpretation since the New Deal, reflects the Constitution's demands for structural flexibility sufficient to adapt substantive laws and institutions to rapidly changing social, economic, and technological conditions. It reflects the comparative inability of the Judiciary to understand either those conditions or the need for new laws and new administrative forms they may create. It reflects the Framers' own aspiration to write a document that would "constitute" a democratic, liberty-protecting form of government that would endure through centuries of change. This understanding led the New Deal Court to reject overly restrictive formalistic interpretations of the Constitution's structural provisions, thereby permitting Congress to enact social and economic legislation that circumstances had led the public to demand. And it led that Court to find in the Constitution authorization for new forms of administration, including independent administrative agencies, with the legal authority flexibly to implement, *i.e.*, to "execute," through adjudication, through rulemaking, and in other ways, the legislation that Congress subsequently enacted.

Where I believe the Court has departed from this basic understanding I have consistently dissented. These decisions set loose an interpretive principle that restricts far too severely the authority of the Federal Government to regulate innumerable relationships between State and citizen. Just as this principle has no logical starting place, I fear that neither does it have any logical stopping point.

Notes and Queries

1. Justice Thomas argues that it would be strange to prohibit Congress from abrogating state sovereignty immunity in Article III judicial proceedings but to permit congressional power to do so through court-like administrative tribunals. What is the basis of his finding that these are analogous proceedings that should fall under the same constitutional limitation? Why does Justice Breyer find fault with this analogy?

2. Another key difference between Justices Thomas and Breyer pertains to the interpretive significance of the growth of the administrative state since the time of the Framers. This leads them to very different conclusions regarding the "18th-century silence" about state immunity in proceedings involving non-judicial tribunals. Which of the two positions do you find to be most faithful to a jurisprudence of originalism?

3. According to Justice Breyer: "An overly restrictive interpretation of the Constitution's structural constraints (unlike its protections of certain basic liberties) will undermine the Constitution's own efforts to achieve its far more basic structural aim, the creation of a representative form of government capable of translating the people's will into effective public action." What is the reasoning that underlies the justice's effort to distinguish between the exercise of judicial review when applied to structural issues as opposed to matters implicating basic liberties? As we will see in later chapters, the distinction drawn by Breyer is one that expresses itself in relation to a number of constitutional provisions, reflecting a fundamental interpretive fault line dividing the justices of the modern Court.

Cooley v. Board of Wardens
53 U.S. 299, 12 How. 299, 13 L.Ed. 996 (1851)

In *Gibbons v. Ogden, infra*, p. 317, the Supreme Court held that a state could not exercise its power over local commerce in such a way as to interfere with the regulation by Congress of commerce among the states. But suppose Congress declines to regulate an aspect of local commerce. May a state then regulate that commerce even if it affects commerce that could otherwise be regulated by Congress? That is the issue here. In 1789, Congress placed the administration of harbors and ports under state control until Congress passed appropriate national legislation. In the absence of further legislation, Pennsylvania passed a law that required all ships entering or leaving the port of Philadelphia either to hire a local pilot or to pay a fine of one-half the pilotage fee. Cooley was fined for not hiring a local pilot. He refused to pay, claiming that the state law impermissibly restrained interstate commerce. The lower courts ruled against Cooley. Opinion of the Court: *Curtis*, Taney, Catron, McKinley, Nelson, Grier. Concurring opinion: *Daniel*. Dissenting opinion: *McLean*, Wayne.

Mr. Justice CURTIS delivered the opinion of the Court.

That the power to regulate commerce includes the regulation of navigation, we consider settled. And when we look to the nature of the service performed by pilots, to the relations which that service and its compensations bear to navigation between the several states, and between the ports of the United States and foreign countries, we are brought to the conclusion, that the regulation of the qualifications of pilots, of the modes and times of offering and rendering their services, of the responsibilities which shall rest upon them, of the powers they shall possess, of the compensation they may demand, and of the penalties by which their rights and duties may be enforced, do constitute regulations of navigation, and consequently of commerce, within the just meaning of this clause of the Constitution. . . .

It becomes necessary, therefore, to consider whether this law of Pennsylvania, being a regulation of commerce, is valid.

. . . [W]e are brought directly and unavoidably to the consideration of the question, whether the grant of the commercial power to Congress, did *per se* deprive the states of all power to regulate pilots. This question has never been decided by this court, nor, in our judgment, has any case depending upon all the considerations which must govern this one, come before this court. The grant of commercial power to Congress does not contain any terms which expressly exclude the states from exercising an authority over its subject-matter. If they are excluded it must be because the nature of the power, thus granted to Congress, requires that a similar authority should not exist in the states. If it were conceded on the one side, that the nature of this power, like that to legislate for the District of Columbia, is absolutely and totally repugnant to the existence of similar power in the states, probably no one would deny that the grant of the power to Congress, as effectually and perfectly excludes the states from all future legislation on the subject, as if express words had been used to exclude them. And on the other hand, if it were admitted that the existence of this power in Congress, like the power of taxation, is compatible with the existence of a similar power in the states, then it would be in conformity with the contemporary exposition of the Constitution (*Federalist*, No. 32), and with the judicial construction, given from time to time by this court, after the most deliberate consideration, to hold that the mere grant of such a power to Congress, did not imply a prohibition on the states to exercise the same power; that it is not the mere existence of such a power, but its exercise by Congress, which may be incompatible with the exercise of the same power by the states, and that the states may legislate in the absence of congressional regulations.

A majority of the court are of opinion that a regulation of pilots is a regulation of commerce, within the grant to Congress of the commercial power, contained in the third clause of the eighth section of the first article of the Constitution.

The diversities of opinion, therefore, which have existed on this subject, have arisen from the different views taken of the nature of this power. But when the nature of a power like this is spoken of, when it is said that the nature of the power requires that it should be exercised exclusively by Congress, it must be intended to refer to the subjects of that power, and to say they are of such a nature as to require exclusive legislation by Congress. Now the power to regulate commerce, embraces a vast field, containing not only many, but exceedingly various subjects, quite unlike in their nature; some imperatively demanding a single uniform rule, operating equally on the commerce of the United States in every port; and some, like the subject now in question, as imperatively demanding that diversity, which alone can meet the local necessities of navigation.

Either absolutely to affirm, or deny that the nature of this power requires exclusive legislation by Congress, is to lose sight of the nature of the subjects of this power, and to assert concerning all of them, what is really applicable but to a part. Whatever subjects of this power are in their nature national, or admit only of one uniform system, or plan of regulation, may justly be said to be of such a nature as to require exclusive legislation by Congress. That this cannot be affirmed of laws for the regulation of pilots and pilotage is plain. The act of 1789 contains a clear and authoritative declaration by the first Congress, that the nature of this subject is such, that until Congress should find it necessary to exert its power, it should be left to the legislation of the states; that it is local and not national; that it is likely to be the best provided for, not by one system, or plan of regulations, but by as many as the legislative discretion of the several states should deem applicable to the local peculiarities of the ports within their limits.

Viewed in this light, so much of this act of 1789 as declares that pilots shall continue to be regulated "by such laws as the states may respectively hereafter enact for that purpose," instead of being held to be inoperative, as an attempt to confer on the states a power to legislate, of which the Constitution had deprived them, is allowed an appropriate and important signification. It manifests the understanding of Congress, at the outset of the government, that the nature of this subject is not such as to require its exclusive legislation. The practice of the states, and of the national government, has been in conformity with this declaration, from the origin of the national government to this time; and the nature of the subject when examined, is such as to leave no doubt of the superior fitness and propriety, not to say the absolute necessity, of different systems of regulation, drawn from local knowledge and experience, and confined to local wants. How then can we say, that by the mere grant of power to regulate commerce, the states are deprived of all the power to legislate on this subject, because from the nature of the power the legislation of Congress must be exclusive. This would be to affirm that the nature of the power is in any case, something different from the nature of the subject to which, in such case, the power extends, and that the nature of the power necessarily demands, in all cases, exclusive legislation by Congress, while the nature of one of the subjects of that power, not only does not require such exclusive legislation, but may be best provided for by many different systems enacted by the states, in conformity with the circumstances of the ports within their limits. In construing an instrument designed for the formation of a government, and in determining the extent of one of its important grants of power to legislate, we can make no such distinction between the nature of the power and the nature of the subject on which that power was intended practically to operate, nor consider the grant more extensive by affirming of the power, what is not true of its subject now in question.

It is the opinion of a majority of the court that the mere grant to Congress of the power to regulate commerce, did not deprive the states of power to regulate pilots, and that although Congress has legislated on this subject, its legislation manifests an intention, with a single exception, not to regulate this subject, but to leave its regulation to the several states. To these precise questions, which are all we are called on to decide, this opinion must be understood to be confined. It does not extend to the question what other subjects, under the commercial power, are within the exclusive control of Congress, or may be regulated by the states in the absence of all congressional legislation; nor to the general question, how far any regulation of a subject by Congress may be deemed to operate as an exclusion of all legislation by the states upon the same subject. We decide the precise questions before us, upon what we deem sound principles, applicable to this particular subject in the state in which the legislation of Congress has left it. We go no further.

We are of opinion that this state law was enacted by virtue of a power, residing in the state to legislate; that it is not in conflict with any law of Congress; that it does not interfere with any system which Congress has established by making regulations, or by intentionally leaving individuals to their own unrestricted action; that this law is therefore valid, and the judgment of the Supreme Court of Pennsylvania in each case must be affirmed.

Notes and Queries

1. Read *Gibbons v. Ogden* in chapter 7. Can *Cooley* be reconciled with *Gibbons?*

2. Should the fact that Congress expressly allowed states to impose their own regulations matter constitutionally—i.e., was the congressional statute itself unconstitutional? Does the existence of these different standards place too great a burden on interstate commerce? Or does it merely signal that Congress felt that "local peculiarities," best known by state governments, must be taken into account?

3. Would Pennsylvania's regulations have violated the commerce clause if Congress had not explicitly permitted the states to have different standards? Should Congress have the power to delegate regulation of interstate commerce to the states?

4. Should the absence of congressional guidance mean that states can act as they wish? Or could it mean that Congress thinks the activity should not be regulated, and it implicitly prohibits the states from enacting such regulations?

5. What conception of local and state community is implied in the majority opinion? Is the existence of many different standards in many different states destructive of national economic unity? Of local community? Why should we even consider the nation to comprise a single economic unit?

Southern Pacific Company v. State of Arizona
325 U.S. 761, 65 S.Ct. 1515, 89 L.Ed. 1915 (1945)

Arizona's Train Limit Law of 1912 made it unlawful for any person or corporation to operate within the state a railroad train with more than fourteen passenger cars or more than seventy freight cars. The law was a safety measure designed to prevent accident owing to the "slack action" of cars on long trains. In 1940 Arizona sued the Southern Pacific Company for its repeated violations of the law. The company admitted the offenses but maintained that the law violated the Constitution. The trial court ruled in favor of the company, but the state supreme court reversed.

Opinion of the Court: *Stone*, Reed, Frankfurter, Murphy, Jackson, Burton. Concurring opinion: *Rutledge.* Dissenting opinions: *Black*, Douglas.

Mr. Chief Justice STONE delivered the opinion of the Court.

Congress, in enacting legislation within its constitutional authority over interstate commerce, will not be deemed to have intended to strike down a state statute designed to protect the health and safety of the public unless its purpose to do so is clearly manifested, or unless the state law, in terms or in its practical administration, conflicts with the Act of Congress, or plainly and palpably infringes its policy.

Although the commerce clause conferred on the national government power to regulate commerce, its possession of the power does not exclude all state power of regulation. . . . [I]t has been recognized that, in the absence of conflicting legislation by Congress, there is a residuum of power in the state to make laws governing matters of local concern which nevertheless in some measure affect interstate commerce or even, to some extent, regulate it. Thus the states may regulate matters which, because of their number and diversity, may never be adequately dealt with by Congress. When the regulation of matters of local concern is local in character and effect, and its impact on the national commerce does not seriously interfere with its operation, and the consequent incentive to deal with them nationally is slight, such regulation has been generally held to be within state authority.

But ever since *Gibbons v. Ogden* [1824], the states have not been deemed to have authority to impede substantially the free flow of commerce from state to state, or to regulate those phases of the national commerce which, because of the need of national uniformity, demand that their regulation, if any, be prescribed by a single authority.

In the application of these principles some enactments may be found to be plainly within and others plainly without state power. But between these extremes lies the infinite variety of cases in which regulation of local matters may also operate as a regulation of commerce, in which reconciliation of the conflicting claims of state and national power is to be attained only by some appraisal and accommodation of the competing demands of the state and national interests involved.

Hence the matters for ultimate determination here are the nature and extent of the burden which the state regulation of interstate trains, adopted as a safety measure, imposes on interstate commerce, and whether the relative weights of the state and national interests involved are such as to make inapplicable the rule, generally observed, that the free flow of interstate commerce and its freedom from local restraints in matters requiring uniformity of regulation are interests safeguarded by the commerce clause from state interference.

The findings show that the operation of long trains, that is trains of more than fourteen passenger and more than seventy freight cars, is standard practice over the main lines of the railroads of the United States, and that, if the length of trains is to be regulated at all, national uniformity in the regulation adopted, such as only Congress can prescribe, is practically indispensable to the operation of an efficient and economical national railway system. On many railroads passenger trains of more than seventy cars are operated, and on some systems freight trains are run ranging from one hundred and twenty-five to one hundred and sixty cars in length. Outside of Arizona, where the length of trains is not restricted, appellant runs a substantial proportion of long trains. In 1939 on its comparable route for through traffic through Utah and Nevada from 66 to 85% of its freight trains were over 70 cars in length and over 43% of its passenger trains included more than fourteen passenger cars.

In Arizona, approximately 93% of the freight traffic and 95% of the passenger traffic is interstate. Because of the Train Limit Law appellant is required to haul over 30% more trains in Arizona than would otherwise have been necessary. The record shows a definite relationship between operating costs and the length of trains, the increase in length resulting in a reduction of operating costs per car. The additional cost of operation of trains complying with the Train Limit Law in Arizona amounts for the two railroads traversing that state to about $1,000,000 a year. The reduction in train lengths also impedes efficient operation. More locomotives and more manpower are required; the necessary conversion and reconversion of train lengths at terminals and the delay caused by breaking up and remaking long trains upon entering and leaving the state in order to comply with the law, delays the traffic and diminishes its volume moved in a given time, especially when traffic is heavy.

The unchallenged findings leave no doubt that the Arizona Train Limit Law imposes a serious burden on the interstate commerce conducted by appellant. It materially impedes the movement of appellant's interstate trains through that state and interposes a substantial obstruction to the national policy proclaimed by Congress, to promote adequate, economical and efficient railway transportation service. . . . Enforcement of the law in Arizona, while train lengths remain unregulated or are regulated by varying standards in other states, must inevitably result in an impairment of uniformity of efficient railroad operation because the railroads are subjected to regulation which is not uniform in its application. Compliance with a state statute limiting train lengths requires interstate trains of a length lawful in other states to be broken up and reconstituted as they enter each state according as it may impose varying limitations upon train lengths. The alternative is for the carrier to conform to the lowest train limit restriction of any of the states through which its trains pass, whose laws thus control the carriers' operations both within and without the regulating state.

If one state may regulate train lengths, so may all the others, and they need not prescribe the same maximum limitation. The practical effect of such regulation is to control train operations beyond the boundaries of the state exacting it because of the necessity of breaking up and reassembling long trains at the nearest terminal points before entering and after leaving the regulating state. The serious impediment to the free flow of commerce by the local regulation of train lengths and the practical necessity that such regulation, if any, must be prescribed by a single body having a nation-wide authority are apparent.

The trial court found that the Arizona law had no reasonable relation to safety, and made train operation more dangerous.

The principal source of danger of accident from increased length of trains is the resulting increase of "slack action" of the train. Slack action is the amount of free movement of one car before it transmits its motion to an adjoining coupled car.

. . . The length of the train increases the slack since the slack action of a train is the total of the free movement between its several cars. The amount of slack action has some effect on the severity of the shock of train movements, and on freight trains sometimes results in injuries to operatives, which most frequently occur to occupants of the caboose. The amount and severity of slack action, however, are not wholly dependent upon the length of the train, as they may be affected by the mode and conditions of operation as to grades, speed, and load.

. . . The accident rate in Arizona is much higher than on comparable lines elsewhere, where there is no regulation of length of trains. The record lends support to the trial court's conclusion that the train length limitation increased rather than diminished the number of accidents. This is shown by comparison of appellant's operations in Arizona with those in Nevada, and by comparison of operations of appellant and of the Santa Fe Railroad in Arizona with those of the same roads in New Mexico, and by like comparison between appellant's operations in Arizona and operations throughout the country.

We think, as the trial court found, that the Arizona Train Limit Law, viewed as a safety measure, affords at most slight and dubious advantage, if any, over unregulated train lengths. . . . Its undoubted effect on the commerce is the regulation, without securing uniformity, of the length of trains operated in interstate commerce, which lack is itself a primary cause of preventing the free flow of commerce by delaying it and by substantially increasing its cost and impairing its efficiency.

Here we conclude that the state does go too far. Its regulation of train lengths, admittedly obstructive to interstate train operation, and having a seriously adverse effect on transportation efficiency and economy, passes beyond what is plainly essential for safety since it does not appear that it will lessen rather than increase the danger of accident. Its attempted regulation of the operation of interstate trains cannot establish nation-wide control such as is essential to the maintenance of an efficient transportation system, which Congress alone can prescribe. The state interest cannot be preserved at the expense of the national interest by an enactment which regulates interstate train lengths without securing such control, which is a matter of national concern. To this the interest of the state here asserted is subordinate.

. . . Here examination of all the relevant factors makes it plain that the state interest is outweighed by the interest of the nation in an adequate, economical and efficient railway transportation service, which must prevail.

Mr. Justice BLACK, dissenting.

In *Hennington v. Georgia* [1896], a case which involved the power of a state to regulate interstate traffic, this Court said: "The whole theory of our government, federal and state, is hostile to the idea that questions of legislative authority may depend . . . upon opinions of judges as to the wisdom or want of wisdom in the enactment of laws under powers clearly conferred upon the legislature." What the Court decides today is that it is unwise governmental policy to regulate the length of trains. I am therefore constrained to note my dissent.

. . . [T]he "findings" of the state court do not authorize today's decision. That court did not find that there is no unusual danger from slack movements in long trains. It did decide on disputed evidence that the long train "slack movement" dangers were more than offset by prospective dangers as a result of running a larger number of short trains, since many people might be hurt at grade crossings. There was undoubtedly some evidence before the state court from which it could have reached such a conclusion. There was undoubtedly as much evidence before it which would have justified a different conclusion.

Under those circumstances, the determination of

whether it is in the interest of society for the length of trains to be governmentally regulated is a matter of public policy. Someone must fix that policy—either the Congress, or the state, or the courts. A century and a half of constitutional history and government admonishes this Court to leave that choice to the elected legislative representatives of the people themselves, where it properly belongs both on democratic principles and the requirements of efficient government.

When we finally get down to the gist of what the Court today actually decides, it is this: Even though more railroad employees will be injured by "slack action" movements on long trains than on short trains, there must be no regulation of this danger in the absence of "uniform regulations." That means that no one can legislate against this danger except the Congress; and even though the Congress is perfectly content to leave the matter to the different state legislatures, this Court, on the ground of "lack of uniformity," will require it to make an express avowal of that fact before it will permit a state to guard against that admitted danger.

We are not left in doubt as to why, as against the potential peril of injuries to employees, the Court tips the scales on the side of "uniformity." For the evil it finds in a lack of uniformity is that it (1) delays interstate commerce, (2) increases its cost and (3) impairs its efficiency. All three of these boil down to the same thing, and that is that running shorter trains would increase the cost of railroad operations. The "burden" on commerce reduces itself to mere cost because there was no finding, and no evidence to support a finding, that by the expenditure of sufficient sums of money, the railroads could not enable themselves to carry goods and passengers just as quickly and efficiently with short trains as with long trains. Thus the conclusion that a requirement for long trains will "burden interstate commerce" is a mere euphemism for the statement that a requirement for long trains will increase the cost of railroad operations. . . .

. . . I would affirm the judgment of the Supreme Court of Arizona.

Notes and Queries

1. This case seems to present a classic conflict between the principles of judicial supremacy and democracy. Is it clear, however, that Justices Stone and Black can be identified with one or the other of these principles?

2. Was the state's interest in public safety accorded sufficient weight in this case? How is the legitimate state interest in safety to be balanced against the burden on interstate commerce?

3. Does the text or the structure of the Constitution provide any guidance to how this balance should be carried out? Is any balancing test necessarily a subjective product of the will of a majority of justices? Is such balancing nonetheless necessary?

4. Are Justice Black's objections effectively met by the majority? How closely would he examine state justifications for economic regulation? Is his reasoning more consistent with the concept of federalism?

City of Philadelphia v. New Jersey

437 U.S. 617, 98 S.Ct. 2531, 57 L.Ed.2d 475 (1978)

A New Jersey statue prohibited the importation of most solid or liquid waste that originated or was collected outside the state. Operators of private landfills in New Jersey and several cities with contracts with these operators challenged the statute, claiming that it discriminated against interstate commerce. The Supreme Court of New Jersey upheld the law. Opinion of the Court: *Stewart*, Brennan, White, Marshall, Blackmun, Powell, Stevens. Dissenting opinion: *Rehnquist*, Burger.

Mr. Justice STEWART delivered the opinion of the Court.

Before it addressed the merits of the appellants' claim, the New Jersey Supreme Court questioned whether the interstate movement of those wastes banned by ch. 363 is "commerce" at all within the meaning of the Commerce Clause. Any doubts on that score should be laid to rest at the outset.

The state court expressed the view that there may be two definitions of "commerce" for constitutional purposes. When relied on "to support some exertion of federal control or regulation," the Commerce Clause permits "a very sweeping concept" of commerce. But when relied on "to strike down or restrict state legislation," that Clause and the term "commerce" have a "much more confined . . . reach."

We think the state court misread our cases, and thus erred in assuming that they require a two-tiered definition of commerce. In saying that innately harmful articles "are not legitimate subject of trade and commerce," the *Bowman* Court [referring to *Bowman v. Chicago & Northwestern R. Co.* (1888)] was stating its conclusion, not the starting point of its reasoning. All objects of interstate trade merit Commerce Clause protection; none is excluded by definition at the outset. . . . [T]he Court [has] held simply that because the articles' worth in interstate commerce was far outweighed by the dangers inhering in their very movement, States could prohibit their transportation across state lines. Hence, we reject the state court's suggestion that the banning of "valueless" out-of-state wastes by ch. 363 implicates no constitutional protection. Just as Congress has power to regulate the interstate movement of these wastes, States are not free from constitutional scrutiny when they restrict that movement.

Although the Constitution gives Congress the power to regulate commerce among the States, many subjects of potential federal regulation under that power inevitably escape congressional attention "because of their local character and their number and diversity." In the absence of federal legislation, these subjects are open to control by the States so long as they act within the restraints imposed by the Commerce Clause itself. The bounds of these restraints appear nowhere in the words of the Commerce Clause, but have emerged gradually in the decisions of this Court giving effect to its basic purpose. . . .

The opinions of the Court through the years have reflected an alertness to the evils of "economic isolation" and protectionism, while at the same time recognizing that incidental burdens on interstate commerce may be unavoidable when a State legislates to safeguard the health and safety of its people. Thus, where simple economic protectionism is effected by state legislation, a virtually *per se* rule of invalidity has been erected. . . .

The crucial inquiry, therefore, must be directed to determining whether ch. 363 is basically a protectionist measure, or whether it can fairly be viewed as a law directed to legitimate local concerns, with effects upon interstate commerce that are only incidental.

The New Jersey law at issue in this case falls squarely within the area that the Commerce Clause puts off limits to state regulation. On its face, it imposes on out-of-state commercial interests the full burden of conserving the State's remaining landfill space.

The appellees argue that not all laws which facially discriminate against out-of-state commerce are forbidden protectionist regulations. In particular, they point to quarantine laws, which this Court has repeatedly upheld even though they appear to single out interstate commerce for special treatment.

It is true that certain quarantine laws have not been considered forbidden protectionist measures, even though they were directed against out-of-state commerce. But those quarantine laws banned the importation of articles such as diseased livestock that required destruction as soon as possible because their very movement risked contagion and other evils. Those laws thus did not discriminate against interstate commerce as such, but simply prevented traffic in noxious articles, whatever their origin.

The New Jersey statute is not such a quarantine law. There has been no claim here that the very movement of waste into or through New Jersey endangers health, or that waste must be disposed of as soon and as close to its point of generation as possible. The harms caused by waste are said to arise after its disposal in landfill sites, and at that point, as New Jersey concedes, there is no basis to distinguish out-of-state waste from domestic waste. If one is inherently harmful, so is the other. Yet New Jersey has banned the former while leaving its landfill sites open to the latter. The New Jersey law blocks the importation of waste in an obvious effort to saddle those outside the State with the entire burden of slowing the flow of refuse into New Jersey's remaining landfill sites. That legislative effort is clearly impermissible under the Commerce Clause of the Constitution.

Today, cities in Pennsylvania and New York find it expedient or necessary to send their waste into New Jersey for disposal, and New Jersey claims the right to close its borders to such traffic. Tomorrow, cities in New Jersey may find it expedient or necessary to send their waste into Pennsylvania or New York for disposal, and those States might then claim the right to close their borders. The Commerce Clause will protect New Jersey in the future, just as it protects her neighbors now, from efforts by one State to isolate itself in the stream of interstate commerce from a problem shared by all. The judgment is

Reversed.

Mr. Justice REHNQUIST, with whom The Chief Justice joins, dissenting.

The question presented in this case is whether New Jersey must also continue to receive and dispose of solid waste from neighboring States, even though these will inexorably increase the health problems discussed above. The Court answers this question in the affirmative. New Jersey must either prohibit all landfill operations, leaving itself to cast about for a presently nonexistent solution to the serious problem of disposing of the waste generated within its own borders, or it must accept waste from every portion of the United States, thereby multiplying the health and safety problems which would result if it dealt only with such wastes generated within the State. Because past precedents establish that the Commerce Clause does not present appellees with such a Hobson's choice, I dissent.

. . . Under [prior cases], New Jersey may require germ-infected rags or diseased meat to be disposed of as best as possible within the State, but at the same time prohibit the importation of such items for disposal at the facilities that are set up within New Jersey for disposal of such material generated within the State. The physical fact of life that New Jersey must somehow dispose of its own noxious items does not mean that it must serve as a depository for those of every other State. Similarly, New Jersey should be free under our past precedents to prohibit the importation of solid waste because of the health and safety problems that such waste poses to its citizens. The fact that New Jersey continues to, and indeed must continue to, dispose of its own solid waste does not mean that New Jersey may not prohibit the importation of even more solid waste into the State. I simply see no way to distinguish solid waste, on the record of this case, from germ-infected rags, diseased meat, and other noxious items.

. . . According to the Court, the New Jersey law is distinguishable from these other laws, and invalid, because the concern of New Jersey is not with the movement of solid waste but with the present inability to safely dispose of it once it reaches its destination.

. . . [T]he Court implies that the challenged laws must be invalidated because New Jersey has left its landfills open to domestic waste. But, as the Court notes, this Court has repeatedly upheld quarantine laws "even though they appear to single out interstate commerce for special treatment." The fact that New Jersey has left its landfill sites open for domestic waste does not, of course, mean that solid waste is not innately harmful. Nor does it mean that New Jersey prohibits importation of solid waste for reasons other than the health and safety of its population. New Jersey must out of sheer necessity treat and dispose of its solid waste in some fashion, just as it must treat New Jersey cattle suffering from hoof-and-mouth disease. It does not follow that New Jersey must, under the Commerce Clause, accept solid waste or diseased cattle from outside its borders and thereby exacerbate its problems.

The Supreme Court of New Jersey expressly found that ch. 363 was passed "to preserve the health of New Jersey residents by keeping their exposure to solid waste and landfill areas to a minimum." The Court points to absolutely no evidence that would contradict this finding by the New Jersey Supreme Court. Because I find no basis for distinguishing the laws under challenge here from our past cases upholding state laws that prohibit the importation of items that could endanger the population of the State, I dissent.

Notes and Queries

1. What interest does New Jersey claim its regulation advances? Did the Court recognize this interest as legitimate? Why, then, did the Court strike down the law?

2. How does the Court connect the impact of this legislation to the commerce clause? How does the court show that the New Jersey legislation produces an unconstitutional "economic isolation"? What would be the effect of allowing such legislation according to the majority's claim?

3. Why does Justice Rehnquist assert that the majority opinion offers the state a Hobson's choice? If the regulation were strictly motivated by a concern about waste, why were no restrictions placed on the in-state production and disposal of waste?

4. On the other hand, consider the broader policy implications of *Philadelphia*. Would a decision for New Jersey have prompted Philadelphia or Pennsylvania to develop new technologies of waste disposal? Might a decision for New Jersey have also prompted Congress to deal more readily with the neglected problem of waste disposal nationwide? Might the Court's fixation on "legal" federalism in *Philadelphia* have inhibited the development of a "democratic" solution to the problem of waste disposal in America?

Baldwin v. Fish and Game Commission of Montana

436 U.S. 371; 98 S.Ct. 1852; 56 L.Ed.2d 354 (1978)

Montana residents were able to purchase a state elk-hunting license for $9 a year, while out-of-state residents who wanted to hunt elk in Montana were required to purchase a combination hunting and fishing license for $225 a year. A group of hunters from Minnesota, who had previously hunted elk in Montana, challenged the constitutionality of Montana's licensing scheme under the privileges and immunities clause of Article 4, sec. 2. A

three-judge federal district court denied relief. Opinion of the Court: *Blackmun*, Burger, Powell, Rehnquist, Stevens, Stewart. Concurring opinion: *Burger*. Dissenting opinion: *Brennan*, Marshall, *White*.

Mr. Justice BLACKMUN delivered the opinion of the Court.

Appellants strongly urge here that the Montana licensing scheme for the hunting of elk violates the Privileges and Immunities Clause of Art. IV, s 2, of our Constitution. That Clause is not one the contours of which have been precisely shaped by the process and wear of constant litigation and judicial interpretation over the years since 1789. . . . We are, nevertheless, not without some pronouncements by this Court as to the Clause's significance and reach.

When the Privileges and Immunities Clause has been applied to specific cases, it has been interpreted to prevent a State from imposing unreasonable burdens on citizens of other States in their pursuit of common callings within the State, in the ownership and disposition of privately held property within the State, and in access to the courts of the State.

It has not been suggested, however, that state citizenship or residency may never be used by a State to distinguish among persons. Suffrage, for example, always has been understood to be tied to an individual's identification with a particular State. No one would suggest that the Privileges and Immunities Clause requires a State to open its polls to a person who declines to assert that the State is the only one where he claims a right to vote. The same is true as to qualification for an elective office of the State. Nor must a State always apply all its laws or all its services equally to anyone, resident or nonresident, who may request it so to do. Some distinctions between residents and nonresidents merely reflect the fact that this is a Nation composed of individual States, and are permitted; other distinctions are prohibited because they hinder the formation, the purpose, or the development of a single Union of those States. Only with respect to those "privileges" and "immunities" bearing upon the vitality of the Nation as a single entity must the State treat all citizens, resident and nonresident, equally. Here we must decide into which category falls a distinction with respect to access to recreational big-game hunting.

Many of the early cases embrace the concept that the States had complete ownership over wildlife within their boundaries, and, as well, the power to preserve this bounty for their citizens alone. It was enough to say "that in regulating the use of the common property of the citizens of [a] state, the legislature is [not] bound to extend to the citizens of all the other states the same advantages as are secured to their own citizens." *Corfield v. Coryell* [1825]. It appears to have been generally accepted that although the States were obligated to treat all those within their territory equally in most respects, they were not obliged to share those things they held in trust for their own people. In *Corfield*, Mr. Justice Washington, sitting as Circuit Justice, although recognizing that the States may not interfere with the "right of a citizen of one state to pass through, or to reside in any other state, for purposes of trade, agriculture, professional pursuits, or otherwise; to claim the benefit of the writ of habeas corpus; to institute

and maintain actions of any kind in the courts of the state; to take, hold and dispose of property, either real or personal," nonetheless concluded that access to oyster beds determined to be owned by New Jersey could be limited to New Jersey residents. This holding, and the conception of state sovereignty upon which it relied, formed the basis for similar decisions during later years of the 19th century.

In more recent years, however, the Court has recognized that the States' interest in regulating and controlling those things they claim to "own," including wildlife, is by no means absolute. States may not compel the confinement of the benefits of their resources, even their wildlife, to their own people whenever such hoarding and confinement impedes interstate commerce.

Appellants contend that the doctrine on which *Corfield* relied has no remaining vitality. We do not agree. . . . The fact that the State's control over wildlife is not exclusive and absolute in the face of federal regulation and certain federally protected interests does not compel the conclusion that it is meaningless in their absence

Appellants have demonstrated nothing to convince us that we should completely reject the Court's earlier decisions. In his opinion in *Coryell*, Mr. Justice Washington, although he seemingly relied on notions of "natural rights" when he considered the reach of the Privileges and Immunities Clause, included in his list of situations, in which he believed the States would be obligated to treat each other's residents equally, only those where a nonresident sought to engage in an essential activity or exercise a basic right. He himself used the term "fundamental," in the modern as well as the "natural right" sense. . . . With respect to such basic and essential activities, interference with which would frustrate the purposes of the formation of the Union, the States must treat residents and nonresidents without unnecessary distinctions.

Does the distinction made by Montana between residents and nonresidents in establishing access to elk hunting threaten a basic right in a way that offends the Privileges and Immunities Clause? Merely to ask the question seems to provide the answer. . . . Elk hunting by nonresidents in Montana is a recreation and a sport. In itself—wholly apart from license fees—it is costly and obviously available only to the wealthy nonresident or to the one so taken with the sport that he sacrifices other values in order to indulge in it and to enjoy what it offers. It is not a means to the nonresident's livelihood. The mastery of the animal and the trophy are the ends that are sought; appellants are not totally excluded from these. The elk supply, which has been entrusted to the care of the State by the people of Montana, is finite and must be carefully tended in order to be preserved.

Appellants' interest in sharing this limited resource on more equal terms with Montana residents simply does not fall within the purview of the Privileges and Immunities Clause. Equality in access to Montana elk is not basic to the maintenance or well-being of the Union. . . . We do not decide the full range of activities that are sufficiently basic to the livelihood of the Nation that the States may not interfere with a nonresident's participation therein without similarly interfering with a resident's participation. Whatever rights or activities may be "fundamental" under the Privileges and Immunities Clause, we are persuaded, and hold, that elk hunting by nonresidents in Montana is not one of them. . . .

Mr. Chief Justice BURGER, concurring.

In joining the Court's opinion, I write separately only to emphasize the significance of Montana's special interest in its elk population and to point out the limits of the Court's holding.

The doctrine that a State "owns" the wildlife within its borders as trustee for its citizens is admittedly a legal anachronism of sorts. . . . But, as noted in the Court's opinion, and contrary to the implications of the dissent, the doctrine is not completely obsolete. It manifests the State's special interest in regulating and preserving wildlife for the benefit of its citizens.

[This Court has] made clear that the Privileges and Immunities Clause does not prevent a State from preferring its own citizens in granting public access to natural resources in which they have a special interest.

It is the special interest of Montana citizens in its elk that permits Montana to charge nonresident hunters higher license fees without offending the Privileges and Immunities Clause. The Court does not hold that the Clause permits a State to give its residents preferred access to recreational activities offered for sale by private parties. Indeed it acknowledges that the Clause requires equality with respect to privileges "bearing upon the vitality of the Nation as a single entity." It seems clear that those basic privileges include "all the privileges of trade and commerce" which were protected in the fourth article of the Articles of Confederation. The Clause assures noncitizens the opportunity to purchase goods and services on the same basis as citizens; it confers the same protection upon the buyer of luxury goods as upon the buyer of bread.

Mr. Justice BRENNAN, with whom Mr. Justice WHITE and Mr. Justice MARSHALL join, dissenting.

Far more troublesome than the Court's narrow holding—elk hunting in Montana is not a privilege or immunity entitled to protection under Art. IV, s. 2, cl. 1, of the Constitution—is the rationale of the holding that Montana's elk-hunting licensing scheme passes constitutional muster. The Court concludes that because elk hunting is not a "basic and essential activit[y]," interference with which would frustrate the purposes of the formation of the Union," . . . the Privileges and Immunities Clause of Art. IV, s. 2—"The Citizens of each State shall be entitled to all Privileges and Immunities of Citizens in the several States"—does not prevent Montana from irrationally, wantonly, and even invidiously discriminating against nonresidents seeking to enjoy natural treasures it alone among the 50 States possesses. I cannot agree that the Privileges and Immunities Clause is so impotent a guarantee that such discrimination remains wholly beyond the purview of that provision.

I think the time has come to confirm explicitly that which has been implicit in our modern privileges and immunities decisions, namely that an inquiry into whether a given right is "fundamental" has no place in our analysis of whether a State's discrimination against nonresidents—who "are not represented in the [discriminating] State's legislative halls,"—violates the Clause. Rather, our primary concern is the State's justification for its discrimination. . . . [A] State's discrimination against nonresidents is permissible where (1) the presence or activity of nonresidents is the source or cause of the problem or effect with which the State seeks to deal, and (2) the discrimination practiced against nonresidents bears a substantial relation to the problem they present.

It is clear that under a proper privileges and immunities analysis Montana's discriminatory treatment of nonresident big-game hunters in this case must fall. . . . There are three possible justifications for charging nonresident elk hunters an amount at least 7.5 times the fee imposed on resident big-game hunters. The first is conservation. . . . [T]here is nothing in the record to indicate that the influx of nonresident hunters created a special danger to Montana's elk or to any of its other wildlife species.

Moreover, if Montana's discriminatorily high big-game license fee is an outgrowth of general conservation policy to discourage elk hunting, this too fails as a basis for the licensing scheme. Montana makes no effort similarly to inhibit its own residents.

The second possible justification for the fee differential . . . is a cost justification. . . . The licensing scheme, appellants contend, is simply an attempt by Montana to shift the costs of its conservation efforts, however commendable they may be, onto the shoulders of nonresidents who are powerless to help themselves at the ballot box. The District Court agreed, finding that "[o]n a consideration of [the] evidence . . . and with due regard to the presumption of constitutionality . . . the ratio of 7.5 to 1 cannot be justi-fied on any basis of cost allocation." . . . Montana's attempt to cost-justify its discriminatory licensing practices thus fails under the second prong of a correct privileges and immunities analysis—that which requires the discrimina-tion a State visits upon nonresidents to bear a substantial relation to the problem or burden they pose.

The third possible justification for Montana's licensing scheme, . . . is actually no justification at all, but simply an assertion that a State "owns" the wildlife within its borders in trust for its citizens and may therefore do with it what it pleases.

In unjustifiably discriminating against nonresident elk hunters, Montana has not "exercised its police power in conformity with the . . . Constitution." The State's police power interest in its wildlife cannot override the appel-lants' constitutionally protected privileges and immunities right. I respectfully dissent and would reverse.

Notes and Queries

1. How does the Court distinguish between interests that are "fundamental" under the privileges and immuni-ties clause and those that are not? Does the Constitution offer any guidance? Does the privileges and immunities clause protect only those activities or resources that are "basic to the maintenance or well-being of the Union"?

2. Does the distinction between fundamental and non-fundamental interests in fact elevate local or parochial definitions of community over a national definition of community?

3. Could Montana under *Baldwin* exclude nonresi-dents altogether from hunting elk within the state?

Chapter 7

Congressional Powers

The fundamental defect of the Confederation, wrote Alexander Hamilton in 1780, "is a want of power in Congress."[1] He argued that "Congress should have complete sovereignty in all that relates to war, peace, trade, finance, and to the management of foreign affairs."[2] For the purpose of creating "a more perfect union," and over the strong objections of the anti-Federalists, Article I conferred upon the national government primary—but not complete—authority over these realms of public policy. Article I incorporates most of Congress' powers and in terms noticeably more specific than those conferred on the judiciary (Article III) or the executive branch (Article II). Yet, as the cases in this chapter illustrate, the scope and range of these powers remain disputed. The dispute, of course, relates to our discussion in chapter 2 of the necessity (i.e., the "why and what") of constitutional interpretation.

Among the most disputed of Congress's powers is its authority "to regulate commerce . . . among the several states," commonly called the power to regulate interstate commerce. This clause has played an important role in binding the nation together as an integrated economic unit, but it has also been critical in determining the extent of congressional power generally. Over the decades, however, the commerce clause has been subject alternately to broad and narrow interpretation. These varying interpretations have often corresponded to the ebb and flow of American economic and political development. The Court's abrupt change in *NLRB v. Jones and Laughlin Steel Corporation* (1937, reprinted later in the chapter) is one prominent example of these cycles of change. The decision should be viewed against the backdrop of the growth in multistate corporate enterprise as well as within the context of the 1936 presidential election and Roosevelt's plan to pack the Supreme Court with justices favorable to the New Deal. *United States v. Lopez* (1995, reprinted later in the chapter) is the most recent turning point in the interpretation of federal power under the commerce clause.

---

[1] Letter from Alexander Hamilton to James Duane, 3 September 1780 in Philip B. Kurland and Ralph Lerner, eds., *The Founder's Constitution* (Chicago: The University of Chicago Press, 1987) I: 150.

[2] Ibid., 153.

Lopez commands our attention because it resurrects and reenacts the debates among the Constitution's Framers over the allocation of national and state authority. The case also fixes our attention on another of our themes, the tension between judicial review and democracy in America.

Regulating Interstate Commerce

The commerce clause raises several interpretive and normative questions. How, for example, is commerce to be defined? What constitutes commerce among the several states? What are the proper functions and powers of the respective state and federal governments under the commerce clause? Does the change and growth of the nation's increasingly capitalist, commercial economy require a change in traditional ideas of what governmental structures have the power to regulate commerce? What weight should original intent, current values, or modern conditions of trade have in construing the commerce clause? Should constitutional interpreters hold fast to the more restrictive founding idea of what constitutes commerce among the states so as to avoid one of the Founders' fears, namely, a tyrannical national government? (The Founders, for their part, also feared the impotence of the Articles of Confederation.) Should they take account of a changing interdependent national economy that affects more than one state? If the states do not possess enough power to control commercial activities implicating more than a single state, should control then pass to the federal government? Should federal power extend to noncommercial activities with an indirect or remote relationship to commerce?

Overlapping these queries are broader questions of democratic theory. When is it proper for the judicial branch to override decisions on commercial or economic matters forged in the national political process? Scholars such as Jesse Choper have argued that because the states play such a significant role in the composition and selection of the national government, the federal courts should not decide constitutional questions respecting the ultimate power of the national government relative to the states.[3] Would the same consideration apply when political majorities at the state level enact legislation impinging on commerce when no conflicting federal law exists? Should the federal courts interdict such laws merely because they independently conclude that a state has regulated interstate trade in violation of the commerce clause itself? Finally, how much responsibility under the Constitution do Congress and the Court have in assuring that its exercise of the commerce power does not interfere with the reserved powers of the states?

Marshall's Textualism

All treatments of the commerce clause begin with John Marshall's interpretation of its meaning in the seminal case of *Gibbons v. Ogden* (1824, reprinted later in the chapter). His *Gibbons* opinion, like that of *McCulloch v. Maryland*, belongs in the pantheon of great essays on American federalism. Its ruling—that New York's state-granted steamboat monopoly was unconstitutional because it conflicted with a federal coasting statute—is less important for present purposes than its definition of commerce and the scope of the power to regulate it. Commerce, Marshall declared, comprehends not only navigation between the ports of different states—the specific

---

[3] Jesse Choper, *Judicial Review and the National Political Process: A Functional Reconsideration of the Role of the Supreme Court* (Chicago: The University of Chicago Press, 1980), 2.

activity at issue in *Gibbons*—but "every species of commercial intercourse." According to Marshall, as long as any aspect of commerce implicates or involves more than one state, such as transportation or the exchange of commodities across state lines, Congress may regulate it. The power to *regulate*, however, is equally broad. "This power, like all others vested in congress," wrote Marshall, "is complete in itself, may be exercised to its utmost extent, and acknowledges no limitations, other than are prescribed in the constitution." Marshall conceded, as in *McCulloch*, that the national government is "limited to specified objects," but the power to regulate those objects—interstate commerce being one of them—is "vested in congress as absolutely as it would be in a single [unitary] government."

Marshall's doctrine of national supremacy with respect to the power clauses of Article I was not meant to deprive the states of their rightful authority over their internal affairs. Whereas commerce *among* the states is clearly subject to congressional legislation, commerce *within* the states, said Marshall, is subject to state regulation. Marshall also conceded that the state's police power extends to "inspection laws, quarantine laws, and health laws of every description" even though they "may have . . . considerable influence on commerce." It was Justice William Johnson, not Marshall, who in *Gibbons* posited Congress's exclusive authority over commerce and denied any significant difference between commerce among and within the states. This power, in Johnson's words, "can reside but in one potentate; and hence, the grant of this power carries with it the whole subject, leaving nothing for the state to act upon."

Marshall's disagreement with Johnson may have been more political than jurisprudential. Against the backdrop of a fierce national debate over the slave trade, Marshall seemed unwilling to make any grand doctrinal pronouncement on the full scope of federal or state authority over commerce. Any such pronouncement would have stoked the flames of the emerging national conflict over slavery and exposed the Supreme Court to political retaliation. (Southerners would have reacted bitterly to any decision giving Congress sweeping power over commerce; such power would have validated Congress's control of the slave trade within and among the states.) It was sufficient for the purpose at hand simply to strike down New York's law because it contravened a federal statute on the same subject. Future generations of justices, oscillating between judicial pragmatism and formalism, would have to work out the implications of the middle road Marshall sought to map out between Johnson's nationalism and state claims to concurrent authority over commerce.

Post-*Gibbons* Checks on National Power

When Roger Brooke Taney, a Jacksonian Democrat, became Chief Justice in 1836, many thought he would proceed to demolish the constitutional edifice of judicial sovereignty and federal supremacy that Marshall had so deftly—and incompletely—constructed. But he held firmly to the principle of judicial review and only refined the jurisprudence of federal supremacy. Taney, whose tenure lasted until his death in 1864, presided over the Supreme Court when the states were vigorously reacting to the challenges and evils of pre-industrial capitalism. (For additional details see chapter 10.) Although his Court sustained many local regulations of business and commerce in ways that Marshall would not have approved, it left intact the basic structure of Marshall's nation-state jurisprudence. As for judicial review, Taney built on Marshall's gains, performing so well "that not even the monumental indiscretion of the *Dred Scott* decision could quite destroy the judicial imperium."[4] Together with the modifications in the field of federal-state relations, Taney's decisions set the stage for the era of judicial vigilance in support of capitalism and free enterprise.

Later in the nineteenth and well into the twentieth century, the Supreme Court returned to the dual federalism implicit in the states' rights account of the Constitution. It often used the commerce clause as a weapon to limit the ability of the federal government to regulate the national economy. These years corresponded roughly with the gilded age of American politics.[5] The gospel of wealth ruled the land, businessmen equated freedom with absolute economic liberty, and judges protected the rights of contract and property with a vengeance. Between 1888 and 1937, as noted in chapter 10, the federal judiciary itself zealously defended *laissez-faire* capitalism and corporate autonomy. The constitutionalism of economic liberty that reached its zenith in *Lochner v. New York* (1905), which restricted state power, found echoes in commerce clause cases such as *United States v. E. C. Knight Co.* (1895, reprinted later in the chapter) and its progeny. The tension between federal and state authority was most acute here as the Court narrowed the scope of national authority in the interest of state sovereignty. (In *E. C. Knight*, the Court held that national regulatory power did not extend to "local" activities such as manufacturing or production.)

At the same time, however, we observe strong countervailing trends in support of a more magnanimous view of the commerce power. *Champion v. Ames* (1903, reprinted later in the chapter) initiated one of these trends. Known as the *Lottery Case*, *Champion* sustained a federal statute that had little to do with interstate commerce as such. Rather, it was designed to achieve a police power purpose in support of state efforts to suppress disfavored activities, here gambling, having no immediate relationship to commerce. The Court ruled that Congress could assist the states in rooting out certain viruses threatening national morals by blocking their entrance into the bloodstream of interstate commerce. "As a state may, for the purpose of guarding the morals of its own people, forbid all sales of lottery tickets within its limits," the Court declared, "so Congress, for the purpose of guarding the people of the United States against the 'widespread pestilence of lotteries,' and to protect the commerce which concerns all the states, may prohibit the carrying of lottery tickets from one state to another." In the years ahead, the Supreme Court would rely on *Champion* to sustain congressional efforts to keep the channels of commerce free of other "pollutants" such as prostitution, pornography, adulterated foods, and misbranded products.[6]

Two other lines of authority helped to counterbalance the dual federalism implicit in decisions such as *E. C. Knight*. One line begins with the so-called *Shreveport* case,[7] in which the Supreme Court sustained an order requiring the Texas Railroad Commission to bring its intrastate shipment rates into line with higher interstate rates fixed by the Interstate Commerce Commission. By this time, trains had transformed the nation into a single economic unit. They were common instruments of interstate traffic and so closely and substantially related to intrastate rail shipments, declared

---

[4] Robert G. McCloskey, *The American Supreme Court*, rev. by Sanford Levinson (Chicago: University of Chicago Press, 1994), 56.

[5] See Ralph Henry Gabriel, *The Course of American Democratic Thought* (New York: Greenwood Press, 1986), chap. 13, 151–169.

[6] See *Hoke v. United States*, 227 U.S. 308 (1913) and *Hippolite Egg Co. v. United States*, 220 U.S. 45 (1911), which have also been applied to immoral activity of a noncommercial kind. See *Caminetti v. United States*, 242 U.S. 470 (1917) and *Cleveland v. United States*, 329 U.S. 14 (1946).

[7] *Houston, East and West Texas Ry. v. United States*, 234 U.S. 342 (1914).

the Court, that Congress could regulate the latter when necessary to protect the former against local discriminatory ratemaking. *Swift & Co. v. United States* (1905), on the other hand, marks the start of a related line of authority.[8] *Swift* sustained the federal regulation of transactions in the stockyards of Chicago and other midwestern cities because the cattle shipped in from out of state and slaughtered there were still in the stream of commerce. The meats processed and packaged in the stockyards were to be shipped and sold to dealers and consumers in still other states. So the interstate journey had not yet ended. Accordingly, Congress could regulate the sales practices of stockyard dealers so as to immunize the interstate market against local monopolies.

E. C. Knight is prototypical of those pre-1937 cases that disabled the national government from dealing with the abuses of an unregulated market economy, just as it represented a return to what was thought to be the original vision of the Constitution's Framers. The sugar monopoly at issue in *Knight* could not be regulated by Congress because manufacturing was declared a local activity unrelated to the exchange of commodities in interstate commerce. In addition, the monopoly's effect on interstate commerce was considered to be indirect rather than direct and thus outside the compass of congressional control. The Court's majority reached a similar conclusion in *Hammer v. Dagenhart* (1918, reprinted later in the chapter). Congress sought to strike at the evil of child labor by prohibiting the interstate transportation of goods produced by underage children. The court labored to distinguish this case from *Champion*, arguing that the particular goods involved here, unlike lottery tickets, were harmless. In any event, said the Court, the evil sought to be eliminated—i.e, the exploitation of children—was strictly local and thus subject to the exclusive jurisdiction of the state. On the other hand, as the dissents argued, a state's decision not to prohibit child labor could frustrate a national or shared policy by giving that state a competitive economic advantage.

The Supreme Court carried this reasoning to new heights in *Carter v. Carter Coal Co.* (1936).[9] The Bituminous Coal Conservation Act of 1935 was one of several New Deal measures designed to rebuild and stabilize the American economy in a period of industrial crisis. It sought to regulate wages and hours of work in the nation's coal mines. Despite the importance of coal to the national economy, the Court nullifed the act because the *production* of coal, like labor relations in the coal industry, was a local activity with no more than an *indirect* effect on commerce. The Court implied that if the effect on commerce had been *direct*, the activity would be subject to congressional regulation. Insensitive to considerations of degree, the Court announced that if one ton of coal can be said to have but an indirect effect on commerce, the effect does not become direct by multiplying the tonnage. With this decision, like several others handed down in 1935 and 1936, the Supreme Court cut the heart out of President Roosevelt's program of economic recovery.[10]

Carter raises serious questions about the relationship between institutional competence and the structural design of the Constitution. Jesse Choper has urged the Supreme Court to regard as nonjusticiable federal-state conflicts grounded in the ar-

---

[8] See 196 U.S. 375 (1905) and *Stafford v. Wallace*, 258 U.S. 495 (1922).

[9] 298 U.S. 238 (1936).

[10] See, for example, *Schechter Poultry Corporation v. United States*, 295 U.S. 495 (1935); *United States v. Butler*, 297 U.S. 1 (1936); and *Railroad Retirement Board v. Alton R.R.*, 295 U.S. 330 (1935). These cases nullified, respectively, the National Industrial Recovery Act, the Agricultural Adjustment Act, and the Railroad Retirement Act.

gument that federal law interferes with the rights of the states. Such disputes, he argues, raise "issues of practicability" and "effectiveness of governmental levels" and thus should be resolved by the political branches. He writes: "Whatever the [judiciary's] special competence in adjudicating disputes over individual rights, when the fundamental constitutional issue turns on the relative competence of different levels of government to deal with societal problems, the courts are no more inherently capable of correct judgment than are the companion federal branches." Indeed, he continues, "the judiciary may well be less capable than the national legislature or executive in such inquiries, given both the highly pragmatic nature of federal-state questions and the forceful representation of the states in the national political process."[11] This argument, rooted in democratic theory, finds support in *Garcia v. San Antonio Metropolitan Transit Authority* (1985, reprinted later in the chapter).

Modern Commerce Clause Jurisprudence

The Court's allegiance to *Carter* and its limited view of congressional power over commerce ended in 1937. Some commentators believed—probably mistakenly—that the change occurred in response to President Roosevelt's plan to pack the Supreme Court with justices committed to the New Deal. (The plan called for the appointment of a new member of the Court for every justice over the age of 70 who refused to retire.) Whether true or not, the famous "switch in time that saved nine" occurred when the Court decided to uphold the National Labor Relations Act in *NLRB v. Jones & Laughlin Steel Corporation* (1937, reprinted later in the chapter).[12] Far more sensitive than *Carter* to matters of degree, *NLRB* found that the unfair labor practices regulated by the federal law interrupted commerce so greatly as to burden it *directly*. While *NLRB* adhered to the analytical pattern of the Court's pre-1937 cases, it soon became clear that the line between local and national would no longer hold up in an increasingly complex economy. It was swiftly abandoned, along with the direct-indirect standard. Now Congress could regulate *any* local activity having a substantial economic effect on interstate commerce.

Wickard v. Filburn (1942, reprinted later in the chapter) took a giant step forward by allowing Congress to reach even the trivial actions of a single farmer if these actions, taken cumulatively with those of many others similarly situated, have a substantial impact on interstate commerce. In an effort to stabilize the agricultural economy, the Agricultural Adjustment Act of 1938 established a national acreage allotment for wheat and penalized farmers for growing wheat in excess of their assigned quotas. Filburn, a small Ohio farmer, planted wheat in excess of his allotment but used the excess for his own family. Nevertheless, the Court sustained the fine levied against him because even the personal consumption of the wheat grown on one's own property would affect the marketing of wheat generally. The Agricultural Adjustment Act was thus a valid exercise of the commerce power. *Wickard's* "cumulative effects" doctrine pushed the commerce power to its limits, for almost any local economic activity seemed open to regulation under its logic.

Heart of Atlanta Motel, Inc. v. United States (1964, reprinted later in the chapter), also represents another expansion of the commerce power. *Wickard*, as noted, in-

---

[11] Jesse Choper, *The Scope of National Power vis-à-vis the State: The Dispensability of Judicial Review*, 86 Yale Law Journal 1556–57 (1977).

[12] *NLRB* was foreshadowed a month earlier by *West Coast Hotel Co. v. Parrish* (1937) in which the Court by the same vote sustained a state minimum wage law for women and children. It thus overruled *Adkins v. Children's Hospital*, 261 U.S. 525 (1923), a decision which had nullified a similar statute because it violated freedom of contract.

volved congressional regulation of *economic* activity. *Heart of Atlanta*, by contrast, validated the use of the commerce power for the purpose of achieving a moral end, namely, the prohibition of racial discrimination. Title II of the Civil Rights Act of 1964 bans racial discrimination in public accommodations related to interstate commerce. That this section of the Civil Rights Act of 1964 sought to deal with a moral wrong, said the Court, does not invalidate the enactment if Congress has rational grounds for believing that racial discrimination "has a disruptive effect on commercial inter-course." Even conceding that the hotel operation was purely local, "if it is interstate commerce that feels the pinch," said the Court, "it does not matter how local the operation that applies the squeeze."[13] But Congress had no hard data on the magnitude of the pinch. Anecdotal evidence of racial discrimination in motels along interstate highways was sufficient to supply the rational basis for the law's passage. *Katzenbach v. McClung* (1964) extended the application of the Civil Rights Act to Ollie's Barbecue, a family-owned restaurant located within the city of Birmingham, Alabama, some distance from an interstate highway. Nevertheless, Ollie's Barbecue was reachable through the federal commerce power because 46 percent of the meat the restaurant sold to local customers "was bought from a local supplier who had procured it from outside the state."[14] After *Wickard*, *Atlanta*, and *McClung*, the reach of congressional power under the commerce clause seemed well-nigh unlimited.

New-Found Limits on Congressional Power

On 24 June 1976 by a five to four vote, the Supreme Court struck down a federal statute that extended the maximum hours and minimum wage provisions of the Fair Labor Standards Act (FLSA) to most state and local employees. *National League of Cities v. Usery* (1976, reprinted later in the chapter), wrote Justice Brennan in dissent, "repudiates principles governing judicial interpretation of our Constitution settled since the time of Chief Justice John Marshall."[15] Not since 1936 had the Supreme Court found unconstitutional an exercise of the federal commerce power. The story of *Usery* and its repudiation just nine years later in *Garcia v. San Antonio Metropolitan Transit Authority* is a fascinating tale of doctrinal warfare on the Supreme Court. But the dispute also triggered a fierce debate over the constitutional role of the federal judiciary in commerce clause cases. The highlights of the dispute are worth examining, and we will do so by retracing the path of the four cases in table 7.1 below.

TABLE 7.1 *Alignment on the Supreme Court*

Wirtz (1968)		*Fry* (1975)		*Usery* (1976)		*Garcia* (1985)	
Harlan	+	Marshall	+	Rehnquist	+	Blackmun	+
Black	+	Burger	+	Burger	+	Brennan	+
Brennan	+	Brennan	+	Powell	+	White	+
White	+	White	+	Stewart	+	Marshall	+
Fortas	+	Blackmun	+	Blackmun	+	Stevens	+
Warren	+	Powell	+	Brennan	−	Powell	−
Douglas	−	Stewart	+	White	−	Burger	−
Stewart	−	Douglas	x	Marshall	−	O'Connor	−
Marshall	o	Rehnquist	−	Stevens	−	Rehnquist	−

Legend: + = in the majority; − = in dissent; o = nonparticipating; x = review improvidently granted

[13] 379 U.S. 241, 258 (1964).

[14] 379 U.S. 294, 296 (1964).

[15] 426 U.S. 833, 857 (1976).

The Rise and Fall of a Constitutional Doctrine

Congress's power clearly extends to nonstate activities and private businesses affecting or affected by interstate commerce. But may Congress subject a state to the same legislation applicable to private parties? The Supreme Court had already answered this question in 1936. *United States v. California* had ruled that a state-owned railroad running between two points within a single state is subject to the terms of the Federal Safety Appliance Act.[16] Whether state-run or not, said the Court, the railroad is a common carrier engaged in interstate trade and thus subject to congressional regulation. The state argued, on the other hand, that by regulating the railroad it was performing a public function in its sovereign capacity as a state; accordingly, the railroad lay outside the scope of federal control. Relying on *Shreveport* and the *Stockyard* cases, the Court noted simply that a state—no less than an individual—is within Congress' reach when its activity substantially affects interstate commerce. Chief Justice Stone, speaking for the Court, dismissed the state's "sovereignty" argument by asserting that "the sovereign power of the state is necessarily diminished to the extent of the grant of power to the Federal Government in the Constitution."[17]

When *Maryland v. Wirtz* (1968) was decided, Stone's view seemed solidly entrenched in American law.[18] But Maryland and twenty-seven other states challenged the validity of congressional amendments extending the Fair Labor Standards Act (FLSA) to employees of state hospitals and public schools. A 1941 decision had overruled *Hammer v. Dagenhart* (1918)[19]—a case that struck down a federal statute (Federal Child Labor Act) prohibiting the shipment in interstate commerce of goods produced in factories that employed children under the age of fourteen—and upheld FLSA as a valid means of curtailing the industrial strife that often interferes with the free flow of commerce. But could FLSA be amended to reach *state* employees? For six of the *Wirtz* justices, the answer was an easy "yes." Because the commerce power is plenary, as Chief Justice Marshall insisted in *Gibbons v. Ogden* (1824), regulations affecting interstate commerce may cover *any* enterprise, activity, or employee related to commerce. In short, as in other post-1937 cases, the *Wirtz* Court conferred constitutional status on its vision of the national economy as an organic unity.

Seven years later, in *Fry v. United States,*[20] the Supreme Court relied on *Wirtz* to sustain a special program of wage and salary controls that applied to government employees as well as workers in the private economy. (Congress enacted the Economic Stabilization Act of 1970 during an economic crisis.) *Fry*'s most notable feature, however, was Justice Rehnquist's lone dissent. Already known for his strong views in favor of state sovereignty, Rehnquist drew upon dual federalist lines of thought in several old federal tax cases to mount a skillful assault on the doctrinal basis of *Wirtz*. Rehnquist had dramatically shifted the Court's interpretive perspective. The question for him was not whether Article I had authorized this exercise of the federal commerce power, but rather whether Congress had invaded a province of state sovereignty under the Tenth Amendment. He was even able to draw support from the liberal Justice William O. Douglas, whose dissent in *Wirtz* had labelled FLSA's appli-

---

[16] 297 U.S. 275.

[17] Ibid., at 184.

[18] 392 U.S. 183 (1968).

[19] *United States v. Darby*, 312 U.S. 100 (1941).

[20] 421 U.S. 542 (1975).

cation to state employees as "a serious invasion of state sovereignty . . . [in]consistent with our constitutional federalism."[21]

Rehnquist's opinion set the stage for the equally dramatic reversal of *Wirtz* in *Usery*. Even allowing for the different circumstances behind *Fry* and *Usery*, it was truly amazing to find Rehnquist's lone dissent in 1975 carrying the day in 1976. Congress had amended FLSA once again, now to extend its reach to nearly all the employees of the states and their political subdivisions. Rehnquist did not deny that the wages and hours of state employees affected interstate commerce. In his view, however, the legislation was directed against the "States as States," displacing them "in areas of [their] traditional governmental functions," thus violating the Tenth Amendment. The decision had potentially revolutionary implications, and from the scathing words of Justice Brennan's dissent, it was clear that the majority opinion had profoundly influenced the court's commerce clause jurisprudence.

Overlaying the doctrinal division on the *Usery* Court was the equally intense conflict among the justices over the role of the judiciary in federal commerce clause cases. Justice Brennan rebuked the majority for its "patent usurpation of the role reserved for the political process." Worse, he wrote, is "the startling restructuring of our federal system, and the role . . . create[d] therein for the federal judiciary." Justice Blackmun, on the other hand, was unwilling to read the majority opinion "so despairingly"—as if the Court had reverted to the conceptual reasoning of its pre-1937 jurisprudence. He stressed what he thought was the Court's attempt to balance state and federal interests. His own view was that the Court had merely concluded in the particular circumstances of *Usery* that the state's vital interest in structuring the wages of its employees outweighed the asserted national interest in setting those wages. Blackmun tried to soothe the dissenters by suggesting that with respect, for example, to federal environmental legislation, the balance of interests would favor the federal government.

Nevertheless, as might have been anticipated, *Usery* triggered scores of constitutional challenges against other federal laws regulating various kinds of state activities, enterprises, or functions. In each of the cases reaching the Supreme Court, the federal act was sustained, with Blackmun almost always providing the deciding vote. Blackmun seemed determined to confine *Usery* to its particular facts, concluding in these other instances that the activity in question failed to qualify as a "traditional governmental function" worthy of protection under the Tenth Amendment.[22] Finally, frustrated by its inability to clearly distinguish traditional from non-traditional state functions—an uncertainty reflected by the inconsistent results among the lower federal courts on this question—the Court gave up altogether in *Garcia*, consigning *Usery* to the grave just nine years after its birth. Interestingly, it was Justice Blackmun, the fifth critical vote in *Usery*, who wrote the majority opinion in *Garcia*.

The doctrinal results in *Usery* and *Garcia* demonstrate how the method of structural interpretation can yield different outcomes. As for *Garcia*, however, the result seems less important than the tension it reflects between democracy and judicial review. In overruling *Usery*, the five-person majority announced that "[t]he political process ensures that laws that unduly burden the States will not be promulgated,"

---

[21] 392 U. S. 183, 201.

[22] See, for example, *Hodel v. Virginia Surface Mining Association*, 452 U.S. 264 (1981) upholding a federal statute regulating a state-owned strip mining operation; *Federal Energy Regulatory Commission v. Mississippi*, 456 U.S.742 (1982) upholding a federal utility regulatory act; and *EEOC v. Wyoming*, 460 U.S. 226 (1983) sustaining a federal age discrimination in employment act over a law on mandatory retirement for state employees.

for "the principal and basic limit on the federal commerce power is that inherent in all congressional action—the built-in restraints that our system provides through state participation in federal governmental action." According to this majoritarian-democratic view, the states would find their protection in the indirect influence they exert over the Senate, House of Representatives, and the presidency "by their control of electoral qualifications and their role in Presidential elections." Justice Powell, joined by Chief Justice Burger and Justices Rehnquist and O'Connor in dissent, adopted a constitutionalist perspective, arguing, *inter alia*, that state participation in the election of the President and members of Congress is insufficient to protect vital state interests, in part because of the "hydraulic pressure inherent within each of the separate branches to exceed the limits of its power." As Justice O'Connor wrote in a separate dissent, if federalism as the Framers cultivated it "is to remain meaningful, this Court cannot abdicate its constitutional responsibility to oversee the Federal Government's compliance with its duty to respect the legitimate interests of the States."

A Return to State Autonomy

State autonomy returned with a vengeance in *United States v. Lopez* (1995, reprinted later in the chapter). Writing for a five to four majority, as he did in *Usery*, Chief Justice Rehnquist invalidated the Gun-Free School Zones Act (1990) making it a federal crime "for any individual knowingly to possess a firearm at a place that [he or she] knows, or has reasonable cause to believe, is a school zone." For the first time in sixty years, a general law enacted by Congress under the commerce clause, and not directed against state activity, failed to receive the Court's approval. Until *Lopez*, established doctrine held that Congress could regulate any intrastate activity having a *substantial effect* on interstate commerce and that any law regulating such an activity would receive the Court's blessing if Congress could show that it had a *rational basis* for believing that the activity regulated affected interstate commerce. Indeed, these standards of judgment furnished Congress with a license to federalize a number of crimes for the purpose allegedly of cutting down on interstate criminal activity.[23]

In reexamining the line of cases beginning with *Jones & Laughlin Steel* (1937), however, the *Lopez* Court raised doubts about the scope of Congress' power to regulate interstate commerce. First, the Court determined for itself whether a *substantial* relationship existed between the regulated activity and interstate commerce. Previous cases such as *Wickard* and *Atlanta Hotel* suggested that this was a matter for Congress to decide. Second, and relatedly, the Court required Congress to show more than simply a "rational basis" for regulating a subject or activity supposedly related to commerce. Now Congress would have to produce findings demonstrating the substantiality of the relationship. In the Court's assessment, no such findings were available with respect to the Gun-Free Zones Act. Finally, the Court emphasized that Congress' power over commerce extends mainly to commercial or economic activity. Central to the decision in *Lopez* was, in the Court's words, "the noneconomic, criminal nature of the [regulated] conduct."

At least with regard to criminal activity, the *Lopez* Court seemed resolved to halt any further conversion of the commerce clause into "a general police power traditionally retained by the States." In enacting the "gun-possession" law, said the Court, Congress had regulated a purely local activity under the pretext of regulating com-

---

[23] See, for example, *Perez v. United States*, 402 U.S. 146 (1971), which sustained provisions of the Consumer Credit Protection Act prohibiting purely intrastate "loan sharking" activity.

merce. Thus the old doctrinal distinction between national and local activity was brought back to life. Chief Justice Rehnquist claimed that it had never expired. In support of the claim, he invoked *Gibbons*, *Jones & Laughlin Steel*, and similar cases discussed in this introduction. But the justices in the minority, citing and reviewing the same cases, saw the statute as one rationally and substantially related to the interstate gun market and therefore subject to congressional regulation.

Some commentators regarded *Lopez* as a revolutionary case. Yet when viewed through the prism of American constitutional history, *Lopez* could be said to represent, as one commentator has pointed out, "an act of interpretive fidelity" by which he meant a reading of the Constitution that returns to the framers' original understanding of the federal-state relationship. The dissenting opinion, according to this analysis, is by contrast "a textualist account" that seeks an "understanding of the [Constitution] that is most compelling in the current context." Both approaches represent "dominant modalities of constitutional interpretation."[24] In the originalist account, the framers could not have imagined that federal power would reach gun possession by a private individual within the confines of a single state. But a reading of the constitutional text in light of an increasingly unified national economy easily lends itself to the view that Congress is indeed empowered to regulate every activity of social life that affects this economy. In the end, these interpretive approaches seem driven by distinct visions of the American economy. One vision—the originalist—sees the economy in territorial terms where state and national interests are discernible and distinguishable, whereas the other—the textualist—envisions the economy as a single organic unit that belies any such division. As a matter of constitutional interpretation, then, one may doubt whether constitutional doctrine as such yields any right answer to the question *Lopez* poses.

If there was any doubt that *Lopez*—like *Usery*—would be confined to its particular facts, *United States v. Morrison* (2000, reprinted later in the chapter) set it to rest. *Morrison*, when combined with the 11th Amendment cases discussed in chapter 4, signaled the emergence of a major change in the constitutional jurisprudence of federal-state relations.[25] *Morrison* involved a challenge to the validity of the Violence Against Women Act of 1994, which provided a federal civil remedy for victims of gender-motivated violence. The petitioner was a female student assaulted and repeatedly raped by members of Virginia Tech's varsity football team. (The case reached the Supreme Court after a divided federal court of appeals had invalidated the statute on constitutional grounds.) Chief Justice Rehnquist, writing for the same five-person *Lopez* majority, concluded that crimes of violence against women is a local activity having no substantial effect on interstate commerce. The federal statute was therefore unconstitutional.

How far was the Court retreating from its previous case law? The majority accepted the broad range of congressional power established in prior cases. Recapitulating the teaching of *Jones & Laughlin Steel* and related cases, Chief Justice Rehnquist observed that this power extends not only to regulating the channels and instrumentalities of commerce as well as persons and things in interstate commerce, but also intrastate activities that substantially affect interstate commerce. Yet as wide as this power is, said the Chief Justice, it "is not without effective bounds."[26] He repeated the mantra

---

[24] Lawrence Lessig, *Translating Federalism: Lopez v. United States*, 1995, The Supreme Court Review 126–128 (1996).

[25] 529 U.S. 598 (2000).

[26] Ibid., 608.

of *Lopez*, namely, that any regulated intrastate activity would require congressional evidence that the activity affected interstate commerce *substantially*. *Morrison* differed from *Lopez* in that Congress had assembled "numerous findings regarding the serious [economic] impact that gender-motivated violence has on victims and their families." Nevertheless, taking up the gauntlet, the Chief Justice declared: "Whether particular operations affect interstate commerce sufficiently to come under the constitutional power of Congress to regulate them is ultimately a judicial rather than a legislative question, and can be settled finally only by this Court."[27] For the Chief Justice, often known for his support of legislative majorities, this was a bold assertion of judicial power.

The congressional findings at issue in *Morrison* had been based on calculations of the nationwide, aggregated impact of gender-motivated violence on employment, production, and consumption. The justices in the majority were unimpressed because of what they regarded as the fundamentally local and noneconomic character of the regulated conduct. If aggregated impact is to be the standard of judgment, they said, what is to keep Congress from regulating subjects such as family relations or marriage and divorce, areas of American life clearly within the domain of state and local authority? The Court characterized *Wickard* as a "the most far reaching example of Commerce Clause authority over intrastate activity,"[28] but conceded that at least there, unlike here, economic activity was involved. Justice Thomas would have gone further than other justices in the majority. "[I]n my view," he wrote, "the very notion of a 'substantial effects' test under the Commerce Clause is inconsistent with the original understanding of Congress' powers and with this Court's early Commerce Clause cases. By continuing to apply this rootless and malleable standard, however circumscribed, the Court has encouraged the Federal Government to persist in its view that the Commerce Clause has virtually no limits."[29]

The dissenting justices (Souter, joined by Stevens, Ginsburg, and Breyer), looking at the same Founding history and case law, advanced traditional arguments rooted in democratic theory and institutional competence. *Morrison's* "fundamental defect," they argued, "is the majority's rejection of the Founders' considered judgment that politics, not judicial review, should mediate between state and national interests [in the field of interstate commerce]."[30] The dissenters were surely right in saying that the Violence Against Women Act "would have passed muster between *Wickard* in 1942 and *Lopez* in 1995, a period in which the law enjoyed a stable understanding of congressional power under the Commerce Clause." They went on to question the Court's assertion of "a uniquely judicial competence" in this field, arguing that factual inquiries about the relationship between a regulated activity and interstate commerce are fundamentally the business of Congress, leaving the Court with the sole responsibility of determining the rationality of the ensuing legislation. The dissenters also rebuked the Court for resurrecting the "formalistic distinction" between economic and noneconomic activities and of reviving the notion of traditional and autonomous state spheres of action.

Only one member of the Court stands between the majority and minority views. Accordingly, the fate of the new departure in constitutional doctrine inaugurated by *Lopez* and *Morrison* is likely to depend on the next one or two appointees to the Supreme Court.

---

[27] Ibid., 614.

[28] Ibid., 610.

[29] Ibid., 627.

[30] Ibid., 647.

Taxing and Spending Power

Levying taxes is among government's most awesome powers. In the United States, it even exceeds the reach of the commerce power. The power to regulate commerce, as *Lopez* instructs, must have *some* connection to interstate traffic or activity. The taxing and spending power, by contrast, may touch any object or activity, local or not, so long as the taxes are imposed uniformly throughout the nation and the spending serves the general welfare. In addition to this rule of uniformity, the Constitution prohibits any tax on exports and provides that direct taxes can only be apportioned among the states according to population. The "direct" tax clause was rendered a virtual nullity when the 16th Amendment, ratified in 1913, empowered Congress "to lay and collect taxes on incomes, from whatsoever source, without apportionment among the several States."[31]

Apart from the limits just mentioned, Article I, Section 8, clause 1, confers on Congress the general power "to lay and collect taxes [and] pay the debts and provide for the common defense and general welfare of the United States" (Article I, Section 8). This power has constituted a weapon that rivals the commerce clause in its contribution to the expansion of federal authority in our time. In reviewing the exercise of this power, the Supreme Court would wrestle once again with the perennial tension between democracy and constitutionalism as well as the competing claims of nation and state.

This tension surfaced early on in *Bailey v. Drexel Furniture Company* (1922), which nullifed a federal tax on factories employing children.[32] The question was whether a federal tax could be justified if its effect and purpose were palpably regulatory rather than fiscal. The *Bailey* Court answered in the negative. The main purpose of the statute, said the Court, was not to raise revenue but to stop the employment of children. Additionally, as in *Hammer v. Dagenhart*, the court found that the regulation of employment was a state function within the reservations of the Tenth Amendment.

From 1937 to the present, however, the Court would revert to the spirit of some of its pre-*Bailey* decisions by deferring to Congress' judgment on the need for federal tax legislation. As in *McCray v. United States* (1904),[33] which upheld a federal excise tax on oleomargarine colored like butter, the Court would refuse to inquire into the existence of some hidden regulatory motive. A federal tax statute would be valid if on its face it levied a tax no matter what the degree of its effect in discouraging certain practices or activities. In *United States v. Kahriger* (1953), for example, the Court sustained a federal excise tax on gambling—designed clearly to penalize the business of wagering—because *objectively* it qualified as a tax measure that produced revenue. "Unless there are provisions, extraneous to any tax need," said the Supreme Court, "courts are without authority to limit the exercise of the taxing power." A lawful power could of course be exerted for an unlawful purpose, but "under our constitutional system," as the *McCray* court said, the remedy for such abuses of power lies not with the judiciary but in the people. Interestingly, this perspective lacks judicial support with respect to congressional regulation of interstate commerce.

---

[31] The Sixteenth Amendment was ratified in the aftermath of *Pollock v. Farmer's Loan & Trust Company*, 157 U.S. 429 (1895), which invalidated a federal tax on real estate as an unapportioned direct tax.

[32] 259 U.S. 20 (1922).

[33] 195 U.S. 27 (1904). See also *United States v. Doremus*, 249 U.S. 86 (1919) upholding the Narcotic Drug Act, which imposed a special tax on the manufacture or sale of opium or coca leaves or their derivatives.

Congress, as noted, may tax and spend "for the general welfare." The meaning of the general welfare clause has been vigorously debated ever since James Madison and Alexander Hamilton locked horns over its scope. Madison, taking the narrow view, maintained that the taxing and spending power could only be used to accomplish the specific objectives enumerated in the Constitution. Hamilton, taking the broader view, held that the clause served as an independent source of federal power. In short, Hamilton maintained, Congress could tax and spend for any purpose so long as by doing so it advanced the general welfare. In *United States v. Butler* (1936, reprinted later in the chapter), the Supreme Court accepted Hamilton's expansive view. Still in its pre–New Deal "dual federalist" mode, the *Butler* court struck down Congress' attempt to limit agricultural output by paying farmers to take acreage out of production with funds derived from a tax on food processors. The tax was invalid, ruled the Court, because the money was being spent not for the general welfare but for a local purpose, namely production, wholly within the jurisdiction of the states.

Butler featured the often quoted dissenting opinion of Justice Stone, who reminded his brothers of an important principle of judicial review that he thought the majority had ignored. Courts, he wrote, "are only concerned with the power to enact statutes, not with their wisdom," and that "for the removal of unwise [legislation] appeal lies not to the courts but to the ballot box and to the processes of democratic government." The Court eventually came around to Stone's position. Except for the reservation laid out in *South Dakota v. Dole* (1987), the Court no longer regards the Tenth Amendment as a significant limit on the spending power. In addition, the Court has given up on any independent attempt to define the "general welfare"; contrary to its readiness to mark out the limits of interstate commerce, it defers instead to Congress' determination about what the general welfare includes.

Today the spending power justifies a wide variety of federal programs ranging from highway construction to Medicare and caring for the poor. In fact, Congress has used the spending power to influence the policies and practices of local governments as well as private establishments. Congress does so by attaching conditions to the receipt of federal money. For example, a public or private university may be denied federal funds if it discriminates on the basis of race in any of its programs or activities.[34] Indeed, they may be required to meet specified affirmative action goals in the hiring of women and minorities as a condition for continuing to receive federal funds.

South Dakota v. Dole (1987, reprinted later in the chapter) is one of the most recent challenges to the exercise of the spending power. Here the question was whether Congress could withhold a percentage of the highway funds to which a state would be entitled if the legislature of that state fails to adopt a minimum drinking age law. Thus, the main question before the Court was whether Congress could regulate indirectly through the spending power what it could not regulate directly under its enumerated authority. Chief Justice Rehnquist, writing for the majority, sustained the federal statute because the means chosen to deal with the problem of highway safety "were reasonably calculated to advance the general welfare." The new wrinkle in *Dole* seems to be the Court's willingness, at least at the edges of constitutional legality, to decide for itself what, in fact, advances the general welfare. *Dole* also revived the Tenth Amendment. The opinion made clear, and as Justice O'Connor argued even more forcefully in dissent, that while Congress may use the power of the purse to induce the states to adopt policies they would otherwise reject, it may not compel them to adopt such policies. If they succumb to the allure of

---

[34] See *Bob Jones University v. United States*, 461 U.S. 574 (1983).

federal dollars, they must abide by the conditions Congress imposes. But the states must be left with the option of rejecting federal funding in the interest of their reserved powers.

Additional Congressional Powers

Congress possesses a large number of powers outside of Article I. For example, Article III authorizes Congress to create a system of inferior federal courts; Article IV confers on Congress the power to make rules for territories and property belonging to the United States; Article II empowers the Senate to participate in the important treaty-making process discussed in chapter 5; and the 16th Amendment, as already noted, grants Congress the power to lay and collect taxes on incomes. In addition, various amendments to the Constitution, including the Reconstruction Amendments, empower Congress to enforce their mandates by appropriate legislation. In fact, Congress justified the Violence Against Women Act not only under the authority of the commerce clause, but also as an exercise of its remedial power under Section 5 of the Fourteenth Amendment. Section 5 declares that Congress may "enforce, by appropriate legislation," the constitutional guarantee that no state shall deprive any person of "life, liberty, or property without due process of law." This power constitutes the basis of many federal civil rights laws. But as chapter 14 ("The Equal Protection Clause and Racial Discrimination") points out, the enforcement power of Section 5 applies to *state* conduct and not to purely private activity. *Morrison* rejected the "state action" argument because the law directed its force against private individuals rather than the state. The enforcement provisions of the several amendments to the Constitution nevertheless constitute an awesome reservoir of federal power.

Comparative Perspectives

Since the United States has a federal constitution, common sense dictates that it be compared with other federal systems. In this brief comparative note, we confine our attention to Canada and Germany. The constitutions of these nations divide authority between nation and state and grant the judiciary the authority to resolve conflicts between levels of government. In addition, each constitution includes words and phrases similar to the American commerce clause. Finally, as several of the features in the cases reproduced below show, the content of the commerce power depends as much on judicial interpretation of the text as on the text of the constitution itself.

According to Section 91 of the Canadian Constitution, as shown in Comparative Note 7.1 "the exclusive Legislative Authority of the Parliament of Canada extends to . . . the Regulation of Trade and Commerce."[35] Section 91 lists twenty-eight other subjects or topics over which the national government has exclusive jurisdiction while the provinces enjoy equally exclusive jurisdiction over other specified classes of subjects. The dominion or national government, however, is not confined to its enumerated powers; Parliament is empowered "to make laws for the peace, order, and good government of Canada in relation to all matters not coming . . . [within the exclusive jurisdiction of the] Provinces." Thus, under the Canadian Constitution, unlike the American, the national government is one of reserved powers, whereas the states (provinces) are confined to their delegated powers.

What is so interesting about the Canadian commerce power and other powers—

---

[35] Constitution Act, 1867, Section 91 (2) (formerly, the British North American Act, 1867).

such as the power to raise and spend money—that Section 91 gives the dominion government is that the Canadian founders set out deliberately to correct what they saw as a weakness in the U.S. Constitution—a system of divided power that left too much sovereignty to the states, thus planting the seeds of the Civil War. John Macdonald, often regarded as Canada's Alexander Hamilton, observed that "the primary error at the formation of [the U.S.] constitution was that each state reserved for itself all sovereign rights, save the small portion delegated. We must reverse this process by strengthening the General Government and conferring on the [provinces] only such power as may be required for local purposes."[36] But in an ironic twist of fate, the judiciary of each country read the commerce power of its respective constitution in a way that seemed to contradict the terms of the original text.

Whereas the American Supreme Court turned a strong federal instrument into one possessing unitary features, the Canadian Supreme Court turned the centralizing language of its Constitution into something resembling a dual federalist system. Although in recent decades the Canadian Supreme Court has expanded the meaning of "trade and commerce," it often construes these terms to the advantage of the provinces. Canadian laws dealing with agriculture, fair competition, and food and drug standards that would have been sustained under the American commerce power have been invalidated as *ultra vires* under Canada's trade and commerce power.[37] Another prominent example is the field of labor-management relations, an area judicially seen in Canada as a matter relating to "property and civil rights," subjects within the exclusive jurisdiction of the provinces.[38] The term "trade" in the trade and commerce clause has also been given a narrowing construction; the Court sanctions national legislation that is concerned with trade in general and throughout the country, but not laws that regulate a single trade within a province or even throughout the country. Similarly, the term "regulate," unlike Chief Justice Marshall's broad definition, permits only a *regulatory* scheme overseen by a national regulatory agency. Accordingly, as Comparative Note 7.6 suggests, the power to regulate trade and commerce does not support a national law to discourage an unfair business practice through a civil damage suit brought by a private party. These examples show that, in Canada, provincial rights serve as a significant limit on the national trade and commerce power. By contrast, in the United States—with possibly the single exception of *Lopez*—the reserved power clause of the Tenth Amendment has ceased to be a limit on the national commerce power.

How does one explain the differing constructions of the Canadian and American commerce clauses? By the intent of the framers? We have seen that intent was basically ignored in both countries. By the constitutional text? One could argue that Canada has been more faithful to the constitutional text in as much as it expressly confers on the provinces jurisdiction over "all Matters of a merely local or private Nature in the Province."[39] This provision, however, determines the meaning of trade and

---

[36] Quoted in Alexander Smith, *The Commerce Power in Canada and the United States* (Toronto: Butterworths, 1963), p. 15.

[37] See, for example, federal statutes establishing a grading system for agricultural products in *Dominion Stores v. The Queen*, 1 S.C.R. 844 (1980); setting national standards on the composition and quality of goods in *Labatt Breweries of Can. Ltd. v. A.G. Can*, 1 S.C.R. 914 (1980); and regulating unfair business practices and providing a civil remedy for engaging in such practice in *McDonald v. Vapor Canada*, 2 S.C.R. 134 (1977).

[38] See *Northern Telecom Ltd. v. Communications Workers of Canada*, 1 S.C.R. 115 (1980). National power over employee-employer relations extends only to those industries or enterprises—e.g., banks, inland fisheries, and the postal service—falling within the dominion's exclusive jurisdiction.

[39] Can. Const. Act, 1967, sec. 92 (16).

commerce no more or no less than any other subject contained within the sphere of provincial powers. Consider whether the different doctrinal approaches of the two tribunals simply represent pragmatic judgments about how to balance state and federal authority. Are their respective doctrinal formulations driven by independent judicial images of how a federal system ought to operate? Such images, however, are not fixed in time or space, and even on the same tribunal the judicial image is rarely unanimous. Just as American dissenting opinions offer highly federalized views of the nation-state relationship, Canadian dissenting opinions offer highly centralized views of that relationship, perhaps suggesting far more indeterminacy in constitutional interpretation than many textualists would be willing to admit.

In recent years, Canada has made some attempts to move away from its version of "dual federalism." The Charlottetown Agreement (1992), for example, included a passage committing Canada to the preservation and development of its social and economic union. This provision might have given new life to the trade and commerce clause, especially when viewed in light of Section 121 of the Constitution Act of 1867, which provides for a common market. (Section 121 reads: "All Articles of Growth, Produce, or Manufacture of any one of the Provinces shall, from and after the Union, be admitted free into each of the other Provinces.") Two years earlier, Justice La Forest of the Canadian Supreme Court wrote, "The concept of Canada as a single country comprising what one would now call a common market was basic to the [original] Confederation arrangements, and the drafters of the *British North American Act* attempted to pull down the existing internal barriers that restricted movement within the country."[40] Canadians, however, rejected the Charlottetown Agreement in a national referendum and, as one Canadian scholar notes, "the full impact of s. 121 on presently existing trade barriers, and its relation to the Trade and Commerce power has yet to be developed by the courts."[41]

In Germany's Basic Law, we find that there is no general commerce power as in the United States and Canadian constitutions, but rather a catalogue of subjects that embrace activities such as transportation, labor relations, and the marketing of food, drink, and tobacco. Perhaps the advantage of a twentieth-century constitution such as the Basic Law is that it specifies those subjects and activities of commerce that the national government is empowered to regulate, either exclusively or concurrently. These subjects include telecommunications, federal railroads, labor relations, agricultural production, air transportation, the free movement and exchange of goods, the production and utilization of nuclear energy, the construction and maintenance of long distance highways, and economic matters relating to mining, industry, crafts, commerce, banking, stock exchanges, and private insurance. While these terms require interpretation no less than the more general words and phrases of the Basic Law, the textual detail seems to provide the Constitutional Court with more guidance in defining the nature and scope of national power than does the American or Canadian constitution.

The prolixity of the Basic Law may account for the highly active judicial role, as noted in chapter 6, in defining the boundary between national and state authority. Because the national government enjoys such a monopoly of policymaking power, the Federal Constitutional Court seems determined to protect and fortify those powers that have been reserved to the states. For example, in one of its most notable decisions, the Court declared unconstitutional the creation of a national television

---

[40] *Black v. Law Society of Alberta*, 1 S.C.R. 591, at 609 (1989).

[41] Joseph Eliot Magnet, *Constitutional Law of Canada* (Cowansville, Quebec: Yvon Blais Inc., 1993), 304.

station because it invaded the states' reserved power over cultural affairs, notwithstanding the national government's exclusive jurisdiction over "telecommunications." As one observer of the Constitutional Court has noted, "the German approach contrast sharply with Justice Stone's familiar insistence that the tenth amendment's reservation to the states of all powers not granted to the federal government was a mere 'truism.'"[42]

In shifting the scene to the power to tax and spend, we find that the Basic Law, like many other modern constitutions and unlike the United States Constitution, devotes numerous provisions to the field of public finance. Most of these provisions are devoted to the apportionment of revenue between the national and state governments. For present purposes, it is sufficient to note that the national government has exclusive authority over export and import taxes. In addition, Article 106 of the Basic Law reserves several tax sources to the national government, among them customs duties, certain excise taxes, and income and corporation surtaxes. As in the United States, tax statutes may be enacted for social purposes not directly related to the production of revenue.

The spending power of the national government, while broad, is nevertheless more limited than in the United States, at least where grants in aid to states and localities are concerned. In the *Financial Subsidies Case* (1976), for example, the Court reviewed Bavaria's complaint that an urban renewal program interfered with the state's autonomy. Summarizing this and another constitutional case, David P. Currie writes:

> . . . [I]n order to preserve state autonomy, the Court continued, implementation of the grant program must be left essentially to the states. The Federation might spend money to rebuild cities, but the Länder [states] must be free to determine where and how to do it. Since the urban renewal law could be construed to leave the choice of individual projects principally to the states, it was upheld; a second program that did not meet this requirement was struck down the next year. Thus, unlike the modern Supreme Court, the German court polices federal spending to prevent usurpation of state or local authority by the attachment of conditions to the enjoyment of largesse.[43]

The relative activism of Germany's Federal Constitutional Court in this field also contrasts with the Supreme Court's relatively restrained position in *South Dakota v. Dole* (1987). It is probable that *Dole*, like *Garcia v. San Antonio Metropolitan Transit Authority* (1985) would have been decided differently in the hands of the Federal Constitutional Court.

Selected Bibliography

Barber, Sotirios. National League of Cities v. Usery: *New Meaning for the Tenth Amendment.* 1976 Supreme Court Review 161 (1977).

Choper, Jesse H. *Judicial Review and the National Political-Process: A Functional Reconsideration of the Role of the Supreme Court.* Chicago: University of Chicago Press, 1980.

[42] David P. Currie, *The Constitution of the Federal Republic of Germany* (Chicago: University of Chicago Press, 1994), 38.

[43] Ibid., 58.

Corwin, Edward S. "The Passing of Dual Federalism." In Robert G. McCloskey, ed., *Essays in Constitutional Law.* New York: Vintage, 1957.

———. *The Commerce Power Versus States Rights.* Princeton, N.J.: Princeton University Press, 1936.

Epstein, Richard A. *The Proper Scope of the Commerce Power,* 73 Virginia Law Review 1387 (1987).

The Federalist, Nos. 30–36, 41–42, 56.

Frankfurter, Felix. *The Commerce Clause Under Marshall, Taney, and Waite.* Chapel Hill, N.C.: University of North Carolina Press, 1937.

Hovenkamp, Herbert. *Judicial Restraint and Constitutional Federalism.* 96 Columbia Law Review 2213 (1996).

Kramer, Larry. *Putting the Politics Back Into the Political Safeguards of Federalism.* 100 Columbia Law Review 215 (2000).

MacDonald, Vincent C. *The Constitution in a Changing World,* 26 Canadian Bar Review 21 (1948).

McCoy, Thomas R., and Barry Friedmann. *Conditional Spending: Federalism's Trojan Horse,* 1988 Supreme Court Review 85–128 (1988).

Michelman, Frank J. *States' Rights and States' Roles: the Permutations of Sovereignty in National League of Cities v. Usery.* 86 Yale Law Journal 1165 (1977).

Noonan, John T., Jr. *Narrowing the Nation's Power.* Berkeley: University of California Press, 2002.

Rosenthal, Albert J. Constitutional Federal Spending and the Constitution. 39 *Stanford Law Review* 1103 (1987)

Smith, Stephen. *State Autonomy After Garcia: Will the Political Process Protect States' Interests?* 71 Iowa Law Review 1527 (1986).

Symposium: Major Issues in Federalism. 38 Arizona Law Review 793 (1996).

Van Alystyne, William. *Federalism, Congress, the States and the Tenth Amendment: Adrift in the Cellophane Sea.* 1987 Duke Law Journal 769 (1987).

Selected Comparative Bibliography

Blair, Philip M. *Federalism and Judicial Review in West Germany.* Oxford: Clarendon Press, 1981.

Cairns, Alan C. *Charter versus Federalism: The Dilemmas of Constitutional Reform.* Montreal: McGill-Queen's University Press, 1992.

Jeffery, Charlie (ed.). *Recasting German Federalism: The Legacies of Unification.* London: Pinter, 1999.

Jeffery, Charlie and Savigear, Peter. *German Federalism Today.* New York: St. Martin's Press, 1991.

Goldstein, Leslie Friedman. *Constituting Federal Sovereignty.* Baltimore: The Johns Hopkins University Press, 2001.

McWhinney, Edward et al. *Federalism-in-the-Making: Contemporary Canadian and German Constitutionalism.* Dordrecht: Kluwer Academic Publishers, 1992.

Smith, Alexander. *The Commerce Power in Canada and the United States.* Toronto: Butterworth & Co. Ltd., 1963.

Gibbons v. Ogden

22 U.S. (9 Wheat.) 1, 6 L. Ed. 23 (1824)

In 1808 Robert Fulton and Robert R. Livingston, pioneers in the development of the steamboat, received from the New York legislature an exclusive right to operate steamboats on the state's streams and waters. Later Aron Ogden secured from Fulton and Livingston the exclusive right to engage in steam navigation across the Hudson River between New York and New Jersey. Thomas Gibbons, however, was navigating a steamboat of his own on the same waters with a license secured under the Federal Coasting Act of 1893. Ogden sued Gibbons under the steamboat monopoly law. The New York courts upheld Ogden's claim and the New York statute. Opinion of the Court: *Marshall,* Todd, Duval, Story, Thompson. Concurring opinion: *Johnson.*

Mr. Chief Justice MARSHALL delivered the opinion of the Court.

The state of New York maintains the constitutionality of these laws; and their legislature, their council of revision, and their judges, have repeatedly concurred in this opinion. It is supported by great names—by names which have all the titles to consideration that virtue, intelligence and office can bestow. No tribunal can approach the decision of this question without feeling a just and real respect for that opinion which is sustained by such authority; but it is the province of this court, while it respects, not to bow to it implicitly; and the judges must exercise, in the examination of the subject, that understanding which Providence has bestowed upon them, with that independence which the people of the United States expect from this department of the government.

As preliminary to the very able discussions of the constitution, which we have heard from the bar, and as having some influence on its construction, reference has been made to the political situation of these States, anterior to its formation. It has been said, that they were sovereign, were completely independent, and were connected with each other only by a league. This is true. But, when these allied sovereigns converted their league into a government, when they converted their Congress of Ambassadors, deputed to deliberate on their common concerns, and to recommend measures of general utility, into a Legislature, empowered to enact laws on the most interesting

Comparative Note 7.1

U.S. Constitution, Art. I, Sec. 8, cl. 3

The Congress shall have the power to regulate commerce . . . among the several states.

Commonwealth of Australia Constitution Act (1900)

Sec. 51. The Parliament shall . . . have power to make laws for the peace, order, and good government of the Commonwealth with respect to:

(i) Trade and commerce with other countries, and among the States . . .

(ii) Taxation; but so as not to discriminate between states or parts of states.

Sec. 92. On the imposition of uniform duties of customs, trade, commerce, and intercourse among the states, whether by means of internal carriage or ocean navigation, shall be absolutely free. . . .

Constitution Act, 1867 (Canada)

Sec. 91 . . . . [E]xclusive legislative authority of the Parliament of Canada extends to all matters coming within the classes of subjects next hereinafter enumerated; that is to say . . . 2. The regulation of trade and commerce.

Basic Law of Germany

Art. 73. The Federation shall have exclusive power in respect of: . . .

5. unity of customs and trading area [and] free movement of goods, . . .

6. air transport;

6a. the operation of railways wholly or majority-owned by the Federation, the construction, maintenance and operation of the infrastructure of the federal railways . . .

Art. 74. The Federation shall have concurrent legislative power over . . .

11. economic affairs (mining, industry, energy, crafts, trades, commerce, banking, the stock exchange system and private insurance);

12. labor relations, including . . . industrial safety . . . as well as social security and unemployment insurance . . .

16. measures to prevent abuse of economic power;

17. promotion of agricultural production and forestry; . . .

22. road traffic, motor transport, construction and maintenance of roads for long-distance traffic. . . .

---

subjects, the whole character in which the States appear, underwent a change, the extent of which must be determined by a fair consideration of the instrument by which that change was effected.

This instrument contains an enumeration of powers expressly granted by the people to their government. It has been said, that these powers ought to be construed strictly. But why ought they to be so construed? Is there one sentence in the constitution which gives countenance to this rule? In the last of the enumerated powers, that which grants, expressly, the means for carrying all others into execution, Congress is authorized "to make all laws which shall be necessary and proper" for the purpose. But this limitation on the means which may be used, is not extended to the powers which are conferred; nor is there one sentence in the constitution, which has been pointed out by the gentlemen of the bar, or which we have been able to discern, that prescribes this rule. We do not, therefore, think ourselves justified in adopting it. What do gentlemen mean, by a strict construction? If they contend only

against that enlarged construction, which would extend words beyond their natural and obvious import, we might question the application of the term, but should not controvert the principle. If they contend for that narrow construction which, in support of some theory not to be found in the constitution, would deny to the government those powers which the words of the grant, as usually understood, import, and which are consistent with the general views and objects of the instrument; for that narrow construction, which would cripple the government, and render it unequal to the object for which it is declared to be instituted, and to which the powers given, as fairly understood, render it competent; then we cannot perceive the propriety of this strict construction, nor adopt it as the rule by which the constitution is to be expounded. . . .

The words are, "Congress shall have power to regulate commerce with foreign nations, and among the several States, and with the Indian tribes."

The subject to be regulated is commerce; and our constitution being, as was aptly said at the bar, one of enumeration, and not of definition, to ascertain the extent of the power, it becomes necessary to settle the meaning of the word. The counsel for the appellee would limit it to traffic, to buying and selling, or the interchange of commodities, and do not admit that it comprehends navigation. This would restrict a general term, applicable to many objects, to one of its significations. Commerce, undoubted, is traffic, but it is something more: it is intercourse. It describes the commercial intercourse between nations, and parts of nations, in all its branches, and is regulated by prescribing rules for carrying on that intercourse. The mind can scarcely conceive a system for regulating commerce between nations, which shall exclude all laws concerning navigation, which shall be silent on the admission of the vessels of the one nation into the ports of the other, and be confined to prescribing rules for the conduct of individuals, in the actual employment of buying and selling, or of barter.

If commerce does not include navigation, the government of the Union has no direct power over that subject, and can make no law prescribing what shall constitute American vessels, or requiring that they shall be navigated by American seamen. Yet this power has been exercised from the commencement of the government, has been exercised with the consent of all, and has been understood by all to be a commercial regulation. All America understands, and has uniformly understood, the word "commerce," to comprehend navigation. It was so understood, and must have been so understood, when the constitution was framed. The power over commerce, including navigation, was one of the primary objects for which the people of America adopted their government, and must have been contemplated in forming it. The convention must have used the word in that sense, because all have understood it in that sense; and the attempt to restrict it comes too late.

The word used in the constitution, then, comprehends, and has been always understood to comprehend, navigation within its meaning; and a power to regulate navigation, is as expressly granted, as if that term had been added to the word "commerce." To what commerce does this power extend? The constitution informs us, to commerce "with foreign nations, and among the several States, and with the Indian tribes." It has, we believe, been universally admitted, that these words comprehend every species of commercial intercourse between the United States and foreign nations. No sort of trade can be carried on between this country and any other, to which this power does not extend. . . .

If this be the admitted meaning of the word, in its application to foreign nations, it must carry the same meaning throughout the sentence, and remain a unit, unless there be some plain intelligible cause which alters it. The subject to which the power is next applied, is to commerce "among the several States." The word "among" means intermingled with. A thing which is among others, is intermingled with them. Commerce among the States, cannot stop at the external boundary line of each State, but may be introduced into the interior. It is not intended to say that these words comprehend that commerce, which is completely internal, which is carried on between man and man in a State, or between different parts of the same State, and which does not extend to or affect other States. Such a power would be inconvenient, and is certainly unnecessary.

Comprehensive as the word "among" is, it may very properly be restricted to that commerce which concerns more States than one. The phrase is not one which would probably have been selected to indicate the completely interior traffic of a State, because it is not an apt phrase for that purpose; and the enumeration of the particular classes of commerce, to which the power was to be extended, would not have been made, had the intention been to extend the power to every description. The enumeration presupposes something not enumerated; and that something, if we regard the language or the subject of the sentence, must be the exclusively internal commerce of a State. The genius and character of the whole government seem to be, that its action is to be applied to all the external concerns of the nation, and to those internal concerns which affect the States generally; but not to those which are completely within a particular state, which do not affect other states, and with which it is not necessary to interfere, for the purpose of executing some of the general powers of the government. The completely internal commerce of a State, then, may be considered as reserved for the State itself.

But, in regulating commerce with foreign nations, the power of Congress does not stop at the jurisdictional lines of the several States. It would be a very useless power, if it could not pass those lines. The commerce of the United States with foreign nations, is that of the whole United States. Every district has a right to participate in it. The deep streams which penetrate our country in every direction, pass through the interior of almost every State in the Union, and furnish the means of exercising this right. If Congress has the power to regulate it, that power must be exercised whenever the subject exists. If it exists within the States, if a foreign voyage may commence or terminate at a port within a State, then the power of Congress may be exercised within a State.

This principle is, if possible, still more clear, when applied to commerce "among the several States." They either join each other, in which case they are separated by a mathematical line, or they are remote from each other, in which case other States lie between them. What is commerce "among" them; and how is it to be conducted? Can a trading expedition between two adjoining States, commence and terminate outside of each? And if the trading intercourse be between two States remote from each other, must it not commence in one, terminate in the other, and probably pass through a third? . . . The power of Congress, then, whatever it may be, must be exercised within the territorial jurisdiction of the several States. . . .

We are now arrived at the inquiry—What is this power? It is the power to regulate; that is, to prescribe the rule by which commerce is to be governed. This power, like all others vested in Congress, is complete in itself, may be exercised to its utmost extent, and acknowledges no limitations, other than are prescribed in the constitution. These are expressed in plain terms, and do not affect the questions which arise in this case, or which have been discussed at the bar. If, as has always been understood, the sovereignty of Congress, though limited to specified objects, is plenary as to those objects, the power over commerce with foreign nations, and among the several States, is vested in Congress as absolutely as it would be in a single government, having in its constitution the same restrictions on the exercise of the power as are found in the constitution of the United States. The wisdom and the discretion of Congress, their identity with the people, and the influence which their constituents possess at elections, are, in this, as in many other instances, as that, for example, of declaring war, the sole restraints on which they have relied, to secure them from its abuse. They are the restraints on which the people must often rely solely, in all representative governments.

But it has been urged with great earnestness, that, although the power of Congress to regulate commerce with foreign nations, and among the several States, be co-extensive with the subject itself, and have no other limits than are prescribed in the constitution, yet the States may severally exercise the same power, within their respective jurisdictions. . . .

The grant of the power to lay and collect taxes is, like the power to regulate commerce, made in general terms, and has never been understood to interfere with the exercise of the same power by the State; and hence has been drawn an argument which has been applied to the question under consideration. But the two grants are not, it is conceived, similar in their terms or their nature. Although many of the powers formerly exercised by the States, are transferred to the government of the Union, yet the State

governments remain, and constitute a most important part of our system. The power of taxation is indispensable to their existence, and is a power which, in its own nature, is capable of residing in, and being exercised by, different authorities at the same time. We are accustomed to see it placed, for different purposes, in different hands. Taxation is the simple operation of taking small portions from a perpetually accumulating mass, susceptible of almost infinite division; and a power in one to take what is necessary for certain purposes, is not, in its nature, incompatible with a power in another to take what is necessary for other purposes. Congress is authorized to lay and collect taxes, to pay the debts, and provide for the common defence and general welfare of the United States. This does not interfere with the power of the States to tax for the support of their own governments; nor is the exercise of that power by the States, an exercise of any portion of the power that is granted to the United States. In imposing taxes for State purposes, they are not doing what Congress is empowered to do. Congress is not empowered to tax for those purposes which are within the exclusive province of the States. When, then, each government exercises the power of taxation, neither is exercising the power of the other. But, when a State proceeds to regulate commerce with foreign nations, or among the several States, it is exercising the very power that is granted to Congress, and is doing the very thing which Congress is authorized to do. There is no analogy, then, between the power of taxation and the power of regulating commerce.

In discussing the question, whether this power is still in the States, in the case under consideration, we may dismiss from it the inquiry, whether it is surrendered by the mere grant to Congress, or is retained until Congress shall exercise the power. We may dismiss that inquiry, because it has been exercised, and the regulations which Congress deemed it proper to make, are now in full operation. The sole question is, can a State regulate commerce with foreign nations and among the States, while Congress is regulating it?

But, the inspection laws are said to be regulations of commerce, and are certainly recognised in the constitution, as being passed in the exercise of a power remaining with the States. That inspection laws may have a remote and considerable influence on commerce, will not be denied; but that a power to regulate commerce is the source from which the right to pass them is derived, cannot be admitted. The object of inspection laws, is to improve the quality of articles produced by the labour of a country; to fit them for exportation; or, it may be, for domestic use. They act upon the subject before it becomes an article of foreign commerce, or of commerce among the States, and prepare it for that purpose. They form a portion of that immense mass of legislation, which embraces every thing within the territory of a State, not surrendered to the general government: all which can be most advantageously exercised by the States themselves. Inspection laws, quarantine laws, health laws of every description, as well as laws for regulating the internal commerce of a State, and those which respect turnpike roads, ferries [and so forth] are component parts of this mass.

No direct general power over these objects is granted to Congress; and, consequently, they remain subject to State legislation. If the legislative power of the Union can reach them, it must be for national purposes; it must be where the power is expressly given for a special purpose, or is clearly incidental to some power which is expressly given. It is obvious, that the government of the Union, in the exercise of its express powers, that, for example, of regulating commerce with foreign nations and among the States, may use means that may also be employed by a State, in the exercise of its acknowledged powers; that, for example, of regulating commerce within the State. . . .

In our complex system, presenting the rare and difficult scheme of one general government, whose action extends over the whole, but which possesses only certain enumerated powers; and of numerous state governments, which retain and exercise all powers not delegated to the Union, contests respecting power must arise. Were it even otherwise, the measures taken by the respective governments to execute their acknowledged powers, would often be of the same description, and might, sometimes, interfere. This, however, does not prove that the one is exercising, or has a right to exercise, the powers of the other.

Since, however, in exercising the power of regulating their own purely internal affairs, whether of trading or police, the States may sometimes enact laws, the validity of which depends on their interfering with, and being contrary to, an act of Congress passed in pursuance of the constitution, the Court will enter upon the inquiry, whether the laws of New York, as expounded by the highest tribunal of that State, have, in their application to this case, come into collision with an act of Congress, and deprived a citizen of a right to which that act entitles him. Should this collision exist, it will be immaterial whether those laws were passed in virtue of a concurrent power "to regulate commerce with foreign nations and among the several States," or, in virtue of a power to regulate their domestic trade and police. In one case and the other, the acts of New York must yield to the law of Congress; and the decision sustaining the privilege they confer, against a right given by a law of the Union, must be erroneous.

This opinion has been frequently expressed in this Court, and is founded, as well on the nature of the government as on the words of the constitution. In argument, however, it has been contended, that if a law passed by a State, in the exercise of its acknowledged sovereignty, comes into conflict with a law passed by Congress in pursuance of the constitution, they affect the subject, and each other, like equal opposing powers.

But the framers of our constitution foresaw this state of things, and provided for it, by declaring the supremacy not only of itself, but of the laws made in pursuance of it. The nullity of any act, inconsistent with the constitution, is produced by the declaration, that the constitution is the supreme law. The appropriate application of that part of the clause which confers the same supremacy on laws and treaties, is to such acts of the State Legislatures as do not transcend their powers, but, though enacted in the execution of acknowledged State powers, interfere with, or are contrary to the laws of Congress, made in pursuance of the constitution, or some treaty made under the authority of the United States. In every such case, the act of Congress, or the treaty, is supreme; and the law of the State, though enacted in the exercise of powers not controverted, must yield to it. . . .

But all inquiry into this subject seems to the Court to be put completely at rest, by the act already mentioned, entitled, "An act for the enrolling and licensing of steam boats."

This act authorizes a steam boat employed, or intended to be employed, only in a river or bay of the United States, owned wholly or in part by an alien, resident within the United States, to be enrolled and licensed as if the same belonged to a citizen of the United States.

This act demonstrates the opinion of Congress, that steam boats may be enrolled and licensed, in common with vessels using sails. They are, of course, entitled to the same privileges, and can no more be restrained from navigating waters, and entering ports which are free to such vessels, than if they were wafted on their voyage by the winds, instead of being propelled by the agency of fire. The one element may be as legitimately used as the other, for every commercial purpose authorized by the laws of the Union; and the act of a State inhibiting the use of either to any vessel having a license under the act of Congress, comes, we think, in direct collision with that act.

Mr. Justice JOHNSON, concurring.

In attempts to construe the constitution, I have never found much benefit resulting from the inquiry, whether the whole; or any part of it, is to be construed strictly or liberally. The simple, classical, precise, yet comprehensive language in which it is couched, leaves, at most, but very little latitude for construction; and when its intent and meaning are discovered, nothing remains but to execute the will of those who made it, in the best manner to effect the purposes intended. The great and paramount purpose was, to unite the mass of wealth and power, for the protection of the humblest individual; his rights, civil and political, his interests and prosperity, are the sole end; the rest are nothing but the means. . . .

The history of the times will . . . sustain the opinion, that the grant of power over commerce, if intended to be commensurate with the evils existing, and the purpose of remedying those evils, could be only commensurate with the power of the states over the subject. . . .

. . . But what was that power? The states were, unquestionably, supreme; and each possessed that power over commerce, which is acknowledged to reside in every sovereign state. . . . The power of a sovereign state over commerce, therefore, amounts to nothing more than a power to limit and restrain it at pleasure. And since the power to prescribe the limits to its freedom, necessarily implies the power to determine what shall remain unrestrained, it follows, that the power must be exclusive: it can reside but in one potentate; and hence, the grant of power carries with it the whole subject, leaving nothing for the state to act upon.

Notes and Queries

1. In chapter 2 we described the competing approaches to constitutional interpretation, such as originalism, textu-alism, structuralism, and prudentialism. Which of these approaches does Marshall follow in *Gibbons?* Is this case really a debate over the meaning of the words in the Constitution or is some larger value or theory at work here?

2. Consult the constitutional provisions of the four federal systems in Comparative Note 7.1. Would Marshall have had an easier time justifying the result in *Gibbons* under the foreign constitutions? What does Marshall's opinion say about the determinacy or indeterminacy of a constitutional text?

3. What limits, if any, does Marshall impose on Congress' power to regulate commerce? Are they similar to—or different from—the limits on federal power articulated in *McCulloch* (chapter 6)?

4. How does Justice Johnson's analysis of federal power under the commerce clause differ from Marshall's? Whose opinion is the most persuasive? Does Marshall's vision of the national political community differ from Johnson's? In what way?

5. The Court wrote that the definition of the word "commerce" must include navigation because it was so understood when the Constitution was written. Does this appeal to original understanding sufficiently account for the great commercial and industrial change that had occurred between the framing and 1824, when *Gibbons* was decided?

6. The Court also wrote that "all America understands, and has uniformly understood, the word 'commerce,' to comprehend navigation." Should the definition of constitutional terms depend upon popular understanding of those terms? Why or why not?

United States v. E. C. Knight Co. et al.

156 U.S. 1, 15 S. Ct. 249, 39 L. Ed. 325 (1895)

The American Sugar Refining Company, which purchased the stock of E. C. Knight and three other companies in Philadelphia, obtained control over the bulk of the nation's sugar refining business. The U.S. government sued E. C. Knight and the other companies for violating the Sherman Antitrust Act of 1890. The act made it illegal to monopolize or restrain interstate commerce by means of any contract, combination, or conspiracy. The lower federal courts refused to cancel the agreements, holding that the activity engaged in by the companies did not constitute interstate commerce. The Supreme Court did not strike the statute, but interpreted its reach narrowly so as to save it. Opinion of the Court: *Fuller*, Field, Gray, Brewer, Brown, Shiras, White, Peckham. Dissenting opinion: *Harlan.*

Mr. Chief Justice FULLER delivered the opinion of the Court.

The fundamental question is whether, conceding that the existence of a monopoly in manufacture is established by the evidence, that monopoly can be directly suppressed under the act of congress in the mode attempted by this bill.

It cannot be denied that the power of a state to protect the lives, health, and property of its citizens, and to preserve good order and the public morals, "the power to govern men and things within the limits of its dominion," is a power originally and always belonging to the States, not surrendered by them to the general government, nor directly restrained by the constitution of the United States, and essentially exclusive. . . . The constitution does not

Comparative Note 7.2

[In this case Chief Justice Dixon handed down an influential opinion interpreting Sec. 51 (I) of the Australian Constitution. For the text of Sec. 51 (I) see Comparative Note 7.1.]

The distinction which is drawn between inter-State trade and domestic trade of a State for the purpose of the power conferred upon the Parliament by s. 51 (1) to make laws with respect to trade and commerce with other countries and among the States may well be considered artificial and unsuitable to modern times. But it is a distinction adopted by the Constitution and it must be observed however much inter-dependency may

now exist between the two divisions of trade and commerce which the Constitution thus distinguishes. A legislative power, however, with respect to any subject matter contains within itself authority over whatever is incidental to the subject matter of the power and enables the legislature to include within laws made in pursuance of the power provisions which can only be justified as ancillary or incidental. But even in the application of this principle . . . the distinction which the Constitution makes between the two branches of trade and commerce must be maintained.

SOURCE: *Wragg v. South Wales* (1953), 88 C.L.R. 353.

provide that interstate commerce shall be free, but, by the grant of this exclusive power to regulate it, it was left free, except as congress might impose restraints. Therefore it has been determined that the failure of congress to exercise this exclusive power in any case is an expression of its will that the subject shall be free from restrictions or impositions upon it by the several States, and if a law passed by a State in the exercise of its acknowledged powers comes into conflict with that will, the congress and the state cannot occupy the position of equal opposing sovereignties, because the constitution declares its supremacy, and that of the laws passed in pursuance thereof; and that which is not supreme must yield to that which is supreme. . . . That which belongs to commerce is within the jurisdiction of the United States, but that which does not belong to commerce is within the jurisdiction of the police power of the State.

The argument is that the power to control the manufacture of refined sugar is a monopoly over a necessary of life, to the enjoyment of which by a large part of the population of the United States interstate commerce is indispensable, and that, therefore, the general government, in the exercise of the power to regulate commerce, may repress such monopoly directly, and set aside the instruments which have created it. But this argument cannot be confined to necessaries of life merely, and must include all articles of general consumption. Doubtless the power to control the manufacture of a given thing involves, in a certain sense, the control of its disposition, but this is a secondary, and not the primary, sense; and, although the exercise of that power may result in bringing the operation of commerce into play, it does not control it, and af-

fects it only incidentally and indirectly. Commerce succeeds to manufacture, and is not a part of it. The power to regulate commerce is the power to prescribe the rule by which commerce shall be governed, and is a power independent of the power to suppress monopoly. But it may operate in repression of monopoly whenever that comes within the rules by which commerce is governed, or whenever the transaction is itself a monopoly of commerce.

It is vital that the independence of the commercial power and of the police power, and the delimitation between them, however sometimes perplexing, should always be recognized and observed, for, while the one furnishes the strongest bond of union, the other is essential to the preservation of the autonomy of the States as required by our dual form of government; and acknowledged evils, however grave and urgent they may appear to be, had better be borne, than the risk be run, in the effort to suppress them, of more serious consequences by resort to expedients of even doubtful constitutionality.

It will be perceived how far-reaching the proposition is that the power of dealing with a monopoly directly may be exercised by the general government whenever interstate or international commerce may be ultimately affected. The regulation of commerce applies to the subjects of commerce, and not to matters of internal police. Contracts to buy, sell, or exchange goods to be transported among the several States, the transportation and its instrumentalities, and articles bought, sold, or exchanged for the purposes of such transit among the States, or put in the way of transit, may be regulated; but this is because they form part of interstate trade or commerce. The fact that an article is manufactured for export to another State does not of itself make it an article of interstate commerce, and the intent of the manufacturer does not determine the time when the article or product passes from the control of the State and belongs to commerce. . . .

Contracts, combinations, or conspiracies to control domestic enterprise in manufacture, agriculture, mining, production in all its forms, or to raise or lower prices or wages, might unquestionably tend to restrain external as well as domestic trade, but the restraint would be an indirect result, however inevitable, and whatever its extent, and such result would not necessarily determine the object of the contract, combination, or conspiracy.

. . . Slight reflection will show that, if the national power extends to all contracts and combinations in manufacture, agriculture, mining, and other productive industries, whose ultimate result may affect external commerce, comparatively little of business operations and affairs would be left for state control.

It was in the light of well-settled principles that the act of July 2, 1890, was framed. Congress did not attempt thereby to assert the power to deal with monopoly directly as such. . . . [W]hat the law struck at was combinations, contracts, and conspiracies to monopolize trade and commerce among the several States or with foreign nations; but the contracts and acts of the defendants related exclusively to the acquisition of the Philadelphia refineries and the business of sugar refining in Pennsylvania, and bore no direct relation to commerce between the States or with foreign nations. The object was manifestly private gain in the manufacture of the commodity, but not through control of interstate or foreign commerce. It is true that the bill alleged that the products of these refineries were sold and distributed among the several states, and that all the companies were engaged in trade or commerce with the several states and with foreign nations; but this was no more than to say that trade and commerce served manufacture to fulfill its function. Sugar was refined for sale, and sales were probably made at Philadelphia for consumption, and undoubtedly for resale by the first purchasers throughout Pennsylvania and other states, and refined sugar was also forwarded by the companies to other states for sale. Nevertheless it does not follow that an attempt to monopolize, or the actual monopoly of, the manufacture was an attempt, whether executory or consummated, to monopolize commerce, even though, in order to dispose of the product, the instrumentality of commerce was necessarily invoked. There was nothing in the proofs to indicate any intention to put a restraint upon trade or commerce, and the fact, as we have seen, that trade or commerce might be indirectly affected, was not enough to entitle complainants to a decree. . . .

Decree affirmed.

Mr. Justice HARLAN, dissenting.

The court holds it to be vital in our system of government to recognize and give effect to both the commercial power of the nation and the police powers of the States, to the end that the Union be strengthened, and the autonomy of the States preserved. In this view I entirely concur. Undoubtedly, the preservation of the just authority of the States is an object of deep concern to every lover of his country. No greater calamity could befall our free institutions than the destruction of that authority, by whatever means such a result might be accomplished. . . . But it is equally true that the preservation of the just authority of the general government is essential as well to the safety of the States as to the attainment of the important ends for which that government was ordained by the people of the United States; and the destruction of *that* authority would be fatal to the peace and well-being of the American people. The Constitution, which enumerates the powers committed to the nation for objects of interest to the people of all the states, should not, therefore, be subjected to an interpretation so rigid, technical, and narrow that those objects cannot be accomplished. . . .

Congress is invested with power to regulate commerce with foreign nations and among the several states. . . . It is the settled doctrine of this court that interstate commerce embraces something more than the mere physical transportation of articles of property, and the vehicles or vessels by which such transportation is effected. . . . It includes the purchase and sale of articles that are intended to be transported from one state to another,—every species of commercial intercourse among the states and with foreign nations.

If it be true that a *combination* of corporations or individuals may, so far as the power of congress is concerned, subject interstate trade, in any of its stages, to unlawful restraints, the conclusion is inevitable that the Constitution has failed to accomplish one primary object of the Union, which was to place commerce *among the States* under the control of the common government of all the people, and thereby relieve or protect it against burdens or restrictions imposed, by whatever authority, for the benefit of particular localities or special interests.

The fundamental inquiry in this case is, what, in a legal sense, is an unlawful restraint of trade? . . .

In my judgment, the citizens of the several States composing the Union are entitled of right to buy goods in the State where they are manufactured, or in any other State, without being confronted by an illegal combination whose business extends throughout the whole country, which, by the law everywhere, is an enemy to the public interests, and which prevents such buying, except at prices arbitrarily fixed by it. . . . Whatever improperly obstructs the free course of interstate intercourse and trade, as involved in the buying and selling of articles to be carried from one State to another, may be reached by Congress under its authority to regulate commerce among the states. The exercise of that authority so as to make trade among the states in all recognized articles of commerce absolutely free from unreasonable or illegal restrictions imposed by combinations is justified by an express grant of power to congress, and would redound to the welfare of the whole country. I am unable to perceive that any such result would imperil the autonomy of the states, especially as that result cannot be attained through the action of any one State.

Notes and Queries

1. Chief Justice Fuller wrote that "Commerce succeeds to manufacture and is not a part of it." Where does this distinction come from? Is it implicit in the definition of commerce? Does Fuller trace it to the intent of the Founders or to the original understanding of the commerce clause? Is it a necessary consequence of the Tenth Amendment or of federalism itself?

2. Is Fuller's argument compatible with Marshall's reasoning in *Gibbons?* (Marshall had acknowledged the state's police power jurisdiction over its internal affairs.)

3. Is Justice Harlan's interpretation of the commmerce clause more firmly based in the Constitution? What does he see as the purpose of the clause? Of the Constitution as a whole? What place would he allow for democratic regulation of individual and corporate property?

4. Should the economic changes that took place in the one hundred years between the ratification of the Constitution and this case influence how the commerce clause should be interpreted? Why or why not?

Champion v. Ames
188 U.S. 321, 23 S. Ct. 321, 47 L. Ed. 492 (1903)

In 1895 Congress passed a statute that prohibited the shipment of lottery tickets in interstate commerce or through the U.S. mail. W. F. Champion was arrested and held for trial in federal district court for having used the Wells-Fargo Express Company to ship a package containing lottery tickets issued by the Pan-American Lottery Company. He then sued out a writ of habeas corpus against a U.S. Marshal on the ground that the act under which he was to be tried was unconstitutional and void. Opinion of the Court: *Harlan*, Holmes, McKenna, White, Brown. Dissenting opinion: *Fuller*, Brewer, Shiras, Peckham.

Mr. Justice HARLAN delivered the opinion of the court.

The appellant insists that the carrying of lottery tickets from one State to another State by an express company engaged in carrying freight and packages from State to State, although such tickets may be contained in a box or package, does not constitute, and cannot by any act of Congress be legally made to constitute, *commerce* among the States within the meaning of the clause of the Constitution of the United States providing that Congress shall have power "to regulate commerce with foreign nations, and among the several states, and with the Indian tribes;" consequently, that Congress cannot make it an offense to cause such tickets to be carried from one State to another.

The Government insists that express companies, when engaged, for hire, in the business of transportation from one State to another, are instrumentalities of commerce among the States; that the carrying of lottery tickets from one State to another is commerce which Congress may regulate; and that as a means of executing the power to regulate interstate commerce Congress may make it an offense against the United States to cause lottery tickets to be carried from one State to another.

The questions presented by these opposing contentions are of great moment, and are entitled to receive, as they have received, the most careful consideration.

What is the import of the word "commerce" as used in the Constitution? It is not defined by that instrument. Undoubtedly, the carrying from one State to another by independent carriers of things or commodities that are ordinary subjects of traffic, and which have in themselves a recognized value in money, constitutes interstate commerce. But does not commerce among the several States include something more? Does not the carrying from one State to another, by independent carriers, of lottery tickets that entitle the holder to the payment of a certain amount of money therein specified also constitute commerce among the States?

The leading case under the commerce clause of the Constitution is *Gibbons v. Ogden* [1824]. Referring to that clause, Chief Justice Marshall said: "The subject to be regulated is commerce; and our Constitution being, as was aptly said at the bar, one of enumeration, and not of definition, to ascertain the extent of the power it becomes necessary to settle the meaning of the word. . . . Commerce, undoubtedly, is traffic, but it is something more; it is intercourse. It describes the commercial intercourse between nations and parts of nations, in all its branches, and is regulated by prescribing rules for carrying on that intercourse. . . ."

Again: "We are now arrived at the inquiry—What is this power? It is the power to regulate; that is, to prescribe the rule by which commerce is to be governed. This power, like all others vested in Congress, is *complete in itself,* may be exercised *to its utmost extent,* and acknowledges *no limitations, other than are prescribed in the Constitution."* . . .

This reference to prior adjudications could be extended if it were necessary to do so. The cases cited . . . show that commerce among the states embraces navigation, intercourse, communication, traffic, the transit of persons, and the transmission of messages by telegraph. They also show that the power to regulate commerce among the several states is vested in Congress as absolutely as it would be in a single government, having in its constitution the same restrictions on the exercise of the power as are found in the Constitution of the United States; that such power is plenary, complete in itself, and may be exerted by Congress to its utmost extent, subject *only* to such limitations as the Constitution imposes upon the exercise of the powers granted by it; and that in determining the character of the regulations to be adopted Congress has a large discretion which is not to be controlled by the courts, simply because, in their opinion, such regulations could be employed.

We come, then, to inquire whether there is any solid foundation upon which to rest the contention that Congress may not regulate the carrying of lottery tickets from one state to another, at least by corporations or companies whose business it is, for hire, to carry tangible property from one State to another. We are of opinion that lottery tickets are subjects of traffic, and therefore are subjects of commerce, and the regulation of the carriage of such tickets from State to State, at least by independent carriers, is a regulation of commerce among the several States. But it is said that the statute in question does not regulate the carrying of lottery tickets from State to State, but by punishing those who cause them to be so carried Congress in effect prohibits such carrying; that in respect of the carrying from one state to another of articles or things that are, in fact, or according to usage in business, the subjects of

commerce, the authority given Congress was not to *prohibit,* but only to *regulate.* . . .

If a State, when considering legislation for the suppression of lotteries within its own limits, may properly take into view the evils that inhere in the raising of money, in that mode, why may not Congress, invested with the power to regulate commerce among the several States, provide that such commerce shall not be polluted by the carrying of lottery tickets from one State to another? In this connection it must not be forgotten that the power of Congress to regulate commerce among the states is plenary, is complete in itself, and is subject to no limitations except such as may be found in the Constitution. What provision in that instrument can be regarded as limiting the exercise of the power granted? . . . If it be said that the act of 1895 is inconsistent with the Tenth Amendment, reserving to the states respectively, or to the people, the powers not delegated to the United States, the answer is that the power to regulate commerce among the states has been expressly delegated to Congress.

Besides, Congress, by that act, does not assume to interfere with traffic or commerce in lottery tickets carried on exclusively within the limits of any State, but has in view only commerce of that kind among the several States. It has not assumed to interfere with the completely internal affairs of any State, and has only legislated in respect of a matter which concerns the people of the United States. As a State may, for the purpose of guarding the morals of its own people, forbid all sales of lottery tickets within its limits, so Congress, for the purpose of guarding the people of the United States against the "widespread pestilence of lotteries" and to protect the commerce which concerns all the States, may prohibit the carrying of lottery tickets from one State to another. In legislating upon the subject of the traffic in lottery tickets, as carried on through interstate commerce, Congress only supplemented the action of those States—perhaps all of them—which, for the protection of the public morals, prohibit the drawing of lotteries, as well as the sale or circulation of lottery tickets, within their respective limits. It said, in effect, that it would not permit the declared policy of the States, which sought to protect their people against the mischiefs of the lottery business, to be overthrown or disregarded by the agency of interstate commerce. We should hesitate long before adjudging that an evil of such appalling character, carried on through interstate commerce, cannot be met and crushed by the only power competent to that end. . . .

It is said, however, that if, in order to suppress lotteries carried on through interstate commerce, Congress may exclude lottery tickets from such commerce, that principle leads necessarily to the conclusion that Congress may arbitrarily exclude from commerce among the states any article, commodity, or thing, of whatever kind or nature, or however useful or valuable, which it may choose, no matter with what motive, to declare shall not be carried from one State to another. It will be time enough to consider the constitutionality of such legislation when we must do so. The present case does not require the court to declare the full extent of the power that Congress may exercise in the regulation of commerce among the States. We may, however, repeat, in this connection, what the court has heretofore said, that the power of Congress to regulate commerce among the States, although plenary, cannot be deemed arbitrary, since it is subject to such limitations or restrictions as are prescribed by the Constitution. . . .

The whole subject is too important, and the questions suggested by its consideration are too difficult of solution, to justify any attempt to lay down a rule for determining in advance the validity of every statute that may be enacted under the commerce clause. We decide nothing more in the present case than that lottery tickets are subjects of traffic among those who choose to sell or buy them; that the carriage of such tickets by independent carriers from one state to another is therefore interstate commerce; that under its power to regulate commerce among the several States Congress—subject to the limitations imposed by the Constitution upon the exercise of the powers granted—has plenary authority over such commerce, and may prohibit the carriage of such tickets from State to State; and that legislation to that end, and of that character, is not inconsistent with any limitation or restriction imposed upon the exercise of the powers granted to Congress.

The judgment is affirmed.

Mr. Chief Justice FULLER, dissenting.

The power of the State to impose restraints and burdens on persons and property in conservation and promotion of the public health, good order, and prosperity is a power originally and always belonging to the States, not surrendered by them to the general government, nor directly restrained by the Constitution of the United States, and essentially exclusive, and the suppression of lotteries as a harmful business falls within this power, commonly called, of police.

It is urged, however, that because Congress is empowered to regulate commerce between the several States, it, therefore, may suppress lotteries by prohibiting the carriage of lottery matter. Congress may, indeed, make all laws necessary and proper for carrying the powers granted to it into execution, and doubtless an act prohibiting the carriage of lottery matter would be necessary and

proper to the execution of a power to suppress lotteries; but that power belongs to the states and not to Congress. To hold that Congress has general police power would be to hold that it may accomplish objects not intrusted to the General Government, and to defeat the operation of the Tenth Amendment, declaring that "the powers not delegated to the United States by the Constitution, nor prohibited by it to the states, are reserved to the states respectively, or to the people." . . .

. . . To say that the mere carrying of an article which is not an article of commerce in and of itself nevertheless becomes such the moment it is to be transported from one state to another, is to transform a non-commercial article into a commercial one simply because it is transported. I cannot conceive that any such result can properly follow. It would be to say that everything is an article of commerce the moment it is taken to be transported from place to place, and of interstate commerce if from State to State. An invitation to dine, or to take a drive, or a note of introduction, all become articles of commerce under the ruling in this case, by being deposited with an express company for transportation. This in effect breaks down all the differences between that which is, and that which is not, an article of commerce, and the necessary consequence is to take from the States all jurisdiction over the subject so far as interstate communication is concerned. It is a long step in the direction of wiping out all traces of state lines, and the creation of a centralized government.

Does the grant to Congress of the power to regulate interstate commerce impart the absolute power to prohibit it?

The power to prohibit the transportation of diseased animals and infected goods over railroads or on steamboats is an entirely different thing, for they would be in themselves injurious to the transaction of interstate commerce, and, moreover, are essentially commercial in their nature. And the exclusion of diseased persons rests on different ground, for nobody would pretend that persons could be kept off the trains because they were going from one State to another to engage in the lottery business. However enticing that business may be, we do not understand these pieces of paper themselves can communicate bad principles by contact.

In my opinion the act in question in the particular under consideration is invalid, and the judgments below ought to be reversed.

Notes and Queries

1. Is the use of federal power at issue in *Champion* consistent with Chief Justice Marshall's analysis in *Gib-*

bons? How is *Champion* to be squared with *E. C. Knight*? Has the commerce clause been used here as a pretext to regulate a subject unrelated to commerce? What other provisions of the Constitution might support the exercise of the federal power that has been exercised here? Would the Preamble be of any help?

2. There seems little doubt that the congressional legislation at issue in *Champion* was in the national interest. Does the Constitution, however, confer on the federal government the power to regulate matters in the national interest? If so, what function does the Tenth Amendment serve?

3. In his opinion for the Court, Justice Harlan noted that the plenary power of Congress to regulate commerce is not arbitrary because "it is subject to such limitations or restrictions as are prescribed by the Constitution." What are those limits?

Hammer v. Dagenhart
247 U.S. 251, 38 S. Ct. 529, 62 L. Ed. 1101 (1918)

The Federal Child Labor Act of 1916 prohibited the transportation in interstate commerce of products made in any mill, factory, or manufacturing establishment in which children under fourteen years of age were employed or in which children between fourteen and sixteen were employed to work more than eight hours a day or more than six days a week. Dagenhart brought suit on behalf of himself and his two minor sons who were employed in a North Carolina cotton mill. The government appealed when the federal district court struck down the statute. Opinion of the Court: *Day*, White, VanDevanter, Pitney, McReynolds. Dissenting opinion: *Holmes*, McKenna, Brandeis, Clarke.

Mr. Justice DAY delivered the opinion of the Court.

The controlling question for decision is: Is it within the authority of Congress in regulating commerce among the States to prohibit the transportation in interstate commerce of manufactured goods, the product of a factory in which, within thirty days prior to their removal therefrom, children under the age of fourteen have been employed or permitted to work, or children between the ages of fourteen and sixteen years have been employed or permitted to work more than eight hours in any day, or more than six days in any week, or after the hour of 7 o'clock p. m., or before the hour of 6 o'clock a. m.?

The power essential to the passage of this act, the government contends, is found in the commerce clause of the Constitution which authorizes Congress to regulate commerce with foreign nations and among the States.

In *Gibbons v. Ogden*, Chief Justice Marshall, speaking for this court, and defining the extent and nature of the commerce power, said, "It is the power to regulate, that is, to prescribe the rule by which commerce is to be governed." In other words, the power is one to control the means by which commerce is carried on, which is directly the contrary of the assumed right to forbid commerce from moving and thus destroy it as to particular commodities. But it is insisted that adjudged cases in this court [e.g., *Champion v. Ames*] establish the doctrine that the power to regulate given to Congress incidentally includes the authority to prohibit the movement of ordinary commodities and therefore that the subject is not open for discussion. The cases demonstrate the contrary. They rest upon the character of the particular subjects dealt with and the fact that the scope of governmental authority, state or national, possessed over them is such that the authority to prohibit is as to them but the exertion of the power to regulate.

In [earlier cases] the use of interstate transportation was necessary to the accomplishment of harmful results. In other words, although the power over interstate transportation was to regulate, that could only be accomplished by prohibiting the use of the facilities of interstate commerce to effect the evil intended.

This element is wanting in the present case. The thing intended to be accomplished by this statute is the denial of the facilities of interstate commerce to those manufacturers in the states who employ children within the prohibited ages. The act in its effect does not regulate transportation among the States, but aims to standardize the ages at which children may be employed in mining and manufacturing within the States. The goods shipped are of themselves harmless. The act permits them to be freely shipped after thirty days from the time of their removal from the factory. When offered for shipment, and before transportation begins, the labor of their production is over, and the mere fact that they were intended for interstate commerce transportation does not make their production subject to federal control under the commerce power.

Over interstate transportation, or its incidents, the regulatory power of Congress is ample, but the production of articles, intended for interstate commerce, is a matter of local regulation. . . . If it were otherwise, all manufacture intended for interstate shipment would be brought under

Comparative Note 7.3

[The Industrial Disputes Act of 1907 was designed to deal with work stoppages and labor disputes in some of Canada's most vital industries. The act was regarded as "emergency" legislation enacted pursuant to the Canadian government's power "to make laws for the peace, order and good government of Canada." The privy council declared the act invalid as a violation of the Constitution (i.e., the British North American Act, 1867).]

Whatever else may be the effect of this enactment, it is clear that it is one which could have been passed, so far as any Province was concerned, by the Provincial Legislature under the powers concerned by s. 92 of the [Constitution]. For its provisions were concerned directly with the civil rights of both employers and employed in the Province. . . . The Dominion parliament has, under the initial words of s. 91, a general power to make laws for Canada. But these laws are not to relate to the classes of subjects assigned to the Provinces by s. 92, unless their enactment falls under heads spe-

cifically assigned to the Dominion Parliament by the enumeration in s. 91. . . .

. . . [T]he invocation of the specific power in s. 91 to regulate trade and commerce [does not] assist the Dominion contention. . . . [We cannot accept] the general principle that the mere fact that Dominion legislation is for the general advantage of Canada, or is such that it will meet a mere want which is felt throughout the Dominion, renders it competent if it cannot be brought within the heads enumerated specifically in s. 91. . . . No doubt there may be cases arising out of some extraordinary peril to the national life of Canada, as a whole, such as the cases arising out of a war, where legislation is required of an order that passes beyond the heads of exclusive Provincial competency. Such cases may be dealt with under the words at the commencement of s. 91, conferring general powers in relation to peace, order, and good government, simply because such cases are not otherwise provided for. But instances of this . . . are highly exceptional.

Source: *Toronto Electric Commissioners v. Snider*, In the Privy Council [1925] A.C. 396; II Olmstead 394.

---

federal control to the practical exclusion of the authority of the States, a result certainly not contemplated by the framers of the Constitution when they vested in Congress the authority to regulate commerce among the States.

It is further contended that the authority of Congress may be exerted to control interstate commerce in the shipment of childmade goods because of the effect of the circulation of such goods in other States where the evil of this class of labor has been recognized by local legislation, and the right to thus employ child labor has been more rigorously restrained than in the State of production. In other words, that the unfair competition, thus engendered, may be controlled by closing the channels of interstate commerce to manufacturers in those states where the local laws do not meet what Congress deems to be the more just standard of other States.

There is no power vested in Congress to require the States to exercise their police power so as to prevent possible unfair competition. Many causes may co-operate to give one State, by reason of local laws or conditions, an economic advantage over others. The commerce clause was not intended to give to Congress a general authority to equalize such conditions. . . .

The grant of power of Congress over the subject of in-

terstate commerce was to enable it to regulate such commerce, and not to give it authority to control the States in their exercise of the police power over local trade and manufacture.

The grant of authority over a purely federal matter was not intended to destroy the local power always existing and carefully reserved to the States in the Tenth Amendment to the Constitution.

A statute must be judged by its natural and reasonable effect. The control by Congress over interstate commerce cannot authorize the exercise of authority not entrusted to it by the Constitution. The maintenance of the authority of the States over matters purely local is as essential to the preservation of our institutions as is the conservation of the supremacy of the federal power in all matters entrusted to the nation by the federal Constitution.

In interpreting the Constitution it must never be forgotten that the Nation is made up of States to which are entrusted the powers of local government. And to them and to the people the powers not expressly delegated to the national government are reserved. . . . To sustain this statute would not be in our judgment a recognition of the lawful exertion of congressional authority over interstate commerce, but would sanction an invasion by the federal power of the control of a matter purely local in its character, and over which no authority has been delegated to Congress in conferring the power to regulate commerce among the States.

In our view the necessary effect of this act is, by means of a prohibition against the movement in interstate commerce of ordinary commercial commodities to regulate the hours of labor of children in factories and mines within the States, a purely state authority. Thus the act in a two-fold sense is repugnant to the Constitution. It not only transcends the authority delegated to Congress over commerce but also exerts a power as to a purely local matter to which the federal authority does not extend. The far reaching result of upholding the act cannot be more plainly indicated than by pointing out that if Congress can thus regulate matters entrusted to local authority by prohibition of the movement of commodities in interstate commerce, all freedom of commerce will be at an end, and the power of the States over local matters may be eliminated, and thus our system of government be practically destroyed.

For these reasons we hold that this law exceeds the constitutional authority of Congress. It follows that the decree of the District Court must be.

Affirmed.

Mr. Justice HOLMES, dissenting.

The first step in my argument is to make plain what no one is likely to dispute—that the statute in question is within the power expressly given to Congress if considered only as to its immediate effects and that if invalid it is so only upon some collateral ground. The statute confines itself to prohibiting the carriage of certain goods in interstate or foreign commerce. Congress is given power to regulate such commerce in unqualified terms. It would not be argued today that the power to regulate does not include the power to prohibit. Regulation means the prohibition of something, and when interstate commerce is the matter to be regulated I cannot doubt that the regulation may prohibit any part of such commerce that Congress sees fit to forbid. . . .

The question then is narrowed to whether the exercise of its otherwise constitutional power by Congress can be pronounced unconstitutional because of its possible reaction upon the conduct of the States in a matter upon which I have admitted that they are free from direct control. I should have thought that that matter had been disposed of so fully as to leave no room for doubt. I should have thought that the most conspicuous decisions of this Court had made it clear that the power to regulate commerce and other constitutional powers could not be cut down or

qualified by the fact that it might interfere with the carrying out of the domestic policy of any State.

The notion that prohibition is any less prohibition when applied to things now thought evil I do not understand. But if there is any matter upon which civilized countries have agreed—far more unanimously than they have with regard to intoxicants and some other matters over which this country is now emotionally aroused—it is the evil of premature and excessive child labor. I should have thought that if we were to introduce our own moral conceptions where in my opinion they do not belong, this was preeminently a case for upholding the exercise of all its powers by the United States.

But I had thought that the propriety of the exercise of a power admitted to exist in some cases was for the consideration of Congress alone and that this Court always had disavowed the right to intrude its judgment upon questions of policy or morals. It is not for this Court to pronounce when prohibition is necessary to regulation if it ever may be necessary—to say that it is permissible as against strong drink but not as against the product of ruined lives.

The act does not meddle with anything belonging to the States. They may regulate their internal affairs and their domestic commerce as they like. But when they seek to send their products across the State line they are no longer within their rights. If there were no Constitution and no Congress their power to cross the line would depend upon their neighbors. Under the Constitution such commerce belongs not to the States but to Congress to regulate. It may carry out its views of public policy whatever indirect effect they may have upon the activities of the States. Instead of being encountered by a prohibitive tariff at her boundaries the State encounters the public policy of the United States which it is for Congress to express. The public policy of the United States is shaped with a view to the benefit of the nation as a whole. If, as has been the case within the memory of men still living, a State should take a different view of the propriety of sustaining a lottery from that which generally prevails, I cannot believe that the fact would require a different decision from that reached in *Champion v. Ames*. Yet in that case it would be said with quite as much force as in this that Congress was attempting to intermeddle with the State's domestic affairs. The national welfare as understood by Congress may require a different attitude within its sphere from that of some self-seeking State. It seems to me entirely constitutional for Congress to enforce its understanding by all the means at its command.

Notes and Queries

1. Justice Day wrote that to the states and the people "the powers not expressly delegated to the national government are reserved." Is this what the Tenth Amendment actually says? The Founders consciously omitted the word "expressly" when they drafted the amendment. Does adding it change anything? Would it affect the relationship between the Tenth Amendment and the necessary and proper clause?

2. In its effort to distinguish this case from others, the Court distinguished between evil and nonevil products. Is the distinction fairly traceable to the commerce clause or to the Constitution more generally?

3. Justice Day also distinguished between local manufacture and interstate shipping. Is this distinction implicit in the commerce clause? In the Tenth Amendment? In dual federalism?

4. Can the Court's opinion in *Hammer* be reconciled with the decision in *E. C. Knight*? How? Can it be squared with the Court's opinion in *Champion*?

5. Holmes remarked that "this Court always had disavowed the right to intrude [on Congress'] judgment upon questions of policy or morals." Did the Court ignore its disavowal in *Hammer*? When does the Court cross the line from constitutional interpretation to ordinary policymaking? Is it possible to clearly distinguish the two?

6. *Hammer v. Dagenhart* was overruled by *United States v. Darby*, 312 U.S. 100 (1941). *Hammer* is nevertheless important because it showed how narrowly the Su-

preme Court interpreted the scope of Congress' power over interstate commerce at the time of the decision. *Hammer* should also be seen in tandem with numerous decisions of the Supreme Court that struck down congressional statutes designed to deal with the economic depression of the 1930s. Notable among these cases was *Schechter Poultry Corporation v. United States* (1935), a case we have already visited in regard to the doctrine of nondelegation (see chapter 4). But *Schechter* also struck down the National Industrial Recovery Act for exceeding Congress' power under the commerce clause. The Court acknowledged "the grave national crisis with which Congress was confronted," but went on to say that "[e]xtraordinary conditions do not create or enlarge constitutional power." The Court continued:

> The Constitution established a national government with powers deemed to be adequate, as they have proved to be both in war and peace, but these powers of the national government are limited by the constitutional grants. Those who act under these grants are not at liberty to transcend the imposed limits because they believe that more or different power is necessary. Such assertions of extraconstitutional authority were anticipated and precluded by the explicit terms of the Tenth Amendment.

Are the terms of the Tenth Amendment as explicit as the Court suggests?

7. Compare *Hammer* to the Privy Council decision in Comparative Note 7.3. Do *Hammer* and *Snider* follow the same approach to constitutional interpretation?

National Labor Relations Board v. Jones & Laughlin Steel Corporation

301 U.S. 1, 57 S. Ct. 615, 81 L. Ed. 893 (1937)

The National Labor Relations Act of 1935 gave employees the right to organize unions and to bargain collectively through representatives of their own choosing. It established the National Labor Relations Board (NLRB) to investigate and prevent specified "unfair labor practices" that affect interstate commerce. The declared policy behind the law was to eliminate the sources of obstruction to the free flow of commerce, among them the refusal by employers to recognize unions or to accept collective bargaining.

The NLRB investigated charges of anti-union activity against the Jones and Laughlin Steel Corporation, the

fourth largest producer of steel in the United States. The corporation was charged with dismissing union officials and discriminating against union members in its hiring and tenure policies. The NLRB sustained the charges and ordered the corporation to cease and desist from its discriminatory activity. The Board petitioned the circuit court of appeals to enforce the order when Jones and Laughlin failed to comply. The court denied the petition, holding the NLRB's order beyond the scope of federal power. Opinion of the Court: *Hughes*, Brandeis, Stone, Roberts, Cardozo. Dissenting opinion: *McReynolds*, VanDevanter, Sutherland, Butler.

Mr. Chief Justice HUGHES delivered the opinion of the Court.

First. The Scope of the Act.—The act is challenged in its entirety as an attempt to regulate all industry, thus invading the reserved powers of the States over their local con-

Comparative Note 7.4

[Australia's Air Navigation Act of 1920 authorized the Governor General to make regulations for the control of air navigation in the Commonwealth and the territories. The regulations extended to flying operations within the limits of a single state. The issue before the High Court was whether the Commonwealth Parliament has power to regulate intrastate—as opposed to interstate and foreign—air navigation.]

Latham C. J. The illustrations which have been given indicate the difficulties of any double control of aviation and might well be used to support the contention that it is wise or expedient that there should be a single control of this subject matter. Considerations of wisdom or expediency cannot, however, control the natural construction of statutory language. The Constitution gives to the Commonwealth Parliament power over inter-State and foreign trade and commerce, although these subjects are obviously in many respects very difficult to separate from each other. . . . Although foreign and inter-State trade and commerce may be closely associated with intra-state trade and commerce, the court has uniformly held that the distinction drawn by the Constitution must be fully recognized, and that the power to deal with the former subject does not involve an incidental power to deal with the latter subject. It is true that in the United States of America a similar contention has been approved by the Supreme Court in such cases as *Southern Railway Co. v. United States*, where the court found that there was such a close or direct relation or connection between the inter-State and intra-State traffic when moving over the same railroad [as to make it nearly impossible to regulate the former without regulating the latter.] The decisions of this court, however, have definitely declined to adopt such a principle, and have therefore left the problem . . . to be solved by some form of cooperation between the Commonwealth and the States.

SOURCE: *R v. Burgess; Ex parte Henry* (1936) 55 C.L.R. 608, 628–629.

cerns. It is asserted that the references in the Act to interstate and foreign commerce are colorable at best; that the Act is not a true regulation of such commerce or of matters which directly affect it, but on the contrary has the fundamental object of placing under the compulsory supervision of the federal government all industrial labor relations within the nation. . . .

The grant of authority to the Board does not purport to extend to the relationship between all industrial employees and employers. Its terms do not impose collective bargaining upon all industry regardless of effects upon interstate or foreign commerce. It purports to reach only what may be deemed to burden or obstruct that commerce and, thus qualified, it must be construed as contemplating the exercise of control within constitutional bounds. It is a familiar principle that acts which directly burden or obstruct interstate or foreign commerce, or its free flow, are within the reach of the congressional power. Acts having that effect are not rendered immune because they grow out of labor disputes. It is the effect upon commerce, not the source of the injury, which is the criterion. Whether or not particular action does affect commerce in such a close and intimate fashion as to be subject to federal control, and hence to lie within the authority conferred upon the Board, is left by the statute to be determined as individual cases arise. . . .

Second. The unfair labor practices in question. . . .

. . . [I]n its present application, the statute goes no further than to safeguard the right of employees to self-organization and to select representatives of their own choosing for collective bargaining or other mutual protection without restraint or coercion by their employer.

That is a fundamental right. Employees have as clear a right to organize and select their representatives for lawful purposes as the respondent has to organize its business and select its own officers and agents. Discrimination and coercion to prevent the free exercise of the right of employees to self-organization and representation is a proper subject for condemnation by competent legislative authority. . . . Hence the prohibition by Congress of interference with the selection of representatives for the purpose of negotiation and conference between employers and employees, "instead of being an invasion of the constitutional right of either, was based on the recognition of the rights of both." . . .

Third. The application of the Act to Employees Engaged in Production.—The Principle Involved.—Respondent says that, whatever may be said of employees engaged in interstate commerce, the industrial relations and activities in the manufacturing department of respondent's enterprise are not subject to federal regulation. The argument rests upon the proposition that manufacturing in itself is not commerce.

. . . The congressional authority to protect interstate commerce from burdens and obstructions is not limited to transactions which can be deemed to be an essential part of a "flow" of interstate or foreign commerce. Burdens and obstructions may be due to injurious action springing from other sources. . . . Although activities may be intrastate in character when separately considered, if they have such a close and substantial relation to interstate commerce that their control is essential or appropriate to protect that commerce from burdens and obstructions, Congress cannot be denied the power to exercise that control. Undoubtedly the scope of this power must be considered in the light of our dual system of government and may not be extended so as to embrace effects upon interstate commerce so indirect and remote that to embrace them, in view of our complex society, would effectually obliterate the distinction between what is national and what is local and create a completely centralized government. The question is necessarily one of degree. . . .

It is thus apparent that the fact that the employees here concerned were engaged in production is not determinative. The question remains as to the effect upon interstate commerce of the labor practice involved. . . .

Fourth. Effects of the Unfair Labor Practice in Respondent's Enterprise.—Giving full weight to respondent's contention with respect to a break in the complete continuity of the "stream of commerce" by reason of respondent's manufacturing operations, the fact remains that the stoppage of those operations by industrial strife would have a most serious effect upon interstate commerce. In view of respondent's far-flung activities, it is idle to say that the effect would be indirect or remote. It is obvious that it would be immediate and might be catastrophic. We are asked to shut our eyes to the plainest facts of our national life and to deal with the question of direct and indirect effects in an intellectual vacuum. Because there may be but indirect and remote effects upon interstate commerce in connection with a host of local enterprises throughout the country, it does not follow that other industrial activities do not have such a close and intimate relation to interstate commerce as to make the presence of industrial strife a matter of the most urgent national concern. When industries organize themselves on a national scale, making their relation to interstate commerce the dominant factor in their activities, how can it be maintained that their industrial labor relations constitute a forbidden field into which Congress may not enter when it is

necessary to protect interstate commerce from the paralyzing consequences of industrial war? We have often said that interstate commerce itself is a practical conception. It is equally true that interferences with that commerce must be appraised by a judgment that does not ignore actual experience.

Experience has abundantly demonstrated that the recognition of the right of employees to self-organization and to have representatives of their own choosing for the purpose of collective bargaining is often an essential condition of industrial peace. Refusal to confer and negotiate has been one of the most prolific causes of strife. This is such an outstanding fact in the history of labor disturbances that it is a proper subject of judicial notice and requires no citation of instances. . . .

Our conclusion is that the order of the Board was within its competency and that the act is valid as here applied. The judgment of the Circuit Court of Appeals is reversed and the cause is remanded for further proceedings in conformity with this opinion. It is so ordered.

Reversed and remanded.

Mr. Justice McREYNOLDS delivered the following dissenting opinion.

. . . Six District Courts, on the authority of *Schechter*'s and *Carter*'s Cases, have held that the Board has no authority to regulate relations between employers and employees engaged in local production. No decision or judicial opinion to the contrary has been cited, and we find none. Every consideration brought forward to uphold the act before us was applicable to support the acts held unconstitutional in causes decided within two years. And the lower courts rightly deemed them controlling.

Any effect on interstate commerce by the discharge of employees shown here would be indirect and remote in the highest degree, as consideration of the facts will show. In [this case] ten men out of ten thousand were discharged; in the other cases only a few. The immediate effect in the factory may be to create discontent among all those employed and a strike may follow, which, in turn, may result in reducing production, which ultimately may reduce the volume of goods moving in interstate commerce. By this chain of indirect and progressively remote events we finally reach the evil with which it is said the legislation under consideration undertakes to deal. A more remote and indirect interference with interstate commerce or a more definite invasion of the powers reserved to the states is difficult, if not impossible, to imagine. . . . The Constitution still recognizes the existence of states with indestructible powers; the Tenth Amendment was supposed to put them beyond controversy.

We are told that Congress may protect the "stream of commerce" and that one who buys raw material without the state, manufactures it therein, and ships the output to another state is in that stream. Therefore it is said he may be prevented from doing anything which may interfere with its flow. . . . There is no ground on which reasonably to hold that refusal by a manufacturer, whose raw materials come from states other than that of his factory and whose products are regularly carried to other states, to bargain collectively with employees in his manufacturing plant, directly affects interstate commerce. . . . Whatever effect any cause of discontent may ultimately have upon commerce is far too indirect to justify congressional regulation. . . .

That Congress has power by appropriate means, not prohibited by the Constitution, to prevent direct and material interference with the conduct of interstate commerce is settled doctrine. But the interference struck at must be direct and material, not some mere possibility contingent on wholly uncertain events; and there must be no impairment of rights guaranteed. A state by taxation on property may indirectly but seriously affect the cost of transportation; it may not lay a direct tax upon the receipts from interstate transportation. The first is an indirect effect, the other direct. . . .

The things inhibited by the Labor Act relate to the man-agement of a manufacturing plant—something distinct from commerce and subject to the authority of the state. And this may not be abridged because of some vague possibility of distant interference with commerce. . . .

It seems clear to us that Congress has transcended the powers granted.

Notes and Queries

1. The respondent argued that manufacturing is not commerce. How did the Court respond to this distinction? Was its reading of the commerce clause influenced by national economic conditions? Is Chief Justice Hughes' opinion consistent with the Court's approach in *E. C. Knight*?

2. *Jones & Laughlin* was a turning point in the Supreme Court's commerce clause jurisprudence. From then on the Court rarely questioned Congress's exercise of the commerce power. In Canada and Australia, however, the higher courts would continue to hold fast to their restricted view of the national power over trade and commerce. See in particular Comparative Note 7.5. What explains the different approaches of the American and Australian courts? (For the relevant constitutional provisions, see Comparative Note 7.1.) What do the American and Australian cases tell you about the process of constitutional interpretation?

Wickard v. Filburn
317 U.S. 111, 63 S. Ct. 82, 87 L. Ed. 122 (1942)

The Agricultural Adjustment Act of 1938 limited the amount of acreage that individual farmers could devote to the production of wheat. The act, which purported to be a regulation of interstate commerce, was designed to stabilize the price of wheat in the national market. Filburn, an Ohio farmer, was fined for raising wheat in excess of the quota allotted to him under the act. He defended himself on the grounds that the excess wheat he had grown on his farm was for his own home consumption and not intended for shipment in interstate commerce. The government appealed after a federal district court had enjoined the collection of the fine. Opinion of the Court: *Jackson*, Stone, Roberts, Black, Reed, Frankfurter, Douglas, Murphy, Byrnes

Mr. Justice JACKSON delivered the opinion of the Court.

It is urged that under the Commerce Clause of the Constitution, Article I, s 8, clause 3, Congress does not possess the power it has in this instance sought to exercise. The question would merit little consideration since our decision in *United States v. Darby* [1941] . . . , sustaining the federal power to regulate production of goods for commerce, except for the fact that this Act extends federal regulation to production not intended in any part for commerce but wholly for consumption on the farm. . . .

Appellee says that this is a regulation of production and consumption of wheat. Such activities are, he urges, beyond the reach of Congressional power under the Commerce Clause, since they are local in character, and their effects upon interstate commerce are at most "indirect." In answer the Government argues that the statute regulates neither production nor consumption, but only marketing; and, in the alternative, that if the Act does go beyond the regulation of marketing it is sustainable as a "necessary and proper" implementation of the power of Congress over interstate commerce.

Whether the subject of the regulation in question was "production," "consumption," or "marketing" is . . . not material for purposes of deciding the question of federal power before us. That an activity is of local character may help in a doubtful case to determine whether Congress

Comparative Note 7.5

[As noted in Comparative Note 7.1, Australia's Constitution provides that Parliament shall have power to make laws with respect to "trade and commerce with other countries and among the states," terms almost identical to the American Commerce Clause. In *Airlines of New South Wales v. New South Wales*, however, the Australian High Court interpreted these words much more restrictively than the post-1936 Supreme Court. The case involved air navigation regulations which applied to "all air navigation within Australian territory"—that is, to both interstate and intrastate air navigation. In the following extract, Justice Kitto explicitly rejected the expansive view of the commerce power adopted in the United States.]

I pause to [note our traditional] stand against the introduction into Australian constitutional law of some of the vague standards which at times have been accepted in relation to the reach of the commerce power under the Constitution of the United States and have resulted in a greatly diminished importance in that country of the distinction between inter-State and intra-State commerce. . . . Thus it is held, upon consideration of economic effects, that the reach of the commerce power extends to "those intra-State activities which in a substantial way interfere with or obstruct the exercise of the granted power": . . . *Wickard v. Filburn*.

The establishment of these criteria in the United States has evoked in that country itself criticisms of which we would do well to take notice. . . . The Australian union is one of dual federalism, and until the Par-

liament and the people see fit to change it, a true federation it must remain. This Court is entrusted with the preservation of constitutional distinctions, and it both fails in its task and exceeds its authority if it discards them, however out of touch with practical conceptions or with modern conditions they may appear to be in some or all of their applications. To import the doctrine of the American cases into the law of the Australian Constitution would in my opinion be an error. The Constitution supplies its own criteria of legislative power.

. . . [The test] is . . . a question as to whether, when the factual situation in which the law operates is understood, the law by its operation upon the intra-State section of the relevant form of commerce is seen to operate also upon the actual conduct of an activity or collection of activities in respect of which federal power exists, e.g., the actual carrying on of activities forming part of the overseas and inter-State sections of that form of commerce.

[Justice Kitto went on to say that a "merely consequential" effect of intrastate activity on interstate trade is not sufficient to extend federal power to the state. But he went on to sustain the Acts' constitutionality because, given the nature of modern air navigation, there was a "real possibility of physical interference"—as distinct from a "consequential effect"—with interstate air navigation if federal regulations did not extend to the state level.]

Source: (1965) 113 C.L.R. 54, 113–117.

---

intended to reach it. The same consideration might help in determining whether in the absence of Congressional action it would be permissible for the state to exert its power on the subject matter, even though in so doing it to some degree affected interstate commerce. But even if appellee's activity be local though it may not be regarded as commerce, it may still, whatever its nature, be reached by Congress if it exerts a substantial economic effect on interstate commerce and this irrespective of whether such effect is what might at some earlier time have been defined as "direct" or "indirect."

The effect of consumption of homegrown wheat on interstate commerce is due to the fact that it constitutes the most variable factor in the disappearance of the wheat

crop. Consumption on the farm where grown appears to vary in an amount greater than 20 per cent of average production. The total amount of wheat consumed as food varies but relatively little, and use as seed is relatively constant.

The maintenance by government regulation of a price for wheat undoubtedly can be accomplished as effectively by sustaining or increasing the demand as by limiting the supply. The effect of the statute before us is to restrict the amount which may be produced for market and the extent as well to which one may forestall resort to the market by producing to meet his own needs. That appellee's own contribution to the demand for wheat may be trivial by itself is not enough to remove him from the scope of federal regulation where, as here, his contribution, taken together with that of many others similarly situated, is far from trivial.

It is well established by decisions of this Court that the power to regulate commerce includes the power to regulate the prices at which commodities in that commerce are dealt in and practices affecting such prices. One of the primary purposes of the Act in question was to increase the market price of wheat and to that end to limit the volume thereof that could affect the market. It can hardly be denied that a factor of such volume and variability as home-consumed wheat would have a substantial influence on price and market conditions. . . . This record leaves us in no doubt that Congress may properly have considered that wheat consumed on the farm where grown, if wholly outside the scheme of regulation, would have a substantial effect in defeating and obstructing its purpose to stimulate trade therein at increased prices.

It is said, however, that this Act, forcing some farmers into the market to buy what they could provide for themselves, is an unfair promotion of the markets and prices of specializing wheat growers. It is of the essence of regulation that it lays a restraining hand on the self-interest of the regulated and that advantages from the regulation commonly fall to others. The conflicts of economic interest between the regulated and those who advantage by it are wisely left under our system to resolution by the Congress under its more flexible and responsible legislative process. Such conflicts rarely lend themselves to judicial determination. And with the wisdom, workability, or fairness, of the plan of regulation we have nothing to do.

Reversed.

Notes and Queries

1. Is Justice Jackson's argument in favor of the regulatory statute in *Wickard* merely a "pretext" for the regulation of other activity reserved exclusively to the states? Do you find the "cumulative effects" feature of the case convincing? Recall that the farmer involved in this case consumed the wheat for his family's private use.

2. Are there any limitations on the exercise of the commerce power after *Wickard*? Compare Jackson's reasoning with the Australian High Court's opinion in Comparative Notes 7.4 and 7.5. Might the U.S. Supreme Court have plausibly advanced a similar argument against federal regulation in *Wickard*?

3. Should the Tenth Amendment constitute a bar to the kind of federal regulation imposed in *Wickard*? In this connection, see *United States v. Darby* (1941), decided shortly before *Wickard*. In *Darby*, Justice Stone asserted that the Tenth Amendment "states but a truism that all is retained which has not been surrendered. There is nothing in the history of its adoption to suggest that it was more than declaratory of the relationship between the national and state governments as it had been established by the Constitution before the Amendment." Do you agree?

4. The Court claimed that it had nothing to do with whether the regulation in this case was wise, workable, or fair. Is this disinterest a constitutional mandate? Is it grounded in an understanding about the nature and limits of judicial authority in a constitutional democracy?

5. Is it possible to square the Court's claim of disinterest with its earlier observation that the cumulative effects of personal wheat consumption might have a "substantial" impact on interstate commerce?

Heart of Atlanta Motel, Inc. v. United States
379 U.S. 241, 85 S. Ct. 348, 13 L. Ed.2d 258 (1964)

The Civil Rights Act of 1964 prohibited discrimination based on race, color, relgion, or national origin in public accommodations whose operations affect interstate commerce. The Heart of Atlanta Motel, which was readily accessible to interstate highways and 75 percent of whose guests were from states other than Georgia, refused to comply with the statute. The motel sought a declaratory judgment, claiming that the public accommodations section (Title II) of the act violated the Constitution. A three-judge federal district court upheld the section as a legitimate exercise of the federal commerce power. Opinion of the Court: *Clark*, Warren, Black, Douglas, Harlan, Brennan, Stewart, White, Goldberg. Concurring opinions: *Black*, *Douglas*.

Mr. Justice CLARK delivered the opinion of the Court.

It is admitted that the operation of the motel brings it within the provisions of s 201(a) of the Act and that appellant refused to provide lodging for transient Negroes because of their race or color and that it intends to continue that policy unless restrained.

The sole question posed is, therefore, the constitutionality of the Civil Rights Act of 1964 as applied to these facts. The legislative history of the Act indicates that Congress based the Act on s 5 and the Equal Protection Clause of the Fourteenth Amendment as well as its power to regu-

Comparative Note 7.6

[Section 7(e) of Canada's Federal Tax Marks Act proscribed misleading and antisocial business practices and provided for both civil and criminal remedies for its violation. The main issue here is whether this is a valid exercise of the "trade and commerce" power under s.91(2). In declaring the provisions at issue unconstitutional, Chief Justice Laskin identifies the conditions that any federal act enacted pursuant to s.92 (2) must fulfill.]

The plain fact is that s.7(e) is not a regulation, nor is it concerned with trade as a whole nor with general trade and commerce. In a loose sense every legal prescription is regulatory, even the prescriptions of the *Criminal Code*, but I do not read s.92(2) as in itself authorizing federal legislation that merely creates a statutory tort, enforceable by private action, and applicable, as here, to the entire range of business relationships in any activity, whether the activity be itself within or beyond federal legislative authority.

What is evident here is that the Parliament of Canada has simply extended or intensified existing common and civil law delictual liability by statute which at the same time has prescribed the usual civil remedies open to an aggrieved person. The Parliament of Canada can no more acquire legislative jurisdiction by supplementing existing tort liability, cognizable in provincial Courts as reflective of provincial competence, than the provincial Legislatures can acquire legislative jurisdiction by supplementing the federal criminal law.

. . . The provision is not directed to trade but to the ethical conduct of persons engaged in trade or in business, and, in my view, such a detached provision cannot survive alone unconnected to a general regulatory scheme to govern trading relations going beyond merely local concern. Even on the footing of being concerned with practices in the conduct of trade, its private enforcement by civil action gives it a local cast because it is as applicable in its terms to local or intra-provincial competitions as it is to competitors in inter-provincial trade.

SOURCE: *MacDonald v. Vapour Can. Ltd*. In the Supreme Court of Canada [1977] 2 S.C.R. 134.

---

late interstate commerce under Art. I, s 8, cl. 3, of the Constitution. . . .

While the Act as adopted carried no congressional findings the record of its passage through each house is replete with evidence of the burdens that discrimination by race or color places upon interstate commerce. This testimony included the fact that our people have become increasingly mobile with millions of people of all races traveling from State to State; that Negroes in particular have been the subject of discrimination in transient accommodations, having to travel great distances to secure the same; that often they have been unable to obtain accommodations and have had to call upon friends to put them up overnight, and that these conditions had become so acute as to require the listing of available lodging for Negroes in a special guidebook which was itself "dramatic testimony to the difficulties" Negroes encounter in travel. . . . This testimony indicated a qualitative as well as quantitative effect on interstate travel by Negroes. The former was the obvious impairment of the Negro traveler's pleasure and convenience that resulted when he continually was uncertain of finding lodging. As for the latter, there was evidence that this uncertainty stemming from racial discrimination had the effect of discouraging travel on the part of a substantial portion of the Negro community. . . . [T]he voluminous testimony presents overwhelming evidence that discrimination by hotels and motels impedes interstate travel.

That Congress was legislating against moral wrongs in many of these areas rendered its enactments no less valid. In framing Title II of this Act Congress was also dealing with what it considered a moral problem. But that fact does not detract from the overwhelming evidence of the disruptive effect that racial discrimination has had on commercial intercourse. It was this burden which empowered Congress to enact appropriate legislation, and, given this basis for the exercise of its power, Congress was not restricted by the fact that the particular obstruction to interstate commerce with which it was dealing was also deemed a moral and social wrong.

It is said that the operation of the motel here is of a purely local character. But, assuming this to be true, "[i]f it is interstate commerce that feels the pinch, it does not matter how local the operation which applies the squeeze." . . . Thus the power of Congress to promote interstate commerce also includes the power to regulate the local incidents thereof, including local activities in both the States of origin and destination, which might have a substantial and harmful effect upon that commerce. One need only examine the evidence which we have discussed above to see that Congress may—as it has—prohibit racial discrimination by motels serving travelers, however "local" their operations may appear.

We, therefore, conclude that the action of the Congress in the adoption of the Act as applied here to a motel which concededly serves interstate travelers is within the power granted it by the Commerce Clause of the Constitution, as interpreted by this Court for 140 years. It may be argued that Congress could have pursued other methods to eliminate the distinctions it found in interstate commerce caused by racial discrimination. But this is a matter of policy that rests entirely with the Congress not with the courts. How obstructions in commerce may be removed—what means are to be employed—is within the sound and exclusive discretion of the Congress. It is subject only to one caveat—that the means chosen by it must be reasonably adapted to the end permitted by the Constitution. We cannot say that its choice here was not so adapted. The Constitution requires no more.

Affirmed.

Mr. Justice BLACK, concurring.

[In the following extract Justice Black refers to "Ollie's Barbecue," a restaurant located in a residential section of Birmingham, Alabama, some distance away from the nearest interstate highway. This restaurant was also charged with violating the public accommodations section of the Civil Rights Act. In *Katzenback v. McClung*, 379 U.S. 294, decided on the same day as *Atlanta Motel*, the Court held that Ollie's Barbecue was also within the reach of the statute because a substantial percentage of its supplies came from out of state.]

. . . The foregoing facts are more than enough, in my judgment, to show that Congress acting within its discretion and judgment has power under the Commerce Clause and the Necessary and Proper Clause to bar racial discrimination in the Heart of Atlanta Motel and Ollie's Barbeque. I recognize that every remote, possible, speculative effect on commerce should not be accepted as an adequate constitutional ground to uproot and throw into the discard all our traditional distinctions between what is purely local, and therefore controlled by state laws, and what affects the national interest and is therefore subject to control by federal laws. I recognize too that some isolated and remote lunchroom which sells only to local people and buys almost all its supplies in the locality may possibly be beyond the reach of the power of Congress to regulate commerce, just as such an establishment is not covered by the present Act. But in deciding the constitutional power of

Congress in cases like the two before us we do not consider the effect on interstate commerce of only one isolated, individual, local event, without regard to the fact that this single local event when added to many others of as similar nature may impose a burden on interstate commerce by reducing its volume or distorting its flow.

Mr. Justice DOUGLAS, concurring.

Though I join the Court's opinions, I am somewhat reluctant here . . . to rest solely on the Commerce Clause. My reluctance is not due to any conviction that Congress lacks power to regulate commerce in the interests of human rights. It is rather my belief that the right of people to be free of state action that discriminates against them because of race, like the "right of persons to move freely from State to State occupies a more protected position in our constitutional system than does the movement of cattle, fruit, steel and coal across state lines." . . .

Hence I would prefer to rest on the assertion of legislative power contained in s 5 of the Fourteenth Amendment which states: "The Congress shall have power to enforce, by appropriate legislation, the provisions of this article"—a power which the Court concedes was exercised at least in part in this Act.

A decision based on the Fourteenth Amendment would have a more settling effect, making unnecessary litigation over whether a particular restaurant or inn is within the commerce definitions of the Act or whether a particular customer is an interstate traveler. Under my construction, the Act would apply to all customers in all the enumerated places of public accommodation. And that construction would put an end to all obstructionist strategies and finally close one door on a bitter chapter in American history.

Notes and Queries

1. Justice Clark wrote that "voluminous testimony presents overwhelming evidence that discrimination by hotels and motels impedes interstate travel." Is there a difference between activity that "impedes interstate travel" and activity that "affects" interstate commerce? The testimony referred to by Justice Clark concerned mainly noneconomic activity, namely, personal travel.

2. The Court conceded that Congress might have chosen other means to eliminate racial discrimination. What other means did Congress have at its disposal? The Court had struck down earlier efforts by Congress to prohibit private acts of discrimination in *The Civil Rights Cases* (1883, reprinted in chapter 14). The Kennedy Administration feared that those cases might impede civil rights legislation predicated on the Reconstruction Amendments, and

they successfully sought to have the legislation justified upon the congressional power to regulate matters that "affect" interstate commerce. Justice Douglas suggested in his concurrence that Congress might have relied upon the equal protection clause. Do you agree?

3. In what ways does this case resemble *Champion v. Ames*? Should the Court permit Congress to use its power

to regulate interstate commerce to advance noncommercial ends, such as ending the moral vice of racial discrimination? To advance the ends of other constitutional provisions? Why or why not? Do these distinctions ultimately matter?

4. How would the statute have fared under the Canadian Constitution? See Comparative Note 7.6.

National League of Cities v. Usery

426 U.S. 833, 96 S. Ct. 2465, 49 L. Ed.2d 245 (1976)

In this case several cities and states sued in federal district court to test the validity of 1974 amendments to the Fair Labor Standards Act extending the statutory minimum wage and maximum hour provisions to employees of states and their political subdivisions. They argued that these provisions violated the principle of state sovereignty under the Tenth Amendment. A federal district court, following the decision in *Maryland v. Wirtz,* dismissed the suit, and the case was appealed to the Supreme Court. Opinion of the Court: *Rehnquist*, Burger, Powell, Stewart. Concurring opinion: *Blackmun*. Dissenting Opinions: *Brennan*, White, Marshall, *Stevens*.

Mr. Justice REHNQUIST delivered the opinion of the Court.

Nearly 40 years ago Congress enacted the Fair Labor Standards Act [which was upheld] as a valid exercise of congressional authority under the commerce power in *United States v. Darby.* . . . The original Fair Labor Standards Act passed in 1938 specifically excluded the State and their political subdivisions from its coverage. . . .

In a series of amendments beginning in 1961 Congress began to extend the provisions of the Fair Labor Standards Act to some types of public employees. The 1961 amendments to the Act extended its coverage to persons who were employed in "enterprises" engaged in commerce or in the production of goods for commerce. And in 1966, with the amendment of the definition of employers under the Act, the exemption heretofore extended to the States and their political subdivisions was removed with respect to employees of state hospitals, institutions, and schools. We nevertheless sustained the validity of the combined effect of these two amendments in *Maryland v. Wirtz* (1968). . . . [W]e have decided that the "far-reaching implications of *Wirtz* should be overruled, and that the judgment of the District Court must be reversed."

It is established beyond peradventure that the Com-

merce Clause of Art. I of the Constitution is a grant of plenary authority to Congress. That authority is, in the words of Mr. Chief Justice Marshall in *Gibbons v. Ogden* "the power to regulate; that is, to prescribe the rule by which commerce is to be governed." . . .

Congressional power over areas of private endeavor, even when its exercise may pre-empt express state-law determinations contrary to the result which has commended itself to the collective wisdom of Congress, has been held to be limited only by the requirement that "the means chosen by (Congress) must be reasonably adapted to the end permitted by the Constitution." *Heart of Atlanta Hotel v. United States* [1964].

Appellants in no way challenge these decisions establishing the breadth of authority granted Congress under the commerce power. Their contention, on the contrary, is that when Congress seeks to regulate directly the activities of States as public employers, it transgresses an affirmative limitation on the exercise of its power akin to other commerce power affirmative limitations contained in the Constitution. . . .

This Court has never doubted that there are limits upon the power of Congress to override state sovereignty even when exercising its otherwise plenary powers to tax or to regulate commerce which are conferred by Art. I of the Constitution. In *Wirtz*, for example, the Court took care to assure the appellants that it had "ample power to prevent . . . 'the utter destruction of the State as a sovereign political entity,'" which they feared. Appellee Secretary in this case, both in his brief and upon oral argument, has agreed that our federal system of government imposes definite limits upon the authority of Congress to regulate the activities of the States as States by means of the commerce power. In *Fry* [*v. United States* (1975)], the Court recognized that an express declaration of this limitation is found in the Tenth Amendment: "While the Tenth Amendment has been characterized as a 'truism,' stating merely that 'all is retained which has not been surrendered,' *United States v. Darby* (1941), it is not without significance. The Amendment expressly declares the constitutional policy that Congress may not exercise power in a fashion that impairs the

States' integrity or their ability to function effectively in a federal system." . . .

The expressions in these more recent cases trace back to earlier decisions of this Court recognizing the essential role of the States in our federal system of government. Mr. Chief Justice Chase, perhaps because of the particular time at which he occupied that office, had occasion more than once to speak for the Court on this point. In *Texas v. White* (1869), he declared that "[t]he Constitution, in all its provisions, looks to an indestructible Union, composed of indestructible States." . . .

It is one thing to recognize the authority of Congress to enact laws regulating individual businesses necessarily subject to the dual sovereignty of the government of the Nation and of the State in which they reside. It is quite another to uphold a similar exercise of congressional authority directed, not to private citizens, but to the States as States. We have repeatedly recognized that there are attributes of sovereignty attaching to every state government which may not be impaired by Congress, not because Congress may lack an affirmative grant of legislative authority to reach the matter, but because the Constitution prohibits it from exercising the authority in that manner. . . .

One undoubted attribute of state sovereignty is the States' power to determine the wages which shall be paid to those whom they employ in order to carry out their governmental functions, what hours those persons will work, and what compensation will be provided where these employees may be called upon to work overtime. The question we must resolve here, then, is whether these determinations are "functions essential to separate and independent existence," so that Congress may not abrogate the States' otherwise plenary authority to make them.

Quite apart from the substantial costs imposed upon the States and their political subdivisions, the Act displaces state policies regarding the manner in which they will structure delivery of those governmental services which their citizens require. The Act, speaking directly to the States qua States, requires that they shall pay all but an extremely limited minority of their employees the minimum wage rates currently chosen by Congress. It may well be that as a matter of economic policy it would be desirable that States, just as private employers, comply with these minimum wage requirements. But it cannot be gainsaid that the federal requirement directly supplants the considered policy choices of the States' elected officials and administrators as to how they wish to structure pay scales in state employment. The State might wish to employ persons with little or no training, or those who wish to work on a casual basis, or those who for some

other reason do not possess minimum employment requirements, and pay them less than the federally prescribed minimum wage. It may wish to offer part-time or summer employment to teenagers at a figure less than the minimum wage, and if unable to do so may decline to offer such employment at all. But the Act would forbid such choices by the States. The only "discretion" left to them under the Act is either to attempt to increase their revenue to meet the additional financial burden imposed upon them by paying congressionally prescribed wages to their existing complement of employees, or to reduce that complement to a number which can be paid the federal minimum wage without increasing revenue.

Our examination of the effect of the 1974 amendments, as sought to be extended to the States and their political subdivisions, satisfies us that both the minimum wage and the maximum hour provisions will impermissibly interfere with the integral governmental functions of these bodies. . . . If Congress may withdraw from the States the authority to make those fundamental employment decisions upon which their systems for performance of these functions must rest, we think there would be little left of the States' "separate and independent existence." . . . [T]he dispositive factor is that Congress has attempted to exercise its Commerce Clause authority to prescribe minimum wages and maximum hours to be paid by the States in their capacities as sovereign governments. In so doing, Congress has sought to wield its power in a fashion that would impair the States' "ability to function effectively in a federal system." This exercise of congressional authority does not comport with the federal system of government embodied in the Constitution. We hold that insofar as the challenged amendments operate to directly displace the States' freedom to structure integral operations in areas of traditional governmental functions, they are not within the authority granted Congress by Art. I, s 8, cl. 3.

With respect to the Court's decision in *Wirtz*, we reach a different conclusion. Both appellee and the District Court thought that decision required rejection of appellants' claims. Appellants, in turn, advance several arguments by which they seek to distinguish the facts before the Court in *Wirtz* from those presented by the 1974 amendments to the Act. There are undoubtedly factual distinctions between the two situations, but in view of the conclusions expressed earlier in this opinion we do not believe the reasoning in *Wirtz* may any longer be regarded as authoritative.

Mr. Justice BLACKMUN, concurring.

. . . Although I am not untroubled by certain possible implications of the Court's opinion—some of them suggested by the dissents—I do not read the opinion so despairingly as does my Brother Brennan. In my view, the result with respect to the statute under challenge here is necessarily correct. I may misinterpret the Court's opinion, but it seems to me that it adopts a balancing approach, and does not outlaw federal power in areas such as environmental protection, where the federal interest is demonstrably greater and where state facility compliance with imposed federal standards would be essential. With this understanding on my part of the Court's opinion, I join it.

Mr. Justice BRENNAN, with whom Mr. Justice WHITE and Mr. Justice MARSHALL join, dissenting. . . .

The Court concedes, as of course it must, that Congress enacted the 1975 amendments pursuant to its exclusive power under Art. I, s 8, cl. 3, of the Constitution "[t]o regulate Commerce . . . among the several States." It must therefore be surprising that my Brethren should choose this bicentennial year of our independence to repudiate principles governing judicial interpretation of our Constitution settled since the time of Mr. Chief Justice John Marshall, discarding his postulate that the Constitution contemplates that restraints upon exercise by Congress of its plenary commerce power lie in the political process and not in the judicial process. For 152 years ago Mr. Chief Justice Marshall enunciated that principle to which, until today, his successors on this Court have been faithful. . . .

My Brethren do not successfully obscure today's patent usurpation of the role reserved for the political process by their purported discovery in the Constitution of a restraint derived from sovereignty of the States on Congress' exercise of the commerce power. Mr. Chief Justice Marshall recognized that limitations "prescribed in the constitution," *Gibbons v. Ogden* [1824], restrain Congress' exercise of the power. Thus laws within the commerce power may not infringe individual liberties protected by the First Amendment. . . . But there is no restraint based on state sovereignty requiring or permitting judicial enforcement anywhere expressed in the Constitution; our decisions over the last century and a half have explicitly rejected the existence of any such restraint on the commerce power.

My Brethren thus have today manufactured an abstraction without substance, founded neither in the words of the Constitution nor on precedent. An abstraction having such profoundly pernicious consequences is not made less so by characterizing the 1974 amendments as legislation directed against the "States Qua States." . . . [M]y Brethren make no claim that the 1974 amendments are not regulations of "commerce"; rather they overrule *Wirtz* in disagreement with historic principles that *United States v. California* [1936] reaffirmed: "[W]hile the commerce power has limits, valid general regulations of commerce do not cease to be regulations of commerce because a State is involved. If a State is engaging in economic activities that are validly regulated by the Federal Government when engaged in by private persons, the State too may be forced to conform its activities to federal regulation." Clearly, therefore, my Brethren are also repudiating the long line of our precedents holding that a judicial finding that Congress has not unreasonably regulated a subject matter of "commerce" brings to an end the judicial role. . . .

The reliance of my Brethren upon the Tenth Amendment as "an express declaration of [a state sovereignty] limitation," not only suggests that they overrule governing decisions of this Court that address this question but must astound scholars of the Constitution. . . .

My Brethren purport to find support for their novel state-sovereignty doctrine in the concurring opinion of Mr. Chief Justice Stone in *New York v. United States* [1946]. That reliance is plainly misplaced. That case presented the question whether the Constitution either required immunity of New York State's mineral water business from federal taxation or denied to the Federal Government power to lay the tax. The Court sustained the federal tax. Mr. Chief Justice Stone observed in his concurring opinion that "a federal tax which is not discriminatory as to the subject matter may nevertheless so affect the State, merely because it is a State that is being taxed, as to interfere unduly with the State's performance of its sovereign functions of government." But the Chief Justice was addressing not the question of a state-sovereignty restraint upon the exercise of the commerce power, but rather the principle of implied immunity of the States and Federal Government from taxation by the other: "The counterpart of such undue interference has been recognized since Marshall's day as the implied immunity of each of the dual sovereignties of our constitutional system from taxation by others."

. . . [M]ore significant for our purposes is . . . *United States v. California*, a case concerned with Congress' power to regulate commerce. . . . *California* directly presented the question whether any state-sovereignty restraint precluded application of the Federal Safety Appliance Act to a state owned and operated railroad. The State argued "that as the state is operating the railroad without profit, for the purpose of facilitating the commerce of the port, and is using the net proceeds of operation for harbor improvement, . . . it is engaged in performing a public function in its sovereign capacity and for that reason cannot constitutionally be subjected to the provisions of the federal act." Mr. Justice Stone rejected the contention in an opinion for a unanimous Court. His rationale is a complete refutation of today's holding:

> That in operating its railroad [the State] is acting within a power reserved to the states cannot be doubted. . . . The only question we need consider is whether the exercise of that power, in whatever capacity, must be in subordination to the power to regulate interstate commerce, which has been granted specifically to the national government.
>
> The sovereign power of the states is necessarily diminished to the extent of the grants of power to the federal government in the Constitution.

My Brethren do more than turn aside longstanding constitutional jurisprudence that emphatically rejects today's conclusion. More alarming is the startling restructuring of our federal system, and the role they create therein for the federal judiciary. This Court is simply not at liberty to erect a mirror of its own conception of a desirable governmental structure. . . .

It is unacceptable that the judicial process should be thought superior to the political process in this area. Under the Constitution the Judiciary has no role to play beyond finding that Congress has not made an unreasonable legislative judgment respecting what is "commerce." My Brother Blackmun suggests that controlling judicial supervision of the relationship between the States and our National Government by use of a balancing approach diminishes the ominous implications of today's decision. Such an approach, however, is a thinly veiled rationalization for judicial supervision of a policy judgment that our system of government reserves to Congress.

Judicial restraint in this area merely recognizes that the political branches of our Government are structured to protect the interests of the States, as well as the Nation as a whole, and that the States are fully able to protect their own interests in the premises. Congress is constituted of representatives in both the Senate and House elected from the States. *The Federalist* No. 45 (J. Madison). Decisions upon the extent of federal intervention under the Commerce Clause into the affairs of the States are in that sense decisions of the States themselves. Judicial redistribution of powers granted the National Government by the terms of the Constitution violates the fundamental tenet of our federalism that the extent of federal intervention into the States' affairs in the exercise of delegated powers shall be determined by the States' exercise of political power through their representatives in Congress. There is no reason whatever to suppose that in enacting the 1974 amendments Congress, even if it might extensively obliterate state sovereignty by fully exercising its plenary power respecting commerce, had any purpose to do so. Surely the presumption must be to the contrary. Any realistic assessment of our federal political system, dominated as it is by representatives of the people elected from the States, yields the conclusion that it is highly unlikely that those representatives will ever be motivated to disregard totally the concerns of these States. *The Federalist* No. 46. Certainly this was the premise upon which the Constitution, as authoritatively explicated in *Gibbons v. Ogden*, was founded. Indeed, though the States are represented in the National Government, national interests are not similarly represented in the States' political processes. . . .

We are left then with a catastrophic judicial body blow at Congress' power under the Commerce Clause. Even if Congress may nevertheless accomplish its objectives for example, by conditioning grants of federal funds upon compliance with federal minimum wage and overtime standards, there is an ominous portent of disruption of our constitutional structure implicit in today's mischievous decision. I dissent.

Notes and Queries

1. In *Maryland v. Wirtz*, Justice Harlan conceded that the "power to regulate commerce though broad indeed, has limits." What are those limits? Are there any limits short of "the utter destruction of the State as a sovereign political entity"? See also *Texas v. White*, 7 Wall. 700 (1869).

2. What understanding of judicial power does the majority in *National League of Cities* adopt? Is that understanding premised upon a view of the proper relationship between the states and the national government? How does it differ from the dissent's view of judicial power? Why, according to Brennan, "is it unacceptable that the judicial process should be thought superior to the political process in this area"?

3. What explains *National League's* apparent retreat from the Court's post–New Deal deference to congressional economic legislation? What interpretation of the Constitution as a whole, and the Tenth Amendment in particular, does it advance?

4. How would you describe the differing approaches of Rehnquist, Blackmun, and Brennan in *National League*? Do these approaches really dictate the result of their reasoning? Or are their opinions driven by their larger visions of the Constitution? If so, what are these visions?

5. Suppose in the interest of promoting greater safety on the nation's highways, Congress were to pass a law requiring a federal license of any person wishing to operate an automobile on any highway in the United States.

The statute would have the effect of displacing the states in the issuance of drivers' licenses. Would *National League* be of any help in deciding whether such a statute would survive constitutional analysis?

6. *National League of Cities* provided the stimulus for other challenges to the federal regulation of state activities arguably within the ambit of a traditional governmental function. In each of these challenges the Court sustained the federal regulation, distinguishing *National League of Cities* and limiting it largely to its distinctive facts. See, for example, *Hodel v. Virginia Surface Mining & Reclamation Assn.*, 452 U.S. 264 (1981, upholding national surface mining standards throughout the states); *Transportation Union v. Long Island R. Co.*, 455 U.S. 678 (1982, upholding the application of the Railway Labor Act to a state-owned railroad); *Federal Energy Regulatory Commission v. Mississippi*, 456 U.S. 742 (1982, upholding the Public Utilities Regulatory Policies Act as applied to state public utility companies); and *Equal Employment Opportunity Commission v. Wyoming*, 460 U.S. 226 (1983, sustaining the application of the Federal Age Discrimination Act to state employees). At the same time, lower federal courts seemed hopelessly divided over what state activities were traditional governmental functions and thus within the protection of *National Cities*. The controversy on and off the Supreme Court over the reach of *National League of Cities* reached its climax in *Garcia v. San Antonio Metropolitan Transit Authority*, where the Court reconsidered its decision in the earlier case.

Garcia v. San Antonio Metropolitan Transit Authority
469 U.S. 528, 105 S. Ct. 1005, 83 L. Ed.2d 1016 (1985)

The San Antonio Metropolitan Transit Authority (SAMTA) is a public mass transit authority that is a major provider of transportation in the San Antonio, Texas, metropolitan area. In 1979, the Wage and Hour Administration of the Department of Labor issued an opinion that SAMTA's operations are not immune from the minimum wage and overtime requirements of the Fair Labor Standards Act (FLSA). SAMTA filed an action in federal district court, seeking declaratory relief. The district court held that a municipally owned mass transit is a traditional governmental function within the meaning of *National League of Cities* and thus exempt from the terms of the FLSA. Opinion of the Court: *Blackmun*, Brennan, Marshall, Stevens, White. Dissenting opinions: *Powell*, Burger, *O'Connor*, *Rehnquist*.

Justice BLACKMUN delivered the opinion of the Court.

We revisit in these cases an issue raised in *National League of Cities v. Usery* [1976]. In that litigation, this Court, by a sharply divided vote, ruled that the Commerce Clause does not empower Congress to enforce the minimum-wage and overtime provisions of the Fair Labor Standards Act (FLSA) against the States "in areas of traditional governmental functions." Although *National League of Cities* supplied some examples of "traditional governmental functions," it did not offer a general explanation of how a "traditional" function is to be distinguished from a "nontraditional" one. Since then, federal and state courts have struggled with the task, thus imposed, of identifying a traditional function for purposes of state immunity under the Commerce Clause.

In the present cases, a Federal District Court concluded that municipal ownership and operation of a mass-transit system is a traditional governmental function and thus, under *National League of Cities*, is exempt from the obligations imposed by the FLSA. Faced with the identical question, three Federal Courts of Appeals and one state appellate court have reached the opposite conclusion.

Our examination of this "function" standard applied in these and other cases over the last eight years now persuades us that the attempt to draw the boundaries of state regulatory immunity in terms of "traditional governmental functions" is not only unworkable but is also inconsistent with established principles of federalism and, indeed, with those very federalism principles on which *National League of Cities* purported to rest. That case, accordingly, is overruled.

The controversy in the present cases has focused on the . . . requirement . . . that the challenged federal statute trench on "traditional governmental functions." The District Court voiced a common concern: "Despite the abundance of adjectives, identifying which particular state functions are immune remains difficult." Just how troublesome the task has been is revealed by the results reached in other federal cases. Thus, courts have held that regulating ambulance services, licensing automobile drivers, operating a municipal airport, performing solid waste disposal, and operating a highway authority are functions protected under *National League of Cities*. At the same time, courts have held that issuance of industrial development bonds, regulation of intrastate natural gas sales, regulation of traffic on public roads, regulation of air transportation, operation of a telephone system, leasing and sale of natural gas, operation of a mental health facility and provision of in-house domestic services for the aged and handicapped are not entitled to immunity. We find it difficult, if not impossible, to identify an organizing principle that places each of the cases in the first group on one side of a line and each of the cases in the second group on the other side. The constitutional distinction between licensing drivers and regulating traffic, for example, or between operating a highway authority and operating a mental health facility, is elusive at best.

We believe, however, that there is a more fundamental problem at work here, a problem that explains why the Court was never able to provide a basis for the governmental/proprietary distinction in the intergovernmental tax-immunity cases and why an attempt to draw similar distinctions with respect to federal regulatory authority under *National League of Cities* is unlikely to succeed regardless of how the distinctions are phrased. The problem is that neither the governmental/proprietary distinction nor any other that purports to separate out important governmental functions can be faithful to the role of federalism in a democratic society. The essence of our federal system is that within the realm of authority left open to them under the Constitution, the States must be equally free to engage in any activity that their citizens choose for the common weal, no matter how unorthodox or unnecessary anyone else—including the judiciary—deems state involvement to be. Any rule of state immunity that looks to the "traditional," "integral," or "necessary" nature of governmental functions inevitably invites an unelected federal judiciary to make decisions about which state policies it favors and which ones it dislikes. . . .

We therefore now reject, as unsound in principle and unworkable in practice, a rule of state immunity from federal regulation that turns on a judicial appraisal of whether a particular governmental function is "integral" or "traditional." Any such rule leads to inconsistent results at the same time that it disserves principles of democratic self-governance, and it breeds inconsistency precisely because it is divorced from those principles. If there are to be limits on the Federal Government's power to interfere with state functions—as undoubtedly there are—we must look elsewhere to find them. . . .

The central theme of *National League of Cities* was that the States occupy a special position in our constitutional system and that the scope of Congress' authority under the Commerce Clause must reflect that position. . . .

What has proved problematic is not the perception that the Constitution's federal structure imposes limitations on the Commerce Clause, but rather the nature and content of those limitations. . . .

We doubt that courts ultimately can identify principled constitutional limitations on the scope of Congress' commerce clause powers over the States merely by relying on *a priori* definitions of state sovereignty. In part, this is because of the elusiveness of objective criteria for "fundamental" elements of state sovereignty, a problem we have witnessed in the search for "traditional governmental functions." There is, however, a more fundamental reason: the sovereignty of the States is limited by the Constitution itself. A variety of sovereign powers, for example, are withdrawn from the States by Article I, s 10. Section 8 of the same Article works an equally sharp contraction of state sovereignty by authorizing Congress to exercise a wide range of legislative powers and (in conjunction with the Supremacy Clause of Article VI) to displace contrary state legislation. By providing for final review of questions of federal law in this Court, Article III curtails the sovereign power of the States' judiciaries to make authoritative determinations of law. Finally, the developed application, through the Fourteenth Amendment, of the greater part of the Bill of Rights to the States limits the sovereign authority that States otherwise would possess to legislate with respect to their citizens and to conduct their own affairs.

The States unquestionably do "retai[n] a significant measure of sovereign authority." . . . They do so, however, only to the extent that the Constitution has not divested them of their original powers and transferred those powers to the Federal Government. In the words of James Madison to the Members of the First Congress: "Interference with the power of the States was no constitutional criterion of the power of Congress. If the power was not given, Congress could not exercise it; if given, they might exercise it, although it should interfere with the laws, or even the Constitution of the States." . . .

As a result, to say that the Constitution assumes the continued role of the States is to say little about the nature of that role. Only recently, this Court recognized that the purpose of the constitutional immunity recognized in *National League of Cities* is not to preserve "a sacred province of state autonomy." With rare exceptions, like the guarantee, in Article IV, s 3, of state territorial integrity, the Constitution does not carve out express elements of state sovereignty that Congress may not employ its delegated powers to displace. . . . The power of the Federal Government is a "power to be respected" as well, and the fact that the States remain sovereign as to all powers not vested in Congress or denied them by the Constitution offers no guidance about where the frontier between state and federal power lies. In short, we have no license to employ freestanding conceptions of state sovereignty when measuring congressional authority under the Commerce Clause.

When we look for the States' "residuary and inviolable sovereignty," in the shape of the constitutional scheme rather than in predetermined notions of sovereign power, a different measure of state sovereignty emerges. Apart from the limitation on federal authority inherent in the delegated nature of Congress' Article I powers, the principal means chosen by the Framers to ensure the role of the States in the federal system lies in the structure of the Federal Government itself. It is no novelty to observe that the composition of the Federal Government was designed in large part to protect the States from overreaching by Congress. The Framers thus gave the States a role in the selection both of the Executive and the Legislative Branches of the Federal Government. The States were vested with indirect influence over the House of Representatives and the Presidency by their control of electoral qualifications and their role in Presidential elections. U.S. Const., Art. I, s 2, and Art. II, s 1. They were given more direct influence in the Senate, where each State received equal representation and each Senator was to be selected by the legislature of his State. Art. I, s 3. The significance attached to the States' equal representation in the Senate is underscored by the prohibition of any constitutional amendment divesting a State of equal representation without the State's consent. Art. V.

The extent to which the structure of the Federal Government itself was relied on to insulate the interests of the States is evident in the views of the Framers. James Madison explained that the Federal Government "will partake sufficiently of the spirit [of the States], to be disinclined to invade the rights of the individual States, or the prerogatives of their governments." *Federalist* No. 46. In short, the Framers chose to rely on a federal system in which special restraints on federal power over the States inhered principally in the workings of the National Government itself, rather than in discrete limitations on the objects of federal authority. State sovereign interests, then, are more properly protected by procedural safeguards inherent in the structure of the federal system than by judicially created limitations on federal power.

We realize that changes in the structure of the Federal Government have taken place since 1789, not the least of which has been the substitution of popular election of Senators by the adoption of the Seventeenth Amendment in 1913, and that these changes may work to alter the influence of the States in the federal political process. Nonetheless, against this background, we are convinced that the fundamental limitation that the constitutional scheme imposes on the Commerce Clause to protect the "States as States" is one of process rather than one of result. Any substantive restraint on the exercise of Commerce Clause powers must find its justification in the procedural nature of this basic limitation, and it must be tailored to compensate for possible failings in the national political process rather than to dictate a "sacred province of state autonomy." . . . Insofar as the present cases are concerned, then, we need go no further than to state that we perceive nothing in the overtime and minimum-wage requirements of the FLSA, as applied to SAMTA, that is destructive of state sovereignty or violative of any constitutional provision. . . .

In these cases, the status of public mass transit simply underscores the extent to which the structural protections of the Constitution insulate the States from federally imposed burdens. When Congress first subjected state mass-transit systems to FLSA obligations in 1966, and when it expanded those obligations in 1974, it simultaneously provided extensive funding for state and local mass transit. . . . In short, Congress has not simply placed a financial burden on the shoulders of States and localities that operate mass-transit systems, but has provided substantial countervailing financial assistance as well, assistance that may leave individual mass-transit systems better off than they would have been had Congress never intervened at all in the area. Congress' treatment of public mass transit reinforces our conviction that the national political process systematically protects States from the risk of having their functions in that area handicapped by Commerce Clause regulation.

This analysis makes clear that Congress' action in affording SAMTA employees the protections of the wage and hour provisions of the FLSA contravened no affirmative limit on Congress' power under the Commerce Clause. The judgment of the District Court therefore must be reversed.

Justice POWELL, with whom the Chief Justice, Justice REHNQUIST, and Justice O'CONNOR join, dissenting.

The Court today, in its 5–4 decision, overrules *National League of Cities v. Usery* [1976], a case in which we held that Congress lacked authority to impose the requirements of the Fair Labor Standards Act on state and local governments. Because I believe this decision substantially alters the federal system embodied in the Constitution, I dissent.

Whatever effect the Court's decision may have in weakening the application of *stare decisis*, it is likely to be less important than what the Court has done to the Constitution itself. A unique feature of the United States is the *fed-*

eral system of government guaranteed by the Constitution and implicit in the very name of our country. Despite some genuflecting in the Court's opinion to the concept of federalism, today's decision effectively reduces the Tenth Amendment to meaningless rhetoric when Congress acts pursuant to the Commerce Clause. . . .

To leave no doubt about its intention, the Court renounces its decision in *National League of Cities* because it "inevitably invites an unelected federal judiciary to make decisions about which state policies it favors and which ones it dislikes." In other words, the extent to which the States may exercise their authority, when Congress purports to act under the Commerce Clause, henceforth is to be determined from time to time by political decisions made by members of the Federal Government, decisions the Court says will not be subject to judicial review. I note that it does not seem to have occurred to the Court that it—an unelected majority of five Justices—today rejects almost 200 years of the understanding of the constitutional status of federalism. In doing so, there is only a single passing reference to the Tenth Amendment. Nor is so much as a dictum of any court cited in support of the view that the role of the States in the federal system may depend upon the grace of elected federal officials, rather than on the Constitution as interpreted by this Court.

Today's opinion does not explain how the States' role in the electoral process guarantees that particular exercises of the Commerce Clause power will not infringe on residual state sovereignty. Members of Congress are elected from the various States, but once in office they are Members of the Federal Government. Although the States participate in the Electoral College, this is hardly a reason to view the President as a representative of the States' interest against federal encroachment. We noted recently "[t]he hydraulic pressure inherent within each of the outer limits of its power." The Court offers no reason to think that this pressure will not operate when Congress seeks to invoke its powers under the Commerce Clause, notwithstanding the electoral role of the States. . . .

The Framers believed that the separate sphere of sovereignty reserved to the States would ensure that the States would serve as an effective "counterpoise" to the power of the Federal Government. The States would serve this essential role because they would attract and retain the loyalty of their citizens. The roots of such loyalty, the Founders thought, were found in the objects peculiar to state government. For example, Hamilton argued that the States "regulat[e] all those personal interests and familiar concerns to which the sensibility of individuals is more immediately awake." *The Federalist* No. 17. Thus, he

maintained that the people would perceive the States as "the immediate and visible guardian of life and property," a fact which "contributes more than any other circumstance to impressing upon the minds of the people affection, esteem and reverence towards the government." . . .

Thus, the harm to the States that results from federal overreaching under the Commerce Clause is not simply a matter of dollars and cents. Nor is it a matter of the wisdom or folly of certain policy choices. Rather, by usurping functions traditionally performed by the States, federal overreaching under the Commerce Clause undermines the constitutionally mandated balance of power between the States and the Federal Government, a balance designed to protect our fundamental liberties. . . .

In *National League of Cities*, we spoke of fire prevention, police protection, sanitation, and public health as "typical of [the services] performed by state and local governments in discharging their dual functions of administering the public law and furnishing public services." . . . Not only are these activities remote from any normal concept of interstate commerce, they are also activities that epitomize the concerns of local, democratic self-government. In emphasizing the need to protect traditional governmental functions, we identified the kinds of activities engaged in by state and local governments that affect the everyday lives of citizens. These are services that people are in a position to understand and evaluate, and in a democracy, have the right to oversee. We recognized that "it is functions such as these which governments are created to provide . . ." and that the States and local governments are better able than the National Government to perform them.

The Court maintains that the standard approved in *National League of Cities* "disserves principles of democratic self-governance." In reaching this conclusion, the Court looks myopically only to persons elected to positions in the Federal Government. It disregards entirely the far more effective role of democratic self-government at the state and local levels. . . . [Federal] legislation is drafted primarily by the staffs of the congressional committees. . . . Federal departments and agencies customarily are authorized to write regulations. . . . The administration and regulation and enforcement of federal laws and regulations necessarily are largely in the hands of staff and civil service employees. These employees may have little or no knowledge of the States and localities that will be affected by the statutes and regulations for which they are responsible. In any case, they hardly are as accessible and responsive as those who occupy analogous positions in state and local governments.

In drawing this contrast, I imply no criticism of these federal employees or the officials who are ultimately in charge. The great majority are conscientious and faithful to their duties. My point is simply that members of the immense federal bureaucracy are not elected, know less about the services traditionally rendered by States and localities, and are inevitably less responsive to recipients of such services, than are state legislatures, city councils, boards of supervisors, and state and local commissions, boards, and agencies. It is at these state and local levels— not in Washington as the Court so mistakenly thinks—that "democratic self-government" is best exemplified.

The Court emphasizes that municipal operation of an intracity mass transit system is relatively new in the life of our country. It nevertheless is a classic example of the type of service traditionally provided by local government. It is local by definition. It is indistinguishable in principle from the traditional services of providing and maintaining streets, public lighting, traffic control, water, and sewerage systems. Services of this kind are precisely those with which citizens are more "familiarly and minutely conversant." *The Federalist* No. 46 . . . State and local officials of course must be intimately familiar with these services and sensitive to their quality as well as cost. Such officials also know that their constituents and the press respond to the adequacy, fair distribution, and cost of these services. It is this kind of state and local control and accountability that the Framers understood would insure the vitality and preservation of the federal system that the Constitution explicitly requires.

Justice REHNQUIST, dissenting.

I join both Justice Powell's and Justice O'Connor's thoughtful dissents. Justice Powell's reference to the "balancing test" approved in *National League of Cities* is not identical with the language in that case, which recognized that Congress could not act under its commerce power to infringe on certain fundamental aspects of state sovereignty that are essential to "the States' separate and independent existence." Nor is either test, or Justice O'Connor's suggested approach, precisely congruent with Justice Blackmun's views in 1976, when he spoke of a balancing approach which did not outlaw federal power in areas "where the federal interest is demonstrably greater." But under any one of these approaches the judgment in these cases should be affirmed, and I do not think it incumbent on those of us in dissent to spell out further the fine points of a principle that will, I am confident, in time again, command the support of a majority of this Court.

Justice O'CONNOR, with whom Justice POWELL and Justice REHNQUIST join, dissenting.

The Court today surveys the battle scene of federalism and sounds a retreat. Like Justice Powell, I would prefer to hold the field and, at the very least, render a little aid to the wounded. I join Justice Powell's opinion. I also write separately to note my fundamental disagreement with the majority's views of federalism and the duty of this Court.

In my view, federalism cannot be reduced to the weak "essence" distilled by the majority today. There is more to federalism than the nature of the constraints that can be imposed on the States in "the realm of authority left open to them by the Constitution." The central issue of federalism, of course, is whether any realm is left open to the States by the Constitution—whether any area remains in which a State may act free of federal interference. . . . The true "essence" of federalism is that the States *as States* have legitimate interests which the National Government is bound to respect even though its laws are supreme. . . . If federalism so conceived and so carefully cultivated by the Framers of our Constitution is to remain meaningful, this Court cannot abdicate its constitutional responsibility to oversee the Federal Government's compliance with its duty to respect the legitimate interests of the States. . . .

In the decades since ratification of the Constitution, interstate economic activity has steadily expanded. Industrialization, coupled with advances in transportation and communications, has created a national economy in which virtually every activity occurring within the borders of a State plays a part. The expansion and integration of the national economy brought with it a coordinate expansion in the scope of national problems. This Court has been increasingly generous in its interpretation of the commerce power of Congress, primarily to assure that the National Government would be able to deal with national economic problems. . . .

It is worth recalling the cited passage in *McCulloch v. Maryland* [1819] that lies at the source of the recent expansion of the commerce power. "Let the end be legitimate, let it be within the scope of the constitution," Chief Justice Marshall said, "and all means which are appropriate, which are plainly adapted to that end, which are not prohibited, but consist with the letter *and spirit* of the constitution, are constitutional [emphasis added]." The spirit of the Tenth Amendment, of course, is that the States will retain their integrity in a system in which the laws of the United States are nevertheless supreme.

It is not enough that the "end be legitimate"; the means to that end chosen by Congress must not contravene the spirit of the Constitution. Thus many of this Court's decisions acknowledge that the means by which national power is exercised must take into account concerns for state autonomy. . . . The operative language of these cases varies, but the underlying principle is consistent: state autonomy is a relevant factor in assessing the means by which Congress exercises its powers. . . .

The problems of federalism in an integrated national economy are capable of more responsible resolution than holding that the States as States retain no status apart from that which Congress chooses to let them retain. The proper resolution, I suggest, lies in weighing state autonomy as a factor in the balance when interpreting the means by which Congress can exercise its authority on the States as States. . . .

It has been difficult for this Court to craft bright lines defining the scope of the state autonomy protected by *National League of Cities*. Such difficulty is to be expected whenever constitutional concerns as important as federalism and the effectiveness of the commerce power come into conflict. Regardless of the difficulty, it is and will remain the duty of this Court to reconcile these concerns in the final instance. That the Court shuns the task today by appealing to the "essence of federalism" can provide scant comfort to those who believe our federal system requires something more than a unitary, centralized government. I would not shirk the duty acknowledged by *National League of Cities* and its progeny.

Notes and Queries

1. What method or methods of constitutional interpretation did Justice Blackmun use in his majority opinion?

Do they differ from the approach used by Chief Justice Rehnquist?

2. Are the various opinions in this case premised, at bottom, on different visions of American federalism? Or are they premised on different understandings about the proper role of courts in giving life to these visions?

3. In her dissent, Justice O'Connor suggested that judicial withdrawal from the "battle scene" of federalism leaves the states without effective protection from the centralizing tendencies of the national government. Is "constitutional protection" for the states synonymous with "judicial" protection? How would the majority respond? Consider *Federalist* 39, where Madison wrote that the federal government will be "disinclined to invade" the rights of the states. Do you agree?

4. Justice Rehnquist ended his dissent with these words: ". . . I do not think it incumbent on those of us in dissent to spell out further the fine points of a principle that will, I am confident, in time again command the support of a majority of this Court." Since writing these words, Chief Justice Burger and Justices Brennan, Blackmun, White, and Powell have been replaced. Yet *Garcia* still stands. Does Rehnquist's dissent suggest that in the final analysis what drives constitutional decision making is not law but ideology? Is the question itself a proper one?

United States v. Lopez
514 U.S. 547, 115 S. Ct. 1624, 131 L. Ed. 2d 626 (1995)

Alfonso Lopez, Jr., a twelfth-grade student, was indicted and convicted of knowingly possessing a firearm at a school zone in violation of the Gun-Free School Zones Act of 1990. The act makes it a federal offense "for any individual knowingly to possess a firearm at a place that the individual knows, or has reasonable cause to believe, is a school zone." It defines a school zone as in or on the grounds of a public, parochial, or private school or within a distance of one thousand feet from the school grounds. Lopez appealed, claiming that the act exceeded Congress' power under the commerce clause. The U.S. Court of Appeals agreed and reversed the district court. Opinion of the Court: *Rehnquist*, Kennedy, O'Connor, Scalia, Thomas. Concurring opinions: *Kennedy, Thomas*. Dissenting opinions: *Stevens, Souter, Breyer*, Ginsburg.

CHIEF JUSTICE REHNQUIST delivered the opinion of the Court.

We start with first principles. The Constitution creates a Federal Government of enumerated powers. . . . The Court, through Chief Justice Marshall, first defined the nature of Congress's commerce power in *Gibbons v. Ogden* [1824]. . . . The commerce power "is the power to regulate; that is, to prescribe the rule by which commerce is to be governed. This power, like all others vested in Congress, is complete in itself, may be exercised to its utmost extent, and acknowledges no limitations, other than are prescribed in the constitution." The *Gibbons* Court, however, acknowledged that limitations on the commerce power are inherent in the very language of the Commerce Clause:

It is not intended to say that these words comprehend that commerce, which is completely internal, which is carried on between man and man in a State, or between different parts of the same State, and which does not extend to or affect other States. Such a power would be inconvenient, and is certainly unnecessary.

Comprehensive as the word "among" is, it may very

Comparative Note 7.7

[Article 74 (11) of Germany's Basic Law grants the federation concurrent authority over "economic matters (mining, industry, supply of power, crafts, trades, commerce, banking, stock exchanges, and private insurance)." In 1965 the federal government, acting under this authority, passed a law designed to protect the professional title of "engineer" by specifying the educational and occupational standards with which all persons using the title must comply. Three persons whose prior training did not satisfy these requirements challenged the validity of the statute, arguing that it was not within the federal government's power to regulate "economic matters." The following extract is from the decision of the Federal Constitutional Court.]

2. The subject regulated by the Engineer Act does not involve a law relating to "economic matters" within the meaning of Article 74 (11). In contrast to the Reich Constitution of 1871 and the Weimar Constitution, the Basic Law forbids a broad interpretation of the provisions conferring authority on the federal government. Article 30 underscores the jurisdictional primacy of the states. Article 70 (1) makes this clear by providing that the states enjoy the right to legislate to the extent that the Basic Law does not confer legislative power on the federation. The federation is limited to the enumerated powers specified in Articles 73 through 75.

"Economic matters" within the meaning of Article 74 (11) extend to regulations of economic life and to commercial activities as such, particularly to the processes of production, manufacturing, and distribution of goods. Regulations pertaining to economic competition and consumer protection are also "economic matters" within the meaning of the Basic Law. . . . The Engineer Act, however, does not cover these processes. . . . The federal government lacks authority to pass the Engineer Act because the law is not connected to a subject matter within its express authority under the Basic Law. . . . The argument that a national uniform policy on the use of the title "engineer" is feasible does not sufficiently warrant an [expanded interpretation] of federal power.

SOURCE: Engineer's Case (1969), German Federal Constitutional Court, in Kommers, *Constitutional Jurisprudence*, 2nd ed., 87.

---

properly be restricted to that commerce which concerns more States than one. . . . The enumeration presupposes something not enumerated; and that something, if we regard the language or the subject of the sentence, must be the exclusively internal commerce of a State.

[*NLRB v. Jones & Laughlin Steel Corp.* (1937), *United States v. Darby* (1941), and *Wickard v. Filburn* (1942)] ushered in an era of Commerce Clause jurisprudence that greatly expanded the previously defined authority of Congress under that Clause. In part, this was a recognition of the great changes that had occurred in the way business was carried on in this country. Enterprises that had once been local or at most regional in nature had become national in scope. . . .

But even these modern-era precedents which have expanded congressional power under the Commerce Clause confirm that this power is subject to outer limits. In *Jones & Laughlin Steel*, the Court warned that the scope of the interstate commerce power "must be considered in the light of our dual system of government and may not be extended so as to embrace effects upon interstate commerce so indirect and remote that to embrace them, in view of our complex society, would effectually obliterate the dis-

tinction between what is national and what is local and create a completely centralized government." . . . Since that time, the Court has heeded that warning and undertaken to decide whether a rational basis existed for concluding that a regulated activity sufficiently affected interstate commerce.

Consistent with this structure, we have identified three broad categories of activity that Congress may regulate under its commerce power. First, Congress may regulate the use of the channels of interstate commerce. Second, Congress is empowered to regulate and protect the instrumentalities of interstate commerce, or persons or things in interstate commerce, even though the threat may come only from intrastate activities. Finally, Congress' commerce authority includes the power to regulate those activities having a substantial relation to interstate commerce. . . .

We now turn to consider the power of Congress, in the light of this framework, to enact [the Act before us]. The first two categories of authority may be quickly disposed of: [The Act] is not a regulation of the use of the channels of interstate commerce, nor is it an attempt to prohibit the interstate transportation of a commodity through the channels of commerce; nor can [the Act] be justified as a regulation of an activity that substantially affects interstate commerce.

First, we have upheld a wide variety of congressional Acts regulating intrastate economic activity where we have concluded that the activity substantially affected interstate commerce. . . . [These examples show that] where economic activity substantially affects interstate commerce, legislation regulating that activity will be sustained.

The Government's essential contention, in fine, is that we may determine here that [the Act] is valid because possession of a firearm in a local school zone does indeed substantially affect interstate commerce. The Government argues that possession of a firearm in a school zone may result in violent crime and that violent crime can be expected to affect the functioning of the national economy in two ways. First, the costs of violent crime are substantial, and, through the mechanism of insurance, those costs are spread throughout the population. Second, violent crime reduces the willingness of individuals to travel to areas within the country that are perceived to be unsafe. The Government also argues that the presence of guns in schools poses a substantial threat to the educational process by threatening the learning environment. A handicapped educational process, in turn, will result in a less productive citizenry. That, in turn, would have an adverse effect on the Nation's economic well being. As a result, the Government argues that Congress could rationally have concluded that [the Act] substantially affects interstate commerce.

We pause to consider the implications of the Government's arguments. The Government admits, under its "costs of crime" reasoning, that Congress could regulate not only all violent crime, but all activities that might lead to violent crime, regardless of how tenuously they relate to interstate commerce. Similarly, under the Government's "national productivity" reasoning, Congress could regulate any activity that it found was related to the economic productivity of individual citizens: family law (including marriage, divorce, and child custody), for example. Under the theories that the Government presents . . . it is difficult to perceive any limitation on federal power, even in areas such as criminal law enforcement or education where States historically have been sovereign. Thus, if we were to accept the Government's arguments, we are hard-pressed to posit any activity by an individual that Congress is without power to regulate.

Justice Breyer rejects our reading of precedent and argues that "Congress . . . could rationally conclude that schools fall on the commercial side of the line." Again, Justice Breyer's rationale lacks any real limits because, depending on the level of generality, any activity can be looked upon as commercial. Under the dissent's rationale, Congress could just as easily look at child rearing as "fall[-ing] on the commercial side of the line" because it provides a "valuable service—namely, to equip [children] with the skills they need to survive in life and, more specifically, in the workplace." We do not doubt that Congress has authority under the Commerce Clause to regulate numerous commercial activities that substantially affect interstate commerce and also affect the educational process. That authority, though broad, does not include the authority to regulate each and every aspect of local schools.

To uphold the Government's contentions here, we would have to pile inference upon inference in a manner that would bid fair to convert congressional authority under the Commerce Clause to a general police power of the sort retained by the States. Admittedly, some of our prior cases have taken long steps down that road, giving great deference to congressional action. The broad language in [past] opinions has suggested the possibility of additional expansion, but we decline here to proceed any further. To do so would require us to conclude that the Constitution's enumeration of powers does not presuppose something not enumerated, and that there never will be a distinction between what is truly national and what is truly local. This we are unwilling to do. For the foregoing reasons the judgment of the Court of Appeals is Affirmed.

Justice THOMAS, concurring.

The Court today properly concludes that the Commerce Clause does not grant Congress the authority to prohibit gun possession within 1,000 feet of a school, as it attempted to do in the Gun-Free School Zones Act of 1990. Although I join the majority, I write separately to observe that our case law has drifted far from the original understanding of the Commerce Clause. In a future case, we ought to temper our Commerce Clause jurisprudence in a manner that both makes sense of our more recent case law and is more faithful to the original understanding of that Clause.

. . . [I]t seems to me that the power to regulate "commerce" can by no means encompass authority over mere gun possession, any more than it empowers the Federal Government to regulate marriage, littering, or cruelty to animals, throughout the 50 States. Our Constitution quite properly leaves such matters to the individual States, notwithstanding these activities' effects on interstate commerce. Any interpretation of the Commerce Clause that even suggests that Congress could regulate such matters is in need of reexamination.

[*E. C. Knight* (1895), *Schechter* (1935), *Carter Coal Co.* (1936), and related cases] all establish a simple point: from the time of the ratification of the Constitution to the mid-1930's, it was widely understood that the Constitution granted Congress only limited powers, notwithstanding the Commerce Clause. Moreover, there was no question that activities wholly separated from business, such as gun possession, were beyond the reach of the commerce power. If anything, the "wrong turn" was the Court's dramatic departure in the 1930's from a century and a half of precedent.

Justice BREYER, with whom Justice STEVENS, Justice SOUTER, and Justice GINSBURG join, dissenting.

The issue in this case is whether the Commerce Clause authorizes Congress to enact a statute that makes it a crime to possess a gun in, or near, a school. In my view, the statute falls well within the scope of the commerce power as this Court has understood that power over the last half-century.

I

In reaching this conclusion, I apply three basic principles of Commerce Clause interpretation. First, the power to "regulate Commerce . . . among the several States" encompasses the power to regulate local activities insofar as they significantly affect interstate commerce. See *Gibbons v. Ogden* (1824), *Wickard v. Filburn* (1942).

Second, in determining whether a local activity will likely have a significant effect upon interstate commerce, a court must consider, not the effect of an individual act (a single instance of gun possession), but rather the cumulative effect of all similar instances (i.e, the effect of all guns possessed in or near schools). . . .

Third, the Constitution requires us to judge the connection between a regulated activity and interstate commerce, not directly, but at one remove. Courts must give Congress a degree of leeway in determining the existence of a significant factual connection between the regulated activity and interstate commerce—both because the Constitution delegates the commerce power directly to Congress and because the determination requires an empirical judgment of a kind that a legislature is more likely than a court to make with accuracy. The traditional words "rational basis" capture this leeway. Thus, the specific question before us, as the Court recognizes, is not whether the "regulated activity sufficiently affected interstate commerce," but, rather, whether Congress could have had "*a rational basis*" for so concluding.

II

Applying these principles to the case at hand, we must ask whether Congress could have had a *rational basis* for finding a significant (or substantial) connection between gun-related school violence and interstate commerce. . . . As long as one views the commerce connection, not as a "technical legal conception," but as "a practical one," the answer to this question must be yes. Numerous reports and studies—generated both inside and outside government—make clear that Congress could reasonably have found the empirical connection that its law, implicitly or explicitly, asserts.

. . . Congress obviously could have thought that guns and learning are mutually exclusive. And, Congress could therefore have found a substantial educational problem—teachers unable to teach, students unable to learn—and concluded that guns near schools contribute substantially to the size and scope of that problem.

Having found that guns in schools significantly undermine the quality of education in our Nation's classrooms, Congress could also have found, given the effect of education upon interstate and foreign commerce, that gun-related violence in and around schools is a commercial, as well as a human, problem. . . .

In recent years the link between secondary education and business has strengthened, becoming both more direct and more important. . . . Increasing global competition also has made primary and secondary education economically more important. . . . Finally, there is evidence that, today more than ever, many firms base their location decisions upon the presence, or absence, of a work force with a basic education.

The economic links I have just sketched seem fairly obvious. Why then is it not equally obvious, in light of those links, that a widespread, serious, and substantial physical threat to teaching and learning also substantially threatens the commerce to which that teaching and learning is inextricably tied? . . . The only question, then, is whether the latter threat is (to use the majority's terminology) "substantial." And, the evidence of (1) the *extent* of the gun-related violence problem, (2) the *extent* of the resulting negative effect on classroom learning and (3) the extent of the consequent negative commercial effects when taken together, indicate a threat to trade and commerce that is "substantial." At the very least, Congress could rationally have concluded that the links are "substantial."

To hold this statute constitutional is not to "obliterate" the "distinction of what is national and what is local," nor is it to hold that the Commerce Clause permits the Federal Government to "regulate any activity that it found was related to the economic productivity of individual citizens," to regulate "marriage, divorce, and child custody," or to regulate any and all aspects of education. . . .

In sum, a holding that the particular statute before us falls within the commerce power would not expand the scope of that Clause. Rather, it simply would apply preexisting law to changing economic circumstances. It would recognize that, in today's economic world, gun-related violence near the classroom makes a significant difference to our economic, as well as our social, well being. In accordance with well-accepted precedent, such a holding would permit Congress "to act in terms of economic . . . realities," would interpret the commerce power as "an affirmative power commensurate with national needs," and would acknowledge that the "commerce clause does not operate so as to render the nation powerless to defend itself against economic forces that Congress decrees inimical or destructive of the national economy."

Notes and Queries

1. What standards does Chief Justice Rehnquist propose for distinguishing between "what is truly national" and "what is truly local"? Do those standards find their source in the constitutional text? In the original understanding of the commerce clause and the Tenth Amend-

ment? In contemporary judicial understanding about the marketplace?

2. What is the original understanding of the commerce clause to which Justice Thomas refers? Is that understanding outdated in light of two centuries of economic development? If it is outdated, should the judiciary interpret it in ways that make it relevant for contemporary conditions? Is Justice Thomas suggesting that the Court's decisions striking down significant parts of the New Deal, as in *Schechter* and *Hammer*, were correctly decided after all?

3. What understanding of judicial power does the dissent by Justice Breyer adopt? Does the "rational basis" standard mean, in practice, that the Court will exercise no supervision over the commerce clause?

4. Justice Breyer insists that to uphold the statute in this case "is not to 'obliterate' the distinction" between what is national and what is local. Do you agree? What criteria does he offer to help us make the distinction?

5. Suppose we were to find that the Texas delegation in the U.S. Congress voted unanimously against the Gun-Free Zone law. Would this reality favor the majority opinion? Suppose, on the other hand, that Congress had vigorously debated the constitutionality of the law, concluding that it did not offend the values implicit in the Tenth Amendment. Would this reality argue for a passive judicial role?

United States v. Morrison
529 U.S. 598, 120 S.Ct. 1740, 146 L.Ed.2d 658 (2000)

Christy Brzonkala enrolled at Virginia Polytechnic Institute (Virginia Tech) in 1994. In September of that year she met Antonio Morrison and James Crawford, both fellow students and members of Virginia Tech's varsity football team. Minutes after the meeting Morrison and Crawford assaulted and repeatedly raped her. Brzonkala sued her attackers under the Violence Against Women Act. The statute, passed by Congress in 1994, declared that "all persons within the United States shall have the right to be free from crimes of violence motivated by gender" and provided a civil action for damages against violators of the statute. Lower federal courts invalidated the statute on constitutional grounds. The Supreme Court granted certiorari to consider two issues: Whether the Violence Against Women Act went beyond Congress' power to regulate commerce and whether it exceeded Congress' authority under Section 5 of the Fourteenth Amendment. The extracts below are confined to the Court's interpretation of the commerce power. Opinion of the Court: *Rehnquist,*

O'Connor, Scalia, Kennedy, Thomas. Concurring opinion: *Thomas.* Dissenting opinions: *Souter,* Stevens, Ginsburg, *Breyer.*

Chief Justice REHNQUIST delivered the opinion of the Court.

In these cases we consider the constitutionality of 42 U.S.C. s. 13981 which provides a federal civil remedy for the victims of gender-motivated violence. The United States Court of Appeals for the Fourth Circuit, sitting en banc, struck down s.13981 because it concluded that Congress lacked constitutional authority to enact the section's civil remedy.

Section 13981 was part of the Violence Against Women Act of 1994. It states that "[a]ll persons within the United States shall have the right to be free from crimes of violence motivated by gender." To enforce that right, subsection (c) declares: "A person (including a person who acts under color of any statute, ordinance, regulation, custom, or usage of any State) who commits a crime of violence motivated by gender and thus deprives another of the right declared in subsection (b) of this section shall be

Comparative Note 7.8

[Canada's *Combines Investigation Act* (1970) creates a federal civil remedy against any business which engages in anti-competitive practices. Because the creation of civil causes of action are within the domain of the provinces, the Act was challenged as an invalid exercise of the national government's power to regulate "trade and commerce." The following extracts are from Chief Justice Dickson's opinion upholding the law.]

[There are] three hallmarks of validity for legislation under the . . . trade and commerce power. First, the impugned legislation . . . must be part of a general regulatory scheme. Second, the scheme must be monitored by the continuing oversight of a regulatory agency. Third, the legislation must be concerned with trade as a whole rather than with a particular industry. . . .

In determining the proper test it should be remembered that in a federal system it is inevitable that, in pursuing valid objectives, the legislation of each level of government will impact occasionally on the sphere of power of the other level of government; . . . Thus a certain degree of judicial restraint in proposing strict tests which will result in striking down such legislation is appropriate. . . . As the seriousness of the encroachment on provincial powers varies, so does the test required to ensure that an appropriate constitutional balance is maintained. . . . [The] criteria [mentioned] share a common theme: all three are indications that the scheme of regulation is national in scope and that local regulation would be inadequate. The Act is quite clearly concerned with the regulation of trade in general, rather than with the regulation of a particular industry or commodity. . . . [The] purpose of the Act is to ensure the existence of a healthy level of competition in the Canadian economy. The deleterious effects of anti-competitive practices transcend provincial boundaries. Competition is not an issue of purely local concern but one of crucial importance for the national economy.

Source: *General Motors of Canada Ltd. V. City National Leasing et al.,* 58 D.L.R. (4th) 268ff (1989).

---

liable to the party injured, in an action for the recovery of compensatory and punitive damages, injunctive and declaratory relief, and such other relief as a court may deem appropriate."

Every law enacted by Congress must be based on one or more of its powers enumerated in the Constitution. "The powers of the legislature are defined and limited; and that those limits may not be mistaken or forgotten, the constitution is written." Congress explicitly identified the sources of federal authority on which it relied in enacting s.13981. It said that a "federal civil rights cause of action" is established "[p]ursuant to the affirmative power of Congress . . . under section 5 of the Fourteenth Amendment to the Constitution [and] under section 8 of Article I of the Constitution." We address Congress' authority to enact this remedy under [section 8].

As we observed in *[United States v.] Lopez,* modern Commerce Clause jurisprudence has "identified three broad categories of activity that Congress may regulate under its commerce power." "First, Congress may regulate the use of the channels of interstate commerce." "Second, Congress is empowered to regulate and protect the instrumentalities of interstate commerce, or persons or things in interstate commerce, even though the threat may come only from intrastate activities." "Finally, Congress' commerce authority includes the power to regulate those activities having a substantial relation to interstate commerce, . . . *i.e.,* those activities that substantially affect interstate commerce."

Petitioners do not contend that these cases fall within either of the first two of these categories of Commerce Clause regulation. They seek to sustain s.13981 as a regulation of activity that substantially affects interstate commerce.

Since *Lopez* most recently canvassed and clarified our case law governing this third category of Commerce Clause regulation, it provides the proper framework for conducting the required analysis of s.13981. In *Lopez,* we held that the Gun-Free School Zones Act of 1990, which made it a federal crime to knowingly possess a firearm in a school zone, exceeded Congress' authority under the Commerce Clause.

Several significant considerations contributed to our decision. First, we observed that s.922(q) was "a criminal statute that by its terms has nothing to do with 'commerce' or any sort of economic enterprise, however broadly one might define those terms." But a fair reading of *Lopez* shows that the noneconomic, criminal nature of the conduct at issue was central to our decision in that case. The second consideration that we found important in analyzing s.922(q) was that the statute contained "no express jurisdictional element which might limit its reach to a discrete set of firearm possessions that additionally have an explicit connection with or effect on interstate commerce." Third, we noted that neither s.922(q) " 'nor its legislative history contain[s] express congressional findings regarding the effects upon interstate commerce of gun possession in a school zone.' " Finally, our decision in *Lopez* rested in part on the fact that the link between gun possession and a substantial effect on interstate commerce was attenuated.

We rejected these "costs of crime" and "national productivity" arguments because they would permit Congress to "regulate not only all violent crime, but all activities that might lead to violent crime, regardless of how tenuously they relate to interstate commerce."

With these principles underlying our Commerce Clause jurisprudence as reference points, the proper resolution of the present cases is clear. Gender-motivated crimes of violence are not, in any sense of the phrase, economic activity. While we need not adopt a categorical rule against aggregating the effects of any noneconomic activity in order to decide these cases, thus far in our Nation's history our cases have upheld Commerce Clause regulation of intrastate activity only where that activity is economic in nature.

Like the Gun-Free School Zones Act at issue in *Lopez*, s.13981 contains no jurisdictional element establishing that the federal cause of action is in pursuance of Congress' power to regulate interstate commerce. Although *Lopez* makes clear that such a jurisdictional element would lend support to the argument that s.13981 is sufficiently tied to interstate commerce, Congress elected to cast s.13981's remedy over a wider, and more purely intrastate, body of violent crime.

In contrast with the lack of congressional findings that we faced in *Lopez*, s.13981 *is* supported by numerous findings regarding the serious impact that gender-motivated violence has on victims and their families. But the existence of congressional findings is not sufficient, by itself, to sustain the constitutionality of Commerce Clause legislation. As we stated in *Lopez*, "[S]imply because Congress may conclude that a particular activity substantially affects interstate commerce does not necessarily make it so."

In these cases, Congress' findings are substantially weakened by the fact that they rely so heavily on a method of reasoning that we have already rejected as unworkable if we are to maintain the Constitution's enumer-ation of powers. Congress found that gender-motivated violence affects interstate commerce "by deterring potential victims from traveling interstate, from engaging in employment in interstate business, and from transacting with business, and in places involved in interstate commerce; . . . by diminishing national productivity, increasing medical and other costs, and decreasing the supply of and the demand for interstate products."

Given these findings and petitioners' arguments, the concern that we expressed in *Lopez* that Congress might use the Commerce Clause to completely obliterate the Constitution's distinction between national and local authority seems well founded. The reasoning that petitioners advance seeks to follow the but-for causal chain from the initial occurrence of violent crime (the suppression of which has always been the prime object of the States' police power) to every attenuated effect upon interstate commerce. If accepted, petitioners' reasoning would allow Congress to regulate any crime as long as the nationwide, aggregated impact of that crime has substantial effects on employment, production, transit, or consumption. Indeed, if Congress may regulate gender-motivated violence, it would be able to regulate murder or any other type of violence since gender-motivated violence, as a subset of all violent crime, is certain to have lesser economic impacts than the larger class of which it is a part.

Petitioners' reasoning, moreover, will not limit Congress to regulating violence but may, as we suggested in *Lopez*, be applied equally as well to family law and other areas of traditional state regulation since the aggregate effect of marriage, divorce, and childrearing on the national economy is undoubtedly significant. Congress may have recognized this specter when it expressly precluded s.13981 from being used in the family law context.

We accordingly reject the argument that Congress may regulate noneconomic, violent criminal conduct based solely on that conduct's aggregate effect on interstate commerce. The Constitution requires a distinction between what is truly national and what is truly local. . . .

[W]e conclude that the Commerce Clause does not provide Congress with authority to enact s.13981, we address petitioners' alternative argument that the section's civil remedy should be upheld as an exercise of Congress' remedial power under s.5 of the Fourteenth Amendment. As noted above, Congress expressly invoked the Fourteenth Amendment as a source of authority to enact s.13981.

Justice THOMAS, concurring.

The majority opinion correctly applies our decision in *United States* v. *Lopez,* and I join it in full. I write separately only to express my view that the very notion of a "substantial effects" test under the Commerce Clause is inconsistent with the original understanding of Congress' powers and with this Court's early Commerce Clause cases. By continuing to apply this rootless and malleable standard, however circumscribed, the Court has encouraged the Federal Government to persist in its view that the Commerce Clause has virtually no limits. Until this Court replaces its existing Commerce Clause jurisprudence with a standard more consistent with the original understanding, we will continue to see Congress appropriating state police powers under the guise of regulating commerce.

Justice SOUTER, with whom Justice STEVENS, Justice GINSBURG, and Justice BREYER join, dissenting.

The Court says both that it leaves Commerce Clause precedent undisturbed and that the Civil Rights Remedy of the Violence Against Women Act of 1994, exceeds Congress's power under that Clause. I find the claims irreconcilable and respectfully dissent.

Our cases, which remain at least nominally undisturbed, stand for the following propositions. Congress has the power to legislate with regard to activity that, in the aggregate, has a substantial effect on interstate commerce. The fact of such a substantial effect is not an issue for the courts in the first instance, but for the Congress, whose institutional capacity for gathering evidence and taking testimony far exceeds ours. By passing legislation, Congress indicates its conclusion, whether explicitly or not, that facts support its exercise of the commerce power. The business of the courts is to review the congressional assessment, not for soundness but simply for the rationality of concluding that a jurisdictional basis exists in fact. Any explicit findings that Congress chooses to make, though not dispositive of the question of rationality, may advance judicial review by identifying factual authority on which Congress relied. Applying those propositions in these cases can lead to only one conclusion.

One obvious difference from *Lopez* is the mountain of data assembled by Congress, here showing the effects of violence against women on interstate commerce. Passage of the Act in 1994 was preceded by four years of hearings, which included testimony from physicians and law professors; from survivors of rape and domestic violence; and from representatives of state law enforcement and private business. The record includes reports on gender bias from task forces in 21 States, and we have the benefit of specific factual findings in the eight separate Reports issued by Congress and its committees over the long course leading to enactment.

. . . Congress found that "crimes of violence motivated by gender have a substantial adverse effect on interstate commerce, by deterring potential victims from traveling interstate, from engaging in employment in interstate business, and from transacting with business, and in places involved, in interstate commerce . . . [,] by diminishing national productivity, increasing medical and other costs, and decreasing the supply of and the demand for interstate products. . . ."

Congress thereby explicitly stated the predicate for the exercise of its Commerce Clause power. Is its conclusion irrational in view of the data amassed? True, the methodology of particular studies may be challenged, and some of the figures arrived at may be disputed. But the sufficiency of the evidence before Congress to provide a rational basis for the finding cannot seriously be questioned. ("The Constitution gives to Congress the role of weighing conflicting evidence in the legislative process.")

The Act would have passed muster at any time between *Wickard* in 1942 and *Lopez* in 1995, a period in which the law enjoyed a stable understanding that congressional power under the Commerce Clause, complemented by the authority of the Necessary and Proper Clause, Art. I. s.8 cl. 18, extended to all activity that, when aggregated, has a substantial effect on interstate commerce. As already noted, this understanding was secure even against the turmoil at the passage of the Civil Rights Act of 1964, in the aftermath of which the Court not only reaffirmed the cumulative effects and rational basis features of the substantial effects test, but declined to limit the commerce power through a formal distinction between legislation focused on "commerce" and statutes addressing "moral and social wrong[s]."

The fact that the Act does not pass muster before the Court today is therefore proof, to a degree that *Lopez* was not, that the Court's nominal adherence to the substantial effects test is merely that. Although a new jurisprudence has not emerged with any distinctness, it is clear that some congressional conclusions about obviously substantial, cumulative effects on commerce are being assigned lesser values than the once-stable doctrine would assign them. These devaluations are accomplished not by any express repudiation of the substantial effects test or its application through the aggregation of individual conduct, but by supplanting rational basis scrutiny with a new criterion of review.

This new characterization of substantial effects has no support in our cases (the self-fulfilling prophecies of *Lopez* aside), least of all those the majority cites. Perhaps this explains why the majority is not content to rest on its cited precedent but claims a textual justification for moving toward its new system of congressional deference subject to selective discounts.

The Court finds it relevant that the statute addresses conduct traditionally subject to state prohibition under domestic criminal law, a fact said to have some heightened significance when the violent conduct in question is not itself aimed directly at interstate commerce or its instrumentalities. Again, history seems to be recycling, for the theory of traditional state concern as grounding a limiting principle has been rejected previously, and more than once.

The objection to reviving traditional state spheres of action as a consideration in commerce analysis, however, not only rests on the portent of incoherence, but is compounded by a further defect just as fundamental. The defect, in essence, is the majority's rejection of the Founders' considered judgment that politics, not judicial review, should mediate between state and national interests as the strength and legislative jurisdiction of the National Government inevitably increased through the expected growth of the national economy.

Politics as the moderator of the congressional employment of the commerce power was the theme many years later in *Wickard,* for after the Court acknowledged the breadth of the *Gibbons* formulation it invoked Chief Justice Marshall yet again in adding that "[h]e made emphatic the embracing and penetrating nature of this power by warning that effective restraints on its exercise must proceed from political rather than judicial processes."

As with "conflicts of economic interest," so with supposed conflicts of sovereign political interests implicated by the Commerce Clause: the Constitution remits them to politics.

All of this convinces me that today's ebb of the commerce power rests on error, and at the same time leads me to doubt that the majority's view will prove to be enduring law.

Justice BREYER, with whom Justice STEVENS joins, and with whom Justice SOUTER and Justice GINSBURG join as to Part I—A, dissenting.

No one denies the importance of the Constitution's federalist principles. Its state/federal division of authority protects liberty—both by restricting the burdens that government can impose from a distance and by facilitating citizen participation in government that is closer to home. The question is how the judiciary can best implement that original federalist understanding where the Commerce Clause is at issue.

The majority holds that the federal commerce power does not extend to such "noneconomic" activities as "noneconomic, violent criminal conduct" that significantly affects interstate commerce only if we "aggregate" the interstate "effect[s]" of individual instances. Justice Souter explains why history, precedent, and legal logic militate against the majority's approach. I agree and join his opinion. I add that the majority's holding illustrates the difficulty of finding a workable judicial Commerce Clause touchstone—a set of comprehensible interpretive rules that courts might use to impose some meaningful limit, but not too great a limit, upon the scope of the legislative authority that the Commerce Clause delegates to Congress.

Consider the problems. The "economic/noneconomic" distinction is not easy to apply. Does the local street corner mugger engage in "economic" activity or "noneconomic" activity when he mugs for money? Would evidence that desire for economic domination underlies many brutal crimes against women save the present statute?

The line becomes yet harder to draw given the need for exceptions. The Court itself would permit Congress to aggregate, hence regulate, "noneconomic" activity taking place at economic establishments. And it would permit Congress to regulate where that regulation is "an essential part of a larger regulation of economic activity, in which the regulatory scheme could be undercut unless the intrastate activity were regulated." Given the former exception, can Congress simply rewrite the present law and limit its application to restaurants, hotels, perhaps universities, and other places of public accommodation? Given the latter exception, can Congress save the present law by including it, or much of it, in a broader "Safe Transport" or "Workplace Safety" act?

More important, why should we give critical constitutional importance to the economic, or noneconomic, nature of an interstate-commerce-affecting *cause*? If chemical emanations through indirect environmental change cause identical, severe commercial harm outside a State, why should it matter whether local factories or home fireplaces release them? The Constitution itself refers only to Congress' power to "regulate Commerce . . . among the several States," and to make laws "necessary and proper" to implement that power. Art. I, s.8, cls. 3, 18. The language says nothing about either the local nature, or the economic nature, of an interstate-commerce-affecting cause.

This Court has long held that only the interstate commercial effects, not the local nature of the cause, are constitutionally relevant. Nothing in the Constitution's language, or that of earlier cases prior to *Lopez,* explains why the Court should ignore one highly relevant characteristic of an interstate-commerce-affecting cause (how "local" it is), while placing critical constitutional weight upon a different, less obviously relevant, feature (how "economic" it is).

The majority . . . is . . . concerned with what it sees as an important . . . consideration. To determine the lawfulness of statutes simply by asking whether Congress could reasonably have found that *aggregated* local instances significantly affect interstate commerce will allow Congress to regulate almost anything. Virtually all local activity, when instances are aggregated, can have "substantial effects on employment, production, transit, or consumption." Hence Congress could "regulate any crime," and perhaps "marriage, divorce, and childrearing" as well, obliterating the "Constitution's distinction between national and local authority."

This consideration, however, while serious, does not reflect a jurisprudential defect, so much as it reflects a practical reality. We live in a Nation knit together by two centuries of scientific, technological, commercial, and environmental change. Those changes, taken together, mean that virtually every kind of activity, no matter how local, genuinely can affect commerce, or its conditions, outside the State—at least when considered in the aggregate. And that fact makes it close to impossible for courts to develop meaningful subject-matter categories that would exclude some kinds of local activities from ordinary Commerce Clause "aggregation" rules without, at the same time, depriving Congress of the power to regulate activities that have a genuine and important effect upon interstate commerce.

Since judges cannot change the world, the "defect" means that, within the bounds of the rational, Congress, not the courts, must remain primarily responsible for striking the appropriate state/federal balance.

I would also note that Congress, when it enacted the statute, followed procedures that help to protect the federalism values at stake. It provided adequate notice to the States of its intent to legislate in an "are[a] of traditional state regulation." And in response, attorneys general in the overwhelming majority of States (38) supported congressional legislation, telling Congress that "[o]ur experience as Attorneys General strengthens our belief that the problem of violence against women is a national one, requiring federal attention, federal leadership, and federal funds."

I continue to agree with Justice Souter that the Court's traditional "rational basis" approach is sufficient. But I recognize that the law in this area is unstable and that time and experience may demonstrate both the unworkability of the majority's rules and the superiority of Congress' own procedural approach—in which case the law may evolve towards a rule that, in certain difficult Commerce Clause cases, takes account of the thoroughness with which Congress has considered the federalism issue.

For these reasons . . . this statute falls well within Congress's Commerce Clause authority, and I dissent from the Court's contrary conclusion.

Notes and Queries

1. Can *Morrison* be reconciled with *Wickard v. Filburn* and *Heart of Atlanta Motel, Inc. v. United States*? In *Atlanta Motel*, Justice Black wrote: "I recognize that every remote, possible, speculative effect on commerce should not be accepted as an adequate constitutional ground to uproot and throw into discard all our traditional distinctions between what is purely local, and therefore controlled by state laws, and what affects the national interest and is therefore subject to control by federal laws." Have the dissenting justices abandoned Black's view of the limits on the exercise of the commerce power?

2. Chief Justice Rehnquist differentiates between economic and noneconomic activities, a distinction that Justice Breyer says is hard to draw. Is the distinction a meaningful one in assessing the reach of congressional power over interstate commerce in the 21st century?

3. Justice Thomas would do away with the "substantial effects" test because it "is inconsistent with the original understanding of Congress' powers and with this Court's early Commerce Clause cases." Does John Marshall's opinion in *Gibbons v. Ogden* support Thomas' view of "original understanding"? As for Marshall, this is how he defined the commerce power in *Gibbons*: "The power [to regulate commerce], like all others vested in Congress is complete in itself, may be exercised to its utmost extent, and acknowledges no limitations, other than are prescribed in the constitution." Is the majority opinion in *Morrison* (and *Lopez*) consistent with Marshall's definition of the commerce power?

4. Justice Souter, dissenting, points out—citing James Wilson, John Marshall, and James Madison in particular—that it was the "Founders' considered judgment that politics, not judicial review, should mediate between state and national interests as the strength and legislative jurisdiction of the National Government inevitably increased through the expected growth of the national economy." What then is the source of the historical disagreement between Justices Souter and Thomas?

5. In *Narrowing the Nation's Power* (2000), Judge John T. Noonan Jr. writes: [H]istorical examples showed how misguided and how ineffectual had been attempts by the Supreme Court between 1887 and 1937 to create categorical enclaves exempt from the commerce power. These at-

tempts included cases holding that mining, [production, manufacturing, and labor relations were] not commerce between the states. . . . They included the long, sustained, quixotic effort by the court to distinguish between direct and indirect effects on commerce and to hold that only activities 'directly' affecting commerce could be regulated by Congress. Some of these categories had set out a sharp, clear concept, only for the concept in the course of time to prove inadequate to measure the interstate impact of industry. . . . Adherence to the categories had produced the constitutional confrontation with the New Deal and the judicial crisis of 1937. The court now was taking 'a step toward recapturing the prior mistakes.'" Do *Lopez* and *Morrison* recapture these "prior mistakes"? Or do they set out a reasonable basis for a new and workable theory of state autonomy?

United States v. Butler
297 U.S. 1, 56 S.Ct. 312, 80 L.Ed. 477 (1936)

The Agricultural Adjustment Act of 1933 was a New Deal measure designed to stabilize farm prices by maintaining a balance between the production and consumption of agricultural products. The act authorized the secretary of agriculture to reduce the acreage devoted to agricultural production. Farmers who took their acreage out of production through agreement with producers were to be compensated with funds raised by a processing tax levied on certain agricultural products. Following Butler's refusal to pay the processing tax, a federal district court found the taxes valid and ordered them paid. The court of appeals reversed, and the government appealed. Opinion of the Court: *Roberts*, Hughes, VanDevanter, McReynolds, Sutherland, Butler. Dissenting opinion: *Stone*, Brandeis, Cardozo.

Mr. Justice ROBERTS delivered the opinion of the Court.

. . . The government asserts that even if the respondents may question the propriety of the appropriation embodied in the statute, their attack must fail because Article I, s 8 of the Constitution, authorizes the contemplated expenditure of the funds raised by the tax. This contention presents the great and the controlling question in the case. We approach its decision with a sense of our grave responsibility to render judgment in accordance with the principles established for the governance of all three branches of the government.

There should be no misunderstanding as to the function of this court in such a case. It is sometimes said that the court assumes a power to overrule or control the action of the people's representatives. This is a misconception. The Constitution is the supreme law of the land ordained and established by the people. All legislation must conform to the principles it lays down. When an act of Congress is appropriately challenged in the courts as not conforming to the constitutional mandate, the judicial branch of the government has only one duty; to lay the article of the Constitution which is invoked beside the statute which is challenged and to decide whether the latter squares with the former. All the court does, or can do, is to announce its considered judgment upon the question. The only power it has, if such it may be called, is the power of judgment. This court neither approves nor condemns any legislative policy. Its delicate and difficult office is to ascertain and declare whether the legislation is in accordance with, or in contravention of, the provisions of the Constitution; and, having done that, its duty ends.

The question is not what power the federal government ought to have, but what powers in fact have been given by the people. It hardly seems necessary to reiterate that ours is a dual form of government; that in every state there are two governments—the State and the United States. Each State has all governmental powers save such as the people, by their Constitution, have conferred upon the United States, denied to the states, or reserved to themselves. The federal union is a government of delegated powers. It has only such as are expressly conferred upon it and such as are reasonably to be implied from those granted. In this respect we differ radically from nations where all legislative power, without restriction or limitation, is vested in a parliament or other legislative body subject to no restrictions except the discretion of its members.

Article I, s 8, of the Constitution, vests sundry powers in the Congress. But two of its clauses have any bearing upon the validity of the statute under review.

The clause thought to authorize the legislation, the first, confers upon the Congress power "to lay and collect Taxes, Duties, Imposts and Excises, to pay the Debts and provide for the common Defense and general Welfare of the United States." It is not contended that this provision grants power to regulate agricultural production upon the theory that such legislation would promote the general welfare. The government concedes that the phrase "to provide for the general welfare" qualifies the power "to lay and collect taxes." The view that the clause grants

Comparative Note 7.9

[In this case, the Privy Council struck down Canada's Employment and Social Security Act of 1935, the Dominion's equivalent of American "New Deal" legislation. Designed to alleviate the problem of unemployment, the Act established an unemployment insurance scheme to be paid for out of federal funds. The parliament passed the statute under its residual power to provide for the peace, order, and good government of Canada. In holding the act unconstitutional, the Privy Council affirmed the decision of the Canadian Supreme Court.]

Lord Atkin . . . There can be no doubt that, *prima facie,* provisions as to insurance of this kind, especially where they affect the contract of employment, fall within the class of property and civil rights in the Province, and would be within the exclusive competence of the Provincial Legislature.

. . . A strong appeal [in support of the Act has been] made on the ground of the special importance of unemployment insurance in Canada at the time of, and for some time previous to, the passing of the Act. . . . It is sufficient to say that the present Act does not purport to deal with any special emergency. . . .

It only remains to deal with the argument . . . that the legislation can be supported under [the Dominion's power to raise] money by any mode or system of taxation. . . .

That the Dominion may impose taxation for the purpose of creating a fund for special purposes . . . could not as a general proposition be denied. . . . But assuming that the Dominion has collected by means of taxation [an unemployment insurance] fund, it by no means follows that any legislation which disposes of it is necessarily within Dominion competence. [The legislation may still] encroach upon the classes of subjects which are reserved to Provincial competence. It is not necessary that it should be a colourable device, or a pretense. If on the true view of the legislation it is found that in reality in pith and substance the legislation invades civil rights within the Province . . . the legislation will be invalid. . . . In the present case, their Lordships agreed with the majority of the Supreme Court in holding that in pith and substance this Act is an insurance Act affecting the civil rights of employers and employed in each Province.

SOURCE: *Attorney General of Canada v. Attorney General of Ontario,* In the Privy Council [1937] A.C. 355; III Olmstead 207.

---

power to provide for the general welfare, independently of the taxing power, has never been authoritatively accepted. Mr. Justice Story points out that, if it were adopted, "it is obvious that under color of the generality of the words, to 'provide for the common defense and general welfare,' the government of the United States is, in reality, a government of general and unlimited powers, notwithstanding the subsequent enumeration of specific powers." The true construction undoubtedly is that the only thing granted is the power to tax for the purpose of providing funds for payment of the nation's debts and making provision for the general welfare.

Nevertheless, the Government asserts that warrant is found in this clause for the adoption of the Agricultural Adjustment Act. The argument is that Congress may appropriate and authorize the spending of moneys for the "general welfare"; that the phrase should be liberally construed to cover anything conducive to national welfare; that decision as to what will promote such welfare rests with Congress alone, and the courts may not review its determination; and, finally, that the appropriation under

attack was in fact for the general welfare of the United States.

The Congress is expressly empowered to lay taxes to provide for the general welfare. Funds in the Treasury as a result of taxation may be expended only through appropriation. Article I, s 9, cl. 7. They can never accomplish the objects for which they were collected, unless the power to appropriate is as broad as the power to tax. The necessary implication from the terms of the grant is that the public funds may be appropriated "to provide for the general welfare of the United States." These words cannot be meaningless, else they would not have been used. The conclusion must be that they were intended to limit and define the granted power to raise and to expend money. How shall they be construed to effectuate the intent of the instrument?

Since the foundation of the nation, sharp differences of opinion have persisted as to the true interpretation of the phrase. Madison asserted it amounted to no more than a reference to the other powers enumerated in the subsequent clauses of the same section; that, as the United

States is a government of limited and enumerated powers, the grant of power to tax and spend for the general national welfare must be confined to the enumerated legislative fields committed to the Congress. In this view the phrase is mere tautology, for taxation and appropriation are or may be necessary incidents of the exercise of any of the enumerated legislative powers. Hamilton, on the other hand, maintained the clause confers a power separate and distinct from those later enumerated, is not restricted in meaning by the grant of them, and Congress consequently has a substantive power to tax and to appropriate, limited only by the requirement that it shall be exercised to provide for the general welfare of the United States. Each contention has had the support of those whose views are entitled to weight. This court has noticed the question, but has never found it necessary to decide which is the true construction. Mr. Justice Story, in his Commentaries, espouses the Hamiltonian position. We shall not review the writings of public men and commentators or discuss the legislative practice. Study of all these leads us to conclude that the reading advocated by Mr. Justice Story is the correct one. While, therefore, the power to tax is not unlimited, its confines are set in the clause which confers it, and not in those of section 8 which bestow and define the legislative powers of the Congress. It results that the power of Congress to authorize expenditure of public moneys for public purposes is not limited by the direct grants of legislative power found in the Constitution.

But the adoption of the broader construction leaves the power to spend subject to limitations. . . . Story says that if the tax be not proposed for the common defense or general welfare, but for other objects wholly extraneous, it would be wholly indefensible upon constitutional principles. And he makes it clear that the powers of taxation and appropriation extend only to matters of national, as distinguished from local, welfare.

We are not now required to ascertain the scope of the phrase "general welfare of the United States" or to determine whether an appropriation in aid of agriculture falls within it. Wholly apart from that question, another principle embedded in our Constitution prohibits the enforcement of the Agricultural Adjustment Act. The act invades the reserved rights of the states. It is a statutory plan to regulate and control agricultural production, a matter beyond the powers delegated to the federal government. The tax, the appropriation of the funds raised, and the direction for their disbursement, are but parts of the plan. They are but means to an unconstitutional end.

From the accepted doctrine that the United States is a government of delegated powers, it follows that those not expressly granted, or reasonably to be implied from such as are conferred, are reserved to the states or to the people. To forestall any suggestion to the contrary, the Tenth Amendment was adopted. The same proposition, otherwise stated, is that powers not granted are prohibited. None to regulate agricultural production is given, and therefore legislation by Congress for that purpose is forbidden.

It is an established principle that the attainment of a prohibited end may not be accomplished under the pretext of the exertion of powers which are granted. . . . The power of taxation, which is expressly granted, may, of course, be adopted as a means to carry into operation another power also expressly granted. But resort to the taxing power to effectuate an end which is not legitimate, not within the scope of the Constitution, is obviously inadmissible.

If the taxing power may not be used as the instrument to enforce a regulation of matters of state concern with respect to which the Congress has no authority to interfere, may it, as in the present case, be employed to raise the money necessary to purchase a compliance which the Congress is powerless to command? The government asserts that whatever might be said against the validity of the plan, if compulsory, it is constitutionally sound because the end is accomplished by voluntary co-operation. . . . The regulation is not in fact voluntary. The farmer, of course, may refuse to comply, but the price of such refusal is the loss of benefits. The amount offered is intended to be sufficient to exert pressure on him to agree to the proposed regulation. The power to confer or withhold unlimited benefits is the power to coerce or destroy. . . .

But if the plan were one for purely voluntary co-operation it would stand no better so far as federal power is concerned. At best, it is a scheme for purchasing with federal funds submission to federal regulation of a subject reserved to the states. . . .

Congress has no power to enforce its commands on the farmer to the ends sought by the Agricultural Adjustment Act. It must follow that it may not indirectly accomplish those ends by taxing and spending to purchase compliance. The Constitution and the entire plan of our government negative any such use of the power to tax and to spend as the act undertakes to authorize. It does not help to declare that local conditions throughout the nation have created a situation of national concern; for this is but to say that whenever there is a widespread similarity of local conditions, Congress may ignore constitutional limitations upon its own powers and usurp those reserved to the states. If, in lieu of compulsory regulation of subjects within the states' reserved jurisdiction, which is prohibited, the Congress could invoke the taxing and spending power as a means to accomplish the same end, clause 1 of section 8 of Article I would become the instrument for total subversion of the governmental powers reserved to the individual states.

If the act before us is a proper exercise of the federal taxing power, evidently the regulation of all industry throughout the United States may be accomplished by similar exercises of the same power. It would be possible to exact money from one branch of an industry and pay it to another branch in every field of activity which lies within the province of the states. The mere threat of such a procedure might well induce the surrender of rights and the compliance with federal regulation as the price of continuance in business. . . .

The judgment is affirmed.

Mr. Justice STONE, dissenting.

The power of courts to declare a statute unconstitutional is subject to two guiding principles of decisions which ought never to be absent from judicial consciousness. One is that courts are concerned only with the power to enact statutes, not with their wisdom. The other is that while unconstitutional exercise of power by the executive and legislative branches of the government is subject to judicial restraint, the only check upon our own exercise of power is our own sense of self-restraint. For the removal of unwise laws from the statute books appeal lies, not to the courts, but to the ballot and to the processes of democratic government.

The constitutional power of Congress to levy an excise tax upon the processing of agricultural products is not questioned. The present levy is held invalid, not for any want of power in Congress to lay such a tax to defray public expenditures, including those for the general welfare, but because the use to which its proceeds are put is disapproved.

As the present depressed state of agriculture is nation wide in its extent and effects, there is no basis for saying that the expenditure of public money in aid of farmers is not within the specifically granted power of Congress to levy taxes to "provide for the general welfare." The opinion of the Court does not declare otherwise. . . .

It is with these preliminary and hardly controverted matters in mind that we should direct our attention to the pivot on which the decision of the Court is made to turn. It is that a levy unquestionably within the taxing power of Congress may be treated as invalid because it is a step in a plan to regulate agricultural production and is thus a forbidden infringement of state power. The levy is not any the less an exercise of taxing power because it is intended to defray an expenditure for the general welfare rather than for some other support of government. Nor is the levy and collection of the tax pointed to as effecting the regulation. While all federal taxes inevitably have some influence on the internal economy of the states, it is not contended that the levy of a processing tax upon manufacturers using agricultural products as a raw material has any perceptible regulatory effect upon either their production or manufacture. . . . Here regulation, if any there be, is accomplished not by the tax, but by the method by which its proceeds are expended, and would equally be accomplished by any like use of public funds, regardless of their source.

It is upon the contention that state power is infringed by purchased regulation of agricultural production that chief reliance is placed. It is insisted that, while the Constitution gives to Congress, in specific and unambiguous terms, the power to tax and spend, the power is subject to limitations which do not find their origin in any express provision of the Constitution and to which other expressly delegated powers are not subject.

Such a limitation is contradictory and destructive of the power to appropriate for the public welfare, and is incapable of practical application. The spending power of Congress is in addition to the legislative power and not subordinate to it. This independent grant of the power of the purse, and its very nature, involving in its exercise the duty to insure expenditure within the granted power, presuppose freedom of selection among divers ends and aims, and the capacity to impose such conditions as will render the choice effective. It is a contradiction in terms to say that there is power to spend for the national welfare, while rejecting any power to impose conditions reasonably adapted to the attainment of the end which alone would justify the expenditure.

A tortured construction of the Constitution is not to be justified by recourse to extreme examples of reckless congressional spending which might occur if courts could not prevent—expenditures which, even if they could be thought to effect any national purpose, would be possible only by action of a legislature lost to all sense of public responsibility. Such suppositions are addressed to the mind accustomed to believe that it is the business of courts to sit in judgement on the wisdom of legislative action. Courts are not the only agency of government that must be assumed to have capacity to govern. Congress and the courts both unhappily may falter or be mistaken in the performance of their constitutional duty. But interpretation of our great charter of government which proceeds on any assumption that the responsibility for the preservation of our institutions is the exclusive concern of any one of the three branches of government, or that it alone can save them from destruction is far more likely, in the long run, "to obliterate the constituent members" of "an indestructible union of indestructible states" than the frank recognition that language, even of a constitution, may mean what it says: that the power to tax and spend includes the power to relieve a nationwide economic maladjustment by conditional gifts of money.

Notes and Queries

1. In his opinion for the Court, Justice Roberts describes the process of constitutional interpretation as a "power of judgment." The Court, he wrote, "has only one duty, to lay the article of the Constitution which is invoked beside the statute which is challenged and to decide whether the latter squares with the former." Do you agree? Recall our discussion in chapter 2. Is this a theory of interpretation, or is Roberts denying that interpretation is necessary?

2. In the introduction to this chapter, we argued that the Court's opinion validated the expansive, Hamiltonian reading of the spending power. Is that expansive reading consistent with the result in the case? Why or why not?

3. In 1937, following the Supreme Court's change of attitude towards the New Deal legislation, the Court sustained major provisions of the Social Security Act of 1935. In *Steward Machine Co. v. Davis*, 301 U.S. 548 (1937), the Court upheld an unemployment compensation scheme involving a tax on employers of eight or more persons and grants to the states to assist them in administering the compensation program. In *Helvering v. Davis*, 301 U.S. 619 (1937), the Court upheld the federal social security program. The law laid a special income tax on employees to be deducted from their wages and paid by their employers. The Court declared here, as in *Steward*, that the Social Security Act was a valid exercise of federal authority and did not invade the power of the states under the Tenth Amendment. Another question that arose in these cases was whether the federal taxes and expenditures served the "general welfare" within the meaning of Article I, Section 8. In *Butler* the Court had made an independent assessment of the meaning of these terms. In *Helvering* the Court took—and has taken ever since—the position that "the discretion [to define the meaning of these terms] belong to Congress, unless the choice is clearly wrong, a display of arbitrary power [and] not an exercise of judgment." "[T]he concept of the general welfare is not static," said the Court. "Needs that were narrow or parochial a century ago may be interwoven in our day with the well-being of the nation. What is critical or urgent changes with the times," and thus it is best to leave the decision to Congress as to whether the general welfare is involved. But if it is appropriate to leave the definition of the "general welfare" to Congress, why is it not equally appropriate to leave the definition of the term "commerce" to Congress?

South Dakota v. Dole
483 U.S. 203, 107 S. Ct. 2793, 97 L. Ed.2d 171 (1987)

Congress, in an effort to reduce highway accidents, enacted the National Minimum Drinking Age Amendments of 1984. In passing the statute, Congress tried to induce the states to establish a uniform drinking age of twenty-one years. The statute was designed to stop young people from commuting to border states where the drinking age was lower than twenty-one. It was also based on the finding that young people who drink and drive cause a disproportionate number of automobile accidents. The statute directs the secretary of transportation to withhold a percentage of otherwise allocable federal highway funds from those states in which persons less than twenty-one years of age are lawfully permitted to purchase or possess any alcoholic beverage. South Dakota, which permits persons nineteen years of age or older to purchase beer containing up to 3.2 percent alcohol, sued the secretary of transportation, claiming that the statute exceeded Congress' spending power and violated the Twenty-First Amendment. The district court ruled against the state, and the court of appeals affirmed. Opinion of the Court: *Rehnquist*, White, Marshall, Blackmun, Powell, Stevens, Scalia. Dissenting opinions: *Brennan, O'Connor.*

Chief Justice REHNQUIST delivered the opinion of the Court.

. . . [W]e need not decide in this case whether [the Twenty-first] Amendment would prohibit an attempt by Congress to legislate directly a national minimum drinking age. Here, Congress has acted indirectly under its spending power to encourage uniformity in the States' drinking ages. As we explain below, we find this legislative effort within constitutional bounds even if Congress may not regulate drinking ages directly.

The Constitution empowers Congress to "lay and collect Taxes, Duties, Imposts, and Excises, to pay the Debts and provide for the common Defence and general Welfare of the United States." Art. I, s 8, cl. 1. Incident to this power, Congress may attach conditions on the receipt of federal funds, and has repeatedly employed the power "to further broad policy objectives by conditioning receipt of federal moneys upon compliance by the recipient with federal statutory and administrative directives." . . . The breadth of this power was made clear in *United States v. Butler* [1936], where the Court, resolving a longstanding debate over the scope of the Spending Clause, determined that "the power of Congress to authorize expenditure of public moneys for public purposes is not limited by the direct grants of legislative power found in the Constitution." Thus, objectives not thought to be within Article I's "enumerated legislative fields," may nevertheless be attained through the use of the spending power and the conditional grant of federal funds.

We can readily conclude that the provision is designed to serve the general welfare, especially in light of the fact that "the concept of welfare or the opposite is shaped by Congress." Congress found that the differing drinking ages in the States created particular incentives for young persons to combine their desire to drink with their ability to drive, and that this interstate problem required a national solution. The means it chose to address this dangerous situation were reasonably calculated to advance the general welfare. The conditions upon which States receive the funds, moreover, could not be more clearly stated by Congress. And the State itself, rather than challenging the germaneness of the condition to federal purposes, admits that it "has never contended that the congressional action was . . . unrelated to a national concern in the absence of the Twenty-first Amendment." . . . Indeed, the condition imposed by Congress is directly related to one of the main purposes for which highway funds are expended—safe interstate travel. . . .

Our decisions have recognized that in some circumstances the financial inducement offered by Congress might be so coercive as to pass the point at which "pressure turns into compulsion." Here, however, Congress has directed only that a State desiring to establish a minimum drinking age lower than 21 lose a relatively small percentage of certain federal highway funds. Petitioner contends that the coercive nature of this program is evident from the degree of success it has achieved. We cannot conclude, however, that a conditional grant of federal money of this sort is unconstitutional simply by reason of its success in achieving the congressional objective.

Here Congress has offered relatively mild encouragement to the States to enact higher minimum drinking ages than they would otherwise choose. But the enactment of such laws remains the prerogative of the States not merely in theory but in fact. Even if Congress might lack the power to impose a national minimum drinking age directly, we conclude that encouragement to state action

found in s 158 is a valid use of the spending power. Accordingly, the judgment of the Court of Appeals is

Affirmed.

Justice O'CONNOR, dissenting.

My disagreement with the Court is relatively narrow on the spending power issue: it is a disagreement about the application of a principle rather than a disagreement on the principle itself. I agree with the Court that Congress may attach conditions on the receipt of federal funds to further "the federal interest in particular national projects or programs." I also subscribe to the established proposition that the reach of the spending power "is not limited by the direct grants of legislative power found in the Constitution." *United States v. Butler* (1936).

Finally, I agree that there are four separate types of limitations on the spending power: the expenditure must be for the general welfare, the conditions imposed must be unambiguous, they must be reasonably related to the purpose of the expenditure, and the legislation may not violate any independent constitutional provision. Insofar as two of those limitations are concerned, the Court is clearly correct that s. 158 is wholly unobjectionable. Establishment of a national minimum drinking age certainly fits within the broad concept of the general welfare and the statute is entirely unambiguous. I am also willing to assume, arguendo, that the Twenty-first Amendment does not constitute an "independent constitutional bar" to a spending condition. . . .

We have repeatedly said that Congress may condition grants under the spending power only in ways reasonably related to the purpose of the federal program. In my view, establishment of a minimum drinking age of 21 is not sufficiently related to interstate highway construction to justify so conditioning funds appropriated for that purpose.

The Court reasons that Congress wishes that the roads it builds may be used safely, that drunken drivers threaten highway safety, and that young people are more likely to drive while under the influence of alcohol under existing law than would be the case if there were a uniform national drinking age of 21. It hardly needs saying, however, that if the purpose of s 158 is to deter drunken driving, it is far too over and under-inclusive. It is over-inclusive because it stops teenagers from drinking even when they are not about to drive on interstate highways. It is under-inclusive because teenagers pose only a small part of the drunken driving problem in this Nation.

When Congress appropriates money to build a highway, it is entitled to insist that the highway be a safe one. But it is not entitled to insist as a condition of the use of highway funds that the State impose or change regulations in other areas of the State's social and economic life because of an attenuated or tangential relationship to highway use or safety. Indeed, if the rule were otherwise, the Congress could effectively regulate almost any area of a State's social, political, or economic life on the theory that use of the interstate transportation system is somehow enhanced. . . .

There is a clear place at which the Court can draw the line between permissible and impermissible conditions on federal grants. It is the line identified in the Brief for the National Conference of State Legislatures et al. as Amici Curiae:

Congress has the power to spend for the general welfare, it has the power to legislate only for delegated purposes. . . . The appropriate inquiry, then, is whether the spending requirement or prohibition is a condition on a grant or whether it is regulation. The difference turns on whether the requirement specifies in some way how the money should be spent, so that Congress' intent in making the grant will be effectuated. Congress has no power under the Spending Clause to impose requirements on a grant that go beyond specifying how the money should be spent. A requirement that is not such a specification is not a condition, but a regulation, which is valid only if it falls within one of Congress' delegated regulatory powers.

While [United States v.] Butler's authority is questionable insofar as it assumes that Congress has no regulatory power over farm production, its discussion of the spending power and its description of both the power's breadth and its limitations remain sound. The Court's decision in Butler also properly recognizes the gravity of the task of appropriately limiting the spending power. If the spending power is to be limited only by Congress' notion of the general welfare, the reality, given the vast financial resources of the Federal Government, is that the Spending Clause gives "power to the Congress to tear down the barriers, to invade the states' jurisdiction, and to become a parliament of the whole people, subject to no restrictions save such as are self-imposed." This, of course, as Butler held, was not the Framers' plan and it is not the meaning of the Spending Clause. . . .

Notes and Queries

1. How does the Court distinguish between "relatively mild encouragement" and coercion? Does the spending power suggest such a distinction? If not, why is the distinction important?

2. Justice Rehnquist, as noted in earlier chapters, is an ardent defender of the independence and integrity of the states. His dissenting opinion in *City of Philadelphia v. New Jersey* (1978) and his majority opinion in *National League of Cities v. Usery* (1976) manifest his devotion to the rights of the states. What then explains his position in favor of the national government in *Dole*?

3. What is the difference between persuasion and an "unconstitutional condition"?

Chapter 8

Voting and Political Representation

The central focus of this chapter is the relationship between democracy and constitutionalism, one of the major themes running through this book. Democracy of course can be defined in two ways. One way envisions it as a set of substantive commitments to core values such as liberty, equality, and human dignity. The more conventional view defines it as a set of formal institutions within and through which the people govern themselves. These institutions include voting mechanisms of various kinds, ballot access requirements, territorial-based legislative districting, campaign finance laws, rules governing participation in political party activities, and other regulations that structure the American political process. Yet the substantive and formal aspects of democracy are interdependent. Liberty and equality can hardly be realized if cumbersome registration procedures or other electoral barriers make it difficult to vote. The same is true if representative institutions are unresponsive to public opinion or fail to represent significant segments of the community. Constitutionalism enters the picture when it seeks to organize these institutions and procedures in the interest of liberty, equality, and dignity.

In recent decades, the Supreme Court has steadily expanded its vigilance over the electoral process and other features of our formal democracy. *Bush v. Gore* (reprinted later in the chapter), the controversial case that decided the presidential election of 2000, is the most dramatic example of the broad reading the Court has given to specified clauses of the Constitution and to its own role in the American political process. That the presidential election was resolved judicially instead of politically triggered a major national debate not only over *what* the Constitution means, but also over *who* should interpret it. The cases featured in this chapter prompt several important queries about the nature of our polity. Who are the "people" entitled to vote for political representatives? What vision of the body politic should inform the scope and meaning of representation? Does fair and effective representation include group as well as individual voting rights? Are minority communities entitled as a matter of right to a limited number of legislative seats? What is the purpose of legislative apportionment? To maximize party competition? To insure the representation of organic or natural communities held together by common values and interests? Or to construct political communities marked by diversity and heterogeneity? These queries raise related issues of constitutional design, ones we explore along the way by examining the Constitution's electoral structures (or lack thereof) in the light of democratic theory and by comparing American electoral practices and procedures with those of other advanced constitutional democracies.

The Constitutional Framework and Political Participation

The original Constitution created what James Madison characterized as a "republic." In *The Federalist* 10, he distinguished sharply between a democracy and a republic. By the former, he meant a "pure democracy . . . consisting of a small number of citizens, who assemble and administer the government in person."[1] By the latter, he meant "a government in which the scheme of representation takes place [in an extended territorial] sphere." The larger this sphere and the greater the variety of interests and parties in it, said Madison, the less probable it is "that a majority of the whole will have a common motive to invade the rights of other citizens." In short, he concluded, representation in a large-scale republic like the United States has the effect of "refin[ing] and enlarg[ing] the public views, by passing them through the medium of a chosen body of citizens, whose wisdom may best discern the true interest of their country, and whose patriotism and love of justice will be least likely to sacrifice it to temporary or partial considerations."[2] Notwithstanding the Madisonian distinction between a "republic" and a "democracy," Americans today employ these terms synonymously. Republican institutions are in fact forms of representative democracy.

The original republican design, however, consisted of a number of undemocratic elements. The first of these was the Constitution's failure to define the rights of suffrage. This was left up to the states with the consequence that women and African-Americans were deprived of the right to vote well into the 20th century. The institution of slavery was worse, having withdrawn from its victims all rights of citizenship. African-Americans were excluded from "we the people of the United States" who had established "the more perfect Union" ordained by the Constitution. It took a civil war and several constitutional amendments to redress this injustice.

A second feature of the original design that from today's perspective was profoundly undemocratic—and, arguably, still is—was the provision for equal state representation in the United States Senate. This was the price the Founders were willing to pay for the adoption of the Constitution. But it meant that smaller states with a minority of the American people could—and often would—override the wishes of states representing the majority. In addition, senators were to be chosen not by the people but by their state legislatures, a method of selection that would insure, as Robert A. Dahl writes, "that senators would be less responsive to popular majorities and perhaps more sensitive to the needs of property holders."[3] The Founders, who were profoundly suspicious of majority factions and the undiluted impulse of sudden

---

[1] Clinton Rossiter (ed.), *The Federalist Papers*, Kessler Introduction and Notes (New York: Penguin Putnam Inc., 1999), 49.

[2] Ibid., 134.

[3] Robert A. Dahl, *How Democratic Is the American Constitution?* (New Haven: Yale University Press, 2001), 17.

passions, sought to establish a nonpopular legislative body that would reflect "the cool and deliberate sense of the community."

For similar reasons, the Founders rejected the popular election of the President. But they also rejected a proposal to have the President elected by Congress. Instead, they wanted a chief executive free of both popular majorities and congressional control. Their solution was the creation of "electors" equal to the whole number of a state's senators and representatives in Congress, and appointed "in such manner as the Legislature [in each state] may direct."[4] Again, the states would play a crucial role. Equally important, the electors would be "composed of men of exceptional wisdom and virtue who would choose the chief executive unswayed by popular opinion."[5] Had the states provided for the popular election of electors, as is the case today, the electoral college could have claimed a measure of democratic legitimacy. But most states assigned the task of choosing electors to their legislatures, resulting in the selection of presidential electors known less for their wisdom and virtue than for their loyalty to legislative cabals committed to—or captured by—particular candidates. The electoral college failed to work as the framers expected, and one major mechanical flaw had to be repaired as early as 1804 with the passage of the Twelfth Amendment.[6] Later on, as indicated, the states would chose their electors by popular vote, but the resulting elections would be skewed by the practice of giving all of a state's electoral votes to the candidate winning the most votes, a scheme that in several instances, including the year 2000, produced a president who failed to receive a majority of popular votes. This "winner-take-all" system virtually disenfranchises the losers which, as some commentators claim, may be one of the causes of low voter turnouts in presidential elections.

Even the charter of liberty known as the Fourteenth Amendment once deprived large segments of the population from participation in the electoral process. By threatening to reduce a state's representation in Congress proportionate to its denial of the vote to its "male inhabitants," the Amendment's second paragraph permitted the states to continue their refusal to extend the franchise to women. (Originally, feminists opposed the "male inhabitants" language of the Fourteenth Amendment. Ironically, decades later, they would be the Amendment's ultimate beneficiaries.) Similarly, it allowed the states to deny the vote to persons convicted of a crime. These provisions, along with the Supreme Court's narrow interpretation of the Amendment generally,[7] left the states with a lot of slack to determine who could vote. The Supreme Court obliged by sustaining these restrictions. In upholding the validity of Missouri's denial of the right to vote to women, the Court said that "the Constitution of the United States does not confer the right of suffrage upon anyone."[8] Many states also denied the right of suffrage to ex-felons and paupers. By approving of these and other exclusions, the Supreme Court removed whole categories of persons from membership in the political community.

---

[4] U.S. Const., Art. II, sec. 1.

[5] Dahl, *How Democratic*, 16–17.

[6] In the original design, electors were not required to cast ballots separately for President and Vice President. This resulted in a deadlocked electoral vote in 1800, requiring 36 ballots in the House of Representatives before Jefferson obtained a majority of House votes. The Twelfth Amendment required the President and Vice President to be chosen in distinct ballots.

[7] Relevant here are *The Slaughter-House Cases*, 83 U.S. 36 (1873, reprinted in chapter 9) and *The Civil Rights Cases*, 109 U.S. 3 (1883, reprinted in chapter 14). The former placed most of the "privileges and immunities" of citizenship under state regulation, whereas the latter ruled that the Fourteenth Amendment bans only state—not private—discrimination.

[8] *Minor v. Happersett*, 21 Wall. (88 U.S.) 162 (1875).

Yet, over the decades, the original Madisonian republic evolved into a more popular democracy. No fewer than eleven of the seventeen constitutional amendments ratified since 1791—the year of the adoption of the Bill of Rights—have served to further democratize the American political system. The most important of these deal with the right to vote. The Fifteen, Nineteenth, and Twenty-sixth Amendments, ratified respectively in 1870, 1919, and 1971, bar the United States or any state from denying or abridging the right to vote on account of race, sex, or age. The Twenty-fourth Amendment, ratified in 1964, bars state governments from conditioning the right to vote in *federal* elections on the payment of any tax. Decades earlier, in 1913, the Seventeenth Amendment required the popular election of U.S. Senators. The Twenty-second Amendment, which prevents a president from seeking a third term, was the only instance in which the electoral rights of the people could be said to have been reduced.

Despite the promise of these amendments, African Americans in particular struggled long and hard to vindicate their rights of suffrage. The Supreme Court was part of the problem, mainly because the justices limited the reach of the Fourteenth Amendment.[9] In a series of decisions known as the *White Primary Cases*, the Court refused to strike down Southern state laws prohibiting African Americans from participating in primary elections. In *Newberry v. United States* (1921) the Court held that primaries were "in no real sense part of the manner of holding elections." There was no state action as such, and thus Congress was barred from doing anything about it. Because winning the Democratic Party's primary was tantamount to winning the general election in the solidly Democratic South, this practice effectively negated African Americans' right to vote. In *Nixon v. Herndon* (1927), the Court had found a legally required white primary to be "a direct and obvious infringement" of the Fourteenth Amendment. Instead of enacting another law, Texas Democrats responded by passing a simple party resolution that limited primary participation to whites. In *Grovey v. Townsend* (1935), the Court concluded that this obvious subterfuge was just enough to escape the limits of the Equal Protection Clause. In short, primaries were not a substantial part of the electoral process and political parties were essentially private organizations, free from the restraints of equal protection. But in *Smith v. Allwright* (1944), the Court changed its mind, ruling that a political party is "an agency of the state" when conducting a primary election. Now Texas resorted to still another strategy to keep African Americans from voting; they turned the entire primary system over to what were called "Jaybird Associations" or self-governing voluntary clubs. Once again, in 1953, the Court found state action, thus ending all further efforts in Texas to keep African Americans from voting in state primary elections.[10]

By now, the Supreme Court was beginning meticulously to scrutinize other state laws inhibiting the effective exercise of the franchise. In a series of cases decided in the 1960s and beyond, the Court struck down literacy tests, residence requirements, and other election practices regarded as invidiously discriminatory or unreasonably burdensome. State poll taxes were among these invalidated election practices.[11] The Court's vigilance even extended to barring state and local governments from conditioning suffrage on presumptions about the degree of knowledge voters may possess on controverted political issues or about the intensity of their interest in special purpose elections such as those held in school or water districts. Here too, as in other

---

[9] See note 7 above.

[10] See *Terry v. Adams*, 345 U.S. 461 (1953).

[11] *Harper v. Virginia State Board of Elections*, 383 U.S. 663 (1966).

areas of American constitutional law, competing images of democracy contended for supremacy in the judicial mind. Should political participation be organized around particular communities of shared interests or values—a republican conception of democracy—or include all *bona fide* residents within a given electoral unit regardless of their interests, affiliations, or length of residence in the community—a liberal or individualistic view of democracy.

The Apportionment Revolution

Does federal judicial power extend to reviewing the fairness of state and federal legislative districts marked by significant disparities in population? Until the early 1960s the Supreme Court said "no." *Colegrove v. Green* (1946) reflected the prevailing judicial attitude. Illinois had failed to redraw its congressional district boundaries in over forty years, notwithstanding vast population disparities among election districts. State voters challenged these disparities as a violation of equal protection. Justice Frankfurter, writing for the plurality in *Colegrove*, declined to embroil the judiciary in what he described as "an essentially political contest . . . dressed up in the abstract phrases of the law."[12] Partisanship is at its most intense in the remapping of legislative districts and for that reason alone, Frankfurter argued, the courts should refuse to interfere. Malapportionment in Illinois was a harm suffered by the people of that state and repairing the wrong was up to them. Justice Black, strongly dissenting, condemned the state's "rotton borough" system as a violation of equal voting rights, suggesting that the right to cast a ballot is meaningless if that ballot is undervalued relative to a ballot cast by a voter in a less populated district.

Baker v. Carr (1962, reprinted in chapter 3), described as "perhaps the most profoundly destabilizing opinion in the Supreme Court's history,"[13] marked an epoch-making change in the Court's perspective. Legislative districts throughout the country were severely malapportioned because of the states' failure to re-map these districts in the light of shifting population patterns. Population imbalances were also caused by the traditional state practice of basing representation on geographic districting, often for the purpose of conferring equal representation on particular governmental units analogous to the "federal" plan of representation in the United States Senate. *Baker* involved a challenge to Tennessee's grossly malapportioned state legislative districts. Fully aware of the controversy the case would generate if it went against the state, Justice Brennan, speaking for a seven-person majority, proceeded cautiously. He simply concluded, without offering guidelines for revising legislative district lines, that the voting rights asserted by the petitioners can be judicially vindicated under the Equal Protection Clause of the Fourteenth Amendment,"[14] thus rejecting the long-held view that apportionment actions of this kind are non-justiciable "political questions."

Justice Frankfurter, in one of his most animated dissents, deplored the Court's exercise of "destructively novel judicial power" which in his view represented "a massive repudiation of the experience of our whole past."[15] There was little question that the Supreme Court had embarked upon a revolutionary path. But whether this exercise of novel judicial power was destructive of the democratic process was highly

---

[12] 328 U.S. 549, 554.

[13] Samuel Issacharoff et al., *The Law of Democracy* (Westbury, N.Y.: The Foundation Press, 1998), 134.

[14] 369 U.S. 186,

[15] Ibid., 267.

debated. The Court might have decided the case under the constitutional command that the United States "guarantee to every State in this Union a Republican form of Government." Under this clause, the Court might have tossed the ball back to the states, instructing them to devise their own solutions in accordance with general republican—or democratic—principles.

In 1964, however, the Court rejected this approach by driving a stake through the heart of electoral districting patterns all over the country. In three landmark cases, the Court held that legislative districts must be based solely on population. In *Reynolds v. Sims* (1964, reprinted in this chapter), Chief Justice Warren wrote:

> *Legislatures represent people, not trees or acres. Legislators are elected by voters, not farms or cities or economic interests. As long as ours is a representative form of government, and our legislatures are those instruments of government elected directly by and directly representative of the people, the right to elect legislators in a free and unimpaired fashion is the backbone of our political system.*[16]

Accordingly, speaking for eight members of the Court, Warren ruled that "[f]ull and effective participation by all citizens in state government requires . . . that each citizen have an equally effective voice in the election of members of the state legislature." In short, state legislative districts must be, "as nearly as is practicable," equal in population. The Court went on to find the "federal analogy inapposite and irrelevant to state legislative schemes." Representation in both houses of a state legislature would have to be based solely on population.

Wesberry v. Sanders, the second in this trilogy of cases, shifted the scene to congressional districts. Overruling *Colegrove v. Green*, *Wesberry* held that Article I, Section 2, of the Constitution, providing for the election of representatives by the "people of the several states," also requires the application of the "one person-one vote" rule.[17] Finally, in *Lucas v. The Forty-Fourth General Assembly of the State of Colorado*, the Court even struck down an apportionment plan that had recently been adopted by an overwhelming popular vote in a statewide referendum. The plan recognized population as a prime, but not controlling, factor in the apportionment of Colorado's senate. Geography, compactness, contiguity of territory, and country lines also entered the equation. But the Court was unyielding: "An individual's constitutionally protected right to cast an equally weighted vote cannot be denied even by a vote of a majority of a State's electorate."[18] These cases would eventually change the face of legislatures throughout the country.

The Supreme Court had embarked upon no less than a bold exercise in constitutional design. But the exercise elicited enormous criticism on and off the bench. Justice Stewart's forceful dissent in *Lucas* captures the gist of the criticism. Several theories of representative government, he noted, have enjoyed good pedigree in the history of political thought and even in American political history. For this reason, Stewart could "not join in the fabrication of a constitutional mandate which imports and forever freezes one theory of political thought into our Constitution, and forever denies to every State any opportunity for enlightened and progressive innovation in the design of its democratic institutions."[19] *Effective* political representation, he argued, cannot ignore the "interests and aspirations of diverse groups of people." His

---

[16] 377 U.S. 533, 562.

[17] 376 U.S. 1.

[18] 377 U.S. 713, 736.

[19] Ibid.

vision of democracy seems to approximate the view of the Canadian Supreme Court expressed in Comparative Note 8.1. "Representative government," he wrote, "is a process of accommodating group interests through democratic institutional arrangements," ones that need not rely exclusively on equal representation for equal numbers of people.

The theory of group representation sounded in Stewart's dissent found a strong echo in later cases, and the Court soon came to realize that mathematical exactitude could not be defended over all other considerations. In *Gaffney v. Cummings*, for example, the Court rejected as "invidiously discriminatory under the Fourteenth Amendment" an apportionment plan that "would achieve a rough approximation of the statewide strengths of the Democratic and Republican Parties."[20] The Court described as "politically mindless" any districting scheme for state legislators limited to census data without regard for the "political strength of any group or party." In *Karcher v. Daggett*, the Court even approved small deviations from the equal population standard for the sake of "making districts compact, respecting municipal boundaries, preserving cores of prior districts, and avoiding contests between incumbent Representatives."[21] *Karcher*, however, made clear that the Constitution's Article I, Section 2, which refers to the election of representatives by the "people of the several states," requires virtually absolute population equality for the apportionment of *congressional* legislative districts.

Finally, *Davis v. Bandemer* (1986, reprinted in this chapter) raised the question whether judicial review would actually extend to partisan gerrymanders.[22] Here a state legislature adhered to the one person–one vote rule of apportionment but gerrymandered districts in such a way as to underrepresent the statewide voting strength of the Democratic Party. In short, could a *political group* suffer invidious discrimination under the Constitution? Although a plurality emphasized the primacy of equal population in remapping districts, it ruled that any electoral system that consistently degrades "a group of voters' influence on the political process as a whole" would offend the Equal Protection Clause.[23] The Court broke new ground by declaring such cases justiciable. In the present case, however, the plurality concluded that the mere lack of proportional representation in one or two elections does not constitute unconstitutional discrimination. To make out such a case requires a "threshold showing of discriminatory vote dilution." Otherwise, said the plurality, these cases "would invite judicial interference in legislative districting whenever a political party suffers at the polls."[24] Disagreeing, Justice O'Connor, joined by Chief Justice Burger and Justice Rehnquist, held that all partisan gerrymandering claims of the major political parties should be regarded as nonjusticiable political questions best left to legislatures.

Justices Powell and Stevens, on the other hand, took the strongest position in favor of judicial intervention. For them any deliberate or arbitrary distortion of populations or political subdivision lines for the purpose of depriving certain voters "of an equal opportunity to participate in the State's legislative processes" is arguably unconstitutional, and they faulted the plurality for not developing standards that would clearly identify such gerrymanders. "The concept of representation," they

---

[20] 412 U.S. 735, 752 (1973).

[21] 462 U.S. 725, 740 (1983).

[22] 478 U.S. 109.

[23] Ibid., 132.

[24] Ibid., 142.

noted, "necessarily applies to groups: groups of voters elect representatives, individual voters do not."[25] Adding a new twist to the one person–one vote rule, they remarked, "While population disparities do dilute the weight of individual voters, their discriminatory effect is felt only when those individual votes are combined."[26] When, therefore, these individual votes are recombined to deprive a particular group of fair and effective representation, a serious constitutional issue is presented. Comparative Note 8.2 features a related view of "fair and effective" representation.

The most volatile apportionment issue in the 1990s was racial gerrymandering. Could a legislature re-map districts so as to elect minority representatives? To comply with the Federal Voting Rights Act, as interpreted by the Attorney General, North Carolina created two majority-black districts the contours of which were compared to a "bug splattered on a windshield." In *Shaw v. Reno* (1993, reprinted in this chapter), a narrow majority of five justices invalidated the plan as an "odious" classification based on race, one that "bears an uncomfortable resemblance to political apartheid."[27] Any plan, said the Court, that "disregards traditional districting principles such as compactness, contiguity, and respect for political subdivisions" merely for the purpose of creating minority populated districts "reinforces the perception that members of the same racial group . . . think alike, share the same political interests, and will prefer the same candidates at the polls."[28] The four justices in dissent (White, Blackmun, Stevens, and Souter) denied that the state's plan involved any attempt to discriminate against white voters or to deny them fair representation. This 5–4 alignment held up three years later when *Shaw II* declared North Carolina's revised plan unconstitutional because race was still found to have been the state legislature's "predominant consideration" in determining a majority-black district's shape and placement.[29]

Shaw I led to devastating criticism off as well as on the Court. One critique went so far as to suggest that *Shaw* was the "equivalent for the civil rights jurisprudence of our generation to what *Plessy v. Ferguson* and *Dred Scott v. Sandford* were for earlier generations."[30] More cautious critics, however, tended to question the empirical assumptions of *Shaw*, noting the absence of evidence that would show that race-conscious districting promotes racial bloc voting or prompts representatives to confine their representation to the "racial bloc" that presumably elects them. And, as Justice White remarked in *Gaffney*, the Court had never struck down an apportionment plan simply because districting principles such as compactness and contiguity were ignored.

Shaw I gave rise to judicial assaults on similar minority-created congressional districts in Georgia and Texas. In both cases, the same five-person majority struck down the districting plans as racial gerrymanders in violation of the Fourteenth Amendment.[31] Again, race was found to be the primary motive in mapping the districts under scrutiny. *Hunt v. Cromartie* (1999, reprinted in this chapter), finally, challenged still another revised North Carolina district shaped in snakelike form. But now

---

[25] Ibid., 167.

[26] Ibid.

[27] 509 U.S. 630, 647.

[28] Ibid.

[29] *Shaw v. Hunt,* 517 U.S. 899 (1996).

[30] Leon Higginbotham, Jr., Gregory A. Clarick, and Marcella David, *Shaw v. Reno: A Mirage of Good Intentions with Devastating Racial Consequences,* 62 Fordham Law Review 1603 (1994).

[31] See, respectively, *Miller v. Johnson,* 515 U.S. 900 (1995) and *Bush v. Vera,* 517 U.S. 952 (1996).

the Court announced its readiness to approve a plan that is race-neutral on its face and in the absence of proof that "race was the predominant factor motivating the legislature's districting decision."[32] North Carolina's saga ended with *Cromartie II* (2001), when the Supreme Court reversed as "clearly erroneous" a federal district court's factual conclusion that the North Carolina legislature used race as the "predominant factor" in drawing the boundaries of a congressional district.[33] Justice Breyer, writing for the majority, reemphasized what the Court had said in *Bush v. Vera*, namely, that a facially neutral redistricting law is likely to be upheld unless the law is unexplainable on grounds other than race.[34] In short, majority-minority districts—i.e., districts in which a racial minority constitutes a majority of voters—are valid if the state can offer a legitimate *political* reason for its districting decision. Race may be a motivating factor in drawing district lines, but politics must be the driving force behind the decision. Accordingly, *Cromartie II* stands for the proposition that majority-minority districts can be created in situations where there is a high correlation between race and party preference and where the emphasis on the latter is designed to achieve balanced legislative representation, in short a political result.

Georgia v. Ashcroft (2003), the most recent development in this field, endorsed a new approach to racial redistricting. The Voting Rights Act of 1965, as construed by the Justice Department, had prohibited certain states from reducing the percentage of minority voters in a legislative district. The assumption behind the policy was that African American candidates could only win in "safe" districts where they constitute the majority of voters. *Ashcroft's* ruling, led by Justice O'Connor, announced that states may now choose to create "influence" or "coalition" districts "where minority voters may not be able to elect a candidate of choice but can play a substantial, if not decisive, role in the electoral process."[35] The Court appeared to be influenced by the fact that Georgia's Democratic Party and African American leaders supported the creation of "coalition" districts on the theory that minority voters would have more political leverage if they could influence the outcome in many districts, as opposed to a districting scheme that concentrates African American voters in fewer districts. The 5 to 4 alignment in the case contained a note of irony. The same five justices who ruled in favor of Republican George W. Bush for president in 2000 voted to support the Democratic position in *Ashcroft*, while the four justices in dissent supported the Bush Administration.

Political Parties and Elections

The Constitution's framers greeted political parties with hostility. They equated parties with the "factions" against which James Madison railed in *Federalist 10*. This hostility toward parties manifested itself structurally in institutions such as federalism, bicameralism, separation of powers, and checks and balances, all features calculated to prevent government's capture by a single group or a combination of groups. Indeed, President Washington used the occasion of his *Farewell Address* to renew the Founders' caution against the evil of party. "The common and continual mischief of the spirit of party," he warned, "are sufficient to make it the interest and duty of a wise people to discourage and restrain it." The thought behind the comment was

---

[32] 526 U.S. 541 (1999)

[33] *Hunt v. Cromartie*, 121 S. Ct. 1452 (2001).

[34] 517 U.S. 952 (1996).

[35] 71 U.S.L.W. 4545, 4551–2 (2003).

that a politically informed and virtuous people would elect independent-minded representatives dedicated to the common good of the whole people and not to any part of them organized around particular interests.

The Founders' perspective could not last in an advanced modern democracy, and the Constitution's discouragement of parties could not check their inevitability. Democracy is built on competition and, as the early conflict between the Federalists and Jeffersonians show, meaningful elections can only take place when voters are given a choice between policies, programs, and candidates. Political parties provide this choice by aggregating interests, nominating candidates, mobilizing the electorate, managing campaigns, and organizing the government. Parties out of power play an equally important role. They keep the ruling party "honest" by scrutinizing its policies, auditing its behavior, demanding transparency, insisting on accountability, and advancing an alternative agenda, all in the interest of responsible party government.

Unlike many parliamentary democracies, the United States has been aptly described as a two-party system. Third parties and independent candidates have not fared well in American politics. They have occasionally captured a city government or a state governorship, and they have influenced the outcome of presidential elections, as did Ralph Nader's party—The Greens—in 2000. American election law, however, is stacked against them. The single-member-district-winner-take-all arrangement makes it highly improbable that any third party or independent candidate will win enough votes to enter any of the nation's major legislative bodies.[36] In addition, the two-party system has managed to entrench itself though statutory policies such as bans on write-in votes, ballot access restrictions, high petition requirements, excessive candidate filing fees, and prohibitions on multiparty or "fusion" candidacies.

The Supreme Court has struck down these laws when they *substantially* limit the choice of candidates, burden voters' ability to voice their preferences, or interfere with the right to associate with others in support of a candidate. Yet the Court has sustained reasonable restrictions on access to the ballot when designed to cut down on "voter confusion, ballot over-crowding, and the presence of frivolous candidacies."[37] The Court has also acknowledged the "strong interest [of the states] in the stability of their political systems," permitting them "to enact reasonable election regulations that may, in practice, favor the traditional two-party system, and that temper the destabilizing effects of party-splintering and excessive factionalism."[38] In *William v. Rhodes*, on the other hand, the Court invalidated Ohio's restrictive ballot access procedure because of its tendency to give Republicans and Democrats "a complete monopoly" over elections. By denying the Ohio American Independent Party a place on the presidential ballot, declared the Court, Ohio had stifled the marketplace of ideas "at the core of our electoral process and of the First Amendment freedoms."[39]

But to what extent may state law limit a party's discretion to organize itself, con-

---

[36] Consider the fact that in 2003 only one of the Senate's 100 members was an independent, and he was elected to the Senate as a Republican only to declare his independent status during his term of office. As for other elections, Bradley Smith reports that of "20,000 elections for state legislators from 1982 to 1988, only three [were] won by members of a party other than the Democrats and Republicans." Note, *Judicial Protection of Ballot-Access Rights: Third Parties Need Not Apply,* 28 Harvard Journal of Legislation 167, 171 (1991).

[37] *Munro v. Socialist Workers Party,* 479 U.S. 189 (1986).

[38] *Timmons v. Twin Cities Area New Party,* 117 S.Ct. 1364 (1997).

[39] 393 U. S. 23 (1968).

duct its affairs, and select its leaders? Our constitutional case law has tried delicately to balance a party's right to associational freedom against the equally important right of citizens to vote for candidates of their choice. Accordingly, the Court has approved regulations designed to keep elections fair and honest. On the other hand, it has struck down bans on party endorsements in primary elections while upholding a party's right to open or close such elections to independent voters or nonparty members.[40] In *California Democratic Party v. Jones* (2000), the Court invalidated California's open primary system because it allowed nonparty members to determine party policy in violation of freedom of speech and political association.[41]. Similarly, in *Duke v. Massey*, a lower federal court ruled in favor of party leaders who removed David Duke, a well-known racist, from the list of candidates in Georgia's Republican presidential primary. The Court ruled that a state has a "compelling interest [in] protecting a political party's right to exclude persons with 'adverse political principles.' "[42]

An important presidential primary election case is *Democratic Party of the U.S. v. Wisconsin* (1981, reprinted in this chapter), in which the Democratic Party challenged Wisconsin's open primary for selecting and binding the delegates to the national party convention. The Court refused to rule on the merits of open versus closed presidential primaries for selecting delegates to a national convention. The Court conceded that Wisconsin may open "its Democratic preference primary to voters who do not publicly declare their party affiliation," but went on to assert that it could not "bind the National Party to honor the binding primary results" in defiance of national party rules. The Court could discover no compelling reason that would authorize the state to impair a party's need to build a more effective and responsible party in the interest of associational freedom. But this case was not merely a clash between a national party and a state rule. *Wisconsin* is interesting because Wisconsin's Democratic Party supported the state rule. So the case could be redefined as a conflict between national and state parties, prompting one to ask whether the Court should have intervened in an intraparty dispute in the first place.

Money and Politics

Campaign finance regulation is one of the most contested and complex areas of contemporary election law. The history of such regulation, at both federal and state levels, begins around 1910. The laws have taken a number of forms. They have sought mainly and variously to bar corporations, unions, and other organizations from contributing to election campaigns, to curtail the influence of large individual contributors, to require the disclosure of campaign contributions, to limit over-all spending on elections, and to provide for their public financing. Most of these policies have been designed to reduce the role of big money as a corrupting influence on elections and to promote the equalization of electoral competition by giving meaning to the principle of one person–one vote. But each of these purposes has been subverted by loopholes as well as by ingenuous circumventions of the law, not to mention early decisions of the Supreme Court invalidating the application of campaign finance regulation to nominating conventions and primary elections.[43]

---

[40] See *Rosario v. Rockefeller*, 410 U.S. 572 (1973) and *Tashjian v. Republican Party of Connecticut*, 479 U.S. 208 (1986).

[41] 530 U.S. 567

[42] 87 F.3d 1226 (11th Cir. 1996).

[43] See, for example, *Newberry v. United States*, 256 U.S. 232 (1921). Twenty years later *Newberry* was reversed in *United States v. Classic*, 313 U.S. 299 (1941).

The contemporary era of campaign finance regulation begins with the Federal Election Campaign Act of 1971 (FECA). The law was enacted in partial response to the burgeoning costs of federal elections, owing especially to the increasing use of television advertising. Three years later, following revelations of widespread corruption in the 1972 presidential election campaign, Congress passed several amendments to FECA. Described by a lower federal court as "the most comprehensive reform legislation [ever] passed by Congress concerning the election of the President, Vice-President, and members of Congress," these amendments established limits on the size of contributions in federal elections by individuals, political parties, or Political Action Committees (PACs); imposed ceilings on the total amount that particular candidates could spend in a federal election; and limited the use of a candidate's personal or family funds. To offset the latter, the 1974 amendments established the first system of public funding for presidential elections. In addition, they required that contributions and expenditures above certain thresholds be reported and publicly disclosed. Finally, Congress created the Federal Election Commission (FEC) to enforce this complex regulatory scheme.

In an orchestrated effort to prevent the FECA amendments from going into effect in the 1976 campaign, an unusual coalition of political parties, interest groups, and candidates for federal office challenged their constitutionality. The Act's contribution and expenditure limits, they contended, violated their right to freedom of speech as guaranteed by the First Amendment. The Supreme Court rendered its judgment in *Buckley v. Valeo* (1976, reprinted later in the chapter), the length and complexity of which matched the intensity of the controversy it generated. In a divided *per curiam* opinion, the Court upheld the Act's provision limiting contributions but struck down its limits on *expenditures* by individuals, groups, and candidates. Concluding that the risk of corruption is far greater in *giving* than in *spending* money, the Court ruled that restrictions on expenditures are a substantial and direct restraint on the quantity and diversity of political speech. Neither the mere possibility of corruption nor the pursuit of equality was sufficiently compelling to justify any abridgement of "unfettered political speech." As the Court put it: "[T]he concept that government may restrict the speech of some elements of our society in order to enhance the relative voice of others is wholly foreign to the First Amendment, which was designed to 'secure the widest possible dissemination of information from diverse and antagonistic sources,' and 'to assure unfettered interchange of ideas for the bringing about of political and social changes desired by the people.' "[44]

This decision was anything but self-evident. It flowed less from the text of the First Amendment than from the Supreme Court's normative vision of political democracy. Madison's *Federalist* 10 seems to have been elevated into America's reigning public philosophy. Factions, which we would now call pressure groups, are essential to liberty. In this pluralistic model of democracy, they are not qualitatively superior to political parties. They, like parties, are the progenitors of political organization and communication. To limit them is to constrain the "unfettered exchange of ideas," much as governmental regulation is said to constrain the normal functioning of the market economy. A very different perspective, as we shall see later on, prevails in some other constitutional democracies.

A generation later, the national debate triggered by *Buckley* rolled on in the judiciary as well as the halls of Congress. *Buckley's* legacy has been called a "Thirty Years

---

[44] 424 U.S. 48–49 (1976).

War between campaign finance controls and First Amendment freedoms."[45] The war produced an endless stream of argument by political scientists and legal scholars attacking or defending the Supreme Court's empirical assumptions about the effect of contributions and spending limits on freedom of speech, electoral competition, and minor political parties. One consequence, however, of the loopholes created by *Buckley* was the rising prominence of "soft money" in election campaigns. Soft money referred mainly to funds contributed or expended for voter registration drives, get-out-the-vote campaigns, issue advocacy, and other non-candidate related activities. ("Hard" money, by contrast, directly supported candidates or their campaigns.) Soft money donations to the two main political parties in the 1990s skyrocketed from $45 million in 1988 to $495.1 million in 1999–2000, accounting for 40 percent of party fund-raising.[46] The donors were mainly corporations, unions, political action committees and other large contributors, leading to charges that these gifts were influencing elections in corrupting ways. Huge pots of soft money pouring into party headquarters prompted doubts that a bright line could be drawn between non-candidate and candidate-related political financing or between contributions and expenditures. Soft money, as noted below, was the principal target of the controversial Bipartisan Campaign Act of 2002.

Meanwhile, in the intervening years, the Supreme Court had several opportunities to revisit *Buckley*. Generally, the Court has continued to adhere to *Buckley's* distinction between expenditure and contribution limits,[47] although increasingly struggling to differentiate between them. Three justices who have joined the Court since 1986 (Kennedy, Scalia, and Thomas) would overrule *Buckley*. These three have argued, not unpersuasively, that contribution limits are as repressive of free speech as limits on expenditures.[48] Justices Stevens, Ginsburg, and Breyer, on the other hand, would submit all campaign finance regulation to a lower standard of review than required by the First Amendment. Justice Stevens, for example, makes this simple point: "Money is property; it is not speech."[49] Accordingly, restrictions on the use of money do not require as high a standard of review as restrictions on speech as such. The balancing test advocated by the dissenting justices would in all probability result in upholding reasonable federal and state restrictions on contributions and expenditures.

Two Colorado cases constitute the latest chapter in the *Buckley* saga. In *Colorado Republican Federal Campaign Committee v. Federal Election Commission*, the Colorado Republican Party challenged the dollar limit on what it could spend in the state's

---

[45] Joel M. Gora, *The Legacy of* Buckley v. Valeo, 2 Election Law Journal 55 (2003).

[46] Richard Briffault, *Soft Money Reform and the Constitution,* 1 Election Law Journal 344–345 (2002).

[47] See *Federal Election Commission v. Massachusetts Citizens for Life*, 479 U.S. 238 (1986, striking down a FECA ban on direct expenditures of corporate funds to a non-profit political group concerned with electing candidates to political office). But in *Austin v. Michigan Chamber of Commerce*, 494 U.S. 652 (1990), the Court seemed to plow new ground. *Austin* sustained the state's ban on independent corporate expenditures on behalf of or in opposition to the election of a candidate because the statute was carefully tailored to prevent the political corruption stemming from "the corrosive and distorting effects of immense aggregations of wealth that are accumulated with the help of the corporate form and that have little or no correlation to the public's support for the corporation's political ideas." What made this case different from ordinary corporate expenditures segregated for or keyed to the promotion of political views was the non-political character of many of the Chamber's activities, together with the many non-political reasons why business groups join the Chamber. Accordingly, the statute "ensures that expenditures reflect actual public support for the political ideas espoused by corporations."

[48] See *Nixon v. Shrink Missouri Government PAC*, 528 U.S. 377 (2000).

[49] Id., 398.

senatorial election of 1986. The principal opinion ruled that spending limits set by the FEC were unconstitutional as applied to independent expenditures not "coordinated" with a candidate or his or her campaign. Accordingly, the Court rejected the FEC's position that any party expenditure in connection with a particular election for federal office was presumed to be coordinated with the party's candidate. Excess money had been spent for radio advertisements attacking the Democratic Party's candidate long before the Republican candidate had been selected, resulting in no coordinated spending. Earlier cases had already decided that coordinated spending by individuals and non-party groups often took the form of "disguised contributions," thus subjecting them to regulation. Left undecided in *Colorado I* was whether the congressional effort to limit coordinated expenditures by *political parties* controverted the First Amendment.

Federal Election Commission v. Colorado Republican Campaign Committee (*Colorado II*) (2001) answered this question. Colorado's Republican Party argued that any limit on a party's coordinated expenditures imposes a "unique First Amendment burden," triggering the highest degree of judicial scrutiny. After all, parties are candidate-oriented organizations and candidates ordinarily share their party's policy goals. Accordingly, money spent to promote a party's policy goals is money necessarily spent in support of its candidates. Such spending, the argument continued, has less potential for corruption than the coordinated expenditures of individuals and nonparty groups. Justice Souter, speaking for the majority, rejected this reasoning, holding that "a party's coordinated expenditures, unlike expenditures truly independent, may be restricted to minimize circumventions of contribution limits."[50] In the Court's mind, Congress had sustained its burden of showing that coordinated spending by a party should be limited because it is the "functional" equivalent of a contribution. Why? Because "unlimited expenditures coordinated with a candidate would induce individual and other nonparty contributors to give to the party in order to finance coordinated spending for a favored candidate beyond the contribution limits binding on them."[51] Four dissenting justices insisted that *Buckley* should be overruled.

The controversy over *Buckley* and the Supreme Court's refusal to abandon its basic distinction between contributions and expenditures has not deterred campaign finance reformers from pressing for further efforts to reduce the influence of big money in elections. After a seven-year congressional fight, their efforts led to the Bipartisan Campaign Reform Act of 2002. As its chief sponsor, Senator John McCain of Arizona, said: "Twenty-five years after Watergate, the electoral system is [still] out of control. Our elections are awash in money which is flowing into the system at record levels. . . . Something must be done."[52] The Reform Act bans "soft money" donations by labor unions, corporations, and individuals to political parties for the purpose of influencing federal elections. Its other provisions include a ban on issue advertising in support of a specific candidate within sixty days of a general election. The treasuries of large organizations can no longer be used, wrote McCain, "to finance campaign advertisements masquerading as 'issue discussion.'"[53] To compensate for these prohibitions, the Reform Act raises FECA's ceilings on "hard money" contributions from individuals and political action committees. The new law, as Sena-

---

[50] *Federal Election Commission v. Colorado Republican Federal Campaign Committee*, 121 S. Ct. 2351, 2371 (2001).

[51] Ibid., 2361.

[52] *Congressional Record*, S-384, January 21, 1997.

[53] John S. McCain, *Free Air Time: The Continuing Reform Battle*, 2 Electoral Law Journal 171 (2003).

tor McCain noted, "puts teeth back into [our campaign finance] laws."[54] The constitutionality of these provisions was a central issue in the congressional debate, so much so that the Act authorized its immediate review in the federal courts.

The invitation to sue was taken up promptly by more than 80 plaintiffs, including strange bedfellows such as the Republican National Committee, California's Democratic Party, National Rifle Association, American Civil Liberties Union, and the Christian Coalition, all of whom argued that the Act's soft money limits were an unconstitutional invasion of free speech. On May 2, 2003, a three-judge federal district court awarded them a significant victory by striking down the Act's prohibitions on soft money contributions and expenditures for non-candidate purposes, but the court sustained the validity of provisions that barred political parties from using unlimited donations for candidate or issue-oriented purposes. A dissenting judge would have invalidated the entire ban on soft money.

On December 10, 2003, finally, and splitting 5 to 4, the Supreme Court delivered what many regarded as a stunning decision. In the most important political spending case since *Buckley v. Valeo*, the Court upheld all the major provisions of the Reform Act.[55] The decision could change the game of national politics. First, the Court blurred the line between contributions and expenditures. Unlimited contributions of soft money, said the lead opinion, can easily be diverted into expenditures on behalf of candidates. Second, corruption or the appearance thereof was defined as more than "cash for votes." It now includes the "[selling] of access to federal candidates and office holders," along with the "suggestion that money buys influence in congress." McConnell was anything but doctrinally neat. It seemed to rest heavily on the intuitive feeling, shared by many, that money counts in politics, and that its influence leads to the appearance of corruption that Congress is authorized to regulate. As evidence of the undue influence of soft money contributions, the Court cited Congress' failure to enact crucial legislation in the areas of tort reform and tobacco legislation. Four justices (Scalia, Kennedy, Thomas, and Rehnquist) wrote separate dissents. Justice Scalia captured the core of the dissents in noting that McConnell "is a sad day for the freedom of speech."

Soon after the decision came down, campaign reformers set their sights on other targets. One proposed reform would lower the cost of television and radio broadcasting by candidates and require stations to allocate significant time-slots for candidate-centered or issue-centered programming, as is the case in other advanced democracies. Another proposal is a voucher system, to be financed out of broadcasting profits, that would allow federal candidates to debate one another on radio or television or present their views in some related format, all for the purpose of reducing the advantage of incumbency and promoting electoral competition.

Actually, *McConnell* might have been anticipated by the Supreme Court's earlier ruling in *Federal Election Commission v. Beaumont* (2003) holding that FECA's ban on direct corporate contributions in federal elections applied to nonprofit advocacy corporations. Here the nonprofit corporation was a tax-exempt anti-abortion organization. A direct ban on its contributions in federal elections, said the majority, does not violate freedom of speech, as the Fourth Circuit Court of Appeals had ruled. Nonprofit advocacy corporations, like business corporations, said the majority, can be regulated by closely drawn statutes to prevent potential corruption from large political war chests to evade individual contribution limits.[56] Justices Scalia and

---

[54] Ibid.

[55] *McConnell v. Federal Election Commission,* 2003 WL 22900467 (U.S., Dec. 10, 2003)

[56] 71 U.S.L.W. 4451.

Thomas, dissenting, denied that the statute was narrowly tailored to achieve a relevant compelling interest.

Bush v. Gore

The presidential election of 2000 showed that the American electoral process is seriously flawed. For the first time in American history, the Supreme Court decided who would be the next President of the United States. Political democracies do not choose their leaders by judicial fiat. They elect them, usually by political majorities. Given the institutional constraints within which Americans select their chief executive, however, presidents are often elected by pluralities rather than majorities. By itself, this may be one of the flaws in the design of our electoral institutions. In addition, as a formal constitutional matter, presidents are not elected by the voters at all. They are chosen—as was the original intent—by electors appointed in turn as directed by the state legislatures, and their number in each state is equal to the number of persons representing the state in Congress. Originally, legislatures chose the electors. But early on they provided for their popular election. To maximize their influence, the states also adopted the policy of giving all their electoral votes to the presidential candidate winning the popular vote. The necessary majority is 270 votes.[57] If no candidate receives a majority, the election shifts to the House of Representatives, where each state has one vote. When this happens, a majority of the states is necessary to elect the president.

This system of selecting electors and counting electoral votes means that a president who wins the popular vote may fall short of a majority in the electoral college. In the last 125 years, this has happened only twice, in 1888 and 2000. Grover Cleveland won a close popular contest with Benjamin Harrison in 1888 but lost the electoral vote by a margin of 233 to 168. No controversy erupted over that election except for the criticism aimed at the electoral college system itself. The 2000 election was a different story. It ranks as one of the most controversial elections in American history. Its outcome was unknown until the Supreme Court awarded the presidency to George W. Bush on 12 December 2000, a full five weeks after the November election. The story of the election is a complicated political and legal drama that highlights once again the clash between constitutionalism and democracy. In this short space, we can only recount the *essential* details that culminated in the presidential election case known as *Bush v. Gore (Bush II)* (2000, reprinted later in this chapter).

The 2000 election, the results of which are presented in table 8.1, was one of the closest in the nation's history. Florida was the site of an electrifying showdown between Albert Gore and George W. Bush, respectively the Democratic and Republican

TABLE 8.1 *Presidential Election Results, 2000*

Candidate	Party	Popular Vote		Electoral Vote	
Bush	Republican	50,459,624	47.87%	271	50.4%
Gore	Democratic	51,003,238	48.38	266	49.4
Nader	Green	2,882,985	2.74	0	0
Buchanan	Reform	449,120	0.43	0	0
Browne	Libertarian	384,440	0.36	0	0
Other		232,922	0.22	0	0

[57] Altogether, there are 538 electoral votes, a number equal to 100 U.S. Senators, 435 members of the House of Representatives, and the 3 electors chosen by the District of Columbia.

candidates for President. After the last votes were counted, Bush's lead was less than one-half of 1 percent out of 5.8 million votes cast, triggering under state law an automatic machine recount, which pared Bush's lead down to a few hundred votes. In the light of this narrow margin, voting irregularities in the form of "undervotes," "overvotes," and "no votes" prompted the Gore campaign to request hand recounts in four counties in which most of the anomalies occurred.[58] A rash of federal and state lawsuits followed, with Bush suing to halt the recounts and Gore countersuing to continue them. The legal joust ended with a Florida Supreme Court decision to extend the hand-counting of the votes to 26 November, eight days after the state's statutory deadline for certifying the election results. All of this maneuvering was being played out against the backdrop of assertions about the motives of a state government dominated by Republicans and a state judiciary dominated by Democrats.

Bush's lawyers carried the legal battle to the U.S. Supreme Court which, on Monday, December 4, set aside the Florida Supreme Court's decision to extend the deadline for a manual recount and remanded the case back to Florida for consideration of several issues.[59] In particular, the Florida court was asked to clarify the standard to be used in determining the "intent of the voter" in the hand recounts. Another critical issue was whether the high court had changed the state's electoral appointment procedures in violation of Article II, Section 1, Clause 2 of the Constitution. This clause authorizes the states to appoint electors "in such manner as the *legislature* may direct" (emphasis added). The question was whether a *judicial* decision may change or qualify a state's *statutory* procedures for counting, recounting, and certifying its electoral votes. Under Florida law, the election results were to have been certified to Congress by 14 November. But Florida's law, like its constitution, is subject to interpretation by state courts, and there was language in both designed to provide for the proper counting of all votes in a presidential election. The issue boiled down to whether the state's Supreme Court could change certain dates and procedures in the interest of seeking greater clarification of the voters' intent.

Also implicated was the so-called "safe harbor" provision of the Electoral Count Act, passed by Congress in 1887. This provision allows the states to resolve electoral controversies without federal interference if the electors are chosen under "laws enacted prior to [election day]" and if the selection process is completed six days prior to the meeting of the electoral college.[60] In this instance, the electoral college was to meet on 6 January 2001, more than enough time, Gore's lawyers argued in agreement with Florida's Supreme Court, to finish the manual recount. They also argued that the "laws" enacted prior to the election included judicial rulings interpreting them. Failing to sail safely into the harbor by the prescribed date would invite a congressional resolution of the conflict.

The last chapter of this legal clash began on 8 December when, with Bush still ahead in votes by a razor-thin margin, Florida's Supreme Court, in a 4 to 3 decision, ordered a statewide manual recount of all votes cast, a decision Bush's campaign immediately appealed to the U.S. Supreme Court. On the same day, Florida's legisla-

---

[58] The so-called "undervotes" resulted from machine ballots insufficiently punched to clearly record the voter's choice. In addition, some confusing ballot designs, such as Palm Beach County's punch card "butterfly" ballot, misled voters into voting for a candidate other than the one they thought they were choosing. Other anomalies caused "overvotes" or ballots containing more than one vote for president. Still other ballots contained no vote for president, another possible consequence of voter confusion.

[59] *Bush v. Palm Beach County Canvassing Board (Bush I),* 530 U.S. 70 (2000).

[60] 3 *United States Code*, Section 5.

ture, attempting to seize the initiative from the judiciary, began a special session to consider appointing 25 Bush electors. Two days later, Bush and Gore presented their arguments before the Supreme Court. On 13 December, in a 5 to 4 decision, the Court overturned the Florida court's decision, saying that time had run out for any determination of a new standard to govern a statewide manual recount. The game was over. The next day, around 9 P.M., Gore conceded the election, with Florida's 25 electoral votes going to Bush. When the air cleared, Florida had given 2,912,790 (48.85%) votes to Bush and 2,912,253 (48.84%) to Gore, a winning margin of 537, a virtual tie in the light of the total vote cast. Ralph Nader, the main third party candidate, corralled 97,488 (1.63%) votes.

In striking down the Florida court's judgment, the Supreme Court held, in its 5 to 4 *per curiam* opinion, that the mandated recount violated the Equal Protection Clause. It did so because no uniform standard had been laid down for determining legal from illegal votes, leaving open the possibility of differential standards being used in different counties of the state. The Court appeared to expand the teaching of the apportionment cases by saying that "the right to vote is protected in more than the initial allocation of the franchise." Now equal protection applies "as well to the manner of its exercise," for "[h]aving once granted the right to vote on equal terms, the State may not, by later arbitrary and disparate treatment, value one person's vote over that of another."[61] In addition, the majority ruled that any attempt to meet the "safe harbor" deadline would be futile because insufficient time remained to work out a viable plan to meet the minimal requirements of equal protection under law. Chief Justice Rehnquist, Justices Scalia and Thomas concurring, expressed the view that the reversal of the Florida Supreme Court's decision was also required by Article II, Section 1, Clause 2, of the Constitution.

For many observers, *Bush II* was an exercise in blatant partisanship. They complained that the five justices who favored Bush (Rehnquist, O'Connor, Scalia, Thomas, and Kennedy) abandoned their usual posture of deferring to state court judgments to reach a preferred political result. Some academic lawyers bolstered this view by tearing the decision apart on doctrinal and historical grounds. *Bush II* nevertheless had its articulate defenders, among them scholar-judge Richard Posner who argued that judicial intervention was necessary to avoid a national crisis.[62] Still others felt, as did Justices Breyer and Souter in dissent, that the Florida Supreme Court's failure to provide "a uniform, specific standard to guide the recounts" was a legitimate equal protection issue.

As noted earlier, *Bush II* was a classic conflict between democracy and constitutionalism. It was equally an historic conflict between state and federal authority. The justices in dissent (Breyer, Stevens, Ginsburg, and Souter) argued that the states had the primary responsibility of selecting presidential electors and that sufficient time remained for the Florida recount to have been carried out under established and non-arbitrary rules of law. Other commentators thought *Bush II* presented a political question unfit for judicial resolution.[63] Had Florida not been able to appoint the electors on schedule, the controversy under existing law would have been resolved, democratically, by Congress. Democracy of course can be a messy business. It is

---

[61] 531 U.S. 104–105.

[62] Richard A. Posner, "Florida 2000: A Legal and Statistical Analysis of the Election Deadlock and the Ensuing Litigation," 2000 *Supreme Court Review* 1–60 (2001).

[63] See, for example, Erwin Chemerinsky, Bush v. Gore *Was Not Justiciable,* 76 Notre Dame Law Review 1093–1112 (2001).

disorderly, partisan, and unpredictable. Constitutional rulings, by contrast, are neat, clean, and stabilizing. Some commentators have suggested that *Bush II* represented a general distrust of democratic institutions and, like the apportionment decisions themselves, a "part of a broader pattern in which the current Court increasingly resists the use of democratic processes to address issues of democracy itself."[64]

Comparative Perspectives

We live in an age of democracy, prompting many to wonder whether the electoral college, adopted in the 18th century, is appropriate for the 21st century. Foreign observers, Europeans in particular, were appalled to learn that the presidential candidate who had won the most popular votes in 2000 had lost the election. They had to be told that voters do not directly elect the President of the United States. According to *Bush II*, individual citizens even lack a federal constitutional right to elect the electors "unless and until the state legislature chooses a state-wide election as the means to implement its power to appoint members of the electoral college."[65] The electoral college—an anti-majoritarian institution—is unique among the world's advanced democracies. All such democracies elect their presidents or first ministers by popular or parliamentary majorities. In presidential systems such as France, Poland, and Argentina, a candidate is required to obtain an overall majority of votes cast, failing which a runoff takes place between the two candidates winning the largest number of votes on the first ballot. In parliamentary democracies, by contrast, legislatures—usually the popularly elected lower chamber—choose their national political leaders. This, the parliamentary model, was available to Americans at the time of the Founding when several governors were elected by their state legislatures. But the Founders rejected this model—along with that of popular election—in the light of their resolve to place legislative and executive authority in mutually exclusive hands.[66]

The American electoral system differs from most of the world's democracies in still another respect. Americans elect their legislators in single-member districts (SMD) where the candidate with the most votes wins, a stratagem that often results in plurality winners. But most parliamentary democracies elect their legislators under systems of proportional representation (PR), as in Israel and 12 Western European democracies. According to Robert Dahl's analysis of 22 countries that have been steadily democratic since 1950, no fewer than 18 have PR systems of one kind or another.[67] (The exceptions are Canada, France, United Kingdom, and the United States.) The popu-

---

[64] See Samuel Issacharoff, Pamela S. Karlan, and Richard H. Pildes, *The Law of Democracy*, Revised Second Edition (New York: Foundation Press, 2002), 317.

[65] Ibid., 104.

[66] The electoral college nevertheless has its champions. They claim that it reinforces the federal system by requiring broad support throughout the country, giving individual states a heavy stake in the election of the president. The present system also seems to enhance the status of minority communities in large states such as New York, California, and Illinois because these minorities often hold the balance of power in a winner-take-all system, resulting in the additional benefit, its defenders hold, that politics in America is less likely to be polarized along ideological lines. Relatedly, by encouraging a two-party system, the electoral college, they say, produces a stable, durable government. Yet the practice of allocating all of a state's electoral vote to the presidential candidate winning the most votes—often less than a majority—virtually disenfranchises the losers. The winner-take-all system could be remedied without a constitutional amendment if electoral votes were distributed by congressional district outcomes. But this change would still permit the election of a minority president.

[67] Dahl, *How Democratic,* 164.

larity of PR in the democratic world was underlined more recently when New Zealand, in 1993, replaced its SMD system with a PR plan. Even in England, pressure is mounting to adopt some form of PR given the current system's failure to ensure that the party winning a majority of votes secures the majority of parliamentary seats, not to mention the inability of third parties to win seats proportionate to their voting strength in the country as a whole.[68]

Any change in the American electoral system, however, would be likely to modify the party system. As many political scientists have pointed out, SMD schemes, such as those in the United States and England, tend to reflect and reinforce a two-party system, whereas PR countries usually reflect and reinforce multi-party systems. But this is not an iron-clad relationship. SMD systems exist in France and Canada, yet third parties consistently win seats in their respective parliaments. So whether Americans would be willing to borrow a PR design from abroad would depend on their satisfaction or frustration with two-party government. (Unlike changing the electoral college, modifying the SMD election system would not require a constitutional amendment.)

As an aside, it might be interesting to imagine what the political alignment in the U.S. House of Representatives would have been if its 435 members had been chosen by PR on the basis of the presidential election returns in 2000. In reflecting on the results tabulated in table 8.2, students might ask whether the balance of power enjoyed by Ralph Nader's Green Party would have produced a more responsive and responsible politics. The question leads one to consider the relative advantages of SMD and PR. It is said that the former produces a more stable government than the latter, although PR produces a greater measure of representative fairness. Many PR countries have tried to overcome the problem of stability by imposing a voting threshold—often 5 percent—as a way of keeping splinter parties out of the legislature. If the 5 percent barrier had applied to our imaginary House election, no minority party would have been represented in 2000. So it is possible for two parties to predominate in a PR system. As the German experience has shown, the PR 5 percent rule helped to promote political stability by keeping all but one minor party out of parliament for most of the post-war decades.

Germany is especially noteworthy because its election system is among the world's most admired plans of political representation, variations of which have been copied by other countries, including, most recently, New Zealand. Germany's two-ballot system of modified proportional representation (MPR) combines single-member districts with PR, with 50 percent of 598 members of parliament being

TABLE 8.2 *Election 2000 by Proportional Representation*

Candidate	Party	Percent of Vote	House Seats
Gore	Democratic	48.38	211
Bush	Republican	47.87	208
Nader	Green	2.74	12
Buchanan	Reform	.43	2
Browne	Libertarian	.36	1
Other		.22	1
Total:		100.00	435

---

[68] See the discussion of electoral reform in Vernon Bogdanor, *Power and the People* (Suffolk: St. Edmundsbury Press, Ltd., 1997), 53–93, and Robert Alexander, *The Voice of the People: A Constitution for Tomorrow* (London: Weidenfeld & Nicolson, 1997), 64–68.

elected under each ballot. On the first ballot, voters record their district choice; on the second, they vote for a party list that includes the names of those candidates nominated by their respective parties, and this ballot determines the number of parliamentary seats allocated to a party. In short, each party retains all the districts seats it has won, but then list seats are added to give each party the number of parliamentary seats proportionate to its share of the popular vote. Even if a party fails to win a single district seat, it still receives list seats proportionate to its popular vote if it breaks the 5 percent barrier. So Germany combines the strengths of the two systems, reputedly achieving both stability and fairness. As for the principle of proportionality, it has evolved into a constituent principle of Germany's political order. Actually, any attempt to abolish PR would be suspect under Germany's Constitution.

Regulations governing access to the ballot also vary considerably when viewed comparatively. Unlike the United States, where the First Amendment is broadly protective of the rights of political parties to compete in elections regardless of their substantive beliefs and commitments, many democracies permit (or encourage) participation to be limited on the basis of ideological criteria. In Germany, for example, political parties opposed to democracy are unconstitutional. Also prohibited are associations "directed against the constitutional order or the concept of international understanding."[69] Similarly, in Israel and India, national election commissions have the authority to disqualify parties or candidates for their failure to comply with legal requirements respecting the content of electoral appeals. While these determinants are reviewable by the courts in these two polities, they provide governmental officials with powers that may seem quite extraordinary when viewed through the prism of the American experience.

In Israel, the Central Elections Committee may exclude a political party from the ballot if it denies the "existence of the State of Israel as the state of the Jewish people." Such had been the long-standing practice of the Committee, but until 1988 its mandate for doing so had always been obscure at best. In an important case in 1984, the Supreme Court had cited the absence of explicit statutory language authorizing exclusions by the Committee as the basis for overturning decisions banning both an anti-Zionist Arab party and a racist anti-Arab party. The legislature then amended the Basic Law to make explicit what had previously existed mainly in policy assumptions deduced from regime principles. Soon thereafter, the Central Elections Committee excluded a party (the Progressive List for Peace) from Knesset elections; while the ruling was reversed by the Court because of a finding of insufficient evidence of culpability, a majority made it clear that a disqualification would be valid if properly substantiated by the facts.[70] Thus, section 7A of the amended Basic Law (which also allows for removal of extremist Jewish parties that deny the "democratic nature of the state") formally—that is, constitutionally—establishes that electoral participation is predicated on the acceptance of certain substantive principles that constitute the essence of the polity.

In Germany, electoral participation is also predicated on the acceptance of democratic principles. In fact, Germany's Federal Constitutional Court has defined the Federal Republic as a "militant democracy"—that is, a democracy that will not tolerate, as in the Weimar Republic, the enemies of democracy. The concept has roots in the language of the Basic Law itself. Article 21 (1) declares that "political parties shall participate in the formation of the political will of the people," but specifies that

---

[69] Basic Law of the Federal Republic of Germany (1949), art. 9 (2).

[70] *Ben Shalom v. Central Committee for the Elections of the Twelfth Knesset.* 43 (4) P.D. 221 (1988).

"their internal organization shall conform to democratic principles." More importantly, under the terms of Article 21 (2), political parties shall be declared unconstitutional if "by reason of their aims or the behavior of their adherents, [they] seek to impair or abolish the free democratic order or to endanger the existence of the Federal Republic of Germany." Political parties, however, may not be banned on the whim of established governments. This power resides in the Federal Constitutional Court and only pursuant to a petition from the Federal Government or one of the houses of parliament. So far only two parties have been declared unconstitutional, a neo-Nazi party in 1952 and the Communist Party of Germany in 1956. More recent attempts to ban the allegedly "neo-Nazi," anti-immigrant National Democratic Party have failed to win the Court's approval.

In India, the constitutional commitment to secularism sets limits on electoral participation. The conduct of Indian elections is governed by the Representation of the People Act, a foundational enactment passed in 1951 that includes a "corrupt practices" provision. For Americans, a statutory invocation of corruption in the regulatory context of campaign behavior has only one meaning: the improper use of money to secure electoral advantage. In India the term has broader application and includes the inappropriate use of speech to advance one's electoral prospects. Specifically, the law forbids "the appeal by a candidate or his agent to vote or refrain from voting for any person on the ground of his religion, race, caste, community, or language or the use of, or appeal to, religious symbols for the furtherance of the prospects of the election of that candidate." In a group of cases (collectively known as the Hindutva Cases) decided in 1996, the Supreme Court upheld the constitutionality of the provision. It reasoned: "No democratic political and social order, in which the conditions of freedom and their progressive expansion for all make some regulations of all activities imperative, could endure without an agreement on the basic essentials which unite and hold citizens together despite all the differences of religion, race, caste, community, culture, creed, and language."[71] Thus, any victorious candidate involved in such corruption could have his or her election overturned by the Election Commission. Corruption here implies more than just the betrayal of the public trust for private benefit, but embraces a view perhaps best expressed in Montesquieu's observation that "The corruption of every government generally begins with that of its principles. [Montesquieu, *The Spirit of the Laws* (New York: Hafner Publishing, 1966), p. 109.]"

The subjects of the remaining paragraphs are campaign finance regulation and the apportionment of legislative districts. The comparative literature on these topics is vast, so we must confine ourselves here to selective judicial cases that contrast significantly with American constitutional policy. As for apportionment, foreign constitutional courts, as Comparative Notes 8.1 and 8.2 indicate, are less disposed to insist on arithmetic equality among districts than the U.S. Supreme Court. Foreign courts are more inclined to strike a balance between equality, effective government, and fairness of representation. This is the posture of Australia's High Court, even in the face of a constitutional text requiring legislators to be "directly chosen by the people." The Court points out that even in equally apportioned districts the value of a vote may be affected "in such a way as to allow one party in a two party system to return a majority of representatives with less than a majority of total votes."[72] Interestingly, and appropriately, the Court went on to say that the problem of disproportion

---

[71] *Probhoo v. Kunte*, 1 Sup Ct 130, 149 (1996).

[72] *McGinty v. Western Australia*, 186 C.L.R. 140 (1996).

and malapportionment—a central issue of American constitutional law—would largely disappear in a system of proportional representation.

Canada offers still another example of an approach at variance with the American. Although Section 3 of its Charter of Rights and Liberties confers on "every citizen" the right to vote in federal and state (i.e., provincial) elections, the Canadian Supreme Court has declared that the "purpose of [this] right . . . is not equality of voting power but the right to 'effective representation.'"[73] The Court noted that "equity" as well as "equality" was among the factors to be weighed in an apportionment scheme and that this might well include "practical considerations, such as social and physical geography." These and similar decisions handed down by the high courts of other nations (among them, Germany, England, and Japan) suggest that there are other paths to popular democracy apart from the one chosen by the United States Supreme Court.

In turning, finally, to campaign finance, one finds that political spending is a serious problem in all advanced democracies, and the solutions to the problem are as varied as the regimes themselves. These solutions range from the imposition of limits on campaign contributions and expenditures, as in the United States, to the public funding of political parties, as in several parliamentary democracies, including Israel and Australia. But whether these differences and the variations within them correspond to given structures of government or of party competition must await further comparative research. More important for the limited purpose of this essay are the differing visions of democracy informing constitutional cases on political finance. It will suffice here to compare *Buckley v. Valeo* with related cases in Canada and Germany.

In *Libman v. Quebec A.G.* (1997),[74] several interest groups and political parties challenged the constitutional validity of provincial spending limits in referendum campaigns under the free speech and association provisions of Canada's Charter of Rights and Freedoms. The Referendum Act, a provincial statute, provided for the public financing of referendum campaigns while restricting the amounts individuals and groups can contribute and spend on such campaigns. As the Supreme Court noted, the Act sought "to guarantee the democratic nature of referendums by promoting equality between the options submitted by the government and seeking to promote free and informed voting" and thus "to prevent the most affluent members of society from exerting a disproportionate influence by dominating the referendum debate through access to greater resources." These regulations, said the Court, "are designed to preserve the confidence of the electorate in a democratic process that it knows will not be dominated by the power of money."[75]

Although invalidating the Referendum Act as a disproportionate means for the achievement of a legitimate end, the *Libman* opinion contrasted sharply with the absolutist tenor of *Buckley*. *Libman* accepted, as *Buckley* did not, the principle of limits on electoral expenditures. Speech, however fundamentally precious in Canada's free and democratic society, would not trump all other competing values. "The principle of electoral fairness," said a unanimous tribunal, "flows directly from a principle entrenched in the Constitution: that of the political equality of citizens." Electoral fairness, said the Court, "presupposes that certain rights of freedom can legitimately be restricted in the name of a healthy electoral democracy. Elections are

---

[73] *Reference Re Provincial Electoral Boundaries (Sask.),* 2 S.C.R. 158 [1991].

[74] 151 D.L.R. (4th) 385 [1997].

[75] Ibid, 407–408.

fair and equitable," continued the Court, "only if all the citizens are reasonably informed of all possible choices and if parties and candidates are given a reasonable opportunity to present their positions so that election discourse is not dominated by those with access to greater financial resources."[76] Canada's electoral democracy accordingly requires some compromise among the values of fairness, equity, and freedom of speech.

Buckley v. Valeo, by contrast, highlights the fundamental importance of "unfettered freedom of speech" that the Supreme Court has transposed into the reigning value of the American constitutional order. One commentator, inspired by Theodore Lowi's analysis of American pluralism in *The End of Liberalism*, writes: "If both [Canada and the United States] are polities and, by Aristotle's definition, a mixture of oligarchic and democratic elements, we find that the Canadian definition of equality pushes the Canadian polity more toward the democratic pole, while the American moves the United States toward the oligarchic pole."[77] The suggestion is that *Buckley* incorporates a *laissez-faire* view of speech analogous to the older American ideology of free market capitalism. Thus, regulating the marketplace of ideas, like controls over the market economy, is to distort its natural operation. Students might reflect on whether the Canadian view could be easily incorporated into American constitutional doctrine or whether *Buckley's* ruggedly pluralistic model of democracy projects a more accurate view of political reality in America.

Owing to its party-centered focus, Germany's constitutional law of political finance furnishes another sharp contrast to American judicial policy. Actually, Germany's Federal Constitutional Court (FCC) has been more active in this field than either the Canadian or United States Supreme Court. In Germany, however, the constitutional text has served as the basis for judicializing the broad contours of party politics. Article 21 of the Basic Law provides that "political parties shall participate in forming the political will of the people. They may be freely established. Their internal organization shall conform to democratic principles. They shall publicly account for the sources and use of their funds and for their assets." From this text, the first in German history to acknowledge the legitimacy of political parties, the FCC has fashioned an elaborate theory of the "party state" (*Parteienstaat*), one that acknowledges parties as the chief agents of political representation in a parliamentary democracy and, more importantly for our purposes, as "integral units of the constitutional state."

In short, as Comparative Note 8.3 underscores, the FCC regards parties as more than voluntary units of civil society. Because they are fundamentally charged with organizing the "will" of the German people and responsible for representing that will in parliament, they are also, at least for electoral purposes, part of the state's constitutional structure of democracy, even entitling the parties to public financial support. As for elections, Article 21 has been interpreted in tandem with Article 38 which declares that members of parliament "shall be elected in general, direct, free, equal and secret elections" and that "[t]hey shall be representatives of the whole people [and] bound . . . only by their conscience." In the FCC's jurisprudence, these provisions have been interpreted to require, as in Canadian constitutional law, not only fair and effective, as opposed to strictly equal, representation, but also equal treatment of political parties under Germany's system of modified proportional representation.

---

[76] Ibid., 410. See Comparative Note 8.5.

[77] Jodi Cockerill, "Constituting Equality: A Comparative Analysis of *Buckley v. Valeo* and *Libman v. Quebec AG*," (unpublished manuscript, 1998), 3.

Apart from the public funding cases discussed below, the FCC has insisted on equal opportunity for political parties in four major decisions. First, as indicated in Comparative Note 8.3, the Court has required publicly owned radio and television stations to allocate blocs of air time, during an election campaign, to minor parties, along with the major parliamentary parties, proportionate to their strength in the area within reach of the stations. Second, in the well-known *Official Propaganda Case* (1977), the FCC invalidated the official distribution of pamphlets and brochures praising the record and advancing the cause of the Social Democratic–dominated coalition government as a violation of electoral equality and majority rule during the 1976 federal election campaign. Third, in the first all-German election following reunification, the FCC required that the PR 5 percent rule be applied separately in East and West Germany to give minor East German parties, especially the Party of Democratic Socialism, the reformed Communist Party, a fighting chance to enter the national parliament, which it succeeded in doing. Finally, early on in 1958, the Court ruled unconstitutional a federal tax provision allowing citizens to deduct from their net taxable income a portion of their donations to political parties. Social Democrats challenged the provision because, they alleged, it favored political parties supported by corporations and wealthy individuals. The FCC agreed, declaring that the tax code offended the basic right of political parties to equal opportunity.[78] It is hard to imagine the U.S. Supreme Court, "activist" as it is, deciding the radio and tax deduction cases in the same way.

In the *Tax Deduction Case*, the FCC acknowledged the financial plight of political parties and their need for funds if they were to play the important role envisioned by the Basic Law's framers. The Court then suggested that the state might constitutionally fund political parties and election campaigns as a means of ensuring effective competition among the parties and of diminishing their dependence on special interest groups. Funding would be appropriate, said the Court, because parties during election campaigns serve as "constitutional organs" functioning as vital links between state and society. Parliament took the cue and immediately passed funding legislation that by the late 1990s was costing German taxpayers nearly $500 million per federal election campaign, amounting to about $8.05 per voter.[79]

Germany's Political Parties Act sets maximum amounts that the parties may receive for a given election campaign and the money is distributed on the basis of the number of valid votes cast for each party list (i.e., the second ballot vote). The FCC, however, has kept a tight rein on these expenditures to make sure that the money is being spent in accordance with constitutional standards and that no party is left out of the equation. In fact, the Court struck down the Party Finance Act of 1959 for excluding the funding of parties unrepresented in the national parliament. In a later decision, the FCC even ordered parliament to finance, to the extent allowable under the distribution formula, parties receiving as little as 0.5 percent of the national vote. An equalitarian constitutional policy of this nature would be well-nigh impossible under current ruling American constitutional law.

It might be noted in conclusion, however, that the FCC's perspective on political parties and elections generally is grounded in Germany's political history, a history

---

[78] See, respectively, the decisions of the Federal Constitutional Court in Donald P. Kommers, *The Constitutional Jurisprudence of the Federal Republic of Germany*, 2nd ed. (Durham, N.C.: Duke University Press, 1997), 201, 177, 187, and 215.

[79] Karl-Heinz Nassmacher, "Political Finance in West Central Europe (Austria, Germany, Switzerland)" in Nassmacher (ed.), *Foundations of Democracy*, 2nd ed. (Baden-Baden: Nomos Verlagsgesellschaft, 2001), 93.

that represents "a unique synthesis of Western parliamentarianism and the German state tradition."[80] The conception of a political party as a "constitutional organ" entitled to public funding for the role it plays in the electoral process would run against the grain of the American constitutional view that parties are unofficial organizations fully dependent, and properly so, on voluntary contributions. Still, German constitutionalism has lessons to teach about the meaning of equality as it affects the electoral process.

Selected Bibliography

Briffault, Richard. *Soft Money Reform and the Constitution.* 1 Election Law Journal 343–360 (2002).

Chemerinsky, Erwin. Bush v. Gore *Was Not Justiciable.* 76 *Notre Dame Law Review* 1093–1112 (2001).

Dahl, Robert A. *How Democratic is the American Constitution.* New Haven: Yale University Press, 2001.

Dahl, Robert A. *On Democracy.* New Haven: Yale University Press, 1998.

Deadlock: The Inside Story of America's Closest Election by the Political Staff of the *Washington Post.* Washington, D.C.: The Washington Post Company, 2001.

Dionne, E. J. Jr. and William Kristol (eds.). *Bush v. Gore.* Washington, D.C.: The Brookings Institution, 2001.

Election Law Journal. A new publication devoted to the study of elections and the electoral process.

Epstein, Richard A. *In Such Manner as the Legislature Thereof May Direct: The Outcome in* Bush v. Gore *Defended.* 68 University of Chicago Law Review 613 (2001).

Gais, Thomas. *Improper Influence: Campaign Finance Law, Political Interest Groups, and the Problem of Equality.* Ann Arbor: University of Michigan Press, 1996.

Gillman, Howard. *The Votes That Counted: How the Court Decided the 2000 Presidential Election.* Chicago: The University of Chicago Press, 2001.

Gormley, Ken, *Racial Mind-Game and Reapportionment: When Can Race be Considered (Legitimately) in Redistricting?* 4 University of Pennsylvania Journal of Constitutional Law 735–799 (2002)

Krotoszynski, Ronald J. Jr. An Epitaphios *for Neutral Principles in Constitutional Law:* Bush v. Gore *and the Emerging Jurisprudence of* Oprah! 90 The Georgetown Law Journal 2087–2141.

Lazare, Daniel. *The Frozen Republic: How the Constitution is Paralyzing Democracy.* New York: Harcourt Brace & Company, 1996.

Mann, Thomas E. *Linking Knowledge and Action: Political Science and Campaign Finance Reform.* 1 Perspectives on Politics 69–83 (March 2003).

McConnell, Michael M. *The Redistricting Cases: Original Mistakes and Current Controversies.* 24 Harvard Journal of Law and Public Policy 103–117 (2000–2001).

McDonald, Laughlin. *A Voting Rights Odyssey: Black Enfranchisement in Georgia.* New York: Cambridge University Press, 2003.

Pippen, J., S. Bowler, and T. Donovan. *Election Reform and Direct Democracy: Campaign Finance Regulations in the American States.* 6 American Politics Research 599–582 (2002).

Rakove, Jack N. (Ed.). *The Unfinished Election of 2000.* New York: Basic Books, 2001.

Redish, Martin H. *Free Speech and the Flawed Postulates of Campaign Finance Reform.* 3 University of Pennsylvania Journal of Constitutional Law 783 (1999).

Smith, Bradley A. *Unfree Speech: The Folly of Campaign Finance Reform.* Princeton: Princeton University Press, 2001.

Symposium on Campaign Finance Reform. 94 Columbia Law Review 1125 (1994)

Wright, J. Skelley. *Politics and the Constitution: Is Money Speech?* 85 Yale Law Journal 1001 (1976).

Selected Comparative Bibliography

Courtney, John C. *Commissioned Ridings: Designing Canada's Electoral Districts.* Montreal and Kingston: McGill-Queen's University Press, 2001.

Grofman, Bernard and Arend Lijphart. *The Evolution of Electoral and Party Systems in the Nordic Countries.* New York: Agathon Press, 2002.

Hogan, G.W. *Federal Republic of Germany, Ireland, and the United Kingdom: Three European Approaches to Political Campaign Regulation.* 21 Capital University Law Review 501–543 (1992).

Lee, Frances E. and Bruce I. Oppenheimer. *Sizing Up the Senate: The Unequal Consequences of Equal Representation.* Chicago: The University of Chicago Press, 1999.

Nassmacher, Karl-Heinz (ed). Comparative Political Finance

---

[80] Michaela Richter, "The Basic Law and the Democratic Party State: Constitutional Theory and Political Practice" in *Cornerstone of Democracy: The West German Grundgesetz, 1949–89,* Occasional Paper No. 13 (Washington, D.C.: German Historical Institute, 1995), 37.

in Established Democracies in Nassmacher (ed.) *Foundations for Democracy*. Baden-Baden: Nomos Verlagsgesellschaft, 2001.

Young, Lisa and William Cross. *The Rise of Plebiscitary Democracy in Canadian Political Parties*. 6 Party Politics 673–699 (2002).

Reynolds v. Sims

377 U.S. 533, 84 S. Ct. 1362, 12 L. Ed. 2d 506 (1964)

In 1961, and for the first time since the 1900 census, Alabama reapportioned its legislature in accordance with state constitutional requirements, one of which provided that the House of Representatives consist of 105 members. Under the 1961 plan, each of the state's 67 counties would receive one representative, while the election of the remaining members would be based on population. The one representative per county formula, however, gave some advantage to less populated areas. The plan was challenged as a violation of the Fourteenth Amendment's Equal Protection Clause. Opinion of the Court: *Warren*, Black, Brennan, Douglas, Goldberg, White. Concurring opinion: *Clark*, Stewart. Dissenting opinion: *Harlan*.

Mr. Chief Justice WARREN delivered the opinion of the Court.

A predominant consideration in determining whether a State's legislative apportionment scheme constitutes an invidious discrimination violative of rights asserted under the Equal Protection Clause is that the rights allegedly impaired are individual and personal in nature. As stated by the Court in *United States v. Bathgate*, 246 U.S. 220, 227 (1918), "[t]he right to vote is personal. . . ." While the result of a court decision in a state legislative apportionment controversy may be to require the restructuring of the geographical distribution of seats in a state legislature, the judicial focus must be concentrated upon ascertaining whether there has been any discrimination against certain of the State's citizens which constitutes an impermissible impairment of their constitutionally protected right to vote. . . . Undoubtedly, the right of suffrage is a fundamental matter in a free and democratic society. Especially since the right to exercise the franchise in a free and unimpaired manner is preservative of other basic civil and political rights, any alleged infringement of the right of citizens to vote must be carefully and meticulously scrutinized. . . .

Legislators represent people, not trees or acres. Legislators are elected by voters, not farms or cities or economic interests. As long as ours is a representative form of government, and our legislatures are those instruments of government elected directly by and directly representative

of the people, the right to elect legislators in a free and unimpaired fashion is a bedrock of our political system. . . . [I]f a State should provide that the votes of citizens in one part of the State should be given two times, or five times, or 10 times the weight of votes of citizens in another part of the State, it could hardly be contended that the right to vote of those residing in the disfavored areas had not been effectively diluted. . . . Of course, the effect of state legislative districting schemes which give the same number of representatives to unequal numbers of constituents is identical. Overweighting and overvaluation . . . has the certain effect of dilution and undervaluation of the votes of those living there. The resulting discrimination against those individual voters living in disfavored areas is easily demonstrable mathematically. Their right to vote is simply not the same right to vote as that of those living in a favored part of the State. Two, five, or 10 of them must vote before the effect of their voting is equivalent to that of their favored neighbor. Weighting the votes of citizens differently, by any method or means, merely because of where they happen to reside, hardly seems justifiable. . . .

State legislatures are, historically, the fountainhead of representative government in this country. . . . But representative government is in essence self-government through the medium of elected representatives of the people, and each and every citizen has an inalienable right to full and effective participation in the political processes of his State's legislative bodies. Most citizens can achieve this participation only as qualified voters through the election of legislators to represent them. Full and effective participation by all citizens in state government requires, therefore, that each citizen have an equally effective voice in the election of members of his state legislature. Modern and viable state government needs, and the Constitution demands, no less.

Logically, in a society ostensibly grounded on representative government, it would seem reasonable that a majority of the people of a State could elect a majority of that State's legislators. To conclude differently, and to sanction minority control of state legislative bodies, would appear to deny majority rights in a way that far surpasses any possible denial of minority rights that might otherwise be thought to result. Since legislatures are responsible for enacting laws by which all citizens are to be governed, they

Comparative Note 8.1

[Proposed changes in Saskatchewan's electoral districts were challenged as infringing Section 3 of the Charter of Rights and Freedoms. (According to Section 3, "Every citizen of Canada has the right to vote in an election of members of the House of Commons or of a legislative assembly and to be qualified for membership therein.") The redistribution of seats deviated significantly from a pure population standard, resulting in the underrepresentation of urban areas.]

The content of the Charter's right to vote is to be determined in a broad and purposive way, having regard to historical and social context. The broader philosophy underlying the historical development of the right to vote must be sought and practical considerations, such as social and physical geography, must be borne in mind. The Court, most importantly, must be guided by the ideal of a "free and democratic society" upon which the Charter is founded. The purpose of the right to vote enshrined in s. 3 of the Charter is not equality of voting power per se but the right to "effective representation." The right to vote therefore comprises many factors, of which equity is but one. The section does not guarantee equality of voting power.

Relative parity of voting power is a prime condition of effective representation. Deviations from absolute voter parity, however, may be justified on the grounds of practical impossibility or the provision of more effective representation. Factors like geography, community history, community interests and minority representation may need to be taken into account to ensure that our legislative assemblies effectively represent the diversity of our social mosaic. Beyond this, dilution of one citizen's vote as compared with another's should not be countenanced.

SOURCE: *Reference Re Provincial Electoral Boundaries (Sask.)*, 2 S.C.R. 158 (1991).

---

should be bodies which are collectively responsive to the popular will. And the concept of equal protection has been traditionally viewed as requiring the uniform treatment of persons standing in the same relation to the governmental action questioned or challenged. With respect to the allocation of legislative representation, all voters, as citizens of a State, stand in the same relation regardless of where they live. . . . Since the achieving of fair and effective representation for all citizens is concededly the basic aim of legislative apportionment, we conclude that the Equal Protection Clause guarantees the opportunity for equal participation by all voters in the election of state legislators. Diluting the weight of votes because of place of residence impairs basic constitutional rights under the Fourteenth Amendment just as much as invidious discriminations based upon factors such as race, or economic status. Our constitutional system amply provides for the protection of minorities by means other than giving them majority control of state legislatures. And the democratic ideals of equality and majority rule, which have served this Nation so well in the past, are hardly of any less significant for the present and the future.

We are told that the matter of apportioning representation in a state legislature is a complex and many-faceted one. We are advised that States can rationally consider factors other than population in apportioning legislative representation. We are admonished not to restrict the power of the States to impose differing views as to political philosophy on their citizens. We are cautioned about the dangers of entering into political thickets and mathematical quagmires. Our answer is this: a denial of constitutionally protected rights demands judicial protection; our oath and our office require no less of us. . . .

To the extent that a citizen's right to vote is debased, he is that much less a citizen. The fact that an individual lives here or there is not a legitimate reason for overweighting or diluting the efficacy of his vote. The complexions of societies and civilizations change, often with amazing rapidity. A nation once primarily rural in character becomes predominantly urban. Representation schemes once fair and equitable become archaic and outdated. But the basic principle of representative government remains, and must remain, unchanged—the weight of a citizen's vote cannot be made to depend on where he lives. Population is, of necessity, the starting point for consideration and the controlling criterion for judgment in legislative apportionment controversies. A citizen, a qualified voter, is no more nor no less so because he lives in the city or on the farm. This is the clear and strong command of our Constitution's Equal Protection Clause. This is an essential part of the concept of a government of laws and not men. This is at the heart of Lincoln's vision of "government of the people, by the people, [and] for the people." The Equal Protection Clause demands no less than substantially equal state legislative representation for all citizens, of all places as well as of all races.

We hold that, as a basic constitutional standard, the Equal Protection Clause requires that the seats in both houses of a bicameral state legislature must be apportioned on a population basis. Simply stated, an individual's right to vote for state legislators is unconstitutionally impaired when its weight is in a substantial fashion diluted when compared with votes of citizens living in other parts of the State. . . .

Mr. Justice HARLAN, dissenting.

The Court's constitutional discussion . . . is remarkable . . . for its failure to address itself at all to the Fourteenth Amendment as a whole or to the legislative history of the Amendment pertinent to the matter at hand. Stripped of aphorisms, the Court's argument boils down to the assertion that appellees' right to vote has been invidiously "debased" or "diluted" by systems of apportionment which entitle them to vote for fewer legislators than other voters, an assertion which is tied to the Equal Protection Clause only by the constitutionally frail tautology that "equal" means "equal."

Had the Court paused to probe more deeply into the matter, it would have found that the Equal Protection Clause was never intended to inhibit the States in choosing any democratic method they pleased for the apportionment of their legislatures.

The Court's elaboration of its new "constitutional" doctrine indicates how far—and how unwisely—it has strayed from the appropriate bounds of its authority. The consequence of today's decision is that in all but the handful of States which may already satisfy the new requirements the local District Court or, it may be, the state courts, are given blanket authority and the constitutional duty to supervise apportionment of the State Legislatures. It is difficult to imagine a more intolerable and inappropriate interference by the judiciary with the independent legislatures of the States. . . .

. . . [T]he Court declares it unconstitutional for a State to give effective consideration to any of the following in establishing legislative districts:

(1) history;
(2) "economic or other sorts of group interests";
(3) area;
(4) geographical considerations;
(5) a desire "to insure effective representation for sparsely settled areas";

(6) "availability of access of citizens to their representatives";
(7) theories of bicameralism (except those approved by the Court);
(8) occupation;
(9) "an attempt to balance urban and rural power";
(10) the preference of a majority of voters in the State. . . .

I know of no principle of logic or practical or theoretical politics, still less any constitutional principle, which establishes all or any of these exclusions. Certain it is that the Court's opinion does not establish them. So far as the Court says anything at all on this score, it says only that "legislators represent people, not trees or acres"; that "citizens, not history or economic interests, cast votes"; that "people, not land or trees or pastures, vote." All this may be conceded. But it is surely equally obvious, and, in the context of elections, more meaningful to note that people are not ciphers and that legislators can represent their electors only by speaking for their interests—economic, social, political—many of which do reflect the place where the electors live.

. . . What is done today deepens my conviction that judicial entry into this realm is profoundly ill-advised and constitutionally impermissible. As I have said before, I believe that the vitality of our political system, on which in the last analysis all else depends, is weakened by reliance on the judiciary for political reform; in time a complacent body politic may result.

Notes and Queries

1. Chief Justice Warren notes that the one person–one vote standard "is the clear and strong command of our Constitution's Equal Protection Clause." How does he know this? Does Lincoln's vision of government "of the people, by the people, [and] for the people"—the line Warren quotes—really embody strict population equality in political representation? Could the "people" be more effectively represented by other means?

2. What vision of politics seems to be incorporated into the one person–one vote principle? Is it compatible with the conception of democracy as expressed in *Federalist No. 10*?

3. The constitutions of other advanced democracies such as Germany and Canada are based on the principle of popular democracy and provide for the direct, popular election of their legislators. Yet their highest constitutional tribunals have not imposed a rigid rule of one person–one vote on their electoral systems. Why not?

4. In the introductory essay, we noted that Colorado's voters had approved in a popular referendum a plan of representation that established one state legislative chamber based on population and the other based on governmental units. In fact, the plan was approved by a popular majority in all of the state's counties. Yet the Supreme Court declared that "the fact that a challenged legislative apportionment plan was approved by the electorate is without federal constitutional significance." Do you find this reason convincing in the light of the structures and relationships embedded in the U.S. Constitution itself?

5. Can you think of circumstances where the equal population standard might actually undermine the equal voting power of residents in a particular district. Think, for example, of legislative districts in which a disproportionately large number of residents are ineligible to vote, such as minors, ex-felons, and immigrants.

Davis v. Bandemer
478 U.S. 109, 106 S. Ct. 2797, 92 L. Ed. 2d 85 (1986)

In 1981, the Republican-controlled Indiana legislature enacted a new districting plan. Indiana Democrats challenged the act as an unconstitutional political gerrymander. The November 1982 elections provided them with some evidence for their claim, as the statewide percentage of votes obtained by Democrats was several points greater than the percentage of seats won in the state legislature. A federal district court found the redistricting plan unconstitutional, and the Supreme Court took the case on appeal. Opinion of the Court: *White*, Brennan, Marshall, Blackmun. Concurring in the judgment: *Chief Justice Burger*, *O'Connor*, Rehnquist. Concurring in part and dissenting in part: *Powell*, Stevens.

Justice WHITE announced the judgment of the Court and delivered the opinion of the Court as to Part II and an opinion as to Parts I, III, and IV, in which Justice BRENNAN, Justice MARSHALL, and Justice BLACKMUN join.

. . . The District Court held that, because any apportionment scheme that purposely prevents proportional representation is unconstitutional, Democratic voters need only show that their proportionate voting influence has been adversely affected. Our cases, however, clearly foreclose any claim that the Constitution requires proportional representation, or that legislatures in reapportioning must draw district lines to come as near as possible to allocating seats to the contending parties in proportion to what their anticipated statewide vote will be. . . .

[. . .]These holdings rest on a conviction that the mere fact that a particular apportionment scheme makes it more difficult for a particular group in a particular district to elect the representatives of its choice does not render that scheme constitutionally infirm. This conviction, in turn, stems from a perception that the power to influence the political process is not limited to winning elections. An individual or a group of individuals who votes for a losing candidate is usually deemed to be adequately represented by the winning candidate, and to have as much opportunity to influence that candidate as other voters in the district. We cannot presume in such a situation, without actual proof to the contrary, that the candidate elected will entirely ignore the interests of those voters. This is true even in a safe district where the losing group loses election after election. Thus, a group's electoral power is not unconstitutionally diminished by the simple fact of an apportionment scheme that makes winning elections more difficult, and a failure of proportional representation alone does not constitute impermissible discrimination under the Equal Protection Clause.

As with individual districts, where unconstitutional vote dilution is alleged in the form of statewide political gerrymandering, the mere lack of proportional representation will not be sufficient to prove unconstitutional discrimination. Again, without specific supporting evidence, a court cannot presume in such a case that those who are elected will disregard the disproportionately underrepresented group. Rather, unconstitutional discrimination occurs only when the electoral system is arranged in a manner that will consistently degrade a voter's or a group of voters' influence on the political process as a whole.

Although this is a somewhat different formulation than we have previously used in describing unconstitutional vote dilution in an individual district, the focus of both of these inquiries is essentially the same. In both contexts, the question is whether a particular group has been unconstitutionally denied its chance to effectively influence the political process. In a challenge to an individual district, this inquiry focuses on the opportunity of members of the group to participate in party deliberations in the slating and nomination of candidates, their opportunity to register and vote, and hence their chance to directly influence the election returns and to secure the attention of the winning candidate. Statewide, however, the inquiry centers on the voters' direct or indirect influence on the

Comparative Note 8.2

[In organizing the first all-German election following reunification in 1990, the Federal Parliament (Bundestag) provided that the election would take place under West Germany's two-ballot MPR system requiring a political party to obtain 5 percent of the vote to gain entry into parliament. East Germany, by contrast, in its one free election since the collapse of communism, followed a single-ballot system of pure PR. East German leaders objected to the application of the 5 percent rule because the political reform groups that played so critical a role in bringing down the regime were unlikely to scale this barrier. In this first all-German election, the Federal Constitutional Court required the 5 percent rule to be applied separately in East and West Germany. In the course of its decision, the Court considered the meaning of equality in a system of competitive political parties.]

Parties are charged with the primary responsibility of organizing citizens into political groups for electoral purposes. In the field of elections and voting, formal equality includes the principle of formal equal opportunity, namely, the opportunity of political parties and voter organizations to compete for electoral support. This right of equal opportunity derives from the constitutional status of [political] parties, the freedom to form political parties, and the principle of a multiparty system which is associated with the concept of a free democracy. The principle of equal opportunity governs the election proper as well as the campaign. Democracy cannot function—as a matter of principle—if the parties are unable to enter an election campaign under the same legal circumstances. In regulating the process of forming the political will of the people, the legislature operates under strict limits. It may not undermine the equal opportunity of parties or voter associations. Differential treatment of parties and voter associations is constitutionally prohibited. . . .

The very purpose of proportional representation is to have government realistically reflect the political will of the electorate. Such a system may result in splintering the electorate, making it difficult or impossible to form a stable parliamentary majority. . . . As a rule, a threshold of 5 percent is constitutionally unobjectionable. This court emphasized early on that the compatibility [of the 5 percent threshold] with equality in voting cannot be determined abstractly. . . . But one thing is certain: a deviation from the customary [5 percent rule]—even if only a temporary deviation—may be necessary if the circumstances internal to the state have essentially changed; for instance, if shortly before an election the electoral territory is expanded to include territories that have had a different political structure.

SOURCE: *National Unity Election Case* (Germany 1990), 82 BverfGE 322.

---

elections of the state legislature as a whole. And, as in individual district cases, an equal protection violation may be found only where the electoral system substantially disadvantages certain voters in their opportunity to influence the political process effectively. In this context, such a finding of unconstitutionality must be supported by evidence of continued frustration of the will of a majority of the voters or effective denial to a minority of voters of a fair chance to influence the political process. . . .

Relying on a single election to prove unconstitutional discrimination is unsatisfactory. The District Court observed, and the parties do not disagree, that Indiana is a swing State. Voters sometimes prefer Democratic candidates, and sometimes Republican. The District Court did not find that, because of the 1981 Act, the Democrats could not, in one of the next few elections, secure a sufficient vote to take control of the assembly. Indeed, the District Court declined to hold that the 1982 election results

were the predictable consequences of the 1981 Act, and expressly refused to hold that those results were a reliable prediction of future ones. The District Court did not ask by what percentage the statewide Democratic vote would have had to increase to control either the House or the Senate. The appellants argue here, without a persuasive response from the appellees, that, had the Democratic candidates received an additional few percentage points of the votes cast statewide, they would have obtained a majority of the seats in both houses. Nor was there any finding that the 1981 reapportionment would consign the Democrats to a minority status in the Assembly throughout the 1980's, or that the Democrats would have no hope of doing any better in the reapportionment that would occur after the 1990 census. Without findings of this nature, the District Court erred in concluding that the 1981 Act violated the Equal Protection Clause.

In sum, we hold that political gerrymandering cases are

properly justiciable under the Equal Protection Clause. We also conclude, however, that a threshold showing of discriminatory vote dilution is required for a prima facie case of an equal protection violation. In this case, the findings made by the District Court of an adverse effect on the appellees do not surmount the threshold requirement. Consequently, the judgment of the District Court is Reversed.

Chief Justice BURGER, concurring in the judgment.

It is not surprising that citizens who are troubled by gerrymandering turn first to the courts for redress. De Tocqueville, that perceptive commentator on our country, observed that "[s]carcely any question arises in the United States which does not become, sooner or later, a subject of judicial debate." What I question is the Court's urge to craft a judicial remedy for this perceived "injustice." In my view, the Framers of the Constitution envisioned quite a different scheme. They placed responsibility for correction of such flaws in the people, relying on them to influence their elected representatives. . . .

Justice O'CONNOR, with whom Chief Justice BURGER and Justice REHNQUIST join, concurring in the judgment.

Today the Court holds that claims of political gerrymandering lodged by members of one of the political parties that make up our two-party system are justiciable under the Equal Protection Clause of the Fourteenth Amendment. Nothing in our precedents compels us to take this step, and there is every reason not to do so. I would hold that the partisan gerrymandering claims of major political parties raise a nonjusticiable political question that the judiciary should leave to the legislative branch, as the Framers of the Constitution unquestionably intended. Accordingly, I would reverse the District Court's judgment on the grounds that appellees' claim is nonjusticiable.

There can be little doubt that the emergence of a strong and stable two-party system in this country has contributed enormously to sound and effective government. The preservation and health of our political institutions, state and federal, depends to no small extent on the continued vitality of our two-party system, which permits both stability and measured change. The opportunity to control the drawing of electoral boundaries through the legislative process of apportionment is a critical and traditional part of politics in the United States, and one that plays no small role in fostering active participation in the political parties at every level. Thus, the legislative business of apportionment is fundamentally a political affair, and challenges to the manner in which an apportionment has been carried out—by the very parties that are responsible for this proc-

ess—present a political question in the truest sense of the term.

To turn these matters over to the federal judiciary is to inject the courts into the most heated partisan issues. It is predictable that the courts will respond by moving away from the nebulous standard a plurality of the Court fashions today and toward some form of rough proportional representation for all political groups. The consequences of this shift will be as immense as they are unfortunate. I do not believe, and the Court offers not a shred of evidence to suggest, that the Framers of the Constitution intended the judicial power to encompass the making of such fundamental choices about how this Nation is to be governed. Nor do I believe that the proportional representation towards which the Court's expansion of equal protection doctrine will lead is consistent with our history, our traditions, or our political institutions. . . .

The step taken today is a momentous one which, if followed in the future, can only lead to political instability and judicial malaise. If members of the major political parties are protected by the Equal Protection Clause from dilution of their voting strength, then members of every identifiable group that possesses distinctive interests and tends to vote on the basis of those interests should be able to bring similar claims. Federal courts will have no alternative but to attempt to recreate the complex process of legislative apportionment in the context of adversary litigation in order to reconcile the competing claims of political, religious, ethnic, racial, occupational, and socioeconomic groups. Even if there were some way of limiting such claims to organized political parties, the fact remains that the losing party or the losing group of legislators in every reapportionment will now be invited to fight the battle anew in federal court. Apportionment is so important to legislators and political parties that the burden of proof the plurality places on political gerrymandering plaintiffs is unlikely to deter the routine lodging of such complaints. . . .

In my view, where a racial minority group is . . . vulnerable to exclusion from the political process, individual voters who belong to that group enjoy some measure of protection against intentional dilution of their group voting strength by means of racial gerrymandering. As a matter of past history and present reality, there is a direct and immediate relationship between the racial minority's group voting strength in a particular community and the individual rights of its members to vote and to participate in the political process. In these circumstances, the stronger nexus between individual rights and group interests, and the greater warrant the Equal Protection Clause gives the federal courts to intervene for protection against racial discrimination, suffice to render racial gerrymandering claims justiciable. . . .

Clearly, members of the Democratic and Republican Parties cannot claim that they are a discrete and insular group vulnerable to exclusion from the political process by some dominant group: these political parties are the dominant groups, and the Court has offered no reason to believe that they are incapable of fending for themselves through the political process. . . . [E]ach major party presumably has ample weapons at its disposal to conduct the partisan struggle that often leads to a partisan apportionment, but also often leads to a bipartisan one. There is no proof before us that political gerrymandering is an evil that cannot be checked or cured by the people or by the parties themselves. Absent such proof, I see no basis for concluding that there is a need, let alone a constitutional basis, for judicial intervention. . . .

Justice POWELL, with whom Justice STEVENS joins, concurring in part and dissenting in part.

The Equal Protection Clause guarantees citizens that their State will govern them impartially. In the context of redistricting, that guarantee is of critical importance, because the franchise provides most citizens their only voice in the legislative process. Since the contours of a voting district powerfully may affect citizens' ability to exercise influence through their vote, district lines should be determined in accordance with neutral and legitimate criteria. When deciding where those lines will fall, the State should treat its voters as standing in the same position, regardless of their political beliefs or party affiliation. . . .

In conclusion, I want to make clear the limits of the standard that I believe the Equal Protection Clause imposes on legislators engaged in redistricting. Traditionally, the determination of electoral districts within a State has been a matter left to the legislative branch of the state government. Apart from the doctrine of separation of powers and the federal system prescribed by the Constitution, federal judges are ill-equipped generally to review legislative decisions respecting redistricting. As the Court's opinion

makes clear, however, our precedents hold that a colorable claim of discriminatory gerrymandering presents a justiciable controversy under the Equal Protection Clause. Federal courts, in exercising their duty to adjudicate such claims, should impose a heavy burden of proof on those who allege that a redistricting plan violates the Constitution. . . . [T]his case presents a paradigm example of unconstitutional discrimination against the members of a political party that happened to be out of power. . . .

Accordingly, I would affirm the judgment of the District Court.

Notes and Queries

1. Justice O'Connor suggests that she would uphold districting that diluted the voting power of a racial minority, but rejects a similar claim by one of the major parties. What is the constitutional rationale behind this distinction? How is the democratic process more compromised in the case of racial gerrymandering than it is in political gerrymandering between the two major parties?

2. Justice O'Connor also suggests that the damage done to major parties through redistricting will right itself without judicial intervention. If redistricting had to rely on the political process alone, how could we be sure that certain ideological groups would not be relegated to permanent minority status?

3. Justices Powell and Stevens effectively argue that an apportionment should reflect the popular strength of the political parties represented in the legislature. How exactly is this to be determined by courts of law? As indicated in the introductory essay to this chapter, the problem of disproportionality would disappear if the United States, like most European countries, adopted a system of proportional representation, except that PR might stimulate the emergence of third parties. Justice O'Connor, on the other hand, notes that "[t]he preservation and health of our political institutions, state and federal, depends to no small extent on the continued vitality of our two-party system, which permits both stability and measured change." Is she right about this?

Shaw v. Reno

509 U.S. 630, 113 S. Ct. 2816, 125 L. Ed. 2d 411 (1993)

Following the 1990 census, North Carolina was awarded an increase from eleven to twelve congressional seats. The state legislature redrafted the boundaries for electoral districts in a manner designed to protect the eleven incumbents and to make the new district a majority–African

American district. (North Carolina had not elected an African American congressional representative since Reconstruction.) The Attorney General, as directed by the Voting Rights Act of 1965, reviewed the plan. She rejected it, finding that the state could draw the boundaries in a way that would create two majority African American districts. The legislature created the new district, 160 miles long, stretching much of the length and just the width of Interstate 85. Five residents challenged the plan, claiming it was a racial gerrymander in violation of the Equal Protection Clause of the Fourteenth Amendment. Opinion of the Court: *O'Connor*, Kennedy, Rehnquist, Scalia, Thomas. Dissenting opinions: *White*, Blackmun, Stevens; *Blackmun*; *Stevens*; *Souter*.

Justice O'CONNOR delivered the opinion of the Court.

This case involves two of the most complex and sensitive issues this Court has faced in recent years: the meaning of the constitutional "right" to vote, and the propriety of race-based state legislation designed to benefit members of historically disadvantaged racial minority groups. . . . Appellants allege that the revised plan, which contains district boundary lines of dramatically irregular shape, constitutes an unconstitutional racial gerrymander. The question before us is whether appellants have stated a cognizable claim.

The first of the two majority-black districts contained in the revised plan, District 1, is somewhat hook shaped. Centered in the northeast portion of the State, it moves southward until it tapers to a narrow band; then, with finger-like extensions, it reaches far into the southern-most part of the State near the South Carolina border. District 1 has been compared to a "Rorschach ink-blot test," and a "bug splattered on a windshield."

The second majority-black district, District 12, is even more unusually shaped. It is approximately 160 miles long and, for much of its length, no wider than the I-85 corridor. It winds in snakelike fashion through tobacco country, financial centers, and manufacturing areas "until it gobbles in enough enclaves of black neighborhoods." Northbound and southbound drivers on I-85 sometimes find themselves in separate districts in one county, only to "trade" districts when they enter the next county. Of the 10 counties through which District 12 passes, 5 are cut into 3 different districts; even towns are divided. At one point the district remains contiguous only because it intersects at a single point with two other districts before crossing over them. One state legislator has remarked that "[i]f you drove down the interstate with both car doors open, you'd kill most of the people in the district." The district has inspired poetry: "Ask not for whom the line is drawn; it is drawn to avoid thee."

The Attorney General did not object to the General Assembly's revised plan. But numerous North Carolinians did. The North Carolina Republican Party and individual voters brought suit in Federal District Court, alleging that the plan constituted an unconstitutional political gerrymander under *Davis v. Bandemer* (1986). . . .

Appellants alleged not that the revised plan constituted a political gerrymander, nor that it violated the "one person, one vote" principle, see *Reynolds v. Sims* (1964), but that the State had created an unconstitutional *racial* gerrymander. . . .

They alleged that the General Assembly deliberately "create[d] two Congressional Districts in which a majority of black voters was concentrated arbitrarily—without regard to any other considerations, such as compactness, contiguousness, geographical boundaries, or political sub-divisions" with the purpose "to create Congressional districts along racial lines" and to assure the election of two black representatives to Congress. . . . Our focus is on appellants' claim that the State engaged in unconstitutional racial gerrymandering. That argument strikes a powerful historical chord: It is unsettling how closely the North Carolina plan resembles the most egregious racial gerrymanders of the past.

An understanding of the nature of appellants' claim is critical to our resolution of the case. In their complaint, appellants did not claim that the General Assembly's reapportionment plan unconstitutionally "diluted" white voting strength. They did not even claim to be white. Rather, appellants' complaint alleged that the deliberate segregation of voters into separate districts on the basis of race violated their constitutional right to participate in a "color-blind" electoral process.

Despite their invocation of the ideal of a "color-blind" Constitution, see *Plessy v. Ferguson* (1896) (Harlan, J., dissenting), appellants appear to concede that race-conscious redistricting is not always unconstitutional. That concession is wise: This Court never has held that race-conscious state decisionmaking is impermissible in *all* circumstances. What appellants object to is redistricting legislation that is so extremely irregular on its face that it rationally can be viewed only as an effort to segregate the races for purposes of voting, without regard for traditional districting principles and without sufficiently compelling justification. For the reasons that follow, we conclude that appellants have stated a claim upon which relief can be granted under the Equal Protection Clause.

. . . Classifications of citizens solely on the basis of race "are by their very nature odious to a free people whose institutions are founded upon the doctrine of equality." *Hirabayashi v. United States* (1943), *Loving v. Virginia* (1967). They threaten to stigmatize individuals by reason of their membership in a racial group and to incite racial hostility. Accordingly, we have held that the Fourteenth Amendment requires state legislation that expressly distinguishes among citizens because of their race to be narrowly tailored to further a compelling governmental interest.

These principles apply not only to legislation that contains explicit racial distinctions, but also to those "rare" statutes that, although race neutral, are, on their face, "unexplainable on grounds other than race.". . . .

Put differently, we believe that reapportionment is one area in which appearances do matter. A reapportionment plan that includes in one district individuals who belong to the same race, but who are otherwise widely separated by geographical and political boundaries, and who may have little in common with one another but the color of their skin, bears an uncomfortable resemblance to political apartheid. It reinforces the perception that members of the same racial group—regardless of their age, education, economic status, or the community in which they live— think alike, share the same political interests, and will prefer the same candidates at the polls. We have rejected such perceptions elsewhere as impermissible racial stereotypes. By perpetuating such notions, a racial gerrymander may exacerbate the very patterns of racial bloc voting that majority-minority districting is sometimes said to counteract.

The message that such districting sends to elected representatives is equally pernicious. When a district obviously is created solely to effectuate the perceived common interests of one racial group, elected officials are more likely to believe that their primary obligation is to represent only the members of that group, rather than their constituency as a whole. This is altogether antithetical to our system of representative democracy. As Justice Douglas explained in his dissent in *Wright v. Rockefeller* nearly 30 years ago:

Here the individual is important, not his race, his creed, or his color. The principle of equality is at war with the notion that District A must be represented by a Negro, as it is with the notion that District B must be represented by a Caucasian, District C by a Jew, District D by a Catholic, and so on. . . . That system, by whatever name it is called, is a divisive force in a community, emphasizing differences between candidates and voters that are irrelevant in the constitutional sense. . . .

When racial or religious lines are drawn by the State, the multiracial, multi-religious communities that our Constitution seeks to weld together as one become separatist; antagonisms that relate to race or to religion rather than to political issues are generated; communities seek not the best representative but the best racial or religious partisan. Since that system is at war with the democratic ideal, it should find no footing here.

For these reasons, we conclude that a plaintiff challenging a reapportionment statute under the Equal Protection Clause may state a claim by alleging that the legislation, though race-neutral on its face, rationally cannot be understood as anything other than an effort to separate voters into different districts on the basis of race, and that the separation lacks sufficient justification. It is unnecessary for us to decide whether or how a reapportionment plan that, on its face, can be explained in nonracial terms successfully could be challenged. Thus, we express no view as to whether "the intentional creation of majority-minority districts, without more," always gives rise to an equal protection claim. We hold only that, on the facts of this case, appellants have stated a claim sufficient to defeat the state appellees' motion to dismiss.

Racial classifications of any sort pose the risk of lasting harm to our society. They reinforce the belief, held by too many for too much of our history, that individuals should be judged by the color of their skin. Racial classifications with respect to voting carry particular dangers. Racial gerrymandering, even for remedial purposes, may balkanize us into competing racial factions; it threatens to carry us further from the goal of a political system in which race no longer matters—a goal that the Fourteenth and Fifteenth Amendments embody, and to which the Nation continues to aspire. It is for these reasons that race-based districting by our state legislatures demands close judicial scrutiny.

In this case, the Attorney General suggested that North Carolina could have created a reasonably compact second majority-minority district in the south-central to southeastern part of the State. We express no view as to whether appellants successfully could have challenged such a district under the Fourteenth Amendment. We also do not decide whether appellants' complaint stated a claim under constitutional provisions other than the Fourteenth Amendment. Today we hold only that appellants have stated a claim under the Equal Protection Clause by alleging that the North Carolina General Assembly adopted a reapportionment scheme so irrational on its face that it can be understood only as an effort to segregate voters into separate voting districts because of their race, and that the separation lacks sufficient justification. If the allegation of racial gerrymandering remains uncontradicted, the District Court further must determine whether the North Carolina plan is narrowly tailored to further a compelling governmental interest. Accordingly, we reverse the judgment of the District Court and remand the case for further proceedings consistent with this opinion.

It is so ordered.

Justice WHITE, with whom Justice BLACKMUN and Justice STEVENS join, dissenting.

The grounds for my disagreement with the majority are simply stated: Appellants have not presented a cognizable claim, because they have not alleged a cognizable injury. To date, we have held that only two types of state voting practices could give rise to a constitutional claim. The first involves direct and outright deprivation of the right to vote, for example by means of a poll tax or literacy test. Plainly, this variety is not implicated by appellants' allegations and need not detain us further. The second type of unconstitutional practice is that which "affects the political strength of various groups," in violation of the Equal Protection Clause. As for this latter category, we have insisted that members of the political or racial group demonstrated that the challenged action have the intent and effect of unduly diminishing their influence on the political process. Although this severe burden has limited the number of successful suits, it was adopted for sound reasons.

The central explanation has to do with the nature of the redistricting process. As the majority recognizes, "redistricting differs from other kinds of state decisionmaking in that the legislature always is aware of race when it draws district lines, just as it is aware of age, economic status, religious and political persuasion, and a variety of other demographic factors." "Being aware," in this context, is shorthand for "taking into account," and it hardly can be doubted that legislators routinely engage in the business of making electoral predictions based on group characteristics—racial, ethnic, and the like.

[L]ike bloc-voting by race, [the racial composition of a geographic area] too is a fact of life, well known to those responsible for drawing electoral district lines. These lawmakers are quite aware that the districts they create will have a white or a black majority; and with each new district comes the unavoidable choice as to the racial composition of the district. *Beer v. United States* (1976) (White, J., dissenting).

Redistricting plans also reflect group interests and inevitably are conceived with partisan aims in mind. To allow judicial interference whenever this occurs would be to invite constant and unmanageable intrusion. Moreover, a group's power to affect the political process does not automatically dissipate by virtue of an electoral loss. Accordingly, we have asked that an identifiable group demonstrate more than mere lack of success at the polls to make out a successful gerrymandering claim.

. . . [I]t strains credulity to suggest that North Carolina's purpose in creating a second majority-minority district was to discriminate against members of the majority group by "impair[ing] or burden[ing their] opportunity . . . to participate in the political process." The State has made no mystery of its intent, which was to respond to the Attorney General's objections, by improving the minority group's prospects of electing a candidate of its choice. I doubt that this constitutes a discriminatory purpose as defined in the Court's equal protection cases—i.e., an intent to aggravate "the unequal distribution of electoral power." But even assuming that it does, there is no question that appellants have not alleged the requisite discriminatory effects. Whites constitute roughly 76% of the total population and 79% of the voting age population in North Carolina. Yet, under the State's plan, they still constitute a voting majority in 10 (or 83%) of the 12 congressional districts. Though they might be dissatisfied at the prospect of casting a vote for a losing candidate—a lot shared by many, including a disproportionate number of minority voters—surely they cannot complain of discriminatory intent.

Lacking support in any of the Court's precedents, the majority's novel type of claim also makes no sense. As I understand the theory that is put forth, a redistricting plan that uses race to "segregate" voters by drawing "uncouth" lines is harmful in a way that a plan that uses race to distribute voters differently is not, for the former "bears an uncomfortable resemblance to political apartheid." This distinction is untenable.

Racial gerrymanders come in various shades: At-large voting schemes, the fragmentation of a minority group among various districts "so that it is a majority in none," otherwise known as "cracking," the "stacking" of "a large minority population concentration . . . with a larger white population," and, finally, the "concentration of [minority voters] into districts where they constitute an excessive majority." . . . In each instance, race is consciously utilized by the legislature for electoral purposes; in each instance, we have put the plaintiff challenging the district lines to the burden of demonstrating that the plan was meant to, and did in fact, exclude an identifiable racial group from participation in the political process.

Not so, apparently, when the districting "segregates" by drawing odd-shaped lines. In that case, we are told, such proof no longer is needed. Instead, it is the State that must rebut the allegation that race was taken into account, a fact that, together with the legislators' consideration of ethnic, religious, and other group characteristics, I had thought we practically took for granted. . . . Part of the explanation for the majority's approach has to do, perhaps, with the emotions stirred by words such as "segregation" and "political apartheid." But their loose and imprecise use by today's majority has, I fear, led it astray. The consideration of race in "segregation" cases is no different than in other race-conscious districting; from the standpoint of the affected groups, moreover, the line-drawings all act in similar fashion. A plan that "segregates" being functionally indistinguishable from any of the other varieties of gerrymandering, we should be consistent in what we require from a claimant: proof of discriminatory purpose and effect.

The other part of the majority's explanation of its holding is related to its simultaneous discomfort and fascination with irregularly shaped districts. Lack of compactness or contiguity, like uncouth district lines, certainly is a helpful indicator that some form of gerrymandering (racial or other) might have taken place and that "something may be amiss." Disregard for geographic divisions and compactness often goes hand in hand with partisan gerrymandering.

But while district irregularities may provide strong indicia of a potential gerrymander, they do no more than that. In particular, they have no bearing on whether the plan ultimately is found to violate the Constitution. Given two districts drawn on similar, race-based grounds, the one does not become more injurious than the other simply by virtue of being snake-like, at least so far as the Constitution is concerned and absent any evidence of differential racial impact. The majority's contrary view is perplexing in light of its concession that "compactness or attractiveness has never been held to constitute an independent federal constitutional requirement for state legislative districts." It is shortsighted as well, for a regularly shaped district can just as effectively effectuate racially discriminatory gerrymandering as an odd-shaped one. By focusing on looks rather than impact, the majority "immediately casts attention in the wrong direction—toward superficialities of shape and size, rather than toward the political realities of district composition."

Limited by its own terms to cases involving unusually shaped districts, the Court's approach nonetheless will unnecessarily hinder to some extent a State's voluntary effort to ensure a modicum of minority representation. This will be true in areas where the minority population is geographically dispersed. It will also be true where the minority population is not scattered but, for reasons unrelated to race—for example, incumbency protection—the State would rather not create the majority-minority district in its most "obvious" location. When, as is the case here, the creation of a majority-minority district does not unfairly minimize the voting power of any other group, the Constitution does not justify, much less mandate, such obstruction. . . .

Although I disagree with the holding that appellants' claim is cognizable, the Court's discussion of the level of scrutiny it requires warrants a few comments. I have no doubt that a State's compliance with the Voting Rights Act clearly constitutes a compelling interest. Here, the Attorney General objected to the State's plan on the ground that it failed to draw a second majority-minority district for what appeared to be pretextual reasons. Rather than challenge this conclusion, North Carolina chose to draw the second district. . . .

Justice BLACKMUN, dissenting.

. . . It is particularly ironic that the case in which today's majority chooses to abandon settled law and to recognize for the first time this "analytically distinct" constitutional claim, is a challenge by white voters to the plan under which North Carolina has sent black representatives to Congress for the first time since Reconstruction. I dissent.

Justice STEVENS, dissenting.

For the reasons stated by Justice White, the decision of the District Court should be affirmed. . . . I believe that the Equal Protection Clause is violated when the State creates the kind of uncouth district boundaries seen in *Karcher v. Daggett* (1983), *Gomillion v. Lightfoot* (1960), and this case, for the sole purpose of making it more difficult for members of a minority group to win an election. The duty to govern impartially is abused when a group with power over the electoral process defines electoral boundaries solely to enhance its own political strength at the expense of the weaker group. That duty, however, is not violated when the majority acts to facilitate the election of a member of a group that lacks such power because it remains underrepresented in the state legislature—whether that group is defined by political affiliation, by common economic interests, or by religious, ethnic, or racial characteristics. The difference between constitutional and unconstitutional gerrymanders has nothing to do with whether they are based on assumptions about the groups they affect, but whether their purpose is to enhance the power of the group in control of the districting process at the expense of any minority group, and thereby to strengthen the unequal distribution of electoral power. . . .

Finally, we must ask whether otherwise permissible redistricting to benefit an underrepresented minority group becomes impermissible when the minority group is defined by its race. The Court today answers the question in the affirmative, and its answer is wrong. If it is permissible to draw boundaries to provide adequate representation for rural voters, for union members, for Hasidic Jews, for Polish Americans, or for Republicans, it necessarily follows that it is permissible to do the same thing for members of the very minority group whose history in the United States gave birth to the Equal Protection Clause. A contrary conclusion could only be described as perverse.

Notes and Queries

1. What, exactly, is the right supposedly violated by North Carolina's redistricting? Is it that the action constitutes a "racial gerrymander"? Where does the Constitution prohibit racial gerrymanders? Is it the right of voters to participate in "a color-blind electoral process"? Where does the Constitution guarantee that right?

2. The majority concluded that it was possible that a racial gerrymander could harm voters, even if, as in this case, it did not seem to dilute voting strength. What kinds of harm did the majority think are possible? How did the dissents respond to these claims of harm?

3. Assume the State does not contradict the claim that the gerrymander was drawn along lines of race. What test will the Court use to assess the constitutionality of the district? What interests will North Carolina advance to justify its decision? Are those interests compelling? Why or why not?

4. In *Miller v. Johnson* (1995), the Court held that the "use of race as a predominant factor" in the determination of district boundaries in Georgia was presumptively unconstitutional under strict scrutiny. A year later in *Shaw v. Hunt* (1996), the Court again emphasized that a redistricting plan (this time in North Carolina) in which race is "a predominate consideration" are subject to strict scrutiny. In both *Miller* and *Shaw* the Court found that the plans were not saved by the presence of a compelling state interest.

Hunt v. Cromartie
526 U.S. 541, 143 L. Ed. 2d 731, 119 S. Ct. 1545 (1999)

In *Hunt* the Supreme Court was asked for a third time to address the constitutionality of North Carolina's Twelfth Congressional District. First reviewed in *Shaw v. Reno* (*Shaw I*), the district was 160 miles long, often little wider than the highway it followed, and it was challenged as a racial gerrymander subject to equal protection scrutiny. The Court ruled that racial gerrymanders did raise justiciable claims, and remanded the case to the District Court to determine whether the district was, in fact, a racial gerrymander. The District Court concluded that the district was drawn with race as its predominant concern, and was, therefore, unconstitutional. In *Shaw v. Hunt* (*Shaw II*) the Supreme Court concurred. In response the state redrew the district. It was again challenged as unconstitutional. The District Court granted motion for summary judgment, concluding, without hearing the state's explanation, that the district's odd shape and majority-black character conclusively showed that the district was created through racial gerrymandering. In *Hunt* the Supreme Court was asked to rule on the appropriateness of the lower Court's conclusion for summary judgment, and whether there might be at least a plausible non-racial explanation for the district's composition that at least merited a hearing in District Court. Opinion of the Court: *Thomas*, Rehnquist, O'Connor, Scalia, Kennedy. Concurring opinion: *Stevens*, Souter, Ginsburg, Breyer.

Justice THOMAS delivered the opinion of the Court.

Our decisions have established that all laws that classify citizens on the basis of race, including racially gerryman-

dered districting schemes, are constitutionally suspect and must be strictly scrutinized. . . .

Districting legislation ordinarily, if not always, classifies tracts of land, precincts, or census blocks, and is race-neutral on its face. North Carolina's 1997 plan was not atypical; appellees, therefore, were required to prove that District 12 was drawn with an impermissible racial motive—in this context, strict scrutiny applies if race was the "predominant factor" motivating the legislature's districting decision. . . .

Appellees offered only circumstantial evidence in support of their claim. Their evidence included maps of District 12, showing its size, shape, and alleged lack of continuity. They also submitted evidence of the district's low scores with respect to traditional measures of compactness and expert affidavit testimony explaining that this statistical evidence proved the State had ignored traditional districting criteria in crafting the new Twelfth District. Appellees further claimed that the State had disrespected political subdivisions and communities of interest. . . .

Appellees also presented statistical and demographic evidence with respect to the precincts that were included within District 12 and those that were placed in neighboring districts. . . . This evidence tended to show that, in several instances, the State had excluded precincts that had a lower percentage of black population but were as Democratic (in terms of registered voters) as the precinct inside District 12.

Viewed *in toto*, appellees' evidence tends to support an inference that the State drew its district lines with an impermissible racial motive—even though they presented no direct evidence of intent.

The District Court nevertheless was only partially correct in stating that the material facts before it were uncontroverted. The legislature's motivation is itself a factual question. Appellants asserted that the General Assembly drew its district lines with the intent to make District 12 a strong Democratic district. In support, they presented the after-the-fact affidavit testimony of the two members of the General Assembly responsible for developing the State's 1997 plan. Those legislators further stated that, in crafting their districting law, they attempted to protect incumbents, to adhere to traditional districting criteria, and to preserve the existing partisan balance in the State's congressional delegation, which in 1997 was composed of six Republicans and six Democrats.

More important, we think, was the affidavit of an expert, Dr. David W. Peterson. He reviewed racial demographics, party registration, and election result data. . . . He recognized "a strong correlation between racial composition and party preference" so that "in precincts with high black representation, there is a correspondingly high tendency for voters to favor the Democratic Party" but that "[i]n precincts with low black representation, there is much more variation in party preference, and the fraction of registered voters favoring Democrats is substantially lower." Because of this significant correlation, the data tended to support both a political and racial hypothesis. Therefore, Peterson focused on "divergent boundary segments," those where blacks were greater inside District 12 but Democrats were greater outside and those where blacks were greater outside the district but Democrats were greater inside. He concluded that the State included the more heavily Democratic precinct much more often than the more heavily black precinct, and therefore, that the data as a whole supported a political explanation at least as well as, and somewhat better than, a racial explanation.

Peterson's analysis of District 12's divergent boundary segments and his affidavit testimony that District 12 displays a high correlation between race and partisanship support an inference that the General Assembly did no more than create a district of strong partisan Democrats. . . .

. . . Our prior decisions have made clear that a jurisdiction may engage in constitutional political gerrymandering, even if it so happens that the most loyal Democrats happen to be black Democrats and even if the State were conscious of that fact. Evidence that blacks constitute even a supermajority in one congressional district while amounting to less than a plurality in a neighboring district

will not, by itself, suffice to prove that a jurisdiction was motivated by race in drawing its district lines when the evidence also shows a high correlation between race and party preference.

Justice STEVENS, with whom Justice SOUTER, Justice GINSBURG and Justice BREYER join, concurring in the judgment.

. . . The Court concludes that evidence submitted to the District Court on behalf of the State made it inappropriate for that Court to grant appellees' motion for summary judgment. I agree with that conclusion, but write separately to emphasize the importance of two undisputed matters of fact that are firmly established by the historical record and confirmed by the record in this case.

First, bizarre configuration is the traditional hallmark of the political gerrymander. . . . As we learned in *Gomillion* v. *Lightfoot*, a racial gerrymander may have an equally "uncouth" shape. Thus, the shape of the congressional district at issue in this case provides strong evidence that either political or racial factors motivated its architects, but sheds no light on the question of which set of factors was more responsible for subordinating any of the State's "traditional" districting principles.

Second, as the Presidential campaigns conducted by Strom Thurmond in 1948 and by George Wallace in 1968, and the Senate campaigns conducted more recently by Jesse Helms, have demonstrated, a great many registered Democrats in the South do not always vote for Democratic candidates in federal elections. The Congressional Quarterly recently recorded the fact that in North Carolina "Democratic voter registration edges . . . no longer translat[e] into success in statewide or national races. In recent years, conservative white Democrats have gravitated toward Republican candidates." This voting pattern has proven to be particularly pronounced in voting districts that contain more than about one-third African-American residents. There was no need for expert testimony to establish the proposition that "in North Carolina, party registration and party preference do not always correspond."

The record supports the conclusion that the most loyal Democrats living near the borders of District 12 "happen to be black Democrats," and I have no doubt that the legislature was conscious of that fact when it enacted this apportionment plan. But everyone agrees that that fact is not sufficient to invalidate the district.

Accordingly, appellees' evidence may include nothing more than (i) a bizarre shape, which is equally consistent with either political or racial motivation, (ii) registration data, which are virtually irrelevant when actual voting results were available and which point in a different direction, and (iii) knowledge of the racial composition of the district. Because we do not have before us the question whether the District Court erred in denying the State's motion for summary judgment, I need not decide whether that circumstantial evidence even raises an inference of improper motive. It is sufficient at this stage of the proceedings to join in the Court's judgment of reversal, which I do.

Notes and Queries

1. Justice Thomas contends that the Court will uphold facially race-neutral districting, absent evidence that race was the predominant factor in the drawing of the District. Why does he reject the District Court's conclusion in this case? What is the alternative explanation for the district's shape?

2. Does *Cromartie* represent the Court's increasing concern for equity and fairness in the apportionment of legislative districts? Can you imagine situations where the achievement of equity and fairness might require some qualification of the one person–one vote standard? Do cases such as *Bandemer, Shaw,* and *Cromartie* reinforce the warning of Justice Frankfurter that the judiciary should never have entered the "political thicket" of legislative apportionment?

3. Would proportional representation (PR) insure greater African-American representation in Congress—or a state legislature—than the single-member-district system? PR could lead to the rise of a third party organized around African-American interests. Would such a system improve the position of African-Americans in American politics? Would it help to maximize voting turnout among African-Americans? Would it fragment American politics in dangerous ways?

Democratic Party of the United States v. Wisconsin
450 U.S. 107, 67 L. Ed. 2d 82, 101 S. Ct. 1010 (1981)

Rule 2A of the Democratic Party's Selection Rules for its 1980 National Convention stated: "Participation in the delegate selection process in primaries or caucuses shall be restricted to Democratic voters only who publicly declare their party preference and have that preference publicly recorded." Wisconsin's election laws allowed non-Democrats (independents and persons registered in other parties) to vote in the Democratic primary. The National Party initially rejected the Wisconsin delegates bound by the open primary, and this decision was challenged in the Wisconsin Supreme Court. The Party defended its refusal to seat the delegates based on its right to political association protected by the First and Fourteenth Amendments. The Wisconsin Court concluded that the primary plan did not impermissibly violate that right. The United States Supreme Court took the case on appeal. Opinion of the Court: *Stewart,* Burger, Brennan, White, Marshall, Stevens. Dissenting opinion: *Powell,* Blackmun, Rehnquist.

Justice STEWART delivered the opinion of the Court.

Rule 2A can be traced to efforts of the National Party to study and reform its nominating procedures and internal structure after the 1968 Democratic National Convention. The Convention . . . directed the Democratic National Committee (DNC) to establish a Commission on Party Structure and Delegate Selection (McGovern/Fraser Com-

mission). This Commission concluded that a major problem faced by the Party was that rank-and-file Party members had been underrepresented at its Convention, and that the Party should "find methods which would guarantee every American who claims a stake in the Democratic Party the opportunity to make his judgment felt in the presidential nominating process." The Commission stressed that Party nominating procedures should be as open and accessible as possible to all persons who wished to join the Party, but expressed the concern that "a full opportunity for all Democrats to participate is diluted if members of other political parties are allowed to participate in the selection of delegates to the Democratic National Convention."

The 1972 Democratic National Convention also established a Commission on Delegate Selection and Party Structure (Mikulski Commission). This Commission reiterated many of the principles announced by the McGovern/Fraser Commission, but went further to propose binding rules directing state parties to restrict participation in the delegate selection process to Democratic voters.

In 1975, the Party established yet another commission to review its nominating procedures, the Commission on Presidential Nomination and Party Structure (Winograd Commission). This Commission was particularly concerned with what it believed to be the dilution of the voting strength of Party members in States sponsoring open or "crossover" primaries. Indeed, the Commission based its concern in part on a study of voting behavior in Wisconsin's open primary.

[A] study assessing the Wisconsin Democratic primaries

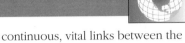

Comparative Note 8.3

[The following extracts are from Germany's Law on Political Parties.]

Article 1. Constitutional Status and Functions of the Parties

(1) Political parties form a constitutionally integral part of a free and democratic system of government. Their free and continuous participation in the formation of the political will of the people enables them to discharge the public tasks which are incumbent upon them pursuant to the Basic Law and they undertake to fulfill to the best of their ability.

(2) The parties shall participate in the formation of the political will of the people in all fields of public life, in particular by:—

    a. bringing their influence to bear on the shaping of public opinion; inspiring and furthering political education; . . .

    b. exercising an influence on political trends in parliament and government;

    c. initiating their defined political aims in the national decision-making processes; and

    d. ensuring continuous, vital links between the people and the public authorities.

(3) The parties shall define their aims in the form of political manifestos. . . .

Article 5. Equality of Treatment

(1) Where a public authority provides facilities or other public services for use by a party, it must accord equal treatment to all other parties. The scale of such facilities and services may be graduated to conform with the importance of the parties to the minimum extent needed for the achievement of their aims. . . .

Article 18. Principles and Extent of Public Financing

(1) The State shall grant the parties funds to partly finance their general activities pursuant to the Basic law. The criteria for the distribution of public funds shall be the parties' performance in European, national and state elections, the sum of its membership contributions and the amount of donations received.

Source: Political Parties Act of 24 July 1967, as amended 31 January 1994 (Federal Law Gazette, 149).

from 1964 to 1972, found that crossover voters comprised 26% to 34% of the primary voters; that the voting patterns of crossover voters differed significantly from those of participants who identified themselves as Democrats; and that crossover voters altered the composition of the delegate slate chosen from Wisconsin. The Winograd Commission thus recommended that the Party strengthen its rules against crossover voting, predicting that continued crossover voting "could result in a convention delegation which did not fairly reflect the division of preferences among Democratic identifiers in the electorate." And it specifically recommended that "participation in the delegate selection process in primaries or caucuses . . . be restricted to Democratic voters only who publicly declare their party preference and have that preference publicly recorded."

The question in this case is not whether Wisconsin may conduct an open primary election if it chooses to do so, or whether the National Party may require Wisconsin to limit its primary election to publicly declared Democrats. Rather, the question is whether, once Wisconsin has opened its Democratic Presidential preference primary to

voters who do not publicly declare their party affiliation, it may then bind the National Party to honor the binding primary results, even though those results were reached in a manner contrary to National Party rules.

. . . The issue is whether the State may compel the National Party to seat a delegation chosen in a way that violates the rules of the Party. . . .

Here, the members of the National Party, speaking through their rules, chose to define their associational rights by limiting those who could participate in the processes leading to the selection of delegates to their National Convention. On several occasions this Court has recognized that the inclusion of persons unaffiliated with a political party may seriously distort its collective decisions—thus impairing the party's essential functions—and that political parties may accordingly protect themselves from intrusion by those with adverse political principles. . . .

The State argues that its law places only a minor burden on the National Party. The National Party argues that the burden is substantial, because it prevents the Party from "screen[ing] out those whose affiliation is . . . slight, tenuous, or fleeting," and that such screening is essential to build a more effective and responsible Party. But it is not for the courts to mediate the merits of this dispute. For even if the State were correct a State, or a court, may not constitutionally substitute its own judgment for that of the Party. A political party's choice among the various ways of determining the makeup of a State's delegation to the party's national convention is protected by the Constitution. And as is true of all expressions of First Amendment freedoms, the courts may not interfere on the ground that they view a particular expression as unwise or irrational.

We must consider, finally, whether the State has compelling interests that justify the imposition of its will upon the appellants. . . . The State asserts a compelling interest in preserving the overall integrity of the electoral process, providing secrecy of the ballot, increasing voter participation in primaries, and preventing harassment of voters. But all those interests go to the conduct of the Presidential preference primary—not to the imposition of voting requirements upon those who, in a separate process, are eventually selected as delegates. Therefore, the interests advanced by the State do not justify its substantial intrusion into the associational freedom of members of the National Party.

The State has a substantial interest in the manner in which its elections are conducted, and the National Party has a substantial interest in the manner in which the delegates to its National Convention are selected. But these interests are not incompatible, and to the limited extent they clash in this case, both interests can be preserved. The National Party rules do not forbid Wisconsin to conduct an open primary. But if Wisconsin does open its primary, it cannot require that Wisconsin delegates to the National Party Convention vote there in accordance with the primary results, if to do so would violate Party rules. Since the Wisconsin Supreme Court has declared that the National Party cannot disqualify delegates who are bound to vote in accordance with the results of the Wisconsin open primary, its judgment is reversed.

Justice POWELL, with whom Justice BLACKMUN and Justice REHNQUIST join, dissenting.

. . . Because I believe that this law does not impose a substantial burden on the associational freedom of the National Party, and actually promotes the free political activity of the citizens of Wisconsin, I dissent. . . .

It goes without saying that nomination of a candidate for President is a principal function performed by a national political party, and Wisconsin has, to an extent, regulated the terms on which a citizen may become a "member" of the group of people permitted to influence that decision. If appellant National Party were an organization with a particular ideological orientation or political mission, perhaps this regulation would present a different question. In such a case, the state law might well open the organization to participation by persons with incompatible beliefs and interfere with the associational rights of its founders.

The Democratic Party, however, is not organized around the achievement of defined ideological goals. . . . It can hardly be denied that this Party generally has been composed of various elements reflecting most of the American Political spectrum. The Party does take positions on public issues, but these positions vary from time to time, and there never has been a serious effort to establish for the Party a monolithic ideological identity by excluding all those with differing views. As a result, it is hard to see what the Democratic Party has to fear from an open primary plan. Wisconsin's law may influence to some extent the outcome of a primary contest by allowing participation by voters who are unwilling to affiliate with the Party publicly. It is unlikely, however, that this influence will produce a delegation with preferences that differ from those represented by a substantial number of delegates from other parts of the country. Moreover, it seems reasonable to conclude that, insofar as the major parties do have ideological identities, an open primary merely allows relatively independent voters to cast their lot with the party that speaks to their present concerns. By attracting participation by relatively independent-minded voters, the Wisconsin plan arguably may enlarge the support for a party at the general election.

It is significant that the Democratic Party of Wisconsin, which represents those citizens of Wisconsin willing to take part publicly in Party affairs, is here *defending* the state law. . . . In addition, the National Party apparently is quite willing to accept public affiliation immediately before primary voting, which some States permit. As Party affiliation becomes this easy for a voter to change in order to participate in a particular primary election, the difference between open and closed primaries loses its practical significance.

In sum, I would hold that the National Party has failed to make a sufficient showing of a burden on its associational rights.

The Court does not dispute that the State serves important interests by its open primary plan. Instead the Court argues that these interests are irrelevant because they do not support a requirement that the outcome of the primary be binding on delegates chosen for the convention. This argument, however, is premised on the unstated assumption that a non-binding primary would be an adequate mechanism for pursuing the state interests involved. This assumption is unsupportable because the very purpose of a Presidential primary, as enunciated as early as 1903 when Wisconsin passed its first primary law, was to give control over the nomination process to individual voters. Wisconsin cannot do this, and still pursue the interests underlying an open primary, without making the open primary binding. . . .

Here, Wisconsin has attempted to ensure that the prospect of public party affiliation will not inhibit voters from participating in a Democratic primary. . . . The State of Wisconsin has determined that some voters are deterred from participation by a public affiliation requirement, and the validity of that concern is not something that we should second-guess.

Notes and Queries

1. Justice Stewart argues that "it is not for the courts to mediate the merits of this dispute. For even if the state were correct a State, or a court, may not constitutionally substitute its own judgment for that of the [National] Party." Is this a democratic or a constitutionalist perspective?

2. Is it possible, in the words of Justice Stewart, "to build a more effective and responsible Party" in a system of open primary elections? The study of Wisconsin Democratic primaries cited by Justice Stewart showed that Republican voters often crossed over to vote for the Democratic candidate least likely to win in the general election. Would strategic voting of this kind undermine the building of an effective and responsible party system?

3. Rule 2A was developed by the Democratic Party after the 1968 and 1972 Democratic Conventions to address a perceived failure in the candidate selection process. The dissenters suggest that the associational right to restrict state delegates to those bound by closed primaries is not substantial enough to outweigh the state's interest in an open primary. What happened at those conventions that might have led the National Party to seek these reforms?

4. The dissenters suggest that the associational right asserted by the National Party is hollow because the major parties have never had defined ideologies. Is this an accurate assessment?

5. The Democratic Party sought to prevent delegates chosen through open primaries to secure the nomination of more representative candidates. The dissent argues, however, that "an open primary merely allows relatively independent voters to cast their lot with the party that speaks to their present concerns." They assert that a process that incorporates independent voters might in fact create a more mainstream and representative candidate. Is it necessarily true that non-affiliated citizens will help to select a better candidate for any one party? Moreover, is it accurate to conclude that an open primary will "merely" attract independent voters? Consider recent elections. What might occur if registered Republicans or Greens decided to vote in a Democratic primary?

Buckley v. Valeo
424 U.S. 1, 46 L. Ed. 2d 659, 96 S. Ct. 612 (1976)

The Federal Election Campaign Act of 1971 (amended in 1974 following the Watergate scandal's revelations of widespread corruption in the 1972 presidential campaign) regulated contributions to candidates, regulated expenditures by individuals and groups "relative to a clearly identified candidate," limited expenditures by candidates themselves, required detailed accounting and reporting of contributions in excess of $10, and established provisions for the federal funding of presidential campaigns. These provisions were challenged as violating the First Amendment. Congress defended its actions as reasonable regulations of campaigns for the legitimate purpose of removing corruption and its appearance. Opinion of the Court: *Per Curiam* (Burger, Brennan, Stewart, White, Marshall, Blackmun, Powell, Rehnquist). Concurring in part and dissenting in part: *Burger, White, Marshall,* Rehnquist. Not participating: Stevens.

PER CURIAM.

. . . In appellants' view, limiting the use of money for political purposes constitutes a restriction on communication violative of the First Amendment, since virtually all meaningful political communications in the modern setting involve the expenditure of money. Further, they argue that the reporting and disclosure provisions of the Act unconstitutionally impinge on their right to freedom of association. . . .

I. Contribution and Expenditure Limitations

The constitutional power of Congress to regulate federal elections is well established and is not questioned by any of the parties in this case. Thus, the critical constitutional questions presented here go not to the basic power of Congress to legislate in this area, but to whether the specific legislation that Congress has enacted interferes with First Amendment freedoms. . . .

Comparative Note 8.4

[Quebec's Referendum Act provided for the public funding of referendum campaigns and established national committees to regulate the expenditures up to certain amounts. Because of the severity of these limits, the Canadian Supreme Court declared the Act to be an unjustified restriction on freedom of speech and association. Under the proportionality test built into Section 1 of the Canadian Charter of Rights and Freedoms, the government must show that a regulation is carefully tailored so that rights are impaired no more than necessary in a free and democratic society. Yet the Court made clear that as a matter of principle, independent expenditures can be limited for the purpose of reducing the influence of money in the electoral process. The following extract differs significantly from the tenor of *Buckley v. Valeo*.]

. . . Since political expression is at the very heart of freedom of expression, it should normally benefit from a high degree of constitutional protection, that is, the courts should generally apply a high standard of justification to legislation that infringes the freedom of political expression.

What is the situation in the case at bar? In answering this question, the legislature's objective, namely to enhance the exercise of the right to vote, must be borne in mind. Thus, while the impugned provisions do in a way restrict one of the most basic forms of expression, namely political expression, the legislature must be accorded a certain deference to enable it to arbitrate between the democratic values of freedom of expression and referendum fairness. The latter is related to the very values the *Canadian Charter* seeks to protect, in particular the political equality of citizens that is at the heart of a free and democratic society. The impugned provisions impose a balance between the financial resources available to the proponents of each option in order to ensure that the vote by the people will be free and informed and that the discourse of each option can be heard. To attain this objective, the legislature had to try to strike a balance between absolute freedom of individual expression and equality among the different expressions for the benefit of all. From this point of view, the impugned provisions are therefore not purely restrictive of freedom of expression. Their primary purpose is to promote political expression by ensuring an equal dissemination of points of view and thereby truly respecting democratic institutions.

. . . It is clear from our analysis that protecting the fairness of referendum campaigns is a laudable objective that will *necessarily* involve certain restrictions on freedom of expression. Freedom of political expression, so dear to our democratic tradition, would lose much value if it could only be exercised in a context in which the economic power of the most affluent members of society constituted the ultimate guidepost of our political choices. Nor would it be much better served by a system that undermined the confidence of citizens in the referendum process.

Source: *Libman v. Quebec (Attorney General)*, 151 D.L.R. (4th) 416 [1997].

A. General Principles

The Act's contribution and expenditure limitations operate in an area of the most fundamental First Amendment activities. Discussion of public issues and debate on the qualifications of candidates are integral to the operation of the system of government established by our Constitution. . . . In upholding the constitutional validity of the Act's contribution and expenditure provisions on the ground that those provisions should be viewed as regulating conduct, not speech, the Court of Appeals relied upon *United States v. O'Brien*. The *O'Brien* case involved a defendant's claim that the First Amendment prohibited his prosecution for burning his draft card because his act was "symbolic speech" engaged in as a "demonstration against the war and against the draft." On the assumption that "the alleged communicative element in O'Brien's conduct [was] sufficient to bring into play the First Amendment," the Court sustained the conviction because it found "a sufficiently important governmental interest in regulating the non-speech element" that was "unrelated to the suppression of free expression" and that had an "incidental restriction on alleged First Amendment Freedoms . . . no greater than [was] essential to the furtherance of that interest." The Court expressly emphasized that *O'Brien* was not a case "where the alleged governmental interest in regulating conduct arises in some measure because the communication allegedly integral to the conduct is itself thought to be harmful."

We cannot share the view that the present Act's contribution and expenditure limitations are comparable to the restrictions on conduct upheld in *O'Brien*. The expenditure of money simply cannot be equated with such conduct as destruction of a draft card. . . . Even if the categorization of the expenditure of money as conduct were accepted, the limitations challenged here would not meet the *O'Brien* test because the governmental interests advanced in support of the Act involve "suppressing communication." The interests served by the Act include restricting the voices of people and interest groups who have money to spend and reducing the overall scope of federal election campaigns. . . .

A restriction on the amount of money a person or group can spend on political communication during a campaign necessarily reduces the quantity of expression by restricting the number of issues discussed, the depth of their exploration, and the size of the audience reached. This is because virtually every means of communicating ideas in today's mass society requires the expenditure of money. The distribution of the humblest handbill or leaflet entails printing, paper, and circulation costs. Speeches and rallies generally necessitate hiring a hall and publicizing the event. The electorate's increasing dependence on television, radio, and other mass media for news and information has made these expensive modes of communication indispensable instruments of effective political speech.

The expenditure limitations contained in the Act represent substantial rather than merely theoretical restraints on the quantity and diversity of political speech. The $1,000 ceiling on spending "relative to a clearly identified candidate," would appear to exclude all citizens and groups except candidates, political parties, and the institutional press from any significant use of the most effective modes of communication. . . .

By contrast with a limitation upon expenditures for political expression, a limitation upon the amount that any one person or group may contribute to a candidate or political committee entails only a marginal restriction upon the contributor's ability to engage in free communication. A contribution serves as a general expression of support for the candidate and his views, but does not communicate the underlying basis for the support. The quantity of communication by the contributor does not increase perceptibly with the size of his contribution, since the expression rests solely on the undifferentiated, symbolic act of contributing. At most, the size of the contribution provides a very rough index of the intensity of the contributor's support for the candidate. A limitation on the amount of money a person may give to a candidate or campaign organization thus involves little direct restraint on his political communication, for it permits the symbolic expression of support evidenced by a contribution but does not in

any way infringe the contributor's freedom to discuss candidates and issues. While contributions may result in political expression if spent by a candidate or an association to present views to the voters, the transformation of contributions into political debate involves speech by someone other than the contributor.

Given the important role of contributions in financing political campaigns, contribution restrictions could have a severe impact on political dialogue if the limitations prevented candidates and political committees from amassing the resources necessary for effective advocacy. There is no indication, however, that the contribution limitations imposed by the Act would have any dramatic adverse effect on the funding of campaigns and political associations. The overall effect of the Act's contribution ceilings is merely to require candidates and political committees to raise funds from a greater number of persons and to compel people who would otherwise contribute amounts greater than the statutory limits to expend such funds on direct political expression, rather than to reduce the total amount of money potentially available to promote political expression. . . .

In sum, although the Act's contribution and expenditure limitations both implicate fundamental First Amendment interests, its expenditure ceilings impose significantly more severe restrictions on protected freedoms of political expression and association than do its limitations on financial contributions. . . .

B. Contribution Limitations

[T]he primary interest served by the limitations and, indeed, by the Act as a whole, is the prevention of corruption and the appearance of corruption spawned by the real or imagined coercive influence of large financial contributions on candidates' positions and on their actions if elected to office. Two "ancillary" interests underlying the Act are also allegedly furthered by the $1,000 limits on contributions. First, the limits serve to mute the voices of affluent persons and groups in the election process and thereby to equalize the relative ability of all citizens to affect the outcome of elections. Second, it is argued, the ceilings may to some extent act as a brake on the skyrocketing cost of political campaigns and thereby serve to open the political system more widely to candidates without access to sources of large amounts of money.

It is unnecessary to look beyond the Act's primary purpose—to limit the actuality and appearance of corruption resulting from large individual financial contributions—in order to find a constitutionally sufficient justification for the $1,000 contribution limitation. Under a system of private financing of elections, a candidate lacking immense personal or family wealth must depend on financial contributions from others to provide the resources necessary to conduct a successful campaign. The increasing importance of the communications media and sophisticated mass-mailing and polling operations to effective campaigning make the raising of large sums of money an ever more essential ingredient of an effective candidacy. To the extent that large contributions are given to secure a political quid pro quo from current and potential office holders, the integrity of our system of representative democracy is undermined.

Apart from these First Amendment concerns, appellants argue that the contribution limitations work such an invidious discrimination between incumbents and challengers that the statutory provisions must be declared unconstitutional on their face. . . .

There is no such evidence to support the claim that the contribution limitations in themselves discriminate against major-party challengers to incumbents. Challengers can and often do defeat incumbents in federal elections. . . . And, to the extent that incumbents generally are more likely than challengers to attract very large contributions, the Act's $1,000 ceiling has the practical effect of benefitting challengers as a class. . . .

The charge of discrimination against minor-party and independent candidates is more troubling, but the record provides no basis for concluding that the Act invidiously disadvantages such candidates. . . .

C. Expenditure Limitations

The Act's expenditure ceilings impose direct and substantial restraints on the quantity of political speech. . . . It is clear that a primary effect of these expenditure limitations is to restrict the quantity of campaign speech by individuals, groups, and candidates. . . .

1. The $1,000 Limitation on Expenditures "Relative to a Clearly Identified Candidate"

Section 608 (e) (1) provides that "[n]o person may make any expenditure . . . relative to a clearly identified candidate during a calendar year which, when added to all other expenditures made by such person during the year advocating the election or defeat of such candidate, exceeds $1,000." The plain effect is to prohibit all individuals, who are neither candidates nor owners of institutional press facilities, and all groups, except political parties and campaign organizations, from voicing their views "relative to a clearly identified candidate" through means that entail aggregate expenditures of more than $1,000 during a calendar year. The provision would make it a federal criminal offense for a person or association to place a single one-

quarter page advertisement "relative to a clearly identified candidate" in a major metropolitan newspaper. . . .

We find that the governmental interest in preventing corruption and the appearance of corruption is inadequate to justify 608 (e) (1)'s ceiling on independent expenditures. . . . [A]ssuming . . . that large independent expenditures pose the same dangers of actual or apparent quid pro quo arrangements as do large contributions, 608 (e) (1) does not provide an answer that sufficiently relates to the elimination of those dangers. Unlike the contribution limitations' total ban on the giving of large amounts of money to candidates, 608 (e) (1) prevents only some large expenditures. So long as persons and groups eschew expenditures that in express terms advocate the election or defeat of a clearly identified candidate, they are free to spend as much as they want to promote the candidate and his views. . . . It would naively underestimate the ingenuity and resourcefulness of persons and groups desiring to buy influence to believe that they would have much difficulty devising expenditures that skirted the restriction on express advocacy of election or defeat but nevertheless benefitted the candidate's campaign. . . .

While the independent expenditure ceiling thus fails to serve any substantial governmental interest in stemming the reality or appearance of corruption in the electoral process, it heavily burdens core First Amendment expression. . . . Advocacy of the election or defeat of candidates for federal office is no less entitled to protection under the First Amendment than the discussion of political policy generally or advocacy of the passage or defeat of legislation.

It is argued, however, that the ancillary governmental interest in equalizing the relative ability of individuals and groups to influence the outcome of elections serves to justify the limitation on express advocacy of the election or defeat of candidates imposed by sec. 608 (e) (1)'s expenditure ceilings. But the concept that government may restrict the speech of some elements of our society in order to enhance the relative voice of others is wholly foreign to the First Amendment, which was designed "to secure the widest possible dissemination of information from diverse and antagonistic sources," and "to assure unfettered interchange of ideas for the bringing about of political and social changes desired by the people." The First Amendment's protection against governmental abridgment of free expression cannot properly be made to depend on a person's financial ability to engage in public discussion. . . .

2. Limitation on Expenditures by Candidates from Personal or Family Resources

The Act also sets limits on expenditures by a candidate "from his personal funds, or the personal funds of his immediate family, in connection with his campaigns during any calendar year." . . .

The ceiling on personal expenditures by candidates on their own behalf, like the limitations on independent expenditures . . . imposes a substantial restraint on the ability of persons to engage in protected First Amendment expression. The candidate, no less than any other person, has a First Amendment right to engage in the discussion of public issues and vigorously and tirelessly to advocate his own election and the election of other candidates.

II. Reporting and Disclosure Requirements

A. General Principles

. . . [W]e have repeatedly found that compelled disclosure, in itself, can seriously infringe on privacy of association and belief guaranteed by the First Amendment.

It is undoubtedly true that public disclosure of contributions to candidates and political parties will deter some individuals who otherwise might contribute. In some instances, disclosure may even expose contributors to harassment or retaliation. These are not insignificant burdens on individual rights, and they must be weighed carefully against the interests which Congress has sought to promote by this legislation.

III. Public Financing of Presidential Election Campaigns

. . . [T]he Constitution does not require Congress to treat all declared candidates the same for public financing purposes. . . . Since the Presidential elections of 1856 and 1860, when the Whigs were replaced as a major party by the Republicans, no third party has posed a credible threat to the two major parties in Presidential elections. Third parties have been completely incapable of matching the major parties' ability to raise money and win elections. Congress was, of course, aware of this fact of American life, and thus was justified in providing both major parties full funding and all other parties only a percentage of the major-party entitlement. . . .

Conclusion

In summary, we sustain the individual contribution limits, the disclosure and reporting provisions, and the public financing scheme. We conclude, however, that the limitations on campaign expenditures, on independent expenditures by individuals and groups, and on expenditures by

a candidate from his personal funds are constitutionally infirm. . . .

Mr. Chief Justice BURGER, concurring in part and dissenting in part.

. . . In my view, the Act's disclosure scheme is impermissibly broad and violative of the First Amendment as it relates to reporting contributions in excess of $10 and $100. The contribution limitations infringe on First Amendment liberties and suffer from the same infirmities that the Court correctly sees in the expenditure ceilings. The system for public financing of Presidential campaigns is, in my judgment, an impermissible intrusion by the Government into the traditionally private political process.

More broadly, the Court's result does violence to the intent of Congress in this comprehensive scheme of campaign finance. By dissecting the Act bit by bit, and casting off vital parts, the Court fails to recognize that the whole of this Act is greater than the sum of its parts. Congress intended to regulate all aspects of federal campaign finances, but what remains after today's holding leaves no more than a shadow of what Congress contemplated. I question whether the residue leaves a workable program.

Disclosure Provisions

Disclosure is, in principle, the salutary and constitutional remedy for most of the ills Congress was seeking to alleviate. I therefore agree fully with the broad proposition that public disclosure of contributions by individuals and by entities—particularly corporations and labor unions—is an effective means of revealing the type of political support that is sometimes coupled with expectations of special favors or rewards. That disclosure impinges on First Amendment rights is conceded by the Court, but given the objectives to which disclosure is directed, I agree that the need for disclosure outweighs individual constitutional claims.

Contribution and Expenditure Limits

I agree fully with that part of the Court's opinion that holds unconstitutional the limitations the Act puts on campaign expenditures which "place substantial and direct restrictions on the ability of candidates, citizens, and associations to engage in protected political expression, restrictions that the First Amendment cannot tolerate." Yet when it approves similarly stringent limitations on contributions, the Court ignores the reasons it finds so persuasive in the context of expenditures. For me contributions and expenditures are two sides of the same First Amendment coin.

By limiting campaign contributions, the Act restricts the

amount of money that will be spent on political activity—and does so directly. . . . Limiting contributions, as a practical matter, will limit expenditures and will put an effective ceiling on the amount of political activity and debate that the Government will permit to take place. . . .

The Court's attempt to distinguish the communication inherent in political contributions from the speech aspects of political expenditures simply "will not wash." We do little but engage in word games unless we recognize that people—candidates and contributors—spend money on political activity because they wish to communicate ideas, and their constitutional interest in doing so is precisely the same whether they or someone else utters the words. . . .

Public Financing

Since the turn of this century when the idea of Government subsidies for political campaigns first was broached, there has been no lack of realization that the use of funds from the public treasury to subsidize political activity of private individuals would produce substantial and profound questions about the nature of our democratic society. . . .

I would . . . fault the Court for not adequately analyzing and meeting head on the issue of whether public financial assistance to the private political activity of individual citizens and parties is a legitimate expenditure of public funds. The public monies at issue here are not being employed simply to police the integrity of the electoral process or to provide a forum for the use of all participants in the political dialogue, as would, for example, be the case if free broadcast time were granted. Rather, we are confronted with the Government's actual financing, out of general revenues, a segment of the political debate itself. . . .

. . . [T]he scheme approved by the Court today invidiously discriminates against minor parties. . . . The fact that there have been few drastic realignments in our basic two-party structure in 200 years is no constitutional justification for freezing the status quo of the present major parties at the expense of such future political movements. . . . In short, I see grave risks in legislation, enacted by incumbents of the major political parties, which distinctly disadvantages minor parties or independent candidates. This Court has, until today, been particularly cautious when dealing with enactments that tend to perpetuate those who control legislative power. . . .

Mr. Justice WHITE, concurring in part and dissenting in part.

The disclosure requirements and the limitations on contributions and expenditures are challenged as invalid abridgments of the right of free speech protected by the First Amendment. I would reject these challenges. I agree with the Court's conclusion and much of its opinion with respect to sustaining the disclosure provisions. I am also in agreement with the Court's judgment upholding the limitations on contributions. I dissent, however, from the Court's view that the expenditure limitations violate the First Amendment.

Proceeding from the maxim that "money talks," the Court finds that the expenditure limitations will seriously curtail political expression by candidates and interfere substantially with their chances for election. The Court concludes that the Constitution denies Congress the power to limit campaign expenses; federal candidates—and I would suppose state candidates, too—are to have the constitutional right to raise and spend unlimited amounts of money in quest of their own election. . . .

[A]s it should be unnecessary to point out, money is not always equivalent to or used for speech, even in the context of political campaigns. I accept the reality that communicating with potential voters is the heart of an election campaign and that widespread communication has become very expensive. There are, however, many expensive campaign activities that are not themselves communicative or remotely related to speech. Furthermore, campaigns differ among themselves. Some seem to spend much less money than others and yet communicate as much as or more than those supported by enormous bureaucracies with unlimited financing. . . .

I have little doubt . . . that limiting the total that can be spent will ease the candidate's understandable obsession with fundraising, and so free him and his staff to communicate in more places and ways unconnected with the fundraising function. There is nothing objectionable—indeed it seems to me a weighty interest in favor of the provision—in the attempt to insulate the political expression of federal candidates from the influence inevitably exerted by the endless job of raising increasingly large sums of money. I regret that the Court has returned them all to the treadmill.

Mr. Justice MARSHALL, concurring in part and dissenting in part.

One of the points on which all Members of the Court agree is that money is essential for effective communication in a political campaign. It would appear to follow that the candidate with a substantial personal fortune at his disposal is off to a significant "headstart." Of course, the less wealthy candidate can potentially overcome the disparity in resources through contributions from others. But ability to generate contributions may itself depend upon a showing of a financial base for the campaign or some demonstration of pre-existing support, which in turn is facilitated by expenditures of substantial personal sums. Thus the wealthy candidate's immediate access to a substantial personal fortune may give him an initial advantage that his less wealthy opponent can never overcome. And even if the advantage can be overcome, the perception that personal wealth wins elections may not only discourage potential candidates without significant personal wealth from entering the political arena, but also undermine public confidence in the integrity of the electoral process.

The concern that candidacy for public office not become, or appear to become, the exclusive province of the wealthy assumes heightened significance when one considers the impact of 608 (b), which the Court today upholds. That provision prohibits contributions from individuals and groups to candidates in excess of $1,000, and contributions from political committees in excess of $5,000. While the limitations on contributions are neutral in the sense that all candidates are foreclosed from accepting large contributions, there can be no question that large contributions generally mean more to the candidate without a substantial personal fortune to spend on his campaign. Large contributions are the less wealthy candidate's only hope of countering the wealthy candidate's immediate access to substantial sums of money. With that option removed, the less wealthy candidate is without the means to match the large initial expenditures of money of which the wealthy candidate is capable. In short, the limitations on contributions put a premium on a candidate's personal wealth. . . .

Notes and Queries

1. A number of First Amendment challenges have been brought against the Federal Election Campaign Act. Can you identify the varying constitutional arguments used against the limits on political contributions and expenditures (whether by private individuals, campaigns, groups, or the candidates themselves) and the public funding of presidential campaigns? Other than diminishing corruption and its appearance, what additional ends are sought by the legislation?

2. Is the expenditure of money for political purposes speech or conduct? A U.S. Court of Appeals upheld both expenditures and contributions limits on the theory of *United States v. O'Brien* (reprinted in chapter 12), the draft-card burning case. The appeals court claimed that spending money was conduct similar to burning draft cards and therefore capable of being regulated in the in-

terest of important public values. Rejecting the comparison, the Court said that it "has never suggested that the dependence of a communication on the expenditure of money operates itself to introduce a nonspeech element or to reduce the exacting scrutiny required by the First Amendment," to which Federal District Judge J. Skelly Wright responded as follows: "I am bound to say that this passage performs a judicial sleight of hand. The real question in the case was: Can the use of *money* be regulated, by analogy, to conduct such as draft-card burning, where there is an undoubted incidental effect on *speech*? However, what the Court asked was whether *pure speech* can be regulated where there is some incidental effect on *money*. Naturally the answer to the Court's question was 'No.' But this left untouched the real question in the case. The Court riveted its attention on what the money could buy—be it communication, or communication mixed with conduct. Yet the campaign reform law did not dictate what could be bought. It focused exclusively on the giving and spending itself. In short, the Court turned the congressional telescope around and looked through the wrong end." See *Politics and the Constitution: Is Money Speech?* 85 Yale Law Journal 1000–01 (1976).

3. In the same article, Judge Wright wrote: "[T]he effectiveness of political speakers is not necessarily diminished by reasonable contribution and expenditure ceilings. The giving and spending restrictions may cause candidates and other individuals to rely more on less expensive means of communication. But there is no reason to believe that such a shift in means reduces the number of issues discussed in a campaign. And by forcing candidates to put more emphasis on local organizing or leafletting or door-to-door canvassing and less on full-page ads and television commercials, the restrictions may well generate deeper exploration of the issues raised. . . . All similarly situated competition [would] face the same constraints." Ibid., 1012. How persuasive is this argument? Wright wrote these words in 1976. Have changes since then in the world of communication rendered his view as relevant today?

4. Justice Marshall contends that the Court's upholding of limitations on contributions, coupled with its striking of limits on personal expenditures, will have the perverse effect of further privileging personal wealth in the electoral system, therefore undermining the reformist impulses of the Congress. How would such a system undermine the electoral chances for lesser-known, and less wealthy candidates? How would a removal of contribution ceilings change the primary process? Would their removal advantage or disadvantage major party incumbents; encourage or discourage third party and major party challengers?

Federal Election Commission v. Colorado Republican Federal Campaign Committee

533 U.S. 431, 121 S. Ct. 2351, 150 L. Ed. 2d 461 (2001)

In *Federal Election Commission v. Colorado Republican Federal Campaign Committee* (*Colorado I*), the Supreme Court held that the spending limits on a political party's independent expenditures were unconstitutional. It remanded the case for further consideration of whether all limits on party expenditures, including expenditures coordinated with the candidate, violated the First Amendment. On this second question the District Court found for the Republican Party. The U.S. Court of Appeals affirmed. Opinion of the Court: *Souter*, Stevens, O'Connor, Ginsburg, Breyer. Dissenting opinion: *Thomas*, Scalia, Kennedy, Rehnquist.

Justice SOUTER delivered the opinion of the Court.

The Party's argument that its coordinated spending, like its independent spending, should be left free from restriction under the *Buckley* line of cases boils down to this: because a party's most important speech is aimed at electing candidates and is itself expressed through those candidates, any limit on party support for a candidate imposes a unique First Amendment burden. The point of organizing a party, the argument goes, is to run a successful candidate who shares the party's policy goals. Therefore, while a campaign contribution is only one of several ways that individuals and nonparty groups speak and associate politically, financial support of candidates is essential to the nature of political parties as we know them. And coordination with a candidate is a party's natural way of operating, not merely an option that can easily be avoided. Limitation of any party expenditure coordinated with a candidate, the Party contends, is therefore a serious, rather than incidental, imposition on the party's speech and associative purpose, and that justifies a stricter level of scrutiny than we have applied to analogous limits on individuals and nonparty groups. But whatever level of scrutiny is applied, the Party goes on to argue, the burden on a party reflects a fatal mismatch between the effects of limiting coordinated party expenditures and the prevention of corruption or the appearance of it. . . .

When we look directly at a party's function in getting and spending money, it would ignore reality to think that the party role is adequately described by speaking generally of electing particular candidates. The money parties spend comes from contributors with their own personal interests. PACs, for example, are frequent party contributors who (according to one of the Party's own experts) "do not pursue the same objectives in electoral politics" that parties do. PACs "are most concerned with advancing their narrow interest[s]" and therefore "provide support to candidates who share their views, regardless of party affiliation." In fact, many PACs naturally express their narrow interests by contributing to both parties during the same electoral cycle, and sometimes even directly to two competing candidates in the same election. Parties are thus necessarily the instruments of some contributors whose object is not to support the party's message or to elect party candidates across the board, but rather to support a specific candidate for the sake of a position on one, narrow issue, or even to support any candidate who will be obliged to the contributors.

Parties thus perform functions more complex than simply electing candidates; whether they like it or not, they act as agents for spending on behalf of those who seek to produce obligated officeholders. It is this party role, which functionally unites parties with other self-interested political actors, that the Party Expenditure Provision targets. This party role, accordingly, provides good reason to view limits on coordinated spending by parties through the same lens applied to such spending by donors, like PACs, that can use parties as conduits for contributions meant to place candidates under obligation. . . .

The Party's arguments for being treated differently from other political actors subject to limitation on political spending under the Act do not pan out. Despite decades of limitation on coordinated spending, parties have not been rendered useless. In reality, parties continue to organize to elect candidates, and also function for the benefit of donors whose object is to place candidates under obligation, a fact that parties cannot escape. Indeed, parties' capacity to concentrate power to elect is the very capacity that apparently opens them to exploitation as channels for circumventing contribution and coordinated spending limits binding on other political players. And some of these players could marshal the same power and sophistication for the same electoral objectives as political parties themselves. . . .

Since there is no recent experience with unlimited coordinated spending, the question is whether experience under the present law confirms a serious threat of abuse from the unlimited coordinated party spending as the Government contends. It clearly does. Despite years of

Comparative Note 8.5

[England's Representation of the People Act (1983) places limits on the amount of money that individual persons may spend in support of a parliamentary candidate. A citizen charged and convicted for violating the Act appealed to the European Court of Human Rights. Although the Court held, 14 votes to 6, that the restriction in question—here a ban on expenditures of more than 5 pounds—was disproportionate to the aim pursued, it recognized the legitimacy of the state's interest in controlling campaign expenditures.]

42. Free elections and freedom of expression, particularly freedom of political debate, together form the bedrock of any democratic system. The two rights are interrelated and operate to reinforce each other: for example, as the Court has observed in the past, freedom of expression is one of the "conditions" necessary to "ensure the free expression of opinion of the people in the choice of the legislature." For this reason, it is particularly important in the period preceding an election that opinions and information of all kinds are permitted to circulate freely.

43. Nonetheless, in certain circumstances the two rights may come into conflict and it may be considered necessary, in the period preceding or during an election, to place certain restrictions, of a type which would not usually be acceptable, on freedom of expression, in order to secure the "free expression of the opinion of the people in the choice of the legislature." The Court recognizes that, in striking the balance between these two rights, the Contracting States have a margin of appreciation, as they do generally with regard to the organization of their electoral systems.

[In his dissenting opinion, Justice Valticos wrote: "There is something slightly ridiculous in seeking to give the British Government lessons in how to hold elections and run a democracy; above all, it is wrong to seek the repeal of a provision aimed at influencing the way people vote and at preventing candidates with substantial financial resources ultimately gaining an advantage over other less well-off candidates."]

SOURCE: *Bowman v. United Kingdom*, 26 E.H.R.R. 1, 18 and 22 (1998).

---

enforcement of the challenged limits, substantial evidence demonstrates how candidates, donors, and parties test the limits of the current law, and it shows beyond serious doubt how contribution limits would be eroded if inducement to circumvent them were enhanced by declaring parties' coordinated spending wide open.

Under the Act, a donor is limited to $2,000 in contributions to one candidate in a given election cycle. The same donor may give as much as another $20,000 each year to a national party committee supporting the candidate. What a realist would expect to occur has occurred. Donors give to the party with the tacit understanding that the favored candidate will benefit.

Although the understanding between donor and party may involve no definite commitment and may be tacit on the donor's part, the frequency of the practice and the volume of money involved has required some manner of informal bookkeeping by the recipient. In the Democratic Party, at least, the method is known as "tallying," a system that helps to connect donors to candidates through the accommodation of a party. . . .

While this evidence rules out denying the potential for corruption by circumvention, the Party does try to mini-

mize the threat. It says that most contributions to parties are small, with negligible corrupting momentum to be carried through the party conduit. But some contributions are not small; they can go up to $20,000, and the record shows that even under present law substantial donations turn the parties into matchmakers whose special meetings and receptions give the donors the chance to get their points across to the candidates. . . .

We hold that a party's coordinated expenditures, unlike expenditures truly independent, may be restricted to minimize circumvention of contribution limits. We therefore reject the Party's facial challenge and, accordingly, reverse the judgment of the United States Court of Appeals for the Tenth Circuit.

It is so ordered.

Justice THOMAS, with whom Justice SCALIA and Justice KENNEDY join, and with whom Chief Justice REHNQUIST joins as to Part II, dissenting.

As an initial matter, I continue to believe that *Buckley* v. *Valeo* should be overruled. I remain baffled that this Court has extended the most generous First Amendment safeguards to filing lawsuits, wearing profane jackets, and exhibiting drive-in movies with nudity, but has offered only tepid protection to the core speech and associational rights that our Founders sought to defend. . . .

We need not, however, overrule *Buckley* and apply strict scrutiny in order to hold the Party Expenditure Provision unconstitutional. . . .

. . . Restricting contributions by individuals and political committees may, under *Buckley*, entail only a "marginal restriction," but the same cannot be said about limitations on political parties. Political parties and their candidates are "inextricably intertwined" in the conduct of an election. *Colorado I.* A party nominates its candidate; a candidate often is identified by party affiliation throughout the election and on the ballot; and a party's public image is largely defined by what its candidates say and do. Most importantly, a party's success or failure depends in large part on whether its candidates get elected. Because of this unity of interest, it is natural for a party and its candidate to work together and consult with one another during the course of the election. . . .

The Court nevertheless concludes that these concerns of inhibiting party speech are rendered "implausible" by the nearly 30 years of history in which coordinated spending has been statutorily limited. . . . I am unpersuaded by the Court's attempts to downplay the extent of the burden on political parties' First Amendment rights. First, the Court does not examine the record or the findings of the District Court, but instead relies wholly on the "observ[a-tions]" of the "political scientists" who happen to have written an *amicus* brief in support of the petitioner. I find more convincing, and more relevant, the record evidence that the parties have developed, which, as noted above, indicates that parties have suffered as a result of the Party Expenditure Provision. Second, we have never before upheld a limitation on speech simply because speakers have coped with the limitation for 30 years. And finally, if the passage of time were relevant to the constitutional inquiry, I would wonder why the Court adopted a "30-year" rule rather than the possible countervailing "200-year" rule. For nearly 200 years, this country had congressional elections without limitations on coordinated expenditures by political parties. Nowhere does the Court suggest that these elections were not "functional," or that they were marred by corruption.

The Court's only other response to the argument that parties are linked to candidates and that breaking this link would impose significant costs on speech is no response at all. The Court contends that parties are not organized simply to "elec[t] particular candidates" as evidenced by the fact that many political action committees donate money to both parties and sometimes even opposing can-

didates. According to the Court, "[p]arties are thus necessarily the instruments of some contributors whose object is not to support the party's message or to elect party candidates across the board." There are two flaws in the Court's analysis. First, no one argues that a party's role is merely to get particular candidates elected. Surely, among other reasons, parties also exist to develop and promote a platform. The point is simply that parties and candidates have shared interests, that it is natural for them to work together, and that breaking the connection between parties and their candidates inhibits the promotion of the party's message. Second, the mere fact that some donors contribute to both parties and their candidates does not necessarily imply that the donors control the parties or their candidates. It certainly does not mean that the parties are mere "instruments" or "agents," of the donors. Indeed, if a party receives money from donors on both sides of an issue, how can it be a tool of both donors? If the Green Party were to receive a donation from an industry that pollutes, would the Green Party necessarily become, through no choice of its own, an instrument of the polluters? The Court proffers no evidence that parties have become pawns of wealthy contributors. Parties might be the target of the speech of donors, but that does not suggest that parties are influenced (let alone improperly influenced) by the speech. Thus, the Court offers no explanation for why political parties should be treated the same as individuals and political committees.

Considering that we have never upheld an expenditure limitation against political parties, I would posit that substantial evidence is necessary to justify the infringement of parties' First Amendment interests. . . . The Government does not, and indeed cannot, point to any congressional findings suggesting that the Party Expenditure Provision is necessary, or even helpful, in reducing corruption or the perception of corruption. . . .

The dearth of evidence is unsurprising in light of the unique relationship between a political party and its candidates: "The very aim of a political party is to influence its candidate's stance on issues and, if the candidate takes office or is reelected, his votes." *Colorado I.* If coordinated expenditures help achieve this aim, the achievement "does not . . . constitute 'a subversion of the political process.'" It is simply the essence of our Nation's party system of government. One can speak of an individual citizen or a political action committee corrupting or coercing a candidate, but "[w]hat could it mean for a party to 'corrupt' its candidate or to exercise 'coercive' influence over him?"

Even if the Government had presented evidence that the Party Expenditure Provision affects corruption, the statute still would be unconstitutional, because there are better tailored alternatives for addressing the corruption. In addition to bribery laws and disclosure laws, the Government has two options that would not entail the restriction of political parties' First Amendment rights.

First, the Government could enforce the earmarking rule of 2 U.S.C. s. 441a(a)(8), under which contributions that "are in any way earmarked or otherwise directed through an intermediary or conduit to [a] candidate" are treated as contributions to the candidate. Vigilant enforcement of this provision is a precise response to the Court's circumvention concerns. . . .

. . . [T]here is a second, well-tailored option for combating corruption that does not entail the reduction of parties' First Amendment freedoms. The heart of the Court's circumvention argument is that, whereas individuals can donate only $2,000 to a candidate in a given election cycle, they can donate $20,000 to the national committees of a political party, an amount that is allegedly large enough to corrupt the candidate. If indeed $20,000 is enough to corrupt a candidate (an assumption that seems implausible on its face and is, in any event, unsupported by any evidence), the proper response is to lower the cap. That way, the speech restriction is directed at the source of the alleged corruption—the individual donor—and not the party. . . .

In my view, it makes no sense to contravene a political party's core First Amendment rights because of what a third party might unlawfully try to do. Instead of broadly restricting political parties' speech, the Government should have pursued better-tailored alternatives for combating the alleged corruption.

Notes and Queries

1. Justice Souter argues that the Government's defense of limitations on party contributions is justified by its desire to limit the corruption of candidates by individual contributions to the party. He suggests that large individual contributions to the parties, contributions which are limited to $20,000, might tie candidates to the special interests of the donor's. In dissent Justice Thomas argues that no evidence was provided to show that the existence of large contributions to parties corrupts candidates, and that such corruption is implausible. Who is right? Justice Souter thinks that these large contributions will undermine the general good in favor of special interests. Is it reasonable to think that a candidate will be bound by such a contribution?

2. Justice Souter seems to suggest that political parties play a unique role in the American political order. He nevertheless claims that the "argument for [their] being treated differently from other political actors subject to limitation on political spending under the Act do not pan out." Parties, Souter maintains, "act as agents for spending on behalf of those who seek to produce obligated office holders. It is this role, which functionally unites parties with other self-interested political actors, that the Party Expenditure Provision targets." Would his argument lose its cogency if American political parties were more disciplined and exercised more control over the policy positions of their candidates?

3. This case, like related decisions, features an analysis of the role and nature of political parties in America. Compare the analysis of the majority and dissenting opinions. Neither the majority nor dissenting opinion cites any study of parties by a political scientist. Would the majority opinion have been crafted differently had the Court consulted the political science literature? How different?

4. Does Souter's idea of a political party differ from the theory of party responsibility advanced in *Democratic Party of the United States v. Wisconsin?*

Bush v. Gore
531 U.S. 98, 148 L. Ed. 2d 388, 121 S. Ct. 525 (2000)

On 8 November 2000, one day following the presidential election, the Florida Division of Elections reported that Governor George Bush had defeated Vice President Albert Gore in the state by less than 2,000 votes of nearly 6,000,000 cast. Given the close margin, Florida law required an automatic machine recount of the ballots. Following the mandatory recount, Bush retained the lead, though it had diminished. Objecting to numerous irregularities in the counting of votes, Gore sought manual recounts in four Florida counties. A rash of federal and state lawsuits followed, with Bush suing to stop the recounts and Gore countersuing to have them continued. Finally, the Florida Supreme Court decided to extend the hand-counting of the votes until November 26, eight days after the state's statutory deadline for certifying the election results to Congress. Bush challenged this decision and the Supreme Court granted certiorari. (For additional details, see the section on *Bush v. Gore* in the introductory essay.) Opinion of the Court: *Per curiam.* Concurring opinion: *Rehnquist.* Dissenting opinions: *Steven, Souter, Breyer, Ginsburg.*

PER CURIAM.
The petition presents the following questions: whether

the Florida Supreme Court established new standards for resolving Presidential election contests, thereby violating Art. I, s. 1, cl. 2, of the United States Constitution . . . and whether the use of standardless manual recounts violates the Equal Protection and Due Process Clauses. With respect to the equal protection question, we find a violation of the Equal Protection Clause.

Much of the controversy seems to revolve around ballot cards designed to be perforated by a stylus but which, either through error or deliberate omission, have not been perforated with sufficient precision for a machine to count them. In some cases a piece of the card—a chad—is hanging, say by two corners. In other cases there is no separation at all, just an indentation.

The Florida Supreme Court has ordered that the intent of the voter be discerned from such ballots. . . . This is unobjectionable as an abstract proposition and a starting principle. The problem inheres in the absence of specific standards to ensure its equal application. The formulation of uniform rules to determine intent based on these recurring circumstances is practicable and, we conclude, necessary.

The want of those rules here has led to unequal evaluation of ballots in various respects. . . .

The record provides some examples. A monitor in Miami-Dade County testified at trial that he observed that three members of the county canvassing board applied different standards in defining a legal vote. And testimony at trial also revealed that at least one county changed its evaluative standards during the counting process. Palm Beach County, for example, began the process with a 1990 guideline which precluded counting completely attached chads, switched to a rule that considered a vote to be legal if any light could be seen through a chad, changed back to the 1990 rule, and then abandoned any pretense of a *per se* rule, only to have a court order that the county consider dimpled chads legal. This is not a process with sufficient guarantees of equal treatment. . . .

The State Supreme Court ratified this uneven treatment. . . .

In addition, the recounts in these three counties were not limited to so-called undervotes but extended to all of the ballots. The distinction has real consequences. A manual recount of all ballots identifies not only those ballots which show no vote but also those which contain more than one, the so-called overvotes. Neither category will be counted by the machine. This is not a trivial concern. At oral argument, respondents estimated there are as many as 110,000 overvotes statewide. As a result, the citizen whose ballot was not read by a machine because he failed to vote for a candidate in a way readable by a machine

may still have his vote counted in a manual recount; on the other hand, the citizen who marks two candidates in a way discernable by the machine will not have the same opportunity to have his vote count, even if a manual examination of the ballot would reveal the requisite indicia of intent. Furthermore, the citizen who marks two candidates, only one of which is discernable by the machine, will have his vote counted even though it should have been read as an invalid ballot. The State Supreme Court's inclusion of vote counts based on these variant standards exemplifies concerns with the remedial processes that were under way.

That brings the analysis to yet a further equal protection problem. The votes certified by the court included a partial total from one county, Miami-Dade. The Florida Supreme Court's decision thus gives no assurance that the recounts included in a final certification must be complete. . . .

In addition to these difficulties the actual process by which the votes were to be counted under the Florida Supreme Court's decision raises further concerns. That order did not specify who would recount the ballots. The county canvassing boards were forced to pull together ad hoc teams comprised of judges from various Circuits who had no previous training in handling and interpreting ballots. . . .

The recount process, in its features here described, is inconsistent with the minimum procedures necessary to protect the fundamental right of each voter in the special instance of a statewide recount under the authority of a single state judicial officer. Our consideration is limited to the present circumstances, for the problem of equal protection in election processes generally presents many complexities.

The question before the Court is not whether local entities, in the exercise of their expertise, may develop different systems for implementing elections. Instead, we are presented with a situation where a state court with the power to assure uniformity has ordered a statewide recount with minimal procedural safeguards. When a court orders a statewide remedy, there must be at least some assurance that the rudimentary requirements of equal treatment and fundamental fairness are satisfied. . . .

The Supreme Court of Florida has said that the legislature intended the State's electors to "participat[e] fully in the federal electoral process," as provided in 3 U.S.C. s. 5. . . . That statute, in turn, requires that any controversy or contest that is designed to lead to a conclusive selection of electors be completed by December 12. That date is upon us, and there is no recount procedure in place under the State Supreme Court's order that comports with minimal constitutional standards. Because it is evident that any recount seeking to meet the December 12 date will be unconstitutional for the reasons we have discussed, we reverse the judgment of the Supreme Court of Florida ordering a recount to proceed.

Seven Justices of the Court agree that there are constitutional problems with the recount ordered by the Florida Supreme Court that demand a remedy. The only disagreement is as to the remedy. Because the Florida Supreme Court has said that the Florida Legislature intended to obtain the safe-harbor benefits of 3 U.S.C. s. 5, Justice Breyer's proposed remedy—remanding to the Florida Supreme Court for its ordering of a constitutionally proper contest until December 18—contemplates action in violation of the Florida election code. . . .

None are more conscious of the vital limits on judicial authority than are the members of this Court, and none stand more in admiration of the Constitution's design to leave the selection of the President to the people, through their legislatures, and to the political sphere. When contending parties invoke the process of the courts, however, it becomes our unsought responsibility to resolve the federal and constitutional issues the judicial system has been forced to confront.

The judgment of the Supreme Court of Florida is reversed, and the case is remanded for further proceedings not inconsistent with this opinion. . . .

Chief Justice REHNQUIST, with whom Justice SCALIA and Justice THOMAS join, concurring.

We join the *per curiam* opinion. We write separately because we believe there are additional grounds that require us to reverse the Florida Supreme Court's decision.

We deal here not with an ordinary election, but with an election for the President of the United States. . . .

In most cases, comity and respect for federalism compel us to defer to the decisions of state courts on issues of state law. That practice reflects our understanding that the decisions of state courts are definitive pronouncements of the will of the States as sovereigns. Of course, in ordinary cases, the distribution of powers among the branches of a State's government raises no questions of federal constitutional law, subject to the requirement that the government be republican in character. But there are a few exceptional cases in which the Constitution imposes a duty or confers a power on a particular branch of a State's government. This is one of them. Article II, s. 1, cl. 2, provides that "[e]ach State shall appoint, in such Manner as the *Legislature* thereof may direct," electors for President and Vice President. (Emphasis added). . . .

In Florida, the legislature had chosen to hold statewide elections to appoint the State's 25 electors. Importantly, the legislature has delegated the authority to run the elections and to oversee election disputes to the Secretary of State (Secretary), and to state circuit courts. Isolated sections of the code may well admit of more than one interpretation, but the general coherence of the legislative scheme may not be altered by judicial interpretation so as to wholly change the statutorily provided apportionment of responsibility among these various bodies. In any election but a Presidential election, the Florida Supreme Court can give as little or as much deference to Florida's executives as it chooses, so far as Article II is concerned, and this Court will have no cause to question the court's actions. But, with respect to a Presidential election, the court must be both mindful of the legislature's role under Article II in choosing the manner of appointing electors and deferential to those bodies expressly empowered by the legislature to carry out its constitutional mandate.

. . . Though we generally defer to state courts on the interpretation of state law there are of course areas in which the Constitution requires this Court to undertake an independent, if still deferential, analysis of state law. . . .

This inquiry does not imply a disrespect for state *courts*, but rather a respect for the constitutionally prescribed role of state *legislatures*. To attach definitive weight to the pronouncement of a state court, when the very question at issue is whether the court has actually departed from the statutory meaning, would be to abdicate our responsibility to enforce the explicit requirements of Article II. . . .

Justice STEVENS, with whom Justice GINSBURG and Justice BREYER join, dissenting.

The federal questions that ultimately emerged in this case are not substantial. . . .

Admittedly, the use of differing substandards for determining voter intent in different counties employing similar voting systems may raise serious concerns. Those concerns are alleviated—if not eliminated—by the fact that a single impartial magistrate will ultimately adjudicate all objections arising from the recount process. . . .

. . . [N]either in this case, nor in its earlier opinion . . . did the Florida Supreme Court make any substantive change in Florida electoral law. Its decisions were rooted in long-established precedent and were consistent with the relevant statutory provisions, taken as a whole. It did what courts do—it decided the case before it in light of the legislature's intent to leave no legally cast vote uncounted. . . . If we assume—as I do—that the members of that court and the judges who would have carried out its mandate are impartial, its decision does not even raise a colorable federal question.

What must underlie petitioners' entire federal assault on the Florida election procedures is an unstated lack of confidence in the impartiality and capacity of the state judges who would make the critical decisions if the vote count were to proceed. Otherwise, their position is wholly without merit. The endorsement of that position by the majority of this Court can only lend credence to the most cynical appraisal of the work of judges throughout the land. It is confidence in the men and women who administer the judicial system that is the true backbone of the rule of law. Time will one day heal the wound to that confidence that will be inflicted by today's decision. One thing, however, is certain. Although we may never know with complete certainty the identity of the winner of this year's Presidential election, the identity of the loser is perfectly clear. It is the Nation's confidence in the judge as an impartial guardian of the rule of law.

I respectfully dissent.

Justice GINSBURG, with whom Justice STEVENS joins, and with whom Justice SOUTER and Justice BREYER join as to Part I, dissenting.

The Chief Justice acknowledges that provisions of Florida's Election Code "may well admit of more than one interpretation." But instead of respecting the state high court's province to say what the State's Election Code means, the Chief Justice maintains that Florida's Supreme Court has veered so far from the ordinary practice of judicial review that what it did cannot properly be called judging. . . . I might join The Chief Justice were it my commission to interpret Florida law. But disagreement with the Florida court's interpretation of its own State's law does not warrant the conclusion that the justices of that court have legislated. There is no cause here . . . to upset their reasoned interpretation of Florida law. . . .

The extraordinary setting of this case has obscured the ordinary principle that dictates its proper resolution: Federal courts defer to state high courts' interpretations of their state's own law. This principle reflects the core of federalism, on which all agree. . . . The Chief Justice's solicitude for the Florida Legislature comes at the expense of the more fundamental solicitude we owe to the legislature's sovereign. Were the other members of this Court as mindful as they generally are of our system of dual sovereignty, they would affirm the judgment of the Florida Supreme Court. . . .

I dissent.

Justice SOUTER, with whom Justice BREYER joins and with whom Justice STEVENS and Justice GINSBURG join with regard to all but Part C, dissenting.

It is only on the third issue before us that there is a meritorious argument for relief, as this Court's *Per Curiam* opinion recognizes. It is an issue that might well have been dealt with adequately by the Florida courts if the state proceedings had not been interrupted, and if not disposed of at the state level it could have been considered by the Congress in any electoral vote dispute. . . .

Petitioners have raised an equal protection claim. . . . It is true that the Equal Protection Clause does not forbid the use of a variety of voting mechanisms within a jurisdiction, even though different mechanisms will have different levels of effectiveness in recording voters' intentions; local variety can be justified by concerns about cost, the potential value of innovation, and so on. But evidence in the record here suggests that a different order of disparity obtains under rules for determining a voter's intent that have been applied (and could continue to be applied) to identical types of ballots used in identical brands of machines and exhibiting identical physical characteristics (such as "hanging" or "dimpled" chads). I can conceive of no legitimate state interest served by these differing treatments of the expressions of voters' fundamental rights. The differences appear wholly arbitrary.

In deciding what to do about this, we should take account of the fact that electoral votes are due to be cast in six days. I would therefore remand the case to the courts of Florida with instructions to establish uniform standards for evaluating the several types of ballots that have prompted differing treatments, to be applied within and among counties when passing on such identical ballots in any further recounting (or successive recounting) that the courts might order.

Unlike the majority, I see no warrant for this Court to assume that Florida could not possibly comply with this requirement before the date set for the meeting of electors, December 18. . . .

I respectfully dissent.

Justice BREYER, with whom Justice STEVENS and Justice GINSBURG join except as to Part I-A-1, and with whom Justice SOUTER joins as to Part I, dissenting.

Of course, the selection of the President is of fundamental national importance. But that importance is political, not legal. And this Court should resist the temptation unnecessarily to resolve tangential legal disputes, where doing so threatens to determine the outcome of the election. The Constitution and federal statutes themselves make clear that restraint is appropriate. They set forth a road map of how to resolve disputes about electors, even after an election as close as this one. That road map foresees resolution of electoral disputes by *state* courts. But it nowhere provides for involvement by the United States Supreme Court.

To the contrary, the Twelfth Amendment commits to Congress the authority and responsibility to count electoral votes. A federal statute, the Electoral Count Act, enacted after the close 1876 Hayes-Tilden Presidential election, specifies that, after States have tried to resolve disputes (through "judicial" or other means), Congress is the body primarily authorized to resolve remaining disputes. The legislative history of the Act makes clear its intent to commit the power to resolve such disputes to Congress, rather than the courts. . . .

The decision by both the Constitution's Framers and the 1886 Congress to minimize this Court's role in resolving close federal presidential elections is as wise as it is clear. However awkward or difficult it may be for Congress to resolve difficult electoral disputes, Congress, being a political body, expresses the people's will far more accurately than does an unelected Court. And the people's will is what elections are about.

Moreover, Congress was fully aware of the danger that would arise should it ask judges, unarmed with appropriate legal standards, to resolve a hotly contested Presidential election contest. Just after the 1876 Presidential election, Florida, South Carolina, and Louisiana each sent two slates of electors to Washington. Without these States, Tilden, the Democrat, had 184 electoral votes, one short of the number required to win the Presidency. With those States, Hayes, his Republican opponent, would have had 185. In order to choose between the two slates of electors, Congress decided to appoint an electoral commission composed of five Senators, five Representatives, and five Supreme Court Justices. Initially the Commission was to be evenly divided between Republicans and Democrats, with Justice David Davis, an Independent, to possess the decisive vote. However, when at the last minute the Illinois Legislature elected Justice Davis to the United States Senate, the final position on the Commission was filled by Supreme Court Justice Joseph P. Bradley.

The Commission divided along partisan lines, and the responsibility to cast the deciding vote fell to Justice Bradley. He decided to accept the votes by the Republican electors, and thereby awarded the Presidency to Hayes.

Justice Bradley immediately became the subject of vociferous attacks. Bradley was accused of accepting bribes, of being captured by railroad interests, and of an eleventh-hour change in position. . . . For present purposes, the relevance of this history lies in the fact that the participation in the work of the electoral commission by five Justices, including Justice Bradley, did not lend that process

greater legitimacy. Nor did it assure the public that the process had worked fairly, guided by the law. Rather, it simply embroiled Members of the Court in partisan conflict, thereby undermining respect for the judicial process. . . .

This history may help to explain why I think it not only legally wrong, but also most unfortunate, for the Court simply to have terminated the Florida recount. . . .

. . . [I]n this highly politicized matter, the appearance of a split decision runs the risk of undermining the public's confidence in the Court itself. That confidence is a public treasure. It has been built slowly over many years. . . . It is a vitally necessary ingredient of any successful effort to protect basic liberty and, indeed, the rule of law itself. We run no risk of returning to the days when a President (responding to this Court's efforts to protect the Cherokee Indians) might have said, "John Marshall has made his decision; now let him enforce it!" But we do risk a self-inflicted wound—a wound that may harm not just the Court, but the Nation.

. . . What it does today, the Court should have left undone. I would repair the damage done as best we now can, by permitting the Florida recount to continue under uniform standards.

I respectfully dissent.

Notes and Queries

1. The *Per Curiam* opinion concludes with a statement suggesting that the justices' hand was forced. But did they really have to decide this case? On what grounds might they have decided to reject the case? Is there any evidence to show, as many commentators have suggested, that *Bush v. Gore* was an exercise of naked political partisanship?

2. Constitutional scholars such as Laurence Tribe and Cass Sunstein have pointed to the *Per Curiam* opinion as evidence that the conservative aspiration to originalist interpretation and judicial restraint was merely a guise for the majority's own activism. They point to the failure of the *Per Curiam* justices to apply the Equal Protection Clause in other cases, and even in other cases involving election irregularities. Is this assessment correct? How many of the justices concluded that the Florida recount did implicate equal protection guarantees?

3. Justice Souter suggests that the Court should have allowed the political process time to work, and that the Constitution lodged the adjudication of such disputes in the Congress. If the Supreme Court had allowed the recount to go forward in Florida, how would the dispute have been resolved in Congress?

4. Justice Breyer argues that "the people's will is what elections are about," and therefore, the Court should not have resolved the election controversy. Does his claim implicate other aspects of the presidential selection apparatus in the Constitution? Does the electoral college undermine the people's will? Would a resolution of the dispute by Congress undermine the popular will any less than a resolution of the dispute by the Court?

Part Three

Liberty, Community, and Constitutional Interpretation under the Bill of Rights

Considered in its totality, and not simply provision by provision, a bill of rights sketches the broad outlines of the relationship between liberty and community. A bill of rights is a blueprint, less a list of protected liberties than an overall vision of the ideal relationship between liberty and community.[1] In this larger, autobiographical sense, a bill of rights indicates how conflicts between liberty and community should be conceived and, to some extent, reconciled. It expresses the "dominant ideas concerning the relations between the individual citizen and the government."[2]

This pattern of ordered liberty, and the delicate balance between public interest and private right it seeks to achieve, is reflected in every part of the American Bill of Rights. Individual provisions, such as the First Amendment, express in broad terms how the Framers sought to balance specific liberties and the public interest. Similarly, the due process clauses of the Fifth and Fourteenth Amendments do not guarantee absolute or unrestricted rights to liberty and property, but only that government may not deprive a person of them without due process of law.[3] Their very language assumes the state may regulate individual liberties in the public interest.

A bill of rights, therefore, is important not only for the specific protections it promises, but also for what it tells us about larger issues of constitutional politics. Implicit in a bill of rights are assumptions about human nature, the source and scope of individual rights, and the relationship of the individual

---

[1] As Donald Lutz has written, the Framers saw the Bill of Rights as "the statement of broad principles rather than as a set of legally enforceable rights." As quoted in James A. Henretta, *The Nineteenth-Century Revolution in Civil Liberties: From "Rights in Property" to "Property in Rights."* 19 This Constitution 13 (Fall 1991).

[2] Carl J. Friedrich, *Constitutional Government and Democracy.* rev. ed. (Boston: Ginn and Company, 1950), 160.

[3] What due process of law requires of state authorities before they may regulate or infringe upon a right is another question. Some scholars, notably John Hart Ely, believe the due process clause of the Fourteenth Amendment imposes only procedural restrictions. *Democracy and Distrust: A Theory of Judicial Review.* (Cambridge: Harvard University Press, 1980), 18–22. Other scholars argue the clause has a "substantive" component, or that there is, in addition to "procedural due process," a type of "substantive due process." See Laurence H. Tribe, *Constitutional Choices.* (Cambridge: Harvard University Press, 1985), 10–11.

and community. The American Bill of Rights does not so much resolve these issues as it raises them.

Consider the most basic of questions: From where does individual liberty originate? The Preamble to the Constitution states only that "We the People . . . to secure the Blessings of Liberty to ourselves and our Posterity, do ordain and establish this Constitution. . . ." But nowhere does the text suggest the source of the Blessings of Liberty, which has led scholars and judges to look for evidence elsewhere. The Declaration of Independence, for example, asserts "That all men are created equal, that they are endowed by their creator with certain unalienable rights; [and] that among these are life, liberty & the pursuit of happiness. . . ."

Implicit in this dramatic assertion of human equality are important claims about the nature and origin of constitutional liberties, as well as of the limits of governmental power. The phrase, "endowed by their creator with certain unalienable rights," for example, suggests that "human rights . . . do not depend on history, but on the laws of nature and nature's God."[4] We possess rights because we are human, not because others have chosen to give them to us or because we have given them to ourselves in a social contract. The source of human liberties is natural and pre-constitutional. Constitutional liberties therefore precede, not only in historical time but also in political theory, both the Declaration of Independence and the Constitution of 1787.

The Declaration of Independence, then, may have considerable significance for how we understand the Constitution and the Bill of Rights. The Declaration asserts that we possess certain inalienable rights. The Constitution *recognizes* and seeks to protect them by imposing limits on both the objects and the means of governmental power. We possess these liberties, and governments must respect them, not because they are "in" the Constitution, whether explicitly or implicitly, but because such rights derive from nature.

Whatever the Founders may have thought about the relationship between the Declaration and the Constitution of 1787, many scholars and Supreme Court justices now reject the premise that there are "natural rights." Like John Hart Ely, many judges have concluded that "The idea [of natural law] is a discredited one in our society . . . and for good reason."[5] The good reason is that "natural law" is so hopelessly vague that we doubt its utility as a way of discerning the Constitution's meaning. "At various times," Ely notes, "judges have argued that natural law says nothing at all about the propriety of slavery, while others have insisted that no conception of natural law could possibly authorize such a practice." In a case included in the next chapter, *Adamson v. California* (1947), Justice Black further noted that the imprecision of natural law as a source of constitutional meaning would endow "this Court . . . with boundless power . . . periodically to expand and contract constitutional standards to conform to the Court's conception of . . . 'civilized decency' and 'fundamental liberty and justice.' "

Scholars and judges who reject the natural law theory of the Declaration argue that the Constitution itself, or rather, the agreement that secured it, is the basis of our liberties. The Constitution does more than simply recognize or recite liberties, it *creates* and thus is the very source of those liberties. The Constitution, therefore, "con-

---

[4] Edward J. Erler, *The American Polity: Essays on the Theory and Practice of Constitutional Government.* (New York: Crane Russak, 1991), xi.

[5] Ely, supra note 3, at 50.

sists of a complex of value judgments the framers wrote into the text of the Constitution and thereby constitutionalized."[6]

This controversy is not simply a theoretical argument among medieval scholars cloistered from the real world of constitutional law. Disputes over the source of liberty are important for understanding two vital issues in constitutional interpretation. As we shall see in chapter 9, whether we need a Bill of Rights, and how far it should extend (to the national government only, or to the states as well) will be influenced by our answers to the questions of source and scope.

Differences between competing accounts of the source of individual liberty also manifest themselves in everyday practical disputes between the rights of individuals and the powers of the community. Expansive conceptions of the right to property, as we shall see in chapter 10, or of privacy, as we shall see in chapter 11, inevitably run up against communal interests in the regulation of those rights. Should the right to property include the right to use one's backyard as a landfill for toxic waste? Should the right to liberty include the right of adults to have sexual relations with members of the same sex?

The answers to these questions should indicate the extent to which constitutional interpretation involves reconciling individual liberty and the rights of the larger community. If the community is the source of liberty and property—if, in other words, those rights exist because they are the product of democratic agreement—then the community's authority to regulate them is arguably greater than it is if such rights have an existence independent of the Constitution.

This has important consequences for constitutional interpretation. If the Bill of Rights is the source of liberty, then there is little warrant, some argue, for judges to "find" or "infer" additional constitutional rights. If additional or implied rights exist, then they do so only because and when the community chooses to recognize them through the process of constitutional amendment. If, however, the Bill of Rights acknowledges that liberty is derived from nature, or the human condition, then there may be some justification for judicial efforts to infer additional rights not expressly mentioned in the Bill of Rights.

Hence, the second issue concerns who possesses the constitutional authority to resolve such disputes. It is a part of any constitution's function to mark the boundaries between state and society, but constitutions typically speak with imprecision. The "majestic generalities" of constitutional texts require interpretation. But interpretation by whom? Who should fix the boundaries between liberty and community? How one approaches the question of who decides will be influenced by the approach one uses to understand the founding. As we saw in chapter 2, those who favor the democratic or republican interpretations of the founding will be more apt to favor an allocation of interpretive authority to the popular, representative institutions, which can be democratically controlled. Constitutionalists will be more likely to want to remove at least some areas of constitutional interpretation from popular institutions, for fear of majority tyranny and faction. In earlier chapters we distinguished between constitutional review and judicial review. These two conceptions of interpretative authority gave rise to the positions of departmentalism, typically favored by republicans and anti-Federalists, and judicial supremacy, typically favored by the Federalists. In the chapters that follow, we will see how questions concerning interpretive authority continue to influence the process of interpretation itself.

---

[6] Michael J. Perry, *The Constitution, the Courts, and Human Rights.* (New Haven: Yale University Press, 1982), 10.

Bills of Rights in Other Constitutions

The American Constitution is relatively silent about the source of liberty. Most foreign constitutions, in contrast, include explicit claims about the source of individual liberties and of the state's responsibility to recognize and protect them. The Basic Law of Germany, for example, "reflects a conscious ordering of individual freedoms and public interests. It resounds with the language of human freedom, but a freedom restrained by certain political values, community norms, and ethical principles."[7]

The German Basic Law states clearly that humans possess liberty because it is an inalienable human right, not because the state, or our fellow citizens, have given it to us. Article 1 of the Basic Law thus *recognizes* that individuals possess liberties, but it is not the source of those liberties. As if to emphasize its importance, Article 1 of the Basic Law states "The dignity of man shall be inviolable. To respect and protect it shall be the duty of all state authority. The German people therefore acknowledge inviolable and inalienable human rights as the basis of every community, of peace and of justice in the world."[8]

Similarly, in *McGee v. Attorney General and Revenue Commissioners* (1974), the Irish Supreme Court declared that:

> *Articles 41, 42, and 43 [of the Irish Constitution] emphatically reject the theory that there are no rights without laws, no rights contrary to the law and no rights anterior to the law. They indicate that justice is placed above the law and acknowledge that natural or human rights are not created by law but that the Constitution confirms their existence and gives them protection. The individual has natural or human rights over which the state has no authority.*

Article 97 of the Japanese Constitution takes a somewhat different, if related tack. It states that:

> *The fundamental human rights by this Constitution guaranteed to the people of Japan are fruits of the age-old struggle of man to be free; they have survived the many exacting tests for durability and are conferred upon this and future generations in trust, to be held for all time inviolate.*

Every bill of rights is unique in some ways, but there are also similarities, especially in post–World War II constitutions. The list of liberties expressly protected is usually more expansive than the American Bill of Rights. It is common, for example, to find explicitly protected rights to privacy, and guarantees of equality based on gender as well as race. Twentieth-century constitutions are also likely to protect "social rights" that the American Bill of Rights fails to mention. These "social rights" include rights to work, as well as rights to various types of social welfare, such as health care, education, and subsistence.

In contrast to the stark, typically unqualified language of the American Constitution, many other constitutions are far less likely to use the absolutist language of the

---

[7] Donald P. Kommers, *The Jurisprudence of Free Speech in the U.S. and the Federal Republic of Germany,* 53 Southern California Law Review 677 (1980).

[8] The German Bill of Rights also adopts a theory of human rights that gives those rights superior political status. The Basic Law's Bill of Rights appears in the first twenty articles of the text. In contrast, the Weimar Constitution had put its list of liberties at the end of the text. Article 79 of the Basic Law further underscores the importance of Article 1 and respect for human dignity by providing that "Amendments of this Basic Law affecting . . . the basic principles laid down in Articles 1 and 20, shall be inadmissible." Article 19 states that "the essential content of a basic right [may not be] encroached upon."

American Bill of Rights, and correspondingly more likely to qualify rights with duties. Thus constitutions in other states often couple provisions for individual liberties with governmental authority to restrict those liberties in the public interest. Article 5 of the German Basic Law, for example, guarantees freedom of expression. It states "There shall be no censorship." It adds, however, that "These rights are limited by the provisions of the general laws, the provisions of law for the protection of youth, and by the right to inviolability of personal honor." Even more importantly, Article 18 of the Basic Law provides that "Whoever abuses freedom of expression of opinion, in particular of the press, freedom of teaching, freedom of assembly, freedom of association, privacy of posts and telecommunications, or the right of asylum in order to combat the free democratic order, shall forfeit these basic rights."

Similarly, Section 1 of the Canadian Charter of Rights, the general limitations clause, provides that every guarantee in the Charter is subject "to such reasonable limits prescribed by law as can be demonstrably justified in a free and democratic society." As Peter Hogg has concluded, "Section one makes clear that a law limiting a Charter Right is valid, if the law is a 'reasonable' one that can be reasonably justified in a free and democratic society."[9] Article 2 of the Italian Constitution also stresses the interdependence of individual and community. In it, "The Republic recognizes and guarantees the inviolable rights of man, both as an individual and in the social organizations wherein his personality is developed, and it requires the performance of fundamental duties of political, economic, and social solidarity." Article 4 likewise guarantees all citizens a right to work, but couples it with "the duty of exercising . . . an activity or pursuit that contributes to the material or spiritual progress of society."

In sum, the American Bill of Rights is inescapably individualistic at heart, especially when compared to the bills of rights of most other constitutional democracies. In this sense, the image of the human person implicit in the Bill of Rights is that of the autonomous, free individual who exists in a state of tension with the larger community. By way of contrast, consider the opinion of the German Federal Constitutional Court in *The Investment Aid Case* (1954):

> *The image of man in the Basic Law is not that of an isolated, sovereign individual. On the contrary, the Basic Law has resolved the tension between individual and society in favor of coordination and interdependence with the community without touching the intrinsic value of the person.*[10]

Conclusion

In every case that arises under the Bill of Rights, we must reconcile our desire for individual liberty with the need for public order, personal autonomy with the needs of the community. Of course, the process of constitutional interpretation under the First Amendment is in some ways unique to that provision, as interpretation of the Fifth Amendment is unique to it.

This uniqueness is a consequence of constitutional draftsmanship: The language and purpose of the First Amendment differ from the Fifth, which in turn differ from the Fourteenth. The tendency to focus on the uniqueness of specific constitutional provisions, sometimes called "clause-bound interpretivism," is a consequence of a written constitution that "picks out" certain individual liberties for special protection.

---

[9] Peter W. Hogg, *Constitutional Law of Canada*. 3d ed. (Toronto: The Carswell Company Limited, 1985), 801–02.

[10] *Investment Aid Case*, 4 BVerfGE 7 (1954).

It is a convenient way of understanding particular problems in constitutional law. It is, moreover, the way books in constitutional law are organized, and how courses in constitutional law are usually taught.

For organizational convenience, we utilize that approach in the following chapters. We want to emphasize again, however, that inherent in individual cases and isolated provisions are common problems of constitutional interpretation, some of which we have discussed here. Recognition of those common problems is an important part of the process of constitutional interpretation, both in the United States and in other constitutional democracies.

Chapter 9

The Bill of Rights, Incorporation, and Capital Punishment

The relationship between liberty and community, or between individual liberty and the public good, is one of the inescapable features of political life. It appears in every polity, in matters as profound as the death penalty, and in ordinary activities like applying for a driver's license. If we were perfectly free to do as we like, anyone could drive, whether licensed or not. But the public has important interests, such as the safety and welfare of the community, which lead it to override individual liberty and create a licensing system. When the state acts on the basis of one of these public interests it exercises its police power, or "the power to protect the health, safety, morals and welfare of the people."[1] Much of politics in any society consists in determining what restrictions on liberty are permissible. The relationship between liberty and community is especially complex in constitutional democracies, however, because they are committed simultaneously to the preservation of individual liberty, human dignity, and to majoritarian rule.

In a simple democracy, unencumbered by constitutional limits, restrictions on individual liberty need only satisfy the *process* required to make law. Any law passed according to the proper majoritarian procedures, regardless of its content, is legitimate.[2] The primacy of form over substance should be no surprise. At its core, democracy is a theory of empowerment and not of limitations. In contrast, constitutionalists seek to protect individual liberty from arbitrary or capricious governmental power. Constitutionalists believe power is always prone to abuse no matter who wields it; they hold that some individual liberties may not be abridged even by a majority. Because constitutionalists share with democrats a commitment to self-government, one of these liberties is the right to participate in politics. Unlike democrats, however, constitutionalists do not consider this liberty necessarily pre-eminent or the only one immune from majoritarian infringement. They seek not only to empower majorities, but also to protect "the self in its dignity and

---

[1] *West Coast Hotel v. Parrish*, 300 U.S. 379 (1937).

[2] Some scholars would argue that even in a pure democracy, there may be no laws that would dismantle the structure of democracy itself. See Michael Walzer, *Philosophy and Democracy*, 9 Political Theory 379, 383 (1981).

worth."[3] Thus constitutional democracies allow majorities to rule while simultaneously limiting their power. In this way they hope to reconcile individual liberty and the public good, or "the permanent and aggregate interests of the community," in the words of the Founders.[4] As James Madison wrote in *Federalist* 10, "To secure the public good and private rights . . . and at the same time to preserve the spirit and form of popular government, is then the great object to which our inquiries are directed."

One device for achieving that goal is a bill of rights. As we saw in chapter 8, however, it is not the only, or perhaps even the most important, mechanism.[5] Indeed, most of the delegates at the Philadelphia Convention did not think a bill of rights was necessary. When George Mason, senior delegate from Virginia, proposed that one be drafted, the delegates rejected his suggestion. Only about half of the new American states included a bill of rights in their constitutions. The Articles of Confederation also omitted a bill of rights.

Constitutional Theory and the Need for a Bill of Rights

Constitutional theory no more supplied a reason for including one than did experience. Many of the Constitution's principal authors, including Madison and Hamilton, argued that a bill of rights would be at best superfluous and at worst dangerous. It would be superfluous because, in the words of James Bowdoin, "The Constitution itself is a bill of rights."[6] This was the classical understanding of constitutional government: the Constitution is a grant of enumerated powers from the sovereign people to the government, which depends for its authority upon popular consent. Powers not granted to the government remain with the people (a philosophy later made explicit in the Tenth Amendment). Thus the national government's only authority to interfere with individual liberty was delegated by the people in the Constitution. A bill of rights would be dangerous because, by restating the truism that powers not surrendered are retained by the people, it might create confusion about the source of governmental authority. As Hamilton explained in *Federalist* 84, "[B]ills of rights . . . are not only unnecessary . . . but would even be dangerous. They would contain various exceptions to powers which are not granted; and, on this very account, would afford a colorable pretext to claim more than were granted. For why declare that things shall not be done which there is not power to do?"

Like Hamilton, Madison worried that incompleteness might lead to the conclusion that government could properly abridge any liberties not included in a list of liberties. Moreover, no such list could hope to be complete—the passage of time would reveal the imperfect foresight of its authors. Madison also warned that bills of rights were based on a naive view of human nature. Writing to Thomas Jefferson, he argued that mere "parchment barriers" would not restrain a majority or government intent on subverting individual liberty. "[E]xperience proves the inefficacy of a bill of rights on those occasions when its controul is most needed," he wrote. "Repeated violations of those parchment barriers have been committed by overbearing majorities in every

---

[3] Carl J. Friedrich, *Transcendent Justice*. (Durham: Duke University Press, 1964), 16.

[4] Clinton Rossiter (ed.), *The Federalist Papers*. (New York: New American Library, 1961). See nos. 10, 45, 78, 80, and 89. References to *The Federalist Papers* are from this edition.

[5] The Australian Constitution has no bill of rights, nor did the Canadian until recently.

[6] Quoted in Philip B. Kurland and Ralph Lerner (eds.), *The Founder's Constitution*. (Chicago: University of Chicago Press, 1987), I: 426.

state."[7] Other delegates argued that a bill of rights might handicap the ability of the national government to act with energy in those areas where it was authorized to govern. The Framers sought to achieve two equally important goals: to limit government to protect liberty and property, and to create a central government strong enough to overcome the weakness and parochialism that had plagued the Union under the Articles of Confederation. A bill of rights, some feared, might leave the government so limited that it would be unable to secure the public good.

The unamended text of the Constitution does contain a few important limitations on majoritarian government, such as ones concerning habeas corpus or property rights, provisions not unlike the parchment barriers of a bill of rights. Even so, the Framers did not rely primarily on these for the protection of liberty. Madison's argument in *Federalist* 10 illustrates their approach to the problem. The chief threat to liberty in a democracy, argued Madison, was "faction," by which he meant "a number of citizens, whether amounting to a majority or minority of the whole, who are united and actuated by some common impulse of passion, or of interest, adverse to the rights of other citizens, or to the permanent and aggregate interests of the community." An inevitable consequence of democracy, faction could be controlled in two ways, either by "removing its cause" or "controlling its effects." Because the former would require denying people liberty to associate and pursue their ends, it represented a "remedy . . . worse than the disease." Therefore, Madison concluded, one must try to control the effects of faction.

The Founders' primary strategy for accomplishing this was the creation of a large, geographically diverse republic, since a large republic would encourage the development of a wide variety of local interests. "Extend the sphere," wrote Madison, "and you take in a greater variety of parties and interests; you make it less probable that a majority of the whole will have a common motive to invade the rights of other citizens; or if such a common motive exists, it will be more difficult for all who feel it to discover their own strength. . . ." In the face of such diversity, only very large and stable popular majorities could sustain themselves for long. Moreover, in a republic, the process of representation itself would help moderate factions. Representation would "refine and enlarge the public views, by passing them through the medium of a chosen body of citizens, whose wisdom may best discern the true interest of their country, and whose patriotism and love of justice will be least likely to sacrifice it to temporary or partial considerations."

Finally, the *Federalist* also shows that the Founders sought to protect liberty through proper constitutional design and institutional structure. As we saw in chapters 4 and 6, they hoped that separation of powers, checks and balances, and federalism would limit the ability of any one governmental institution to act capriciously. Any exercise of real power would require the cooperation of other branches, each primarily concerned with the preservation of its own autonomy and power. Any faction bent on threatening liberty would thus find it necessary to control not only the legislature or the presidency, but both.

Omission of a bill of rights quickly became one of the central issues in the debates over ratification. Many of the anti-Federalist opponents of the Constitution were classical republicans. They considered the chief purpose of good government to be the promotion and protection of virtue among its citizens. Their preference for small,

---

[7] Letter of James Madison to Thomas Jefferson, 17 October 1788. Reprinted in Michael Kammen (ed.), *The Origins of the American Constitution: A Documentary History.* (New York: Penguin Books, 1986), 367–71.

local communities and their corresponding fear of Madison's "enlarged republic" indicate that they desired the political liberty to govern themselves in those small communities, free from national interference. A bill of rights could further that goal. A guarantee of religious liberty, for example, might prevent the national government from establishing a religion to replace the establishments erected by the various states.[8]

Thomas Jefferson advanced what eventually became three of the strongest arguments in support of a bill of rights. First, sharing with the Federalists a dim view of human nature, he argued that "a bill of rights is what the people are entitled to against every government on earth . . . and what no just government should refuse, or rest on inference."[9] Parchment barriers might not restrain government, but the permanence gained through the written word might remind governors and governed alike of the limits on power and the value of liberty. Second, and relatedly, Jefferson and other anti-Federalists believed that a written bill of rights could be a vital tool in the education of citizens into the ways of constitutional democracy. Finally, Jefferson suggested to Madison that a bill of rights might put "a legal check . . . in the hands of the judiciary."[10] It is unclear whether Jefferson really thought a written bill of rights authorized judicial review,[11] but his observation proved remarkably accurate.

Such arguments persuaded ratification conventions in Virginia and New York, as well as in Massachusetts, South Carolina, and New Hampshire, to favor "conditional" ratification of the Constitution: ratification in return for the promise of amendments to protect individual liberties. Despite their opposition, both Madison and Hamilton eventually agreed to submit a bill of rights to the first Congress. Introducing the amendments to the House of Representatives on 8 June 1789, Madison said that, though he still thought them unnecessary, he had "always conceived, that in a certain form, and to a certain extent, such a provision was neither improper nor altogether useless."[12] Congressional debate consolidated and reduced Madison's proposals to twelve amendments, ten of which were ratified by 15 December 1791.[13]

Passage of the Bill of Rights did not quiet all controversy. The language of the amendments left open the question of whether they applied to the federal government only, or to the states as well.[14] Inherent in the question were two very different conceptions of liberty and community. Madison and others thought the Bill of Rights should apply to both levels of government because they believed the states were at

---

[8] See Leonard Levy, *The Establishment Clause: Religion and the First Amendment*. (New York: Macmillan Publishing Company, 1986), 75–77.

[9] Kammen, supra note 7, 376–78.

[10] Ibid.

[11] Recall our discussion in chapter 3 of Jefferson's departmentalist theory of constitutional review, which did not deny the possibility of judicial review but did subordinate it to the larger practice of constitutional review, carried out not only by the courts but by all three branches of the national government.

[12] Speech Placing the Proposed Bill of Rights before the House of Representatives, 8 June 1789.

[13] Massachusetts, Connecticut, and Georgia did not ratify the amendments until the sesquicentennial of the Constitution in 1939. The two proposals not ratified concerned congressional representation and a provision that would have prevented Congress from voting on congressional salary increases.

[14] As Michael W. McConnell has observed in a perceptive essay, "The natural inclination is to think that individual 'rights' must be protected against 'the state'—that is, against government in general. . . . Yet it is striking how many important rights in the Constitution . . . are protected by their terms against one level or branch of government and not against the others." "Contract Rights and Property Rights: A Case Study in the Relationship between Individual Liberties and Constitutional Structure," in Ellen Frankel Paul and Howard Dickman [eds.], *Liberty, Property, and the Foundations of the American Constitution*. (Albany: State University of New York, 1989), 141.

least as likely to abuse power and threaten liberty as the federal government. Most anti-Federalists, by contrast, feared encroachment by the national government and sought to protect states from its overbearing power. They believed the proximity of state and local governments to their citizens, coupled with political liberty, made local interference with individual rights unlikely. They therefore argued that the Bill of Rights applied only to the national government.[15]

The Supreme Court took up this question in *Barron v. Baltimore* (1833, reprinted later in the chapter). Baltimore had dredged a harbor, thus rendering Barron's wharf useless. Barron sued the city, claiming that its action constituted an unlawful taking of property in violation of the Fifth Amendment. In resolving the case, Chief Justice Marshall—arguing on the basis of constitutional theory and history—first distinguished between constitution-making at the state and national levels. Because the national government is one of enumerated powers, argued Marshall, it possesses only those powers explicitly granted and whatever is fairly implied by them. The Bill of Rights reflected the Founders' fears that the new government might try to exceed those powers. "The constitution," wrote Marshall, "was ordained and established by the people of the United States for themselves, for their own government, and not for the government of the individual states." Each state established a constitution for itself, and in that constitution, provided such "limitations and restrictions on the powers of its particular government, as its judgment dictated." Next, arguing from the constitutional text, Marshall conceded that parts of the original Constitution did profess to operate on the states directly, such as Article I, Section 10. But because the Bill of Rights, by contrast, did not include such language, Marshall argued that when the Framers sought to restrict the states, they said so explicitly. Because he could find no reason "for departing from this safe and judicious course, in framing the amendments," Marshall concluded that the Bill of Rights was meant to apply only to the national government.

Barron v. Baltimore is an important case, with lasting effects on the development of the Supreme Court's jurisprudence. It made clear that the liberties contained in the Bill of Rights did not protect citizens against actions taken by state governments. It protected certain freedoms against federal infringement, but any state could restrict those freedoms unless prohibited from doing so by its own state constitution.

The Reconstruction Amendments and the Bill of Rights

The persistence of slavery and the Civil War shattered the nation's confidence in the ability or willingness of state governments to protect the liberties of all citizens. In 1868, following the Civil War, Congress ratified the Thirteenth, Fourteenth, and Fifteenth Amendments to the Constitution (the Reconstruction Amendments). The Thirteenth prohibits slavery and involuntary servitude, and the Fifteenth ensures that the

---

[15] The same concerns influenced debate over the proposed language of the Tenth Amendment. Anti-Federalists wanted it to read, "The powers not *expressly* delegated to the United States . . . are reserved to the States respectively, or to the people." The Federalists succeeded in deleting the word "expressly." Thus drafted, the Amendment did not prohibit the general government from exercising implied powers, thought by many Federalists to be the natural reading of the necessary and proper clause of Article I and the cornerstone of a strong national government.

right of United States citizens to vote may not be abridged because of race or color.[16] The centerpiece of the Reconstruction Amendments, however, is the Fourteenth. A congressional response to the Supreme Court's decision in *Dred Scott v. Sandford* (1856) that the Fifth Amendment protected ownership of slaves because they were property, the Fourteenth Amendment in particular sought to correct *Dred Scott* in three ways. First, it made the freed slaves citizens and protected the "privileges and immunites of citizens of the United States" against infringement by the states; second, it protected due process of law against infringement by the states; and third, it prohibited states from depriving people of "the equal protection of the laws."[17]

But the Fourteenth Amendment did much more than simply correct *Dred Scott*, important though that was. The Reconstruction Amendments worked a fundamental transformation in the relationship between the federal government and the states in the field of civil liberties. The dominant view at the founding, cemented by *Barron*, was that the Bill of Rights applied only against the national government, leaving the states free to settle upon the terms of their own powers and limitations.[18] The Fourteenth Amendment reflects Madison's earlier fear that individual liberties might be restricted by the states as well as by the national government. Indeed, all three of the Reconstruction Amendments rested upon a different conception of which level of government, local or national, should take responsibility for protecting civil liberties. These amendments, and a series of civil rights acts in the 1860s and 1870s, were evidence of Congress' suspicion of the states and its belief that the federal government could more safely be entrusted with this task. This philosophy is perhaps best represented in Section 5 of the Fourteenth Amendment, which provides that "Congress shall have the power to enforce . . . the provisions of this article."

The Fourteenth Amendment and the Incorporation Doctrine

Inspired by the philosophy that animated the Reconstruction Amendments, some constitutional lawyers soon began to ask whether the Fourteenth Amendment should force reconsideration of *Barron*. Did the Fourteenth Amendment make the Bill of Rights applicable to the states? It is certainly possible to read at least part of the Amendment as doing just that: The privileges and immunities clause provides that "[n]o state shall make or enforce any law which shall abridge the privileges or immunities of citizens of the United States." The critical issue, of course, is the definition of "privileges and immunities." Is it a shorthand for the guarantees included in the first ten amendments?

The Supreme Court first considered this question in the *Slaughter-House Cases*

---

[16] Some scholars have argued that the Reconstruction Amendments, by embracing fully the concept of human equality, represent the full constitutionalization of the Declaration of Independence, which had been compromised by slavery at the founding. The Reconstruction Amendments are thus, in this view, an integral part of our efforts to become "a more perfect Union." See, for example, Edward J. Erler, *The American Polity*. (New York: Crane Russak, 1991), 4–8.

[17] Whereas the privileges and immunities clause speaks of the privileges and immunities of *citizens*, the due process and equal protection clauses apply, significantly, to *persons*.

[18] As Laurence Tribe notes, "The nineteenth century legal mind grasped the concept of federalism by visualizing two coextensive spheres, one defining the power of the federal government, the other that of states. . . . Historically, a large part of the states' sphere consisted in the power and duty to guard the rights and privileges of the citizen. . . .'" *American Constitutional Law*. 2d ed. (Mineola, New York: Foundation Press, 1988), 552.

(1873, reprinted later in the chapter). At issue was whether a monopoly in New Orleans on the butchering of livestock violated the rights of butchers employed elsewhere. The butchers argued that the monopoly, created by the state legislature, violated their right to pursue a legal occupation, supposedly protected by the privileges and immunities clause of the Fourteenth Amendment. The Court's resolution of this issue is a magnificent example of how constitutional interpretation is intertwined with the three normative themes we identified in the introduction: the conflict between federal and state power; the conflict between representative democracy (political majoritarianism) and constitutionalism (limits on majorities); and the conflict between the individual and the community. *Slaughter-House* involved all three of these tensions.

Writing for the Court, Justice Miller held that the Fourteenth Amendment recognized two types of citizenship: citizenship of one's own state, and citizenship of the United States. By creating citizenship of the United States and granting it to newly-freed slaves, and by forbidding states to deny citizens the privileges and immunities of United States citizenship, the Fourteenth Amendment had overturned *Dred Scott*. But, Miller continued, the privileges and immunities of federal citizenship—citizenship of the United States—are not identical to those of state citizenship. Each citizenship protects a set of privileges and immunities peculiar to itself. The Framers of the amendment did not intend it to interfere with the privileges and immunities of state citizenship, but only to protect the privileges and immunities of national citizenship against hostile state action.[19] Because the right to pursue an occupation was a privilege of state and not federal citizenship, Miller concluded, states could regulate it as they wished.

Plainly evident in Miller's clever (if less than obvious) interpretation is a vision of states, and their responsibility for civil liberties, at odds with the vision reflected in the Fourteenth Amendment. In Miller's view, the amendment was not intended to alter the states' role as primary custodians of individual liberty, possessing considerable autonomy to regulate the affairs of their own citizens. Others disagreed. Justice Swayne, in dissent, conceded that the interpretation Miller refused to embrace would be revolutionary in its impact on the relationship between the states and the federal government. But, he wrote, "Fairly construed these amendments may be said to rise to the dignity of a new Magna Charta." Moreover, Justice Field argued that if the majority's interpretation was correct—if the Fourteenth Amendment merely restated the relationship between state and federal responsibility for protecting civil liberties that existed before the Civil War—then the amendment "was a vain and idle enactment, which accomplished nothing, and most unnecessarily excited Congress and the people on its passage." An amendment so unremarkable in theory and benign in effect would have been unlikely to create such controversy in Congress.

Slaughter-House put to rest the possibility that the privileges and immunities clause might serve as the basis for applying the Bill of Rights to the states. Yet in less than thirty years the spirit of the *Slaughter-House* dissents became law, and today most of the first ten amendments do apply against the states. How did this happen? The "doctrine of incorporation" allowed the federal courts to apply most of the provisions of the Bill of Rights to the states by reading (or "incorporating") those protections into the due process clause of the Fourteenth Amendment, and not through the privileges and immunities clause. Even though it does not say so, courts now inter-

---

[19] One might note in response that these were already protected through the Supremacy Clause of Article VI.

pret the Fourteenth Amendment to mean ". . . Nor shall any state deprive any person of life, liberty, and property, without due process of law, as defined by the first eight amendments to the Constitution." Linguistically, and perhaps conceptually, the process of incorporation is awkward and untidy, an unfortunate consequence of *Slaughter-House*. Nevertheless, its effect on the relationship between the states and the federal government, and on the power of the federal judiciary, has been dramatic.

The Court's deliberations reveal four basic approaches to the incorporation doctrine. Implicit in each is a particular vision of the relationship between liberty and community, as well as of the relationship between the states and the federal government. Likewise, each rests upon a particular understanding of the limits of judicial power in a constitutional democracy.

The Fundamental Fairness Doctrine

Most of the early cases involving incorporation dealt with the First Amendment. In *Hurtado v. California* (1884), the Court rejected the claim that the due process clause incorporated the Fifth Amendment.[20] Nevertheless, the Court did concede that the due process clause was a general guarantee of fairness, prohibiting the states from interfering with "fundamental principles of liberty and justice." The Court built on this interpretation in *Holden v. Hardy* (1898) by concluding that the due process clause, though not incorporating the entire Bill of Rights, protects "traditional notions" of due process and fundamental fairness. In *Twining v. New Jersey* (1908), the Court refused to incorporate the Fifth Amendment's protection against self-incrimination, but it admitted,

> It is possible that some of the personal rights safeguarded by the first eight Amendments against National action may also be safeguarded against state action, because a denial of them would be a denial of due process of law. If this is so, it is not because these rights are enumerated in the first eight Amendments, but because they are of such a nature that they are included in the conception of due process of law.

Finally, in *Gitlow v. New York* (1925), the Court followed through on its earlier suggestions by ruling that the due process clause did incorporate the First Amendment's guarantee of freedom of speech.

By the 1930s the case law concerning the incorporation of the Bill of Rights was confused. The Court confronted the mess in *Palko v. Connecticut* (1937, reprinted later in the chapter), when it ruled that the Fourteenth Amendment did not make the double jeopardy clause applicable to the states. Palko argued that "[w]hatever would be a violation of the original bill of rights . . . if done by the federal government is . . . equally unlawful by the force of the Fourteenth Amendment if done by a state." Although the Court rejected the argument, Justice Cardozo conceded that some provisions of the Bill of Rights had been made applicable to the states. Was there some principled way of distinguishing between those cases in which the Court had applied a part of the Bill of Rights to the states and those in which it had refused to do so? "The line of division may seem to be wavering and broken," wrote Cardozo, but "reflection and analysis" disclosed a "rationalizing principle." The due process clause

[20] The Court eventually reversed this judgment. It incorporated free speech in *Gitlow v. New York* (1925); freedom of the press in *Near v. Minnesota* (1931); free exercise of religion in *Hamilton v. Regents* (1934); and no establishment in *Everson v. Ewing Township* (1947).

incorporates those parts of the Bill of Rights "so rooted in the traditions and conscience of our people as to be ranked fundamental" or which are "the very essence of a scheme of ordered liberty." Double jeopardy was not one of those provisions.[21]

In sum, the fundamental fairness doctrine, restated in *Palko*, insisted the due process clause did not incorporate the entire Bill of Rights, but only those parts of it essential to ordered liberty. The due process clause might include guarantees similar to those of the first eight amendments, but it certainly did not include every provision. In some ways, then, the fundamental fairness doctrine yields a due process clause that is both less expansive than the Bill of Rights (since some of those rights may not be protected) and more expansive (since fairness may require protections not explicitly included in the first eight amendments). As Justice Harlan, dissenting in *Duncan v. Louisiana* (1968, reprinted later in the chapter), said, "[T]he first section of the Fourteenth Amendment was meant neither to incorporate, nor to be limited to, the specific guarantees of the first eight Amendments. . . ." Instead it "requires that those procedures be fundamentally fair in all respects." To require more than that would be to put a "straitjacket" on the states and their administration of civil and criminal law.[22] As we shall see when we consider the death penalty cases, this concern for federalism and the limits of judicial power—which we also saw in *Slaughter-House* and *Hurtado*—continues to influence the Court.

Total Incorporation

One might argue that the due process clause makes every provision of the Bill of Rights applicable to the states. The foremost proponent of this view, called total incorporation, was Justice Hugo Black. Black insisted—probably mistakenly—that original intent required this position.[23] But his attraction to total incorporation also rested on a particular understanding of the limits of judicial power in a constitutional democracy. Any alternative approach, he argued, gave judges unwarranted and unprincipled discretion in deciding which, if any, of the Bill of Rights applied to the states. In *Duncan*, Black responded forcefully to Harlan's support for the fundamental fairness doctrine:

> *Thus [in Harlan's approach] the Due Process Clause is treated as prescribing no specific and clearly ascertainable constitutional command that judges must obey in interpreting the Constitution, but rather as leaving judges free to decide at any particular time whether a particular rule or judicial formulation embodies an "immutable principle of free government" or is "implicit in the concept of ordered liberty," or whether certain conduct "shocks the judge's conscience" or runs counter to some other similar, undefined and undefinable standard. . . . It is impossible for me to believe that such unconfined power is given to judges in our Constitution that is a written one in order to limit governmental power.*

Black routinely chastised Harlan for this position, claiming that its inherent subjectivity—where did Harlan find these additional restraints upon state governments, since

---

[21] The Court's refusal to apply the double jeopardy clause to the states reflected its treatment of the criminal procedure provisions of the Bill of Rights more generally. These were not incorporated until after 1961, when the Court found "essential" the search and seizure clauses of the Fourth Amendment in *Mapp v. Ohio* (1961).

[22] See also Harlan's concurrence in *Ker v. California* (1963).

[23] See his dissent in *Adamson v. California* (1947). For evidence that Black was probably wrong about the intent of those who wrote the Fourteenth Amendment, see, for example, Charles Fairman, *Does the Fourteenth Amendment Incorporate the Bill of Rights? The Original Understanding*, 2 Stanford Law Review 5 (1949).

the text itself was silent on the matter?—gave extraordinary and unaccountable power to nonelected judges. It allowed them, once freed from the specific restraints in the Bill of Rights, to remake the states in whatever image they chose.

Justice Harlan argued in response that total incorporation was at best an illusory restraint on judicial power, since most of the so-called specific restraints on interpretation found in the Bill of Rights were every bit as vague as due process and therefore could not effectively limit judicial discretion. Justice Felix Frankfurter also reacted to Black's argument that fundamental fairness left judges free to depart from the text:

> *Judicial review . . . inescapably imposes on this Court an exercise of judgment upon the whole course of the proceedings in order to ascertain whether they offend those canons of decency and fairness which express the notions of justice of English-speaking people. . . . These standards of justice are not authoritatively formulated anywhere as though they were prescriptions in a pharmacopeia. But neither does the application of the Due Process Clause imply that judges are wholly at large. The judicial judgment in applying the [clause] must move within accepted notions of justice and is not to be based upon the idiosyncracies of a merely personal judgment.*

Frankfurter also complained in *Adamson v. California* (1947, reprinted later in the chapter) that "[a] construction which gives to due process no independent function but turns it into a summary of the specific provisions of the Bill of Rights [would] deprive the States of opportunity for reforms in legal process designed for extending the area of freedom." Black responded simply, "I am not bothered by the argument [about federalism]. . . . I have never believed that under the guise of federalism the States should be able to experiment with the protections afforded our citizens through the Bill of Rights. . . ."

Total Incorporation "Plus"

Favored by Justices Douglas and Murphy, total incorporation plus holds that the due process clause fully incorporates the Bill of Rights as well as other nonexplicit and evolving rights. Dissenting in *Poe v. Ullman* (1961), Douglas wrote, "Though I believe that "due process" as used in the Fourteenth Amendment includes all of the first eight Amendments, I do not think it is restricted and confined to them." This approach shares with total incorporation the view that the due process clause is a shorthand for the first eight amendments, but it goes substantially beyond it. Some justices, especially Black, thought that Douglas' willingness to include nonexplicit, implied rights reopened the possibility of unprincipled judicial subjectivity and therefore offered no improvement over the fundamental fairness approach. With that in mind, compare Douglas' position quoted above to Harlan's dissent in the same case: "[I]t is not the particular enumeration of rights in the first eight Amendments which spells out the reach of . . . due process, but rather . . . those concepts which are considered to embrace those rights which are fundamental; which belong to the citizens of all free governments. . . ."

Selective Incorporation

A majority of the justices who have considered the issue have ruled that the due process clause incorporates some but not all of the Bill of Rights. The doctrine of selective incorporation resembles the fundamental fairness doctrine in its willingness to distinguish what is essential to due process from what is not. Both doctrines protect under the due process clause only those rights that are "fundamental to ordered liberty." There is, however, one important difference between the positions. Whereas judges following the fundamental fairness approach would incorporate only the particular part of a constitutional guarantee involved in the specific case at hand, proponents of selective incorporation look less to the particulars of the case and instead determine whether the guarantee as a whole should apply to the states.

The doctrine of selective incorporation eventually resulted in the piecemeal incorporation of nearly every provision of the Bill of Rights—in part because Justice Black, unable to win a majority for total incorporation, was willing to support selective incorporation as the next best alternative. Dissenting in *Adamson*, Black wrote that "if the choice must be between the selective process of the *Palko* decision applying some of the Bill of Rights to the States, or the *Twining* rule applying none of them, I would choose the *Palko* selective process. . . ." Thus the position favored by Justice Black has become law in fact, if not in theory.

Black's criticism of selective incorporation was mild compared to that of Justice Harlan, who called it "an uneasy and illogical compromise among the views of various justices on how the Due Process Clause should be interpreted." In the same opinion in *Duncan*, Harlan criticized selective incorporation for equating "fundamental" with "old, much praised, and found in the Bill of Rights." Finally, reflecting the concern for federalism he had expressed in earlier cases, Harlan wrote that "neither history, nor sense, supports using the Fourteenth Amendment to put the states in a constitutional straitjacket with respect to their own development in the administration of criminal or civil law."[24]

The incorporation doctrine dramatically transformed American constitutional law and "altered fundamentally the nature of the federal system."[25] Implicit in each of the approaches to incorporation is a particular vision of the relationship between liberty and community. Proponents of full incorporation argue for the dominance of national standards and the need for uniformity in local communities. Justices who favor the fundamental fairness approach or selective incorporation are willing to sacrifice some degree of national uniformity for greater flexibility within local communities. These are still live questions, as the Court's continuing struggle with the jot-for-jot theory indicates.[26]

The debate over incorporation thus involved competing understandings of constitutional interpretation, the role of the states in a federal system, and the proper role of judges in a constitutional democracy. It also illustrates how questions concerning individual liberties are also questions about federalism and the limits of judicial power. This helps to explain the conviction with which different justices held their views on the meaning and proper interpretation of the due process clause. Much of

[24] We shall see in chapter 11 that selective incorporation is intricately related to the concept of fundamental rights. The fundamental rights doctrine, following *Palko*, holds that there are two classes of constitutional liberties. Some liberties are fundamental because "they are the very essence of a scheme of ordered liberty." Some liberties, however, are not essential and hence not fundamental. A state may use its police powers to interfere with fundamental rights only when it has a "compelling reason" to do so (see, for example, *San Antonio v. Rodriguez* [1973]). A state may regulate nonfundamental rights so long as its action is rational, rather than compelling.

[25] Richard C. Cortner, *The Supreme Court and the Second Bill of Rights: The Fourteenth Amendment and the Nationalization of the Bill of Rights.* (Madison: University of Wisconsin Press, 1981), 291.

[26] In 1985, Attorney General Edwin Meese publicly criticized the incorporation doctrine, calling its intellectual foundation "shaky" and complaining that the doctrine had damaged the states as independent constitutional actors. For a criticism of Meese's speech, see Michael Kent Curtis, *No State Shall Abridge: The Fourteenth Amendment and the Bill of Rights.* (Durham, NC: Duke University Press, 1986).

the rhetoric surrounding incorporation occurred not in dissents, but in concurring opinions. Often judicial disagreement over the proper method of interpretation had no effect on the outcome of the case. At stake were federal-state relations and the power of the federal judiciary to oversee those relations, issues that transcended specific results in specific cases.

Continuing Incorporation Problems

The process of selective incorporation resulted in the application to the states of nearly every provision of the Bill of Rights (see table 9.1). There remains some question, however, about whether any particular guarantee applies with equal force or in precisely the same way against the states and the national government. That they might mean somewhat different things was a logical, if not inevitable, result of the fundamental fairness approach. A determination that fairness requires the incorporation of a provision of the Bill of Rights would not necessarily mean that it also re-

TABLE 9.1 *I. Selected Supreme Court Decisions on Selective Incorporation*

Constitutional Provision	Case
First Amendment	
Speech & Press	Gitlow v. New York (1925)
Free Exercise	Cantwell v. Connecticut (1940)
Establishment	Everson v. Board of Education (1947)
Fourth Amendment	
Search & Seizure	Wolf v. Colorado (1949)
Exclusionary Rule	Mapp v. Ohio (1961)
Fifth Amendment	
Self-incrimination	Malloy v. Hogan (1964)
Double jeopardy	Benton v. Maryland (1969)
Sixth Amendment	
Public trial	In re Oliver (1948)
Right to counsel (felony)	Gideon v. Wainwright (1963)
Right to counsel (misdemeanor w/jail)	Argersinger v. Hamlin (1972)
Speedy trial	Klopfer v. North Carolina (1967)
Jury trial	Duncan v. Louisiana (1968)
Eighth Amendment	
Cruel & unusual punishment	Louisiana v. Resweber (1947)
Ninth Amendment	
Implied Rights	
Privacy	Griswold v. Connecticut (1965)

II. Unincorporated Provisions of the Bill of Rights

Second Amendment	
right to keep and bear arms	
Third Amendment	
no quartering of soldiers	
Fifth Amendment	
right to a grand jury hearing	
Seventh Amendment	
right to trial by jury in civil cases	
Eighth Amendment	
right to be free of excessive fines	

quires the application of the entire set of requirements that the Court has determined are applicable to the national government under that provision.

In *Mapp v. Ohio* (1961) a majority of the Court seemed to insist that incorporation of a right did include the full range of requirements that had been developed under the provision. More recent cases, however, suggest that the issue is not fully settled.[27] Writing in a long concurrence in *Williams v. Florida* (1970), Harlan complained that, because judges recognized the states' need for a little "elbow room," the "jot-for-jot" theory of incorporation had led to the diminution of federal rights. "These decisions," he wrote, "demonstrate that the difference between a [*Palko*] 'due process' approach [and] 'selective incorporation' is not an abstract [one]. The 'backlash' in [this case] exposes the malaise, for [here] the Court dilutes a federal guarantee in order to reconcile the logic of 'incorporation,' the jot-for-jot and case-for-case application of the federal right to the States, with the reality of federalism."

As *Mapp* and *Williams* intimate, much of the Court's long discussion about incorporation occurred in the context of whether the criminal procedure provisions of the Bill of Rights should apply to the states. Traditionally, the states had possessed nearly complete autonomy in the areas of criminal law and procedure. The effects of incorporation would be most apparent in these cases. Consequently, they provided the occasion for an extended series of judicial discussions about the merits of incorporation. These decisions are important also because they often involve the Court's initial efforts to give the provisions in question an expansive interpretation. But they factor just as importantly in those cases where the Court has sought to restrict their reach, as we shall see when we examine the Court's longstanding and complex jurisprudence surrounding cruel and unusual punishment.

The Bill of Rights and Capital Punishment

Justice Stewart, concurring in *Furman v. Georgia* (1972), observed "The penalty of death differs from all other forms of criminal punishment, not in degree but in kind. . . . [I]t is unique . . . in its absolute renunciation of all that is embodied in our concept of humanity." A majority of the Court—and apparently a majority of American citizens—has never agreed, however, that the death penalty is by definition cruel and unusual. Nevertheless, Justice Stewart was unquestionably correct when he suggested death is different: In a constitutional democracy, committed to the dignity of the human person, a decision to sentence a person to death implicates moral values and constitutional principles of the highest order.

The United States Supreme Court has not always seemed to recognize the enormity of capital punishment. In *Louisiana v. Resweber* (1947), for example, the Court agreed that the ban against cruel and unusual punishments applied to the states. Nevertheless, it ruled that a young African-American man was not subjected to cruel and unusual punishment when he was made to face the electric chair a second time because it had malfunctioned the first time. The majority wrote

> *The fact that an unforeseeable accident prevented the prompt consummation of the sentence cannot, it seems to us, add an element of cruelty to a subsequent execution. . . . The situation of the unfortunate victim of this accident is just as*

---

[27] See, for instance, *Williams v. Florida* (1970, holding that the Sixth Amendment's requirement of trial by jury did not mandate a twelve-person jury) and *Apodaca v. Oregon* (1972, holding that the Sixth Amendment did not require unanimous jury verdicts in state courts).

though he had suffered the identical amount of mental anguish and physical pain in any other occurrence, such as, for example, a fire in the cell block. . . .

Justice Burton, dissenting, argued that "Although the failure of the first attempt, in the present case, was unintended, the reapplication of the electric current will be intentional. How many deliberate and intentional reapplications of electric current does it take to produce a cruel, unusual and unconstitutional punishment?"

If there is one distinguishing feature of the Court's death penalty jurisprudence, it is the persistence and intensity of disagreement over its constitutionality. If *Resweber* foreshadowed that controversy, the Supreme Court's decision in *Furman v. Georgia* (1972) cemented it. A sharply divided Court concluded that Georgia's death penalty violated the Eighth Amendment, but could not agree why. Justice Stewart was not the only justice to write separately in *Furman. Every* member of the Court issued an opinion. Only Justices Brennan and Marshall directly addressed the question on the merits, concluding that the death penalty must always be unconstitutional. Three other justices (Douglas, White, and Stewart) did not go so far, ruling instead that the statute in question was unconstitutional because it gave the jury too great a discretion to impose or to withhold the penalty, thus making its imposition capricious. Four other justices dissented, leaving Chief Justice Burger to conclude, "Since there is no majority of the Court . . . the future of capital punishment in this country has been left in limbo. . . . If today's opinions demonstrate nothing else, they starkly show that this is an area where legislatures can act far more effectively than courts."

Following *Furman*, well over 30 states adopted new death penalty laws, and every new decision evokes a similar flurry of activity in the states. States that maintained or reinstituted the penalty argued that it serves several important purposes, including those of deterrence and retribution. Advocates also argue that capital punishment can be an appropriate "expression of society's moral outrage at particularly offensive conduct." (Justice Stewart in *Gregg v. Georgia* [1976, reprinted later in the chapter.])

The *Furman* Court's insistence upon changes in the administration of the death penalty, coupled with its inability to agree upon the reasons why Georgia's system amounted to cruel and unusual punishment, initiated an ongoing dialogue among federal courts and state legislatures about when the death penalty can pass constitutional muster. That dialogue has lasted some thirty years, and shows no sign of ending. For the most part, these new statutes attempted to constrain the jury's decision to impose death by imposing new procedural guidelines, such as bifurcated proceedings—one to determine guilt, and a second for sentencing.

The Court considered some of these in the leading case of *Gregg v. Georgia*. Once again, the Court could not find a majority voice. Writing for a plurality, Justice Stewart wrote, "We now hold that the punishment of death does not invariably violate the Constitution. . . . And a heavy burden rests on those who would attack the judgment of the representatives of the people." Even so, the Court did presume to cabin the death penalty with a number of important restrictions, because "the death penalty must [comport] with the basic concept of human dignity at the core of the [Eighth] Amendment." Mandatory death penalty schemes, the plurality concluded, are by definition unconstitutional—the sentencing authority, judge or jury, must have the option to reject death. Similarly, the plurality noted that the sentencing authority must be "given adequate information and guidance. As a general proposition these concerns are best met by a bifurcated proceeding. . . ." In an impassioned dissent, Justice Brennan challenged the plurality's insistence upon deference to the political process, writing that ". . . This Court inescapably has the duty, as the ultimate arbiter of the meaning of the Constitution, to say whether . . . 'moral concepts' require us to hold" that the death penalty is cruel and unusual. "I emphasize only that foremost among the 'moral concepts' recognized in our cases and inherent in the Clause is . . . that the State . . . must treat its citizens in a manner consistent with their intrinsic worth as human beings. . . ."

Since *Gregg*, the Court and the states have continued to tinker with the administration of the death penalty, but the Court has steadfastly refused to revisit the fundamental question of whether the death penalty, *per se*, violates the Eighth Amendment.[28] The Court has, however, placed several additional limitations on the practice. So, for example, in *Coker v. Georgia* (1977), the Court invalidated the death penalty for the crime of rape, and in *Enmund v. Florida* (1982), it ruled that capital punishment could not be imposed on an individual who had driven a getaway car, but had not actually participated in a murder that took place as part of the same crime. In *Pulley v. Harris* (1984), the Court rejected a claim that the Eighth Amendment requires state appellate courts to conduct reviews of death penalty cases to ensure "proportionality" in sentencing. The Court has ruled also that the penalty may not be imposed upon defendants younger than 15 at the time of their crime, *Thompson v. Oklahoma* (1988), but that it can be imposed upon defendants who had committed crimes when they were sixteen and seventeen. *Stanford v. Kentucky* (1989). However, the state may not execute any person found to be mentally retarded. *Atkins v. Virginia* (2002, reprinted later in the chapter).

Who Gets the Death Penalty?

As long ago as *Furman* (1972), some justices had complained that the imposition of the death penalty was racially biased. "It would seem to be incontestable," Justice Douglas wrote, "that the death penalty inflicted on one defendant is 'unusual' if it discriminates against him by reason of his race, religion, wealth, social position, or class, or if it is imposed under a procedure that gives room for the play of such prejudices." Justice Douglas knew all too well, though, that the long history of the death penalty in the United States was at least partly a sorrowful history of racial discrimination. Under Jim Crow, some states had made a rape committed by a white man punishable by a prison term; the same crime, committed by a black man against a white woman, was punishable by death.

A quick look at the demographics of death row might lead one to conclude that racial discrimination continues to haunt the death penalty. In 2002, there were just over 300 persons on death row in the United States, nearly a third of them in Texas, California, and Florida.[29] Over 98 percent are male, 56 percent are white, 35 percent are black, 7 percent are Hispanic, and 2 percent are of other racial backgrounds.[30]

In *McCleskey v. Kemp* (1987, reprinted later in the chapter), the Court considered a claim of racial discrimination by Warren McCleskey—an African-American sentenced to death for killing a policeman during an armed robbery. McCleskey's attorneys presented statistical studies that African-Americans who murdered white victims

---

[28] In April 2002, U.S. District Court Judge Jed S. Rakoff did conclude that the Federal Death Penalty Act is unconstitutional because the death penalty violates the cruel and unusual punishments clause. The judge concluded that the "fully foreseeable" risk that enforcement of the death penalty will result in the execution of "a meaningful number of innocent people" violates "substantive due process."

[29] Twelve states do not have the death penalty. They are: Alaska, Hawaii, Iowa, Maine, Massachusetts, Michigan, Minnesota, North Dakota, Rhode Island, Vermont, West Virginia, and Wisconsin. There is also no death penalty in the District of Columbia.

[30] Death Penalty Information Center. http://www.deathpenaltyinfo.org

were substantially more likely to receive the death penalty than whites who murdered blacks. In his opinion for the Court, though, Justice Powell concluded that "At most . . . ," the evidence presented "indicates a discrepancy that appears to correlate with race. Apparent disparities in sentencing are an inevitable part of our criminal justice system. . . ." And, echoing recurrent fears about the limits of judicial power, Powell noted, "McCleskey's arguments are best presented to the legislative bodies. It is not the responsibility—or indeed even the right—of this Court to determine the appropriate punishment for particular crimes. . . ." In response, Justice Brennan wrote "to reject McCleskey's powerful evidence on this basis is to ignore the qualitatively different character of the death penalty and the particular repugnance of racial discrimination. . . ."

Continuing Death Penalty Issues: Does Innocence Matter?

In *Herrera v. Collins* (1993), the Court ruled that a prisoner's claim of "actual innocence," standing alone, is not a sufficient ground for habeas corpus relief because federal courts "sit to correct constitutional violations, not factual errors."[31]

Suppose we know that some persons, innocent of the crimes for which they are convicted, will be put to death. Should the failure of any system of capital punishment to execute only the guilty matter constitutionally? In January 2003, just days before his term was to end, Illinois Governor George Ryan commuted the sentences of all 167 death row inmates in the state's prisons. Ryan noted that nearly half of the state's 300 capital cases had been reversed for new trials or resentencing, and that thirty-three defendants had been represented by attorneys who were later suspended or disbarred. And whatever the Court had concluded in *Kemp*, Governor Ryan was disturbed to learn that more than two-thirds of the inmates on death row were African Americans. Perhaps most troubling, the Governor concluded that "there is not a doubt in my mind that the number of innocent men freed from our Death Row stands at 17. . . . That is an absolute embarrassment [and] nothing short of a catastrophic failure." The governor concluded, "Our capital system is haunted by the demon of error. . . . [Some] will say that I am usurping the decisions of judges and juries and state legislators. . . . Even if the exercise of my power becomes my burden I will bear it. Our Constitution compels it."

Summary

Governor Ryan's impassioned speech—and the outraged response it drew in some quarters—illustrates the depth of feeling and emotion that continue to surround the debate over the death penalty in the United States. The Court is not immune from that passion. In *Callins v. Collins* (1994), the Supreme Court denied a petition for certiorari by Bruce Edward Callins, sentenced to death by a Texas jury. Callins had shot a man in the neck during a robbery; the victim soon bled to death. Callins ultimately appealed, claiming ineffective assistance of counsel.[32]

---

[31] But see *United States v. Quinones*, (U.S.D.C, SDNY, 2002), where District Judge Rakoff concluded that *Herrera* is limited because Herrera's proffer of actual innocence was not truly persuasive.

[32] In *Wiggins v. Smith* (26 June 2003), the Court reversed the sentence of Maryland death row inmate Kevin Wiggins on the basis of inadequate representation by his original trial attorneys. Standard procedure in Maryland at the time of the trial included preparation of a "social history" report that would contain mitigation investigations regarding the case. In this case, however, the report was not prepared or even requested. Justice O'Connor, writing for the court, remarked that "[a]ny reasonably competent attorney

The Court voted 8 to 1—Justice Blackmun dissenting—to deny the petition. In his opinion, an emotional Justice Blackmun stated,

> *from this day forward, I no longer shall tinker with the machinery of death. . . . Rather than continue to coddle the Court's delusion that the desired level of fairness has been achieved and the need for regulation eviscerated, I feel morally and intellectually obligated simply to concede that the death penalty experiment has failed. . . . The basic question—does the system accurately and consistently determine which defendants 'deserve' to die?—cannot be answered in the affirmative. . . . The path the Court has chosen lessens us all. I dissent.*

Blackmun's poignant dissent provoked an equally impassioned response by Justice Scalia. He noted that Justice Blackmun's opinion "often refers to 'intellectual, moral and personal' perceptions, but never to the text and tradition of the Constitution. It is the latter rather than former that ought to control. . . . Convictions in opposition to the death penalty are often passionate and deeply held. That would be no excuse for reading them into a Constitution that does not contain them. . . ."

As the heated discussion between Justice Scalia and Blackmun should make clear, disagreement over the constitutionality of the death penalty is also a dispute about the requirements of human dignity, and about purposes and limits of judicial power. Indeed, it is a dispute about the nature and meaning of the Constitution itself.

Comparative Perspectives

The first thing to note about the death penalty in comparative perspective is that most constitutional democracies have abolished it. By law or by practice, approximately 100 countries prohibit capital punishment. There is no death penalty, for example, in Canada, France, Germany, Ireland, Italy, Kenya, South Africa, and Sweden. On the other hand, Afghanistan, China, Iran, the Republic of Congo, Cuba, Egypt, India, Japan, Jordan, North and South Korea, Libya, Syria, Taiwan, and the United States do have the death penalty. In 2001, 90 percent of all reported executions occurred in China, Iran, Saudi Arabia and the USA.[33] The United States is one of only approximately six countries that authorize the death penalty for offenders under the age of 18.[34] As one critic has noted, "the countries that most vigorously employ the death penalty are generally ones that the United States has the least in common with politically, economically, or socially . . . , as they are the least democratic and the worst human rights abusers in the world."[35]

Suppose America's prolific use of the death penalty is a case of American "excep-

---

would have realized that pursuing such leads was necessary to making an informed choice among possible defenses, particularly given the apparent absence of aggravating factors from Wiggins' background." The Court concluded that the "performance of Wiggins' attorneys at sentencing violated his Sixth Amendment right to effective assistance of counsel."

[33] http://www.web.amnesty.org/rmp/dplibrary.nsf/index?openview

[34] The other countries are Iran, Nigeria, Pakistan, Saudi Arabia, and Yemen.

[35] Carol S. Steiker, *Capital Punishment and American Exceptionalism*, 81 Oregon Law Review 97 (2002). Professor Steiker's pioneering work seeks to answer an important question: What accounts for this gross discrepancy in the use of capital punishment between the United States and the rest of the countries we consider to be our "peers" in so many other respects? Steiker's nuanced analysis suggests there are a number of reasons—but one was the Court's decision in *Furman* to regulate, rather than to abolish capital punishment. This "choice helped to legitimize and stabilize the practice of capital punishment in the United States." Moreover, the decision "created an impediment to American acceptance of capital punishment as a violation of international human rights law. . . ."

tionalism," as some scholars have argued. Should the practices of other countries matter to constitutional analysis in the United States? Consider Justice Scalia's remarks in his opinion for the plurality in *Stanford v. Kentucky* (1989), where he wrote "We emphasize that it is *American* conceptions of decency that are dispositive, rejecting the contention . . . that the sentencing practices of other countries are relevant." In dissent, Justice Brennan disagreed, writing "Our cases recognize that objective indicators of contemporary standards of decency in the form of legislation in other countries is also of relevance. . . . Within the world community, the imposition of the death penalty for juvenile crimes appears to be overwhelmingly disapproved." Perhaps because the difference between the United States and other constitutional democracies is so stark, dispute about the relevance of comparative constitutional practices has become a staple in American death penalty jurisprudence, figuring prominently, for example, in the Court's opinion in *Atkins v. Virginia* (2002, reprinted later in the chapter.) Thus, Justice Scalia, dissenting, argued that "[I]rrelevant are the practices of the 'world community'. . . . We must never forget that it is a Constitution for the United States of America that we are expounding. . . ."

This kind of debate over the appropriateness of constitutional borrowing (see chapter 2), is especially interesting in light of the Eighth Amendment's reference to "unusual" in the "cruel and unusual punishments" clause. It also takes on added significance in light of the increasing globalization of liberal democratic institutions, a phenomenon we discussed in chapter 2.

The Death Penalty and Judicial Power

In some countries, the death penalty is prohibited clearly and explicitly in the constitutional text.[36] In other countries, the prohibition is a function of judicial decision. Two of the most important decisions are by the constitutional courts of South Africa and Hungary. The decision by the Hungarian Constitutional Court is perhaps the clearest example of how issues of judicial power are wrapped up in the death penalty: The Court's decision—striking down the death penalty—was its very first. Perhaps more surprising, the decision did not follow a lower court decision sentencing an offender to death. Instead, the Court acted upon a complaint filed by a law professor, who had argued that the penalty violated Article 54(1) of the Constitution. That article provides that "everyone has the inherent right to life and human dignity. . . . And no one shall be subject to torture or to cruel and inhumane or degrading treatment or punishment. . . . " No other provision mentioned the death penalty. One commentator has suggested that the decision can be explained as a condition for Hungary's entry into the European Union.[37]

The South African Constitution, like the Hungarian, does not mention the death penalty. In *State v. Makwanyane* (1995), the Constitutional Court noted that the silence of the South African constitution was "not accidental," but instead reflected a "Solomonic" decision by the founders to leave the decision to the court. Relevant provisions of the Constitution included Article 9, which provides that every person

---

[36] "Out of the 69 countries in the world which have to date abolished the death penalty for all crimes, at least 38 have prohibited it in their constitutions, often on human rights grounds. The latest to do so is Luxembourg, which amended its constitution in April 1999 to prohibit the death penalty. Nine other countries have constitutional provisions which limit the crimes for which the death penalty can be imposed." http://www.web.amnesty.org/rmp/dplibrary.nsf/index?openview

[37] George P. Fletcher, *Searching for the Rule of Law in the Wake of Communism,* 1992 Brigham Young University Law Review 145, 159.

has the right to life; Article 10, which provides that everyone has the right to dignity; and Article 11(2), which prohibits "cruel, unhuman, or degrading treatment or punishment."

In accordance with its Constitution, which instructs the Court "to consider international law" and permits it to consider foreign law (see our discussion of "borrowing" in chapter 2), the Court began its opinion with a detailed discussion of the death penalty in the United States, as well as decisions by the European Court of Human Rights, the Constitutional Court of Hungary, and several other countries, including India and Japan. It noted, too, that comparable bills of rights would have especial importance until South Africa developed its own indigenous jurisprudence. Nevertheless, the Court also made clear that comparative materials, while instructional, do not necessarily provide definitive answers to questions about the interpretation of the South African Bill of Rights. A sophisticated understanding of constitutional borrowing must account for the kinds of situations and circumstances where the better approach would be to reject foreign experience as an appropriate model of constitutional development.

The Court began its review of comparative materials by observing that

Today, capital punishment has been abolished as a penalty for murder either specifically or in practice by almost half the countries of the world including the democracies of Europe and our neighbouring countries, Namibia, Mozambique and Angola. In most of those countries where it is retained, as the Amnesty International statistics show, it is seldom used.

The Court's most detailed discussion, however, was of the history of the death penalty in the American Supreme Court. It concluded that American

jurisprudence has not resolved the dilemma arising from the fact that the Constitution prohibits cruel and unusual punishments, but also permits, and contemplates that there will be capital punishment. The acceptance by a majority of the United States Supreme Court of the proposition that capital punishment is not per se unconstitutional, but that in certain circumstances it may be arbitrary, and thus unconstitutional, has led to endless litigation. Considerable expense and interminable delays result from the exceptionally-high standard of procedural fairness set by the United States courts in attempting to avoid arbitrary decisions. The difficulties that have been experienced in following this path, to which Justice Blackmun and Justice Scalia have both referred, but from which they have drawn different conclusions, persuade me that we should not follow this route.

The Court noted that its decision was also intricately caught up with questions about the limits of judicial power in a constitutional democracy. Echoing Justice Brennan's remarks in *Gregg,*

This Court cannot allow itself to be diverted from its duty to act as an independent arbiter of the Constitution by making choices on the basis that they will find favour with the public. Justice Powell's comment in his dissent in Furman v Georgia *bears repetition: But however one may assess amorphous ebb and flow of public opinion generally on this volatile issue, this type of inquiry lies at the periphery—not the core—of the judicial process in constitutional cases. The assessment of popular opinion is essentially a legislative, and not a judicial, function. . . .*[38]

---

[38] Compare the decision by the Hungarian Court, after noting that "social sentiments" often favor the death penalty: "The Constitutional Court, however, does not hunt for popularity in society; its only competence is to ensure the coherence and constitutionality of the legal system. . . ."

TABLE 9.2

Part A lists several countries whose constitutions prohibit the death penalty, with quotations from the relevant articles.

Part B lists several countries whose constitutions limit the scope of the death penalty, with quotations from the relevant articles.

A. Constitutions which Prohibit the Death Penalty

Country	*Title of constitution*	*Text*
AUSTRIA	Federal Constitutional Law of the Republic of Austria (1920, as amended in 1968)	Article 85 states: "The death penalty is abolished."
COLOMBIA	Constitution of Colombia (1991)	Article 11 states: "The right to life is inviolable. There will be no death penalty."
COSTA RICA	Constitution of the Republic of Costa Rica (1949)	Article 21 states: "Human life is inviolable." Article 21 is included under Title IV, "Individual Rights and Guarantees."
CROATIA	Constitution of the Republic of Croatia (1990)	Article 21 states: "Every human being shall have the right to life. In the Republic of Croatia there shall be no death penalty."
CZECH REPUBLIC	Charter of Fundamental Rights and Freedoms (1992)	Article 6, dealing with the right to life, states: ". . . (3) There shall be no death penalty."
ECUADOR	Constitution of the Republic of Ecuador (1979, as codified in 1998)	Article 23 states in part: ". . . the State recognizes and guarantees all people the following: (1) The inviolability of life. There is no death penalty. . . ."
FINLAND	Constitution Act of Finland (1919, as amended in 1995)	Section 6 states in part: "Everyone shall have the right to life and personal liberty, physical integrity and security of person. No one shall be sentenced to death, tortured or otherwise treated in a degrading manner."
GERMANY	Basic Law of the Federal Republic of Germany (1949)	Article 102 states: "The death penalty is abolished."
LUXEMBOURG	Constitution of the Grand Duchy of Luxembourg of 17 October 1868 (as amended on 29 April 1999)	Article 18 states: "The death penalty cannot be established." Article 18 is included in Chapter II, "People of Luxembourg and their Rights."
MOZAMBIQUE	Constitution of the Republic of Mozambique (1990)	Article 70 states: "1. All citizens shall have the right to life. All shall have the right to physical integrity and may not be subjected to torture or to cruel or inhuman treatment. 2. In the Republic of Mozambique there shall be no death penalty."
NETHERLANDS	Constitution of the Kingdom of the Netherlands (1983)	Article 114 states: "Capital punishment may not be imposed."

TABLE 9.2 Continued.

NICARAGUA	Constitution of the Republic of Nicaragua (1987)	Article 23 states: "The right to life is inviolable and inherent to the human person. In Nicaragua there is no death penalty."
PANAMA	Constitution of the Republic of Panama (1972)	Article 30 states: "There is no death penalty." Article 30 is included under Title III, "Individual and Social Rights and Duties."
PORTUGAL	Constitution of the Portuguese Republic (1976)	Article 24 states: "1. Human life is inviolable. 2. In no case shall the death penalty be applied."
ROMANIA	Constitution of Romania (1991)	Article 22(3) states: "Capital punishment is prohibited." Article 22 is entitled "The Right to Life and to Physical and Mental Well-being."
SLOVAK REPUBLIC	Constitution of the Slovak Republic of 3 September 1992	Article 15, dealing with the right to life, states: ". . . (3) The death penalty shall be inadmissable. . . ."
SLOVENIA	Constitution of the Republic of Slovenia (1991)	Article 17 states: "Human life is inviolable. There shall be no death penalty in Slovenia."
SWEDEN	Instrument of Government (1975)	Article 4 states: "There shall be no capital punishment." Article 4 is included under Chapter 2, "Fundamental Rights and Freedoms."
URUGUAY	Constitution of the Oriental Republic of Uruguay (1966)	Article 26 states in part: "The death penalty shall not be applied to anyone." Article 26 is included under Section II, "Rights, Duties and Guarantees."
VENEZUELA	Constitution of the Republic of Venezuela (1961)	Article 58 states: "The right to life is inviolable. No law may establish the death penalty, nor may any authority apply it."

B. Constitutions which Restrict the Scope of the Death Penalty

Country	*Title of constitution*	*Text*
ARGENTINA	Constitution of the Argentine Nation (1994)	Article 18 states in part: "The penalty of death for political offences, all kinds of torture, and flogging, are forever abolished."
BRAZIL	Constitution of the Federative Republic of Brazil (1988)	Article 5, XLVII states in part: "There will be no penalties of: a) death, except in cases of declared war as defined in Article 84, XIX." Article 5, XLVII is included under Title II, "Fundamental Rights and Guarantees."

TABLE 9.2   Continued.

EL SALVADOR	Constitution of the Republic of El Salvador (1983)	Article 27 states in part: "The death penalty may be imposed only in cases provided by military laws during a state of international war." Article 27 is included under Title II, "Fundamental Rights and Guarantees of the Person."
GREECE	Constitution of Greece (1975)	Article 7(3) states in part: "The death penalty shall not be imposed for political crimes, unless these are composite." Article 7 is included under Part II, "Individual and Social Rights."
ITALY	Constitution of the Republic of Italy of 27 December 1947	Article 27 states in part: "The death penalty is not admitted except in cases specified by military laws in time of war." Article 27 is included under Title I, Part One, "Rights and Duties of Private Citizens."
MEXICO	Constitution of the United States of Mexico (1917)	Article 22 prohibits torture and specific cruel punishments and states: "The death penalty is . . . prohibited for political crimes and, in relation to other crimes, can only be imposed for treason during international war, parricide, murder that is committed treacherously, with premeditation or against a defenceless person, arson, kidnapping, banditry, piracy and grave military offences."
PERU	Constitution of the Republic of Peru (1993)	Article 140 states: "The death penalty may only be applied for the crime of treason in time of war, and of terrorism, in accordance with national laws and international treaties to which Peru is party."
SPAIN	Spanish Constitution (1978)	Article 15 states: "All have the right to life and physical and moral integrity and in no case may they be subjected to torture or inhuman or degrading punishment or treatment. The death penalty is abolished except in those cases which may be established by military penal law in times of war."

SOURCE: http://web.amnesty.org/ai.nsf/Index/ACT500051999?OpenDocument&of=THEMES\DEATH+PENALTY

The Court thus declined to follow the United States' model, concluding instead that the constitutional value of human dignity, coupled with Article 11(2), prohibited capital punishment as a "serious impairment of human dignity." The Court concluded,

> *The rights to life and dignity are the most important of all human rights, and the source of all other personal rights. . . . By committing ourselves to a society founded on the recognition of human rights we are required to value these two rights above all others. And this must be demonstrated by the State in everything that it does, including the way it punishes criminals. This is not achieved by objectifying murderers and putting them to death to serve as an example to others in the expectation that they might possibly be deterred thereby.*[39]

The Court also noted that the Canadian Court had similarly recognized the value of human dignity in the well-known case of *Kindler v. Canada* (1992). In *Kindler*, three of seven judges concluded that the death penalty is cruel and unusual, in part because "it is the supreme indignity to the individual, . . . [and] the absolute and irrevocable castration. . . ." Nevertheless, a majority concluded that the Canadian Constitution did not prohibit the government from extraditing Kindler to the United States without first seeking assurance that Kindler would not be given the death penalty.[40]

In its review of foreign case law, the Court observed also that "similar issues were debated by the European Court of Human Rights" in *Soering v. United Kingdom* (1989). *Soering* also involved extradition to the United States of a defendant facing capital punishment. Detained in England, Soering was a suspect in the murder of his girlfriend's parents in Virginia. Soering argued that, if extradited, he would be subject to inhuman and degrading treatment in violation of Article 3 of the European Convention on Human Rights. Article 2 of the Convention similarly protects the right to life, but makes an exception for executions "following [the] conviction of a crime for which this penalty is provided by law." A blanket prohibition of capital punishment under Article 3 would thus conflict with Article 2. Consequently the Court ruled that the death penalty is not absolutely contrary to the Convention, but must satisfy the conditions set forth in Article 3. These included a requirement of proportionality and acceptable conditions of detention. The Court ruled that in this case, Soering's extradition would not satisfy those conditions. Soering, the Court concluded, was impaired mentally, a youth (18 at the time of the offense), and might be on death row for as long as eight years, which might itself possibly amount to cruel and unusual punishment.

Conclusion

Justice Stewart was right: Death is different. And when seen in a comparative perspective, it becomes clear that America is different, too. The constitutional courts of

---

[39] The Court also embarked upon a long review of capital punishment in India, Canada and other countries. It concluded that in India, the relevant constitutional provisions were worded differently, and that the founders had "specifically contemplated and sanctioned" the death penalty.

[40] In *Minister v. Burns* (2001), the Canadian Court reconsidered the issue in *Kindler*, concluding that the "basic tenets" of fundamental justice had not changed since *Kindler*, "but their application in particular cases . . . must take note of factual developments in Canada and in relevant foreign jurisdictions." The Court then concluded that the balance, which had "tilted in favour of extradition without reassurances in *Kindler . . .* now tilts against the constitutionality of such an outcome."

other advanced industrial democracies have concluded that the constitutional values of life, liberty, and dignity compel them, even in the absence of a clear constitutional command, and even in the face of public opposition, to condemn the death penalty. Should these decisions have any relevance for constitutional interpretation in the United States? The justices of the American Supreme Court ask the question with increasing frequency, especially in the area of capital punishment. They have yet to come to a consensus, but just to ask the question is to engage, once again, the most fundamental of constitutional issues: Who are we, and what do we believe?

Selected Bibliography

Acker, James R., R. M. Bohm, and C. Lanier, eds., 1998. *America's Experiment with Capital Punishment: Reflections on the Past, Present, and Future of the Ultimate Penal Sanction*. Durham: Carolina Academic Press.

Amar, Akhil Reed, 1999. *Intratextualism*. Harvard Law Review 112: 747.

———. 1999. *Continuing the Conversation*. University of Richmond Law Review 33: 579

———. 1996. *Did the Fourteenth Amendment Incorporate the Bill of Rights Against States?* Harvard Journal of Law & Public Policy 19: 443.

Arkes, Hadley. 1990. *Beyond the Constitution*. Princeton: Princeton University Press.

Aynes, Richard L. 1999. *Commentary on Akhil Reed Amar's The Bill of Rights: Creation and Reconstruction: Refined Incorporation and the Fourteenth Amendment*. University of Richmond Law Review 33: 289.

Baldus, David, G. Woodruff, and C. Pulaski, Jr., 1990. *Equal Justice and the Death Penalty*. Boston: Northeastern University Press.

Banner, Stuart. 2002. *The Death Penalty: An American History*. Cambridge: Harvard University Press.

Becker, Theodore. 1941. *The Declaration of Independence: A Study in the History of Political Ideas*. New York: Alfred A. Knopf.

Bedau, Hugo Adam, ed., 1997. *The Death Penalty in America: Current Controversies*. Oxford: Oxford University Press.

Berger, Raoul. 1997. *Government by Judiciary: The Transforming of the Fourteenth Amendment*. Indianapolis: Liberty Fund, Inc.

———1982. *Death Penalties: The Supreme Court's Obstacle Course*. Cambridge: Harvard University Press.

Berns, Walter. 1979. *For Capital Punishment: Crime and the Morality of the Death Penalty*. New York: Basic Books.

Black, Charles, L. 1975. *Capital Punishment: The Inevitability of Caprice and Mistake*. New York: W.W. Norton.

Cogan, Neil. 1997. *The Complete Bill of Rights: The Drafts, Debates, Sources, and Origins*. New York: Oxford University Press.

Cortner, Richard C. 1981. *The Supreme Court and the Second Bill of Rights: The Fourteenth Amendment and the Nationalization of the Bill of Rights*. Madison: University of Wisconsin Press.

Corwin, Edward S. 1948. *Liberty Against Government*. Baton Rouge, La.: Louisiana State University Press.

Curtis, Michael Kent. 1986. *No State Shall Abridge: The Fourteenth Amendment and the Bill of Rights*. Durham: Duke University Press.

Dorf, Michael C. 2002. *Equal Protection Incorporation*. Virginia Law Review 88: 951.

Eidelberg, Paul. 1968. *The Philosophy of the American Constitution*. New York: Free Press.

Ely, John Hart. 1980. *Democracy and Distrust: A Theory of Judicial Review*. Cambridge, Mass.: Harvard University Press.

Erler, Edward J. 1991. *The American Polity: Essays on the Theory and Practice of Constitutional Government*. New York: Crane Russak.

Gerber, Rudolph J. 1999. *Cruel and Usual: Our Criminal Justice System*. Westport: Praeger Publishers.

Haines, Herbert H. 1996. *Against Capital Punishment: The Anti-Death Penalty Movement in America, 1972–1994*. New York: Oxford University Press.

Kammen, Michael. 1986. *The Origins of the American Constitution: A Documentary History*. New York: Penguin Books.

Kennedy, Randall L., 1988. *McKleskey v. Kemp: Rule, Capital Punishment, and the Supreme Court*. Harvard Law Review 101: 1388.

Latzer, Barry, ed. 1997. *Death Penalty Cases: Leading U.S. Supreme Court Cases on Capital Punishment*. Woburn, MA: Butterworth-Heinemann.

Levy, Leonard. 1999. *Origins of the Bill of Rights*. New Haven: Yale University Press.

McDonald, Forrest. 1985. *Novus Ordo Seclorum*. Lawrence: University Press of Kansas.

Perry, Michael. 1982. *The Constitution, the Court, and Human Rights*. New Haven, CT.: Yale University Press.

Russell, Gregory D. 1994. *The Death Penalty and Racial Bias: Overturning Supreme Court Assumptions*. Westport, Greenwood Press.

Sarat, Austin, ed. 1998. *The Killing State: Capital Punishment in Law, Politics, and Culture.* New York: Oxford University Press.

————. 2001. *When the State Kills: Capital Punishment and the American Condition.* Princeton: Princeton University Press.

Simmons, Brent E. 2001. *The Invincibility of Constitutional Error: The Rehnquist Court's States' Rights Assault on Four- teenth Amendment Protections of Individual Rights.* Seton Hall Constitutional Law Journal 11: 259.

Smith, Christopher E. 1997. *The Rehnquist Court and Crimi- nal Punishment.* NY: Garland Press.

Tribe, Laurence. 1985. *Constitutional Choices.* Cambridge, Mass.: Harvard University Press.

Van den Haag, Ernest and John P. Conrad. 1983. *The Death Penalty: A Debate.* NY: Putman Press.

Vila, Bryan and Cynthia Morris, eds. 1997. *Capital Punish- ment in the United States: A Documentary History.* West- port, CT: Greenwood Publishing Group.

Wildenthal, Bryan H. 2000. *The Lost Compromise: Reassessing the Early Understanding in Court and Congress on Incor- poration of the Bill of Rights in the Fourteenth Amendment.* Ohio State Law Journal 61: 1051.

Wong-Ervin, Koren Wai. 1998. *The Second Amendment and the Incorporation Conundrum: Towards a Workable Juris- prudence.* Hastings Law Journal 50: 177.

Wood, Gordon. 1969. *The Creation of the American Republic 1776–1787.* New York: W.W. Norton & Company.

Selected Comparative Bibliography

Friedrich, Carl J. 1950. *Constitutional Government and De- mocracy.* rev. ed. Boston, Mass.: Ginn and Company.

Hood, Roger. 1989. *The Death Penalty: A World Wide Per- spective.* New York: Oxford University Press.

Hood, Roger et al. 1999. *The Death Penalty—Abolition in Eu- rope.* Council of Europe Publishing.

Kaufman-Osborn, Timothy V., 2002. *From Noose to Needle: Capital Punishment and the Late Liberal State.* Ann Arbor: University of Michigan Press.

Schabas, William A. 1996. *The Death Penalty As Cruel Treat- ment and Torture: Capital Punishment Challenged in the World's Courts.* Boston: Northeastern University Press.

Barron v. Baltimore

32 U.S. 243, 7 Pet. 243, 8 L.Ed. 672 (1833)

In paving its streets, the city of Baltimore had diverted the flow of several streams, resulting in deposits of sand and gravel near Barron's wharf. Baltimore's activity deprived Barron of the use of his wharf, whereupon he sued the city, claiming that its action violated the clause of the Fifth Amendment that proclaims "no person shall . . . be de- prived of life, liberty, or property, without due process of law; nor shall private property be taken for public use, without just compensation." Opinion of the Court: *Mar- shall,* Duvall, Johnson, McLean, Story, Thompson. Not Participating: Baldwin.

Mr. Chief Justice MARSHALL delivered the opinion of the Court.

The question thus presented is, we think, of great impor- tance, but not of much difficulty.

The constitution was ordained and established by the people of the United States for themselves, for their own government, and not for the government of the individual states. Each state established a constitution for itself, and in that constitution, provided such limitations and restric- tions on the powers of its particular government, as its judgment dictated. The people of the United States framed such a government for the United States as they supposed best adapted to their situation and best calculated to pro- mote their interests. The powers they conferred on this government were to be exercised by itself; and the limita- tions on power, if expressed in general terms, are natu- rally, and, we think, necessarily, applicable to the government created by the instrument. They are limita- tions of power granted in the instrument itself; not of dis- tinct governments, framed by different persons and for different purposes.

If these propositions be correct, the fifth amendment must be understood as restraining the power of the gen- eral government, not as applicable to the states. In their several constitutions, they have imposed such restrictions on their respective governments, as their own wisdom suggested; such as they deemed most proper for them- selves. It is a subject on which they judge exclusively, and with which others interfere no further than they are sup- posed to have a common interest.

The counsel for the plaintiff . . . insists, that the constitu- tion was intended to secure the people of the several states against the undue exercise of power by their respec- tive state governments; as well as against that which might be attempted by their general government. In support of this argument he relies on the inhibitions contained in the tenth section of the first article.

We think that section affords a strong, if not a conclu- sive, argument in support of the opinion already indicated by the court.

The preceding section contains restrictions which are obviously intended for the exclusive purpose of restraining the exercise of power by the departments of the general government. Some of them use language applicable only to congress; others are expressed in general terms. The third clause, for example, declares, that "no bill of attainder or ex post facto law shall be passed." No language can be more general; yet the demonstration is complete, that it applies solely to the government of the United States. . . .

If the original constitution, in the ninth and tenth sections of the first article, draws this plain and marked line of discrimination between the limitations it imposes on the powers of the general government, and on those of the state; if, in every inhibition intended to act on state power, words are employed, which directly express that intent; some strong reason must be assigned for departing from this safe and judicious course, in framing the amendments, before that departure can be assumed.

We search in vain for that reason.

Had the framers of these amendments intended them to be limitations on the powers of the state governments, they would have imitated the framers of the original constitution, and have expressed that intention. Had congress engaged in the extraordinary occupation of improving the constitutions of the several states, by affording the people additional protection from the exercise of power by their own governments, in matters which concerned themselves alone, they would have declared this purpose in plain and intelligible language.

But it is universally understood, it is a part of the history of the day, that the great revolution which established the constitution of the United States, was not effected without immense opposition. Serious fears were extensively entertained, that those powers which the patriot statesmen, who then watched over the interests of our country, deemed essential to union, and to the attainment of those invaluable objects for which union was sought, might be exercised in a manner dangerous to liberty. In almost every convention by which the constitution was adopted, amendments to guard against the abuse of power were recommended. These amendments demanded security against the apprehended encroachments of the general government—not against those of the local governments.

In compliance with a sentiment thus generally expressed, to quiet fears thus extensively entertained, amendments were proposed by the required majority in congress, and adopted by the states. These amendments contain no expression indicating an intention to apply them to the state governments. This court cannot so apply them.

We are of opinion, that the provision in the fifth amendment to the constitution, declaring that private property shall be taken for public use, without just compensation, is intended solely as a limitation on the exercise of power by the government of the United States, and is not applicable to the legislation of the states. We are, therefore, of opinion, that there is no repugnancy between the several acts of the general assembly of Maryland . . . and the constitution of the United States. This court, therefore, has no jurisdiction of the cause, and it is dismissed.

Notes and Queries

1. The Court concluded that the question raised in this case was, as Marshall wrote, "not of much difficulty." But consider: Only two provisions of the Bill of Rights apply explicitly to the national government—the First, which mentions Congress, and the Seventh, which is addressed to the federal judiciary—whereas the others are written in general terms. Why shouldn't we infer that the Founders intended the Bill of Rights to apply to the states, except on those two occasions when they took great care to say so?

2. Is Marshall's opinion based on a particular understanding of the relationship between the national government and the states? Consider the opinion of Laurence Tribe, who argues that *Barron* is "a concession to state power." Tribe contends that implicit in *Barron* is the belief that respect for the principle of federalism and state's rights was for the Founders a necessary part of what it meant to protect liberty. *American Constitutional Law.* (Mineola: New York, 1988), 3. The influence of federalism on interpretation of the Bill of Rights is a recurrent theme in this chapter.

3. What approaches to constitutional interpretation does Marshall use in *Barron?* To what extent does he rely upon historical context? Structural reasoning? Political theory? Words of the Constitution?

4. Does Marshall regard the Bill of Rights more as a list of individual liberties, or rather as a set of restrictions on the actions of certain levels of government? What is the difference?

5. Would Madison and Hamilton agree with Marshall's argument about the reach of federal power? Would most anti-Federalists agree with Marshall's decision?

[The Slaughter-House Cases] Butchers' Benevolent Association of New Orleans v. Crescent City Live-Stock Landing and Slaughter-House Company

83 U.S. 36, 16 Wall. 36, 21 L.Ed. 394 (1873)

In 1869 the Louisina legislature, controlled by northern "carpetbag" interests and amid charges that its members had been bribed and corrupted, granted a monopoly to a single slaughter-house company to shelter and slaughter animals within the city of New Orleans. (The monopoly had been granted against the backdrop of a cholera epidemic.) The monopoly put several competing firms out of business and prevented hundreds of butchers from engaging in their occupation. These firms and butchers attacked the validity of the statute under the Thirteenth and Fourteenth Amendments. Opinion of the Court: *Miller*, Clifford, Davis, Hunt, Strong. Dissenting opinions: *Bradley, Field*, Chase, *Swayne*.

Mr. Justice MILLER . . . delivered the opinion of the Court.

The plaintiffs . . . allege that the statute is a violation of the Constitution of the United States in these several particulars:

That it creates an involuntary servitude forbidden by the thirteenth article of amendment;

That it abridges the privileges and immunities of citizens of the United States;

That it denies to the plaintiffs the equal protection of the laws; and,

That it deprives them of their property without due process of law; contrary to the provisions of the first section of the fourteenth article of amendment.

This court is thus called upon for the first time to give construction to these articles.

We do not conceal from ourselves the great responsibility which this duty devolves upon us. No questions so far-reaching and pervading in their consequences, so profoundly interesting to the people of this country, and so important in their bearing upon the relations of the United States, and of the several States to each other and to the citizens of the States and of the United States, have been before this court during the official life of any of its present members. . . .

The most cursory glance at these [three amendments] discloses a unity of purpose, when taken in connection with the history of the times, which cannot fail to have an important bearing on any question of doubt concerning their true meaning. Nor can such doubts, when any reasonably exist, be safely and rationally solved without a reference to that history; for in it is found the occasion and the necessity for recurring again to the great source of power in this country, the people of the States, for additional guarantees of human rights; additional powers to the Federal government; additional restraints upon those of the States. Fortunately that history is fresh within the memory of us all. . . .

We repeat, then, in the light of this recapitulation of events, almost too recent to be called history, but which are familiar to us all; and on the most casual examination of the language of these amendments, no one can fail to be impressed with the one pervading purpose found in them all . . . ; we mean the freedom of the slave race, the security and firm establishment of that freedom, and the protection of the newly-made freeman and citizen from the oppressions of those who had formerly exercised unlimited dominion over him. It is true that only the fifteenth amendment, in terms, mentions the negro by speaking of his color and his slavery. But it is just as true that each of the other articles was addressed to the grievances of that race. . . .

We do not say that no one else but the negro can share in this protection. Both the language and spirit of these articles are to have their fair and just weight in any question of construction. . . . But what we do say, and what we wish to be understood is, that in any fair and just construction of any section or phrase of these amendments, it is necessary to look to the purpose which we have said was the pervading spirit of them all, the evil which they were designed to remedy, and the process of continued addition to the Constitution, until that purpose was supposed to be accomplished, as far as constitutional law can accomplish it.

The first section of the fourteenth article . . . opens with a definition of citizenship—not only citizenship of the United States, but citizenship of the States. No such definition was previously found in the Constitution, nor had any attempt been made to define it by act of Congress. . . . But it had been held by this court, in the celebrated *Dred Scott* case, only a few years before the outbreak of the civil war, that a man of African descent, whether a slave or not, was not and could not be a citizen of a State or of the United States. This decision, while it met the condemnation of some of the ablest statesmen and constitutional lawyers of the country, had never been overruled; and if it was to be accepted as a constitutional limitation of the right of citizenship, then all the negro race who had recently been made freemen, were still, not only not citizens, but were incapable of becoming so by anything short of an amendment to the Constitution.

To remove this difficulty primarily, and to establish a clear and comprehensive definition of citizenship which should declare what should constitute citizenship of the United States, and also citizenship of a State, the first clause of the first section was framed.

"All persons born or naturalized in the United States, and subject to the jurisdiction thereof, are citizens of the United States and of the State wherein they reside."

The first observation we have to make on this clause is, that it puts at rest both the questions which we stated to have been the subject of differences of opinion. It declares that persons may be citizens of the United States without regard to their citizenship of a particular State, and it overturns the *Dred Scott* decision by making all persons born within the United States and subject to its jurisdiction citizens of the United States. That its main purpose was to establish the citizenship of the negro can admit of no doubt. . . .

The next observation is more important in . . . the present case. It is, that the distinction between citizenship of the United States and citizenship of a State is clearly recognized and established. Not only may a man be a citizen of the United States without being a citizen of a State, but an important element is necessary to convert the former into the latter. He must reside within the State to make him a citizen of it, but it is only necessary that he should be born or naturalized in the United States to be a citizen of the Union.

It is quite clear, then, that there is a citizenship of the United States, and a citizenship of a State, which are distinct from each other, and which depend upon different characteristics or circumstances in the individual.

. . . The argument, however, in favor of the plaintiffs rests wholly on the assumption that the citizenship is the same, and the privileges and immunities guaranteed by the clause are the same.

The language is, "No State shall make or enforce any law which shall abridge the privileges or immunities of *citizens of the United States.*" It is a little remarkable, if this clause was intended as a protection to the citizen of a State against the legislative power of his own State, that the word citizen of the State should be left out when it is so carefully used, and used in contradistinction to citizens of the United States, in the very sentence which precedes it. It is too clear for argument that the change in phraseology was adopted understandingly and with a purpose.

Of the privileges and immunities of the citizen of the United States, and of the privileges and immunities of the citizen of the State, and what they respectively are, we will presently consider; but we wish to state here that it is only the former which are placed by this clause under the protection of the Federal Constitution, and that the latter, whatever they may be, are not intended to have any additional protection by this paragraph of the amendment. . . .

In the Constitution of the United States . . . the corresponding provision is found in section two of the fourth article, in the following words: "The citizens of each State shall be entitled to all the privileges and immunities of citizens of the several States."

There can be but little question that the purpose of both these provisions is the same, and that the privileges and immunities intended are the same in each. . . .

Fortunately we are not without judicial construction of this clause of the Constitution. The first and the leading case on the subject is that of *Corfield v. Coryell* (1823), decided by Mr. Justice Washington in the Circuit Court. . . .

> The inquiry [he says] is, what are the privileges and immunities of citizens of the several States? We feel no hesitation in confining these expressions to those privileges and immunities which are fundamental; which belong of right to the citizens of all free governments, and which have at all times been enjoyed by citizens of the several States which compose this Union, from the time of their becoming free, independent, and sovereign. What these fundamental principles are, it would be more tedious than difficult to enumerate. They may all, however, be comprehended under the following general heads: protection by the government, with the right to acquire and possess property of every kind, and to pursue and obtain happiness and safety, subject, nevertheless, to such restraints as the government may prescribe for the general good of the whole.

This definition of the privileges and immunities of citizens of the States is adopted in the main by this court in . . . *Ward v. The State of Maryland* (1871). . . .

In . . . *Paul v. Virginia* (1869), the [U.S.] Supreme Court, in expounding this clause of the Constitution, says that "the privileges and immunities secured to citizens of each State in the several states . . . are those privileges and immunities which are common to the citizens in the latter States under their constitutions and laws by virtue of their being citizens."

The constitutional provision there alluded to did not create those rights, which it called privileges and immunities of citizens of the States. It threw around them in that clause no security for the citizen of the State in which they were claimed or exercised. Nor did it profess to control the power of the State governments over the rights of its own citizens.

Its sole purpose was to declare to the several States, that whatever those rights, as you grant or establish them to your own citizens, or as you limit or qualify, or impose restrictions on their exercise, the same, neither more nor less, shall be the measure of the rights of citizens of other States within your jurisdiction.

It would be the vainest show of learning to attempt to prove by citations of authority, that up to the adoption of the recent amendments, no claim or pretence was set up that those rights depended on the Federal government for their existence or protection, beyond the very few express limitations which the Federal Constitution imposed upon the States—such, for instance, as the prohibition against ex post facto laws, bills of attainder, and laws impairing the obligation of contracts. But with the exception of these and a few other restrictions, the entire domain of the privileges and immunities of citizens of the States . . . lay within the constitutional and legislative power of the States, and without that of the Federal government. Was it the purpose of the fourteenth amendment, by the simple declaration that no State should make or enforce any law which shall abridge the privileges and immunities of *citizens of the United States*, to transfer the security and protection of all the civil rights which we have mentioned, from the States to the Federal government? And where it is declared that Congress shall have the power to enforce that article, was it intended to bring within the power of Congress the entire domain of civil rights heretofore belonging exclusively to the States?

All this and more must follow, if the proposition of the plaintiffs in error be sound. For not only are these rights subject to the control of Congress whenever in its discretion any of them are supposed to be abridged by State legislation, but that body may also pass laws in advance, limiting and restricting the exercise of legislative power by the States, in their most ordinary and usual functions, as in its judgment it may think proper on all such subjects. And still further, such a construction . . . would constitute this court a perpetual censor upon all legislation of the States, on the civil rights of their own citizens, with authority to nullify such as it did not approve as consistent with those rights, as they existed at the time of the adoption of this amendment. The argument we admit is not always the most conclusive which is drawn from the consequences urged against the adoption of a particular construction of an instrument. But when, as in the case before us, these consequences are so serious, so far-reaching and pervad-

ing, so great a departure from the structure and spirit of our institutions; when the effect is to fetter and degrade the State governments by subjecting them to the control of Congress, in the exercise of powers heretofore universally conceded to them of the most ordinary and fundamental character; when in fact it radically changes the whole theory of the relations of the State and Federal governments to each other and of both these governments to the people; the argument has a force that is irresistible, in the absence of language which expresses such a purpose too clearly to admit of doubt.

We are convinced that no such results were intended by the Congress which proposed these amendments, nor by the legislatures of the States which ratified them.

Having shown that the privileges and immunities relied on in the argument are those which belong to citizens of the States as such, and that they are left to the State governments for security and protection, and not by this article placed under the special care of the Federal government, we may hold ourselves excused from defining the privileges and immunities of citizens of the United States which no State can abridge, until some case involving those privileges may make it necessary to do so.

But lest it should be said that no such privileges and immunities are to be found if those we have been considering are excluded, we venture to suggest some which owe their existence to the Federal government, its National character, its Constitution, or its laws.

One of these is well described in . . . *Crandall v. Nevada* (1868). It is . . . the right of the citizen of this great country, protected by implied guarantees of its Constitution, "to come to the seat of government to assert any claim he may have upon that government, to transact any business he may have with it, to seek its protection, to share its offices, to engage in administering its functions. He has the right of free access to its seaports . . . , to the subtreasuries, land offices, and courts of justice in the several States. . . ."

Another privilege of a citizen of the United States is to demand the care and protection of the Federal government over his life, liberty, and property when on the high seas or within the jurisdiction of a foreign government. . . . The right to peaceably assemble and petition for redress of grievances, the privilege of the writ of habeas corpus, are rights of the citizen guaranteed by the Federal Constitution. The right to use the navigable waters of the United States, however they may penetrate the territory of the several States, all rights secured to our citizens by treaties with foreign nations, are dependent upon citizenship of the United States, and not citizenship of a State. One of these privileges is conferred by the very article under consideration. It is that a citizen of the United States can, of his own volition, become a citizen of any State of the Union by a bona fide residence therein, with the same rights as other citizens of that State. To these may be added the rights secured by the thirteenth and fifteenth articles of amendment, and by the other clause of the fourteenth, next to be considered.

But it is useless to pursue this branch of the inquiry, since we are of opinion that the rights claimed by these plaintiffs . . . if they have any existence, are not privileges and immunities of citizens of the United States within the meaning of the clause of the fourteenth amendment under consideration.

The argument has not been much pressed in these cases that the defendant's charter deprives the plaintiffs of their property without due process of law, or that it denies to them the equal protection of the law. . . .

We are not without judicial interpretation . . . of the meaning of this clause. And it is sufficient to say that under no construction of that provision that we have ever seen, or any that we deem admissible, can the restraint imposed by . . . Louisiana upon the exercise of their trade by the butchers of New Orleans be held to be a deprivation of property within the meaning of that provision.

The adoption of the first eleven amendments to the Constitution so soon after the original instrument was accepted, shows a prevailing sense of danger at that time from the Federal power. And it cannot be denied that such a jealousy continued to exist with many patriotic men until the breaking out of the late civil war. It was then discovered that the true danger to the perpetuity of the Union was in the capacity of the State organizations to combine and concentrate all the powers of the State, and of contiguous States, for a determined resistance to the General Government.

Unquestionably this has given great force to the argument, and added largely to the number of those who believe in the necessity of a strong National government.

But, however pervading this sentiment, and however it may have contributed to the adoption of the amendments we have been considering, we do not see in those amendments any purpose to destroy the main features of the general system. Under the pressure of all the excited feeling growing out of the war, our statesmen have still believed that the existence of the State with powers for domestic and local government, including the regulation of civil rights—the rights of person and of property—was essential to the perfect working of our complex form of government, though they have thought proper to impose additional limitations on the States, and to confer additional power on that of the Nation.

But whatever fluctuations may be seen in the history of public opinion on this subject during the period of our national existence, we think it will be found that this court, so far as its functions required, has always held with a steady and an even hand the balance between State and Federal power, and we trust that such may continue to be the history of its relation to that subject so long as it shall have duties to perform which demand of it a construction of the Constitution. . . .

The judgments of the Supreme Court of Louisiana in these cases are AFFIRMED.

Mr. Justice FIELD, dissenting.

The question presented is . . . one of the gravest importance, not merely to the parties here, but to the whole country. It is nothing less than the question whether the recent amendments to the Federal Constitution protect the citizens of the United States against the deprivation of their common rights by State legislation. In my judgment the fourteenth amendment does afford such protection, and was so intended by the Congress which framed and the States which adopted it.

The first clause of the fourteenth amendment . . . recognizes in express terms, if it does not create, citizens of the United States, and it makes their citizenship dependent upon the place of their birth, or the fact of their adoption, and not upon the constitution or laws of any State or the condition of their ancestry. A citizen of a State is now only a citizen of the United States residing in that State. The fundamental rights, privileges, and immunities which belong to him as a free man and a free citizen, now belong to him as a citizen of the United States, and are not dependent upon his citizenship of any State. The exercise of these rights and privileges, and the degree of enjoyment received from such exercise, are always more or less affected by the condition and the local institutions of the State, or city, or town where he resides. They are thus affected in a State by the wisdom of its laws, the ability of its officers, the efficiency of its magistrates, the education and morals of its people, and by many other considerations. This is a result which follows from the constitution of society, and can never be avoided, but in no other way can they be affected by the action of the State, or by the residence of the citizen therein. They do not derive their existence from its legislation, and cannot be destroyed by its power.

The amendment does not attempt to confer any new privileges or immunities upon citizens, or to enumerate or define those already existing. It assumes that there are such privileges and immunities which belong of right to citizens as such, and ordains that they shall not be abridged by State legislation. If this inhibition has no reference to privileges and immunities of this character, but only refers . . . to such privileges and immunities as were before its adoption specially designated in the Constitution or necessarily implied as belonging to citizens of the United States, it was a vain and idle enactment, which accomplished nothing, and most unnecessarily excited Congress and the people on its passage. With privileges and immunities thus designated or implied no State could ever have interfered by its laws, and no new constitutional provision was required to inhibit such interference. The supremacy of the Constitution and the laws of the United States always controlled any State legislation of that character. But if the amendment refers to the natural and inalienable rights which belong to all citizens, the inhibition has a profound significance and consequence.

What, then, are the privileges and immunities which are secured against abridgment by State legislation?

In the first section of the Civil Rights Act Congress has given its interpretation to these terms, or at least has stated some of the rights which, in its judgment, these terms include; it has there declared that they include the right "to make and enforce contracts, to sue, be parties and give evidence, to inherit, purchase, lease, sell, hold, and convey real and personal property, and to full and equal benefit of all laws and proceedings for the security of person and property." That act . . . was passed before the fourteenth amendment, but the amendment was adopted . . . to obviate objections to the act, or, speaking more accurately . . . to obviate objections to legislation of a similar character, extending the protection of the National government over the common rights of all citizens of the United States. Accordingly, after its ratification, Congress re-enacted the act under the belief that whatever doubts may have previously existed of its validity, they were removed by the amendment.

What the clause in question [Article IV] did for the protection of the citizens of one State against hostile and discriminating legislation of other States, the fourteenth amendment does for the protection of every citizen of the United States against hostile and discriminating legislation against him in favor of others, whether they reside in the same or in different States. If under the fourth article of the Constitution equality of privileges and immunities is secured between citizens of different States, under the fourteenth amendment the same equality is secured between citizens of the United States.

It will not be pretended that under the fourth article of the Constitution any State could create a monopoly in any known trade or manufacture in favor of her own citizens, or any portion of them, which would exclude an equal participation in the trade or manufacture monopolized by citizens of other States. . . .

Now, what the clause in question does for the protection of citizens of one State against the creation of monopolies in favor of citizens of other States, the fourteenth amendment does for the protection of every citizen of the United States against the creation of any monopoly whatever. The privileges and immunities of citizens of the United States, of every one of them, is secured against abridgment in any form by any State. The fourteenth amendment places them under the guardianship of the National authority. All monopolies in any known trade or manufacture are an invasion of these privileges, for they encroach upon the liberty of citizens to acquire property and pursue happiness, and were held void at common law. . . .

The common law of England is the basis of the jurisprudence of the United States. It was brought to this country by the colonists, together with the English statutes, and was established here so far as it was applicable to their condition. That law and the benefit of such of the English statutes as existed at the time of their colonization, and which they had by experience found to be applicable to their circumstances, were claimed by the Congress of the United Colonies in 1774 as a part of their "indubitable rights and liberties." Of the statutes, the benefits of which was thus claimed, the statute of James I against monopolies was one of the most important. And when the Colonies separated from the mother country no privilege was more fully recognized or more completely incorporated into the fundamental law of the country than that every free subject in the British empire was entitled to pursue his happiness by following any of the known established trades and occupations of the country. . . . The immortal document which proclaimed the independence of the country declared as self-evident truths that the Creator had endowed all men "with certain inalienable rights, and that among these are life, liberty, and the pursuit of happiness; and that to secure these rights governments are instituted among men."

This equality of right, with exemption from all disparaging and partial enactments, in the lawful pursuits of life, throughout the whole country, is the distinguishing privilege of citizens of the United States. To them, everywhere, all pursuits, all professions, all avocations are open without other restrictions than such as are imposed equally upon all others of the same age, sex, and condition. The State may prescribe such regulations for every pursuit and calling of life as will promote the public health, secure the good order and advance the general prosperity of society, but when once prescribed, the pursuit or calling must be free to be followed by every citizen who is within the conditions designated, and will conform to the regulations. This is the fundamental idea upon which our institutions rest, and unless adhered to in the legislation of the country our government will be a republic only in name. The fourteenth amendment, in my judgment, makes it essential to the validity of the legislation of every State that this equality of rights should be respected. . . . That only is a free government, in the American sense of the term, under which the inalienable right of every citizen to pursue his happiness is unrestrained, except by just, equal, and impartial laws.

I am authorized by the Chief Justice, Mr. Justice Swayne, and Mr. Justice Bradley, to state that they concur with me in this dissenting opinion.

Mr. Justice BRADLEY, also dissenting.

It is contended that this prohibition abridges the privileges and immunities of citizens of the United States . . . ; and whether it does so or not is the simple question in this case. And the solution of this question depends upon the solution of two other questions, to wit:

First. Is it one of the rights and privileges of a citizen of the United States to pursue such civil employment as he may choose to adopt, subject to such reasonable regulations as may be prescribed by law?

Secondly. Is a monopoly, or exclusive right, given to one person to the exclusion of all others, to keep slaughter-houses . . . a reasonable regulation of that employment which the legislature has a right to impose?

The first of these questions is one of vast importance, and lies at the very foundations of our government. The question is now settled by the fourteenth amendment itself, that citizenship of the United States is the primary citizenship in this country; and that State citizenship is secondary and derivative, depending upon citizenship of the United States and the citizen's place of residence. The States have not now, if they ever had, any power to restrict their citizenship to any classes or persons. A citizen of the United States has a perfect constitutional right to go to and reside in any State he chooses, and to claim citizenship therein, and an equality of rights with every other citizen; and the whole power of the nation is pledged to sustain him in that right. He is not bound to cringe to any superior, or to pray for any act of grace, as a means of enjoying all the rights and privileges enjoyed by other citizens. And when the spirit of lawlessness, mob violence, and sectional hate can be so completely repressed as to give full practical effect to this right, we shall be a happier nation, and a more prosperous one than we now are. Citizenship of the United States ought to be, and, according to the

Constitution, is, a sure and undoubted title to equal rights in any and every State in this Union, subject to such regulations as the legislature may rightfully prescribe. If a man be denied full equality before the law, he is denied one of the essential rights of citizenship as a citizen of the United States.

Every citizen, then, being primarily a citizen of the United States, and, secondarily, a citizen of the State where he resides, what, in general, are the privileges and immunities of a citizen of the United States? Is the right, liberty, or privilege of choosing any lawful employment one of them?

This seems to me to be the essential question before us for consideration. And in my judgment, the right of any citizen to follow whatever lawful employment he chooses to adopt (submitting himself to all lawful regulations) is one of his most valuable rights, and one which the legislature of a State cannot invade, whether restrained by its own constitution or not. . . .

I think sufficient has been said to show that citizenship is not an empty name, but that, in this country at least, it has connected with it certain incidental rights, privileges, and immunities of the greatest importance. And to say that these rights and immunities attach only to State citizenship, and not to citizenship of the United States, appears to me to evince a very narrow and insufficient estimate of constitutional history and the rights of men, not to say the rights of the American people. . . .

But we are not bound to resort to implication, or to the constitutional history of England, to find an authoritative declaration of some of the most important privileges and immunities of citizens of the United States. It is in the Constitution itself. The Constitution, it is true, as it stood prior to the recent amendments, specifies, in terms, only a few of the personal privileges and immunities of citizens, but they are very comprehensive in their character. The States were merely prohibited from passing bills of attainder, ex post facto laws, laws impairing the obligation of contracts, and perhaps one or two more. But others of the greatest consequence were enumerated, although they were only secured, in express terms, from invasion by the Federal government; such as the right of habeas corpus, the right of trial by jury, of free exercise of religious worship, the right of free speech and a free press, the right peaceably to assemble for the discussion of public measures, the right to be secure against unreasonable searches and seizures, and above all, and including almost all the rest, the right of not being deprived of life, liberty, or property, without due process of law. These, and still others are specified in the original Constitution, or in the early amendments of it, as among the privileges and immunities of citizens of the United States, or, what is still stronger for the force of the argument, the rights of all persons, whether citizens or not.

But even if the Constitution were silent, the fundamental privileges and immunities of citizens, as such, would be no less real and no less inviolable than they now are. . . . Their very citizenship conferred these privileges, if they did not possess them before. And these privileges they would enjoy whether they were citizens of any State or not. . . .

The granting of monopolies, or exclusive privileges to individuals or corporations, is an invasion of the right of others to choose a lawful calling, and an infringement of personal liberty. . . .

Lastly: Can the Federal courts administer relief to citizens of the United States whose privileges and immunities have been abridged by a State? Of this I entertain no doubt. Prior to the fourteenth amendment this could not be done, except in a few instances, for the want of the requisite authority.

As the great mass of citizens of the United States were also citizens of individual States, many of their general privileges and immunities would be the same in the one capacity as in the other. Having this double citizenship, and the great body of municipal laws intended for the protection of person and property being the laws of the State, and no provision being made, and no machinery provided by the Constitution, except in a few specified cases, for any interference by the General Government between a State and its citizens, the protection of the citizen in the enjoyment of his fundamental privileges and immunities (except where a citizen of one State went into another State) was largely left to State laws and State courts, where they will still continue to be left unless actually invaded by the unconstitutional acts or delinquency of the State governments themselves.

Admitting, therefore, that formerly the States were not prohibited from infringing any of the fundamental privileges and immunities of citizens of the United States, except in a few specified cases, that cannot be said now, since the adoption of the fourteenth amendment. In my judgment, it was the intention of the people of this country in adopting that amendment to provide National security against violation by the States of the fundamental rights of the citizen.

But great fears are expressed that this construction of the amendment will lead to enactments by Congress interfering with the internal affairs of the States, and establishing therein civil and criminal codes of law for the government of the citizens, and thus abolishing the State governments in everything but name; or else, that it will lead the Federal courts to draw to their cognizance the supervision of State tribunals on every subject of judicial inquiry, on the plea of ascertaining whether the privileges and immunities of citizens have not been abridged.

In my judgment no such practical inconveniences would arise. Very little, if any, legislation on the part of Congress would be required to carry the amendment into effect. Like the prohibition against passing a law impairing the obligation of a contract, it would execute itself. . . . The great question is, What is the true construction of the amendment? When once we find that, we shall find the means of giving it effect. The argument from inconvenience ought not to have a very controlling influence in questions of this sort. The National will and National interest are of far greater importance.

Mr. Justice SWAYNE, dissenting.

The first eleven amendments to the Constitution were intended to be checks and limitations upon the government which that instrument called into existence. They had their origin in a spirit of jealousy on the part of the States, which existed when the Constitution was adopted. The first ten were proposed in 1789 by the first Congress at its first session after the organization of the government. The eleventh was proposed in 1794, and the twelfth in 1803. . . .

These [three] amendments are a new departure, and mark an important epoch in the constitutional history of the country. They trench directly upon the power of the States, and deeply affect those bodies. They are, in this respect, at the opposite pole from the first eleven.

Fairly construed these amendments may be said to rise to the dignity of a new Magna Charta. . . .

The first section of the fourteenth amendment is alone involved in the consideration of these cases. No searching analysis is necessary to eliminate its meaning. Its language is intelligible and direct. Nothing can be more transparent. Every word employed has an established signification. There is no room for construction. There is nothing to construe. Elaboration may obscure, but cannot make clearer, the intent and purpose sought to be carried out. . . .

These amendments are all consequences of the late civil war. The prejudices and apprehension as to the central government which prevailed when the Constitution was adopted were dispelled by the light of experience. The public mind became satisfied that there was less danger of tyranny in the head than of anarchy and tyranny in the members. The provisions of this section are all eminently conservative in their character. They are a bulwark of defence, and can never be made an engine of oppression.

The language employed is unqualified in its scope. There is no exception in its terms, and there can be properly none in their application. By the language "citizens of the United States" was meant all such citizens; and by "any person" was meant all persons within the jurisdiction of the State. No distinction is intimated on account of race or color. This court has no authority to interpolate a limitation that is neither expressed nor implied. Our duty is to execute the law, not to make it. The protection provided was not intended to be confined to those of any particular race or class, but to embrace equally all races, classes, and conditions of men. It is objected that the power conferred is novel and large. The answer is that the novelty was known and the measure deliberately adopted. The power is beneficent in its nature, and cannot be abused. It is such as should exist in every well-ordered system of polity. Where could it be more appropriately lodged than in the hands to which it is confided? It is necessary to enable the government of the nation to secure to every one within its jurisdiction the rights and privileges enumerated, which, according to the plainest considerations of reason and justice and the fundamental principles of the social compact, all are entitled to enjoy. Without such authority any government claiming to be national is glaringly defective. The construction adopted by the majority of my brethren is, in my judgment, much too narrow. It defeats, by a limitation not anticipated, the intent of those by whom the instrument was framed and of those by whom it was adopted. To the extent of that limitation it turns, as it were, what was meant for bread into a stone. By the Constitution, as it stood before the war, ample protection was given against oppression by the Union, but little was given against wrong and oppression by the States. That want was intended to be supplied by this amendment. Against the former this court has been called upon more than once to interpose. Authority of the same amplitude was intended to be conferred as to the latter. But this arm of our jurisdiction is, in these cases, stricken down by the judgment just given. Nowhere, than in this court, ought the will of the nation, as thus expressed, to be more liberally construed or more cordially executed. This determination of the majority seems to me to lie far in the other direction.

I earnestly hope that the consequences to follow may prove less serious and far-reaching than the minority fear they will be.

Notes and Queries

1. Do we need a Bill of Rights? As we mentioned in the introduction to this chapter, the Philadelphia Convention produced a Constitution that did not include a bill of rights. Opponents of the proposal considered the omission a crucial defect. Consider, for example, this extract from the *Letters of Brutus*, #2, 1 November 1787.

> Those who have governed have been found in all ages ever active to enlarge their powers and abridge the public liberty. This has induced the people in all countries, where any sense of freedom remained, to fix barriers against the encroachments of their rulers. . . . I presume, to an American, than (sic), that this principle is a fundamental one. . . . It is therefore the more astonishing, that this grand security, to the right of the people, is not found in this constitution.

In response, Hamilton wrote in *Federalist* 84 that a bill of rights, rather than restraining the federal government, would actually provide opportunities for its expansion.

> I go further, and affirm that bills of rights, in the sense and in the extent in which they are contended for, are not only unnecessary in the proposed constitution, but would even be dangerous. They would contain various exceptions to powers which are not granted; and on this very account, would afford a colourable pretext to claim more than were granted. For why declare that things shall not be done which there is no power to do?

Which position do you find more persuasive?

2. In his dissent, Justice Field wrote that by virtue of the Fourteenth Amendment, "The privileges and immunities of citizens of the United States, of every one of them, is secured against abridgment in any form by any state." As we saw, however, the early advocates of a bill of rights were more fearful of the national government than of state governments. Why were the proponents of a bill of rights not equally concerned with state infringements of liberty?

3. To what extent does the Fourteenth Amendment reflect fear not of the national government but rather of the states? Would such a fear, if recognized by the Fourteenth Amendment, reflect a profound or revolutionary change in our understanding of the relationship of citizens to the states? Of the relationship between the federal governments and the states? Is this the change Justice Swayne had in mind when he called the Reconstruction Amendments "a new departure, and . . . an important epoch in the constitutional history of the country"?

4. How does Miller appeal to the intent of the Framers of the Reconstruction Amendments? What distinction does he draw from this intent? If his interpretation is correct, how great a change in federal-state relations was brought about by these Amendments?

5. Note that Justice Field, dissenting, appealed to "principles of morality" and "inherent rights" to maintain that

all the common rights of citizenship were contained in the meaning of the "privileges or immunities of citizens of the United States." Does this appeal have any basis in the history or the text of the Constitution? If not, then what—if anything—legitimates the appeal to such principles or rights?

Palko v. Connecticut
302 U.S. 319, 58 S.Ct. 149, 82 L.Ed. 288 (1937)

Palko was indicted and tried for first degree murder, but a jury found him guilty of second-degree murder and he was given a life sentence. A Connecticut statute, however, permitted the state to appeal rulings and decisions "upon all questions of law arising on the trial of criminal cases." The state appealed and a new trial was ordered. Palko was found guilty and sentenced to death. Palko appealed, arguing that the second trial violated the double jeopardy clause of the Fifth Amendment. Opinion of the Court: *Cardozo*, Black, Brandeis, Hughes, McReynolds, Roberts, Stone, Sutherland. Dissenting opinion: *Butler*.

Mr. Justice CARDOZO delivered the opinion of the Court.

1. The execution of the sentence will not deprive appellant of his life without the process of law assured to him by the Fourteenth Amendment of the Federal Constitution.

The argument for appellant is that whatever is forbidden by the Fifth Amendment is forbidden by the Fourteenth also. The Fifth Amendment, which is not directed to the States, but solely to the federal government, creates immunity from double jeopardy. No person shall be "subject for the same offense to be twice put in jeopardy of life or limb." The Fourteenth Amendment ordains, "nor shall any State deprive any person of life, liberty, or property, without due process of law." To retry a defendant, though under one indictment and only one, subjects him, it is said, to double jeopardy in violation of the Fifth Amendment, if the prosecution is one on behalf of the United States. From this the consequence is said to follow that there is a denial of life or liberty without due process of law, if the prosecution is one on behalf of the People of a state. . . .

. . . Right-minded men . . . could reasonably, even if mistakenly, believe that a second trial was lawful in prosecutions subject to the Fifth Amendment, if it was all in the same case. Even more plainly, right-minded men could reasonably believe that in espousing that conclusion they were not favoring a practice repugnant to the conscience of mankind. Is double jeopardy in such circumstances, if double jeopardy it must be called, a denial of due process forbidden to the States? The tyranny of labels . . . must not lead us to leap to a conclusion that a word which in one set of facts may stand for oppression or enormity is of like effect in every other.

We have said that in appellant's view the Fourteenth Amendment is to be taken as embodying the prohibitions of the Fifth. His thesis is even broader. Whatever would be a violation of the original bill of rights (Amendments I to VIII) if done by the federal government is now equally unlawful by force of the Fourteenth Amendment if done by a state. There is no such general rule.

The Fifth Amendment provides, among other things, that no person shall be held to answer for a capital or otherwise infamous crime unless on presentment or indictment of a grand jury. This court has held that, in prosecutions by a state, presentment or indictment by a grand jury may give way to informations at the instance of a public officer. *Hurtado v. California* (1884). The Fifth Amendment provides also that no person shall be compelled in any criminal case to be a witness against himself. This court has said that, in prosecutions by a state, the exemption will fail if the state elects to end it. *Twining v. New Jersey* (1908). The Sixth Amendment calls for a jury trial in criminal cases and the Seventh for a jury trial in civil cases at common law where the value in controversy shall exceed $20. This court has ruled that consistently with those amendments trial by jury may be modified by a state or abolished altogether.

On the other hand, the due process clause of the Fourteenth Amendment may make it unlawful for a state to abridge by its statutes the freedom of speech which the First Amendment safeguards against encroachment by the Congress, *De Jonge v. Oregon* (1937); *Herndon v. Lowry* (1937); or the like freedom of the press *Grosjean v. American Press Co.* (1936); *Near v. Minnesota* (1931); or the free exercise of religion, *Pierce v. Society of Sisters* (1925); or the right of peaceable assembly, without which speech would be unduly trammeled, *De Jonge*; *Herndon*; or the right of one accused of crime to the benefit of counsel *Powell v. Alabama* (1932). In these and other situations immunities that are valid as against the federal government by force of the specific pledges of particular amendments have been found to be implicit in the concept of ordered liberty, and thus, through the Fourteenth Amendment, become valid as against the states.

The line of division may seem to be wavering and broken if there is a hasty catalogue of the cases on the one side and the other. Reflection and analysis will induce a different view. There emerges the perception of a rationalizing principle which gives to discrete instances a proper order and coherence. The right to trial by jury and the immunity from prosecution except as the result of an indictment may have value and importance. Even so, they are not of the very essence of a scheme of ordered liberty. To abolish them is not to violate a "principle of justice so rooted in the traditions and conscience of our people as to be ranked as fundamental." *Snyder.* Few would be so narrow or provincial as to maintain that a fair and enlightened system of justice would be impossible without them. What is true of jury trials and indictments is true also, as the cases show, of the immunity from compulsory self-incrimination. This too might be lost, and justice still be done. . . . Justice, however, would not perish if the accused were subject to a duty to respond to orderly inquiry. The exclusion of these immunities and privileges from the privileges and immunities protected against the action of the States has not been arbitrary or casual. It has been dictated by a study and appreciation of the meaning, the essential implications, of liberty itself.

We reach a different plane of social and moral values when we pass to the privileges and immunities that have been taken over from the earlier articles of the Federal Bill of Rights and brought within the Fourteenth Amendment by a process of absorption. These in their origin were effective against the federal government alone. If the Fourteenth Amendment has absorbed them, the process of absorption has had its source in the belief that neither liberty nor justice would exist if they were sacrificed. *Twining.* This is true, for illustration, of freedom of thought and speech. Of that freedom one may say that it is the matrix, the indispensable condition, of nearly every other form of freedom. With rare aberrations a pervasive recognition of that truth can be traced in our history, political and legal. So it has come about that the domain of liberty, withdrawn by the Fourteenth Amendment from encroachment by the states, has been enlarged by latter-day judgments to include liberty of the mind as well as liberty of action. The extension became, indeed, a logical imperative when once it was recognized, as long ago it was, that liberty is something more than exemption from physical restraint, and that even in the field of substantive rights and duties the legislative judgment, if oppressive and arbitrary, may be overridden by the courts. . . . Fundamental too in the concept of due process, and so in that of liberty, is the thought that condemnation shall be rendered only after trial. . . .

Our survey of the cases serves, we think, to justify the statement that the dividing line between them, if not unfaltering throughout its course, has been true for the most part to a unifying principle. On which side of the line the case made out by the appellant has appropriate location must be the next inquiry and the final one. Is that kind of double jeopardy to which the statute has subjected him a hardship so acute and shocking that our policy will not endure it? Does it violate those "fundamental principles of liberty and justice which lie at the base of all our civil and political institutions"? *Hebert v. Louisiana* (1926). The answer surely must be "no." What the answer would have to be if the state were permitted after a trial free from error to try the accused over again or to bring another case against him, we have no occasion to consider. We deal with the statute before us and no other. The state is not attempting to wear the accused out by a multitude of cases with accumulated trials. It asks no more than this, that the case against him shall go on until there shall be a trial free from the corrosion of substantial legal error. . . . This is not cruelty at all, nor even vexation in any immoderate degree. If the trial had been infected with error adverse to the accused, there might have been review at his instance, and as often as necessary to purge the vicious taint. A reciprocal privilege, subject at all times to the discretion of the presiding judge, . . . has now been granted to the state. There is here no seismic innovation. The edifice of justice stands, its symmetry, to many, greater than before.

The judgment is affirmed.

Mr. Justice BUTLER dissents.

Notes and Queries

1. The specific holding in *Palko* was overruled in *Benton v. Maryland*, 395 U.S. 784 (1969). Nevertheless, *Palko* remains influential for its suggestion that some liberties are of the "very essence of ordered liberty." This test has strongly influenced the development of the incorporation doctrine and the Court's fundamental rights jurisprudence.

2. The plaintiff argued "whatever would be a violation of the original Bill of Rights if done by the federal government is now equally unlawful by force of the Fourteenth Amendment if done by a state." But there is no written directive in the text of the Constitution that tells us that a violation of the first eight (or ten?) amendments by a state is unconstitutional because it violates the due process clause of the Fourteenth Amendment. As Justice Cardozo indicated, however, in some cases the Court had held that certain provisions of the Bill of Rights did apply to the states, where others did not.

Although the precedents seemed "wavering and bro- ken," Justice Cardozo argued that in fact the Court had utilized a "rationalizing principle" to distinguish the cases. Put simply, some of the provisions of the Bill of Rights are "of the very essence of a scheme of ordered liberty," and some are not. Only the former apply to the states.

How does the Court know which rights are essential to ordered liberty? Does the constitutional text offer any guidance? What criteria did Justice Cardozo propose for determining which liberties are so essential, and those that are not? Can we trace those criteria back to the Constitu- tion? Or is the determination of what is "fundamental" in- evitably just a function of a judge's personal opinion? This is a difficulty that influenced the development of the incor- poration doctrine long after *Palko*, as we shall see in the cases that follow. See Hadley Arkes, *Beyond the Constitu- tion.* (Princeton, Princeton University Press, 1990), 159– 168.

3. Until very recently, *Palko* was one of a mere handful of cases to make comparisons to other constitutional de- mocracies. In footnote #1, the Court noted that bans against compulsory self-incrimination are a part of estab- lished criminal procedure in continental Europe, and that double jeopardy "is not everywhere forbidden." Does this suggest that a liberty must be "universal" or widely shared among constitutional democracies to rank as "essential to the very essence of ordered liberty"? Scholars of compara- tive constitutional law typically refer to these shared val- ues as "the common core" of liberties protected by constitutional states. Should the recognition of a liberty in other constitutions influence the "significance" of that liberty in the American Constitution?

As the doctrine of incorporation developed, a signifi- cant difference between *Palko*'s use of comparative mate- rials and their use by later Courts appeared. In the fundamental fairness approach, the concept of "ordered liberty," proposed in *Palko*, was reduced to the question of whether a "fair and enlightened system of justice" would be "impossible" without a particular right. In con- trast, the selective incorporation doctrine, developed in *Cohen* and described in the introduction to this chapter, "proceeds upon the . . . assumption that state criminal processes are not imaginary and theoretical schemes but actual systems bearing virtually every characteristic of the common-law system that has been developing contempo- raneously in England and in this country." *Duncan v. Lou- isiana,* (1968). Hence, the focus should be less on the traditions of European legal systems, or on those of "civi- lized peoples," and more on Anglo-American traditions. As we shall see later in the chapter, this debate has been rekindled in recent cases concerning the death penalty.

Adamson v. California

332 U.S. 46, 67 S.Ct. 1672, 91 L.Ed. 1903 (1947)

California's constitution allowed prosecuting attorneys and trial judges to comment on a defendant's failure to testify at trial. As a result, juries were permitted to consider a defendant's silence in reaching a decision on his or her guilt. Adamson, charged with murder, refused to testify at his trial. The prosecutor suggested to the jury that his si- lence was evidence of guilt. Adamson was convicted and sentenced to death, a sentence upheld by the state su- preme court. He appealed to the Supreme Court, claiming that the prosecutor's argument violated the self-incrimination clause of the Fifth Amendment. Opinion of the Court: *Reed*, Burton, Frankfurter, Jackson, Vinson. Concurring opinion: *Frankfurter*. Dissenting opinions: *Black*, Doug- las, *Murphy*, Rutledge.

Mr. Justice REED delivered the opinion of the Court.

. . . [A]ppellant urges that the provision of the Fifth Amend- ment that no person "shall be compelled in any criminal case to be a witness against himself" is a fundamental na- tional privilege or immunity protected against state abridg- ment by the Fourteenth Amendment or a privilege or immunity secured, through the Fourteenth Amendment, against deprivation by state action because it is a personal right, enumerated in the federal Bill of Rights.

. . . Therefore, appellant argues, the due process clause of the Fourteenth Amendment protects his privilege against self-incrimination. The due process clause of the Fourteenth Amendment, however, does not draw all the rights of the federal Bill of Rights under its protection. That contention was made and rejected in *Palko v. Connecticut.* . . . It was rejected with citation of the cases excluding several of the rights, protected by the Bill of Rights, against infringement by the National Government. Nothing has been called to our attention that either the framers of the Fourteenth Amendment or the states that adopted intended its due process clause to draw within its scope the earlier amendments to the Constitution. *Palko* held that such provisions of the Bill of Rights as were "im- plicit in the concept of ordered liberty," . . . became secure from state interference by the clause. But it held nothing more.

Specifically, the due process clause does not protect, by virtue of its mere existence, the accused's freedom from giving testimony by compulsion in state trials that is secured to him against federal interference by the Fifth Amendment. For a state to require testimony from an accused is not necessarily a breach of a state's obligation to give a fair trial. Therefore, we must examine the effect of the California law applied in this trial to see whether the comment on failure to testify violates the protection against state action that the due process clause does grant to an accused. The due process clause forbids compulsion to testify by fear of hurt, torture or exhaustion. It forbids any other type of coercion that falls within the scope of due process. California follows Anglo-American legal tradition in excusing defendants in criminal prosecutions from compulsory testimony. That is a matter of legal policy and not because of the requirements of due process under the Fourteenth Amendment. So our inquiry is directed, not at the broad question of the constitutionality of compulsory testimony from the accused under the due process clause, but to the constitutionality of the provision of the California law that permits comment upon his failure to testify. It is, of course, logically possible that while an accused might be required, under appropriate penalties, to submit himself as a witness without a violation of due process, comment by judge or jury on inferences to be drawn from his failure to testify, in jurisdictions where an accused's privilege against self-incrimination is protected, might deny due process. For example, a statute might declare that a permitted refusal to testify would compel an acceptance of the truth of the prosecution's evidence.

. . . For a state to require testimony from an accused is not necessarily a breach of a state's obligation to give a fair trial. Therefore, we must examine the effect of the California law . . . to see whether the comment on failure to testify violates the protection . . . that the due process clause does grant to an accused.

Generally, comment on the failure of an accused to testify is forbidden in American jurisdictions. . . . California, however, is one of a few states that permit limited comment upon a defendant's failure to testify. That permission is narrow. . . . The California law . . . authorizes comment by court and counsel upon the "failure of the defendant to explain or to deny by his testimony any evidence or facts in the case against him." This does not involve any presumption, rebuttable or irrebuttable, either of guilt or of the truth of any fact, that is offered in evidence. . . . It allows inferences to be drawn from proven facts. Because of this clause, the court can direct the jury's attention to whatever evidence there may be that a defendant could deny and the prosecution can argue as to inferences that may be drawn from the accused's failure to testify. . . .

California has prescribed a method for advising the jury in the search for truth. However sound may be the legislative conclusion that an accused should not be compelled in any criminal case to be a witness against himself, we see no reason why comment should not be made upon his silence. . . .

AFFIRMED.

Mr. Justice FRANKFURTER, concurring.

. . . Sensible and justminded men, in important affairs of life, deem it significant that a man remains silent when confronted with serious and responsible evidence against himself which it is within his power to contradict. The notion that to allow jurors to do that which sensible and rightminded men do every day violates the "immutable principles of justice" as conceived by a civilized society is to trivialize the importance of "due process."

For historical reasons a limited immunity from the common duty to testify was written into the Federal Bill of Rights, and I am prepared to agree that, as part of that immunity, comment on the failure of an accused to take the witness stand is forbidden in federal prosecutions. It is so, of course, by explicit act of Congress. . . . But to suggest that such a limitation can be drawn out of "due process" in its protection of ultimate decency in a civilized society is to suggest that the Due Process Clause fastened fetters of unreason upon the States. . . .

Between the incorporation of the Fourteenth Amendment into the Constitution and the beginning of the present membership of the Court—a period of 70 years—the scope of that Amendment was passed upon by 43 judges. Of all these judges, only one, who may respectfully be called an eccentric exception, ever indicated the belief that the Fourteenth Amendment was a shorthand summary of the first eight Amendments theretofore limiting only the Federal Government, and that due process incorporated those eight Amendments as restrictions upon the powers of the States. . . .

Those reading the English language with the meaning which it ordinarily conveys, those conversant with the political and legal history of the concept of due process, those sensitive to the relations of the States to the central government as well as the relation of some of the provisions of the Bill of Rights to the process of justice, would hardly recognize the Fourteenth Amendment as a cover for the various explicit provisions of the first eight Amendments. Some of these are enduring reflections of experience with human nature, while some express the restricted views of Eighteenth-Century England regarding the best methods for the ascertainment of facts. The notion that the Fourteenth Amendment was a covert way of imposing upon the States all the rules which it seemed important to Eighteenth Century statesmen to write into the Federal Amendments, was rejected by judges who were themselves witnesses of the process by which the Fourteenth Amendment became part of the Constitution. Arguments that may now be adduced to prove that the first eight Amendments were concealed within the historic phrasing of the Fourteenth Amendment were not unknown at the time of its adoption. A surer estimate of their bearing was possible for judges at the time than distorting distance is likely to vouchsafe. Any evidence of design or purpose not contemporaneously known could hardly have influenced those who ratified the Amendment. . . .

. . . There is suggested merely a selective incorporation of the first eight Amendments into the Fourteenth Amendment. Some are in and some are out, but we are left in the dark as to which are in and which are out. Nor are we given the calculus for determining which go in and which stay out. If the basis of selection is merely that those provisions of the first eight Amendments are incorporated which commend themselves to individual justices as indispensable to the dignity and happiness of a free man, we are thrown back to a merely subjective test. The protection against unreasonable search and seizure might have primacy for one judge, while trial by a jury of 12 for every claim above $20 might appear to another as an ultimate need in a free society. In the history of thought "natural law" has a much longer and much better founded meaning and justification than such subjective selection of the first eight Amendments for incorporation into the Fourteenth. If all that is meant is that due process contains within itself certain minimal standards which are "of the very essence of a scheme of ordered liberty," *Palko v. Connecticut*, putting upon this Court the duty of applying these standards from time to time, then we have merely arrived at the insight which our predecessors long ago expressed. . . . This guidance bids us to be duly mindful of the heritage of the past, with its great lessons of how liberties are won and how they are lost. As judges charged with the delicate task of subjecting the government of a continent to the Rule of Law we must be particularly mindful that it is "a constitution we are expounding," so that it should not be imprisoned in what are merely legal forms even though they have the sanction of the Eighteenth Century.

It may not be amiss to restate the pervasive function of the Fourteenth Amendment in exacting from the States observance of basic liberties. . . . The Amendment neither comprehends the specific provisions by which the founders deemed it appropriate to restrict the federal government nor is it confined to them. The Due Process Clause of the Fourteenth Amendment has an independent potency, precisely as does the Due Process Clause of the Fifth Amendment in relation to the Federal Government. It ought not to require argument to reject the notion that due process of law meant one thing in the Fifth Amendment and another in the Fourteenth. . . .

A construction which gives to due process no independent function but turns it into a summary of the specific provisions of the Bill of Rights would, as has been noted, tear up by the roots much of the fabric of law in the several States, and would deprive the States of opportunity for reforms in legal process designed for extending the area of freedom. It would assume that no other abuses would reveal themselves in the course of time than those which had become manifest in 1791. Such a view not only disregards the historic meaning of "due process." It leads inevitably to a warped construction of specific provisions of the Bill of Rights to bring within their scope conduct clearly condemned by due process but not easily fitting into the pigeon-holes of the specific provisions. It seems pretty late in the day to suggest that a phrase so laden with historic meaning should be given an improvised content consisting of some but not all of the provisions of the first eight Amendments, selected on an undefined basis, with improvisation of content for the provisions so selected.

. . . The relevant question is whether the criminal proceedings which resulted in conviction deprived the accused of the due process of law to which the United States Constitution entitled him. Judicial review of that guaranty of the Fourteenth Amendment inescapably imposes upon this Court an exercise of judgment upon the whole course of the proceedings in order to ascertain whether they offend those canons of decency and fairness which express the notions of justice of English-speaking peoples even toward those charged with the most heinous offenses. These standards of justice are not authoritatively formulated anywhere as though they were prescriptions in a pharmacopoeia. But neither does the application of the Due Process Clause imply that judges are wholly at large. The judicial judgment in applying the Due Process Clause must move within the limits of accepted notions of justice and is not to be based upon the idiosyncrasies of a merely personal judgment. The fact that judges among themselves may differ whether in a particular case a trial offends accepted notions of justice is not disproof that general rather than idiosyncratic standards are applied. An important safeguard against such merely individual judgment is an alert deference to the judgment of the State court under review.

Mr. Justice MURPHY, with whom Mr. Justice RUTLEDGE concurs, dissenting.

While in substantial agreement with the views of Mr. Justice Black, I have one reservation and one addition to make.

I agree that the specific guarantees of the Bill of Rights should be carried over intact into the first section of the Fourteenth Amendment. But I am not prepared to say that the latter is entirely and necessarily limited by the Bill of Rights. Occasions may arise where a proceeding falls so far short of conforming to fundamental standards of procedure as to warrant constitutional condemnation in terms of a lack of due process despite the absence of a specific provision in the Bill of Rights. . . .

Mr. Justice BLACK, dissenting.

This decision reasserts a constitutional theory spelled out in *Twining v. New Jersey* (1908), that this Court is endowed by the Constitution with boundless power under "natural law" periodically to expand and contract constitutional standards to conform to the Court's conception of what at a particular time constitutes "civilized decency" and "fundamental liberty and justice. . . ."

. . . I would not reaffirm the *Twining* decision. I think that decision and the "natural law" theory of the Constitution upon which it relies degrade the constitutional safeguards of the Bill of Rights and simultaneously appropriate for this Court a broad power which we are not authorized by the Constitution to exercise. . . .

My study of the historical events that culminated in the Fourteenth Amendment, and the expressions of those who sponsored and favored, as well as those who opposed its submission and passage, persuades me that one of the chief objects that the provisions of the Amendment's first section, separately, and as a whole, were intended to accomplish was to make the Bill of Rights, applicable to the states. With full knowledge of the import of the *Barron* decision, the framers and backers of the Fourteenth Amendment proclaimed its purpose to be to overturn the constitutional rule that case had announced. This historical purpose has never received full consideration or exposition in any opinion of this Court interpreting the Amendment.

For this reason, I am attaching to this dissent, an appendix which contains a resume, by no means complete, of the Amendment's history. In my judgment that history conclusively demonstrates that the language of the first section of the Fourteenth Amendment, taken as a whole, was thought by those responsible for its submission to the people, and by those who opposed its submission, sufficiently explicit to guarantee that thereafter no state could deprive its citizens of the privileges and protections of the Bill of Rights. . . . And I further contend that the "natural

law" formula which the Court uses to reach its conclusion in this case should be abandoned as an incongruous excrescence on our Constitution. I believe that formula to be itself a violation of our Constitution, in that it subtly conveys to courts, at the expense of legislatures, ultimate power over public policies in fields where no specific provision of the Constitution limits legislative power. . . .

. . . I cannot consider the Bill of Rights to be an outworn 18th Century 'strait jacket'. . . . Its provisions may be thought outdated abstractions by some. And it is true that they were designed to meet ancient evils. But they are the same kind of human evils that have emerged from century to century wherever excessive power is sought by the few at the expense of the many. In my judgment the people of no nation can lose their liberty so long as a Bill of Rights like ours survives and its basic purposes are conscientiously interpreted, enforced and respected so as to afford continuous protection against old, as well as new, devices and practices which might thwart those purposes. I fear to see the consequences of the Court's practice of substituting its own concepts of decency and fundamental justice for the language of the Bill of Rights as its point of departure in interpreting and enforcing that Bill of Rights. If the choice must be between the selective process of the *Palko* decision applying some of the Bill of Rights to the States, or the *Twining* rule applying none of them, I would choose the *Palko* selective process. But rather than accept either of these choices. I would follow what I believe was the original purpose of the Fourteenth Amendment—to extend to all the people of the nation the complete protection of the Bill of Rights. To hold that this Court can determine what, if any, provisions of the Bill of Rights will be enforced, and if so to what degree, is to frustrate the great design of a written Constitution.

Conceding the possibility that this Court is now wise enough to improve on the Bill of Rights by substituting natural law concepts for the Bill of Rights, I think the possibility is entirely too speculative to agree to take that course. I would therefore hold in this case that the full protection of the Fifth Amendment's proscription against compelled testimony must be afforded by California. This I would do because of reliance upon the original purpose of the Fourteenth Amendment.

It is an illusory apprehension that literal application of some or all of the provisions of the Bill of Rights to the States would unwisely increase the sum total of the powers of this Court to invalidate state legislation. The Federal Government has not been harmfully burdened by the requirement that enforcement of federal laws affecting civil liberty conform literally to the Bill of Rights. Who would advocate its repeal? It must be conceded, of course, that the natural-law-due-process formula, which the Court today reaffirms, has been interpreted to limit substantially this Court's power to prevent state violations of the individual civil liberties guaranteed by the Bill of Rights. But this formula also has been used in the past and can be used in the future, to license this Court, in considering regulatory legislation, to roam at large in the broad expanses of policy and morals and to trespass, all too freely, on the legislative domain of the States as well as the Federal Government.

Mr. Justice Douglas joins in this opinion.

Notes and Queries

1. In a doctrinal sense, *Adamson* reaffirmed Justice Cardozo's approach in *Palko*. In a larger sense, though, both cases raise questions about the methodology of constitutional interpretation and why justices sometimes disagree about those methods. Indeed, clearly articulated in *Adamson* are the three major positions developed by various justices on the question of incorporation.

Justice Black's opinion, for example, represents the strongest challenge to selective incorporation. Black insisted that Frankfurter's use of selective incorporation, like appeals to natural law, wrongly entrusted judges with unprincipled discretion to "expand and contract constitutional standards to conform to the Court's conception of . . . civilized decency. . . ." Does Black's advocacy of total incorporation avoid the perils of judicial subjectivity that led him to reject selective incorporation? Justice Harlan thought not, observing in several cases that the "so-called specific" provisions of the Bill of Rights were themselves written in vague and general language that demanded interpretation.

Black also wrote

the "natural law" formula which the Court uses to reach its conclusion in this case should be abandoned as an incongruous excrescence on our Constitution. I believe that formula to be itself a violation of our Constitution, in that it subtly conveys to courts, at the expense of legislatures, ultimate power over public policies in fields where no specific provision of the Constitution limits legislative power. . . .

Black's impassioned appeal is reminiscent of Brutus, who predicted that

The judicial power will operate to effect, in the most certain, but yet silent and imperceptible manner, what is evidently the tendency of the constitution—I mean,

an entire subversion of the legislative, executive, and judicial power of the individual states. . . . That the judicial power of the United States, will lean strongly in favour of the general government, and will give such an explanation to the constitution, as will favour an extension of its own jurisdiction, is very evident.

In response to Black, Frankfurter argued that

Judicial review . . . inescapably imposes upon this Court an exercise of judgment upon the . . . proceedings . . . to ascertain whether they offend those canons of decency and fairness which express the notions of justice of English-speaking peoples. . . . These standards of justice are not authoritatively formulated anywhere as though they were prescriptions in a pharmacopoeia. But neither does the application of the Due Process Clause imply that judges are wholly at large. . . .

Does Frankfurter's insistence that judges will not draw upon their own subjective preferences in interpreting the due process clause adequately respond to Black's challenge? Does it respond to Brutus' prediction about the transference of power from states to the federal judiciary?

2. In "Do We Have an Unwritten Constitution," 27 Stanford Law Review (1975), Thomas C. Grey describes the interpretive debate in *Adamson* as a battle between a "pure interpretivist" model and a "broader interpretive model." According to Grey, Justice Black is a pure interpretivist who stressed the need for fidelity to the constitutional text. The broader model differs from the pure interpretivist model in its

acceptance of the Court's additional role as the expounder of basic national ideals of individual liberty and fair treatment, even when the content of these ideals is not expressed as a matter of positive law in the written Constitution. It must at once be conceded that such a role for our courts is more difficult to justify than is the role assigned by the pure interpretivist model. Why, one asks, are the courts better able to discern and articulate basic national ideals than are the people's politically responsible representatives?

How, if at all, can this question be answered?

4. Assuming the task itself is proper, why should the Court limit its inquiry into the "canons of decency and fairness" to the experience of English-speaking peoples? Recall that in *Palko*, Justice Cardozo utilized the traditions of continental Europe and elsewhere to conclude protections against double jeopardy were not "essential to a scheme of ordered liberty."

Rochin v. California

342 U.S. 165, 72 S. Ct. 205, 96 L. Ed. 183 (1952)

Three police officers, suspecting Rochin was selling drugs, entered his home and forced their way into the bedroom occupied by him and his wife. When asked about two capsules lying on a bedside table, Rochin put them in his mouth. After an unsuccessful struggle to extract them by force, the officers took him to a hospital, where doctors acting under orders from the police pumped his stomach against his will. He vomited two capsules of morphine. These were admitted in evidence over his objection and he was convicted in a state court of violating a state law forbidding possession of morphine. Opinion of the Court: *Frankfurter*, Vinson, Reed, Jackson, Burton, Clark. Concurring: *Black*, *Douglas*.

Mr. Justice FRANKFURTER delivered the opinion of the Court.

In our federal system the administration of criminal justice is predominantly committed to the care of the States. The power to define crimes belongs to Congress only as an appropriate means of carrying into execution its limited grant of legislative powers. U.S. Const., Art. I, 8, cl. 18. Broadly speaking, crimes in the United States are what the laws of the individual States make them, subject to the limitations of Art. I, 10, cl. 1, in the original Constitution, prohibiting bills of attainder and ex post facto laws, and of the Thirteenth and Fourteenth Amendments.

These limitations, in the main, concern not restrictions upon the powers of the States to define crime, except in the restricted area where federal authority has preempted the field, but restrictions upon the manner in which the States may enforce their penal codes. Accordingly, in reviewing a State criminal conviction under a claim of right guaranteed by the Due Process Clause of the Fourteenth Amendment, from which is derived the most far-reaching and most frequent federal basis of challenging State criminal justice, "we must be deeply mindful of the responsibilities of the States for the enforcement of criminal laws, and exercise with due humility our merely negative function in subjecting convictions from state courts to the very narrow scrutiny which the Due Process Clause of the Fourteenth Amendment authorizes."

Due process of law, "itself a historical product," is not to be turned into a destructive dogma against the States in the administration of their systems of criminal justice.

However, this Court too has its responsibility. Regard for the requirements of the Due Process Clause "inescapably imposes upon this Court an exercise of judgment upon the whole course of the proceedings [resulting in a conviction] in order to ascertain whether they offend those canons of decency and fairness which express the notions of justice of English-speaking peoples even toward those charged with the most heinous offenses." These standards of justice are not authoritatively formulated anywhere as though they were specifics. Due process of law is a summarized constitutional guarantee of respect for those personal immunities which, as Mr. Justice Cardozo twice wrote for the Court, are "so rooted in the traditions and conscience of our people as to be ranked as fundamental," *Snyder v. Massachusetts* (1934) or are "implicit in the concept of ordered liberty." *Palko v. Connecticut* (1937).

The Court's function in the observance of this settled conception of the Due Process Clause does not leave us without adequate guides in subjecting State criminal procedures to constitutional judgment. In dealing not with the machinery of government but with human rights, the absence of formal exactitude, or want of fixity of meaning, is not an unusual or even regrettable attribute of constitutional provisions. Words being symbols do not speak without a gloss. On the one hand the gloss may be the deposit of history, whereby a term gains technical content. Thus the requirements of the Sixth and Seventh Amendments for trial by jury in the federal courts have a rigid meaning. No changes or chances can alter the content of the verbal symbol of "jury"—a body of twelve men who must reach a unanimous conclusion if the verdict is to go against the defendant. On the other hand, the gloss of some of the verbal symbols of the Constitution does not give them a fixed technical content. It exacts a continuing process of application.

When the gloss has thus not been fixed but is a function of the process of judgment, the judgment is bound to fall differently at different times and differently at the same time through different judges. Even more specific provisions, such as the guaranty of freedom of speech and the detailed protection against unreasonable searches and seizures, have inevitably evoked as sharp divisions in this Court as the least specific and most comprehensive protection of liberties, the Due Process Clause.

The vague contours of the Due Process Clause do not leave judges at large. We may not draw on our merely personal and private notions and disregard the limits that bind judges in their judicial function. Even though the concept of due process of law is not final and fixed, these limits are derived from considerations that are fused in the whole nature of our judicial process. See Cardozo, *The Nature of the Judicial Process; The Growth of the Law; The Paradoxes of Legal Science*. These are considerations deeply rooted in reason and in the compelling traditions of the legal profession. The Due Process Clause places upon this Court the duty of exercising a judgment, within the narrow confines of judicial power in reviewing State convictions, upon interests of society pushing in opposite directions.

Due process of law thus conceived is not to be derided as resort to a revival of "natural law." To believe that this judicial exercise of judgment could be avoided by freezing "due process of law" at some fixed stage of time or thought is to suggest that the most important aspect of constitutional adjudication is a function for inanimate machines and not for judges, for whom the independence safeguarded by Article III of the Constitution was designed and who are presumably guided by established standards of judicial behavior. Even cybernetics has not yet made that haughty claim. To practice the requisite detachment and to achieve sufficient objectivity no doubt demands of judges the habit of self-discipline and self-criticism, incertitude that one's own views are incontestable and alert tolerance toward views not shared. But these are precisely the presuppositions of our judicial process. They are precisely the qualities society has a right to expect from those entrusted with ultimate judicial power.

Restraints on our jurisdiction are self-imposed only in the sense that there is from our decisions no immediate appeal short of impeachment or constitutional amendment. But that does not make due process of law a matter of judicial caprice. The faculties of the Due Process Clause may be indefinite and vague, but the mode of their ascertainment is not self-willed. In each case "due process of law" requires an evaluation based on a disinterested inquiry pursued in the spirit of science, on a balanced order of facts exactly and fairly stated, on the detached consideration of conflicting claims, on a judgment not ad hoc and episodic but duly mindful of reconciling the needs both of continuity and of change in a progressive society.

Applying these general considerations to the circumstances of the present case, we are compelled to conclude that the proceedings by which this conviction was obtained do more than offend some fastidious squeamishness or private sentimentalism about combatting crime too energetically. This is conduct that shocks the conscience. Illegally breaking into the privacy of the petitioner, the struggle to open his mouth and remove what was there, the forcible extraction of his stomach's contents—this course of proceeding by agents of government to obtain evidence is bound to offend even hardened sensibilities. They are methods too close to the rack and the screw to permit of constitutional differentiation.

It has long since ceased to be true that due process of law is heedless of the means by which otherwise relevant and credible evidence is obtained. . . . These decisions are not arbitrary exceptions to the comprehensive right of States to fashion their own rules of evidence for criminal trials. They are not sports in our constitutional law but applications of a general principle. They are only instances of the general requirement that States in their prosecutions respect certain decencies of civilized conduct. Due process of law, as a historic and generative principle, precludes defining, and thereby confining, these standards of conduct more precisely than to say that convictions cannot be brought about by methods that offend "a sense of justice." It would be a stultification of the responsibility which the course of constitutional history has cast upon this Court to hold that in order to convict a man the police cannot extract by force what is in his mind but can extract what is in his stomach. . . .

Use of involuntary verbal confessions in State criminal trials is constitutionally obnoxious not only because of their unreliability. They are inadmissible under the Due Process Clause even though statements contained in them may be independently established as true. Coerced confessions offend the community's sense of fair play and decency. So here, to sanction the brutal conduct which naturally enough was condemned by the court whose judgment is before us, would be to afford brutality the cloak of law. Nothing would be more calculated to discredit law and thereby to brutalize the temper of a society. . . .

We are not unmindful that hypothetical situations can be conjured up, shading imperceptibly from the circumstances of this case and by gradations producing practical differences despite seemingly logical extensions. But the Constitution is "intended to preserve practical and substantial rights, not to maintain theories."

On the facts of this case the conviction of the petitioner has been obtained by methods that offend the Due Process Clause. The judgment below must be

Reversed.

MR. JUSTICE MINTON took no part in the consideration or decision of this case.

MR. JUSTICE BLACK, concurring.

Adamson v. California (1947) sets out reasons for my belief that state as well as federal courts and law enforcement officers must obey the Fifth Amendment's command that "No person . . . shall be compelled in any criminal case to be a witness against himself." I think a person is compelled to be a witness against himself not only when he is compelled to testify, but also when as here, incriminating evidence is forcibly taken from him by a contrivance of modern science. . . .

In the view of a majority of the Court, however, the Fifth Amendment imposes no restraint of any kind on the states. They nevertheless hold that California's use of this evidence violated the Due Process Clause of the Fourteenth Amendment. Since they hold as I do in this case, I regret my inability to accept their interpretation without protest. But I believe that faithful adherence to the specific guarantees in the Bill of Rights insures a more permanent protection of individual liberty than that which can be afforded by the nebulous standards stated by the majority.

What the majority hold is that the Due Process Clause empowers this Court to nullify any state law if its application "shocks the conscience," offends "a sense of justice" or runs counter to the "decencies of civilized conduct." The majority emphasize that these statements do not refer to their own consciences or to their senses of justice and decency. For we are told that "we may not draw on our merely personal and private notions"; our judgment must be grounded on "considerations deeply rooted in reason and in the compelling traditions of the legal profession." We are further admonished to measure the validity of state practices, not by our reason, or by the traditions of the legal profession, but by "the community's sense of fair play and decency"; by the "traditions and conscience of our people"; or by "those canons of decency and fairness which express the notions of justice of English-speaking peoples." These canons are made necessary, it is said, because of "interests of society pushing in opposite directions."

If the Due Process Clause does vest this Court with such unlimited power to invalidate laws, I am still in doubt as to why we should consider only the notions of English-speaking peoples to determine what are immutable and fundamental principles of justice. Moreover, one may well ask what avenues of investigation are open to discover "canons" of conduct so universally favored that this Court should write them into the Constitution? All we are told is that the discovery must be made by an "evaluation based on a disinterested inquiry pursued in the spirit of science, on a balanced order of facts."

Some constitutional provisions are stated in absolute and unqualified language such, for illustration, as the First Amendment stating that no law shall be passed prohibiting the free exercise of religion or abridging the freedom of speech or press. Other constitutional provisions do require courts to choose between competing policies, such as the Fourth Amendment which, by its terms, necessitates a judicial decision as to what is an "unreasonable" search or seizure. There is, however, no express constitutional language granting judicial power to invalidate every state law of every kind deemed "unreasonable" or contrary to the Court's notion of civilized decencies. . . . Of even graver concern, however, is the use of the philosophy to nullify the Bill of Rights. I long ago concluded that the accordion-like qualities of this philosophy must inevitably imperil all the individual liberty safeguards specifically enumerated in the Bill of Rights. . . .

MR. JUSTICE DOUGLAS, concurring.

As an original matter it might be debatable whether the provision in the Fifth Amendment that no person "shall be compelled in any criminal case to be a witness against himself" serves the ends of justice. Not all civilized legal procedures recognize it. But the choice was made by the Framers, a choice which sets a standard for legal trials in this country. The Framers made it a standard of due process for prosecutions by the Federal Government. If it is a requirement of due process for a trial in the federal courthouse, it is impossible for me to say it is not a requirement of due process for a trial in the state courthouse. . . . Of course an accused can be compelled to be present at the trial, to stand, to sit, to turn this way or that, and to try on a cap or a coat. But I think that words taken from his lips, capsules taken from his stomach, blood taken from his veins are all inadmissible provided they are taken from him without his consent. They are inadmissible because of the command of the Fifth Amendment.

That is an unequivocal, definite and workable rule of evidence for state and federal courts. But we cannot in fairness free the state courts from that command and yet excoriate them for flouting the "decencies of civilized conduct" when they admit the evidence. That is to make the rule turn not on the Constitution but on the idiosyncrasies of the judges who sit here.

Notes and Queries

1. In *Breithaupt v. Abram* (1957), the Court found it was neither "brutal" nor "offensive" to take a blood sample from a suspected drunken driver while he was unconscious. In *Schmerber v. California* (1966), the Court sustained the constitutionality of a blood test taken against the expressed will of a suspect. Are these cases different in any meaningful way from *Rochin*? Do they support Justice Black's claim that the Court's approach in *Rochin* was purely subjective? Would deciding these cases on grounds of self-incrimination, as Black urged in *Adamson*, eliminate judicial subjectivity?

2. Germany's Federal Constitutional Court has imposed severe limits on the technical methods that can be em-

ployed in any penetration of the human body. In the *Pneumoencephalography Case* (1963), the Court invalidated a court-ordered puncture of a person's vertebral canal for the purpose of testing his responsibility for a crime. Certain administrative courts in Germany have also invalidated the polygraph test in criminal investigations.

To attach a person to a machine for the purpose of eliciting the truth, these courts have suggested, is an inadmissible invasion of a person's innermost self and a violation of human dignity. Donald P. Kommers, *The Constitutional Jurisprudence of the Federal Republic of Germany.* 2d ed. (Durham: Duke University Press, 1997), 332.

Duncan v. Louisiana
391 U.S. 145, 88 S.Ct. 1444, 20 L.Ed.2d 491 (1968)

Gary Duncan, a nineteen-year-old African American, was convicted of simple battery in Louisiana, a misdemeanor punishable by a maximum sentence of two years' imprisonment and a $300 fine. The judge denied Duncan's request for a trial by jury under a state constitutional provision that granted jury trials only in cases in which capital punishment or imprisonment at hard physical labor could be imposed. After exhausting his state remedies, Duncan appealed to the Supreme Court, claiming that the denial of a jury trial violated rights guaranteed to him by the United States Constitution. Opinion of the Court: *White*, Black, Brennan, Douglas, Fortas, Marshall, Warren. Concurring opinion: *Black*, Douglas, *Fortas*. Dissenting opinions: *Harlan*, Stewart.

Mr. Justice WHITE delivered the opinion of the Court.

The test for determining whether a right extended by the Fifth and Sixth Amendments with respect to federal criminal proceedings is also protected against state action by the Fourteenth Amendment has been phrased in a variety of ways in the opinions of this Court. The question has been asked whether a right is among those "fundamental principles of liberty and justice which lie at the base of all our civil and political institutions," . . . whether it is "basic in our system of jurisprudence," . . . and whether it is "a fundamental right, essential to a fair trial." . . . The claim before us is that the right to trial by jury guaranteed by the Sixth Amendment meets these tests. The position of Louisiana, on the other hand, is that the Constitution imposes upon the States no duty to give a jury trial in any criminal case, regardless of the seriousness of the crime or the size of the punishment which may be imposed. Because we believe that trial by jury in criminal cases is fundamental to the American scheme of justice, we hold that the Fourteenth Amendment guarantees a right of jury trial in all criminal cases which—were they to be tried in a federal court—would come within the Sixth Amendment's guarantee. Since we consider the appeal before us to be

such a case, we hold that the Constitution was violated when appellant's demand for jury trial was refused.

The guarantees of jury trial in the Federal and State Constitutions reflect a profound judgment about the way in which law should be enforced and justice administered. A right to jury trial is granted to criminal defendants in order to prevent oppression by the Government. Those who wrote our constitutions knew from history and experience that it was necessary to protect against unfounded criminal charges brought to eliminate enemies and against judges too responsive to the voice of higher authority. The framers of the constitutions strove to create an independent judiciary but insisted upon further protection against arbitrary action. Providing an accused with the right to be tried by a jury of his peers gave him an inestimable safeguard against the corrupt or overzealous prosecutor and against the compliant, biased, or eccentric judge. If the defendant preferred the common-sense judgment of a jury to the more tutored but perhaps less sympathetic reaction of the single judge, he was to have it. Beyond this, the jury trial provisions in the Federal and State Constitutions reflect a fundamental decision about the exercise of official power—a reluctance to entrust plenary powers over the life and liberty of the citizen to one judge or to a group of judges. Fear of unchecked power, so typical of our State and Federal Governments in other respects, found expression in the criminal law in this insistence upon community participation in the determination of guilt or innocence. The deep commitment of the Nation to the right of jury trial in serious criminal cases as a defense against arbitrary law enforcement qualifies for protection under the Due Process Clause of the Fourteenth Amendment, and must therefore be respected by the States.

II

Louisiana's final contention is that even if it must grant jury trials in serious criminal cases, the conviction before us is valid and constitutional because here the petitioner was tried for simple battery and was sentenced to only 60 days in the parish prison. We are not persuaded. It is doubtless true that there is a category of petty crimes or offenses which is not subject to the Sixth Amendment jury trial provision and should not be subject to the Fourteenth Amendment jury trial requirement here applied to the States. Crimes carrying possible penalties up to six months do not require a jury trial if they otherwise qualify as petty offenses. . . . But the penalty authorized for a particular crime is of major relevance in determining whether it is serious or not and may in itself, if severe enough, subject the trial to the mandates of the Sixth Amendment. . . . The penalty authorized by the law of the locality may be taken "as a gauge of its social and ethical judgments." . . . In the case before us the Legislature of Louisiana has made simple battery a criminal offense punishable by imprisonment for up to two years and a fine. The question, then, is whether a crime carrying such a penalty is an offense which Louisiana may insist on trying without a jury.

We think not. . . . Of course the boundaries of the petty offense category have always been ill-defined, if not ambulatory. In the absence of an explicit constitutional provision, the definitional task necessarily falls on the courts, which must either pass upon the validity of legislative attempts to identify those petty offenses which are exempt from jury trial or, where the legislature has not addressed itself to the problem, themselves face the question in the first instance. In either case it is necessary to draw a line in the spectrum of crime, separating petty from serious infractions. This process, although essential, cannot be wholly satisfactory, for it requires attaching different consequences to events which, when they lie near the line, actually differ very little.

. . . In the federal system, petty offenses are defined as those punishable by no more than six months in prison and a $500 fine. In 49 of the 50 States crimes subject to trial without a jury, which occasionally include simple battery, are punishable by no more than one year in jail. Moreover, in the late 18th century in America crimes triable without a jury were for the most part punishable by no more than a six-month prison term, although there appear to have been exceptions to this rule. We need not, however, settle in this case the exact location of the line between petty offenses and serious crimes. It is sufficient for our purposes to hold that a crime punishable by two years in prison is, based on past and contemporary standards in this country, a serious crime and not a petty offense. Consequently, appellant was entitled to a jury trial and it was error to deny it.

The judgment below is reversed and the case is remanded for proceedings not inconsistent with this opinion. Reversed and remanded.

Mr. Justice BLACK, with whom Mr. Justice DOUGLAS joins, concurring.

While I do not wish at this time to discuss at length my disagreement with Brother Harlan's [opinion] . . . I do want to point out what appears to me to be the basic difference between us. His view . . . is that "due process is an evolving concept" and therefore that it entails a "gradual process of judicial inclusion and exclusion" to ascertain those "immutable principles of free government which no member of the Union may disregard." Thus the Due Process Clause is treated as prescribing no specific and clearly ascertainable constitutional command that judges must obey in interpreting the Constitution, but rather as leaving judges free to decide at any particular time whether a particular rule or judicial formulation embodies an "immutable principl(e) of free government" or is "implicit in the concept of ordered liberty," or whether certain conduct "shocks the judge's conscience" or runs counter to some other similar, undefined and undefinable standard. Thus due process, according to my Brother Harlan, is to be a phrase with no permanent meaning, but one which is found to shift from time to time in accordance with judges' predilections and understandings of what is best for the country. If due process means this, the Fourteenth Amendment, in my opinion, might as well have been written that "no person shall be deprived of life, liberty or property except by laws that the judges of the United States Supreme Court shall find to be consistent with the immutable principles of free government." It is impossible for me to believe that such unconfined power is given to judges in our Constitution that is a written one in order to limit governmental power.

Another tenet of the *Twining* doctrine as restated by my Brother Harlan is that "due process of law requires only fundamental fairness." But the "fundamental fairness" test is one on a par with that of shocking the conscience of the Court. Each of such tests depends entirely on the particular judge's idea of ethics and morals instead of requiring him to depend on the boundaries fixed by the written words of the Constitution. Nothing in the history of the phrase "due process of law" suggests that constitutional controls are to depend on any particular judge's sense of values. . . .

Finally I want to add that I am not bothered by the argument that applying the Bill of Rights to the States "according to the same standards that protect those personal rights against federal encroachment," interferes with our concept of federalism in that it may prevent States from trying novel social and economic experiments. I have never believed that under the guise of federalism the States should be able to experiment with the protections afforded our citizens through the Bill of Rights. . . . It seems to me totally inconsistent to advocate on the one hand, the power of this Court to strike down any state law or practice which it finds "unreasonable" or "unfair" and, on the other hand, urge that the States be given maximum power to develop their own laws and procedures. . . .

In closing I want to emphasize that I believe as strongly as ever that the Fourteenth Amendment was intended to make the Bill of Rights applicable to the States. I have been willing to support the selective incorporation doctrine, however, as an alternative, although perhaps less historically supportable than complete incorporation. The selective incorporation process, if used properly, does limit the Supreme Court in the Fourteenth Amendment field to specific Bill of Rights' protections only and keeps judges from roaming at will in their own notions of what policies outside the Bill of Rights are desirable and what are not. And, most importantly for me, the selective incorporation process has the virtue of having already worked to make most of the Bill of Rights' protections applicable to the States.

Mr. Justice FORTAS, concurring.

I would make these points clear today. Neither logic nor history nor the intent of the draftsmen of the Fourteenth Amendment can possibly be said to require that the Sixth Amendment or its jury trial provision be applied to the States together with the total gloss that this Court's decisions have supplied. The draftsmen of the Fourteenth Amendment intended what they said, not more or less: that no State shall deprive any person of life, liberty, or property without due process of law. It is ultimately the duty of this Court to interpret, to ascribe specific meaning to this phrase. There is no reason whatever for us to conclude that, in so doing, we are bound slavishly to follow not only the Sixth Amendment but all of its bag and baggage, however securely or insecurely affixed they may be by law and precedent to federal proceedings. To take this course . . . would be not only unnecessary but mischievous because it would inflict a serious blow upon the principle of federalism. The Due Process Clause commands us to apply its great standard to state court proceedings to assure basis fairness. It does not command us rigidly and arbitrarily to impose the exact pattern of federal proceedings upon the 50 States. On the contrary, the Constitution's command, in my view, is that in our insistence upon state observance of due process, we should, so far as possible, allow the greatest latitude for state differences. It requires, within the limits of the lofty basic standards that it prescribes for the States as well as the Federal Government, maximum opportunity for diversity and minimal imposition of uniformity of method and detail upon the States.

Our Constitution sets up a federal union, not a monolith. . . .

. . . Jury trial is more than a principle of justice applicable to individual cases. It is a system of administration of the business of the State. While . . . the right of jury trial is fundamental, it does not follow that the particulars of according that right must be uniform. We should be ready to welcome state variations which do not impair—indeed, which may advance—the theory and purpose of trial by jury.

Mr. Justice HARLAN, whom Mr. Justice STEWART joins, dissenting.

Every American jurisdiction provides for trial by jury in criminal cases. The question before us is not whether jury trial is an ancient institution, which it is; nor whether it plays a significant role in the administration of criminal justice, which it does; nor whether it will endure, which it shall. The question in this case is whether the State of Louisiana, which provides trial by jury for all felonies, is prohibited by the Constitution from trying charges of simple battery to the court alone. In my view, the answer to that question, mandated alike by our constitutional history and by the longer history of trial by jury, is clearly "no."

The Court's approach to this case is an uneasy and illogical compromise among the views of various Justices on how the Due Process Clause should be interpreted. The Court does not say that those who framed the Fourteenth Amendment intended to make the Sixth Amendment applicable to the States. And the Court concedes that it finds nothing unfair about the procedure by which the present appellant was tried. Nevertheless, the Court reverses his conviction: it holds, for some reason not apparent to me, that the Due Process Clause incorporates the particular clause of the Sixth Amendment that requires trial by jury in federal criminal cases—including, as I read its opinion, the sometimes trivial accompanying baggage of judicial interpretation in federal contexts. . . .

I

A few members of the Court have taken the position that the intention of those who drafted the first section of the Fourteenth Amendment was simply, and exclusively, to make the provisions of the first eight Amendments applicable to state action. This view has never been accepted by this Court. In my view, often expressed elsewhere, the first section of the Fourteenth Amendment was meant neither to incorporate, nor to be limited to, the specific guarantees of the first eight Amendments. . . . In short, neither history, nor sense, supports using the Fourteenth Amendment to put the States in a constitutional straitjacket with respect to their own development in the administration of criminal or civil law.

Although I therefore fundamentally disagree with the total incorporation view of the Fourteenth Amendment, it seems to me that such a position does at least have the virtue, lacking in the Court's selective incorporation approach, of internal consistency: we look to the Bill of Rights, word for word, clause for clause, precedent for precedent because, it is said, the men who wrote the Amendment wanted it that way. For those who do not accept this "history," a different source of "intermediate premises" must be found. The Bill of Rights is not necessarily irrelevant to the search for guidance in interpreting the Fourteenth Amendment, but the reason for and the nature of its relevance must be articulated.

Apart from the approach taken by the absolute incorporationists, I can see only one method of analysis that has any internal logic. That is to start with the words "liberty" and "due process of law" and attempt to define them in a way that accords with American traditions and our system of government. This approach, involving a much more discriminating process of adjudication than does "incorporation," is, albeit difficult, the one that was followed throughout the 19th and most of the present century. It entails a "gradual process of judicial inclusion and exclusion," seeking, with due recognition of constitutional tolerance for state experimentation and disparity, to ascertain those "immutable principles of justice which inhere in the very idea of free government which no member of the Union may disregard." . . .

The relationship of the Bill of Rights to this "gradual process" seems to me to be twofold. In the first place it has long been clear that the Due Process Clause imposes some restrictions on state action that parallel Bill of Rights restrictions on federal action. Second, and more important than this accidental overlap, is the fact that the Bill of Rights is evidence, at various points, of the content Americans find in the term "liberty" and of American standards of fundamental fairness.

Today's Court still remains unwilling to accept the total incorporationists' view of the history of the Fourteenth Amendment. This, if accepted, would afford a cogent reason for applying the Sixth Amendment to the States. The Court is also, apparently, unwilling to face the task of determining whether denial of trial by jury in the situation before us, or in other situations, is fundamentally unfair. Consequently, the Court has compromised on the ease of the incorporationist position, without its internal logic. It has simply assumed that the question before us is whether the Jury Trial Clause of the Sixth Amendment should be incorporated into the Fourteenth, jot-for-jot and case-for-

case, or ignored. Then the Court merely declares that the clause in question is "in" rather than "out." . . .

II

Since, as I see it, the Court has not even come to grips with the issues in this case, it is necessary to start from the beginning. When a criminal defendant contends that his state conviction lacked "due process of law," the question before this Court, in my view, is whether he was denied any element of fundamental procedural fairness. . . .

The argument that jury trial is not a requisite of due process is quite simple. The central proposition of *Palko* . . . is that "due process of law" requires only that criminal trials be fundamentally fair. As stated above, apart from the theory that it was historically intended as a mere shorthand for the Bill of Rights, I do not see what else "due process of law" can intelligibly be thought to mean. If due process of law requires only fundamental fairness, then the inquiry in each case must be whether a state trial process was a fair one. The Court has held, properly I think, that in an adversary process it is a requisite of fairness, for which there is no adequate substitute, that a criminal defendant be afforded a right to counsel and to cross-examine opposing witnesses. But it simply has not been demonstrated, nor, I think, can it be demonstrated, that trial by jury is the only fair means of resolving issues of fact. . . .

In sum, there is a wide range of views on the desirability of trial by jury, and on the ways to make it most effective when it is used; there is also considerable variation from State to State in local conditions such as the size of the criminal caseload, the ease or difficulty of summoning jurors, and other trial conditions bearing on fairness. We have before us, therefore, an almost perfect example of a situation in which the celebrated dictum of Mr. Justice Brandeis should be invoked. It is, he said, "one of the happy incidents of the federal system that a single courageous state may, if its citizens choose, serve as a laboratory. . . ." This Court, other courts, and the political process are available to correct any experiments in criminal procedure that prove fundamentally unfair to defendants. That is not what is being done today: instead, and quite without reason, the Court has chosen to impose upon every State one means of trying criminal cases; it is a good means, but it is not the only fair means, and it is not demonstrably better than the alternatives States might devise. . . .

Notes and Queries

1. *Duncan* raises an important issue: Do the provisions of the Bill of Rights apply in exactly the same way against

the states as they do against the federal government? At first appearance, it might seem strange that a single provision could mean different things, depending upon which level of government it is applied against. Justices who argued that they should not, such as Harlan and Fortas, in essence argued that the demands of federalism—a cardinal constitutional value—must influence the interpretation of the Bill of Rights. Are you persuaded that the meaning of specific provisions in the text should be influenced by overarching constitutional values, such as federalism or separation of powers? Are there other values in constitutional interpretation—such as uniformity—that should outweigh the value of federalism? How are judges to weigh these values?

2. Justice White held that "trial by jury in criminal cases is fundamental to the American scheme of justice. . . ." In *Palko*, however, the Court made explicit reference to the traditions of continental Europe, and in *Rochin*, Justice Frankfurter appealed to the notions of "English speaking peoples. . . ." Which is the better formulation, and why?

3. The problem of incorporation is unique to the United States, and it stems from the ambiguity surrounding the scope and reach of the Fourteenth Amendment. The ambiguity was underlined by the absence of language specifying the content of the amendment's broad phrases. In addition, as we have seen, the Supreme Court declined initially to accept the view that the Fourteenth Amendment dramatically changed the nature of American federalism. Foreign constitutions typically present no such difficulty. Their provisions on fundamental rights were written for unitary governments or apply uniformly to local and national governments in federal and confederal systems. Or, alternatively, they make very clear the rights that are to be applied to a particular level of government.

The exercise of judicial review in Switzerland presents an interesting contrast to the United States. Swiss courts are empowered to control the constitutionality of cantonal (i.e., state) law but not federal law,[41] whereas in the United States the Bill of Rights applied to the federal government and by interpretation, as this chapter has pointed out, to state governments through a process of selective incorporation. One further difference between the two systems is that while American judges may annul legislation in conflict with the Bill of Rights, Swiss judges may not; they can only refuse to enforce such laws. Like the Supreme Court, however, Switzerland's highest tribunal, the Federal Court, has recognized nonwritten constitutional rights—e.g., "personal liberty, freedom of opinion, [and] the right to a previous hearing"[42]—as fundamental to a democratic society based on the rule of law.

The significance of the American incorporation cases is the extent to which the Supreme Court relies on comparative law—particularly English and Roman law—for determining whether a state criminal trial practice is fundamentally unfair and thus forbidden by the due process clause of the Fourteenth Amendment. In *Duncan v. Louisiana* (1968), the Court turned away from this approach. "Because we believe that trial by jury in criminal cases is fundamental to the American scheme of justice," wrote Justice White for the majority, "we hold that the Fourteenth Amendment guarantees a right of jury trial in all criminal cases which—were they to be tried in a federal court—would come within the Sixth Amendment's guarantee."

In deciding *Duncan*, the Supreme Court invoked the history of the common law and its importance to the American community; in short, the Court used an approach that, as Robert E. Rodes, Jr. notes, "developed out of the spirit of a given people, the *Volksgeist*." The *Volksgeist* as a source of legal validity has been harshly criticized by legal theorists, but as Rodes writes in reference to *Duncan*, "it is difficult to see what the Supreme Court . . . has in mind if not a *Volksgeist* when it holds that an American accused of a serious crime cannot have a fair trial if he is denied a jury, whereas everyone else in the world can."[43] In emphasizing the overriding significance of American traditions, then, *Duncan* departed from the view espoused in *Hurtado* and *Twining* that "due process of law" requires only that criminal practices or procedures be fundamentally fair.

---

[41] See A.R. Brewer-Carias, *Judicial Review in Comparative Perspective* (Cambridge: Cambridge University Press, 1989), 271–74.

[42] Ibid, at 107.

[43] Robert E. Rodes, Jr. *The Legal Enterprise.* (Port Washington, N.Y.: Kennikat Press, 1976), 19.

Gregg v. Georgia

428 U.S. 153, 96 S.Ct. 2909, 49 L.Ed.2d 859 (1976)

Just before Thanksgiving in 1973, Troy Gregg and a companion were hitchhiking on a Florida highway. Fred Simmons and Bill Moore picked them up. The next morning Moore and Simmons were found in the brush just off the road in Gwinnet County, Georgia. A Georgia court tried and convicted Troy Gregg on two counts each of armed robbery and murder. Following *Furman v. Georgia*, the court then held a separate proceeding to determine what sentence should be applied. The jury, applying a state law that directed it to consider extenuating, aggravating, and mitigating factors, found beyond a reasonable doubt that there was at least one aggravating factor and sentenced Gregg to death. Gregg appealed, claiming that the death penalty violates the cruel and unusual punishment clause of the Eighth Amendment. Judgment of the Court: *Stewart*, Powell, Stevens. Concurring in the judgment: *White*, Burger, Rehnquist; *Blackmun*. Dissenting opinions: *Brennan; Marshall*.

Judgment of the Court, and opinion of Mr. Justice STEWART, Mr. Justice POWELL, and Mr. Justice STEVENS, announced by Mr. Justice STEWART.

The issue in this case is whether the imposition of the sentence of death for the crime of murder under the law of Georgia violates the Eighth and Fourteenth Amendments.

I. . . .

II. . . .

III

We address initially the basic contention that the punishment of death for the crime of murder is, under all circumstances, "cruel and unusual" in violation of the Eighth and Fourteenth Amendments of the Constitution. In Part IV of this opinion, we will consider the sentence of death imposed under the Georgia statutes at issue in this case.

The Court on a number of occasions has both assumed and asserted the constitutionality of capital punishment. In several cases that assumption provided a necessary foundation for the decision, as the Court was asked to decide whether a particular method of carrying out a capital sentence would be allowed to stand under the Eighth Amendment. But until *Furman v. Georgia* (1972), the Court never confronted squarely the fundamental claim that the punishment of death always, regardless of the offense or the procedure followed in im-

posing the sentence, is cruel and unusual punishment in violation of the Constitution. Although this issue was presented and addressed in *Furman*, it was not resolved by the Court. Four Justices would have held that capital punishment is not unconstitutional per se; two Justices would have reached the opposite conclusion; and three Justices, while agreeing that the statutes then before the Court were invalid as applied, left open the question whether such punishment may ever be imposed. We now hold that the punishment of death does not invariably violate the Constitution.

A

In the earliest cases raising Eighth Amendment claims, the Court focused on particular methods of execution to determine whether they were too cruel to pass constitutional muster. The constitutionality of the sentence of death itself was not at issue, and the criterion used to evaluate the mode of execution was its similarity to "torture" and other "barbarous" methods. . . .

But the Court has not confined the prohibition embodied in the Eighth Amendment to "barbarous" methods that were generally outlawed in the 18th century. Instead, the Amendment has been interpreted in a flexible and dynamic manner. The Court early recognized that "a principle to be vital, must be capable of wider application than the mischief which gave it birth." *Weems v. United States*, (1910). Thus the Clause forbidding "cruel and unusual" punishments "is not fastened to the obsolete but may acquire meaning as public opinion becomes enlightened by a humane justice."

Later, in *Trop v. Dulles* (1958), the Court reviewed the constitutionality of the punishment of denationalization imposed upon a soldier who escaped from an Army stockade and became a deserter for one day. Although the concept of proportionality was not the basis of the holding, the plurality observed in dicta that "(f)ines, imprisonment and even execution may be imposed depending upon the enormity of the crime."

It is clear from the foregoing precedents that the Eighth Amendment has not been regarded as a static concept. As Mr. Chief Justice Warren said, in an oft-quoted phrase, "(t)he Amendment must draw its meaning from the evolving standards of decency that mark the progress of a maturing society." *Trop v. Dulles* (1958). Thus, an assessment of contemporary values concerning the infliction of a challenged sanction is relevant to the application of the Eighth Amendment. As we develop below more fully, . . . this assessment does not call for a subjective judgment. It requires, rather, that we look to objective indicia that reflect the public attitude toward a given sanction.

But our cases also make clear that public perceptions of standards of decency with respect to criminal sanctions are not conclusive. A penalty also must accord with "the dignity of man," which is the "basic concept underlying the Eighth Amendment." *Trop v. Dulles* (1958). This means, at least, that the punishment not be "excessive." When a form of punishment in the abstract (in this case, whether capital punishment may ever be imposed as a sanction for murder) rather than in the particular (the propriety of death as a penalty to be applied to a specific defendant for a specific crime) is under consideration, the inquiry into "excessiveness" has two aspects. First, the punishment must not involve the unnecessary and wanton infliction of pain. . . . Second, the punishment must not be grossly out of proportion to the severity of the crime.

B

Of course, the requirements of the Eighth Amendment must be applied with an awareness of the limited role to be played by the courts. This does not mean that judges have no role to play, for the Eighth Amendment is a restraint upon the exercise of legislative power. . . .

But, while we have an obligation to insure that constitutional bounds are not overreached, we may not act as judges as we might as legislators. .

Courts are not representative bodies. They are not designed to be a good reflex of a democratic society. Their judgment is best informed, and therefore most depend-

able, within narrow limits. Their essential quality is detachment, founded on independence. History teaches that the independence of the judiciary is jeopardized when courts become embroiled in the passions of the day and assume primary responsibility in choosing between competing political, economic and social pressures. *Dennis v. United States* (1951) (Frankfurter, J., concurring in affirmance of judgment).

Therefore, in assessing a punishment selected by a democratically elected legislature against the constitutional measure, we presume its validity. We may not require the legislature to select the least severe penalty possible so long as the penalty selected is not cruelly inhumane or disproportionate to the crime involved. And a heavy burden rests on those who would attack the judgment of the representatives of the people.

In the discussion to this point we have sought to identify the principles and considerations that guide a court in addressing an Eighth Amendment claim. We now consider specifically whether the sentence of death for the crime of murder is a per se violation of the Eighth and Fourteenth Amendments to the Constitution. We note first that history and precedent strongly support a negative answer to this question.

The imposition of the death penalty for the crime of murder has a long history of acceptance both in the United States and in England. The common-law rule imposed a mandatory death sentence on all convicted murderers. . . . And the penalty continued to be used into the 20th century by most American States, although the

---

Comparative Note 9.1

[President Arthur Chaskalson of the Constitutional Court of South Africa in declaring unconstitutional the death penalty in that country.]

Public opinion may have some relevance to the enquiry, but, in itself, it is no substitute for the duty vested in the Courts to interpret the Constitution and to uphold its provisions without fear or favour. If public opinion were to be decisive, there would be no need for constitutional adjudication. The protection of rights could then be left to Parliament, which has a mandate from the public, and is answerable to the public for the way its mandate is exercised. . . . The very reason for

establishing the new legal order, and for vesting the power of judicial review of all legislation in the courts, was to protect the rights of minorities and others who cannot protect their rights adequately through the democratic process. Those who are entitled to claim this protection include the social outcasts and marginalised people of our society. It is only if there is a willingness to protect the worst and weakest amongst us that all of us can be secure that our own rights will be protected.

SOURCE: *The State v. Makwanyane and Mchunu* (1995), (3) S.A. 391.

breadth of the common-law rule was diminished, initially by narrowing the class of murders to be punished by death and subsequently by widespread adoption of laws expressly granting juries the discretion to recommend mercy. It is apparent from the text of the Constitution itself that the existence of capital punishment was accepted by the Framers. At the time the Eighth Amendment was ratified, capital punishment was a common sanction in every State. Indeed, the First Congress of the United States enacted legislation providing death as the penalty for specified crimes. . . . The Fifth Amendment, adopted at the same time as the Eighth, contemplated the continued existence of the capital sanction by imposing certain limits on the prosecution of capital cases: "No person shall be held to answer for a capital, or otherwise infamous crime, unless on a presentment or indictment of a Grand Jury. . . ; nor shall any person be subject for the same offense to be twice put in jeopardy of life or limb; . . . nor be deprived of life, liberty, or property, without due process of law. . . ." And the Fourteenth Amendment, adopted over three-quarters of a century later, similarly contemplates the existence of the capital sanction in providing that no State shall deprive any person of "life, liberty, or property" without due process of law.

For nearly two centuries, this Court, repeatedly and often expressly, has recognized that capital punishment is not invalid per se.

Four years ago, the petitioners in *Furman* and its companion cases predicated their argument primarily upon the asserted proposition that standards of decency had evolved to the point where capital punishment no longer could be tolerated. The petitioners in those cases said, in effect, that the evolutionary process had come to an end, and that standards of decency required that the Eighth Amendment be construed finally as prohibiting capital punishment for any crime regardless of its depravity and impact on society. This view was accepted by two Justices. Three other Justices were unwilling to go so far; focusing on the procedures by which convicted defendants were selected for the death penalty rather than on the actual punishment inflicted, they joined in the conclusion that the statutes before the Court were constitutionally invalid.

The petitioners in the capital cases before the Court today renew the "standards of decency" argument, but developments during the four years since *Furman* have undercut substantially the assumptions upon which their argument rested. Despite the continuing debate, dating back to the 19th century, over the morality and utility of capital punishment, it is now evident that a large proportion of American society continues to regard it as an ap-

propriate and necessary criminal sanction. The most marked indication of society's endorsement of the death penalty for murder is the legislative response to *Furman*. The legislatures of at least 35 States have enacted new statutes that provide for the death penalty for at least some crimes that result in the death of another person. And the Congress of the United States, in 1974, enacted a statute providing the death penalty for aircraft piracy that results in death. These recently adopted statutes have attempted to address the concerns expressed by the Court in *Furman* primarily (i) by specifying the factors to be weighed and the procedures to be followed in deciding when to impose a capital sentence, or (ii) by making the death penalty mandatory for specified crimes. But all of the post-*Furman* statutes make clear that capital punishment itself has not been rejected by the elected representatives of the people.

The jury also is a significant and reliable objective index of contemporary values because it is so directly involved. . . . The Court has said that "one of the most important functions any jury can perform in making . . . a selection (between life imprisonment and death for a defendant convicted in a capital case) is to maintain a link between contemporary community values and the penal system." *Witherspoon v. Illinois* (1968). It may be true that evolving standards have influenced juries in recent decades to be more discriminating in imposing the sentence of death. But the relative infrequency of jury verdicts imposing the death sentence does not indicate rejection of capital punishment per se. Rather, the reluctance of juries in many cases to impose the sentence may well reflect the humane feeling that this most irrevocable of sanctions should be reserved for a small number of extreme cases. . . . Indeed, the actions of juries in many States since *Furman* are fully compatible with the legislative judgments, reflected in the new statutes, as to the continued utility and necessity of capital punishment in appropriate cases. At the close of 1974 at least 254 persons had been sentenced to death since *Furman*, and by the end of March 1976, more than 460 persons were subject to death sentences.

As we have seen, however, the Eighth Amendment demands more than that a challenged punishment be acceptable to contemporary society. The Court also must ask whether it comports with the basic concept of human dignity at the core of the Amendment. . . . Although we cannot "invalidate a category of penalties because we deem less severe penalties adequate to serve the ends of penology," *Furman v. Georgia* (Powell, J., dissenting), the sanction imposed cannot be so totally without penological justification that it results in the gratuitous infliction of

Comparative Note 9.2

[In this case, the Supreme Court of Canada considered an extradition request by the United States for two Canadian citizens wanted for aggravated first degree murders committed in Washington State. The Canadian Minister of Justice approved the request without seeking a condition that the men would not face the death penalty.]

a) Principles of Criminal Justice as Applied in Canada

The death penalty has been rejected as an acceptable element of criminal justice by the Canadian people, speaking through their elected federal representatives, after years of protracted debate. Canada has not executed anyone since 1962. Parliament abolished the last legal vestiges of the death penalty in 1998 (An Act to Amend the National Defence Act, S.C. 1998, c. 35) some seven years after the decisions of this Court in *Kindler and Ng*. In his letter to the respondents, the Minister of Justice emphasized that "in Canada, Parliament has decided that capital punishment is not an appropriate penalty for crimes committed here, and I am firmly committed to that position."

While government policy at any particular moment may or may not be consistent with principles of fundamental justice, the fact that successive governments and Parliaments over a period of almost 40 years have refused to inflict the death penalty reflects, we believe, a fundamental Canadian principle about the appropriate limits of the criminal justice system.

We are not called upon in this appeal to determine whether capital punishment would, if authorised by the Canadian Parliament, violate s. 12 of the Charter ("cruel and unusual treatment or punishment"), and if so in what circumstances. It is, however, incontestable that capital punishment, whether or not it violates s. 12 of the Charter, and whether or not it could be upheld under s. 1, engages the underlying values of the prohibition against cruel and unusual punishment. It is final. It is irreversible. Its imposition has been described as arbitrary. Its deterrent value has been doubted. Its implementation necessarily causes psychological and physical suffering. It has been rejected by the Canadian Parliament for offences committed within Canada. Its potential imposition in this case is thus a factor that weighs against extradition without assurances.

SOURCE: *Minister of Justice, Appellant v. Glen Sebastian Burns and Atif Ahmad Rafay,* 2001 S.C.C. 7.

---

suffering. . . . The death penalty is said to serve two principal social purposes: retribution and deterrence of capital crimes by prospective offenders.

In part, capital punishment is an expression of society's moral outrage at particularly offensive conduct. This function may be unappealing to many, but it is essential in an ordered society that asks its citizens to rely on legal processes rather than self-help to vindicate their wrongs.

"The instinct for retribution is part of the nature of man, and channeling that instinct in the administration of criminal justice serves an important purpose in promoting the stability of a society governed by law. When people begin to believe that organized society is unwilling or unable to impose upon criminal offenders the punishment they 'deserve,' then there are sown the seeds of anarchy of self-help, vigilante justice, and lynch law." *Furman v. Georgia* (Stewart, J., concurring). "Retribution is no longer the dominant objective of the criminal law," *Williams v. New York* (1949), but neither is it a forbidden objective nor one inconsistent with our respect for the dignity of men. . . . Indeed, the decision that capital punishment may be the appropriate sanction in extreme cases is an expression of the community's belief that certain crimes are themselves so grievous an affront to humanity that the only adequate response may be the penalty of death.

Statistical attempts to evaluate the worth of the death penalty as a deterrent to crimes by potential offenders have occasioned a great deal of debate. The results simply have been inconclusive. . . . Although some of the studies suggest that the death penalty may not function as a significantly greater deterrent than lesser penalties, there is no convincing empirical evidence either supporting or refuting this view. We may nevertheless assume safely that there are murderers, such as those who act in passion, for whom the threat of death has little or no deterrent effect. But for many others, the death penalty undoubtedly is a significant deterrent. There are carefully contemplated murders, such as murder for hire, where the possible penalty of death may well enter into the cold calculus that precedes the decision to act. And there are some categories of murder, such as murder by a life prisoner, where other sanctions may not be adequate.

Comparative Note 9.3

Today in Hungary, social sentiments towards criminals often call for retaining capital punishment. It is quite common, however, that such sentiments are also directed towards crimes which are not threatened with capital punishment, as for example in the case of fatal car accidents when they demand death for the person who caused death. The Constitutional Court, however, does not hunt for popularity in society; its only competence is to ensure the coherence and constitutionality of the legal system: deprivation of life by the State is forbidden even according to the strict text of our Constitution and may not be justified by the constitutional principles of criminal law either.

SOURCE: *The Capital Punishment Decision*, reprinted in Laszlo Solyom and Georg Brunner, *Constitutional Judiciary in a New Democracy.* (Ann Arbor: University of Michigan Press, 2000), 138.

The value of capital punishment as a deterrent of crime is a complex factual issue the resolution of which properly rests with the legislatures, which can evaluate the results of statistical studies in terms of their own local conditions and with a flexibility of approach that is not available to the courts. . . . Indeed, many of the post-*Furman* statutes reflect just such a responsible effort to define those crimes and those criminals for which capital punishment is most probably an effective deterrent. In sum, we cannot say that the judgment of the Georgia Legislature that capital punishment may be necessary in some cases is clearly wrong. Considerations of federalism, as well as respect for the ability of a legislature to evaluate, in terms of its particular State, the moral consensus concerning the death penalty and its social utility as a sanction, require us to conclude, in the absence of more convincing evidence, that the infliction of death as a punishment for murder is not without justification and thus is not unconstitutionally severe. Finally, we must consider whether the punishment of death is disproportionate in relation to the crime for which it is imposed. There is no question that death as a punishment is unique in its severity and irrevocability. . . . When a defendant's life is at stake, the Court has been particularly sensitive to insure that every safeguard is observed. . . . But we are concerned here only with the imposition of capital punishment for the crime of murder, and when a life has been taken deliberately by the offender, we cannot say that the punishment is invariably disproportionate to the crime. It is an extreme sanction, suitable to the most extreme of crimes.

We hold that the death penalty is not a form of punishment that may never be imposed, regardless of the circumstances of the offense, regardless of the character of the offender, and regardless of the procedure followed in reaching the decision to impose it.

IV

We now consider whether Georgia may impose the death penalty on the petitioner in this case.

A

While *Furman* did not hold that the infliction of the death penalty per se violates the Constitution's ban on cruel and unusual punishments, it did recognize that the penalty of death is different in kind from any other punishment imposed under our system of criminal justice. Because of the uniqueness of the death penalty, *Furman* held that it could not be imposed under sentencing procedures that created a substantial risk that it would be inflicted in an arbitrary and capricious manner.

In summary, the concerns expressed in *Furman* that the penalty of death not be imposed in an arbitrary or capricious manner can be met by a carefully drafted statute that ensures that the sentencing authority is given adequate information and guidance. As a general proposition these concerns are best met by a system that provides for a bifurcated proceeding at which the sentencing authority is apprised of the information relevant to the imposition of sentence and provided with standards to guide its use of the information.

B

In short, Georgia's new sentencing procedures require as a prerequisite to the imposition of the death penalty, specific jury findings as to the circumstances of the crime or the character of the defendant. Moreover, to guard further against a situation comparable to that presented in *Furman*, the Supreme Court of Georgia compares each death sentence with the sentences imposed on similarly situated defendants to ensure that the sentence of death in a particular case is not disproportionate. On their face these procedures seem to satisfy the concerns of *Furman*. No longer should there be "no meaningful basis for distinguishing the few cases in which (the death penalty) is imposed from the many cases in which it is not."

V

The basic concern of *Furman* centered on those defendants who were being condemned to death capriciously and arbitrarily. Under the procedures before the Court in that case, sentencing authorities were not directed to give attention to the nature or circumstances of the crime committed or to the character or record of the defendant. Left unguided, juries imposed the death sentence in a way that could only be called freakish. The new Georgia sentencing procedures, by contrast, focus the jury's attention on the particularized nature of the crime and the particularized characteristics of the individual defendant. While the jury is permitted to consider any aggravating or mitigating circumstances, it must find and identify at least one statutory aggravating factor before it may impose a penalty of death. In this way the jury's discretion is channeled. No longer can a jury wantonly and freakishly impose the death sentence; it is always circumscribed by the legislative guidelines. In addition, the review function of the Supreme Court of Georgia affords additional assurance that the concerns that prompted our decision in *Furman* are not present to any significant degree in the Georgia procedure applied here.

For the reasons expressed in this opinion, we hold that the statutory system under which Gregg was sentenced to death does not violate the Constitution. Accordingly, the judgment of the Georgia Supreme Court is affirmed. It is so ordered.

Mr. Justice WHITE, with whom The Chief Justice and Mr. Justice REHNQUIST join, concurring in the judgment.

Statement of The Chief Justice and Mr. Justice REHNQUIST.

Mr. Justice BLACKMUN, concurring in the judgment.

Mr. Justice BRENNAN, dissenting.

. . . Death for whatever crime and under all circumstances "is truly an awesome punishment. The calculated killing of a human being by the State involves, by its very nature, a denial of the executed person's humanity. . . ." Death is not only an unusually severe punishment, unusual in its pain, in its finalty, and its in enormity, but it serves no penal purpose more effectively than a less severe punishment; therefore the principle inherent in the Clause that prohibits pointless infliction of excessive punishment when less severe punishment can adequately achieve the same purpose invalidates the punishment.

The fatal constitutional infirmity in the punishment of death is that it treats "members of the human race as non-humans, as objects to be toyed with and discarded. [The death penalty] is thus inconsistent with the fundamental premise of the Clause that even the vilest criminal remains a human being possessed of common human dignity." . . . I therefore would hold, on that ground alone, that death is today a cruel and unusual punishment prohibited by the Clause.

Mr. Justice MARSHALL, dissenting.

In *Furman* I concluded that the death penalty is constitutionally invalid for two reasons. First, the death penalty is excessive. . . . And second, the American people, fully informed as to the purposes of the death penalty and its liabilities would in my view reject it as morally unacceptable.

Since the decision in *Furman*, the legislatures of 35 States have since enacted new statutes authorizing the imposition of death for certain crimes. . . . I would be less than candid if I did not acknowledge that these developments have a significant bearing on a realistic assessment of the moral acceptability of the death penalty to the American people. But if the constitutionality of the death penalty turns, as I have urged, on the opinion of an *informed* citizenry, then even the enactment of new death statutes cannot be viewed as conclusive.

Even assuming, however, that the post-*Furman* enactment of statutes . . . renders the prediction of the views of an informed citizenry an uncertain basis for a constitutional decision, the enactment of those statutes has no bearing whatsoever on the conclusion that the death penalty is unconstitutional because it is excessive.

The two purposes that sustain the death penalty as non-excessive in the Court's view are general detterrence and retribution. . . . The evidence I reviewed in *Furman* remains convincing, in my view, that "capital punishment is not necessary as a deterrent to crime in our society." The justification for the death penalty must be found elsewhere.

The other principal purpose said to be served by the death penalty is retribution. The notion that retribution can serve as a moral justification for the sanction of death finds credence in the opinion of my Brothers Stewart, Powell, and Stevens. . . . It is this notion that I find to be the most disturbing aspect of today's decision. . . . To be sustained under the Eighth Amendment, the death penalty

Comparative Note 9.4

[South Africa's Constitutional Court held that the death penalty violates the country's interim Constitution even though it contains no express provision against the death penalty. The judgment of the eleven-person tribunal was unanimous. The following extracts are from the opinion of Arthur Chaskalson, the Court's president.]

The United States jurisprudence has not resolved the [death penalty] dilemma arising from the fact that the Constitution prohibits cruel and unusual punishment, but also . . . contemplates that there will be capital punishment. The acceptance by the majority of the U.S. Supreme Court . . . that capital punishment is not per se unconstitutional, but that in certain circumstances it may be arbitrary, and thus unconstitutional, has led to endless litigation. . . . The difficulties that have been experienced in following [the American] path . . . persuade me that we should not follow this route.

Although the United States Constitution does not contain a specific guarantee of human dignity, it has been accepted by the U.S. Supreme Court that the concept of human dignity is at the core of the . . . "cruel and unusual punishment" [clause] . . : For Justice Brennan, this was decisive of the question in *Gregg v. Georgia*. The fatal constitutional infirmity in the punishment of death is that it treats "members of the human race as nonhumans, as objects to be toyed with and discarded." . . .

Under our constitutional order the right to human dignity is specifically guaranteed. It can only be limited by legislation which passes the stringent test of being "necessary." The weight given to human dignity by Justice Brennan is wholly consistent with the values of our Constitution and the new order established by it. It is also consistent with the approach to extreme punishments followed by courts in other countries.

SOURCE: *The State v. Makwanyane and Mchunu,* South African Constitutional Court, 6 June 1995.

must "[comport] with the basic concept of human dignity at the core of the Amendment."

Notes and Queries

1. At the founding, all thirteen states permitted the death penalty for some criminal offenses. The constitutional text itself is largely, but not completely, silent on the issue. The Fifth Amendment, for example, makes references to capital crimes and the deprivation of life without due process of law.

Should the Court consider the colonial history of capital punishment in determining whether the death penalty is unconstitutional? The rationale for an affirmative answer would seem to rest upon an originalist or an intentionalist view of constitutional interpretation, would it not? That is, because the Founders did not think the death penalty unconstitutional, the Court should defer to their judgment. What understanding of constitutional change is implicit in this approach? Of judicial power?

2. At no time has the Supreme Court found the death penalty per se unconstitutional. In *Wilkerson v. Utah* (1878), the Court upheld execution by firing squad (but noted that such punishments as "torture, being disembowelled alive, beheaded, quartered, or burned alive . . ."

would be cruel and unusual), and in *In re Kemmler* (1890), it approved execution by electrocution.

In *Furman v. Georgia* (1972), the Court struck down a Georgia law that allowed juries essentially unlimited discretion in deciding whether to impose the death penalty. *Gregg* was based on a revised version of that law, designed to overcome the faults specified in *Furman*. Thirty-five other states had also revised their laws after *Furman*. The Court has since refused to reconsider the constitutionality of the death penalty as a general issue, and indeed in several cases has upheld state procedures designed to expedite the often lengthy process of imposing the sentence. Moreover, in *McKleskey v. Kemp* (1987, reprinted later in the chapter), the Court rejected claims, based on statistical studies, that Georgia's system discriminated on the basis of the race of the murder victim. And in *Stanford v. Kentucky* (1989), the Court sustained a state statute that authorized the death penalty for crimes committed when a person was 16 or 17 years of age.

In 1994, Justice Blackmun announced that notwithstanding his opinion in *Furman*,

From this day forward, I no longer shall tinker with the machinery of death. For more than 20 years I have endeavored—indeed, I have struggled—along with a majority of this Court, to develop procedural and substantive rules that would lend more than the mere appearance of fairness to the death penalty endeavor. Rather than continue to coddle the Court's delusion that the desired level of fairness has been achieved . . . , I feel morally and intellectually obligated simply to concede that the death penalty experiment has failed. It is virtually self-evident to me now that no combination of procedural rules or substantive regulations ever can save the death penalty from its inherent constitutional deficiencies.

In response, Justice Scalia noted that Blackmun's explanation "often refers to 'intellectual, moral, and personal' perceptions, but never to the text and tradition of the Constitution. It is the latter rather than the former that ought to control." Later, Scalia concluded that "Convictions in opposition to the death penalty are often passionate and deeply held. That would be no excuse for reading them into a Constitution that does not contain them."

Absent a clear textual provision so indicating, is it obvious that the "text and tradition" of the Constitution do not mandate procedural fairness in the application of the death penalty? On the other hand, how is the Court to determine what is fair or how much "fairness" is required?

3. The plurality opinion by Justice Stewart noted that "[T]he Eighth Amendment demands more than that a challenged punishment must be acceptable to contemporary society. The Court also must ask whether it comports with the basic concept of human dignity at the core of the Amendment. . . ." Is it obvious that a commitment to human dignity is at the core of the Eighth Amendment? What does that commitment actually require of us? Is there any way for a judge to decide what human dignity permits or prohibits besides appealing to his or her own sense of values and morality? Or are there some components of dignity that all, or most, of "us" would agree are essential?

How are we to define "us"? Is the relevant community the state? The United States? The family of constitutional democracies? As you consider this question, remember that most of the individual states permit the death penalty for at least some cases. On the other hand, the great majority of constitutional democracies forbid the death penalty.

The best discussion of this question, in the context of "American exceptionalism," is by Carol Steiker, *Capital Punishment and American Exceptionalism*, 81 Oregon Law Review 97 (2002). The question has also been a matter of great dispute among the justices themselves. See, for example, the Court's decision in *Stanford v. Kentucky* (1989), and, more recently, *Atkins v. Virginia* (2002, reprinted later in the chapter).

4. What significance does Justice Stewart attach to the efforts of states to rewrite their capital punishment laws after *Furman?* Is this a method of interpretation that relies upon appeals to public opinion? In *Trop v. Dulles* (1958), Chief Justice Warren argued that the Eighth Amendment should take its meaning from "evolving standards of decency"? Is this position the same as the Court's in *Gregg?* Or should we understand Justice Stewart's comments as a statement about the importance of federalism and judicial power for issues concerning individual liberty?

5. Just beneath the surface in debates over the death penalty hide hoary questions about the relationship of the individual to the community and what responsibilities membership in a community entails. Similarly, the constitutionality of the death penalty leads us to ask questions about human dignity and personality. Other constitutional texts and courts have not been reluctant to address these issues explicitly. See table 9.2.

In addition, the Court's decision in *Gregg* has been the subject of much commentary by other constitutional courts. The South African Court, for example, observed that

The United States jurisprudence has not resolved the dilemma arising from the fact that the Constitution prohibits cruel and unusual punishments, but also permits, and contemplates that there will be capital punishment. The acceptance by a majority of the United States Supreme Court of the proposition that capital punishment is not per se unconstitutional, has led to endless litigation. . . . The difficulties that have been experienced in following this path . . . persuade me that we should not follow this route.

What does the South African Court's opinion suggest about the limits of constitutional borrowing?

McCleskey v. Kemp
481 U.S. 279, 107 S. Ct. 1756, 95 L. Ed. 2d 262 (1987)

McCleskey, a black man, was convicted of murdering a white police officer during the course of an armed robbery. The jury recommended that he be sentenced to

death, and the court followed the jury's recommendation. McCleskey filed a petition for a writ of habeas corpus, in which he claimed that the state's capital sentencing process was administered in a racially discriminatory manner in violation of the Eighth and Fourteenth Amendments. In support of his claim, the accused proffered an elaborate statistical study of almost twenty-five hundred capital punishment cases in Georgia, indicating that, even after taking account of numerous nonracial variables, defendants charged with killing whites were 4.3 times as likely to receive a death sentence as defendants charged with killing blacks, and that black defendants were 1.1 times as likely to receive a death sentence as other defendants. The district court dismissed the habeas corpus petition. McCleskey filed a cert petition with the Supreme Court. Opinion: *Powell*, Rehnquist, White, O'Connor, Scalia. Dissenting opinion: *Brennan*, Marshall, Blackmun, Stevens; *Blackmun*, Marshall, Stevens, Brennan; *Stevens*, Blackmun.

Mr. Justice POWELL delivered the opinion of the Court.

This case presents the question whether a complex statistical study that indicates a risk that racial considerations enter into capital sentencing determinations proves that petitioner McCleskey's capital sentence is unconstitutional under the Eighth or Fourteenth Amendment.

. . . In support of his claim, McCleskey proffered a statistical study performed by Professors David C. Baldus, Charles Pulaski, and George Woodworth (the Baldus study) that purports to show a disparity in the imposition of the death sentence in Georgia based on the race of the murder victim and, to a lesser extent, the race of the defendant. The Baldus study is actually two sophisticated statistical studies that examine over 2,000 murder cases that occurred in Georgia during the 1970's. The raw numbers collected by Professor Baldus indicate that defendants charged with killing white persons received the death penalty in 11% of the cases, but defendants charged with killing blacks received the death penalty in only 1% of the cases. The raw numbers also indicate a reverse racial disparity according to the race of the defendant: 4% of the black defendants received the death penalty, as opposed to 7% of the white defendants.

Baldus also divided the cases according to the combination of the race of the defendant and the race of the victim. He found that the death penalty was assessed in 22% of the cases involving black defendants and white victims; 8% of the cases involving white defendants and white victims; 1% of the cases involving black defendants and black victims; and 3% of the cases involving white defendants and black victims. Similarly, Baldus found that prosecutors sought the death penalty in 70% of the cases involving black defendants and white victims; 32% of the cases involving white defendants and white victims; 15% of the cases involving black defendants and black victims; and 19% of the cases involving white defendants and black victims.

Baldus subjected his data to an extensive analysis, taking account of 230 variables that could have explained the disparities on nonracial grounds. One of his models concludes that, even after taking account of 39 nonracial variables, defendants charged with killing white victims were 4.3 times as likely to receive a death sentence as defendants charged with killing blacks. According to this model, black defendants were 1.1 times as likely to receive a death sentence as other defendants. Thus, the Baldus study indicates that black defendants, such as McCleskey, who kill white victims have the greatest likelihood of receiving the death penalty.

McCleskey's first claim is that the Georgia capital punishment statute violates the Equal Protection Clause of the Fourteenth Amendment. He argues that race has infected the administration of Georgia's statute in two ways: persons who murder whites are more likely to be sentenced to death than persons who murder blacks, and black murderers are more likely to be sentenced to death than white murderers. As a black defendant who killed a white victim, McCleskey claims that the Baldus study demonstrates that he was discriminated against because of his race and because of the race of his victim. In its broadest form, McCleskey's claim of discrimination extends to every actor in the Georgia capital sentencing process, from the prosecutor who sought the death penalty and the jury that imposed the sentence, to the State itself that enacted the capital punishment statute and allows it to remain in effect despite its allegedly discriminatory application. We agree with the Court of Appeals, and every other court that has considered such a challenge, that this claim must fail.

Our analysis begins with the basic principle that a defendant who alleges an equal protection violation has the burden of proving "the existence of purposeful discrimination." A corollary to this principle is that a criminal defendant must prove that the purposeful discrimination "had a discriminatory effect" on him. Thus, to prevail under the Equal Protection Clause, McCleskey must prove that the decisionmakers in his case acted with discriminatory purpose. He offers no evidence specific to his own case that would support an inference that racial considerations played a part in his sentence. Instead, he relies solely on the Baldus study. McCleskey argues that the Baldus study compels an inference that his sentence rests on purposeful discrimination. McCleskey's claim that these statistics are sufficient proof of discrimination, without regard to the facts of a particular case, would extend to all capital cases in Georgia, at least where the victim was white and the defendant is black.

Finally, McCleskey's statistical proffer must be viewed in the context of his challenge. McCleskey challenges decisions at the heart of the State's criminal justice system. "One of society's most basic tasks is that of protecting the lives of its citizens and one of the most basic ways in which it achieves the task is through criminal laws against murder." *Gregg v. Georgia* (1976) (White, J., concurring). Implementation of these laws necessarily requires discretionary judgments. Because discretion is essential to the criminal justice process, we would demand exceptionally clear proof before we would infer that the discretion has been abused. The unique nature of the decisions at issue in this case also counsels against adopting such an inference from the disparities indicated by the Baldus study. Accordingly, we hold that the Baldus study is clearly insufficient to support an inference that any of the decisionmakers in McCleskey's case acted with discriminatory purpose.

McCleskey also suggests that the Baldus study proves that the State as a whole has acted with a discriminatory purpose. He appears to argue that the State has violated the Equal Protection Clause by adopting the capital punishment statute and allowing it to remain in force despite its allegedly discriminatory application. But "discriminatory purpose" . . . implies more than intent as volition or intent as awareness of consequences. It implies that the decisionmaker, in this case a state legislature, selected or reaffirmed a particular course of action at least in part "because of," not merely "in spite of," its adverse effects upon an identifiable group. For this claim to prevail, McCleskey would have to prove that the Georgia Legislature enacted or maintained the death penalty statute because of an anticipated racially discriminatory effect. In *Gregg v. Georgia*, this Court found that the Georgia capital sentencing system could operate in a fair and neutral manner. There was no evidence then, and there is none now, that the Georgia Legislature enacted the capital punishment statute to further a racially discriminatory purpose.

Nor has McCleskey demonstrated that the legislature maintains the capital punishment statute because of the racially disproportionate impact suggested by the Baldus study. As legislatures necessarily have wide discretion in the choice of criminal laws and penalties, and as there were legitimate reasons for the Georgia Legislature to adopt and maintain capital punishment, we will not infer a discriminatory purpose on the part of the State of Georgia. Accordingly, we reject McCleskey's equal protection claims.

McCleskey also argues that the Baldus study demonstrates that the Georgia capital sentencing system violates the Eighth Amendment. We begin our analysis of this claim by reviewing the restrictions on death sentences established by our prior decisions under that Amendment.

The Eighth Amendment prohibits infliction of "cruel and unusual punishments." This Court's early Eighth Amendment cases examined only the "particular methods of execution to determine whether they were too cruel to pass constitutional muster." *Gregg v. Georgia* (1976). Subsequently, the Court recognized that the constitutional prohibition against cruel and unusual punishments "is not fastened to the obsolete but may acquire meaning as public opinion becomes enlightened by a humane justice." *Weems v. United States*, (1910).

Chief Justice Warren, writing for the plurality in *Trop v. Dulles* (1958), acknowledged the constitutionality of capital punishment. In his view, the "basic concept underlying the Eighth Amendment" in this area is that the penalty must accord with "the dignity of man." In applying this mandate, we have been guided by his statement that "the Amendment must draw its meaning from the evolving standards of decency that mark the progress of a maturing society." Thus, our constitutional decisions have been informed by "contemporary values concerning the infliction of a challenged sanction," *Gregg*. In assessing contemporary values, we have eschewed subjective judgment, and instead have sought to ascertain "objective indicia that reflect the public attitude toward a given sanction." First among these indicia are the decisions of state legislatures, "because the . . . legislative judgment weighs heavily in ascertaining" contemporary standards. . . . We also have been guided by the sentencing decisions of juries, because they are "a significant and reliable objective index of contemporary values." Most of our recent decisions as to the constitutionality of the death penalty for a particular crime have rested on such an examination of contemporary values.

In light of our precedents under the Eighth Amendment, McCleskey cannot argue successfully that his sentence is "disproportionate to the crime in the traditional sense." See *Pulley v. Harris* (1984). . . . McCleskey argues that the sentence in his case is disproportionate to the sentences in other murder cases.

Although our decision in *Gregg* as to the facial validity of the Georgia capital punishment statute appears to foreclose McCleskey's disproportionality argument, he further contends that the Georgia capital punishment system is arbitrary and capricious in application, and therefore his sentence is excessive, because racial considerations may influence capital sentencing decisions in Georgia. We now address this claim.

To evaluate McCleskey's challenge, we must examine exactly what the Baldus study may show. Even Professor

Baldus does not contend that his statistics prove that race enters into any capital sentencing decisions or that race was a factor in McCleskey's particular case. Statistics at most may show only a likelihood that a particular factor entered into some decisions. There is, of course, some risk of racial prejudice influencing a jury's decision in a criminal case. There are similar risks that other kinds of prejudice will influence other criminal trials. The question "is at what point that risk becomes constitutionally unacceptable. . . ." McCleskey asks us to accept the likelihood allegedly shown by the Baldus study as the constitutional measure of an unacceptable risk of racial prejudice influencing capital sentencing decisions. This we decline to do.

McCleskey's argument that the Constitution condemns the discretion allowed decisionmakers in the Georgia capital sentencing system is antithetical to the fundamental role of discretion in our criminal justice system. Discretion in the criminal justice system offers substantial benefits to the criminal defendant. Not only can a jury decline to impose the death sentence, it can decline to convict or choose to convict of a lesser offense. Whereas decisions against a defendant's interest may be reversed by the trial judge or on appeal, these discretionary exercises of leniency are final and unreviewable.

. . . Where the discretion that is fundamental to our criminal process is involved, we decline to assume that what is unexplained is invidious. In light of the safeguards designed to minimize racial bias in the process, the fundamental value of jury trial in our criminal justice system, and the benefits that discretion provides to criminal defendants, we hold that the Baldus study does not demonstrate a constitutionally significant risk of racial bias affecting the Georgia capital sentencing process of uniformity against the necessity for the exercise of discretion.

Two additional concerns inform our decision in this case. First, McCleskey's claim, taken to its logical conclusion, throws into serious question the principles that underlie our entire criminal justice system. The Eighth Amendment is not limited in application to capital punishment, but applies to all penalties. *Solem v. Helm* (1983). . . . Thus, if we accepted McCleskey's claim that racial bias has impermissibly tainted the capital sentencing decision, we could soon be faced with similar claims as to other types of penalty. Moreover, the claim that his sentence rests on the irrelevant factor of race easily could be extended to apply to claims based on unexplained discrepancies that correlate to membership in other minority groups, and even to gender. Similarly, since McCleskey's claim relates to the race of his victim, other claims could apply with equally logical force to statistical disparities that correlate with the race or sex of other actors in the criminal justice system, such as defense attorneys or judges. Also, there is no logical reason that such a claim need be limited to racial or sexual bias. If arbitrary and capricious punishment is the touchstone under the Eighth Amendment, such a claim could—at least in theory—be based upon any arbitrary variable, such as the defendant's facial characteristics, or the physical attractiveness of the defendant or the victim, that some statistical study indicates may be influential in jury decisionmaking. As these examples illustrate, there is no limiting principle to the type of challenge brought by McCleskey. The Constitution does not require that a State eliminate any demonstrable disparity that correlates with a potentially irrelevant factor in order to operate a criminal justice system that includes capital punishment. As have we stated specifically in the context of capital punishment, the Constitution does not "plac[e] totally unrealistic conditions on its use." *Gregg.*

Second, McCleskey's arguments are best presented to the legislative bodies. It is not the responsibility—or indeed even the right—of this Court to determine the appropriate punishment for particular crimes. It is the legislatures, the elected representatives of the people, that are "constituted to respond to the will and consequently the moral values of the people." *Furman.* (Burger, C. J., dissenting.) Legislatures also are better qualified to weigh and "evaluate the results of statistical studies in terms of their own local conditions and with a flexibility of approach that is not available to the courts Capital punishment is now the law in more than two-thirds of our States. It is the ultimate duty of courts to determine on a case-by-case basis whether these laws are applied consistently with the Constitution. Despite McCleskey's wide-ranging arguments that basically challenge the validity of capital punishment in our multiracial society, the only question before us is whether in his case, the law of Georgia was properly applied. We agree with the District Court and the Court of Appeals for the Eleventh Circuit that this was carefully and correctly done in this case.

Justice BRENNAN, with whom Justice MARSHALL joins, and with whom Justice BLACKMUN and Justice STEVENS join in part, dissenting.

Adhering to my view that the death penalty is in all circumstances cruel and unusual punishment forbidden by the Eighth and Fourteenth Amendments, I would vacate the decision below insofar as it left undisturbed the death sentence imposed in this case.

At some point in this case, Warren McCleskey doubtless asked his lawyer whether a jury was likely to sentence him to die. A candid reply to this question would have been disturbing. First, counsel would have to tell Mc-Cleskey that few of the details of the crime or of Mc-Cleskey's past criminal conduct were more important than the fact that his victim was white. Furthermore, counsel would feel bound to tell McCleskey that defendants charged with killing white victims in Georgia are 4.3 times as likely to be sentenced to death as defendants charged with killing blacks. In addition, frankness would compel the disclosure that it was more likely than not that the race of McCleskey's victim would determine whether he received a death sentence: 6 of every 11 defendants convicted of killing a white person would not have received the death penalty if their victims had been black, while, among defendants with aggravating and mitigating factors comparable to McCleskey's, 20 of every 34 would not have been sentenced to die if their victims had been black. Finally, the assessment would not be complete without the information that cases involving black defendants and white victims are more likely to result in a death sentence than cases featuring any other racial combination of defendant and victim. The story could be told in a variety of ways, but McCleskey could not fail to grasp its essential narrative line: there was a significant chance that race would play a prominent role in determining if he lived or died.

The Court today holds that Warren McCleskey's sentence was constitutionally imposed. It finds no fault in a system in which lawyers must tell their clients that race casts a large shadow on the capital sentencing process. The Court arrives at this conclusion by stating that the Baldus study cannot "prove that race enters into any capital sentencing decisions or that race was a factor in McCleskey's particular case." (emphasis in original) Since, according to Professor Baldus, we cannot say "to a moral certainty" that race influenced a decision, we can identify only "a likelihood that a particular factor entered into some decisions," and "a discrepancy that appears to correlate with race." This "likelihood" and "discrepancy," holds the Court, is insufficient to establish a constitutional violation. The Court reaches this conclusion by placing four factors on the scales opposite McCleskey's evidence: the desire to encourage sentencing discretion, the existence of "statutory safeguards" in the Georgia scheme, the fear of encouraging widespread challenges to other sentencing decisions, and the limits of the judicial role. The Court's evaluation of the significance of petitioner's evidence is fundamentally at odds with our consistent concern for rationality in capital sentencing, and the considerations that the majority invokes to discount that evidence cannot justify ignoring its force.

Defendants challenging their death sentences thus never have had to prove that impermissible considerations have actually infected sentencing decisions. We have required instead that they establish that the system under which they were sentenced posed a significant risk of such an occurrence. McCleskey's claim does differ, however, in one respect from these earlier cases: it is the first to base a challenge not on speculation about how a system might operate, but on empirical documentation of how it does operate.

The Court assumes the statistical validity of the Baldus study, and acknowledges that McCleskey has demonstrated a risk that racial prejudice plays a role in capital sentencing in Georgia. . . . Nonetheless, it finds the probability of prejudice insufficient to create constitutional concern. Close analysis of the Baldus study, however, in light of both statistical principles and human experience, reveals that the risk that race influenced McCleskey's sentence is intolerable by any imaginable standard.

The Baldus study indicates that, after taking into account some 230 nonracial factors that might legitimately influence a sentencer, the jury more likely than not would have spared McCleskey's life had his victim been black. The study distinguishes between those cases in which (1) the jury exercises virtually no discretion because the strength or weakness of aggravating factors usually suggests that only one outcome is appropriate; and (2) cases reflecting an "intermediate" level of aggravation, in which the jury has considerable discretion in choosing a sentence. McCleskey's case falls into the intermediate range. In such cases, death is imposed in 34% of white-victim crimes and 14% of black-victim crimes, a difference of 139% in the rate of imposition of the death penalty. In other words, just under 59%—almost 6 in 10—defendants comparable to McCleskey would not have received the death penalty if their victims had been black.

Furthermore, even examination of the sentencing system as a whole, factoring in those cases in which the jury exercises little discretion, indicates the influence of race on capital sentencing. For the Georgia system as a whole, race accounts for a six percentage point difference in the rate at which capital punishment is imposed. Since death is imposed in 11% of all white-victim cases, the rate in comparably aggravated black-victim cases is 5%. The rate of capital sentencing in a white-victim case is thus 120% greater than the rate in a black-victim case. Put another way, over half—55%—of defendants in white-victim crimes in Georgia would not have been sentenced to die if their victims had been black. Of the more than 200 variables potentially relevant to a sentencing decision, race of the victim is a powerful explanation for variation in death sentence rates—as powerful as nonracial aggravating factors such as a prior murder conviction or acting as the principal planner of the homicide.

These adjusted figures are only the most conservative indication of the risk that race will influence the death sentences of defendants in Georgia. Data unadjusted for the mitigating or aggravating effect of other factors show an even more pronounced disparity by race. The capital sentencing rate for all white-victim cases was almost 11 times greater than the rate for black-victim cases. Furthermore, blacks who kill whites are sentenced to death at nearly 22 times the rate of blacks who kill blacks, and more than 7 times the rate of whites who kill blacks. In addition, prosecutors seek the death penalty for 70% of black defendants with white victims, but for only 15% of black defendants with black victims, and only 19% of white defendants with black victims. Since our decision upholding the Georgia capital sentencing system in *Gregg*, the State has executed seven persons. All of the seven were convicted of killing whites, and six of the seven executed were black. Such execution figures are especially striking in light of the fact that, during the period encompassed by the Baldus study, only 9.2% of Georgia homicides involved black defendants and white victims, while 60.7% involved black victims.

The statistical evidence in this case thus relentlessly documents the risk that McCleskey's sentence was influenced by racial considerations. . . . In determining whether this risk is acceptable, our judgment must be shaped by the awareness that "the risk of racial prejudice infecting a capital sentencing proceeding is especially serious in light of the complete finality of the death sentence," and that "it is of vital importance to the defendant and to the community that any decision to impose the death sentence be, and appear to be, based on reason rather than caprice or emotion." . . . Surely, we should not be willing to take a person's life if the chance that his death sentence was irrationally imposed is more likely than not. In light of the gravity of the interest at stake, petitioner's statistics on their face are a powerful demonstration of the type of risk that our Eighth Amendment jurisprudence has consistently condemned.

Evaluation of McCleskey's evidence cannot rest solely on the numbers themselves. We must also ask whether the conclusion suggested by those numbers is consonant with our understanding of history and human experience. Georgia's legacy of a race-conscious criminal justice system, as well as this Court's own recognition of the persistent danger that racial attitudes may affect criminal proceedings, indicates that McCleskey's claim is not a fanciful product of mere statistical artifice.

History and its continuing legacy thus buttress the pro-

bative force of McCleskey's statistics. Formal dual criminal laws may no longer be in effect, and intentional discrimination may no longer be prominent. Nonetheless, as we acknowledged in *Turner*, "subtle, less consciously held racial attitudes" continue to be of concern, and the Georgia system gives such attitudes considerable room to operate. The conclusions drawn from McCleskey's statistical evidence are therefore consistent with the lessons of social experience.

The majority thus misreads our Eighth Amendment jurisprudence in concluding that McCleskey has not demonstrated a degree of risk sufficient to raise constitutional concern. The determination of the significance of his evidence is at its core an exercise in human moral judgment, not a mechanical statistical analysis. It must first and foremost be informed by awareness of the fact that death is irrevocable, and that as a result "the qualitative difference of death from all other punishments requires a greater degree of scrutiny of the capital sentencing determination." For this reason, we have demanded a uniquely high degree of rationality in imposing the death penalty. A capital sentencing system in which race more likely than not plays a role does not meet this standard. It is true that every nuance of decision cannot be statistically captured, nor can any individual judgment be plumbed with absolute certainty. Yet the fact that we must always act without the illumination of complete knowledge cannot induce paralysis when we confront what is literally an issue of life and death. Sentencing data, history, and experience all counsel that Georgia has provided insufficient assurance of the heightened rationality we have required in order to take a human life.

In fairness, the Court's fear that McCleskey's claim is an invitation to descend a slippery slope also rests on the realization that any humanly imposed system of penalties will exhibit some imperfection. Yet to reject McCleskey's powerful evidence on this basis is to ignore both the qualitatively different character of the death penalty and the particular repugnance of racial discrimination, considerations which may properly be taken into account in determining whether various punishments are "cruel and unusual." Furthermore, it fails to take account of the unprecedented refinement and strength of the Baldus study.

The Court's projection of apocalyptic consequences for criminal sentencing is thus greatly exaggerated. The Court can indulge in such speculation only by ignoring its own jurisprudence demanding the highest scrutiny on issues of death and race. As a result, it fails to do justice to a claim in which both those elements are intertwined—an occasion calling for the most sensitive inquiry a court can conduct. Despite its acceptance of the validity of Warren Mc-

Cleskey's evidence, the Court is willing to let his death sentence stand because it fears that we cannot successfully define a different standard for lesser punishments. This fear is baseless.

Finally, the Court justifies its rejection of McCleskey's claim by cautioning against usurpation of the legislatures' role in devising and monitoring criminal punishment. The Court is, of course, correct to emphasize the gravity of constitutional intervention and the importance that it be sparingly employed. The fact that "capital punishment is now the law in more than two thirds of our States," however, does not diminish the fact that capital punishment is the most awesome act that a State can perform. The judiciary's role in this society counts for little if the use of governmental power to extinguish life does not elicit close scrutiny. It is true that society has a legitimate interest in punishment. Yet, as Alexander Bickel wrote:

> It is a premise we deduce not merely from the fact of a written constitution but from the history of the race, and ultimately as a moral judgment of the good society, that government should serve not only what we conceive from time to time to be our immediate material needs but also certain enduring values. This in part is what is meant by government under law. *The Least Dangerous Branch* 24 (1962).

Our commitment to these values requires fidelity to them even when there is temptation to ignore them. Such temptation is especially apt to arise in criminal matters, for those granted constitutional protection in this context are those whom society finds most menacing and opprobrious. Even less sympathetic are those we consider for the sentence of death, for execution "is a way of saying, 'You are not fit for this world, take your chance elsewhere.'"

Justice BLACKMUN, with whom Justice MARSHALL and Justice STEVENS join, and with whom Justice BRENNAN joins in all but Part IV-B, dissenting.

Notes and Queries

1. Does the 8th Amendment require evidence of racial discrimination in McCleskey's case? How could this be shown? Or should McCleskey be required to show, instead, that racial discrimination is a general part of the death penalty system in Georgia? Is there a constitutional reason to prefer one position over another?

2. Justice Powell wrote that "in assessing contemporary values, we have eschewed subjective judgment, and instead have sought to ascertain 'objective indicia' that reflect the public attitude toward a given sanction." Do such criteria exist? Are "public attidudes" the same thing as "contemporary values"? Why is the "public attitude" relevant in assessing the constitutionality of the death penalty?

3. The majority concluded that accepting McCleskey's claim, taken to its logical conclusion, would throw "into serious question the principles that underlie our entire justice system." What are those principles? Assume the majority is correct: Is that a legitimate reason for denying McCleskey relief?

4. Justice Powell also echoed a recurrent and important theme in death penalty jurisprudence—deference to legislative authorities. Thus, he wrote, "McCleskey's arguments are best presented to the legislative bodies. It is not the responsibility—or even the right—of this Court to determine the appropriate punishment for particular crimes. It is the legislatures, the elected repesentatives of the people, that are 'constituted to respond to the will and consequently the moral values of the people.'"

Compare the decision of the South African Constitutional Court in *State v. Makwanyane* (1995)(Comparative Note 9.1) There, the Court argued that

> Public opinion may have some relevance to the enquiry, but in itself, it is no substitute for the duty vested in the Courts to interpret the Constitution and to uphold its provisions without fear or favour. If public opinion were to be decisive there would be no need for constitutional adjudication. . . . The very reason for . . . vesting the power of judicial review of all legislation in the courts, was to protect the rights of minorities and others who cannot protect their rights adequately through the democratic process. . . . This Court cannot allow itself to be diverted from its duty to act as an independent arbiter of the Constitution by making choices on the basis that they will find favour with the public.

5. In his dissent, Justice Brennan argued that the "judiciary's role in this society counts for little if the use of the governmental power to extinguish life does not elicit close scrutiny." What role for the judiciary does Justive Brennan envision? Can that role be squared with the democratic underpinnings of our constitutional democracy?

Atkins v. Virginia

536 U.S. 304, 122 S. Ct. 2242, 153 L. Ed. 2d 335 (2002)

On 16 August 1996, Atkins and William Jones, armed with a semiautomatic handgun, abducted Eric Nesbitt, robbed him, drove him to an automated teller machine in his pickup truck where cameras recorded their withdrawal of additional cash, then took him to an isolated location where he was shot eight times and killed. Atkins was convicted of capital murder by a Virginia jury and sentenced to death. Atkins appealed, claiming that he could not be sentenced to death because he was mentally retarded. Opinion of the Court: *Stevens*, O'Connor, Kennedy, Souter, Ginsberg, Breyer. Dissenting opinion: *Rehnquist*, Scalia, Thomas; *Scalia*, Rehnquist, Thomas.

Justice STEVENS delivered the opinion of the Court.

Those mentally retarded persons who meet the law's requirements for criminal responsibility should be tried and punished when they commit crimes. Because of their disabilities in areas of reasoning, judgment, and control of their impulses, however, they do not act with the level of moral culpability that characterizes the most serious adult criminal conduct. Moreover, their impairments can jeopardize the reliability and fairness of capital proceedings against mentally retarded defendants. Presumably for these reasons, in the 13 years since we decided *Penry v. Lynaugh* (1989), the American public, legislators, scholars, and judges have deliberated over the question whether the death penalty should ever be imposed on a mentally retarded criminal. The consensus reflected in those deliberations informs our answer to the question presented by this case: whether such executions are "cruel and unusual punishments" prohibited by the Eighth Amendment to the Federal Constitution.

. . . Guided by our approach in these cases, we shall first review the judgment of legislatures that have addressed the suitability of imposing the death penalty on the mentally retarded and then consider reasons for agreeing or disagreeing with their judgment.

The parties have not called our attention to any state legislative consideration of the suitability of imposing the death penalty on mentally retarded offenders prior to 1986. In that year, the public reaction to the execution of a mentally retarded murderer in Georgia apparently led to the enactment of the first state statute prohibiting such executions. In 1988, when Congress enacted legislation reinstating the federal death penalty, it expressly provided that a "sentence of death shall not be carried out upon a person who is mentally retarded." In 1989, Maryland enacted a similar prohibition. It was in that year that we decided *Penry*, and concluded that those two state enactments, "even when added to the 14 States that have rejected capital punishment completely, do not provide sufficient evidence at present of a national consensus."

Much has changed since then. Responding to the national attention received by the Bowden execution and our decision in *Penry*, state legislatures across the country began to address the issue. In 1990 Kentucky and Tennessee enacted statutes similar to those in Georgia and Maryland, as did New Mexico in 1991, and Arkansas, Colorado, Washington, Indiana, and Kansas in 1993 and 1994. In 1995, when New York reinstated its death penalty, it emulated the Federal Government by expressly exempting the mentally retarded. Nebraska followed suit in 1998. There appear to have been no similar enactments during the next two years, but in 2000 and 2001 six more States— South Dakota, Arizona, Connecticut, Florida, Missouri, and North Carolina—joined the procession. The Texas Legislature unanimously adopted a similar bill, and bills have passed at least one house in other States, including Virginia and Nevada.

It is not so much the number of these States that is significant, but the consistency of the direction of change. Given the well-known fact that anticrime legislation is far more popular than legislation providing protections for persons guilty of violent crime, the large number of States prohibiting the execution of mentally retarded persons (and the complete absence of States passing legislation reinstating the power to conduct such executions) provides powerful evidence that today our society views mentally retarded offenders as categorically less culpable than the average criminal. The evidence carries even greater force when it is noted that the legislatures that have addressed the issue have voted overwhelmingly in favor of the prohibition. Moreover, even in those States that allow the execution of mentally retarded offenders, the practice is uncommon. . . . The practice, therefore, has become truly unusual, and it is fair to say that a national consensus has developed against it.[44]

---

[44] Footnote by the court: Additional evidence makes it clear that this legislative judgment reflects a much broader social and professional consensus. For example, several organizations with germane expertise have adopted official positions opposing the imposition of the death penalty upon a mentally retarded offender. See Brief for American Psychological Association et al. as *Amici Curiae*; Brief for AAMR et al. as *Amici Curiae*. In addition, representatives of widely diverse religious communities in the United States, reflecting Christian, Jewish, Muslim, and Buddhist traditions, have filed an amicus curiae brief explaining that even though their views about the death penalty differ, they all "share a conviction that the execution of persons with mental retardation cannot be morally justified." See Brief for United

Comparative Note 9.5

The existence of an international trend against the death penalty is useful in testing our values against those of comparable jurisdictions. This trend against the death penalty supports some relevant conclusions. First, criminal justice, according to international standards, is moving in the direction of abolition of the death penalty. Second, the trend is more pronounced among democratic states with systems of criminal justice comparable to our own. The United States (or those parts of it that have retained the death penalty) is the exception, although of course it is an important exception. Third, the trend to abolition in the democracies, particularly the Western democracies, mirrors and

perhaps corroborates the principles of fundamental justice that led to the rejection of the death penalty in Canada. . . .

The recent and continuing disclosures of wrongful convictions for murder in Canada, the United States and the United Kingdom provide tragic testimony to the fallibility of the legal system, despite its elaborate safeguards for the protection of the innocent. When fugitives are sought to be tried for murder by a retentionist state, however similar in other respects to our own legal system, this history weighs powerfully in the balance against extradition without assurances.

SOURCE: *Minister of Justice, Appellant v. Glen Sebastian Burns and Atif Ahmad Rafay*, 2001 S.C.C. 7.

To the extent there is serious disagreement about the execution of mentally retarded offenders, it is in determining which offenders are in fact retarded. In this case, for instance, the Commonwealth of Virginia disputes that Atkins suffers from mental retardation. Not all people who claim to be mentally retarded will be so impaired as to fall within the range of mentally retarded offenders about whom there is a national consensus. As was our approach in *Ford v. Wainwright* (1986), with regard to insanity, "we leave to the State[s] the task of developing appropriate ways to enforce the constitutional restriction upon its execution of sentences."

This consensus unquestionably reflects widespread judgment about the relative culpability of mentally retarded offenders, and the relationship between mental retardation and the penological purposes served by the death penalty. Additionally, it suggests that some characteristics of mental retardation undermine the strength of the procedural protections that our capital jurisprudence steadfastly guards.

In light of these deficiencies, our death penalty jurispru-

dence provides two reasons consistent with the legislative consensus that the mentally retarded should be categorically excluded from execution. First, there is a serious question as to whether either justification that we have recognized as a basis for the death penalty applies to mentally retarded offenders.

With respect to retribution—the interest in seeing that the offender gets his "just desserts"—the severity of the appropriate punishment necessarily depends on the culpability of the offender. Since *Gregg*, our jurisprudence has consistently confined the imposition of the death penalty to a narrow category of the most serious crimes. . . . If the culpability of the average murderer is insufficient to justify the most extreme sanction available to the State, the lesser culpability of the mentally retarded offender surely does not merit that form of retribution. Thus, pursuant to our narrowing jurisprudence, which seeks to ensure that only the most deserving of execution are put to death, an exclusion for the mentally retarded is appropriate.

With respect to deterrence—the interest in preventing capital crimes by prospective offenders—"it seems likely that 'capital punishment can serve as a deterrent only when murder is the result of premeditation and deliberation.'" Exempting the mentally retarded from that punishment will not affect the "cold calculus that precedes the decision" of other potential murderers. Indeed, that sort of calculus is at the opposite end of the spectrum from behavior of mentally retarded offenders. The theory of deterrence in capital sentencing is predicated upon the notion that the increased severity of the punishment will inhibit criminal actors from carrying out murderous con-

States Catholic Conference et al. as *Amici Curiae* in *McCarver v. North Carolina*, O. T. 2001, No. 00–8727, p. 2. Moreover, within the world community, the imposition of the death penalty for crimes committed by mentally retarded offenders is overwhelmingly disapproved. Brief for The European Union as *Amicus Curiae* in *McCarver v. North Carolina*, O. T. 2001, No. 00–8727, p. 4. Finally, polling data shows a widespread consensus among Americans, even those who support the death penalty, that executing the mentally retarded is wrong. R. Bonner & S. Rimer, "Executing the Mentally Retarded Even as Laws Begin to Shift," *N. Y. Times*, Aug. 7, 2

duct. Yet it is the same cognitive and behavioral impairments that make these defendants less morally culpable—for example, the diminished ability to understand and process information, to learn from experience, to engage in logical reasoning, or to control impulses—that also make it less likely that they can process the information of the possibility of execution as a penalty and, as a result, control their conduct based upon that information. Nor will exempting the mentally retarded from execution lessen the deterrent effect of the death penalty with respect to offenders who are not mentally retarded.

Our independent evaluation of the issue reveals no reason to disagree with the judgment of "the legislatures that have recently addressed the matter" and concluded that death is not a suitable punishment for a mentally retarded criminal. We are not persuaded that the execution of mentally retarded criminals will measurably advance the deterrent or the retributive purpose of the death penalty. Construing and applying the Eighth Amendment in the light of our "evolving standards of decency," we therefore conclude that such punishment is excessive and that the Constitution "places a substantive restriction on the State's power to take the life" of a mentally retarded offender.

The judgment of the Virginia Supreme Court is reversed and the case is remanded for further proceedings not inconsistent with this opinion.

It is so ordered.

Chief Justice REHNQUIST, with whom Justice SCALIA and Justice THOMAS join, dissenting.

The question presented by this case is whether a national consensus deprives Virginia of the constitutional power to impose the death penalty on capital murder defendants like petitioner, i.e., those defendants who indisputably are competent to stand trial, aware of the punishment they are about to suffer and why, and whose mental retardation has been found an insufficiently compelling reason to lessen their individual responsibility for the crime. The Court pronounces the punishment cruel and unusual primarily because 18 States recently have passed laws limiting the death eligibility of certain defendants based on mental retardation alone, despite the fact that the laws of 19 other States besides Virginia continue to leave the question of proper punishment to the individuated consideration of sentencing judges or juries familiar with the particular offender and his or her crime.

I write separately, however, to call attention to the defects in the Court's decision to place weight on foreign laws, the views of professional and religious organizations, and opinion polls in reaching its conclusion. The Court's suggestion that these sources are relevant to the constitutional question finds little support in our precedents and, in my view, is antithetical to considerations of federalism, which instruct that any "permanent prohibition upon all units of democratic government must [be apparent] in the operative acts (laws and the application of laws) that the people have approved." *Stanford v. Kentucky* (1989). The Court's uncritical acceptance of the opinion poll data brought to our attention, moreover, warrants additional comment, because we lack sufficient information to conclude that the surveys were conducted in accordance with generally accepted scientific principles or are capable of supporting valid empirical inferences about the issue before us.

In making determinations about whether a punishment is "cruel and unusual" under the evolving standards of decency embraced by the Eighth Amendment, we have emphasized that legislation is the "clearest and most reliable objective evidence of contemporary values." The reason we ascribe primacy to legislative enactments follows from the constitutional role legislatures play in expressing policy of a State. And because the specifications of punishments are "peculiarly questions of legislative policy," our cases have cautioned against using "the aegis of the Cruel and Unusual Punishment Clause" to cut off the normal democratic processes.

In my view, these two sources—the work product of legislatures and sentencing jury determinations—ought to be the sole indicators by which courts ascertain the contemporary American conceptions of decency for purposes of the Eighth Amendment. They are the only objective indicia of contemporary values firmly supported by our precedents. More importantly, however, they can be reconciled with the undeniable precepts that the democratic branches of government and individual sentencing juries are, by design, better suited than courts to evaluating and giving effect to the complex societal and moral considerations that inform the selection of publicly acceptable criminal punishments.

In reaching its conclusion today, the Court does not take notice of the fact that neither petitioner nor his *amici* have adduced any comprehensive statistics that would conclusively prove (or disprove) whether juries routinely consider death a disproportionate punishment for mentally retarded offenders like petitioner. Instead, it adverts to the fact that other countries have disapproved imposition of the death penalty for crimes committed by mentally retarded offenders. . . . I fail to see, however, how the views of other countries regarding the punishment of their citizens provide any support for the Court's ultimate determination. While it is true that some of our prior opinions have looked to "the climate of international opinion," we have since explicitly rejected the idea that the sentencing practices of other countries could "serve to establish the first Eighth Amendment prerequisite, that [a] practice is accepted among our people." *Stanford* (emphasizing that "American conceptions of decency . . . are dispositive") (emphasis in original).

Stanford's reasoning makes perfectly good sense, and the Court offers no basis to question it. For if it is evidence of a national consensus for which we are looking, then the viewpoints of other countries simply are not relevant.

To further buttress its appraisal of contemporary societal values, the Court marshals public opinion poll results and evidence that several professional organizations and religious groups have adopted official positions opposing the imposition of the death penalty upon mentally retarded offenders. In my view, none should be accorded any weight on the Eighth Amendment scale when the elected representatives of a State's populace have not deemed them persuasive enough to prompt legislative action. . . . For the Court to rely on such data today serves only to illustrate its willingness to proscribe by judicial fiat—at the behest of private organizations speaking only for themselves—a punishment about which no across-the-board consensus has developed through the workings of normal democratic processes in the laboratories of the States.

Even if I were to accept the legitimacy of the Court's decision to reach beyond the product of legislatures and practices of sentencing juries to discern a national standard of decency, I would take issue with the blind-faith credence it accords the opinion polls brought to our attention. An extensive body of social science literature describes how methodological and other errors can affect the reliability and validity of estimates about the opinions and attitudes of a population derived from various sampling techniques.

There are strong reasons for limiting our inquiry into what constitutes an evolving standard of decency under the Eighth Amendment to the laws passed by legislatures and the practices of sentencing juries in America. Here, the Court goes beyond these well-established objective indicators of contemporary values. It finds "further support to [its] conclusion" that a national consensus has developed against imposing the death penalty on all mentally retarded defendants in international opinion, the views of professional and religious organizations, and opinion polls not demonstrated to be reliable.

Believing this view to be seriously mistaken, I dissent.

Justice SCALIA, with whom the CHIEF JUSTICE and Justice THOMAS join, dissenting.

Today's decision is the pinnacle of our Eighth Amendment death-is-different jurisprudence. Not only does it, like all

of that jurisprudence, find no support in the text or history of the Eighth Amendment; it does not even have support in current social attitudes regarding the conditions that render an otherwise just death penalty inappropriate. Seldom has an opinion of this Court rested so obviously upon nothing but the personal views of its members.

Under our Eighth Amendment jurisprudence, a punishment is "cruel and unusual" if it falls within one of two categories: "those modes or acts of punishment that had been considered cruel and unusual at the time that the Bill of Rights was adopted," and modes of punishment that are inconsistent with modern "standards of decency," as evinced by objective indicia, the most important of which is "legislation enacted by the country's legislatures. . . ."

The Court makes no pretense that execution of the mildly mentally retarded would have been considered "cruel and unusual" in 1791. Only the severely or profoundly mentally retarded, commonly known as "idiots," enjoyed any special status under the law at that time.

The Court is left to argue, therefore, that execution of the mildly retarded is inconsistent with the "evolving standards of decency that mark the progress of a maturing society." *Trop v. Dulles* (1958). Before today, our opinions consistently emphasized that Eighth Amendment judgments regarding the existence of social "standards" "should be informed by objective factors to the maximum possible extent" and "should not be, or appear to be, merely the subjective views of individual Justices. . . ."

The Court pays lip service to these precedents as it miraculously extracts a "national consensus" forbidding execution of the mentally retarded, from the fact that 18 States—less than half (47%) of the 38 States that permit capital punishment (for whom the issue exists)—have very recently enacted legislation barring execution of the mentally retarded. Even that 47% figure is a distorted one. If one is to say, as the Court does today, that all executions of the mentally retarded are so morally repugnant as to violate our national "standards of decency," surely the "consensus" it points to must be one that has set its righteous face against all such executions. Not 18 States, but only seven—18% of death penalty jurisdictions—have legislation of that scope. Eleven of those that the Court counts enacted statutes prohibiting execution of mentally retarded defendants convicted after, or convicted of crimes committed after, the effective date of the legislation; those already on death row, or consigned there before the statute's effective date, or even (in those States using the date of the crime as the criterion of retroactivity) tried in the future for murders committed many years ago, could be put to death. That is not a statement of absolute moral repugnance, but one of current preference between two tolerable approaches.

But let us accept, for the sake of argument, the Court's faulty count. That bare number of States alone—18—should be enough to convince any reasonable person that no "national consensus" exists. How is it possible that agreement among 47% of the death penalty jurisdictions amounts to "consensus"?

The Court attempts to bolster its embarrassingly feeble evidence of "consensus" with the following: "It is not so much the number of these States that is significant, but the consistency of the direction of change." But in what other direction could we possibly see change? Given that 14 years ago all the death penalty statutes included the mentally retarded, any change (except precipitate undoing of what had just been done) was bound to be in the one direction the Court finds significant enough to overcome the lack of real consensus. That is to say, to be accurate the Court's "consistency-of-the-direction-of-change" point should be recast into the following unimpressive observation: "No State has yet undone its exemption of the mentally retarded, one for as long as 14 whole years." In any event, reliance upon "trends," even those of much longer duration than a mere 14 years, is a perilous basis for constitutional adjudication.

But the Prize for the Court's Most Feeble Effort to fabri-cate "national consensus" must go to its appeal (de-servedly relegated to a footnote) to the views of assorted professional and religious organizations, members of the so-called "world community," and respondents to opinion polls. I agree with the Chief Justice, (dissenting opinion), that the views of professional and religious organizations and the results of opinion polls are irrelevant. Equally irrelevant are the practices of the "world community," whose notions of justice are (thankfully) not always those of our people. "We must never forget that it is a Constitution for the United States of America that we are expounding. . . . [W]here there is not first a settled consensus among our own people, the views of other nations, however enlightened the Justices of this Court may think them to be, cannot be imposed upon Americans through the Constitution."

Beyond the empty talk of a "national consensus," the Court gives us a brief glimpse of what really underlies today's decision: pretension to a power confined neither by the moral sentiments originally enshrined in the Eighth Amendment (its original meaning) nor even by the current moral sentiments of the American people. "[T]he Constitution," the Court says, "contemplates that in the end our own judgment will be brought to bear on the question of the acceptability of the death penalty under the Eighth Amendment." . . . The arrogance of this assumption of

Comparative Note 9.6

In the course of the arguments addressed to us, we were referred to books and articles on the death sentence, and to judgments dealing with challenges made to capital punishment in the courts of other countries and in international tribunals. The international and foreign authorities are of value because they analyse arguments for and against the death sentence and show how courts of other jurisdictions have dealt with this vexed issue. For that reason alone they require our attention. They may also have to be considered because of their relevance to section 35(1) of the Constitution, which states:

In interpreting the provisions of this Chapter a
Court of law shall promote the values, which underlie
An open and democratic society based on freedom and
Equality and shall, where applicable, have regard to
Public international law applicable to the

Protection of the rights entrenched in this Chapter,
And may have regard to comparable foreign case law.

Our Constitution expresses the right to life in an unqualified form, and prescribes the criteria that have to be met for the limitation of entrenched rights, including the prohibition of legislation that negates the essential content of an entrenched right. In dealing with comparative law, we must bear in mind that we are required to construe the South African Constitution, and not an international instrument or the constitution of some foreign country, and that this has to be done with due regard to our legal system, our history and circumstances, and the structure and language of our own Constitution. We can derive assistance from public international law and foreign case law, but we are in no way bound to follow it. . . .

SOURCE: *State v. Makwanyane and Mchunu*, (1995) (3) S.A. 391.

power takes one's breath away. And it explains, of course, why the Court can be so cavalier about the evidence of consensus. It is just a game, after all. "[I]n the end," it is the feelings and intuition of a majority of the Justices that count—"the perceptions of decency, or of penology, or of mercy, entertained . . . by a majority of the small and unrepresentative segment of our society that sits on this Court."

I respectfully dissent.

Notes and Queries

1. *Atkins* rehearses an increasingly familiar argument among the justices about whether and when it is appropriate for the United States Supreme Court to make use of comparative materials. It reminds us, too, that the debate typically occurs in the context of concerns about the limits of judicial power. Consider footnote 21 of the majority's opinion: Of what relevance, precisely, is the Court's reference to the views of the "world community"?

Consider, too, Chief Justice Rehnquist's remarks: "*Stanford's* reasoning makes perfectly good sense, and the Court offers no basis to question it. For if it is evidence of a national consensus for which we are looking, then the viewpoints of other countries simply are not relevant. . . ." Do you agree with the Chief Justice?

2. Why does the majority expend so much effort on trying to prove that there is a national consensus against imposing the death penalty on mentally diminished offenders? Was its argument persuasive? In dissent, Justice Scalia strongly criticized the majority's conclusion that such a consensus exists. Do you agree with Justice Scalia that the majority opinion is a "pretension to a power confined neither by the moral sentiments originally enshrined in the Eighth Amendment . . . nor even by the current moral sentiments of the American people"?

3. In his dissent, the Chief wrote that "In my view, these two sources—the work product of legislatures and sentencing jury determinations—ought to be the sole indicators by which courts ascertain the contemporary American conceptions of decency for purposes of the Eighth Amendment. . . . They can be reconciled with the undeniable precepts that the democratic branches of government . . . are by design, better suited than courts to evaluating and giving effect to the . . . moral considerations that inform" the death penalty.

Chapter 10

Liberty and Property

One of the Constitution's central purposes, according to the Preamble, is to secure the "Blessings of Liberty." The Constitution does not fix these blessings with any specificity, but any careful examination of the rights and liberties it protects, together with other sources such as the Declaration of Independence, the *Federalist Papers*, and the Framers' correspondence, discloses that the pursuit of property was first among the Blessings of Liberty. Indeed, the unamended constitutional text (before the Bill of Rights) is riddled with references to and protections for property. These provisions are usually written in highly individualistic language, leaving no room for governmental regulation, especially when compared to similar provisions in the constitutions of other countries.

This individualistic language, however, is misleading in two respects. First, property rights in the United States have never been absolute. The authority of the national and state governments to interfere with private property has waxed and waned, but there has never been a time when the Supreme Court did not permit some restrictions on property through the states' police powers. Second, because the Founders' conceptions of liberty and property were very complex, the nature of property rights in the American system has been less individualistic than the constitutional text might suggest. In the lexicon of the Founders, liberty and property often appear interchangeable; James Madison, for example, wrote that "a man has property in his opinions and the free communication of them, . . . in his religious opinions, and in the profession and practice dictated by them. . . . In a word, as a man is said to have a right to his property, he may be equally said to have a property in his rights."[1]

When the Founders spoke of liberty, then, they meant not a single right, capable of precise definition, but rather an expansive collection of related

---

[1] "Property," *National Gazette*, 29 March 1792; reprinted in Marvin Meyers (ed.), *The Mind of the Founder*. (Indianapolis: Bobbs-Merrill, 1973), 243–44. For a caution about equating liberty and property, however, see Michael Kammen, "The Rights of Property and Property in Rights: The Problematic Nature of 'Property' in the Political Thought of the Founders and the Early Republic," in Ellen Frankel Paul and Howard Dickman (eds), *Liberty, Property, and the Foundations of the American Constitution* (Albany: State University of New York Press, 1989), 5.

"liberties," especially the right to property and the right (of propertied men) to participate in the affairs of governance. As Forrest McDonald notes, "Neither liberty nor property was a right, singular; each was a complex and subtle combination of many rights, power, and duties, distributed among individuals, society, and the state."[2]

Both Federalists and anti-Federalists—agreeing that the association between liberty and community centered chiefly on the right to property—"expressed concerns about the protection of property under the new government" of 1787.[3] Inherent differences about the meaning and purpose of property, however, soon appeared in disputes about how best to secure it. This led to conflict over the relative roles of the state and national governments in safeguarding liberty. Jefferson and the anti-Federalists argued that the safest protection for liberty and property was self-governance in small, local, and predominantly agrarian communities. Implicit in the Jeffersonian vision is the belief that virtue and fraternity are centrally connected to direct participation in the shared political life of one's community. The prerequisite for this direct participation was ownership of property, which guaranteed personal independence and liberty. To attain these ends, Jefferson even proposed, in his draft constitution for Virginia, that every citizen who did not already own land should be given fifty acres.

Hamilton, Madison, and the Federalists were equally certain that the pursuit of liberty meant the pursuit of property and that property was both a source of liberty and a sign of virtue. Madison wrote in *Federalist* 10 that "the first object of government" was to protect "the diversity in the faculties of men from which the rights of property originate."[4] Secure possession of property *was* the goal of the pursuit of liberty and the first end of all legitimate governments. The Federalists likewise believed that "threats against liberty will be felt first as threats against property rights—in the form of unjust taxes, the impairment of the obligations of contracts, or other disfranchisments of property rights."[5] Threats to property were thus the first and most obvious danger to liberty itself.

But the Federalists also believed that "the greatest danger to the personal rights and liberties of the people, including their right to property, came from factional majorities of the people themselves."[6] They therefore saw in local communities, not comfort for property, but only insecurity. Madison claimed in *Federalist* 10 that the chief threat to liberty consisted in the existence of "faction," which he defined as "a number of citizens, whether amounting to a majority or minority of the whole, who are united and actuated by some common impulse of passion, or of interest, adverse to the rights of other citizens, or to the permanent and aggregate interests of the community." Because small communities could be easily dominated by a faction, Madison argued that the surest relief from faction consisted in the promotion of diverse interests in the population. This could best be achieved in a large, extensive republic, a conclusion the anti-Federalists feared.

Protection for property, broadly defined, was thus a goal shared by Federalists and anti-Federalists alike and was a central purpose of the new constitutional order. On the floor of the Philadelphia Convention, Madison noted that among the reasons for a new constitution was "the necessity of providing more effectually for the secur-

---

[2] Forrest McDonald, *Novus Ordo Seclorum*. (Lawrence, KS: University Press of Kansas, 1985), 13.

[3] Kammen, supra note 1, 9.

[4] Clinton Rossiter, ed., *The Federalist Papers*. (New York: New American Library, 1961), #10.

[5] Edward J. Erler, *The American Polity*. (New York: Crane Russak, 1991), 29.

[6] Gordon S. Wood, "Preface," in Paul and Dickman, supra note 1, xiii.

ity of private rights. . . . Interferences with these were evils which had, perhaps more than anything else, produced this convention."[7] Many of the delegates believed property was insecure under the Articles of Confederation, which largely left regulation and protection of property to the various state governments. Each state was free to coin its own money, to set trade and tariff policies for itself, to favor its own commerce, and to penalize the commerce of other states. Many of the state legislatures, dominated by majorities of debtors, systematically discriminated against commercial interests. Shay's Rebellion in western Massachusetts also heightened the fears of many delegates.

The Constitution they produced reflected their fears. Notwithstanding claims that no bill of rights would be necessary to protect individual liberties (see the discussion in chapter 9), the text included several specific protections for property and contract rights. Most important was Article I, Section 10, which provides that "[n]o State shall . . . pass any . . . ex post facto law or laws impairing the obligation of contracts. . . ." Unlike the provisions of the first eight amendments, Article I, Section 10 operates directly on the states, further underscoring the delegates' fears of state interference with private property. Other provisions included limitations on the state's authority to levy taxes, to regulate interstate commerce, to coin money, and to enact bankruptcy laws.

One might see these provisions as the effort of a prosperous commercial class to protect its own interests against the masses of democratically inclined debtors. Charles Beard, in a famous study, concluded that the Founders were elitist men of wealth who sought to protect their possessions and status by limiting the power of majorities to interfere with property and contractual obligations.[8] More recently, Sheldon Wolin and Michael Parenti (among others) have advanced a somewhat different version of this argument. They claim the Framers, despite their rhetoric of consent and democracy, constructed a form a government that, through such devices as separation of powers, checks and balances, and representation, largely removed "the people" from the business of governance.[9]

Anti-democratic interpretations of the Constitution's concern for property dismiss the intimate connection the Framers saw between property and liberty. They also obscure the relationship anti-Federalists saw between personal independence and political virtue. "Dependence," wrote Jefferson, "begets subservience and venality [and] suffocates the germ of virtue. . . ."[10] Only the possession of property, especially land, could secure the independence necessary for free political participation.

Proponents of the civic republican interpretation of the Founding argue that although the Framers meant to protect private liberty and property, they sought also to promote public virtue. By "virtue," republicans meant "the capacity of individuals to willingly sacrifice self-interest for the public good or to identify their self-interest with the public good." From this perspective, the cardinal purpose of the new constitutional order should be to create communities in which "virtue" could flourish. What

---

[7] Max Farrand (ed.), *The Records of the Federal Convention of 1787.* (New Haven: Yale University Press, 1937), I: 33–4.

[8] Charles Beard, *An Economic Interpretation of the Constitution.* (New York: MacMillan, 1913).

[9] Sheldon S. Wolin, *The Presence of the Past: Essays on the State and the Constitution.* (Baltimore: Johns Hopkins University Press, 1989); and Michael Parenti, "The Constitution as an Elitist Document," in Richard Goldwin and William Schambra (eds), *How Democratic is the Constitution?* (Washington: American Enterprise Institute, 1980), 47.

[10] Notes on Virginia (1782), reprinted in Andrew A. Lipscomb, Jr. (ed.), *The Writings of Thomas Jefferson.* (Washington, D.C.: The Thomas Jefferson Memorial Association, 1903), II: 229.

distinguishes the republican interpretation from others is the claim that the Framers sought to build a political society in which virtue could be the guiding principle. . . ."[11] In the civic republican tradition, then, the pursuit and promotion of virtue necessitated, at least occasionally, the subordination of private interests to the public good.

As these debates suggest, the Founders' conceptions of liberty and property were expansive and complex. Property was understood to be closely connected to *all* individual liberties, including political liberty. Though less concerned with public virtue, liberals shared with Jeffersonians the belief that the protection of property was, as Locke had written, "the great and chief end" of society and the best guarantor of liberty, both personal and political. For this reason, and because both conservatives and progressives have found support for their arguments in the Constitution, the "role played by economic concerns in America's constitutional debates has . . . been exceedingly complex."[12]

The Contracts Clause and the Vested Rights Doctrine

Article I, Section 10 of the Constitution provides, "No State shall . . . pass any . . . Law impairing the Obligation of Contracts. . . ." Aside from the Bill of Rights, it is the clearest and most important expression of concern for private property in the constitutional text. In the nation's early years, the contracts clause gave rise to many of the Supreme Court's most important decisions. These cases involve one of the central issues of constitutional law: the relationship between individual liberty (in this case the right to property) and the community's right to regulate it in the public interest. This conflict raises difficult questions about the nature and source of property rights and, no less important, about the Supreme Court's role in policing the boundaries between individual liberty and the public good.

The Supreme Court's first interpretation of the contracts clause partially frustrated the Framers' efforts to protect property against debtor-controlled state legislatures. In *Calder v. Bull* (1798, reprinted later in the chapter), the Connecticut legislature set aside a state probate court judgment awarding an inheritance to one party by passing a law that effectively awarded the property to the other party. The retroactive character of the state legislation invited claims that the state had passed an *ex post facto* law, or one that changed the rules after the fact to reach the opposite result. Justice Chase's opinion for the Supreme Court denied that the prohibition of *ex post facto* laws protected private property from regulation by state legislatures. Chase held more narrowly that the prohibition applied only to criminal laws that punish actions legal at the time they were committed, or that increase retroactively the punishment for specific crimes. Because the Connecticut law had done neither, it was not an *ex post facto* law.

Despite this result, much of Chase's opinion reads like a sermon on the sacred right to private property. Using the language of natural law, Chase appealed to "certain vital principles in our free Republican government, which will determine and overrule an apparent and flagrant abuse of legislative power" such as "a law that

---

[11] John R. Bauer, *The Political Thought of the Framers: Ambiguities and Interpretations,* 20 Perspectives on Political Science (Winter 1991), 11, 13

[12] Rogers M. Smith, *Liberalism and American Constitutional Law.* (Cambridge: Harvard University Press, 1985), 139.

takes property from A, and gives it to B." Chase, therefore, could not accept "the omnipotence of a state legislature, or that it is absolute and without controul; although its authority should not be expressly restrained by the constitution. . . ." The vital principles restraining legislatures were thus *not* included in the text of the Constitution; rather, they resided in "the general principles of law and reason."

Only in the very last paragraph of his opinion did Chase embrace a conception of private property that left it vulnerable to state legislatures. "It seems to me," he concluded, "that the *right of property*, in its origin, could only arise from *compact express*, or *implied*, and I think it is the better opinion, that the *right*, as well as the *modes*, or *manner*, of acquiring property . . . is conferred by society . . . and is always subject to the rules prescribed by *positive* law. . . ."

In his concurring opinion, Justice Iredell rejected Chase's appeal to general principles not found in the constitutional text, noting, "It is true, that some speculative jurists have held, that a legislative act against natural justice . . . must be void; but I cannot think that . . . any court of justice would possess a power to declare it so. . . . The ideas of natural justice are regulated by no fixed standard; the ablest and purest men have differed on the subject. . . ."

As this last exchange suggests, the real significance of *Calder* is not what it had to say about *ex post facto* or even about property as such, but rather that it initiated a debate about constitutional interpretation that remains as intense and relevant today as in 1798—i.e., between positivism and "natural law." As we shall see in this and the chapters that follow, the division in *Calder* remains the great fault line in the Supreme Court.

The Marshall Court (1801–35) shared Chase's belief that judges possessed authority to overrule state legislatures even absent a specific provision in the constitutional text. Marshall, however, was even less inclined than Chase to admit the power of positive law to regulate private property. In two important decisions, the Marshall Court went far to make private property immune from regulation by the state. Most dramatic was *Fletcher v. Peck* (1810, reprinted later in the chapter), in which Chief Justice Marshall declared unconstitutional an act by the Georgia legislature annulling an earlier session's patently fraudulent sale of the Yazoo land tract to private investors.[13] Marshall held that the state's original sale was a contract within the meaning of Article I, Section 10 (a conclusion probably not foreseen by the Founders, who in all likelihood meant the provision to apply only to private contracts). Consequently, the second legislative act, setting aside the sale, violated the constitutional prohibition against impairment of contracts. In the last paragraph of his opinion, Marshall went so far as to write that "Georgia was restrained, either by general principles which are common to our free institutions, or by the particular provisions of the constitution of the United States. . . ." Justice Johnson went even further in his concurring opinion, noting "I do not hesitate to declare that a state does not possess the power of revoking its own grants. But I do it, on a general principle, on the reason and nature of things; a principle which will impose laws even on the Deity. . . ."

This language is reminiscent of Chase's appeal in *Calder* to "certain vital republican principles." Notably absent in *Fletcher*, though, is *Calder*'s stress on the socially created and limited nature of property. On the contrary, in *Fletcher* the right to property acquired nearly transcendent status, protected by principles of natural justice. *Fletcher* thus represents the highwater mark of protection of property through the

---

[13] The best account of the scandal is C. Peter McGrath, *Yazoo: The Case of Fletcher v. Peck.* (New York: W.W. Norton & Co., Inc., 1966).

doctrine of natural or "vested rights." Vested rights were liberties whose source was the doctrine of "inalienability" suggested by the Declaration of Independence, or the very nature of republican government (as Justice Chase had insisted in *Calder*), rather than positive law. These principles have force whether or not the Constitution expressly incorporates them.

The Marshall Court built on *Fletcher* in *Dartmouth College v. Woodward* (1819). In this case, Marshall first determined that the charter of Dartmouth College was a contract within the meaning of Article I. "Surely," he stated, "in this transaction [the college charter] every ingredient of a complete and legitimate contract is to be found." The question remaining was whether a public, corporate charter should be excluded from the terms of Article I, Section 10.[14] Marshall admitted,

> *It is more than possible, that the preservation of rights of this description was not particularly in the view of the framers of the constitution, when that clause was introduced into that instrument. . . . But although a particular and a rare case may not, in itself, be of sufficient magnitude to induce a rule, yet it must be governed by the rule . . . unless some plain and strong reason for excluding it can be given.*

Marshall could find no such reason. His insistence that any ambiguity in the charter must be interpreted in a way that defended the property right against the state shows clearly the paramount status of property for the Marshall Court.

Not long after *Fletcher* and *Dartmouth*, changes in the Court's membership and leadership, and resulting changes in ideology, led the Court to begin dismantling the wall of protection it had erected. *Charles River Bridge Company v. Warren Bridge* (1837, reprinted later in the chapter) best illustrates the change. Massachusetts contracted with a private corporation in 1785 to build a toll bridge across the Charles River. When the state contracted with another company in 1828 to build a second bridge next to the first one—which would eliminate tolls once costs had been recovered—the first company sued, claiming the new contract impaired the contract of 1785. The Supreme Court first heard argument in 1831, and John Marshall favored following *Fletcher* and *Dartmouth*. Internal divisions, however, forced the Court to order reargument, and by the time the case was decided in 1837, Roger Taney had succeeded Marshall as Chief Justice.

In *Fletcher* the Marshall Court had spoken of the natural right to private property, "inherent in the very nature of things." In *Charles River Bridge* the Taney Court (1836–64) stressed instead the state's interest in regulating property for the common good. Chief Justice Taney, writing for the Court, repeatedly underscored the necessity of interpreting the contracts clause in a way that does not unduly restrict the state's authority to encourage public works and improvements. Making frequent use of what we might call public policy arguments, Taney emphasized not the "natural" or "sacred" right of property, but rather the interests and rights of the community. He noted, "[T]he object and end of all government is to promote the happiness and prosperity of the community. . . . While the rights of private property are sacredly guarded, we must not forget that the community also have rights, and that the happiness and well being of every citizen depends on their faithful preservation."

In dissent, Justice Story, the last and closest of Marshall's intellectual companions, met Taney on the same ground. He argued that "for my own part, I can conceive of

---

[14] There was little doubt that the contracts clause prohibited state interference with private contracts. The Court held so in *Sturges v. Crowinshield* (1819).

no surer plan to arrest all public improvements, founded on private capital and enterprise, than to make the outlay of the capital uncertain. . . ." Following *Dartmouth*, Story insisted that contractual ambiguities should be resolved in favor of the individual's right to private property. As Story's reply suggests, at issue were "two different models of economic development."[15] Story's opinion rests on a highly individualistic conception of property, while Taney's opinion embodies a more communal vision. Whereas Story, like the Marshall Court, stressed the need for the security of private property, Taney emphasized the community's interest in developing property for the public good. Both, however, defended their understanding of property on the basis of its ability to serve the community.

The same tension between public and private interests appears in *Home Building & Loan v. Blaisdell* (1934, reprinted later in the chapter). In *Blaisdell*, the Court upheld a Minnesota law that temporarily prohibited creditors from foreclosing on debtors who were behind in making mortgage payments on their homes. Chief Justice Hughes, in his majority opinion, conceded the law probably violated the Framers' understanding of the contracts clause. Nevertheless, borrowing from a draft opinion circulated but never published by Justice Cardozo,[16] Hughes wrote:

> *But full recognition of the occasion and general purpose of the clause does not suffice to fix its precise scope. . . . With a growing recognition of public needs and the relation of individual right to public security, the court has sought to prevent the perversion of the clause through its use as an instrument to throttle the capacity of the States to protect their fundamental interests.*

Dissenting, Justice Sutherland responded, "A provision of the Constitution, it is hardly necessary to say, does not admit of two distinctly opposite interpretations. It does not mean one thing at one time and an entirely different thing at another time."

Both Hughes and Sutherland claimed to interpret the contracts clause as the Framers had intended. Initially, Sutherland's approach may appear more faithful to original intent. The clearest evidence of what the Framers intended, he would argue, is what they said: "As nearly as possible we should place ourselves in the condition of those who framed and adopted it." Cardozo and Hughes, however, focused less on the words and more on the *purpose* of the clause. As one of us has argued, "there was a deeper intent, which was to promote the conditions of economic stability."[17] Although one might distinguish between *intent* and *purpose*, the point is that reliance on superficial conceptions of "Framer's intent" may frustrate the underlying purposes of specific constitutional provisions. The majority in *Blaisdell* was prepared to sanction action inconsistent with the literal words of the contracts clause to secure a result consistent with its purpose.

A more recent case, *United States Trust Company v. New Jersey* (1977), suggests the contracts clause may yet have life. The laws that gave the New York Port Authority power to operate a commuter railroad in 1962 specifically provided that bonds issued to pay for the railroad's construction had to be paid in full before the Port Authority could use the revenue pledged for their security to offset general expenses.

---

[15] Morton J. Horwitz, *The Transformation of American Law, 1780–1860.* (Cambridge: Harvard University Press, 1977), 134.

[16] Professor Alpheus Mason of Princeton University found a draft of Cardozo's opinion in Chief Justice Stone's private papers, which are located at the Library of Congress. For a discussion, see Walter F. Murphy et al., *American Constitutional Interpretation*, 3d ed., (Westbury, NY: Foundation Press, 2003), 226.

[17] Gary J. Jacobsohn, *Pragmatism, Statesmanship, and the Supreme Court.* (Ithaca: Cornell University Press, 1977), 188.

When New York and New Jersey repealed those provisions in 1973–74, a bond-holder challenged their actions. To the surprise of many, the Court held the repeal did violate the contracts clause. Justice Blackmun, writing for the majority, noted, "Whether or not the protection of contract rights comports with current views of wise public policy, the Contracts Clause remains a part of our written Constitution." In dissent, Justice Brennan complained,

> *Today's decision . . . remolds the Contract Clause into a potent instrument for overseeing important policy determinations of the state legislature. At the same time, by creating a constitutional safe haven for property rights embedded in a contract, the decision substantially distorts modern constitutional jurisprudence governing regulation of private economic interests.*

Since the decision in *United States Trust Company,* the Court has done little to revive the contracts clause.[18] Regardless of the clause's current doctrinal status, however, cases under it inevitably raise vital questions about the relation between liberty and community and about the Court's own role in supervising the relationship, questions which remain on the Court's agenda.

The Rise and Fall of Economic Due Process

Much of the tension between private property and the state's police powers originally centered on the contracts clause, but the *Slaughter-House Cases* demonstrate that such disputes also involve the due process clauses of the Fifth and Fourteenth Amendments, which guarantee that no citizen shall be deprived of property without due process of law. It should come as no surprise that concerns about economic liberty appear in both doctrinal lines: in the nineteenth century and early into the twentieth, economic liberty was the architectonic value of American society. *Slaughter-House* also indicates that property involves more than just land or physical possessions; it also includes the right to contract with others for the purpose of transferring and disposing of property, broadly understood.

The importance of the due process clause as a vehicle for protecting property rights increased as the reach of the contracts clause diminished. In the late nineteenth century, however, as *Slaughter-House* made clear, the due process clause of the Fourteenth Amendment offered no greater protection for property rights than did Article I, Section 10.

Munn v. Illinois (1877, reprinted later in the chapter), like *Slaughter-House,* favored police powers over private property. *Munn* involved a challenge to the Illinois legislature's power to fix rates for grain storage in privately owned grain elevators. Two aspects of the case stand out. First, Chief Justice Waite's majority opinion asserted that "property . . . become[s] clothed with a public interest when used in a manner to make it of public consequence, and affect the community at large." Because grain storage is an economic activity with significant public consequences, the Court upheld the state's exercise of its regulatory powers. Justice Field, who had dissented in *Slaughter-House,* complained in dissent the decision was "subversive of the rights of property. . . . The legislation in question is nothing less than a bold assertion of absolute power by the State to control at its discretion the property and business of the citizen. . . ."

---

[18] But see *Allied Steel Co. v. Spannaus* (1978). For a discussion, see Bernard Schwartz, *Old Wine in New Bottles: The Renaissance of the Contracts Clause,* 1979 Supreme Court Review 95.

Here we see again the conflict that surfaced in *Charles River Bridge* forty years earlier. Waite's majority opinion stressed the communal nature of all individual liberties and therefore the authority of legislatures to regulate property. Field's dissent, on the other hand, like Story's earlier, rested upon a more individualistic conception of the public good that emphasized the sanctity and security of private property.

The second important aspect of *Munn* was the Court's explicit ruling that the determination of what was reasonable compensation for the use of private property was a legislative decision and not, as the owners had argued, a judicial matter. "For protection against abuses by legislatures the people must resort to the polls," wrote Waite, "not to the courts" (though he did admit that with regard to purely private contracts "what is reasonable must be ascertained judicially"). Justice Field, however, gave judicial power under the due process clause broader scope, arguing that the absence of judicial supervision gave "unrestrained license to legislative will. . . ." Hence, he concluded, "If this be sound law, if there be no protection, either in the principles upon which our republican government be founded, or in the prohibitions of the Constitution against such invasion of private rights, all property and business in the State are held at the mercy of a majority of its legislature."[19]

Munn galvanized commercial interests to organize in opposition to state regulation and to promote the doctrine of laissez-faire government. The American Bar Association, for example, founded in 1878, was formed with the express purpose of getting the case overturned. Together with significant changes in the Court's membership, this growing and powerful ideological movement soon began to influence judicial interpretation of the due process clause. This new direction became evident in *Mugler v. Kansas* (1887), when the Court warned that any exercise of the police power must have "a real or substantial relation" to its object. Justice Harlan, moreover, cautioned that judges would not be "misled by mere pretences" but would instead "look at the substance of things." The Court moved even further from *Munn* in *Chicago, Milwaukee, and St. Paul Railway Co. v. Minnesota* (1890), holding that a state law regulating rate-making was unconstitutional because it did not provide for judicial review of the rate-making process. In direct contrast to *Munn*, the Court concluded that the question of the "reasonableness" of the rates was "eminently a question for judicial investigation."[20]

The rise of substantive due process reached full expression in *Allgeyer v. Louisiana* (1897). Writing for the Court, Justice Peckham offered an expansive definition of liberty of contract, concluding,

> *The liberty mentioned [in the Fourteenth Amendment] . . . is deemed to embrace the right of the citizen to be free in the enjoyment of all his faculties; to be free to use them in all lawful ways; to live and work where he will; to earn his livelihood by any lawful calling; to pursue any livelihood or avocation, and for that purpose to enter into all contracts which may be proper, necessary, and essential to his carrying out to a successful conclusion the purposes above mentioned.*

Allgeyer shows that the Court's use of laissez-faire and economic due process rested upon a conception of civil liberties in which property and contract rights were central to personal autonomy and personhood. Although it did not overrule *Munn*, *Allgeyer* abandoned the communitarian spirit that had animated it, embracing instead the indi-

---

[19] Meanwhile, Justice Field actively sought his party's nomination for President. For a brief description of his candidacy and of his efforts to increase the Court's size to 21 members, see Howard J. Graham, *Everyman's Constitution*. (Madison: State Historical Society of Wisconsin, 1968), 137–44.

[20] See also *Smyth v. Ames* (1898).

vidualism of Field's earlier dissent, together with its expansive implications for judicial power.

The most prominent example of substantive economic due process, so-called because of the Court's use of the due process clause to protect the substantive rights of property and contract in *Allgeyer* and other cases, was *Lochner v. New York* (1905, reprinted later in the chapter). In *Lochner*, Justice Peckham's opinion for a 5 to 4 majority held that a New York law regulating working conditions of bakers unconstitutionally infringed upon the right of employer and employees to contract. Calling such regulations "mere meddlesome interferences" with the right to contract, the majority could find "no reasonable ground for interfering with the liberty of person or the right of free contract, by determining the hours of labor, in the occupation of a baker." In dissent, Justice Holmes replied, "This case is decided upon an economic theory which a large part of the country does not entertain. . . . [A] constitution is not intended to embody a particular economic theory, whether of paternalism and the organic relation of the citizen to the State or of laissez-faire."

Whereas in *Munn* and *Slaughter-House* the Court had ruled that the determination of reasonableness was a decision for state legislatures, the *Lochner* Court, ruling instead that reasonableness was for judicial determination, now assumed the role of "perpetual censor" on state economic activity that Justice Miller, writing in *Slaughter-House*, had feared. (As we saw in earlier chapters, the Court pursued a similar course in its commerce clause decisions.)[21]

The *Lochner* philosophy governed two other important cases. In *Coppage v. Kansas* (1915), the Court considered the conviction of a man arrested for violating the state's "yellow dog" law. A yellow dog contract required employees to agree, if hired, that they would not join a labor union. In striking down the law as a violation of the right to contract, Justice Pitney observed that "an interference . . . so serious as that now under consideration . . . must be deemed to be arbitrary, unless it be supportable as a reasonable exercise of the police power of the State." The state's effort to redress the obviously unequal bargaining positions of employers and employees was not such a reasonable exercise, he continued, because

> *wherever the right of private property exists, there must and will be inequalities of fortune. . . . [But it] is from the nature of things impossible to uphold freedom of contract and the right of private property without at the same time recognizing as legitimate those inequalities of fortune that are the necessary result of the exercise of those rights.*

Holmes dissented again, repeating his insistence in *Lochner* that the wisdom of the law was not relevant to its constitutionality.

In *Adkins v. Children's Hospital* (1923), the Court ruled that a minimum wage law for women in the Dictirct of Columbia violated the due process clause. Acknowledging that in *Muller v. Oregon* (1908) it had upheld a law limiting the number of hours women could work per day, the Court noted that the country had since adopted the

---

[21] Although the Court vigorously protected the rights of property and contract, it did not extend such aggressive scrutiny to other liberties, or even to property and contract when the rights of women were involved. See *Muller v. Oregon* (1908), upholding a state law that limited the number of hours women could work per day; *Bunting v. Oregon* (1917), upholding a state law that established a maximum ten-hour day for factory workers; *Jacobson v. Massachusetts* (1905), upholding a state law requiring vaccination against smallpox; and *Buck v. Bell* (1927), in which Justice Holmes, declaring that "three generations of imbeciles is enough," rejected the claim that compulsory sterilization violated Carrie Buck's rights to due process and equal protection.

Nineteenth Amendment. Women therefore no longer occupied a position of "substantial civil inferiority." Consequently, protective laws of the sort upheld in earlier cases could no longer interfere with a woman's liberty of contract if such interference would be unconstitutional when applied to males. And in language that moved beyond even the test of "reasonableness" promulgated in the *Mugler-Allgeyer-Lochner* line of cases, Justice Sutherland wrote that "freedom of contract is . . . the general rule and restraint the exception; and the exercise of legislative authority to abridge it can be justified only by the existence of exceptional circumstances." Dissenting, a puzzled Holmes confessed "that I do not understand the principle on which the power to fix a minimum for the wages of women can be denied by those who admit the power to fix a maximum for their hours of work. . . . The bargain is equally affected whichever half you regulate." Holmes again insisted, "The criterion of constitutionality is not whether we believe the law to be for the public good."

The Decline of Economic Due Process

The Great Depression and President Roosevelt's New Deal presented substantial challenges to economic due process and the federal judiciary's protection of laissez-faire economics. Though gradually moving away from the doctrinaire position of *Lochner*, the Court continued to strike down major parts of the New Deal, notably in *Schechter Poultry Corporation v. United States* (1935), *United States v. Butler* (1936), and *Carter v. Carter Coal Company* (1936). Popular belief has it that the Court's dramatic reversal of course was a consequence of President Roosevelt's "court-packing" plan, a proposal that justices over the age of seventy be given six months to retire and that the president be entitled to appoint a new justice to serve alongside any justice who kept his seat. The principal evidence for this myth is Justice Roberts' vote against state regulation in *Morehead v. New York* (1936) to his vote to sustain it one year later in *West Coast Hotel v. Parrish* (1937, reprinted later in the chapter). In fact, though, Justice Roberts changed his mind in late 1936, well before Roosevelt announced his ill-fated plan to "save the court from hardened judicial arteries."

The Court's gradual repudiation of economic due process had started three years earlier in *Nebbia v. New York* (1934). Upholding a New York statute establishing price controls for milk sold at grocery stores, the Court noted, "The due process clause makes no mention of sales or prices any more than it speaks of business or contract. . . ." The Court likewise adopted the spirit of Holmes' *Lochner* dissent: "With the wisdom of the policy . . . the Courts are both incompetent and unauthorized to deal."

The Court's retreat from economic due process reached full steam in *West Coast Hotel*, in which it upheld a Washington state law establishing a minimum wage and overruled *Adkins*. Chief Justice Hughes, writing of the liberty of contract so important in *Lochner*, noted that "the liberty safeguarded is liberty in a social organization which requires the protection of law against the evils which menace the health, safety, morals and welfare of the people." In direct contrast to Peckham's opinion in *Lochner*, Hughes insisted, "Even if the wisdom of the policy . . . is debatable . . . still the legislature is entitled to its judgment." Only Justice Sutherland in dissent protested that "the Washington statute . . . is in every substantial respect identical with the statute involved in the *Adkins* case. . . ." And taking the Chief Justice to task again, as he had earlier in *Blaisdell*, Sutherland complained "The defense of the . . . law is made upon grounds which were discountenanced by the makers of the Constitution and have many times been rejected by this Court. . . . With due regard for the processes of logical thinking, it legitimately cannot be urged that conditions which produced the rule may now be invoked to destroy it."

West Coast Hotel signaled the end of economic due process and aggressive judicial scrutiny of state and federal economic activity. By 1963, in *Ferguson v. Skrupa* the Court could pointedly observe, "The doctrine that prevailed in *Lochner* . . . and like cases—that due process authorizes courts to hold laws unconstitutional when they believe the legislature has acted unwisely—has long since been discarded." And in *Hawaii Housing Authority v. Midkiff* (1984), Justice O'Connor wrote that the Court would invalidate a state's exercise of its police power to regulate private property only if it were not "rationally related to a conceivable public purpose. . . ." In *Midkiff* we see a Court much more solicitous of the public interest in regulating property than we do in decisions embodying economic due process or asserting the doctrine of vested rights. The change represents a fundamentally different conception of the relationship between individual liberty and community interests, and of how private property affects that relationship. It also rests upon an understanding of judicial power that reduces the role of courts in balancing those two interests, and instead entrusts most such decisions to legislatures.

The Takings Clause and Due Process

The Court's rejection of economic due process, like its abandonment of the contracts clause, has meant that the right to property, arguably the most important of rights at the Founding, is substantially less important than it once was as a foundation for personal autonomy or as a "fence to liberty." Even so, a few recent cases arising under the takings clause of the Fifth Amendment suggest that the right to property may yet have a future. The clause provides simply that private property may not "be taken for public use, without just compensation." Both the federal government and the states have long held a power of eminent domain, or the authority to "take" private property, either for a public use or because the property poses a threat to the public welfare. The power is essentially legislative in character, and for much of its history the Supreme Court has been unwilling to closely supervise its use.

In a series of recent cases, however, the Court has suggested that it might begin to use somewhat more rigorous scrutiny than the simple rationality test in determining when a "taking" has occurred under the just compensation clause of the Fifth Amendment.[22] In *Nollan v. California Coastal Committee* (1987), the Court considered the constitutionality of a decision by a coastal commission to condition a permit to replace a small beach cottage with a larger home with a requirement that the owners grant the public an easement across the property to the beach. The homeowners claimed the easement constituted a taking. Writing for the majority, Justice Scalia held that the easement did constitute a taking for which the homeowners must be compensated. Justice Scalia concluded that in this case, there was a "lack of nexus" between the purpose of the condition and the "probable impact" of the actual condition. The Court seemed to suggest that something more than simple rationality might be required in takings cases, but the opinion was not completely clear about what an alternative test might look like.

In *Lucas v. South Carolina Coastal Council* (1992) the Court stated that it would

---

[22] See Richard Epstein, *Takings: Private Property and the Power of Eminent Domain.* (Cambridge: Harvard University Press, 1985); and Cass Sunstein, *Interest Groups in American Public Law,* 38 Stanford Law Review 29 (1985).

require local officials to "do more than proffer the legislature's declaration" as a reason for regulation. In striking down a decision by South Carolina to prohibit further beachfront development, the Court, again in an opinion by Justice Scalia, also ruled that a state decision that deprives a property owner of "all economically beneficial use," means it must compensate the owner, no matter how important the public interest in such regulation may be. Similarly, in *Dolan v. Tigard* (1994), the Court required local officials to actually bring forth evidence of a connection between the regulations it imposed and the conditions that gave rise to them. In both *Lucas* and *Dolan*, the Court used the rationality test, but it appeared to shift the burden of proof to local authorities. And in both cases, the majority's approach provoked animated dissents. In *Nollan*, for example, Justice Brennan complained that the Court's new-found insistence upon a "precise accounting system" had "given appellants a windfall at the expense of the public." Justice Blackmun concluded that "Even the wisest lawyers would have to acknowledge great uncertainty about the scope of this Court's takings jurisprudence. . . ." Blackmun was less circumspect in *Lucas*, announcing that "Today the Court has launched a missile to kill a mouse." Justice Stevens, also in dissent, concluded that Justice Scalia's majority opinion had established a rule that "is an unsound and unwise addition to the law and the Court's formulation of the exception to that rule is too rigid and too narrow."

The debate came to the fore again in the recent case of *Tahoe-Sierra Preservation Council v. Tahoe Regional Planning Agency* (2002, reprinted later in the chapter). In this case, the Court addressed a series of local statutes that placed moratoria on the owners of certain property while the states of Nevada and California formulated a land-use plan for the area. The owners claimed this moratoria necessarily constituted a "temporary" taking under *Lucas*. The Court refused to go so far, ruling that cases like *Lucas* and *Tahoe* must be decided on a case by case basis. In this case, no taking had occurred. This time in dissent, Justices Thomas and Scalia argued that "A taking is exactly what occurred in this case. . . . The Court assures [the landowners] that a 'temporary prohibition on economic use' cannot be a taking because 'logically . . . the property will recover as soon as the prohibition is lifted.' But the 'logical' assurance that a 'temporary restriction . . . merely causes a diminution in value,' is cold comfort to the property owners. . . . After all, 'in the long run, we are all dead.'"

In light of these cases, and the Court's seeming inability to agree upon a rule to govern them, we cannot say for certain whether the Court's fear of economic due process will continue to result in little or no protection for property rights. Whatever the status of property, and notwithstanding the repudiation of economic due process, the Court has been willing to use substantive due process to protect other liberties, such as privacy and personal autonomy, as we shall see in chapter 11.

Comparative Perspectives

Most constitutions include specific protections for individual liberty and private property.[23] These protections usually include corresponding duties or obligations, or are phrased so as to acknowledge that both liberty and property have social dimensions. It is often in these provisions that theories of human personality and visions of the

---

[23] The Canadian Charter protects liberty, but does not in express terms protect property. Article 1(a) of the Canadian Bill of Rights, a statutory enactment, does protect private property, but its legal status is not clear.

proper relationship between state and society are most visible. Rights to property are consequently among the most useful and important for discerning how constitutional democracies reconcile their twin commitments to liberty and community. And as the South African Constitutional Court has written they are also, and for some of the same reasons, "notoriously difficult to interpret. . . ."[24]

A review of some of these provisions suggests that an understanding of liberty and property as the fulcrum between the competing demands of individual and community is much too simplistic. It ignores the subtle way in which property shapes community by defining the condition of individuals *in* society. It also ignores the ways in which community defines the nature of property. Rights to property and the state's police powers, rather than simply conflicting, are mutually interdependent.

Section 25 of the South African Constitution, for example, provides that

> *No one may be deprived of property except in terms of law of general application, and no law may permit arbitrary deprivation of property.*
>> *(2) Property may be expropriated only in terms of law of general application*
>>> *(a) for a public purpose or in the public interest; and*
>>> *(b) subject to compensation, the amount of which and the time and manner of payment of which have either been agreed to by those affected or decided or approved by a court.*

The same section indicates that "the public interest includes the nation's commitment to land reform, and to reforms to bring about equitable access to all South Africa's natural resources. . . ."

The German Basic Law likewise guarantees the right to property and couples it with certain social obligations. Article 14 states, "Property and the right of inheritance are guaranteed." Subsection 14(2), however, qualifies the right by declaring, "Property imposes duties. Its use should also serve the public weal." Similarly, Article 15, which states that land and natural resources may be transferred to public ownership, clearly reflects a vision of property that subordinates its private and individualistic

---

Comparative Note 10.1

Every natural or legal person is entitled to the peaceful enjoyment of his possessions. No one shall be deprived of his possessions except in the public interest and subject to the conditions provided by law and by the general principles of international law [European Convention for the Protection of Human Rights, Protocol No. 1 (1952), Article 1.]

Everyone has the right to freely possess, use, and dispose of his or her property. Restrictions shall be provided by law. Property shall not be used contrary to the public interest. [Constitution of the Republic of Estonia (1996), Sec. 32 (2).]

A social market economy, based on the freedom of economic activity, private ownership, and solidarity, dialogue and cooperation between social partners, shall be the basis of the economic system of the Republic of Poland. [Constitution of the Republic of Poland (1997), Article 20.]

Property may be expropriated only in terms of law of general application . . . for public purposes or in the public interest; . . . the public interest includes the nation's commitment to land reform, and to reforms to bring about equitable access to all South Africa's natural resources; . . . [Constitution of the Republic of South Africa (1996), Article 25 (2) and (4) [a].]

---

[24] *First National Bank of South Africa Limited v. Commissioner for South African Revenue Services* CCT 19/01 (2002).

dimensions to the public good. In the *Hamburg Flood Control Case* (1968), the Federal Constitutional Court stated, "The Basic Law establishes that in the recurring tension between the property interest of the individual and the needs of the public, the public interest may, in case of conflict, take precedence over the legally guaranteed position of the individual. . . ."

Article 29 of the Japanese Constitution begins by claiming, "The right to own or hold property may not be carried on so as to conflict with the public interest, or in a manner prejudicial to safety or liberty, or the dignity of man." Section 2 qualifies the right, however, by stating that "Property rights shall be defined by law, in conformity with the public welfare." Likewise, Article 41 of the Italian Constitution provides that "Private enterprise in the economic field shall be free." But "it may not be carried on so as to conflict with the public interest, or in a manner prejudicial to safety or liberty, or the dignity of man." Article 42 continues, "Private property is recognized and guaranteed by law, which determines the manner of its acquisition and enjoyment and its limits, in order to assure its social function and render it accessible to all."[25]

Ireland's Constitution plainly reflects the influence of Catholic social thought. Article 43 "acknowledges that man, in virtue of his rational being, has the natural right, antecedent to positive law, to the private ownership of external goods." It cautions, though, "that the exercise of [the right] ought, in civil society, to be regulated by the principles of social justice."

As these provisions indicate, the problems that characterize the relationship between property and the public good in the United States are a familiar feature of most constitutional democracies. Many twentieth-century constitutions also provide explicitly for a variety of "social rights," which typically include the right to a job, to education, and to various forms of social welfare. The German Basic Law, for example, incorporates as an overarching constitutional value the concept of the "social welfare state," which "places social rights on the same footing as civil rights."[26] The Irish Constitution is more specific, promising to "safeguard with special care the economic interests of the weaker sections of the community, and, where necessary, to contribute to support of the infirm, the widow, the orphan, and the aged." Article 25 of the Japanese Constitution states that "all people shall have the right to maintain the minimum standards of wholesome and cultured living."[27] In other instances, the right to property is coupled with qualifications that refer back to the particular needs and histories of the state in question. The South African provisions, for example, indicate that the state must take "reasonable legislative and other measures" to remediate inequities that are a "result of past discriminatory laws or practices. . . ."

In contrast, the American Constitution is considerably less expansive. The Bill of Rights does not define liberty or property, and it does not explicitly guarantee "social rights" of the kind common to other constitutions. Arguments that such rights should be protected in the United States often rely on claims that they are, in fact, "property" and thus protected by the Fifth and Fourteenth Amendments. Nor does the American

---

[25] Contrast this language with Justice Chase's opinion in *Calder v. Bull* (1798).

[26] Donald P. Kommers, *The Constitutional Jurisprudence of the Federal Republic of Germany.* (2d ed. Durham, N.C.: Duke University Press, 1997), 241.

[27] In the *Minimum Standards of Wholesome and Cultured Living Case* (1948), the Japanese Supreme Court dismissed a claim that governmental rationing policies violated Article 25: "[T]he nation must assume . . . responsibility broadly toward all the people; this is a governmental function. But the state does not bear such an obligation concretely and materially toward the people as individuals. In other words, this provision does not directly bestow on the people as individuals such a concrete and material right in respect to the nation . . . ." See also the *Asahi Tuberculosis Case* (1967).

Bill of Rights couple its explicit protections for liberty and property with detailed or specific reservations in the public interest. Nevertheless, as we have seen, the Supreme Court has tended to find some of these qualifications implicit in the right itself.

Rights to Property and Occupational Liberty

A related issue, implicit but not directly addressed in *Slaughter-House*, is whether the Fourteenth Amendment guarantees individual freedom of occupational choice. The Constitution is silent on the point, but in *Allgeyer* the Court ruled that liberty includes freedom "to live and work where [one] will; to earn [one's] livelihood by any lawful calling; [and] to pursue any livelihood or avocation. . . ." And in *Meyer v. Nebraska* (1923) the Court suggested that liberty included the right "to engage in any of the common occupations of life." Since its rejection of economic due process in the 1930s, however, the Court has been largely inactive in this area (though not entirely—see *Williamson & Lee Optical* [1955] and *Ferguson* [1963]).

The connection between occupational liberty and property is also an issue in most other constitutional democracies. Twentieth-century constitutions typically offer explicit protection for occupational liberties and subsistence rights. Article 12(1) of the German Basic Law, for example, declares, "All Germans shall have the right freely to choose their trade, occupation, or profession, their place of work, and their place of training." In the *Pharmacy Case* (1958), the Federal Constitutional Court ruled unconstitutional a Bavarian statute that restricted the number of licensed pharmacies in local communities. An individual denied a license filed a constitutional complaint, arguing that the statute violated Article 12(1).

The Federal Court observed that Article 12(1) is the state's recognition that "[w]ork . . . [has] a relationship to the human personality as a whole: It is a relationship that shapes and completes the individual over a lifetime . . . ; it is the foundation of a person's existence through which that person simultaneously contributes to the total social product. . . ." The Court thus recognized that occupational choices shape both individual and community. Consequently, "The legislature is . . . empowered to make regulations affecting either the choice or the practice of a profession. The more a regulatory power is directed to the choice . . . , the narrower are its limits; the more it is directed to the practice of a profession, the broader are its limits. . . ."

In *Sumiyoshi v. Governor of Hiroshima* (1975), the Supreme Court of Japan found parts of the Pharmaceutical Affairs Law unconstitutional because they contravened Article 22 of the Japanese Constitution. Article 22 declares that an individual has the right "to choose [an] occupation to the extent that it does not interfere with the public welfare." Sumiyoshi owned three drugstores. The government rejected his application for a fourth because he sought to operate it within one hundred meters of one of his competitors, in violation of the Pharmaceutical Affairs Law. The Court first noted that occupational choice is a "social activity" that necessitates restrictions in the public interest. Such restrictions are constitutionally acceptable only if they are "necessary and reasonable measures for an important public interest. . . ."

The relationship between liberty and property is especially interesting in Canada. Section 7 of the Charter expressly protects liberty, but does not mention property at all. The Canadian Supreme Court has nevertheless had to consider whether some forms of occupational rights—rights easily subsumed under the label "property"—might be protected as liberty under Section 7. In the case of *In re Wilson* (1988), the Court noted,

> *Liberty within the meaning of S. 7 is not confined to mere freedom from bodily restraint. It does not, however, extend to protect property or pure economic rights.*

It may embrace individual freedom of movement, including the right to choose one's occupation and where to pursue it, subject to the right of the state to impose, in accordance with the principles of fundamental justice, legitimate and reasonable restrictions on the activities of individuals. . . .[28]

In Canada, therefore, the right to liberty may extend to activities that other constitutional democracies protect under the rubric of property rights. This reminds us that there are intimate connections between liberty and property, a theme we shall see also in the following chapters.

The cases of India and Israel make for an interesting comparison, in part because in both countries the Founders were, in many instances, committed socialists. And in both cases, the evolution of property rights has been intricately caught up with the evolution of judicial power. In India, for example, the struggle over constitutional rights to private property has been a constant in the evolution of the constitutional polity and the role of the courts. The Constitution of 1949 contained several safeguards: First, Article 19(1)(f) guaranteed the right to acquire property subject to reasonable restrictions to serve the public welfare. (This provision was later repealed.) Another clause, [Art. 31 (1)], guarantees that no person shall be deprived of property except under authority of law. This clause was intended as a protection against executive appropriations of property and was not intended to limit the authority of the legislature. Finally, Article 31(2) provides that the acquisition of private property by the State may be done only for a public purpose and in conjunction with just compensation. (Subsequent amendments, however, made it easier for the State to acquire property without full compensation.) But the courts have fought (more strenuously in some periods than others) over the years to protect private property in spite of the effort embodied in the new constitutional language to facilitate national planning and development.

The rise in the powers of the Supreme Court in Israel was made possible by the adoption in 1992 of two basic laws (Basic Law: Human Dignity and Liberty and Basic Law: Freedom of Occupation). As rewritten in 1994, the latter provides that "Every Israel national or resident has the right to engage in any occupation, profession or trade." It further states that "There shall be no violation of the freedom of occupation except by a law that accords with the values of the State of Israel, enacted for a proper purpose and to an extent no greater than required, or by such a law enacted with explicit authorization therein." It should be noted that this basic law (in Israel, of course, there is no formal written comprehensive constitution) is different from most, in that it is entrenched, that is to say, it cannot be altered except by a basic law passed by a majority of the members of the Knesset. This in turn provides the Court with additional authority to exercise its newly legitimated power of judicial review over the actions of the legislature. Indeed, one frequently articulated criticism of the Court in recent years is that its newly acquired (by judicial say-so) authority was designed to protect private property against State invasions, and that its efforts to this point demonstrate much greater commitment to protect rights of property than other kinds of rights. In other words, this criticism suggests the "constitutional revolution" in Israel was all about facilitating the neo-liberal economic agenda of the country's propertied interests.

---

[28] In *In re Fernandes and Director of Social Services Winnipeg Central* (1992), on the other hand, the Manitoba Court of Appeal concluded that Section 7 did not protect "[t]he desire to live in a particular setting. . . ." The plaintiff Fernandes had complained that a decision by the Director of Social Services to deny his application to return to his residence (with public aid), and instead to maintain him in a hospital, violated Section 7.

Selected Bibliography

Ackerman, Bruce. 1973. *Private Property and the Constitution.* New Haven: Yale University Press.

Becker, Theodore. 1941. *The Declaration of Independence: A Study in the History of Political Ideas.* New York: Alfred A. Knopf.

Brigham, John. 1989. "Constitutional Property: The Double Standard and Beyond," in Michael W. McCann and Gerald L. Houseman, *Judging the Constitution: Critical Essays on Judicial Lawmaking.* Glenview, Ill.: Scott, Foresman & Company.

Buckley, F. H. (ed.). 1999. *The Fall and Rise of Freedom of Contract.* Durham, NC: Duke University Press.

Corwin, Edward S. 1948. *Liberty Against Government.* Baton Rouge, La.: Louisiana State University Press.

Currie, David. 1985. *The Constitution in the Supreme Court: The Protection of Economic Interests.* University of Chicago Law Review 52: 324.

Eidelberg, Paul. 1968. *The Philosophy of the American Constitution.* New York: Free Press.

Ely, John Hart. 1980. *Democracy and Distrust: A Theory of Judicial Review.* Cambridge, Mass.: Harvard University Press.

Ely, Richard. 1992. *The Guardian of Every Other Right: The Constitutional History of Property Rights.* New York: Oxford University Press.

Epstein, Richard. 1985. *Takings: Private Property and the Power of Eminent Domain.* Cambridge, Mass.: Harvard University Press.

Epstein, Richard A. (ed.). 2000. *Modern Understandings of Liberty and Property.* New York: Garland Publishing.

Erler, Edward J. 1991. *The American Polity: Essays on the Theory and Practice of Constitutional Government.* New York: Crane Russak.

Goldwin, Robert A. and William A. Schambra. 1982. *How Capitalistic Is the Constitution?* Washington: American Enterprise Institute.

Hart, John F. 2001. *Land Use Law in the Early Republic and the Original Meaning of the Takings Clause.* Northwestern University Law Review 94: 1099.

Herber, Dan. 2002. *Surviving the View Through the* Lochner *Looking Glass:* Tahoe-Sierra *and the Case for Upholding Development Moratoria.* Minnesota Law Review 86: 913.

Horwitz, Morton. 1977. *The Transformation of American Law, 1780–1860.* Cambridge, Mass.: Harvard University Press.

McDonald, Forrest. 1985. *Novus Ordo Seclorum.* Lawrence: University Press of Kansas.

McGrath, Peter. 1966. *Yazoo: Land and Politics in the New Republic: The Case of Fletcher v. Peck.* Providence: Brown University Press.

Merrill, Thomas W. 2000. *The Landscape of Constitutional Property.* Virginia Law Review 86: 885.

Paul, Ellen Frankel and Howard Dickman. 1989. *Liberty, Property and the Foundations of the American Constitution.* Albany: SUNY Press.

Pennock, Roland J. and John W. Chapman, eds. 1980. *Property.* (Nomos, vol. XXII). New York: New York University Press.

Perry, Michael. *The Constitution, the Court, and Human Rights.* New Haven, CT.: Yale University Press, 1982.

Rose, Carol M. 1994. *Property and Persuasion: Essays on the History, Theory, and Rhetoric of Ownership.* Boulder: Westview Press, Inc.

Scheiber, Harry M. 1998. *The State and Freedom of Contract.* Stanford, Calif.: Stanford University Press.

Siegan, Bernard H. 2001. *Property Rights: From Magna Carta to the Fourteenth Amendment.* New Brunswick, N.J.: Social Philosophy and Policy Foundation: Transaction Publishers.

———. 1980. *Economic Liberties and the Constitution.* Chicago: University of Chicago Press.

Tribe, Laurence. 1985. *Constitutional Choices.* Cambridge, Mass.: Harvard University Press.

White, G. Edward. 2000. *The Constitution and the New Deal.* Cambridge, Mass.: Harvard University Press.

Wood, Gordon. 1969. *The Creation of the American Republic 1776–1787.* New York: W.W. Norton & Company.

Wright, Benjamin. 1938. *The Contracts Clause of the Constitution.* Cambridge, Mass.: Harvard University Press.

Selected Comparative Bibiliography

Alexander, Gregory S. 2003. *Property as a Fundamental Constitutional Right? The German Example,* Cornell Law Review 88: 733.

Friedrich, Carl J. 1950. *Constitutional Government and Democracy.* rev. ed. Boston, Mass.: Ginn and Company.

Jacobsohn, Gary Jeffrey. 2002. *The Wheel of Law: India's Secularism in Comparative Constitutional Context.* Princeton: Princeton University Press.

Kommers, Donald P. 1997. *The Constitutional Jurisprudence of the Federal Republic of Germany.* 2d ed. Durham, N.C.: Duke University Press, 1997.

Michalowski, Sabine and Lorna Woods. 1999. *German Constitutional Law: The Protection of Civil Liberties.* Aldershot: Dartmouth Publishing Company.

Solyom, Laszlo. 1994. *The Hungarian Constitutional Court and Social Change.* Yale Journal of International Law 19:233.

Sunstein, Cass, "On Property and Constitutionalism," in Rosenfeld, Michael, ed. 1994. *Constitutionalism, Identity, Difference, and Legitimacy.* Durham: Duke University Press, 1994.

Calder v. Bull

3 U.S. 386, 3 Dall. 386, 1 L. Ed. 648 (1798)

In March 1793, a probate court in Hartford awarded Calder an estate that Bull had claimed under a will that had not been properly recorded. After failing to enter a timely appeal to the court's ruling, Bull persuaded the Connecticut legislature to pass a law setting aside the decree of the probate court and granting a new hearing, which awarded the estate to Bull. Opinion of the Court: *Chase, Patterson, Iredell, Cushing.* Not participating: Ellsworth, Wilson

Mr. Justice CHASE, concurring in the result.

It appears to me a self-evident proposition, that the several State Legislatures retain all the powers of legislation, delegated to them by the State Constitutions; which are not EXPRESSLY taken away by the Constitution of the United States. . . . All the powers delegated by the people of the United States to the Federal Government are defined, and NO CONSTRUCTIVE powers can be exercised by it, and all the powers that remain in the State Governments are indefinite. . . .

The sole enquiry is, whether this resolution or law of Connecticut, having such operation, is an *ex post facto* law, within the prohibition of the Federal Constitution?

. . . I cannot subscribe to the omnipotence of a State Legislature, or that it is absolute and without control; although its authority should not be expressly restrained by the Constitution, or fundamental law, of the State. The people of the United States erected their Constitutions, or forms of government, to establish justice, to promote the general welfare, to secure the blessings of liberty; and to protect their persons and property from violence. The purposes for which men enter into society will determine the nature and terms of the social compact; and as they are the foundation of the legislative power, they will decide what are the proper objects of it: The nature, and ends of legislative power will limit the exercise of it. This fundamental principle flows from the very nature of our free Republican governments, that no man should be compelled to do what the laws do not require; nor to refrain from acts which the laws permit. There are acts which the Federal, or State, Legislature cannot do, without exceeding their authority. There are certain vital principles in our free Republican governments, which will determine and over-rule an apparent and flagrant abuse of legislative power; as to authorize manifest injustice by positive law; or to take away that security for personal liberty, or private property, for the protection whereof the government was

established. An ACT of the Legislature (for I cannot call it a law) contrary to the great first principles of the social compact, cannot be considered a rightful exercise of legislative authority. The obligation of a law in governments established on express compact, and on republican principles, must be determined by the nature of the power, on which it is founded. A few instances will suffice to explain what I mean. A law that punished a citizen for an innocent action, or, in other words, for an act, which, when done, was in violation of no existing law; a law that destroys, or impairs, the lawful private contracts of citizens; a law that makes a man a Judge in his own cause; or a law that takes property from A. and gives it to B. It is against all reason and justice, for a people to entrust a Legislature with SUCH powers; and, therefore, it cannot be presumed that they have done it. The genius, the nature, and the spirit, of our State Governments, amount to a prohibition of such acts of legislation; and the general principles of law and reason forbid them. The Legislature may enjoin, permit, forbid, and punish; they may declare new crimes; and establish rules of conduct for all its citizens in future cases; they may command what is right, and prohibit what is wrong; but they cannot change innocence into guilt; or punish innocence as a crime; or violate the right of an antecedent lawful private contract; or the right of private property. To maintain that our Federal, or State, Legislature possesses such powers, if they had not been expressly restrained; would, in my opinion, be a political heresy, altogether inadmissible in our free republican governments.

The Constitution of the United States, article 1, section 9, prohibits the Legislature of the United States from passing any *ex post facto* law; and, in section 10, lays several restrictions on the authority of the Legislatures of the several states; and, among them, "that no state shall pass any *ex post facto* law." . . .

I will state what laws I consider ex post facto laws, within the words and the intent of the prohibition. 1st. Every law that makes an action, done before the passing of the law, and which was innocent when done, criminal; and punishes such action. 2nd. Every law that aggravates a crime, or makes it greater than it was, when committed. 3rd. Every law that changes the punishment, and inflicts a greater punishment, than the law annexed to the crime, when committed. 4th. Every law that alters the legal rules of evidence, and receives less, or different, testimony, than the law required at the time of the commission of the offence, in order to convict the offender. All these, and similar laws, are manifestly unjust and oppressive. In my opinion, the true distinction is between *ex post facto* laws, and retrospective laws. Every *ex post facto* law must necessarily be retrospective; but every retrospective law is not an *ex post facto* law: The former, only, are prohibited. Every law that takes away, or impairs, rights vested, agreeably to existing laws, is retrospective, and is generally unjust; and may be oppressive; and it is a good general rule, that a law should have no retrospect: but there are cases in which laws may justly, and for the benefit of the community, and also of individuals, relate to a time antecedent to their commencement; as statutes of oblivion, or of pardon. They are certainly retrospective, and literally both concerning, and after, the facts committed. But I do not consider any law *ex post facto*, within the prohibition, that mollifies the rigor of the criminal law; but only those that create, or aggravate, the crime; or increase the punishment, or change the rules of evidence, for the purpose of conviction. . . . There is a great and apparent difference between making an UNLAWFUL act LAWFUL; and the making an innocent action criminal, and punishing it as a CRIME. The expressions "ex post facto laws," are technical, they had been in use long before the Revolution, and had acquired an appropriate meaning, by legislators, lawyers, and authors. The celebrated and judicious Sir William Blackstone, in his *Commentaries*, considers an *ex post facto* law precisely in the same light I have done. His opinion is confirmed by his successor, Mr. Wooddeson; and by the author of *The Federalist*, who I esteem superior to both, for his extensive and accurate knowledge of the true principles of Government. . . . If the term *ex post facto* law is to be construed to include and to prohibit the enacting any law after a fact, it will greatly restrict the power of the federal and state legislatures; and the consequences of such a construction may not be foreseen.

It is not to be presumed, that the federal or state legislatures will pass laws to deprive citizens of rights vested in them by existing laws; unless for the benefit of the whole community; and on making full satisfaction. The restraint against making any ex post facto laws was not considered, by the framers of the constitution, as extending to prohibit the depriving a citizen even of a vested right to property; or the provision, "that private property should not be taken for PUBLIC use, without just compensation," was unnecessary.

It seems to me, that the *right* of property, in its origin, could only arise from *compact express*, or *implied*, and I think it the better opinion, that the *right*, as well as the *mode*, or *manner*, of acquiring property, and of alienating or transferring, inheriting, or transmitting it, is conferred by society; is regulated by civil institution, and is always subject to the rules prescribed by *positive* law.

I am of opinion, that the decree of the Supreme Court of Errors of Connecticut be affirmed, with costs.

PATERSON, Justice.

IREDELL, Justice.

If . . . a government, composed of Legislative, Executive and Judicial departments, were established, by a Constitution, which imposed no limits on the legislative power, the consequence would inevitably be, that whatever the legislative power chose to enact, would be lawfully enacted, and the judicial power could never interpose to pronounce it void. It is true, that some speculative jurists have held, that a legislative act against natural justice must, in itself, be void; but I cannot think that, under such a government, any Court of Justice would possess a power to declare it so. Sir William Blackstone, having put the strong case of an act of Parliament, which should authorise a man to try his own cause, explicitly adds, that even in that case, "there is no court that has power to defeat the intent of the Legislature, when couched in such evident and express words, as leave no doubt whether it was the intent of the Legislature, or no."

In order, therefore, to guard against so great an evil, it has been the policy of all the American states, which have, individually, framed their state constitutions since the revolution, and of the people of the United States, when they framed the Federal Constitution, to define with precision the objects of the legislative power, and to restrain its exercise within marked and settled boundaries. If any act of Congress, or of the Legislature of a state, violates those constitutional provisions, it is unquestionably void; though, I admit, that as the authority to declare it void is of a delicate and awful nature, the Court will never resort to that authority, but in a clear and urgent case. If, on the other hand, the Legislature of the Union, or the Legislature of any member of the Union, shall pass a law, within the general scope of their constitutional power, the Court cannot pronounce it to be void, merely because it is, in their judgment, contrary to the principles of natural justice. The ideas of natural justice are regulated by no fixed standard: the ablest and the purest men have differed upon the subject; and all that the Court could properly say, in such an event, would be, that the Legislature (possessed of an equal right of opinion) had passed an act which, in the opinion of the judges, was inconsistent with the abstract principles of natural justice. There are then but two lights, in which the subject can be viewed: 1st. If the Legislature pursue the authority delegated to them, their acts are valid. 2nd. If they transgress the boundaries of that authority, their acts are invalid. In the former case, they exercise the discretion vested in them by the people, to whom alone they are responsible for the faithful discharge of their trust: but in the latter case, they violate a fundamental law, which must be our guide, whenever we are called upon as judges to determine the validity of a legislative act.

Still, however, in the present instance, the act or resolution of the Legislature of Connecticut, cannot be regarded as an *ex post facto* law; for, the true construction of the prohibition extends to criminal, not to civil, cases.

The policy, the reason and humanity, of the prohibition, do not . . . extend to civil cases, to cases that merely affect the private property of citizens. Some of the most necessary and important acts of Legislation are, on the contrary, founded upon the principle, that private rights must yield to public exigencies. Highways are run through private grounds. Fortifications, Light-houses, and other public edifices, are necessarily sometimes built upon the soil owned by individuals. In such, and similar cases, if the owners should refuse voluntarily to accommodate the public, they must be constrained, as far as the public necessities require; and justice is done, by allowing them a reasonable equivalent. Without the possession of this power the operations of Government would often be obstructed, and society itself would be endangered. It is not sufficient to urge, that the power may be abused, for, such is the nature of all power, such is the tendency of every human institution. . . . We must be content to limit power where we can, and where we cannot, consistently with its use, we must be content to repose a salutary confidence. It is our consolation that there never existed a Government, in ancient or modern times, more free from danger in this respect, than the Governments of America.

CUSHING, Justice.

The case appears to me to be clear of all difficulty, taken either way. If the act is a judicial act, it is not touched by the Federal Constitution: and, if it is a legislative act, it is maintained and justified by the ancient and uniform practice of the state of Connecticut. JUDGMENT affirmed.

Notes and Queries

1. *Calder's* narrow understanding of the *ex post facto* clause as limited to issues of criminal law was roundly criticized at the time. Nevertheless, the decision has not been overruled. There is some reason to think the Founders meant to include protection for property in the *ex post facto* clause. In *Federalist* 44, Madison wrote

> Bills of attainder, ex post facto laws, and laws impairing the obligation of contracts, are contrary to the first principles of the social compact, and to every principle of sound legislation. The two former are expressly prohib-

ited by the declarations prefixed to some of the State Constitutions, and all of them are prohibited by the spirit and scope of these fundamental charters. Our own experience has taught us nevertheless, that additional fences against these dangers ought not to be admitted. Very properly therefore have the Convention added this constitutional bulwark in favor of personal security and private rights. . . . [The American people] have seen with regret and with indignation, that sudden changes and legislative interferences in cases affecting personal rights, become jobs in the hands of enterprizing and influential speculators; and snares to the more industrious and less informed part of the community.

To what, exactly, does Madison attribute the "insecurity of titles"?

2. Justices Chase and Iredell both stressed the social dimensions of the right to property. Notwithstanding expansive references to "vital republican principles" that would control the action of a legislature even in the absence of an explicit constitutional limitation, Chase wrote that "the *right* of property . . . could arise only from *contract express*, or implied . . . the *modes*, or *manner*, of acquiring property, and of alienating or transferring, inheriting, or transmitting it, is conferred by society . . . and is always subject to the rules prescribed by *positive* law." Likewise, Iredell wrote that "Some of the most necessary and important acts of Legislation are . . . founded upon the principle, that private rights must yield to public exigencies."

Compare these statements with the Article 14 of the German Basic Law, which provides that "Property and the right of inheritance are guaranteed." Article 14(2) qualifies the right, however, by providing that "Property imposes duties. Its use should also serve the public weal." The Irish Constitution of 1937 underscores even more explicitly the community's interest in private property. Article 43 guarantees that the state will pass no law to abolish private property. The Article further provides, though, that "the exercise of property rights ought, in civil society, to be regulated by the principles of social justice. . . ." Consequently, the state may regulate property rights "with a view to reconciling their exercise with the exigencies of the common good."

As we observed in the introduction to this chapter, most constitutional texts include an explicit set of protections for property rights, as well as mention the qualifications that attach to the right. An important exception is the Canadian Charter of Rights, which fails to include a specific protection for property rights. Some scholars have suggested that Section 7 of the Charter, which guarantees the "security of the person," might include a person's capacity to satisfy basic economic needs, and hence should protect at least some property interests. For a discussion, see Peter W. Hogg, *Constitutional Law of Canada.* 3d ed., (Toronto: The Carswell Company, Ltd., 1992), 1023.

3. In some ways, the debate between Justices Chase and Iredell foreshadows the interchange by Justices Black and Frankfurter over natural law in the incorporation controversy. Chase found in natural law, or "vital republican principles," much as Frankfurter later did with due process (see the discussion of the incorporation controversy in chapter 9), a valuable source of constitutional meaning. Justice Iredell, as did Justice Black a century later, complained about the uncertainty and subjectivity of judicial appeals to such vague and indeterminate sources.

4. Justice Chase located the right to property in natural law or the social compact, independent of any specific protection in the constitutional text. Justice Iredell admitted that property might well find its authority in such principles, but denied that these principles can authorize a court to declare state action unconstitutional—the Court's powers instead must be grounded firmly in the text. Did the sources and methods of constitutional interpretation have an important bearing on their understanding of judicial power in a constitutional democracy?

5. Which opinion best captures the sense of property outlined in *Federalist* 10?

Fletcher v. Peck

10 U.S. 87, 6 Cranch 87, 3 L. Ed. 162 (1810)

In 1795, land speculators bribed the members of the Georgia legislature to sell them more than 35 million acres of state-owned land at 1 1/2 cents per acre. Outraged Georgians voted out most of the corrupt legislators, and in 1796 the state legislature revoked the land sales. In the intervening year, however, the lands had been reconveyed to other buyers. Peck, a Massachusetts resident, derived his title from such a purchaser. Peck then sold the land to Fletcher, a resident of New Hampshire, under a deed which certified the authenticity of the original conveyance. A federal court found the original Georgia statute valid and the act of revocation invalid, whereupon Fletcher appealed to the Supreme Court. Opinion of the Court: *Marshall*, Johnson, Livingston, Todd, Washington. Concurring opinion: *Johnson.* Not participating: Chase, Cushing.

Mr. Chief Justice MARSHALL delivered the opinion of the Court.

The question, whether a law be void for its repugnancy to the constitution, is, at all times, a question of much delicacy, which ought seldom, if ever, to be decided in the affirmative, in a doubtful case. The court, when impelled by duty to render such a judgment, would be unworthy of its station, could it be unmindful of the solemn obligations which that station imposes. But it is not on slight implication and vague conjecture that the legislature is to be pronounced to have transcended its powers, and its acts to be considered as void. The opposition between the constitution and the law should be such that the judge feels a clear and strong conviction of their incompatibility with each other.

In this case the court can perceive no such opposition. If the majority of the legislature be corrupted, it may well be doubted, whether it be within the province of the judiciary to control their conduct, and, if less than a majority act from impure motives, the principle by which judicial interference would be regulated, is not clearly discerned.

Whatever difficulties this subject might present, when viewed under aspects of which it may be susceptible, this court can perceive none in the particular pleadings now under consideration.

If a suit be brought to set aside a conveyance obtained by fraud, and the fraud be clearly proved, the conveyance will be set aside, as between the parties; but the rights of third persons, who are purchasers without notice, for a valuable consideration, cannot be disregarded. Titles, which, according to every legal test, are perfect, are acquired with that confidence which is inspired by the opinion that the purchaser is safe. If there be any concealed defect, arising from the conduct of those who had held the property long before he acquired it, of which he had no notice, that concealed defect cannot be set up against him. He has paid his money for a title good at law, he is innocent, whatever may be the guilt of others, and equity will not subject him to the penalties attached to that guilt. All titles would be insecure, and the intercourse between man and man would be very seriously obstructed, if this principle be overturned. . . .

Is the power of the legislature competent to the annihilation of such title, and to a resumption of the property thus held?

The principle asserted is, that one legislature is competent to repeal any act which a former legislature was competent to pass; and that one legislature cannot abridge the powers of a succeeding legislature. The correctness of this principle, so far as respects general legislation, can never be controverted. But, if an act be done under a law, a succeeding legislature cannot undo it. The past cannot be recalled by the most absolute power.

When, then, a law is in its nature a contract, a repeal of the law cannot divest those rights.

It may well be doubted whether the nature of society and of government does not prescribe some limits to the legislative power; and, if any be prescribed, where are they to be found, if the property of an individual, fairly and honestly acquired, may be seized without compensation.

To the legislature all legislative power is granted; but the question, whether the act of transferring the property of an individual to the public, be in the nature of the legislative power, is well worthy of serious reflection. It is the peculiar province of the legislature to prescribe general rules for the government of society; the application of those rules to individuals in society would seem to be the duty of other departments. How far the power of giving the law may involve every other power, in cases where the constitution is silent, never has been, and perhaps never can be, definitely stated.

The validity of this rescinding act, then, might well be doubted, were Georgia a single sovereign power. But Georgia cannot be viewed as a single, unconnected, sovereign power, on whose legislature no other restrictions are imposed than may be found in its own constitution. She is a part of a large empire; she is a member of the American union; and that union has a constitution the supremacy of which all acknowledge, and which imposes limits to the legislatures of the several states, which none claim a right to pass. The constitution of the United States declares that no state shall pass any bill of attainder, *ex post facto* law, or law impairing the obligation of contracts.

Does the case now under consideration come within this prohibitory section of the constitution?

In considering this very interesting question, we immediately ask ourselves what is a contract? Is a grant a contract? A contract is a compact between two or more parties, and is either executory or executed. . . . The contract between Georgia and the purchasers was executed by the grant. A contract executed . . . contains obligations binding on the parties. A grant, in its own nature, amounts to an extinguishment of the right of the grantor, and implies a contract not to reassert that right. A party is, therefore, always estopped by his own grant.

Since, then, in fact, a grant is a contract executed, the obligation of which still continues, and since the constitu-

tion uses the general term contract . . . it must be construed to comprehend [a grant]. . . .

If, under a fair construction the constitution, grants are comprehended under the terms contracts, is a grant from the state excluded from the operation of the provision? The words themselves contain no such distinction. They are general, and are applicable to contracts of every description. If contracts made with the state are to be exempted from their operation, the exception must arise from the character of the contracting party, not from the words which are employed.

Whatever respect might have been felt for the state sovereignties, it is not to be disguised that the framers of the constitution viewed, with some apprehension, the violent acts which might grow out of the feelings of the moment; and that the people of the United States, in adopting that instrument, have manifested a determination to shield themselves and their property from the effects of those sudden and strong passions to which men are exposed. The restrictions on the legislative power of the states are obviously founded in this sentiment; and the constitution of the United States contains what may be deemed a bill of rights for the people of each state. . . .

What motive, then, for implying, in words which import a general prohibition to impair the obligation of contracts, an exception in favour of the right to impair the obligation of those contracts into which the state may enter?

The state legislatures can pass no *ex post facto* law. An *ex post facto* law is one which renders an act punishable in a manner in which it was not punishable when it was committed. Such a law may inflict penalties on the person, or may inflict pecuniary penalties which swell the public treasury. The legislature is then prohibited from passing a law by which a man's estate, or any part of it, shall be seized for a crime which was not declared, by some previous law, to render him liable to that punishment. Why, then, should violence be done to the natural meaning of words for the purpose of leaving to the legislature the power of seizing, for public use, the estate of an individual in the form of a law annulling the title by which he holds that estate? The court can perceive no sufficient grounds for making this distinction. This rescinding act would have the effect of an *ex post facto* law. It forfeits the estate of Fletcher for a crime not committed by himself, but by those from whom he purchased. This cannot be effected in the form of an *ex post facto* law, or bill of attainder; why, then, is it allowable in the form of a law annulling the original grant?

It is, then, the unanimous opinion of the court, that . . . the estate having passed into the hands of a purchaser for a valuable consideration, without notice, the state of Georgia was restrained, either by general principles which are common to our free institutions, or by the particular provisions of the constitution of the United States, from passing a law whereby the estate of the plaintiff in the premises so purchased could be constitutionally and legally impaired and rendered null and void.

JOHNSON, J.

In this case I entertain . . . an opinion different from that which has been delivered by the court.

I do not hesitate to declare that a state does not possess the power of revoking its own grants. But I do it on a general principle, on the reason and nature of things: a principle which will impose laws even on the Deity.

A contrary opinion can only be maintained upon the ground that no existing legislature can abridge the powers of those which will succeed it. . . .

. . . When the legislature have once conveyed their interest or property in any subject to the individual, they have lost all control over it; have nothing to act upon; it has passed from them; is vested in the individual; becomes intimately blended with his existence, as essentially so as the blood that circulates through his system. The government may indeed demand of him the one or the other, not because they are not his, but because whatever is his is his country's.

I have thrown out these ideas that I may have it distinctly understood that my opinion on this point is not founded on the provision in the constitution of the United States, relative to laws impairing the obligation of contracts. It is much to be regretted that words of less equivocal signification, had not been adopted in that article of the constitution. There is reason to believe, from the letters of Publius, which are well-known to be entitled to the highest respect, that the object of the convention was to afford a general protection to individual rights against the acts of the state legislatures.

Notes and Queries

1. The Yazoo Land Frauds were a wide-ranging scandal that involved many of the elite members of early American politics. Peck was represented by John Quincy Adams,

Federalist and future president. Fletcher was represented by Luther Martin, a member of the Constitutional Convention of 1787 who became a leading Anti-Federalist and would later argue for the state of Maryland in *McCulloch v. Maryland*. Chief Justice Marshall himself had been involved in the controversy before joining the Court: as a Member of Congress, he had supported a proposal to compensate landowners for losses associated with the insecurity of the Yazoo titles.

2. Are the principles found by Marshall and Johnson similar to those articulated by Chase in *Calder v. Bull*? How do they differ? Does the decision in *Fletcher* allow for greater or lesser government regulation of property rights?

3. If it were not for the decision in *Calder*, *Fletcher* might have been decided upon the basis of the *ex post facto* clause. That option foreclosed, Chief Justice Marshall turned to the contracts clause as a way to protect the right to property. But does the contracts clause cover public, as well as private contracts? The language offered no clear answer, but the Founders probably had meant the provision to apply only to private contracts, and not those to which the state is itself a party. On the other hand, Alexander Hamilton thought the provision did apply to such contracts—or, at least he thought so when asked by the Yazoo Land Companies for legal advice. Following Hamilton (as he had in *Marbury*), Marshall ruled that it did. Unwilling to rest upon those grounds alone, though, Marshall also insisted that Georgia was restrained "by general principles which are common to our free institutions," as well as by the contracts clause. Justice Johnson went further, declaring that the principle that restricted the state was "a general principle" that bound even "the Deity."

What are these principles? How did Marshall and Johnson find them? Are they in the text of the Constitution (implicitly or explicitly)? Would these principles alone, without the contracts clause, be adequate to defend their decision?

4. *Fletcher* represents the highwater mark of protection for property. Only 25 years after *Fletcher*, in *Charles River Bridge Company v. Warren Bridge* (1837, reprinted later in the chapter), the Court began to emphasize the public interest in property over the security of the private right.

Charles River Bridge Company v. Warren Bridge
36 U.S. 420, 11 Pet. 420, 9 L. Ed. 773 (1837)

In 1785, Massachusetts incorporated "The Proprietors of the Charles River Bridge," authorizing the company to build and operate a toll bridge between Boston and

Charlestown. In 1792, the contract was extended for seventy years. In 1828, however, the legislature incorporated another company and authorized it to build another bridge—the Warren Bridge—across the Charles River, one which eventually would be free of tolls. The original bridge company filed suit against the state, claiming that the franchise to build a second bridge impaired their contract with the state and was thus unconstitutional. Opinion of the Court: *Taney*, Baldwin, Barbour, McLean, Wayne. Concurring opinion: *McLean*. Dissenting opinions: *Story*, *Thompson*.

Mr. Chief Justice TANEY delivered the opinion of the Court.

The questions involved in this case are of the gravest character, and the court have given to them the most anxious and deliberate consideration. The value of the right claimed by the plaintiffs is large in amount; and many persons may, no doubt, be seriously affected in their pecuniary interests, by any decision which the court may pronounce; and the questions which have been raised as to the power of the several states, in relation to the corporations they have chartered, are pregnant with important consequences; not only to the individuals who are concerned in the corporate franchises, but to the communities in which they exist. The court are fully sensible, that it is their duty, in exercising the high powers conferred on them by the constitution of the United States, to deal with these great and extensive interests, with the utmost caution; guarding, so far as they have the power to do so, the rights of the property, and at the same time, carefully abstaining from any encroachment on the rights reserved to the states.

The plaintiffs insist, mainly, upon two grounds: 1st. That by virtue of the grant of 1650, Harvard College was entitled, in perpetuity, to the right of keeping a ferry between Charlestown and Boston; that this right was exclusive; and that the legislature had not the power to establish another ferry on the same line of travel, because it would infringe the rights of the college; and that these rights, upon the erection of the bridge in the place of the ferry . . . were transferred to, and became vested in The Proprietors of the Charles River Bridge, 2d. That independently of the ferry-right, the acts of the legislature would not authorize another bridge, and especially, a free one, by the side of this, and placed in the same line of travel, whereby the franchise granted to the Proprietors of the Charles River Bridge should be rendered of no value; and that the law authorizing the erection of the Warren bridge in 1828, impairs the obligation of one or both of these contracts.

Much has been said in the argument of the principles of construction by which this law is to be expounded, and what undertakings, on the part of the state, may be implied. The court think there can be no serious difficulty on that head. It is the grant of certain franchises, by the public, to a private corporation, and in a matter where the public interest is concerned. The rule of construction in such cases is well settled, both in England, and by the

decisions of our own tribunals. In the case of the *Proprietors of the Sturbridge Canal v. Wheeley and others, et al.,* the court say,

The canal having been made under an act of parliament, the rights of the plaintiffs are derived entirely from that act. This, like many other cases, is a bargain between a company of adventurers and the public, the terms of which are expressed in the statute; and the rule of construction in all such cases, is now fully established to be this—that any ambiguity in the terms of the contract, must operate against the adventurers, and in favor of the public, and the plaintiffs can claim nothing that is not clearly given them by the act.

Borrowing, as we have done, our system of jurisprudence from the English law; and have adopted, in every other case, civil and criminal, its rules for the construction of statutes; is there anything in our local situation, or in the nature of our political institutions, which should lead us to depart from the principle, where corporations are concerned? . . . Can any good reason be assigned, for excepting this particular class of cases from the operation of the general principle; and for introducing a new and adverse rule of construction, in favor of corporations. We think not. . . .

But we are not now left to determine, for the first time, the rules by which public grants are to be construed in this country. The subject has already been considered in this court; and the rule of construction, above stated, fully established. In the case of the *United States v Arredondo*, the leading cases upon this subject are collected . . . and the principle recognized, that in grants by the public, nothing passes by implication. . . .

. . . But the object and end of all government is to promote the happiness and prosperity of the community by which it is established; and it can never be assumed, that the government intended to diminish its power of accomplishing the end for which it was created. And in a country like ours, free, active and enterprising, continually advancing in numbers and wealth, new channels of communication are daily found necessary, both for travel and trade, and are essential to the comfort, convenience and prosperity of the people. A state ought never to be presumed to surrender this power, because, like the taxing power, the whole community have an interest in preserving it undiminished. And when a corporation alleges, that a State has surrendered for seventy years its power of improvement and public accommodation, in a great and important line of travel . . . the community have a right to insist "that its abandonment ought not to be presumed, in a case in which a deliberate purpose of the state to abandon it does not appear." The continued existence of a government would be of no great value, if, by implications and presumptions, it was disarmed of the powers necessary to accomplish the ends of its creation, and the functions it was designed to perform, transferred to the hands of privileged corporations . . . While the rights of private property are sacredly guarded, we must not forget, that the community also have rights, and that the happiness and well-being of every citizen depends on their faithful preservation.

Adopting the rule of construction above stated as the settled one, we proceed to apply it to the charter of 1785, to the proprietors of the Charles River Bridge. This act of incorporation is in the usual form, and the privileges such as are commonly given to corporations of that kind. It confers on them the ordinary faculties of a corporation, for the purpose of building the bridge; and establishes certain rates of toll, which the company are authorized to take: this is the whole grant. There is no exclusive privilege given to them over the waters of Charles River, above or below their bridge; no right to erect another bridge themselves, nor to prevent other persons from erecting one, no engagement from the state, that another shall not be erected; and no undertaking not to sanction competition, nor to make improvements that may diminish the amount of its income. Upon all these subject, the charter is silent; and nothing is said in it about a line of travel, so much insisted on in the argument, in which they are to have exclusive privileges. . . .

. . . If a contract on that subject can be gathered from the charter, it must be by implication; and cannot be found in the words used. Can such an agreement be implied? The rule of construction before stated is an answer to the question: in charters of this description, no rights are taken from the public, or given to the corporation, beyond those which the words of the charter, by their natural and proper construction, purport to convey.

Indeed, the practice and usage of almost every state in the Union . . . is opposed to the doctrine contended for on the part of the plaintiffs in error. Turnpike roads have been made in succession, on the same line of travel; the later ones interfering materially with the profits of the first. These corporations have, in some instances, been utterly ruined by the introduction of newer and better modes of transportation and that the franchise of the turnpike corporation is not worth preserving. Yet in none of these cases have the corporation supposed that their privileges were invaded, or any contract violated on the part of the state . . . We cannot deal thus with the rights reserved to the states; and by legal intendments and mere technical reasoning, take away from them any portion of that power over their own internal police and improvement, which is so necessary to their well-being and prosperity.

And what would be the fruits of this doctrine of implied contracts, on the part of the states, and of property in a line of travel, by a corporation, if it would now be sanctioned by this court? To what results would it lead us? If it is to be found in the charter to this bridge, the same process of reasoning must discover it, in the various acts which have been passed, within the last forty years, for turnpike companies. . . . Let it once be understood, that such charters carry with them these implied contracts, and give the unknown and undefined property in a line of travelling; and you will soon find the old turnpike corporations awakening from their sleep, and calling upon this court to put down the improvements which have taken their place. The millions of property which have been invested in railroads and canals, upon lines of travel which had been before occupied by turnpike corporations, will be put in jeopardy. We shall be thrown back to the improvements of the last century, and obliged to stand still, until the claims of the old turnpike corporations shall be satisfied; and they shall consent to permit these states to avail themselves of the lights of modern science, and to partake of the benefit of those improvements which are now adding to the wealth and prosperity, and the convenience and comfort, of every other part of the civilized world. Nor is this all. This court will find itself compelled to fix, by some arbitrary rule, the width of this new kind of property in a line of travel; for if such a right of property exists, we have no lights to guide us in marking out its extent, unless, indeed, we resort to the old feudal grants, and to the exclusive rights of ferries, by prescription, between towns; and are prepared to decide that when a turnpike road from one town to another, had been made, no railroad or canal, between there two points, could afterwards be established. This court are not prepared to sanction principles which must lead to such results.

The judgment of the supreme judicial court of the commonwealth of Massachusetts . . . must . . . be affirmed.

McLEAN, Justice.

. . . The new bridge, while tolls were charged, lessened the profits of the old one about one-half, or two-thirds; and now that it is a free bridge by law, the tolls received by the complainants are merely nominal. On what principle of law, can such an act be sustained? Are rights acquired under a solemn contract with the legislature, held by a more uncertain tenure than other rights? Is the legislative power so omnipotent in such cases, as to resume what it has granted, without compensation? It will scarcely be contended, that if the legislature may do this, indirectly, it may not do it directly. If it may do it through the instrumentality of the Warren Bridge company, it may dispense with that instrumentality.

But it is said, that any check to the exercise of this discretion by the legislature, will operate against the advance of improvements. Will not a different effect be produced? If every bridge or turnpike company were liable to have their property wrested from them, under an act of the legislature, without compensation, could much value be attached to such property? Would prudent men expend their funds in making such improvements? Can it be considered as an injurious check to legislation, that private property shall not be taken for public purposes, without compensation? This restriction is imposed by the federal constitution, and by the constitutions of the respective states.

The spirit of internal improvement pervades the whole country. There is, perhaps, no state in the Union, where important public works, such as turnpike roads, canals, railroads, bridges, & c., are not either contemplated, or in a state of rapid progression. These cannot be carried on, without the frequent exercise of the power to appropriate private property for public use. Vested rights are daily divested by this exercise of the eminent domain. And if, in all these case, this court can act as a court of supervision for the correction of errors, its power may be invoked in numberless instances. . . . For, if this court can take jurisdiction on the ground, every individual whose property has been taken, has a constitutional right to the judgment of this court, whether compensation has been made in the mode required by the constitution of the state. . . .

. . . To revise these cases, would carve out for this court a new jurisdiction, not contemplated by the constitution, and which cannot be safely exercised.

There are considerations which grow out of our admirable system of government, that should lead the judicial tribunals both of the federal and state governments to mutual forbearance, in the exercise of doubtful powers. The boundaries of their respective jurisdictions can never, perhaps, be so clearly defined, on certain questions, as to free them from doubt. This remark is peculiarly applicable to the federal tribunals, whose powers are delegated, and consequently, limited. The strength of our political system consists in its harmony; and this can only be preserved, by a strict observance of the respective powers of the state and federal government. Believing that this court has no jurisdiction in this case I am in favor of dismissing the bill, for want of jurisdiction.

STORY, Justice, dissenting.

The present . . . is not the case of a royal grant, but of a legislative grant, by a public statute. The rules of the com-

mon law in relation to royal grants have, therefore, in reality, nothing to do with the case. We are to give this act of incorporation a rational and fair construction, according to the general rules which govern in all cases of the exposition of public statutes. We are to ascertain the legislative intent; and that once ascertained, it is our duty to give it a full and liberal operation. The books are full of cases to this effect, if indeed, so plain a principle of common sense and common justice stood in any need of authority to support it. . . .

I admit, that were the terms of a grant to impose burdens upon the public, or to create a restraint injurious to the public interest, there is sound reason for interpreting the terms, if ambiguous, in favor of the public. But at the same time, I insist, that there is not the slightest reason for saying, even in such a case, that the grant is not to be construed favorably to the grantee, so as to secure him in the enjoyment of what is actually granted. . . .

. . . Our legislatures neither have, nor affect to have, any royal prerogatives. There is no provision in the constitution authorizing their grants to be construed differently from the grants of private persons, in regard to the like subject matter. The policy of the common law, which gave the crown so many exclusive privileges and extraordinary claims . . . was founded, in a good measure, if not altogether, upon the divine right of kings, or, at least, upon a sense of their exalted dignity and pre-eminence over all subjects. . . . Parliamentary grants never enjoyed any such privileges. . . .

But it has been argued, that if grants of this nature are to be construed liberally, as conferring any exclusive rights on the grantees, it will interpose an effectual barrier against all general improvements of the country. For my own part, I can conceive of no surer plan to arrest all public improvements, founded on private capital and enterprise, than to make the outlay of that capital uncertain and questionable, both as to security and as to productiveness. No man will hazard his capital in any enterprise, in which, if there is to be a loss, it must be borne exclusively by himself; and if there is success, he has not the slightest security of enjoying the rewards of that success, for a single moment.

THOMPSON, Justice, dissenting.

. . . I concur entirely in all the principles and reasonings contained in Justice Story's opinion.

Notes and Queries

1. The 1828 election of Andrew Jackson to the presidency signaled the end of the Federalists' dominance in national politics. Chief Justice Taney replaced Marshall in 1836, thus signaling a similar change in the Court's con-

tract clause jurisprudence. Marshall had elevated the right to property to paramount status; as we have seen, the Marshall Court typically protected property against state regulation. Chief Justice Taney's approach in *Charles River Bridge*, in contrast, emphasized the state's police powers and the public interest in regulating property. One small point best illustrates the change in emphasis: In *Dartmouth College*, Marshall had ruled that ambiguities in public contracts should be resolved in favor of the property owner. Taney ruled instead that they should be resolved in favor of the public.

2. On a more basic level, the contrast between *Dartmouth College* and *Charles River Bridge*, or between Chief Justice Taney's opinion and Justice Story's dissent, is between two different conceptions of private property and the state. Marshall and Story stressed the need for security of property (or capital), insisting that undue state regulation unwisely put the burden of risk in capital development on private parties. Taney, however, stressed that the need for commercial development required an expansive conception of state police powers. As Morton Horwitz observed in *The Transformation of American Law, 1780–1860* (Cambridge: Harvard University Press, 1977), this case "represented the last great contest in America between two different models of economic development" (p. 31).

3. Is security of contract necessary for economic stability and securing investment? In *Federalist* 10, Madison wrote "Complaints are every where heard from our most considerate and virtuous citizens . . . that our governments are too unstable; that the public good is disregarded in the conflicts of rival parties; and that measures are too often decided, not according to the rules of justice, and the rights of the minor party; but by the superior force of an interested and over-bearing majority." Defenders of the Articles of Confederation replied that "what government has not some law in favour of debtors? . . . we are not worse than other people in that respect which we most condemn." *Agrippa #*3, 30 November 1787.

At the Virginia ratifying convention, John Marshall again complained that the present government "takes away the incitements to industry, by rendering property insecure and unprotected." Story's dissent makes the same argument. Is the argument persuasive? Is it appropriate for the Court to weigh these kinds of policy arguments?

4. How does the location of the property right given in *Charles River Bridge* depart from that expressed in the *Fletcher* and *Dartmouth College* cases? Does this change affect who will win a dispute between individual property rights and the desires of the community?

5. How do these different readings reflect different understandings of the relation between individual private property rights and the public good? Does Taney's opinion in this case come closer to Chase's in *Calder v. Bull* or to Iredell's?

Home Building & Loan Association v. Blaisdell

290 US 398, 54 S. Ct. 231, 78 L. Ed. 413 (1934)

In 1933, in the midst of the Great Depression, Minnesota enacted the Mortgage Moratorium Act, which regulated the foreclosure of property mortgaged to financial institutions. The statute authorized courts, upon the application of a debtor, to postpone the foreclosure of mortgages and to extend the period of redemption from a foreclosure sale. Minnesota's highest court sustained the statute, and the case reached the Supreme Court on appeal. Opinion of the Court: *Hughes*, Brandeis, Cardozo, Roberts, Stone. Dissenting Opinion: *Sutherland*, Butler, McReynolds, Van Devanter.

Mr. Chief Justice HUGHES delivered the opinion of the Court.

[We must decide] whether the provision for this temporary and conditional relief exceeds the power of the State by reason of the clause in the Federal Constitution prohibiting impairment of the obligations of contracts. . . .

Emergency does not create power. Emergency does not increase granted power or remove or diminish the restrictions imposed upon power granted or reserved. The Constitution was adopted in a period of grave emergency. Its grants of power to the federal government and its limitations of the power of the States were determined in the light of emergency, and they are not altered by emergency. . . .

While emergency does not create power, emergency may furnish the occasion for the exercise of power. . . . The constitutional question presented in the light of an emergency is whether the power possessed embraces the particular exercise of it in response to particular conditions. Thus, the war power of the federal government is not created by the emergency of war, but it is a power given to meet that emergency. . . . But where constitutional grants and limitations of power are set forth in general clauses, which afford a broad outline, the process of construction is essential to fill in the details. That is true of the contract clause. The necessity of construction is not obviated by the fact that the contract clause is associated in the same section with other and more specific prohibitions. Even the grouping of subjects in the same clause may not require the same application to each of the subjects, regardless of differences in their nature.

In the construction of the contract clause, the debates in the Constitutional Convention are of little aid. But the reasons which led to the adoption of that clause, and of the other prohibitions of Section 10 of Article 1, are not left in doubt, and have frequently been described with eloquent emphasis. The widespread distress following the revolutionary period and the plight of debtors had called forth in the States an ignoble array of legislative schemes for the defeat of creditors and the invasion of contractual obligations. Legislative interferences had been so numerous and extreme that the confidence essential to prosperous trade had been undermined and the utter destruction of credit was threatened. . . . It was necessary to interpose the restraining power of a central authority in order to secure the foundations even of "private faith." . . .

But full recognition of the occasion and general purpose of the clause does not suffice to fix its precise scope. Nor does an examination of the details of prior legislation in the States yield criteria which can be considered controlling. To ascertain the scope of the constitutional prohibition, we examine the course of judicial decisions in its application. These put it beyond question that the prohibition is not an absolute and is not to be read with literal exactness like a mathematical formula. . . .

. . . Chief Justice Marshall pointed out the distinction between obligation and remedy. In *Sturges v. Crowninshield* (1819) [he said] "The distinction between the obligation of a contract, and the remedy given by the legislature to enforce that obligation, has been taken at the bar, and exists in the nature of things. Without impairing the obligation of the contract, the remedy may certainly be modified as the wisdom of the nation shall direct." And in *Von Hoffman v. City of Quincy* (1867), the general statement above quoted was limited by the further observation that

It is competent for the States to change the form of the remedy, or to modify it otherwise, as they may see fit, provided no substantial right secured by the contract is thereby impaired. No attempt has been made to fix definitely the line between alterations of the remedy, which are to be deemed legitimate, and those which, under the form of modifying the remedy, impair substantial rights. Every case must be determined upon its own circumstances. . . .

And Chief Justice Waite, quoting this language in *Antoni v. Greenhow* (1883), added: "In all such cases the question becomes therefore, one of reasonableness, and of that the legislature is primarily the judge."

Not only is the constitutional provision qualified by the measure of control which the state retains over remedial processes, but the state also continues to possess authority to safeguard the vital interests of its people. It does not matter that legislation appropriate to that end "has the result of modifying or abrogating contracts already in effect." *Stephenson v. Binford* (1932). Not only are existing laws read into contracts in order to fix obligations as between the parties, but the reservation of essential attributes of sovereign power is also read into contracts as a postulate of the legal order. The policy of protecting contracts against impairment presupposes the maintenance of a government by virtue of which contractual relations are worth while—a government which retains adequate authority to secure the peace and good order of society. This principle of harmonizing the constitutional prohibition with the necessary residuum of state power has had progressive recognition in the decisions of this Court.

Undoubtedly, whatever is reserved of state power must be consistent with the fair intent of the constitutional limitation of that power. The reserved power cannot be construed so as to destroy the limitation, nor is the limitation to be construed to destroy the reserved power in its essential aspects. They must be construed in harmony with each other. . . . But it does not follow that conditions may not arise in which a temporary restraint of enforcement may be consistent with the spirit and purpose of the constitutional provision and thus be found to be within the range of the reserved power of the state to protect the vital interests of the community. . . .

It is manifest from this review of our decisions that there has been a growing appreciation of public needs and of the necessity of finding ground for a rational compromise between individual rights and public welfare. The settlement and consequent contraction of the public domain, the pressure of a constantly increasing density of population, the interrelation of the activities of our people and the complexity of our economic interests, have inevitably led to an increased use of the organization of society in order to protect the very bases of individual opportunity. Where, in earlier days, it was thought that only the concerns of individuals or of classes were involved, and that those of the state itself were touched only remotely, it has later been found that the fundamental interests of the state are directly affected; and that the question is no longer merely that of one party to a contract as against another, but of the use of reasonable means to safeguard the economic structure upon which the good of all depends.

It is no answer to say that this public need was not apprehended a century ago, or to insist that what the provision of the Constitution meant to the vision of that day it must mean to the vision of our time. If by the statement that what the Constitution meant at the time of its adoption it means to-day, it is intended to say that the great clauses of the Constitution must be confined to the interpretation which the framers, with the conditions and outlook of their time, would have placed upon them, the statement carries its own refutation. It was to guard against such a narrow conception that Chief Justice Marshall uttered the memorable warning: "We must never forget, that it is a constitution we are expounding" (*McCulloch v. Maryland* [1819]); "a constitution intended to endure for ages to come, and, consequently, to be adapted to the various crises of human affairs." . . . When we are dealing with the words of the Constitution, said this Court in *Missouri v. Holland* (1920), "we must realize that they have called into life a being the development of which could not have been foreseen completely by the most gifted of its begetters. . . . The case before us must be considered in the light of our whole experience and not merely in that of what was said a hundred years ago."

Nor is it helpful to attempt to draw a fine distinction between the intended meaning of the words of the Constitution and their intended application. When we consider the contract clause and the decisions which have expounded it in harmony with the essential reserved power of the states to protect the security of their peoples, we find no warrant for the conclusion that the clause has been warped by these decisions from its proper significance or that the founders of our government would have interpreted the clause differently had they had occasion to assume that responsibility in the conditions of the later day. The vast body of law which has been developed was unknown to the fathers, but it is believed to have preserved the essential content and the spirit of the Constitution. With a growing recognition of public needs and the relation of individual right to public security, the court has sought to prevent the perversion of the clause through its use as an instrument to throttle the capacity of the states to protect their fundamental interests. This development is a growth from the seeds which the fathers planted.

We are of the opinion that the Minnesota statute as here applied does not violate the contract clause of the Federal Constitution. Whether the legislation is wise or unwise as a matter of policy is a question with which we are not concerned.

Judgment affirmed.

Mr. Justice SUTHERLAND, dissenting.

A provision of the Constitution, it is hardly necessary to say, does not admit of two distinctly opposite interpretations. It does not mean one thing at one time and an entirely different thing at another time. If the contract impairment clause, when framed and adopted, meant that the terms of a contract for the payment of money could not be altered *in invitum* by a state statute enacted for the relief of hardly pressed debtors to the end and with the effect of postponing payment or enforcement during and because of an economic or financial emergency, it is but to state the obvious to say that it means the same now. This view, at once so rational in its application to the written word, and so necessary to the stability of constitutional principles, though from time to time challenged, has never, unless recently, been put within the realm of doubt by the decisions of this court. . . .

The provisions of the Federal Constitution, undoubtedly, are pliable in the sense that in appropriate cases they have the capacity of bringing within their grasp every new condition which falls within their meaning. But, their meaning is changeless; it is only their application which is extensible. Constitutional grants of power and restrictions upon the exercise of power are not flexible as the doctrines of the common law are flexible. These doctrines, upon the principles of the common law itself, modify or abrogate themselves whenever they are or whenever they become plainly unsuited to different or changed conditions. . . .

The whole aim of construction, as applied to a provision of the Constitution, is to discover the meaning, to ascertain and give effect to the intent of its framers and the people who adopted it. The necessities which gave rise to the provision, the controversies which preceded, as well as the conflicts of opinion which were settled by its adoption, are matters to be considered to enable us to arrive at a correct result. . . . The history of the times, the state of things existing when the provision was framed and adopted should be looked to in order to ascertain the mischief and the remedy. As nearly as possible we should place ourselves in the condition of those who framed and adopted it. And, if the meaning be at all doubtful, the doubt should be resolved, wherever reasonably possible to do so, in a way to forward the evident purpose with which the provision was adopted.

An application of these principles to the question under review removes any doubt, if otherwise there would be any, that the contract impairment clause denies to the several states the power to mitigate hard consequences resulting to debtors from financial or economic exigencies by an impairment of the obligation of contracts of indebtedness. A candid consideration of the history and circumstances which led up to and accompanied the framing and adoption of this clause will demonstrate conclusively that it was framed and adopted with the specific and studied purpose of preventing legislation designed to relieve debtors *especially* in time of financial distress. . . .

The present exigency is nothing new. From the beginning of our existence as a nation, periods of depression, of industrial failure, of financial distress, of unpaid and unpayable indebtedness, have alternated with years of plenty. The vital lesson that expenditure beyond income begets poverty, that public or private extravagance, financed by promises to pay, either must end in complete or partial repudiation or the promises be fulfilled by self-denial and painful effort, though constantly taught by bitter experience, seems never to be learned; and the attempt by legislative devices to shift the misfortune of the debtor to the shoulders of the creditor without coming into conflict with the contract impairment clause has been persistent and oft-repeated.

The defense of the Minnesota law is made upon grounds which were discountenanced by the makers of the Constitution and have many times been rejected by this Court. That defense should not now succeed because it constitutes an effort to overthrow the constitutional provision by an appeal to facts and circumstances identical with those which brought it into existence. With due regard for the processes of logical thinking, it legitimately cannot be urged that conditions which produced the rule may now be invoked to destroy it.

The Minnesota statute either impairs the obligation of contracts or it does not. If it does not, the occasion to which it relates becomes immaterial. . . . If it does, the emergency no more furnishes a proper occasion for its exercise than if the emergency were non-existent. . . .

I quite agree with the opinion of the Court that whether the legislation under review is wise or unwise is a matter with which we have nothing to do. Whether it is likely to work well or work ill presents a question entirely irrelevant to the issue. The only legitimate inquiry we can make is whether it is constitutional. If it is not, its virtues, if it have any, cannot save it; if it is, its faults cannot be invoked to accomplish its destruction. If the provisions of the Constitution be not upheld when they pinch as well as when they comfort, they may as well be abandoned. Being unable to reach any other conclusion than that the Minnesota statute infringes the constitutional restriction under review, I have no choice but to say so.

I am authorized to say that Mr. Justice Van Devanter, Mr. Justice McReynolds, and Mr. Justice Butler concur in this opinion.

Notes and Queries

1. As is often the case, the majority and dissenting opinions in *Blaisdell* disagreed on far more than just the proper result. Chief Justice Hughes' opinion for the Court, borrowing heavily from an opinion circulated but unpublished by Justice Cardozo, emphasized the need to interpret the contracts clause as just one part of a larger Constitution. Hence, the majority focused less on the words of Article I, Section 10, which seemed at first glance to prohibit the state's action, and more on its purpose—read here as being the promotion of the economic welfare of the state as a whole. Justice Sutherland's dissent denied that the meaning of constitutional provisions could change as dramatically as it seemed to here. (Would the majority have agreed that the meaning of the clause had changed?) The opinions in *Blaisdell* thus make clear that methods of constitutional interpretation, whether appeals to intent, purpose, or social policy, are often related to questions of constitutional change. What method of interpretation did the majority use? Did that method accept the possibility that the meaning of a constitutional provision can change as times change? What method of interpretation did Justice Sutherland employ? How did Justice Sutherland think we should cope with the problem of change?

2. *Blaisdell* raises interesting questions about the use of Framers' intent and appeals to purpose as methods of constitutional interpretation. Sutherland argued that "as nearly as possible we should place ourselves in the condition of those who framed and adopted" the contracts clause. In cases of doubt, he suggested, we should interpret the clause "in a way to forward the evident purpose" of the provision. Both Sutherland and the majority, however, claimed that their interpretation of the clause was faithful to its "purpose." Who was right?

What was the purpose of the clause? Simply to prohibit state interference with contracts? Or, as Gary Jacobsohn has argued, was there a "deeper" purpose, "to promote the conditions of economic stability"? *Pragmatism, Statesmanship, and the Supreme Court* (New York: Cornell University Press, 1977), 188.

3. The Court's opinion in *Blaisdell* seemed to signal the death of the contracts clause as a significant source of protection for private property, much as Justice Sutherland feared it would. No Court in the past half-century has sought seriously to revitalize the contracts clause. Nevertheless, at least one recent case indicates that there may yet be life in Article I, Section 10. In *United States Trust Co. v. New Jersey* (1977), the Court wrote that "the Contract Clause remains a part of our written Constitution. . . ."

United States Trust involved a 1962 agreement between

New York and New Jersey to improve the port of New York. In particular, the agreement limited the ability of the Port Agreement to subsidize railway transportation from the revenue generated by bonds floated by the Port Authority. Twelve years later, under great financial distress, New York and New Jersey repealed the 1962 agreement. A bank brought suit on behalf of the bondholders, alleging that the repeal violated the states' contract with them.

Justice Blackmun's majority opinion ruled in favor of the bank, concluding that repeal of the 1962 agreement was neither "necessary" nor "reasonable in light of the surrounding circumstances." In dissent, Justice Brennan expressed astonishment and dismay that the majority had revived the contracts clause. "I might understand, though I could not accept, this revival of the Contract Clause were it in accordance with some coherent and constructive view of public policy.... The justification for today's decision, therefore, remains a mystery to me...." Recounting the history of the Court's efforts to protect property against state regulation, Brennan concluded that "this Court should have learned long ago that the Constitution—be it through the Contract or Due Process Clause—can actively intrude into such economic and policy matters only if my Brethren are prepared to bear enormous institutional and social costs."

Munn v. Illinois
94 U.S. 113, 4 Otto 113, 24 L. Ed. 77 (1876)

In response to a downturn in grain prices and widespread fear of the monopolistic practices of railroads and storage companies, in 1871 the Illinois state legislature passed a law regulating grain warehouses and fixing grain storage prices. Munn and Scott were convicted of operating their grain elevator without a license. The defendants admitted the facts charged but alleged that the statute requiring such a license was unconstitutional because it attempted to fix maximum rates for storage. This, they claimed, deprived them of their property in violation of the Fifth and Fourteenth Amendments. Opinion of the Court: *Waite*, Bradley, Clifford, Davis, Hunt, Miller, Swayne. Dissenting opinions: *Field*, Strong.

Mr. Chief Justice WAITE delivered the opinion of the Court.

Every statute is presumed to be constitutional. The courts ought not to declare one to be unconstitutional, unless it is clearly so. If there is doubt, the expressed will of the legislature should be sustained.

The Constitution contains no definition of the word "deprive," as used in the Fourteenth Amendment. To determine its signification, therefore, it is necessary to ascertain the effect which usage has given it, when employed in the same or a like connection. While this provision of the amendment [the due process clause] is new in the Constitution of the United States, as a limitation upon the powers of the States, it is old as a principle of civilized government. It is found in the Magna Charta, and, in substance if not in form, in nearly or quite all the constitutions that have been from time to time adopted by the several States of the Union. By the Fifth Amendment, it was introduced into the Constitution of the United States as a limitation upon the powers of the national government, and by the Fourteenth, as a guaranty against any encroachment upon an acknowledged right of citizenship by the legislatures of the States.

When one becomes a member of society, he necessarily parts with some rights or privileges which, as an individual not affected by his relations to others, he might retain. "A body politic," as aptly defined in the preamble of the Constitution of Massachusetts, "is a social compact by which the whole people covenants with each citizen, and each citizen with the whole people, that all shall be governed by certain laws for the common good." This does not confer power upon the whole people to control rights which are purely and exclusively private; but it does authorize the establishment of laws requiring each citizen to so conduct himself, and so use his own property, as not unnecessarily to injure another. This is the very essence of government.... From this source come the police powers, which, as was said by Mr. Chief Justice Taney in the *License Cases* (1847) "are nothing more or less than the powers of government inherent in every sovereignty, ... that is to say, ... the power to govern men and things." Under these powers the government regulates the conduct of its citizens one towards another, and the manner in which each shall use his own property, when such regulation becomes necessary for the public good. In their exercise it has been customary in England from time immemorial, and in this country from its first colonization, to regulate ferries, common carriers, hackmen, bakers, millers, wharfingers, innkeepers, &c., and in so doing to fix a maximum of charge to be made for services rendered, accommodations furnished, and articles sold.... [I]t has never yet been successfully contended that such legislation came within any of the constitutional prohibitions against interference with private property. With the Fifth Amendment in force, Congress, in 1820, conferred power upon the city of Washington "to regulate . . . the rates of wharfage at private wharves, . . . the sweeping of chimneys, and to fix the rates of fees therefor, . . . and the weight and quality of bread," "to make the rates of hauling by cartmen, wagoners, carmen, and daymen, and the rates of commission of auctioneers." . . .

From this it is apparent that, down to the time of the adoption of the Fourteenth Amendment, it was not supposed that statutes regulating the use, or even the price of the use, of private property necessarily deprived an owner of his property without due process of law. Under some circumstances they may, but not under all. The amendment does not change the law in this particular: it simply prevents the States from doing that which will operate as such a deprivation.

This brings us to inquire as to the principles upon which this power of regulation rests. . . .

. . . Looking, then, to the common law, from whence came the right which the Constitution protects, we find that when private property is "affected with a public interest, it ceases to be *juris privati* only." This was said by Lord Chief Justice Hale more than two hundred years ago . . . and has been accepted without objection as an essential element in the law of property ever since. Property does become clothed with a public interest when used in a manner to make it of public consequence, and affect the community at large. When, therefore, one devotes his property to a use in which the public has an interest, he, in effect, grants to the public an interest in that use, and must submit to be controlled by the public for the common good, to the extent of the interest he has thus created. He may withdraw his grant by discontinuing the use; but, so long as he maintains the use, he must submit to the control.

. . . Enough has already been said to show that, when private property is devoted to a public use, it is subject to public regulation. It remains only to ascertain whether the warehouses of these plaintiffs . . . and the business which is carried on there, come within the operation of this principle.

. . . [I]t appears that

the great producing region of the West and North-west sends its grain by water and rail to Chicago, where the greater part of it is shipped by vessel for transportation to the seaboard by the Great Lakes, and some of it is forwarded by railway to the Eastern ports. . . . It has been found impossible to preserve each owner's grain separate, and this has given rise to a system of inspec-

tion and grading, by which the grain of different owners is mixed, and receipts issued for the number of bushels which are negotiable, and redeemable in like kind, upon demand. . . . [T]he ownership has . . . been by private individuals, who have embarked their capital and devoted their industry to such business as a private pursuit.

Under such circumstances it is difficult to see why, if the common carrier, or the miller, or the ferryman, or the innkeeper, or the wharfinger, or the baker, or the cartman, or the hackney-coachman, pursues a public employment and exercises "a sort of public office," these plaintiffs in error do not. They stand . . . in the very "gateway of commerce," and take toll from all who pass. Their business most certainly "tends to a common charge, and is become a thing of public interest and use. . . ." Certainly, if any business can be clothed "with a public interest and ceases to be *juris privati* only," this has been.

. . . For our purposes we must assume that, if a state of facts could exist that would justify such legislation, it actually did exist when the statute now under consideration was passed. For us the question is one of power, not of expediency. If no state of circumstances could exist to justify such a statute, then we may declare this one void, because in excess of the legislative power of the State. But if it could, we must presume it did. Of the propriety of legislative interference within the scope of legislative power, the legislature is the exclusive judge.

Neither is it a matter of any moment that no precedent can be found for a statute precisely like this. It is conceded that the business is one of recent origin, that its growth has been rapid, and that it is already of great importance. And it must also be conceded that it is a business in which the whole public has a direct and positive interest. It presents, therefore, a case for the application of a long-known and well-established principle in social science, and this statute simply extends the law so as to meet this new development of commercial progress. There is no attempt to compel these owners to grant the public an interest in their property, but to declare their obligations, if they use it in this particular manner.

It is insisted, however, that the owner of property is entitled to a reasonable compensation for its use, even though it be clothed with a public interest, and that what is reasonable is a judicial and not a legislative question.

As has already been shown, the practice has been otherwise. In countries where the common law prevails, it has been customary from time immemorial for the legislature to declare what shall be a reasonable compensation under such circumstances. . . . Undoubtedly, in mere private contracts, relating to matters in which the public has no interest, what is reasonable must be ascertained judicially. But this is because the legislature has no control over such a contract. . . .

Rights of property which have been created by the common law cannot be taken away without due process; but the law itself, as a rule of conduct, may be changed at the will, or even at the whim, of the legislature, unless prevented by constitutional limitations. . . .

We know that this is a power which may be abused; but that is no argument against its existence. For protection against abuses by legislatures the people must resort to the polls, not to the courts.

Judgment Affirmed.

Mr. Justice FIELD, dissenting.

. . . The principle upon which the opinion of the majority proceeds is, in my judgment, subversive of the rights of private property, heretofore believed to be protected by constitutional guaranties against legislative interference. . . .

The declaration of the [Illinois] Constitution of 1870, that private buildings used for private purposes shall be deemed public institutions, does not make them so. The receipt and storage of grain in a building erected by private means for that purpose does not constitute the building a public warehouse. There is no magic in the language, though used by a constitutional convention, which can change a private business into a public one, or alter the character of the building in which the business is transacted. A tailor's or a shoemaker's shop would still retain its private character, even though the assembled wisdom of the State should declare, by organic act or legislative ordinance, that such a place was a public workshop, and that the workmen were public tailors or public shoemakers. One might as well attempt to change the nature of colors, by giving them a new designation. The defendants were no more public warehousemen . . . than the merchant who sells his merchandise to the public is a public merchant, or the blacksmith who shoes horses for the public is a public blacksmith; and it was a strange notion that by calling them so they would be brought under legislative control.

. . . When Sir Matthew Hale, and the sages of the law in his day, spoke of property as affected by a public interest, and ceasing from that cause to be *juris privati* solely, that is, ceasing to be held merely in private right, they referred to property dedicated by the owner to public uses, or to property the use of which was granted by the government, or in connection with which special privileges were conferred. Unless the property was thus dedicated, or some right bestowed by the government was held with the property, either by specific grant or by prescription of

so long a time as to imply a grant originally, the property was not affected by any public interest so as to be taken out of the category of property held in private right. But it is not in any such sense that the terms "clothing property with a public interest" are used in this case. From the nature of the business under consideration—the storage of grain—which, in any sense in which the words can be used, is a private business, in which the public are interested only as they are interested in the storage of other products of the soil, or in articles of manufacture, it is clear that the court intended to declare that, whenever one devotes his property to a business which is useful to the public,—"affects the community at large,"—the legislature can regulate the compensation which the owner may receive for its use, and for his own services in connection with it. . . .

If this be sound law, if there be no protection, either in the principles upon which our republican government is founded, or in the prohibitions of the Constitution against such invasion of private rights, all property and all business in the State are held at the mercy of a majority of its legislature. The public has no greater interest in the use of buildings for the storage of grain than it has in the use of buildings for the residences of families, nor, indeed, any thing like so great an interest; and, according to the doctrine announced, the legislature may fix the rent of all tenements used for residences, without reference to the cost of their erection. If the owner does not like the rates prescribed, he may cease renting his houses. He has granted to the public, says the court, an interest in the use of the buildings, and "he may withdraw his grant by discontinuing the use; but, so long as he maintains the use, he must submit to the control." . . . [T]here is hardly an enterprise or business engaging the attention and labor of any considerable portion of the community, in which the public has not an interest in the sense in which that term is used by the court in its opinion; and the doctrine which allows the legislature to interfere with and regulate the charges which the owners of property thus employed shall make for its use, that is, the rates at which all these different kinds of business shall be carried on, has never before been asserted, so far as I am aware, by any judicial tribunal in the United States.

. . . The [Fourteenth Amendment] places property under the same protection as life and liberty. Except by due process of law, no State can deprive any person of either. The provision has been supposed to secure to every individual the essential conditions for the pursuit of happiness; and for that reason has not been heretofore, and should never be, construed in any narrow or restricted sense.

No State "shall deprive any person of life, liberty, or property without due process of law," says the Fourteenth Amendment to the Constitution. By the term "life," as here used, something more is meant than mere animal existence. The inhibition against its deprivation extends to all those limbs and faculties by which life is enjoyed. The provision equally prohibits the mutilation of the body by the amputation of an arm or leg, or the putting out of an eye, or the destruction of any other organ of the body through which the soul communicates with the outer world. The deprivation not only of life, but of whatever God has given to every one with life, for its growth and enjoyment, is prohibited by the provision in question, if its efficacy be not frittered away by judicial decision.

By the term "liberty" . . . something more is meant than mere freedom from physical restraint or the bounds of a prison. It means freedom to go where one may choose, and to act in such manner, not inconsistent with the equal rights of others, as his judgment may dictate for the promotion of his happiness; that is, to pursue such callings and avocations as may be most suitable to develop his capacities, and give to them their highest enjoyment.

The same liberal construction which is required for the protection of life and liberty, in all particulars in which life and liberty are of any value, should be applied to the protection of private property. If the legislature of a State, under pretence of providing for the public good, or for any other reason, can determine, against the consent of the owner, the uses to which private property shall be devoted, or the prices which the owner shall receive for its uses, it can deprive him of the property as completely as by a special act for its confiscation or destruction. . . .

. . . The legislation in question is nothing less than a bold assertion of absolute power by the State to control at its discretion the property and business of the citizen, and fix the compensation he shall receive. The will of the legislature is made the condition upon which the owner shall receive the fruits of his property and the just reward of his labor, industry, and enterprise. "That government," says Story, "can scarcely be deemed to be free where the rights of property are left solely dependent upon the will of a legislative body without any restraint. The fundamental maxims of a free government seem to require that the rights of personal liberty and private property should be held sacred." *Wilkeson v. Leland* (1829). The decision of the court in this case gives unrestrained license to legislative will. . . .

. . . But I deny the power of any legislature under our government to fix the price which one shall receive for his property of any kind. If the power can be exercised as to one article, it may as to all articles, and the prices of every thing, from a calico gown to a city mansion, may be the subject of legislative direction.

I am of opinion that the judgment of the Supreme Court of Illinois should be reversed.

Mr. Justice STRONG.

. . . I concur in what [Justice Field] has said.

Notes and Queries

1. Why did Chief Justice Waite conclude that the Court should defer to the state legislature on the issue of reasonable compensation? Is there anything in the Court's opinion that suggests possible exceptions to the rule of judicial deference?

Notwithstanding *Munn's* rule of deference, in *Chicago, Milwaukee, and St. Paul Railway Co. v. Minnesota* (1890), the Court concluded that "The question of the reasonableness of a rate of charge for transportation by a railroad company, involving as it does the element of reasonableness both as regards the company and as regards the public, is eminently a question for judicial investigation, requiring due process of law for its determination." Is there any way to reconcile this quote with the conclusion in *Munn?*

2. In *The Constitution Besieged: The Rise and Demise of Lochner Era Police Powers Jurisprudence* (Durham: Duke University Press, 1993), 68–69, Howard Gillman noted that

> In his opinion upholding the regulation, Chief Justice Morrison R. Waite emphasized the long-standing principle that a person's rights and liberties are subordinate to the general welfare. . . . Justice Waite and the majority decided this case upon the principle that it is "the very essence of government to regulate the conduct of its citizens towards another, and the manner in which each shall use his own property, when such regulation becomes necessary for the general good."

From where in the Constitution did the Court derive this principle? Does Justice Waite's explication of "deprive" as used in the Fourteenth Amendment provide a sufficient textual basis for the decision? Or does the majority's understanding of the Constitution depend upon other methods of interpretation?

3. Justice Waite argued that "When one becomes a member of society, he necessarily parts with some rights or privileges which, as an individual not affected by his relations to others, he might retain." What rights and liberties might Waite be referring to? Waite also noted "This does not confer power upon the whole people to control

Comparative Note 10.2

[A German consumer-protection statute banned the sale of foodstuffs that might be confused with products made of chocolate. The statute was successfully invoked against a company selling a product coated with chocolate. Germany's Federal Constitutional Court invalidated the statute as applied.]

In deciding whether an [economic] regulation which limits the practice of a trade is consistent with the principle of proportionality, we must take into account the discretion which the legislature has—within the framework of its authority—in the sphere of commercial activity. The Basic Law grants the legislature wide latitude in setting economic policy and devising the means necessary to implement it. In the instant case, however, the legislature [by banning the sale of the affected product] has exceeded the proper bounds of its discretion, for

less restrictive means can easily achieve the purpose of . . . protecting the consumer from deception. . . . Nor do other considerations justify the competitive edge given here to pure chocolate products. If a case involves possible confusion between milk and margarine products, then the legislature may indeed adopt measures in the public interest for maintaining a productive farm economy—thus serving a purpose beyond the immediate goal of consumer protection. In the instant case, however, no justifiable grounds exist for [imposing] a broader restriction than is needed to safeguard the consumer from false labeling. Thus [the regulator] should only take measures which are necessary for the protection of the consumer. To accomplish this end it would have been enough to require proper labeling.

SOURCE: *Chocolate Candy Case* (1980) from Kommers, *Constitutional Jurisprudence*, 279–80.

rights which are purely and exclusively private. . . ." Are any rights "purely and exclusively" private? Which ones, and why?

4. *Munn* highlights the public interest in private property, notwithstanding the absence of clear language in the constitutional text legitimating that interest. Other constitutional documents usually emphasize the interdependence of private right and public interest. Section 25 of the South African Constitution, for example, provides that

(1) No one may be deprived of property except in terms of law of general application, and no law may permit arbitrary deprivation of property.
(2) Property may be expropriated only in terms of law of general application—
    (a) for a public purpose or in the public interest . . .
(4) For the purposes of this section—
    (a) the public interest includes the nation's commitment to land reform, and to reforms to bring about equitable access to all South Africa's natural resources. . . .

In a recent case, the South African Constitutional Court emphasized that Section 25 must be considered in its his-

torical context, including "the need for and aim at redressing one of the most enduring legacies of racial discrimination . . . namely the grossly unequal distribution of land. . . ." See Comparative Note 10.6.

The German Basic Law also stresses the connections between individual rights and social imperatives. Article 14 (1) of the German Basic Law indicates that "Property and the right of inheritance are guaranteed. . . ." Article 19 (2) further protects property by noting that "In no case may the essential content of a basic right be encroached upon." Section (2), however also states that "Property imposes duties. Its use should also serve the public weal."

In the *Hamburg Flood Control Case* (1968), the Federal Constitutional Court was asked to declare unconstitutional the Dikes and Embankments Act of 1964, which Hamburg had passed after widespread flooding in 1962. The Act classified some formerly private property as "dikeland," made it public, and compensated the owners. Although it acknowledged that "property is an elemental constitutional right . . ." and that "its function is to . . . enable [an individual] to lead a self-governing life," the Court upheld the Dikes Act. "The Basic Law," the Court held, "establishes that in the recurring tension between the property interest of the individual and the needs of the public, the public interest may, in case of conflict, take precedence over the legally guaranteed position of the individual. . . ."

Lochner v. New York

198 U.S. 45, 25 S. Ct. 539, 49 L. Ed. 937 (1905)

In 1897 the New York legislature enacted a labor law, which provided that no employee shall be required or permitted to work in a bakery or confectionary establishment more than sixty hours in any one week or more than ten hours in any one day. Lochner, an employer, was fined for violating the law. He contested the fine, arguing that the law unconstitutionally interfered with his right, as well as the right of his employees, to liberty under the Fourteenth Amendment. The New York courts upheld his conviction. Opinion of the Court: *Peckham*, Brewer, Brown, Fuller, McKenna. Dissenting opinions: *Harlan*, Day, White, *Holmes*.

Mr. Justice PECKHAM delivered the opinion of the Court.

The mandate of the statute, that "no employee shall be required or permitted to work," is the substantial equivalent of an enactment that "no employee shall contract or agree to work," more than ten hours per day; and, as there is no provision for special emergencies, the statute is mandatory in all cases. It is not an act merely fixing the number of hours which shall constitute a legal day's work, but an absolute prohibition upon the employer permitting, under any circumstances, more than ten hours' work to be done in his establishment. The employee may desire to earn the extra money which would arise from his working more than the prescribed time, but this statute forbids the employer from permitting the employee to earn it.

The statute necessarily interferes with the right of contract between the employer and employees, concerning the number of hours in which the latter may labor in the bakery of the employer. The general right to make a contract in relation to his business is part of the liberty of the individual protected by the 14th Amendment of the Federal Constitution. *Allgeyer v. Louisiana* (1897). Under that provision no state can deprive any person of life, liberty, or property without due process of law. The right to purchase or to sell labor is part of the liberty protected by this amendment, unless there are circumstances which exclude the right. There are, however, certain powers, existing in the sovereignty of each state in the Union, somewhat vaguely termed police powers, the exact description and limitation of which have not been attempted by the courts. Those powers, broadly stated, and without, at present, any attempt at a more specific limitation, relate to the safety, health, morals, and general welfare of the public. Both property and liberty are held on such reason-

able conditions as may be imposed by the governing power of the state in the exercise of those powers, and with such conditions the 14th Amendment was not designed to interfere. *Mugler v. Kansas* (1887); *In re Kemmler* (1878); *Crowley v. Christianson* (1890); *In re Converse* (1891).

The State, therefore, has power to prevent the individual from making certain kinds of contracts. . . . Contracts in violation of a statute . . . or a contract to let one's property for immoral purposes, or to do any other unlawful act, could obtain no protection from the Federal Constitution. . . .

This Court has recognized the existence and upheld the exercise of the police powers of the States in many cases. . . .

It must, of course, be conceded that there is a limit to the valid exercise of the police power by the state. There is no dispute concerning this general proposition. Otherwise the 14th Amendment would have no efficacy and the legislatures of the states would have unbounded power, and it would be enough to say that any piece of legislation was enacted to conserve the morals, the health, or the safety of the people; such legislation would be valid, no matter how absolutely without foundation the claim might be. The claim of the police power would be a mere pretext—become another and delusive name for the supreme sovereignty of the state to be exercised free from constitutional restraint. This is not contended for. In every case that comes before this court, therefore, where legislation of this character is concerned, and where the protection of the Federal Constitution is sought, the question necessarily arises: Is this a fair, reasonable, and appropriate exercise of the police power of the State, or is it an unreasonable, unnecessary, and arbitrary interference with the right of the individual to his personal liberty, or to enter into those contracts in relation to labor which may seem to him appropriate or necessary for the support of himself and his family? Of course the liberty of contract relating to labor includes both parties to it. The one has as much right to purchase as the other to sell labor.

This is not a question of substituting the judgment of the court for that of the legislature. If the act be within the power of the state it is valid, although the judgment of the court might be totally opposed to the enactment of such a law. But the question would still remain: Is it within the police power of the state? and that question must be answered by the court.

. . . There is no reasonable ground for interfering with the liberty of person or the right of free contract, by determining the hours of labor, in the occupation of a baker.

There is no contention that bakers as a class are not equal in intelligence and capacity to men in other trades or manual occupations, or that they are not able to assert their rights and care for themselves without the protecting arm of the State, interfering with their independence of judgment and of action. They are in no sense wards of the State. . . . [W]e think that a law like the one before us involves neither the safety, the morals nor the welfare of the public, and that the interest of the public is not in the slightest degree affected by such an act. . . . Clean and wholesome bread does not depend upon whether the baker works but ten hours per day or only sixty hours a week. . . .

It is a question of which of two powers or rights shall prevail—the power of the State to legislate or the right of the individual to liberty of person and freedom of contract. . . .

. . . We think that there can be no fair doubt that the trade of a baker, in and of itself, is not an unhealthy one to that degree which would authorize the legislature to interfere with the right to labor, and with the right of free contract on the part of the individual, either as employer or employee. In looking through statistics regarding all trades and occupations, it may be true that the trade of a baker does not appear to be as healthy as some other trades, and is also vastly more healthy than still others. To the common understanding the trade of a baker has never been regarded as an unhealthy one. Very likely physicians would not recommend the exercise of that or of any other trade as a remedy for ill health. Some occupations are

more healthy than others, but we think there are none which might not come under the power of the legislature to supervise and control the hours of working therein, if the mere fact that the occupation is not absolutely and perfectly healthy is to confer that right upon the legislative department of the government. It might be safely affirmed that almost all occupations more or less affect the health. There must be more than the mere fact of the possible existence of some small amount of unhealthiness to warrant legislative interference with liberty. It is unfortunately true that labor, even in any department, may possibly carry with it the seeds of unhealthiness. But are we all, on that account, at the mercy of legislative majorities? A printer, a tinsmith, a locksmith, a carpenter, a cabinetmaker, a dry goods clerk, a bank's, a lawyer's, or a physician's clerk, or a clerk in almost any kind of business, would all come under the power of the legislature, on this assumption. . . .

We mention these extreme cases because the contention is extreme. We do not believe in the soundness of the views which uphold this law. On the contrary, we think that such a law as this, although passed in the assumed exercise of the police power, and as relating to the public health, or the health of the employees named, is not within that power, and is invalid. The act is . . . an illegal interference with the rights of individuals, both employers and employees, to make contracts regarding labor upon such terms as they may think best, or which they may agree upon with the other parties to such contracts. Statutes of the nature of that under review, limiting the hours

---

Comparative Note 10.3

As part of fundamental human rights, Article 22 (1) of the Constitution guarantees the freedom of occupation. The freedom of occupation to be protected should be construed broadly and generally to include the freedom of business. Furthermore, the Constitution can be said to establish an economic structure based on the free economic activities of individual citizens. However, the Constitution does not purport to guarantee to the individual citizen an absolute and unrestricted freedom of economic activities; each citizen can enjoy this freedom so long as "it does not violate the public welfare." It is clear from the above provisions of the Constitution that freedom can be restricted to meet the demands of the public welfare.

When the free economic activities of individual citizens do varied damage and must be faced for the sake of safety and order in society and the public interest, legal restrictions against such economic activities based on the above paragraph are allowable insofar as they are rational and necessary in order to alleviate or possibly to solve these problems. Not only that, but taking other provisions of the Constitution into account, the Constitution as a whole is designed to achieve balanced, harmonious development of the social economy in compliance with the ideas of the welfare state, and . . . clearly guarantees the right to a livelihood of all the people.

SOURCE: *Marushin Industries, Inc. v. Japan (1972)* from Beer and Itoh, *Constitutional Case Law of Japan,* 185.

Comparative Note 10.4

[In this case, the South African Constitutional Court considered the constitutionality of a statute that authorized an official to sell a person's property to satisfy a debt owed to another, without a prior judgment or authorization by a court. The appellant, whose property was seized, challenged the statute as a violation of Section 25 of the South African Constitution. In this extract, the Court considers the meaning of the word "arbitrary" in Section 25(1), which provides that "No law may permit arbitrary deprivation of property."]

The word "arbitrary," depending on its statutory context, may only impose a low level of judicial scrutiny, requiring nothing more than the absence of bias or bad faith to satisfy such scrutiny. For example, it has been held to mean "capricious or proceeding merely from the will and not based on reason or principle." But context is all-important. . . . Context is crucial, both in the sense that the concept "arbitrary" appears in a constitution, and in the sense that it must be construed as part of a comprehensive and coherent Bill of Rights in a comprehensive and coherent constitution. This is certainly all part of the context.

Yet context goes further and would include the particular international jurisprudential context in which the Constitution came into existence and presently functions. Section 39(1) of the Constitution provides that a court, when interpreting the Bill of Rights, "must consider international law" and "may consider foreign law." At the same time one should never lose sight of the historical context in which the property clause came into existence. The background is one of conquest, as a consequence of which there was a taking of land in circumstances which, to this day, are a source of pain and tension. As already mentioned, the purpose of section 25 is not merely to protect private property but also to advance the public interest in relation to property. Thus it is necessary not only to have regard to foreign law, but also to the peculiar circumstances of our own history and the provisions of our Constitution.

In its context "arbitrary," as used in section 25, is not limited to non-rational deprivations, in the sense of there being no rational connection between means and ends. It refers to a wider concept and a broader controlling principle that is more demanding than an enquiry into mere rationality.

SOURCE: *First National Bank of SA, Limited v. Commissioner for South African Revenue Services*, CCT 19/01 (16 May 2002).

---

in which grown and intelligent men may labor to earn their living, are mere meddlesome interferences with the rights of the individual, and they are not asked from condemnation by the claim that they are passed in the exercise of the police power and upon the subject of the health of the individual whose rights are interfered with, unless there be some fair ground, reasonable in and of itself, to say that there is material danger to the public health, or to the health of the employees, if the hours of labor are not curtailed. . . .

This interference on the part of the legislatures of the several states with the ordinary trades and occupations of the people seems to be on the increase. . . .

It is impossible for us to shut our eyes to the fact that many of the laws of this character, while passed under what is claimed to be the police power for the purpose of protecting the public health or welfare, are, in reality, passed from other motives. We are justified in saying so when, from the character of the law and the subject upon which it legislates, it is apparent that the public health or welfare bears but the most remote relation to the law. The

purpose of a statute must be determined from the natural and legal effect of the language employed; and whether it is or is not repugnant to the Constitution of the United States must be determined from the natural effect of such statutes when put into operation, and not from their proclaimed purpose. . . .

It seems to us that the real object and purpose were simply to regulate the hours of labor between the master and his employees (all being men, *sui juris*), in a private business, not dangerous in any degree to morals, or in any real and substantial degree to the health of the employees. Under such circumstances the freedom of master and employee to contract with each other in relation to their employment, and in defining the same, cannot be prohibited or interfered with, without violating the Federal Constitution.

Reversed.

Mr. Justice HARLAN (with whom Mr. Justice WHITE and Mr. Justice DAY concurred) dissenting.

Granting . . . that there is a liberty of contract which cannot be violated even under the sanction of direct legislative enactment, but assuming, as according to settled law we may assume, that such liberty of contract is subject to such regulations as the state may reasonably prescribe for the common good and the well-being of society, what are the conditions under which the judiciary may declare such regulations to be in excess of legislative authority and void? Upon this point there is no room for dispute; for the rule is universal that a legislative enactment, Federal or state, is never to be disregarded or held invalid unless it be, beyond question, plainly and palpably in excess of legislative power. . . . If there be doubt as to the validity of the statute, that doubt must therefore be resolved in favor of its validity, and the courts must keep their hands off, leaving the legislature to meet the responsibility for unwise legislation. If the end which the legislature seeks to accomplish be one to which its power extends, and if the means employed to that end, although not the wisest or best, are yet not plainly and palpably unauthorized by law, then the court cannot interfere. In other words, when the validity of a statute is questioned, the burden of proof, so to speak, is upon those who assert it to be unconstitutional. *McCulloch v. Maryland*, (1819).

Let these principles be applied to the present case. . . .

It is plain that this statute was enacted in order to protect the physical well-being of those who work in bakery and confectionery establishments. It may be that the statute had its origin, in part, in the belief that employers and employees in such establishments were not upon an equal footing, and that the necessities of the latter often compelled them to submit to such exactions as unduly taxed their strength. Be this as it may, the statute must be taken as expressing the belief of the people of New York that, as a general rule, and in the case of the average man, labor in excess of sixty hours during a week in such establishments may endanger the health of those who thus labor. Whether or not this be wise legislation it is not the province of the court to inquire. Under our systems of government the courts are not concerned with the wisdom or policy of legislation. . . . But when this inquiry is entered upon I find it impossible, in view of common experience, to say that there is here no real or substantial relation between the means employed by the state and the end sought to be accomplished by its legislation. . . . Nor can I say that the statute has no appropriate or direct connection with that protection to health which each state owes to her citizens . . . ; or that it is not promotive of the health of the employees in question . . . or that the regulation prescribed by the state is utterly unreasonable and extravagant or wholly arbitrary. . . . Still less can I say that the statute is, beyond question, a plain, palpable invasion of rights secured by the fundamental law. Therefore I submit that this court will transcend its functions if it assumes to annul the statute of New York.

Mr. Justice HOLMES dissenting.

This case is decided upon an economic theory which a large part of the country does not entertain. If it were a question whether I agreed with that theory, I should desire to study it further and long before making up my mind. But I do not conceive that to be my duty, because I strongly believe that my agreement or disagreement has nothing to do with the right of a majority to embody their opinions in law. It is settled by various decisions of this court that state constitutions and state laws may regulate life in many ways which we as legislators might think as injudicious, or if you like as tyrannical, as this, and which, equally with this, interfere with the liberty to contract. Sunday laws and usury laws are ancient examples. . . . The liberty of the citizen to do as he likes so long as he does not interfere with the liberty of others to do the same, which has been a shibboleth for some well-known writers, is interfered with by school laws, by the Postoffice, by every state or municipal institution which takes his money for purposes thought desirable, whether he likes it or not. The 14th Amendment does not enact Mr. Herbert Spencer's *Social Statics*. The other day we sustained the Massachusetts vaccination law. *Jacobson v. Massachusetts* (1905). . . . But a Constitution is not intended to embody a particular economic theory, whether of paternalism and the organic relation of the citizen to the state or of laissez faire. It is made for people of fundamentally differing views, and the accident of our finding certain opinions natural and familiar, or novel, and even shocking, ought not to conclude our judgment upon the question whether statutes embodying them conflict with the Constitution of the United States.

General propositions do not decide concrete cases. The decision will depend on a judgment or intuition more subtle than any articulate major premise. But I think that the proposition just stated, if it is accepted, will carry us far toward the end. Every opinion tends to become a law. I think that the word "liberty," in the 14th Amendment, is perverted when it is held to prevent the natural outcome of a dominant opinion, unless it can be said that a rational and fair man necessarily would admit that the statute proposed would infringe fundamental principles as they have been understood by the traditions of our people and our law. It does not need research to show that no such sweeping condemnation can be passed upon the statute before us. A reasonable man might think it a proper measure on the score of health. Men whom I certainly could not pronounce unreasonable would uphold it as a first installment of a general regulation of the hours of work. . . .

Notes and Queries

1. Few decisions in American constitutional law are as sharply criticized as *Lochner*. But consider: What, exactly, is wrong with *Lochner*? Was the Court wrong to protect property and liberty against the police power of the state? Was *Lochner* wrong because the Court's judgment about what constituted wise public policy was wrong? Or was *Lochner* wrong because the Court substituted its own views about what constitutes sound public policy for the legislature's judgment? What, if anything, is wrong with judicial second-guessing of legislative policy decisions?

2. Justice Holmes' insistence that the Constitution "does not embody a particular economic theory" is oft-quoted. Is Holmes correct? It is true that the American Constitution makes no explicit reference to particular economic theories, but its protection of private property and contractual rights, some would argue, clearly anticipates a capitalistic economy of some sort. And as *Lochner* itself made clear, in the late 1800s and early 1900s the Court was convinced that the Constitution privileged laissez-faire capitalism.

Consider this response to Holmes, offered by Howard Gillman in *The Constitution Besieged*:

> And while the Constitution was not intended to embody a particular economic program, it most certainly rested on clearly articulated assumptions about the proper relationship between state and society, and it was on that basis that the majority struck down the act. Holmes's unprecedented admonition that judges ought to respect the "right of majority to embody their opinions in law" and let the "natural outcome of a dominant opinion" prevail amounted to an abdication of judicial responsibility that was as unacceptable to his peers as it would be today if the same was said about the Court's approach to racial classifications.

3. Holmes wrote that "liberty, in the Fourteenth Amendment, is perverted when it is held to prevent the natural outcome of a dominant opinion, unless it can be said that a rational and fair man necessarily would admit that the statute proposed would infringe fundamental principles. . . ." What are some examples of these fundamental principles? Are they derived from the Constitution? Isn't an appeal to them necessarily anti-democratic? Why or why not?

What source of authority is there for judicial imposition upon the democratic legislative process in the face of constitutional silence on the matter at hand? Is there ever a time when the Constitution demands judicial deference to the legislative will on questions affecting individual liberties?

4. The German Basic Law declares that Germany is a *Sozialstaat*, a social welfare state. As Donald P. Kommers notes, "The principle of the social welfare state is of particular importance here because it establishes the boundaries and infuses the meaning of all economic rights created by the Basic Law."[29] Are those boundaries sufficiently elastic to accommodate Holmes' statement of economic neutrality? In the *Investment Aid Case* (1954), the Federal Constitutional Court said "The Basic Law neither guarantees the neutrality of the executive or legislative power in economic matters nor does it guarantee a 'social market economy.' . . ." Moreover, "Although the present economic and social order is . . . consistent with the Basic Law, it is by no means the only one possible."

Although it professes neutrality, the *Investment Aid Case* does not mean that the economic organization of the state is entirely free of constitutional restraints. Article XIX's insistence that no law may encroach upon a basic right suggests that whatever the economic organization of the state, it must respect Article XIV's provisions for private property.

5. The American Constitution says little about the economic organization of the state. The German Basic Law institutes a social welfare state and market economy, while acknowledging in Article XV that land, natural resources and means of production may, "for purposes of socialization be transferred to public ownership. . . ." The Irish Constitution of 1937 is somewhat less hospitable to market economies. Article 42.3 provides that private property "ought in civil society to be regulated by principles of social justice. . . . The State, accordingly, may . . . delimit by law the exercise of [property] with a view to reconciling [its] exercise with the exigencies of the common good."

---

[29] Kommers, 241.

West Coast Hotel v. Parrish

300 U.S. 379, 57 S. Ct. 578, 81 L. Ed. 703 (1937)

In 1913, the state of Washington enacted a minimum wage law for women and minors "to [protect] them from conditions of labor which might have a pernicious effect on their health and morals." Parrish sued her employer, the West Coast Hotel, for the difference between what she had been paid and what she should have been paid under the statute. Lower state courts ruled in favor of the hotel, finding the law unconstitutional, but the state Supreme Court upheld the law. Opinion of the Court: *Hughes*, Brandeis, Cardozo, Roberts, Stone. Dissenting opinions: *Sutherland*, Butler, McReynolds, Van Devanter

Mr. Chief Justice HUGHES delivered the opinion of the Court.

The appellant conducts a hotel. The appellee Elsie Parrish was employed as a chambermaid and (with her husband) brought this suit to recover the difference between the wages paid her and the minimum wage fixed pursuant to the state law. The minimum wage was $14.50 per week of 48 hours. The appellant challenged the act as repugnant to the due process clause of the Fourteenth Amendment of the Constitution of the United States. The Supreme Court of the state, reversing the trial court, sustained the statute. . . . The case is here on appeal.

The appellant relies upon the decision of this Court in *Adkins v. Children's Hospital* (1923), which held invalid the District of Columbia Minimum Wage Act which was attacked under the due process clause of the Fifth Amendment. . . . [C]ounsel for the appellees attempted to distinguish the *Adkins Case* upon the ground that the appellee was employed in a hotel and that the business of an innkeeper was affected with a public interest. That effort at distinction is obviously futile. . . .

The recent case of *Morehead v. New York* (1936) came here on certiorari to the New York court which had held the New York minimum wage act for women to be invalid. A minority of this Court thought that the New York statute was distinguishable in a material feature from that involved in the *Adkins Case*. . . . But the Court of Appeals of New York had said that it found no material difference between the two statutes and this Court held that the "meaning of the statute" as fixed by the decision of the state court "must be accepted here as if the meaning had been specifically expressed in the enactment." That view led to the affirmance by this Court of the judgment in the *Morehead Case*, as the Court considered that the only question before it was whether the *Adkins Case* was distinguishable and that reconsideration of that decision had not been sought. . . .

We think that the question which was not deemed to be open in the *Morehead Case* is open and is necessarily presented here. The Supreme Court of Washington has upheld the minimum wage statute of that state. It has decided that the statute is a reasonable exercise of the police power of the state. In reaching that conclusion, the state court has invoked principles long established by this Court in the application of the Fourteenth Amendment. The state court has refused to regard the decision in the *Adkins Case* as determinative and has pointed to our decisions both before and since that case as justifying its position. We are of the opinion that this ruling of the state court demands on our part a re-examination of the *Adkins Case*. The importance of the question, in which many states having similar laws are concerned, the close division by which the decision in the *Adkins Case* was reached, and the economic conditions which have supervened, and in the light of which the reasonableness of the exercise of the protective power of the state must be considered, make it not only appropriate, but we think imperative, that in deciding the present case the subject should receive fresh consideration.

The principle which must control our decision is not in doubt. The constitutional provision invoked is the due process clause of the Fourteenth Amendment governing the states, as the due process clause invoked in the *Adkins Case* governed Congress. In each case the violation alleged by those attacking minimum wage regulation for women is deprivation of freedom of contract. What is this freedom? The Constitution does not speak of freedom of contract. It speaks of liberty and prohibits the deprivation of liberty without due process of law. In prohibiting that deprivation, the Constitution does not recognize an absolute and uncontrollable liberty. Liberty in each of its phases has its history and connotation. But the liberty safeguarded is liberty in a social organization which requires the protection of law against the evils which menace the health, safety, morals, and welfare of the people. Liberty under the Constitution is thus necessarily subject to the restraints of due process, and regulation which is reasonable in relation to its subject and is adopted in the interests of the community is due process.

This essential limitation of liberty in general governs freedom of contract in particular. More than twenty-five years ago we set forth the applicable principle in these words:

[f]reedom of contract is a qualified, and not an absolute, right. There is no absolute freedom to do as one wills

Comparative Note 10.5

[Article 12, paragraph 1, of the German Constitution reads in part: "All Germans have the right freely to choose their trade, occupation, or profession." The following extract is taken from a decision striking down a Bavarian statute limiting the number of licensed pharmacists permitted to operate in a given geographical area.]

Article 12 (1) protects the citizen's freedom in an area of particular importance to a modern society based on the division of labor. Every individual has the right to take up any activity which he believes himself prepared to undertake as a "profession"—that is, to make [the activity] the very basis of his life. . . . [Article 12 (1)] guarantees the individual more than just the freedom to engage independently in a trade. To be sure, the basic right aims at the protection of economically meaningful work, but it views work as a "vocation"

(*Beruf*). Work in this sense is seen in terms of its relationship to the human personality as a whole: It is a relationship that shapes and completes the individual over a lifetime of devoted activity; it is the foundation of a person's existence through which that person simultaneously contributes to the total social product.

. . . The more legislation affects the choice of a profession, the more limited is the regulatory power. This interpretation accords with the basic concepts of the Constitution and the image of the human person founded on those concepts. The choice of an occupation is an act of self-determination, of the free will of the individual; it must be protected as much as possible from state encroachment. In practicing an occupation, however, the individual immediately affects the life of society; this aspect of [vocational activity] is subject to regulation in the interest of others and of society.

Source: *Pharmacy Case (1958)* from Kommers, *Constitutional Jurisprudence,* 274, 275–76.

or to contract as one chooses. The guaranty of liberty does not withdraw from legislative supervision that wide department of activity which consists of the making of contracts, or deny to government the power to provide restrictive safeguards. Liberty implies the absence of arbitrary restraint, not immunity from reasonable regulations and prohibitions imposed in the interests of the community. *Chicago, B & Q R. Co. v. McGuire* (1911).

The point that has been strongly stressed that adult employees should be deemed competent to make their own contracts was decisively met nearly forty years ago in *Holden v. Hardy* (1898), where we pointed out the inequality in the footing of the parties. We said "The legislature has also recognized the fact, which the experience of legislators in many states has corroborated, that the proprietors of these establishments and their operatives do not stand upon an equality, and that their interests are, to a certain extent, conflicting. The former naturally desire to obtain as much labor as possible from their employees, while the latter are often induced by the fear of discharge to conform to regulations which their judgment, fairly exercised, would pronounce to be detrimental to their health or strength." In other words, the proprietors lay down the rules, and the laborers are practically constrained to obey them. In such cases self-interest is often an unsafe guide, and the legislature may properly interpose its authority.

And we added that the fact "that both parties are of full age, and competent to contract, does not necessarily deprive the State of the power to interfere, where the parties do not stand upon an equality, or where the public health demands that one party to the contract shall be protected against himself." "The State still retains an interest in his welfare, however reckless he may be. The whole is no greater than the sum of all parts, and when the individual health, safety, and welfare are sacrificed or neglected, the State must suffer."

It is manifest that this established principle is peculiarly applicable in relation to the employment of women in whose protection the state has a special interest. That phase of the subject received elaborate consideration in *Muller v. Oregon* (1908), where the constitutional authority of the state to limit the working hours of women was sustained. We emphasized the consideration that "woman's physical structure and the performance of maternal functions place her at a disadvantage in the struggle for subsistence" and that her physical well being "becomes an object of public interest and care in order to preserve the strength and vigor of the race." We emphasized the need of protecting women against oppression despite her possession of contractual rights. . . .

This array of precedents and the principles they applied were thought by the dissenting Justices in the *Adkins Case* to demand that the minimum wage statute be sustained.

The validity of the distinction made by the Court between a minimum wage and a maximum of hours in limiting liberty of contract was especially challenged. That challenge persists and is without any satisfactory answer. As Chief Justice Taft observed: "In absolute freedom of contract the one term is as important as the other, for both enter equally into the consideration given and received, a restriction as to the one is not any greater in essence than the other, and is of the same kind. One is the multiplier and the other the multiplicand." . . .

The minimum wage to be paid under the Washington statute is fixed after full consideration by representatives of employers, employees, and the public. It may be assumed that the minimum wage is fixed in consideration of the services that are performed in the particular occupations under normal conditions. . . . The statement of Mr. Justice Holmes in the *Adkins Case* is pertinent: "This statute does not compel anybody to pay anything. It simply forbids employment at rates below those fixed as the minimum requirement of health and right living. It is safe to assume that women will not be employed at even the lowest wages allowed unless they earn them, or unless the employer's business can sustain the burden. . . ."

We think that the views thus expressed are sound and that the decision in the *Adkins Case* was a departure from the true application of the principles governing the regulation by the state of the relation of employer and employed. Those principles have been reenforced by our subsequent decisions. Thus in *Radice v. New York* (1924), we sustained the New York statute which restricted the employment of women in restaurants at night. . . . In *Nebbia v. New York* (1934), dealing with the New York statute providing for minimum prices for milk, the general subject of the regulation of the use of private property and of the making of private contracts received an exhaustive examination, and we again declared that if such laws "have a reasonable relation to a proper legislative purpose, and are neither arbitrary nor discriminatory, the requirements of due process are satisfied"; that "with the wisdom of the policy adopted, with the adequacy or practicability of the law enacted to forward it, the courts are both incompetent and unauthorized to deal"; that "times without number we have said that the Legislature is primarily the judge of the necessity of such an enactment, that every possible presumption is in favor of its validity, and that though the court may hold views inconsistent with the wisdom of the law, it may not be annulled unless palpably in excess of legislative power."

With full recognition of the earnestness and vigor which characterize the prevailing opinion in the *Adkins Case*, we find it impossible to reconcile that ruling with these well-considered declarations. What can be closer to the public interest than the health of women and their protection from unscrupulous and overreaching employers? And if the protection of women is a legitimate end of the exercise of state power, how can it be said that the requirement of the payment of a minimum wage fairly fixed in order to meet the very necessities of existence is not an admissible means to that end? . . . The adoption of similar requirements by many states evidences a deepseated conviction both as to the presence of the evil and as to the means adapted to check it. Legislative response to that conviction cannot be regarded as arbitrary or capricious and that is all we have to decide. Even if the wisdom of the policy be regarded as debatable and its effects uncertain, still the Legislature is entitled to its judgment.

There is an additional and compelling consideration which recent economic experience has brought into a strong light. The exploitation of a class of workers who are in an unequal position with respect to bargaining power and are thus relatively defenseless against the denial of a living wage is not only detrimental to their health and well being, but casts a direct burden for their support upon the community. What these workers lose in wages the taxpayers are called upon to pay. The bare cost of living must be met. We may take judicial notice of the unparalleled demands for relief which arose during the recent period of depression and still continue to an alarming extent despite the degree of economic recovery which has been achieved. . . . The community is not bound to provide what is in effect a subsidy for unconscionable employers. The community may direct its law-making power to correct the abuse which springs from their selfish disregard of the public interest. The argument that the legislation in question constitutes an arbitrary discrimination, because it does not extend to men, is unavailing. This Court has frequently held that the legislative authority, acting within its proper field, is not bound to extend its regulation to all cases which it might possibly reach. The Legislature "is free to recognize degrees of harm and it may confine its restrictions to those classes of cases where the need is deemed to be clearest." . . .

Our conclusion is that the case of *Adkins v. Children's Hospital* should be, and it is, overruled. The judgment of the Supreme Court of the state of Washington is affirmed. Affirmed.

Mr. Justice SUTHERLAND, dissenting.

Mr. Justice Van Devanter, Mr. Justice McReynolds, Mr. Justice Butler, and I think the judgment of the court below should be reversed. . . .

Under our form of government, where the written Constitution, by its own terms, is the supreme law, some agency, of necessity, must have the power to say the final word as to the validity of a statute assailed as unconstitutional. The Constitution makes it clear that the power has been intrusted to this court when the question arises in a controversy within its jurisdiction; and so long as the power remains there, its exercise cannot be avoided without betrayal of the trust.

It has been pointed out many times, as in the *Adkins Case*, that this judicial duty is one of gravity and delicacy; and that rational doubts must be resolved in favor of the constitutionality of the statute. But whose doubts, and by whom resolved? Undoubtedly it is the duty of a member of the court, in the process of reaching a right conclusion, to give due weight to the opposing views of his associates; but in the end, the question which he must answer is not whether such views seem sound to those who entertain them, but whether they convince him that the statute is constitutional or engender in his mind a rational doubt upon that issue. The oath which he takes as a judge is not a composite oath, but an individual one. And in passing upon the validity of a statute, he discharges a duty imposed upon him, which cannot be consummated justly by an automatic acceptance of the views of others which have neither convinced, nor created a reasonable doubt in, his mind. If upon a question so important he thus surrender his deliberate judgment, he stands forsworn. He cannot subordinate his convictions to that extent and keep faith with his oath or retain his judicial and moral independence.

The suggestion that the only check upon the exercise of the judicial power . . . is the judge's own faculty of self-restraint, is both ill considered and mischievous. Self-restraint belongs in the domain of will and not of judgment. The check upon the judge is that imposed by his oath of office, by the Constitution, and by his own conscientious and informed convictions; and since he has the duty to make up his own mind and adjudge accordingly, it is hard to see how there could be any other restraint. . . .

It is urged that the question involved should now receive fresh consideration, among other reasons, because of "the economic conditions which have supervened"; but the meaning of the Constitution does not change with the ebb and flow of economic events. We frequently are told in more general words that the Constitution must be construed in the light of the present. If by that it is meant that the Constitution is made up of living words that apply to every new condition which they include, the statement is quite true. But to say, if that be intended, that the words of the Constitution mean today what they did not mean when written—that is, that they do not apply to a situation

now to which they would have applied then—is to rob that instrument of the essential element which continues it in force as the people have made it until they, and not their official agents, have made it otherwise.

The judicial function is that of interpretation; it does not include the power of amendment under the guise of interpretation. To miss the point of difference between the two is to miss all that the phrase "supreme law of the land" stands for and to convert what was intended as inescapable and enduring mandates into mere moral reflections. If the Constitution, intelligently and reasonably construed in the light of these principles, stands in the way of desirable legislation, the blame must rest upon that instrument, and not upon the court for enforcing it according to its terms. The remedy in that situation—and the only true remedy—is to amend the Constitution. . . .

The people by their Constitution created three separate, distinct, independent, and coequal departments of government. The governmental structure rests, and was intended to rest, not upon any one or upon any two, but upon all three of these fundamental pillars. It seems unnecessary to repeat, what so often has been said, that the powers of these departments are different and are to be exercised independently. The differences clearly and definitely appear in the Constitution. Each of the departments is an agent of its creator; and one department is not and cannot be the agent of another. Each is answerable to its creator for what it does, and not to another agent. The view, therefore, of the Executive and of Congress that an act is constitutional is persuasive in a high degree; but it is not controlling.

Coming, then, to a consideration of the Washington statute, it first is to be observed that it is in every substantial respect identical with the statute involved in the *Adkins Case*. Such vices as existed in the latter are present in the former. And if the *Adkins Case* was properly decided, as we who join in this opinion think it was, it necessarily follows that the Washington statute is invalid.

In support of minimum-wage legislation, it has been urged, on the one hand, that great benefits will result in favor of underpaid labor, and, on the other hand, that the danger of such legislation is that the minimum will tend to become the maximum and thus bring down the earnings of the more efficient toward the level of the less-efficient employees. But with these speculations we have nothing to do. We are concerned only with the question of constitutionality. . . .

An appeal to the principle that the Legislature is free to recognize degrees of harm and confine its restrictions accordingly, is but to beg the question, which is—Since the contractual rights of men and women are the same, does the legislation here involved, by restricting only the rights of women to make contracts as to wages, create an arbitrary discrimination? We think it does. Difference of sex affords no reasonable ground for making a restriction applicable to the wage contracts of all working women from which like contracts of all working men are left free. Certainly a suggestion that the bargaining ability of the average woman is not equal to that of the average man would lack substance. The ability to make a fair bargain, as every one knows, does not depend upon sex.

Notes and Queries

1. *Parrish* was decided in the midst of controversy over President Roosevelt's Court-packing plan. The Court's decision to overrule *Adkins* removed much of the immediate impetus for the plan, however, and thus contributed to the "switch in time that saved nine." The issue died completely when, shortly after *Parrish*, Justice Willis Van Devanter retired, thus affording Roosevelt his first appointment to the Court.

2. *Lochner*, of course, depended upon a particular understanding of the relationship between the individual and the community, in which the liberty of the individual must be protected against the community's efforts to constrain that liberty, whether for the public's good or for the individual's own good. Contrast the language in *Lochner* about protecting the individual with this statement from *West Coast Hotel*:

> The exploitation of a class of workers who are in an unequal bargaining position with respect to bargaining power . . . is not only detrimental to their health and well being but casts a direct burden for their support upon the community.

How does this understanding of the relationship between individual liberty and the public good differ from *Lochner's*?

3. The dissent argued that "the meaning of the Constitution does not change with the ebb and flow of economic events" and that "to say . . . that the words of the Constitution mean today what they did not mean when written . . . is to rob that instrument of the essential element which continues it in force as the people have made it until they, and not their official agents, have made it otherwise. . . ." The majority, the dissent argued, had not so much interpreted as it had amended the Constitution: "The judicial function is that of interpretation; it does not include the power of amendment under the guise of interpretation."

What distinguishes acceptable "interpretation" from unacceptable "amendment"? When, if ever, do political, economic, and social change legitimate judicial "amendment" of the Constitution?

Tahoe-Sierra Preservation Council, Inc. v. Tahoe Regional Planning Agency

535 U.S. 302, 122 S. Ct. 1465, 152 L. Ed. 2d 517 (2002)

The Lake Tahoe Basin falls within the states of California and Nevada. The two states created the Tahoe Regional Planning Agency (TRPA). The TRPA imposed two moratoria in 1981–1984, the first of about 24 months and an ensuing one of about another 8 months, on virtually all residential development in the area subject to the TRPA's jurisdiction, until the TRPA adopted a new and comprehensive land-use plan in 1984. The plaintiffs, an association of persons who owned real estate in the area, challenged the moratoria, claiming that they constituted a taking of their property without just compensation. A District Court ordered the TRPA to pay damages to many of the affected landowners with respect to the two moratoria, as, among other matters, the District Court found that (1) even though the property of these landowners retained some value during the period of the two moratoria, the landowners were temporarily deprived of all economically viable use of their land; and (2) the two moratoria therefore constituted categorical takings, for purposes of the takings clause. On appeal, a panel of the United States Court of Appeals for the Ninth Circuit concluded that because the moratoria had only a temporary impact on the landowners' fee interest in the affected properties, no categorical taking occurred. Opinion of the Court: *Stevens*, Breyer, Ginsburg, Kennedy, O'Connor, Souter. Dissenting opinion: *Rehnquist*, Scalia, Thomas; *Thomas*, Scalia.

Justice STEVENS delivered the opinion of the Court.

The question presented is whether a moratorium on development imposed during the process of devising a comprehensive land-use plan constitutes a per se taking of property requiring compensation under the Takings Clause of the United States Constitution. . . .

Petitioners make only a facial attack on Ordinance 81–5 and Resolution 83–21. They contend that the mere enactment of a temporary regulation that, while in effect, denies a property owner all viable economic use of her property gives rise to an unqualified constitutional obligation to compensate her for the value of its use during that period. Hence, they "face an uphill battle," *Keystone Bituminous Coal Assn. v. DeBenedictis* (1987), that is made especially steep by their desire for a categorical rule requiring compensation whenever the government imposes such a moratorium on development.

Under their proposed rule, there is no need to evaluate the landowners' investment-backed expectations, the actual impact of the regulation on any individual, the importance of the public interest served by the regulation, or the reasons for imposing the temporary restriction. For petitioners, it is enough that a regulation imposes a temporary deprivation—no matter how brief—of all economically viable use to trigger a per se rule that a taking has occurred. . . .

We shall first explain why our cases do not support their proposed categorical rule—indeed, fairly read, they implicitly reject it. . . . In our view the answer to the abstract question whether a temporary moratorium effects a taking is neither "yes, always" nor "no, never"; the answer depends upon the particular circumstances of the case. Resisting "the temptation to adopt what amount to per se rules in either direction," *Palazzolo v. Rhode Island*, (2001) (O'Connor, J., concurring), we conclude that the circumstances in this case are best analyzed within the *Penn Central* framework.

The text of the Fifth Amendment itself provides a basis for drawing a distinction between physical takings and regulatory takings. Its plain language requires the payment of compensation whenever the government acquires private property for a public purpose, whether the acquisition is the result of a condemnation proceeding or a physical appropriation. But the Constitution contains no comparable reference to regulations that prohibit a property owner from making certain uses of her private property. Our jurisprudence involving condemnations and physical takings is as old as the Republic and, for the most part, involves the straightforward application of *per se* rules. Our regulatory takings jurisprudence, in contrast, is of more recent vintage and is characterized by "essentially ad hoc, factual inquiries. . . ."

In determining whether government action affecting property is an unconstitutional deprivation of ownership rights under the Just Compensation Clause, a court must interpret the word "taken." When the government condemns or physically appropriates the property, the fact of a taking is typically obvious and undisputed. When, however, the owner contends a taking has occurred because a law or regulation imposes restrictions so severe that they are tantamount to a condemnation or appropriation, the

predicate of a taking is not self-evident, and the analysis is more complex.

When the government physically takes possession of an interest in property for some public purpose, it has a categorical duty to compensate the former owner, regardless of whether the interest that is taken constitutes an entire parcel or merely a part thereof. Thus, compensation is mandated when a leasehold is taken and the government occupies the property for its own purposes, even though that use is temporary. Similarly, when the government appropriates part of a rooftop in order to provide cable TV access for apartment tenants, or when its planes use private airspace to approach a government airport, it is required to pay for that share no matter how small. But a government regulation that merely prohibits landlords from evicting tenants unwilling to pay a higher rent, that bans certain private uses of a portion of an owner's property, or that forbids the private use of certain airspace, *Penn Central Transp. Co. v. New York City* (1978), does not constitute a categorical taking. "The first category of cases requires courts to apply a clear rule; the second necessarily entails complex factual assessments of the purposes and economic effects of government actions."

This longstanding distinction between acquisitions of property for public use, on the one hand, and regulations prohibiting private uses, on the other, makes it inappropriate to treat cases involving physical takings as controlling precedents for the evaluation of a claim that there has been a "regulatory taking," and vice versa. For the same reason that we do not ask whether a physical appropriation advances a substantial government interest or whether it deprives the owner of all economically valuable use, we do not apply our precedent from the physical takings context to regulatory takings claims. Land-use regulations are ubiquitous and most of them impact property values in some tangential way—often in completely unanticipated ways. Treating them all as *per se* takings would transform government regulation into a luxury few governments could afford. By contrast, physical appropriations are relatively rare, easily identified, and usually represent a greater affront to individual property rights. . . .

Perhaps recognizing this fundamental distinction, petitioners wisely do not place all their emphasis on analogies to physical takings cases. Instead, they rely principally on our decision in *Lucas v. South Carolina Coastal Council* (1992)—a regulatory takings case that, nevertheless, applied a categorical rule—to argue that the *Penn Central* framework is inapplicable here. A brief review of some of the cases that led to our decision in *Lucas*, however, will

Comparative Note 10.6

[In this case, the South African Constitutional Court considered the constitutionality of a statute that authorized an official to sell a person's property to satisfy a debt owed to another, without a prior judgment or authorization by a court. The appellant, whose property was seized, challenged the statute as a violation of Section 25 of the South African Constitution.]

Constitutional property clauses are notoriously difficult to interpret and it is unlikely that the interpretation of section 25 of the Constitution will be wholly spared these problems. A court is therefore fortunate, at this relatively early stage of section 25 jurisprudence, to have at its disposal a considerable body of work produced by South African scholars in the field. In this judgment heavy reliance is placed on such work and the assistance derived therefrom gratefully acknowledged.

Section 25 embodies a negative protection of property and does not expressly guarantee the right to acquire, hold and dispose of property. . . .

The subsections which have specifically to be interpreted in the present case must not be construed in isolation, but in the context of the other provisions of section 25 and their historical context, and indeed in the context of the Constitution as a whole. Subsections (4) to (9) all, in one way or another, underline the need for and aim at redressing one of the most enduring legacies of racial discrimination in the past, namely the grossly unequal distribution of land in South Africa. The details of these provisions are not directly relevant to the present case, but ought to be borne in mind whenever section 25 is being construed, because they emphasise that under the 1996 Constitution the protection of property as an individual right is not absolute but subject to societal considerations.

The purpose of section 25 has to be seen both as protecting existing private property rights as well as serving the public interest, mainly in the sphere of land reform but not limited thereto, and also as striking a proportionate balance between these two functions.

SOURCE: *First National Bank of SA, Limited v. Commissioner for South African Revenue Services*, CCT 19/01 (16 May 2002).

---

help to explain why the holding in that case does not answer the question presented here.

. . . [O]ur decision in *Lucas* is not dispositive of the question presented. Although *Lucas* endorsed and applied a categorical rule, it was not the one that petitioners propose. . . .

The categorical rule that we applied in *Lucas* states that compensation is required when a regulation deprives an owner of "all economically beneficial uses" of his land. Under that rule, a statute that "wholly eliminated the value" of Lucas' fee simple title clearly qualified as a taking. But our holding was limited to "the extraordinary circumstance when no productive or economically beneficial use of land is permitted." The emphasis on the word "no" in the text of the opinion was, in effect, reiterated in a footnote explaining that the categorical rule would not apply if the diminution in value were 95% instead of 100%. Anything less than a "complete elimination of value," or a "total loss," the Court acknowledged, would require the kind of analysis applied in *Penn Central.*

Certainly, our holding that the permanent "obliteration of the value" of a fee simple estate constitutes a categorical taking does not answer the question whether a regula-

tion prohibiting any economic use of land for a 32-month period has the same legal effect. Petitioners seek to bring this case under the rule announced in *Lucas* by arguing that we can effectively sever a 32-month segment from the remainder of each landowner's fee simple estate, and then ask whether that segment has been taken in its entirety by the moratoria. Of course, defining the property interest taken in terms of the very regulation being challenged is circular. With property so divided, every delay would become a total ban; the moratorium and the normal permit process alike would constitute categorical takings.

An interest in real property is defined by the metes and bounds that describe its geographic dimensions and the term of years that describes the temporal aspect of the owner's interest. Both dimensions must be considered if the interest is to be viewed in its entirety. Hence, a permanent deprivation of the owner's use of the entire area is a taking of "the parcel as a whole," whereas a temporary restriction that merely causes a diminution in value is not. Logically, a fee simple estate cannot be rendered valueless by a temporary prohibition on economic use, because the property will recover value as soon as the prohibition is lifted. . . . Mere fluctuations in value during the process of governmental decisionmaking, absent extraordinary delay, are "incidents of ownership. They cannot be considered as a 'taking' in the constitutional sense . . ."

Neither *Lucas* . . . nor any of our other regulatory takings cases compels us to accept petitioners' categorical submission. In fact, these cases make clear that the categorical rule in *Lucas* was carved out for the "extraordinary case" in which a regulation permanently deprives property of all value; the default rule remains that, in the regulatory taking context, we require a more fact specific inquiry. Nevertheless, we will consider whether the interest in protecting individual property owners from bearing public burdens "which, in all fairness and justice, should be borne by the public as a whole," justifies creating a new rule for these circumstances.

. . . [T]he ultimate constitutional question is whether the concepts of "fairness and justice" that underlie the Takings Clause will be better served by one of these categorical rules or by a *Penn Central* inquiry into all of the relevant circumstances in particular cases. From that perspective, the extreme categorical rule that any deprivation of all economic use, no matter how brief, constitutes a compensable taking surely cannot be sustained. Petitioners' broad submission would apply to numerous "normal delays in obtaining building permits, changes in zoning ordinances, variances, and the like," as well as to orders temporarily prohibiting access to crime scenes, businesses that violate health codes, fire-damaged buildings, or other areas that we cannot now foresee. Such a rule would undoubtedly require changes in numerous practices that have long been considered permissible exercises of the police power. . . . A rule that required compensation for every delay in the use of property would render routine government processes prohibitively expensive or encourage

hasty decisionmaking. Such an important change in the law should be the product of legislative rulemaking rather than adjudication. . . .

In rejecting petitioners' *per se* rule, we do not hold that the temporary nature of a land-use restriction precludes finding that it effects a taking; we simply recognize that it should not be given exclusive significance one way or the other.

A narrower rule that excluded the normal delays associated with processing permits, or that covered only delays of more than a year, would certainly have a less severe impact on prevailing practices, but it would still impose serious financial constraints on the planning process. Unlike the "extraordinary circumstance" in which the government deprives a property owner of all economic use, moratoria like Ordinance 81–5 and Resolution 83–21 are used widely among land-use planners to preserve the status quo while formulating a more permanent development strategy. . . . Yet even the weak version of petitioners' categorical rule would treat these interim measures as takings regardless of the good faith of the planners, the reasonable expectations of the landowners, or the actual impact of the moratorium on property values.

The interest in facilitating informed decisionmaking by regulatory agencies counsels against adopting a *per se* rule that would impose such severe costs on their deliberations. Otherwise, the financial constraints of compensating property owners during a moratorium may force officials to rush through the planning process or to abandon the practice altogether. To the extent that communities are forced to abandon using moratoria, landowners will have incentives to develop their property quickly be-

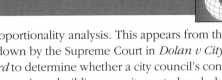

Comparative Note 10.7

There is broad support in other jurisdictions for an approach based on some concept of proportionality when dealing with deprivation of property, although the context and analytical methodology are not the same as under our Constitution. It is useful to consider approaches followed in other democratic systems before attempting to conclude what "arbitrary" deprivation means under section 25 of our Constitution.

Although the concept of proportionality is seldom used by name when American courts determine the takings issue, the courts do appear to employ some sort

of proportionality analysis. This appears from the test laid down by the Supreme Court in *Dolan v City of Tigard* to determine whether a city council's conditions for approving a building permit exacted such dedications of land as to amount to an impermissible taking, notwithstanding the clear relationship between such conditions and the council's legitimate government purpose. Rehnquist CJ, who delivered the opinion of the Court, laid down a "rough proportionality" test to decide individual cases. . . .

SOURCE: *First National Bank of SA, Limited v. Commissioner for South African Revenue Services*, CCT 19/01 (16 May 2002).

fore a comprehensive plan can be enacted, thereby fostering inefficient and ill-conceived growth.

It may well be true that any moratorium that lasts for more than one year should be viewed with special skepticism. But given the fact that the District Court found that the 32 months required by TRPA to formulate the 1984 Regional Plan was not unreasonable, we could not possibly conclude that every delay of over one year is constitutionally unacceptable. Formulating a general rule of this kind is a suitable task for state legislatures. In our view, the duration of the restriction is one of the important factors that a court must consider in the appraisal of a regulatory takings claim, but with respect to that factor as with respect to other factors, the "temptation to adopt what amount to *per se* rules in either direction must be resisted." There may be moratoria that last longer than one year which interfere with reasonable investment-backed expectations, but as the District Court's opinion illustrates, petitioners' proposed rule is simply "too blunt an instrument," for identifying those cases. We conclude, therefore, that the interest in "fairness and justice" will be best served by relying on the familiar *Penn Central* approach when deciding cases like this, rather than by attempting to craft a new categorical rule.

Accordingly, the judgment of the Court of Appeals is affirmed.

Chief Justice REHNQUIST, with whom Justice SCALIA and Justice THOMAS join, dissenting.

For over half a decade petitioners were prohibited from building homes, or any other structures, on their land. Because the Takings Clause requires the government to pay compensation when it deprives owners of all economically viable use of their land, see *Lucas v. South Carolina Coastal Council* (1992), and because a ban on all development lasting almost six years does not resemble any traditional land-use planning device, I dissent.

. . . *Lucas* reaffirmed our "frequently expressed" view that "when the owner of real property has been called upon to sacrifice all economically beneficial uses in the name of the common good, that is, to leave his property economically idle, he has suffered a taking. . . . " But the Court refuses to apply *Lucas* on the ground that the deprivation was "temporary."

Neither the Takings Clause nor our case law supports such a distinction. For one thing, a distinction between "temporary" and "permanent" prohibitions is tenuous. The "temporary" prohibition in this case that the Court finds is not a taking lasted almost six years. The "permanent" prohibition that the Court held to be a taking in *Lucas* lasted less than two years.

The "permanent" prohibition in *Lucas* lasted less than

two years because the law, as it often does, changed. . . . Under the Court's decision today, the takings question turns entirely on the initial label given a regulation, a label that is often without much meaning. There is every incentive for government to simply label any prohibition on development "temporary," or to fix a set number of years. As in this case, this initial designation does not preclude the government from repeatedly extending the "temporary" prohibition into a long-term ban on all development. The Court now holds that such a designation by the government is conclusive even though in fact the moratorium greatly exceeds the time initially specified. Apparently, the Court would not view even a 10-year moratorium as a taking under *Lucas* because the moratorium is not "permanent. . . ."

More fundamentally, even if a practical distinction between temporary and permanent deprivations were plausible, to treat the two differently in terms of takings law would be at odds with the justification for the *Lucas* rule. The *Lucas* rule is derived from the fact that a "total deprivation of use is, from the landowner's point of view, the equivalent of a physical appropriation." The regulation in *Lucas* was the "practical equivalence" of a long-term physical appropriation, i.e., a condemnation, so the Fifth Amendment required compensation. The "practical equivalence," from the landowner's point of view, of a "temporary" ban on all economic use is a forced leasehold.

Instead of acknowledging the "practical equivalence" of this case and a condemned leasehold, the Court analogizes to other areas of takings law in which we have distinguished between regulations and physical appropriations. But whatever basis there is for such distinctions in those contexts does not apply when a regulation deprives a landowner of all economically beneficial use of his land. In addition to the "practical equivalence" from the landowner's perspective of such a regulation and a physical appropriation, we have held that a regulation denying all productive use of land does not implicate the traditional justification for differentiating between regulations and physical appropriations. In "the extraordinary circumstance when no productive or economically beneficial use of land is permitted," it is less likely that "the legislature is simply 'adjusting the benefits and burdens of economic life' in a manner that secures an 'average reciprocity of advantage' to everyone concerned, and more likely that the property is being pressed into some form of public service under the guise of mitigating serious public harm. . . ."

The Court also reads *Lucas* as being fundamentally concerned with value, rather than with the denial of "all economically beneficial or productive use of land." But *Lucas* repeatedly discusses its holding as applying where "no productive or economically beneficial use of land is permitted." Moreover, the Court's position that value is the *sine qua non* of the *Lucas* rule proves too much. Surely, the land at issue in *Lucas* retained some market value based on the contingency, which soon came to fruition, that the development ban would be amended.

The Court worries that applying *Lucas* here compels finding that an array of traditional, short-term, land-use planning devices are takings. But since the beginning of our regulatory takings jurisprudence, we have recognized that property rights "are enjoyed under an implied limitation." Thus, in *Lucas*, after holding that the regulation prohibiting all economically beneficial use of the coastal land came within our categorical takings rule, we nonetheless inquired into whether such a result "inhered in the title itself, in the restrictions that background principles of the State's law of property and nuisance already place upon land ownership." Because the regulation at issue in *Lucas* purported to be permanent, or at least long term, we concluded that the only implied limitation of state property law that could achieve a similar long-term deprivation of all economic use would be something "achieved in the courts—by adjacent landowners (or other uniquely affected persons) under the State's law of private nuisance, or by the State under its complementary power to abate nuisances that affect the public generally, or otherwise."

When a regulation merely delays a final land use decision, we have recognized that there are other background principles of state property law that prevent the delay from being deemed a taking. . . . Zoning regulations existed as far back as colonial Boston, and New York City enacted the first comprehensive zoning ordinance in 1916. . . . Thus, the short-term delays attendant to zoning and permit regimes are a longstanding feature of state property law and part of a landowner's reasonable investment-backed expectations.

But a moratorium prohibiting all economic use for a period of six years is not one of the longstanding, implied limitations of state property law.

But this case does not require us to decide as a categorical matter whether moratoria prohibiting all economic use are an implied limitation of state property law, because the duration of this "moratorium" far exceeds that of ordinary moratoria. As the Court recognizes, state statutes authorizing the issuance of moratoria often limit the moratoria's duration. . . . Indeed, it has long been understood that moratoria on development exceeding these short time periods are not a legitimate planning device.

Because the prohibition on development of nearly six years in this case cannot be said to resemble any "implied limitation" of state property law, it is a taking that requires compensation. . . .

Justice THOMAS, with whom Justice SCALIA joins, dissenting.

A taking is exactly what occurred in this case. No one seriously doubts that the land use regulations at issue rendered petitioners' land unsusceptible of any economically beneficial use. This was true at the inception of the moratorium, and it remains true today. These individuals and families were deprived of the opportunity to build single-family homes as permanent, retirement, or vacation residences on land upon which such construction was authorized when purchased. The Court assures them that "a temporary prohibition on economic use" cannot be a taking because "logically . . . the property will recover value as soon as the prohibition is lifted." But the "logical" assurance that a "temporary restriction . . . merely causes a diminution in value," is cold comfort to the property owners in this case or any other. After all, "in the long run we are all dead." John Maynard Keynes, *Monetary Reform* 88 (1924).

I would hold that regulations prohibiting all productive uses of property are subject to *Lucas*' per se rule, regardless of whether the property so burdened retains theoretical useful life and value if, and when, the "temporary" moratorium is lifted. To my mind, such potential future value bears on the amount of compensation due and has nothing to do with the question whether there was a taking in the first place. It is regrettable that the Court has charted a markedly different path today.

Notes and Queries

1. Is the Court's opinion in this case consistent with its ruling in *Lucas v. South Carolina Coastal Council* (1992)? If not, how does it differ? Do these differences rest upon different understandings about what "property" means? About the relationship between individual liberty, the community, and how (if?) property should mediate that relationship?

2. The majority noted that "land-use regulations are ubiquitous and most of them impact property values in some tangential way—often in completely unanticipated ways. Treating them all as per se takings would transform government regulation into a luxury few governments could afford." What method of constitutional interpretation does such reasoning reflect?

3. In his dissent, the Chief Justice argued that the takings clause does not "support" a distinction between temporary and permanent prohibitions on land use. If such a distinction does not exist, then are all land use regulations potentially takings? How did the Chief respond to such concerns?

Chapter 11

Fundamental Rights: Privacy and Personhood

E very constitutional democracy must reconcile the tensions that inhere in its simultaneous commitments to individual liberty and the good of the community. As we saw in the introduction to part III, our Bill of Rights, when taken as a whole and not simply provision by provision, charts the boundaries of the relationship between liberty and community. For the Founders, and throughout much of our constitutional history, the tensions between these two values manifest themselves most clearly in the Supreme Court's consideration of rights to property. We continue our examination of the relationship between liberty and community in this chapter, but our focus broadens to a study of the development of the constitutional right to privacy and related fundamental rights. Like the right to property, the constitutional right to privacy is a battleground for the competing interests of liberty and community. Should the community have a say in determining what responsibilities, if any, a woman has toward the fetus she carries? Does the right to privacy protect a women's right to reproductive autonomy? Is the moral sense of the community reason enough to prohibit certain sexual practices? Implicit in these questions, and in the many others surrounding "privacy," are fundamental notions of personhood, personality, and the state.

From our perspective, discussion concerning the right to privacy raises many of the issues that discussion over property rights did for earlier generations, including questions of constitutional interpretation and judicial power. As we consider those questions, we shall see that an analysis focusing only on the tensions between privacy and community is too simplistic. In a more important sense privacy and community are interdependent. Underlying the right to privacy, at least as developed by the Supreme Court, is a vision of moral individualism that stresses self-determination and autonomy. Developed from classical conceptions of western liberalism, this understanding of privacy emphasizes individuality and self-reliance, or the separation of self from society.[1]

As we saw in our examination of property, however, American constitu-

---

[1] For an interesting discussion of autonomy as a constitutional interest, see Rogers M. Smith, *The Constitution and Autonomy*, 60 Tex. L. Rev. 175 (1982).

tional history also holds a countervailing understanding of individual liberty and community that emphasizes the extent to which "individuals" are undeniably social creatures who flourish as moral and political agents only in community with others. Justice Scalia drew on this tradition in writing that "Our society prohibits, and all human societies have prohibited, certain activities not because they harm others, but because they are considered immoral."[2] In the United States, as in all constitutional democracies, individualistic conceptions of privacy must wrestle with a long-standing tradition of social and moral regulation. Moreover, and especially in modern nation-states, the many interests that fall under the general rubric of "privacy"—such as protecting information about ourselves or making certain decisions free of state interference—are profoundly influenced by society and the state. The desirability of privacy in a complex and large social setting is easy to appreciate, but it may be nearly impossible to achieve.

The issues we consider in this chapter also highlight questions about the nature of constitutional interpretation and judicial power. These two questions go hand in hand. The constitutional text includes several explicit protections for the right to property. In contrast, the textual sources for a constitutional right to privacy are more obscure. Unlike property, then, the right to privacy is essentially a creation of judicial interpretation. Questions about the "legitimacy" of the right, as well as questions about the propriety of the Court's development of the right to privacy, continue to play an important role in constitutional politics.

In the following materials, we consider these problems and how the Court and other political actors have dealt with them. We begin with the development of substantive due process and noneconomic liberties before the second World War. We then consider the post–World War II development of substantive due process, including the rights to privacy and abortion.

Finally, we will explore how other constitutional states have dealt with the rights to liberty and privacy. Unlike the American Constitution, which includes no explicit protection for privacy or autonomy (except insofar as such values are necessary parts of liberty or property), many twentieth-century constitutions do contain explicit provisions to secure liberty, privacy, and related interests. As is true with their approach to other civil liberties, these constitutions typically couple protections for individual liberties with corresponding obligations and duties. In some instances this does not lead to much difference in the ways in which constitutional issues involving liberty and privacy get resolved in the courts, and indeed American adjudication is often cited by foreign tribunals despite the distinctions between the United States and other nations in the language of their respective constitutional texts. Often, as we shall see, the differences in result are pronounced, reflecting not just alternative legal constructions, but salient disparities in political culture, history, and tradition. Whether these disparities are such that they preclude serious efforts by the American Supreme Court at cross-national borrowing has, for better or worse, rarely been put to the test, although the subject has been of increasing debate among the justices as we saw in our earlier examination of the death penalty in chapter 9.

The Early Development of Noneconomic Substantive Due Process

As we saw in chapter 10, the decline of substantive due process as a source of protection for economic liberties was fast and dramatic. Pilloried as the illegitimate triumph

---

[2] *Barnes v. Glen Theatre, Inc.*, 501 U.S. 560 (1991).

of judicial opinion over majoritarian politics, the Court's use of substantive due process is now discredited as "Lochnerizing," to be avoided at all costs.[3] Curiously, however, the Court continues to use substantive due process to protect a variety of interests and values that are noneconomic, such as privacy or procreation. Much of contemporary constitutional law scholarship struggles to explain why substantive due process protection is wrong for economic interests, but might be permissible for these other interests.[4]

The Court's use of substantive due process for noneconomic interests has been one of the defining features of American constitutional law in the past half century, but the practice originated contemporaneously with the rise of economic due process. There have always been two distinct strands of substantive due process—one concerned solely with economic liberties, the other concerned more broadly with a great variety of personal liberties, some textually specific and others only hinted at by the constitutional document. In *Meyer v. Nebraska* (1923, reprinted later in the chapter), for example, the Court ruled that the liberty clause of the Fourteenth Amendment protects the rights of public school teachers to teach languages other than English. In his opinion for the Court, Justice McReynolds observed that

> *While this Court has not attempted to define with exactness the liberty thus guaranteed, the term has received much consideration and some things have been definitely stated. Without doubt [liberty] denotes not merely freedom from bodily restraint but also the right of the individual to contract, to engage in any of the common occupations of life, to acquire useful knowledge, to marry, establish a home and bring up children, to worship God . . . , and generally to enjoy those privileges long recognized at common law as essential to the orderly pursuit of happiness. . . .*

Similarly, in *Pierce v. Society of Sisters* (1925), McReynolds concluded for a majority that an Oregon law requiring a public school education for children ages eight to sixteen "unreasonably interferes with the liberty of parents and guardians to direct the upbringing and education of children under their control."

In both *Pierce* and *Meyer* the Court protected "implied" interests under the general umbrella of "liberty." Like *Lochner*, the decisions in *Meyer* and *Pierce* protected these implied interests against allegedly "unreasonable" state action. As a matter of interpretative methodology, the three cases seem indistinguishable. *Lochner* is discredited, but *Meyer* and *Pierce* remain good law. The Court's use of substantive due process to protect a wide variety of implied and noneconomic liberties has thus survived the demise of *Lochner*.

Carolene Products: Justifying Judicial Protection of Noneconomic Due Process

There are no obvious reasons why substantive due process protection might be warranted for some liberties and not for others. Justice Holmes, for example, dissented as vigorously in *Meyer* as he did in *Lochner*. In both cases, Holmes argued, the Court

---

[3] See, e.g., Howard Gillman, *The Constitution Besieged: The Rise and Demise of Lochner Era Police Power Jurisprudence.* (Durham: Duke University Press, 1994).

[4] The literature on this problem is enormous. Some of the better works are listed in the bibliography to this chapter. Prominent among them is John Hart Ely, *Democracy and Distrust: A Theory of Judicial Review.* (Cambridge: Harvard University Press, 1980).

was simply substituting its own judgment of what constituted good, or reasonable, public policy for the judgment of the legislature.

The constitutional text itself seems to offer no warrant for giving certain constitutional rights more aggressive judicial protection than others. After some early doubt, Justice Frankfurter finally concluded "I do not think there is a second-class citizenship among the different clauses inhabiting the Constitution."[5] As the Court's initial protection of property suggested, however, reasons to prefer some liberties over others may be found elsewhere, such as constitutional history or political theory. The Court's early protection for property, for example, was often premised upon appeals to political theory, as in *Calder* and *Fletcher*. At other times, as the Court insisted in *Blaisdell,* some liberties are said to be superior to others on the basis of claims that the Constitution should be interpreted in light of its evident purpose or purposes, an inquiry that must be informed by the realities of our world no less than those of the Founders.

Justice Stone was among the first to decide that the Court's retreat from economic due process did not mean, necessarily, that the Court could not aggressively protect noneconomic liberties. Stone's suggestion appeared in a footnote in his opinion for the Court in *United States v. Carolene Products* (1938, reprinted later in the chapter). In this otherwise insignificant case, the Court sustained the Filled Milk Act of 1923, which prohibited the interstate shipment of skimmed milk that included non-milk fat or oils. The Court reaffirmed its newfound unwillingness to supervise economic policy decisions, concluding that so long as the legislation was rational it was constitutional.

In footnote four, however, Justice Stone indicated that the "rational basis" test the Court applied to economic legislation might not apply to some other forms of legislation. He identified three distinct areas in which the Court might carve out a more pronounced role for judicial review. The first paragraph of the note argues that the Court may waive the presumption of constitutionality when legislation, on its face, appears to contravene one of the Bill of Rights (unless, of course, it contravenes the Fifth Amendment's protection of property). The second paragraph hints at judicial protection for the liberties that make the political system work, such as voting rights, rights to political information, or restraints upon political organizations and rights to assembly. The third paragraph implies a role for the Court as a defender of unpopular minorities and groups unable to protect themselves through the ordinary operation of the political process.

Much of the doctrinal and theoretical development of constitutional law in the United States over the past half century is foreshadowed by footnote four.[6] As we shall see in this and later chapters, the Court has subjected all three sorts of legislation to "more searching" judicial scrutiny, just as it once subjected legislation concerning property rights to more searching scrutiny.

In adopting the path mapped out by Justice Stone, the Court rejected an alternative course, first proposed by James Bradley Thayer, and later advocated by Justice Frankfurter.[7] In a pioneering article entitled, "The Origin and Scope of the American Doc-

---

[5] Felix Frankfurter to Justice Stanley Reed, February 7, 1956, in Bernard Schwartz, *Super Chief: Earl Warren and His Supreme Court.* (New York: New York University Press, 1983), p. 190.

[6] Major works of constitutional theory that build on footnote four include John Hart Ely, *Democracy and Distrust,* supra note 4; Bruce Ackerman, *Beyond Carolene Products,* 98 Harv. L. Rev. 713 (1985).

[7] Although he first embraced footnote four, Justice Frankfurter later concluded, "that there is no warrant in the constitutional basis of this Court's authority for attributing different roles to it depending upon the nature of the challenge to the legislation. Our power does not vary according to the particular provision of the Bill of Rights which is invoked." *West Virginia v. Barnette,* 319 U.S. 624 (dissenting op.)

trine of Constitutional Law,"[8] Thayer argued the Court should declare legislation unconstitutional only "when those who have the right to make laws have not merely made a mistake, but have made a very clear one,—so clear that it is not open to rational question." Thayer justified judicial deference by stressing the relationship between the people and their legislative representatives. Ultimately, protection for constitutional liberties rests not with courts, he argued, but rather with the people and their elected representatives. Consequently, Thayer's doctrine of judicial deference is based essentially on democratic grounds. Respect for the power of legislative majorities and the demands of democratic political theory, Thayer concluded, demanded a careful appreciation of the proper limits of judicial power in a democracy.

Thayer's justification for limited judicial review, unlike footnote four, acknowledged no distinction between types of legislation or liberty. As you read *Carolene Products* and the cases following it, consider what grounds Stone offered for adopting the Thayer doctrine of deference for some liberties but not for others. Are they based in the constitutional text or in a more general understanding of the constitutional order? Are they based on a particular conception of judicial power in a constitutional democracy? Are they based, like Thayer's argument, on the political theory of democracy, albeit a somewhat different understanding of how democracy works and what it demands of judges?

Early Applications of *Carolene Products*: *Buck, Skinner,* and Rights to Procreation

Prior to *Carolene Products,* the Court only occasionally protected individual liberty against a state's use of its police powers to protect the public good. More common were cases like *Jacobson v. Massachusetts* (1905), where the Court sustained a forced smallpox vaccination law over Jacobson's claim that the vaccination violated "his bodily integrity" and the "inherent right of every freeman" to control his own body. In 1927, the Court rejected a similar claim in the case of *Buck v. Bell.* Justice Holmes wrote for the Court that "Carrie Buck is a feeble minded white woman who was committed to the State mental hospital. She was the daughter of a feeble minded mother in the same institution, and the mother of an illegitimate feeble minded child."[9] Buck's employer had Carrie committed so she could be sterilized, as permitted under Virginia law, and then return to her work.

After reviewing the protections for patients in the Virginia statute, which included a hearing and the appointment of a guardian, Holmes concluded that "The attack is not upon the procedure but upon the substantive law. It seems to be contended that in no circumstances could such an order be justified. It certainly is contended that the order cannot be justified upon the existing grounds." The Court disagreed, noting that "In view of the general declarations of the legislature . . . obviously we cannot say as a matter of law that the grounds do not exist, and if they exist they justify the result."[10] Citing *Jacobson,* Holmes continued, "The principle that sustains compulsory

---

[8] 7 Harvard Law Review 129 (1893)

[9] This was not true. The only evidence of the daughter's mental capacity was a comment by a state social worker who testified that "the look of [the seven month old] baby . . . is not quite normal, but just what it is, I can't tell." Later the child did moderately well in her elementary school classes.

[10] *Buck* has generated a wealth of commentary, both academic and popular, including a made-for-television movie in 1994 entitled "Against Her Will." Among the best scholarly studies are Walter Berns, *Buck v. Bell: Due Process of Law?* 6 Western Political Quarterly 672 (1953); J. Smith & K. Nelson, *The Sterilization of Carrie Buck* (New Jersey: New Horizon Press, 1989); Stephen Jay Gould, *Carrie Buck's Daughter,* 2 Constitutional Commentary 331 (1985).

vaccination is broad enough to cover cutting the Fallopian tubes. Three generations of imbeciles are enough."[11]

The Court was presented with an opportunity to reconsider *Buck* in 1942, just four years after *Carolene Products*. Convicted twice of armed robbery and once for stealing chickens, Jack Skinner had also run afoul of an Oklahoma statute that required the sterilization of habitual criminals (persons convicted twice or more for crimes involving "moral turpitude"). The statute guaranteed a hearing, but limited it to the issue of whether the defendant could be sterilized "without detriment to his or her general health."

Skinner challenged the law, claiming first that its procedural safeguards were insufficient, and second that the substance of the law was also unconstitutional. Without addressing the differences between the procedures in *Buck* and Skinner's case, Justice Douglas found the law unconstitutional as a violation of the equal protection clause of the Fourteenth Amendment.[12] The Oklahoma statute distinguished between embezzlement and larceny. Both offenses are felonies, but Oklahoma determined (for reasons not immediately apparent to anyone else) that only larceny involves moral turpitude. Consequently, Justice Douglas noted, a person who stole more than twenty dollars thrice from an employer and a stranger who did the same are both felons. But only the latter could be sterilized. This, according to the Court, "is a clear, pointed, unmistakable discrimination."

Justice Douglas also observed, in language notable for its absence in *Buck*, that "This case touches a sensitive and important area of human rights. Oklahoma deprives certain individuals of a right which is basic to the perpetuation of a race—the right to have offspring. . . ." In cases involving "one of the basic civil rights of man," Douglas argued, the Court must use "strict scrutiny" to ensure that the classification drawn by the state is essential. Justice Stone, architect of footnote four, agreed that more searching judicial scrutiny was warranted in this case, but not because the statute offended the equal protection clause. Instead, Stone concluded that "a law which condemns, without hearing, all the individuals of a class to so harsh a measure . . . is lacking in the first principles of due process."

Although the justices disagreed about why the Oklahoma statute violated the Constitution, they unanimously agreed that the "presumption of constitutionality" rule that prevailed in cases concerning economic liberties was inappropriate in *Skinner*. In this respect, *Skinner v. Oklahoma* (1942, reprinted later in the chapter) represents an early and partial realization of Stone's vision for the Court in *Carolene Products*, a vision that understood the relationship between courts and legislatures in a particular way. In *Jacobson* and *Buck* the Court had announced its unwillingness to examine in detail the sufficiency of the evidence the legislature had relied upon to make public policy. In *Skinner*, though, the Court was less inclined to accept such evidence at face value. In his concurrence, Justice Stone stated instead that "[T]he State does not contend—nor can there be any pretense—that either common knowledge or experience, or scientific investigation, has given assurance that the criminal tenden-

---

[11] Only Pierce Butler dissented, for reasons he did not state. The story has it that at least one Harvard law professor used to describe the case as "Three generations of imbeciles are enough, Justice Butler dissenting." The story, unfortunately, gives some indication of how noncontroversial *Buck* was when decided. The eugenics movement was then a powerful force in American society, as evidenced by the fact that over thirty states had similar laws by the 1930s. By 1935, there had been approximately 20,000 forced sterilizations in the United States. See Gould, supra note 10, at 332.

[12] Justice Holmes dismissed the equal protection challenge in *Buck*, curtly observing that appeals to the equal protection clause are "the usual last resort of constitutional arguments."

cies of any class of habitual offenders are universally or even generally inheritable." Finally, and no less importantly, *Skinner* also represents the continued development of the strand of judicial protection for noneconomic liberties begun by *Meyer* and *Pierce*.

Substantive Due Process: The Development of a Constitutional Right to Privacy

For the founders, the right to property marked the point where liberty and community intersected. Property, defined not only in terms of one's material possessions but also as one's domain over one's self, represented a place where private rights and the public good existed not only in a state of tension, but interdependence. One of the chief aims of good government was to facilitate the pursuit of property, not simply for financial gain, but also because property was essential to personal autonomy and the development of a virtuous citizenry. Hence the purpose and the very definition of property were in some ways public matters.[13]

Even so, the concept of property has always included an element of refuge from community and public light. Indeed, the very idea of autonomy, a chief commodity of property, implies a sense of separation and perhaps occasional estrangement from a larger community. The sense of estrangement, or separation, is of even greater significance when we recognize that it is often very difficult to distinguish a "legitimate" community interest from the naked exercise of state power.

In a physical sense, refuge as a part of the right to property means the right to exclude others from one's property. In an intangible sense, refuge also means the right to escape the attention of others or to keep details about one's self private.[14] The distinction between these two aspects of refuge is important because it suggests there is an aspect of privacy untethered from traditional conceptions of property as a possession or place and tied more to an element of personal liberty.[15] Both emphasize the ways in which privacy covers a diverse collection of varied interests and how those interests mark the boundaries of the individual and community.

Early Efforts to Construct a Constitutional Right to Privacy

There is no explicit provision in the constitutional text that protects a comprehensive right to privacy. Nevertheless, some concern for privacy does appear in several places, including the Fourth Amendment, which protects against unreasonable searches and seizures, and the Fifth Amendment's protection against self-incrimination, as well as in its protection for private property. Other aspects of privacy intersect with the First Amendment's freedom of association.

The Court's earliest decisions on privacy tended to emphasize privacy as a right to exclude others from one's property, thus underscoring the intimate connection between property and privacy. In *Olmstead v. United States* (1928), for example, the Court ruled that the Fourth Amendment did not prohibit the use of wiretaps of private telephone conversations secured by the government without an actual trespass onto

---

[13] See the introduction to chapter 10.

[14] This is a kind of "informational" privacy. See Alan Westin, *Privacy and Freedom*. (New York: Atheneum, 1967).

[15] See Ernest Van Den Haag, "On Privacy," in J. Roland Pennock and John W. Chapman, eds., *Privacy*. (New York: Atherton Press, 1971).

Olmstead's property. In a well-known dissent, Justice Brandeis argued for a more expansive conception of constitutional privacy, one free of property and place:

> *The protection guaranteed . . . is much broader in scope. The makers of our Constitution undertook to secure conditions favorable to the pursuit of happiness. They recognized the significance of man's spiritual nature, of his feelings and of his intellect. . . . They conferred, as against the government, the right to be let alone—the most comprehensive of rights and the right most valued by civilized men. To protect that right, every unjustifiable intrusion by the government upon the privacy of an individual, whatever the means employed, must be deemed a violation of the Fourth Amendment.*[16]

Notwithstanding Brandeis' dissent, the Court continued to stress the necessity of a property interest in privacy cases until the 1960s.

The first significant change, and a landmark case in the development of a general right to privacy, came in *Griswold v. Connecticut* (1965, reprinted later in the chapter). *Griswold* is important not simply because it began the emancipation of privacy from property, but also, and no less significantly, because it reignited the debate over the Court's use of substantive due process. *Griswold* was the culmination of a string of test cases designed to challenge the constitutionality of a Connecticut law that made it a crime to use or to counsel others about birth control. Estelle Griswold, director of Planned Parenthood in the state, and Dr. Lee Buxton, the medical director of a clinic at Yale, were arrested for providing such information to married couples. They were each fined one hundred dollars.

The appellants contended that the statute violated a constitutional right to privacy, grounded largely in the due process clause of the Fourteenth Amendment. At oral argument the Court explored the obvious difficulties with the argument. In response to the Court's concern about finding the right in the due process clause, Griswold's attorney insisted that

> *it is not broad due process in the sense in which the issue was raised in the 1930s. In the first place, this is not a regulation which deals with economic or commercial matters. It is a regulation that touches upon individual rights: the right to protect life and health, the right of advancing scientific knowledge, the right to have children voluntarily. And therefore, we say we are not asking this Court to revive* Lochner v. New York, *or to overrule* Nebbia *or* West Coast Hotel.
>
> *THE COURT: It sounds to me like you're asking us to follow the constitutional philosophy of that case.*
>
> *APPELLANTS: No, Your Honor. We are asking you to follow the philosophy of* Meyer v. Nebraska *and* Pierce v. Society of Sisters. . . .

In his opinion for the Court, Justice Douglas confronted *Lochner*: "Overtones of some arguments suggest that *Lochner v. New York* should be our guide. But we decline that invitation. . . ." Instead, Douglas argued that "specific guarantees in the Bill of Rights have penumbras, formed by emanations from those guarantees that help give them life and substance."

According to the majority, some of the specific guarantees in the Bill of Rights thus

---

[16] Brandeis' eloquent opinion recalls an article he had coauthored with Samuel Warren, a law school classmate and business associate, over a quarter century before *Olmstead*. Samuel D. Warren and Louis D. Brandeis, *The Right to Privacy*, 4 Harvard Law Review 193 (1890). Most commentators argue that the article played a critical role in persuading courts to recognize privacy as a legally protectable interest. William C. Prosser, *Privacy*, 48 California Law Review 383 (1960).

create "zones of privacy." These guarantees included the First, Third, Fourth, and Fifth Amendments. "The present case, then, concerns a relationship lying within the zone of privacy created by several constitutional guarantees." Later in the opinion Justice Douglas moved even further from the text, saying "We deal with a right of privacy older than the Bill of Rights. . . ." To allow the state to regulate "the sacred precincts of the marital bedroom" would be "repulsive to the notions of privacy surrounding the marriage relationship."

The dissents in *Griswold* were quick to point out the majority's inventiveness. Justice Stewart observed that "In the course of its opinion the Court refers to no less than six Amendments to the Constitution . . . [but] does not say which . . . , if any, it thinks is infringed by this . . . law." Justice Black added "I get nowhere in this case by talk about a constitutional right to privacy as an emanation from one or more constitutional provisions. I like my privacy as well as the next one, but I am neverthe-less compelled to admit that government has a right to invade it unless prohibited by some specific constitutional provision. . . ."

As we saw in our discussion of *Griswold* in chapter 2, the Court's imprecision in identifying the source of the right to privacy makes it is possible to read *Griswold* in several ways. Read one way, the case marks a dramatic change in the Court's privacy jurisprudence, since it focuses on the privacy that surrounds the marital relationship. This is a conception of privacy that attaches to people, or to socially sanctioned institutions, such as marriage or the family, and not so much to places.[17] On the other hand, the opinion stresses the sanctity of the "marital bedroom" and the repulsive-ness of allowing the state to enter such places.

In *Eisenstadt v. Baird* (1972), the Court rejected both of these readings. In his opinion for the Court, Justice Brennan concluded that "the rights [to privacy] must be the same for married and unmarried alike. . . . It is true that in *Griswold* the right of privacy in question inhered in the marital relationship. Yet the married couple is not an independent entity with a mind and heart of its own, but an association of two individuals each with a separate intellectual and emotional makeup. If the right to privacy means anything, it is the right of the individual, married or single, to be free from unwarranted governmental intrusion into matters affecting a person as the decision whether to bear or beget a child."

Justice Brennan's language in *Eisenstadt* is important for two reasons. First, he made clear that the new right to privacy was independent of the privacy interest generated by the right to exclude inherent in the right to property. Justice Brennan finally loosened privacy from its Fourth Amendment moorings. Second, Brennan in-dicated that privacy is an *individual* right, and not one tied only to the marital rela-tionship as a social institution. Together, then, *Griswold* and *Eisenstadt* yield a right to privacy that protects at least some individual decisions from interference by the state. This represented an important expansion of privacy.

Griswold and *Eisenstadt* raise important issues, first of constitutional interpreta-tion, and second of judicial power. Critics of both cases complained that the Court's construction of the right to privacy was dangerously removed from any fair reading of the constitutional text. Consider Judge Bork's testimony at his confirmation hear-ings before the Senate Committee on the Judiciary: "Let me repeat about this created, generalized and undefined right of privacy in *Griswold*. Aside from the fact that the right was not derived by Justice Douglas, in any traditional mode of constitutional

---

[17] In *Katz v. United States* (1967), the Court further distanced privacy from property by noting that the privacy component of the Fourth Amendment "protects people, not places. . . ."

analysis, there is this. The right was not—we do not know what it is. We do not know what it covers. It can strike at random."[18]

Consequently, Bork and others argued, there can be no principled limitations upon the breadth or scope of the new right. Such criticisms are reminiscent of those directed against *Lochner*. In all three cases, questions about the legitimacy of the Court's interpretation of the Constitution coincide with questions about the proper extent of judicial power. Justices Black and Stewart, in particular, argued that the values inherent in democracy—that power should be exercised by the people and their accountable representatives—require a Court far more cautious than the one that ruled in cases like *Griswold*. These criticisms intensified as the Court began to expand the range of interests protected by the right to privacy.

Roe v. Wade: Privacy and Abortion

Few topics in American constitutional law are as emotionally charged, and as doctrinally confused, as is the discussion of abortion rights. *Roe v. Wade* (1973, reprinted later in the chapter) and its progeny are controversial because of the sensitive and important moral and political issues abortion involves. The doctrinal confusion that surrounds the constitutional dimensions of abortion raises these same concerns, as well as unruly questions of judicial power.[19]

Roe involved a challenge to a Texas criminal statute that prohibited abortion at any point in a pregnancy except if necessary to save the life of the mother. A companion case, *Doe v. Bolton*, involved a Georgia statute requiring that all abortions first win the approval of a "hospital abortion committee." It also required that all abortions be performed in hospitals. In 1970, Jane Roe (a pseudonym) was twenty-five, unmarried, and pregnant. Her doctor advised her that abortion was illegal in Texas. Roe then contacted an attorney, who filed a class-action suit in a state court on behalf of Roe and all other women "similarly situated." Roe asked the Court to declare the Texas statute unconstitutional as a violation of her constitutional right to privacy.

In his opinion for a 7–2 majority, Justice Blackmun agreed that the constitutional right to privacy, "whether it be found in the Fourteenth Amendment's concept of personal liberty and restrictions on state action, as we feel it is, or, as the District Court determined, in the Ninth Amendment . . . is broad enough to encompass a woman's decision whether or not to terminate her pregnancy." Roe had argued that her right was absolute and thus entirely free of state regulation. The majority concluded instead that the new right, while not absolute, was "fundamental." Texas could limit the right, provided those limits were justified by a "compelling state interest" and were "narrowly drawn" to achieve those interests alone.

The state claimed it had two such interests. First, it argued that it had a compelling interest, one that should outweigh the woman's right to privacy, in protecting the life of the unborn fetus. Second, it asserted an equally compelling interest in protecting the health and safety of the mother. Blackmun rejected the first altogether, denying that the Court had to resolve the question of when life begins, but concluding that a fetus is not a "person" in a constitutional sense. The Court did concede, however, that the states do have an interest in protecting "potential" life, an interest that becomes compelling at the point of fetal viability outside the mother's womb.

---

[18] Transcript of Senate Hearings Before the Committee on the Judiciary, 100th Congress, First Session. *The Nomination of Robert A. Bork to be Associate Justice of the Supreme Court of the United States*. Part 1, (Washington, D.C., Government Printing Office, 1989), p. 150.

[19] For readings, please consult the bibliography at the end of this chapter.

The Court conceded also that the state has an interest in protecting maternal health. The strength of that interest, and consequently the state's authority to regulate abortion, increases as the pregnancy continues. In the first trimester, where the risks of abortion as a medical procedure are minimal, the state's authority is correspondingly small. In the second and third trimesters the state's authority increases in direct proportion to the increase in risk.

In dissent, Justice White anticipated one of the major criticisms of *Roe*. White argued that the majority had simply announced "a new right . . . with scarcely any reason or authority for its action. . . ." Critics of *Roe* have complained that the Court's discussion of the right to privacy's source is cavalier. Similarly, some critics complain that the conception of privacy advanced in *Roe* is endlessly expansive and without principled or coherent limits.[20] What does privacy protect, and what does it exclude? The Court simply announced, with no justification whatsoever, that privacy includes a decision of whether to terminate a pregnancy. Moreover, critics claim, the Court's insistence that it need not resolve the difficult question of when life begins is nonsensical: If the fetus is a life, is it not apparent that its right to life must trump the mother's right to privacy?

Justice Rehnquist raised objections to the Court's decision to see abortion as implicating a privacy interest. "A transaction resulting in an operation such as this is not 'private' in the ordinary usage of that word," he observed. Given the undeniable necessity of involving others in such a decision, how can we say that the decision implicates a privacy interest? And recalling the origin of privacy in the right to exclude inherent in private property, Rehnquist added that "Nor is the 'privacy' that the Court finds here even a distant relative from the searches and seizures protected by the Fourth Amendment. . . ."

As Justice Rehnquist noted, the right to privacy protected in *Roe* is arguably of a different character than those cases in which the Court found a privacy interest inherent in property rights. In this respect, *Roe*, building on *Eisenstadt*, marks the full liberation of privacy from property as a constitutional right. Together, *Roe* and *Eisenstadt* yield a conception of privacy that protects a range of individual interests and personal choices. The immunity of these personal decisions from state regulation derives not from the place where such decisions occur, whether in the home or some equally "private" place, but rather from their centrality to conceptions of individual autonomy and self-determination.

A second set of criticisms relates to issues of judicial power and accountability. As Justice White complained in his angry dissent, the Court's decision seems to many critics to be indistinguishable from *Lochner*—a raw, unprincipled exercise of judicial power. "[The] judgment is an improvident and extravagant exercise of the power of judicial review. . . . This issue, for the most part, should be left with the people and to the political processes the people have devised to govern their affairs." In a single decision, the argument runs, the Court set aside the work of several state legislatures and, no less important, constituted itself an ongoing censor over the efforts of various states to settle the controversy over abortion through democratic channels.

The impropriety of the Court's oversight is underscored, for some, by the lack of a clear, constitutional basis for the existence of a right to an abortion. As Ely noted, the Court "is under an obligation to trace its premises to the charter from which it

---

[20] See, e.g., John Hart Ely, *The Wages of Crying Wolf: A Comment on* Roe v. Wade, 82 Yale Law Journal 920 (1973); Louis Henkin, *Privacy and Autonomy,* 74 Columbia Law Review 1410 (1974); Jeb Rubenfeld, *The Right of Privacy,* 102 Harvard Law Review 737 (1989).

derives its authority. A neutral and durable principle may be a thing of beauty and joy forever. But if it lacks connection with any value the Constitution marks as special, it is not a constitutional principle and the Court has no business imposing it."[21]

> *The Constitution has little to say about contract, less about abortion, and those who would speculate about which the framers would have been more likely to protect may not be pleased with the answer. The Court continues to disavow the philosophy of* Lochner. *Yet . . . it is candidly impossible to regard* Roe *as the product of anything else. . . .*[22]

Justice Rehnquist agreed, claiming that the *Roe* was indistinguishable from *Lochner* and its ilk. As you read *Roe* and the cases that follow it, pay especial attention to the Court's efforts to answer this question, and the extent to which it successfully traces its arguments to the "Constitution," however defined.

Consider also the following questions. What right, precisely, did *Roe* vindicate? A right of self-determination? The right of women to participate as equals in the full life of the community?[23] Of sexual liberty? Of lifestyle? Is the issue in *Roe* less about privacy than reproductive autonomy? Less about autonomy than about the question of when life begins and who decides? Or is the question, ultimately, about who has the authority to decide who is and is not a member of the community we share? If *Roe* does involve such questions, then is it clear that some issues in constitutional interpretation must also be issues of political theory and moral philosophy?[24]

Abortion Litigation After *Roe*

Recent abortion cases have highlighted the issues of judicial power and accountability. Recall that *Roe* did not completely prohibit the states from regulating abortion. The states may control abortions, provided their interests, or goals, are "compelling" and "narrowly drawn" to promote only those interests. After *Roe* several states rewrote their abortion laws to see what regulations would survive the Court's scrutiny. In *Planned Parenthood of Central Missouri v. Danforth* (1976), the Court struck down a state law requiring minors to obtain the consent of their parents and wives to obtain the consent of their husbands before an abortion. In *Bellotti v. Baird* (1979), the Court also struck down a Massachusetts law that required unmarried pregnant minors to obtain parental consent, or alternatively, to obtain authorization from a judge. Four years later, in *Planned Parenthood v. Ashcroft* (1983), the Court appeared to modify its position by sustaining a state law requiring parental consent for "unemancipated" minors, coupled with a provision that allowed some minors alternatively to obtain a judge's approval.

In the same year, though, in *Akron v. Akron Center for Reproductive Health* (1983), the Court reaffirmed its decision in *Roe*, stating that "the doctrine of *stare decisis*, while perhaps never entirely persuasive on a constitutional question, is a doctrine that demands respect in a society governed by the rule of law. We respect it today and reaffirm *Roe*." In a strong dissent, Justice O'Connor argued that "the *Roe*

---

[21] John Hart Ely, "The Wages of Crying Wolf," p. 949.

[22] Ibid., p. 939.

[23] See Mark Graber, "Interpreting Abortion," in *Feminist Jurisprudence*. (Lanham, MD.: Rowman & Littlefield Pubs., 1992), p. 190.

[24] See, for example, Ronald Dworkin, *Taking Rights Seriously*. (Cambridge: Harvard University Press, 1977), p. 149 ff.

framework . . . is clearly on a collision course with itself. . . . The *Roe* framework is inherently tied to the state of medical technology that exists whenever particular litigation ensues." As Justice O'Connor noted, in the ten years after *Roe* medical technology had advanced the point of fetal viability closer to the moment of conception, while simultaneously making the procedure safer during a more advanced pregnancy. The state's interest in fetal life, therefore, grew more compelling earlier in the pregnancy, whereas its interest in maternal health grew weaker.

In *Webster v. Reproductive Health Services* (1989), Justice Rehnquist, writing for a plurality, advanced a similar criticism, noting the trimester framework constructed in *Roe* is "hardly consistent with the notion of a Constitution cast in general terms, as ours is, and usually speaking in general principles. . . ." According to Rehnquist, the trimester framework was a work of judicial invention, an unacceptable exercise of judicial power. Nevertheless, the plurality concluded that "This case . . . affords us no occasion to revisit the holding of *[Roe]* and we leave it undisturbed." In her concurrence, Justice O'Connor added that the case "cannot provide a basis for reevaluating *Roe.*" Nevertheless, *Webster* did represent a significant change from *Roe*, because now a plurality of the Court held that the states' interest in protecting potential human life began at conception, and not at "the point of viability. . . ."

In an angry concurrence, Justice Scalia commented that "the outcome of today's case will doubtless be heralded as a triumph of judicial statesmanship. It is not that, unless it is statesmanlike needlessly to prolong this Court's self-awarded sovereignty over a field where it has little proper business. . . ." Scalia also accused the plurality of acting irresponsibly in not overruling *Roe* outright. Scalia singled Justice O'Connor for special mention, stating that her "assertion that a 'fundamental rule of judicial restraint' requires us to avoid reconsidering *Roe* cannot be taken seriously."

Justice Blackmun, concurring in part and dissenting in part, shared Scalia's concern about the "deceptive fashion" in which the plurality sought to "return to the States virtually unfettered authority to control" a woman's decision whether to have an abortion. "For today, at least," Justice Blackmun concluded, "the law of abortion stands undisturbed. For today, the women of this Nation still retain the liberty to control their destinies. But the signs are evident and very ominous, and a chill wind blows. I dissent."

The justices continued their angry exchanges in *Planned Parenthood of Southeastern Pennsylvania v. Casey* (1992, reprinted later in the chapter). Writing for a three person plurality, Justice O'Connor again declined the government's invitation to overrule *Roe*, largely on grounds of judicial self-restraint. "Liberty finds no refuge in a jurisprudence of doubt. . . . After considering the fundamental constitutional questions resolved by *Roe*, principles of institutional integrity, and the rule of *stare decisis*, we are led to conclude this: the essential holding of *Roe v. Wade* should be retained. . . ." O'Connor concluded that "a decision to overrule *Roe's* essential holding . . . would address error, if error there was, at the cost of both profound and unnecessary damage to the Court's legitimacy, and to the Nation's commitment to the rule of law."[25]

Although the plurality declined to overrule *Roe*, it did work substantial changes in the regulatory framework surrounding abortion. O'Connor rejected the trimester framework, finding that it was not "part of the essential holding of *Roe.*" Moreover,

---

[25] For an interesting analysis of the possible impact on pregnant women if *Roe* is overruled, see John Kaplan, *Abortion as a Vice Crime: A "What If" Story,"* 51 Law & Contemporary Problems 151 (1988).

the plurality refused to apply the compelling state interest test as the measure of the state's constitutionality, writing instead that restrictions on abortion should be held unconstitutional only when they impose an "undue burden on a woman's ability" to make the decision.

Justice Blackmun, concurring in part and dissenting in part, said "I do not underestimate the significance of today's joint opinion." He called the opinion by O'Connor, Kennedy, and Souter "an act of personal courage and constitutional principle," although he argued that "*Roe*'s requirement of strict scrutiny as implemented through a trimester framework should not be disturbed."

Justice Scalia was less impressed. In a sharply worded dissent remarkable for its candor, Scalia argued that "to portray *Roe* as a statesmanlike 'settlement' of a divisive issue, a jurisprudential Peace of Westphalia that is worth preserving, is nothing less than Orwellian. . . ." Instead, *Roe* had created a national politics "plagued by abortion protests, national abortion lobbying [and] abortion marches on Congress. . . ." Moreover, *Roe* created a "vast new class of abortion consumers and abortion proponents by eliminating the moral opprobrium that had attached to the act. . . ."

Webster and *Casey* illustrate how issues of constitutional interpretation and judicial power coincide. The plurality's insistence on respect for precedent in *Casey*, for example, is both a way of interpreting the Constitution and a way of understanding judicial power. On a doctrinal level, *Casey* promised a continued and contentious role for the Court in overseeing state efforts to regulate abortion. Future cases would surely involve additional state regulations, each of which the Court would have to address on a case by case basis.

The first of such regulations found its way to the Court in *Stenberg v. Carhart* (2000, reprinted later in the chapter), a case concerning Nebraska's ban on partial-birth abortion, a procedure twice outlawed by bills of Congress and twice vetoed by President Clinton. In a 5–4 decision filled with medical minutia and painfully graphic detail, the Court struck down the Nebraska statute as a violation of the abortion right established in *Roe* and reaffirmed (and redefined) in *Casey*. Applying, rather than revisiting, the principles established in those cases, Justice Breyer declared the Nebraska ban unconstitutional for two reasons: it lacked "the requisite exception for the 'preservation of the . . . health of the mother,'" and it imposed "an 'undue burden' on a woman's ability to choose an abortion." Describing a procedure that many view as dangerously close to infanticide in a manner he admitted might have seemed "clinically cold or callous to some," Justice Breyer—supported by Justice O'Connor's vigorous concurrence—emphasized the need for a health exception. The "State may promote but not endanger a woman's health when it regulates the methods of abortion." Furthermore, he reasoned, the ban on partial-birth abortion had the "effect of placing a substantial obstacle in the path of a woman seeking an abortion of a nonviable fetus" and, thus, according to *Casey*, amounted to an "undue burden" upon a woman's right to choose.

Yet the application of *Casey* proved to be a matter of substantial dispute. In a decision with eight separate opinions (only Justice Souter did not write for himself), eight members of the Court—including Chief Justice Rehnquist and Justice Thomas—seemed to concede that *Casey* was the governing precedent at hand. Though the Chief Justice frankly stated that he continued "to believe [*Casey*] is wrongly decided," and Justice Thomas rejected the notion that "*Casey*'s fabricated undue-burden standard merits adherence," only Justice Scalia explicitly argued for an overruling of *Casey*. Unlike Justice Thomas and Justice Kennedy, each of whom objected that the majority opinion misapplied and misinterpreted *Casey*, Justice Scalia found the Court's decision in *Stenberg* to be "*Casey*'s logical and entirely predictable consequence." He even expressed optimism that *Stenberg* would "one day . . . be assigned its rightful place in the history of this Court's jurisprudence beside *Korematsu* and *Dred Scott*," two cases widely considered the Court's most egregious errors. Ridiculing the "undue burden" test as "ultimately standardless," Justice Scalia argued that the Court, "armed with neither constitutional text nor accepted tradition," simply cannot resolve the controversy generated by the issue of abortion. Justice Kennedy, a member of the *Casey* plurality, emphatically disagreed, claiming that a "proper understanding of *Casey*"—one where the States are given "an important constitutional role in defining their interests"—was not meant to yield the result provided in *Stenberg*. Believing that the Nebraska statute denied "no woman a safe abortion," and that judges are "ill-equipped to evaluate the relative worth of particular surgical procedures," he saw *Stenberg* as a betrayal of his own joint opinion in *Casey*, which allowed, in his view, states to "forbid a procedure many decent and civilized people find so abhorrent."

Stenberg, a case involving an issue that deeply fractured the American public, was decided, perhaps appropriately, by a deeply fractured Court. Only Chief Justice Rehnquist remains from the Court that decided *Roe* thirty years ago, yet the shockwaves from that decision continue to reverberate through the Court today. Nearly every term there is a challenge to the abortion right, a further attempt to reaffirm, repudiate, or redefine *Roe* and its progeny. The storm shows no sign of abating, and with the Court seemingly deadlocked at 5–4—with the architects of *Casey*'s joint opinion themselves split as to what that precedent allows—the issue of abortion may very well rest in the hands of those justices who are considering retirement.

In addition to efforts to impose regulations on abortion, the federal government has attempted to regulate abortion through constraints on federal funding. In *Maher v. Roe* (1977), the Court upheld a state regulation that denied Medicaid benefits to women wanting an abortion, except in cases certified by a physician to be "medically necessary." In *Harris v. McRae* (1980), the Court likewise upheld the so-called Hyde Amendment, which forbade the use of federal monies to fund nontherapeutic abortions. Justice Stewart wrote that "[i]t simply does not follow that a woman's freedom of choice carries with it a constitutional entitlement to the financial resources to avail herself of the full range of protected choices. . . ."

Federal funding was also at issue in *Rust v. Sullivan* (1991). In 1987, the Department of Health and Human Services issued a regulation barring birth control clinics receiving federal monies from providing information to clients about abortion services. The Court upheld the restriction, finding that it violated neither the right to privacy nor freedom of speech. Writing for the majority, Chief Justice Rehnquist concluded that the "Government can, without violating the Constitution, selectively fund a program to encourage certain activities it believes to be in the public interest, without at the same time funding an alternate program which seeks to deal with the problem in another way." Dissenting, Justices Blackmun and Marshall complained that the regulations "suppressed speech favorable to abortion" and "compels anti-abortion speech. . . ." The effect was to "place . . . formidable obstacles in the path . . . of freedom of choice . . ." by "suppressing medically pertinent information and injecting a restrictive ideological message. . . ."

As we shall see in the next chapter, the right to free speech has figured prominently in the struggles over abortion in another way: regulations restricting a person's right to approach other persons in the vicinity of a health care facility. Whether the state has the authority to protect women from unwanted encounters at a moment when they are likely to bear the physical and/or emotional stress typically attendant the decision to seek an abortion, is a question difficult to separate from the set of deeply divisive moral questions concerning abortion itself.

Substantive Due Process and Other Liberty Interests

The right to liberty, like property, is less a single right than a collection of diverse interests. There is no general right to liberty that admits of a universal or comprehensive definition. Instead, liberty is an umbrella that covers more specific interests, whether of procreation, abortion, marriage, or sexuality. As a consequence, constitutional interpretation tends to center on questions about which of these more specific interests "liberty" actually encompasses and which ones it does not. As you read the cases in this chapter, you should consider the reasons the Court offers for protecting some interests and not others. Are those reasons fairly traceable to the Constitution?

What Is Liberty?

As a society committed to constitutional democracy, we value liberty because it embodies the concepts of choice, autonomy, and self-direction. We consider these essential to self-government, both as a community and as individuals. Even so, we have seen repeatedly that individual liberty must be bounded by restraints that account for the shared interests of the community. Sometimes, then, the community, in the exercise of its police powers, must have the constitutional authority to interfere with individual liberty. Are there also times when the community—or the state—should be under a positive obligation to help us to attain the conditions that allow us to exercise our liberty in meaningful ways? Some philosophers find it useful to distinguish between "negative" liberty, or "freedom from" something, and "positive" liberty, or the "freedom to" do something.[26]

Which of these understandings of liberty does the Constitution protect? Implicit in the question are competing visions of the Constitution, as well as of the relationship between the state and the individual. Most commentators have assumed that the Constitution, grounded in classical notions of Lockean liberalism, protects only negative liberty.[27] The language and structure of the due process clauses, which conceive of freedom in terms of a prohibition against governmental interference ("nor shall any State deprive any person of life, liberty, or property, without due process of law") seem to support this position.

The Court addressed this important issue in the case of *DeShaney v. Winnebago County Department of Social Services* (1989, reprinted later in the chapter). The facts in *DeShaney* are distressing. In the early spring of 1984, Joshua DeShaney was beaten so badly by his father, Randy DeShaney, that he fell into a coma. Joshua suffered extensive brain damage and is profoundly retarded. He will spend the rest of his life in an institution.

Randy DeShaney had beaten his son for several years. Two years before the final beating, DeShaney's second wife had called the Winnebago County Department of

---

[26] See, for example, Isaiah Berlin, *Four Essays on Liberty*. (London: Oxford University Press, 1969). For a criticism of the distinction, see Gerald C. McCallum, Jr., *Negative and Positive Freedom*, 76 Philosophical Rev. 320 (1967).

[27] See, for example, David P. Currie, *Positive and Negative Constitutional Rights*, 53 University of Chicago Law Review 864 (1986).

Social Services (DSS). In 1983 Joshua was treated several times in hospital emergency rooms for suspicious injuries. Each time the authorities notified DSS. On one such occasion the DSS took Joshua out of his father's custody, but the agency returned him to his father just three days later. A social worker assigned to the case visited the DeShaney home nearly two dozen times over the next year but did nothing to protect Joshua. Inexplicably, she acknowledged "I just knew the phone would ring some day and Joshua would be dead."

Joshua's mother sued the DSS, alleging that its failure to protect her son deprived him of his liberty without due process of law in violation of the Fourteenth Amendment. A majority of the Court did not agree. Writing for the Court, Chief Justice Rehnquist admitted "The facts of this case are undeniably tragic." The purpose of the due process clause, however, is "to protect the people from the State, not to ensure that the State protects them from each other." Moreover, "nothing in the language of the Due Process Clause itself requires the State to protect the life . . . of its citizens against invasion by private actors." In this case, the harm done to Joshua DeShaney, Rehnquist concluded, was committed by his father alone, and not by the state.

In response to the plaintiff's claim that the State had a special obligation to protect Joshua because it knew of the danger to him, the Court conceded that "in certain limited circumstances the Constitution imposes . . . affirmative duties of care and protection. . . ." Those circumstances, the Court held, did not apply here. Although the state "may have been aware of the dangers Joshua faced, it played no part in their creation [and did nothing] to render him any more vulnerable to them."

In dissent, Justice Brennan complained that the majority focused on the wrong question: "No one . . . has asked the Court to proclaim that, as a general matter, the Constitution safeguards positive as well as negative liberties." The majority's decision to address that question—and its predetermined answer to it—led inescapably to the conclusion that the state had no duty to protect. But it was not obvious that Joshua's claim should be conceived in terms of the State's inaction. Instead, Brennan argued, the Court should have focused on the steps the State *did* take and how those steps put Joshua in a worse position. Justice Blackmun was harsher, complaining that the majority, in a "pretense," had retreated "into a sterile formalism which prevents it from recognizing either the facts of the case before it or the legal norms that should apply to those facts. . . . Poor Joshua!"

The *DeShaney* Court's unwillingness to read due process broadly to cover "positive liberty" was in large measure a consequence of its fear of further judicial "expansion of the Due Process Clause. . . ." Similar concerns about constitutional interpretation and the limits of judicial power characterize the Court's consideration of other liberty interests.

Liberty and "Unconventional" Sexual Practices

Such fears are especially prominent in cases, such as *Bowers v. Hardwick* (1986, reprinted later in the chapter), and *Village of Belle Terre v. Boraas* (1974), where the Court refused to extend privacy to cover so-called "unconventional" sexual practices or "alternative" lifestyles. In *Bowers*, the Court ruled that the right to privacy does not prohibit states from making consensual sodomy between same-sex partners a criminal offense.[28] Writing for the majority, Justice White concluded that "there is no fun-

---

[28] For discussions of this case, see, e.g., Richard D. Mohr, *Gays/Justice: A Study of Ethics, Society and Law.* (New York: Columbia University Press, 1988); Earl M. Maltz, *The Court, the Academy, and the Constitution: A Comment on Bowers v. Hardwick and Its Critics,* 1989 Brigham Young University L. Rev. 59 (1989);

damental right [of] homosexuals to engage in sodomy." In part, the majority based its conclusion on grounds that protection for homosexual conduct is not "deeply rooted in this nation's history and traditions." Moreover, Justice White, echoing his dissent in *Roe*, argued that the Court should be reluctant "to expand the substantive reach of the Due Process Clause," for in doing so, "the Judiciary necessarily takes to itself further authority to govern the country. . . ."[29]

In his dissent Justice Blackmun described the interest involved in *Bowers* in very different terms. Whereas the majority framed the issue as whether the right to privacy includes a "right to engage in sodomy," Justice Blackmun thought the issue was about the right to be let alone and to self-determination. Reading the Court's earlier privacy cases broadly, Blackmun concluded that "We protect those rights not because they contribute, in some direct and material way, to the general public welfare, but because they form so central a part of an individual's life."[30]

Bowers is important because it demonstrated that the Court has been unable to develop a method or procedure for determining conclusively what privacy includes and excludes. As the dispute between the majority and Justice Blackmun suggests, constitutional interpretation in cases that involve "privacy" is profoundly influenced by how one conceptualizes the interest involved. This in turn influences, and is influenced by, the way one sees the role of precedent in constitutional interpretation, as well as one's understanding of the relationship between the individual and the community and the power of the Court to oversee the terms of that relationship.

All of these issues were in play again seventeen years later when the Court revisited its holding in *Bowers*. In a much anticipated case, *Lawrence v. Texas* (2003, reprinted later in the chapter), a majority overruled the earlier controversial decision, and in so doing set the stage for what is likely to be a protracted legal and political struggle over the rights of gays and lesbians in such areas as marriage, adoption, and custody. The 6–3 decision striking down Texas' anti-sodomy law was not a surprise to Court-watchers, although the breadth and directness of its affirmation of a right of privacy for homosexuals was startling to many observers. Some saw it as a case analogous to *Brown v. Board of Education*, overturning a widely discredited decision and establishing a new legal day for a minority long the object of societal discrimination.

The law in *Lawrence* was different from *Bowers* in one important respect: unlike the statute in Georgia, the Texas law (similar to those of three other states) banned sodomy between same-sex partners but did not criminalize the same acts when performed by heterosexuals. This difference meant that the law could be overturned on equal protection grounds without disturbing the *Bowers* precedent. Only one justice—Justice O'Connor (who had joined the *Bowers* majority)—took this route. Thus she argued that "The Texas statute makes homosexuals unequal in the eyes of the

---

Norman Vieira, *Hardwick and the Right of Privacy*, 55 University of Chicago Law Review 1181 (1988); Thomas B. Stoddard, Bowers v. Hardwick: *Precedent by Personal Predilection*, 54 University of Chicago Law Review 648 (1987); Mark F. Kohler, *History, Homosexuals, and Homophobia: The Judicial Intolerance of* Bowers v. Hardwick, 19 Connecticut Law Review 129 (1986); David A. J. Richards, *Homosexuality and the Constitutional Right to Privacy*, 8 N.Y.U. Review of Law & Social Change 311 (1979).

[29] Justice Powell joined the majority. After he retired, he told a group of law students at New York University he "probably made a mistake" in *Bowers*. He also said that it "was not a major case, and one of the reasons I voted the way I did was the case was a frivolous case just to see what the Court would do. . . ." *Washington Post,* October 26, 1990, p. A-3.

[30] Compare Blackmun's description of the right with Kenneth L. Karst, *The Freedom of Intimate Association,* 89 Yale Law Journal 624 (1980).

law by making particular conduct—and only that conduct—subject to criminal sanction." This effort, she maintained, fails the Court's minimal rational basis review, as the state's purported interest in promoting morality cannot be sustained as applied to only one group of people. Moral disapproval expressed in such a discriminatory way cannot escape the inference that "the disadvantage imposed is born of animosity toward the class of persons affected." As such, she held, it is unnecessary to determine whether an anti-sodomy law that is neutral in effect and application violates the Fourteenth Amendment's Due Process Clause.

But Justice Kennedy's opinion of the Court made precisely that determination, ruling emphatically that the Texas statute was in clear violation of the liberty guaranteed under the Constitution. Its opening paragraph laid out the libertarian theme that would be the motif of the entire opinion: "Liberty presumes an autonomy of self that includes freedom of thought, belief, expression, and certain intimate conduct." This presumption required a reconsideration of the holding in *Bowers*, which of course had been premised on a radically different view that privileged the authority of the community in establishing moral limits to the varieties of intimate association. In a frontal attack on the earlier decision, Justice Kennedy was (unlike the *Brown* Court's overruling of *Plessy v. Ferguson*) unambiguous in asserting that the majority in *Bowers* had gotten it wrong. "To say that the issue in *Bowers* was simply the right to engage in certain sexual conduct demeans the claim the individual put forward, just as it would demean a married couple were it to be said marriage is simply about the right to have sexual intercourse." Among the reasons why, according to the Court, that precedent could no longer stand, was one that had not figured in 1986, the fact that trans-national norms of constitutional understanding argued in favor of the liberty interest asserted in the case. In the end, the ruling in *Lawrence* was based on the majority's perception that the law in question "demeans the lives of homosexual persons."

Whether it did or not was, to state it mildly, of little concern to Justice Scalia. In a bitter dissent he accused the majority of inappropriately taking sides in a culture war that should be fought out in the democratic arena. His opinion contrasted the Court's overruling of *Bowers* with its refusal in *Casey* to abandon the precedent in *Roe v. Wade* on the ground—now revealed to be less principled than what its authors insisted at the time—that "Liberty finds no refuge in a jurisprudence of doubt." He saw no legitimate reason to discard the correctness of the underlying principle in *Bowers*, that the law is reasonable when it seeks to enforce the moral choices of the majority. Indeed, in an observation that some of the supporters of the Court's ruling can only hope to be true, he saw the overturning of the earlier holding as entailing "a massive disruption of the current social order," placing in doubt the validity of numerous regulations of popularly designated immoral conduct. Dismissing as fundamentally flawed in its constitutional premises the majority's reliance on an "emerging awareness" that conduct pertaining to sex should be protected against criminal prosecution, Justice Scalia renewed his now familiar indictment of the judicial use of non-American materials. "The Court's discussion of . . . foreign views . . . is . . . meaningless dicta." In this case it was, according to the justice, also "dangerous dicta," in part because it played into the hands of "the agenda promoted by some homosexual activists directed at eliminating the moral opprobrium that has traditionally attached to homosexual conduct." In anticipation of the legal battles that lie ahead, he perceived in the logic of the Court's libertarian position the "judicial imposition of homosexual marriage." And as if to highlight the deep division on the Court with respect to this issue, he pointed out that the appropriate response to the Court's denial of where its logic leads was: "Do not believe it."

Substantive Due Process and the Family

Similar issues trouble the Court's efforts to decide whether "privacy" protects a wide range of interests that are not primarily sexual in nature. In *Moore v. East Cleveland* (1977, reprinted later in the chapter), the Court narrowly struck down an ordinance that prohibited, under its definition of immediate family, a grandmother from living in the same house with her son and two of her grandchildren (who were first cousins). The Court wrote that "when the government intrudes on choices concerning family living arrangements, [we] must examine carefully the importance of the governmental interests advanced. . . ." Justice Stevens agreed with the result, but characterized the issue as "whether [the] ordinance is a permissible restriction on appellant's right to use her own property as she sees fit," thus underscoring the connection between property and privacy. In dissent, Justice Stewart admitted that several cases do appear to protect "what might broadly be termed 'private family life,'" including *Roe, Griswold, Pierce,* and *Meyer.* Nevertheless, he concluded that "appellant's desire to share a single-dwelling unit . . . can hardly be equated with any of the interests protected in the cases just cited."

The spirit of Stewart's dissent claimed the Court in *Michael H. v. Gerald D.* (1989, reprinted later in the chapter), where the Court found no fundamental right on the part of a biological father (not married to the mother) to be guaranteed visits with his child. The Court emphasized the primacy of the nuclear family as a valid state interest in sustaining a California statute that created a legal presumption that a child born to a married woman is a product of the marriage. In determining whether the father's interest reached the status of a fundamental right, Justice Scalia, following *Palko, Griswold,* and *Bowers,* concluded the interest must "be so rooted in the traditions and conscience of our people as to be ranked as fundamental. . . . Thus, the legal issue in this case reduces to whether the relationship [in this case] has been treated as a protected family unit under the historic practices of our society. . . . We think it impossible to find that it has. In fact, quite to the contrary, our traditions have protected the marital family . . . against the sort of claim Michael asserts. . . ."

In dissent, Justice Brennan argued that "The plurality's interpretive method is more than novel; it is misguided. . . . In construing the Fourteenth Amendment to offer shelter only to those interests specifically protected by historical practice . . . , the plurality ignores the kind of society in which our Constitution exists. We are not an assimilative, homogeneous society. . . . In a community such as ours, 'liberty' must include the freedom not to conform."

The fundamental rights of parents would find their way back to the Court in *Troxel v. Granville* (2000, reprinted later in the chapter), a case involving Washington's third-party visitation statute. Though the Court in *Troxel* repeatedly noted its recognition of the "changing realities of the American family"—including the types of associations the Court had previously acknowledged in *Moore*—the result was an endorsement of the traditional family. In a decision governed only by a plurality of four and including six separate opinions (including three solo dissents), the Court struck down the Washington statute. It thus denied a set of grandparents increased visitation time with their deceased son's children as an unconstitutional infringement on parents' fundamental rights to rear their children. Despite the fact that similar statutes existed in all 50 states, Justice O'Connor's plurality opinion relied on a series of precedents (from *Meyer* to *Pierce* to *Wisconsin v. Yoder*) to sketch a parental due process right to "make decisions concerning the care, custody, and control of her daughters."

In separate concurrences, Justices Souter and Thomas joined the holding of the

Court while critiquing its rationale. Justice Souter would have preferred to go further than the plurality by declaring the "any person, any time" visitation statute unconstitutional on its face rather than merely as applied in the specific instance at hand. Justice Thomas, in a brief concurrence, voiced disapproval with the other Justices' failure to articulate strict scrutiny as "the appropriate standard of review" in such a case. And in individual dissents, Justices Stevens, Scalia, and Kennedy disagreed with the plurality's willingness to replace the judgment of popularly elected legislatures with those of appointed judges. Justice Stevens, in particular, much like Justice Douglas in *Wisconsin v. Yoder*, expressed concern for the rights of the children themselves. Each of the six opinions paid lip service to the bonds that children establish with non-parental figures such as grandparents, yet only three were willing to say that the importance of such bonds was significant enough to overcome the fundamental rights of parents.

Nonetheless, the decision generated unhappiness among both grandparents-rights and parents-rights activists—the former criticizing the Court for not understanding the value of their function in the lives of the children they care for, the latter accusing the Court of leaving the door open for future abrogation of fundamental parental rights.

This lack of enthusiasm for the result in *Troxel* also reflects the confusion about the family that is endemic to American constitutional law. "Neither the text of the Constitution nor settled cultural patterns effectively determine the scope of childhood or the parameters of the parent-child relationship."[31] Thus the Court's ambivalent support for the nuclear model of the family is understandable in light of its own development of a decidedly individualist jurisprudence of fundamental rights, as well as its recognition over the years of the multiple patterns of familial development that have come to fill the American social landscape. Unlike constitutions that seek to define the relations that make up the family, the silence of the American document on this vital subject leaves adjudication in this area more dependent on the uncertainties of judicial interpretation. As such, the standing of the individual—whether parent or child—in relation to the small community that is the family is likely to remain unstable in the foreseeable future.

Substantive Due Process and Rights Concerning the Quality of Life

Privacy issues often include questions about the quality of life. Cases concerning an individual's right to refuse medical treatment have appeared with increasing frequency in the past two decades. In the well-known case of *In re Quinlan* (1976), for example, the New Jersey Supreme Court decided that the right to privacy included a right on the part of Quinlan to be removed from a respirator and for her family to decline other life-maintaining procedures.

In *Cruzan v. Director, Missouri Health Department* (1990), the Supreme Court upheld a state statute that required "clear and convincing" evidence of a person's desire to refuse life-prolonging treatment. Justice Rehnquist, writing for the Court, assumed the due process clause includes a right to refuse such treatment. Nevertheless, the state's interests, first, in preserving life, and second, in safeguarding Nancy Cruzan's "personal element of choice," were sufficiently strong to justify the imposition of stringent evidentiary requirements. In dissent, Justice Stevens argued that

---

[31] Janet L. Dolgin, *The Constitutional As Family Arbiter: A Moral in the Mess?*, 102 Columbia Law Review, 366.

"However commendable may be the State's interest in human life, it cannot pursue that interest by appropriating Nancy Cruzan's life as a symbol for its own purposes."

In *Washington v. Glucksberg* (1997, reprinted later in the chapter), the Court addressed the related issue of physician-assisted suicide. In his opinion for the Court, Chief Justice Rehnquist weighed a claimed liberty of "personal choice by a mentally competent, terminally ill adult to commit physician-assisted suicide" against "our Nation's history, legal traditions, and practices." The Court concluded that bans in the states against suicide and assisted-suicide are "longstanding expressions of the States' commitment to the protection and preservation of human life." Consequently, the Court was unwilling to find a fundamental right to assisted suicide. It thus measured Washington State's ban against the rationality test. The Court had little difficulty identifying a number of rational state interests to support the ban, including a state's "unqualified interest in the preservation of human life."

Whether the outcome in *Glucksberg* is, as one leading commentator described it, a "repudiation of *Roe's* constitutional methodology,"[32] is certainly contestable. But it does represent a victory for induction over deduction, in the sense that most members of the Court felt more comfortable addressing the substantive issue in the case from an experiential, traditionalist approach, rather than from a more philosophically grounded orientation that reasons from general theoretical propositions. Thus they did not follow the path suggested in an unusual amicus curiae brief submitted by six leading moral philosophers supporting Glucksberg on the basis of carefully reasoned ethical principles. On the other hand, while denying a claim to a general "right to die," the Court left open, in Justice O'Connor's words, the "narrower question whether a mentally competent person who is experiencing great suffering has a constitutionally cognizable interest in controlling the circumstances of his or her imminent death." It was a prudential—or in Sunstein's term, minimalist—decision that left considerable space for further democratic deliberation.

Glucksberg and *Cruzan* nicely illustrate how cases that involve the right to privacy implicate theories of human personality and the relationship between individual self-determination and our status as members of larger communities. What obligations do we have to ourselves, and to others, in questions about life and death? What obligations does the state have, whether to individuals or to the community? Are there principled ways for judges to answer such questions, ways that derive from the Constitution? Or should judges defer to legislatures in such cases, recognizing, as Justice Scalia argued in dissent, that the information and materials necessary to resolve such issues "are neither set forth in the Constitution nor known to the nine Justices of this Court any better than they are known to nine people picked at random from the Kansas City telephone directory. . . ."

Comparative Perspectives

There are many ways to approach the relationship between liberty and community. The American Constitution tends to use the language of classical liberalism, which privileges individual autonomy, whether through property or privacy. Even in the American case, however, the demands of community sometimes necessitate limitations on liberty.

The German Basic Law is a good example of the way many twentieth-century

[32] Michael W. McConnell, *The Right To Die and the Jurisprudence of Tradition,* 1997 Utah Law Review 665 (1997).

constitutions understand the complex interrelationship between private and public dimensions of individuals in the social order. Article 1 of the Basic Law provides "The dignity of man shall be inviolable," and Article 2 further states that "Everyone shall have the right to the free development of personality insofar as he does not violate the rights of others or offend against the constitutional order or the moral code." Article 2 explicitly recognizes, therefore, as Article 1 does implicitly, that individual self-determination must be a principal value in any constitutional democracy. In this respect, the German Basic Law, like most western constitutions, affords special status and protection to the individual.

On the other hand, Article 2 also acknowledges the undeniable interdependence of the individual and of the community in which he or she is a member. Moreover, Articles 1 and 2 must be interpreted in light of Article 20, which provides that Germany is "a democratic and social federal state." Article 20 thus reinforces the image of the individual inherent in Articles 1 and 2, described by the Federal Constitutional Court:

The image of man in the Basic Law is not that of an isolated, sovereign individual; rather, the Basic Law has decided in favor of a relationship between an individual and community in the sense of a person's dependence on and commitment to the community, without infringing upon a person's individual value.[33]

As Donald Kommers has concluded, "[The German Court] envisions society as more than a collection of individuals moved by self-interest, calculation, or the manipulation of others. . . . It defends freedom as individual self-determination but attaches nearly equal weight to the social values of participation, communication, and civility."[34] Individuality—or privacy, or the development of free personality—takes shape and develops partly as a consequence of, and in reaction to, our interactions with other people. As property is both defined by and a refuge from society, so too is human individuality.

In American constitutional law, the doctrine of substantive due process has yielded a number of judicially discovered fundamental rights not explicitly protected in the constitutional document, such as the right to marry or to raise children. Constitutional texts in other countries, in part because most are products of the twentieth century, are more likely to offer explicit protection for a wider range of interests. The Irish Constitution, for instance, has an article specifically on the rights of the family, as do the Greek and German constitutions. Thus, Article 41.1 provides: "1. The State recognises the Family as the natural primary and fundamental unit of Society, and as a moral institution possessing inalienable and imprescriptible rights, antecedent and superior to all positive law. 2. The State, therefore, guarantees to protect the family in its constitution and authority, as the necessary basis of social order and as indispensable to the welfare of the Nation and the State." These provisions are notable for their inclusion within the protective ambit of natural law constitutional language, as well as their designation of the family as a corporate entity entitled to rights separate from the claims of its individual members. In both regards, they reflect a constitutional treatment of the family markedly different from the American experience, where one is unlikely to encounter a Supreme Court opinion expressing the follow-

---

[33] *The Investment Aid Case*, 4 BVerfGE 7 (1954)

[34] Donald P. Kommers, *The Constitutional Jurisprudence of the Federal Republic of Germany* (Durham: Duke University Press, 1989), p. 313.

ing point of view. "[T]he rights in Art. 41.1.1 are those which can properly be said to belong to the institution itself as distinct from the personal rights which each individual member might enjoy by virtue of membership of the family. No doubt if the rights of the unit were threatened or infringed any member of the family could move the court to uphold them, but the cause of action would then be the threat to the rights granted as a unit, and not to those of its individual members."[35]

Several other constitutions also protect a wide range of rights and interests at best implicit in the American Constitution. The Canadian Charter, for example, protects life and liberty, and the "security of the person" in Section 7. Most commentators assume the phrase "life and liberty" encompasses more than just freedom from physical restraint or physical security, but extends also to some of the same types of "substantive" interests, such as the right to marry, to raise children, to choose a profession, and so on, that are subsumed under liberty in the American Constitution.[36] Article 12 (2) of South Africa's Constitution (1996) guarantees "the right to bodily and psychological integrity, which includes the right (a) to make decisions concerning reproduction." According to Article 36 (1), however, this and all other guaranteed rights may be limited by measures that are "reasonable and justifiable in an open and democratic society."

The Japanese Constitution protects the right to liberty in Article 13, which provides that "all of the people shall be respected as individuals. Their right to life, liberty, and the pursuit of happiness shall, to the extent it does not interfere with the public welfare, be the supreme consideration in legislation. . . ." Article 22 guarantees freedom to choose an occupation and residence, Article 23 guarantees academic freedom, Article 24 guarantees the right to marriage, and Article 25 provides that "all people shall have the right to maintain the minimum standards of wholesome and cultured living." Other provisions protect rights to free (compulsory) education, the right (and obligation) to work, and of laborers to bargain collectively. Article 12 provides that the Japanese people must "always be responsible for utilizing [their rights] for the public welfare."

In similar fashion, the Indian Constitution contains a long list of substantive entitlements, many of which are contained in a section headed "Fundamental Rights." These include many of the guarantees familiar to Americans, as well as a few—such as the abolition of untouchability—that are peculiar to India. A separate section—Part IV—consists of a list of "directive principles of State policy" that does not confer upon citizens any enforceable rights; rather it enumerates social goals that become, in the language of Article 37, "the duty of the State to apply . . . in making laws." Under this category one finds such provisions as "the right to an adequate means of livelihood" and the "right to work, to education and to public assistance in cases of unemployment."

This arrangement, borrowed in significant measure from the Irish Constitution, highlights the dilemma involved in the judicial enforcement of "positive" rights, a genre of constitutional entitlements often requiring substantial commitments of economic resources for their fulfillment. Thus the problem faced by many countries so committed is that the material preconditions for court mandated enjoyment of affirmative fundamental rights may not exist, which then threatens the legitimacy of a legal system seemingly built on hollow promises. By enumerating rights in the lan-

---

[35] *Murray v. Ireland,* [1985] ILRM 542 at 547.

[36] See for example, Peter W. Hogg, *Constitutional Law of Canada* (Toronto: Carswell Company Limited, 1985), p. 744–745.

guage of goals, which entails carving out a special nonjusticiable space for them, the Indian Constitution represents itself as an aspirational document in a manner that is much more explicit than any such claim that could be advanced about the American Constitution by interpreters so inclined. The directive principles serve a kind of hortatory role in constitutional interpretation, inviting judges to seize opportunities to move the polity in specific ways without forcing them to expend political capital in the unrealistic pursuit of an overly ambitious and expansive regime of rights.

Privacy and Abortion in Other Constitutional Democracies

It should be no surprise that many twentieth-century constitutions are somewhat more specific about the right to privacy than is the American text. Individual privacy and autonomy are endemic problems in mass societies. And since they are problems that raise fundamental issues about the relationship of the individual to the state—issues central to the very nature of constitutional democracy—it is both understandable and proper that contemporary constitutions should address these issues.

As we have seen, concern for individual autonomy is at the centerpiece of the German constitutional order. More particular provisions for privacy include Articles 10 and 13. Article 10 protects the privacy of posts and telecommunications, again provided that their use does not threaten the security of the state or the democratic order. Article 13, acknowledging the connection between privacy and property, protects the "inviolability" of the home.

In the United States, the right to privacy covers a wide range of substantive interests and activities. Nevertheless, it sometimes seems as though the controversy surrounding the right to privacy is essentially a controversy about the right to an abortion. Certainly the abortion cases can serve as a valuable prism through which to assess privacy as a constitutional value. A comparative analysis of privacy and abortion law can facilitate that assessment, especially since American constitutional law on abortion is distinctive in some important respects. As Mary Ann Glendon has observed,

> *When American abortion law is viewed in comparative perspective, it presents several unique features. Not only do we have less regulation of abortion than any other western nation, but we provide less public support for maternity and child raising. And, to a greater extent than in any other country, our courts have shut down the legislative process of bargaining, education, and persuasion on the abortion issue.*[37]

To appreciate the contrast, consider that in its landmark abortion case the Hungarian Constitutional Court organized its ruling around a referral of the decision on the legal status of the fetus back to Parliament. Without any compelling constitutional answer to the question of the legal status of the fetus, the Court, in the view of the author of its opinion, "made it clear that Parliament shall determine the indications for a lawful abortion."[38] In the end, the legislature legalized abortion in "crisis situations" of the mother, a decision that is reviewable by the Court. "[T]he essential question will no longer be the (legal) status of humans but rather the balancing of interests

---

[37] Mary Ann Glendon, *Abortion and Divorce in Western Law* (Cambridge: Harvard University Press, 1987), p. 2.

[38] Laszlo Solyom and Georg Brunner, *Constitutional Democracy in a New Democracy: The Hungarian Constitutional Court* (Ann Arbor: The University of Michigan Press, 2000), p. 7.

between the objective protection of life and the mother's right to privacy, especially whether the 'crisis' indication is definite enough."[39] Moreover, apropos Glendon's observation, the Court has shown its commitment to governmental support for child-rearing by invalidating an earlier severing of maternal and child care benefits.

Perhaps the two best known foreign decisions on abortion are those by the German and Canadian constitutional courts. Both provoked considerable controversy, but neither decision caused as much turmoil as *Roe*. As you consider these cases, you may want to ask why the political consequences in Canada and Germany differed from those in the United States. Are those differences a consequence of political culture? Or can we trace them more directly to differences of constitutional interpretation and doctrine?

Canadian law allowed a woman to procure an abortion if her pregnancy "would be likely to endanger her life or health." This entitlement, however, was encumbered by regulations that restricted access to an abortion and caused significant delays in procuring it. (One of these regulations required that an abortion be certified by a therapeutic abortion committee of three doctors in an approved hospital.) Because of its serious procedural flaws, Canada's Supreme Court struck down the entire statute, reasoning that it interfered with the mother's "security of the person" in violation of the "principles of fundamental justice." Section 7 of the Charter of Rights and Liberties provides that "everyone has the right to life, liberty and security of the person and the right not to be deprived thereof except in accordance with the principles of fundamental justice."

Canada's Supreme Court, unlike the U.S. Supreme Court, declined to explore "the broadest implications" of Section 7. Thus their decision was, in Cass Sunstein's terminology, significantly more "minimalist" than was the ruling by their American counterpart in *Roe*. Although three of the justices agreed that the law-related delays in procuring an abortion interfered with a woman's liberty to secure medical treatment, the majority ruled that it would be up to the legislature to correct the procedural deficiencies in the law and at the same time to balance the state's interest in the preservation of the fetus against the woman's liberty interest in terminating her pregnancy. Counsel and one dissenting opinion strongly advised the Court to follow the American decision in *Roe v. Wade*. Chief Justice Dickson, however, declined to do so, remarking, in language reminiscent of Justice Scalia's dismissal of foreign legal precedents (see chapter 2), that "we do our own Constitution a disservice to simply allow the American debate to define the issue for us."

The German approach did grapple directly with the question of fetal life. In 1974, Germany relaxed its criminal provisions regulating abortion. Under the new law, abortions before the twelfth week were permissible, provided the woman agreed to prior counseling and the abortion was performed by a licensed physician. After the twelfth week, abortions were permissible only in the event of serious danger to the woman or in the likelihood that irreversible, serious damage had affected the fetus. These conditions would almost certainly be unconstitutional under the original *Roe* framework.

Five German states and 193 members of the German parliament challenged the new law, claiming that the liberal policy for first trimester abortions violated the fetus' right to human dignity and to life under Articles 1 and 2(2) of the Basic Law. On the other hand, a restrictive policy might violate a woman's right to the free development of personality in Article 1. The Federal Constitutional Court found the statute uncon-

---

[39] Ibid., p. 8.

stitutional, arguing that together, Articles 1 and 2 make life the highest value in the constitutional order. A woman's right to autonomy and privacy, the Court argued, is also an important constitutional value, but one necessarily subordinate to the protection of life. In the Court's opinion, "the obligation of the state to furnish protection is comprehensive. . . . Human life represents a supreme value within the constitutional order . . . ; it is the vital basis of . . . human dignity and the prerequisite of all other basic rights." Because the fetus has a right to life under the Basic Law, the Court continued, "termination of pregnancy has a social dimension which makes it accessible to and in need of state regulation. . . . It is true that the right of the woman freely to develop her personality also lays claim to recognition and protection. . . . But this right is not given without limitation—the rights of others, the constitutional order, and moral law limit it."

In 1992, the German Bundestag passed a new abortion statute. Shortly thereafter the law was challenged in the Constitutional Court. In its much anticipated decision, the Court ruled that the state's interest in preserving the value of unborn life required that the state make abortion illegal. The Court also ruled, however, that the state need not punish the act, though illegal, if the abortion occurs in the first three months of the pregnancy and "after the State had had an opportunity to try to get the pregnant woman to change her mind."[40] The Court's opinion, like *Casey* did with *Roe*, began with a review of its earlier decision. And like *Casey*, the Court reaffirmed the central meaning of its earlier holding.

Interestingly, the German Court did not conclude that it alone knew best how to accommodate these competing interests. Instead, such questions "are left in large measure to the legislator and in general are removed from review by a constitutional court." As a consequence, legislative efforts to regulate abortion in Germany take place in an environment considerably freer of judicially imposed restraints and oversight than in the United States. Some commentators, such as Mary Ann Glendon, believe that "the Bundestag was able to work out a compromise typical of that reached at this stage . . . by most other Western democracies," but not by the United States.[41]

The German decisions differ from the Supreme Court's in a few additional important respects. Unlike the American Court, the Federal Constitutional Court characterized the fetus, after the fourteenth week, as "developing life." Consequently, the German Court faced squarely the question of how to reconcile the constitutional values of life and privacy. In contrast, the American Supreme Court had no need to resolve the issue, since the fetus was determined to be neither a person nor life in a constitutional sense. Moreover, the two decisions invoke somewhat different understandings of "privacy." In *Roe*, privacy is demonstrably an individualistic concept, as was also made clear in *Eisenstadt*. The German Court employed a concept of privacy more inclined to stress the communal and social aspects of abortion, one that "emphasizes the connections among the woman, developing life, and the larger community."[42] It is a mistake to think that the German Court imposes a particular moral vision upon the individual woman while the American Court leaves such decisions to the individual. Instead, a careful analysis of the two cases makes clear that to claim

---

[40] Donald P. Kommers, *The Constitutional Law of Abortion in Germany: Should Americans Pay Attention?* 10 Journal of Contemporary Health Law & Policy 1, 17 (1994).

[41] Glendon, *Abortion and Divorce in Western Law*, p. 34. For a criticism, see Laurence Tribe, *Abortion: The Clash of Absolutes*. p. 74.

[42] Glendon, *Abortion and Divorce in Western Law*, p. 35.

that a decision to abort is "private" is itself a moral claim. Did the Supreme Court recognize these alternative claims? Did it provide a reasoned justification for choosing one over the other?

Some of the differences between the two opinions are therefore related to the alternative meanings privacy takes in Germany and the United States. As we saw, privacy in the United States is essentially about refuge from, and the exclusion of, others—it is about the right to be let alone. In Germany, however, "privacy" has a social dimension that emphasizes the ways in which individuals are members of larger communities and are shaped by those communities.

Roe, of course, raised contentious issues about the proper role of the Court in the American political process. Similar questions followed the decisions in Canada and Germany, albeit with less urgency. In Canada, Article 7 provides that all deprivations of life, liberty, and security must accord with "the principles of fundamental justice." Do such principles include matters of procedural justice alone, or do they also include substantive principles? If they do include the latter, then the potential scope of judicial review under Article 7 is substantial. In *Morgentaler*, Justice Dickson concluded that "in the present case, I do not believe it is necessary . . . to tread the fine line between substantive review and the adjudication of public policy." Questions about the extent of judicial power arise also in Germany. In their dissent in the abortion case, Justices Rupp, Brunneck and Simon argued that the Constitutional Court had exceeded its authority. In language reminiscent of Justice White's dissent in *Roe*, they argued that "The decision in this matter is the legislature's responsibility."

A comparative perspective on questions of liberty and privacy makes clear the extent to which issues relating to such terms acquire meaning by virtue of the larger political, social, and moral orders of which they are a part. A comparative analysis also highlights the different understandings and approaches of courts in giving constitutional meaning to these values. Courts in different countries will differ in how constrained they feel by what is distinctive in their sociopolitical culture in assessing their ability to profit from the experience of others. But there is little doubt that as students of constitutional law we can only benefit from an awareness of the great variability in conceptual understanding that characterizes the practice of fundamental rights.

Selected Bibliography

Allen, Anita. *Uneasy Access: Privacy for Women in a Free Society.* (Totowa, N.J.: Rowman & Littlefield, 1988.)

Arkes, Hadley. *First Things: An Inquiry Into the First Principles of Morals and Justice.* Princeton: Princeton University Press, 1986.

———. *Natural Rights and the Right To Choose.* Cambridge: Cambridge University Press, 2002.

Barnett, Randy E., ed. *The Rights Retained By the People: The History and Meaning of the Ninth Amendment.* Fairfax, Va.: George Mason University Press, 1989.

Barnett, Walter. *Sexual Freedom and the Constitution.* Albuquerque, N.M.: University of New Mexico Press, 1973.

Brill, Alinda. *Nobody's Business: Paradoxes of Privacy.* Reading: Addison-Wesley Publishing Co., 1990.

Craig, Barbara Hinkson and David M. O'Brien. *Abortion in American Politics.* Chatham, NJ: Chatham House Publishers, 1993.

Dworkin, Ronald. *Life's Dominion.* New York: Alfred A Knopf, 1993.

Ely, John Hart. *Democracy and Distrust: A Theory of Judicial Review.* Cambridge: Harvard University Press, 1980.

The Wages of Crying Wolf: A Comment on Roe v. Wade, 82 Yale L. J. 920 (1973).

Fried, Charles, *Privacy,* 77 Yale L. J. 475 (1968).

Galston, William. *Liberal Purposes.* New York: Cambridge University Press, 1991.

Garrow, David J. *Liberty and Sexuality: The Right to Privacy and the Making of Roe v. Wade.* New York: Macmillan, 1994.

Gillman, Howard. *The Constitution Besieged: The Rise and Demise of Lochner Era Police Power Jurisprudence.* Durham: Duke University Press, 1994.

Ginsburg, Ruth Bader, *Some Thoughts On Autonomy and Equality In relation To* Roe v. Wade, 63 North Carolina Law Review 375 (1985).

Hart, H. L. A., *Law, Liberty, and Morality.* New York: Vintage Books, 1963.

Harvard Law Review, eds. *Sexual Orientation and the Law.* Cambridge: Harvard University Press, 1990.

Hauerwas, Stanley. *A Community of Character.* Notre Dame: University of Notre Dame Press, 1981.

Henkin, Louis, *Privacy and Autonomy,* 74 Colum. L. Rev. 1410 (1974).

Hixon, Richard E. *Privacy in a Public Society: Human Rights in Conflict.* New York: Oxford University Press, 1987.

Innes, Julie C. *Privacy, Intimacy, and Isolation.* New York: Oxford University Press, 1992.

Kammen, Michael. *Spheres of Liberty: Changing Perceptions of Liberty in America.* Ithaca: Cornell University Press, 1986.

Karst, Kenneth, *The Freedom of Intimate Association,* 89 Yale L. J. 624 (1980).

Macedo, Stephen. *Liberal Virtues.* New York: Oxford University Press, 1990.

Mensch, Elizabeth and Alan Freeman. *The Politics of Virtue: Is Abortion Debatable?* Durham: Duke University Press, 1993.

Mill, John. *On Privacy.* New York: Appleton-Century-Crofts, 1947.

Minow, Martha, *Which Question: Which Lie? Reflections on the Physician-Assisted Suicide Cases,* 1997 Supreme Court Review 1.

O'Brien, David M. *Privacy, Law, and Public Policy.* New York: Praeger, 1979.

Packard, Vance. *The Naked Society.* New York: David McKay Co., 1964.

Pennock, Roland & John W. Chapman, eds. *Privacy.* New York: Atherton Press, 1971.

Richards, David A. J. *Toleration and the Constitution.* New York: Oxford University Press, 1986.

Rubenfeld, Jed, *The Right of Privacy,* 102 Harv. L. Rev. 737 (1989).

Rubin, Eva R. *Abortion. Politics, and the Courts: Roe v. Wade and Its Aftermath.* New York: Greenwood, 1987.

Samar, Vincent J. *The Right to Privacy: Gays, Lesbians, and the Constitution.* Philadelphia: Temple University Press, 1991.

Smith, Rogers, M., *The Constitution and Autonomy,* 60 Tex. L. Rev. 175 (1982).

Stoddard, Thomas B., Bowers v. Hardwick: *Precedent by Personal Predilection,* 54 U. of Chi. L. Rev. 648 (1987).

Sunstein, Cass, *The Right to Die,* 106 Yale Law Journal 1123 (1997).

Tribe, Laurence. *Abortion: The Clash of Absolutes.* New York: Norton Publishing Co., 1990.

Warren, Samuel D. & Louis D. Brandeis, *The Right to Privacy,* 4 Harv. L. Rev. 193 (1890).

Westin, Alan. *Privacy and Freedom.* New York: Athaneum, 1967.

Selected Comparative Bibliography

Conkle, Daniel O., *Canada's* Roe: *the Canadian Abortion Decision and Its Implications for American Constitutional Law and Theory,* 6 Constitutional Commentary 299 (1989).

Devlin, Patrick, *The Enforcement of Morals.* (1965).

Gavison, Ruth, *Privacy and the Limits of Law,* 89 Yale L. J. 421 (1980).

Glendon, Mary Ann. *Abortion and Divorce in Western Law.* Cambridge: Harvard University Press, 1987.

Hogg, Peter W. *Constitutional Law of Canada.* 3rd ed. Toronto: Carswell Company Limited, 1985.

Kelly, John Maurice. *Fundamental Rights in the Irish Law and Constitution.* Dublin: Allen Figgis and Co., Ltd., 1961.

Kommers, Donald P. *The Constitutional Jurisprudence of the Federal Republic of Germany,* Durham: Duke University Press, 1989.

Walls, M., and D. Bergin. *The Law of Divorce in Ireland.* Bristol: Jordans, 1997.

United States v. Carolene Products

304 U.S. 144, 58 S. Ct. 778, 82 L. Ed. 1234 (1938)

In 1923 Congress passed the Filled Milk Act, which prohibited the interstate shipment of skimmed milk that included fat or oils that looked like cream but were not derived from milk. Carolene Products was indicted for shipping such a product across state lines. At trial, the company responded that the Act was an unconstitutional extension of Congress' power to regulate interstate commerce. Opinion of the Court: *Stone,* Brandeis, Hughes, Roberts. Concurring opinions: *Black, Butler.* Dissenting opinion: *McReynolds.* Not participating: Cardozo, Reed.

Mr. Justice STONE delivered the opinion of the Court.

[Footnote #4 of the Court]: There may be narrower scope for operation of the presumption of constitutionality when legislation appears on its face to be within a specific prohibition of the Constitution, such as those of the first ten amendments, which are deemed equally specific when held to be embraced within the Fourteenth. . . .

It is unnecessary to consider now whether legislation which restricts those political processes which can ordinarily be expected to bring about repeal of undesirable legislation, is to be subjected to more exacting judicial scrutiny under the general prohibitions of the Fourteenth Amendment than are most other types of legislation.

Nor need we inquire whether similar considerations enter into the review of statutes directed at particular religious, or national, or racial minorities, whether prejudices against discrete and insular minorities may be a special condition, which tends seriously to curtail the operation of those political processes ordinarily thought to be relied upon to protect minorities, and which may call for a correspondingly more searching judicial inquiry.

Notes and Queries

1. How does Stone distinguish between economic and civil liberties? What is the basis for the Court's general pol-icy of deference? What are the three areas in which more aggressive judicial scrutiny of legislation may be warranted?

2. Is there a basis for Stone's distinction in the text of the Constitution? If not, from where is it derived? Are different justifications necessary for each of the "preferred" areas? Are these justifications consistent with one another?

3. Which theory of incorporation does footnote four most closely approximate?

4. Much of the academic community embraced footnote four. Felix Frankfurter, then a professor at Harvard Law School, complimented Stone. But later as a Supreme Court Justice, Frankfurter criticized the doctrine of "preferred freedoms" in *West Virginia v. Barnette* (1943), stating that "the Constitution does not give us greater veto power when dealing with one 'phase' of liberty than with another."

Meyer v. Nebraska

262 U.S. 390, 43 S. Ct. 625, 67 L. Ed. 1042 (1923)

After World War I, a number of states sought to promote isolationism by prohibiting the teaching of foreign languages in elementary schools. Meyer, a teacher in a Nebraska parochial school, was arrested for teaching German to a young boy. Meyer appealed, claiming the law infringed on his Fourteenth Amendment right to liberty. State courts upheld the statute. Opinion of the Court: *McReynolds*, Brandeis, Butler, Day, McKenna, Van Devanter, Taft. Dissenting without opinion: Holmes, Sutherland.

Mr. Justice McREYNOLDS delivered the opinion of the Court.

The problem for our determination is whether the statute as construed and applied unreasonably infringes the liberty guaranteed to the plaintiff in error by the Fourteenth Amendment: "No state . . . shall deprive any person of life, liberty or property without due process of law."

While this Court has not attempted to define with exactness the liberty thus guaranteed, the term has received much consideration and some of the included things have been definitely stated. Without doubt, it denotes not merely freedom from bodily restraint but also the right of the individual to contract, to engage in any of the common occupations of life, to acquire useful knowledge, to marry, establish a home and bring up children, to worship God according to the dictates of his own conscience, and generally to enjoy those privileges long recognized at common law as essential to the orderly pursuit of happiness by free men. *Slaughter-House Cases* (1873); *Allgeyer v. Louisiana* (1897); *Lochner v. New York* (1905); *Adkins v. Children's Hospital* (1923). The established doctrine is that this liberty may not be interfered with, under the guise of protecting the public interest, by legislative action which is arbitrary or without reasonable relation to some purpose within the competency of the state to effect. Determination by the Legislature of what constitutes proper exercise of police power is not final or conclusive but is subject to supervision by the courts.

The American people have always regarded education and acquisition of knowledge as matters of supreme importance which should be diligently promoted. . . . Corresponding to the right of control, it is the natural duty of the parent to give his children education suitable to their station in life; and nearly all the States, including Nebraska, enforce this obligation by compulsory laws.

Practically, education of the young is only possible in schools conducted by especially qualified persons who devote themselves thereto. The calling always has been regarded as useful and honorable, essential, indeed, to the public welfare. Mere knowledge of the German language cannot reasonably be regarded as harmful. Heretofore it has been commonly looked upon as helpful and desirable. Plaintiff in error taught this language in school as part of his occupation. His right thus to teach and the right of parents to engage him so to instruct their children, we think, are within the liberty of the Amendment.

The challenged statute forbids the teaching in school of any subject except in English; also the teaching of any other language until the pupil has attained and successfully passed the eighth grade, which is not usually accomplished before the age of twelve. . . . Latin, Greek, Hebrew are not proscribed; but German, French, Spanish, Italian, and every other alien speech are within the ban. Evidently the Legislature has attempted materially to interfere with the calling of modern language teachers, with the opportunities of pupils to acquire knowledge, and with the power of parents to control the education of their own.

It is said the purpose of the legislation was to promote civic development by inhibiting training and education of the immature in foreign tongues and ideals before they could learn English and acquire American ideals, and "that the English language should be and become the mother tongue of all children reared in this state." It is also affirmed that the foreign born population is very large, that certain communities commonly use foreign words, follow foreign leaders, move in a foreign atmosphere, and that the children are thereby hindered from becoming citizens of the most useful type and the public safety is imperiled.

That the state may do much, go very far, indeed, in order to improve the quality of its citizens, physically, mentally and morally, is clear; but the individual has certain fundamental rights which must be respected. The protection of the Constitution extends to all, to those who speak other languages as well as to those born with English on the tongue. Perhaps it would be highly advantageous if all had ready understanding of our ordinary speech, but this cannot be coerced by methods which conflict with the Constitution—a desirable end cannot be promoted by prohibited means.

For the welfare of his Ideal Commonwealth, Plato suggested a law which should provide:

That the wives of our guardians are to be common, and their children are to be common, and no parent is to know his own child, nor any child his parent. . . . The proper officers will take the offspring of the good parents to the pen or fold, and there they will deposit them with certain nurses who dwell in a separate quarter; but

the offspring of the inferior, or of the better when they chance to be deformed, will be put away in some mysterious, unknown place, as they should be.

In order to submerge the individual and develop ideal citizens, Sparta assembled the males at seven into barracks and intrusted their subsequent education and training to official guardians. Although such measures have been deliberately approved by men of great genius their ideas touching the relation between individual and state were wholly different from those upon which our institutions rest; and it hardly will be affirmed that any Legislature could impose such restrictions upon the people of a state without doing violence to both letter and spirit of the Constitution.

The desire of the Legislature to foster a homogeneous people with American ideals prepared readily to understand current discussions of civic matters is easy to appreciate. Unfortunate experiences during the late war and aversion toward every character of truculent adversaries were certainly enough to quicken that aspiration. But the means adopted, we think, exceed the limitations upon the power of the state and conflict with rights assured to plaintiff in error. The interference is plain enough and no adequate reason therefore in time of peace and domestic tranquility has been shown.

The power of the State to compel attendance at some school and to make reasonable regulations for all schools, including a requirement that they shall give instructions in English, is not questioned. . . . No emergency has arisen which renders knowledge by a child of some other language other than English so clearly harmful as to justify its inhibition with the consequent infringement of rights long freely enjoyed. We are constrained to conclude that the statute as applied is arbitrary and without reasonable relation to any end within the competency of the State.

. . . It is well known that proficiency in a foreign language seldom comes to one not instructed at an early age, and experience shows that this is not injurious to the health, morals or understanding of the ordinary child.

The judgment of the court below must be reversed and the cause remanded for further proceedings not inconsistent with this opinion. Reversed.

Mr. Justice HOLMES and Mr. Justice SUTHERLAND, dissenting.

We all agree . . . that it is desirable that all the citizens of the United States should speak a common tongue, and therefore that the end aimed at by the statute is a lawful and proper one. The only question is whether the means adopted deprive teachers of the liberty secured to them by the Fourteenth Amendment. . . . I cannot bring my mind to believe that in some circumstances and circumstances existing it is said in Nebraska, the statute might not be regarded as a reasonable or even necessary method of reaching the desired result. . . . But if it is reasonable it is not an undue restriction of the liberty either of teacher or scholar. No one would doubt that a teacher might be forbidden to teach many things, and the only criterion of his liberty under the Constitution that I can think of is "whether, considering the end in view, the statute passes the bounds of reason and assumes the character of a merely arbitrary fiat." *Purity Extract & Tonic Co. v. Lynch* (1912). *Hebe v. Shaw* (1919). *Jacob Ruppert v. Caffey* (1920). I think I appreciate the objection to the law but it appears to me to present a question upon which men reasonably might differ and therefore I am unable to say that the Constitution . . . prevents the experiment from being tried. . . .

Notes and Queries

1. Why isn't *Meyer* a First Amendment case, rather than a liberty–due process case?

2. Justice McReynold's definition of "liberty" is wonderfully expansive. What authority does he offer for his definition? How does he know, "without a doubt," that liberty protects the right to contract, to engage in a common occupation, to acquire useful knowledge, to marry and to raise children, and to worship God? Are these "natural" rights? Are they fairly implied by the word "liberty"? Does McReynolds appeal to history? To tradition? To the intent of the Founders? To contemporary moral standards?

Consider also: Did McReynolds "interpret" the Fourteenth Amendment? Or did he simply rely upon his personal sense of what constitutes good law?

3. Why did Justice Holmes dissent? Did he disagree with the majority's definition of liberty, or with the Court's willingness to supervise the legislative process? Are the two issues related? You may wish to compare this opinion with his dissent in *Lochner* (1905).

4. In his opinion, Justice McReynolds referred to the "communalism" of Sparta and the city of speech in Plato's *Republic*, but he distinguished those types of societies from our own. "Although such measures have been deliberately approved by men of great genius their ideas touching the relation between individual and state were wholly different from those upon which our institutions rest; and it hardly will be affirmed that any Legislature could impose such restrictions upon the people of a state without doing violence to both letter and spirit of the Constitution."

What is the relationship between individuals and the state upon which our institutions rest? Where is that relationship found in the "letter" of the Constitution? Where (and how) is it found in the spirit of the Constitution?

5. As we mentioned in the introduction to this chapter, *Meyer* represents a strand of substantive due process for noneconomic liberties. Unlike *Lochner*, however, *Meyer* remains good law. As you consider the cases that follow *Meyer*, you should ask whether there are defensible constitutional reasons for the disparate fates of *Meyer* and *Lochner*.

Skinner v. Oklahoma
316 U.S. 535, 62 S. Ct. 1110, 86 L. Ed. 1655 (1942)

In 1935, the state of Oklahoma classified certain crimes, not concerning political offenses, embezzlement, or violations of tax laws or prohibition, as involving "moral turpitude." The law permitted the state to sterilize "habitual criminals," defined as those convicted three or more times for crimes involving moral turpitude. The law provided defendants with notice and a hearing before the procedure, but the hearing was limited to the question of whether the defendant could be sterilized without harm to his health. Skinner had been convicted in 1929 of armed robbery and in 1926 of stealing chickens. In 1934, he was again convicted of armed robbery. After passage of the law, Skinner was scheduled to be sterilized. He challenged the law, claiming it violated the equal protection and liberty clauses of the Fourteenth Amendment and that it constituted "cruel and unusual punishment" prohibited by the Eighth Amendment. State courts upheld the law. Opinion of the Court: *Douglas*, Black, Byrnes, Frankfurter, Murphy, Reed, Roberts. Concurring opinions: *Stone*, *Jackson*.

Mr. Justice DOUGLAS delivered the opinion of the Court.

This case touches a sensitive and important area of human rights. Oklahoma deprives certain individuals of a right which is basic to the perpetuation of a race—the right to have offspring. . . .

Several objections to the constitutionality of the Act have been pressed upon us. It is urged that the Act cannot be sustained as an exercise of the police power in view of the state of scientific authorities respecting inheritability of criminal traits. It is argued that due process is lacking because under this Act, unlike the act upheld in *Buck v. Bell*, the defendant is given no opportunity to be heard on the issue as to whether he is the probable potential parent of socially undesirable offspring. It is also suggested that the Act is penal in character and that the sterilization provided for is cruel and unusual punishment and violative of the Fourteenth Amendment. We pass those points without intimating an opinion on them, for there is a feature of the Act which clearly condemns it. That is its failure to meet the requirements of the equal protection clause of the Fourteenth Amendment.

We do not stop to point out all of the inequalities in this Act. A few examples will suffice. In Oklahoma grand larceny is a felony. Larceny is grand larceny when the property taken exceeds $20 in value. Embezzlement is punishable "in the manner prescribed for feloniously stealing property of the value of that embezzled." Hence he who embezzles property worth more than $20 is guilty of a felony. A clerk who appropriates over $20 from his employer's till and a stranger who steals the same amount are thus both guilty of felonies. If the latter repeats his act and is convicted three times, he may be sterilized. But the clerk is not subject to the pains and penalties of the Act no matter how large his embezzlements nor how frequent his convictions. A person who enters a chicken coop and steals chickens commits a felony; and he may be sterilized if he is thrice convicted. If, however, he is a bailee of the property and fraudulently appropriates it, he is an embezzler. Hence no matter how habitual his proclivities for embezzlement are and no matter how often his conviction, he may not be sterilized. Thus the nature of the two crimes is intrinsically the same and they are punishable in the same manner. . . .

It was stated in *Buck v. Bell*, supra, that the claim that state legislation violates the equal protection clause of the Fourteenth Amendment is "the usual last resort of constitutional arguments." Under our constitutional system the States in determining the reach and scope of particular legislation need not provide "abstract symmetry." They may mark and set apart the classes and types of problems according to the needs and as dictated or suggested by experience. It was in that connection that Mr. Justice Holmes, speaking for the Court in *Bain Peanut Co. v. Pinson*, stated, "We must remember that the machinery of government would not work if it were not allowed a little play in its joints." . . . Thus, if we had here only a question as to a State's classification of crimes, such as embezzlement or larceny, no substantial federal question would be raised. . . .

But the instant legislation runs afoul of the equal protection clause, though we give Oklahoma that large defer-ence which the rule of the foregoing cases requires. We are dealing here with legislation which involves one of the basic civil rights of man. Marriage and procreation are fundamental to the very existence and survival of the race. The power to sterilize, if exercised, may have subtle, far-reaching and devastating effects. In evil or reckless hands it can cause races or types which are inimical to the dominant group to wither and disappear. There is no redemption for the individual whom the law touches. Any experiment which the State conducts is to his irreparable injury. He is forever deprived of a basic liberty. We mention these matters not to reexamine the scope of the police power of the States. We advert to them merely in emphasis of our view that strict scrutiny of the classification which a State makes in a sterilization law is essential, lest unwittingly or otherwise invidious discriminations are made against groups or types of individuals in violation of the constitutional guaranty of just and equal laws. The guaranty of "equal protection of the laws is a pledge of the protection of equal laws." When the law lays an unequal hand on those who have committed intrinsically the same quality of offense and sterilizes one and not the other, it has made as an invidious a discrimination as if it had selected a particular race or nationality for oppressive treatment. [Sterilization] of those who have thrice committed grand larceny with immunity for those who are embezzlers is a clear, pointed, unmistakable discrimination. Oklahoma makes no attempt to say that he who commits larceny by trespass or trick or fraud has biologically inheritable traits which he who commits embezzlement lacks. . . . We have not the slightest basis for inferring that line has any significance in eugenics nor that the inheritability of criminal traits follows the neat legal distinctions which the law has marked between those two offenses. In terms of fines and imprisonment the crimes of larceny and embezzlement rate the same under the Oklahoma code. Only when it comes to sterilization are the pains and penalties of the law different. The equal protection clause would indeed be a formula of empty words if such conspicuously artificial lines could be drawn. In *Buck v. Bell*, the Virginia statute was upheld though it applied only to feebleminded persons in institutions of the State. But it was pointed out that "so far as the operations enable those who otherwise must be kept confined to be returned to the world, and thus open the asylum to others, the equality aimed at will be more nearly reached." Here there is no such saving feature. Embezzlers are forever free. Those who steal or take in other ways are not. . . .

Reversed.

Mr. Chief Justice STONE concurring.

I concur in the result, but I am not persuaded that we are aided in reaching it by recourse to the equal protection clause.

If Oklahoma may resort generally to the sterilization of criminals on the assumption that their propensities are transmissible to future generations by inheritance, I seriously doubt that the equal protection clause requires it to apply the measure to all criminals in the first instance, or to none.

Moreover, if we must presume that the legislature knows—what science has been unable to ascertain—that the criminal tendencies of any class of habitual offenders are transmissible regardless of the varying mental characteristics of its individuals, I should suppose that we must likewise presume that the legislature, in its wisdom, knows that the criminal tendencies of some classes of offenders are more likely to be transmitted than those of others. And so I think the real question we have to consider is not one of equal protection, but whether the wholesale condemnation of a class to such an invasion of personal liberty, without opportunity to any individual to show that his is not the type of case which would justify resort to it, satisfies the demands of due process.

There are limits to the extent to which the presumption of constitutionality can be pressed, especially where the liberty of the person is concerned (see *United States v. Carolene Products Co.*) and where the presumption is resorted to only to dispense with a procedure which the ordinary dictates of prudence would seem to demand for the protection of the individual from arbitrary action. Although petitioner here was given a hearing to ascertain whether sterilization would be detrimental to his health, he was given none to discover whether his criminal tendencies are of an inheritable type. Undoubtedly a state may, after appropriate inquiry, constitutionally interfere with the personal liberty of the individual to prevent the transmission by inheritance of his socially injurious tendencies. *Buck v. Bell.* But until now we have not been called upon to say that it may do so without giving him a hearing and opportunity to challenge the existence as to him of the only facts which could justify so drastic a measure.

Science has found and the law has recognized that there are certain types of mental deficiency associated with delinquency which are inheritable. But the State does not contend—nor can there be any pretense—that either common knowledge or experience, or scientific investigation, has given assurance that the criminal tendencies of any class of habitual offenders are universally or even generally inheritable. In such circumstances, inquiry whether such is the fact in the case of any particular individual cannot rightly be dispensed with. Whether the procedure by which a statute carries its mandate into execution satisfies due process is a matter of judicial cognizance. A law which condemns, without hearing, all the individuals of a class to so harsh a measure as the present because some or even many merit condemnation, is lacking in the first principles of due process. And so, while the state may protect itself from the demonstrably inheritable tendencies of the individual which are injurious to society, the most elementary notions of due process would seem to require it to take appropriate steps to safeguard the liberty of the individual by affording him, before he is condemned to an irreparable injury in his person, some opportunity to show that he is without such inheritable tendencies. . . .

Mr. Justice JACKSON, concurring.

I also think the present plan to sterilize the individual in pursuit of a eugenic plan to eliminate from the race characteristics that are only vaguely identified and which in our present state of knowledge are uncertain as to transmissibility presents other constitutional questions of gravity. This Court has sustained such an experiment with respect to an imbecile, a person with definite and observable characteristics where the condition had persisted through three generations and afforded grounds for the belief that it was transmissible and would continue to manifest itself in generations to come. *Buck v. Bell.*

There are limits to the extent to which a legislatively represented majority may conduct biological experiments at the expense of the dignity and personality and natural powers of a minority—even those who have been guilty of what the majority define as crimes. But this Act falls down before reaching this problem, which I mention only to avoid the implication that such a question may not exist because not discussed. On it I would also reserve judgment.

Notes and Queries

1. In *Buck v. Bell* (1927), the Court refused to invalidate a Virginia law that provided for the sterilization of mentally retarded individuals in state institutions. Carrie Buck, who had been raped by her employer's son, was sterilized. Her guardian challenged the law, claiming it violated Carrie's rights to liberty and the equal protection clause. Writing for the majority, Justice Holmes sustained the law, finding it a valid exercise of the state's police power to protect the community against the costs associ-

ated with the genetic transmission of defects. "Three generations of imbeciles are enough," concluded Holmes.

2. The Virginia and Oklahoma statutes were not unique. Early in the twentieth century many intellectuals and public officials, Justice Holmes included, favored compulsory sterilization as a public policy. See, for example, Harry Hamilton Laughlin, *Eugenical Sterilization in the United States* (Chicago: Psychopathic Laboratory of the Municipal Court of Chicago, 1922). By one estimate, more than thirty states had forced sterilization laws by the 1930s, and by 1935, there had been over 20,000 forced sterilizations in the United States, most in Virginia and in California. See, e.g, Stephen Jay Gould, *Carrie Buck's Daughter*, 2 Constitutional Commentary 331 (1985); Paul A. Lombardo, *Three Generations, No Imbeciles: New Light on Buck v. Bell*, 60 New York University Law Review 30 (1985); Clement Vose, *Constitutional Change: Politics and Supreme Court Litigation Since 1907* (Lexington, Mass: Lexington Books, 1972).

3. At first glance, *Skinner* seems difficult to reconcile with *Buck* (1927). Are the differences in result a consequence of gender? After all, Skinner was male, and his impending sterilization may have seemed to an all-male Court more serious than Buck's. Or is the difference one of constitutional strategy? Justice Holmes dismissed Buck's equal protection argument without discussion. Justice Douglas, however, relied almost exclusively on the equal protection clause, a decision criticized by Justice Stone.

Do the differences between *Buck* and *Skinner* have less to do with gender than the evolution of constitutional jurisprudence? Recall that *Buck* precedes *Carolene Products* by over 10 years, whereas *Skinner* is among the first important civil liberties cases to follow footnote four. How, if at all, did *Carolene Products* influence the Court's decision in *Skinner*?

4. If, as Justice Stone argued, the state may "constitu-

tionally interfere with the personal liberty of the individual to prevent the transmission by inheritance of his socially injurious tendencies," and if the state defines what is "socially injurious," then does the distinction between what is private and what is public disappear? How can the civil liberties of "discrete and insular" minorities be protected if the majority may intrude upon them whenever it finds certain behavior "socially injurious"? Does footnote four suggest an answer to this question?

Justice Jackson wrote: "There are limits to the extent to which a legislatively represented majority may conduct biological experiments at the expense of the dignity and personality and natural powers of a minority—even those who have been guilty of what the majority defines as crimes." What are those limits? Are they contained in the letter or the spirit of the Constitution? Or are they "a normative premise upon which Western constitutionalism is founded"? See John E. Finn, *Constitutions in Crisis: Political Violence and the Rule of Law* (New York: Oxford University Press, 1991), 36.

5. It is not uncommon for the constitutions of other democracies to state explicitly that certain values, such as respect for human dignity (at best implicit in the United States Constitution) are protected. Consider Articles 1 and 2 of the German Basic Law: Article 1(1). "The dignity of man shall be inviolable. To respect and protect it shall be the duty of all state authority." Article 2(1). "Everyone shall have the right to the free development of his personality insofar as he does not violate the rights of others or offend against the constitutional order or the moral code." Article 3 of the Italian Constitution "recognizes and guarantees the inviolable rights of man, both as an individual and in the social organizations wherein his personality is developed. . . ." Article 13 of the Japanese Constitution provides simply that "All of the people shall be respected as individuals."

Griswold v. Connecticut
381 U.S. 479, 85 S. Ct. 1678, 14 L. Ed. 2d 510 (1965)

Griswold, the Executive Director of Planned Parenthood of Connecticut, distributed contraceptives in violation of an 1879 state law. Between 1923 and 1963, more than 25 bills had been introduced in the state legislature to overturn the birth control ban, but all were defeated. She did so publicly, notifying local law enforcement officials of her action in advance. The state fined her $100. Griswold appealed, claiming the law violated her Fourteenth Amendment rights to liberty and due process. Opinion of

the Court: *Douglas*, Brennan, Clark, Goldberg, Harlan, Warren, White. Concurring opinions: *Goldberg, Harlan, White.* Dissenting opinions: *Black, Stewart.*

Mr. Justice DOUGLAS delivered the opinion of the Court.

Coming to the merits, we are met with a wide range of questions that implicate the Due Process Clause of the Fourteenth Amendment. Overtones of some arguments suggest that *Lochner v. State of New York* (1905), should be our guide. But we decline that invitation as we did in *West Coast Hotel Co. v. Parrish* (1937). We do not sit as a super-legislature to determine the wisdom, need, and

Comparative Note 11.1

[In *McGee v. Attorney General* (1974), the Irish Supreme Court ruled unconstitutional an Irish statute that prohibited the importation of contraceptives into Ireland. The plaintiff had claimed that the law violated Article 41 of the Constitution (which recognizes the family "as a moral institution possessing inalienable and imprescriptible rights) by intruding upon a private family decision affecting a married couple. She also invoked Article 44, which guarantees to every citizen freedom of conscience and the free profession and practice of religion, subject to public order and morality.]

The individual has natural and human rights over which the State has no authority; and the family, as the natural primary and fundamental unit group of society, has rights as such which the State cannot control. . . . [T]he rights of a married couple to decide how many

children, if any, they will have are matters outside the reach of positive law where the means employed to implement such decisions do not impinge upon the common good or destroy or endanger human life. . . .

In my opinion, s17 of the Act of 1935, in so far as it unreasonably restricts the availability of contraceptives for use within marriage, is inconsistent with the provisions of Article 41 of the Constitution for being an unjustified invasion of the privacy of husband and wife in their sexual relations with one another. . . .

It was submitted that social conscience, as distinct from religious conscience, falls within the ambit of Article 44. I do not think that is so. The whole context in which the question of conscience appears in Article 44 is one dealing with the exercise of religion and the free profession and practice of religion.

Source: Opinion of Justice Walsh, *McGee v. The Attorney General*, IR 284 at 298 (1974).

---

propriety of laws that touch economic problems, business affairs, or social conditions. This law, however, operates directly on an intimate relation of husband and wife and their physician's role in one aspect of that relation.

The association of people is not mentioned in the Constitution nor in the Bill of Rights. The right to educate a child in a school of the parents' choice—whether public or private or parochial—is also not mentioned. Nor is the right to study any particular subject or any foreign language. Yet the First Amendment has been construed to include certain of those rights.

By *Pierce v. Society of Sisters* (1925), the right to educate one's children as one chooses is made applicable to the States by the force of the First and Fourteenth Amendments. By *Meyer v. State of Nebraska* (1923), the same dignity is given the right to study the German language in a private school. In other words, the State may not, consistently with the spirit of the First Amendment, contract the spectrum of available knowledge. The right of freedom of speech and press includes not only the right to utter or to print, but the right to distribute, the right to receive, the right to read and freedom of inquiry, freedom of thought, and freedom to teach—indeed the freedom of the entire university community. Without those peripheral rights the specific rights would be less secure. And so we reaffirm the principle of the *Pierce* and the *Meyer* cases.

In *NAACP v. State of Alabama* (1958), we protected the

"freedom to associate and privacy in one's associations," noting that freedom of association was a peripheral First Amendment right. Disclosure of membership lists of a constitutionally valid association, we held, was invalid "as entailing the likelihood of a substantial restraint upon the exercise by petitioner's members of their right to freedom of association." Ibid. In other words, the First Amendment has a penumbra where privacy is protected from governmental intrusion. In like context, we have protected forms of "association" that are not political in the customary sense but pertain to the social, legal, and economic benefit of the members. In *Schware v. Board of Bar Examiners* (1957), we held it not permissible to bar a lawyer from practice, because he had once been a member of the Communist Party. The man's "association with that Party" was not shown to be "anything more than a political faith in a political party" and was not action of a kind proving bad moral character. . . .

Those cases involved more than the "right of assembly"—a right that extends to all irrespective of their race or idealogy. . . . The right of "association," like the right of belief (*West Virginia State Board of Education v. Barnette* [1943]), is more than the right to attend a meeting; it includes the right to express one's attitudes or philosophies by membership in a group or by affiliation with it or by other lawful means. Association in that context is a form of expression of opinion; and while it is not expressly included in the First Amendment its existence is necessary in making the express guarantees fully meaningful.

The foregoing cases suggest that specific guarantees in the Bill of Rights have penumbras, formed by emanations from those guarantees that help give them life and substance. See *Poe v. Ullman* (1961, dissenting opinion). Various guarantees create zones of privacy. The right of association contained in the penumbra of the First Amendment is one, as we have seen. The Third Amendment in its prohibition against the quartering of soldiers "in any house" in time of peace without the consent of the owner is another facet of that privacy. The Fourth Amendment explicitly affirms the "right of the people to be secure in their persons, houses, papers, and effects, against unreasonable searches and seizures." The Fifth Amendment in its Self-Incrimination Clause enables the citizen to create a zone of privacy which government may not force him to surrender to his detriment. The Ninth Amendment provides: "The enumeration in the Constitution, of certain rights, shall not be construed to deny or disparage others retained by the people."

The Fourth and Fifth Amendments were described in *Boyd v. United States* (1886), as protection against all governmental invasions "of the sanctity of a man's home and the privacies of life." We recently referred in *Mapp v. Ohio* (1961) to the Fourth Amendment as creating a "right to privacy, no less important than any other right carefully and particularly reserved to the people."

We have had many controversies over these penumbral rights of "privacy and repose." These cases bear witness that the right of privacy which presses for recognition here is a legitimate one.

The present case, then, concerns a relationship lying within the zone of privacy created by several fundamental constitutional guarantees. And it concerns a law which, in forbidding the use of contraceptives rather than regulating their manufacture or sale, seeks to achieve its goals by means having a maximum destructive impact upon that relationship. Such a law cannot stand in light of the familiar principle, so often applied by this Court, that a "governmental purpose to control or prevent activities constitutionally subject to state regulation may not be achieved by means which sweep unnecessarily broadly and thereby invade the area of protected freedoms." Would we allow the police to search the sacred precincts of marital bedrooms for telltale signs of the use of contraceptives? The very idea is repulsive to the notions of privacy surrounding the marriage relationship.

We deal with a right of privacy older than the Bill of Rights—older than our political parties, older than our school system. Marriage is a coming together for better or for worse, hopefully enduring, and intimate to the degree of being sacred. It is an association that promotes a way of life, not causes; a harmony in living, not political faiths; a bilateral loyalty, not commercial or social projects. Yet it is an association for as noble a purpose as any involved in our prior decisions.

Reversed.

Mr. Justice GOLDBERG, whom the Chief Justice and Mr. Justice BRENNAN join, concurring.

I agree with the Court that Connecticut's birth-control law unconstitutionally intrudes upon the right of marital privacy, and I join in its opinion and judgment. Although I have not accepted the view that "due process" as used in the Fourteenth Amendment includes all of the first eight Amendments, I do agree that the concept of liberty protects those personal rights that are fundamental, and is not confined to the specific terms of the Bill of Rights. My conclusion that the concept of liberty is not so restricted and that it embraces the right of marital privacy though that right is not mentioned explicitly in the Constitution is supported both by numerous decisions of this Court, referred to in the Court's opinion, and by the language and history of the Ninth Amendment. In reaching the conclusion that the right of marital privacy is protected, as being within the protected penumbra of specific guarantees of the Bill of Rights, the Court refers to the Ninth Amendment, I add these words to emphasize the relevance of that Amendment to the Court's holding.

The Court stated many years ago that the Due Process Clause protects those liberties that are "so rooted in the traditions and conscience of our people as to be ranked as fundamental." And, in *Meyer v. State of Nebraska* (1923), the Court, referring to the Fourteenth Amendment, stated: "While this court has not attempted to define with exactness the liberty thus guaranteed, the term has received much consideration and some of the included things have been definitely stated. Without doubt, it denotes not merely freedom from bodily restraint but also (for example,) the right . . . to marry, establish a home and bring up children. . . ." This Court, in a series of decisions, has held that the Fourteenth Amendment absorbs and applies to the States those specifics of the first eight amendments which express fundamental personal rights. The language and history of the Ninth Amendment reveal that the Framers of the Constitution believed that there are additional fundamental rights, protected from governmental infringement, which exist alongside those fundamental rights specifically mentioned in the first eight constitutional amendments.

The Ninth Amendment reads, "The enumeration in the

Constitution, of certain rights, shall not be construed to deny or disparage others retained by the people." The Amendment is almost entirely the work of James Madison. It was introduced in Congress by him and passed the House and Senate with little or no debate and virtually no change in language. It was proffered to quiet expressed fears that a bill of specifically enumerated rights could not be sufficiently broad to cover all essential rights and that the specific mention of certain rights would be interpreted as a denial that others were protected.

In presenting the proposed Amendment, Madison said:

It has been objected also against a bill of rights, that, by enumerating particular exceptions to the grant of power, it would disparage those rights which were not placed in that enumeration; and it might follow by implication, that those rights which were not singled out, were intended to be assigned into the hands of the General Government, and were consequently insecure. This is one of the most plausible arguments I have ever heard urged against the admission of a bill of rights into this system; but, I conceive, that it may be guarded against. I have attempted it, as gentlemen may see by turning to the last clause of the fourth resolution (the Ninth Amendment).

Mr. Justice Story wrote of this argument against a bill of rights and the meaning of the Ninth Amendment: "In regard to . . . [a] suggestion, that the affirmance of certain rights might disparage others, or might lead to argumentative implications in favor of other powers, it might be sufficient to say that such a course of reasoning could never be sustained upon any solid basis. . . . But a conclusive answer is, that such an attempt may be interdicted (as it has been) by a positive declaration in such a bill of rights that the enumeration of certain rights shall not be construed to deny or disparage others retained by the people." . . . He further stated, referring to the Ninth Amendment:

This clause was manifestly introduced to prevent any perverse or ingenious misapplication of the well known maxim, that an affirmation in particular cases implies a negation in all others; and, *e converso*, that a negation in particular cases implies an affirmation in all others. . . .

These statements of Madison and Story make clear that the Framers did not intend that the first eight amendments be construed to exhaust the basic and fundamental rights which the Constitution guaranteed to the people.

While this Court has had little occasion to interpret the Ninth Amendment, "[i]t cannot be presumed that any clause in the constitution is intended to be without effect."

Marbury v. Madison (1803). In interpreting the Constitution, "real effect should be given to all the words it uses." The Ninth Amendment to the Constitution may be regarded by some as a recent discovery and may be forgotten by others, but since 1791 it has been a basic part of the Constitution which we are sworn to uphold. To hold that a right so basic and fundamental and so deeprooted in our society as the right of privacy in marriage may be infringed because that right is not guaranteed in so many words by the first eight amendments to the Constitution is to ignore the Ninth Amendment and to give it no effect whatsoever. Moreover, a judicial construction that this fundamental right is not protected by the Constitution because it is not mentioned in explicit terms by one of the first eight amendments or elsewhere in the Constitution would violate the Ninth Amendment, which specifically states that "[t]he enumeration in the Constitution, of certain rights, shall not be *construed* to deny or disparage others retained by the people." (Emphasis added.)

A dissenting opinion suggests that my interpretation of the Ninth Amendment somehow "broaden(s) the powers of this Court." . . . With all due respect, I believe that it misses the import of what I am saying. I do not take the position of my Brother Black in his dissent in *Adamson v. People of State of California* (1947), that the entire Bill of Rights is incorporated in the Fourteenth Amendment, and I do not mean to imply that the Ninth Amendment is applied against the States by the Fourteenth. Nor do I mean to state that the Ninth Amendment constitutes an independent source of rights protected from infringement by either the States or the Federal Government. Rather, the Ninth Amendment shows a belief of the Constitution's authors that fundamental rights exist that are not expressly enumerated in the first eight amendments and an intent that the list of rights included there not be deemed exhaustive. As any student of this Court's opinions knows, this Court has held, often unanimously, that the Fifth and Fourteenth Amendments protect certain fundamental personal liberties from abridgment by the Federal Government or the States. . . . The Ninth Amendment simply shows the intent of the Constitution's authors that other fundamental personal rights should not be denied such protection or disparaged in any other way simply because they are not specifically listed in the first eight constitutional amendments. I do not see how this broadens the authority of the Court; rather it serves to support what this Court has been doing in protecting fundamental rights.

Nor am I turning somersaults with history in arguing that the Ninth Amendment is relevant in a case dealing with a State's infringement of a fundamental right. While the Ninth Amendment—and indeed the entire Bill of

Rights—originally concerned restrictions upon federal power, the subsequently enacted Fourteenth Amendment prohibits the States as well from abridging fundamental personal liberties. And, the Ninth Amendment, in indicating that not all such liberties are specifically mentioned in the first eight amendments, is surely relevant in showing the existence of other fundamental personal rights, now protected from state, as well as federal, infringement. In sum, the Ninth Amendment simply lends strong support to the view that the "liberty" protected by the Fifth and Fourteenth Amendments from infringement by the Federal Government or the States is not restricted to rights specifically mentioned in the first eight amendments.

. . . While it may shock some of my Brethren that the Court today holds that the Constitution protects the right of marital privacy, in my view it is far more shocking to believe that the personal liberty guaranteed by the Constitution does not include protection against such totalitarian limitation of family size, which is at complete variance with our constitutional concepts. Yet, if upon a showing of a slender basis of rationality, a law outlawing voluntary birth control by married persons is valid, then, by the same reasoning, a law requiring compulsory birth control also would seem to be valid. In my view, however, both types of law would unjustifiably intrude upon rights of marital privacy which are constitutionally protected.

In sum, I believe that the right of privacy in the marital relation is fundamental and basic—a personal right "retained by the people" within the meaning of the Ninth Amendment. Connecticut cannot constitutionally abridge this fundamental right, which is protected by the Fourteenth Amendment from infringement by the States. I agree with the Court that petitioners' convictions must therefore be reversed.

Mr. Justice HARLAN, concurring in the judgment.

I fully agree with the judgment of reversal, but find myself unable to join the Court's opinion. The reason is that it seems to me to evince an approach to this case very much like that taken by my Brothers Black and Stewart in dissent, namely: the Due Process Clause of the Fourteenth Amendment does not touch this Connecticut statute unless the enactment is found to violate some right assured by the letter or penumbra of the Bill of Rights.

In other words, what I find implicit in the Court's opinion is that the "incorporation" doctrine may be used to *restrict* the reach of Fourteenth Amendment Due Process. For me this is just as unacceptable constitutional doctrine as is the use of the "incorporation" approach to *impose* upon the States all the requirements of the Bill of Rights.

In my view, the proper constitutional inquiry in this case is whether this Connecticut statute infringes the Due Process Clause of the Fourteenth Amendment because the enactment violates basic values "implicit in the concept of ordered liberty," *Palko v. State of Connecticut* (1937). I believe that it does. While the relevant inquiry may be aided by resort to one or more of the provisions of the Bill of Rights, it is not dependent on them or any of their radiations. The Due Process Clause of the Fourteenth Amendment stands, in my opinion, on its own bottom.

A further observation seems in order respecting the justification of my Brothers Black and Stewart for their "incorporation" approach to this case. Their approach does not rest on historical reasons, which are of course wholly lacking, but on the thesis that by limiting the content of the Due Process Clause of the Fourteenth Amendment to the protection of rights which can be found elsewhere in the Constitution, in this instance in the Bill of Rights, judges will thus be confined to "interpretation" of specific constitutional provisions, and will thereby be restrained from introducing their own notions of constitutional right and wrong into the "vague contours of the Due Process Clause." *Rochin v. People of State of California* (1952).

. . . While I could not more heartily agree that judicial "self restraint" is an indispensable ingredient of sound constitutional adjudication, I do submit that the formula suggested for achieving it is more hollow than real. "Specific" provisions of the Constitution, no less than "due process," lend themselves as readily to "personal" interpretations by judges whose constitutional outlook is simply to keep the Constitution in supposed "tune with the times."

Judicial self-restraint will not, I suggest, be brought about in the "due process" area by the historically unfounded incorporation formula long advanced by my Brother Black, and now in part espoused by my Brother Stewart. It will be achieved in this area, as in other constitutional areas, only by continual insistence upon respect for the teachings of history, solid recognition of the basic values that underlie our society, and wise appreciation of the great roles that the doctrines of federalism and separation of powers have played in establishing and preserving American freedoms. Adherence to these principles will not, of course, obviate all constitutional differences of opinion among judges, nor should it. Their continued recognition will, however, go farther toward keeping most judges from roaming at large in the constitutional field than will the interpolation into the Constitution of an artificial and largely illusory restriction on the content of the Due Process Clause.

Mr. Justice WHITE, concurring in the judgment.

Mr. Justice BLACK, with whom Mr. Justice STEWART joins, dissenting.

I agree with my Brother Stewart's dissenting opinion. And like him I do not to any extent whatever base my view that this Connecticut law is constitutional on a belief that the law is wise or that its policy is a good one. In order that there may be no room at all to doubt why I vote as I do, I feel constrained to add that the law is every bit as offensive to me as it is my Brethren of the majority and my Brothers Harlan, White and Goldberg who, reciting reasons why it is offensive to them, hold it unconstitutional. There is no single one of the graphic and eloquent strictures and criticisms fired at the policy of this Connecticut law either by the Court's opinion or by those of my concurring Brethren to which I cannot subscribe—except their conclusion that the evil qualities they see in the law make it unconstitutional.

The Court talks about a constitutional "right of privacy" as though there is some constitutional provision or provisions forbidding any law ever to be passed which might abridge the "privacy" of individuals. But there is not. There are, of course, guarantees in certain specific constitutional provisions which are designed in part to protect privacy at certain times and places with respect to certain activities. Such, for example, is the Fourth Amendment's guarantee against "unreasonable searches and seizures." But I think it belittles that Amendment to talk about it as though it protects nothing but "privacy." To treat it that way is to give it a niggardly interpretation, not the kind of liberal reading I think any Bill of Rights provision should be given. The average man would very likely not have his feelings soothed any more by having his property seized openly than by having it seized privately and by stealth. He simply wants his property left alone. And a person can be just as much, if not more, irritated, annoyed and injured by an unceremonious public arrest by a policeman as he is by a seizure in the privacy of his office or home.

One of the most effective ways of diluting or expanding a constitutionally guaranteed right is to substitute for the crucial word or words of a constitutional guarantee another word or words, more or less flexible and more or less restricted in meaning. This fact is well illustrated by the use of the term "right of privacy" as a comprehensive substitute for the Fourth Amendment's guarantee against "unreasonable searches and seizures." "Privacy" is a broad, abstract and ambiguous concept which can easily be shrunken in meaning but which can also, on the other hand, easily be interpreted as a constitutional ban against many things other than searches and seizures. I have ex-

pressed the view many times that First Amendment freedoms, for example, have suffered from a failure of the courts to stick to the simple language of the First Amendment in construing it, instead of invoking multitudes of words substituted for those the Framers used. For these reasons I get nowhere in this case by talk about a constitutional "right of privacy" as an emanation from one or more constitutional provisions. I like my privacy as well as the next one, but I am nevertheless compelled to admit that government has a right to invade it unless prohibited by some specific constitutional provision. For these reasons I cannot agree with the Court's judgment and the reasons it gives for holding this Connecticut law unconstitutional.

My Brother Goldberg has adopted the recent discovery that the Ninth Amendment as well as the Due Process Clause can be used by this Court as authority to strike down all state legislation which this Court thinks violates "fundamental principles of liberty and justice," or is contrary to the "traditions and (collective) conscience of our people." He also states, without proof satisfactory to me, that in making decisions on this basis judges will not consider "their personal and private notions." One may ask how they can avoid considering them. Our Court certainly has no machinery with which to take a Gallup Poll. And the scientific miracles of this age have not yet produced a gadget which the Court can use to determine what traditions are rooted in the "(collective) conscience of our people." Moreover, one would certainly have to look far beyond the language of the Ninth Amendment to find that the Framers vested in this Court any such awesome veto powers over lawmaking, either by the States or by the Congress. Nor does anything in the history of the Amendment offer any support for such a shocking doctrine. The whole history of the adoption of the Constitution and Bill of Rights points the other way, and the very material quoted by my Brother Goldberg shows that the Ninth Amendment was intended to protect against the idea that "by enumerating particular exceptions to the grant of power" to the Federal Government, "those rights which were not singled out, were intended to be assigned into the hands of the General Government (the United States), and were consequently insecure." That Amendment was passed, not to broaden the powers of this Court or any other department of "the General Government," but, as every student of history knows, to assure the people that the Constitution in all its provisions was intended to limit the Federal Government to the powers granted expressly or by necessary implication. If any broad, unlimited power to hold laws unconstitutional because they offend what this Court conceives to be the "(collective) conscience of our people" is vested in this Court by the Ninth

Amendment, the Fourteenth Amendment, or any other provision of the Constitution, it was not given by the Framers, but rather has been bestowed on the Court by the Court. . . .

I realize that many good and able men have eloquently spoken and written, sometimes in rhapsodical strains, about the duty of this Court to keep the Constitution in tune with the times. The idea is that the Constitution must be changed from time to time and that this Court is charged with a duty to make those changes. For myself, I must with all deference reject that philosophy. The Constitution makers knew the need for change and provided for it. Amendments suggested by the people's elected representatives can be submitted to the people or their selected agents for ratification. That method of change was good for our Fathers, and being somewhat old fashioned I must add it is good enough for me. And so, I cannot rely on the Due Process Clause or the Ninth Amendment or any mysterious and uncertain natural law concept as a reason for striking down this state law. The Due Process Clause with an "arbitrary and capricious" or "shocking to the conscience" formula was liberally used by this Court to strike down economic legislation in the early decades of this century, threatening, many people thought, the tranquility and stability of the Nation. See, e.g., *Lochner v. State of New York* (1905). That formula, based on subjective considerations of "natural justice," is no less dangerous when used to enforce this Court's views about personal rights than those about economic rights. I had thought that we had laid that formula, as a means for striking down state legislation, to rest once and for all in cases like *West Coast Hotel Co. v. Parrish* (1937). . . .

In 1798, when this Court was asked to hold another Connecticut law unconstitutional, Justice Iredell said:

[I]t has been the policy of all the American states, which have, individually, framed their state constitutions since the revolution, and of the people of the United States, when they framed the Federal Constitution, to define with precision the objects of the legislative power, and to restrain its exercise within marked and settled boundaries. If any act of Congress, or of the Legislature of a state, violates those constitutional provisions, it is unquestionably void; though, I admit, that as the authority to declare it void is of a delicate and awful nature, the Court will never resort to that authority, but in a clear and urgent case. If, on the other hand, the Legislature of the Union, or the Legislature of any member of the Union, shall pass a law, within the general scope of their constitutional power, the Court cannot pronounce it to be void, merely because it is, in their judgment,

contrary to the principles of natural justice. The ideas of natural justice are regulated by no fixed standard: the ablest and the purest men have differed upon the subject; and all that the Court could properly say, in such an event, would be, that the Legislature (possessed of an equal right of opinion) had passed an act which, in the opinion of the judges, was inconsistent with the abstract principles of natural justice. *Calder v. Bull* (1798).

I would adhere to that constitutional philosophy in passing on this Connecticut law today. . . .

Mr. Justice STEWART, whom Mr. Justice BLACK joins, dissenting.

Since 1879 Connecticut has had on its books a law which forbids the use of contraceptives by anyone. I think this is an uncommonly silly law. As a practical matter, the law is obviously unenforceable, except in the oblique context of the present case. As a philosophical matter, I believe the use of contraceptives in the relationship of marriage should be left to personal and private choice, based upon each individual's moral, ethical, and religious beliefs. As a matter of social policy, I think professional counsel about methods of birth control should be available to all, so that each individual's choice can be meaningfully made. But we are not asked in this case to say whether we think this law is unwise, or even asinine. We are asked to hold that it violates the United States Constitution. And that I cannot do.

In the course of its opinion the Court refers to no less than six Amendments to the Constitution: the First, the Third, the Fourth, the Fifth, the Ninth, and the Fourteenth. But the Court does not say which of these Amendments, if any, it thinks is infringed by this Connecticut law.

We *are* told that the Due Process Clause of the Fourteenth Amendment is not, as such, the "guide" in this case. With that much I agree. There is no claim that this law, duly enacted by the Connecticut Legislature, is unconstitutionally vague. There is no claim that the appellants were denied any of the elements of procedural due process at their trial, so as to make their convictions constitutionally invalid. And, as the Court says, the day has long passed since the Due Process Clause was regarded as a proper instrument for determining "the wisdom, need, and propriety" of state laws. . . .

The Court also quotes the Ninth Amendment, and my Brother Goldberg's concurring opinion relies heavily upon it. But to say that the Ninth Amendment has anything to do with this case is to turn somersaults with history. The Ninth Amendment, like its companion the Tenth, which this Court held "states but a truism that all is retained which has not been surrendered," was framed by James Madison and adopted by the States simply to make clear that the adoption of the Bill of Rights did not alter the plan that the Federal Government was to be a government of express and limited powers, and that all rights and powers not delegated to it were retained by the people and the individual States. Until today no member of this Court has ever suggested that the Ninth Amendment meant anything else, and the idea that a federal court could ever use the Ninth Amendment to annul a law passed by the elected representatives of the people of the State of Connecticut would have caused James Madison no little wonder.

What provision of the Constitution, then, does make this state law invalid? The Court says it is the right of privacy "created by several fundamental constitutional guarantees." With all deference, I can find no such general right of privacy in the Bill of Rights, in any other part of the Constitution, or in any case ever before decided by this Court.

Notes and Queries

1. As noted in the introduction to this chapter, *Griswold* renewed debate over the Court's use of substantive due process. Justice Douglas insisted the Court was not following *Lochner*. How persuasive is the majority's claim that its discussion of a constitutional right to privacy is not a repetition of *Lochner v. New York*? What safeguards does the majority offer against the fear that its constitutional interpretation is little more than personal opinion? Was Justice Black correct in accusing the Court of having resuscitated the "natural law due process philosophy" that *Lochner* symbolizes? What are the differences between the majority opinion and Justice Harlan's concurrence? What are the differences between the majority opinion and Justice Goldberg's concurrence?

2. From where in the Constitution does the Court derive the right to privacy? Justice Douglas' reference to "penumbras and emanations" has been heavily criticized as too far removed from the text, as a creation of the Court, rather than a fair reading of the Constitution. Would the opinion be more or less persuasive if the Court had simply said that "privacy" is an "implied" right? For criticisms of the majority's approach, see Thomas Kauper, *Penumbras, Peripheries, Emanations, Things Fundamental and Things Forgotten*, 64 Michigan Law Review 235 (1965); John Hart Ely, *The Supreme Court, 1977 Term—Foreword: On Discovering Fundamental Values*, 92 Harvard Law Review 5 (1978); Robert H. Bork, *Neutral Principles and Some First Amendment Problems*," 47 Indiana Law Journal 1 (1971).

3. What is the significance of Justice Douglas's great emphasis on the sanctity of marriage and "the intimate relation of husband and wife"? Does this emphasis suggest that the right to privacy in *Griswold* attaches to the marital relationship, or that it is a right of marital privacy? Does it suggest that privacy is a right that attaches to "socially sanctioned" institutions? Elsewhere in the opinion, Justice Douglas referred to the "notions of privacy surrounding the marital relationship." Does this further support the claim that the right to privacy protected is marital privacy?

Does *Griswold* mark the emancipation of privacy from property rights? Or does it also suggest that privacy is tied to the home? Consider Justice Douglas' query about enforcement of the statute: "Would we allow the police to search the sacred precincts of marital bedrooms? . . ."

4. Justice Goldberg preferred to strike the Connecticut law on the basis of the Ninth Amendment. Justice Harlan, on the other hand, argued that its unconstitutionality should be premised on the due process clause. Why did they seek constitutional bases for their decisions other than "penumbras and emanations"? Do they succeed in overcoming the problems they found in the majority's analysis?

How would you interpret the phrase "retained by the people" in the Ninth Amendment? Are those rights "natural"? Or are they simply whatever additional rights are granted or recognized by the states in their own constitutions?

How did Goldberg make sense of the Ninth Amendment? Did he suggest that the right to privacy is protected by the Ninth Amendment? Or did he use it as a way "of reading" the other provisions of the Bill of Rights? Is there any meaningful difference between these two approaches?

How would Justices Black and Stewart interpret the Ninth Amendment? Doesn't the amendment outrightly reject the "plain words" method of constitutional interpretation that Justice Black embraces?

For reading on the Ninth Amendment, see Thomas McAfee, *The Original Meaning of the Ninth Amendment*, 90 Columbia Law Review 1215 (1990); Randy Barnett, *Reconceiving the Ninth Amendment*, 74 Cornell Law Review 1 (1988); Russell Caplan, *The History and Meaning of the Ninth Amendment*, 69 Virginia Law Review 223 (1983).

5. In *Eisenstadt v. Baird (1972)*, the Court was presented with an opportunity to clarify the nature of the privacy right it found in *Griswold*. Writing for the Court, Justice Brennan (who had urged Justice Douglas to concentrate on the marital relationship in *Griswold*), said that

It is true that in *Griswold* the right of privacy . . . inhered in the marital relationship. Yet the marital couple is not an independent entity with a mind and heart of its own, but an association of two individuals each with a separate intellectual and emotional make-up. If the right of privacy means anything, it is the right of the individual, married or single, to be free from unwarranted governmental intrusion into matters so fundamentally affecting a person as the decision whether to bear or beget a child.

Eisenstadt, presumably, makes clear that the right to privacy does attach to individuals, and not alone to places or relationships. Does it also limit privacy to issues surrounding contraception and procreation?

6. Consider the excerpt from the opinion by Justice Walsh in Comparative Note 11.1. In one respect it resembles the ruling in *Griswold* very closely, in that it provides a constitutional justification for a right to use contracep-tives by people in a marital relationship. Indeed, to the extent that the right affirmed is tied to constitutional language that explicitly protects "the institution of marriage," it can be viewed as a guarantee more solidly based than the right recognized by the American Supreme Court. But notice that the same opinion rejects the claim to exercise this right as an expression of individual conscience. How then, if at all, could the right to contraceptives be made applicable to an unmarried person? In *Eisenstadt v. Baird*, the American Court extended the right to married and un-married people alike, making clear that access to contra-ceptives was not to be tethered to marriage as a social institution. Do you think that this extension could have been achieved if the American Constitution, like the Irish, expressed an explicit and unambiguous endorsement of traditional marriage and family? In other words, can more be less, such that, as in this instance, the provision of fam-ily rights might be taken to limit the reach of unenumer-ated rights?

Roe v. Wade
410 U.S. 113, 93 S. Ct. 705, 35 L. Ed. 2d 147 (1973)

As one of the most restrictive abortion laws in the nation, the Texas law, passed in 1858, prohibited abortion unless it was necessary to save the life of the mother. Roe, un-married and pregnant, challenged the law. She claimed it violated her constitutional right to privacy and the equal protection clause of the Fourteenth Amendment. Opinion of the Court: *Blackmun*, Burger, Brennan, Douglas, Mar-shall, Powell, Stewart. Concurring opinions: *Burger, Douglas, Stewart*. Dissenting opinions: *Rehnquist, White*.

Mr. Justice BLACKMUN delivered the opinion of the Court.

We forthwith acknowledge our awareness of the sensitive and emotional nature of the abortion controversy, of the vigorous opposing views, even among physicians, and of the deep and seemingly absolute convictions that the sub-ject inspires. One's philosophy, one's experiences, one's exposure to the raw edges of human existence, one's reli-gious training, one's attitudes toward life and family and their values, and the moral standards one establishes and seeks to observe, are all likely to influence and to color one's thinking and conclusions about abortion. In addi-tion, population growth, pollution, poverty, and racial overtones tend to complicate and not to simplify the problem.

Our task, of course, is to resolve the issue by constitu-tional measurement, free of emotion and of predilection. We seek earnestly to do this, and, because we do, we have inquired into, and in this opinion place some emphasis upon, medical and medical-legal history and what that history reveals about man's attitudes toward the abortion procedure over the centuries. We bear in mind, too, Mr. Justice Holmes' admonition in his now-vindicated dissent in *Lochner v. New York* (1905): "[The Constitution] is made for people of fundamentally differing views, and the acci-dent of our finding certain opinions natural and familiar, or novel, and even shocking, ought not to conclude our judgment upon the question whether statutes embodying them conflict with the Constitution of the United States."

The principal thrust of appellant's attack on the Texas statutes is that they improperly invade a right, said to be possessed by the pregnant woman, to choose to terminate her pregnancy. Appellant would discover this right in the concept of personal "liberty" embodied in the Fourteenth Amendment's Due Process Clause; or in personal marital, familial, and sexual privacy said to be protected by the Bill of Rights or its penumbras, or among those rights reserved to the people by the Ninth Amendment. Before addressing this claim, we feel it desirable briefly to survey, in several aspects, the history of abortion, for such insight as that history may afford us, and then to examine the state pur-poses and interests behind the criminal abortion laws.

VI

It perhaps is not generally appreciated that the restrictive criminal abortion laws in effect in a majority of States

Comparative Note 11.2

[In this case, Germany's Federal Constitutional Court struck down a liberalized abortion statute as violative of the right "to life and the principle of human dignity.]

In interpreting Article 2 (2) [1] of the Basic Law, one must proceed from its wording: "Everyone shall have the right to life. . . ." Life in the sense of the developmental existence of a human individual begins, according to established biological-physiological findings, on the fourteenth day after conception (i.e., implantation or individuation). The developmental process thus begun is a continuous one which manifests no sharp demarcation and does not permit any precise delineation of the various developmental stages of human life. . . . Wherever human life exists, it merits human dignity; whether the subject of this dignity is conscious of it and knows how to safeguard it is not of decisive moment. . . .

No compromise is possible that would both guarantee the protection of unborn life and concede to the pregnant woman the freedom of terminating the pregnancy, because termination of pregnancy always means destruction of the prenatal life. In the ensuing balancing process, both constitutional values must be perceived in their relation to human dignity as the center of the Constitution's value system. . . .

From time immemorial it has been the task of the criminal law to protect the elementary values of community life. In the preceding passages [we] established that the life of every individual human being is among the most important legal values. The termination of a pregnancy irrevocably destroys human life that has come into being. [It] is an act of killing. . . .

[Yet] it would appear unreasonable to expect [a woman] to continue her pregnancy if the termination proves to be necessary to "avert a danger to the life" of the pregnant woman "or the danger of a grave injury to her health." In this case her own "right to life and physical inviolability" are at stake, and she cannot be expected to sacrifice it for the unborn life. In addition, the legislature may refrain from imposing penal sanctions for abortions in other cases where pregnancy would subject the woman to extraordinary burdens. . . .

SOURCE: *Abortion Case I* (1975) in Kommers, *Constitutional Jurisprudence*, 336–46.

---

today are of relatively recent vintage. Those laws, generally proscribing abortion or its attempt at any time during pregnancy except when necessary to preserve the pregnant woman's life, are not of ancient or even of common-law origin. Instead, they derive from statutory changes effected, for the most part, in the latter half of the 19th century.

1. Ancient attitudes. These are not capable of precise determination. We are told that at the time of the Persian Empire abortifacients were known and that criminal abortions were severely punished. We are also told, however, that abortion was practiced in Greek times as well as in the Roman Era, and that "it was resorted to without scruple." The Ephesian, Soranos, often described as the greatest of the ancient gynecologists, appears to have been generally opposed to Rome's prevailing free-abortion practices. He found it necessary to think first of the life of the mother, and he resorted to abortion when, upon this standard, he felt the procedure advisable. Greek and Roman law afforded little protection to the unborn. If abortion was prosecuted in some places, it seems to have been based on a concept of a violation of the father's right to his offspring. Ancient religion did not bar abortion.

2. The Hippocratic Oath. What then of the famous Oath that has stood so long as the ethical guide of the medical profession and that bears the name of the great Greek (460(?)-377(?) B.C.), who has been described as the Father of Medicine, the "wisest and the greatest practitioner of his art," and the "most important and most complete medical personality of antiquity," who dominated the medical schools of his time, and who typified the sum of the medical knowledge of the past? The Oath varies somewhat according to the particular translation, but in any translation the content is clear: "I will give no deadly medicine to anyone if asked, nor suggest any such counsel; and in like manner I will not give to a woman a pessary to produce abortion," or "I will neither give a deadly drug to anybody if asked for it, nor will I make a suggestion to this effect. Similarly, I will not give to a woman an abortive remedy."

Although the Oath is not mentioned in any of the principal briefs in this case, it represents the apex of the development of strict ethical concepts in medicine, and its influence endures to this day. Why did not the authority of Hippocrates dissuade abortion practice in his time and that of Rome? The late Dr. Edelstein provides us with a theory: The Oath was not uncontested even in Hippocrates' day; only the Pythagorean school of philosophers frowned upon the related act of suicide. Most Greek thinkers, on the other hand, commended abortion, at least prior to viability. See Plato, *Republic*, V, 461; Aristotle, *Politics*, VII, 1335b 25. For the Pythagoreans, however, it was a matter of dogma. For them the embryo was animate from the moment of conception, and abortion meant destruction of a living being. The abortion clause of the Oath, therefore, "echoes Pythagorean doctrines," and "[i]n no other stratum of Greek opinion were such views held or proposed in the same spirit of uncompromising austerity."

3. The common law. It is undisputed that at common law, abortion performed before "quickening"—the first recognizable movement of the fetus in utero, appearing usually from the 16th to the 18th week of pregnancy—was not an indictable offense. The absence of a common-law crime for pre-quickening abortion appears to have developed from a confluence of earlier philosophical, theological, and civil and canon law concepts of when life begins. These disciplines variously approached the question in terms of the point at which the embryo or fetus became "formed" or recognizably human, or in terms of when a "person" came into being, that is, infused with a "soul" or "animated." A loose consensus evolved in early English law that these events occurred at some point between conception and live birth. This was "mediate animation." Although Christian theology and the canon law came to fix the point of animation at 40 days for a male and 80 days for a female, a view that persisted until the 19th century, there was otherwise little agreement about the precise time of formation or animation. There was agreement, however, that prior to this point the fetus was to be regarded as part of the mother, and its destruction, therefore, was not homicide. Due to continued uncertainty about the precise time when animation occurred, to the lack of any empirical basis for the 40–80-day view, and perhaps to Aquinas' definition of movement as one of the two first principles of life, Bracton focused upon quickening as the critical point. The significance of quickening was echoed by later common-law scholars and found its way into the received common law in this country.

Whether abortion of a quick fetus was a felony at common law, or even a lesser crime, is still disputed. Bracton, writing early in the 13th century, thought it homicide. But the later and predominant view, following the great common-law scholars, has been that it was, at most, a lesser offense. In a frequently cited passage, Coke took the position that abortion of a woman "quick with childe" is "a great misprision, and no murder." Blackstone followed, saying that while abortion after quickening had once been considered manslaughter (though not murder), "modern

law" took a less severe view. A recent review of the common-law precedents argues, however, that those precedents contradict Coke and that even post-quickening abortion was never established as a common-law crime. This is of some importance because while most American courts ruled, in holding or dictum, that abortion of an unquickened fetus was not criminal under their received common law, others followed Coke in stating that abortion of a quick fetus was a "misprision," a term they translated to mean "misdemeanor." That their reliance on Coke on this aspect of the law was uncritical and, apparently in all the reported cases, dictum (due probably to the paucity of common-law prosecutions for post-quickening abortion), makes it now appear doubtful that abortion was ever firmly established as a common-law crime even with respect to the destruction of a quick fetus.

It is thus apparent that at common law, at the time of the adoption of our Constitution, and throughout the major portion of the 19th century, abortion was viewed with less disfavor than under most American statutes currently in effect. Phrasing it another way, a woman enjoyed a substantially broader right to terminate a pregnancy than she does in most States today. At least with respect to the early stage of pregnancy, and very possibly without such a limitation, the opportunity to make this choice was present in this country well into the 19th century. Even later, the law continued for some time to treat less punitively an abortion procured in early pregnancy. . . .

6. The position of the American Medical Association. The anti-abortion mood prevalent in this country in the late 19th century was shared by the medical profession. Indeed, the attitude of the profession may have played a significant role in the enactment of stringent criminal abortion legislation during that period.

VII

Three reasons have been advanced to explain historically the enactment of criminal abortion laws in the 19th century and to justify their continued existence. It has been argued occasionally that these laws were the product of a Victorian social concern to discourage illicit sexual conduct. Texas, however, does not advance this justification in the present case, and it appears that no court or commentator has taken the argument seriously. The appellants and *amici* contend, moreover, that this is not a proper state purpose at all and suggest that, if it were, the Texas statutes are overbroad in protecting it since the law fails to distinguish between married and unwed mothers.

A second reason is concerned with abortion as a medical procedure. When most criminal abortion laws were first enacted, the procedure was a hazardous one for the woman. This was particularly true prior to the development of antisepsis. Antiseptic techniques, of course, were based on discoveries by Lister, Pasteur, and others first announced in 1867, but were not generally accepted and employed until about the turn of the century. Abortion mortality was high. Even after 1900, and perhaps until as late as the development of antibiotics in the 1940s, standard modern techniques such as dilation and curettage were not nearly so safe as they are today. Thus, it has been argued that a State's real concern in enacting a criminal abortion law was to protect the pregnant woman, that is, to restrain her from submitting to a procedure that placed her life in serious jeopardy.

Modern medical techniques have altered this situation. Appellants and various *amici* refer to medical data indicating that abortion in early pregnancy, that is, prior to the end of the first trimester, although not without its risk, is now relatively safe. Mortality rates for women undergoing early abortions, where the procedure is legal, appear to be as low as or lower than the rates for normal childbirth. Consequently, any interest of the State in protecting the woman from an inherently hazardous procedure, except when it would be equally dangerous for her to forgo it, has largely disappeared. Of course, important state interests in the areas of health and medical standards do remain. The State has a legitimate interest in seeing to it that abortion, like any other medical procedure, is performed under circumstances that insure maximum safety for the patient. This interest obviously extends at least to the performing physician and his staff, to the facilities involved, to the availability of after-care, and to adequate provision for any complication or emergency that might arise. The prevalence of high mortality rates at illegal "abortion mills" strengthens, rather than weakens, the State's interest in regulating the conditions under which abortions are performed. Moreover, the risk to the woman increases as her pregnancy continues. Thus, the State retains a definite interest in protecting the woman's own health and safety when an abortion is proposed at a late stage of pregnancy.

The third reason is the State's interest—some phrase it in terms of duty—in protecting prenatal life. Some of the argument for this justification rests on the theory that a new human life is present from the moment of conception. The State's interest and general obligation to protect life then extends, it is argued, to prenatal life. Only when the life of the pregnant mother herself is at stake, balanced against the life she carries within her, should the interest of the embryo or fetus not prevail. Logically, of course, a legitimate state interest in this area need not stand or fall on acceptance of the belief that life begins at conception or at some other point prior to live birth. In assessing the State's interest, recognition may be given to the less rigid claim that as long as at least potential life is involved, the State may assert interests beyond the protection of the pregnant woman alone.

VIII

The Constitution does not explicitly mention any right of privacy. In a line of decisions, however, going back perhaps as far as [1891], the Court has recognized that a right of personal privacy, or a guarantee of certain areas or zones of privacy, does exist under the Constitution. In varying contexts, the Court or individual Justices have, indeed, found at least the roots of that right in the First Amendment, in the Fourth and Fifth Amendments, in the penumbras of the Bill of Rights, in the Ninth Amendment, or in the concept of liberty guaranteed by the first section of the Fourteenth Amendment. These decisions make it clear that only personal rights that can be deemed "fundamental" or "implicit in the concept of ordered liberty," are included in this guarantee of personal privacy. They also make it clear that the right has some extension to activities relating to marriage, procreation, contraception, family relationships, and child rearing and education.

This right of privacy, whether it be founded in the Fourteenth Amendment's concept of personal liberty and restrictions upon state action, as we feel it is, or, as the District Court determined, in the Ninth Amendment's reservation of rights to the people, is broad enough to encompass a woman's decision whether or not to terminate her pregnancy. The detriment that the State would impose upon the pregnant woman by denying this choice altogether is apparent. Specific and direct harm medically diagnosable even in early pregnancy may be involved. Maternity, or additional offspring, may force upon the woman a distressful life and future. Psychological harm may be imminent. Mental and physical health may be taxed by child care. There is also the distress, for all concerned, associated with the unwanted child, and there is the problem of bringing a child into a family already unable, psychologically and otherwise, to care for it. In other cases, as in this one, the additional difficulties and continuing stigma of unwed motherhood may be involved. All these are factors the woman and her responsible physician necessarily will consider in consultation.

On the basis of elements such as these, appellant and some *amici* argue that the woman's right is absolute and that she is entitled to terminate her pregnancy at whatever time, in whatever way, and for whatever reason she alone chooses. With this we do not agree. Appellant's arguments that Texas either has no valid interest at all in regulating the abortion decision, or no interest strong enough to support any limitation upon the woman's sole determination, are unpersuasive. The Court's decisions recognizing a right of privacy also acknowledge that some state regulation in areas protected by that right is appropriate. As noted above, a State may properly assert important interests in safeguarding health, in maintaining medical standards, and in protecting potential life. At some point in pregnancy, these respective interests become sufficiently compelling to sustain regulation of the factors that govern the abortion decision. The privacy right involved, therefore, cannot be said to be absolute. In fact, it is not clear to us that the claim asserted by some *amici* that one has an unlimited right to do with one's body as one pleases bears a close relationship to the right of privacy previously articulated in the Court's decisions. The Court has refused to recognize an unlimited right of this kind in the past. *Jacobson v. Massachusetts* (1905); *Buck v. Bell* (1927).

We, therefore, conclude that the right of personal privacy includes the abortion decision, but that this right is not unqualified and must be considered against important state interests in regulation.

Although the results [of lower court decisions] are divided, most of these courts have agreed that the right of privacy, however based, is broad enough to cover the abortion decision; that the right, nonetheless, is not absolute and is subject to some limitations; and that at some point the state interests as to protection of health, medical standards, and prenatal life, become dominant. We agree with this approach.

Where certain "fundamental rights" are involved, the Court has held that regulation limiting these rights may be justified only by a "compelling state interest," and that legislative enactments must be narrowly drawn to express only the legitimate state interests at stake.

A. The appellee and certain *amici* argue that the fetus is a "person" within the language and meaning of the Fourteenth Amendment. In support of this, they outline at length and in detail the well-known facts of fetal development. If this suggestion of personhood is established, the appellant's case, of course, collapses, for the fetus' right to life would then be guaranteed specifically by the Amendment. The appellant conceded as much on reargument. On the other hand, the appellee conceded on reargument that no case could be cited that holds that a fetus is a person within the meaning of the Fourteenth Amendment.

The Constitution does not define "person" in so many words. Section 1 of the Fourteenth Amendment contains three references to "person." The first, in defining "citizens," speaks of "persons born or naturalized in the United States." The word also appears both in the Due Process Clause and in the Equal Protection Clause. "Per-

son" is used in other places in the Constitution: in the listing of qualifications for Representatives and Senators, Art. I, s. 2, cl. 2, and s. 3, cl. 3; in the Apportionment Clause, Art. I, s. 2, cl. 3; in the Migration and Importation provision, Art. I, s. 9, cl. 1; in the Emolument Clause, Art, I, s. 9, cl. 8; in the Electros provisions, Art. II, s. 1, cl. 2, and the superseded cl. 3; in the provision outlining qualifications for the office of President, Art. II, s 1, cl. 5; in the Extradition provisions, Art. IV, s. 2, cl. 2, and the superseded Fugitive Slave Clause 3; and in the Fifth, Twelfth, and Twenty-second Amendments, as well as in ss. 2 and 3 of the Fourteenth Amendment. But in nearly all these instances, the use of the word is such that it has application only postnatally. None indicates, with any assurance, that it has any possible prenatal application.

All this, together with our observation . . . that throughout the major portion of the 19th century prevailing legal abortion practices were far freer than they are today, persuades us that the word "person," as used in the Fourteenth Amendment, does not include the unborn. . . . This conclusion, however, does not of itself fully answer the contentions raised by Texas, and we pass on to other considerations.

B. The pregnant woman cannot be isolated in her privacy. She carries an embryo and, later, a fetus, if one accepts the medical definitions of the developing young in the human uterus. The situation therefore is inherently different from marital intimacy, or bedroom possession of obscene material, or marriage, or procreation, or education, with which *Eisenstadt* and *Griswold, Stanley, Loving, Skinner* and *Pierce* and *Meyer* were respectively concerned. As we have intimated above, it is reasonable and appropriate for a State to decide that at some point in time another interest, that of health of the mother or that of potential human life, becomes significantly involved. The woman's privacy is no longer sole and any right of privacy she possesses must be measured accordingly.

Texas urges that, apart from the Fourteenth Amendment, life begins at conception and is present throughout pregnancy, and that, therefore, the State has a compelling interest in protecting that life from and after conception. We need not resolve the difficult question of when life begins. When those trained in the respective disciplines of medicine, philosophy, and theology are unable to arrive at any consensus, the judiciary, at this point in the development of man's knowledge, is not in a position to speculate as to the answer.

It should be sufficient to note briefly the wide divergence of thinking on this most sensitive and difficult question. . . .

X

In view of all this, we do not agree that, by adopting one theory of life, Texas may override the rights of the pregnant woman that are at stake. We repeat, however, that the State does have an important and legitimate interest in preserving and protecting the health of the pregnant woman, whether she be a resident of the State or a non-resident who seeks medical consultation and treatment there, and that it has still another important and legitimate interest in protecting the potentiality of human life. These interests are separate and distinct. Each grows in substantiality as the woman approaches term and, at a point during pregnancy, each becomes "compelling."

With respect to the State's important and legitimate interest in the health of the mother, the "compelling" point, in the light of present medical knowledge, is at approximately the end of the first trimester. This is so because of the now-established medical fact . . . that until the end of the first trimester mortality in abortion may be less than mortality in normal childbirth. It follows that, from and after this point, a State may regulate the abortion procedure to the extent that the regulation reasonably relates to the preservation and protection of maternal health. Examples of permissible state regulation in this area are requirements as to the qualifications of the person who is to perform the abortion; as to the licensure of that person; as to the facility in which the procedure is to be performed, that is, whether it must be a hospital or may be a clinic or some other place of less-than-hospital status; as to the licensing of the facility; and the like.

This means, on the other hand, that, for the period of pregnancy prior to this "compelling" point, the attending physician, in consultation with his patient, is free to determine, without regulation by the State, that, in his medical judgment, the patient's pregnancy should be terminated. If that decision is reached, the judgment may be effectuated by an abortion free of interference by the State.

With respect to the State's important and legitimate interest in potential life, the "compelling" point is at viability. This is so because the fetus then presumably has the capability of meaningful life outside the mother's womb. State regulation protective of fetal life after viability thus has both logical and biological justifications. If the State is interested in protecting fetal life after viability, it may go so far as to proscribe abortion during that period, except when it is necessary to preserve the life or health of the mother.

Measured against these standards, Art. 1196 of the Texas Penal Code, in restricting legal abortions to those "procured or attempted by medical advice for the purpose of saving the life of the mother," sweeps too broadly. The statute makes no distinction between abortions performed early in pregnancy and those performed later, and it limits to a single reason, "saving" the mother's life, the legal justification for the procedure. The statute, therefore, cannot survive the constitutional attack made upon it here.

To summarize and to repeat:

1. A state criminal abortion statute of the current Texas type, that excepts from criminality only a life-saving procedure on behalf of the mother, without regard to pregnancy stage and without recognition of the other interests involved, is violative of the Due Process Clause of the Fourteenth Amendment.

   (a) For the stage prior to approximately the end of the first trimester, the abortion decision and its effectuation must be left to the medical judgment of the pregnant woman's attending physician.

   (b) For the stage subsequent to approximately the end of the first trimester, the State, in promoting its interest in the health of the mother, may, if it chooses, regulate the abortion procedure in ways that are reasonably related to maternal health.

   (c) For the stage subsequent to viability, the State in promoting its interest in the potentiality of human life may, if it chooses, regulate, and even proscribe, abortion except where it is necessary, in appropriate medical judgment, for the preservation of the life or health of the mother.

This holding, we feel, is consistent with the relative weights of the respective interests involved, with the lessons and examples of medical and legal history, with the lenity of the common law, and with the demands of the profound problems of the present day. The decision leaves the State free to place increasing restrictions on abortion as the period of pregnancy lengthens, so long as those restrictions are tailored to the recognized state interests. The decision vindicates the right of the physician to administer medical treatment according to his professional judgment up to the points where important state interests provide compelling justifications for intervention. Up to those points, the abortion decision in all its aspects is inherently, and primarily, a medical decision, and basic responsibility for it must rest with the physician. If an individual practitioner abuses the privilege of exercising proper medical judgment, the usual remedies, judicial and intra-professional, are available.

Affirmed in part and reversed in part.

Mr. Chief Justice BURGER, concurring. . . .

Mr. Justice DOUGLAS, concurring. . . .

Mr. Justice STEWART, concurring. . . .

Mr. Justice WHITE, with whom Mr. Justice REHNQUIST joins, dissenting.

. . . I find nothing in the language or the history of the Constitution to support the Court's judgment. The Court simply fashions and announces a new constitutional right for pregnant mothers and, with scarcely any reason or authority for its action, invests that right with sufficient substance to override most existing state abortion statutes. The upshot is that the people and the legislatures of the 50 States are constitutionally disentitled to weigh the relative importance of the continued existence and development of the fetus on the one hand against a spectrum of possible impacts on the mother on the other hand. As an exercise of raw judicial power, the Court perhaps has authority to do what it does today; but in my view its judgment is an improvident and extravagant exercise of the power of judicial review. . . .

The Court apparently values the convenience of the pregnant mother more than the continued existence and development of the life or potential life which she carries. Whether or not I might agree with that marshalling of values, I can in no event join the Court's judgment because I find no constitutional warrant for imposing such an order of priorities on the people and legislatures of the States. . . . This issue, for the most part, should be left with the people and to the political processes the people have devised to govern their affairs.

Mr. Justice REHNQUIST, dissenting.

. . . I would reach a conclusion opposite to that reached by the Court. I have difficulty in concluding, as the Court does, that the right of "privacy" is involved in this case. Texas, by the statute here challenged, bars the performance of a medical abortion by a licensed physician on a plaintiff such as Roe. A transaction resulting in an operation such as this is not "private" in the ordinary usage of that word. Nor is the "privacy" that the Court finds here even a distant relative of the freedom from searches and seizures protected by the Fourth Amendment to the Constitution, which the Court has referred to as embodying a right to privacy.

If the Court means by the term "privacy" no more than that the claim of a person to be free from unwanted state regulation of consensual transactions may be a form of "liberty" protected by the Fourteenth Amendment, there is no doubt that similar claims have been upheld in our

earlier decisions on the basis of that liberty. I agree with the statement of Mr. Justice Stewart in his concurring opinion that the "liberty," against deprivation of which without due process the Fourteenth Amendment protects, embraces more than the rights found in the Bill of Rights. But that liberty is not guaranteed absolutely against deprivation, only against deprivation without due process of law. The test traditionally applied in the area of social and economic legislation is whether or not a law such as that challenged has a rational relation to a valid state objective. . . . The Due Process Clause of the Fourteenth Amendment undoubtedly does place a limit, albeit a broad one, on legislative power to enact laws such as this. If the Texas statute were to prohibit an abortion even where the mother's life is in jeopardy, I have little doubt that such a statute would lack a rational relation to a valid state objective under the test stated in *Williamson v. Lee Optical Co.* (1955). But the Court's sweeping invalidation of any restrictions on abortion during the first trimester is impossible to justify under that standard, and the conscious weighing of competing factors that the Court's opinion apparently substitutes for the established test is far more appropriate to a legislative judgment than to a judicial one.

The Court eschews the history of the Fourteenth Amendment in its reliance on the "compelling state interest" test. . . . But the Court adds a new wrinkle to this test by transposing it from the legal considerations associated with the Equal Protection Clause of the Fourteenth Amendment to this case arising under the Due Process Clause of the Fourteenth Amendment. Unless I misapprehend the consequences of this transplanting of the "compelling state interest test," the Court's opinion will accomplish the seemingly impossible feat of leaving this area of the law more confused than it found it.

While the Court's opinion quotes from the dissent of Mr. Justice Holmes in *Lochner v. New York* (1905), the result it reaches is more closely attuned to the majority opinion of Mr. Justice Peckham in that case. As in *Lochner* and similar cases applying substantive due process standards to economic and social welfare legislation, the adoption of the compelling state interest standard will inevitably require this Court to examine the legislative policies and pass on the wisdom of these policies in the very process of deciding whether a particular state interest put forward may or may not be "compelling." The decision here to break pregnancy into three distinct terms and to outline the permissible restrictions the State may impose in each one, for example, partakes more of judicial legislation than it does of a determination of the intent of the drafters of the Fourteenth Amendment.

The fact that a majority of the States reflecting, after all, the majority sentiment in those States, have had restrictions on abortions for at least a century is a strong indication, it seems to me, that the asserted right to an abortion is not "so rooted in the traditions and conscience of our people as to be ranked as fundamental." Even today, when society's views on abortion are changing, the very existence of the debate is evidence that the "right" to an abortion is not so universally accepted as the appellant would have us believe.

To reach its result, the Court necessarily has had to find within the Scope of the Fourteenth Amendment a right that was apparently completely unknown to the drafters of the Amendment. As early as 1821, the first state law dealing directly with abortion was enacted by the Connecticut Legislature. By the time of the adoption of the Fourteenth Amendment in 1868, there were at least 36 laws enacted by state or territorial legislatures limiting abortion. . . .

There apparently was no question concerning the validity of this provision or of any of the other state statutes when the Fourteenth Amendment was adopted. The only conclusion possible from this history is that the drafters did not intend to have the Fourteenth Amendment withdraw from the States the power to legislate with respect to this matter.

Notes and Queries

1. The Court's decision in *Roe* touched off a national controversy over the politics of abortion that shows no signs of abating. Similarly, *Roe* sparked a continuing debate among scholars about the legitimacy of privacy as a constitutional right and the role of the Court in the political process. Nearly a quarter century after the decision, perhaps we should reconsider why the decision is so controversial. What, precisely, does *Roe* stand for?

Is the issue in *Roe* about whether we, males and females alike, have the right to control our bodies? Is the issue whether women should be autonomous with regard to decisions they make about matters of reproduction? Or is the issue about the question of when life begins? About whether a fetus is a "person" in a constitutional sense? About patriarchy and gender discrimination? On the last, see Catharine MacKinnon, "Roe v. Wade: A Study in Male Ideology," in Jay L. Garfield, ed., *Abortion: Moral and Legal Perspectives* (Amherst, Mass.: University Of Massachusetts Press, 1984).

Alternatively, the issues in *Roe* might have more to do with the question of who bears responsibility for addressing such momentous matters. Should questions about reproductive autonomy be left solely with individuals, or

does the community (or the state) have a legitimate interest in such decisions? Is a woman's relationship with the fetus a matter over which a community ought to have some say, perhaps because such issues raise questions about the conditions of membership in the community?

As is obvious from the various opinions in *Roe* and our questions here, much of the controversy surrounding the case revolves around the role of the Supreme Court in the abortion controversy. The dissents by Justices White and Rehnquist castigate the majority for its "usurpation" of the legislative process and the powers of the people acting through their state governments. Clearly such criticisms, shared by many students of the Constitution, rest upon a particular understanding of the relationship between the democratic process and judicial protection of individual liberties. Do the opinions in *Roe* address this tension satisfactorily?

Roe also nicely illustrates how individual liberties are tied to issues of constitutional structure and architecture. Justice White, for example, complained that "The upshot [of the majority's decision] is that the people and the legislatures of the 50 States are constitutionally disentitled to weigh the relative importance of the continued existence and development of the fetus, on the one hand, against a spectrum of possible impacts on the mother, on the other hand. . . ." Implicit in Justice White's criticism is concern for the constitutional value of federalism. *Roe* essentially deprives the states of the ability to take part in a continuing public dialogue over the issues raised by abortion. Remember that prior to *Roe*, many states had already relaxed their tough anti-abortion laws. Would that trend have continued absent *Roe?* See Eric Uslander and Ronald Weber, *Public Support for Pro-Choice Abortion Policies in the Nation and States: Changes and Stability After the* Roe *and* Doe *Decisions*, 77 Michigan Law Review 1172 (1979). Instead, such dialogue is effectively superseded by *Roe*, thus foreclosing, critics argue, the possibility of a public compromise over issues of controversy.

But given the complexity of the issues, and their undeniable emotional impact, is it really possible to expect that public dialogue could reach an understanding of the issues? As you ponder this question, you may want to consider how the constitutional courts of other countries have dealt with abortion.

2. The majority stated that it could find no provision in the Constitution, or case in American constitutional jurisprudence, that treated a fetus as a "person." Is the definition of "personhood" predominantly a legal question? John Noonan, writing in *The Root and Branch of* Roe v. Wade, 63 Nebraska Law Review 668–69 (1984), noted that according to the famous legal philosopher Hans Kelsen,

a person is simply a construct of the law. . . . Personhood depends on recognition by the law. . . . There is one massive phenomenon in the history of our country that might be invoked to support Kelsen's point of view. That phenomenon is the way a very large class of human beings were treated prior to the enactment of the thirteenth and fourteenth amendments. . . . To put it bluntly, law was the medium and lawyers were the agents responsible for turning one class of beings into property.

Is Noonan's analogy to the American law of slavery an appropriate one?

3. Justice Blackmun wrote that "This right of privacy . . . is broad enough to encompass a woman's decision whether or not to terminate her pregnancy." Whether the right to privacy was broad enough to encompass such a decision was, of course, one of the central questions in *Roe*. How did Justice Blackmun justify the majority's conclusion? Did he rely on the text? Did he appeal to the intent of the Founders? To history? To the moral judgment of the community?

How would you determine whether the Constitution protects the right to an abortion? What sources would you appeal to in your effort?

4. Would we want to consult the abortion decisions of other constitutional courts? Can they help us to understand the competing constitutional values that inhere in abortion and how we might reconcile those values? Do they help us to see the implicit judgments and philosophical assumptions we make in the way we frame the issues? Do they offer insight about the nature of judicial power and the roles courts can play in settling constitutional controversies? Or are the constitutions and political cultures of other societies simply too far removed from our own to offer any guidance at all?

As we mentioned in the introduction to this chapter, two of the best known foreign decisions come from the German and Canadian Constitutional Courts. In the *German Abortion Case* (1975) (see Comparative Note 11.2 on page 596), the Federal Constitutional Court ruled that the Basic Law imposes very strict limitations upon the right to an abortion. Unlike the American Supreme Court, which was unwilling to consider the question of when life begins, the German Court determined that the fetus is "developing life," and thus must be protected under Articles 1 and 2(2) of the Basic Law. The German Court thus faced squarely the tension between the competing constitu-

tional rights of the fetus and the mother, a contest the American Court could purport to avoid. Moreover, the American and German Courts conceived of the right to "privacy" in somewhat different ways. The Supreme Court, as we have seen, stressed the highly individualistic nature of privacy, thus yielding an understanding of the right that seeks to protect the woman's right to make decisions free of unwarranted public regulation. The Federal Constitutional Court, in contrast, emphasized the extent to which all individual liberties, including privacy, take place and must be influenced by society at large.

As we have seen, one of the primary criticisms of *Roe* is its inhibition of the legislative process as a way of securing public agreement about the issues raised by abortion. In contrast, the German decision affords the legislature great, but not unlimited, discretion in formulating public policy on abortion.

In *Morgentaler v. The Queen* (1988), the Canadian Supreme Court concluded that a federal statute prohibiting most abortions (there was an exception in cases where a committee of three doctors certified that an abortion was necessary to protect the health or life of the mother) violated Section 7 of the Constitution. Section 7 provides that "everyone has the right to life, liberty and security of the person and the right not to be deprived thereof except in accordance with the principles of fundamental justice." The Court concluded that the statute violates the "security of the person" because this security includes the protection of bodily integrity.

Like the American Court, the Canadian Court thought it unnecessary to determine whether the fetus has an independent right to life under Section 7. Instead, its role was to weigh the balance struck by Parliament in seeking to protect the interest of the fetus as against the interests of the pregnant woman.

5. How does Blackmun relate *Roe* to *Griswold*? Is this connection a proper one? Why does White, who joined the majority in *Griswold*, dissent in *Roe*?

6. Why does Justice Blackmun say that the Court need not determine when life begins? Do the dissenters think the court should have tried to answer this question? Should the Court have tried to do so?

7. Is White correct in charging the majority with announcing "a new right . . . with scarcely any reason or authority for its action"?

8. Justices White and Rehnquist criticize the majority for its "usurpation" of the legislative process. On what theory of democracy does this reasoning depend? Do the opinions in *Roe* address this problem satisfactorily?

Planned Parenthood of Southeastern Pennsylvania v. Casey

505 U.S. 833, 112 S. Ct. 2791, 120 L. Ed. 2d 674 (1992)

In 1988 and 1989 Pennsylvania enacted a number of changes to its abortion law. These included requirements that there be a twenty-four-hour waiting period before all abortions, that minors receive parental consent (with a judicial bypass procedure), that all women give informed consent before the procedure took place (acknowledging information about the effects and risks of abortion), and that married women inform their husbands that they intended to have an abortion. Planned Parenthood sued in federal court, claiming these restrictions were unconstitutional and inconsistent with the ruling in *Roe*. The District Court agreed, but on appeal the Circuit Court reversed, finding all the provisions constitutional except for spousal notification.

Judgment of the Court and opinion of the Court in part: *O'Connor, Kennedy, Souter*. Concurring in the opinion in part and the judgment in part and dissenting in part: *Blackmun, Stevens*. Concurring in the judgment in part and dissenting in part: *Rehnquist*, Scalia, Thomas, White; *Scalia*, Rehnquist, Thomas, White.

Justice O'CONNOR, Justice KENNEDY and Justice SOUTER announced the judgment of the Court and delivered the opinion of the Court with respect to Parts I, II, III, V-A, V-C and VI, an opinion with respect to Part V-E in which Justice STEVENS joins, and an opinion with respect to Parts IV, V-B, V-D.

I

Liberty finds no refuge in a jurisprudence of doubt. Yet 19 years after our holding that the Constitution protects a woman's right to terminate her pregnancy in its early stages, *Roe v. Wade*, that definition of liberty is still questioned. Joining the respondents as *amicus curiae*, the United States, as it has done in five other cases in the last decade, again asks us to overrule *Roe*.

. . . [A]t oral argument in this Court, the attorney for the parties challenging the statute took the position that none of the enactments can be upheld without overruling *Roe v. Wade*. We disagree with that analysis; but we acknowledge that our decisions after *Roe* cast doubt upon the meaning and reach of its holding. Further, the Chief Justice admits that he would overrule the central holding of *Roe* and adopt the rational relationship test as the sole criterion of constitutionality. State and federal courts as well as legislatures throughout the Union must have guidance as they seek to address this subject in conformance with the Constitution. Given these premises, we find it imperative to review once more the principles that define the rights of the woman and the legitimate authority of the State respecting the termination of pregnancies by abortion procedures.

After considering the fundamental constitutional questions resolved by *Roe*, principles of institutional integrity, and the rule of *stare decisis*, we are led to conclude this: the essential holding of *Roe v. Wade* should be retained and once again reaffirmed.

It must be stated at the outset and with clarity that *Roe*'s essential holding, the holding we reaffirm, has three parts. First is a recognition of the right of the woman to choose to have an abortion before viability and to obtain it without undue interference from the State. Before viability, the State's interests are not strong enough to support a prohibition of abortion or the imposition of a substantial obstacle to the woman's effective right to elect the procedure. Second is a confirmation of the State's power to restrict abortions after fetal viability, if the law contains exceptions for pregnancies which endanger a woman's life or health. And third is the principle that the State has legitimate interests from the outset of the pregnancy in protecting the health of the woman and the life of the fetus that may become a child. These principles do not contradict one another; and we adhere to each.

II

. . . Our law affords constitutional protection to personal decisions relating to marriage, procreation, contraception, family relationships, child rearing, and education. Our cases recognize "the right of the individual, married or single, to be free from unwarranted governmental intrusion into matters so fundamentally affecting a person as the decision whether to bear or beget a child." Our precedents "have respected the private realm of family life which the state cannot enter." These matters, involving the most intimate and personal choices a person may make in a lifetime, choices central to personal dignity and autonomy, are central to the liberty protected by the Fourteenth Amendment. At the heart of liberty is the right to define one's own concept of existence, of meaning, of the universe, and of the mystery of human life. Beliefs about these matters could not define the attributes of personhood were they formed under compulsion of the State.

These considerations begin our analysis of the woman's interest in terminating her pregnancy but cannot end it, for this reason: though the abortion decision may origi-

Comparative Note 11.3

Two conflicting developments regarding the concept of humankind compels a determination of the fetus' legal capacity. Both developments alter the traditional thinking about the fetus.

On the one hand, abortion has reached a historically unprecedented magnitude, having become one of the main forms of contraception, while its associated health risks have become less significant. . . . The decriminalization of abortion has commenced. Social movements press for the total liberalization of abortion. Confronted by the practice of abortion on a mass scale . . . , the public's misgivings about the fetus' disposal are being laid to rest. . . .

On the other hand, as a result of scientific progress there is no longer a bright line separating the fetus from the "human being." Biological, and especially genetic opinions maintain that human life is a uniform progression from conception, not from birth, to death. Within this progression several stages can be distinguished, with birth not necessarily being the most important di-

viding line during the early stages of human life. The social position of the fetus also changes. It partakes increasingly of society on account of its independent physical presence and attributes, rather than on the basis of its impending social position. . . . This transformation means that the conception of the fetus as a person will become increasingly self-evident in society's consciousness.

It is the legislature who must evaluate the ethical and scientific viewpoints about the fetus, weigh the changing conceptualizations in the context of social trends opposed to such change, and decide whether these changing conceptualizations should be mirrored in the law.

But in this decision the Constitutional Court express[es] no opinion on the substantive issues surrounding abortion. . . . There is ample time for the legislature to make its determination and enact law about abortion and the legal status of the fetus.

SOURCE: *Hungarian Abortion Case* (1991), *East European Case Reporter of Constitutional Law, Vol. 1* (1994). (Den Bosch: The Netherlands, 1994), 19–20, 23, 28.

---

nate within the zone of conscience and belief, it is more than a philosophic exercise. Abortion is a unique act. It is an act fraught with consequences for others: for the woman who must live with the implications of her decision; for the persons who perform and assist in the procedure; for the spouse, family, and society which must confront the knowledge that these procedures exist, procedures some deem nothing short of an act of violence against innocent human life; and, depending on one's beliefs, for the life or potential life that is aborted. Though abortion is conduct, it does not follow that the State is entitled to proscribe it in all instances. That is because the liberty of the woman is at stake in a sense unique to the human condition and so unique to the law. . . . Her suffering is too intimate and personal for the state to insist, without more, upon its own vision of the woman's role, however dominant that vision has been in the course of our history and our culture. The destiny of the woman must be shaped to a large extent on her own conception of her spiritual imperatives and her place in society.

While we appreciate the weight of the arguments made on behalf of the State in the case before us, arguments which in their ultimate formulation conclude that *Roe*

should be overruled, the reservations any of us may have in reaffirming the central holding of *Roe* are outweighed by the explication of individual liberty we have given combined with the force of *stare decisis*. We turn now to that doctrine.

III

A

The obligation to follow precedent begins with necessity, and a contrary necessity marks its outer limit. With Cardozo, we recognize that no judicial system could do society's work if it eyed each issue afresh in every case that raised it. See B. Cardozo, *The Nature of the Judicial Process* 149 (1921). Indeed, the very concept of the rule of law underlying our own Constitution requires such continuity over time that a respect for precedent is, by definition, indispensable. . . . At the other extreme, a different necessity would make itself felt if a prior judicial ruling should come to be seen so clearly as error that its enforcement was for that very reason doomed.

Even when the decision to overrule a prior case is not, as in the rare, latter instance, virtually foreordained, it is

Comparative Note 11.4

[A new abortion law that the all-German parliament was obliged to pass after the country's unification decriminalized abortions obtained during the first three months of pregnancy by declaring such abortions as "not illegal." In its 1993 decision, the Federal Constitutional Court held that unless an abortion is "justified" by certain indications specified by law, it must be declared illegal even though the state need not criminally punish such an abortion. The Court insisted that the state adopt counseling procedures and social policies that would encourage women to carry their pregnancies to term.]

The state must impose rules of conduct to protect unborn life by means of legal obligations, prohibitions, or duties to act or refrain from acting. These rules must also apply to the protection of the unborn child from its mother, regardless of the state of this relationship of duality in unity *[Zweiheit in Einheit]*. [But] the unborn child can only be protected from its mother if the legislature prohibit an abortion and imposes a legal duty on the mother to carry the child to term. . . .

Moreover, [the state must also protect unborn life] against invasion by third parties, not the least of whom are people within the pregnant woman's family or social circle. These individuals may threaten the unborn child directly or indirectly by denying the pregnant woman the assistance they owe her, creating difficulties for her because of the pregnancy, or pressuring her to terminate the pregnancy.

These [legislatively created] rules of conduct cannot be simply voluntary; they must be imposed by law. The right to life is embodied in the norms of the Basic Law. [This right is special] and thus requires special binding rules for its effective realization. [Criminal] penalties, however, are not the only possible sanctions, although they may sway individuals to respect and obey the requirements of law.

The legislature has the responsibility of determining the nature and scope of the required protection. . . .

SOURCE: *Abortion Case II (1993)* in Kommers, *Constitutional Jurisprudence*, 351–53.

---

common wisdom that the rule of *stare decisis* is not an "inexorable command," and certainly it is not such in every constitutional case. . . . Rather, when this Court reexamines a prior holding, its judgment is customarily informed by a series of prudential and pragmatic considerations designed to test the consistency of overruling a prior decision with the ideal of the rule of law, and to gauge the respective costs of reaffirming and overruling a prior case. Thus, for example, we may ask whether the rule has proved to be intolerable simply in defying practical workability, whether the rule is subject to a kind of reliance that would lend a special hardship to the consequences of overruling and add inequity to the cost of repudiation, whether related principles of law have so far developed as to have left the old rule no more than a remnant of abandoned doctrine, or whether facts have so changed or come to be seen so differently, as to have robbed the old rule of significant application or justification.

So in this case we may inquire whether *Roe's* central rule has been found unworkable; whether the rule's limitation on state power could be removed without serious inequity to those who have relied upon it or significant damage to the stability of the society governed by the rule in question; whether the law's growth in the intervening years has left *Roe's* central rule a doctrinal anachronism discounted by society; and whether *Roe's* premises of fact have so far changed in the ensuing two decades as to render its central holding somehow irrelevant or unjustifiable in dealing with the issue it addressed.

1. Although *Roe* has engendered opposition, it has in no sense proven "unworkable," representing as it does a simple limitation beyond which a state law is unenforceable. While *Roe* has, of course, required judicial assessment of state laws affecting the exercise of the choice guaranteed against government infringement, and although the need for such review will remain as a consequence of today's decision, the required determinations fall within judicial competence.

2. The inquiry into reliance counts the cost of a rule's repudiation as it would fall on those who have relied reasonably on the rule's continued application. . . .

. . . The ability of women to participate equally in the economic and social life of the Nation has been facilitated by their ability to control their reproductive lives. The Constitution serves human values, and while the effect of reliance on *Roe* cannot be exactly measured, neither can the certain cost of overruling *Roe* for people who have ordered their thinking and living around that case be dismissed.

3. No evolution of legal principle has left *Roe*'s doctrinal footings weaker than they were in 1973. No development of constitutional law since the case was decided has implicitly or explicitly left *Roe* behind as a mere survivor of obsolete constitutional thinking. . . .

The *Roe* Court itself placed its holding in the succession of cases most prominently exemplified by *Griswold*. When it is so seen, *Roe* is clearly in no jeopardy, since subsequent constitutional developments have neither disturbed, nor do they threaten to diminish, the scope of recognized protection accorded to the liberty relating to intimate relationships, the family and decisions about whether or not to beget or bear a child. See, e.g., *Carey*; *Moore v. City of East Cleveland* (1977).

. . . [O]ne could classify *Roe* as *sui generis*. If the case is so viewed, then there clearly has been no erosion of its central determination. The original holding . . . was expressly reaffirmed by a majority of six in 1983, see *Akron v. Akron Center for Reproductive Health, Inc.* (1983) *(Akron I),* and by a majority of five in 1986, see *Thornburgh v. American College of Obstetricians and Gynecologists* (1986). . . . More recently, in *Webster v. Reproductive Health Services* (1989) . . . a majority of the Court either decided to reaffirm or declined to address the constitutional validity of the central holding of *Roe*.

4. We have seen how time has overtaken some of *Roe*'s factual assumptions: advances in maternal health care allow for abortions safe to the mother later in pregnancy than was true in 1973, and advances in neonatal care have advanced viability to a point somewhat earlier. But these facts go only to the scheme of time limits on the realization of competing interests, and the divergences from the factual premises of 1973 have no bearing on the validity of *Roe*'s central holding, that viability marks the earliest point at which the State's interest in fetal life is constitutionally adequate to justify a legislative ban on nontherapeutic abortions.

. . . The soundness or unsoundness of that constitutional judgment in no sense turns on whether viability occurs at approximately 28 weeks, as was usual at the time of *Roe*, at 23 to 24 weeks, as it sometimes does today, or at some moment even slightly earlier in pregnancy, as it may if fetal respiratory capacity can somehow be enhanced in the future. Whenever it may occur, the attainment of viability may continue to serve as the critical fact, just as it has done since *Roe* was decided; which is to say that no change in *Roe*'s factual underpin-

ning has left its central holding obsolete, and none supports an argument for overruling it.

5. The sum of the precedential inquiry to this point shows *Roe*'s underpinnings unweakened in any way affecting its central holding. While it has engendered disapproval, it has not been unworkable. An entire generation has come of age free to assume *Roe*'s concept of liberty in defining the capacity of women to act in society, and to make reproductive decisions; no erosion of principle going to liberty or personal autonomy has left *Roe*'s central holding a doctrinal remnant; *Roe* portends no developments at odds with other precedent for the analysis of personal liberty; and no changes of fact have rendered viability more or less appropriate as the point at which the balance of interests tips. Within the bounds of normal *stare decisis* analysis, then, and subject to the considerations on which it customarily turns, the stronger argument is for affirming *Roe*'s central holding, with whatever degree of personal reluctance any of us may have, not for overruling it.

B

In a less significant case, *stare decisis* analysis could, and would, stop at the point we have reached. But the sustained and widespread debate *Roe* has provoked calls for some comparison between that case and others of comparable dimension that have responded to national controversies and taken on the impress of the controversies addressed. Only two such decisional lines from the past century present themselves for examination, and in each instance the result reached by the Court accorded with the principles we apply today.

The first example is that line of cases identified with *Lochner v. New York*, which imposed substantive limitations on legislation limiting economic autonomy in favor of health and welfare regulation, adopting, in Justice Holmes' view, the theory of laissez-faire. . . . The facts upon which the earlier case had premised a constitutional resolution of social controversy had proved to be untrue, and history's demonstration of their untruth not only justified but required the new choice of constitutional principle that *West Coast Hotel* announced. Of course, it was true that the Court lost something by its misperception, or its lack of prescience, and the Court-packing crisis only magnified the loss; but the clear demonstration that the facts of economic life were different from those previously assumed warranted the repudiation of the old law.

The second comparison that 20th century history invites is with the cases employing the separate-but-equal rule for applying the Fourteenth Amendment's equal protection guarantee. They began with *Plessy v. Ferguson* (1896), holding that legislatively mandated racial segregation in public transportation works no denial of equal protection, rejecting the argument that racial separation enforced by the legal machinery of American society treats the black race as inferior. The *Plessy* Court considered "the underlying fallacy of the plaintiff's argument to consist in the assumption that the enforced separation of the two races stamps the colored race with a badge of inferiority. If this be so, it is not by reason of anything found in the act, but solely because the colored race chooses to put that construction upon it." Whether, as a matter of historical fact, the Justices in the *Plessy* majority believed this or not, this understanding of the implication of segregation was the stated justification for the Court's opinion. But this understanding of the facts and the rule it was stated to justify were repudiated in *Brown v. Board of Education* (1954). . . .

The Court in *Brown* addressed these facts of life by observing that whatever may have been the understanding in *Plessy*'s time of the power of segregation to stigmatize those who were segregated with a "badge of inferiority," it was clear by 1954 that legally sanctioned segregation had just such an effect, to the point that racially separate public educational facilities were deemed inherently unequal. Society's understanding of the facts upon which a constitutional ruling was sought in 1954 was thus fundamentally different from the basis claimed for the decision in 1896. While we think *Plessy* was wrong the day it was decided, we must also recognize that the *Plessy* Court's explanation for its decision was so clearly at odds with the facts apparent to the Court in 1954 that the decision to reexamine *Plessy* was on this ground alone not only justified but required.

West Coast Hotel and *Brown* each rested on facts, or an understanding of facts, changed from those which furnished the claimed justifications for the earlier constitutional resolutions. Each case was comprehensible as the Court's response to facts that the country could understand, or had come to understand already, but which the Court of an earlier day, as its own declarations disclosed, had not been able to perceive. As the decisions were thus comprehensible they were also defensible, not merely as the victories of one doctrinal school over another by dint of numbers (victories though they were), but as applications of constitutional principle to facts as they had not been seen by the Court before. In constitutional adjudication as elsewhere in life, changed circumstances may impose new obligations, and the thoughtful part of the Nation could accept each decision to overrule a prior case as a response to the Court's constitutional duty.

Because the case before us presents no such occasion it could be seen as no such response.

. . . Because neither the factual underpinnings of *Roe*'s central holding nor our understanding of it has changed (and because no other indication of weakened precedent has been shown) the Court could not pretend to be reexamining the prior law with any justification beyond a present doctrinal disposition to come out differently from the Court of 1973. To overrule prior law for no other reason than that would run counter to the view repeated in our cases, that a decision to overrule should rest on some special reason over and above the belief that a prior case was wrongly decided.

C

. . . The root of American governmental power is revealed most clearly in the instance of the power conferred by the Constitution upon the Judiciary of the United States and specifically upon this Court. As Americans of each succeeding generation are rightly told, the Court cannot buy support for its decisions by spending money and, except to a minor degree, it cannot independently coerce obedience to its decrees. The Court's power lies, rather, in its legitimacy, a product of substance and perception that shows itself in the people's acceptance of the Judiciary as fit to determine what the Nation's law means and to declare what it demands.

The underlying substance of this legitimacy is of course the warrant for the Court's decisions in the Constitution and the lesser sources of legal principle on which the Court draws. That substance is expressed in the Court's opinions, and our contemporary understanding is such that a decision without principled justification would be no judicial act at all. But even when justification is furnished by apposite legal principle, something more is required. Because not every conscientious claim of principled justification will be accepted as such, the justification claimed must be beyond dispute. The Court must take care to speak and act in ways that allow people to accept its decisions on the terms the Court claims for them, as grounded truly in principle, not as compromises with social and political pressures having, as such, no bearing on the principled choices that the Court is obliged to make. Thus, the Court's legitimacy depends on making legally principled decisions under circumstances in which their principled character is sufficiently plausible to be accepted by the Nation.

The need for principled action to be perceived as such is implicated to some degree whenever this, or any other appellate court, overrules a prior case. This is not to say, of course, that this Court cannot give a perfectly satisfactory explanation in most cases. People understand that some of the Constitution's language is hard to fathom and that the Court's Justices are sometimes able to perceive significant facts or to understand principles of law that eluded their predecessors and that justify departures from existing decisions. . . .

. . . Where, in the performance of its judicial duties, the Court decides a case in such a way as to resolve the sort of intensely divisive controversy reflected in *Roe* and those rare, comparable cases, its decision has a dimension that the resolution of the normal case does not carry. It is the dimension present whenever the Court's interpretation of the Constitution calls the contending sides of a national controversy to end their national division by accepting a common mandate rooted in the Constitution.

The Court is not asked to do this very often, having thus addressed the Nation only twice in our lifetime, in the decisions of *Brown* and *Roe*. But when the Court does act in this way, its decision requires an equally rare precedential force to counter the inevitable efforts to overturn it and to thwart its implementation. Some of those efforts may be mere unprincipled emotional reactions; others may proceed from principles worthy of profound respect. But whatever the premises of opposition may be, only the most convincing justification under accepted standards of precedent could suffice to demonstrate that a later decision overruling the first was anything but a surrender to political pressure, and an unjustified repudiation of the principle on which the Court staked its authority in the first instance. So to overrule under fire in the absence of the most compelling reason to reexamine a watershed decision would subvert the Court's legitimacy beyond any serious question.

. . . The promise of constancy, once given, binds its maker for as long as the power to stand by the decision survives and the understanding of the issue has not changed so fundamentally as to render the commitment obsolete. From the obligation of this promise this Court cannot and should not assume any exemption when duty requires it to decide a case in conformance with the Constitution. A willing breach of it would be nothing less than a breach of faith, and no Court that broke its faith with the people could sensibly expect credit for principle in the decision by which it did that.

It is true that diminished legitimacy may be restored, but only slowly. Unlike the political branches, a Court thus weakened could not seek to regain its position with a new mandate from the voters, and even if the Court could somehow go to the polls, the loss of its principled character could not be retrieved by the casting of so many votes. Like the character of an individual, the legitimacy of the

Court must be earned over time. So, indeed, must be the character of a Nation of people who aspire to live according to the rule of law. Their belief in themselves as such a people is not readily separable from their understanding of the Court invested with the authority to decide their constitutional cases and speak before all others for their constitutional ideals. If the Court's legitimacy should be undermined, then, so would the country be in its very ability to see itself through its constitutional ideals. The Court's concern with legitimacy is not for the sake of the Court but for the sake of the Nation to which it is responsible.

The Court's duty in the present case is clear. In 1973, it confronted the already-divisive issue of governmental power to limit personal choice to undergo abortion, for which it provided a new resolution based on the due process guaranteed by the Fourteenth Amendment. Whether or not a new social consensus is developing on that issue, its divisiveness is no less today than in 1973, and pressure to overrule the decision, like pressure to retain it, has grown only more intense. A decision to overrule *Roe*'s essential holding under the existing circumstances would address error, if error there was, at the cost of both profound and unnecessary damage to the Court's legitimacy, and to the Nation's commitment to the rule of law. It is therefore imperative to adhere to the essence of *Roe*'s original decision, and we do so today.

IV

From what we have said so far it follows that it is a constitutional liberty of the woman to have some freedom to terminate her pregnancy. We conclude that the basic decision in *Roe* was based on a constitutional analysis which we cannot now repudiate. The woman's liberty is not so unlimited, however, that from the outset the State cannot show its concern for the life of the unborn, and at a later point in fetal development the State's interest in life has sufficient force so that the right of the woman to terminate the pregnancy can be restricted. . . .

Yet it must be remembered that *Roe v. Wade* speaks with clarity in establishing not only the woman's liberty but also the State's "important and legitimate interest in potential life." That portion of the decision in *Roe* has been given too little acknowledgement and implementation by the Court in its subsequent cases. Those cases decided that any regulation touching upon the abortion decision must survive strict scrutiny, to be sustained only if drawn in narrow terms to further a compelling state interest. Not all of the cases decided under that formulation can be reconciled with the holding in *Roe* itself that the State has legitimate interests in the health of the woman and in protecting the potential life within her. In resolving this tension, we choose to rely upon *Roe*, as against the later cases.

. . . Measures aimed at ensuring that a woman's choice contemplates the consequences for the fetus do not necessarily interfere with the right recognized in *Roe*, although those measures have been found to be inconsistent with the rigid trimester framework announced in that case. A logical reading of the central holding in *Roe* itself, and a necessary reconciliation of the liberty of the woman and the interest of the State in promoting prenatal life, require, in our view, that we abandon the trimester framework as a rigid prohibition on all previability regulation aimed at the protection of fetal life. The trimester framework suffers from these basic flaws: in its formulation it misconceives the nature of the pregnant woman's interest; and in practice it undervalues the State's interest in potential life, as recognized in *Roe*.

As our jurisprudence relating to all liberties save perhaps abortion has recognized, not every law which makes a right more difficult to exercise is, *ipso facto*, an infringement of that right. . . .

. . . Numerous forms of state regulation might have the incidental effect of increasing the cost or decreasing the availability of medical care, whether for abortion or any other medical procedure. The fact that a law which serves a valid purpose, one not designed to strike at the right itself, has the incidental effect of making it more difficult or more expensive to procure an abortion cannot be enough to invalidate it. Only where state regulation imposes an undue burden on a woman's ability to make this decision does the power of the State reach into the heart of the liberty protected by the Due Process Clause. . . .

The very notion that the State has a substantial interest in potential life leads to the conclusion that not all regulations must be deemed unwarranted. Not all burdens on the right to decide whether to terminate a pregnancy will be undue. In our view, the undue burden standard is the appropriate means of reconciling the states' interest with the woman's constitutionally protected liberty.

. . . Because we set forth a standard of general application to which we intend to adhere, it is important to clarify what is meant by an undue burden. A finding of an undue burden is a shorthand for the conclusion that a state regulation has the purpose or effect of placing a substantial obstacle in the path of a woman seeking an abortion of a nonviable fetus. A statute with this purpose is invalid because the means chosen by the State to further the interest in potential life must be calculated to inform the woman's free choice, not hinder it. And a statute which, while furthering the interest in potential life or some other valid state interest, has the effect of placing a substantial obstacle in the path of a woman's choice cannot be considered a permissible means of serving its legitimate ends. . . .

. . . Regulations designed to foster the health of a woman seeking an abortion are valid if they do not constitute an undue burden.

Even when jurists reason from shared premises, some disagreement is inevitable. That is to be expected in the application of any legal standard which must accommodate life's complexity. We do not expect it to be otherwise with respect to the undue burden standard. We give this summary:

(a) To protect the central right recognized by *Roe v. Wade* while at the same time accommodating the State's profound interest in potential life, we will employ the undue burden analysis as explained in this opinion. An undue burden exists . . . if its purpose or effect is to place a substantial obstacle in the path of a woman seeking an abortion before the fetus attains viability.

(b) We reject the rigid trimester framework of *Roe v. Wade*. To promote the State's profound interest in potential life, throughout pregnancy the State may take measures to ensure that the woman's choice is informed, and measures designed to advance this interest will not be invalidated as long as their purpose is to persuade the woman to choose childbirth over abortion. These measures must not be an undue burden on the right.

(c) As with any medical procedure, the State may enact regulations to further the health or safety of a woman seeking an abortion. Unnecessary health regulations that have the purpose or effect of presenting a substantial obstacle to a woman seeking an abortion impose an undue burden on the right.

(d) Our adoption of the undue burden analysis does not disturb the central holding of *Roe v. Wade*, and we reaffirm that holding. Regardless of whether exceptions are made for particular circumstances, a State may not prohibit any woman from making the ultimate decision to terminate her pregnancy before viability.

(e) We also reaffirm *Roe's* holding that "subsequent to viability, the State in promoting its interest in the potentiality of human life may, if it chooses, regulate, and even proscribe, abortion except where it is necessary, in appropriate medical judgment, for the preservation of the life or health of the mother."

These principles control our assessment of the Pennsylvania statute, and we now turn to the issue of the validity of its challenged provisions.

V

[The Court sustained the definition of "medical emergency," the twenty-four-hour waiting period, and the parental consent requirement. The Court struck down the spousal notification requirement and the record and reporting requirement that provided for notification to a spouse.]

VI

Our Constitution is a covenant running from the first generation of Americans to us and then to future generations. It is a coherent succession. Each generation must learn anew that the Constitution's written terms embody ideas and aspirations that must survive more ages than one. We accept our responsibility not to retreat from interpreting the full meaning of the covenant in light of all of our precedents. We invoke it once again to define the freedom guaranteed by the Constitution's own promise, the promise of liberty.

Justice STEVENS, concurring in part and dissenting in part.

I

The Court is unquestionably correct in concluding that the doctrine of *stare decisis* has controlling significance in a case of this kind, notwithstanding an individual justice's concerns about the merits. The central holding of *Roe v. Wade*, has been a "part of our law" for almost two decades. It was a natural sequel to the protection of individual liberty established in *Griswold v. Connecticut*. The societal costs of overruling *Roe* at this late date would be enormous. *Roe* is an integral part of a correct understanding of both the concept of liberty and the basic equality of men and women.

II

My disagreement with the joint opinion begins with its understanding of the trimester framework established in *Roe*. Contrary to the suggestion of the joint opinion, *ante*, at 2823, it is not a "contradiction" to recognize that the State may have a legitimate interest in potential human life and, at the same time, to conclude that interest does not justify the regulation of abortion before viability (although other interests, such as maternal health, may). The fact that the State's interest is legitimate does not tell us when, if ever, that interest outweighs the pregnant woman's interest in personal liberty. It is appropriate, therefore, to consider more carefully the nature of the interests at stake.

First, it is clear that, in order to be legitimate, the State's interest must be secular; consistent with the First Amendment the State may not promote a theological or sectarian interest. Moreover, as discussed above, the state interest in potential human life is not an interest *in loco parentis*, for the fetus is not a person.

Identifying the State's interests—which the States rarely articulate with any precision—makes clear that the interest in protecting potential life is not grounded in the Constitution. It is, instead, an indirect interest supported by both humanitarian and pragmatic concerns. Many of our citizens believe that any abortion reflects an unacceptable disrespect for potential human life and that the performance of more than a million abortions each year is intolerable; many find third-trimester abortions performed when the fetus is approaching personhood particularly offensive. The State has a legitimate interest in minimizing such offense. The State may also have a broader interest in expanding the population, believing society would benefit from the services of additional productive citizens—or that the potential human lives might include the occasional Mozart or Curie. These are the kinds of concerns that comprise the State's interest in potential human life.

Justice BLACKMUN, concurring in part, concurring in the judgment in part, and dissenting in part. I join parts I, II, III, V-A, V-C, and VI of the joint opinion of Justices O'CONNOR, KENNEDY, and SOUTER

Three years ago, in *Webster v. Reproductive Health Serv.*, four Members of this Court appeared poised to "cas[t] into darkness the hopes and visions of every woman in this country" who had come to believe that the Constitution guaranteed her the right to reproductive choice. All that remained between the promise of *Roe* and the darkness of the plurality was a single, flickering flame. Decisions since *Webster* gave little reason to hope that this flame would cast much light. But now, just when so many expected the darkness to fall, the flame has grown bright.

I do not underestimate the significance of today's joint opinion. Yet I remain steadfast in my belief that the right to reproductive choice is entitled to the full protection afforded by this Court before *Webster*. And I fear for the darkness as four Justices anxiously await the single vote necessary to extinguish the light.

I

Make no mistake, the joint opinion of Justices O'Connor, Kennedy, and Souter is an act of personal courage and constitutional principle. In contrast to previous decisions in which Justices O'Connor and Kennedy postponed reconsideration of *Roe v. Wade*, the authors of the joint opinion today join Justice Stevens and me in concluding that "the essential holding of *Roe* should be retained and once again reaffirmed." In brief, five Members of this Court today recognize that "the Constitution protects a woman's right to terminate her pregnancy in its early stages."

A fervent view of individual liberty and the force of *stare decisis* have led the Court to this conclusion. Today a majority reaffirms that the Due Process Clause of the Fourteenth Amendment establishes "a realm of personal liberty which the government may not enter,"—a realm whose outer limits cannot be determined by interpretations of the Constitution that focus only on the specific practices of States at the time the Fourteenth Amendment was adopted. . . . Finally, the Court today recognizes that in the case of abortion, "the liberty of the woman is at stake in a sense unique to the human condition and so unique to the law. The mother who carries a child to full term is subject to anxieties, to physical constraints, to pain that only she must bear."

The Court's reaffirmation of *Roe*'s central holding is also based on the force of *stare decisis*. "[N]o erosion of principle going to liberty or personal autonomy has left *Roe*'s central holding a doctrinal remnant; *Roe* portends no developments at odds with other precedent for the analysis of personal liberty; and no changes of fact have rendered viability more or less appropriate as the point at which the balance of interests tips." Indeed, the Court acknowledges that *Roe*'s limitation on state power could not be removed "without serious inequity to those who have relied upon it or significant damage to the stability of the society governed by the rule in question." . . . What has happened today should serve as a model for future Justices and a warning to all who have tried to turn this Court into yet another political branch. In striking down the Pennsylvania statute's spousal notification requirement, the Court has established a framework for evaluating abortion regulations that responds to the social context of women facing issues of reproductive choice. . . . In determining the burden imposed by the challenged regulation, the Court inquires whether the regulation's "purpose or effect is to place a substantial obstacle in the path of a woman seeking an abortion before the fetus attains viability." The Court reaffirms: "The proper focus of constitutional inquiry is the group for whom the law is a restriction, not the group for whom the law is irrelevant." . . .

II. . . .

III

At long last, The Chief Justice and those who have joined him admit it. Gone are the contentions that the issue need not be (or has not been) considered. There, on the first page, for all to see, is what was expected: "We believe that *Roe* was wrongly decided, and that it can and should be overruled consistently with our traditional approach to *stare decisis* in constitutional cases." If there is much reason to applaud the advances made by the joint opinion today, there is far more to fear from The Chief Justice's opinion.

The Chief Justice's criticism of *Roe* follows from his stunted conception of individual liberty. While recognizing that the Due Process Clause protects more than simple physical liberty, he then goes on to construe this Court's personal-liberty cases as establishing only a laundry list of particular rights, rather than a principled account of how these particular rights are grounded in a more general right of privacy. This constricted view is reinforced by The Chief Justice's exclusive reliance on tradition as a source of fundamental rights. He argues that the record in favor of a right to abortion is no stronger than the record in *Michael H. v. Gerald D.* (1989), where the plurality found no fundamental right to visitation privileges by an adulterous father, or in *Bowers v. Hardwick* (1986), where the Court found no fundamental right to engage in homosexual sodomy, or in a case involving the "firing of a gun . . . into another person's body." In The Chief Justice's world, a woman considering whether to terminate a pregnancy is entitled to no more protection than adulterers, murderers, and so-called "sexual deviates." Given The Chief Justice's exclusive reliance on tradition, people using contraceptives seem the next likely candidate for his list of outcasts.

Even more shocking than The Chief Justice's cramped notion of individual liberty is his complete omission of any discussion of the effects that compelled childbirth and motherhood have on women's lives. The only expression of concern with women's health is purely instrumental— for The Chief Justice, only women's psychological health is a concern, and only to the extent that he assumes that every woman who decides to have an abortion does so without serious consideration of the moral implications of their decision. In short, The Chief Justice's view of the State's compelling interest in maternal health has less to do with health than it does with compelling women to be maternal.

Nor does The Chief Justice give any serious consideration to the doctrine of *stare decisis*. For The Chief Justice, the facts that gave rise to *Roe* are surprisingly simple: "women become pregnant, there is a point somewhere, depending on medical technology, where a fetus becomes viable, and women give birth to children." This characterization of the issue thus allows The Chief Justice quickly to discard the joint opinion's reliance argument by asserting that "reproductive planning could take . . . virtually immediate account of a decision overruling *Roe*." (internal quotations omitted).

The Chief Justice's narrow conception of individual liberty and *stare decisis* leads him to propose the same standard of review proposed by the plurality in *Webster*. "States may regulate abortion procedures in ways rationally related to a legitimate state interest. . . ." The Chief Justice then further weakens the test by providing an insurmountable requirement for facial challenges: petitioners must "show that no set of circumstances exists under which the [provision] would be valid." . . .

But, we are reassured, there is always the protection of the democratic process. While there is much to be praised about our democracy, our country since its founding has recognized that there are certain fundamental liberties that are not to be left to the whims of an election. A woman's right to reproductive choice is one of those fundamental liberties. Accordingly, that liberty need not seek refuge at the ballot box.

IV

In one sense, the Court's approach is worlds apart from that of The Chief Justice and Justice Scalia. And yet, in another sense, the distance between the two approaches is short—the distance is but a single vote.

I am 83 years old. I cannot remain on this Court forever, and when I do step down, the confirmation process for my successor well may focus on the issue before us today. That, I regret, may be exactly where the choice between the two worlds will be made.

Chief Justice REHNQUIST, with whom Justice WHITE, Justice SCALIA, and Justice THOMAS join, concurring in the judgment in part and dissenting in part.

The joint opinion, following its newly-minted variation on *stare decisis*, retains the outer shell of *Roe v. Wade*, but beats a wholesale retreat from the substance of that case. We believe that *Roe* was wrongly decided, and that it can and should be overruled consistently with our traditional approach to *stare decisis* in constitutional cases. We would adopt the approach of the plurality in *Webster v. Reproductive Health Services,* and uphold the challenged provisions of the Pennsylvania statute in their entirety.

I

. . . Unfortunately for those who must apply this Court's decisions, the reexamination undertaken today leaves the Court no less divided than beforehand. Although they reject the trimester framework that formed the underpinning of *Roe*, Justices O'Connor, Kennedy, and Souter adopt a revised undue burden standard to analyze the challenged regulations. We conclude, however, that such an outcome is an unjustified constitutional compromise, one which leaves the Court in a position to closely scrutinize all types of abortion regulations despite the fact that it lacks the power to do so under the Constitution.*

II

The joint opinion of Justices O'Connor, Kennedy, and Souter cannot bring itself to say that *Roe* was correct as an original matter, but the authors are of the view that "the immediate question is not the soundness of *Roe*'s resolution of the issue, but the precedential force that must be accorded to its holding." Instead of claiming that *Roe* was correct as a matter of original constitutional interpretation, the opinion therefore contains an elaborate discussion of *stare decisis*. . . .

. . . Whatever the "central holding" of *Roe* that is left after the joint opinion finishes dissecting it is surely not the result of that principle. While purporting to adhere to precedent, the joint opinion instead revises it. *Roe* continues to exist, but only in the way a storefront on a western movie set exists: a mere facade to give the illusion of reality. . . .

In our view, authentic principles of *stare decisis* do not require that any portion of the reasoning in *Roe* be kept intact. "*Stare decisis* is not . . . a universal, inexorable command," especially in cases involving the interpretation of the Federal Constitution. Erroneous decisions in such constitutional cases are uniquely durable because correction through legislative action, save for constitutional amendment, is impossible. It is therefore our duty to reconsider constitutional interpretations that "depar[t] from a proper understanding" of the Constitution. . . .

But the joint opinion goes on to state that when the Court "resolve[s] the sort of intensely divisive controversy reflected in *Roe* and those rare, comparable cases," its decision is exempt from reconsideration under established principles of *stare decisis*. . . . This is truly a novel principle, one which is contrary to both the Court's historical practice and to the Court's traditional willingness to toler-

---

*Two years after *Roe*, the West German constitutional court, by contrast, struck down a law liberalizing access to abortion on the grounds that life developing within the womb is constitutionally protected. Judgment of February 25, 1975, 39 BVerfGE 1 (translated in Jonas & Gorby, *West German Abortion Decision: A Contrast to* Roe v. Wade, 9 J. Marshall J.Prac. & Proc. 605 (1976)). In 1988, the Canadian Supreme Court followed reasoning similar to that of *Roe* in striking down a law which restricted abortion. *Morgentaler v. Queen*, 1 S.C.R. 30, 44 D.L.R. 4th 385 (1988). [Footnote by the Court]

ate criticism of its opinions. Under this principle, when the Court has ruled on a divisive issue, it is apparently prevented from overruling that decision for the sole reason that it was incorrect, *unless opposition to the original decision has died away.*

The first difficulty with this principle lies in its assumption that cases which are "intensely divisive" can be readily distinguished from those that are not. . . . In addition, because the Court's duty is to ignore public opinion on issues that come before it, its members are in perhaps the worst position to judge whether a decision divides the Nation deeply enough to justify such uncommon protection. . . .

. . . The Judicial Branch derives its legitimacy, not from following public opinion, but from deciding by its best lights whether legislative enactments of the popular branches of Government comport with the Constitution. The doctrine of *stare decisis* is an adjunct of this duty, and should be no more subject to the vagaries of public opinion than is the basic judicial task.

. . . The decision in *Roe* has engendered large demonstrations, including repeated marches on this Court and on Congress, both in opposition to and in support of that opinion. A decision either way on *Roe* can therefore be perceived as favoring one group or the other. But this perceived dilemma arises only if one assumes, as the joint opinion does, that the Court should make its decisions with a view toward speculative public perceptions. . . .

IV

For the reasons stated, we therefore would hold that each of the challenged provisions of the Pennsylvania statute is consistent with the Constitution. It bears emphasis that our conclusion in this regard does not carry with it any necessary approval of these regulations. Our task is, as always, to decide only whether the challenged provisions of a law comport with the United States Constitution. If, as we believe, these do, their wisdom as a matter of public policy is for the people of Pennsylvania to decide.

Justice SCALIA, with whom THE CHIEF JUSTICE, Justice WHITE, and Justice THOMAS join, concurring in the judgment in part and dissenting in part.

My views on this matter are unchanged. . . . The States may, if they wish, permit abortion-on-demand, but the Constitution does not require them to do so. The permissibility of abortion, and the limitations upon it, are to be resolved like most important questions in our democracy: by citizens trying to persuade one another and then voting. As the Court acknowledges, "where reasonable people disagree the government can adopt one position or

the other." The Court is correct in adding the qualification that this "assumes a state of affairs in which the choice does not intrude upon a protected liberty,"—but the crucial part of that qualification is the penultimate word. A State's choice between two positions on which reasonable people can disagree is constitutional even when (as is often the case) it intrudes upon a "liberty" in the absolute sense. Laws against bigamy, for example—which entire societies of reasonable people disagree with—intrude upon men and women's liberty to marry and live with one another. But bigamy happens not to be a liberty specially "protected" by the Constitution.

That is, quite simply, the issue in this case: not whether the power of a woman to abort her unborn child is a "liberty" in the absolute sense; or even whether it is a liberty of great importance to many women. Of course it is both. The issue is whether it is a liberty protected by the Constitution of the United States. I am sure it is not. I reach that conclusion not because of anything so exalted as my views concerning the "concept of existence, of meaning, of the universe, and of the mystery of human life." Rather, I reach it for the same reason I reach the conclusion that bigamy is not constitutionally protected—because of two simple facts: (1) the Constitution says absolutely nothing about it, and (2) the longstanding traditions of American society have permitted it to be legally proscribed.

The ultimately standardless nature of the "undue burden" inquiry is a reflection of the underlying fact that the concept has no principled or coherent legal basis. As The Chief Justice points out, *Roe's* strict-scrutiny standard "at least had a recognized basis in constitutional law at the time *Roe* was decided," while "[t]he same cannot be said for the 'undue burden' standard, which is created largely out of whole cloth by the authors of the joint opinion." The joint opinion is flatly wrong in asserting that "our jurisprudence relating to all liberties save perhaps abortion has recognized" the permissibility of laws that do not impose an "undue burden."

To the extent that I can discern *any* meaningful content in the "undue burden" standard as applied in the joint opinion, it appears to be that a State may not regulate abortion in such a way as to reduce significantly its incidence. . . . The imperial judiciary lives. It is instructive to compare the Nietzschean vision of us unelected, life-termed judges—leading a Volk who will be "tested by following," and whose very "belief in themselves" is mystically bound up in their "understanding" of a Court that "speak[s] before all others for their constitutional ideals"—with the somewhat more modest role envisioned for these lawyers by the Founders. . . .

I cannot agree with, indeed I am appalled by, the

Court's suggestion that the decision whether to stand by an erroneous constitutional decision must be strongly influenced—against overruling, no less—by the substantial and continuing public opposition the decision has generated. The Court's judgment that any other course would "subvert the Court's legitimacy" must be another consequence of reading the error-filled history book that described the deeply divided country brought together by *Roe*. In my history-book, the Court was covered with dishonor and deprived of legitimacy by *Dred Scott v. Sandford* (1856), an erroneous (and widely opposed) opinion that it did not abandon, rather than by *West Coast Hotel Co. v. Parrish*, which produced the famous "switch in time" from the Court's erroneous (and widely opposed) constitutional opposition to the social measures of the New Deal. (Both *Dred Scott* and one line of the cases resisting the New Deal rested upon the concept of "substantive due process" that the Court praises and employs today. Indeed, *Dred Scott* was "very possibly the first application of substantive due process in the Supreme Court, the original precedent for *Lochner v. New York* and *Roe v. Wade*." (D. Currie, *The Constitution in the Supreme Court* 271 [1985]) [footnotes omitted].)

But whether it would "subvert the Court's legitimacy" or not, the notion that we would decide a case differently from the way we otherwise would have in order to show that we can stand firm against public disapproval is frightening. It is a bad enough idea, even in the head of someone like me, who believes that the text of the Constitution, and our traditions, say what they say and there is no fiddling with them. But when it is in the mind of a Court that believes the Constitution has an evolving meaning, that the Ninth Amendment's reference to "othe[r]" rights is not a disclaimer, but a charter for action, and that the function of this Court is to "speak before all others for [the people's] constitutional ideals" unrestrained by meaningful text or tradition—then the notion that the Court must adhere to a decision for as long as the decision faces "great opposition" and the Court is "under fire" acquires a character of almost czarist arrogance. We are offended by these marchers who descend upon us, every year on the anniversary of *Roe*, to protest our saying that the Constitution requires what our society has never thought the Constitution requires. These people who refuse to be "tested by following" must be taught a lesson. We have no Cossacks, but at least we can stubbornly refuse to abandon an erroneous opinion that we might otherwise change—to show how little they intimidate us.

In truth, I am as distressed as the Court is—and expressed my distress several years ago,—about the "political pressure" directed to the Court: the marches, the mail,

the protests aimed at inducing us to change our opinions. How upsetting it is, that so many of our citizens (good people, not lawless ones, on both sides of this abortion issue, and on various sides of other issues as well) think that we Justices should properly take into account their views, as though we were engaged not in ascertaining an objective law but in determining some kind of social consensus. The Court would profit, I think, from giving less attention to the fact of this distressing phenomenon, and more attention to the cause of it. That cause permeates today's opinion: a new mode of constitutional adjudication that relies not upon text and traditional practice to determine the law, but upon what the Court calls "reasoned judgment," which turns out to be nothing but philosophical predilection and moral intuition. All manner of "liberties," the Court tells us, inhere in the Constitution and are enforceable by this Court—not just those mentioned in the text or established in the traditions of our society. Why even the Ninth Amendment—which says only that "[t]he enumeration in the Constitution of certain rights shall not be construed to deny or disparage others retained by the people"—is, despite our contrary understanding for almost 200 years, a literally boundless source of additional, unnamed, unhinted-at "rights," definable and enforceable by us, through "reasoned judgment."

What makes all this relevant to the bothersome application of "political pressure" against the Court are the twin facts that the American people love democracy and the American people are not fools. As long as this Court thought (and the people thought) that we Justices were doing essentially lawyers' work up here—reading text and discerning our society's traditional understanding of that text—the public pretty much left us alone. Texts and traditions are facts to study, not convictions to demonstrate about. But if in reality our process of constitutional adjudication consists primarily of making value judgments; if we can ignore a long and clear tradition clarifying an ambiguous text . . . ; if, as I say, our pronouncement of constitutional law rests primarily on value judgments, then a free and intelligent people's attitude towards us can be expected to be (ought to be) quite different. The people know that their value judgments are quite as good as those taught in any law school—maybe better. If, indeed, the "liberties" protected by the Constitution are, as the Court says, undefined and unbounded, then the people should demonstrate, to protest that we do not implement their values instead of ours. Not only that, but confirmation hearings for new Justices should deteriorate into question-and-answer sessions in which Senators go through a list of their constituents' most favored and most disfavored alleged constitutional rights, and seek the nominee's commitment to support or oppose them. Value judgments, after all, should be voted on, not dictated; and if our Constitution has somehow accidently committed them to the Supreme Court, at least we can have a sort of plebiscite each time a new nominee to that body is put forward. Justice Blackmun not only regards this prospect with equanimity, he solicits it.

There is a poignant aspect to today's opinion. Its length, and what might be called its epic tone, suggest that its authors believe they are bringing to an end a troublesome era in the history of our Nation and of our Court. . . .

. . . Quite to the contrary, by foreclosing all democratic outlet for the deep passions this issue arouses, by banishing the issue from the political forum that gives all participants, even the losers, the satisfaction of a fair hearing and an honest fight, by continuing the imposition of a rigid national rule instead of allowing for regional differences, the Court merely prolongs and intensifies the anguish.

We should get out of this area, where we have no right to be, and where we do neither ourselves nor the country any good by remaining.

Notes and Queries

1. What is the significance of Justice O'Connor's characterization of the right to an abortion as a "significant liberty interest," and not as a fundamental right? Is it true that her opinion leaves the "essential holding of *Roe v. Wade* . . . retained and once again reaffirmed"? Or is the Chief Justice correct in his assessment that under the plurality opinion, "*Roe* continues to exist, but only in the way a storefront on a western movie set exists. . . ."?

2. The plurality wrote that "At the heart of liberty is the right to define one's own concept of existence, of meaning, of the universe, and of the mystery of human life. Beliefs about these matters could not define the attributes of personhood were they formed under the compulsion of the State." What understanding of the relationship between individual liberty and community animates these remarks? What conception of human personality underlies them? Does the plurality mean to suggest that the State—or the community—have no legitimate interest in the constitution of human personality?

3. *Casey* illustrates the interplay between methods of

constitutional interpretation and conceptions of judicial power. Does respect for precedent imply an expansive or a limited role for the Court, or does it depend upon the nature of the controversy involved? Is it appropriate for a Court to let concern for its own authority and legitimacy influence how it interprets the Constitution? How do the joint opinions and the dissents understand and utilize "tradition" as a way of interpreting the Constitution?

Does the Court's power reside "in its legitimacy," as the plurality wrote? Is that legitimacy solely or even primarily found in "principled justification," as grounded "truly in principle, not as compromises with social and political pressures having, as such, no bearing on the principled choices the Court is obliged to make"? Does *Roe* satisfy this test of legitimacy? Does *Casey*? How would you respond to Justice Scalia's remark that "whether it would 'subvert the Court's legitimacy' or not, the notion that we would decide a case differently from the way we otherwise would have in order to show that we can stand firm against public disapproval is frightening"?

Justices O'Connor and Rehnquist, for example, ground judicial legitimacy, and respect for precedent, in very different sources. O'Connor points to "reliance" and "workability" as major considerations. Are these appropriate considerations? Should our definition of the Constitution bow to what works? Why or why not? Justice Rehnquist, in contrast, argues that "The Judicial Branch derives its legitimacy, not from following public opinion, but from deciding by its best lights whether legislative enactments of the popular branches . . . comport with the Constitution." What does it mean to say something does or does not "comport" with the Constitution?

Which of these arguments is most persuasive, and why?

4. What are the implications of *Casey* for the role of the Court in overseeing the politics of abortion? Did the Court expand its supervisory role over state efforts to regulate abortion, or did it retreat?

Consider also the questions *Casey* raises concerning the proper extent of judicial power in a constitutional democracy, questions we raised earlier in chapter 3. Is *Casey* an even more expansive use of judicial power than *Roe*?

5. Which state restrictions did the Court uphold as consistent with *Roe*? What was the Court's reasoning? Is it significant that all the justices could concur with some part of the plurality opinion?

Stenberg v. Carhart

530 U.S. 914 (2000)

In 1999, the State of Nebraska passed a statute that banned "partial birth abortions," unless necessary to save the life of the mother. The statute defined a partial birth abortion as a "procedure in which the person performing the abortion partially delivers vaginally a living unborn child before killing the unborn child. . . ." The law made the crime a felony and provided for the automatic revocation of a convicted doctor's state license to practice medicine. Dr. Leroy Carhart, a physician who performed abortions, challenged the law.

This decision was handed down on the same day as *Hill v. Colorado*, a decision involving a Colorado statute aimed at curbing the activities of protesters outside of abortion clinics. Though the cases both have the abortion debate as a backdrop, they involve different constitutional questions. Still, in *Hill* Justices Kennedy and Scalia, particularly Kennedy, direct their attention to the opinions in *Stenberg* and *Casey*. It would be worthwhile to skip ahead to *Hill* and consider the dissents in light of the *Stenberg* decision.

Opinion of the Court: *Breyer*, Stevens, O'Connor, Souter, Ginsburg. Concurring opinions: Stevens; O'Connor; Ginsburg. Dissenting opinions: *Rhenquist*; *Scalia*; *Kennedy*, Rhenquist; *Thomas*, Rhenquist, Scalia.

Justice BREYER delivered the opinion of the Court.

We again consider the right to an abortion. We understand the controversial nature of the problem. Millions of Americans believe that life begins at conception and consequently that an abortion is akin to causing the death of an innocent child; they recoil at the thought of a law that would permit it. Other millions fear that a law that forbids abortion would condemn many American women to lives that lack dignity, depriving them of equal liberty and leading those with least resources to undergo illegal abortions with the attendant risks of death and suffering. Taking account of these virtually irreconcilable points of view, aware that constitutional law must govern a society whose different members sincerely hold directly opposing views, and considering the matter in light of the Constitution's guarantees of fundamental individual liberty, this Court, in the course of a generation, has determined and then redetermined that the Constitution offers basic protection to the woman's right to choose. *Roe v. Wade* (1973); *Planned Parenthood of Southeastern Pa. v. Casey* (1992). We shall not revisit those legal principles. Rather, we apply them to the circumstances of this case.

Three established principles determine the issue before us. We shall set them forth in the language of the joint opinion in *Casey*. First, before "viability . . . the woman has a right to choose to terminate her pregnancy."

Second, "a law designed to further the State's interest in fetal life which imposes an undue burden on the woman's decision before fetal viability" is unconstitutional. An "undue burden is . . . shorthand for the conclusion that a state regulation has the purpose or effect of placing a substantial obstacle in the path of a woman seeking an abortion of a nonviable fetus."

Third, "subsequent to viability, the State in promoting its interest in the potentiality of human life may, if it chooses, regulate, and even proscribe, abortion except where it is necessary, in appropriate medical judgment, for the preservation of the life or health of the mother." (quoting *Roe v. Wade*).

We apply these principles to a Nebraska law banning "partial birth abortion." The statute reads as follows:

"No partial birth abortion shall be performed in this state, unless such procedure is necessary to save the life of the mother whose life is endangered by a physical disorder, physical illness, or physical injury, including a life-endangering physical condition caused by or arising from the pregnancy itself

The statute defines "partial birth abortion" as: "an abortion procedure in which the person performing the abortion partially delivers vaginally a living unborn child before killing the unborn child and completing the delivery."

It further defines "partially delivers vaginally a living unborn child before killing the unborn child" to mean "deliberately and intentionally delivering into the vagina a living unborn child, or a substantial portion thereof, for the purpose of performing a procedure that the person performing such procedure knows will kill the unborn child and does kill the unborn child."

· · ·

II

The question before us is whether Nebraska's statute, making criminal the performance of a "partial birth abortion," violates the Federal Constitution, as interpreted in *Planned Parenthood of Southeastern Pa. v. Casey* (1992), and *Roe v. Wade* (1973). We conclude that it does for at least two independent reasons. First, the law lacks any exception "for the preservation of the . . . health of the mother." *Casey.* Second, it "imposes an undue burden on a woman's ability" to choose a D&E abortion, thereby unduly burdening the right to choose abortion itself. *Ibid.* We shall discuss each of these reasons in turn.

A

The *Casey* joint opinion reiterated what the Court held in *Roe;* that "subsequent to viability, the State in promoting its interest in the potentiality of human life may, if it chooses, regulate, and even proscribe, abortion *except where it is necessary, in appropriate medical judgment, for the preservation of the life or health of the mother.*"

The fact that Nebraska's law applies both pre- and post-viability aggravates the constitutional problem presented. The State's interest in regulating abortion previability is considerably weaker than postviability. Since the law requires a health exception in order to validate even a post-viability abortion regulation, it at a minimum requires the same in respect to previability regulation.

The quoted standard also depends on the state regulations "promoting [the State's] interest in the potentiality of human life." The Nebraska law, of course, does not directly further an interest "in the potentiality of human life" by saving the fetus in question from destruction, as it regulates only a *method* of performing abortion. Nebraska describes its interests differently. It says the law "show[s] concern for the life of the unborn," "prevent[s] cruelty to partially born children," and "preserve[s] the integrity of the medical profession." Brief for Petitioners. But we cannot see how the interest-related differences could make any difference to the question at hand, namely, the application of the "health" requirement.

Consequently, the governing standard requires an exception "where it is necessary, in appropriate medical judgment for the preservation of the life or health of the mother," *Casey,* for this Court has made clear that a State may promote but not endanger a woman's health when it regulates the methods of abortion. *Thornburgh v. American College of Obstetricians and Gynecologists* (1986); *Colautti v. Franklin* (1979); *Danforth; Doe v. Bolton* (1973).

Justice Thomas says that the cases just cited limit this principle to situations where the pregnancy *itself* creates a threat to health. He is wrong. The cited cases, reaffirmed in *Casey,* recognize that a State cannot subject women's health to significant risks both in that context, *and also* where state regulations force women to use riskier methods of abortion. Our cases have repeatedly invalidated statutes that in the process of regulating the *methods* of abortion, imposed significant health risks. They make clear that a risk to a women's health is the same whether it happens to arise from regulating a particular method of abortion, or from barring abortion entirely. Our holding does not go beyond those cases, as ratified in *Casey.* . . .

4 . . .

In sum, Nebraska has not convinced us that a health exception is "never necessary to preserve the health of women." Rather, a statute that altogether forbids D&X creates a significant health risk. The statute consequently must contain a health exception. This is not to say, as Justice Thomas and Justice Kennedy claim, that a State is prohibited from proscribing an abortion procedure whenever a particular physician deems the procedure preferable. By no means must a State grant physicians "unfettered discretion" in their selection of abortion methods. (Kennedy, J., dissenting.) But where substantial medical authority supports the proposition that banning a particular abortion procedure could endanger women's health, *Casey* requires the statute to include a health exception when the procedure is "necessary, in appropriate medical judgment, for the preservation of the life or health of the mother." Requiring such an exception in this case is no departure from *Casey,* but simply a straightforward application of its holding.

B

The Eighth Circuit found the Nebraska statute unconstitutional because, in *Casey's* words, it has the "effect of placing a substantial obstacle in the path of a woman seeking an abortion of a nonviable fetus." It thereby places an "undue burden" upon a woman's right to terminate her pregnancy before viability. Nebraska does not deny that the statute imposes an "undue burden" *if* it applies to the more commonly used D&E procedure as well as to D&X. And we agree with the Eighth Circuit that it does so apply. . . .

In sum, using this law some present prosecutors and future Attorneys General may choose to pursue physicians who use D&E procedures, the most commonly used method for performing previability second trimester abortions. All those who perform abortion procedures using that method must fear prosecution, conviction, and imprisonment. The result is an undue burden upon a woman's right to make an abortion decision. We must consequently find the statute unconstitutional.

The judgment of the Court of Appeals is Affirmed.

Justice STEVENS, with whom Justice GINSBURG joins, concurring.

Although much ink is spilled today describing the gruesome nature of late-term abortion procedures, that rhetoric does not provide me a *reason* to believe that the procedure Nebraska here claims it seeks to ban is more brutal, more gruesome, or less respectful of "potential life" than the equally gruesome procedure Nebraska claims it still allows. Justice Ginsburg and Judge Posner have, I believe, correctly diagnosed the underlying reason for the enactment of this legislation—a reason that also explains much of the Court's rhetoric directed at an objective that extends well beyond the narrow issue that this case presents. The rhetoric is almost, but not quite, loud enough to obscure the quiet fact that during the past 27 years, the central holding of *Roe v. Wade* (1973), has been endorsed by all but 4 of the 17 Justices who have addressed the issue. That holding—that the word "liberty" in the *Fourteenth Amendment* includes a woman's right to make this difficult and extremely personal decision— makes it impossible for me to understand how a State has any legitimate interest in requiring a doctor to follow any procedure other than the one that he or she reasonably believes will best protect the woman in her exercise of this constitutional liberty. But one need not even approach this view today to conclude that Nebraska's law must fall. For the notion that either of these two equally gruesome procedures performed at this late stage of gestation is more akin to infanticide than the other, or that the State furthers any legitimate interest by banning one but not the other, is simply irrational.

Justice O'CONNOR, concurring.

The issue of abortion is one of the most contentious and controversial in contemporary American society. It presents extraordinarily difficult questions that, as the Court recognizes, involve "virtually irreconcilable points of view." *Ante,* at 1. The specific question we face today is whether Nebraska's attempt to proscribe a particular method of abortion, commonly known as "partial-birth abortion," is constitutional. For the reasons stated in the Court's opinion, I agree that Nebraska's statute cannot be reconciled with our decision in *Planned Parenthood of Southeastern Pa. v. Casey* (1992), and is therefore unconstitutional. I write separately to emphasize the following points.

First, the Nebraska statute is inconsistent with *Casey* because it lacks an exception for those instances when the banned procedure is necessary to preserve the health of the mother. Importantly, Nebraska's own statutory scheme underscores this constitutional infirmity. As we held in *Casey,* prior to viability "the woman has a right to choose to terminate her pregnancy." After the fetus has become viable, States may substantially regulate and even proscribe abortion, but any such regulation or proscription must contain an exception for instances "where it is necessary, in appropriate medical judgment, for the preservation of the life or health of the mother." Nebraska has

recognized this constitutional limitation in its separate statute generally proscribing postviability abortions. That statute provides that "[n]o abortion shall be performed after the time at which, in the sound medical judgment of the attending physician, the unborn child clearly appears to have reached viability, *except when necessary to preserve the life or health of the mother."* Because even a postviability proscription of abortion would be invalid absent a health exception, Nebraska's ban on previability partial-birth abortions, under the circumstances presented here, must include a health exception as well, since the State's interest in regulating abortions before viability is "considerably weaker" than after viability. The statute at issue here, however, only excepts those procedures "necessary to save the life of the mother whose life is endangered by a physical disorder, physical illness, or physical injury." This lack of a health exception necessarily renders the statute unconstitutional. . . .

Second, Nebraska's statute is unconstitutional on the alternative and independent ground that it imposes an undue burden on a woman's right to choose to terminate her pregnancy before viability. Nebraska's ban covers not just the dilation and extraction (D&X) procedure, but also the dilation and evacuation (D&E) procedure, "the most commonly used method for performing previability second trimester abortions." The statute defines the banned procedure as "deliberately and intentionally delivering into the vagina a living unborn child, *or a substantial portion thereof,* for the purpose of performing a procedure that the person performing such procedure knows will kill the unborn child and does kill the unborn child." As the Court explains, the medical evidence establishes that the D&E procedure is included in this definition. Thus, it is not possible to interpret the statute's language as applying only to the D&X procedure . . . by proscribing the most commonly used method for previability second trimester abortions . . . the statute . . . imposes an undue burden on a woman's right to terminate her pregnancy prior to viability.

It is important to note that, unlike Nebraska, some other States have enacted statutes more narrowly tailored to proscribing the D&X procedure alone. Some of those statutes have done so by specifically excluding from their coverage the most common methods of abortion, such as the D&E and vacuum aspiration procedures. . . .

If Nebraska's statute limited its application to the D&X procedure and included an exception for the life and health of the mother, the question presented would be quite different than the one we face today. As we held in *Casey,* an abortion regulation constitutes an undue burden if it "has the purpose or effect of placing a substantial obstacle in the path of a woman seeking an abortion of a nonviable fetus." If there were adequate alternative methods for a woman safely to obtain an abortion before viability, it is unlikely that prohibiting the D&X procedure alone would "amount in practical terms to a substantial obstacle to a woman seeking an abortion." Thus, a ban on partial-birth abortion that only proscribed the D&X method of abortion and that included an exception to preserve the life and health of the mother would be constitutional in my view.

Nebraska's statute, however, does not meet these criteria. It contains no exception for when the procedure, in appropriate medical judgment, is necessary to preserve the health of the mother; and it proscribes not only the D&X procedure but also the D&E procedure, the most commonly used method for previability second trimester abortions, thus making it an undue burden on a woman's right to terminate her pregnancy. For these reasons, I agree with the Court that Nebraska's law is unconstitutional.

Justice GINSBURG, with whom Justice STEVENS joins, concurring.

I write separately only to stress that amidst all the emotional uproar caused by an abortion case, we should not lose sight of the character of Nebraska's "partial birth abortion" law. As the Court observes, this law does not save any fetus from destruction, for it targets only "a *method* of performing abortion." Nor does the statute seek to protect the lives or health of pregnant women. Moreover, as Justice Stevens points out, *ante*, at 1 (concurring opinion), the most common method of performing previability second trimester abortions is no less distressing or susceptible to gruesome description. . . .

A state regulation that "has the purpose or effect of placing a substantial obstacle in the path of a woman seeking an abortion of a nonviable fetus" violates the Constitution. *Planned Parenthood of Southeastern Pa. v. Casey* (1992). Such an obstacle exists if the State stops a woman from choosing the procedure her doctor "reasonably believes will best protect the woman in [the] exercise of [her] constitutional liberty." (Stevens, J., concurring.) Again as stated by Chief Judge Posner, "if a statute burdens constitutional rights and all that can be said on its behalf is that it is the vehicle that legislators have chosen for expressing their hostility to those rights, the burden is undue." *Hope Clinic*, 195 F.3d, at 881.

Justice SCALIA, dissenting.

I am optimistic enough to believe that, one day, *Stenberg v. Carhart* will be assigned its rightful place in the history

of this Court's jurisprudence beside *Korematsu* and *Dred Scott*. The method of killing a human child—one cannot even accurately say an entirely unborn human child—proscribed by this statute is so horrible that the most clinical description of it evokes a shudder of revulsion. And the Court must know (as most state legislatures banning this procedure have concluded) that demanding a "health exception"—which requires the abortionist to assure himself that, in his expert medical judgment, this method is, in the case at hand, marginally safer than others (how can one prove the contrary beyond a reasonable doubt?)—is to give live-birth abortion free rein. The notion that the Constitution of the United States, designed, among other things, "to establish Justice, insure domestic Tranquility, . . . and secure the Blessings of Liberty to ourselves and our Posterity," prohibits the States from simply banning this visibly brutal means of eliminating our half-born posterity is quite simply absurd.

Even so, I had not intended to write separately here until the focus of the other separate writings (including the one I have joined) gave me cause to fear that this case might be taken to stand for an error different from the one that it actually exemplifies. Because of the Court's practice of publishing dissents in the order of the seniority of their authors, this writing will appear in the reports before those others, but the reader will not comprehend what follows unless he reads them first.

* * *

The two lengthy dissents in this case have, appropriately enough, set out to establish that today's result does not follow from this Court's most recent pronouncement on the matter of abortion, *Planned Parenthood of Southeastern Pa. v. Casey* (1992). It would be unfortunate, however, if those who disagree with the result were induced to regard it as merely a regrettable misapplication of *Casey*. It is not that, but is *Casey's* logical and entirely predictable consequence. To be sure, the Court's construction of this statute so as to make it include procedures other than live-birth abortion involves not only a disregard of fair meaning, but an abandonment of the principle that even ambiguous statutes should be interpreted in such fashion as to render them valid rather than void. *Casey* does not permit *that* jurisprudential novelty—which must be chalked up to the Court's inclination to bend the rules when any effort to limit abortion, or even to speak in opposition to abortion, is at issue. It is of a piece, in other words, with *Hill v. Colorado*, also decided today.

But the Court gives a second and independent reason for invalidating this humane (not to say anti-barbarian) law: That it fails to allow an exception for the situation in which the abortionist believes that this live-birth method of destroying the child might be safer for the woman. (As pointed out by Justice Thomas, and elaborated upon by Justice Kennedy, there is no good reason to believe this is ever the case, but—who knows?—it sometime *might* be.)

I have joined Justice Thomas's dissent because I agree that today's decision is an "unprecedented expansio[n]" of our prior cases, "is not mandated" by *Casey's* "undue burden" test, and can even be called (though this pushes me to the limit of my belief) "obviously irreconcilable with *Casey's* explication of what its undue-burden standard requires." But I never put much stock in *Casey's* explication of the inexplicable. In the last analysis, my judgment that *Casey* does not support today's tragic result can be traced to the fact that what I consider to be an "undue burden" is different from what the majority considers to be an "undue burden"—a conclusion that can not be demonstrated true or false by factual inquiry or legal reasoning. It is a value judgment, dependent upon how much one respects (or believes society ought to respect) the life of a partially delivered fetus, and how much one respects (or believes society ought to respect) the freedom of the woman who gave it life to kill it. Evidently, the five Justices in today's majority value the former less, or the latter more, (or both), than the four of us in dissent. Case closed. There is no cause for anyone who believes in *Casey* to feel betrayed by this outcome. It has been arrived at by precisely the process *Casey* promised—a democratic vote by nine lawyers, not on the question whether the text of the Constitution has anything to say about this subject (it obviously does not); nor even on the question (also appropriate for lawyers) whether the legal traditions of the American people would have sustained such a limitation upon abortion (they obviously would); but upon the pure policy question whether this limitation upon abortion is "undue"—*i.e.*, goes too far.

In my dissent in *Casey*, I wrote that the "undue burden" test made law by the joint opinion created a standard that was "as doubtful in application as it is unprincipled in origin"; "hopelessly unworkable in practice"; "ultimately standardless." Today's decision is the proof. As long as we are debating this issue of necessity for a health-of-the-mother exception on the basis of *Casey*, it is really quite impossible for us dissenters to contend that the majority is *wrong* on the law—any more than it could be said that one is *wrong in law* to support or oppose the death penalty, or to support or oppose mandatory minimum sentences. The most that we can honestly say is that we disagree with the majority on their policy-judgment-couched-as-law. And those who believe that a 5-to-4 vote on a policy matter by unelected lawyers should not overcome the judgment of 30 state legislatures have a problem, not with the *application* of *Casey*, but with its *existence*. *Casey* must be overruled.

While I am in an I-told-you-so mood, I must recall my bemusement, in *Casey*, at the joint opinion's expressed belief that *Roe v. Wade* had "call[ed] the contending sides of a national controversy to end their national division by accepting a common mandate rooted in the Constitution," and that the decision in *Casey* would ratify that happy truce. It seemed to me, quite to the contrary, that "*Roe* fanned into life an issue that has inflamed our national politics in general, and has obscured with its smoke the selection of Justices to this Court in particular, ever since"; and that, "by keeping us in the abortion-umpiring business, it is the perpetuation of that disruption, rather than of any *Pax Roeana*, that the Court's new majority decrees." Today's decision, that the Constitution of the United States prevents the prohibition of a horrible mode of abortion, will be greeted by a firestorm of criticism—as well it should. I cannot understand why those who *acknowledge* that, in the opening words of Justice O'Connor's concurrence, "[t]he issue of abortion is one of the most contentious and controversial in contemporary American society," *ante*, at 1, persist in the belief that this Court, armed with neither constitutional text nor accepted tradition, can resolve that contention and controversy rather than be consumed by it. If only for the sake of its own preservation, the Court should return this matter to the people—where the Constitution, by its silence on the subject, left it—and let *them* decide, State by State, whether this practice should be allowed. *Casey* must be overruled.

Justice KENNEDY, with whom The Chief Justice joins, dissenting.

For close to two decades after *Roe v. Wade* (1973), the Court gave but slight weight to the interests of the separate States when their legislatures sought to address persisting concerns raised by the existence of a woman's right to elect an abortion in defined circumstances. When the Court reaffirmed the essential holding of *Roe*, a central premise was that the States retain a critical and legitimate role in legislating on the subject of abortion, as limited by the woman's right the Court restated and again guaranteed. *Planned Parenthood of Southeastern Pa. v. Casey* (1992). The political processes of the State are not to be foreclosed from enacting laws to promote the life of the unborn and to ensure respect for all human life and its potential. The State's constitutional authority is a vital means for citizens to address these grave and serious issues, as they must if we are to progress in knowledge and understanding and in the attainment of some degree of consensus.

The Court's decision today, in my submission, repudiates this understanding by invalidating a statute advancing critical state interests, even though the law denies no woman the right to choose an abortion and places no undue burden upon the right. The legislation is well within the State's competence to enact. Having concluded Nebraska's law survives the scrutiny dictated by a proper understanding of *Casey*, I dissent from the judgment invalidating it.

I

The Court's failure to accord any weight to Nebraska's interest in prohibiting partial-birth abortion is erroneous and undermines its discussion and holding. The Court's approach in this regard is revealed by its description of the abortion methods at issue, which the Court is correct to describe as "clinically cold or callous." The majority views the procedures from the perspective of the abortionist, rather than from the perspective of a society shocked when confronted with a new method of ending human life. Words invoked by the majority, such as "transcervical procedures," "[o]smotic dilators," "instrumental disarticulation," and "paracervical block," may be accurate and are to some extent necessary, *ante*, at 5–6; but for citizens who seek to know why laws on this subject have been enacted across the Nation, the words are insufficient. Repeated references to sources understandable only to a trained physician may obscure matters for persons not trained in medical terminology . . .

Casey is premised on the States having an important constitutional role in defining their interests in the abortion debate. It is only with this principle in mind that Nebraska's interests can be given proper weight. The State's brief describes its interests as including concern for the life of the unborn and "for the partially-born," in preserving the integrity of the medical profession, and in "erecting a barrier to infanticide." A review of *Casey* demonstrates the legitimacy of these policies. The Court should say so.

States may take sides in the abortion debate and come down on the side of life, even life in the unborn:

"Even in the earliest stages of pregnancy, the State may enact rules and regulations designed to encourage [a woman] to know that there are philosophic and social arguments of great weight that can be brought to bear in favor of continuing the pregnancy to full term and that there are procedures and institutions to allow adoption of unwanted children as well as a certain degree of state assistance if the mother chooses to raise the child herself."

States also have an interest in forbidding medical procedures which, in the State's reasonable determination, might cause the medical profession or society as a whole to become insensitive, even disdainful, to life, including life in the human fetus. Abortion, *Casey* held, has consequences beyond the woman and her fetus. The States' interests in regulating are of concomitant extension. *Casey* recognized that abortion is, "fraught with consequences for . . . the persons who perform and assist in the procedure [and for] society which must confront the knowledge that these procedures exist, procedures some deem nothing short of an act of violence against innocent human life." *Ibid.*, at 852.

A State may take measures to ensure the medical profession and its members are viewed as healers, sustained by a compassionate and rigorous ethic and cognizant of the dignity and value of human life, even life which cannot survive without the assistance of others. Ibid.; *Washington v. Glucksberg* (1997).

Casey demonstrates that the interests asserted by the State are legitimate and recognized by law. . . . Rendering express what is only implicit in the majority opinion, Justice Stevens and Justice Ginsburg are forthright in declaring that the two procedures are indistinguishable and that Nebraska has acted both irrationally and without a proper purpose in enacting the law. The issue is not whether members of the judiciary can see a difference between the two procedures. It is whether Nebraska can. The Court's refusal to recognize Nebraska's right to declare a moral difference between the procedures is a dispiriting disclosure of the illogic and illegitimacy of the Court's approach to the entire case. . . .

It ill-serves the Court, its institutional position, and the constitutional sources it seeks to invoke to refuse to issue a forthright affirmation of Nebraska's right to declare that critical moral differences exist between the two procedures. The natural birth process has been appropriated; yet the Court refuses to hear the State's voice in defining its interests in its law. The Court's holding contradicts *Casey's* assurance that the State's constitutional position in the realm of promoting respect for life is more than marginal.

II . . .

Courts are ill-equipped to evaluate the relative worth of particular surgical procedures. The legislatures of the several States have superior factfinding capabilities in this regard. In an earlier case, Justice O'Connor had explained that the general rule extends to abortion cases, writing that the Court is not suited to be "the Nation's *ex officio* medical board with powers to approve or disapprove medical and operative practices and standards throughout the

United States." "Irrespective of the difficulty of the task, legislatures, with their superior factfinding capabilities, are certainly better able to make the necessary judgments than are courts." Nebraska's judgment here must stand.

In deferring to the physician's judgment, the Court turns back to cases decided in the wake of *Roe*, cases which gave a physician's treatment decisions controlling weight. Before it was repudiated by *Casey*, the approach of deferring to physicians had reached its apex in *Akron, supra*, where the Court held an informed consent requirement was unconstitutional. The law challenged in *Akron* required the abortionist to inform the woman of the status of her pregnancy, the development of her fetus, the date of possible viability, the physical and emotional complications that may result from an abortion, and the availability of agencies to provide assistance and information. The physician was also required to advise the woman of the risks associated with the abortion technique to be employed and other information. The law was invalidated based on the physician's right to practice medicine in the way he or she saw fit; for, according to the *Akron* Court, "[i]t remains primarily the responsibility of the physician to ensure that appropriate information is conveyed to his patient, depending on her particular circumstances." Dispositive for the Court was that the law was an "intrusion upon the discretion of the pregnant woman's physician." The physician was placed in an "undesired and uncomfortable straitjacket." The Court's decision today echoes the *Akron* Court's deference to a physician's right to practice medicine in the way he sees fit.

The Court, of course, does not wish to cite *Akron*; yet the Court's holding is indistinguishable from the reasoning in *Akron* that *Casey* repudiated. No doubt exists that today's holding is based on a physician-first view which finds its primary support in that now-discredited case. Rather than exalting the right of a physician to practice medicine with unfettered discretion, *Casey* recognized: "Whatever constitutional status the doctor-patient relation may have as a general matter, in the present context it is derivative of the woman's position." *Casey* discussed the informed consent requirement struck down in *Akron* and held *Akron* was wrong. . . .

IV

Ignoring substantial medical and ethical opinion, the Court substitutes its own judgment for the judgment of Nebraska and some 30 other States and sweeps the law away. The Court's holding stems from misunderstanding the record, misinterpretation of *Casey*, outright refusal to respect the law of a State, and statutory construction in conflict with settled rules. The decision nullifies a law ex-

pressing the will of the people of Nebraska that medical procedures must be governed by moral principles having their foundation in the intrinsic value of human life, including life of the unborn. Through their law the people of Nebraska were forthright in confronting an issue of immense moral consequence. The State chose to forbid a procedure many decent and civilized people find so abhorrent as to be among the most serious of crimes against human life, while the State still protected the woman's autonomous right of choice as reaffirmed in *Casey*. The Court closes its eyes to these profound concerns.

From the decision, the reasoning, and the judgment, I dissent.

Justice THOMAS, with whom The Chief Justice and Justice SCALIA join, dissenting.

In 1973, this Court struck down an Act of the Texas Legislature that had been in effect since 1857, thereby rendering unconstitutional abortion statutes in dozens of States. *Roe v. Wade*. As some of my colleagues on the Court, past and present, ably demonstrated, that decision was grievously wrong. Abortion is a unique act, in which a woman's exercise of control over her own body ends, depending on one's view, human life or potential human life. Nothing in our Federal Constitution deprives the people of this country of the right to determine whether the consequences of abortion to the fetus and to society outweigh the burden of an unwanted pregnancy on the mother. Although a State *may* permit abortion, nothing in the Constitution dictates that a State *must* do so. . . .

. . . Although in *Casey* the separate opinions of The Chief Justice and Justice Scalia urging the Court to overrule *Roe* did not command a majority, seven Members of that Court, including six Members sitting today, acknowledged that States have a legitimate role in regulating abortion and recognized the States' interest in respecting fetal life at all stages of development. The joint opinion authored by Justices O'Connor, Kennedy, and Souter concluded that prior case law "went too far" in "undervalu[ing] the State's interest in potential life" and in "striking down . . . some abortion regulations which in no real sense deprived women of the ultimate decision." *Roe* and subsequent cases, according to the joint opinion, had wrongly "treat[ed] all governmental attempts to influence a woman's decision on behalf of the potential life within her as unwarranted," a treatment that was "incompatible with the recognition that there is a substantial state interest in potential life throughout pregnancy." Accordingly, the joint opinion held that so long as state regulation of abortion furthers legitimate interests—that is, interests not designed to strike at the right itself—the regulation is invalid only if it imposes an undue burden on a woman's ability to obtain an abortion, meaning that it places a *substantial obstacle* in the woman's path.

. . . The standard is a product of its authors' own philosophical views about abortion, and it should go without saying that it has no origins in or relationship to the Constitution and is, consequently, as illegitimate as the standard it purported to replace. Even assuming, however, as I will for the remainder of this dissent, that *Casey's* fabricated undue-burden standard merits adherence (which it does not), today's decision is extraordinary. Today, the Court inexplicably holds that the States cannot constitutionally prohibit a method of abortion that millions find hard to distinguish from infanticide and that the Court hesitates even to describe. This holding cannot be reconciled with *Casey's* undue-burden standard, as that standard was explained to us by the authors of the joint opinion, and the majority hardly pretends otherwise. In striking down this statute—which expresses a profound and legitimate respect for fetal life and which leaves unimpeded several other safe forms of abortion—the majority opinion gives the lie to the promise of *Casey* that regulations that do no more than "express profound respect for the life of the unborn are permitted, if they are not a substantial obstacle to the woman's exercise of the right to choose" whether or not to have an abortion. Today's decision is so obviously irreconcilable with *Casey's* explication of what its undue-burden standard requires, let alone the Constitution, that it should be seen for what it is, a reinstitution of the pre-*Webster* abortion-on-demand era in which the mere invocation of "abortion rights" trumps any contrary societal interest. If this statute is unconstitutional under *Casey*, then *Casey* meant nothing at all, and the Court should candidly admit it.

To reach its decision, the majority must take a series of indefensible steps. The majority must first disregard the principles that this Court follows in every context but abortion: We interpret statutes according to their plain meaning and we do not strike down statutes susceptible of a narrowing construction. The majority also must disregard the very constitutional standard it purports to employ, and then displace the considered judgment of the people of Nebraska and 29 other States. The majority's decision is lamentable, because of the result the majority reaches, the illogical steps the majority takes to reach it, and because it portends a return to an era I had thought we had at last abandoned. . . .

IV

Having resolved that Nebraska's partial birth abortion statute permits doctors to perform D&E abortions, the ques-

tion remains whether a State can constitutionally prohibit the partial birth abortion procedure without a health exception. Although the majority and Justice O'Connor purport to rely on the standard articulated in the *Casey* joint opinion in concluding that a State may not, they in fact disregard it entirely.

A

Though Justices O'Connor, Kennedy, and Souter declined in *Casey*, on the ground of *stare decisis*, to reconsider whether abortion enjoys any constitutional protection, *Casey* professed to be, in part, a repudiation of *Roe* and its progeny. The *Casey* joint opinion expressly noted that prior case law had undervalued the State's interest in potential life, and had invalidated regulations of abortion that "in no real sense deprived women of the ultimate decision." The joint opinion repeatedly recognized the States' weighty interest in this area. And, the joint opinion expressed repeatedly the States' legitimate role in regulating abortion procedures. According to the joint opinion, "The fact that a law which serves a valid purpose, one not designed to strike at the right itself, has the incidental effect of making it more difficult or more expensive to procure an abortion cannot be enough to invalidate it."

The *Casey* joint opinion therefore adopted the standard: "Only where state regulation imposes an undue burden on a woman's ability to make this decision does the power of the State reach into the heart of the liberty protected by the Due Process Clause." A regulation imposes an "undue burden" only if it "has the effect of placing a substantial obstacle in the path of a woman's choice."

B

There is no question that the State of Nebraska has a valid interest—one not designed to strike at the right itself—in prohibiting partial birth abortion. *Casey* itself noted that States may "express profound respect for the life of the unborn." States may, without a doubt, express this profound respect by prohibiting a procedure that approaches infanticide, and thereby dehumanizes the fetus and trivializes human life. The AMA has recognized that this procedure is "ethically different from other destructive abortion techniques because the fetus, normally twenty weeks or longer in gestation, is killed *outside* the womb. The 'partial birth' gives the fetus an autonomy which separates it from the right of the woman to choose treatments for her own body." Thirty States have concurred with this view. . . .

The question whether States have a legitimate interest in banning the procedure does not require additional authority. In a civilized society, the answer is too obvious, and the contrary arguments too offensive to merit further discussion.

C

The next question, therefore, is whether the Nebraska statute is unconstitutional because it does not contain an exception that would allow use of the procedure whenever "necessary in appropriate medical judgment, for the preservation of the . . . health of the mother." According to the majority, such a health exception is required here because there is a "division of opinion among some medical experts over whether D&X is generally safer [than D& E], and an absence of controlled medical studies that would help answer these medical questions." In other words, unless a State can conclusively establish that an abortion procedure is no safer than other procedures, the State cannot regulate that procedure without including a health exception. Justice O'Connor agrees. The rule set forth by the majority and Justice O'Connor dramatically expands on our prior abortion cases and threatens to undo *any* state regulation of abortion procedures.

The majority and Justice O'Connor suggest that their rule is dictated by a straightforward application of *Roe* and *Casey*. But that is simply not true. In *Roe* and *Casey*, the Court stated that the State may "regulate, and even proscribe, abortion except where it is necessary, in appropriate medical judgment, for the preservation of the life or health of the mother." *Casey* said that a health exception must be available if "*continuing her pregnancy* would constitute a threat" to the woman. Under these cases, if a State seeks to prohibit abortion, even if only temporarily or under particular circumstances, as *Casey* says that it may, the State must make an exception for cases in which the life or health of the mother is endangered by continuing the pregnancy. These cases addressed only the situation in which a woman must obtain an abortion because of some threat to her health from continued pregnancy. But *Roe* and *Casey* say nothing at all about cases in which a physician considers one prohibited method of abortion to be preferable to permissible methods. Today's majority and Justice O'Connor twist *Roe* and *Casey* to apply to the situation in which a woman desires—for whatever reason—an abortion and wishes to obtain the abortion by some particular method. In other words, the majority and Justice O'Connor fail to distinguish between cases in which health concerns require a woman to obtain an abortion and cases in which health concerns cause a woman who desires an abortion (for whatever reason) to prefer one method over another. . . .

D

The majority assiduously avoids addressing the *actual* standard articulated in *Casey*—whether prohibiting partial birth abortion without a health exception poses a substantial obstacle to obtaining an abortion. And for good reason: Such an obstacle does not exist. There are two essential reasons why the Court cannot identify a substantial obstacle. First, the Court cannot identify any real, much less substantial, barrier to any woman's ability to obtain an abortion. And second, the Court cannot demonstrate that any such obstacle would affect a sufficient number of women to justify invalidating the statute on its face. . . .

2 . . .

* * *

We were reassured repeatedly in *Casey* that not all regulations of abortion are unwarranted and that the States may express profound respect for fetal life. Under *Casey*, the regulation before us today should easily pass constitutional muster. But the Court's abortion jurisprudence is a particularly virulent strain of constitutional exegesis. And so today we are told that 30 States are prohibited from banning one rarely used form of abortion that they believe to border on infanticide. It is clear that the Constitution does not compel this result.

I respectfully dissent.

Notes and Queries

1. The ruling in *Stenberg* produced a wave of revulsion among abortion opponents that was, however predictable (note Justice Scalia's anticipation of a "firestorm of criticism"), notable by its depth and intensity. The Court was seen as having placed its imprimatur on, in Justice Scalia's words, a "method of killing a human child." His explicit equation of the outcome with the Court's decisions in *Korematsu* and *Dred Scott* signaled what he saw as the historic magnitude of the Court's moral failure. Off of the Court, this argument was elaborated by critics of the decision. Thus Hadley Arkes wrote: "With the opinion in *Stenberg*, Breyer and his colleagues brought themselves to the threshold of accepting infanticide outright, and it takes but the shortest step to cross that threshold. Whether it was the design of the judges or not, the decision in *Stenberg* did indeed form a design, and the effect of that design was to prepare the public mind for an acceptance of infanticide, unfolding in the gentlest way, step by step." *Natural Rights and the Right to Choose* (Cambridge University Press, 2002), 243. This parallels Lincoln's critique of Chief Justice Taney's opinion in *Dred Scott*, which in-

sisted that the ruling, which applied only to territories, had prepared the public mind for a future Court decision that would declare as unconstitutional any effort by a state to ban slavery from within its borders. Do you see any merit in this argument? Is there any danger that the Court might actually support a right to engage in infanticide?

2. The critical question for the Court to decide was whether the Nebraska statute was reconcilable with the decision in *Casey*. Much of the disagreement surrounding the issue of its consistency or lack thereof with the earlier ruling pertained to the application of the undue burden test. Do you agree with the Justice most identified with that test, Justice O'Connor, that the statute was unconstitutional because it imposed "an undue burden on a woman's right to choose to terminate her pregnancy before viability"? Or do you agree with her co-author in *Casey's* joint opinion, Justice Kennedy, that under the earlier case "The political processes of the State are not to be foreclosed from enacting laws to promote the life of the unborn and to ensure respect for all human life and its potential"?

3. How should the Court ascertain whether a banned procedure is necessary to preserve the health of the mother? What weight should it attach to the determination of the specific attending physician as opposed to the official position of an organization like the American Medical Association? What, in other words, is "appropriate medical judgment"?

4. One of the consequences of the decision in *Stenberg* was an energizing of legislative efforts to ban "partial-birth" abortions. Bills authorizing the outlawing of the procedure were vetoed by President Clinton on two occasions. With a new alignment of political forces in Washington, one much more sympathetic to the prolife position, a national ban on D & X abortions has been passed into law ("Partial Birth Abortion Ban Act of 2003"). It is inevitable that the Supreme Court will revisit the issue in the near future. Assuming that is the case, and assuming further that the makeup of the Court that will hear the case is the same as the Court that decided *Stenberg*, is it also inevitable that a federal law that fails to address the problems cited in the Nebraska law will be declared unconstitutional? Is there any reason for according the Congress more deference than the states?

DeShaney v. Winnebago County Department of Social Services

489 U.S. 189, 109 S. Ct. 998, 103 L. Ed. 2d 249 (1989)

Randy DeShaney had beaten his son Joshua for many years. In spring of 1984, Joshua's father beat him so badly that Joshua fell into a coma and suffered extensive brain damage. He is retarded and will spend the rest of his life in institutions. Upon hearing the news, the social worker acknowledged that "I just knew the phone would ring some day and Joshua would be dead." Joshua's mother sued the DSS, alleging that its failure to protect her son by removing him from his father's custody deprived him of liberty in violation of the Fourteenth Amendment. Lower courts ruled against her. Opinion of the Court: *Rehnquist*, Kennedy, O'Connor, Scalia, Stevens, White. Dissenting opinions: *Brennan*, Marshall, *Blackmun*.

Mr. Chief Justice REHNQUIST delivered the opinion of the Court.

The facts of this case are undeniably tragic. Petitioner Joshua DeShaney was born in 1979. In 1980, a Wyoming court granted his parents a divorce and awarded custody of Joshua to his father, Randy DeShaney, . . . [who] shortly thereafter moved to . . . Wisconsin, taking the infant Joshua with him. There he entered into a second marriage, which also ended in divorce.

The Winnebago County authorities first learned that Joshua DeShaney might be a victim of child abuse in January 1982, when his father's second wife complained to the police, at the time of their divorce, that he had previously "hit the boy causing marks and [was] a prime case for child abuse." The Winnebago County Department of Social Services (DSS) interviewed the father, but he denied the accusations, and DSS did not pursue them further. In January 1983, Joshua was admitted to a local hospital with multiple bruises and abrasions. The examining physician suspected child abuse and notified DSS, which immediately obtained an order from a Wisconsin juvenile court placing Joshua in the temporary custody of the hospital. Three days later, the county convened an ad hoc "Child Protection Team"—consisting of a pediatrician, a psychologist, a police detective, the county's lawyer, several DSS caseworkers, and various hospital personnel—to consider Joshua's situation. At this meeting, the Team decided that there was insufficient evidence of child abuse to retain Joshua in the custody of the court. . . .

Based on the recommendation . . . the juvenile court dismissed the child protection case and returned Joshua to the custody of his father. A month later, emergency room personnel called the DSS caseworker handling Joshua's case to report that he had once again been treated for suspicious injuries. The caseworker concluded that there was no basis for action. For the next six months, the caseworker made monthly visits to the DeShaney home, during which she observed a number of suspicious injuries on Joshua's head. . . . The caseworker dutifully recorded these incidents in her files, along with her continuing suspicions that someone in the DeShaney household was physically abusing Joshua, but she did nothing more. In November 1983, the emergency room notified DSS that Joshua had been treated once again for injuries that they believed to be caused by child abuse. On the caseworker's next two visits to the DeShaney home, she was told that Joshua was too ill to see her. Still DSS took no action.

In March 1984, Randy DeShaney beat 4-year old Joshua so severely that he fell into a life-threatening coma. . . . Joshua did not die, but he suffered brain damage so severe that he is expected to spend the rest of his life confined to an institution for the profoundly retarded. Randy DeShaney was subsequently tried and convicted of child abuse.

. . . The complaint [by Joshua's mother] alleged that respondents had deprived Joshua of his liberty without due process of law . . . by failing to protect him against a risk of violence at his father's hands of which they knew or should have known. . . .

II

The Due Process Clause of the Fourteenth Amendment provides that "[n]o State shall . . . deprive any person of life, liberty, or property, without due process of law." Petitioners contend that the State deprived Joshua of his liberty interest in "free[dom] from . . . unjustified intrusions on personal security," by failing to provide him with adequate protection against his father's violence. The claim is one invoking the substantive rather than procedural component of the Due Process Clause; petitioners do not claim that the State denied Joshua protection without according him appropriate procedural safeguards, but that it was categorically obligated to protect him in these circumstances.

But nothing in the language of the Due Process Clause itself requires the State to protect the life, liberty, and property of its citizens against invasion by private actors. The Clause is phrased as a limitation on the State's power to act, not as a guarantee of certain minimal levels of safety and security. It forbids the State itself to deprive individuals of life, liberty, or property without "due process of law," but its language cannot fairly be extended to impose an affirmative obligation on the State to ensure that those interests do not come to harm through other means. Nor does history support such an expansive reading of the constitutional text. Like its counterpart in the Fifth Amend-

ment, the Due Process Clause of the Fourteenth Amendment was intended to prevent government "from abusing [its] power, or employing it as an instrument of oppression.". . . . Its purpose was to protect the people from the State, not to ensure that the State protected them from each other. The Framers were content to leave the extent of governmental obligation in the latter area to the democratic political processes.

Consistent with these principles, our cases have recognized that the Due Process Clauses generally confer no affirmative right to governmental aid, even where such aid may be necessary to secure life, liberty, or property interests of which the government itself may not deprive the individual. As we said in *Harris v. McRae*, "[a]lthough the liberty protected by the Due Process Clause affords protection against unwarranted government interference, it does not confer an entitlement to such [governmental aid] as may be necessary to realize all the advantages of that freedom." If the Due Process Clause does not require the State to provide its citizens with particular protective services, it follows that the State cannot be held liable under the Clause for injuries that could have been averted had it chosen to provide them. As a general matter, then, we conclude that a State's failure to protect an individual against private violence simply does not constitute a violation of the Due Process Clause.

Petitioners contend, however, that even if the Due Process Clause imposes no affirmative obligation on the State to provide the general public with adequate protective services, such a duty may arise out of certain "special relationships" created or assumed by the State with respect to particular individuals. Petitioners argue that such a "special relationship" existed here because the State knew that Joshua faced a special danger of abuse at his father's hands, and specifically proclaimed, by word and by deed, its intention to protect him against that danger.

Having actually undertaken to protect Joshua from this danger—which petitioners concede the State played no part in creating—the State acquired an affirmative "duty," enforceable through the Due Process Clause, to do so in a reasonably competent fashion. Its failure to discharge that duty, so the argument goes, was an abuse of governmental power that so "shocks the conscience," *Rochin v. California* (1952) as to constitute a substantive due process violation.

We reject this argument. It is true that in certain limited circumstances the Constitution imposes upon the State affirmative duties of care and protection with respect to particular individuals. In *Estelle v. Gamble* (1976), we recognized that the Eighth Amendment's prohibition against cruel and unusual punishment, made applicable to the States through the Fourteenth Amendment's Due Process Clause, requires the State to provide adequate medical care to incarcerated prisoners. We reasoned that because the prisoner is unable "by reason of the deprivation of his liberty [to] care for himself," it is only "just" that the State be required to care for him.

In *Youngberg v. Romeo* (1982), we extended this analysis beyond the Eighth Amendment setting, holding that the substantive component of the Fourteenth Amendment's Due Process Clause requires the State to provide involuntarily committed mental patients with such services as are necessary to ensure their "reasonable safety" from themselves and others. As we explained, "[i]f it is cruel and unusual punishment to hold convicted criminals in unsafe conditions, it must be unconstitutional [under the Due Process Clause] to confine the involuntarily committed—who may not be punished at all—in unsafe conditions."

But these cases afford petitioners no help. Taken together, they stand only for the proposition that when the State takes a person into its custody and holds him there against his will, the Constitution imposes upon it a corresponding duty to assume some responsibility for his safety and general well-being. The rationale for this principle is simple enough: when the State by the affirmative exercise of its power so restrains an individual's liberty that it renders him unable to care for himself, and at the same time fails to provide for his basic human needs—e.g., food, clothing, shelter, medical care, and reasonable safety—it transgresses the substantive limits on state action set by the Eighth Amendment and the Due Process Clause. The affirmative duty to protect arises not from the State's knowledge of the individual's predicament or from its expressions of intent to help him, but from the limitation which it has imposed on his freedom to act on his own behalf. In the substantive due process analysis, it is the State's affirmative act of restraining the individual's freedom to act on his own behalf—through incarceration, institutionalization, or other similar restraint of personal liberty—which is the "deprivation of liberty" triggering the protections of the Due Process Clause, not its failure to act to protect his liberty interests against harms inflicted by other means.

The *Estelle-Youngberg* analysis simply has no applicability in the present case. Petitioners concede that the harms Joshua suffered did not occur while he was in the State's custody, but while he was in the custody of his natural father, who was in no sense a state actor. While the State may have been aware of the dangers that Joshua faced in the free world, it played no part in their creation, nor did it do anything to render him any more vulnerable to them. That the State once took temporary custody of Joshua does not alter the analysis, for when it returned him to his father's custody, it placed him in no worse position than that in which he would have been had it not acted at all; the State does not become the permanent guarantor of an individual's safety by having once offered him shelter. Under these circumstances, the State had no constitutional duty to protect Joshua.

It may well be that, by voluntarily undertaking to protect Joshua against a danger it concededly played no part in creating, the State acquired a duty under state tort law to provide him with adequate protection against that danger. But the claim here is based on the Due Process Clause of the Fourteenth Amendment, which, as we have said many times, does not transform every tort committed by a state actor into a constitutional violation. A State may, through its courts and legislatures, impose such affirmative duties of care and protection upon its agents as it wishes. But not "all common-law duties owed by government actors were . . . constitutionalized by the Fourteenth Amendment." Because, as explained above, the State had no constitutional duty to protect Joshua against his father's violence, its failure to do so—though calamitous in hindsight—simply does not constitute a violation of the Due Process Clause.

Judges and lawyers, like other humans, are moved by natural sympathy in a case like this to find a way for Joshua and his mother to receive adequate compensation for the grievous harm inflicted upon them. But before yielding to that impulse, it is well to remember once again that the harm was inflicted not by the State of Wisconsin, but by Joshua's father. The most that can be said of the state functionaries in this case is that they stood by and did nothing when suspicious circumstances dictated a more active role for them. In defense of them it must also be said that had they moved too soon to take custody of the son away from the father, they would likely have been met with charges of improperly intruding into the parent-child relationship, charges based on the same Due Process Clause that forms the basis for the present charge of failure to provide adequate protection.

The people of Wisconsin may well prefer a system of liability which would place upon the State and its officials the responsibility for failure to act in situations such as the present one. They may create such a system, if they do not have it already, by changing the tort law of the State in accordance with the regular law-making process. But they should not have it thrust upon them by this Court's expansion of the Due Process Clause of the Fourteenth Amendment.

AFFIRMED.

Justice BRENNAN, with whom Justice MARSHALL and Justice BLACKMUN join, dissenting.

It may well be, as the Court decides, that the Due Process Clause as construed by our prior cases creates no general right to basic governmental services. That, however, is not the question presented here; indeed, that question was not raised in the complaint, urged on appeal, presented in the petition for certiorari, or addressed in the briefs on the merits. No one, in short, has asked the Court to proclaim that, as a general matter, the Constitution safeguards positive as well as negative liberties.

This is more than a quibble over dicta; it is a point about perspective, having substantive ramifications. In a constitutional setting that distinguishes sharply between action and inaction, one's characterization of the misconduct alleged under s 1983 may effectively decide the case. Thus, by leading off with a discussion (and rejection) of the idea that the Constitution imposes on the States an affirmative duty to take basic care of their citizens, the Court foreshadows—perhaps even preordains—its conclusion that no duty existed even on the specific facts before us. . . .

The Court's baseline is the absence of positive rights in the Constitution and a concomitant suspicion of any claim that seems to depend on such rights. From this perspective, the DeShaneys' claim is first and foremost about inaction (the failure, here, of respondents to take steps to protect Joshua), and only tangentially about action (the establishment of a state program specifically designed to help children like Joshua). And from this perspective, holding these Wisconsin officials liable—where the only difference between this case and one involving a general claim to protective services is Wisconsin's establishment and operation of a program to protect children—would seem to punish an effort that we should seek to promote.

I would begin from the opposite direction. I would focus first on the action that Wisconsin has taken with respect to Joshua and children like him, rather than on the actions that the State failed to take. Such a method is not new to this Court. Both *Estelle v. Gamble* (1976) and *Youngberg v. Romeo* (1982), began by emphasizing that the States had confined J.W. Gamble to prison and Nicholas Romeo to a psychiatric hospital. This initial action rendered these people helpless to help themselves or to seek help from persons unconnected to the government. . . .

. . . Unlike the Court, therefore, I am unable to see in *Youngberg* a neat and decisive divide between action and inaction.

Moreover, to the Court, the only fact that seems to count as an "affirmative act of restraining the individual's freedom to act on his own behalf" is direct physical control. I would not, however, give *Youngberg* and *Estelle* such a stingy scope. I would recognize, as the Court apparently cannot, that "the State's knowledge of [an] individual's predicament [and] its expressions of intent to help him" can amount to a "limitation of his freedom to act on his own behalf" or to obtain help from others. Thus, I would read *Youngberg* and *Estelle* to stand for the much more generous proposition that, if a State cuts off private sources of aid and then refuses aid itself, it cannot wash its hands of the harm that results from its inaction.

Wisconsin has established a child-welfare system specifically designed to help children like Joshua. Wisconsin law places upon the local departments of social services such as respondent (DSS or Department) a duty to investigate reported instances of child abuse. . . . While other governmental bodies and private persons are largely responsible for the reporting of possible cases of child abuse, . . . Wisconsin law channels all such reports to the local departments of social services for evaluation and, if necessary, further action. . . . Even when it is the sheriff's office or police department that receives a report of suspected child abuse, that report is referred to local social services departments for action; the only exception to this occurs when the reporter fears for the child's immediate safety. In this way, Wisconsin law invites—indeed, directs—citizens and other governmental entities to depend on local departments of social services such as respondent to protect children from abuse.

In these circumstances, a private citizen, or even a person working in a government agency other than DSS, would doubtless feel that her job was done as soon as she had reported her suspicions of child abuse to DSS. Through its child-welfare program, in other words, the State of Wisconsin has relieved ordinary citizens and governmental bodies other than the Department of any sense of obligation to do anything more than report their suspicions of child abuse to DSS. If DSS ignores or dismisses these suspicions, no one will step in to fill the gap. Wisconsin's child-protection program thus effectively confined Joshua DeShaney within the walls of Randy DeShaney's violent home until such time as DSS took action to remove him. Conceivably, then, children like Joshua are made worse off by the existence of this program when the persons and entities charged with carrying it out fail to do their jobs.

It simply belies reality, therefore, to contend that the State "stood by and did nothing" with respect to Joshua. Through its child-protection program, the State actively interfered in Joshua's life and, by virtue of this intervention, acquired ever more certain knowledge that Joshua was in grave danger. . . .

As the Court today reminds us, "the Due Process Clause of the Fourteenth Amendment was intended to prevent government 'from abusing [its] power, or employing it as an instrument of oppression.'" My disagreement with the Court arises from its failure to see that inaction can be every bit as abusive of power as action, that oppression can result when a State undertakes a vital duty and then ignores it. Today's opinion construes the Due Process Clause to permit a State to displace private sources of protection and then, at the critical moment, to shrug its shoulders and turn away from the harm that it has promised to try to prevent. Because I cannot agree that our Constitution is indifferent to such indifference, I respectfully dissent.

Justice BLACKMUN, dissenting.

Today, the Court purports to be the dispassionate oracle of the law, unmoved by "natural sympathy." But, in this pretense, the Court itself retreats into a sterile formalism which prevents it from recognizing either the facts of the case before it or the legal norms that should apply to those facts. As Justice Brennan demonstrates, the facts here involve not mere passivity, but active state intervention in the life of Joshua DeShaney—intervention that triggered a fundamental duty to aid the boy once the State learned of the severe danger to which he was exposed.

The Court fails to recognize this duty because it attempts to draw a sharp and rigid line between action and inaction. But such formalistic reasoning has no place in the interpretation of the broad and stirring clauses of the Fourteenth Amendment. Indeed, I submit that these clauses were designed, at least in part, to undo the formalistic legal reasoning that infected antebellum jurisprudence, which the late Professor Robert Cover analyzed so effectively in his significant work entitled *Justice Accused* (1975).

Like the antebellum judges who denied relief to fugitive slaves, the Court today claims that its decision, however harsh, is compelled by existing legal doctrine. On the contrary, the question presented by this case is an open one, and our Fourteenth Amendment precedents may be read more broadly or narrowly depending upon how one chooses to read them. Faced with the choice, I would adopt a "sympathetic" reading, one which comports with dictates of fundamental justice and recognizes that compassion need not be exiled from the province of judging. . . .

Poor Joshua! Victim of repeated attacks by an irresponsible, bullying, cowardly, and intemperate father, and abandoned by respondents who placed him in a dangerous predicament and who knew or learned what was going on, and yet did essentially nothing except, as the Court revealingly observes, "dutifully recorded these incidents in [their] files." It is a sad commentary upon American life, and constitutional principles—so full of late of patriotic fervor and proud proclamations about "liberty and justice for all," that this child, Joshua DeShaney, now is assigned to live out the remainder of his life profoundly retarded. Joshua and his mother, as petitioners here, deserve—but now are denied by this Court—the opportunity to have the facts of their case considered in the light of the constitutional protection that 42 U.S.C. s 1983 is meant to provide.

Notes and Queries

1. According to Joshua's mother, how, precisely, did the state deprive her son of his liberty? Is the state under a general obligation, fairly derived from the Constitution, to protect its citizens from one another? Can such a duty be squared with the language of the due process clause?

What vision of the relationship between the individual and the state does the due process clause—as interpreted by the majority—embody? Is this vision consistent with the Constitution as a whole? Does it incorporate a particular understanding of judicial power?

In the introduction to this chapter we distinguished between "positive" and "negative" liberty. Is this a useful distinction? Is it a useful way of considering what obligations the Constitution imposes, or on whom it imposes them? See Isaiah Berlin, *Four Essays on Liberty* (London: Oxford University Press, 1969); Susan Bandes, *The Negative Constitution: A Critique*, 88 Michigan Law Review 2271 (1990); David P. Currie, *Positive and Negative Constitutional Rights*, 53 University of Chicago Law Review 864 (1986).

2. What might be the consequences of a decision that the state *is* under a constitutional obligation to protect citizens from one another? Is it appropriate for a court to consider potential consequences when it interprets the Constitution? Why or why not?

3. Is this case about the state's inaction, as the majority claimed, or about the insufficiency of the actions the state *did* take, as Justice Brennan argued in dissent? Is this simply a semantic difference, or are there important differences of constitutional theory between these two formulations? How would you respond to Justice Blackmun's claim that the majority's sharp distinction between action and inaction is "formalistic legal reasoning"? Is there an alternative kind of reasoning, or way of interpreting the Constitution, that does not reduce to the personal sentiment of individual judges? Is Blackmun's impas-

sioned reference to "Poor Joshua" appropriate in a judicial decision? Why or why not?

4. In "The State Action Paradox," Louis M. Seidman and Mark Tushnet write that "Like Chief Justice Rehnquist, Justice Brennan looks for state action, rather than arguing that the state should be held liable for failure to act. Why does Justice Brennan choose to argue around the state action requirement, rather than directly confront it?" Elsewhere in the same piece, they conclude that "each of the three *DeShaney* opinions is, in its own way, unconvincing. None provides a persuasive theory for sorting the public form the private." Is there any way to trace that kind of theory back to the Constitution? *Remnants of Belief* (New York: Oxford University Press, 1996), 55, 61.

5. The petitioners also claimed the state had a duty to protect Joshua because the state knew of the danger to him. Is the state's failure to act when it should have acted a *constitutional* defect? Why?

Moore v. East Cleveland
431 U.S. 494, 97 S. Ct. 1932, 52 L. Ed. 2d 531 (1977)

Moore, a resident of East Cleveland, Ohio, shared her house with her son and two grandsons, who were first cousins. A city ordinance stated that only a single family could reside in a single dwelling. As defined under the ordinance the Moores did not qualify as a single family. Moore appealed her conviction under the ordinance, claiming that it violated the due process clause of the Fourteenth Amendment. State courts ruled in favor of the city. Judgment of the Court: *Powell,* Brennan, Marshall, Blackmun. Concurring in the judgment: *Stevens.* Concurring opinion: *Brennan.* Dissenting opinions: *Burger, Stewart,* Rehnquist, *White.*

Mr. Justice POWELL announced the judgment of the Court and delivered an opinion in which Mr. Justice BRENNAN, Mr. Justice MARSHALL, and Mr. Justice BLACKMUN joined.

The city argues that our decision in *Village of Belle Terre v. Boraas* (1974), requires us to sustain the ordinance attacked here. Belle Terre, like East Cleveland, imposed limits on the types of groups that could occupy a single dwelling unit. Applying the constitutional standard announced in this Court's leading land-use case, *Euclid v.*

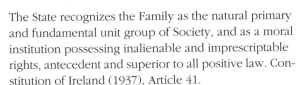

Comparative Note 11.5

The State recognizes the Family as the natural primary and fundamental unit group of Society, and as a moral institution possessing inalienable and imprescriptable rights, antecedent and superior to all positive law. Constitution of Ireland (1937), Article 41.

The family is the basic nucleus of society. It is formed on the basis of natural rights or legal ties, through the free decision of a man and woman to contract matrimony or through the responsible resolve to comply with it. The state and society guarantee the integral protection of the family. Constitution of Colombia (1991), Article 42.

Marriage, being a union of a man and a woman, as well as the family, motherhood, and parenthood, shall be placed under the protection and care of the Republic of Poland. Constitution of the Republic of Poland (1997), Article 18.

In the Republic of Hungary, mothers are entitled to special care and protection before and after childbirth, in accordance with special regulations. Constitution of Hungary (1990), Section 67(2).

Marriage and the family shall enjoy the special protection of the state. Germany's Basic Law (1949), Article 6(1).

Men and women of marriageable age have the right to marry and to found a family, according to the national laws governing the exercise of this right. European Convention on Human Rights (1951), Article 12.

Marriage shall be based only on the mutual consent of both sexes and it shall be maintained through mutual cooperation with the equal rights of husband and wife as a basis. Constitution of Japan (1947), Article 24.

The family is the natural and fundamental group unit of society and is entitled to protection by society and the State. International Covenant on Civil and Political Rights (1966), Article 1.

Every person has the right to establish a family, the basic element of society, and to receive protection therefore. American Declaration of the Rights and Duties of Man (1948), Article VI.

Ambler Realty Co. (1926), we sustained the *Belle Terre* ordinance on the ground that it bore a rational relationship to permissible state objectives.

But one overriding factor sets this case apart from Belle Terre. The ordinance there affected only unrelated individuals. It expressly allowed all who were related by "blood, adoption, or marriage" to live together, and in sustaining the ordinance we were careful to note that it promoted "family needs" and "family values." East Cleveland, in contrast, has chosen to regulate the occupancy of its housing by slicing deeply into the family itself. This is no mere incidental result of the ordinance. On its face it selects certain categories of relatives who may live together and declares that others may not. In particular, it makes a crime of a grandmother's choice to live with her grandson in circumstances like those presented here.

When a city undertakes such intrusive regulation of the family, neither *Belle Terre* nor *Euclid* governs; the usual judicial deference to the legislature is inappropriate. "This Court has long recognized that freedom of personal choice in matters of marriage and family life is one of the liberties protected by the Due Process Clause of the Fourteenth Amendment." *Cleveland Board of Education v. LaFleur*, (1974). A host of cases, tracing their lineage to *Meyer v. Nebraska* (1923), and *Pierce v. Society of Sisters* (1925), have consistently acknowledged a "private realm of family life which the state cannot enter." Of course, the family is not beyond regulation. But when the government intrudes on choices concerning family living arrangements, this Court must examine carefully the importance of the governmental interests advanced and the extent to which they are served by the challenged regulation.

When thus examined, this ordinance cannot survive. The city seeks to justify it as a means of preventing overcrowding, minimizing traffic and parking congestion, and avoiding an undue financial burden on East Cleveland's school system. Although these are legitimate goals, the ordinance before us serves them marginally, at best. For example, the ordinance permits any family consisting only of husband, wife, and unmarried children to live together, even if the family contains a half dozen licensed drivers, each with his or her own car. At the same time it forbids an adult brother and sister to share a household, even if both faithfully use public transportation. The ordinance would permit a grandmother to live with a single dependent son and children, even if his school-age children number a dozen, yet it forces Mrs. Moore to find another dwelling for her grandson John, simply because of the presence of his uncle and cousin in the same household. . . .

II

The city would distinguish the cases based on *Meyer* and *Pierce*. It points out that none of them "gives grandmothers any fundamental rights with respect to grandsons," and suggests that any constitutional right to live together as a family extends only to the nuclear family—essentially a couple and their dependent children. To be sure, these cases did not expressly consider the family relationship presented here. They were immediately concerned with freedom of choice with respect to childbearing, or with the rights of parents to the custody and companionship of their own children, or with traditional parental authority in matters of child rearing and education. But unless we close our eyes to the basic reasons why certain rights associated with the family have been accorded shelter under the Fourteenth Amendment's Due Process Clause, we cannot avoid applying the force and rationale of these precedents to the family choice involved in this case.

Understanding those reasons requires careful attention to this Court's function under the Due Process Clause. Mr. Justice Harlan described it eloquently:

> Due process has not been reduced to any formula; its content cannot be determined by reference to any code. The best that can be said is that through the course of this Court's decisions it has represented the balance which our Nation, built upon postulates of respect for the liberty of the individual, has struck between that liberty and the demands of organized society. If the supplying of content to this Constitutional concept has of necessity been a rational process, it certainly has not been one where judges have felt free to roam where unguided speculation might take them. The balance of which I speak is the balance struck by this country, having regard to what history teaches are the traditions from which it developed as well as the traditions from which it broke. That tradition is a living thing. A decision of this Court which radically departs from it could not long survive, while a decision which builds on what has survived is likely to be sound. No formula could serve as a substitute, in this area, for judgment and restraint.
>
> . . . [T]he full scope of the liberty guaranteed by the Due Process Clause cannot be found in or limited by the precise terms of the specific guarantees elsewhere provided in the Constitution. This "liberty" is not a series of isolated points pricked out in terms of the taking of property; the freedom of speech, press, and religion; the right to keep and bear arms; the freedom from unreasonable searches and seizures; and so on. It is a rational continuum which, broadly speaking, includes a

freedom from all substantial arbitrary impositions and purposeless restraints, and which also recognizes, what a reasonable and sensitive judgment must, that certain interests require particularly careful scrutiny of the state needs asserted to justify their abridgment. . . .

Substantive due process has at times been a treacherous field for this Court. There *are* risks when the judicial branch gives enhanced protection to certain substantive liberties without the guidance of the more specific provisions of the Bill of Rights. As the history of the *Lochner* era demonstrates, there is reason for concern lest the only limits to such judicial intervention become the predilections of those who happen at the time to be Members of this Court. That history counsels caution and restraint. But it does not counsel abandonment, nor does it require what the city urges here: cutting off any protection of family rights at the first convenient, if arbitrary boundary—the boundary of the nuclear family.

Appropriate limits on substantive due process come not from drawing arbitrary lines but rather from careful "respect for the teachings of history [and], solid recognition of the basic values that underlie our society. *Griswold v. Connecticut* (1965) (Harlan, J., concurring). Our decisions establish that the Constitution protects the sanctity of the family precisely because the institution of the family is deeply rooted in this Nation's history and tradition. It is through the family that we inculcate and pass down many of our most cherished values, moral and cultural.

Ours is by no means a tradition limited to respect for the bonds uniting the members of the nuclear family. The tradition of uncles, aunts, cousins, and especially grandparents sharing a household along with parents and children has roots equally venerable and equally deserving of constitutional recognition. Over the years millions of our citizens have grown up in just such an environment, and most, surely, have profited from it. Even if conditions of modern society have brought about a decline in extended family households, they have not erased the accumulated wisdom of civilization, gained over the centuries and honored throughout our history, that supports a larger conception of the family. Out of choice, necessity, or a sense of family responsibility, it has been common for close relatives to draw together and participate in the duties and the satisfactions of a common home. Decisions concerning child rearing, which *Yoder, Meyer, Pierce* and other cases have recognized as entitled to constitutional protection, long have been shared with grandparents or other relatives who occupy the same household—indeed who may take on major responsibility for the rearing of the children. Especially in times of adversity, such as the death of a spouse or economic need, the broader family has tended to come together for mutual sustenance and to maintain or rebuild a secure home life. This is apparently what happened here.

Whether or not such a household is established because of personal tragedy, the choice of relatives in this degree of kinship to live together may not lightly be denied by the State. *Pierce* struck down an Oregon law requiring all children to attend the State's public schools, holding that the Constitution "excludes any general power of the State to standardize its children by forcing them to accept instruction from public teachers only." By the same token the Constitution prevents East Cleveland from standardizing its children and its adults by forcing all to live in certain narrowly defined family patterns. Reversed.

Mr. Justice BRENNAN, with whom Mr. Justice MARSHALL joins, concurring.

. . . I do not question that a municipality may constitutionally zone to alleviate noise and traffic congestion and to prevent overcrowded and unsafe living conditions, in short to enact reasonable land-use restrictions in furtherance of the legitimate objectives East Cleveland claims for its ordinance. But the zoning power is not a license for local communities to enact senseless and arbitrary restrictions which cut deeply into private areas of protected family life. East Cleveland may not constitutionally define "family" as essentially confined to parents and the parents' own children. The plurality's opinion conclusively demonstrates that classifying family patterns in this eccentric way is not a rational means of achieving the ends East Cleveland claims for its ordinance, and further that the ordinance unconstitutionally abridges the "freedom of personal choice in matters of . . . family life [that] is one of the liberties protected by the Due Process Clause of the Fourteenth Amendment." *Cleveland Board of Education v. LaFleur* (1974). I write only to underscore the cultural myopia of the arbitrary boundary drawn by the East Cleveland ordinance in the light of the tradition of the American home that has been a feature of our society since our beginning as a Nation—the "tradition" in the plurality's words, "of uncles, aunts, cousins, and especially grandparents sharing a household along with parents and children. . . ." The line drawn by this ordinance displays a depressing insensitivity toward the economic and emotional needs of a very large part of our society.

In today's America, the "nuclear family" is the pattern so often found in much of white suburbia. J. Vander Zanden, *Sociology: A Systematic Approach* 322 (3d ed. 1975). The Constitution cannot be interpreted, however, to tolerate the imposition by government upon the rest of us of white suburbia's preference in patterns of family living. The "extended family" that provided generations of early Americans with social services and economic and emotional support in times of hardship, and was the beachhead for successive waves of immigrants who populated our cities, remains not merely still a pervasive living pattern, but under the goad of brutal economic necessity, a prominent pattern—virtually a means of survival—for large numbers of the poor and deprived minorities of our society. For them compelled pooling of scant resources requires compelled sharing of a household.

The "extended" form is especially familiar among black families. We may suppose that this reflects the truism that black citizens, like generations of white immigrants before them, have been victims of economic and other disadvantages that would worsen if they were compelled to abandon extended, for nuclear, living patterns. Even in husband and wife households, 13% of black families compared with 3% of white families include relatives under 18 years old, in addition to the couple's own children. In black households whose head is an elderly woman, as in this case, the contrast is even more striking: 48% of such black households, compared with 10% of counterpart white households, include related minor children not offspring of the head of the household.*

The extended family often plays an important role in the rearing of young black children whose parents must work. Many such children frequently "spend all of their growing-up years in the care of extended kin. . . . Often children are 'given' to their grandparents, who rear them to adulthood. . . . Many children normally grow up in a three-generation household and they absorb the influences of grandmother and grandfather as well as mother and father." J. Ladner, *Tomorrow's Tomorrow: The Black Woman* 60 (1972).

I do not wish to be understood as implying that East Cleveland's enforcement of its ordinance is motivated by a racially discriminatory purpose: The record of this case would not support that implication. But the prominence of other than nuclear families among ethnic and racial mi-

nority groups, including our black citizens, surely demonstrates that the "extended family" pattern remains a vital tenet of our society. It suffices that in prohibiting this pattern of family living as a means of achieving its objectives, appellee city has chosen a device that deeply intrudes into family associational rights that historically have been central, and today remain central, to a large proportion of our population.

Mr. Justice STEVENS, concurring in the judgment.

In my judgment the critical question presented by this case is whether East Cleveland's housing ordinance is a permissible restriction on appellant's right to use her own property as she sees fit.

Long before the original States adopted the Constitution, the common law protected an owner's right to decide how best to use his own property. This basic right has always been limited by the law of nuisance which proscribes uses that impair the enjoyment of other property in the vicinity. But the question whether an individual owner's use could be further limited by a municipality's comprehensive zoning plan was not finally decided until this century.

There appears to be no precedent for an ordinance which excludes any of an owner's relatives from the group of persons who may occupy his residence on a permanent basis. Nor does there appear to be any justification for such a restriction on an owner's use of his property. The city has failed totally to explain the need for a rule which would allow a homeowner to have two grandchildren live with her if they are brothers, but not if they are cousins. Since this ordinance has not been shown to have any "substantial relation to the public health, safety, morals, or general welfare" of the city of East Cleveland, and since it cuts so deeply into a fundamental right normally associated with the ownership of residential property—that of an owner to decide who may reside on his or her property—it must fall under the limited standard of review of zoning decisions which this Court preserved in *Euclid* and *Nectow.* Under that standard, East Cleveland's unprecedented ordinance constitutes a taking of property without due process and without just compensation.

For these reasons, I concur in the Court's judgment.

Mr. Chief Justice BURGER, dissenting. . . . .

Mr. Justice STEWART, with whom Mr. Justice REHNQUIST joins, dissenting.

To suggest that the biological fact of common ancestry necessarily gives related persons constitutional rights of association superior to those of unrelated persons is to

---

*Within the black lower-class it has been quite common for several generations, or parts of the kin, to live together under one roof. Often a maternal grandmother is the acknowledged head of this type of household which has given rise to the term "matrifocal" to describe lower-class black family patterns. See J. Scanzoni, *The Black Family in Modern Society* 134 (1971); see also Anderson, "The Pains and Pleasures of Old Black Folks", *Ebony* 123, 128–130 (Mar. 1973). See generally E. Frazier, *The Negro Family in the United States* (1939); Lewis, "The Changing Negro Family", in E. Ginzberg, ed., *The Nation's Children* 108 (1960). [Footnote by the Court]

misunderstand the nature of the associational freedoms that the Constitution has been understood to protect. Freedom of association has been constitutionally recognized because it is often indispensable to effectuation of explicit First Amendment guarantees. But the scope of the associational right, until now, at least, has been limited to the constitutional need that created it; obviously not every "association" is for First Amendment purposes or serves to promote the ideological freedom that the First Amendment was designed to protect.

The "association" in this case is not for any purpose relating to the promotion of speech, assembly, the press, or religion. And wherever the outer boundaries of constitutional protection of freedom of association may eventually turn out to be, they surely do not extend to those who assert no interest other than the gratification, convenience, and economy of sharing the same residence.

The appellant is considerably closer to the constitutional mark in asserting that the East Cleveland ordinance intrudes upon "the private realm of family life which the state cannot enter." *Prince v. Massachusetts* (1944). Several decisions of the Court have identified specific aspects of what might broadly be termed "private family life" that are constitutionally protected against state interference.

Although the appellant's desire to share a single-dwelling unit also involves "private family life" in a sense, that desire can hardly be equated with any of the interests protected in the cases just cited. The ordinance about which the appellant complains did not impede her choice to have or not to have children, and it did not dictate to her how her own children were to be nurtured and reared. The ordinance clearly does not prevent parents from living together or living with their unemancipated offspring.

But even though the Court's previous cases are not directly in point, the appellant contends that the importance of the "extended family" in American society requires us to hold that her decision to share her residence with her grandsons may not be interfered with by the State. This decision, like the decisions involved in bearing and raising children, is said to be an aspect of "family life" also entitled to substantive protection under the Constitution. Without pausing to inquire how far under this argument an "extended family" might extend, I cannot agree. When the Court has found that the Fourteenth Amendment placed a substantive limitation on a State's power to regulate, it has been in those rare cases in which the personal interests at issue have been deemed "implicit in the concept of ordered liberty.'"

The interest that the appellant may have in permanently sharing a single kitchen and a suite of contiguous rooms with some of her relatives simply does not rise to that level. To equate this interest with the fundamental decisions to marry and to bear and raise children is to extend the limited substantive contours of the Due Process Clause beyond recognition.

Viewed in the light of these principles, I do not think East Cleveland's definition of "family" offends the Constitution. The city has undisputed power to ordain single-family residential occupancy. And that power plainly carries with it the power to say what a "family" is. Here the city has defined "family" to include not only father, mother, and dependent children, but several other close relatives as well. The definition is rationally designed to carry out the legitimate governmental purposes identified in the *Belle Terre* opinion: "The police power is not confined to elimination of filth, stench, and unhealthy places. It is ample to lay out zones where family values, youth values, and the blessings of the quiet seclusion and clean air make the area a sanctuary for people."

Mr. Justice WHITE, dissenting. . . .

. . . That the Court has ample precedent for the creation of new constitutional rights should not lead it to repeat the process at will. The Judiciary, including this Court is the most vulnerable and comes nearest to illegitimacy when it deals with judge-made constitutional law having little or no cognizable roots in the language or even the design of the Constitution. Realizing that the present construction of the Due Process Clause represents a major judicial gloss on its terms, as well as on the anticipation of the Framers, and that much of the underpinning for the broad, substantive application of the Clause disappeared in the conflict between the Executive and the Judiciary in the 1930's and 1940's, the Court should be extremely reluctant to breathe still further substantive content into the Due Process Clause so as to strike down legislation adopted by a State or city to promote its welfare. Whenever the Judiciary does so, it unavoidably pre-empts for itself another part of the governance of the country without express constitutional authority. . . .

. . . Under our cases, the Due Process Clause extends substantial protection to various phases of family life, but none requires that the claim made here be sustained. I cannot believe that the interest in residing with more than one set of grandchildren is one that calls for any kind of heightened protection under the Due Process Clause. To say that one has a personal right to live with all, rather than some, of one's grandchildren and that this right is implicit in ordered liberty is, as my Brother Stewart says, "to extend the limited substantive contours of the Due Process Clause beyond recognition." The present claim is hardly one of which it could be said that "neither liberty nor justice would exist if [it] were sacrificed."

Mrs. Moore's interest in having the offspring of more than one dependent son live with her qualifies as a liberty protected by the Due Process Clause; but, because of the nature of that particular interest, the demands of the Clause are satisfied once the Court is assured that the challenged proscription is the product of a duly enacted or promulgated statute, ordinance, or regulation and that it is not wholly lacking in purpose or utility.

Notes and Queries

1. Moore lost her case in the state courts, which had followed the Supreme Court case of *Village of Belle Terre v. Boraas* (1974). In that case, the Court upheld a city ordinance that restricted single-family residences to "families" that comprised one or more persons related by blood, adoption, or marriage. In the absence of a "family," the law prohibited more than two unrelated persons from sharing a house. A landlord who had leased a single dwelling to six unrelated students at SUNY-Stony Brook was charged with violating the ordinance. In an opinion by Justice Douglas, the Court upheld the law, calling it a reasonable effort to promote "family values" and to secure "the blessings of quiet seclusion and clean air [that] make the area a sanctuary for people."

Why aren't the same values sufficient to save the city of East Cleveland's statute? Does the difference between *Belle Terre* and *Moore* rest in the difference between "families" and the living arrangements of persons who are unrelated? Why are those differences significant as a matter of constitutional interpretation? Does the Constitution offer some special protection for the family? Why? You may wish to compare Justice Powell's opinion in *Moore* with Justice Douglas's majority opinion in *Griswold*.

2. According to Justice Powell, why does the Constitution protect "the sanctity of the family"? Does he respond persuasively to Justice White's complaints about the Court's use of substantive due process?

3. Justice Stewart argued that freedom of association applies only to matters that "promote the ideological freedom that the First Amendment was designed to protect. The association in this case is not for any purpose relating to the promotion of speech, assembly, the press, or religion." From where in the Constitution does Justice Stewart infer this limitation on freedom of association? Does he provide any instruction about how we are to determine what types of association will qualify and which will not? How would Justice Stewart respond, for example, to the claim that patterns of family life, and choices about which sorts of families are desirable and which are not, are inescapably political and "ideological"?

Consider a similar argument by Judge Bork: "Constitutional protection should be accorded only to speech that is explicitly political. . . . All other forms of speech raise only issues of human gratification and their protection against legislative regulation involves the judge in making decisions of the sort made in *Griswold v. Connecticut*." Are choices about family life simple choices of "gratification"? Would it matter if we knew that East Cleveland passed its law to facilitate the process of gentrification in poorer, ethnic neighborhoods? Doesn't Justice Brennan's opinion suggest that this process, and the development of cultural ideals about family life more generally, involve patently political issues?

4. Why isn't this case about the right to property, as Justice Stevens argued?

Troxel v. Granville
536 U.S. 57, 147 L Ed 49, 120 S Ct 2054 (2000)

Section 26.10.160(3) of Washington State's Revised Code permitted "any person" to petition a state court for child visitation rights "at any time." Visitation could then be ordered if the court concluded it might "serve the best interest of the child." Under this provision, Jenifer and Gary Troxel petitioned a Washington Superior Court for the right to visit their grandchildren. Their son, Brad Troxel, and the grandchildren's mother, Tommie Granville, had ended their relationship (they were never married), but the grandchildren were still routinely brought by Brad to visit them. After his death Granville informed the Troxels that future visits would be short and limited to once a month. The Troxels sought visitation rights in state court. When the Superior Court ordered visitation for the grandparents, Tommie Granville appealed to the Washington Supreme Court, which concluded that the visitation scheme unconstitutionally interfered with the right of parents to rear their children. Opinion of the Court: *O'Connor*, Rehnquist, Ginsburg, Breyer. Concurring opinions: *Souter*, *Thomas*. Dissenting opinions: *Stevens*, *Scalia*, Kennedy.

Justice O'CONNOR announced the judgment of the Court and delivered an opinion, in which The Chief Justice, Justice GINSBURG, and Justice BREYER join.

The demographic changes of the past century make it difficult to speak of an average American family. The composition of families varies greatly from household to household.

The nationwide enactment of nonparental visitation statutes is assuredly due, in some part, to the States' recognition of these changing realities of the American family. Because grandparents and other relatives undertake duties of a parental nature in many households, States have sought to ensure the welfare of the children therein by protecting the relationships those children form with such third parties. The States' nonparental visitation statutes are further supported by a recognition, which varies from State to State, that children should have the opportunity to benefit from relationships with statutorily specified persons—for example, their grandparents. The extension of statutory rights in this area to persons other than a child's parents, however, comes with an obvious cost. For example, the State's recognition of an independent third-party interest in a child can place a substantial burden on the traditional parent-child relationship.

The *Fourteenth Amendment* provides that no State shall "deprive any person of life, liberty, or property, without due process of law." We have long recognized that the Amendment's Due Process Clause, like its *Fifth Amendment* counterpart, "guarantees more than fair process." *Washington v. Glucksberg* (1997). The Clause also includes a substantive component that "provides heightened protection against government interference with certain fundamental rights and liberty interests."

The liberty interest at issue in this case—the interest of parents in the care, custody, and control of their children—is perhaps the oldest of the fundamental liberty interests recognized by this Court.

Section 26.10.160(3), as applied to Granville and her family in this case, unconstitutionally infringes on that fundamental parental right. The Washington nonparental visitation statute is breathtakingly broad. According to the statute's text, "*[a]ny person* may petition the court for visitation rights *at any time*," and the court may grant such visitation rights whenever "visitation may serve *the best interest of the child*." s.26.10.160(3) (emphases added). . . . [A] parent's decision that visitation would not be in the child's best interest is accorded no deference. . . . Instead, the Washington statute places the best-interest determination solely in the hands of the judge. . . . Thus, in practical effect, in the State of Washington a court can disregard and overturn *any* decision by a fit custodial parent concerning visitation whenever a third party affected by the decision files a visitation petition, based solely on the judge's determination of the child's best interests.

Turning to the facts of this case, the record reveals that the Superior Court's order was based on precisely the type of mere disagreement we have just described and nothing more. The Superior Court's order was not founded on any special factors that might justify the State's interference with Granville's fundamental right to make decisions concerning the rearing of her two daughters.

The problem here is not that the Washington Superior Court intervened, but that when it did so, it gave no special weight at all to Granville's determination of her daughters' best interests.

The decisional framework employed by the Superior Court directly contravened the traditional presumption that a fit parent will act in the best interest of his or her child. In that respect, the court's presumption failed to provide any protection for Granville's fundamental constitutional right to make decisions concerning the rearing of her own daughters. In an ideal world, parents might always seek to cultivate the bonds between grandparents and their grandchildren. Needless to say, however, our world is far from perfect, and in it the decision whether such an intergenerational relationship would be beneficial in any specific case is for the parent to make in the first instance. And, if a fit parent's decision of the kind at issue here becomes subject to judicial review, the court must accord at least some special weight to the parent's own determination.

Finally, we note that there is no allegation that Granville ever sought to cut off visitation entirely. Rather, the present dispute originated when Granville informed the Troxels that she would prefer to restrict their visitation with Isabelle and Natalie to one short visit per month and special holidays.

Considered together with the Superior Court's reasons for awarding visitation to the Troxels, the combination of these factors demonstrates that the visitation order in this case was an unconstitutional infringement on Granville's fundamental right to make decisions concerning the care, custody, and control of her two daughters.

Because we rest our decision on the sweeping breadth of s.26.10.160(3) and the application of that broad, unlimited power in this case, we do not consider the primary constitutional question passed on by the Washington Supreme Court—whether the Due Process Clause requires all nonparental visitation statutes to include a showing of harm or potential harm to the child as a condition precedent to granting visitation. We do not, and need not, define today the precise scope of the parental due process right in the visitation context. . . . Because much state-court adjudication in this context occurs on a case-by-case basis, we would be hesitant to hold that specific nonparental visitation statutes violate the Due Process Clause as a *per se* matter.

Accordingly, the judgment of the Washington Supreme Court is affirmed.

Justice SOUTER, concurring in the judgment.

I concur in the judgment affirming the decision of the Supreme Court of Washington, whose facial invalidation of its own state statute is consistent with this Court's prior cases addressing the substantive interests at stake. I would say no more.

We have long recognized that a parent's interests in the nurture, upbringing, companionship, care, and custody of children are generally protected by the Due Process Clause of the Fourteenth Amendment.

On the basis of this settled principle, the Supreme Court of Washington invalidated its statute because it authorized a contested visitation order at the intrusive behest of any person at any time subject only to a best-interests-of-the-child standard.

Since I do not question the power of a State's highest court to construe its domestic statute and to apply a demanding standard when ruling on its facial constitutionality, this for me is the end of the case. I would simply affirm the decision of the Supreme Court of Washington that its statute, authorizing courts to grant visitation rights to any person at any time, is unconstitutional. I therefore respectfully concur in the judgment.

Justice THOMAS, concurring in the judgment.

. . . I agree with the plurality that this Court's recognition of a fundamental right of parents to direct the upbringing of their children resolves this case. Our decision in *Pierce v. Society of Sisters* (1925), holds that parents have a fundamental constitutional right to rear their children, including the right to determine who shall educate and socialize them. . . . I would apply strict scrutiny to infringements of fundamental rights. Here, the State of Washington lacks even a legitimate governmental interest—to say nothing of a compelling one—in second-guessing a fit parent's decision regarding visitation with third parties. On this basis, I would affirm the judgment below.

Justice SCALIA, dissenting.

In my view, a right of parents to direct the upbringing of their children is among the "unalienable Rights" with which the Declaration of Independence proclaims "all Men . . . are endowed by their Creator." And in my view that right is also among the "othe[r] [rights] retained by the people" which the Ninth Amendment says the Constitution's enumeration of rights "shall not be construed to deny or disparage." The Declaration of Independence, however, is not a legal prescription conferring powers upon the courts; and the Constitution's refusal to "deny or disparage" other rights is far removed from affirming any one of them, and even farther removed from authorizing judges to identify what they might be, and to enforce the judges' list against laws duly enacted by the people. Consequently, while I would think it entirely compatible with the commitment to representative democracy set forth in the founding documents to argue, in legislative chambers or in electoral campaigns, that the state has *no power* to interfere with parents' authority over the rearing of their children, I do not believe that the power which the Constitution confers upon me *as a judge* entitles me to deny legal effect to laws that (in my view) infringe upon what is (in my view) that unenumerated right.

Judicial vindication of "parental rights" under a Constitution that does not even mention them requires . . . not only a judicially crafted definition of parents, but also—unless, as no one believes, the parental rights are to be absolute—judicially approved assessments of "harm to the child" and judicially defined gradations of other persons (grandparents, extended family, adoptive family in an adoption later found to be invalid, long-term guardians, etc.) who may have some claim against the wishes of the parents. If we embrace this unenumerated right, I think it obvious—whether we affirm or reverse the judgment here, or remand as Justice Stevens or Justice Kennedy would do—that we will be ushering in a new regime of judicially prescribed, and federally prescribed, family law. I have no reason to believe that federal judges will be better at this than state legislatures; and state legislatures have the great advantages of doing harm in a more circumscribed area, of being able to correct their mistakes in a flash, and of being removable by the people.

For these reasons, I would reverse the judgment below.

Justice STEVENS, dissenting.

Cases like this do not present a bipolar struggle between the parents and the State over who has final authority to determine what is in a child's best interests. There is at a minimum a third individual, whose interests are implicated in every case to which the statute applies—the child.

. . . . My colleagues are of course correct to recognize that the right of a parent to maintain a relationship with his or her child is among the interests included most often in the constellation of liberties protected through the Fourteenth Amendment. Our cases leave no doubt that parents have a fundamental liberty interest in caring for and guiding their children, and a corresponding privacy interest—absent exceptional circumstances—in doing so without the undue interference of strangers to them and to their child.

Despite this Court's repeated recognition of these significant parental liberty interests, these interests have never been seen to be without limits.

A parent's rights with respect to her child have thus never been regarded as absolute, but rather are limited by the existence of an actual, developed relationship with a child, and are tied to the presence or absence of some embodiment of family. These limitations have arisen, not simply out of the definition of parenthood itself, but because of this Court's assumption that a parent's interests in a child must be balanced against the State's long-recognized interests as *parens patriae*, and, critically, the child's own complementary interest in preserving relationships that serve her welfare and protection.

While this Court has not yet had occasion to elucidate the nature of a child's liberty interests in preserving established familial or family-like bonds, it seems to me extremely likely that, to the extent parents and families have fundamental liberty interests in preserving such intimate relationships, so, too, do children have these interests, and so, too, must their interests be balanced in the equation. At a minimum, our prior cases recognizing that children are, generally speaking, constitutionally protected actors require that this Court reject any suggestion that when it comes to parental rights, children are so much chattel. The constitutional protection against arbitrary state interference with parental rights should not be extended to prevent the States from protecting children against the arbitrary exercise of parental authority that is not in fact motivated by an interest in the welfare of the child.

This is not, of course, to suggest that a child's liberty interest in maintaining contact with a particular individual is to be treated invariably as on a par with that child's parents' contrary interests.

But presumptions notwithstanding, we should recognize that there may be circumstances in which a child has a stronger interest at stake than mere protection from serious harm caused by the termination of visitation by a "person" other than a parent. The almost infinite variety of family relationships that pervade our ever-changing society strongly counsel against the creation by this Court of a constitutional rule that treats a biological parent's liberty interest in the care and supervision of her child as an isolated right that may be exercised arbitrarily. It is indisputably the business of the States, rather than a federal court employing a national standard, to assess in the first instance the relative importance of the conflicting interests that give rise to disputes such as this. Far from guaranteeing that parents' interests will be trammeled in the sweep of cases arising under the statute, the Washington law merely gives an individual—with whom a child may have an established relationship—the procedural right to ask the State to act as arbiter, through the entirely well-known best-interests standard, between the parent's protected interests and the child's. It seems clear to me that the Due Process Clause of the Fourteenth Amendment leaves room for States to consider the impact on a child of possibly arbitrary parental decisions that neither serve nor are motivated by the best interests of the child.

Accordingly, I respectfully dissent.

Notes and Queries

1. How would you assess the strength of the state's case for intervention in the context of third-party visits? Is it stronger or weaker than it was in *Meyer v. Nebraska*, where parental rights to make decisions about children free from state interference were emphatically upheld? Why does the Court place so much reliance on the rulings in *Meyer* and *Pierce*?

2. Consider the following critical analysis of the result in *Troxel*. "It is easy to see the appeal the middle holds for the Court: It recognizes some special authority in parents but allows the state to police how that authority is exercised. In application, however, the middle ground is standardless, offering no clear, principled basis on which to distinguish appropriate from inappropriate state interference. As a result, courts are left to make family law policy absent the constraints of either meaningful standards or the democratic process, and children can be expected to suffer a triple loss: they lose the individualized expertise of their parents and the community-wide expertise of democratic lawmaking, and in their place they gain the additional harm associated with this ongoing constitutional litigation." Emily Buss, *Adrift in the Middle: Parental Rights After* Troxel v. Granville, Supreme Court Review 2000. The criticism reflects the Court's reluctance to adopt a strong form of parental rights or to relegate these types of disputes to the democratic process. Often the Court's work is praised when it embraces a case-by-case, incremental approach that maximizes available options in complex policy arenas. Can you think of a persuasive reason why a more principled, less flexible approach might be advisable in this particular arena of concern?

3. Justice O'Connor's plurality opinion presents three contrasting models of the family, a reflection perhaps of the confusion in contemporary society over the changing scope and permutations of the family. As outlined by Janet Dolgin ("The Constitution as Family Arbiter: A Moral in the Mess?"), these models may be described as individual-

ist, nuclear, and extended-kin. The first assumes the autonomy of family members in relation to each other, the second subordinates the personhood of children to the care of presumptively devoted parents of opposite gender, and the third emphasizes the importance of a loosely structured community of relatives, including grandparents. (The Court's decision in *Moore v. City of East Cleveland* was predicated on this third model of the family.) Which of these models is preferred by the Court and why?

4. Why does Justice Stevens dissent in this case? To what extent is it because of his preference for a model of the family that differs from that of the other justices?

5. According to Justice Scalia, "a right of parents to direct the upbringing of their children is among the 'unalienable Rights' with which the Declaration of Independence

proclaims 'all Men . . . are endowed by their Creator.'" However, he went on to say that "The Declaration of Independence . . . is not a legal prescription conferring powers upon the courts. . . . Consequently . . . I do not believe that the power which the Constitution confers upon me *as a judge* entitles me to deny legal effect to laws that (in my view) infringe upon what is (in my view) that unenumerated right." He thus gave voice to his textualist interpretive theory, while affirming his allegiance to a theory of justice predicated on the existence of natural rights principles. Were Justice Scalia a member of the Irish Supreme Court, he would not have to distinguish between jurisprudence and justice. Thus, Article 41 reads: "The State recognizes the Family . . . as a moral institution possessing inalienable and imprescriptible rights, antecedent and superior to all positive law." Do you think Justice Scalia would be happier sitting on the Irish Court?

Bowers v. Hardwick

478 U.S. 186, 106 S. Ct. 2841, 92 L. Ed. 2d 140 (1986)

Hardwick was arrested for violating a Georgia law prohibiting sodomy. If convicted, he would have faced up to twenty years in prison. Hardwick challenged the law, claiming it violated his constitutional rights to privacy, expression and association. The federal district court rejected his claim, but the circuit court reversed. The state then appealed. Opinion of the Court: *White,* Burger, Powell, O'Connor, Rehnquist. Concurring opinions: Burger, Powell. Dissenting opinions: *Blackmun,* Brennan, Marshall, *Stevens.*

Mr. Justice WHITE delivered the opinion of the Court.

This case does not require a judgment on whether laws against sodomy between consenting adults in general, or between homosexuals in particular, are wise or desirable. It raises no question about the right or propriety of state legislative decisions to repeal their laws that criminalize homosexual sodomy, or of state court decisions invalidating those laws on state constitutional grounds. The issue presented is whether the Federal Constitution confers a fundamental right upon homosexuals to engage in sodomy and hence invalidates the laws of the many States that still make such conduct illegal and have done so for a very long time. The case also calls for some judgment about the limits of the Court's role in carrying out its constitutional mandate.

We first register our disagreement with the Court of Appeals and with respondent that the Court's prior cases

have construed the Constitution to confer a right of privacy that extends to homosexual sodomy and for all intents and purposes have decided this case. The reach of this line of cases was sketched in *Carey v. Population Services International* (1977). *Pierce v. Society of Sisters* (1925), and *Meyer v. Nebraska* (1923), were described as dealing with child rearing and education; *Prince v. Massachusetts* (1944), with family relationships; *Skinner v. Oklahoma* (1942), with procreation; *Loving v. Virginia* (1967), with marriage; *Griswold v. Connecticut* (1965), and *Eisenstadt v. Baird* (1972), with contraception; and *Roe v. Wade* (1973) with abortion. The latter three cases were interpreted as construing the Due Process Clause of the Fourteenth Amendment to confer a fundamental individual right to decide whether or not to beget or bear a child.

. . . Accepting the decisions in these cases and the above description of them, we think it evident that none of the rights announced in those cases bears any resemblance to the claimed constitutional right of homosexuals to engage in acts of sodomy that is asserted in this case. No connection between family, marriage, or procreation on the one hand and homosexual activity on the other has been demonstrated, either by the Court of Appeals or by respondent. Moreover, any claim that these cases nevertheless stand for the proposition that any kind of private sexual conduct between consenting adults is constitutionally insulated from state proscription is unsupportable. Indeed, the Court's opinion in *Carey* twice asserted that the privacy right, which the *Griswold* line of cases found to be one of the protections provided by the Due Process Clause, did not reach so far.

Precedent aside, however, respondent would have us

Comparative Note 11.6

[Article 8 of The European Convention on Human Rights declares: "Everyone has the right to respect for his private and family life. . . ." Jeffrey Dudgeon, a thirty-five-year-old homosexual, challenged Northern Ireland's law punishing certain homosexual acts between consenting adult males, claiming an unjustified interference with his right to respect for his private life.]

According to the Court's case-law, a restriction on a Convention right [must be justified] as "necessary in a democratic society." [It cannot be so justified] unless, amongst other things, it is proportionate to the legitimate aim pursued. [I]n assessing the requirements of the protection of morals in Northern Ireland, the contested measures must be seen in the context of Northern Irish society. The fact that similar measures are not considered necessary in other parts of the United Kingdom or in other member States of the Council of Europe does not mean that they cannot be necessary in Northern Ireland. . . .

[The Court concluded, however, that in the context of Northern Irish society, there was no pressing necessity to pass this law and that it was not proportionate to the aim pursued.]

The Convention right affected by the impugned legislation protects an essentially private manifestation of the human personality. As compared with the era when [the statute] was enacted, there is now a better understanding . . . of homosexual behavior to the extent that in the great majority of the member States of the Council of Europe it is no longer considered to be necessary or appropriate to treat homosexual practices of the kind now in question as in themselves a matter to which the sanctions of the criminal law should be applied; the Court cannot overlook the marked changes which have occurred in this regard in the domestic law of the member States. . . . In Northern Ireland itself, the authorities have refrained in recent years from enforcing the law in respect of private homosexual acts between consenting males over the age of 21 years capable of valid consent. No evidence has been adduced to show that this has been injurious to moral standards in Northern Ireland or that there has been any public demand for stricter enforcement of the law.

[The Court held, 15 to 4, that there was a violation of Article 8.]

SOURCE: *Dudgeon v. United Kingdom,* Judgment of the European Commission on Human Rights, (hereinafter E.H.R.R. 4149 [1981].

---

announce, as the Court of Appeals did, a fundamental right to engage in homosexual sodomy. This we are quite unwilling to do. It is true that despite the language of the Due Process Clauses of the Fifth and Fourteenth Amendments, which appears to focus only on the processes by which life, liberty, or property is taken, the cases are legion in which those Clauses have been interpreted to have substantive content, subsuming rights that to a great extent are immune from federal or state regulation or proscription. Among such cases are those recognizing rights that have little or no textual support in the constitutional language. *Meyer, Prince,* and *Pierce* fall in this category, as do the privacy cases from *Griswold* to *Carey.*

Striving to assure itself and the public that announcing rights not readily identifiable in the Constitution's text involves much more than the imposition of the Justices' own choice of values on the States and the Federal Government, the Court has sought to identify the nature of the rights qualifying for heightened judicial protection. In *Palko v. Connecticut* (1937), it was said that this category includes those fundamental liberties that are "implicit in

the concept of ordered liberty," such that "neither liberty nor justice would exist if [they] were sacrificed." A different description of fundamental liberties appeared in *Moore v. East Cleveland* (1977), (opinion of Powell, J.), where they are characterized as those liberties that are "deeply rooted in this Nation's history and tradition."

It is obvious to us that neither of these formulations would extend a fundamental right to homosexuals to engage in acts of consensual sodomy. Proscriptions against that conduct have ancient roots. . . . Sodomy was a criminal offense at common law and was forbidden by the laws of the original thirteen States when they ratified the Bill of Rights. In 1868, when the Fourteenth Amendment was ratified, all but 5 of the 37 States in the Union had criminal sodomy laws. In fact, until 1961, all 50 States outlawed sodomy, and today, 24 States and the District of Columbia continue to provide criminal penalties for sodomy performed in private and between consenting adults. Against this background, to claim that a right to engage in such conduct is "deeply rooted in this Nation's history and tradition" or "implicit in the concept of ordered liberty" is, at best, facetious. Nor are we inclined to take a more expansive view of our authority to discover new fundamental rights imbedded in the Due Process Clause. The Court is most vulnerable and comes nearest to illegitimacy when it deals with judge-made constitutional law having little or no cognizable roots in the language or design of the Constitution. That this is so was painfully demonstrated by the face-off between the Executive and the Court in the 1930's, which resulted in the repudiation of much of the substantive gloss that the Court had placed on the Due Process Clause of the Fifth and Fourteenth Amendments. There should be, therefore, great resistance to expand the substantive reach of those Clauses, particularly if it requires redefining the category of rights deemed to be fundamental. Otherwise, the Judiciary necessarily takes to itself further authority to govern the country without express constitutional authority. The claimed right pressed on us today falls far short of overcoming this resistance.

Respondent, however, asserts that the result should be different where the homosexual conduct occurs in the privacy of the home. He relies on *Stanley v. Georgia* (1969), where the Court held that the First Amendment prevents conviction for possessing and reading obscene material in the privacy of his home: "If the First Amendment means anything, it means that a State has no business telling a man, sitting alone in his house, what books he may read or what films he may watch."

Stanley did protect conduct that would not have been protected outside the home, and it partially prevented the enforcement of state obscenity laws; but the decision was firmly grounded in the First Amendment. The right pressed upon us here has no similar support in the text of the Constitution, and it does not qualify for recognition under the prevailing principles for construing the Fourteenth Amendment. Its limits are also difficult to discern. Plainly enough, otherwise illegal conduct is not always immunized whenever it occurs in the home. Victimless crimes, such as the possession and use of illegal drugs do not escape the law where they are committed at home. *Stanley* itself recognized that its holding offered no protection for the possession in the home of drugs, firearms, or stolen goods. And if respondent's submission is limited to the voluntary sexual conduct between consenting adults, it would be difficult, except by fiat, to limit the claimed right to homosexual conduct while leaving exposed to prosecution adultery, incest, and other sexual crimes even though they are committed in the home. We are unwilling to start down that road.

Even if the conduct at issue here is not a fundamental right, respondent asserts that there must be a rational basis for the law and that there is none in this case other than the presumed belief of a majority of the electorate in Georgia that homosexual sodomy is immoral and unacceptable. This is said to be an inadequate rationale to support the law. The law, however, is constantly based on notions of morality, and if all laws representing essentially moral choices are to be invalidated under the Due Process Clause, the courts will be very busy indeed. Even respondent makes no such claim, but insists that majority sentiments about the morality of homosexuality should be declared inadequate. We do not agree, and are unpersuaded that the sodomy laws of some 25 States should be invalidated on this basis.

Accordingly, the judgment of the Court of Appeals is Reversed.

Chief Justice BURGER, concurring.

I join the Court's opinion, but I write separately to underscore my view that in constitutional terms there is no such thing as a fundamental right to commit homosexual sodomy.

As the Court notes, the proscriptions against sodomy have very "ancient roots." Decisions of individuals relating to homosexual conduct have been subject to state intervention throughout the history of Western Civilization. Condemnation of those practices is firmly rooted in Judaeo-Christian moral and ethical standards. Homosexual sodomy was a capital crime under Roman law. During the English Reformation when powers of the ecclesiastical courts were transferred to the King's Courts, the first English statute criminalizing sodomy was passed. Blackstone described "the infamous crime against nature" as an offense of "deeper malignity" than rape, an heinous act "the very mention of which is a disgrace to human nature," and "a crime not fit to be named."

The common law of England, including its prohibition of sodomy, became the received law of Georgia and the other Colonies. In 1816 the Georgia Legislature passed the statute at issue here, and that statute has been continuously in force in one form or another since that time. To hold that the act of homosexual sodomy is somehow protected as a fundamental right would be to cast aside millennia of moral teaching.

This is essentially not a question of personal "preferences" but rather of the legislative authority of the State. I find nothing in the Constitution depriving a State of the power to enact the statute challenged here.

Justice POWELL, concurring.

. . . I agree with the Court that there is no fundamental right—i.e., no substantive right under the Due Process Clause—such as that claimed by respondent, and found to exist by the Court of Appeals. This is not to suggest, however, that respondent may not be protected by the Eighth Amendment of the Constitution. The Georgia statute at issue in this case . . . authorizes a court to imprison a person for up to 20 years for a single private, consensual act of sodomy. In my view, a prison sentence for such conduct—certainly a sentence of long duration—would create a serious Eighth Amendment issue. Under the Georgia statute a single act of sodomy, even in the private setting of a home, is a felony comparable in terms of the possible sentence imposed to serious felonies such as aggravated battery, first degree arson, and robbery.

In this case, however, respondent has not been tried, much less convicted and sentenced. Moreover, respondent has not raised the Eighth Amendment issue below. For these reasons this constitutional argument is not before us.

Justice BLACKMUN, with whom Justice BRENNAN, Justice MARSHALL, and Justice STEVENS join, dissenting.

This case is no more about "a fundamental right to engage in homosexual sodomy," as the Court purports to declare, than *Stanley v. Georgia* (1969), was about a fundamental right to watch obscene movies, or *Katz v. United States* (1967), was about a fundamental right to place interstate bets from a telephone booth. Rather, this case is about "the most comprehensive of rights and the right most valued by civilized men," namely, "the right to be let alone." *Olmstead v. United States*, (1928), (Brandeis, J., dissenting).

The statute at issue denies individuals the right to decide for themselves whether to engage in particular forms of private, consensual sexual activity. The Court concludes that [it] is valid essentially because "the laws of . . . many States . . . still make such conduct illegal and have done so for a very long time." But the fact that the moral judgments expressed by statutes like [this] may be "natural and familiar . . . ought not to conclude our judgment upon the question whether statutes embodying them conflict with the Constitution of the United States." *Roe v. Wade*, (1973), quoting *Lochner v. New York,* (1905), (Holmes, J., dissenting). Like Justice Holmes, I believe that "[i]t is revolting to have no better reason for a rule of law than that it was laid down in the time of Henry IV. It is still more revolting if the grounds upon which it was laid down have vanished long since, and the rule simply persists from blind imitation of the past." I believe we must analyze respondent's claim in the light of the values that underlie the constitutional right to privacy. If that right means anything, it means that, before Georgia can prosecute its citizens for making choices about the most intimate aspects of their lives, it must do more than assert that the choice they have made is an "abominable crime not fit to be named among Christians."

I . . .

. . . First, the Court's almost obsessive focus on homosexual activity is particularly hard to justify in light of the broad language Georgia has used. Unlike the Court, the Georgia Legislature has not proceeded on the assumption that homosexuals are so different from other citizens that their lives may be controlled in a way that would not be tolerated if it limited the choices of those other citizens. Rather, Georgia has provided that "[a] person commits the offense of sodomy when he performs or submits to any sexual act involving the sex organs of one person and the mouth or anus of another." The sex or status of the persons who engage in the act is irrelevant as a matter of state law. In fact, to the extent I can discern a legislative purpose for Georgia's 1968 enactment of s 16–6-2, that purpose seems to have been to broaden the coverage of the law to reach heterosexual as well as homosexual activity. [Hardwick's] claim that [the statute] involves an unconstitutional intrusion into his privacy and his right of intimate association does not depend in any way on his sexual orientation.

Second, I disagree with the Court's refusal to consider whether [the statute] runs afoul of the Eighth or Ninth Amendments or the Equal Protection Clause of the Fourteenth Amendment. . . . [N]either the Eighth Amendment nor the Equal Protection Clause is so clearly irrelevant that a claim resting on either provision should be peremptorily dismissed. The Court's cramped reading of the issue before it makes for a short opinion, but it does little to make for a persuasive one.

II . . .

"Our cases long have recognized that the Constitution embodies a promise that a certain private sphere of individual liberty will be kept largely beyond the reach of government." . . . In construing the right to privacy, the Court has proceeded along two somewhat distinct, albeit complementary, lines. First, it has recognized a privacy interest with reference to certain decisions that are properly for the individual to make. E.g., *Roe v. Wade*, (1973); *Pierce v. Society of Sisters*, (1925). Second, it has recognized a privacy interest with reference to certain places without regard for the particular activities in which the individuals who occupy them are engaged. The case before us implicates both the decisional and the spatial aspects of the right to privacy.

A

The Court concludes today that none of our prior cases dealing with various decisions that individuals are entitled to make free of governmental interference "bears any resemblance to the claimed constitutional right of homosexuals to engage in acts of sodomy that is asserted in this case." While it is true that these cases may be characterized by their connection to protection of the family, the Court's conclusion that they extend no further than this boundary ignores the warning in *Moore v. East Cleveland* (1977), against "clos[ing] our eyes to the basic reasons why certain rights associated with the family have been accorded shelter under the Fourteenth Amendment's Due Process Clause." We protect those rights not because they contribute, in some direct and material way, to the general public welfare, but because they form so central a part of an individual's life. "[T]he concept of privacy embodies the 'moral fact that a person belongs to himself and not others nor to society as a whole.'" *Thornburgh v. American Coll. of Obst. & Gyn.* (1986) (Stevens, J., concurring), quoting Fried, Correspondence, 6 *Phil. & Pub. Affairs* 288–289 (1977). And so we protect the decision whether to marry precisely because marriage "is an association that promotes a way of life, not causes; a harmony in living, not political faiths; a bilateral loyalty, not commercial or social projects." *Griswold v. Connecticut* (1965). We protect the decision whether to have a child because parenthood alters so dramatically an individual's self-definition, not because of demographic considerations or the Bible's command to be fruitful and multiply. And we protect the family because it contributes so powerfully to the happiness of individuals, not because of a preference for stereotypical households. . . .

Only the most willful blindness could obscure the fact that sexual intimacy is "a sensitive, key relationship of human existence, central to family life, community welfare, and the development of human personality." The fact that individuals define themselves in a significant way through their intimate sexual relationships with others suggests, in a Nation as diverse as ours, that there may be many "right" ways of conducting those relationships, and that much of the richness of a relationship will come from the freedom an individual has to choose the form and nature of these intensely personal bonds.

In a variety of circumstances we have recognized that a necessary corollary of giving individuals freedom to choose how to conduct their lives is acceptance of the fact that different individuals will make different choices. . . . The Court claims that its decision today merely refuses to recognize a fundamental right to engage in homosexual sodomy; what the Court really has refused to recognize is the fundamental interest all individuals have in controlling the nature of their intimate associations with others.

B

The behavior for which Hardwick faces prosecution occurred in his own home, a place to which the Fourth Amendment attaches special significance. The Court's treatment of this aspect of the case is symptomatic of its overall refusal to consider the broad principles that have informed our treatment of privacy in specific cases. Just as the right to privacy is more than the mere aggregation of a number of entitlements to engage in specific behavior, so too, protecting the physical integrity of the home is more than merely a means of protecting specific activities that often take place there. . . .

. . . I cannot agree with the Court's statement that "[the] right pressed upon us here has no . . . support in the text of the Constitution." Indeed, the right of an individual to conduct intimate relations in the intimacy of his or her own home seems to me to be the heart of the Constitution's protection of privacy.

III . . .

The core of petitioner's defense . . . , however, is that respondent and others who engage in the conduct prohibited . . . interfere with Georgia's exercise of the "right of the Nation and of the States to maintain a decent society." Essentially, petitioner argues, and the Court agrees, that the fact that the acts described . . . "for hundreds of years, if not thousands, have been uniformly condemned as immoral" is a sufficient reason to permit a State to ban them today.

I cannot agree that either the length of time a majority has held its convictions or the passions with which it defends them can withdraw legislation from this Court's scrutiny. . . . As Justice Jackson wrote so eloquently for the Court in *West Virginia Board of Education v. Barnette* (1943), "we apply the limitations of the Constitution with no fear that freedom to be intellectually and spiritually diverse or even contrary will disintegrate the social organization. . . . [F]reedom to differ is not limited to things that do not matter much. That would be a mere shadow of freedom. The test of its substance is the right to differ as to things that touch the heart of the existing order." It is precisely because the issue raised by this case touches the heart of what makes individuals what they are that we should be especially sensitive to the rights of those whose choices upset the majority.

The assertion that "traditional Judeo-Christian values proscribe" the conduct involved, cannot provide an adequate justification for [this law]. That certain, but by no means all, religious groups condemn the behavior at issue gives the State no license to impose their judgments on the entire citizenry. The legitimacy of secular legislation depends instead on whether the State can advance some justification for its law beyond its conformity to religious doctrine. . . . [F]ar from buttressing his case, petitioner's invocation of Leviticus, Romans, St. Thomas Aquinas, and sodomy's heretical status during the Middle Ages undermines his suggestion that [the statute] represents a legitimate use of secular coercive power. A State can no more punish private behavior because of religious intolerance than it can punish such behavior because of racial animus. "The Constitution cannot control such prejudices, but neither can it tolerate them. Private biases may be outside the reach of the law, but the law cannot, directly or indirectly give them effect." *Palmore v. Sidoti* (1984). . . . No matter how uncomfortable a certain group may make the majority of this Court, we have held that "[m]ere public intolerance or animosity cannot constitutionally justify the deprivation of a person's physical liberty."

Nor can [the statute] be justified as a "morally neutral" exercise of Georgia's power to "protect the public environment." Certainly, some private behavior can affect the fabric of society as a whole. Reasonable people may differ about whether particular sexual acts are moral or immoral, but "we have ample evidence for believing that people will not abandon morality, will not think any better of murder, cruelty and dishonesty, merely because some private sexual practice which they abominate is not punished by the law." Petitioner and the Court fail to see the difference between laws that protect public sensibilities and those that enforce private morality. Statutes banning public sexual activity are entirely consistent with protecting the individual's liberty interest in decisions concerning sexual relations: the same recognition that those decisions are intensely private which justifies protecting them from governmental interference can justify protecting individuals from unwilling exposure to the sexual activities of others. But the mere fact that intimate behavior may be punished when it takes place in public cannot dictate how States can regulate intimate behavior that occurs in intimate places. . . .

This case involves no real interference with the rights of others, for the mere knowledge that other individuals do not adhere to one's value system cannot be a legally cognizable interest, . . . let alone an interest that can justify invading the houses, hearts, and minds of citizens who choose to live their lives differently.

IV

It took but three years for the Court to see the error in its analysis in *Minersville School District v. Gobitis* (1940),

and to recognize that the threat to national cohesion posed by a refusal to salute the flag was vastly outweighed by the threat to those same values posed by compelling such a salute. I can only hope that here, too, the Court soon will reconsider its analysis and conclude that depriving individuals of the right to choose for themselves how to conduct their intimate relationships poses a far greater threat to the values most deeply rooted in our Nation's history than tolerance of nonconformity could ever do. Because I think the Court today betrays those values, I dissent.

Justice STEVENS, with whom Justice BRENNAN and Justice MARSHALL join, dissenting.

Like the statute that is challenged in this case, the rationale of the Court's opinion applies equally to the prohibited conduct regardless of whether the parties who engage in it are married or unmarried, or are of the same or different sexes. Sodomy was condemned as an odious and sinful type of behavior during the formative period of the common law. That condemnation was equally damning for heterosexual and homosexual sodomy. Moreover, it provided no special exemption for married couples. The license to cohabit and to produce legitimate offspring simply did not include any permission to engage in sexual conduct that was considered a "crime against nature."

The history of the Georgia statute before us clearly reveals this traditional prohibition of heterosexual, as well as homosexual, sodomy. Indeed, at one point in the 20th century, Georgia's law was construed to permit certain sexual conduct between homosexual women even though such conduct was prohibited between heterosexuals. The history of the statutes cited by the majority as proof for the proposition that sodomy is not constitutionally protected, similarly reveals a prohibition on heterosexual, as well as homosexual, sodomy.

Because the Georgia statute expresses the traditional view that sodomy is an immoral kind of conduct regardless of the identity of the persons who engage in it, I believe that a proper analysis of its constitutionality requires consideration of two questions: First, may a State totally prohibit the described conduct by means of a neutral law applying without exception to all persons subject to its jurisdiction? If not, may the State save the statute by announcing that it will only enforce the law against homosexuals? The two questions merit separate discussion.

I

Our prior cases make two propositions abundantly clear. First, the fact that the governing majority in a State has traditionally viewed a particular practice as immoral is not a sufficient reason for upholding a law prohibiting the practice; neither history nor tradition could save a law prohibiting miscegenation from constitutional attack. Second, individual decisions by married persons, concerning the intimacies of their physical relationship, even when not intended to produce offspring, are a form of "liberty" protected by the Due Process Clause of the Fourteenth Amendment. *Griswold v. Connecticut* (1965). Moreover, this protection extends to intimate choices by unmarried as well as married persons. *Carey v. Population Services International* (1977); *Eisenstadt v. Baird* (1972).

Society has every right to encourage its individual members to follow particular traditions in expressing affection for one another and in gratifying their personal desires. It, of course, may prohibit an individual from imposing his will on another to satisfy his own selfish interests. It may also prevent an individual from interfering with, or violating, a legally sanctioned and protected relationship, such as marriage. And it may explain the relative advantages and disadvantages of different forms of intimate expression. But when individual married couples are isolated from observation by others, the way in which they voluntarily choose to conduct their intimate relations is a matter for them—not the State—to decide. The essential "liberty" that animated the development of the law in cases like *Griswold, Eisenstadt,* and *Carey* surely embraces the right to engage in nonreproductive, sexual conduct that others may consider offensive or immoral. . . .

II

If the Georgia statute cannot be enforced as it is written—if the conduct it seeks to prohibit is a protected form of liberty for the vast majority of Georgia's citizens—the State must assume the burden of justifying a selective application of its law. Either the persons to whom Georgia seeks to apply its statute do not have the same interest in "liberty" that others have, or there must be a reason why the State may be permitted to apply a generally applicable law to certain persons that it does not apply to others. The first possibility is plainly unacceptable. Although the meaning of the principle that "all men are created equal" is not always clear, it surely must mean that every free citizen has the same interest in "liberty" that the members of the majority share. From the standpoint of the individual, the homosexual and the heterosexual have the same interest in deciding how he will live his own life, and, more narrowly, how he will conduct himself in his personal and voluntary associations with his companions. State intrusion into the private conduct of either is equally burdensome.

The second possibility is similarly unacceptable. A policy of selective application must be supported by a neutral and legitimate interest—something more substantial than a habitual dislike for, or ignorance about, the disfavored group. Neither the State nor the Court has identified any such interest in this case. The Court has posited as a justification for the Georgia statute "the presumed belief of a majority of the electorate in Georgia that homosexual sodomy is immoral and unacceptable." But the Georgia electorate has expressed no such belief—instead, its representatives enacted a law that presumably reflects the belief that all sodomy is immoral and unacceptable. Unless the Court is prepared to conclude that such a law is constitutional, it may not rely on the work product of the Georgia Legislature to support its holding. For the Georgia statute does not single out homosexuals as a separate class meriting special disfavored treatment. . . .

I respectfully dissent.

Notes and Queries

1. In 1961, Illinois became the first state to decriminalize acts of sodomy. By 1975, just about half of the states, Georgia not included, had decriminalized consensual sodomy. Is the Court's decision in *Bowers* likely to affect how states approach issues of sexuality and public policy in the future? As of 1990, state supreme courts in Texas, Michigan, and Kentucky struck down state laws against sodomy on the basis of their state constitutions.

2. Questions of sexuality raise profound moral, philosophical, and institutional questions in the American constitutional order. Is the Court's opinion sufficiently attentive to these questions? Justice Blackmun, for instance, says that this case "touches the heart of what makes individuals what they are." What does make a person who he or she is? Is society a collection of self-made individuals, or is the relationship between society and the individual more complex and interdependent? Why should society be disallowed from expressing its collective opinion about the preferred constitution of the individual?

3. The majority opinion and the dissent by Justice Blackmun frame the issue in *Bowers* in very different ways. Does that in turn influence how they interpret precedent? At an earlier stage in the proceedings, Hardwick was joined in his complaint by "John and Mary Doe," a married couple who alleged that fear of prosecution under the law infringed upon the privacy of their sexual relationship. Does Justice White's description of the issue as "whether the Federal Constitution confers a fundamental right upon homosexuals to engage in sodomy" leave open

the possibility that the same law, applied to heterosexuals, would violate the Constitution?

4. According to the majority, what role should the moral standards of the community play in determining what is and is not protected by the right to privacy? Is this understanding compatible with the Court's other privacy cases? With footnote four in *Carolene Products*? Are the limits on privacy generated in *Bowers* applicable to other sexual practices, or to the sexual practices of heterosexuals?

5. What role does an appeal to history play in the majority's analysis? Why does Justice White refer to the long history and the "ancient roots" of state sodomy laws? Justice Blackmun, in contrast, said that he could not "agree that either the length of time a majority has held its convictions or the passion with which it defends them can withdraw legislation from this Court's scrutiny." As we have seen, however, appeals to history and tradition are a common method of constitutional interpretation. Is there a principled way to determine when such appeals are acceptable and when they are not? Does Justice Blackmun offer a way?

Chief Justice Burger argued that to overturn state laws against sodomy would be to "cast aside a millennia of moral teaching." Does the Constitution incorporate that moral teaching? Would we accept similar arguments about the inherent, natural, and ancient history of the inferiority of some races to others, or of one sex to another?

6. Is it possible, much less desirable, for a community to entirely foreswear collective opinions on moral issues? Could one argue that to disfranchise the community from making moral decisions is to deprive it of a part of the power of self-governance? And why isn't the claim that moral decisions should be left to the individual itself a claim about morality and power? If so, then isn't the question raised by cases like *Bowers* not whether the community or the individual should be entrusted with the power to decide questions of morality, but rather which moral position the community should embrace?

7. The majority in *Bowers* seemed concerned with the integrity of the Court as an institution and utilized this concern in sustaining the anti-sodomy law: "The Court is most vulnerable and comes nearest to illegitimacy when it deals with judge-made constitutional law having little or no cognizable roots in the language or design of the Constitution. . . . There should be, therefore, great resistance to expand the substantive reach of those clauses, particularly if it requires redefining the category of rights to be deemed fundamental. Otherwise, the Judiciary takes to itself further authority to govern the country without express constitutional authority."

Should one criteria for principled interpretation of the Constitution be whether or not the Court's integrity will be weakened by a particular result in a particular case? Shouldn't the Court's first concern be to find the "correct" interpretation of the Constitution, irrespective of the consequences?

8. In *The Homosexuality Case*, 6BVerfGE 389 (1957), the Federal Constitutional Court heard a challenge to a German statute that prohibited homosexuality. The petitioners claimed that the statute violated Article 2(1) of the Basic Law, which guarantees the free development of personality. The Court conceded that the "free development of one's personality . . . also extends to the sexual sphere." The Court further noted, however, that the right is also limited, so that an individual may not "infringe the rights of others or offend against the constitutional order or the moral code."

The Court further concluded that "Homosexual activity clearly offends against the moral code. . . . But it is difficult to determine the validity of a moral code. A judge's personal sense of morality cannot be decisive . . . , nor can opinions of individual groups among the people suffice." After reviewing the history of the proscription against homosexuality in German law, the Court concluded that the statute did not violate Article 2(1).

9. Comparative Note 11.6 contains an extract from an opinion by the European Court, striking down Northern Ireland's provision punishing certain homosexual acts between consenting adult males. Does the Court's analysis differ in any significant way from *Bowers*? Would the introduction of a "proportionality principle" in the *Bowers* analysis affect the result?

Lawrence v. Texas

123 S. Ct 1406, 155 L. Ed 2d 376 (2003)

Responding to a reported weapons disturbance in a private residence, Houston police entered Lawrence's apartment and saw him and another adult man engaging in a private, consensual sexual act. The men were arrested and convicted of deviate sexual intercourse in violation of a Texas statute forbidding two persons of the same sex to engage in certain intimate sexual conduct. In affirming, the State Court of Appeals held that the statute was not unconstitutional under the Due Process Clause of the Fourteenth Amendment. The court considered *Bowers v. Hardwick* (1986) controlling on that point.

Comparative Note 11.7

[In 1999, the South African Constitutional Court decided an important sodomy case. An excerpt from Justice Albie Sachs' opinion follows.]

In My View, the common-law crime of sodomy constitutes an infringement of the right to dignity which is a cornerstone of our Constitution. Its importance is further emphasized by the role accorded to it in section 36 of the Constitution which provides that:

> "The rights in the Bill of Rights may be limited only in terms of law of general application to the extent that the limitation is reasonable and justifiable in an open and democratic society based on human dignity, equality and freedom. . . ."

Dignity is a difficult concept to capture in precise terms. At its least, it is clear that the constitutional protection of dignity requires us to acknowledge the value and worth of all individuals as members of our society. The common-law prohibition on sodomy criminalizes all sexual intercourse per anum between men: regardless of the relationship of the couple who engage therein,

of the age of such couple, of the place where it occurs, or indeed of any other circumstances whatsoever. In so doing, it punishes a form of sexual conduct which is identified by our broader society with homosexuals. Its symbolic effect is to state that in the eyes of our legal system all gay men are criminals. The stigma thus attached to a significant portion of our population is manifest. But the harm imposed by the criminal law is far more symbolic. As a result of the criminal offense, gay men are at risk of arrest, prosecution and conviction of the offense of sodomy simply because they seek to engage in sexual conduct which is part of their experience of being human. Just as apartheid legislation rendered the lives of couples of different racial groups perpetually at risk, the sodomy offense builds insecurity and vulnerability into the daily lives of gay men. There can be no doubt that the existence of a law which punishes a form of sexual expression for gay men degrades and devalues gay men in our broader society. As such it is a palpable invasion of their dignity and a breach of section 10 of the Constitution.

SOURCE: *National Coalition For Gay and Lesbian Equality v. Minister of Justice and Others*, 1999 (1) SALR 6 (CC), in Norman Dorsen, et al., eds., *Comparative Constitutionalism: Cases and Materials* (St. Paul: Thomson/West, 2003), p. 613.

Kennedy, J., delivered the opinion of the Court, in which Stevens, Souter, Ginsburg, and Breyer, JJ., joined. O'Connor, J., filed an opinion concurring in the judgment. Scalia, J., filed a dissenting opinion, in which Rehnquist, C. J., and Thomas, J., joined. Thomas, J., filed a dissenting opinion.

Justice KENNEDY delivered the opinion of the Court.

Liberty protects the person from unwarranted government intrusions into a dwelling or other private places. In our tradition the State is not omnipresent in the home. And there are other spheres of our lives and existence, outside the home, where the State should not be a dominant presence. Freedom extends beyond spatial bounds. Liberty presumes an autonomy of self that includes freedom of thought, belief, expression, and certain intimate conduct. The instant case involves liberty of the person both in its spatial and more transcendent dimensions.

I

The question before the Court is the validity of a Texas statute making it a crime for two persons of the same sex to engage in certain intimate sexual conduct. . . .

II

We conclude the case should be resolved by determining whether the petitioners were free as adults to engage in the private conduct in the exercise of their liberty under the Due Process Clause of the Fourteenth Amendment to the Constitution. For this inquiry we deem it necessary to reconsider the Court's holding in *Bowers*. . . .

The facts in *Bowers* had some similarities to the instant case. A police officer, whose right to enter seems not to have been in question, observed Hardwick, in his own bedroom, engaging in intimate sexual conduct with another adult male. The conduct was in violation of a Georgia statute making it a criminal offense to engage in sodomy. One difference between the two cases is that the Georgia statute prohibited the conduct whether or not the participants were of the same sex, while the Texas statute, as we have seen, applies only to participants of the same sex. Hardwick was not prosecuted, but he brought an action in federal court to declare the state statute invalid. He alleged he was a practicing homosexual and that the criminal prohibition violated rights guaranteed to him by the Constitution. The Court, in an opinion by Justice White, sustained the Georgia law. Chief Justice Burger and Justice Powell joined the opinion of the Court and filed separate, concurring opinions. Four Justices dissented.

The Court began its substantive discussion in *Bowers* as follows: "The issue presented is whether the Federal Constitution confers a fundamental right upon homosexuals to engage in sodomy and hence invalidates the laws of the many States that still make such conduct illegal and have done so for a very long time." That statement, we now conclude, discloses the Court's own failure to appreciate the extent of the liberty at stake. To say that the issue in Bowers was simply the right to engage in certain sexual conduct demeans the claim the individual put forward, just as it would demean a married couple were it to be said marriage is simply about the right to have sexual intercourse. The laws involved in *Bowers* and here are, to be sure, statutes that purport to do no more than prohibit a particular sexual act. Their penalties and purposes, though, have more far-reaching consequences, touching upon the most private human conduct, sexual behavior, and in the most private of places, the home. The statutes do seek to control a personal relationship that, whether or not entitled to formal recognition in the law, is within the liberty of persons to choose without being punished as criminals.

This, as a general rule, should counsel against attempts by the State, or a court, to define the meaning of the relationship or to set its boundaries absent injury to a person or abuse of an institution the law protects. It suffices for us to acknowledge that adults may choose to enter upon this relationship in the confines of their homes and their own private lives and still retain their dignity as free persons. When sexuality finds overt expression in intimate conduct with another person, the conduct can be but one element in a personal bond that is more enduring. The liberty protected by the Constitution allows homosexual persons the right to make this choice.

Having misapprehended the claim of liberty there presented to it, and thus stating the claim to be whether there is a fundamental right to engage in consensual sodomy, the *Bowers* Court said: "Proscriptions against that conduct have ancient roots." In academic writings, and in many of the scholarly amicus briefs filed to assist the Court in this case, there are fundamental criticisms of the historical premises relied upon by the majority and concurring opinions in *Bowers*. We need not enter this debate in the attempt to reach a definitive historical judgment, but . . . counsel against adopting the definitive conclusions upon which *Bowers* placed such reliance. . . .

In summary, the historical grounds relied upon in *Bowers* are more complex than the majority opinion and the concurring opinion by Chief Justice Burger indicate. Their historical premises are not without doubt and, at the very least, are overstated.

It must be acknowledged, of course, that the Court in *Bowers* was making the broader point that for centuries there have been powerful voices to condemn homosexual conduct as immoral. The condemnation has been shaped by religious beliefs, conceptions of right and acceptable behavior, and respect for the traditional family. For many persons these are not trivial concerns but profound and deep convictions accepted as ethical and moral principles to which they aspire and which thus determine the course of their lives. These considerations do not answer the question before us, however. The issue is whether the majority may use the power of the State to enforce these views on the whole society through operation of the criminal law. "Our obligation is to define the liberty of all, not to mandate our own moral code." (*Planned Parenthood of Southeastern Pa. v. Casey*, 1992).

Chief Justice Burger joined the opinion for the Court in *Bowers* and further explained his views as follows: "Decisions of individuals relating to homosexual conduct have been subject to state intervention throughout the history of Western civilization. Condemnation of those practices is firmly rooted in Judeo-Christian moral and ethical standards." As with Justice White's assumptions about history, scholarship casts some doubt on the sweeping nature of the statement by Chief Justice Burger as it pertains to private homosexual conduct between consenting adults. In all events we think that our laws and traditions in the past half century are of most relevance here. These references show an emerging awareness that liberty gives substantial protection to adult persons in deciding how to conduct their private lives in matters pertaining to sex. "[H]istory and tradition are the starting point but not in all cases the ending point of the substantive due process inquiry." (*County of Sacramento v. Lewis*, 1998).

The sweeping references by Chief Justice Burger to the history of Western civilization and to Judeo-Christian moral and ethical standards did not take account of other authorities pointing in an opposite direction. A committee advising the British Parliament recommended in 1957 repeal of laws punishing homosexual conduct. Parliament enacted the substance of those recommendations 10 years later.

Of even more importance, almost five years before *Bowers* was decided the European Court of Human Rights considered a case with parallels to *Bowers* and to today's case. An adult male resident in Northern Ireland alleged he was a practicing homosexual who desired to engage in consensual homosexual conduct. The laws of Northern Ireland forbade him that right. He alleged that he had been questioned, his home had been searched, and he feared criminal prosecution. The court held that the laws proscribing the conduct were invalid under the European Convention on Human Rights. Authoritative in all countries that are members of the Council of Europe (21 nations then, 45 nations now), the decision is at odds with the premise in Bowers that the claim put forward was insubstantial in our Western civilization.

In our own constitutional system the deficiencies in *Bowers* became even more apparent in the years following its announcement. The 25 States with laws prohibiting the relevant conduct referenced in the Bowers decision are reduced now to 13, of which 4 enforce their laws only against homosexual conduct. In those States where sodomy is still proscribed, whether for same-sex or heterosexual conduct, there is a pattern of nonenforcement with respect to consenting adults acting in private. The State of Texas admitted in 1994 that as of that date it had not prosecuted anyone under those circumstances.

Two principal cases decided after *Bowers* cast its holding into even more doubt. In *Planned Parenthood of Southeastern Pa. v. Casey* (1992), the Court reaffirmed the substantive force of the liberty protected by the Due Process Clause. The *Casey* decision again confirmed that our laws and tradition afford constitutional protection to personal decisions relating to marriage, procreation, contraception, family relationships, child rearing, and education. In explaining the respect the Constitution demands for the autonomy of the person in making these choices, we stated as follows:

"These matters, involving the most intimate and personal choices a person may make in a lifetime, choices central to personal dignity and autonomy, are central to the liberty protected by the Fourteenth Amendment. At the heart of liberty is the right to define one's own concept of existence, of meaning, of the universe, and of the mystery of human life. Beliefs about these matters could not define the attributes of personhood were they formed under compulsion of the State."

Persons in a homosexual relationship may seek auton-

omy for these purposes, just as heterosexual persons do. The decision in *Bowers* would deny them this right.

The second post-*Bowers* case of principal relevance is *Romer v. Evans* (1996). There the Court struck down class-based legislation directed at homosexuals as a violation of the Equal Protection Clause. *Romer* invalidated an amendment to Colorado's constitution which named as a solitary class persons who were homosexuals, lesbians, or bisexual either by "orientation, conduct, practices or relationships," and deprived them of protection under state antidiscrimination laws. We concluded that the provision was "born of animosity toward the class of persons affected" and further that it had no rational relation to a legitimate governmental purpose.

As an alternative argument in this case, counsel for the petitioners and some amici contend that *Romer* provides the basis for declaring the Texas statute invalid under the Equal Protection Clause. That is a tenable argument, but we conclude the instant case requires us to address whether *Bowers* itself has continuing validity. Were we to hold the statute invalid under the Equal Protection Clause some might question whether a prohibition would be valid if drawn differently, say, to prohibit the conduct both between same-sex and different-sex participants.

Equality of treatment and the due process right to demand respect for conduct protected by the substantive guarantee of liberty are linked in important respects, and a decision on the latter point advances both interests. If protected conduct is made criminal and the law which does so remains unexamined for its substantive validity, its stigma might remain even if it were not enforceable as drawn for equal protection reasons. When homosexual conduct is made criminal by the law of the State, that declaration in and of itself is an invitation to subject homosexual persons to discrimination both in the public and in the private spheres. The central holding of *Bowers* has been brought in question by this case, and it should be addressed. Its continuance as precedent demeans the lives of homosexual persons. . . .

The foundations of *Bowers* have sustained serious erosion from our recent decisions in *Casey* and *Romer*. When our precedent has been thus weakened, criticism from other sources is of greater significance. In the United States criticism of *Bowers* has been substantial and continuing, disapproving of its reasoning in all respects, not just as to its historical assumptions. The courts of five different States have declined to follow it in interpreting provisions in their own state constitutions parallel to the Due Process Clause of the Fourteenth Amendment.

To the extent *Bowers* relied on values we share with a wider civilization, it should be noted that the reasoning and holding in *Bowers* have been rejected elsewhere. The European Court of Human Rights has followed not *Bowers* but its own decision in *Dudgeon v. United Kingdom* (1981). Other nations, too, have taken action consistent with an affirmation of the protected right of homosexual adults to engage in intimate, consensual conduct. The right the petitioners seek in this case has been accepted as an integral part of human freedom in many other countries. There has been no showing that in this country the governmental interest in circumscribing personal choice is somehow more legitimate or urgent.

The doctrine of stare decisis is essential to the respect accorded to the judgments of the Court and to the stability of the law. It is not, however, an inexorable command. In *Casey* we noted that when a Court is asked to overrule a precedent recognizing a constitutional liberty interest, individual or societal reliance on the existence of that liberty cautions with particular strength against reversing course. The holding in *Bowers*, however, has not induced detrimental reliance comparable to some instances where recognized individual rights are involved. Indeed, there has been no individual or societal reliance on *Bowers* of the sort that could counsel against overturning its holding once there are compelling reasons to do so. *Bowers* itself causes uncertainty, for the precedents before and after its issuance contradict its central holding. . . .

Bowers was not correct when it was decided, and it is not correct today. It ought not to remain binding precedent. *Bowers v. Hardwick* should be and now is overruled.

The present case does not involve minors. It does not involve persons who might be injured or coerced or who are situated in relationships where consent might not easily be refused. It does not involve public conduct or prostitution. It does not involve whether the government must give formal recognition to any relationship that homosexual persons seek to enter. The case does involve two adults who, with full and mutual consent from each other, engaged in sexual practices common to a homosexual lifestyle. The petitioners are entitled to respect for their private lives. The State cannot demean their existence or control their destiny by making their private sexual conduct a crime. Their right to liberty under the Due Process Clause gives them the full right to engage in their conduct without intervention of the government. "It is a promise of the Constitution that there is a realm of personal liberty which the government may not enter." (*Casey*). The Texas statute furthers no legitimate state interest which can justify its intrusion into the personal and private life of the individual.

Had those who drew and ratified the Due Process Clauses of the Fifth Amendment or the Fourteenth Amendment known the components of liberty in its manifold possibilities, they might have been more specific. They did not presume to have this insight. They knew times can blind us to certain truths and later generations can see that laws once thought necessary and proper in fact serve only to oppress. As the Constitution endures, persons in every generation can invoke its principles in their own search for greater freedom.

The judgment of the Court of Appeals for the Texas Fourteenth District is reversed, and the case is remanded for further proceedings not inconsistent with this opinion.

It is so ordered.

Justice O'CONNOR, concurring in the judgment.

The Court today overrules *Bowers v. Hardwick*. I joined *Bowers*, and do not join the Court in overruling it. Nevertheless, I agree with the Court that Texas' statute banning same-sex sodomy is unconstitutional. Rather than relying on the substantive component of the Fourteenth Amendment's Due Process Clause, as the Court does, I base my conclusion on the Fourteenth Amendment's Equal Protection Clause. . . .

We have been most likely to apply rational basis review to hold a law unconstitutional under the Equal Protection Clause where, as here, the challenged legislation inhibits personal relationships. In *Department of Agriculture v. Moreno* (1973), for example, we held that a law preventing those households containing an individual unrelated to any other member of the household from receiving food stamps violated equal protection because the purpose of the law was to "discriminate against hippies." The asserted governmental interest in preventing food stamp fraud was not deemed sufficient to satisfy rational basis review. In *Eisenstadt v. Baird* (1972), we refused to sanction a law that discriminated between married and unmarried persons by prohibiting the distribution of contraceptives to single persons. Likewise, in *Cleburne v. Cleburne Living Center* (1985), we held that it was irrational for a State to require a home for the mentally disabled to obtain a special use permit when other residences—like fraternity houses and apartment buildings—did not have to obtain such a permit. And in *Romer v. Evans*, we disallowed a state statute that "impos[ed] a broad and undifferentiated disability on a single named group"—specifically, homosexuals. The dissent apparently agrees that if these cases have stare decisis effect, Texas' sodomy law would not pass scrutiny under the Equal Protection Clause, regardless of the type of rational basis review that we apply.

The statute at issue here makes sodomy a crime only if

a person "engages in deviate sexual intercourse with another individual of the same sex." Sodomy between opposite-sex partners, however, is not a crime in Texas. That is, Texas treats the same conduct differently based solely on the participants. Those harmed by this law are people who have a same-sex sexual orientation and thus are more likely to engage in behavior prohibited by s.21.06.

The Texas statute makes homosexuals unequal in the eyes of the law by making particular conduct—and only that conduct—subject to criminal sanction. It appears that prosecutions under Texas' sodomy law are rare. This case shows, however, that prosecutions under s.21.06 do occur. And while the penalty imposed on petitioners in this case was relatively minor, the consequences of conviction are not. As the Court notes, petitioners' convictions, if upheld, would disqualify them from or restrict their ability to engage in a variety of professions, including medicine, athletic training, and interior design. Indeed, were petitioners to move to one of four States, their convictions would require them to register as sex offenders to local law enforcement.

And the effect of Texas' sodomy law is not just limited to the threat of prosecution or consequence of conviction. Texas' sodomy law brands all homosexuals as criminals, thereby making it more difficult for homosexuals to be treated in the same manner as everyone else. Indeed, Texas itself has previously acknowledged the collateral effects of the law, stipulating in a prior challenge to this action that the law "legally sanctions discrimination against [homosexuals] in a variety of ways unrelated to the criminal law," including in the areas of "employment, family issues, and housing." (*State v. Morales, Texas,* 1994).

Texas attempts to justify its law, and the effects of the law, by arguing that the statute satisfies rational basis review because it furthers the legitimate governmental interest of the promotion of morality. In *Bowers,* we held that a state law criminalizing sodomy as applied to homosexual couples did not violate substantive due process. We rejected the argument that no rational basis existed to justify the law, pointing to the government's interest in promoting morality. The only question in front of the Court in *Bowers* was whether the substantive component of the Due Process Clause protected a right to engage in homosexual sodomy. *Bowers* did not hold that moral disapproval of a group is a rational basis under the Equal Protection Clause to criminalize homosexual sodomy when heterosexual sodomy is not punished.

This case raises a different issue than *Bowers*: whether, under the Equal Protection Clause, moral disapproval is a legitimate state interest to justify by itself a statute that bans homosexual sodomy, but not heterosexual sodomy.

It is not. Moral disapproval of this group, like a bare desire to harm the group, is an interest that is insufficient to satisfy rational basis review under the Equal Protection Clause. Indeed, we have never held that moral disapproval, without any other asserted state interest, is a sufficient rationale under the Equal Protection Clause to justify a law that discriminates among groups of persons.

Moral disapproval of a group cannot be a legitimate governmental interest under the Equal Protection Clause because legal classifications must not be "drawn for the purpose of disadvantaging the group burdened by the law." Texas' invocation of moral disapproval as a legitimate state interest proves nothing more than Texas' desire to criminalize homosexual sodomy. But the Equal Protection Clause prevents a State from creating "a classification of persons undertaken for its own sake." And because Texas so rarely enforces its sodomy law as applied to private, consensual acts, the law serves more as a statement of dislike and disapproval against homosexuals than as a tool to stop criminal behavior. The Texas sodomy law "raise[s] the inevitable inference that the disadvantage imposed is born of animosity toward the class of persons affected."

Texas argues, however, that the sodomy law does not discriminate against homosexual persons. Instead, the State maintains that the law discriminates only against homosexual conduct. While it is true that the law applies only to conduct, the conduct targeted by this law is conduct that is closely correlated with being homosexual. Under such circumstances, Texas' sodomy law is targeted at more than conduct. It is instead directed toward gay persons as a class. "After all, there can hardly be more palpable discrimination against a class than making the conduct that defines the class criminal." (Scalia, J., dissenting). When a State makes homosexual conduct criminal, and not "deviate sexual intercourse" committed by persons of different sexes, "that declaration in and of itself is an invitation to subject homosexual persons to discrimination both in the public and in the private spheres." . . .

A State can of course assign certain consequences to a violation of its criminal law. But the State cannot single out one identifiable class of citizens for punishment that does not apply to everyone else, with moral disapproval as the only asserted state interest for the law. The Texas sodomy statute subjects homosexuals to "a lifelong penalty and stigma. A legislative classification that threatens the creation of an underclass . . . cannot be reconciled with" the Equal Protection Clause. (*Plyler v. Doe,* 1982).

Whether a sodomy law that is neutral both in effect and application would violate the substantive component of the Due Process Clause is an issue that need not be decided today. I am confident, however, that so long as the Equal Protection Clause requires a sodomy law to apply equally to the private consensual conduct of homosexuals and heterosexuals alike, such a law would not long stand in our democratic society. In the words of Justice Jackson:

"The framers of the Constitution knew, and we should not forget today, that there is no more effective practical guaranty against arbitrary and unreasonable government than to require that the principles of law which officials would impose upon a minority be imposed generally. Conversely, nothing opens the door to arbitrary action so effectively as to allow those officials to pick and choose only a few to whom they will apply legislation and thus to escape the political retribution that might be visited upon them if larger numbers were affected." (*Railway Express Agency, Inc. v. New York*, 1949)

That this law as applied to private, consensual conduct is unconstitutional under the Equal Protection Clause does not mean that other laws distinguishing between heterosexuals and homosexuals would similarly fail under rational basis review. Texas cannot assert any legitimate state interest here, such as national security or preserving the traditional institution of marriage. Unlike the moral disapproval of same-sex relations—the asserted state interest in this case—other reasons exist to promote the institution of marriage beyond mere moral disapproval of an excluded group.

A law branding one class of persons as criminal solely based on the State's moral disapproval of that class and the conduct associated with that class runs contrary to the values of the Constitution and the Equal Protection Clause, under any standard of review. I therefore concur in the Court's judgment that Texas' sodomy law banning "deviate sexual intercourse" between consenting adults of the same sex, but not between consenting adults of different sexes, is unconstitutional.

Justice SCALIA, with whom THE CHIEF JUSTICE and Justice THOMAS join, dissenting.

"Liberty finds no refuge in a jurisprudence of doubt." (*Casey*). That was the Court's sententious response, barely more than a decade ago, to those seeking to overrule *Roe v. Wade* (1973). The Court's response today, to those who have engaged in a 17-year crusade to overrule *Bowers v. Hardwick*, is very different. The need for stability and certainty presents no barrier.

Most of the rest of today's opinion has no relevance to its actual holding—that the Texas statute "furthers no legitimate state interest which can justify" its application to petitioners under rational-basis review. Though there is discussion of "fundamental proposition[s]" and "funda-mental decisions," nowhere does the Court's opinion declare that homosexual sodomy is a "fundamental right" under the Due Process Clause; nor does it subject the Texas law to the standard of review that would be appropriate (strict scrutiny) if homosexual sodomy were a "fundamental right." Thus, while overruling the outcome of *Bowers*, the Court leaves strangely untouched its central legal conclusion: "[R]espondent would have us announce . . . a fundamental right to engage in homosexual sodomy. This we are quite unwilling to do." Instead the Court simply describes petitioners' conduct as "an exercise of their liberty"—which it undoubtedly is—and proceeds to apply an unheard-of form of rational-basis review that will have far-reaching implications beyond this case.

I

I begin with the Court's surprising readiness to reconsider a decision rendered a mere 17 years ago in *Bowers v. Hardwick*. I do not myself believe in rigid adherence to stare decisis in constitutional cases; but I do believe that we should be consistent rather than manipulative in invoking the doctrine. Today's opinions in support of reversal do not bother to distinguish—or indeed, even bother to mention—the paean to stare decisis coauthored by three Members of today's majority in *Planned Parenthood v. Casey*. There, when stare decisis meant preservation of judicially invented abortion rights, the widespread criticism of *Roe* was strong reason to reaffirm it:

"Where, in the performance of its judicial duties, the Court decides a case in such a way as to resolve the sort of intensely divisive controversy reflected in *Roe*[,] . . . its decision has a dimension that the resolution of the normal case does not carry. . . . [T]o overrule under fire in the absence of the most compelling reason . . . would subvert the Court's legitimacy beyond any serious question."

Today, however, the widespread opposition to *Bowers*, a decision resolving an issue as "intensely divisive" as the issue in *Roe*, is offered as a reason in favor of overruling it. Gone, too, is any "enquiry" (of the sort conducted in *Casey*) into whether the decision sought to be overruled has "proven 'unworkable.'"

Today's approach to stare decisis invites us to overrule an erroneously decided precedent (including an "intensely divisive" decision) if: (1) its foundations have been "eroded" by subsequent decisions; (2) it has been subject to "substantial and continuing" criticism; and (3) it has not induced "individual or societal reliance" that counsels against overturning. The problem is that *Roe* itself—which today's majority surely has no disposition to overrule—satisfies these conditions to at least the same degree as *Bowers*. . . .

I do not quarrel with the Court's claim that *Romer v. Evans* "eroded" the "foundations" of *Bowers'* rational-basis holding. But *Roe* and *Casey* have been equally "eroded" by *Washington v. Glucksberg* (1997), which held that only fundamental rights which are "deeply rooted in this Nation's history and tradition" qualify for anything other than rational basis scrutiny under the doctrine of "substantive due process." *Roe* and *Casey*, of course, subjected the restriction of abortion to heightened scrutiny without even attempting to establish that the freedom to abort was rooted in this Nation's tradition. . . .

. . . It seems to me that the "societal reliance" on the principles confirmed in *Bowers* and discarded today has been overwhelming. Countless judicial decisions and legislative enactments have relied on the ancient proposition that a governing majority's belief that certain sexual behavior is "immoral and unacceptable" constitutes a rational basis for regulation. State laws against bigamy, same-sex marriage, adult incest, prostitution, masturbation, adultery, fornication, bestiality, and obscenity are likewise sustainable only in light of *Bowers'* validation of laws based on moral choices. Every single one of these laws is called into question by today's decision; the Court makes no effort to cabin the scope of its decision to exclude them from its holding. The impossibility of distinguishing homosexuality from other traditional "morals" offenses is precisely why *Bowers* rejected the rational-basis challenge. "The law," it said, "is constantly based on notions of morality, and if all laws representing essentially moral choices are to be invalidated under the Due Process Clause, the courts will be very busy indeed."

What a massive disruption of the current social order, therefore, the overruling of *Bowers* entails. Not so the overruling of *Roe*, which would simply have restored the regime that existed for centuries before 1973, in which the permissibility of and restrictions upon abortion were determined legislatively State-by-State. *Casey*, however, chose to base its stare decisis determination on a different "sort" of reliance. "[P]eople," it said, "have organized intimate relationships and made choices that define their views of themselves and their places in society, in reliance on the availability of abortion in the event that contraception should fail." This falsely assumes that the consequence of overruling *Roe* would have been to make abortion unlawful. It would not; it would merely have permitted the States to do so. Many States would unquestionably have declined to prohibit abortion, and others would not have prohibited it within six months (after which the most significant reliance interests would have expired). Even for persons in States other than these, the choice would not have been between abortion and childbirth,

but between abortion nearby and abortion in a neighboring State.

To tell the truth, it does not surprise me, and should surprise no one, that the Court has chosen today to revise the standards of stare decisis set forth in *Casey*. It has thereby exposed *Casey*'s extraordinary deference to precedent for the result-oriented expedient that it is.

II

Having decided that it need not adhere to stare decisis, the Court still must establish that *Bowers* was wrongly decided and that the Texas statute, as applied to petitioners, is unconstitutional.

Texas Penal Code Ann. s.21.06(a) (2003) undoubtedly imposes constraints on liberty. So do laws prohibiting prostitution, recreational use of heroin, and, for that matter, working more than 60 hours per week in a bakery. But there is no right to "liberty" under the Due Process Clause, though today's opinion repeatedly makes that claim. The Fourteenth Amendment expressly allows States to deprive their citizens of "liberty," so long as "due process of law" is provided:

"No state shall . . . deprive any person of life, liberty, or property, without due process of law."

Our opinions applying the doctrine known as "substantive due process" hold that the Due Process Clause prohibits States from infringing fundamental liberty interests, unless the infringement is narrowly tailored to serve a compelling state interest. We have held repeatedly, in cases the Court today does not overrule, that only fundamental rights qualify for this so-called "heightened scrutiny" protection—that is, rights which are "deeply rooted in this Nation's history and tradition." All other liberty interests may be abridged or abrogated pursuant to a validly enacted state law if that law is rationally related to a legitimate state interest.

Bowers held, first, that criminal prohibitions of homosexual sodomy are not subject to heightened scrutiny because they do not implicate a "fundamental right" under the Due Process Clause. Noting that "[p]roscriptions against that conduct have ancient roots," that "[s]odomy was a criminal offense at common law and was forbidden by the laws of the original 13 States when they ratified the Bill of Rights," and that many States had retained their bans on sodomy, *Bowers* concluded that a right to engage in homosexual sodomy was not "deeply rooted in this Nation's history and tradition."

The Court today does not overrule this holding. Not once does it describe homosexual sodomy as a "fundamental right" or a "fundamental liberty interest," nor does it subject the Texas statute to strict scrutiny. Instead, having failed to establish that the right to homosexual sodomy is "deeply rooted in this Nation's history and tradition," the Court concludes that the application of Texas's statute to petitioners' conduct fails the rational basis test, and overrules *Bowers*' holding to the contrary. "The Texas statute furthers no legitimate state interest which can justify its intrusion into the personal and private life of the individual."

I shall address that rational-basis holding presently. First, however, I address some aspersions that the Court casts upon *Bowers*' conclusion that homosexual sodomy is not a "fundamental right"—even though, as I have said, the Court does not have the boldness to reverse that conclusion. . . .

. . . *Bowers*' conclusion that homosexual sodomy is not a fundamental right "deeply rooted in this Nation's history and tradition" is utterly unassailable.

Realizing that fact, the Court instead says: "[W]e think that our laws and traditions in the past half century are of most relevance here. These references show an emerging awareness that liberty gives substantial protection to adult persons in deciding how to conduct their private lives in matters pertaining to sex." Apart from the fact that such an "emerging awareness" does not establish a "fundamental right," the statement is factually false. States continue to prosecute all sorts of crimes by adults "in matters pertaining to sex": prostitution, adult incest, adultery, obscenity, and child pornography. Sodomy laws, too, have been enforced "in the past half century," in which there have been 134 reported cases involving prosecutions for consensual, adult, homosexual sodomy. In relying, for evidence of an "emerging recognition," upon the American Law Institute's 1955 recommendation not to criminalize "consensual sexual relations conducted in private," the Court ignores the fact that this recommendation was "a point of resistance in most of the states that considered adopting the Model Penal Code."

In any event, an "emerging awareness" is by definition not "deeply rooted in this Nation's history and tradition[s]," as we have said "fundamental right" status requires. Constitutional entitlements do not spring into existence because some States choose to lessen or eliminate criminal sanctions on certain behavior. Much less do they spring into existence, as the Court seems to believe, because *foreign nations* decriminalize conduct. The *Bowers* majority opinion *never* relied on "values we share with a wider civilization," but rather rejected the claimed right to sodomy on the ground that such a right was not "deeply rooted in *this Nation's* history and tradition," (emphasis added). *Bowers*' rational-basis holding is likewise devoid of any reliance on the views of a "wider civiliza-

tion." The Court's discussion of these foreign views (ignoring, of course, the many countries that have retained criminal prohibitions on sodomy) is therefore meaningless dicta. Dangerous dicta, however, since "this Court . . . should not impose foreign moods, fads, or fashions on Americans." (*Foster v. Florida*, 2002).

IV

I turn now to the ground on which the Court squarely rests its holding: the contention that there is no rational basis for the law here under attack. This proposition is so out of accord with our jurisprudence—indeed, with the jurisprudence of *any* society we know—that it requires little discussion.

The Texas statute undeniably seeks to further the belief of its citizens that certain forms of sexual behavior are "immoral and unacceptable,"—the same interest furthered by criminal laws against fornication, bigamy, adultery, adult incest, bestiality, and obscenity. *Bowers* held that this *was* a legitimate state interest. The Court today reaches the opposite conclusion. The Texas statute, it says, "furthers *no legitimate state interest* which can justify its intrusion into the personal and private life of the individual," (emphasis added). The Court embraces instead Justice Stevens' declaration in his *Bowers* dissent, that "the fact that the governing majority in a State has traditionally viewed a particular practice as immoral is not a sufficient reason for upholding a law prohibiting the practice." This effectively decrees the end of all morals legislation. If, as the Court asserts, the promotion of majoritarian sexual morality is not even a *legitimate* state interest, none of the above-mentioned laws can survive rational-basis review. . . .

Justice O'Connor argues that the discrimination in this law which must be justified is not its discrimination with regard to the sex of the partner but its discrimination with regard to the sexual proclivity of the principal actor.

"While it is true that the law applies only to conduct, the conduct targeted by this law is conduct that is closely correlated with being homosexual. Under such circumstances, Texas' sodomy law is targeted at more than conduct. It is instead directed toward gay persons as a class."

Of course the same could be said of any law. A law against public nudity targets "the conduct that is closely correlated with being a nudist," and hence "is targeted at more than conduct"; it is "directed toward nudists as a class." But be that as it may. Even if the Texas law does deny equal protection to "homosexuals as a class," that denial still does not need to be justified by anything more than a rational basis, which our cases show is satisfied by the enforcement of traditional notions of sexual morality.

Justice O'Connor simply decrees application of "a more

searching form of rational basis review" to the Texas statute. The cases she cites do not recognize such a standard, and reach their conclusions only after finding, as required by conventional rational-basis analysis, that no conceivable legitimate state interest supports the classification at issue. Nor does Justice O'Connor explain precisely what her "more searching form" of rational-basis review consists of. It must at least mean, however, that laws exhibiting "'a . . . desire to harm a politically unpopular group,'" are invalid even though there may be a conceivable rational basis to support them.

This reasoning leaves on pretty shaky grounds state laws limiting marriage to opposite-sex couples. Justice O'Connor seeks to preserve them by the conclusory statement that "preserving the traditional institution of marriage" is a legitimate state interest. But "preserving the traditional institution of marriage" is just a kinder way of describing the State's moral disapproval of same-sex couples. Texas's interest in s.21.06 could be recast in similarly euphemistic terms: "preserving the traditional sexual mores of our society." In the jurisprudence Justice O'Connor has seemingly created, judges can validate laws by characterizing them as "preserving the traditions of society" (good); or invalidate them by characterizing them as "expressing moral disapproval" (bad).

* * *

Today's opinion is the product of a Court, which is the product of a law-profession culture, that has largely signed on to the so-called homosexual agenda, by which I mean the agenda promoted by some homosexual activists directed at eliminating the moral opprobrium that has traditionally attached to homosexual conduct. I noted in an earlier opinion the fact that the American Association of Law Schools (to which any reputable law school must seek to belong) excludes from membership any school that refuses to ban from its job-interview facilities a law firm (no matter how small) that does not wish to hire as a prospective partner a person who openly engages in homosexual conduct.

One of the most revealing statements in today's opinion is the Court's grim warning that the criminalization of homosexual conduct is "an invitation to subject homosexual persons to discrimination both in the public and in the private spheres." It is clear from this that the Court has taken sides in the culture war, departing from its role of assuring, as neutral observer, that the democratic rules of engagement are observed. Many Americans do not want persons who openly engage in homosexual conduct as partners in their business, as scoutmasters for their children, as teachers in their children's schools, or as boarders in their home. They view this as protecting themselves and their families from a lifestyle that they believe to be immoral and destructive. The Court views it as "discrimination" which it is the function of our judgments to deter. So imbued is the Court with the law profession's anti-anti-homosexual culture, that it is seemingly unaware that the attitudes of that culture are not obviously "mainstream"; that in most States what the Court calls "discrimination" against those who engage in homosexual acts is perfectly legal; that proposals to ban such "discrimination" under Title VII have repeatedly been rejected by Congress; that in some cases such "discrimination" is mandated by federal statute; and that in some cases such "discrimination" is a constitutional right.

Let me be clear that I have nothing against homosexuals, or any other group, promoting their agenda through normal democratic means. Social perceptions of sexual and other morality change over time, and every group has the right to persuade its fellow citizens that its view of such matters is the best. That homosexuals have achieved some success in that enterprise is attested to by the fact that Texas is one of the few remaining States that criminalize private, consensual homosexual acts. But persuading one's fellow citizens is one thing, and imposing one's views in absence of democratic majority will is something else. I would no more require a State to criminalize homosexual acts—or, for that matter, display any moral disapprobation of them—than I would forbid it to do so. What Texas has chosen to do is well within the range of traditional democratic action, and its hand should not be stayed through the invention of a brand-new "constitutional right" by a Court that is impatient of democratic change. It is indeed true that "later generations can see that laws once thought necessary and proper in fact serve only to oppress"; and when that happens, later generations can repeal those laws. But it is the premise of our system that those judgments are to be made by the people, and not imposed by a governing caste that knows best.

One of the benefits of leaving regulation of this matter to the people rather than to the courts is that the people, unlike judges, need not carry things to their logical conclusion. The people may feel that their disapprobation of homosexual conduct is strong enough to disallow homosexual marriage, but not strong enough to criminalize private homosexual acts—and may legislate accordingly. The Court today pretends that it possesses a similar freedom of action, so that that we need not fear judicial imposition of homosexual marriage, as has recently occurred in Canada (in a decision that the Canadian Government has chosen not to appeal). At the end of its opinion—after having laid waste the foundations of our rational-basis jurisprudence—the Court says that the present case "does not involve whether the government must give formal recognition to any relationship that homosexual persons seek to enter." Do not believe it. More illuminating than this bald, unreasoned disclaimer is the progression of thought displayed by an earlier passage in the Court's opinion, which notes the constitutional protections afforded to "personal decisions relating to *marriage*, procreation, contraception, family relationships, child rearing, and education," and then declares that "[p]ersons in a homosexual relationship may seek autonomy for these purposes, just as heterosexual persons do," (emphasis added). Today's opinion dismantles the structure of constitutional law that has permitted a distinction to be made between heterosexual and homosexual unions, insofar as formal recognition in marriage is concerned. If moral disapprobation of homosexual conduct is "no legitimate state interest" for purposes of proscribing that conduct; and if, as the Court coos (casting aside all pretense of neutrality), "[w]hen sexuality finds overt expression in intimate conduct with another person, the conduct can be but one element in a personal bond that is more enduring"; what justification could there possibly be for denying the benefits of marriage to homosexual couples exercising "[t]he liberty protected by the Constitution"? Surely not the encouragement of procreation, since the sterile and the elderly are allowed to marry. This case "does not involve" the issue of homosexual marriage only if one entertains the belief that principle and logic have nothing to do with the decisions of this Court. Many will hope that, as the Court comfortingly assures us, this is so.

The matters appropriate for this Court's resolution are only three: Texas's prohibition of sodomy neither infringes a "fundamental right" (which the Court does not dispute), nor is unsupported by a rational relation to what the Constitution considers a legitimate state interest, nor denies the equal protection of the laws. I dissent.

Justice THOMAS, dissenting.

I join Justice Scalia's dissenting opinion. I write separately to note that the law before the Court today "is . . . uncommonly silly." (*Griswold v. Connecticut*, 1965). If I were a member of the Texas Legislature, I would vote to repeal it. Punishing someone for expressing his sexual preference through noncommercial consensual conduct with another adult does not appear to be a worthy way to expend valuable law enforcement resources.

Notwithstanding this, I recognize that as a member of this Court I am not empowered to help petitioners and others similarly situated. My duty, rather, is to "decide cases 'agreeably to the Constitution and laws of the United States.'" And, just like Justice Stewart, I "can find [neither in the Bill of Rights nor any other part of the Constitution a] general right of privacy," or as the Court terms it today, the "liberty of the person both in its spatial and more transcendent dimensions."

Notes and Queries

1. *Lawrence* invites comparison to the abortion decision in *Planned Parenthood of Southeastern Pa. v. Casey* for at least two reasons. In both cases, the controlling opinions are informed by a strong libertarian commitment, made clear in Justice Kennedy's quoting from *Casey* that "Our obligation is to define the liberty of all, not to mandate our own moral code." And in both cases much attention was directed to the question of whether the Court should follow a landmark controversial precedent. A significant part of Justice Scalia's dissent was devoted to a critique of the Court's reversal of *Bowers* on the grounds of its alleged failure to follow the *Casey* plurality's criteria for following or abandoning precedents. How persuasive is this critique? Should judges determined to uphold the central holding in *Roe v. Wade* have been more respectful of the principle of *stare decisis* in *Lawrence*?

2. The majority opinion was noteworthy for its heavy reliance on foreign sources, most notably the ruling by the European Court of Human Rights, which we refer to in our introduction. "There has been no showing that in this country the governmental interest in circumscribing personal choice is somehow more legitimate or urgent." Should the fact that a number of other countries provide more protection for the privacy rights of homosexuals weigh heavily on judicial consideration of these rights in the United States? Should, for example, the fact (alluded to in Justice Scalia's dissent) that a Canadian court removed a ban on same-sex marriages have any bearing on how an American court addresses that issue when it is presented for judicial resolution?

3. The Court cites as evidence of the deficiencies in *Bowers* the fact that since that decision the number of states with laws prohibiting sodomy has markedly declined. But could it not be argued that such evidence is more supportive of the alternative view that the democratic process is working and thus should not be short-circuited by judicial rulings foreclosing legislative solutions? One of the likely effects of *Lawrence* is that it will energize political opposition to gay rights. In this regard, one should note (see, for example, Gerald Rosenberg's *The Hollow Hope*) how important *Roe v. Wade* was to the mobilization of anti-abortion politics. Do you see any dif-

ferences in the way these two issues are likely to play out in the aftermath of the Court's rulings?

4. In his 1999 book, *One Case At a Time: Judicial Minimalism On the Supreme Court*, Cass Sunstein wrote: "Suppose . . . that the ban on same-sex marriage is challenged on equal protection grounds. Even if judges find the challenge plausible in its substance, there is much reason for caution on the part of the courts. An immediate judicial vindication of the principle could well jeopardize important interests. It could galvanize opposition. It could weaken the antidiscrimination movement as that movement is operating in democratic arenas" (p. 161). Much of the immediate response to *Lawrence* involved speculation about the future response of the Court to just such a challenge. Do you find in Justice O'Connor's equal protection argument a convincing basis for constitutionally requiring same-sex marriages? If so, do you agree with Sunstein that prudence (see chapter 2) dictates caution in extending it to the institution of marriage?

Michael H. v. Gerald D.
491 U.S. 110, 109 S. Ct. 2333, 105 L. Ed. 2d 91 (1989)

The facts of the case are summarized in Justice Scalia's opinion. Judgment of the Court: *Scalia*, Rehnquist, O'Connor, Kennedy. Concurring opinion: *O'Connor*. Concurring in the judgment: *Stevens*. Dissenting opinions: *Brennan*, Marshall, Blackmun, *White*.

Justice SCALIA announced the judgment of the Court and delivered an opinion.

Under California law, a child born to a married woman living with her husband is presumed to be a child of the marriage. The presumption of legitimacy may be rebutted only by the husband or wife, and then only in limited circumstances. The instant appeal presents the claim that this presumption infringes upon the due process rights of a man who wishes to establish his paternity of a child born to the wife of another man, and the claim that it infringes upon the constitutional right of the child to maintain a relationship with her natural father.

I

The facts of this case are, we must hope, extraordinary. On May 9, 1976, in Las Vegas, Nevada, Carole D., an international model, and Gerald D., a top executive in a French oil company, were married. The couple established a home in Playa del Rey, California in which they resided as husband and wife when one or the other was not out of the country on business. In the summer of 1978, Carole became involved in an adulterous affair with a neighbor, Michael H. In September 1980, she conceived a child, Victoria D., who was born on May 11, 1981. Gerald was listed

---

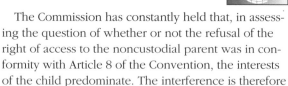

Comparative Note 11.8

[Hendricks, a divorced father, complained about court decisions denying him access to his child because of the mother's refusal, one premised on the need for the child's harmonious development. The following extracts are from the decision of the European Commission on Human Rights.]

The Commission [realizes] that the natural link between a parent and child is of fundamental importance and that, where the actual "family life" in the sense of "living together" has come to an end, continued contact between them is desirable and should in principle remain possible. Respect for family life within the meaning of Article 8 [of the European Convention] thus implies that this contact should not be denied unless there are strong reasons [justifying the] interference.

The Commission has constantly held that, in assessing the question of whether or not the refusal of the right of access to the noncustodial parent was in conformity with Article 8 of the Convention, the interests of the child predominate. The interference is therefore justified where it has been made for the protection of the health of the child.

[Considering the evidence and the decisions below] it follows that the interference with the applicant's right to respect for his family life, being proportionate to the legitimate aim pursued, was justified under Article 8 (2) as being necessary in a democratic society for the protection of the rights and freedoms of another person, namely the child concerned.

SOURCE: *Hendricks v. Netherlands*, Judgment of the European Commission on Human Rights, 5 E.H.R.R. 223 (1982).

as father on the birth certificate and has always held Victoria out to the world as his daughter. Soon after delivery of the child, however, Carole informed Michael that she believed he might be the father.

In the first three years of her life, Victoria remained always with Carole, but found herself within a variety of quasi-family units. In October 1981, Gerald moved to New York City to pursue his business interests, but Carole chose to remain in California. The end of that month, Carole and Michael had blood tests of themselves and Victoria, which showed a 98.07% probability that Michael was Victoria's father. In January 1982, Carole visited Michael in St. Thomas, where his primary business interests were based. There Michael held Victoria out as his child. In March, however, Carole left Michael and returned to California, where she took up residence with yet another man, Scott K. Later that spring, and again in the summer, Carole and Victoria spent time with Gerald in New York City, as well as on vacation in Europe. In the fall, they returned to Scott in California.

In November 1982, rebuffed in his attempts to visit Victoria, Michael filed a filiation action in California Superior Court to establish his paternity and right to visitation. In March 1983, the court appointed an attorney and guardian ad litem to represent Victoria's interests. Victoria then filed a cross-complaint asserting that if she had more than one psychological or de facto father, she was entitled to maintain her filial relationship, with all of the attendant rights, duties, and obligations, with both. In May 1983, Carole filed a motion for summary judgment. During this period, from March through July of 1983, Carole was again living with Gerald in New York. In August, however, she returned to California, became involved once again with Michael, and instructed her attorneys to remove the summary judgment motion from the calendar. For the ensuing eight months, when Michael was not in St. Thomas he lived with Carole and Victoria in Carole's apartment in Los Angeles, and held Victoria out as his daughter. In April 1984, Carole and Michael signed a stipulation that Michael was Victoria's natural father. Carole left Michael the next month, however, and instructed her attorneys not to file the stipulation. In June 1984, Carole reconciled with Gerald and joined him in New York, where they now live with Victoria and two other children since born into the marriage.

In May 1984, Michael and Victoria, through her guardian ad litem, sought visitation rights for Michael *pendente lite.* To assist in determining whether visitation would be in Victoria's best interests, the Superior Court appointed a psychologist to evaluate Victoria, Gerald, Michael, and Carole. The psychologist recommended that Carole retain sole custody, but that Michael be allowed continued contact with Victoria pursuant to a restricted visitation schedule. The court concurred and ordered that Michael be provided with limited visitation privileges. . . .

Before us, Michael and Victoria both raise equal protection and due process challenges. We do not reach Michael's equal protection claim, however, as it was neither raised nor passed upon below. . . .

II

The California statute that is the subject of this litigation is, in substance, more than a century old. . . .

III

We address first the claims of Michael. At the outset, it is necessary to clarify what he sought and what he was denied. California law, like nature itself, makes no provision for dual fatherhood. Michael was seeking to be declared the father of Victoria. The immediate benefit he evidently sought to obtain from that status was visitation rights. . . . But if Michael were successful in being declared the father, other rights would follow—most importantly, the right to be considered as the parent who should have custody, a status which "embrace[s] the sum of parental rights with respect to the rearing of a child, including the child's care; the right to the child's services and earnings; the right to direct the child's activities; the right to make decisions regarding the control, education, and health of the child; and the right, as well as the duty, to prepare the child for additional obligations, which includes the teaching of moral standards, religious beliefs, and elements of good citizenship." All parental rights, including visitation, were automatically denied by denying Michael status as the father. . . .

Michael contends as a matter of substantive due process that because he has established a parental relationship with Victoria, protection of Gerald's and Carole's marital union is an insufficient state interest to support termination of that relationship. This argument is, of course, predicated on the assertion that Michael has a constitutionally protected liberty interest in his relationship with Victoria.

It is an established part of our constitutional jurisprudence that the term "liberty" in the Due Process Clause extends beyond freedom from physical restraint. See, e.g., *Pierce v. Society of Sisters* (1925); *Meyer v. Nebraska* (1923). Without that core textual meaning as a limitation, defining the scope of the Due Process Clause "has at times been a treacherous field for this Court," giving "reason for concern lest the only limits to . . . judicial intervention become the predilections of those who happen at the time to be Members of this Court." *Moore v. East Cleveland*

(1977). The need for restraint has been cogently expressed by Justice White:

> That the Court has ample precedent for the creation of new constitutional rights should not lead it to repeat the process at will. The Judiciary, including this Court, is the most vulnerable and comes nearest to illegitimacy when it deals with judge-made constitutional law having little or no cognizable roots in the language or even the design of the Constitution. Realizing that the present construction of the Due Process Clause represents a major judicial gloss on its terms, as well as on the anticipation of the Framers, the Court should be extremely reluctant to breathe still further substantive content into the Due Process Clause so as to strike down legislation adopted by a State or city to promote its welfare. Whenever the Judiciary does so, it unavoidably pre-empts for itself another part of the governance of the country without express constitutional authority. *Moore* (dissenting opinion).

In an attempt to limit and guide interpretation of the Clause, we have insisted not merely that the interest denominated as a "liberty" be "fundamental" (a concept that, in isolation, is hard to objectify), but also that it be an interest traditionally protected by our society. As we have put it, the Due Process Clause affords only those protections "so rooted in the traditions and conscience of our people as to be ranked as fundamental." Our cases reflect "continual insistence upon respect for the teachings of history [and] solid recognition of the basic values that underlie our society." *Griswold v. Connecticut* (1965) (Harlan, J., concurring in judgment).

This insistence that the asserted liberty interest be rooted in history and tradition is evident, as elsewhere, in our cases according constitutional protection to certain parental rights. Michael reads the landmark case of *Stanley v. Illinois* (1972), as establishing that a liberty interest is created by biological fatherhood plus an established parental relationship—factors that exist in the present case as well. We think that distorts the rationale of those cases. As we view them, they rest not upon such isolated factors but upon the historic respect—indeed, sanctity would not be too strong a term—traditionally accorded to the relationships that develop within the unitary family.

In *Stanley*, for example, we forbade the destruction of such a family when, upon the death of the mother, the state had sought to remove children from the custody of a father who had lived with and supported them and their mother for 18 years. As Justice Powell stated for the plurality in *Moore v. East Cleveland*, "Our decisions establish that the Constitution protects the sanctity of the family pre-

cisely because the institution of the family is deeply rooted in this Nation's history and tradition."

Thus, the legal issue in the present case reduces to whether the relationship between persons in the situation of Michael and Victoria has been treated as a protected family unit under the historic practices of our society, or whether on any other basis it has been accorded special protection. We think it impossible to find that it has. In fact, quite to the contrary, our traditions have protected the marital family (Gerald, Carole, and the child they acknowledge to be theirs) against the sort of claim Michael asserts.

We have found nothing in the older sources, nor in the older cases, addressing specifically the power of the natural father to assert parental rights over a child born into a woman's existing marriage with another man. Since it is Michael's burden to establish that such a power (at least where the natural father has established a relationship with the child) is so deeply embedded within our traditions as to be a fundamental right, the lack of evidence alone might defeat his case. But the evidence shows that even in modern times—when, as we have noted, the rigid protection of the marital family has in other respects been relaxed—the ability of a person in Michael's position to claim paternity has not been generally acknowledged. . . .

Moreover, even if it were clear that one in Michael's position generally possesses, and has generally always possessed, standing to challenge the marital child's legitimacy, that would still not establish Michael's case. As noted earlier, what is at issue here is not entitlement to a state pronouncement that Victoria was begotten by Michael. It is no conceivable denial of constitutional right for a State to decline to declare facts unless some legal consequence hinges upon the requested declaration.

What Michael asserts here is a right to have himself declared the natural father and thereby to obtain parental prerogatives. What he must establish, therefore, is not that our society has traditionally allowed a natural father in his circumstances to establish paternity, but that it has traditionally accorded such a father parental rights, or at least has not traditionally denied them. Even if the law in all States had always been that the entire world could challenge the marital presumption and obtain a declaration as to who was the natural father, that would not advance Michael's claim. Thus, it is ultimately irrelevant, even for purposes of determining current social attitudes towards the alleged substantive right Michael asserts, that the present law in a number of States appears to allow the natural father—including the natural father who has not established a relationship with the child—the theoretical power to rebut the marital presumption. . . . What counts is whether the States in fact award substantive parental rights to the natural father of a child conceived within and born into an extant marital union that wishes to embrace the child. We are not aware of a single case, old or new, that has done so. This is not the stuff of which fundamental rights qualifying as liberty interests are made.*

We do not accept Justice Brennan's criticism that this result "squashes" the liberty that consists of "the freedom not to conform." . . . It seems to us that reflects the erroneous view that there is only one side to this controversy—that one disposition can expand a "liberty" of sorts without contracting an equivalent "liberty" on the other side. Such a happy choice is rarely available. Here, to provide protection to an adulterous natural father is to deny protection to a marital father, and vice versa. If Michael has a "freedom not to conform" (whatever that means), Gerald must equivalently have a "freedom to conform." One of them will pay a price for asserting that "freedom"—Michael by being unable to act as father of the child he has adulterously begotten, or Gerald by being unable to preserve the integrity of the traditional family unit he and Victoria have established. Our disposition

---

*Justice Brennan criticizes our methodology in using historical traditions specifically relating to the rights of an adulterous father, rather than inquiring more generally "whether parenthood is an interest that historically has received our attention and protection." There seems to us no basis for the contention that this methodology is "novel[l]." For example, in *Bowers v. Hardwick* (1986), we noted that at the time the Fourteenth Amendment was ratified all but 5 of the 37 States had criminal sodomy laws . . . and we concluded from that record . . . that "to claim that the right to engage in such conduct is 'deeply rooted in this Nation's history and tradition' or 'implicit in the concept of ordered liberty' is, at best, facetious." In *Roe v. Wade* (1973), we spent about a fifth of our opinion negating the proposition that there was a longstanding tradition of laws proscribing abortion.

We do not understand why, having rejected our focus upon the societal tradition regarding the natural father's rights vis-à-vis a child whose mother is married to another man, Justice Brennan would choose to focus instead upon "parenthood." Why should the relevant category not be even more general—perhaps "family relationships"; or "personal relationships"; or even "emotional attachments in general"? Though the dissent has no basis for the level of generality it would select, we do: We refer to the most specific level at which a relevant tradition protecting, or denying protection to, the asserted right can be identified. . . .

One would think that Justice Brennan would appreciate the value of consulting the most specific tradition available, since he acknowledges that "[e]ven if we can agree . . . that 'family' and 'parenthood' are part of the good life, it is absurd to assume that we can agree on the content of those terms and destructive to pretend that we do." Because such general traditions provide such imprecise guidance, they permit judges to dictate rather than discern the society's views. . . . [Footnote by the Court]

does not choose between these two "freedoms," but leaves that to the people of California. Justice Brennan's approach chooses one of them as the constitutional imperative, on no apparent basis except that the unconventional is to be preferred.

IV

We have never had occasion to decide whether a child has a liberty interest, symmetrical with that of her parent, in maintaining her filial relationship. We need not do so here because, even assuming that such a right exists, Victoria's claim must fail. Victoria's due process challenge is, if anything, weaker than Michael's. Her basic claim is not that California has erred in preventing her from establishing that Michael, not Gerald, should stand as her legal father. Rather, she claims a due process right to maintain filial relationships with both Michael and Gerald. This assertion merits little discussion, for, whatever the merits of the guardian ad litem's belief that such an arrangement can be of great psychological benefit to a child, the claim that a State must recognize multiple fatherhood has no support in the history or traditions of this country.

Moreover, even if we were to construe Victoria's argument as forwarding the lesser proposition that, whatever her status vis-à-vis Gerald, she has a liberty interest in maintaining a filial relationship with her natural father, Michael, we find that, at best, her claim is the obverse of Michael's and fails for the same reasons.

Victoria claims in addition that her equal protection rights have been violated because, unlike her mother and presumed father, she had no opportunity to rebut the presumption of her legitimacy. We find this argument wholly without merit. We reject, at the outset, Victoria's suggestion that her equal protection challenge must be assessed under a standard of strict scrutiny because, in denying her the right to maintain a filial relationship with Michael, the State is discriminating against her on the basis of her illegitimacy. . . . Illegitimacy is a legal construct, not a natural trait. Under California law, Victoria is not illegitimate, and she is treated in the same manner as all other legitimate children: she is entitled to maintain a filial relationship with her legal parents.

We apply, therefore, the ordinary "rational relationship" test to Victoria's equal protection challenge. The primary rationale underlying s 621's limitation on those who may rebut the presumption of legitimacy is a concern that allowing persons other than the husband or wife to do so may undermine the integrity of the marital union. When the husband or wife contests the legitimacy of their child, the stability of the marriage has already been shaken. In contrast, allowing a claim of illegitimacy to be pressed by the child—or, more accurately, by a court-appointed guardian ad litem—may well disrupt an otherwise peaceful union. Since it pursues a legitimate end by rational means, California's decision to treat Victoria differently from her parents is not a denial of equal protection.

The judgment of the California Court of Appeal is Affirmed.

Justice O'CONNOR, with whom Justice KENNEDY joins, concurring in part.

I concur in all but footnote 6 of Justice Scalia's opinion. This footnote sketches a mode of historical analysis to be used when identifying liberty interests protected by the Due Process Clause . . . that may be somewhat inconsistent with our past decisions in this area. On occasion the Court has characterized relevant traditions protecting asserted rights at levels of generality that might not be "the most specific level" available. I would not foreclose the unanticipated by the prior imposition of a single mode of historical analysis.

Justice STEVENS, concurring in the judgment.

As I understand this case, it raises two different questions about the validity of California's statutory scheme. First, is [the law] unconstitutional because it prevents Michael and Victoria from obtaining a judicial determination that he is her biological father—even if no legal rights would be affected by that determination? Second, does the California statute deny appellants a fair opportunity to prove that Victoria's best interests would be served by granting Michael visitation rights? On the first issue I agree with Justice Scalia that the Federal Constitution imposes no obligation upon a State to "declare facts unless some legal consequence hinges upon the requested declaration."

On the second issue I do not agree with Justice Scalia's analysis. He seems to reject the possibility that a natural father might ever have a constitutionally protected interest in his relationship with a child whose mother was married to and cohabiting with another man at the time of the child's conception and birth. I think cases like *Stanley v. Illinois* (1972), and *Caban v. Mohammed* (1979), demonstrate that enduring "family" relationships may develop in unconventional settings. I therefore would not foreclose the possibility that a constitutionally protected relationship between a natural father and his child might exist in a case like this. Indeed, I am willing to assume for the purpose of deciding this case that Michael's relationship with Victoria is strong enough to give him a constitutional right to try to convince a trial judge that Victoria's best interest would be served by granting him visitation rights.

I am satisfied, however, that the California statute, as applied in this case, gave him that opportunity.

Justice BRENNAN, with whom Justice MARSHALL and Justice BLACKMUN join, dissenting.

In a case that has yielded so many opinions as has this one, it is fruitful to begin by emphasizing the common ground shared by a majority of this Court. Five Members of the Court refuse to foreclose "the possibility that a natural father might ever have a constitutionally protected interest in his relationship with a child whose mother was married to and cohabiting with another man at the time of the child's conception and birth." Five Justices agree that the flaw inhering in a conclusive presumption that terminates a constitutionally protected interest without any hearing whatsoever is a procedural one. Four Members of the Court agree that Michael H. has a liberty interest in his relationship with Victoria, and one assumes for purposes of this case that he does.

In contrast, only two Members of the Court fully endorse Justice Scalia's view of the proper method of analyzing questions arising under the Due Process Clause. Nevertheless, because the plurality opinion's exclusively historical analysis portends a significant and unfortunate departure from our prior cases and from sound constitutional decisionmaking, I devote a substantial portion of my discussion to it.

I

Once we recognized that the "liberty" protected by the Due Process Clause of the Fourteenth Amendment encompasses more than freedom from bodily restraint, today's plurality opinion emphasizes, the concept was cut loose from one natural limitation on its meaning. This innovation paved the way, so the plurality hints, for judges to substitute their own preferences for those of elected officials. Dissatisfied with this supposedly unbridled and uncertain state of affairs, the plurality casts about for another limitation on the concept of liberty.

It finds this limitation in "tradition." Apparently oblivious to the fact that this concept can be as malleable and as elusive as "liberty" itself, the plurality pretends that tradition places a discernible border around the Constitution. The pretense is seductive; it would be comforting to believe that a search for "tradition" involves nothing more idiosyncratic or complicated than poring through dusty volumes on American history. Yet, as Justice White observed in his dissent in *Moore v. East Cleveland* (1977), "What the deeply rooted traditions of the country are is arguable." Indeed, wherever I would begin to look for an interest "deeply rooted in the country's traditions," one thing is certain: I would not stop (as does the plurality) at *Bracton,* or *Blackstone,* or *Kent,* or even the *American Law Reports* in conducting my search. Because reasonable people can disagree about the content of particular traditions, and because they can disagree even about which traditions are relevant to the definition of "liberty," the plurality has not found the objective boundary that it seeks.

Even if we could agree, moreover, on the content and significance of particular traditions, we still would be forced to identify the point at which a tradition becomes firm enough to be relevant to our definition of liberty and the moment at which it becomes too obsolete to be relevant any longer. The plurality supplies no objective means by which we might make these determinations. Indeed, as soon as the plurality sees signs that the tradition upon which it bases its decision (the laws denying putative fathers like Michael standing to assert paternity) is crumbling, it shifts ground and says that the case has nothing to do with that tradition, after all. "What is at issue here," the plurality asserts after canvassing the law on paternity suits, "is not entitlement to a state pronouncement that Victoria was begotten by Michael." . . . But that is precisely what is at issue here, and the plurality's last-minute denial of this fact dramatically illustrates the subjectivity of its own analysis.

It is ironic that an approach so utterly dependent on tradition is so indifferent to our precedents. Citing barely a handful of this Court's numerous decisions defining the scope of the liberty protected by the Due Process Clause to support its reliance on tradition, the plurality acts as though English legal treatises and the *American Law Reports* always have provided the sole source for our constitutional principles. They have not. Just as common-law notions no longer define the "property" that the Constitution protects, neither do they circumscribe the "liberty" that it guarantees. On the contrary, " '[l]iberty' and 'property' are broad and majestic terms. They are among the '[g]reat [constitutional] concepts . . . purposely left to gather meaning from experience. . . . [T]hey relate to the whole domain of social and economic fact, and the statesmen who founded this Nation knew too well that only a stagnant society remains unchanged.' " *Board of Regents of State Colleges v. Roth* (1972), quoting *National Ins. Co. v. Tidewater Co.* (1949) (Frankfurter, J., dissenting).

It is not that tradition has been irrelevant to our prior decisions. Throughout our decisionmaking in this important area runs the theme that certain interests and practices—freedom from physical restraint, marriage, childbearing, childrearing, and others—form the core of our definition of "liberty." Our solicitude for these interests is partly the result of the fact that the Due Process Clause would seem an empty promise if it did not protect them, and partly the result of the historical and traditional importance of these interests in our society. In deciding cases arising under the Due Process Clause, therefore, we have considered whether the concrete limitation under consideration impermissibly impinges upon one of these more generalized interests.

Today's plurality, however, does not ask whether parenthood is an interest that historically has received our attention and protection; the answer to that question is too clear for dispute. Instead, the plurality asks whether the specific variety of parenthood under consideration—a natural father's relationship with a child whose mother is married to another man—has enjoyed such protection.

If we had looked to tradition with such specificity in past cases, many a decision would have reached a different result. Surely the use of contraceptives by unmarried couples, . . . or even by married couples; the freedom from corporal punishment in schools; the freedom from an arbitrary transfer from a prison to a psychiatric institution; and even the right to raise one's natural but illegitimate children, were not "interest[s] traditionally protected by our society," at the time of their consideration by this Court. If we had asked, therefore, in *Eisenstadt, Griswold, Ingraham, Vitek,* or *Stanley* itself whether the specific interest under consideration had been traditionally protected, the answer would have been a resounding "no." That we did not ask this question in those cases highlights the novelty of the interpretive method that the plurality opinion employs today.

The plurality's interpretive method is more than novel; it is misguided. It ignores the good reasons for limiting the role of "tradition" in interpreting the Constitution's deliberately capacious language. In the plurality's constitutional universe, we may not take notice of the fact that the original reasons for the conclusive presumption of paternity are out of place in a world in which blood tests can prove virtually beyond a shadow of a doubt who sired a particular child and in which the fact of illegitimacy no longer plays the burdensome and stigmatizing role it once did. Nor, in the plurality's world, may we deny "tradition" its full scope by pointing out that the rationale for the conventional rule has changed over the years, as has the rationale for [the California law]; instead, our task is simply to identify a rule denying the asserted interest and not to ask whether the basis for that rule—which is the true reflection of the values undergirding it—has changed too often or too recently to call the rule embodying that rationale a "tradition." Moreover, by describing the decisive question as whether Michael and Victoria's interest is one that has been "traditionally protected by our society," rather than one that society traditionally has thought important (with or without protecting it), and by suggesting that our sole function is to "discern the society's views," . . . the plurality acts as if the only purpose of the Due Process Clause is to confirm the importance of interests already protected by a majority of the States. Transforming the protection afforded by the Due Process Clause into a redundancy mocks those who, with care and purpose, wrote the Fourteenth Amendment.

In construing the Fourteenth Amendment to offer shelter only to those interests specifically protected by historical practice, moreover, the plurality ignores the kind of society in which our Constitution exists. We are not an assimilative, homogeneous society, but a facilitative, pluralistic one, in which we must be willing to abide someone else's unfamiliar or even repellant practice because the same tolerant impulse protects our own idiosyncrasies. Even if we can agree, therefore, that "family" and "parenthood" are part of the good life, it is absurd to assume that we can agree on the content of those terms and destructive to pretend that we do. In a community such as ours, "liberty" must include the freedom not to conform. The plurality today squashes this freedom by requiring specific approval from history before protecting anything in the name of liberty.

The document that the plurality construes today is unfamiliar to me. It is not the living charter that I have taken to be our Constitution; it is instead a stagnant, archaic, hidebound document steeped in the prejudices and superstitions of a time long past. This Constitution does not recognize that times change, does not see that sometimes a practice or rule outlives its foundations. I cannot accept an interpretive method that does such violence to the charter that I am bound by oath to uphold.

II

The plurality's reworking of our interpretive approach is all the more troubling because it is unnecessary. This is not a case in which we face a "new" kind of interest, one that requires us to consider for the first time whether the Constitution protects it. On the contrary, we confront an interest—that of a parent and child in their relationship with each other—that was among the first that this Court acknowledged in its cases defining the "liberty" protected by the Constitution, see, e.g., *Meyer v. Nebraska* (1923), *Skinner v. Oklahoma* (1942), *Prince v. Massachusetts* (1944), and I think I am safe in saying that no one doubts the wisdom or validity of those decisions. Where the interest under consideration is a parent-child relationship, we need not ask, over and over again, whether that interest is one that society traditionally protects.

Thus, to describe the issue in this case as whether the relationship existing between Michael and Victoria "has been treated as a protected family unit under the historic practices of our society, or whether on any other basis it has been accorded special protection," is to reinvent the wheel. The better approach—indeed, the one commanded by our prior cases and by common sense—is to ask whether the specific parent-child relationship under consideration is close enough to the interests that we already have protected to be deemed an aspect of "liberty" as well. On the facts before us, therefore, the question is not what "level of generality" should be used to describe the relationship between Michael and Victoria, but whether the relationship under consideration is sufficiently substantial to qualify as a liberty interest under our prior cases.

The plurality's focus on the "unitary family" conflates the question whether a liberty interest exists with the question what procedures may be used to terminate or curtail it. It is no coincidence that we never before have looked at the relationship that the unwed father seeks to disrupt, rather than the one he seeks to preserve, in determining whether he has a liberty interest in his relationship with his child. To do otherwise is to allow the State's interest in terminating the relationship to play a role in defining the "liberty" that is protected by the Constitution. According to our established framework under the Due Process Clause, however, we first ask whether the person claiming constitutional protection has an interest that the Constitution recognizes; if we find that she does, we next consider the State's interest in limiting the extent of the procedures that will attend the deprivation of that interest. By stressing the need to preserve the "unitary family" and by focusing not just on the relationship between Michael and Victoria but on their "situation" as well, today's plurality opinion takes both of these steps at once.

The plurality has wedged itself between a rock and a hard place. If it limits its holding to those situations in which a wife and husband wish to raise the child together, then it necessarily takes the State's interest into account in defining "liberty"; yet if it extends that approach to circumstances in which the marital union already has been dissolved, then it may no longer rely on the State's asserted interest in protecting the "unitary family" in denying that Michael and Victoria have been deprived of liberty. . . .

III . . .

B

The question before us, therefore, is whether California has an interest so powerful that it justifies granting Michael no hearing before terminating his parental rights.

"Many controversies have raged about the cryptic and abstract words of the Due Process Clause but there can be no doubt that at a minimum they require that deprivation of life, liberty or property by adjudication be preceded by notice and opportunity for hearing appropriate to the nature of the case." *Mullane v. Central Hanover Bank & Trust Co.* (1950). When a State seeks to limit the procedures that will attend the deprivation of a constitutionally protected interest, it is only the State's interest in streamlining procedures that is relevant. A State may not, in other words, justify abbreviated procedures on the ground that it wishes to pay welfare benefits to fewer people or wants to reduce the number of tenured professors on its payroll. It would be strange indeed if a State could curtail procedures with the explanation that it was hostile to the underlying, constitutionally protected interest.

The purported state interests here, however, stem primarily from the State's antagonism to Michael and Victoria's constitutionally protected interest in their relationship with each other and not from any desire to streamline procedures. Gerald D. explains that s 621 promotes marriage, maintains the relationship between the child and presumed father, and protects the integrity and privacy of the matrimonial family. It is not, however, s 621, but the best-interest principle, that protects a stable marital relationship and maintains the relationship between the child and presumed father. These interests are implicated by the determination of who gets parental rights, not by the determination of who is the father; in the hearing that Michael seeks, parental rights are not the issue. Of the objectives that Gerald stresses, therefore, only the preservation of family privacy is promoted by the refusal to hold a hearing itself. Yet s 621 furthers even this objective only partially. . . .

IV

The atmosphere surrounding today's decision is one of make-believe. Beginning with the suggestion that the situation confronting us here does not repeat itself every day in every corner of the country, moving on to the claim that it is tradition alone that supplies the details of the liberty that the Constitution protects, and passing finally to the notion that the Court always has recognized a cramped vision of "the family," today's decision lets stand California's pronouncement that Michael—whom blood tests show to a 98 percent probability to be Victoria's father—is not Victoria's father. When and if the Court awakes to reality, it will find a world very different from the one it expects.

Justice WHITE, with whom Justice BRENNAN joins, dissenting. . . .

"The emphasis of the Due Process Clause is on 'process.'" *Moore v. East Cleveland* (1977) (White, J., dissenting). I fail to see the fairness in the process established by the State of California and endorsed by the Court today. Michael H. has evidence which demonstrates that he is the father of young Victoria. Yet he is blocked by the State from presenting that evidence to a court. As a result, he is foreclosed from establishing his paternity and is ultimately precluded, by the State, from developing a relationship with his child. "A fundamental requirement of due process is 'the opportunity to be heard.' . . . It is an opportunity which must be granted at a meaningful time and in a meaningful manner." *Armstrong v. Manzo* (1965). I fail to see how appellant was granted any meaningful opportunity to be heard when he was precluded at the very outset from introducing evidence which would support his assertion of paternity. Michael H. has never been afforded an opportunity to present his case in any meaningful manner.

As the Court has said: "The significance of the biological connection is that it offers the natural father an opportunity that no other male possesses to develop a relationship with his offspring. If he grasps that opportunity and accepts some measure of responsibility for the child's future, he may enjoy the blessings of the parent-child relationship and make uniquely valuable contributions to the child's development." It is as if this passage was addressed to Michael H. Yet the plurality today recants. Michael H. eagerly grasped the opportunity to have a relationship with his daughter (he lived with her; he declared her to be his child; he provided financial support for her) and still, with today's opinion, his opportunity has vanished. He has been rendered a stranger to his child. Because [the law], as applied, should be held unconstitutional under the Due Process Clause of the Fourteenth Amendment, I respectfully dissent.

Notes and Queries

1. What is the constitutional issue in this case? Is it, as the plurality wrote, whether an adulterous father has a right to visits with his child if he is not married to the child's mother? Is it whether the state can favor certain types of family arrangements and discourage others? Is it about moral conceptions of illegitimacy and the sanctity of marriage? Or is it, as Justice Brennan argued, about "the freedom not to conform"?

2. Does this case establish that a father has a substantive liberty interest in raising his biological child? If so, what interest of the state is sufficiently strong to overcome that right? What interest, precisely, does the state seek to protect in this case?

3. What role do history and tradition play in the plurali-

ty's analysis? How does the plurality define history and tradition? How does Justice Brennan define tradition?

Justice Scalia concluded that the relationship between Michael and Victoria has not been treated as "a protected family unit under the historic practices of our society. . . ." Does this mean that an individual's choices about family life are entitled to constitutional protection only if they conform to the majority's beliefs about what constitutes a "real" family? Is the Court's respect for history and tradition related to a particular understanding of judicial power? Is that understanding consistent with *Carolene*

Products? Doesn't any appeal to "historic practices" as a way of defining what is a protected liberty rest upon hidden, majoritarian assumptions about the proper relationship of individuals to each other and to the community?

4. Recall Justice Scalia's claim that "The facts of this case are, we must hope, extraordinary." Is this kind of judicial commentary appropriate? Does it suggest an unwillingness or inability to appreciate cultural difference?

5. Does the child have any rights in this case? What are they?

Washington v. Glucksberg
65 USLW 4669, 117 S. Ct. 2258, 138 L. Ed. 2d 772 (1997)

Washington state law makes it a felony to "aid another person to attempt suicide." Four physicians, claiming that they would assist certain terminal patients in ending their lives but for the law, sought to have the statute declared unconstitutional; they were joined in their suit by three gravely ill patients. Relying primarily on *Planned Parenthood of Southeastern Pa. v. Casey* (1992) and *Cruzan v. Dir., Mo. Dept. of Health* (1990), they claimed that the prohibition violated the liberty of a mentally competent, terminally ill person, to commit physician-assisted suicide. A United States District Court agreed, concluding that Washington's assisted-suicide ban is unconstitutional because it places an undue burden on the exercise of that constitutionally protected liberty interest. The Circuit Court affirmed. Opinion of the Court: *Rehnquist*, O'Connor, Scalia, Kennedy, Thomas. Concurring opinion: *O'Connor*, Ginsburg, Breyer. Concurring in the judgment: *Stevens, Souter, Ginsburg, Breyer*.

Chief Justice REHNQUIST delivered the opinion of the Court.

The question presented in this case is whether Washington's prohibition against "caus[ing]" or "aid[ing]" a suicide offends the Fourteenth Amendment to the United States Constitution. We hold that it does not.

It has always been a crime to assist a suicide in the State of Washington. . . .

The plaintiffs asserted "the existence of a liberty interest protected by the Fourteenth Amendment which extends to a personal choice by a mentally competent, terminally ill adult to commit physician-assisted suicide." Relying primarily on *Planned Parenthood v. Casey* (1992), and *Cruzan v. Director, Missouri Dept. of Health* (1990), the District Court agreed, and concluded that Washington's

assisted-suicide ban is unconstitutional because it "places an undue burden on the exercise of [that] constitutionally protected liberty interest." . . .

A panel of the Court of Appeals for the Ninth Circuit reversed, emphasizing that "[i]n the two hundred and five years of our existence no constitutional right to aid in killing oneself has ever been asserted and upheld by a court of final jurisdiction." The Ninth Circuit reheard the case *en banc*, reversed the panel's decision, and affirmed the District Court. Like the District Court, the en banc Court of Appeals emphasized our *Casey* and *Cruzan* decisions. The court also discussed what it described as "historical" and "current societal attitudes" toward suicide and assisted suicide, and concluded that "the Constitution encompasses a due process liberty interest in controlling the time and manner of one's death—that there is, in short, a constitutionally-recognized 'right to die.'" After "[w]eighing and then balancing" this interest against Washington's various interests, the court held that the State's assisted-suicide ban was unconstitutional "as applied to terminally ill competent adults who wish to hasten their deaths with medication prescribed by their physicians. . . ." We granted certiorari, and now reverse.

We begin, as we do in all due-process cases, by examining our Nation's history, legal traditions, and practices. See, e.g., *Casey, Cruzan, Moore v. East Cleveland*. In almost every State—indeed, in almost every western democracy—it is a crime to assist a suicide. The States' assisted-suicide bans are not innovations. Rather, they are longstanding expressions of the States' commitment to the protection and preservation of all human life. Indeed, opposition to and condemnation of suicide—and, therefore, of assisting suicide—are consistent and enduring themes of our philosophical, legal, and cultural heritages.

More specifically, for over 700 years, the Anglo-American common-law tradition has punished or otherwise disapproved of both suicide and assisting suicide. . . .

Comparative Note 11.9

[Colombia imposed a prison sentence of six months to three years on any person "who kills another out of mercy [or] intense suffering due to . . . grave or incurable illness." Colombia's Constitutional Court struck down the law as applied to doctors in assisted suicide cases.]

The duty of the state to protect life should be compatible with respect for human dignity and the free development of personality. For this reason, the Court feels that with regard to terminally ill persons who experience intense suffering, the State's duty [to protect life] yields when faced with the informed consent of a patient who wishes to die in a dignified manner. In effect, in this case, the duty of the state weakens considerably given the fact that death, in the light of medical reports, is inevitable in a relatively short time. . . . The fundamental right to live in a dignified way implies then the right to die with dignity, since to condemn a person to prolong his existence for a short time when he [chooses otherwise] and suffers profound pain is equivalent not only to cruel and inhuman treatment forbidden by the Constitution (Article 12), but also an annulment of his dignity and autonomy as a moral agent.

Justice Carlos Gaviria Diaz (dissenting): In my view, euthanasia applied to a terminally ill person with his fragile and weak consent is unconstitutional. It affects the universal humanitarian right to life, it constitutes a crime contrary to the dignity of the human person and the prevalence of an erroneous conception of the free development of the personality that in the fundamental Constitution was never established as an absolute right, but rather limited by the rights of others and the juridical order (Article 16 of the Political Constitution of 1991).

SOURCE: *Euthanasia Case*, Constitutional Court of Colombia, 18 June 1997. (Typescript, translated by Geraldine Ameriks.)

For the most part, the early American colonies adopted the common-law approach. . . .

Over time, however, the American colonies abolished these harsh common-law penalties. . . . [H]owever . . . the movement away from the common law's harsh sanctions did not represent an acceptance of suicide; rather . . . this change reflected the growing consensus that it was unfair to punish the suicide's family for his wrongdoing. . . .

That suicide remained a grievous, though nonfelonious, wrong is confirmed by the fact that colonial and early state legislatures and courts did not retreat from prohibiting assisting suicide. . . . And the prohibitions against assisting suicide never contained exceptions for those who were near death. . . .

Though deeply rooted, the States' assisted-suicide bans have in recent years been reexamined and, generally, reaffirmed. Because of advances in medicine and technology, Americans today are increasingly likely to die in institutions, from chronic illnesses. Public concern and democratic action are therefore sharply focused on how best to protect dignity and independence at the end of life, with the result that there have been many significant changes in state laws and in the attitudes these laws reflect. Many States, for example, now permit "living wills," surrogate health-care decisionmaking, and the withdrawal or refusal of life-sustaining medical treatment. At the same time,

however, voters and legislators continue for the most part to reaffirm their States' prohibitions on assisting suicide.

The Washington statute at issue in this case was enacted in 1975 as part of a revision of that State's criminal code. Four years later, Washington passed its Natural Death Act, which specifically stated that the "withholding or withdrawal of life-sustaining treatment . . . shall not, for any purpose, constitute a suicide" and that "[n]othing in this chapter shall be construed to condone, authorize, or approve mercy killing. . . ." In 1991, Washington voters rejected a ballot initiative which, had it passed, would have permitted a form of physician-assisted suicide. Washington then added a provision to the Natural Death Act expressly excluding physician-assisted suicide. Also, on April 30, 1997, President Clinton signed the Federal Assisted Suicide Funding Restriction Act of 1997, which prohibits the use of federal funds in support of physician-assisted suicide.*

---

*Other countries are embroiled in similar debates: The Supreme Court of Canada recently rejected a claim that the Canadian Charter of Rights and Freedoms establishes a fundamental right to assisted suicide, *Rodriguez v. British Columbia* (Attorney General), 107 D.L.R. (4th) 342 (1993); the British House of Lords Select Committee on Medical Ethics refused to recommend any change in Great Britain's assisted-suicide prohibition, House of Lords, Session 1993–94

Thus, the States are currently engaged in serious, thoughtful examinations of physician-assisted suicide and other similar issues. . . .

Attitudes toward suicide itself have changed since *Bracton*, but our laws have consistently condemned, and continue to prohibit, assisting suicide. Despite changes in medical technology and notwithstanding an increased emphasis on the importance of end-of-life decisionmaking, we have not retreated from this prohibition. Against this backdrop of history, tradition, and practice, we now turn to respondents' constitutional claim.

The Due Process Clause guarantees more than fair process, and the "liberty" it protects includes more than the absence of physical restraint. The Clause also provides heightened protection against government interference with certain fundamental rights and liberty interests. In a long line of cases, we have held that, in addition to the specific freedoms protected by the Bill of Rights, the "liberty" specially protected by the Due Process Clause includes the rights to marry, *Loving v. Virginia* (1967); to have children, *Skinner v. Oklahoma ex rel. Williamson* (1942); to direct the education and upbringing of one's children, *Meyer v. Nebraska* (1923); *Pierce v. Society of Sisters* (1925); to marital privacy, *Griswold v. Connecticut* (1965); to use contraception, ibid; *Eisenstadt v. Baird* (1972); to bodily integrity, *Rochin v. California* (1952), and to abortion, *Casey, supra*. We have also assumed, and strongly suggested, that the Due Process Clause protects the traditional right to refuse unwanted lifesaving medical treatment. *Cruzan.*

But we "ha[ve] always been reluctant to expand the concept of substantive due process because guideposts

for responsible decisionmaking in this unchartered area are scarce and open-ended." By extending constitutional protection to an asserted right or liberty interest, we, to a great extent, place the matter outside the arena of public debate and legislative action. We must therefore "exercise the utmost care whenever we are asked to break new ground in this field," lest the liberty protected by the Due Process Clause be subtly transformed into the policy preferences of the members of this Court.

Our established method of substantive-due-process analysis has two primary features: First, we have regularly observed that the Due Process Clause specially protects those fundamental rights and liberties which are, objectively, "deeply rooted in this Nation's history and tradition," and "implicit in the concept of ordered liberty," such that "neither liberty nor justice would exist if they were sacrificed," *Palko v. Connecticut* (1937). Second, we have required in substantive-due-process cases a "careful description" of the asserted fundamental liberty interest. Our Nation's history, legal traditions, and practices thus provide the crucial "guideposts for responsible decision-making," that direct and restrain our exposition of the Due Process Clause. As we stated recently . . . , the Fourteenth Amendment "forbids the government to infringe . . . 'fundamental' liberty interests at all, no matter what process is provided, unless the infringement is narrowly tailored to serve a compelling state interest."

Justice Souter, relying on Justice Harlan's dissenting opinion in *Poe v. Ullman*, would largely abandon this restrained methodology, and instead ask "whether [Washington's] statute sets up one of those 'arbitrary impositions' or 'purposeless restraints' at odds with the Due Process Clause of the Fourteenth Amendment." In our view, however, the development of this Court's substantive-due-process jurisprudence, described briefly above, has been a process whereby the outlines of the "liberty" specially protected by the Fourteenth Amendment—never fully clarified, to be sure, and perhaps not capable of being fully clarified—have at least been carefully refined by concrete examples involving fundamental rights found to be deeply rooted in our legal tradition. This approach tends to rein in the subjective elements that are necessarily present in due-process judicial review. In addition, by establishing a threshold requirement—that a challenged state action implicate a fundamental right—before requiring more than a reasonable relation to a legitimate state interest to justify the action, it avoids the need for complex balancing of competing interests in every case.

Turning to the claim at issue here, the Court of Appeals stated that "[p]roperly analyzed, the first issue to be resolved is whether there is a liberty interest in determining

Report of the Select Committee on Medical Ethics, 12 *Issues in Law & Med.* 193, 202 (1996) ("We identify no circumstances in which assisted suicide should be permitted"); New Zealand's Parliament rejected a proposed "Death With Dignity Bill" that would have legalized physician-assisted suicide in August 1995, Graeme, "MPs Throw out Euthanasia Bill," *The Dominion* (Wellington), Aug. 17, 1995, p. 1; and the Northern Territory of Australia legalized assisted suicide and voluntary euthanasia in 1995. See Shenon, "Australian Doctors Get Right to Assist Suicide", *N.Y. Times*, July 28, 1995, p. A8. As of February 1997, three persons had ended their lives with physician assistance in the Northern Territory. Mydans, "Assisted Suicide: Australia Faces a Grim Reality," *N.Y. Times*, Febr. 2, 1997, p. A3. On March 24, 1997, however, the Australian Senate voted to overturn the Northern Territory's law. Thornhill, "Australia Repeals Euthanasia Law," *Washington Post*, March 25, 1997, p. A14; see Euthanasia Laws Act 1997, No. 17, 1997 (Austl.). On the other hand, on May 20, 1997, Colombia's Constitutional Court legalized voluntary euthanasia for terminally ill people. Sentencia No. C-239/97 (*Corte Constitucional*, Mayo 20, 1997); see Colombia's "Top Court Legalizes Euthanasia," *Orlando Sentinel*, May 22, 1997. p. A18. [Footnote by the Court]

the time and manner of one's death," or, in other words, "[i]s there a right to die?" Similarly, respondents assert a "liberty to choose how to die" and a right to "control of one's final days," and describe the asserted liberty as "the right to choose a humane, dignified death," and "the liberty to shape death." As noted above, we have a tradition of carefully formulating the interest at stake in substantive-due-process cases. For example, although *Cruzan* is often described as a "right to die" case, we were, in fact, more precise: we assumed that the Constitution granted competent persons a "constitutionally protected right to refuse lifesaving hydration and nutrition." The Washington statute at issue in this case prohibits "aid[ing] another person to attempt suicide," and, thus, the question before us is whether the "liberty" specially protected by the Due Process Clause includes a right to commit suicide which itself includes a right to assistance in doing so.

We now inquire whether this asserted right has any place in our Nation's traditions. Here, as discussed above, we are confronted with a consistent and almost universal tradition that has long rejected the asserted right, and continues explicitly to reject it today, even for terminally ill, mentally competent adults. To hold for respondents, we would have to reverse centuries of legal doctrine and practice, and strike down the considered policy choice of almost every State.

Respondents contend, however, that the liberty interest they assert is consistent with this Court's substantive-due-process line of cases, if not with this Nation's history and practice. Pointing to *Casey* and *Cruzan*, respondents read our jurisprudence in this area as reflecting a general tradition of "self-sovereignty," and as teaching that the "liberty" protected by the Due Process Clause includes "basic and intimate exercises of personal autonomy." According to respondents, our liberty jurisprudence, and the broad, individualistic principles it reflects, protects the "liberty of competent, terminally ill adults to make end-of-life decisions free of undue government interference." The question presented in this case, however, is whether the protections of the Due Process Clause include a right to commit suicide with another's assistance. With this "careful description" of respondents' claim in mind, we turn to *Casey* and *Cruzan*.

Respondents contend that in *Cruzan* we "acknowledged that competent, dying persons have the right to direct the removal of life-sustaining medical treatment and thus hasten death," and that "the constitutional principle behind recognizing the patient's liberty to direct the withdrawal of artificial life support applies at least as strongly to the choice to hasten impending death by consuming lethal medication." Similarly, the Court of Appeals concluded that "*Cruzan*, by recognizing a liberty interest that includes the refusal of artificial provision of life-sustaining food and water, necessarily recognize[d] a liberty interest in hastening one's own death."

The right assumed in *Cruzan*, however, was not simply deduced from abstract concepts of personal autonomy. Given the common-law rule that forced medication was a battery, and the long legal tradition protecting the decision to refuse unwanted medical treatment, our assumption was entirely consistent with this Nation's history and constitutional traditions. The decision to commit suicide with the assistance of another may be just as personal and profound as the decision to refuse unwanted medical treatment, but it has never enjoyed similar legal protection. Indeed, the two acts are widely and reasonably regarded as quite distinct. In *Cruzan* itself, we recognized that most States outlawed assisted suicide—and even more do today—and we certainly gave no intimation that the right to refuse unwanted medical treatment could be somehow transmuted into a right to assistance in committing suicide.

Respondents also rely on *Casey*. . . . [T]he opinion discussed in some detail this Court's substantive-due-process tradition of interpreting the Due Process Clause to protect certain fundamental rights and "personal decisions relating to marriage, procreation, contraception, family relationships, child rearing, and education," and noted that many of those rights and liberties "involv[e] the most intimate and personal choices a person may make in a lifetime."

The Court of Appeals, like the District Court, found *Casey* "highly instructive" and "almost prescriptive" for determining "what liberty interest may inhere in a terminally ill person's choice to commit suicide":

> Like the decision of whether or not to have an abortion, the decision how and when to die is one of "the most intimate and personal choices a person may make in a lifetime," a choice "central to personal dignity and autonomy."

Similarly, respondents emphasize the statement in *Casey* that:

> At the heart of liberty is the right to define one's own concept of existence, of meaning, of the universe, and of the mystery of human life. Beliefs about these matters could not define the attributes of personhood were they formed under compulsion of the State.

By choosing this language, the Court's opinion in *Casey* described, in a general way and in light of our prior cases, those personal activities and decisions that this Court has identified as so deeply rooted in our history and traditions, or so fundamental to our concept of constitutionally ordered liberty, that they are protected by the Fourteenth Amendment. The opinion moved from the recognition that liberty necessarily includes freedom of conscience and belief about ultimate considerations to the observation that "though the abortion decision may originate within the zone of conscience and belief, it is more than a philosophic exercise." That many of the rights and liberties protected by the Due Process Clause sound in personal autonomy does not warrant the sweeping conclusion that any and all important, intimate, and personal decisions are so protected, *San Antonio Independent School Dist. v. Rodriguez* (1973), and *Casey* did not suggest otherwise.

The history of the law's treatment of assisted suicide in this country has been and continues to be one of the rejection of nearly all efforts to permit it. That being the case, our decisions lead us to conclude that the asserted "right" to assistance in committing suicide is not a fundamental liberty interest protected by the Due Process Clause. The Constitution also requires, however, that Washington's assisted-suicide ban be rationally related to legitimate government interests. See *Heller v. Doe* (1993). This requirement is unquestionably met here. . . .

First, Washington has an "unqualified interest in the preservation of human life." *Cruzan*. The State's prohibition on assisted suicide, like all homicide laws, both reflects and advances its commitment to this interest. This interest is symbolic and aspirational as well as practical:

> While suicide is no longer prohibited or penalized, the ban against assisted suicide and euthanasia shores up the notion of limits in human relationships. It reflects the gravity with which we view the decision to take one's own life or the life of another, and our reluctance to encourage or promote these decisions.

Relatedly, all admit that suicide is a serious public-health problem, especially among persons in otherwise vulnerable groups. The State has an interest in preventing suicide, and in studying, identifying, and treating its causes.

Those who attempt suicide—terminally ill or not—often suffer from depression or other mental disorders. Research indicates, however, that many people who request physician-assisted suicide withdraw that request if their depression and pain are treated. . . . Thus, legal physician-assisted suicide could make it more difficult for the State to protect depressed or mentally ill persons, or those who are suffering from untreated pain, from suicidal impulses.

The State also has an interest in protecting the integrity and ethics of the medical profession. In contrast to the Court of Appeals' conclusion that "the integrity of the medical profession would [not] be threatened in any way by [physician-assisted suicide]," the American Medical Association, like many other medical and physicians' groups, has concluded that "[p]hysician-assisted suicide is fundamentally incompatible with the physician's role as healer." And physician-assisted suicide could, it is argued, undermine the trust that is essential to the doctor-patient relationship by blurring the time-honored line between healing and harming.

Next, the State has an interest in protecting vulnerable groups—including the poor, the elderly, and disabled persons—from abuse, neglect, and mistakes. The Court of Appeals dismissed the State's concern that disadvantaged persons might be pressured into physician-assisted suicide as "ludicrous on its face." We have recognized, however, the real risk of subtle coercion and undue influence in end-of-life situations. *Cruzan*. Similarly, the New York Task Force warned that "[l]egalizing physician-assisted suicide would pose profound risks to many individuals who are ill and vulnerable. . . . The risk of harm is greatest for the many individuals in our society whose autonomy and well-being are already compromised by poverty, lack of access to good medical care, advanced age, or membership in a stigmatized social group." If physician-assisted suicide were permitted, many might resort to it to spare their families the substantial financial burden of end-of-life health-care costs.

The State's interest here goes beyond protecting the vulnerable from coercion; it extends to protecting disabled and terminally ill people from prejudice, negative and inaccurate stereotypes, and "societal indifference." The State's assisted-suicide ban reflects and reinforces its policy that the lives of terminally ill, disabled, and elderly people must be no less valued than the lives of the young and healthy, and that a seriously disabled person's suicidal impulses should be interpreted and treated the same way as anyone else's. See New York Task Force 101–102; Physician-Assisted Suicide and Euthanasia in the Netherlands: A Report of Chairman Charles T. Canady, at 9, 20 (discussing prejudice toward the disabled and the negative messages euthanasia and assisted suicide send to handicapped patients).

Finally, the State may fear that permitting assisted suicide will start it down the path to voluntary and perhaps even involuntary euthanasia. The Court of Appeals struck down Washington's assisted-suicide ban only "as applied to competent, terminally ill adults who wish to hasten their deaths by obtaining medication prescribed by their doctors." Washington insists, however, that the impact of the court's decision will not and cannot be so limited. If suicide is protected as a matter of constitutional right, it is argued, "every man and woman in the United States must enjoy it." The Court of Appeals' decision, and its expansive reasoning, provide ample support for the State's concerns. The court noted, for example, that the "decision of a duly appointed surrogate decision maker is for all legal purposes the decision of the patient himself," that "in some instances, the patient may be unable to self-administer the drugs and . . . administration by the physician . . . may be the only way the patient may be able to receive them," and that not only physicians, but also family members and loved ones, will inevitably participate in assisting suicide. Thus, it turns out that what is couched as a limited right to "physician-assisted suicide" is likely, in effect, a much broader license, which could prove extremely difficult to police and contain. Washington's ban on assisting suicide prevents such erosion.

This concern is further supported by evidence about the practice of euthanasia in the Netherlands. The Dutch government's own study revealed that in 1990, there were 2,300 cases of voluntary euthanasia (defined as "the deliberate termination of another's life at his request"), 400 cases of assisted suicide, and more than 1,000 cases of euthanasia without an explicit request. In addition to these latter 1,000 cases, the study found an additional 4,941 cases where physicians administered lethal morphine overdoses without the patients' explicit consent. Physician-Assisted Suicide and Euthanasia in the Netherlands: A Report of Chairman Charles T. Canady, at 12–13 (citing Dutch study). This study suggests that, despite the existence of various reporting procedures, euthanasia in the Netherlands has not been limited to competent, terminally ill adults who are enduring physical suffering, and that regulation of the practice may not have prevented abuses in cases involving vulnerable persons, including severely disabled neonates and elderly persons suffering from dementia. . . . Washington, like most other States, reasonably ensures against this risk by banning, rather than regulating, assisting suicide.

We need not weigh exactly the relative strengths of these various interests. They are unquestionably important and legitimate, and Washington's ban on assisted suicide is at least reasonably related to their promotion and protection. We therefore hold that Wash. Rev. Code s 9A.36.060(1) (1994) does not violate the Fourteenth Amendment, either on its face or "as applied to competent, terminally ill adults who wish to hasten their deaths by obtaining medication prescribed by their doctors."

Throughout the Nation, Americans are engaged in an earnest and profound debate about the morality, legality, and practicality of physician-assisted suicide. Our holding permits this debate to continue, as it should in a democratic society. The decision of the *en banc* Court of Appeals is reversed, and the case is remanded for further proceedings consistent with this opinion.

Justice O'CONNOR, concurring.

Death will be different for each of us. For many, the last days will be spent in physical pain and perhaps the despair that accompanies physical deterioration and a loss of control of basic bodily and mental functions. Some will seek medication to alleviate that pain and other symptoms.

The Court frames the issue in this case as whether the Due Process Clause of the Constitution protects a "right to commit suicide which itself includes a right to assistance in doing so," and concludes that our Nation's history, legal traditions, and practices do not support the existence of such a right. I join the Court's opinions because I agree that there is no generalized right to "commit suicide." But respondents urge us to address the narrower question whether a mentally competent person who is experiencing great suffering has a constitutionally cognizable interest in controlling the circumstances of his or her imminent death. I see no need to reach that question in the context of the facial challenges to the New York and Washington laws at issue here. The parties and *amici* agree that in these States a patient who is suffering from a terminal illness and who is experiencing great pain has no legal barriers to obtaining medication, from qualified physicians, to alleviate that suffering, even to the point of causing unconsciousness and hastening death. In this light, even assuming that we would recognize such an interest, I agree that the State's interests in protecting those who are not truly competent or facing imminent death, or those whose decisions to hasten death would not truly be voluntary, are sufficiently weighty to justify a prohibition against physician-assisted suicide.

Every one of us at some point may be affected by our own or a family member's terminal illness. There is no reason to think the democratic process will not strike the proper balance between the interests of terminally ill, mentally competent individuals who would seek to end their suffering and the State's interests in protecting those who might seek to end life mistakenly or under pressure. As the Court recognizes, States are presently undertaking extensive and serious evaluation of physician-assisted suicide and other related issues. In such circumstances, "the . . . challenging task of crafting appropriate procedures for safeguarding . . . liberty interests is entrusted to the 'laboratory' of the States . . . in the first instance." *Cruzan v. Director, Mo. Dept. of Health* (1990).

In sum, there is no need to address the question whether suffering patients have a constitutionally cognizable interest in obtaining relief from the suffering that they may experience in the last days of their lives. There is no dispute that dying patients in Washington and New York can obtain palliative care, even when doing so would hasten their deaths. The difficulty in defining terminal illness and the risk that a dying patient's request for assistance in ending his or her life might not be truly voluntary justifies the prohibitions on assisted suicide we uphold here.

Justice STEVENS, concurring in the judgments.

The Court ends its opinion with the important observation that our holding today is fully consistent with a continuation of the vigorous debate about the "morality, legality, and practicality of physician-assisted suicide" in a democratic society. Ante, at 32. I write separately to make it clear that there is also room for further debate about the limits that the Constitution places on the power of the States to punish the practice.

The morality, legality, and practicality of capital punishment have been the subject of debate for many years. In 1976, this Court upheld the constitutionality of the practice in cases coming to us from Georgia [*Gregg v. Georgia* (1976)], Florida [*Proffitt v. Florida* (1976)] and Texas [*Jurek v. Texas* (1976)]. In those cases we concluded that a State does have the power to place a lesser value on some lives than on others; there is no absolute requirement that a State treat all human life as having an equal right to preservation. Because the state legislatures had sufficiently narrowed the category of lives that the State could terminate, and had enacted special procedures to ensure that the defendant belonged in that limited category, we concluded that the statutes were not unconstitutional on their face. In later cases coming to us from each of those States, however, we found that some applications of the statutes were unconstitutional.

Today, the Court decides that Washington's statute prohibiting assisted suicide is not invalid "on its face," that is to say, in all or most cases in which it might be applied. That holding, however, does not foreclose the possibility that some applications of the statute might well be invalid.

History and tradition provide ample support for refusing to recognize an open-ended constitutional right to commit suicide. Much more than the State's paternalistic interest in protecting the individual from the irrevocable consequences of an ill-advised decision motivated by temporary concerns is at stake. There is truth in John Donne's observation that "No man is an island." The State has an interest in preserving and fostering the benefits that every human being may provide to the community—a community that thrives on the exchange of ideas, expressions of affection, shared memories and humorous incidents as well as on the material contributions that its members create and support. The value to others of a person's life is far too precious to allow the individual to claim a constitutional entitlement to complete autonomy in making a decision to end that life. Thus, I fully agree with the Court that the "liberty" protected by the Due Process Clause does not include a categorical "right to commit suicide which itself includes a right to assistance in doing so."

But just as our conclusion that capital punishment is not always unconstitutional did not preclude later decisions holding that it is sometimes impermissibly cruel, so is it equally clear that a decision upholding a general statutory prohibition of assisted suicide does not mean that every possible application of the statute would be valid. A State, like Washington, that has authorized the death penalty and thereby has concluded that the sanctity of human life does not require that it always be preserved, must acknowledge that there are situations in which an interest in hastening death is legitimate. Indeed, not only is that interest sometimes legitimate, I am also convinced that there are times when it is entitled to constitutional protection.

The state interests supporting a general rule banning the practice of physician-assisted suicide do not have the same force in all cases. First and foremost of these interests is the "unqualified interest in the preservation of human life," which is equated with "the sanctity of life." That interest not only justifies—it commands—maximum protection of every individual's interest in remaining alive, which in turn commands the same protection for decisions about whether to commence or to terminate life-support systems or to administer pain medication that may hasten death. Properly viewed, however, this interest is not a collective interest that should always outweigh the interests of a person who because of pain, incapacity, or sedation finds her life intolerable, but rather, an aspect of individual freedom.

Many terminally ill people find their lives meaningful even if filled with pain or dependence on others. Some find value in living through suffering; some have an abiding desire to witness particular events in their families' lives; many believe it a sin to hasten death. Individuals of different religious faiths make different judgments and choices about whether to live on under such circumstances. There are those who will want to continue aggressive treatment; those who would prefer terminal sedation; and those who will seek withdrawal from life-support systems and death by gradual starvation and dehydration. Although as a general matter the State's interest in the contributions each person may make to society outweighs the person's interest in ending her life, this interest does not have the same force for a terminally ill patient faced not with the choice of whether to live, only of how to die. Allowing the individual, rather than the State, to make judgments "about the 'quality' of life that a particular individual may enjoy" does not mean that the lives of terminally-ill, disabled people have less value than the lives of those who are healthy. Rather, it gives proper recognition to the individual's interest in choosing a final chapter that accords with her life story, rather than one that demeans her values and poisons memories of her.

Similarly, the State's legitimate interests in preventing suicide, protecting the vulnerable from coercion and abuse, and preventing euthanasia are less significant in this context. I agree that the State has a compelling interest in preventing persons from committing suicide because of depression, or coercion by third parties. But the State's legitimate interest in preventing abuse does not apply to an individual who is not victimized by abuse, who is not suffering from depression, and who makes a rational and voluntary decision to seek assistance in dying. Although, as the New York Task Force report discusses, diagnosing depression and other mental illness is not always easy, mental health workers and other professionals expert in working with dying patients can help patients cope with depression and pain, and help patients assess their options.

The final major interest asserted by the State is its interest in preserving the traditional integrity of the medical profession. The fear is that a rule permitting physicians to assist in suicide is inconsistent with the perception that they serve their patients solely as healers. But for some patients, it would be a physician's refusal to dispense medication to ease their suffering and make their death tolerable and dignified that would be inconsistent with the healing role. . . .

Justice SOUTER, concurring in the judgment.

. . . I conclude that the statute's application to the doctors has not been shown to be unconstitutional, but I write separately to give my reasons for analyzing the substantive due process claims as I do, and for rejecting this one.

The analogies between the abortion cases and this one are several. Even though the State has a legitimate interest in discouraging abortion, the Court recognized a woman's right to a physician's counsel and care. Like the decision to commit suicide, the decision to abort potential life can be made irresponsibly and under the influence of others, and yet the Court has held in the abortion cases that physi-

cians are fit assistants. Without physician assistance in abortion, the woman's right would have too often amounted to nothing more than a right to self-mutilation, and without a physician to assist in the suicide of the dying, the patient's right will often be confined to crude methods of causing death, most shocking and painful to the decedent's survivors.

In my judgment, the importance of the individual interest here, as within that class of "certain interests" demanding careful scrutiny of the State's contrary claim, see *Poe*, cannot be gainsaid. Whether that interest might in some circumstances, or at some time, be seen as "fundamental" to the degree entitled to prevail is not, however, a conclusion that I need draw here, for I am satisfied that the State's interests described in the following section are sufficiently serious to defeat the present claim that its law is arbitrary or purposeless.

The State has put forward several interests to justify the Washington law as applied to physicians treating terminally ill patients, even those competent to make responsible choices: protecting life generally, discouraging suicide even if knowing and voluntary, and protecting terminally ill patients from involuntary suicide and euthanasia, both voluntary and nonvoluntary.

It is not necessary to discuss the exact strengths of the first two claims of justification in the present circumstances, for the third is dispositive for me. That third justification is different from the first two, for it addresses specific features of respondents' claim, and it opposes that claim not with a moral judgment contrary to respondents', but with a recognized state interest in the protection of nonresponsible individuals and those who do not stand in relation either to death or to their physicians as do the patients whom respondents describe. The State claims interests in protecting patients from mistakenly and involuntarily deciding to end their lives, and in guarding against both voluntary and involuntary euthanasia. Leaving aside any difficulties in coming to a clear concept of imminent death, mistaken decisions may result from inadequate palliative care or a terminal prognosis that turns out to be error; coercion and abuse may stem from the large medical bills that family members cannot bear or unreimbursed hospitals decline to shoulder. Voluntary and involuntary euthanasia may result once doctors are authorized to prescribe lethal medication in the first instance, for they might find it pointless to distinguish between patients who administer their own fatal drugs and those who wish not to, and their compassion for those who suffer may obscure the distinction between those who ask for death and those who may be unable to request it. The argument is that a progression would occur, obscuring the line between the ill and the dying, and between the responsible and the unduly influenced, until ultimately doctors and perhaps others would abuse a limited freedom to aid suicides by yielding to the impulse to end another's suffering under conditions going beyond the narrow limits the respondents propose. The State thus argues, essentially, that respondents' claim is not as narrow as it sounds, simply because no recognition of the interest they assert could be limited to vindicating those interests and affecting no others. The State says that the claim, in practical effect, would entail consequences that the State could, without doubt, legitimately act to prevent.

The State, however, goes further, to argue that dependence on the vigilance of physicians will not be enough. First, the lines proposed here (particularly the requirement of a knowing and voluntary decision by the patient) would be more difficult to draw than the lines that have limited other recently recognized due process rights. Limiting a state from prosecuting use of artificial contraceptives by married couples posed no practical threat to the State's capacity to regulate contraceptives in other ways that were assumed at the time of *Poe* to be legitimate; the trimester measurements of *Roe* and the viability determination of *Casey* were easy to make with a real degree of certainty. But the knowing and responsible mind is harder to assess. Second, this difficulty could become the greater by combining with another fact within the realm of plausibility, that physicians simply would not be assiduous to preserve the line. They have compassion, and those who would be willing to assist in suicide at all might be the most susceptible to the wishes of a patient, whether the patient were technically quite responsible or not. Physicians, and their hospitals, have their own financial incentives, too, in this new age of managed care. Whether acting from compassion or under some other influence, a physician who would provide a drug for a patient to administer might well go the further step of administering the drug himself; so, the barrier between assisted suicide and euthanasia could become porous, and the line between voluntary and involuntary euthanasia as well. The case for the slippery slope is fairly made out here, not because recognizing one due process right would leave a court with no principled basis to avoid recognizing another, but because there is a plausible case that the right claimed would not be readily containable by reference to facts about the mind that are matters of difficult judgment, or by gatekeepers who are subject to temptation, noble or not.

Respondents propose an answer to all this, the answer of state regulation with teeth. Legislation proposed in several States, for example, would authorize physician-assisted suicide but require two qualified physicians to confirm the patient's diagnosis, prognosis, and competence; and would mandate that the patient make repeated requests witnessed by at least two others over a specified time span; and would impose reporting requirements and criminal penalties for various acts of coercion.

But at least at this moment there are reasons for caution in predicting the effectiveness of the teeth proposed. Respondents' proposals, as it turns out, sound much like the guidelines now in place in the Netherlands, the only place where experience with physician-assisted suicide and euthanasia has yielded empirical evidence about how such regulations might affect actual practice. Dutch physicians must engage in consultation before proceeding, and must decide whether the patient's decision is voluntary, well considered, and stable, whether the request to die is enduring and made more than once, and whether the patient's future will involve unacceptable suffering. There is, however, a substantial dispute today about what the Dutch experience shows. Some commentators marshall evidence that the Dutch guidelines have in practice failed to protect patients from involuntary euthanasia and have been violated with impunity. This evidence is contested. The day may come when we can say with some assurance which side is right, but for now it is the substantiality of the factual disagreement, and the alternatives for resolving it, that matter. They are, for me, dispositive of the due process claim at this time.

I take it that the basic concept of judicial review with its possible displacement of legislative judgment bars any finding that a legislature has acted arbitrarily when the following conditions are met: there is a serious factual controversy over the feasibility of recognizing the claimed right without at the same time making it impossible for the State to engage in an undoubtedly legitimate exercise of power; facts necessary to resolve the controversy are not readily ascertainable through the judicial process; but they are more readily subject to discovery through legislative factfinding and experimentation. It is assumed in this case, and must be, that a State's interest in protecting those unable to make responsible decisions and those who make no decisions at all entitles the State to bar aid to any but a knowing and responsible person intending suicide, and to prohibit euthanasia. . . .

The capacity of the State to protect the others if respondents were to prevail is, however, subject to some genuine question, underscored by the responsible disagreement over the basic facts of the Dutch experience. This factual controversy is not open to a judicial resolution with any substantial degree of assurance at this time.

Legislatures, on the other hand, have superior opportunities to obtain the facts necessary for a judgment about the present controversy. Not only do they have more flexible mechanisms for factfinding than the Judiciary, but their mechanisms include the power to experiment, moving forward and pulling back as facts emerge within their own jurisdictions. There is, indeed, good reason to suppose that in the absence of a judgment for respondents here, just such experimentation will be attempted in some of the States.

I do not decide here what the significance might be of legislative foot-dragging in ascertaining the facts going to the State's argument that the right in question could not be confined as claimed. Sometimes a court may be bound to act regardless of the institutional preferability of the political branches as forums for addressing constitutional claims. Now, it is enough to say that our examination of legislative reasonableness should consider the fact that the Legislature of the State of Washington is no more obviously at fault than this Court is in being uncertain about what would happen if respondents prevailed today. We therefore have a clear question about which institution, a legislature or a court, is relatively more competent to deal with an emerging issue as to which facts currently unknown could be dispositive. The answer has to be, for the reasons already stated, that the legislative process is to be preferred. There is a closely related further reason as well.

One must bear in mind that the nature of the right claimed, if recognized as one constitutionally required, would differ in no essential way from other constitutional rights guaranteed by enumeration or derived from some more definite textual source than "due process." An unenumerated right should not therefore be recognized, with the effect of displacing the legislative ordering of things, without the assurance that its recognition would prove as durable as the recognition of those other rights differently derived. To recognize a right of lesser promise would simply create a constitutional regime too uncertain to bring with it the expectation of finality that is one of this Court's central obligations in making constitutional decisions.

Legislatures, however, are not so constrained. The experimentation that should be out of the question in constitutional adjudication displacing legislative judgments is entirely proper, as well as highly desirable, when the legislative power addresses an emerging issue like assisted suicide. The Court should accordingly stay its hand to allow reasonable legislative consideration. While I do not decide for all time that respondents' claim should not be recognized, I acknowledge the legislative institutional competence as the better one to deal with that claim at this time.

Justice GINSBURG. . . .

Justice BREYER, concurring in the judgments.

I believe that Justice O'Connor's views, which I share, have greater legal significance than the Court's opinion suggests. I join her separate opinion, except insofar as it joins the majority. And I concur in the judgments. I shall briefly explain how I differ from the Court.

I agree with the Court . . . that the articulated state interests justify the distinction drawn between physician assisted suicide and withdrawal of life-support. I also agree with the Court that the critical question in both of the cases before us is whether "the 'liberty' specially protected by the Due Process Clause includes a right" of the sort that the respondents assert. I do not agree, however, with the Court's formulation of that claimed "liberty" interest. The Court describes it as a "right to commit suicide with another's assistance." But I would not reject the respondents' claim without considering a different formulation, for which our legal tradition may provide greater support. That formulation would use words roughly like a "right to die with dignity." But irrespective of the exact words used, at its core would lie personal control over the manner of death, professional medical assistance, and the avoidance of unnecessary and severe physical suffering—combined.

I do not believe, however, that this Court need or now should decide whether or not such a right is "fundamental." That is because, in my view, the avoidance of severe physical pain (connected with death) would have to comprise an essential part of any successful claim and because, as Justice O'Connor points out, the laws before us do not force a dying person to undergo that kind of pain. Rather, the laws of New York and of Washington do not prohibit doctors from providing patients with drugs sufficient to control pain despite the risk that those drugs themselves will kill. And under these circumstances the laws of New York and Washington would overcome any remaining significant interests and would be justified, regardless.

Medical technology, we are repeatedly told, makes the administration of pain-relieving drugs sufficient, except for a very few individuals for whom the ineffectiveness of pain control medicines can mean, not pain, but the need for sedation which can end in a coma. We are also told that there are many instances in which patients do not receive the palliative care that, in principle, is available, but that is so for institutional reasons or inadequacies or obstacles, which would seem possible to overcome, and which do not include a prohibitive set of laws.

This legal circumstance means that the state laws before us do not infringe directly upon the (assumed) central interest (what I have called the core of the interest in dying with dignity) as, by way of contrast, the state anticontraceptive laws at issue in *Poe* did interfere with the central interest there at stake—by bringing the State's police powers to bear upon the marital bedroom.

Were the legal circumstances different—for example, were state law to prevent the provision of palliative care, including the administration of drugs as needed to avoid pain at the end of life—then the law's impact upon serious and otherwise unavoidable physical pain (accompanying death) would be more directly at issue. And as Justice O'Connor suggests, the Court might have to revisit its conclusions in these cases.

Notes and Queries

1. How did the majority describe the liberty interest in this case? How else might it be described? Is there a constitutionally grounded reason—perhaps one based in a particular understanding of judicial power and majoritarian politics—to prefer an expansive or a narrow formulation of the question in this case?

2. Why does the Court begin in its analysis with an inquiry into history and tradition? Is this interpretive approach to the meaning of due process consistent with the plurality opinion in *Michael H.*? With Justice Cardozo's opinion in *Palko*? How does the majority's analysis of due process differ—if at all—from Justice Souter's analysis?

3. What understanding of the relationship between individual liberty and community interests animates the majority's opinion? Is it consistent with the Court's substantive due process jurisprudence in the past, as represented by cases like *Meyer, Griswold, Roe,* and *Cruzan*? Is that opinion grounded in classical understandings of western liberalism? In classical or civic republican approaches to community?

Alternatively, is the Court's opinion grounded less in philosophical understandings about liberty and community and more in institutional understandings about the proper balance between judicial and legislative power?

4. What is the significance of the Court's analysis of the Dutch experience with physician-assisted suicide? How does the majority use this information? How does Justice Souter use it? Are their treatments consistent with the Court's reception of medical evidence in *Jacobson*? Is it appropriate for the Court to refer to this material? Why or why not?

5. Should there be a constitutionally cognizable difference between physical pain and other types of suffering at the end of life? Justice O'Connor suggests that the fact that the state laws do not prohibit physicians from giving pain medication, even to the point of hastening death, saves them from being unconstitutional. Justice Breyer suggests that the right to death with dignity can be protected as long as the dying individual is free from severe physical pain. Justice Souter, on the other hand, implies that a dying person might legitimately choose to end her own life in order to preserve her dignity, even if she is not in severe physical pain.

6. The majority opinions in *Glucksberg* suggest that the state's interest in protecting the disabled includes more than protecting them from coercion, "it extends to protecting disabled and terminally ill people from prejudice, negative and inaccurate stereotypes, and 'societal indifference.'" How does a law prohibiting physician-assisted suicide contribute to that broader interest?

7. In his concurrence, Justice Stevens wants to a) recognize that the State has the power to place a lesser value on some lives than others; and b) maintain that allowing physician-assisted suicide for the terminally ill and disabled "does not mean that the lives of terminally-ill, disabled people have less value than the lives of those who are healthy." Are these two goals compatible?

8. In a companion case, *Vacco v. Quill* (1977), the Court considered whether a New York law making it a crime to aid another to commit or attempt suicide violates the equal protection clause when patients may refuse life-saving treatment. In his opinion for the Court, Chief Justice Rehnquist concluded that the differential treatment does not violate the equal protection clause, saying that "the distinction between assisting suicide and withdrawing life-sustaining treatment, a distinction widely recognized and endorsed in the medical profession, and in our legal traditions, is both important and logical; it is certainly rational."

9. The Colombia *Euthanasia Case* (see Comparative Note 11.9) elicited strong dissenting opinions. Justice Jose Gregario Hernandez Galinda noted that "only Holland, the State of Oregon in the United States and Australia have legalized euthanasia and only then under the severest of regulations. Moreover, I understand that Australia later abolished that measure." In the hierarchy of rights, he wrote, the right to life, which is declared to be "inviolate" under the Columbian Constitution, trumps the right of individuals "to unrestricted development of their identity (Article 16)." Justice Martha V. Sachia Mendez developed a similar argument, suggesting that the Court has invented a new concept of "dignity" that ignores the reality of death. Human dignity, she wrote, "does not exhaust itself [in the notion] of autonomy. It embraces a more generous concept of humanity that covers its decline until its final end. . . . Human pain summons solidarity and requires answers from the community. . . . [E]xcessive suffering by

itself cannot dissolve the essential ties of sociability that are expressed in the prohibition not to kill." Can you define the competing conceptions of human dignity at the basis of the majority and dissenting opinions?

Nearly all of the dissenting justices faulted the Court for its attempt to decide the point at which a physician would be criminally responsible for terminating the life of a patient "oppressed by intense suffering." Justice Sachia Mendez wrote "that this is a subject that should be defined through the political process and its institutional channels. . . ." Does the disagreement on the Colombian Court underscore the prudence of the cautious approach taken by the U.S. Supreme Court in assisted suicide cases?

Chapter 12

Freedom of Speech

"Congress shall make no law . . . abridging the freedom of speech, or of the press." From these sparse words of the First Amendment the Supreme Court has created a huge and complicated jurisprudence, a body of case law that begins with *Schenck v. United States* (1919) but which, for the most part, is a post-1950 phenonemon. The cases featured in this chapter command attention because they highlight recurring themes in American constitutional law. As noted in previous chapters, these themes engage the judicial effort to reconcile the tension between democracy and constitutionalism, on the one hand, and between the values of liberty and community, on the other. The Supreme Court is not alone in dealing with these seemingly insoluble tensions. Constitutional courts exercising the power of judicial review around the world have faced and are facing similar problems of interpretation and goverance.

The First Amendment: An Interpretive Problem

Original Intent

In construing the language of the First Amendment, the Supreme Court seldom appeals to its original history, in part because there is a paucity of proof about what the Framers meant by the speech clauses. One thing that can be said for sure is that the Founders fought against prior censorship of the press. As Leonard Levy has pointed out in a thorough study of these origins, the Founders held firm to the prevailing Blackstonian position that while it would be wrong for the state to interfere with the freedom of editors in advance of publication, the press could properly be sued for injuries sustained as a result of publication.[1] Whether, as some scholars contend, the

---

[1] See Leonard Levy, *Legacy of Suppression: Freedom of Speech and Press in Early American History* (Cambridge: The Belknap Press of Harvard University Press, 1960), pp. 13–15 and 214–248. Zechariah Chafee took a broader view of the orginal intent behind the speech clauses. In *Free Speech in the United States* (Cambridge: Harvard University Press, 1941), pp. 27–35, he argued that the Founders had accepted a broad Miltonian faith in freedom of expression well beyond their objection to prior censorship and seditious libel. Levy's meticulous research, however, appears to support the founding generation's more limited conception of free speech. In a revised version of *Legacy of Suppression*, Levy recanted some of his earlier views about the suppressive impulses of the Framers, but he reaffirmed that freedom of political

Founders also intended to abolish the common law crime of seditious libel—i.e., a written communication critical of the government or its agents—remains in dispute.[2] Yet even if the historical record could show precisely what the Founders meant by free speech and press, any attempt in our own day to restrict the interpretation of these terms to their eighteenth-century meaning would be unacceptable. Indeed, most originalists would probably so conclude. Americans in the twenty-first century define liberty more broadly than their forebears.

Justice Hugo Black, on the other hand, saw the Founders' original intention embedded in the literal language of the speech clauses. "[T]he First Amendment's unequivocal command," he declared, "shows that the men who drafted our Bill of Rights did all the 'balancing' that was to be done in this field."[3] "No law," he insisted, means *no law*. Black's view, however, never commanded more than one or two votes on the Supreme Court, largely because any such "absolutist" perspective would have invalidated many widely accepted restrictions on speech, restrictions that reflect the complexity of the relationship between individual liberty and the interests of the community.

Text, Theory, and Purpose

If looking backward to historical intent provides little guidance in discerning the meaning of free speech, the dictionary gives us even less help. The words "freedom" and "speech" are potentially boundless. Hence, they demand *interpretation*. In interpreting the First Amendment, the Supreme Court almost of necessity had to look forward to the broad purposes of its language, and it did so in the light of various theories or arguments advanced in justification of the speech and press clauses. These justifications include self-government, individual self-fulfillment, and the attainment of truth. Each of these rationales is embedded deeply in our political history and intellectual tradition. The argument from self-government expresses the view that representative democracy would be impossible without the consent and participation of an active citizenry.[4] The argument from self-realization regards speech as central to rational inquiry and the development of the human personality.[5] Finally, the argument from truth, derived from J. S. Mill's *On Liberty*, rests on the proposition that truth is most likely to emerge only when confronted by its refutation in an arena of free and open debate.[6] Of course, each of these arguments begs further questions: What do we mean by participation in a society where political access is experienced unequally? Is the self that is to be realized whatever one chooses it to mean, or is there a distinctively human self, one that has meaning independent of the choice of the individual? Are all truths of equal standing in a regime founded on the existence of certain self-evident truths? Depending on the answers to these questions, the same rationales for promoting free speech can form the basis for counter-rationales for its limitation.

Resort to sophisticated theories would seem unnecessary to justify the high prior-

---

discourse at the time of the founding stopped short of seditious libel. See *Emergence of a Free Press* (Oxford: Oxford University Press, 1985).

[2] See David Anderson, *The Origins of the Press Clause*, 30 UCLA Law Review 493–496 (1983).

[3] *Konigsberg v. State Bar of California*, 366 U.S. 36, 61 (1961).

[4] *Time Inc., v. Hill*, 385 U.S. 374 (1967).

[5] See *Whitney v. California*, 274 U.S 357 (1927) (Brandeis, concurring.)

[6] *Red Lion Broadcasting Co. v. Federal Communications Commission*, 395 U.S. 367 (1969).

ity accorded speech in our constitutional system. Freedom of speech serves other purposes more modest and direct than philosophical or structural arguments from democracy, autonomy, and truth. One such purpose emphasizes the "checking value" of free speech and press. On this view, the main function of the speech and press clauses is to arrest "the inherent tendency of government officials to abuse the power entrusted to them."[7] Others have suggested free speech serves as a safety valve for the release of energy that might otherwise be directed toward subversion or violence. Still other values said to be served by the speech and press clauses are self-reliance, nonconformity, and tolerance for opposing views.[8]

It may be useful to point out that the First Amendment forbids laws curtailing *freedom* of speech, not speech itself. The interpretive problem is to define what this freedom means. Does it include speech that offends people or puts them in harm's way? Justice Holmes once remarked that freedom of speech would not extend to falsely shouting "fire" in a crowded theater. Holmes' case is easy, however; punishing the false cry of "fire" that would injure or trample people to death in a rush for the exits would invite little argument. But would freedom of speech extend to derogatory remarks about a racial or religious group or untrue statements about the public re-cord of a legislative representative? For the sake of what values or interests would government be justified in limiting such speech? Unlike many of the constitutions of other advanced liberal democracies, the United States Constitution fails to specify what these limits are. And so the Supreme Court has been left to its own devices when confronted with constitutional challenges to rules or regulations that impinge upon freedom of speech or press.

Balancing versus Absolutism

As the cases in this chapter illustrate, non-constitutional social interests—e.g., reputa-tion, privacy, repose, or public morality—have often prevailed over countervailing claims to freedom of speech. In deciding whether a speech interest should win over a countervailing non-constitutional social value, the Supreme Court often engages in *ad hoc* balancing. Here judges carefully weigh the conflicting claims of individual and community in the light of a particular set of facts and without much regard for general theorizing, precisely the kind of balancing act that the absolutists say is im-permissible under the "no law" decree of the First Amendment. *Ad hoc* balancing, however, is not always a matter of weighing individual rights against community interests. When the Court balances competing community interests, such as the com-munity's interest in receiving information against its interest in peaceful neighbor-hoods, the outcome depends on the weight the Court decides to attach to each interest, and this is not always certain.

Over the years the Supreme Court has gravitated to the poles of both absolutism and balancing. Severe criticism has greeted both approaches: absolutism because it allows freedom of speech to trump all competing values; balancing because the case-by-case approach is too particularized to provide any coherent theory of constitu-tional interpretation. As for absolutism, Justice Black had an ingenious if not ingenu-ous way of getting around the dubious implications of his literalism. If taken literally,

---

[7] Vincent Blasi, *The Checking Value in First Amendment Theory,* 1977 A.B.F. Res. J. 538.

[8] See especially Lee C. Bollinger, *The Tolerant Society* (New York: Oxford University Press, 1986) and Steven H. Shiffrin, *The First Amendment, Democracy, and Romance* (Princeton: Princeton University Press, 1993).

the "no law" language of the First Amendment would mean that you could not have laws punishing blackmail, criminal solicitation, fraud, or dozens of other commonly accepted restrictions on speech, including some aspects of contract and securities law, not to mention the clamps the National Labor Relations Act puts on the speech of employers when their workers are holding a union election. To get out of this quandary, Black, like the Court itself on numerous occasions, sharply distinguished between speech and conduct. But the speech-conduct distinction lacks credibility because the outcome of any given case depends on how narrowly or broadly judges choose to define speech, and this approach, like *ad hoc* balancing, produces uncertain results.

One could of course subscribe to absolutism and still give little protection to speech, a situation dramatized by *Cohen v. California* (1971, reprinted later in the chapter). The issue in *Cohen* was whether a person could be punished for "offensive conduct" by appearing in public with an abusive epithet ("Fuck the Draft") emblazoned on the back of his jacket. In this case five justices voted to reverse the conviction because it rested "solely upon 'speech.'" Yet four dissenting justices saw "mainly conduct and little speech" in what Justice Blackmun (Justice Black concurring) called "Cohen's absurd and immature antic." The disagreement highlights the fact that the absolutist's interpretive task is not as easy as it may first appear; thus distinguishing speech from antics requires definitional dexterity. Today, however, in light of recent "symbolic" speech and "expressive" conduct cases,[9] the speech-conduct distinction appears to have lost much of its vitality. (Further discussion follows in the upcoming sections.)

Definitional Balancing

More firmly entrenched in our First Amendment jurisprudence is the so-called "categorical" or "definitional" approach to the First Amendment, one that fuses elements of absolutism and balancing. When using this approach, the Supreme Court confers extraordinary—almost absolute—protection upon the expression of ideas affecting politics or society. In other instances, where artistic or scientific speech may be involved, some of the justices are inclined to rank the speech in terms of its informational value. If the speech ranks low in terms of importance, the community's interest in suppressing the speech may trump the individual's interest in hearing or uttering it. But when things such as "fighting words" or obscene speech are concerned, the Court categorically defines such speech as "nonspeech" and declares them unworthy of First Amendment protection. The seminal case here is *Chaplinsky v. New Hampshire* (1942, reprinted later in the chapter). Writing for a unanimous Court, Justice Murphy said:

> *There are certain well-defined and narrowly limited classes of speech, the prevention and punishment of which has never been thought to raise any constitutional problem. These include the lewd and the obscene, the profane, the libelous, and the insulting or "fighting words"—those which by their very utterance inflict injury or tend to incite an immediate breach of peace. It has been observed that such utterances are no essential part of any exposition of ideas, and are of such slight social value as a step to truth that any benefit that may be derived from them is clearly outweighed by the social interest in law and order.[10]*

---

[9] See *United States v. O'Brien* and *Texas v. Johnson* (reprinted later in the chapter).

[10] 315 U.S. 568, 86 L. Ed. 1031 (1942).

Justice Murphy thus elaborated a two-track theory of speech. On one track, speech would almost always merit protection but on the other it would almost always remain unprotected. Unprotected speech, it would seem, is unprotected *because*, contrary to what the majority said in *Cohen v. California*, it corrupts public discourse and offends deep-seated community values.

Categorical analysis is not free of problems, however. The Supreme Court still has to determine the degree of protection that it will accord even legitimate speech in specific fact-situations. The categorical approach also begs crucial definitional and theoretical questions. For example, the Supreme Court is virtually unanimous in categorizing obscenity as unprotected speech but often hopelessly divided over how to define it. In addition, as the quotation from *Chaplinsky* and the discussion to follow indicates, speech is often graded for its value in furthering democracy, individual autonomy, or the discovery of truth, but these theories cannot be fully reconciled and in any case provide no sure basis for resolving troublesome conflicts between free speech claims and highly valued social interests. As a consequence, the Court has had to construct a maze of doctrinal rules and tests for measuring the legitimacy of restrictions on speech, the result of which, according to one noted free speech scholar, "is a body of law complicated enough to inspire comparisons with the Internal Revenue Code."[11]

Speech, Conduct, and Time-Place-Manner (TPM) Restrictions

One conventional way of teasing some order out of the Court's interpretive approach is to distinguish between its treatment of laws regulating the *content* of speech itself and those purporting to regulate *conduct*. With regard to content, we can distinguish between three types of restrictions on speech: content-neutral, content-based, and viewpoint-based. A content-neutral regulation is one that seeks to achieve a valid public purpose unrelated to expression but whose secondary effect is to regulate or ban speech altogether. An example would be a city's ban on the posting of any and all signs on public property. The ban's purpose would be to improve the appearance of the environment.[12] A content-based restriction would be a general regulation banning the expression of all points of view relating to a particular topic of speech.[13] An example would be a ban on political campaigning on a military base; the ban would apply to all political viewpoints, whether Republican, Democratic, Communist, or Fascist. The third category is a viewpoint-based restriction. Here government places its stamp of approval on one side of an issue or argument, forbidding the expression of other points of view.

Varying tests have been applied to each of these categories. Content-neutral regulations are the least suspect and most likely to be upheld unless it can be shown that the burden on speech is substantial and no alternative means of communication are available. Content-based regulations, on the other hand, are reviewed with far greater judicial scrutiny, expressing a pervading and historic mistrust of official censorship. Yet these regulations may also survive constitutional analysis if justified by an important public purpose. In some contexts, even viewpoint-based restrictions on speech

---

[11] See Shiffren, *The First Amendment, Democracy, and Romance*, p. 3.

[12] See *Los Angeles City Council v. Taxpayers for Vincent*, 466 US 789 (1984).

[13] Other examples of content-based restrictions are regulations forbidding civil servants from taking part in political campaigns or ordinances that bar sexually explicit movies to be shown in a given locality. With respect to the latter, see *Renton v. Playtime Theatres, Inc.*, 475 U.S. 41 (1986).

are permissible, especially when government attaches speech restrictions to the use of public funds.[14] Ironically, a content-based restriction on speech—e.g., barring any kind of political demonstration adjacent to a public school during class hours[15]— often calls for a higher degree of scrutiny than a content-neutral restriction—e.g., a ban on the posting of signs on *all* public property[16]—even though the latter may constrain speech more than the former.

By contrast, regulations of conduct impinging on speech are presumptively valid and thus subject to a less severe standard of review. Such regulations—they are also content-neutral—often restrict the time, place, or manner of protected speech. Examples of such restrictions are laws against handbill distribution in residential neighborhoods, raucous emissions of sound trucks after a certain hour, and political campaigning within a certain distance of a voting booth.[17] In assessing the validity of these TPM regulations, the Court balances the general interest of the community—in these cases to keep the streets clean, protect privacy and repose, and prevent the intimidation of voters—against the interests of the individual. In such situations, the community (i.e., the government) usually wins, provided the restrictions are justified without reference to the content of the regulated speech, are narrowly tailored to serve a significant governmental interest, and leave open ample alternative channels for communicating the information. That it does is not surprising given the imbalance in favor of the community that such a weighing of interests typically projects, in contrast to what might result were the individual interest framed in a way that more explicitly indicated its importance to the broader interest of the community.

Symbolic Speech and Expressive Conduct

The distinction between content and conduct is elusive, particularly when "speech" and "nonspeech" elements unite in a single course of action. An action, activity, or conduct may be motivated by an expressive purpose. Some high profile examples include burning the flag, mutilating a draft card, sleeping overnight in a public park, or wearing a black armband. If these actions constitute symbolic protests against American military policy, compulsory draft registration, homelessness, or war in a distant country, then speech is clearly implicated. And if a ban on these activities is *intended* to suppress the message, the restriction would be suspect, thus warranting intensive judicial review.

But here again a problem rears its head. Motivational analysis is not an exact science, and for the judiciary to assume the worst about the legislature's intent would undermine the respect the judiciary normally owes to legislative judgments. In addition, government can ordinarily marshal legitimate reasons for content-neutral regulations of the kind mentioned. The camping and draft card restrictions, for example, may be justified by the need, respectively, to foster the health and safety of park

---

[14] In *Rust v. Sullivan,* 114 L. ed 2d 233 (1991), the Supreme Court upheld a provision of the Public Health Services Act that prohibits recipients—mainly clinics and doctors engaged in family planning—of funds under the Act from advocating abortion as a method of family planning. See also *Perry Educational Association v. Perry Local Educator's Association,* 460 U.S. 37 (1983), in which a public school allowed its mail boxes to be used by a union representing the school district's teachers, but excluding a rival union.

[15] *Grayned v. Rockford,* 408 U.S. 104 (1972).

[16] *Los Angeles City Council*

[17] See, respectively, *Schneider v. New Jersey,* 308 U.S. 147 (1939), *Ward v. Rock Against Racism,* 491 U.S. 781 (1989), and *Burson v. Freeman,* 119 L. Ed2 5 (1992).

users and to preserve important public records.[18] The result in these and analogous cases depends on how heavy a thumb individual justices are willing to place on the state or individual side of the scale in applying the three-part test mentioned in the previous section.

In *United States v. O'Brien* (1968, reprinted later in the chapter), the Court worked out a four-part test for determining the validity of legislation that regulates *expressive* conduct. The defendant in *O'Brien* had burned his draft registration card in public as a protest against the Vietnam War in the face of a federal law making it a crime to deliberately destroy one's draft card. A federal law or any regulation like it—i.e., one combining speech and nonspeech elements—said the Court, is justified if it is within the constitutional power of government; if it furthers an important governmental interest; if that interest is unrelated to the suppression of speech; and if the incidental restriction on speech is no greater than necessary to further that interest. The government passed the test in *O'Brien*; the draft was enacted pursuant to a valid power of Congress; the preservation of draft cards was vital to administering the selective service system; on the face of the statute there was no intent to prohibit speech; and interference with speech was no greater than necessary to achieve the objective.

This brief account of the interpretive problems facing the Supreme Court in resolving free speech issues in a complex society is far from exhaustive. It suggests, however, that no single interpretive theory is available to guide the Court in its deliberations. The lack of guidance is particularly acute with regard to the respective weights that should be accorded to individual and community interests in the ever-present balancing process in which the Court appears to be engaged. In the absence of such interpretive guidance, the Court has settled for certain doctrinal frameworks created for the purpose of according speech, in various and complex situations, its rightful place on our scale of constitutional values.

Speech and the Polity: Normative Issues

The cases featured in this chapter invoke normative themes that pervade much of contemporary American constitutional law. In these and related cases, the Supreme Court has had to struggle with the tension between liberty and community as well as that between democracy and judicial supremacy within our constitutional tradition. This tradition, however, has not spoken with a single voice. As pointed out earlier in this book, Americans are the heirs of rival traditions. One of these traditions, associated with classical republican virtues, celebrates social discipline, communal loyalty, and commitment to the common good. The other, associated with early Federalist thought, emphasizes the sovereign self, acquisitive individualism, and the privatization of life and society. Defining the "rivalry" in this way probably exaggerates the differences between these traditions. We wish merely to suggest here that much of our free speech jurisprudence can be understood as a playing out of the tension between the two sets of values.[19]

---

[18] See *Clark v. Community For Creative Non-Violence,* 468 U.S. 288 (1984) and *United States v. O'Brien,* 391 U.S. 367 (1968).

[19] Jean Bethke Elshtain prefers to call the rivalry an "ambiguity." She continues: "It is an ambiguity encoded in the Constitution and the Bill of Rights, in a simultaneous commitment to a 'we' and to a protection of the 'one,' and it is at once and the same time a source of strength and a cause for concern. Current individualist and communitarian debates are *not*, therefore, engagements between traditionalists and anti-traditionalists, or between liberals and restorationists. Rather, the intensity of, and interest in, this discussion is best understood as a contestation over the appropriation of the tradition itself. The Founders were Enlightenment figures who rejected traditions embodied in monarchical absolutism, but they also thought in some very traditional ways: Natural law and natural right were not their invention. Preoccupied from time to time with classical republican precedents, the Federalists and Anti-Federalists struggled with a

Internal Security and Advocacy of Unlawful Conduct

When is the nation or community entitled to protect itself against subversive speech that advocates illegal action or arguably endangers the security of the United States? *Schenck v. United States* (1919, reprinted later in the chapter), in which the Supreme Court sustained the conviction of persons charged with distributing pamphlets encouraging resistance to military conscription under the Espionage Act of 1917, set forth the famous "clear and present danger" test. Justice Holmes, writing for a unanimous Court, said:

> . . . *[T]he character of every act depends upon the circumstances in which it is done. . . . [The] question in every case is whether the words used are used in such circumstances and are of such a nature as to create a clear and present danger that they will bring about the substantive evils that Congress has a right to prevent. It is a question of proximity and degree.*

As the following discussion shows, the clear and present danger test has a checkered history in calibrating where the line should be drawn between protected and unprotected speech. In the absence of any precise definition of "clear" and "present," different judges applying the test to similar sets of facts could easily come to different results.[20]

Over the years, the clear and present danger test underwent various formulations. In *Gitlow v. New York*, the Court transposed the standard into what amounted to a "bad tendency" test. In sustaining the application of New York's criminal anarchy statute to the militant advocacy of political strikes, the *Gitlow* Court simply deferred to the New York legislature's judgment that certain words, in and of themselves, tended to endanger the state's security. Holmes, joined by Brandeis, dissented because in his view no "present" danger existed.

Brandeis seemed to revise the test in *Whitney v. California* (1927). "The fact that speech is likely to result in some violence," he argued, "is not enough to justify its suppression. There must be the probability of serious injury to the State."[21] This view in which Holmes concurred, came close to being regnant in the ensuing years. In the 1950s, however, when anticommunist sentiment ran strong in the country, the Court reaffirmed its deferential posture toward legislative efforts to put down totalitarian movements. The pivotal case is *Dennis v. United States* (1951, reprinted later in the chapter). Now the standard was "whether the gravity of the 'evil,' discounted by its improbability, justifies such invasion of free speech as is necessary to avoid the danger."[22] As Chief Justice Vinson wrote, government is not reduced to "helplessness in the face of preparation for revolution," no matter how far off the putsch might be.

As the 1950s came to a close, and under the leadership of Chief Justice Warren, the Court returned to the Brandeis-Holmes version of the First Amendment. *Yates v.*

---

general fund of ideas, a repertoire of stock concerns and understandings much as contemporary interlocutors do." See " 'In Common Together': Unity, Diversity, and Civic Virtue" in Robert E. Calvert (ed.), *The Constitution of the People* (Lawrence, Kansas: University Press of Kansas, 1991), p. 65.

[20] Actually, the test yielded different results in Holmes' own hands. He sustained the conviction in *Schenck* even though the record showed little evidence of the damage, real or potential, caused by the antidraft flyers. In *Abrams v. United States*, decided a few months later, Holmes dissented from a decision sustaining the conviction of other antiwar propagandists in the absence of any present danger of immediate evil. See 250 US 616, 628.

[21] 274 US 357 (1927).

[22] 341 US 494; 95 L. ed 1137 (1951).

United States (1957) and *Noto v. United States* (1961), which distinguished sharply between advocacy of illegal action and advocacy in the realm of ideas,[23] lighted the way to *Brandenburg v. Ohio* (1969, reprinted later in the chapter), the case that incorporates the most up-to-date restatement of the clear and present danger doctrine. In a *per curiam* opinion reversing the conviction of a Ku Klux Klan leader under Ohio's criminal syndicalism statute, the Court declared that the "guarantees of free speech and free press do not permit a State to forbid or proscribe advocacy of the use of force or of law violation except where such advocacy is directed to inciting or producing imminent lawless action and is likely to incite or produce such action."

Even as it appeared to expand the boundaries of free speech, perhaps beyond the limits of any other constitutional democracy in the world, the *Brandenburg* test is not without its own problems. The terms "advocacy," "inciting," "imminent," and "likely to incite" are still in need of definition, and judges may differ on the emphasis they place on (1) the actual words used in a speech, (2) the intent of the speaker, (3) the context of the speech, and (4) the seriousness (or lack thereof) of a particular lawless action. Justice Douglas, who concurred in *Brandenburg*, was unimpressed with the Court's performance. Reverting to a seeming absolutism, he could see "no place in the regime of the First Amendment for any 'clear and present danger' test whether strict or tight as some would make it or free-wheeling as the Court in *Dennis* rephrased it." Nevertheless, the upshot of the *Brandenburg* test is the wide protection it gives to political speech of almost any kind.

The illegal advocacy cases raise the perennial issue of how competing interests are to be assessed and what role the judiciary should play in reviewing the political assessment. In *Dennis* the Court suggested that any balancing is to be done mainly by the legislature and that if the legislation is reasonable the courts should defer to its judgment. *Brandenburg* and the Brandeis-Holmes vision of the First Amendment reject this view of the judiciary's role. These standards elevate speech—certainly political speech—into a preferred freedom, requiring the highest level of judicial scrutiny. As in the defamation cases discussed later, this level of scrutiny is often justified by arguments based on democratic theory and the necessity to preserve an uninhibited marketplace of ideas in the interest of truth. Brandeis added still another justification in his *Whitney* concurrence. Drawing upon classical republican theory, he emphasized the importance of speech to civic virtue, reasoned deliberation, and a participatory republic. Hence in his view "public discussion is a political duty" and "the greatest menace to freedom is an inert people." As Pnina Lahav noted, Brandeis believed that persons are "social beings" with an "organic sense of belonging" to the commonwealth, and thus "committed to the public good" through the faculty of speech.[24]

Defamation and Privacy

The broad protection accorded to political speech in *Brandenberg* was foreshadowed by the Court's historic decision in *New York Times Co. v. Sullivan* (1964, reprinted later in the chapter). Prior to *Sullivan*, public officials could sue newspapers

---

[23] See respectively 354 US 298 and 367 US 290. But see *Scales v. United States*, 367 US 203 (1961), where the Court extended the application of the Smith Act to knowing membership in an organization advocating the overthrow of the national government.

[24] *Holmes and Brandeis: Libertarian and Republican Justifications of Free Speech*, 4 Journal of Law and Politics 451, 460 (1987).

and other critics under state libel laws for defamatory utterances and false statements of fact directed toward their official conduct. In overturning a long-established policy against the protection of such utterances, the Court announced that in the future public officials could recover damages for a falsehood relating to their official conduct only if they can show that the utterance was made with "actual malice" or with the knowledge that it was made "with reckless disregard [of the truth]." In laying down this rule, the Court sought to prevent the states from converting their defamation laws into laws against seditious libel.

Justice Brennan, writing for seven of his brethren, ranked speech superior to the social values of personal honor and reputation, whether of public officials or of the offices they hold. Arguments based on both self-government and truth grounded *Sullivan*. Brennan noted that "we consider this case against the background of a profound national commitment to the principle that debate on public issues should be uninhibited, robust, and wide-open, and that it may well include vehement, caustic, and sometimes unpleasantly sharp attacks on government and public officials." The Court pointed out that "erroneous statement is inevitable in free debate" and freedom of expression needs "breathing space" to survive; any other rule, said Brennan, would lead to "self-censorship" of the press, deter would-be critics of official conduct, and dampen the vigor of public debate. As for truth, the Court invoked no less a figure than John Stuart Mill, citing with approval his argument that even false statements contribute to public debate because then truth emerges more vigorously and clearly "by its collision with error."[25]

While praised by some as "an occasion for dancing in the streets,"[26] *Sullivan* invited considerable criticism for its elevation of speech over the countervailing values of truth, human dignity, and the integrity of public discussion. The criticism intensified when the Court extended the *Sullivan* privilege to cover public figures such as football coaches, celebrities, and even private persons voluntarily or involuntarily caught up in a matter of public interest,[27] even though the utterances in such cases may not relate directly to governmental affairs. Justice Brennan, however, was not unmindful of the important social values that underlie state defamation laws; after all, "[s]ociety has a pervasive interest in preventing and redressing attacks upon reputation,"[28] a concern Justice Stewart traced to "our basic concept of the essential dignity and worth of every human being."[29] Justice Brennan, however, was unwilling to limit the *Sullivan* rule to *political* discussion. Still writing for the majority in 1971, he argued that free speech "must embrace all issues about which information is needed . . . to enable the members of society to cope with the exigencies of their period."[30] In his hands, the *Sullivan* rule would extend to all matters of public discussion.

By 1974, however, a deeply fractured Court limited a newspaper's constitutional privilege against liability for a false statement of fact.[31] At least where the injury is

---

[25] See John Stuart Mill, "On Liberty," in John Garvey, *The First Amendment: A Reader* (St. Paul, Minn.: West Publishing Co., 1992), 59.

[26] See Harry Kalven, Jr. *The* New York Times *Case: A Note on The Central Meaning of the First Amendment,* 1964 The Supreme Court Review 221, note 125.

[27] See *Curtis Publishing Co. v. Butts* and *Associated Press v. Walker,* 388 US 130 (1967), *Time, Inc. v. Hill,* 385 US 374 (1967), and *Time, Inc. v. Firestone,* 424 US 448 (1976).

[28] *Rosenblatt v. Baer,* 383 US 75, 86 (1965).

[29] Ibid., at 92.

[30] *Rosenbloom v. Metromedia,* 403 US 29, 41 (1971).

[31] *Gertz v. Robert Welch, Inc.* 418 US 323 (1974).

inflicted on a private person caught up in a matter of public interest, the Court shifted its emphasis to the dignitarian argument advanced by Justice Stewart. The shift owed much to the new Nixon appointees (Chief Justice Burger and Justices Powell and Blackmun). Although Justice Powell, writing for a plurality, noted that "there is no such thing as a false idea,"[32] he went on to say that "there is no constitutional value in false statements of fact." Why? Because "[n]either the intentional lie nor the careless error materially advances society's interest in 'uninhibited, robust, and wide-open' debate on public issues."[33] Justice Brennan dissented.

Although, as we shall see, the Court began increasingly, from the mid-1970s to the present, linking the protection of speech to its perceived value, it continued to immunize the mass media against liability for their criticism of public figures and public officials. Chief Justice Rehnquist, expressing the opinion of seven of the Court's members, extended the *Sullivan* privilege even to the publication of a parody intended to inflict emotional harm on its victim. In what the Court acknowledged as "doubtless gross and repugnant in the eyes of most," *Hustler* magazine had depicted Jerry Falwell, a minister well-known for his leadership of the "Moral Majority," in a drunken incestuous relationship with his mother. Even devastating satire of this description deserves protection, said the Court; otherwise, political cartoonists and satirists would run the risk of having to prove in court that they did not speak out of hatred. The constitutional vision of the polity emerging from *Hustler* and related cases stands in marked contrast to the image of a deliberative assembly often associated with republican political theory.[34]

Offensive Talk, Fighting Words, and Hate Speech

May a liberal society suppress racist propaganda or hate talk directed at particular groups? May it regulate the use of epithets or words that offend, hurt, or shock members of an audience or others who hear the message? May it punish communicative acts contemptuous of cherished national symbols? The Supreme Court of the United States has grappled with each of these issues in recent years, and more often than not freedom of expression has emerged victorious. The cases are important because once again they highlight the tension between freedom of speech and society's interest in protecting values such as civility, social morality, and public order. They are also in the public eye in view of the slash and burn rhetoric so common in America today, ranging from the charges of murder hurled against doctors who perform abortions to the National Rifle Association's assault on government officials as jack-booted stormtroopers.

The tension between freedom of speech and civility surfaced dramatically in *Beauharnais v. Illinois* (1952) and *Chaplinsky v. New Hampshire* (1942), the two cases that mark the beginning of the Court's effort to deal with offensive talk and hate speech. In *Beauharnais* a divided Court sustained a statute making it a crime to defame any class of persons based on race or creed as criminal, unchaste, or lacking in virtue in such a way as to expose persons in the class to derision and ridicule or which causes a breach of the peace. Ever conscious of its institutional role, the majority noted that it would be "arrant dogmatism" for the Court to deny a state legislature a choice of policy in dealing with "obstinate social issues" and that it is reasonable

---

[32] Ibid., at 339.

[33] Ibid., at 340.

[34] *Hustler Magazine v. Falwell*, 485 US 46 (1988).

for a legislature to conclude that the dignity accorded a person in society may well depend on the reputation of the group to which he or she belongs.

Beauharnais drew upon *Chaplinsky* for support. The latter laid down the doctrine that "fighting words," which do not enjoy the protection of the First Amendment, include "the lewd and obscene, the profane, the libelous, and the insulting." Such words tend "by their very utterance" to "inflict injury" or "incite to an immediate breach of the peace," and since they contribute nothing to the expression of ideas or truth, their value is outweighed by the "social interest in order and morality."[35] In a related case, the Court announced that "[r]esort to epithets or personal abuse is not in any sense communication of information or opinion safeguarded by the Constitution."[36]

To see where *Chaplinsky* and *Beauharnais* stand today, we briefly cite more recent decisions. *Cohen v. California* (1971, reprinted later in the chapter), and *Skokie v. National Socialist Party* (1978) are benchmarks in the Court's contemporary approach to group defamation and offensive speech as noted earlier. *Cohen* reversed the conviction of a young person who used vulgar language in a public place. Here the Court seemed to vindicate no less than the principle of *expressive* individualism inherent in the notion of personal autonomy. Justice Harlan, writing for the majority, spoke of the "emotive" as well as the "cognitive" function of speech and reminded his readers that "one man's vulgarity is another's lyric." While his opinion purported to follow *Chaplinsky*, it is noteworthy that the earlier decision's concern for "the social interest in order and morality" was reduced in the later decision to a concern only for order. Justice Blackmun, joined by Chief Justice Burger and Justice Black, found Cohen's "speech" little more than an "absurd and immature antic" and thus "well within the sphere of *Chaplinsky*." But these justices, too, showed little inclination to mount a defense of the communitarian interest in good taste and morality.

In *Skokie*, the Supreme Court denied *certiorari* in a case in which the Illinois Supreme Court, invoking *Cohen*, permitted members of the American Nazi Party to demonstrate in a heavily populated Jewish community and to display the swastika.[37] Both the display and the demonstration, said the Court, are "symbolic expression[s] of thought" within the protection of the First Amendment and "may not be prohibited merely because the ideas are themselves offensive to some of their hearers." Years later, in *Texas v. Johnson* (1989, reprinted later in the chapter), the Court struck down the conviction of a person who had burned and insulted the national flag in violation of Texas's law prohibiting the "desecration of venerated objects." In a 5 to 4 opinion, the Court said that the conviction could not stand because, in seeking to preserve the flag as a symbol of national unity, Texas had interfered with the content of a message intended to offend, invite dispute, and create dissatisfaction with American military policy. The Court also distinguished the case from *Chaplinsky* since the flag burning incident did not qualify as an insult directed at particular persons, thus inviting retaliation.

When *Cohen* and *Johnson* are considered in tandem with *Sullivan* and *Brandenburg*, one may wonder how much vitality *Beauharnais* and *Chaplinsky* still possess. The Court's construction of the First Amendment absolutely bars any official interference with the communication of an idea, no matter how offensive, unless the state meets *Brandenburg*'s "incitement" test or justifies the interference by some other

---

[35] 315 US 568 at 572.

[36] *Cantwell v. Connecticut,* 310 US 296 (1940).

[37] 373 N.E. 2d 21, 69 Ill. 2d 605 (1978).

"compelling" state interest. Some commentators such as Steven H. Shiffrin, however, have found the judicial focus on ideas misplaced. The point may well have been illustrated by Chief Justice Rehnquist in *Texas v. Johnson* when he described the flag burning incident as "an inarticulate grunt" rather than the passing on of an idea. According to Shriffrin, this emphasis on ideas takes the romance out of the First Amendment. Its free speech provisions, he argues, should be seen "as a cultural symbol to encourage dissent,"[38] protecting all forms of rebelliousness and nonconformity, whether they convey ideas or not.

That said, Justice Brennan's central point in the Texas case is unmistakably about tolerance of disturbingly provocative *ideas*. "If there is any bedrock principle underlying the First Amendment, it is that the government may not prohibit the expression of an idea simply because society finds the idea itself offensive or disagreeable." This principle was sorely tested in *R.A.V. v. City of St. Paul* (1992, reprinted later in the chapter), a critical hate speech case involving the effort of a local community to resolve the conflict between the ideals of freedom and equality. The Supreme Court, however, found its attempt to mediate the balance between these values overbroad and thus at odds with the First Amendment. St. Paul's ordinance was aimed at the display of bias-motivated symbols and abusive rhetoric that arouse anger on the basis of race, religion, or gender. As construed by Minnesota's Supreme Court, the ordinance fell within *Chaplinsky's* "fighting words" exception to freedom of speech and was narrowly tailored to achieve this objective. While the Court was unanimous in striking down the law, Justice Scalia spoke for only a bare majority in finding that the statute unconstitutionally engaged in viewpoint discrimination because it disfavored only those fighting words related to the topics just mentioned. This, said Scalia, amounted to censorship, and while the ordinance promoted a compelling interest in protecting certain groups from discrimination it was not reasonably designed to bring about this result.

R.A.V. was revisited by the Court in 2003 in *Virginia v. Black*, in which a divided Court upheld Virginia's right to make it a felony "for any person . . . with the intent of intimidating any person or group . . . to burn . . . a cross on the property of another, a highway or other public place." Justice O'Connor wrote in her opinion of the (fragmented) Court: "The First Amendment permits Virginia to outlaw cross burnings done with the intent to intimidate because burning a cross is a particularly virulent form of intimidation. Instead of prohibiting all intimidating messages, Virginia may choose to regulate this subset of intimidating messages in light of cross burning's long and pernicious history as a signal of impending violence. Thus, just as a State may regulate only that obscenity which is the most obscene due to its prurient content, so too may a State choose to prohibit only those forms of intimidation that are most likely to inspire fear of bodily harm. A ban on cross burning carried out with the intent to intimidate is fully consistent with our holding in *R. A. V.* and is proscribable under the First Amendment."[39]

R.A.V. still casts considerable doubt on the validity of state efforts to ban language or displays that create an intimidating or demeaning environment in education or the workplace. One of the most comprehensive of these codes was adopted by the University of Michigan. It banned "[a]ny behavior, verbal or physical, that stigmatizes

---

[38] See Shiffren, p. 6.

[39] *Virginia v. Black* 123 S. Ct. 1536, at p. 1549–50 (2003). In this case, however, the specific conviction was overturned because the Court found another part of the statute, in which "[a]ny such burning . . . shall be prima facie evidence of an intent to intimidate a person or group," to be unconstitutional.

. . . an individual on the basis of race, ethnicity, religion, sex, sexual orientation, creed, national origin, ancestry, age, marital status, handicap or Vietnam-era veteran status." Citing *Brandenburg, Chaplinsky,* and *Texas v. Johnson,* a federal district court struck down the code, holding that it swept too broadly by banning speech fully protected by the Constitution. To survive constitutional analysis, said the lower court, the state would have to craft a much narrower code aimed at abusive epithets causing direct harm to particular individuals.[40] The court sounded a familiar refrain in reminding Americans that speech may not be banned merely because it offends or shocks. But it also reminded them (as was illustrated in the Virginia cross-burning case) that the traditional rationales for protecting speech may provide less than satisfactory support for defending speech that is less about the communication of ideas than it is about the vilification and intimidation of targeted groups of vulnerable people.

Indecency and Obscenity

In *Roth v. United States* (1957), the Supreme Court reaffirmed the view that obscenity is unprotected speech under the First Amendment. But the standard laid down in *Roth* for defining obscenity caused more difficulties than it resolved,[41] for the justices were hopelessly divided over its meaning and application. By 1964, in *Jacobellis v. Ohio* (1964),[42] the Court had protected virtually everything under the *Roth* rule except hard-core pornography. By now, a national community standard was being applied and no work was to be proscribed unless it was "utterly without social importance." Still the problem of definition lingered, and the Court could not agree on an opinion to buttress its decisions nullifying state and local restrictions on the production and distribution of obscene materials.

With *Miller v. California* (1973, reprinted later in the chapter), this picture changed. Now, for the first time, a majority of the justices agreed on a standard more supportive of state and local efforts "to maintain a decent society."[43] The emerging majority seemed more open to the view that the "crass commercial exploitation of sex" tended to debase "family life, community welfare, and the development of the human personality."[44] Environmental arguments fortified these communitarian and dignitarian concerns; localities could now legitimately control the "secondary effects" (e.g., deterioration resulting from pandering, prostitution, and crime) in the interest of preserving the tone and quality of urban life. In fact, establishments like adult theatres were being singled out for the content of their showings, and the Court treated the regulation of such establishments as a time, place, and manner restriction on speech, thus imposing a less severe test than the states would otherwise have had to meet under ordinary content-based legislation.[45]

In the meanwhile, Justice Stevens had begun to gather support for his latter-day

---

[40] *Doe v. University of Michigan,* 721 F.Supp. 852 (E.D.Mich, 1989).

[41] According to *Roth,* a thing is obscene if the average person applying contemporary community standards finds that "the dominant theme taken as a whole appeals to a prurient interest" [i.e., a morbid interest in sex] 354 US 476.

[42] 378 US184 (1964).

[43] The quoted words are from Chief Justice Warren's dissenting opinion, ibid., at 199.

[44] *Paris Adult Theatre I v. Slaton,* 413 US 49 (1973).

[45] See See *Young v. American Mini Theatres, Inc.,* 427 U.S. 50 (1976) and *Renton v. Playtime Theatres, Inc.,* 475 U.S. 41 (1986).

effort to grade speech in terms of its social, political, or artistic value, in effect reviving *Chaplinsky* by allowing the states to regulate "low-value" speech in the interest of order and morality. This view manifested itself even in indecent—as opposed to obscene—speech cases as when the Court sustained an FCC ruling against a daytime radio broadcast of comedian George Carlin's "Seven Dirty Words" monologue. In a hard jab at Carlin and the radio station, Stevens remarked that when "a pig has entered the parlor, the exercise of [the FCC's] regulatory power does not depend on proof that the pig is obscene."[46] In the Internet case, *Reno v. American Civil Liberties Union* (1997), however, Justice Stevens' majority opinion held that a federal law prohibiting the knowing transmission of obscene or indecent messages to recipients under eighteen years of age is unconstitutional. The breadth of the statutory prohibition and the nature of the Internet as "a unique and wholly new medium of worldwide human communication" was at the basis of the distinction between this case and previous decisions sustaining the ban on obscene or indecent material on radio and television.

Subsequent cases involving pornography on the Internet have given the Court (and the nation) a glimpse into some of the unique jurisprudential questions that this new medium might engender. In *Ashcroft v. Free Speech Coalition* (2002), for example, the Court, in a 6 to 3 decision (with Chief Justice Rehnquist and Justices O'Connor and Scalia dissenting), struck down key provisions of the Child Pornography Protection Act (CPPA) of 1996 regulating "virtual child pornography." Recognizing the broad range of artistic and literary creations that have been inspired by the themes of teenage sexual activity (including William Shakespeare's *Romeo and Juliet* and the 2000 Academy Award–winning film *American Beauty*), the Court refused, in effect, to punish individuals for appearing to depict something that they are not, in fact, actually depicting. Justice Kennedy's opinion for the Court relied upon the test for obscene materials set forth in *Miller*. He distinguished the case from *Ferber v. New York* (1982—determining that, in keeping with the State's interest in protecting children from exploitation, pornography depicting children can be regulated whether or not the images are obscene) by the fact that children were not at all involved in production.

The conflict between social morality and individual expression stood out in sharp relief in *Barnes v. Glen Theatre, Inc.* (1991). Here the Court sustained Indiana's public indecency statute as applied to nude dancing as entertainment. The decision was 5 to 4. Three of the justices in the majority (Rehnquist, Kennedy, and O'Connor) agreed that nonobscene nude dancing was "expressive" conduct but found that the statute had met the O'Brien test. Applying a far less restrictive standard, Justice Scalia thought the community's moral opposition to nude dancing furnished a *reasonable* basis for the legislation. Justice Souter, on the other hand, saw the statute as a legitimate regulation of nude dancing's secondary effects.[47]

The bare majority and fragmented precedent of *Barnes*, however, provided Justice Souter—along with the rest of the Court—with an opportunity to reconsider the secondary effects doctrine in *City of Erie v. Pap's A. M.* (2000, reprinted later in the chapter). Crafting an ordinance similar to the Indiana law upheld in *Barnes*, the city of Erie, Pennsylvania, made it an offense to "knowingly or intentionally appear in public in a 'state of nudity.'" Reaffirming *Barnes* with a 6 to 3 decision, the Court, speaking through Justice O'Connor, viewed the ordinance as a content-neutral regu-

---

[46] *Federal Communications Comm'n v. Pacifica Foundation,* 438 US 726 (1978).

[47] 115 L. ed2 504.

lation unrelated to the suppression of expression. "It does not target nudity that contains an erotic message; rather it bans all public nudity, regardless of whether that nudity is accompanied by expressive activity." Thus, the Court reasoned, Erie need only meet the intermediate level of scrutiny for symbolic speech established by *O'Brien* rather than the strict scrutiny required by *Johnson*. Having already determined the ordinance to have only a "*de minimis*" effect on expression falling only within the "outer ambit" of the First Amendment, the Court gave relatively little pause in finding the Erie ordinance satisfactory to each prong of *O'Brien*'s four-part test for determining the constitutionality of restrictions on symbolic speech. In the Court's view, Erie was justified in combating the deleterious secondary effects of nudity.

In separate opinions, Justice Stevens (joined by Justice Ginsburg) and Justice Souter (concurring in part and dissenting in part) criticized different aspects of the plurality opinion. Justice Stevens' blistering dissent accused Justice O'Connor of concluding that "admittedly trivial advancements of a State's interest may provide the basis for censorship." First, he took issue with the use of the secondary effects doctrine to legitimate a total ban on a type of expression[48]—"The fact that this censorship may have a laudable ulterior purpose cannot mean that censorship is not censorship." Next, he questioned the plurality's collapsing of the incidental burdens doctrine (used when speech and nonspeech elements are combined) and the secondary effects doctrine, contending that Erie cannot simultaneously claim that it did not aim to restrict speech (as the incidental burdens doctrine requires) and that it aimed to restrict the secondary effects of speech. Finally, he examined the legislative history of the Erie City Council concerning the ordinance at hand to show the "censorial purpose" of the regulation of nudity. According to Justice Stevens, the case began and ended with the recognition that nude dancing is a type of expressive conduct protected by the First Amendment. Thus, for the Court to assume that "the regulation of the nudity component of nude dancing is unrelated to the message conveyed by nude dances" and to believe that such regulation will have any noticeable impact on secondary effects amounts to "nothing short of a titanic surrender to the implausible."

Justice Souter, on the other hand, did not question the plurality's approach to the case but merely its result. Agreeing that the intermediate scrutiny of *O'Brien* is the correct standard, he wondered whether Erie might have attempted, as the fourth prong of *O'Brien* requires, a less restrictive means of combating secondary effects. Additionally, Justice Souter found himself disturbed by Erie's lack of an "evidentiary basis" for the ills it attempted to regulate and for the cure it attempted to put forth, the same evidentiary basis he had failed to call for in his *Barnes* concurrence. "I may not be less ignorant of nude dancing than I was nine years ago, but I have come to believe that a government most toe the mark more carefully than I first insisted."

The last and most dramatic chapter in the fight against obscenity originates in the feminist movement, particularly as represented by Andrea Dworkin and Catherine MacKinnon. These two women inspired the passage of Indianapolis's Anti-Pornography Ordinance (1984; see query 7 after *Miller v. California*).[49] The ordinance defines pornography as "a systematic *practice* of exploitation and subordination based on sex" (emphasis added), causing women physical and psychological harm and re-

---

[48] Justice Stevens cites two previous cases—*Young v. American Mini Theatres, Inc.* (1976) and *Renton v. Playtime Theatres, Inc.* (1986)—to show how the original use of the secondary effects doctrine was to rationalize restricting zoning laws rather than total bans on expression.

[49] Not all feminists, however, agree. See Nadine Strossen's effort to marshal a feminist argument against the censorship of pornography in *Defending Pornography: Free Speech, Sex, and the Fight for Women's Rights* (New York: Scribner, 1995).

stricting their opportunities in society. Redefining pornography as discrimination rather than speech would lay the basis for arguing that what the state is doing is regulating action and preventing harm instead of controlling the marketplace of ideas.

Up to now, in part owing to the disputed relationship between pornography and harm, the judiciary has steadfastly refused to accept this argument. While it has received considerably support in legal academic circles, the courts have not been sympathetic to the effort to reconceptualize the problem of pornography. In *American Booksellers Association, Inc. v. Hudnut* (1985), the Seventh Circuit Court of Appeals declared the Indianapolis statute unconstitutional on the basis of its viewpoint discrimination. Interestingly, the opinion by Judge Easterbrook accepted the premises underlying the legislation, that pornographic depictions tend to perpetuate subordination of women. But the acceptance proved fatal to the law, since it only demonstrated the power of pornography as speech. Indeed, the irony of the feminist campaign to politicize pornography by highlighting its effects on the structures of power in society is this: that in effectively removing this variety of expression from the category of low-value speech, and in fact elevating it to the most protected constitutional domain—political speech—the proponents of this novel approach have probably made it increasingly unlikely that statutory restrictions will be upheld.

New Frontiers of Speech

The last two decades have witnessed a large number of significant developments in American free speech jurisprudence and considerable rethinking of older doctrine, on and off the Court. The First Amendment, as always, continues to be seen as the core of American democracy, but speech is also seen, increasingly, as a major source of social problems and indeed of American democracy itself. Books by Catharine MacKinnon, Stanley Fish, and Cass R. Sunstein are one sign of the new thinking about our First Amendment jurisprudence.[50] MacKinnon's book is on the cusp of the feminist campaign to redefine pornography as discrimination; Fish's disquisition defends the speech codes adopted by a number of American universities; Sunstein's book proposes "a New Deal for speech" in an extended argument that would orient speech toward the achievement of social equality and deliberative democracy. All this comes at a time when the Supreme Court itself is struggling to shape new First Amendment doctrine for a complex social and political order.

A major change in the Supreme Court's recent jurisprudence is the "largely untold story" of "[t]he extraordinary transformation of the First Amendment from a principle [rooted in deliberative democracy] into a celebration of [a deregulated economic market]."[51] The *Virginia Pharmacy Case* (1976) appeared to signal the beginning of this development. Before 1976 commercial speech was unprotected, largely because the typical advertisement could not be justified by an argument from democracy or as a contribution to the exposition of ideas. In *Pharmacy*, however, the Court defended the consumer's interest in the "free flow of commercial information."[52] In our society, said the Court, goods are allocated by individual choices in a free enterprise system

---

[50] See respectively *Only Words* (Cambridge, Mass.: Harvard University Press, 1993), *There's No Such Thing As Free Speech* (New York: Oxford University Press, 1993), and *Democracy and the Problem of Free Speech* (New York: The Free Press, 1993).

[51] See *Problem of Free Speech*, ibid., p. xviii.

[52] *Virginia State Board of Pharmacy v. Virginia Citizens Consumer Council*, 425 US 748 (1976).

and if the public is to be aware of these choices, and to make enlightened decisions in the marketplace, they must have access to information about them. Commercial speech, however, receives less protection than political speech; the state remains free to regulate commercial speech to ensure the flow of truthful and legitimate information.

From the mid-1970s onward, the Court also extended the protection of the First Amendment to corporate promotional advertising and began taking a jaundiced view of state efforts to control the influence of wealth in politics. In *First National Bank v. Bellotti* (1978), for example, the Court invalidated a statute prohibiting banks and business corporations from making contributions or expenditures to influence the vote in certain referenda.[53] In *Central Hudson Gas & Elec. Corp. v. Public Service Comm'n* (1980), and more recently in *Florida Bar v. Went For It, Inc.* (1995), the Court ruled that commercial speech is subject to "intermediate scrutiny." Commercial speech that is neither misleading or concerning unlawful activity must be regulated if it satisfies a three-prong test: First, "the government must assert a substantial interest . . . ; second, [it] must demonstrate that the restriction . . . directly and materially advances that interest; and third, the regulation must be 'narrowly drawn.'"[54]

Buckley v. Valeo (1976) foreshadowed *Bellotti*. In *Valeo* the Court struck down the provisions of the Federal Election Campaign Act that placed a limit on the amount of money that any one person or organization could spend in support of a particular candidate for Congress. The Court virtually equated money with speech and found that Congress's effort to lessen the influence of wealth in political campaigns and to equalize the chances of political candidates were insufficiently compelling reasons for limiting the volume and quantity of speech that large expenditures would cast into the marketplace of ideas.

At the same time, the Court broadened the freedom of newspaper and broadcasters to deny access to their facilities. Here the conflict between speech and press was most acute. In two critical cases the Court struck down Florida's "right of reply" statute and sustained CBS's right to refuse paid editorial announcements.[55] More recently, the Court declined to extend the notion of the public forum to include televised political debates by allowing a public television station to exclude a congressional candidate who had failed to create "appreciable public interest" in his candidacy.[56] These cases departed from the "fairness" rule—a rule requiring broadcasters who present views on controversial issues to grant access to persons with opposing views—upheld in *Red Lion Broadcasting Co., v. FCC* (1969) in which the Court recognized the state's interest in regulating broadcast monopolies and preserving diversity in the mass media. "It is the purpose of the First Amendment to preserve an uninhibited marketplace of ideas . . . rather than to countenance monopolization of that market." The Court went on to say that "[i]t is the right of the public to receive suitable access to social, political, esthetic, moral, and other ideas and experiences which is crucial here."[57] In 1987, however, the FCC rescinded the fairness rule, claiming in part that "[t]he First Amendment was adopted to protect the people *not from journalists, but from government.*"

---

[53] 435 US 765f (1978). See also *Central Hudson Gas and Elec. Corp. v. Public Service Comm'n*, 447 US 557 (1980).

[54] *Florida Bar*, quoting *Central Hudson* at 564–65.

[55] *Miami Herald Publishing Co. v. Tornillo*, 418 US 241 (1974) and *Columbia Broadcasting System, Inc. v. Democratic National Committee*, 412 US 94 (1973).

[56] *Arkansas Educational Television Commission v. Forbes*, 523 U.S. 666 (1998).

[57] 395 US 367 (1969).

That government itself has become the real threat to freedom of speech in American society today is a proposition that many are beginning to question. Government can and has served as a liberating rather than a restraining force in the marketplace of ideas, as when it lends its support to the arts, humanities, and the sciences, or when it acts as an educator, counselor, librarian, or museum director. Yet when underwriting these activities through the taxing power or when operating publicly owned facilities for specified purposes, there is always the danger that government may act as censor. The extent to which in disposing of its own resources government may prefer some activities, projects, values, and ideas to the exclusion of others is a matter of increasing dispute and is clearly at the frontier of our constitutional law.

A final development worth mentioning here—one clearly related to the "economic market" cases just discussed—is the change wrought by the Supreme Court in "public forum" doctrine. For decades street, sidewalks, and public parks have been regarded as traditional public forums in which people were free, subject of course to reasonable TPM restrictions, to demonstrate or to disseminate information and opinion. In 1968, the Supreme Court extended this principle to a privately owned shopping center, holding that shopping malls open to the public are the functional equivalent of a city business district or a town commercial center.[58] In *Dudgens v. NLRB* (1976), however, the Court appeared to recoil from this precedent by allowing the owners of businesses within such centers to bar access to groups picketing or speaking against their labor policies or business practices.[59]

Whether access to public property for speech purposes is permitted depends largely on how government decides to characterize the property. If government designates public property for specific uses, speech activities incompatible with these declared uses may be barred.[60] More problematical are facilities such as an airport, a major focus of traffic and communication today. Should government be allowed to ban face-to-face solicitation or leaflet distribution in such places? A deeply divided Court sustained the ban.[61] In *Madsen v. Woman's Health Center* (1994), where freedom of speech and the state's interest in public safety and order collided in savage fashion, the Court even sustained the establishment of a buffer zone on a public street from which demonstrators against abortion clinics were excluded. Both decisions were hard cases, with the Court in substantial disagreement not only over standards of judicial review, but over where to draw the delicate line between community and liberty.

Similar disagreements pervaded the Court's decision in *Hill v. Colorado* (2000, reprinted later in the chapter), another case concerning abortion demonstrators and buffer zones around abortion clinics. The latest in a line of cases descending from *Madsen* (upholding a fixed buffer zone) and *Schenck v. Pro-Choice Network of Western New York* (1997—again upholding a fixed buffer zone but striking down a "floating"[62] buffer zone), *Hill* involved a Colorado statute that regulated protesting within

---

[58] *Amalgamated Food Employees Union v. Logan Valley Plaza, Inc.,* 391 US 308 (1968).

[59] 424 US 507 (1976).

[60] An example of such a restriction would be a ban on political campaigning on military bases. See *Greer v. Spock,* 424 US 828 (1976).

[61] *International Society for Krishna Consciousness, Inc., v. Lee,* 112 S. Ct. 2701 (1992).

[62] The designation "floating" as applied to abortion clinic buffer zones refers to the notion that individuals entering abortion clinics carry with them a bubble, in effect, where no protestor may enter. Accordingly, the buffer zone is "floating" because it travels with the patient rather than remains stationary with regard to a doorway, sidewalk, or other landmark. Under the "floating" standard, it is possible for a protestor to violate the buffer zone merely by standing still if the patient—in attempting to enter or exit the clinic— walks by the protestor at a distance smaller than the buffer zone provides.

100 feet of the entrance of any health care facility, by making it unlawful to "knowingly approach" within eight feet of another person, without consent, in order to orally protest, counsel, or pass out handbills. Writing for a 6 to 3 majority, Justice Stevens engaged in a "delicate balancing" of the speech rights of the protestors against the "unwilling listener's interest in avoiding unwanted communication" (an aspect of Justice Brandeis' broader "right to be let alone") to sustain the statute as a legitimate exercise of Colorado's police power. Since it applied to "all demonstrators whether or not the demonstration concerns abortion, and whether they oppose or support the woman who has made an abortion decision," yet left "open ample channels for communication," the statute met both the content neutrality and "narrowly tailored" requirements of the *Ward v. Rock Against Racism* (1989) test for time-place-manner restrictions. "Under this statute, absolutely no channel of communication is foreclosed. No speaker is silenced. And no message is prohibited."

Dissenting separately, Justice Scalia (joined by Justice Thomas) and Justice Kennedy accused the majority (which included Chief Justice Rehnquist) of allowing the abortion issue to bias their interpretation of the First Amendment. Both dissents lambasted the majority for failing to see how the Colorado law's "predictable and intended operation" made it undeniably content-based, with Justice Scalia citing such neglect as proof that "utter absurdity . . . is no obstacle in abortion cases." Justice Kennedy further criticized the prophylaxis that Justice Stevens praised by reminding the Court that "[o]verbreadth is a constitutional flaw, not a saving feature." Far from seeing, as the majority did, a valid, content-neutral, narrowly tailored, time-place-manner restriction, at least three justices viewed the Colorado statute as a restriction on the type of uninhibited and robust expression that "ought to be at the heart of civilized discourse."

The controversy surrounding public facilities and speech activities is hardly restricted to acts of protesting. In many instances, the First Amendment is implicated in disputes over public funding of different speech activities. Often such cases arise within the framework of public educational institutions—colleges and universities that, to many scholars, present the purest context for the application of the Court's decades-old "marketplace" metaphor. In *Board of Regents of the University of Wisconsin System v. Southworth* (2000), the Court entertained precisely that notion. *Southworth* involved a claim that the University's activity taxation and allocation system, which effectively used a student's money to fund extracurricular groups whose activities he did not support, was a violation of free speech rights. Speaking for a unanimous Court, Justice Kennedy disagreed. The First Amendment, he reasoned, permits public educational facilities to use a student tax in encouraging extracurricular speech, provided that the program for collecting and allocating such funds is viewpoint neutral. Deferring to the University's claim that the funds are administered in a viewpoint-neutral manner, the Court upheld the basic structure of the program but struck down one aspect of the allocation scheme—a provision that allows extracurricular organizations to obtain funding (or lose funding, for that matter) through a student referendum—as a substitution of majority will for the constitutionally-mandated standard of viewpoint neutrality. *Southworth* represents a relatively easy case, one in which each member of the Court interpreted the Constitution through the same contextual lens: the "vast, unexplored bounds" of institutions of higher learning.

These decisions are even more complicated when, as in cases like *Rosenberger v. University of Virginia* (1995), two or more constitutional provisions seem to pull in different directions. In this case, a state university's decision to dent funding to a student-run religious publication obviously implicated the First Amendment's speech guarantees. One of the university's defenses, however (discussed more fully in the next chapter), was that it was required to deny funding to satisfy the demands of the no establishment clause. Applying *Rosenberger* in *Good News Club et al. v. Milford Central School* (2001, reprinted in the next chapter), the Court held that public school districts cannot deny religious groups the opportunity to meet on their property while allowing other non-religious groups to do so. Such action, the Court reasoned, was viewpoint discrimination and unconstitutional abridgement of the groups' freedom of speech. As in *Rosenberger*, a majority of the Court dismissed the notion that compliance with the Establishment Clause necessitated a restriction on speech.

The Freedom of Association

How far does the First Amendment extend to protect formal groups or organizations rather than just individuals? And how much weight should organizational rights be accorded when in conflict with other rights? These are the issues the Court must confront in freedom of association cases. First articulated as "an inseparable aspect" of the liberty guaranteed by the Fourteenth Amendment in *NAACP v. Alabama* (1958), freedom of association refers to the right of a group of individuals to "engage in association for the advancement of beliefs and ideas." (A year earlier, in *Sweezy v. New Hampshire*, the Court had indicated that "[O]ur form of government is built on the premise that every citizen shall have the right to engage in political expression and association. This right was enshrined in the First Amendment of the Bill of Rights."[63])

The Court has developed the "freedom of expressive association" much as it did the right to privacy in *Griswold v. Connecticut* (1965): as a penumbral emanation from other guarantees, specifically, as suggested in *Sweezy*, the First Amendment. Viewed as a corollary to—and necessary element of—the explicit First Amendment rights of speech, religion, petition, and assembly, associational rights protect the rights of groups of individuals who share common values and goals and who wish to express such values and goals in a particular way. The right, though, is hardly absolute. Indeed, when juxtaposed with other rights, the Court has traditionally shown the associational right to be a fairly weak defense against charges of discrimination. As free association cases have increasingly come to involve disputes over discriminatory membership practices and exclusionary group activities, the Court has had opportunities to clarify the nature and depth of freedom of expressive association.

In a series of decisions in the 1980s, the Court rejected the claim that freedom of association legitimates all-male clubs from discriminating against women.[64] At issue in these cases are human rights or public accommodation laws—much like the part of the Civil Rights Act of 1964 at issue in racial discrimination cases like *Heart of Atlanta Motel, Inc. v. United States* (1964)—that forbid discrimination in places of public accommodation (such as hotels, restaurants, parks, schools, etc.) on the basis of, among other characteristics, race, gender, age, or national origin. But while the Court has been clear in stating that free association claims are not sufficient to justify

---

[63] 354 U.S. 234 (1957), at 250.

[64] *Roberts v. United States Jaycees*, 468 U.S. 609 (1984); *Board of Directors of Rotary International v. Rotary Club of Duarte*, 481 U.S. 537 (1987); *New York Club Association, Inc. v. City of New York*, 487 U.S. 1 (1989).

discrimination based on certain traits (race and gender, for example), it has been more circumspect in extending this principle to other minority groups.

The rights of homosexuals, in particular, have a checkered history before the Court. After denying a right to engage in consensual homosexual sodomy,[65] striking down a state constitutional amendment forbidding political or legal protection of homosexuals,[66] and granting a parade organizer the right to refuse to allow a homosexual pride group to march,[67] the Court was faced with a conflict between the equality rights of homosexuals and free association rights in *Boy Scouts of America v. Dale* (2000, reprinted later in the chapter). In a bitterly divided 5 to 4 decision, the Court chose free association. The case arose when a former Scoutmaster brought suit against the Boy Scouts, claiming that the organization's dismissal of him based on his sexual orientation was a violation of New Jersey's public accommodations law. Writing for the majority in striking down the law as a violation of the First Amendment freedom of association, Chief Justice Rehnquist disagreed. "Forcing a group to accept certain members may impair the ability of the group to express those views, and only those views, that it intends to express." Citing the need for the Court to defer to groups' own preference regarding their principles and standards, the Court accepted the Boy Scouts' determination that homosexuality was "inconsistent" with certain values embodied by the organization, specifically the demand that Scouts and Scoutmasters be "morally straight" and "clean." The First Amendment, Chief Justice Rehnquist declared, "protects expression, be it of the popular variety or not."

Writing in dissent for himself as well as Justices Souter, Ginsburg, and Breyer, Justice Stevens reminded the majority that the Court's previous decisions "have squarely held that a State's antidiscrimination law does not violate a group's right to associate simply because the law conflicts with that group's exclusionary membership policy." He examined the Boy Scouts' statements and documents for any mention of homosexuality, and found none. "In short, Boy Scouts of America is simply silent on homosexuality. There is no shared goal or collective effort to foster a belief about homosexuality at all—let alone one that is significantly burdened by admitting homosexuals." In sharp disagreement with the majority's deference to the Boy Scouts and what he perceived as their personal biases against homosexuality, Justice Stevens ended his dissent as he began it, with a warning from Justice Brandeis to "ever be on our guard, lest we erect our prejudices into legal principles."

The result in *Dale* illustrates the tension in liberal constitutionalism between formal equality and associational freedom. Thus, as Tocqueville famously argued in fervent support of associations in democratic regimes, "[F]reedom of association has become a necessary guarantee against the tyranny of the majority."[68] Chief Justice Rehnquist's opinion may thus be seen as a Tocquevillian defense of unpopular opinion (although in this case the views expressed may not in reality be so unpopular). On the other hand, Tocqueville also "doubt[ed] that there is in any country, in any period, in which it would not be wise to set bounds for freedom of association."[69] Justice Stevens' opinion was surely written in the spirit of this observation, as he saw constitutional boundaries to enforce against the illiberal possibilities of associational freedom.

[65] *Bowers v. Hardwick*, 478 U.S. 186 (1986).

[66] *Romer v. Evans*, 517 U.S. 620 (1996).

[67] *Hurley v. Irish-American Gay Group of Boston*, 515 U.S. 557 (1995).

[68] Alexis de Tocqueville, *Democracy In America* (Chicago: The University of Chicago Press, 2000), 183.

[69] Ibid., 500.

Comparative Perspectives

We have noticed that the boundaries of free expression in the United States are expansive, and that the First Amendment endorses a regime of speech that is uninhibited, robust, and wide-open. Speech may not be suppressed unless it falls into an unprotected category of expression or is of such "low value" in the marketplace of ideas that it can be regulated in the public interest. We have also found that restrictions on "high-value" speech are reviewed with "strict scrutiny," rendering such limitations almost always invalid unless the state can demonstrate convincingly that more speech is inadequate to avoid the evil or danger sought to be regulated. Finally, we have noticed that the Constitution lacks specific guidelines for interpreting the broad phrases of the First Amendment. As a consequence, the Supreme Court has had to resort to common-law principles or abstract philosophical arguments to justify its various and varying approaches to the interpretation of the speech clauses.

Not surprisingly, the highly developed American jurisprudence of free speech has often served as a point of departure for high courts in other constitutional polities. But the transplantation of First Amendment approaches and solutions has been very selective, as revealed in crossnational comparisons that invariably show the United States on the far libertarian end of a spectrum of expressive freedom.[70] For example, many nations have laws against incitement to racial hatred; but the American antipathy to this sort of a prohibition is so strong that at international conventions on racial discrimination, the United States highlights its extreme position by refusing to accept any interpretation that would require it to ban racist speech in contravention of the First Amendment.

In constitutional terms, the American emphasis on viewpoint-neutrality and the autonomy of the speaker contrasts sharply with other democracies, where, for example, the right to give offense is afforded decidedly less legal protection, and where a more sympathetic official solicitude for the virtues of civility prevails. Judges in countries such as Israel, who borrow extensively from American constitutional experience, sometimes find that their disagreements hinge largely upon how much separation—rather than whether there needs to be any separation at all—should distance their own position from that of the Americans. As in all cases of borrowing, the reluctance to endorse a systematic appropriation of any given legal approach by one system from another reflects more than the presence of alternative constitutional arrangements; more significant are the contrasting sociopolitical and ideological environments within which the judiciaries of the different nations adjudicate. Thus in India, for example, the explicit constitutional commitment to social reconstruction produces judicial decisions that are more viewpoint-specific than one is accustomed to seeing in the United States. Hence the egalitarian rationale for free speech: "This liberty [freedom of speech] may be regarded as an autonomous and fundamental good and its value gets support from the need to develop our evolving society from [an] unequal past to a vigorous homogeneous egalitarian order in which each gets equality of status and of opportunity; social, economic and political justice with dig-

---

[70] Consider this excerpt from a South African case. "The United States Constitution stands as a monument to the vision and the libertarian aspirations of the Founding fathers; and the First Amendment in particular to the values endorsed by all who cherish freedom. But they paint eighteenth-century insights in broad, bold strokes. The language is simple, terse and direct, the injunctions unqualified and the style peremptory. Our Constitution is a wholly different kind of instrument. . . . [I]t is infinitely more explicit, more detailed, more balanced, more carefully phrased and counterpoised. . . ." *S. v. Mamabolo*, 2001 (3) SALR 409 (CC), at 40.

nity of person so as to build an integrated and united Bharat. Transformation for that strong social restructure would be secured when channels for free discussion are wide open. . . ."[71]

By way of further illustration consider an important free speech case in Israel, where the Supreme Court justice best known in that country for using citations of American cases and jurisprudence, had this to say in response to an official ban on a march through an Arab neighborhood proposed by a notorious anti-Arab political leader. "A near certainty that the feelings of a religious or ethnic minority be really and harshly hurt, by publication of a deviant speech, is enough to justify limiting that speech. Therefore . . . it would be justified to prevent a demonstration of Petitioners, if it intends to pass through Arab populated areas, and a near certainty of a real injury exists because of the racist content of Petitioners' message."[72] Contrast this group-sensitive, viewpoint-specific sentiment with the view of a United States District Court, which in deciding eight years earlier in favor of the American Nazis' right to parade through a Jewish neighborhood in Skokie, Illinois, announced: "We live in a society that is very conscious of racial and religious differences, in which open discussion of important public issues will often require reference to racial and religious groups, often in terms which members of those groups, and others, would consider insulting and degrading. . . . The [Supreme] Court has made it clear that speech may not be punished merely because it offends."[73] The different approaches suggest what we have pointed out in previous chapters, that the benefits of comparative constitutional law depend on the successful adaptation of foreign experience to local circumstances. Thus the Israeli Court adapted the American requirement of imminence in the "clear and present danger" test to derive a "near certainty" test, and then applied the new standard to a problem—hate speech—that poses very different challenges in Israel than in the United States.

Israel is notable for its lack of a formal written constitution, but as we turn our attention to the more conventional model of modern democratic constitutions, we find interpretative guidelines rooted in the fundamental text itself, one consequence of which is to limit judicial discretion in establishing the boundaries of speech. Nearly all of these constitutions, like the U.S. Constitution, establish freedom of speech as a core value of their respective polities. Typically, however, they link freedom of expression to duties and responsibilities. Among these duties is respect for the rights of others, including the protection of every person's dignity, a constitutional principle with implications for what persons may say or write about other persons or how they are visually portrayed. Modern constitutions also include reservation clauses enumerating the purposes for which speech may be regulated. Finally, these constitutions define speech with greater particularity than does the U.S. Constitution.

Representative examples of these more detailed constitutions are Germany's Basic Law, the European Convention for the Protection of Human Rights and Fundamental Freedoms, and the Indian Constitution. Freedom of expression as guaranteed by the European Convention includes the right "to hold opinions and to receive and impart information and ideas without interference by public authority." The Convention also makes clear that these provisions do not "prevent States from requiring the licensing of broadcasting, television or cinema enterprises." Germany's Basic Law, on the other

---

[71] *Dr. D. C. Saxena v. Hon'ble The Chief Justice of India* (1997).

[72] Justice Aharon Barak, in *Kahane v. Broadcasting Authority*, 41 (3) P.D. 255, 295–96 (1986).

[73] *Collin v. Smith*, 447 F. Supp. 676, 691,697 (1978).

hand, protects no fewer than ten speech rights. They include "the right freely to express and disseminate [one's] opinion orally, in writing or visually and to obtain information from generally available sources." They also include "freedom of the press and freedom of reporting through audio-visual media," not to mention freedom of "art and scholarship, research and teaching." Capping the list is the command, "There shall be no censorship." The exercise of these rights, however, depends on the observance of certain principles of political obligation; freedom of expression, like other basic rights, may be forfeited under the Basic Law if used "to undermine the free democratic basic order." India's charter provides more generally for "freedom of speech and expression," but then is quite specific in its enumeration of constitutional limitations, which include: defamation; contempt of court; decency or morality; security of the State; friendly relations with foreign States; incitement to an offence; public order; and maintenance of the sovereignty and integrity of India. As its Supreme Court has pointed out: "[F]or the very protection of these liberties the society must arm itself with certain powers. What the Constitution, therefore, attempts to do in declaring the rights of the people is to strike a balance between individual liberty and social security."[74]

In a similar fashion, the European Convention declares that "[t]he exercise of these freedoms [of expression] carries with it [certain] responsibilities" and then proceeds to enumerate the purposes in the interest of which speech may be restricted, regulated, or penalized. These interests include national security or public safety; prevention of disorder or the disclosure of confidential information; protection of health, morals, or reputation or rights of others; and the maintenance of the authority and impartiality of the judiciary. The Basic Law, on the other hand, provides that freedom of speech is "subject to limitations embodied in the provisions of general legislation, statutory provisions for the protection of young persons and the citizen's right to personal honor." In both jurisdictions, however, freedom of speech is the norm and any regulation thereof must be justified as a legitimate exception to the general rule. Moreover, any restriction on speech must be prescribed by law, apply generally and, in the case of Germany, may not negate the "essential content" of the basic right.

Speech, like other rights in liberal constitutions, also finds considerable protection in so-called "democratic necessity" clauses. Such clauses are found, for example, in the democratic constitutions of Eastern Europe's post-communist states and in the new Constitution (1996) of the Republic of South Africa. Typical is the clause in the latter's constitution: Entrenched rights may be limited "only to the extent that [they are] reasonable and justifiable in an open and democratic society based on freedom and equality."[75] The phrase is far from new, however. The European Convention, like other mid-twentieth century democratic constitutions, allows regulations of speech—and other basic rights as well—but only for specified purposes, as just noted, and again only to the extent "necessary in a democratic society."[76] Similar wording appears in Canada's Charter of Rights and Freedoms (1982), which actually begins with a general limitation clause. Section 1 of the Charter "guarantees the rights and freedoms set out [in the Charter] subject only to such reasonable limits prescribed by law as can be demonstrably justified in a free and democratic society."

As this language may suggest, modern constitutions, while including guarantees of personal rights, are heavily oriented toward the creation and preservation of repre-

---

[74] *Gopalan v. State of Madras*, (1950) S.C.R. 88 (253–54).

[75] Sec. 33 (1), Act No. 200 (1993).

[76] European Convention, art. 10 (2).

sentative democracy. Consequently, they are "more closely connected with a view about the desirability of an informed electorate than . . . with nineteenth-century liberal theories concerning the discovery of truth."[77] This particular view is sharply etched into Germany's Basic Law. Like South Africa's Constitution, it incorporates the unamendable principle of a representative and multi-party democracy. The Basic Law, however, also endorses the concept of a "militant democracy," one that finds its most vigorous expression in the provision that bans antidemocratic political parties as unconstitutional, reflecting the Basic Law's intolerance of democracy's enemies. Germany's standards for declaring parties unconstitutional would fail Holmes' "clear and present danger" as well as the *Brandenburg* test for determining the validity of restrictions on political speech. Yet Germany's Constitutional Court has described political speech as "absolutely basic to a liberal-democratic constitutional order" and has protected such speech with corresponding vigilance.

Modern democratic constitutions, as written and interpreted, also vigorously protect other categories of speech. Works of art and scholarship, as we have seen, enjoy protection under the Basic Law and can only be limited by some competing value in the constitution itself. The *Mephisto Case*, in which the Federal Constitutional Court sustained the validity of an injunction against the publication of a novel whose protagonist was based on the life of a famous actor still in the memory of many persons, was an inquiry into the limits of artistic freedom. The Court found that artistic freedom is not an unlimited right but, like all rights guaranteed by the Basic Law, is limited by the "value order established in the Basic Law," at the very top of which is found the principle of "human dignity" which the state is duty bound to "respect and protect" under Article 1 of the Basic Law. "Because a work of art acts not only as an aesthetic reality but also exists in the social world," said the Court, "an artist's use of personal data about people in his environment can affect their rights to societal respect and esteem."

The protection accorded to personal honor and reputation is approaching the level of a transnational constitutional and moral consensus. The Universal Declaration of Human Rights (1948) bans all "arbitrary . . . attacks upon a person's honor and reputation." Poland's new Constitution (1997) declares that "everyone shall have the right to legal protection of his honor and good reputation." Estonia's Constitution (1996) also states that "no one's honor or good name shall be defamed." Similar provisions appear in dozens of new constitutions written since 1990, all in the interest of protecting personal dignity. (See Comparative Note 12.5)

American students of constitutional law may be struck by this emphasis on the importance of "human dignity" and the state's duty to protect it, even against claims of liberty or freedom of speech. The express constitutional right to have one's dignity respected does not imply the radical individualism seemingly implied in *Cohen v. California*, but rather an individualism construed as responsible freedom exercised within a framework of social discipline. Here dignity lives in obvious tension with liberty and thus, in some situations, as the *Mephisto Case* shows, dignity may trump liberty when it conflicts with the latter, whereas in the United States liberty usually trumps claims based on dignity.

The tension between these two values is apparent even in constitutions characterized by the absence of any express mention of a dignity interest. In a landmark case in Israel involving a libel suit against an influential newspaper, the Supreme Court, relying heavily on *New York Times Company v. Sullivan*, ruled in favor of the news-

---

[77] Eric Berendt, *Freedom of Speech* (Oxford: Clarendon Press 1985), p. 4.

paper.[78] Yet in a reconsideration of the case several years later, the Court reversed itself in an opinion in which the author cautioned against "being taken in by the American decision in *New York Times*."[79] He found the American inattention to reputation to be a sufficiently weighty reason to resist doctrinal transplantation from the United States to Israel, a place where, for historical reasons, the constitutional soil is much more receptive to the interest in dignity that is subsumed in reputational considerations. As the Israeli Chief Justice has written, "The freedom of speech ends where the right to reputation begins. . . ."[80]

It would of course be very misleading to suggest that dignity is an unimportant principle in American constitutionalism. All constitutional democracies may be said to be rooted ultimately in the principle of human dignity, whether expressed or implied in their fundamental law. The notion of dignity, however, and the vision of the human person on which it is based, may differ from one constitution to another, just as the terms "equality" and "democracy" may convey different realities under constitutions designed as much as the American one for advanced, liberal, secular, and pluralistic democracies. In addition, the way in which these values are reconciled or balanced may differ from one society to another.

The different ways in which these values are reconciled or balanced are manifest in *R. v. Keegstra* (1990) and *R. v. Butler* (1992),[81] two Canadian cases involving hate speech and pornography. These two decisions are in stark contrast to *R.A.V. v. City of St. Paul* and *American Booksellers Association v. Hudnut*. *Butler* was a landmark case because a majority of Canadian justices sustained an obscenity statute on the basis of legislative findings that such material causes harm to women as individuals and also "wreaks social damage in that a significant portion of the population is humiliated by its gross misrepresentations." *Keegstra*, on the other hand, sustained a statute criminalizing the willful promotion of hatred against an identifiable group. Here the law was applied to a high school teacher who made vicious anti-Semitic remarks in the classroom. The Court found that such utterances caused real harm to members of the maligned group and affected the larger society as well. "Such consequences," said the Court, "bear heavily in a nation that prides itself on tolerance and the fostering of human dignity through, among other things, respect for the many racial, religious and cultural groups in our society." In the United States, the invocation of "tolerance" may well have cut the other way (as it did in *Skokie*), protecting, as Holmes once said, the ideas that we hate.

The Charter, however, contains an interpretive provision that is quite different from anything found in the U.S. Constitution. "This charter shall be interpreted," reads Section 27, "in a manner consistent with the preservation and enhancement of the multi-cultural heritage of Canadians." The Court found that the hate speech at issue in *Keegstra* was incompatible with this directive. Hate speech was also found to offend the principle of equality as defined and elaborated in the Charter. To buttress its decision the Court also cited Canada's obligation under international human rights law to enact legislation banning racist and related hate propaganda. Interestingly, the Canadian Supreme Court found equivalent American constitutional cases persuasive but not dispositive. Chief Justice Brian Dickson admitted that "the Ameri-

---

[78] *Electric Company v. Ha'aretz* (I), 31 (2) P.D. 281 (1974).

[79] *Electric Company v. Ha'aretz* (II), 32 (3) P.D. 337, 343 (1978)

[80] Aharon Barak, "Foreword: A Judge On Judging: The Role of a Supreme Court In a Democracy," 116 *Harvard Law Review* 16, 96 (2002).

[81] See respectively 3 C.R.R. (2nd) 193 (1990) and 89 D.L.R. (4th) 449 (1992).

can experience [is] tremendously helpful in coming to [our] own conclusions," but doubted that Canadian constitutional theory could easily absorb the "various categorizations and guiding rules generated by American law." Where the Charter "operates to accentuate a uniquely Canadian vision of a free and democratic society," he said, "we must not hesitate to depart from the path taken in the United States."

The vision Chief Justice Dickson speaks of, however, is not unique to Canada. Germany's Constitutional Court, in the *Holocaust Denial Case* (1994), sustained a statute punishing the denial of the Holocaust and the presence of gas chambers in Auschwitz. Here the Constitutional Court distinguished between the expression of opinions and "demonstrably untrue statements of fact." A free and democratic society, suggested the Court, must protect the former but not the latter, particularly when untruths of the kind uttered here effectively invade the "right of [Jews to their] personality."[82] The Court has also emphasized the importance of truth-telling in attacks on public officials and well-known personalities. While robust and even offensive speech is carefully guarded under the Basic Law, especially when it qualifies as political speech, the values often stressed by the Court are those of democratic participation, effective communication, and civility. Contrary to the vision of the polity projected in *New York Times Company v. Sullivan*, the German vision faintly resembles the polity of early American republican theory.

One of the most significant developments in Canadian constitutional thought is the doubt that *Keegstra* casts on the Miltonian faith, which the U.S. Supreme Court appears not to have abandoned, in truth's ability to triumph over falsehood. The Court cited with approval the report of a Special Committee on Hate Propaganda in Canada (the Cohen Committee). In pointing to modern advertising and the "triumphs of impudent propaganda such as Hitler's . . . the individual is [often] swayed and even swept away by hysterical, emotional appeals [and w]e act irresponsibly if we ignore the way in which emotion can drive reason from the field." For this reason, Canada seems also to tolerate a greater measure of control over commercial advertising, just as in Germany and some other constitutional democracies, government is seen, not as an enemy of free speech, but a guarantor of it, particularly when laws are passed to limit monopolies in the electronic media, to require balanced programming on radio and television, to afford individuals a "right of reply" when attacked by newspapers, and to prescribe public funding of political campaigns.

And yet, perhaps surprisingly, at least in Canada's case, speech under the Charter is more broadly defined than in the United States. When Chief Justice Dickson spoke negatively about "categorization" in American free speech doctrine, he was referring to the Supreme Court's tendency to divide speech into categories, giving protection to some categories while withdrawing it from others. Thus, for example, as we have seen, fighting words and obscenity are not "speech" within the meaning of the First Amendment. The Canadian Supreme Court, by contrast, in both *Keegstra* and *Butler*, ruled that hate propaganda and obscenity are constitutionally protected speech. The Court made clear that even degrading, dehumanizing, and hateful speech is "speech" within the meaning of Section 2 of the Charter of Rights. A judicial declaration of this nature would be the end of the matter in the United States. It is only the beginning of analysis under the foreign constitutions considered in this section.

---

[82] Judgment of April 13, 1994, 1 BvR 23/94. Several months earlier, however, the Constitutional Court struck down a conviction of a person convicted of distributing a book denying Germany's responsibility for the Second World War. This utterance, said the Court, was an expression of an opinion protected by freedom of speech. Judgment of January 11, 1994, 1 BvR 434/87.

Once again Canada is representative of the process of decision followed in speech and other fundamental rights cases. The Canadian Supreme Court's function is one of weighing and balancing. A judicial finding by the Supreme Court—or for that matter by the European Court of Human Rights—that a law infringes a right or freedom does not mandate that the law must fall. If the limit imposed on the right is "reasonable" and "can be demonstrably justified in a free and democratic society" (under section 1 of the Charter), the law is valid. Principles of rationality and proportionality govern here, and they relate to both ends and means. As to ends, it must be shown that a law limiting a speech right must serve an overriding public interest and be "pressing and substantial" in a democratic society.

As we have seen, weighing different interests against expressive freedom also permeates American free speech law, although judges tend to be much less explicit and open in their balancing jurisprudence. Rarely, for example, do we find the same degree of self-consciousness about the judicial role that is often observed abroad, as illustrated in this excerpt from an Israeli Supreme Court opinion. "A social principle (such as freedom of expression) does not have 'absolute' weight. The weight of a social principle is always relative. The status of a fundamental principle is always determined relative to other principles, with which it may conflict. The weight of the freedom of speech relative to the freedom of movement is different from its weight relative to judicial integrity, both of these are different from the weight of the freedom of speech relative to reputation or privacy, and all of these are different from the weight of the freedom of speech relative to the public interest in security and safety."[83] In the end, of course, how all of these competing interests get balanced will vary from country to country according to local circumstances. The appeal of comparative law lies in its potential for expanding judicial horizons to the point where judges can at least assess their own emphases in the light of alternative experience. Or as has been well put by the author of the above opinion, "As judges, we must . . . examine whether there is anything in the historical development and social conditions that makes the local and the foreign system different enough to render interpretive inspiration impracticable."[84]

Selected Bibliography

Abel, Richard, *Speech and Respect* (London: Stevens & Sons/ Sweet & Maxwell, 1994).

Berns, Walter, *The First Amendment and the Future of American Democracy* (New York: Basic Books, 1976).

Bollinger, Lee C., *The Tolerant Society* (New York: Oxford University Press, 1986.

Bork, Robert, *Neutral Principles and Some First Amendment Problems,* 47 Indiana Law Journal 1–35 (1971).

Chafee, Zechariah, Jr., *Free Speech in the United States* (Cambridge: Harvard University Press, 1942).

Downs, Donald A., *Nazis in Skokie: Freedom, Community, and the First Amendment* (Notre Dame: University of Notre Dame Press, 1985).

Eberle, Edward J., *Hate Speech, Offensive Speech, and Public Discourse in America,* 29 Wake Forest Law Review 1135– 1213 (1994).

Emerson, Thomas I., *The System of Freedom of Expression* (New York: Random House, 1970).

Fish, Stanley, *There's No Such Thing As Free Speech: And It's a Good Thing Too* (New York: Oxford University Press, 1993).

Graber, Mark A., *Transforming Free Speech: The Ambiguous Legacy of Civil Libertarianism* (Berkeley: University of California Press, 1991).

Greenawalt, Kent, *Fighting Words* (Princeton: Princeton University Press, 1995).

---

[83] *Re'em Eng'g Contractors Ltd. V. Municipality of Upper Nazareth,* 47(5) P.D. 189, 211 (1992).

[84] Barak, *Foreword: A Judge On Judging,* 113.

Kalven, Harry, Jr., *A Worthy Tradition: Freedom of Speech in America* (New York: Harper & Row, 1988).

Levy, Leonard W., *Emergence of a Free Press* (New York: Oxford University Press, 1985).

MacKinnon, Catharine A., *Only Words* (Cambridge: Harvard University Press, 1993).

Meiklejohn, Alexander, *Political Freedom: The Constitutional Power of the People* (New York: Oxford University Press, 1965).

"On Liberty" in J. S. Mill, *Utilitarianism, Liberty and Representative Government* (London: J. M. Dent & Sons, 1910).

Rabban, David, *Free Speech In Its Forgotten Years* (New York: Cambridge University Press, 1997).

Schauer, Frederick, *Free Speech: A Philosophical Inquiry* (Cambridge: Cambridge University Press, 1982).

Shriffen, Steven H., *The First Amendment, Democracy, and Romance* (Princeton: Princeton University Press, 1990).

Strossen, Nadine, *Defending Pornography: Free Speech, Sex, and the Fight for Women's Rights* (New York: Scribner, 1995).

Sunstein, Cass R., *Democracy and the Problem of Free Speech* (New York: The Free Press, 1993).

Selected Comparative Bibliography

Barendt, Eric, *Freedom of Speech* (Oxford: Clarendon Press, 1985).

Greenawalt, Kent, *Free Speech in the United States and Canada,* 55 Law and Contemporary Problems 5 (1992).

Kommers, Donald P., *The Jurisprudence of Free Speech in the United States and the Federal Republic of Germany,* 53 Southern California Law Review 657 (1980).

Lahav, Pnina, *American Influence on Israel's Jurisprudence of Free Speech,* 9 Hastings Constitutional Law Quarterly 21–108, (1990).

Peleg, Ilan, ed., *Patterns of Censorship Around the World* (Boulder: Westview Press, 1993).

Schneiderman, David (ed.), *Freedom of Expression and the Charter* (Thompson Professional Publishing Canada, 1991).

Schenck v. United States

249 U.S. 47, 39 S.Ct. 247, 63 L.Ed. 470 (1919)

Charles Schenck was indicted and convicted for violating provisions of the Espionage Act of 1917. As general secretary of the Socialist Party, he was charged with conspiring to cause and attempting to cause insubordination in the military and naval forces of the United States. At the time, the United States was involved in the First World War, and Schenck printed and mailed an anti-war circular to fifteen thousand men eligible for the draft. The mailing alleged that conscription was a violation of the Thirteenth Amendment and urged draftees to "assert" their rights. Opinion of the Court: *Holmes,* White, McKenna, Day, Van Devanter, Pitney, McReynolds, Brandeis, Clarke.

Justice HOLMES delivered the opinion of the Court.

The document in question upon its first printed side recited the first section of the Thirteenth Amendment, said that the idea embodied in it was violated by the Conscription Act and that a conscript is little better than a convict. In impassioned language it intimated that conscription was despotism in its worst form and a monstrous wrong against humanity in the interest of Wall Street's chosen few. It said "Do not submit to intimidation," but in form at least confined itself to peaceful measures such as a petition for the repeal of the act. The other and later printed side of the sheet was headed "Assert Your Rights." It stated reasons for alleging that any one violated the Constitution when he refused to recognize "your right to as-

sert your opposition to the draft," and went on "If you do not assert and support your rights, you are helping to deny or disparage rights which it is the solemn duty of all citizens and residents of the United States to retain." It described the arguments on the other side as coming from cunning politicians and a mercenary capitalist press, and even silent consent to the conscription law as helping to support an infamous conspiracy. It denied the power to send our citizens away to foreign shores to shoot up the people of other lands, and added that words could not express the condemnation such cold-blooded ruthlessness deserves, &c., &c., winding up "You must do your share to maintain, support and uphold the rights of the people of this country." Of course the documents would not have been sent unless it had been intended to have some effect, and we do not see what effect it could be expected to have upon persons subject to the draft except to influence them to obstruct the carrying of it out. The defendants do not deny that the jury might find against them on this point.

But it is said, suppose that that was the tendency of this circular, it is protected by the First Amendment to the Constitution. Two of the strongest expressions are said to be quoted respectively from well-known public men. It well may be that the prohibition of laws abridging the freedom of speech is not confined to previous restraints, although to prevent them may have been the main purpose. . . . We admit that in many places and in ordinary times the defendants in saying all that was said in the circular would have been within their constitutional rights. But the character of every act depends upon the circumstances in which it is done. The most stringent protection of free speech would not protect a man in falsely shouting fire in a theatre and causing a panic. It does not even protect a man from an injunction against uttering words that may have all the effect of force. The question in every case is whether the words used are used in such circumstances and are of such a nature as to create a clear and present danger that they will bring about the substantive evils that Congress has a right to prevent. It is a question of proximity and degree. When a nation is at war many things that might be said in time of peace are such a hindrance to its effort that their utterance will not be endured so long as men fight and that no Court could regard them as protected by any constitutional right. It seems to be admitted that if an actual obstruction of the recruiting service were proved, liability for words that produced that effect might be enforced. The statute of 1917 . . . punishes conspiracies to obstruct as well as actual obstruction. If the act, (speaking, or circulating a paper) its tendency and the intent with which it is done are the same, we perceive no ground for saying that success alone warrants making the act a crime. . . .

Judgments affirmed.

Notes and Queries

1. *Gitlow v. New York* (1925) illustrates another stage in the career of the "clear and present danger" doctrine outlined in *Schenck*. The defendant in *Gitlow* was convicted of violating a New York law which forbade advocacy "by word of mouth or writing" of "criminal anarchy."

Gitlow had published a document called "The Left-Wing Manifesto" which called for "industrial revolution" and a "general strike" to bring down the "parliamentary state." The Court, in a 7 to 2 decision, upheld the conviction. The distinctive aspect of this law was that, unlike the law in *Schenck*, it actually forbad certain types of *speech* distinct from *action*.

Justice Sanford wrote for the majority:

That utterances inciting to the overthrow of organized government by unlawful means, present a sufficient danger of substantive evil to bring their punishment within the range of legislative discretion, is clear. Such utterances, by their very nature, involve danger to the public peace and to the security of the state. They threaten breaches of the peace and ultimate revolution. And the immediate danger is none the less real and substantial because the effect of a given utterance cannot be accurately foreseen. The state cannot reasonably be required to measure the danger from every such utterance in the nice balance of a jeweler's scale. A single revolutionary spark may kindle a fire that, smoldering for a time, may burst into a sweeping and destructive conflagration. It cannot be said that the state is acting arbitrarily or unreasonably when in the exercise of its judgment as to the measures necessary to protect the public peace and safety, it seeks to extinguish the spark without waiting until it has enkindled the flame or blazed into the conflagration.

In *Gitlow*, then, Justice Sanford upheld the right of the legislature to determine that "utterances of a specified

---

Comparative Note 12.1

[In 1953, the Minister of Interior in Israel suspended two communist newspapers for publishing articles containing material which, in the opinion of the Minister, was likely to endanger the public peace. He acted under authority of the Press Ordinance, an enactment first passed under the British Mandate and then maintained after establishment of the State of Israel. In this first, and still most famous, Israeli free speech case, Justice Shimon Agranat, an American educated jurist, wrote the opinion of the Court overturning the Minister's ruling. The excerpt that follows appears after the opinion reviews American cases in some detail, beginning with Justice Holmes' views in *Schenck*.]

The guiding principle ought always to be: is it probable that as a consequence of the publication, a danger to the public peace has been disclosed; the bare tendency in that direction in the matter published will not suffice to fulfill that requirement. Moreover, the Minister of Interior is bound to estimate the effect of the matter published on the public peace only according to the standard of what is reasonable in the light of the surrounding circumstances: and in that estimation, the length of time likely to pass between the publication and the consequential event which constitutes the harm to the public peace is liable to be an important factor, though not necessarily a decisive one.

SOURCE: *"Kol Ha'am" Co. Ltd. V. Minister of Interior*, 7 P.D. 871 (1953).

character" could be punished because of their *tendency* to bring about the danger of substantive evil.

Justice Holmes dissented, arguing that his "clear and present danger" test should have been invoked in this case and that if it had been, the law in question would have failed to pass constitutional muster. His dissent foreshadowed later decisions:

It is said that this manifesto was more than a theory, that it was an incitement. Every idea is an incitement. It offers itself for belief and if believed it is acted on unless some other belief outweighs it or some failure of energy stifles the movement at its birth. The only difference between the expression of an opinion and an incitement in the narrower sense is the speaker's enthusiasm for the result. Eloquence may set fire to reason. But whatever may be thought of the redundant discourse before us it had no chance of starting a present conflagration. If in the long run the beliefs expressed in proletarian dictatorship are destined to be accepted by the dominant forces of the community, the only meaning of free speech is that they should be given their chance and have their way.

2. Do you agree with Justice Holmes' contention that the only meaning of free speech is to allow "beliefs expressed in proletarian dictatorship" to have their way if in the long run such beliefs are "destined to be accepted by the dominant forces of the community"? Some have suggested that Holmes' constitutional policy would render the state wholly defenseless in the face of sworn enemies. Why must the state wait for an "immediate threat of conflagration" before it can justify the suppression of speech? Why should a democracy protect the enemies of democracy?

3. Consider this provision of Germany's Basic Law: "Whoever abuses freedom of expression . . . in order to combat the free democratic basic order shall forfeit [this] basic [liberty]" (Article 18). In a similar fashion, the Basic Law declares that political parties "which by reason of their aims or the behavior of their adherents seek to impair or abolish the free democratic order . . . shall be unconstitutional" (Article 21 [2]). Bear in mind that these provisions are part of what is generally regarded as one of the most progressive and liberal of western democratic constitutions. What is to be said on behalf of the German formula for seeking to preserve both freedom of speech and democracy? Can one be saved without the other?

4. We might ask ourselves whether Justice Brandeis achieved a better balance between liberty and order in his landmark concurring opinion in *Whitney v. California* (1927), an opinion widely acclaimed for its eloquence as much as for its stirring defense of liberty. Although Brandeis voted with the majority in upholding the application of California's Criminal Syndicalism Act against a person who participated in communist activities, he wrote:

Those who won our independence believed that the final end of the State was to make men free to develop their faculties; and that in its government the deliberative forces should prevail over the arbitrary. . . . They believed liberty to be the secret of happiness and courage to be the secret of liberty. They believed that freedom to think as you will and to speak as you think are means indispensable to the discovery and spread of political truth . . . that without free speech the assembly discussion would be futile; that the greatest menace to freedom is an inert people; that public discussion is a political duty; . . .

Fear of serious injury cannot alone justify suppression of free speech and assembly. Men feared witches and burnt women. It is the function of speech to free men from the bondage of irrational fears. To justify suppression of free speech there must be reasonable ground to fear that serious evil will result if free speech is practiced. There must be reasonable ground to believe that the danger apprehended is imminent. There must be reasonable ground to believe that the evil to be prevented is a serious one. Every denunciation of existing law tends in some measure to increase the probability that there will be violation of it. Condonation of a breach enhances the probability. . . .

If there be time to expose through discussion the falsehood and fallacies, to avert the evil by the process of education, the remedy to be applied is more speech, not enforced silence. Only an emergency can justify repression. Such must be the rule if authority is to be reconciled with freedom. . . .

5. Concerning the passage from Brandeis, Robert F. Nagel writes: "This depiction is much admired, but it is as troubling as it is beautiful. This people—the "they" repeatedly referred to—was, according to Brandeis, those who won American independence and who adopted the first amendment. Yet Brandeis offers almost no historical evidence and, thus, suggests that the truth of his claims is self-evident and beyond debate. He does not qualify or complicate his picture of the dispositions of our forefathers to take account even of well-known facts, for example, that some patriots ran in mobs beating their political opponents in the streets, and that prosecutions for seditious libel occurred in the nineteenth century. . . . A poetic endorsement of rationality and the search for truth is cavalier of facts and designed to establish a political mythol-

ogy. See *Judicial Power and American Character* (Oxford: Oxford University Press, 1994), 99–100. Does Nagel have a point?

6. Compare the dissent of Holmes in *Gitlow* and the concurrence of Brandeis in *Whitney*. What is it about speech as a distinctive human activity that accords it special protection according to these two justices, and how is it that they differ from the majority opinions? Are the disputes simply matters of fact or is something deeper involved?

7. Consider the excerpt from the opinion by Justice Agranat in Comparative Note 12.1. In what ways is the formulation developed by the Israeli justice similar to the test announced by Justice Holmes in *Schenck*, and in what ways is it different? The Ordinance under which the suspension of the newspapers in that case occurred authorizes suspending a publication "if any matter appearing in a newspaper is, in the opinion of the Minister of Interior, likely to endanger the public peace." As you read the remaining cases in this chapter, ask yourself whether such a law would be constitutional in the United States.

Dennis v. United States

341 U.S. 494, 71 S.Ct. 857, 95 L.Ed. 1137 (1951)

In 1948 Eugene Dennis and ten other leaders of the Communist Party of the United States were convicted of violating the Smith Act after a sensational nine-month trial. The Smith Act, passed by Congress in 1940, made it illegal to "advocate, abet, advise, or teach the duty, necessity, desirability, or propriety of overthrowing or destroying any government in the United States by force or violence." The Court of Appeals affirmed the convictions. The Supreme Court limited its grant of certiorari to two questions: Whether the Smith Act, inherently or as construed and applied, violates the First Amendment's protection of speech, or the First and Fifth Amendments because of indefiniteness. Opinion of the Court: *Vinson*, Reed, Burton, Minton. Concurring opinions: *Frankfurter, Jackson*. Dissenting opinions: *Black, Douglas*. Not participating: Clark.

Chief Justice VINSON announced the judgment of the Court and an opinion in which Justice REED, Justice BURTON and Justice MINTON join.

The obvious purpose of the statute is to protect existing Government, not from change by peaceable, lawful and constitutional means, but from change by violence, revolution and terrorism. That it is within the *power* of the Congress to protect the Government of the United States from armed rebellion is a proposition which requires little discussion. Whatever theoretical merit there may be to the argument that there is a "right" to rebellion against dictatorial governments is without force where the existing structure of the government provides for peaceful and orderly change. We reject any principle of governmental helplessness in the face of preparation for revolution, which principle, carried to its logical conclusion, must lead to anarchy. No one could conceive that it is not within the power of Congress to prohibit acts intended to overthrow the Government by force and violence. The question with which we are concerned here is not whether Congress has such *power*, but whether the *power* which it has employed conflicts with the First and Fifth Amendments to the Constitution.

One of the bases for the contention that the means which Congress has employed are invalid takes the form of an attack on the face of the statute on the grounds that by its terms it prohibits academic discussion of the merits of Marxism-Leninism, that it stifles ideas and is contrary to all concepts of a free speech and a free press. . . .

The very language of the Smith Act negates the interpretation which petitioners would have us impose on that Act. It is directed at advocacy, not discussion. Thus, the trial judge properly charged the jury that they could not convict if they found that petitioners did "no more than pursue peaceful studies and discussions or teaching and advocacy in the realm of ideas." He further charged that it was not unlawful "to conduct in an American college or university a course explaining the philosophical theories set forth in the books which have been placed in evidence." Such a charge is in strict accord with the statutory language, and illustrates the meaning to be placed on those words. Congress did not intend to eradicate the free discussion of political theories, to destroy the traditional rights of Americans to discuss and evaluate ideas without fear of governmental sanction. Rather Congress was concerned with the very kind of activity in which the evidence showed these petitioners engaged.

. . . Speech is not an absolute, above and beyond control by the legislature when its judgment, subject to review here, is that certain kinds of speech are so undesirable as to warrant criminal sanction. Nothing is more certain in modern society than the principle that there are no absolutes, that a name, a phrase, a standard has meaning only when associated with the considerations which gave birth to the nomenclature. To those who would paralyze our

Comparative Note 12.2

[In 1956, Germany's Federal Constitutional Court ruled that the Communist Party was unconstitutional. The decision was based on the provision of Article 21 of the Basic Law which declares that "parties which by reason of their aims or the behavior of their adherents seek to impair or abolish the free democratic basic order . . . shall be unconstitutional."]

In a free democracy, the dignity of man is the supreme value. It is inviolate and must be respected by the state. . . . The free democratic order also deduces from the idea of man's dignity and freedom the task of insuring that justice and humanity exist in relationships among citizens themselves. This duty includes preventing exploitation of one individual by another. . . .

. . . [Communist Party] statements . . . [are] a smear campaign intended to disparage the constitutional order of the federal republic. Its prestige is to be diminished, the people's confidence in the value order established by it is to be shaken. . . . A party . . . must acknowledge other political parties as competitors in a constant struggle for the best political system. . . . These implications mean that the minimum obligation of each political party in a liberal democratic state is to recognize . . . the supreme constitutional values as binding on itself, to contribute to strengthening their prestige with the people, and at least to refrain from any disparagement, abuse, and calumny of this order. A party which consciously, constantly, and with premeditation wages a campaign of defamation and mockery of these values and the order they embody wants to impair or even eliminate this order. It is inconceivable that such a party could be constitutionally called upon to participate in forming the political will in a free democracy. . . .

SOURCE: *Communist Party Case* (1956), Murphy and Tanenhaus, *Comparative Constitutional Law*, 621–26.

Government in the face of impending threat by encasing it in a semantic straitjacket we must reply that all concepts are relative.

In this case we are squarely presented with the application of the "clear and present danger" test, and must decide what that phrase imports. . . . Overthrow of the Government by force and violence is certainly a substantial enough interest for the Government to limit speech. Indeed, this is the ultimate value of any society, for if a society cannot protect its very structure from armed internal attack, it must follow that no subordinate value can be protected. If, then, this interest may be protected, the literal problem which is presented is what has been meant by the use of the phrase "clear and present danger" of the utterances bringing about the evil within the power of Congress to punish.

Obviously, the words cannot mean that before the Government may act, it must wait until the putsch is about to be executed, the plans have been laid and the signal is awaited. If Government is aware that a group aiming at its overthrow is attempting to indoctrinate its members and to commit them to a course whereby they will strike when the leaders feel the circumstances permit, action by the Government is required. The argument that there is no need for Government to concern itself, for Government is strong, it possesses ample powers to put down a rebellion, it may defeat the revolution with ease needs no answer. For that is not the question. Certainly an attempt to overthrow the Government by force, even though doomed from the outset because of inadequate numbers or power of the revolutionists, is a sufficient evil for Congress to prevent. The damage which such attempts create both physically and politically to a nation makes it impossible to measure the validity in terms of the probability of success, or the immediacy of a successful attempt. In the instant case the trial judge charged the jury that they could not convict unless they found that petitioners intended to overthrow the Government "as speedily as circumstances would permit." This does not mean, and could not properly mean, that they would not strike until there was certainty of success. What was meant was that the revolutionists would strike when they thought the time was ripe. We must therefore reject the contention that success or probability of success is the criterion.

Chief Judge Learned Hand, writing for the majority below, interpreted the phrase as follows: "In each case [courts] must ask whether the gravity of the 'evil,' discounted by its improbability, justifies such invasion of free speech as is necessary to avoid the danger." We adopt this statement of the rule. As articulated by Chief Judge Hand, it is as succinct and inclusive as any other we might devise at this time. It takes into consideration those factors which we deem relevant, and relates their significances. More we cannot expect from words.

Likewise, we are in accord with the court below, which affirmed the trial court's finding that the requisite danger existed. The mere fact that from the period 1945 to 1948 petitioners' activities did not result in an attempt to overthrow the Government by force and violence is of course no answer to the fact that there was a group that was ready to make the attempt. The formation by petitioners of such a highly organized conspiracy, with rigidly disciplined members subject to call when the leaders, these petitioners, felt that the time had come for action, coupled with the inflammable nature of world conditions, similar uprisings in other countries, and the touch-and-go nature of our relations with countries with whom petitioners were in the very least ideologically attuned, convince us that their convictions were justified on this score. And this analysis disposes of the contention that a conspiracy to advocate, as distinguished from the advocacy itself, cannot be constitutionally restrained, because it comprises only the preparation. It is the existence of the conspiracy which creates the danger. . . .

There remains to be discussed the question of vagueness—whether the statute as we have interpreted it is too vague, not sufficiently advising those who would speak of the limitations upon their activity. It is urged that such vagueness contravenes the First and Fifth Amendments. This argument is particularly nonpersuasive when presented by petitioners, who, the jury found, intended to overthrow the Government as speedily as circumstances would permit. . . .

We agree that the standard as defined is not a neat, mathematical formulary. Like all verbalizations it is subject to criticism on the score of indefiniteness. But petitioners themselves contend that the verbalization "clear and present danger" is the proper standard. We see no difference, from the standpoint of vagueness, whether the standard of "clear and present danger" is one contained in *haec verba* within the statute, or whether it is the judicial measure of constitutional applicability. We have shown the indeterminate standard the phrase necessarily connotes. We do not think we have rendered that standard any more indefinite by our attempt to sum up the factors which are included within its scope. We think it well serves to indicate to those who would advocate constitutionally prohibited conduct that there is a line beyond which they may not go—a line which they, in full knowledge of what they intend and the circumstances in which their activity takes place, will well appreciate and understand. . . .

We hold that [sections] 2 (a) (1), 2 (a) (3) and 3 of the Smith Act do not inherently, or as construed or applied in the instant case, violate the First Amendment and other provisions of the Bill of Rights, or the First and Fifth Amendments because of indefiniteness. Petitioners intended to overthrow the Government of the United States as speedily as the circumstances would permit. Their conspiracy to organize the Communist Party and to teach and advocate the overthrow of the Government of the United States by force and violence created a "clear and present danger" of an attempt to overthrow the Government by force and violence. They were properly and constitutionally convicted for violation of the Smith Act. The judgments of conviction are affirmed.

Justice FRANKFURTER, concurring in affirmance of the judgment.

. . . Free speech is subject to prohibition of those abuses of expression which a civilized society may forbid. As in the case of every other provision of the Constitution that is not crystallized by the nature of its technical concepts, the fact that the First Amendment is not self-defining and self-enforcing neither impairs its usefulness nor compels its paralysis as a living instrument.

Absolute rules would inevitably lead to absolute exceptions, and such exceptions would eventually corrode the rules. The demands of free speech in a democratic society as well as the interest in national security are better served by candid and informed weighing of the competing interests, within the confines of the judicial process, than by announcing dogmas too inflexible for the non-Euclidian problems to be solved.

But how are competing interests to be assessed? Since they are not subject to quantitative ascertainment, the issue necessarily resolves itself into asking, who is to make the adjustment?—who is to balance the relevant factors and ascertain which interest is in the circumstances to prevail? Full responsibility for the choice cannot be given to the courts. Courts are not representative bodies. They are not designed to be a good reflex of a democratic society. Their judgment is best informed, and therefore most dependable, within narrow limits. Their essential quality is detachment, founded on independence. History teaches that the independence of the judiciary is jeopardized when courts become embroiled in the passions of the day and assume primary responsibility in choosing between competing political, economic and social pressures.

Primary responsibility for adjusting the interests which compete in the situation before us of necessity belongs to the Congress. The nature of the power to be exercised by this Court has been delineated in decisions not charged with the emotional appeal of situations such as that now before us. We are to set aside the judgment of those whose duty it is to legislate only if there is no reasonable basis for it. We are to determine whether a statute is sufficiently definite to meet the constitutional requirements of due process, and whether it respects the safeguards against undue concentration of authority secured by separation of power. We must assure fairness of procedure, allowing full scope to governmental discretion but mindful of its impact on individuals in the context of the problem involved. And, of course, the proceedings in a particular case before us must have the warrant of substantial proof. Beyond these powers we must not go; we must scrupulously observe the narrow limits of judicial authority even though self-restraint is alone set over us. Above all we must remember that this Court's power of judicial review is not "an exercise of the powers of a super-legislature." . . .

In reviewing statutes which restrict freedoms protected by the First Amendment, we have emphasized the close relation which those freedoms bear to maintenance of a free society. . . . Some members of the Court—and at times a majority—have done more. They have suggested that our function in reviewing statutes restricting freedom of expression differs sharply from our normal duty in sitting in judgment on legislation. It has been said that such statutes "must be justified by clear public interest, threatened not doubtfully or remotely, but by clear and present danger. The rational connection between the remedy provided and the evil to be curbed, which in other contexts might support legislation against attack on due process grounds, will not suffice." It has been suggested, with the casualness of a footnote, that such legislation is not presumptively valid, see *United States v. Carolene Products Co.* [1938], n. 4, and it has been weightily reiterated that freedom of speech has a "preferred position" among constitutional safeguards. *Kovacs v. Cooper* [1949].

The precise meaning intended to be conveyed by these phrases need not now be pursued. It is enough to note that they have recurred in the Court's opinions, and their cumulative force has, not without justification, engendered belief that there is a constitutional principle, expressed by those attractive but imprecise words, prohibiting restriction upon utterance unless it creates a situation of "imminent" peril against which legislation may guard. It is on this body of the Court's pronouncements that the defendants' argument here is based.

In all fairness, the argument cannot be met by reinterpreting the Court's frequent use of "clear" and "present" to mean an entertainable "probability." In giving this meaning to the phrase "clear and present danger," the Court of Appeals was fastidiously confining the rhetoric of opinions to the exact scope of what was decided by them. We have greater responsibility for having given constitu-

tional support, over repeated protests, to uncritical libertarian generalities.

The defendants have been convicted of conspiring to organize a party of persons who advocate the overthrow of the Government by force and violence. The jury has found that the object of the conspiracy is advocacy as "a rule or principle of action," "by language reasonably and ordinarily calculated to incite persons to such action," and with the intent to cause the overthrow "as speedily as circumstances would permit."

On any scale of values which we have hitherto recognized, speech of this sort ranks low.

These general considerations underlie decision of the case before us.

On the one hand is the interest in security. . . .

On the other hand is the interest in free speech. . . .

It is not for us to decide how we would adjust the clash of interests which this case presents were the primary responsibility for reconciling it ours. Congress has determined that the danger created by advocacy of overthrow justifies the ensuing restriction on freedom of speech. The determination was made after due deliberation, and the seriousness of the congressional purpose is attested by the volume of legislation passed to effectuate the same ends.

Can we then say that the judgment Congress exercised was denied it by the Constitution? Can we establish a constitutional doctrine which forbids the elected representatives of the people to make this choice? Can we hold that the First Amendment deprives Congress of what it deemed necessary for the Government's protection?

To make validity of legislation depend on judicial reading of events still in the womb of time—a forecast, that is, of the outcome of forces at best appreciated only with knowledge of the topmost secrets of nations—is to charge the judiciary with duties beyond its equipment. We do not expect courts to pronounce historic verdicts on bygone events. Even historians have conflicting views to this day on the origins and conduct of the French Revolution, or, for that matter, varying interpretations of "the glorious Revolution" of 1688. It is as absurd to be confident that we can measure the present clash of forces and their outcome as to ask us to read history still enveloped in clouds of controversy.

Justice JACKSON, concurring.

This prosecution is the latest of never-ending, because never successful, quests for some legal formula that will secure an existing order against revolutionary radicalism. It requires us to reappraise, in the light of our own times and conditions, constitutional doctrines devised under other circumstances to strike a balance between authority and liberty.

Activity here charged to be criminal is conspiracy—that defendants conspired to teach and advocate, and to organize the Communist Party to teach and advocate, overthrow and destruction of the Government by force and violence. There is no charge of actual violence or attempt at overthrow.

The principal reliance of the defense in this Court is that the conviction cannot stand under the Constitution because the conspiracy of these defendants presents no "clear and present danger" of imminent or foreseeable overthrow. . . .

The "clear and present danger" test was an innovation by Mr. Justice Holmes in the *Schenck* case, reiterated and refined by him and Mr. Justice Brandeis in later cases, all arising before the era of World War II revealed the subtlety and efficacy of modernized revolutionary techniques used by totalitarian parties. In those cases, they were faced with convictions under so-called criminal syndicalism statutes aimed at anarchists but which, loosely construed, had been applied to punish socialism, pacifism, and left-wing ideologies, the charges often resting on far-fetched inferences which, if true, would establish only technical or trivial violations. They proposed "clear and present danger" as a test for the sufficiency of evidence in particular cases.

I would save it, unmodified, for application as a "rule of reason" in the kind of case for which it was devised. When the issue is criminality of a hot-headed speech on a street corner, or circulation of a few incendiary pamphlets, or parading by some zealots behind a red flag, or refusal of a handful of school children to salute our flag, it is not beyond the capacity of the judicial process to gather, comprehend, and weigh the necessary materials for decision whether it is a clear and present danger of substantive evil or a harmless letting off of steam. It is not a prophecy, for the danger in such cases has matured by the time of trial or it was never present. The test applies and has meaning where a conviction is sought to be based on a speech or writing which does not directly or explicitly advocate a crime but to which such tendency is sought to be attributed by construction or by implication from external circumstances. The formula in such cases favors freedoms that are vital to our society, and, even if sometimes applied too generously, the consequences cannot be grave. But its recent expansion has extended, in particular to Communists, unprecedented immunities. Unless we are to hold our Government captive in a judge-made verbal trap, we must approach the problem of a well-organized, nation-wide conspiracy, such as I have described, as realistically as our predecessors faced the trivialities that were being prosecuted until they were checked with a rule of reason.

I think reason is lacking for applying that test to this case.

Justice BLACK, dissenting.

. . .

At the outset I want to emphasize what the crime involved in this case is, and what it is not. These petitioners were not charged with an attempt to overthrow the Government. They were not charged with overt acts of any kind designed to overthrow the Government. They were not even charged with saying anything or writing anything designed to overthrow the Government. The charge was that they agreed to assemble and to talk and publish certain ideas at a later date: The indictment is that they conspired to organize the Communist Party and to use speech or newspapers and other publications in the future to teach and advocate the forcible overthrow of the Government. No matter how it is worded, this is a virulent form of prior censorship of speech and press, which I believe the First Amendment forbids. I would hold Section 3 of the Smith Act authorizing this prior restraint unconstitutional on its face and as applied.

But let us assume, contrary to all constitutional ideas of fair criminal procedure, that petitioners although not indicted for the crime of actual advocacy, may be punished for it. Even on this radical assumption, the other opinions in this case show that the only way to affirm these convictions is to repudiate directly or indirectly the established "clear and present danger" rule. This the Court does in a way which greatly restricts the protections afforded by the First Amendment. The opinions for affirmance indicate that the chief reason for jettisoning the rule is the expressed fear that advocacy of Communist doctrine endangers the safety of the Republic. Undoubtedly, a governmental policy of unfettered communication of ideas does entail dangers. To the Founders of this Nation, however, the benefits derived from free expression were worth the risk. They embodied this philosophy in the First Amendment's command that "Congress shall make no law . . . abridging the freedom of speech, or of the press. . . ." I have always believed that the First Amendment is the keystone of our Government, that the freedoms it guarantees provide the best insurance against destruction of all freedom. At least as to speech in the realm of public matters, I believe that the "clear and present danger" test does not "mark the furthermost constitutional boundaries of protected expression" but does "no more than recognize a minimum compulsion of the Bill of Rights."

Justice DOUGLAS, dissenting.

If this were a case where those who claimed protection under the First Amendment were teaching the techniques of sabotage, the assassination of the President, the filching of documents from public files, the planting of bombs, the art of street warfare, and the like, I would have no doubts. The freedom to speak is not absolute; the teaching of methods of terror and other seditious conduct should be beyond the pale along with obscenity and immorality. This case was argued as if those were the facts. The argument imported much seditious conduct into the record. That is easy and it has popular appeal, for the activities of Communists in plotting and scheming against the free world are common knowledge. But the fact is that no such evidence was introduced at the trial. There is a statute which makes a seditious conspiracy unlawful. Petitioners, however, were not charged with a "conspiracy to overthrow" the Government. They were charged with a conspiracy to form a party and groups and assemblies of people who teach and advocate the overthrow of our Government by force or violence and with a conspiracy to advocate and teach its overthrow by force and violence. It may well be that indoctrination in the techniques of terror to destroy the Government would be indictable under either statute. But the teaching which is condemned here is of a different character.

So far as the present record is concerned, what petitioners did was to organize people to teach and themselves teach the Marxist-Leninist doctrine contained chiefly in four books: Stalin, *Foundations of Leninism* (1924); Marx and Engels, *Manifesto of the Communist Party* (1848); Lenin, *The State and Revolution* (1917); *History of the Communist Party of the Soviet Union* (B.) (1939).

Those books are to Soviet Communism what *Mein Kampf* was to Nazism. If they are understood, the ugliness of Communism is revealed, its deceit and cunning are exposed, the nature of its activities becomes apparent, and the chances of its success less likely. That is not, of course, the reason why petitioners chose these books for their classrooms. They are fervent Communists to whom these volumes are gospel. They preached the creed with the hope that some day it would be acted upon.

The opinion of the Court does not outlaw these texts nor condemn them to the fire, as the Communists do literature offensive to their creed. But if the books themselves are not outlawed, if they can lawfully remain on library shelves, by what reasoning does their use in a classroom become a crime? It would not be a crime under the Act to introduce these books to a class, though that would be teaching what the creed of violent overthrow of the Government is. The Act, as construed, requires the element of intent—that those who teach the creed believe in it. The crime then depends not on what is taught but on who the teacher is. That is to make freedom of speech turn not on what is said, but on the intent with which it is said. Once we start down that road we enter territory dangerous to the liberties of every citizen. . . .

The vice of treating speech as the equivalent of overt acts of a treasonable or seditious character is emphasized by a concurring opinion, which by invoking the law of conspiracy makes speech do service for deeds which are dangerous to society. The doctrine of conspiracy has served divers and oppressive purposes and in its broad reach can be made to do great evil. But never until today has anyone seriously thought that the ancient law of conspiracy could constitutionally be used to turn speech into seditious conduct. Yet that is precisely what is suggested. I repeat that we deal here with speech alone, not with speech plus acts of sabotage or unlawful conduct. Not a single seditious act is charged in the indictment. To make a lawful speech unlawful because two men conceive it is to raise the law of conspiracy to appalling proportions. That course is to make a radical break with the past and to violate one of the cardinal principles of our constitutional scheme.

Free speech has occupied an exalted position because of the high service it has given our society. Its protection is essential to the very existence of a democracy. The airing of ideas releases pressures which otherwise might become destructive. When ideas compete in the market for acceptance, full and free discussion exposes the false and they gain few adherents. Full and free discussion even of ideas we hate encourages the testing of our own prejudices and preconceptions. Full and free discussion keeps a society from becoming stagnant and unprepared for the stresses and strains that work to tear all civilizations apart.

* * *

Free speech—the glory of our system of government—should not be sacrificed on anything less than plain and objective proof of danger that the evil advocated is imminent. On this record no one can say that petitioners and their converts are in such a strategic position as to have even the slightest chance of achieving their aims.

The First Amendment provides that "Congress shall make no law . . . abridging the freedom of speech." The Constitution provides no exception. This does not mean, however, that the Nation need hold its hand until it is in such weakened condition that there is no time to protect itself from incitement to revolution. Seditious conduct can always be punished. But the command of the First Amendment is so clear that we should not allow Congress to call a halt to free speech except in the extreme case of peril from the speech itself. The First Amendment makes confidence in the common sense of our people and in their maturity of judgment the great postulate of our democracy. Its philosophy is that violence is rarely, if ever, stopped by denying civil liberties to those advocating resort to force. The First Amendment reflects the philosophy of Jefferson "that it is time enough for the rightful purposes of civil government, for its officers to interfere when principles break out into overt acts against peace and good order." The political censor has no place in our public debates. Unless and until extreme and necessitous circumstances are shown, our aim should be to keep speech unfettered and to allow the processes of law to be invoked only when the provocateurs among us move from speech to action.

Vishinsky wrote in 1938 in *The Law of the Soviet State*, "In our state, naturally, there is and can be no place for freedom of speech, press, and so on for the foes of socialism."

Our concern should be that we accept no such standard for the United States. Our faith should be that our people will never give support to these advocates of revolution, so long as we remain loyal to the purposes for which our Nation was founded.

Notes and Queries

1. In *Yates v. U.S.* (1957) fourteen "second-tier" leaders of the Communist Party were convicted under the same Smith Act that was at issue in *Dennis*. Justice Harlan, however, refined the doctrine of *Dennis* so as to nullify the convictions. He did this in two ways: first, he used a particularly narrow interpretive strategy to construe the word "organize" in the Act as meaning "form or establish" rather than the broader meaning taken by the government which understood "organizing" as a "continuing process." Since the Communist Party was "organized" no later than 1945, the three-year statute of limitations had run out and the defendants could not be charged. Second, he argued that the holding in *Dennis* had been misconstrued, and he outlined a distinction between "advocacy of forcible overthrow as an abstract doctrine and advocacy of action to that end." Harlan continued:

The essence of the *Dennis* holding was that indoctrination of a group in preparation for future violent action,

as well as exhortation to immediate action, by advocacy found to be directed to "action for the accomplishment" of forcible overthrow, to violence as "a rule or principle of action," and employing "language of incitement," is not constitutionally protected when the group is of sufficient size and cohesiveness, is sufficiently oriented towards action, and other circumstances are such as reasonably to justify apprehension that action will occur. This is quite a different thing from the view of the District Court here that mere doctrinal justification of forcible overthrow, if engaged in with the intent to accomplish overthrow, is punishable *per se* under the Smith Act. That sort of advocacy, even though uttered with the hope that it may ultimately lead to violent revolution, is too remote from concrete action to be regarded as the kind of indoctrination preparatory to action which was condemned in *Dennis.*

2. Justice Jackson's concurrence in *Dennis* is similar to his dissent in an earlier case, *Terminiello v. Chicago* 337 U.S. 1 (1949). In that case the Court overturned the conviction of a man who had been charged with disturbing the peace by giving a speech which condemned various political and racial groups. The hall in which he spoke was packed and an angry crowd protested outside. Jackson wrote: "This court has gone far toward accepting the doctrine that civil liberty means the removal of all restraints from these crowds and that all local attempts to maintain order are impairments of the liberty of the citizen. The choice is between liberty with order or anarchy without either. There is danger that, if the Court does not temper its doctrinaire logic with a little practical wisdom, it will convert the constitutional Bill of Rights into a suicide pact." Compare this with Frankfurter's concurring opinion in *Dennis* and Douglas's dissent. Douglas expresses a profound faith in the inevitable vindication of the truth if all ideas are freely exchanged. Jackson seems doubtful about this. Why might this be? Does the history of the twentieth century offer any instructive examples which could support Jackson's case?

3. Article 21 of Germany's Basic Law provides as follows: "[Political parties which by reason of their aims or the conduct of their adherents seek to impair or do away with the free democratic basic order or threaten the existence of the Federal Republic of Germany shall be unconstitutional." (See Comparative Note 12.2.) Would this provision pass muster under *Dennis*? Under the U.S. Constitution?

Brandenburg v. Ohio

395 U.S. 444, 89 S.Ct. 1827, 23 L.Ed.2d 430 (1969)

Charles Brandenburg, a leader of the Ku Klux Klan, was convicted under Ohio's Criminal Syndicalism Statute for "advocating . . . the duty, necessity, or propriety of crime, sabotage, violence, or unlawful methods of terrorism as a means of accomplishing industrial or political reform." The basis of the charge was local television news coverage showing a meeting of hooded figures, some of whom carried firearms. One of the speakers, who was not armed, threatened to "march on Congress, four hundred thousand strong." "We're not a revengent organization," he said, "but if our President, our Congress, our Supreme Court, continues to suppress the white, Caucasian race, it's possible that there might have to be some revengeance taken." An appeal was taken to the Supreme Court after the Supreme Court of Ohio dismissed Brandenburg's appeal. Opinion of the Court *per curiam*: Warren, Black, Douglas, Harlan, Brennan, Stewart, White, Fortas, Marshall. Concurring opinions: *Black, Douglas.*

PER CURIAM

* * *

The Ohio Criminal Syndicalism Statute was enacted in 1919. From 1917 to 1920, identical or quite similar laws were adopted by 20 States and two territories. In 1927, this Court sustained the constitutionality of California's Criminal Syndicalism Act, the text of which is quite similar to that of the laws of Ohio. *Whitney v. California* [1927]. The Court upheld the statute on the ground that, without more, "advocating" violent means to effect political and economic change involves such danger to the security of the State that the State may outlaw it. But *Whitney* has been thoroughly discredited by later decisions. These later decisions have fashioned the principle that the constitutional guarantees of free speech and free press do not permit a State to forbid or proscribe advocacy of the use of force or of law violation except where such advocacy is directed to inciting or producing imminent lawless action and is likely to incite or produce such action. As we said in *Noto v. United States*, [1961], "the mere abstract teaching . . . of the moral propriety or even moral necessity for a resort to force and violence, is not the same as preparing a group for violent action and steeling it to such action." A statute which fails to draw this distinction impermissibly intrudes upon the freedoms guaranteed by the First and Fourteenth Amendments. It sweeps within its condemnation speech which our Constitution has immunized from governmental control.

Measured by this test, Ohio's Criminal Syndicalism Act cannot be sustained. The Act punishes persons who "advocate or teach the duty, necessity, or propriety" of violence "as a means of accomplishing industrial or political reform"; or who publish or circulate or display any book or paper containing such advocacy; or who "justify" the commission of violent acts "with intent to exemplify, spread or advocate the propriety of the doctrines of criminal syndicalism"; or who "voluntarily assemble" with a group formed "to teach or advocate the doctrines of criminal syndicalism." Neither the indictment nor the trial judge's instructions to the jury in any way refined the statute's bald definition of the crime in terms of mere advocacy not distinguished from incitement to imminent lawless action.

Accordingly, we are here confronted with a statute which, by its own words and as applied, purports to punish mere advocacy and to forbid, on pain of criminal punishment, assembly with others merely to advocate the described type of action. Such a statute falls within the condemnation of the First and Fourteenth Amendments. The contrary teaching of *Whitney v. California*, *supra*, cannot be supported, and that decision is therefore overruled.

Reversed.

Justice DOUGLAS, concurring.

While I join the opinion of the Court, I desire to enter a caveat. . . .

I see no place in the regime of the First Amendment for any "clear and present danger" test, whether strict and tight as some would make it, or free-wheeling as the Court in *Dennis* rephrased it.

When one reads the opinions closely and sees when and how the "clear and present danger" test has been applied, great misgivings are aroused. First, the threats were often loud but always puny and made serious only by judges so wedded to the status quo that critical analysis made them nervous. Second, the test was so twisted and perverted in *Dennis* as to make the trial of those teachers of Marxism an all-out political trial which was part and parcel of the cold war that has eroded substantial parts of the First Amendment.

Action is often a method of expression and within the protection of the First Amendment.

One's beliefs have long been thought to be sanctuaries which government could not invade. . . .

The line between what is permissible and not subject to control and what may be made impermissible and subject to regulation is the line between ideas and overt acts.

The example usually given by those who would punish

Comparative Note 12.3

[After an important case in which the Hungarian Constitutional Court had established free speech as privileged within the hierarchy of protected rights, Parliament, asserting that it had conformed to the requirements of the Court's ruling, restored the crime of incitement. The newly amended Criminal Code now provided: 1) that anyone who, before a large public audience, incites hatred against the Hungarian nation, any other nationality, people, religion, or race or certain groups among the population commits an offence punishable by up to three years' imprisonment; 2) anyone in the same circumstances who uses an offensive or denigrating expression, or commits similar acts, against the groups above, commits an offence punishable by up to one year's imprisonment, corrective training or a fine. In 1992 the Constitutional Court upheld the first part of the law and found the second unconstitutional.]

To afford constitutional protection to the incitement of hatred against certain groups under the guise of the freedom of expression and freedom of press would present an indissoluble contradiction with the value system and political orientation expressed in the Constitution: the democratic rule of law, the equality of human beings, equality of dignity, as well as the prohibition of discrimination, the freedom of religion and conscience, the protection of national and ethnic minorities—as recognized by the various articles of the Constitution. . . .

Incitement to hatred is the negation of this aforenoted content, the emotional preparation for the use of violence. It is an abuse of the freedom of expression; it is an intolerant classification of a group, which is the characteristic of dictatorships, not democracies. To tolerate the exercise of the freedom of expression and freedom of the press in a way which art. 269(1) prohibits would contradict the requirements springing from the democratic rule of law. . . .

The emphatic expression of disapproval and condemnation of such behavior, the fortification of those democratic ideas and values which are attacked by the perpetrators of these activities, and the restoration of the violated legal and moral order require the application of the instruments of criminal law.

[The Court went on to strike down the second part of the law, concluding that, standing alone, "denigration" was an insufficient basis for restricting speech without violating the "requirement of ideological neutrality."]

SOURCE: Hungarian Incitement to Hate Case (1992) (Reprinted in Laszlo Solyom and Georg Brunner, *Constitutional Judiciary in a New Democracy* (Ann Arbor: The University of Michigan Press, 2000), 231.

---

speech is the case of one who falsely shouts fire in a crowded theatre.

This is, however, a classic case where speech is brigaded with action. . . . They are indeed inseparable and a prosecution can be launched for the overt acts actually caused. Apart from rare instances of that kind, speech is, I think, immune from prosecution. Certainly there is no constitutional line between advocacy of abstract ideas as in *Yates* [*v. United States* (1957)] and advocacy of political action as in *Scales* [*v. United States* (1961)]. The quality of advocacy turns on the depth of the conviction; and government has no power to invade that sanctuary of belief and conscience.

Notes and Queries

1. How does the "imminent lawless action" test of *Brandenburg* differ from the "clear and present danger" test in *Schenck*?

2. Compare the methods of interpretation of Douglas's concurring opinion in *Brandenburg* with Frankfurter's concurrence in *Dennis*. How does Douglas's method of "absolute" standards differ from Frankfurter's attempt at balancing constitutional values?

3. Section 80a of the German Criminal Code punishes incitement to a war of aggression. The relevant section reads: "Whoever, within the area of applicability of this Code, in a meeting or by the distribution of writings, publicly incites to a war of aggression, shall be punished by imprisonment from three months to five years." Would this statute survive constitutional analysis in the United States?

4. In *Dennis*, Justice Frankfurter asked: "But how are competing interests to be assessed? Since they are not subject to quantitative ascertainment, the issue necessarily resolves itself into asking, who is to make the adjustment?—Who is to balance the relevant factors and ascer-

tain which interest is in the circumstances to prevail? Full responsibility for the choice cannot be given to the courts. Courts are not representative bodies. They are not designed to be a good reflex of a democratic society. Their judgment is best informed, and therefore most dependable, within narrow limits. . . ." How is the tension between majority rule and judicial supremacy to be resolved in matters of public order and national security? What are these "narrow limits" of judicial power mentioned by Frankfurter?

5. Could Mark Antony be convicted under *Brandenburg* for his famous "Lend me your ears" speech before the citizens of Rome over the mutilated body of Julius Caesar?

6. After *Brandenburg*, where would we wish to draw the line in the following situations between permissible and impermissible speech?

a. discussing the pros and cons of draft resistance

b. advocating draft resistance as a general principle

c. burning the flag in public as a protest against the draft

d. mailing leaflets to prospective draftees, encouraging them not to register for the draft

e. burning draft cards in symbolic protest against the draft

f. occupying a federal building in symbolic protest against the draft

g. pouring blood over draft board records

7. Consider the excerpt from the Hungarian Constitutional Court's decision in the Incitement to Hate Case in Comparative Note 12.3. Would the statute at issue there survive constitutional analysis in the United States? In that opinion the Court relied on the language of a turn of the century judicial opinion, which said: "[C]riticism, disapproval, objections or, indeed, offensive declarations do not constitute incitement; incitement occurs only when the expression, comments, etc., address not reason but seek to influence the world of emotions and are capable of arousing passions and hostile feelings. For the concept of incitement it is totally immaterial whether the stated facts are true or not; what matters is that they, true or false, are capable of arousing hatred." This reference is manifest in the Court's emphasis in its opinion on "the emotional preparation for the use of violence." Could these expressed concerns fit within the doctrinal parameters of the American Court's opinion in *Brandenburg*? If yes, how so? If no, speculate as to the possible reasons why a Hungarian Court would approach the issue of incitement differently from an American Court.

New York Times Co. v. United States

403 U.S. 713, 91 S.Ct. 2140, 29 L.Ed.2d 822 (1971)

In June 1971 the *New York Times* began publishing extracts from a classified study of U.S. involvement in the Vietnam War commissioned by the Department of Defense in 1967 (the so-called "Pentagon Papers"). The *Times* obtained the documents from Daniel Ellsberg, a former Pentagon official. After the *Times* disregarded a request by the Department of Justice to suspend publication of the excerpts, Attorney General John Mitchell obtained a temporary restraining order enjoining the paper to stop publishing the material on grounds that it endangered national security. A similar injunction was placed on the *Washington Post*, which had also begun publishing parts of the documents. Both newspapers appealed to the Supreme Court which heard oral arguments the next day. Just four days later the Court handed down its decision. Opinion of the Court *per curiam*: *Black*, Douglas, Brennan, Stewart, White, Marshall. Separate opinions: *Black, Douglas, Brennan, Stewart, White, Burger, Harlan, Blackmun.*

PER CURIAM

"Any system of prior restraints of expression comes to this Court bearing a heavy presumption against its constitutional validity." *Bantam Books, Inc. v. Sullivan*, (1963); see also *Near v. Minnesota*, (1931). The Government "thus carries a heavy burden of showing justification for the imposition of such a restraint." *Organization for a Better Austin v. Keefe*, (1971). The District Court for the Southern District of New York in the *New York Times* case and the District Court for the District of Columbia and the Court of Appeals for the District of Columbia Circuit in the *Washington Post* case held that the Government had not met that burden. We agree.

So ordered.

Justice BLACK, with whom Justice DOUGLAS joins, concurring.

I adhere to the view that the Government's case against the *Washington Post* should have been dismissed and that the injunction against the *New York Times* should have been vacated without oral argument when the cases were first presented to this Court. I believe that every moment's continuance of the injunctions against these newspapers amounts to a flagrant, indefensible, and continuing viola-

Comparative Note 12.4

[The famed Indian writer and political activist, Arundhati Roy, wrote an article in a popular magazine condemning the construction of a dam for its allegedly adverse environmental impact, which included the displacement of hundreds of thousands of people from their ancestral homes. She was charged with using the article to misrepresent the proceedings of a court that had approved the construction. Her conviction for contempt of court was heard by the Supreme Court of India.]

This Court . . . has pointed out that a free and healthy Press is indispensable to the function of a true democracy but, at the same time, cautioned that the freedom of Press is not absolute, unlimited and unfettered at all times and in all circumstances. . . .

Nobody has a right to denigrate [an]other's right of person and reputation. Bonafide criticism of any system or institution including the judiciary cannot be objected to as healthy and constructive criticism are tools to augment forensic tools for improving its function. . . .

The legislature appears to have kept in mind to bring the law on the subject into line with modern trends of thinking in other countries without ignoring the ground realities and prevalent socio-economic system in India, the vast majority of whose people are poor, ignorant, uneducated, easily liable to be misled, but who . . . have the tremendous faith in the Dispensers of Justice. . . .

The well-known proposition of law is that it punishes the archer as soon as the arrow is shot no matter if it misses to hit the target. The respondent is proved to have shot the arrow, intended to damage the institution of the judiciary and thereby weaken the faith of the public in general and if such an attempt is not prevented, disastrous consequences are likely to follow resulting in the destruction of [the] rule of law, the expected norm of any civilized society.

SOURCE: *In Re: Arundhati Roy* 06/03/2002

---

tion of the First Amendment. Furthermore, after oral argument, I agree completely that we must affirm the judgment of the Court of Appeals for the District of Columbia Circuit and reverse the judgment of the Court of Appeals for the Second Circuit for the reasons stated by my Brothers Douglas and Brennan. In my view it is unfortunate that some of my Brethren are apparently willing to hold that the publication of news may sometimes be enjoined. Such a holding would make a shambles of the First Amendment.

In the First Amendment the Founding Fathers gave the free press the protection it must have to fulfill its essential role in our democracy. The press was to serve the governed, not the governors. The Government's power to censor the press was abolished so that the press would remain forever free to censure the Government. The press was protected so that it could bare the secrets of government and inform the people. Only a free and unrestrained press can effectively expose deception in government. And paramount among the responsibilities of a free press is the duty to prevent any part of the government from deceiving the people and sending them off to distant lands to die of foreign fevers and foreign shot and shell. In my view, far from deserving condemnation for their courageous reporting, the *New York Times*, the *Washington Post*, and other newspapers should be commended for serving the purpose that the Founding Fathers saw so clearly. In revealing the workings of government that led to the Vietnam war, the newspapers nobly did precisely that which the Founders hoped and trusted they would do.

The Government's case here is based on premises entirely different from those that guided the Framers of the First Amendment. . . . And the Government argues in its brief that in spite of the First Amendment, "the authority of the Executive Department to protect the nation against publication of information whose disclosure would endanger the national security stems from two interrelated sources: the constitutional power of the President over the conduct of foreign affairs and his authority as Commander-in-Chief."

In other words, we are asked to hold that despite the First Amendment's emphatic command, the Executive Branch, the Congress, and the Judiciary can make laws enjoining publication of current news and abridging freedom of the press in the name of "national security." The Government does not even attempt to rely on any act of Congress. Instead it makes the bold and dangerously far-reaching contention that the courts should take it upon themselves to "make" a law abridging freedom of the press in the name of equity, presidential power and national security, even when the representatives of the people in Congress have adhered to the command of the First Amendment and refused to make such a law. To find that the President has "inherent power" to halt the publication of news by resort to the courts would wipe out the First Amendment and destroy the fundamental liberty and security of the very people the Government hopes to make "secure." No one can read the history of the adoption of the First Amendment without being convinced beyond any doubt that it was injunctions like those sought here that Madison and his collaborators intended to outlaw in this Nation for all time.

Justice DOUGLAS, with whom Justice BLACK joins, concurring.

While I join the opinion of the Court I believe it necessary to express my views more fully.

It should be noted at the outset that the First Amendment provides that "Congress shall make no law . . . abridging the freedom of speech, or of the press." That leaves, in my view, no room for governmental restraint on the press.

The power to wage war is "the power to wage war successfully." But the war power stems from a declaration of war. The Constitution by Art. I, Section 8, gives Congress, not the President, power "to declare War." Nowhere are presidential wars authorized. We need not decide therefore what leveling effect the war power of Congress might have.

These disclosures may have a serious impact. But that is no basis for sanctioning a previous restraint on the press. . . .

The Government says that it has inherent powers to go into court and obtain an injunction to protect the national interest, which in this case is alleged to be national security.

Near v. Minnesota [1931] repudiated that expansive doctrine in no uncertain terms.

The dominant purpose of the First Amendment was to prohibit the widespread practice of governmental suppression of embarrassing information. It is common knowledge that the First Amendment was adopted against the widespread use of the common law of seditious libel to punish the dissemination of material that is embarrassing to the powers-that-be. The present cases will, I think, go down in history as the most dramatic illustration of that principle. A debate of large proportions goes on in the Nation over our posture in Vietnam. That debate antedated the disclosure of the contents of the present documents. The latter are highly relevant to the debate in progress.

Secrecy in government is fundamentally anti-democratic, perpetuating bureaucratic errors. Open debate and discussion of public issues are vital to our national health. On public questions there should be "uninhibited, robust, and wide-open" debate.

Justice BRENNAN, concurring.

The error that has pervaded these cases from the outset was the granting of any injunctive relief whatsoever, interim or otherwise. The entire thrust of the Government's claim throughout these cases has been that publication of the material sought to be enjoined "could," or "might," or "may" prejudice the national interest in various ways. But the First Amendment tolerates absolutely no prior judicial restraints of the press predicated upon surmise or conjecture that untoward consequences may result. Our cases, it is true, have indicated that there is a single, extremely narrow class of cases in which the First Amendment's ban on prior judicial restraint may be overridden. Our cases have thus far indicated that such cases may arise only when the Nation "is at war," during which times "no one would question but that a government might prevent actual obstruction to its recruiting service or the publication of the sailing dates of transports or the number and location of troops. . . ." "The chief purpose of [the First Amendment's] guaranty [is] to prevent previous restraints upon publication." *Near v. Minnesota*, *supra*, at 713. Thus, only governmental allegation and proof that publication must inevitably, directly, and immediately cause the occurrence of an event kindred to imperiling the safety of a transport already at sea can support even the issuance of an interim restraining order. In no event may mere conclusions be sufficient: for if the Executive Branch seeks judicial aid in preventing publication, it must inevitably submit the basis upon which that aid is sought to scrutiny by the judiciary. And therefore, every restraint issued in this case, whatever its form, has violated the First Amendment—and not less so because that restraint was justified as necessary to afford the courts an opportunity to examine the claim more thoroughly. Unless and until the Government has clearly made out its case, the First Amendment commands that no injunction may issue.

Justice STEWART, with whom Justice WHITE joins, concurring.

In the governmental structure created by our Constitution, the Executive is endowed with enormous power in the two related areas of national defense and international relations. This power, largely unchecked by the Legislative and Judicial branches, has been pressed to the very hilt since the advent of the nuclear missile age. For better or for worse, the simple fact is that a President of the United States possesses vastly greater constitutional independence in these two vital areas of power than does, say, a prime minister of a country with a parliamentary form of government.

In the absence of the governmental checks and balances present in other areas of our national life, the only effective restraint upon executive policy and power in the areas of national defense and international affairs may lie in an enlightened citizenry—in an informed and critical public opinion which alone can here protect the values of democratic government. For this reason, it is perhaps here that a press that is alert, aware, and free most vitally serves the basic purpose of the First Amendment. For without an informed and free press there cannot be an enlightened people.

Yet it is elementary that the successful conduct of international diplomacy and the maintenance of an effective national defense require both confidentiality and secrecy. Other nations can hardly deal with this Nation in an atmosphere of mutual trust unless they can be assured that their confidences will be kept. And within our own executive departments, the development of considered and intelligent international policies would be impossible if those charged with their formulation could not communicate with each other freely, frankly, and in confidence. In the area of basic national defense the frequent need for absolute secrecy is, of course, self-evident.

I think there can be but one answer to this dilemma, if dilemma it be. The responsibility must be where the power is. If the Constitution gives the Executive a large degree of unshared power in the conduct of foreign affairs and the maintenance of our national defense, then under the Constitution the Executive must have the largely unshared duty to determine and preserve the degree of internal security necessary to exercise that power successfully. It is an awesome responsibility, requiring judgment and wisdom of a high order. I should suppose that moral, political, and practical considerations would dictate that a very first principle of that wisdom would be an insistence upon avoiding secrecy for its own sake. For when everything is classified, then nothing is classified, and the system becomes one to be disregarded by the cynical or the careless, and to be manipulated by those intent on self-protection or self-promotion. I should suppose, in short, that the hallmark of a truly effective internal security system would be the maximum possible disclosure, recognizing that secrecy can best be preserved only when credibility is truly maintained. But be that as it may, it is

clear to me that it is the constitutional duty of the Executive—as a matter of sovereign prerogative and not as a matter of law as the courts know law—through the promulgation and enforcement of executive regulations, to protect the confidentiality necessary to carry out its responsibilities in the fields of international relations and national defense.

This is not to say that Congress and the courts have no role to play. Undoubtedly Congress has the power to enact specific and appropriate criminal laws to protect government property and preserve government secrets. Congress has passed such laws, and several of them are of very colorable relevance to the apparent circumstances of these cases. And if a criminal prosecution is instituted, it will be the responsibility of the courts to decide the applicability of the criminal law under which the charge is brought. Moreover, if Congress should pass a specific law authorizing civil proceedings in this field, the courts would likewise have the duty to decide the constitutionality of such a law as well as its applicability to the facts proved.

But in the cases before us we are asked neither to construe specific regulations nor to apply specific laws. We are asked, instead, to perform a function that the Constitution gave to the Executive, not the Judiciary. We are asked, quite simply, to prevent the publication by two newspapers of material that the Executive Branch insists should not, in the national interest, be published. I am convinced that the Executive is correct with respect to some of the documents involved. But I cannot say that disclosure of any of them will surely result in direct, immediate, and irreparable damage to our Nation or its people. That being so, there can under the First Amendment be but one judicial resolution of the issues before us. I join the judgments of the Court.

Justice WHITE, with whom Justice STEWART joins, concurring.

I concur in today's judgments, but only because of the concededly extraordinary protection against prior restraints enjoyed by the press under our constitutional system. I do not say that in no circumstances would the First Amendment permit an injunction against publishing information about government plans or operations. Nor, after examining the materials the Government characterizes as the most sensitive and destructive, can I deny that revelation of these documents will do substantial damage to public interests. Indeed, I am confident that their disclosure will have that result. But I nevertheless agree that the United States has not satisfied the very heavy burden that it must meet to warrant an injunction against publication in these cases, at least in the absence of express and appropriately limited congressional authorization for prior restraints in circumstances such as these.

The Government's position is simply stated: The responsibility of the Executive for the conduct of the foreign affairs and for the security of the Nation is so basic that the President is entitled to an injunction against publication of a newspaper story whenever he can convince a court that the information to be revealed threatens "grave and irreparable" injury to the public interest; and the injunction should issue whether or not the material to be published is classified, whether or not publication would be lawful under relevant criminal statutes enacted by Congress, and regardless of the circumstances by which the newspaper came into possession of the information.

At least in the absence of legislation by Congress, based on its own investigations and findings, I am quite unable to agree that the inherent powers of the Executive and the courts reach so far as to authorize remedies having such sweeping potential for inhibiting publications by the press. Much of the difficulty inheres in the "grave and irreparable danger" standard suggested by the United States. If the United States were to have judgment under such a standard in these cases, our decision would be of little guidance to other courts in other cases, for the material at issue here would not be available from the Court's opinion or from public records, nor would it be published by the press. Indeed, even today where we hold that the United States has not met its burden, the material remains sealed in court records and it is properly not discussed in today's opinions. Moreover, because the material poses substantial dangers to national interests and because of the hazards of criminal sanctions, a responsible press may choose never to publish the more sensitive materials. To sustain the Government in these cases would start the courts down a long and hazardous road that I am not willing to travel, at least without congressional guidance and direction.

Chief Justice BURGER, dissenting.

So clear are the constitutional limitations on prior restraint against expression, that from the time of *Near v. Minnesota* [1931] until recently in *Organization for a Better Austin v. Keefe* [1971] we have had little occasion to be concerned with cases involving prior restraints against news reporting on matters of public interest. There is, therefore, little variation among the members of the Court in terms of resistance to prior restraints against publication. Adherence to this basic constitutional principle, however, does not make these cases simple. In these cases, the imperative of a free and unfettered press comes into collision with another imperative, the effective functioning of a complex modern government and specifically the effective exercise of certain constitutional powers of the Executive. Only those who view the First Amendment as an absolute in all circumstances—a view I respect, but reject—can find such cases as these to be simple or easy. . . .

It is not disputed that the *Times* has had unauthorized possession of the documents for three to four months, during which it has had its expert analysts studying them, presumably digesting them and preparing the material for publication. During all of this time, the *Times*, presumably in its capacity as trustee of the public's "right to know," has held up publication for purposes it considered proper and thus public knowledge was delayed. No doubt this was for a good reason; the analysis of 7,000 pages of complex material drawn from a vastly greater volume of material would inevitably take time and the writing of good news stories takes time. But why should the United States Government, from whom this information was illegally acquired by someone, along with all the counsel, trial judges, and appellate judges be placed under needless pressure? After these months of deferral, the alleged "right to know" has somehow and suddenly become a right that must be vindicated *instanter*.

Would it have been unreasonable, since the newspaper could anticipate the Government's objections to release of secret material, to give the Government an opportunity to review the entire collection and determine whether agreement could be reached on publication? Stolen or not, if security was not in fact jeopardized, much of the material could no doubt have been declassified, since it spans a period ending in 1968. With such an approach—one that great newspapers have in the past practiced and stated editorially to be the duty of an honorable press—the newspapers and Government might well have narrowed the area of disagreement as to what was and was not publishable, leaving the remainder to be resolved in orderly litigation, if necessary. To me it is hardly believable that a newspaper long regarded as a great institution in American life would fail to perform one of the basic and simple duties of every citizen with respect to the discovery or possession of stolen property or secret government documents. That duty, I had thought—perhaps naively—was to report forthwith, to responsible public officers. This duty rests on taxi drivers, Justices, and the *New York Times*. The course followed by the *Times*, whether so calculated or not, removed any possibility of orderly litigation of the issues. If the action of the judges up to now has been correct, that result is sheer happenstance.

Our grant of the writ of certiorari before final judgment in the *Times* case aborted the trial in the District Court before it had made a complete record pursuant to the mandate of the Court of Appeals for the Second Circuit.

The consequence of all this melancholy series of events is that we literally do not know what we are acting on. As I see it, we have been forced to deal with litigation concerning rights of great magnitude without an adequate record, and surely without time for adequate treatment either in the prior proceedings or in this Court. It is interesting to note that counsel on both sides, in oral argument before this Court, were frequently unable to respond to questions on factual points. Not surprisingly they pointed out that they had been working literally "around the clock" and simply were unable to review the documents that give rise to these cases and were not familiar with them. This Court is in no better posture. I agree generally with Mr. Justice Harlan and Mr. Justice Blackmun but I am not prepared to reach the merits.

Justice HARLAN, with whom the Chief Justice and Justice BLACKMUN join, dissenting.

It is plain to me that the scope of the judicial function in passing upon the activities of the Executive Branch of the Government in the field of foreign affairs is very narrowly restricted. This view is, I think, dictated by the concept of separation of powers upon which our constitutional system rests.

From this constitutional primacy in the field of foreign affairs, it seems to me that certain conclusions necessarily follow. Some of these were stated concisely by President Washington, declining the request of the House of Representatives for the papers leading up to the negotiation of the Jay Treaty:

> The nature of foreign negotiations requires caution, and their success must often depend on secrecy; and even when brought to a conclusion a full disclosure of all the measures, demands, or eventual concessions which may have been proposed or contemplated would be extremely impolitic; for this might have a pernicious influence on future negotiations, or produce immediate inconveniences, perhaps danger and mischief, in relation to other powers.

The power to evaluate the "pernicious influence" of premature disclosure is not, however, lodged in the Executive alone. I agree that, in performance of its duty to protect the values of the First Amendment against political pressures, the judiciary must review the initial Executive determination to the point of satisfying itself that the subject matter of the dispute does lie within the proper compass of the President's foreign relations power. Constitutional considerations forbid "a complete aban-

donment of judicial control." Moreover, the judiciary may properly insist that the determination that disclosure of the subject matter would irreparably impair the national security be made by the head of the Executive Department concerned—here the Secretary of State or the Secretary of Defense—after actual personal consideration by that officer. This safeguard is required in the analogous area of executive claims of privilege for secrets of state.

But in my judgment the judiciary may not properly go beyond these two inquiries and redetermine for itself the probable impact of disclosure on the national security. . . .

Even if there is some room for the judiciary to override the executive determination, it is plain that the scope of review must be exceedingly narrow. I can see no indication in the opinions of either the District Court or the Court of Appeals in the *Post* litigation that the conclusions of the Executive were given even the deference owing to an administrative agency, much less that owing to a co-equal branch of the Government operating within the field of its constitutional prerogative.

Accordingly, I would vacate the judgment of the Court of Appeals for the District of Columbia Circuit on this ground and remand the case for further proceedings in the District Court. Before the commencement of such further proceedings, due opportunity should be afforded the Government for procuring from the Secretary of State or the Secretary of Defense or both an expression of their views on the issue of national security. The ensuing review by the District Court should be in accordance with the views expressed in this opinion. And for the reasons stated above I would affirm the judgment of the Court of Appeals for the Second Circuit.

Notes and Queries

1. What conception of judicial power animates the various opinions in this case? Are they grounded in understandings about the nature and limits of judicial expertise? In larger understandings about the limits of judicial power in a democratic state? In considerations of prudence?

2. What reasons did the government advance for wanting to suppress publication of the papers? On what basis did the Court reject them? Is there a meaningful difference between an appeal to national security and fear of embarrassment? Are there ever times when publication should be suppressed simply because publicity will reflect unfavorably on the government or its officials? Are respect for the dignity of political institutions and governmental officials unimportant constitutional values?

3. Frequently, the opposing sides in a constitutional dispute even disagree over the central question at issue,

that is, over the nature of the disagreement itself. Is this case really about (a) prior restraint of the press, or (b) the executive branch's authority over national security? How does the way one frames the question influence the outcome of the case? What are the respective roles of absolute standards versus balancing of constitutional values and interests?

4. A crucial aspect of *New York Times* is how much deference a court should give to the legislature and executive branches in matters relating to security and public order. It is often said that the President is representative of *all* the people. Should the representative character of the presidency be a factor in the extent of a court's review of a presidential action? Suppose, too, that there is evidence showing that the President has conscientiously considered the constitutional implications of his actions in the security field. Would this be an added reason for judicial deference to presidential action? Is the Supreme Court's judgment about constitutionality superior to that of the President in the security field? Is there any such thing as a "right" answer in this field? Is the right answer to be found in the democratic process or in some judicial theory independent of process?

5. Consider the Indian Supreme Court opinion in Comparative Note 12.4. Would the American Supreme Court have upheld a conviction in a similar case? How persuasive is the Court's claim that in ruling in such cases it is necessary to take into account the realities of the socioeconomic system?

Chaplinsky v. New Hampshire
315 U.S. 568, 62 S.Ct. 766, 86 L.Ed. 1031 (1942)

Chaplinsky, a member of the Jehovah's Witnesses, was convicted under a New Hampshire statute forbidding the use of "any offensive, derisive or annoying word to any other person who is lawfully in any street or other public place," or with intent to "deride, offend, or annoy him." Chaplinsky became embroiled in a disturbance while distributing religious literature on a busy street. When a policeman arrived, who had come to investigate reports of a riot, Chaplinsky called him a "racketeer" and a "fascist." Chaplinsky appealed his conviction on grounds that the statute was invalid under the Fourteenth Amendment's incorporation of the First Amendment's protection of freedom of speech, of the press, and of worship. Opinion of the Court: *Murphy*, Black, Reed, Frankfurter, Douglas, Byrnes, Stone, Jackson.

Justice MURPHY delivered the opinion of the Court.

It is now clear that "Freedom of speech and freedom of the press, which are protected by the First Amendment from infringement by Congress, are among the fundamental personal rights and liberties which are protected by the Fourteenth Amendment from invasion by state action." Freedom of worship is similarly sheltered.

Appellant assails the statute as a violation of all three freedoms, speech, press and worship, but only an attack on the basis of free speech is warranted. The spoken, not the written, word is involved. And we cannot conceive that cursing a public officer is the exercise of religion in any sense of the term. But even if the activities of the appellant which preceded the incident could be viewed as religious in character, and therefore entitled to the protection of the Fourteenth Amendment, they would not cloak him with immunity from the legal consequences for concomitant acts committed in violation of a valid criminal statute. We turn, therefore, to an examination of the statute itself.

Allowing the broadest scope to the language and purpose of the Fourteenth Amendment, it is well understood that the right of free speech is not absolute at all times and under all circumstances. There are certain well-defined and narrowly limited classes of speech, the prevention and punishment of which have never been thought to raise any constitutional problem. These include the lewd and obscene, the profane, the libelous, and the insulting or "fighting" words—those which by their very utterance inflict injury or tend to incite an immediate breach of the peace. It has been well observed that such utterances are no essential part of any exposition of ideas, and are of such slight social value as a step to truth that any benefit that may be derived from them is clearly outweighed by the social interest in order and morality. "Resort to epithets or personal abuse is not in any proper sense communication of information or opinion safeguarded by the Constitution, and its punishment as a criminal act would raise no question under that instrument."

The state statute here challenged comes to us authoritatively construed by the highest court of New Hampshire. It has two provisions—the first relates to words or names addressed to another in a public place; the second refers to noises and exclamations. The court said: "The two provisions are distinct. One may stand separately from the other. Assuming, without holding, that the second were unconstitutional, the first could stand if constitutional." We accept that construction of severability and limit our consideration to the first provision of the statute.

On the authority of its earlier decisions, the state court declared that the statute's purpose was to preserve the public peace, no words being "forbidden except such as have a direct tendency to cause acts of violence by the persons to whom, individually, the remark is addressed." It was further said: "The word 'offensive' is not to be defined in terms of what a particular addressee thinks. . . . The test is what men of common intelligence would understand would be words likely to cause an average addressee to fight. . . . The English language has a number of words and expressions which by general consent are 'fighting words' when said without a disarming smile. . . . Such words, as ordinary men know, are likely to cause a fight. So are threatening, profane or obscene revilings. Derisive and annoying words can be taken as coming within the purview of the statute as heretofore interpreted only when they have this characteristic of plainly tending to excite the addressee to a breach of the peace. . . . The statute, as construed, does no more than prohibit the face-to-face words plainly likely to cause a breach of the peace by the addressee, words whose speaking constitutes a breach of the peace by the speaker—including 'classical fighting words', words in current use less 'classical' but equally likely to cause violence, and other disorderly words, including profanity, obscenity and threats."

We are unable to say that the limited scope of the statute as thus construed contravenes the Constitutional right of free expression. It is a statute narrowly drawn and limited to define and punish specific conduct lying within the domain of state power, the use in a public place of words likely to cause a breach of the peace. This conclusion necessarily disposes of appellant's contention that the statute is so vague and indefinite as to render a conviction thereunder a violation of due process. A statute punishing verbal acts, carefully drawn so as not unduly to impair liberty of expression, is not too vague for a criminal law.

Nor can we say that the application of the statute to the facts disclosed by the record substantially or unreasonably impinges upon the privilege of free speech. Argument is unnecessary to demonstrate that the appellations "damned racketeer" and "damned Fascist" are epithets likely to provoke the average person to retaliation, and thereby cause a breach of the peace.

The refusal of the state court to admit evidence of provocation and evidence bearing on the truth or falsity of the utterances, is open to no Constitutional objection. Whether the facts sought to be proved by such evidence constitute a defense to the charge, or may be shown in mitigation, are questions for the state court to determine. Our function is fulfilled by a determination that the challenged statute, on its face and as applied, does not contravene the Fourteenth Amendment.

Affirmed.

Notes and Queries

1. Does the "fighting words" doctrine outlined in *Chaplinsky* require the Court to develop a theory of speech with which to discern the relative importance of any type of utterance balanced against "social interest in order and morality"? Could such a theory be found in the Constitution?

2. The First Amendment's response to abusive remarks is not really clear. Is it social violence that is feared? Damage to the ethos of the community? The possibility of responsive violence on the part of an individual? Should a speaker be protected if he is *trying* to provoke a fight? Would it make a difference to whom the abusive remarks are addressed? What if the person addressed is not a police officer but rather someone unable physically to respond to an abusive epithet? Can any provocation of the nature engaged in by Chaplinsky be justified by the classic arguments in favor of free speech?

United States v. O'Brien
391 U.S. 367, 88 S.Ct. 1673, 20 L.Ed.2d 672 (1968)

In March of 1966, David O'Brien and three others burned their Selective Service registration certificates (commonly known as "draft cards") on the steps of the South Boston Courthouse. O'Brien was arrested by agents of the F.B.I., tried, and convicted under the Universal Military Training and Service Act of 1948 which forbade forging, altering, knowingly destroying, mutilating, or in any manner changing one's Selective Service Certificate. At trial, O'Brien said that he publicly burned his draft card as a protest against the war in Vietnam and the draft itself. O'Brien appealed his conviction which was then overturned by the First Circuit Court of Appeals which held that the law unconstitutionally abridged the freedom of speech. Another federal appeals court, however, sustained the law, and the Supreme Court agreed to decide the issue.

Chief Justice WARREN delivered the opinion of the Court.

O'Brien first argues that the 1965 Amendment is unconstitutional as applied to him because his act of burning his

Comparative Note 12.5

Sec. 90a. Defamation of the State and its symbols

(1) Whoever publicly, in a meeting or by the distribution of writings:

1. insults or maliciously maligns the Federal Republic of Germany or one of its *Länder* [states] or its constitutional order . . . shall be punished by up to three years' imprisonment or by fine.

Sec. 187a. Malicious gossip and criminal libel and slander against persons in political life

(1) Whoever publicly, in a meeting, or by the distribution of writings, commits the offense of malicious gossip against a person active in the political life of the nation from motives related to the victim's position in public life, and if the offense is likely to significantly reduce his effectiveness as a politician, imprisonment from three months to five years shall be imposed.

Sec. 189. Defamation of the memory of the dead

Whoever blackens the memory of the dead shall be punished by up to two years' imprisonment or by fine.

Source: *The Penal Code 3 of the Federal Republic of Germany* (trans. Joseph J. Darby) (London: Sweet & Maxwell Limited, 1987).

---

registration certificate was protected "symbolic speech" within the First Amendment. His argument is that the freedom of expression which the First Amendment guarantees includes all modes of "communication of ideas by conduct," and that his conduct is within this definition because he did it in "demonstration against the war and against the draft."

We cannot accept the view that an apparently limitless variety of conduct can be labeled "speech" whenever the person engaging in the conduct intends thereby to express an idea. However, even on the assumption that the alleged communicative element in O'Brien's conduct is sufficient to bring into play the First Amendment, it does not necessarily follow that the destruction of a registration certificate is constitutionally protected activity. This Court has held that when "speech" and "nonspeech" elements are combined in the same course of conduct, a sufficiently important governmental interest in regulating the nonspeech element can justify incidental limitations on First Amendment freedoms. To characterize the quality of the governmental interest which must appear, the Court has employed a variety of descriptive terms: compelling; substantial; subordinating; paramount; cogent; strong. Whatever imprecision inheres in these terms, we think it clear that a government regulation is sufficiently justified if it is within the constitutional power of the Government; if it furthers an important or substantial governmental interest; if the governmental interest is unrelated to the suppression of free expression; and if the incidental restriction on alleged First Amendment freedoms is no greater than is essential to the furtherance of that interest. We find that the 1965 Amendment to S. 12 (b)(3) of the Universal Military Training and Service Act meets all of these requirements, and consequently that O'Brien can be constitutionally convicted for violating it.

The constitutional power of Congress to raise and support armies and to make all laws necessary and proper to that end is broad and sweeping. The power of Congress to classify and conscript manpower for military service is "beyond question." Pursuant to this power, Congress may establish a system of registration for individuals liable for training and service, and may require such individuals within reason to cooperate in the registration system. The issuance of certificates indicating the registration and eligibility classification of individuals is a legitimate and substantial administrative aid in the functioning of this system. And legislation to insure the continuing availability of issued certificates serves a legitimate and substantial purpose in the system's administration.

O'Brien's argument to the contrary is necessarily premised upon his unrealistic characterization of Selective Service certificates. He essentially adopts the position that such certificates are so many pieces of paper designed to notify registrants of their registration or classification, to be retained or tossed in the wastebasket according to the convenience or taste of the registrant. Once the registrant has received notification, according to this view, there is no reason for him to retain the certificate. O'Brien notes that most of the information on a registration certificate serves no notification purpose at all; the registrant hardly needs to be told his address and physical characteristics. We agree that the registration certificate contains much information of which the registrant needs no notification. This circumstance, however, does not lead to the conclusion that the certificate serves no purpose, but that, like the classification certificate, it serves purposes in addition to initial notification. Many of these purposes would be defeated by the certificates' destruction or mutilation. Among these are:

1. The registration certificate serves as proof that the individual described thereon has registered for the draft. . . .

2. The information supplied on the certificates facilitates communication between registrants and local boards, simplifying the system and benefiting all concerned. . . .

3. Both certificates carry continual reminders that the registrant must notify his local board of any change of address, and other specified changes in his status. The smooth functioning of the system requires that local boards be continually aware of the status and whereabouts of registrants, and the destruction of certificates deprives the system of a potentially useful notice device.

4. The regulatory scheme involving Selective Service certificates includes clearly valid prohibitions against the alteration, forgery, or similar deceptive misuse of certificates. The destruction or mutilation of certificates obviously increases the difficulty of detecting and tracing abuses such as these. Further, a mutilated certificate might itself be used for deceptive purposes.

The many functions performed by Selective Service certificates establish beyond doubt that Congress has a legitimate and substantial interest in preventing their wanton and unrestrained destruction and assuring their continuing availability by punishing people who knowingly and wilfully destroy or mutilate them. And we are unpersuaded that the pre-existence of the nonpossession regulations in any way negates this interest.

In the absence of a question as to multiple punishment, it has never been suggested that there is anything improper in Congress' providing alternative statutory avenues of prosecution to assure the effective protection of one and the same interest. Here, the pre-existing avenue of prosecution was not even statutory. Regulations may be modified or revoked from time to time by administrative discretion. Certainly, the Congress may change or supplement a regulation.

Equally important, a comparison of the regulations with the 1965 Amendment indicates that they protect overlapping but not identical governmental interests, and that they reach somewhat different classes of wrongdoers. The gravamen of the offense defined by the statute is the deliberate rendering of certificates unavailable for the various purposes which they may serve. Whether registrants keep their certificates in their personal possession at all times, as required by the regulations, is of no particular concern under the 1965 Amendment, as long as they do not muti-

late or destroy the certificates so as to render them unavailable. Although as we note below we are not concerned here with the nonpossession regulations, it is not inappropriate to observe that the essential elements of nonpossession are not identical with those of mutilation or destruction. Finally, the 1965 Amendment, like S. 12 (b) which it amended, is concerned with abuses involving any issued Selective Service certificates, not only with the registrant's own certificates. The knowing destruction or mutilation of someone else's certificates would therefore violate the statute but not the nonpossession regulations.

We think it apparent that the continuing availability to each registrant of his Selective Service certificates substantially furthers the smooth and proper functioning of the system that Congress has established to raise armies. We think it also apparent that the Nation has a vital interest in having a system for raising armies that functions with maximum efficiency and is capable of easily and quickly responding to continually changing circumstances. For these reasons, the Government has a substantial interest in assuring the continuing availability of issued Selective Service certificates.

It is equally clear that the 1965 Amendment specifically protects this substantial governmental interest. We perceive no alternative means that would more precisely and narrowly assure the continuing availability of issued Selective Service certificates than a law which prohibits their willful mutilation or destruction. The 1965 Amendment prohibits such conduct and does nothing more. In other words, both the governmental interest and the operation of the 1965 Amendment are limited to the noncommunicative aspect of O'Brien's conduct. The governmental interest and the scope of the 1965 Amendment are limited to preventing harm to the smooth and efficient functioning of the Selective Service System. When O'Brien deliberately rendered unavailable his registration certificate, he willfully frustrated this governmental interest. For this noncommunicative impact of his conduct, and for nothing else, he was convicted.

The case at bar is therefore unlike one where the alleged governmental interest in regulating conduct arises in some measure because the communication allegedly integral to the conduct is itself thought to be harmful. . . .

In conclusion, we find that because of the Government's substantial interest in assuring the continuing availability of issued Selective Service certificates, because amended S. 462 (b) is an appropriately narrow means of protecting this interest and condemns only the independent noncommunicative impact of conduct within its reach, and because the noncommunicative impact of O'Brien's act of burning his registration certificate frustrated the Government's interest, a sufficient governmental interest has been shown to justify O'Brien's conviction.

O'Brien finally argues that the 1965 Amendment is unconstitutional as enacted because what he calls the "purpose" of Congress was "to suppress freedom of speech." We reject this argument because under settled principles the purpose of Congress, as O'Brien uses that term, is not a basis for declaring this legislation unconstitutional.

It is a familiar principle of constitutional law that this Court will not strike down an otherwise constitutional statute on the basis of an alleged illicit legislative motive. . . .

Inquiries into congressional motives or purposes are a hazardous matter. When the issue is simply the interpretation of legislation, the Court will look to statements by legislators for guidance as to the purpose of the legislature, because the benefit to sound decision-making in this circumstance is thought sufficient to risk the possibility of misreading Congress' purpose. It is entirely a different matter when we are asked to void a statute that is, under well-settled criteria, constitutional on its face, on the basis of what fewer than a handful of Congressmen said about it. What motivates one legislator to make a speech about a statute is not necessarily what motivates scores of others to enact it, and the stakes are sufficiently high for us to eschew guesswork. We decline to void essentially on the ground that it is unwise legislation which Congress had the undoubted power to enact and which could be reenacted in its exact form if the same or another legislator made a "wiser" speech about it.

It is so ordered.

Justice HARLAN, concurring.

* * *

I wish to make explicit my understanding that this passage does not foreclose consideration of First Amendment claims in those rare instances when an "incidental" restriction upon expression, imposed by a regulation which furthers an "important or substantial" governmental interest and satisfies the Court's other criteria, in practice has the effect of entirely preventing a "speaker" from reaching a significant audience with whom he could not otherwise lawfully communicate. This is not such a case, since O'Brien manifestly could have conveyed his message in many ways other than by burning his draft card.

Notes and Queries

1. The Court lays down a four-part test for determining when speech combined with conduct can be suppressed. The governmental interest must be *substantial*; the conduct involved must be *incidental*; and it must be no greater than *essential* to further the government's interest. How does the Court determine the meaning of the italicized terms? Can these judgments be anything but subjective? The Court admits that the term "substantial" is imprecise. Does this imprecision account for the fact that the Court weighed in on the side of the federal statute?

2. The majority in *O'Brien* insisted that it would not inquire into legislative motive. What reasons did the majority offer for this refusal? Are those reasons grounded in a particular vision of judicial power? Are there times when a judicial inquiry into the motives of other actors would be appropriate?

Cohen v. California
403 U.S. 15, 91 S.Ct. 1780, 29 L.Ed.2d 284 (1971)

Paul Robert Cohen was convicted in the Los Angeles Municipal Court for wearing a jacket, while in the corridor of a county courthouse, emblazoned with the words, "Fuck the Draft." He was charged under a provision of California's Penal Code which prohibits "maliciously and willfully disturb[ing] the peace or quiet of any neighborhood or person . . . by . . . offensive conduct." California's Supreme Court denied review. Opinion of the Court: *Harlan*, Douglas, Brennan, Stewart, Marshall, White. Dissenting opinion: *Blackmun*, Burger, Black.

Justice HARLAN delivered the opinion of the Court.

In order to lay hands on the precise issue which this case involves, it is useful first to canvass various matters which this record does not present.

The conviction quite clearly rests upon the asserted offensiveness of the words Cohen used to convey his message to the public. The only "conduct" which the State sought to punish is the fact of communication. Thus, we deal here with a conviction resting solely upon "speech," not upon any separately identifiable conduct which allegedly was intended by Cohen to be perceived by others as expressive of particular views but which, on its face, does not necessarily convey any message and hence arguably could be regulated without effectively repressing Cohen's ability to express himself. Further, the State certainly lacks power to punish Cohen for the underlying content of the message the inscription conveyed. At least so long as there is no showing of an intent to incite disobedience to or disruption of the draft, Cohen could not, consistently with the First and Fourteenth Amendments, be punished for asserting the evident position on the inutility or immorality of the draft his jacket reflected.

Comparative Note 12.6

The constitutional principles of the Basic Law embrace the respect and protection of human dignity. The free human person and his dignity are the highest values of the constitutional order. The state in all of its forms is obliged to respect and defend it. This is based on the conception of man as a spiritual-moral being endowed with the freedom to determine and develop himself. This freedom within the meaning of the Basic law is not that of an isolated and self-regarding individual but rather [that] of a person related to and bound by the community. In the light of this community-boundedness it cannot be "in principle unlimited." The individual must allow those limits on his freedom of action that the legislature deems necessary in the interest of the community's social life. . . .

SOURCE: *Life Imprisonment Case* (1977), in Kommers, *Constitutional Jurisprudence*, 307–8.

Appellant's conviction, then, rests squarely upon his exercise of the "freedom of speech" protected from arbitrary governmental interference by the Constitution and can be justified, if at all, only as a valid regulation of the manner in which he exercised that freedom, not as a permissible prohibition on the substantive message it conveys. This does not end the inquiry, of course, for the First and Fourteenth Amendments have never been thought to give absolute protection to every individual to speak whenever or wherever he pleases, or to use any form of address in any circumstances that he chooses. In this vein, too, however, we think it important to note that several issues typically associated with such problems are not presented here.

In the first place, Cohen was tried under a statute applicable throughout the entire State. Any attempt to support this conviction on the ground that the statute seeks to preserve an appropriately decorous atmosphere in the courthouse where Cohen was arrested must fail in the absence of any language in the statute that would have put appellant on notice that certain kinds of otherwise permissible speech or conduct would nevertheless, under California law, not be tolerated in certain places. No fair reading of the phrase "offensive conduct" can be said sufficiently to inform the ordinary person that distinctions between certain locations are thereby created.

In the second place, as it comes to us, this case cannot be said to fall within those relatively few categories of instances where prior decisions have established the power of government to deal more comprehensively with certain forms of individual expression simply upon a showing that such a form was employed. This is not, for example, an obscenity case. Whatever else may be necessary to give rise to the States' broader power to prohibit obscene expression, such expression must be, in some significant way, erotic. It cannot plausibly be maintained that this vulgar allusion to the Selective Service System would conjure up such psychic stimulation in anyone likely to be confronted with Cohen's crudely defaced jacket.

This Court has also held that the States are free to ban the simple use, without a demonstration of additional justifying circumstances, of so-called "fighting words," those personally abusive epithets which, when addressed to the ordinary citizen, are, as a matter of common knowledge, inherently likely to provoke violent reaction *Chaplinsky v. New Hampshire* (1942). While the four-letter word displayed by Cohen in relation to the draft is not uncommonly employed in a personally provocative fashion, in this instance it was clearly not "directed to the person of the hearer." No individual actually or likely to be present could reasonably have regarded the words on appellant's jacket as a direct personal insult. Nor do we have here an instance of the exercise of the State's police power to prevent a speaker from intentionally provoking a given group to hostile reaction. There is, as noted above, no showing that anyone who saw Cohen was in fact violently aroused or that appellant intended such a result.

Finally, in arguments before this Court much has been made of the claim that Cohen's distasteful mode of expression was thrust upon unwilling or unsuspecting viewers, and that the State might therefore legitimately act as it did in order to protect the sensitive from otherwise unavoidable exposure to appellant's crude form of protest. Of course, the mere presumed presence of unwitting listeners or viewers does not serve automatically to justify curtailing all speech capable of giving offense. While this Court has recognized that government may properly act in many situations to prohibit intrusion into the privacy of the home of unwelcome views and ideas which cannot be totally banned from the public dialogue, we have at the same time consistently stressed that "we are often 'captives' outside the sanctuary of the home and subject to objectionable speech." The ability of government, consonant with the Constitution, to shut off discourse solely to protect others from hearing it is, in other words, dependent upon a showing that substantial privacy interests are being invaded in an essentially intolerable manner. Any broader view of this authority would effectively empower a majority to silence dissidents simply as a matter of personal predilections.

In this regard, persons confronted with Cohen's jacket were in a quite different posture than, say, those subjected to the raucous emissions of sound trucks blaring outside their residences. Those in the Los Angeles courthouse could effectively avoid further bombardment of their sensibilities simply by averting their eyes. And, while it may be that one has a more substantial claim to a recognizable privacy interest when walking through a courthouse corridor than, for example, strolling through Central Park, surely it is nothing like the interest in being free from unwanted expression in the confines of one's own home. Given the subtlety and complexity of the factors involved, if Cohen's "speech" was otherwise entitled to constitutional protection, we do not think the fact that some unwilling "listeners" in a public building may have been briefly exposed to it can serve to justify this breach of the peace conviction where, as here, there was no evidence that persons powerless to avoid appellant's conduct did in fact object to it, and where that portion of the statute upon which Cohen's conviction rests evinces no concern, either on its face or as construed by the California courts, with the special plight of the captive auditor, but, instead, indiscriminately sweeps within its prohibitions all "offensive conduct" that disturbs "any neighborhood or person."

Against this background, the issue flushed by this case stands out in bold relief. It is whether California can excise, as "offensive conduct," one particular scurrilous epithet from the public discourse, either upon the theory of the court below that its use is inherently likely to cause violent reaction or upon a more general assertion that the States, acting as guardians of public morality, may properly remove this offensive word from the public vocabulary.

The rationale of the California court is plainly untenable. At most it reflects an "undifferentiated fear or apprehension of disturbance [which] is not enough to overcome the right to freedom of expression." We have been shown no evidence that substantial numbers of citizens are standing ready to strike out physically at whoever may assault their sensibilities with execrations like that uttered by Cohen. There may be some persons about with such lawless and violent proclivities, but that is an insufficient base upon which to erect, consistently with constitutional val-

ues, a governmental power to force persons who wish to ventilate their dissident views into avoiding particular forms of expression. The argument amounts to little more than the self-defeating proposition that to avoid physical censorship of one who has not sought to provoke such a response by a hypothetical coterie of the violent and lawless, the States may more appropriately effectuate that censorship themselves.

Admittedly, it is not so obvious that the First and Fourteenth Amendments must be taken to disable the States from punishing public utterance of this unseemly expletive in order to maintain what they regard as a suitable level of discourse within the body politic. We think, however, that examination and reflection will reveal the shortcomings of a contrary viewpoint.

At the outset, we cannot overemphasize that, in our judgment, most situations where the State has a justifiable interest in regulating speech will fall within one or more of the various established exceptions, discussed above but not applicable here, to the usual rule that governmental bodies may not prescribe the form or content of individual expression. Equally important to our conclusion is the constitutional backdrop against which our decision must be made. The constitutional right of free expression is powerful medicine in a society as diverse and populous as ours. It is designed and intended to remove governmental restraints from the arena of public discussion, putting the decision as to what views shall be voiced largely into the hands of each of us, in the hope that use of such freedom will ultimately produce a more capable citizenry and more perfect polity and in the belief that no other approach would comport with the premise of individual dignity and choice upon which our political system rests.

To many, the immediate consequence of this freedom may often appear to be only verbal tumult, discord, and even offensive utterance. These are, however, within established limits, in truth necessary side effects of the broader enduring values which the process of open debate permits us to achieve. That the air may at times seem filled with verbal cacophony is, in this sense not a sign of weakness but of strength. We cannot lose sight of the fact that, in what otherwise might seem a trifling and annoying instance of individual distasteful abuse of a privilege, these fundamental societal values are truly implicated. That is why "wholly neutral futilities . . . come under the protection of free speech as fully as do Keats' poems or Donne's sermons," and why "so long as the means are peaceful, the communication need not meet standards of acceptability."

Against this perception of the constitutional policies involved, we discern certain more particularized considerations that peculiarly call for reversal of this conviction. First, the principle contended for by the State seems inherently boundless. How is one to distinguish this from any other offensive word? Surely the State has no right to cleanse public debate to the point where it is grammatically palatable to the most squeamish among us. Yet no readily ascertainable general principle exists for stopping short of that result were we to affirm the judgment below. For, while the particular four-letter word being litigated here is perhaps more distasteful than most others of its genre, it is nevertheless often true that one man's vulgarity is another's lyric. Indeed, we think it is largely because governmental officials cannot make principled distinctions in this area that the Constitution leaves matters of taste and style so largely to the individual.

Additionally, we cannot overlook the fact, because it is well illustrated by the episode involved here, that much linguistic expression serves a dual communicative function: it conveys not only ideas capable of relatively precise, detached explication, but otherwise inexpressible emotions as well. In fact, words are often chosen as much for their emotive as their cognitive force. We cannot sanction the view that the Constitution, while solicitous of the cognitive content of individual speech, has little or no regard for that emotive function which, practically speaking, may often be the more important element of the overall message sought to be communicated. Indeed, as Mr. Justice Frankfurter has said, "one of the prerogatives of American citizenship is the right to criticize public men and measures—and that means not only informed and responsible criticism but the freedom to speak foolishly and without moderation."

Finally, and in the same vein, we cannot indulge the facile assumption that one can forbid particular words without also running a substantial risk of suppressing ideas in the process. Indeed, governments might soon seize upon the censorship of particular words as a convenient guise for banning the expression of unpopular views. We have been able, as noted above, to discern little social benefit that might result from running the risk of opening the door to such grave results.

It is, in sum, our judgment that, absent a more particularized and compelling reason for its actions, the State may not, consistently with the First and Fourteenth Amendments, make the simple public display here involved of this single four-letter expletive a criminal offense. Because that is the only arguably sustainable rationale for the conviction here at issue, the judgment below must be

Reversed.

Justice BLACKMUN, with whom THE CHIEF JUSTICE and Mr. Justice BLACK join.

Cohen's absurd and immature antic, in my view, was mainly conduct and little speech. . . . Further, the case appears to me to be well within the sphere of *Chaplinsky v. New Hampshire*, where Mr. Justice Murphy, a known champion of First Amendment freedoms, wrote for a unanimous bench. As a consequence, this Court's agonizing over First Amendment values seems misplaced and unnecessary.

Notes and Queries

1. Why did the phrase on Cohen's jacket *not* constitute "fighting words"? Why did it not constitute "obscenity"?

2. In his criticism of *Cohen*, Archibald Cox—the Harvard Law School Professor who represented the *New York Times* in the Pentagon Papers Case (*New York Times Company v. United States*)—wrote:

> Surely the State has power to regulate the decorum of judicial proceedings, and I would suppose that the power includes the preservation of dignity by barring words spoken to be offensive though not relevant to the issues. The State may do this because dignity is conducive to reasoned justice and also builds respect. . . . What then about public discourse? Is there no State interest in the level at which public discourse is conducted? Granting that the State can do little to protect moral and aesthetic sensibilities or to raise the level of public discourse, does it follow that the State must allow exhibitionists and other persons trading upon our lower prurient instincts to inflict themselves upon the public consciousness and dull its sensibilities? One wonders, too, whether the Supreme Court in extending the protection of the First Amendment to sheer vulgarity, useful only in its ability to shock, does not give vulgarities an imprimatur which contributes to the lowering of public discourse. The moral influence of the Supreme Court's opinions reaches far beyond the limits of its decrees. May not its amoral influence be similarly extended? *The Role of the Supreme Court in American Government* (Oxford University Press, 1976), 47–48.

Do Cox's comments represent a liberal argument against the result in *Cohen*?

3. Do you agree with Justice Harlan's statement that "one man's vulgarity is another's lyric"? Is this moral relativism in the extreme? Are there no objective standards for determining what Professor Cox describes as "offensive" language?

4. Justice Harlan also noted: "That the air may at times seem filled with verbal cacophony is not a sign of weakness, but of strength." Is this the image of democracy that

Americans would wish to project in their constitutional law? Does "verbal cacophony" bear any relation at all to Madison's notion of a deliberative democracy or to Holmes' truth-discovery function of the marketplace of ideas?

5. What theory of liberty is at the root of *Cohen?* Do the extracts in Comparative Notes 12.6 and 12.7 incorporate a different vision of liberty?

New York Times Co. v. Sullivan

376 U.S. 254, 84 S.Ct. 710, 11 L.Ed.2d 686 (1964)

In March 1960 the *New York Times* ran an advertisement, paid for by civil rights activists and signed by 68 prominent citizens, which alleged police misconduct during civil rights protests in Montgomery, Alabama. The advertisement contained several inaccuracies and L. B. Sullivan, an elected commissioner of the City of Montgomery, sued the *Times* and four of the signers for libel. While Sullivan's name did not appear in the ad, he claimed that the charges were directed at him as the official charged with supervision of the police department. The jury awarded Sullivan $500,000 in damages. The judgment was affirmed by the Supreme Court of Alabama. Opinion of the Court: *Brennan*, Warren, Clark, Harlan, Stewart, White. Concurring opinions: *Black, Goldberg*, Douglas.

Justice BRENNAN delivered the opinion of the Court.

We are required in this case to determine for the first time the extent to which the constitutional protections for speech and press limit a State's power to award damages in a libel action brought by a public official against critics of his official conduct. . . .

Under Alabama law as applied in this case, a publication is "libelous per se" if the words "tend to injure a person . . . in his reputation" or to "bring [him] into public contempt"; the trial court stated that the standard was met if the words are such as to "injure him in his public office, or impute misconduct to him in his office, or want of official integrity, or want of fidelity to a public trust. . . ." Once "libel per se" has been established, the defendant has no defense as to stated facts unless he can persuade the jury that they were true in all their particulars. . . . Unless he can discharge the burden of proving truth, general damages are presumed, and may be awarded without proof of pecuniary injury. . . .

The question before us is whether this rule of liability, as applied to an action brought by a public official against critics of his official conduct, abridges the freedom of speech and of the press that is guaranteed by the First and Fourteenth Amendments.

. . . [W]e consider this case against the background of a profound national commitment to the principle that debate on public issues should be uninhibited, robust, and wide-open, and that it may well include vehement, caustic, and sometimes unpleasantly sharp attacks on government and public officials. The present advertisement, as an expression of grievance and protest on one of the major public issues of our time, would seem clearly to qualify for the constitutional protection. The question is whether it forfeits that protection by the falsity of some of its factual statements and by its alleged defamation of respondent.

Authoritative interpretations of the First Amendment guarantees have consistently refused to recognize an exception for any test of truth—whether administered by judges, juries, or administrative officials—and especially one that puts the burden of proving truth on the speaker. The constitutional protection does not turn upon "the truth, popularity, or social utility of the ideas and beliefs which are offered." . . . [The Court has recognized] [t]hat erroneous statement is inevitable in free debate, and that it must be protected if the freedoms of expression are to have the "breathing space" that they "need . . . to survive." . . .

Injury to official reputation affords no more warrant for repressing speech that would otherwise be free than does factual error. Where judicial officers are involved, this Court has held that concern for the dignity and reputation of the courts does not justify the punishment as criminal contempt of criticism of the judge or his decision. This is true even though the utterance contains "half-truths" and "misinformation." Such repression can be justified, if at all, only by a clear and present danger of the obstruction of justice. If judges are to be treated as "men of fortitude, able to thrive in a hardy climate," surely the same must be true of other government officials, such as elected city commissioners. Criticism of their official conduct does not lose its constitutional protection merely because it is effective criticism and hence diminishes their official reputations.

If neither factual error nor defamatory content suffices to remove the constitutional shield from criticism of official conduct, the combination of the two elements is no less inadequate. This is the lesson to be drawn from the

Comparative Note 12.7

[Heinrich Boll, a renowned author, brought suit against a well-known commentator for telling a television audience that the author had helped to lay the groundwork for political terrorism in Germany. He quoted Boll as having characterized the state as a "dung heap defended with ratlike rage by the remnants of rotten power." Boll claimed he had not used these words and that his honor had been impugned by the broadcast.]

The attacks upon the complainant in the commentary were of such a nature as to impair his constitutionally guaranteed general right to an intimate sphere. Among other things this right includes personal honor and the right to one's own words; it also protects the bearer of these rights against having statements attributed to him which he did not make and which impair his self-defined claim to social recognition.

The individual may also invoke his right to personality to the extent that his statements are falsified, distorted, or rendered inaccurate. . . . As the Federal Supreme Court explained, a quotation does not involve the discussion of the critic's subjective opinion but rather a fact for which the person being criticized must be held accountable. For this reason a quotation used as evidence of criticism is an especially potent weapon in the battle of opinion: Unlike the easily recognizable

expression of an opinion this particular quotation is perceived as a fact, with the same power [of a fact] to convince and persuade. If the quotation is incorrect, distorted, or false, then it encroaches that much more upon the speaker's right to an intimate sphere, because he is thus led onto the battlefield as a witness against himself.

Because value judgments are so much at issue in public discussion, freedom of speech must be allowed in the interest of furthering the formation of public opinion and without regard to the content of individual judgments. But this protection does not extend to false statements of fact. Incorrect information does not merit protection under the rubric of freedom of opinion, because it does not contribute to the constitutionally guaranteed process of forming public opinion.

. . . [Yet] the duty to tell the truth cannot be enforced in such a way as to jeopardize the process of forming public opinion. An exaggerated emphasis upon the duty to tell the truth . . . could restrict and even cripple the media by preventing them . . . from fulfilling their function . . . But neither democracy nor the task of forming public opinion will suffer if the media are required to quote [someone] correctly.

SOURCE: *Boll Case* (1980), in Kommers, *Constitutional Jurisprudence*, 421–22.

---

great controversy over the Sedition Act of 1798, which first crystallized a national awareness of the central meaning of the First Amendment. That statute made it a crime, punishable by a $5,000 fine and five years in prison, "if any person shall write, print, utter or publish . . . any false, scandalous and malicious writing or writings against the government of the United States, or either house of the Congress . . . , or the President . . . , with intent to defame . . . or to bring them, or either of them, into contempt or disrepute; or to excite against them, or either or any of them, the hatred of the good people of the United States." The Act allowed the defendant the defense of truth, and provided that the jury were to be judges both of the law and the facts. Despite these qualifications, the Act was vigorously condemned as unconstitutional in an attack joined in by Jefferson and Madison. . . .

Although the Sedition Act was never tested in this Court, the attack upon its validity has carried the day in the court of history. Fines levied in its prosecution were repaid by

Act of Congress on the ground that it was unconstitutional. . . .

There is no force in respondent's argument that the constitutional limitations implicit in the history of the Sedition Act apply only to Congress and not to the States. It is true that the First Amendment was originally addressed only to action by the Federal Government, and that Jefferson, for one, while denying the power of Congress "to control the freedom of the press," recognized such a power in the States. But this distinction was eliminated with the adoption of the Fourteenth Amendment and the application to the States of the First Amendment's restrictions.

What a State may not constitutionally bring about by means of a criminal statute is likewise beyond the reach of its civil law of libel. The fear of damage awards under a rule such as that invoked by the Alabama courts here may be markedly more inhibiting than the fear of prosecution under a criminal statute. Alabama, for example, has a criminal libel law which subjects to prosecution "any person who speaks, writes, or prints of and concerning another any accusation falsely and maliciously importing the commission by such person of a felony, or any other indictable offense involving moral turpitude," and which allows as punishment upon conviction a fine not exceeding $500 and a prison sentence of six months. Presumably a person charged with violation of this statute enjoys ordinary criminal-law safeguards such as the requirements of an indictment and of proof beyond a reasonable doubt. These safeguards are not available to the defendant in a civil action. The judgment awarded in this case—without the need for any proof of actual pecuniary loss—was one thousand times greater than the maximum fine provided by the Alabama criminal statute, and one hundred times greater than that provided by the Sedition Act. . . . Whether or not a newspaper can survive a succession of such judgments, the pall of fear and timidity imposed upon those who would give voice to public criticism is an atmosphere in which the First Amendment freedoms cannot survive. Plainly the Alabama law of civil libel is "a form of regulation that creates hazards to protected freedoms markedly greater than those that attend reliance upon the criminal law."

The state rule of law is not saved by its allowance of the defense of truth. . . . A rule compelling the critic of official conduct to guarantee the truth of all his factual assertions—and to do so on pain of libel judgments virtually unlimited in amount—leads to a comparable "self-censorship." Allowance of the defense of truth, with the burden of proving it on the defendant, does not mean that only false speech will be deterred. Even courts accepting this defense as an adequate safeguard have recognized the difficulties of adducing legal proofs that the alleged libel was true in all its factual particulars. Under such a rule, would-be critics of official conduct may be deterred from voicing their criticism, even though it is believed to be true and even though it is in fact true, because of doubt whether it can be proved in court or fear of the expense of having to do so. They tend to make only statements which "steer far wider of the unlawful zone." The rule thus dampens the vigor and limits the variety of public debate. It is inconsistent with the First and Fourteenth Amendments.

The constitutional guarantees require, we think, a federal rule that prohibits a public official from recovering damages for a defamatory falsehood relating to his official conduct unless he proves that the statement was made with "actual malice"—that is, with knowledge that it was false or with reckless disregard of whether it was false or not. . . .

We hold today that the Constitution delimits a State's power to award damages for libel in actions brought by public officials against critics of their official conduct. Since this is such an action, the rule requiring proof of actual malice is applicable. . . .

Applying these standards, we consider that the proof presented to show actual malice lacks the convincing clarity which the constitutional standard demands, and hence that it would not constitutionally sustain the judgment for respondent under the proper rule of law. The case of the individual petitioners requires little discussion. Even assuming that they could constitutionally be found to have authorized the use of their names on the advertisement, there was no evidence whatever that they were aware of any erroneous statements or were in any way reckless in that regard. The judgment against them is thus without constitutional support.

As to the *Times*, we similarly conclude that the facts do not support a finding of actual malice. . . .

Reversed and remanded.

Justice BLACK, with whom Justice DOUGLAS joins, concurring.

I concur in reversing this half-million-dollar judgment against the New York Times Company and the four individual defendants. In reversing the Court holds that "the Constitution delimits a State's power to award damages for libel in actions brought by public officials against critics of their official conduct." I base my vote to reverse on the belief that the First and Fourteenth Amendments not merely "delimit" a State's power to award damages to "public officials against critics of their official conduct" but completely prohibit a State from exercising such a power. The Court goes on to hold that a State can subject such critics to damages if "actual malice" can be proved against them. "Malice," even as defined by the Court, is an elusive, abstract concept, hard to prove and hard to disprove. The requirement that malice be proved provides at best an evanescent protection for the right critically to discuss public affairs and certainly does not measure up to the sturdy safeguard embodied in the First Amendment. Unlike the Court, therefore, I vote to reverse exclusively on the ground that the *Times* and the individual defendants had an absolute, unconditional constitutional right to publish in the *Times* advertisement their criticisms of the Montgomery agencies and officials. . . .

Notes and Queries

1. Does the value of truth play any role in the right to criticize public officials? What are the implications of this for political debate in the United States?

2. Do you agree with Justice Brennan that this country

has had a "profound national commitment to the principle that debate on public issues should be uninhibited, robust, and wide-open"? Is this an accurate description of American public life in the 1990s?

3. Justice Brennan notes that "erroneous" statements are inevitable in free debate. But what is wrong about requiring journalists and others to check their factual statements about politicians—and, by implication, other public figures—before they publish, broadcast, or otherwise disseminate such statements? Brennan notes that anything other than the malice rule would cause journalists to en-

gage in self-censorship. Is this an assumption or an empirical fact?

4. What vision of society and the polity is at the root of the Court's opinion? Does the excerpt in Comparative Note 12.7 espouse a different vision of the polity?

5. Germany's Federal Constitutional Court has repeatedly declared that human dignity is the core value of the Basic Law. Similarly, it has been suggested that the core value of American constitutionalism is liberty. Do these contrasting values explain the difference between the American and German outcomes?

The Sedition Act of 1798

An Act in addition to the act, entitled "An act for the punishment of certain crimes against the United States."

SEC. 1 Be it enacted . . . , That if any persons shall unlawfully combine or conspire together, with intent to oppose any measure or measures of the government of the United States, which are or shall be directed by proper authority, or to impede the operation of any law of the United States, or to intimidate or prevent any person holding a place or office in or under the government of the United States, from undertaking, performing or executing his trust or duty; and if any person or persons, with intent as aforesaid, shall counsel, advise or attempt to procure any insurrection, riot, unlawful assembly, or combination, whether such conspiracy, threatening, counsel, advice, or attempt shall have the proposed effect or not, he or they shall be deemed guilty of a high misdemeanor, and on conviction, before any court of the United States having jurisdiction thereof, shall be punished by a fine not exceeding five thousand dollars, and by imprisonment during a term not less than six months nor exceeding five years; and further, at the discretion of the court may be holden to find sureties for his good behaviour in such sum, and for such time, as the said court may direct.

SEC. 2. That if any person shall write, print, utter, or publish, or shall cause or procure to be written, printed, uttered or published, or shall knowingly and willingly assist or aid in writing, printing, uttering or publishing any

false, scandalous and malicious writing or writings against the government of the United States, or either house of the Congress of the United States, or the President of the United States, with intent to defame the said government, or either house of the said Congress, or the said President, or to bring them, or either of them, into contempt or disrepute; or to excite against them, or either or any of them, the hatred of the good people of the United States, or to excite any unlawful combinations therein, for opposing or resisting any law of the United States, or any act of the President of the United States, done in pursuance of any such law, or of the powers in him vested by the constitution of the United States, or to resist, oppose, or defeat any such law or act, or to aid, encourage or abet any hostile designs of any foreign nation against the United States, their people or government, then such person, being thereof convicted before any court of the United States having jurisdiction thereof, shall be punished by a fine not exceeding two thousand dollars, and by imprisonment not exceeding two years.

SEC. 3. That if any person shall be prosecuted under this act, for the writing or publishing any libel aforesaid, it shall be lawful for the defendant, upon the trial of the cause, to give in evidence in his defence, the truth of the matter contained in the publication charged as a libel. And the jury who shall try the cause, shall have a right to determine the law and the fact, under the direction of the court, as in other cases.

SEC. 4. That this act shall continue to be in force until March 3, 1801, and no longer. . . .

Texas v. Johnson
491 U.S. 397, 109 S.Ct. 2533, 105 L.Ed.2d 342 (1989)

During the 1984 Republican National Convention, Gregory Lee Johnson burned an American flag in front of Dal-

las City Hall. The flag burning was part of a large demonstration protesting policies of the Reagan administration and several Dallas-based corporations. During the course of the protest, Johnson doused the flag with kerosene and set the flag on fire as demonstrators chanted,

Comparative Note 12.8

[Section 90a (1) of Germany's Criminal Code punishes anyone who "disparages the colors, the flag . . . or the anthem of the Federal Republic of Germany or one of its regional states." In the case from which the extracts are drawn, a bookstore owner sold an antimilitary tract which included a photo montage showing a soldier urinating on Germany's national flag.]

[The conviction] violates the freedom of art within the meaning of Article 5 (3). This decision, however, does not actually stand in the way of punishing someone [who actually disparages the flag within the meaning of Section 90]. As a free state, the Federal Republic of Germany relies on the identification of its citizens with the basic values that the flag represents. . . . [The] state's colors laid down in Article 22 [of the Basic Law] stand for the free democratic constitutional order.

. . . The flag serves as an important symbol of [political] integration by means of the values it represents. Its disparagement can thus impair the state's essential au-

thority. [But these] state symbols enjoy constitutional protection only to the extent that they represent the *fundamental values* of the Federal Republic [emphasis added]. . . .

In the light of Article 5 (3), however, the protection of these symbols must not result in immunizing the state [or its military establishment] against criticism or even disapproval.

[The Federal Constitutional Court faulted the lower court for misinterpreting the photo collage as an attack on the flag and for failing adequately to balance the value of artistic freedom against the value protected by Sec. 90a.]

. . . The collage is [really] to be classified as a caricature and thus as a satiric portrayal. . . . [R]ather, the caricature expresses primarily an anti-militaristic . . . tendency . . . and thereby disapproval, if not abhorrence, of military service.

SOURCE: *Flag Desecration Case* (Germany, 1990), 81 BverfGe 278.

"America, the red, white, and blue, we spit on you." Johnson was later convicted of violating a Texas law against the desecration of venerated objects and sentenced to one year in prison and a $2,000 fine. Although the Texas Court of Criminal Appeals ruled that the desecration statute could be upheld as a legitimate means of protecting the public peace, it held that the statute as applied violated the free speech guarantee of the First Amendment. Opinion of the Court: *Brennan*, Marshall, Blackmun, Scalia, Kennedy. Concurring opinion: *Kennedy*. Dissenting opinions: *Rehnquist*, White, O'Connor, *Stevens*.

Justice BRENNAN delivered the opinion of the Court.

After publicly burning an American flag as a means of political protest, Gregory Lee Johnson was convicted of desecrating a flag in violation of Texas law. This case presents the question whether his conviction is consistent with the First Amendment. We hold that it is not. . . .

Johnson was convicted of flag desecration for burning the flag rather than for uttering insulting words. This fact somewhat complicates our consideration of his conviction under the First Amendment. We must first determine whether Johnson's burning of the flag constituted expressive conduct, permitting him to invoke the First Amendment in challenging his conviction. If his conduct was

expressive, we next decide whether the State's regulation is related to the suppression of free expression. If the State's regulation is not related to expression, then the less stringent standard we announced in *United States v. O'Brien* for regulations of noncommunicative conduct controls. . . . If it is, then we are outside of *O'Brien's* test, and we must ask whether this interest justifies Johnson's conviction under a more demanding standard. A third possibility is that the State's asserted interest is simply not implicated on these facts, and in that event the interest drops out of the picture.

The First Amendment literally forbids the abridgment only of "speech," but we have long recognized that its protection does not end at the spoken or written word. While we have rejected "the view that an apparently limitless variety of conduct can be labeled 'speech' whenever the person engaging in the conduct intends thereby to express an idea," we have acknowledged that conduct may be "sufficiently imbued with elements of communication to fall within the scope of the First and Fourteenth Amendments."

In deciding whether particular conduct possesses sufficient communicative elements to bring the First Amendment into play, we have asked whether "[a]n intent to convey a particularized message was present, and [whether] the likelihood was great that the message would be understood by those who viewed it." Hence, we have recognized the expressive nature of students' wearing of black armbands to protest American military involvement in Vietnam; of a sit-in by blacks in a "whites only" area to protest segregation; of the wearing of American military uniforms in a dramatic presentation criticizing American involvement in Vietnam; and of picketing about a wide variety of causes.

Especially pertinent to this case are our decisions recognizing the communicative nature of conduct relating to flags. Attaching a peace sign to the flag; refusing to salute the flag; and displaying a red flag, we have held, all may find shelter under the First Amendment. That we have had little difficulty identifying an expressive element in conduct relating to flags should not be surprising. The very purpose of a national flag is to serve as a symbol of our country; it is, one might say, "the one visible manifestation of two hundred years of nationhood." . . . Pregnant with expressive content, the flag as readily signifies this Nation as does the combination of letters found in "America."

The State of Texas conceded for purposes of its oral argument in this case that Johnson's conduct was expressive conduct, and this concession seems to us as prudent as was Washington's in *Spence*. Johnson burned an American flag as part—indeed, as the culmination—of a political demonstration that coincided with the convening of the Republican Party and its renomination of Ronald Reagan for President. The expressive, overtly political nature of this conduct was both intentional and overwhelmingly apparent. At his trial, Johnson explained his reasons for burning the flag as follows: "The American Flag was burned as Ronald Reagan was being renominated as President. And a more powerful statement of symbolic speech, whether you agree with it or not, couldn't have been made at that time. It's quite a just position [juxtaposition]. We had new patriotism and no patriotism." In these circumstances, Johnson's burning of the flag was conduct "sufficiently imbued with elements of communication" to implicate the First Amendment.

The government generally has a freer hand in restricting expressive conduct than it has in restricting the written or spoken word. It may not, however, proscribe particular conduct because it has expressive elements. "[W]hat might be termed the more generalized guarantee of freedom of expression makes the communicative nature of conduct an inadequate basis for singling out that conduct for proscription. A law directed at the communicative nature of conduct must, like a law directed at speech itself, be justified by the substantial showing of need that the First Amendment requires." It is, in short, not simply the verbal

or nonverbal nature of the expression, but the governmental interest at stake, that helps to determine whether a restriction on that expression is valid.

Thus, although we have recognized that where "'speech' and 'nonspeech' elements are combined in the same course of conduct, a sufficiently important governmental interest in regulating the nonspeech element can justify incidental limitations on First Amendment freedoms," we have limited the applicability of *O'Brien's* relatively lenient standard to those cases in which "the governmental interest is unrelated to the suppression of free expression." In stating, moreover, that *O'Brien's* test "in the last analysis is little, if any, different from the standard applied to time, place, or manner restrictions," we have highlighted the requirement that the governmental interest in question be unconnected to expression in order to come under *O'Brien's* less demanding rule.

In order to decide whether *O'Brien's* test applies here, therefore, we must decide whether Texas has asserted an interest in support of Johnson's conviction that is unrelated to the suppression of expression. If we find that an interest asserted by the State is simply not implicated on the facts before us, we need not ask whether *O'Brien's* test applies. The State offers two separate interests to justify this conviction: preventing breaches of the peace and preserving the flag as a symbol of nationhood and national unity. We hold that the first interest is not implicated on this record and that the second is related to the suppression of expression.

Texas claims that its interest in preventing breaches of the peace justifies Johnson's conviction for flag desecration. However, no disturbance of the peace actually occurred or threatened to occur because of Johnson's burning of the flag. Although the State stresses the disruptive behavior of the protesters during their march toward City Hall, it admits that "no actual breach of the peace occurred at the time of the flag burning or in response to the flag burning." The State's emphasis on the protesters' disorderly actions prior to arriving at City Hall is not only somewhat surprising given that no charges were brought on the basis of this conduct, but it also fails to show that a disturbance of the peace was a likely reaction to Johnson's conduct. The only evidence offered by the State at trial to show the reaction to Johnson's actions was the testimony of several persons who had been seriously offended by the flag burning.

The State's position, therefore, amounts to a claim that an audience that takes serious offense at particular expression is necessarily likely to disturb the peace and that the expression may be prohibited on this basis. Our precedents do not countenance such a presumption. On the contrary, they recognize that a principal "function of free speech under our system of government is to invite dispute. It may indeed best serve its high purpose when it induces a condition of unrest, creates dissatisfaction with conditions as they are, or even stirs people to anger." It would be odd indeed to conclude both that "if it is the speaker's opinion that gives offense, that consequence is a reason for according it constitutional protection," *and* that the government may ban the expression of certain disagreeable ideas on the unsupported presumption that their very disagreeableness will provoke violence.

Thus, we have not permitted the government to assume that every expression of a provocative idea will incite a riot, but have instead required careful consideration of the actual circumstances surrounding such expression, asking whether the expression "is directed to inciting or producing imminent lawless action and is likely to incite or produce such action." *Brandenburg v. Ohio* (reviewing circumstances surrounding rally and speeches by Ku Klux Klan). To accept Texas' arguments that it need only demonstrate "the potential for a breach of the peace," and that every flag burning necessarily possesses that potential, would be to eviscerate our holding in *Brandenburg.* This we decline to do.

Nor does Johnson's expressive conduct fall within that small class of "fighting words" that are "likely to provoke the average person to retaliation, and thereby cause a breach of the peace" *Chaplinsky v. New Hampshire* (1942). No reasonable onlooker would have regarded Johnson's generalized expression of dissatisfaction with the policies of the Federal Government as a direct personal insult or an invitation to exchange fisticuffs.

We thus conclude that the State's interest in maintaining order is not implicated on these facts. The State need not worry that our holding will disable it from preserving the peace. We do not suggest that the First Amendment forbids a State to prevent "imminent lawless action." And, in fact, Texas already has a statute specifically prohibiting breaches of the peace, which tends to confirm that Texas need not punish this flag desecration in order to keep the peace.

The State also asserts an interest in preserving the flag as a symbol of nationhood and national unity. In *Spence,* we acknowledged that the government's interest in preserving the flag's special symbolic value "is directly related to expression in the context of activity" such as affixing a peace symbol to a flag. We are equally persuaded that this interest is related to expression in the case of Johnson's burning of the flag. The State, apparently, is concerned that such conduct will lead people to believe either that the flag does not stand for nationhood and national unity, but instead reflects other, less positive concepts, or that the concepts reflected in the flag do not in fact exist, that is, that we do not enjoy unity as a Nation. These concerns blossom only when a person's treatment of the flag communicates some message, and thus are related "to the suppression of free expression" within the meaning of *O'Brien.* We are thus outside of *O'Brien*'s test altogether.

It remains to consider whether the State's interest in preserving the flag as a symbol of nationhood and national unity justifies Johnson's conviction.

As in *Spence v. Washington,* "[w]e are confronted with a case of prosecution for the expression of an idea through activity," and "[a]ccordingly, we must examine with particular care the interests advanced by [petitioner] to support its prosecution." Johnson was not, we add, prosecuted for the expression of just any idea; he was prosecuted for his expression of dissatisfaction with the policies of this country, expression situated at the core of our First Amendment values.

Moreover, Johnson was prosecuted because he knew that his politically charged expression would cause "serious offense." If he had burned the flag as a means of disposing of it because it was dirty or torn, he would not have been convicted of flag desecration under this Texas law: federal law designates burning as the preferred means of disposing of a flag "when it is in such condition that it is no longer a fitting emblem for display," and Texas has no quarrel with this means of disposal. The Texas law is thus not aimed at protecting the physical integrity of the flag in all circumstances, but is designed instead to protect it only against impairments that would cause serious offense to others. Texas concedes as much: "Section 42.09(b) reaches only those severe acts of physical abuse of the flag carried out in a way likely to be offensive. The statute mandates intentional or knowing abuse, that is, the kind of mistreatment that is not innocent, but rather is intentionally designed to seriously offend other individuals."

Whether Johnson's treatment of the flag violated Texas law thus depended on the likely communicative impact of his expressive conduct. Our decision in *Boos v. Barry* (1988), *supra,* tells us that this restriction on Johnson's expression is content based. . . .

We must therefore subject the State's asserted interest in preserving the special symbolic character of the flag to "the most exacting scrutiny."

Texas argues that its interest in preserving the flag as a symbol of nationhood and national unity survives this close analysis. Quoting extensively from the writings of this Court chronicling the flag's historic and symbolic role in our society, the State emphasizes the "special place" reserved for the flag in our Nation. The State's argument is not that it has an interest simply in maintaining the flag as a symbol of *something*, no matter what it symbolizes; indeed, if that were the State's position, it would be difficult to see how that interest is endangered by highly symbolic conduct such as Johnson's. Rather, the State's claim is that it has an interest in preserving the flag as a symbol of *nationhood* and *national unity*, a symbol with a determinate range of meanings. According to Texas, if one physically treats the flag in a way that would tend to cast doubt on either the idea that nationhood and national unity are the flag's referents or that national unity actually exists, the message conveyed thereby is a harmful one and therefore may be prohibited.

If there is a bedrock principle underlying the First Amendment, it is that the government may not prohibit the expression of an idea simply because society finds the idea itself offensive or disagreeable.

We have not recognized an exception to this principle even where our flag has been involved. In *Street v. New York* (1969), we held that a State may not criminally punish a person for uttering words critical of the flag. Rejecting the argument that the conviction could be sustained on the ground that Street had "failed to show the respect for our national symbol which may properly be demanded of every citizen," we concluded that "the constitutionally guaranteed 'freedom to be intellectually . . . diverse or even contrary,' and the 'right to differ as to things that touch the heart of the existing order,' encompass the freedom to express publicly one's opinions about our flag, including those opinions which are defiant or contemptuous." Nor may the government, we have held, compel conduct that would evince respect for the flag. "To sustain the compulsory flag salute we are required to say that a Bill of Rights which guards the individual's right to speak his own mind, left it open to public authorities to compel him to utter what is not in his mind."

In holding in *Barnette* that the Constitution did not leave this course open to the government, Justice Jackson described one of our society's defining principles in words deserving of their frequent repetition: "If there is any fixed star in our constitutional constellation, it is that no official, high or petty, can prescribe what shall be orthodox in politics, nationalism, religion, or other matters of opinion or force citizens to confess by word or act their faith therein." . . .

In short, nothing in our precedents suggests that a State may foster its own view of the flag by prohibiting expressive conduct relating to it. To bring its argument outside our precedents, Texas attempts to convince us that even if its interest in preserving the flag's symbolic role does not

allow it to prohibit words or some expressive conduct critical of the flag, it does permit it to forbid the outright destruction of the flag. The State's argument cannot depend here on the distinction between written or spoken words and nonverbal conduct. That distinction, we have shown, is of no moment where the nonverbal conduct is expressive, as it is here, and where the regulation of that conduct is related to expression, as it is here. . . .

Texas' focus on the precise nature of Johnson's expression, moreover, misses the point of our prior decisions: their enduring lesson, that the government may not prohibit expression simply because it disagrees with its message, is not dependent on the particular mode in which one chooses to express an idea. If we were to hold that a State may forbid flag burning wherever it is likely to endanger the flag's symbolic role, but allow it wherever burning a flag promotes that role—as where, for example, a person ceremoniously burns a dirty flag—we would be saying that when it comes to impairing the flag's physical integrity, the flag itself may be used as a symbol—as a substitute for the written or spoken word or a "short cut from mind to mind"—only in one direction. We would be permitting a State to "prescribe what shall be orthodox" by saying that one may burn the flag to convey one's attitude toward it and its referents only if one does not endanger the flag's representation of nationhood and national unity.

We never before have held that the Government may ensure that a symbol be used to express only one view of that symbol or its referents. . . .

To conclude that the government may permit designated symbols to be used to communicate only a limited set of messages would be to enter territory having no discernible or defensible boundaries. Could the government, on this theory, prohibit the burning of state flags? Of copies of the Presidential seal? Of the Constitution? In evaluating these choices under the First Amendment, how would we decide which symbols were sufficiently special to warrant this unique status? To do so, we would be forced to consult our own political preferences, and impose them on the citizenry, in the very way that the First Amendment forbids us to do.

There is, moreover, no indication—either in the text of the Constitution or in our cases interpreting it—that a separate juridical category exists for the American flag alone. Indeed, we would not be surprised to learn that the persons who framed our Constitution and wrote the Amendment that we now construe were not known for their reverence for the Union Jack. The First Amendment does not guarantee that other concepts virtually sacred to our Nation as a whole—such as the principle that discrimination on the basis of race is odious and destructive—will go unquestioned in the market-place of ideas. We decline, therefore, to create for the flag an exception to the joust of principles protected by the First Amendment.

It is not the State's ends, but its means, to which we object. It cannot be gainsaid that there is a special place reserved for the flag in this Nation, and thus we do not doubt that the government has a legitimate interest in making efforts to "preserv[e] the national flag as an unalloyed symbol of our country." We reject the suggestion, urged at oral argument by counsel for Johnson, that the government lacks "any state interest whatsoever" in regulating the manner in which the flag may be displayed. Congress has, for example, enacted precatory regulations describing the proper treatment of the flag, and we cast no doubt on the legitimacy of its interest in making such recommendations. To say that the government has an interest in encouraging proper treatment of the flag, however, is not to say that it may criminally punish a person for burning a flag as a means of political protest. "National unity as an end which officials may foster by persuasion and example is not in question. The problem is whether under our Constitution compulsion as here employed is a permissible means for its achievement."

We are fortified in today's conclusion by our conviction that forbidding criminal punishment for conduct such as Johnson's will not endanger the special role played by our flag or the feelings it inspires.

We are tempted to say, in fact, that the flag's deservedly cherished place in our community will be strengthened, not weakened, by our holding today. Our decision is a reaffirmation of the principles of freedom and inclusiveness that the flag best reflects, and of the conviction that our toleration of criticism such as Johnson's is a sign and source of our strength. Indeed, one of the proudest images of our flag, the one immortalized in our own national anthem, is of the bombardment it survived at Fort McHenry. It is the Nation's resilience, not its rigidity, that Texas sees reflected in the flag—and it is that resilience that we reassert today.

The way to preserve the flag's special role is not to punish those who feel differently about these matters. It is to persuade them that they are wrong. "To courageous, self-reliant men, with confidence in the power of free and fearless reasoning applied through the processes of popular government, no danger flowing from speech can be deemed clear and present, unless the incidence of the evil apprehended is so imminent that it may befall before there is opportunity for full discussion. If there be time to expose through discussion the falsehood and fallacies, to avert the evil by the processes of education, the remedy

to be applied is more speech, not enforced silence." *Whitney v. California* (1927). And, precisely because it is our flag that is involved, one's response to the flag burner may exploit the uniquely persuasive power of the flag itself. We can imagine no more appropriate response to burning a flag than waving one's own, no better way to counter a flag burner's message than by saluting the flag that burns, no surer means of preserving the dignity even of the flag that burned than by—as one witness here did—according its remains a respectful burial. We do not consecrate the flag by punishing its desecration, for in doing so we dilute the freedom that this cherished emblem represents.

Affirmed.

Justice KENNEDY, concurring.

I write not to qualify the words Justice Brennan chooses so well, for he says with power all that is necessary to explain our ruling. I join his opinion without reservation, but with a keen sense that this case, like others before us from time to time, exacts its personal toll. This prompts me to add to our pages these few remarks.

The case before us illustrates better than most that the judicial power is often difficult in its exercise. We cannot here ask another Branch to share responsibility, as when the argument is made that a statute is flawed or incomplete. For we are presented with a clear and simple statute to be judged against a pure command of the Constitution. The outcome can be laid at no door but ours.

The hard fact is that sometimes we must make decisions we do not like. We make them because they are right, right in the sense that the law and the Constitution, as we see them, compel the result. And so great is our commitment to the process that, except in the rare case, we do not pause to express distaste for the result, perhaps for fear of undermining a valued principle that dictates the decision. This is one of those rare cases.

Our colleagues in dissent advance powerful arguments why respondent may be convicted for his expression, reminding us that among those who will be dismayed by our holding will be some who have had the singular honor of carrying the flag in battle. And I agree that the flag holds a lonely place of honor in an age when absolutes are distrusted and simple truths are burdened by unneeded apologetics.

With all respect to those views, I do not believe the Constitution gives us the right to rule as the dissenting Members of the Court urge, however painful this judgment is to announce. Though symbols often are what we ourselves make of them, the flag is constant in expressing beliefs Americans share, beliefs in law and peace and that freedom which sustains the human spirit. The case here today forces recognition of the costs to which those beliefs commit us. It is poignant but fundamental that the flag protects those who hold it in contempt.

For all the record shows, this respondent was not a philosopher and perhaps did not even possess the ability to comprehend how repellent his statements must be to the Republic itself. But whether or not he could appreciate the enormity of the offense he gave, the fact remains that his acts were speech, in both the technical and the fundamental meaning of the Constitution. So I agree with the Court that he must go free.

Chief Justice REHNQUIST, with whom Justice WHITE and Justice O'CONNOR join, dissenting.

In holding this Texas statute unconstitutional, the Court ignores Justice Holmes' familiar aphorism that "a page of history is worth a volume of logic." For more than 200 years, the American flag has occupied a unique position as the symbol of our Nation, a uniqueness that justifies a governmental prohibition against flag burning in the way respondent Johnson did here.

At the time of the American Revolution, the flag served to unify the Thirteen Colonies at home, while obtaining recognition of national sovereignty abroad. Ralph Waldo Emerson's "Concord Hymn" describes the first skirmishes of the Revolutionary War in these lines:

By the rude bridge that arched the flood
Their flag to April's breeze unfurled,
Here once the embattled farmers stood
And fired the shot heard round the world.

The American flag played a central role in our Nation's most tragic conflict, when the North fought against the South. The lowering of the American flag at Fort Sumter was viewed as the start of the war. . . .

In the First and Second World Wars, thousands of our countrymen died on foreign soil fighting for the American cause. At Iwo Jima in the Second World War, United States Marines fought hand to hand against thousands of Japanese. By the time the Marines reached the top of Mount Suribachi, they raised a piece of pipe upright and from one end fluttered a flag. That ascent had cost nearly 6,000 American lives. The Iwo Jima Memorial in Arlington National Cemetery memorializes that event. . . .

During the Korean war, the successful amphibious landing of American troops at Inchon was marked by the raising of an American flag within an hour of the event. Impetus for the enactment of the Federal Flag Desecration Statute in 1967 came from the impact of flag burnings in the United States on troop morale in Vietnam. . . .

The flag symbolizes the Nation in peace as well as in war. It signifies our national presence on battleships, airplanes, military installations, and public buildings from the United States Capitol to the thousands of county courthouses and city halls throughout the country. Two flags are prominently placed in our courtroom. Countless flags are placed by the graves of loved ones each year on what was first called Decoration Day, and is now called Memorial Day. The flag is traditionally placed on the casket of deceased members of the Armed Forces, and it is later given to the deceased's family. Congress has provided that the flag be flown at half-staff upon the death of the President, Vice President, and other government officials "as a mark of respect to their memory." The flag identifies United States merchant ships, and "[t]he laws of the Union protect our commerce wherever the flag of the country may float."

No other American symbol has been as universally honored as the flag. In 1931, Congress declared "The Star-Spangled Banner" to be our national anthem. In 1949, Congress declared June 14th to be Flag Day. In 1987, John Philip Sousa's "The Stars and Stripes Forever" was designated as the national march. Congress has also established "The Pledge of Allegiance to the Flag" and the manner of its deliverance. The flag has appeared as the principal symbol on approximately 33 United States postal stamps and in the design of at least 43 more, more times than any other symbol.

Both Congress and the States have enacted numerous laws regulating misuse of the American flag. Until 1967, Congress left the regulation of misuse of the flag up to the States. Now, however, 18 U. S. C. Section 700(a) provides that:

Whoever knowingly casts contempt upon any flag of the United States by publicly mutilating, defacing, defiling, burning, or trampling upon it shall be fined not more than $ 1,000 or imprisoned for not more than one year, or both.

Congress has also prescribed, *inter alia*, detailed rules for the design of the flag, the time and occasion of flag's display, the position and manner of its display, respect for the flag, and conduct during hoisting, lowering, and passing of the flag. With the exception of Alaska and Wyoming, all of the States now have statutes prohibiting the burning of the flag. . . .

The American flag, then, throughout more than 200 years of our history, has come to be the visible symbol embodying our Nation. It does not represent the views of any particular political party, and it does not represent any particular political philosophy. The flag is not simply another "idea" or "point of view" competing for recognition in the marketplace of ideas. Millions and millions of Americans regard it with an almost mystical reverence regardless of what sort of social, political, or philosophical beliefs they may have. I cannot agree that the First Amendment invalidates the Act of Congress, and the laws of 48 of the 50 States, which make criminal the public burning of the flag.

But the Court insists that the Texas statute prohibiting the public burning of the American flag infringes on respondent Johnson's freedom of expression. Such freedom, of course, is not absolute. In *Chaplinsky v. New Hampshire* (1942), a unanimous Court upheld Chaplinsky's conviction under a state statute that made it unlawful to "address any offensive, derisive or annoying word to any person who is lawfully in any street or other public place." . . .

Here it may equally well be said that the public burning of the American flag by Johnson was no essential part of any exposition of ideas, and at the same time it had a tendency to incite a breach of the peace. Johnson was free to make any verbal denunciation of the flag that he wished; indeed, he was free to burn the flag in private. He could publicly burn other symbols of the Government or effigies of political leaders. He did lead a march through the streets of Dallas, and conducted a rally in front of the Dallas City Hall. He engaged in a "die-in" to protest nuclear weapons. He shouted out various slogans during the march, including: "Reagan, Mondale which will it be? Either one means World War III"; "Ronald Reagan, killer of the hour, Perfect example of U.S. power"; and "red, white and blue, we spit on you, you stand for plunder, you will go under." For none of these acts was he arrested or prosecuted; it was only when he proceeded to burn publicly an American flag stolen from its rightful owner that he violated the Texas statute.

The Court could not, and did not, say that Chaplinsky's utterances were not expressive phrases—they clearly and succinctly conveyed an extremely low opinion of the addressee. The same may be said of Johnson's public burning of the flag in this case; it obviously did convey Johnson's bitter dislike of his country. But his act, like Chaplinsky's provocative words, conveyed nothing that could not have been conveyed and was not conveyed just as forcefully in a dozen different ways. As with "fighting words," so with flag burning, for purposes of the First Amendment: It is "no essential part of any exposition of ideas, and [is] of such slight social value as a step to truth that any benefit that may be derived from [it] is clearly outweighed" by the public interest in avoiding a probable breach of the peace. The highest courts of several States have upheld state statutes prohibiting the public burning of the flag on the grounds that it is so inherently inflammatory that it may cause a breach of public order.

The result of the Texas statute is obviously to deny one in Johnson's frame of mind one of many means of "symbolic speech." Far from being a case of "one picture being worth a thousand words," flag burning is the equivalent of an inarticulate grunt or roar that, it seems fair to say, is most likely to be indulged in not to express any particular idea, but to antagonize others. The Texas statute deprived Johnson of only one rather inarticulate symbolic form of protest—a form of protest that was profoundly offensive to many—and left him with a full panoply of other symbols and every conceivable form of verbal expression to express his deep disapproval of national policy. Thus, in no way can it be said that Texas is punishing him because his hearers—or any other group of people—were profoundly opposed to the message that he sought to convey. Such opposition is no proper basis for restricting speech or expression under the First Amendment. It was Johnson's use of this particular symbol, and not the idea that he sought to convey by it or by his many other expressions, for which he was punished. . . .

The Court concludes its opinion with a regrettably patronizing civics lecture, presumably addressed to the Members of both Houses of Congress, the members of the 48 state legislatures that enacted prohibitions against flag burning, and the troops fighting under that flag in Vietnam who objected to its being burned: "The way to preserve the flag's special role is not to punish those who feel differently about these matters. It is to persuade them that they are wrong." The Court's role as the final expositor of the Constitution is well established, but its role as a Platonic guardian admonishing those responsible to public opinion as if they were truant schoolchildren has no similar place in our system of government. The cry of "no taxation without representation" animated those who revolted against the English Crown to found our Nation—the idea that those who submitted to government should have some say as to what kind of laws would be passed. Surely one of the high purposes of a democratic society is to legislate against conduct that is regarded as evil and profoundly offensive to the majority of people—whether it be murder, embezzlement, pollution, or flag burning.

Our Constitution wisely places limits on powers of legislative majorities to act, but the declaration of such limits by this Court "is, at all times, a question of much delicacy, which ought seldom, if ever, to be decided in the affirmative, in a doubtful case." Uncritical extension of constitutional protection to the burning of the flag risks the frustration of the very purpose for which organized governments are instituted. The Court decides that the American flag is just another symbol, about which not only must opinions pro and con be tolerated, but for which the most minimal public respect may not be enjoined. The government may conscript men into the Armed Forces where they must fight and perhaps die for the flag, but the government may not prohibit the public burning of the banner under which they fight. I would uphold the Texas statute as applied in this case.

Justice STEVENS, dissenting.

As the Court analyzes this case, it presents the question whether the State of Texas, or indeed the Federal Government, has the power to prohibit the public desecration of the American flag. The question is unique. In my judgment rules that apply to a host of other symbols, such as state flags, armbands, or various privately promoted emblems of political or commercial identity, are not necessarily controlling. Even if flag burning could be considered just another species of symbolic speech under the logical application of the rules that the Court has developed in its interpretation of the First Amendment in other contexts, this case has an intangible dimension that makes those rules inapplicable.

A country's flag is a symbol of more than "nationhood and national unity." It also signifies the ideas that characterize the society that has chosen that emblem as well as the special history that has animated the growth and power of those ideas. The fleurs-de-lis and the tricolor both symbolized "nationhood and national unity," but they had vastly different meanings. The message conveyed by some flags—the swastika, for example—may survive long after it has outlived its usefulness as a symbol of regimented unity in a particular nation.

So it is with the American flag. It is more than a proud symbol of the courage, the determination, and the gifts of nature that transformed 13 fledgling Colonies into a world power. It is a symbol of freedom, of equal opportunity, of religious tolerance, and of good will for other peoples who share our aspirations. The symbol carries its message to dissidents both at home and abroad who may have no interest at all in our national unity or survival.

The value of the flag as a symbol cannot be measured. Even so, I have no doubt that the interest in preserving that value for the future is both significant and legitimate. Conceivably that value will be enhanced by the Court's conclusion that our national commitment to free expression is so strong that even the United States as ultimate guarantor of that freedom is without power to prohibit the desecration of its unique symbol. But I am unpersuaded. The creation of a federal right to post bulletin boards and

graffiti on the Washington Monument might enlarge the market for free expression, but at a cost I would not pay. Similarly, in my considered judgment, sanctioning the public desecration of the flag will tarnish its value—both for those who cherish the ideas for which it waves and for those who desire to don the robes of martyrdom by burning it. That tarnish is not justified by the trivial burden on free expression occasioned by requiring that an available, alternative mode of expression—including uttering words critical of the flag—be employed.

It is appropriate to emphasize certain propositions that are not implicated by this case. The statutory prohibition of flag desecration does not "prescribe what shall be orthodox in politics, nationalism, religion, or other matters of opinion or force citizens to confess by word or act their faith therein." The statute does not compel any conduct or any profession of respect for any idea or any symbol.

Nor does the statute violate "the government's paramount obligation of neutrality in its regulation of protected communication." The content of respondent's message has no relevance whatsoever to the case. The concept of "desecration" does not turn on the substance of the message the actor intends to convey, but rather on whether those who view the act will take serious offense. Accordingly, one intending to convey a message of respect for the flag by burning it in a public square might nonetheless be guilty of desecration if he knows that others—perhaps simply because they misperceive the intended message—will be seriously offended. Indeed, even if the actor knows that all possible witnesses will understand that he intends to send a message of respect, he might still be guilty of desecration if he also knows that this understanding does not lessen the offense taken by some of those witnesses. Thus, this is not a case in which the fact that "it is the speaker's opinion that gives offense" provides a special "reason for according it constitutional protection." The case has nothing to do with "disagreeable ideas." It involves disagreeable conduct that, in my opinion, diminishes the value of an important national asset.

The Court is therefore quite wrong in blandly asserting that respondent "was prosecuted for his expression of dissatisfaction with the policies of this country, expression situated at the core of our First Amendment values." Respondent was prosecuted because of the method he chose to express his dissatisfaction with those policies. Had he chosen to spray-paint—or perhaps convey with a motion picture projector—his message of dissatisfaction on the facade of the Lincoln Memorial, there would be no question about the power of the Government to prohibit his means of expression. The prohibition would be supported by the legitimate interest in preserving the quality of an important national asset. Though the asset at stake in this case is intangible, given its unique value, the same interest supports a prohibition on the desecration of the American flag.

The ideas of liberty and equality have been an irresistible force in motivating leaders like Patrick Henry, Susan B. Anthony, and Abraham Lincoln, schoolteachers like Nathan Hale and Booker T. Washington, the Philippine Scouts who fought at Bataan, and the soldiers who scaled the bluff at Omaha Beach. If those ideas are worth fighting for—and our history demonstrates that they are—it cannot be true that the flag that uniquely symbolizes their power is not itself worthy of protection from unnecessary desecration.

I respectfully dissent.

Notes and Queries

1. *Texas v. Johnson* is a nice example of how the Court applies its doctrinal "tests" to subsequent cases. This case turns on the application of the "O'Brien" test (spelled out in the *O'Brien* case printed earlier). What kind of interpretive approach would have to be applied to reach the result advocated by Chief Justice Rehnquist? Would it involve the kind of balancing advocated by Frankfurter in earlier free speech cases?

2. Does the Court's notion of "symbolic speech" as enunciated in *O'Brien, Tinker,* and *Johnson* depart from the understanding of speech in earlier free speech cases, specifically *Chaplinsky*?

3. What *idea* actually was Johnson trying to communicate by burning the flag? Justice Rehnquist analogized his action to an "inarticulate grunt." Was the act of burning the flag more than that? Or should protest pure and simple, even if it does not communicate a distinct message, be reason enough to protect the symbolic act?

4. Germany's criminal code includes the following provision:

Sec. 90a

(2) Whoever removes, destroys, renders useless or unrecognizable or commits an insulting act with respect to a publicly displayed flag of the Federal Republic of Germany or of one of its states or national insignia of the Federal Republic of Germany or of one of its states which has been publicly installed by the authorities shall be punished by up to three years' imprisonment or by fine.

Would this provision survive constitutional analysis in the United States?

5. Is the integrity of the community at issue in the flag burning case? The flag after all is a visible symbol of social being. It shelters the memory and character of a moral community, one designed by the Constitution to live in perpetuity. Doesn't the protection of the flag insure that the community will outlive individuals who happen to be alive at a particular moment in time? Along the same lines, doesn't the national community have the right to insist that Americans respect the flag, that if there is any one thing that we can or should agree upon it is this, particularly since the very meaning of America is symbolized by the flag? Or is the meaning of America our freedom to disagree on or about *any* institution, idea, convention, or symbol, however cherished, loved, or sacred?

6. In response to the Supreme Court's decision in *Johnson,* Congress passed the Flag Protection Act of 1989. In the process of doing so, the constitutional issues were revisited and debated at length. Congress also tried to cure what the *Johnson* Court regarded as the fatal flaw in the Texas statute. The statute was flawed because Texas sought to protect the flag "only against impairment that would cause serious offense to others." The congressional statute, on the other hand, sought merely to protect the "physical integrity of the flag" and thus made it a crime for anyone to knowingly deface, mutilate, burn, or trample on the U.S. flag. In *United States v. Eichman* (1990), however, the Court struck down the federal law by the same vote and for the same reason as in *Johnson.* Should the Court have deferred to the congressional judgment in view of the legislative debate in the aftermath of *Johnson*? Is there any reason for granting greater judicial deference to Congress in this respect than to a state?

R.A.V. v. City of St. Paul
505 U.S. 377, 112 S.Ct. 2538, 120 L.Ed.2d 305 (1992)

R.A.V. and several other teenagers burned a cross on the lawn of an African American family before dawn on the morning of 21 June 1990. R.A.V. was charged with violating a city ordinance which forbade placing "on public or private property a symbol, object, appellation, characterization, or graffiti, including, but not limited to, a burning cross or Nazi swastika, which one knows or has reasonable grounds to know arouses anger, alarm or resentment in others on the basis of race, color, creed, religion, or

Comparative Note 12.9

[The following extract is from a Canadian Supreme Court case sustaining the validity of a statute criminalizing the willful promotion of hate against an identifiable group. Here the law was applied to a high school teacher who uttered hateful anti-Semitic comments before his students.] Chief Justice Dickson, writing for the majority.

. . . [T]he presence of hate propaganda in Canada is sufficiently substantial to warrant concern. Disquiet caused by the existence of such material is not simply the product of its offensiveness, however, but stems from the very real harm which it causes. Essentially, there are two sorts of injury caused by hate propaganda. First, there is harm done to members of the target group. It is indisputable that the emotional damage caused by words may be of grave psychological and social consequence. . . . [W]ords and writings that willfully promote hatred can constitute a serious attack on persons belonging to a racial or religious group, and in this regard the Cohen Committee notes that these persons are humiliated and degraded.

. . . The derision, hostility and abuse encouraged by hate propaganda therefore have a severely negative impact on the individual's sense of self-worth and acceptance. . . .

A second harmful effect of hate propaganda which is of pressing and substantial concern is its influence upon society at large. . . . It is thus not inconceivable that the active dissemination of hate propaganda can attract individuals to its cause, and in the process create serious discord between various cultural groups in society. . . .

. . . [G]iven the unparalleled vigour with which hate propaganda repudiates and undermines democratic values, and in particular its condemnation of the view that all citizens need to be treated with equal respect and dignity so as to make participation in the political process meaningful, I am unable to see the protection of such expression as integral to the democratic ideal so central to [the guarantee of free speech].

. . . I am of the opinion that hate propaganda contributes little to the aspirations of Canadians or Canada in either the quest for truth, the promotion of individual self-development or the protection and fostering of a vibrant democracy where the participation of all individuals is accepted and encouraged.

SOURCE: *R. v.* Keegstra, 3 Canadian Rights Reporter (2ⁿᵈ) 194 (1990).

---

gender. . . .” The trial court dismissed the case on grounds that the ordinance was overly broad and impermissibly content-based, thus violating the First Amendment. The Minnesota Supreme Court, however, reversed on grounds that the ordinance was permissible if interpreted to forbid only expressions which could be interpreted as “fighting words” under the doctrine of *Chaplinsky v. New Hampshire* (1942). Opinion of the Court: *Scalia*, Rehnquist, Kennedy, Souter, Thomas. Concurring opinions: *White*, Blackmun, O'Connor, Stevens (in part) and *Stevens* (in part).

Justice SCALIA delivered the opinion of the Court.

Assuming, arguendo, that all of the expression reached by the ordinance is proscribable under the “fighting words” doctrine, we nonetheless conclude that the ordinance is facially unconstitutional in that it prohibits otherwise permitted speech solely on the basis of the subjects the speech addresses.

The First Amendment generally prevents government from proscribing speech, or even expressive conduct, be-cause of disapproval of the ideas expressed. Content-based regulations are presumptively invalid. From 1791 to the present, however, our society, like other free but civilized societies, has permitted restrictions upon the content of speech in a few limited areas, which are “of such slight social value as a step to truth that any benefit that may be derived from them is clearly outweighed by the social interest in order and morality.” *Chaplinsky.*

We have sometimes said that these categories of expression are “not within the area of constitutionally protected speech,” *Roth; Beauharnais; Chaplinsky,* or that the “protection of the First Amendment does not extend” to them. Such statements must be taken in context, however, and are no more literally true than is the occasionally repeated shorthand characterizing obscenity “as not being speech at all.” What they mean is that these areas of speech can, consistently with the First Amendment, be regulated *because of their constitutionally proscribable content* (obscenity, defamation, etc.)—not that they are categories of speech entirely invisible to the Constitution, so that they may be made the vehicles for content discrimination unre-

Comparative Note 12.10

[Germany's Federal Supreme Court sustained the validity of a law penalizing the denial of the Holocaust over the objection that the law violated freedom of speech. Later the Federal Constitutional Court sustained the decision of the Supreme Court. Extracts from both tribunals are reproduced.]

The historical fact itself that human beings were singled out according to the criteria of the so-called "Nuremberg Acts" and were robbed of their individuality for the purpose of extermination puts Jews living in the Federal Republic into a special personal relationship vis-à-vis their fellow citizens; what happened is also present in this relationship today. It is part of their personal self-perception to be comprehended as belonging to a group of people who stand out by virtue of their fate and in relation to whom there is a special moral responsibility on the part of all others and that this is a part of their dignity. Respect for this self-perception is virtually, for each individual, one of the guarantees against repetition of this kind of discrimination and forms a basic condition of their life in the Federal Republic. Whoever seeks to deny these events denies, vis-à-vis each individual, the personal worth due to each one. For the person concerned this means continuing discrimination against the group to which he belongs and, as part of that group, against himself.

Source: Judgment of Federal Supreme Court, 75 BGHZ 160 (1994). Author's translation.

The probibited utterance that there was no persecution of the Jews during the Third Reich is a representation of fact that is demonstrably untrue in the light of innumerable eye-witness accounts and documents, of the findings of the courts in numerous criminal cases and of historical analysis. Taken on its own, a statement having this content therefore does not enjoy the protection of freedom of expression. Therein lies an important difference between denying the persecution of the Jews during the Third Reich and denying German guilt in respect of the outbreak of the Second World War—the subject of our decision handed down by the Federal Constitutional Court on January 11, 1994. Utterances concerning guilt and responsibility for historical events are always complex evaluations that cannot be reduced to representations of fact, while the denial of an event itself will normally have the character of a representation of fact.

Source: Judgment of April 13, 1994, 90 BverfGE 241. Author's translation.

---

lated to their distinctively proscribable content. Thus, the government may proscribe libel; but it may not make the further content discrimination of proscribing only libel critical of the government.

The proposition that a particular instance of speech can be proscribable on the basis of one feature (e.g., obscenity) but not on the basis of another (e.g., opposition to the city government) is commonplace, and has found application in many contexts. We have long held, for example, that nonverbal expressive activity can be banned because of the action it entails, but not because of the ideas it expresses—so that burning a flag in violation of an ordinance against outdoor fires could be punishable, whereas burning a flag in violation of an ordinance against dishonoring the flag is not. Similarly, we have upheld reasonable "time, place, or manner" restrictions, but only if they are "justified without reference to the content of the regulated

speech." And just as the power to proscribe particular speech on the basis of a noncontent element (e.g., noise) does not entail the power to proscribe the same speech on the basis of a content element; so also, the power to proscribe it on the basis of one content element (e.g., obscenity) does not entail the power to proscribe it on the basis of other content elements.

Even the prohibition against content discrimination that we assert the First Amendment requires is not absolute. It applies differently in the context of proscribable speech than in the area of fully protected speech. The rationale of the general prohibition, after all, is that content discrimination "raises the specter that the Government may effectively drive certain ideas or viewpoints from the marketplace." But content discrimination among various instances of a class of proscribable speech often does not pose this threat.

When the basis for the content discrimination consists entirely of the very reason the entire class of speech at issue is proscribable, no significant danger of idea or viewpoint discrimination exists. Such a reason, having been adjudged neutral enough to support exclusion of the entire class of speech from First Amendment protection, is also neutral enough to form the basis of distinction within the class. To illustrate: A State might choose to prohibit only that obscenity which is the most patently offensive in its prurience—i.e., that which involves the most lascivious displays of sexual activity. But it may not prohibit, for example, only that obscenity which includes offensive *political* messages. And the Federal Government can criminalize only those threats of violence that are directed against the President—since the reasons why threats of violence are outside the First Amendment (protecting individuals from the fear of violence, from the disruption that fear engenders, and from the possibility that the threatened violence will occur) have special force when applied to the person of the President. But the Federal Government may not criminalize only those threats against the President that mention his policy on aid to inner cities. . . .

II

Applying these principles to the St. Paul ordinance, we conclude that, even as narrowly construed by the Minnesota Supreme Court, the ordinance is facially unconstitutional. Although the phrase in the ordinance, "arouses anger, alarm or resentment in others," has been limited by the Minnesota Supreme Court's construction to reach only those symbols or displays that amount to "fighting words," the remaining, unmodified terms make clear that the ordinance applies only to "fighting words" that insult, or provoke violence, "on the basis of race, color, creed, religion or gender." Displays containing abusive invective, no matter how vicious or severe, are permissible unless they are addressed to one of the specified disfavored topics. Those who wish to use "fighting words" in connection with other ideas—to express hostility, for example, on the basis of political affiliation, union membership, or homosexuality—are not covered. The First Amendment does not permit St. Paul to impose special prohibitions on those speakers who express views on disfavored subjects.

In its practical operation, moreover, the ordinance goes even beyond mere content discrimination, to actual viewpoint discrimination. Displays containing some words—odious racial epithets, for example—would be prohibited to proponents of all views. But "fighting words" that do not themselves invoke race, color, creed, religion, or gender—aspersions upon a person's mother, for example—would seemingly be usable *ad libitum* in the placards of

those arguing *in favor* of racial, color, etc. tolerance and equality, but could not be used by that speaker's opponents.

One could hold up a sign saying, for example, that all "anti-Catholic bigots" are misbegotten; but not that all "papists" are, for that would insult and provoke violence "on the basis of religion." St. Paul has no such authority to license one side of a debate to fight freestyle, while requiring the other to follow Marquis of Queensbury Rules.

What we have here, it must be emphasized, is not a prohibition of fighting words that are directed at certain persons or groups (which would be facially valid if it met the requirements of the Equal Protection Clause); but rather, a prohibition of fighting words that contain (as the Minnesota Supreme Court repeatedly emphasized) messages of "bias-motivated" hatred and in particular, as applied to this case, messages "based on virulent notions of racial supremacy." One must wholeheartedly agree with the Minnesota Supreme Court that "it is the responsibility, even the obligation, of diverse communities to confront such notions in whatever form they appear," but the manner of that confrontation cannot consist of selective limitations upon speech. St. Paul's brief asserts that a general "fighting words" law would not meet the city's needs because only a content-specific measure can communicate to minority groups that the "group hatred" aspect of such speech "is not condoned by the majority." The point of the First Amendment is that majority preferences must be expressed in some fashion other than silencing speech on the basis of its content. . . .

Finally, St. Paul and its *amici* defend the conclusion of the Minnesota Supreme Court that, even if the ordinance regulates expression based on hostility towards its protected ideological content, this discrimination is nonetheless justified because it is narrowly tailored to serve compelling state interests. Specifically, they assert that the ordinance helps to ensure the basic human rights of members of groups that have historically been subjected to discrimination, including the right of such group members to live in peace where they wish. We do not doubt that these interests are compelling, and that the ordinance can be said to promote them. But the "danger of censorship" presented by a facially content-based statute requires that that weapon be employed only where it is "*necessary* to serve the asserted [compelling] interest." The existence of adequate content-neutral alternatives thus "undercuts significantly" any defense of such a statute, casting considerable doubt on the government's protestations that "the asserted justification is in fact an accurate description of the purpose and effect of the law." The dispositive question in this case, therefore, is whether content discrimination is reasonably necessary to achieve St. Paul's compelling interests; it plainly is not. An ordinance not limited to the favored topics, for example, would have precisely the same beneficial effect. In fact the only interest distinctively served by the content limitation is that of displaying the city council's special hostility towards the particular biases thus singled out. That is precisely what the First Amendment forbids. The politicians of St. Paul are entitled to express that hostility—but not through the means of imposing unique limitations upon speakers who (however benightedly) disagree.

Let there be no mistake about our belief that burning a cross in someone's front yard is reprehensible. But St. Paul has sufficient means at its disposal to prevent such behavior without adding the First Amendment to the fire.

The judgment of the Minnesota Supreme Court is reversed, and the case is remanded for proceedings not inconsistent with this opinion.

It is so ordered.

Justice WHITE, with whom Justice BLACKMUN and Justice O'CONNOR join, and with whom Justice STEVENS joins except as to Part I(A), concurring in the judgment.

I agree with the majority that the judgment of the Minnesota Supreme Court should be reversed. However, our agreement ends there.

This case could easily be decided within the contours of established First Amendment law by holding, as petitioner argues, that the St. Paul ordinance is fatally overbroad because it criminalizes not only unprotected expression but expression protected by the First Amendment. See Part II, *infra*. Instead, "finding it unnecessary" to consider the questions upon which we granted review, the Court holds the ordinance facially unconstitutional on a ground that was never presented to the Minnesota Supreme Court, a ground that has not been briefed by the parties before this Court, a ground that requires serious departures from the teaching of prior cases. . . .

I

A

This Court's decisions have plainly stated that expression falling within certain limited categories so lacks the values the First Amendment was designed to protect that the Constitution affords no protection to that expression. *Chaplinsky.*

Thus, as the majority concedes, this Court has long held certain discrete categories of expression to be proscribable on the basis of their content. For instance, the Court

has held that the individual who falsely shouts "fire" in a crowded theatre may not claim the protection of the First Amendment. The Court has concluded that neither child pornography, nor obscenity, is protected by the First Amendment. And the Court has observed that, "leaving aside the special considerations when public officials [and public figures] are the target, a libelous publication is not protected by the Constitution."

All of these categories are content based. But the Court has held that the First Amendment does not apply to them because their expressive content is worthless or of de minimis value to society. *Chaplinsky.* This categorical approach has provided a principled and narrowly focused means for distinguishing between expression that the government may regulate freely and that which it may regulate on the basis of content only upon a showing of compelling need.

Today, however, the Court announces that earlier Courts did not mean their repeated statements that certain categories of expression are "not within the area of constitutionally protected speech." The present Court submits that such clear statements "must be taken in context" and are not "literally true."

To the contrary, those statements meant precisely what they said: The categorical approach is a firmly entrenched part of our First Amendment jurisprudence. Indeed, the Court in *Roth* reviewed the guarantees of freedom of expression in effect at the time of the ratification of the Constitution and concluded, "in light of this history, it is apparent that the unconditional phrasing of the First Amendment was not intended to protect every utterance."

Nevertheless, the majority holds that the First Amendment protects those narrow categories of expression long held to be undeserving of First Amendment protection—at least to the extent that lawmakers may not regulate some fighting words more strictly than others because of their content. The Court announces that such content-based distinctions violate the First Amendment because "the government may not regulate use based on hostility—or favoritism—towards the underlying message expressed." Should the government want to criminalize certain fighting words, the Court now requires it to criminalize all fighting words.

To borrow a phrase, "Such a simplistic, all-or-nothing-at-all approach to First Amendment protection is at odds with common sense and with our jurisprudence as well." It is inconsistent to hold that the government may proscribe an entire category of speech because the content of that speech is evil, *Ferber,* but that the government may not treat a subset of that category differently without violating the First Amendment; the content of the subset is by definition worthless and undeserving of constitutional protection.

The majority's observation that fighting words are quite expressive indeed is no answer. Fighting words are not a means of exchanging views, rallying supporters, or registering a protest; they are directed against individuals to provoke violence or to inflict injury. Therefore, a ban on all fighting words or on a subset of the fighting words category would restrict only the social evil of hate speech, without creating the danger of driving viewpoints from the marketplace.

Therefore, the Court's insistence on inventing its brand of First Amendment underinclusiveness puzzles me. The overbreadth doctrine has the redeeming virtue of attempting to avoid the chilling of protected expression, but the Court's new "underbreadth" creation serves no desirable function. Instead, it permits, indeed invites, the continuation of expressive conduct that in this case is evil and worthless in First Amendment terms, until the city of St. Paul cures the underbreadth by adding to its ordinance a catch-all phrase such as "and all other fighting words that may constitutionally be subject to this ordinance."

Any contribution of this holding to First Amendment jurisprudence is surely a negative one, since it necessarily signals that expressions of violence, such as the message of intimidation and racial hatred conveyed by burning a cross on someone's lawn, are of sufficient value to outweigh the social interest in order and morality that has traditionally placed such fighting words outside the First Amendment. Indeed, by characterizing fighting words as a form of "debate," the majority legitimates hate speech as a form of public discussion. . . .

I agree with petitioner that the ordinance is invalid on its face. Although the ordinance as construed reaches categories of speech that are constitutionally unprotected, it also criminalizes a substantial amount of expression that—however repugnant—is shielded by the First Amendment.

In attempting to narrow the scope of the St. Paul antibias ordinance, the Minnesota Supreme Court relied upon two of the categories of speech and expressive conduct that fall outside the First Amendment's protective sphere: words that incite "imminent lawless action" and "fighting" words. The Minnesota Supreme Court erred in its application of the *Chaplinsky* fighting words test and consequently interpreted the St. Paul ordinance in a fashion that rendered the ordinance facially overbroad.

In construing the St. Paul ordinance, the Minnesota Supreme Court drew upon the definition of fighting words that appears in *Chaplinsky*—words "which by their very utterance inflict injury or tend to incite an immediate

breach of the peace." However, the Minnesota court was far from clear in identifying the "injuries" inflicted by the expression that St. Paul sought to regulate. Indeed, the Minnesota court emphasized (tracking the language of the ordinance) that "the ordinance censors only those displays that one knows or should know will create anger, alarm or resentment based on racial, ethnic, gender or religious bias." I therefore understand the court to have ruled that St. Paul may constitutionally prohibit expression that "by its very utterance" causes "anger, alarm or resentment."

Our fighting words cases have made clear, however, that such generalized reactions are not sufficient to strip expression of its constitutional protection. The mere fact that expressive activity causes hurt feelings, offense, or resentment does not render the expression unprotected.

In the First Amendment context, "criminal statutes must be scrutinized with particular care; those that make unlawful a substantial amount of constitutionally protected conduct may be held facially invalid even if they also have legitimate application." The St. Paul antibias ordinance is such a law. Although the ordinance reaches conduct that is unprotected, it also makes criminal expressive conduct that causes only hurt feelings, offense, or resentment, and is protected by the First Amendment. The ordinance is therefore fatally overbroad and invalid on its face.

III

Today, the Court has disregarded two established principles of First Amendment law without providing a coherent replacement theory. Its decision is an arid, doctrinaire interpretation, driven by the frequently irresistible impulse of judges to tinker with the First Amendment. The decision is mischievous at best and will surely confuse the lower courts. I join the judgment, but not the folly of the opinion.

Notes and Queries

1. In *Beauharnais v. Illinois* (1952) the Court ruled on the constitutionality of an Illinois law which forbade exhibitions, or publications which portrayed "depravity, criminality, unchastity or lack of virtue of a class of citizens, of any race, color, creed, or religion" which exposed such groups to "contempt, derision, or obloquy or which is productive of breach of the peace or riots." Beauharnais had printed and distributed a pamphlet urging the enactment of segregationist laws and denouncing African Americans. The law he was charged under was similar to statutes against criminal libel against individuals. In the opinion of the Court, Justice Frankfurter wrote:

. . . if an utterance directed at an individual may be the object of criminal sanctions, we cannot deny to a State the power to punish the same utterance directed at a defined group, unless we can say that this is a willful and purposeless restriction unrelated to the peace and well-being of the State.

In this case, Frankfurter concluded that the history of racial strife in Illinois was ample justification for the state's action:

In the face of this history and its frequent obligato of extreme racial and religious propaganda, we would deny experience to say that the Illinois legislature was without reason in seeking ways to curb false and malicious defamation of racial and religious groups, made in public places and by means calculated to have a powerful emotional impact on those to whom it was presented.

Justice Douglas' dissent was characteristically strong:

The First Amendment is couched in absolute terms—freedom of speech shall not be abridged. . . . Yet recently the Court . . . has engrafted the right of regulation onto the First Amendment by placing in the hands of the legislative branch the right to regulate "within reasonable limits" the right of free speech. This to me is an ominous and alarming trend. The free trade in ideas which the Framers of the Constitution visualized disappears. In its place there is substituted a new orthodoxy—an orthodoxy that changes with the whims of the age or the day, an orthodoxy which the majority by solemn judgment proclaims to be essential to the safety, morality or health of society. Free speech in the constitutional sense disappears. Limits are drawn—limits dictated by expediency, political opinion, prejudices or some other desideratum of legislative action.

Douglas went on to support his "absolute" view with observations about human nature:

Intemperate speech is a distinctive characteristic of man. Hot heads blow off and release destructive energy in the process. They shout and rave, exaggerating weaknesses, magnifying error, viewing with alarm. So it has been from the beginning; so it will be throughout time. The Framers of the Constitution knew human nature as well as we do. They too had lived in dangerous days; they too knew the suffocating influence of orthodoxy and standardized thought. They weighed the compulsions for restrained speech and thought against the abuses of liberty. They chose liberty. That should be

our choice today no matter how distasteful to us the pamphlet of Beauharnais may be.

2. The decision in *R.A.V.* itself was joined by all of the justices and yet there are four separate and lengthy opinions, most of which are highly critical of Justice Scalia's Opinion of the Court. What is the disagreement within the agreement?

3. How are the constitutional values at issue in *R.A.V.* similar to or different from those in *Beauharnais?*

4. Of what importance do you think variations in constitutional language are in deciding constitutional issues such as those raised in *R.A.V.?* The Canadian Charter guarantees "freedom of thought, belief, opinion and expression, including freedom of the press and other media of communication" but "subject only to such reasonable limits prescribed by law as can be demonstrably justified in a free and democratic society." Under Germany's Basic Law, "Everyone has the right freely to express and to disseminate his opinion by speech [and] writing" but this right may be limited "by the right to the inviolability of personal honor." The Japanese Constitution guarantees "freedom of speech, press and all other forms of expression" but "[the Japanese people] shall refrain from any abuse of these freedoms and rights and shall always be responsible for utilizing them for the public welfare." Suppose the U.S. Supreme Court had decided *R.A.V.* under the language of one or another of these foreign constitutions. Would it have reached the same result? If so, what does this tell us about the importance of a constitutional text? About the process of constitutional interpretation?

5. International human rights law requires that racist excitement be excluded from the protective ambit of freedom of expression. The European Convention for the Protection of Human Rights governs the policy of some thirty European nations. The Convention itself does not require the suppression of hate propaganda. But laws penalizing racist speech have been upheld by the European Court and justified as legitimate means for protecting aggrieved minorities and furthering the value of equality. These developments appear to represent a growing consensus in the international community. Should this consensus guide the deliberations of the U.S. Supreme Court?

6. Whether hate speech can be validly suppressed may depend on the basic value informing a constitution. We noted in the introductory essay that the fundamental value informing the U.S. Constitution is liberty, just as dignity might be said to be the primary value of the Basic Law and fraternity of the Canadian Charter. The architectonic or all-embracing value that informs a constitution as a whole may explain why courts of judicial review, in inter-

preting similar language, produce widely varying results. Is liberty the all-embracing value of the United States Constitution? Under what circumstances would the concept of "dignity" trump it in a constitutional case?

7. Wisconsin's "hate crimes" statute provides for an enhanced penalty when a person convicted of an aggravated battery chooses his victim because of his race. A Wisconsin court sentenced Todd Mitchell to four years in prison under the statute, instead of the ordinary maximum prison term of two years. In *Wisconsin v. Mitchell*, 508 U.S. 476 (1993), Chief Justice Rehnquist, writing for a unanimous Court, distinguished this case from *R.A.V.* since the St. Paul ordinance was explicitly directed at speech, whereas here the statute was aimed at conduct unprotected by the First Amendment. In addition, motive played the same role here as it did under federal and state antidiscrimination laws, which the court had upheld against a constitutional challenge.

Hill v. Colorado
530 U.S. 703, 120 U.S. S.Ct. 2480 (2000)

In 1999 Colorado enacted a statute that criminalized the act of "knowingly approach[ing] another person within eight feet of such person, unless such other person consents, for the purpose of passing leaflet or handbill to, displaying a sign to, or engaging in oral protest, education, or counseling with such other person in the public way or sidewalk area within a radius of one hundred feet from any entrance door to a health care facility." The statute's preamble states the legislature's purpose as restricting "a person's right to protest or counsel against certain medical procedures." Petitioners claimed that the statute was a facially invalid infringement of First Amendment speech rights. The state of Colorado defended the statute as a narrowly tailored Time/Place/Manner restriction.

Opinion of the Court: *Stevens*. Concurring opinion: *Souter*. Dissent opinions: *Scalia; Kennedy*.

Justice STEVENS delivered the opinion of the Court. . . .

II . . .

The right to free speech, of course, includes the right to attempt to persuade others to change their views, and may not be curtailed simply because the speaker's message may be offensive to his audience. But the protection afforded to offensive messages does not always embrace offensive speech that is so intrusive that the unwilling audience cannot avoid it. . . . Even in a public forum, one of the reasons we tolerate a protester's right to wear a jacket expressing his opposition to government policy in vulgar language is because offended viewers can "effectively avoid further bombardment of their sensibilities simply by averting their eyes." *Cohen v. California* (1971). . . .

The unwilling listener's interest in avoiding unwanted communication has been repeatedly identified in our cases. It is an aspect of the broader "right to be let alone" that one of our wisest Justices characterized as "the most comprehensive of rights and the right most valued by civilized men." *Olmstead v. United States* (1928) (Brandeis, J., dissenting). . . .

It is that right, as well as the right of "passage without obstruction," that the Colorado statute legitimately seeks to protect. The restrictions imposed by the Colorado statute only apply to communications that interfere with these rights rather than those that involve willing listeners.

. . . The dissenters, however, appear to consider recognizing any of the interests of unwilling listeners—let alone balancing those interests against the rights of speakers—to be unconstitutional. Our cases do not support this view.

III

All four of the state court opinions upholding the validity of this statute concluded that it is a content-neutral time, place, and manner regulation. . . .

Petitioners nevertheless argue that the statute is not content neutral insofar as it applies to some oral communication. The statute applies to all persons who "knowingly approach" within eight feet of another for the purpose of leafletting or displaying signs; for such persons, the content of their oral statements is irrelevant. With respect to persons who are neither leafletters nor sign carriers, however, the statute does not apply unless their approach is "for the purpose of . . . engaging in oral protest, education, or counseling." Petitioners contend that an individual near a health care facility who knowingly approaches a pedestrian to say "good morning" or to randomly recite lines from a novel would not be subject to the statute's restrictions. Because the content of the oral statements made by an approaching speaker must sometimes be examined to determine whether the knowing approach is covered by the statute, petitioners argue that the law is "content-based." . . .

The Colorado statute's regulation . . . places no restrictions on—and clearly does not prohibit—either a particular viewpoint or any subject matter that may be discussed by a speaker. Rather, it simply establishes a minor place restriction on an extremely broad category of communications with unwilling listeners. Instead of drawing distinctions based on the subject that the approaching speaker may wish to address, the statute applies equally to used car salesmen, animal rights activists, fundraisers, environmentalists, and missionaries. Each can attempt to educate unwilling listeners on any subject, but without consent may not approach within eight feet to do so.

Similarly, the contention that a statute is "viewpoint based" simply because its enactment was motivated by the conduct of the partisans on one side of a debate is without support. (Kennedy, J., dissenting) . . .

IV

. . . We already have noted that the statute serves governmental interests that are significant and legitimate and that the restrictions are content neutral. We are likewise persuaded that the statute is "narrowly tailored" to serve those interests and that it leaves open ample alternative channels for communication. As we have emphasized on more than one occasion, when a content-neutral regulation does not entirely foreclose any means of communication, it may satisfy the tailoring requirement even though it is not the least restrictive or least intrusive means of serving the statutory goal.

. . . The 8 foot separation between the speaker and the audience should not have any adverse impact on the readers' ability to read signs displayed by demonstrators. . . .

It is . . . not clear that the statute's restrictions will necessarily impede, rather than assist, the speakers' efforts to communicate their messages. The statute might encourage the most aggressive and vociferous protesters to moderate their confrontational and harassing conduct, and thereby make it easier for thoughtful and law-abiding sidewalk counselors like petitioners to make themselves heard. But whether or not the 8 foot interval is the best possible accommodation of the competing interests at stake, we must accord a measure of deference to the judgment of the Colorado Legislature. . . .

The burden on the ability to distribute handbills is more serious because it seems possible that an 8 foot interval could hinder the ability of a leafletter to deliver handbills to some unwilling recipients. The statute does not, however, prevent a leafletter from simply standing near the path of oncoming pedestrians and proffering his or her material, which the pedestrians can easily accept. . . .

. . . States and municipalities plainly have a substantial interest in controlling the activity around certain public and private places. . . .

Persons who are attempting to enter health care facilities—for any purpose—are often in particularly vulnera-

ble physical and emotional conditions. The State of Colorado has responded to its substantial and legitimate interest in protecting these persons from unwanted encounters, confrontations, and even assaults by enacting an exceedingly modest restriction on the speakers' ability to approach.

Justice Kennedy, however, argues that the statute leaves petitioners without adequate means of communication. This is a considerable overstatement. The statute seeks to protect those who wish to enter health care facilities, many of whom may be under special physical or emotional stress, from close physical approaches by demonstrators. In doing so, the statute takes a prophylactic approach; it forbids all unwelcome demonstrators to come closer than eight feet. We recognize that by doing so, it will sometimes inhibit a demonstrator whose approach in fact would have proved harmless. But the statute's prophylactic aspect is justified by the great difficulty of protecting, say, a pregnant woman from physical harassment with legal rules that focus exclusively on the individual impact of each instance of behavior, demanding in each case an accurate characterization (as harassing or not harassing) of each individual movement within the 8-foot boundary. Such individualized characterization of each individual movement is often difficult to make accurately. A bright-line prophylactic rule may be the best way to provide protection, and, at the same time, by offering clear guidance and avoiding subjectivity, to protect speech itself. . . .

This restriction is thus reasonable and narrowly tailored. . . .

Justice SOUTER, with whom Justice O'CONNOR, Justice GINSBURG, and Justice BREYER join, concurring.

I join the opinion of the Court and add this further word. The key to determining whether [the statute] makes a content-based distinction between varieties of speech lies in understanding that content-based discriminations are subject to strict scrutiny because they place the weight of government behind the disparagement or suppression of some messages, whether or not with the effect of approving or promoting others. . . . Thus the government is held to a very exacting and rarely satisfied standard when it disfavors the discussion of particular subjects or particular viewpoints within a given subject matter.

Concern about employing the power of the State to suppress discussion of a subject or a point of view is not, however, raised in the same way when a law addresses not the content of speech but the circumstances of its delivery. . . . Unless regulation limited to the details of a speaker's delivery results in removing a subject or view-point from effective discourse (or otherwise fails to advance a significant public interest in a way narrowly fitted to that objective), a reasonable restriction intended to affect only the time, place, or manner of speaking is perfectly valid. . . .

. . . The facts overwhelmingly demonstrate the validity of subsection (3) as a content-neutral regulation imposed solely to regulate the manner in which speakers may conduct themselves within 100 feet of the entrance of a health care facility. . . .

This is not to say that enforcement of the approach restriction will have no effect on speech; of course it will make some difference. The effect of speech is a product of ideas and circumstances, and time, place, and manner are circumstances. The question is simply whether the ostensible reason for regulating the circumstances is really something about the ideas. Here, the evidence indicates that the ostensible reason is the true reason. The fact that speech by a stationary speaker is untouched by this statute shows that the reason for its restriction on approaches goes to the approaches, not to the content of the speech of those approaching. What is prohibited is a close encounter when the person addressed does not want to get close. So, the intended recipient can stay far enough away to prevent the whispered argument, mitigate some of the physical shock of the shouted denunciation, and avoid the unwanted handbill. But the content of the message will survive on any sign readable at eight feet and in any statement audible from that slight distance. Hence the implausibility of any claim that an anti-abortion message, not the behavior of protesters, is what is being singled out. . . .

Justice SCALIA, with whom Justice THOMAS joins, dissenting.

The Court today concludes that a regulation requiring speakers on the public thoroughfares bordering medical facilities to speak from a distance of eight feet is "not a 'regulation of speech,'" but "a regulation of the places where some speech may occur"; and that a regulation directed to only certain categories of speech (protest, education, and counseling) is not "content-based." For these reasons, it says, the regulation is immune from the exacting scrutiny we apply to content-based suppression of speech in the public forum. The Court then determines that the regulation survives the less rigorous scrutiny afforded content-neutral time, place, and manner restrictions because it is narrowly tailored to serve a government interest—protection of citizens' "right to be let alone"—that has explicitly been disclaimed by the State, probably for the reason that, as a basis for suppressing peaceful pri-

vate expression, it is patently incompatible with the guarantees of the *First Amendment*.

None of these remarkable conclusions should come as a surprise. . . . Having deprived abortion opponents of the political right to persuade the electorate that abortion should be restricted by law, the Court today continues and expands its assault upon their individual right to persuade women contemplating abortion that what they are doing is wrong. Because, like the rest of our abortion jurisprudence, today's decision is in stark contradiction of the constitutional principles we apply in all other contexts, I dissent.

I

. . . Whatever may be said about the restrictions on the other types of expressive activity, the regulation as it applies to oral communications is obviously and undeniably content-based. A speaker wishing to approach another for the purpose of communicating *any* message except one of protest, education, or counseling may do so without first securing the other's consent. . . . I have no doubt that this regulation would be deemed content-based *in an instant* if the case before us involved antiwar protesters, or union members seeking to "educate" the public about the reasons for their strike. . . .

. . . The Court's confident assurance that the statute poses no special threat to First Amendment freedoms because it applies alike to "used car salesmen, animal rights activists, fundraisers, environmentalists, and missionaries," is a wonderful replication (except for its lack of sarcasm) of Anatole France's observation that "[t]he law, in its majestic equality, forbids the rich as well as the poor to sleep under bridges. . . ." This Colorado law is no more targeted at used car salesmen, animal rights activists, fund raisers, environmentalists, and missionaries than French vagrancy law was targeted at the rich. We know what the Colorado legislators, by their careful selection of content ("protest, education, and counseling"), were taking aim at, for they set it forth in the statute itself: the "right to protest or counsel *against* certain medical procedures" on the sidewalks and streets surrounding health care facilities. (emphasis added) . . .

. . . [I]t blinks reality to regard this statute, in its application to oral communications, as anything other than a content-based restriction upon speech in the public forum. As such, it must survive that stringent mode of constitutional analysis our cases refer to as "strict scrutiny," which requires that the restriction be narrowly tailored to serve a compelling state interest. Since the Court does not even attempt to support the regulation under this standard, I shall discuss it only briefly. Suffice it to say that if protecting people from unwelcome communications (the governmental interest the Court posits) is a compelling state interest, the First Amendment is a dead letter. And if (as I shall discuss at greater length below) forbidding peaceful, nonthreatening, but uninvited speech from a distance closer than eight feet is a "narrowly tailored" means of preventing the obstruction of entrance to medical facilities (the governmental interest the State asserts) narrow tailoring must refer not to the standards of Versace, but to those of Omar the tentmaker. . . .

II

As the Court explains, under our precedents even a content-neutral, time, place, and manner restriction must be narrowly tailored to advance a significant state interest, and must leave open ample alternative means of communication. . . .

This requires us to determine, first, what *is* the significant interest the State seeks to advance? . . . Colorado has identified in the text of the statute itself the interest it sought to advance: to ensure that the State's citizens may "obtain medical counseling and treatment in an unobstructed manner" by "preventing the willful obstruction of a person's access to medical counseling and treatment at a health care facility." In its brief here, the State repeatedly confirms the interest squarely identified in the statute under review. . . . The Court nevertheless concludes that the Colorado provision is narrowly tailored to serve . . . *the State's interest in protecting its citizens' rights to be let alone from unwanted speech.*

Indeed, the situation is even more bizarre than that. The interest that the Court makes the linchpin of its analysis was not only unasserted by the State; it is not only completely *different* from the interest that the statute specifically sets forth; it was explicitly *disclaimed* by the State in its brief before this Court, and characterized as a "straw interest" *petitioners* served up in the hope of discrediting the State's case. . . . We may thus add to the lengthening list of "firsts" generated by this Court's relentlessly pro-abortion jurisprudence, the first case in which, in order to sustain a statute, the Court has relied upon a governmental interest not only unasserted by the State, but positively repudiated. . . .

A . . .

To support the legitimacy of its self-invented state interest, the Court relies upon a bon mot in a 1928 dissent. . . . It characterizes the "unwilling listener's interest in avoiding unwanted communication" as an "aspect of the broader 'right to be let alone'" Justice Brandeis coined in his dissent in *Olmstead v. United States.* The amusing feature is

that even this slim reed contradicts rather than supports the Court's position. The right to be let alone that Justice Brandeis identified was a right the Constitution "conferred, *as against the government*"; it was *that* right, not some generalized "common-law right" or "interest" to be free from hearing the unwanted opinions of one's fellow citizens, which he called the "most comprehensive" and "most valued by civilized men." (emphasis added). To the extent that there can be gleaned from our cases a "right to be let alone" in the sense that Justice Brandeis intended, it is the right of the *speaker* in the public forum to be free from government interference of the sort Colorado has imposed here. . . .

B

I turn now to the real state interest at issue here—the one set forth in the statute and asserted in Colorado's brief: the preservation of unimpeded access to health care facilities. We need look no further than subsection (2) of the statute to see what a provision would look like that is narrowly tailored to serve *that* interest. Under the terms of that subsection, any person who "knowingly obstructs, detains, hinders, impedes, or blocks another person's entry to or exit from a health care facility" is subject to criminal and civil liability. It is possible, I suppose, that subsection (2) of the Colorado statute will leave unrestricted some expressive activity that, if engaged in from within eight feet, may be sufficiently harassing as to have the effect of impeding access to health care facilities. In subsection (3), however, the State of Colorado has prohibited a vast amount of speech that cannot possibly be thought to correspond to that evil.

To begin with, the 8-foot buffer zone attaches to *every* person on the public way or sidewalk within 100 feet of the entrance of a medical facility, regardless of whether that person is seeking to enter or exit the facility. . . .

The Court makes no attempt to justify on the facts this blatant violation of the narrow-tailoring principle. . . .

The burdens this law imposes upon the right to speak are substantial, despite an attempt to minimize them that is not even embarrassed to make the suggestion that they might actually "assist . . . the speakers' efforts to communicate their messages. . . ." It seriously asserts, for example, that the 8-foot zone allows a speaker to communicate at a "normal conversational distance." I have certainly held conversations at a distance of eight feet seated in the quiet of my chambers, but I have never walked along the public sidewalk—and have not seen others do so—"conversing" at an 8-foot remove. The suggestion is absurd. So is the suggestion that the opponents of abortion can take comfort in the fact that the statute "places no limitation on the number of speakers or the noise level, including the use of amplification equipment." That is good enough, I suppose, for "protesting"; but the Court must know that most of the "counseling" and "educating" likely to take place outside a health care facility cannot be done at a distance and at a high-decibel level. The availability of a powerful amplification system will be of little help to the woman who hopes to forge, in the last moments before another of her sex is to have an abortion, a bond of concern and intimacy that might enable her to persuade the woman to change her mind and heart. The counselor may wish to walk alongside and to say, sympathetically and as softly as the circumstances allow, something like: "My dear, I know what you are going through. I've been through it myself. You're not alone and you do not have to do this. There are other alternatives. Will you let me help you? May I show you a picture of what your child looks like at this stage of her human development?" The Court would have us believe that this can be done effectively—yea, perhaps even *more* effectively—by shouting through a bullhorn at a distance of eight feet.

The Court seems prepared, if only for a moment to take seriously the magnitude of the burden the statute imposes on simple handbilling and leafletting. That concern is fleeting, however, since it is promptly assuaged by the realization that a leafletter may, without violating the statute, stand "near the path" of oncoming pedestrians and make his "proffe[r] . . . , which the pedestrians can easily accept." It does not take a veteran labor organizer to recognize although, surely any would, that leafletting will be rendered utterly ineffectual by a requirement that the leafletter obtain from each subject permission to approach, or else man a stationary post and wait for passersby voluntarily to approach an outstretched hand. That simply is not how it is done, and the Court knows it—or should. . . .

. . . [T]he law before us here enacts a broad prophylactic restriction. . . . Such prophylactic restrictions in the *First Amendment* context—even when they are content-neutral—are not permissible. . . . [T]he Court, in responding to Justice Kennedy, abandoned any pretense at compliance with that doctrine, and acknowledged—indeed, boasted—that the statute it approves "takes a prophylactic approach," and adopts "[a] bright-line prophylactic rule." I scarcely know how to respond to such an unabashed repudiation of our *First Amendment* doctrine. Prophylaxis is the antithesis of narrow tailoring . . .

* * *

It is interesting to compare the present decision, which *upholds* an utterly bizarre proabortion "request to approach" provision of Colorado law, with *Stenberg*, also an-

nounced today, which *strikes down* a live-birth abortion prohibition adopted by 30 States and twice passed by both Houses of Congress (though vetoed both times by the President). The present case disregards the State's own assertion of the purpose of its proabortion law, and posits instead a purpose that the Court believes will be more likely to render the law *constitutional. Stenberg* rejects the State's assertion of the very meaning of its antiabortion law, and declares instead a meaning that will render the law *un*constitutional. The present case *rejects* overbreadth challenges to a proabortion law that regulates speech, on grounds that have no support in our prior jurisprudence and that instead amount to a total repudiation of the doctrine of overbreadth. *Stenberg applies* overbreadth analysis to an antiabortion law that has nothing to do with speech, even though until eight years ago overbreadth was unquestionably the exclusive preserve of the *First Amendment*.

Does the deck seem stacked? You bet. As I have suggested throughout this opinion, today's decision is not an isolated distortion of our traditional constitutional principles, but is one of many aggressively proabortion novelties announced by the Court in recent years. Today's distortions, however, are particularly blatant. Restrictive views of the *First Amendment* that have been in dissent since the 1930's suddenly find themselves in the majority. "Uninhibited, robust, and wide open" debate is replaced by the power of the state to protect an unheard-of "right to be let alone" on the public streets. I dissent.

Justice KENNEDY, dissenting.

The Court's holding contradicts more than a half century of well-established *First Amendment* principles. For the first time, the Court approves a law which bars a private citizen from passing a message, in a peaceful manner and on a profound moral issue, to a fellow citizen on a public sidewalk. If from this time forward the Court repeats its grave errors of analysis, we shall have no longer the proud tradition of free and open discourse in a public forum. In my view, Justice Scalia's First Amendment analysis is correct and mandates outright reversal. In addition to undermining established First Amendment principles, the Court's decision conflicts with the essence of the joint opinion in *Planned Parenthood of Southeastern Pa. v. Casey* (1992). . . .

I . . .

A . . .

. . . The liberty of a society is measured in part by what its citizens are free to discuss among themselves. Colorado's scheme of disfavored-speech zones on public streets and sidewalks, and the Court's opinion validating them, are antithetical to our entire First Amendment tradition. To say that one citizen can approach another to ask the time or the weather forecast or the directions to Main Street but not to initiate discussion on one of the most basic moral and political issues in all of contemporary discourse, a question touching profound ideas in philosophy and theology, is an astonishing view of the First Amendment. For the majority to examine the statute under rules applicable to content-neutral regulations is an affront to First Amendment teachings. . . .

III . . .

. . . Laws punishing speech which protests the lawfulness or morality of the government's own policy are the essence of the tyrannical power the First Amendment guards against. We must remember that, by decree of this Court in discharging our duty to interpret the Constitution, any plea to the government to outlaw some abortions will be to no effect. See *Planned Parenthood of Southeastern Pa. v. Casey* (1992). Absent the ability to ask the government to intervene, citizens who oppose abortion must seek to convince their fellow citizens of the moral imperative of their cause. . . .

The means of expression at stake here are of controlling importance. Citizens desiring to impart messages to women considering abortions likely do not have resources to use the mainstream media for their message, much less resources to locate women contemplating the option of abortion. Lacking the aid of the government or the media, they seek to resort to the time honored method of leafleting and the display of signs. . . .

Colorado's excuse, and the Court's excuse, for the serious burden imposed upon the right to leaflet or to discuss is that it occurs at the wrong place. Again, Colorado and the Court have it just backwards. For these protestors the 100-foot zone in which young women enter a building is not just the last place where the message can be communicated. It likely is the only place. It is the location where the Court should expend its utmost effort to vindicate free speech, not to burden or suppress it.

Perhaps the leaflet will contain a picture of an unborn child, a picture the speaker thinks vital to the message. One of the arguments by the proponents of abortion, I had thought, was that a young woman might have been so uninformed that she did not know how to avoid pregnancy. The speakers in this case seek to ask the same uninformed woman, or indeed any woman who is considering an abortion, to understand and to contemplate the nature of the life she carries within her. To re-

strict the right of the speaker to hand her a leaflet, to hold a sign, or to speak quietly is for the Court to deny the neutrality that must be the first principle of the First Amendment. In this respect I am in full agreement with Justice Scalia's explanation of the insult the Court gives when it tells us these grave moral matters can be discussed just as well through a bullhorn. It would be remiss, moreover, not to observe the profound difference a leaflet can have in a woman's decisionmaking process. . . .

There are, no doubt, women who would testify that abortion was necessary and unregretted. The point here is simply that speech makes a difference, as it must when acts of lasting significance and profound moral consequence are being contemplated. The majority reaches a contrary conclusion only by disregarding settled free speech principles. In doing so it delivers a grave wound to the First Amendment as well as to the essential reasoning in the joint opinion in *Casey,* a concern to which I now turn.

IV

In *Planned Parenthood of Southeastern Pa. v. Casey,* the Court reaffirmed its prior holding that the Constitution protects a woman's right to terminate her pregnancy in its early stages. The joint opinion in *Casey* considered the woman's liberty interest and principles of *stare decisis,* but took care to recognize the gravity of the personal decision: "[Abortion] is an act fraught with consequences for others: for the woman who must live with the implications of her decision; for the persons who perform and assist in the procedure; for the spouse, family, and society which must confront the knowledge that these procedures exist, procedures some deem nothing short of an act of violence against innocent human life; and, depending on one's beliefs, for the life or potential life that is aborted."

The Court now strikes at the heart of the reasoned, careful balance I had believed was the basis for the joint opinion in *Casey.* The vital principle of the opinion was that in defined instances the woman's decision whether to abort her child was in its essence a moral one, a choice the State could not dictate. Foreclosed from using the machinery of government to ban abortions in early term, those who oppose it are remitted to debate the issue in its moral dimensions. In a cruel way, the Court today turns its back on that balance. It in effect tells us the moral debate is not so important after all and can be conducted just as well through a bullhorn from an 8-foot distance as it can through a peaceful, face-to-face exchange of a leaflet. The lack of care with which the Court sustains the Colorado statute reflects a most troubling abdication of our responsibility to enforce the First Amendment.

There runs through our First Amendment theory a concept of immediacy, the idea that thoughts and pleas and petitions must not be lost with the passage of time. In a fleeting existence we have but little time to find truth through discourse. No better illustration of the immediacy of speech, of the urgency of persuasion, of the preciousness of time, is presented than in this case. Here the citizens who claim First Amendment protection seek it for speech which, if it is to be effective, must take place at the very time and place a grievous moral wrong, in their view, is about to occur. The Court tears away from the protesters the guarantees of the First Amendment when they most need it. So committed is the Court to its course that it denies these protesters, in the face of what they consider to be one of life's gravest moral crises, even the opportunity to try to offer a fellow citizen a little pamphlet, a handheld paper seeking to reach a higher law.

I dissent.

Notes and Queries

1. *Hill* was decided on the same day as *Stenberg v. Carhart*, the so-called partial-birth abortion case. The coupling of these cases was noted by Justice Scalia, who described the Court's ruling in *Hill* as part of "our abortion jurisprudence." Indeed, it is not difficult to discern a common subtext in the various opinions of the Court, one driven by the national controversy over abortion. How is this subtext manifested in the actual texts of the opinions? The minority justices in effect charge the majority with hypocrisy for the latter's tolerance of abortion-sympathetic restrictions on free speech. Are they in turn vulnerable to the same charge, given that Justices Scalia, Rehnquist, and Kennedy had previously upheld (in *Rust v. Sullivan*) federal regulations forbidding doctors *within* clinics to counsel patients about abortions?

2. Justice Stevens writes of "the unwilling listener's interest in avoiding unwanted communication." He identifies this interest as part of the broader "right to be let alone," which was first articulated by Justice Brandeis in a case (*Olmstead v. United States*) that is important in the Court's developing jurisprudence of privacy. Does one, however, have a right to privacy when one ventures into a public space? Do you agree with Justice Scalia that in the public forum it is the right of the *speaker* that needs protection from governmental interference, as opposed to that of the listener, who must accept the reality that she may be required to hear uncomfortable messages?

3. Justice Souter's insistence that the Colorado statute was content-neutral was challenged both on and off of the Court. One critical commentary cited "abundant evidence in *Hill* that . . . the complete text, operation, and discriminatory function of the statute revealed an intent to restrict one particular kind of speech, namely anti-abortion speech." Jamin B. Raskin and Clark L. LeBlanc, *Disfavored Speech About Favored Rights:* Hill v. Colorado, *the Vanishing Public Forum and the Need For an Objective Speech Discrimination Test,* 51 American University Law Review 179, p. 212. The critique goes on to advocate that restrictions on speech be analyzed to discover their "social meaning" as a way of testing the claims of neutrality that supporters of such restrictions often assert in their defense. Do you agree? Should the Court engage in an independent historical/sociological inquiry to determine the constitutionality of a law?

4. Is Justice Kennedy correct in finding an inconsistency between the judgment in this case and the ruling in *Casey*? Does the fact that the Court upheld the right of a woman to obtain an abortion require that she be forced to listen to those imploring her to refrain from exercising that right?

Miller v. California
413 U.S. 15, 93 S.Ct. 2607, 37 L.Ed.2d 419 (1973)

The defendant was convicted of mailing unsolicited advertising brochures containing pictures and drawings of sexually explicit materials in violation of a California statute making it a misdemeanor to distribute such materials. The trial court instructed the jury to evaluate the materials by the contemporary community standards of California. The previous test for determining obscenity was laid down in *Roth v. United States*, 354 U.S. 476 (1957). The *Roth* test was "whether to the average person, applying contemporary community standards, the dominant theme taken as a whole appeals to a prurient interest." In applying this test, the Supreme Court identified "community" with a national rather than a local standard, making it extremely difficult for any obscenity statute to survive constitutional analysis. The California conviction was affirmed on appeal. Opinion of the Court: *Berger*, White, Blackmun, Powell, Rehnquist. Dissenting opinions: *Brennan*, Stewart, Marshall; *Douglas*.

Chief Justice BURGER delivered the opinion of the Court.

Comparative Note 12.11

[In 1960, the Japanese Supreme Court rejected an appeal from a publisher convicted of selling an obscene publication. The publication was the novel *Lady Chatterly's Lover*. The following extract is from the opinion sustaining the conviction.]

As a general rule, the possession, irrespective of differences of civilization, race, clime, and history, of a sense of shame is a fundamental characteristic that sets man apart from the beasts. Shame, compassion, and reverence are the most fundamental emotions that man possesses. . . . These emotions constitute the foundation of universal morality.

The existence of the sense of shame is especially striking in respect to sexual desire. Sexual desire in itself is not evil; it is the instinct with which man is provided for the preservation of the species, that is, for the continuation and development of the family and of human society. That men possess this in common with other animals is a natural aspect of mankind. Consequently, the spirituality existent in man, namely, his nobility, is conscious of a feeling of revulsion toward it.

This is, of course, the sense of shame. This emotion is not to be discerned in animals. There may be situations in which it is lacking or rare in certain spiritually undeveloped or ill individual human beings or in certain special societies, but it exists beyond question, if one observes humanity in general. For example, even in uncivilized societies the custom of complete exposure of the sexual organs is extremely rare and, again, there is no such thing as the public performance of the sex act. In short, the nonpublic nature of the sex act, which characterizes man alone, is a natural manifestation of the sense of shame that has its origin in human nature. This sense of shame must be respected, and any rejection of it as a form of hypocrisy runs counter to human nature. Thus, the existence of the sense of shame, in company with reason, controls the sexual life of man, which is difficult to restrain, so that it will not fall into licentiousness and, no matter how civilized a society may be, contributes to the maintenance of order and morality in respect to sex.

Source: *Court and Constitution in Japan: Selected Supreme Court Decisions 1948–60*, ed. John M. Maki (Seattle: University of Washington Press, 1964), 3–37.

I

This case involves the application of a State's criminal obscenity statute to a situation in which sexually explicit materials have been thrust by aggressive sales action upon unwilling recipients who had in no way indicated any desire to receive such materials. . . .

* * *

II

This much has been categorically settled by the Court, that obscene material is unprotected by the First Amendment. "The First and Fourteenth Amendments have never been treated as absolutes." We acknowledge, however, the inherent dangers of undertaking to regulate any form of expression. State statutes designed to regulate obscene materials must be carefully limited. As a result, we now confine the permissible scope of such regulation to works which depict or describe sexual conduct. That conduct must be specifically defined by the applicable state law, as written or authoritatively construed. A state offense must also be limited to works which, taken as a whole, appeal to the prurient interest in sex, which portray sexual conduct in a patently offensive way, and which, taken as a whole, do not have serious literary, artistic, political, or scientific value.

The basic guidelines for the trier of fact must be: (a) whether "the average person, applying contemporary community standards" would find that the work, taken as a whole, appeals to the prurient interest; (b) whether the work depicts or describes, in a patently offensive way, sexual conduct specifically defined by the applicable state law; and (c) whether the work, taken as a whole, lacks serious literary, artistic, political, or scientific value. . . . If a state law that regulates obscene material is thus limited, as written or construed, the First Amendment values applicable to the States through the Fourteenth Amendment are adequately protected by the ultimate power of appellate courts to conduct an independent review of constitutional claims when necessary.

We emphasize that it is not our function to propose regulatory schemes for the States. That must await their concrete legislative efforts. It is possible, however, to give a few plain examples of what a state statute could define for regulation under part (b) of the standard announced in this opinion, *supra*:

(a) Patently offensive representations or descriptions of ultimate sexual acts, normal or perverted, actual or simulated.

(b) Patently offensive representations or descriptions of masturbation, excretory functions, and lewd exhibition of the genitals.

Sex and nudity may not be exploited without limit by films or pictures exhibited or sold in places of public accommodation any more than live sex and nudity can be exhibited or sold without limit in such public places. At a minimum, prurient, patently offensive depiction or description of sexual conduct must have serious literary, artistic, political, or scientific value to merit First Amendment protection. For example, medical books for the education of physicians and related personnel necessarily use graphic illustrations and descriptions of human anatomy. In resolving the inevitably sensitive questions of fact and law, we must continue to rely on the jury system, accompanied by the safeguards that judges, rules of evidence, presumption of innocence, and other protective features provide, as we do with rape, murder, and a host of other offenses against society and its individual members.

Justice Brennan, author of the [earlier] opinions of the Court, or the plurality opinions . . . has abandoned his former position and now maintains that no formulation of this Court, the Congress, or the States can adequately distinguish obscene material unprotected by the First Amendment from protected expression (dissenting in *Paris Adult Theatre I v. Slaton*). Paradoxically, Mr. Justice Brennan indicates that suppression of unprotected obscene material is permissible to avoid exposure to unconsenting adults, as in this case, and to juveniles, although he gives no indication of how the division between protected and nonprotected materials may be drawn with greater precision for these purposes than for regulation of commercial exposure to consenting adults only. Nor does he indicate where in the Constitution he finds the authority to distinguish between a willing "adult" one month past the state law age of majority and a willing "juvenile" one month younger.

Under the holdings announced today, no one will be subject to prosecution for the sale or exposure of obscene materials unless these materials depict or describe patently offensive "hard core" sexual conduct specifically defined by the regulating state law, as written or construed. We are satisfied that these specific prerequisites will provide fair notice to a dealer in such materials that his public and commercial activities may bring prosecution. If the inability to define regulated materials with ultimate, godlike precision altogether removes the power of the States

or the Congress to regulate, then "hard core" pornography may be exposed without limit to the juvenile, the passerby, and the consenting adult alike, as, indeed, Mr. Justice Douglas contends. . . . In this belief, however, Mr. Justice Douglas now stands alone.

III

Under a National Constitution, fundamental First Amendment limitations on the powers of the States do not vary from community to community, but this does not mean that there are, or should or can be, fixed, uniform national standards of precisely what appeals to the "prurient interest" or is "patently offensive." These are essentially questions of fact, and our Nation is simply too big and too diverse for this Court to reasonably expect that such standards could be articulated for all 50 States in a single formulation, even assuming the prerequisite consensus exists. When triers of fact are asked to decide whether "the average person, applying contemporary community standards" would consider certain materials "prurient," it would be unrealistic to require that the answer be based on some abstract formulation. The adversary system, with lay jurors as the usual ultimate fact finders in criminal prosecutions, has historically permitted triers of fact to draw on the standards of their community, guided always by limiting instructions on the law. To require a State to structure obscenity proceedings around evidence of a national "community standard" would be an exercise in futility. . . .

We conclude that neither the State's alleged failure to offer evidence of "national standards," nor the trial court's charge that the jury consider state community standards, were constitutional errors. Nothing in the First Amendment requires that a jury must consider hypothetical and unascertainable "national standards" when attempting to determine whether certain materials are obscene as a matter of fact. . . .

It is neither realistic nor constitutionally sound to read the First Amendment as requiring that the people of Maine or Mississippi accept public depiction of conduct found tolerable in Las Vegas, or New York City. People in different States vary in their tastes and attitudes, and this diversity is not to be strangled by the absolutism of imposed uniformity. . . . We hold that the requirement that the jury evaluate the materials with reference to "contemporary standards of the State of California" serves this protective purpose and is constitutionally adequate.

IV

The dissenting Justices sound the alarm of repression. But, in our view, to equate the free and robust exchange of ideas and political debate with commercial exploitation of obscene material demeans the grand conception of the First Amendment and its high purposes in the historic struggle for freedom. . . . The First Amendment protects works which, taken as a whole, have serious literary, artistic, political, or scientific value, regardless of whether the government or a majority of the people approve of the ideas these works represent. "The protection given speech and press was fashioned to assure unfettered interchange of ideas for the bringing about of political and social changes desired by the people." But the public portrayal of hard-core sexual conduct for its own sake, and for the ensuing commercial gain, is a different matter.

There is no evidence, empirical or historical, that the stern 19th century American censorship of public distribution and display of material relating to sex in any way limited or affected expression of serious literary, artistic, political, or scientific ideas. On the contrary, it is beyond any question that the era following Thomas Jefferson to Theodore Roosevelt was an "extraordinarily vigorous period," not just in economics and politics, but in belles lettres and in "the outlying fields of social and political philosophies." We do not see the harsh hand of censorship of ideas—good or bad, sound or unsound—and "repression" of political liberty lurking in every state regulation of commercial exploitation of human interest in sex.

In sum, we (a) reaffirm the *Roth* holding that obscene material is not protected by the First Amendment; (b) hold that such material can be regulated by the States, subject to the specific safeguards enunciated above, without a showing that the material is "utterly without redeeming social value"; and (c) hold that obscenity is to be determined by applying "contemporary community standards," not "national standards." . . .

Vacated and remanded.

Justice DOUGLAS, dissenting.

Today the Court retreats from the earlier formulations of the constitutional test and undertakes to make new definitions. This effort, like the earlier ones, is earnest and well intentioned. The difficulty is that we do not deal with constitutional terms, since "obscenity" is not mentioned in the Constitution or Bill of Rights. And the First Amendment makes no such exception from "the press" which it undertakes to protect nor, as I have said on other occasions, is an exception necessarily implied, for there was no recognized exception to the free press at the time the Bill of Rights was adopted which treated "obscene" publications differently from other types of papers, magazines, and books. So there are no constitutional guidelines for

deciding what is and what is not "obscene." The Court is at large because we deal with tastes and standards of literature. What shocks me may be sustenance for my neighbor. What causes one person to boil up in rage over one pamphlet or movie may reflect only his neurosis, not shared by others. We deal here with a regime of censorship which, if adopted, should be done by constitutional amendment after full debate by the people.

Obscenity cases usually generate tremendous emotional outbursts. They have no business being in the courts. If a constitutional amendment authorized censorship, the censor would probably be an administrative agency. Then criminal prosecutions could follow as, if, and when publishers defied the censor and sold their literature. Under that regime a publisher would know when he was on dangerous ground. Under the present regime—whether the old standards or the new ones are used—the criminal law becomes a trap. A brand new test would put a publisher behind bars under a new law improvised by the courts after the publication. That . . . has all the evils of an *ex post facto* law.

My contention is that until a civil proceeding has placed a tract beyond the pale, no criminal prosecution should be sustained. . . .

II

If a specific book, play, paper, or motion picture has in a civil proceeding been condemned as obscene and review of that finding has been completed, and thereafter a person publishes, shows, or displays that particular book or film, then a vague law has been made specific. There would remain the underlying question whether the First Amendment allows an implied exception in the case of obscenity. I do not think it does and my views on the issue have been stated over and over again. But at least a criminal prosecution brought at that juncture would not violate the time-honored void-for-vagueness test.

No such protective procedure has been designed by California in this case. Obscenity—which even we cannot define with precision—is a hodge-podge. To send men to jail for violating standards they cannot understand, construe, and apply is a monstrous thing to do in a Nation dedicated to fair trials and due process.

III

The idea that the First Amendment permits government to ban publications that are "offensive" to some people puts an ominous gloss on freedom of the press. That test would make it possible to ban any paper or any journal or magazine in some benighted place. The First Amendment was designed "to invite dispute," to induce "a condition of unrest," to "create dissatisfaction with conditions as they are," and even to stir "people to anger." The idea that the First Amendment permits punishment for ideas that are "offensive" to the particular judge or jury sitting in judgment is astounding. No greater leveler of speech or literature has ever been designed. To give the power to the censor, as we do today, is to make a sharp and radical break with the traditions of a free society. The First Amendment was not fashioned as a vehicle for dispensing tranquilizers to the people. Its prime function was to keep debate open to "offensive" as well as to "staid" people. The tendency throughout history has been to subdue the individual and to exalt the power of government. The use of the standard "offensive" gives authority to government that cuts the very vitals out of the First Amendment. As is intimated by the Court's opinion, the materials before us may be garbage. But so is much of what is said in political campaigns, in the daily press, on TV, or over the radio. By reason of the First Amendment—and solely because of it—speakers and publishers have not been threatened or subdued because their thoughts and ideas may be "offensive" to some.

If there are to be restraints on what is obscene, then a constitutional amendment should be the way of achieving the end. There are societies where religion and mathematics are the only free segments. It would be a dark day for America if that were our destiny. But the people can make it such if they choose to write obscenity into the Constitution and define it.

We deal with highly emotional, not rational, questions. To many the Song of Solomon is obscene. I do not think we, the judges, were ever given the constitutional power to make definitions of obscenity. If it is to be defined, let the people debate and decide by a constitutional amendment what they want to ban as obscene and what standards they want the legislatures and the courts to apply. Perhaps the people will decide that the path towards a mature, integrated society requires that all ideas competing for acceptance must have no censor. Perhaps they will decide otherwise. Whatever the choice, the courts will have some guidelines. Now we have none except our own predilections.

Justice BRENNAN, with whom Justice STEWART and Justice MARSHALL join, dissenting.

Notes and Queries

1. In *Paris Adult Theatre I v. Slaton* (1973), decided on the same day as *Miller*, the Court upheld a Georgia statute which outlawed "hard-core" pornography. The opinion of the Court was argued in the same terms as the opinion in *Miller*. In his dissent, Justice Brennan argued that it was not possible to distinguish "obscene" sexually oriented material which does not merit constitutional protection under the First Amendment, from nonobscene sexually oriented material that cannot be suppressed. He urged the Court to abandon its attempts to define obscenity, writing:

> Like the proscription of abortions, the effort to suppress obscenity is predicated on unprovable, although strongly held, assumptions about human behavior, morality, sex, and religion. The existence of these assumptions cannot validate a statute that substantially undermines the guarantees of the First Amendment, any more than the existence of similar assumptions on the issue of abortion can validate a statute that infringes the constitutionally protected privacy interests of a pregnant woman. . . . For if a State, in an effort to maintain or create a particular moral tone, may prescribe what its citizens cannot read or cannot see, then it would seem to follow that in pursuit of the same objective a State could decree that its citizens must read certain books or must view certain films. . . .
>
> In short, while I cannot say that the interests of the State—apart from the question of juveniles and unconsenting adults—are trivial or nonexistent, I am compelled to conclude that these interests cannot justify the substantial damage to constitutional rights and to this nation's judicial machinery that inevitably results from State efforts to bar the distribution even of unprotected material to consenting adults. . . .

2. Compare the logic of *Miller* with the logic of *Brandenburg, Cohen*, and *New York Times Company v. Sullivan*. Was *Miller* decided on ground consistent with the other decisions? What kind of harm does obscene material cause?

3. The tension between liberty and community loom large in obscenity cases. These terms however are not self-defining. What does the Supreme Court have in mind when referring to liberty? Abstract individualism? Radical autonomy? A community-centered individual? There are also different understandings of community. A community could be national or local. It could refer generally to the civic culture or to a neighborhood, religious group, or some other network of social relations. How does a court decide which of these community orientations is reflected in a restriction on speech? How much judicial deference is owing to local majorities responsible for the adoption of such restrictions? Would or should the degree of judicial deference hinge on the deliberative quality of the debate

preceding their adoption? On the quality or extent of the representative assembly adopting the restrictions?

4. *Miller* raises important questions not only about the tension between liberty and community, but also about the boundaries and definition of community. What reasons does the Court offer for entrusting decisions about pornography to smaller, local communities? Do those reasons rest upon a particular understanding of what "community" means or the values it promotes? What are the arguments for making the relevant community the nation rather than the municipality? Do they too rest upon a particular understanding of community?

5. In Germany and some other foreign jurisdictions, obscenity would be judged by the standard of human dignity. The majority opinion in *Slaton* includes the following passage: "The sum of experience, including that of the past two decades, affords an ample basis for legislatures to conclude that a sensitive, key relationship of human existence, central to family life, community welfare, and the development of the human personality, can be debased and distorted by crass commercial exploitation of sex. Nothing in the Constitution prohibits a State from reaching such a conclusion and acting on it legislatively simply because there is no conclusive evidence or empirical data." Is this fundamentally a dignitarian argument?

6. Are the majority and dissenting opinions in *Miller*

based on different conceptions of personhood or the human personality? Compare the two opinions with the extract from the Canadian Supreme Court in Comparative Note 12.9.

7. In 1984, the City Council of Indianapolis passed an ordinance redefining pornography as follows:

Pornography is a discriminatory practice based on sex because its effect is to deny women equal opportunities in society. Pornography is a systematic practice of exploitation and subordination based on sex which differentially harms women. The bigotry and contempt it promotes, with the acts of aggression it fosters, harm women's opportunities for equality of rights in employment, education, access to and use of public accommodations, and acquisition of real property, and contribute significantly to restricting women in particular from full exercise of citizenship and participation in public life, including neighborhoods.

The Supreme Court summarily affirmed a federal appeals court decision striking down the ordinance as violative of the First Amendment. *American Booksellers Association, Inc. v. Hudnut*, 771 F. 2d 323. aff'd 475 U.S. 1001 (7th Cir. 1985). The Canadian Supreme Court appears to have accepted the "harm" theory categorically rejected in *Hudnut*. (See Comparative Note 12.12).

City of Erie v. Pap's A.M.
529 U.S. 277, 146 L Ed 2d 265, 120 S Ct 1382 (2000)

When Erie, Pennsylvania enacted an ordinance banning public nudity, Pap's A.M., the owner of a nude dancing establishment, challenged the statute as a violation of the First Amendment right to freedom of expression. In 1991 the Supreme Court had upheld a similar Indiana ordinance in *Barnes v. Glen Theatre*, but in spite of that decision, the Pennsylvania Supreme Court determined that the Erie ordinance did violate a right to free expression. Judgment of the Court: *O'Connor*, Rehnquist, Kennedy, Breyer. Concurring opinions: *Scalia*, Thomas. Concurring in part and dissenting in part: *Souter.* Dissenting opinions: *Stevens*, Ginsburg.

Justice O'CONNOR announced the judgment of the Court and delivered the opinion of the Court with respect to Parts I and II, and an opinion with respect to Parts III and IV, in which The Chief Justice, Justice KENNEDY, and Justice BREYER join.

Being "in a state of nudity" is not an inherently expressive condition. As we explained in *Barnes*, however, nude

dancing of the type at issue here is expressive conduct, although we think that it falls only within the outer ambit of the First Amendment's protection.

To determine what level of scrutiny applies to the ordinance at issue here, we must decide "whether the State's regulation is related to the suppression of expression." *Texas v. Johnson* (1989); see also *United States v. O'Brien* (1968). If the governmental purpose in enacting the regulation is unrelated to the suppression of expression, then the regulation need only satisfy the "less stringent" standard from *O'Brien* for evaluating restrictions on symbolic speech. If the government interest is related to the content of the expression, however, then the regulation falls outside the scope of the *O'Brien* test and must be justified under a more demanding standard.

In *Barnes*, we analyzed an almost identical statute, holding that Indiana's public nudity ban did not violate the First Amendment, although no five Members of the Court agreed on a single rationale for that conclusion. We now clarify that government restrictions on public nudity such as the ordinance at issue here should be evaluated under the framework set forth in *O'Brien* for content-neutral restrictions on symbolic speech.

Comparative Note 12.12

[In this case, the Canadian Supreme Court sustained an obscenity statute on grounds largely rejected by the United States Circuit Court of Appeals in *American Booksellers Ass. v. Hudnut*.]

Justice Sopinka, writing for the majority.

. . . To impose a certain standard of public and sexual morality, solely because it reflects the conventions of a given community, is inimical to the exercise and enjoyment of individual freedoms, which form the basis of our social contract. . . . On the other hand, I cannot agree with the suggestion of the appellant that Parliament does not have the right to legislate on the basis of some fundamental conception of morality for the purposes of safeguarding the values which are integral to a free and democratic society.

In my view . . . the overriding objective of [the obscenity statute] is not moral disapprobation but the avoidance of harm to society. . . . The harm was described in the following way by the [MacGuigan Report]:

. . . *The effect of this type of material is to reinforce male-female stereotypes to the detriment of both sexes. It attempts to make degradation, humiliation,*

victimization, and violence in human relationships appear normal and acceptable. A society which holds that egalitarianism, non-violence, consensualism, and mutuality are basic to any human interaction . . .

The message of obscenity which degrades and dehumanizes is analogous to that of hate propaganda. . . . While a direct link between obscenity and harm to society may be difficult, if not impossible, to establish, it is reasonable to presume that exposure to images bears a causal relationship to changes in attitudes and beliefs. . . .

The objective of the legislation . . . is of fundamental importance in a free and democratic society. It is aimed at avoiding harm, which Parliament has reasonably concluded will be caused directly or indirectly, to individuals, groups such as women and children, and consequently to society as a whole, by the distribution of these [hard core pornographic] materials. It thus seeks to enhance respect for all members of society, and non-violence and equality in their relations with each other.

SOURCE: *R. v. Butler* (1992) 89 D.L.R. (4th) 449.

The city of Erie argues that the ordinance is a content-neutral restriction that is reviewable under *O'Brien* because the ordinance bans conduct, not speech; specifically, public nudity. Respondent counters that the ordinance targets nude dancing and, as such, is aimed specifically at suppressing expression, making the ordinance a content-based restriction that must be subjected to strict scrutiny.

The ordinance here, like the statute in *Barnes*, is on its face a general prohibition on public nudity. By its terms, the ordinance regulates conduct alone. It does not target nudity that contains an erotic message; rather, it bans all public nudity, regardless of whether that nudity is accompanied by expressive activity.

. . . In that sense, this case is similar to *O'Brien*. O'Brien burned his draft registration card as a public statement of his antiwar views, and he was convicted under a statute making it a crime to knowingly mutilate or destroy such a card. This Court rejected his claim that the statute violated his First Amendment rights, reasoning that the law punished him for the "noncommunicative impact of his conduct, and for nothing else." In other words, the Government regulation prohibiting the destruction of draft cards was aimed at maintaining the integrity of the Selective Service System and not at suppressing the message of draft resistance that O'Brien sought to convey by burning his draft card. So too here, the ordinance prohibiting public nudity is aimed at combating crime and other negative secondary effects caused by the presence of adult entertainment establishments like Kandyland and not at suppressing the erotic message conveyed by this type of nude dancing. Put another way, the ordinance does not attempt to regulate the primary effects of the expression, *i.e.*, the effect on the audience of watching nude erotic dancing, but rather the secondary effects, such as the impacts on public health, safety, and welfare. . . .

Although the Pennsylvania Supreme Court acknowledged that one goal of the ordinance was to combat the negative secondary effects associated with nude dancing establishments, the court concluded that the ordinance was nevertheless content based, relying on Justice White's position in dissent in *Barnes* for the proposition that a ban of this type *necessarily* has the purpose of suppressing the erotic message of the dance. . . . A majority of the Court rejected that view in *Barnes*, and we do so again here.

Even if we had not already rejected the view that a ban on public nudity is necessarily related to the suppression of the erotic message of nude dancing, we would do so now because the premise of such a view is flawed. The State's interest in preventing harmful secondary effects is not related to the suppression of expression. In trying to control the secondary effects of nude dancing, the ordinance seeks to deter crime and the other deleterious effects caused by the presence of such an establishment in the neighborhood.

Similarly, even if Erie's public nudity ban has some minimal effect on the erotic message by muting that portion of the expression that occurs when the last stitch is dropped, the dancers at Kandyland and other such establishments are free to perform wearing pasties and G-strings. Any effect on the overall expression is *de minimis*. . . . If States are to be able to regulate secondary effects, then *de minimis* intrusions on expression such as those at issue here cannot be sufficient to render the ordinance content based.

We conclude that Erie's asserted interest in combating the negative secondary effects associated with adult entertainment establishments like Kandyland is unrelated to the suppression of the erotic message conveyed by nude dancing. The ordinance prohibiting public nudity is therefore valid if it satisfies the four-factor test from *O'Brien* for evaluating restrictions on symbolic speech.

Applying that standard here, we conclude that Erie's ordinance is justified under *O'Brien*. The first factor of the *O'Brien* test is whether the government regulation is within the constitutional power of the government to enact. Here, Erie's efforts to protect public health and safety are clearly within the city's police powers. The second factor is whether the regulation furthers an important or substantial government interest. The asserted interests of regulating conduct through a public nudity ban and of combating the harmful secondary effects associated with nude dancing are undeniably important.

Finally, it is worth repeating that Erie's ordinance is on its face a content neutral restriction that regulates conduct, not First Amendment expression. And the government should have sufficient leeway to justify such a law based on secondary effects.

As to the second point—whether the regulation furthers the government interest—it is evident that, since crime and other public health and safety problems are caused by the presence of nude dancing establishments like Kandyland, a ban on such nude dancing would further Erie's interest in preventing such secondary effects.

The ordinance also satisfies *O'Brien*'s third factor, that the government interest is unrelated to the suppression of free expression, as discussed. The fourth and final *O'Brien* factor—that the restriction is no greater than is essential to the furtherance of the government interest—is satisfied as well. The ordinance regulates conduct, and any incidental impact on the expressive element of nude dancing is *de minimis*.

We hold, therefore, that Erie's ordinance is a content-neutral regulation that is valid under *O'Brien*. Accordingly, the judgment of the Pennsylvania Supreme Court is reversed, and the case is remanded for further proceedings not inconsistent with this opinion.

Justice SCALIA, with whom Justice THOMAS joins, concurring in the judgment.

. . . I agree that the decision of the Pennsylvania Supreme Court must be reversed, but disagree with the mode of analysis the Court has applied.

. . . In *Barnes*, I voted to uphold the challenged Indiana statute "not because it survives some lower level of First Amendment scrutiny, but because, as a general law regulating conduct and not specifically directed at expression, it is not subject to First Amendment scrutiny at all." Erie's ordinance, too, by its terms prohibits not merely nude dancing, but the act—irrespective of whether it is engaged in for expressive purposes—of going nude in public.

Moreover, even were I to conclude that the city of Erie had specifically singled out the activity of nude dancing, I still would not find that this regulation violated the First Amendment unless I could be persuaded (as on this record I cannot) that it was the communicative character of nude dancing that prompted the ban. When conduct other than speech itself is regulated, it is my view that the First Amendment is violated only "[w]here the government prohibits conduct precisely because of its communicative attributes." *Barnes*. Here, even if one hypothesizes that the city's object was to suppress only nude dancing, that would not establish an intent to suppress what (if anything) nude dancing communicates. I do not feel the need, as the Court does, to identify some "secondary effects" associated with nude dancing that the city could properly seek to eliminate. (I am highly skeptical, to tell the truth, that the addition of pasties and G-strings will at all reduce the tendency of establishments such as Kandyland to attract crime and prostitution, and hence to foster sexually transmitted disease.) The traditional power of government to foster good morals (*bonos mores*), and the acceptability of the traditional judgment (if Erie wishes to endorse it) that nude public dancing *itself* is immoral, have not been repealed by the First Amendment.

Justice SOUTER, concurring in part and dissenting in part.

I . . . agree with the analytical approach that the plurality employs in deciding this case. Erie's stated interest in combating the secondary effects associated with nude dancing establishments is an interest unrelated to the suppression of expression under *United States v. O'Brien,* and the city's regulation is thus properly considered under the *O'Brien* standards. I do not believe, however, that the current record allows us to say that the city has made a sufficient evidentiary showing to sustain its regulation. . . .

In several recent cases, we have confronted the need for factual justifications to satisfy intermediate scrutiny under the First Amendment. Those cases do not identify with any specificity a particular quantum of evidence, nor do I seek to do so in this brief concurrence. What the cases do make plain, however, is that application of an intermediate scrutiny test to a government's asserted rationale for regulation of expressive activity demands some factual justification to connect that rationale with the regulation in issue.

The upshot of these cases is that intermediate scrutiny requires a regulating government to make some demonstration of an evidentiary basis for the harm it claims to flow from the expressive activity, and for the alleviation expected from the restriction imposed. . . . What is clear is that the evidence of reliance must be a matter of demonstrated fact, not speculative supposition.

By these standards, the record before us today is deficient in its failure to reveal any evidence on which Erie may have relied, either for the seriousness of the threatened harm or for the efficacy of its chosen remedy. . . . As to current fact, the city council's closest approach to an evidentiary record on secondary effects and their causes was the statement of one councilor, during the debate over the ordinance, who spoke of increases in sex crimes in a way that might be construed as a reference to secondary effects. But that reference came at the end of a litany of concerns ("free condoms in schools, drive-by shootings, abortions, suicide machines" and declining student achievement test scores) that do not seem to be secondary effects of nude dancing.

There is one point, however, on which an evidentiary record is not quite so hard to find, but it hurts, not helps, the city. The final *O'Brien* requirement is that the incidental speech restriction be shown to be no greater than essential to achieve the government's legitimate purpose. To deal with this issue, we have to ask what basis there is to think that the city would be unsuccessful in countering any secondary effects by the significantly lesser restriction of zoning to control the location of nude dancing, thus allowing for efficient law enforcement, restricting effects on property values, and limiting exposure of the public. The record shows that for 23 years there has been a zoning ordinance on the books to regulate the location of establishments like Kandyland, but the city has not enforced it.

The record before us now does not permit the conclusion that Erie's ordinance is reasonably designed to mitigate real harms. This does not mean that the required showing cannot be made, only that, on this record, Erie has not made it. I would remand to give it the opportunity to do so. Accordingly, although I join with the plurality in adopting the *O'Brien* test, I respectfully dissent from the Court's disposition of the case.

Justice STEVENS, with whom Justice GINSBURG joins, dissenting.

Far more important than the question whether nude dancing is entitled to the protection of the First Amendment are the dramatic changes in legal doctrine that the Court endorses today. Until now, the "secondary effects" of commercial enterprises featuring indecent entertainment have justified only the regulation of their location. For the first time, the Court has now held that such effects may justify the total suppression of protected speech.

The Court's use of the secondary effects rationale to permit a total ban has grave implications for basic free speech principles. Ordinarily, laws regulating the primary effects of speech, *i.e.,* the intended persuasive effects caused by the speech, are presumptively invalid. Under today's opinion, a State may totally ban speech based on its secondary effects . . . yet the regulation is not presumptively invalid.

The Court's mishandling of our secondary effects cases is not limited to its approval of a total ban. It compounds that error by dramatically reducing the degree to which the State's interest must be furthered by the restriction imposed on speech, and by ignoring the critical difference between secondary effects caused by speech and the incidental effects on speech that may be caused by a regulation of conduct.

In what can most delicately be characterized as an enormous understatement, the plurality concedes that "requiring dancers to wear pasties and G-strings may not greatly reduce these secondary effects." To believe that the mandatory addition of pasties and a G-string will have *any* kind of noticeable impact on secondary effects requires nothing short of a titanic surrender to the implausible.

Correct analysis of the issue in this case should begin with the proposition that nude dancing is a species of expressive conduct that is protected by the First Amendment. . . . [N]ude dancing fits well within a broad, cultural tradition recognized as expressive in nature and entitled to First Amendment protection. The nudity of the dancer is both a component of the protected expression and the specific target of the ordinance. It is pure sophistry to reason from the premise that the regulation of the nudity component of nude dancing is unrelated to the message conveyed by nude dancers.

Notes and Queries

1. Do you agree that the ban on public nudity is no different from the ban on burning draft registration cards in *United States v. O'Brien*? Or is Justice Souter correct in finding that even under the intermediate scrutiny standard, there must be an evidentiary basis for the harm that is claimed to flow from an expressive activity, and that the two cases are distinguishable on that basis?

2. In her opinion for the Court, Justice O'Connor indicated that the "Court will not strike down an otherwise constitutional statute on the basis of an alleged illicit legislative motive." By contrast, in arguing that the ordinance in question was unconstitutional censorship of expression, Justice Stevens' dissenting opinion quotes a lawmaker to the effect that the banning of public nudity was specifically targeted at the problem of adult entertainment. How much weight should be attached to such evidence,

as opposed to the specific language of the statute? (Note, though, that the preamble to the Erie ordinance does in fact articulate this purpose.) As we will see in the next chapter, Justice Stevens' opinion in *Wallace v. Jaffree* uses the same approach to establish the intent behind a law. What are the strengths and weaknesses of this approach? Can motive be ignored in determining a law's constitutionality?

3. One critique of the Court's ruling in *Pap's* suggests the following: "Since this form of entertainment is not popular among the American majority, is not considered to be 'high-value' speech, and arguably provides limited stand-alone contributions to American society as a whole, it is only in the very minds of its particular audience that this uniquely erotic expression has its desired effect. As such, the plurality allows a plainly majoritarian attack on unpopular speech to be disguised by jurisprudential smoke and mirrors." Christopher Thomas Leahy, "The First Amendment Gone Awry: City of Erie v. Pap's A.M., Ailing Analytical Structures, and the Suppression of Protected Speech," 150 *University of Pennsylvania Law Review* 1021, 1074. The "smoke and mirrors" refers to the Court's use of the secondary effects doctrine, which in this case led, for the first time, to a total ban on a form of expression, as opposed to the imposition of a time, place, or manner restriction. Why, however, should a majority not be able to ban a unique form of low-value expression that is thought to have effects on the quality of community life that, in its estimation, are decidedly negative? Is Justice Scalia correct in affirming that a community may determine "that nude public dancing *itself* is immoral," and that such a determination may justify banning it under "the traditional power of government to foster good morals"?

Boy Scouts of America v. Dale
530 U.S. 640, 147 L Ed 554, 120 S Ct 2446 (2000)

James Dale, an accomplished member of the Cub Scouts and Boy Scouts since 1978, applied for adult membership in the organization in 1989 and was named the assistant scoutmaster of the Monmouth Council (New Jersey) Troop 73. At about the same time Dale began attending Rutgers University, where he became co-president of the Rutgers University Lesbian/Gay Alliance. While at a seminar addressing the psychological needs of lesbian and gay teenagers, Dale was interviewed by a local newspaper, and he emphasized the need for gay role models for teens. When the interview was published, the Boy Scouts revoked his membership. Davis challenged this action in New Jersey Superior Court, alleging that the Scouts' action violated a

New Jersey public accommodations statute that prohibited discrimination on the basis of sexual orientation. When the New Jersey Supreme Court found that the Boy Scouts was a public accommodation subject to the anti-discrimination statute, the Scouts countered that the statute violated the organization's First Amendment right to expressive association. Opinion of the Court: *Rehnquist*, O'Connor, Scalia, Kennedy, Thomas. Dissenting opinions: *Stevens*, Souter, Ginsburg, Breyer; *Souter*, Ginsburg, Breyer

Chief Justice REHNQUIST delivered the opinion of the Court.

In *Roberts v. United States Jaycees* (1984), we observed that "implicit in the right to engage in activities protected by the First Amendment" is "a corresponding right to asso-

Comparative Note 12.13

[Article 19 of the Indian Constitution: Protection of certain rights regarding freedom of speech, etc.—All citizens shall have the right—

. . . .

(c) to form associations or unions;

. . . .

(4) Nothing in sub-clause (c) of the said clause shall affect the operation of any existing law in so far as it imposes, or prevent the State from making any law imposing, in the interests of the sovereignty and integrity of India or public order or morality, reasonable restrictions on the exercise of the right conferred by the said sub-clause.]

Exercising the right to form an association may curtail the freedom to express views against its activities. For example, a person joining an association to promote adoptions cannot express anti-adoption views. He may lose his membership. Some restriction on one's rights may be necessary to protect another's rights in a given situation. Proper exercise of rights may have, implicit in them, certain restrictions. The rights must be harmoniously construed so that they are properly promoted with the minimum of such implied and necessary restrictions.

SOURCE: *M. H. Devendrappa v. the Karnataka State Small Industries Development Corporation (1998).*

---

ciate with others in pursuit of a wide variety of political, social, economic, educational, religious, and cultural ends." This right is crucial in preventing the majority from imposing its views on groups that would rather express other, perhaps unpopular, ideas.

The forced inclusion of an unwanted person in a group infringes the group's freedom of expressive association if the presence of that person affects in a significant way the group's ability to advocate public or private viewpoints.

Given that the Boy Scouts engages in expressive activity, we must determine whether the forced inclusion of Dale as an assistant scoutmaster would significantly affect the Boy Scouts' ability to advocate public or private viewpoints. This inquiry necessarily requires us first to explore, to a limited extent, the nature of the Boy Scouts' view of homosexuality.

. . . The Boy Scouts asserts that homosexual conduct is inconsistent with the values embodied in the Scout Oath and Law, particularly with the values represented by the terms "morally straight" and "clean."

. . . [T]he Scout Oath and Law do not expressly mention sexuality or sexual orientation. And the terms "morally straight" and "clean" are by no means self-defining. Different people would attribute to those terms very different meanings. For example, some people may believe that engaging in homosexual conduct is not at odds with being "morally straight" and "clean." And others may believe that engaging in homosexual conduct is contrary to being "morally straight" and "clean." The Boy Scouts says it falls within the latter category.

The New Jersey Supreme Court analyzed the Boy Scouts' beliefs and found that the "exclusion of members solely on the basis of their sexual orientation is inconsistent with Boy Scouts' commitment to a diverse and 'representative' membership . . . [and] contradicts Boy Scouts' overarching objective to reach 'all eligible youth.'" The court concluded that the exclusion of members like Dale "appears antithetical to the organization's goals and philosophy." But our cases reject this sort of inquiry; it is not the role of the courts to reject a group's expressed values because they disagree with those values or find them internally inconsistent.

The Boy Scouts asserts that it "teach[es] that homosexual conduct is not morally straight," and that it does "not want to promote homosexual conduct as a legitimate form of behavior." We accept the Boy Scouts' assertion. We need not inquire further to determine the nature of the Boy Scouts' expression with respect to homosexuality.

We must then determine whether Dale's presence as an assistant scoutmaster would significantly burden the Boy Scouts' desire to not "promote homosexual conduct as a legitimate form of behavior." As we give deference to an association's assertions regarding the nature of its expression, we must also give deference to an association's view of what would impair its expression. That is not to say that an expressive association can erect a shield against antidiscrimination laws simply by asserting that mere acceptance of a member from a particular group would impair its message. But here Dale, by his own admission, is one of a group of gay Scouts who have "become leaders in their community and are open and honest about their sexual orientation." Dale was the copresident of a gay and lesbian organization at college and remains a gay rights activist. Dale's presence in the Boy Scouts would, at the very least, force the organization to send a message, both to the youth members and the world, that the Boy Scouts accepts homosexual conduct as a legitimate form of behavior.

Having determined that the Boy Scouts is an expressive association and that the forced inclusion of Dale would significantly affect its expression, we inquire whether the application of New Jersey's public accommodations law to require that the Boy Scouts accept Dale as an assistant scoutmaster runs afoul of the Scouts' freedom of expressive association. We conclude that it does.

We are not, as we must not be, guided by our views of whether the Boy Scouts' teachings with respect to homosexual conduct are right or wrong; public or judicial disapproval of a tenet of an organization's expression does not justify the State's effort to compel the organization to accept members where such acceptance would derogate from the organization's expressive message.

The judgment of the New Jersey Supreme Court is reversed, and the cause remanded for further proceedings not inconsistent with this opinion.

Justice STEVENS, with whom Justice SOUTER, Justice GINSBURG and Justice BREYER join, dissenting.

In this case, Boy Scouts of America contends that it teaches the young boys who are Scouts that homosexuality is immoral. Consequently, it argues, it would violate its right to associate to force it to admit homosexuals as members, as doing so would be at odds with its own shared goals and values. This contention, quite plainly, requires us to look at what, exactly, are the values that BSA actually teaches.

To bolster its claim that its shared goals include teaching that homosexuality is wrong, BSA directs our attention to two terms appearing in the Scout Oath and Law. The first is the phrase "morally straight," which appears in the Oath . . . ; the second term is the word "clean," which appears in a list of 12 characteristics together comprising the Scout Law.

It is plain as the light of day that neither one of these principles—"morally straight" and "clean"—says the slightest thing about homosexuality. Indeed, neither term in the Boy Scouts' Law and Oath expresses any position whatsoever on sexual matters.

. . . The relevant question is whether the mere inclusion of the person at issue would "impose any serious burden," "affect in any significant way," or be "a substantial restraint upon" the organization's "shared goals," "basic goals," or "collective effort to foster beliefs." Accordingly,

it is necessary to examine what, exactly, are BSA's shared goals and the degree to which its expressive activities would be burdened, affected, or restrained by including homosexuals. See *Roberts v. United States Jaycees* (1984) and *Board of Directors of Rotary Int'l v. Rotary Club of Duarte* (1987).

The evidence before this Court makes it exceptionally clear that BSA has, at most, simply adopted an exclusionary membership policy and has no shared goal of disapproving of homosexuality. BSA's mission statement and federal charter say nothing on the matter; its official membership policy is silent; its Scout Oath and Law—and accompanying definitions—are devoid of any view on the topic; its guidance for Scouts and Scoutmasters on sexuality declare that such matters are "not construed to be Scouting's proper area," but are the province of a Scout's parents and pastor; and BSA's posture respecting religion tolerates a wide variety of views on the issue of homosexuality. Moreover, there is simply no evidence that BSA otherwise teaches anything in this area, or that it instructs Scouts on matters involving homosexuality in ways not conveyed in the Boy Scout or Scoutmaster Handbooks. In short, Boy Scouts of America is simply silent on homosexuality. There is no shared goal or collective effort to foster a belief about homosexuality at all—let alone one that is significantly burdened by admitting homosexuals.

The majority pretermits this entire analysis. It finds that BSA in fact "teach[es] that homosexual conduct is not morally straight." This conclusion, remarkably, rests entirely on statements in BSA's briefs. Moreover, the majority insists that we must "give deference to an association's assertions regarding the nature of its expression" and "we must also give deference to an association's view of what would impair its expression." So long as the record "contains written evidence" to support a group's bare assertion, "[w]e need not inquire further." Once the organization "asserts" that it engages in particular expression, "[w]e cannot doubt" the truth of that assertion.

This is an astounding view of the law. I am unaware of any previous instance in which our analysis of the scope of a constitutional right was determined by looking at what a litigant asserts in his or her brief and inquiring no further. . . . It is an odd form of independent review that consists of deferring entirely to whatever a litigant claims. But the majority insists that our inquiry must be "limited," because "it is not the role of the courts to reject a group's expressed values because they disagree with those values or find them internally inconsistent."

But nothing in our cases calls for this Court to do any such thing. An organization can adopt the message of its choice, and it is not this Court's place to disagree with it.

But we must inquire whether the group is, in fact, expressing a message (whatever it may be) and whether that message (if one is expressed) is significantly affected by a State's antidiscrimination law. More critically, that inquiry requires our *independent* analysis, rather than deference to a group's litigating posture. Reflection on the subject dictates that such an inquiry is required.

There is, of course, a valid concern that a court's independent review may run the risk of paying too little heed to an organization's sincerely held views. But unless one is prepared to turn the right to associate into a free pass out of antidiscrimination laws, an independent inquiry is a necessity.

Even if BSA's right to associate argument fails, it nonetheless might have a First Amendment right to refrain from including debate and dialogue about homosexuality as part of its mission to instill values in Scouts. . . . Dale's right to advocate certain beliefs in a public forum or in a private debate does not include a right to advocate these ideas when he is working as a Scoutmaster. And BSA cannot be compelled to include a message about homosexuality among the values it actually chooses to teach its Scouts, if it would prefer to remain silent on that subject.

In its briefs, BSA implies, even if it does not directly argue, that Dale would use his Scoutmaster position as a "bully pulpit" to convey immoral messages to his troop, and therefore his inclusion in the group would compel BSA to include a message it does not want to impart. Even though the majority does not endorse that argument, I think it is important to explain why it lacks merit, before considering the argument the majority does accept.

BSA has not contended, nor does the record support, that Dale had ever advocated a view on homosexuality to his troop before his membership was revoked. Accordingly, BSA's revocation could only have been based on an assumption that he would do so in the future. But the only information BSA had at the time it revoked Dale's membership was a newspaper article describing a seminar at Rutgers University on the topic of homosexual teenagers that Dale attended.

To be sure, the article did say that Dale was co-president of the Lesbian/Gay Alliance at Rutgers University, and that group presumably engages in advocacy regarding homosexual issues. But surely many members of BSA engage in expressive activities outside of their troop, and surely BSA does not want all of that expression to be carried on inside the troop.

The majority, though, does not rest its conclusion on the claim that Dale will use his position as a bully pulpit. Rather, it contends that Dale's mere presence among the Boy Scouts will itself force the group to convey a message about homosexuality—even if Dale has no intention of doing so.

The only apparent explanation for the majority's holding . . . is that homosexuals are simply so different from the rest of society that their presence alone—unlike any other individual's—should be singled out for special First Amendment treatment. Under the majority's reasoning, an openly gay male is irreversibly affixed with the label "homosexual." That label, even though unseen, communicates a message that permits his exclusion wherever he goes. His openness is the sole and sufficient justification for his ostracism. Though unintended, reliance on such a justification is tantamount to a constitutionally prescribed symbol of inferiority.

Unfavorable opinions about homosexuals "have ancient roots." *Bowers v. Hardwick* (1986). Like equally atavistic opinions about certain racial groups, those roots have been nourished by sectarian doctrine. Over the years, however, interaction with real people, rather than mere adherence to traditional ways of thinking about members of unfamiliar classes, have modified those opinions. A few examples: The American Psychiatric Association's and the American Psychological Association's removal of "homosexuality" from their lists of mental disorders; a move toward greater understanding within some religious communities; Justice Blackmun's classic opinion in *Bowers;* Georgia's invalidation of the statute upheld in *Bowers;* and New Jersey's enactment of the provision at issue in this case. Indeed, the past month alone has witnessed some remarkable changes in attitudes about homosexuals.

That such prejudices are still prevalent and that they have caused serious and tangible harm to countless members of the class New Jersey seeks to protect are established matters of fact that neither the Boy Scouts nor the Court disputes. That harm can only be aggravated by the creation of a constitutional shield for a policy that is itself the product of a habitual way of thinking about strangers. As Justice Brandeis so wisely advised, "we must be ever on our guard, lest we erect our prejudices into legal principles."

If we would guide by the light of reason, we must let our minds be bold. I respectfully dissent.

Justice SOUTER, with whom Justice GINSBURG and Justice BREYER join, dissenting.

I join Justice Stevens's dissent but add this further word. . . . Justice Stevens describes the changing attitudes toward gay people and notes a parallel with the decline of stereotypical thinking about race and gender. . . . The fact that we are cognizant of this laudable decline in stereotypical thinking on homosexuality should not, however, be taken to control the resolution of this case.

The right of expressive association does not . . . turn on the popularity of the views advanced by a group that claims protection. Whether the group appears to this Court to be in the vanguard or rearguard of social thinking is irrelevant to the group's rights.

Notes and Queries

1. According to Chief Justice Rehnquist: "Forcing a group to accept certain members may impair the ability of the group to express those views, and only those views, that it intends to express. Thus 'freedom of association plainly presupposes a freedom not to associate.'" Do you agree that the freedom of association necessarily implies a freedom of disassociation? If it does, should that freedom outweigh the state's interest in enforcing its anti-discrimination laws?

2. How persuasive is the Court in its finding that the Boy Scouts have a message on the subject of homosexuality? Does it matter that not all members of the association share the views about homosexuality that the Court recognizes as an acceptable reason for the exclusion of Dale from the Boy Scouts?

3. One commentator has written that "The Scouts [are] situated no differently than a tax protester, who is also prevented from communicating a message he does not want to communicate and who is also forced, much as the Scouts are, to send a message he does not want to send—support for the United States government." Jed Rubenfeld, *The First Amendment's Purpose,* 53 Stanford Law Review 767 (2001). Do you agree that these examples are indistinguishable for First Amendment purposes? Do you further agree that "individuals should not obtain a First Amendment 'pass' from generally applicable conduct laws just because they want to break the law for expressive reasons"? As we shall see in chapter 13, this issue of exemption from laws of general applicability is central to the Court's interpretation of the First Amendment's free exercise clause.

4. Justice Stevens argued that "it is exceedingly difficult to believe that BSA . . . adopts a single particular religious or moral philosophy when it comes to sexual orientation." Why shouldn't the Boy Scouts' statement before the Court that they do not wish to express the message Dale personifies be sufficient to win its case? Of what relevance, then, is Justice Stevens' inquiry into whether the association actually teaches anything about homosexuality? In other words, how deferential should the Court be to how an association characterizes itself in a legal submission?

Chapter 13

Freedom of Religion in Public and Private Life

The relationship between matters of the soul and matters of state is a subject of intense controversy in most nations. Every polity must reconcile the demands of religious faith (and denial) with the beliefs of others, as well as with the collective welfare of the community. In the United States and most other constitutional democracies, religion and politics make for an especially perplexing mix. Problems arise because such states seek to respect an individual's right to autonomy in matters of religious persuasion as well as the majority's right to govern.

Consider two sorts of problems. First, under what conditions, if any, may a majority of the community express its beliefs in public places, such as schools? In the controversial case of *Newdow v. U.S. Congress* (2002), the Ninth Circuit Court of Appeals ruled that a congressional statute (passed in 1954) that added the words "under God" to the pledge of allegiance is unconstitutional. Agreeing with Newdow that the pledge violated the establishment clause, the circuit court concluded the pledge "conveyed a message of state endorsement of a religious belief."[1] The decision caused a hailstorm of controversy. House Majority Leader Tom DeLay, for example, announced plans to remove the federal courts' jurisdiction to rule on the constitutionality of the words "under God" in the Pledge: "Congress for so long has been lax in standing up for the Constitution. There are ways to express ourselves. . . . [W]e could limit the jurisdiction of the judicial branch."

A second set of problems concerns under what conditions, if any, a community may regulate or prohibit the religious beliefs and practices of individual citizens or religious groups. Should parents be permitted to withhold medical treatment, such as a blood transfusion, from their children if it violates a principle of their religion? Should a society be permitted to prohibit polygamy if it offends the moral sensibilities of a majority? The religion clauses of the First Amendment, perhaps more clearly than any other part of the constitutional document, illuminate the themes central to our exploration of American constitutional law. They raise difficult and important issues of constitutional interpretation and judicial power, issues that cannot be fully

---

[1] As we write this, the Supreme Court has agreed to review the case in the 2003–04 term.

understood without an appreciation of the political, philosophical—and sometimes theological—ideas that stand behind and inform those clauses and the Constitution as a whole.[2]

Much of American colonial history is a story about the struggle between demands for religious conformity and religious freedom.[3] It is therefore surprising that the unamended text of the Philadelphia Constitution says almost nothing about freedom of religion. Article VI provides that "no religious Test shall ever be required as a Qualification to any Office or public Trust under the United States." This is an important and novel guarantee of religious freedom, especially since many of the States did have religious tests for office.[4] In Massachusetts and Maryland, for example, only Christians could hold the office of governor, and in some others the post was reserved to Protestants. Standing alone, however, Article VI hardly amounts to a sweeping guarantee of religious freedom.

The absence of an explicit guarantee of religious freedom was a major objection to the Constitution's ratification in several states. As we saw in chapter 9, the proponents of conditional ratification eventually forced Madison and Hamilton to promise to introduce a proposed bill of rights in the first Congress. Concerning religion, Madison's draft provided "The civil rights of none shall be abridged on account of religious belief or worship, nor shall any national religion be established, nor shall the full and equal rights of conscience be in any manner, or any pretext, infringed." As finally ratified, the First Amendment includes two provisions for religious freedom. The establishment clause provides that "Congress shall make no law respecting an establishment of religion." The free exercise clause further guarantees that Congress shall make no law "prohibiting the free exercise" of religion.[5]

Constitutional Interpretation and the Religion Clauses of the First Amendment

In recent years, a deeply divided Court has hinted at sweeping changes in the long-settled doctrines that make up freedom of religion jurisprudence. A moment's reflection should make clear why there is so much confusion and disagreement within the Court. First, and most immediate, any guarantee of religious freedom in a diverse and complex society requires an appreciation of the ways in which religious beliefs will be intertwined with, and sometimes in conflict with, the political, cultural, and moral

---

[2] Historically a commitment to constitutionalism has usually "expressed larger religious and moral ideas of covenant" with a just God, "who limits His power on terms of our free and rational consent. . . ." "[O]ur covenant with the state . . . limits its power by political and/or constitutional constraints of respect for our rights. . . . In the West, therefore, the development of constitutionalism cannot be understood historically absent an appreciation of its roots in political and religious thought more generally." David A. J. Richards, *Toleration and the Constitution.* (New York: Oxford University Press, 1986), 68, 101–02. Carl J. Friedrich, *Transcendent Justice.* (Durham: Duke University Press, 1964).

[3] Many of us are inclined to think of America's colonial heritage as a struggle to break away from the suffocating religious conformity of Europe, and of England in particular. Having won religious freedom for themselves, however, some colonists were less eager to extend it to others. Roger Williams' flight to Rhode Island to escape religious persecution in Massachusetts was indicative of the relative absence of religious freedom in some colonies. Many colonies had official, or established, religions, and most required a profession of belief to hold office or to vote.

[4] The Supreme Court found this requirement unconstitutional in *Torasco v. Watkins*, 367 U.S. 488 (1961).

[5] The primary source of these provisions is Madison, who had publicly campaigned for religious toleration in Virginia in 1785. In his "Memorial and Remonstrance Against Religious Assessments," Madison argued for the complete independence of religion and the state.

beliefs of other persons. In such a society, religion must compete, if it does not act in concert with, a wide variety of other sources, including public schools and the state itself, as an influence on an individual's development. And in some ways, the very diversity of religious beliefs that the religion clauses promote causes problems. Religious freedom as a means of achieving diversity has proven remarkably success- ful in the United States. By one estimate, there are well over 250 major churches in the United States, and scores of smaller groups.[6] The variety and diversity of religious expression in the United States greatly increases the opportunities for religious con- flict, whether among religions, or between the community and particular religious beliefs. In part because of the clause itself, and in part because of the complex inter- relationship between religion, individual identity, and the state in the 21st century, the Court's jurisprudence on freedom of religion is very much in a state of flux.

Some of the interpretative difficulties surrounding the religion clauses are common to other provisions in the Bill of Rights. Here, as elsewhere, appeals to Framers' intent must cope with an ambiguous historical record. When the Founders prohibited laws respecting an establishment of religion, did they intend, in Jefferson's words, to erect a "wall of separation" between church and state? Sometimes called the "separationist position," advocates of the Jeffersonian wall of separation argue that the Founders intended the establishment clause to prohibit completely any kind of state support, direct or indirect, for religion.[7] Or did they mean only to prohibit the common Euro- pean practice, then followed by some American states, of creating an official state religion? Proponents of the "accommodationist position" argue the latter, observing that the Founders did not foresee a state hostile to religion in general.[8] The purpose of the First Amendment, they argue, was to forbid the government from favoring one religion over another, but it does not require complete neutrality, or hostility, toward all forms of religion.[9]

The American Supreme Court has largely constructed a jurisprudence that em- braces the Lockean privatization of religion. The claim that religion is a private mat- ter, though, is a hallmark of Protestant theology. It less easily characterizes the religious thought of Roman Catholicism and orthodox Judaism, for example, or of Hindu and Muslim religious beliefs, which are more likely to stress the communal and public aspects of religious belief and practice. In some other constitutional de- mocracies, such as Germany, Italy, Ireland, and to a lesser extent Canada, constitu- tional courts have been less eager to embrace the claim that religion is a private affair.

The Lockean position was embraced by Thomas Paine and Thomas Jefferson, who closely linked religious toleration with notions of free expression. And many of the cases we shall consider in this chapter make little or no mention of religion directly, instead treating the issues as matters of freedom of expression. What explains this tendency to subsume religion questions under issues of expression? One answer suggests the tendency can be explained as a legacy of our Lockean constitutionalism: Removal of religion to the private sphere is both a sign of and has contributed to the

---

[6]Leo Rosten, *Religions in America: Ferment and Faith in Age of Crisis.* (New York: Simon & Schuster, 1963).

[7]*Everson v. Board of Education*, 330 U.S. 1 (1947); See also Leonard W. Levy, *The Establishment Clause: Religion and the First Amendment.* (New York: Macmillan Co., 1986).

[8]*Marsh v. Chambers*, 463 U.S. 783 (1983).

[9]See, for example, Michael J. Malbin, *Religion and Politics: The Intentions of the Authors of the First Amendment.* (Washington, D.C.: American Enterprise Institute, 1981), 13–17.

Court's inability or unwillingness to reconcile democracy and religion. Moreover, the tendency to assimilate religious claims into the speech clause has two consequences. First, it sidesteps any need to define religion. Second, and more importantly, it denies or obscures the distinctive importance of religion to public life and the independent content of the religion clauses.[10]

Why, then, did the Founders make special mention of religion? Appeals to the purposes of the religion clauses require us first to determine why we desire religious liberty. Freedom of religion is important to constitutional democracies for several reasons. As we have seen, self-determination and individual judgment lie at the heart of Lockean democratic theory. In seeking to limit government, Locke expanded the private domain, and included in that domain is religion. The privatization of religion, of course, had several justifications, including genuine respect for personal autonomy as well as removal from the public domain of an enduring source of civil conflict. In addition, constitutionalism's concern for self-determination and individual autonomy seem self-evidently to require some measure of freedom in matters of religious belief and expression. Although religion and religious belief are "expression," they are "of a special kind; [they] rise above ordinary expression because [they] deal with the innermost convictions of the human person. . . ."[11]

Freedom of religion is also a constitutional imperative because, like freedom of expression, it serves a larger social and political purpose. The political theory of liberalism embraced by Madison in *Federalist* 10 values toleration and diversity in civil society as a guard against the tyranny of faction. Freedom of religion, like freedom of expression, is an end in itself, but it is also a means of protecting and preserving constitutional democracy from social and political unrest. Other Founders, such as George Washington and John Adams, sought to protect religious freedom because they believed it "was an essential cornerstone for morality, civic virtue and democratic government."[12] Others have argued that religious freedom is as much a means of protecting religion as of protecting the state. Roger Williams' flight to Rhode Island prompted a defense of separation of church and state grounded not in the needs of the state, but rather upon the sanctity of religious belief. Religion, Williams argued, would be corrupted by politics if not made immune from it.[13]

The Problem of Definition: What Is Religion?

What does "religion" mean? The difficulty in defining religion, like so many of the other issues we have considered, raises thorny questions about the nature and limits of judicial power. Should the Court defer to individual judgments about what is protected religious belief? Or should the Court decide for itself what religion means? Can the Court assume this authority without inevitably trampling on the religious beliefs of minority groups? These are open questions in the Court's freedom of religion jurisprudence.

Read literally, the First Amendment prohibits only Congress from interfering with

---

[10] See, for example, John H. Garvey, *Free Exercise and the Values of Religious Liberty,* 18 Connecticut Law Review 779 (1986).

[11] Donald P. Kommers, *The Constitutional Jurisprudence of the Federal Republic of Germany.* 2d ed. (Durham: Duke University Press, 1997), 443.

[12] See Arlin Adams and Charles Emmerich, *A Nation Dedicated to Religious Liberty: The Constitutional Heritage of the Religion Clauses.* (Philadelphia: University of Pennsylvania Press, 1990), 26.

[13] See Mark DeWolfe Howe, *The Garden and the Wilderness: Religion and Government in American History.* (Chicago: University of Chicago Press, 1965).

religious liberty. Even after the amendment was ratified the states were free, within the confines of Article VI, to regulate religious liberty as they chose; religious oaths and established religions in the states persisted until well into the twentieth century. In *Cantwell v. Connecticut* (1940), though, the Court incorporated the free exercise clause. The establishment clause followed just seven years later, in *Everson v. Board of Education* (1947, reprinted later in the chapter). Hence, most of the Court's work on freedom of religion is a product of the twentieth century and mainly of the period following the Second World War, when many foreign constitutional courts were developing their own constitutional law of religious freedom.

Two decisions in the late nineteenth century, however, foreshadowed most of the important conceptual and interpretive difficulties in this area. In *Reynolds v. United States* (1878), the Court unanimously upheld a congressional statute that prohibited polygamy in United States territories. The statute was an obvious effort to harass the Mormons, who had migrated to Utah to escape persecution, some of it grounded in religious bigotry, and some of it a reaction to the heady political aspirations of Mormon elders in other states. In response to the Mormons' claim that the law interfered with their freedom of religious exercise, the Court observed that "Laws are made for the government of actions, and while they cannot interfere with mere religious belief and opinions, they may with practices."

Evident in *Reynolds*, and soon afterward in *Davis v. Beason* (1890, reprinted later in the chapter), was an underlying hostility to some, if not most, of the tenets of Mormon faith. In *Davis*, Justice Field argued that "The term 'religion' has reference to one's views of his relations to his Creator, and to the obligations they impose of reverence for his being and character, and of obedience to his will." Field then concluded, "To call their advocacy a tenet of religion is to offend the common sense of mankind."

In rejecting a Mormon "tenet of faith," the Court reserved to itself the final authority to define what religion means in the First Amendment. Is this an appropriate exercise of judicial authority? On the one hand, the term "religion" in the First Amendment seems to demand interpretation by someone, much as "speech" requires interpretation for purposes of free expression. But is it clear that the power should rest with the Court? How is the Court to determine what actually counts as a religious value? Should it appeal to the convictions of the majority or to "the common sense of mankind"? Should it appeal to history or tradition to distinguish "real" from "false" religions?

Alternatively, should the Court simply accept as "religion" whatever is sincerely held as a religious belief? In *United States v. Ballard* (1944), the Court considered this question in a mail fraud case involving members of the "I am" religion. Founded by Guy Ballard, the religion claimed its members were "divine messengers" with the power to heal physical ailments. The government arrested Ballard's widow and son for making "fraudulent claims." (The possibility that religion may be a front for fraud is hardly unique to the United States. In recent years, for example, German authorities have attempted to regulate the Church of Scientology, claiming that it is fraudulent and misleading.)

In his opinion for the Court, Justice Douglas stated that the jury was prohibited from considering "the truth or verity of respondents' religious doctrines or beliefs. [If] one could be sent to jail because a jury in a hostile environment found [his] teaching false, little indeed would be left of religious freedom." Hence, freedom of religion means sometimes accepting views that would seem "incredible, if not preposterous, to most people." In *Fowler v. Rhode Island* (1953), the Court concluded again "It is no business of courts to say that what is a religious practice or activity for one group is not religion under the protection of the First Amendment." Similarly, in *Thomas v. Review Board* (1981), the Court said, "Courts are not arbiters of scriptural interpretation." Perhaps it was inevitable the Court would cede over at least some of the power of definition to individuals. The alternative would embroil the Court in endless cases about whether one set or another of allegedly religious beliefs was authentic or fake. Would it be possible for the Court to craft a "neutral" principle (of the sort discussed in chapter 2) to decide such cases?

Nevertheless, the Court has not totally withdrawn from the practice of determining what constitutes a religious belief. In *Wisconsin v. Yoder* (1972, reprinted later in the chapter), the Court emphasized that

> *a way of life, however virtuous and admirable, may not be interposed as a barrier . . . if it is based on purely secular considerations; to have the protection of the Religion Clauses, the claims must be rooted in religious belief. . . . Thus, if the Amish asserted their claims because of their subjective evaluation and rejection of the contemporary secular values accepted by the majority, much as Thoreau rejected the social values of his time . . . , their claims would not rest on a religious basis. Thoreau's choice was philosophical and personal rather than religious.*

Questions about the definition of religion are also complicated by the presence of two guarantees of religious freedom in the First Amendment. In the preceding cases, for example, the Court considered the definition of religion for purposes of the Free Exercise Clause. Should the same definition hold for establishment cases? Consider Justice Rutledge's dissent in *Everson*: "'Religion' appears only once in the [First] Amendment. But the word governs two prohibitions and governs them alike. It does not have two meanings, one narrow to forbid an 'establishment' and another, much broader, for securing 'the free exercise thereof.'"

There is an obvious appeal to Rutledge's approach. On the other hand, can a single definition do justice to the wide range of different problems the two clauses raise? The foregoing cases developed a fairly expansive definition of religion for the free exercise clause. As we saw, this expansive notion, if not required by the free exercise clause, *is* sympathetic to the broader notions of autonomy and freedom of conscience, and of religious pluralism, that inform religious liberty. But is it clear that a similarly expansive definition of religion is appropriate for the establishment clause? In answering this question, we must again consider the purposes of the clause, as well as the realities of the contemporary welfare state. An expansive definition of religion under the establishment provision might render unconstitutional a great many governmental programs designed to aid children in public and private schools, or concerning the distribution of welfare and unemployment benefits.[14] In this way, an expansive definition of religion under the establishment clause is likely to frustrate the purposes we sought to achieve by defining religion broadly under the free exercise clause.

The Establishment Clause: Strict Separation or Accommodation?

At the founding, state established religions were common both in Europe and in the American colonies. Similarly, there was widespread discrimination against Roman

---

[14]Laurence Tribe, *American Constitutional Law*, 3d ed., (Mineola, N.Y.: Foundation Press, 2000), vol. II, chapter 14.

Catholics, Jews, and "dissenting" Protestants in the new world. In four states, the office of governor was restricted to Protestants; two others, Massachusetts and Maryland, required their governors to be Christians. Maryland required officeholders to profess a belief in God until 1961.[15] Given this history, there is little doubt the Founders meant the establishment clause to prohibit the national government from establishing an official religion.[16] Beyond this point, however, the meaning of the establishment clause generates more conflict than consensus.

One disagreement concerns whether the clause requires government neutrality to all forms of religious belief and nonbelief, or simply prohibits it from favoring one religion over another. The former position, sometimes called the separationist position, envisions a state wholly neutral toward all religions and without preference to religion over irreligion. As developed by Philip Kurland, its leading proponent, the doctrine requires that "the freedom and separation clauses should be read as a single precept that government cannot utilize religion as a standard for action or inaction because these clauses prohibit classification in terms of religion either to confer a benefit or to impose a burden."[17] The latter, the accommodationist position, argues for a narrower interpretation that would allow at least some forms of nonpreferential governmental aid to religion.[18]

Until recently, the Supreme Court firmly embraced the separationist position, insisting, in Jefferson's terminology, upon a "wall of separation" between church and state. In *Everson v. Board of Education* (1947, reprinted later in the chapter), the Supreme Court considered the constitutionality of a state program that used public funds to provide transportation of students to parochial schools. The plaintiffs argued that public aid to these students constituted aid to the religion, or tended to "establish" the religion. In a literal sense, of course, such aid cannot be said to "establish" a religion. It does, however, tend to favor religion by using public monies and resources to facilitate attendance at parochial schools.

Hence, the question in this case, and in the great majority of establishment clause cases, is how to distinguish between acceptable and unacceptable "cooperation" between the state and religion. In *Everson*, the Court upheld the cooperation on grounds that its primary purpose was secular and intended to benefit the school children, thus giving rise to a doctrinal approach to establishment issues called the "child benefit theory." More importantly, the Court firmly embraced the separationist reading of the establishment clause, writing, "The First Amendment has erected a wall between church and state. That wall must be kept high and impregnable. We could not approve the slightest breach."[19] Justice Jackson, dissenting, noted the contrast between the majority's absolutist language and the somewhat softer result: "The case which irresistibly comes to mind as the most fitting precedent is that of Julia who, according to Byron's reports, 'whispering I will ne'er consent,' consented." In dissent, Justice Rutledge advanced a view that called for complete separation, writing

---

[15] The Court declared this unconstitutional in *Torasco v. Watkins*, 367 U.S. 488 (1961).

[16] For a discussion, see, Leonard W. Levy, *The Establishment Clause: Religion and the First Amendment.* (New York: Macmillan, 1986), 75ff.

[17] Philip B. Kurland, *Of Church and State and the Supreme Court,* 29 University of Chicago Law Review 1 (1961).

[18] Levy, supra note 16. C. Herman Pritchett, *Constitutional Civil Liberties.* (Englewood Cliffs, N.J.: Englewood Cliffs, 1984), 145–46.

[19] For an analysis of Justice Black's reading of constitutional history, see Robert Cord, *Separation of Church and State: Historical Fact and Current Fiction.* (New York: Lambeth Press, 1982).

that the purpose of the Amendment "was broader than separating church and state in [a] narrow sense. It was to create a complete and permanent separation of the spheres of religious activity and civil authority by comprehensively forbidding every form of public aid or support for religion." In recent years, Rutledge's call for a complete and permanent separation has been embraced by Justice Stevens, among others.

One year later, in *McCollum v. Illinois* (1948), the Court struck a program permitting public school students to attend weekly religious classes on school premises. Unlike *Everson*, ruled the Court, the primary purpose of the released time program was not secular. Nor were children the primary beneficiaries of the aid; instead, the program sought to aid religion. On the other hand, in *Zorach v. Clauson* (1952), the Court upheld a released time program for students who attended religious programs off the school premises, observing, "We are a religious people whose institutions presuppose a Supreme Being. . . . When the state encourages religious instruction or co-operates with religious authorities by adjusting the schedule of public events to sectarian needs, it follows the best of our traditions."

The apparent inconsistency in the results of these cases seems to many observers to be the distinguishing characteristic of establishment jurisprudence.[20] Since 1971, the Court has tried to articulate a clear and consistent test for distinguishing between acceptable accommodations and aid to religion and unconstitutional establishment. In *Lemon v. Kurtzman* (1971, reprinted later in the chapter), Chief Justice Burger, writing for the Court, announced a three-part test. Governmental aid will pass constitutional muster if (1) it has a valid secular purpose; (2) its primary effect is neither to advance nor inhibit religion; and (3) it does not lead to "excessive government entanglement" with religion. The policy at issue in *Lemon*—a state program that contributed to the salaries of teachers in private schools who taught secular subjects—failed the test because it led to excessive entanglement. Concern about excessive entanglement led the Court to "examine the character and purposes of the institutions which are benefited, the nature of the aid that the State provides, and the resulting relationship between the government and the religious authority." The policy, the Court concluded, would necessitate "comprehensive and continuing surveillance," and included "divisive political potential" along religious lines.

The *Lemon* test has been the primary analytical tool in establishment cases for the past two decades. In a series of recent cases, however, several members of the Court, especially Justices Rehnquist, O'Connor, and Scalia, have suggested that it rests on a mistaken understanding of the establishment clause and should be abandoned.[21] Justices Rehnquist and Scalia have argued repeatedly that "the wall of separation" understanding of the establishment clause is wrong as a matter of history. In their view, the clause is not violated when government accommodates religion. As a consequence, as the Chief Justice explained in *Lee*, the appropriate test for establishment cases is not *Lemon*, but rather the so-called "coercion" test: "at a minimum, the Constitution guarantees that government may not coerce anyone to support or participate in religion or its exercise, or otherwise to act in a way which establishes a state religion or religious faith, or tends to do so." Justice O'Connor, in contrast, has argued in favor of an "endorsement" test. Writing in *Lynch v. Donnelly* (1984, reprinted later in the chapter), O'Connor explained that government "may run afoul" of the

---

[20] Tribe, supra note 14, at chapter 14.

[21] See, for example, Chief Justice Rehnquist's dissent in *Wallace v. Jaffree* (1985).

establishment clause in two ways. "One is excessive government entanglement. . . . The second and more direct infringement is government endorsement or disapproval of religion. Endorsement sends a message to nonadherents that they are outsiders, not full members of the political community. . . ."

To date, the Court has been unable or unwilling to decide which of the above approaches is the appropriate way to consider establishment cases. In the recent case of *Santa Fe Independent School District v. Doe* (2000) the Court applied all three tests in striking down a school district policy that permitted students to lead a prayer before high school football games.

Religious Education and Observances in Public Schools

As the foregoing decisions suggest, some of the most difficult problems in establishment clause jurisprudence have involved the nation's public and private schools. This should not be a surprise: Until recently primary school education was more the business of churches and private organizations than the state. This close connection underscores the extent to which education and religion contribute to human personality. Given the importance of both religion and education to individual self-development, as well as to the welfare of the community, it was inevitable that the nation's schools would become a staging point for the establishment clause. As Justice Rutledge observed in his dissent in *Everson*, "Two great drives are constantly in motion to abridge, in the name of education, the complete division of religion and civil authority. . . . One is to introduce religious education and observances into the public schools. The other, to obtain public funds for the aid and support of various private religious schools. . . ."

Prayer in the Schools

Few Supreme Court decisions have proved as controversial for so long a time as *Engel v. Vitale* (1962, reprinted later in the chapter) and *School District of Abington Township v. Schempp* (1963). In *Engel*, the Court invalidated a practice in the New York schools of reciting a short prayer at the opening of the school day. Writing for the Court, Justice Black concluded that the establishment clause "must at least mean that [it] is no part of the business of government to compose official prayers for any group of the American people to recite as a part of a religious program carried on by government." In *Schempp* the Court struck down Bible reading and the saying of the Lord's Prayer in class. In both cases the Court concluded that the challenged practices served sacred rather than secular purposes. The Court's insistence upon the presence of a secular purpose, however, means that the Constitution does not preclude the study of religion or the Bible "when presented objectively as part of a secular program of education."

Engel and *Schempp* initiated a volatile debate on school prayer that has continued undiminished for four decades. Many schools ignored the Court's ruling in *Engel*; obligatory prayers in public schools continued in parts of the country for many years and still do in some parts of the South. Republican candidate Barry Goldwater made the rulings a key part of his 1964 presidential campaign, complaining, as did Ronald Reagan in the 1980s, that the Court had "ruled against God." Nearly every session of Congress in the past thirty years has witnessed proposals to strip the Court of its appellate jurisdiction over school prayer issues, or to amend the Constitution to permit the practice.[22]

---

[22] Edward Keynes and Randall K. Miller, *The Court vs. Congress: Prayer, Busing, and Abortion.* (Durham: Duke University Press, 1989), 174–205.

The continuing controversy over school prayer has kept it on the Court's agenda, thus illustrating how constitutional interpretation by judges is often just a part of an ongoing constitutional dialogue with the other branches and the states. As we saw, in *Santa Fe*, the Court struck down student-led prayers before public high school football games, and earlier, in *Lee v. Weisman* (1992, reprinted later in the chapter) the Court found unconstitutional the recitation of a "nondenominational" prayer at public high school graduation ceremonies. In *Wallace v. Jaffree* (1985, reprinted later in the chapter), the Court struck down an Alabama statute that required a one-minute "moment of silence" at the beginning of the school day. Alabama was one of over two dozen states to experiment with a moment of silence statute in the 1970s and '80s. Relying heavily on the legislative history of the statute, the Court concluded that the undeniable purpose of the statute was to promote religion. Presumably, a moment of silence whose primary purpose is secular—perhaps to help students to focus attention on their studies that day—would be constitutionally acceptable.

Wallace is also important for Chief Justice Rehnquist's detailed and explicit rejection of the "separationist" understanding of the establishment clause. Calling appeals to Jefferson's wall of separation a "mistaken understanding of constitutional history," the Chief Justice concluded that the clause does "not require government neutrality between religion and irreligion nor [does] it prohibit the federal government from providing non-discriminatory aid to religion. There is simply no historical foundation for the proposition that the Framers intended to build the 'wall of separation' that was constitutionalized in *Everson*."[23]

The School Curriculum

Should a majority of the community be entitled to oversee and participate in that development? Is it possible to argue that the parents' free exercise of religion should encompass the right to express and affirm their faith in public and social institutions?[24] Would recognition of that right tend to "establish" religion, or does it merely account for or accommodate religious belief? Would this accommodation interfere with the free exercise rights of parents and children who disagreed?

In *Edwards v. Aguillard* (1987, reprinted later in the chapter), the Court considered such questions in a case involving a new twist on the evolution controversy. Reacting to a widespread sense that the "secular humanism" of public schools was detrimental to the spiritual health of Christian students, Louisiana required its public schools to teach "creation science," or the scientific basis for the theory of Genesis, alongside evolutionary theory. Again using the *Lemon* test, Justice Brennan, writing for the majority, concluded that creation science was meant, "to advance the religious viewpoint that a supernatural being created human-kind," and in so doing "advances a religious doctrine. . . ." In dissent, Justice Scalia argued that the secular purpose of the act was "to ensure that students would be free to decide for themselves how life began, based upon a fair and balanced presentation of the scientific evidence."[25]

---

[23] The Chief Justice relied upon the scholarly work of Malbin and Cord, supra. For a criticism of Rehnquist's use of history, see Levy, note 6.

[24] You should contrast the American school prayer cases with decisions in Germany and Canada, discussed on pages 791–92.

[25] In 1993 a high school biology teacher in California sued his employer, the school district, alleging that the district's requirement that he teach the theory of evolution violated the religion clauses of the First Amendment because evolution "is a religious belief system." In *Peloza v. Capistrano Unified School District* (1994), the Circuit Court ruled that "secular humanism" is not a religion and dismissed the claim.

Public Aid for Private Religious Schools

The constitutionality of public aid to parochial schools has been an issue since *Everson*, where the Court upheld a subsidy for the costs of student transport to parochial schools. Since then, the Court has upheld plans that provide free textbooks for secular subjects,[26] though it rejected a subsidy for teacher salaries in *Lemon*. The Court also upset tuition grant subsidies in *Committee for Public Education v. Nyquist* (1973), but approved state subsidies for books and tests, though not field trips, in *Meek v. Pittinger* (1975) and *Wolman v. Walter* (1977). In *Mitchell v. Helms* (2000), however, the Court ruled in favor of a federal program that provided aid for public school districts that purchased curricular materials and then lent them to private schools. Chief Justice Rehnquist's opinion for the Court concluded that such aid, even if not for books alone, did not amount to an establishment of religion, thus overruling the decisions in *Meeks* and *Wolman*.

In the important case of *Zelman v. Simmons-Harris* (2002, reprinted later in the chapter), the Court revisited the issue in *Nyquist*. *Zelman* concerned a voucher system instituted in Cleveland, Ohio. Under the system, certain low-income families received vouchers from the state that they could use to send their children to elementary schools of their own choice, public or private, religious or not. In the 1999–2000 academic year, 96 percent of the families receiving vouchers sent their children to private, religious schools. Writing for the majority, Chief Justice Rehnquist held that the voucher program did not violate the establishment clause, in part because the program had a secular purpose: to provide educational opportunity to students who would otherwise have to attend Cleveland's "failing" public schools. Moreover, because all schools were included in the program, the program was "neutral" toward religion. In his dissent, Justice Stevens called the decision "profoundly misguided" and alluded to the continuing problems of religious conflict in "the Balkans, Northern Ireland, and the Middle East." Justices Breyer and Souter likewise warned that the decision is likely to be a source of divisiveness. "If the divisiveness . . . is to be avoided in the short term," concluded Justice Souter, "it will be avoided only by action of the political branches at the state and national levels."

The Court has also continued to review cases involving the allocation of and access to school resources, as well as the use of federal funds. In *Grand Rapids School District v. Ball* (1985), the Court invalidated a "shared time" program that used public monies to fund after-school remedial classes for private school students. In *Bowen v. Kendrick* (1988), however, the Court sustained the Adolescent Family Life Act, which permits religious organizations to use federal money to advise students on sexual issues. And in *Rosenberger v. University of Virginia* (1995), the Court ruled that a University's refusal to fund a religious publication by a religious group, when it funded other student publications, amounted to discrimination on the basis of religious expression. Similarly, in *Good News Club et al. v. Milford Central School* (2001, reprinted later in the chapter), the Court invalidated a decision by a local school board that had prohibited the club from using school space, after hours, for its meetings. Noting that the board had let other organizations and members of the public use the space, the Court ruled that the establishment clause did not provide a defense for the school board. The principle of "neutral accommodation" meant that the board must allow religious organizations equal access to the space, so long as attendance was voluntary and not under school sponsorship.

---

[26] *Board of Education v. Allen*, 392 U.S. 236 (1968).

As these cases should make clear, much of the Court's establishment clause jurisprudence is fact-driven. Despite the *Lemon* test, or perhaps because of it, as critics charge, the results seem to defy easy categorization or explanation. Is there a "neutral" constitutional principle that can explain these cases or provide a more reliable guide to interpretation? Can these cases be explained by a principle that forbids and fears governmental "endorsement" or "symbolic identification"?[27] How would the adoption of the "accommodationist" perspective on the establishment clause affect the Court's decisions in these cases?

Other Establishment Clause Issues

Given the great diversity of religious belief in the United States, and the expansive, if not intrusive nature of the modern state, establishment clause issues can appear in a great variety of situations. In the past half-century, the Court has considered the constitutionality of Sunday Closing laws,[28] the constitutionality of tax exemptions for church property,[29] and the opening of state legislative sessions with prayers.[30]

Among the more controversial establishment cases are those involving state-sponsored nativity scenes during the Christmas holidays. Cases involving religious holidays, especially those celebrated by majority sects and religions, vividly illustrate the two different approaches to the establishment clause we have considered. Implicit in those approaches are two very different understandings about the role of religion in the public life of the community. The separationist position, which insists upon a high wall of separation between church and state, would prohibit all aid to religion, even if such aid were nonpreferential among religions. It envisions a public sphere wholly cleansed of religion. The accommodationist position, as we have seen, prohibits only preferential treatment among religions; it would, in other words, seek to have the state accommodate religion, or acknowledge the important role of religion in civil society. On this understanding, freedom of religion is a positive liberty, a freedom *to* more than a freedom *from*. The crèche cases show how the two approaches can yield dramatically different results.

In *Lynch v. Donnelly* (1984, reprinted later in the chapter), the Court upheld a display of a crèche in an annual Christmas display because it was a part of a larger presentation, the primary purpose of which was the celebration of a holiday that had religious but also secular importance. In *Allegheny County v. American Civil Liberties Union* (1989), the Court ruled that a display of a crèche with a banner bearing a religious slogan and clearly sponsored by the Catholic Church did violate the establishment clause, since its primary purpose, under the *Lemon* test, was to advance religion. In the same case, however, the Court permitted a display of a menorah, located beside a Christmas tree and other holiday ornaments. In this instance the Court found, as it had in *Lynch*, that the primary purpose of the spectacle was secular.

Allegheny shows a Court deeply divided on the most basic sorts of questions concerning the establishment clause. Justice Blackmun's plurality opinion utilized the *Lemon* test. Justice Kennedy, joined by Justices Rehnquist, White, and Scalia, proposed an alternative to *Lemon*. The new test would permit governmental accommo-

---

[27] See, for example, Justice O'Connor's concurrence in *Lynch v. Donnelly* (1984, reprinted later in the chapter).

[28] *Braunfeld v. Brown*, 366 U.S. 599 (1961).

[29] *Walz v. Tax Commission*, 397 U.S. 664 (1970).

[30] *Marsh v. Chambers*, 463 U.S. 783 (1983).

dations of religion, but would disallow "coercion" or "significant" expenditures of public money. In a recent case involving establishment and the public schools, the Court again debated the utility of the *Lemon* test. Writing for the Court in *Board of Education v. Kiryas Joel* (1994), Justice Souter completely avoided any mention of the *Lemon* test, prompting Justice Blackmun to restate his commitment to *Lemon*. In her concurrence, Justice O'Connor applauded the move away from *Lemon*, as did Justice Scalia in his dissent. To replace *Lemon*, Justice Scalia offered a test that would emphasize "fidelity to the longstanding traditions of our people. . . ." Does Scalia's test rely on a different understanding of the proper scope of judicial power than the *Lemon* test?

The Free Exercise Clause

Liberalism's demand for tolerance seems to require freedom of conscience in a constitutional democracy. Like freedom of expression, therefore, a guarantee of religious freedom is an essential part of the American constitutional order. It is also a common feature in other constitutional democracies, even in those that favor particular or established state religions.

In part because expression and religion are so closely related, many of the cases that involve free exercise issues rest instead on freedom of expression. In *West Virginia v. Barnette* (1943, reprinted later in the chapter), for example, the Court considered claims by Jehovah's Witnesses that compulsory flag salute laws violated a religious precept as speech issues. And in a number of cases involving the Jehovah's Witnesses, the Court struck down as "prior restraint" or censorship municipal laws that sought to prohibit the Witnesses from making public speeches or soliciting from house to house.[31]

As is true with the establishment clause, there is at least one undisputed understanding of the free exercise clause: The state may not punish individuals for holding or rejecting particular religious beliefs. Thus, one of the purposes of the free exercise clause is the protection of individual autonomy in matters of faith. As we have seen, liberalism also prizes tolerance and diversity. Indeed, one of the purposes of free exercise is pluralism and tolerance in religious belief. Consequently, the free exercise clause, like the establishment clause, also has as one of its chief purposes the prevention of social and political unrest that usually accompanies religious conflict.

An additional source of interpretive difficulty should be familiar by now. Every exercise of an "individual" liberty takes place in a larger community. An individual's right to believe what he or she wants is as near an absolute liberty as exists in the United States. When one acts on that belief, however, he or she is more likely to bump up against the rights of others or of the community. At what point should the community's interest in public order, be it protecting children, animals, or a shared moral sense, restrict an individual's freedom of belief?

Should a claim of free exercise excuse practices, for instance, that offend the moral or religious sensibilities of the community, such as polygamy? In *Reynolds* and *Davis*, the Court said no. Should a claim of free exercise immunize the use of illegal drugs if done as a part of a religious ceremony? In *Employment Div. v. Smith* (1990, reprinted later in the chapter), the Court said no, finding that an Oregon drug law that forbade members of the Native American Church from using small amounts of peyote

---

[31] See, e.g., *Cantwell v. Connecticut*, 310 U.S. 296 (1940); *Murdock v. Pennsylvania*, 319 U.S. 105 (1943); *West Virginia v. Barnette*, 319 U.S. 624 (1943).

during a service did not represent "an attempt to regulate religious beliefs [or] the communication of religious beliefs."

In both cases the Court distinguished between freedom of belief and of practice. The distinction between belief and action is obvious enough, though one may wonder how valuable freedom of belief is without a corresponding liberty to act on it. But can we clearly distinguish between belief and practice? Assuming we can make the distinction work, we are still left with difficult questions of application. Does the distinction sufficiently respect the rights of individuals? Does it recognize or respect the rights of religious communities or communities of faith, and not just of individuals? For what reasons may society rightfully regulate a religious practice? Is physical harm to individuals reason enough? What if the individual knowingly and willingly accepts the risk of harm? What about threats to public safety or health? Is harm to the sensibilities of majoritarian religious or cultural beliefs sufficient reason to restrict religious practice?

As these questions suggest, the distinction between belief and action leaves unresolved the major difficulty in making sense of the free exercise clause: Which actions warrant immunity, which can be regulated, and why? The belief-action distinction tells us nothing about the circumstances under which various communal interests are sufficiently strong to outweigh the countervailing interest in religious liberty. Nor does it clearly distinguish—if it should—between actions that are primarily celebratory or liturgical, as in *Smith* or in *Church of the Lukumi Babalu Aye, Inc. v. Hialeah* (1993, reprinted later in the chapter) and actions that are incidental to worship or primarily secular in nature.

Taken together, *Reynolds, Davis* and *Smith* established what is called the "secular regulation" rule. The rule provides that secular regulations that do not purposely burden religion do not offend the free exercise clause. It will thus invalidate laws purposely designed to regulate religion, but it does not require the accommodation of religion. Without more, the rule leaves open the possible regulation of an enormous range of religious behavior. In other words, it weighs the balance between freedom of religious practice and the community's right to govern itself dramatically in favor of the community.[32] As C. Herman Pritchett has observed, "While the secular regulation rule is appealing in its simplicity and apparent evenhandedness, in application it may prove senselessly harsh. . . ."[33] On the other hand, cases like *Davis* highlight the tension in constitutionalism between claims of conscience and the need for strict legal equality.

In part to weigh the balance more toward claims of conscience, the Court ruled in *Sherbert v. Verner* (1963) that a secular regulation that "substantially burdens" a religious practice must be justified by "a compelling governmental interest." This is a test we have encountered in other areas, such as the right to privacy. In this case its use led to the unconstitutionality of a state law that denied Sherbert unemployment compensation because as a Seventh Day Adventist she refused to accept a job that required her to work on Saturday. But in light of Justice Scalia's opinion for the Court

---

[32] On the other hand, some feminist scholars argue that traditional "rights analysis" represents a masculine, or conflictual, way of understanding the relationship between the individual and the community. A feminist approach, they argue, would start not with the needs of individuals but rather with those of communities; when in conflict, resolution should be sought in terms of accommodating preferences, instead of determining who wins and who loses. See, for example, Suzanna Sherry, *Civic Virtue and the Feminine Voice in Constitutional Adjudication*, 73 Virginia Law Review 543 (1980); Martha Minow, *The Supreme Court 1986 Term—Forward: Justice Engendered*, 101 Harvard Law Review 10 (1987).

[33] Pritchett, supra note 18, 137.

in *Smith,* arguing that accommodation is not constitutionally required, the viability of the *Sherbert* rule is uncertain. Some scholars have argued that *Smith* marks a dramatic change in the Court's free exercise jurisprudence.[34] Indeed, one concluded that the Court's opinion "is troubling, bordering on shocking. . . ."[35] The arguments begun in *Smith* have continued unabated, both inside and outside the Court. In several cases various members of the Court have argued boisterously about the *Smith* rule, most notably in *Lee v. Weisman* (1992) and *Hialeah* (1993).

The argument has not been only inside the Court. Following the Court's decision in *Smith* (1990), which seemed to many observers to substantially curtail free exercise rights, Congress reacted by passing the Religious Freedom Restoration Act of 1993. Acting under its Section 5 enforcement powers in the Fourteenth Amendment, Congress sought to "restore the compelling state interest test" in all free exercise cases. In *Boerne v. Flores* (1997, reprinted later in the chapter), the Court struck down the act, claiming that it sought not to enforce Fourteenth Amendment liberties but instead to "alter the meaning of the free exercise clause. . . ." *Boerne* is a dramatic example of how constitutional law is an ongoing dialogue, not only about *what* the Constitution means but also, and no less important, about *who* gets to decide what it means.

Free Exercise and the Public Schools

To what extent should public schools be required to respect the religious beliefs and practices of schoolchildren and their parents? The question requires us to consider again the claims of religious liberty in light of a community's undoubted interest in the education of its citizens. And again, the problem is made more urgent, if not more difficult, by the great diversity of religious belief in the United States. As we saw, a frequent complaint of the Court's work in this area is that an exemption for one religion, if made available to all, will overburden the educational process, as well as tend to "establish" the religion in question. But such practices almost always implicate the free exercise rights of individuals as well.

On one level, the difficulties of free exercise in the classroom have to do with a community's desire for collective self-expression and the undoubted importance of public rituals in creating and sustaining a political community. But such rituals may sometimes give rise to social and political pressures to conform to secular norms even at the cost of suppression of an individual's (and the community of faith in which the individual is a member) religious identity and belief.

It is just such a conflict that explains at least some of the controversy surrounding *Newdow v. U.S. Congress* (2002). The Court has on more than one occasion considered the volatile constitutional issues raised by patriotic observances in public schools. In *Minersville v. Gobitis* (1940), for example, the town of Minersville, Pennsylvania, defended its practice of requiring a flag-salute in classrooms as an exercise of the police power to promote patriotism among the students. Minersville's custom was just a part of a larger national campaign, begun in 1919 and pressed by the American Legion, the Veterans of Foreign Wars, the Daughters of the American Revolution, and the Ku Klux Klan, to "foster one hundred per cent Americanism."[36]

---

[34] See especially, Michael McConnell, *Free Exercise Revisionism and the* Smith *Decision,* 57 University of Chicago Law Review 1109 (1990).

[35] Ibid.

[36] As quoted in Peter Irons, *The Courage of Their Convictions.* (New York: Penguin Books, 1988), 16.

The Gobitis children were expelled from public schools when they refused, based on the religious beliefs of the Jehovah's Witnesses, to salute the flag. A nearly unanimous Court (only Justice Stone dissented) concluded that the flag salute was a constitutionally defensible exercise of the police power. Writing for the Court, Justice Frankfurter acknowledged that "every possible leeway should be given to the claims of religious faith," but nevertheless concluded that the law's purpose was secular and legitimate. Indeed, Frankfurter noted, the state's interest is "inferior to none in the hierarchy of legal values. National unity is the basis of national security." Moreover,

> to insist that, though the ceremony may be required, exceptional immunity must be given to dissidents, is to maintain that there is no basis for a legislative judgment that such an exemption might introduce elements of difficulty into the school discipline, might cast doubts in the minds of the other children. . . .

Justice Frankfurter's opinion struck a familiar chord about the nature and limits of judicial authority in a constitutional democracy. In free exercise cases no less than others, constitutional interpretation and issues about judicial power go hand in hand.

Gobitis unleashed "a wave of persecution against the Witnesses, and the ruling was rather generally condemned in the press."[37] Two years later, in *Jones v. Opelika* (1942), three Justices (Black, Douglas, and Murphy), announced they had erred in *Gobitis*. The following year, in *West Virginia v. Barnette* (1943, reprinted later in the chapter), a new majority led by Justice Jackson (later to be chief prosecutor at the Nuremberg war trials), overruled *Gobitis*, saying "The sole conflict is between authority and rights of the individual. . . . Freedom to differ is not limited to things that do not matter much. That would be a mere shadow of freedom. The test of its substance is the right to differ as to things that touch the heart of the existing order." Dissenting, Justice Frankfurter argued that "The state is not shut out from a domain because the individual conscience may deny the state's claim. . . . One may have the right to practice one's religion and at the same time owe the duty of formal obedience to laws that run counter to one's beliefs. . . ."

Newdow, Gobitis and *Barnette* involved religious objections to a specific practice in the public schools. Well before *Gobitis,* Mennonite and Amish children had also refused to salute the flag and were expelled for their religious convictions. Conflict between the state and the Amish reached a new height in *Wisconsin v. Yoder* (1972, reprinted later in the chapter). In this case, Old Order Amish sought an exemption from a law that required parents to send their children to school until they turned sixteen. The Amish argued that education beyond the eighth grade was unnecessary, since their children would be educated in the ways of the Amish. Moreover, education in secular schools would expose their children to influences that would contradict their religious beliefs.

All nine justices concluded that the state law, although secular in purpose, would have a profoundly negative influence on the Amish community, especially since the adolescent children were at "a crucial . . . stage of development. . . . As the record so strongly shows, the values and programs of the modern secondary school are in sharp conflict with the fundamental mode of life mandated by the Amish religion. . . ." Consequently, following *Sherbert,* the public school requirement could stand only if it furthered a compelling state interest. The Court admitted that compulsory education "is necessary to prepare citizens to participate effectively and intelligently in our open political system," but concluded that "an additional one or two

---

[37] Pritchett, supra note 18, 136.

years of formal high school for Amish children in place of their long-established program of informal vocational education would do little to serve those interests."

Whatever one thinks of the outcome, *Yoder* raises several difficult questions. Can the decision be squared with an understanding of the First Amendment that requires government neutrality toward religion? Or did the Court simply make a special rule for the Amish? Is there an alternative understanding of freedom of religion, besides the push to neutrality, which can justify the result in *Yoder*? Do tolerance and a commitment to religious pluralism, for example, sometimes command the state to act in ways that are not hostile or destructive of religious communities? Can we reconcile *Yoder* with *Davis* and *Reynolds*? On the other hand, can the case be squared with *Smith*? Recall that earlier we considered whether the Lockean foundations of liberal constitutionalism had inhibited the development in our jurisprudence of a conception of religion that reconciled the independent value of religion as a constitutional value distinct from that of expression and speech. Does *Yoder* move in that direction by acknowledging the roles that communities of faith play in the polity? Finally, is this an instance where assigning different purposes to the free exercise clause may lead to substantially different outcomes? How should the Court choose between these competing purposes? Is there a way to reconcile them?

Free Exercise and the Military

Pressures to conform are nowhere more profound than in military organizations. As a consequence, claims of free exercise have frequently conflicted with military rules and regulations. The most obvious of these conflicts involve claims of conscientious objection to military service. In *U.S. v. Seeger* (1965), the Court concluded that statutory language requiring objectors to base their objection on a "belief in relation to a Supreme Being . . . but not including essentially political, sociological, or philosophical views . . ." did not require a belief in God but instead only "a broader concept of a power or being, or a faith to which all else is subordinate or upon which all else is ultimately dependent." In *Welsh v. United States* (1970), the Court further ruled that beliefs held "with the strength of more traditional religious convictions" would be sufficient to satisfy statutory rules. Is it possible to reconcile the Court's expansive reading of these statutes with its definition of religion in *Yoder*?

In these cases, the Court was asked to consider the constitutionality of exemptions to military service based on a federal statute. The Court has never held, however, that the religion clauses offer an independent ground for conscientious objection.[38] Would such an exemption be required under *Sherbert* or *Yoder*? In *Goldman v. Weinberger* (1986), the Court upheld an Air Force regulation that prohibited soldiers and officers from wearing nonsanctioned headwear. Goldman sought an exemption, claiming that his wearing of a yarmulke was protected by the free exercise clause. The Court disagreed, noting that "when evaluating whether military needs justify a particular restriction on religiously motivated conduct, courts must give great deference to the professional judgment of military authorities. . . ." Here the Court decided that it must defer to the military's judgment that the regulation was necessary to foster *esprit de corps* and "the subordination of personal preferences and identities in favor of the overall group mission." In so ruling, the Court declined to use the compelling state interest test set forth in *Sherbert*.

---

[38] See *Selective Draft Law Cases*, 245 U.S. 366 (1918).

Reconciling the Establishment and Free Exercise Clauses

In a great many cases, the religion clauses work in tandem to secure religious freedom. In some cases, however, they appear to be at odds. "The problem is that too much coercion may deny free exercise, while exemption from coercion in response to religious objections may be favoritism amounting to establishment."[39] As Justice Stewart noted in *School District of Abington Township v. Schempp* (1963), the military's use of federal monies to pay chaplains might well violate the establishment clause. But "a lonely soldier stationed at some faraway outpost could surely complain that a government which did *not* provide him the opportunity for pastoral guidance was affirmatively prohibiting the free exercise of his religion."

Or consider *Yoder*: Assume the Court was correct in holding that Wisconsin's compulsory education laws violated the free exercise rights of the Amish. The state must then exempt the Amish. Doesn't that tend to "aid" or establish the Amish religion? On the other hand, isn't that aid, in service of religious pluralism, a part of the very purpose of the free exercise clause?

In such instances, should our aim be to reconcile the clauses, or to give each full expression, even if in doing so they appear to conflict with one another? One possibility is to insist upon "neutrality" as the standard for interpreting the free exercise clause. As we saw, though, a strict adherence to the rule of neutrality is likely to work against our desire for religious tolerance and diversity by imposing a hardship on some religious communities, such as the Mormons or the Amish. Indeed, on this reading, *Yoder* was wrongly decided. It led to conflict with the establishment clause because it violated the demand of neutrality by making an exception for the Amish. Another possibility is to suggest that "aid" to religion, if nondiscriminatory, is not establishment; in other words, we might adopt the accommodationist reading of the establishment clause. This approach, however, privileges religion over irreligion. In doing so, doesn't it compromise our commitment to individual autonomy in matters of belief and nonbelief?

Comparative Perspectives

The constitutions of most western democracies include guarantees of religious freedom. The reasons for such guarantees are not difficult to find. Religious strife is a part not only of the history of the United States, but also of most constitutional democracies. Be it discrimination against Mormons and Jehovah's Witnesses in the United States, against Canada's French Catholic Quebecois, or against German Jews, most constitutional states have some practical experience with the disruptive effects of religious bigotry.

The desire for social peace alone is enough to explain the proliferation of constitutional guarantees of religious freedom. Matters of religion also evoke ideals of autonomy and tolerance that transcend the constitutional traditions and cultures of any specific state. A commitment to constitutionalism itself, then, also explains the appearance of religious freedom guarantees in a great many constitutional documents.

A widely shared commitment to religious freedom does not mean, however, that there are no substantial differences between constitutional democracies. Every society will seek to realize these values in its own way. In each of the countries we shall

---

[39] Pritchett, supra note 18, 133.

consider, the role of religion in public and private life is unique. The constitutional courts of these countries, while borrowing freely from the work of other courts, must struggle to articulate a coherent and complete vision of the role of religion that fits their communities. The United States Supreme Court has found it difficult, if not impossible, to forge such a vision. A comparative perspective cannot supply a distinctively American vision of religion in public affairs, but it can help to illuminate the choices and constraints we face.

Establishment in Comparative Perspective

Earlier we noted that the Founders' distinctive contribution to religious freedom was the establishment clause of the First Amendment. Two centuries ago it was not uncommon for states to favor or establish certain religions. The close historical relationship between altar and throne has profoundly influenced the constitutional development of several countries, including Germany, Canada, Japan, and Ireland. Although each of these countries guarantees free exercise, in all of them the relationship of church to state is also formally recognized in some way.

"Strong historical forces have molded the practice of church-state relations in . . . Germany," notes one commentator.[40] The Basic Law "embraces a complicated scheme of church-state relations."[41] Chief among those concepts is that of official neutrality. But neutrality does not mean, as it might in the United States, complete nonintervention or hostility toward religion in public affairs. The Basic Law incorporates Articles 136, 137, 138, 139, and 141 of the Weimar Constitution; together, these articles envision for churches a prominent role in the private and public life of Germans. Article 137(1) prohibits the establishment of a "state church," but also recognizes churches as "religious bodies under public law" and gives them the power "to levy taxes" for religious activities. The Basic Law also permits religious instruction in public schools, largely as an adjunct of free exercise and the right of parents under Article 7(2) to determine whether their children "shall receive religious instruction" in public schools. Moreover, Article 7(3) guarantees churches direction over religious instruction in public school studies.

Unlike establishment clause jurisprudence in the United States, these articles push more toward cooperation than to hostility. In the German *School Prayer Case* (1979), for example, the Federal Constitutional Court found no constitutional bar to voluntary prayer in public schools. Indeed, the Court's decision adopted an approach to religious freedom that incorporates not only freedom from state interference, or a negative liberty, but also a positive freedom, the right to express one's belief in the larger community. The latter, as developed by the Federal Constitutional Court, "implies an obligation on the part of the state to create a social order in which it is possible for the religious personality to develop and flourish."[42]

The Court qualified the positive freedom by requiring schools to "guarantee the dissenting pupil the right to decide freely and without compulsion whether to participate in the prayer." After reviewing the various ways a student could avoid prayer, the Court admitted that

> *whenever the class prays, each of these alternatives will have the effect of distinguishing the pupil in question from the praying pupils—especially if only one pupil*

---

[40] Kommers, supra note 11, at 504.

[41] Ibid., at 444.

[42] Ibid., at 461.

*profes*ses *other beliefs. This distinction could be an unbearable one for the person concerned if it should place him in the role of an outsider and serve to discriminate against him. . . . This is especially true of the younger schoolchild, who is hardly capable of critically asserting himself against his environment. Nonetheless, one cannot assume that abstaining from school prayer will generally or even in a substantial number of cases force a dissenting student into an unbearable position as an outsider.*

In contrast, in *Zylerberg v. Sudbury Board of Education* (1988), the Canadian Supreme Court found that a statute permitting religious instruction (with a release option for students who chose not to participate) did violate the Charter of Rights. The Court noted, in sharp contrast to the reasoning of the German Court, that "the exemption imposes a penalty on pupils from religious minorities who utilize it by stigmatizing them as nonconformists and setting them apart from their fellow students who are members of the dominant religion."

The *School Prayer Case* and *Zylerberg* provide an interesting contrast with the absolutism of the American Supreme Court's decisions in *Engel v. Vitale* and *Schempp.* The German approach to the relationship between establishment and free exercise differs in fundamental ways from the American cases. For the German Court, the freedom to pray in schools is a part of the positive freedom of religion to make positive affirmations of one's faith, whereas in the United States, the Court approached prayer in school as a "freedom from" establishment issue. In contrast to the stark individualism that characterizes the American cases, the German Court advanced a concept of religious neutrality that embraced accommodation for the religious values of the community.

This model of cooperation between the state and religion is common in other constitutional democracies, including Ireland, Italy, and Canada. Section 2(a) of the Canadian Charter, for example, does not include an establishment provision. Presumably, then, governmental aid to churches and to denominational schools, which have a long history in parts of Canada, survive the Charter, though they would violate the First Amendment.[43] In *Metropolitan Toronto Board of Education v. Attorney General of Ontario* (1987), the Supreme Court of Canada ruled that a provincial statute providing for the full funding of Catholic high schools did not violate the Charter.

Free Exercise in Comparative Perspective

The great majority of the world's constitutions include a guarantee of freedom of conscience and religion. Article 4 of the Basic Law, for example, provides that

  (1) Freedom of faith, of conscience, and freedom of creed, religious or ideological, shall be inviolable.
  (2) The undisturbed practice of religion is guaranteed.
  (3) No one may be compelled to take up arms against his conscience.

Other provisions include Article 3(3), which declares that persons may not be favored or disfavored because of their faith or religious opinions. Article 136 bans compulsory disclosure of one's religious convictions or participation in a religious exercise. It also prohibits mandatory religious oaths. A unique provision, Article 4(3),

---

[43] See, Peter W. Hogg, *Constitutional Law in Canada.* 3rd ed. (Toronto: Carswell, 1992).

provides that "No one may be compelled against his conscience to perform service in war involving the use of arms."[44]

Similarly, Section 2 of the Canadian Charter protects "freedom of conscience and religion," and Article 20 of the Japanese Constitution provides that "Freedom of religion is guaranteed to all. . . . No person shall be compelled to take part in any religious acts, celebration, rite or practice. The state and its organs shall refrain from religious education or any other religious activity."

The Indian Constitution in Article 25 provides that "Subject to public order, morality and health and to the other provisions of this Part, all persons are equally entitled to freedom of conscience and the right freely to profess, practice and propagate religion." The other provisions, however, are very significant; one of them stipulating that the guarantee of religious freedom shall not prevent the State from enacting any law "providing for social welfare." Thus with admirable clarity the document guarantees to all Indians a broad right to religious freedom, only to declare that this right is subject to substantial possible limitation. The language, though, evinces a clear founding purpose that seeks to reconcile the securing of religious freedom with the achievement of social justice.

The Italian Constitution makes special references to the Catholic Church, as did the Irish Constitution before amended, but both specifically guarantee free exercise. Article 19 of the Italian Constitution, for example, states "Everyone shall have the right freely to profess his own religious faith . . . and to worship in private or in public, providing that the rites do not offend against public decency." The qualification—that religious practices must not offend public decency—is a familiar caution in most constitutional texts. In the Irish case of *Corway v. Independent Newspapers (Ireland) Limited* (1999), the Supreme Court of Ireland considered whether a political cartoon in a newspaper amounted to blasphemy of the Catholic Church—a violation, in other words, of an Irish statute and of Article 40.6.1 of the Irish Constitution, which provides: "The publication or utterance of blasphemous matter is an offence which shall be punishable in accordance with law." Elsewhere, however, Article 44 of the Constitution guarantees "freedom of conscience and the free profession and practice of religion." After reviewing this and other provisions in the Constitution, the Court concluded that the cartoon "may indeed have been in very bad taste," but that it "is difficult to see how the common law crime as blasphemy . . . could survive in such a constitutional framework."

Defining Religion

As in the United States, issues surrounding freedom of religious exercise in other constitutional democracies tend to center first on the definition of religion. Section 2 of the Canadian Charter refers explicitly to rights of conscience, suggesting that it protects a wide range of beliefs that might not, strictly speaking, qualify as "religious." The German Federal Constitutional Court has likewise tended toward an expansive understanding of "religion," as indicated in the excerpt from the *Rumpelkammer Case* (1968)(Comparative Note 13.11). In this case, the Court observed that "[T]he exercise of religion includes not only worship and practices . . . but also religious education and ceremonies of nonestablished religions and atheists as well as other expressions of religious and ideological life."

---

[44] Donald P. Kommers has noted that "Most commentators regard this freedom, as does the Constitutional Court itself, as a concrete manifestation of the general 'freedom of conscience' secured by paragraph 1 of Article 4." Kommers, supra note 11, 458.

A second issue concerns the tension between individual freedom and the community's interest in the health, safety, and welfare of society at large. The guarantee of religious freedom in the Canadian Charter, like the other guarantees of individual liberty, is subject to the limitations clause in Section 1. As we saw in earlier chapters, Section 1 circumscribes liberties by subjecting them to "such reasonable limits prescribed by law as can be demonstrably justified in a free and democratic society." Section 2 is also subject to the "override" provision of Section 33, which provides that Parliament may exempt an act of legislation from the demands of Section 2 by including a statement that the statute is to operate independent of the clause.

The language of the Basic Law, in contrast to the Canadian Charter, suggests a near absolute ban on regulations concerning the free exercise of religion, for the reservations that typically appear in other provisions of the Basic Law do not attend the religion clauses. Nevertheless, the Federal Constitutional Court has acknowledged the legitimacy of some regulations on the free exercise of religion, as opposed to freedom of belief itself. Thus, as the Court observed in the *Blood Transfusion Case* (1971), "The freedom guaranteed by Article 4(1) . . . , like all fundamental rights, has as its point of departure the view of man in the Constitution, i.e., man as a responsible personality, developing freely within the social community. These community ties of the individual recognized by the Constitution impose formal limits on even those fundamental rights which are guaranteed unreservedly."

In India, on the other hand, the very explicitness of the constitutional recognition (especially in Article 25) that far-reaching social reform required attention to the critical role of religion in Indian life, suggests why judges in that polity are often quite willing to uphold regulations that may impinge on religious freedom. To facilitate their task, however, they have been much more active than their American counterparts in entering the thicket of theological disputation, distinguishing essential from nonessential religious activity. Once a contested practice is relegated to the latter category it becomes much easier to uphold State regulations that limit religious liberty in the interest of egalitarian social objectives. Attempting to isolate what is integral to religion from what is not is to tread on very dangerous ground—which is why American judges studiously avoid doing so—but in a constitutional polity where religion is widely experienced as a way of life, judges do not have the luxury of sidestepping such questions. Both India and the United States are committed to the free exercise of religion, but they express the commitment in different ways; most importantly, the fact that critical elements of the social structure in India are inextricably entwined with religion renders the possibilities of any meaningful social reform unimaginable without the direct intervention of the State in the spiritual domain.

Like the American Supreme Court, then, the constitutional courts of democracies have struggled with the distinction between belief and practice, with maintaining respect for an individual's right to practice a belief while acknowledging the rights of the community. Their efforts, like our own, require an appreciation of the many ways individual liberty is influenced by the larger social and political environments within which individuals exist. In the Canadian case of *British Columbia College of Teachers v. Trinity Western University and Lindquist et al.* (2001), the Canadian Supreme Court wrote extensively on the belief-conduct distinction. The case involved a decision by a provincial accrediting board to deny Trinity Western's application to assume full responsibility for a teacher-training program it had previously shared with another institution. The accrediting board denied the request, finding that Trinity's evangelical, Christian perspective included discriminatory practices "contrary to the public interest." In particular, the board was concerned about statements in the University's Code of Behavior that stated that certain activities, such as drunkenness, cheating, involvement in the occult, pornography, and homosexual behavior, are "biblically condemned."

The Supreme Court reversed the decision, ruling that "A truly free society is one which can accommodate a wide variety of beliefs, diversity of tastes and pursuits, customs and codes of conduct. . . . The essence of the concept of freedom of religion is the right to entertain such religious beliefs as a person chooses. . . . But the concept means more than that. Freedom can be primarily characterized by the absence of coercion or constraint. . . ." The Court continued, however, by noting, "freedom of religion, like any freedom, is not absolute. It is inherently limited by the rights and freedoms of others. . . . The proper place to draw the line in cases like the one at bar is generally between belief and conduct. The freedom to hold beliefs is broader than the freedom to act on them." In this case, the Court ruled, the code was a statement of belief, and there was not sufficient evidence that the University had acted or would act in discriminatory fashion. The Court's finding asks us to consider again the nature of the relationship between what we believe and how we act, and in so doing reminds us that cases involving freedom of religion go to the core of what it means to live in a constitutional democracy.

Selected Bibliography

Alley, Robert. ed. 1988. *The Supreme Court on Church and State*. New York: Oxford University Press.

Carter, Lief. 1991. *Constitutional Interpretation: Cases in Law and Religion*. New York: Longman.

Carter, Stephen L. 1993. *The Culture of Disbelief: How American Law and Politics Trivialize Religious Devotion*. New York: Basic Books.

Choper, Jesse H. 1995. *Securing Religious Liberty: Principles for Judicial Interpretation of the Religion Clauses*. Chicago: University of Chicago Press.

Cookson, Catherine. 2001. *Regulating Religion: The Courts and the Free Exercise Clause*. Oxford; New York: Oxford University Press.

Craycraft, Kenneth R. Jr. 1999. *The American Myth of Religious Freedom*. Dallas, Texas: Spence Publishing Company.

Dreisbach, Daniel L. 2002. *Thomas Jefferson and the Wall of Separation Between Church and State*. New York: New York University Press.

Edge, Peter W. and Graham Harvey, eds. 2000. *Law and Religion in Contemporary Society: Communities, Individualism, and the State*. Burlington, VT: Ashgate Publishing Co.

Epps, Garrett. 2001. *To an Unknown God: Religious Freedom on Trial*. New York: St. Martin's Press.

Feldman, Noah. 2002. *The Intellectual Origins of the Establishment Clause*. New York University Law Review 77: 346.

Feldman, Stephen M. 1997. *Please Don't Wish Me a Merry Christmas: A Critical History of the Separation of Church and State*. New York: New York University.

Fisher, Louis. 2002. *Religious Liberty in America: Political Safeguards*. Lawrence: University Press of Kansas.

Formicola, Jo Renee, and Hubert Morken. 1997. *Everson Revisited: Religion, Education, and Law at the Crossroads*. Lanham, MD: Rowman & Littlefield.

French, Rebecca Redwood. 1999. *From Yoder to Yoda: Models of Traditional, Modern, and Postmodern Religion in U.S. Constitutional Law*. Arizona Law Review 41: 49.

Glenn, Charles L. 2000. *The Ambiguous Embrace: Government and Faith-Based Schools and Social Agencies*. Princeton, NJ: Princeton University Press.

Greenwalt, Kent. 1984. *Religion as a Concept in Constitutional Law*. Catholic University Law Review 72: 753.

Guliuzza, Frank III. 2000. *Over the Wall: Protecting Religious Expression in the Public Square*. Albany, N.Y.: State University of New York Press.

Hall, Timothy L. 1998. *The Believer's First Amendment Separating Church and State: Roger Williams and Religious Liberty*. University of Illinois Press.

Hamburger, Phillip. 2002. *Separation of Church and State*. Cambridge, Mass.: Harvard University Press.

Howe, Mark Dewolfe. 1965. *The Garden and the Wilderness*. Chicago: University of Chicago Press.

Hutson, James H. 2000. *Religion and the New Republic: Faith in the Founding of America*. Lanham, MD: Rowman & Littlefield.

Kramnick, Isaac, and R. Laurence Moore. 1997. *The Godless Constitution: The Case Against Religious Correctness*. New York: W.W. Norton & Co.

Kurland, Philip. 1961. *Of Church and State and the Supreme Court*. University of Chicago Law Review 29: 1.

———. 1962. *Religion and the Law*. Chicago: Aldine.

Lee, Francis Graham. 2002. *Church-State Relations*. Westport, Conn.: Greenwood Press.

Levy, Leonard W. 1986. *The Establishment Clause: Religion and the First Amendment.* New York: Macmillan Press.

Malbin, Michael. 1978. *Religion and Politics.* Washington, D.C.: American Enterprise Institute.

Mazur, Eric Michael. 1999. *The Americanization of Religious Minorities: Confronting the Constitutional Order.* Baltimore: The John Hopkins University Press.

McLaren, John and Harold Coward, eds. 1999. *Religious Conscience, the State, and the Law: Historical Contexts and Contemporary Significance.* Albany: State University of New York Press.

McConnell, Michael W., John H. Garvey, and Thomas C. Berg. 2002. *Religion and the Constitution.* New York: Aspen Law & Business.

McConnell, Michael. 1990. *The Origins and Historical Understanding of Free Exercise of Religion.* Harvard Law Review 103: 1409.

———. 1990. *Free Exercise Revisionism and the* Smith *Decision.* University of Chicago Law Review 57:1109.

Monsma, Stephen V., ed. 2002. *Church-State Relations in Crisis: Debating Neutrality.* Lanham, MD: Rowman & Littlefield.

Noonan, John T. Jr. 1998. *The Lustre of Our Country: The American Experience of Religious Freedom.* Berkeley: The University of California Press.

Perry, Michael J. 1985. *The Authority of Text, Tradition, and Reason: A Theory of Constitutional Interpretation,* Southern California Law Review. 58: 221.

Ravitch, Frank S. 1999. *School Prayer and Discrimination: the Civil Rights of Religious Minorities and Dissenters.* Boston: Northeastern University Press.

Richards, David A. J. 1986. *Toleration and the Constitution.* New York: Oxford University Press.

Segers, Mary C., ed. 2002. *Piety, Politics, and Pluralism: Religion, the Courts, and the 2000 Election.* Oxford: Rowman & Littlefield.

Smith, Steven D. 1995. *Foreordained Failure: The Quest for a Constitutional Principle of Religious Freedom.* New York: Oxford University Press.

Sorauf, Frank. 1970. *The Wall of Separation: The Constitutional Politics of Church and State.* Princeton: Princeton University Press.

Stronks, Julia K. 2002. *Law, Religion, and Public Policy: A Commentary on First Amendment Jurisprudence.* Lanham, MD: Lexington Books.

Sullivan, Kathleen, 1992. *Religion and Liberal Democracy.* University of Chicago Law Review 59: 195.

Symposium, 1990. *Religious Dimensions of American Constitutionalism.* Emory Law Journal 39: 1.

Symposium, 2003. *Religion in the Public Square.* Notre Dame Journal of Law, Ethics, & Public Policy 17: 307.

Tushnet, Mark. *Red, White, and Blue.* 1988. Cambridge: Harvard University Press.

———. 1987. *Religion and Theories of Constitutional Interpretation,* Loyola Law Review 33: 221.

Selected Comparative Bibliography

Arzt, Donna. 1991. *Religious Freedom in a Religious State: The Case of Israel in Comparative Constitutional Perspective,* Wisconsin International Law Journal 1991: 9.

Beschle, Donald L. 2002. *Does the Establishment Clause Matter? Non-Establishment Principles in the United States and Canada.* University of Pennsylvania Journal of Constitutional Law 4: 451.

Dhavan, Rajeev. 1987. *Religious Freedom in India,* American Journal of Comparative Law. 1987: 35.

du Plessis, Lourens. 2001. *Freedom of or Freedom from Religion? An Overview of Issues Pertinent to the Constitutional Protection of Religious Rights and Freedom in "the New South Africa."* Brigham Young University Law Review 2001: 439.

Englard, Itzhak. 1987. *Law and Religion in Israel,* American Journal of Comparative Law 1987: 35.

Evans, Carolyn. 2001. *Freedom of Religion Under the European Convention on Human Rights.* Oxford; New York: Oxford University Press.

Evans, Malcolm D. 1997. *Religious Liberty and International Law in Europe.* Cambridge; New York: Cambridge University Press.

Garlicki, Leszek Lech. 2001. *Perspectives on Freedom of Conscience and Religion in the Jurisprudence of Constitutional Courts.* Brigham Young University Law Review 2001: 467.

Jacobsohn, Gary Jeffrey. 2002. *The Wheel of Law: India's Secularism in Comparative Constitutional Context.* Princeton: Princeton University Press.

Monsma, Stephen V. and J. Christopher Soper. 1997. *The Challenge of Pluralism: Church and State in Five Democracies.* Lanham: Rowman & Littlefield.

Muehlhoff, Inke. 2000. *Freedom of Religion in Public Schools in Germany and in the United States.* Georgia Journal of International and Comparative Law 28: 405.

O'Brien, David M. with Yasuo Ohkoshi. 1996. *To Dream of Dreams: Religious Freedom and Constitutional Politics in Postwar Japan.* Honolulu: University of Hawaii Press.

Rosenblum, Nancy L., ed. 2000. *Demands of Faith: Religious Accommodation in Pluralist Democracies.* Princeton, New Jersey: Princeton University Pres.

Sedler, Robert A. 1988. *The Constitutional Protection of Freedom of Religion, Expression, and Association in Canada and the United States,* Case Western University Journal of International Law 20: 577.

Shetreet, Shimon. 1999. *State and Religion: Funding of Religious Institutions—The Case of Israel in Comparative Perspective.* Notre Dame Journal of Legal Ethics and Public Law 13: 421.

Thiersten, Joel, and Yahya R. Kamalipour. 2002. *Religion, Law, and Freedom: A Global Perspective.* Westport, Conn.: Praeger.

van der Vyver, Johan D. 2000. *State-Sponsored Proselytization: A South African Experience.* Emory International Law Journal 14: 779.

Wuerth, Ingrid Brunk. 1998. *Private Religious Choice in German and American Constitutional Law: Government Funding and Government Religious Speech.* Vanderbilt Journal of Transnational Law 31: 1127.

Everson v. Board of Education

330 U.S. 1, 67 S. Ct. 504, 91 L. Ed. 711 (1947)

There is a long history of state and local assistance to parochial schools in the United States. Before *Everson* and the incorporation of the establishment clause, most of the cases challenging public assistance to parochial schools occurred in state courts. In 1941, New Jersey passed a statute that permitted local communities to subsidize bus transportation for students attending private schools. Everson, a resident in a town that had voted to subsidize transportation to local Catholic schools, sued the town, claiming that the subsidy violated the establishment clause. Earlier, in the case of *Cochran v. Louisiana Board of Education* (1930), the Supreme Court upheld a state statute that allowed public authorities to provide textbooks to children in parochial school. The Court also denied that the establishment clause applied to the states. Opinion of the Court: *Black*, Vinson, Reed, Douglas, Murphy. Dissenting opinions: *Jackson, Rutledge*, Frankfurter, Burton.

Justice BLACK delivered the opinion of the Court.

The New Jersey statute is challenged as a "law respecting an establishment of religion." The First Amendment, as made applicable to the states by the Fourteenth, . . . commands that a state "shall make no law respecting an establishment of religion, or prohibiting the free exercise thereof. . . ." These words of the First Amendment reflected in the minds of early Americans a vivid mental picture of conditions and practices which they fervently wished to stamp out in order to preserve liberty for themselves and for their posterity. Doubtless their goal has not been entirely reached; but so far has the Nation moved toward it that the expression "law respecting an establishment of religion," probably does not so vividly remind present-day Americans of the evils, fears, and political problems that caused that expression to be written into our Bill of Rights. Whether this New Jersey law is one respecting an "establishment of religion" requires an understanding of the meaning of that language, particularly with respect to the imposition of taxes. Once again, therefore, it is not inappropriate briefly to review the background and environment of the period in which that constitutional language was fashioned and adopted.

A large proportion of the early settlers of this country came here from Europe to escape the bondage of laws which compelled them to support and attend government-favored churches. The centuries immediately before and contemporaneous with the colonization of America had been filled with turmoil, civil strife, and persecutions, generated in large part by established sects determined to maintain their absolute political and religious supremacy. With the power of government supporting them, at various times and places, Catholics had persecuted Protestants, Protestants had persecuted Catholics, Protestant sects had persecuted other Protestant sects, Catholics of one shade of belief had persecuted Catholics of another shade of belief, and all of these had from time to time persecuted Jews. In efforts to force loyalty to whatever religious group happened to be on top and in league with the government of a particular time and place, men and women had been fined, cast in jail, cruelly tortured, and killed. Among the offenses for which these punishments had been inflicted were such things as speaking disrespectfully of the views of ministers of government-established churches, non-attendance at those churches, expressions of non-belief in their doctrines, and failure to pay taxes and tithes to support them.

These practices of the old world were transplanted to and began to thrive in the soil of the new America. The very charters granted by the English Crown to the individuals and companies designated to make the laws which would control the destinies of the colonials authorized these individuals and companies to erect religious establishments which all, whether believers or non-believers, would be required to support and attend. An exercise of this authority was accompanied by a repetition of many of the old-world practices and persecutions. . . .

The meaning and scope of the First Amendment, preventing establishment of religion or prohibiting the free exercise thereof, in the light of its history and the evils it was designed forever to suppress, have been several times elaborated by the decisions of this Court prior to the application of the First Amendment to the states by the Fourteenth. The broad meaning given the Amendment by these earlier cases has been accepted by this Court in its decisions concerning an individual's religious freedom rendered since the Fourteenth Amendment was interpreted to make the prohibitions of the First applicable to state action abridging religious freedom. There is every reason to give the same application and broad interpretation to the "establishment of religion" clause. . . .

The "establishment of religion" clause of the First Amendment means at least this: Neither a state nor the Federal Government can set up a church. Neither can pass laws which aid one religion, aid all religions, or prefer one religion over another. Neither can force nor influence a person to go to or to remain away from church against his will or force him to profess a belief or disbelief in any religion. No person can be punished for entertaining or professing religious beliefs or disbeliefs, for church attendance or non-attendance. No tax in any amount, large or small, can be levied to support any religious activities or institutions, whatever they may be called, or whatever form they may adopt to teach or practice religion. Neither a state nor the Federal Government can, openly or secretly, participate in the affairs of any religious organizations or groups and vice versa. In the words of Jefferson, the clause against establishment of religion by law was intended to erect "a wall of separation between church and State."

We must consider the New Jersey statute in accordance with the foregoing limitations imposed by the First Amendment. But we must not strike that state statute down if it is within the State's constitutional power even though it approaches the verge of that power. . . . New Jersey cannot consistently with the "establishment of religion" clause of the First Amendment contribute tax-raised funds to the support of an institution which teaches the tenets and faith of any church. On the other hand, other language of the amendment commands that New Jersey cannot hamper its citizens in the free exercise of their own religion. Consequently, it cannot exclude individual Catholics, Lutherans, Mohammedans, Baptists, Jews, Methodists, Non-believers, Presbyterians, or the members of any other faith, because of their faith, or lack of it, from receiving the benefits of public welfare legislation. While we do not mean to intimate that a state could not provide transportation only to children attending public schools, we must be careful, in protecting the citizens of New Jersey against state-established churches, to be sure that we do not inadvertently prohibit New Jersey from extending its general state law benefits to all its citizens without regard to their religious belief.

Measured by these standards, we cannot say that the First Amendment prohibits New Jersey from spending tax-raised funds to pay the bus fares of parochial school pupils as a part of a general program under which it pays the fares of pupils attending public and other schools. It is undoubtedly true that children are helped to get to church schools. There is even a possibility that some of the children might not be sent to the church schools if the parents were compelled to pay their children's bus fares out of their own pockets when transportation to a public school would have been paid for by the State. The same possibility exists where the state requires a local transit company to provide reduced fares to school children including those attending parochial schools, or where a municipally owned transportation system undertakes to carry all school children free of charge. Moreover, state-paid policemen, detailed to protect children going to and from church schools from the very real hazards of traffic, would serve much the same purpose and accomplish much the same result as state provisions intended to guarantee free transportation of a kind which the state deems to be best for the school children's welfare. And parents might refuse to risk their children to the serious danger of traffic accidents going to and from parochial schools, the approaches to which were not protected by policemen. Similarly, parents might be reluctant to permit their children to attend schools which the state had cut off from such general government services as ordinary police and fire protection, connections for sewage disposal, public highways and sidewalks. Of course, cutting off church schools from these services, so separate and so indisputably marked off from the religious function, would make it far more difficult for the schools to operate. But such is obviously not the purpose of the First Amendment. That Amendment requires the state to be a neutral in its relations with groups of religious believers and non-believers; it does not require the state to be their adversary. State power is no more to be used so as to handicap religions than it is to favor them.

This Court has said that parents may, in the discharge of their duty under state compulsory education laws, send their children to a religious rather than a public school if the school meets the secular educational requirements which the state has power to impose. . . . It appears that these parochial schools meet New Jersey's requirements. The State contributes no money to the schools. It does not support them. Its legislation, as applied, does no more than provide a general program to help parents get their children, regardless of their religion, safely and expeditiously to and from accredited schools.

The First Amendment has erected a wall between church and state. That wall must be kept high and impregnable. We could not approve the slightest breach. New Jersey has not breached it here.

Affirmed.

Comparative Note 13.1

[The secularity of the state is a cardinal principle of French constitutionalism. Socialist members of parliament challenged the constitutionality of a law under which private schools, mainly Catholic, received state funding, including payment for teachers' salaries.]

1. Considering that, according to article 1 of the *loi* [law] complementing the *loi* of 31 December 1959, as amended by the *loi* of 1 June 1971 on the freedom of education, teachers entrusted with the task of teaching in a private establishment linked to the State by a contract of association are obliged to respect the specific character of that establishment;

2. Considering that . . . the safeguarding of the specific character of an establishment linked to the State by contract . . . merely implements the principle of freedom of education;

3. Considering that this principle . . . constitutes one of the fundamental principles recognized by the laws of the Republic . . . and on which the Constitution of 1958 conferred constitutional value;

4. Considering that the affirmation by the same Preamble to the 1946 Constitution, that "the organization of free and secular education is a duty of the State," does not exclude the existence of private education, nor the granting of State aid to such education in circumstances defined by law . . . [and]

5. Considering that . . . according to the terms of article 10 of the Declaration of the Rights of Man and of the Citizen of 1789, "No one may be troubled on account of his opinions or religion, provided that their expression does not infringe public policy . . ." The Preamble to the 1946 Constitution [carried over into the 1958 Constitution] affirms that "No one may be harmed in his work or employment on account of his origins, opinions, or beliefs"; that freedom of conscience must be regarded as one of the fundamental principles recognized by the laws of the Republic. . . .

SOURCE: Decision No. 77–87 of 23 November 1977, French Constitutional Council in John Bell, *French Constitutional Law* (Oxford: Clarendon Press, 1992), 319–20.

Justice JACKSON, dissenting.

I find myself, contrary to first impressions, unable to join in this decision. I have a sympathy, though it is not ideological, with Catholic citizens who are compelled by law to pay taxes for public schools, and also feel constrained by conscience and discipline to support other schools for their own children. Such relief to them as this case involves is not in itself a serious burden to taxpayers and I had assumed it to be as little serious in principle. Study of this case convinces me otherwise. The Court's opinion marshals every argument in favor of state aid and puts the case in its most favorable light, but much of its reasoning confirms my conclusions that there are no good grounds upon which to support the present legislation. In fact, the undertones of the opinion, advocating complete and uncompromising separation of Church from State, seem utterly discordant with its conclusion yielding support to their commingling in educational matters. The case which irresistibly comes to mind as the most fitting precedent is that of Julia who, according to Byron's reports, "whispering 'I will ne'er consent,'—consented."

This policy of our Federal Constitution has never been wholly pleasing to most religious groups. They all are quick to invoke its protections; they all are irked when they feel its restraints. This Court has gone a long way, if not an unreasonable way, to hold that public business of such paramount importance as maintenance of public order, protection of the privacy of the home, and taxation may not be pursued by a state in a way that even indirectly will interfere with religious proselyting.

But we cannot have it both ways. Religious teaching cannot be a private affair when the state seeks to impose regulations which infringe on it indirectly, and a public affair when it comes to taxing citizens of one faith to aid another, or those of no faith to aid all. If these principles seem harsh in prohibiting aid to Catholic education, it must not be forgotten that it is the same Constitution that alone assures Catholics the right to maintain these schools at all when predominant local sentiment would forbid them. . . . Nor should I think that those who have done so well without this aid would want to see this separation between Church and State broken down. If the state may aid these religious schools, it may therefore regulate them. Many groups have sought aid from tax funds only to find that it carried political controls with it. Indeed this Court has declared that "It is hardly lack of due process for the Government to regulate that which it subsidizes."

But in any event, the great purposes of the Constitution do not depend on the approval or convenience of those they restrain. I cannot read the history of the struggle to separate political from ecclesiastical affairs, well summarized in the opinion of Mr. Justice Rutledge in which I generally concur, without a conviction that the Court today is unconsciously giving the clock's hands a backward turn.

Justice FRANKFURTER joins in this opinion.

Justice RUTLEDGE, with whom Justice FRANKFURTER, Justice JACKSON and Justice BURTON agree, dissenting.

No one conscious of religious values can be unsympathetic toward the burden which our constitutional separation puts on parents who desire religious instruction mixed with secular for their children. They pay taxes for others' children's education, at the same time the added cost of instruction for their own. Nor can one happily see benefits denied to children which others receive, because in conscience they or their parents for them desire a different kind of training others do not demand.

But if those feelings should prevail, there would be an end to our historic constitutional policy and command. No more unjust or discriminatory in fact is it to deny attendants at religious schools the cost of their transportation than it is to deny them tuitions, sustenance for their teachers, or any other educational expense which others receive at public cost. Hardship in fact there is which none can blink. But, for assuring to those who undergo it the greater, the most comprehensive freedom, it is one written by design and firm intent into our basic law.

Of course discrimination in the legal sense does not exist. The child attending the religious school has the same right as any other to attend the public school. But he forgoes exercising it because the same guaranty which assures this freedom forbids the public school or any agency of the state to give or aid him in securing the religious instruction he seeks.

Were he to accept the common school, he would be the first to protest the teaching there of any creed or faith not his own. And it is precisely for the reason that their atmosphere is wholly secular that children are not sent to public schools under the *Pierce* doctrine. But that is a constitutional necessity, because we have staked the very existence of our country on the faith that complete separation between the state and religion is best for the state and best for religion.

That policy necessarily entails hardship upon persons who forego the right to educational advantages the state can supply in order to secure others it is precluded from giving. Indeed this may hamper the parent and the child forced by conscience to that choice. But it does not make the state unneutral to withhold what the Constitution forbids it to give. On the contrary it is only by observing the prohibition rigidly that the state can maintain its neutrality and avoid partisanship in the dissensions inevitable when sect opposes sect over demands for public moneys to further religious education, teaching or training in any form or degree, directly or indirectly. Like St. Paul's freedom, religious liberty with a great price must be bought. And for those who exercise it most fully, by insisting upon religious education for their children mixed with secular, by the terms of our Constitution the price is greater than for others.

Notes and Queries

1. Justice Black's opinion for the Court relied heavily on the history of religious freedom and the First Amendment to interpret the establishment clause. History, Justice Black concluded, showed that the Founders envisioned a wall of separation between church and state.

Is history ever as instructive, or as clear, as Justice Black insisted? Many scholars have concluded that Black's historical analysis is incomplete or misleading. Robert Cord, for example, thinks the historical record suggests the Founders were not opposed to nondiscriminatory aid to religion in general. *Separation of Church and State* (New York: Lambeth Press, 1982). And as we saw in the introduction to this chapter, many scholars think appeals to "history" reveal a great variety of approaches to the relationship between church and state, including traditions that feared the influence of the state on religion. See, for example, Mark DeWolfe Howe, *The Garden and the Wilderness* (Chicago: University of Chicago Press, 1965).

2. As we shall see later in this chapter, scholarly disputes with Justice Black's interpretation of history have led some justices to argue for the dismantling of the wall of separation built in *Everson*. See, for example, Chief Justice Rehnquist's opinion in *Wallace v. Jaffree* (1985).

3. What, if anything, do such disagreements about the meaning of history suggest about its use in constitutional interpretation? Should disagreement about the historical record disqualify appeals to history? Assume, on the other hand, that we can agree about the lesson of history—assume, for example, that we could agree that the history of the establishment clause reveals that the Founders would plainly have opposed any state aid to religion.

Should that lesson determine the meaning of the establishment clause for our time?

4. Would interpretation be easier if we forsook history and relied instead on appeals to the purpose(s) of the establishment clause? What "purpose" would support the Court's opinion in *Everson?*

5. The majority, following Jefferson, claimed there must

be a wall of separation between church and state. Nevertheless, the Court upheld the New Jersey statute. Is Justice Jackson's conclusion that the Court breached the wall it had created in *Everson* correct? Is it possible to reconcile the Court's rhetoric with its holding? Should the wall of separation distinguish between substantial and incidental aid to religion?

Engel v. Vitale
370 U.S. 421, 82 S. Ct. 1261, 8 L.Ed. 2d 601 (1962)

In the 1950s, the New York Board of Regents authorized local school districts to require children to say a short prayer it had composed. No school district had to mandate the prayer, but no other prayer was permissible. The parents of ten students, some Jewish, some Unitarian, and some nonbelievers, challenged the prayer as an establishment of religion. As the case proceeded some of the families received anti-Semitic threats and threats against their lives. Opinion of the Court: *Black*, Warren, Clark, Harlan, Brennan. Concurring opinion: *Douglas.* Dissenting opinion: *Stewart.* Not participating: *Frankfurter, White.*

Justice BLACK delivered the opinion of the Court.

We think that by using its public school system to encourage recitation of the Regents' prayer, the State of New York has adopted a practice wholly inconsistent with the Establishment Clause. There can, of course, be no doubt that New York's program of daily classroom invocation of God's blessings as prescribed in the Regents' prayer is a religious activity. . . .

The petitioners contend among other things that the state laws requiring or permitting use of the Regents' prayer must be struck down as a violation of the Establishment Clause because that prayer was composed by governmental officials as a part of a governmental program to further religious beliefs. For this reason, petitioners argue, the State's use of the Regents' prayer in its public school system breaches the constitutional wall of separation between Church and State. We agree with that contention since we think that the constitutional prohibition against laws respecting an establishment of religion must at least mean that in this country it is no part of the business of government to compose official prayers for any group of the American people to recite as a part of a religious program carried on by government.

There can be no doubt that New York's state prayer program officially establishes the religious beliefs embodied in the Regents' prayer. The respondents' argument to the

contrary, which is largely based upon the contention that the Regents' prayer is "non-denominational" and the fact that the program, as modified and approved by state courts, does not require all pupils to recite the prayer but permits those who wish to do so to remain silent or be excused from the room, ignores the essential nature of the program's constitutional defects. Neither the fact that the prayer may be denominationally neutral nor the fact that its observance on the part of the students is voluntary can serve to free it from the limitations of the Establishment Clause, as it might from the Free Exercise Clause, of the First Amendment, both of which are operative against the States by virtue of the Fourteenth Amendment. Although these two clauses may in certain instances overlap, they forbid two quite different kinds of governmental encroachment upon religious freedom. The Establishment Clause, unlike the Free Exercise Clause, does not depend upon any showing of direct governmental compulsion and is violated by the enactment of laws which establish an official religion whether those laws operate directly to coerce nonobserving individuals or not. This is not to say, of course, that laws officially prescribing a particular form of religious worship do not involve coercion of such individuals. When the power, prestige and financial support of government is placed behind a particular religious belief, the indirect coercive pressure upon religious minorities to conform to the prevailing officially approved religion is plain. But the purposes underlying the Establishment Clause go much further than that. Its first and most immediate purpose rested on the belief that a union of government and religion tends to destroy government and to degrade religion. The history of governmentally established religion, both in England and in this country, showed that whenever government had allied itself with one particular form of religion, the inevitable result had been that it had incurred the hatred, disrespect and even contempt of those who held contrary beliefs. That same history shows that many people had lost their respect for any religion that had relied upon the support of government to spread its faith. The Establishment Clause thus stands as an expression of principle on the part of the

Founders of our Constitution that religion is too personal, too sacred, too holy, to permit its "unhallowed perversion" by a civil magistrate. Another purpose of the Establishment Clause rested upon an awareness of the historical fact that governmentally established religions and religious persecutions go hand in hand. . . . The New York laws officially prescribing the Regents' prayer are inconsistent both with the purposes of the Establishment Clause and with the Establishment Clause itself.

It has been argued that to apply the Constitution in such a way as to prohibit state laws respecting an establishment of religious services in public schools is to indicate a hostility toward religion or toward prayer. Nothing, of course, could be more wrong. . . . It is neither sacrilegious nor antireligious to say that each separate government in this country should stay out of the business of writing or sanctioning official prayers and leave that purely religious function to the people themselves and to those the people choose to look to for religious guidance. . . .

. . . To those who may subscribe to the view that be-cause the Regents' official prayer is so brief and general there can be no danger to religious freedom in its governmental establishment, however, it may be appropriate to say in the words of James Madison, the author of the First Amendment:

It is proper to take alarm at the first experiment on our liberties. . . . Who does not see that the same authority which can establish Christianity, in exclusion of all other Religions, may establish with the same ease any particular sect of Christians, in exclusion of all other Sects? That the same authority which can force a citizen to contribute three pence only of his property for the support of any one establishment, may force him to conform to any other establishment in all cases whatsoever?

The judgment of the Court of Appeals of New York is reversed and the cause remanded for further proceedings not inconsistent with this opinion.

Reversed and remanded.

Comparative Note 13.2

[This decision consolidated two German cases. In the first case a parent complained that an administrative decision prohibiting voluntary prayer in public schools violated his child's right to exercise his religion in public. In the second case, the complainant claimed that being "forced" to pray in school—here an interdenominational public school—violated the child's right to religious liberty.]

2. The problem of school prayer must first be seen in the broader framework of whether religious references are ever permissible in (compulsory) interdenominational state schools, or whether the state within its authority to structure the school system is confined to making religious or ideological references in religion classes, which are expressly guaranteed in Article 7(3) of the Basic Law.

The school prayer at issue in this constitutional complaint represents a supradenominational (ecumenical) invocation of God based on Christian beliefs. . . . Even in its transdenominational form, prayer is connected to the truth of a belief; . . . [Still] voluntary participation [in prayer] remains within the scope of creative freedom granted to the states as bearers of supreme authority in school matters [under Article 7(1)].

Article 4 of the Basic Law grants not only freedom of belief but also the external freedom publicly to acknowledge one's belief. . . . [T]he state must balance this affirmative freedom to worship as expressed by permitting school prayer with the negative freedom of confession of other parents and pupils opposed to school prayer. . . . [Schools] may achieve this balance by guaranteeing that participation be voluntary for pupils and teachers. . . . As a rule a pupil can find an acceptable way to avoid participating in the prayer so as to decide with complete freedom not to participate.

Admittedly . . . each of these alternatives will have the effect of distinguishing the pupil in question from the praying pupils—especially if the pupil professes other beliefs. . . . Nonetheless, one cannot assume that abstaining from school prayer will generally or even in a substantial number of cases force a dissenting pupil into an unbearable position as an outsider. An assessment of the conditions under which the prayer is to occur, the function that the teacher has in connection with this exercise, and the actual conditions in the school leads us to conclude that we need not fear discrimination against a pupil who does not participate in the prayer. . . .

SOURCE: *School Prayer Case* (1979) in Kommers, *Constitutional Jurisprudence*, 467–70.

Justice FRANKFURTER took no part in the decision of this case.

Justice WHITE took no part in the consideration or decision of this case.

Justice DOUGLAS, concurring.

It is customary in deciding a constitutional question to treat it in its narrowest form. Yet at times the setting of the question gives it a form and content which no abstract treatment could give. The point for decision is whether the Government can constitutionally finance a religious exercise. Our system at the federal and state levels is presently honeycombed with such financing. Nevertheless, I think it is an unconstitutional undertaking whatever form it takes.

. . . The First Amendment leaves the Government in a position not of hostility to religion but of neutrality. The philosophy is that the atheist or agnostic—the nonbeliever—is entitled to go his own way. The philosophy is that if government interferes in matters spiritual, it will be a divisive force. The First Amendment teaches that a government neutral in the field of religion better serves all religious interests.

Justice STEWART, dissenting.

. . . The Court today decides that in permitting this brief nondenominational prayer the school board has violated the Constitution of the United States. I think this decision is wrong. . . . With all respect, I think the Court has misapplied a great constitutional principle. I cannot see how an "official religion" is established by letting those who want to say a prayer say it. On the contrary, I think that to deny the wish of these school children to join in reciting this prayer is to deny them the opportunity of sharing in the spiritual heritage of our Nation.

At the opening of each day's Session of this Court we stand, while one of our officials invokes the protection of God. Since the days of John Marshall our Crier has said, "God save the United States and this Honorable Court." Both the Senate and the House of Representatives open their daily Sessions with prayer. Each of our Presidents, from George Washington to John F. Kennedy, has upon assuming his Office asked the protection and help of God.

Countless similar examples could be listed, but there is no need to belabor the obvious. It was all summed up by this Court just ten years ago in a single sentence: "We are a religious people whose institutions presuppose a Supreme Being."

I do not believe that this Court, or the Congress, or the President has by the actions and practices I have mentioned established an "official religion" in violation of the Constitution. And I do not believe the State of New York has done so in this case. What each has done has been to recognize and to follow the deeply entrenched and highly cherished spiritual traditions of our Nation—traditions which come down to us from those who almost two hundred years ago avowed their "firm Reliance on the Protection of divine Providence" when they proclaimed the freedom and independence of this brave new world.

I dissent.

Notes and Queries

1. Public reaction to the Court's decision was swift and angry. Critics complained that the Court had taken God out of the schools, cries that intensified a year later, when the Court announced its opinion in *School District of Abington v. Schempp* (1963). In this case, the Court invalidated Bible reading practices and the recitation of the Lord's Prayer during classroom time. Several members of Congress reacted by threatening to strip the Court of its appellate jurisdiction. Representative George Andrews, of Alabama, complained that "They put the Negroes in the schools and now they've driven God out." (*New York Times,* 26 June 1962, 1)

2. In *Lee v. Weisman* (1992, reprinted later in the chapter), the Court considered the constitutionality of a commencement ceremony benediction at a public high school in Providence, Rhode Island. As a part of the graduation ceremony, a school principal invited a member of the local clergy to say a short prayer.

Justice Kennedy's opinion for the Court found the practice unconstitutional because, as a practical matter, it compelled the participation of the students. Dissenting, Justice Scalia argued that "The deeper flaw in the Court's opinion does not lie in its wrong answer to the question whether there was state-induced 'peer pressure' coercion; it lies, rather, in the Court's making violation of the establishment clause hinge on such a precious question. The coercion that was a hallmark of historical establishments of religion was coercion of religious orthodoxy and of financial support *by force of law and threat of penalty*" (emphasis in original).

3. Some members of Congress proposed a constitutional amendment to overturn the school prayer decisions; the proposal was defeated in the Senate in 1966. Even so, every new session of Congress includes a similar proposal, and various presidential candidates, including Barry Goldwater and Ronald Reagan, have made the return of school prayer a prominent part of their campaigns. In 1984 President Reagan acted on the pledge, introducing in Congress another amendment, which provided "Nothing in this Constitution shall be construed to prohibit indi-

vidual or group prayer in public schools or other public institutions. No person shall be required by the United States or by any State to participate in prayer. Neither the United States or any State shall compose the words of any prayer to be said in public schools." The proposed amendment achieved a majority of 56 votes, but was 11 shy of the two-thirds necessary to advance it. In response, Senator Helms of North Carolina promised that "[W]e have just begun to fight. Round 1 is over, but so long as I am in the Senate there will be many more rounds. . . ." Helms was right. The congressional elections of 1994, which resulted in the Republican control of both Houses of Congress for the first time in a half-century, led to renewed calls for a school prayer amendment.

4. As we shall see, many states reacted to *Engel* and *Schempp* by requiring a "moment of silence" at the beginning of the school day. The Court considered the constitutionality of one such plan in *Wallace v. Jaffree* (1985, reprinted later in this chapter).

Somewhat more successful have been efforts to ensure the equal access of religious groups to public facilities. In *Widmar v. Vincent* (1981) and *Westside Community Board of Education v. Mergens* (1990), for example, the Court upheld legislation that requires equal access to all schools that receive federal funds. More recently, in *Good News Club v. Milford* (2000, reprinted later in the chapter), a deeply divided Court reiterated its position that such access does not amount to a violation of the establishment clause.

5. What was the constitutional difficulty in *Engel?* Was it the mere presence of prayer in the schools? Is there a constitutional difference between voluntary and mandatory prayer? Or was the difficulty a function of the prayer's composition by state authorities?

6. In *Zylberberg v. Director of Education of Sudbury Board of Education* 52 D.L.R. (4th) 587 (1988), the Court of Appeals for Ontario was asked to assess the constitutionality of the singing of *O Canada* and the saying of the Lord's Prayer in the Sudbury public schools. At a parent's request, a child could be excused from the exercises, and no child was required to participate in them.

"On its face," the Court concluded, the practice violated the guarantee of religious freedom in the Canadian Constitution. The Court went on to consider, however, whether the provisions that allowed children not to participate could save the practice. The Court concluded that "the reality is that [the practice] imposes on religious minorities a compulsion to conform to the religious practices of the majority. . . . The peer pressure and the class-room norms to which children are acutely sensitive, in our opinion, are real and pervasive and operate to compel members of religious minorities to conform with majority religious practices."

Compare the American and Canadian decisions with the German Constitutional Court's decision in the *School Prayer Case*, 52 BVerfGE 223 (1979)(Comparative Note 13.2).

Lemon v. Kurtzman
403 U.S. 602, 91 S. Ct. 2105, 29 L. Ed. 2d 745 (1971)

In this consolidated case the Court again considered the constitutionality of state aid to church-related schools. In one case, Pennsylvania reimbursed such schools for the costs of teachers' salaries, books, and other "secular services," defined as courses in mathematics, physical education, science, and foreign languages; the state spent over $5 million per year under the program. In another case, Rhode Island supplemented teacher salaries to 15 percent if those teachers taught secular subjects. Alton Lemon sued Kurtzman, Pennsylvania's superintendent of schools, the state treasurer, and seven schools receiving aid, claiming that the aid violated the establishment clause. Opinion of the Court: *Burger*, Black, Douglas, Harlan, Stewart, Blackmun. Concurring opinions: *Douglas*, Black; *Brennan*. Dissenting opinion: White. Not participating: *Marshall*.

Chief Justice BURGER delivered the opinion of the Court.

In *Everson v. Board of Education* (1947), this Court upheld a state statute that reimbursed the parents of parochial school children for bus transportation expenses. There Mr. Justice Black, writing for the majority, suggested that the decision carried to "the verge" of forbidden territory. . . . Candor compels acknowledgement . . . that we can only dimly perceive the lines of demarcation in this extraordinarily sensitive area of constitutional law.

The language of the Religion Clauses of the First Amendment is at best opaque, particularly when compared with other portions of the Amendment. Its authors did not simply prohibit the establishment of a state church or a state religion, an area history shows they regarded as very important and fraught with great dangers. Instead they commanded that there should be "no law respecting an establishment of religion." A law may be one "respecting" the forbidden objective while falling short of its total realization. A law "respecting" the proscribed result, that is, the establishment of religion, is not always easily identifiable as one violative of the Clause. A given law might not establish a state religion but nevertheless be one "respecting" that end in the sense of being a step that could lead to such establishment and hence offend the First Amendment.

Every analysis in this area must begin with consideration of the cumulative criteria developed by the Court over many years. Three such tests may be gleaned from our cases. First, the statute must have a secular legislative purpose; second, its principal or primary effect must be one that neither advances nor inhibits religion . . . ; finally, the statute must not foster "an excessive government entanglement with religion."

Inquiry into the legislative purposes of the Pennsylvania and Rhode Island statutes affords no basis for a conclusion that the legislative intent was to advance religion. On the contrary, the statutes themselves clearly state that they are intended to enhance the quality of the secular education in all schools covered by the compulsory attendance laws. There is no reason to believe the legislatures meant anything else. . . .

. . . The legislatures of Rhode Island and Pennsylvania have concluded that secular and religious education are identifiable and separable. In the abstract we have no quarrel with this conclusion.

The two legislatures, however, have also recognized that church-related elementary and secondary schools have a significant religious mission and that a substantial portion of their activities is religiously oriented. They have therefore sought to create statutory restrictions designed to guarantee the separation between secular and religious educational functions and to ensure that State financial aid supports only the former. . . . We need not decide whether these legislative precautions restrict the principal or primary effect of the programs to the point where they do not offend the Religion Clauses, for we conclude that the cumulative impact of the entire relationship arising under the statutes in each State involves excessive entanglement between government and religion.

Our prior holdings do not call for total separation between church and state; total separation is not possible in an absolute sense. Some relationship between government and religious organizations is inevitable. . . . Fire inspections, building and zoning regulations, and state requirements under compulsory school-attendance laws are examples of necessary and permissible contacts. . . . Judicial caveats against entanglement must recognize that the line of separation, far from being a "wall," is a blurred, indistinct, and variable barrier depending on all the circumstances of a particular relationship.

This is not to suggest, however, that we are to engage in a legalistic minuet in which precise rules and forms must govern. A true minuet is a matter of pure form and style, the observance of which is itself the substantive end. Here we examine the form of the relationship for the light that it casts on the substance.

In order to determine whether the government entanglement with religion is excessive, we must examine the character and purposes of the institutions that are benefited, the nature of the aid that the State provides, and the resulting relationship between the government and the religious authority. . . . Here we find that both statutes foster an impermissible degree of entanglement.

The Rhode Island Program

The church schools involved in the program are located close to parish churches. . . . The school buildings contain identifying religious symbols such as crosses on the exterior and crucifixes, and religious paintings and statues either in the classrooms or hallways. Although only approximately 30 minutes a day are devoted to direct religious instruction, there are religiously oriented extracurricular activities. Approximately two-thirds of the teachers in these schools are nuns of various religious orders. Their dedicated efforts provide an atmosphere in which religious instruction and religious vocations are natural and proper parts of life in such schools. . . .

. . . This process of inculcating religious doctrine is, of course, enhanced by the impressionable age of the pupils, in primary schools particularly. In short, parochial schools involve substantial religious activity and purpose.

The substantial religious character of these church-related schools gives rise to entangling church-state relationships of the kind the Religion Clauses sought to avoid. . . .

The dangers and corresponding entanglements are enhanced by the particular form of aid that the Rhode Island Act provides. Our decisions from *Everson* to *Allen* have permitted the States to provide church-related schools with secular, neutral, or nonideological services, facilities, or materials. Bus transportation, school lunches, public health services, and secular textbooks supplied in common to all students were not thought to offend the Establishment Clause. . . .

In *Allen* the Court refused to make assumptions, on a meager record, about the religious content of the textbooks that the State would be asked to provide. We cannot, however, refuse here to recognize that teachers have a substantially different ideological character from books. In terms of potential for involving some aspect of faith or morals in secular subjects, a textbook's content is ascertainable, but a teacher's handling of a subject is not. We cannot ignore the danger that a teacher under religious

Comparative Note 13.3

[Ontario's Retail Business Holidays Act prohibited retail stores from being open on certain holidays (e.g., Christmas, New Year's Day, Canada Day, Good Friday) and on Sundays except for stores with fewer than seven employees which remained closed the preceding Saturday. The declared purpose of the Act was to provide uniform holidays for retail workers. In *McGowan v. Maryland* (1961), the U.S. Supreme Court upheld a similar law. Unlike the U.S. Court, the Canadian Supreme Court found that the law infringed freedom of religion, but that is was justifiable under s. 1 of the Charter of Rights and Freedoms.]

In *Big M Drug Mart* the court noted the use by the majority of the [U.S.] Supreme Court of a concept of "shifting legislative purpose," whereby the purpose underlying the laws was seen to have shifted from religious to secular concerns. The majority of the U.S. Supreme Court thereby sustained the legislation from attack under the "establishment clause." . . . This court declined to import the "shifting purpose" doctrine into Canadian jurisprudence and the purpose of the *Lord's Day Act* was consequently held, in *Big M Drug Mart,* to infringe the right to be free from conforming to religious dogma.

Two requirements must be satisfied to establish that a limit [on a fundamental right] is reasonable and demonstrably justified in a free and democratic society [under the terms of s. 7]. First, the legislative objective which the limitation is designed to promote must be of sufficient importance to warrant overriding a constitutional right. It must bear on a "pressing and substantial concern." Secondly, the means chosen to attain those objectives must be proportional or appropriate to the ends. The proportionality requirement, in turn, normally has three aspects: the limiting measures must be carefully designed, or rationally connected, to the objective; they must impair the right as little as possible; and their effects must not so severely trench on individual or group rights that the legislative objective, albeit important, is, nevertheless, outweighed by the abridgement of rights. The court stated that the nature of the proportionality test would vary depending on the circumstances. Both in articulating the standard of proof and in describing the criteria comprising the proportionality [test] the court has been careful to avoid rigid and inflexible standards.

Source: *Edwards Books and Art Ltd. et al. v. The Queen.* (1986) In the Supreme Court of Canada 35 D.L.R. (4th).

---

control and discipline poses to the separation of the religious from the purely secular aspects of pre-college education. The conflict of functions inheres in the situation.

In our view the record shows these dangers are present to a substantial degree. . . .

Several teachers testified, however, that they did not inject religion into their secular classes. . . . But what has been recounted suggests the potential if not actual hazards of this form of state aid. The teacher is employed by a religious organization, subject to the direction and discipline of religious authorities, and works in a system dedicated to rearing children in a particular faith. These controls are not lessened by the fact that most of the lay teachers are of the Catholic faith. Inevitably some of a teacher's responsibilities hover on the border between secular and religious orientation.

We need not and do not assume that teachers in parochial schools will be guilty of bad faith or any conscious design to evade the limitations imposed by the statute and the First Amendment. We simply recognize that a dedi-

cated religious person, teaching in a school affiliated with his or her faith and operated to inculcate its tenets, will inevitably experience great difficulty in remaining religiously neutral. Doctrines and faith are not inculcated or advanced by neutrals. With the best of intentions such a teacher would find it hard to make a total separation between secular teaching and religious doctrine. . . . Further difficulties are inherent in the combination of religious discipline and the possibility of disagreement between teacher and religious authorities over the meaning of the statutory restrictions.

. . . The Rhode Island Legislature has not, and could not, provide state aid on the basis of a mere assumption that secular teachers under religious discipline can avoid conflicts. The State must be certain, given the Religion Clauses, that subsidized teachers do not inculcate religion—indeed the State here has undertaken to do so. To ensure that no trespass occurs, the State has therefore carefully conditioned its aid with pervasive restrictions. . . .

A comprehensive, discriminating, and continuing state

surveillance will inevitably be required to ensure that these restrictions are obeyed and the First Amendment otherwise respected. Unlike a book, a teacher cannot be inspected once so as to determine the extent and intent of his or her personal beliefs and subjective acceptance of the limitations imposed by the First Amendment. These prophylactic contacts will involve excessive and enduring entanglement between state and church.

There is another area of entanglement in the Rhode Island program that gives concern. The statute excludes teachers employed by nonpublic schools whose average per-pupil expenditures on secular education equal or exceed the comparable figures for public schools. In the event that the total expenditures of an otherwise eligible school exceed this norm, the program requires the government to examine the school's records in order to determine how much of the total expenditures is attributable to secular education and how much to religious activity. This kind of state inspection and evaluation of the religious content of a religious organization is fraught with the sort of entanglement that the Constitution forbids. It is a relationship pregnant with dangers of excessive government direction of church schools and hence of churches. . . .

The Pennsylvania Program

. . . [T]he very restrictions and surveillance necessary to ensure that teachers play a strictly nonideological role give rise to entanglements between church and state. The Pennsylvania statute, like that of Rhode Island, fosters this kind of relationship. . . .

The Pennsylvania statute, moreover, has the further defect of providing state financial aid directly to the church-related school. This factor distinguishes both *Everson* and *Allen*, for in both those cases the Court was careful to point out that state aid was provided to the student and his parents—not to the church-related school. . . . The history of government grants of a continuing cash subsidy indicates that such programs have almost always been accompanied by varying measures of control and surveillance. The government cash grants before us now provide no basis for predicting that comprehensive measures of surveillance and controls will not follow. . . .

A broader base of entanglement of yet a different character is presented by the divisive political potential of these state programs. In a community where such a large number of pupils are served by church-related schools, it can be assumed that state assistance will entail considerable political activity. Partisans of parochial schools, understandably concerned with rising costs and sincerely dedicated to both the religious and secular educational missions of their schools, will inevitably champion this

cause and promote political action to achieve their goals. Those who oppose state aid, whether for constitutional, religious, or fiscal reasons, will inevitably respond and employ all of the usual political campaign techniques to prevail. Candidates will be forced to declare and voters to choose. It would be unrealistic to ignore the fact that many people confronted with issues of this kind will find their votes aligned with their faith.

Ordinarily political debate and division, however vigorous or even partisan, are normal and healthy manifestations of our democratic system of government, but political division along religious lines was one of the principal evils against which the First Amendment was intended to protect. . . . The potential divisiveness of such conflict is a threat to the normal political process. . . . It conflicts with our whole history and tradition to permit questions of the Religion Clauses to assume such importance in our legislatures and in our elections that they could divert attention from the myriad issues and problems that confront every level of government. . . . The history of many countries attests to the hazards of religion's intruding into the political arena or of political power intruding into the legitimate and free exercise of religious belief.

The potential for political divisiveness related to religious belief and practice is aggravated in these two statutory programs by the need for continuing annual appropriations and the likelihood of larger and larger demands as costs and populations grow. . . .

We have already noted that modern governmental programs have self-perpetuating and self-expanding propensities. These internal pressures are only enhanced when the schemes involve institutions whose legitimate needs are growing and whose interests have substantial political support. Nor can we fail to see that in constitutional adjudication some steps, which when taken were thought to approach "the verge," have become the platform for yet further steps. A certain momentum develops in constitutional theory and it can be a "downhill thrust" easily set in motion but difficult to retard or stop. . . . The dangers are increased by the difficulty of perceiving in advance exactly where the "verge" of the precipice lies. As well as constituting an independent evil against which the Religion Clauses were intended to protect, involvement or entanglement between government and religion serves as a warning signal.

. . . Under our system the choice has been made that government is to be entirely excluded from the area of religious instruction and churches excluded from the affairs of government. The Constitution decrees that religion must be a private matter for the individual, the family, and the institutions of private choice, and that while some involvement and entanglement are inevitable, lines must be drawn.

The judgment of the Rhode Island District Court is affirmed. The judgment of the Pennsylvania District Court is reversed, and the case is remanded for further proceedings consistent with this opinion.

Mr. Justice WHITE, dissenting.

Our prior cases have recognized the dual role of parochial schools in American society: they perform both religious and secular functions. It is enough for me that the States and the Federal Government are financing a separable secular function of overriding importance in order to sustain the legislation here challenged. That religion and private interests other than education may substantially benefit does not convert these laws into impermissible establishments of religion.

. . . Where a state program seeks to ensure the proper education of its young, in private as well as public schools, free exercise considerations at least counsel against refusing support for students attending parochial schools simply because in that setting they are also being instructed in the tenets of faith they are constitutionally free to practice. . . .

The Court thus creates an insoluble paradox for the State and the parochial schools. The State cannot finance secular instruction if it permits religion to be taught in the same classroom; but if it exacts a promise that religion not be so taught—a promise the school and its teachers are quite willing and on this record able to give—and enforces it, it is then entangled in the "no establishment" aspect of the Court's Establishment Clause jurisprudence. . . .

Mr. Justice MARSHALL took no part in the consideration or decision of [*Lemon*].

Notes and Queries

1. *Lemon* was the first in a long line of cases concerning the extent to which states may use public monies to aid parochial schools. To aid analysis, the Court proposed a three part test: "First, the statute must have a secular legislative purpose; second, its principal or primary effect must be one that neither advances nor inhibits religion . . . ; finally, the statute must not foster 'an excessive government entanglement with religion.'" Is this test grounded in the text of the First Amendment? Is it grounded in an understanding of the purposes of the Amendment? In history and tradition?

2. Chief Justice Burger noted that "a broader base of entanglement . . . is presented by the divisive potential" of state aid programs. Is the potential for divisiveness a valid judicial concern, and is the Court any better equipped to assess that potential than legislatures? Several members of the Court have expressed concern about such issues; see, for example, the discussion in *Zelman v. Simmons-Harris* (2002, reprinted later in the chapter).

3. Critics of the *Lemon* test complain that it has led to a wide variety of seemingly inconsistent results. The Court has permitted the funding of school lunch programs in parochial schools because their primary purpose is nutritional. Likewise, public support for tuition reimbursements for parents and teacher salary supplements for nonreligious subjects, as well as certain types of limited support for various sorts of instructional materials, is constitutionally permissible. On the other hand, the Court has invalidated other tuition reimbursement programs and support for field trips.

4. As other cases in this chapter, such as *Wallace* and *Lynch*, indicate, the continued vitality of the *Lemon* test is a matter of some doubt. What, precisely, is wrong with the *Lemon* test? Is it simply wrong to hope that the complexities of the relationship between state and religion can be reduced to a single test?

5. Compare the Canadian Court's approach in Comparative Note 13.3 to the U.S. Supreme Court's decisions in *Lemon* and *Aguillard*. Would adoption of a constitutional provision similar to Section 7 of the Canadian Constitution yield different results in these cases? Would it lead to greater consistency in this area?

Lynch v. Donnelly
465 U.S. 668, 104 S.Ct. 1355, 79 L.Ed.2d 604 (1984)

Like many cities, Pawtucket, Rhode Island, celebrates the Christmas season by erecting a holiday display. Pawtucket's display, located on a park owned by a nonprofit organization, includes reindeer, a Christmas tree, and similar symbols, as well as a crèche that features life-sized statues of Mary, Joseph, Jesus, the shepards, and the three wise men. The display itself is owned by the city and displayed at the public's expense. A Rhode Island affiliate of the American Civil Liberties Union filed suit in a district court, alleging that the city's display of the crèche violated the establishment clause. The district and circuit courts agreed with the ACLU. The Solicitor General of the United States, in an *amicus* brief to the Supreme Court, argued that prohibiting the display would be an act of "cultural censorship." Opinion of the Court: *Burger*, Rehnquist, White, Powell, O'Connor. Concurring opinion: *O'Connor*. Dissenting opinions: *Brennan*, Marshall, Blackmun, Stevens; *Blackmun*, Stevens.

The Chief Justice delivered the opinion of the Court.

A

This Court has explained that the purpose of the Establishment and Free Exercise Clauses of the First Amendment is "to prevent, as far as possible, the intrusion of either [the church or the state] into the precincts of the other." *Lemon v. Kurtzman*, (1971). At the same time, however, the Court has recognized that "total separation is not possible in an absolute sense. Some relationship between government and religious organizations is inevitable." In every Establishment Clause case, we must reconcile the inescapable tension between the objective of preventing unnecessary intrusion of either the church or the state upon the other, and the reality that, as the Court has so often noted, total separation of the two is not possible. The Court has sometimes described the Religion Clauses as erecting a "wall" between church and state, see, e.g., *Everson v. Board of Education*, (1947). The concept of a "wall" of separation is a useful figure of speech probably deriving from views of Thomas Jefferson. The metaphor has served as a reminder that the Establishment Clause forbids an established church or anything approaching it. But the metaphor itself is not a wholly accurate description of the practical aspects of the relationship that in fact exists between church and state.

No significant segment of our society and no institution within it can exist in a vacuum or in total or absolute isolation from all the other parts, much less from government. "It has never been thought either possible or desirable to enforce a regime of total separation. . . ." *Committee for Public Education & Religious Liberty v. Nyquist* (1973), nor does the Constitution require complete separation of church and state; it affirmatively mandates accommodation, not merely tolerance, of all religions, and forbids hostility toward any.

Anything less would require the "callous indifference" we have said was never intended by the Establishment Clause. Indeed, we have observed, such hostility would bring us into "war with our national tradition as embodied in the First Amendment's guaranty of the free exercise of religion."

• • •

B

The Court's interpretation of the Establishment Clause has comported with what history reveals was the contemporaneous understanding of its guarantees. A significant example of the contemporaneous understanding of that Clause is found in the events of the first week of the First Session of the First Congress in 1789. In the very week that Congress approved the Establishment Clause as part of the Bill of Rights for submission to the states, it enacted legislation providing for paid chaplains for the House and Senate. . . .

C

There is an unbroken history of official acknowledgment by all three branches of government of the role of religion in American life from at least 1789. Seldom in our opinions was this more affirmatively expressed than in Justice Douglas' opinion for the Court validating a program allowing release of public school students from classes to attend off-campus religious exercises. Rejecting a claim that the program violated the Establishment Clause, the Court asserted pointedly: "We are a religious people whose institutions presuppose a Supreme Being." *Zorach v. Clauson* (1952).

III

This history may help explain why the Court consistently has declined to take a rigid, absolutist view of the Establishment Clause. We have refused "to construe the Religion Clauses with a literalness that would undermine the ultimate constitutional objective as illuminated by history." In our modern, complex society, whose traditions and constitutional underpinnings rest on and encourage diversity and pluralism in all areas, an absolutist approach in applying the Establishment Clause is simplistic and has been uniformly rejected by the Court. Rather than mechanically invalidating all governmental conduct or statutes that confer benefits or give special recognition to religion in general or to one faith—as an absolutist approach would dictate—the Court has scrutinized challenged legislation or official conduct to determine whether, in reality, it establishes a religion or religious faith, or tends to do so. . . .

In each case, the inquiry calls for line drawing; no fixed, per se rule can be framed. The Establishment Clause like the Due Process Clauses is not a precise, detailed provision in a legal code capable of ready application. The purpose of the Establishment Clause "was to state an objective, not to write a statute." The line between permissible relationships and those barred by the Clause can no more be straight and unwavering than due process can be defined in a single stroke or phrase or test. The Clause erects a "blurred, indistinct, and variable barrier depending on all the circumstances of a particular relationship."

In the line-drawing process we have often found it useful to inquire whether the challenged law or conduct has a secular purpose, whether its principal or primary effect is to advance or inhibit religion, and whether it creates an excessive entanglement of government with religion. *Lemon*. But, we have repeatedly emphasized our unwillingness to be confined to any single test or criterion in this sensitive area. . . .

In this case, the focus of our inquiry must be on the crèche in the context of the Christmas season. . . . Focus exclusively on the religious component of any activity would inevitably lead to its invalidation under the Establishment Clause. The Court has invalidated legislation or governmental action on the ground that a secular purpose was lacking, but only when it has concluded there was no question that the statute or activity was motivated wholly by religious considerations. Even where the benefits to religion were substantial . . . , we saw a secular purpose and no conflict with the Establishment Clause.

The District Court inferred from the religious nature of the crèche that the City has no secular purpose for the display. In so doing, it rejected the City's claim that its reasons for including the crèche are essentially the same as its reasons for sponsoring the display as a whole. The District Court plainly erred by focusing almost exclusively on the crèche. When viewed in the proper context of the Christmas Holiday season, it is apparent that, on this record, there is insufficient evidence to establish that the inclusion of the crèche is a purposeful or surreptitious effort to express some kind of subtle governmental advocacy of a particular religious message. In a pluralistic society a variety of motives and purposes are implicated. The City, like the Congresses and Presidents, however, has principally taken note of a significant historical religious event long celebrated in the Western World. The crèche in the display depicts the historical origins of this traditional event long recognized as a National Holiday.

The narrow question is whether there is a secular purpose for Pawtucket's display of the crèche. The display is sponsored by the City to celebrate the Holiday and to depict the origins of that Holiday. These are legitimate secular purposes. The District Court's inference, drawn from the religious nature of the crèche, that the City has no secular purpose was, on this record, clearly erroneous.

We are unable to discern a greater aid to religion deriving from inclusion of the crèche than from these benefits and endorsements previously held not violative of the Establishment Clause. What was said about the legislative prayers in *Marsh*, and implied about the Sunday Closing Laws in *McGowan* is true of the City's inclusion of the crèche: its "reason or effect merely happens to coincide or harmonize with the tenets of some . . . religions." This case differs significantly from *Larkin v. Grendel's Den*, and

McCollum, where religion was substantially aided. In *Grendel's Den*, important governmental power—a licensing veto authority—had been vested in churches. In *McCollum*, government had made religious instruction available in public school classrooms; the State had not only used the public school buildings for the teaching of religion, it had "afford[ed] sectarian groups an invaluable aid . . . [by] provid[ing] pupils for their religious classes through use of the State's compulsory public school machinery."

No comparable benefit to religion is discernible here. The dissent asserts some observers may perceive that the City has aligned itself with the Christian faith by including a Christian symbol in its display and that this serves to advance religion. We can assume . . . the display advances religion in a sense; but our precedents plainly contemplate that on occasion some advancement of religion will result from governmental action. The Court has made it abundantly clear, however, that "not every law that confers an 'indirect,' 'remote,' or 'incidental' benefit upon [religion] is, for that reason alone, constitutionally invalid." Here, whatever benefit to one faith or religion or to all religions, is indirect, remote and incidental; display of the crèche is no more an advancement or endorsement of religion than the Congressional and Executive recognition of the origins of the Holiday itself as "Christ's Mass," or the exhibition of literally hundreds of religious paintings in governmentally supported museums.

IV

Justice Brennan describes the crèche as a "re-creation of an event that lies at the heart of Christian faith." The crèche, like a painting, is passive; admittedly it is a reminder of the origins of Christmas. Even the traditional, purely secular displays extant at Christmas, with or without a crèche, would inevitably recall the religious nature of the Holiday. The display engenders a friendly community spirit of good will in keeping with the season. The crèche may well have special meaning to those whose faith includes the celebration of religious masses, but none who sense the origins of the Christmas celebration would fail to be aware of its religious implications. That the display brings people into the central city, and serves commercial interests and benefits merchants and their employees, does not, as the dissent points out, determine the character of the display. That a prayer invoking Divine guidance in Congress is preceded and followed by debate and partisan conflict over taxes, budgets, national defense, and myriad mundane subjects, for example, has never been thought to demean or taint the sacredness of the invocation.

Comparative Note 13.4

[On the occasion of constructing a city gymnasium, the city held a Shinto groundbreaking ceremony conducted by Shinto priests. A city assemblyman challenged the ceremony, claiming that it was a religious activity in violation of the Japanese Constitution.]

Thus, the [Japanese] Constitution [strives] for a secular and religiously neutral state by taking as its ideal the total separation of religion and the State. . . . Yet religion has a multifaceted social side that brings it into contact with many aspects of social life . . . [that makes impossible] a total separation of religion and the State. . . .

Furthermore, to attempt total separation would . . . lead to anomalous situations such as, for example, questioning the propriety of extending to religiously affiliated schools the financial assistance given to private schools in general. . . . Ironically, to deny such subsidies would impose a disadvantage on these entities simply because of their religious nature and would inevitably result in invidious discrimination because of religion. . . .

. . . [A]lthough it is true that a *Shinto* groundbreaking ceremony has its origin in a religious ceremony intended to pacify the earth god *(tochi no kami),* and thereby to insure a firm foundation for the building and safe construction, there can be no doubt that this religious significance has weakened gradually over time. Even though a present-day groundbreaking ceremony might feature some prayer-like behavior, generally these affairs have become nothing more than ritual formalities in the construction industry almost completely devoid of religious significance. Most people would evaluate the ceremony, even when conducted in accord with established religious practice, as a secularized ritual without religious meaning. The groundbreaking in the case was conducted as a *Shinto* religious ceremony, but for most citizens and the mayor of Tsu City and others involved in sponsoring the groundbreaking, this was a secular event inasmuch as the function in question was no different from the standard ritual practiced over many years.

Source: *Kakunaga v. Sekiguchi* (1977), in Beer and Itoh, *Constitutional Case Law of Japan,* 480, 482.

Of course the crèche is identified with one religious faith but no more so than the examples we have set out from prior cases in which we found no conflict with the Establishment Clause. It would be ironic, however, if the inclusion of a single symbol of a particular historic religious event, as part of a celebration acknowledged in the Western World for 20 centuries, and in this country by the people, by the Executive Branch, by the Congress, and the courts for two centuries, would so "taint" the City's exhibit as to render it violative of the Establishment Clause. To forbid the use of this one passive symbol—the crèche—at the very time people are taking note of the season with Christmas hymns and carols in public schools and other public places, and while the Congress and Legislatures open sessions with prayers by paid chaplains would be a stilted over-reaction contrary to our history and to our holdings. If the presence of the crèche in this display violates the Establishment Clause, a host of other forms of taking official note of Christmas, and of our religious heritage, are equally offensive to the Constitution. The Court has acknowledged that the "fears and political problems" that gave rise to the Religion Clauses in the 18th century are of far less concern today.

We are unable to perceive the Archbishop of Canterbury, the Vicar of Rome, or other powerful religious leaders behind every public acknowledgment of the religious heritage long officially recognized by the three constitutional branches of government. Any notion that these symbols pose a real danger of establishment of a state church is far-fetched indeed.

V . . .

VI

We hold that, notwithstanding the religious significance of the crèche, the City of Pawtucket has not violated the Establishment Clause of the First Amendment. Accordingly, the judgment of the Court of Appeals is reversed.

It is so ordered.

Justice O'CONNOR, concurring.

I concur in the opinion of the Court. I write separately to suggest a clarification of our Establishment Clause doctrine. The suggested approach leads to the same result in this case as that taken by the Court, and the Court's opinion, as I read it, is consistent with my analysis.

The Establishment Clause prohibits government from making adherence to a religion relevant in any way to a person's standing in the political community. Government can run afoul of that prohibition in two principal ways. One is excessive entanglement with religious institutions, which may interfere with the independence of the institutions, give the institutions access to government or governmental powers not fully shared by nonadherents of the religion, and foster the creation of political constituencies defined along religious lines. The second and more direct infringement is government endorsement or disapproval of religion. Endorsement sends a message to nonadherents that they are outsiders, not full members of the political community, and an accompanying message to adherents that they are insiders, favored members of the political community. Disapproval sends the opposite message.

Our prior cases have used the three-part test articulated in *Lemon v. Kurtzman* (1971), as a guide to detecting these two forms of unconstitutional government action. It has never been entirely clear, however, how the three parts of the test relate to the principles enshrined in the Establishment Clause. Focusing on institutional entanglement and on endorsement or disapproval of religion clarifies the *Lemon* test as an analytical device.

The central issue in this case is whether Pawtucket has endorsed Christianity by its display of the crèche. To answer that question, we must examine both what Pawtucket intended to communicate in displaying the crèche and what message the City's display actually conveyed. The purpose and effect prongs of the *Lemon* test represent these two aspects of the meaning of the City's action.

The meaning of a statement to its audience depends both upon the intention of the speaker and on the "objective" meaning of the statement in the community. Some listeners need not rely solely upon the words themselves in discerning the speaker's intent: they can judge intent by, for example, examining the context of the statement or asking questions of the speaker. Other listeners do not have or will not seek access to such evidence of intent. They will rely instead on the words themselves; for them the message actually conveyed may be something not actually intended. If the audience is large, as it always is when government "speaks" by word or deed, some portion of the audience will inevitably receive a message determined by the "objective" content of the statement, and some portion will inevitably receive the intended message. Examination of both . . . is therefore necessary to determine whether the action carries a forbidden meaning.

The purpose prong of the *Lemon* test asks whether government's actual purpose is to endorse or disapprove of religion. The effect prong asks whether, irrespective of government's actual purpose, the practice under review in fact conveys a message of endorsement or disapproval. An affirmative answer to either question should render the challenged practice invalid.

Focusing on the evil of government endorsement or disapproval of religion makes clear that the effect prong of the *Lemon* test is properly interpreted not to require invalidation of a government practice merely because it in fact causes, even as a primary effect, advancement or inhibition of religion. . . . What is crucial is that a government practice not have the effect of communicating a message of government endorsement or disapproval of religion. It is only practices having that effect, whether intentionally or unintentionally, that make religion relevant, in reality or public perception, to status in the political community.

Pawtucket's display of its crèche, I believe, does not communicate a message that the government intends to endorse the Christian beliefs represented by the crèche. Although the religious and indeed sectarian significance of the crèche, as the District Court found, is not neutralized by the setting, the overall holiday setting changes what viewers may fairly understand to be the purpose of the display—as a typical museum setting, though not neutralizing the religious content of a religious painting, negates any message of endorsement of that content. The display celebrates a public holiday, and no one contends that declaration of that holiday is understood to be an endorsement of religion. The holiday itself has very strong secular components and traditions. Government celebration of the holiday, which is extremely common, generally is not understood to endorse the religious content of the holiday, just as government celebration of Thanksgiving is not so understood. The crèche is a traditional symbol of the holiday that is very commonly displayed along with purely secular symbols, as it was in Pawtucket.

These features combine to make the government's display of the crèche in this particular physical setting no more an endorsement of religion than such governmental "acknowledgments" of religion as legislative prayers of the type approved in *Marsh* v. *Chambers* (1983), government declaration of Thanksgiving as a public holiday, printing of "In God We Trust" on coins, and opening court sessions with "God save the United States and this honorable court." Those government acknowledgments of religion serve, in the only ways reasonably possible in our culture, the legitimate secular purposes of solemnizing public occasions, expressing confidence in the future, and encouraging the recognition of what is worthy of appreciation in society. For that reason, and because of their history and ubiquity, those practices are not understood as conveying government approval of particular religious beliefs. The display of the crèche likewise serves a secular purpose—celebration of a public holiday with traditional symbols. It cannot fairly be understood to convey a message of government endorsement of religion. It is significant in this regard that the crèche display apparently caused no political divisiveness prior to the filing of this lawsuit, although Pawtucket had incorporated the crèche in its annual Christmas display for some years. For these reasons, I conclude that Pawtucket's display of the crèche does not have the effect of communicating endorsement of Christianity.

Justice BRENNAN, with whom Justice MARSHALL, Justice BLACKMUN and Justice STEVENS join, dissenting.

The principles announced in the compact phrases of the Religion Clauses have, as the Court today reminds us . . . , proven difficult to apply. Faced with that uncertainty, the Court properly looks for guidance to the settled test announced in *Lemon v. Kurtzman* for assessing whether a challenged governmental practice involves an impermissible step toward the establishment of religion. Applying that test to this case, the Court reaches an essentially narrow result which turns largely upon the particular holiday context in which the City of Pawtucket's nativity scene appeared. The Court's decision implicitly leaves open questions concerning the constitutionality of the public display on public property of a crèche standing alone, or the public display of other distinctively religious symbols such as a cross. Despite the narrow contours of the Court's opinion, our precedents in my view compel the holding that Pawtucket's inclusion of a life-sized display depicting the biblical description of the birth of Christ as part of its annual Christmas celebration is unconstitutional. Nothing in the history of such practices or the setting in which the City's crèche is presented obscures or diminishes the plain fact that Pawtucket's action amounts to an impermissible governmental endorsement of a particular faith.

I

B

The Court advances two principal arguments to support its conclusion that the Pawtucket crèche satisfies the *Lemon* test. Neither is persuasive.

First. The Court, by focusing on the holiday "context" in which the nativity scene appeared, seeks to explain away the clear religious import of the crèche and the findings of the District Court that most observers understood

the crèche as both a symbol of Christian beliefs and a symbol of the City's support for those beliefs. Thus, although the Court concedes that the City's inclusion of the nativity scene plainly serves "to depict the origins" of Christmas as a "significant historical religious event," and that the crèche "is identified with one religious faith," we are nevertheless expected to believe that Pawtucket's use of the crèche does not signal the City's support for the sectarian symbolism that the nativity scene evokes. The effect of the crèche, of course, must be gauged not only by its inherent religious significance but also by the overall setting in which it appears. But it blinks reality to claim, as the Court does, that by including such a distinctively religious object as the crèche in its Christmas display, Pawtucket has done no more than make use of a "traditional" symbol of the holiday, and has thereby purged the crèche of its religious content and conferred only an "incidental and indirect" benefit on religion.

The Court's struggle to ignore the clear religious effect of the crèche seems to me misguided for several reasons. In the first place, the City has positioned the crèche in a central and highly visible location within the Hodgson Park display. The District Court's findings in this regard are unambiguous: "[D]espite the small amount of ground covered by the crèche, viewers would not regard the crèche as an insignificant part of the display. It is an almost life sized tableau marked off by a white picket fence. Furthermore, its location lends the crèche significance. The crèche faces the Roosevelt Avenue bus stops and access stairs where the bulk of the display is placed. Moreover, the crèche is near two of the most enticing parts of the display for children—Santa's house and the talking wishing well. Although the Court recognizes that one cannot see the crèche from all possible vantage points, it is clear from the City's own photos that people standing at the two bus shelters and looking down at the display will see the crèche centrally and prominently positioned."

Moreover, the City has done nothing to disclaim government approval of the religious significance of the crèche, to suggest that the crèche represents only one religious symbol among many others that might be included in a seasonal display truly aimed at providing a wide catalogue of ethnic and religious celebrations, or to disassociate itself from the religious content of the crèche. . . .

Third, we have consistently acknowledged that an otherwise secular setting alone does not suffice to justify a governmental practice that has the effect of aiding religion. . . .

Finally, and most importantly, even in the context of Pawtucket's seasonal celebration, the crèche retains a specifically Christian religious meaning. I refuse to accept the notion implicit in today's decision that non-Christians would find that the religious content of the crèche is eliminated by the fact that it appears as part of the City's otherwise secular celebration of the Christmas holiday. The nativity scene is clearly distinct in its purpose and effect from the rest of the Hodgson Park display for the simple reason that it is the only one rooted in a biblical account of Christ's birth. It is the chief symbol of the characteristically Christian belief that a divine Savior was brought into the world and that the purpose of this miraculous birth was to illuminate a path toward salvation and redemption. For Christians, that path is exclusive, precious and holy. But for those who do not share these beliefs, the symbolic reenactment of the birth of a divine being who has been miraculously incarnated as a man stands as a dramatic reminder of their differences with Christian faith. When government appears to sponsor such religiously inspired views, we cannot say that the practice is "'so separate and so indisputably marked off from the religious function,' that [it] may fairly be viewed as reflect[ing] a neutral posture toward religious institutions." *Nyquist.* To be so excluded on religious grounds by one's elected government is an insult and an injury that, until today, could not be countenanced by the Establishment Clause. . . .

Second. The Court also attempts to justify the crèche by entertaining a beguilingly simple, yet faulty syllogism. The Court begins by noting that government may recognize Christmas day as a public holiday; the Court then asserts that the crèche is nothing more than a traditional element of Christmas celebrations; and it concludes that the inclusion of a crèche as part of a government's annual Christmas celebration is constitutionally permissible. The Court apparently believes that once it finds that the designation of Christmas as a public holiday is constitutionally acceptable, it is then free to conclude that virtually every form of governmental association with the celebration of the holiday is also constitutional. The vice of this dangerously superficial argument is that it overlooks the fact that the Christmas holiday in our national culture contains both secular and sectarian elements. To say that government may recognize the holiday's traditional, secular elements of gift giving, public festivities and community spirit, does not mean that government may indiscriminately embrace the distinctively sectarian aspects of the holiday. Indeed, in its eagerness to approve the crèche, the Court has advanced a rationale so simplistic that it would appear to allow the Mayor of Pawtucket to participate in the celebration of a Christmas mass, since this would be just another unobjectionable way for the City to "celebrate the holiday."

The inclusion of a crèche in Pawtucket's otherwise sec-

ular celebration of Christmas clearly violates these principles. Unlike such secular figures as Santa Claus, reindeer and carolers, a nativity scene represents far more than a mere "traditional" symbol of Christmas. The essence of the crèche's symbolic purpose and effect is to prompt the observer to experience a sense of simple awe and wonder appropriate to the contemplation of one of the central elements of Christian dogma—that God sent His son into the world to be a Messiah.

Contrary to the Court's suggestion, the crèche is far from a mere representation of a "particular historic religious event." It is, instead, best understood as a mystical recreation of an event that lies at the heart of Christian faith. To suggest, as the Court does, that such a symbol is merely "traditional" and therefore no different from Santa's house or reindeer is not only offensive to those for whom the crèche has profound significance, but insulting to those who insist for religious or personal reasons that the story of Christ is in no sense a part of "history" nor an unavoidable element of our national "heritage."

II

Although the Court's relaxed application of the *Lemon* test to Pawtucket's crèche is regrettable, it is at least understandable and properly limited to the particular facts of this case. The Court's opinion, however, also sounds a broader and more troubling theme. Invoking the celebration of Thanksgiving as a public holiday, the legend "In God We Trust" on our coins, and the proclamation "God save the United States and this Honorable Court" at the opening of judicial sessions, the Court asserts, without explanation, that Pawtucket's inclusion of a crèche in its annual Christmas display poses no more of a threat to Establishment Clause values than these other official "acknowledgments" of religion.

Intuition tells us that some official "acknowledgment" is inevitable in a religious society if government is not to adopt a stilted indifference to the religious life of the people. It is equally true, however, that if government is to remain scrupulously neutral in matters of religious conscience, as our Constitution requires, then it must avoid those overly broad acknowledgments of religious practices that may imply governmental favoritism toward one set of religious beliefs. This does not mean, of course, that public officials may not take account, when necessary, of the separate existence and significance of the religious institutions and practices in the society they govern. Should government choose to incorporate some arguably religious element into its public ceremonies, that acknowledgment must be impartial; it must not tend to promote one faith or handicap another; and it should not sponsor religion generally over non-religion. . . .

III

. . . [T]he City's action should be recognized for what it is: a coercive, though perhaps small, step toward establishing the sectarian preferences of the majority at the expense of the minority, accomplished by placing public facilities and funds in support of the religious symbolism and theological tidings that the crèche conveys.

I dissent.

Justice BLACKMUN, with whom Justice STEVENS joins, dissenting.

Notes and Queries

1. Does the majority's opinion in *Lynch* rest upon the accommodationist or the separationist understanding of the establishment clause? How does the opinion justify its choice?

2. Is the majority's use of the *Lemon* test consistent with the way it has used it in other cases, such as *Jaffree*? What is the secular purpose of the crèche display?

3. The Solicitor General's *amicus* brief argued that for the Court to prohibit the display would be an act of "cultural censorship." Is there a constitutionally significant difference between religion and culture? What is it? What is the difference, if any, between a state's recognition of the religious character of a people and the establishment of religion?

4. In *Allegheny County v. American Civil Liberties Union* (1989) the Court heard yet another crèche case. A slim majority concluded that a display of a crèche in a courthouse, standing alone, did violate the establishment clause. The presence of an 18-foot-high menorah outside the building was permissible, however, because that display included a Christmas tree and a sign extolling the virtues of liberty. In one case, Justice Blackmun wrote for the majority, the state had "endorsed" religion; in the latter, and in *Lynch*, it had not.

In dissent, Justice Kennedy proposed an alternative analysis, writing that "Non-coercive government action within the realm of flexible accommodation or passive acknowledgment of existing symbols" would be constitu-

tional "unless it benefits religion in a way more direct and more substantial than practices that are accepted in our national heritage." Using this test, Kennedy found both displays in *Allegheny* permissible.

The majority rejected Kennedy's test, complaining that

Although Justice Kennedy repeatedly accuses the Court of harboring a "latent" hostility or "callous indifference" toward religion, nothing could be further from the truth, and the accusations could be said to be as offensive as they are abused. Justice Kennedy apparently has misperceived a respect for religious pluralism, a respect commanded by the Constitution, as hostility or indifference to religion. No misperception could be more antithetical to the values embodied in the Establishment Clause.

5. Justice Brennan tells us that "if government is to remain scrupulously neutral . . . as our Constitution requires, then it must avoid those overly broad acknowledgements of religious practices that may imply favoritism toward one set of religious beliefs." He adds: "Should government choose to incorporate some arguably religious element into its public ceremonies, that acknowledgement must be impartial . . . and it should not sponsor religion generally over nonreligion." Suppose a president schedules a Mass or attends a religious service in the White House? Would this violate Brennan's standard?

6. In *Kakunaga v. Sekiguchi* (1977) (Comparative Note 13.4), the Japanese Supreme Court considered the constitutionality of a ground-breaking ceremony for a new city gymnasium conducted by four Shinto Priests. The Court noted that Article 20 of the Constitution represents an effort to achieve "a secular and religiously neutral State by taking as its ideal the total separation of religion and the State." Nevertheless, "an actual system of government that attempts a total separation of religion and the State is virtually impossible."

In upholding the constitutionality of the ceremony, the Court observed that "[A]lthough it is true that a Shinto ground breaking ceremony has its origin in a religious ceremony . . . there can be no doubt that this religious significance has weakened gradually over time. . . . Most people would evaluate the ceremony, even when conducted in accord with established religious practice, as a secularized ritual without religious meaning."

Edwards v. Aguillard

482 U.S. 578, 107 S. Ct. 2573, 96 L.Ed. 2d 510 (1987)

As a part of the continuing battle against "secular human-ism" in the public schools, the Louisiana legislature passed a "Balanced Treatment for Creation-Science and Evolution-Science in Public School Instruction Act." The statute provided that evolution could not be taught in the public schools unless it was accompanied by lessons in creation science. Donald Aguillard and the parents of other children in public schools brought suit against the Governor and other public officials. They argued that the creation science statute violated the establishment clause. Opinion of the Court: *Brennan*, Blackmun, Marshall, Powell, Stevens, O'Connor. Concurring opinions: *Powell*, O'Connor; *White*. Dissenting opinion: *Scalia*, Rehnquist.

Justice BRENNAN delivered the opinion of the Court.

The question for decision is whether Louisiana's "Bal-anced Treatment for Creation-Science and Evolution-Sci-ence in Public School Instruction" Act (Creationism Act), . . . is facially invalid as violative of the Establishment Clause of the First Amendment.

The Court has been particularly vigilant in monitoring compliance with the Establishment Clause in elementary and secondary schools. Families entrust public schools with the education of their children, but condition their trust on the understanding that the classroom will not pur-posely be used to advance religious views that may con-flict with the private beliefs of the student and his or her family. Students in such institutions are impressionable and their attendance is involuntary. . . . The State exerts great authority and coercive power through mandatory at-tendance requirements, and because of the students' emu-lation of teachers as role models and the children's susceptibility to peer pressure. . . . Furthermore, "the pub-lic school is at once the symbol of our democracy and the most pervasive means for promoting our common des-tiny. In no activity of the State is it more vital to keep out divisive forces than in its schools. . . ."

Therefore, in employing the three-pronged *Lemon* test, we must do so mindful of the particular concerns that arise in the context of public elementary and secondary schools. We now turn to the evaluation of the Act under the *Lemon* test.

Lemon's prong focuses on the purpose that animated adoption of the Act. A governmental intention to promote religion is clear when the State enacts a law to serve a religious purpose. This intention may be evidenced by promotion of religion in general, . . . or by advancement of a particular religious belief . . . If the law was enacted for the purpose of endorsing religion, "no consideration of the second or third criteria [of *Lemon*] is necessary." In this case, appellants have identified no clear secular pur-pose for the Louisiana Act.

True, the Act's stated purpose is to protect academic freedom. This phrase might, in common parlance, be un-derstood as referring to enhancing the freedom of teach-ers to teach what they will. . . . Even if "academic freedom" is read to mean "teaching all of the evidence" with respect to the origin of human beings, the Act does not further this purpose. The goal of providing a more comprehensive science curriculum is not furthered either by outlawing the teaching of evolution or by requiring the teaching of creation science.

While the Court is normally deferential to a State's artic-ulation of a secular purpose, it is required that the state-ment of such purpose be sincere and not a sham. . . . As Justice O'Connor stated in *Wallace*: "It is not a trivial mat-ter, however, to require that the legislature manifest a sec-ular purpose and omit all sectarian endorsements from its laws. That requirement is precisely tailored to the Estab-lishment Clause's purpose of assuring that Government not intentionally endorse religion or a religious practice."

It is clear from the legislative history that the purpose of the legislative sponsor, Senator Bill Keith, was to narrow the science curriculum. During the legislative hearings, Senator Keith stated: "My preference would be that nei-ther [creationism nor evolution] be taught." . . . Such a ban on teaching does not promote—indeed, it undermines— the provision of a comprehensive scientific education.

It is equally clear that requiring schools to teach cre-ation science with evolution does not advance academic freedom. The Act does not grant teachers a flexibility that they did not already possess to supplant the present sci-ence curriculum with the presentation of theories, besides evolution, about the origin of life. Indeed, the Court of Appeals found that no law prohibited Louisiana public school teachers from teaching any scientific theory. . . . As the president of the Louisiana Science Teachers Associa-tion testified, "any scientific concept that's based on estab-lished fact can be included in our curriculum already, and no legislation allowing this is necessary." . . . The Act pro-vides Louisiana schoolteachers with no new authority. Thus the stated purpose is not furthered by it.

Furthermore, the goal of basic "fairness" is hardly fur-thered by the Act's discriminatory preference for the teaching of creation science and against the teaching of evolution. While requiring that curriculum guides be de-veloped for creation science, the Act says nothing of comparable guides for evolution. . . . Similarly, resource services are supplied for creation science but not for evolution. . . . Only "creation scientists" can serve on the panel that supplies the resource services. The Act forbids school boards to discriminate against anyone who "chooses to be a creation-scientist" or to teach "creationism," but fails to protect those who choose to teach evolution or any other noncreation science theory, or who refuse to teach creation science.

If the Louisiana Legislature's purpose was solely to maximize the comprehensiveness and effectiveness of science instruction, it would have encouraged the teaching of all scientific theories about the origins of humankind. . . . But under the Act's requirements, teachers who were once free to teach any and all facets of this subject are now unable to do so. Moreover, the Act fails even to ensure that creation science will be taught, but instead requires the teaching of this theory only when the theory of evolution is taught. Thus we agree with the Court of Appeals' conclusion that the Act does not serve to protect academic freedom, but has the distinctly different purpose of discrediting "evolution by counterbalancing its teaching at every turn with the teaching of creationism. . . ."

. . . [W]e need not be blind in this case to the legislature's preeminent religious purpose in enacting this statute. There is a historic and contemporaneous link between the teachings of certain religious denominations and the teaching of evolution. It was this link that concerned the Court in *Epperson v. Arkansas* (1968), which also involved a facial challenge to a statute regulating the teaching of evolution. In that case, the Court reviewed an Arkansas statute that made it unlawful for an instructor to teach evolution or to use a textbook that referred to this scientific theory. Although the Arkansas antievolution law did not explicitly state its predominate religious purpose, the Court could not ignore that "the statute was a product of the upsurge of 'fundamentalist' religious fervor" that has long viewed this particular scientific theory as contradicting the literal interpretation of the Bible. . . . After reviewing the history of antievolution statutes, the Court determined that "there can be no doubt that the motivation for the [Arkansas] law was the same [as other antievolution statutes]: to suppress the teaching of a theory which, it was thought, 'denied' the divine creation of man." . . . The Court found that there can be no legitimate state interest in protecting particular religions from scientific views "distasteful to them," . . . and concluded "that the First Amendment does not permit the State to require that teaching and learning must be tailored to the principles or prohibitions of any religious sect or dogma."

These same historic and contemporaneous antagonisms

between the teachings of certain religious denominations and the teaching of evolution are present in this case. The preeminent purpose of the Louisiana Legislature was clearly to advance the religious viewpoint that a supernatural being created humankind. The term "creation science" was defined as embracing this particular religious doctrine by those responsible for the passage of the Creationism Act. Senator Keith's leading expert on creation science, Edward Boudreaux, testified at the legislative hearings that the theory of creation science included belief in the existence of a supernatural creator. . . . Senator Keith also cited testimony from other experts to support the creation-science view that "a creator [was] responsible for the universe and everything in it." . . . The legislative history therefore reveals that the term "creation science," as contemplated by the legislature that adopted this Act, embodies the religious belief that a supernatural creator was responsible for the creation of humankind.

In this case, the purpose of the Creationism Act was to restructure the science curriculum to conform with a particular religious viewpoint. Out of many possible science subjects taught in the public schools, the legislature chose to affect the teaching of the one scientific theory that historically has been opposed by certain religious sects. As in *Epperson*, the legislature passed the Act to give preference to those religious groups which have as one of their tenets the creation of humankind by a divine creator. . . . [T]he Creationism Act is designed either to promote the theory of creation science which embodies a particular religious tenet by requiring that creation science be taught whenever evolution is taught or to prohibit the teaching of a scientific theory disfavored by certain religious sects by forbidding the teaching of evolution when creation science is not also taught. The Establishment Clause, however, "forbids alike the preference of a religious doctrine or the prohibition of theory which is deemed antagonistic to a particular dogma." Because the primary purpose of the Creationism Act is to advance a particular religious belief, the Act endorses religion in violation of the First Amendment.

We do not imply that a legislature could never require that scientific critiques of prevailing scientific theories be taught. Indeed, the Court acknowledged in *Stone* that its decision forbidding the posting of the Ten Commandments did not mean that no use could ever be made of the Ten Commandments, or that the Ten Commandments played an exclusively religious role in the history of Western Civilization. . . . In a similar way, teaching a variety of scientific theories about the origins of humankind to schoolchildren might be validly done with the clear secular intent of enhancing the effectiveness of science instruction. But because the primary purpose of the Creationism Act is to endorse a particular religious doctrine, the Act furthers religion in violation of the Establishment Clause.

The Louisiana Creationism Act advances a religious doctrine by requiring either the banishment of the theory of evolution from public school classrooms or the presentation of a religious viewpoint that rejects evolution in its entirety. The Act violates the Establishment Clause of the First Amendment because it seeks to employ the symbolic and financial support of government to achieve a religious purpose. The judgment of the Court of Appeals therefore is Affirmed.

Justice SCALIA, with whom The Chief Justice joins, dissenting.

Even if I agreed with the questionable premise that legislation can be invalidated under the Establishment Clause on the basis of its motivation alone, without regard to its effects, I would still find no justification for today's decision. The Louisiana legislators who passed the "Balanced Treatment for Creation-Science and Evolution-Science Act" (Balanced Treatment Act), . . . each of whom had sworn to support the Constitution, were well aware of the potential Establishment Clause problems and considered that aspect of the legislation with great care. After seven hearings and several months of study, resulting in substantial revision of the original proposal, they approved the Act overwhelmingly and specifically articulated the secular purpose they meant it to serve. Although the record contains abundant evidence of the sincerity of that purpose (the only issue pertinent to this case), the Court today holds, essentially on the basis of "its visceral knowledge regarding what must have motivated the legislators," . . . that the members of the Louisiana Legislature knowingly violated their oaths and then lied about it. I dissent. Had requirements of the Balanced Treatment Act that are not apparent on its face been clarified by an interpretation of the Louisiana Supreme Court, or by the manner of its implementation, the Act might well be found unconstitutional; but the question of its constitutionality cannot rightly be disposed of on the gallop, by impugning the motives of its supporters.

. . . Thus, the majority's invalidation of the Balanced Treatment Act is defensible only if the record indicates that the Louisiana Legislature had no secular purpose.

It is important to stress that the purpose forbidden by *Lemon* is the purpose to "advance religion." . . . Our cases in no way imply that the Establishment Clause forbids legislators merely to act upon their religious convictions. We surely would not strike down a law providing money to feed the hungry or shelter the homeless if it could be dem-

onstrated that, but for the religious beliefs of the legislators, the funds would not have been approved. Also, political activism by the religiously motivated is part of our heritage. Notwithstanding the majority's implication to the contrary, . . . we do not presume that the sole purpose of a law is to advance religion merely because it was supported strongly by organized religions or by adherents of particular faiths. . . . To do so would deprive religious men and women of their right to participate in the political process. Today's religious activism may give us the Balanced Treatment Act, but yesterday's resulted in the abolition of slavery, and tomorrow's may bring relief for famine victims.

Similarly, we will not presume that a law's purpose is to advance religion merely because it "happens to coincide or harmonize with the tenets of some or all religions," . . . or because it benefits religion, even substantially. . . . Thus, the fact that creation science coincides with the beliefs of certain religions, a fact upon which the majority relies heavily, does not itself justify invalidation of the Act.

We have relatively little information upon which to judge the motives of those who supported the Act. About the only direct evidence is the statute itself and transcripts of the seven committee hearings at which it was considered. Unfortunately, several of those hearings were sparsely attended, and the legislators who were present revealed little about their motives. We have no committee reports, no floor debates, no remarks inserted into the legislative history, no statement from the Governor, and no postenactment statements or testimony from the bill's sponsor or any other legislators. . . . Nevertheless, there is ample evidence that the majority is wrong in holding that the Balanced Treatment Act is without secular purpose.

. . . The Louisiana Legislature explicitly set forth its secular purpose ("protecting academic freedom") in the very text of the Act. . . . We have in the past repeatedly relied upon or deferred to such expressions. . . .

The Court seeks to evade the force of this expression of purpose by stubbornly misinterpreting it, and then finding that the provisions of the Act do not advance that misinterpreted purpose, thereby showing it to be a sham. The Court first surmises that "academic freedom" means "enhancing the freedom of teachers to teach what they will," even though "academic freedom" in that sense has little scope in the structured elementary and secondary curriculums with which the Act is concerned. Alternatively, the Court suggests that it might mean "maximiz[ing] the comprehensiveness and effectiveness of science instruction," though that is an exceedingly strange interpretation of the words, and one that is refuted on the very face of the statute. . . . Had the Court devoted to this central question of the meaning of the legislatively expressed purpose a small fraction of the research into legislative history that produced its quotations of religiously motivated statements by individual legislators, it would have discerned quite readily what "academic freedom" meant: students' freedom from indoctrination. The legislature wanted to ensure that students would be free to decide for themselves how life began, based upon a fair and balanced presentation of the scientific evidence—that is, to protect "the right of each [student] voluntarily to determine what to believe (and what not to believe) free of any coercive pressures from the State." The legislature did not care whether the topic of origins was taught; it simply wished to ensure that when the topic was taught, students would receive "all of the evidence."

The Act's reference to "creation" is not convincing evidence of religious purpose. The Act defines creation science as "scientific evidenc[e]," . . . and Senator Keith and his witnesses repeatedly stressed that the subject can and should be presented without religious content. . . . We have no basis on the record to conclude that creation science need be anything other than a collection of scientific data supporting the theory that life abruptly appeared on earth. . . . Creation science, its proponents insist, no more must explain whence life came than evolution must explain whence came the inanimate materials from which it says life evolved. . . . Senator Keith suggested this when he referred to "a creator however you define a creator."

Because I believe that the Balanced Treatment Act had a secular purpose, which is all the first component of the *Lemon* test requires, I would reverse the judgment of the Court of Appeals and remand for further consideration.

Our cases interpreting and applying the purpose test have made such a maze of the Establishment Clause that even the most conscientious governmental officials can only guess what motives will be held unconstitutional. We have said essentially the following: Government may not act with the purpose of advancing religion, except when forced to do so by the Free Exercise Clause (which is now and then); or when eliminating existing governmental hostility to religion (which exists sometimes); or even when merely accommodating governmentally uninhibited religious practices, except that at some point (it is unclear where) intentional accommodation results in the fostering of religion, which is of course unconstitutional.

But the difficulty of knowing what vitiating purpose one is looking for is as nothing compared with the difficulty of knowing how or where to find it. For while it is possible to discern the objective "purpose" of a statute (i.e., the public good at which its provisions appear to be directed), or even the formal motivation for a statute where that is

explicitly set forth (as it was, to no avail, here), discerning the subjective motivation of those enacting the statute is, to be honest, almost always an impossible task. The number of possible motivations, to begin with, is not binary, or indeed even finite. In the present case, for example, a particular legislator need not have voted for the Act either because he wanted to foster religion or because he wanted to improve education. He may have thought the bill would provide jobs for his district, or may have wanted to make amends with a faction of his party he had alienated on another vote, or he may have been a close friend of the bill's sponsor, or he may have been repaying a favor he owed the Majority Leader, or he may have hoped the Governor would appreciate his vote and make a fundraising appearance for him, or he may have been pressured to vote for a bill he disliked by a wealthy contributor or by a flood of constituent mail, or he may have been seeking favorable publicity, or he may have been reluctant to hurt the feelings of a loyal staff member who worked on the bill, or he may have been settling an old score with a legislator who opposed the bill, or he may have been mad at his wife who opposed the bill, or he may have been intoxicated and utterly unmotivated when the vote was called, or he may have accidentally voted "yes" instead of "no," or, of course, he may have had (and very likely did have) a combination of some of the above and many other motivations. To look for the sole purpose of even a single legislator is probably to look for something that does not exist.

Given the many hazards involved in assessing the subjective intent of governmental decisionmakers, the first prong of *Lemon* is defensible, I think, only if the text of the Establishment Clause demands it. That is surely not the case. The Clause states that "Congress shall make no law respecting an establishment of religion." One could argue, I suppose, that any time Congress acts with the intent of advancing religion, it has enacted a "law respecting an establishment of religion"; but far from being an unavoidable reading, it is quite an unnatural one. . . .

. . . I think it time that we sacrifice some "flexibility" for "clarity and predictability." Abandoning *Lemon's* purpose test—a test which exacerbates the tension between the Free Exercise and Establishment Clauses, has no basis in the language or history of the Amendment, and, as today's decision shows, has wonderfully flexible consequences—would be a good place to start.

Notes and Queries

1. As in *Wallace v. Jaffree* (1985, reprinted later in the chapter), the relevance of legislative motivation is a critical

issue in *Edwards*. Does *Lemon* require a judicial inquiry into legislative motivation, as Justice Scalia argued in dissent? How can any court accurately assess "motivation," given the probable great number of different motives held by different legislators? How is any court to distinguish between sincere expressions of a secular purpose and shams? What vision of the relationship between the legislature and the judiciary does the Court adopt? Does the majority opinion offer any insight into these questions?

2. Did the majority conclude—explicitly or implicitly—that creation science is not good science? If so, is this an appropriate activity for judges? Could it be avoided?

3. In the introduction we saw that the Court has tended toward an expansive definition of religion, especially in free exercise cases, and has largely adopted a posture of deference to individual definitions of the religion. Does this suggest that the Court should defer to the judgment of others that "secular humanism" is a religion? Lower fed-eral courts have typically rejected this option. See, e.g., *Peloza v. Capistrano Unified School District*, 37 F.3d 517 (9th Cir. 1994); *Mozert v. Hawkins County Bd. of Ed.*, 827 F.2d 1058 (6th Cir. 1987).

4. The majority concluded that "In this case, the purpose of the Creationism Act was to restructure the science curriculum to *conform* with a particular religious viewpoint." (our emphasis) Would it matter if instead of "to conform" we substituted "to include"? How would the dissent approach this question? Does the answer depend upon the purpose of the establishment clause? In other words, do the separationist and accommodationist perspectives yield different answers?

5. Is it fair of the majority to conclude that the statute's purpose is simply to advance religion? Are there any secular purposes it might advance? What should the Court do if it can find both secular and nonsecular purposes to the Act?

Wallace v. Jaffree
472 U.S. 38, 105 S.Ct. 2479, 86 L.Ed.2d 29, (1985)

In reaction to *Engel* and *Schempp*, many states began to enact legislation that permitted a "moment of silence" at the beginning of the day in public schools; by the late 1970s, almost half of the states had such legislation. In 1981, Alabama amended its moment of silence law to authorize a moment of silence "for meditation or voluntary prayer." Ishmael Jaffree, a father to two children in the second grade and a third in kindergarten in Alabama's public schools, claimed that the law violated the establishment clause. In an extraordinary opinion, the District Court ruled for Alabama, finding, in contrast to *Everson*, that the establishment clause does not prohibit the states from establishing religion. Opinion of the Court: *Stevens*, Brennan, Marshall, Blackmun, Powell. Concurring opinions: *Powell*; *O'Connor*. Dissenting opinions: *Burger*; *White*; *Rehnquist*.

Justice STEVENS delivered the opinion of the Court.

When the Court has been called upon to construe the breadth of the Establishment Clause, it has examined the criteria developed over a period of many years. Thus, in *Lemon v. Kurtzman* (1971), we wrote: "Every analysis in this area must begin with consideration of the cumulative criteria developed by the Court over many years. Three such tests may be gleaned from our cases. First, the statute must have a secular legislative purpose; second, its principal or primary effect must be one that neither advances nor inhibits religion; finally, the statute must not foster 'an excessive government entanglement with religion.'"

It is the first of these three criteria that is most plainly implicated by this case. As the District Court correctly recognized, no consideration of the second or third criteria is necessary if a statute does not have a clearly secular purpose. For even though a statute that is motivated in part by a religious purpose may satisfy the first criterion, the First Amendment requires that a statute must be invalidated if it is entirely motivated by a purpose to advance religion.

In applying the purpose test, it is appropriate to ask "whether government's actual purpose is to endorse or disapprove of religion." In this case, the answer to that question is dispositive. For the record not only provides us with an unambiguous affirmative answer, but it also reveals that the enactment of s 16-1-20.1 was not motivated by any clearly secular purpose—indeed, the statute had no secular purpose.

IV

The sponsor of the bill that became s 16-1-20.1, Senator Donald Holmes, inserted into the legislative record—apparently without dissent—a statement indicating that the legislation was an "effort to return voluntary prayer" to the public schools. Later Senator Holmes confirmed this purpose before the District Court. In response to the question whether he had any purpose for the legislation other than returning voluntary prayer to public schools, he stated: "No, I did not have no other purpose in mind." The State did not present evidence of any secular purpose.

The legislative intent to return prayer to the public schools is, of course, quite different from merely protecting every student's right to engage in voluntary prayer during an appropriate moment of silence during the schooldays. The 1978 statute already protected that right, containing nothing that prevented any student from engaging in voluntary prayer during a silent minute of meditation. Appellants have not identified any secular purpose that was not fully served by s 16-1-20 before the enactment of s 16-1-20.1. Thus, only two conclusions are consistent with the text of s 16-1-20.1: (1) the statute was enacted to convey a message of state endorsement and promotion of prayer; or (2) the statute was enacted for no purpose. No one suggests that the statute was nothing but a meaningless or irrational act.

The legislature enacted s 16-1- 20.1, despite the existence of s 16-1-20 for the sole purpose of expressing the State's endorsement of prayer activities for one minute at the beginning of each schoolday. The addition of "or voluntary prayer" indicates that the State intended to characterize prayer as a favored practice. Such an endorsement is not consistent with the established principle that the government must pursue a course of complete neutrality toward religion.

The judgment of the Court of Appeals is affirmed.

It is so ordered.

Justice POWELL, concurring.

Justice O'CONNOR, concurring in the judgment.

Nothing in the United States Constitution as interpreted by this Court or in the laws of the State of Alabama prohibits public school students from voluntarily praying at any time before, during, or after the school day. . . .

I agree with the judgment of the Court that, in light of the findings of the courts below and the history of its enactment, s 16-1-20.1 of the Alabama Code violates the Establishment Clause of the First Amendment. In my view, there can be little doubt that the purpose and likely effect of this subsequent enactment is to endorse and sponsor voluntary prayer in the public schools. I write separately to identify the peculiar features of the Alabama law that render it invalid, and to explain why moment of silence laws in other States do not necessarily manifest the same infirmity. I also write to explain why neither history nor the Free Exercise Clause of the First Amendment validates the Alabama law struck down by the Court today.

A state-sponsored moment of silence in the public schools is different from state-sponsored vocal prayer or Bible reading. First, a moment of silence is not inherently religious. Silence, unlike prayer or Bible reading, need not be associated with a religious exercise. Second, a pupil who participates in a moment of silence need not compromise his or her beliefs. During a moment of silence, a student who objects to prayer is left to his or her own thoughts, and is not compelled to listen to the prayers or thoughts of others. For these simple reasons, a moment of silence statute does not stand or fall under the Establishment Clause according to how the Court regards vocal prayer or Bible reading. Scholars and at least one Member of this Court have recognized the distinction and suggested that a moment of silence in public schools would be constitutional. As a general matter, I agree. It is difficult to discern a serious threat to religious liberty from a room of silent, thoughtful schoolchildren.

By mandating a moment of silence, a State does not necessarily endorse any activity that might occur during the period. . . . Nonetheless, it is also possible that a moment of silence statute, either as drafted or as actually implemented, could effectively favor the child who prays over the child who does not. For example, the message of endorsement would seem inescapable if the teacher exhorts children to use the designated time to pray. Similarly, the face of the statute or its legislative history may clearly establish that it seeks to encourage or promote voluntary prayer over other alternatives, rather than merely provide a quiet moment that may be dedicated to prayer by those so inclined. The crucial question is whether the State has conveyed or attempted to convey the message that children should use the moment of silence for prayer.

Before reviewing Alabama's moment of silence law to determine whether it endorses prayer, some general observations on the proper scope of the inquiry are in order. First, the inquiry into the purpose of the legislature in enacting a moment of silence law should be deferential and limited. . . . .

Perhaps because I am new to the struggle, I am not ready to abandon all aspects of the *Lemon* test. I do believe, however, that the standards announced in *Lemon* should be reexamined and refined in order to make them more useful. . . . We must strive to do more than erect a constitutional "signpost" to be followed or ignored in a particular case as our predilections may dictate. Instead, our goal should be "to frame a principle that is not only grounded in the history and language of the first amendment, but one that is also capable of consistent application to the relevant problems." Last Term, I proposed a refinement of the *Lemon* test with this goal in mind. *Lynch v. Donnelly* (1984).

. . . Direct government action endorsing religion or a particular religious practice is invalid under this approach because "it sends a message to nonadherents that they are outsiders, not full members of the political community, and an accompanying message to adherents that they are insiders, favored members of the political community." Under this view, *Lemon's* inquiry as to the purpose and effect of a statute requires courts to examine whether government's purpose is to endorse religion and whether the statute actually conveys a message of endorsement.

The endorsement test does not preclude government from acknowledging religion or from taking religion into account in making law and policy. . . .

. . . Since there is arguably a secular pedagogical value to a moment of silence in public schools, courts should find an improper purpose behind such a statute only if the statute on its face, in its official legislative history, or in its interpretation by a responsible administrative agency suggests it has the primary purpose of endorsing prayer. . . .

The analysis above suggests that moment of silence laws in many States should pass Establishment Clause scrutiny because they do not favor the child who chooses to pray during a moment of silence over the child who chooses to meditate or reflect. Alabama Code s 16-1-20.1 (Supp.1984) does not stand on the same footing. However deferentially one examines its text and legislative history, however objectively one views the message attempted to be conveyed to the public, the conclusion is unavoidable that the purpose of the statute is to endorse prayer in public schools. I accordingly agree with the Court of Appeals, that the Alabama statute has a purpose which is in violation of the Establishment Clause, and cannot be upheld.

The Court does not hold that the Establishment Clause is so hostile to religion that it precludes the States from affording schoolchildren an opportunity for voluntary silent prayer. To the contrary, the moment of silence statutes of many States should satisfy the Establishment Clause standard we have here applied. The Court holds only that Alabama has intentionally crossed the line between creating a quiet moment during which those so inclined may pray, and affirmatively endorsing the particular religious practice of prayer. This line may be a fine one, but our precedents and the principles of religious liberty require that we draw it. In my view, the judgment of the Court of Appeals must be affirmed.

Chief Justice BURGER, dissenting.

Some who trouble to read the opinions in these cases will find it ironic—perhaps even bizarre—that on the very day we heard arguments in the cases, the Court's session opened with an invocation for Divine protection. . . .

Inevitably some wag is bound to say that the Court's holding today reflects a belief that the historic practice of the Congress and this Court is justified because members of the Judiciary and Congress are more in need of Divine guidance than are schoolchildren. Still others will say that all this controversy is "much ado about nothing," since no power on earth—including this Court and Congress—can stop any teacher from opening the school day with a moment of silence for pupils to meditate, to plan their day—or to pray if they voluntarily elect to do so.

Justice WHITE, dissenting.

Justice REHNQUIST, dissenting.

Thirty-eight years ago this Court, in *Everson v. Board of Education* (1947), summarized its exegesis of Establishment Clause doctrine thus: "In the words of Jefferson, the clause against establishment of religion by law was intended to erect 'a wall of separation between church and State.' *Reynolds v. United States.*" This language from *Reynolds*, a case involving the Free Exercise Clause of the First Amendment rather than the Establishment Clause, quoted from Thomas Jefferson's letter to the Danbury Baptist Association the phrase "I contemplate with sovereign reverence that act of the whole American people which declared that their legislature should 'make no law respecting an establishment of religion, or prohibiting the free exercise thereof,' thus building a wall of separation between church and State."

It is impossible to build sound constitutional doctrine upon a mistaken understanding of constitutional history, but unfortunately the Establishment Clause has been expressly freighted with Jefferson's misleading metaphor for nearly 40 years. Thomas Jefferson was of course in France at the time the constitutional Amendments known as the Bill of Rights were passed by Congress and ratified by the States. His letter to the Danbury Baptist Association was a short note of courtesy, written 14 years after the Amendments were passed by Congress. He would seem to any detached observer as a less than ideal source of contemporary history as to the meaning of the Religion Clauses of the First Amendment.

Jefferson's fellow Virginian, James Madison, with whom he was joined in the battle for the enactment of the Virginia Statute of Religious Liberty of 1786, did play as large a part as anyone in the drafting of the Bill of Rights. He had two advantages over Jefferson in this regard: he was present in the United States, and he was a leading Member of the First Congress. But when we turn to the record of the proceedings in the First Congress leading up to the adoption of the Establishment Clause of the Constitution, including Madison's significant contributions thereto, we see a far different picture of its purpose than the highly simplified "wall of separation between church and State."

Comparative Note 13.5

[In this case the Federal Constitutional Court considered a challenge to a Bavarian school regulation requiring a cross in every classroom by followers of the anthroposophical philosophy of life taught by Rudolph Steiner.]

Art. 4(1) Basic Law protects freedom of religion. The decision for or against a faith is according to it a matter for the individual, not the State. The State may neither prescribe nor forbid a faith or religion. Freedom of religion does not however mean just the freedom to have a faith, but also the freedom to live and act in accordance with one's religious convictions. In particular, freedom of religion guarantees participation in acts of worship a faith prescribes or is expressed in. This implies, conversely, the freedom to stay away from acts of worship of a faith not shared. This freedom relates similarly to the symbols in which a faith or religion presents itself. Art. 4(1) Basic Law leaves it to the individual to decide what religious symbols in which a faith or religion presents itself. . . . Certainly, in a society, that allows room for differing religious convictions, the individual has no right to be spared from other manifestations of faith, acts of worship or religious symbols. This is however to be distinguished from a situation created by the State where the individual is exposed without possibility of escape to the influence of a particular faith, to the acts through which it is manifested and to the symbols in which it is presented.

Art. 4(1) Basic Law does not however confine itself to barring the State from intervening in the religious convictions . . . of individuals or of religious communities. Instead, it further imposes the duty on it to guarantee room for them to operate in which the personality can develop in the philosophical and religious area and to protect them against attacks or obstruction by adherents of other religious tendencies or competing religious groups. Art. 4(1) Basic Law, however, does not confer on the individual or on religious communities any entitlement in principle to give expression to their religious conviction with State support. On the contrary . . . the Basic Law implies the principle of state neutrality towards the various religions. . . . The State . . . can guarantee peaceful coexistence only if it itself maintains neutrality in questions of belief. It may thus not itself endanger religious peace in a society. . . .

Even a State that comprehensively guarantees religious freedom and thereby commits itself to religious and philosophical neutrality cannot divest itself of the culturally conveyed, historically rooted values, convictions and attitudes on which the cohesion of society is based. . . . The Christian faith and the Christian churches have in this connection, however one may today wish to assess their heritage, been of overwhelming decisive force. The traditions of thought, mental experiences and patterns of conduct deriving from them cannot be a matter of indifference for the State. This is particularly true for schools, where the cultural foundations of society are principally handed down and renewed.

[The Court went on to conclude that the crucifix "symbolizes the essential core" of the Christian faith and that its affixation in State elementary schools violates Art. 4(1) of the Basic Law.]

The affixation of the cross cannot be justified from the positive religious freedom of parents and pupils of the Christian faith. . . . Positive religious freedom is due to all parents and pupils equally, not just the Christian ones.

SOURCE: *Classroom Crucifixion Case* (1995), in 17 *Human Rights Law Journal* 458 (1996).

On the basis of the record of these proceedings in the House of Representatives, James Madison was undoubtedly the most important architect among the Members of the House of the Amendments which became the Bill of Rights, but it was James Madison speaking as an advocate of sensible legislative compromise, not as an advocate of incorporating the Virginia Statute of Religious Liberty into the United States Constitution. . . . His original language "nor shall any national religion be established" obviously does not conform to the "wall of separation" between church and State idea which latter-day commentators have ascribed to him. His explanation on the floor of the meaning of his language—"that Congress should not establish a religion, and enforce the legal observation of it by law" is of the same ilk. When he replied to Huntington in the debate over the proposal which came from the Select Committee of the House, he urged that the language "no religion shall be established by law" should be amended by inserting the word "national" in front of the word "religion."

It seems indisputable from these glimpses of Madison's thinking, as reflected by actions on the floor of the House in 1789, that he saw the Amendment as designed to prohibit the establishment of a national religion, and perhaps to prevent discrimination among sects. He did not see it as requiring neutrality on the part of government between religion and irreligion. Thus the Court's opinion in *Everson*—while correct in bracketing Madison and Jefferson together in their exertions in their home State leading to the enactment of the Virginia Statute of Religious Liberty—is totally incorrect in suggesting that Madison carried these views onto the floor of the United States House of Representatives when he proposed the language which would ultimately become the Bill of Rights.

. . . And its repetition in varying forms in succeeding opinions of the Court can give it no more authority than it possesses as a matter of fact; *stare decisis* may bind courts as to matters of law, but it cannot bind them as to matters of history.

Joseph Story, a Member of this Court from 1811 to 1845, and during much of that time a professor at the Harvard Law School, published by far the most comprehensive treatise on the United States Constitution that had then appeared. Volume 2 of *Story's Commentaries on the Constitution of the United States* 630–632 (5th ed. 1891) discussed the meaning of the Establishment Clause of the First Amendment this way: "Probably at the time of the adoption of the Constitution, and of the amendment to it now under consideration [First Amendment], the general if not the universal sentiment in America was, that Christianity ought to receive encouragement from the State so far as was not incompatible with the private rights of conscience and the freedom of religious worship. An attempt to level all religions, and to make it a matter of state policy to hold all in utter indifference, would have created universal disapprobation, if not universal indignation."

It would seem from this evidence that the Establishment Clause of the First Amendment had acquired a well-accepted meaning: it forbade establishment of a national religion, and forbade preference among religious sects or denominations. Indeed, the first American dictionary defined the word "establishment" as "the act of establishing, founding, ratifying or ordaining," such as in "[t]he episcopal form of religion, so called, in England." N. Webster, *American Dictionary of the English Language* (1st ed. 1828).

The Establishment Clause did not require government neutrality between religion and irreligion nor did it prohibit the Federal Government from providing nondiscriminatory aid to religion. There is simply no historical foundation for the proposition that the Framers intended to build the "wall of separation" that was constitutionalized in *Everson*. Notwithstanding the absence of a historical basis for this theory of rigid separation, the wall idea might well have served as a useful albeit misguided analytical concept, had it led this Court to unified and principled results in Establishment Clause cases.

The opposite, unfortunately, has been true; in the 38 years since *Everson* our Establishment Clause cases have been neither principled nor unified. Our recent opinions, many of them hopelessly divided pluralities, have with embarrassing candor conceded that the "wall of separation" is merely a "blurred, indistinct, and variable barrier," which "is not wholly accurate" and can only be "dimly perceived."

Whether due to its lack of historical support or its practical unworkability, the *Everson* "wall" has proved all but useless as a guide to sound constitutional adjudication. It illustrates only too well the wisdom of Benjamin Cardozo's observation that "[m]etaphors in law are to be narrowly watched, for starting as devices to liberate thought, they end often by enslaving it."

But the greatest injury of the "wall" notion is its mischievous diversion of judges from the actual intentions of the drafters of the Bill of Rights. The "crucible of litigation" is well adapted to adjudicating factual disputes on the basis of testimony presented in court, but no amount of repetition of historical errors in judicial opinions can make the errors true. The "wall of separation between church and State" is a metaphor based on bad history, a metaphor which has proved useless as a guide to judging. It should be frankly and explicitly abandoned.

These difficulties arise because the *Lemon* test has no more grounding in the history of the First Amendment than does the wall theory upon which it rests. The three-part test represents a determined effort to craft a workable rule from a historically faulty doctrine; but the rule can only be as sound as the doctrine it attempts to service. The three-part test has simply not provided adequate standards for deciding Establishment Clause cases, as this Court has slowly come to realize. Even worse, the *Lemon* test has caused this Court to fracture into unworkable plurality opinions, depending upon how each of the three factors applies to a certain state action. . . .

If a constitutional theory has no basis in the history of the amendment it seeks to interpret, is difficult to apply and yields unprincipled results, I see little use in it. The "crucible of litigation" has produced only consistent unpredictability, and today's effort is just a continuation of "the Sisyphean task of trying to patch together the 'blurred, indistinct and variable barrier' described in *Lemon v. Kurtzman*." We have done much straining since 1947, but still we admit that we can only "dimly perceive" the *Everson* wall. Our perception has been clouded not by the Constitution but by the mists of an unnecessary metaphor. The true meaning of the Establishment Clause can only be seen in its history. As drafters of our Bill of Rights, the Framers inscribed the principles that control today. Any deviation from their intentions frustrates the permanence of that Charter and will only lead to the type of unprincipled decisionmaking that has plagued our Establishment Clause cases since *Everson*.

The Framers intended the Establishment Clause to prohibit the designation of any church as a "national" one. The Clause was also designed to stop the Federal Government from asserting a preference for one religious denomination or sect over others. Given the "incorporation" of the Establishment Clause as against the States via the Fourteenth Amendment in *Everson*, States are prohibited as well from establishing a religion or discriminating between sects. As its history abundantly shows, however, nothing in the Establishment Clause requires government to be strictly neutral between religion and irreligion, nor does that Clause prohibit Congress or the States from pursuing legitimate secular ends through nondiscriminatory sectarian means.

The Court strikes down the Alabama statute because the State wished to "characterize prayer as a favored practice." It would come as much of a shock to those who drafted the Bill of Rights as it will to a large number of thoughtful Americans today to learn that the Constitution, as construed by the majority, prohibits the Alabama Legislature from "endorsing" prayer. George Washington himself, at the request of the very Congress which passed the Bill of Rights, proclaimed a day of "public thanksgiving and prayer, to be observed by acknowledging with grateful hearts the many and signal favors of Almighty God." History must judge whether it was the Father of his Country in 1789, or a majority of the Court today, which has strayed from the meaning of the Establishment Clause.

The State surely has a secular interest in regulating the manner in which public schools are conducted. Nothing in the Establishment Clause of the First Amendment, properly understood, prohibits any such generalized "endorsement" of prayer. I would therefore reverse the judgment of the Court of Appeals.

Notes and Queries

1. What role does legislative history play in the majority's analysis? Do you agree with Justice O'Connor's suggestion that even under the majority's opinion, some "moment of silence" laws might survive constitutional scrutiny? Doesn't this kind of reliance on legislative history invite the Court to scrutinize the "motives" of a legislature, a practice it typically forswears?

2. How does the Court utilize the "purpose" prong of the *Lemon* test?

3. Justice Rehnquist's impassioned dissent relies heavily on the history of the establishment clause to reject the "wall of separation" metaphor. Note his insistence that "The true meaning of the Establishment Clause can only be seen in its history."

As you know by now, constitutional history is rarely unambiguous. How, if at all, should Justice Rehnquist account for scholarly disagreement over the history of the religious freedom guarantees? Should dispute about the lessons of history disqualify "history" as a method of constitutional interpretation?

Is "history" a smokescreen? Aren't the justices really arguing about what the Framers intended? Or are they arguing, instead, about what the purpose of the clause is? Are there concrete differences of result if we reframe the dispute in these ways?

4. Is this case, as Chief Justice Burger lamented, "much ado about nothing . . ."? Why or why not?

Lee v. Weisman
505 U.S. 577, 112 S.Ct. 2649, 120 L.Ed.2d 467 (1992)

Robert Lee, the principal of Bishop Middle School, invited Rabbi Leslie Gutterman to offer an invocation and benediction at the school's graduation ceremony. The request was not at all unusual—the public schools in Providence, Rhode Island, had long followed the practice. Rabbi Gutterman was asked to follow a set of guidelines for civic occasions prepared by the National Conference of Christians and Jews. Among other things, the guidelines recommended that public prayers should be prepared with "inclusiveness and sensitivity." Daniel Weisman, the father of a graduating student, sought a restraining order in a United States District Court. He complained that the practice violated the establishment clause of the First Amendment. The District Court and the Circuit Court agreed. Opinion of the Court: *Kennedy*, Blackmun, Stevens, O'Connor, Souter. Concurring opinions: *Blackmun*, Stevens, O'Connor; *Souter*, Stevens, O'Connor. Dissenting opinion: *Scalia*, Rehnquist, White, Thomas.

Justice KENNEDY delivered the opinion of the Court.

The school board (and the United States, which supports it as *amicus curiae*) argued that these short prayers and others like them at graduation exercises are of profound meaning to many students and parents throughout this country who consider that due respect and acknowledgment for divine guidance and for the deepest spiritual aspirations of our people ought to be expressed at an event as important in life as a graduation. We assume this to be so in addressing the difficult case now before us, for the significance of the prayers lies also at the heart of Daniel and Deborah Weisman's case.

These dominant facts mark and control the confines of our decision: State officials direct the performance of a formal religious exercise at promotional and graduation ceremonies for secondary schools. Even for those students who object to the religious exercise, their attendance and participation in the state-sponsored religious activity are in a fair and real sense obligatory, though the school district does not require attendance as a condition for receipt of the diploma.

The principle that government may accommodate the free exercise of religion does not supersede the fundamental limitations imposed by the Establishment Clause. It is beyond dispute that, at a minimum, the Constitution guarantees that government may not coerce anyone to support or participate in religion or its exercise, or otherwise act in a way which "establishes a [state] religion or religious faith, or tends to do so." The State's involvement in the school prayers challenged today violates these central principles.

That involvement is as troubling as it is undenied. A school official, the principal, decided that an invocation and a benediction should be given; this is a choice attributable to the State, and from a constitutional perspective it is as if a state statute decreed that the prayers must occur. The principal chose the religious participant, here a rabbi, and that choice is also attributable to the State. The reason for the choice of a rabbi is not disclosed by the record, but the potential for divisiveness over the choice of a particular member of the clergy to conduct the ceremony is apparent. Divisiveness, of course, can attend any state decision respecting religions, and neither its existence nor its potential necessarily invalidates the State's attempts to accommodate religion in all cases. The potential for divisiveness is of particular relevance here though, because it centers around an overt religious exercise in a secondary school environment where, as we discuss below, subtle coercive pressures exist and where the stu-

dent had no real alternative which would have allowed her to avoid the fact or appearance of participation.

The State's role did not end with the decision to include a prayer and with the choice of a clergyman. Principal Lee provided Rabbi Gutterman with a copy of the "Guidelines for Civic Occasions," and advised him that his prayers should be nonsectarian. Through these means the principal directed and controlled the content of the prayers. Even if the only sanction for ignoring the instructions were that the rabbi would not be invited back, we think no religious representative who valued his or her continued reputation and effectiveness in the community would incur the State's displeasure in this regard. It is a cornerstone principle of our Establishment Clause jurisprudence that "it is no part of the business of government to compose official prayers for any group of the American people to recite as a part of a religious program carried on by government," *Engel v. Vitale* (1962), and that is what the school officials attempted to do.

Petitioners argue, and we find nothing in the case to refute it, that the directions for the content of the prayers were a good-faith attempt by the school to ensure that the sectarianism which is so often the flashpoint for religious animosity be removed from the graduation ceremony. The concern is understandable, as a prayer which uses ideas or images identified with a particular religion may foster a different sort of sectarian rivalry than an invocation or benediction in terms more neutral. The school's explanation, however, does not resolve the dilemma caused by its participation. The question is not the good faith of the school in attempting to make the prayer acceptable to most persons, but the legitimacy of its undertaking that enterprise at all when the object is to produce a prayer to be used in a formal religious exercise which students, for all practical purposes, are obliged to attend.

We are asked to recognize the existence of a practice of nonsectarian prayer, prayer within the embrace of what is known as the Judeo-Christian tradition, prayer which is more acceptable than one which, for example, makes explicit references to the God of Israel, or to Jesus Christ, or to a patron saint. . . . If common ground can be defined which permits once conflicting faiths to express the shared conviction that there is an ethic and a morality which transcend human invention, the sense of community and purpose sought by all decent societies might be advanced. But though the First Amendment does not allow the government to stifle prayers which aspire to these ends, neither does it permit the government to undertake that task for itself.

The First Amendment's Religion Clauses mean that religious beliefs and religious expression are too precious to be either proscribed or prescribed by the State. The design of the Constitution is that preservation and transmission of religious beliefs and worship is a responsibility and a choice committed to the private sphere, which itself is promised freedom to pursue that mission. It must not be forgotten then, that while concern must be given to define the protection granted to an objector or a dissenting nonbeliever, these same Clauses exist to protect religion from government interference.

These concerns have particular application in the case of school officials, whose effort to monitor prayer will be perceived by the students as inducing a participation they might otherwise reject. Though the efforts of the school officials in this case to find common ground appear to have been a good-faith attempt to recognize the common aspects of religions and not the divisive ones, our precedents do not permit school officials to assist in composing prayers as an incident to a formal exercise for their students. And these same precedents caution us to measure the idea of a civic religion against the central meaning of the Religion Clauses of the First Amendment, which is that all creeds must be tolerated and none favored. The suggestion that government may establish an official or civic religion as a means of avoiding the establishment of a religion with more specific creeds strikes us as a contradiction that cannot be accepted.

The degree of school involvement here made it clear that the graduation prayers bore the imprint of the State and thus put school-age children who objected in an untenable position. We turn our attention now to consider the position of the students, both those who desired the prayer and she who did not.

To endure the speech of false ideas or offensive content and then to counter it is part of learning how to live in a pluralistic society, a society which insists upon open discourse towards the end of a tolerant citizenry. And tolerance presupposes some mutuality of obligation. It is argued that our constitutional vision of a free society requires confidence in our own ability to accept or reject ideas of which we do not approve, and that prayer at a high school graduation does nothing more than offer a choice. By the time they are seniors, high school students no doubt have been required to attend classes and assemblies and to complete assignments exposing them to ideas they find distasteful or immoral or absurd or all of these. Against this background, students may consider it an odd measure of justice to be subjected during the course of their educations to ideas deemed offensive and irreligious, but to be denied a brief, formal prayer ceremony that the school offers in return. This argument cannot prevail,

however. It overlooks a fundamental dynamic of the Constitution.

The First Amendment protects speech and religion by quite different mechanisms. Speech is protected by ensuring its full expression even when the government participates, for the very object of some of our most important speech is to persuade the government to adopt an idea as its own. The method for protecting freedom of worship and freedom of conscience in religious matters is quite the reverse. In religious debate or expression the government is not a prime participant, for the Framers deemed religious establishment antithetical to the freedom of all. The Free Exercise Clause embraces a freedom of conscience and worship that has close parallels in the speech provisions of the First Amendment, but the Establishment Clause is a specific prohibition on forms of state intervention in religious affairs with no precise counterpart in the speech provisions. *Buckley v. Valeo* (1976). The explanation lies in the lesson of history that was and is the inspiration for the Establishment Clause, the lesson that in the hands of government what might begin as a tolerant expression of religious views may end in a policy to indoctrinate and coerce. A state-created orthodoxy puts at grave risk that freedom of belief and conscience which are the sole assurance that religious faith is real, not imposed.

The lessons of the First Amendment are as urgent in the modern world as in the 18th century when it was written. One timeless lesson is that if citizens are subjected to state-sponsored religious exercises, the State disavows its own duty to guard and respect that sphere of inviolable conscience and belief which is the mark of a free people. To compromise that principle today would be to deny our own tradition and forfeit our standing to urge others to secure the protections of that tradition for themselves.

As we have observed before, there are heightened concerns with protecting freedom of conscience from subtle coercive pressure in the elementary and secondary public schools. See, e.g., *School Dist. of Abington v. Schempp* (1963) (Goldberg, J., concurring); *Edwards v. Aguillard* (1987); *Board of Ed. of Westside Community Schools v. Mergens* (1990) (Kennedy, J., concurring). Our decisions in *Engel v. Vitale*, and *School Dist. of Abington*, recognize, among other things, that prayer exercises in public schools carry a particular risk of indirect coercion. The concern may not be limited to the context of schools, but it is most pronounced there. What to most believers may seem nothing more than a reasonable request that the nonbeliever respect their religious practices, in a school context may appear to the nonbeliever or dissenter to be an attempt to employ the machinery of the State to enforce a religious orthodoxy.

We need not look beyond the circumstances of this case to see the phenomenon at work. The undeniable fact is that the school district's supervision and control of a high school graduation ceremony places public pressure, as well as peer pressure, on attending students to stand as a group or, at least, maintain respectful silence during the invocation and benediction. This pressure, though subtle and indirect, can be as real as any overt compulsion. Of course, in our culture standing or remaining silent can signify adherence to a view or simple respect for the views of others. And no doubt some persons who have no desire to join a prayer have little objection to standing as a sign of respect for those who do. But for the dissenter of high school age, who has a reasonable perception that she is being forced by the State to pray in a manner her conscience will not allow, the injury is no less real. There can be no doubt that for many, if not most, of the students at the graduation, the act of standing or remaining silent was an expression of participation in the rabbi's prayer. That was the very point of the religious exercise. It is of little comfort to a dissenter, then, to be told that for her the act of standing or remaining in silence signifies mere respect, rather than participation. What matters is that, given our social conventions, a reasonable dissenter in this milieu could believe that the group exercise signified her own participation or approval of it.

Finding no violation under these circumstances would place objectors in the dilemma of participating, with all that implies, or protesting. We do not address whether that choice is acceptable if the affected citizens are mature adults, but we think the State may not, consistent with the Establishment Clause, place primary and secondary school children in this position. Research in psychology supports the common assumption that adolescents are often susceptible to pressure from their peers towards conformity, and that the influence is strongest in matters of social convention. . . . To recognize that the choice imposed by the State constitutes an unacceptable constraint only acknowledges that the government may no more use social pressure to enforce orthodoxy than it may use more direct means.

The injury caused by the government's action, and the reason why Daniel and Deborah Weisman object to it, is that the State, in a school setting, in effect required participation in a religious exercise. It is, we concede, a brief exercise during which the individual can concentrate on joining its message, meditate on her own religion, or let her mind wander. But the embarrassment and the intrusion of the religious exercise cannot be refuted by arguing that these prayers, and similar ones to be said in the future, are of a *de minimis* character. To do so would be an affront to the rabbi who offered them and to all those for whom the prayers were an essential and profound recognition of divine authority. And for the same reason, we think that the intrusion is greater than the two minutes or so of time consumed for prayers like these. Assuming, as we must, that the prayers were offensive to the student and the parent who now object, the intrusion was both real and, in the context of a secondary school, a violation of the objectors' rights. That the intrusion was in the course of promulgating religion that sought to be civic or nonsectarian rather than pertaining to one sect does not lessen the offense or isolation to the objectors. At best it narrows their number, at worst increases their sense of isolation and affront.

There was a stipulation in the District Court that attendance at graduation and promotional ceremonies is voluntary. Petitioners and the United States, as *amicus,* made this a center point of the case, arguing that the option of not attending the graduation excuses any inducement or coercion in the ceremony itself. The argument lacks all persuasion. Law reaches past formalism. And to say a teenage student has a real choice not to attend her high school graduation is formalistic in the extreme. True, Deborah could elect not to attend commencement without renouncing her diploma; but we shall not allow the case to turn on this point. Everyone knows that in our society and in our culture high school graduation is one of life's most significant occasions. A school rule which excuses attendance is beside the point. Attendance may not be required by official decree, yet it is apparent that a student is not free to absent herself from the graduation exercise in any real sense of the term "voluntary," for absence would require forfeiture of those intangible benefits which have motivated the student through youth and all her high school years. Graduation is a time for family and those closest to the student to celebrate success and express mutual wishes of gratitude and respect, all to the end of impressing upon the young person the role that it is his or her right and duty to assume in the community and all of its diverse parts.

The importance of the event is the point the school district and the United States rely upon to argue that a formal prayer ought to be permitted, but it becomes one of the principal reasons why their argument must fail. Their contention, one of considerable force were it not for the constitutional constraints applied to state action, is that the prayers are an essential part of these ceremonies because for many persons an occasion of this significance lacks meaning if there is no recognition, however brief, that human achievements cannot be understood apart from their spiritual essence. We think the Government's position that this interest suffices to force students to choose between compliance or forfeiture demonstrates fundamental inconsistency in its argumentation. It fails to acknowledge that what for many of Deborah's classmates and their parents was a spiritual imperative was for Daniel and Deborah Weisman religious conformance compelled by the State. While in some societies the wishes of the majority might prevail, the Establishment Clause of the First Amendment is addressed to this contingency and rejects the balance urged upon us. The Constitution forbids the State to exact religious conformity from a student as the price of attending her own high school graduation. This is the calculus the Constitution commands.

The Government's argument gives insufficient recognition to the real conflict of conscience faced by the young student. The essence of the Government's position is that with regard to a civic, social occasion of this importance it is the objector, not the majority, who must take unilateral and private action to avoid compromising religious scruples, hereby electing to miss the graduation exercise. This turns conventional First Amendment analysis on its head. It is a tenet of the First Amendment that the State cannot require one of its citizens to forfeit his or her rights and benefits as the price of resisting conformance to state-sponsored religious practice. To say that a student must remain apart from the ceremony at the opening invocation and closing benediction is to risk compelling conformity in an environment analogous to the classroom setting, where we have said the risk of compulsion is especially high. Just as in *Engel v. Vitale* and *School Dist. of Abington v. Schempp*, where we found that provisions within the challenged legislation permitting a student to be voluntarily excused from attendance or participation in the daily prayers did not shield those practices from invalidation, the fact that attendance at the graduation ceremonies is voluntary in a legal sense does not save the religious exercise. . . .

We do not hold that every state action implicating religion is invalid if one or a few citizens find it offensive. People may take offense at all manner of religious as well as nonreligious messages, but offense alone does not in every case show a violation. We know too that sometimes to endure social isolation or even anger may be the price of conscience or nonconformity. But, by any reading of our cases, the conformity required of the student in this case was too high an exaction to withstand the test of the Establishment Clause. The prayer exercises in this case are especially improper because the State has in every practical sense compelled attendance and participation in an explicit religious exercise at an event of singular impor-

tance to every student, one the objecting student had no real alternative to avoid.

Our society would be less than true to its heritage if it lacked abiding concern for the values of its young people, and we acknowledge the profound belief of adherents to many faiths that there must be a place in the student's life for precepts of a morality higher even than the law we today enforce. We express no hostility to those aspirations, nor would our oath permit us to do so. A relentless and all-pervasive attempt to exclude religion from every aspect of public life could itself become inconsistent with the Constitution. We recognize that, at graduation time and throughout the course of the educational process, there will be instances when religious values, religious practices, and religious persons will have some interaction with the public schools and their students. But these matters, often questions of accommodation of religion, are not before us. The sole question presented is whether a religious exercise may be conducted at a graduation ceremony in circumstances where, as we have found, young graduates who object are induced to conform. No holding by this Court suggests that a school can persuade or compel a student to participate in a religious exercise. That is being done here, and it is forbidden by the Establishment Clause of the First Amendment.

For the reasons we have stated, the judgment of the Court of Appeals is

Affirmed.

Justice BLACKMUN, with whom Justice STEVENS and Justice O'CONNOR join, concurring.

Nearly half a century of review and refinement of Establishment Clause jurisprudence has distilled one clear understanding: Government may neither promote nor affiliate itself with any religious doctrine or organization, nor may it obtrude itself in the internal affairs of any religious institution. The application of these principles to the present case mandates the decision reached today by the Court.

Application of these principles to the facts of this case is straightforward. There can be "no doubt" that the "invocation of God's blessings" delivered at Nathan Bishop Middle School "is a religious activity." In the words of *Engel*, the Rabbi's prayer "is a solemn avowal of divine faith and supplication for the blessings of the Almighty. The nature of such a prayer has always been religious." The question then is whether the government has "plac[ed] its official stamp of approval" on the prayer. As the Court ably demonstrates, when the government "compose[s] official prayers," selects the member of the clergy to deliver the prayer, has the prayer delivered at a public school event that is planned, supervised and given by school officials, and pressures students to attend and participate in the prayer, there can be no doubt that the government is advancing and promoting religion. As our prior decisions teach us, it is this that the Constitution prohibits.

I join the Court's opinion today because I find nothing in it inconsistent with the essential precepts of the Establishment Clause developed in our precedents. The Court holds that the graduation prayer is unconstitutional because the State "in effect required participation in a religious exercise." Although our precedents make clear that proof of government coercion is not necessary to prove an Establishment Clause violation, it is sufficient. Government pressure to participate in a religious activity is an obvious indication that the government is endorsing or promoting religion.

But it is not enough that the government restrain from compelling religious practices: It must not engage in them either. The Court repeatedly has recognized that a violation of the Establishment Clause is not predicated on coercion. The Establishment Clause proscribes public schools from "conveying or attempting to convey a message that religion or a particular religious belief is favored or preferred," *County of Allegheny v. American Civil Liberties Union, Greater Pittsburgh Chapter* (1989), even if the schools do not actually "impos[e] pressure upon a student to participate in a religious activity."

The scope of the Establishment Clause's prohibitions developed in our case law derives from the Clause's purposes. The First Amendment encompasses two distinct guarantees—the government shall make no law respecting an establishment of religion or prohibiting the free exercise thereof—both with the common purpose of securing religious liberty. Through vigorous enforcement of both Clauses, we "promote and assure the fullest possible scope of religious liberty and tolerance for all and . . . nurture the conditions which secure the best hope of attainment of that end."

Our decisions have gone beyond prohibiting coercion, however, because the Court has recognized that "the fullest possible scope of religious liberty," entails more than freedom from coercion. The Establishment Clause protects religious liberty on a grand scale; it is a social compact that guarantees for generations a democracy and a strong religious community—both essential to safeguarding religious liberty. "Our fathers seem to have been perfectly sincere in their belief that the members of the Church would be more patriotic, and the citizens of the State more religious, by keeping their respective functions entirely separate."

The mixing of government and religion can be a threat to free government, even if no one is forced to participate. When the government puts its imprimatur on a particular religion, it conveys a message of exclusion to all those who do not adhere to the favored beliefs. A government cannot be premised on the belief that all persons are created equal when it asserts that God prefers some. . . .

When the government arrogates to itself a role in religious affairs, it abandons its obligation as guarantor of democracy. Democracy requires the nourishment of dialog and dissent, while religious faith puts its trust in an ultimate divine authority above all human deliberation. When the government appropriates religious truth, it "transforms rational debate into theological decree." Those who disagree no longer are questioning the policy judgment of the elected but the rules of a higher authority who is beyond reproach. . . .

It is these understandings and fears that underlie our Establishment Clause jurisprudence. We have believed that religious freedom cannot exist in the absence of a free democratic government, and that such a government cannot endure when there is fusion between religion and the political regime. We have believed that religious freedom cannot thrive in the absence of a vibrant religious community and that such a community cannot prosper when it is bound to the secular. And we have believed that these were the animating principles behind the adoption of the Establishment Clause. To that end, our cases have prohibited government endorsement of religion, its sponsorship, and active involvement in religion, whether or not citizens were coerced to conform.

Justice SOUTER, with whom Justice STEVENS and Justice O'CONNOR join, concurring.

I join the whole of the Court's opinion, and fully agree that prayers at public school graduation ceremonies indirectly coerce religious observance. I write separately nonetheless on two issues of Establishment Clause analysis that underlie my independent resolution of this case: whether the Clause applies to governmental practices that do not favor one religion or denomination over others, and whether state coercion of religious conformity, over and above state endorsement of religious exercise or belief, is a necessary element of an Establishment Clause violation.

Some have challenged this precedent by reading the Establishment Clause to permit "nonpreferential" state promotion of religion. The challengers argue that, as originally understood by the Framers, "[t]he Establishment Clause did not require government neutrality between religion and irreligion nor did it prohibit the Federal Government from providing nondiscriminatory aid to religion." . . . While a case has been made for this position, it is not so convincing as to warrant reconsideration of our settled law; indeed, I find in the history of the Clause's textual development a more powerful argument supporting the Court's jurisprudence following *Everson.*

What we thus know of the Framers' experience underscores the observation of one prominent commentator, that confining the Establishment Clause to a prohibition on preferential aid "requires a premise that the Framers were extraordinarily bad drafters—that they believed one thing but adopted language that said something substantially different, and that they did so after repeatedly attending to the choice of language." . . . We must presume, since there is no conclusive evidence to the contrary, that the Framers embraced the significance of their textual judgment. Thus, on balance, history neither contradicts nor warrants reconsideration of the settled principle that the Establishment Clause forbids support for religion in general no less than support for one religion or some.

While these considerations are, for me, sufficient to reject the nonpreferentialist position, one further concern animates my judgment. In many contexts, including this one, nonpreferentialism requires some distinction between "sectarian" religious practices and those that would be, by some measure, ecumenical enough to pass Establishment Clause muster. Simply by requiring the enquiry, nonpreferentialists invite the courts to engage in comparative theology. I can hardly imagine a subject less amenable to the competence of the federal judiciary, or more deliberately to be avoided where possible.

This case is nicely in point. Since the nonpreferentiality of a prayer must be judged by its text, Justice Blackmun pertinently observes that Rabbi Gutterman drew his exhortation "[t]o do justly, to love mercy, to walk humbly" straight from the King James version of Micah, ch. 6, v. 8. At some undefinable point, the similarities between a state-sponsored prayer and the sacred text of a specific religion would so closely identify the former with the latter that even a nonpreferentialist would have to concede a breach of the Establishment Clause. And even if Micah's thought is sufficiently generic for most believers, it still embodies a straightforwardly theistic premise, and so does the rabbi's prayer. Many Americans who consider themselves religious are not theistic; some, like several of the Framers, are deists who would question Rabbi Gutterman's plea for divine advancement of the country's political and moral good. Thus, a nonpreferentialist who would condemn subjecting public school graduates to, say, the Anglican liturgy would still need to explain why the government's preference for theistic over nontheistic religion is constitutional.

Nor does it solve the problem to say that the State should promote a "diversity" of religious views; that position would necessarily compel the government and, inevitably, the courts to make wholly inappropriate judgments about the number of religions the State should sponsor and the relative frequency with which it should sponsor each. In fact, the prospect would be even worse than that. As Madison observed in criticizing religious Presidential proclamations, the practice of sponsoring religious messages tends, over time, "to narrow the recommendation to the standard of the predominant sect." We have not changed much since the days of Madison, and the judiciary should not willingly enter the political arena to battle the centripetal force leading from religious pluralism to official preference for the faith with the most votes.

Our precedents may not always have drawn perfectly straight lines. They simply cannot, however, support the position that a showing of coercion is necessary to a successful Establishment Clause claim.

Like the provisions about "due" process and "unreasonable" searches and seizures, the constitutional language forbidding laws "respecting an establishment of religion" is not pellucid. But virtually everyone acknowledges that the Clause bans more than formal establishments of religion in the traditional sense, that is, massive state support for religion through, among other means, comprehensive schemes of taxation. This much follows from the Framers' explicit rejection of simpler provisions prohibiting either the establishment of a religion or laws "establishing religion" in favor of the broader ban on laws "respecting an establishment of religion."

While some argue that the Framers added the word "respecting" simply to foreclose federal interference with state establishments of religion, the language sweeps more broadly than that. In Madison's words, the Clause in its final form forbids "everything like" a national religious establishment, and, after incorporation, it forbids "everything like" a state religious establishment. The sweep is broad enough that Madison himself characterized congressional provisions for legislative and military chaplains as unconstitutional "establishments."

While petitioners insist that the prohibition extends only to the "coercive" features and incidents of establishment, they cannot easily square that claim with the constitutional text. The First Amendment forbids not just laws "respecting an establishment of religion," but also those "prohibiting the free exercise thereof." Yet laws that coerce nonadherents to "support or participate in any religion or its exercise," would virtually by definition violate their right to religious free exercise. See *Employment Div., Dept. of Human Resources of Ore. v. Smith* (1990). Thus, a literal application of the coercion test would render the

Establishment Clause a virtual nullity, as petitioners' counsel essentially conceded at oral argument. . . .

While we may be unable to know for certain what the Framers meant by the Clause, we do know that, around the time of its ratification, a respectable body of opinion supported a considerably broader reading than petitioners urge upon us. This consistency with the textual considerations is enough to preclude fundamentally reexamining our settled law, and I am accordingly left with the task of considering whether the state practice at issue here violates our traditional understanding of the Clause's proscriptions.

While the Establishment Clause's concept of neutrality is not self-revealing, our recent cases have invested it with specific content: the State may not favor or endorse either religion generally over nonreligion or one religion over others. . . . This principle against favoritism and endorsement has become the foundation of Establishment Clause jurisprudence, ensuring that religious belief is irrelevant to every citizen's standing in the political community, and protecting religion from the demeaning effects of any governmental embrace. . . . Now, as in the early Republic, "religion & Govt. will both exist in greater purity, the less they are mixed together." Letter from J. Madison to E. Livingston (July 10, 1822). . . . Our aspiration to religious liberty, embodied in the First Amendment, permits no other standard. . . .

In everyday life, we routinely accommodate religious beliefs that we do not share. A Christian inviting an Orthodox Jew to lunch might take pains to choose a kosher restaurant; an atheist in a hurry might yield the right of way to an Amish man steering a horse-drawn carriage. In so acting, we express respect for, but not endorsement of, the fundamental values of others. We act without expressing a position on the theological merit of those values or of religious belief in general, and no one perceives us to have taken such a position.

The government may act likewise. Most religions encourage devotional practices that are at once crucial to the lives of believers and idiosyncratic in the eyes of nonadherents. By definition, secular rules of general application are drawn from the nonadherent's vantage and, consequently, fail to take such practices into account. Yet when enforcement of such rules cuts across religious sensibilities, as it often does, it puts those affected to the choice of taking sides between God and government. In such circumstances, accommodating religion reveals nothing beyond a recognition that general rules can unnecessarily offend the religious conscience when they offend the conscience of secular society not at all.

Whatever else may define the scope of accommodation permissible under the Establishment Clause, one requirement is clear: accommodation must lift a discernible burden on the free exercise of religion. Concern for the position of religious individuals in the modern regulatory State cannot justify official solicitude for a religious practice unburdened by general rules; such gratuitous largesse would effectively favor religion over disbelief. By these lights one easily sees that, in sponsoring the graduation prayers at issue here, the State has crossed the line from permissible accommodation to unconstitutional establishment.

Religious students cannot complain that omitting prayers from their graduation ceremony would, in any realistic sense, "burden" their spiritual callings. To be sure, many of them invest this rite of passage with spiritual significance, but they may express their religious feelings about it before and after the ceremony. They may even organize a privately sponsored baccalaureate if they desire the company of likeminded students. Because they accordingly have no need for the machinery of the State to affirm their beliefs, the government's sponsorship of prayer at the graduation ceremony is most reasonably understood as an official endorsement of religion and, in this instance, of theistic religion. One may fairly say, as one commentator has suggested, that the government brought prayer into the ceremony "precisely because some people want a symbolic affirmation that government approves and endorses their religion, and because many of the people who want this affirmation place little or no value on the costs to religious minorities."

Petitioners would deflect this conclusion by arguing that graduation prayers are no different from Presidential religious proclamations and similar official "acknowledgments" of religion in public life. But religious invocations in Thanksgiving Day addresses and the like, rarely noticed, ignored without effort, conveyed over an impersonal medium, and directed at no one in particular, inhabit a pallid zone worlds apart from official prayers delivered to a captive audience of public school students and their families. Madison himself respected the difference between the trivial and the serious in constitutional practice. Realizing that his contemporaries were unlikely to take the Establishment Clause seriously enough to forgo a legislative chaplainship, he suggested that "[r]ather than let this step beyond the landmarks of power have the effect of a legitimate precedent, it will be better to apply to it the legal aphorism *de minimis non curat lex*. . . ." But that logic permits no winking at the practice in question here. When public school officials, armed with the State's authority, convey an endorsement of religion to their students, they strike near the core of the Establishment

Clause. However "ceremonial" their messages may be, they are flatly unconstitutional.

Justice SCALIA, with whom The Chief Justice, Justice WHITE, and Justice THOMAS join, dissenting.

Three Terms ago, I joined an opinion recognizing that the Establishment Clause must be construed in light of the "[g]overnment policies of accommodation, acknowledgment, and support for religion [that] are an accepted part of our political and cultural heritage." That opinion affirmed that "the meaning of the Clause is to be determined by reference to historical practices and understandings." It said that "[a] test for implementing the protections of the Establishment Clause that, if applied with consistency, would invalidate longstanding traditions cannot be a proper reading of the Clause." *County of Allegheny v. American Civil Liberties Union, Greater Pittsburgh Chapter* (1989) (Kennedy, J., concurring in judgment in part and dissenting in part).

These views of course prevent me from joining today's opinion, which is conspicuously bereft of any reference to history. In holding that the Establishment Clause prohibits invocations and benedictions at public-school graduation ceremonies, the Court—with nary a mention that what it is doing lays waste a tradition that is as old as public-school graduation ceremonies themselves, and that is a component of an even more longstanding American tradition of nonsectarian prayer to God at public celebrations generally. As its instrument of destruction, the bulldozer of its social engineering, the Court invents a boundless, and boundlessly manipulable, test of psychological coercion. . . . Today's opinion shows more forcefully than volumes of argumentation why our Nation's protection, that fortress which is our Constitution, cannot possibly rest upon the changeable philosophical predilections of the Justices of this Court, but must have deep foundations in the historic practices of our people. . . .

The history and tradition of our Nation are replete with public ceremonies featuring prayers of thanksgiving and petition. Illustrations of this point have been amply provided in our prior opinions, but since the Court is so oblivious to our history as to suggest that the Constitution restricts "preservation and transmission of religious beliefs . . . to the private sphere," it appears necessary to provide another brief account.

From our Nation's origin, prayer has been a prominent part of governmental ceremonies and proclamations. The Declaration of Independence, the document marking our birth as a separate people, "appeal[ed] to the Supreme Judge of the world for the rectitude of our intentions" and avowed "a firm reliance on the protection of divine Providence." In his first inaugural address, after swearing his oath of office on a Bible, George Washington deliberately made a prayer a part of his first official act as President.

In addition to this general tradition of prayer at public ceremonies, there exists a more specific tradition of invocations and benedictions at public school graduation exercises. . . . As the Court obliquely acknowledges in describing the "customary features" of high school graduations, and as respondents do not contest, the invocation and benediction have long been recognized to be "as traditional as any other parts of the [school] graduation program and are widely established."

The Court presumably would separate graduation invocations and benedictions from other instances of public "preservation and transmission of religious beliefs" on the ground that they involve "psychological coercion." I find it a sufficient embarrassment that our Establishment Clause jurisprudence regarding holiday displays, has come to "requir[e] scrutiny more commonly associated with interior decorators than with the judiciary." But interior decorating is a rock-hard science compared to psychology practiced by amateurs. . . . The Court's argument that state officials have "coerced" students to take part in the invocation and benediction at graduation ceremonies is, not to put too fine a point on it, incoherent. . . .

The Court declares that students' "attendance and participation in the [invocation and benediction] are in a fair and real sense obligatory." But what exactly is this "fair and real sense"? According to the Court, students at graduation who want "to avoid the fact or appearance of participation," in the invocation and benediction are psychologically obligated by "public pressure, as well as peer pressure, . . . to stand as a group or, at least, maintain respectful silence" during those prayers. This assertion—the very linchpin of the Court's opinion—is almost as intriguing for what it does not say as for what it says. It does not say, for example, that students are psychologically coerced to bow their heads, place their hands in a Durer-like prayer position, pay attention to the prayers, utter "Amen," or in fact pray. (Perhaps further intensive psychological research remains to be done on these matters.) It claims only that students are psychologically coerced "to stand . . . or, at least, maintain respectful silence." Both halves of this disjunctive (both of which must amount to the fact or appearance of participation in prayer if the Court's analysis is to survive on its own terms) merit particular attention.

To begin with the latter: The Court's notion that a student who simply sits in "respectful silence" during the invocation and benediction (when all others are standing) has somehow joined—or would somehow be perceived as having joined—in the prayers is nothing short of ludicrous. We indeed live in a vulgar age. But surely "our social conventions," have not coarsened to the point that anyone who does not stand on his chair and shout obscenities can reasonably be deemed to have assented to everything said in his presence. Since the Court does not dispute that students exposed to prayer at graduation ceremonies retain (despite "subtle coercive pressures") the free will to sit, there is absolutely no basis for the Court's decision. It is fanciful enough to say that "a reasonable dissenter," standing head erect in a class of bowed heads, "could believe that the group exercise signified her own participation or approval of it." It is beyond the absurd to say that she could entertain such a belief while pointedly declining to rise.

But let us assume the very worst, that the nonparticipating graduate is "subtly coerced" to stand! Even that half of the disjunctive does not remotely establish a "participation" (or an "appearance of participation") in a religious exercise. The Court acknowledges that "in our culture standing . . . can signify adherence to a view or simple respect for the views of others." (Much more often the latter than the former, I think, except perhaps in the proverbial town meeting, where one votes by standing.) But if it is a permissible inference that one who is standing is doing so simply out of respect for the prayers of others that are in progress, then how can it possibly be said that a "reasonable dissenter . . . could believe that the group exercise signified her own participation or approval"? Quite obviously, it cannot. I may add, moreover, that maintaining respect for the religious observances of others is a fundamental civic virtue that government (including the public schools) can and should cultivate—so that even if it were the case that the displaying of such respect might be mistaken for taking part in the prayer, I would deny that the dissenter's interest in avoiding even the false appearance of participation constitutionally trumps the government's interest in fostering respect for religion generally.

I also find it odd that the Court concludes that high school graduates may not be subjected to this supposed psychological coercion, yet refrains from addressing whether "mature adults" may. I had thought that the reason graduation from high school is regarded as so significant an event is that it is generally associated with transition from adolescence to young adulthood. Many graduating seniors, of course, are old enough to vote. Why, then, does the Court treat them as though they were first-graders? Will we soon have a jurisprudence that distinguishes between mature and immature adults?

The other "dominant fac[t]" identified by the Court is

that "[s]tate officials direct the performance of a formal religious exercise" at school graduation ceremonies. "Direct[ing] the performance of a formal religious exercise" has a sound of liturgy to it, summoning up images of the principal directing acolytes where to carry the cross, or showing the rabbi where to unroll the Torah. A Court professing to be engaged in a "delicate and fact-sensitive" line-drawing, would better describe what it means as "prescribing the content of an invocation and benediction." But even that would be false. All the record shows is that principals of the Providence public schools, acting within their delegated authority, have invited clergy to deliver invocations and benedictions at graduations; and that Principal Lee invited Rabbi Gutterman, provided him a two-page pamphlet, prepared by the National Conference of Christians and Jews, giving general advice on inclusive prayer for civic occasions, and advised him that his prayers at graduation should be nonsectarian. How these facts can fairly be transformed into the charges that Principal Lee "directed and controlled the content of [Rabbi Gutterman's] prayer," that school officials "monitor prayer," and attempted to "compose official prayers," and that the "government involvement with religious activity in this case is pervasive," is difficult to fathom.

These distortions of the record are, of course, not harmless error: without them the Court's solemn assertion that the school officials could reasonably be perceived to be "enforc[ing] a religious orthodoxy," would ring as hollow as it ought.

The deeper flaw in the Court's opinion does not lie in its wrong answer to the question whether there was state-induced "peer-pressure" coercion; it lies, rather, in the Court's making violation of the Establishment Clause hinge on such a precious question. The coercion that was a hallmark of historical establishments of religion was coercion of religious orthodoxy and of financial support by force of law and threat of penalty. Typically, attendance at the state church was required; only clergy of the official church could lawfully perform sacraments; and dissenters, if tolerated, faced an array of civil disabilities.

The Establishment Clause was adopted to prohibit such an establishment of religion at the federal level (and to protect state establishments of religion from federal interference). I will further acknowledge for the sake of argument that, as some scholars have argued, by 1790 the term "establishment" had acquired an additional meaning—"financial support of religion generally, by public taxation"—that reflected the development of "general or multiple" establishments, not limited to a single church. But that would still be an establishment coerced by force of law. And I will further concede that our constitutional tradition, from the Declaration of Independence and the first inaugural address of Washington . . . , down to the present day, has, with a few aberrations, ruled out of order government-sponsored endorsement of religion—even when no legal coercion is present, and indeed even when no ersatz, "peer-pressure" psycho-coercion is present—where the endorsement is sectarian, in the sense of specifying details upon which men and women who believe in a benevolent, omnipotent Creator and Ruler of the world are known to differ (for example, the divinity of Christ). But there is simply no support for the proposition that the officially sponsored nondenominational invocation and benediction read by Rabbi Gutterman—with no one legally coerced to recite them—violated the Constitution of the United States. To the contrary, they are so characteristically American they could have come from the pen of George Washington or Abraham Lincoln himself.

This historical discussion places in revealing perspective the Court's extravagant claim that the State has "for all practical purposes," and "in every practical sense," compelled students to participate in prayers at graduation. Beyond the fact, stipulated to by the parties, that attendance at graduation is voluntary, there is nothing in the record to indicate that failure of attending students to take part in the invocation or benediction was subject to any penalty or discipline. Contrast this with, for example, the facts of *Barnette*: Schoolchildren were required by law to recite the Pledge of Allegiance; failure to do so resulted in expulsion, threatened the expelled child with the prospect of being sent to a reformatory for criminally inclined juveniles, and subjected his parents to prosecution (and incarceration) for causing delinquency. To characterize the "subtle coercive pressures," allegedly present here as the "practical" equivalent of the legal sanctions in *Barnette* is . . . well, let me just say it is not a "delicate and fact-sensitive" analysis.

Our Religion Clause jurisprudence has become bedeviled (so to speak) by reliance on formulaic abstractions that are not derived from, but positively conflict with, our long-accepted constitutional traditions. Foremost among these has been the so-called *Lemon* test, which has received well-earned criticism from many Members of this Court. The Court today demonstrates the irrelevance of *Lemon* by essentially ignoring it, and the interment of that case may be the one happy byproduct of the Court's otherwise lamentable decision. Unfortunately, however, the Court has replaced *Lemon* with its psycho-coercion test, which suffers the double disability of having no roots whatever in our people's historic practice, and being as infinitely expandable as the reasons for psychotherapy itself.

Another happy aspect of the case is that it is only a jurisprudential disaster and not a practical one. Given the odd basis for the Court's decision, invocations and benedictions will be able to be given at public school graduations next June, as they have for the past century and a half, so long as school authorities make clear that anyone who abstains from screaming in protest does not necessarily participate in the prayers. All that is seemingly needed is an announcement, or perhaps a written insertion at the beginning of the graduation program, to the effect that, while all are asked to rise for the invocation and benediction, none is compelled to join in them, nor will be assumed, by rising, to have done so. That obvious fact recited, the graduates and their parents may proceed to thank God, as Americans have always done, for the blessings He has generously bestowed on them and on their country.

The reader has been told much in this case about the personal interest of Mr. Weisman and his daughter, and very little about the personal interests on the other side. They are not inconsequential. Church and state would not be such a difficult subject if religion were, as the Court apparently thinks it to be, some purely personal avocation that can be indulged entirely in secret, like pornography, in the privacy of one's room. For most believers it is not that, and has never been. Religious men and women of almost all denominations have felt it necessary to acknowledge and beseech the blessing of God as a people, and not just as individuals, because they believe in the "protection of divine Providence," as the Declaration of Independence put it, not just for individuals but for societies; because they believe God to be, as Washington's first Thanksgiving Proclamation put it, the "Great Lord and Ruler of Nations." One can believe in the effectiveness of such public worship, or one can deprecate and deride it. But the longstanding American tradition of prayer at official ceremonies displays with unmistakable clarity that the Establishment Clause does not forbid the government to accommodate it.

The narrow context of the present case involves a community's celebration of one of the milestones in its young citizens' lives, and it is a bold step for this Court to seek to banish from that occasion, and from thousands of similar celebrations throughout this land, the expression of gratitude to God that a majority of the community wishes to make. The issue before us today is not the abstract philosophical question whether the alternative of frustrating this desire of a religious majority is to be preferred over the alternative of imposing "psychological coercion," or a feeling of exclusion, upon nonbelievers. Rather, the question is whether a mandatory choice in favor of the former has been imposed by the United States Constitution. As the age-old practices of our people show, the answer to that question is not at all in doubt.

I must add one final observation: The Founders of our Republic knew the fearsome potential of sectarian religious belief to generate civil dissension and civil strife. And they also knew that nothing, absolutely nothing, is so inclined to foster among religious believers of various faiths a toleration—no, an affection—for one another than voluntarily joining in prayer together, to the God whom they all worship and seek. Needless to say, no one should be compelled to do that, but it is a shame to deprive our public culture of the opportunity, and indeed the encouragement, for people to do it voluntarily. The Baptist or Catholic who heard and joined in the simple and inspiring prayers of Rabbi Gutterman on this official and patriotic occasion was inoculated from religious bigotry and prejudice in a manner that cannot be replicated. To deprive our society of that important unifying mechanism, in order to spare the nonbeliever what seems to me the minimal inconvenience of standing or even sitting in respectful nonparticipation, is as senseless in policy as it is unsupported in law.

For the foregoing reasons, I dissent.

Notes and Queries

1. Did the majority employ the *Lemon* test? Did it modify it? Or, as Justice Scalia claims, did it replace *Lemon* with a "psycho-coercion" test?

2. What does the majority mean by the term "coercion"? In what sense, if any, were students who attended the ceremony "coerced"? Contrast the majority's use of the term with Justice Scalia's understanding of "coercion." Does the text of the Constitution—or any other source of constitutional meaning, such as originalism, or the purpose(s) of the First Amendment—give us any reason to prefer one definition to another?

3. The majority opinion, Justice Souter's concurrence, and Justice Scalia's dissent all claim to rely on "tradition" to support their interpretation of the Constitution. What are we to make of a method of interpretation that leaves judges free to disagree with each other so widely? What, precisely, do the justices disagree over? Do they find different meanings in the same tradition, or do they identify different traditions? Or do they disagree about how much weight we should attach to tradition?

4. In his concurrence, Justice Blackmun argued that "When the government arrogates to itself a role in religious affairs, it abandons its obligations as guarantor of democracy." In what sense is the government—or the Supreme Court—a guarantor of democracy? What understanding of judicial power is implicit in this claim? Is that understanding supported by the constitutional text? By history?

5. What understanding of the relationship between individual liberty and community interests does the majority embrace? How does it differ from Justice Scalia's?

6. The Court approaches the question in *Lee* from the perspective of the individual students who wish not to participate in a religious ceremony. In other words, it seeks to protect the negative religious liberty of nonparticipants. In so doing, doesn't the Court do damage to another understanding of religious liberty, one that emphasizes the positive expression of faith? Does the Constitution give us a reason to prefer one approach to religious liberty to the other?

7. In *Santa Fe Independent School District v. Doe* (2000), the Court considered a challenge by Mormon and Catholic students at a Santa Fe high school to a longstanding school policy of having a student lead a prayer over the public address system before varsity football games. After the suit was filed, the school district changed the policy, which authorized two student elections—the first to determine whether "invocations" should be delivered before the games, and the second to select a spokesperson to deliver them. The 6–3 majority, led by Justice Stevens, concluded that the practice did violate the Establishment Clause and in so doing reaffirmed the decision in *Lee*. In dissent, Chief Justice Rehnquist again criticized the *Lemon* test, noting that in *Lee* the Court "did not feel compelled" to apply it. The Chief Justice also distinguished Lee, noting that in *Lee* the speech was "directed and controlled," whereas in this case it was "selected or created by a student." Does the distinction matter? Why?

Good News Club et al. v. Milford Central School

533 U.S. 98, 121 S. Ct. 2093, 150 L. Ed. 2d 151 (2001)

The Milford school district adopted a policy that allowed members of the public to use school facilities after hours, within certain conditions. The Good News Club, a private Christian organization, sought to use space at the Milford Central School to hold their meetings. The superintendent denied the request because in his view the Club's meetings were the "equivalent of religious worship," and thus prohibited by the policy, which barred the use of the school "for religious purposes." Opinion by: *Thomas*, Rehnquist, O'Connor, Scalia, Kennedy, Breyer (in part); Concurring opinion: *Scalia*; *Breyer* (in part); Dissenting opinion: *Stevens*; *Souter*, Ginsburg.

Justice THOMAS delivered the opinion of the Court.

This case presents two questions. The first question is whether Milford Central School violated the free speech rights of the Good News Club when it excluded the Club from meeting after hours at the school. The second question is whether any such violation is justified by Milford's concern that permitting the Club's activities would violate the Establishment Clause. We conclude that Milford's restriction violates the Club's free speech rights and that no Establishment Clause concern justifies that violation.

II

The standards that we apply to determine whether a State has unconstitutionally excluded a private speaker from use of a public forum depend on the nature of the forum. If the forum is a traditional or open public forum, the State's restrictions on speech are subject to stricter scrutiny than are restrictions in a limited public forum. . . . [W]e simply will assume that Milford operates a limited public forum.

When the State establishes a limited public forum, the State is not required to and does not allow persons to engage in every type of speech. The State may be justified "in reserving [its forum] for certain groups or for the discussion of certain topics." *Rosenberger v. Rector and Visitors of Univ. of Va* (1995). The State's power to restrict speech, however, is not without limits. The restriction must not discriminate against speech on the basis of viewpoint, and the restriction must be "reasonable in light of the purpose served by the forum. . . ."

III

Applying this test, we first address whether the exclusion constituted viewpoint discrimination. We are guided in our analysis by two of our prior opinions, *Lamb's Chapel* and *Rosenberger*. In *Lamb's Chapel*, we held that a school district violated the Free Speech Clause of the First Amendment when it excluded a private group from presenting films at the school based solely on the films' discussions of family values from a religious perspective. Likewise, in *Rosenberger*, we held that a university's refusal to fund a student publication because the publication addressed issues from a religious perspective violated the Free Speech Clause. Concluding that Milford's exclusion of the Good News Club based on its religious nature is indistinguishable from the exclusions in these cases, we hold that the exclusion constitutes viewpoint discrimination. Because the restriction is viewpoint discriminatory, we need not decide whether it is unreasonable in light of the purposes served by the forum.

Milford has opened its limited public forum to activities that serve a variety of purposes, including events "pertaining to the welfare of the community." Milford interprets its policy to permit discussions of subjects such as child rearing, and of "the development of character and morals from a religious perspective." For example, this policy would allow someone to use Aesop's Fables to teach children moral values. Additionally, a group could sponsor a debate on whether there should be a constitutional amendment to permit prayer in public schools, and the Boy Scouts could meet "to influence a boy's character, development and spiritual growth." In short, any group that "promote[s] the moral and character development of children" is eligible to use the school building.

Just as there is no question that teaching morals and character development to children is a permissible purpose under Milford's policy, it is clear that the Club teaches morals and character development to children. For example, no one disputes that the Club instructs children to overcome feelings of jealousy, to treat others well regardless of how they treat the children, and to be obedient, even if it does so in a nonsecular way. Nonetheless, because Milford found the Club's activities to be religious in nature—"the equivalent of religious instruction itself,"—it excluded the Club from use of its facilities.

. . . [W]e find it quite clear that Milford engaged in viewpoint discrimination when it excluded the Club from the after school forum.

Like the church in *Lamb's Chapel*, the Club seeks to address a subject otherwise permitted under the rule, the teaching of morals and character, from a religious standpoint. Certainly, one could have characterized the film presentations in *Lamb's Chapel* as a religious use. . . . And one easily could conclude that the films' purpose to instruct that "society's slide toward humanism . . . can only be counterbalanced by a loving home where Christian values are instilled from an early age" was "quintessentially religious." The only apparent difference between the activity of *Lamb's Chapel* and the activities of the Good News Club is that the Club chooses to teach moral lessons from a Christian perspective through live storytelling and prayer, whereas *Lamb's Chapel* taught lessons through films. This distinction is inconsequential.

Our opinion in *Rosenberger* also is dispositive. In *Rosenberger*, a student organization at the University of Virginia was denied funding for printing expenses because its publication, *Wide Awake,* offered a Christian viewpoint. Just as the Club emphasizes the role of Christianity in students' morals and character, *Wide Awake* "challenge[d] Christians to live, in word and deed, according to the faith they proclaim and . . . encourage[d] students to consider what a personal relationship with Jesus Christ means." Because the university "select[ed] for disfavored treatment those student journalistic efforts with religious editorial viewpoints," we held that the denial of funding was unconstitutional. Although in *Rosenberger* there was no prohibition on religion as a subject matter, our holding did not rely on this factor. Instead, we concluded simply that the university's denial of funding to print *Wide Awake* was viewpoint discrimination.

We disagree that something that is "quintessentially religious" or "decidedly religious in nature" cannot also be characterized properly as the teaching of morals and character development from a particular viewpoint. . . . What matters for purposes of the Free Speech Clause is that we can see no logical difference in kind between the invocation of Christianity by the Club and the invocation of teamwork, loyalty, or patriotism by other associations to provide a foundation for their lessons. . . . [W]e reaffirm our holdings in *Lamb's Chapel* and *Rosenberger* that speech discussing otherwise permissible subjects cannot be excluded from a limited public forum on the ground that the subject is discussed from a religious viewpoint. Thus, we conclude that Milford's exclusion of the Club from use of the school, pursuant to its community use policy, constitutes impermissible viewpoint discrimination.

IV

Milford argues that, even if its restriction constitutes viewpoint discrimination, its interest in not violating the Establishment Clause outweighs the Club's interest in gaining equal access to the school's facilities. In other words, according to Milford, its restriction was required to avoid violating the Establishment Clause. We disagree.

We have said that a state interest in avoiding an Establishment Clause violation "may be characterized as compelling," and therefore may justify content-based discrimination. *Widmar v. Vincent* (1981). However, it is not clear whether a State's interest in avoiding an Establishment Clause violation would justify viewpoint discrimination. We need not, however, confront the issue in this case, because we conclude that the school has no valid Establishment Clause interest.

We rejected Establishment Clause defenses similar to Milford's in two previous free speech cases, *Lamb's Chapel* and *Widmar*. . . .

The Establishment Clause defense fares no better in this case. As in *Lamb's Chapel*, the Club's meetings were held after school hours, not sponsored by the school, and open to any student who obtained parental consent, not just to Club members. As in *Widmar*, Milford made its forum available to other organizations. The Club's activities are materially indistinguishable from those in *Lamb's Chapel* and *Widmar*.

Milford attempts to distinguish *Lamb's Chapel* and *Widmar* by emphasizing that Milford's policy involves elementary school children. According to Milford, children will perceive that the school is endorsing the Club and will feel coercive pressure to participate, because the Club's activities take place on school grounds, even though they occur during nonschool hours. This argument is unpersuasive.

First, we have held that "a significant factor in upholding governmental programs in the face of Establishment Clause attack is their neutrality towards religion." *Rosenberger*. Milford's implication that granting access to the Club would do damage to the neutrality principle defies logic. For the "guarantee of neutrality is respected, not offended, when the government, following neutral criteria and evenhanded policies, extends benefits to recipients whose ideologies and viewpoints, including religious ones, are broad and diverse." *Rosenberger*. The Good News Club seeks nothing more than to be treated neutrally and given access to speak about the same topics as are other groups. Because allowing the Club to speak on school grounds would ensure neutrality, not threaten it, Milford faces an uphill battle in arguing that the Establishment Clause compels it to exclude the Good News Club.

Second, to the extent we consider whether the community would feel coercive pressure to engage in the Club's activities, the relevant community would be the parents, not the elementary school children. It is the parents who choose whether their children will attend the Good News Club meetings. Because the children cannot attend without their parents' permission, they cannot be coerced into engaging in the Good News Club's religious activities. Milford does not suggest that the parents of elementary school children would be confused about whether the school was endorsing religion. Nor do we believe that such an argument could be reasonably advanced.

Third, whatever significance we may have assigned in the Establishment Clause context to the suggestion that elementary school children are more impressionable than adults, we have never extended our Establishment Clause jurisprudence to foreclose private religious conduct during nonschool hours merely because it takes place on school premises where elementary school children may be present.

Equally unsupportive is *Edwards v. Aguillard* (1987), in which we held that a Louisiana law that proscribed the teaching of evolution as part of the public school curriculum, unless accompanied by a lesson on creationism, violated the Establishment Clause. In *Edwards*, we mentioned that students are susceptible to pressure in the classroom, particularly given their possible reliance on teachers as role models. But we did not discuss this concern in our application of the law to the facts. Moreover, we did note that mandatory attendance requirements meant that State advancement of religion in a school would be particularly harshly felt by impressionable students. But we did not suggest that, when the school was not actually advancing religion, the impressionability of students would be relevant to the Establishment Clause issue.

Fourth, even if we were to consider the possible misperceptions by schoolchildren in deciding whether Milford's permitting the Club's activities would violate the Establishment Clause, the facts of this case simply do not support Milford's conclusion. There is no evidence that young children are permitted to loiter outside classrooms after the school day has ended. Surely even young children are aware of events for which their parents must sign permission forms. The meetings were held in a combined high school resource room and middle school special education room, not in an elementary school classroom. The instructors are not schoolteachers. And the children in the group are not all the same age as in the normal classroom setting; their ages range from 6 to 12. In sum, these circumstances simply do not support the theory that small children would perceive endorsement here.

Finally, even if we were to inquire into the minds of schoolchildren in this case, we cannot say the danger that children would misperceive the endorsement of religion is any greater than the danger that they would perceive a hostility toward the religious viewpoint if the Club were excluded from the public forum. This concern is particularly acute given the reality that Milford's building is not

used only for elementary school children. . . . There may be as many, if not more, upperclassmen than elementary school children who occupy the school after hours. For that matter, members of the public writ large are permitted in the school after hours pursuant to the community use policy. Any bystander could conceivably be aware of the school's use policy and its exclusion of the Good News Club, and could suffer as much from viewpoint discrimination as elementary school children could suffer from perceived endorsement.

We cannot operate, as Milford would have us do, under the assumption that any risk that small children would perceive endorsement should counsel in favor of excluding the Club's religious activity. We decline to employ Establishment Clause jurisprudence using a modified heckler's veto, in which a group's religious activity can be proscribed on the basis of what the youngest members of the audience might misperceive. . . . There are countervailing constitutional concerns related to rights of other individuals in the community. In this case, those countervailing concerns are the free speech rights of the Club and its members. And, we have already found that those rights have been violated, not merely perceived to have been violated, by the school's actions toward the Club.

Accordingly, we conclude that permitting the Club to meet on the school's premises would not have violated the Establishment Clause.

The judgment of the Court of Appeals is reversed, and the case is remanded for further proceedings consistent with this opinion.

It is so ordered.

Justice SCALIA, concurring.

I join the Court's opinion but write separately to explain further my views on two issues.

First, I join Part IV of the Court's opinion, regarding the Establishment Clause issue, with the understanding that its consideration of coercive pressure, and perceptions of endorsement, "to the extent" that the law makes such factors relevant, is consistent with the belief (which I hold) that in this case that extent is zero. As to coercive pressure: Physical coercion is not at issue here; and so-called "peer pressure," if it can even be considered coercion, is, when it arises from private activities, one of the attendant consequences of a freedom of association that is constitutionally protected. . . . What is at play here is not coercion, but the compulsion of ideas—and the private right to exert and receive that compulsion (or to have one's children receive it) is protected by the Free Speech and Free Exercise Clauses, not banned by the Establishment Clause. A priest has as much liberty to proselytize as a patriot.

As to endorsement, I have previously written that "[r]eligious expression cannot violate the Establishment Clause where it (1) is purely private and (2) occurs in a traditional or designated public forum, publicly announced and open to all on equal terms." *Capitol Square Review and Advisory Bd. v. Pinette* (1995). The same is true of private speech that occurs in a limited public forum, publicly announced, whose boundaries are not drawn to favor religious groups but instead permit a cross-section of uses.

From no other group does respondent require the sterility of speech that it demands of petitioners. The Boy Scouts could undoubtedly buttress their exhortations to keep "morally straight" and live "clean" lives, see *Boy Scouts of America v. Dale* (2000), by giving reasons why that is a good idea—because parents want and expect it, because it will make the scouts "better" and "more successful" people, because it will emulate such admired past Scouts as former President Gerald Ford. The Club, however, may only discuss morals and character, and cannot give its reasons why they should be fostered—because God wants and expects it, because it will make the Club members "saintly" people, and because it emulates Jesus Christ. The Club may not, in other words, independently discuss the religious premise on which its views are based—that God exists and His assistance is necessary to morality. It may not defend the premise, and it absolutely must not seek to persuade the children that the premise is true. The children must, so to say, take it on faith. This is blatant viewpoint discrimination. Just as calls to character based on patriotism will go unanswered if the listeners do not believe their country is good and just, calls to moral behavior based on God's will are useless if the listeners do not believe that God exists. Effectiveness in presenting a viewpoint rests on the persuasiveness with which the speaker defends his premise—and in respondent's facilities every premise but a religious one may be defended.

The dissenters emphasize that the religious speech used by the Club as the foundation for its views on morals and character is not just any type of religious speech—although they cannot agree exactly what type of religious speech it is. In Justice Stevens' view, it is speech "aimed principally at proselytizing or inculcating belief in a particular religious faith. . . ." This does not, to begin with, distinguish *Rosenberger*, which also involved proselytizing speech, as the above quotations show. But in addition, it does not distinguish the Club's activities from those of the other groups using respondent's forum—which have not, as Justice Stevens suggests, been restricted to roundtable "discussions" of moral issues. Those groups may seek to inculcate children with their beliefs, and they may furthermore "recruit others to join their respective groups." The

Club must therefore have liberty to do the same. . . . even if, as Justice Stevens fears without support in the record, its actions may prove (shudder!) divisive.

Justice BREYER, concurring in part.

Justice STEVENS, dissenting.

The Milford Central School has invited the public to use its facilities for educational and recreational purposes, but not for "religious purposes." Speech for "religious purposes" may reasonably be understood to encompass three different categories. First, there is religious speech that is simply speech about a particular topic from a religious point of view. . . . Second, there is religious speech that amounts to worship, or its equivalent. . . . Third, there is an intermediate category that is aimed principally at proselytizing or inculcating belief in a particular religious faith.

The novel question that this case presents concerns the constitutionality of a public school's attempt to limit the scope of a public forum it has created. More specifically, the question is whether a school can, consistently with the First Amendment, create a limited public forum that admits the first type of religious speech without allowing the other two.

Distinguishing speech from a religious viewpoint, on the one hand, from religious proselytizing, on the other, is comparable to distinguishing meetings to discuss political issues from meetings whose principal purpose is to recruit new members to join a political organization. If a school decides to authorize after school discussions of current events in its classrooms, it may not exclude people from expressing their views simply because it dislikes their particular political opinions. But must it therefore allow organized political groups—for example, the Democratic Party, the Libertarian Party, or the Ku Klux Klan—to hold meetings, the principal purpose of which is not to discuss the current-events topic from their own unique point of view but rather to recruit others to join their respective groups? I think not. Such recruiting meetings may introduce divisiveness and tend to separate young children into cliques that undermine the school's educational mission.

School officials may reasonably believe that evangelical meetings designed to convert children to a particular religious faith pose the same risk. And, just as a school may allow meetings to discuss current events from a political perspective without also allowing organized political recruitment, so too can a school allow discussion of topics such as moral development from a religious (or nonreligious) perspective without thereby opening its forum to religious proselytizing or worship.

It is clear that, by "religious purposes," the school district did not intend to exclude all speech from a religious point of view. Instead, it sought only to exclude religious speech whose principal goal is to "promote the gospel." In other words, the school sought to allow the first type of religious speech while excluding the second and third types. As long as this is done in an even handed manner, I see no constitutional violation in such an effort. The line between the various categories of religious speech may be difficult to draw, but I think that the distinctions are valid, and that a school, particularly an elementary school, must be permitted to draw them.

This case is undoubtedly close. Nonetheless, regardless of whether the Good News Club's activities amount to "worship," it does seem clear, based on the facts in the record, that the school district correctly classified those activities as falling within the third category of religious speech and therefore beyond the scope of the school's limited public forum. In short, I am persuaded that the school district could (and did) permissibly exclude from its limited public forum proselytizing religious speech that does not rise to the level of actual worship. I would therefore affirm the judgment of the Court of Appeals.

Accordingly, I respectfully dissent.

Justice SOUTER, with whom Justice GINSBURG joins, dissenting.

It is beyond question that Good News intends to use the public school premises not for the mere discussion of a subject from a particular, Christian point of view, but for an evangelical service of worship calling children to commit themselves in an act of Christian conversion. The majority avoids this reality only by resorting to the bland and general characterization of Good News's activity as "teaching of morals and character, from a religious standpoint." If the majority's statement ignores reality, as it surely does, then today's holding may be understood only in equally generic terms. Otherwise, indeed, this case would stand for the remarkable proposition that any public school opened for civic meetings must be opened for use as a church, synagogue, or mosque.

Notes and Queries

1. In *Widmar v. Vincent* (1981), the Court acknowledged that a state's interest in avoiding a violation of the establishment clause might be "compelling." In *Good News*, however, the Court said that it is "not clear whether a State's interest in avoiding an Establishment Clause violation would justify viewpoint discrimination." Is it possible to reconcile these two positions? Or did the Court suggest that there is never a justification for viewpoint discrimination?

2. Is the majority opinion guided by *Lemon?* If not, what doctrinal approach did the majority use?

3. In dissent, Justice Stevens distinguished between three different types of religious speech. Is the distinction grounded in the Constitution, however narrowly or broadly defined? Is it a useful analytical device?

Zelman, Superintendent of Public Instruction of Ohio v. Simmons-Harris

536 U.S. 639, 122 S. Ct. 2460, 153 L. Ed. 2d 604 (2002)

Ohio provides financial assistance to families in any school district that is or has been "under federal court order requiring supervision and operational management of the district by the state superintendent." Cleveland is the only Ohio school district to fall within that category. The program provides two basic kinds of assistance to parents of children in a covered district. First, it provides tuition aid for students in kindergarten through third grade, expanding each year through eighth grade, to attend a public or private school of their parent's choosing. Second, the program provides tutorial aid for students who choose to remain enrolled in public school. Under the program, 96 percent of the students participating in the scholarship program were enrolled in religiously affiliated schools. Opinion by: *Rehnquist*, O'Connor, Scalia, Kennedy, Thomas; Concurring opinion: *O'Connor*, Thomas; Dissenting opinion: *Stevens*; *Souter*, Ginsburg, Breyer; *Breyer*, Stevens, Souter.

Chief Justice REHNQUIST delivered the opinion of the Court.

The State of Ohio has established a pilot program designed to provide educational choices to families with children who reside in the Cleveland City School District. The question presented is whether this program offends the Establishment Clause of the United States Constitution. We hold that it does not.

The Establishment Clause of the First Amendment, applied to the States through the Fourteenth Amendment, prevents a State from enacting laws that have the "purpose" or "effect" of advancing or inhibiting religion. There is no dispute that the program challenged here was enacted for the valid secular purpose of providing educational assistance to poor children in a demonstrably failing public school system. Thus, the question presented is whether the Ohio program nonetheless has the forbidden "effect" of advancing or inhibiting religion.

To answer that question, our decisions have drawn a consistent distinction between government programs that provide aid directly to religious schools, and programs of true private choice, in which government aid reaches religious schools only as a result of the genuine and independent choices of private individuals. While our jurisprudence with respect to the constitutionality of direct aid programs has "changed significantly" over the past two decades, our jurisprudence with respect to true private choice programs has remained consistent and unbroken. Three times we have confronted Establishment Clause challenges to neutral government programs that provide aid directly to a broad class of individuals, who, in turn, direct the aid to religious schools or institutions of their own choosing. Three times we have rejected such challenges.

In *Mueller*, we rejected an Establishment Clause challenge to a Minnesota program authorizing tax deductions for various educational expenses, including private school tuition costs, even though the great majority of the program's beneficiaries (96%) were parents of children in religious schools. We began by focusing on the class of beneficiaries, finding that because the class included "all parents," including parents with "children [who] attend nonsectarian private schools or sectarian private schools," the program was "not readily subject to challenge under the Establishment Clause. . . ." Then, viewing the program as a whole, we emphasized the principle of private choice, noting that public funds were made available to religious schools "only as a result of numerous, private choices of individual parents of school-age children." This, we said, ensured that "'no imprimatur of state approval' can be deemed to have been conferred on any particular religion, or on religion generally." We thus found it irrelevant to the constitutional inquiry that the vast majority of beneficiaries were parents of children in religious schools.

In *Witters*, we used identical reasoning to reject an Establishment Clause challenge to a vocational scholarship program that provided tuition aid to a student studying at a religious institution to become a pastor. Looking at the program as a whole, we observed that "[a]ny aid . . . that ultimately flows to religious institutions does so only as a result of the genuinely independent and private choices of aid recipients."

Finally, in *Zobrest*, we applied *Mueller* and *Witters* to reject an Establishment Clause challenge to a federal program that permitted sign-language interpreters to assist deaf children enrolled in religious schools. . . . Looking once again to the challenged program as a whole, we observed that the program "distributes benefits neutrally to any child qualifying as 'disabled.'" Its "primary beneficiaries," we said, were "disabled children, not sectarian schools."

Mueller, *Witters*, and *Zobrest* thus make clear that where a government aid program is neutral with respect to religion, and provides assistance directly to a broad class of citizens who, in turn, direct government aid to religious schools wholly as a result of their own genuine and independent private choice, the program is not readily subject to challenge under the Establishment Clause. A program that shares these features permits government aid to reach religious institutions only by way of the deliberate choices of numerous individual recipients. The incidental advancement of a religious mission, or the perceived endorsement of a religious message, is reasonably attributable to the individual recipient, not to the government, whose role ends with the disbursement of benefits. . . . It is precisely for these reasons that we have never found a program of true private choice to offend the Establishment Clause.

We believe that the program challenged here is a program of true private choice, consistent with *Mueller*, *Witters*, and *Zobrest*, and thus constitutional. As was true in those cases, the Ohio program is neutral in all respects toward religion. It is part of a general and multifaceted undertaking by the State of Ohio to provide educational opportunities to the children of a failed school district. It confers educational assistance directly to a broad class of individuals defined without reference to religion, i.e., any parent of a school-age child who resides in the Cleveland City School District. The program permits the participation of all schools within the district, religious or nonreligious. Adjacent public schools also may participate and have a financial incentive to do so. Program benefits are available to participating families on neutral terms, with no reference to religion. The only preference stated anywhere in the program is a preference for low-income families, who receive greater assistance and are given priority for admission at participating schools.

There are no "financial incentive[s]" that "ske[w]" the program toward religious schools. . . . The program here in fact creates financial disincentives for religious schools, with private schools receiving only half the government assistance given to community schools and one-third the assistance given to magnet schools. Adjacent public schools, should any choose to accept program students, are also eligible to receive two to three times the state funding of a private religious school. Families too have a financial disincentive to choose a private religious school over other schools. Parents that choose to participate in the scholarship program and then to enroll their children in a private school (religious or nonreligious) must copay a portion of the school's tuition. Families that choose a community school, magnet school, or traditional public school pay nothing. Although such features of the program are not necessary to its constitutionality, they clearly dispel the claim that the program "creates . . . financial incentive[s] for parents to choose a sectarian school."

Respondents suggest that even without a financial incentive for parents to choose a religious school, the program creates a "public perception that the State is endorsing religious practices and beliefs." But we have repeatedly recognized that no reasonable observer would think a neutral program of private choice, where state aid reaches religious schools solely as a result of the numerous independent decisions of private individuals, carries with it the imprimatur of government endorsement. The argument is particularly misplaced here since "the reasonable observer in the endorsement inquiry must be deemed aware" of the "history and context" underlying a challenged program. *Good News Club v. Milford Central School* (2001). Any objective observer familiar with the full history and context of the Ohio program would reasonably view it as one aspect of a broader undertaking to assist poor children in failed schools, not as an endorsement of religious schooling in general.

There also is no evidence that the program fails to provide genuine opportunities for Cleveland parents to select secular educational options for their school-age children. Cleveland schoolchildren enjoy a range of educational choices: They may remain in public school as before, remain in public school with publicly funded tutoring aid, obtain a scholarship and choose a religious school, obtain a scholarship and choose a nonreligious private school, enroll in a community school, or enroll in a magnet school. That 46 of the 56 private schools now participating in the program are religious schools does not condemn it as a violation of the Establishment Clause. The Establishment Clause question is whether Ohio is coercing parents into sending their children to religious schools, and that question must be answered by evaluating all options Ohio provides Cleveland schoolchildren, only one of which is to obtain a program scholarship and then choose a religious school.

Justice Souter speculates that because more private religious schools currently participate in the program, the program itself must somehow discourage the participation of private nonreligious schools. But Cleveland's preponderance of religiously affiliated private schools certainly did not arise as a result of the program; it is a phenomenon common to many American cities. Indeed, by all accounts the program has captured a remarkable cross-section of private schools, religious and nonreligious. It is true that 82% of Cleveland's participating private schools are religious schools, but it is also true that 81% of private schools in Ohio are religious schools. To attribute constitutional significance to this figure, moreover, would lead to the absurd result that a neutral school-choice program might be permissible in some parts of Ohio, but not in inner-city Cleveland, where Ohio has deemed such programs most sorely needed, but where the preponderance of religious schools happens to be greater. Likewise, an identical private choice program might be constitutional in some States, such as Maine or Utah, where less than 45% of private schools are religious schools, but not in other States, such as Nebraska or Kansas, where over 90% of private schools are religious schools.

Respondents and Justice Souter claim that even if we do not focus on the number of participating schools that are religious schools, we should attach constitutional significance to the fact that 96% of scholarship recipients have enrolled in religious schools. They claim that this alone proves parents lack genuine choice, even if no parent has ever said so. We need not consider this argument in detail, since it was flatly rejected in *Mueller*, where we found it irrelevant that 96% of parents taking deductions for tuition expenses paid tuition at religious schools. Indeed, we have recently found it irrelevant even to the constitutionality of a direct aid program that a vast majority of program benefits went to religious schools. The constitutionality of a neutral educational aid program simply does not turn on whether and why, in a particular area, at a particular time, most private schools are run by religious organizations, or most recipients choose to use the aid at a religious school.

In sum, the Ohio program is entirely neutral with respect to religion. It provides benefits directly to a wide spectrum of individuals, defined only by financial need and residence in a particular school district. It permits such individuals to exercise genuine choice among options public and private, secular and religious. The program is therefore a program of true private choice. In keeping with an unbroken line of decisions rejecting challenges to similar programs, we hold that the program does not offend the Establishment Clause.

The judgment of the Court of Appeals is reversed.

It is so ordered.

Justice O'CONNOR, concurring.

While I join the Court's opinion, I write separately for two reasons. First, although the Court takes an important step, I do not believe that today's decision, when considered in light of other longstanding government programs that impact religious organizations and our prior Establishment Clause jurisprudence, marks a dramatic break from the past. Second, given the emphasis the Court places on verifying that parents of voucher students in religious schools have exercised "true private choice," I think it is worth elaborating on the Court's conclusion that this inquiry should consider all reasonable educational alternatives to religious schools that are available to parents. To do otherwise is to ignore how the educational system in Cleveland actually functions.

These cases are different from prior indirect aid cases in part because a significant portion of the funds appropriated for the voucher program reach religious schools without restrictions on the use of these funds. The share of public resources that reach religious schools is not, however, as significant as respondents suggest.

Even if one assumes that all voucher students came from low-income families and that each voucher student used up the entire $2,250 voucher, at most $8.2 million of public funds flowed to religious schools under the voucher program in 1999–2000. Although just over one-half as many students attended community schools as religious private schools on the state fisc, the State spent over $1 million more—$9.4 million—on students in community schools than on students in religious private schools because per-pupil aid to community schools is more than double the per-pupil aid to private schools under the voucher program. Moreover, the amount spent on religious private schools is minor compared to the $114.8 million the State spent on students in the Cleveland magnet schools.

Against this background, the support that the Cleveland voucher program provides religious institutions is neither substantial nor atypical of existing government programs. While this observation is not intended to justify the Cleveland voucher program under the Establishment Clause it places in broader perspective alarmist claims about implications of the Cleveland program and the Court's decision in these cases.

Nor does today's decision signal a major departure from this Court's prior Establishment Clause jurisprudence. A central tool in our analysis of cases in this area has been the *Lemon* test. As originally formulated, a statute passed this test only if it had "a secular legislative purpose," if its "principal or primary effect" was one that "neither ad-

vance[d] nor inhibit[ed] religion," and if it did "not foster an excessive government entanglement with religion." *Lemon v. Kurtzman* (1971). . . . In *Agostini v. Felton*, (1997), we folded the entanglement inquiry into the primary effect inquiry. This made sense because both inquiries rely on the same evidence, and the degree of entanglement has implications for whether a statute advances or inhibits religion.

The Court's opinion in these cases focuses on a narrow question related to the *Lemon* test: how to apply the primary effects prong in indirect aid cases? Specifically, it clarifies the basic inquiry when trying to determine whether a program that distributes aid to beneficiaries, rather than directly to service providers, has the primary effect of advancing or inhibiting religion. . . . Courts are instructed to consider two factors: first, whether the program administers aid in a neutral fashion, without differentiation based on the religious status of beneficiaries or providers of services; second, and more importantly, whether beneficiaries of indirect aid have a genuine choice among religious and nonreligious organizations when determining the organization to which they will direct that aid. If the answer to either query is "no," the program should be struck down under the Establishment Clause.

There is little question in my mind that the Cleveland voucher program is neutral as between religious schools and nonreligious schools. Justice Souter rejects the Court's notion of neutrality, proposing that the neutrality of a program should be gauged not by the opportunities it presents but rather by its effects. In particular, a "neutrality test . . . [should] focus on a category of aid that may be directed to religious as well as secular schools, and ask whether the scheme favors a religious direction." Justice Souter doubts that the Cleveland program is neutral under this view. He surmises that the cap on tuition that voucher schools may charge low-income students encourages these students to attend religious rather than nonreligious private voucher schools. But Justice Souter's notion of neutrality is inconsistent with that in our case law. As we put it in *Agostini*, government aid must be "made available to both religious and secular beneficiaries on a non-discriminatory basis."

I do not agree that the nonreligious schools have failed to provide Cleveland parents reasonable alternatives to religious schools in the voucher program.

Justice THOMAS, concurring.

Frederick Douglass once said that "[e]ducation . . . means emancipation. It means light and liberty. It means the uplifting of the soul of man into the glorious light of truth, the light by which men can only be made free." Today many of our inner-city public schools deny emancipation to urban minority students. Despite this Court's observation nearly 50 years ago in *Brown v. Board of Education,* that "it is doubtful that any child may reasonably be expected to succeed in life if he is denied the opportunity of an education," urban children have been forced into a system that continually fails them. These cases present an example of such failures. Besieged by escalating financial problems and declining academic achievement, the Cleveland City School District was in the midst of an academic emergency when Ohio enacted its scholarship program.

The Fourteenth Amendment fundamentally restructured the relationship between individuals and the States and ensured that States would not deprive citizens of liberty without due process of law. It guarantees citizenship to all individuals born or naturalized in the United States and provides that "[n]o State shall make or enforce any law which shall abridge the privileges; nor shall any State deprive any person of life, liberty, or property, without due process of law; nor deny to any person within its jurisdiction the equal protection of the laws.". . . . When rights are incorporated against the States through the Fourteenth Amendment they should advance, not constrain, individual liberty.

Consequently, in the context of the Establishment Clause, it may well be that state action should be evaluated on different terms than similar action by the Federal Government. "States, while bound to observe strict neutrality, should be freer to experiment with involvement [in religion]—on a neutral basis—than the Federal Government." Thus, while the Federal Government may "make no law respecting an establishment of religion," the States may pass laws that include or touch on religious matters so long as these laws do not impede free exercise rights or any other individual religious liberty interest. By considering the particular religious liberty right alleged to be invaded by a State, federal courts can strike a proper balance between the demands of the Fourteenth Amendment on the one hand and the federalism prerogatives of States on the other.

Whatever the textual and historical merits of incorporating the Establishment Clause, I can accept that the Fourteenth Amendment protects religious liberty rights. But I cannot accept its use to oppose neutral programs of school choice through the incorporation of the Establishment Clause. There would be a tragic irony in converting the Fourteenth Amendment's guarantee of individual liberty into a prohibition on the exercise of educational choice.

The wisdom of allowing States greater latitude in dealing with matters of religion and education can be easily appreciated in this context. Respondents advocate using the Fourteenth Amendment to handcuff the State's ability to experiment with education. But without education one can hardly exercise the civic, political, and personal freedoms conferred by the Fourteenth Amendment. Faced with a severe educational crisis, the State of Ohio enacted wide-ranging educational reform that allows voluntary participation of private and religious schools in educating poor urban children otherwise condemned to failing public schools. The program does not force any individual to submit to religious indoctrination or education. It simply gives parents a greater choice as to where and in what manner to educate their children. This is a choice that those with greater means have routinely exercised.

Although one of the purposes of public schools was to promote democracy and a more egalitarian culture, failing urban public schools disproportionately affect minority children most in need of educational opportunity. At the time of Reconstruction, blacks considered public education "a matter of personal liberation and a necessary function of a free society." J. Anderson, *Education of Blacks in the South,* 1860–1935, p. 18 (1988). Today, however, the promise of public school education has failed poor inner-city blacks. While in theory providing education to everyone, the quality of public schools varies significantly across districts. Just as blacks supported public education during Reconstruction, many blacks and other minorities now support school choice programs because they provide the greatest educational opportunities for their children in struggling communities. Opponents of the program raise formalistic concerns about the Establishment Clause but ignore the core purposes of the Fourteenth Amendment.

While the romanticized ideal of universal public education resonates with the cognoscenti who oppose vouchers, poor urban families just want the best education for their children, who will certainly need it to function in our high-tech and advanced society. As Thomas Sowell noted 30 years ago: "Most black people have faced too many grim, concrete problems to be romantics. They want and need certain tangible results, which can be achieved only by developing certain specific abilities." *Black Education: Myths and Tragedies* 228 (1972). The same is true today. An individual's life prospects increase dramatically with each successfully completed phase of education. For instance, a black high school dropout earns just over $13,500, but with a high school degree the average income is almost $21,000. Blacks with a bachelor's degree have an average annual income of about $37,500, and $75,500 with a professional degree. The failure to provide education to poor urban children perpetuates a vicious cycle of poverty, dependence, criminality, and alienation that continues for the remainder of their lives. If society cannot end racial discrimination, at least it can arm minorities with the education to defend themselves from some of discrimination's effects.

. . . [S]chool choice programs that involve religious schools appear unconstitutional only to those who would twist the Fourteenth Amendment against itself by expansively incorporating the Establishment Clause. Converting the Fourteenth Amendment from a guarantee of opportunity to an obstacle against education reform distorts our constitutional values and disserves those in the greatest need.

As Frederick Douglass poignantly noted "no greater benefit can be bestowed upon a long benighted people, than giving to them, as we are here earnestly this day endeavoring to do, the means of an education."

Justice STEVENS, dissenting.

Is a law that authorizes the use of public funds to pay for the indoctrination of thousands of grammar school children in particular religious faiths a "law respecting an establishment of religion" within the meaning of the First Amendment? In answering that question, I think we should ignore three factual matters that are discussed at length by my colleagues.

First, the severe educational crisis that confronted the Cleveland City School District when Ohio enacted its voucher program is not a matter that should affect our appraisal of its constitutionality.

Second, the wide range of choices that have been made available to students within the public school system has no bearing on the question whether the State may pay the tuition for students who wish to reject public education entirely and attend private schools that will provide them with a sectarian education. The fact that the vast majority of the voucher recipients who have entirely rejected public education receive religious indoctrination at state expense does, however, support the claim that the law is one "respecting an establishment of religion."

Third, the voluntary character of the private choice to prefer a parochial education over an education in the public school system seems to me quite irrelevant to the question whether the government's choice to pay for religious indoctrination is constitutionally permissible. Today, however, the Court seems to have decided that the mere fact that a family that cannot afford a private education wants its children educated in a parochial school is a sufficient justification for this use of public funds.

For the reasons stated by Justice Souter and Justice

Breyer, I am convinced that the Court's decision is profoundly misguided. Admittedly, in reaching that conclusion I have been influenced by my understanding of the impact of religious strife on the decisions of our forbears to migrate to this continent, and on the decisions of neighbors in the Balkans, Northern Ireland, and the Middle East to mistrust one another. Whenever we remove a brick from the wall that was designed to separate religion and government, we increase the risk of religious strife and weaken the foundation of our democracy.

I respectfully dissent.

Justice SOUTER, with whom Justice STEVENS, Justice GINSBURG, and Justice BREYER join, dissenting.

If there were an excuse for giving short shrift to the Establishment Clause, it would probably apply here. But there is no excuse. Constitutional limitations are placed on government to preserve constitutional values in hard cases, like these. "[C]onstitutional lines have to be drawn, and on one side of every one of them is an otherwise sympathetic case that provokes impatience with the Constitution and with the line. But constitutional lines are the price of constitutional government." *Agostini v. Felton* (1997) (Souter, J., dissenting). I therefore respectfully dissent. . . .

How can a Court consistently leave *Everson* on the books and approve the Ohio vouchers? The answer is that it cannot. It is only by ignoring *Everson* that the majority can claim to rest on traditional law in its invocation of neutral aid provisions and private choice to sanction the Ohio law. It is, moreover, only by ignoring the meaning of neutrality and private choice themselves that the majority can even pretend to rest today's decision on those criteria.

Although it has taken half a century since *Everson* to reach the majority's twin standards of neutrality and free choice, the facts show that, in the majority's hands, even these criteria cannot convincingly legitimize the Ohio scheme.

Consider first the criterion of neutrality. As recently as two Terms ago, a majority of the Court recognized that neutrality conceived of as evenhandedness toward aid recipients had never been treated as alone sufficient to satisfy the Establishment Clause. . . . But at least in its limited significance, formal neutrality seemed to serve some purpose. Today, however, the majority employs the neutrality criterion in a way that renders it impossible to understand.

Neutrality in this sense refers, of course, to evenhandedness in setting eligibility as between potential religious and secular recipients of public money.

In order to apply the neutrality test, then, it makes sense to focus on a category of aid that may be directed to religious as well as secular schools, and ask whether the scheme favors a religious direction. Here, one would ask whether the voucher provisions, allowing for as much as $2,250 toward private school tuition (or a grant to a public school in an adjacent district), were written in a way that skewed the scheme toward benefiting religious schools.

This, however, is not what the majority asks. . . . The majority looks not to the provisions for tuition vouchers, but to every provision for educational opportunity. . . . The majority then finds confirmation that "participation of all schools" satisfies neutrality by noting that the better part of total state educational expenditure goes to public schools, thus showing there is no favor of religion.

The illogic is patent. If regular, public schools (which can get no voucher payments) "participate" in a voucher scheme with schools that can, and public expenditure is still predominantly on public schools, then the majority's reasoning would find neutrality in a scheme of vouchers available for private tuition in districts with no secular private schools at all. . . .

The majority addresses the issue of choice the same way it addresses neutrality, by asking whether recipients or potential recipients of voucher aid have a choice of public schools among secular alternatives to religious schools. Again, however, the majority asks the wrong question and misapplies the criterion. . . . The question is whether the private hand is genuinely free to send the money in either a secular direction or a religious one. The majority now has transformed this question about private choice in channeling aid into a question about selecting from examples of state spending (on education) including direct spending on magnet and community public schools that goes through no private hands and could never reach a religious school under any circumstance. When the choice test is transformed from where to spend the money to where to go to school, it is cut loose from its very purpose.

If, contrary to the majority, we ask the right question about genuine choice to use the vouchers, the answer shows that something is influencing choices in a way that aims the money in a religious direction: of 56 private schools in the district participating in the voucher program (only 53 of which accepted voucher students in 1999–2000), 46 of them are religious; 96.6% of all voucher recipients go to religious schools, only 3.4% to nonreligious ones. Unfortunately for the majority position, there is no explanation for this that suggests the religious direction results simply from free choices by parents.

There is, in any case, no way to interpret the 96.6% of current voucher money going to religious schools as reflecting a free and genuine choice by the families that apply for vouchers. The 96.6% reflects, instead, the fact

that too few nonreligious school desks are available and few but religious schools can afford to accept more than a handful of voucher students. . . . And it is entirely irrelevant that the State did not deliberately design the network of private schools for the sake of channeling money into religious institutions. The criterion is one of genuinely free choice on the part of the private individuals who choose, and a Hobson's choice is not a choice, whatever the reason for being Hobsonian.

It is virtually superfluous to point out that every objective underlying the prohibition of religious establishment is betrayed by this scheme, but something has to be said about the enormity of the violation. I anticipated these objectives earlier, in discussing *Everson,* which cataloged them, the first being respect for freedom of conscience. Jefferson described it as the idea that no one "shall be compelled to . . . support any religious worship, place, or ministry whatsoever," even a "teacher of his own religious persuasion," and Madison thought it violated by any "authority which can force a citizen to contribute three pence . . . of his property for the support of any . . . establishment." *Memorial and Remonstrance.* Madison's objection to three pence has simply been lost in the majority's formalism.

As for the second objective, to save religion from its own corruption, Madison wrote of the "experience . . . that ecclesiastical establishments, instead of maintaining the purity and efficacy of Religion, have had a contrary operation."

The risk is already being realized. In Ohio, for example, a condition of receiving government money under the program is that participating religious schools may not "discriminate on the basis of . . . religion," which means the school may not give admission preferences to children who are members of the patron faith; children of a parish are generally consigned to the same admission lotteries as non-believers.

When government aid goes up, so does reliance on it; the only thing likely to go down is independence. . . . A day will come when religious schools will learn what political leverage can do, just as Ohio's politicians are now getting a lesson in the leverage exercised by religion.

Justice Breyer has addressed this issue in his own dissenting opinion, which I join, and here it is enough to say that the intensity of the expectable friction can be gauged by realizing that the scramble for money will energize not only contending sectarians, but taxpayers who take their liberty of conscience seriously. Religious teaching at taxpayer expense simply cannot be cordoned from taxpayer politics, and every major religion currently espouses social positions that provoke intense opposition. Not all taxpaying Protestant citizens, for example, will be content to underwrite the teaching of the Roman Catholic Church condemning the death penalty. Nor will all of America's Muslims acquiesce in paying for the endorsement of the religious Zionism taught in many religious Jewish schools, which combines "a nationalistic sentiment" in support of Israel with a "deeply religious" element. Nor will every secular taxpayer be content to support Muslim views on differential treatment of the sexes, or, for that matter, to fund the espousal of a wife's obligation of obedience to her husband, presumably taught in any schools adopting the articles of faith of the Southern Baptist Convention. Views like these, and innumerable others, have been safe in the sectarian pulpits and classrooms of this Nation not only because the Free Exercise Clause protects them directly, but because the ban on supporting religious establishment has protected free exercise, by keeping it relatively private. With the arrival of vouchers in religious schools, that privacy will go, and along with it will go confidence that religious disagreement will stay moderate.

If the divisiveness permitted by today's majority is to be avoided in the short term, it will be avoided only by action of the political branches at the state and national levels. Legislatures not driven to desperation by the problems of public education may be able to see the threat in vouchers negotiable in sectarian schools. Perhaps even cities with problems like Cleveland's will perceive the danger, now that they know a federal court will not save them from it.

My own course as a judge on the Court cannot, however, simply be to hope that the political branches will save us from the consequences of the majority's decision. *Everson's* statement is still the touchstone of sound law, even though the reality is that in the matter of educational aid the Establishment Clause has largely been read away. True, the majority has not approved vouchers for religious schools alone, or aid earmarked for religious instruction. But no scheme so clumsy will ever get before us, and in the cases that we may see, like these, the Establishment Clause is largely silenced. I do not have the option to leave it silent, and I hope that a future Court will reconsider today's dramatic departure from basic Establishment Clause principle.

Justice BREYER, with whom Justice STEVENS and Justice SOUTER join, dissenting.

I write separately . . . to emphasize the risk that publicly financed voucher programs pose in terms of religiously based social conflict. I do so because I believe that the Establishment Clause concern for protecting the Nation's social fabric from religious conflict poses an overriding obstacle to the implementation of this well-intentioned

school voucher program. And by explaining the nature of the concern, I hope to demonstrate why, in my view, "parental choice" cannot significantly alleviate the constitutional problem.

The First Amendment begins with a prohibition, that "Congress shall make no law respecting an establishment of religion," and a guarantee, that the government shall not prohibit "the free exercise thereof." These Clauses embody an understanding, reached in the 17th century after decades of religious war, that liberty and social stability demand a religious tolerance that respects the religious views of all citizens, permits those citizens to "worship God in their own way," and allows all families to "teach their children and to form their characters" as they wish. The Clauses reflect the Framers' vision of an American Nation free of the religious strife that had long plagued the nations of Europe. . . . Whatever the Framers might have thought about particular 18th century school funding practices, they undeniably intended an interpretation of the Religion Clauses that would implement this basic First Amendment objective.

In part for this reason, the Court's 20th century Establishment Clause cases—both those limiting the practice of religion in public schools and those limiting the public funding of private religious education—focused directly upon social conflict, potentially created when government becomes involved in religious education. In *Engel v. Vitale* (1962), the Court held that the Establishment Clause forbids prayer in public elementary and secondary schools. It did so in part because it recognized the "anguish, hardship and bitter strife that could come when zealous religious groups struggl[e] with one another to obtain the Government's stamp of approval."

When it decided these 20th century Establishment Clause cases, the Court did not deny that an earlier American society might have found a less clear-cut church/state separation compatible with social tranquility. Indeed, historians point out that during the early years of the Republic, American schools—including the first public schools—were Protestant in character. Their students recited Protestant prayers, read the King James version of the Bible, and learned Protestant religious ideals. Those practices may have wrongly discriminated against members of minority religions, but given the small number of such individuals, the teaching of Protestant religions in schools did not threaten serious social conflict.

The 20th century Court was fully aware, however, that immigration and growth had changed American society dramatically since its early years. By 1850, 1.6 million Catholics lived in America, and by 1900 that number rose to 12 million. There were similar percentage increases in the Jewish population. Not surprisingly, with this increase in numbers, members of non-Protestant religions, particularly Catholics, began to resist the Protestant domination of the public schools. Scholars report that by the mid-19th century religious conflict over matters such as Bible reading "grew intense," as Catholics resisted and Protestants fought back to preserve their domination. In some States "Catholic students suffered beatings or expulsions for refusing to read from the Protestant Bible, and crowds . . . rioted over whether Catholic children could be released from the classroom during Bible reading."

The 20th century Court was also aware that political efforts to right the wrong of discrimination against religious minorities in primary education had failed; in fact they had exacerbated religious conflict. Catholics sought equal government support for the education of their children in the form of aid for private Catholic schools. But the "Protestant position" on this matter, scholars report, "was that public schools must be 'nonsectarian' (which was usually understood to allow Bible reading and other Protestant observances) and public money must not support 'sectarian' schools (which in practical terms meant Catholic)." And this sentiment played a significant role in creating a movement that sought to amend several state constitutions (often successfully), and to amend the United States Constitution (unsuccessfully) to make certain that government would not help pay for "sectarian" (i.e., Catholic) schooling for children.

These historical circumstances suggest that the Court, applying the Establishment Clause through the Fourteenth Amendment to 20th century American society, faced an interpretive dilemma that was in part practical. The Court appreciated the religious diversity of contemporary American society. It realized that the status quo favored some religions at the expense of others. And it understood the Establishment Clause to prohibit (among other things) any such favoritism. Yet how did the Clause achieve that objective? Did it simply require the government to give each religion an equal chance to introduce religion into the primary schools—a kind of "equal opportunity" approach to the interpretation of the Establishment Clause? Or, did that Clause avoid government favoritism of some religions by insisting upon "separation"—that the government achieve equal treatment by removing itself from the business of providing religious education for children? This interpretive choice arose in respect both to religious activities in public schools and government aid to private education.

In both areas the Court concluded that the Establishment Clause required "separation," in part because an "equal opportunity" approach was not workable. With respect to religious activities in the public schools, how

could the Clause require public primary and secondary school teachers, when reading prayers or the Bible, only to treat all religions alike? In many places there were too many religions, too diverse a set of religious practices, too many whose spiritual beliefs denied the virtue of formal religious training. This diversity made it difficult, if not impossible, to devise meaningful forms of "equal treatment" by providing an "equal opportunity" for all to introduce their own religious practices into the public schools.

With respect to government aid to private education, did not history show that efforts to obtain equivalent funding for the private education of children whose parents did not hold popular religious beliefs only exacerbated religious strife?

The principle underlying these cases—avoiding religiously based social conflict—remains of great concern. As religiously diverse as America had become when the Court decided its major 20th century Establishment Clause cases, we are exponentially more diverse today. America boasts more than 55 different religious groups and subgroups with a significant number of members. Major religions include, among others, Protestants, Catholics, Jews, Muslims, Buddhists, Hindus, and Sikhs. And several of these major religions contain different subsidiary sects with different religious beliefs. Newer Christian immigrant groups are "expressing their Christianity in languages, customs, and independent churches that are barely recognizable, and often controversial, for European-ancestry Catholics and Protestants."

Under these modern-day circumstances, how is the "equal opportunity" principle to work—without risking the "struggle of sect against sect" against which Justice Rutledge warned? School voucher programs finance the religious education of the young. And, if widely adopted, they may well provide billions of dollars that will do so. Why will different religions not become concerned about, and seek to influence, the criteria used to channel this money to religious schools? Why will they not want to examine the implementation of the programs that provide this money—to determine, for example, whether implementation has biased a program toward or against particular sects, or whether recipient religious schools are adequately fulfilling a program's criteria? If so, just how is the State to resolve the resulting controversies without provoking legitimate fears of the kinds of religious favoritism that, in so religiously diverse a Nation, threaten social dissension?

How are state officials to adjudicate claims that one religion or another is advocating, for example, civil disobedience in response to unjust laws, the use of illegal drugs in a religious ceremony, or resort to force to call attention to what it views as an immoral social practice? What kind of public hearing will there be in response to claims that one religion or another is continuing to teach a view of history that casts members of other religions in the worst possible light? How will the public react to government funding for schools that take controversial religious positions on topics that are of current popular interest—say, the conflict in the Middle East or the war on terrorism? Yet any major funding program for primary religious education will require criteria. And the selection of those criteria, as well as their application, inevitably pose problems that are divisive. Efforts to respond to these problems not only will seriously entangle church and state, see *Lemon*, but also will promote division among religious groups, as one group or another fears (often legitimately) that it will receive unfair treatment at the hands of the government.

I recognize that other nations, for example Great Britain and France, have in the past reconciled religious school funding and religious freedom without creating serious strife. Yet British and French societies are religiously more homogeneous—and it bears noting that recent waves of immigration have begun to create problems of social division there as well.

In a society as religiously diverse as ours, the Court has recognized that we must rely on the Religion Clauses of the First Amendment to protect against religious strife, particularly when what is at issue is an area as central to religious belief as the shaping, through primary education, of the next generation's minds and spirits.

I do not believe that the "parental choice" aspect of the voucher program sufficiently offsets the concerns I have mentioned. Parental choice cannot help the taxpayer who does not want to finance the religious education of children. It will not always help the parent who may see little real choice between inadequate nonsectarian public education and adequate education at a school whose religious teachings are contrary to his own. It will not satisfy religious minorities unable to participate because they are too few in number to support the creation of their own private schools. It will not satisfy groups whose religious beliefs preclude them from participating in a government-sponsored program, and who may well feel ignored as government funds primarily support the education of children in the doctrines of the dominant religions. And it does little to ameliorate the entanglement problems or the related problems of social division.

I fear that this present departure from the Court's earlier understanding risks creating a form of religiously based conflict potentially harmful to the Nation's social fabric. Because I believe the Establishment Clause was written in part to avoid this kind of conflict, and for reasons set forth

by Justice Souter and Justice Stevens, I respectfully dissent.

Notes and Queries

1. Most other constitutional democracies are more favorably disposed to nonpreferential government support for religion than the United States. This fact could provide justices like Rehnquist and Scalia with support for their view that the First Amendment is no bar to parochial schools benefiting from state-sponsored financial assistance. Nevertheless, Chief Justice Rehnquist, the author of the majority opinion, makes no mention of European democracies where such assistance has been found constitutional. It was left to a dissenter in the case, Justice Breyer, to say, in effect, that "our society is not Europe's." "I recognize that other nations, for example Great Britain and France, have in the past reconciled religious school funding without creating serious strife. Yet British and French societies are religiously more homogeneous."

2. Justice O'Connor, in her concurring opinion, denied that "today's decision signal[s] a major departure" from prior establishment clause jurisprudence. Do you agree?

3. Quoting Madison, Justice Souter wrote that one of the purposes of the establishment clause was "to save religion from its own corruption." In Souter's view, the risk of compromise to religion itself is "already being realized" in the Ohio scheme. Assume, for purposes of argument, that there is a risk inherent in such programs that religions will compromise their purity and their independence. Is weighing the risk a political or a judicial function?

4. Do you agree with the dissent's prediction that the Ohio policy will likely result in social unrest and divisiveness? Is an appeal to these kinds of consequences a legitimate part of constitutional interpretation?

5. Justice Souter's dissent also reminds us there are important issues of judicial power involved in these cases. "If the divisiveness . . . is to be avoided in the short term," he wrote, "it will be avoided only by the action of the political branches. . . . My own course as a judge on the Court cannot, however, simply be to hope that the political branches will save us from the consequences of the majority's decision." What understanding of democratic politics and judicial power inheres in the phrase, "My own course as a judge on the Court"?

5. In his dissent, Justice Breyer also described how the Court's interpretation of the establishment clause was concerned with "avoiding religiously based social conflict." But couldn't one argue that the great diversity of religious beliefs in the United States is at least partly a consequence of the Court's interpretation of both the establishment and

free exercise clauses? In other words, in its quest to protect religion, the Court has been willing to recognize as "religious" a seemingly innumerable set of beliefs and practices. Doesn't the push to diversity in fact increase the chances of collisions among religions and between the state and religion, a point at least hinted at in Justice Breyer's reference to Britain and France as "religiously more homogeneous"?

5. In his concurrence, Justice Thomas wrote that "in the context of the establishment clause, it may well be that state action should be evaluated on different terms than similar action by the federal government." Why? Because "when rights are incorporated" they "should advance, not constrain, individual liberty"? Because courts should "strike a proper balance between the demands of the Fourteenth Amendment . . . and the federalism prerogatives of the States"?

7. Justice Thomas wrote eloquently about how failing public schools disproportionately affect minority schoolchildren. "If society cannot end racial discrimination, at least it can arm minorities with the education to defend themselves from some of discrimination's effects. . . ." Although he does not cast the question in these terms, does the equal protection clause of the Fourteenth Amendment trump the establishment clause? Or, to phrase the question in terms similar to those used in *Widmar v. Vincent* (1981) and *Good News Club* (2001), would a state interest in avoiding a violation of the establishment clause constitute a "compelling state interest"? Or, does a compelling state interest in remedying the effects of racial discrimination justify what would otherwise be a violation of the establishment clause?

Davis v. Beason

133 U.S. 333, 10 S.Ct. 299, 33 L.Ed. 637 (1890)

As part of a long-standing campaign to harass Mormons, a campaign motivated in part by religious bigotry and in part based on the lofty political aspirations of some Church elders, the Territory of Idaho enacted a law limiting the right to vote to males who had not been convicted of certain crimes or to males who swore an oath that they did not practice polygamy and were not a member of any organization that "advises, counsels, or encourages" anyone to commit bigamy or polygamy. Opinion of the Court: *Field*, Fuller, Miller, Bradley, Harlan, Gray, Blatchford, Lamar, Brewer.

Mr. Justice FIELD . . . delivered the opinion of the Court.

. . . Bigamy and polygamy are crimes by the laws of all civilized and Christian countries. They are crimes by the laws of the United States, and they are crimes by the laws of Idaho. They tend to destroy the purity of the marriage relation, to disturb the peace of families, to degrade woman, and to debase man. Few crimes are more pernicious to the best interests of society, and receive more general or more deserved punishment. To extend exemption from punishment for such crimes would be to shock the moral judgment of the community. To call their advocacy a tenet of religion is to offend the common sense of mankind. If they are crimes, then to teach, advise, and counsel their practice is to aid in their commission, and such teaching and counseling are themselves criminal,

and proper subjects of punishment, as aiding and abetting crime are in all other cases.

The term "religion" has reference to one's views of his relations to his Creator, and to the obligations they impose of reverence for his being and character, and of obedience to his will. It is often confounded with the *cultus* or form of worship of a particular sect, but is distinguishable from the latter. The first amendment to the constitution, in declaring that congress shall make no law respecting the establishment of religion or forbidding the free exercise thereof, was intended to allow every one under the jurisdiction of the United States to entertain such notions respecting his relations to his Maker and the duties they impose as may be approved by his judgment and conscience, and to exhibit his sentiments in such form of worship as he may think proper, not injurious to the equal rights of others, and to prohibit legislation for the support of any religious tenets, or the modes of worship of any sect. The oppressive measures adopted, and the cruelties and punishments inflicted, by the governments of Europe for many ages, to compel parties to conform in their religious beliefs and modes of worship, to the views of the most numerous sect, and the folly of attempting in that way to control the mental operations of persons, and enforce an outward conformity to a prescribed standard, led to the adoption of the amendment in question. It was never intended or supposed that the amendment could be invoked as a protection against legislation for the punishment of acts inimical to the peace, good order, and morals of society. With man's relations to his Maker and the obligations he may think they impose, and the manner in

Comparative Note 13.6

[In this case, the Canadian Supreme Court considered whether a teacher-training program run by an evangelical, Christian university, which included in its standard of conduct prohibitions against homosexual behavior, was protected by freedom of religion.]

In our opinion, this is a case where any potential conflict should be resolved through the proper delineation of the rights and values involved. In essence, properly defining the scope of the rights avoids a conflict in this case. Neither freedom of religion nor the guarantee against discrimination based on sexual orientation is absolute. As L'Heureux-Dube J. stated in *P. (D.) v. S. (C.)*, [1993], writing for the majority on this point:

> As the Court has reiterated many times, freedom of religion, like any freedom, is not absolute. It is inherently limited by the rights and freedoms of others. Whereas parents are free to choose and practise the religion of their choice, such activities can and must be restricted when they are against the child's best interests, without thereby infringing the parents' freedom of religion. . . .

In addition, the Charter must be read as a whole, so that one right is not privileged at the expense of another. As Lamer C.J. stated for the majority of this Court in *Dagenais v. Canadian Broadcasting Corp.*, [1994]:

> A hierarchical approach to rights, which places some over others, must be avoided, both when inter-

preting the Charter and when developing the common law. When the protected rights of two individuals come into conflict . . . Charter principles require a balance to be achieved that fully respects the importance of both sets of rights. . . .

Students attending TWU are free to adopt personal rules of conduct based on their religious beliefs provided they do not interfere with the rights of others. Their freedom of religion is not accommodated if the consequence of its exercise is the denial of the right of full participation in society. Clearly, the restriction on freedom of religion must be justified by evidence that the exercise of this freedom of religion will, in the circumstances of this case, have a detrimental impact on the school system.

Instead, the proper place to draw the line in cases like the one at bar is generally between belief and conduct. The freedom to hold beliefs is broader than the freedom to act on them. Absent concrete evidence that training teachers at TWU fosters discrimination in the public schools of B.C., the freedom of individuals to adhere to certain religious beliefs while at TWU should be respected. The BCCT, rightfully, does not require public universities with teacher education programs to screen out applicants who hold sexist, racist or homophobic beliefs. For better or for worse, tolerance of divergent beliefs is a hallmark of a democratic society.

Source: *British Columbia College of Teachers v. Trinity Western University and Donna Gail Lindquist*, 2001 Can. Sup. Ct. 2001 SCC 31.

which an expression shall be made by him of his belief on those subjects, no interference can be permitted, provided always the laws of society, designed to secure its peace and prosperity, and the morals of its people, are not interfered with. However free the exercise of religion may be, it must be subordinate to the criminal laws of the country, passed with reference to actions regarded by general consent as properly the subjects of punitive legislation. There have been sects which denied as a part of their religious tenets that there should be any marriage tie, and advocated promiscuous intercourse of the sexes, as prompted by the passions of its members. And history discloses the fact that the necessity of human sacrifices, on special occasions, has been a tenet of many sects. Should a sect of either of these kinds ever find its way into this country,

swift punishment would follow the carrying into effect of its doctrines, and no heed would be given to the pretense that, as religious beliefs, their supporters could be protected in their exercise by the constitution of the United States. Probably never before in the history of this country has it been seriously contended that the whole punitive power of the government for acts, recognized by the general consent of the Christian world in modern times as proper matters for prohibitory legislation, must be suspended in order that the tenets of a religious sect encouraging crime without hindrance. . . .

. . . [T]he only question which remains is whether those who make polygamy a part of their religion are excepted from the operation of the statute. If they are, then those who do not make polygamy a part of their religious belief

Comparative Note 13.7

[In this case, the Indian Supreme Court considered the constitutionality of a statute that criminalized bigamous marriages among Hindus. The Act was challenged as a violation of Articles 14, 15 (concerning equality) and 25 of the Constitution. Article 25 guarantees freedom of conscience and the right freely to profess, practice, and propagate religion.]

Now a sharp distinction must be drawn between religious faith and religious practices. What the State protects is religious faith and belief. If religious practices run counter to public order, morality or health or a policy of social welfare . . . , then the religious practices must give way before the good of the people of the State as a whole. A very interesting and instructive case is to be found in the American Reports, viz, *Davis v. Beason* (1890). . . .

. . . [T]he right of the State to legislate on questions relating to marriage cannot be disputed. Marriage is undoubtedly a social institution in which the State is vitally interested. Although there may not be universal recognition of the fact, still a very large volume of opinion in the world today admits that monogamy is a very desirable and praiseworthy institution. . . .

Source: *The State of Bombay v. Narasu Appa*, 39 A.I.R. 84 (1952).

may be found guilty and punished, while those who do must be acquitted and go free. This would be introducing a new element into criminal law. Laws are made for the government of actions, and while they cannot interfere with mere religious belief and opinions, they may with practices. . . . Can a man excuse his practices to the contrary, because of his religious belief? To permit this would be to make the professed doctrines of religious belief superior to the law of the land, and in effect to permit every citizen to become a law unto himself. Government could exist only in name under such circumstances. . . .

It is assumed by counsel of the petitioner that, because no mode of worship can be established, or religious tenets enforced, in this country, therefore any form of worship may be followed, and any tenets, however destructive of society, may be held and advocated, if asserted to be a part of the religious doctrines of those advocating and practicing them. But nothing is further from the truth. While legislation for the establishment of a religion is forbidden, and its free exercise permitted, it does not follow that everything which may be so called can be tolerated. Crime is not the less odious because sanctioned by what any particular sect may designate as religion.

Notes and Queries

1. Twelve years earlier, in *Reynolds v. United States* (1878), the Court upheld a federal law that prohibited po-

Comparative Note 13.8

[Rule 27 of the Indian Government Servants Conduct Rules provided that a government employee cannot marry a second wife during the presence of the first wife without the permission of the state government. Ram Prasad argued that the rule violated Article 25 of the Indian Constitution because it interfered with a principle according to the Hindu Dharam Shastras that a man cannot attain salvation without a son.]

The question, therefore, to be considered is whether the right to marry a second wife in the presence of the first wife can be regarded as a religious belief. . . . The

other question which is to be considered is whether such a religious belief is contrary to public order. . . .

The acts done in pursuance of a particular belief are as much a part of the religion as belief itself, but that to my mind does not lay down that polygamy . . . is an essential part of the Hindu religion. The presence of a son may be essential to achieve religious salvation but that does not necessarily mean that in the presence of a wife who has a living female child and there being a right to adopt, a second marriage is so obligatory so as to form part of the Hindu religion. . . .

Source: *Ram Prasad v. State of Bombay*, A.I.R. SC. 853 (1962).

lygamy in the territories. The Court wrote that "while [laws] cannot interfere with mere religious belief and opinions, they may with practices." Did the law at issue in *Davis* interfere with a religious practice, as opposed to a "mere" religious belief? Is the distinction between belief and action a fair reading of the text of the First Amendment? Does it satisfy the purpose(s) of the free exercise clause? Is the distinction workable? Compare the Court's treatment of the belief-action distinction with the approach of the Canadian Court in Comparative Note 13.6, and with the Indian Court's decision, reprinted in Comparative Note 13.7.

2. Justice Field's opinion for the Court states that "the term 'religion' has reference to one's views of his relations to his Creator, and to the obligations they impose of reverence for his being and character, and of obedience to his will." What is the source of this definition? Does Field find it in the Constitution, however defined? Does he find it in "the general consent of the Christian world"? Is that an appropriate source? What understanding of judicial power is implicit in Justice Field's definition?

3. Consider also a second issue of judicial power: The statute in this case effectively conditioned the right of political participation upon conformity to a majoritarian tenet of religious faith. How, if not through democratic channels, can a religious minority protect itself against such action? Should the Court have assumed the role of protecting this minority from the political process?

West Virginia v. Barnette
319 U.S. 624, 63 S.Ct. 1178, 87 L.Ed. 1628 (1943)

In *Minersville v. Gobitis* (1940), the Court upheld a decision by a local school board to require students to salute the flag against a challenge by Jehovah's Witnesses. *Minersville* unleashed a wave of persecution against Jehovah's Witnesses and other religious minorities. The Department of Justice alone received hundreds of reports within two weeks of the decision, including reports of the burning of Witnesses' meeting places as well as beatings and castrations. Just two years after the decision, in *Jones v. Opelika* (1942), Justices Black, Douglas, and Murphy announced that they had erred in *Gobitis*. In the meantime, Justice Jackson had replaced Hughes, and Justice Rutledge had succeeded McReynolds. Both Jackson and Rutledge were thought to be hostile to *Gobitis*. Following *Minersville,* the West Virginia legislature required all schools to include courses in history and civics and on the Constitutions of the United States and of the State. *Barnette* involved a decision by a local Board of Education to adopt a resolution requiring all students to salute the flag, and noting that refusal to do so would be "regarded as an act of insubordination, and [would] be dealt with accordingly." Opinion of the Court: *Jackson*, Stone, Black, Douglas, Murphy, Rutledge. Concurring opinions: *Black, Douglas.* Dissenting opinions: *Roberts*, Reed; *Frankfurter.*

Justice JACKSON delivered the opinion of the Court.

The freedom asserted by these appellees does not bring them into collision with rights asserted by any other individual. It is such conflicts which most frequently require intervention of the State to determine where the rights of one end and those of another begin. But the refusal of these persons to participate in the ceremony does not interfere with or deny rights of others to do so. Nor is there any question in this case that their behavior is peaceable and orderly. The sole conflict is between authority and rights of the individual. The State asserts power to condition access to public education on making a prescribed sign and profession and at the same time to coerce attendance by punishing both parent and child. The latter stands on a right of self-determination in matters that touch individual opinion and personal attitude.

The very purpose of a Bill of Rights was to withdraw certain subjects from the vicissitudes of political controversy, to place them beyond the reach of majorities and officials and to establish them as legal principles to be applied by the courts. One's right to life, liberty, and property, to free speech, a free press, freedom of worship and assembly, and other fundamental rights may not be submitted to vote; they depend on the outcome of no elections.

Struggles to coerce uniformity of sentiment in support of some end thought essential to their time and country have been waged by many good as well as by evil men. Nationalism is a relatively recent phenomenon but at other times and places the ends have been racial or territorial security, support of a dynasty or regime, and particular plans for saving souls. As first and moderate methods to attain unity have failed, those bent on its accomplishment must resort to an ever-increasing severity. As governmental pressure toward unity becomes greater, so strife becomes more bitter as to whose unity it shall be. Probably no deeper division of our people could proceed from any provocation than from finding it necessary to choose what doctrine and whose program public educational officials shall compel youth to unite in embracing. Ultimate futility of such attempts to compel coherence is the lesson of every such effort from the Roman drive to stamp out Christianity as a disturber of its pagan unity, the Inquisition, as a means to religious and dynastic unity, the Siberian exiles as a means to Russian unity, down to the fast failing efforts of our present totalitarian enemies. Those who begin coercive elimination of dissent soon find themselves exterminating dissenters. Compulsory unification of opinion achieves only the unanimity of the graveyard.

It seems trite but necessary to say that the First Amendment to our Constitution was designed to avoid these ends by avoiding these beginnings. There is no mysticism in the American concept of the State or of the nature or origin of its authority. We set up government by consent of the governed, and the Bill of Rights denies those in power any legal opportunity to coerce that consent. Authority here is to be controlled by public opinion, not public opinion by authority.

The case is made difficult not because the principles of its decision are obscure but because the flag involved is our own. Nevertheless, we apply the limitations of the Constitution with no fear that freedom to be intellectually and spiritually diverse or even contrary will disintegrate the social organization. To believe that patriotism will not flourish if patriotic ceremonies are voluntary and spontaneous instead of a compulsory routine is to make an unflattering estimate of the appeal of our institutions to free minds. We can have intellectual individualism and the rich cultural diversities that we owe to exceptional minds only at the price of occasional eccentricity and abnormal attitudes. When they are so harmless to others or to the State as those we deal with here, the price is not too great. But freedom to differ is not limited to things that do not matter much. That would be a mere shadow of freedom. The test of its substance is the right to differ as to things that touch the heart of the existing order.

If there is any fixed star in our constitutional constellation, it is that no official, high or petty, can prescribe what shall be orthodox in politics, nationalism, religion, or other matters of opinion or force citizens to confess by word or act their faith therein. If there are any circumstances which permit an exception, they do not now occur to us.

We think the action of the local authorities in compelling the flag salute and pledge transcends constitutional limitations on their power and invades the sphere of intellect and spirit which it is the purpose of the First Amendment to our Constitution to reserve from all official control.

The decision of this Court in *Minersville School District v. Gobitis* and the holdings of those few per curiam decisions which preceded and foreshadowed it are overruled, and the judgment enjoining enforcement of the West Virginia Regulation is

Affirmed.

Justice ROBERTS and Justice REED adhere to the views expressed by the Court in *Minersville School District v. Gobitis,* and are of the opinion that the judgment below should be reversed.

Justice BLACK and Justice DOUGLAS, concurring.

We are substantially in agreement with the opinion just read, but since we originally joined with the Court in the *Gobitis* case, it is appropriate that we make a brief statement of reasons for our change of view.

Reluctance to make the Federal Constitution a rigid bar against state regulation of conduct thought inimical to the public welfare was the controlling influence which moved us to consent to the *Gobitis* decision. Long reflection convinced us that although the principle is sound, its application in the particular case was wrong. We believe that the statute before us fails to accord full scope to the freedom of religion secured to the appellees by the First and Fourteenth Amendments.

No well-ordered society can leave to the individuals an absolute right to make final decisions, unassailable by the State, as to everything they will or will not do. The First Amendment does not go so far. Religious faiths, honestly held, do not free individuals from responsibility to conduct themselves obediently to laws which are either imperatively necessary to protect society as a whole from grave and pressingly imminent dangers or which, without any general prohibition, merely regulate time, place or manner of religious activity. Decision as to the constitutionality of particular laws which strike at the substance of religious tenets and practices must be made by this Court. The duty is a solemn one, and in meeting it we cannot say that a failure, because of religious scruples, to assume a particular physical position and to repeat the words of a patriotic formula creates a grave danger to the nation. Such a statutory exaction is a form of test oath, and the test oath has always been abhorrent in the United States.

Words uttered under coercion are proof of loyalty to nothing but self-interest. Love of country must spring from willing hearts and free minds, inspired by a fair administration of wise laws enacted by the people's elected representatives within the bounds of express constitutional prohibitions. These laws must, to be consistent with the First Amendment, permit the widest toleration of conflicting viewpoints consistent with a society of free men.

Neither our domestic tranquility in peace nor our martial effort in war depend on compelling little children to participate in a ceremony which ends in nothing for them but a fear of spiritual condemnation. If, as we think, their fears are groundless, time and reason are the proper antidotes for their errors. The ceremonial, when enforced against conscientious objectors, more likely to defeat than to serve its high purpose, is a handy implement for disguised religious persecution. As such, it is inconsistent with our Constitution's plan and purpose.

Justice MURPHY, concurring.

. . . Without wishing to disparage the purposes and intentions of those who hope to inculcate sentiments of loyalty and patriotism by requiring a declaration of allegiance as a feature of public education, or unduly belittle the benefits that may accrue therefrom, I am impelled to conclude that such a requirement is not essential to the maintenance of effective government and orderly society. To many it is deeply distasteful to join in a public chorus of affirmation of private belief. By some, including the members of this sect, it is apparently regarded as incompatible with a primary religious obligation and therefore a restriction on religious freedom. Official compulsion to affirm what is contrary to one's religious beliefs is the antithesis of freedom of worship which, it is well to recall, was achieved in this country only after what Jefferson characterized as the "severest contests in which I have ever been engaged."

Justice FRANKFURTER, dissenting.

One who belongs to the most vilified and persecuted minority in history is not likely to be insensible to the freedoms guaranteed by our Constitution. Were my purely personal attitude relevant I should wholeheartedly associate myself with the general libertarian views in the Court's opinion, representing as they do the thought and action of a lifetime. But as judges we are neither Jew nor Gentile, neither Catholic nor agnostic. We owe equal attachment to the Constitution and are equally bound by our judicial obligations whether we derive our citizenship from the earliest or the latest immigrants to these shores. As a member of this Court I am not justified in writing my private notions of policy into the Constitution, no matter how deeply I may cherish them or how mischievous I may deem their disregard. The duty of a judge who must decide which of two claims before the Court shall prevail, that of a State to enact and enforce laws within its general competence or that of an individual to refuse obedience because of the demands of his conscience, is not that of the ordinary person. It can never be emphasized too much that one's own opinion about the wisdom or evil of a law should be excluded altogether when one is doing one's

duty on the bench. The only opinion of our own even looking in that direction that is material is our opinion whether legislators could in reason have enacted such a law. In the light of all the circumstances, including the history of this question in this Court, it would require more daring than I possess to deny that reasonable legislators could have taken the action which is before us for review. Most unwillingly, therefore, I must differ from my brethren with regard to legislation like this. I cannot bring my mind to believe that the "liberty" secured by the Due Process Clause gives this Court authority to deny to the State of West Virginia the attainment of that which we all recognize as a legitimate legislative end namely, the promotion of good citizenship, by the means here chosen.

Not so long ago we were admonished that "the only check upon our own exercise of power is our own sense of self-restraint. For the removal of unwise laws from the statute books appeal lies not to the courts but to the ballot and to the processes of democratic government." . . . We have been told that generalities do not decide concrete cases. But the intensity with which a general principle is held may determine a particular issue, and whether we put first things first may decide a specific controversy.

The admonition that judicial self-restraint alone limits arbitrary exercise of our authority is relevant every time we are asked to nullify legislation. The Constitution does not give us greater veto power when dealing with one phase of "liberty" than with another, or when dealing with grade school regulations than with college regulations that offend conscience. In neither situation is our function comparable to that of a legislature or are we free to act as though we were a super-legislature. Judicial self-restraint is equally necessary whenever an exercise of political or legislative power is challenged. There is no warrant in the constitutional basis of this Court's authority for attributing different roles to it depending upon the nature of the challenge to the legislation. Our power does not vary according to the particular provision of the Bill of Rights which is invoked. The right not to have property taken without just compensation has, so far as the scope of judicial power is concerned, the same constitutional dignity as the right to be protected against unreasonable searches and seizures, and the latter has no less claim than freedom of the press or freedom of speech or religious freedom. In no instance is this Court the primary protector of the particular liberty that is invoked. This Court has recognized, what hardly could be denied, that all the provisions of the first ten Amendments are "specific" prohibitions. *United States v. Carolene Products* (1938). But each specific Amendment, insofar as embraced within the Fourteenth Amendment, must be equally respected, and the function of this Court does not differ in passing on the constitutionality of legislation challenged under different Amendments.

. . . [R]esponsibility for legislation lies with legislatures, answerable as they are directly to the people, and this Court's only and very narrow function is to determine whether within the broad grant of authority vested in legislatures they have exercised a judgment for which reasonable justification can be offered. . . . The reason why from the beginning even the narrow judicial authority to nullify legislation has been viewed with a jealous eye is that it serves to prevent the full play of the democratic process.

This is no dry, technical matter. It cuts deeply into one's conception of the democratic process—it concerns no less the practical differences between the means for making these accommodations that are open to courts and to legislatures. A court can only strike down. . . . It cannot modify or qualify, it cannot make exceptions to a general requirement. And it strikes down not merely for a day. At least the finding of unconstitutionality ought not to have ephemeral significance unless the Constitution is to be reduced to the fugitive importance of mere legislation. . . .

Law is concerned with external behavior and not with the inner life of man. It rests in large measure upon compulsion. Socrates lives in history partly because he gave his life for the conviction that duty of obedience to secular law does not presuppose consent to its enactment or belief in its virtue. . . . The state is not shut out from a domain because the individual conscience may deny the state's claim. . . .

One's conception of the Constitution cannot be severed from one's conception of a judge's function in applying it. The Court has no reason for existence if it merely reflects the pressures of the day. Our system is built on the faith that men set apart for this special function, freed from the influences of immediacy and from the deflections of worldly ambition, will become able to take a view of longer range than the period of responsibility entrusted to Congress and legislatures. . . .

Of course patriotism can not be enforced by the flag salute. But neither can the liberal spirit be enforced by judicial invalidation of illiberal legislation. Our constant preoccupation with the constitutionality of legislation rather than with its wisdom tends to preoccupation of the American mind with a false value. The tendency of focusing attention on constitutionality is to make constitutionality synonymous with wisdom, to regard a law as all right if it is constitutional. Such an attitude is a great enemy of liberalism. Particularly in legislation affecting freedom of thought and freedom of speech much which should offend a free-spirited society is constitutional. Reliance for

the most precious interests of civilization, therefore, must be found outside of their vindication in courts of law. Only a persistent positive translation of the faith of a free society into the convictions and habits and actions of a community is the ultimate reliance against unabated temptations to fetter the human spirit.

Notes and Queries

1. In his opinion for the Court, Justice Jackson wrote that "[W]e act in these matters not by authority of our competence but by force of our commissions." In dissent, Justice Frankfurter responded that "[R]esponsibility for legislation lies with legislatures, answerable as they are directly to the people, and this Court's only and very narrow function is to determine whether within the broad grant of authority vested in legislatures they have exercised a judgment for which reasonable justification can be offered. . . ." Which of these two different understandings of the role of the judiciary in a constitutional democracy is best supported by the constitutional text? Which is best supported by the political theory(ies) of the Constitution?

2. In their concurrence, Justices Black and Douglas admitted that "Religious faiths, honestly held, do not free individuals from responsibility to conduct themselves obediently to laws which are either imperatively necessary to protect society as a whole from grave and pressingly imminent dangers. . . ." To which branch of government is such a decision entrusted? Why? How would Justice Frankfurter answer this question?

3. Did Justice Frankfurter reject the philosophy of *Carolene Products*? If so, why? Is his objection grounded in the language or the nature of the constitutional document? In a particular approach to the role of the Supreme Court in a constitutional democracy? Would you agree that the "liberal spirit [cannot] be enforced by judicial invalidation of illiberal legislation"?

4. In *Wooley v. Maynard* (1977), the Court overturned a New Hampshire man's conviction for defacing a license plate on an automobile. A Jehovah's Witness, the man objected to the phrase "Live Free or Die." The Court, borrowing from *Barnette*, concluded that "the right of freedom of thought . . . includes both the right to speak freely and the right to refrain from speaking at all."

5. In *Bijoe Emmanuel v. The State of Kerala*, A.I.R. 1987 S.C. 748, the Indian Supreme Court considered the objections of Jehovah's Witnesses, enrolled in local schools, to the singing of the national anthem "Jana Gana Mana." Three children, Bijoe, Binu Mol, and Bindu Emmanuel, were expelled. They appealed, claiming that their expul-

sion violated Article 19(1)(a) of the Indian Constitution, which guarantees freedom of speech and expression, as well as Article 25(1), which guarantees freedom of conscience and religion. In its opinion striking down the practice, the Court noted that "[O]ur tradition teaches tolerance; our philosophy preaches tolerance; our constitution practises tolerance; let us not dilute it."

6. In the *Religious Oath Case*, 33 BVerfGE 23 (1972), the German Federal Constitutional Court was asked to set aside a conviction of an evangelical pastor. The pastor, a witness in a criminal case, had refused to be sworn in because, in his view, Jesus Christ's Sermon on the Mount prohibited him from doing so. The Constitutional Court overturned his conviction, noting that "The fundamental right of religious freedom under Article 4(1) of the Basic Law protects the complainant's convictions. . . . The interest of the governmental community in an efficiently functioning administration of the law . . . should not be undervalued. . . . But accepting a decision [not to be sworn in] based on someone's conviction that swearing an oath is not permissible in an individual case does not impair this interest. . . ." In dissent, Justice v. Schlabrendorff concluded that the pastor's understanding of the Sermon on the Mount was flawed. "A citizen who, according to his own statement, ascribes to the Christian belief and makes an obvious misinterpretation has no claim to the protection of Article 4 of the Basic Law."

Wisconsin v. Yoder

406 U.S. 205, 92 S. Ct. 1526, 32 L.Ed. 2d 15 (1972)

The Amish are a self-sufficient religious community who rely primarily on agriculture to sustain themselves. They reject the materialism of the modern world and interact with it only to the extent necessary. Three members of the Old Amish Order in New Glarus, Wisconsin, were convicted for violating the state's compulsory education law. The members had refused to send their 14- and 15-year-old children to public school; state law required attendance until the age of 16. Refusing to defend themselves in legal proceedings, the Amish were represented by an outside group of lawyers and professionals sympathetic to their plight. Opinion of the Court: *Burger*, Brennan, Marshall, White, Stewart, Blackmun. Dissenting opinion: *Douglas*. Not participating: *Rehnquist, Powell.*

Chief Justice BURGER delivered the opinion of the Court.

There is no doubt as to the power of a State . . . to impose reasonable regulations for the control and duration of basic education. See. e.g., *Pierce v. Society of Sisters* (1925). Providing public schools ranks at the very apex of the function of a State. Yet even this paramount responsibility was, in *Pierce*, made to yield to the right of parents to provide an equivalent education in a privately operated system. . . . As that case suggests, the values of parental direction of the religious upbringing and education of their children in their early and formative years have a high place in our society. . . . Thus, a State's interest in universal education . . . is not totally free from a balancing process when it impinges on fundamental rights and interests. . . .

Amish objection to formal education beyond the eighth grade is firmly grounded in these central religious concepts. They object to the high school, and higher education generally, because the values they teach are in marked variance with Amish values and the Amish way of life; they view secondary school education as an impermissible exposure of their children to a "worldly" influence in conflict with their beliefs. The high school tends to emphasize intellectual and scientific accomplishments, self-distinction, competitiveness, worldly success, and social life with other students. Amish society emphasizes informal learning-through-doing; a life of "goodness," rather than a life of intellect; wisdom, rather than technical knowledge; community welfare, rather than competition; and separation from, rather than integration with, contemporary worldly society.

Formal high school education beyond the eighth grade is contrary to Amish beliefs, not only because it places Amish children in an environment hostile to Amish beliefs with increasing emphasis on competition in class work and sports and with pressure to conform to the styles, manners, and ways of the peer group, but also because it takes them away from their community, physically and emotionally, during the crucial and formative adolescent period of life. During this period, the children must acquire Amish attitudes favoring manual work and self-reliance and the specific skills needed to perform the adult role of an Amish farmer or housewife. They must learn to enjoy physical labor. Once a child has learned basic reading, writing, and elementary mathematics, these traits, skills, and attitudes admittedly fall within the category of those best learned through example and "doing" rather than in a classroom. And, at this time in life, the Amish child must also grow in his faith and his relationship to the Amish community if he is to be prepared to accept the heavy obligations imposed by adult baptism. . . .

The Amish do not object to elementary education through the first eight grades as a general proposition because they agree that their children must have basic skills in the "three R's" in order to read the Bible, to be good farmers and citizens, and to be able to deal with non-Amish people when necessary in the course of daily affairs. They view such a basic education as acceptable because it does not significantly expose their children to worldly values or interfere with their development in the Amish community during the crucial adolescent period. . . . In the Amish belief higher learning tends to develop values they reject as influences that alienate man from God.

On the basis of such considerations, Dr. Hostetler testified that compulsory high school attendance could not only result in great psychological harm to Amish children, because of the conflicts it would produce, but would also, in his opinion, ultimately result in the destruction of the Old Order Amish church community as it exists in the United States today. . . . [Another expert witness] described their system of learning through doing the skills directly relevant to their adult roles in the Amish community as "ideal" and perhaps superior to ordinary high school education. The evidence also showed that the Amish have an excellent record as law-abiding and generally self-sufficient members of society.

. . . [A] State's interest in universal education, however highly we rank it, is not totally free from a balancing process when it impinges on fundamental rights and interests, such as those specifically protected by the Free Exercise Clause of the First Amendment.

It follows that in order for Wisconsin to compel school attendance beyond the eighth grade against a claim that such attendance interferes with the practice of a legitimate religious belief, it must appear either that the State does not deny the free exercise of religious belief by its requirement, or that there is a state interest of sufficient magnitude to override the interest claiming protection under the Free Exercise Clause. . . .

The essence of all that has been said and written on the subject is that only those interests of the highest order and those not otherwise served can overbalance legitimate claims to the free exercise of religion. We can accept it as settled, therefore, that, however strong the State's interest in universal compulsory education, it is by no means absolute to the exclusion or subordination of all other interests.

. . . In evaluating those claims we must be careful to determine whether the Amish religious faith and their mode of life are, as they claim, inseparable and interdependent. A way of life, however virtuous and admirable, may not be interposed as a barrier to reasonable state regulation of education if it is based on purely secular considerations; to have the protection of the Religion Clauses, the claims must be rooted in religious belief. Although a determination of what is a "religious" belief or practice entitled to constitutional protection may present a most delicate question, the very concept of ordered liberty precludes allowing every person to make his own standards on matters of conduct in which society as a whole has important interests. Thus, if the Amish asserted their claims because of their subjective evaluation and rejection of the contemporary secular values accepted by the majority, much as Thoreau rejected the social values of his time and isolated himself at Walden Pond, their claims would not rest on a religious basis. Thoreau's choice was philosophical and personal rather than religious, and such belief does not rise to the demands of the Religion Clauses.

Giving no weight to such secular considerations, however, we see that the record in this case abundantly supports the claim that the traditional way of life of the Amish is not merely a matter of personal preference, but one of deep religious conviction, shared by an organized group, and intimately related to daily living. . . . [T]he unchallenged testimony of acknowledged experts in education and religious history, almost 300 years of consistent practice, and strong evidence of a sustained faith pervading and regulating respondents' entire mode of life support the claim that enforcement of the State's requirement of compulsory formal education after the eighth grade would gravely endanger if not destroy the free exercise of respondents' religious beliefs. . . .

We turn, then, to the State's broader contention that its interest in its system of compulsory education is so compelling that even the established religious practices of the Amish must give way. Where fundamental claims of religious freedom are at stake, however, we cannot accept such a sweeping claim; despite its admitted validity in the generality of cases, we must searchingly examine the interests that the State seeks to promote by its requirement for compulsory education to age 16, and the impediment to those objectives that would flow from recognizing the claimed Amish exemption.

The State advances two primary arguments in support of its system of compulsory education. It notes, as Thomas Jefferson pointed out early in our history, that some degree of education is necessary to prepare citizens to participate effectively and intelligently in our open political system if we are to preserve freedom and independence. Further, education prepares individuals to be self-reliant and self-sufficient participants in society. We accept these propositions.

However, the evidence adduced by the Amish in this case is persuasively to the effect that an additional one or two years of formal high school for Amish children in place of their long-established program of informal vocational education would do little to serve those interests. . . . It is one thing to say that compulsory education for a year or two beyond the eighth grade may be necessary when its goal is the preparation of the child for life in modern society as the majority live, but it is quite another if the goal of education be viewed as the preparation of the child for life in the separated agrarian community that is the keystone of the Amish faith.

Contrary to the suggestion of the dissenting opinion of Justice Douglas, our holding today in no degree depends on the assertion of the religious interest of the child as contrasted with that of the parents. It is the parents who are subject to prosecution here for failing to cause their children to attend school, and it is their right of free exercise, not that of their children, that must determine Wisconsin's power to impose criminal penalties on the parent. The dissent argues that a child who expresses a desire to attend public high school in conflict with the wishes of his parents should not be prevented from doing so. There is no reason for the Court to consider that point since it is not an issue in the case. The children are not parties to this litigation. The State has at no point tried this case on the theory that respondents were preventing their children from attending school against their expressed desires, and indeed the record is to the contrary. . . .

Our holding in no way determines the proper resolution of possible competing interests of parents, children, and the State in an appropriate state court proceeding in which the power of the State is asserted on the theory that Amish parents are preventing their minor children from attending high school despite their expressed desires to the contrary. Recognition of the claim of the State in such a proceeding would, of course, call into question traditional concepts of parental control over the religious upbringing and education of their minor children recognized in this Court's past decisions. It is clear that such an intrusion by a State into family decisions in the area of religious training would give rise to grave questions of religious freedom. . . . On this record we neither reach nor decide those issues.

For the reasons stated we hold, with the Supreme Court of Wisconsin, that the First and Fourteenth Amendments prevent the State from compelling respondents to cause their children to attend formal high school to age 16.

Affirmed.

Justice POWELL and Justice REHNQUIST took no part in the consideration or decision of this case.

Justice STEWART, with whom Justice BRENNAN joins, concurring.

This case in no way involves any questions regarding the right of the children of Amish parents to attend public high schools, or any other institutions of learning, if they wish to do so. As the Court points out, there is no suggestion whatever in the record that the religious beliefs of the children here concerned differ in any way from those of their parents. Only one of the children testified. The last two questions and answers on her cross-examination accurately sum up her testimony:

Q. So I take it then, Frieda, the only reason you are not going to school, and did not go to school since last September, is because of your religion?
A. Yes.
Q. That is the only reason?
A. Yes.

It is clear to me, therefore, that this record simply does not present the interesting and important issue discussed in . . . the dissenting opinion of Justice Douglas. With this observation, I join the opinion and the judgment of the Court.

Justice DOUGLAS, dissenting in part.

. . . The Court's analysis assumes that the only interests at stake in the case are those of the Amish parents on the one hand, and those of the State on the other. The difficulty with this approach is that, despite the Court's claim, the parents are seeking to vindicate not only their own free exercise claims, but also those of their high-school-age children.

. . . If the parents in this case are allowed a religious exemption, the inevitable effect is to impose the parents' notions of religious duty upon their children. Where the child is mature enough to express potentially conflicting desires, it would be an invasion of the child's rights to permit such an imposition without canvassing his views. . . . As the child has no other effective forum, it is in this litigation that his rights should be considered. And, if an Amish child desires to attend high school, and is mature enough to have that desire respected, the State may well be able to override the parents' religiously motivated objections.

Religion is an individual experience. It is not necessary, nor even appropriate, for every Amish child to express his views on the subject in a prosecution of a single adult. These, however, are the views of the child whose parent is the subject of the suit. Frieda Yoder has in fact testified that her own religious views are opposed to high-school education. I therefore join the judgment of the Court as to respondent Jonas Yoder. But Frieda Yoder's views may not be those of [the other children whose parents are involved here]. . . .

On this important and vital matter of education, I think the children should be entitled to be heard. While the parents, absent dissent, normally speak for the entire family, the education of the child is a matter on which the child will often have decided views. He may want to be a pianist or an astronaut or an oceanographer. To do so he will have to break from the Amish tradition.

It is the future of the student, not the future of the parents, that is imperiled by today's decision. If a parent keeps his child out of school beyond the grade school, then the child will be forever barred from entry into the new and amazing world of diversity that we have today. The child may decide that that is the preferred course, or he may rebel. It is the student's judgment, not his parents', that is essential if we are to give full meaning to what we have said about the Bill of Rights and of the right of students to be masters of their own destiny. If he is harnessed to the Amish way of life by those in authority over him and if his education is truncated, his entire life may be stunted and deformed. The child, therefore, should be given an opportunity to be heard before the State gives the exemption which we honor today.

Notes and Queries

1. What is the significance of the Court's extensive reliance on the distinctive and long history of the Amish in this country? Did the Court review this history to determine whether the Amish's beliefs were "religious" for purposes of the First Amendment? Or was the Court signaling to other potential claimants that it will not routinely excuse or exempt religious organizations from "facially" neutral state laws?

Consider, for example, a sanctuary established in the late 1980s and professing the religious values and beliefs of the Reverend Sung Myung Moon. Would the Court be as quick to protect those beliefs, given the absence of a long history similar to that of the Amish? Why is such a history important? Does it suggest sincerity of belief?

Is sincerity a necessary component of what constitutes religion? How does the Court define religion? Is the Court's definition derived in any significant way from the Constitution itself? From the Framers' intent? From history or tradition? What is the difference between a "religious" belief and a "philosophical and personal belief"?

2. Did the Court depart from the general idea that the religion clauses require the government to be neutral toward religion? Why is the exception made for the Amish in *Yoder* not an "establishment" of religion? The Court dismissed the problem in a footnote, observing that "Accommodating the religious beliefs of the Amish can hardly be characterized as sponsorship or active involvement." But hasn't the Court demanded strict neutrality toward religion? Is *Yoder* consistent with a strictly neutral policy of compulsory education?

Does this suggest that *Yoder* is best understood as promoting a concept of religion that values religious pluralism and diversity? Is that necessarily an accommodationist reading of the religion clauses? Doesn't it conflict with the separationist approach to the establishment clause? How should the Court choose between these different interpretations?

3. Why is the state's interest in public education not sufficiently compelling to overcome the fundamental right in this case? Is it because the children are "partly" educated and will likely return to the Amish community? Would the state's interest be stronger if it could demonstrate that a "significant" number of Amish children will leave their communities at the age of majority?

Consider, too, the precise nature of the right involved in this case. Is it free exercise? The right of parents to supervise the education of their children? The right of the children to determine for themselves their religious commitments, as Justice Douglas wrote? Or is the right a collective one, a right (perhaps a liberty right?) of insular religious communities to maintain themselves in a pluralistic and secular society? See Robert M. Cover, *Foreword: Nomos and Narrative*, 97 Harvard Law Review 26 (1983); Stanley Hauerwas, *Faith in the Republic: A Frances Lewis Law Center Conversation*, 45 Washington and Lee Law Review 471 (1988).

4. In *United States v. Lee* (1982), the Court refused to exempt the Amish from social security taxes, even though "the Amish consider it sinful not to provide for their own elderly and are therefore religiously opposed to the national social security system." In this case, the Court found that the government's interest in mandatory participation was compelling. The Court worried also that an exemption for the Amish might lead other groups to ask for exemptions.

5. As *Yoder* indicates, the values children are exposed to and learn in school may sometimes conflict with the religious and moral instruction they receive from their parents. In the *Interdenominational School Case*, 41 BVerfGE 29 (1975), the parents of children in the German state of Baden-Württemberg challenged the constitutionality of the state's decision to establish Christian interdenominational schools as the uniform type of public grade school.

Article 7(5) of the Basic Law affords to states the right to establish interdenominational, denominational, or ideological schools.

The Court concluded that "Article 4 of the Basic Law protects the negative as well as the positive manifestation of religious freedom against encroachments by the state. This freedom especially affects the organization of those areas of life which, because of their social necessity or political aims, are not left to the free play of social forces but have been taken into the care of the state." The Court continued that "In the instant case the complainant's request to keep the education of their children free from all religious influences . . . must inevitably conflict with the desire of other citizens to afford their children a religious education. . . ."

In balancing these conflicting claims, the Court concluded that the state was not absolutely prohibited from incorporating Christian principles in the school system. Nevertheless, the state was obligated to "choose a type of school which, insofar as it can influence childrens' decisions concerning faith and conscience, contains only a minimum of coercive elements." Consequently, the Court elaborated, the state could not demand a commitment to the principles of Christianity.

In *Kjeldsen, Busk Madsen and Perderson v. Denmark* (7 Dec. 1976), the parents of children in Denmark's primary schools objected to compulsory sex education. They filed a complaint with the European Commission of Human Rights, charging that the requirement violated Article 2 of Protocol 1, which provides that "No person shall be denied the right to education. In the exercise of any functions which it assumes in relation to education and to teaching, the State shall respect the right of parents to ensure such education and teaching is in conformity with their own religious and philosophical convictions."

The Court found for Denmark, ruling that "Examination of the legislation . . . establishes . . . that it in no way amounts to an attempt at indoctrination aimed at advocating a specific kind of sexual behaviour. It does not make a point of exalting sex or inciting pupils to indulge precociously in practices that are dangerous for their stability, health or future or that many parents consider reprehensible. Further, it does not affect the right of parents to enlighten and advise their children. . . ." Hence, "the disputed legislation in itself no way offends the applicants' religious and philosophical convictions to the extent forbidden by . . . Article 2. . . ."

Sherbert v. Verner
374 U.S. 398, 83 S.Ct. 1790, 10 L.Ed.2d 965 (1963)

Adell Sherbert was fired from her job in a textile mill because she refused to work on Saturdays, the sabbath day of the Seventh-Day Adventist Church. She also refused to accept other jobs for the same reason. Because she would not accept these new jobs, the South Carolina Employment Security Commission denied her application for unemployment benefits. She challenged the ruling. A trial court and the state Supreme Court upheld the Commission's ruling. Opinion of the Court: *Brennan*, Clark, Warren, Black, Goldberg. Concurring opinions: *Douglas*; *Stewart*. Dissenting opinion: *Harlan*, White.

Mr. Justice BRENNAN delivered the opinion of the Court.

We turn first to the question whether the disqualification for benefits imposes any burden on the free exercise of appellant's religion. We think it is clear that it does. In a sense the consequences of such a disqualification to religious principles and practices may be only an indirect result of welfare legislation within the State's general competence to enact; it is true that no criminal sanctions directly compel appellant to work a six-day week. But this is only the beginning, not the end, of our inquiry.

Here not only is it apparent that appellant's declared ineligibility for benefits derives solely from the practice of her religion, but the pressure upon her to forego that practice is unmistakable. The ruling forces her to choose between following the precepts of her religion and forfeiting benefits, on the one hand, and abandoning one of the precepts of her religion in order to accept work, on the other hand. Governmental imposition of such a choice puts the same kind of burden upon the free exercise of religion as would a fine imposed against appellant for her Saturday worship.

Nor may the South Carolina court's construction of the statute be saved from constitutional infirmity on the ground that unemployment compensation benefits are not appellant's "right" but merely a "privilege." It is too late in the day to doubt that the liberties of religion and expression may be infringed by the denial of or placing of conditions upon a benefit or privilege. . . . [T]o condition the availability of benefits upon this appellant's willingness to violate a cardinal principle of her religious faith effectively penalizes the free exercise of her constitutional liberties.

Significantly South Carolina expressly saves the Sunday worshipper from having to make the kind of choice which we here hold infringes the Sabbatarian's religious liberty. When in times of "national emergency" the textile plants are authorized by the State Commissioner of Labor to operate on Sunday, "no employee shall be required to work on Sunday who is conscientiously opposed to Sunday work; and if any employee should refuse to work on Sunday on account of conscientious objections he or she shall not jeopardize his or her seniority by such refusal or be discriminated against in any other manner." No question of the disqualification of a Sunday worshipper for benefits is likely to arise, since we cannot suppose that an employer will discharge him in violation of this statute. The unconstitutionality of the disqualification of the Sabbatarian is thus compounded by the religious discrimination which South Carolina's general statutory scheme necessarily effects.

· · ·

III

We must next consider whether some compelling state interest enforced in the eligibility provisions of the South Carolina statute justifies the substantial infringement of appellant's First Amendment right. It is basic that no showing merely of a rational relationship to some colorable state interest would suffice; in this highly sensitive constitutional area, "(o)nly the gravest abuses, endangering paramount interest, give occasion for permissible limitation." No such abuse or danger has been advanced in the present case. The appellees suggest no more than a possibility that the filing of fraudulent claims by unscrupulous claimants feigning religious objections to Saturday work might not only dilute the unemployment compensation fund but also hinder the scheduling by employers of necessary Saturday work. But that possibility is not apposite here because no such objection appears to have been made before the South Carolina Supreme Court, and we are unwilling to assess the importance of an asserted state interest without the views of the state court. Nor, if the contention had been made below, would the record appear to sustain it; there is no proof whatever to warrant such fears of malingering or deceit as those which the respondents now advance. Even if consideration of such evidence is not foreclosed by the prohibition against judicial inquiry into the truth or falsity of religious beliefs,—a question as to which we intimate no view since it is not before us—it is highly doubtful whether such evidence would be sufficient to warrant a substantial infringement of religious liberties. For even if the possibility of spurious claims did threaten to dilute the fund and disrupt the scheduling of work, it would plainly be incumbent upon the appellees to demonstrate that no alternative forms of

regulation would combat such abuses without infringing First Amendment rights. . . .

IV

In holding as we do, plainly we are not fostering the "establishment" of the Seventh-day Adventist religion in South Carolina, for the extension of unemployment benefits to Sabbatarians in common with Sunday worshippers reflects nothing more than the governmental obligation of neutrality in the face of religious differences, and does not represent that involvement of religious with secular institutions which it is the object of the Establishment Clause to forestall.

Nor does the recognition of the appellant's right to unemployment benefits under the state statute serve to abridge any other person's religious liberties. Nor do we, by our decision today, declare the existence of a constitutional right to unemployment benefits on the part of all persons whose religious convictions are the cause of their unemployment. This is not a case in which an employee's religious convictions serve to make him a nonproductive member of society. . . . Finally, nothing we say today constrains the States to adopt any particular form or scheme of unemployment compensation. Our holding today is only that South Carolina may not constitutionally apply the eligibility provisions so as to constrain a worker to abandon his religious convictions respecting the day of rest. This holding but reaffirms a principle that we announced a decade and a half ago, namely that no State may "exclude individual Catholics, Lutherans, Mohammedans, Baptists, Jews, Methodists, Non-believers, Presbyterians, or the members of any other faith, because of their faith, or lack of it, from receiving the benefits of public welfare legislation."

. . . The judgment of the South Carolina Supreme Court is reversed and the case is remanded for further proceedings not inconsistent with this opinion. It is so ordered. Reversed and remanded.

Mr. Justice DOUGLAS, concurring.

Mr. Justice STEWART, concurring in the result.

. . . . I cannot join the Court's opinion. This case presents a double-barreled dilemma, which in all candor I think the Court's opinion has not succeeded in papering over. The dilemma ought to be resolved. . . .

I am convinced that no liberty is more essential to the continued vitality of the free society which our Constitution guarantees than is the religious liberty protected by the Free Exercise Clause explicit in the First Amendment and imbedded in the Fourteenth. And I regret that on occasion, and specifically in *Braunfeld v. Brown* . . . , the Court has shown what has seemed to me a distressing insensitivity to the appropriate demands of this constitutional guarantee. By contrast I think that the Court's approach to the Establishment Clause has on occasion, and specifically in *Engel, Schempp* and *Murray,* been not only insensitive, but positively wooden, and that the Court has accorded to the Establishment Clause a meaning which neither the words, the history, nor the intention of the authors of that specific constitutional provision even remotely suggests. But my views as to the correctness of the Court's decisions in these cases are beside the point here. The point is that the decisions are on the books. And the result is that there are many situations where legitimate claims under the Free Exercise Clause will run into head-on collision with the Court's insensitive and sterile construction of the Establishment Clause. The controversy now before us is clearly such a case. . . .

If the appellant's refusal to work on Saturdays were based on indolence, or on a compulsive desire to watch the Saturday television programs, no one would say that South Carolina could not hold that she was not "available for work" within the meaning of its statute. That being so, the Establishment Clause as construed by this Court not only permits but affirmatively requires South Carolina equally to deny the appellant's claim for unemployment compensation when her refusal to work on Saturdays is based upon her religious creed. . . .

To require South Carolina to so administer its laws as to pay public money to the appellant under the circumstances of this case is thus clearly to require the State to violate the Establishment Clause as construed by this Court. This poses no problem for me, because I think the Court's mechanistic concept of the Establishment Clause is historically unsound and constitutionally wrong. I think the process of constitutional decision in the area of the relationships between government and religion demands considerably more than the invocation of broad-brushed rhetoric of the kind I have quoted. And I think that the guarantee of religious liberty embodied in the Free Exercise Clause affirmatively requires government to create an atmosphere of hospitality and accommodation to individual belief or disbelief. In short, I think our Constitution commands the positive protection by government of religious freedom—not only for a minority, however small—not only for the majority, however large—but for each of us.

Mr. Justice HARLAN, whom Mr. Justice WHITE joins, dissenting.

. . . What the Court is holding is that if the State chooses to condition unemployment compensation on the appli-

cant's availability for work, it is constitutionally compelled to carve out an exception—and to provide benefits—for those whose unavailability is due to their religious convictions. Such a holding has particular significance in two respects.

First, despite the Court's protestations to the contrary, the decision necessarily overrules *Braunfeld v. Brown,* which held that it did not offend the "Free Exercise" Clause of the Constitution for a State to forbid a Sabbatarian to do business on Sunday. The secular purpose of the statute before us today is even clearer than that involved in *Braunfeld.* And just as in *Braunfeld*—where exceptions to the Sunday closing laws for Sabbatarians would have been inconsistent with the purpose to achieve a uniform day of rest and would have required case-by-case inquiry into religious beliefs—so here, an exception to the rules of eligibility based on religious convictions would necessitate judicial examination of those convictions and would be at odds with the limited purpose of the statute to smooth out the economy during periods of industrial instability. . . .

Second, the implications of the present decision are far more troublesome than its apparently narrow dimensions would indicate at first glance. The meaning of today's holding, as already noted, is that the State must furnish unemployment benefits to one who is unavailable for work if the unavailability stems from the exercise of religious convictions. The State, in other words, must single out for financial assistance those whose behavior is religiously motivated, even though it denies such assistance to others whose identical behavior (in this case, inability to work on Saturdays) is not religiously motivated. It has been suggested that such singling out of religious conduct for special treatment may violate the constitutional limitations on state action. . . . My own view, however, is that at least under the circumstances of this case it would be a permissible accommodation of religion for the State, if it chose to do so, to create an exception to its eligibility requirements for persons like the appellant. The constitutional obligation of "neutrality," is not so narrow a channel that the slightest deviation from an absolutely straight course leads to condemnation. There are too many instances in which no such course can be charted, too many areas in which the pervasive activities of the State justify some special provision for religion to prevent it from being submerged by an all-embracing secularism. The State violates its obligation of neutrality when, for example, it mandates a daily religious exercise in its public schools, with all the attendant pressures on the school children that such an exercise entails. But there is, I believe, enough flexibility in the Constitution to permit a legislative judgment accommodating an unemployment compensation law to the exercise of religious beliefs such as appellant's.

For very much the same reasons, however, I cannot subscribe to the conclusion that the State is constitutionally compelled to carve out an exception to its general rule of eligibility in the present case. Those situations in which the Constitution may require special treatment on account of religion are, in my view, few and far between, and this view is amply supported by the course of constitutional litigation in this area. Such compulsion in the present case is particularly inappropriate in light of the indirect, remote, and insubstantial effect of the decision below on the exercise of appellant's religion and in light of the direct financial assistance to religion that today's decision requires. For these reasons I respectfully dissent from the opinion and judgment of the Court.

Notes and Queries

1. The majority's decision in *Sherbert* recognized that the "secular regulation" rule could work a great hardship on many individuals with sincerely held religious beliefs. Partly to offset that possibility, the Court concluded that a secular regulation that "substantially burdens" a religious practice must be justified by a compelling state interest. Doesn't this rule depart from the requirement of strict neutrality by requiring the state sometimes to make exceptions based on religious principles? Isn't such a decision incompatible with the Court's establishment clause jurisprudence? Or is the departure from neutrality required by

an approach to the free exercise clause that promotes religious pluralism and tolerance?

2. In *Thomas v. Review Board* (1981), the Court again ruled that to deny unemployment benefits to a worker who quit his job for religious reasons, the state must demonstrate a compelling interest. And in 1989, the Court ruled that benefits could not be denied to a worker whose refusal to work on Sundays was based on a sincere religious belief, even though the worker belonged to no organized religion. In dissent, Justice Rehnquist argued that an exemption for Thomas, as for Sherbert, conflicted with the Court's establishment clause jurisprudence. He urged that *Sherbert* be overruled. In *Lyng v. Northwest Indian Cemetery Protective Association* (1988), Justice O'Connor, writing for the Court, explained that the compelling state interest test was appropriate only when there is governmental coercion or penalties on the free exercise of religion. Incidental effects on religion, even if seriously disruptive, are measured by the less strict rationality test. Hence, in this case, the Court upheld a plan by the U.S. Forest Service to permit timber harvesting in an area of a national forest sacred to several Indian tribes.

Can the Court's decision in *Lyng* to abandon the compelling state interest test, even though there is clear evidence of a burden on religion, be reconciled with *Sherbert*? Does it rest on a different understanding of the relationship between the state and religion?

3. In dissent, Justice Stewart complained that the Court had "papered over" the conflict in this case between the Establishment and Free Exercise clauses. How would Justice Stewart reconcile the conflict?

Church of the Lukumi Babalu Aye, Inc. v. Hialeah

508 U.S. 520, 113 S.Ct. 2217, 124 L.Ed.2d 472 (1993)

The Santeria religion (the "way of the Saints") combines elements of Catholicism and traditional African religious practices, one of which involves ritual animal sacrifice and the subsequent cooking and eating of the animals. The religion was brought to the United States most often by exiles from the Cuban revolution; there are at least 50,000 practitioners in South Florida today. One Santerian church, the Church of Lukumi Babula Aye, rented land in Hialeah, Florida, with the intention of establishing a place to worship. Some of the local residents, however, objected, and the City Council responded in an "emergency session" by adopting several ordinances that, together, made cruelty to animals a criminal offense, prohibited rit-

ual animal sacrifice "not for the primary purpose of food consumption" and exempting licensed slaughterhouses. The Church filed suit in a U.S. District Court, complaining that the new statutes violated the Church's right to free exercise of religion. The District Court ruled for Hialeah, and the appellate court affirmed that ruling. Opinion of the Court: *Kennedy*, Stevens, joined in part by Rehnquist, White, Scalia, Souter, Thomas. Concurring in the opinion part and in the judgment: *Scalia*, Rehnquist; *Souter*. Concurring in the judgment: *Blackmun*, O'Connor.

Justice KENNEDY delivered the opinion of the Court, except as to Part II-A-2.

The principle that government may not enact laws that suppress religious belief or practice is so well understood that few violations are recorded in our opinions. Concerned that this fundamental nonpersecution principle of the First Amendment was implicated here, however, we granted certiorari.

Our review confirms that the laws in question were enacted by officials who did not understand, failed to perceive, or chose to ignore the fact that their official actions violated the Nation's essential commitment to religious freedom. The challenged laws had an impermissible object; and in all events the principle of general applicability was violated because the secular ends asserted in defense of the laws were pursued only with respect to conduct motivated by religious beliefs. We invalidate the challenged enactments and reverse the judgment of the Court of Appeals.

. . . The city does not argue that Santeria is not a "religion" within the meaning of the First Amendment. Nor could it. Although the practice of animal sacrifice may seem abhorrent to some, "religious beliefs need not be acceptable, logical, consistent, or comprehensible to others in order to merit First Amendment protection." *Thomas v. Review Bd. of Indiana Employment Security Div.* (1981). Given the historical association between animal sacrifice and religious worship, petitioners' assertion that animal sacrifice is an integral part of their religion "cannot be deemed bizarre or incredible." *Frazee v. Illinois Dept. of Employment Security,* (1989). Neither the city nor the courts below, moreover, have questioned the sincerity of petitioners' professed desire to conduct animal sacrifices for religious reasons. We must consider petitioners' First Amendment claim.

In addressing the constitutional protection for free exercise of religion, our cases establish the general proposition that a law that is neutral and of general applicability need not be justified by a compelling governmental interest even if the law has the incidental effect of burdening a particular religious practice. *Employment Div., Dept. of Human Resources of Ore. v. Smith.* Neutrality and general applicability are interrelated, and, as becomes apparent in this case, failure to satisfy one requirement is a likely indication that the other has not been satisfied. A law failing to satisfy these requirements must be justified by a compelling governmental interest and must be narrowly tailored to advance that interest. These ordinances fail to satisfy the *Smith* requirements. We begin by discussing neutrality.

At a minimum, the protections of the Free Exercise Clause pertain if the law at issue discriminates against some or all religious beliefs or regulates or prohibits conduct because it is undertaken for religious reasons. Indeed, it was "historical instances of religious persecution and intolerance that gave concern to those who drafted the Free Exercise Clause." These principles, though not

often at issue in our Free Exercise Clause cases, have played a role in some. In *McDaniel v. Paty* (1978), for example, we invalidated a State law that disqualified members of the clergy from holding certain public offices, because it "impose[d] special disabilities on the basis of . . . religious status." On the same principle, in *Fowler v. Rhode Island* (1953), we found that a municipal ordinance was applied in an unconstitutional manner when interpreted to prohibit preaching in a public park by a Jehovah's Witness but to permit preaching during the course of a Catholic mass or Protestant church service. . . .

The record in this case compels the conclusion that suppression of the central element of the Santeria worship service was the object of the ordinances. First, though use of the words "sacrifice" and "ritual" does not compel a finding of improper targeting of the Santeria religion, the choice of these words is support for our conclusion. There are further respects in which the text of the city council's enactments discloses the improper attempt to target Santeria. Resolution 87–66, adopted June 9, 1987, recited that "residents and citizens of the City of Hialeah have expressed their concern that certain religions may propose to engage in practices which are inconsistent with public morals, peace or safety," and "reiterate[d]" the city's commitment to prohibit "any and all [such] acts of any and all religious groups." No one suggests, and on this record it cannot be maintained, that city officials had in mind a religion other than Santeria.

It is a necessary conclusion that almost the only conduct subject to Ordinances 87-40, 87-52, and 87-71 is the religious exercise of Santeria church members. The texts show that they were drafted in tandem to achieve this result. We begin with Ordinance 87-71. It prohibits the sacrifice of animals, but defines sacrifice as "to unnecessarily kill . . . an animal in a public or private ritual or ceremony not for the primary purpose of food consumption." The definition excludes almost all killings of animals except for religious sacrifice, and the primary purpose requirement narrows the proscribed category even further, in particular by exempting kosher slaughter. . . . We need not discuss whether this differential treatment of two religions is itself an independent constitutional violation. It suffices to recite this feature of the law as support for our conclusion that Santeria alone was the exclusive legislative concern. The net result of the gerrymander is that few if any killings of animals are prohibited other than Santeria sacrifice, which is proscribed because it occurs during a ritual or ceremony and its primary purpose is to make an offering to the orishas, not food consumption. Indeed, careful drafting ensured that, although Santeria sacrifice is

Comparative Note 13.9

[The Indian states of Bihar and Uttar Pradesh passed laws banning the slaughter of "all categories of animals of the species bovine cattle." Several Muslim petitioners challenged these statutes, claiming that because sacrificing cows is sanctioned by their religion the laws violate the free exercise of their religion in violation of Article 25 of the Indian Constitution. Article 25 reads: "Subject to public order, morality and health and to the other provisions of this Part, all persons are equally entitled to freedom of conscience and the right freely to profess, practice and propagate religion."]

. . . [T]he sole purpose of these enactments is to secure the preservation, protection and improvement of stock . . . in the interest of the general public. . . .

What, then, we inquire, are the materials placed before us to substantiate the claim that the sacrifice of a cow is enjoined or sanctioned by Islam? The materials before us are extremely meagre and it is surprising that on a matter of this description the allegations in the petition should be so vague. . . .

. . . No affidavit has been filed by any person specially competent to expound the relevant tenets of Islam. No reference is made in the petition to any particular Surah of the Holy Quran which, in terms, requires the sacrifice of a cow. . . . While the petitioners claim that the sacrifice of a cow is essential, the State denies the obligatory nature of the religious practice. The fact, emphasized by the respondents, cannot be disputed, namely, that many Mussalmans do not sacrifice a cow on the Bakr Id Day. It is part of the known history of India that the Moghul Emperor Babar saw the wisdom of prohibiting the slaughter of cows as and by way of religious sacrifice and directed his son Humayun to follow this example. Similarly, Emperors Akbar, Jehangir, and Ahmad Shah, it is said, prohibited cow slaughter. . . . Three of the members of the Gosamvardhan Enquiry Committee set up by the Uttar Pradesh Government [—all of them Muslims—] concurred in . . . the total ban on slaughter of cows. We have . . . no material on the record before us which will enable us to say, in the face of the foregoing facts, that the sacrifice of a cow on that day is an obligatory overt act for a Mussalman to exhibit his religious belief and idea. In the premises, it is not possible for us to uphold this [religious] claim of the petitioners.

Source: *M. H. Quareshi v. The State of Bihar,* Supreme Court of India, 1958 A.I.R. 731.

---

prohibited, killings that are no more necessary or humane in almost all other circumstances are unpunished.

Operating in similar fashion is Ordinance 87-52, which prohibits the "possess[ion], sacrifice, or slaughter" of an animal with the "inten[t] to use such animal for food purposes." This prohibition, extending to the keeping of an animal as well as the killing itself, applies if the animal is killed in "any type of ritual" and there is an intent to use the animal for food, whether or not it is in fact consumed for food. The ordinance exempts, however, "any licensed [food] establishment" with regard to "any animals which are specifically raised for food purposes," if the activity is permitted by zoning and other laws. This exception, too, seems intended to cover kosher slaughter. Again, the burden of the ordinance, in practical terms, falls on Santeria adherents but almost no others. . . .

We also find significant evidence of the ordinances' improper targeting of Santeria sacrifice in the fact that they proscribe more religious conduct than is necessary to achieve their stated ends. It is not unreasonable to infer, at least when there are no persuasive indications to the contrary, that a law which visits "gratuitous restrictions" on religious conduct, seeks not to effectuate the stated governmental interests, but to suppress the conduct because of its religious motivation.

The legitimate governmental interests in protecting the public health and preventing cruelty to animals could be addressed by restrictions stopping far short of a flat prohibition of all Santeria sacrificial practice. If improper disposal, not the sacrifice itself, is the harm to be prevented, the city could have imposed a general regulation on the disposal of organic garbage. It did not do so. Indeed, counsel for the city conceded at oral argument that, under the ordinances, Santeria sacrifices would be illegal even if they occurred in licensed, inspected, and zoned slaughterhouses. Thus, these broad ordinances prohibit Santeria sacrifice even when it does not threaten the city's interest in the public health. The District Court accepted the argument that narrower regulation would be unenforceable because of the secrecy in the Santeria rituals and the lack of any central religious authority to require compliance with secular disposal regulations. It is difficult to under-

Comparative Note 13.10

[Germany's Animal Protection Act of 1986 contains a general ban on slaughtering warm-blooded animals without previously stunning them. Sec. 4a (1) reads: "A warm-blooded animal may only be slaughtered if it was stunned before the draining of its blood begins." Sec. 4a (2), however, provides an exemption against stunning but "only to the extent necessary" to meet the needs of religious groups whose beliefs "prescribe ritual slaughtering or prohibit the consumption of the meat of animals that were not ritually slaughtered." Administrative authorities denied the exemption to a Turkish citizen, a "pious Sunnitic Muslim" who operated a butcher shop, on the ground that ritual slaughtering prior to the consumption of meat was not "mandatorily prohibited by the highest representatives of Sunnitic Islam." The butcher filed a constitutional complaint in the Federal Constitutional Court, alleging in part that the denial of the exemption violated his rights to personality and religious freedom under the Basic Law.]

[The complainant charges]:

1. Slaughtering without previously stunning the animal is of central importance in the Islamic religion. Its ritual character does not only result from the fact that the obligation of ritual slaughtering can be directly inferred from the Koran. The manner of ritual slaughtering is also precisely determined. The ban on ritual slaughtering therefore constitutes an encroachment upon the fundamental right that is guaranteed by Article 4.1 and 4.2 of the Basic Law. . . .

The constitutional complaint is well-founded. . . .

For the complainant, however, ritual slaughtering is not only a means for *obtaining and* preparing meat for his Muslim customers and for himself. It is . . . also an expression of a basic religious attitude that for the *complainant as* a pious Sunnitic Muslim, includes the obligation to perform the slaughtering in accordance with the rules of his religion, which he regards as binding. . . .

The ban does not only concern the Muslim butcher but also his customers. When they demand meat of animals that were ritually slaughtered, this is obviously based on the fact that they are convinced that their faith prohibits them, in a binding manner, from eating other meat. If they were required to, basically, forgo the con-

sumption of meat, this would not sufficiently take the eating habits in the Federal Republic of Germany into consideration. In Germany, meat is a common food, and it can hardly be regarded as reasonable to involuntarily renounce its consumption. It is true that the consumption of imported meat makes such renunciation dispensable; however, due to the fact that in this case, the personal contact to the butcher and the confidence that goes with such contact do not exist, the consumption of imported meat is fraught with the insecurity whether the meat really complies with the commandments of Islam.

These consequences for pious Muslim butchers and their pious customers must be weighed against the fact that the protection of animals constitutes a public interest that is attached high importance among the population. The parliament has taken this into consideration by not regarding animals as objects but as fellow creatures, which also feel pain, and by intending to protect them by special laws. . . .

Under these circumstances, an exemption from the mandatory stunning of warm-blooded animals before their blood is drained cannot be precluded if the intention connected with this exemption is to facilitate, on the one hand, the practice of a profession with a religious character, which is protected by fundamental rights, and, on the other hand, the observation of religious dietary laws by the customers of the person who practices the occupation in question. Without such exemptions, the fundamental rights of those who want to perform slaughtering without stunning as their occupation would be unreasonably restricted, and the interests of the protection of animals would, without a sufficient constitutional justification, be given priority in a one-sided manner. What is necessary instead is a regulation that, in a balanced manner, takes into consideration: (1) the fundamental rights that are affected; and (2) the aims of a protection of animals that is based on ethical principles.

[The lower court's] interpretation . . . prevents a butcher from exercising his occupation who intends to perform ritual slaughtering because he, with a view to the faith that he and his customers adhere to, wants to ensure their supply with the meat of animals that were slaughtered without being stunned. This is an unreasonable burden for the persons concerned, which, in a one-sided manner, only takes the interests of the protection of animals into account.

This result, however, can be avoided by interpreting the legal elements "religious group" and "mandatory provisions" in a manner that takes the fundamental right under Article 2.1 in conjunction with Articles 4.1 and 4.2 of the Basic Law into account.

Indirectly, this interpretation has consequences also when it comes to dealing with the concept of "mandatory provisions" that prohibit the members of the religious group in question from the consumption of the meat of animals that were not ritually slaughtered. The

competent authorities, and in the case of disputes, the courts, are to examine and to decide whether the religious group in question complies with this prerequisite, because this is the legal element that is required for the grant of the exceptional permission that is sought. In the case of a religion that, as Islam does, takes different views as regards mandatory ritual slaughtering, the point of reference of such an examination is not necessarily Islam as a whole or the Sunnitic or Shiitic persuasions of this religion. The question whether mandatory provisions exist is to be answered with a view to the specific religious group in question, which may also exist within such a persuasion.

Source: *Ritual Slaughter Case*, German Federal Constitutional Court, 1 BvR 1783/99 (2002).

---

stand, however, how a prohibition of the sacrifices themselves, which occur in private, is enforceable if a ban on improper disposal, which occurs in public, is not. The neutrality of a law is suspect if First Amendment freedoms are curtailed to prevent isolated collateral harms not themselves prohibited by direct regulation.

Under similar analysis, narrower regulation would achieve the city's interest in preventing cruelty to animals. With regard to the city's interest in ensuring the adequate care of animals, regulation of conditions and treatment, regardless of why an animal is kept, is the logical response to the city's concern, not a prohibition on possession for the purpose of sacrifice. The same is true for the city's interest in prohibiting cruel methods of killing. . . . If the city has a real concern that other methods are less humane, however, the subject of the regulation should be the method of slaughter itself, not a religious classification that is said to bear some general relation to it.

In determining if the object of a law is a neutral one under the Free Exercise Clause, we can also find guidance in our equal protection cases. . . . Here, as in equal protection cases, we may determine the city council's object from both direct and circumstantial evidence. Relevant evidence includes, among other things, the historical background of the decision under challenge, the specific series of events leading to the enactment or official policy in question, and the legislative or administrative history, including contemporaneous statements made by members of the decisionmaking body. These objective factors bear on the question of discriminatory object.

That the ordinances were enacted "because of," not merely "in spite of," their suppression of Santeria religious practice is revealed by the events preceding their enact-

ment. Although respondent claimed at oral argument that it had experienced significant problems resulting from the sacrifice of animals within the city before the announced opening of the Church, the city council made no attempt to address the supposed problem before its meeting in June 1987, just weeks after the Church announced plans to open. The minutes and taped excerpts of the June 9 session, both of which are in the record, evidence significant hostility exhibited by residents, members of the city council, and other city officials toward the Santeria religion and its practice of animal sacrifice. The public crowd that attended the June 9 meetings interrupted statements by council members critical of Santeria with cheers and the brief comments of Pichardo with taunts. When Councilman Martinez, a supporter of the ordinances, stated that in prerevolution Cuba "people were put in jail for practicing this religion," the audience applauded.

Other statements by members of the city council were in a similar vein. . . .

In sum, the neutrality inquiry leads to one conclusion: The ordinances had as their object the suppression of religion. The pattern we have recited discloses animosity to Santeria adherents and their religious practices; the ordinances by their own terms target this religious exercise; the texts of the ordinances were gerrymandered with care to proscribe religious killings of animals but to exclude almost all secular killings; and the ordinances suppress much more religious conduct than is necessary in order to achieve the legitimate ends asserted in their defense. These ordinances are not neutral, and the court below committed clear error in failing to reach this conclusion.

We turn next to a second requirement of the Free Exercise Clause, the rule that laws burdening religious practice must be of general applicability. All laws are selective to some extent, but categories of selection are of paramount concern when a law has the incidental effect of burdening religious practice. The Free Exercise Clause "protect[s] religious observers against unequal treatment," and inequality results when a legislature decides that the governmental interests it seeks to advance are worthy of being pursued only against conduct with a religious motivation.

The principle that government, in pursuit of legitimate interests, cannot in a selective manner impose burdens only on conduct motivated by religious belief is essential to the protection of the rights guaranteed by the Free Exercise Clause. The principle underlying the general applicability requirement has parallels in our First Amendment jurisprudence. In this case we need not define with precision the standard used to evaluate whether a prohibition is of general application, for these ordinances fall well below the minimum standard necessary to protect First Amendment rights.

Respondent claims that Ordinances 87-40, 87-52, and 87-71 advance two interests: protecting the public health and preventing cruelty to animals. The ordinances are underinclusive for those ends. They fail to prohibit nonreligious conduct that endangers these interests in a similar or greater degree than Santeria sacrifice does. The underinclusion is substantial, not inconsequential. Despite the city's proffered interest in preventing cruelty to animals, the ordinances are drafted with care to forbid few killings but those occasioned by religious sacrifice. Many types of animal deaths or kills for nonreligious reasons are either not prohibited or approved by express provision. . . .

The city concedes that "neither the State of Florida nor the City has enacted a generally applicable ban on the killing of animals." It asserts, however, that animal sacrifice is "different" from the animal killings that are permitted by law. According to the city, it is "self-evident" that killing animals for food is "important"; the eradication of insects and pests is "obviously justified"; and the euthanasia of excess animals "makes sense." These *ipse dixits* do not explain why religion alone must bear the burden of the ordinances, when many of these secular killings fall within the city's interest in preventing the cruel treatment of animals.

The ordinances are also underinclusive with regard to the city's interest in public health, which is threatened by the disposal of animal carcasses in open public places and the consumption of uninspected meat. . . . Neither interest is pursued by respondent with regard to conduct that is not motivated by religious conviction. The health risks posed by the improper disposal of animal carcasses are

the same whether Santeria sacrifice or some nonreligious killing preceded it. The city does not, however, prohibit hunters from bringing their kill to their houses, nor does it regulate disposal after their activity. Despite substantial testimony at trial that the same public health hazards result from improper disposal of garbage by restaurants, restaurants are outside the scope of the ordinances. Improper disposal is a general problem that causes substantial health risks, but which respondent addresses only when it results from religious exercise.

The ordinances are underinclusive as well with regard to the health risk posed by consumption of uninspected meat. Under the city's ordinances, hunters may eat their kill and fishermen may eat their catch without undergoing governmental inspection. Likewise, state law requires inspection of meat that is sold but exempts meat from animals raised for the use of the owner and "members of his household and nonpaying guests and employees." The asserted interest in inspected meat is not pursued in contexts similar to that of religious animal sacrifice. . . .

We conclude, in sum, that each of Hialeah's ordinances pursues the city's governmental interests only against conduct motivated by religious belief. . . . This precise evil is what the requirement of general applicability is designed to prevent.

A law burdening religious practice that is not neutral or not of general application must undergo the most rigorous of scrutiny. To satisfy the commands of the First Amendment, a law restrictive of religious practice must advance "interests of the highest order" and must be narrowly tailored in pursuit of those interests. The compelling interest standard that we apply once a law fails to meet the *Smith* requirements is not "water[ed] . . . down" but "really means what it says." *Employment Div., Dept. of Human Resources of Ore. v. Smith* (1990). A law that targets religious conduct for distinctive treatment or advances legitimate governmental interests only against conduct with a religious motivation will survive strict scrutiny only in rare cases. It follows from what we have already said that these ordinances cannot withstand this scrutiny. . . .

The Free Exercise Clause commits government itself to religious tolerance, and upon even slight suspicion that proposals for state intervention stem from animosity to religion or distrust of its practices, all officials must pause to remember their own high duty to the Constitution and to the rights it secures. Those in office must be resolute in resisting importunate demands and must ensure that the sole reasons for imposing the burdens of law and regulation are secular. Legislators may not devise mechanisms, overt or disguised, designed to persecute or oppress a religion or its practices. The laws here in question were enacted contrary to these constitutional principles, and they are void.

Reversed.

Justice SCALIA, with whom The Chief Justice joins, concurring in part and concurring in the judgment.

I do not join section [Part II-A and Part II-B] because it departs from the opinion's general focus on the object of the laws at issue to consider the subjective motivation of the lawmakers, i.e., whether the Hialeah City Council actually intended to disfavor the religion of Santeria. As I have noted elsewhere, it is virtually impossible to determine the singular "motive" of a collective legislative body, see, e.g., *Edwards v. Aguillard* (1987) (dissenting opinion), and this Court has a long tradition of refraining from such inquiries.

Perhaps there are contexts in which determination of legislative motive must be undertaken. But I do not think that is true of analysis under the First Amendment (or the Fourteenth, to the extent it incorporates the First). The First Amendment does not refer to the purposes for which legislators enact laws, but to the effects of the laws enacted: "Congress shall make no law . . . prohibiting the free exercise [of religion]. . . ." This does not put us in the business of invalidating laws by reason of the evil motives of their authors. Had the Hialeah City Council set out resolutely to suppress the practices of Santeria, but ineptly adopted ordinances that failed to do so, I do not see how those laws could be said to "prohibi[t] the free exercise" of religion. Nor, in my view, does it matter that a legislature consists entirely of the pure-hearted, if the law it enacts in fact singles out a religious practice for special burdens. Had the ordinances here been passed with no motive on the part of any councilman except the ardent desire to prevent cruelty to animals (as might in fact have been the case), they would nonetheless be invalid.

Justice SOUTER, concurring in part and concurring in the judgment.

This case turns on a principle about which there is no disagreement, that the Free Exercise Clause bars government action aimed at suppressing religious belief or practice. The Court holds that Hialeah's animal-sacrifice laws violate that principle, and I concur in that holding without reservation.

Because prohibiting religious exercise is the object of the laws at hand, this case does not present the more difficult issue addressed in our last free-exercise case, *Employment Div., Dept. of Human Resources of Ore. v. Smith* (1990), which announced the rule that a "neutral, generally applicable" law does not run afoul of the Free Exer-

cise Clause even when it prohibits religious exercise in effect. The Court today refers to that rule *in dicta,* and despite my general agreement with the Court's opinion I do not join Part II, where the dicta appear, for I have doubts about whether the *Smith* rule merits adherence. I write separately to explain why the *Smith* rule is not germane to this case and to express my view that, in a case presenting the issue, the Court should re-examine the rule *Smith* declared.

According to *Smith*, if prohibiting the exercise of religion results from enforcing a "neutral, generally applicable" law, the Free Exercise Clause has not been offended. I call this the *Smith* rule to distinguish it from the noncontroversial principle, also expressed in *Smith* though established long before, that the Free Exercise Clause is offended when prohibiting religious exercise results from a law that is not neutral or generally applicable. It is this noncontroversial principle, that the Free Exercise Clause requires neutrality and general applicability, that is at issue here. But before turning to the relationship of *Smith* to this case, it will help to get the terms in order, for the significance of the *Smith* rule is not only in its statement that the Free Exercise Clause requires no more than "neutrality" and "general applicability," but also in its adoption of a particular, narrow conception of free-exercise neutrality. . . .

While general applicability is, for the most part, self-explanatory, free-exercise neutrality is not self-revealing. A law that is religion neutral on its face or in its purpose may lack neutrality in its effect by forbidding something that religion requires or requiring something that religion forbids. A secular law, applicable to all, that prohibits consumption of alcohol, for example, will affect members of religions that require the use of wine differently from members of other religions and nonbelievers, disproportionately burdening the practice of, say, Catholicism or Judaism. Without an exemption for sacramental wine, Prohibition may fail the test of religion neutrality.

It does not necessarily follow from that observation, of course, that the First Amendment requires an exemption from Prohibition; that depends on the meaning of neutrality as the Free Exercise Clause embraces it. The point here is the unremarkable one that our common notion of neutrality is broad enough to cover not merely what might be called formal neutrality, which as a free-exercise requirement would only bar laws with an object to discriminate against religion, but also what might be called substantive neutrality, which, in addition to demanding a secular object, would generally require government to accommodate religious differences by exempting religious practices from formally neutral laws. If the Free Exercise Clause secures only protection against deliberate discrimination, a formal requirement will exhaust the Clause's neutrality command; if the Free Exercise Clause, rather, safeguards a right to engage in religious activity free from unnecessary governmental interference, the Clause requires substantive, as well as formal, neutrality.

Though *Smith* used the term "neutrality" without a modifier, the rule it announced plainly assumes that free-exercise neutrality is of the formal sort. Distinguishing between laws whose "object" is to prohibit religious exercise and those that prohibit religious exercise as an "incidental effect," *Smith* placed only the former within the reaches of the Free Exercise Clause; the latter, laws that satisfy formal neutrality, *Smith* would subject to no free-exercise scrutiny at all, even when they prohibit religious exercise in application. The four Justices who rejected the *Smith* rule, by contrast, read the Free Exercise Clause as embracing what I have termed substantive neutrality. The enforcement of a law "neutral on its face," they said, may "nonetheless offend [the Free Exercise Clause's] requirement for government neutrality if it unduly burdens the free exercise of religion." The rule these Justices saw as flowing from free-exercise neutrality, in contrast to the *Smith* rule, "requir[es] the government to justify any substantial burden on religiously motivated conduct by a compelling state interest and by means narrowly tailored to achieve that interest."

The proposition for which the *Smith* rule stands, then, is that formal neutrality, along with general applicability, are sufficient conditions for constitutionality under the Free Exercise Clause. That proposition is not at issue in this case, however, for Hialeah's animal-sacrifice ordinances are not neutral under any definition, any more than they are generally applicable. This case, rather, involves the noncontroversial principle repeated in *Smith,* that formal neutrality and general applicability are necessary conditions for free-exercise constitutionality. It is only "this fundamental nonpersecution principle of the First Amendment [that is] implicated here," and it is to that principle that the Court adverts when it holds that Hialeah's ordinances "fail to satisfy the *Smith* requirements." . . . In applying that principle the Court does not tread on troublesome ground. . . .

Since holding in 1940 that the Free Exercise Clause applies to the States, the Court repeatedly has stated that the Clause sets strict limits on the government's power to burden religious exercise, whether it is a law's object to do so or its unanticipated effect. *Smith* responded to these statements by suggesting that the Court did not really mean what it said, detecting in at least the most recent opinions a lack of commitment to the compelling-interest test in the context of formally neutral laws. But even if the Court's commitment were that palid, it would argue only for moderating the language of the test, not for eliminating constitutional scrutiny altogether. In any event, I would have trouble concluding that the Court has not meant what it has said in more than a dozen cases over several decades, particularly when in the same period it repeatedly applied the compelling-interest test to require exemptions, even in a case decided the year before *Smith.* In sum, it seems to me difficult to escape the conclusion that, whatever *Smith's* virtues, they do not include a comfortable fit with settled law. . . .

This is not the place to explore the history that a century of free-exercise opinions have overlooked, and it is enough to note that, when the opportunity to reexamine *Smith* presents itself, we may consider recent scholarship raising serious questions about the *Smith* rule's consonance with the original understanding and purpose of the Free Exercise Clause. There appears to be a strong argument from the Clause's development in the First Congress, from its origins in the post-Revolution state constitutions and pre-Revolution colonial charters, and from the philosophy of rights to which the Framers adhered, that the Clause was originally understood to preserve a right to engage in activities necessary to fulfill one's duty to one's God, unless those activities threatened the rights of others or the serious needs of the State. If, as this scholarship suggests, the Free Exercise Clause's original "purpose [was] to secure religious liberty in the individual by prohibiting any invasions thereof by civil authority," then there would be powerful reason to interpret the Clause to accord with its natural reading, as applying to all laws prohibiting religious exercise in fact, not just those aimed at its prohibition, and to hold the neutrality needed to implement such a purpose to be the substantive neutrality of our pre-*Smith* cases, not the formal neutrality sufficient for constitutionality under *Smith.*

The scholarship on the original understanding of the Free Exercise Clause is, to be sure, not uniform. And there are differences of opinion as to the weight appropriately accorded original meaning. But whether or not one considers the original designs of the Clause binding, the interpretive significance of those designs surely ranks in the hierarchy of issues to be explored in resolving the tension inherent in free-exercise law as it stands today.

The extent to which the Free Exercise Clause requires government to refrain from impeding religious exercise defines nothing less than the respective relationships in our constitutional democracy of the individual to government and to God. "Neutral, generally applicable" laws, drafted as they are from the perspective of the nonadherent, have the unavoidable potential of putting the believer to a choice between God and government. Our cases now present competing answers to the question when government, while pursuing secular ends, may compel disobedience to what one believes religion commands. The case before us is rightly decided without resolving the existing tension, which remains for another day when it may be squarely faced.

Justice BLACKMUN, with whom Justice O'CONNOR joins, concurring in the judgment.

. . . I write separately to emphasize that the First Amendment's protection of religion extends beyond those rare occasions on which the government explicitly targets religion (or a particular religion) for disfavored treatment, as is done in this case. In my view, a statute that burdens the free exercise of religion "may stand only if the law in general, and the State's refusal to allow a religious exemption in particular, are justified by a compelling interest that cannot be served by less restrictive means." *Employment Div., Dept. of Human Resources of Ore. v. Smith* (1990) (dissenting opinion). The Court, however, applies a different test. It applies the test announced in *Smith*, under which "a law that is neutral and of general applicability need not be justified by a compelling governmental interest even if the law has the incidental effect of burdening a particular religious practice." I continue to believe that *Smith* was wrongly decided, because it ignored the value of religious freedom as an affirmative individual liberty and treated the Free Exercise Clause as no more than an antidiscrimination principle. Thus, while I agree with the result the Court reaches in this case, I arrive at that result by a different route.

When a law discriminates against religion as such, as do the ordinances in this case, it automatically will fail strict scrutiny under *Sherbert v. Verner* (1963). This is true because a law that targets religious practice for disfavored treatment both burdens the free exercise of religion and, by definition, is not precisely tailored to a compelling governmental interest.

Thus, unlike the majority, I do not believe that "[a] law burdening religious practice that is not neutral or not of general application must undergo the most rigorous of scrutiny." In my view, regulation that targets religion in this way, ipso facto, fails strict scrutiny. It is for this reason that a statute that explicitly restricts religious practices violates the First Amendment. It is only in the rare case that a state or local legislature will enact a law directly burdening religious practice as such. Because respondent here does single out religion in this way, the present case is an easy one to decide.

Notes and Queries

1. In *Employment Div. v. Smith* (1990, reprinted next), the Court ruled that "neutral" laws of "general applicability" need not be justified by a compelling state interest, even if they have the "incidental effect" of burdening a religious practice. Does the majority opinion by Justice Kennedy apply the *Smith* test in this case?

2. The Court found easily that the city's action in this case was not neutral. But does Justice Kennedy say anything about what "neutrality" means?

3. The majority spends a great deal of time actually examining the local ordinances, finding that their purpose was plainly to burden the Santeria religion. Is it appropriate for the Court to consider the "motivations" of a legislature or a city council? Justice Scalia thought not. Why?

4. Assume the city had acted without an improper motive. Assume, in other words, that the city did not have as its primary purpose the "suppression" of the Santeria religion. Would its secular purposes be sufficient, under *Smith*, to save its ordinances?

5. In several places the Court suggests that the city's claims that it acted to pursue legitimate secular puposes fails because it might have pursued those ends through "narrower" legislation. Is this the same thing as requiring the city to pursue the "least restrictive alternative"? If so, hasn't the Court in fact applied strict scrutiny?

Employment Division v. Smith
494 U.S. 872, 110 S.Ct. 1595, 108 L.Ed. 2d 876 (1990)

Consuming small amounts of peyote, a cactus that includes mescaline, is a common practice in certain Native American religious ceremonies. Oregon's controlled substance law, however, prohibits the possession or use of peyote. The law includes no exceptions for religious ceremonies. In 1964, the California Supreme Court, in *People*

v. Woody, held that the state could not enforce a similar statute against individuals who had taken peyote as a part of a Navaho religious ritual. Alfred Smith and Galen Black, members of the Native American Church, were dismissed from their jobs as counselors at a private drug rehabilitation clinic because they admitted to taking peyote. Their applications for unemployment benefits were denied because they had been dismissed for "job-related misconduct." The Oregon Supreme Court upheld the decision.

Opinion of the Court: *Scalia*, Kennedy, White, Stevens, Rehnquist. Concurring in the judgment: *O'Connor*; joining in part, Brennan, Marshall, Blackmun. Dissenting opinion: *Blackmun*, Brennan, Marshall.

Justice SCALIA delivered the opinion of the Court.

This case requires us to decide whether the Free Exercise Clause of the First Amendment permits the State of Oregon to include religiously inspired peyote use within the reach of its general criminal prohibition on use of that drug, and thus permits the State to deny unemployment benefits to persons dismissed from their jobs because of such religiously inspired use.

. . . The free exercise of religion means, first and foremost, the right to believe and profess whatever religious doctrine one desires. Thus, the First Amendment obviously excludes all "governmental regulation of religious beliefs as such." . . . The government may not compel affirmation of religious belief, . . . punish the expression of religious doctrines it believes to be false, . . . impose special disabilities on the basis of religious views or religious status, . . . or lend its power to one or the other side in controversies over religious authority or dogma.

But the "exercise of religion" often involves not only belief and profession but the performance of (or abstention from) physical acts: assembling with others for a worship service, participating in sacramental use of bread and wine, proselytizing, abstaining from certain foods or certain modes of transportation. It would be true, we think (though no case of ours has involved the point), that a State would be "prohibiting the free exercise [of religion]" if it sought to ban such acts or abstentions only when they are engaged in for religious reasons, or only because of the religious belief that they display. It would doubtless be unconstitutional, for example, to ban the casting of "statues that are to be used for worship purposes," or to prohibit bowing down before a golden calf.

Respondents in the present case, however, seek to carry the meaning of "prohibiting the free exercise [of religion]" one large step further. They contend that their religious motivation for using peyote places them beyond the reach of a criminal law that is not specifically directed at their religious practice, and that is concededly constitutional as applied to those who use the drug for other reasons. They assert, in other words, that "prohibiting the free exercise [of religion]" includes requiring any individual to observe a generally applicable law that requires (or forbids) the performance of an act that his religious belief forbids (or requires). As a textual matter, we do not think the words must be given that meaning. It is no more necessary to regard the collection of a general tax, for example, as

"prohibiting the free exercise [of religion]" by those citizens who believe support of organized government to be sinful, than it is to regard the same tax as "abridging the freedom . . . of the press" of those publishing companies that must pay the tax as a condition of staying in business. It is a permissible reading of the text, in the one case as in the other, to say that if prohibiting the exercise of religion (or burdening the activity of printing) is not the object of the tax but merely the incidental effect of a generally applicable and otherwise valid provision, the First Amendment has not been offended.

Our decisions reveal that the latter reading is the correct one. We have never held that an individual's religious beliefs excuse him from compliance with an otherwise valid law prohibiting conduct that the State is free to regulate. On the contrary, the record of more than a century of our free exercise jurisprudence contradicts that proposition. As described succinctly by Justice Frankfurter in *Minersville*, "Conscientious scruples have not, in the course of the long struggle for religious toleration, relieved the individual from obedience to a general law not aimed at the promotion or restriction of religious beliefs. The mere possession of religious convictions which contradict the relevant concerns of a political society does not relieve the citizen from the discharge of political responsibilities (footnote omitted)." We first had occasion to assert that principle in *Reynolds v. United States* (1878), where we rejected the claim that criminal laws against polygamy could not be constitutionally applied to those whose religion commanded the practice. "Laws," we said, "are made for the government of actions, and while they cannot interfere with mere religious belief and opinions, they may with practices. . . . Can a man excuse his practices to the contrary because of his religious belief? To permit this would be to make the professed doctrines of religious belief superior to the law of the land, and in effect to permit every citizen to become a law unto himself."

Subsequent decisions have consistently held that the right of free exercise does not relieve an individual of the obligation to comply with a "valid and neutral law of general applicability on the ground that the law proscribes (or prescribes) conduct that his religion prescribes (or proscribes)." In *Prince v. Massachusetts* (1944), we held that a mother could be prosecuted under the child labor laws for using her children to dispense literature in the streets, her religious motivation notwithstanding. We found no constitutional infirmity in "excluding [these children] from doing there what no other children may do." In *Braunfeld v. Brown* (1961), we upheld Sunday-closing laws against the claim that they burdened the religious practices of persons whose religions compelled them to refrain from

Comparative Note 13.11

[In this case, Germany's Federal Constitutional Court characterized a charitable collection as falling within the protection afforded to religious freedom in the Basic Law. In the following extract the Court comments on the distinction between religious beliefs and conduct.]

2. a) The fundamental right to the free exercise of religion [Article 2 (2) of the Basic Law] . . . not only embraces the personal freedom to believe or not to believe, i.e., to profess a faith, to keep it secret, or renounce a former belief and uphold another, but also includes the freedom to worship publicly, to proselytize, and to compete openly with other religions. . . .

Accordingly, the exercise of religion includes not only worship and practices such as the observance of

religious customs like Sunday services, church collections, prayers, reception of the sacraments, processions, display of church flags, and the ringing of the church bells, but also religious education, ceremonies of non-established religions and atheists as well as other expressions of religious and ideological life.

b) The basic right secured by Article 4 (1) and (2) of the Basic Law is accorded not only to established churches, religious communities and associations united by a particular creed, but also to associations only partially devoted to fostering the religious or ideological life of their members. It is essential only that the organization be directed toward the attainment of a religious goal [such as a charitable collection for the poor motivated by Gospel values]. . . .

SOURCE: *Rumpelkammer Case* (1968) in Kommers, *Constitutional Jurisprudence,* 446.

---

work on other days. In *Gillette v. United States* (1871), we sustained the military Selective Service System against the claim that it violated free exercise by conscripting persons who opposed a particular war on religious grounds.

Our most recent decision involving a neutral, generally applicable regulatory law that compelled activity forbidden by an individual's religion was *United States v. Lee* (1982). There, an Amish employer, on behalf of himself and his employees, sought exemption from collection and payment of Social Security taxes on the ground that the Amish faith prohibited participation in governmental support programs. We rejected the claim that an exemption was constitutionally required. There would be no way, we observed, to distinguish the Amish believer's objection to Social Security taxes from the religious objections that others might have to the collection or use of other taxes. . . .

The only decisions in which we have held that the First Amendment bars application of a neutral, generally applicable law to religiously motivated action have involved not the Free Exercise Clause alone, but the Free Exercise Clause in conjunction with other constitutional protections, such as freedom of speech and of the press. . . . And it is easy to envision a case in which a challenge on freedom of association grounds would likewise be reinforced by Free Exercise Clause concerns.

The present case does not present such a hybrid situation, but a free exercise claim unconnected with any communicative activity or parental right. Respondents urge us to hold, quite simply, that when otherwise prohibitable

conduct is accompanied by religious convictions, not only the convictions but the conduct itself must be free from governmental regulation. We have never held that, and decline to do so now.

Respondents argue that . . . the claim for a religious exemption must be evaluated under the balancing test set forth in *Sherbert*. . . . In recent years we have abstained from applying the *Sherbert* test (outside the unemployment compensation field) at all. . . .

Even if we were inclined to breathe into *Sherbert* some life beyond the unemployment compensation field, we would not apply it to require exemptions from a generally applicable criminal law. . . . We conclude today that the sounder approach . . . is to hold the test inapplicable to such challenges. . . . To make an individual's obligation to obey such a law contingent upon the law's coincidence with his religious beliefs, except where the State's interest is "compelling" . . . contradicts both constitutional tradition and common sense.

The "compelling governmental interest" requirement seems benign, because it is familiar. . . . But using it as the standard that must be met before the government may accord different treatment on the basis of race . . . or before the government may regulate the content of speech . . . , is not remotely comparable to using it for the purpose asserted here. . . . What it produces in those other fields—equality of treatment, and an unrestricted flow of contending speech—are constitutional norms; what it would produce here—a private right to ignore generally applicable laws—is a constitutional anomaly.

Nor is it possible to limit the impact of respondents' proposal by requiring a "compelling state interest" only when the conduct prohibited is "central" to the individual's religion. It is no more appropriate for judges to determine the "centrality" of religious beliefs before applying a "compelling state interest" test in the free exercise field, than it would be for them to determine the "importance" of ideas before applying [the test] in the free speech field. . . .

Values that are protected against government interference through enshrinement in the Bill of Rights are not thereby banished from the political process. Just as a society that believes in the negative protection accorded to the press by the First Amendment is likely to enact laws that affirmatively foster the dissemination of the printed word, so also a society that believes in the negative protection accorded to religious belief can be expected to be solicitous of that value in its legislation as well. It is therefore not surprising that a number of States have made an exception to their drug laws for sacramental peyote use. . . . But to say that a nondiscriminatory religious-practice exemption is permitted, or even that it is desirable, is not to say that it is constitutionally required, and that the appropriate occasions for its creation can be discerned by the courts. It may fairly be said that leaving accommodation to the political process will place at a relative disadvantage those religious practices that are not widely engaged in; but that unavoidable consequence of democratic government must be preferred to a system in which each conscience is a law unto itself or in which judges weigh the social importance of all laws against the centrality of all religious beliefs.

Because respondents' ingestion of peyote was prohibited under Oregon law, and because that prohibition is constitutional, Oregon may, consistent with the Free Exercise Clause, deny respondents unemployment compensation when their dismissal results from use of the drug. The decision of the Oregon Supreme Court is accordingly reversed.

It is so ordered.

Justice O'CONNOR, with whom Justice BRENNAN, Justice MARSHALL, and Justice BLACKMUN join as to Parts I and II, concurring in the judgment.

. . . Because the First Amendment does not distinguish between religious belief and religious conduct, conduct motivated by sincere religious belief, like the belief itself, must be at least presumptively protected by the Free Exercise Clause.

The Court today, however, interprets the Clause to permit the government to prohibit, without justification, conduct mandated by an individual's religious beliefs, so long as that prohibition is generally applicable. . . . But a law that prohibits certain conduct—conduct that happens to be an act of worship for someone—manifestly does prohibit that person's free exercise of his religion. A person who is barred from engaging in religiously motivated conduct is barred from freely exercising his religion. Moreover, that person is barred from freely exercising his religion regardless of whether the law prohibits the conduct only when engaged in for religious reasons, only by members of that religion, or by all persons. It is difficult to deny that a law that prohibits religiously motivated conduct, even if the law is generally applicable, does not at least implicate First Amendment concerns.

To say that a person's right to free exercise has been burdened, of course, does not mean that he has an absolute right to engage in the conduct. Under our established First Amendment jurisprudence, we have recognized that the freedom to act, unlike the freedom to believe, cannot be absolute. . . . Instead, we have respected both the First Amendment's express textual mandate and the governmental interest in regulation of conduct by requiring the government to justify any substantial burden on religiously motivated conduct by a compelling state interest and by means narrowly tailored to achieve that interest. . . . The compelling interest test effectuates the First Amendment's command that religious liberty is an independent liberty, that it occupies a preferred position, and that the Court will not permit encroachments upon this liberty, whether direct or indirect, unless required by clear and compelling governmental interests "of the highest order." "Only an especially important governmental interest pursued by narrowly tailored means can justify exacting a sacrifice of First Amendment freedoms as the price for an equal share of the rights, benefits, and privileges enjoyed by other citizens."

The Court today gives no convincing reason to depart from settled First Amendment jurisprudence. . . . The Court's parade of horribles not only fails as a reason for discarding the compelling state interest test, it instead demonstrates just the opposite: that courts have been quite capable of applying our free exercise jurisprudence to strike sensible balances between religious liberty and compelling state interests.

Finally, the Court today suggests that the disfavoring of minority religions is an "unavoidable consequence" under our system of government and that accommodation of such religions must be left to the political process.

In my view, however, the essence of a free exercise claim is relief from a burden imposed by government on religious practices or beliefs, whether the burden is imposed directly through laws that prohibit or compel specific religious practices, or indirectly through laws that, in effect, make abandonment of one's own religion or conformity to the religious beliefs of others the price of an equal place in the civil community. . . . A State that makes criminal an individual's religiously motivated conduct burdens that individual's free exercise of religion in the severest manner possible, for it "results in the choice to the individual of either abandoning his religious principle or facing criminal prosecution." I would have thought it beyond argument that such laws implicate free exercise concerns.

. . . The compelling interest test reflects the First Amendment's mandate of preserving religious liberty to the fullest extent possible in a pluralistic society. . . .

The Court's holding today not only misreads settled First Amendment precedent; it appears to be unnecessary to this case. I would reach the same result applying our established free exercise jurisprudence.

There is no dispute that Oregon's criminal prohibition of peyote places a severe burden on the ability of respondents to freely exercise their religion. Peyote is a sacrament of the Native American Church and is regarded as vital to respondents' ability to practice their religion. . . . Under Oregon law, as construed by that State's highest court, members of the Native American Church must choose between carrying out the ritual embodying their religious beliefs and avoidance of criminal prosecution. That choice is, in my view, more than sufficient to trigger First Amendment scrutiny.

. . . [T]he critical question in this case is whether exempting respondents from the State's general criminal prohibition "will unduly interfere with fulfillment of the governmental interest." . . . Although the question is close, I would conclude that uniform application of Oregon's criminal prohibition is "essential to accomplish," . . . its overriding interest in preventing the physical harm caused by the use of a Schedule I controlled substance. Oregon's criminal prohibition represents that State's judgment that the possession and use of controlled substances, even by only one person, is inherently harmful and dangerous. Because the health effects caused by the use of controlled substances exist regardless of the motivation of the user, the use of such substances, even for religious purposes, violates the very purpose of the laws that prohibit them. . . . Moreover, in view of the societal interest in preventing trafficking in controlled substances, uniform application of the criminal prohibition at issue is essential to the effectiveness of Oregon's stated interest in preventing any possession of peyote.

For these reasons, I believe that granting a selective exemption in this case would seriously impair Oregon's compelling interest in prohibiting possession of peyote by its citizens. Under such circumstances, the Free Exercise Clause does not require the State to accommodate respondents' religiously motivated conduct.

Justice BLACKMUN, with whom Justice BRENNAN and Justice MARSHALL join, dissenting.

This Court over the years painstakingly has developed a consistent and exacting standard to test the constitutionality of a state statute that burdens the free exercise of religion. Such a statute may stand only if the law in general, and the State's refusal to allow a religious exemption in particular, are justified by a compelling state interest that cannot be served by less restrictive means.

Until today, I thought this was a settled and inviolate principle. . . . The majority, however, perfunctorily dismisses it as a "constitutional anomaly."

It is not the State's broad interest in fighting the critical "war on drugs" that must be weighed against respondents' claim, but the State's narrow interest in refusing to make an exception for the religious, ceremonial use of peyote. . . .

The State proclaims an interest in protecting the health and safety of its citizens from the dangers of unlawful drugs. It offers, however, no evidence that the religious use of peyote has ever harmed anyone. The factual findings of other courts cast doubt on the State's assumption that religious use of peyote is harmful. The fact that peyote is classified as a Schedule I controlled substance does not, by itself, show that any and all uses of peyote, in any circumstance, are inherently harmful and dangerous. The Federal Government, which created the classifications of unlawful drugs from which Oregon's drug laws are derived, apparently does not find peyote so dangerous as to preclude an exemption for religious use. Moreover, other Schedule I drugs have lawful uses.

The carefully circumscribed ritual context in which respondents used peyote is far removed from the irresponsible and unrestricted recreational use of unlawful drugs. The Native American Church's internal restrictions on, and supervision of, its members' use of peyote substantially obviate the State's health and safety concerns.

The State also seeks to support its refusal to make an exception for religious use of peyote by invoking its interest in abolishing drug trafficking. There is, however, practically no illegal traffic in peyote. . . .

Finally, the State argues that granting an exception for religious peyote use would erode its interest in the uniform, fair, and certain enforcement of its drug laws. The

State fears that, if it grants an exemption for religious peyote use, a flood of other claims to religious exemptions will follow. It would then be placed in a dilemma, it says, between allowing a patchwork of exemptions that would hinder its law enforcement efforts, and risking a violation of the Establishment Clause by arbitrarily limiting its religious exemptions. This argument, however, could be made in almost any free exercise case. . . . This Court, however, consistently has rejected similar arguments in past free exercise cases, and it should do so here as well.

The State's apprehension of a flood of other religious claims is purely speculative. Almost half the States, and the Federal Government, have maintained an exemption for religious peyote use for many years, and apparently have not found themselves overwhelmed by claims to other religious exemptions. Allowing an exemption for religious peyote use would not necessarily oblige the State to grant a similar exemption to other religious groups. The unusual circumstances that make the religious use of peyote compatible with the State's interests in health and safety and in preventing drug trafficking would not apply to other religious claims. Some religions, for example, might not restrict drug use to a limited ceremonial context, as does the Native American Church. . . . Some religious claims involve drugs such as marijuana and heroin, in which there is significant illegal traffic, with its attendant greed and violence, so that it would be difficult to grant a religious exemption without seriously compromising law enforcement efforts. That the State might grant an exemption for religious peyote use, but deny other religious claims arising in different circumstances, would not violate the Establishment Clause. Though the State must treat all religions equally, and not favor one over another, this obligation is fulfilled by the uniform application of the "compelling interest" test to all free exercise claims, not by reaching uniform results as to all claims. A showing that religious peyote use does not unduly interfere with the State's interests is "one that probably few other religious groups or sects could make"; . . . this does not mean that an exemption limited to peyote use is tantamount to an establishment of religion.

For these reasons, I conclude that Oregon's interest in enforcing its drug laws against religious use of peyote is not sufficiently compelling to outweigh respondents' right to the free exercise of their religion. Since the State could not constitutionally enforce its criminal prohibition against respondents, the interests underlying the State's drug laws cannot justify its denial of unemployment benefits. Absent such justification, the State's regulatory interest in denying benefits for religiously motivated "misconduct" is indistinguishable from the state interests this Court has rejected in

Frazee, Hobbie, Thomas, and *Sherbert.* The State of Oregon cannot, consistently with the Free Exercise Clause, deny respondents unemployment benefits.

I dissent.

Notes and Queries

1. Is Justice Scalia's majority opinion consistent with *Sherbert?* Or does it represent a rejection of the *Sherbert* rule, as Justice Blackmun claimed in his dissent? Did Justice Scalia reject the use of the compelling state interest test? Or did he conclude that the state's interest in this case is compelling?

Does *Smith* signal the end of constitutionally required accommodations for free exercise?

2. Would an exception for the Native American Church constitute an "establishment" of religion? Or would it simply recognize that "The concept of worship extends to ritual and ceremonial acts giving direct expression of belief, as well as various practices integral to such acts. . . ." See General Comment No 22 (44) by the United Nations Human Rights Committee on Article 18 of the International Covenant on Civil and Political Rights (1993), 233. Does this suggest that the Court should distinguish between liturgical action and other sorts of action? What would be the effect of such a distinction in *Smith?*

3. Justice Scalia wrote that "It may fairly be said that leaving accommodation to the political process will place at a relative disadvantage those religious practices that are not widely engaged in; but that unavoidable consequence of democratic government must be preferred to a system in which conscience is a law unto itself or in which judges weigh the social importance of all laws against the centrality of all religious beliefs."

Is this assertion reminiscent more of *Minersville v. Gobitis* or *West Virginia v. Barnette?* What understanding of judicial authority is implicit in Scalia's opinion? What understanding does he reject? Would he reject *Carolene Products?*

Can a role of judicial deference to legislative choices be squared with the underlying logic of the free exercise clause? For a trenchant criticism of the majority's opinion, see Michael McConnell, *Free Exercise Revisionism and the* Smith *Decision,* 57 University of Chicago Law Review 1109 (1990). McConnell concludes that Justice Scalia's opinion misunderstands both the history and the purpose of the free exercise clause. The clause, he writes, "singles out a particular category of human activities for particular protection, a protection that is most often needed by practitioners of non-mainstream faiths who lack the ability to protect themselves in the political sphere. . . ." Is McConnell's argument simply a restatement of footnote 4 in *Carolene Products*? How would Justice Scalia respond to McConnell?

4. Justice Scalia noted that in this case the claim of religious liberty was "unconnected with any communicative activity or parental right," thus distinguishing it from other cases where the Court had seemed to carve out religious exceptions to otherwise valid laws. Does this suggest that a law that tramples on a single constitutional liberty is less offensive than one that tramples on many liberties? Or is Justice Scalia suggesting something else? Is he suggesting that there is a hierarchy of constitutional liberties? Isn't that an essential part of the logic of *Carolene Products*?

Boerne v. Flores
521 U.S. 507, 117 S.Ct. 2157, 138 L.Ed. 2d 624 (1997)

St. Peter Catholic Church, in San Antonio, Texas, found that its building was too small to seat all of its parishioners. It sought to enlarge the building, but the city denied its request for a building permit because the church was located in an historic district. The Church sued, claiming that the denial violated the Religious Freedom Restoration Act of 1993, the major provisions of which are included in the Court's opinion. The primary purpose of the Act, enacted by Congress under its Section 5 powers of the Fourteenth Amendment, was to reinstate the compelling state interest that had prevailed before the Court's decision in *Smith*. The District Court found that the Act was unconstitutional because Congress had exceeded the scope of its authority under Section 5 of the Fourteenth Amendment. The Circuit Court reversed. Opinion of the Court: *Kennedy*, Rehnquist, Stevens, Thomas, Ginsburg. Concurring in part: *Scalia*, Stevens. Dissenting opinions: *O'Connor*, Breyer; *Souter*; Breyer.

Justice KENNEDY delivered the opinion of the Court.

Congress enacted RFRA in direct response to the Court's decision in *Employment Div., Dept. of Human Resources of Ore. v. Smith* (1990). There we considered a Free Exercise Clause claim brought by members of the Native American Church who were denied unemployment benefits when they lost their jobs because they had used peyote. Their practice was to ingest peyote for sacramental purposes, and they challenged an Oregon statute of general applicability which made use of the drug criminal. In evaluating the claim, we declined to apply the balancing test set forth in *Sherbert v. Verner*, (1963), under which we would have asked whether Oregon's prohibition substantially burdened a religious practice and, if it did, whether the burden was justified by a compelling government interest. We stated:

[G]overnment's ability to enforce generally applicable prohibitions of socially harmful conduct . . . cannot depend on measuring the effects of a governmental action on a religious objector's spiritual development. To make an individual's obligation to obey such a law contingent upon the law's coincidence with his religious beliefs, except where the State's interest is "compelling" . . . contradicts both constitutional tradition and common sense.

The application of the *Sherbert* test, the *Smith* decision explained, would have produced an anomaly in the law, a constitutional right to ignore neutral laws of general applicability. The anomaly would have been accentuated, the Court reasoned, by the difficulty of determining whether a particular practice was central to an individual's religion. We explained, moreover, that it "is not within the judicial ken to question the centrality of particular beliefs or practices to a faith, or the validity of particular litigants' interpretations of those creeds."

The only instances where a neutral, generally applicable law had failed to pass constitutional muster, the *Smith* Court noted, were cases in which other constitutional protections were at stake. In *Wisconsin v. Yoder* (1972), for example, we invalidated Wisconsin's mandatory school-attendance law as applied to Amish parents who refused on religious grounds to send their children to school. That case implicated not only the right to the free exercise of religion but also the right of parents to control their children's education.

The *Smith* decision acknowledged the Court had employed the *Sherbert* test in considering free exercise challenges to state unemployment compensation rules on three occasions where the balance had tipped in favor of the individual. *Sherbert*; *Thomas v. Review Bd. of Indiana Employment Security Div.* (1981); *Hobbie v. Unemployment Appeals Comm'n of Fla.* (1987). Those cases, the Court explained, stand for "the proposition that where the State has in place a system of individual exemptions, it may not refuse to extend that system to cases of religious hardship without compelling reason." By contrast, where a general prohibition, such as Oregon's, is at issue, "the sounder approach, and the approach in accord with the vast majority of our precedents, is to hold the test inapplicable to [free exercise] challenges." *Smith* held that neutral, generally applicable laws may be applied to religious practices even when not supported by a compelling governmental interest.

These points of constitutional interpretation were debated by Members of Congress in hearings and floor debates. Many criticized the Court's reasoning, and this disagreement resulted in the passage of RFRA. Congress announced:

(1) [T]he framers of the Constitution, recognizing free exercise of religion as an unalienable right, secured its protection in the First Amendment to the Constitution;

(2) laws "neutral" toward religion may burden religious exercise as surely as laws intended to interfere with religious exercise;

(3) governments should not substantially burden religious exercise without compelling justification;

(4) in *Employment Division v. Smith*, (1990), the Supreme Court virtually eliminated the requirement that the government justify burdens on religious exercise imposed by laws neutral toward religion; and

(5) the compelling interest test as set forth in prior Federal court rulings is a workable test for striking sensible balances between religious liberty and competing prior governmental interests.

The Act's stated purposes are:

(1) to restore the compelling interest test as set forth in *Sherbert v. Verner*, (1963) and *Wisconsin v. Yoder*, (1972) and to guarantee its application in all cases where free exercise of religion is substantially burdened; and

(2) to provide a claim or defense to persons whose religious exercise is substantially burdened by government.

RFRA prohibits "[g]overnment" from "substantially burden[ing]" a person's exercise of religion even if the burden results from a rule of general applicability unless the government can demonstrate the burden "(1) is in furtherance of a compelling governmental interest; and (2) is the least restrictive means of furthering that compelling governmental interest." The Act's mandate applies to any "branch, department, agency, instrumentality, and official (or other person acting under color of law) of the United States," as well as to any "State, or . . . subdivision of a State." The Act's universal coverage is confirmed in s. 2000bb-3(a), under which RFRA "applies to all Federal and State law, and the implementation of that law, whether statutory or otherwise, and whether adopted before or after [RFRA's enactment]."

Under our Constitution, the Federal Government is one of enumerated powers. *McCulloch v. Maryland* (1819); see also *The Federalist* No. 45, p. 292 (C. Rossiter ed., 1961) (J. Madison). The judicial authority to determine the constitutionality of laws, in cases and controversies, is based on the premise that the "powers of the legislature are defined and limited; and that those limits may not be mistaken, or forgotten, the constitution is written." *Marbury v. Madison* (1803).

Congress relied on its Fourteenth Amendment enforcement power in enacting the most far reaching and substantial of RFRA's provisions, those which impose its requirements on the States. See Religious Freedom Restoration Act of 1993, S.Rep. No. 103–111, pp. 13–14 (1993) (Senate Report); H.R.Rep. No. 103–88, p. 9 (1993) (House Report). The Fourteenth Amendment provides, in relevant part:

Section 1. . . . No State shall make or enforce any law which shall abridge the privileges or immunities of citizens of the United States; nor shall any State deprive any person of life, liberty, or property, without due process of law; nor deny to any person within its jurisdiction the equal protection of the laws.

Section 5. The Congress shall have power to enforce, by appropriate legislation, the provisions of this article.

The parties disagree over whether RFRA is a proper exercise of Congress's s. 5 power "to enforce" by "appropriate legislation" the constitutional guarantee that no State shall deprive any person of "life, liberty, or property, without due process of law" nor deny any person "equal protection of the laws."

. . . Congress, it is said, is only protecting by legislation one of the liberties guaranteed by the Fourteenth Amendment's Due Process Clause, the free exercise of religion, beyond what is necessary under *Smith*. It is said the congressional decision to dispense with proof of deliberate or overt discrimination and instead concentrate on a law's effects accords with the settled understanding that s. 5 includes the power to enact legislation designed to prevent as well as remedy constitutional violations. It is further contended that Congress's s. 5 power is not limited to remedial or preventive legislation.

It is also true, however, that "[a]s broad as the congressional enforcement power is, it is not unlimited." In assessing the breadth of s. 5's enforcement power, we begin with its text. Congress has been given the power "to enforce" the "provisions of this article." We agree with respondent, of course, that Congress can enact legislation under s. 5 enforcing the constitutional right to the free exercise of religion. The "provisions of this article," to which s. 5 refers, include the Due Process Clause of the Fourteenth Amendment. Congress' power to enforce the Free Exercise Clause follows from our holding in *Cantwell v. Connecticut* (1940), that the "fundamental concept of liberty embodied in [the Fourteenth Amendment's Due Process Clause] embraces the liberties guaranteed by the First Amendment."

Congress' power under s. 5, however, extends only to "enforc[ing]" the provisions of the Fourteenth Amendment. The Court has described this power as "remedial," *South Carolina v. Katzenbach* (1966). The design of the Amendment and the text of s. 5 are inconsistent with the suggestion that Congress has the power to decree the substance of the Fourteenth Amendment's restrictions on the States. Legislation which alters the meaning of the Free Exercise Clause cannot be said to be enforcing the Clause. Congress does not enforce a constitutional right by changing what the right is. It has been given the power "to enforce," not the power to determine what constitutes a constitutional violation. Were it not so, what Congress would be enforcing would no longer be, in any meaningful sense, the "provisions of [the Fourteenth Amendment]."

While the line between measures that remedy or prevent unconstitutional actions and measures that make a substantive change in the governing law is not easy to discern, and Congress must have wide latitude in determining where it lies, the distinction exists and must be observed. There must be a congruence and proportionality between the injury to be prevented or remedied and the means adopted to that end. Lacking such a connection, legislation may become substantive in operation and effect. History and our case law support drawing the distinction, one apparent from the text of the Amendment.

The Fourteenth Amendment's history confirms the remedial, rather than substantive, nature of the Enforcement Clause. . . .

The design of the Fourteenth Amendment has proved significant also in maintaining the traditional separation of powers between Congress and the Judiciary. The first eight Amendments to the Constitution set forth self-executing prohibitions on governmental action, and this Court has had primary authority to interpret those prohibitions. The Bingham draft, some thought, departed from that tradition by vesting in Congress primary power to interpret and elaborate on the meaning of the new Amendment through legislation. Under it, "Congress, and not the courts, was to judge whether or not any of the privileges or immunities were not secured to citizens in the several States." While this separation of powers aspect did not occasion the widespread resistance which was caused by the proposal's threat to the federal balance, it nonetheless attracted the attention of various Members. As enacted, the Fourteenth Amendment confers substantive rights against the States which, like the provisions of the Bill of Rights, are self-executing. The power to interpret the Constitution in a case or controversy remains in the Judiciary.

The remedial and preventive nature of Congress' enforcement power, and the limitation inherent in the power, were confirmed in our earliest cases on the Fourteenth Amendment. In the *Civil Rights Cases* (1883), the Court invalidated sections of the Civil Rights Act of 1875 which prescribed criminal penalties for denying to any person "the full enjoyment of" public accommodations and conveyances, on the grounds that it exceeded Congress' power by seeking to regulate private conduct. The Enforcement Clause, the Court said, did not authorize Congress to pass "general legislation upon the rights of the citizen, but corrective legislation; that is, such as may be necessary and proper for counteracting such laws as the States may adopt or enforce, and which, by the amendment, they are prohibited from making or enforcing. . . ." The power to "legislate generally upon" life, liberty, and property, as opposed to the "power to provide modes of redress" against offensive state action, was "repugnant" to the Constitution. Although the specific holdings of these early cases might have been superseded or modified, their treatment of Congress' s. 5 power as corrective or preventive, not definitional, has not been questioned.

Recent cases have continued to revolve around the question of whether s. 5 legislation can be considered remedial. . . .

Any suggestion that Congress has a substantive, nonremedial power under the Fourteenth Amendment is not supported by our case law. In *Oregon v. Mitchell* (1970), a majority of the Court concluded Congress had exceeded its enforcement powers by enacting legislation lowering the minimum age of voters from 21 to 18 in state and local elections. The five Members of the Court who reached this conclusion explained that the legislation intruded into an area reserved by the Constitution to the States.

If Congress could define its own powers by altering the Fourteenth Amendment's meaning, no longer would the Constitution be "superior paramount law, unchangeable by ordinary means." It would be "on a level with ordinary legislative acts, and, like other acts, . . . alterable when the legislature shall please to alter it." *Marbury v. Madison* (1803). Under this approach, it is difficult to conceive of a principle that would limit congressional power. Shifting legislative majorities could change the Constitution and effectively circumvent the difficult and detailed amendment process contained in Article V.

We now turn to consider whether RFRA can be considered enforcement legislation under s. 5 of the Fourteenth Amendment.

Respondent contends that RFRA is a proper exercise of Congress' remedial or preventive power. The Act, it is said, is a reasonable means of protecting the free exercise of religion as defined by *Smith*. It prevents and remedies laws which are enacted with the unconstitutional object of targeting religious beliefs and practices. *Church of the Lukumi Babalu Aye, Inc. v. Hialeah* (1993). To avoid the difficulty of proving such violations, it is said, Congress can simply invalidate any law which imposes a substantial burden on a religious practice unless it is justified by a compelling interest and is the least restrictive means of accomplishing that interest. If Congress can prohibit laws with discriminatory effects in order to prevent racial discrimination in violation of the Equal Protection Clause, then it can do the same . . . to promote religious liberty.

While preventive rules are sometimes appropriate remedial measures, there must be a congruence between the means used and the ends to be achieved. The appropriateness of remedial measures must be considered in light of the evil presented. Strong measures appropriate to address one harm may be an unwarranted response to another, lesser one.

Regardless of the state of the legislative record, RFRA cannot be considered remedial, preventive legislation, if those terms are to have any meaning. RFRA is so out of proportion to a supposed remedial or preventive object that it cannot be understood as responsive to, or designed to prevent, unconstitutional behavior. It appears, instead, to attempt a substantive change in constitutional protections. Preventive measures prohibiting certain types of laws may be appropriate when there is reason to believe that many of the laws affected by the congressional enactment have a significant likelihood of being unconstitutional.

RFRA is not so confined. Sweeping coverage ensures its intrusion at every level of government, displacing laws and prohibiting official actions of almost every description and regardless of subject matter. . . . Any law is subject to challenge at any time by any individual who alleges a substantial burden on his or her free exercise of religion, The stringent test RFRA demands of state laws reflects a lack of proportionality or congruence between the means adopted and the legitimate end to be achieved. If an objector can show a substantial burden on his free exercise, the State must demonstrate a compelling governmental interest and show that the law is the least restrictive means of furthering its interest. Claims that a law substantially burdens someone's exercise of religion will often be difficult to contest. Requiring a State to demonstrate a compelling interest and show that it has adopted the least restrictive means of achieving that interest is the most demanding test known to constitutional law. If " 'compelling interest' really means what it says . . . many laws will not meet the test. . . . [The test] would open the prospect of constitutionally required religious exemptions from civic obligations of almost every conceivable kind." Laws valid under *Smith* would fall under RFRA without regard to whether they had the object of stifling or punishing free exercise. We make these observations not to reargue the position of the majority in *Smith* but to illustrate the substantive alteration of its holding attempted by RFRA. Even assuming RFRA would be interpreted in effect to mandate some lesser test, say one equivalent to intermediate scrutiny, the statute nevertheless would require searching judicial scrutiny of state law with the attendant likelihood of invalidation. This is a considerable congressional intrusion into the States' traditional prerogatives and general authority to regulate for the health and welfare of their citizens.

The substantial costs RFRA exacts, both in practical terms of imposing a heavy litigation burden on the States and in terms of curtailing their traditional general regulatory power, far exceed any pattern or practice of unconstitutional conduct under the Free Exercise Clause as interpreted in *Smith*. Simply put, RFRA is not designed to identify and counteract state laws likely to be unconstitutional because of their treatment of religion. In most cases, the state laws to which RFRA applies are not ones which will have been motivated by religious bigotry. If a state law disproportionately burdened a particular class of religious observers, this circumstance might be evidence of an impermissible legislative motive. RFRA's substantial burden test, however, is not even a discriminatory effects or disparate impact test. It is a reality of the modern regulatory state that numerous state laws, such as the zoning regulations at issue here, impose a substantial burden on a large class of individuals. When the exercise of religion has been burdened in an incidental way by a law of general application, it does not follow that the persons affected have been burdened any more than other citizens, let alone burdened because of their religious beliefs. In addition, the Act imposes in every case a least restrictive means requirement—a requirement that was not used in the pre-*Smith* jurisprudence RFRA purported to codify—which also indicates that the legislation is broader than is appropriate if the goal is to prevent and remedy constitutional violations.

When Congress acts within its sphere of power and responsibilities, it has not just the right but the duty to make its own informed judgment on the meaning and force of the Constitution. This has been clear from the early days of the Republic. In 1789, when a Member of the House of Representatives objected to a debate on the constitutionality of legislation based on the theory that "it would be officious" to consider the constitutionality of a measure that did not affect the House, James Madison explained that "it is incontrovertibly of as much importance to this branch of the Government as to any other, that the constitution should be preserved entire. It is our duty." 1 Annals of Congress 500 (1789). Were it otherwise, we would not afford Congress the presumption of validity its enactments now enjoy.

Our national experience teaches that the Constitution is preserved best when each part of the government respects both the Constitution and the proper actions and determinations of the other branches. When the Court has interpreted the Constitution, it has acted within the province of the Judicial Branch, which embraces the duty to say what the law is. When the political branches of the Government act against the background of a judicial interpretation of the Constitution already issued, it must be understood that in later cases and controversies the Court will treat its precedents with the respect due them under settled principles, including *stare decisis*, and contrary expectations must be disappointed. RFRA was designed to control cases and controversies, such as the one before us; but as the provisions of the federal statute here invoked are beyond congressional authority, it is this Court's precedent, not RFRA, which must control.

It is for Congress in the first instance to "determin[e] whether and what legislation is needed to secure the guarantees of the Fourteenth Amendment," and its conclusions are entitled to much deference. Congress' discretion is not unlimited, however, and the courts retain the power, as they have since *Marbury v. Madison*, to determine if Congress has exceeded its authority under the Constitution. Broad as the power of Congress is under the Enforcement Clause of the Fourteenth Amendment, RFRA contradicts vital principles necessary to maintain separation of powers and the federal balance. The judgment of the Court of Appeals sustaining the Act's constitutionality is reversed.

It is so ordered.

Justice STEVENS, concurring.

In my opinion, the Religious Freedom Restoration Act of 1993 (RFRA) is a "law respecting an establishment of reli-gion" that violates the First Amendment to the Constitution.

If the historic landmark on the hill in Boerne happened to be a museum or an art gallery owned by an atheist, it would not be eligible for an exemption from the city ordinances that forbid an enlargement of the structure. Because the landmark is owned by the Catholic Church, it is claimed that RFRA gives its owner a federal statutory entitlement to an exemption from a generally applicable, neutral civil law. Whether the Church would actually prevail under the statute or not, the statute has provided the Church with a legal weapon that no atheist or agnostic can obtain. This governmental preference for religion, as opposed to irreligion, is forbidden by the First Amendment. *Wallace v. Jaffree* (1985).

Justice SCALIA, with whom Justice STEVENS joins, concurring in part.

I write to respond briefly to the claim of Justice O'Connor's dissent (hereinafter "the dissent") that historical materials support a result contrary to the one reached in *Employment Div., Dept. of Human Resources of Ore. v. Smith* (1990). We held in *Smith* that the Constitution's Free Exercise Clause "does not relieve an individual of the obligation to comply with a 'valid and neutral law of general applicability on the ground that the law proscribes (or prescribes) conduct that his religion prescribes (or proscribes).'" The material that the dissent claims is at odds with *Smith* either has little to say about the issue or is in fact more consistent with *Smith* than with the dissent's interpretation of the Free Exercise Clause. The dissent's extravagant claim that the historical record shows *Smith* to have been wrong should be compared with the assessment of the most prominent scholarly critic of *Smith*, who, after an extensive review of the historical record, was willing to venture no more than that "constitutionally compelled exemptions [from generally applicable laws regulating conduct] were within the contemplation of the framers and ratifiers as a possible interpretation of the free exercise clause." Michael McConnell, *The Origins and Historical Understanding of Free Exercise of Religion*, 103 Harvard Law Review 1409, 1415 (1990) (emphasis added); see also Hamburger, *A Constitutional Right of Religious Exemption: An Historical Perspective*, 60 George Washington Law Review 915 (1992).

I have limited this response to the new items of "historical evidence" brought forward by today's dissent. (The dissent's claim that "[b]efore *Smith*, our free exercise cases were generally in keeping" with the dissent's view, is adequately answered in *Smith* itself.) The historical evidence marshaled by the dissent cannot fairly be said to demonstrate the correctness of *Smith*; but it is more supportive of that conclusion than destructive of it. And, to return to a point I made earlier, that evidence is not compatible with any theory I am familiar with that has been proposed as an alternative to *Smith*. The dissent's approach has, of course, great popular attraction. Who can possibly be against the abstract proposition that government should not, even in its general, nondiscriminatory laws, place unreasonable burdens upon religious practice? Unfortunately, however, that abstract proposition must ultimately be reduced to concrete cases. The issue presented by *Smith* is, quite simply, whether the people, through their elected representatives, or rather this Court, shall control the outcome of those concrete cases. For example, shall it be the determination of this Court, or rather of the people, whether (as the dissent apparently believes,) church construction will be exempt from zoning laws? The historical evidence put forward by the dissent does nothing to undermine the conclusion we reached in *Smith*: It shall be the people.

Justice O'CONNOR, with whom Justice BREYER joins except as to a portion of Part I, dissenting.

I dissent from the Court's disposition of this case. I agree with the Court that the issue before us is whether the Religious Freedom Restoration Act (RFRA) is a proper exercise of Congress' power to enforce s. 5 of the Fourteenth Amendment. But as a yardstick for measuring the constitutionality of RFRA, the Court uses its holding in *Employment Div., Dept. of Human Resources of Ore. v. Smith* (1990), the decision that prompted Congress to enact RFRA as a means of more rigorously enforcing the Free Exercise Clause. I remain of the view that *Smith* was wrongly decided, and I would use this case to reexamine the Court's holding there. . . . If the Court were to correct the misinterpretation of the Free Exercise Clause set forth in *Smith*, it would simultaneously put our First Amendment jurisprudence back on course and allay the legitimate concerns of a majority in Congress who believed that *Smith* improperly restricted religious liberty. We would then be in a position to review RFRA in light of a proper interpretation of the Free Exercise Clause.

I agree with much of the reasoning set forth in Part III-A of the Court's opinion. Indeed, if I agreed with the Court's standard in *Smith*, I would join the opinion. As the Court's careful and thorough historical analysis shows, Congress lacks the "power to decree the substance of the Fourteenth Amendment's restrictions on the States." Rather, its power under s. 5 of the Fourteenth Amendment extends only to enforcing the Amendment's provisions. In short,

Congress lacks the ability independently to define or expand the scope of constitutional rights by statute. Accordingly, whether Congress has exceeded its s. 5 powers turns on whether there is a "congruence and proportionality between the injury to be prevented or remedied and the means adopted to that end." This recognition does not, of course, in any way diminish Congress' obligation to draw its own conclusions regarding the Constitution's meaning. Congress, no less than this Court, is called upon to consider the requirements of the Constitution and to act in accordance with its dictates. But when it enacts legislation in furtherance of its delegated powers, Congress must make its judgments consistent with this Court's exposition of the Constitution and with the limits placed on its legislative authority by provisions such as the Fourteenth Amendment.

The Court's analysis of whether RFRA is a constitutional exercise of Congress' s. 5 power, set forth in Part III-B of its opinion, is premised on the assumption that *Smith* correctly interprets the Free Exercise Clause. This is an assumption that I do not accept. I continue to believe that *Smith* adopted an improper standard for deciding free exercise claims. In *Smith*, five Members of this Court—without briefing or argument on the issue— interpreted the Free Exercise Clause to permit the government to prohibit, without justification, conduct mandated by an individual's religious beliefs, so long as the prohibition is generally applicable. Contrary to the Court's holding in that case, however, the Free Exercise Clause is not simply an antidiscrimination principle that protects only against those laws that single out religious practice for unfavorable treatment. Rather, the Clause is best understood as an affirmative guarantee of the right to participate in religious practices and conduct without impermissible governmental interference, even when such conduct conflicts with a neutral, generally applicable law. Before *Smith*, our free exercise cases were generally in keeping with this idea: where a law substantially burdened religiously motivated conduct—regardless whether it was specifically targeted at religion or applied generally—we required government to justify that law with a compelling state interest and to use means narrowly tailored to achieve that interest.

The Court's rejection of this principle in *Smith* is supported neither by precedent nor . . . by history. The decision has harmed religious liberty. . . . [L]ower courts applying *Smith* no longer find necessary a searching judicial inquiry into the possibility of reasonably accommodating religious practice.

Accordingly, I believe that we should reexamine our

holding in *Smith*, and do so in this very case. In its place, I would return to a rule that requires government to justify any substantial burden on religiously motivated conduct by a compelling state interest and to impose that burden only by means narrowly tailored to achieve that interest.

The historical evidence casts doubt on the Court's current interpretation of the Free Exercise Clause. The record instead reveals that its drafters and ratifiers more likely viewed the Free Exercise Clause as a guarantee that government may not unnecessarily hinder believers from freely practicing their religion, a position consistent with our pre-*Smith* jurisprudence.

The Religion Clauses of the Constitution represent a profound commitment to religious liberty. Our Nation's Founders conceived of a Republic receptive to voluntary religious expression, not of a secular society in which religious expression is tolerated only when it does not conflict with a generally applicable law. As the historical sources discussed above show, the Free Exercise Clause is properly understood as an affirmative guarantee of the right to participate in religious activities without impermissible governmental interference, even where a believer's conduct is in tension with a law of general application. Certainly, it is in no way anomalous to accord heightened protection to a right identified in the text of the First Amendment. For example, it has long been the Court's position that freedom of speech—a right enumerated only a few words after the right to free exercise—has special constitutional status. Given the centrality of freedom of speech and religion to the American concept of personal liberty, it is altogether reasonable to conclude that both should be treated with the highest degree of respect.

Although it may provide a bright line, the rule the Court declared in *Smith* does not faithfully serve the purpose of the Constitution. Accordingly, I believe that it is essential for the Court to reconsider its holding in *Smith*—and to do so in this very case. I would therefore direct the parties to brief this issue and set the case for reargument.

I respectfully dissent from the Court's disposition of this case.

Justice SOUTER, dissenting.

To decide whether the Fourteenth Amendment gives Congress sufficient power to enact the Religious Freedom Restoration Act, the Court measures the legislation against the free-exercise standard of *Employment Div., Dept. of Human Resources of Ore. v. Smith* (1990). . . . I have serious doubts about the precedential value of the *Smith* rule and its entitlement to adherence. These doubts are intensified today by the historical arguments going to the original understanding of the Free Exercise Clause presented in

Justice O'Connor's opinion, which raises very substantial issues about the soundness of the *Smith* rule. But without briefing and argument on the merits of that rule (which this Court has never had in any case, including *Smith* itself), I am not now prepared to join Justice O'Connor in rejecting it or the majority in assuming it to be correct. . . . I would therefore dismiss the writ of certiorari as improvidently granted, and I accordingly dissent from the Court's disposition of this case.

Justice BREYER, dissenting.

Notes and Queries

1. As we saw, at issue in *Smith* was a basic contest between democratic theory and the powers of communities to regulate themselves, and constitutionalism's concern for individual liberty. Justice Scalia's opinion for the majority in *Smith* expressed a clear preference for democratic values by evidencing great respect for the democratic process. On the other hand, the Religious Freedom Restoration Act seems to offer far greater protection for individual liberty. What are we to make of the fact that in this case, it is Congress, and not the Court, that has assumed the role of guarantor of constitutional liberty?

2. The most fundamental issue raised by the Act and the Court's decision in *Boerne* is, of course, who should interpret the Constitution. Does Justice Kennedy's opinion for the Court fully address that question? What is the Court's answer to it? Does the Court's distinction between "substantive" and "remedial" legislation speak to this issue?

3. In the Act, Congress presumably sought to tell federal judges that they must apply a particular test—in this case, the tougher, pre-*Smith* test—to assess free exercise cases. Could Congress instruct those same judges to apply a weaker test? See *Kaztenbach v. Morgan*, 384 U.S. 641 (1966).

4. Is *Boerne* a free exercise case or a federalism case? How—if at all—do concerns about the proper prerogatives of states influence the Court's opinion?

5. Justice Kennedy wrote that "If Congress could define its own powers by altering the Fourteenth Amendment's meaning, no longer would the Constitution be 'superior paramount law, unchangeable by ordinary means.'" Did Congress define its own powers in the Restoration Act? Similarly, Justice Kennedy said several times that Congress had changed the meaning of the Free Exercise Clause. Do you agree?

6. Justice Stevens argued that the Act was an unconstitutional establishment of religion. Does his opinion rest

on a particular view of the relationship between the free exercise and no establishment clauses? Was it appropriate for the majority to assess the constitutionality of the Act by the *Smith* standard, especially since that standard was the subject of dispute? Justice O'Connor suggests that it was not. What standard would she use?

Chapter 14

The Equal Protection Clause and Racial Discrimination

*E*quality has always been one of the ideals of the American constitutional order. "We hold these truths to be self-evident," wrote Jefferson in the Declaration of Independence, "that all men are created equal." The Declaration was founded on a bedrock principle of democracy: legitimate government is based upon popular consent. This insistence on consent reflects the Founders' recognition of the equal moral worth of all human beings. Equality is central not only to democracy, but to constitutionalism as well. Constitutionalism's respect for the dignity and autonomy of the individual is evident in its emphasis upon limited government and protection for individual liberty. Madison drew the connection between equality and protection for individual liberty when he introduced a draft of the Bill of Rights to the first Congress, saying, "It may be said, in some circumstances, [that the proposed amendments] do no more than state the perfect equality of mankind. This, to be sure, is an absolute truth."[1]

The original constitution, however, did not reflect this absolute truth. Even though several constitutional provisions, such as the prohibition on titles of nobility (Art. I, Sec. 9) and the full faith and credit clause (Art. IV) implied a commitment to the political equality envisioned in the Declaration, several other provisions represented concessions to the evil of slavery, a practice that some of the Founders were determined to preserve and that others tolerated as the necessary price for union. Indeed, fundamental disagreement over slavery may be one of the reasons why the Constitution did not include an explicit guarantee of equality until the Fourteenth Amendment was ratified in 1868.

The Fourteenth Amendment guarantees that "[n]o State shall make or enforce any law which shall . . . deny to any person within its jurisdiction the equal protection to the law." This chapter takes up the equal protection clause as it relates to racial issues. Owing to the history of slavery and discrimination in America, these issues have represented the strongest challenge to the Fourteenth Amendment's promise of equality. Here more than anywhere else the disparity between constitutional ideal and constitutional

---

[1] 1 Annals of Congress 454 (June 8, 1789).

practice is clearest. Equality is a value we aspire to and a condition we rarely achieve. Our failures, no less than our successes, teach us about the real meaning and limits of equality. As a consequence, constitutional interpretation in this area, perhaps more than in any other, is an exercise in cultural self-definition, involving questions about who "we" are as well as what "we" believe.[2]

Interpreting Equality

When does a state deny a person equal protection under the terms of the Fourteenth Amendment? Public laws and regulations customarily divide people into groups. In doing so, they either confer a benefit or impose a burden. As noted in greater detail in chapter 15, these laws and regulations often classify people for specified purposes on the basis of attributes such as age, residence, income, aptitude, occupation, marital status, and numberless other features that mark some people off from others. The Fourteenth Amendment itself offers little guidance about what makes a classification—a particular discrimination—unconstitutional. Its language is remarkably and deliberately inclusive—nowhere, for example, does it suggest that it forbids only racial discrimination. Nor does it suggest that other forms of discrimination are not covered. Here, as elsewhere, the Constitution speaks in majestic generalities. How, then, should we determine what equality means? As we shall see, the Court's interpretation of the Equal Protection Clause has been heavily influenced by its particular history and its close connection with the problem of racial discrimination.

Prior to the late 1930s, the Court rarely used the Equal Protection Clause to strike down governmental policies. Race-based legislation was the exception. Even though the Fourteenth Amendment was written in general language, the *Slaughter-House Cases* (reprinted in chapter 9) advanced the theory, based on the Court's reading of original intent, that it should be applied mainly to emancipated African Americans.[3] "We doubt very much," said the Court, "whether any action of a state not directed by way of discrimination against the negroes as a class, or on account of their race, will ever be held to come within the purview of this provision."[4] With this dubious reading of the background and significance of the Fourteenth Amendment, the Supreme Court refused seriously to consider the validity of legal classifications based on factors other than race. Even as late as 1927, Justice Holmes disparaged the use of the Equal Protection Clause by remarking that "[it is] the usual last resort of constitutional arguments."[5]

In early cases, the Court adopted the rationality test for assessing the validity of legislative line-drawing based on race. In short, a state could "discriminate" as long as the discrimination (i.e., the line-drawing) rationally advanced a legitimate state purpose. The practical effect of the rationality test was of course to deny the promise of equal protection by allowing legislatures to base policy on appeals to a public opinion demanding separation of the races. In *Carolene Products* (1938, reprinted in chapter 11), however, the Court hinted that it would subject certain types of state action to more "searching" inquiry. The final paragraph of *Carolene*'s footnote four

---

[2] For a discussion of how equal protection involves questions of cultural self-definition, see Kenneth L. Karst, *Belonging to America: Equal Citizenship and the Constitution* (New Haven: Yale University Press, 1989).

[3] 83 U.S. 36 (1873).

[4] *Slaughter-House Cases*, 83 U.S. (16 Wall.) 36, 81 (1872).

[5] *Buck v. Bell*, 274 U.S. 200, 208 (1927).

suggested that stricter scrutiny would be appropriate for legislation directed at "discrete and insular" religious, national, or racial minorities and which interfered with the political processes normally relied upon to protect those minorities.

In *Korematsu v. United States* (1944, reprinted in chapter 5) the Court cautiously began to build on footnote four, stating that "all legal restrictions which curtail the civil rights of a single racial group are immediately suspect." Even though the Court upheld the internment challenged in *Korematsu*, that case inaugurated a jurisprudence that finds in the Equal Protection Clause many different tests for determining a law's constitutionality. Since that time the Court has continued to subject legislation to different tests under the Equal Protection Clause depending on the nature of the classification. Invidious racial classifications are always "suspect," and the state must show that such a classification advances a "compelling state interest" and is "narrowly tailored to achieve its purposes." Very few statutes survive this strict judicial scrutiny. Nonsuspect classifications, on the other hand, such as those involving property or economic regulation, remain subject to the rationality test and are therefore very rarely overturned. To understand how and why race became a suspect classification, we now turn to examine the constitutional history of race in the United States.

Racial Discrimination and the Supreme Court

The Declaration of Independence is premised upon a belief in the equal moral worth of all people, a belief with roots in Lockean political theory, the common law, and the Judeo-Christian tradition. The Declaration was also evidence of Americans' inability to translate that ideal into practice. In earlier drafts of the document, Jefferson (who opposed slavery in principle despite being a slaveowner in fact) had accused the British king of waging

> *cruel war against human nature itself, violating its most sacred rights of life and liberty in the persons of a distant people who never offended him, captivating & carrying them into slavery in another hemisphere or to incur miserable death in their transportation thither. . . . Determined to keep open a market where Men should be bought and sold, he has prostituted his negative for suppressing every legislative attempt to prohibit or restrain this execrable commerce.*

This language was omitted from the final draft because South Carolina and Georgia objected to it.

Slavery and the Constitution

The 1790 census already counted 697,000 slaves in the U.S., out of a total population of 3.9 million. In several southern states, slaves accounted for more than 20 percent of the population. Especially in the South, these large numbers of slaves played a significant role in the social, political, and economic life of the new nation. In spite of this, northern areas witnessed a growing movement toward abolition—Pennsylvania and Maryland abolished slavery in 1780, Connecticut and Rhode Island four years later, New York a year after that, and New Jersey in 1786. These divisions of opinion ensured that slavery would be a critical issue at the Constitutional Convention.[6]

---

[6] Paul Finkelman, *An Imperfect Union: Slavery, Federalism, and Comity* (Chapel Hill: University of North Carolina Press, 1981).

Although the word "slavery" never appears in the Constitution, a number of oblique references to it reveal that the issue was never far from the surface of debate. One such reference occurs in Article V, which provided that there could be no amendment to the first and fourth clauses of Article I, Section 9, before 1808; those clauses in turn declared that the "Migration or Importation of such Persons as any of the States now existing shall think proper to admit" could not be prohibited by Congress before 1808. Article IV, in another veiled reference to slavery, contained the fugitive slave clause, providing that persons "held to service or labor" in one state should be returned to that state if they escaped and were captured elsewhere. Still another example was the clause of Article I which counted slaves as three-fifths of a person for determining the apportionment of taxes and state representation in Congress.[7] This concession gave southern states somewhat increased representation at the cost of higher taxes.

Although Congress formally prohibited the slave trade in 1808, it continued illegally for many years. And the expansion of the Union made it inevitable that slavery would continue to play a prominent role in national politics. Slavery became a major issue in the early 1800s when Congress sought to ban the expansion of slavery into the territories. Although the prevailing opinion in the Supreme Court was that the states were free to deal with slavery as they wished, Congress' power over slavery in the territories seemed clear from the language of Article IV, Section 3. It declared: "The Congress shall have power to dispose of and make needful rules and regulations respecting the Territory or other Property belonging to the United States." Accordingly, as early as 1805, Congress prohibited slavery in several Northwest territories. But when Congress sought to ban any further introduction of slaves into Missouri—a slave territory—as a condition of statehood, a major North-South conflict erupted, with several states threatening secession as a consequence. The conflict led to the famous—or infamous—Compromise of 1820, admitting Missouri as a slave and Maine as a free state (thus preserving the two camps' equality in the Senate) and prohibiting slavery in the Louisiana Territory north of latitude 36' 30".

The compromise was short-lived. Angry passions over slavery flared up again soon. With the Missouri Compromise in mind, John Q. Adams remarked, "I take it for granted that the present question is a mere preamble—a title-page to a great, tragic volume."[8] At the urging of President Buchanan and other politicians who wanted the slavery issue resolved as a matter of law, the Supreme Court went on to write leading chapters in this "tragic volume." The chapters were known as *Prigg v. Pennsylvania* (1842) and *Dred Scott v. Sandford* (1856, reprinted later in this chapter). *Prigg* hurled the court into the fire of the fugitive slave controversy. As noted earlier, Article IV, Section 2, of the Constitution, required the return of slaves escaping into another state, a policy that Congress had sought to enforce with the passage of the Fugitive Slave Act in 1793. Several states, including Pennsylvania, devised strategies to aid escaping slaves. Pennsylvania prohibited the forcible return of fugitive slaves unless their owners or their agents could legally prove that the persons apprehended were in fact their "property." In striking the statute as a violation of the Fugitive Slave Act,[9] the *Prigg* Court, instead of settling the federal-state controversy,

---

[7] Southern states originally demanded that slaves be counted as full persons for these purposes, but this was unacceptable to antislavery northern interests. They insisted on reducing the number of slaves to be counted for tax and representation purposes. That the three-fifths clause was motivated by antislavery sentiments makes it no less a blot on the edifice of American constitutionalism.

[8] Samuel E. Morison and Henry S. Commager, *The Growth of the American Republic*, 5th ed. (New York: Oxford University Press, 1962): 444.

[9] 41 U.S. (16 Pet.) 536. A few years later, in 1847, the Court upheld the federal government's power to enact the Fugitive Slave Act. *Jones v. Van Zandt*, 5 Howard 215.

as many had hoped, merely inflamed the passions of Americans unwilling to put up with what they regarded as a grave constitutional evil.

Prigg dramatically illustrates the tense and complex relationship between law and morality. Did Justice Story, the author of the opinion and a towering figure in the history of American law, compromise his moral principles to enforce an immoral constitutional provision? Motives are hard to discern in the opinion-writing of a justice, but Story, like Chief Justice Marshall, was an ardent nationalist, and his determination to enhance the power of the national government may itself have included a moral strategy. He may well have sustained Congress' exclusive control over fugitive slaves, which in the 1840s would serve the interest of slave owners but which he might have understood would ultimately enhance the prospects of freedom. In fact, it was the congressional abolition of slavery in the Northwest Territory that gave rise to *Dred Scott v. Sandford*, the next chapter in this woeful tale.

Dred Scott brought the slavery controversy to a boil. The issue was whether Scott, a Missouri slave who had traveled with his owner to the free state of Illinois, remained a slave or had become free by virtue of the move. Chief Justice Taney, writing for the Court, ruled that Scott was still a slave. The decision turned on whether Scott was a citizen, possessing the right to sue his owner in a federal court. "The question," Taney wrote, "is simply this: Can a negro, whose ancestors were imported into this country and sold as slaves, become a member of the political community formed and brought into existence by the Constitution of the United States . . . ?" Professing an unwillingness to assess "the justice or injustice" of the matter, Taney concluded that when the Constitution was ratified, African Americans, whether free or slaves, were not citizens. In support of this view he referred extensively to the Founders' attitudes toward African Americans, declaring that they could not have been regarded at that time "as fellow-citizens and members of the sovereignty," for they were "a class of beings whom they had . . . stigmatized . . . and upon whom they had impressed such deep and enduring marks of inferiority and degradation." Taney also observed that African Americans "had for more than a century . . . been regarded as beings of an inferior order, . . . [and] they had no rights which the white man was bound to respect."

Had Taney ended the case there, declaring simply that Scott was not and could not be a citizen of Missouri within the meaning of citizenship as defined by the Constitution, the decision would have been little more than a footnote in a sad chapter of American constitutional history. But he went on to conclude that African Americans, having been bought and sold as "articles of merchandise," are the property of their owners. Accordingly, they—the owners—are entitled to protection under the Due Process Clause of the Fifth Amendment. Hence Congress could not interfere with the slave trade because doing so would infringe on the property rights of slave owners. From this conclusion it was but a short step for the Court to declare the Missouri Compromise unconstitutional. The Court thus transformed the Constitution and the vision of the union of "We the People," "which by its original terms had evaded and at best accommodated slavery, into a prohibition of federal interference with and an endorsement of the institution."[10]

Critics of the Court complain that it should not have sought to settle judicially what had not been settled politically. Yet President Buchanan had encouraged the Court to do just that, saying in his inaugural address that slavery in the territories "was a judicial question, which legitimately belongs to the Supreme Court, before whom it

---

[10] Donald P. Lively, *The Constitution and Race* (New York: Praeger, 1992), p. 29.

is now pending and will, it is understood, be speedily settled." He was, of course, wrong. Just four years later the country was engulfed in civil war. Far from settling the matter, the Court's opinion galvanized northern abolitionists and reopened fundamental questions about the constitutional order and the nature of the American community.[11] Among these questions were issues concerning who should interpret the Constitution. Whereas Buchanan had sought a final settlement from the Court, President Lincoln, in his 1861 inaugural address (reprinted in appendix C), challenged that authority.

> *I do not forget the position assumed by some, that constitutional questions are to be decided by the Supreme Court; nor do I deny that such decisions must be binding in any case, upon the parties to a suit, as to the object of that suit, while they are also entitled to very high respect and consideration, in all parallel cases, by all other departments of the government. . . . [A]t the same time the candid citizen must confess that if the policy of the government, upon vital questions, affecting the whole people, is to be irrevocably fixed by decisions of the Supreme Court, the instant they are made, in ordinary litigation between parties, in personal actions, the people will have ceased, to be their own rulers, having, to that extent, practically resigned their government, into the hands of that eminent tribunal.*

This question of who possessed final authority to interpret the Constitution was not just one of abstract constitutional theory. The Court's opinion in *Dred Scott*, if unchallenged, would have meant the spread of slavery throughout the territories, which was patently unacceptable to Lincoln and northern abolitionists.

Another fundamental constitutional issue raised by the war concerned the nature of the Union and the question of secession. Seven states had seceded by the time of Lincoln's inauguration, forming the new Confederate States of America, with its own constitution. The constitutional theory of secession rested upon a particular understanding of the larger constitutional order.[12] Southern states argued that the Union was a consensual agreement between sovereign states free to withdraw from it if the national government, in their view, exceeded its lawful authority. Responding in his inaugural address, Lincoln claimed the Union was older than the Constitution and was perpetual in nature. On this theory, the independent states created neither the Union nor the Constitution; rather, the sovereign people were the source of both. Moreover, because the Union was perpetual, a state's consent, once given, could not be revoked. After the war, in *Texas v. White* (1869), the Court affirmed the constitutional theory upon which the North's victory had been based: It declared that "[t]he Constitution, in all its provisions, looks to an indestructible Union, composed of indestructible states." *Texas v. White* thus consolidated the constitutional settlement occasioned by the Civil War. That settlement rested upon a dramatic change in the relationship between the states and the national government, especially concerning the protection of civil liberties.

---

[11] At the heart of the abolitionist movement was a debate over the Constitution itself. Some abolitionists, such as Frederick Douglass, thought the Constitution was distinctly pro-slavery, "a covenant with death and an agreement with hell" requiring major structural changes. Others, such as Lysander Spooner, considered it an inherently anti-slavery text, albeit one that included, for reasons of political necessity, accommodations to the practice.

[12] The theory of secession was preceded by the doctrine of nullification, developed earlier by Jefferson and especially John Calhoun (in his *Discourses on the Constitution of the United States*), which claimed that states could "nullify" a Supreme Court ruling with which they disagreed.

Civil War Amendments, Jim Crow, and Separate but Equal

The most obvious evidence of this change was the addition of the Thirteenth, Fourteenth, and Fifteenth Amendments (the Reconstruction Amendments), adopted respectively in 1865, 1868, and 1870. The Thirteenth prohibits slavery and involuntary servitude; the Fourteenth requires the states to protect the privileges and immunities of citizenship and to guarantee all persons due process of law and the equal protection of the laws; and the Fifteenth provides that the right to vote cannot be abridged on account of race, color, or previous condition of servitude. Furthermore, by explicitly authorizing Congress to enforce their provisions "by appropriate legislation," these amendments embraced an understanding of federalism that envisions a national government strong enough to demand from the states respect for the civil and constitutional rights of citizens.

In practice, however, these amendments promised far more than they delivered. Immediately after the Reconstruction Acts were ratified, many southern states adopted repressive "black codes" discriminating against African Americans. In response, Congress passed the Civil Rights Act of 1866 declaring all persons born in the United States to be citizens and providing that all citizens shall have the same legal rights as white persons, including the right to buy and sell property. This was followed by the Civil Rights Act of 1875, which prohibited discrimination based on race in hotels and other places of public accommodation. But when interpreted by the Supreme Court, these laws turned out to have little bite. Along with the amendments on which they were based, these laws were narrowly construed to the disadvantage of African Americans. For example, when the Supreme Court considered the 1875 law in the *Civil Rights Cases* (1883, reprinted later in the chapter) it found that the Fourteenth Amendment prohibited only state, not private, acts of racial discrimination.

The Supreme Court narrowed the application of the Fifteenth Amendment in a similar fashion. Literary tests, poll taxes, and white primaries were employed throughout the South to deny the voting rights of African Americans, but the Court did little to stop such abuses. In cases like *Giles v. Harris* (1913) and *Guinn v. United States* (1915), the Court upheld literacy tests as reasonable qualifications on the right to vote. Not until after World War II did the Court—again following Congress' lead—begin to give the amendment teeth in cases such as *Katzenbach v. Morgan* (1966), which finally recognized that some states had been using literacy tests to deny equal protection to racial minorities.

The Fourteenth Amendment with its due process and equal protection, was by most accounts designed to constitutionalize, and thus to nationalize, all the basic rights of American citizens. Congressman John Bingham, who drafted the amendment, explained that it rests on "the great democratic idea that all men, before the law, are equal in respect of those rights of person which God gives and no man or state may rightfully take away, except as forfeiture for crime."[13] The Court first addressed the meaning of "equal protection" in the *Slaughter-House Cases* (1873, reprinted in chapter 9). Writing for the Court, Justice Miller concluded that the main purpose of the amendment was to secure "the freedom of the slave race, the security of and firm establishment of that freedom, and the protection of the newly-made free man and citizen from the oppressions of those who had formerly exercised unlimited

---

[13] Quoted in Robert S. Peck, *The Bill of Rights and the Politics of Interpretation* (St. Paul: West Publishing Company, 1992), p. 145.

dominion over him." The Court's insistence on the importance of this purpose kept it, early on, from extending its reach to other forms of discrimination.

The "Negro rights theory" of the Fourteenth Amendment was foreshadowed in the important case of *Strauder v. West Virginia* (1880, reprinted later in the chapter). *Strauder* struck down a West Virginia law forbidding blacks to serve on juries. Writing for the Court, Justice Strong said that the Amendment "was designed to assure to the colored race the enjoyment of all the civil rights that under the law are enjoyed by white persons, and to give to that race the protection of the general government, in that enjoyment, whenever it should be denied by the States." He concluded that the right to sit on juries is a legal right that must be made available to African Americans as well as whites. Similarly, in *Yick Wo v. Hopkins* (1886), the Court invalidated a San Francisco ordinance requiring special permission to operate a laundry in a building not made of brick or stone. Though facially neutral, the law in fact discriminated against Chinese establishments: two hundred Chinese men applied for permission and were all refused, while all Caucasian applications but one were accepted. The Court noted that "though the law itself be fair on its face and impartial in appearance, yet, if it is applied and administered . . . with an evil eye and an unequal hand, so as practically to make unjust and illegal discriminations between persons in similar circumstances . . . the denial of equal justice is still within the prohibition of the Constitution." By looking at the reality of racial discrimination, the Court sought to make good on the promise of racial equality.

On the whole, though, *Strauder* and *Yick Wo* represented the exception rather than the norm. More common were cases denying the promise of equal protection. Foremost among these was *Plessy v. Ferguson* (1896, reprinted later in the chapter), in which the Court upheld the doctrine of "separate but equal." *Plessy* sustained a Louisiana law requiring separate railroad cars for whites and blacks. Writing for a 7–1 majority, Justice Brown admitted the Fourteenth Amendment was meant "to enforce the absolute equality of the two races before the law." But in the nature of things, he declared, "it could not have been intended to abolish distinctions based upon color, or to enforce social, as distinguished from political equality, or a commingling of the two races upon terms unsatisfactory to either." The Court concluded that "reasonable" statutes enacted "not for the annoyance or oppression of a particular class" did not violate the Equal Protection Clause. Justice Harlan, standing alone, disagreed. In one of the Court's most notable dissents, he wrote: "[I]n view of the Constitution, in the eye of the law, there is in this country no superior, dominant, ruling class of citizens. There is no caste here. Our constitution is color-blind. . ." Thus *any* law classifying persons by race would in his view violate the Constitution.

Doctrinally, the *Plessy* majority indicated the Court would judge equal protection claims against the lowly rationality test, deferring to the judgments of state legislatures about what were "reasonable" racial classifications. Practically, this approach profoundly slowed progress toward racial equality. Whatever its intent, *Plessy* had given "separate but equal" the constitutional stamp of approval. What followed was a system of virtual apartheid in some parts of the country, and less formal but pervasive discrimination in others. Voter registration of blacks dropped precipitously. And degrading "Jim Crow" laws, demanding racial separation in nearly every area of human interaction, became the economic reality behind the words "separate but equal."[14]

But separate was never equal, a fact nowhere more apparent than in public education. It was in this area that civil rights advocates proceeded slowly and carefully to

---

[14] For a detailed description of the horrors of Jim Crow, see C. Vann Woodward, *The Strange Career of Jim Crow* (New York: Oxford University Press, 1966).

attack the separate but equal doctrine. In the 1930s, the National Association for the Advancement of Colored People (NAACP), led by Thurgood Marshall, began a systematic campaign for school desegregation.[15] They aimed initially not at overturning *Plessy,* but rather at making good on the "equal" part of separate but equal, hoping that the enormous cost to the states of providing genuinely equal facilities "would eventually destroy segregation." As Marshall later explained the strategy,

> *[T]he university level was the best place to begin. . . . In the first place, at the university level no provision for negro education was a rule rather than the exception. Then, too, the difficulties incident to providing equal educational opportunities even within the concept of the separate but equal doctrine were insurmountable. To provide separate medical schools, law schools, engineering schools, and graduate schools with all the variety of offerings available at most state universities would be an almost financial impossibility.*[16]

The first significant victory appeared in *Missouri ex rel. Gaines v. Canada* (1938). Missouri, which lacked a separate law school for minorities, had denied Gaines, an African American man, admission to its public university law school. It offered instead to pay his tuition in another state. The Court found this violated equal protection, ruling that the duty to provide a separate but equal education could not "be cast by one state upon another." Though it was the first federal case to insist that separate but equal actually required some kind of equality, *Gaines* did not challenge the constitutional premise of *Plessy,* which effectively held that equality was possible within a framework of separation. Indeed, the limits of *Gaines* became clear ten years later in *Sipuel v. Board of Regents* (1948), in which Oklahoma denied an African American man admission to its state law school. This time, Marshall and the NAACP argued that separate was inherently unequal, an argument they would repeat six years later in *Brown v. Board of Education* (reprinted later in the chapter). Though the Court was not yet ready to accept this argument, it did demand that Oklahoma either admit African Americans to the state law school or open a separate school for them.

The NAACP continued its attack. In *Sweatt v. Painter* (1950) it challenged the refusal of Texas—which *did* have a separate law school for African Americans—to admit an African American man to its law school for whites. Now the NAACP introduced expert testimony—again foreshadowing *Brown*—demonstrating that segregated education was necessarily unequal, even if the state equalized physical resources. This time the existence of separate facilities was not enough to quiet the equal protection claim. The Court noted the presence of inequalities, notwithstanding the existence of separate schools. The school for whites (to no one's surprise) had a stronger faculty, a better library, and better physical facilities. All of this, of course, could still be made equal if the state were willing to spend the necessary money. Even more important, therefore, was the Court's willingness to consider intangible inequalities, such as the difference between the two schools in prestige and academic reputation, the importance of alumni organizations, tradition, and professional opportunities.

Sweatt presaged the fall of the separate but equal doctrine, but the Court had not yet discarded it. Nor did it seem likely to do so soon. As Marshall and others noted, the emotional hold of separate but equal in higher education was insignificant compared to its importance in elementary education.

---

[15] The NAACP's decision to begin a litigation strategy is described in Richard Kluger, *Simple Justice* (New York: Alfred A. Knopf, 1976).

[16] See Lively, *supra* note 10, at 99.

Brown and the Evolution of Equal Protection

In 1951, Linda Brown was a third-grade student in Topeka, Kansas. She walked over a mile to and from the "colored" school each day. Her father, Oliver Brown, sought to have her enrolled in a nearby school reserved for whites. When the school refused, Brown, with the help of the NAACP, sued the Board of Education, directly attacking the principle of separate but equal.

Though *Sweatt* had prepared the way for a direct attack on *Plessy*, success in *Brown* depended on two additional factors. The first involved the practical reality of who sits on the Court. The Court first heard oral argument in 1952, and was likely to split 5 to 4 in favor of Brown, with at least two presumed dissenters, Justices Vinson and Reed, strongly committed to affirming *Plessy*. Justice Frankfurter, not the only one to fear the consequences of such a badly split vote, suggested the Court re-hear the case in the 1953 term. This the Court did, asking the lawyers to concentrate on the question of whether the framers of the Fourteenth Amendment had intended it to prohibit racial discrimination in public elementary school education. One month before the new term began, Chief Justice Vinson—probably the most committed potential dissenter—died, thus prompting Frankfurter to remark, "This is the first indication that I have ever had that there is a God."[17] President Eisenhower named Earl Warren, governor of California and a political rival in his presidential campaign, to replace Vinson.

Nearly every account of *Brown* attributes the unanimous opinion of the Court to Warren's remarkable leadership, which was doubtless critical to the result. But a second factor, the evolution of equal protection jurisprudence in other areas, gave Warren and the NAACP a canvas to paint on. In *Carolene Products* (1938, reprinted in chapter 11), the Court had already hinted that it might more closely review legislation directed against "discrete and insular" racial, ethnic, or religious minorities. And *Korematsu* (1944, reprinted in chapter 5) repeated the promise of strict scrutiny for racial classifications when the Court announced that "all legal restrictions which curtail the civil rights of a single racial group are immediately suspect." Together, these cases provided a basis for a more searching judicial review of racial classifications than the deferential posture assumed by the Court in *Plessy*.

Chief Justice Warren read the Court's opinion, notable for its brevity and clarity, to a packed gallery on 17 May 1954. He began by noting that reargument in 1953 centered on the intention of the framers of the Fourteenth Amendment. After reading the briefs and hearing the arguments, the Court concluded there was no reliable evidence about what the Framers had intended the Equal Protection Clause to mean for public education. In approaching the problem, the Court wrote, "we cannot turn the clock back to 1868 when the Amendment was adopted, or even to 1896, when *Plessy v. Ferguson* was written." Rather, public education must be seen in the light of its "critical place in American life" and its role "in the performance of our most basic public responsibilities, even service in the armed forces. It is the very foundation of good citizenship. Today," continued the Court, "[education] is a principal instrument in awakening the child to cultural values, in preparing him later for professional training, and in helping him to adjust normally to his environment."

This insistence on the importance of education to the constitutional order, both as an instrument of democracy and as key to individual self-development, provided the

---

[17] Quoted in Bernard Schwartz, *A History of the Supreme Court* (New York: Oxford University Press, 1993), 286.

practical justification for the Court's unwillingness to defer to legislative decisions about what constituted "reasonable" racial classifications. In strictly scrutinizing the effect of segregation on children attending public schools, and drawing upon social science data supplied by the NAACP, the Court underscored the harmful effects of racial segregation, finding that legally enforced racial separation "has a tendency to [retard] the educational and mental development of Negro children and to deprive them of some of the benefits they would receive in a racial[ly] integrated school system." Segregation, declared the Court, "generates a feeling of inferiority" in African American children "that may affect their hearts and minds in a way unlikely ever to be undone." "Separate educational facilities," concluded the Court, "are inherently unequal."

Bolling v. Sharpe, finally, a companion case to *Brown*, merits attention because it incorporates the concept of equal protection into the Due Process Clause of the Fifth Amendment. *Bolling* involved racial segregation in the District of Columbia which is under the jurisdiction of the national government and therefore governed by the Fifth instead of the Fourteenth Amendment. But the Fifth contains no guarantee of equal protection; it says simply that government may not deprive a person of liberty without due process of law. The unanimous Court opined that it would be unthinkable to invalidate segregation in the states but not in the nation's capital. Moreover, said the Court, the concepts of equal protection and due process of law are interrelated. The justices did not mean to "imply that the two are always interchangeable phrases" but, they concluded, "discrimination may be so unjustifiable as to be violative of due process,"[18] a view predicated on Justice Harlan's reasoning in *Plessy*.

The *Brown* opinion, like *Bolling*, was short and to the point. But its central argument was (perhaps deliberately) obscure as to whether it was mandating desegregation or integration. The Court simply acknowledged that *Brown's* implementation would cause "problems of considerable complexity." It addressed some of these problems the next term, in *Brown v. Board of Education II* (1955), when it advised local officials to desegregate "as soon as possible" and with "all deliberate speed." Here the Court retreated to its usual course of deference, writing that desegregation policies were primarily the responsibility of local authorities, subject, however, to review by federal courts to ensure good faith compliance.

Southern officials seized upon *Brown II* as an excuse to delay desegregation indefinitely. Some openly defied the Court, refusing to comply with its decision, most notoriously when Arkansas Governor Orval Faubus defied three separate judicial orders to desegregate a Little Rock high school, ultimately leading President Eisenhower to send in the National Guard. The state's resistance to federal authority resulted in *Cooper v. Aaron* (1958, reprinted in chapter 3), the case that settled two issues, namely, that the Supreme Court has the last word on what the Constitution means and that state officials are bound by its pronouncements on the meaning of American federalism.

Resistance to judicial authority continued, however. Several southern states had published a "Manifesto," in which they claimed the authority to "nullify" the decision, in part because the Court's decision "constitutes a deliberate, palpable, and dangerous" effort to prohibit the states from exercising "certain rights and powers never surrendered by them. . . ." As more and more states passed statutes designed in various ways to stonewall and avoid desegregation, the Court became increasingly exasperated. In *Green v. New Kent County* (1968) it ordered a school district "to

[18] 347 U.S. 497, 499 (1954).

come forward with a plan that promises realistically to work, and promises realistically to work *now*." One year later, in *Alexander v. Holmes County Board of Education* (1969), Justice Brennan wrote that "all deliberate speed [is no longer] constitutionally permissible" and that segregated schooling must stop "at once."

There has also been much scholarly criticism of *Brown*. Some focuses on the Court's use of social science data to establish psychological harm resulting from separate education. Chief Justice Warren would later deny that social science had played much of a role in the Court's decision. Other critics have focused on the Court's failure to address the associational rights of students opposed to integration. Still others have argued that the decision went beyond the intentions of the Fourteenth Amendment's framers, who tolerated segregated schools long after the Amendment's ratification. Recently some critics of *Brown* have claimed that the decision is itself racist, arguing that the premise of "equal opportunity" so central to the case is a myth that helps perpetuate the subordination of African Americans, or that the decision's "individualistic" perspective neglects systemic and pervasive social discrimination, enabling white elites to delude themselves into thinking they have done enough to combat racism.[19]

Implementing *Brown* raised important questions about the scope of judicial power. What judicial decrees were permissible in dismantling school systems segregated by the force of law? In *Swann v. Charlotte-Mecklenburg Bd. of Education* (1971), the Supreme Court ruled unanimously that lower federal courts may take a number of steps to begin the transition to a racially non-discriminatory school system. Among these were school busing, redrawing school attendance zones, and the limited use of mathematical white-black ratios. At the same time, in *North Carolina Bd. of Ed. v. Swann*, it struck down a North Carolina law forbidding busing. And then, for the first time, in *Keyes v. School District No. 1, Denver, Colorado* (1973, reprinted later in the chapter), the Court began to consider the legitimacy of school segregation outside the South. Here the schools were segregated not by any law on the books but by the accident of housing patterns and population movements. The constitutional problem was whether there was any difference between segregation by law (*de jure*) and segregation in fact (*de facto*). It was over this question that the Supreme Court's unanimity broke down. The *Keyes* Court found that step-by-step decisions made by school officials over time, such as where to build new schools or close old ones, constituted *de jure* discrimination if these decisions tended to perpetuate the continuation of segregated schools, but the Court also made clear that *de facto* segregation alone, in the absence of any showing of discrimination, did not violate the Fourteenth Amendment. Justice Rehnquist dissented from the broad ruling of the majority while Justices Douglas and Powell declared that for purposes of the Equal Protection Clause, there is "no difference between *de jure* and *de facto* segregation."

One year later, in *Milliken v. Bradley* (1974, reprinted later in the chapter), the justices divided 5 to 4 in rejecting a Detroit desegregation plan that tried to eliminate discrimination by ordering busing across city and district lines to the suburbs. The plan went too far, according to the Court, because there had been no actual showing of *de jure* discrimination in the suburbs, no showing, that is, that the suburban districts (as opposed to the city) had violated the Constitution. Therefore, ruled the Court, the remedial order of the lower court had to be confined to the city, which

---

[19] See Sidney Wilhelm, *The Supreme Court: A Citadel for White Supremacy*, 79 Michigan Law Review 847 (1981); Charles Lawrence, *Justice or Just Us: Racism and the Role of Ideology*, 35 Stanford Law Review 831 (1983).

was overwhelmingly African American. Justice Douglas, in a bitter dissent, held that "we are now in a dramatic retreat from the 7-to-1 decision in 1896 that Blacks could be segregated in public facilities, provided they receive equal treatment." The Court's difficulties in addressing the busing issue remind us that efforts to combat legal discrimination often run up against obstacles posed by social and cultural discrimination, raising questions about the capacity of the judiciary effectively to deal with such discrimination.[20]

Although *Brown* ended *de jure* discrimination in public schools, it did not address discrimination in other areas of public life. Immediately following *Brown*, the federal courts struck down segregation in a variety of other areas, including on public buses, at public beaches, and public parks. In most of these cases, the Supreme Court simply affirmed the holdings of lower courts, instead of issuing broad opinions as in *Brown*. Some critics have charged that these decisions underscored one of the weaknesses of *Brown*. In short, the Court's emphasis on the critical importance of education in *Brown* made the extension of *Brown* to these other cases and areas of community life less than obvious. These later decisions would have been consistent with Justice Harlan's view in *Plessy* that the Constitution is color-blind, resulting in the prohibition of any law that classifies persons on the basis of race. The *Brown* Court, however, was unwilling to go that far.

The *Civil Rights Cases* (1883, reprinted later in the chapter) is a precedent of major importance, and it has complicated the history of American equal protection jurisprudence. Whether Congress' power to enforce the provisions of the Fourteenth Amendment could only be exercised against positive acts of state discrimination, as the Court ruled, is still debated among historians. (Many of the representatives who voted for the Civil Rights Act of 1875 were the same persons who drafted the Fourteenth Amendment.) The real question, however, is what constitutes "state action" for Fourteenth Amendment purposes. As noted, this was a major issue in many of the segregation cases. It is the principal issue in *Shelley v. Kraemer* (1948, reprinted later in the chapter) and *Palmare v. Sidoti* (1984, reprinted later in the chapter). Taken together, all the cases discussed so far suggest that invidious racial classifications are unconstitutional. Another example of such a classification was Virginia's miscegenation statute. In *Loving v. Virginia* (1967), the Court struck down the statute, labeling the ban on racial intermarriage as invidious and thus incapable of being justified, under the standard of strict scrutiny, by any compelling purpose the state might invoke. With this decision the Supreme Court had given notice that all such classifications are presumptively unconstitutional.

Affirmative Action and Equality

Before *Brown*, the Court's equal protection jurisprudence tended to concentrate on legislative classifications that were malign or invidious in intent or effect. Affirmative action programs, however, raise different questions because they seek to atone for the effects of historic discrimination against minorities. Accordingly, affirmative action programs classify on the basis of race to benefit minorities instead of harming them. Does the remedial or benign purpose of these policies suggest the need for

---

[20] For a treatment of the criticism which ultimately persuaded the Court that busing was an inappropriate means to integrated schools, see Gary Orfield, *Must We Bus? Segregated Schools and National Policy* (Washington, DC: Brookings Institution, 1978).

a special judicial test? Or should they be treated as identical to invidious forms of discrimination because, whatever their purpose, they continue to utilize racial classifications and in some cases may harm whites (the problem of "reverse discrimination")?

One answer open to the Court would be to conclude, as Justice Stevens argued early on, that there is only one equal protection clause, and accordingly to consider affirmative action programs just as it would consider forms of invidious discrimination. All legislative efforts at classification, whether "benign" or "remedial," would be subject to a single standard of judicial review. Powerful arguments support this approach. It provides a welcome degree of doctrinal consistency and simplicity. We saw in chapter 2 that consistency and simplicity are an important part of principled constitutional interpretation. Moreover, this approach frees the Court from having to make problematic assessments of the merit of various public policies or from engaging in troublesome evaluations of legislative motive, the difficulty of which has often led to claims that such inquiries are not appropriate for courts. Perhaps most important, using a single test gives substance to Justice Harlan's claim in *Plessy* that "our Constitution is color blind." Different levels of judicial scrutiny for affirmative action programs, based on who is harmed or helped by such programs, seem to deny Harlan's claim by giving race a central place in the Court's analytical framework.

On the other hand, the effect of a single test would be to render most affirmative action programs of doubtful constitutionality, since they likely would be considered under strict scrutiny. Moreover, it is not clear that the reasons that gave rise to the strict scrutiny test—reasons derived from footnote four of *Carolene Products*—apply with equal force to remedial legislation. Footnote four pointed to the necessity of judicial protection for "discrete and insular" minorities that cannot fully avail themselves of the political process. But the people "harmed" by affirmative action programs may not share that political disability.[21] The most important objection to a single test, however, is that it fails to account for a long and sordid history of constitutionally-sanctioned discrimination. Though Harlan's *Plessy* dissent may represent an appealing constitutional ideal, in practice the Constitution has never been color blind. It has always been used to permit racial inequalities. Critics therefore contend that a doctrinal insistence upon formal equality fails to consider, and indeed masks, longstanding practical inequalities sanctioned by the Constitution. In the words of Justice Blackmun, "In order to get beyond race, we must first take account of race. There is no other way."[22] On this understanding, a commitment to merely formal equality betrays the underlying purposes and aspirations of the equal protection clause.

The Court's first sustained consideration of these issues came in *Regents of the University of California v. Bakke* (1978, reprinted later in the chapter). Allan Bakke, a white man, was twice denied admission to the University of California's medical school at Davis, despite having a higher grade point average and better MCAT scores than a number of applicants admitted under a special program which reserved 16 spaces out of a class of 100 for "economically and/or culturally disadvantaged" persons or members of certain racial minorities. Bakke claimed that the special program

---

[21] See Richard Lempert, *The Force of Irony: On the Morality of Affirmative Action and* United Steelworkers v. Weber, 95 Ethics 86 (1984); John Hart Ely, *The Constitutionality of Reverse Racial Discrimination*, 41 University of Chicago Law Review 723 (1974); Bruce Ackerman, *Beyond Carolene Products*, 98 Harvard Law Review 713 (1985).

[22] Opinon of Justice Blackmun in *Regents of the University of California v. Bakke*, 438 U.S. 265 (1978).

violated the equal protection clause by discriminating against him on the basis of his race.

The Court concluded that the special program was unconstitutional, and Bakke was admitted to Davis. But the Court did not rule that race was a prohibited factor in admissions decisions. Four justices, in an opinion by Justice Stevens, argued that the Davis plan violated Title VI of the Civil Rights Act of 1964, which prohibits racial discrimination in any program or activity receiving federal financial assistance. They declined to decide whether the Equal Protection Clause prohibits or protects affirmative action programs. Four other justices, in an opinion by Justice Brennan, concluded that the plan satisfied both Title VI and the equal protection clause. Following the logic of *Carolene Products*, they argued that remedial racial classifications should not be subject to strict scrutiny. They argued instead for an intermediate test, one demanding more than mere rationality but less than strict scrutiny. Remedial classifications, Brennan wrote, "must serve important governmental objectives and must be substantially related to achievement of those objectives."

The decisive and most enduring opinion in *Bakke* was the judgment of Justice Powell. Powell held that the Davis program violated both Title VI and the Equal Protection Clause. "Equal protection cannot mean one thing when applied to one individual," he argued, "and something else when applied to a person of another color." Hence, a program like Davis's, which prefers "members of any one group for no reason other than race or ethnic origin is discrimination for its own sake. This the Constitution forbids." But Powell did not say that the Equal Protection Clause always forbids any consideration of race. Sometimes, he wrote, race may be "a 'plus' in a particular applicant's file." An admissions committee may therefore consider an applicant's "potential contribution to diversity" as long as race is not the decisive factor. Powell did, however, insist that the appropriate standard of judicial review for even these plans was strict scrutiny, not some less stringent test. He thus rejected the notion that racial discrimination is ever benign and argued that it would never be constitutional to remedy past discrimination by putting the burden on persons, like Bakke, who had played no part in it. In sum, Powell's opinion leads to the unconstitutionality of strict racial quotas, but it does not insist upon a "color-blind" equal protection clause.

In the years following *Bakke*, the nation witnessed a fierce debate over the merits of official affirmative action plans. No less intense was the joust on the Supreme Court. A series of decisions handed down between 1978 and 1995—some upholding, some striking down racial preferences—revealed cleavages on the Court as deep as those dividing the general public.[23] The debate centered on whether "benign" racial classifications should be vetted with the same degree of scrutiny as "invidious" ones. In applying strict scrutiny to cities and states, the Supreme Court ruled that remedial programs must be narrowly tailored to compensate identifiable victims of past governmental discrimination. Yet the Court reviewed some *federal* programs under the Fifth Amendment with far less scrutiny, saying in effect that Congress possesses broader authority than the states to deal with the general effects of societal discrimination. Disturbed by the Court's tendency to uphold "benign" federal programs by applying a standard less than strict scrutiny, Justice Kennedy, echoing the views of three colleagues, remarked, "I regret that after a century of judicial opinions we inter-

---

[23] These cases involved local or national "set-aside" programs reserving a percentage of jobs, contracts, or licenses for minority persons or businesses, all for the purpose of overcoming the effects of past discrimination. See especially *Wygant v. Jackson Bd. Of Education*, 476 U.S. 267 (1986), *Fullilove v. Klutznick*, 448 U.S. 448 (1980), *City of Richmond v. Croson*, 488 U.S. 469 (1989), and *Metro Broadcasting, Inc. v. Federal Communications Commission*, 497 U.S. 547 (1990).

pret the Constitution to do no more than move us from 'separate but equal' to 'unequal but benign.'"

Finally, in *Adarand Constructors, Inc. v. Pena* (1995, reprinted later in the chapter), and for the first time, a majority ruled that "all racial classifications, imposed by whatever federal, state, or local actor, must be analyzed by a reviewing court under strict scrutiny." In the interest of "consistency" and "congruence," declared the Court, all such classifications, whether invidious or benign, "are constitutional only if they are narrowly tailored measures that further compelling governmental interests." The dissenting justices faulted the majority for failing to recognize the moral difference between invidious and benign classifications. (Justice Stevens, one of the dissenters, had qualified his earlier stance advocating a single standard of equal protection review.) In response, the majority pointed out that all race-based programs are suspect and should trigger no less than strict scrutiny review. Yet *Adarand* conveyed the message that some affirmative action programs would pass constitutional muster. But which ones? And could the equal protection clause or the equal protection component of the Fifth Amendment be employed to defend the rights of groups as well as individuals? The Court's uncertainty over these and related questions is ultimately a consequence of the race-specific history of the Fourteenth Amendment and our collective inability to articulate a vision of equality that accounts for the long history of racial discrimination against minorities and surpasses that history.

Adarand marked a temporary halt to the Supreme Court's effort to define the boundaries of equality on the field of affirmative action. By 2002, however, affirmative action was back in the news, the focus returning, for the first time since *Bakke*, to American higher education. Pending in the Supreme Court were two cases involving the University of Michigan. In the first, a rejected applicant challenged Michigan's "point system" for achieving racial and ethnic diversity in its undergraduate College of Literature, Science, and the Arts. Unlike California in *Bakke*, the University did not admit a set number of minorities under a separate admissions system. Instead, Michigan awarded uniform points to a list of factors taken into account in a single admissions process, except that under-represented minorities received an automatic advantage of 20 points, with 100 needed to guarantee admission, a system resulting in the admission of every qualified minority applicant.

In the second case, Michigan's law school denied admission to a qualified white woman who claimed that she had been discriminated against on the basis of race. The law school sought to achieve diversity among its students through compliance with *Bakke* where, it will be recalled, Justice Powell validated the use of race as one factor among many that may be taken into account for the purpose of attaining a diverse student body. Left unanswered by *Bakke*, however, was whether diversity ranks as a *compelling* state interest that justifies a race-conscious admissions program, an issue that divided lower federal courts in the 1990s amid what appeared to be a rising anti-affirmative action mood in the country. Perhaps emboldened by these factors, the plaintiff challenged *any* use of race in university admissions as well as the objective of diversity as compelling for equal protection purposes. Major colleges and universities joined an *amicus* brief in support of Michigan, whereas the Bush Administration intervened on the side of the plaintiffs. How the Supreme Court would decide these cases was far from certain as much of America, the universities in particular, nervously awaited decision day.

The day arrived on 23 June 2003. In *Grutter v. Bollinger* (2003, reprinted later in the chapter), the Supreme Court, by a 5 to 4 vote, even as it employed the language of strict scrutiny analysis, upheld the constitutionality of the law school's admission policy. Justice O'Connor, writing for the majority, ruled that the policy was narrowly tailored to achieve a *compelling* governmental interest in the attainment of racial diversity. What saved the program was the "highly individualized, holistic review of each applicant's file, giving serious consideration to all the ways an applicant might contribute to a diverse educational environment." The majority distinguished this program from the one invalidated in *Bakke*. There a forbidden racial quota was employed; here, by contrast, race was "used in a flexible, nonmechanical way."

Grutter also appeared to differ from *Bakke* in its emphasis on securing the future rather than remedying the past. Universities, Justice O'Connor noted, play a significant role in our constitutional culture, for their job is "to cultivate a set of leaders with legitimacy in the eyes of the citizenry" and to open the path of "leadership . . . to talented and qualified individuals of every race and ethnicity." Still another fascinating aspect of the opinion was Justice O'Connor's prediction that "25 years from now, the use of racial preferences will no longer be necessary to further the interest approved today." All four justices in dissent (Rehnquist, Kennedy, Thomas, and Scalia) wrote separate opinions, ranging from Rehnquist's questioning of the empirical assumptions behind the majority's "narrow tailoring" analysis to Justice Thomas' objection to any use of race in university admissions.

In *Gratz v. Bollinger* (2003), on the other hand, the Court by a vote of 6 to 3 struck down Michigan's point system. Here Justices O'Connor and Breyer joined the four dissenters in *Grutter* to invalidate the system as the functional equivalent of a racial quota. University spokespersons were nevertheless elated. Mary Sue Coleman, president of the University of Michigan, welcomed the Court's principal ruling, namely, that race-conscious admissions programs are a legitimate means of achieving racial and ethnic diversity in higher education. Michigan's point system, she said, could easily be modified to accord with the ruling in *Gratz*.[24] In dissent, however, Justice Scalia warned that the debate over affirmative action is far from over. The "*Gratz-Grutter* split double header," he wrote, "seems perversely designed to prolong the controversy and the litigation." Time will determine whether he is right or wrong.

Private Discrimination and the State Action Doctrine

The words of the Fourteenth Amendment—"No State shall deny. . . ."—seem to make explicit what is only implicit in the Bill of Rights: the constitutional guarantee is only against the states. Accordingly, as all the cases so far discussed in this chapter show, the equal protection clause prohibits only public acts of discrimination. Purely private discrimination may violate various federal or state civil rights statutes, but it does not offend the Fourteenth Amendment because it does not involve "state action." What exactly is the difference between private and state action? In its efforts to construct a sphere of individual autonomy, or an area of private life free from state regulation, the state action doctrine highlights the relationship between individual and community that we have stressed throughout this book. How are we to balance—and who should balance—the desire for liberty with our commitment to equality?

In the *Civil Rights Cases* (1883, reprinted later in the chapter), the Court struck down a congressional civil rights statute outlawing racial discrimination by private citizens in all public accommodations. The Fourteenth Amendment, wrote the Court, "does not authorize Congress to create a mode of municipal law for the regulation of private rights; but to provide modes of redress against the operation of State laws, and the action of State officers." Congressional power under Section 5 of the amendment, argued the Court, was limited by the terms of Section 1, which clearly referred

---

[24] *New York Times*, June 24, 2003, A1.

to the action of states. In short, congressional laws to enforce the provisions of Section 1 may only be directed to affirmative acts of state discrimination.

Justice Harlan, in dissent, foreshadowed the development of state action jurisprudence. The Civil Rights Act of 1875 had prohibited discrimination on the nation's railroads (among other places). Was it clear, he asked, that such discrimination was exclusively or even predominantly private? Harlan argued that the close connections between government and the railroads—substantial public subsidies, coupled with frequent use of the state's power of eminent domain to help build the railroads—made them "public instrumentalities" and meant that state action was an undeniable part of the practice of discrimination. Since the *Civil Rights Cases*, the Court's work has focused on what constitutes state action and what, if anything, is purely private discrimination. Determining how closely the state must be involved in "private" discrimination has proved so complicated that, in the words of Charles Black, "the phrase 'state action' [is] a term of art in our constitutional law."[25]

The Court first considered this problem in the *White Primary Cases*, already discussed in chapter 8. As we saw there, state efforts to privatize elections were an obvious subterfuge to deny African Americans the right to vote; accordingly, these efforts could not escape the limits of the Equal Protection Clause. Much more difficult was judicially determining whether state action is present in activities in which the state is only indirectly involved. Is state action present when a private restaurant located on property leased to it by a public parking facility discriminates on the basis of race? Is such action present when a state grants a liquor license to a private club that prohibits African Americans from becoming members? *Shelley v. Kraemer* (1948) and *Palmore v. Sidoti* (1984), both of which are reprinted in this chapter, prompt an additional—and crucial—inquiry: To what extent may courts, in resolving disputes between private parties, base their decisions on the prejudices of these parties? In *Sidoti*, the Supreme Court noted that the "Constitution cannot control such prejudices but neither can it tolerate them. Private biases may be outside the reach of the law, but the law cannot, directly or indirectly, give them effect." This brings us full circle from *Plessy*, where the Court thought it clear that the legislature could "act with reference to the established usages, customs and traditions of the people, and with a view to the promotion of their comfort."

Comparative Perspectives

The American civil rights movements of the past few decades are just part of a larger international movement after World War II to secure human dignity and the basic rights of all persons. Appeals to equality have played a central part in this development. The Universal Declaration of Human Rights, adopted by the General Assembly of the United Nations in 1948, and subsequent international covenants for the protection of civil, political, social, and economic rights all embrace the principle of nondiscrimination. This is stated most fully in Articles 26 and 27 of the International Covenant on Civil and Political Rights:

> *Article 26. All persons are equal before the law and are entitled without any discrimination to the equal protection of the law. In this respect, the laws shall prohibit any discrimination and guarantee to all persons equal and effective protection against discrimination on any ground such as race, colour, sex, lan-*

---

[25] "State Action," in Kenneth L. Karst (ed.), *Civil Rights and Equality* (New York: Macmillan Publishing Co., 1989), 44.

guage, religion, political or other opinion, national or social origin, property, birth or other status.

Article 27 promises that in those states in which ethnic, religious or linguistic minorities exist, persons belonging to such minorities shall not be denied the right, in community with other members of their group, to enjoy their own culture, to profess and practice their own religion, or to use their own language.

Most of the national constitutions drafted after the Second World War reflect these international developments in human rights law. Article 3(1) of Germany's Basic Law, for example, states, "All persons shall be equal before the law." Paragraph 2 goes on to declare, "Men and women shall have equal rights," and paragraph 3 provides, "No one may be prejudiced or favoured because of his sex, his parentage, his race, his language, his homeland and origin, his faith, or his religious or political opinions." This provision may also be enforced in private legal relationships. For example, a person dismissed from his or her employment on account of race or religion would have a constitutional cause of action against the employer, a possibility that stems from an early pronouncement by the Federal Constitutional Court that the Basic Law influences the interpretation of laws covering private legal relationships. In the United States, by contrast, state action is required for a constitutional violation.

Although the Canadian Charter of Rights does not apply to private action, it defines equality in similarly broad terms. Section 15 declares, "Every individual is equal before and under the law and has the right to the equal protection and equal benefit of the law without discrimination based on race, national or ethnic origin, colour, religion, sex, age or mental or physical disability." These four different ways of expressing equality were intended "to reverse the restrictive interpretation placed by the Supreme Court of Canada on the phrase 'equality before the law' . . . used in the Canadian Bill of Rights."[26] Americans will note with interest that the Canadian decisions the Charter sought to circumvent were similar to the American Supreme Court's decisions limiting the reach of the equal protection clause.

Most twentieth-century constitutions include guarantees of equal protection of the laws and prohibit discrimination based on race. Often they contain more specific provisions reflecting their countries' unique histories. Canada, for example, has long wrestled with discrimination based on language and ethnic heritage. The Charter therefore grants protection to linguistic minorities and even commits the nation to the perpetuation of a multi-cultural society. To ensure that Canadian courts understand this, Section 27 states, "This Charter shall be interpreted in a manner consistent with the preservation and enhancement of the multicultural heritage of Canadians." This emphasis on the rights and prerogatives of linguistic and cultural groups is very different from the individualism that pervades American equal protection jurisprudence.

The drafters of the Canadian Charter of Rights, aware of American constitutional controversy over affirmative action, expressly protected such policies against challenges under their general equality clause. Section 15(2) provides, "Subsection (1) does not preclude any law, program or activity that has as its object the amelioration of conditions of disadvantaged individuals or groups including those that are disadvantaged because of race, national or ethnic origin, colour, religion, sex, age or mental or physical disability." Similar provisions appear in various international human rights documents, including the Convention Concerning Discrimination in Respect to

---

[26] Peter Hogg, *Constitutional Law of Canada* (Toronto: Carswell, 1992), 1158–9.

Employment and Occupation (1958) and the International Convention on the Elimination of All Forms of Racial Discrimination (1965). Interestingly, India's constitution was amended in 1951 to incorporate an affirmative action clause after the Indian Supreme Court had declared that the state was powerless to provide special educational advantages for backward communities.[27] Article 9 of South Africa's new Constitution, finally, permits parliament to adopt "measures designed to protect or advance persons, or categories of persons, disadvantaged by unfair discrimination." This provision, like the others just mentioned, removes all doubts about the validity of affirmative actions laws designed to help minority groups.

As we saw, the Fourteenth Amendment guarantees equal protection without specifying what kinds of discrimination are prohibited. The Supreme Court's equal protection jurisprudence has thus been heavily influenced by appeals to intent, history, and thorny questions about race. As a consequence, much of the Court's early work in interpreting the equal protection clause struggled over questions about the scope and breadth of the clause. Equal protection provisions in 20th-century constitutions typically speak with greater precision. They prohibit discrimination on various grounds and thus enable constitutional courts to surpass many of the race-specific problems that characterize the Supreme Court's jurisprudence. These provisions also typically rest upon understandings of equality that are not as individualistic as they are in the United States. The Canadian emphasis on the prerogatives of linguistic and cultural groups, for example, stands in stark contrast to the individualistic ethos that pervades American equal protection jurisprudence.

The Supreme Court could find guidance in the methodology used by most other constitutional courts in their interpretation of the general concept of equality. The principle of proportionality commonly applied by the European Court of Human Rights and the high tribunals of Canada and several European constitutional courts furnishes one guideline. These courts have not produced the kind of debilitating arguments over levels of judicial scrutiny displayed in the American decisions. These courts do not interpret the constitutional text as much as they require governments to justify that a given classification is appropriate and necessary to attain the objective sought. The anomaly of American equal protection law stems in part, as we have seen, from the Constitution's silence about the meaning of discrimination. Yet, even outside the scope of the express prohibitions against discrimination in modern constitutions, the constitutional case law of foreign courts has resulted in the nullification of statutes and regulations likely to have survived constitutional review in the United States.

Selected Bibliography

Baer, Judith A. *Equality Under the Constitution.* Ithaca: Cornell University Press, 1984.

Bell, Derrick. *Race, Racism and American Law.* 4th ed. 2000.

Berger, Raoul. *Government by Judiciary: The Transformation of the Fourteenth Amendment.* Cambridge: Harvard University Press, 1977.

Berman, Daniel. *It Is So Ordered: The Supreme Court Rules on School Desegregation.* New York: W.W. Norton, 1966.

Carter, Stephen. *Reflections of an Affirmative Action Baby.* New York: Basic Books, 1991.

Ely, John Hart. *Democracy and Distrust.* Cambridge: Harvard University Press, 1980.

[27] See *State of Madras v. Chamaham Dorairajan,* A.I.R. 1951 S.C. 226. The new provision of the Indian Constitution (Article 15 [4]) provides: "Nothing in this article . . . shall prevent the state from making any special provision for the advancement of any socially and educationally backward classes of citizens or for the Scheduled Castes and the Scheduled Tribes."

Ezorsky, Gertrude. *Racism and Justice: The Case for Affirmative Action*. Ithaca: Cornell University Press, 1991.

Farber, Daniel. *Lincoln's Constitution*. Chicago: University of Chicago Press, 2003.

Fiscus, Ronald J. *The Constitutional Logic of Affirmative Action*. Durham: Duke University Press, 1992.

Fiss, Owen. *Groups and the Equal Protection Clause*. 5 Phil. & Pub. Aff. 107 (1976).

Gibson, Dale. *The Law of the Charter: Equality Rights*. Toronto: Carswell Press, 1990.

Glazer, Nathan. *Affirmative Discrimination: Ethnic Inequality and Public Policy*. New York: Basic Books, 1975.

Karst, Kenneth. *Belonging to America*. New Haven: Yale University Press, 1987.

Kluger, Richard. *Simple Justice: The History of Brown v. Board of Education and Black America's Struggle for Equality*. New York: Knopf, 1976.

Kull, Andrew. *The Color-Blind Constitution*. Cambridge: Harvard University Press, 1992.

Lively, Donald E. *The Constitution and Race*. New York: Praeger Press, 1992.

Lofgren, Charles A. *The Plessy Case: A Legal-Historical Interpretation*. New York: Oxford University Press, 1986.

Myrdal, Gunner. *An American Dilemma: The Negro Problem and Modern Democracy*. New York: Harper & Row, 1944.

Nieman, Donald G. *Promises to Keep: African-Americans and the Constitutional Order, 1776 to Present*. New York: Oxford University Press, 1991.

Pennock, J. Roland and John W. Chapman, eds., *Equality*. New York: Lieber-Alberton, 1967.

Pole, J. R. *The Pursuit of Equality in American History*. 2d ed. Berkeley: University of California Press, 1993.

Rosenberg, Gerald N. *The Hollow Hope: Can Courts Bring About Social Change?* Chicago: University of Chicago Press, 1991.

Seidman, Louis M. *Constitutional Law: Equal Protection*. New York: Foundation Press, 2003.

TenBroek, Jacobus. *Equal Under Law*. Berkeley: University of California Press, 1965.

Tussman, Joseph and Jacobus TenBroek. *The Equal Protection of the Laws*. 37 Cal. L. Rev. 341 (1949).

Vose, Clement E. *Caucasians Only: The Supreme Court, the NAACP, and the Restrictive Covenant Cases*. Berkeley: University of California Press, 1959.

West, Robin. *Progressive Constitutionalism: Reconstructing the Fourteenth Amendment*. Durham: Duke University Press, 1994.

Wilkinson, J. Harvie III. *From Brown to Bakke*. New York: Oxford University Press, 1979.

Wolters, Raymond. *The Burden of Brown*. Knoxville: University of Tennessee Press, 1984.

Woodward, C. Vann. *The Strange Career of Jim Crow*. New York: Oxford University Press, 1966.

Selected Comparative Bibliography

Beytagh, Francis X. *Equal Protection: U.S. and Ireland*. 18 Irish Jurist 56, 220 (1983).

Favoreau, Louis. *The Principle of Equality in the Jurisprudence of the* Conseil Constitutionnel. 21 Capital Univ. L. Rev. 165 (1992).

Harris, David. *Equality, Equality Rights and Discrimination Under the Charter of Rights and Freedoms*. 21 Univ. of British Columbia L. Rev. 65 (1988).

Klein, Eckart. "The Principle of Equality and Its Protection in the Federal Republic of Germany," in T. Koopmans, *Constitutional Protection of Equality*. Leyden: A.W. Sijthoff, 1975.

Kushnick, Louis. *Race, Class and Struggle: Essays on Racism and Inequality in Britain, the US and Western Europe*. London: Rivers Oram Press, 1998.

Parikh, Sunita. *The Politics of Preference: Democratic Institutions and Affirmative Action in the United States and India*. Ann Arbor: University of Michigan Press, 1997.

Tomatsu, Hidenari. *Equal Protection of the Law*. Symposium on Japan, 53 Law & Contemp. Prob. 109 (1990).

Upham, Frank. *Law and Social Change in PostWar Japan*. Cambridge: Harvard University Press, 1987.

Dred Scott v. Sandford

60 U.S. 393, 19 How. 393, 15 L. Ed. 691 (1856)

Dred Scott, a slave, belonged to Dr. Emerson, a U.S. Army surgeon stationed in Missouri. In 1834 Emerson was transferred to Rock Island, Illinois, a state that forbade slavery, yet he took Scott with him. Later Emerson was transferred to Fort Snelling in what is now Minnesota, a free territory under the Missouri Compromise of 1820, and he again took Scott with him. Emerson and Scott returned to Missouri in 1838. In 1846, Dred Scott sued for his freedom in a Missouri state court because he was brought into and had resided in a free territory. Scott won the initial case, but the Missouri Supreme Court reversed the judgment. Unsatisfied, abolitionists arranged a fictitious sale of Scott to John Sandford, a resident of New York and a relative of Emerson, so that the Federal Circuit Court could assert jurisdiction because of diversity of citizenship. The Circuit Court ruled against Scott, and the decision was appealed to the Supreme Court on a writ of error. Opinion of the Court: *Taney*, Campbell, Catron, Grier, Nelson, Wayne. Concurring opinions: *Campbell, Catron, Grier, Nelson, Wayne*. Dissenting opinions: *Curtis, McLean*.

Mr. Chief Justice TANEY delivered the opinion of the Court.

The question is simply this: Can a negro, whose ancestors were imported into this country, and sold as slaves, become a member of the political community formed and brought into existence by the Constitution of the United States, and as such become entitled to all the rights, and privileges, and immunities, guaranteed by that instrument to the citizen? One of which rights is the privilege of suing in a court of the United States in the cases specified in the Constitution.

It will be observed, that the plea applies to that class of persons only whose ancestors were negroes of the African race, and imported into this country, and sold and held as slaves. The only matter in issue before the court, therefore, is, whether the descendants of such slaves, when they shall be emancipated, or who are born of parents who had become free before their birth, are citizens of a State, in the sense in which the word citizen is used in the Constitution of the United States. And this being the only matter in dispute on the pleadings, the court must be understood as speaking in this opinion of that class only, that is, of those persons who are the descendants of Africans who were imported into this country, and sold as slaves. . . .

The words "people of the United States" and "citizens" are synonymous terms, and mean the same thing. They both describe the political body who, according to our republican institutions, form the sovereignty, and who hold the power and conduct the Government through their representatives. They are what we familiarly call the "sovereign people," and every citizen is one of this people, and a constituent member of this sovereignty. The question before us is, whether the class of persons described in the plea in abatement compose a portion of this people, and are constituent members of this sovereignty? We think they are not, and that they are not included, and were not intended to be included, under the word "citizens" in the Constitution, and can therefore claim none of the rights and privileges which that instrument provides for and secures to citizens of the United States. On the contrary, they were at that time considered as a subordinate and inferior class of beings, who had been subjugated by the dominant race, and, whether emancipated or not, yet remained subject to their authority, and had no rights or privileges but such as those who held the power and the Government might choose to grant them.

It is not the province of the court to decide upon the justice or injustice, the policy or impolicy, of these laws. The decision of that question belonged to the political or law-making power; to those who formed the sovereignty and framed the Constitution. The duty of the court is, to interpret the instrument they have framed, with the best

lights we can obtain on the subject, and to administer it as we find it, according to its true intent and meaning when it was adopted.

In discussing this question, we must not confound the rights of citizenship which a State may confer within its own limits, and the rights of citizenship as a member of the Union. It does not by any means follow, because he has all the rights and privileges of a citizen of a State, that he must be a citizen of the United States. He may have all of the rights and privileges of the citizen of a State, and yet not be entitled to the rights and privileges of a citizen in any other State. For, previous to the adoption of the Constitution of the United States, every State had the undoubted right to confer on whomsoever it pleased the character of citizen, and to endow him with all its rights. But this character of course was confined to the boundaries of the State, and gave him no rights or privileges in other States beyond those secured to him by the laws of nations and the comity of States. Nor have the several States surrendered the power of conferring these rights and privileges by adopting the Constitution of the United States. Each State may still confer them upon an alien, or any one it thinks proper, or upon any class or description of persons; yet he would not be a citizen in the sense in which that word is used in the Constitution of the United States, nor entitled to sue as such in one of its courts, nor to the privileges and immunities of a citizen in the other States. The rights which he would acquire would be restricted to the State which gave them. The Constitution has conferred on Congress the right to establish an uniform rule of naturalization, and this right is evidently exclusive, and has always been held by this court to be so. Consequently, no State, since the adoption of the Constitution, can by naturalizing an alien, invest him with the rights and privileges secured to a citizen of a State under the Federal Government, although, so far as the State alone was concerned, he would undoubtedly be entitled to the rights of a citizen, and clothed with all the rights and immunities which the Constitution and laws of the State attached to that character.

It is very clear, therefore, that no State can, by any act or law of its own, passed since the adoption of the Constitution, introduce a new member into the political community created by the Constitution of the United States. It cannot make him a member of this community by making him a member of its own. And for the same reason it cannot introduce any person, or description of persons, who were not intended to be embraced in this new political family, which the Constitution brought into existence, but were intended to be excluded from it.

The question then arises, whether the provisions of the

Constitution, in relation to the personal rights and privileges to which the citizen of a State should be entitled, embraced the negro African race, at that time in this country, or who might afterwards be imported, who had then or should afterwards be made free in any State; and to put it in the power of a single State to make him a citizen of the United States, and endow him with the full rights of citizenship in every other State without their consent? Does the Constitution of the United States act upon him whenever he shall be made free under the laws of a State, and raised there to the rank of a citizen, and immediately cloth him with all the privileges of a citizen in every other State, and in its own courts?

The court thinks the affirmative of these propositions cannot be maintained. And if it cannot, the plaintiff in error could not be a citizen of the State of Missouri, within the meaning of the Constitution of the United States, and, consequently, was not entitled to sue in its courts.

It is true, every person, and every class and description of persons, who were at the time of the adoption of the Constitution recognized as citizens in the several States, became also citizens of this new political body; but none other; it was formed by them, and for them and their posterity, but for no one else. And the personal rights and privileges guarantied to citizens of this new sovereignty were intended to embrace those only who were then members of the several State communities, or who should afterwards by birthright or otherwise become members, according to the provisions of the Constitution and the principles on which it was founded. It was the union of those who were at that time members of distinct and separate political communities into one political family, whose power, for certain specified purposes, was to extend over the whole territory of the United States. And it gave to each citizen rights and privileges outside of his State which he did not before possess, and placed him in every other State upon a perfect equality with its own citizens as to rights of person and rights of property; it made him a citizen of the United States.

It becomes necessary, therefore, to determine who were citizens of the several States when the Constitution was adopted. . . .

And in order to do this, we must recur to the Governments and institutions of the thirteen colonies, when they separated from Great Britain and formed new sovereignties, and took their places in the family of independent nations. We must inquire who, at that time, were recognized as the people or citizens of a State, whose rights and liberties had been outraged by the English Government; and who declared their independence, and assumed the

powers of Government to defend their rights by force of arms.

In the opinion of the court, the legislation and histories of the times, and the language used in the Declaration of Independence, show, that neither the class of persons who had been imported as slaves, nor their descendants, whether they had become free or not, were then acknowledged as a part of the people, nor intended to be included in the general words used in that memorable instrument.

It is difficult at this day to realize the state of public opinion in relation to that unfortunate race, which prevailed in the civilized and enlightened portions of the world at the time of the Declaration of Independence, and when the Constitution of the United States was framed and adopted. But the public history of every European nation displays it in a manner too plain to be mistaken.

They had for more than a century before been regarded as beings of an inferior order, and altogether unfit to associate with the white race, either in social or political relations; and so far inferior, that they had no rights which the white man was bound to respect; and that the negro might justly and lawfully be reduced to slavery for his benefit. He was bought and sold, and treated as an ordinary article of merchandise and traffic, whenever a profit could be made by it. This opinion was at that time fixed and universal in the civilized portion of the white race. It was regarded as an axiom in morals as well as in politics, which no one thought of disputing, or supposed to be open to dispute; and men in every grade and position in society daily and habitually acted upon it in their private pursuits, as well as in matters of public concern, without doubting for a moment the correctness of this opinion.

And in no nation was this opinion more firmly fixed or more uniformly acted upon than by the English Government and English people. They not only seized them on the coast of Africa, and sold them or held them in slavery for their own use; but they took them as ordinary articles of merchandise to every country where they could make a profit on them, and were far more extensively engaged in this commerce than any other nation in the world. . . .

The legislation of the different colonies furnishes positive and indisputable proof of this fact. It would be tedious, in this opinion, to enumerate the various laws they passed upon this subject. . . .

The legislation of the States therefore shows, in a manner not to be mistaken, the inferior and subject condition of that race at the time the Constitution was adopted, and long afterwards, throughout the thirteen States by which that instrument was framed; and it is hardly consistent with the respect due to these States, to suppose that they regarded at that time, as fellow-citizens and members of the sovereignty, a class of beings whom they had thus stigmatized; whom, as we are bound, out of respect to the State sovereignties, to assume they had deemed it just and necessary thus to stigmatize, and upon whom they had impressed such deep and enduring marks of inferiority and degradation; or, that when they met in convention to form the Constitution, they looked upon them as a portion of their constituents, or designed to include them in the provisions so carefully inserted for the security and protection of the liberties and rights of their citizens. It cannot be supposed that they intended to secure to them rights, and privileges, and rank, in the new political body throughout the Union, which every one of them denied within the limits of its own dominion. More especially, it cannot be believed that the large slaveholding States regarded them as included in the word citizens, or would have consented to a Constitution which might compel them to receive them in that character from another State. For if they were so received, and entitled to the privileges and immunities of citizens, it would exempt them from the operation of the special laws and from the police regulations which they considered to be necessary for their own safety. It would give to persons of the negro race, who were recognized as citizens in any one State of the Union, the right to enter every other State whenever they pleased, singly or in companies, without pass or passport, and without obstruction, to sojourn there as long as they pleased, to go where they pleased at every hour of the day or night without molestation, unless they committed some violation of law for which a white man would be punished; and it would give them the full liberty of speech in public and in private upon all subjects upon which its own citizens might speak; to hold public meetings upon political affairs, and to keep and carry arms wherever they went. And all of this would be done in the face of the subject race of the same color, both free and slaves, and inevitably producing discontent and insubordination among them, and endangering the peace and safety of the State. . . .

Undoubtedly, a person may be a citizen, that is, a member of the community who form the sovereignty, although he exercises no share of the political power, and is incapacitated from holding particular offices. Women and minors, who form a part of the political family, cannot vote; and when a property qualification is required to vote or hold a particular office, those who have not the necessary qualification cannot vote or hold the office, yet they are citizens.

So, too, a person may be entitled to vote by the law of the State, who is not a citizen even of the State itself. And in some of the States of the Union foreigners not naturalized are allowed to vote. And the State may give the right to free negroes and mulattoes, but that does not make them citizens of the State, and still less of the United States. And the provision in the Constitution giving privileges and immunities in other States, does not apply to them.

Neither does it apply to a person who, being the citizen of a State, migrates to another State. For then he becomes subject to the laws of the State in which he lives, and he is no longer a citizen of the State from which he removed. And the State in which he resides may then, unquestionably, determine his status or condition, and place him among the class of persons who are not recognized as citizens, but belong to an inferior and subject race; and may deny him the privileges and immunities enjoyed by its citizens. . . .

No one, we presume, supposes that any change in public opinion or feeling, in relation to this unfortunate race, in the civilized nations of Europe or in this country, should induce the court to give to the words of the Constitution a more liberal construction in their favor than they were intended to bear when the instrument was framed and adopted. Such an argument would be altogether inadmissible in any tribunal called on to interpret it. If any of its provisions are deemed unjust, there is a mode prescribed in the instrument itself by which it may be amended; but while it remains unaltered, it must be construed now as it was understood at the time of its adoption. It is not only the same in words, but the same in meaning, and delegates the same powers to the Government, and reserves and secures the same rights and privileges to the citizen; and as long as it continues to exist in its present form, it speaks not only in the same words, but with the same meaning and intent with which it spoke when it came from the hands of its framers, and was voted on and adopted by the people of the United States. Any other rule of construction would abrogate the judicial character of this court, and make it the mere reflex of the popular opinion or passion of the day. This court was not created by the Constitution for such purposes. Higher and graver trusts have been confided to it, and it must not falter in the path of duty.

What the construction was at that time, we think can hardly admit of doubt. We have the language of the Declaration of Independence and of the Articles of Confederation, in addition to the plain words of the Constitution itself; we have the legislation of the different States, before, about the time, and since, the Constitution was adopted; we have the legislation of Congress, from the time of its adoption to a recent period; and we have the constant and uniform action of the Executive Department, all concurring together, and leading to the same result.

And if anything in relation to the construction of the Constitution can be regarded as settled, it is that which we now give to the word "citizen" and the word "people."

And upon a full and careful consideration of the subject, the court is of opinion, that . . . Dred Scott was not a citizen of Missouri within the meaning of the Constitution of the United States, and not entitled as such to sue in its courts; and, consequently, that the Circuit Court had no jurisdiction of the case. . . .

Notes and Queries

1. Why does Chief Justice Taney say that African Americans have no standing to sue in federal court? What methods of interpretation does he employ to arrive at this conclusion?

2. *Dred Scott* is generally regarded as the Court's most disastrous decision. But why? Because the Court decided to resolve the issue of Scott's citizenship? Because it declared Scott a non-citizen? Or because it held that African Americans could never become citizens of the United States?

3. Taney rested his decision heavily on the original intent of the Founding Fathers. But original intent, like textual arguments, has long been regarded as a legitimate approach to constitutional interpretation. Can Taney be faulted if indeed he was using conventional methods of interpretation in this case? Or if he was indeed convinced that the Founders had no intention of granting citizenship to African Americans?

4. Is *Dred Scott* an example of good judicial reasoning that nevertheless leads to a grave constitutional evil? Was William Lloyd Garrison right in concluding that the Constitution was "an agreement with death and a covenant with hell"? What does a constitutional interpreter do when confronted with constitutional language that seems to lead to a bad result? Is *Dred Scott* such a case?

Strauder v. West Virginia
100 U.S. (10 Otto.) 303, 25 L. Ed. 664 (1880)

Strauder, an African American man, was indicted for murder in West Virginia in 1874. Before his trial in a state court, he presented a motion for removal to the United States Circuit Court. His reason for removal was that West Virginia law forbade African Americans from serving on either a grand or petit jury, in violation of the equal protection of the laws guaranteed by the Fourteenth Amendment. The West Virginia court denied his motion and subsequently convicted him. Strauder appealed to the Supreme Court. Opinion of the Court: *Strong*, Waite, Swayne, Miller, Bradley, Hunt, Harlan. Dissenting opinions: *Clifford, Field*.

Mr. Justice STRONG delivered the opinion of the Court.

. . . [T]he . . . question is not whether a colored man, when an indictment has been preferred against him, has a right to a grand or a petit jury composed in whole or in part of persons of his own race or color, but it is whether, in the composition or selection of jurors by whom he is to be indicted or tried, all persons of his race or color may be excluded by law, solely because of their race or color, so that by no possibility can any colored man sit upon the jury.

The question [is] important, for [it] demand[s] a construction of the recent amendments of the Constitution. If the defendant has a right to have a jury selected for the trial of his case without discrimination against all persons of his race or color, because of their race or color, the right, if not created, is protected by those amendments, and the legislation of Congress under them. The Fourteenth Amendment ordains that "all persons born or naturalized in the United States and subject to the jurisdiction thereof are citizens of the United States and of the State wherein they reside. No State shall make or enforce any laws which shall abridge the privileges or immunities of citizens of the United States, nor shall any State deprive any person of life, liberty, or property, without due process of law, nor deny to any person within its jurisdiction the equal protection of the laws."

This is one of a series of constitutional provisions having a common purpose; namely, securing to a race recently emancipated, a race that through many generations had been held in slavery, all the civil rights that the superior race enjoy. The true spirit and meaning of the amendments . . . cannot be understood without keeping in view the history of the times when they were adopted, and the general objects they plainly sought to accomplish. At the time when they were incorporated into the Constitution, it required little knowledge of human nature to anticipate that those who had long been regarded as an inferior and subject race would, when suddenly raised to the rank of citizenship, be looked upon with jealousy and positive dislike, and that State laws might be enacted or enforced to perpetuate the distinctions that had before existed. Discriminations against them had been habitual. It was well known that in some States laws making such discrimina-

Comparative Note 14.1

American Declaration of the Rights and Duties of Man (1948)

Section 11. All persons are equal before the law and have the right and duties established in this Declaration, without distinction as to race, sex, language, creed or any other factor.

Canadian Charter of Rights (1982)

[Title 61] Equality Rights

Section 15 [General Equality, No Discrimination].

(1) Every individual is equal before the law and under the law and has the right to the equal protection and equal benefit of the law without discrimination based on age, national or ethnic origin, colour, religion, sex, age, or mental or physical disability.

(2) Subsection (1) does not preclude any law, program or activity that has as its object the amelioration of conditions of disadvantaged individuals or groups including those that are disadvantaged because of race, national or ethnic origin, colour, religion, sex, age, or mental or physical disability.

European Convention for the Protection of Human Rights and Fundamental Freedoms (1950)

Article 14.

The enjoyment of the rights and freedoms set forth in this Convention shall be secured without discrimination on any ground such as sex, race, colour, language, religion, political or other opinion, national or social origin, association with a national minority, property, birth or other status.

Indian Constitution (1950)

Article number 14.

Equality before law—The State shall not deny to any person equality before the law or the equal protection of the laws within the territory of India.

Article number 15.

Prohibition of discrimination on grounds of religion, race, caste, sex or place of birth—

(1) State shall not discriminate against any citizen on grounds only of religion, race, caste, sex, place of birth or any of them.

(2) No citizen shall, on ground only of religion, race, caste, sex, place of birth or any of them be subject to any disability, liability, restriction or condition with regard to—

(1) access to shops, public restaurants, hotels and places of public entertainment; or

(2) the use of wells, tanks, bathing ghats, roads and places of public resort maintained whole or partly out of State funds or dedicated to the use of general public.

(3) Nothing in this article shall prevent the State from making any special provision for women and children.

(4) Nothing in this article or in clause (2) of article 29 shall prevent the State from making any special provision for the advancement of any socially and educationally backward classes of citizens or for the Scheduled Castes and the Scheduled Tribes.

South African Constitution (1996)

Section 1. The Republic of South Africa is one sovereign democratic state founded on the following values: (b) Non-racialism and non-sexism.

Section 9 Equality.

(1) Every one is equal before the law and has the right to equal protection and benefit of the law.

(2) Equality includes the full and equal enjoyment of all rights and freedoms. To promote the achievement of equality, legislative and other measures designed to protect or advance persons, or categories of persons, disadvantaged by unfair discrimination may be taken.

(3) The state may not unfairly discriminate directly or indirectly against anyone on one or more grounds, including race, gender, sex, pregnancy, marital status, ethnic or social origin, colour, sexual orientation, age, disability, religion, conscience, belief, culture, language and birth.

(4) No person may unfairly discriminate directly or indirectly against anyone on one or more grounds in terms of subsection (3). National legislation must be enacted to prevent or prohibit unfair discrimination.

(5) Discrimination on one or more of the grounds listed in subsection (3) is unfair unless it is established that the discrimination is fair.

tions then existed, and others might well be expected. The colored race, as a race, was abject and ignorant, and in that condition was unfitted to command the respect of those who had superior intelligence. Their training had left them mere children, and as such they needed the protection which a wise government extends to those who are unable to protect themselves. They especially needed protection against unfriendly action in the States where they were resident. It was in view of these considerations the Fourteenth Amendment was framed and adopted. It was designed to assure to the colored race the enjoyment of all the civil rights that under the law are enjoyed by white persons, and to give to that race the protection of the general government, in that enjoyment, whenever it should be denied by the States. It not only gave citizenship and the privileges of citizenship to persons of color, but it denied to any State the power to withhold from them the equal protection of the laws, and authorized Congress to enforce its provisions by appropriate legislation. . . .

If this is the spirit and meaning of the amendment, whether it means more or not, it is to be construed liberally, to carry out the purposes of its framers. It ordains that no State shall make or enforce any laws which shall abridge the privileges or immunities of citizens of the United States (evidently referring to the newly made citizens, who, being citizens of the United States, are declared to be also citizens of the State in which they reside). It ordains that no State shall deprive any person of life, liberty, or property, without due process of law, or deny to any person within its jurisdiction the equal protection of the laws. What is this but declaring that the law in the States shall be the same for the black as for the white; that all persons, whether colored or white, shall stand equal before the laws of the States, and, in regard to the colored race, for whose protection the amendment was primarily designed, that no discrimination shall be made against them by law because of their color? The words of the amendment, it is true, are prohibitory, but they contain a necessary implication of a positive immunity, or right, most valuable to the colored race—the right to exemption from unfriendly legislation against them distinctively as colored—exemption from legal discriminations, implying inferiority in civil society, lessening the security of their enjoyment of the rights which others enjoy, and discriminations which are steps towards reducing them to the condition of a subject race.

That the West Virginia statute respecting juries . . . is such a discrimination ought not to be doubted. Nor would it be if the persons excluded by it were white men. If in those States where the colored people constitute a major-

ity of the entire population a law should be enacted excluding all white men from jury service, thus denying to them the privilege of participating equally with the blacks in the administration of justice, we apprehend no one would be heard to claim that it would not be a denial to white men of the equal protection of the laws. Nor if a law should be passed excluding all naturalized Celtic Irishmen, would there by any doubt of its inconsistency with the spirit of the amendment. The very fact that colored people are singled out and expressly denied by a statute all right to participate in the administration of the law, as jurors, because of their color, though they are citizens, and may be in other respects fully qualified, is practically a brand upon them, affixed by the law, an assertion of their inferiority, and a stimulant to that race prejudice which is an impediment to securing to individuals of the race that equal justice which the law aims to secure to all others. . . . The very idea of a jury is a body of men composed of the peers or equals of the person whose rights it is selected or summoned to determine; that is, of his neighbors, fellows, associates, persons having the same legal status in society as that which he holds. . . . It is well known that prejudices often exist against particular classes in the community, which sway the judgment of jurors, and which, therefore, operate in some cases to deny to persons of those classes the full enjoyment of that protection which others enjoy. . . . The framers of the constitutional amendment must have known full well the existence of such prejudice and its likelihood to continue against the manumitted slaves and their race, and that knowledge was doubtless a motive that led to the amendment. By their manumission and citizenship the colored race became entitled to the equal protection of the laws of the States in which they resided; and the apprehension that through prejudice they might be denied that equal protection, that is, that there might be discrimination against them, was the inducement to bestow upon the national government the power to enforce the provision that no State shall deny to them the equal protection of the laws. Without the apprehended existence of prejudice that portion of the amendment would have been unnecessary, and it might have been left to the States to extend equality of protection.

In view of these considerations, it is hard to see why the statute of West Virginia should not be regarded as discriminating against a colored man when he is put upon trial for an alleged criminal offence against the State. It is not easy to comprehend how it can be said that while every white man is entitled to a trial by a jury selected from persons of his own race or color, or, rather, selected without discrimination against his color, and a negro is not, the latter is equally protected by the law with the former. Is not protection of life and liberty against race or color prejudice, a right, a legal right, under the constitutional amendment? And how can it be maintained that compelling a colored man to submit to a trial for his life by a jury drawn from a panel from which the State has expressly excluded every man of his race, because of color alone, however well qualified in other respects, is not a denial to him of equal legal protection?

We do not say that within the limits from which it is not excluded by the amendment a State may not prescribe the qualifications of its jurors, and in so doing make discriminations. It may confine the selection to males, to freeholders, to citizens, to persons within certain ages, or to persons having educational qualifications. We do not believe the Fourteenth Amendment was ever intended to prohibit this. Looking at its history, it is clear it had no such purpose. Its aim was against discrimination because of race or color. . . . We are not now called upon to affirm or deny that it had other purposes.

The Fourteenth Amendment makes no attempt to enumerate the rights it is designed to protect. It speaks in general terms, and those are as comprehensive as possible. Its language is prohibitory; but every prohibition implies the existence of rights and immunities, prominent among which is an immunity from inequality of legal protection, either for life, liberty, or property. Any State action that denies this immunity to a colored man is in conflict with the Constitution.

The judgment of the Supreme Court of West Virginia will be reversed, and the case remitted with instructions to reverse the judgment of the Circuit Court of Ohio county; and it is

So ordered.

Mr. Justice FIELD and Mr. Justice CLIFFORD dissent.

Notes and Queries

1. In the *Slaughter-House Cases* the Court had emphasized the Fourteenth Amendment's purpose of ending racial discrimination sanctioned by law. That emphasis appears also in *Strauder*, but the Court went out of its way not to limit its concept of racial discrimination to discrimination against African-Americans, noting that laws directed against "all naturalized Celtic Irishmen" would also fall within the "spirit of the amendment." What is the spirit of the Amendment? How did the Court determine what the spirit of the Amendment is? In *Hernandez v. Texas*, 347 U.S. 475 (1954), the Court ruled that discrimination in jury selection against Mexican-Americans also violated the Fourteenth Amendment.

2. Strauder was an African American. Would it matter if he had made the same claim—that the law discriminated against African Americans—if he had been white? Does it depend upon whether the class discriminates on the basis of a racial classification, or rather against certain racial classes? Does the answer depend upon a particular understanding of "equality"? In *Peters v. Kiff*, 407 U.S. 493 (1972), the Court overturned the conviction of a white man who claimed that blacks had been excluded from the federal grand jury that indicted him and the petit jury that convicted him. The Court contended that the arbitrary exclusion of any racial group from jury service violates the Fourteenth Amendment.

3. Compare the Court's statement in *Strauder* that the discrimination against African Americans is "practically a brand upon them" and "an assertion of inferiority" with the claim in *Plessy*—decided 16 years after *Strauder*—that racial discrimination imposed no "badge of inferiority" unless it was "because the colored race chooses to put that construction upon it." Is there a constitutional reason—and not a reason based on one's own preferences—to prefer one formulation to the other?

4. What method of interpretation did Justice Strong think was required under the Fourteenth Amendment? What reasons did he offer to support that method? Did the Court use the same method in *Slaughter-House*?

Plessy v. Ferguson
163 U.S. 537, 165 S. Ct. 1138, 41 L. Ed. 256 (1896)

Plessy, a Louisiana man of mixed race (one-eighth African American and seven-eighths Caucasian), bought a first-class train ticket from New Orleans to Covington, Louisiana. As he was boarding the train onto a coach reserved for whites, the conductor ordered him onto a coach assigned to non-whites. Under the Louisiana law at that time, railway companies were required to provide separate but equal accommodations for their passengers either by separate coaches or by erecting partitions inside the coaches. Officers of the trains were required to assign each passenger to the coach in which the officer felt he or she belonged. Encouraged by local civil rights groups who wanted to challenge the law, Plessy brought this suit after he refused to sit in the compartment to which he was assigned, was ejected from the train, and jailed for his refusal. Opinion of the Court: *Brown*, Field, Fuller, Gray, Peckham, Shiras, White. Dissenting opinion: *Harlan*. Not participating: *Brewer*.

Mr. Justice BROWN delivered the opinion of the Court.

That [the Louisiana law] does not conflict with the Thirteenth Amendment, which abolished slavery and involuntary servitude, except as a punishment for crime, is too clear for argument. Slavery implies involuntary servitude—a state of bondage; the ownership of mankind as a chattel, or, at least, the control of the labor and services of one man for the benefit of another, and the absence of a legal right to the disposal of his own person, property, and services. . . . It was intimated, however, [in the *Slaughter-House Cases*] that this amendment was regarded by the statesmen of that day as insufficient to protect the colored race from certain laws which had been enacted in the Southern states, imposing upon the colored race onerous disabilities and burdens, and curtailing their rights in the pursuit of life, liberty, and property to such an extent that their freedom was of little value; and that the Fourteenth Amendment was devised to meet this exigency.

A statute which implies merely a legal distinction between the white and colored races—a distinction which is founded in the color of the two races, and which must always exist so long as white men are distinguished from the other race by color—has no tendency to destroy the legal equality of the two races, or re-establish a state of involuntary servitude. . . .

By the Fourteenth Amendment, all persons born or naturalized in the United States, and subject to the jurisdiction thereof, are made citizens of the United States and of the state wherein they reside; and the states are forbidden from making or enforcing any law which shall abridge the privileges or immunities of citizens of the United States, or shall deprive any person of life, liberty, or property without due process of law, or deny to any person within their jurisdiction the equal protection of the laws.

The proper construction of this amendment was first called to the attention of this court in the *Slaughter-House Cases* (1873). . . . The case did not call for any expression of opinion as to the exact rights it was intended to secure to the colored race, but it was said generally that its main purpose was to establish the citizenship of the negro, to give definitions of citizenship of the United States and of the states, and to protect from the hostile legislation of the states the privileges and immunities of citizens of the United States, as distinguished from those of citizens of the States.

The object of the amendment was undoubtedly to enforce the absolute equality of the two races before the law, but, in the nature of things, it could not have been intended to abolish distinctions based upon color, or to enforce social, as distinguished from political, equality, or a commingling of the two races upon terms unsatisfactory to either. Laws permitting, and even requiring, their separation, in places where they are liable to be brought into contact, do not necessarily imply the inferiority of either race to the other, and have been generally, if not universally, recognized as within the competency of the state legislatures in the exercise of their police power. The most common instance of this is connected with the establishment of separate schools for white and colored children, which have been held to be a valid exercise of the legislative power even by courts of states where the political rights of the colored race have been longest and most earnestly enforced. . . .

One of the earliest of these cases is that of *Roberts v. Boston* (1849), in which the Supreme Judicial Court of Massachusetts held that the general school committee of Boston had power to make provision for the instruction of colored children in separate schools established exclusively for them, and to prohibit their attendance upon the other schools. "The great principle," said Chief Justice Shaw . . .

> Is that by the constitution and laws of Massachusetts, all persons without distinction of age, sex, birth, or color, origin or condition, are equal before the law. . . . But, when this great principle comes to be applied to the actual and various conditions of persons in society, it will not warrant the assertion, that men and women are legally clothed with the same civil and political powers, and that children and adults are legally to have the same functions and be subject to the same treatment; but only that the rights of all, as they are settled and regulated by law, are equally entitled to the paternal consideration and protections of the law for their maintenance and security.

Laws forbidding the intermarriage of the two races may be said in a technical sense to interfere with the freedom of contract, and yet have been universally recognized as within the police power of the State. . . .

While we think the enforced separation of the races, as applied to the internal commerce of the state, neither abridges the privileges or immunities of the colored man, deprives him of his property without due process of law, nor denies him the equal protection of the laws, within the meaning of the Fourteenth Amendment, we are not prepared to say that the conductor, in assigning passengers to the coaches according to their race, does not act at his peril, or that the provision of the second section of the act that denies to the passenger compensation in damages for a refusal to receive him into the coach in which he properly belongs is a valid exercise of the legislative power. Indeed, we understand it to be conceded by the state's attorney that such part of the act as exempts from liability the railway company and its officers is unconstitutional. The power to assign to a particular coach obviously implies the power to determine to which race the passenger belongs, as well as the power to determine who, under the laws of the particular state, is to be deemed a white, and who a colored, person. . . .

It is claimed by the plaintiff . . . that, in any mixed community, the reputation of belonging to the dominant race, in this instance the white race, is *property*, in the same sense that a right of action or of inheritance is property. Conceding this to be so, for the purposes of this case, we are unable to see how this statute deprives him of, or in any way affects his right to, such property. If he be a white man, and assigned to a colored coach, he may have his action for damages against the company for being deprived of his so-called "property." Upon the other hand, if he be a colored man, and be so assigned, he has been deprived of no property, since he is not lawfully entitled to the reputation of being a white man.

In this connection, it is also suggested by the learned counsel for the plaintiff . . . that the same argument that will justify the state legislature in requiring railways to provide separate accommodations for the two races will also authorize them to require separate cars to be provided for people whose hair is of a certain color, or who are aliens, or who belong to certain nationalities, or to enact laws requiring colored people to walk upon one side of the street, and white people upon the other, or requiring white men's houses to be painted white, and colored men's black, or their vehicles or business signs to be of different colors, upon the theory that one side of the street is as good as the other, or that a house or vehicle of one color is as good as one of another color. The reply to all this is that every exercise of the police power must be reasonable, and extend only to such laws as are enacted in good faith for the promotion of the public good, and not for the annoyance or oppression of a particular class. . . .

So far, then, as a conflict with the Fourteenth Amendment is concerned, the case reduces itself to the question whether the statute of Louisiana is a reasonable regulation, and with respect to this there must necessarily be a large discretion on the part of the legislature. In determining the question of reasonableness, it is at liberty to act with reference to the established usages, customs, and tra-

ditions of the people, and with a view to the promotion of their comfort, and the preservation of the public peace and good order. Gauged by this standard, we cannot say that a law which authorizes or even requires the separation of the two races in public conveyances is unreasonable, or more obnoxious to the Fourteenth Amendment than the acts of congress requiring separate schools for colored children in the District of Columbia, the constitutionality of which does not seem to have been questioned, or the corresponding acts of state legislatures.

We consider the underlying fallacy of the plaintiff's argument to consist in the assumption that the enforced separation of the two races stamps the colored race with a badge of inferiority. If this be so, it is not by reason of anything found in the act, but solely because the colored race chooses to put that construction upon it. The argument necessarily assumes that if, as has been more than once the case, and is not unlikely to be so again, the colored race should become the dominant power in the state legislature, and should enact a law in precisely similar terms, it would thereby relegate the white race to an inferior position. We imagine that the white race, at least, would not acquiesce in this assumption. The argument also assumes that social prejudices may be overcome by legislation, and that equal rights cannot be secured to the negro except by an enforced commingling of the two races. We cannot accept this proposition. If the two races are to meet upon terms of social equality, it must be the result of natural affinities, a mutual appreciation of each other's merits, and a voluntary consent of individuals. . . . Legislation is powerless to eradicate racial instincts, or to abolish distinctions based upon physical differences, and the attempt to do so can only result in accentuating the difficulties of the present situation. If the civil and political rights of both races be equal, one cannot be inferior to the other civilly or politically. If one race be inferior to the other socially, the constitution of the United States cannot put them upon the same plane.

The judgment of the court below is therefore affirmed.

Mr. Justice BREWER did not hear the argument or participate in the decision of this case.

Mr. Justice HARLAN dissenting.

In respect of civil rights, common to all citizens, the Constitution of the United States does not, I think, permit any public authority to know the race of those entitled to be protected in the enjoyment of such rights. Every true man has pride of race, and under appropriate circumstances, when the rights of others, his equals before the law, are not to be affected, it is his privilege to express such pride and to take such action based upon it as to him seems proper. But I deny that any legislative body or judicial tribunal may have regard to the race of citizens when the civil rights of those citizens are involved. Indeed, such legislation as that here in question is inconsistent not only with that equality of rights which pertains to citizenship, national and state, but with the personal liberty enjoyed by every one within the United States.

The Thirteenth Amendment does not permit the withholding or the deprivation of any right necessarily inhering in freedom. It not only struck down the institution of slavery as previously existing in the United States, but it prevents the imposition of any burdens or disabilities that constitute badges of slavery or servitude. It decreed universal civil freedom in this country. This court has so adjudged. But, that amendment having been found inadequate to the protection of the rights of those who had been in slavery, it was followed by the Fourteenth Amendment, which added greatly to the dignity and glory of American citizenship, and to the security of personal liberty. . . . These two amendments, if enforced according to their true intent and meaning, will protect all the civil rights that pertain to freedom and citizenship. Finally, and to the end that no citizen should be denied, on account of his race, the privilege of participating in the political control of his country, it was declared by the Fifteenth Amendment that "the right of citizens of the United States to vote shall not be denied or abridged by the United States or by any state on account of race, color or previous condition of servitude."

These notable additions to the fundamental law were welcomed by the friends of liberty throughout the world. They removed the race line from our governmental systems. They had, as this court has said, a common purpose, namely, to secure "to a race recently emancipated, a race that through many generations have been held in slavery, all the civil rights that the superior race enjoy." They declared, in legal effect, this court has further said, "that the law in the states shall be the same for the black as for the white; that all persons, whether colored or white, shall stand equal before the laws of the states; and in regard to the colored race, for whose protection the amendment was primarily designed, that no discrimination shall be made against them by law because of their color." We also said: "The words of the amendment, it is true, are prohibitory, but they contain a necessary implication of a positive immunity or right, most valuable to the colored race—the right to exemption from unfriendly legislation against them distinctively as colored; exemption from legal discriminations, implying inferiority in civil society, lessening the security of their enjoyment of the rights which others

enjoy; and discriminations which are steps towards reducing them to the condition of a subject race." . . .

It was said in argument that the statute of Louisiana does not discriminate against either race, but prescribes a rule applicable alike to white and colored citizens. But this argument does not meet the difficulty. Every one knows that the statute in question had its origin in the purpose, not so much to exclude white persons from railroad cars occupied by blacks, as to exclude colored people from coaches occupied by or assigned to white persons. Railroad corporations of Louisiana did not make discrimination among whites in the matter of accommodation for travelers. The thing to accomplish was, under the guise of giving equal accommodation for whites and blacks, to compel the latter to keep to themselves while traveling in railroad passenger coaches. No one would be so wanting in candor as to assert the contrary. The fundamental objection, therefore, to the statute, is that it interferes with the personal freedom of citizens. . . . If a white man and a black man choose to occupy the same public conveyance on a public highway, it is their right to do so; and no government, proceeding alone on grounds of race, can prevent it without infringing the personal liberty of each.

It is one thing for railroad carriers to furnish, or to be required by law to furnish, equal accommodations for all whom they are under a legal duty to carry. It is quite another thing for government to forbid citizens of the white and black races from traveling in the same public conveyance, and to punish officers of railroad companies for permitting persons of the two races to occupy the same passenger coach. If a state can prescribe, as a rule of civil conduct, that whites and blacks shall not travel as passengers in the same railroad coach, why may it not so regulate the use of the streets of its cities and towns as to compel white citizens to keep on one side of a street, and black citizens to keep on the other? Why may it not, upon like grounds, punish whites and blacks who ride together in street cars or in open vehicles on a public road or street? Why may it not require sheriffs to assign whites to one side of a court room, and blacks to the other? And why may it not also prohibit the commingling of the two races in the galleries of legislative halls or in public assemblages convened for the consideration of the political questions of the day? Further, if this statute of Louisiana is consistent with the personal liberty of citizens, why may not the state require the separation in railroad coaches of native and naturalized citizens of the United States, or of Protestants and Roman Catholics?

The answer given at the argument to these questions was that regulations of the kind they suggest would be unreasonable, and could not, therefore, stand before the law. Is it meant that the determination of questions of legislative power depends upon the inquiry whether the statute whose validity is questioned is, in the judgment of the courts, a reasonable one, taking all the circumstances into consideration? A statute may be unreasonable merely because a sound public policy forbade its enactment. But I do not understand that the courts have anything to do with the policy or expediency of legislation. A statute may be valid, and yet, upon grounds of public policy, may well be characterized as unreasonable. . . . There is a dangerous tendency in these latter days to enlarge the functions of the courts, by means of judicial interference with the will of the people as expressed by the legislature. Our institutions have the distinguishing characteristic that the three departments of government are co-ordinate and separate. Each must keep within the limits defined by the constitution. And the courts best discharge their duty by executing the will of the law-making power, constitutionally expressed, leaving the results of legislation to be dealt with by the people through their representatives. Statutes must always have a reasonable construction. Sometimes they are to be construed strictly, sometimes literally, in order to carry out the legislative will. But, however construed, the intent of the legislature is to be respected if the particular statute in question is valid, although the courts, looking at the public interests, may conceive the statute to be both unreasonable and impolitic. If the power exists to enact a statute, that ends the matter so far as the courts are concerned. . . .

The white race deems itself to be the dominant race in this country. And so it is, in prestige, in achievements, in education, in wealth, and in power. So, I doubt not, it will continue to be for all time, if it remains true to its great heritage, and holds fast to the principles of constitutional liberty. But in view of the constitution, in the eye of the law, there is in this country no superior, dominant, ruling class of citizens. There is no caste here. Our constitution is color-blind, and neither knows nor tolerates classes among citizens. In respect of civil rights, all citizens are equal before the law. The humblest is the peer of the most powerful. The law regards man as man, and takes no account of his surroundings or of his color when his civil rights as guaranteed by the supreme law of the land are involved. It is therefore to be regretted that this high tribunal, the final expositor of the fundamental law of the land, has reached the conclusion that it is competent for a state to regulate the enjoyment by citizens of their civil rights solely upon the basis of race.

In my opinion, the judgment this day rendered will, in time, prove to be quite as pernicious as the decision made by this tribunal in the *Dred Scott Case.* It was adjudged in that case that the descendants of Africans who were imported into this country, and sold as slaves, were not included nor intended to be included under the word "citizens" in the constitution, and could not claim any of the rights and privileges which that instrument provided for and secured to citizens of the United States; that, at the time of the adoption of the constitution, they were "considered as a subordinate and inferior class of beings, who had been subjugated by the dominant race, and, whether emancipated or not, yet remained subject to their authority, and had no rights or privileges but such as those who held the power and the government might choose to grant them." The recent amendments of the constitution, it was supposed, had eradicated these principles from our institutions. But it seems that we have yet, in some of the states, a dominant race—a superior class of citizens,—which assumes to regulate the enjoyment of civil rights, common to all citizens, upon the basis of race. The present decision, it may well be apprehended, will not only stimulate aggressions, more or less brutal and irritating, upon the admitted rights of colored citizens, but will encourage the belief that it is possible, by means of state enactments, to defeat the beneficent purposes which the people of the United States had in view when they adopted the recent amendments of the constitution, by one of which the blacks of this country were made citizens of the United States and of the states in which they respectively reside, and whose privileges and immunities, as citizens, the states are forbidden to abridge. Sixty millions of whites are in no danger from the presence here of eight millions of blacks. The destinies of the two races, in this country, are indissolubly linked together, and the interests of both require that the common government of all shall not permit the seeds of race hate to be planted under the sanction of law. What can more certainly arouse race hate, what more certainly create and perpetuate a feeling of distrust between these races, than state enactments which, in fact, proceed on the ground that colored citizens are so inferior and degraded that they cannot be allowed to sit in public coaches occupied by white citizens? That, as all will admit, is the real meaning of such legislation as was enacted in Louisiana. . . .

The arbitrary separation of citizens, on the basis of race, while they are on a public highway, is a badge of servitude wholly inconsistent with the civil freedom and the equality before the law established by the constitution. It cannot be justified upon any legal grounds.

If evils will result from the commingling of the two races upon public highways established for the benefit of all, they will be infinitely less than those that will surely come from state legislation regulating the enjoyment of civil rights upon the basis of race. We boast of the freedom enjoyed by our people above all other peoples. But it is difficult to reconcile that boast with a state of the law which, practically, puts the brand of servitude and degradation upon a large class of our fellow citizens—our equals before the law. The thin disguise of "equal" accommodations for passengers in railroad coaches will not mislead any one, nor atone for the wrong this day done.

For the reason stated, I am constrained to withhold my assent from the opinion and judgment of the majority.

Notes and Queries

1. As we mentioned in the introduction to this chapter, the equal protection clause raises important issues concerning judicial power and democratic theory. When should the Court defer to legislative decisions on the sorts of classifications best suited to the community? Respect for democratic theory, and a cautious appreciation of the limits of judicial power, have led some commentators, such as James Bradley Thayer, to argue that the Court should respect legislative choices so long as they are rational. On the other hand, the vision of judicial power outlined in footnote 4 of *Carolene Products* rests on an understanding that democratic theory sometimes exists in tension with constitutionalism's concern for human dignity and equality.

In *Plessy* the Court firmly embraced the deferential standard of review advocated by Thayer, writing that the legislature "must necessarily be [afforded] a large discretion" to determine whether a particular regulation was "reasonable." The Court further added that the legislature was "at liberty to act with reference to the established usages, customs, and traditions of the people. . . ." What "reasonable" state interest did the law in this case promote? Should the Court defer to established usages and traditions if they are inherently racist?

2. The majority opinion insisted that social equality and legal equality are not the same thing. "Legislation is powerless to eradicate racial instincts or to abolish distinctions based upon physical differences. . . . If one race be inferior to the other socially, the Constitution of the United States cannot put them upon the same plane. . . ." Do you agree with the Court?

3. Perhaps the most complete analysis of *Plessy* is in Charles Lofgren, *The Plessy Case*. (New York: Oxford University Press, 1987). Lofgren reports that, contrary to its notoriety today, *Plessy* was virtually ignored by the public and constitutional law scholars alike when it was decided. What, if anything, does this suggest about racial segregation in the late nineteenth and early twentieth centuries?

4. Did *Plessy* hold that racial segregation was constitutionally permissible if it did not rest on assumptions of inferiority? If so, could not the Court have used *Plessy* to strike down the elaborate system of Jim Crow that followed its decision? Similarly, did the Court hold that racial segregation is permissible if what is separate is also equal? Exactly where in his opinion for the majority did Justice Brown insist that what was separate must still be equal? As we shall see in the other cases reprinted in this chapter, the NAACP eventually used this part of *Plessy* to dismantle Jim Crow, by forcing the Court to insist, as it did not for many decades following its decision, upon some measure of actual equality.

5. *Plessy* has been described as a manifestation of bad law, bad history, and bad sociology. In what sense is this true, and do you agree?

Brown v. Board of Education of Topeka
347 U.S. 483, 74 S. Ct. 686, 98 L. Ed. 873 (1954)

In Kansas, South Carolina, Virginia, and Delaware, African-American schoolchildren sought admission to all-white public schools. Each state had laws prohibiting the integration of the public schools, and in each case except Delaware, the district court denied the childrens' admission based on the "separate but equal" doctrine formulated in *Plessy v. Ferguson* (1896), which stated that equal treatment is provided when both races are provided substantially equal facilities even though the facilities are separate. The district court of Delaware adhered to the doctrine but found the white schools to be substantially superior and therefore ordered that the black students be admitted to the white schools. Opinion of the Court: *Warren*, Black, Burton, Clark, Douglas, Frankfurter, Jackson, Minton, Reed.

Mr. Chief Justice WARREN delivered the opinion of the Court.

The plaintiffs contend that segregated public schools are not "equal" and cannot be made "equal," and that hence they are deprived of the equal protection of the laws. . . .

Reargument was largely devoted to the circumstances surrounding the adoption of the Fourteenth Amendment in 1868. It covered exhaustively consideration of the Amendment in Congress, ratification by the states, then existing practices in racial segregation, and the views of

Comparative Note 14.2

[In *The Queen v. Drybones*, (1970) S.C.R. 282, the Canadian Supreme Court considered a provision of the Canadian Indian Act that made it a crime, punishable by a minimum fine of $10 and a maximum jail sentence of ninety days, for an Indian to be drunk "off a reserve." In contrast, it was a crime for whites to be drunk only in a public place. The maximum incarceration was for thirty days. Joe Drybones was convicted under the act and appealed, claiming that the provision violated section 1(b) of the statutory Bill of Rights, which guaranteed "the right of the individual to equality before the law and the protection of the law."]

In his judgment for the Court, Justice Ritchie wrote:

the right which is here at issue is "the right of the individual to equality before the law and the protection of the law."...

...[Without attempting any exhaustive definition of "equality before the law" I think that [the provision] means at least that no individual or group of individuals is to be treated more harshly than another under that law, and I am therefore of the opinion that an individual is denied equality before the law if it is made an offense punishable at law, on

account of his race, for him to do something which his fellow Canadians are free to do without having committed any offense or having been made subject to any penalty....

In a separate opinion, Justice Hall wrote:

The concept that the Canadian Bill of Rights is operative in the face of a law in Canada only when that law does not give equality to all persons within the class to whom that particular law extends or relates ... is analogous to the position taken by the Supreme Court of the United States in Plessy v. Ferguson *and which was wholly rejected by the same Court in its historic desegregation judgment* Brown v. Board of Education. ...

The social situations in Brown v. Board of Education *and in the instant case are, of course, very different, but the basic philosophic content is the same. The Canadian Bill of Rights is not fulfilled if it merely equates Indians with Indians in terms of equality before the law, but can have validity and meaning only when ... it is seen to repudiate discrimination in every law of Canada by reason of race, national origin, colour, religion or sex.*

---

proponents and opponents of the Amendment. This discussion and our own investigation convince us that, although these sources cast some light, it is not enough to resolve the problem with which we are faced. At best, they are inconclusive. The most avid proponents of the post-War Amendments undoubtedly intended them to remove all legal distinctions among "all persons born or naturalized in the United States." Their opponents, just as certainly, were antagonistic to both the letter and the spirit of the Amendments and wished them to have the most limited effect. What others in Congress and the state legislatures had in mind cannot be determined with any degree of certainty.

An additional reason for the inconclusive nature of the Amendment's history, with respect to segregated schools, is the status of public education at that time. In the South, the movement toward free common schools, supported by general taxation, had not yet taken hold. Education of white children was largely in the hands of private groups. Education of Negroes was almost nonexistent, and practically all of the race were illiterate. In fact, any education

of Negroes was forbidden by law in some states. Today, in contrast, many Negroes have achieved outstanding success in the arts and sciences as well as in the business and professional world. It is true that public school education at the time of the Amendment had advanced further in the North, but the effect of the Amendment on Northern States was generally ignored in the congressional debates. Even in the North, the conditions of public education did not approximate those existing today. The curriculum was usually rudimentary; ungraded schools were common in rural areas; the school term was but three months a year in many states, and compulsory school attendance was virtually unknown. As a consequence, it is not surprising that there should be so little in the history of the Fourteenth Amendment relating to its intended effect on public education.

In the first cases in this Court construing the Fourteenth Amendment, decided shortly after its adoption, the Court interpreted it as proscribing all state-imposed discriminations against the Negro race. The doctrine of "separate but equal" did not make its appearance in this court until 1896 in the case of *Plessy v. Ferguson*, involving not education but transportation. American courts have since labored with the doctrine for over half a century. In this Court, there have been six cases involving the "separate but equal" doctrine in the field of public education. In more recent cases, all on the graduate school level, inequality was found in that specific benefits enjoyed by white students were denied to Negro students of the same educational qualifications. In none of these cases was it necessary to re-examine the doctrine to grant relief to the Negro plaintiff. And . . . the Court expressly reserved decision on the question whether *Plessy v. Ferguson* should be held inapplicable to public education.

In the instant cases, that question is directly presented. Here, unlike *Sweatt v. Painter* (1950), there are findings below that the Negro and white schools involved have been equalized, or are being equalized, with respect to buildings, curricula, qualifications and salaries of teachers, and other "tangible" factors. Our decision, therefore, cannot turn on merely a comparison of these tangible factors in the Negro and white schools involved in each of the cases. We must look instead to the effect of segregation itself on public education.

In approaching this problem, we cannot turn the clock back to 1868 when the Amendment was adopted, or even to 1896 when *Plessy v. Ferguson* was written. We must consider public education in the light of its full development and its present place in American life throughout the Nation. Only in this way can it be determined if segregation in public schools deprives these plaintiffs of the equal protection of the laws.

Today, education is perhaps the most important function of state and local governments. Compulsory school attendance laws and the great expenditures for education both demonstrate our recognition of the importance of education to our democratic society. It is required in the performance of our most basic public responsibilities, even service in the armed forces. It is the very foundation of good citizenship. Today it is a principal instrument in awakening the child to cultural values, in preparing him for later professional training, and in helping him to adjust normally to his environment. In these days, it is doubtful that any child may reasonably be expected to succeed in life if he is denied the opportunity of an education. Such an opportunity, where the state has undertaken to provide it, is a right which must be made available to all on equal terms.

We come then to the question presented: Does segregation of children in public schools solely on the basis of race, even though the physical facilities and other "tangible" factors may be equal, deprive the children of the minority group of equal educational opportunities? We believe that it does.

In *Sweatt v. Painter*, in finding that a segregated law school for Negroes could not provide them equal educational opportunities, this Court relied in large part on "those qualities which are incapable of objective measurement but which make for greatness in a law school." In *McLaurin v. Oklahoma State Regents* (1950), the Court, in requiring that a Negro admitted to a white graduate school be treated like all other students, again resorted to intangible considerations: ". . . his ability to study, to engage in discussions and exchange views with other students, and, in general, to learn his profession." Such considerations apply with added force to children in grade and high schools. To separate them from others of similar age and qualifications solely because of their race generates a feeling of inferiority as to their status in the community that may affect their hearts and minds in a way unlikely ever to be undone. The effect of this separation on their educational opportunities was well stated by a finding in the Kansas case by a court which nevertheless felt compelled to rule against the Negro plaintiffs:

> Segregation of white and colored children in public schools has a detrimental effect upon the colored children. The impact is greater when it has the sanction of the law; for the policy of separating the races is usually interpreted as denoting the inferiority of the negro group. A sense of inferiority affects the motivation of a child to learn. Segregation with the sanction of law, therefore, has a tendency to (retard) the educational and mental development of Negro children and to deprive them of some of the benefits they would receive in a racial[ly] integrated school system.

Whatever may have been the extent of psychological knowledge at the time of *Plessy v. Ferguson*, this finding is amply supported by modern authority.* Any language in *Plessy v. Ferguson* contrary to this finding is rejected.

We conclude that in the field of public education the doctrine of "separate but equal" has no place. Separate

---

*K.B. Clark, *Effect of Prejudice and Discrimination on Personality Development* (Midcentury White House Conference on Children and Youth, 1950), Witmer and Kotinsky, *Personality in the Making* (1952), c. VI; Deutscher and Chein, *The Psychological Effects of Enforced Segregation: A Survey of Social Science Opinion*, 26 J. Psychol. 259 (1948); Chein, *What are the Psychological Effects of Segregation Under Conditions of Equal Facilities?*, 3 Int. J. Opinion and Attitude Res. 229 (1949); Brameld, *Educational Costs, in Discrimination and National Welfare* (MacIver, ed., 1949), 44–48; Frazier, *The Negro in the United States* (1949), 674–81. And see generally Myrdal, *An American Dilemma* (1944). [Footnote by the Court.]

educational facilities are inherently unequal. Therefore, we hold that the plaintiffs and others similarly situated for whom the actions have been brought are, by reason of the segregation complained of, deprived of the equal protection of the laws guaranteed by the Fourteenth Amendment. This disposition makes unnecessary any discussion whether such segregation also violates the Due Process Clause of the Fourteenth Amendment.

Because these are class actions, because of the wide applicability of this decision, and because of the great variety of local conditions, the formulation of decrees in these cases presents problems of considerable complexity. On reargument, the consideration of appropriate relief was necessarily subordinated to the primary question—the constitutionality of segregation in public education. We have now announced that such segregation is a denial of the equal protection of the laws. In order that we may have the full assistance of the parties in formulating decrees, the cases will be restored to the docket, and the parties are requested to present further argument. . . .

It is so ordered.

Notes and Queries

1. In a second case, *Brown v. Board of Education II* (1955), the Court considered the question of how to give effect to *Brown I*. Noting that "Full implementation of [*Brown I*] may require solution of varied local school problems," the Court remanded the cases to the lower courts, which it charged with primary responsibility for fashioning relief decrees. It then ordered the district courts to "enter such orders and decrees consistent with this opinion as are necessary and proper to admit to public schools on racially nondiscriminatory basis with all deliberate speed the parties to these cases."

There has been much debate about what the Court meant by "all deliberate speed." Justice Frankfurter, who penned the phrase, later complained that its use in Chief Justice Warren's unanimous opinion in *Brown II* had changed its meaning. Warren, for his part, later came to believe that "he had been sold a bill of goods" by Frankfurter. Justice Black reportedly objected to the phrase, and later concluded that "It seems to me, probably, with all due deference to the opinion and my brethren, all of them, that it would have been better—maybe—I don't say positively—not to have that sentence." (1969 *Congressional Quarterly Weekly Report* 7.)

Whatever the Court's intent, Southern officials found in the phrase all the excuse they needed to evade *Brown I*. Reaction to the Court's decision in *Brown*, especially in the South, was predictably hostile. Ninety-six congressmen, and nearly every Southern representative, signed a resolution condemning the decision. In part, the resolution read that "We regard the decision . . . as clear abuse of judicial power. It climaxes a trend in the Federal judiciary undertaking to legislate, in derogation of the authority of Congress, and to encroach upon the reserved rights of the states and the people. . . . This unwarranted exercise of power by the court, contrary to the Constitution, is creating chaos and confusion in the states primarily affected."

Eight southern legislatures (Alabama, Arkansas, Florida, Georgia, Louisiana, Mississippi, South Carolina, and Virginia) also passed a "nullification" resolution, which declared that the states possessed constitutional authority to "nullify" a Supreme Court decision. The Court responded in *Cooper v. Aaron*, (1958), stating that

> Article 6 . . . makes the Constitution the "supreme Law of the Land." . . . [*Marbury*] declared the basic principle that the federal judiciary is supreme in the exposition of the law of the Constitution. . . . It follows that the interpretation of the Fourteenth Amendment enunciated by this Court in the *Brown* Case is the supreme law of the land, and Article 6 of the Constitution makes it of binding effect on the States "any Thing in the Constitution or Laws of any State to the Contrary notwithstanding."

What understanding of judicial power is inherent in *Cooper*? Is it the same position the Court adopted in *Marbury v. Madison*?

2. Of what relevance was the Founders' intent to the Court's decision? Consider the following argument:

> Suppose that we turned back the clock so that we could talk to the framers of the Fourteenth Amendment. If we asked them whether the amendment outlawed segregation in public schools, they would answer "No." [But the framers] had in mind a relatively new and peripheral social institution. [In] contrast they thought that freedom of contract was extremely important . . . and they certainly wanted to outlaw racial discrimination with respect to this freedom. Returning to 1954 and the question for the Court in *Brown*, we might . . . challenge the interpretivists with their own weapons. [Public] education as it exists today . . . is in fact the functional equivalent not of public education in 1868, but of freedom of contract in 1868. . . .

Mark Tushnet, *Following the Rules Laid Down: A Critique of Interpretivism and Neutral Principles*, 96 Harvard Law Review 781, 800 (1983).

3. In presenting his case to the Court, Thurgood Marshall relied in part on the work of Dr. Kenneth Clark, pro-

fessor of psychology at Columbia University, to show that separate but equal damaged the self-esteem of black schoolchildren. Clark conducted tests asking children to distinguish between "nice" and "bad" dolls, and "pretty" from "ugly" dolls. Both black and white children consistently identified the pretty and nice dolls as pink-skinned. And both black and white children consistently described black-skinned dolls as ugly and bad. Clark concluded from this data that even young black children were conscious of their racial identity and suffered from poor self-esteem because of it.

The Court referred to Clark's work in a footnote as support for its conclusion that "Segregation of white and colored children in public schools has a detrimental effect upon the colored children." Some critics, such as Herbert Weschler, criticized the Court for relying upon "social science," complaining that in doing so the Court had failed to rely upon "a neutral constitutional principle" of the sort we considered in chapter 2.

After *Brown*, pro-segregationists tried to argue that feelings of inferiority were more likely to result from integration than segregation. In *Stell v. Savannah-Chatham County Bd. of Ed.*, 220 F.Supp. 667 (S.D.Ga. 1963), a district court concluded, after reviewing studies of student test scores, that the failure of black students to perform as well as whites "would create serious psychological problems of frustration on the part of the Negro child," and would lead to "substantial and irremovable psychological injury. . . ." On appeal, a unanimous Circuit Court reversed. 333 F.2d 55 (5th Cir. 1964).

4. Was *Brown* a racist decision? Consider this observation by Derrick Bell:

[The] decision in *Brown* to break with the Court's long-held position . . . cannot be understood without some consideration of the decision's value to whites [able] to see the economic and political advantages at home and abroad that would accompany the abandonment of segregation. [*Brown* provided] immediate credibility to America's struggle with Communist countries to win the hearts and minds of emerging third world people [and] offered much needed reassurance to American Blacks.

Brown v. Board of Education and the Interest-Convergence Dilemma, 93 Harvard Law Review 518, 524 (1980).

5. Did *Brown* change anything? Most children in the United States continue to attend heavily segregated public schools. Residential housing patterns, coupled with the historic insistence of localized schooling, are largely responsible for segregated schools.

Keyes v. School District No. 1, Denver, Colorado

413 U.S. 189, 93 S. Ct. 2686, 37 L. Ed. 2d. 548 (1973)

In *Swann v. Charlotte-Mecklenburg Board of Education* (1971), the Court ruled that in areas where there had been *de jure* segregation—segregation imposed and maintained by the force of law—school authorities must take positive action to create an integrated, single school system. Although admitting that the kinds of remedies that might be necessary to achieve integration—including busing—might be "administratively awkward, inconvenient, and even bizarre in some situations and may impose burdens on some," the Court concluded that such remedies were required in the face of *de jure* discrimination. The facts in *Keyes* are summarized in Justice Brennan's opinion for the Court. Opinion of the Court: *Brennan*, Douglas, Stewart, Marshall, Blackmun. Concurring opinion: *Douglas*. Concurring in part and dissenting in part: *Powell*. Dissenting opinion: *Rehnquist*. Not participating: White.

Mr. Justice BRENNAN delivered the opinion of the Court.

This school desegregation case concerns the Denver, Colorado, school system. That system has never been operated under a constitutional or statutory provision that mandated or permitted racial segregation in public education. Rather, the gravamen of this action, brought . . . by parents of Denver schoolchildren, is that the respondent School Board alone, by use of various techniques such as the manipulation of student attendance zones, school site selection and a neighborhood school policy, created or maintained racially or ethnically (or both racially and ethnically) segregated schools throughout the school district, entitling petitioners to a decree directing desegregation of the entire school district.

. . . [T]he [District] court concluded that its finding of a purposeful and systematic program of racial segregation affecting thousands of students in the Park Hill area did not, in itself, impose on the School Board an affirmative duty to eliminate segregation throughout the school district. Instead, the court fractionated the district and held that petitioners had to make a fresh showing of *de jure* segregation in each area of the city for which they sought relief. Moreover, the District Court held that its finding of intentional segregation in Park Hill was not in any sense material to the question of segregative intent in other areas of the city. Under this restrictive approach, the District Court concluded that petitioners' evidence of intentionally discriminatory School Board action in areas of the district other than Park Hill was insufficient to "dictate the conclusion that this is *de jure* segregation which calls for an all-out effort to desegregate. It is more like *de facto* segregation, with respect to which the rule is that the court cannot order desegregation in order to provide a better balance."

Nevertheless, the District Court went on to hold that the proofs established that the segregated core city schools were educationally inferior to the predominantly "white" or "Anglo" schools in other parts of the district—that is, "separate facilities . . . unequal in the quality of education provided." Thus, the court held that, under the doctrine of *Plessy v. Ferguson* (1896), respondent School Board constitutionally "must at a minimum . . . offer an equal educational opportunity," and, therefore, although all-out desegregation "could not be decreed, . . . the only feasible and constitutionally acceptable program—the only program which furnishes anything approaching substantial equality—is a system of desegregation and integration which provides compensatory education in an integrated environment." The District Court then formulated a varied remedial plan to that end which was incorporated in the Final Decree.

. . . In our view, the . . . question that requires our decision at this time is . . . whether the District Court and the Court of Appeals applied an incorrect legal standard in addressing petitioners' contention that respondent School Board engaged in an unconstitutional policy of deliberate segregation in the core city schools. Our conclusion is that those courts did not apply the correct standard in addressing that contention.

Petitioners apparently concede for the purposes of this case that in the case of a school system like Denver's, where no statutory dual system has ever existed, plaintiffs must prove not only that segregated schooling exists but also that it was brought about or maintained by intentional state action. . . . Respondent argues, however, that a finding of state-imposed segregation as to a substantial portion of the school system can be viewed in isolation from the rest of the district, and that even if state-imposed segregation does exist in a substantial part of the Denver school system, it does not follow that the District Court could predicate on that fact a finding that the entire school system is a dual system. We do not agree. We have never suggested that plaintiffs in school desegregation cases must bear the burden of proving the elements of *de jure* segregation as to each and every school or each and every student within the school system. Rather, we have held that where plaintiffs prove that a current condition of seg-

regated schooling exists within a school district where a dual system was compelled or authorized by statute at the time of our decision in *Brown v. Board of Education* (1954) (*Brown I*), the State automatically assumes an affirmative duty "to effectuate a transition to a racially nondiscriminatory school system," *Brown v. Board of Education* (1955) (*Brown II*), that is, to eliminate from the public schools within their school system "all vestiges of state-imposed segregation." *Swann v. Charlotte-Mecklenburg Board of Education* (1971).

This is not a case, however, where a statutory dual system has ever existed. Nevertheless, where plaintiffs prove that the school authorities have carried out a systematic program of segregation affecting a substantial portion of the students, schools, teachers, and facilities within the school system, it is only common sense to conclude that there exists a predicate for a finding of the existence of a dual school system. Several considerations support this conclusion. First, it is obvious that a practice of concentrating Negroes in certain schools by structuring attendance zones or designating "feeder" schools on the basis of race has the reciprocal effect of keeping other nearby schools predominantly white. Similarly, the practice of building a school—such as the Barrett Elementary School in this case—to a certain size and in a certain location, "with conscious knowledge that it would be a segregated school," has a substantial reciprocal effect on the racial composition of other nearby schools. So also, the use of mobile classrooms, the drafting of student transfer policies, the transportation of students, and the assignment of faculty and staff, on racially identifiable bases, have the clear effect of earmarking schools according to their racial composition, and this, in turn, together with the elements of student assignment and school construction, may have a profound reciprocal effect on the racial composition of residential neighborhoods within a metropolitan area, thereby causing further racial concentration within the schools. We recognized this in *Swann* when we said:

> They [school authorities] must decide questions of location and capacity in light of population growth, finances, land values, site availability, through an almost endless list of factors to be considered. The result of this will be a decision which, when combined with one technique or another of student assignment, will determine the racial composition of the student body in each school in the system. Over the long run, the consequences of the choices will be far reaching. People gravitate toward school facilities, just as schools are located in response to the needs of people. The location of schools may thus influence the patterns of residential

development of a metropolitan area and have important impact on composition of inner-city neighborhoods.

In the past, choices in this respect have been used as a potent weapon for creating or maintaining a state-segregated school system. In addition to the classic pattern of building schools specifically intended for Negro or white students, school authorities have sometimes, since *Brown*, closed schools which appeared likely to become racially mixed through changes in neighborhood residential patterns. This was sometimes accompanied by building new schools in the areas of white suburban expansion farthest from Negro population centers in order to maintain the separation of the races with a minimum departure from the formal principles of "neighborhood zoning." Such a policy does more than simply influence the short-run composition of the student body of a new school. It may well promote segregated residential patterns which, when combined with "neighborhood zoning," further lock the school system into the mold of separation of the races. Upon a proper showing a district court may consider this in fashioning a remedy.

In short, common sense dictates the conclusion that racially inspired school board actions have an impact beyond the particular schools that are the subjects of those actions. This is not to say, of course, that there can never be a case in which the geographical structure of, or the natural boundaries within, a school district may have the effect of dividing the district into separate, identifiable and unrelated units. Such a determination is essentially a question of fact to be resolved by the trial court in the first instance, but such cases must be rare. In the absence of such a determination, proof of state-imposed segregation in a substantial portion of the district will suffice to support a finding by the trial court of the existence of a dual system. Of course, where that finding is made, as in cases involving statutory dual systems, the school authorities have an affirmative duty "to effectuate a transition to a racially nondiscriminatory school system." *Brown II* (1955).

On the question of segregative intent, petitioners presented evidence tending to show that the Board, through its actions over a period of years, intentionally created and maintained the segregated character of the core city schools. Respondents countered this evidence by arguing that the segregation in these schools is the result of a racially neutral "neighborhood school policy" and that the acts of which petitioners complain are explicable within the bounds of that policy. Accepting the School Board's explanation, the District Court and the Court of Appeals

agreed that a finding of *de jure* segregation as to the core city schools was not permissible since petitioners had failed to prove "(1) a racially discriminatory purpose and (2) a causal relationship between the acts complained of and the racial imbalance admittedly existing in those schools." This assessment of petitioners' proof was clearly incorrect.

Although petitioners had already proved the existence of intentional school segregation in the Park Hill schools, this crucial finding was totally ignored when attention turned to the core city schools. Plainly, a finding of intentional segregation as to a portion of a school system is not devoid of probative value in assessing the school authorities' intent with respect to other parts of the same school system. On the contrary where, as here, the case involves one school board, a finding of intentional segregation on its part in one portion of a school system is highly relevant to the issue of the board's intent with respect to the other segregated schools in the system. . . .

Applying these principles in the special context of school desegregation cases, we hold that a finding of intentionally segregative school board actions in a meaningful portion of a school system, as in this case, creates a presumption that other segregated schooling within the system is not adventitious. It establishes, in other words, a *prima facie* case of unlawful segregative design on the part of school authorities, and shifts to those authorities the burden of proving that other segregated schools within the system are not also the result of intentionally segregative actions. . . . We emphasize that the differentiating factor between *de jure* segregation and so-called *de facto* segregation to which we referred in *Swann* is purpose or intent to segregate. Where school authorities have been found to have practiced purposeful segregation in part of a school system, they may be expected to oppose system-wide desegregation, as did the respondents in this case, on the ground that their purposefully segregative actions were isolated and individual events, thus leaving plaintiffs with the burden of proving otherwise. But at that point where an intentionally segregative policy is practiced in a meaningful or significant segment of a school system, as in this case, the school authorities cannot be heard to argue that plaintiffs have proved only "isolated and individual" unlawfully segregative actions. In that circumstance, it is both fair and reasonable to require that the school authorities bear the burden of showing that their actions as to other segregated schools within the system were not also motivated by segregative intent.

The respondent School Board invoked at trial its "neighborhood school policy" as explaining racial and ethnic concentrations within the core city schools, arguing that since the core city area population had long been Negro and Hispano, the concentrations were necessarily the result of residential patterns and not of purposefully segregative policies. We have no occasion to consider in this case whether a "neighborhood school policy" of itself will justify racial or ethnic concentrations in the absence of a finding that school authorities have committed acts constituting *de jure* segregation. It is enough that we hold that the mere assertion of such a policy is not dispositive where, as in this case, the school authorities have been found to have practiced *de jure* segregation in a meaningful portion of the school system by techniques that indicate that the "neighborhood school" concept has not been maintained free of manipulation. Our observations in *Swann* are particularly instructive on this score:

> Absent a constitutional violation there would be no basis for judicially ordering assignment of students on a racial basis. All things being equal, with no history of discrimination, it might well be desirable to assign pupils to schools nearest their homes. But all things are not equal in a system that has been deliberately constructed and maintained to enforce racial segregation. . . .

The judgment of the Court of Appeals is modified to vacate instead of reverse the parts of the Final Decree that concern the core city schools, and the case is remanded to the District Court for further proceedings consistent with this opinion.

It is so ordered.

Mr. Chief Justice BURGER concurs in the result.

Mr. Justice DOUGLAS, concurring.

While I join the opinion of the Court, I agree with my Brother Powell that there is, for the purposes of the Equal Protection Clause of the Fourteenth Amendment as applied to the school cases, no difference between *de facto* and *de jure* segregation. The school board is a state agency and the lines that it draws, the locations it selects for school sites, the allocation it makes of students, the budgets it prepares are state action for Fourteenth Amendment purposes.

. . . I think it is time to state that there is no constitutional difference between *de jure* and *de facto* segregation, for each is the product of state actions or policies. If a "neighborhood" or "geographical" unit has been created along racial lines by reason of the play of restrictive covenants that restrict certain areas to "the elite," leaving the "undesirables" to move elsewhere, there is state action in the

constitutional sense because the force of law is placed behind those covenants.

There is state action in the constitutional sense when public funds are dispersed by urban development agencies to build racial ghettoes.

Where the school district is racially mixed and the races are segregated in separate schools, where black teachers are assigned almost exclusively to black schools where the school board closed existing schools located in fringe areas and built new schools in black areas and in distant white areas, where the school board continued the "neighborhood" school policy at the elementary level, these actions constitute state action. They are of a kind quite distinct from the classical *de jure* type of school segregation. Yet calling them *de facto* is a misnomer, as they are only more subtle types of state action that create or maintain a wholly or partially segregated school system.

When a State forces, aids, or abets, or helps create a racial "neighborhood," it is a travesty of justice to treat that neighborhood as sacrosanct in the sense that its creation is free from the taint of state action.

The Constitution and Bill of Rights have described the design of a pluralistic society. The individual has the right to seek such companions as he desires. But a State is barred from creating by one device or another ghettoes that determine the school one is compelled to attend.

Mr. Justice POWELL concurring in part and dissenting in part.

This is the first school desegregation case to reach this Court which involves a major city outside the South. It comes from Denver, Colorado, a city and a State which have not operated public schools under constitutional or statutory provisions which mandated or permitted racial segregation. Nor has it been argued that any other legislative actions (such as zoning and housing laws) contributed to the segregation which is at issue. The Court has inquired only to what extent the Denver public school authorities may have contributed to the school segregation which is acknowledged to exist in Denver.

The situation in Denver is generally comparable to that in other large cities across the country in which there is a substantial minority population and where desegregation has not been ordered by the federal courts. There is segregation in the schools of many of these cities fully as pervasive as that in southern cities prior to the desegregation decrees of the past decade and a half. The focus of the school desegregation problem has now shifted from the South to the country as a whole. Unwilling and foot-dragging as the process was in most places, substantial progress toward achieving integration has been made in

Southern States. No comparable progress has been made in many nonsouthern cities with large minority populations primarily because of the *de facto/de jure* distinction nurtured by the courts and accepted complacently by many of the same voices which denounced the evils of segregated schools in the South. But if our national concern is for those who attend such schools, rather than for perpetuating a legalism rooted in history rather than present reality, we must recognize that the evil of operating separate schools is no less in Denver than in Atlanta.

In my view we should abandon a distinction which long since has outlived its time, and formulate constitutional principles of national rather than merely regional application. When *Brown I* was decided, the distinction between *de jure* and *de facto* segregation was consistent with the limited constitutional rationale of that case. The situation confronting the Court, largely confined to the Southern States, was officially imposed racial segregation in the schools extending back for many years and usually embodied in constitutional and statutory provisions.

The great contribution of *Brown I* was its holding in unmistakable terms that the Fourteenth Amendment forbids state-compelled or state-authorized segregation of public schools. Although some of the language was more expansive, the holding in *Brown I* was essentially negative: It was impermissible under the Constitution for the States, or their instrumentalities to force children to attend segregated schools. The forbidden action was *de jure*, and the opinion in *Brown I* was construed—for some years and by many courts—as requiring only state neutrality, allowing "freedom of choice" as to schools to be attended so long as the State itself assured that the choice was genuinely free of official restraint.

But the doctrine of *Brown I*, as amplified by *Brown II* (1955), did not retain its original meaning. In a series of decisions extending from 1954 to 1971 the concept of state neutrality was transformed into the present constitutional doctrine requiring affirmative state action to desegregate school systems. The keystone case was *Green v. County School Board* (1968), where school boards were declared to have "the affirmative duty to take whatever steps might be necessary to convert to a unitary system in which racial discrimination would be eliminated root and branch." The school system before the Court in *Green* was operating in a rural and sparsely settled county where there were no concentrations of white and black populations, no neighborhood school system (there were only two schools in the county), and none of the problems of an urbanized school district. The Court properly identified the freedom-of-choice program there as a subterfuge, and the language in *Green* imposing an affirmative duty to convert to a uni-

tary system was appropriate on the facts before the Court. There was however reason to question to what extent this duty would apply in the vastly different factual setting of a large city with extensive areas of residential segregation, presenting problems and calling for solutions quite different from those in the rural setting of New Kent County, Virginia.

But the doubt as to whether the affirmative-duty concept would flower into a new constitutional principle of general application was laid to rest by *Swann v. Charlotte-Mecklenburg Board of Education* (1971), in which the duty articulated in *Green* was applied to the urban school system of metropolitan Charlotte, North Carolina. In describing the residential patterns in Charlotte, the Court noted the "familiar phenomenon" in the metropolitan areas of minority groups being "concentrated in one part of the city," and acknowledged that:

> Rural areas accustomed for half a century to the consolidated school systems implemented by bus transportation could make adjustments more readily than metropolitan areas with dense and shifting population, numerous schools, congested and complex traffic patterns.

Despite this recognition of a fundamentally different problem from that involved in *Green*, the Court nevertheless held that the affirmative-duty rule of *Green* was applicable, and prescribed for a metropolitan school system with 107 schools and some 84,000 pupils essentially the same remedy—elimination of segregation "root and branch"—which had been formulated for the two schools and 1,300 pupils of New Kent County.

In *Swann*, the Court further noted it was concerned only with States having "a long history" of officially imposed segregation and the duty of school authorities in those States to implement *Brown I*. In so doing, the Court refrained from even considering whether the evolution of constitutional doctrine from *Brown I* to *Green/Swann* undercut whatever logic once supported the *de facto/de jure* distinction. In imposing on metropolitan southern school districts an affirmative duty, entailing largescale transportation of pupils, to eliminate segregation in the schools, the Court required these districts to alleviate conditions which in large part did not result from historic, state-imposed *de jure* segregation. Rather, the familiar root cause of segregated schools in all the biracial metropolitan areas of our country is essentially the same: one of segregated residential and migratory patterns the impact of which on the racial composition of the schools was often perpetuated and rarely ameliorated by action of public school authorities. This is a national, not a southern, phenomenon. And it is largely unrelated to whether a particular State had or did not have segregative school laws.

Whereas *Brown I* rightly decreed the elimination of state-imposed segregation in that particular section of the country where it did exist, *Swann* imposed obligations on southern school districts to eliminate conditions which are not regionally unique but are similar both in origin and effect to conditions in the rest of the country. As the remedial obligations of *Swann* extend far beyond the elimination of the outgrowths of the state-imposed segregation outlawed in *Brown*, the rationale of *Swann* points inevitably toward a uniform, constitutional approach to our national problem of school segregation.

The Court's decision today, while adhering to the *de jure/de facto* distinction, will require the application of the *Green/Swann* doctrine of "affirmative duty" to the Denver School Board despite the absence of any history of state-mandated school segregation. The only evidence of a constitutional violation was found in various decisions of the School Board. I concur in the Court's position that the public school authorities are the responsible agency of the State, and that if the affirmative-duty doctrine is sound constitutional law for Charlotte, it is equally so for Denver. I would not, however, perpetuate the *de jure/de facto* distinction nor would I leave to petitioners the initial tortuous effort of identifying "segregative acts" and deducing "segregative intent." I would hold, quite simply, that where segregated public schools exist within a school district to a substantial degree, there is a *prima facie* case that the duly constituted public authorities (I will usually refer to them collectively as the "school board") are sufficiently responsible to warrant imposing upon them a nationally applicable burden to demonstrate they nevertheless are operating a genuinely integrated school system. . . .

There is thus no reason as a matter of constitutional principle to adhere to the *de jure/de facto* distinction in school desegregation cases. In addition, there are reasons of policy and prudent judicial administration which point strongly toward the adoption of a uniform national rule. The litigation heretofore centered in the South already is surfacing in other regions. The decision of the Court today, emphasizing as it does the elusive element of segregative intent, will invite numerous desegregation suits in which there can be little hope of uniformity of result. . . . In a pluralistic society such as ours, it is essential that no racial minority feel demeaned or discriminated against and that students of all races learn to play, work, and co-operate with one another in their common pursuits and endeavors. Nothing in this opinion is meant to discourage school boards from exceeding minimal constitutional standards in promoting the values of an integrated school experience.

A constitutional requirement of extensive student transportation solely to achieve integration presents a vastly more complex problem. It promises, on the one hand, a greater degree of actual desegregation, while it infringes on what may fairly be regarded as other important community aspirations and personal rights. Such a requirement is also likely to divert attention and resources from the foremost goal of any school system: the best quality education for all pupils. The Equal Protection Clause does, indeed, command that racial discrimination not be tolerated in the decisions of public school authorities. But it does not require that school authorities undertake widespread student transportation solely for the sake of maximizing integration.

This obviously does not mean that bus transportation has no place in public school systems or is not a permissible means in the desegregative process. The transporting of school children is as old as public education, and in rural and some suburban settings it is as indispensable as the providing of books. . . . There is a significant difference, however, in transportation plans voluntarily initiated by local school boards for educational purposes and those imposed by a federal court. The former usually represent a necessary or convenient means of access to the school nearest home; the latter often require lengthy trips for no purpose other than to further integration. Yet the Court in *Swann* was unquestionably right in describing bus transportation as "one tool of school desegregation." The crucial issue is when, under what circumstances, and to what extent such transportation may appropriately be ordered. The answer to this turns—as it does so often in the law—upon a sound exercise of discretion under the circumstances.

Appellants, however, pose the question of whether the neighborhood system of pupil placement, fairly administered without racial bias, comports with the requirements of equal opportunity if it nevertheless results in the creation of schools with predominantly or even exclusively Negro pupils. The neighborhood system is in wide use throughout the nation and has been for many years the basis of school administration. This is so because it is acknowledged to have several valuable aspects which are an aid to education, such as minimization of safety hazards to children in reaching school, economy of cost in reducing transportation needs, ease of pupil placement and administration through the use of neutral, easily determined standards, and better home-school communication.

Neighborhood school systems, neutrally administered,

reflect the deeply felt desire of citizens for a sense of community in their public education. Public schools have been a traditional source of strength to our Nation, and that strength may derive in part from the identification of many schools with the personal features of the surrounding neighborhood.

Community support, interest, and dedication to public schools may well run higher with a neighborhood attendance pattern: distance may encourage disinterest. Many citizens sense today a decline in the intimacy of our institutions—home, church, and school—which has caused a concomitant decline in the unity and communal spirit of our people. I pass no judgment on this viewpoint, but I do believe that this Court should be wary of compelling in the name of constitutional law what may seem to many a dissolution in the traditional, more personal fabric of their public schools.

Closely related to the concept of a community and neighborhood education, are those rights and duties parents have with respect to the education of their children. The law has long recognized the parental duty to nurture, support, and provide for the welfare of children, including their education. . . .

Up to this point I have focused mainly on the personal interests of parents and children which a community may believe to be best protected by a neighborhood system of schools. But broader considerations lead me to question just as seriously any remedial requirement of extensive student transportation solely to further integration. Any such requirement is certain to fall disproportionately on the school districts of our country, depending on their degree of urbanization, financial resources, and their racial composition. . . .

Finally, courts in requiring so far-reaching a remedy as student transportation solely to maximize integration, risk setting in motion unpredictable and unmanageable social consequences. No one can estimate the extent to which dismantling neighborhood education will hasten an exodus to private schools, leaving public school systems the preserve of the disadvantaged of both races. Or guess how much impetus such dismantlement gives the movement from inner city to suburb, and the further geographical separation of the races. Nor do we know to what degree this remedy may cause deterioration of community and parental support of public schools, or divert attention from the paramount goal of quality in education to a perennially divisive debate over who is to be transported where.

The problem addressed in this opinion has perplexed courts, school officials, other public authorities, and students of public education for nearly two decades. The

problem, especially since it has focused on the "busing issue," has profoundly disquieted the public wherever extensive transportation has been ordered. I make no pretense of knowing the best answers. Yet, the issue in this and like cases comes to this Court as one of constitutional law. As to this issue, I have no doubt whatever. There is nothing in the Constitution, its history, or—until recently—in the jurisprudence of this Court that mandates the employment of forced transportation of young and teenage children to achieve a single interest, as important as that interest may be. We have strayed, quite far as I view it, from the rationale of *Brown I* and *II*. . . .

I urge a return to this rationale. This would result, as emphasized above, in no prohibition on court-ordered student transportation in furtherance of desegregation. But it would require that the legitimate community interests in neighborhood school systems be accorded far greater respect. In the balancing of interests so appropriate to a fair and just equitable decree, transportation orders should be applied with special caution to any proposal as disruptive of family life and interests—and ultimately of education itself—as extensive transportation of elementary-age children solely for desegregation purposes. As a minimum, this Court should not require school boards to engage in the unnecessary transportation away from their neighborhoods of elementary age children. It is at this age level that neighborhood education performs its most vital role. It is with respect to children of tender years that the greatest concern exists for their physical and psychological health. It is also here, at the elementary school, that the rights of parents and children are most sharply implicated.

It is well to remember that the course we are running is a long one and the goal sought in the end—so often overlooked—is the best possible educational opportunity for all children. Communities deserve the freedom and the incentive to turn their attention and energies to this goal of quality education, free from protracted and debilitating battles over court-ordered student transportation. . . .

Mr. Justice REHNQUIST, dissenting.

The Court notes at the outset of its opinion the differences between the claims made by the plaintiffs in this case and the classical "*de jure*" type of claims made by plaintiffs in cases such as *Brown v. Board of Education* (1954), and its progeny. I think the similarities and differences, not only in the claims, but in the nature of the constitutional violation, deserve somewhat more attention than the Court gives them.

. . . It is quite possible, of course, that a school district purporting to adopt racially neutral boundary zones might, with respect to every such zone, invidiously discriminate against minorities, so as to produce substantially the same result as was produced by the statutorily decreed segregation involved in *Brown*. If that were the case, the consequences would necessarily have to be the same as were the consequences in *Brown*. But, in the absence of a statute requiring segregation, there must necessarily be the sort of factual inquiry which was unnecessary in those jurisdictions where racial mixing in the schools was forbidden by law.

. . . The Court has taken a long leap in this area of constitutional law in equating the district-wide consequences of gerrymandering individual attendance zones in a district where separation of the races was never required by law with statutes or ordinances in other jurisdictions which did so require. It then adds to this potpourri a confusing enunciation of evidentiary rules in order to make it more likely that the trial court will on remand reach the result which the Court apparently wants it to reach. Since I believe neither of these steps is justified by prior decisions of this Court, I dissent.

Mr. Justice WHITE took no part in the decision of this case.

Notes and Queries

1. *Keyes* was the first school desegregation case that did not involve the South. No one denied that the Denver school system was segregated. Here, however, and in much of the rest of the country, school segregation was *de facto* rather than *de jure*. No official state or municipal policy mandated segregation by race. The Court was thus faced with a case that gave it an opportunity to decide whether *de facto* discrimination, alone, violated the equal protection clause. How did the Court's majority opinion respond to that opportunity?

2. In their separate opinions, Justices Douglas and Powell argued for an end to the *de jure/de facto* distinc-

tion. Do you agree? What would be gained by dropping the distinction? Would anything be lost? Do you agree with Justice Powell's argument that the distinction impedes the development of a "uniform, constitutional approach to our national problem of school desegregation"? Why do we need a uniform approach?

3. Recall the Court's decision in *Brown*. Are the reasons that the Court offered in *Brown* for concluding that separate but equal in elementary schools is unconstitutional tied in any way to whether the discrimination from *Brown* was *de jure*? Does *de jure* discrimination have a more negative impact than *de facto* discrimination on the self-esteem of minority students? Does *de jure* discrimination stigmatize more than *de facto* discrimination? Why or why not?

Does *Keyes* suggest some confusion in the Court about what *Brown* meant? Consider Justice Powell's observation that the Court transformed *Brown* from a decision that required "state neutrality . . . into the present constitutional doctrine requiring affirmative state action to desegregate the school systems."

4. In addition to his comments on the *de jure/de facto* distinction, Justice Powell addressed the issue of remedies at some length in his opinion. Reaction to the Court's approval of an expansive system of busing in *Swann* had, predictably, led to many proposals in Congress to restrict or prohibit busing. The Education Amendments of 1974, although claiming not to be a limit on "the authority of the courts of the United States," nevertheless set forth a list of remedies, in order of priority, that federal courts and agencies were to consult in devising desegregation plans. What countervailing interests did Justice Powell offer in support of "neighborhood schooling"? Are those interests grounded in the constitutional text or in the larger constitutional order? Do they reflect an understanding of community that the Constitution should protect? Are Justice Powell's comments on community also premised upon a particular understanding of judicial power?

Milliken v. Bradley
418 U.S. 717, 94 S. Ct. 3112, 41 L. Ed. 2d 1069 (1974)

In *Brown v. Board of Education*, 349 U.S. 294 (1955) (*Brown* II), the Supreme Court began the process of fashioning remedies for the school segregation problem. Noncompliance and evasion were common reactions to the decision. In Detroit a district court found that city school officials had created "optional attendance" zones that allowed students the choice of attending one of two high

schools in their district. The primary effect of this program was to allow white students to avoid predominantly African-American schools. The Court also found that the Detroit School Board had bused African-American children to predominantly African-American schools, even though they were farther away than predominantly white schools with available space. Practices such as these led the court to construct a remedy that would rectify the constitutional violations of the Detroit city officials. The Court came up with a plan that bused Detroit students outside the Detroit

School District into adjacent or nearby school districts, even though the court admitted that suburban school districts had not engaged in any constitutionally invalid practices. Opinion of the Court: *Burger*, Blackmun, Powell, Rehnquist, Stewart. Concurring opinion: *Stewart*. Dissenting opinions: *Douglas*, Marshall, Brennan, *White*.

Mr. Chief Justice BURGER delivered the opinion of the Court.

We granted certiorari in these consolidated cases to determine whether a federal court may impose a multidistrict, areawide remedy to a single district *de jure* segregation problem absent any finding that the other included school districts have failed to operate unitary school systems within their districts, absent any claim or finding that the boundary lines of any affected school district were established with the purpose of fostering racial segregation in public schools, absent any finding that the included districts committed acts which effected segregation within the other school districts, and absent a meaningful opportunity of the included neighboring school districts to present evidence or be heard on the propriety of a multidistrict remedy. . . .

Viewing the record as a whole, it seems clear that the District Court and the Court of Appeals shifted the primary focus from a Detroit remedy to the metropolitan area only because of their conclusion that total desegregation of Detroit would not produce the racial balance which they perceived as desirable. Both courts proceeded on an assumption that the Detroit schools could not be truly desegregated—in their view of what constituted desegregation—unless the racial composition of the student body of each school substantially reflected the racial composition of the population of the metropolitan area as a whole. The metropolitan area was then defined as Detroit plus 53 of the outlying school districts. . . .

Here the District Court's approach to what constituted "actual desegregation" raises the fundamental question . . . as to the circumstances in which a federal court may order desegregation relief that embraces more than a single school district. The court's analytical starting point was its conclusion that school district lines are no more than arbitrary lines on a map drawn "for political convenience." Boundary lines may be bridged where there has been a constitutional violation calling for interdistrict relief, but the notion that school district lines may be casually ignored or treated as a mere administrative convenience is contrary to the history of public education in our country. No single tradition in public education is more deeply rooted than local control over the operation of schools; local autonomy has long been thought essen-

tial both to the maintenance of community concern and support for public schools and to the quality of the educational process. . . .

The Michigan educational structure involved in this case, in common with most States, provides for a large measure of local control, and a review of the scope and character of these local powers indicates the extent to which the interdistrict remedy approved by the two courts could disrupt and alter the structure of public education in Michigan. The metropolitan remedy would require, in effect, consolidation of 54 independent school districts historically administered as separate units into a vast new super school district. Entirely apart from the logistical and other serious problems attending large-scale transportation of students, the consolidation would give rise to an array of other problems in financing and operating this new school system. Some of the more obvious questions would be: What would be the status and authority of the present popularly elected school boards? Would the children of Detroit be within the jurisdiction and operating control of a school board elected by the parents and residents of other districts? What board or boards would levy taxes for school operations? . . . What provisions would be made for financing? . . . What body would determine that portion of the curricula now left to the discretion of local school boards? . . .

Of course, no state law is above the Constitution. School district lines and the present laws with respect to local control, are not sacrosanct and if they conflict with the Fourteenth Amendment federal courts have a duty to prescribe appropriate remedies. . . . But our prior holdings have been confined to violations and remedies within a single school district. We therefore turn to address, for the first time, the validity of a remedy mandating cross-district or interdistrict consolidation to remedy a condition of segregation found to exist in only one district.

The controlling principle consistently expounded in our holdings is that the scope of the remedy is determined by the nature and extent of the constitutional violation. Before the boundaries of separate and autonomous school districts may be set aside by consolidating the separate units for remedial purposes or by imposing a cross-district remedy, it must first be shown that there has been a constitutional violation within one district that produces a significant segregative effect in another district. Specifically, it must be shown that racially discriminatory acts of the state or local school districts, or of a single school district have been a substantial cause of interdistrict segregation. Thus an interdistrict remedy might be in order where the racially discriminatory acts of one or more school districts caused racial segregation in an adjacent district, or where district lines have been deliberately drawn on the basis of race. In such circumstances an interdistrict remedy would be appropriate to eliminate the interdistrict segregation directly caused by the constitutional violation. Conversely, without an interdistrict violation and interdistrict effect, there is no constitutional wrong calling for an interdistrict remedy.

The record before us, voluminous as it is, contains evidence of *de jure* segregated conditions only in the Detroit schools; indeed, that was the theory on which the litigation was initially based and on which the District Court took evidence. With no showing of significant violation by the 53 outlying school districts and no evidence of any interdistrict violation or effect, the court went beyond the original theory of the case as framed by the pleadings and mandated a metropolitan area remedy. To approve the remedy ordered by the court would impose on the outlying districts, not shown to have committed any constitutional violation, a wholly impermissible remedy based on a standard not hinted at in *Brown I* and *II* or any holding of this Court.

The constitutional right of the Negro respondents residing in Detroit is to attend a unitary school system in that district. Unless petitioners drew the district lines in a discriminatory fashion or arranged for white students residing in the Detroit district to attend schools in Oakland and Macomb Counties, they were under no constitutional duty to make provisions for Negro students to do so. The view of the dissenters, that the existence of a dual system in Detroit can be made the basis for a decree requiring cross-district transportation of pupils, cannot be supported on the grounds that it represents merely the devising of a suitably flexible remedy for the violation of rights already established by our prior decisions. It can be supported only by drastic expansion of the constitutional right itself, an expansion without any support in either constitutional principle or precedent.

In dissent Mr. Justice White and Mr. Justice Marshall undertake to demonstrate that agencies having statewide authority participated in maintaining the dual school system found to exist in Detroit. They are apparently of the view that once such participation is shown, the District Court should have a relatively free hand to reconstruct school districts outside of Detroit in fashioning relief. . . . The difference between us rises instead from established doctrine laid down by our cases. . . . Terms such as "unitary" and "dual" systems and "racially identifiable schools," have meaning, and the necessary federal authority to remedy the constitutional wrong is firmly established. But the remedy is necessarily designed, as all remedies are, to restore the victims of discriminatory conduct to the position

they would have occupied in the absence of such conduct. Disparate treatment of White and Negro students occurred within the Detroit school system, and not elsewhere, and on this record the remedy must be limited to that system.

. . . Accepting, *arguendo*, the correctness of the finding [by the lower court] of state responsibility for the segregated conditions within the city of Detroit, it does not follow that an interdistrict remedy is constitutionally justified or required. . . . The boundaries of the Detroit School District, which are coterminus with the boundaries of the city of Detroit, were established over a century ago by neutral legislation when the city was incorporated; there is no evidence in the record, nor is there any suggestion by the respondents, that either the original boundaries . . . were established for the purpose of creating, maintaining or perpetuating segregation of races. . . .

We conclude that the relief ordered by the District Court and affirmed by the Court of Appeals was based upon an erroneous standard and was unsupported by record evidence that acts of the outlying districts effected the discrimination found to exist in the schools of Detroit. Accordingly, the judgment of the Court of Appeals is reversed and the case is remanded for further proceedings consistent with this opinion leading to prompt formulation of a decree directed to eliminating the segregation found to exist in Detroit city schools, a remedy which has been delayed since 1970.

Reversed and remanded.

Mr. Justice STEWART, concurring.

The opinion of the Court convincingly demonstrates, that traditions of local control of schools, together with the difficulty of a judicially supervised restructuring of local administration of schools, render improper and inequitable such an interdistrict response to a constitutional violation found to have occurred only within a single school district.

This is not to say, however, that an interdistrict remedy of the sort approved by the Court of Appeals would not be proper, or even necessary, in other factual situations. Were it to be shown, for example, that state officials had contributed to the separation of the races by drawing or redrawing school district lines, or by purposeful racially discriminatory use of state housing or zoning laws, then a decree calling for transfer of pupils across district lines or for restructuring of district lines might well be appropriate.

Mr. Justice DOUGLAS, dissenting.

Today's decision . . . means that there is no violation of the Equal Protection Clause though the schools are segregated by race and though the black schools are not only "separate" but "inferior."

So far as equal protection is concerned we are now in a dramatic retreat from the 7-to-1 decision in 1896 that Blacks could be segregated in public facilities, provided they receive equal treatment.

. . . It is conceivable that ghettos develop on their own without any hint of state action. But since Michigan by one device or another has over the years created black school districts and white school districts, the task of equity is to provide a unitary system for the affected area where, as here, the State washes its hands of its own creations.

Mr. Justice WHITE, with whom Mr. Justice DOUGLAS, Mr. Justice BRENNAN, and Mr. Justice MARSHALL join, dissenting.

Regretfully, and for several reasons, I can join neither the Court's judgment nor its opinion. The core of my disagreement is that deliberate acts of segregation and their consequences will go unremedied, not because a remedy would be infeasible or unreasonable in terms of the usual criteria governing school desegregation cases, but because an effective remedy would cause what the Court considers to be undue administrative inconvenience to the State. The result is that the State of Michigan, the entity at which the Fourteenth Amendment is directed, has successfully insulated itself from its duty to provide effective desegregation remedies by vesting sufficient power over its public schools in its local school districts. If this is the case in Michigan, it will be the case in most States.

There are undoubted practical as well as legal limits to the remedial powers of federal courts in school desegregation cases. The Court has made it clear that the achievement of any particular degree of racial balance in the school system is not required by the Constitution; nor may it be the primary focus of a court in devising an acceptable remedy for *de jure* segregation. A variety of procedures and techniques are available to a district court engrossed in fashioning remedies in a case such as this; but the courts must keep in mind that they are dealing with the process of *educating* the young, including the very young. The task is not to devise a system of pains and penalties to punish constitutional violations brought to light. Rather, it is to desegregate an *educational* system in which the races have been kept apart, without, at the same time, losing sight of the central *educational* function of the schools.

Viewed in this light, remedies calling for school zoning, pairing, and pupil assignments, become more and more suspect as they require that schoolchildren spend more and more time in buses going to and from school and that more and more educational dollars be diverted to transportation systems. Manifestly, these considerations are of immediate and urgent concern when the issue is the desegregation of a city school system where residential patterns are predominantly segregated and the respective areas occupied by blacks and whites are heavily populated and geographically extensive. Thus, if one postulates a metropolitan school system covering a sufficiently large area, with the population evenly divided between whites and Negroes and with the races occupying identifiable residential areas, there will be very real practical limits on the extent to which racially identifiable schools can be eliminated within the school district. It is also apparent that the larger the proportion of Negroes in the area, the more difficult it would be to avoid having a substantial number of all-black or nearly all-black schools.

I am surprised that the Court, sitting at this distance from the State of Michigan, claims better insight than the Court of Appeals and the District Court as to whether an interdistrict remedy for equal protection violations practiced by the State of Michigan would involve undue difficulties for the State in the management of its public schools.

I am even more mystified as to how the Court can ignore the legal reality that the constitutional violations, even if occurring locally, were committed by governmental entities for which the State is responsible and that it is the State that must respond to the command of the Fourteenth Amendment. An interdistrict remedy for the infringements that occurred in this case is well within the confines and powers of the State, which is the governmental entity ultimately responsible for desegregating its schools. . . .

The result reached by the Court certainly cannot be supported by the theory that the configuration of local governmental units is immune from alteration when necessary to redress constitutional violations. In addition to the well-established principles already noted, the Court has elsewhere required the public bodies of a State to restructure the State's political subdivisions to remedy infringements of the constitutional rights of certain members of its populace, notably in the reapportionment cases. . . .

Nor does the Court's conclusion follow from the talismanic invocation of the desirability of local control over education. Local autonomy over school affairs, in the sense of the community's participation in the decisions affecting the education of its children, is, of course, an important interest. But presently constituted school district lines do not delimit fixed and unchangeable areas of a local educational community. If restructuring is required to meet constitutional requirements, local authority may simply be redefined in terms of whatever configuration is adopted, with the parents of the children attending schools in the newly demarcated district or attendance zone continuing their participation in the policy management of the schools with which they are concerned most directly. . . .

Finally, I remain wholly unpersuaded by the Court's assertion that "the remedy is necessarily designed, as all remedies are, to restore the victims of discriminatory conduct to the position they would have occupied in the absence of such conduct." . . . Surely the Court's remedy will not restore to the Negro community, stigmatized as it was by the dual school system, what it would have enjoyed over all or most of this period if the remedy is confined to present-day Detroit; for the maximum remedy available within that area will leave many of the schools almost totally black, and the system itself will be predominantly black and will become increasingly so. Moreover, when a State has engaged in acts of official segregation over a lengthy period of time, as in the case before us, it is unrealistic to suppose that the children who were victims of the State's unconstitutional conduct could now be provided the benefits of which they were wrongfully deprived. Nor can the benefits which accrue to school systems in which schoolchildren have not been officially segregated, and to the communities supporting such school systems, be fully and immediately restored after a substantial period of unlawful segregation. The education of children of different races in a desegregated environment has unhappily been lost, along with the social, economic, and political advantages which accompany a desegregated school system as compared with an unconstitutionally segregated system. . . .

I am therefore constrained to record my disagreement and dissent.

Mr. Justice MARSHALL, with whom Mr. Justice DOUGLAS, Mr. Justice BRENNAN, and Mr. Justice WHITE join, dissenting.

I cannot subscribe to this emasculation of our constitutional guarantee of equal protection of the laws and must respectfully dissent. Our precedents, in my view, firmly establish that where, as here, state-imposed segregation has been demonstrated, it becomes the duty of the State to eliminate root and branch all vestiges of racial discrimination and to achieve the greatest possible degree of actual desegregation. . . .

The rights at issue in this case are too fundamental to be abridged on grounds as superficial as those relied on by the majority today. We deal here with the right of all of our children, whatever their race, to an equal start in life

and to an equal opportunity to reach their full potential as citizens. Those children who have been denied that right in the past deserve better than to see fences thrown up to deny them that right in the future. Our Nation, I fear, will be ill served by the Court's refusal to remedy separate and unequal education, for unless our children begin to learn together, there is little hope that our people will ever learn to live together.

Nor can it be said that the State is free from any responsibility for the disparity between the racial makeup of Detroit and its surrounding suburbs. The State's creation, through *de jure* acts of segregation, of a growing core of all-Negro schools inevitably acted as a magnet to attract Negroes . . . [and] inevitably helped drive whites to other areas of the city or to the suburbs. . . .

The State must also bear part of the blame for the white flight to the suburbs which would be forthcoming from a Detroit-only decree and would render such a remedy ineffective. . . . Indeed, by limiting the District Court to a Detroit-only remedy and allowing that flight to the suburbs to succeed, the Court today allows the State to profit from its own wrong and to perpetuate for years to come the separation of the races it achieved in the past by purposeful state action.

Desegregation is not and was never expected to be an easy task. Racial attitudes ingrained in our Nation's childhood and adolescence are not quickly thrown aside in its middle years. But just as the inconvenience of some cannot be allowed to stand in the way of the rights of others, so public opposition, no matter how strident, cannot be permitted to divert this Court from the enforcement of the constitutional principles at issue in this case. Today's holding, I fear, is more a reflection of a perceived public mood that we have gone far enough in enforcing the Constitution's guarantee of equal justice than it is the product of neutral principles of law. In the short run, it may seem to be the easier course to allow our great metropolitan areas to be divided up each into two cities—one white, the other black—but it is a course, I predict, our people will ultimately regret. I dissent.

Notes and Queries

1. In a second decision, *Milliken II*, 433 U.S. 267 (1977), the Supreme Court ruled that lower federal courts may "order remedial education programs as a part of a school desegregation decree," because the remedy is appropriate to the violation "if [it] is tailored to cure the '*condition*' that offends the Constitution." The Court ruled in response to a district court decision, following the remand in *Milliken*

I, that rejected busing in favor of extensive remedial education programs.

2. When *Milliken* was decided, nearly one-half of all nonwhite schoolchildren in the United States lived in the nation's thirty largest school districts, all of them urban. When you consider *Milliken* together with *San Antonio Independent School District v. Rodriguez* (1973, reprinted in chapter 15), is it really possible *ever* to have equal education for urban minorities? *Milliken* essentially means that you cannot have interdistrict remedies in most cases (owing to the difficulty of showing *de jure* discrimination in the suburbs), while *Rodriguez* says that virtually all-minority school districts do not have to be (indeed they are not) funded equally. Does this mean that we have reached the point of having separate (*Milliken*) and unequal (*Rodriguez*) schools?

3. What understanding of judicial power does the majority opinion use? Does the decision turn on the distinction between *de jure* and *de facto* discrimination? Or does it turn on respect for federalism and the importance of local control of public education?

4. Is *Milliken* faithful to the pith and substance of *Brown v. Board of Education*? Does it misconstrue *Brown*? What, in fact, did *Brown* rule? Did it rule that white children must go to school with black children in "desegregated" schools? Here is the Court saying that all-black schools are okay so long as the state takes measures that would bring the deprived black children up to where they would have been scholastically had it not been for a law-supported pattern of racial discrimination?

5. Justice Douglas argued that the Court's decision represented "a dramatic retreat" from *Plessy*. Do you agree?

6. In his dissent, Justice White argued that despite its importance, local control over education, "in the sense of the community's participation in the decisions affecting the education of its children," is less important a constitutional value than the mandate of equality. What reasons did Justice White offer to support that calculation? What reasons did the majority offer for rejecting his assessment?

7. Justice Marshall wrote in his dissent that the court's decision was "more a reflection of a perceived public mood" than "the product of neutral principles of law." Do you agree? Is there a neutral principle (see chapter 2) that could support the majority's conclusion? What neutral principle would support Justice Marshall's position?

The Civil Rights Cases
109 U.S. 3, 3 S. Ct. 18, 27 L. Ed. 2d 835 (1883)

The Court consolidated five cases that involved the Civil Rights Act of 1875, which made it a criminal misdemeanor to deny the enjoyment or use of hotels, public transportation and theaters on the basis of race. The defendants alleged that the Act was unconstitutional because it purported to prohibit private acts of discrimination as well as state-mandated discrimination. Opinion of the Court: *Bradley*, Waite, Field, Miller, Woods, Matthews, Gray, Blatchford. Dissenting opinion: *Harlan*.

Mr. Justice BRADLEY delivered the opinion of the Court.

These cases are all founded on the first and second sections of the act of congress known as the "Civil Rights Act," passed March 1, 1875, entitled "An act to protect all citizens in their civil and legal rights." . . .

. . . [I]t is the purpose of the law to declare that, in the enjoyment of the accommodations and privileges of inns, public conveyances, theaters, and other places of public amusement, no distinction shall be made between citizens of different race or color, or between those who have, and those who have not, been slaves. Its effect is to declare that in all inns, public conveyances, and places of amuse-ment, colored citizens, whether formerly slaves or not, and citizens of other races, shall have the same accommodations and privileges in all inns, public conveyances, and places of amusement, as are enjoyed by white citizens; and vice versa. The second section makes it a penal offense for any person to deny to any citizen of any race or color, regardless of previous servitude, any of the accommodations or privileges mentioned in the first section.

The first section of the Fourteenth Amendment—which is the one relied on—after declaring who shall be citizens of the United States, and of the several states, is prohibitory in its character, and prohibitory upon the States. . . .

It is State action of a particular character that is prohibited. Individual invasion of individual rights is not the subject-matter of the amendment. It has a deeper and broader scope. It nullifies and makes void all State legislation, and State action of every kind, which impairs the privileges and immunities of citizens of the United States, or which injures them in life, liberty, or property without due process of law, or which denies to any of them the equal protection of the laws. . . . [T]he last section of the amendment invests Congress with power to enforce it by appropriate legislation. To enforce what? To enforce the prohibition. To adopt appropriate legislation for correcting the effects of such prohibited State law and State acts, and thus to render them effectually null, void, and innocuous. This is

Comparative Note 14.3

[In this case the Supreme Court, Bophuthatswana Provincial Division, considered an action brought by four foreign nationals who had been denied promotion at the University of Bophuthatswana. They claimed that they had been discriminated against by virtue of their status as aliens, in violation of Section 8(2) of the 1993 South African Constitution (since replaced with the 1996 Constitution), which prohibited discrimination on the basis of social origin. Among the issues raised by the case was the question of whether the fundamental rights applied vertically, or only between the State and the individual, or also horizontally, between private entities. The following extracts are from the opinion by Justice Friedman.]

Friedman, JP:. . . .

(1) United States

In United States law, most of the protections for the individual rights and liberties enshrined in the Constitution apply only to the actions of governmental agencies. . . .

If the rights in terms of the Constitution are to be extended to private conduct "State action" is required.

(2) Germany

The position in Germany has been summarized as follows:

> The Bill of Rights in the basic law (Constitution) . . . as a general rule, has been held to have mediate (indirect), and not immediate (direct), *Drittwirkung*; that is to say, the restraints emanating from the constitutional rights and freedoms of the individual apply to the powers of governmental administration and legislation only and do not govern the rights and duties of a person in private law relations, but when interpreting all legislation, including acts regulating matters of private law, the Courts are required to take cognizance of the provisions of the Bill of Rights and as far as possible to give such legislation a meaning that coincides with the juridical values embodied in the Constitution.

(3) Canada

In the important case of *Retail, Wholesale and Department Store Union Local 580 v. Dolphin Delivery Ltd.* (1987) 33 DLR (4th) 174 the Canadian Supreme Court . . . found that the Charter did not apply, as the case involved private parties and there was no governmental action.

This decision has been severely criticised not only in Canada but in other countries as well as being contrary to the Spirit of the Charter.

(7) South Africa

In order to ascertain whether the fundamental rights . . . are to be applied vertically or horizontally or in both instances it is necessary to determine the intention of the framers of the Constitution.

The Constitution seeks to restructure the legal, social and economic order of this society and country. . . .

A mere cursory glance at these constitutional principles makes it clear that the object thereof is to safeguard and entrench the enshrined values of equality and freedom, and to protect the fundamental rights in terms of a justiciable bill of rights. . . .

The values contained in the constitutional principles . . . which are, as stated herein, "cast in stone," as well as those requiring national unity and reconciliation, point to an interpretation wider than a vertical one. The objectives of the Constitution in remodeling South African society and the body politic . . . embraces a wider application than the vertical dimension only. It is not only a question of the relationship between the State and the individual, but also between corporations, clubs, local authorities, educational institutions, etcetera and the individual. The horizontal application of the fundamental rights need to be applied to deal with inequalities and racial discrimination in society, and to advance, cause and develop a democratic society.

In considering the application of the fundamental rights, it is imperative that we think the provisions through to their factual consequences. . . . A vertical application means that the Constitution protects fundamental rights and freedoms only against invasion by the State and not from abuse by our neighbors and fellow citizens. Consequently private power remains relatively unbridled. . . . There is the provision in the constitution of equality before the law. At its minimum the Constitution commands evenhanded justice that forbids discrimination.

Source: *Baloro and Others v. University of Bophuthatswana and Others* (1995, BLCR 1018 B).

the legislative power conferred upon Congress, and this is the whole of it. . . .

And so in the present case, until some State law has been passed, or some State action through its officers or agents has been taken, adverse to the rights of citizens sought to be protected by the Fourteenth Amendment, no legislation of the United States under said Amendment, nor any proceeding under such legislation, can be called into activity, for the prohibitions of the amendment are against State laws and acts done under State authority. Of course, legislation may, and should be, provided in advance to meet the exigency when it arises; but it should be adapted to the mischief and wrong which the Amendment was intended to provide against; and that is, State laws, or State action of some kind, adverse to the rights of the citizen secured by the Amendment. Such legislation cannot properly cover the whole domain of rights appertaining to life, liberty and property, defining them and providing for their vindication. That would be to establish a code of municipal law regulative of all private rights between man and man in society. It would be to make Congress take the place of the State legislatures and to supersede them. . . .

An inspection of the law shows that it makes no reference whatever to any supposed or apprehended violation of the Fourteenth Amendment on the part of the States. It is not predicated on any such view. It proceeds *ex directo* to declare that certain acts committed by individuals shall be deemed offenses, and shall be prosecuted and punished by proceedings in the courts of the United States. It does not profess to be corrective of any constitutional wrong committed by the States; it does not make its operation to depend upon any such wrong committed. . . . In other words, it steps into the domain of local jurisprudence, and lays down rules for the conduct of individuals in society towards each other, and imposes sanctions for the enforcement of those rules, without referring in any manner to any supposed action of the state or its authorities.

If this legislation is appropriate for enforcing the prohibitions of the Amendment, it is difficult to see where it is to stop. Why may not Congress, with equal show of authority, enact a code of laws for the enforcement and vindication of all rights of life, liberty, and property? If it is supposable that the States may deprive persons of life, liberty, and property without due process of law, (and the Amendment itself does suppose this) why should not Congress proceed at once to prescribe due process of law for the protection of every one of these fundamental rights, in every possible case, as well as to prescribe equal privileges in inns, public conveyances, and theaters. The truth is that the implication of a power to legislate in this manner is based upon the assumption that if the States are forbidden to legislate or act in a particular way on a particular subject, and power is conferred upon Congress to enforce the prohibition, this gives Congress power to legislate generally upon that subject, and not merely power to provide modes of redress against such State legislation or action. The assumption is certainly unsound. It is repugnant to the Tenth Amendment of the Constitution, which declares that powers not delegated to the United States by the Constitution, nor prohibited by it to the States, are reserved to the states respectively or to the people.

. . . The wrongful act of an individual, unsupported by any such authority, is simply a private wrong, or a crime of that individual; an invasion of the rights of the injured party, it is true, whether they affect his person, his property, or his reputation; but if not sanctioned in some way by the State, or not done under State authority, his rights remain in full force, and may presumably be vindicated by resort to the laws of the State for redress. . . .

If the principles of interpretation which we have laid down are correct, as we deem them to be . . . it is clear that the law in question cannot be sustained by any grant of legislative power made to Congress by the Fourteenth Amendment. . . .

But the power of Congress to adopt direct and primary, as distinguished from corrective, legislation on the subject in hand, is sought, in the second place, from the Thirteenth Amendment, which abolishes slavery. This Amendment declares "that neither slavery, nor involuntary servitude, except as a punishment for crime, whereof the party shall have been duly convicted, shall exist within the United States, or any place subject to their jurisdiction"; and it gives congress power to enforce the amendment by appropriate legislation. . . .

. . . And such legislation may be primary and direct in its character; for the amendment is not a mere prohibition of state laws establishing or upholding slavery, but an absolute declaration that slavery or involuntary servitude shall not exist in any part of the United States.

. . . Conceding the major proposition to be true, that congress has a right to enact all necessary and proper laws for the obliteration and prevention of slavery, with all its badges and incidents, is the minor proposition also true, that the denial to any person of admission to the accommodations and privileges of an inn, a public conveyance, or a theater, does subject that person to any form of servitude, or tend to fasten upon him any badge of slavery? If it does not, then power to pass the law is not found in the Thirteenth Amendment.

The long existence of African slavery in this country

gave us very distinct notions of what it was, and what were its necessary incidents. Compulsory service of the slave for the benefit of the master, restraint of his movements except by the master's will, disability to hold property, to make contracts, to have a standing in court, to be a witness against a white person, and such like burdens and incapacities were the inseparable incidents of the institution. Severer punishments for crimes were imposed on the slave than on free persons guilty of the same offenses. Congress, as we have seen, by the Civil Rights Bill of 1866, passed in view of the Thirteenth Amendment, before the fourteenth was adopted, undertook to wipe out these burdens and disabilities, the necessary incidents of slavery. . . . [A]t that time . . . Congress did not assume, under the authority given by the Thirteenth Amendment, to adjust what may be called the social rights of men and races in the community; but only to declare and vindicate those fundamental rights which appertain to the essence of citizenship, and the enjoyment or deprivation of which constitutes the essential distinction between freedom and slavery.

. . . Can the act of a mere individual, the owner of the inn, the public conveyance, or place of amusement, refusing the accommodation, be justly regarded as imposing any badge of slavery or servitude upon the applicant, or only as inflicting an ordinary civil injury, properly cognizable by the laws of the State, and presumably subject to redress by those laws until the contrary appears?

After giving to these questions all the consideration which their importance demands, we are forced to the conclusion that such an act of refusal has nothing to do with slavery or involuntary servitude, and that if it is violative of any right of the party, his redress is to be sought under the laws of the State; or, if those laws are adverse to his rights and do not protect him, his remedy will be found in the corrective legislation which Congress has adopted, or may adopt, for counteracting the effect of State laws, or State action, prohibited by the Fourteenth Amendment. It would be running the slavery argument into the ground to make it apply to every act of discrimination which a person may see fit . . .

When a man has emerged from slavery, and by the aid of beneficent legislation has shaken off the inseparable concomitants of that state, there must be some stage in the progress of his elevation when he takes the rank of a mere citizen, and ceases to be the special favorite of the laws, and when his rights as a citizen, or a man, are to be protected in the ordinary modes by which other men's rights are protected. There were thousands of free colored people in this country before the abolition of slavery, enjoying all the essential rights of life, liberty, and property the same as white citizens; yet no one, at that time, thought that it was any invasion of their personal status as freemen because they were not admitted to all the privileges enjoyed by white citizens, or because they were subjected to discriminations in the enjoyment of accommodations in inns, public conveyances, and places of amusement. Mere discriminations on account of race or color were not regarded as badges of slavery. If, since that time, the enjoyment of equal rights in all these respects has become established by constitutional enactment, it is not by force of the Thirteenth Amendment, (which merely abolishes slavery) but by force of the Fourteenth and Fifteenth Amendments.

On the whole, we are of opinion that no countenance of authority for the passage of the law in question can be found in either the Thirteenth or Fourteenth Amendment of the Constitution; and no other ground of authority for its passage being suggested, it must necessarily be declared void, at least so far as its operation in the several states is concerned.

Mr. Justice HARLAN dissenting.

The opinion in these cases proceeds, it seems to me, upon grounds entirely too narrow and artificial. The substance and spirit of the recent amendments of the Constitution have been sacrificed by a subtle and ingenious verbal criticism. . . .

. . . I do not contend that the Thirteenth Amendment invests congress with authority, by legislation, to regulate the entire body of the civil rights which citizens enjoy, or may enjoy, in the several States. But I do hold that since slavery, as the court has repeatedly declared, was the moving or principal cause of the adoption of that Amendment, and since that institution rested wholly upon the inferiority, as a race, of those held in bondage, their freedom necessarily involved immunity from, and protection against, all discrimination against them, because of their race, in respect of such civil rights as belong to freemen of other races. Congress, therefore, under its express power to enforce that Amendment, by appropriate legislation, may enact laws to protect that people against the deprivation, on account of their race, of any civil rights enjoyed by other freemen in the same State; and such legislation may be of a direct and primary character, operating upon states, their officers and agents, and also upon, at least, such individuals and corporations as exercise public functions and wield power and authority under the State.

. . . [Congress] does not . . . assume to prescribe the general conditions and limitations under which inns, public conveyances, and places of public amusement shall be conducted or managed. It simply declares in effect that since the nation has established universal freedom in this country for all time, there shall be no discrimination, based merely upon race or color, in respect of the legal rights in the accommodations and advantages of public conveyances, inns, and places of public amusement.

I am of opinion that such discrimination . . . is a badge of servitude, the imposition of which Congress may prevent under its power, through appropriate legislation, to enforce the Thirteenth Amendment; and consequently, without reference to its enlarged power under the Fourteenth Amendment, the [Civil Rights Act of 1875] is not, in my judgment, repugnant to the Constitution.

It remains now to consider these cases with reference to the power Congress has possessed since the adoption of the Fourteenth Amendment. . . .

. . . [W]hat was secured to colored citizens of the United States—as between them and their respective states—by the grant to them of State citizenship? With what rights, privileges, or immunities did this grant from the nation invest them? There is one, if there be no others— exemption from race discrimination in respect of any civil right belonging to citizens of the white race in the same State. That, surely, is their constitutional privilege when within the jurisdiction of other States. And such must be their constitutional right, in their own State, unless the recent amendments be "splendid baubles," thrown out to delude those who deserved fair and generous treatment at the hands of the nation. Citizenship in this country necessarily imports equality of civil rights among citizens of every race in the same State. It is fundamental in American citizenship that, in respect of such rights, there shall be no discrimination by the State, or its officers, or by individuals, or corporations exercising public functions or authority, against any citizen because of his race or previous condition of servitude. . . .

If, then, exemption from discrimination in respect of civil rights is a new constitutional right, secured by the grant of State citizenship to colored citizens of the United States, why may not the nation, by means of its own legislation of a primary direct character, guard, protect, and enforce that right? It is a right and privilege which the Nation conferred. It did not come from the States in which those colored citizens reside. It has been the established doctrine of this court during all its history, accepted as vital to the national supremacy, that Congress, in the absence of a positive delegation of power to the State Legislatures, may by legislation enforce and protect any right derived from or created by the National Constitution. . . .

It was said of the case of *Dred Scott v. Sandford* that this court in that case overruled the action of two generations,

virtually inserted a new clause in the Constitution, changed its character, and made a new departure in the workings of the Federal Government. I may be permitted to say that if the recent Amendments are so construed that Congress may not, in its own discretion, and independently of the action or non-action of the States, provide, by legislation of a primary and direct character, for the security of rights created by the National Constitution; if it be adjudged that the obligation to protect the fundamental privileges and immunities granted by the Fourteenth Amendment to citizens residing in the several States, rests, primarily, not on the Nation, but on the States; if it be further adjudged that individuals and corporations exercising public functions may, without liability to direct primary legislation on the part of Congress, make the race of citizens the ground for denying them that equality of civil rights which the Constitution ordains as a principle of republican citizenship,—then, not only the foundations upon which the national supremacy has always securely rested will be materially disturbed, but we shall enter upon an era of constitutional law, when the rights of freedom and American citizenship cannot receive from the nation that efficient protection which heretofore was accorded to slavery and the rights of the master.

. . . I agree that government has nothing to do with social, as distinguished from technically legal, rights of individuals. No government ever has brought, or ever can bring, its people into social intercourse against their wishes. . . . What I affirm is that no State, nor the officers of any State, nor any corporation or individual wielding power under State authority for the public benefit or the public convenience, can, consistently either with the freedom established by the fundamental law, or with that equality of civil rights which now belongs to every citizen, discriminate against freemen or citizens, in their civil rights, because of their race, or because they once labored under disabilities imposed upon them as a race. The rights which Congress, by the act of 1875, endeavored to secure and protect are legal, not social, rights. . . .

My brethren say that when a man has emerged from slavery, and by the aid of beneficent legislation has shaken off the inseparable concomitants of that state, there must be some stage in the progress of his elevation when he takes the rank of a mere citizen, and ceases to be the special favorite of the laws, and when his rights as a citizen, or a man, are to be protected in the ordinary modes by which other men's rights are protected. It is, I submit, scarcely just to say that the colored race has been the special favorite of the laws. What the nation, through Congress, has sought to accomplish in reference to that race is, what had already been done in every State in the Union for the white race, to secure and protect rights belonging to them as freemen and citizens; nothing more.

The one underlying purpose of congressional legislation has been to enable the black race to take the rank of mere citizens. The difficulty has been to compel a recognition of their legal right to take that rank, and to secure the enjoyment of privileges belonging, under the law, to them as a component part of the people for whose welfare and happiness government is ordained. At every step in this direction the nation has been confronted with class tyranny. . . . If the constitutional amendments be enforced, according to the intent with which, as I conceive, they were adopted, there cannot be, in this republic, any class of human beings in practical subjection to another class, with power in the latter to dole out to the former just such privileges as they may choose to grant. . . .

For the reasons stated I feel constrained to withhold my assent to the opinion of the court.

Notes and Queries

1. The Civil War signalled momentous changes in the constitutional order of the United States. The Reconstruction Amendments were the most obvious of those changes, reflecting a renewed commitment to the protection of human equality and the abolition of racial discrimination by law. As we saw in the introduction, however, the Reconstruction Amendments also represented a fundamental revolution in the relationship between the states and the federal government. The enforcement powers granted to Congress in the new amendments envisioned a dramatic and ongoing role for the federal government in supervising the states.

In the *Civil Rights Cases* the Court voiced its discomfort with the nationalizing trends that both caused and were accelerated by the Reconstruction Amendments. Hence, the Court's narrow interpretation of the Thirteenth Amendment was premised upon its insistence that the Amendment could not have meant to empower Congress to act on subjects "which are within the domain of state legislation. . . . It does not authorize Congress to create a code of municipal law for regulation of private rights."

Assume that the Court understood the revolutionary change that the Reconstruction Amendments effected in the relationship between the states and the national government. Was it obligated to give full effect to the Amendments as reflecting the will of the sovereign people as represented by Congress? Can we imagine a situation in which the Court should not give effect to a constitutional amendment properly passed, perhaps because the amendment is fundamentally incompatible with the overarching constitutional order? Consider the opinion of the German Federal Constitutional Court in the *Southwest Case* (1951):

An individual constitutional provision cannot be considered as an isolated clause and interpreted alone. A constitution has an inner unity, and the meaning of any one part is linked to that of other provisions. Taken as a unit, a constitution reflects certain overarching principles and fundamental decisions to which individual provisions are subordinate. . . . [I]t follows that any constitutional provision must be interpreted in such a way that it is compatible with those elementary principles and with the basic decisions of the framers of the Constitution.

What assumptions does this make about judicial power? About the relationship between constitutionalism and democracy? How does the Court's opinion in the *Southwest Case* differ, if at all, from the approach the Supreme Court used in the *Civil Rights Cases*?

2. The Court insisted that the Fourteenth Amendment does not touch "private" acts of racial discrimination, but is instead limited to "state action." The distinction may seem obvious at first glance, but as Justice Harlan's dissent should make clear, it is not always so easy to distinguish between "purely private" acts of racial discrimination and state action. In *The Civil Rights Cases*, for example, states had used their substantial police powers to promote the development of railroads. Was it so clear that discrimination by the railroads was entirely private? Could not the state have used its substantial resources to entice railroads into nondiscrimination?

As we saw in the introduction, the Court has developed an elaborate and sometimes confusing jurisprudence to determine when the presence of the state is sufficiently "close" to private discrimination to satisfy the state action requirement. At no time, however, has the Court seriously reconsidered the desirability or necessity of the state action requirement itself. This might be unfortunate, for two reasons. First, in practical terms, of course, the doctrine sanctioned, if it did not encourage, "an enormous network of racial exclusion and humiliation, characterizing both North and South." "State Action," by Charles L. Black, Jr., in *Civil Rights and Equality*. Introduction by Kenneth L. Karst (New York: Macmillan Publishing Co., 1989), 47. Second, and at a more abstract level, the state action doctrine demonstrates the vagueness of concepts central to the liberal constitutional state, such as the distinction between state and society, as well as between the public and private spheres. The integrity of these distinctions is essential to liberal constitutionalism; the state action doctrine shows us how difficult it can be to give practical effect and meaning to those concepts.

Shelley v. Kraemer
334 U.S. 1, 68 S. Ct. 836, 92 L. Ed. 1161 (1948)

The Shelleys, an African-American family, purchased a home in St. Louis in 1945. However, thirty out of the thirty-nine residents in the Shelley's new neighborhood had signed and recorded an agreement restricting the sale of property in the vicinity to white families. Such agreements, known formally as "restrictive covenants" and informally as "whites only clauses," were common throughout the country. Some of the property owners brought this suit when the Shelleys bought the house. The Supreme Court of Missouri upheld the restrictive covenant. A similar case arose in Michigan and the Michigan Supreme Court upheld the restrictive agreement as well. Opinion of the Court: *Vinson*, Black, Burton, Douglas, Frankfurter, Murphy. Not participating: Jackson, Reed, Rutledge.

Mr. Chief Justice VINSON delivered the opinion of the Court.

These cases present for our consideration questions relating to the validity of court enforcement of private agreements, generally described as restrictive covenants, which have as their purpose the exclusion of persons of designated race or color from the ownership or occupancy of real property. . . .

It is well, at the outset, to scrutinize the terms of the restrictive agreements involved in these cases. In the Missouri case, the covenant declares that no part of the affected property shall be "occupied by any person not of the Caucasian race, it being intended hereby to restrict the use of said property . . . against the occupancy as owners or tenants of any portion of said property for resident or other purpose by people of the Negro or Mongolian Race." Not only does the restriction seek to proscribe use and occupancy of the affected properties by members of the excluded class, but as construed by the Missouri courts, the agreement requires that title of any person who uses his property in violation of the restriction shall be divested. The restriction of the covenant in the Michigan case seeks to bar occupancy by persons of the excluded class. It provides that "[t]his property shall not be used or occupied by any person or persons except those of the Caucasian race."

It should be observed that these covenants do not seek to proscribe any particular use of the affected properties. Use of the properties for residential occupancy, as such, is not forbidden. The restrictions of these agreements, rather, are directed toward a designated class of persons and seek to determine who may and who may not own or make use of the properties for residential purposes. The excluded class is defined wholly in terms of race or color; "simply that and nothing more."

It cannot be doubted that among the civil rights intended to be protected from discriminatory state action by the Fourteenth Amendment are the rights to acquire, enjoy, own and dispose of property. Equality in the enjoyment of property rights was regarded by the framers of that Amendment as an essential pre-condition to the realization of other basic civil rights and liberties which the Amendment was intended to guarantee. . . .

It is likewise clear that restrictions on the right of occupancy of the sort sought to be created by the private agreements in these cases could not be squared with the requirements of the Fourteenth Amendment if imposed by state statute or local ordinance. . . .

But the present cases . . . do not involve action by state legislatures or city councils. Here the particular patterns of discrimination and the areas in which the restrictions are to operate, are determined, in the first instance, by the terms of agreements among private individuals. Participation of the State consists in the enforcement of the restrictions so defined. The crucial issue with which we are here confronted is whether this distinction removes these cases from the operation of the prohibitory provisions of the Fourteenth Amendment.

Since the decision of this Court in the *Civil Rights Cases* (1883), the principle has become firmly embedded in our constitutional law that the action inhibited by the first section of the Fourteenth Amendment is only such action as may fairly be said to be that of the States. That Amendment erects no shield against merely private conduct, however discriminatory or wrongful.

We conclude, therefore, that the restrictive agreements standing alone cannot be regarded as a violation of any rights guaranteed to petitioners by the Fourteenth Amendment. So long as the purposes of those agreements are effectuated by voluntary adherence to their terms, it would appear clear that there has been no action by the State and the provisions of the Amendment have not been violated.

But here there was more. These are cases in which the purposes of the agreements were secured only by judicial enforcement by state courts of the restrictive terms of the agreements. The respondents urge that judicial enforcement of private agreements does not amount to state action; or, in any event, the participation of the State is so attenuated in character as not to amount to state action within the meaning of the Fourteenth Amendment. Finally, it is suggested, even if the States in these cases may be deemed to have acted in the constitutional sense, their action did not deprive petitioners of rights guaranteed by the Fourteenth Amendment. We move to a consideration of these matters.

That the action of state courts and of judicial officers in their official capacities is to be regarded as action of the State within the meaning of the Fourteenth Amendment, is a proposition which has long been established by decisions of this Court. . . .

The short of the matter is that from the time of the adoption of the Fourteenth Amendment until the present, it has been the consistent ruling of this Court that the action of the States to which the Amendment has reference, includes action of state courts and state judicial officials. Although, in construing the terms of the Fourteenth Amendment, differences have from time to time been expressed as to whether particular types of state action may be said to offend the Amendment's prohibitory provisions, it has never been suggested that state court action is immunized from the operation of those provisions simply because the act is that of the judicial branch of the state government. . . .

We have no doubt that there has been state action in these cases in the full and complete sense of the phrase. The undisputed facts disclose that petitioners were willing purchasers of properties upon which they desired to establish homes. The owners of the properties were willing sellers; and contracts of sale were accordingly consummated. It is clear that but for the active intervention of the state courts, supported by the full panoply of state power, petitioners would have been free to occupy the properties in question without restraint.

These are not cases, as has been suggested, in which the States have merely abstained from action, leaving private individuals free to impose such discriminations as they see fit. Rather, these are cases in which the States have made available to such individuals the full coercive power of government to deny to petitioners, on the grounds of race or color, the enjoyment of property rights in premises which petitioners are willing and financially able to acquire and which the grantors are willing to sell. The difference between judicial enforcement and nonenforcement of the restrictive covenants is the difference to petitioners between being denied rights of property available to other members of the community and being accorded full enjoyment of those rights on an equal footing.

The enforcement of the restrictive agreements by the state courts in these cases was directed pursuant to the common-law policy of the States as formulated by those courts in earlier decisions. . . . We have noted that previous decisions of this Court have established the proposition that judicial action is not immunized from the operation of the Fourteenth Amendment simply because it is taken pursuant to the state's common-law policy. Nor is the Amendment ineffective simply because the particular pattern of discrimination, which the State has enforced, was defined initially by the terms of a private agreement. State action, as that phrase is understood for the purposes of the Fourteenth Amendment, refers to exertions of state power in all forms. And when the effect of that action is to deny rights subject to the protection of the Fourteenth Amendment, it is the obligation of this Court to enforce the constitutional commands.

We hold that in granting judicial enforcement of the restrictive agreements in these cases, the States have denied petitioners the equal protection of the laws and that, therefore, the action of the state courts cannot stand. . . .

Respondents urge, however, that since the state courts stand ready to enforce restrictive covenants excluding white persons from the ownership or occupancy of property covered by such agreements, enforcement of covenants excluding colored persons may not be deemed a denial of equal protection of the laws to the colored persons who are thereby affected. This contention does not bear scrutiny. The parties have directed our attention to no case in which a court, state or federal, has been called upon to enforce a covenant excluding members of the white majority from ownership or occupancy of real property on grounds of race or color. But there are more fundamental considerations. The rights created by the first section of the Fourteenth Amendment are, by its terms, guaranteed to the individual. The rights established are personal rights. It is, therefore, no answer to these petitioners to say that the courts may also be induced to deny white persons rights of ownership and occupancy on grounds of race or color. Equal protection of the laws is not achieved through indiscriminate imposition of inequalities. . . .

The historical context in which the Fourteenth Amendment became a part of the Constitution should not be forgotten. Whatever else the framers sought to achieve, it is clear that the matter of primary concern was the establishment of equality in the enjoyment of basic civil and political rights and the preservation of those rights from discriminatory action on the part of the States based on considerations of race or color. Seventy-five years ago this Court announced that the provisions of the Amendment are to be construed with this fundamental purpose in mind. Upon full consideration, we have concluded that in these cases the States have acted to deny petitioners the equal protection of the laws guaranteed by the Fourteenth

Amendment. Having so decided, we find it unnecessary to consider whether petitioners have also been deprived of property without due process of law or denied privileges and immunities of citizens of the United States.

For the reasons stated, the judgment of the Supreme Court of Missouri and the judgment of the Supreme Court of Michigan must be reversed.

Mr. Justice REED, Mr. Justice JACKSON, and Mr. Justice RUTLEDGE took no part in the consideration or decision of these cases.

Notes and Queries

1. Restrictive racial covenants were common not only in the southern United States, but also in the North. For many years, they proved an effective way to maintain discrimination in housing, even though the Civil Rights Act of 1866 guaranteed minorities the right to purchase and sell property. A presidential commission studying the effects of restrictive covenants concluded just a few months before *Shelley* that the practice had hampered federal efforts to clean up urban slums.

2. *Shelley*, like the *Civil Rights Cases*, raises important state action issues. What acts of private discrimination, if any, do not ultimately depend upon some sort of support—or toleration—by the state? Consider the following: Should a homeowner be permitted to keep people off his property for any reason at all, including a person's race? If so—and remember such a decision might be protected by the First Amendment's freedom of association—then may the homeowner avail himself of the help of the police if the person refuses to leave? May a business owner exclude whomever he or she wants from the business, for any reason, including race? See *Bell v. Maryland* (1964). You may recall that one of the aims of the state action doctrine is to protect individual autonomy by carving out a sphere of life free from state regulation. How are we to balance the desire for autonomy with our commitment to equality? Consider the following conclusion by Henkin, "If the competing claims of liberty and the possibility that they may sometimes prevail are recognized, [*Shelley*] must be given a limited reading. . . . [T]here are circumstances where the discriminator can invoke a protected liberty which is not constitutionally inferior to the claim of equal protection." What might those circumstances be?

3. For nearly two decades following *Shelley*, the Court found state action in every case where it was at issue. In *Evans v. Abney* (1970), however, the Burger Court found no state action in a decision to return land to the donors, who had given the land to the city in a will with the proviso that the land, to be used as a public park, could be used by whites only. And in *Palmer v. Thompson* (1971), a majority upheld a decision by the city of Jackson, Mississippi, to close (instead of desegregating) its public swimming pools.

4. Only six justices heard this case. Justices Jackson, Reed, and Rutledge recused themselves, probably because each owned property that included a restrictive covenant. The issue surfaced again many years later, when Senate hearings on the promotion of Justice Rehnquist to Chief Justice disclosed that Rehnquist also owned property with a restrictive covenant.

Palmore v. Sidoti

466 U.S. 429, 104 S. Ct. 1829, 80 L. Ed. 2d 421 (1984)

Linda and Anthony Sidoti, a white couple, were divorced in 1980; Linda was awarded custody of their 3-year-old daughter. In 1981, Linda married Clarence Palmore Jr., an African American man, whereupon Anthony Sidoti sued for custody of his daughter. Although Anthony had made several allegations of instances in which his daughter had not properly been cared for, the Florida court found them to be unsubstantiated. Nevertheless, the court concluded that it would serve the child's best interests by awarding custody to Anthony, stating that Linda had chosen a lifestyle for herself and her child that was unacceptable to both Anthony and to society. Although Anthony's resentment of Linda's choice to marry interracially was not enough to award him custody, the court found that Linda's daughter would suffer social stigmatization if she remained with Linda and Clarence: "This Court feels that despite the strides that have been made in bettering relations between the races in this country, it is inevitable that . . . [the child] will, if allowed to remain in her present situation and attain school age . . . be more vulnerable to peer pressures, [and] suffer from the social stigmatization that is sure to come." Opinion of the Court: *Burger*, Blackmun, Brennan, Marshall, O'Connor, Powell, Rehnquist, Stevens, White.

Chief Justice BURGER delivered the opinion of the Court.

The judgment of a state court determining or reviewing a child custody decision is not ordinarily a likely candidate for review by this Court. However, the court's opinion, after stating that the "father's evident resentment of the mother's choice of a black partner is not sufficient" to deprive her of custody, then turns to what it regarded as the damaging impact on the child from remaining in a racially-mixed household. This raises important federal concerns arising from the Constitution's commitment to eradicating discrimination based on race.

The Florida court did not focus directly on the parental qualifications of the natural mother or her present husband, or indeed on the father's qualifications to have custody of the child. The court found that "there is no issue as to either party's devotion to the child, adequacy of housing facilities, or respect[a]bility of the new spouse of either parent." This, taken with the absence of any negative finding as to the quality of the care provided by the mother, constitutes a rejection of any claim of petitioner's unfitness to continue the custody of her child.

The court correctly stated that the child's welfare was the controlling factor. But that court was entirely candid and made no effort to place its holding on any ground other than race. Taking the court's findings and rationale at face value, it is clear that the outcome would have been different had petitioner married a Caucasian male of similar respectability.

A core purpose of the Fourteenth Amendment was to do away with all governmentally-imposed discrimination based on race. Classifying persons according to their race is more likely to reflect racial prejudice than legitimate public concerns; the race, not the person, dictates the category. Such classifications are subject to the most exacting scrutiny; to pass constitutional muster, they must be justified by a compelling governmental interest and must be "necessary . . . to the accomplishment" of its legitimate purpose.

The State, of course, has a duty of the highest order to protect the interests of minor children, particularly those of tender years. In common with most states, Florida law mandates that custody determinations be made in the best interests of the children involved. The goal of granting custody based on the best interests of the child is indisputably a substantial governmental interest for purposes of the Equal Protection Clause.

It would ignore reality to suggest that racial and ethnic prejudices do not exist or that all manifestations of those prejudices have been eliminated. There is a risk that a child living with a step-parent of a different race may be subject to a variety of pressures and stresses not present if the child were living with parents of the same racial or ethnic origin.

The question, however, is whether the reality of private biases and the possible injury they might inflict are permissible considerations for removal of an infant child from the custody of its natural mother. We have little difficulty concluding that they are not. The Constitution cannot control such prejudices but neither can it tolerate them. Private biases may be outside the reach of the law, but the law cannot, directly or indirectly, give them effect. "Public officials sworn to uphold the Constitution may not avoid a constitutional duty by bowing to the hypothetical effects of private racial prejudice that they assume to be both widely and deeply held."

This is by no means the first time that acknowledged racial prejudice has been invoked to justify racial classifications. In *Buchanan v. Warley* (1917), for example, this Court invalidated a Kentucky law forbidding Negroes from buying homes in white neighborhoods.

It is urged that this proposed segregation will promote the public peace by preventing race conflicts. Desirable as this is, and important as is the preservation of the public peace, this aim cannot be accomplished by laws or ordinances which deny rights created or protected by the Federal Constitution.

Whatever problems racially-mixed households may pose for children in 1984 can no more support a denial of constitutional rights than could the stresses that residential integration was thought to entail in 1917. The effects of racial prejudice, however real, cannot justify a racial classification removing an infant child from the custody of its natural mother found to be an appropriate person to have such custody.

The judgment of the District Court of Appeal is reversed.

It is so ordered.

Notes and Queries

1. Is the nature of "state action" in *Sidoti* different from that found in *Shelley*? (After all, psychological harm was a major consideration in *Brown v. Board of Education*.)

2. Contrast *Palmore* with *Brown* and *Shelley*. What if the father's counsel had been able to demonstrate to the Court that detailed empirical studies demonstrated that children who grow up in mixed race households suffer psychological harm? Or imagine a situation where a white couple's decision to adopt an African-American child was set aside on the grounds that minority children should be placed with adoptive parents of their own race? Such was the position adopted by the Black Association of Child Welfare Workers in 1972. Would a state law reflecting that position survive constitutional scrutiny?

Regents of the University of California v. Bakke

438 U.S. 265, 98 S. Ct. 2733, 57 L. Ed. 2d 750 (1978)

The Medical School at the University of California-Davis had two separate admissions programs—one for regular admissions and one for special admissions. The regular admissions track required a candidate to have a minimum of a 2.5 GPA or the school would not consider the application. Then, after evaluating the candidate's MCAT score, letters of recommendation and extracurricular activities, along with the candidate's performance in an interview with the admissions committee, the candidate was either accepted or rejected. The special admissions program, on the other hand, asked on the application whether the candidate wished to be considered "economically and/or educationally disadvantaged" and was a member of a "minority group." If an applicant met these two qualifications, he or she would be rated in a similar manner as the regular group but were not mandated to meet the 2.5 GPA requirement and were not ranked against candidates in the general admissions program. In 1973 and 1974, the faculty committee set the number of special admissions at 16, thereby making 16 seats in the first-year class unavailable to white applicants. Alan Bakke was a white candidate for the entering class of both 1973 and 1974. Despite high MCAT scores, he was rejected for admission. In both years, special applicants were admitted with significantly lower scores. After his second rejection, he brought this action claiming the admissions program excluded him based on his race in violation of the Equal Protection Clause. Judgment of the Court: *Powell.* Concurring in part and dissenting in part: *Brennan*, Blackmun, Marshall, White. Concurring in part and dissenting in part: *Stevens*, Burger, Rehnquist, Stewart.

Mr. Justice POWELL announced the judgment of the Court.

. . . It is settled beyond question that the "rights created by the first section of the Fourteenth Amendment are, by its terms, guaranteed to the individual. The rights established are personal rights." The guarantee of equal protection cannot mean one thing when applied to one individual and something else when applied to a person of another color. If both are not accorded the same protection, then it is not equal.

Nevertheless, petitioner argues that the court below erred in applying strict scrutiny to the special admissions program because white males . . . are not a "discrete and insular minority" requiring extraordinary protection from the majoritarian political process. This rationale, however, has never been invoked in our decisions as a prerequisite to subjecting racial or ethnic distinctions to strict scrutiny. Nor has this Court held that discreteness and insularity constitute necessary preconditions to a holding that a particular classification is invidious. These characteristics may be relevant in deciding whether or not to add new types of classifications to the list of "suspect" categories or whether a particular classification survives close examination. Racial and ethnic classifications, however, are subject to stringent examination without regard to these additional characteristics. *Korematsu v. United States* (1944).

Although many of the Framers of the Fourteenth Amendment conceived of its primary function as bridging the vast distance between members of the Negro race and the white "majority," the Amendment itself was framed in universal terms, without reference to color, ethnic origin, or condition of prior servitude. As this Court recently remarked in interpreting the 1866 Civil Rights Act to extend to claims of racial discrimination against white persons, "the 39th Congress was intent upon establishing in the federal law a broader principle than would have been necessary simply to meet the particular and immediate plight of the newly freed Negro slaves." And that legislation was specifically broadened in 1870 to ensure that "all persons," not merely "citizens," would enjoy equal rights under the law. Indeed, it is not unlikely that among the Framers were many who would have applauded a reading of the Equal Protection Clause that states a principle of universal application and is responsive to the racial, ethnic, and cultural diversity of the Nation.

Petitioner urges us to adopt for the first time a more restrictive view of the Equal Protection Clause and hold that discrimination against members of the white "majority" cannot be suspect if its purpose can be characterized as "benign." The clock of our liberties, however, cannot be turned back to 1868. It is far too late to argue that the guarantee of equal protection to all persons permits the recognition of special wards entitled to a degree of protection greater than that accorded others. "The Fourteenth Amendment is not directed solely against discrimination due to a 'two-class theory'—that is, based upon differences between 'white' and Negro."

Once the artificial line of a "two-class theory" of the Fourteenth Amendment is put aside, the difficulties entailed in varying the level of judicial review according to a perceived "preferred" status of a particular racial or ethnic minority are intractable. The concepts of "majority" and "minority" necessarily reflect temporary arrangements and

Comparative Note 14.4

[Section 15 (1) of the Canadian Charter of Rights and Freedoms provides: "Every individual is equal before and under the law and has the right to the equal protection and equal benefit of the law without discrimination based on race, national or ethnic origin, colour, religion, sex, age or mental or physical disability." Section 15 (2) declares: "Subsection (1) does not preclude any law, program or activity that has as its object the amelioration of conditions of disadvantaged individuals or groups including those that are disadvantaged because of race, national or ethnic origin, colour, religion, sex, age or mental or physical disability."]

. . . [T]he text of s. 15 offered some clues to its scope that were missing from its counterparts in the Canadian Bill of Rights and the [U.S.] fourteenth amendment. The listed grounds of "race, national or ethnic origin, colour, religion, sex, age or mental or physical disability" pointed to personal characteristics of individuals which could not be changed (or could not easily be changed),

and which have often been the targets of prejudice and stereotyping. The reference in subsection (2) (the affirmative action clause) to "disadvantaged individuals or groups" suggested that the role of s. 15 was to correct discrimination against disadvantaged individuals or groups. These references suggested that the purpose of s. 15 was not to eliminate all unfairness from our laws, let alone all classifications that could not be rationally defended, but rather to eliminate discrimination based on immutable personal characteristics. These considerations led the Court in *Andrews* to interpret s. 15 as a prohibition of discrimination, and to define discrimination as disadvantage caused by the classifications listed in s. 15 and analogous classifications. This has the merit of avoiding any inquiry into the abstract concept of equality, and the further merit of excluding from equality review those statutes that do not employ the listed classifications, or analogous classifications.

SOURCE: Hogg, *Constitutional Law of Canada*, 4th ed. (1997), 1244.

---

political judgments. As observed above, the white "majority" itself is composed of various minority groups, most of which can lay claim to a history of prior discrimination at the hands of the State and private individuals. Not all of these groups can receive preferential treatment and corresponding judicial tolerance of distinctions drawn in terms of race and nationality, for then the only "majority" left would be a new minority of white Anglo-Saxon Protestants. There is no principled basis for deciding which groups would merit "heightened judicial solicitude" and which would not. Courts would be asked to evaluate the extent of the prejudice and consequent harm suffered by various minority groups. Those whose societal injury is thought to exceed some arbitrary level of tolerability then would be entitled to preferential classifications at the expense of individuals belonging to other groups. Those classifications would be free from exacting judicial scrutiny. As these preferences began to have their desired effect, and the consequences of past discrimination were undone, new judicial rankings would be necessary. The kind of variable sociological and political analysis necessary to produce such rankings simply does not lie within the judicial competence—even if they otherwise were politically feasible and socially desirable.

Moreover, there are serious problems of justice con-

nected with the idea of preference itself. First, it may not always be clear that a so-called preference is in fact benign. Courts may be asked to validate burdens imposed upon individual members of a particular group in order to advance the group's general interest. Nothing in the Constitution supports the notion that individuals may be asked to suffer otherwise impermissible burdens in order to enhance the societal standing of their ethnic groups. Second, preferential programs may only reinforce common stereotypes holding that certain groups are unable to achieve success without special protection based on a factor having no relationship to individual worth. Third, there is a measure of inequity in forcing innocent persons in respondent's position to bear the burdens of redressing grievances not of their making.

By hitching the meaning of the Equal Protection Clause to these transitory considerations, we would be holding, as a constitutional principle, that judicial scrutiny of classifications touching on racial and ethnic background may vary with the ebb and flow of political forces. Disparate constitutional tolerance of such classifications well may serve to exacerbate racial and ethnic antagonisms rather than alleviate them. Also, the mutability of a constitutional principle, based upon shifting political and social judgments, undermines the chances for consistent application

Comparative Note 14.5

[In this case the Indian Supreme Court considered the constitutionality of an admissions program at Punjab University that reserved 64 of 150 spots in morning and evening law classes for disadvantaged castes, tribes, "backward classes," the physically handicapped, outstanding forceman and deference personnel. The remaining 86 seats in the morning class were open to all qualified applicants. The remaining seats in the evening class were restricted to "regular employees of government/semi-government institutions, affiliated colleges, statutory corporations and government companies." The appellants, who worked in the private sector, claimed that the restriction on admissions into the evening class violated Article 14 of the Indian Constitution.]

Dutt, J. . . .

It is now well settled that Article 14 forbids class legislation, but does not forbid reasonable classification. Whether a classification is a permissible classification under Art. 14 or not, two conditions must be satisfied, namely (1) that the classification must be founded on an intelligible differentia which distinguishes persons or things that are grouped together from others left out of the group, and (2) that the differentia must have a rational nexus to the object sought to be achieved. . . .

It is difficult to accept the contention that the Government employees or the employees of semi-Government or other institutions . . . stand on a different footing from the employees of private concerns, in so far as the question of admission to evening classes is concerned. It is true that the service conditions of employees of Government/semi-Government institutions etc. are different, and they may have greater security of service, but that hardly matters for the purpose of admission in the evening classes. The test is whether the employees of private establishments are equally in a disadvantageous position like the employees of Government/

semi-Government institutions etc, in attending morning classes. . . . To exclude the employees of private establishments will not, therefore, satisfy the test of intelligible differentia that distinguishes the employees of Government/semi-Government institutions etc. grouped together from the employees of private establishments. It is true that a classification need not be made with mathematical precision but if there is little or no difference between the persons or things which have been grouped together and those left out of the group, in that case the classification cannot be said to be a reasonable one. . . .

But, the next important question is even if the restriction . . . is removed . . . whether reservation of a certain percent of seats in the evening classes for the employees will be justified and reasonable. . . . The university, being an autonomous body, must be accessible, and such access must be based on the principle that those who are the most meritorious must be preferred to those who are less meritorious. This principle is, however, subject to the provision of Art. 15 of the Constitution which allows positive discrimination, despite the merit principle, on the basis that the equality clause will not be meaningful unless equal opportunity is given to such classes enumerated by Article 15 by giving them preferential treatment.

. . . [It] would be unreasonable to assume that in enacting Art. 15(4), Parliament intended to provide that where the advancement of the backward classes or the Scheduled Castes and Scheduled Tribes was concerned, the fundamental rights of the citizens constituting the rest of the society were to be completely and absolutely ignored. . . . Thus, the provision of Art. 15(4) does not contemplate to reserve all the seats or the majority of the seats in an educational institution at the cost of the rest of the society. . . .

SOURCE: *Deepak Sibal v. Punjab University*, A.I.R. (1989) S.C. 903.

---

of the Constitution from one generation to the next, a critical feature of its coherent interpretation. . . .

If it is the individual who is entitled to judicial protection . . . rather than the individual only because of his membership in a particular group, then constitutional standards may be applied consistently. Political judgments regarding the necessity for the particular classification may

be weighed in the constitutional balance . . . but the standard of justification will remain constant. This is as it should be, since those political judgments are the product of rough compromise struck by contending groups within the democratic process. When they touch upon an individual's race or ethnic background, he is entitled to a judicial determination that the burden he is asked to bear on that basis is precisely tailored to serve a compelling governmental interest. . . .

We have held that in "order to justify the use of a suspect classification, a State must show that its purpose or interest is both constitutionally permissible and substantial, and that its use of the classification is 'necessary . . . to the accomplishment' of its purpose or the safeguarding of its interest." The special admissions program purports to serve the purposes of: (i) "reducing the historic deficit of traditionally disfavored minorities in medical schools and in the medical profession"; (ii) countering the effects of societal discrimination; (iii) increasing the number of physicians who will practice in communities currently undeserved; and (iv) obtaining the educational benefits that flow from an ethnically diverse student body. It is necessary to decide which, if any, of these purposes is substantial enough to support the use of a suspect classification.

If petitioner's purpose is to assure within its student body some specified percentage of a particular group merely because of its race or ethnic origin, such a preferential purpose must be rejected not as insubstantial but as facially invalid. Preferring members of any one group for no reason other than race or ethnic origin is discrimination for its own sake. This the Constitution forbids.

The State certainly has a legitimate and substantial interest in ameliorating, or eliminating where feasible, the disabling effects of identified discrimination. The line of school desegregation cases, commencing with *Brown*, attests to the importance of this state goal and the commitment of the judiciary to affirm all lawful means toward its attainment. In the school cases, the States were required by court order to redress the wrongs worked by specific instances of racial discrimination. That goal was far more focused than the remedying of the effects of "societal discrimination," an amorphous concept of injury that may be ageless in its reach into the past.

Hence, the purpose of helping certain groups whom the faculty of the Davis Medical School perceived as victims of "societal discrimination" does not justify a classification that imposes disadvantages upon persons like respondent, who bear no responsibility for whatever harm the beneficiaries of the special admissions program are thought to have suffered. To hold otherwise would be to convert a remedy heretofore reserved for violations of legal rights into a privilege that all institutions throughout the Nation could grant at their pleasure to whatever groups are perceived as victims of societal discrimination. That is a step we have never approved.

Petitioner identifies, as another purpose of its program, improving the delivery of health-care services to communities currently underserved. It may be assumed that in some situations a State's interest in facilitating the health care of its citizens is sufficiently compelling to support the use of a suspect classification. But there is virtually no evidence in the record indicating that petitioner's special admissions program is either needed or geared to promote that goal.

The fourth goal asserted by petitioner is the attainment of a diverse student body. This clearly is a constitutionally permissible goal for an institution of higher education. Academic freedom, though not a specifically enumerated constitutional right, long has been viewed as a special concern of the First Amendment. The freedom of a university to make its own judgments as to education includes the selection of its student body. . . .

Thus, in arguing that its universities must be accorded the right to select those students who will contribute the most to the "robust exchange of ideas," petitioner invokes a countervailing constitutional interest, that of the First Amendment. In this light, petitioner must be viewed as seeking to achieve a goal that is of paramount importance in the fulfillment of its mission.

It may be argued that there is greater force to these views at the undergraduate level than in a medical school where the training is centered primarily on professional competency. But even at the graduate level, our tradition and experience lend support to the view that the contribution of diversity is substantial. . . . Physicians serve a heterogeneous population. An otherwise qualified medical student with a particular background—whether it be ethnic, geographic, culturally advantaged or disadvantaged—may bring to a professional school of medicine experiences, outlooks, and ideas that enrich the training of its student body and better equip its graduates to render with understanding their vital service to humanity.

Ethnic diversity, however, is only one element in a range of factors a university properly may consider in attaining the goal of a heterogeneous student body. Although a university must have wide discretion in making the sensitive judgments as to who should be admitted, constitutional limitations protecting individual rights may not be disregarded. Respondent urges—and the courts below have held—that petitioner's dual admissions program is a racial classification that impermissibly infringes his rights under the Fourteenth Amendment. As the interest of diversity is compelling in the context of a university's admissions program, the question remains whether the program's racial classification is necessary to promote this interest.

It may be assumed that the reservation of a specified number of seats in each class for individuals from the preferred ethnic groups would contribute to the attainment of considerable ethnic diversity in the student body. But petitioner's argument that this is the only effective means of serving the interest of diversity is seriously flawed. In a most fundamental sense the argument misconceives the nature of the state interest that would justify consideration of race or ethnic background. It is not an interest in simple ethnic diversity, in which a specified percentage of the student body is in effect guaranteed to be members of selected ethnic groups, with the remaining percentage an undifferentiated aggregation of students. The diversity that furthers a compelling state interest encompasses a far broader array of qualifications and characteristics of which racial or ethnic origin is but a single though important element. Petitioner's special admissions program, focused solely on ethnic diversity, would hinder rather than further attainment of genuine diversity.

The experience of other university admissions programs which take race into account . . . demonstrates that the assignment of a fixed number of places to a minority group is not a necessary means toward that end. An illuminating example is found in the Harvard College program:

> In recent years Harvard College has expanded the concept of diversity to include students from disadvantaged economic, racial and ethnic groups. . . .
>
> In practice, this new definition of diversity has meant that race has been a factor in some admission decisions. . . . A farm boy from Idaho can bring something . . . that a Bostonian cannot offer. Similarly, a black student can usually bring something that a white person cannot offer. . . .

In such an admissions program, race or ethnic background may be deemed a "plus" in a particular applicant's file, yet it does not insulate the individual from comparison with all other candidates for the available seats. The file of a particular black applicant may be examined for his potential contribution to diversity without the factor of race being decisive when compared, for example, with that of an applicant identified as an Italian-American if the latter is thought to exhibit qualities more likely to promote beneficial educational pluralism. Such qualities could include exceptional personal talents, unique work or service experience, leadership potential, maturity, demonstrated compassion, a history of overcoming disadvantage, ability to communicate with the poor, or other qualifications deemed important. In short, an admissions program operated in this way is flexible enough to consider all pertinent elements of diversity in light of the particular qualifications of each applicant, and to place them on the same footing for consideration, although not necessarily according them the same weight. Indeed, the weight attributed

to a particular quality may vary from year to year depending upon the "mix" both of the student body and the applicants for the incoming class.

This kind of program treats each applicant as an individual in the admissions process. The applicant who loses out on the last available seat to another candidate receiving a "plus" on the basis of ethnic background will not have been foreclosed from all consideration for that seat simply because he was not the right color or had the wrong surname. It would mean only that his combined qualifications, which may have included similar nonobjective factors, did not outweigh those of the other applicant. His qualifications would have been weighed fairly and competitively, and he would have no basis to complain of unequal treatment under the Fourteenth Amendment.

It has been suggested that an admissions program which considers race only as one factor is simply a subtle and more sophisticated—but no less effective—means of according racial preference than the Davis program. A facial intent to discriminate, however, is evident in petitioner's preference program and not denied in this case. No such facial infirmity exists in an admissions program where race or ethnic background is simply one element—to be weighed fairly against other elements—in the selection process. And a court would not assume that a university, professing to employ a facially nondiscriminatory admissions policy, would operate it as a cover for the functional equivalent of a quota system. In short, good faith would be presumed in the absence of a showing to the contrary in the manner permitted by our cases.

. . . The fatal flaw in petitioner's preferential program is its disregard of individual rights as guaranteed by the Fourteenth Amendment. Such rights are not absolute. But when a State's distribution of benefits or imposition of burdens hinges on ancestry or the color of a person's skin, that individual is entitled to a demonstration that the challenged classification is necessary to promote a substantial state interest. Petitioner has failed to carry this burden. For this reason, that portion of the California court's judgment holding petitioner's special admissions program invalid under the Fourteenth Amendment must be affirmed.

In enjoining petitioner from ever considering the race of any applicant, however, the courts below failed to recognize that the State has a substantial interest that legitimately may be served by a properly devised admissions program involving the competitive consideration of race and ethnic origin. For this reason, so much of the California court's judgment as enjoins petitioner from any consideration of the race of any applicant must be reversed.

Opinion of Mr. Justice BRENNAN, Mr. Justice WHITE, Mr. Justice MARSHALL, and Mr. Justice BLACKMUN,

concurring in the judgment in part and dissenting in part.

. . . [C]laims that law must be "color-blind" or that the datum of race is no longer relevant to public policy must be seen as aspiration rather than as description of reality. This is not to denigrate aspiration; for reality rebukes us that race has too often been used by those who would stigmatize and oppress minorities. Yet we cannot—and, as we shall demonstrate, need not under our Constitution . . . let color blindness become myopia which masks the reality that many "created equal" have been treated within our lifetimes as inferior both by the law and by their fellow citizens.

The assertion of human equality is closely associated with the proposition that differences in color or creed, birth or status, are neither significant nor relevant to the way in which persons should be treated. Nonetheless, the position that such factors must be "constitutionally an irrelevance," summed up by the shorthand phrase "[o]ur Constitution is color-blind," has never been adopted by this Court as the proper meaning of the Equal Protection Clause. Indeed, we have expressly rejected this proposition on a number of occasions.

Our cases have always implied that an "overriding statutory purpose," could be found that would justify racial classifications. . . .

Accordingly, we turn to the problem of articulating what our role should be in reviewing state action that expressly classifies by race.

Unquestionably we have held that a government practice or statute which restricts "fundamental rights" or which contains "suspect classifications" is to be subjected to "strict scrutiny" and can be justified only if it furthers a compelling governmental purpose and, even then, only if no less restrictive alternative is available. But no fundamental right is involved here. Nor do whites as a class have any of the "traditional indicia of suspectness: the class is not saddled with such disabilities, or subjected to such a history of purposeful unequal treatment, or relegated to such a position of political powerlessness as to command extraordinary protection from the majoritarian political process." *San Antonio v. Rodriguez* (1973). See *Carolene Products*, n. 4 (1938).

On the other hand . . . this case . . . should [not] be analyzed by applying the very loose rational-basis standard of review that is the very least that is always applied in equal protection cases. . . . [A] number of considerations . . . lead us to conclude that racial classifications designed to serve remedial purposes "must serve important governmental objectives and must be substantially related to achievement of those objectives." *Craig v. Boren* (1976).

First, race, like "gender-based classifications too often [has] been inexcusably utilized to stereotype and stigmatize politically powerless segments of society." . . .

Second, race, like gender and illegitimacy, . . . is an immutable characteristic which its possessors are powerless to escape or set aside. . . .

In sum, because of the significant risk that racial classifications established for ostensibly benign purposes can be misused . . . to justify such a classification an important and articulated purpose for its use must be shown. In addition, any statute must be stricken that stigmatizes any group or that singles out those least well represented in the political process to bear the brunt of a benign program. . . .

Davis' articulated purpose of remedying the effects of past societal discrimination is, under our cases, sufficiently important to justify the use of race-conscious admissions programs where there is a sound basis for concluding that minority underrepresentation is substantial and chronic, and that the handicap of past discrimination is impeding access of minorities to the Medical School. . . .

[T]he conclusion that state educational institutions may constitutionally adopt admissions programs designed to avoid exclusion of historically disadvantaged minorities, even when such programs explicitly take race into account, finds direct support in our cases construing congressional legislation designed to overcome the present effects of past discrimination. Congress can and has outlawed actions which have a disproportionately adverse and unjustified impact upon members of racial minorities and has required or authorized race-conscious action to put individuals disadvantaged by such impact in the position they otherwise might have enjoyed. Such relief does not require as a predicate proof that recipients of preferential advancement have been individually discriminated against; it is enough that each recipient is within a general class of persons likely to have been the victims of discrimination. Nor is it an objection to such relief that preference for minorities will upset the settled expectations of nonminorities. In addition, we have held that Congress, to remove barriers to equal opportunity, can and has required employers to use test criteria that fairly reflect the qualifications of minority applicants vis-à-vis nonminority applicants, even if this means interpreting the qualifications of an applicant in light of his race.

It is not even claimed that Davis' program in any way operates to stigmatize or single out any discrete and insular, or even any identifiable, nonminority group. Nor will harm comparable to that imposed upon racial minorities by exclusion or separation on grounds of race be the likely result of the program. It does not, for example, establish an exclusive preserve for minority students apart from and exclusive of whites. Rather, its purpose is to overcome the effects of segregation by bringing the races together. True, whites are excluded from participation in the special admissions program, but this fact only operates to reduce the number of whites to be admitted in the regular admissions program in order to permit admission of a reasonable percentage—less than their proportion of the California population—of otherwise underrepresented qualified minority applicants.

Nor was Bakke in any sense stamped as inferior by the Medical School's rejection of him. . . . Unlike discrimination against racial minorities, the use of racial preferences for remedial purposes does not inflict a pervasive injury upon individual whites in the sense that wherever they go or whatever they do there is a significant likelihood that they will be treated as second-class citizens because of their color. This distinction does not mean that the exclusion of a white resulting from the preferential use of race is not sufficiently serious to require justification; but it does mean that the injury inflicted by such a policy is not distinguishable from disadvantages caused by a wide range of government actions, none of which has ever been thought impermissible for that reason alone.

. . . Nor can the program reasonably be regarded as stigmatizing the program's beneficiaries or their race as inferior. The Davis program does not simply advance less qualified applicants; rather, it compensates applicants, who it is uncontested are fully qualified to study medicine, for educational disadvantages which it was reasonable to conclude were a product of state-fostered discrimination. Once admitted, these students must satisfy the same degree requirements as regularly admitted students; they are taught by the same faculty in the same classes; and their performance is evaluated by the same standards by which regularly admitted students are judged. Under these circumstances, their performance and degrees must be regarded equally with the regularly admitted students with whom they compete for standing. Since minority graduates cannot justifiably be regarded as less well qualified than nonminority graduates by virtue of the special admissions program, there is no reasonable basis to conclude that minority graduates at schools using such programs would be stigmatized as inferior by the existence of such programs.

. . . Davis considers on an individual basis each applicant's personal history whether he or she has likely been disadvantaged by racial discrimination. The record makes clear that only minority applicants likely to have been isolated from the mainstream of American life are considered in the special program; other minority applicants are eligible only through the regular admissions program. True, the procedure by which disadvantage is detected is informal, but we have never insisted that educators conduct their affairs through adjudicatory proceedings, and such insistence here is misplaced. A case-by-case inquiry into the extent to which each individual applicant has been affected, either directly or indirectly, by racial discrimination, would seem to be, as a practical matter, virtually impossible, despite the fact that there are excellent reasons for concluding that such effects generally exist. When individual measurement is impossible or extremely impractical, there is nothing to prevent a State from using categorical means to achieve its ends, at least where the category is closely related to the goal. And it is clear from our cases that specific proof that a person has been victimized by discrimination is not a necessary predicate to offering him relief where the probability of victimization is great.

Mr. Justice MARSHALL, concurring in part and dissenting in part.

I agree with the judgment of the Court only insofar as it permits a university to consider the race of an applicant in making admissions decisions. I do not agree that petitioner's admissions program violates the Constitution. For it must be remembered that, during most of the past 200 years, the Constitution as interpreted by this Court did not prohibit the most ingenious and pervasive forms of discrimination against the Negro. Now, when a State acts to remedy the effects of that legacy of discrimination, I cannot believe that this same Constitution stands as a barrier. . . .

The position of the Negro today in America is the tragic but inevitable consequence of centuries of unequal treatment. Measured by any benchmark of comfort or achievement, meaningful equality remains a distant dream for the Negro. . . .

It is because of a legacy of unequal treatment that we now must permit the institutions of this society to give consideration to race in making decisions about who will hold the positions of influence, affluence, and prestige in America. For far too long, the doors to those positions have been shut to Negroes. If we are ever to become a fully integrated society, one in which the color of a person's skin will not determine the opportunities available to him or her, we must be willing to take steps to open those doors. I do not believe that anyone can truly look into America's past and still find that a remedy for the effects of that past is impermissible.

Mr. Justice BLACKMUN. . . .

I suspect that it would be impossible to arrange an affirmative action program in a racially neutral way and have it successful. To ask that this be so is to demand the impossible. In order to get beyond racism, we must first take account of race. There is no other way. And in order to treat some persons equally, we must treat them differently. We cannot—we dare not—let the Equal Protection Clause perpetuate racial supremacy.

Mr. Justice STEVENS, with whom The Chief Justice, Mr. Justice STEWART, and Mr. Justice REHNQUIST join, concurring in the judgment in part and dissenting in part.

It is always important at the outset to focus precisely on the controversy before the Court. It is particularly important to do so in this case because correct identification of the issues will determine whether it is necessary or appropriate to express any opinion about the legal status of any admissions program other than petitioner's.

Section 601 of the Civil Rights Act of 1964, 78 Stat. 252, 42 U.S.C. s 2000d, provides: "No person in the United States shall, on the ground of race, color, or national origin, be excluded from participation in, be denied the benefits of, or be subjected to discrimination under any program or activity receiving Federal financial assistance."

The University, through its special admissions policy, excluded Bakke from participation in its program of medical education because of his race. The University also acknowledges that it was, and still is, receiving federal financial assistance. The plain language of the statute therefore requires affirmance of the judgment below. A different result cannot be justified unless that language misstates the actual intent of the Congress that enacted the statute or the statute is not enforceable in a private action. Neither conclusion is warranted.

. . . Accordingly, I concur in the Court's judgment insofar as it affirms the judgment of the Supreme Court of California. To the extent that it purports to do anything else, I respectfully dissent.

Notes and Queries

1. In an earlier case, *DeFunis v. Odegaard* (1974), the Court managed to avoid a ruling on affirmative action programs in higher education. Marco DeFunis, a white man, had been denied admission to the law school at the University of Washington. The school had, however, admitted 36 of 37 African-American, Hispanic, Indian, and Filipino applicants with lower LSAT scores. DeFunis sued the law school in a state court, which ordered the school to admit him. By the time the case got to the Supreme Court, DeFunis was in his third and final year of law school. The University agreed to let him finish, no matter the outcome of the case, leading the Supreme Court to conclude that the case was moot. Partly as a consequence of this ruling, Alan Bakke was forced to stay out of medical school while his case was pending.

2. How, precisely, did the Davis plan discriminate against Bakke? Was he denied an "equal" opportunity to compete for admission? If so, how?

3. There was no majority opinion for the Court in *Bakke*. Instead, the Court divided into six opinions. Four justices (the Brennan group) were prepared to uphold the constitutionality of Davis' affirmative action plan. Four justices (the Burger group) believed that the plan violated Title VI of the Civil Rights Act of 1964. Justice Powell provided the fifth vote to strike the plan. Did Powell hold that all affirmative actions are unconstitutional? If not, what would distinguish a constitutionally acceptable plan from the Davis plan? In other words, what is the holding in *Bakke?*

4. In addition to their disagreement over the merit of the Davis plan, the Brennan group and Justice Powell disagreed over the standard of scrutiny the Court should use to review affirmative action plans. What reasons did Justice Brennan offer for subjecting "remedial" legislation to a less stringent test than "strict scrutiny"? Is Brennan's opinion consistent with the rationale for strict judicial scrutiny offered by the Court in *Carolene Products?*

In contrast to strict scrutiny or some other standard of review, consider the following quotation from the Canadian Supreme Court in the case of *R. v. Oakes* (1986):

To establish that a limit [on a basic right] is reasonable and demonstrably justified in a free and democratic society, two central criteria must be satisfied. First, the objective, which the measures responsible for a limit on a *Charter* right or freedom are designed to serve, must be "of sufficient importance to warrant overriding a constitutionally protected right or freedom." . . . Second, once a sufficiently significant objective is recognized, then the party invoking section 1 must show that the means chosen are reasonable and demonstrably justified. This involves "a form of proportionality test": . . . There are . . . three important components of a proportionality test. First, the measures adopted must be carefully designed to achieve the objective in question. They must not be arbitrary, unfair or based on irrational considerations. In short, they must be rationally connected to the objective. Second, the means, even if rationally connected to the objective in this first sense, should impair "as little as possible" the right or freedom in question. . . . Third, there must be proportionality between the *effects* of the measures which are responsible for limiting the *Charter* right or freedom, and the objective which has been identified as of "sufficient importance."

Would this method of review yield a different result in *Bakke*?

5. Why did Justice Powell insist that all forms of racial discrimination must be subjected to the same test? Is the concept of equality implicit in Justice Powell's opinion the same one implicit in Justice Brennan's? Is Powell's understanding, in which he insisted that the Constitution must be colorblind, also implicit in his opinion?

Adarand Constructors, Inc. v. Pena

515 U.S. 200, 115 S. Ct. 2097, 132 L. Ed. 2d 158 (1995)

Most federal contracting programs include "set-aside" provisions, or clauses that encourage the primary contractor to subcontract a part of the contract to businesses owned by "socially and economically disadvantaged" persons. In this case, a contractor in the highway construction industry subcontracted part of the contract to a firm owned by a Hispanic. Adarand Constructors, a white-owned company, challenged the set-aside program as a violation of the equal protection clause of the Fourteenth Amendment. Judgment of the Court: *O'Connor*, Rehnquist, Scalia, Kennedy, Thomas. Concurring in part and concurring in the judgment: *Scalia; Thomas*. Dissenting opinions: *Stevens, Ginsburg*, Breyer, *Souter*.

Justice O'CONNOR announced the judgment of the Court and delivered an opinion with respect to Parts I, II, III-A, III-B, III-D, and IV, which is for the Court except insofar as it might be inconsistent with the views expressed in Justice SCALIA's concurrence, and an opinion with respect to Part III-C in which Justice KENNEDY joins.

[The Government] urge that "[t]he Subcontracting Compensation Clause program is . . . a program based on disadvantage, not on race," and thus that it is subject only to "the most relaxed judicial scrutiny." To the extent that the statutes and regulations involved in this case are race neutral, we agree. Respondents concede, however, that "the race-based rebuttable presumption used in some certification determinations under the Subcontracting Compensation Clause" is subject to some heightened level of scrutiny. The parties disagree as to what that level should be. (We note, incidentally, that this case concerns only classifications based explicitly on race, and presents none of the additional difficulties posed by laws that, although facially race neutral, result in racially disproportionate im-

pact and are motivated by a racially discriminatory purpose.)

Adarand's claim arises under the Fifth Amendment to the Constitution, which provides that "No person shall . . . be deprived of life, liberty, or property, without due process of law." Although this Court has always understood that Clause to provide some measure of protection against *arbitrary* treatment by the Federal Government, it is not as explicit a guarantee of equal treatment as the Fourteenth Amendment, which provides that "No State shall . . . deny to any person within its jurisdiction the equal protection of the laws." Our cases have accorded varying degrees of significance to the difference in the language of those two Clauses. We think it necessary to revisit the issue here.

In *Bolling v. Sharpe* (1954), the Court for the first time explicitly questioned the existence of any difference between the obligations of the Federal Government and the States to avoid racial classifications. *Bolling* did note that "[t]he 'equal protection of the laws' is a more explicit safeguard of prohibited unfairness than 'due process of law,'" . . . But *Bolling* then concluded that, "[i]n view of [the] decision that the Constitution prohibits the states from maintaining racially segregated public schools, it would be unthinkable that the same Constitution would impose a lesser duty on the Federal Government."

Bolling's facts concerned school desegregation, but its reasoning was not so limited. The Court's observations that "[d]istinctions between citizens solely because of their ancestry are by their very nature odious," *Hirabayashi*, that "all legal restrictions which curtail the civil rights of a single racial group are immediately suspect," *Korematsu*, carry no less force in the context of federal action than in the context of action by the States—indeed, they first appeared in cases concerning action by the Federal Government. *Bolling* relied on those observations, and reiterated "that the Constitution of the United States, in its present form, forbids, so far as civil and political rights are concerned, discrimination by the General Government, or by the States, against any citizen because of his race." . . .

Comparative Note 14.6

In the United States, the enshrinement in the Declaration of Independence and the Constitution of the ideals of equality and equal opportunity for all individuals conflicted with the practice of slavery and then discrimination to create what Gunnar Myrdal called "the American Dilemma" (1944). This dilemma, which had influenced politics since the United States became independent from Britain, provided the grounds on which proponents of civil rights could argue that African Americans were entitled to equal treatment under the laws and its effects were cited to support activist policies such as preferences and compensation for past wrongs.

But the importance of equality of opportunity was difficult to separate from the liberal emphasis on the individual, which was at least as deeply entrenched an ideological concept as that of equality and equal opportunity. While social groups were protected in both reality and in law, the recurrent emphasis on the individual as the primary unit of politics meant that affirmative action, which selected individuals using the criterion of group membership, was vulnerable to the criticism that it violated a crucial tenet of American political philosophy by rewarding groups at the expense of individuals. . . .

In India, the primacy of equality and equal opportunity found its analogy in an opposite situation, the caste structure. The ideology of caste as a religious and social organizing principle legitimated the unequal treatment of low castes and untouchables. But the colonization of India by the British challenged the supremacy of caste ideology in two ways: first, it gave prominence to the ideals (though not the practice) of liberalism, individualism, and equality; and second, British rule undermined the high-caste argument that those who were at the top of the political and social hierarchy somehow deserved to be there. . . .

. . . Caste ideology reinforced the dominance of group over individual identity, which gave support to the group-based orientation of the policy [of affirmative action], but privileging low castes and especially untouchables went against the fundamental tenets of caste doctrine. Similarly, the newer but increasingly powerful philosophies of individualism and equality presented ideological problems for affirmative action, but the growing commitment to equality and equal opportunity made the historical oppression of low castes and untouchables more problematic. . . .

Source: Sunita Parikh, *The Politics of Preference: Democratic Institutions and Affirmative Action in the United States and India* (Ann Arbor: University of Michigan Press, 1997), 32–33.

The Court's application of that general principle to the case before it, and the resulting imposition on the Federal Government of an obligation equivalent to that of the States, followed as a matter of course.

Later cases in contexts other than school desegregation did not distinguish between the duties of the States and the Federal Government to avoid racial classifications. . . .

Most of the cases discussed above involved classifications burdening groups that have suffered discrimination in our society. In 1978, the Court confronted the question whether race-based governmental action designed to benefit such groups should also be subject to "the most rigid scrutiny." *Regents of Univ. of Cal. v. Bakke* (1978), involved an equal protection challenge to a state-run medical school's practice of reserving a number of spaces in its entering class for minority students. The petitioners argued that "strict scrutiny" should apply only to "classifications that disadvantage 'discrete and insular minorities.'"

Bakke did not produce an opinion for the Court, but Justice Powell's opinion announcing the Court's judgment rejected the argument. In a passage joined by Justice White, Justice Powell wrote that "[t]he guarantee of equal protection cannot mean one thing when applied to one individual and something else when applied to a person of another color." He concluded that "[r]acial and ethnic distinctions of any sort are inherently suspect and thus call for the most exacting judicial examination." On the other hand, four Justices in *Bakke* would have applied a less stringent standard of review to racial classifications "designed to further remedial purposes." And four Justices thought the case should be decided on statutory grounds.

Two years after *Bakke*, the Court faced another challenge to remedial race-based action, this time involving action undertaken by the Federal Government. In *Fullilove v. Klutznick*, (1980), the Court upheld Congress' inclusion of a 10% set-aside for minority-owned businesses

Comparative Note 14.7

Liberalism and the cult of the individual helped shape the American vision of equality. This vision is apparent from the earliest days of the American experience. Our Revolution, unlike that of the French, was not based on class struggle, and our notion of equality was not an economic one. . . .

The French historical experience has been different than ours and has resulted in a different notion of legal equality. . . . Post-Revolutionary society was inspired by the political ideology of Rousseau, which posited a relationship between the individual and the state very different than that found in America. . . . In contrast to the liberal concept of society as exercising minimal control over the individual, Rousseau's vision implied extensive control over the individual, but as a positive rather than a negative force; . . . In the ideal society, a strong state directed by the collective will of its citizens is a force for moral good and an avenue to liberty.

. . . Equality in France meant not that the state would cease to meddle in the lives of its citizens, but that it would actively insure their equality. . . .

The goal is not inherent equality, but equalization of a citizen's place in society. "If men are equal in law, let them be equal in fact; if they are equal at the start, let them be equal at the finish." In this, the French notion of equality is more result-oriented than its American counterpart. It is also more sensitive to the injustice of economic inequalities. In France, "if the difference in human conditions legitimizes different rules, it also justifies, in a social Republic, provisions which correct the most shocking social inequalities; violating formal equality to attain true equality also serves equality.

Source: Cynthia A. Vroom, *Equal Protection Versus the Principle of Equality: American and French Views on Equality in the Law,* 21 Capital University Law Review 201–207·(1992).

in the Public Works Employment Act of 1977. As in *Bakke,* there was no opinion for the Court. Chief Justice Burger, in an opinion joined by Justices White and Powell, observed that "[a]ny preference based on racial or ethnic criteria must necessarily receive a most searching examination to make sure that it does not conflict with constitutional guarantees." That opinion, however, "d[id] not adopt, either expressly or implicitly, the formulas of analysis articulated in such cases as (*Bakke*)." It employed instead a two-part test which asked, first, "whether the objectives of th[e] legislation are within the power of Congress," and second, "whether the limited use of racial and ethnic criteria, in the context presented, is a constitutionally permissible means for achieving the congressional objectives." It then upheld the program under that test, adding at the end of the opinion that the program also "would survive judicial review under either 'test' articulated in the several *Bakke* opinions." Justice Powell wrote separately to express his view that the plurality opinion had essentially applied "strict scrutiny" as described in his *Bakke* opinion—i.e., it had determined that the set-aside was "a necessary means of advancing a compelling governmental interest"—and had done so correctly. Justice Stewart (joined by then-Justice Rehnquist) dissented, arguing that the Constitution required the Federal Government to meet the same strict standard as the States when enacting racial classifications, and that the program before

the Court failed that standard. Justice Stevens also dissented, arguing that "[r]acial classifications are simply too pernicious to permit any but the most exact connection between justification and classification," and that the program before the Court could not be characterized "as a 'narrowly tailored' remedial measure." Justice Marshall (joined by Justices Brennan and Blackmun) concurred in the judgment, reiterating the view of four Justices in *Bakke* that any race-based governmental action designed to "remed[y] the present effects of past racial discrimination" should be upheld if it was "substantially related" to the achievement of an "important governmental objective"— i.e., such action should be subjected only to what we now call "intermediate scrutiny."

In *Wygant v. Jackson Bd. of Ed.,* the Court considered a Fourteenth Amendment challenge to another form of remedial racial classification. The issue in *Wygant* was whether a school board could adopt race-based preferences in determining which teachers to lay off. Justice Powell's plurality opinion observed that "the level of scrutiny does not change merely because the challenged classification operates against a group that historically has not been subject to governmental discrimination," and stated the two-part inquiry as "whether the layoff provision is supported by a compelling state purpose and whether the means chosen to accomplish that purpose are narrowly tailored." In other words, "racial classifications of any sort must be subjected to 'strict scrutiny.'" The plurality then concluded that the school board's interest in "providing minority role models for its minority students, as an attempt to alleviate the effects of societal discrimination," was not a compelling interest that could justify the use of a racial classification. It added that "[s]ocietal discrimination, without more, is too amorphous a basis for imposing a racially classified remedy," and insisted instead that "a public employer . . . must ensure that, before it embarks on an affirmative-action program, it has convincing evidence that remedial action is warranted. That is, it must have sufficient evidence to justify the conclusion that there has been prior discrimination." . . .

The Court's failure to produce a majority opinion in *Bakke, Fullilove,* and *Wygant* left unresolved the proper analysis for remedial race-based governmental action. Lower courts found this lack of guidance unsettling.

The Court resolved the issue, at least in part, in 1989. *Richmond v. J.A. Croson Co.,* (1989), concerned a city's determination that 30% of its contracting work should go to minority-owned businesses. A majority of the Court in *Croson* held that "the standard of review under the Equal Protection Clause is not dependent on the race of those burdened or benefited by a particular classification," and that the single standard of review for racial classifications should be "strict scrutiny."

With *Croson,* the Court finally agreed that the Fourteenth Amendment requires strict scrutiny of all race-based action by state and local governments. But *Croson* of course had no occasion to declare what standard of review the Fifth Amendment requires for such action taken by the Federal Government. *Croson* observed simply that the Court's "treatment of an exercise of congressional power in *Fullilove* cannot be dispositive here," because *Croson's* facts did not implicate Congress' broad power under s. 5 of the Fourteenth Amendment. On the other hand, the Court subsequently indicated that *Croson* had at least some bearing on federal race-based action when it vacated a decision upholding such action and remanded for further consideration in light of *Croson.* Thus, some uncertainty persisted with respect to the standard of review for federal racial classifications.

Despite lingering uncertainty in the details, however, the Court's cases through *Croson* had established three general propositions with respect to governmental racial classifications. First, skepticism: "[A]ny preference based on racial or ethnic criteria must necessarily receive a most searching examination." . . . Second, consistency: "The standard of review under the Equal Protection Clause is not dependent on the race of those burdened or benefited by a particular classification," i.e., all racial classifications

reviewable under the Equal Protection Clause must be strictly scrutinized. And third, congruence: "Equal protection analysis in the Fifth Amendment area is the same as that under the Fourteenth Amendment." Taken together, these three propositions lead to the conclusion that any person, of whatever race, has the right to demand that any governmental actor subject to the Constitution justify any racial classification subjecting that person to unequal treatment under the strictest judicial scrutiny. . . .

A year later, however, the Court took a surprising turn. *Metro Broadcasting, Inc. v. FCC,* (1990), involved a Fifth Amendment challenge to two race-based policies of the Federal Communications Commission (FCC). In *Metro Broadcasting,* the Court repudiated the long-held notion that "it would be unthinkable that the same Constitution would impose a lesser duty on the Federal Government" than it does on a State to afford equal protection of the laws. It did so by holding that "benign" federal racial classifications need only satisfy intermediate scrutiny, even though *Croson* had recently concluded that such classifications enacted by a State must satisfy strict scrutiny. "[B]enign" federal racial classifications, the Court said, "—even if those measures are not 'remedial' in the sense of being designed to compensate victims of past governmental or societal discrimination—are constitutionally permissible to the extent that they serve *important* governmental objectives within the power of Congress and are *substantially related* to achievement of those objectives." The Court did not explain how to tell whether a racial classification should be deemed "benign," other than to express "confiden[ce]" that an 'examination of the legislative scheme and its history' will separate benign measures from other types of racial classifications."

By adopting intermediate scrutiny as the standard of review for congressionally mandated "benign" racial classifications, *Metro Broadcasting* departed from prior cases in two significant respects. First, it turned its back on *Croson's* explanation of why strict scrutiny of all governmental racial classifications is essential:

Absent searching judicial inquiry into the justification for such race-based measures, there is simply no way of determining what classifications are "benign" or "remedial" and what classifications are in fact motivated by illegitimate notions of racial inferiority or simple racial politics. Indeed, the purpose of strict scrutiny is to "smoke out" illegitimate uses of race by assuring that the legislative body is pursuing a goal important enough to warrant use of a highly suspect tool. The test also ensures that the means chosen "fit" this compelling goal so closely that there is little or no possibility that the motive for the classification was illegitimate racial prejudice or stereotype.

We adhere to that view today, despite the surface appeal of holding "benign" racial classifications to a lower standard, because "it may not always be clear that a so-called preference is in fact benign."

Second, *Metro Broadcasting* squarely rejected one of the three propositions established by the Court's earlier equal protection cases, namely, congruence between the standards applicable to federal and state racial classifications, and in so doing also undermined the other two—skepticism of all racial classifications and consistency of treatment irrespective of the race of the burdened or benefited group. Under *Metro Broadcasting,* certain racial classifications ("benign" ones enacted by the Federal Government) should be treated less skeptically than others; and the race of the benefited group is critical to the determination of which standard of review to apply. *Metro Broadcasting* was thus a significant departure from much of what had come before it.

The three propositions undermined by *Metro Broadcasting* all derive from the basic principle that the Fifth and Fourteenth Amendments to the Constitution protect persons, not groups. It follows from that principle that all governmental action based on race—a classification long recognized as "in most circumstances irrelevant and therefore prohibited,"—should be subjected to detailed judicial inquiry to ensure that the personal right to equal protection of the laws has not been infringed. These ideas have long been central to this Court's understanding of equal protection, and holding "benign" state and federal racial classifications to different standards does not square with them. "[A] free people whose institutions are founded upon the doctrine of equality," should tolerate no retreat from the principle that government may treat people differently because of their race only for the most compelling reasons. Accordingly, we hold today that all racial classifications, imposed by whatever federal, state, or local governmental actor, must be analyzed by a reviewing court under strict scrutiny. In other words, such classifications are constitutional only if they are narrowly tailored measures that further compelling governmental interests. To the extent that *Metro Broadcasting* is inconsistent with that holding, it is overruled.

In dissent, Justice Stevens criticizes us for "deliver[ing] a disconcerting lecture about the evils of governmental racial classifications." With respect, we believe his criticisms reflect a serious misunderstanding of our opinion.

Justice Stevens concurs in our view that courts should take a skeptical view of all governmental racial classifica-

tions. He also allows that "[n]othing is inherently wrong with applying a single standard to fundamentally different situations, as long as that standard takes relevant differences into account." What he fails to recognize is that strict scrutiny *does* take "relevant differences" into account—indeed, that is its fundamental purpose. The point of carefully examining the interest asserted by the government in support of a racial classification, and the evidence offered to show that the classification is needed, is precisely to distinguish legitimate from illegitimate uses of race in governmental decisionmaking. And Justice Stevens concedes that "some cases may be difficult to classify," all the more reason, in our view, to examine all racial classifications carefully. Strict scrutiny does not "trea[t] dissimilar race-based decisions as though they were equally objectionable," to the contrary, it evaluates carefully all governmental race-based decisions in order to decide which are constitutionally objectionable and which are not. By requiring strict scrutiny of racial classifications, we require courts to make sure that a governmental classification based on race, which "so seldom provide[s] a relevant basis for disparate treatment," is legitimate, before permitting unequal treatment based on race to proceed.

Justice Stevens chides us for our "supposed inability to differentiate between 'invidious' and 'benign' discrimination," because it is in his view sufficient that "people understand the difference between good intentions and bad." But, as we have just explained, the point of strict scrutiny is to "differentiate between" permissible and impermissible governmental use of race. And Justice Stevens himself has already explained in his dissent in *Fullilove* why "good intentions" alone are not enough to sustain a supposedly "benign" racial classification:

> [E]ven though it is not the actual predicate for this legislation, a statute of this kind inevitably is perceived by many as resting on an assumption that those who are granted this special preference are less qualified in some respect that is identified purely by their race. Because that perception—especially when fostered by the Congress of the United States—can only exacerbate rather than reduce racial prejudice, it will delay the time when race will become a truly irrelevant, or at least insignificant, factor. Unless Congress clearly articulates the need and basis for a racial classification, and also tailors the classification to its justification, the Court should not uphold this kind of statute.

These passages make a persuasive case for requiring strict scrutiny of congressional racial classifications.

Justice Stevens also claims that we have ignored any difference between federal and state legislatures. But requiring that Congress, like the States, enact racial classifications only when doing so is necessary to further a "compelling interest" does not contravene any principle of appropriate respect for a coequal branch of the Government. It is true that various Members of this Court have taken different views of the authority s. 5 of the Fourteenth Amendment confers upon Congress to deal with the problem of racial discrimination, and the extent to which courts should defer to Congress' exercise of that authority. We need not, and do not, address these differences today. For now, it is enough to observe that Justice Stevens' suggestion that any Member of this Court has repudiated in this case his or her previously expressed views on the subject, is incorrect.

. . . *Metro Broadcasting*'s untenable distinction between state and federal racial classifications lacks support in our precedents, and undermines the fundamental principle of equal protection as a personal right. In this case, as between that principle and "its later misapplications," the principle must prevail.

Our action today makes explicit what Justice Powell thought implicit in the *Fullilove* lead opinion: Federal racial classifications, like those of a State, must serve a compelling governmental interest, and must be narrowly tailored to further that interest. Of course, it follows that to the extent (if any) that *Fullilove* held federal racial classifications to be subject to a less rigorous standard, it is no longer controlling. But we need not decide today whether the program upheld in *Fullilove* would survive strict scrutiny as our more recent cases have defined it.

Because our decision today alters the playing field in some important respects, we think it best to remand the case to the lower courts for further consideration in light of the principles we have announced. . . .

Accordingly, the judgment of the Court of Appeals is vacated, and the case is remanded for further proceedings consistent with this opinion.

It is so ordered.

Justice SCALIA, concurring in part and concurring in the judgment.

I join the opinion of the Court, except Part III-C, and except insofar as it may be inconsistent with the following: In my view, government can never have a "compelling interest" in discriminating on the basis of race in order to "make up" for past racial discrimination in the opposite direction. See *Richmond v. J.A. Croson Co.*, (1989) (Scalia, J., concurring in judgment). Individuals who have been wronged by unlawful racial discrimination should be made whole; but under our Constitution there can be no such thing as either a creditor or a debtor race. That con-

cept is alien to the Constitution's focus upon the individual, see Amdt. 14, s. 1 ("[N]or shall any State . . . deny to any person" the equal protection of the laws), and its rejection of dispositions based on race, see Amdt. 15, s. 1 (prohibiting abridgment of the right to vote "on account of race"), or based on blood, see Art. III, s. 3 ("[N]o Attainder of Treason shall work Corruption of Blood"); Art. I, s. 9, cl. 8 ("No Title of Nobility shall be granted by the United States"). To pursue the concept of racial entitlement—even for the most admirable and benign of purposes—is to reinforce and preserve for future mischief the way of thinking that produced race slavery, race privilege and race hatred. In the eyes of government, we are just one race here. It is American.

Justice THOMAS, concurring in part and concurring in the judgment.

I agree with the majority's conclusion that strict scrutiny applies to *all* government classifications based on race. I write separately, however, to express my disagreement with the premise underlying Justice Stevens' and Justice Ginsburg's dissents: that there is a racial paternalism exception to the principle of equal protection. I believe that there is a "moral [and] constitutional equivalence," (Stevens, J., dissenting), between laws designed to subjugate a race and those that distribute benefits on the basis of race in order to foster some current notion of equality. Government cannot make us equal; it can only recognize, respect, and protect us as equal before the law.

That these programs may have been motivated, in part, by good intentions cannot provide refuge from the principle that under our Constitution, the government may not make distinctions on the basis of race. As far as the Constitution is concerned, it is irrelevant whether a government's racial classifications are drawn by those who wish to oppress a race or by those who have a sincere desire to help those thought to be disadvantaged. There can be no doubt that the paternalism that appears to lie at the heart of this program is at war with the principle of inherent equality that underlies and infuses our Constitution. See Declaration of Independence ("We hold these truths to be self-evident, that all men are created equal, that they are endowed by their Creator with certain unalienable Rights, that among these are Life, Liberty, and the pursuit of Happiness").

These programs not only raise grave constitutional questions, they also undermine the moral basis of the equal protection principle. Purchased at the price of immeasurable human suffering, the equal protection principle reflects our Nation's understanding that such classifications ultimately have a destructive impact on the individual and our society. Unquestionably, "[i]nvidious [racial] discrimination is an engine of oppression." It is also true that "[r]emedial" racial preferences may reflect "a desire to foster equality in society." But there can be no doubt that racial paternalism and its unintended consequences can be as poisonous and pernicious as any other form of discrimination. So-called "benign" discrimination teaches many that because of chronic and apparently immutable handicaps, minorities cannot compete with them without their patronizing indulgence. Inevitably, such programs engender attitudes of superiority or, alternatively, provoke resentment among those who believe that they have been wronged by the government's use of race. These programs stamp minorities with a badge of inferiority and may cause them to develop dependencies or to adopt an attitude that they are "entitled" to preferences. . . .

In my mind, government-sponsored racial discrimination based on benign prejudice is just as noxious as discrimination inspired by malicious prejudice. In each instance, it is racial discrimination, plain and simple.

Justice STEVENS, with whom Justice GINSBURG joins, dissenting.

Instead of deciding this case in accordance with controlling precedent, the Court today delivers a disconcerting lecture about the evils of governmental racial classifications. For its text the Court has selected three propositions, represented by the bywords "skepticism," "consistency," and "congruence." I shall comment on each of these propositions, then add a few words about *stare decisis,* and finally explain why I believe this Court has a duty to affirm the judgment of the Court of Appeals.

The Court's concept of skepticism is, at least in principle, a good statement of law and of common sense. Undoubtedly, a court should be wary of a governmental decision that relies upon a racial classification. "Because racial characteristics so seldom provide a relevant basis for disparate treatment, and because classifications based on race are potentially so harmful to the entire body politic," a reviewing court must satisfy itself that the reasons for any such classification are "clearly identified and unquestionably legitimate." *Fullilove v. Klutznick* (1980) (Stevens, J., dissenting). I welcome its renewed endorsement by the Court today. But, as the opinions in *Fullilove* demonstrate, substantial agreement on the standard to be applied in deciding difficult cases does not necessarily lead to agreement on how those cases actually should or will be resolved. In my judgment, because uniform standards are often anything but uniform, we should evaluate the Court's comments on "consistency," "congruence," and

stare decisis with the same type of skepticism that the Court advocates for the underlying issue.

The Court's concept of "consistency" assumes that there is no significant difference between a decision by the majority to impose a special burden on the members of a minority race and a decision by the majority to provide a benefit to certain members of that minority notwithstanding its incidental burden on some members of the majority. In my opinion that assumption is untenable. There is no moral or constitutional equivalence between a policy that is designed to perpetuate a caste system and one that seeks to eradicate racial subordination. Invidious discrimination is an engine of oppression, subjugating a disfavored group to enhance or maintain the power of the majority. Remedial race-based preferences reflect the opposite impulse: a desire to foster equality in society. No sensible conception of the Government's constitutional obligation to "govern impartially," *Hampton v. Mow Sun Wong* (1976), should ignore this distinction.

The consistency that the Court espouses would disregard the difference between a "No Trespassing" sign and a welcome mat. It would treat a Dixiecrat Senator's decision to vote against Thurgood Marshall's confirmation in order to keep African-Americans off the Supreme Court as on a par with President Johnson's evaluation of his nominee's race as a positive factor. It would equate a law that made black citizens ineligible for military service with a program aimed at recruiting black soldiers. An attempt by the majority to exclude members of a minority race from a regulated market is fundamentally different from a subsidy that enables a relatively small group of newcomers to enter that market. An interest in "consistency" does not justify treating differences as though they were similarities.

The Court's explanation for treating dissimilar race-based decisions as though they were equally objectionable is a supposed inability to differentiate between "invidious" and "benign" discrimination. But the term "affirmative action" is common and well understood. Its presence in everyday parlance shows that people understand the difference between good intentions and bad. As with any legal concept, some cases may be difficult to classify, but our equal protection jurisprudence has identified a critical difference between state action that imposes burdens on a disfavored few and state action that benefits the few "in spite of" its adverse effects on the many.

Nothing is inherently wrong with applying a single standard to fundamentally different situations, as long as that standard takes relevant differences into account. For example, if the Court in all equal protection cases were to insist that differential treatment be justified by relevant characteristics of the members of the favored and disfavored classes that provide a legitimate basis for disparate treatment, such a standard would treat dissimilar cases differently while still recognizing that there is, after all, only one Equal Protection Clause. Under such a standard, subsidies for disadvantaged businesses may be constitutional though special taxes on such businesses would be invalid. But a single standard that purports to equate remedial preferences with invidious discrimination cannot be defended in the name of "equal protection."

The Court's concept of "congruence" assumes that there is no significant difference between a decision by the Congress of the United States to adopt an affirmative-action program and such a decision by a State or a municipality. In my opinion that assumption is untenable. It ignores important practical and legal differences between federal and state or local decisionmakers.

Ironically, after all of the time, effort, and paper this Court has expended in differentiating between federal and state affirmative action, the majority today virtually ignores the issue. It provides not a word of direct explanation for its sudden and enormous departure from the reasoning in past cases. Such silence, however, cannot erase the difference between Congress' institutional competence and constitutional authority to overcome historic racial subjugation and the States' lesser power to do so.

Presumably, the majority is now satisfied that its theory of "congruence" between the substantive rights provided by the Fifth and Fourteenth Amendments disposes of the objection based upon divided constitutional powers. But it is one thing to say (as no one seems to dispute) that the Fifth Amendment encompasses a general guarantee of equal protection as broad as that contained within the Fourteenth Amendment. It is another thing entirely to say that Congress' institutional competence and constitutional authority entitles it to no greater deference when it enacts a program designed to foster equality than the deference due a state legislature. The latter is an extraordinary proposition; and, as the foregoing discussion demonstrates, our precedents have rejected it explicitly and repeatedly.

In my judgment, the Court's novel doctrine of "congruence" is seriously misguided. Congressional deliberations about a matter as important as affirmative action should be accorded far greater deference than those of a State or municipality.

The Court's concept of *stare decisis* treats some of the language we have used in explaining our decisions as though it were more important than our actual holdings. In my opinion that treatment is incorrect.

This is the third time in the Court's entire history that it has considered the constitutionality of a federal affirmative-action program. On each of the two prior occasions,

the first in 1980, *Fullilove v. Klutznick,* and the second in 1990, *Metro Broadcasting, Inc. v. FCC,* the Court upheld the program. Today the Court explicitly overrules *Metro Broadcasting* (at least in part), and undermines *Fullilove* by recasting the standard on which it rested and by calling even its holding into question. By way of explanation, Justice O'Connor advises the federal agencies and private parties that have made countless decisions in reliance on those cases that "we do not depart from the fabric of the law; we restore it." A skeptical observer might ask whether this pronouncement is a faithful application of the doctrine of *stare decisis.* . . .

My skeptical scrutiny of the Court's opinion leaves me in dissent. The majority's concept of "consistency" ignores a difference, fundamental to the idea of equal protection, between oppression and assistance. The majority's concept of "congruence" ignores a difference, fundamental to our constitutional system, between the Federal Government and the States. And the majority's concept of *stare decisis* ignores the force of binding precedent. I would affirm the judgment of the Court of Appeals.

Justice SOUTER, with whom Justice GINSBURG and Justice BREYER join, dissenting.

In assessing the degree to which today's holding portends a departure from past practice, it is also worth noting that nothing in today's opinion implies any view of Congress's s. 5 power and the deference due its exercise that differs from the views expressed by the *Fullilove* plurality. The Court simply notes the observation in *Croson* "that the Court's 'treatment of an exercise of congressional power in *Fullilove* cannot be dispositive here,' because *Croson's* facts did not implicate Congress's broad power under s. 5 of the Fourteenth Amendment," and explains that there is disagreement among today's majority about the extent of the s. 5 power. There is therefore no reason to treat the opinion as affecting one way or another the views of s. 5 power, described as "broad," "unique," "unlike [that of] any state or political subdivision." Thus, today's decision should leave s. 5 exactly where it is as the source of an interest of the National Government sufficiently important to satisfy the corresponding requirement of the strict scrutiny test.

Finally, I should say that I do not understand that today's decision will necessarily have any effect on the resolution of an issue that was just as pertinent under *Fullilove's* unlabeled standard as it is under the standard of strict scrutiny now adopted by the Court. The Court has long accepted the view that constitutional authority to remedy past discrimination is not limited to the power to forbid its continuation, but extends to eliminating those effects that would otherwise persist and skew the operation of public systems even in the absence of current intent to practice any discrimination. Indeed, a majority of the Court today reiterates that there are circumstances in which Government may, consistently with the Constitution, adopt programs aimed at remedying the effects of past invidious discrimination.

When the extirpation of lingering discriminatory effects is thought to require a catch-up mechanism, like the racially preferential inducement under the statutes considered here, the result may be that some members of the historically favored race are hurt by that remedial mechanism, however innocent they may be of any personal responsibility for any discriminatory conduct. When this price is considered reasonable, it is in part because it is a price to be paid only temporarily; if the justification for the preference is eliminating the effects of a past practice, the assumption is that the effects will themselves recede into the past, becoming attenuated and finally disappearing. . . .

Justice GINSBURG, with whom Justice BREYER joins, dissenting.

For the reasons stated by Justice Souter, and in view of the attention the political branches are currently giving the matter of affirmative action, I see no compelling cause for the intervention the Court has made in this case. I further agree with Justice Stevens that, in this area, large deference is owed by the Judiciary to "Congress' institutional competence and constitutional authority to overcome historic racial subjugation." I write separately to underscore not the differences the several opinions in this case display, but the considerable field of agreement—the common understandings and concerns—revealed in opinions that together speak for a majority of the Court.

The statutes and regulations at issue, as the Court indicates, were adopted by the political branches in response to an "unfortunate reality": "[t]he unhappy persistence of both the practice and the lingering effects of racial discrimination against minority groups in this country." The United States suffers from those lingering effects because, for most of our Nation's history, the idea that "we are just one race," was not embraced. For generations, our lawmakers and judges were unprepared to say that there is in this land no superior race, no race inferior to any other. . . .

The divisions in this difficult case should not obscure the Court's recognition of the persistence of racial inequality and a majority's acknowledgment of Congress' authority to act affirmatively, not only to end discrimination, but also to counteract discrimination's lingering effects. Those effects, reflective of a system of racial caste only recently ended, are evident in our workplaces, markets, and neigh-

borhoods. Job applicants with identical resumés, qualifications, and interview styles still experience different receptions, depending on their race. White and African-American consumers still encounter different deals. People of color looking for housing still face discriminatory treatment by landlords, real estate agents, and mortgage lenders. Minority entrepreneurs sometimes fail to gain contracts though they are the low bidders, and they are sometimes refused work even after winning contracts. Bias both conscious and unconscious, reflecting traditional and unexamined habits of thought, keeps up barriers that must come down if equal opportunity and nondiscrimination are ever genuinely to become this country's law and practice.

While I would not disturb the programs challenged in this case, and would leave their improvement to the political branches, I see today's decision as one that allows our precedent to evolve, still to be informed by and responsive to changing conditions.

Notes and Queries

1. In *Bolling v. Sharpe* (1954), the Court ruled that it would be "unthinkable" for the federal government to be held to "a lesser duty" than the states with regard to discrimination in public elementary schools. In *Croson*, the Court held that efforts by state and local governments to enact "benign" or remedial racial schemes must satisfy strict scrutiny. In *Metro Broadcasting*, however, the Court ruled that federal efforts to do the same need only pass intermediate scrutiny. Can these disparate decisions be reconciled with the underlying logic of *Bolling*? How did Justice O'Connor deal with this problem?

2. O'Connor's opinion appears to hold that all affirmative action programs must satisfy strict scrutiny. Is it conceivable that efforts to rectify past discrimination will constitute a "compelling" state interest? Justice Scalia insists that the answer to this question must be "no" because "In the eyes of the government, we are just one race here." If remedial efforts do not satisfy the compelling state interest test, what will? In other words, under Justice Scalia's approach, will government ever have an acceptable reason for discriminating on the basis of race?

3. Justice Thomas argues that "there is a moral and constitutional equivalence" between remedial and invidious racial discrimination. Both, he argues, "undermine the moral basis of the equal protection principle." What is that moral principle? How does "benign" discrimination—if there is such a thing, a point Justice Thomas is not likely to concede—undermine the moral principle? Is there a constitutionally relevant difference between "benign" and invidious discrimination?

4. What understanding of federalism does a single requirement of strict scrutiny for state and federal legislation rest upon? Does it account for Section 5 of the Fourteenth Amendment, which gives Congress power to enforce the principle of equal protection of the laws?

5. Justice O'Connor wrote that "Remaining true to an 'intrinsically sounder' doctrine established in prior cases better serves the values of *stare decisis* than would following a more recently decided case inconsistent with the decisions that came before it." Is this understanding of *stare decisis* as a method of interpretation consistent with her decision in *Planned Parenthood v. Casey* (1992)?

6. Justice Stevens argues that O'Connor's opinion fails to account for important differences of constitutional principle between "a decision by representatives of the majority to discriminate against the members of a minority race" and a decision by the same representatives "to impose incidental costs on the majority of their constituents. . . ." What constitutional principle is implicated by this difference? What view of the democratic process undergirds Justice Stevens' approach? Is it consistent with footnote 4 in *Carolene Products* (1938)? Is O'Connor's opinion consistent with footnote 4?

7. Justice Stevens observes that "substantial agreement on the standard to be applied in deciding difficult cases does not necessarily lead to agreement on how those cases actually should or will be resolved." Do you agree? If it is true, then what does this imply about the integrity of constitutional interpretation?

8. In the words of Justice Scalia, "we are just one race here. It is American." Do you agree? Is Justice Scalia's opinion a reassertion of the theory of the "color-blind" Constitution that we saw in Justice Harlan's opinion in *Plessy*?

9. Justice Ginsburg wrote that "in this area, large deference is owed by the Judiciary to Congress' institutional competence and constitutional authority to overcome historic racial subjugation." Why? What is the source of this congressional authority?

Grutter v. Bollinger

539 U.S.——, 123 S. Ct. 2325, 156 L. Ed. 2d 304 (2003)

Grutter v. Bollinger was one of two affirmative action cases involving the University of Michigan and decided by the Supreme Court on June 23, 2003. *Grutter* challenged the use of race as one factor among many in the admission of students to the law school. Other relevant facts are contained in the opinion. (The second case, *Gratz v. Bollinger*, questioned the use of race in the University's undergraduate admissions program. This program, struck down as an unconstitutional quota in violation of the Fourteenth Amendment, automatically awarded 20 points to underrepresented minority applicants among a variety of factors considered in each applicant's file.) *Grutter* sustained the constitutionality of the law school's admission program. Opinion of the Court: *O'Connor*, Stevens, Souter, Ginsburg, Breyer. Concurring opinion: *Ginsburg*. Dissenting opinions: *Rehnquist, Thomas, Scalia, Kennedy*.

Justice O'CONNOR delivered the opinion of the Court.

This case requires us to decide whether the use of race as a factor in student admissions by the University of Michigan Law School is unlawful.

Petitioner Barbara Grutter is a white Michigan resident who applied to the Law School in 1996 with a 3.8 grade point average and 161 LSAT score. The Law School initially placed petitioner on a waiting list, but subsequently rejected her application. In December 1997, petitioner filed suit in the United States District Court for the Eastern District of Michigan against the Law School. . . . Petitioner alleged that respondents discriminated against her on the basis of race in violation of the *Fourteenth Amendment*.

Petitioner further alleged that her application was rejected because the Law School uses race as a "predominant" factor, giving applicants who belong to certain minority groups "a significantly greater chance of admission than students with similar credentials from disfavored racial groups." Petitioner also alleged that respondents "had no compelling interest to justify their use of race in the admissions process." Petitioner requested compensatory and punitive damages, an order requiring the Law School to offer her admission, and an injunction prohibiting the Law School from continuing to discriminate on the basis of race.

In an attempt to quantify the extent to which the Law School actually considers race in making admissions decisions, the parties introduced voluminous evidence at trial. . . .

Dr. Stephen Raudenbush, the Law School's expert, focused on the predicted effect of eliminating race as a factor in the Law School's admission process. . . . He testified that in 2000, 35 percent of underrepresented minority applicants were admitted. Dr. Raudenbush predicted that if race were not considered, only 10 percent of those applicants would have been admitted. Under this scenario, underrepresented minority students would have comprised

Comparative Note 14.8

[In the late 1960s, the Universities of Hamburg and Munich imposed limits on the number of students admitted to their respective medical schools. Numerical limits were imposed because the number of students was beginning to outstrip the capacity of the schools to educate them. The policy resulted in the rejection of qualified applicants. Pursuant to a reference from an administrative court, the Federal Constitutional Court declared that the policy was inconsistent with the Basic Law.]

When the state has created certain educational institutions, claims of access to these institutions may arise from the principle of equality in tandem with Article 12 (1) and with the principle of the state based on social justice. This is especially true when the state has laid claim to a factual monopoly that cannot easily be abandoned, as in the sphere of education, and when participation in governmental services is also an indispensable precondition for the exercise of basic rights as in the field of training for academic professions. In a free social welfare state based on the rule of law, [one] cannot leave it to the limited discretion of governmental agencies to determine the circle of beneficiaries and to exclude some citizens from these privileges, especially since this would result in the [government] steering the choice of a profession. On the contrary, every citizen qualified for university studies has the right to share equally in the opportunity being offered. [This] conclusion flows from the fact that the state offers these services. Therefore, Article 12 (1) [guaranteeing one's right to choose a profession] together with Article 3 (1) [the principle of equality] and the mandate of a social welfare state guarantee any citizen meeting the individual admission requirements the right to be admitted to the [institution of] higher education of his choice.

Source: *Numerus Clausus I Case*, Kommers, *Constitutional Jurisprudence*, 2nd ed., 284–283.

---

4 percent of the entering class in 2000 instead of the actual figure of 14.5 percent.

In the end, the District Court concluded that the Law School's use of race as a factor in admissions decisions was unlawful. Applying strict scrutiny, the District Court determined that the Law School's asserted interest in assembling a diverse student body was not compelling because "the attainment of a racially diverse class . . . was not recognized as such by *Bakke* and is not a remedy for past discrimination." The District Court went on to hold that even if diversity were compelling, the Law School had not narrowly tailored its use of race to further that interest.

Since this Court's splintered decision in *Bakke*, Justice Powell's opinion announcing the judgment of the Court has served as the touchstone for constitutional analysis of race-conscious admissions policies. Public and private universities across the Nation have modeled their own admissions programs on Justice Powell's views on permissible race-conscious policies.

Justice Powell approved the university's use of race to further only one interest: "the attainment of a diverse student body." With the important proviso that "constitutional limitations protecting individual rights may not be disregarded," Justice Powell grounded his analysis in the academic freedom that "long has been viewed as a special concern of the *First Amendment*." . . . In seeking the "right to select those students who will contribute the most to the 'robust exchange of ideas,'" a university seeks "to achieve a goal that is of paramount importance in the fulfillment of its mission." Both "tradition and experience lend support to the view that the contribution of diversity is substantial."

We turn to the question whether the Law School's use of race is justified by a compelling state interest. Before this Court, as they have throughout this litigation, respondents assert only one justification for their use of race in the admissions process: obtaining "the educational benefits that flow from a diverse student body." In other words, the Law School asks us to recognize, in the context of higher education, a compelling state interest in student body diversity. . . . Today, we hold that the Law School has a compelling interest in attaining a diverse student body.

The Law School's educational judgment that such diversity is essential to its educational mission is one to which we defer. The Law School's assessment that diversity will, in fact, yield educational benefits is substantiated by respondents and their *amici*. Our scrutiny of the interest asserted by the Law School is no less strict for taking into account complex educational judgments in an area that lies primarily within the expertise of the university. Our holding today is in keeping with our tradition of giving a degree of deference to a university's academic decisions, within constitutionally prescribed limits.

We have long recognized that, given the important purpose of public education and the expansive freedoms of speech and thought associated with the university environment, universities occupy a special niche in our constitutional tradition. In announcing the principle of student body diversity as a compelling state interest, Justice Powell invoked our cases recognizing a constitutional dimension, grounded in the *First Amendment*, of educational autonomy: "The freedom of a university to make its own judgments as to education includes the selection of its student body." From this premise, Justice Powell reasoned that by claiming "the right to select those students who will contribute the most to the 'robust exchange of ideas,'" a university "seeks to achieve a goal that is of paramount importance in the fulfillment of its mission." Our conclusion that the Law School has a compelling interest in a diverse student body is informed by our view that attaining a diverse student body is at the heart of the Law School's proper institutional mission, and that "good faith" on the part of a university is "presumed" absent "a showing to the contrary."

As part of its goal of "assembling a class that is both exceptionally academically qualified and broadly diverse," the Law School seeks to "enroll a 'critical mass' of minority students." The Law School's interest is not simply "to assure within its student body some specified percentage of a particular group merely because of its race or ethnic origin." That would amount to outright racial balancing, which is patently unconstitutional. Rather, the Law School's concept of critical mass is defined by reference to the educational benefits that diversity is designed to produce.

These benefits are not theoretical but real, as major American businesses have made clear that the skills needed in today's increasingly global marketplace can only be developed through exposure to widely diverse people, cultures, ideas, and viewpoints. What is more, high-ranking retired officers and civilian leaders of the United States military assert that, "based on [their] decades of experience," a "highly qualified, racially diverse officer corps . . . is essential to the military's ability to fulfill its principle mission to provide national security." . . . To fulfill its mission, the military "must be selective in admissions for training and education for the officer corps, *and* it must train and educate a highly qualified, racially diverse officer corps in a racially diverse setting." (emphasis in original). . . .

Individuals with law degrees occupy roughly half the state governorships, more than half the seats in the United States Senate, and more than a third of the seats in the United States House of Representatives. The pattern is even more striking when it comes to highly selective law schools. A handful of these schools accounts for 25 of the 100 United States Senators, 74 United States Courts of Appeals judges, and nearly 200 of the more than 600 United States District Court judges.

In order to cultivate a set of leaders with legitimacy in the eyes of the citizenry, it is necessary that the path to leadership be visibly open to talented and qualified individuals of every race and ethnicity. All members of our heterogeneous society must have confidence in the openness and integrity of the educational institutions that provide this training. As we have recognized, law schools "cannot be effective in isolation from the individuals and institutions with which the law interacts." Access to legal education (and thus the legal profession) must be inclusive of talented and qualified individuals of every race and ethnicity, so that all members of our heterogeneous society may participate in the educational institutions that provide the training and education necessary to succeed in America.

The Law School does not premise its need for critical mass on "any belief that minority students always (or even consistently) express some characteristic minority viewpoint on any issue." To the contrary, diminishing the force of such stereotypes is both a crucial part of the Law School's mission, and one that it cannot accomplish with only token numbers of minority students. . . . The Law School has determined, based on its experience and expertise, that a "critical mass" of underrepresented minorities is necessary to further its compelling interest in securing the educational benefits of a diverse student body.

Even in the limited circumstance when drawing racial distinctions is permissible to further a compelling state interest, government is still "constrained in how it may pursue that end: The means chosen to accomplish the [government's] asserted purpose must be specifically and narrowly framed to accomplish that purpose." The purpose of the narrow tailoring requirement is to ensure that "the means chosen 'fit' . . . the compelling goal so closely that there is little or no possibility that the motive for the classification was illegitimate racial prejudice or stereotype."

Since *Bakke*, we have had no occasion to define the contours of the narrow-tailoring inquiry with respect to race-conscious university admissions programs. That inquiry must be calibrated to fit the distinct issues raised by the use of race to achieve student body diversity in public higher education. Contrary to Justice Kennedy's assertions, we do not "abandon strict scrutiny." Rather, as we have already explained, we adhere to *Adarand*'s teaching that the very purpose of strict scrutiny is to take such "relevant differences into account."

To be narrowly tailored, a race-conscious admissions program cannot use a quota system—it cannot "insulate each category of applicants with certain desired qualifications from competition with all other applicants." Instead, a university may consider race or ethnicity only as a "'plus' in a particular applicant's file," without "insulating the individual from comparison with all other candidates for the available seats." In other words, an admissions program must be "flexible enough to consider all pertinent elements of diversity in light of the particular qualifications of each applicant, and to place them on the same footing for consideration, although not necessarily according them the same weight."

We find that the Law School's admissions program bears the hallmarks of a narrowly tailored plan. As Justice Powell made clear in *Bakke*, truly individualized consideration demands that race be used in a flexible, nonmechanical way. It follows from this mandate that universities cannot establish quotas for members of certain racial groups or put members of those groups on separate admissions tracks. Nor can universities insulate applicants who belong to certain racial or ethnic groups from the competition for admission. Universities can, however, consider race or ethnicity more flexibly as a "plus" factor in the context of individualized consideration of each and every applicant.

We are satisfied that the Law School's admissions program, like the Harvard plan described by Justice Powell, does not operate as a quota. . . .

The Law School's goal of attaining a critical mass of underrepresented minority students does not transform its program into a quota. As the Harvard plan described by Justice Powell recognized, there is of course "some relationship between numbers and achieving the benefits to be derived from a diverse student body, and between numbers and providing a reasonable environment for those students admitted." "Some attention to numbers," without more, does not transform a flexible admissions system into a rigid quota.

That a race-conscious admissions program does not operate as a quota does not, by itself, satisfy the requirement of individualized consideration. When using race as a "plus" factor in university admissions, a university's admissions program must remain flexible enough to ensure that each applicant is evaluated as an individual and not in a way that makes an applicant's race or ethnicity the defining feature of his or her application. The importance of this individualized consideration in the context of a race-conscious admissions program is paramount.

Here, the Law School engages in a highly individualized, holistic review of each applicant's file, giving serious consideration to all the ways an applicant might contribute to a diverse educational environment. The Law School affords this individualized consideration to applicants of all races. There is no policy, either *de jure* or *de facto*, of automatic acceptance or rejection based on any single "soft" variable. Unlike the program at issue in *Gratz v. Bollinger,* the Law School awards no mechanical, predetermined diversity "bonuses" based on race or ethnicity. The Law School's admissions policy "is flexible enough to consider all pertinent elements of diversity in light of the particular qualifications of each applicant, and to place them on the same footing for consideration, although not necessarily according them the same weight."

We agree that, in the context of its individualized inquiry into the possible diversity contributions of all applicants, the Law School's race-conscious admissions program does not unduly harm nonminority applicants. We are mindful, however, that "[a] core purpose of the *Fourteenth Amendment* was to do away with all governmentally imposed discrimination based on race." Accordingly, race-conscious admissions policies must be limited in time. This requirement reflects that racial classifications, however compelling their goals, are potentially so dangerous that they may be employed no more broadly than the interest demands. Enshrining a permanent justification for racial preferences would offend this fundamental equal protection principle. We see no reason to exempt race-conscious admissions programs from the requirement that all governmental use of race must have a logical end point.

We take the Law School at its word that it would "like nothing better than to find a race-neutral admissions formula" and will terminate its race-conscious admissions program as soon as practicable. It has been 25 years since Justice Powell first approved the use of race to further an interest in student body diversity in the context of public higher education. Since that time, the number of minority applicants with high grades and test scores has indeed increased. We expect that 25 years from now, the use of racial preferences will no longer be necessary to further the interest approved today.

In summary, the *Equal Protection Clause* does not prohibit the Law School's narrowly tailored use of race in admissions decisions to further a compelling interest in obtaining the educational benefits that flow from a diverse student body. The judgment of the Court of Appeals for the Sixth Circuit, accordingly, is affirmed.

It is so ordered.

Chief Justice REHNQUIST, with whom Justice SCALIA, Justice KENNEDY, and Justice THOMAS join, dissenting.

I agree with the Court that, "in the limited circumstance when drawing racial distinctions is permissible," the government must ensure that its means are narrowly tailored to achieve a compelling state interest. I do not believe, however, that the University of Michigan Law School's (Law School) means are narrowly tailored to the interest it asserts. The Law School claims it must take the steps it does to achieve a "critical mass" of underrepresented minority students. But its actual program bears no relation to this asserted goal. Stripped of its "critical mass" veil, the Law School's program is revealed as a naked effort to achieve racial balancing.

As we have explained many times, "any preference based on racial or ethnic criteria must necessarily receive a most searching examination." Our cases establish that, in order to withstand this demanding inquiry, respondents must demonstrate that their methods of using race "fit" a compelling state interest "with greater precision than any alternative means."

Although the Court recites the language of our strict scrutiny analysis, its application of that review is unprecedented in its deference.

In practice, the Law School's program bears little or no relation to its asserted goal of achieving "critical mass." Respondents explain that the Law School seeks to accumulate a "critical mass" of *each* underrepresented minority group. But the record demonstrates that the Law School's admissions practices with respect to these groups differ dramatically and cannot be defended under any consistent use of the term "critical mass."

From 1995 through 2000, the Law School admitted between 1,130 and 1,310 students. Of those, between 13 and 19 were Native American, between 91 and 108 were African-Americans, and between 47 and 56 were Hispanic. If the Law School is admitting between 91 and 108 African-Americans in order to achieve "critical mass," thereby preventing African-American students from feeling "isolated or like spokespersons for their race," one would think that a number of the same order of magnitude would be necessary to accomplish the same purpose for Hispanics and Native Americans. Similarly, even if all of the Native American applicants admitted in a given year matriculate, which the record demonstrates is not at all the case, how can this possibly constitute a "critical mass" of Native Americans in a class of over 350 students? In order for this pattern of admission to be consistent with the Law School's explanation of "critical mass," one would have to believe that the objectives of "critical mass" offered by respondents are achieved with only half the number of Hispanics and one-sixth the number of Native Americans as compared to African-Americans. But respondents offer no race-specific reasons for such disparities. Instead, they simply emphasize the importance of achieving "critical mass," without any explanation of why that concept is applied differently among the three underrepresented minority groups.

Only when the "critical mass" label is discarded does a likely explanation for these numbers emerge. The Court states that the Law School's goal of attaining a "critical mass" of underrepresented minority students is not an interest in merely "assuring within its student body some specified percentage of a particular group merely because of its race or ethnic origin." The Court recognizes that such an interest "would amount to outright racial balancing, which is patently unconstitutional." *Ante*, at 17. The Court concludes, however, that the Law School's use of race in admissions, consistent with Justice Powell's opinion in *Bakke*, only pays "some attention to numbers."

But the correlation between the percentage of the Law School's pool of applicants who are members of the three minority groups and the percentage of the admitted applicants who are members of these same groups is far too precise to be dismissed as merely the result of the school paying "some attention to [the] numbers." . . .

I do not believe that the Constitution gives the Law School such free rein in the use of race. The Law School has offered no explanation for its actual admissions practices and, unexplained, we are bound to conclude that the Law School has managed its admissions program, not to achieve a "critical mass," but to extend offers of admission to members of selected minority groups in proportion to their statistical representation in the applicant pool. But this is precisely the type of racial balancing that the Court itself calls "patently unconstitutional."

Finally, I believe that the Law School's program fails strict scrutiny because it is devoid of any reasonably precise time limit on the Law School's use of race in admissions. We have emphasized that we will consider "the planned duration of the remedy" in determining whether a race-conscious program is constitutional. Our previous cases have required some limit on the duration of programs such as this because discrimination on the basis of race is invidious.

Justice THOMAS, with whom Justice SCALIA joins as to Parts I-VII, concurring in part and dissenting in part.

Frederick Douglass, speaking to a group of abolitionists almost 140 years ago, delivered a message lost on today's majority:

"In regard to the colored people, there is always more that is benevolent, I perceive, than just, manifested towards us. What I ask for the negro is not benevolence, not pity, not sympathy, but simply *justice*. The American people have always been anxious to know what they shall do with us. . . . I have had but one answer from the beginning. Do nothing with us! Your doing with us has already played the mischief with us. Do nothing with us! If the apples will not remain on the tree of their own strength, if they are worm-eaten at the core, if they are early ripe and disposed to fall, let them fall! . . . And if the negro cannot stand on his own legs, let him fall also. All I ask is, give him a chance to stand on his own legs! Let him alone! . . . Your interference is doing him positive injury."

Like Douglass, I believe blacks can achieve in every avenue of American life without the meddling of university administrators. Because I wish to see all students succeed whatever their color, I share, in some respect, the sympathies of those who sponsor the type of discrimination advanced by the University of Michigan Law School (Law School). The Constitution does not, however, tolerate institutional devotion to the status quo in admissions policies when such devotion ripens into racial discrimination. Nor does the Constitution countenance the unprecedented deference the Court gives to the Law School, an approach inconsistent with the very concept of "strict scrutiny."

No one would argue that a university could set up a lower general admission standard and then impose heightened requirements only on black applicants. Similarly, a university may not maintain a high admission standard and grant exemptions to favored races. The Law School, of its own choosing, and for its own purposes, maintains an exclusionary admissions system that it knows produces racially disproportionate results. Racial discrimination is not a permissible solution to the self-inflicted wounds of this elitist admissions policy.

The majority upholds the Law School's racial discrimination not by interpreting the people's Constitution, but by responding to a faddish slogan of the cognoscenti. Nevertheless, I concur in part in the Court's opinion. First, I agree with the Court insofar as its decision, which approves of only one racial classification, confirms that further use of race in admissions remains unlawful. Second, I agree with the Court's holding that racial discrimination in higher education admissions will be illegal in 25 years. I respectfully dissent from the remainder of the Court's opinion and the judgment, however, because I believe

that the Law School's current use of race violates the *Equal Protection Clause* and that the Constitution means the same thing today as it will in 300 months.

Dissenting opinions of Justice KENNEDY and SCALIA omitted.

Notes and Queries

1. Justice O'Connor claims to be following the lead of Justice Powell's opinion in *Bakke*. We suggested in the introductory essay that the rationale for affirmative action in higher education has shifted from remedying past discrimination to securing confidence in the future of American institutions. Do you agree?

2. Justice Rehnquist, dissenting, faults the majority for its "unprecedented deference" to the University's affirmative action policy in "the language of strict scrutiny analysis." Is there any warrant for the view that Justice O'Connor applied a lower standard of review in the guise of strict scrutiny review?

3. *Grutter* is the first case to place a specified time limit—25 years—on affirmative action. Is this a prediction or an iron-clad legal principle? And what is the goal behind the 25-year limit? Proportional representation of white, black, and Hispanic students in colleges and universities? Suppose poor school districts, which tend to have more minority students, continue to receive less financial support than middle and upper middle class white districts. Are 25 years enough to eliminate the gap in educational achievement between the races, a gap attributable in large part to social and cultural factors? Will anything really change in 25 years? Consider this comment from a *New York Times* article (Week in Review, 29 June 2003, 1): "In the end, the debate has not changed. Opponents of affirmative action will continue to say that such programs keep the country from focusing on what needs to be done—namely, helping minority students meet higher standards. The supporters of race preferences counter that the country cannot end affirmative action without first fixing the educational system. All agree that unless a commitment is made—by society and minority families themselves—the old arguments will still be around in 25 years."

4. In a moving dissent, Justice Thomas, the only African-American on the Court, writes that "[r]acial discrimination is not a permissible solution to the self-inflicted wounds of this elitist admissions policy." What does Thomas mean by "self-inflicted wounds"? Why does he characterize the policy as "elitist"?

5. Agreeing with the Court's holding that racial discrim-

ination in higher education will be illegal in twenty-five years, Justice Thomas concluded "that the Law School's current use of race violates the *Equal Protection Clause* and that the Constitution means the same thing today as it will in 300 months." Your response?

Chapter 15

Gender Discrimination and Other Claims to Equality

orld War II brought about vast economic and social changes in the United States. The growth of suburbia, the mobility of the population, and the expansion of higher education on a massive scale accompanied these changes. Habits of mind and social values also changed as Americans in untold numbers aspired to personal fulfillment defined largely in terms of material well-being and the equal opportunity to achieve it. Old patterns of social organization and old political structures began to break down under the weight of these new trends. *Brown v. Board of Education* (1954) signaled the collapse of one such pattern,[1] just as *Baker v. Carr* (1962) brought down electoral systems that favored rural over urban and suburban voters.[2] The cry of equality filled the air and, as *Brown* and *Baker* made clear, the Supreme Court was serving notice that it would respond to the cry.

Brown and *Baker* conveyed a message that ran well beyond the demand for racial equality or equal access to the ballot. By nullifying laws embedded in the South's social morality and assuming the power to hear the complaints of voters in malapportioned districts, the Warren Court inspired other groups to seek the judiciary's help in realizing their claims to equality. These groups included women, aliens (legal and illegal), poor people, non-marital children, the handicapped, the aged, gay men and lesbians, and other discriminated-against groups with arguable claims to judicial solicitude under the Equal Protection Clause. Inspired by the increasing emphasis on individual rights in the 1960s and beyond, these groups struggled to eliminate disadvantages they experienced under existing laws and policies. Racial issues and political rights would continue to command the Court's attention, but in the 1960s and beyond equal protection cases would begin to focus more heavily on rights and values unrelated to these concerns.

Conflicts between federal judicial authority and state power and the polarity between liberty and community highlight the cases featured in this chapter. These cases created deep divisions on the Supreme Court, reflecting as much as contributing to the great debate over the reach of federal judicial

---

[1] 347 U.S. 483 (1954).

[2] 369 U.S. 186 (1962).

power. To understand the cases, however, we need to place them in their proper historical and interpretive setting. To do so, we begin with a discussion of equality and governmental line-drawing and then proceed to a brief overview of the Supreme Court's latter-day approach to the interpretation of the Equal Protection Clause. In contrast to the constitutionalism of equality found in other advanced democracies, American equal protection analysis has been heavily influenced, and thus severely limited, by the judicial emphasis on the original purpose of the Fourteenth Amendment.

Legislative Differentiation and the Meaning of Equality

The Declaration of Independence was founded on the proposition that "all men are created equal." Early Americans, however, defined equality in a strictly formal sense. They meant equality under law, which they translated into equality of opportunity, particularly at life's starting gate. Formal equality did not imply equality of result in the ordinary business of life.[3] Once out of life's starting gate, Americans were free to use their faculties to produce a society marked by inequalities of condition and status, many of which were sanctioned and perpetuated by law. Rarely, however, did the Supreme Court use its power to remove these inequalities, in part because the Founders knew that persons were unequally endowed with energy, talent, and ambition, faculties warranting protection, which, wrote Madison, "is the first object of government."[4]

Still the meaning of equality was—and is—sufficiently elastic to accommodate and even to encourage the kind of changes brought about by challenges to the status quo. In western as in American political thought the notion of equality has been central to the idea of justice. For Aristotle as for us the idea of justice—and equality—included the perception that similarly situated persons should be treated similarly. According to this perception, injustice occurs when equals are treated unequally and unequals equally. To say this, however, is platitudinous. In addition, the perception may be mistaken. Justice William Rogers McIntyre of the Canadian Supreme Court writes: "[The Aristotelian perception] is seriously deficient in that it excludes any consideration of the nature of law. If it were to be applied literally, it could be used to justify the Nuremberg laws of Adolf Hitler. Similar treatment was contemplated for all Jews. The similarily situated test would have justified the formalistic separate but equal doctrine of *Plessy v. Ferguson*."[5] The difficulty begins when lawmakers try to determine who should be treated similarly or differently in the light of some policy objective. Differential treatment based on measures such as income, occupation, marital status, place and length of residence, value of property, and the size or nature of a business—the basis of much modern lawmaking—is a normal part of the governing process where political majorities would be expected to have their way. Invariably, however, policies based on such line-drawing raise questions about their compatibility with the norm of equality.

Whether government treats similarly situated persons the same depends, as suggested, on the purpose or reason behind a particular classification. For example, men and women may be similarly situated for some purposes, but not others. Often,

---

[3] See Kenneth L. Karst, *Why Equality Matters*, 17 Georgia Law Review 245, 261–263 (1983).

[4] *The Federalist*, edited by Benjamin Fletcher Wright (New York: Barnes & Noble, Inc., 1996), No. 10, 131.

[5] See *Andrews v. Law Society of British Columbia*, 56 D.L.R. (4th) 1 [1989], 11–12.

however, lawmakers cannot agree on the standard for separating things that are the same from those that are different. Consider a state disability insurance program that pays benefits to private employees temporarily unable to work but excludes from its coverage physical disability resulting from normal pregnancy. Is a woman who is bedridden for two days after a normal childbirth in the same situation as a man bedridden for two days owing to an appendectomy? Has the state discriminated on the basis of sex because the burden of the policy falls entirely on women? Does the policy treat equals unequally in breach of the Aristotelian idea of equality?[6]

On the other hand, why should legislatures be denied the right to draw such lines in accordance with their best political judgment of what constitutes sound public policy? Bear in mind that whenever the state allocates scarce resources, either by conferring a benefit upon some persons or imposing a burden on others, it engages in an inexact science. Whether based on common knowledge of the world, on information gathered from public hearings, or on empirical studies of social, economic, or criminal behavior, legislative decisions are imperfect judgments. James Bradley Thayer once observed that "whatever is rational is constitutional." Unless the legislature makes a clear mistake (i.e., "one not open to rational question"), he wrote, the Court should stay its hand and sustain the legislative judgment.[7] After all, politics almost always intrudes into the legislative process, producing laws evolving out of the give and take of conflict and mediation. Fallibility and partisanship thus combine to produce legislative judgments the fairness of which are often a matter of disagreement among reasonable men and women.[8] This reality raises a central question posed here and in previous chapters: why should the judiciary interfere with reasonable legislative judgments, particularly when they reflect the scheme of life prevailing in the community? But others ask: why should a court of constitutional review be bound by political judgments arguably incompatible with basic rights under the Constitution?

Equal Protection and the Supreme Court: 1938–1960

Prior to 1938, as noted in the previous chapter, the Supreme Court seldom used the equal protection clause to invalidate governmental policies. The year 1938 is important because it inaugurated the Court's policy of applying heightened scrutiny to so-called "suspect" classifications; that is, laws or regulations aimed at "discrete and

---

[6] The Supreme Court grappled with this issue in *Geduldig v. Aiello*. Over the objection of Justices Brennan, Douglas, and Marshall, the majority, speaking through Justice Stewart, ruled that the exclusion of pregnancy from the state's disability insurance system was not "invidious discrimination under the Equal Protection Clause." See 417 U.S. 484, 494 (1974).

[7] *The Origin and Scope of the American Doctrine of Constitutional Law*, 7 Harvard Law Review (1893): 144.

[8] Another example of such a judgment is the gender-based drinking law at issue in *Craig v. Boren* (1976, reprinted in this chapter). In the face of statistics showing that high numbers of traffic deaths involve young men between the ages of eighteen and twenty who drive under the influence of alcohol, a state prohibits the sale of "nonintoxicating" 3.2 beer to males in this age category but omits females from the ban. Clearly, this is an imperfect way of dealing with the problem of alcohol-related driving offenses. The imperfection of the classifying trait—i.e., males eighteen to twenty years of age—is obvious, for it includes many young men in this age category who remain sober behind the wheel and excludes some women of the same age who drive while sotted. In addition, it excludes all persons 21 and above who cause highway deaths while driving under the influence of alcohol. The result is a classification that imposes an undeserved benefit on some persons and an undeserved burden on others. Yet most legislative classifications would seem to suffer from the vice of under- and over-inclusiveness.

insular minorities" unable to rely on the normal political process for their protection.[9] The minorities referred to were mainly racial, and the classification was usually held to be suspect if based on an immutable characteristic and directed against groups marked by their insularity and powerlessness in American society. As for all other statutes, the Court continued to apply a rather low standard of reasonableness that usually resolved itself into one of minimum rationality. Typically, such classifications would be struck down in the name of equal protection only when found to be wholly arbitrary or capricious. If the law or regulation was found to be reasonably connected to a declared purpose or to one the Court itself could imagine, the justices would stay their hands and approve the legislation.[10] This deferential posture in the face of an equal protection challenge accorded with the Court's policy, beginning in 1937, of not using the due process clause of the Fourteenth Amendment as a weapon to nullify regulatory legislation affecting social and economic interests. (Recall, however, that the Court's rejection of *economic* due process did not extend to cases on *personal* rights such as those discussed in chapter 11.)

This limited approach to judicial review was inspired by a conception of politics long dominant in American political science. According to this view, as noted in previous chapters, politics is a pluralistic power struggle. Who gets what, when, and how depends on the bargains and deals pounded out on the anvil of group conflict and persuasion. Majority rule legitimates laws resulting from this process of bargaining and dealing. Any group or coalition of groups capable of getting a majority of legislative votes wins. The losers could be expected to regroup and perhaps deal a winning hand at a later date. Americans tended to identify this process with representative democracy. In such a democracy, the argument continues, the judiciary should defer to legislative judgments so long as the process of decision making in the legislature is fair and the legislature itself is the product of a free and equal election.[11] Manifested here is an interpretive skepticism that doubts the judiciary's capacity to divine the meaning of equality any more objectively than the elected representatives of the people.

What made the years 1938 to 1960 distinctive then was the Supreme Court's two-track approach to the interpretation of the equal protection clause. One track was low, the other high. When on the low track, the Court reviewed laws and administrative acts with minimal scrutiny of means and virtually no scrutiny of ends. The result was usually a decision in favor of the government.[12] The high track, by contrast, applied mainly to classifications based on race and employed strict scrutiny review, an approach that required the state to advance a *compelling* reason—that is, more than a good reason and much more than a reasonable good—for passing the statute and to demonstrate that the classification was narrowly tailored to achieve its designated purpose. Strict scrutiny of both ends and means produced outcomes invariably

---

[9] See *United States v. Carolene Products*, 304 U.S. 144, 153, n. 4

[10] *Railway Express Agency, Inc. v. New York*, 336 U.S. 106 (1949).

[11] For an influential statement of this view see John Ely, *Democracy and Distrust: A Theory of Judicial Review* (Cambridge: Harvard University Press, 1980). For a trenchant criticism of the fairness and equality of representation as practiced in liberal democracies see David Held, "Democracy: From City-States to a Cosmopolitan Order?" in David Held, ed., *Prospects for Democracy* (Stanford, Calif: Stanford University Press, 1993): 13–52. See also Robert Dahl, A *Democratic Dilemma*, 109 Political Science Quarterly 23–34 (1994).

[12] *Morey v. Doud*, 354 U.S. 457 (1957) which held invalid a state law regulating money order firms, but exempting the American Express Company, was the main exception. *Morey*, however, was overruled in *New Orleans v. Duke*, 427 U.S. 297 (1976).

fatal to the challenged legislation. This limited two-tiered approach—one also mirrored in the Court's due process liberty cases—had the curious result of immunizing most laws and administrative acts from any meaningful judicial supervision while cordoning off an extremely narrow band of classifications reserved for devastating critical review.

The 1960s and Beyond

On the eve of the 1960s, equal protection analysis focused almost exclusively on the two-tiered approach. But it did not last for long in the post-*Brown* world of increasing diversity and social change.[13] In the face of such change, the Court decided no longer to limit the Equal Protection Clause to the history of its interpretation, thus shattering the prevailing consensus that had marked judicial analysis prior to 1960. Battle lines formed when some justices showed an increasing willingness—against the backdrop of a growing lack of confidence in the integrity of the American political process—to question legislative judgments based on gender, wealth, alienage, and illegitimacy, regarding them as suspect or nearly so. The simultaneous effort to examine with strict scrutiny legal distinctions impinging on "fundamental rights" other than those explicitly secured by the Constitution deepened the discord. In the 1960s and beyond, as the cases in this chapter illustrate, the Supreme Court would begin to sing in two, three, and occasionally four voices.

The disharmony on the Supreme Court could be traced at least in part to the legacy of the *Slaughter-House Cases* and *Carolene Products*. The former's strict intentionalism and the latter's argument in defense of "discrete and insular minorities" could not easily assimilate groups identified by traits other than race or ethnicity. In addition, because the Court refused to abandon its deferential approach to nonracial classifications, the Court failed to project any real meaning into the concept of equality. Rather, the Court adhered mechanically to the doctrine of formal equality. The only way, then, to breathe new life into the equal protection clause with the least amount of effort and simultaneously to adhere to the legacy of *Slaughter-House* and *Carolene Products*, was to add new levels of judicial review.[14]

Eventually, with respect to classifications based on gender and alienage, the Court settled on an intermediate standard of review—a test that would require the state to advance an *important*, as opposed to a compelling, governmental objective and to demonstrate a *substantial*, as opposed to a mere rational, connection between a classification and its purpose. So now there were three instead of two tracks of equal protection review and before long Justice Thurgood Marshall would urge the adoption of a "sliding scale" approach. Instead of the two or three-tiered approach, Marshall would adjust the intensity of judicial review to the value of the particular interest or individual right limited by the state and the importance of the state's reason for restricting that interest or right. Chief Justice Rehnquist would have none of this; he

---

[13] Edward A. Purcell writes: "By the mid-sixties American society had begun to look significantly different to many citizens. The dashing of hopes created by the Kennedy assassination, an increased awareness of poverty and racism, the sharpening identification of a military-industrial complex, ever growing governmental mendacity, and an apparently endless, pointless, and destructive war all combined to create a profound disillusion with the realities of America." See *The Crisis of Democratic Theory* (1973), p. 267.

[14] An initial strategy was to expand the list of suspect categories, but most of the justices resisted this effort, claiming that groups other than racial minorities failed to meet the indicia of immutability, insularity, and powerlessness. A related effort to apply strict scrutiny review to an expanded list of "fundamental rights" met with equal resistance.

would sustain all reasonable classifications while applying strict scrutiny only to those based on race or national origin.

It should be noted that these various levels, tests, or tiers of review are different ways of talking about when and why judges should or should not defer to legislative judgments or public policies favored by political majorities. Chief Justice Rehnquist's commitment to traditional equal protection principles, Justice Marshall's sliding scale approach, and the intermediate position advocated by other justices illustrate rival approaches to the role of the Court and the interpretation of the Fourteenth Amendment. The Chief Justice comes down on the side of clear and distinct rules—the two-tiered approach—that would serve as a ready set of guidelines for legislators to follow when crafting statutes. Justice Marshall's sliding scale invites the Court to review any number of laws on a case-by-case basis. And the intermediate position would create a category of quasi-suspect classifications warranting heightened but not strict scrutiny review.

In using the equal protection clause as a weapon to challenge an increasing number of legislative classifications, the Supreme Court entered new and perilous territory: new because the justices were now resolving issues without much guidance from history or the literal language of the Constitution; perilous because in second-guessing legislative judgments of fact and value, they were exposing themselves to the charge of willful policymaking. Indeed, by vetting classifications threatening fundamental rights as well as those based on such things as gender, illegitimacy, age, and wealth, the Court propelled itself and much of the country into another debate about the nature and limits of judicial power in America. The debate would repeat the historic and overlapping themes of liberty versus community, judicial supremacy versus majoritarian democracy, and federal versus state power.

Fundamental Interests and Equality

Shapiro v. Thompson (1969, reprinted later in the chapter) offers a dramatic example of federal judicial power overriding state law. Connecticut and Pennsylvania adopted laws denying welfare aid to persons who had not resided within their states for at least a year preceding their application for assistance. Most of the justices conceded that the reasons for establishing the one-year waiting period—for example, to help the states plan their budgets and to encourage new residents to seek immediate employment—were legitimate and reasonable but insufficiently *compelling* to justify the invasion of the fundamental right to travel. Justice Brennan, writing for the majority, seemed to advance two types of argument. On the one hand, even while conceding that the right to travel finds no explicit mention in the Constitution, he regarded this right as a constitutionally protected liberty. In drawing from Justice Stewart's opinion in *United States v. Guest*,[15] however, he also declared that the right to travel is fundamental to the strength of the federal union as such.[16] *Shapiro* solidified the prevailing doctrine that legal classifications impinging upon a *fundamental* right require strict scrutiny, a standard the two states were unable to meet.

The dissenting opinion of Chief Justice Warren, with whom Justice Black joined, showed that the division among the *Shapiro* justices transcended the ideological line between judicial liberals and conservatives. Warren and Black, like Justice Harlan,

---

[15] 383 U.S. 745 (1966).
[16] 394 U.S. 618 at 630.

underscored the insubstantiality of the waiting period as a burden on travel. In their view, the burden was indirect at best, a situation wholly different from previous cases nullifying outright bans on travel. For his part, Justice Harlan saw *Shapiro* as another example of "judicial interference with the state . . . legislative process."[17] In replacing its reasoned judgment for that of the reasoned judgment of local communities, he argued, the Court was devitalizing the states as laboratories of social experimentation. Justice Brennan, on the other hand, invoked a different image of community. "We are citizens of the United States" and "members of the same community"; it is therefore impermissible, he wrote, to deter "poor families in need of assistance" from moving into a state because they consider, "among other factors, the level of a State's public assistance."[18]

Shapiro was foreshadowed by earlier decisions vindicating the right to vote in state elections, the right to marry, and the right to an appellate review of a criminal conviction.[19] Like travel, none of these rights—or interests—enjoyed explicit constitutional protection. What they had in common, however, was their *fundamentality*; they were regarded as crucial to the exercise of citizenship or to the enjoyment of personhood. The Supreme Court would continue to apply strict scrutiny review to each of these rights, particularly when state laws imposed an economic burden on their effective exercise.[20]

Some justices, however, strongly objected to judicial decisions nullifying the imposition of reasonable costs uniformly exacted for state services such as the procurement of a marriage license or a transcript of a criminal trial. In their view, the Court was confusing invidious discrimination with discriminating laws designed to achieve valid public goals. Justice Harlan found *Shapiro* particularly alarming because it appeared to open the door to a spiraling equal protection jurisprudence. Would nutrition, shelter, health care, clean water or other basic necessities of life now swell the list of those fundamental interests worthy of enhanced judicial protection if otherwise reasonable state regulations placed them beyond the reach of people unable to pay for them? Dissenting in *Shapiro*, Justice Harlan expressed a view that would prevail in the 1970s and beyond: "[N]othing . . . entitles this Court to pick out particular human activities, characterize them as 'fundamental,' and give them added protection under an unusually stringent equal protection test."[21]

Within four short years, however, the Court appeared to have shut the door opened by *Shapiro*. In *San Antonio Independent School District v. Rodriguez* (1973, reprinted later in the chapter) a majority of five justices, over the separate dissenting opinions of White, Brennan, and Marshall, not only refused to define the "poor" as

---

[17] Ibid., at 677.

[18] Ibid., at 629–630, 632.

[19] See, respectively, *Griffin v. Illinois*, 351 U.S. 12 (1956), *Harper v. Virginia Bd. of Elections*, 383 U.S. 663 (1966), and *Loving v. Virginia*, 388 U.S. 1 (1967).

[20] This was particularly true with respect to the right to marry. In *Zablocki v. Redhail* (1978), for example, the Court struck down a Wisconsin statute denying a marriage license to one of its residents unless he could show that he had the means to support his out-of-custody minor children for whose welfare he was legally responsible. To prevent some persons from marrying because they are unable to make such a showing, said the Court, violates the norm of equality. In applying strict scrutiny to Wisconsin's law, the Court found, on the basis of its own independent judgment, that the state's substantial interest in making sure that out-of-custody children do not become public charges when the parent enters a new marriage could have been achieved by a far less restrictive means than the present law. See 434 U.S. 374 (1978).

[21] 394 U.S. 618 at 662.

a suspect class; they also declined to include education among the fundamental interests protected by the Constitution. (*Rodriguez* sustained a school financing system resulting in substantial interdistrict disparities in per-pupil expenditures.) Between *Shapiro* and *Rodriguez*, however, Warren Burger had replaced Earl Warren as Chief Justice while Justices Blackmun, Powell, and Rehnquist had replaced Justices Fortas, Black, and Harlan. (Justice Stevens would replace Douglas in 1975.) All four new justices, joined by Justice Stewart, formed the *Rodriguez* majority. Writing for the majority, Justice Powell, echoing the caution sounded by Justice Harlan in *Shapiro*, refused to include education among the fundamental rights protected by the Constitution.

Rodriguez was a crucial case because it represented the end of one major effort to guarantee an environment within which democratic rights could flourish. A new majority—the Nixon Court, as it was then being called—refused to sail into what it regarded as the uncharted waters of socioeconomic rights. Seeking to return the Court to a safer harbor, Justice Powell led the effort to close the door to any expansion of suspect classes or fundamental interests. Actually, *Rodriguez* might have been anticipated by *Lindsey v. Normet* (1972), decided a year earlier, when the Court proclaimed that "the Constitution does not provide judicial remedies for every social and economic ill."[22] *Lindsey* and related cases reinforced the emerging view of the Court's new conservative majority that it was not the Court's business to incorporate a substantive vision of social or economic equality into the Constitution.[23]

Rodriguez was a perfect example of how the tension between constitutionalism and politics affected perspectives on the scope of judicial review. The majority advanced the proposition that an unaccountable judiciary should not override the choices made by an electorally accountable democratic legislature unless those choices contravened an express provision of the Constitution or a right fairly implied from it. The legitimacy of judicial power, they maintained, would depend on the Court's sense of its own self-restraint. Justice Marshall, on the other hand, in perhaps his strongest and most impassioned opinion, dissented, as did Justices Brennan, White, and Douglas. For him, the issue was the legitimacy of political power in America, particularly when that power was exercised to seriously burden economically disadvantaged persons or groups. In this situation, Marshall argued, the Court could not blind itself to social and political realities that impaired the full realization of constitutional values.

Expressing his long-time disagreement with the Court's "rigidified [two-tiered] approach to equal protection analysis," Marshall rejected the majority's dismissal of education as a fundamental interest merely because it could not be found, implicitly or explicitly, in the constitutional text. Sensitive to social context, he stressed the importance of education to the effective exercise of freedom of speech as well as the right to vote. Education, he argued, was therefore a personal interest of constitutional significance, requiring a corresponding level of judicial scrutiny. Given "the constitutional and societal importance of the interest [i.e., education] affected," he concluded, the judiciary could not responsibly consign this interest, consistent with the principle of full and equal citizenship, to the keeping of majoritarian decision making.

Plyler v. Doe (1982, reprinted later in the chapter) adds an interesting footnote to

---

[22] 405 U.S. 56, 74 (denying a tenant's claim to adequate housing).

[23] See *Dandridge v. Williams*, 397 U.S. 471 (1970), which sustained upper limits on welfare payments to large families and *James v. Valtierra*, 402 U.S. 137 (1971) which upheld a California constitutional provision barring a state-sponsored low-income housing project unless approved in a popular referendum.

Rodriguez. It underscored the Court's mixed reaction to educational issues. *Plyler* invalidated a Texas statute denying funds to school districts for the education of children "not legally" admitted into the United States.[24] Although declining to treat undocumented aliens as a suspect class, Justice Brennan, writing for a badly fractured Court, faulted the challenged law because it was "directed against children, and impose[d] its discriminatory burden on the basis of a legal characteristic over which children can have little control. It is thus difficult to conceive of a rational justification for penalizing these children for their presence in the United States." Reflecting on what justice requires, the majority invalidated the Texas law because undocumented children are "persons" within the meaning of the Fourteenth Amendment, underscoring the important point that one does not have to be a citizen or even a legal alien to have a claim on constitutional entitlements. Because the Fourteenth Amendment protects "persons," said Justice Brennan, the state may not arbitrarily deprive undocumented children of the "basic education" accorded to other children. The state's policy, he wrote, "raises the specter of a permanent [underclass] of undocumented residents, [the existence of which] presents most difficult problems for a Nation that prides itself on adherence to principles of equality under law." The Court concluded by saying that "legislation directing the onus of a parent's misconduct [i.e., by entering the country illegally] against his children does not comport with fundamental conceptions of justice."[25] Four justices, led by Chief Justice Burger, dissented, claiming in part that the majority had invaded the state's rightful policy-making role, underscoring once again the lack of agreement over the meaning of equal protection.

Plyler introduced a note of ambiguity with respect to the constitutional status of education. Even while conceding that education is not a fundamental right under the Constitution, Justice Brennan noted that "education has a fundamental role in maintaining the fabric of our society," an opinion shared by Justice Blackmun. Justice Marshall, for his part, continued to insist that education is a fundamental right the state infringement of which must be scrutinized in proportion to its importance. Coupled with *Brown v. Board of Education, Plyler* seems significantly to have elevated the importance of education on the scale of American equal protection values. *Plyler* also seemed to put some teeth into ordinary "rationality" review.

Gender Discrimination

The ideal of civil equality is deeply rooted in our constitutional culture even if Americans have failed to live up to this ideal. On the other hand, certain beliefs and practices have been so embedded in the social culture that Americans often failed to recognize them as unreasonable, arbitrary, or discriminatory. This was particularly true with respect to relationships between men and women. The domination of the former over the latter in most areas of social life was thought to reflect the order of natural morality. Law and the prevailing culture kept women in the home, out of politics, and away from the marketplace. Women finally attained the constitutional right to vote in 1920, but this historic advance in their struggle for political equality fell far short of full partnership with men in the nation's social and economic life.[26]

By mid-century women could still point to a large battery of federal and state

---

[24] 457 U.S. 202 (1982).

[25] Ibid., at 220.

[26] See generally Suzanne M. Marilley, *Woman Suffrage and the Origins of Liberal Feminism in the United States 1820–1920* (Cambridge: Harvard University Press, 1996).

laws—e.g., dealing with occupational choice, conjugal property, social security, disability insurance, and job qualifications—where line-drawing based on gender deprived women of economic opportunity and social independence. Even laws designed to relieve women of burdens such as long hours of work or to protect them against the perils of certain kinds of employment tended to perpetuate traditional views of a woman's place in the larger society, inhibiting her participation in the professional and business world as well as her entry into the political arena.

Gender discrimination was not, however, a one-way street. Men were also its victims. Laws dealing with taxation and social security, child custody and adoption, jury and military service, statutory rape, and the consumption of alcoholic beverages imposed burdens and duties on men not expected of women. In some instances these laws absolved women of duties and burdens required of men. Many of these statutory classifications soon succumbed to the scrutiny of the equal protection clause. Two developments in the 1960s accelerated the scrutiny: One was the creation of the Kennedy Commission on the Status of Women; the other was the addition of gender to the list of impermissible reasons for discrimination under the Civil Rights Act of 1964. As the following discussion shows, however, the gender cases were a centerpiece of the ongoing "great debate" over the intensity and scope of judicial review in the 1970s and beyond.

Reed v. Reed (1971) marked the end of the Court's willing acceptance of legislative classifications based on gender. Here for the first time, and unanimously, the Supreme Court struck down an Idaho statute preferring men over women in the appointment of an administrator of a decedent's estate. Automatically to prefer a male over an equally entitled female administrator, said the Court, "establishes a classification subject to scrutiny under the Equal Protection Clause." In an unusually brief opinion, the Court held that the statute in question was "the very kind of arbitrary legislative choice forbidden by the [Constitution]."[27]

The surprising unanimity of *Reed* evaporated in *Frontiero v. Richardson* (1973, reprinted later in the chapter). *Frontiero* invalidated a federal law denying servicewomen benefits that servicemen were entitled to receive. The case resolved itself, however, into a joust over the meaning of *Reed*. Citing *Reed*, and speaking through Justice Brennan, a plurality of four justices held that laws "based upon sex, like [those] based upon race . . . are inherently suspect, and must therefore be subjected to strict judicial scrutiny."[28] Although voting to invalidate the law in question, Justice Powell, joined by Justices Blackmun and Stewart, denied that *Reed* defined gender as a suspect category. For these justices, the opinion of the *Frontiero* plurality was a bombshell with explosive implications, and they resisted what they regarded as an attempt to expand *Reed*'s rationale. Democratic theory also influenced Powell's opinion. He refused to equate gender with race during the pending struggle for the Equal Rights Amendment (ERA). "If the Amendment is duly adopted," he wrote, "it will represent the will of the people accomplished in the manner prescribed by the Constitution."[29] But failing its passage, he noted, judges would be well advised to follow majoritarian settlements unless found to be irrational or arbitrary. Finally, Justice Rehnquist, adhering to the traditional view that a nonracial classification should be upheld if it has a rational basis, was the lone dissenter.

Frontiero launched the Court into a bruising three-year battle over the standard of

---

[27] 404 U.S. 71, 75, 76.

[28] 411 U.S. 677, 688.

[29] Ibid., at 692.

review to be applied in gender discrimination cases. Brennan, along with Marshall and White, led the fight to identify gender as a suspect class.[30] Often in alliance with Burger, Rehnquist fought a rearguard action on behalf of the traditional equal protection test. Powell, along with Blackmun, Stewart, and Stevens, taking positions ranging from a willingness to view gender as quasi-suspect to a position favorable to putting more sting into the traditional test, occupied the broad middle ground. Finally, in *Craig v. Boren* (1976, reprinted later in the chapter), a majority agreed to regard sex-based classifications as quasi-suspect and subject to an intermediate standard of review. Under this test, sex or gender-based laws would have to be *substantially* related to an *important* governmental interest.

Was this new formulation little more than a play on words? Some members of the Court thought so, some did not. In the Court's lexicon, *substantiality* meant that a legal classification would have to be more than reasonable but less than the almost perfect fit between ends and means required of a suspect classification; *importance* required a purpose less than compelling but more than merely legitimate. Armed with this dialectic of substantiality and importance, the Court struck down many laws and policies based on gender or sex, especially if these laws or policies tended to perpetuate invidious, archaic, and overbroad stereotypes about the relative abilities of men and women. But the justices often differed with one another over the nature and extent of these stereotypes as well as over the meaning and application of the intermediate scrutiny. Whether a gender-based classification served an *important* objective or *substantially* related to a legitimate purpose invited personal judgments of fact and value. Relatedly, intermediate review can be faulted (or praised) for its elasticity; it could be stretched backward to what is little more than a rationality test, as *Rostker v. Goldberg* (1981) (upholding compulsory draft registration for men but not for women) seems to have done, or pushed forward toward strict scrutiny, as *J.E.B. v. Alabama* (1994) (forbidding peremptory challenges by the state to potential jurors on the basis of gender) seemed to do.

A pair of cases decided early in the 1980s illustrate this accordion-like character of intermediate judicial review, for the outcomes could not have been foretold. In *Michael M. v. Superior Court of Sonoma County* (1981), Chief Justice Rehnquist's plurality opinion sustained the constitutionality of California's statutory rape law that punished males for engaging in "unlawful sexual intercourse" with underage females but not females similarly engaged with underage males. Rehnquist found the law substantially related to the state's strong interest in preventing illegitimate teenage pregnancies. Because "the risk of pregnancy itself constitutes a substantial deterrence to young females" and "no similar natural sanctions deter males," the state may, he claimed, "roughly equalize" the deterrents on the sexes by punishing only the male offender. Brennan, joined by White and Marshall, strongly dissented, asserting the state should have been required "to prove that a gender-neutral law would be a less effective deterrent than a gender-based law" in light of suspicions the law had been based on "outmoded sexual stereotypes."

In *Mississippi University for Women v. Hogan* (1982), on the other hand, a five-person majority struck down an admissions policy excluding males from entering the university's nursing school. Justice Blackmun, normally allied with Brennan, White, and Marshall in other discrimination cases, dissented. "I have come to suspect," he wrote, "that it is easy to go too far with rigid rules in this area of claimed sex discrimi-

---

[30] Douglas, who joined Brennan's plurality opinion in *Frontiero*, retired in 1975. Justice John Paul Stevens, appointed by President Ford, replaced him.

nation, and to lose—indeed to destroy—values that mean much to some people by forbidding the State to offer them a choice while not depriving others of an alternative choice."[31] Justice Powell, joined by Rehnquist, also dissented with these stirring words: "The Court's opinion bows deeply to conformity. Left without honor—indeed, held unconstitutional—is an element of diversity that has characterized much of American education and enriched much of American life."

A second university-related case, *United States v. Virginia* (1996, reprinted later in the chapter), invalidated the Virginia Military Institute's all-male admissions policy. Justice Ginsburg, writing for the majority, rejected Virginia's argument that "single-sex education contributes to diversity in educational approaches," largely on the ground that the state had not provided an equal military educational experience for women. Chief Justice Rehnquist, in one of the rare cases where he voted to nullify a gender-based classification, concurred, largely because Virginia, in the light of *Hogan*, had not made an honest effort to set up an equivalent military institution for women. But he also faulted language in the majority opinion that seemed to him to go beyond substantial rationality review. "While the majority adheres to [the intermediate scrutiny test] today," he wrote, "it also says that the States must demonstrate an 'exceedingly persuasive justification' to support a gender-based classification. It is unfortunate that the Court thereby introduces an element of uncertainty respecting the appropriate test." Justice Scalia's impassioned dissent echoed the sentiments of Justice Blackmun in *Hogan*. He not only deplored the Court's willingness to abandon government supported male-only military schools but also its tendency to strike down "one after another of the current preferences of the society . . . into our Basic Law."

As the 1990s ended, the Court was no more unified on the status of gender-based classifications than a generation earlier, a reality underlined in *Nguyen v. Immigration and Naturalization Service* (2001, reprinted later in the chapter). Dividing once again 5 to 4, the Court sustained a gender-based classification relating to the acquisition of citizenship. The federal law in question granted automatic citizenship to non-marital children born outside the United States to a citizen mother and a non-citizen father, but denied citizenship to such children born to a citizen father and a non-citizen mother. Justice Kennedy, writing for the majority, found this distinction between unwed fathers and mothers compatible with the equal protection guarantee embedded in the Fifth Amendment's due process clause. The majority ruled that the federal government had met the standard of scrutiny set forth in *Hogan*, *Virginia*, and related cases. The important governmental objective was the assurance that a biological parent-child relationship exists. "In the case of the mother," wrote Kennedy, "the relationship is verifiable from the birth itself," whereas in the case of the father this is not so. (Paternity would have to be demonstrated in other ways.) Thus, "[f]athers and mothers are not similarly situated with regard to the proof of biological parenthood."

The dissenting justices, interestingly, included the two female members of the Court one of whom—Justice O'Connor—authored the dissent. O'Connor's opinion mounted a blistering assault on the majority's reasoning, mainly for its bland assumption about the parenting roles of mothers and fathers. In the dissenting view, the citizenship law was an "overbroad sex-based generalization" rooted in "the stereotypical notion" that mothers are more likely than fathers to develop a close bond with their children. A gender-neutral statute, combined with DNA tests and other

---

[31] *Mississippi University for Women v. Hogan,* 458 U.S. 718, 734.

evidence of paternity, claimed the dissenters, could just as easily have achieved the government's legitimate interest in verifying the actual formation of a meaningful parent-child relationship.

After reviewing these cases, we find a Court badly splintered in its application of the intermediate standard of review, making it difficult to predict the outcomes of particular cases. The justices are likely to uphold a sex-based classification under the prevailing standard of review when based on archaic stereotypical views of a woman's place in society. But here again the Court seems deeply fractured. Can the discord be explained by false rhetoric? There may be grounds for so concluding. In some instances, as in *Nguyen*, the majority seems to be applying basic rationality review in the guise of intermediate scrutiny, whereas in other instances, as in *Virginia*, the majority seems to be applying the same test in the guise of strict scrutiny. But what does this prove? Perhaps little more than that constitutional interpretation, as we stressed in chapter 2, is invariably and indisputably a matter of judgment by the men and women entrusted with the power of judicial review.

Other Claims to Equality and the Quest for Standards

The tension between democracy and constitutionalism flared up in still other struggles over the proper approach to judicial interpretation. Originally, in several cases handed down in the first half of the twentieth century, the Supreme Court sustained statutes denying resident aliens certain rights as long as there was a reasonable basis for treating them differently than citizens. In the early 1970s, the Court handed down a series of decisions holding that such classifications were inherently suspect and thus subject to close judicial scrutiny.[32] In *Foley v. Connelie* (1978, reprinted later in the chapter), however, the Court declared that not "every statutory exclusion of aliens" would have "to clear the high hurdle of 'strict scrutiny.'" To require such clearance, said the Court, "would obliterate all the distinctions between citizens and aliens and thus depreciate the historic values of citizenship."[33] Alienage, at least for some purposes, was now merely a quasi-suspect category.

As table 15.1 shows, the Supreme Court refused to expand the categories of suspect classifications and fundamental rights significantly despite appeals to do so from constitutional scholars, lower federal courts, and dissenting justices. As we have seen, gender and alienage, once pronounced "suspect," have been accorded quasi-suspect status. Wealth and poverty traveled similar paths. In 1966 the Court proclaimed: "Lines drawn on the basis of wealth or property, like those of race . . . are traditionally disfavored."[34] In 1973, however, *Rodriguez* shut the door on this development. Actually, *Rodriguez* represented the turning point in the Court's strict scrutiny jurisprudence. If the cases featured in this chapter were ordered chronologically rather than topically, the reader would readily see that after 1973, by which time the Court's membership was undergoing significant change, arguments rooted in strict scrutiny jurisprudence were almost uniformly rejected. Sexual orientation might have been added to the list of classifications involving minimal scrutiny but as noted in chapter 11, the doctrinal focus in *Bowers v. Hardwick* (1986) was the due process rather than

---

[32] These decisions struck down state laws barring aliens from certain professions and kinds of employment. See *Graham v. Richardson*, 403 U.S. 365 (1971), *In Re Griffiths*, 413 U.S. 717 (1973), and *Sugarman v. Dougall*, 413 U.S. 634 (1973).

[33] 435 U.S. 291, 295.

[34] *Harper v. Virginia Board of Elections*, 383 U.S. 663, 668 (1966).

TABLE 15.1 *Approaches to Equal Protection Review*

A. Classification		
Selected Traits	**Type**	**Level of Scrutiny**
race	suspect	strict
national origin	suspect	strict
alienage	quasi-suspect	midlevel
sex	quasi-suspect	midlevel
illegitimacy	quasi-suspect	midlevel
economic status	nonsuspect	minimal
age	nonsuspect	minimal
mental retardation	nonsuspect	minimal
B. Claim		
Selected Interests	**Nature**	**Level of Scrutiny**
voting	fundamental	strict
access to courts	fundamental	strict
privacy	fundamental	strict
travel	fundamental	strict
education	nonfundamental	minimal
welfare	nonfundamental	minimal
housing	nonfundamental	minimal
government employment	nonfundamental	minimal

the equal protection clause of the Fourteenth Amendment. In *Romer v. Evans* (1996, reprinted later in the chapter), however, the Court invalidated a Colorado constitutional amendment that barred local governments from enforcing any regulation or conferring any entitlement that grants protected minority status on homosexuals. The amendment was found to deprive homosexuals of their fundamental right to participate in the political process. The Court struck the statute not because homosexuals were regarded as a suspect class, but because the particular classification served no legitimate legislative purpose.

The Court's retrenchment from 1973 onwards did not always spell victory for majoritarian policies. In *Trimble v. Gordon* (1977, reprinted later in the chapter)—another split decision—the Supreme Court struck down an Illinois statute disadvantaging illegitimate children under an intermediate standard of review. (The Court declined, as it had in previous cases, to classify illegitimacy as suspect.) In *Cleburne v. Cleburne Living Center* (1985, reprinted later in the chapter), the Court also struck down a residential zoning restriction as applied to the mentally ill, yet it did so using what seemed to be an enhanced rational basis test. But in *Heller v. Doe* (1993), speaking through Justice Kennedy over the dissents of Justices Souter, Blackmun, and Stevens, the Supreme Court dropped back to the lowest standard of review by upholding a Kentucky statute providing for the involuntary commitment of mentally ill persons.[35]

Finally, the Court could not be induced to classify age as suspect. Here too, as in *Massachusetts Board of Retirement v. Murgia* (1977, reprinted later in the chapter), the Court adamantly insisted on applying minimum rationality. In doing so, it upheld

---

[35] 509 U.S. 312. Here a class of involuntarily committed persons challenged their commitment under a "clear and convincing evidence" standard of proof rather than under the more burdensome standard of "evidence beyond a reasonable doubt." In rejecting the complaint, Justice Kennedy declared that "[A] classification must be upheld . . . if there is any reasonably conceivable state of facts that could provide a rational basis for the classification."

the state's compulsory retirement age of 50 for police officers. Justice Marshall was the lone dissenter in *Murgia*. Underscoring the injustice of a state retirement policy driven by general statistical data on the relationship between age and physical fitness, he would have required the state to engage in individualized testing of persons over 50. Given the importance to the individual of the governmental benefit denied, this would have been a less restrictive means of achieving a physically fit police force. Several years later, the Supreme Court reaffirmed *Murgia* in *Gregory v. Ashcroft* (1991). In upholding Missouri's mandatory retirement for judges at age 70, Justice O'Connor, quoting from *Murgia*, remarked that "a state 'does not violate the Equal Protection Clause merely because the classification made by its laws are imperfect.' "[36]

As already mentioned, this fixation on standards of review remains a source of discord among the Court's members and a source of confusion among students of the Court. Chief Justice Rehnquist continues, as always, to rally around the flag of traditional equal protection review. The ambulatory path taken by the Court in dealing with various kinds of classifications led Rehnquist to exclaim in his *Trimble* dissent that "the Court's decisions [under the equal protection clause] can fairly be described as an endless tinkering with legislative judgments, a series of conclusions unsupported by any central guiding principle."[37] Justice Marshall, although the ideological opposite of Rehnquist, spoke with equal contempt for the Court's "outdated and intellectually disingenuous 'two-tiered' equal protection analysis."[38] His *Rodriquez* and *Murgia* dissents were noted for their advocacy of a sliding scale approach to judicial analysis. With Marshall's departure in 1991, however, no other justice has taken up the cudgel of "sliding scale" review. Yet, as Marshall suggested, the Court has frequently seemed to apply a degree of scrutiny commensurate with the nature of a particular classification and the burden it imposes on the individual.

Justice Stevens, on the other hand, has been a leader in the effort to standardize the approach to equal protection review. He came to the Court in 1975 with no personal stake in the doctrinal baggage that gathered like barnacles around the Fourteenth Amendment's interpretation. Early on in *Craig* (1976), which invalidated Oklahoma's anti-male drinking law, he wrote that "[t]here is only one Equal Protection Clause" and "[i]t requires every State to govern impartially."[39] For him the simple standard of rationality packed enough energy to scuttle the law under review in *Craig* as well as to defeat numerous classifications based on race, gender, alienage, illegitimacy, age, or mental retardation. Years later, in *Cleburne* (1985), he remarked that "the word 'rational'—for me at least—includes elements of legitimacy and neutrality that must always characterize the performance of the sovereign's duty to govern impartially." Impartiality in his hands meant that classifications would have to serve some public purpose transcending the harm they cause to the disadvantaged class.

But whether only one standard of review can account for the very different kinds of issues arguably raised by discrimination based on age and race, say, is a problem Stevens' argument fails to address. The approach of Justice Stevens may be one possible way of resolving the tension between constitutionalism and politics. It bears some

---

[36] 501 U.S. 452 (1991).

[37] 430 U.S. 762, 777 (1977).

[38] *Beal v. Doe*, 432 U.S. 438, 457 (1977).

[39] 429 U.S. 190, 211.

resemblance to an argument advanced by Cass E. Sunstein. Except for a limited number of classifications involving strict scrutiny, intermediate scrutiny, or enhanced rationality review, Sunstein notes, the Court's posture remains one of deference to majoritarian political decisions even if they are little more than "naked preferences" resulting from "an exercise of raw political power."[40] Sunstein would reappropriate the political theory that "reflects the Constitution's roots in civil republicanism and accompanying conceptions of civic virtue." Our system of representative government, he argues, was designed to prohibit naked preferences bludgeoned out of factional conflict. According to this "original Madisonian understanding," he writes, the judicial role should not be confined merely to preserving the integrity of the political process but more fundamentally to ensuring that legislation can be justified by reference to "public values" transcending the particular interests of specific groups.

Comparative Perspectives

By turning our attention to foreign constitutional democracies, we may begin to appreciate some of the crucial differences—and similarities—between American and selected foreign judicial perspectives on equality. As table 15.2 shows, the constitutions of Germany, Canada, Japan, and South Africa, together with the European Convention for the Protection of Human Rights and Fundamental Freedoms, identify the various personal traits on the basis of which *any* discrimination is expressly forbidden. Similar prohibitions appear in other modern constitutions, including those of the newly liberated countries of Eastern Europe.[41] The virtue of these express prohibitions is that they clarify what counts constitutionally as invidious discrimination requiring heightened judicial review. In the Supreme Court's interpretation of the Equal Protection Clause, only two of the twelve items in the tabular list—race and national origin—are regarded as invidious and thus "suspect." And, as we have seen,

TABLE 15.2 *Forbidden Discrimination*

Trait	Germany	Japan[a]	Canada	Europe[b]	South Africa
sex	X	X	X	X	X
race or color	X	X	X	X	X
creed or religion	X	X	X	X	X
language	X		X	X	X
national origin	X		X	X	X
physical disability	X		X		X
social origin				X	X
political opinion	X			X	
age	X		X		X
pregnancy					X
sexual orientation					X
gender					X

[a] Article 14 forbids discrimination on the grounds indicated in "political, economic, or social relations."
[b] Article 14 of the Convention forbids member states from denying guaranteed rights on these grounds.

---

[40] *Naked Preferences and the Constitution*, 84 Columbia Law Review 1689 (1984).

[41] For example, Article 12 of the Constitution of the Republic of Latvia provides: "All persons are equal under the law regardless of race, nationality, sex, language, party affiliation, political and religious persuasion, social, material and occupational standing and origin."

the absence of any such enumeration in the United States Constitution has led to unseemly judicial struggles over what classifications should be assessed with strict or intermediate scrutiny.

The Fourteenth Amendment's failure to specify the kinds of discrimination it forbids is one reason why original intent has played such an important role in the evolution of American equal protection doctrine. Emphasis on the Fourteenth Amendment's historical origin, along with the Fifteenth Amendment's singling out of race as a forbidden limit on the right to vote, largely accounts for the Supreme Court's restraint in interpreting the equal protection clause. In short, the Court found itself trapped in the Constitution's silences on what classifications deserve higher than normal judicial scrutiny. Apart from the nondiscriminatory provision of the Fifteenth Amendment, voting remains the one activity that enjoys explicit protection against denial on the basis of sex (Nineteenth Amendment), economic status (Twenty-fourth Amendment), and age (Twenty-sixth Amendment).

The Supreme Court's more adventurous equal protection decisions of the 1960s and early 1970s were handed down against the backdrop of a global effort, following the Second World War, to constitutionalize democracy and to secure the basic rights of men and women everywhere. American constitutional values played a significant role in the spread of constitutional ideas and institutions abroad.[42] Similarly, ideas emerging from foreign sources, particularly in the decisions of international human rights tribunals and national constitutional courts, were migrating across national borders. Human dignity, defined as nondiscrimination, was a key concept in this emerging constitutional world of rights and liberties. The theme of nondiscriminantion was captured initially in the Universal Declaration of Human Rights adopted by the General Assembly of the United Nations in 1948 and subsequently in international covenants for the protection of civil and political as well as economic, social, and cultural rights. Articles 26 and 27 of the International Covenant on Civil and Political Rights contains one of the broadest definitions of equality to be found in the world's foundational texts. (Article 26, quoted in full in chapter 14, bears repeating):

> *Article 26. All persons are equal before the law and are entitled without any discrimination to the equal protection of the law. In this respect, the law shall prohibit any discrimination and guarantee to all persons equal and effective protection against discrimination on any ground such as race, colour, sex, language, religion, political or other opinion, national or social origin, property, birth or other status.*
>
> *Article 27. In those states in which ethnic, religious or linguistic minorities exist, persons belonging to such minorities shall not be denied the right, in community with the other members of their group, to enjoy their own culture, to profess and practice their own religion, or to use their own language.*

This Covenant, along with the International Covenant of Economic, Social and Cultural Rights, was adopted by the United Nations in 1966. Both entered into force in 1976.[43] Could it be entirely by chance that the high point of the Supreme Court's activism in the equal protection field occurred between these dates? Conversely, as our review of the American cases has shown, the Supreme Court has been cautious

---

[42] See Louis Henkin and Albert J. Rosenthal, eds., *Constitutionalism and Rights* (New York: Columbia University Press, 1990).

[43] The United States attached its signature to both covenants on 5 October 1977. Neither covenant has yet been ratified.

in taking the definition of equality too far beyond the boundaries of its early case law.

Still, to the extent that they embody universal values, foreign constitutions may prompt the Supreme Court to think more deeply about the meaning of equality in America. In this regard, Section 9 of South Africa's 1996 Constitution (reprinted in Comparative Note 15.2) is particularly relevant. Its drafting was influenced in turn by the constitutions of other advanced democracies as well as by international human rights law.[44] Its list of forbidden classifications actually goes beyond that of other constitutions by including gender, pregnancy, and sexual orientation, thus removing any doubt that these traits are related to sex. One recalls in this connection Justice Stewart's observation that California's exclusion of pregnancy from its disability insurance program was not a sex-based classification.[45] In comparing the United States to Germany and Canada—to take these countries as examples—we find notable similarities as well as important differences in the jurisprudence of their highest courts of judicial review. The similarities are most striking in the area of sex-based discrimination, although Germany's Federal Constitutional Court has a much longer and more impressive record of accomplishment in removing sex-based inequalities from the law books. It was not until 1971 that the United States Supreme Court for the first time struck down a legislative classification based on sex and then, as noted earlier in this chapter, the Court struggled for another four years before a majority of its members could agree on a common standard for reviewing such classifications. The serious equal protection jurisprudence of the Canadian Supreme Court, on the other hand, does not begin until the adoption of the Charter of Rights and Liberties in 1982.

The Canadian Supreme Court, however, has decided very few cases involving legal classifications based on sex, largely because legislators, having taken the Charter's ban on such laws seriously, cleansed the law of many of these distinctions. Sex is listed not only as a forbidden basis of discrimination in Section 15 of the Charter; Section 28 goes on to declare that "[n]otwithstanding anything in this Charter, the rights and freedoms referred to in it are guaranteed equally to male and female persons." This language, which is similar to Article 3 (2) of Germany's Basic Law, carried a strong message to lawmakers; in addition, it meant that the Canadian Supreme Court would require a high level of justification for sex-based statutes. Such statutes, incidentally, can be saved under the terms of Section 1, the Charter's main reservation clause. Under this provision, guaranteed rights may be restricted "subject only to such reasonable limits prescribed by law as can be demonstrably justified in a free and democratic society."

A Canadian statute that survived review under the Charter involved a statutory rape law that punished males but not females. The comparable American case is *Michael M. v. Superior Court of Sonoma County* (1981). The party in the Canadian case was a boy under the age of fourteen. In the majority's view, there was no discrimination because the boy was biologically incapable of committing the offense. But a concurring opinion viewed the statute as discriminatory but found it justified under Section 1. The California's statutory rape statute upheld in *Michael M.*, however, would probably not have survived constitutional analysis in Canada; given the ages laid down in the American statute, an argument grounded in biology would not

---

[44] See D. M. Davis, *Constitutional Borrowing: The Influence of Legal Culture and Local History in the Reconstruction of Comparative Influence: The South African Experience*, 1 International Journal of Constitutional Law 181–195 (2003).

[45] *Geduldig v. Aiello*, 417 U.S. 484 (1974).

have been convincing. Plainly, equal protection analysis in Canada differs from the American jurisprudence because of the structural relationship between Sections 1, 15, and 28 of the Charter.

Actually, the record of Germany's Federal Constitutional Court is more comparable to American than to Canadian caselaw. Owing to the Basic Law's explicit ban on sex-based discrimination, the Constitutional Court's scrutiny of sex classifications reaches back to the 1950s. In fact, Article 117 of the Basic Law instructed parliament to remove gender-based classifications in violation of the equality clause of Article 3 (2) by 31 March 1953. Failing this, the Court would take upon itself the task of removing such provisions in appropriate cases. During this early period, however, the Court moved cautiously, sustaining as many gender classifications as it struck down. In one notable instance—the *Homosexuality Case* (1957)—the Court upheld the punishment of homosexual acts between males but not females, mainly on the ground of "expert" testimony that male homosexuality was more dangerous to society than lesbian relationships. It bears noting, however, that West Germany repealed the homosexual statute a few years later and, indeed, if such a statute were reviewed today, the Court in all likelihood would strike it.

In the early years—the late 1950s and 1960s—the Constitutional Court exercised its most vigorous review over sex classifications in the field of marriage and family law, striking down statutes that mirrored the traditional patriarchy of German society. For example, the Court invalidated laws favoring males in matters relating to child rearing and inheritance.[46] The judicial determination to rid the statute books of these distinctions continued later with decisions striking down laws that favored the mother in custody disputes over nonmarital children and fathers in disputes over the surname to be given to marital children.[47]

In both Germany and the United States, and approximately at the same time, the Courts struck down numerous gender-based classifications in social security matters and employment policy. Laws excluding widowers, for example, from old age and survivors' benefits granted to widows on assumptions of female but not male dependency, have not survived constitutional analysis. The Supreme Court and the Federal Constitutional Court have noted that such statutes are based on the stereotypical view that a woman's place is in the home.[48] On the other hand, both tribunals have tended to uphold gender-based social security distinctions—e.g., pension schemes that permit women to collect benefits at an earlier age than men or those which favor women in the computation of wages for old age benefits—when designed to compensate women for the disadvantages they have suffered in the marketplace because of their household and family obligations.[49]

The most notable German decision in the field of employment policy is the *Nocturnal Employment Case* (1992).[50] The case was decided in the spirit of an earlier decision that struck a law that gave a day's paid leave per month to female but not male employees on the assumption that women would need the time off to care for

[46] See 10 BverfGE 59 (1959) and 14 BverfGE 337 (1963).

[47] See Donald P. Kommers, *The Constitutional Jurisprudence of the Federal Republic of Germany.* 2nd ed. (Durham, N.C.: Duke University Press, 1997), 500.

[48] For the United States, see *Califano v. Goldfarb*, 430 U.S. 199 (1977) and *Califano v. Westcott*, 443 U.S. 76 (1979); for Germany, see Judgment of 31 March 1971, 31 BverfGE 1971 and Judgment on 28 January 1987, 74 BverfGE 163.

[49] See Judgment of 12 March 1975, 39 BverfGE 169 and *Califano v. Webster*, 430 U.S. 313 (1977).

[50] 85 BverfGE 191 (1992).

children and household.[51] In a lucid restatement of the theory underlying the Court's interpretation of the equality principle, *Nocturnal Employment* underscored the principle that gender classifications would survive constitutional analysis only in the presence of "indispensably necessary" conditions rooted in objective biological or functional considerations. The biological and functional reasons that heretofore justified a ban on night work for women can no longer support the ban, said the Court. Nor can the statute be saved by its concern for the health and physical safety of women. Night work harms men and women equally, said the Court, and if safety is a concern then the state would be obligated to pass legislation to insure the safety of women. The Court even suggested that company buses be purchased to take women to and from work.

Some gender classifications that have been upheld by the United States Supreme Court would not survive scrutiny in Germany. This is particularly true of distinctions based on pregnancy-related disability benefits, the denial of which the Supreme Court has upheld.[52] In 1977, the Constitutional Court invalidated a state's refusal to hire a teacher for a secondary education position simply because of her advanced pregnancy. In this case, however, the Court construed the Maternity Protection Act through the lens of the Constitution's marriage and family guarantees.[53] Under the Basic Law, the explicit ban on gender discrimination is often interpreted in the light of other key constitutional provisions, including the social state clause of Article 20, the personality clause of Article 2, and the marriage and family clauses of Article 6, an ensemble of social and individual rights that makes it very difficult constitutionally to justify pregnancy-related disadvantages, not to mention other kinds of distinctions based on gender.

In assessing other forbidden classifications, the German and Canadian courts have seldom deviated from the standard used in scrutinizing sex-based laws. Occasionally, however, foreign courts have extended heightened review to legal distinctions based on an irrelevant personal characteristic *analogous* to the forbidden traits expressly listed in the foundational text. In *Egan v. Canada*, for example, involving a social security law that confined its benefits to "spouses in a heterosexual union," the Canadian Supreme Court found that sexual orientation is a "deeply personal characteristic [that] falls within the ambit of s. 15 protection as being analogous to the enumerated grounds." But the Court went on to justify the statute under Section 1 because heterosexual marriage "is the social unit that uniquely has the capacity to procreate children and generally cares for their upbringing, and as such warrants support by Parliament to meet its needs."[54]

Nevertheless, care should be taken not to exaggerate the difference between the judicial methods used by the United States Supreme Court and foreign constitutional courts. The equal protection jurisprudence of the national courts considered in this volume can be organized around the rather rigorously applied principles of rationality and proportionality. What is distinctive about the United States is that only a very narrow range of legislative classifications is subordinated to these tough standards.

---

[51] 52 BverfGE 369 (1979).

[52] See *Geduldig v. Aiello*, note 6 above and *Gilbert v. General Electric Co.*, 429 U.S. 125 (1976). But see *International Union, UAW v. Johnson Controls, Inc.*, 499 U.S. 187 (1991) (striking down a policy that excluded fertile female employees from certain jobs because of concern for the health of any fetus that the woman might conceive).

[53] 44 BverfGE 211 (1977).

[54] [1995] 2 S.C.R. 513.

As for legislative classifications generally—that is, those that are not constitutionally forbidden—foreign standards of judicial review tend also to be more stringent than the minimal rationale often applied by the United States Supreme Court. Whereas the Supreme Court will often assume a reasonable relationship between the measure adopted and its purpose, foreign constitutional tribunals, notably Germany's Federal Constitutional Court and Canada's Supreme Court, have tended independently to examine the objective conditions behind a classification and to require the state to show a substantial connection between the classification and its purpose, an approach followed by the American Supreme Court when reviewing suspect and quasi-suspect classifications.

American variations on equal protection analysis have as much to do with the historical development of equal protection jurisprudence as with the generality of the constitutional text. Given the difficulty in the United States of changing the Constitution itself, the likelihood of a richer textual definition of equality seems remote. But is such a change necessary to import deeper meaning into the Equal Protection Clause? As we pointed out earlier, the concept of equality is not frozen in time. It evolves over time, as it inevitably must, and even foreign courts have not confined forbidden classifications to those actually enumerated in the constitutional text (see Comparative Note 15.9). Foreign constitutions have the advantage of having been drafted in the twentieth century and against the backdrop of increasing human rights consciousness. Perhaps the time has come for American judges to see what lessons if any can be learned from these constitutions.

Selected Bibliography

Baer, Judith A. *Equality Under the Constitution: Reclaiming the Fourteenth Amendment.* Ithaca: Cornell University Press, 1983.

Boland, Tara. *Single-Sex Public Education: Equality v. Choice.* 7 University of Pennsylvania Journal of Constitutional Law 154–172 (1998).

Epstein, Cynthia. *Women in Law.* New York: Basic Books, 1981.

Gerstmann, Evan. *The Constitutional Underclass: Gays, Lesbians and the Failure of the Class-Based Equal Protection.* Chicago: University of Chicago Press, 1999.

Ginsburg, Ruth B. *Constitutional Aspects of Sex-Based Discrimination.* St. Paul, MN: West, 1974.

Hirshman, Linda and Jane E. Larson. *Hard Bargains: The Politics of Sex.* Oxford: Oxford University Press, 1998.

Hull, Elizabeth. *Without Justice for All: The Constitutional Rights of Aliens.* Wesport, Conn.: Greenwood Press, 1985.

Jaffa, Harry V. *Equality and Liberty: Theory and Practice in American Politics.* New York: Oxford University Press, 1989.

Karst, Kenneth L. *Woman's Constitution.* 1984 Duke Law Journal 447 (1984).

Kenn, Lisa and Suzanne B. Golberg. *Strangers to the Law: Gay People on Trial.* Ann Arbor: University of Michigan Press, 1998.

Kirp, David. L., et al., *Justice and Gender.* Cambridge: Harvard University Press, 1989.

Law, Sylvia. *Rethinking Sex and the Constitution.* 132 University of Pennsylvania Law Review 955 (1984).

MacKinnon, Catherine. *Reflections on Sex Equality Under Law.* 100 Yale Law Journal 1281 (1991).

Mezey, Susan. *In Pursuit of Equality: Women, Public Policy, and the Federal Courts.* New York: St. Martin's, 1992.

Rhode, Deborah. *Justice and Gender.* Cambridge: Harvard University Press, 1989.

Sarat, Austin and Thomas R. Kearns, eds. *Identities, Politics, and Rights.* Ann Arbor: University of Michigan Press, 1998.

Seidman, Louis M. *Constitutional Law: Equal Protection of the Law.* New York: Foundation Press, 2003.

Symposium on Sexual Orientation. 9 *Notre Dame Journal of Law, Ethics, and Public Policy* (1995).

Urofsky, Melvin I. *Affirmative Action on Trial.* Lawrence: University Press of Kansas, 1997.

Van Burkleo, Sandra F. *Belonging to the World: Women's Rights and American Constitutional Culture.* Oxford: Oxford University Press, 1997.

West, Robin. *Progressive Constitutionalism: Reconstructing the Fourteenth Amendment.* Durham, N.C.: Duke University Press, 1994.

Wintemute, Robert. *Sexual Orientation and Human Rights.* Oxford: Clarendon Press, 1995.

Selected Comparative Bibliography

Bertelsmann, Klaus and Rust, Ursula. *Equality in Law Between Men and Women in the European Community: Germany.* Dordrecht: Martinus Nijhoff Publishers, 1995.

Galanter, Mark. *Competing Equalities: Law and the Backward Classes in India.* Berkeley: University of California Press, 1984.

Gibson, Dale. *The Law of the Charter: Equality Rights.* Toronto: Carswell, 1990.

Merin, Yuval. *Equality for Same-Sex Couples: The Legal Recognition of Gay Partnerships in Europe and the United States.* Chicago: The University of Chicago Press, 2002.

Peters, Anne. *Women, Quotas and Constitutions: A Comparative Study of Affirmative Action for Women under American, German, European Community and International Law.* The Hague: Kluwer Law International, 1999.

Upham, Frank. *Law and Social Change in Postwar Japan.* Cambridge: Harvard University Press, 1987.

Yogis, John A. et al. *Sexual Orientation and Canadian Law.* Toronto: Edmond Montgomery Publications Limited, 1996.

Shapiro v. Thompson
394 U.S. 618; 89 S. Ct. 1322; 22 L. Ed. 2d 600 (1969)

Vivian Thompson, a 19-year-old unwed mother of one child and pregnant with her second child, moved from Massachusetts to Connecticut to live with her mother, a Hartford resident. Unable to work or to support her children, she applied for welfare under the Aid to Dependent Children program. She was denied assistance because she had not yet resided in the state for a full year. The federal district court invalidated the residence requirement and Connecticut appealed to the Supreme Court. Federal courts had struck down similar residence requirements in Pennsylvania and the District of Columbia. The Supreme Court consolidated these three cases. Opinion of the Court: *Brennan,* Douglas, Stewart, White, Fortas, Marshall. Concurring opinion: *Stewart.* Dissenting opinions: *Warren,* Black, *Harlan.*

Justice BRENNAN delivered the opinion of the Court. . . .

Primarily, appellants justify the waiting-period requirement as a protective device to preserve the fiscal integrity of state public assistance programs. It is asserted that people who require welfare assistance during their first year of residence in a State are likely to become continuing burdens on state welfare programs. Therefore, the argument runs, if such people can be deterred from entering the jurisdiction by denying them welfare benefits during the first year, state programs to assist long-time residents will not be impaired by a substantial influx of indigent newcomers.

There is weighty evidence that exclusion from the jurisdiction of the poor who need or may need relief was the specific objective of these provisions. In the Congress, sponsors of federal legislation to eliminate all residence requirements have been consistently opposed by representatives of state and local welfare agencies who have stressed the fears of the States that elimination of the re-

quirements would result in a heavy influx of individuals into States providing the most generous benefits. . . .

We do not doubt that the one-year waiting-period device is well suited to discourage the influx of poor families in need of assistance. An indigent who desires to migrate, resettle, find a new job, and start a new life will doubtless hesitate if he knows that he must risk making the move without the possibility of falling back on state welfare assistance during his first year of residence, when his need may be most acute. But the purpose of inhibiting migration by needy persons into the State is constitutionally impermissible.

This Court long ago recognized that the nature of our Federal Union and our constitutional concepts of personal liberty unite to require that all citizens be free to travel throughout the length and breadth of our land uninhibited by statutes, rules, or regulations which unreasonably burden or restrict this movement. That proposition was early stated by Chief Justice Taney in the *Passenger Cases*: "For all the great purposes for which the Federal government was formed, we are one people, with one common country. We are all citizens of the United States; and, as members of the same community, must have the right to pass and repass through every part of it without interruption, as freely as in our own States."

We have no occasion to ascribe the source of this right to travel interstate to a particular constitutional provision. It suffices that, as Justice Stewart said for the Court in *United States v. Guest* (1966):

The constitutional right to travel from one State to another . . . occupies a position fundamental to the concept of our Federal Union. It is a right that has been firmly established and repeatedly recognized. . . . [The] right finds no explicit mention in the Constitution. The reason, it has been suggested, is that a right so elementary was conceived from the beginning to be a necessary concomitant of the stronger Union the Constitution created. In any event, freedom to travel throughout the

United States has long been recognized as a basic right under the Constitution. . . .

Alternatively, appellants argue that even if it is impermissible for a State to attempt to deter the entry of all indigents, the challenged classification may be justified as a permissible state attempt to discourage those indigents who would enter the State solely to obtain larger benefits. We observe first that none of the statutes before us is tailored to serve that objective. Rather, the class of barred newcomers is all-inclusive, lumping the great majority who come to the State for other purposes with those who come for the sole purpose of collecting higher benefits. In actual operation, therefore, the three statutes enact what in effect are nonrebuttable presumptions that every applicant for assistance in his first year of residence came to the jurisdiction solely to obtain higher benefits. Nothing whatever in any of these records supplies any basis in fact for such a presumption.

More fundamentally, a State may no more try to fence out those indigents who seek higher welfare benefits than it may try to fence out indigents generally. Implicit in any such distinction is the notion that indigents who enter a State with the hope of securing higher welfare benefits are somehow less deserving than indigents who do not take this consideration into account. But we do not perceive why a mother who is seeking to make a new life for herself and her children should be regarded as less deserving because she considers, among others factors, the level of a State's public assistance. Surely such a mother is no less deserving than a mother who moves into a particular State in order to take advantage of its better educational facilities.

We recognize that a State has a valid interest in preserving the fiscal integrity of its programs. It may legitimately attempt to limit its expenditures, whether for public assistance, public education, or any other program. But a State may not accomplish such a purpose by invidious distinctions between classes of its citizens. It could not, for example, reduce expenditures for education by barring indigent children from its schools. Similarly, in the cases before us, appellants must do more than show that denying welfare benefits to new residents saves money. The saving of welfare costs cannot justify an otherwise invidious classification. . . .

Appellants next advance as justification certain administrative and related governmental objectives allegedly served by the waiting-period requirement. They argue that the requirement (1) facilitates the planning of the welfare budget; (2) provides an objective test of residency; (3) minimizes the opportunity for recipients fraudulently to receive payments from more than one jurisdiction; and (4) encourages early entry of new residents into the labor force.

. . . [We] reject appellants' argument that a mere showing of a rational relationship between the waiting period and these four admittedly permissible state objectives will suffice to justify the classification. . . .

We conclude therefore that appellants in these cases do not use and have no need to use the one-year requirement for the governmental purposes suggested. Thus, even under traditional equal protection tests a classification of welfare applicants according to whether they have lived in the State for one year would seem irrational and unconstitutional. But, of course, the traditional criteria do not apply in these cases. Since the classification here touches on the fundamental right of interstate movement, its constitutionality must be judged by the stricter standard of whether it promotes a *compelling* state interest. Under this standard, the waiting-period requirement clearly violates the Equal Protection Clause.

Justice HARLAN, dissenting.

In upholding the equal protection argument, the Court has applied an equal protection doctrine of relatively recent vintage: the rule that statutory classifications which either are based upon certain "suspect" criteria or affect "fundamental rights" will be held to deny equal protection unless justified by a "compelling" governmental interest.

I think that this branch of the "compelling interest" doctrine is sound when applied to racial classifications, for historically the Equal Protection Clause was largely a product of the desire to eradicate legal distinctions founded upon race. However, I believe that the more recent extensions have been unwise. . . .

The second branch of the "compelling interest" principle is even more troublesome. For it has been held that a statutory classification is subject to the "compelling interest" test if the result of the classification may be to affect a "fundamental right" regardless of the basis of classification. . . . I think this branch of the "compelling interest" doctrine particularly unfortunate and unnecessary. It is unfortunate because it creates an exception which threatens to swallow the standard equal protection rule. Virtually every state statute affects important rights. This Court has repeatedly held, for example, that the traditional equal protection standard is applicable to statutory classifications affecting such fundamental matters as the right to pursue a particular occupation, the right to receive greater or smaller wages or to work more or less hours, and the right to inherit property. Rights such as these are in principle indistinguishable from those involved here, and to ex-

Comparative Note 15.1

Article 3 (Constitution of Italy, 1947)

. . . It is the responsibility of the Republic to remove all obstacles of an economic and social nature which, by limiting the freedom and equality of citizens, prevent the full development of the individual and the participation of all workers in the political, economic, and social organization of the country.

Article 2 (Constitution of Poland, 1997)

The Republic of Poland shall be a democratic state ruled by law and implementing the principles of social justice.

Article 71 (Constitution of Poland, 1997)

The State, in its social and economic policy, shall take into account the good of the family. Families, finding themselves in difficult material and social circumstances—particularly those with many children or a single parent—shall have the right to special assistance from public authorities.

Article 1 (Basic Law of the Federal Republic of Germany, 1949)

The dignity of man is inviolable. To respect and protect it shall be the duty of all public authority.

Article 25 (1) (Universal Declaration of Human Rights, 1948)

Everyone has the right to a standard of living adequate for the health and well-being of himself and of his family, including food, clothing, housing and medical care and necessary social services, and the right to security in the event of unemployment, sickness, disability, widowhood, old age or other lack of livelihood in circumstances beyond his control

---

tend the "compelling interest" rule to all cases in which such rights are affected would go far toward making this Court a "superlegislature." But when a statute affects only matters not mentioned in the Federal Constitution and is not arbitrary or irrational, I must reiterate that I know of nothing which entitles this Court to pick out particular human activities, characterize them as "fundamental," and give them added protection under an unusually stringent equal protection test.

I do not consider that the factors which have been urged to outweigh these considerations are sufficient to render unconstitutional these state and federal enactments. It is said, first, that this Court . . . has acknowledged that the right to travel interstate is a "fundamental" freedom. Second, it is contended that the governmental objectives mentioned above either are ephemeral or could be accomplished by means which do not impinge as heavily on the right to travel, and hence that the requirements are unconstitutional because they "sweep unnecessarily broadly and thereby invade the area of protected freedoms." The appellees claim that welfare payments could be denied those who come primarily to collect welfare by means of less restrictive provisions, such as New York's Welfare Abuses Law; that fraud could be prevented by investigation of individual applicants or by a much shorter residence period; that budgetary predictability is a remote and speculative goal; and that assurance of investment in the community could be obtained by a shorter residence period or by taking into account prior intervals of residence in the jurisdiction.

Taking all of these competing considerations into account, I believe that the balance definitely favors constitutionality. In reaching that conclusion, I do not minimize the importance of the right to travel interstate. However, the impact of residence conditions upon that right is indirect and apparently quite insubstantial. On the other hand, the governmental purposes served by the requirements are legitimate and real, and the residence requirements are clearly suited to their accomplishment. To abolish residence requirements might well discourage highly worthwhile experimentation in the welfare field. The statutes come to us clothed with the authority of Congress and attended by a correspondingly heavy presumption of constitutionality. Moreover, although the appellees assert that the same objectives could have been achieved by less restrictive means, this is an area in which the judiciary should be especially slow to fetter the judgment of Congress and of some 46 state legislatures in the choice of methods. Residence requirements have advantages, such as administrative simplicity and relative certainty, which are not shared by the alternative solutions proposed by the appellees. In these circumstances, I cannot find that the burden imposed by residence requirements upon ability to travel outweighs the governmental interests in their continued employment. Nor do I believe that the period of residence required in these cases—one year—is so excessively long as to justify a finding of unconstitutionality on that score.

I conclude with the following observations. Today's decision, it seems to me, reflects to an unusual degree the current notion that this Court possesses a peculiar wisdom all its own whose capacity to lead this Nation out of its present troubles is contained only by the limits of judicial ingenuity in contriving new constitutional principles to meet each problem as it arises. For anyone who, like myself, believes that it is an essential function of this Court to maintain the constitutional divisions between state and federal authority and among the three branches of the Federal Government, today's decision is a step in the wrong direction. This resurgence of the expansive view of "equal protection" carries the seeds of more judicial interference with the state and federal legislative process, much more indeed than does the judicial application of "due process" according to traditional concepts . . . about which some members of this Court have expressed fears as to its potentialities for setting us judges "at large." I consider it particularly unfortunate that this judicial roadblock to the powers of Congress in this field should occur at the very threshold of the current discussions regarding the "federalizing" of these aspects of welfare relief.

Notes and Queries

1. The *Shapiro* Court ruled that the one-year waiting period imposed as a condition of receiving welfare benefits impinged on the fundamental right to travel. Yet the Court acknowledged that there is no express right to travel in the text of the Constitution. Why then should an argument based on the right to travel be convincing? If the Court is going to invoke rights not mentioned in the Constitution, would it not have been more convincing—and honest—to have rested *Shapiro* on the fundamental right to food, shelter, or perhaps even the preservation of the family unit?

2. What is the interpretive problem in *Shapiro*? Does the problem have anything to do with how the Constitution is perceived? Some justices appear to focus on the words, phrases, and paragraphs of the Constitution. Others seem to view the Constitution as a whole, seeing it mainly as a collection of basic principles. Is this what divides the justices?

3. Undergraduates reading *Shapiro* for the first time are likely to find the Court's opinion abstract, technical, and dry. We are told very little about the lives or circumstances of the real persons affected by the state legislation. Would a recitation of the human suffering caused by these state statutes—the kind of personal narrative you would find in a literary exposition—enliven the controversy and perhaps throw a brighter light on the underlying constitutional issue? To what extent should a justice's own sense of fairness inform his judgment on a constitutional issue like the one presented in *Shapiro*?

4. Although the right to marry, like the right to travel, is "fundamental," *Sosna v. Iowa*, 419 U.S. 393 (1974), sustained an Iowa statute that imposed a one-year residency requirement as a condition for maintaining an action for divorce. The Court distinguished *Sosna* from *Shapiro* because a divorce, unlike welfare payments, was not an urgent necessity, and no serious injury would result by forcing a person to wait a year for relief. Justice Brennan and Marshall dissented, claiming that the court had abandoned the *Shapiro* analysis by not requiring the state to justify its restriction on the fundamental right to divorce and remarry—and on the right to travel—by a compelling governmental interest.

5. More recently, in *Saenz v. Roe*, 526 U.S. 489 (1999), the Court struck down California's durational residency statute limiting the welfare benefits of new residents to the amount they would have received in the state of their former residence. Seven justices struck the statute because it violated the interstate right to travel but not on the authority of *Shapiro*. The Court chose to rest on the privileges and immunities clause of the Fourteenth Amendment, raising questions about *Shapiro's* continued vitality. At the same time, the Court seems to have injected new life into the privileges and immunities clause of the Fourteenth Amendment.

6. See Comparative Note 15.1 for several modern constitutional provisions on social justice and the extract from the Universal Declaration of Human Rights. In addition, Article 20 of Germany's Basic Law defines Germany as "a democratic and *social* federal state" (italics supplied). The Basic Law's Article 6(4) provides that "[e]very mother shall be entitled to the protection and care of the community." Invoking these clauses, along with the human dignity clause of Article 1, Germany's Federal Constitutional Court has repeatedly underscored the fundamentality of these provisions and has often reminded governmental officials of their constitutional duty to establish a just social order. To what extent should these and international human rights standards guide constitutional interpretation in the United States?

San Antonio Independent School District v. Rodriguez

411 U.S. 1; 93 S. Ct. 1278; 36 L. Ed. 2d 16 (1973)

The financing of Texas's public elementary and secondary schools is a product of state and local participation. The state pays about half the cost of such financing, whereas the remaining costs are borne by local school districts through an *ad valorem* tax on property. This system resulted in substantial interdistrict disparities in the amount of money available per student. Mexican-American parents with children in school districts with a low property tax base brought a class action suit on behalf of all other children similarly situated. A federal district court ruled that Texas's school financing system discriminated against the poor on the basis of wealth and denied school children in "underfunded" districts of their fundamental right to an education. Accordingly, ruled the court, the state was required to justify its system under the compelling state interest standard, although here the state had failed even to meet the rational basis test. Opinion of the Court: *Powell*, Blackmun, Burger, Rehnquist, Stewart. Concurring opinion: *Stewart*. Dissenting opinions: *Brennan, Marshall, White*, Douglas.

Justice POWELL delivered the opinion of the Court.

We must decide, first, whether the Texas system of financing public education operates to the disadvantage of some suspect class or impinges upon a fundamental right explicitly or implicitly protected by the Constitution, thereby requiring strict judicial scrutiny. If so, the judgment of the District Court should be affirmed. If not, the Texas scheme must still be examined to determine whether it rationally furthers some legitimate, articulated state purpose and therefore does not constitute an invidious discrimination in violation of the Equal Protection Clause of the Fourteenth Amendment.

We are unable to agree that this case, which in significant aspects is *sui generis*, may be so neatly fitted into the conventional mosaic of constitutional analysis under the Equal Protection Clause. Indeed, for the several reasons that follow, we find neither the suspect-classification nor the fundamental interest analysis persuasive.

The wealth discrimination discovered by the District Court in this case, and by several other courts that have recently struck down school-financing laws in other states, is quite unlike any of the forms of wealth discrimination heretofore reviewed by this Court.

The precedents of this Court provide the proper starting point. The individuals, or groups of individuals, who constituted the class discriminated against in our prior cases shared two distinguishing characteristics: because of their impecunity they were completely unable to pay for some desired benefit, and as a consequence, they sustained an absolute deprivation of a meaningful opportunity to enjoy that benefit. . . .

. . . Even a cursory examination, however, demonstrates that neither of the two distinguishing characteristics of wealth classifications can be found here. First, in support of their charge that the system discriminates against the "poor," appellees have made no effort to demonstrate that it operates to the peculiar disadvantage of any class fairly definable as indigent, or as composed of persons whose incomes are beneath any designated poverty level. Indeed, there is reason to believe that the poorest families are not necessarily clustered in the poorest property districts. . . .

Second, neither appellees nor the District Court addressed the fact that . . . lack of personal resources has not occasioned an absolute deprivation of the desired benefit. The argument here is not that the children in districts having relatively low assessable property values are receiving no public education; rather, it is that they are receiving a poorer quality education than that available to children in districts having more assessable wealth. Apart from the unsettled and disputed question whether the quality of education may be determined by the amount of money expended for it, a sufficient answer to appellees' argument is that, at least where wealth is involved, the Equal Protection Clause does not require absolute equality or precisely equal advantages.

For these two reasons . . . the disadvantaged class is not susceptible of identification in traditional terms.

We thus conclude that the Texas system does not operate to the peculiar disadvantage of any suspect class. But in recognition of the fact that this Court has never heretofore held that wealth discrimination alone provides an adequate basis for invoking strict scrutiny, appellees have not relied solely on this contention. They also assert that the State's system impermissibly interferes with the exercise of a "fundamental" right and that accordingly the prior decisions of this Court require the application of the strict standard of judicial review. . . . It is this question—whether education is a fundamental right, in the sense that it is among the rights and liberties protected by the Constitution—which has so consumed the attention of courts and commentators in recent years.

Nothing this Court holds today in any way detracts from our historic dedication to public education. We are in

Comparative Note 15.2

A. Equality as defined by Section 9 of the South African Constitution (1996)

1. Everyone is equal before the law and has the right to equal protection and benefit of the law.

2. Equality includes the full and equal enjoyment of all rights and freedoms. To promote the achievement of equality, legislative and other measures designed to protect or advance persons, or categories of persons, disadvantaged by unfair discrimination may be taken.

3. The state may not unfairly discriminate directly or indirectly against anyone on one or more grounds, including race, gender, sex, pregnancy, marital status, ethnic origin, colour, sexual orientation, age, disability, religion, conscience, belief, culture, language and birth.

4. No person may unfairly discriminate directly or indirectly against anyone on one or more grounds in terms of subsection 3. National legislation must be enacted to prevent or prohibit unfair discrimination.

5. Discrimination on one or more of the grounds

listed in subsection 3 is unfair unless it is established that the discrimination is fair.

B. Justice J. Kriegler of the South African Constitutional Court described the significance of equality under the South African Constitution as follows:

The importance of equality in the constitutional scheme bears repetition. The South African Constitution is primarily and emphatically an egalitarian constitution. The supreme laws of comparable constitutional states may underscore other principles and rights. But in the light of our own particular history, and our vision for the future, a constitution was written with equality at its centre. Equality is our Constitution's focus and organising principle. The importance of equality rights in the Constitution, and the role of the right to equality in our emerging democracy, must both be understood in order to analyse properly whether a violation of [a] right has occurred.

Source: *President of the Republic of South Africa v. Hugo*, 1997 (4) SA 1 (CC).

---

complete agreement with the conclusion of the three-judge panel below that the "grave significance of education both to the individual and to our society" cannot be doubted. But the importance of a service performed by the State does not determine whether it must be regarded as fundamental for purposes of examination under the Equal Protection Clause. . . .

It is not the province of this Court to create substantive constitutional rights in the name of guaranteeing equal protection of the laws. Thus, the key to discovering whether education is "fundamental" is not to be found in comparisons of the relative societal significance of education as opposed to subsistence or housing. Nor is it to be found by weighing whether education is as important as the right to travel. Rather, the answer lies in assessing whether there is a right to education explicitly or implicitly guaranteed by the Constitution.

Education, of course, is not among the rights afforded explicit protection under our Federal Constitution. Nor do we find any basis for saying it is implicitly so protected. As we have said, the undisputed importance of education will not alone cause this Court to depart from the usual standard for reviewing a State's social and economic legislation. It is appellees' contention, however, that education

is distinguishable from other services and benefits provided by the State because it bears a peculiarly close relationship to other rights and liberties accorded protection under the Constitution. Specifically, they insist that education is itself a fundamental personal right because it is essential to the effective exercise of First Amendment freedoms and to intelligent utilization of the right to vote. In asserting a nexus between speech and education, appellees urge that the right to speak is meaningless unless the speaker is capable of articulating his thoughts intelligently and persuasively. The "marketplace of ideas" is an empty forum for those lacking basic communicative tools. Likewise, they argue that the corollary right to receive information becomes little more than a hollow privilege when the recipient has not been taught to read, assimilate, and utilize available knowledge.

Even if it were conceded that some identifiable quantum of education is a constitutionally protected prerequisite to the meaningful exercise of either right, we have no indication that the present levels of educational expenditure in Texas provide an education that falls short. Whatever merit appellees' argument might have if a State's financing system occasioned an absolute denial of educational opportunities to any of its children, that argument

provides no basis for finding an interference with fundamental rights where only relative differences in spending
levels are involved and where—as is true in the present
case—no charge fairly could be made that the system fails
to provide each child with an opportunity to acquire the
basic minimal skills necessary for the enjoyment of the
rights of speech and of full participation in the political
process.

In sum, to the extent that the Texas system of school
financing results in unequal expenditures between children who happen to reside in different districts, we cannot
say that such disparities are the product of a system that is
so irrational as to be invidiously discriminatory. . . . The
Texas plan is not the result of hurried, ill-conceived legislation. It certainly is not the product of purposeful discrimination against any group or class. . . . The need is
apparent for reform in tax systems which may well have
relied too long and too heavily on the local property
tax. . . . But the ultimate solutions must come from the
lawmakers and from the democratic pressures of those
who elect them.

Reversed.

Mr. Justice WHITE, with whom Mr. Justice DOUGLAS and Mr. Justice BRENNAN join, dissenting. . . .

The Equal Protection Clause permits discriminations between classes but requires that the classification bear
some rational relationship to a permissible object sought
to be attained by the statute. It is not enough that the
Texas system before us seeks to achieve the valid, rational
purpose of maximizing local initiative; the means chosen
by the State must also be rationally related to the end
sought to be achieved. . . .

Neither Texas nor the majority heeds this rule. If the
State aims at maximizing local initiative and local choice,
by permitting school districts to resort to the real property
tax if they choose to do so, it utterly fails in achieving its
purpose in districts with property tax bases so low that
there is little if any opportunity for interested parents, rich
or poor, to augment school district revenues. Requiring
the State to establish only that unequal treatment is in furtherance of a permissible goal, without also requiring the
State to show that the means chosen to effectuate that goal
are rationally related to its achievement, makes equal protection analysis no more than an empty gesture. In my
view, the parents and children in Edgewood, and in like
districts, suffer from an invidious discrimination violative
of the Equal Protection Clause. . . .

Mr. Justice MARSHALL, with whom Mr. Justice DOUGLAS concurs, dissenting.

The Court today decides, in effect, that a State may constitutionally vary the quality of education which it offers its
children in accordance with the amount of taxable wealth
located in the school districts within which they reside. . . .
[T]he majority's holding can only be seen as a retreat from
our historic commitment to equality of educational opportunity and as unsupportable acquiescence in a system
which deprives children in their earliest years of the
chance to reach their full potential as citizens. . . .

In my judgment, the right of every American to an equal
start in life, so far as the provision of a state service as
important as education is concerned, is far too vital to permit state discrimination on grounds as tenuous as those
presented by this record. Nor can I accept the notion that
it is sufficient to remit these appellees to the vagaries of
the political process which, contrary to the majority's suggestion, has proved singularly unsuited to the task of providing a remedy for discrimination. I, for one, am
unsatisfied with the hope of an ultimate "political" solution sometime in the indefinite future while, in the meantime, countless children unjustifiably receive inferior
educations that may affect their hearts and minds in a way
unlikely ever to be undone. I must therefore respectfully
dissent. . . .

To begin, I must once more voice my disagreement with
the Court's rigidified approach to equal protection
analysis. . . .

I therefore cannot accept the majority's labored efforts
to demonstrate that fundamental interests, which call for
strict scrutiny of the challenged classification, encompass
only established rights which we are somehow bound to
recognize from the text of the Constitution itself. To be
sure, some interests which the Court has deemed to be
fundamental for purposes of equal protection analysis are
themselves constitutionally protected rights. . . . But it will
not do to suggest that the "answer" as to whether an interest is fundamental for purposes of equal protection analysis is *always* determined by whether that interest "is a right
. . . explicitly or implicitly guaranteed by the Constitution.

I would like to know where the Constitution guarantees
the right to procreate, or the right to vote in state elections,
or the right to an appeal from a criminal conviction. These
are instances in which, due to the importance of the interests at stake, the Court has displayed a strong concern
with the existence of discriminatory state treatment. But
the Court has never said or indicated that these are interests which independently enjoy fullblown constitutional
protection.

The majority is, of course, correct when it suggests that
the process of determining which interests are fundamental is a difficult one. But I do not think the problem is

insurmountable. And I certainly do not accept the view that the process need necessarily degenerate into an unprincipled, subjective "picking-and-choosing" between various interests or that it must involve this Court in creating "substantive constitutional rights in the name of guaranteeing equal protection of the laws." Although not all fundamental interests are constitutionally guaranteed, the determination of which interests are fundamental should be firmly rooted in the text of the Constitution. The task in every case should be to determine the extent to which constitutionally guaranteed rights are dependent on interests not mentioned in the Constitution. As the nexus between the specific constitutional guarantee and the nonconstitutional interest draws closer, the nonconstitutional interest becomes more fundamental and the degree of judicial scrutiny applied when the interest is infringed on a discriminatory basis must be adjusted accordingly. Thus, it cannot be denied that interests such as procreation, the exercise of the state franchise, and access to criminal appellate processes are not fully guaranteed to the citizen by our Constitution. But these interests have nonetheless been afforded special judicial consideration in the face of discrimination because they are, to some extent, interrelated with constitutional guarantees. Procreation is now understood to be important because of its interaction with the established constitutional right of privacy. The exercise of the state franchise is closely tied to basic civil and political rights inherent in the First Amendment. And access to criminal appellate processes enhances the integrity of the range of rights implicit in the Fourteenth Amendment guarantee of due process of law. Only if we closely protect the related interests from state discrimination do we ultimately ensure the integrity of the constitutional guarantee itself. This is the real lesson that must be taken from our previous decisions involving interests deemed to be fundamental. . . .

In summary, it seems to me inescapably clear that this Court has consistently adjusted the care with which it will review state discrimination in light of the constitutional significance of the interests affected and the invidiousness of the particular classification. . . . [I]f the discrimination inherent in the Texas scheme is scrutinized with the care demanded by the interest and classification present in this case, the unconstitutionality of that scheme is unmistakeable.

Since the Court now suggests that only interests guaranteed by the Constitution are fundamental for purposes of equal protection analysis, and since it rejects the contention that public education is fundamental, it follows that the Court concludes that public education is not constitutionally guaranteed. It is true that this Court has never

deemed the provision of free public education to be required by the Constitution. . . . Nevertheless, the fundamental importance of education is amply indicated by the prior decisions of this Court, by the unique status accorded public education by our society, and by the close relationship between education and some of our most basic constitutional values. . . .

Education directly affects the ability of a child to exercise his First Amendment rights, both as a source and as a receiver of information and ideas, whatever interests he may pursue in life. . . . The opportunity for formal education may not necessarily be the essential determinant of an individual's ability to enjoy throughout his life the rights of free speech and association guaranteed to him by the First Amendment. But such an opportunity may enhance the individual's enjoyment of those rights, not only during but also following school attendance. Thus, in the final analysis, "the pivotal position of education to success in American society and its essential role in opening up to the individual the central experiences of our culture lend it an importance that is undeniable."

The Court seeks solace for its action today in the possibility of legislative reform. The Court's suggestions of legislative redress and experimentation will doubtless be of great comfort to the schoolchildren of Texas' disadvantaged districts, but considering the vested interests of wealthy school districts in the preservation of the status quo, they are worth little more. The possibility of legislative action is, in all events, no answer to this Court's duty under the Constitution to eliminate unjustified state discrimination. In this case we have been presented with an instance of such discrimination, in a particularly invidious form, against an individual interest of large constitutional and practical importance. To support the demonstrated discrimination in the provision of educational opportunity the State has offered a justification which, on analysis, takes on at best an ephemeral character. Thus, I believe that the wide disparities in taxable district property wealth inherent in the local property tax element of the Texas financing scheme render that scheme violative of the Equal Protection Clause.

I would therefore affirm the judgment of the District Court.

Notes and Queries

1. In deciding whether education is a fundamental right, the *Rodriguez* majority revisited the debate between Justices Harlan and Stewart in *Shapiro* about the interpretive role of the Court. Dissenting in *Shapiro*, Justice Harlan wrote that "if the degree of judicial scrutiny of state legisla-

tion fluctuated depending on a majority's view of the importance of the interest affected, we would have gone 'far toward making this court a superlegislature.'" Justice Stewart, however, contended that the majority did "not pick out particular human activities, characterize them as 'fundamental,' and give them added protection . . ." when it applied strict scrutiny analysis to a restriction on the right of interstate travel. Instead the Court in so doing merely recognized an established constitutional right and did its duty by protecting it. What underlying visions of the American constitutional order inform these opposing views of how to interpret the Constitution?

2. In *Cleland v. National College of Business*, 435 U.S. 213 (1978), the Court reiterated its view that the importance of education will not cause it to depart from the traditional standard for reviewing social and economic legislation for purposes of equal protection. In its per curiam opinion, the Court also cited with approval the following language from *Dandridge v. Williams*, 397 U.S. 471 (1970):

Governmental decisions to spend money to improve the general public welfare in one way and not another

are "not confided to the courts. . . ." In enacting legislation of this kind a government does not deny equal protection "merely because the classifications made by its laws are imperfect. If the classification has some 'reasonable basis,' it does not offend the Constitution simply because the classification is not made with mathematical nicety or because in practice it results in some inequality."

How much inequality would have to result before the Court would nullify a legislative classification in the social or economic sphere? Is the Court really *interpreting* the words and phrases of the Constitution when it decides *Rodriguez* and similar cases? If not what is the Court doing?

3. In 1982, eight years after *Rodriguez*, the Supreme Court ruled that Texas could not deny "to undocumented school-age children the free public education that it provides to children who are citizens of the United States or legally admitted aliens." *Plyler v. Doe*, which follows below, contains another perspective on the fundamental character of education.

Plyler v. Doe
457 U.S. 202, 102 S. Ct. 2382, 72 L. Ed. 2nd 786 (1982)

The Texas legislature enacted a statute that withholds from local school districts state funds for the education of children who were not "legally admitted" into the United States. In addition, the statute authorizes local school districts to deny enrollment to these children. Several cases, one a class action suit, were filed in federal district courts in Texas challenging the constitutionality of the law. Opinion of the Court: *Brennan*, Marshall, Blackmun, Powell, Stevens. Concurring opinions: *Marshall, Blackmun, Powell*. Dissenting opinion: *Burger*, White, Rehnquist, O'Connor.

Justice BRENNAN delivered the opinion of the Court.

The question presented by these cases is whether, consistent with the Equal Protection Clause of the Fourteenth Amendment, Texas may deny to undocumented school children the free public education that it provides to children who are citizens of the United States or legally admitted aliens.

In applying the Equal Protection Clause to most forms of state action, we thus seek only the assurance that the classification at issue bears some fair relationship to a legitimate public purpose.

But we would not be faithful to our obligations under the Fourteenth Amendment if we applied so deferential a standard to every classification. . . . With respect to [some] classifications, it is appropriate to enforce the mandate of equal protection by requiring the State to demonstrate that its classification has been precisely tailored to serve a compelling governmental interest. In addition, we have recognized that certain forms of legislative classification, while not facially invidious, nonetheless give rise to recurring constitutional difficulties; in these limited circumstances we have sought the assurance that the classification reflects a reasoned judgment consistent with the ideal of equal protection by inquiring whether it may fairly be viewed as furthering a substantial interest of the State. We turn to a consideration of the standard appropriate for the evaluation of [the challenged law].

Sheer incapability or lax enforcement of the laws barring entry into this country . . . has resulted in the creation of a substantial "shadow population" of illegal immigrants—numbering in the millions—within our borders. This situation raises the specter of a permanent caste of undocumented resident aliens, encouraged by some to remain here as a source of cheap labor, but nevertheless denied the benefits that our society makes available to citizens and lawful residents. The existence of such an underclass presents most difficult problems for a Nation that prides itself on adherence to principles of equality under law.

The children who are plaintiffs in these cases are special members of this underclass. Persuasive arguments support the view that a State may withhold its beneficence from those whose very presence within the United States is the product of their own unlawful conduct. These arguments do not apply with the same force to classifications imposing disabilities on the minor children of such illegal entrants. At the least, those who elect to enter our territory by stealth and in violation of our law should be prepared to bear the consequences, including, but not limited to, deportation. But the children of those illegal entrants are not comparably situated. Their "parents have the ability to conform their conduct to societal norms," and presumably the ability to remove themselves from the State's jurisdiction; but the children who are plaintiffs in these cases "can affect neither their parents' conduct nor their own status." Even if the State found it expedient to control the conduct of adults by acting against their children, legislation directing the onus of a parent's misconduct against his children does not comport with fundamental conceptions of justice.

Public education is not a "right" granted to individuals by the Constitution. But neither is it merely some governmental "benefit" indistinguishable from other forms of social welfare legislation. Both the importance of education in maintaining our basic institutions, and the lasting impact of its deprivation on the life of the child, mark the distinction. The "American people have always regarded education and [the] acquisition of knowledge as matters of supreme importance." We have recognized "the public school as a most vital civic institution for the preservation of a democratic system of government," and as the primary vehicle for transmitting "the values on which our society rests." In addition, education provides the basic tools by which individuals might lead economically productive lives to the benefit of us all. In sum, education has a fundamental role in maintaining the fabric of our society. We cannot ignore the significant social costs borne by our Nation when select groups are denied the means to absorb the values and skills upon which our social order rests.

In addition to the pivotal role of education in sustaining our political and cultural heritage, denial of education to some isolated group of children poses an affront to one of the goals of the Equal Protection Clause: the abolition of governmental barriers presenting unreasonable obstacles to advancement on the basis of individual merit. Paradoxically, by depriving the children of any disfavored group of an education, we foreclose the means by which that group might raise the level of esteem in which it is held by the majority. But more directly, "education prepares individuals to be self-reliant and self-sufficient participants in society." Illiteracy is an enduring disability. The inability to read and write will handicap the individual deprived of a basic education each and every day of his life.

These well-settled principles allow us to determine the proper level of deference to be afforded. Undocumented aliens cannot be treated as a suspect class because their presence in this country in violation of federal law is not a "constitutional irrelevancy." Nor is education a fundamental right; a State need not justify by compelling necessity every variation in the manner in which education is provided to its population. But more is involved in these cases than the abstract question whether [the law] discriminates against a suspect class, or whether education is a fundamental right. [The legislation under review] imposes a lifetime hardship on a discrete class of children not accountable for their disabling status. The stigma of illiteracy will mark them for the rest of their lives. By denying these children a basic education, we deny them the ability to live within the structure of our civic institutions, and foreclose any realistic possibility that they will contribute in even the smallest way to the progress of our Nation. In determining the rationality of [the law], we may appropriately take into account its costs to the Nation and to the innocent children who are its victims. In light of these countervailing costs, the discrimination contained in [the legislation] can hardly be considered rational unless it furthers some substantial goal of the State.

Appellants argue that the classification at issue furthers an interest in the "preservation of the state's limited resources for the education of its lawful residents." Of course, a concern for the preservation of resources standing alone can hardly justify the classification used in allocating those resources. The State must do more than justify its classification with a concise expression of an intention to discriminate. Apart from the asserted state prerogative to act against undocumented children solely on the basis of their undocumented status—an asserted prerogative that carries only minimal force in the circumstances of these cases—we discern three colorable state interests that might support [the challenged law].

First, appellants appear to suggest that the State may seek to protect itself from an influx of illegal immigrants. While a State might have an interest in mitigating the potentially harsh economic effects of sudden shifts in population, [the law] hardly offers an effective method of dealing with an urgent demographic or economic problem. There is no evidence in the record suggesting that illegal entrants impose any significant burden on the State's economy.

Second, while it is apparent that a State may "not . . . reduce expenditures for education by barring [some arbitrarily chosen class of] children from its schools," appellants suggest that undocumented children are appropriately singled out for exclusion because of the special burdens they impose on the State's ability to provide high-quality public education. But the record in no way supports the claim that exclusion of undocumented children is likely to improve the overall quality of education in the State. As the District Court noted, the State failed to offer any "credible supporting evidence that a proportionately small diminution of the funds spent on each child [which might result from devoting some state funds to the education of the excluded group] will have a grave impact on the quality of education." And, after reviewing the State's school financing mechanism, the District Court concluded that barring undocumented children from local schools would not necessarily improve the quality of education provided in those schools. Of course, even if improvement in the quality of education were a likely result of barring some number of children from the schools of the State, the State must support its selection of this group as the appropriate target for exclusion. In terms of educational cost and need, however, undocumented children are "basically indistinguishable" from legally resident alien children.

Finally, appellants suggest that undocumented children are appropriately singled out because their unlawful presence within the United States renders them less likely than other children to remain within the boundaries of the State, and to put their education to productive social or political use within the State. Even assuming that such an interest is legitimate, it is an interest that is most difficult to quantify. The State has no assurance that any child, citizen or not, will employ the education provided by the State within the confines of the State's borders. In any event, the record is clear that many of the undocumented children disabled by this classification will remain in this country indefinitely, and that some will become lawful residents or citizens of the United States. It is difficult to understand precisely what that State hopes to achieve by promoting the creation and perpetuation of a subclass of illiterates within our boundaries, surely adding to the problems and costs of unemployment, welfare, and crime. It is thus clear that whatever savings might be achieved by denying these children an education, they are wholly insubstantial in light of the costs involved to these children, the State, and the Nation.

If the State is to deny a discrete group of innocent children the free public education that it offers to other children residing within its borders, that denial must be justified by a showing that it furthers some substantial state interest. No such showing was made here. Accordingly, the judgment of the Court of Appeals in each of these cases is

Affirmed.

Justice MARSHALL, concurring.

While I join the Court's opinion, I do so without in any way retreating from my opinion in *San Antonio Independent School District v. Rodriguez.* I continue to believe that an individual's interest in education is fundamental, and that this view is amply supported "by the unique status accorded public education by our society, and by the close relationship between education and some of our most basic constitutional values." Furthermore, I believe that the facts of these cases demonstrate the wisdom of rejecting a rigidified approach to equal protection analysis, and of employing an approach that allows for varying levels of scrutiny depending upon "the constitutional and societal importance of the interest adversely affected and the recognized invidiousness of the basis upon which the particular classification is drawn." It continues to be my view that a class-based denial of public education is utterly incompatible with the Equal Protection Clause of the Fourteenth Amendment.

Justice BLACKMUN, concurring.

. . . I believe that the children involved in this litigation "should not be left on the streets uneducated." I write separately, however, because in my view the nature of the interest at stake is crucial to the proper resolution of these cases.

. . . I believe the Court's experience has demonstrated that the *Rodriguez* formulation does not settle every issue of "fundamental rights" arising under the Equal Protection Clause. Only a pedant would insist that there are no meaningful distinctions among the multitude of social and political interests regulated by the States, and *Rodriguez* does not stand for quite so absolute a proposition. To the contrary, *Rodriguez* implicitly acknowledged that certain interests, though not constitutionally guaranteed, must be accorded a special place in equal protection analysis.

In my view, . . . classifications involving the complete denial of education are in a sense unique, for they strike at the heart of equal protection values by involving the State in the creation of permanent class distinctions. In a sense, then, denial of an education is the analogue of denial of the right to vote: the former relegates the individual to second-class social status; the latter places him at a permanent political disadvantage.

Chief Justice BURGER, with whom Justice WHITE, Justice REHNQUIST, and Justice O'CONNOR join, dissenting.

Were it our business to set the Nation's social policy, I would agree without hesitation that it is senseless for an enlightened society to deprive any children—including illegal aliens—of an elementary education. I fully agree that it would be folly—and wrong—to tolerate creation of a segment of society made up of illiterate persons, many having a limited or no command of our language. However, the Constitution does not constitute us as "Platonic Guardians" nor does it vest in this Court the authority to strike down laws because they do not meet our standards of desirable social policy, "wisdom," or "common sense."

The Court's holding today manifests the justly criticized judicial tendency to attempt speedy and wholesale formulation of "remedies" for the failures—or simply the laggard pace—of the political process of our system of government. The Court employs, and in my view abuses the Fourteenth Amendment in an effort to become an omnipotent and omniscient problem solver. That the motives for doing so are noble and compassionate does not alter the fact that the Court distorts our constitutional function to make amends for the defaults of others. . . .

The dispositive issue in these cases, simply put, is whether, for purposes of allocating its finite resources, a state has a legitimate reason to differentiate between persons who are lawfully within the state and those who are unlawfully there. The distinction the State of Texas has drawn—based not only upon its own legitimate interests but on classifications established by the Federal Government in its immigration laws and policies—is not unconstitutional. . . .

Notes and Queries

1. What is the rationale of *Plyler?* Chief Justice Burger suggests that the Court has "patched together bits and pieces of what might be termed quasi-suspect-class and quasi-fundamental rights analysis," thus "spin[ning] out a theory custom-tailored to the facts of [this case]." Is this what Justice Brennan was doing?

2. In *Martinez v. Bynum*, 461 U.S. 321 (1983), decided one year after *Plyler*, the Court in an 8 to 1 decision upheld a Texas statute that authorized local school districts to deny tuition-free admission for a minor who lives apart from a parent or guardian whose presence in the district is for the primary purpose of attending the free public schools. *Martinez* differs from *Plyler* in that the children affected by the law were not bona fide residents of the school district whereas the illegal aliens in *Plyler* actually resided in the school district of their choice. Why should this make a difference in the outcome of the two cases?

3. *Kadrmas v. Dickinson Public Schools*, 487 U.S. 450, decided in 1988, sheds further light on *Plyler*. *Kadrmas* struck down North Dakota's policy of allowing local school boards to charge a user fee for transporting students to and from public schools. The user fee placed a special burden on poor families in certain districts while no fee was imposed in other districts. Justice O'Connor, writing for the majority, sustained the statute over the dissents of four justices (Marshall, Brennan, Stevens, and Blackmun). Rejecting the proposition that education is a "fundamental" right or that the challenged statute discriminated against a "suspect" class, the Court seemed to have followed *Rodriguez* rather than *Plyler*. Justice O'Connor noted that *Plyler* had applied "a heightened level of equal protection scrutiny" to meet the "unique circumstances" of that case. *Kadrmas*, on the other hand, regarded the law as a legitimate or rational means of encouraging local school districts to provide bus service.

Frontiero v. Richardson
411 U.S. 677; 93 S. Ct. 1764; 36 L.Ed. 2d 583 (1973)

This appeal followed a federal district court ruling sustaining the constitutionality of a federal statute providing that a United States serviceman could claim his wife as a "dependent" for purposes of receiving increased living support and medical and dental benefits, regardless of whether she relied on him for support. A servicewoman, however, had to prove that her husband relied on her for over one-half of his support. Lieutenant Sharron Frontiero of the U.S. Air Force brought this action when her application for increased benefits was denied after failing to prove that her husband was a "dependent." Because a federal statute was being challenged, the suit arose under the Due Process Clause of the Fifth Amendment. Opinion of the Court: *Brennan*, Douglas, White, Marshall. Concurring opinion: *Powell*, Blackmun, Burger, Stewart. Dissenting opinion: *Rehnquist*.

Mr. Justice BRENNAN announced the judgment of the Court and an opinion in which Mr. Justice

Comparative Note 15.3

[In 1963, Germany's Federal Constitutional Court sustained a federal statute providing death benefits to a widow without proof of dependency but denying them to a widower unless he could show that his deceased wife was the family's principal wage-earner. In 1975, however, the Court changed its mind on this issue and invalidated the statute.]

In its earlier decision, the Constitutional Court based its decision on the legislative finding that the widow had a greater need for social assistance [than the widower] and on the fact that housework was by law the woman's primary duty. . . . This view has been abandoned. . . . The earlier decision [was appropriate] because of the showing that only 7.5 percent of married women were independently employed. . . . According to [more recent] reports, fully 30 percent of married women are independently employed or in business. . . .

Differential treatment of men and women in respect to survivor's benefits . . . is permissible only if sex-linked biological or functional differences are so crucial in the matter to be regulated that common elements can no longer be recognized or recede completely into the background. . . . In the realm of the *general* equality clause, it suffices that there are objectively rational grounds for a distinction that corresponds with a sense of justice and reveals no arbitrary grouping (italics added). The case is different, however, where the constitution itself [bans discrimination based on sex]. Examination of Art. 3, par. 2 ["Men and women shall have equal rights"] suggests that the challenged provisions of law cannot long be tolerated in their present form. . . .

This decision comes at a time when the earlier understanding of the woman's role in marriage and family has begun to change. . . .

This situation imposes on the legislature a duty to adopt a new provision that will prevent further violations of Art. 3, par. 2. In light of the difficulties we have described, extensive and time-consuming preparatory work will be necessary. The Court assumes, however, that the new regulation must be in effect before the end of the next legislative period. . . .

SOURCE: Federal Constitutional Court, Judgment of March 12, 1975.

DOUGLAS, Mr. Justice WHITE, and Mr. Justice MARSHALL join.

At the outset, appellants contend that classifications based upon sex, like classifications based upon race, alienage, and national origin, are inherently suspect and must therefore be subjected to close judicial scrutiny. We agree and, indeed, find at least implicit support for such an approach in our unanimous decision only last Term in *Reed v. Reed* (1971). . . .

The Court noted [in *Reed v. Reed*] that the Idaho statute "provides that different treatment be accorded to the applicants on the basis of their sex; it thus establishes a classification subject to scrutiny under the Equal Protection Clause." Under "traditional" equal protection analysis, a legislative classification must be sustained unless it is "patently arbitrary" and bears no rational relationship to a legitimate governmental interest. . . .

There can be no doubt that our Nation has had a long and unfortunate history of sex discrimination. Traditionally, such discrimination was rationalized by an attitude of "romantic paternalism" which, in practical effect, put women, not on a pedestal, but in a cage. Indeed, this paternalistic attitude became so firmly rooted in our national consciousness that, exactly 100 years ago, a distinguished member of this Court was able to proclaim:

> Man is, or should be, woman's protector and defender. The natural and proper timidity and delicacy which belongs to the female sex evidently unfits it for many of the occupations of civil life. The constitution of the family organization, which is founded in the divine ordinance, as well as in the nature of things, indicates the domestic sphere as that which properly belongs to the domain and functions of womanhood. The harmony, not to say identity, of interests and views which belong, or should belong, to the family institution is repugnant to the ideas of a woman adopting a distinct and independent career from that of her husband. . . .
>
> . . . The paramount destiny and mission of woman are to fulfill the noble and benign offices of wife and mother. This is the law of the Creator. (*Bradwell v. Illinois* (1873).

As a result of notions such as these, our statute books gradually became laden with gross, stereotyped distinctions between the sexes and, indeed, throughout much of the 19th century the position of women in our society was, in many respects, comparable to that of blacks under the pre–Civil War slave codes. Neither slaves nor women could hold office, serve on juries, or bring suit in their own names, and married women traditionally were denied the legal capacity to hold or convey property or to serve as legal guardians of their own children. And although blacks were guaranteed the right to vote in 1870, women were denied even that right—which is itself "preservative of other basic civil and political rights"—until adoption of the Nineteenth Amendment half a century later.

It is true, of course, that the position of women in America has improved markedly in recent decades. Nevertheless, it can hardly be doubted that, in part because of the high visibility of the sex characteristic, women still face pervasive, although at times more subtle, discrimination in our educational institutions, in the job market and, perhaps most conspicuously, in the political arena. Moreover, since sex, like race and national origin, is an immutable characteristic determined solely by the accident of birth, the imposition of special disabilities upon the members of a particular sex because of their sex would seem to violate "the basic concept of our system that legal burdens should bear some relationship to individual responsibility. . . ." And what differentiates sex from such nonsuspect statuses as intelligence or physical disability, and aligns it with the recognized suspect criteria, is that the sex characteristic frequently bears no relation to ability to perform or contribute to society. As a result, statutory distinctions between the sexes often have the effect of invidiously relegating the entire class of females to inferior legal status without regard to the actual capabilities of its individual members.

We might also note that, over the past decade, Congress has itself manifested an increasing sensitivity to sex-based classifications. In Title VII of the Civil Rights Act of 1964, for example, Congress expressly declared that no employer, labor union, or other organization subject to the provisions of the Act shall discriminate against any individual on the basis of "race, color, religion, sex, or national origin." Similarly, the Equal Pay Act of 1963 provides that no employer covered by the Act "shall discriminate . . . between employees on the basis of *sex*." . . .

With these considerations in mind, we can only conclude that classifications based upon sex, like classifications based upon race, alienage, or national origin, are inherently suspect, and must therefore be subjected to strict judicial scrutiny. Applying the analysis mandated by that stricter standard of review, it is clear that the statutory scheme now before us is constitutionally invalid.

The sole basis of the classification established in the challenged statutes is the sex of the individuals involved. Thus, to this extent at least, it may fairly be said that these statutes command "dissimilar treatment for men and women who are . . . similarly situated."

Moreover, the Government concedes that the differential treatment accorded men and women under these statutes serves no purpose other than mere "administrative convenience." In essence, the Government maintains that, as an empirical matter, wives in our society frequently are dependent upon their husbands, while husbands rarely are dependent upon their wives. Thus, the Government argues that Congress might reasonably have concluded that it would be both cheaper and easier simply conclusively to presume that wives of male members are financially dependent upon their husbands, while burdening female members with the task of establishing dependency in fact.

The Government offers no concrete evidence, however, tending to support its view that such differential treatment in fact saves the Government any money. In order to satisfy the demands of strict judicial scrutiny, the Government must demonstrate, for example, that it is actually cheaper to grant increased benefits with respect to all male members, than it is to determine which male members are in fact entitled to such benefits and to grant increased benefits only to those members whose wives actually meet the dependency requirement. Here, however, there is substantial evidence that, if put to the test, many of the wives of male members would fail to qualify for benefits. And in light of the fact that the dependency determination with respect to the husbands of female members is presently made solely on the basis of affidavits, rather than through the more costly hearing process, the Government's explanation of the statutory scheme is, to say the least, questionable.

In any case, our prior decisions make clear that, although efficacious administration of governmental programs is not without some importance, "the Constitution recognizes higher values than speed and efficiency." And when we enter the realm of "strict judicial scrutiny," there can be no doubt that "administrative convenience" is not a shibboleth, the mere recitation of which dictates constitutionality. . . . On the contrary, any statutory scheme which draws a sharp line between the sexes, solely for the purpose of achieving administrative convenience, necessarily commands "dissimilar treatment for men and women who are . . . similarly situated," and therefore involves the "very kind of arbitrary legislative choice forbidden by the [Constitution]. . . ." We therefore conclude that, by according differential treatment to male and female members of the uniformed services for the sole purpose of achieving administrative convenience, the challenged statutes violate the Due Process Clause of the Fifth Amendment insofar as they require a female member to prove the dependency of her husband.

Reversed.

Mr. Justice POWELL, with whom the Chief Justice and Mr. Justice BLACKMUN join, concurring in the judgment.

I agree that the challenged statutes constitute an unconstitutional discrimination against servicewomen in violation of the Due Process Clause of the Fifth Amendment, but I cannot join the opinion of Justice Brennan, which would hold that all classifications based upon sex, "like classifications based upon race, alienage, and national origin," are "inherently suspect and must therefore be subjected to close judicial scrutiny." It is unnecessary for the Court in this case to characterize sex as a suspect classification, with all of the far-reaching implications of such a holding. *Reed v. Reed* (1971), which abundantly supports our decision today, did not add sex to the narrowly limited group of classifications which are inherently suspect. In my view, we can and should decide this case on the authority of *Reed* and reserve for the future any expansion of its rationale.

There is another, and I find compelling, reason for deferring a general categorizing of sex classifications as invoking the strictest test of judicial scrutiny. The Equal Rights Amendment, which if adopted will resolve the substance of this precise question, has been approved by the Congress and submitted for ratification by the States. If this Amendment is duly adopted, it will represent the will of the people accomplished in the manner prescribed by the Constitution. By acting prematurely and unnecessarily, as I view it, the Court has assumed a decisional responsibility at the very time when state legislatures, functioning within the traditional democratic process, are debating the proposed Amendment. It seems to me that this reaching out to pre-empt by judicial action a major political decision which is currently in process of resolution does not reflect appropriate respect for duly prescribed legislative processes.

There are times when this Court, under our system, cannot avoid a constitutional decision on issues which normally should be resolved by the elected representatives of the people. But democratic institutions are weakened, and confidence in the restraint of the Court is impaired, when we appear unnecessarily to decide sensitive issues of broad social and political importance at the very time they are under consideration within the prescribed constitutional processes.

Notes and Queries

1. As noted in the introductory essay, *Reed v. Reed* (1971) was the first time the Court struck a legislative classification based on gender. (Recall that *Reed* involved a state law giving preference to males as estate administrators.) The Court unanimously invalidated the statute for incorporating an arbitrary classification. In *Frontiero*, however, the Court appears hopelessly divided over the standard of review employed in *Reed*, the dispute taking place between justices committed to strict scrutiny review—the plurarily view in *Frontiero*—and those preferring the "reasonable basis" standard. A majority of five finally settled on a new standard of review in *Craig v. Boren* (1976).

2. Both Justice Brennan, in his opinion, and Justice Powell, in his concurring opinion, advert to the Equal Rights Amendment (ERA) which was passed by Congress in March 1972 but never ratified by the necessary number of state legislatures. Justice Brennan uses the ERA as an indication that Congress considers gender a suspect classification. Justice Powell, however, uses it as an indication that the status of gender is a political question working itself out in the political arena according to the rules of the Constitution. Thus, according to Powell, the Court's pronouncement on the issue is an unwarranted act of judicial interference in the politial process. He almost seems to imply that the dark shadow of *Dred Scott* (1856) looms over the case. Should such political considerations carry weight in constitutional jurisprudence as opposed to the simple merits of the arguments? Should the failure of ERA's ratification influence the interpretation of the Equal Protection Clause? In what way?

3. Recall from the introduction to the chapter the principle that persons who are similarly situated should be treated similarly. Has the Court in *Frontiero* affirmed this concept of fairness by making legislative classifications based on gender disfavored and therefore subject to heightened scrutiny analysis? If so, what criteria did the Court draw upon to determine that both genders are similarly situated?

4. The Court noted that "what differentiates sex from such non-suspect categories as intelligence or physical disability, and aligns it with recognized suspect criteria, is that the sex characteristic frequently bears no relation to

ability to perform or contribute to society." Are classifications based on gender truly aligned with those based on race? Consider that race is suspect because it is *never* indicative of ability and thus triggers strict scrutiny of any such legislative line-drawing. On the other hand, the Court said that gender classifications are suspect because they "*frequently bear* no relation to ability" (italics supplied). Why did the Court phrase the two situations differently? Should it have done so? Does the modified language where gender is concerned foreshadow the Court's retrenchment in *Craig* (reprinted next)?

5. What legitimate state interests might justify a classification based on sex?

Craig v. Boren
429 U.S. 190; 97 S. Ct. 451; 50 L.Ed. 2d 397 (1976)

An Oklahoma statute prohibited the sale of "non-intoxicating" 3.2 percent beer to males under the age of 21 and to women under the age of 18. Craig, a male between 18 and 21 years of age, and Whitener, a liquor store owner, brought this suit claiming the statute violated the Equal Protection Clause of the Fourteenth Amendment. A federal district court upheld the constitutionality of the statute and dismissed the action. Craig and Whitener appealed. Opinion of the Court: *Brennan*, Powell, Stevens, White, Marshall. Concurring opinions: *Powell, Stevens,* Blackmun. Dissenting opinions: *Burger, Rehnquist.*

Justice BRENNAN delivered the opinion of the Court.

To withstand constitutional challenge, previous cases establish that classifications by gender must serve important governmental objectives and must be substantially related to achievement of those objectives. . . .

Reed v. Reed (1971) has also provided the underpinning for decisions that have invalidated statutes employing gender as an inaccurate proxy for other, more germane bases of classification. Hence, "archaic and overbroad" generalizations concerning the financial position of servicewomen and working women could not justify use of a gender line in determining eligibility for certain governmental entitlements. Similarly, increasingly outdated misconceptions concerning the role of females in the home rather than in the "marketplace and world of ideas" were rejected as loose-fitting characterizations incapable of supporting state statutory schemes that were premised upon their accuracy. In light of the weak congruence between gender and the characteristic or trait that gender purported to represent, it was necessary that the legislatures choose either to realign their substantive laws in a gender-neutral fashion, or to adopt procedures for identifying those instances where the sex-centered generalization actually comported with fact. . . .

We accept for purposes of discussion the District Court's identification of the objective underlying [the Oklahoma statute] as the enhancement of traffic safety. Clearly, the protection of public health and safety represents an important function of state and local governments. However, appellees' statistics in our view cannot support the conclusion that the gender-based distinction closely serves to achieve that objective and therefore the distinction cannot under *Reed* withstand equal protection challenge.

The appellees introduced a variety of statistical surveys. First, an analysis of arrest statistics for 1973 demonstrated that 18–20-year-old male arrests for "driving under the influence" and "drunkenness" substantially exceeded female arrests for that same age period. Similarly, youths aged 17–21 were found to be overrepresented among those killed or injured in traffic accidents, with males again numerically exceeding females in this regard. Third, a random roadside survey in Oklahoma City revealed that young males were more inclined to drive and drink beer than were their female counterparts. Fourth, Federal Bureau of Investigation nationwide statistics exhibited a notable increase in arrests for "driving under the influence." Finally, statistical evidence gathered in other jurisdictions, particularly Minnesota and Michigan, was offered to corroborate Oklahoma's experience by indicating the pervasiveness of youthful participation in motor vehicle accidents following the imbibing of alcohol. Conceding that "the case is not free from doubt," the District Court nonetheless concluded that this statistical showing substantiated "a rational basis for the legislative judgment underlying the challenged classification."

Even were this statistical evidence accepted as accurate, it nevertheless offers only a weak answer to the equal protection question presented here. The most focused and relevant of the statistical surveys, arrests of 18–20-year-olds for alcohol-related driving offenses, exemplifies the ultimate unpersuasiveness of this evidentiary record. Viewed in terms of the correlation between sex and the actual activity that Oklahoma seeks to regulate—driving while under the influence of alcohol—the statistics

Comparative Note 15.4

Article 14 (Constitution of Japan, 1947)

All of the people are equal under the law and there shall be no discrimination in political, economic or social relations because of race, creed, sex, social status or family origin.

Article 3 (2) (Basic Law of Germany, 1949)

Men and women shall have equal rights. The state shall seek to ensure equal treatment of men and women and remove existing disadvantages based on sex.

Article 28 (Canadian Charter of Rights and Freedoms, 1982)

Notwithstanding anything in this Charter, the rights and freedoms referred to in it are guaranteed equally to male and female persons.

Article 66 (1) (Constitution of Hungary, 1990)

The Republic of Hungary guarantees the equality of men and women in regard to all civil, political, economic, social and cultural rights.

Article 3 (U.N. Covenant on Economic, Social and Cultural Rights, 1966)

The State Parties to the present Covenant undertake to guarantee that the rights enunciated in the present Covenant will be exercised without discrimination of any kind as to race, color, sex, language, religion . . . birth or other status.

Article 14 (European Convention on Human Rights, 1950)

The enjoyment of the rights and freedoms set forth in this Convention shall be secured without discrimination on any ground such as sex, race, color, language . . . birth or other status.

Article 2 (Convention on Elimination of All Forms of Discrimination Against Women, 1981)

State Parties condemn discrimination against women in all its forms, agree to pursue by all appropriate means and without delay a policy of eliminating discrimination against women and, to this end, undertake:

(a) To embody the principle of equality of men and women in their national constitutions or other appropriate legislation if not yet incorporated therein and to ensure, through law and other appropriate means, the practical realization of this principle.

---

broadly establish that .18% of females and 2% of males in that age group were arrested for that offense. While such a disparity is not trivial in a statistical sense, it hardly can form the basis for employment of a gender line as a classifying device. Certainly if maleness is to serve as a proxy for drinking and driving, a correlation of 2% must be considered an unduly tenuous "fit." . . .

There is no reason to belabor this line of analysis. It is unrealistic to expect either members of the judiciary or state officials to be well versed in the rigors of experimental or statistical technique. But this merely illustrates that proving broad sociological propositions by statistics is a dubious business, and one that inevitably is in tension with the normative philosophy that underlies the Equal Protection Clause. Suffice to say that the showing offered by the appellees does not satisfy us that sex represents a legitimate, accurate proxy for the regulation of drinking and driving. In fact, when it is further recognized that Oklahoma's statute prohibits only the selling of 3.2% beer to young males and not their drinking the beverage once acquired (even after purchase by their 18–20-year-old female companions), the relationship between gender and traffic safety becomes far too tenuous to satisfy Reed's requirement that the gender-based difference be substantially related to achievement of the statutory objective.

We hold, therefore, that under *Reed*, Oklahoma's 3.2% beer statute invidiously discriminates against males 18–20 years of age. . . .

Mr. Justice POWELL, concurring.

With respect to the equal protection standard, I agree that *Reed v. Reed* is the most relevant precedent. But I find it unnecessary, in deciding this case, to read that decision as broadly as some of the Court's language may imply. *Reed* and subsequent cases involving gender-based classifications make clear that the Court subjects such classifications to a more critical examination than is normally applied when "fundamental" constitutional rights and "suspect classes" are not present.

I view this as a relatively easy case. No one questions

the legitimacy or importance of the asserted governmental objective: the promotion of highway safety. The decision of the case turns on whether the state legislature, by the classification it has chosen, has adopted a means that bears a "'fair and substantial relation'" to this objective.

It seems to me that the statistics offered by appellees and relied upon by the District Court do tend generally to support the view that young men drive more, possibly are inclined to drink more, and—for various reasons—are involved in more accidents than young women. Even so, I am not persuaded that these facts and the inferences fairly drawn from them justify this classification based on a three-year age differential between the sexes, and especially one that is so easily circumvented as to be virtually meaningless. Putting it differently, this gender-based classification does not bear a fair and substantial relation to the object of the legislation.

Mr. Justice STEVENS, concurring.

There is only one Equal Protection Clause. It requires every State to govern impartially. It does not direct the courts to apply one standard of review in some cases and a different standard in other cases. Whatever criticism may be leveled at a judicial opinion implying that there are at least three such standards applies with the same force to a double standard.

I am inclined to believe that what has become known as the two-tiered analysis of equal protection claims does not describe a completely logical method of deciding cases, but rather is a method the Court has employed to explain decisions that actually apply a single standard in a reasonably consistent fashion. I also suspect that a careful explanation of the reasons motivating particular decisions may contribute more to an identification of that standard than an attempt to articulate it in all-encompassing terms. It may therefore be appropriate for me to state the principal reasons which persuaded me to join the Court's opinion.

In this case, the classification is not as obnoxious as some the Court has condemned, nor as inoffensive as some the Court has accepted. It is objectionable because it is based on an accident of birth, because it is a mere remnant of the now almost universally rejected tradition of discriminating against males in this age bracket, and because, to the extent it reflects any physical difference between males and females, it is actually perverse. The question then is whether the traffic safety justification put forward by the State is sufficient to make an otherwise offensive classification acceptable.

Mr. Justice STEWART, concurring in the judgment.

The disparity created by these Oklahoma statutes amounts to total irrationality. For the statistics upon which the State now relies, whatever their other shortcomings, wholly fail to prove or even suggest that 3.2% beer is somehow more deleterious when it comes into the hands of a male aged 18–20 than of a female of like age. The disparate statutory treatment of the sexes here, without even a colorably valid justification or explanation, thus amounts to invidious discrimination.

Chief Justice BURGER, dissenting.

. . . Though today's decision does not go so far as to make gender-based classifications "suspect," it makes gender a disfavored classification. Without an independent constitutional basis supporting the right asserted or disfavoring the classification adopted, I can justify no substantive constitutional protection other than the normal protection afforded by the Equal Protection Clause.

The means employed by the Oklahoma Legislature to achieve the objectives sought may not be agreeable to some judges, but since eight Members of the Court think the means not irrational, I see no basis for striking down the statute as violative of the Constitution simply because we find it unwise, unneeded, or possibly even a bit foolish.

Mr. Justice REHNQUIST, dissenting.

The Court's disposition of this case is objectionable on two grounds. First is its conclusion that *men* challenging a gender-based statute which treats them less favorably than women may invoke a more stringent standard of judicial review than pertains to most other types of classifications. Second is the Court's enunciation of this standard, without citation to any source, as being that "classifications by gender must serve *important* governmental objectives and must be *substantially* related to achievement of those objectives." The only redeeming feature of the Court's opinion, to my mind, is that it apparently signals a retreat by those who joined the plurality opinion in *Frontiero v. Richardson*, from their view that sex is a "suspect" classification for purposes of equal protection analysis. I think the Oklahoma statute challenged here need pass only the "rational basis" equal protection analysis and I believe that it is constitutional under that analysis.

Subsequent to *Frontiero*, the Court has declined to hold that sex is a suspect class, . . . and no such holding is imported by the Court's resolution of this case. However, the Court's application here of an elevated or "intermediate" level scrutiny, like that invoked in cases dealing with discrimination against females, raises the question of why the statute here should be treated any differently from countless legislative classifications unrelated to sex which have been upheld under a minimum rationality standard. . . .

Most obviously unavailable to support any kind of special scrutiny in this case, is a history or pattern of past discrimination, such as was relied on by the plurality in *Frontiero* to support its invocation of strict scrutiny. There is no suggestion in the Court's opinion that males in this age group are in any way peculiarly disadvantaged, subject to systematic discriminatory treatment, or otherwise in need of special solicitude from the courts. . . .

The Court does not discuss the nature of the right involved, and there is no reason to believe that it sees the purchase of 3.2 % beer as implicating any important interest, let alone one that is "fundamental" in the constitutional sense of invoking strict scrutiny. . . .

I would have thought that if this Court were to leave anything to decision by the popularly elected branches of the Government, where no constitutional claim other than that of equal protection is invoked, it would be the decision as to what governmental objectives to be achieved by law are "important," and which are not. As for the second part of the Court's new test, the Judicial Branch is probably in no worse position than the Legislative or Executive Branches to determine if there is any rational relationship between a classification and the purpose which it might be thought to serve. But the introduction of the adverb "substantially" requires courts to make subjective judgments as to operational effects, for which neither their expertise nor their access to data fits them. And even if we manage to avoid both confusion and the mirroring of our own preferences in the development of this new doctrine, the thousands of judges in other courts who must interpret the Equal Protection Clause may not be so fortunate. . . .

The Oklahoma Legislature could have believed that 18–20-year-old males drive substantially more, and tend more often to be intoxicated than their female counterparts; that they prefer beer and admit to drinking and driving at a higher rate than females; and that they suffer traffic injuries out of proportion to the part they make up of the population. Under the appropriate rational-basis test for equal protection, it is neither irrational nor arbitrary to bar them from making purchases of 3.2% beer, which purchases might in many cases be made by a young man who immediately returns to his vehicle with the beverage in his possession. The record does not give any good indication of the true proportion of males in the age group who drink

and drive (except that it is no doubt greater than the 2% who are arrested), but whatever it may be I cannot see that the mere purchase right involved could conceivably raise a due process question. There being no violation of either equal protection or due process, the statute should accordingly be upheld.

Notes and Queries

1. In considering what objectives are important and what means are substantially related to such objectives, has the Court extended the reach of equal protection analysis so as to encroach on the domain of the legislature? Has the Court expanded its ability to resolve conflicts between the community and the individual by means of the equal protection clause through *Craig*?

2. What role does statistical evidence play in this case? Can any comparison be made to the sociological evidence used in *Brown*?

3. Justice Rehnquist argues that the statute is rationally related to a permissible purpose. Admitting this, would it still be possible to invalidate Oklahoma's statute without resorting to the language of "substantial rationality" and "important governmental objectives"? Would the answer depend on how you define discrimination? Why not hold that discrimination is present if the classification is not *precisely* tailored to a permissible purpose? Would the Court achieve greater consistency in its case law by adopting this approach in all equal protection cases?

4. Oklahoma's legislature, which presumably speaks for the community at large, might have adopted a policy on traffic safety to avoid the issue of equality altogether. For example, it might have imposed a mandatory five-year prison term on any person causing a traffic accident under the influence of alcohol. Or, alternatively, it might have provided for the permanent cancellation of the offender's driver's license. Such draconian measures, however, would be fiercely debated in any legislature. On the other hand, the legislature might have decided that the institution of a drivers' education program would be a better solution to the problem of highway safety. But this solution might have invited equal controversy. The politically acceptable solution, under these limiting circumstances— that is, the one commanding the support of a political majority—might have been the classification at issue in *Craig*. The legislature might have reasonably thought, given the statistics available to it, that the gender-based statute in this case, although perhaps not the best solution, would help to relieve the pain where the shoe pinches. Does this description of the political process suggest the propriety of judicial restraint in cases such as *Craig*?

5. In his opinion, Justice Stevens wrote that "There is only one Equal Protection Clause. It requires every state to govern impartially. It does not direct the courts to apply one standard of review in some cases and a different standard in other cases." Does the existence of a single equal protection clause really imply that there should be only one standard of review in equal protection cases? Why? Is this push toward a single standard a consequence of a particular method of constitutional interpretation? Is it grounded instead in a particular understanding of judicial power? Assuming that one standard should suffice for all cases, what should the standard be? Finally, does Justice Stevens' observation imply a rejection of footnote 4 of *Carolene Products?*

6. Comparative Note 15.4 lists several national constitutions and international human rights documents that contain explicit provisions against discrimination based on gender. Suppose the U.S. Constitution incorporated similar provisions. Would such constitutional language bar all distinctions based on gender? If not, what gender classifications might be sustained under these provisions? Would any of the gender cases featured in this chapter have been decided differently in the presence of these provisions?

7. In *Frontiero*, Justice Brennan insisted on applying the strict scrutiny test to classifications based on gender. In *Craig* we find him backing off to an intermediate test. Why do you think he gave up on the fight in *Craig?* Might it have had something to do with the fact that the persons discriminated against were men rather than women?

8. In *Rostker v. Goldberg*, 453 U.S. 57 (1981), decided five years after *Craig*, the Supreme Court upheld a United States military service policy that required males but not females to register for possible military service. Speaking for himself and five other justices (Blackmun, Burger, Powell, Stevens, and Stewart), Chief Justice Rehnquist wrote that "[m]en and women, because of the combat restrictions on women, are simply not similarly situated for purposes of a draft or registration for the draft." In so ruling, the Court clearly had institutional considerations in mind. First, the challenged law was an exercise of Congress' power to raise and support armies, requiring in this field, according to the Court, a large measure of deference to congressional choice. Second, the Chief Justice noted that Congress had debated at length—in hearings, floor debate, and in committee—the question of registering women for the draft and the question of the draft exemption's constitutionality. The extensive debate in Congress on these issues, he concluded, demanded judicial restraint. It also showed, according to the Chief Justice, that the exemption for women was not the "accidental byproduct of a traditional way of thinking about women." Justice Marshall in dissent, however, wrote, "The Court today places its imprimatur on one of the most potent remaining public expressions of 'ancient canards about the proper role of women.'" Is Justice Marshall right?

United States v. Virginia
518 U.S. 515 , 135 L. Ed. 2d 735, 116 S.Ct. 2264 (1996)

The Virginia Military Institute is a state-supported, all-male military academy founded in 1839. It is the only state-supported single-sex institution in the state. The United States sued the Institute and the State of Virginia, claiming that the males-only admissions policy violates the equal protection clause of the Fourteenth Amendment. The District Court ruled in favor of VMI, but the appellate court reversed and ordered the state to remedy the violation. VMI responded by proposing to establish a parallel program for women called the Virginia Women's Institute for Leadership at Mary Baldwin College, a private liberal arts school for women. Opinion of the Court: *Ginsburg*, Stevens, O'Connor, Kennedy, Souter, Breyer. Concurring in the judgment: *Rehnquist*. Dissenting opinion: *Scalia*. Not participating: *Thomas*.

Justice GINSBURG delivered the opinion of the Court.

Founded in 1839, VMI is today the sole single-sex school among Virginia's 15 public institutions of higher learning. VMI's distinctive mission is to produce "citizen-soldiers," men prepared for leadership in civilian life and in military service. VMI pursues this mission through pervasive training of a kind not available anywhere else in Virginia. Assigning prime place to character development, VMI uses an "adversative method" modeled on English public schools and once characteristic of military instruction. VMI constantly endeavors to instill physical and mental discipline in its cadets and impart to them a strong moral code. The school's graduates leave VMI with heightened comprehension of their capacity to deal with duress and stress, and a large sense of accomplishment for completing the hazardous course.

Neither the goal of producing citizen-soldiers nor VMI's implementing methodology is inherently unsuitable to women. And the school's impressive record in producing leaders has made admission desirable to some women. Nevertheless, Virginia has elected to preserve exclusively

Comparative Note 15.5

[A supervisor in a cake factory was fined for employing women to wrap cakes at night in violation of a statute forbidding the employment of women as blue-collar workers during the night. The supervisor filed a constitutional complaint with Germany's Federal Constitutional Court, arguing that the statute violated the equality provisions of the Basic Law.]

The constitutional complaint is justified. . . . The prohibition of nocturnal employment of women is incompatible with Article 3 (1) and (2) of the Basic Law. . . .

Not every inequality based on sex offends Article 3 (3). Gender distinctions may be permissible to the extent that they are indispensably necessary to the solution of problems that by their nature can arise only for women or only for men. But this is not such a case.

The prohibition of nocturnal employment was originally based upon the assumption that women laborers were constitutionally more susceptible to harm from

night work than men. Studies in occupational medicine provide no firm basis for this assumption. Working at night is fundamentally harmful to everyone. . . .

The infringement of the ban on discrimination is not justified by the command of Article 3 (2). [Article 3 (2) reads as follows: "Men and women shall have equal rights. The state shall promote the actual implementation of equal rights for women and men and take steps to eliminate disadvantages that now exist."] The prohibition of night work . . . does not promote the goals of this provision. . . . One result of [the existing discrimination] may be that women will continue to be more burdened than men by child rearing and housework in addition to work outside the home, and that the traditional division of labor between the sexes may be further entrenched. To this extent the prohibition of night work impedes the elimination of the social disadvantages suffered by women.

SOURCE: *Nocturnal Employment Case*, 85 BVerfGE 191 (1992) reproduced in Donald P. Kommers, *The Constitutional Jurisprudence of the Federal Republic of Germany* (2d ed. 1997), 291–293.

---

for men the advantages and opportunities a VMI education affords.

In 1990, prompted by a complaint filed with the Attorney General by a female high-school student seeking admission to VMI, the United States sued the Commonwealth of Virginia and VMI, alleging that VMI's exclusively male admission policy violated the Equal Protection Clause of the Fourteenth Amendment. . . .

The District Court ruled in favor of VMI, however, and rejected the equal protection challenge presented by the United States. That court correctly recognized that [in] *Mississippi Univ. For Women v. Hogan* (1982) . . . this Court underscored that a party seeking to uphold government action based on sex must establish an "exceedingly persuasive justification" for the classification. To succeed, the defender of the challenged action must show "at least that the classification serves important governmental objectives and that the discriminatory means employed are substantially related to the achievement of those objectives."

Today's skeptical scrutiny of official action denying rights or opportunities based on sex responds to volumes of history. As a plurality of this Court acknowledged a generation ago, "our Nation has had a long and unfortunate history of sex discrimination." . . .

The heightened review standard our precedent estab-

lishes does not make sex a proscribed classification. Supposed "inherent differences" are no longer accepted as a ground for race or national origin classifications. *Loving v. Virginia* (1967). Physical differences between men and women, however, are enduring: "[T]he two sexes are not fungible; a community made up exclusively of one [sex] is different from a community composed of both." *Ballard v. United States* (1946).

Measuring the record in this case against the review standard just described, we conclude that Virginia has shown no "exceedingly persuasive justification" for excluding all women from the citizen-soldier training afforded by VMI. We therefore affirm the Fourth Circuit's initial judgment, which held that Virginia had violated the Fourteenth Amendment's Equal Protection Clause. Because the remedy proffered by Virginia—the Mary Baldwin VWIL program—does not cure the constitutional violation, i.e., it does not provide equal opportunity, we reverse the Fourth Circuit's final judgment in this case.

The Fourth Circuit initially held that Virginia had advanced no state policy by which it could justify, under equal protection principles, its determination "to afford VMI's unique type of program to men and not to women." Virginia challenges that "liability" ruling and asserts two justifications in defense of VMI's exclusion of women.

First, the Commonwealth contends, "single-sex education provides important education benefits," and the option of single-sex education contributes to "diversity in educational approaches." Second, the Commonwealth argues, "the unique VMI method of character development and leadership training," the school's adversative approach, would have to be modified were VMI to admit women. We consider these two justifications in turn.

Single-sex education affords pedagogical benefits to at least some students, Virginia emphasizes, and that reality is uncontested in this litigation. Similarly, it is not disputed that diversity among public educational institutions can serve the public good. But Virginia has not shown that VMI was established, or has been maintained, with a view to diversifying, by its categorical exclusion of women, educational opportunities within the State. In cases of this genre, our precedent instructs that "benign" justifications proffered in defense of categorical exclusions will not be accepted automatically; a tenable justification must describe actual state purposes, not rationalizations for actions in fact differently grounded.

Mississippi Univ. for Women is immediately in point. There the State asserted, in justification of its exclusion of men from a nursing school, that it was engaging in "educational affirmative action" by "compensat[ing] for discrimination against women." Undertaking a "searching analysis," the Court found no close resemblance between "the alleged objective" and "the actual purpose underlying the discriminatory classification." Pursuing a similar inquiry here, we reach the same conclusion.

Neither recent nor distant history bears out Virginia's alleged pursuit of diversity through single-sex educational options. In 1839, when the Commonwealth established VMI, a range of educational opportunities for men and women was scarcely contemplated. Higher education at the time was considered dangerous for women; reflecting widely held views about women's proper place, the Nation's first universities and colleges—for example, Harvard in Massachusetts, William and Mary in Virginia—admitted only men. VMI was not at all novel in this respect: In admitting no women, VMI followed the lead of the Commonwealth's flagship school, the University of Virginia, founded in 1819. . . .

Virginia describes the current absence of public single-sex higher education for women as "an historical anomaly." But the historical record indicates action more deliberate than anomalous: First, protection of women against higher education; next, schools for women far from equal in resources and stature to schools for men; finally, conversion of the separate schools to coeducation. . . .

In sum, we find no persuasive evidence in this record

that VMI's male-only admission policy "is in furtherance of a state policy of 'diversity.'" No such policy, the Fourth Circuit observed, can be discerned from the movement of all other public colleges and universities in Virginia away from single-sex education. . . . However "liberally" this plan serves the State's sons, it makes no provision whatever for her daughters. That is not *equal* protection.

Virginia next argues that VMI's adversative method of training provides educational benefits that cannot be made available, unmodified, to women. Alterations to accommodate women would necessarily be "radical," so "drastic," Virginia asserts, as to transform, indeed "destroy," VMI's program. Neither sex would be favored by the transformation, Virginia maintains: Men would be deprived of the unique opportunity currently available to them; women would not gain that opportunity because their participation would "eliminat[e] the very aspects of [the] program that distinguish [VMI] from . . . other institutions of higher education in Virginia." . . .

Women's successful entry into the federal military academies, and their participation in the Nation's military forces, indicate that Virginia's fears for the future of VMI may not be solidly grounded. The State's justification for excluding all women from "citizen-soldier" training for which some are qualified, in any event, cannot rank as "exceedingly persuasive," as we have explained and applied the standard. . . .

The State's misunderstanding and, in turn, the District Court's, is apparent from VMI's mission: to produce "citizen-soldiers," individuals "imbued with love of learning, confident in the functions and attitudes of leadership, possessing a high sense of public service, advocates of the American democracy and free enterprise system, and ready . . . to defend their country in time of national peril." Surely that goal is great enough to accommodate women, who today count as citizens in our American democracy equal in stature to men. Just as surely, the State's great goal is not substantially advanced by women's categorical exclusion, in total disregard of their individual merit, from the State's premier "citizen-soldier" corps. . . .

In the second phase of the litigation, Virginia presented its remedial plan—maintain VMI as a male-only college and create VWIL as a separate program for women. . . .

A remedial decree, this Court has said, must closely fit the constitutional violation; it must be shaped to place persons unconstitutionally denied an opportunity or advantage in "the position they would have occupied in the absence of [discrimination]." See *Milliken v. Bradley* (1974). The constitutional violation in this suit is the categorical exclusion of women from an extraordinary educational opportunity afforded men. A proper remedy for an unconstitutional exclusion, we have explained, aims to "eliminate [so far as possible] the discriminatory effects of the past" and to "bar like discrimination in the future." . . .

VWIL affords women no opportunity to experience the rigorous military training for which VMI is famed. ("No other school in Virginia or in the United States, public or private, offers the same kind of rigorous military training as is available at VMI."). Instead, the VWIL program "de-emphasize[s]" military education and uses a "cooperative method" of education "which reinforces self-esteem." VWIL students participate in ROTC and a "largely ceremonial" Virginia Corps of Cadets, but Virginia deliberately did not make VWIL a military institute.

In myriad respects other than military training, VWIL does not qualify as VMI's equal. VWIL's student body, faculty, course offerings, and facilities hardly match VMI's. Nor can the VWIL graduate anticipate the benefits associated with VMI's 157-year history, the school's prestige, and its influential alumni network. . . .

Virginia, in sum, while maintaining VMI for men only, has failed to provide any "comparable single-gender women's institution." Instead, the State has created a VWIL program fairly appraised as a "pale shadow" of VMI in terms of the range of curricular choices and faculty stature, funding, prestige, alumni support and influence. . . .

A prime part of the history of our Constitution, historian Richard Morris recounted, is the story of the extension of constitutional rights and protections to people once ignored or excluded. VMI's story continued as our comprehension of "We the People" expanded. There is no reason to believe that the admission of women capable of all the activities required of VMI cadets would destroy the Institute rather than enhance its capacity to serve the "more perfect Union."

. . . [T]he case is remanded for further proceedings consistent with this opinion. It is so ordered.

Chief Justice REHNQUIST, concurring in the judgment.

The Court holds first that Virginia violates the Equal Protection Clause by maintaining the Virginia Military Institute's (VMI's) all-male admissions policy, and second that establishing the Virginia Women's Institute for Leadership (VWIL) program does not remedy that violation. While I agree with these conclusions, I disagree with the Court's analysis and so I write separately.

Two decades ago in *Craig v. Boren* (1976) we announced that "[t]o withstand constitutional challenge, . . . classifications by gender must serve important govern-

mental objectives and must be substantially related to achievement of those objectives." We have adhered to that standard of scrutiny ever since. While the majority adheres to this test today, *ante,* at 2271, 2275, it also says that the Commonwealth must demonstrate an "exceedingly persuasive justification" to support a gender-based classification. It is unfortunate that the Court thereby introduces an element of uncertainty respecting the appropriate test.

While terms like "important governmental objective" and "substantially related" are hardly models of precision, they have more content and specificity than does the phrase "exceedingly persuasive justification." That phrase is best confined, as it was first used, as an observation on the difficulty of meeting the applicable test, not as a formulation of the test itself. To avoid introducing potential confusion, I would have adhered more closely to our traditional, "firmly established," standard that a gender-based classification "must bear a close and substantial relationship to important governmental objectives."

Our cases dealing with gender discrimination also require that the proffered purpose for the challenged law be the actual purpose. It is on this ground that the Court rejects the first of two justifications Virginia offers for VMI's single-sex admissions policy, namely, the goal of diversity among its public educational institutions. While I ultimately agree that the Commonwealth has not carried the day with this justification, I disagree with the Court's method of analyzing the issue. . . .

. . .

The Court defines the constitutional violation in these cases as "the categorical exclusion of women from an extraordinary educational opportunity afforded to men." By defining the violation in this way, and by emphasizing that a remedy for a constitutional violation must place the victims of discrimination in "the position they would have occupied in the absence of [discrimination]," the Court necessarily implies that the only adequate remedy would be the admission of women to the all-male institution. As the foregoing discussion suggests, I would not define the violation in this way; it is not the "exclusion of women" that violates the Equal Protection Clause, but the maintenance of an all-men school without providing any—much less a comparable—institution for women.

Accordingly, the remedy should not necessarily require either the admission of women to VMI or the creation of a VMI clone for women. An adequate remedy in my opinion might be a demonstration by Virginia that its interest in educating men in a single-sex environment is matched by its interest in educating women in a single-sex institution. To demonstrate such, the Commonwealth does not need to create two institutions with the same number of faculty

Ph.D.'s, similar SAT scores, or comparable athletic fields. Nor would it necessarily require that the women's institution offer the same curriculum as the men's; one could be strong in computer science, the other could be strong in liberal arts. It would be a sufficient remedy, I think, if the two institutions offered the same quality of education and were of the same overall caliber.

If a State decides to create single-sex programs, the State would, I expect, consider the public's interest and demand in designing curricula. And rightfully so. But the State should avoid assuming demand based on stereotypes; it must not assume *a priori,* without evidence, that there would be no interest in a women's school of civil engineering, or in a men's school of nursing. . . .

Justice SCALIA dissenting.

Today the Court shuts down an institution that has served the people of the Commonwealth of Virginia with pride and distinction for over a century and a half. To achieve that desired result, it rejects (contrary to our established practice) the factual findings of two courts below, sweeps aside the precedents of this Court, and ignores the history of our people. As to facts: It explicitly rejects the finding that there exist "gender-based developmental differences" supporting Virginia's restriction of the "adversative" method to only a men's institution, and the finding that the all-male composition of the Virginia Military Institute (VMI) is essential to that institution's character. As to precedent: It drastically revises our established standards for reviewing sex-based classifications. And as to history: It counts for nothing the long tradition, enduring down to the present, of men's military colleges supported by both States and the Federal Government.

Much of the Court's opinion is devoted to deprecating the closed-mindedness of our forebears with regard to women's education, and even with regard to the treatment of women in areas that have nothing to do with education. Closed-minded they were—as every age is, including our own, with regard to matters it cannot guess, because it simply does not consider them debatable. The virtue of a democratic system with a First Amendment is that it readily enables the people, over time, to be persuaded that what they took for granted is not so, and to change their laws accordingly. That system is destroyed if the smug assurances of each age are removed from the democratic process and written into the Constitution. So to counterbalance the Court's criticism of our ancestors, let me say a word in their praise: They left us free to change. The same cannot be said of this most illiberal Court, which has embarked on a course of inscribing one after another of the current preferences of the society (and in some

cases only the counter-majoritarian preferences of the society's law-trained elite) into our Basic Law. Today it enshrines the notion that no substantial educational value is to be served by an all-men's military academy—so that the decision by the people of Virginia to maintain such an institution denies equal protection to women who cannot attend that institution but can attend others. Since it is entirely clear that the Constitution of the United States—the old one—takes no sides in this educational debate, I dissent.

I have no problem with a system of abstract tests such as rational basis, intermediate, and strict scrutiny (though I think we can do better than applying strict scrutiny and intermediate scrutiny whenever we feel like it). Such formulas are essential to evaluating whether the new restrictions that a changing society constantly imposes upon private conduct comport with that "equal protection" our society has always accorded in the past. But in my view the function of this Court is to *preserve* our society's values regarding (among other things) equal protection, not to *revise* them; to prevent backsliding from the degree of restriction the Constitution imposed upon democratic government, not to prescribe, on our own authority, progressively higher degrees. . . . More specifically, it is my view that "when a practice not expressly prohibited by the text of the Bill of Rights bears the endorsement of a long tradition of open, widespread, and unchallenged use that dates back to the beginning of the Republic, we have no proper basis for striking it down.". . .

The all-male constitution of VMI comes squarely within such a governing tradition. Founded by the Commonwealth of Virginia in 1839 and continuously maintained by it since, VMI has always admitted only men. And in that regard it has not been unusual. For almost all of VMI's more than a century and a half of existence, its single-sex status reflected the uniform practice for government-supported military colleges. . . . In other words, the tradition of having government-funded military schools for men is as well rooted in the traditions of this country as the tradition of sending only men into military combat. The people may decide to change the one tradition, like the other, through democratic processes; but the assertion that either tradition has been unconstitutional through the centuries is not law, but politics-smuggled-into-law.

And the same applies, more broadly, to single-sex education in general, which, as I shall discuss, is threatened by today's decision with the cutoff of all state and federal support. Government-run *non*military educational institutions for the two sexes have until very recently also been part of our national tradition. "[It is] [c]oeducation, historically, [that] is a novel educational theory. From grade school through high school, college, and graduate and professional training, much of the Nation's population during much of our history has been educated in sexually segregated classrooms. *Mississippi Univ. For Women v. Hogan* (1982). These traditions may of course be changed by the democratic decisions of the people, as they largely have been.

Today, however, change is forced upon Virginia, and reversion to single-sex education is prohibited nationwide, not by democratic processes but by order of this Court. Even while bemoaning the sorry, bygone days of "fixed notions" concerning women's education, the Court favors current notions so fixedly that it is willing to write them into the Constitution of the United States by application of custom-built "tests." This is not the interpretation of a Constitution, but the creation of one. . . .

Notes and Queries

1. What precisely is the nature of the equal protection violation in this case? Is it, as Justice Ginsburg wrote for the majority, the categorical exclusion of women from "an extraordinary educational opportunity afforded to men"? Or is it, as Justice Rehnquist thought, "the maintenance of an all-men school without providing any—much less a comparable—institution for women"? Does it matter which formulation we adopt? Does it, for example, have an impact on what would constitute an acceptable remedy to the violation? Would the chief justice accept a remedy that the majority would reject?

2. What should be the appropriate test for gender discrimination? In *Mississippi University for Women v. Hogan* (1982), the Court concluded that gender discrimination must pass a test of intermediate scrutiny—that is, the classification "must serve important governmental objectives and . . . the discriminatory means employed [must be] substantially related to the achievement of those objectives." Did Justice Ginsburg utilize this test? Do you agree with Justice Rehnquist's claim that the Court's use of language like "exceedingly persuasive justification" introduced "an element of uncertainty" respecting the appropriate test?

3. Suppose a city decides to create two elite high schools, one for boys and the other for girls, the object being to educate in these schools students of superior ability for the purpose of encouraging them to enter the nation's best colleges and universities. Assume further that both schools are equal in all aspects; but they are segregated by sex on the basis of sociological and psychological studies showing that boys and girls accomplish more academically and learn faster in sex segregated environments. Would these schools be unconstitutional in the light of *Hogan* or the VMI case?

4. Would a state law obligating a married couple to adopt a common family surname or in case of disagreement to give precedence to the husband's name infringe the Equal Protection Clause? This issue caused problems for Germany's Federal Constitutional Court. Notwithstanding an explicit provision in the Basic Law granting equal rights to men and women, the Court in 1988 sustained the requirement of a common family name. Later, however, the Court ruled that giving precedence to the husband's name discriminates against women. In summarizing the decision one commentator wrote: "This discrimination is not justified by any biological differences, nor could it be justified by reference to other limits placed by the Constitution on the equal treatment of men and women. . . . The legislature's requirement for a common family name could be achieved without infringing the principle of equal treatment of men and women." See Rainer Frank, *Germany: Revolution from the Federal Constitutional Court*, 31 University of Louisville Journal of Family Law 347 (1992–93).

5. In *Hogan*, the discrimination was against male students. Does it matter that the discrimination in this case is against women? Should discrimination against women be held to closer judicial scrutiny than discrimination against men? What understanding of "equality" would justify different standards? What understanding of "equality" would command that we use a single standard? Is there a constitutionally grounded reason to prefer one of these conceptions of equality?

6. Justice Scalia wrote that it is "the function of this Court to *preserve* our society's values regarding (among other things) equal protection, not to *revise* them; to prevent backsliding from the degree of restriction the Constitution imposed upon democratic government, not to prescribe, on our own authority, progressively higher degrees." What conception of the relationship between democracy and constitutionalism animates Justice Scalia's view? What understanding of judicial power does it incorporate? How do they differ from the majority's approach? Can we trace these understandings to the Constitution? Can we reconcile them with footnote 4 of *Carolene Products*?

Nguyen v. Immigration and Naturalization Service

533 U.S. 53; 121 S.Ct. 2053; 150 L.Ed.2d 115 (2001).

When Tuan Nguyen, born out of wedlock in Vietnam to a Vietnamese citizen and Joseph Boulais, a United States citizen, pleaded guilty in a Texas state court to two counts of sexual assault on a child, the Immigration and Naturalization Service (INS) initiated deportation proceedings against him. Following the ruling of an immigration judge who ruled Nguyen deportable, and while waiting on appeal, Nguyen obtained an order of parentage from a state court in order to make a citizenship claim and halt his deportation. The review board rejected the citizenship claim because Nguyen failed to comply with the requirements of 8 U.S.C. s. 1409(a)'s citizenship requirements for one born out of wedlock and abroad to a citizen father and a noncitizen mother. Nguyen appealed to the Fifth Circuit, claiming that the regulation violated the Equal Protection Clause by providing different citizenship rules depending on whether the citizen parent is the mother or the father. The Fifth Circuit rejected the claim. Opinion of the Court: *Kennedy*, Rehnquist, Stevens, Scalia, Thomas. Concurring opinion: *Scalia*, Thomas. Dissenting opinion: *O'Connor*, Souter, Ginsburg, Breyer.

Justice KENNEDY delivered the opinion of the Court.

This case presents a question not resolved by a majority of the Court in a case before us three Terms ago. See *Miller v. Albright* (1998) . . .

For a gender-based classification to withstand equal protection scrutiny, it must be established "at least that the [challenged] classification serves 'important governmental objectives and that the discriminatory means employed' are 'substantially related to the achievement of those objectives.'" For reasons to follow, we conclude s. 1409 satisfies this standard. Given that determination, we need not decide whether some lesser degree of scrutiny pertains because the statute implicates Congress' immigration and naturalization power. . . .

The statutory distinction relevant in this case . . . is that s. 1409(a)(4) requires one of three affirmative steps to be taken if the citizen parent is the father, but not if the citizen parent is the mother: legitimation; a declaration of paternity under oath by the father; or a court order of paternity. Congress' decision to impose requirements on unmarried fathers that differ from those on unmarried mothers is based on the significant difference between their respec-

tive relationships to the potential citizen at the time of birth. Specifically, the imposition of the requirement for a paternal relationship, but not a maternal one, is justified by two important governmental objectives. We discuss each in turn.

The first governmental interest to be served is the importance of assuring that a biological parent-child relationship exists. In the case of the mother, the relation is verifiable from the birth itself. The mother's status is documented in most instances by the birth certificate or hospital records and the witnesses who attest to her having given birth.

In the case of the father, the uncontestable fact is that he need not be present at the birth. If he is present, furthermore, that circumstance is not incontrovertible proof of fatherhood. . . . Fathers and mothers are not similarly situated with regard to the proof of biological parenthood. The imposition of a different set of rules for making that legal determination with respect to fathers and mothers is neither surprising nor troublesome from a constitutional perspective. . . .

Petitioners argue that the requirement of s. 1409(a)(1), that a father provide clear and convincing evidence of parentage, is sufficient to achieve the end of establishing paternity, given the sophistication of modern DNA tests. Section 1409(a)(1) does not actually mandate a DNA test, however. The Constitution, moreover, does not require that Congress elect one particular mechanism from among many possible methods of establishing paternity, even if that mechanism arguably might be the most scientifically advanced method. . . .

Finally, to require Congress to speak without reference to the gender of the parent with regard to its objective of ensuring a blood tie between parent and child would be to insist on a hollow neutrality. . . . [C]ongress could have required both mothers and fathers to prove parenthood within 30 days or, for that matter, 18 years, of the child's birth. Given that the mother is always present at birth, but that the father need not be, the facially neutral rule would sometimes require fathers to take additional affirmative steps which would not be required of mothers, whose names will appear on the birth certificate as a result of their presence at the birth, and who will have the benefit of witnesses to the birth to call upon. The issue is not the use of gender specific terms instead of neutral ones. Just as neutral terms can mask discrimination that is unlawful, gender specific terms can mark a permissible distinction. The equal protection question is whether the distinction is lawful. Here, the use of gender specific terms takes into account a biological difference between the parents. The differential treatment is inherent in a sensible statutory scheme, given the unique relationship of the mother to the event of birth.

The second important governmental interest furthered . . . is the determination to ensure that the child and the citizen parent have some demonstrated opportunity or potential to develop not just a relationship that is recognized, as a formal matter, by the law, but one that consists of the real everyday ties that provide a connection between child and citizen parent and, in turn, the United States. In the case of a citizen mother and a child born overseas, the opportunity for a meaningful relationship between citizen parent and child inheres in the very event of birth. . . . The mother knows that the child is in being and is hers and has an initial point of contact with him. There is at least an opportunity for mother and child to develop a real, meaningful relationship.

The same opportunity does not result from the event of birth, as a matter of biological inevitability, in the case of the unwed father. Given the 9-month interval between conception and birth, it is not always certain that a father will know that a child was conceived, nor is it always clear that even the mother will be sure of the father's identity. This fact takes on particular significance in the case of a child born overseas and out of wedlock. One concern in this context has always been with young people, men for the most part, who are on duty with the Armed Forces in foreign countries. . . .

When we turn to the conditions which prevail today, we find that passage of time has produced additional and even more substantial grounds to justify the statutory distinction. The ease of travel and the willingness of Americans to visit foreign countries have resulted in numbers of trips abroad that must be of real concern when we contemplate the prospect of accepting petitioners' argument, which would mandate, contrary to Congress' wishes, citizenship by male parentage subject to no condition save the father's previous length of residence in this country. . . .

Principles of equal protection do not require Congress to ignore this reality. To the contrary, these facts demonstrate the critical importance of the Government's interest in ensuring some opportunity for a tie between citizen father and foreign born child which is a reasonable substitute for the opportunity manifest between mother and child at the time of birth. . . .

Congress is well within its authority in refusing, absent proof of at least the opportunity for the development of a relationship between citizen parent and child, to commit this country to embracing a child as a citizen entitled as of birth to the full protection of the United States, to the abso-lute right to enter its borders, and to full participation in the political process. If citizenship is to be conferred by the unwitting means petitioners urge, so that its acquisition abroad bears little relation to the realities of the child's own ties and allegiances, it is for Congress, not this Court, to make that determination. . . . There is nothing irrational or improper in the recognition that at the moment of birth—a critical event in the statutory scheme and in the whole tradition of citizenship law—the mother's knowledge of the child and the fact of parenthood have been established in a way not guaranteed in the case of the unwed father. This is not a stereotype.

Having concluded that facilitation of a relationship between parent and child is an important governmental interest, the question remains whether the means Congress chose to further its objective—the imposition of certain additional requirements upon an unwed father—substantially relate to that end. Under this test, the means Congress adopted must be sustained. . . .

To fail to acknowledge even our most basic biological differences—such as the fact that a mother must be present at birth but the father need not be—risks making the guarantee of equal protection superficial, and so disserving it. Mechanistic classification of all our differences as stereotypes would operate to obscure those misconceptions and prejudices that are real. The distinction embodied in the statutory scheme here at issue is not marked by misconception and prejudice, nor does it show disrespect for either class. The difference between men and women in relation to the birth process is a real one, and the principle of equal protection does not forbid Congress to address the problem at hand in a manner specific to each gender.

The judgment of the Court of Appeals is Affirmed.

Justice O'CONNOR, with whom Justice SOUTER, Justice GINSBURG, and Justice BREYER join, dissenting.

In a long line of cases spanning nearly three decades, this Court has applied heightened scrutiny to legislative classifications based on sex. The Court today confronts another statute that classifies individuals on the basis of their sex. While the Court invokes heightened scrutiny, the manner in which it explains and applies this standard is a stranger to our precedents. . . .

Sex-based statutes, even when accurately reflecting the way most men or most women behave, deny individuals opportunity. Such generalizations must be viewed not in isolation, but in the context of our Nation's "long and unfortunate history of sex discrimination." Sex-based generalizations both reflect and reinforce "fixed notions concerning the roles and abilities of males and females." *Mississippi Univ. For Women v. Hogan* (1982).

For these reasons, a party who seeks to defend a statute that classifies individuals on the basis of sex "must carry the burden of showing an 'exceedingly persuasive justification' for the classification." *United States v. Virginia* (1996). The defender of the classification meets this burden "only by showing at least that the classification serves 'important governmental objectives.'" *Mississippi Univ. For Women.* Our cases provide significant guidance concerning the meaning of this standard and how a reviewing court is to apply it. This Court's instruction concerning the application of heightened scrutiny to sex-based classifications stands in stark contrast to our elucidation of the rudiments of rational basis review. To begin with, under heightened scrutiny, "[t]he burden of justification is demanding and it rests entirely on [the party defending the classification]." Under rational basis scrutiny, by contrast, the defender of the classification "has no obligation to produce evidence to sustain the rationality of a statutory classification." . . . Heightened scrutiny does not countenance justifications that "rely on overbroad generalizations about the different talents, capacities, or preferences of males and females." These different standards of equal protection review . . . set different bars for the magnitude of the governmental interest that justifies the statutory classification. . . .

The majority concedes that Congress could achieve the goal of assuring a biological parent-child relationship in a sex-neutral fashion, but then, in a surprising turn, dismisses the availability of sex-neutral alternatives as irrelevant. . . .

In our prior cases, the existence of comparable or superior sex-neutral alternatives has been a powerful reason to reject a sex-based classification. The majority, however, turns this principle on its head by denigrating as "hollow" the very neutrality that the law requires. . . . [T]he idea that a mother's presence at birth supplies adequate assurance of an opportunity to develop a relationship while a father's presence at birth does not would appear to rest only on an overbroad sex-based generalization. A mother may not have an opportunity for a relationship if the child is removed from his or her mother on account of alleged abuse or neglect, or if the child and mother are separated by tragedy, such as disaster or war, of the sort apparently present in this case. There is no reason, other than stereotype, to say that fathers who are present at birth lack an opportunity for a relationship on similar terms. . . .

The Court has also failed even to acknowledge the "volumes of history" to which "[t]oday's skeptical scrutiny of official action denying rights or opportunities based on

sex responds." The history of sex discrimination in laws governing the transmission of citizenship and with respect to parental responsibilities for children born out of wedlock counsels at least some circumspection in discerning legislative purpose in this context.

Section 1409 was first enacted as s. 205 of the Nationality Act of 1940. The 1940 Act had been proposed by the President, forwarding a report by a specially convened Committee of Advisors, including the Attorney General. The Committee explained to Congress the rationale for s. 205, whose sex-based classification remains in effect today:

> [T]he Department of State has, at least since 1912, uniformly held that an illegitimate child born abroad of an American mother acquires at birth the nationality of the mother, in the absence of legitimation or adjudication establishing the paternity of the child. This ruling is based . . . on the ground that the mother in such case stands in the place of the father. . . . [U]nder American law the mother has a right to custody and control of such child as against the putative father, and *is bound* to maintain it as its *natural guardian.* This rule seems to be in accord with the old Roman law and with the laws of Spain and France. . . .

Section 1409(a)(4) is thus paradigmatic of a historic regime that left women with responsibility, and freed men from responsibility, for nonmarital children. . . .

No one should mistake the majority's analysis from a careful application of this Court's equal protection jurisprudence concerning sex-based classifications. Today's decision instead represents a deviation from a line of cases in which we have vigilantly applied heightened scrutiny to such classifications to determine whether a constitutional violation has occurred. I trust that the depth and vitality of these precedents will ensure that today's error remains an aberration. I respectfully dissent.

Notes and Queries

1. Justice Kennedy states that "[t]here is nothing irrational or improper in the recognition that at the moment of birth—a critical event in the statutory scheme and in the whole tradition of citizenship law—the mother's knowledge of the child and the fact of parenthood have been established in a way not guaranteed in the case of the unwed father. This is not a stereotype." Do you find this reasoning convincing? Is the majority opinion based on an archaic stereotype, as Justice O'Connor suggests? Can you think of reasons why the two conservative justices differ so fundamentally over the nature of an archaic stereotype?

2. In Comparative Note 15.5 Germany's Federal Constitutional Court remarks: "Gender distinctions may be permissible to the extent that they are indispensably necessary to the solution of problems that by their nature can arise only for women or only for men." Do you agree? Is biology an adequate reason for sex-based classifications? Are women helped or hurt when the state takes into consideration the natural differences between the sexes? Can you think of other biological differences that might warrant such classifications?

3. In *Rostker v. Goldberg*, 453 U.S. 57 (1981), the Court by a 6 to 3 vote upheld a provision of the Military Selective Service Act that subjected men but not women to the military draft. The Court appeared to dismiss the Fifth Amendment due process argument by saying that men and women are not similarly situated with respect to combat. Justice Marshall joined by Justice Brennan in dissent said: "The Court today places its imprimatur on one of the most potent remaining public expressions of 'ancient canards about the proper role of women.'" *Rostker* and *Nguyen* both involved federal as opposed to state legislation. Citizenship, like the military draft, are subjects of paramount national interests and over which Congress has explicit authority under the Constitution. Does this reality explain the result in both *Rostker* and *Nguyen*? As for *Rostker*, why are men and women not similarly situated with respect to combat? *Rostker*, unlike *Nguyen*, did not rest on a biological argument. Is there a biological argument in support of a male-only military draft? And would such an argument illuminate the debate in *United States v. Virginia*?

Foley v. Connelie

435 U.S. 291; 98 S. Ct. 1067; 55 L. Ed. 2d 287 (1978)

Foley, a permanent resident alien, was not allowed to take the competitive examination for the position of New York state trooper because of a New York statute prohibiting any noncitizen from appointment to the state police force. Foley brought suit in district court claiming that the statute excluding aliens from the police force violated the equal protection clause of the Fourteenth Amendment. A federal district court sustained the statute. Opinion of the Court: *Burger*, Stewart, White, Powell, Rehnquist. Concurring opinions: *Stewart*, *Blackmun*. Dissenting opinions; *Marshall*, Brennan, *Stevens*.

Chief Justice BURGER delivered the opinion of the Court.

Appellant claims that the relevant New York statute violates his rights under the Equal Protection Clause.

The decisions of this Court with regard to the rights of aliens living in our society have reflected fine, and often difficult, questions of values. As a Nation we exhibit extraordinary hospitality to those who come to our country, which is not surprising for we have often been described as "a nation of immigrants." Indeed, aliens lawfully residing in this society have many rights which are accorded to noncitizens by few other countries. Our cases generally reflect a close scrutiny of restraints imposed by States on aliens. But we have never suggested that such legislation is inherently invalid, nor have we held that all limitations on aliens are suspect. Rather, beginning with a case which involved the denial of welfare assistance essential to life itself, the Court has treated certain restrictions on aliens with "heightened judicial solicitude," *Graham v. Richardson* (1971), a treatment deemed necessary since aliens—pending their eligibility for citizenship—have no direct voice in the political processes.

It would be inappropriate, however, to require every statutory exclusion of aliens to clear the high hurdle of "strict scrutiny," because to do so would "obliterate all the distinctions between citizens and aliens, and thus depreciate the historic values of citizenship." . . . The act of becoming a citizen is more than a ritual with no content beyond the fanfare of ceremony. A new citizen has become a member of a Nation, part of a people distinct from others. The individual, at that point, belongs to the polity and is entitled to participate in the processes of democratic decisionmaking. Accordingly, we have recognized "a State's historical power to exclude aliens from participation in its democratic political institutions," . . . as part of the sovereign's obligation "to preserve the basic conception of a political community."

The practical consequence of this theory is that "our scrutiny will not be so demanding where we deal with matters firmly within a State's constitutional prerogatives." The State need only justify its classification by a showing of some rational relationship between the interest sought to be protected and the limiting classification. This is not intended to denigrate the valuable contribution of aliens who benefit from our traditional hospitality. It is no more than recognition of the fact that a democratic society is ruled by its people. Thus, it is clear that a State may deny aliens the right to vote, or to run for elective office, for these lie at the heart of our political institutions. Similar considerations support a legislative determination to exclude aliens from jury service. Likewise, we have recog-

Comparative Note 15.6

[In *Andrews v. Law Society of British Columbia*, the Canadian Supreme Court invalidated a provincial statute restricting admission to the bar of British Columbia to Canadian citizens. In the following extract, Justice Wilson comments generally on the identification of discrete and insular minorities.]

Relative to citizens, non-citizens are a group lacking in political power and as such vulnerable to having their interests overlooked and their rights to equal concern and respect violated. They are among "those groups in society to whose needs and wishes elected officials have no apparent interest in attending": see J.H. Ely, *Democracy and Distrust* (1980), at p. 151. Non-citizens, to take only the most obvious example, do not have the right to vote. Their vulnerability to becoming a disadvantaged group in our society is captured by John Stuart Mill's observation in Book III of *On Liberty and Considerations of Representative Government* . . . that "in the absence of its natural defenders, the interests of the excluded is always in danger of being overlooked . . ." I would conclude therefore that non-citizens fall into an analogous category to those specifically enumerated in s. 15. I emphasize, moreover, that this is a determination which is not to be made only in the context of the law which is subject to challenge but rather in the context of the place of the group in the entire social, political and legal fabric of our society. While legislatures must inevitably draw distinctions among the governed, such distinctions should not bring about or reinforce the disadvantage of certain groups and individuals by denying them the rights freely accorded to others.

I believe also that it is important to note that the range of discrete and insular minorities has changed and will continue to change with changing political and social circumstances. For example, Stone J., writing in 1938, was concerned with religious, national and racial minorities. In enumerating the specific grounds in s. 15, the framers of the Charter embraced these concerns in 1982 but also addressed themselves to the difficulties experienced by the disadvantaged on the grounds of ethnic origin, colour, sex, age and physical and mental disability. It can be anticipated that the discrete and insular minorities of tomorrow will include groups not recognized as such today. It is consistent with the constitutional status of s. 15 that it be interpreted with sufficient flexibility to ensure the "unremitting protection" of equality rights in the years to come.

SOURCE: *Andrews v. Law Society of British Columbia* (1989) 56 D.L.R. (4th) 1.

nized that citizenship may be a relevant qualification for fulfilling those "important nonelective executive, legislative, and judicial positions," held by "officers who participate directly in the formulation, execution, or review of broad public policy." This is not because our society seeks to reserve the better jobs to its members. Rather, it is because this country entrusts many of its most important policy responsibilities to these officers, the discretionary exercise of which can often more immediately affect the lives of citizens than even the ballot of a voter or the choice of a legislator. In sum, then, it represents the choice, and right, of the people to be governed by their citizen peers. To effectuate this result, we must necessarily examine each position in question to determine whether it involves discretionary decisionmaking, or execution of policy, which substantially affects members of the political community.

The essence of our holdings to date is that although we extend to aliens the right to education and public welfare, along with the ability to earn a livelihood and engage in

licensed professions, the right to govern is reserved to citizens.

A discussion of the police function is essentially a description of one of the basic functions of government, especially in a complex modern society where police presence is pervasive. The police function fulfills a most fundamental obligation of government to its constituency. Police officers in the ranks do not formulate policy, *per se*, but they are clothed with authority to exercise an almost infinite variety of discretionary powers. The execution of the broad powers vested in them affects members of the public significantly and often in the most sensitive areas of daily life.

Clearly the exercise of police authority calls for a very high degree of judgment and discretion, the abuse or misuse of which can have serious impact on individuals. The office of a policeman is in no sense one of "the common occupations of the community" that the then Mr. Justice Hughes referred to in *Truax v. Raich* [1915]. A policeman vested with the plenary discretionary powers we have described is not to be equated with a private person engaged in routine public employment or other "common occupations of the community" who exercises no broad power over people generally. Indeed, the rationale for the qualified immunity historically granted to the police rests on the difficult and delicate judgments these officers must often make.

In short, it would be as anomalous to conclude that citizens may be subjected to the broad discretionary powers of noncitizen police officers as it would be to say that judicial officers and jurors with power to judge citizens can be aliens. It is not surprising, therefore, that most States expressly confine the employment of police officers to citizens, whom the State may reasonably presume to be more familiar with and sympathetic to American traditions. Police officers very clearly fall within the category of "important nonelective . . . officers who participate directly in the . . . execution . . . of broad public policy." In the enforcement and execution of the laws the police function is one where citizenship bears a rational relationship to the special demands of the particular position. A State may, therefore, consonant with the Constitution, confine the performance of this important public responsibility to citizens of the United States.

Accordingly, the judgment of the District Court is Affirmed.

Mr. Justice STEWART, concurring.

The dissenting opinions convincingly demonstrate that it is difficult if not impossible to reconcile the Court's judgment in this case with the full sweep of the reasoning and authority of some of our past decisions. It is only because I have become increasingly doubtful about the validity of those decisions (in at least some of which I concurred) that I join the opinion of the Court in this case.

Justice MARSHALL, with whom Justice BRENNAN and Justice STEVENS join, dissenting.

Today the Court upholds a law excluding aliens from public employment as state troopers. It bases its decision largely on dictum from *Sugarman v. Dougall*, supra, to the effect that aliens may be barred from holding "state elective or important nonelective executive, legislative, and judicial positions," because persons in these positions "participate directly in the formulation, execution, or review of broad public policy." . . . I do not agree with the Court that state troopers perform functions placing them within this "narro[w] . . . exception" . . . to our usual rule that discrimination against aliens is presumptively unconstitutional. Accordingly I dissent.

Justice STEVENS, with whom Justice BRENNAN joins, dissenting.

. . . What is the group characteristic that justifies the unfavorable treatment of an otherwise qualified individual simply because he is an alien?

No one suggests that aliens as a class lack the intelligence or the courage to serve the public as police officers. The disqualifying characteristic is apparently a foreign allegiance which raises a doubt concerning trustworthiness and loyalty so pervasive that a flat ban against the employment of any alien in any law enforcement position is thought to be justified. But if the integrity of all aliens is suspect, why may not a State deny aliens the right to practice law? Are untrustworthy or disloyal lawyers more tolerable than untrustworthy or disloyal policemen? Or is the legal profession better able to detect such characteristics on an individual basis than is the police department? Unless the Court repudiates its holding in *In re Griffiths* (1973), it must reject any conclusive presumption that aliens, as a class, are disloyal or untrustworthy.

. . . [T]he Court . . . should not uphold a statutory discrimination against aliens, as a class, without expressly identifying the group characteristic that justifies the discrimination. If the unarticulated characteristic is concern about possible disloyalty, it must equally disqualify aliens from the practice of law; yet the Court does not question the continuing vitality of its decision in *Griffiths*. Or if that characteristic is the fact that aliens do not participate in our democratic decisionmaking process, it is irrelevant to eligibility for this category of public service. If there is no group characteristic that explains the discrimination, one can only conclude that it is without any justification that has not already been rejected by the Court.

Notes and Queries

1. In this case the Court seems to be wrestling with the very limits of community and the nature of citizenship. What concept or theory of citizenship (community?) does Chief Justice Burger seem to envision and how is it different from that of Justice Marshall? How much does the text of the Constitution (read as a whole) tell us about this?

2. *Foley* prompts further reflection on the criteria of suspectness set forth in footnote 4 of *Carolene Products* (1938). There the Court suggested that legislation should be reviewed with strict scrutiny if based on an immutable characteristic and aimed at an insular and powerless group in American society. Do these characteristics—that is, immutability, insularity, and powerlessness—adequately define the concept of a "suspect" class? What groups other

than racial or ethnic minorities might be said to possess these characteristics? Would the Supreme Court be prepared to protect them against disadvantages imposed by law? How is insularity and powerlessness in American society to be measured? (Note how these issues troubled the Court years earlier in *San Antonio v. Rodriquez*.)

3. The dissenting justices in *Foley* thought that the Court had backed away from its earlier view that legislative classifications based on alienage are suspect and thus trigger strict scrutiny review. In *Graham v. Richardson* (1971), the Court applied strict scrutiny review in striking down state statutes which denied welfare benefits to resident aliens or to aliens who had not resided in the United States for a given number of years. In this case, however, the Court's reasoning appeared to have been informed by the analysis in *Shapiro v. Thompson* (1969)—the welfare benefit case reproduced earlier in this chapter—and by a countervailing *national* policy in the areas of immigration and naturalization.

Trimble v. Gordon
430 U.S. 762; 97 S. Ct. 1459; 52 L.Ed. 2d 31 (1977)

Deta Mona Trimble was the illegitimate daughter of Jessie Trimble and Sherman Gordon who lived together with Deta Mona. Pursuant to a paternity order entered in 1973, Gordon supported Deta Mona and openly acknowledged her as his child. Gordon died intestate in 1974, leaving an estate worth $2500. A state court excluded Deta Mona as an intestate heir under section 12 of the Illinois Probate Act which allowed illegitimate children to inherit by intestate succession only from their mother, whereas legitimate children were permitted to inherit by intestate succession from both their mother and their father. The Illinois Supreme Court upheld the constitutionality of section 12, citing the state's interest in encouraging family relationships and efficient and accurate disposition of property at death. Deta Mona appealed. Opinion of the Court: *Powell*, Brennan, White, Marshall, Stevens. Dissenting opinions: *Burger*, Stewart, Blackmun, *Rehnquist*.

Justice POWELL delivered the opinion of the Court.

In weighing the constitutional sufficiency of these justifications, we are guided by our previous decisions involving equal protection challenges to laws discriminating on the basis of illegitimacy. "[T]his Court requires, at a minimum, that a statutory classification bear some rational relationship to a legitimate state purpose." *Weber v. Aetna Casualty & Surety Co.* (1972). In this context, the standard just stated is a minimum; the Court sometimes requires more. "Though the latitude given state economic and social regulation is necessarily broad, when state statutory classifications approach sensitive and fundamental personal rights, this Court exercises a stricter scrutiny. . . ."

The Illinois Supreme Court relied in part on the State's purported interest in "the promotion of [legitimate] family relationships." . . .

In a case like this, the Equal Protection Clause requires more than the mere incantation of a proper state purpose. No one disputes the appropriateness of Illinois' concern with the family unit, perhaps the most fundamental social institution of our society. The flaw in the analysis lies elsewhere. As we said in [*Mathews v.*] *Lucas* [1976], the constitutionality of this law "depends upon the character of the discrimination and its relation to legitimate legislative aims." . . . In subsequent decisions, we have expressly considered and rejected the argument that a State may attempt to influence the actions of men and women by imposing sanctions on the children born of their illegitimate relationships.

The Illinois Supreme Court also noted that the decedents whose estates were involved in the consolidated appeals could have left substantial parts of their estates to their illegitimate children by writing a will. . . .

By focusing on the steps that an intestate might have taken to assure some inheritance for his illegitimate children, the analysis loses sight of the essential question: the constitutionality of discrimination against illegitimates in a state intestate succession law. If the decedent had written a will devising property to his illegitimate child, the case no longer would involve intestate succession law at all. Similarly, if the decedent had legitimated the child by marrying the child's mother or by complying with the requirements of some other method of legitimation, the case no longer would involve discrimination against illegitimates. . . .

Finally, appellees urge us to affirm the decision below on the theory that the Illinois Probate Act, including Section 12, mirrors the presumed intentions of the citizens of the State regarding the disposition of their property at death. Individualizing this theory, appellees argue that we must assume that Sherman Gordon knew the disposition of his estate under the Illinois Probate Act and that his failure to make a will shows his approval of that disposition. We need not resolve the question whether presumed intent alone can ever justify discrimination against illegitimates, for we do not think that Section 12 was enacted for

Comparative Note 15.7

[In this case the French Constitutional Council was asked to examine a parliamentary amendment to the Code of Social Security and Health limiting the right of foreign residents to benefits under the code.]

30. Considering that article 24 of the *loi* redrafts article L815–5 of the Code of Social Security, under which "the additional benefit is due to foreigners in application of [European] Community regulations or of reciprocal international agreements";

31. Considering that, with regard to foreigners, the legislature may make specific provisions on condition that it respects international agreements to which France is a party and fundamental freedoms and rights of constitutional value recognized to all who reside in the territory of the Republic;

32. Considering that the additional benefit from the National Solidarity Fund is granted to aged persons, especially those who have become unable to work, who do not have a sum available . . . to assure them a minimum for living; that the allocation of this benefit is subject to a period of residence in France;

33. Considering that to exclude foreigners lawfully resident in France from the enjoyment of the additional benefit if they cannot rely on international agreements or regulations made on that basis, disregards the constitutional principle of equality;

34. Considering that it follows, thus, that article 24 of the referred *loi* has to be declared contrary to the Constitution.

Source: Judgment of the French Constitutional Council, 18 November 1982 in Bell, *French Constitutional Law* 349.

this purpose. . . . [W]e find in Section 12 a primary purpose to provide a system of intestate succession more just to illegitimate children than the prior law, a purpose tempered by a secondary interest in protecting against spurious claims of paternity. In the absence of a more convincing demonstration, we will not hypothesize an additional state purpose that has been ignored by the Illinois Supreme Court.

For the reasons stated above, we conclude that Section 12 of the Illinois Probate Act cannot be squared with the command of the Equal Protection Clause of the Fourteenth Amendment. Accordingly, we reverse the judgment of the Illinois Supreme Court and remand the case for further proceedings not inconsistent with this opinion.

Justice REHNQUIST, dissenting.

The Fourteenth Amendment's prohibition against "any State . . . deny[ing] to any person . . . the equal protection of the laws" is undoubtedly one of the majestic generalities of the Constitution. If, during the period of more than a century since its adoption, this Court had developed a consistent body of doctrine which could reasonably be said to expound the intent of those who drafted and adopted that Clause of the Amendment, there would be no cause for judicial complaint, however unwise or incapable of effective administration one might find those intentions. If, on the other hand, recognizing that those who drafted and adopted this language had rather imprecise notions about what it meant, the Court had evolved a body of doctrine which both was consistent and served some arguably useful purpose, there would likewise be little cause for great dissatisfaction with the existing state of the law.

Unfortunately, more than a century of decisions under this Clause of the Fourteenth Amendment have produced neither of these results. They have instead produced a syndrome wherein this Court seems to regard the Equal Protection Clause as a cat-o'-nine-tails to be kept in the judicial closet as a threat to legislatures which may, in the view of the judiciary, get out of hand and pass "arbitrary," "illogical," or "unreasonable" laws. Except in the area of the law in which the Framers obviously meant it to apply—classifications based on race or on national origin, the first cousin of race—the Court's decisions can fairly be described as an endless tinkering with legislative judgments, a series of conclusions unsupported by any central guiding principle.

. . . But in providing the Court with the duty of enforcing such generalities as the Equal Protection Clause, the Framers of the Civil War Amendments placed it in the position of Adam in the Garden of Eden. As members of a tripartite institution of government which is responsible to no constituency, and which is held back only by its own sense of self-restraint, . . . we are constantly subjected to the human temptation to hold that any law containing a number of imperfections denies equal protection simply because those who drafted it could have made it a fairer or a better law. The Court's opinion in the instant case is no better and no worse than the long series of cases in this line, a line which unfortunately proclaims that the Court has indeed succumbed to the temptation implicit in the Amendment.

The Equal Protection Clause is itself a classic paradox, and makes sense only in the context of a recently fought Civil War. It creates a requirement of equal treatment to be applied to the process of legislation—legislation whose very purpose is to draw lines in such a way that different people are treated differently. The problem presented is one of sorting the legislative distinctions which are acceptable from those which involve invidiously unequal treatment. . . .

The essential problem of the Equal Protection Clause is therefore the one of determining where the courts are to look for guidance in defining "equality" as that word is used in the Fourteenth Amendment. Since the Amendment grew out of the Civil War and the freeing of the slaves, the core prohibition was early held to be aimed at the protection of blacks. If race was an invalid sorting tool where blacks were concerned, it followed logically that it should not be valid where other races were concerned either. A logical, though not inexorable, next step, was the extension of the protection to prohibit classifications resting on national origin.

The presumptive invalidity of all of these classifications has made decisions involving them, for the most part, relatively easy. But when the Court has been required to adjudicate equal protection claims not based on race or national origin, it has faced a much more difficult task. . . .

Illegitimacy, which is involved in this case, has never been held by the Court to be a "suspect classification." Nonetheless, in several opinions of the Court, statements are found which suggest that although illegitimates are not members of a "suspect class," laws which treat them differently from those born in wedlock will receive a more far-reaching scrutiny under the Equal Protection Clause than will other laws regulating economic and social conditions. The Court's opinion today contains language to that effect. In one sense this language is a source of consolation, since it suggests that parts of the Court's analysis used in this case will not be carried over to traditional "rational basis" or "minimum scrutiny" cases. At the same time, though, it is a source of confusion, since the unanswered question remains as to the precise sort of scrutiny to which classifications based on illegitimacy will be subject.

The "difficulty" of the "judicial task" is, I suggest, a self-imposed one, stemming not from the Equal Protection Clause but from the Court's insistence on reading so much into it. I do not see how it can be doubted that the purpose (in the ordinary sense of that word) of the Illinois Legislature in enacting Section 12 of the Illinois Probate Act was to make the language contained in that section a part of the Illinois law. . . .

Here the Illinois Legislature was dealing with a problem of intestate succession of illegitimates from their fathers, which, as the Court concedes, frequently presents difficult problems of proof. The provisions of Illinois Probate Act Section 12, as most recently amended, alleviate some of the difficulties which previously stood in the way of such succession. The fact that the Act in question does not alleviate all of the difficulties, or that it might have gone further than it did, is to me wholly irrelevant under the Equal Protection Clause. The circumstances which justify the distinction between illegitimates and legitimates contained in Section 12 are apparent with no great exercise of imagination; they are stated in the opinion of the Court, though they are there rejected as constitutionally insufficient. Since Illinois' distinction is not mindless and patently irrational, I would affirm the judgment of the Supreme Court of Illinois.

Notes and Queries

1. In his dissent, Justice Rehnquist marshals a not unpersuasive argument on behalf of judicial restraint. He heaps considerable scorn on the Court's use of the Equal Protection Clause as a "cat-o'-nine-tails to be kept in the judicial closet as a threat to legislatures which may, in the view of the judiciary, get out of hand and pass 'arbitrary,' 'illegal,' or 'unreasonable' laws." Instead, Rehnquist argues that the clause should only be applied to classifications based on race or national origin. However, he insists, the Court uses it as grounds for "an endless tinkering with legislative judgments" which has yielded "a series of conclusions unsupported by any central guiding principle." Is he right? Can you discern any guiding principle in the interpretation of this case and the others in this chapter? How would Justice Marshall's "sliding scale" theory play into this? (See Marshall's dissent below in *Massachusetts Board of Retirement v. Murgia.*)

2. Is it clear from the opinion exactly and precisely what standard of review was followed in *Trimble*? How would you describe Justice Powell's approach to constitutional interpretation in this case? A year later, in *Lalli v.*

Lalli, 439 U.S. 259 (1978), the Court sustained a state statute allowing an illegimate child to inherit from an intestate father only if a judicial order had been entered during the father's lifetime. If the state's interest is in the accurate and efficient determination of paternity, why did the state lose in *Trimble* and win in *Lalli*? Can *Trimble* and *Lalli* be reconciled?

3. In his dissent, Chief Justice Rehnquist wrote that "The Equal Protection Clause is itself a classic paradox." Do you agree? Should interpretation of the clause seek to resolve the paradox? How?

Massachusetts Board of Retirement v. Murgia
427 U.S. 307; 96 S. Ct. 2562; 49 L. Ed.2d 520 (1976)

Pursuant to a Massachusetts law requiring mandatory retirement of all police officers at age 50, officer Robert Murgia was forced to leave the police force despite his excellent physical and mental health. The Massachusetts Board of Retirement brought this appeal after a federal district court ruled that the statute could not withstand the rational basis test and therefore was unconstitutional. Per

curiam opinion: Blackmun, Brennan, Burger, Powell, Rehnquist, Stewart, White. Dissenting opinion: *Marshall.* Not participating: Stevens.

PER CURIAM.

. . . [U]niformed state officers [are required to] pass a comprehensive physical examination biennially until age 40. After that, until mandatory retirement at age 50, uniformed officers must pass annually a more rigorous examination, including an electrocardiogram and tests for gastro-intestinal bleeding. Appellee Murgia had passed such an examination four months before he was retired, and there is no dispute that, when he retired, his excellent

---

Comparative Note 15.8

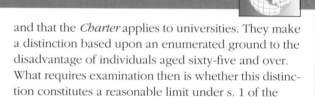

[In this Canadian case, eight professors and a librarian at various universities sought to have a law providing for mandatory retirement at sixty-five years of age declared unconstitutional as a violation of section 15 of the Charter of Rights and Freedoms. The appellants are highly qualified academics. The sole ground for their retirement is that they have reached the mandatory age of sixty-five. The following extract is from the opinion of Justice La Forest of the Supreme Court.]

Assuming the policies of the universities are law, it seems difficult to argue in light of *Andrews* that they are not discriminatory within the meaning of s. 15(1) of the *Charter* since the distinction is based on the enumerated personal characteristic of age. . . . [As we noted in a 1987 case] "[w]ork is one of the most fundamental aspects in a person's life . . . and an essential component of his or her sense of identity, self-worth and emotional well-being." Mandatory retirement takes this away, on the basis of a personal characteristic attributed to an individual solely because [of age].

. . . I therefore have no hesitation in concluding that the policies of the universities violate s. 15 of the *Charter*, on the assumption, of course, that they are "law"

and that the *Charter* applies to universities. They make a distinction based upon an enumerated ground to the disadvantage of individuals aged sixty-five and over. What requires examination then is whether this distinction constitutes a reasonable limit under s. 1 of the *Charter* to the right accorded under s. 15.

Cory, J. [concurring].

. . . I am in agreement with [Justice Wilson's] findings that . . . [these] policies of mandatory retirement are subject to scrutiny under s. 15 and that those policies discriminate on the basis of age and thus contravene s. 15. However, I am in agreement with the conclusion reached by my colleague Justice La Forest that the mandatory retirement policies of the universities come within the scope of s. 1 and thus survive *Charter* scrutiny.

Further, I am in agreement with La Forest J. that, although s. 9(a) of the Ontario *Human Rights Code, 1981*, contravenes s. 15(1) of the *Charter* by discriminating on the basis of age, it is a reasonable limit prescribed by law within the purview of s. 1 of the *Charter*.

SOURCE: *McKinney et al. v. University of Guelph et al.* (1990) 3 S.C.R. 229.

physical and mental health still rendered him capable of performing the duties of a uniformed officer.

The record includes the testimony of three physicians . . . that clearly established that the risk of physical failure, particularly in the cardiovascular system, increases with age, and that the number of individuals in a given age group incapable of performing stress functions increases with the age of the group. . . . The testimony also recognized that particular individuals over 50 could be capable of safely performing the functions of uniformed officers. . . .

In assessing appellee's equal protection claim, the District Court found it unnecessary to apply a strict-scrutiny test, for it determined that the age classification established by the Massachusetts statutory scheme could not in any event withstand a test of rationality. Since there had been no showing that reaching age 50 forecasts even "imminent change" in an officer's physical condition, the District Court held that compulsory retirement at age 50 was irrational under a scheme that assessed the capabilities of officers individually by means of comprehensive annual physical examinations. We agree that rationality is the proper standard by which to test whether compulsory retirement at age 50 violates equal protection. We disagree, however, with the District Court's determination that the age 50 classification is not rationally related to furthering a legitimate state interest.

We need state only briefly our reasons for agreeing that strict scrutiny is not the proper test for determining whether the mandatory retirement provision denies appellee equal protection. *San Antonio School District v. Rodriguez* reaffirmed that equal protection analysis requires strict scrutiny of a legislative classification only when the classification impermissibly interferes with the exercise of a fundamental right or operates to the peculiar disadvantage of a suspect class. Mandatory retirement at age 50 under the Massachusetts statute involves neither situation.

This Court's decisions give no support to the proposition that a right of governmental employment per se is fundamental. Accordingly, we have expressly stated that a standard less than strict scrutiny "has consistently been applied to state legislation restricting the availability of employment opportunities."

Nor does the class of uniformed state police officers over 50 constitute a suspect class for purposes of equal protection analysis. . . . [A] suspect class is one "saddled with such disabilities, or subjected to such a history of purposeful unequal treatment, or relegated to such a position of political powerlessness as to command extraordinary protection from the majoritarian political process." While

the treatment of the aged in this Nation has not been wholly free of discrimination, such persons, unlike, say, those who have been discriminated against on the basis of race or national origin, have not experienced a "history of purposeful unequal treatment" or been subjected to unique disabilities on the basis of stereotyped characteristics not truly indicative of their abilities. The class subject to the compulsory retirement feature of the Massachusetts statute consists of uniformed state police officers over the age of 50. It cannot be said to discriminate only against the elderly. Rather, it draws the line at a certain age in middle life. But even old age does not define a "discrete and insular" group in need of "extraordinary protection from the majoritarian political process." Instead, it marks a stage that each of us will reach if we live out our normal span. Even if the statute could be said to impose a penalty upon a class defined as the aged, it would not impose a distinction sufficiently akin to those classifications that we have found suspect to call for strict judicial scrutiny.

Under the circumstances, it is unnecessary to subject the State's resolution of competing interests in this case to the degree of critical examination that our cases under the Equal Protection Clause recently have characterized as "strict judicial scrutiny."

We turn then to examine this state classification under the rational-basis standard. This inquiry employs a relatively relaxed standard reflecting the Court's awareness that the drawing of lines that create distinctions is peculiarly a legislative task and an unavoidable one. Perfection in making the necessary classifications is neither possible nor necessary. Such action by a legislature is presumed to be valid.

In this case, the Massachusetts statute clearly meets the requirements of the Equal Protection Clause, for the State's classification rationally furthers the purpose identified by the State: Through mandatory retirement at age 50, the legislature seeks to protect the public by assuring physical preparedness of its uniformed police. Since physical ability generally declines with age, mandatory retirement at 50 serves to remove from police service those whose fitness for uniformed work presumptively has diminished with age. This clearly is rationally related to the State's objective. There is no indication that Section 26 (3)(a) has the effect of excluding from service so few officers who are in fact unqualified as to render age 50 a criterion wholly unrelated to the objective of the statute.

That the State chooses not to determine fitness more precisely through individualized testing after age 50 is not to say that the objective of assuring physical fitness is not rationally furthered by a maximum-age limitation. It is only to say that with regard to the interest of all concerned, the State perhaps has not chosen the best means to accomplish this purpose. But where rationality is the test, a State "does not violate the Equal Protection Clause merely because the classifications made by its laws are imperfect."

We do not make light of the substantial economic and psychological effects premature and compulsory retirement can have on an individual; nor do we denigrate the ability of elderly citizens to continue to contribute to society. The problems of retirement have been well documented and are beyond serious dispute. But "[w]e do not decide today that the [Massachusetts statute] is wise, that it best fulfills the relevant social and economic objectives that [Massachusetts] might ideally espouse, or that a more just and humane system could not be devised." . . . We decide only that the system enacted by the Massachusetts Legislature does not deny appellee equal protection of the laws.

The judgment is reversed.

Justice MARSHALL, dissenting.

Although there are signs that its grasp on the law is weakening, the rigid two-tier model still holds sway as the Court's articulated description of the equal protection test. Again, I must object to its perpetuation. The model's two fixed modes of analysis, strict scrutiny and mere rationality, simply do not describe the inquiry the Court has undertaken—or should undertake—in equal protection cases. Rather, the inquiry has been much more sophisticated and the Court should admit as much. It has focused upon the character of the classification in question, the relative importance to individuals in the class discriminated against of the governmental benefits that they do not receive, and the state interests asserted in support of the classification.

Although the Court outwardly adheres to the two-tier model, it has apparently lost interest in recognizing further "fundamental" rights and "suspect" classes. . . . In my view, this result is the natural consequence of the limitations of the Court's traditional equal protection analysis. If a statute invades a "fundamental" right or discriminates against a "suspect" class, it is subject to strict scrutiny. If a statute is subject to strict scrutiny, the statute always, or nearly always, is struck down. Quite obviously, the only critical decision is whether strict scrutiny should be invoked at all. It should be no surprise, then, that the Court is hesitant to expand the number of categories of rights and classes subject to strict scrutiny, when each expansion involves the invalidation of virtually every classification bearing upon a newly covered category.

But however understandable the Court's hesitancy to

invoke strict scrutiny, all remaining legislation should not drop into the bottom tier, and be measured by the mere rationality test. For that test, too, when applied as articulated, leaves little doubt about the outcome; the challenged legislation is always upheld. . . . It cannot be gainsaid that there remain rights, not now classified as "fundamental," that remain vital to the flourishing of a free society, and classes, not now classified as "suspect," that are unfairly burdened by invidious discrimination unrelated to the individual worth of their members. Whatever we call these rights and classes, we simply cannot forgo all judicial protection against discriminatory legislation bearing upon them, but for the rare instances when the legislative choice can be termed "wholly irrelevant" to the legislative goal.

The danger of the Court's verbal adherence to the rigid two-tier test, despite its effective repudiation of that test in the cases, is demonstrated by its efforts here. There is simply no reason why a statute that tells able-bodied police officers, ready and willing to work, that they no longer have the right to earn a living in their chosen profession merely because they are 50 years old should be judged by the same minimal standards of rationality that we use to test economic legislation that discriminates against business interests. Yet, the Court today not only invokes the minimal level of scrutiny, it wrongly adheres to it. Analysis of the three factors I have identified above—the importance of the governmental benefits denied, the character of the class, and the asserted state interests—demonstrates the Court's error.

Whether "fundamental" or not, "the right of the individual . . . to engage in any of the common occupations of life" has been repeatedly recognized by this Court as falling within the concept of liberty guaranteed by the Fourteenth Amendment. . . .

I agree that the purpose of the mandatory retirement law is legitimate, and indeed compelling. The Commonwealth has every reason to assure that its state police officers are of sufficient physical strength and health to perform their jobs. In my view, however, the means chosen, the forced retirement of officers at age 50, is so overinclusive that it must fail.

All potential officers must pass a rigorous physical examination. Until age 40, this same examination must be passed every two years—when the officer re-enlists—and, after age 40, every year. Appellants have conceded that "[w]hen a member passes his re-enlistment or annual physical, he is found to be qualified to perform all of the duties of the Uniformed Branch of the Massachusetts State Police." If a member fails the examination, he is immediately terminated or refused re-enlistment. Thus, the only members of the state police still on the force at age 50 are those who have been determined—repeatedly—by the Commonwealth to be physically fit for the job. Yet, all of these physically fit officers are automatically terminated at age 50. Appellants do not seriously assert that their testing is no longer effective at age 50, nor do they claim that continued testing would serve no purpose because officers over 50 are no longer physically able to perform their jobs. Thus the Commonwealth is in the position of already individually testing its police officers for physical fitness, conceding that such testing is adequate to determine the physical ability of an officer to continue on the job, and conceding that that ability may continue after age 50. In these circumstances, I see no reason at all for automatically terminating those officers who reach the age of 50; indeed, that action seems the height of irrationality.

Accordingly, I conclude that the Commonwealth's mandatory retirement law cannot stand when measured against the significant deprivation the Commonwealth's action works upon the terminated employees. I would affirm the judgment of the District Court.

Notes and Queries

1. *Murgia* recalls our introductory discussion of the politics of legislative classification and the propriety of judicial interference with the political decisions of the legislature. Like other cases in this chapter, however, it also recalls Sunstein's argument that the judiciary should require legislatures to justify their classifications in terms of some legitimate public value.

2. What was the public value at issue in *Murgia?* In the Court's view, the law's objective was to maintain and enhance the physical and mental qualifications of persons working as state troopers. Is this a legitimate public purpose? Even if the legitimacy of the purpose is admitted, the classification is imperfect because there are probably troopers over the age of fifty who are physically and mentally capable of performing their jobs. By the same token, some younger troopers are likely not to be as physically or mentally able as older troopers. Yet as a general rule, and as a matter of common knowledge, age correlates substantially with mental and physical capacity, and legislatures have usually been deemed to have the right to base their decisions on such knowledge. But if individualized treatment is required where gender is concerned, why

should such treatment not be required where age is concerned?

3. Are we sure that a physically fit police force is the only valid public purpose behind the mandatory retirement law? Legislatures are likely to have a number of objectives in mind when voting on bills. With a little imagination, other reasonable objectives can be found to justify mandatory retirement; for example, to give more young people a chance to work for the state or to provide for the orderly turnover of employees, thus insuring some predictability in the administration of a state pension plan. One can see the possibility of judicial manipulation here. What is to prevent the Supreme Court from picking out one purpose for special scrutiny, as Rehnquist charged the Court with doing in *Trimble*, and striking down the statute after finding that particular purpose deficient, thus overlooking other public values the state may have had in mind? On the other hand, as here, the Court has put little or no bite into the equal protection clause. Is the choice facing the Supreme Court one of judicial abdication or a judicial activism that is invariably subjective? Is there a truly objective way *judicially* to determine whether a classification is substantially or reasonably related to a legitimate purpose? Is there a *judicially* objective way of determining whether the purpose is legitimate?

4. Determining when the Supreme Court should overturn the rational choice of the legislature is a major problem for the U.S. Supreme Court. Foreign high courts, such as Canada's Supreme Court and Germany's Federal Constitutional Court, have adopted a strong proportionality test in reviewing *all* legislative classifications. Mere rationality will not suffice. Instead, legislatures are bound by the principle of proportionality. Classification and purpose must be substantially related and the courts will independently examine the legislation to insure that the classification is indeed calculated to bring about the anticipated result. In Canada, for example, mandatory retirement laws have been struck down in the absence of any showing that the classification constitutes the least restrictive means to achieve a statutory purpose. Does the Canadian approach provide the objectivity arguably absent in the American approach to rationality analysis?

5. American and foreign cases implicating the constitutional principle of equality begs a further question: What does it really mean to legislate rationally? Are there competing conceptions of rationality and if so should courts substitute its notion of rationality for that of the legislature?

Cleburne v. Cleburne Living Center

473 U.S. 432; 105 S. Ct. 3249; 87 L. Ed. 2d 313 (1985)

A private citizen bought a house in Cleburne, Texas, which he planned to lease to the Cleburne Living Center (CLC) for the operation of a group home for the mentally retarded. The building was to serve as a home for 13 retarded men and women who were to be supervised by CLC staff members. CLC planned to comply with all state and federal regulations. In the area where the home was located, general permits were granted for nursing homes, homes for the aged, and sanitariums. The city notified CLC that under its zoning regulations a special use permit, renewable annually, would be required for any hospital or home for the feeble-minded. After a hearing, however, the city's planning and zoning commission voted to deny the permit. CLC then filed a suit in federal district court, claiming that the zoning ordinance discriminated against the mentally retarded in violation of the Equal Protection Clause, but the Court of Appeals for the Fifth Circuit reversed, holding that mental retardation was a quasi-suspect classification and that the law should be assessed under intermediate-level scrutiny. Opinion of the Court: *White*, Burger, Powell, Rehnquist, Stevens, O'Connor. Concurring opinon: *Stevens*. Concurring in part and dissenting in part: *Marshall*, Brennan, Blackmun.

Justice WHITE delivered the opinion of the Court.

The Equal Protection Clause of the Fourteenth Amendment commands that no State shall "deny to any person within its jurisdiction the equal protection of the laws," which is essentially a direction that all persons similarly situated should be treated alike. . . . The general rule is that legislation is presumed to be valid and will be sustained if the classification drawn by the statute is rationally related to a legitimate state interest. When social or economic legislation is at issue, the Equal Protection Clause allows the States wide latitude, and the Constitution presumes that even improvident decisions will eventually be rectified by the democratic processes.

The general rule gives way, however, when a statute classifies by race, alienage, or national origin. These factors are so seldom relevant to the achievement of any legitimate state interest that laws grounded in such considerations are deemed to reflect prejudice and antipathy—a view that those in the burdened class are not as worthy or deserving as others. For these reasons and because such discrimination is unlikely to be soon rectified by legislative means, these laws are subjected to strict scrutiny and will be sustained only if they are suitably tailored to serve a compelling state interest. . . .

Against this background, we conclude for several reasons that the Court of Appeals erred in holding mental retardation a quasi-suspect classification calling for a more exacting standard of judicial review than is normally accorded economic and social legislation. . . . How this large and diversified group is to be treated under the law is a difficult and often a technical matter, very much a task for legislators guided by qualified professionals and not by the perhaps ill-informed opinions of the judiciary. Heightened scrutiny inevitably involves substantive judgments about legislative decisions, and we doubt that the predicate for such judicial oversight is present where the classification deals with mental retardation.

Doubtless, there have been and there will continue to be instances of discrimination against the retarded that are in fact invidious, and that are properly subject to judicial correction under constitutional norms. But the appropriate method of reaching such instances is not to create a new quasi-suspect classification and subject all governmental action based on that classification to more searching evaluation. Rather, we should look to the likelihood that governmental action premised on a particular classification is valid as a general matter, not merely to the specifics of the case before us. Because mental retardation is a characteristic that the government may legitimately take into account in a wide range of decisions, and because both State and Federal Governments have recently committed themselves to assisting the retarded, we will not presume that any given legislative action, even one that disadvantages retarded individuals, is rooted in considerations that the Constitution will not tolerate.

Our refusal to recognize the retarded as a quasi-suspect class does not leave them entirely unprotected from invidious discrimination. To withstand equal protection review, legislation that distinguishes between the mentally retarded and others must be rationally related to a legitimate governmental purpose. This standard, we believe, affords government the latitude necessary both to pursue policies designed to assist the retarded in realizing their full potential, and to freely and efficiently engage in activities that burden the retarded in what is essentially an incidental manner. The State may not rely on a classification whose relationship to an asserted goal is so attenuated as to render the distinction arbitrary or irrational. . . .

The constitutional issue is clearly posed. The city does not require a special use permit in an R-3 zone for apartment houses, multiple dwellings, boarding and lodging houses, fraternity or sorority houses, dormitories, apartment hotels, hospitals, sanitariums, nursing homes for convalescents or the aged (other than for the insane or feebleminded or alcoholics or drug addicts), private clubs or fraternal orders, and other specified uses. It does, however, insist on a special permit for the Featherston home, and it does so, as the District Court found, because it would be a facility for the mentally retarded. May the city require the permit for this facility when other care and multiple-dwelling facilities are freely permitted?

. . . Because in our view the record does not reveal any rational basis for believing that the Featherston home would pose any special threat to the city's legitimate interests, we affirm the judgment below insofar as it holds the ordinance invalid as applied in this case.

The District Court found that the City Council's insistence on the permit rested on several factors. First, the Council was concerned with the negative attitude of the majority of property owners located within 200 feet of the Featherston facility, as well as with the fears of elderly residents of the neighborhood. But mere negative attitudes, or fear, unsubstantiated by factors which are properly cognizable in a zoning proceeding, are not permissible bases for treating a home for the mentally retarded differently from apartment houses, multiple dwellings, and the like. . . .

The short of it is that requiring the permit in this case appears to us to rest on an irrational prejudice against the mentally retarded, including those who would occupy the Featherston facility and who would live under the closely supervised and highly regulated conditions expressly provided for by state and federal law.

The judgment of the Court of Appeals is affirmed insofar as it invalidates the zoning ordinance as applied to the Featherston home. . . .

Justice MARSHALL, with whom Justice BRENNAN and Justice BLACKMUN join, concurring in the judgment in part and dissenting in part.

I cannot agree . . . with the way in which the Court reaches its result or with the narrow, as-applied remedy it provides for the city of Cleburne's equal protection violation. The Court holds the ordinance invalid on rational-basis grounds and disclaims that anything special, in the form of heightened scrutiny, is taking place. Yet Cleburne's ordinance surely would be valid under the traditional rational-basis test applicable to economic and commercial regulation. . . .

. . . [T]he Court's heightened-scrutiny discussion is even more puzzling given that Cleburne's ordinance is invalidated only after being subjected to precisely the sort of

probing inquiry associated with heightened scrutiny. To be sure, the Court does not label its handiwork heightened scrutiny, and perhaps the method employed must hereafter be called "second order" rational-basis review rather than "heightened scrutiny." But however labeled, the rational-basis test invoked today is most assuredly not the rational basis test of *Williamson v. Lee Optical* (1955), *Allied Stores v. Bowers* (1959) and their progeny. . . .

The refusal to acknowledge that something more than minimum rationality review is at work here is, in my view, unfortunate in at least two respects. The suggestion that the traditional rational-basis test allows this sort of searching inquiry creates precedent for this Court and lower courts to subject economic and commercial classifications to similar and searching "ordinary" rational-basis review—a small and regrettable step back toward the days of *Lochner v. New York* (1905). Moreover, by failing to articulate the factors that justify today's "second order" rational-basis review, the Court provides no principled foundation for determining when more searching inquiry is to be invoked. . . .

Notes and Queries

1. The Court reiterates in this case "that legislation is presumed to be valid and will be sustained if the classification drawn by the statute is rationally related to a legitimate state interest. When social or economic legislation is at issue, the Equal Protection Clause allows the States wide latitude, and the Constitution presumes that even improvident decisions will eventually be rectified by the democratic process." Does the Constitution presume that improvident legislation will be rectified by the democratic process?

2. *Cleburne* triggered another debate over the standards of judicial review to be used in the equal protection context. What standard of review did Justice White, writing for the majority, actually employ? The Court held that Cleburne's ordinance was invalid on rational-basis grounds. Justice Marshall, however, suggests that here intermediate review masqueraded as rational-basis analysis. "[The] rational basis test invoked today," he wrote, "is most assuredly not the rational-basis test of *Williamson v. Lee Optical*." He continued: "The refusal to acknowledge that something more than minimum rationality review is at work here, in my view . . . unfortunate. . . . The suggestion that the traditional rational-basis test allows this sort of searching inquiry creates precedent for this Court and lower courts to subject economic and commercial classifications to similar and searching 'ordinary' rational-basis review—a small and regrettable step back toward the days of *Lochner v. New York*." Does *Cleburne* revive *Lochner*? Should it?

Romer v. Evans

517 U.S.620, 116 S. Ct. 1620, 134 L. Ed. 2d 855 (1996)

Several cities in Colorado—including Aspen, Boulder and Denver—enacted ordinances specifically to protect the legal rights of homosexuals. In response, a group petitioned the state legislature and finally got on the statewide ballot a referendum on a state constitutional amendment to prohibit and nullify such ordinances. The Amendment, named Amendment 2, stated that no state or division of the state could enforce any regulation whereby homosexual, lesbian or bisexual orientation, conduct, practices or relationships shall constitute or otherwise be the basis of or entitle any person or class of persons to have or claim any minority status, quota preferences, protected status or claim of discrimination. The amendment passed in 1992 by a 54 percent to 46 percent vote. Members of gay rights groups sued, claiming that the amendment denied them equal recourse to the political process and thus equal protection of the laws. The Colorado Supreme Court struck down the amendment, stating that the amendment was subject to strict scrutiny because it infringed the fundamental right of homosexuals to participate in the political process. Opinion of the Court: *Kennedy*, Breyer, Ginsburg, O'Connor, Souter, Stevens. Dissenting opinion: *Scalia*, Rehnquist, Thomas.

Justice KENNEDY delivered the opinion of the Court:

One century ago, the first Justice Harlan admonished this Court that the Constitution "neither knows nor tolerates classes among citizens." (*Plessy v. Ferguson*, 1896). Unheeded then, those words now are understood to state a commitment to the law's neutrality where the rights of persons are at stake. The Equal Protection Clause enforces this principle and today requires us to hold invalid a provision of Colorado's Constitution.

The State's principal argument in defense of Amendment 2 is that it puts gays and lesbians in the same position as all other persons. So, the State says, the measure does no more than deny homosexuals special rights. This reading of the amendment's language is implausible.

Sweeping and comprehensive is the change in legal status effected by this law. Homosexuals, by state decree, are put in a solitary class with respect to transactions and relations in both the private and governmental spheres. The amendment withdraws from homosexuals, but no others, specific legal protection from the injuries caused by discrimination, and it forbids reinstatement of these laws and policies.

Amendment 2 bars homosexuals from securing protection against the injuries that . . . public-accommodations laws address. That in itself is a severe consequence, but there is more. Amendment 2, in addition, nullifies specific legal protections for this targeted class in all transactions in housing, sale of real estate, insurance, health and welfare services, private education, and employment.

Amendment 2's reach may not be limited to specific laws passed for the benefit of gays and lesbians. It is a fair, if not necessary, inference from the broad language of the amendment that it deprives gays and lesbians even of the protection of general laws and policies that prohibit arbitrary discrimination in governmental and private settings.

At some point in the systematic administration of these laws, an official must determine whether homosexuality is an arbitrary and thus forbidden basis for decision. Yet a decision to that effect would itself amount to a policy prohibiting discrimination on the basis of homosexuality, and so would appear to be no more valid under Amendment 2 than the specific prohibitions against discrimination the state court held invalid.

If this consequence follows from Amendment 2, as its broad language suggests, it would compound the constitutional difficulties the law creates. The state court did not decide whether the amendment has this effect, however, and neither need we. In the course of rejecting the argument that Amendment 2 is intended to conserve resources to fight discrimination against suspect classes, the Colorado Supreme Court made the limited observation that the amendment is not intended to affect many antidiscrimination laws protecting non-suspect classes. In our view that does not resolve the issue. In any event, even if, as we doubt, homosexuals could find some safe harbor in laws of general application, we cannot accept the view that Amendment 2's prohibition on specific legal protections does no more than deprive homosexuals of special rights. To the contrary, the amendment imposes a special disability upon those persons alone. Homosexuals are forbidden the safeguards that others enjoy or may seek without constraint. They can obtain specific protection against discrimination only by enlisting the citizenry of Colorado to amend the state constitution or perhaps, on the State's view, by trying to pass helpful laws of general applicability. This is so no matter how local or discrete the harm, no matter how public and widespread the injury. We find nothing special in the protections Amendment 2 withholds. These are protections taken for granted by most people either because they already have them or do not need them; these are protections against exclusion from

Comparative Note 15.9

[Canada's Old Age Security Act conferred a benefit on "spouses in a heterosexual union." A homosexual couple challenged the law as a violation of equality under Section 15 of the Charter of Rights and Liberties. Although ruling that the state satisfied the test of proportionality and met the burden of justification under the Charter's Section 1, the Supreme Court had the following to say about classifications based on sexual orientation.]

The appellants' claim . . . that the Act contravenes s. 15 of the Charter [by] discriminat[ing] on the basis of sexual orientation. To establish that claim, it must first be determined that s. 15's protection of equality with-

out discrimination extends to sexual orientation as a ground analogous to those specifically mentioned in the section. This poses no great hurdle. . . . While I ordinarily have reservations about concessions of constitutional issues, I have no difficulty accepting the appellants' contention that whether or not sexual orientation is based on biological or physiological factors, which may be a matter of some controversy, it is a deeply personal characteristic that is either unchangeable or changeable only at unacceptable personal costs, and so falls within the ambit of s. 15 protection as being analogous to the enumerated grounds. . . .

SOURCE: *Egan v. Canada*, [1995] 2 S.C.R. 513.

---

an almost limitless number of transactions and endeavors that constitute ordinary civic life in a free society.

The Fourteenth Amendment's promise that no person shall be denied the equal protection of the laws must coexist with the practical necessity that most legislation classifies for one purpose or another, with resulting disadvantage to various groups or persons. We have attempted to reconcile the principle with the reality by stating that, if a law neither burdens a fundamental right nor targets a suspect class, we will uphold the legislative classification so long as it bears a rational relation to some legitimate end. . . .

Amendment 2 fails, indeed defies, even this conventional inquiry. First, the amendment has the peculiar property of imposing a broad and undifferentiated disability on a single named group, an exceptional and, as we shall explain, invalid form of legislation. Second, its sheer breadth is so discontinuous with the reasons offered for it that the amendment seems inexplicable by anything but animus toward the class that it affects; it lacks a rational relationship to legitimate state interests.

Taking the first point, even in the ordinary equal protection case calling for the most deferential of standards, we insist on knowing the relation between the classification adopted and the object to be attained. . . . By requiring that the classification bear a rational relationship to an independent and legitimate legislative end, we ensure that classifications are not drawn for the purpose of disadvantaging the group burdened by the law.

Amendment 2 confounds this normal process of judicial review. It is at once too narrow and too broad. It identifies

persons by a single trait and then denies them protection across the board. The resulting disqualification of a class of persons from the right to seek specific protection from the law is unprecedented in our jurisprudence. . . . It is not within our constitutional tradition to enact laws of this sort. Central both to the idea of the rule of law and to our own Constitution's guarantee of equal protection is the principle that government and each of its parts remain open on impartial terms to all who seek its assistance. . . . Respect for this principle explains why laws singling out a certain class of citizens for disfavored legal status or general hardships are rare. A law declaring that in general it shall be more difficult for one group of citizens than for all others to seek aid from the government is itself a denial of equal protection of the laws in the most literal sense.

A second and related point is that laws of the kind now before us raise the inevitable inference that the disadvantage imposed is born of animosity toward the class of persons affected. . . . Even laws enacted for broad and ambitious purposes often can be explained by reference to legitimate public policies which justify the incidental disadvantages they impose on certain persons. Amendment 2, however, in making a general announcement that gays and lesbians shall not have any particular protections from the law, inflicts on them immediate, continuing, and real injuries that outrun and belie any legitimate justifications that may be claimed for it. We conclude that, in addition to the far-reaching deficiencies of Amendment 2 that we have noted, the principles it offends, in another sense, are conventional and venerable; a law must bear a rational relationship to a legitimate governmental purpose, and Amendment 2 does not.

The primary rationale the State offers for Amendment 2 is respect for other citizens' freedom of association, and in particular the liberties of landlords or employers who have personal or religious objections to homosexuality. Colorado also cites its interest in conserving resources to fight discrimination against other groups. The breadth of the Amendment is so far removed from these particular justifications that we find it impossible to credit them. We cannot say that Amendment 2 is directed to any identifiable legitimate purpose or discrete objective. It is a status-based enactment divorced from any factual context from which we could discern a relationship to legitimate state interests; it is a classification of persons undertaken for its own sake, something the Equal Protection Clause does not permit.

We must conclude that Amendment 2 classifies homosexuals not to further a proper legislative end but to make them unequal to everyone else. This Colorado cannot do. A State cannot so deem a class of persons a stranger to its laws. Amendment 2 violates the Equal Protection Clause, and the judgment of the Supreme Court of Colorado is affirmed.

Justice SCALIA, dissenting, with whom the Chief Justice and Justice THOMAS join.

The Court has mistaken a Kulturkampf for a fit of spite. The constitutional amendment before us here is not the manifestation of a "bare . . . desire to harm" homosexuals . . . but is rather a modest attempt by seemingly tolerant Coloradans to preserve traditional sexual mores against the efforts of a politically powerful minority to revise those mores through use of the laws. That objective, and the means chosen to achieve it, are not only unimpeachable under any constitutional doctrine hitherto pronounced (hence the opinion's heavy reliance upon principles of righteousness rather than judicial holdings); they have been specifically approved by the Congress of the United States and by this Court.

In holding that homosexuality cannot be singled out for disfavorable treatment, the Court contradicts a decision, unchallenged here, pronounced only 10 years ago, *Bowers v. Hardwick* (1986), and places the prestige of this institution behind the proposition that opposition to homosexuality is as reprehensible as racial or religious bias. Whether it is or not is precisely the cultural debate that gave rise to the Colorado constitutional amendment (and to the preferential laws against which the amendment was directed). Since the Constitution of the United States says nothing about this subject, it is left to be re-

solved by normal democratic means, including the democratic adoption of provisions in state constitutions. This Court has no business imposing upon all Americans the resolution favored by the elite class from which the Members of this institution are selected, pronouncing that "animosity" toward homosexuality . . . is evil. I vigorously dissent.

Let me first discuss Part II of the Court's opinion, its longest section, which is devoted to rejecting the State's arguments that Amendment 2 "puts gays and lesbians in the same position as all other persons," and "does no more than deny homosexuals special rights."

In reaching this conclusion, the Court considers it unnecessary to decide the validity of the State's argument that Amendment 2 does not deprive homosexuals of the "protection [afforded by] general laws and policies that prohibit arbitrary discrimination in governmental and private settings."

The amendment prohibits *special treatment* of homosexuals, and nothing more. . . .

Despite all of its hand-wringing about the potential effect of Amendment 2 on general antidiscrimination laws, the Court's opinion ultimately does not dispute all this, but assumes it to be true. The only denial of equal treatment it contends homosexuals have suffered is this: They may not obtain *preferential* treatment without amending the state constitution. That is to say, the principle underlying the Court's opinion is that one who is accorded equal treatment under the laws, but cannot as readily as others obtain *preferential* treatment under the laws, has been denied equal protection of the laws. If merely stating this alleged "equal protection" violation does not suffice to refute it, our constitutional jurisprudence has achieved terminal silliness.

. . . [T]here is no doubt of a rational basis for the substance of the prohibition at issue here. The Court's entire novel theory rests upon the proposition that there is something *special*—something that cannot be justified by normal "rational basis" analysis—in making a disadvantaged group (or a nonpreferred group) resort to a higher decision-making level. That proposition finds no support in law or logic.

I turn next to whether there was a legitimate rational basis for the substance of the constitutional amendment—for the prohibition of special protection for homosexuals. It is unsurprising that the Court avoids discussion of this question, since the answer is so obviously yes. The case most relevant to the issue before us today is not even mentioned in the Court's opinion: In *Bowers v. Hardwick* we held that the Constitution does not prohibit what virtually all States had done from the founding of the Republic until very recent years—making homosexual conduct a crime. That holding is unassailable, except by those who think that the Constitution changes to suit current fashions. But in any event it is a given in the present case: Respondents' briefs did not urge overruling *Bowers*, and at oral argument respondents' counsel expressly disavowed any intent to seek such overruling. . . . If it is constitutionally permissible for a State to make homosexual conduct criminal, surely it is constitutionally permissible for a State to enact other laws merely disfavoring homosexual conduct. . . . And a fortiori it is constitutionally permissible for a State to adopt a provision not even disfavoring homosexual conduct, but merely prohibiting all levels of state government from bestowing special protections upon homosexual conduct.

No principle set forth in the Constitution, nor even any imagined by this Court in the past 200 years, prohibits what Colorado has done here. But the case for Colorado is much stronger than that. What it has done is not only unprohibited, but eminently reasonable, with close, congressionally approved precedent in earlier constitutional practice.

First, as to its eminent reasonableness. The Court's opinion contains grim, disapproving hints that Coloradans have been guilty of "animus" or "animosity" toward homosexuality, as though that has been established as Unamerican. Of course it is our moral heritage that one should not hate any human being or class of human beings. But I had thought that one could consider certain conduct reprehensible—murder, for example, or polygamy, or cruelty to animals—and could exhibit even "animus" toward such conduct. Surely that is the only sort of "animus" at issue here: moral disapproval of homosexual conduct, the same sort of moral disapproval that produced the centuries-old criminal laws that we held constitutional in *Bowers*. The Colorado amendment does not, to speak entirely precisely, prohibit giving favored status to people who are *homosexuals*; they can be favored for many reasons—for example, because they are senior citizens or members of racial minorities. But it prohibits giving them favored status *because of their homosexual conduct*—that is, it prohibits favored status for *homosexuality*.

But though Coloradans are, as I say, entitled to be hostile toward homosexual conduct, the fact is that the degree of hostility reflected by Amendment 2 is the smallest conceivable. The Court's portrayal of Coloradans as a society fallen victim to pointless, hate-filled "gay-bashing" is so false as to be comical. Colorado not only is one of the 25 States that have repealed their antisodomy laws, but was among the first to do so. . . . But the society that eliminates criminal punishment for homosexual acts does not necessarily abandon the view that homosexuality is morally wrong and socially harmful; often, abolition simply reflects the view that enforcement of such criminal laws involves unseemly intrusion into the intimate lives of citizens.

There is a problem, however, which arises when criminal sanction of homosexuality is eliminated but moral and social disapprobation of homosexuality is meant to be retained. . . . The problem (a problem, that is, for those who wish to retain social disapprobation of homosexuality) is that, because those who engage in homosexual conduct tend to reside in disproportionate numbers in certain communities, have high disposable income and of course care about homosexual-rights issues much more ardently than the public at large, they possess political power much greater than their numbers, both locally and statewide. Quite understandably, they devote this political power to achieving not merely a grudging social toleration, but full social acceptance, of homosexuality. . . . [H]omosexuals are as entitled to use the legal system for reinforcement of their moral sentiments as are the rest of society. But they are subject to being countered by lawful, democratic countermeasures as well. . . .

Today's opinion has no foundation in American constitutional law, and barely pretends to. The people of Colorado have adopted an entirely reasonable provision which does not even disfavor homosexuals in any substantive sense, but merely denies them preferential treatment. Amendment 2 is designed to prevent piecemeal deterioration of the sexual morality favored by a majority of Coloradans, and is not only an appropriate means to that legitimate end, but a means that Americans have employed before. Striking it down is an act, not of judicial judgment, but of political will. I dissent.

Notes and Queries

1. On what basis does Justice Kennedy strike down the statute? How does his decision differ from that of the Colorado Supreme Court? How does he know the motivation of Colorado voters for enacting the law?

2. What is the dispute in this case? Does Amendment 2 deny homosexuals equal rights, or does it merely withhold from them special rights others do not enjoy?

3. Can *Evans* be reconciled with *Bowers v. Hardwick*? How can one answer Scalia's objection that if criminalizing homosexual conduct is constitutional, then surely Colorado's lesser action is constitutional as well? What does Scalia see as the legitimate state interest advanced by the amendment? Is that interest and the state's action necessarily legitimate just because they are traditional? Does Sc-

alia's reasoning collapse in the light of *Lawrence v. Texas* (overruling *Bowers*)?

4. The Court evidently agrees that "rational basis"—the normal test for compliance with the Equal Protection Clause—is the governing standard. The trial court rejected respondents' argument that homosexuals constitute a "suspect" or "quasi-suspect" class, and respondents elected not to appeal that ruling to the Supreme Court of Colorado. . . . Should homosexuals be considered a suspect or semi-suspect class? Do homosexuals fit the qualifications of a suspect class as articulated in *Carolene Products*? Should that consideration matter?

5. Has the Court really entered the "culture wars" on one side against the other, as Scalia implies? Is the Court's decision a retreat to the jurisprudence of *Lochner*?

6. The following thoughts by Louis Henkin may be an appropriate conclusion to these materials on the equal protection clause:

> United States jurisprudence has struggled for some years with a new refinement of the concept of equal protection. Different levels of scrutiny have been applied where distinctions effect a classification that is suspect or impinge on some fundamental right; in such circumstances the governmental action will be sustained only if it serves a compelling public interest. Which classifications other than race are suspect has hopelessly divided the Supreme Court. The Court has not even begun to refine the other variables, to develop a table of weights for various public interests to determine how compelling they are. Can we find in the international experience and conscience some guidance as to which distinctions should invite stronger scrutiny; which rights are fundamental; which state interests are compelling; and what degree of necessity justifies the infringement of rights?

See "Constitutionalism and Human Rights" in Louis Henkin and Albert J. Rosenthal, eds., *Constitutionalism and Rights: The Influence of the United States Constitution Abroad* (New York: Columbia University Press, 1990), 393.

Declaration of Independence

(Adopted in Congress 4 July 1776)

The Unanimous Declaration of the Thirteen United States of America

When, in the course of human events, it becomes necessary for one people to dissolve the political bonds which have connected them with another, and to assume among the powers of the earth, the separate and equal station to which the laws of nature and of nature's God entitle them, a decent respect to the opinions of mankind requires that they should declare the causes which impel them to the separation.

We hold these truths to be self-evident, that all men are created equal, that they are endowed by their Creator with certain unalienable Rights, that among these are life, liberty and the pursuit of happiness. That to secure these rights, Governments are instituted among Men, deriving their just powers from the consent of the governed. That whenever any form of government becomes destructive to these ends, it is the Right of the People to alter or to abolish it, and to institute new Government, laying its foundation on such principles and organizing its powers in such form, as to them shall seem most likely to effect their Safety and Happiness. Prudence, indeed, will dictate that governments long established should not be changed for light and transient causes; and accordingly all experience hath shown that mankind are more disposed to suffer, while evils are sufferable, than to right themselves by abolishing the forms to which they are accustomed. But when a long train of abuses and usurpations, pursuing invariably the same Object evinces a design to reduce them under absolute despotism, it is their right, it is their duty, to throw off such Government, and to provide new guards for their future security.—Such has been the patient sufferance of these Colonies; and such is now the necessity which constrains them to alter their former Systems of Government. The history of the present King of Great Britain is a history of repeated injuries and usurpations, all having in direct object the establishment of an absolute Tyranny over these States. To prove this, let Facts be submitted to a candid world.

He has refused his Assent to Laws, the most wholesome and necessary for the public good.

He has forbidden his Governors to pass laws of immediate and pressing importance, unless suspended in their operation till his Assent should be obtained; and when so suspended, he has utterly neglected to attend to them.

He has refused to pass other Laws for the accommodation of large districts of people, unless those people would relinquish the right of Representation in the Legislature, a right inestimable to them and formidable to tyrants only.

He has called together legislative bodies at places unusual, uncomfortable, and distant from the depository of their public Records, for the sole purpose of fatiguing them into compliance with his measures.

He has dissolved Representative Houses repeatedly, for opposing with manly firmness his invasions on the rights of the people.

He has refused for a long time, after such dissolutions, to cause others to be elected; whereby the Legislative powers, incapable of Annihilation, have returned to the People at large for their exercise; the state remaining in the meantime exposed to all the dangers of invasion from without, and convulsions within.

He has endeavored to prevent the population of these States; for that purpose obstructing the Laws for Naturalization of Foreigners; refusing to pass others to encourage their migration hither, and raising the conditions of new Appropriations of Lands.

He has obstructed the Administration of Justice, by refusing his Assent to Laws for establishing Judiciary powers.

He has made Judges dependent on his Will alone, for the tenure of their offices, and the amount and payment of their salaries.

He has erected a multitude of New Offices, and sent hither swarms of Officers to harass our people, and eat out their substance.

He has kept among us, in times of peace, Standing Armies without the Consent of our Legislatures.

He has affected to render the Military independent of and superior to Civil Power.

He has combined with others to subject us to a jurisdiction foreign to our constitution, and unacknowledged by our laws; giving his Assent to their Acts of pretended Legislation:

For quartering large bodies of armed troops among us:

For protecting them, by mock Trial, from punishment for any Murders which they should commit on the Inhabitants of these States:

For cutting off our Trade with all parts of the world:

For imposing Taxes on us without our Consent:

For depriving us in many cases, of the benefits of Trial by Jury:

For transporting us beyond Seas to be tried for pretended offenses:

For abolishing the free system of English laws in a neighboring Province, establishing therein an Arbitrary government, and enlarging its Boundaries so as to render it at once an example and fit instrument for introducing the same absolute rule in these Colonies:

For taking away our Charters, abolishing our most valuable Laws, and altering fundamentally the Forms of our Governments:

For suspending our own Legislatures, and declaring themselves invested with power to legislate for us in all cases whatsoever.

He has abdicated Government here, by declaring us out of his protection and waging War against us.

He has plundered our seas, ravaged our Coasts, burned our towns, and destroyed the lives of our people.

He is at this time transporting large Armies of foreign Mercenaries to complete the works of death, desolation and tyranny, already begun with circumstances of Cruelty and perfidy scarcely paralleled in the most barbarous ages, and totaly unworth the Head of a civilized nation.

He has constrained our fellow citizens taken captive on the high seas to bear arms against their country, to become the executioners of their friends and brethren, or to fall themselves by their hands.

He has excited domestic insurrections amongst us, and has endeavored to bring on the inhabitants of our frontiers, the merciless Indian savages, whose known rule of warfare, is undistinguished destruction of all ages, sexes and conditions.

In every stage of these oppressions we have petitioned for redress in the most humble terms: our repeated petitions have been answered only by repeated injury. A prince, whose character is thus marked by every act which may define a tyrant, is unfit to be the ruler of a free people.

Nor have we been wanting in attention to our British brethren. We have warned them from time to time of attempts by their legislature to extend an unwarrantable jurisdiction over us. We have reminded them of the circumstances of our emigration and settlement here. We have appealed to their native justice and magnanimity, and we have conjured them by the ties of our common kindred to disavow these usurpations, which, would inevitably interrupt our connections and correspondence. We must, therefore, acquiesce in the necessity, which denounces our separation, and hold them, as we hold the rest of mankind, enemies in war, in peace friends.

We, therefore, the representatives of the UNITED STATES OF AMERICA, in General Congress, Assembled, appealing to the Supreme Judge of the world for the rectitude of our intentions, do, in the Name, and by the Authority of the good People of these colonies, solemnly publish and declare, That these United Colonies are, and of right ought to be FREE AND INDEPENDENT STATES; that they are Absolved from all allegiance to the British Crown, and that all political connection between them and the State of Great Britain, is and ought to be totally dissolved; and that as Free and Independent States, they have full Power to levy War, conclude Peace, contract Alliances, establish Commerce, and to do all other Acts and Things which Independent States may of right do. And for the support of this declaration, with a firm reliance on the protection of Divine Providence, we mutually pledge to each other our Lives, our Fortunes and our sacred Honor.

The United States Constitution

We the People of the United States, in Order to form a more perfect Union, establish Justice, insure domestic Tranquility, provide for the common defence, promote the general Welfare, and secure the Blessings of Liberty to ourselves and our Posterity, do ordain and establish this Constitution for the United States of America.

Article I

Section 1

All legislative Powers herein granted shall be vested in a Congress of the United States, which shall consist of a Senate and House of Representatives.

Section 2

Clause 1: The House of Representatives shall be composed of Members chosen every second Year by the People of the several States, and the Electors in each State shall have the Qualifications requisite for Electors of the most numerous Branch of the State Legislature.

Clause 2: No Person shall be a Representative who shall not have attained to the Age of twenty five Years, and been seven Years a Citizen of the United States, and who shall not, when elected, be an Inhabitant of that State in which he shall be chosen.

Clause 3: Representatives and direct Taxes shall be apportioned among the several States which may be included within this Union, according to their respective Numbers, which shall be determined by adding to the whole Number of free Persons, including those bound to Service for a Term of Years, and excluding Indians not taxed, three fifths of all other Persons. The actual Enumeration shall be made within three Years after the first Meeting of the Congress of the United States, and within every subsequent Term of ten Years, in such Manner as they shall by Law direct. The Number of Representatives shall not exceed one for every thirty Thousand, but each State shall have at Least one Representative; and until such enumeration shall be made, the State of New Hampshire shall be entitled to chuse three, Massachusetts eight, Rhode-Island and Providence Plantations one, Connecticut five, New-York six, New Jersey four, Pennsylvania eight, Delaware one, Maryland six, Virginia ten, North Carolina five, South Carolina five, and Georgia three.

Clause 4: When vacancies happen in the Representation from any State, the Executive Authority thereof shall issue Writs of Election to fill such Vacancies.

Clause 5: The House of Representatives shall chuse their Speaker and other Officers; and shall have the sole Power of Impeachment.

Section 3

Clause 1: The Senate of the United States shall be composed of two Senators from each State, chosen by the Legislature thereof, for six Years; and each Senator shall have one Vote.

Clause 2: Immediately after they shall be assembled in Consequence of the first Election, they shall be divided as equally as may be into three Classes. The Seats of the Senators of the first Class shall be vacated at the Expiration of the second Year, of the second Class at the Expiration of the fourth Year, and of the third Class at the Expiration of the sixth Year, so that one third may be chosen every second Year; and if Vacancies happen by Resignation, or otherwise, during the Recess of the Legislature of any State, the Executive thereof may make temporary Appointments until the next Meeting of the Legislature, which shall then fill such Vacancies.

Clause 3: No Person shall be a Senator who shall not have attained to the Age of thirty Years, and been nine Years a Citizen of the United States, and who shall not, when elected, be an Inhabitant of that State for which he shall be chosen.

Clause 4: The Vice President of the United States shall be President of the Senate, but shall have no Vote, unless they be equally divided.

Clause 5: The Senate shall chuse their other Officers, and also a President pro tempore, in the Absence of the Vice President, or when he shall exercise the Office of President of the United States.

Clause 6: The Senate shall have the sole Power to try all Impeachments. When sitting for that Purpose, they shall be on Oath or Affirmation. When the President of the United States is tried, the Chief Justice shall preside: And no Person shall be convicted without the Concurrence of two thirds of the Members present.

Clause 7: Judgment in Cases of Impeachment shall not extend further than to removal from Office, and disqualification to hold and enjoy any Office of honor, Trust or Profit under the United States: but the Party convicted shall nevertheless be liable and subject to Indictment, Trial, Judgment and Punishment, according to Law.

Section 4

Clause 1: The Times, Places and Manner of holding Elections for Senators and Representatives, shall be prescribed in each State by the Legislature thereof; but the Congress may at any time by Law make or alter such Regulations, except as to the Places of chusing Senators.

Clause 2: The Congress shall assemble at least once in every Year, and such Meeting shall be on the first Monday in December, unless they shall by Law appoint a different Day.

Section 5

Clause 1: Each House shall be the Judge of the Elections, Returns and Qualifications of its own Members, and a Majority of each shall constitute a Quorum to do Business; but a smaller Number may adjourn from day to day, and may be authorized to compel the Attendance of absent Members, in such Manner, and under such Penalties as each House may provide.

Clause 2: Each House may determine the Rules of its Proceedings, punish its Members for disorderly Behaviour, and, with the Concurrence of two thirds, expel a Member.

Clause 3: Each House shall keep a Journal of its Proceedings, and from time to time publish the same, excepting such Parts as may in their Judgment require Secrecy; and the Yeas and Nays of the Members of either House on any question shall, at the Desire of one fifth of those Present, be entered on the Journal.

Clause 4: Neither House, during the Session of Congress, shall, without the Consent of the other, adjourn for more than three days, nor to any other Place than that in which the two Houses shall be sitting.

Section 6

Clause 1: The Senators and Representatives shall receive a Compensation for their Services, to be ascertained by Law, and paid out of the Treasury of the United States. They shall in all Cases, except Treason, Felony and Breach of the Peace, be privileged from Arrest during their Attendance at the Session of their respective Houses, and in going to and returning from the same; and for any Speech or Debate in either House, they shall not be questioned in any other Place.

Clause 2: No Senator or Representative shall, during the Time for which he was elected, be appointed to any civil Office under the Authority of the United States, which shall have been created, or the Emoluments whereof shall have been encreased during such time; and no Person holding any Office under the United States, shall be a Member of either House during his Continuance in Office.

Section 7

Clause 1: All Bills for raising Revenue shall originate in the House of Representatives; but the Senate may propose or concur with Amendments as on other Bills.

Clause 2: Every Bill which shall have passed the House of Representatives and the Senate, shall, before it become a Law, be presented to the President of the United States; If he approve he shall sign it, but if not he shall return it, with his Objections to that House in which it shall have originated, who shall enter the Objections at large on their Journal, and proceed to reconsider it. If after such Reconsideration two thirds of that House shall agree to pass the Bill, it shall be sent, together with the Objections, to the other House, by which it shall likewise be reconsidered, and if approved by two thirds of that House, it shall become a Law. But in all such Cases the Votes of both Houses shall be determined by yeas and Nays, and the Names of the Persons voting for and against the Bill shall be entered on the Journal of each House respectively. If any Bill shall not be returned by the President within ten Days (Sundays excepted) after it shall have been presented to him, the Same shall be a Law, in like Manner as if he had signed it, unless the Congress by their Adjournment prevent its Return, in which Case it shall not be a Law.

Clause 3: Every Order, Resolution, or Vote to which the Concurrence of the Senate and House of Representatives may be necessary (except on a question of Adjournment) shall be presented to the President of the United States; and before the Same shall take Effect, shall be approved by him, or being disapproved by him, shall be repassed by two thirds of the Senate and House of

Representatives, according to the Rules and Limitations prescribed in the Case of a Bill.

Section 8

Clause 1: The Congress shall have Power To lay and collect Taxes, Duties, Imposts and Excises, to pay the Debts and provide for the common Defence and general Welfare of the United States; but all Duties, Imposts and Excises shall be uniform throughout the United States;

Clause 2: To borrow Money on the credit of the United States;

Clause 3: To regulate Commerce with foreign Nations, and among the several States, and with the Indian Tribes;

Clause 4: To establish an uniform Rule of Naturalization, and uniform Laws on the subject of Bankruptcies throughout the United States;

Clause 5: To coin Money, regulate the Value thereof, and of foreign Coin, and fix the Standard of Weights and Measures;

Clause 6: To provide for the Punishment of counterfeiting the Securities and current Coin of the United States;

Clause 7: To establish Post Offices and post Roads;

Clause 8: To promote the Progress of Science and useful Arts, by securing for limited Times to Authors and Inventors the exclusive Right to their respective Writings and Discoveries;

Clause 9: To constitute Tribunals inferior to the supreme Court;

Clause 10: To define and punish Piracies and Felonies committed on the high Seas, and Offences against the Law of Nations;

Clause 11: To declare War, grant Letters of Marque and Reprisal, and make Rules concerning Captures on Land and Water;

Clause 12: To raise and support Armies, but no Appropriation of Money to that Use shall be for a longer Term than two Years;

Clause 13: To provide and maintain a Navy;

Clause 14: To make Rules for the Government and Regulation of the land and naval Forces;

Clause 15: To provide for calling forth the Militia to execute the Laws of the Union, suppress Insurrections and repel Invasions;

Clause 16: To provide for organizing, arming, and disciplining, the Militia, and for governing such Part of them as may be employed in the Service of the United States, reserving to the States respectively, the Appointment of the Officers, and the Authority of training the Militia according to the discipline prescribed by Congress;

Clause 17: To exercise exclusive Legislation in all Cases whatsoever, over such District (not exceeding ten Miles square) as may, by Cession of particular States, and the Acceptance of Congress, become the Seat of the Government of the United States, and to exercise like Authority over all Places purchased by the Consent of the Legislature of the State in which the Same shall be, for the Erection of Forts, Magazines, Arsenals, dock-Yards, and other needful Buildings;—And

Clause 18: To make all Laws which shall be necessary and proper for carrying into Execution the foregoing Powers, and all other Powers vested by this Constitution in the Government of the United States, or in any Department or Officer thereof.

Section 9

Clause 1: The Migration or Importation of such Persons as any of the States now existing shall think proper to admit, shall not be prohibited by the Congress prior to the Year one thousand eight hundred and eight, but a Tax or duty may be imposed on such Importation, not exceeding ten dollars for each Person.

Clause 2: The Privilege of the Writ of Habeas Corpus shall not be suspended, unless when in Cases of Rebellion or Invasion the public Safety may require it.

Clause 3: No Bill of Attainder or ex post facto Law shall be passed.

Clause 4: No Capitation, or other direct, Tax shall be laid, unless in Proportion to the Census or Enumeration herein before directed to be taken.

Clause 5: No Tax or Duty shall be laid on Articles exported from any State.

Clause 6: No Preference shall be given by any Regulation of Commerce or Revenue to the Ports of one State over those of another: nor shall Vessels bound to, or from, one State, be obliged to enter, clear, or pay Duties in another.

Clause 7: No Money shall be drawn from the Treasury, but in Consequence of Appropriations made by Law; and a regular Statement and Account of the Receipts and Expenditures of all public Money shall be published from time to time.

Clause 8: No Title of Nobility shall be granted by the United States: And no Person holding any Office of Profit or Trust under them, shall, without the Consent of the Congress, accept of any present, Emolument, Office, or Title, of any kind whatever, from any King, Prince, or foreign State.

Section 10

Clause 1: No State shall enter into any Treaty, Alliance, or Confederation; grant Letters of Marque and Reprisal; coin Money; emit Bills of Credit; make any Thing but gold and silver Coin a Tender in Payment of Debts; pass any Bill of Attainder, ex post facto Law, or Law impairing the Obligation of Contracts, or grant any Title of Nobility.

Clause 2: No State shall, without the Consent of the Congress, lay any Imposts or Duties on Imports or Exports, except what may be absolutely necessary for executing its inspection Laws: and the net Produce of all Duties and Imposts, laid by any State on Imports or Exports, shall be for the Use of the Treasury of the United States; and all such Laws shall be subject to the Revision and Controul of the Congress.

Clause 3: No State shall, without the Consent of Congress, lay any Duty of Tonnage, keep Troops, or Ships of War in time of Peace, enter into any Agreement or Compact with another State, or with a foreign Power, or engage in War, unless actually invaded, or in such imminent Danger as will not admit of delay.

Article II

Section 1

Clause 1: The executive Power shall be vested in a President of the United States of America. He shall hold his Office during the Term of four Years, and, together with the Vice President, chosen for the same Term, be elected, as follows

Clause 2: Each State shall appoint, in such Manner as the Legislature thereof may direct, a Number of Electors, equal to the whole Number of Senators and Representatives to which the State may be entitled in the Congress: but no Senator or Representative, or Person holding an Office of Trust or Profit under the United States, shall be appointed an Elector.

Clause 3: The Electors shall meet in their respective States, and vote by Ballot for two Persons, of whom one at least shall not be an Inhabitant of the same State with themselves. And they shall make a List of all the Persons voted for, and of the Number of Votes for each; which List they shall sign and certify, and transmit sealed to the Seat of the Government of the United States, directed to the President of the Senate. The President of the Senate shall, in the Presence of the Senate and House of Representatives, open all the Certificates, and the Votes shall then be counted. The Person having the greatest Number of Votes shall be the President, if such Number be a Majority of the whole Number of Electors appointed; and if there be more than one who have such Majority, and have an equal Number of Votes, then the House of Representatives shall immediately chuse by Ballot one of them for President; and if no Person have a Majority, then from the five highest on the List the said House shall in like Manner chuse the President. But in chusing the President,

the Votes shall be taken by States, the Representation from each State having one Vote; A quorum for this Purpose shall consist of a Member or Members from two thirds of the States, and a Majority of all the States shall be necessary to a Choice. In every Case, after the Choice of the President, the Person having the greatest Number of Votes of the Electors shall be the Vice President. But if there should remain two or more who have equal Votes, the Senate shall chuse from them by Ballot the Vice President.

Clause 4: The Congress may determine the Time of chusing the Electors, and the Day on which they shall give their Votes; which Day shall be the same throughout the United States.

Clause 5: No Person except a natural born Citizen, or a Citizen of the United States, at the time of the Adoption of this Constitution, shall be eligible to the Office of President; neither shall any Person be eligible to that Office who shall not have attained to the Age of thirty five Years, and been fourteen Years a Resident within the United States.

Clause 6: In Case of the Removal of the President from Office, or of his Death, Resignation, or Inability to discharge the Powers and Duties of the said Office, the Same shall devolve on the Vice-President, and the Congress may by Law provide for the Case of Removal, Death, Resignation or Inability, both of the President and Vice President, declaring what Officer shall then act as President, and such Officer shall act accordingly, until the Disability be removed, or a President shall be elected.

Clause 7: The President shall, at stated Times, receive for his Services, a Compensation, which shall neither be encreased nor diminished during the Period for which he shall have been elected, and he shall not receive within that Period any other Emolument from the United States, or any of them.

Clause 8: Before he enter on the Execution of his Office, he shall take the following Oath or Affirmation:—"I do solemnly swear (or affirm) that I will faithfully execute the Office of President of the United States, and will to the best of my Ability, preserve, protect and defend the Constitution of the United States."

Section 2

Clause 1: The President shall be Commander in Chief of the Army and Navy of the United States, and of the Militia of the several States, when called into the actual Service of the United States; he may require the Opinion, in writing, of the principal Officer in each of the executive Departments, upon any Subject relating to the Duties of their respective Offices, and he shall have Power to grant Reprieves and Pardons for Offences against the United States, except in Cases of Impeachment.

Clause 2: He shall have Power, by and with the Advice and Consent of the Senate, to make Treaties, provided two thirds of the Senators present concur; and he shall nominate, and by and with the Advice and Consent of the Senate, shall appoint Ambassadors, other public Ministers and Consuls, Judges of the supreme Court, and all other Officers of the United States, whose Appointments are not herein otherwise provided for, and which shall be established by Law: but the Congress may by Law vest the Appointment of such inferior Officers, as they think proper, in the President alone, in the Courts of Law, or in the Heads of Departments.

Clause 3: The President shall have Power to fill up all Vacancies that may happen during the Recess of the Senate, by granting Commissions which shall expire at the End of their next Session.

Section 3

He shall from time to time give to the Congress Information of the State of the Union, and recommend to their Consideration such Measures as he shall judge necessary and expedient; he may, on extraordinary Occasions, convene both Houses, or either of them, and in Case of Disagreement between them, with Respect to the Time of Adjournment, he may adjourn them to such Time as he shall think proper; he shall receive Ambassadors and other public Ministers; he shall take Care that the Laws be faithfully executed, and shall Commission all the Officers of the United States.

Section 4

The President, Vice President and all civil Officers of the United States, shall be removed from Office on Impeachment for, and Conviction of, Treason, Bribery, or other high Crimes and Misdemeanors.

Article III

Section 1

The judicial Power of the United States, shall be vested in one supreme Court, and in such inferior Courts as the Congress may from time to time ordain and establish. The Judges, both of the supreme and inferior Courts, shall hold their Offices during good Behaviour, and shall, at stated Times, receive for their Services, a Compensation, which shall not be diminished during their Continuance in Office.

Section 2

Clause 1: The judicial Power shall extend to all Cases, in Law and Equity, arising under this Constitution, the Laws of the United States, and Treaties made, or which shall be made, under their Authority;—to all Cases affecting Ambassadors, other public Ministers and Consuls;—to all Cases of admiralty and maritime Jurisdiction;—to Controversies to which the United States shall be a Party;—to Controversies between two or more States;—between a State and Citizens of another State;—between Citizens of different States,—between Citizens of the same State claiming Lands under Grants of different States, and between a State, or the Citizens thereof, and foreign States, Citizens or Subjects.

Clause 2: In all Cases affecting Ambassadors, other public Ministers and Consuls, and those in which a State shall be Party, the supreme Court shall have original Jurisdiction. In all the other Cases before mentioned, the supreme Court shall have appellate Jurisdiction, both as to Law and Fact, with such Exceptions, and under such Regulations as the Congress shall make.

Clause 3: The Trial of all Crimes, except in Cases of Impeachment, shall be by Jury; and such Trial shall be held in the State where the said Crimes shall have been committed; but when not committed within any State, the Trial shall be at such Place or Places as the Congress may by Law have directed.

Section 3

Clause 1: Treason against the United States, shall consist only in levying War against them, or in adhering to their Enemies, giving them Aid and Comfort. No Person shall be convicted of Treason unless on the Testimony of two Witnesses to the same overt Act, or on Confession in open Court.

Clause 2: The Congress shall have Power to declare the Punishment of Treason, but no Attainder of Treason shall work Corruption of Blood, or Forfeiture except during the Life of the Person attainted.

Article IV

Section 1

Full Faith and Credit shall be given in each State to the public Acts, Records, and judicial Proceedings of every other State. And the Congress may by general Laws prescribe the Manner in which such Acts, Records and Proceedings shall be proved, and the Effect thereof.

Section 2

Clause 1: The Citizens of each State shall be entitled to all Privileges and Immunities of Citizens in the several States.

Clause 2: A Person charged in any State with Treason, Felony, or other Crime, who shall flee from Justice, and be found in another State, shall on Demand of the executive Authority of the State from which he fled, be delivered up, to be removed to the State having Jurisdiction of the Crime.

Clause 3: No Person held to Service or Labour in one State, under the Laws thereof, escaping into another, shall, in Consequence of any Law or Regulation therein, be discharged from such Service or Labour, but shall be delivered up on Claim of the Party to whom such Service or Labour may be due.

Section 3

Clause 1: New States may be admitted by the Congress into this Union; but no new State shall be formed or erected within the

Jurisdiction of any other State; nor any State be formed by the Junction of two or more States, or Parts of States, without the Consent of the Legislatures of the States concerned as well as of the Congress.

Clause 2: The Congress shall have Power to dispose of and make all needful Rules and Regulations respecting the Territory or other Property belonging to the United States; and nothing in this Constitution shall be so construed as to Prejudice any Claims of the United States, or of any particular State.

Section 4

The United States shall guarantee to every State in this Union a Republican Form of Government, and shall protect each of them against Invasion; and on Application of the Legislature, or of the Executive (when the Legislature cannot be convened) against domestic Violence.

Article V

The Congress, whenever two thirds of both Houses shall deem it necessary, shall propose Amendments to this Constitution, or, on the Application of the Legislatures of two thirds of the several States, shall call a Convention for proposing Amendments, which, in either Case, shall be valid to all Intents and Purposes, as Part of this Constitution, when ratified by the Legislatures of three fourths of the several States, or by Conventions in three fourths thereof, as the one or the other Mode of Ratification may be proposed by the Congress; Provided that no Amendment which may be made prior to the Year One thousand eight hundred and eight shall in any Manner affect the first and fourth Clauses in the Ninth Section of the first Article; and that no State, without its Consent, shall be deprived of its equal Suffrage in the Senate.

Article VI

Clause 1: All Debts contracted and Engagements entered into, before the Adoption of this Constitution, shall be as valid against the United States under this Constitution, as under the Confederation.

Clause 2: This Constitution, and the Laws of the United States which shall be made in Pursuance thereof; and all Treaties made, or which shall be made, under the Authority of the United States, shall be the supreme Law of the Land; and the Judges in every State shall be bound thereby, any Thing in the Constitution or Laws of any State to the Contrary notwithstanding.

Clause 3: The Senators and Representatives before mentioned, and the Members of the several State Legislatures, and all executive and judicial Officers, both of the United States and of the several States, shall be bound by Oath or Affirmation, to support this Constitution; but no religious Test shall ever be required as a Qualification to any Office or public Trust under the United States.

Article VII

The Ratification of the Conventions of nine States, shall be sufficient for the Establishment of this Constitution between the States so ratifying the Same.

Amendment I (1791)

Congress shall make no law respecting an establishment of religion, or prohibiting the free exercise thereof; or abridging the freedom of speech, or of the press; or the right of the people peaceably to assemble, and to petition the government for a redress of grievances.

Amendment II (1791)

A well regulated militia, being necessary to the security of a free State, the right of the people to keep and bear arms, shall not be infringed.

Amendment III (1791)

No soldier shall, in time of peace be quartered in any house, without the consent of the Owner, nor in time of war, but in a manner to be prescribed by law.

Amendment IV (1791)

The right of the people to be secure in their persons, houses, papers, and effects, against unreasonable searches and seizures, shall not be violated, and no Warrants shall issue, but upon probable cause, supported by Oath or affirmation, and particularly describing the place to be searched, and the persons or things to be seized.

Amendment V (1791)

No person shall be held to answer for a capital, or otherwise infamous crime, unless on a presentment or indictment of a Grand Jury, except in cases arising in the land or naval forces, or in the Militia, when in actual service in time of War or public danger; nor shall any person be subject for the same offense to be twice put in jeopardy of life or limb; nor shall be compelled in any criminal case to be a witness against himself, nor be deprived of life, liberty, or property, without due process of law; nor shall private property be taken for public use, without just compensation.

Amendment VI (1791)

In all criminal prosecutions, the accused shall enjoy the right to a speedy and public trial, by an impartial jury of the state and district wherein the crime shall have been committed, which district shall have been previously ascertained by law, and to be informed of the nature and cause of the accusation; to be confronted with the witnesses against him; to have compulsory process for obtaining witnesses in his favor, and to have the Assistance of Counsel for his defense.

Amendment VII (1791)

In suits at common law, where the value in controversy shall exceed twenty dollars, the right of trial by jury shall be preserved, and no fact tried by a jury, shall be otherwise reexamined in any Court of the United States, than according to the rules of the common law.

Amendment VIII (1791)

Excessive bail shall not be required, nor excessive fines imposed, nor cruel and unusual punishments inflicted.

Amendment IX (1791)

The enumeration in the Constitution, of certain rights, shall not be construed to deny or disparage others retained by the people.

Amendment X (1791)

The powers not delegated to the United States by the Constitution, nor prohibited by it to the states, are reserved to the States respectively, or to the people.

Amendment XI (1795)

The Judicial power of the United States shall not be construed to extend to any suit in law or equity, commenced or prosecuted against one of the United States by Citizens of another State, or by Citizens or Subjects of any Foreign State.

Amendment XII (1804)

The Electors shall meet in their respective states and vote by ballot for President and Vice-President, one of whom, at least, shall not be an inhabitant of the same state with themselves; they shall name in their ballots the person voted for as President, and in distinct ballots the person voted for as Vice-President, and they shall make distinct lists of all persons voted for as President, and of all persons voted for as Vice-President, and of the number of votes for each, which lists they shall sign and certify, and transmit sealed to the seat of the government of the United States, directed to the President of the Senate;—The President of the Senate shall, in the presence of the Senate and House of Representatives, open all the certificates and the votes shall then be counted;—the person having the greatest number of votes for President, shall be the President, if such number be a majority of the whole number of Electors appointed; and if no person have such majority, then from the persons having the highest numbers not exceeding three on the list of those voted for as President,

the House of Representatives shall choose immediately, by ballot, the President. But in choosing the President, the votes shall be taken by states, the representation from each state having one vote; a quorum for this purpose shall consist of a member or members from two-thirds of the states, and a majority of all the states shall be necessary to a choice. And if the House of Representatives shall not choose a President whenever the right of choice shall devolve upon them, before the fourth day of March next following, then the Vice-President shall act as President, as in the case of the death or other constitutional disability of the President. The person having the greatest number of votes as Vice-President, shall be the Vice-President, if such number be a majority of the whole number of Electors appointed, and if no person have a majority, then from the two highest numbers on the list, the Senate shall choose the Vice-President; a quorum for the purpose shall consist of two-thirds of the whole number of Senators, and a majority of the whole number shall be necessary to a choice. But no person constitutionally ineligible to the office of President shall be eligible to that of Vice-President of the United States.

Amendment XIII (1865)

Section 1. Neither slavery nor involuntary servitude, except as a punishment for crime whereof the party shall have been duly convicted, shall exist within the United States, or any place subject to their jurisdiction.

Section 2. Congress shall have power to enforce this article by appropriate legislation.

Amendment XIV (1868)

Section 1. All persons born or naturalized in the United States, and subject to the jurisdiction thereof, are citizens of the United States and of the state wherein they reside. No state shall make or enforce any law which shall abridge the privileges or immunities of citizens of the United States; nor shall any state deprive any person of life, liberty, or property, without due process of law; nor deny to any person within its jurisdiction the equal protection of the laws.

Section 2. Representatives shall be apportioned among the several states according to their respective numbers, counting the whole number of persons in each state, excluding Indians not taxed. But when the right to vote at any election for the choice of electors for President and Vice President of the United States, Representatives in Congress, the executive and judicial officers of a state, or the members of the legislature thereof, is denied to any of the male inhabitants of such state, being twenty-one years of age, and citizens of the United States, or in any way abridged, except for participation in rebellion, or other crime, the basis of representation therein shall be reduced in the proportion which the number of such male citizens shall bear to the whole number of male citizens twenty-one years of age in such state.

Section 3. No person shall be a Senator or Representative in Congress, or elector of President and Vice President, or hold any office, civil or military, under the United States, or under any state, who, having previously taken an oath, as a member of Congress, or as an officer of the United States, or as a member of any state legislature, or as an executive or judicial officer of any state, to support the Constitution of the United States, shall have engaged in insurrection or rebellion against the same, or given aid or comfort to the enemies thereof. But Congress may by a vote of two-thirds of each House, remove such disability.

Section 4. The validity of the public debt of the United States, authorized by law, including debts incurred for payment of pensions and bounties for services in suppressing insurrection or rebellion, shall not be questioned. But neither the United States nor any state shall assume or pay any debt or obligation incurred in aid of insurrection or rebellion against the United States, or any claim for the loss or emancipation of any slave; but all such debts, obligations and claims shall be held illegal and void.

Section 5. The Congress shall have power to enforce, by appropriate legislation, the provisions of this article.

Amendment XV (1870)

Section 1. The right of citizens of the United States to vote shall not be denied or abridged by the United States or by any state on account of race, color, or previous condition of servitude.

Section 2. The Congress shall have power to enforce this article by appropriate legislation.

Amendment XVI (1913)

The Congress shall have power to lay and collect taxes on incomes, from whatever source derived, without apportionment among the several states, and without regard to any census of enumeration.

Amendment XVII (1913)

The Senate of the United States shall be composed of two Senators from each state, elected by the people thereof, for six years; and each Senator shall have one vote. The electors in each state shall have the qualifications requisite for electors of the most numerous branch of the state legislatures.

When vacancies happen in the representation of any state in the Senate, the executive authority of such state shall issue writs of election to fill such vacancies: *Provided,* that the legislature of any State may empower the executive thereof to make temporary appointments until the people fill the vacancies by election as the legislature may direct.

This amendment shall not be so construed as to affect the election or term of any Senator chosen before it becomes valid as part of the Constitution.

Amendment XVIII (1919)

Section 1. After one year from the ratification of this article the manufacture, sale, or transportation of intoxicating liquors within, the importation thereof into, or the exportation thereof from the United States and all territory subject to the jurisdiction thereof for beverage purposes is hereby prohibited.

Section 2. The Congress and the several states shall have concurrent power to enforce this article by appropriate legislation.

Section 3. This article shall be inoperative unless it shall have been ratified as an amendment to the Constitution by the legislatures of the several states, as provided in the Constitution, within seven years from the date of the submission hereof to the states by the Congress.

Amendment XIX (1920)

The right of citizens of the United States to vote shall not be denied or abridged by the United States or by any state on account of sex.

Section 2. The Congress shall have power to enforce this article by appropriate legislation.

Amendment XX (1933)

Section 1. The terms of the President and Vice President shall end at noon on the 20th day of January, and the terms of Senators and Representatives at noon on the 3d day of January, of the years in which such terms would have ended if this article had not been ratified; and the terms of their successors shall then begin.

Section 2. The Congress shall assemble at least once in every year, and such meeting shall begin at noon on the 3d day of January, unless they shall by law appoint a different day.

Section 3. If, at the time fixed for the beginning of the term of the President, the President elect shall have died, the Vice President elect shall become President. If a President shall not have been chosen before the time fixed for the beginning of his term, or if the President elect shall have failed to qualify, then the Vice President elect shall act as President until a President shall have qualified; and the Congress may by law provide for the case wherein neither a President elect nor a Vice President elect shall have qualified, declaring who shall then act as President, or the manner in which one who is to act shall be selected, and such person shall act accordingly until a President or Vice President shall have qualified.

Section 4. The Congress may by law provide for the case of the death of any of the persons from whom the House of Representatives may choose a President whenever the right of choice shall have devolved upon them, and for the case of the death of any of the persons from whom the Senate may choose a Vice President whenever the right of choice shall have devolved upon them.

Section 5. Sections 1 and 2 shall take effect on the 15th day of October following the ratification of this article.

Section 6. This article shall be inoperative unless it shall have been ratified as an amendment to the Constitution by the legislatures of three-fourths of the several states within seven years from the date of its submission.

Amendment XXI (1933)

Section 1. The eighteenth article of amendment to the Constitution of the United States is hereby repealed.

Section 2. The transportation or importation into any state, territory, or possession of the United States for delivery or use therein of intoxicating liquors, in violation of the laws thereof, is hereby prohibited.

Section 3. This article shall be inoperative unless it shall have been ratified as an amendment to the Constitution by conventions in the several states, as provided in the Constitution, within seven years from the date of the submission hereof to the states by the Congress.

Amendment XXII (1951)

Section 1. No person shall be elected to the office of the President more than twice, and no person who has held the office of President, or acted as President, for more than two years of a term to which some other person was elected President shall be elected to the office of the President more than once. But this article shall not apply to any person holding the office of President when this article was proposed by the Congress, and shall not prevent any person who may be holding the office of President, or acting as President, during the term within which this article becomes operative from holding the office of President or acting as President during the remainder of such term.

Section 2. This article shall be inoperative unless it shall have been ratified as an amendment to the Constitution by the legislatures of three-fourths of the several states within seven years from the date of its submission to the states by the Congress.

Amendment XXIII (1961)

Section 1. The District constituting the seat of government of the United States shall appoint in such manner as the Congress may direct:

A number of electors of President and Vice President equal to the whole number of Senators and Representatives in Congress to which the District would be entitled if it were a state, but in no event more than the least populous state; they shall be in addition to those appointed by the states, but they shall be considered, for the purposes of the election of President and Vice President, to be electors appointed by a state; and they shall meet in the District and perform such duties as provided by the twelfth article of amendment.

Section 2. The Congress shall have power to enforce this article by appropriate legislation.

Amendment XXIV (1964)

Section 1. The right of citizens of the United States to vote in any primary or other election for President or Vice President, for electors for President or Vice President, or for Senator or Representative in Congress, shall not be denied or abridged by the United States or any state by reason of failure to pay any poll tax or other tax.

Section 2. The Congress shall have power to enforce this article by appropriate legislation.

Amendment XXV (1967)

Section 1. In case of the removal of the President from office or of his death or resignation, the Vice President shall become President.

Section 2. Whenever there is a vacancy in the office of the Vice President, the President shall nominate a Vice President who shall take office upon confirmation by a majority vote of both Houses of Congress.

Section 3. Whenever the President transmits to the President pro tempore of the Senate and the Speaker of the House of Representatives his written declaration that he is unable to discharge the powers and duties of his office, and until he transmits to them a written declaration to the contrary, such powers and duties shall be discharged by the Vice President as Acting President.

Section 4. Whenever the Vice President and a majority of either the principal officers of the executive departments or of such other body as Congress may by law provide, transmit to the President pro tempore of the Senate and the Speaker of the House of Representatives their written declaration that the President is unable to discharge the powers and duties of his office, the Vice President shall immediately assume the powers and duties of the office as Acting President.

Thereafter, when the President transmits to the President pro tempore of the Senate and the Speaker of the House of Representatives his written declaration that no inability exists, he shall resume the powers and duties of his office unless the Vice President and a majority of either the principal officers of the executive department or of such other body as Congress may by law provide, transmit within four days to the President pro tempore of the Senate and the Speaker of the House of Representatives their written declaration that the President is unable to discharge the powers and duties of his office. Thereupon Congress shall decide the issue, assembling within forty-eight hours for that purpose if not in session. If the Congress, within twenty-one days after receipt of the latter written declaration, or, if Congress is not in session, within twenty-one days after Congress is required to assemble, determines by two-thirds vote of both Houses that the President is unable to discharge the powers and duties of his office, the Vice President shall continue to discharge the same as Acting President; otherwise, the President shall resume the powers and duties of his office.

Amendment XXVI (1971)

Section 1. The right of citizens of the United States, who are 18 years of age or older, to vote, shall not be denied or abridged by the United States or any state on account of age.

Section 2. The Congress shall have the power to enforce this article by appropriate legislation.

Amendment XXVII (1992)*

No law, varying the compensation for services of the Senators and Representatives, shall take effect, until an election of Representatives shall have intervened.

---

*This Amendment was proposed in 1789 as one of the original Bill of Rights. It was not until 1992 that the requisite number of states had ratified the proposal under Article V. In May 1992 the Archivist of the United States certified to Congress that the Amendment had been ratified, notwithstanding serious doubts about the validity of the ratification process and the passage of two centuries between proposal and adoption.

First Inaugural Address

Abraham Lincoln

Fellow citizens of the United States: in compliance with a custom as old as the government itself, I appear before you to address you briefly and to take, in your presence, the oath prescribed by the Constitution of the United States, to be taken by the President "before he enters on the execution of his office."

I do not consider it necessary, at present, for me to discuss those matters of administration about which there is no special anxiety, or excitement.

Apprehension seems to exist among the people of the Southern States that by the accession of a Republican administration their property and their peace and personal security are to be endangered. There has never been any reasonable cause for such apprehension. Indeed, the most ample evidence to the contrary has all the while existed and been open to their inspection. It is found in nearly all the published speeches of him who now addresses you. I do but quote from one of those speeches when I declare that "I have no purpose, directly or indirectly, to interfere with the institution of slavery where it exists. I believe I have no lawful right to do so, and I have no inclination to do so." Those who nominated and elected me did so with full knowledge that I had made this and many similar declarations, and had never recanted them. And, more than this, they placed in the platform for my acceptance, and as a law to themselves and to me, the clear and emphatic resolution which I now read:

> *Resolved: that the maintenance inviolate of the rights of the States, and especially the right of each State to order and control its own domestic institutions according to its own judgment exclusively, is essential to that balance of power on which the perfection and endurance of our political fabric depend, and we denounce the lawless invasion by armed force of the soil of any State or Territory, no matter under what pretext, as among the gravest of crimes.*

I now reiterate these sentiments; and, in doing so, I only press upon the public attention the most conclusive evidence of which the case is susceptible, that the property, peace, and security of no section are to be in any wise endangered by the now incoming administration. I add, too, that all the protection which, consistently with the Constitution and the laws, can be given, will be cheerfully given to all the States when lawfully demanded, for whatever cause—as cheerfully to one section as to another.

There is much controversy about the delivering up of fugitives from service or labor. The clause I now read is as plainly written in the Constitution as any other of its provisions:

> *No person held to service or labor in one State, under the laws thereof, escaping into another, shall in consequence of any law or regulation therein be discharged from such service or labor, but shall be delivered up on claim of the party to whom such service or labor may be due.*

It is scarcely questioned that this provision was intended by those who made it for the reclaiming of what we call fugitive slaves; and the intention of the lawgiver is the law. All members of Congress swear their support to the whole Constitution—to this provision as much as to any other. To the proposition, then, that slaves whose cases come within the terms of this clause "shall be delivered up," their oaths are unanimous. Now, if they would make the effort in good temper, could they not with nearly equal unanimity frame and pass a law by means of which to keep good that unanimous oath?

There is some difference of opinion whether this clause should be enforced by national or by State authority; but surely that difference is not a very material one. If the slave is to be surrendered, it can be of but little consequence to him or to others by which authority it is done. And should any one in any case be content that his oath shall go unkept on a merely unsubstantial controversy as to HOW it shall be kept? Again, in any law upon this subject, ought not all the safeguards of liberty known in civilized and humane jurisprudence to be introduced, so that a free man be not, in any case, surrendered as a slave? And might it not be well at the same time to provide by law for the enforcement of that clause in the Constitution which guarantees that "the citizen of each State shall be entitled to all privileged and immunities of citizens in the several States?"

I take the official oath today with no mental reservations, and with no purpose to construe the Constitution or laws by any hypercritical rules. And while I do not choose now to specify particular acts of Congress as proper to be enforced, I do suggest that it will be much safer for all, both in official and private stations, to conform to and abide by all those acts which stand unrepealed, than to violate any of them, trusting to find impunity in having them held to be unConstitutional.

It is seventy-two years since the first inauguration of a President under our national Constitution. During that period fifteen different and greatly distinguished citizens have, in succession, administered the executive branch of the government. They have conducted it through many perils, and generally with great success. Yet, with all this scope of precedent, I now enter upon the same task for the brief Constitutional term of four years under great and peculiar difficulty. A disruption of the Federal Union, heretofore only menaced, is now formidably attempted.

I hold that, in contemplation of universal law and of the Constitution, the Union of these States is perpetual. Perpetuity is implied, if not expressed, in the fundamental law of all national governments. It is safe to assert that no government proper ever had a provision in its organic law for its own termination. Continue to execute all the express provisions of our National Constitution, and the Union will endure forever—it being impossible to destroy it except by some action not provided for in the instrument itself.

Again, if the United States be not a government proper, but an association of States in the nature of contract merely, can it, as a contract, be peaceably unmade by less than all the parties who made it? One party to a contract may violate it—break it, so to speak; but does it not require all to lawfully rescind it?

Descending from these general principles, we find the proposition that in legal contemplation the Union is perpetual confirmed by the history of the Union itself. The Union is much older than the Constitution. It was formed, in fact, by the Articles of Association in 1774. It was matured and continued by the Declaration of Independence in 1776. It was further matured, and the faith of all the then thirteen States expressly plighted and engaged that it should be perpetual, by the Articles of Confederation in 1778. And, finally, in 1787 one of the declared objects for ordaining and establishing the Constitution was "TO FORM A MORE PERFECT UNION."

But if the destruction of the Union by one or by a part only of the States be lawfully possible, the Union is LESS perfect than before the Constitution, having lost the vital element of perpetuity.

It follows from these views that no State upon its own mere motion can lawfully get out of the Union; that Resolves and Ordinances to that effect are legally void; and that acts of violence, within any State or States, against the authority of the United States, are insurrectionary or revolutionary, according to circumstances.

I therefore consider that, in view of the Constitution and the laws, the Union is unbroken; and to the extent of my ability I shall take care, as the Constitution itself expressly enjoins upon me, that the laws of the Union be faithfully executed in all the States. Doing this I deem to be only a simple duty on my part; and I shall perform it so far as practicable, unless my rightful masters, the American people, shall withhold the requisite means, or in some authoritative manner direct the contrary. I trust this will not be regarded as a menace, but only as the declared purpose of the Union that it WILL Constitutionally defend and maintain itself.

In doing this there needs to be no bloodshed or violence; and there shall be none, unless it be forced upon the national authority. The power confided to me will be used to hold, occupy, and possess the property and places belonging to the government, and to collect the duties and imposts; but beyond what may be necessary for these objects, there will be no invasion, no using of force against or among the people anywhere. Where hostility to the United States, in any interior locality, shall be so great and universal as to prevent competent resident citizens from holding the Federal offices, there will be no attempt to force obnoxious strangers among the people for that object. While the strict legal right may exist in the government to enforce the exercise of these offices, the attempt to do so would be so irritating, and so nearly impracticable withal, that I deem it better to forego for the time the uses of such offices.

The mails, unless repelled, will continue to be furnished in all parts of the Union. So far as possible, the people everywhere shall have that sense of perfect security which is most favorable to calm thought and reflection. The course here indicated will be followed unless current events and experience shall show a modification or change to be proper, and in every case and exigency my best discretion will be exercised according to circumstances actually existing, and with a view and a hope of a peaceful solution of the national troubles and the restoration of fraternal sympathies and affections.

That there are persons in one section or another who seek to destroy the Union at all events, and are glad of any pretext to do it, I will neither affirm nor deny; but if there be such, I need address no word to them. To those, however, who really love the Union may I not speak?

Before entering upon so grave a matter as the destruction of our national fabric, with all its benefits, its memories, and its hopes, would it not be wise to ascertain precisely why we do it? Will you hazard so desperate a step while there is any possibility that any portion of the ills you fly from have no real existence? Will you, while the certain ills you fly to are greater than all the real ones you fly from—will you risk the commission of so fearful a mistake?

All profess to be content in the Union if all Constitutional rights can be maintained. Is it true, then, that any right, plainly written in the Constitution, has been denied? I think not. Happily the human mind is so constituted that no party can reach to the audacity of doing this. Think, if you can, of a single instance in which a plainly written provision of the Constitution has ever been denied. If by the mere force of numbers a majority should deprive a minority of any clearly written Constitutional right, it might, in a moral point of view, justify revolution—certainly would if such a right were a vital one. But such is not our case. All the vital rights of minorities and of individuals are so plainly assured to them by affirmations and negations, guaranties and prohibitions, in the Constitution, that controversies never arise concerning them. But no organic law can ever be framed with a provision specifically applicable to every question which may occur in practical administration. No foresight can anticipate, nor any document of reasonable length contain, express provisions for all possible questions. Shall fugitives from labor be surrendered by national or State authority? The Constitution does not expressly say. May Congress prohibit slavery in the Territories? The Constitution does not expressly say. MUST Congress protect slavery in the Territories? The Constitution does not expressly say.

From questions of this class spring all our constitutional controversies, and we divide upon them into majorities and minorities. If the minority will not acquiesce, the majority must, or the government must cease. There is no other alternative; for continuing the government is acquiescence on one side or the other.

If a minority in such case will secede rather than acquiesce, they make a precedent which in turn will divide and ruin them; for a minority of their own will secede from them whenever a majority refuses to be controlled by such minority. For instance, why may not any portion of a new confederacy a year or two hence arbitrarily secede again, precisely as portions of the present Union now claim to secede from it? All who cherish disunion sentiments are now being educated to the exact temper of doing this.

Is there such perfect identity of interests among the States to compose a new Union, as to produce harmony only, and prevent renewed secession?

Plainly, the central idea of secession is the essence of anarchy. A majority held in restraint by constitutional checks and limitations, and always changing easily with deliberate changes of popular opinions and sentiments, is the only true sovereign of a free people. Whoever rejects it does, of necessity, fly to anarchy or to despotism. Unanimity is impossible; the rule of a minority, as a

permanent arrangement, is wholly inadmissible; so that, rejecting the majority principle, anarchy or despotism in some form is all that is left.

I do not forget the position, assumed by some, that Constitutional questions are to be decided by the Supreme Court; nor do I deny that such decisions must be binding, in any case, upon the parties to a suit, as to the object of that suit, while they are also entitled to very high respect and consideration in all parallel cases by all other departments of the government. And while it is obviously possible that such decision may be erroneous in any given case, still the evil effect following it, being limited to that particular case, with the chance that it may be overruled and never become a precedent for other cases, can better be borne than could the evils of a different practice. At the same time, the candid citizen must confess that if the policy of the government, upon vital questions affecting the whole people, is to be irrevocably fixed by decisions of the Supreme Court, the instant they are made, in ordinary litigation between parties in personal actions, the people will have ceased to be their own rulers, having to that extent practically resigned their government into the hands of that eminent tribunal. Nor is there in this view any assault upon the court or the judges. It is a duty from which they may not shrink to decide cases properly brought before them, and it is no fault of theirs if others seek to turn their decisions to political purposes.

One section of our country believes slavery is RIGHT, and ought to be extended, while the other believes it is WRONG, and ought not to be extended. This is the only substantial dispute. The fugitive-slave clause of the Constitution, and the law for the suppression of the foreign slave-trade, are each as well enforced, perhaps, as any law can ever be in a community where the moral sense of the people imperfectly supports the law itself. The great body of the people abide by the dry legal obligation in both cases, and a few break over in each. This, I think, cannot be perfectly cured; and it would be worse in both cases AFTER the separation of the sections than BEFORE. The foreign slave-trade, now imperfectly suppressed, would be ultimately revived, without restriction, in one section, while fugitive slaves, now only partially surrendered, would not be surrendered at all by the other.

Physically speaking, we cannot separate. We cannot remove our respective sections from each other, nor build an impassable wall between them. A husband and wife may be divorced, and go out of the presence and beyond the reach of each other; but the different parts of our country cannot do this. They cannot but remain face to face, and intercourse, either amicable or hostile, must continue between them. Is it possible, then, to make that intercourse more advantageous or more satisfactory after separation than before? Can aliens make treaties easier than friends can make laws? Can treaties be more faithfully enforced between aliens than laws can among friends? Suppose you go to war, you cannot fight always; and when, after much loss on both sides, and no gain on either, you cease fighting, the identical old questions as to terms of intercourse are again upon you.

This country, with its institutions, belongs to the people who inhabit it. Whenever they shall grow weary of the existing government, they can exercise their CONSTITUTIONAL right of amending it, or their REVOLUTIONARY right to dismember or overthrow it. I cannot be ignorant of the fact that many worthy and patriotic citizens are desirous of having the national Constitution amended. While I make no recommendation of amendments, I fully recognize the rightful authority of the people over the whole subject, to be exercised in either of the modes prescribed in the instrument itself; and I should, under existing circumstances, favor rather than oppose a fair opportunity being afforded the people to act upon it. I will venture to add that to me the convention mode seems preferable, in that it allows amendments to originate with the people themselves, instead of only permitting them to take or reject propositions originated by others not especially chosen for the purpose, and which might not be precisely such as they would wish to either accept or refuse. I understand a proposed amendment to the Constitution—which amendment, however, I have not seen—has passed Congress, to the effect that the Federal Government shall never interfere with the domestic institutions of the States, including that of persons held to service. To avoid misconstruction of what I have said, I depart from my purpose not to speak of particular amendments so far as to say that, holding such a provision to now be implied Constitutional law, I have no objection to its being made express and irrevocable.

The chief magistrate derives all his authority from the people, and they have conferred none upon him to fix terms for the separation of the states. The people themselves can do this also if they choose; but the executive, as such, has nothing to do with it. His duty is to administer the present government, as it came to his hands, and to transmit it, unimpaired by him, to his successor.

Why should there not be a patient confidence in the ultimate justice of the people? Is there any better or equal hope in the world? In our present differences is either party without faith of being in the right? If the Almighty Ruler of Nations, with his eternal truth and justice, be on your side of the North, or on yours of the South, that truth and that justice will surely prevail, by the judgment of this great tribunal, the American people.

By the frame of the government under which we live, this same people have wisely given their public servants but little power for mischief; and have, with equal wisdom, provided for the return of that little to their own hands at very short intervals. While the people retain their virtue and vigilance, no administration, by any extreme of wickedness or folly, can very seriously injure the government in the short space of four years.

My countrymen, one and all, think calmly and WELL upon this whole subject. Nothing valuable can be lost by taking time. If there be an object to HURRY any of you in hot haste to a step which you would never take DELIBERATELY, that object will be frustrated by taking time; but no good object can be frustrated by it. Such of you as are now dissatisfied, still have the old Constitution unimpaired, and, on the sensitive point, the laws of your own framing under it; while the new administration will have no immediate power, if it would, to change either. If it were admitted that you who are dissatisfied hold the right side in the dispute, there still is no single good reason for precipitate action. Intelligence, patriotism, Christianity, and a firm reliance on him who has never yet forsaken this favored land, are still competent to adjust in the best way all our present difficulty.

In YOUR hands, my dissatisfied fellow-countrymen, and not in MINE, is the momentous issue of civil war. The government will not assail YOU. You can have no conflict without being yourselves the aggressors. YOU have no oath registered in heaven to destroy the government, while I shall have the most solemn one to "preserve, protect, and defend it."

I am loathe to close. We are not enemies, but friends. We must not be enemies. Though passion may have strained, it must not break our bonds of affection. The mystic chords of memory, stretching from every battlefield and patriot grave to every living heart and hearthstone all over this broad land, will yet swell the chorus of the Union when again touched, as surely they will be, by the better angels of our nature.

Appendix D

The Gettysburg Address

Abraham Lincoln

Fourscore and seven years ago our Fathers brought forth on this continent, a new nation, conceived in Liberty and dedicated to the proposition that all men are created equal.

Now we are engaged in a great civil war, testing whether that nation or any nation so conceived and so dedicated, can long endure. We are met on a great battlefield of that war. We have come to dedicate a portion of that field as a final resting place for those who here gave their lives that that nation might live. It is altogether fitting and proper that we should do this.

But, in a larger sense, we cannot dedicate—we cannot consecrate—we cannot hallow this ground. The brave men, living and dead, who struggled here, have consecrated it far above our poor power to add or detract. The world will little note, nor long remember, what we say here, but it can never forget what they did here. It is for us the living, rather, to be dedicated here to the unfinished work which they who fought here have thus far so nobly advanced. It is rather for us to be here dedicated to the great task remaining before us—that from these honored dead we take increased devotion to that cause for which they gave the last full measure of devotion—that we here highly resolve that these dead shall not have died in vain—that this nation under God shall have a new birth of freedom—and that government of the people, by the people, for the people shall not perish from the earth.

Understanding Supreme Court Opinions

Constitutional interpretation is not and should not be solely the province of judges. The task of ensuring fidelity to the values of the Constitution is one all governmental officials and citizens must share, a point underscored by Justice Frankfurter's dissent in *West Virginia v. Barnette* (1943). "Reliance for the most precious interests of civilization," he reminded us, "must be found outside of their vindication in courts of law. Only a persistent positive translation of the faith of a free society into the convictions and habits of actions of a community is the ultimate reliance against unabated temptations to fetter the human spirit."

Any citizen of the Constitution, therefore, must have some basic understanding of its rules, principles, and commitments. Judicial opinions construing the Constitution are an obvious and critically important source for learning about those commitments. Unfortunately, their odd form and peculiar cant may make them seem inaccessible to many students.[1] Our experience in teaching these materials has taught us that students may come to understand Supreme Court opinions more quickly and with somewhat less pain if they use some of the following tools.

How to Read an Opinion

A judicial opinion is an act both of explanation and of persuasion. Most opinions purport to explain how the judge or judges arrived at their decision, usually by tracing a series of questions, answers, and arguments from a set beginning to a seemingly inevitable end. In this sense, a judicial opinion helps to assure the accountability of power—a fundamental constitutional imperative—by declaring in public the reasons why a case has been decided in a particular way. An opinion is also an exercise in

persuasion. Difficult cases, at least, often admit of more than one solution; and, any judge who fails to say why his or her solution is preferable to another, no less obvious solution, is a judge who has failed to understand the difference between judicial *power*, or the capacity to reach a decision, and judicial *authority*, or when it is constitutionally appropriate to reach a decision. The latter requires an understanding of the proper nature and limits of judicial power in a constitutional democracy and why a judge has an obligation to tell us why—to persuade us—his or her solution is superior.

The twin purposes of explanation and persuasion suggest that when we read opinions we should remember that they often have more than one purpose—sometimes to settle a contested point of law, sometimes to teach, and sometimes to preach—and more than one audience—sometimes the litigants alone, sometimes the legal academy, and sometimes the entire polity. As you read the opinions, you will also find it helpful to assess them in light of the three themes—interpretive, normative, and comparative—we identified in the introduction. Every opinion, for example, adopts one or more methods of constitutional interpretation. Similarly, in every opinion the justices wrestle—sometimes explicitly, sometimes not—with the political theory and ideals that inform the Constitution and give it meaning.

In every case, then, students should read for the following information:

1. Legal Doctrine. What question of law does the case raise? How do the judges or justices answer that question? What doctrines of law do they utilize or formulate? Does their answer conform to existing legal doctrine or does it change it?
2. Institutional Role. Almost every constitutional case decided by the Supreme Court involves some question about the proper role of the Court in the political process. What understanding of judicial power does the majority embrace? Does the opinion envision a broad or a narrow role for the power of judges? Does that vision rest upon a particular understanding of democratic theory and of the authority of the community to govern

---

[1] Lawrence M. Solan, *The Language of Judges.* (Chicago: University of Chicago Press, 1993); Joseph Goldstein, *The Intelligible Constitution: The Supreme Court's Obligation to Maintain the Constitution as Something We the People Can Understand* (New York: Oxford University Press, 1992).

itself through the means of majoritarian politics? Does it rest upon a particular view about when judges should protect individual liberty from regulation by a majority?

3. Method and Strategies of Constitutional Interpretation. Translating the "majestic generalities" of the Constitution into a practical instrument of governance requires interpretation. What methods and strategies of interpretation do the judges employ? Do they explicitly acknowledge their choices? Do they justify them? What sorts of justifications and evidence does the opinion marshal to support its argument?

4. Commentary on the American Polity. We wrote in the introduction that a course on constitutional law should be a "commentary on the meaning of America." Judicial opinions can be a rich source for such commentary. As you read them, consider what an opinion says about American history, about contemporary politics, about political theory, and about the success or failure of the American experiment.

How to Brief a Case

Seemingly endless generations of first-year law students have spent hours learning the law by "briefing cases." Some of us harbored doubts about the practice and gave it up as soon as we could, but case briefs *can* be an excellent tool for learning how to read judicial opinions. A good brief can help students to focus on what is essential in a case and what is frill. Moreover, a brief can be a useful study tool at the end of semester, when there may be a hundred or more cases to review for a final exam.

A case brief is essentially a short summary, no more than a page or two, of the main features of a case. A typical brief follows a format similar to this:

1. *The Facts.* In the United States the Supreme Court does not decide hypothetical cases or cases that are not ripe. Every case therefore rises in a particular factual context. The facts may or may not have a substantial influence on how the Court decides the case. The facts themselves are sometimes subject to interpretation and a source of disagreement among the justices. The facts should include the statute or policy challenged and the various constitutional provisions implicated in the case.

2. *The Question Presented.* What question of constitutional law does the case present? Frequently a case involves several constitutional provisions and consequently several constitutional questions for resolution. We find it most useful to try to pose the questions in a format that yields a "yes-no" response.

3. *The Holding.* How does the Court answer the questions? Usually the response is contained in the majority opinion, but not infrequently the decisive holding must be constructed through a reading of several different opinions in the case.

4. *The Rationale.* This is a summary and analysis of the reasoning and evidence the Court uses in its decision. What strategies and methods of interpretation does the opinion employ? What kinds of evidence does it muster on behalf of its argument? What are the implications of the opinion for future

cases? How does the Court describe its role in the political process?

5. *Concurring and Dissenting Opinions.* This should also contain a summary and analysis of the various opinions. In what precise ways do the concurring or dissenting opinions agree with or differ from the majority opinion?

6. *Significance of the Case.* Why is the case important? What general principles of constitutional law does this case create, reaffirm, or reject? Students may find it helpful here to consider again the questions we focused upon in "How to Read an Opinion" above. What does this case tell us about the Constitution? What does it tell us about the American polity?

Sample Brief:
Bowers v. Hardwick (1986)

Bowers v. Hardwick
478 U.S. 186, 106 S. Ct. 2841, 92 L. Ed. 2d 140 (1986)

(1) Facts of the Case. Hardwick committed consensual sodomy with another man in private. He was arrested for violating a Georgia law prohibiting sodomy. The law carried a prison term of no less than one year and no more than twenty years. Hardwick challenged the law, claiming it violated his constitutional rights to privacy, expression and association. The federal district court rejected his claim, but the circuit court reversed, finding that Georgia's statute violated Hardwick's rights to private and intimate association. The state appealed to the United States Supreme Court.

(2) The Question Presented.
　　a. Does a statute criminalizing sodomy between consenting adults violate the right to privacy, as protected by the due process clause of the Fourteenth Amendment?
　　b. Does the statute violate the freedom of intimate expression in one's home, as protected by the First Amendment?

(3) The Holding.
　　a. No. The right to privacy does not include a "fundamental right . . . to engage in sodomy. . . ."
　　b. No. The right to intimate expression in one's home does not always make "otherwise illegal conduct" immune from regulation.

(4) The Rationale. (*White*) Nothing in the constitutional text authorizes an individual to commit sodomy. In addition, the Court's prior cases involving a right to privacy involve matters of family, marriage, and procreation. They do not extend to homosexual activity. Moreover, they make clear that private conduct is protected only when the interest or conduct "are implicit in the concept of ordered liberty" (*Palko*) or "deeply rooted in this Nation's history and tradition" (*Moore.*) Protection for homosexual sodomy does not satisfy these criteria; indeed, history and tradition show that sodomy has long been proscribed by the states. Consequently, the Court should be wary of creating a new fundamental right in their absence. Thus, there is no fundamental right to homosexual sodomy. The state must still advance a rational basis

for the proscription of such conduct. Here, the state's rational basis is the protection of majoritarian moral preferences.

(5) Concurring and Dissenting opinions.

    a. Justice Burger, concurring: Proscriptions against sodomy have ancient roots and the state's ban against sodomy is supported by "a millennia of moral teaching. . . ."

    b. Justice Powell, concurring: If he had been convicted, Hardwick might have been imprisoned for twenty years. This might violate the cruel and unusual punishment clause of the Eighth Amendment.

    c. Justice Blackmun, dissenting: This case does not involve a right to homosexual sodomy, but instead whether individuals have a "right to decide for themselves whether to engage in particular forms of private, consensual sexual activity." Prior cases stand for the proposition that individuals have a right to privacy because it forms a central part of an individual's life. Hence the state may interfere with that right only when it has a compelling reason. The protection of a community's shared moral sense is not compelling because there "is no real interference with the rights of others. . . ."

    d. Justice Stevens, dissenting: The Georgia statute applies to heterosexual and homosexual activity alike. Prior cases make it clear that the state may not without a compelling reason interfere with the sexual conduct of unmarried heterosexual adults (*Eisenstadt*). Moreover, Georgia has advanced no interest in selecting out homosexual activity except "habitual dislike for, or ignorance about, the disfavored group."

(6) Significance of the case. *Bowers* is important for several reasons. First, the majority opinion restates the criteria for determining what kinds of activity will be protected by the right to privacy. Second, its reassertion of those criteria is directly related to a specific understanding of the limits of judicial power in a democracy. The majority believes that the Court should not set aside majoritarian preferences absent a clear constitutional warrant for doing so. Similarly, the majority's use of precedent and appeals to history and tradition are informed by this understanding of judicial power. The dissenting opinions embrace a more expansive view of judicial power. Consequently, although they adopt similar methods of interpretation, they reach a different result from the majority. Finally, this case reflects the politics of sexuality and its prominence in the political and cultural life of the nation.

Selected Bibliography

Atiyah, P. S. and Robert S. Summers. *Form and Substance in Anglo-American Law: A Comparative Study of Legal Reasoning, Legal Theory, and Legal Institutions.* (Oxford: Clarendon Press, 1987).

Carter, Lief. *An Introduction to Constitutional Interpretation: Cases in Law and Religion.* (White Plains, N.Y.: Longman, 1991).

Goldstein, Joseph. *The Intelligible Constitution: The Supreme Court's Obligation to Maintain the Constitution as Something We the People Can Understand* (New York: Oxford University Press, 1992).

Levi, Edward H. *An Introduction to Legal Reasoning.* (Chicago: University of Chicago Press, 1948).

Van Geel, T.R. *Understanding Supreme Court Opinions.* 3d ed. (White Plains, N.Y.: Longman, 1991).

Glossary of Terms

abstention: A doctrine that holds that federal courts should not decide issues involving the interpretation of state law until the state's highest court has issued a decision on the question.

acquittal: A finding that a criminal defendant is not guilty.

admiralty: A law or court that pertains to the law of the sea and maritime concerns.

advisory opinion: An opinion by a court issued in a hypothetical or nonadversarial context, or in the absence of a concrete case or controversy.

affidavit: A written statement of facts made before a notary public or similar officer.

affirm: A decision by an appellate court to uphold or confirm a decision by a lower court.

amicus curaie: "Friend of the court"; a person or group, not a party to the case, invited by the court to submit a brief on an issue of concern to that group.

amparo: A procedure by which an individual or party may challenge the constitutionality of a law or policy by claiming a personal and direct harm; common in Latin American legal systems.

appeal: A request asking a higher court to decide whether the trial or lower court decision was correct.

appellant: A person who appeals a judicial decision.

appellate jurisdiction: When a court has the authority to review the judgment and proceedings of an inferior court.

appellee: The party who won the suit in a lower court and against whom an appeal is taken.

apportionment: Distribution of legislative seats entitled to political representation.

arguendo: "For the sake of argument"; assuming something to be true for purposes of argument.

arraignment: A formal proceeding in which the defendant is charged with a crime and must file a plea.

Basic Law: The Constitution of the Federal Republic of Germany.

bench memorandum: A memorandum about a case or an issue of law from a law clerk to a judge.

bench trial: A trial by a judge and without a jury.

bona fide: "In good faith."

Brandeis brief: A lawyer's brief that incorporates a wide variety of nonlegal materials, such as legislative findings, public policy, and social science.

brief: A written argument of law submitted by lawyers that explains to the judges why they should decide the case in their favor.

capital offense: A crime punishable by death.

case and controversy: A matter before a court in which the parties suffer real and direct harm and seek judicial resolution.

certification, writ of: A process where a lower court forwards a case to an appellate court because there are unresolved legal questions on which the lower court needs guidance.

certiorari, writ of: An order issued by the Supreme Court directing the lower court to transmit records for a case the Court has accepted on appeal. The primary means by which the Court sets its docket.

circuit court: An appellate court; in the federal judicial system each court covers several states; in most states their jurisdiction is by county.

civil law: A system of law based primarily on legislation and not on judicial decisions; common in Europe and Latin America. In common law systems, the civil law refers to laws and legal proceedings that are not criminal in nature and which relate to relationships between private persons.

class action: A lawsuit filed by an individual or individuals on behalf of themselves and others "similarly situated."

closed primary: A preliminary election in which the candidate of a political party is selected by the registered voters of that party.

comity: Courtesy; respect owed the various branches and levels of government.

common law: A legal system that is based primarily on judicial decisions rather than legislative action and statutory law.

complaint: A written statement by the plaintiff indicating how he or she has been harmed by the defendant.

concurrent powers: Powers held simultaneously between two or more levels of government.

concurring opinion: An opinion by a judge who agrees with the result reached by the majority but disagrees with all or part of the reasoning.

constitutional court: A court with the authority to review governmental action for its conformity with the constitution; in the United States, these are courts created by or under the authority of Article III.

conviction: A finding of guilt against a criminal defendant.

counsel: The lawyers in a case.

criminal law: The body of law that concerns offenses against the state and which may be penalized by fine or imprisonment.

de facto: In fact or practice.

defendant: The person named in a civil complaint or, in a criminal case, the person accused of the crime.

de jure: In law or official policy.

deposition: An oral statement by a defendant or a witness, usually taken by an attorney, which may later be used at trial.

dicta (*obiter dicta*): Statements by a court that are not strictly necessary to reach or that are not necessarily relevant to the result of the case. Dicta do not have the binding force of precedent.

discovery: The process before trial where attorneys investigate what happened, often by using interrogatories and by taking depositions.

dissenting opinion: An opinion filed by a judge who does not agree with the result reached by the majority of the court.

distinguish: To show why a case differs from another case and thus does not control the result.

diversity jurisdiction: The authority of federal courts to hear cases where the parties are citizens of different (or diverse) states.

docket: A record of court proceedings.

dual federalism: A doctrine of constitutional law that provides that national powers should be construed in ways that do not needlessly invade the authority of the states.

due process: Fair and regular procedure; in the United States, there are two due process clauses, one in the Fifth Amendment and one in the Fourteenth Amendment.

electoral college: The body of electors chosen from each state, usually on the basis of the popular vote, to elect the President and Vice President.

electoral process: Method by which a person is elected to public office.

en banc: "In the bench" or "full bench." Refers to cases where the entire membership of the court participates. In circuit courts, for example, cases are usually decided by a smaller panel of three judges.

equity: A branch of the common law where remedies for harm are governed by rules of justice and fairness and less by strict legal rules and principles.

erga omnes: A decision by a court that binds everyone similarly situated, and not only the parties to the litigation.

error, writ of: A writ sent by a higher court to a lower court instructing it to send the case to the higher court for review for possible error.

ex parte: "From or on one side." A hearing where only one of the sides to a case is present.

ex post facto: "After the fact"; a law that makes something illegal that was not illegal when it was done or which increases the penalty for the act after it has occurred.

federal question jurisdiction: Jurisdiction based on the application of the United States Constitution, acts of Congress, and treaties of the United States.

felony: A crime that carries a penalty of more than a year in prison.

gerrymander: Drawing election district lines in such a way as to favor a particular political party.

grand jury: A panel of citizens that determines whether prosecutors have enough evidence, or probable cause, to believe that an offense has been committed.

Greens: A minority party whose candidate, Ralph Nader, ran for President in 2000.

habeas corpus, writ of: "You have the body"; a writ sent to an officer or official asking him or her to explain why he has authority to detain or imprison a certain individual.

hard money: Financial contributions in direct support of candidates for political office or their campaigns.

impeachment: The constitutional process where the House of Representatives may accuse high officers of the federal government of misconduct. Trial takes place in the Senate.

in camera: "In chambers"; when a hearing or trial is heard by a judge in private chambers.

incidenter: A decentralized method of constitutional review where such authority is shared among many courts and may be considered in any concrete case, without recourse to specialized constitutional procedures.

incorporation: In constitutional doctrine, the process by which various provisions of the Bill of Rights were made applicable to the states through the due process clause of the Fourteenth Amendment.

indictment: A formal charge by a grand jury against a defendant.

in forma pauperis: "In the manner of a pauper." The process where a person sues or appeals or appeals without paying the usual court fees by claiming poverty.

in haec verba: "In these words."

injunction: A judicial order that prohibits or compels the performance of a specific act to prevent irreparable damage or injury.

inter alia: "Among other things."

inter partes: A judicial decision that is binding only upon the parties to the case.

interrogatories: Written questions prepared by an attorney that must be completed, under oath, by the other party during the process of discovery.

ipse dixit: Asserted but not proved.

issue presented: The issue or controversy raised by the facts of the case.

judgment: A final decision by a court in a lawsuit. It usually determines the respective rights and claims of the parties.

judicial review: The authority of a court to review legislation and other governmental action for its conformity with superordinate constitutional provisions.

jurisdiction: The authority of a court to entertain a case.

jurisprudence: The study of law and legal philosophy.

justiciability: Whether a case may appropriately be heard by a court or is suitable for judicial decision.

legislative court: A court created by Congress under its Article I powers; judges on such courts generally do not receive lifetime tenure.

litigant: A party to a lawsuit.

majority opinion: An opinion by a majority of sitting judges or justices.

mandamus, writ of: "We command"; an order by a court to a governmental official directing that official to do something or take a particular course of action.

martial law: A condition where rule by military authorities replaces civilian authorities and courts martial replace civilian courts.

misdemeanor: A criminal offense punishable by less than one year of imprisonment.

modified proportional representation: An electoral system that combines single-member districts with proportional representation.

moot: "Unsettled; undecided." Where the underlying dispute has been resolved or changed so that a judicial resolution of the controversy is not possible or must be hypothetical.

natural law/rights: A system of law or rights based upon "nature" or a deity or higher law that transcends human authority.

open primary: A preliminary election in which any registered voter, Democrat or Republican, may vote in a party's primary to nominate its candidate for the general election

opinion: A written explanation by a judge that sets forth the reasons and legal basis for his or her decision.

opinion of the court: An opinion by a majority of the judges or justices hearing a case.

oral argument: Proceeding where lawyers explain their positions to the court and answer questions from the judges.

original jurisdiction: The authority of a court to hear a case in the first instance or as a trial court.

originalism: A method of constitutional interpretation that seeks the "original" meaning of the constitutional provision in doubt, or the intent of its drafters.

overrule: Where a decision by a court specifically repudiates or supersedes a statement of law made in an earlier case.

panel: A group of appellate judges, usually three, that decide cases. Also, a group of potential jurors.

parties: The litigants in a case, including the plaintiff and the defendant, or, on appeal, the appellants and appellees.

per curiam: "By the Bench"; a collective decision issued by a court where no individual judge or justice claims authorship.

per se: "In or by itself"; in the nature of the thing.

petitioner: The party who seeks a writ or the assistance of the court.

plaintiff: A person who files the complaint in a civil lawsuit.

plea bargain: Where the prosecution and a defendant negotiate a guilty plea in exchange for a reduced charge or sentence.

plurality opinion: An opinion by a group of judges or justices that commands the most votes, but not an absolute majority.

police powers: The powers of a state or local government to protect the "health, safety, welfare, and morals of the community."

political action committee (PAC): An organization formed by a special interest group to raise and contribute money to political candidates or their campaigns.

political-question doctrine: A doctrine that holds that questions that primarily involve political instead of legal issues should not be decided by courts, but instead left to the other branches of government.

positivism: A system of law based upon rules and principles that claim their authority from a "sovereign"; positivism denies the existence of a "higher" law beyond the authority of human law.

precedent: A court decision in an earlier case that is similar to the case at hand.

preemption: A doctrine that holds that issues and matters of concern to both the states and the national government become the prerogative of the national government, once it acts, and thus supersede any action by the states.

presidential elector: A member of the electoral college chosen to elect the President and Vice President.

prima facie: "At first sight"; the evidence needed to establish a case until it is contested by opposing evidence.

primary election: A preliminary election in which a political party's registered voters nominate the candidate who will run in the general election.

principaliter: A method of constitutional review where such power is centralized and is divorced from the underlying factual or legal issue.

procedure: The rules that govern how a lawsuit proceeds. There are different rules for different areas of law and different courts.

proportional representation: An electoral system in which political parties are assigned legislative seats proportionate to their popular vote totals.

prosecute: A decision by the state to charge someone with a crime.

quash: To vacate or annul.

reapportionment: Realignment of legislative district boundaries to reflect changes in population.

record: A full written account of the proceedings in a lawsuit.

recuse: The process by which a judge decides not to participate in a case, usually because he or she has or appears to have a conflict of interest. In the normal course a judge will not set forth the reasons for his or her recusal.

referendum: The process of referring a legislative act or an important public issue to the people for final approval by popular vote.

remand: The process by which an appellate court sends a case back to a lower court for further proceedings.

reserved powers: Powers that remain with the states, as confirmed by the Tenth Amendment.

respondent: The party against whom action is sought or taken.

reverse: When an appellate court sets aside, or overrules, an erroneous decision by a lower court.

ripeness: A requirement that a case must be sufficiently developed factually before it may be heard by a court.

sentence: The punishment for a defendant convicted of a crime.

seriatim: To proceed one after the other or one by one.

single member district system: An electoral system in which legislative seats are assigned to the candidates who win the popular vote, often by a plurality, in their respective districts.

soft money: Funds contributed to or expended for voter registration drives, get-out-the-vote campaigns, issue advocacy, or other noncandidate related activities.

sovereign immunity: A doctrine that holds that the state may not be sued without its consent.

special master: A person appointed by a court to hear evidence, to make findings, and to submit to the court recommendations about how to proceed in light of those findings; usually associated with original jurisdiction.

standing: A doctrine that requires a plaintiff to demonstrate that he or she has a real, direct, and personal interest in a case before the court will hear the case.

stare decisis: "Let the decision stand." The practice of adhering to settled law and prior decisions.

state action: Actions for which the state bears responsibility, either directly or indirectly; a requirement for a judicial remedy under the Fourteenth Amendment

statute: A law passed by a legislature.

stay: To suspend or halt court proceedings.

subpoena: A command to a witness to appear and give testimony.

subpoena duces tecum: A command to a witness to produce documents.

summary judgment: A judicial decision made on the basis of statements and evidence presented for the record without a full trial, and where there is no dispute about the material facts or the law to be applied to the facts.

tort: A civil wrong or breach of a legal duty owed to another person.

vacate: To set aside.

venue: The location or jurisdiction where a case is tried.

verdict: The decision of a jury or a judge.

vested rights: A doctrine holding long-standing property rights must be respected by the government absent an urgent claim of need.

white primary: A preliminary election in which white persons only are permitted to vote.

writ: A written order by a court commanding an individual or a party to comply with its terms.

Chronological Chart of the Justices

Justice (Party)	Term	Appointed By (Party)	Replaced	State	Law School
John Jay (Fed)	1789–95	Washington (Fed)		N.Y.	
John Rutledge (Fed)	1789–91	Washington		S.C.	
William Cushing (Fed)	1789–1810	Washington		Mass.	
James Wilson (Fed)	1789–98	Washington		Penn.	
John Blair (Fed)	1789–95	Washington		Va.	
James Iredell (Fed)	1790–99	Washington		N.C.	
Thomas Johnson (Fed)	1791–93	Washington	Rutledge	Md.	
William Paterson (Fed)	1793–1806	Washington	Johnson	N.J.	
John Rutledge (Fed)	1795	Washington	Jay	S.C.	
Samuel Chase (Fed)	1796–1811	Washington	Blair	Md.	
Oliver Ellsworth (Fed)	1796–1800	Adams (Fed)	Rutledge	Conn.	
Bushrod Washington (Fed)	1798–1829	Adams	Wilson	Pa.	
Alfred Moore (Fed)	1799–1804	Adams	Iredell	N.C.	
John Marshall (Fed)	1801–35	Adams	Ellsworth	Va.	
William Johnson (DR)	1804–34	Jefferson (DR)	Moore	S.C.	
Henry Brockholst Livingston (DR)	1806–23	Jefferson	Paterson	N.Y.	
Thomas Todd (DR)	1807–26	Jefferson	new seat	Ky.	
Gabriel Duvall (DR)	1811–35	Madison (DR)	Chase	Md.	
Joseph Story (DR)	1811–45	Madison	Cushing	Mass.	
Smith Thompson (DR)	1823–43	Monroe (DR)	Livingston	N.Y.	
Robert Trimble (DR)	1826–28	J.Q. Adams (DR)	Todd	Ky.	
John McLean (Dem)	1829–61	Jackson (Dem)	Trimble	Ohio	
Henry Baldwin (Dem)	1830–44	Jackson	Washington	Penn.	
James M. Wayne (Dem)	1835–67	Jackson	Johnson	Ga.	
Roger B. Taney (Dem)	1836–64	Jackson	Marshall	Md.	
Philip B. Barbour (Dem)	1836–41	Jackson	Duval	Va.	
John Catron (Dem)	1837–65	Van Buren (Dem)	new seat	Tenn.	
John McKinley (Dem)	1837–52	Van Buren	new seat	Ky.	
Peter V. Daniel (Dem)	1841–60	Van Buren	Barbour	Va.	
Samuel Nelson (Dem)	1845–72	Tyler (Dem)	Thompson	N.Y.	
Levi Woodbury (Dem)	1845–51	Polk (Dem)	Story	N.H.	
Robert C. Grier (Dem)	1846–70	Polk	Baldwin	Penn.	
Benjamin R. Curtis (Whig)	1851–57	Fillmore (Whig)	Woodbury	Mass.	
John A. Campbell (Dem)	1853–61	Pierce (Dem)	McKinley	Ala.	

Justice (Party)	Term	Appointed By (Party)	Replaced	State	Law School
Nathan Clifford (Dem)	1858–81	Buchanan (Dem)	Curtis	Maine	
Noah H. Swayne (Rep)	1862–81	Lincoln (Rep)	McLean	Ohio	
Samuel F. Miller (Rep)	1862–90	Lincoln	Daniel	Iowa	
David Davis	1862–77	Lincoln	Campbell	Ill.	
Stephen J. Field (Dem)	1863–97	Lincoln	new seat	Calif.	
Salmon P. Chase (Rep)	1864–73	Lincoln	Taney	Ohio	
William Strong (Rep)	1870–80	Grant (Rep)	Grier	Penn.	
Joseph Bradley (Rep)	1870–92	Grant	Wayne	N.J.	
Ward Hunt (Rep)	1872–82	Grant	Nelson	N.Y.	
Morrison Waite (Rep)	1874–88	Grant	Chase	Ohio	
John Marshall Harlan (Rep)	1877–1911	Hayes (Rep)	Davis	Ky.	
William B. Woods (Rep)	1880–87	Hayes	Strong	Ga.	
Stanley Matthews (Rep)	1881–89	Garfield (Rep)	Swayne	Ohio	
Horace Gray (Rep)	1881–1902	Arthur (Rep)	Clifford	Mass.	
Samuel Blatchford (Rep)	1882–93	Arthur	Hunt	N.Y.	
Lucius Q.C. Lamar (Dem)	1888–93	Cleveland (Dem)	Woods	Miss.	
Melville Fuller (Dem)	1888–1910	Cleveland	Waite	Ill.	
David J. Brewer (Rep)	1889–1910	Harrison (Rep)	Matthews	Kan.	
Henry B. Brown (Rep)	1890–1906	Harrison	Miller	Mich.	
George Shiras (Rep)	1892–1903	Harrison	Bradley	Penn.	
Howell E. Jackson (Dem)	1893–95	Harrison	Lamar	Tenn.	
Edward D. White (Dem)	1894–1910	Cleveland (Dem)	Blatchford	La.	
Rufus W. Peckham (Dem)	1895–1909	Cleveland	Jackson	N.Y.	
Joseph McKenna (Rep)	1898–1925	McKinley (Rep)	Field	Calif.	
Oliver Wendell Holmes Jr. (Rep)	1902–32	T. Roosevelt (Rep)	Gray	Mass.	Harvard
William R. Day (Rep)	1903–22	T. Roosevelt	Shiras	Ohio	
William H. Moody (Rep)	1906–10	T. Roosevelt	Brown	Mass.	
Horace H. Lurton (Dem)	1910–16	Taft (Rep)	Peckham	Tenn.	Cumberland
Charles Evans Hughes (Rep)	1910–16	Taft	Brewer	N.Y.	Columbia
Edward D. White (Dem)	1910–21	Taft	Fuller	La.	
Willis Van Devanter (Rep)	1910–37	Taft	White	Wyo.	Cincinnati
Joseph R. Lamar (Dem)	1910–16	Taft	Moody	Ga.	
Mahlon Pitney (Rep)	1912–22	Taft	Harlan	N.J.	
James C. McReynolds (Dem)	1914–40	Wilson (Dem)	Lurton	Tenn.	Virginia
Louis D. Brandeis (Rep)	1916–39	Wilson	Lamar	Mass.	Harvard
John H. Clarke (Dem)	1916–22	Wilson	Hughes	Ohio	
William Howard Taft (Rep)	1921–30	Harding (Rep)	White	Ohio	Cincinnati
George Sutherland (Rep)	1922–38	Harding	Clarke	Utah	
Pierce Butler (Dem)	1922–39	Harding	Day	Minn.	
Edward T. Sanford (Rep)	1922–30	Harding	Pitney	Tenn.	Harvard
Harlan F. Stone (Rep)	1925–41	Coolidge (Rep)	McKenna	N.Y.	Columbia
Charles Evans Hughes (Rep)	1930–41	Hoover (Rep)	Taft	N.Y.	Columbia
Owen J. Roberts (Rep)	1930–45	Hoover	Stanford	Penn.	Pennsylvania
Benjamin Cardozo (Dem)	1932–38	Hoover	Holmes	N.Y.	
Hugo L. Black (Dem)	1937–71	F. Roosevelt (Dem)	Van Devanter	Ala.	Alabama
Stanley F. Reed (Dem)	1938–57	F. Roosevelt	Sutherland	Ky.	
Felix Frankfurter (Ind.)	1939–62	F. Roosevelt	Cardozo	Mass.	Harvard
William O. Douglas (Dem)	1939–75	F. Roosevelt	Brandeis	N.Y.	Columbia
Frank Murphy (Dem)	1940–49	F. Roosevelt	Butler	Mich.	Michigan
James F. Byrnes (Dem)	1941–42	F. Roosevelt	McReynolds	S.C.	
Harlan F. Stone (Rep)	1941–46	F. Roosevelt	Hughes	N.Y.	Columbia
Robert H. Jackson (Dem)	1941–54	F. Roosevelt	Stone	N.Y.	

Justice (Party)	Term	Appointed By (Party)	Replaced	State	Law School
Wiley B. Rutledge (Dem)	1943–49	F. Roosevelt	Byrnes	Iowa	Colorado
Harold H. Burton (Rep)	1945–58	Truman (Dem)	Roberts	Ohio	Harvard
Fred M. Vinson (Dem)	1946–53	Truman	Stone	Ky.	Centre College
Tom C. Clark (Dem)	1949–67	Truman	Murphy	Tex.	Texas
Sherman Minton (Dem)	1949–56	Truman	Rutledge	Ind.	Indiana
Earl Warren (Rep)	1953–69	Eisenhower (Rep)	Vinson	Calif.	California
John Marshall Harlan (Rep)	1955–71	Eisenhower	Jackson	N.Y.	New York Law School
William J. Brennan (Dem)	1956–90	Eisenhower	Minton	N.J.	Harvard
Charles E. Whittaker (Rep)	1957–62	Eisenhower	Reed	Mo.	U. of Kansas City
Potter Stewart (Rep)	1958–1981	Eisenhower	Burton	Ohio	Yale
Byron R. White (Dem)	1962–93	Kennedy (Dem)	Whittaker	Colo.	Yale
Arthur J. Goldberg (Dem)	1962–65	Kennedy	Frankfurter	Ill.	Northwestern
Abe Fortas (Dem)	1965–69	Johnson (Dem)	Goldberg	Tenn.	Yale
Thurgood Marshall (Dem)	1967–91	Johnson	Clark	N.Y.	Howard
Warren E. Burger (Rep)	1969–86	Nixon (Rep)	Warren	Minn.	St. Paul College of Law
Harry A. Blackmun (Rep)	1970–94	Nixon	Fortas	Minn.	Harvard
Lewis Powell Jr. (Dem)	1972–87	Nixon	Black	Va.	Washington & Lee
William H. Rehnquist (Rep)	1972–86	Nixon	Harlan	Ariz.	Stanford
John Paul Stevens (Rep)	1975–	Ford (Rep)	Douglas	Ill.	Northwestern
Sandra Day O'Connor (Rep)	1981–	Reagan (Rep)	Stewart	Ariz.	Stanford
William H. Rehnquist (Rep)	1986–	Reagan	Burger	Ariz.	Stanford
Antonin Scalia (Rep)	1986–	Reagan	Rehnquist	D.C.	Harvard
Anthony M. Kennedy (Rep)	1988–	Reagan	Powell	Calif.	Harvard
David H. Souter (Rep)	1990–	Bush (Rep)	Brennan	N.H.	Harvard
Clarence Thomas (Rep)	1991–	Bush	Marshall	Geor.	Yale
Ruth Bader Ginsburg (Dem)	1993–	Clinton (Dem)	White	D.C.	Columbia
Stephen G. Breyer (Dem)	1994–	Clinton	Blackmun	Mass.	Harvard

Key

Italics = Chief Justice   Dem = Democrat
Fed = Federalist   Rep = Republican
DR = Democratic Republican/Jeffersonian Ind = Independent

Legal Research on the World Wide Web

The Internet is a rich resource for students of constitutional law; the official site of the United States Supreme Court, for example, includes citations to the most recent decisions and information about the Court's rules and procedures. Moreover, students of comparative constitutional law can also find a vast array of materials on the net, including links to foreign constitutions and to the constitutional courts of other countries and jurisdictions.

In the list below we have selected only a very few links. Students who desire a more complete list should first consult all-purpose search engines, such as Google or Yahoo, and then consult similar services that concentrate just on legal materials, such as the ILL database at Cornell University, Findlaw.com, or Lexis-Nexis.

Websites and Internet Resources

American Constitutional Law

http://www.law.cornell.edu/constitution/ constitution.overview.html U.S. (United States Constitution)

http://www.supremecourtus.gov (Supreme Court of the United States)

http://www.law.cornell.edu/supct/ (Cornell Supreme Court Decisions)

http://www.findlaw.com/casecode/supreme.html (Findlaw)

http://oyez.nwu.edu/ (Oyez Oyez Oyez: Oral Recordings of Arguments in important Supreme Court decisions)

http://www.uscourts.gov (Federal Courts Homepage)

Foreign & Comparative Resources/General

http://www.oefre.unibe.ch/law/icl/home.html (International Constitutional Law/World Constitutions)

http://www.law.ualberta.ca/centres/ccs/resource.html#cotw (World Constitutions)

http://oncampus.richmond.edu/~jjones//confinder/const.htm (World Constitutions)

http://www.findlaw.com/01topics/06constitutional/03forconst/ index.html (World Constitutions)

http://www.loc.gov/law/guide/nations.html (Guide to Law Online: Nations of the World)

http://www.hrcr.org/safrica/ (Bills of Rights Comparative Law Materials)

Foreign Constitutional Courts

http://www.echr.coe.int/ (European Court of Human Rights)

http://europa.eu.int/cj/en/index.htm (Court of Justice of the European Communities)

http://www.lib.uchicago.edu/~llou/icc.html (International Criminal Court)

http://www.hcourt.gov.au/ (High Court of Australia)

http://www.scc-csc.gc.ca http://www.solon.org/Constitutions/Canada/English/index.html (Canadian Constitutional Materials)

http://www.conseil-constitutionnel.fr (France Constitutional Council)

http://www.bundesverfassungsgericht.de/ (German Federal Constitutional Court)

http://www.mkab.hu
http://www.law.vill.edu/ceecil/hungary/court.html
(Hungary Constitutional Court)

http://judis.nic.in/ (India Constitutional Court)

http://www.bailii.org/ie/cases/IESC/
(Supreme Court of Ireland decisions)

http://www.court.gov.il/heb/index.htm
(Israel Constitutional Court)

http://www.cortecostituzionale.it/ (Italian Constitutional Court)

http://www.courts.go.jp (Japan Supreme Court)

http://www.trybunal.gov.pl/Eng/index.htm
(Poland Constitutional Tribunal)

http://www.cityline.ru/politika/ks/ksbook.html
(Russia Constitutional Court)

http://www.concourt.gov.za/
(Constitutional Court of South Africa)

http://www.docuweb.ca/sispain/english/politics/court/index.html
(Spain Constitutional Court)

http://www.bailii.org/uk/cases/UKHL/
(United Kingdom House of Lords Decisions)

Appendix I

The Federalist No. 78

The Judiciary Department
Independent Journal
Saturday, June 14, 1788
[Alexander Hamilton]

To the People of the State of New York:

WE PROCEED now to an examination of the judiciary department of the proposed government.

In unfolding the defects of the existing Confederation, the utility and necessity of a federal judicature have been clearly pointed out. It is the less necessary to recapitulate the considerations there urged, as the propriety of the institution in the abstract is not disputed; the only questions which have been raised being relative to the manner of constituting it, and to its extent. To these points, therefore, our observations shall be confined.

The manner of constituting it seems to embrace these several objects: 1st. The mode of appointing the judges. 2d. The tenure by which they are to hold their places. 3d. The partition of the judiciary authority between different courts, and their relations to each other.

First. As to the mode of appointing the judges; this is the same with that of appointing the officers of the Union in general, and has been so fully discussed in the two last numbers, that nothing can be said here which would not be useless repetition.

Second. As to the tenure by which the judges are to hold their places; this chiefly concerns their duration in office; the provisions for their support; the precautions for their responsibility.

According to the plan of the convention, all judges who may be appointed by the United States are to hold their offices *during good behavior*; which is conformable to the most approved of the State constitutions and among the rest, to that of this State. Its propriety having been drawn into question by the adversaries of that plan, is no light symptom of the rage for objection, which disorders their imaginations and judgments. The standard of good behavior for the continuance in office of the judicial magistracy, is certainly one of the most valuable of the modern improvements in the practice of government. In a monarchy it is an excellent barrier to the despotism of the prince; in a republic it is a no less excellent barrier to the encroachments and oppressions of the representative body. And it is the best expedient which can be devised in any government, to secure a steady, upright, and impartial administration of the laws.

Whoever attentively considers the different departments of power must perceive, that, in a government in which they are separated from each other, the judiciary, from the nature of its functions, will always be the least dangerous to the political rights of the Constitution; because it will be least in a capacity to annoy or injure them. The Executive not only dispenses the honors, but holds the sword of the community. The legislature not only commands the purse, but prescribes the rules by which the duties and rights of every citizen are to be regulated. The judiciary, on the contrary, has no influence over either the sword or the purse; no direction either of the strength or of the wealth of the society; and can take no active resolution whatever. It may truly be said to have neither FORCE nor WILL, but merely judgment; and must ultimately depend upon the aid of the executive arm even for the efficacy of its judgments.

This simple view of the matter suggests several important consequences. It proves incontestably, that the judiciary is beyond comparison the weakest of the three departments of power[1]; that it can never attack with success either of the other two; and that all possible care is requisite to enable it to defend itself against their attacks. It equally proves, that though individual oppression may now and then proceed from the courts of justice, the general liberty of the people can never be endangered from that quarter;

1069

I mean so long as the judiciary remains truly distinct from both the legislature and the Executive. For I agree, that "there is no liberty, if the power of judging be not separated from the legislative and executive powers."[2] And it proves, in the last place, that as liberty can have nothing to fear from the judiciary alone, but would have every thing to fear from its union with either of the other departments; that as all the effects of such a union must ensue from a dependence of the former on the latter, notwithstanding a nominal and apparent separation; that as, from the natural feebleness of the judiciary, it is in continual jeopardy of being overpowered, awed, or influenced by its co-ordinate branches; and that as nothing can contribute so much to its firmness and independence as permanency in office, this quality may therefore be justly regarded as an indispensable ingredient in its constitution, and, in a great measure, as the citadel of the public justice and the public security.

The complete independence of the courts of justice is peculiarly essential in a limited Constitution. By a limited Constitution, I understand one which contains certain specified exceptions to the legislative authority; such, for instance, as that it shall pass no bills of attainder, no *ex post facto* laws, and the like. Limitations of this kind can be preserved in practice no other way than through the medium of courts of justice, whose duty it must be to declare all acts contrary to the manifest tenor of the Constitution void. Without this, all the reservations of particular rights or privileges would amount to nothing.

Some perplexity respecting the rights of the courts to pronounce legislative acts void, because contrary to the Constitution, has arisen from an imagination that the doctrine would imply a superiority of the judiciary to the legislative power. It is urged that the authority which can declare the acts of another void, must necessarily be superior to the one whose acts may be declared void. As this doctrine is of great importance in all the American constitutions, a brief discussion of the ground on which it rests cannot be unacceptable.

There is no position which depends on clearer principles, than that every act of a delegated authority, contrary to the tenor of the commission under which it is exercised, is void. No legislative act, therefore, contrary to the Constitution, can be valid. To deny this, would be to affirm, that the deputy is greater than his principal; that the servant is above his master; that the representatives of the people are superior to the people themselves; that men acting by virtue of powers, may do not only what their powers do not authorize, but what they forbid.

If it be said that the legislative body are themselves the constitutional judges of their own powers, and that the construction they put upon them is conclusive upon the other departments, it may be answered, that this cannot be the natural presumption, where it is not to be collected from any particular provisions in the Constitution. It is not otherwise to be supposed, that the Constitution could intend to enable the representatives of the people to substitute their *will* to that of their constituents. It is far more rational to suppose, that the courts were designed to be an intermediate body between the people and the legislature, in order, among other things, to keep the latter within the limits assigned to their authority. The interpretation of the laws is the proper and peculiar province of the courts. A constitution is, in fact, and must be regarded by the judges, as a fundamental law. It therefore belongs to them to ascertain its meaning, as well as the meaning of any particular act proceeding from the legislative body. If there should happen to be an irreconcilable variance between the two, that which has the superior obligation and validity ought, of course, to be preferred; or, in other words, the Constitution ought to be preferred to the statute, the intention of the people to the intention of their agents.

Nor does this conclusion by any means suppose a superiority of the judicial to the legislative power. It only supposes that the power of the people is superior to both; and that where the will of the legislature, declared in its statutes, stands in opposition to that of the people, declared in the Constitution, the judges ought to be governed by the latter rather than the former. They ought to regulate their decisions by the fundamental laws, rather than by those which are not fundamental.

This exercise of judicial discretion, in determining between two contradictory laws, is exemplified in a familiar instance. It not uncommonly happens, that there are two statutes existing at one time, clashing in whole or in part with each other, and neither of them containing any repealing clause or expression. In such a case, it is the province of the courts to liquidate and fix their meaning and operation. So far as they can, by any fair construction, be reconciled to each other, reason and law conspire to dictate that this should be done; where this is impracticable, it becomes a matter of necessity to give effect to one, in exclusion of the other. The rule which has obtained in the courts for determining their relative validity is, that the last in order of time shall be preferred to the first. But this is a mere rule of construction, not derived from any positive law, but from the nature and reason of the thing. It is a rule not enjoined upon the courts by legislative provision, but adopted by themselves, as consonant to truth and propriety, for the direction of their conduct as interpreters of the law. They thought it reasonable, that between the interfering acts of an EQUAL authority, that which was the last indication of its will should have the preference.

But in regard to the interfering acts of a superior and subordinate authority, of an original and derivative power, the nature and reason of the thing indicate the converse of that rule as proper to be followed. They teach us that the prior act of a superior ought to be preferred to the subsequent act of an inferior and subordinate authority; and that accordingly, whenever a particular statute contravenes the Constitution, it will be the duty of the judicial tribunals to adhere to the latter and disregard the former.

It can be of no weight to say that the courts, on the pretense of a repugnancy, may substitute their own pleasure to the constitutional intentions of the legislature. This might as well happen in the case of two contradictory statutes; or it might as well happen in every adjudication upon any single statute. The courts must declare the sense of the law; and if they should be disposed to exercise WILL instead of JUDGMENT, the consequence would equally be the substitution of their pleasure to that of the legislative body. The observation, if it prove any thing, would prove that there ought to be no judges distinct from that body.

If, then, the courts of justice are to be considered as the bulwarks of a limited Constitution against legislative encroachments, this consideration will afford a strong argument for the permanent tenure of judicial offices, since nothing will contribute so much as this to that independent spirit in the judges which must be essential to the faithful performance of so arduous a duty.

This independence of the judges is equally requisite to guard the Constitution and the rights of individuals from the effects of those ill humors, which the arts of designing men, or the influence of particular conjunctures, sometimes disseminate among the people themselves, and which, though they speedily give place to better information, and more deliberate reflection, have a tendency, in the meantime, to occasion dangerous innovations in the government, and serious oppressions of the minor party in the community. Though I trust the friends of the proposed Constitution will never concur with its enemies,[3] in questioning that fundamental principle of republican government, which admits the right of the people to alter or abolish the established Constitution, whenever they find it inconsistent with their happiness, yet it is not to be inferred from this principle, that the representatives of the people, whenever a momentary inclination happens to lay hold of a majority of their constituents, incompatible with the provisions in the existing Constitution, would, on that account, be justifiable in a violation of those provisions; or that the courts would be under a greater obligation to connive at infractions in this shape, than when they had proceeded wholly from the cabals of the representative body. Until the people have, by some solemn and authoritative act, annulled or changed the established form, it is binding upon themselves collectively, as well as individually; and no presumption, or even knowledge, of their sentiments, can warrant their representatives in a departure from it, prior to such an act. But it is easy to see, that it would require an uncommon portion of fortitude in the judges to do their duty as faithful guardians of the Constitution, where legislative invasions of it had been instigated by the major voice of the community.

But it is not with a view to infractions of the Constitution only, that the independence of the judges may be an essential safeguard against the effects of occasional ill humors in the society. These sometimes extend no farther than to the injury of the private rights of particular classes of citizens, by unjust and partial laws. Here also the firmness of the judicial magistracy is of vast importance in mitigating the severity and confining the operation of such laws. It not only serves to moderate the immediate mischiefs of those which may have been passed, but it operates as a check upon the legislative body in passing them; who, perceiving that obstacles to the success of iniquitous intention are to be expected from the scruples of the courts, are in a manner compelled, by the very motives of the injustice they meditate, to qualify their attempts. This is a circumstance calculated to have more influence upon the character of our governments, than but few may be aware of. The benefits of the integrity and moderation of the judiciary have already been felt in more States than one; and though they may have displeased those whose sinister expectations they may have disappointed, they must have commanded the esteem and applause of all the virtuous and disinterested. Considerate men, of every description, ought to prize whatever will tend to beget or fortify that temper in the courts: as no man can be sure that he may not be to-morrow the victim of a spirit of injustice, by which he may be a gainer to-day. And every man must now feel, that the inevitable tendency of such a spirit is to sap the foundations of public and private confidence, and to introduce in its stead universal distrust and distress.

That inflexible and uniform adherence to the rights of the Constitution, and of individuals, which we perceive to be indispensable in the courts of justice, can certainly not be expected from judges who hold their offices by a temporary commission. Periodical appointments, however regulated, or by whomsoever made, would, in some way or other, be fatal to their necessary independence. If the power of making them was committed either to the Executive or legislature, there would be danger of an improper complaisance to the branch which possessed it; if to both, there would be an unwillingness to hazard the displeasure of either; if to the people, or to persons chosen by them for the special purpose, there would be too great a disposition to consult popularity, to justify a reliance that nothing would be consulted but the Constitution and the laws.

There is yet a further and a weightier reason for the permanency of the judicial offices, which is deducible from the nature of the qualifications they require. It has been frequently remarked, with great propriety, that a voluminous code of laws is one of the inconveniences necessarily connected with the advantages of a free government. To avoid an arbitrary discretion in the courts, it is indispensable that they should be bound down by strict rules and precedents, which serve to define and point out their duty in every particular case that comes before them; and it will readily be conceived from the variety of controversies which grow out of the folly and wickedness of mankind, that the records of those precedents must unavoidably swell to a very considerable bulk, and must demand long and laborious study to acquire a competent knowledge of them. Hence it is, that there can be but few men in the society who will have sufficient skill in the laws to qualify them for the stations of judges. And making the proper deductions for the ordinary depravity of human nature, the number must be still smaller of those who unite the requisite integrity with the requisite knowledge. These considerations apprise us, that the government can have no great option between fit character; and that a temporary duration in office, which would naturally discourage such characters from quitting a lucrative line of practice to accept a seat on the bench, would have a tendency to throw the administration of justice into hands less able, and less well qualified, to conduct it with utility and dignity. In the present circumstances of this country, and in those in which it is likely to be for a long time to come, the disadvantages on this score would be greater than they may at first sight appear; but it must be confessed, that they are far inferior to those which present themselves under the other aspects of the subject.

Upon the whole, there can be no room to doubt that the convention acted wisely in copying from the models of those constitutions which have established *good behavior* as the tenure of their judicial offices, in point of duration; and that so far from being blamable on this account, their plan would have been inexcusably defective, if it had wanted this important feature of good government. The experience of Great Britain affords an illustrious comment on the excellence of the institution.

PUBLIUS

1. The celebrated Montesquieu, speaking of them, says: "Of the three powers above mentioned, the judiciary is next to nothing."—*Spirit of Laws.* Vol. I, page 186.

2. *Idem*, page 181.

3. *Vide Protest of the Minority of the Convention of Pennsylvania*, Martin's Speech, etc.

Table of Cases

Cases listed in bold are excerpted in the text; the page numbers of the excerpt are also in bold. Page numbers followed by *f,* n or *t* refer to figures, notes, and tables respectively.

Index

Page numbers followed by *f,* n, or *t* refer to figures, notes, and tables respectively.

About the Authors

Donald P. Kommers received his doctorate from the University of Wisconsin, Madison. He is the Joseph and Elizabeth Robbie Professor of Political Science and concurrent professor of law at the University of Notre Dame. He has published widely in American and comparative constitutional law and politics. His books include *The Constitutional Jurisprudence of the Federal Republic of Germany*, 2nd ed. (1997), and the forthcoming *Black, Red, and Gold: Germany's Constitutional Odyssey*. He was editor of *The Review of Politics* for ten years and for seven years the director of the Notre Dame Law School's Center for Civil and International Human Rights.

John E. Finn is professor of government at Wesleyan University. He received his B.A. in political science from Nasson College, a J.D. from Georgetown University Law Center, and a doctorate in political science from Princeton University. His many publications include *Constitutions in Crisis: Political Violence and the Rule of Law* (1991). He has testified before the House Judiciary Committee on antiterrorism legislation, and has served as a constitutional consultant for Chile and the Ukraine.

Gary J. Jacobsohn received his doctorate from Cornell University. He is Patterson-Banister Professor of Political Science at the University of Texas at Austin. Previously he taught political science for thirty-three years at Williams College. He is the author of several books, including *The Wheel of Law: India's Secularism in Comparative Constitutional Context* (2003), *Apple of Gold: Constitutionalism in Israel and the United States* (1993), *The Supreme Court and the Decline of Constitutional Aspiration* (1986), and *Pragmatism, Statesmanship, and the Supreme Court* (1977). He is a past president of the New England Political Science Association.